THE VOLUME LIBRARY

A Modern, Authoritative Reference for Home and School Use

Clear and Complete • Colorfully Illustrated • Totally Indexed
Special Atlas Section

THE SOUTHWESTERN COMPANY
Nashville, Tennessee

THE VOLUME LIBRARY

ISBN 0-87197-208-5

Printed in the United States of America.

THE VOLUME LIBRARY

PREFACE

What is the Volume Library?

The Volume Library is a respected home reference book that has been published for more than 70 years, bringing knowledge and information to generations of readers. Its 2.5 million words and countless illustrations provide clear introductions to all major fields of study and bring together in two convenient volumes important and hard-to-find information.

The Volume Library, which is revised and updated annually, was designed for interested, well-informed people—students and adults who need an authoritative reference book for their home bookshelves, and parents who want to keep abreast of the subjects their children are studying in school.

Its uses can be summarized in four categories:

- *Learning.* In contrast with many other reference works, *The Volume Library* offers detailed and clear instruction in such practical skills as mathematics and writing. Readers can learn new skills or brush up on old ones without searching out many separate volumes.
- *Reference.* Thousands of important names, dates, places, and events are easily available; they can be looked up quickly and conveniently.
- *Research.* Students, business people, and others who are preparing reports on special subjects will find useful information in clear, understandable form.
- *Browsing.* Many successful people report that their first source of information as young readers was an interesting reference work to pore over while gathering miscellaneous information simply for enjoyment. *The Volume Library* offers introductions to many fields of interest and can often lead even a reluctant learner to further reading in more specialized books, magazines, and other materials.

How is The Volume Library organized?

Each of the 26 subject volumes is complete in itself. The volumes are arranged alphabetically, beginning with ANIMALS and ending with UNITED STATES AND CANADA. In addition, there are a full-color ATLAS of the world and a thorough INDEX, which provides detailed guidance for the use of *The Volume Library.*

Many of the volumes are related. Covering the broad areas of history and geography, for example, are five large volumes, each treating a major region of the world. Six other volumes cover the major subdivisions of science. In a similar way, social studies are considered under such broad volume headings as CHILD AND FAMILY and GOVERNMENT AND LAW. Several volumes outline such important practical fields as business, economics, and technology. Three volumes cover arts and letters, providing histories of painting, sculpture, music, dance, and literature. Finally, two important volumes provide detailed material on practical learning skills. The MATHEMATICS volume gives clear instruction from elementary arithmetic through to geometry and calculus. The LANGUAGE volume considers the skills of speaking, reading, and especially writing. It includes full sections on spelling, grammar, and research for school reports.

The following table shows the relationships of all the volumes and may be helpful for the reader who wants to know where to look first.

History and Geography
- Asia and Australasia
- Europe
- Middle East and Africa
- South and Central America
- United States and Canada
- Atlas

Social Studies
- Child and Family
- Government and Law
- People
- Social Sciences
- Religion and Philosophy

Arts and Letters
- Art
- Literature
- Performing Arts

The Sciences
- Astronomy and Space
- Chemistry and Physics
- Earth Sciences
- Health and Life Sciences
- Animals
- Plants

Practical Arts
- Business and Economics
- Computers
- Food and Agriculture
- Invention and Technology
- Sports and Recreation

Practical Skills
- Language and Family Reading
- Mathematics

How to use The Volume Library

In most encyclopedias, information is broken into small entries and then arranged alphabetically. By contrast, in *The Volume Library* all information on a large topic is found in one place and is described in a way that makes comprehensive sense. This means that a reader with an interest in mathematics, for example, can find a connected account of arithmetic within a few pages; he will not have to look up separate entries on *addition, fractions, measurement,* and so on.

In some cases, of course, a reader will be looking for information that is separated. For example, a reader who has an interest in France will find a long entry on the country in the EUROPE volume, but he will also find an account of French art in the ART volume, of French literature under LITERATURE, of prominent Frenchmen under PEOPLE, and so on. He will even find a brief review of the French language in the LANGUAGE volume. Such a reader will find great usefulness in the INDEX at the back of the book. It is a valuable guide to any researcher seeking to understand the connections and relationships between the many aspects of knowledge in many fields of interest.

Only you, the reader, can decide which of the many attractive features of *The Volume Library* makes it most useful for your purposes. Whether you use it for learning skills, for looking up facts, for research, or for browsing, you will find it a convenient and endlessly fascinating source of knowledge.

TABLE OF CONTENTS

BOOK 1

VOLUME **1**

Animals

VOLUME **2**

Art

VOLUME **3**

Asia and Australasia

VOLUME **4**

Astronomy and Space

VOLUME **5**

Business and Economics

page **265**

VOLUME **6**

Computers

page **347**

VOLUME **7**

Chemistry and Physics

page **397**

VOLUME **8**

Child and Family

page **479**

VOLUME **9**

Earth Sciences

page **545**

VOLUME **10**

Europe

page **627**

VOLUME **11**

Food and Agriculture

page **773**

VOLUME **12**

Government and Law

page **823**

VOLUME **13**

Health and Life Sciences

page **921**

VOLUME **14**

Invention and Technology

VOLUME **15**

Language

BOOK 2

VOLUME **16**

Literature

VOLUME **17**

Mathematics

VOLUME **18**

Middle East and Africa

VOLUME **19**

People

page **1589**

VOLUME **20**

Performing Arts

page **1791**

VOLUME **21**

Plants

page **1857**

VOLUME **22**

Religion and Philosophy

page **1923**

VOLUME **23**

Social Sciences

page **1973**

EDITORIAL STAFF

THE HUDSON GROUP, INC., PLEASANTVILLE, N.Y.

Editor in chief: GORTON CARRUTH
Sponsoring editor: EUGENE EHRLICH
Managing editor: HAYDEN CARRUTH
Art and production: PAM FORDE GRAPHICS
Copy editing and indexing: FELICE LEVY and CYNTHIA CRIPPEN/AEIOU, INC.

Contributors

ACOCELLA, NICHOLAS
M.A. Political writer and columnist.
GOVERNMENT AND LAW.

ADAMS, JANET
Ph.D. Candidate. Instructor, Rhode Island School of Design.
ART.

BAHLMAN, DUDLEY W. R.
Ph.D. Professor of History, and Dean of the Faculty, Williams College.
EUROPE.

BAINER, ROY
M.S. Dean of Engineering, University of California at Davis.
FOOD AND AGRICULTURE.

BAKER, LAURENCE H.
Ph.D. Director, Computing Department, Pioneer Hi-Bred Corn Company.
FOOD AND AGRICULTURE.

BARTELMEZ, ERMINNIE H.
Ph.D. Professor of German, Case Western Reserve University.
LANGUAGE.

BARTH, FRANCES F.
Freelance medical writer.
HEALTH AND LIFE SCIENCES.

BARZANTI, SERGIO
Ph.D. Associate Professor of Social Sciences, Fairleigh Dickinson University.
EUROPE; MIDDLE EAST AND AFRICA.

BAYES, MARJORIE
Ph.D. Clinical psychologist.
CHILD AND FAMILY.

BERLAND, LAURA
B.A. Writer and legal aide.
GOVERNMENT AND LAW.

BERRY, E. WILLARD
Ph.D. Late Professor of Geology, Duke University.
EARTH SCIENCES.

BIRMINGHAM, LLOYD
Freelance educational illustrator.
CHEMISTRY AND PHYSICS; INVENTION AND TECHNOLOGY.

BOARDMAN, FON W.
A.B. Former Vice President and Marketing Director of Oxford University Press, N.Y.; author of books for young people; freelance writer.
FOOD AND AGRICULTURE; PEOPLE; UNITED STATES AND CANADA.

BOCIAN, PHYLLIS R.
B.A. Freelance editor.
CHILD AND FAMILY; LANGUAGE.

BROWN, LEON CARL
Ph.D. Associate Professor of Oriental Studies, Princeton University.
MIDDLE EAST AND AFRICA.

BUNCH, BRYAN H.
B.A. Writer, textbook consultant; former Editor in Chief, American Book Company.
ANIMALS; ASTRONOMY AND SPACE; INVENTION AND TECHNOLOGY; MATHEMATICS; PLANTS; RELIGION; SOCIAL SCIENCES.

BUSHNELL, DAVID
Ph.D. Associate Professor of History, University of Florida.
SOUTH AND CENTRAL AMERICA.

BUTTFIELD, HELEN
A.M. Nature writer and photographer.
PLANTS.

BYAM, GUY R.
M.A. Vice President and Director of Personnel, Bankers Trust Company.
BUSINESS AND FINANCE.

BYERLY, THEODORE C.
Ph.D. Administrator, Cooperative State Research Service, United States Department of Agriculture.
FOOD AND AGRICULTURE.

BYRNES, ROBERT F.
Ph.D. Distinguished Professor of History, Indiana University.
EUROPE.

CAREY, GEORGE W.
Ed.D. Associate Professor of Geography, Teachers College, Columbia University.
SOUTH AND CENTRAL AMERICA.

CARTER, CHARLES H.
Ph.D. Professor of History, Tulane University.
EUROPE.

COHEN, MARSHALL H.
M.A. Economist, U.S. Department of Agriculture.
FOOD AND AGRICULTURE.

COHN-HAFT, LOUIS
Ph.D. Professor of History, Smith College.
EUROPE.

DALRYMPLE, DANA G.
Ph.D. Economist, International Agricultural Development Service, U.S. Department of Agriculture.
FOOD AND AGRICULTURE.

DAVIS, FRANCIS K., JR.
Ph.D. Head, Physics Department, Drexel Institute of Technology.
EARTH SCIENCES.

DELURY, GEORGE
M.A. Political science editor.
GOVERNMENT AND LAW.

DETWILER, SAMUEL B., JR.
M.A. Assistant to the Deputy Administrator for Nutrition, Consumer, and Industrial Use Research, Agricultural Research Service, U.S. Department of Agriculture.
FOOD AND AGRICULTURE.

DICKINSON, RICHARD
M.A. Lecturer and writer on fine arts.
ART.
DIPPEL, JOHN
Ph.D. Freelance writer.
LANGUAGE.
DIRKS, J. EDWARD
Ph.D. Professor of Christian Methods, Yale University Divinity School; Founder and Editor, *Christian Science Quarterly*.
RELIGION AND PHILOSOPHY.
DITTRICK, DIANE K.
M.A. Author and freelance writer on science subjects.
HEALTH AND LIFE SCIENCES.
DOWLING, KENNETH W.
Ph.D. Science Supervisor, State of Wisconsin.
INVENTION AND TECHNOLOGY.
DRAPER, EVERETT T.
M.A. Adjunct Lecturer, LaGuardia Community College, City University of New York.
MATHEMATICS.
DUNBAR, ROBERT G.
Ph.D. Professor of History, Montana State University.
FOOD AND AGRICULTURE.
DUPREE, LOUIS
Ph.D. Research Associate in Anthropology, American Museum of Natural History.
ASIA AND AUSTRALASIA.
EHRLICH, HENRY
B.A. Communications specialist, Assistant Vice President, Citibank.
LANGUAGE.
EMBREE, AINSLIE T.
Ph.D. Associate Professor of History, Columbia University.
ASIA AND AUSTRALASIA.
EMILIANI, CESARE
Ph.D. Professor, Institute of Marine Sciences, University of Miami (Florida).
EARTH SCIENCES.
ENNIS, THOMAS E.
Ph.D. Late Professor of Far Eastern History, West Virginia University.
ASIA AND AUSTRALASIA.
EPPERT, RAY R.
D.Sc., LL.D. Chairman and Chief Executive Officer, Burroughs Corporation.
BUSINESS AND FINANCE.
FABRICANT, MONA
Ed.D. City University of New York.
MATHEMATICS.
FAJARDO, FERNANDO U.
B.S. Chemist, freelance writer.
CHEMISTRY AND PHYSICS.
FELDMAN, ROBERT J.
Freelance writer.
SOUTH AND CENTRAL AMERICA.
FINAN, JOHN J.
Ph.D. Professor of Latin American Studies, School of International Service, The American University.
SOUTH AND CENTRAL AMERICA.
FISCHMAN, JEROME
Ph.D. Associate Professor of History, Adelphi University.
SOUTH AND CENTRAL AMERICA.
FOREMAN W. L.
Director of Public Relations, National Cotton Council of America.
FOOD AND AGRICULTURE.
FRANKLIN, PAULA
B.A. Writer and editor of school and college texts.
SOCIAL SCIENCES.
FUSSELL, G. E.
Formerly in the British Ministry of Agriculture.
FOOD AND AGRICULTURE.
GILBERT, SARA
Freelance writer.
ASIA AND AUSTRALASIA; MIDDLE EAST AND AFRICA.
GOLUB, MARCIA H.
B.A. Freelance writer and editor.
LANGUAGE; LITERATURE; RELIGION AND PHILOSOPHY.
GRAHAM, GORDON F.
B.A. Secretary, National Association of Wool Manufacturers.
FOOD AND AGRICULTURE.
GRIFFIN, CHARLES C.
Ph.D. Professor of History Emeritus, Vassar College.
SOUTH AND CENTRAL AMERICA.
HAMBURG, MORRIS
Ph.D. Professor of Statistics and Operations Research, University of Pennsylvania.
BUSINESS AND FINANCE.
HARRINGTON, JOHN P.
Ph.D. Writer and editor of reference works.
UNITED STATES AND CANADA.
HEIMSATH, CHARLES H.
Ph.D. Professor of South Asian Studies, The School of International Service, The American University.
ASIA AND AUSTRALASIA.
HELLEMANS, ALEXANDER
B.A. Freelance science writer.
ASTRONOMY AND SPACE, CHEMISTRY AND PHYSICS.
HERDER, RONALD
M.A. Adjunct Professor of Music, Manhattanville College.
PERFORMING ARTS.
HERON, S. DUNCAN, JR.
Ph.D. Associate Professor of Geology and Department Chairman, Duke University; Editor in Chief, *Southeastern Geology*.
EARTH SCIENCES.

HESS, CARL W.
Ph.D. Chief, Poultry Research Branch, U.S. Department of Agriculture.
FOOD AND AGRICULTURE.

HESTER, ALBERT S.
B.S. Market Research Analyst, American Cyanamid Company.
FOOD AND AGRICULTURE.

HOOLIHAN, CHRISTOPHER T.
M.A. Former Professor of French and Latin, St. Meinrad College.
LANGUAGE.

HYNEK, J. ALLEN
Ph.D. Professor of Astronomy and Department Chairman, Northwestern University; Director, Dearborn Observatory and Lindheimer Astronomical Research Center.
ASTRONOMY AND SPACE.

INABA, M. G.
Ph.D. Chairman, Department of Geography, Hofstra University.
ASIA AND AUSTRALASIA.

ISSAWI, CHARLES
M.A. Ragnar Nurkse Professor of Economics, Columbia University.
MIDDLE EAST AND AFRICA.

JANOWSKY, OSCAR I.
Ph.D. Professor Emeritus of History, City University of New York; Visiting Professor of History, Brandeis University.
MIDDLE EAST AND AFRICA.

KAHKONEN, SHARON
M.S. Freelance science writer.
INVENTION AND TECHNOLOGY.

KAREL, MARCUS
Ph.D. Associate Professor of Food Engineering, Massachusetts Institute of Technology.
FOOD AND AGRICULTURE.

KISH, GEORGE
Ph.D. Professor of Geography, University of Michigan.
EUROPE.

KLINE, HIBBERD V. B., JR.
Ph.D. Professor and Chairman, Department of Geography, University of Pittsburgh.
MIDDLE EAST AND AFRICA.

KOCZY, FRIEDRICH F.
Ph.D. Late Professor and Chairman, Physical Science Division, Institute of Marine Science, University of Miami.
EARTH SCIENCES.

KOMINUS, NICHOLAS
B.S. Director of Information, United States Cane Sugar Refiners' Association.
FOOD AND AGRICULTURE.

KREN, GEORGE M.
Ph.D. Associate Professor of History, Kansas State University.
EUROPE.

LAGUARDIA, ROBERT.
Freelance writer.
LITERATURE.

LEITH, JAMES A.
Ph.D. Associate Professor of French History, Queen's University, Ontario.
EUROPE.

LEVY, STEPHEN H.
Ph.D. Assistant Professor, Computer and Information Systems, Pace University.
RELIGION AND PHILOSOPHY.

LEY, WILLY
L.H.D. Late Professor, Long Island University.
ASTRONOMY AND SPACE.

LICHTENSTADTER, ILSE
Ph.D., D.Phil.Oxon. Lecturer on Arabic, Center for Middle Eastern Studies, Harvard University.
ASIA AND AUSTRALASIA.

LINDROTH, DAVID
M.F.A. Cartographer and graphic designer.
ASIA AND AUSTRALASIA.

LINDSAY, MICHAEL
M.A. Professor of Far Eastern Studies, American University.
ASIA AND AUSTRALASIA.

LISS, HOWARD.
Freelance writer.
SPORTS AND RECREATION.

LOEWER, H. PETER
B.F.A. Author and illustrator.
ART; CHEMISTRY AND PHYSICS; CHILD AND FAMILY; FOOD AND AGRICULTURE; GOVERNMENT AND LAW; HEALTH AND LIFE SCIENCES; LANGUAGE; MATHEMATICS; PERFORMING ARTS; SOCIAL SCIENCES; SPORTS.

LORIMER, DONALD
B.A. Freelance writer.
ART; CHILD AND FAMILY.

LORIMER, LAWRENCE T.
M.A. Author, editorial consultant.
ART; CHILD AND FAMILY; LANGUAGE; LITERATURE.

MACKAY-SMITH, ALEXANDER
L.L.B. Editor, *The Chronicle of the Horse*.
FOOD AND AGRICULTURE.

MARR, ANNE W.
M.A. Teacher of mathematics and computer science; freelance writer.
INVENTION AND TECHNOLOGY.

McCARTHY, E. JEROME
Ph.D. Professor of Marketing, Michigan State University.
BUSINESS AND FINANCE.

McGREGOR, SAMUEL E.
M.S. Chief, Apiculture Research Branch, Entomology Research Division, U.S. Department of Agriculture.
FOOD AND AGRICULTURE.

McHUGH, JANET
B.A. Writer and editor of school and college texts.
UNITED STATES AND CANADA.

MELAMID, ALEXANDER
Ph.D. Professor of Economics, New York University.
MIDDLE EAST AND AFRICA.

MERRILL, DAVID G.
M.A. Freelance writer.
ASIA AND AUSTRALASIA; EUROPE; MIDDLE EAST AND AFRICA; SOUTH AND CENTRAL AMERICA.

MILLER, PAUL W.
M.B.A. Management Consultant. Department of Management, Western Illinois University.
BUSINESS AND ECONOMICS.

MILNE, LORUS J.
Ph.D. Professor of Zoology, University of New Hampshire.
ANIMALS; PLANTS.

MILNE, MARGERY
Ph.D. Lecturer in Nature Recreation and Zoology, University of New Hampshire.
ANIMALS; PLANTS.

MITCHELL, JOHN W.
Ph.D., D.Sc. Leader, Plant Hormone and Regulator, Pioneering Laboratory, U.S. Department of Agriculture, Crops Research Division.
FOOD AND AGRICULTURE.

MURRY, PAUL B.
Freelance writer.
FOOD AND AGRICULTURE.

MYERS, SARAH K.
Ph.D. Geographer and freelance writer.
INVENTION AND TECHNOLOGY.

NOWELL, CHARLES E.
Ph.D. Professor of History, University of Illinois.
EUROPE.

O'BRIEN, ROBERT
B.A., author.
PERFORMING ARTS.

OLIVER, JOHN E.
M.A. Instructor of Geography, Columbia University.
MIDDLE EAST AND AFRICA.

PAVELIS, GEORGE A.
Ph.D. Chief, Water Resources Branch, Natural Resource Economics Division, U.S. Department of Agriculture.
FOOD AND AGRICULTURE.

PLUMMER, SAMUEL C.
B.A., M.B.A. Freelance writer and editor.
PERFORMING ARTS; SOCIAL SCIENCES.

RANDALL, BERNICE
M.A. Author and editor of educational materials in Spanish and English.
LANGUAGE.

RASMUSSEN, WAYNE D.
Ph.D. Chief, Agriculture History Branch, U.S. Department of Agriculture.
FOOD AND AGRICULTURE.

REILLY, E. M.
Ph.D. Curator Emeritus, Zoology, New York State Museum. Author and freelance writer.
HEALTH AND LIFE SCIENCES.

ROGERS, CHARLES E.
Ph.D. Former Information Officer, U.S. Department of Agriculture.
FOOD AND AGRICULTURE.

ROTBERG, ROBERT I.
D.Phil. Associate Professor of History and Political Science, Massachusetts Institute of Technology.
MIDDLE EAST AND AFRICA.

ROWNEY, DON KARL
Ph.D. Associate Professor of History, Bowling Green State University.
EUROPE.

SACERDOTE, MARC
M.A. Teacher of film animation; freelance writer.
INVENTION AND TECHNOLOGY.

SACKS, RICHARD
Ph.D. Assistant Professor of English and Comparative Literature, Columbia University.
LANGUAGE.

SCOTT, FRANKLIN D.
Ph.D. Professor of History, Northwestern University.
EUROPE.

SCOTT, FREDERICK
M.S. Chemical engineer; Consulting Editor, International Scientific Communications, Inc.
INVENTION AND TECHNOLOGY.

SHANER, DORIS D.
B.A. Vice President, Shaner-Grandelis Associates.
EARTH SCIENCES.

SHERIDAN, BARBARA
B.Sc. Mathematics and physical sciences writer.
MATHEMATICS.

SMITH, DAVID A.
Ph.D. Associate Professor of Geography, State University of New York at Buffalo.
ASIA AND AUSTRALASIA.

STUART, NEIL W.
Ph.D. Research Plant Physiologist, U.S. Department of Agriculture.
FOOD AND AGRICULTURE.

TARAPOR, MAHRUKH.
Freelance writer.
ART.

TESAR, JENNY
M.A. Freelance science and medical writer.
COMPUTERS.

THOMPSON, JOHN M.
Ph.D. Professor of History, Indiana University.
EUROPE.

VAN RIPER, JOSEPH E.
Ph.D. Professor and Chairman, Department of Geography, State University of New York at Binghamton.
EARTH SCIENCES.

VARCHAVER, MARY
B.A. Freelance writer.
PEOPLE.

WAGNER, HARRY L.
B.A. Freelance education writer.
LANGUAGE.

WAHBA, ISAAC J.
Ph.D. Senior Research Chemist, General Mills, Inc.
FOOD AND AGRICULTURE.

WEARNE, ROBERT A.
M.S. Horticulturist, Extension Service, U.S. Department of Agriculture.
FOOD AND AGRICULTURE.

WEBB, KEMPTON E.
Ph.D. Associate Professor of Geography, and Associate Director of Latin American Studies, Columbia University.
SOUTH AND CENTRAL AMERICA.

WEISSMAN, GARY A.
Freelance writer.
MIDDLE EAST AND AFRICA.

WHEELER, DONALD H.
Ph.D. Principal Scientist, General Mills Central Research Laboratories.
FOOD AND AGRICULTURE.

WHITE, DONALD A.
Ph.D. Associate Professor of History, Temple University.
EUROPE.

WHITE, ROBERT M.
Ph.D. Chief, U.S. Weather Bureau; Chief, Meteorological Development Laboratory; Research Associate, Massachusetts Institute of Technology.
EARTH SCIENCES.

WILLIAMS, L. PEARCE
Ph.D. John Stambaugh Professor of History and Chairman, Department of History, Cornell University.
EUROPE.

YARRIS, LYNN
M.A. Science Writer for Lawrence Berkeley Laboratory.
INVENTION AND TECHNOLOGY.

ZOBLER, LEONARD
Ph.D. Professor and Chairman, Department of Geology and Geography, Barnard College, Columbia University.
EARTH SCIENCES.

ZOLBERG, VERA L.
B.A. Assistant Professor of Sociology and Anthropology, St. Xavier College.
MIDDLE EAST AND AFRICA.

VOLUME 16

Literature

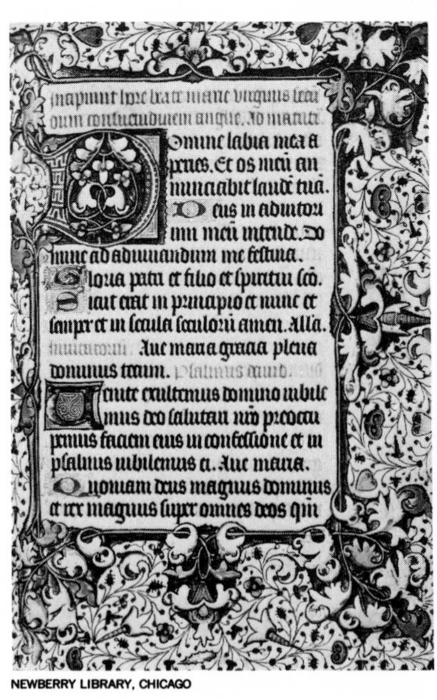

NEWBERRY LIBRARY, CHICAGO

TIME-LINE OF WESTERN LITERATURE

Individual works listed here may be found in the Literature Glossary, page 1297.

	Europe	England
1000	Troubadours *Chanson de Roland*	
1100	*El Cid*	
1200	*Niebelungenlied*	
1300	*Divine Comedy*, Dante *Decameron*, Boccaccio	
1400		*Canterbury Tales*, Chaucer *Morte D'Arthur*, Malory
1500	*Orlando Furioso*, Ariosto *Gargantua*, Rabelais Luther Bible Spanish theater: Lope de Vega	Elizabethan theater: Shakespeare *Faerie Queen*, Spenser
1600	*Don Quixote*, Cervantes French theater: Corneille, Racine, Molière	*Paradise Lost*, Milton
1700	*Candide*, Voltaire French *Encyclopedie* *Young Werther*, Goethe	*Robinson Crusoe*, Defoe *Gulliver's Travels*, Swift *Pamela*, Richardson Dictionary, Samuel Johnson *Songs of Innocence*, Blake *Lyrical Ballads*, Wordsworth and Coleridge

	Russia	Europe	Britain/Ireland	America
1800	*Eugene Onegin*, Pushkin	*Faust*, Goethe *The Red and the Black*, Stendhal	*Pickwick Papers*, Dickens	"Sleepy Hollow," Irving *Essays*, Emerson *The Deerslayer*, Cooper *The Scarlet Letter*, Hawthorne
1850	*War and Peace*, Tolstoy *Brothers Karamazov*, Dostoevski	*Madame Bovary*, Flaubert *Fleurs du Mal*, Baudelaire *Les Miserables*, Hugo *A Doll's House*, Ibsen	*Middlemarch*, G. Eliot	*Walden*, Thoreau *Leaves of Grass*, Whitman *Huckleberry Finn*, Twain *Red Badge of Courage*, Crane
1900	*The Cherry Orchard*, Chekhov	*Dream Play*, Strindberg *Remembrance of Things Past*, Proust *The Trial*, Kafka *Mother Courage*, Brecht	*Ulysses*, Joyce *The Tower*, Yeats *Animal Farm*, Orwell	*The Ambassadors*, James *The Waste Land*, T.S. Eliot *The Great Gatsby*, Fitzgerald *The Sun Also Rises*, Hemingway *The Sound and the Fury*, Faulkner *Grapes of Wrath*, Steinbeck
1950	*Dr. Zhivago*, Pasternak *One Day in the Life of Ivan Denisovich*, Solzhenitsyn	*The Tin Drum*, Grass	*Waiting for Godot*, Beckett	*Death of a Salesman*, Miller "Howl," Ginsberg *100 Years of Solitude*, Garcia Marquez (South America) *Humboldt's Gift*, Bellow
2000				

TOM SAWYER AND HUCKLEBERRY FINN MONUMENT, HANNIBAL, MISSOURI: ERICH HARTMANN/MAGNUM

VOLUME 16
Literature

CHARLES PHELPS CUSHING

VORIES FISHER/GOODMAN THEATRE OF THE ART INSTITUTE OF CHICAGO

FRENCH CULTURAL SERVICES

The first literature predates writing. From widespread Bronze Age farming and shepherding cultures, dating to perhaps 4000 B.C., several prosperous civilizations grew. The most fully developed of these stretched along the Nile River in Egypt; between the Tigris and Euphrates rivers in what is now called the Middle East; along the valley of the Indus River in today's Pakistan; along the islands and shores of the Aegean Sea; and down the Yangtze and Yellow rivers of China.

These civilizations appear to have had many things in common. The major myths that constitute the earliest continuing literature show considerable similarities. For example, many have a god-king who is killed, dismembered, and later resurrected. The god is Osiris in Egypt, Tammuz in Babylonia, Adonis and Dionysus in Greece, and Attis in Phrygia. The god-king's wife (later his mother), who is often the central agent in the god's rebirth or resurrection, has an equally multiple identity. The continuing descent, even today, of this body of myth links modern man with his oldest identity in the birth-death vegetation cycle of life itself.

Many of the early myths also reflect the engineering and astronomical breakthroughs, achieved most notably by the Sumerians (c 3500 and after), that discovered a useful mathematics of proportion and time; these myths were the beginnings of man's ability to control his own destiny. They served also as a source of power for those who understood the mysteries—a narrow class of priests or administrators.

One of the earliest collections of myths is the Babylonian/Assyrian epic of *Gilgamesh*. One of its heroes seeks magic to bring a friend back to life. He fails, and for his presumption is punished with death himself. The story was probably a way of warning men against "playing God." At the same time, it is a first taste of the mixture of skepticism and terror that has characterized man-centered literature ever since.

How to Use this Volume

The Literature Volume is broken into two large sections. The first, beginning on this page, is a narrative history of world literature, with special emphasis on the literatures of the Western world in the last 200 years. Among the features in this section are brief excerpts from the poems of the greatest English and American poets, including Chaucer, Shakespeare, and Walt Whitman.

The second part of the volume is the Literature Glossary, which begins on page 1296. The glossary contains more than 1500 titles, characters, and literary terms. In many cases, it gives brief descriptions of the contents of major works, and it always identifies the author and date.

Authors are *not* listed in the glossary. Their role in literary history may be found in the History of Literature section. In addition, brief biographies of most important authors can be found in the People Volume of the *Volume Library*. The index to the entire *Volume Library* (Volume 28) may also be helpful in finding still other references to writers, works, and characters.

HISTORY OF LITERATURE

Ancient Literature

By the year 2000 B.C. a high level of culture and prosperity were to be found in most of the settled areas of the world. Egypt and the Minoan culture of Crete produced arts of extremely high sophistication and creativity. But beginning c 1500, a series of violent castastrophes shattered this civilized world, destroying the basis of every one of the older cultures but the Egyptian. An almost universal feudal age ensued. Only after 500 years of "darkness" did the true written literatures of the world begin to emerge.

The East

China. China's first surviving documents date to about 1400 B.C. The high level of skill involved suggests written Chinese already had a long history at the time. In the Chou dynasty (1027–256 B.C.), the works ascribed to Confucianism were composed. The legendary Confucius (c 551–479 B.C.) was himself said to be a compiler of the works of earlier days. The Confucian writings we know today are later compilations done during the Han dynasty (202 B.C.–220 A.D.), at the same time as Rome's greatest age. The Five Classics (*Wu Ching*) of Confucius's canon comprise a chronicle of his home state (*Ch'un Chiu*); a system of divination based on numerology and chance (*I Ching*); a book of rituals and government (*Li Chi*); a book of historical documents (*Shu Ching*); and the great classic of Chinese lyric, the *Book of Odes* (*Shi Ching*). The *Book of Odes,* many of them simple folk songs, others concerning private experiences in a violent, feudal time, remains one of the world's most beautiful collections. As Confucius meant it to do, it gives human form to an ethical philosophy far in advance of its time.

The Confucian system was developed further by the teacher Mencius 372?–289? B.C.), whose *Book of Mencius* is the sole surviving collection. The *Tao Te Ching,* ascribed to Lao-tze (604–531 B.C.), and the book of essays, *Chuang-tse,* named after its author

LAO-TZE *helped form Chinese conceptions of religion, philosophy, and literature.*

(c 369–c 286 B.C.), are works representing a philosophy of oneness with the natural opposites of the universe; the philosophy is called Taoism. It is the basis of a major Chinese religion, and its influence has been felt in many Western literatures and religions. During the Han dynasty, the philosophy was codified and explicated by scholars, and it became the basis for much of the future Chinese civilization.

India. The Indus Valley civilization was set back by the catastrophes around 1500 B.C. as well. In the centuries that followed, the region was conquered by the Aryans, an Indo-European people thought to have originated in southern Russia. They assimilated the older civilization and glorified their triumphant history in the masterpieces of Indian religion, the *Vedas.* These massive documents in verse and prose, grouped in four main categories (*Samhita, Brahmana, Aranyaka,* and the prime source of Indian mysticism, *Upanishad*), gave rise in turn to an even more massive body of commentary and explanation. A fifth category, dealing with magic and superstition (*Atharva-Veda*), extended the range even further.

A second major area of Indian literature, that dealing with the life and teachings of the Buddha (c 563–483 B.C.), stemmed from a reaction to the excessive stratification of society imposed by the Vedic priest-rulers. The canon was written down in the Pali and several other dialects in the last two centuries before Christ. The *Jatakas,* or beast-tales, of the Buddha's early lives, set the teachings deep in the tradition of popular narrative.

In the last stage of the Vedic period (c 500–200 B.C.), the *Sutras* were composed. They dealt with every aspect of ritual and of everyday life. At the same time, the Vedic form of Sanskrit, the Indian literary language, was changing to the so-called classical form. Two great heroic epics were written in the classical dialect and they became the centerpieces of Indian secular literature. The *Ramayana* is a vast poetic "family history" of the warring gods. The *Mahabharata,* vaster still, is based on old stories of the lives of royal heroes. The major set-piece of *Mahabharata* is the *Bhagavad-Gita,* which asks Hamlet-like questions about human action and suffering in conflicting circumstances. Its themes have been echoed in the literary productions of many other lands.

The rigid class system of Indian society encouraged a formal, rigidly classical court style in literature. This stifled creativity; and India, for all the richness of its religious genius, never produced the humanist classics that emerged in other areas of the world.

Persia. The period from about 650 to 450 B.C. produced the great teacher of Persian belief, Zoroaster (c 628-c 551 B.C.), in addition to Confucius, Lao-tze, the Buddha, the major Hebrew prophets, and the early Greek philosophers. This period has been called the Age of the Great Teachers.

Zoroastrianism, whose books of law, the *Avesta,* comprise Persia's early literature and contain songs possibly written by the teacher himself, stands out especially. Its stark dualism—darkness against light, good against evil—has reappeared in religion and philosophy ever since. Such a world view is uniquely associated with the production of lyric verse. In Persia, the dualism—and the lyric poetry—survived into the next age, when the ancient civilization assimilated the tenets of Islam.

Greece

The beginnings of Western literature are concerned with religious definition, ethics, and military history. The Western classics differ from those of the East in their focus on man—for his own sake rather than for his divine significance, ethical code, or political identity. The difference appears most clearly in the classical civilizations of the Hellenes, the ancient residents of Greece whose inventions and ideas about the literary arts have carried through the succeeding 3000 years.

ODYSSEUS, *warned that the tempting Sirens are irresistible, has himself tied to the mast of his ship in an episode from the* Odyssey *of Homer.*

Homer and the Hellenes. The great productions of the early Hellenes were two closely related epics, the *Iliad* and the *Odyssey.* They grew out of oral materials and were first written sometime before 700 B.C. They are attributed to a man named Homer, about whom very little is known. As in many such early epics, the beauty of the *Iliad* is not in the invention of the story. That was already fixed by legend. The story concerns the war between the Hellenic states and Troy; historically, such a war may have taken place some centuries earlier, between 1500 and 1000 B.C. The fates of individual characters (Odysseus, Achilles, Hector, Agamemnon, Helen) were fixed in legend as well, and structural devices of oral composition were common to a whole class of singer- or reciter-poets. The early epics used similar descriptive epithets ("rosy-fingered dawn"), told of similar characters and situations, and sought explanations of national destiny in the legends of the past.

Homer represents the single inspiration in the composition of each of the poems (even though two or more poets may have had a hand in the two great works). His genius lay in using traditional materials and devices for new and surprising purposes. Rather than glorifying the Hellenic heroes, he seems to sympathize more with the family of the defeated Trojan hero. Achilles, the petulant hero of the Greek forces, is flawed at best. And Odysseus, the hero of the *Odyssey,* is more fallible than not, surviving only by his resourcefulness and capacity to endure defeat. Odysseus, whose return from the Trojan War took ten adventurous but often painful years, also represents the disaster that the war had been for Greeks and Trojans alike.

The ability to tolerate such contradictions—hero and fallible man, glorious battle, and disastrous war—is a mark of the humanist tradition of Western civilization from this time forward. It appears in no civilization contemporary with Homer, and there is no sign of it before these poems in pre-Hellenic civilizations.

No works, barring the Old and New Testaments, are more essential to the later development of the West: the stories of the separate heroes, events, and gods remain nearly as current in the literature of today as they were in their own time.

The works of Homer, once set, were enacted all over the Hellenic world by traveling performers called the Homeridae. A type of poem called Homeric hymns, composed from Homer's time to the fourth century, tried to imitate the grandeur of the epic in simple, sometimes beautiful celebrations of the gods.

A rival tradition to that of Homer and the Homeridae is that of the didactic poet Hesiod. It begins perhaps 50 or 75 years later than Homer's own time. Hesiod's *Theogony* tells most of what is known about the early Greek gods. His later *Works and Days* goes further. In associating myth with a day-to-day, useful almanac of advice for farmers and merchants, Hesiod bridges the gap between the lives of the gods and the rhythms of everyday life. Hesiod was also the first poet to offer something of his own biography along the way, and to consider the poet's reactions to be an integral part of the making of the poem.

Homer's epics provided the Hellenes with a central identity for the first time, a "school" to which all conformed. Hesiod's more homely works reinforced this sense of identity. But after 650 B.C. the world began to change. Individual city-states, particularly on the Greek islands, were building prosperous commercial cultures of their own. This was Greece's age of great teachers: the philosophers Thales, Anaximander, and Anaximenes in the 500's; then Heraclitus, Pythagoras, Parmenides, and others. These thinkers considered not only ethics, but ultimately the nature of reality, and of meaning itself.

The 600's and 500's saw the development of several interrelated schools of lyric poetry. They survive today only in broken fragments, but these first "serious" lyricists set the forms, and to some extent the subject matter, for the whole classical period—nearly 1000 years. Some of these forms and subjects are still familiar today.

The elegiac couplet, in which the second line slightly syncopates the rhythm of the first, began in the 600's as an exhortation to virtue or military valor. It became the ancients' prime vehicle for expressions of love, hate, sensuality, or grief. As used by Solon, the poet and lawgiver of Athens (c 600), it could express the injustices suffered by the poor or Solon's awareness of the privileges of the rich. Strung together in long chains, the elegiac couplet became the pastoral elegy, a lament for a dead friend portrayed as a shepherd or other innocent victim. Its form, if not its meter, carries all the way to modern times—to the *Lycidas* of Milton or *The Waste Land* of T. S. Eliot.

Other major Hellenic forms were the rushed, passionate iambic, invented in the 600's; the Melic, complicated "private" stanzas employed by Sappho of Lesbos and Alcaeus of Mytilene in the 500's; and the choral ode, first performed at Sparta by Alcman.

The iambic led to the great dramatic poets of the 400's, and less directly, to the lyric poets of Latin, Catullus and Horace. Sappho and Archilochus, the two great lyric poets of Greece, also contributed greatly to later lyric poetry.

The Spartan choral ode grew more complicated over a period of perhaps 75 years. It emerged in Simonides of Ceos (556–468 B.C.), and Pindar

(522?–443 B.C.) as one of the major vehicles of Greek poetry. Pindar's wildly complicated odes, largely in praise of himself, were in great demand at games and other festivals. Simonides, more conservative, was the poet of a new patriotism—it was he who wrote the elegiac epitaph for the Spartans who fell defending Thermopylae: *Stranger, go and tell the Spartans—We're still here, as they told us to be.*

Athens and tragedy. According to tradition, tragedy began with an Attic poet named Thespis, who added an actor to the traditional chorus that chanted or spoke choral lyrics. The new poetry of theater took root in an Athens that had become the most prosperous and most politically advanced of Greek cities. Each of the successive tragic playwrights added new complexities to the form, as if to match the complications in Athens' own increasing maturity.

Much of this great period of drama coincided with the lifetime of the self-willed political leader Pericles (495–429 B.C.). During these years Athens claimed the leadership of a coalition of cities that defeated giant Persia; then, Pericles himself began a catastrophic war with the rival city of Sparta.

The first of the great tragedians, Aeschylus (525–456 B.C.), had himself fought the Persians at Marathon and Salamis. His plays, frequent victors at the drama contests of Athens, are full of the confidence of a great time; among them are *The Persians* (472?); *Seven Against Thebes* (467); *Prometheus Bound* (date uncertain); and *Oresteia,* a trilogy (458).

By contrast, Sophocles (496?–406 B.C.) drew away from plays of civic greatness. He was critical of the state and sought greatness in individuals. The Athens of his long life destroyed much of its own freedom, and eventually lost its political independence through a prolonged state of military emergency. The treachery of the self-interested politician is a running theme in Sophocles' work, though his principal interest is the tragic victim, as in *Antigone* (c 331); *Oedipus Rex* (c 429); *Philoctetes* (409); and *Oedipus at Colonus* (401).

Euripides, the youngest of the three (480?–406 B.C.), seems to have given up on conventional patriotism altogether. He cares about the truth of characters and about the lyric power of his often complex verse. He does not believe in any grander morality than the injustice of human suffering. His plays include *Medea* (431); *Trojan Women* (415); *Electra* (413); and *Bacchae* (405). Nothing like the power of these three playwrights was to be seen again till the time of Shakespeare.

Alongside tragedy, a kind of drama now called Old Comedy was also popular. Aristophanes (448?–380 B.C.) stands out with *The Archanians* (425); *The Clouds* (423); *The Birds* (414); and *Lysistrata* (411). The writers of comedy used a mixture of bawdy humor and pointed topical reference. They mocked social pretension and shabby politics. Their form lasted only as long as Athens' original liberty. It was succeeded by the New Comedy, of which Menander (343?–291? B.C.) is the great exponent. His successful descendants may be seen in the domestic situation comedies of today.

Philosophy and history. Athens contributed other major writers over this period. The *History,* principally of the Persian wars, by Herodotus (484?–426? B.C.), is a first attempt, rich in background information, at comprehensive history. The later *History of the Peloponnesian War* by Thucydides (471?–400? B.C.) is regarded as the first modern history, going far deeper than Herodotus. Thucydides was telling of a tragedy that happened in his own time, yet he remained committed to a dispassionate, complicated view of human nature. The *Anabasis,* a memoir of military adventure, and a collection of anecdotes by the considerably younger Xenophon (434?–355? B.C.), provide color and add to our understanding of the time.

In philosophy, Athens culminated its history of academic humanism with the *Dialogues* of Plato (427–347 B.C.), a literary masterpiece and the central canon for 2000 years of continuity of speculative thought. Three dialogues center on the trial, defense, and death of Plato's teacher, Socrates (*Apology, Crito,* and *Phaedo*). They stand as an indictment of intolerance and as a major expression of agnostic faith. The works of Plato's pupil, Aristotle (384–322 B.C.), date from a time well past Athens' own collapse. They survive almost entirely from a later compilation of pupils' notes. Aristotle's pronouncements on literary theory were to have immense influence during the European Renaissance, almost 2000 years after his death.

The last contribution of Hellenism lay in the rhetoric of its lawyers, including Lysias, Isocrates, and Demosthenes. They tried and failed to rally the Athenians against the Macedon of Philip and Alexander the Great.

Alexandria and Rome

Hellenism proved unable to sustain itself in its homeland, but the classical civilization passed, almost intact, first to Alexandria, the Egyptian capital built by Alexander the Great, and then to a new people, the Romans, and another language, Latin.

The Hellenistic civilization of Alexandria bubbled with fresh ideas, but bore most of its fruit elsewhere. In the period when it had political as well as academic preeminence, it produced

OEDIPUS, *tragic hero of plays by Sophocles, discovers he has unwittingly killed his father and married his mother, as an oracle foretold at his birth.*

GREEK PRESS AND INFORMATION SERVICE

only one great poet, but he is as moving today as he was in his own time. Callimachus (c 265 B.C.) wrote with a strange blend of down-to-earth irony, philological correctness, and formal originality. He resembled a combination of Robert Frost and T. S. Eliot.

Also notable among Callimachus' prolific contemporaries were the slightly older Syracusan, Theocritus, and the somewhat younger Apollonius of Rhodes. The former began the tradition of the pastoral, based on the poet's beloved and rustic Sicily. Apollonius was an Homeric imitator, retelling the story of Jason and the Golden Fleece (*Argonautica*), and updating the heroic epic with a sentimental love story. Both were to have numerous imitators.

The greatest value of Hellenistic culture, however, was that it served the new and powerful Roman state as a window to the past. In fact, during the Roman period, the last major works in classical Greek, all prose, appeared. Among the writers were the Jewish humanist philosopher Philo (20 B.C.–50 A.D.), who anticipated Christianity's later reconciliation of classical philosophy and Old Testament faith, and the historians Josephus (37?–100 A.D.) and Dio Cassius (155?–230? A.D.). The great biographer, Plutarch (46–120 A.D.), produced *Parallel Lives,* which served Shakespeare and many others as the best anecdotal introduction to the Greek and Roman worlds. Latest of all, the literary parodist, Lucian (second century), wrote *True History*, a deliberately absurd romantic novel that is a predecessor to the satires of Rabelais and Jonathan Swift.

The Roman republic. Rome's serious literary works date from the time of Livius Andronicus (c 240 B.C.), who eased his life as a slave by producing plays adapted from the New Comedy into Latin. He also translated the *Odyssey* and generally made the Romans aware of the attractions of the older Greek culture during the time of Rome's great wars against Carthage. The leading military family, the Scipios, led in sponsoring Greek studies and original Latin works.

The comic playwright Plautus (254?–184 B.C.) stands as the major original talent of this time. His New Comedy farces, modeled on the Greek plays (for example, *Amphitryon*; *Menaechmi*; *Miles Gloriosus*; *Pseudolus*), have since served as models themselves for Shakespeare, Molière, and others. The technical innovator Quintus Ennius undertook at the turn of the second century to introduce into Latin verse the elaborate Greek rules of scansion and the hexameter. Called by Vergil the "father of Latin verse," he survives today only in fragments, as does the slightly later Lucilius, orginator of Latin satire.

Many Romans, led by the conservative Cato the Elder (234–149 B.C.), fought the new style, considered weakening to the Roman character. Cato himself wrote in as rude and plainspoken a manner as he could manage. But Rome's triumphs brought the wealth and the slaves that made the weakening inevitable. Some of the slaves, from vastly more cultured backgrounds, provided important reservoirs of "native" talent.

Terence, the second century writer of more sophisticated, if less zesty, comedies (for example, *Phormio*), was a freed slave, born in Carthage. Polybius, (205?–125 B.C.), whose *History*, today surviving in extensive fragments, was a cross-cultural survey of the world, had been a Greek statesmen, and was brought to Rome as a hostage.

A century later, the slave Parthenius of Bithynia opened the techniques of the Hellenistic lyric poets to Latin poets. One of these, Gaius Valerius Catullus, wrote some of the world's most lasting lyrics, serious, scurrilous, and beautiful at once, before a premature death in 54 B.C. A second original master was the didactic poet Lucretius (96?–55 B.C.), whose *De Rerum Natura* included unique anticipations of modern scientific thought. Lucretius also displayed a frenzy for truth-telling, akin to that of the later English visionary, Blake.

In the last stages of the Roman republic, dominated politically by Julius Caesar, the greatest prose came from Caesar himself, clear, interested and alive, describing the military campaigns that opened Western Europe. Other notable prose appeared in the philosophy, orations, and especially the letters of the statesman, Cicero. These later served as a model for a particularly dry style among Renaissance academics.

The biased but informative histories of Sallust (86–34 B.C.) also stand out, as does the encylopedic curiosity of the learned Publius Varro (first century B.C.), whose study of contemporary farming practice was essential for researchers of a later age.

The Augustan age and after. The Roman republic ended with the rise of Caesar's successor, Augustus. A certain kind of spontaneity disappeared from Latin literature. Yet the poets of the empire, beginning with those of Augustus's time, were those that carried to Europe's Middle Ages and became models for writers of the Renaissance.

The greatest of the poets of the Roman Empire was Vergil (Publius Vergilius Maro, 70–19 B.C.), who found his medium early in his *Eclogues* and *Georgics,* modeled on the pastorals of Theocritus and on Hesiod's *Works and Days.* With a young man's fire and a certain gift for mystery and prophecy, Vergil seemed to later Christian readers almost a prophet outside the faith. In his masterpiece, the *Aeneid,* he lifted his target to the model of Homer himself, and sought to create an artificial myth of Rome's greatness. The *Aeneid* has been one of the world's great enduring works. It has nobility and strength of character, despite its sycophantic praise of authority throughout.

But within Vergil's own time the old Roman temperament he celebrated had begun to disappear. For the lyric master, Horace (Quintus Horatius Flaccus, 65–8 B.C.), writing in Augustus's Rome meant adopting a rigidly virtuous stance in his patriotic odes. Fortunately, he exercised more independence in private lyrics praising friendship, wine, and love. The works of the lesser but important Tibullus (54?–18? B.C.), and Propertius (50?–15? B.C.) indicate something of the pressures of the new Roman way of life in their general dissatisfaction, even in sophisticated elegies of love.

Seemingly the most "lightweight" poet of all, Ovid (Publius Ovidius Naso, 43 B.C.–18 A.D.) was the one who caught the spirit of the age. At first a poet of love (*Amores*), he later wrote the *Metamorphoses*, the Latin work most thoroughly mined for ideas, images, and quotes by later cultures. The *Metamorphoses*, a synthesis of myths of the imagination, reflected the creative energy of an age of religious excitement, resonating in Roman mystery cults that sensed an even deeper tumult in the Eastern empire.

After the death of Ovid, exiled for a never-explained violation of the imperial morality, poetic attainment diminished. Several poets important to later generations came from Spain: Seneca the Younger, a philosopher and tragedian whose work influenced Renaissance playwrights and classicists; Seneca's nephew, the young and very talented Lucan, who lost his life in the same year as his uncle (65 A.D.) in a republican conspiracy; and the epigrammatist, Martial (40–104 A.D.).

First century poets of great influence in the Middle Ages included the moral satirist, Persius; and a follower of Vergilian epic, Statius.

The last great Latin poet was Juvenal (60?–140? A.D.), a man from the country who wrote bitter satires about the city's wickedness. Juvenal's poems won a following from many later classicists, reaching down to Dr. Johnson, whose love-hate for London in the 1700's was much like Juvenal's for Rome.

In prose, the later period boasts several important works. Histories of Livy (59 B.C.–17 A.D.) and the great Tacitus (55–117 A.D.); the technical writings of Frontinus (first century A.D.); the inaccurate but pioneering natural science of Pliny the Elder (23–79 A.D.); the letters of Pliny the Younger (62–113 A.D.); and the criticism of rhetoric and literature of Quintilian (c 35–95 A.D.) all stand out.

The Two Bibles

The Hebrew-Christian Bibles represent a tradition of moral and psychological humanism as old as that of the classical world, but centered on man's relation with God. They played the major inspirational role in the history of the West after the collapse of the classical civilization of Greece and Rome after 300 A.D.

The Jewish Scriptures. The early Jews spent more time in slavery than out of it. Their religion concentrated on man's self-respect as it stems from his own conscience. Escape from Egyptian bondage occurred early in the "time of troubles" (after 1500 B.C.). The oldest material in the Bible dates from this time.

From the time of David (c 1012–c 972 B.C.), to a period shortly after the fall of the Northern Kingdom (722 B.C.), at least three major hands may be seen reshaping the material of the ancient legends. Further revisions date from the period of *Deuteronomy* (600's), *Leviticus* (500's), and the century after the return from Babylonian exile (that is, after 537), when a new orthodoxy was established. The text of the *Pentateuch* (the first five books of the Jewish canon—and of the Christian Bible), which with *Joshua* represents the central witness, includes ancient material sometimes left intact, sometimes cut, reorganized, and reshaped, and sometimes amplified with new material that stemmed from rival traditions. Large bodies of interpolation, explanation, and religious, moral, or legal codes, all stemming from the needs and prevailing wisdom of the times, are included as well.

A second body of biblical wisdom grew up over the same ages. The older exemplars (for example, Joshua) were often practical as well as religious leaders. The later prophets (for example, Isaiah and Jeremiah) were Judaism's great teachers of righteousness, as often railing against a Jewish king as against foreign domination. After the writings of the prophets in importance come the works called Holy Writings (*Psalms, Proverbs, Job*), and Scrolls (*Song of Solomon, Lamentations, Daniel*). In these works individual witness, parable, and lyric counted for very nearly as much as the Law, but stood always apart from it.

The New Testament. The Gospels and the associated writings that make up the New Testament occupy a single extended generation of perhaps 150 years.

By the time of the Gospels, the greatest period of creativity in Judaism had long since ended. Aramaic and Greek had replaced Hebrew both as spoken language and as a literary tongue. Fresh thinking in Judaism continued, however. The Apocrypha (valuable works, but not with full religious authority), and such recent discoveries as the Dead Sea Scrolls, give some idea of the kinds of originality involved.

The Christians knew that their teachings promised more, and demanded more, than either classicism or ritual observance had to offer. At a time when the breakdown of civilization made something like Old Testament slavery the universal condition of the Mediterranean peoples, Christianity restored a relationship with a living God irrespective of the government or culture of the day. It did so with an historic Savior of common birth, but of transcending vision, the more believable for the tragic reality of his suffering.

The Gospels told their story artlessly, in simple, everyday Greek. No one has ever translated classical Greek or Latin masterpieces with full satisfaction into the vernacular modern languages. The Bible, on the other hand, translates beautifully, and has essentially created the modern form of several languages. The poetry of ancient Hebrew and the prose of Greek Gospels were written in languages of participation, not exclusion; they were vernacular, not highly structured, literary languages. Christianity demanded the lives of its believers, and offered eternal life in return, promising in the interim the self-respect to live decently, and in good conscience. The acceptance of this revelation transformed society. Nothing that kings or priests or warriors did would ever matter again in quite the same way. This vision, both Jewish and Christian, became, with classical humanism, the second great thread in the new civilization of the West. From the Middle Ages to modern times, the story of literature is woven of these two strands; in all the centuries, they have rarely been far apart, yet they have never lost their own separate identities.

The Middle Ages

Lapsed time photography can present a quickened "movie" of the otherwise imperceptible growth of a galaxy, a weather front, or a tree. The same technique, applied to the first 1500 years after Christ, would show a whirlwind of destruction, all over the world, and then the emergence (particularly in the eighth and ninth centuries, and again in the eleventh through the thirteenth centuries) of thin veneers of culture—in Japan, China, and Islamic nations, and in isolated locations in Europe. The destruction and the gradual rebuilding remade the racial and linguistic map of the human race. The West, hardest hit of all in the early years, emerged at the end of the period with the civilization of the future, based not on the dominance of one group or language, but on diversity itself. Its varied literatures made no firm distinctions between the spoken and the written word. These literatures shared, in varying measures, the classical past, Christianity, and a new stock of Germanic and Celtic history and myth. From these new combinations grew new literatures and a new family of ideas.

The East

China. Po Chü-i (772–846 A.D.) was one of the greatest of the poets of China's classical literary age, during the T'ang dynasty. One of his famous poems tells of the unjust death of a particularly beautiful concubine. A second poem, written after Po Chü-i himself had been banished, tells of hearing a reference to the story in the song of a woman who similarly had once been famous at court. The garments of all who heard, says Po Chü-i, were soiled with tears; not least, the coat of the junior civil servant that he himself had now become.

The poems demonstrate the range of the Chinese style. Their technique of allusion can evoke a history of current catastrophe in a few sentimental references. The poems also demonstrate the range of the Chinese reality. A highly developed and literate civil service existed at the top, with a vast continent of poverty, isolation, and "hillbilly music," as Po Chü-i called it, below.

Many Chinese, like Po Chü-i, knew the miseries of the loss of preferment at court, or of overwork and under-reward while there. Among them are three other famous Chinese poets, Li Po (perhaps 75 years Po Chü-i's senior) and Li Po's contemporaries, Tu Fu and Wang Wei. These poets left the rhymed song forms of the Confucian odes behind, writing by extremely complex rules in a concentrated style.

Their immense popularity, despite the lack of any official status for much of their lives, testifies to the number of similar "minor civil servants" far-flung throughout the land.

Other important Chinese poets include the very early Ts'ao Chih and T'ao Ch'ien; and Han Yü, Li Ho, and Li Yü of the T'ang dynasty.

In the rather more academic Sung dynasty (960–1279), the most famous poet was Su Tung-p'o (1036–1101), who escaped from the growing conservatism of the time with stanza forms very nearly approaching free verse, and used a sharp political tongue that frequently got him into trouble.

As the high world of the serious poet declined, however, the rather lower one of the popular storyteller proliferated. The traditional stories began as folk tales or myths. Each new teller added his own innovations, and as tellers of genius emerged (sometimes classically trained literati, writing anonymously to save face), the tradition spawned popular novels of gaiety, depth, and complexity. *The Romance of the Three Kingdoms,* probably first unraveled in the 14th century, took 200 years to attain its present set form. *All Men Are Brothers,* a realistic treatment of a Robin Hood-like adventure, and the allegory, *Monkey,* date from the same period.

Later still, truly modern novels appeared. The most famous are the *Golden Lotus* (1600's?), the *Dream of the Red Chamber* (1700's), and the *Travels of Lao Ts'an,* by a businessman. Other forms of Chinese literature included the occasional fiction written in the classical form (for example, *Strange Stories from the Liao-chai Studio,* by P'u Sung-ling); the popular opera and theater, based on the same tales as the early novels; and a continuous production of chronicles, encylopedias, and philosophical and similar texts that continued at a high level almost to the modern period.

The Chinese mind in these works remains swift, keen in analysis and characterization, and tuned to the individual nuance, as it had been from the eighth century. Nevertheless, nothing resembling a modern, truly representative literature appeared, until Western influence, beginning in the 1800's, began a national renaissance.

Japan. Japan relates to China as the United States does to Europe—younger, bolder, but very reliant, particularly in its earliest stages, on the older race. Early Japanese literature consists of chronicles, often with mythical elements, relating to Japan's most ancient times. None of these can be traced reliably beyond the fifth century A.D. In early centuries, most literate Japanese wrote in Chinese. Inventing a Japanese written language meant a tortuous reconstruction of Chinese characters for the language.

In the eighth century *Manyóshú,* a collection of some 4500 beautiful poems, forms were set that Japanese poets continued to use until modern times. A roughly contemporary volume contains poems by Japanese poets in Chinese. For the 400 years of the Heian period (794–1192), the precise, always extremely sensitive style of a court aristocracy filled volume after volume of anthology with the perceptions and sentiments of a highly refined people.

In prose, a similar sensitivity was applied, often in writings by women, to the intimate doings and court life of the day. *The Tale of Genji* by Murasaki Shikibu, the *Pillow Book* of Sei Shonagon, and the *Tale of Flowering Fortunes* (author unknown), are the titles of modern translations of fictional and nonfictional works of the period.

After the 1100's, civil and foreign strife paralyzed Japanese literary efforts. Nevertheless this period saw the beginning of several major forms of theater: the Nō tragedy and its accompanying farce, the kyogen. Then, reaching somewhat beyond the immediate period, came the more popular kabuki and the puppet-drama, or ningyo-shibai.

The first of these is a slow-moving, highly ritualized, intellectually demanding performance. Like the Shinto tradition of contemplative worship, it seems to want to show the essence of life by letting contradiction, and time itself, flow of its own nature. Nō has had great influence abroad. The more action-filled, easier to understand kabuki has been, however, since its invention, the favorite of the modern Japanese.

The great figure of puppet theater and kabuki, Chikamatsu Monzaemon (1653–1724), wrote with sometimes terrifying conviction. Well ahead of westerners, he cleared the stage of "nobility" and made low-key, beautiful poetry of the tragedy of contemporary life (as in *The Deaths at Sonezak*).

The 1600's also saw the light haiku form converted to classical purpose by the great innovator, Basho, and his followers. This was also the era when the Tokugawa shogunate (1603–1867) resolutely set Japan against further contact with outsiders, maintaining the nation at a deliberately "feudal" level, but at peace with itself, for the next 200 years.

Islam. While great events in the Far East concerned the West only at a distance, the emergence of Islam in the 600's A.D. confronted the West for many years with a rival, a threat, and, ultimately, an educator. Within the basically Arabic Islamic culture, the special mysticism of the Persian people, writing in their own language and in Arabic as well, provided a unique and lasting influence. So, too, did the confluence of Islamic, Christian, and Jewish influences in Moorish Spain.

Arabic Islam. Prior to Muhammad, Arab peoples had composed aristocratic lyrics in extremely complex verse forms extolling the virtues of the Bedouin warrior caste.

The advent of Muhammad (570–632 A.D.) and the Koran put a temporary stop to such nonreligious verse. By the mid-700's, however, Islam embraced a rich and still growing part of the world. It produced several great centers of culture, most notably at Baghdad, and in the "rebel" caliphate that ruled most of the peninsula that became Spain and Portugal.

The reborn literature remained academic until ibn al-Muqaffa, a Persian, brought Arab prose to life with a translantion of the Indian beast tales, the *Panchatantra* (mid-700's). A generation later the poets abu-Nuwas and abu-al-Atahiyah wrote for the first time of contemporary Arab experience. Prose style flourished in the 800's with the writer of rationalist parables, al-Jahiz. Histories of Muhammad's life and commentary on the Koran produced works, such as those by ibn-Ishaq, al-Bukhari, and at-Tabari, that became foundations of Islamic justice. Works that influenced the West profoundly were those of the Persian physician and Aristotelian philosopher Avicenna (ibn-Sina, 980–1037), and of the Sufi theologian, al-Ghazzali (1058–1111). Among historians, ibn-Khaldun (1332–1406) has a worldwide reputation. The introduction to his world history carefully analyzed historical behavior on principles akin to those of modern sociology.

Throughout this period poetry and its related forms attained a level from which the West was to learn for many centuries. The greatest activity was focused in Baghdad. Some of the most singular talents were those of al-Mutanabbi (915–965), who wrote, he boasted, with an easy force as natural as a lark's; al-Hariri (1054–1122), who almost seems to anticipate James Joyce with his mixture of folk tale simplicity and linguistic invention; and al-Maarri (d. 1057), blind and, like al-Mutanabbi, a Syrian.

To Baghdad, too, belongs much of the provenance of *The Thousand and One Nights,* a work many Muslims consider slight, but which gathers up stories from Arab sources, old Persia, and Muslim Egypt, and so serves as a twelfth to fourteenth century catchall for Islamic magic and romance.

Islam in Spain. Moorish Spain was a world of extraordinary intellectual tolerance, where Arabs, Christians, and Jews taught and learned from each other. Arabic poets such as ibn-Zaydun, ibn-Quzman, and al-Tutili wrote to be sung, not recited, and laid the basis for what became the West's troubador and Renaissance lyric.

The glory of Moorish Spain, however, was the originality of its scholarship. In two works he considered incidental to his monumental comparative history of religions, the philosopher and statesman ibn-Hazm (994–1064), himself a significant poet, laid down a psychology of romantic love, and of the nature of stress and anxiety in the human personality. Nearly contemporary with ibn-Hazm, a philosopher of the East, al-Farabi (870?–950), culminated a long tradition of Muslim scholarship in Platonism and the works of Aristotle with an extensive reconciliation between philosophy and Islam. Avempace (ibn-Bajjah, d. 1138) in Spain carried the argument further and the great philosopher Averroës (ibn Rushd, 1126–1198) carried it to the point of near heresy. Thus the Islamic philosophers (aided by Jews such as Moses Maimonides) brought Aristotle and their own long tradition of learning to the West. In St. Thomas Aquinas, their contributions would become the central philosophic issues of Europe and of the Christian church.

Such influences, in a sense, never ceased. A novel of philosophical self-reliance (*Hayy ibn-Yaqzān*) by ibn-Tufail, Averroës' friend and mentor, emerged later as a mainspring under Daniel Defoe's *Robinson Crusoe.* The poem of a visionary journey to the mountain of Heaven and Hell by the twelfth-century Spanish Sufi poet, ibnu'l-Arabi, provided part of the inspiration and much of the detail for the greatest Christian poem of the next age, Dante's *Divine Comedy.*

Persian Islam. Persia's first literature was the work centered on its great religious teacher, Zoroaster (c 660–c 583 B.C.). Under the dominance of Islam (from the 600's A.D.), Persians gradually recovered the use of their own language and found a major role as the professional administrators of Arab, then Turkic, then Mongol Islamic empires.

The early masterpieces of prose by Islamic Persians in their own tongue are the *Siyāsatnāmeh* of Nizam-al-Mulk and the *Quābūsnāmeh* of Kai Kaus, both written in the 1000's. The first is concerned with the art of the government, and the second with the art of self-cultivation. The *Chahār Maqālah* of Samarqandi (c 1156) is a set of gorgeously written anecdotal biographies of poets. As with the Arabs, historical writing maintained a high level in the works of writers such as Gardizi (1000's), Rashid al-Din (1250?–1318), and Ali Yazdi (d. 1524).

Poets were Persia's chief glory, however, the greatest of them adherents of Sufi mysticism. Firdausi (940?–1020) wrote a national epic, the *Shah Namah,* which is still alive in the word-for-word memory of today's Iranians. Farid ud-din Attar ("Language of Birds," early 1200's), was an allegorist concerned with man's progress toward God; Jami (1414–1492) is revered as a saint. Omar Khayyam (d. c 1123) was

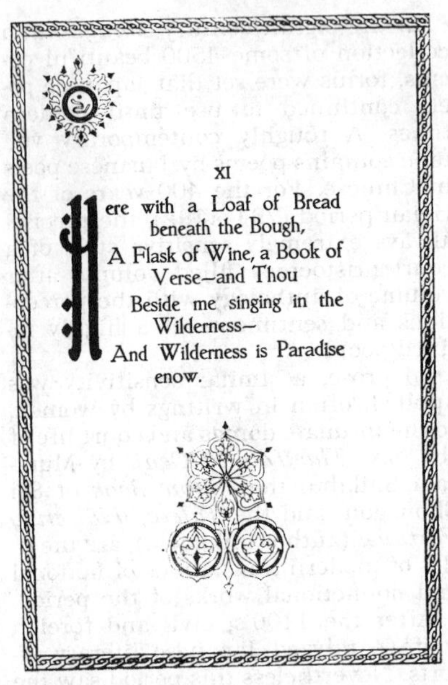
XI
Here with a Loaf of Bread beneath the Bough,
A Flask of Wine, a Book of Verse—and Thou
Beside me singing in the Wilderness—
And Wilderness is Paradise enow.

THE RUBAIYAT, *freely translated by Edward Fitzgerald, became a favorite with Victorians for its lyrical celebration of love and its world-weariness.*

a mathematician whose *Rubaiyat* is famous in the West through an extraordinarily free translation by the Victorian Edward Fitzgerald.

The two great Sufi masters of love lyric were Jalal-ud-din Rumi (1207–1273) and Hafiz (1300's), who was famed for sensuality, though many of his most beautiful poems are of family, death, and the everyday world. These poets of love have had particular influence in the West, and are often considered Islam's greatest poets.

India. The epics derived from the two great chains of Sanskrit legend were discussed in an earlier section. The period to 1100 A.D. was also one of enormous production in Sanskrit court epic and lyric verse. The language itself had become purely literary, not spoken, and the enormous skill and verbal ingenuity of its writers seems cold and academic today.

The Indian drama, in which aristocratic characters spoke Sanskrit and the lower classes spoke the Prakrit dialect, held more interest. The plays of Kaladasa, India's greatest poet (400's?), are still performed. Bhavabhuti (700's), another known playwright, is also among the court poets of greatest force.

The true Indian genius expressed itself most fully in the religions of transcendence and, occasionally, of reform. These religions sought an alternative to the hopelessness of the rigid caste system. For example, the literature of Jainism, written in the Prakrit dialect and in the Pali dialect of the Buddhist scholar Buddhaghosa (400's), has been of enormous influence in both the Eastern and Western worlds.

Indian mysticism includes an identification of religious knowledge with orgiastic release. The twelfth century epic, *The Song of the Cowherd,* represents this erotic ideal.

The folk literature of India boasts what may be the world's largest storehouse of fables, beast tales, and legends. Much of this remains in the oral tradition, but in written collections, the best known of which is the *Panchatantra,* they have become part of Western folklore as well.

From the time of Islamic conquest, Indian classical literature declined. In recent years, the novel, play, and other literary forms of the West have provided a secular beginning on a different and much wider social scale.

The West

The end of the classical period is often dated from the fall of Rome in the time of the barbarian invaders in the 400's. The succeeding centuries are often known as the Dark Ages, yet in these years the new civilization of Northern Europe was slowly establishing itself.

The new culture had many roots. The classical values were obscured, but never quite forgotten. Latin (in a colloquial form) was the language of the church, the one center of learning and memory that persisted through the period. At the same time, the languages and folklores of the earlier European cultures established themselves with new force as the power of Roman civilization diminished greatly.

The last classics. The inspiration of the classical world ran out in the last years of the Roman Empire, yet interest in maintaining the past continued. Athens was a museum of glories long past. Constantinople (now Istanbul, Turkey) became the capital city of the Christian Roman Empire in the 300's. Both encouraged an academic Greek for literary use. Among the works that most appealed to those of the Middle Ages are the *Meditations* (100's) of the intellectual Roman emperor Marcus Aurelius; the genuinely touching *Hero and Leander* (400's) of Musaeus; and a rather seamy epic by Nonnus of Panopolis (*Dionysiaca,* c 450). In addition, the occasional inspired hymnist could touch deep chords of feeling; for example, Romanos in the 500's, the poetess Cassia in the 800's, and Symeon the Mystic (949–1026).

Histories in Greek included the *History of His Own Time* by Procopius (500's) and centuries later the *Alexiad* of Anna Comnena (1083?–1148). For the rest, only a continuing tradition of that resilient form, the epigram, kept the ancient spark alive.

Latin. Latin went on to rather a different history as the backbone, in its late vernacular form (the Vulgate), of the developing West. In its ancient literary form, however, it showed only a few gleams of talent. A "modern" novel of adventure and magical transformations, the so-called *Golden Ass* of Lucius Apuleius, intrigued later readers. So did the Latin letters of Marcus Aurelius, the emperor, and of his former tutor, Fronto. As the Roman Empire reached its end, the principal literary works included the realistic verse paragraphs of Ausonius and the decorative epics of Claudian. The Christian emphasis is evident in the hymns of Venantius Fortunatus, and the anonymous, spectacularly pagan "hymn," *Pervigilium Veneris.*

The last significant classical writer was Boethius (480?–524), whose *The Consolation of Philosophy* served the Middle Ages as an intellectual sourcebook. Later efforts to bring back the classical style would also rely on compilers of texts on grammar, criticism, and philology such as Ambrosius Macrobius and Priscian.

As these few sought to hold on to the ancient forms, the Latin language was developing in new directions. On one hand, it became a basis for a whole family of languages, the ancestor of modern Italian, French, Spanish, and Portuguese. At the same time, Latin itself remained the principal language of the church and of learning throughout Europe.

Although it was far from being a "dead" language, Latin had changed since the days of the classical authors. Most of its speakers had other mother tongues, whether Romance, Germanic, or Celtic. They were not seeking a highly refined and ornate language, but a practical one, and so the Latin Vulgate reflected the different needs of its speakers, evolving a more "natural" and less highly inflected grammar and a more flexible vocabulary.

The great writers in the Vulgate were more theologians and philosophers than literary men, yet the lines between disciplines were not clearly drawn.

The translation of the Bible into the Vulgate by St. Jerome (340?–420) became the important model of the simpler, more immediate form. The new spirit of personal experience and confession, heralded by St. Paul, reappears in the *Confessions* of St. Augustine (354–430), whose spirit is echoed by such modern confessors as Jean Jacques Rousseau and James Joyce.

Profound debates on the nature of authority, philosophical freedom, and the role of secular knowledge accompanied the confessional tradition. From Tertullian and St. Cyprian in the 200's to the great scholastic philosophers of the high Middle Ages (1000–1400), Latin was the language of serious intellectual argument.

NEW YORK PUBLIC LIBRARY

A MEDIEVAL MONK *illuminates a manuscript with miniature paintings.*

As the Middle Ages awoke, its secular tradition awoke too. For a time, the Vulgate competed with the new languages of Europe, and the beginnings of European literature were still in trusty old Latin: the first miracle plays; academic comedies and epics; collections of fables and bestiaries; and an increasing production from usually anonymous lyric poets. These poets—especially the Goliards of the eleventh and twelfth centuries—felt free to use Latin for their own purposes, even cheerfully defying church doctrine.

Much of the documentation of the period, too, is in Latin. In England, for example, in such great historical works as the *Ecclesiastical History of the English Nation,* by the greatest scholar of his day, St. Bede (700's), and in the half-fabulous *History of the Kings of Britain* (c 1135), by Geoffrey of Monmouth, the identity of a new nation was first expressed in the old tongue.

The first modern tongues.

Against the framework of Latin culture and church education, the several Germanic, Romance, and Celtic peoples went through the slow process of learning a "European" identity they had never had before. Four small societies, each of brief duration, were the prophets of modern European society. They were the Anglo-Saxon, the Celtic, the Old Norse, and the Provençal.

Anglo-Saxon. Germans and Celts shared the British Isles from the time that Angles, Saxons, and Jutes began arriving from the European mainland in the 500's. Although often enemies, the peoples seem to have borrowed from each other's folklore and ideas. This seems apparent in the West's first great vernacular poem, the Anglo-Saxon epic, *Beowulf* (700's), the elegiac history of the last hero of a dying Germanic people.

A hundred years later, *The Dream of the Rood* brought Christianity to a new Northern vision. In it the poet relates the history of Christ's passion through the narrative of the tree that became the cross. This device borrows from early Celtic or Germanic; yet it also seems to prefigure the spiritual personification of nature that became, in Wordsworth and others, a major English theme.

These poems stand at the head of a small but very important body of work that occupied the first of Europe's two early literary periods. Other works include *Widsith* (seventh century, the oldest Anglo-Saxon fragment), *Deor,* the *Wanderer,* the *Seafarer,* and epics of the historic battles of Maldon, and Brunaburgh. The few lines that survive from a biblically inspired *Hymn* by Caedmon almost alone suggest a new world view. Sermons and other biblical narratives exist, and the *Anglo-Saxon Chronicle,* begun at the time of King Alfred of Wessex in the ninth century, continued till 1154. The Anglo-Saxon society was strained by repeated attacks of Vikings and Danes and was finally destroyed by the arrival of the Norman French armies in 1066. Only some 250 years later did it emerge in a changed form as modern England.

The Celtic languages. The Celtic people, ancestors of today's Irish and Welsh (among others), once controlled a significant part of Europe. They were driven by succeeding invasions to the edges of the continent (the Breton region of France), to the wilderness regions of Britain (Wales, Cornwall, northern Scotland), and across the water to Ireland.

Celtic literature reaches at least back to the 500's. Among the traditional bards are the Irish Dallán Forgaill and the Welsh Aneurin, Taliesin, Myrddin ("Merlin?"), and Llywarch Hen. The Celtic languages did not produce a major European tongue, although healthy local literatures survive to this day. Their larger impact lay in their treasury of myth and legend, which has enriched the various literatures of Europe in many languages.

The principal legends are related in two major cycles of stories, the Ulster (800's) and the Fenian (1100's); and in the Welsh *Mabinogion* (1000's). The stories gradually center on the mythical court of an actual patriotic hero who brought brief peace in Britain before the Anglo-Saxon invasions. The great leader is identified as King Arthur, and his history grows and develops through successive retellings to become one of the great traditions of European civilization.

In Europe's second period of medieval creativity (eleventh to thirteenth centuries), later versions of the story evolved. These versions became the secular ideal of the new Europe, itself a "table round" of conflicting identities, but of a single pagan and Christian history. New versions of the story continue to flourish to modern times, but they have left their Celtic origins far behind.

Old Norse. As the new European societies first got their cultural legs under them in the eighth and ninth centuries, a new wave of raids and invasions, this time from the Vikings (or Norsemen) of Scandinavia, briefly stopped the awakening.

One small group of Vikings who heavily intermarried with Celts from Scotland and the Hebrides avoided the tyrannizing impact of new Norse kings by settling the small northerly island of Iceland (c 867). It became the first Western constitutional republic (930). In 300 years of independence this tiny nation produced an astonishing literature. Icelanders preserved nearly all there is of pre-Christian Viking and Germanic religion and legend from authentic sources. The *Edda,* by Saemund the Wise, was composed before 1100. The *Prose Edda,* by Snorri Sturluson (1178–1241) is a prose adaptation, together with a discussion of the principles of Norse skaldic verse. The Icelanders also preserved Viking history in an account of Norway by Sturluson (the *Heimskringla)* and the authentic story of the first exploration of America.

But their contribution, like that of the Celts, runs deeper than their surviving texts suggest. The Icelanders represent Europe's first literary expression of the modern frontier temperament. The saga form, an extended chronicle, usually based on historical events, developed a clear narrative prose and an understated feeling for character. Its assumptions (for example, the importance of family and place) far outreach the medieval understanding of human nature.

Provençal. Of all the early creative societies, that of Provence had the greatest immediate influence. A virtually independent region, encompassing the south of modern France, Provence fell under the spell of the inquisitive and opulent culture of Islam. At the same time, its own cultural history dated from the first colonies planted by the Hellenes (from 600 B.C.). Between about 1050 and 1250, while the rest of Europe pursued war and crusades to the Holy Land, Provence was discovering a unique combination of Islamic sensuality and Western puritanism.

The developers of this new sensibility were the *troubadours,* singers of noble birth, more than 400 of whom are known by name. In lyrics of great beauty and freshness, they sang of sexual love of the purest kind, and created an ideal of fervent but hopeless longing for a virtuous and unattainable woman. The nobility of the troubadours added to their appeal; their numbers included not only noblemen but more than one king.

Assisting the troubadours, there were jongleurs, of lower birth, who may have "ghosted" much of the work, but they did not receive the credit. Among them are Bernard de Ventadorn, Bertrand de Born, Peire Vidal, and Arnaut Daniel.

In the north of France, the only slightly less inspired *trouvères* spread the movement in a different dialect. They wrote less true lyric and more extended narrative. They produced one true classic, the epic *Song of Roland,* a romance of Carolingian valor that almost attains the quality of heroic myth. The character of Roland himself would be used over and over again in other European epics, perpetuating the memory of the splendor of Charlemagne's court.

The flowering of Provence ended with the disapproval of the church. Detecting heresy in the region's Christian sects, the church instituted the first Inquisition in 1233. A century of torture and persecution stamped out the heretics—and literary and musical innovation as well.

Other European peoples.

The same centuries that saw the peak of Old Norse and Provençal, and a second peak for Gaelic and Welsh, provided a similar but less concentrated brilliance in other areas of Europe. In nearly all cases, these little flowerings used Celtic myth, Germanic heroic legend, and the new lyricism of the troubadours of Provençal.

Germanic. Early in medieval times, the Swiss Abbey of St. Gall developed a tradition of scholarship, religious writing, and extended chronicle. These bore a long string of progeny in the development of the academic German mind.

Creativity started with the minnesingers, who began by imitating the troubadours, and then developed their own, somewhat more realistic style. The greatest of the minnesingers, Walther von der Vogelweide, preferred requited love to the idealized kind. He wrote with a sense of absolute pitch for the truth of experience and of his characters.

The masterpiece of the period, however, was the *Parzival* of Wolfram von Eschenbach (1170?–1220?). It belongs to the Arthurian tradition, and surpasses every other rendering of the story of the search for the Holy Grail. Wolfram writes from experience of combat as a wandering knight, of the centrality of marriage in human life, and of the connection between pleasure and the ideal in physical love. For all its elements of magical romance, his is among the first works to understand the importance of everyday life to moral experience. This concept was to become one of the West's most important themes.

Among other German works imitative of the French Arthurians, the *Tristan und Isolde* (c 1210) of Gottfried von Strassburg has special importance to later writers. Similarly, the epics from the rather different tradition of Germany's own mythic past, the *Nibelungenlied* and the *Gudrun,* have resonated down through the centuries, appearing in modern dress in the operas of Richard Wagner.

The most original of the late works, however, was the *Meier Helmbrecht,* of Wernher der Gartenaere (c 1250). It tells of a Robin Hood-type character gone wrong—blinded, maimed, rejected by his family, and hanged. This terrifying Middle Ages portrait has been largely verified by later research. Its negative power anticipates the realism that distinguishes much of later German literature.

French. French literature generally served as the model for other European vernaculars. Richest of the old Roman provinces, France had the longest continuing tradition of culture. Its Celtic heritage added a valuable component.

Chrétien de Troyes was the first, most imitated, and most prolific of the Arthurian innovators in the 1100's. In the 1200's, Guillaume de Lorris and Jean de Meung, separated by an over 40-year span, successively composed the two parts of the *Roman de la Rose,* the most celebrated allegory of love in the medieval world. In prose, Geoffroi de Villehardouin, Jean de Joinville, Jean Froissart, and Philippe de Comines, in a succession of histories and personal memoirs over a 300-year period, laid the groundwork for the long history of French clarity and elevation of style. Standard forms of the period, common to most cultures, were the animal fables (as collected in the mock-epic *Reynard the Fox*), the short rhymed pieces sometimes taken from Greek or Latin anecdotes, the religious examples, and the rhymed epics of the *chansons de geste.*

Only one talent reached a surpassing level, however: that of the bedeviled poet François Villon (1431–1463). Villon's combining of his high literary genius with the half-criminal life he led on the Paris streets overshadows everything else of its period. Other significant poets included Rutebeuf, also a writer of miracle plays; Christine de Pisan, an early exponent of women's special viewpoint; and the graceful Charles d'Orleans.

Iberian. The major early work of Spain, the severe, powerful epic, *The Song of the Cid* (twelfth century), deals with El Cid, the great national hero of Spain. Jewish and Moorish lyric constitute Spain's earliest poetry. Later, a body of Provençal-influenced work appeared in Portuguese; later still, both lyric and medieval heroic legend appeared.

As Spain gathered force, important writers emerged late in medieval times: Juan Ruiz (*Libro de Buen Amor,* c 1330); the historian, Pedro

López de Ayala; and the 15th-century poets Inigo López de Mendoza and Juan de Mena. At the very end of the period, past and future crossed paths. The first printed version of *Amadis of Gaul* appeared in 1508; it was a prose romance of great medieval popularity, read until then only in manuscript form. Already in 1499 the novel *La Celestina* by Fernando de Rojas had introduced the exuberant new manner of the Italian Renaissance.

The Renaissance

Flowering in Italy

Between 1250 and 1300 in Italy, the basis of Western thought and literature began to shift in a new direction. This new movement is called the Renaissance (rebirth). Gradually, over the next two centuries, it spread through all of Europe.

In many ways, however, the early Renaissance masters in Italy were the end result—and the most impressive representatives—of the originality of the Middle Ages. Christianity had put the spiritual journey to a new life in God at the center of human existence. The new poets made that journey, too—they were believers rather than skeptics or scoffers. But they saw it in a new and more personal light—not as representatives of Everyman or as mythological knights in search of the Holy Grail, but as individuals.

This spirit of moral individualism paralleled that of the independent Italian cities, which first understood the possibilities of commerce in the new age, and which were often ruled, at least nominally, on a basis of consent of the governed.

Dolce stil nuovo. Frederick II of Sicily (1194–1250) was at once Holy Roman Emperor, German king, and king of Jerusalem. The Islamic, Germanic, and Provençal influences at his court gave birth to a new school of Italian lyric poetry. Cielo dal Camo and Jacopo da Lentini (sometimes credited as inventor of the sonnet) were among the many poets of this style.

One of Frederick's older contemporaries—far from the courtly conventions—was St. Francis of Assisi (1182–1226). The beloved religious mystic enunciated the other major Italian concern of the time, that of personal religious vision. His *Il Cantico della Creature* expressed a faith centered on the humble, not excluding dumb animals. In his follower, Jacopone da Todi, this conscious dedication to simplicity took on a metaphysical exaltation. A similar exaltation entered the lyric of love. Guido Guinnicelli (c 1230–1276) wrote little, but with a special sincerity other poets promptly labeled the *dolce stil nuovo*—the sweet new style.

Guido's *canzone*, beginning *Al cor gentil ripara sempre Amore/Come a la selva augello in la verdura* (Love rests always in the gentle heart/As a bird in the protecting shade of a wood) would be echoed in the lines of Shakespeare, Milton, and Keats; more immediately, its sweetness transformed the sensibilities of Guido's younger contemporaries. Guido Cavalcanti and Guido Orlandi, among many others, writing in the Tuscan dialect, followed Guido in divorcing the spiritual ideal from the forms of knightly service or religious faith. They saw the ideal in the soul of the poet, through the intercession of human love.

Dante. One of the younger poets of this generation was Dante Alighieri (1265–1321). In 1292, he wrote *La Vita Nuova,* a great poem filled with the new sensibility. But this was only a beginning. Through the first two decades of the 1300's, Dante wrote the *Commedia* (known to later generations as *The Divine Comedy*), which was to become one of the cornerstones of Western literature.

The *Commedia* is a visionary journey through Hell, Purgatory, and Heaven. While seeking to attain to knowledge of God's creation, the poem also points in other directions. The

THE INFERNO *of Dante, as illustrated in an early manuscript, shows the tortures of the damned, beset by vicious devils. Dante's hell is divided into various circles, each reserved for those guilty of a particular offense against God. Sins of the spirit, such as pride, are more severely punished than such physical sins as gluttony or sloth.*

NEWBERRY LIBRARY, CHICAGO

NEW YORK PUBLIC LIBRARY

THE DECAMERON *was planned as a cycle of 100 stories told by a group of youths who had fled to the country to escape the Black Death.*

traveler on the journey is clearly Dante himself, experiencing the trip as he tells of it. There are two guides. Through Hell and Purgatory, the great classic poet Vergil leads Dante on his way—a symbol of a new reverence for the ancient classical world. In Paradise, the guide is Dante's beloved, the beautiful Beatrice. She is an ideal symbolizing both divine and human love, a synthesis of religious and secular aspirations.

Dante also uses the *Commedia* to judge every aspect of the life of his home city, Florence, meting out the rewards or punishments deserved by its citizens after death. His concerns are strikingly modern: human psychology, individual responsibility, and love. Dante's God is not quite the God of the church. Rather He is manifest in the perfect geometry of the universe and in the essence of natural beauty (symbolized by a white rose). Dante thus essentially puts humanist principle, rather than church doctrine, at the center of the universe.

Petrarch and Boccaccio.

The generation that followed Dante extended the new approach into other areas of life. The vernacular *I Trionfi* and *Canzoniere* of the poet Petrarch (1304–1374), and the collection of earthy and brilliantly perceptive stories by Giovanni Boccaccio, the *Decameron* (1348–1353), provided examples of the new, man-centered stance that would influence every literature of Europe. Petrarch and Boccaccio were also among the many brilliant classicists of the day. They searched for manuscripts from the ancient past as if for new revelations from the Bible. This emphasis on recovering the classical past led men to hope for a new classical age—a new synthesis of religious and secular, Christian and pagan.

With intellectual discoveries came new critical ideas. As early as 1324 Marsilius of Padua asserted the sovereignty of the governed, not in temporal matters alone, but in religious, too. A hundred years later, the brilliant scholar Lorenzo Valla brought to light many inaccuracies in the Vulgate Bible by comparing it with the Hebrew and Greek originals. This implicitly challenged the view of the Latin Bible as a document fixed, changeless, and beyond criticism.

Perhaps the greatest challenge was in the matter of language itself. The Tuscan dialect of Dante, Petrarch, and Boccaccio—thanks to their brilliance—was established as Italy's literary language for the future. This achievement—the establishment of a vernacular language for literary purposes—was to be repeated over and over in coming centuries in every corner of Europe. Latin was not abandoned; English poets wrote passable Latin verse well into the 1700's. But it never again would serve as the major literary language.

The new classical age—which we know as the Renaissance—would mine the ancient classics for ideas half forgotten. But finding them, it would put them to new "modern" uses. The movement extended far beyond literature. In art, architecture, music, philosophy, and the physical sciences, Renaissance men would confidently bend the works of ancient Greece and Rome to their own purposes.

There was a party of reaction to this new thought and new aesthetic. Renaissance artists and scientists would be banished from their home cities (as was Dante), and even executed for heresy (as was the scientist Giordano Bruno). But by the year 1500, the new trends were irreversible. In the great religious disputes of the 1500's, both sides—the church of Rome and the Northern reformers—were arguing as Renaissance men. The Middle Ages had ended once and for all.

England in the 1300's

England's experience was quite different from Italy's. Conquered by the Norman French in 1066, its literature became a province of the French for generations. By 1300, English writers were just beginning to rediscover their own language as the influence of the Normans diminished. This language was a far cry from the Anglo-Saxon tongue spoken before 1066. It was greatly expanded and strengthened by the addition of thousands of new words from the Norman French—especially abstract words for intellectual uses. And yet it was not French at all; its grammar and its homely everyday words were Germanic. This combination language, owing so much both to the Germanic and the Latin-based French, we call Middle English, but it is recognizable as the basis for the language we speak today.

The earliest works in Middle English date from the 1200's and their concerns are clearly those of the Middle Ages. *The Owl and the Nightingale,* for example, is a debate among the birds on the virtues of sobriety and gaiety. The *Ancren Riwle* is a day-to-day guide for young women about to take up religious meditation. And *Brut* is England's first taste of King Arthur in its own tongue, translated by Layamon from the French. The 1300's were an eventful and often grim age in England. With the rest of Europe, England suffered a disastrous onslaught of the black plague (1348–1349). The Peasants' Revolt (1381) reflected deep social unrest, and the debate over the monarchy, which resulted in the accession of Henry IV in 1399, caused antagonisms that would result in a century of war.

In the last quarter of the century, however, there was a great flowering of literature in the almost-new language. The religious reformer John Wycliffe was instrumental in the preparation of the first (and illegal) English Bible. The second and more authoritative version (1395) was prepared principally by Wycliffe's follower, John Purvey. Defying the courtly French tradition, an otherwise unknown William Langland (1332?–1400) wrote *The Vision of Piers Plowman,* a common man's moral vision in a rough approximation of the old Anglo-Saxon alliterative line. The same line, used more subtly, and set into stanza form, appeared in *The Pearl* and *Sir Gawaine and the Green Knight,* both masterpieces and probably by the same unknown author (c 1390).

Other poets sought to adapt the European line to native purposes. John Gower's *Confessio Amantis* (c 1390) was a moral allegory of impressive power. But the greatest poet of the age, and the first great poet of the language was Geoffrey Chaucer (1340?–1400).

Chaucer. Chaucer was a strange combination of the medieval and the Renaissance. He wrote of an England still in the Middle Ages with affection and understanding. Unlike Dante, he did not put himself at the center of his greatest works, preferring to portray a vast panoply of characters from the England of his time. At the same time, however, Chaucer was an avid disciple of the new Italian writers, particularly Petrarch and Boccaccio.

In his greatest work, *The Canterbury Tales,* he created an English version of Boccaccio's *Decameron*—a series of stories linked together by their tellers. Chaucer's work is in verse rather than prose, however, and his storytellers are filled with life and particularity; they are still recognizable to readers nearly 600 years later. The most famous of the storytellers include the lusty Wife of Bath and the courtly Knight. Each person tells a story appropriate to his character, and the narratives range from the bawdy to the solemn.

Whether considered as the culmination of the Middle Ages or as a premature Renaissance man, Chaucer is the father of English poetry and one of the most winning personalities in world literature.

The larger fortunes of England took another unpredictable turn in the years after Chaucer's death, a turn that isolated Chaucer and cut him off from later English writers. On the one hand, the social chaos of the Wars of the Roses left little time or energy for literature in the 1400's. At the same time, the language itself was undergoing changes that would make Chaucer's poetry seem strange and crude to later readers. When interest in literature revived in the 1500's, the works of Chaucer seemed out of date and out of style. He was admired but rarely imitated, a great master with few direct heirs.

Germany and the Reformation

The period from 1480 to 1530 is one of the great watersheds of history. Exploration opened Africa, India, and America to Europe. Great discoveries were made in the physical sciences. And the world population began an incredible increase that continues into the present century. The spirit of the Italian Renaissance spread through Europe, with each nationality using it in a different way. The values of society and of individuals were transformed as radically as in the early centuries of Christianity.

The secular literary response of Germanic writers to the Italian Renaissance was small. Around 1500, prosperous townfolk produced popular ballads by the thousands; they favored humorous "bits" of narrative, *Schwänke,* in verse or prose. Among the most popular collections were *Nar-*

CHAUCER

Near the end of his long narrative poem *Troilus and Criseyde,* Chaucer sends his "litel book" into the world. He hopes he will live long enough to write something less sad—a "comedye"—and mentions some of the classical writers he admires. In the second verse, he complains that there are too many ways of writing English and hopes that his poem will not be miscopied, but be understood wherever it is read or sung.

Go, litel book, go, litel myn tragedye,
Ther God thi makere yet, er that he dye,
So sende myght to make in som comedye!
But litel book, no makyng thow n'envie,
But subgit be to alle poesye;
And kisse the steppes, where as thow seest pace
Virgile, Ovide, Omer, Lucan, Stace.

And for ther is so gret diversite
In Englissh and in wryting of oure tonge,
So prey I God that none myswrite the,
Ne the mysmetre for defaute of tonge.
And red wherso thow be, or elles songe,
Be thou understonde, God I biseche!
But yet to purpose of my rather speche . . . .

NEW YORK PUBLIC LIBRARY

renschiff or "ship of fools" (1494) by Sebastian Brant, *Till Eulenspiegel,* and the still popular beast fable tradition, *Reinke de Vos* (Reynard the Fox).

The high art and deep personal feelings of minnesingers had shifted, through the imposition of ever more complicated rules and religious content, to the new tradition of *meistersingers,* guild members of accredited skill but rarely of genius. Of the thousands of songs, fables, tales, and plays written by the most illustrious meistersinger, Hans Sachs (1494–1576, subject of the opera by Richard Wagner), only the melodies of some early Lutheran hymns still thrive.

German and Swiss drama, often on religious lines, came to life in the 1500's, but reached no high creative point. Only in 1624 did the poet and critic Martin Opitz help break German verse from imitative Latin styles (*Buch von der Deutschen Poeterey,* 1624).

CULVER PICTURES

GARGANTUA, *the celebrated giant of the works of Rabelais, was famed for his appetites, as the illustration clearly shows.*

The Reformation. On another level, however, the Germanic response to the Italian awakening was revolutionary and shattering. The makers of the Protestant Reformation were learned men who used the tools of early Renaissance scholarship to new ends. As far back as 1415, a Bohemian, Jan Hus, had been burned at the stake for asserting the primacy of Scripture over ecclesiastical authority. Late in the 1400's the great Dutch humanist and scholar, Desiderius Erasmus, writing in Latin and communicating with a wide circle of friends, composed a passionate indictment of corrupt church practices and obscurantism. His editions of Greek and Latin classics set new standards, while his Latin translation of the New Testament, working directly from the Greek text, thoroughly undermined those who rigidly interpreted faith based on the imperfect Vulgate Bible.

In the same era, the German lawyer and scholar, Johann Reuchlin, touched off a pre-Lutheran challenge to authority when he defended the worth of Hebrew classics. Like Erasmus and the English humanist Sir Thomas More, Reuchlin himself remained Catholic, but many of those touched by the controversy were later to join Luther in a reformed church. The Swiss Zwingli and the French John Calvin, both came to Protestant stands from a critical practice learned in humanist scholarship. Philipp Melanchthon, Luther's "right hand," learned at the same font.

Martin Luther himself, while no professed humanist, was a literary genius of idiomatic German who had shaped his intellect on biblical scholarship of the first order. His translation of the Bible (1521–1531), carefully composed in a German that all could read, established a German literary language much as Dante and his contemporaries had created the literary dialect of the Italians. The Luther Bible helped give the many separate German peoples a common identity for the first time. Luther also wrote the first of the great Protestant hymns that were to create a literature of their own.

The same phenomena—translated Bible, inspired hymnody, and the beginnings of a modern literature in their image—occurred in the same period in Denmark and Sweden. Henceforth the Christian literatures of Europe would speak in conflicting voices, with consequences no one has ever quite dispelled.

Renaissance in France

As the Germanic languages spoke for the new, so the Romance languages clung to the old. The impulse to find a rule for literary correctness, even for perfection, stemmed in part from the older societies' dread of rapid change. The threat of religious reform confirmed conservative instincts.

France had as many men of secular talent as Germany had of religious. Yet it often seemed to want to clip the wings of genius before they had fully taken flight. The Huguenot poet, contributor of translated psalms to Calvin's Genevan Psalter, Clément Marot, spent time in prison for his Protestant associations, but he wrote his epigrams, rondeaux, and epistles with a seemingly unaffected lightness and grace. Till his death in 1544, he was the focus of a host of talented disciples and sometime competitors. Among them were Margaret of Navarre, his own and Rabelais' sometime patron. From a related but later school came the author of unusually direct love lyrics, Louise Labé.

The greatest name of 16th-century French lyric, however, is that of Pierre de Ronsard (1524?–1585). With his humanist master, Jean Daurat, and five others, Ronsard formed the Pléiade, named after a group of poets in Hellenist Alexandria. The Pléiade aimed to create classic poetry in the vernacular by deliberately introducing every conceivable technique and form from older examples. The famous sonnet beginning, *Quand vous serez bien vielle, au soir a la chandelle,* shows Ronsard at his best. The image was drawn from ancient authors; yet it kept its freshness into the modern era when Yeats imitated it: *When you are old and grey and full of sleep.* Such imitations (or "thefts") are one of the great wellsprings of literary renewal and may indeed create new masterpieces each time.

Ronsard's collaborators included a much admired lyric poet, Joachim du Bellay, and a playwright, Étienne Jodelle. With their contemporary Robert Garnier, they laid the foundations of serious French theater. Major rivals in Ronsard's own manner included Guillaume du Bartas.

Then came the reaction. The critic Francois de Malherbe demanded a "purer" French and a more logical sentence structure.

In the writing of prose, less inhibited by its shorter tradition, France attained its highest levels. The generation before Ronsard had already produced one of the great individual voices, that of Francois Rabelais (1494?–1553). His *Pantagruel* (1533) and *Gargantua* (1535), and their sequels, novels about a son and father team of giants (inspired by a popular legend), combine an explosive humor with the Renaissance learning of a born genius. A physician, humanist, and random thinker of the widest range, Rabelais lets his narrative wander to speculations of real depth on education, philosophy, or morality one moment, and on the prodigious appetites of his heroes the next.

As with an earlier titan, Lucretius, Rabelais' own vision sometimes seems to overpower him. But the depth and vitality of his first two novels especially have made his special genius a source of delight through the centuries for both intellectual and more popular audiences.

After Rabelais, two other impressive prose pieces made their appearance in the 1500's. *Institutes of the Christian Religion,* a central Protestant text written by a 27-year-old John Calvin (first in Latin, then translated to French), became a model for the closely reasoned, clearly argued advocacy that the French have made their national trademark. At least as brilliant, but of a warmer nature, were the *Essais* of Michel Eyquem de Montaigne (1533–1592). They discover a prose style of tolerance rather than argument. The pleasure of Montaigne is that of time well spent with a wise, infinitely interesting friend, whose only deep commitment is to the virtues of friendship, skepticism, and self-knowledge. Montaigne is among the most influential of world writers.

The century produced great activity in a variety of other fields, including scholarship and translation. The translations of classical authors by Jacques Amyot, best known for his Plutarch's *Lives,* deserve special attention. Montaigne was one of many who credited Amyot with being the great initiator of a beautiful French style.

Italy's Decline

France, whatever its growing principles of orthodoxy, still had its best days ahead of it. The Italy of the period reached its peak and began a long decline. The middle of the 1400's saw a period of great literary promise in the Florence of the Medicis, signaled by the founding (1439) of the academy, with Marsilio Ficino at its head. Among its members were Pico della Mirandola and Leon Battista Alberti, the leading scholars of the time. Later came Lorenzo de Medici himself, a well read man and a talented poet; and Politian (Angelo Poliziano), scholar, author of the first masque, *Orfeo,* and a poet of uncommon sweetness. But before the end of the century, the religious fanatic Savonarola had called down a severe reaction (1481–1498) against the "pagan" learning. The 50 years that followed were to see Italy invaded and impoverished, while the church, terrified of Luther, asserted fierce intellectual discipline. Coincidentally, the recovery of Aristotle's *Poetics* in the mid-1500's seemed to offer "rules of art" by which any new form could be rejected.

A unique history demonstrates this progression. From 1480 the lively Luigi Pulci produced variants (for example, *Il Morgante Maggiore,* 1483) on the old theme of Roland (called Orlando in his Italian incarnation). They anticipated Rabelais with their mixture of brilliance and burlesque. The highly talented Matteo Boiardo spent the years till his death (1494) on another, never finished version, *Orlando Innamorato.* He introduced Arthurian material and made the story, though still lively, an allegory of love. Ludovico Ariosto eventually produced, and rewrote continuously till his death (1533), the version that won fame all over Europe, *Orlando Furioso,* as improbable as a Hollywood spectacular but as fast moving too.

This in turn inspired Torquato Tasso, the one "deep" voice of the four, to attempt a Christian epic of the Crusades, *Jerusalem Delivered* (1575), using Ariosto's stanza, the *ottava rima.* Tasso deliberately used the Aristotelian unities (which muffled rather than freed his talent), but his work was harshly criticized as insufficiently heroic and too profane for the time. A series of subsequent personal tragedies that foreshortened Tasso's career date from this point.

The work of Tasso was to greatly influence such English poets as Spenser, Milton, and Byron in the production of their allegories. Nevertheless, all of the epics of these four Italian writers, unlike their predecessors of Dante's age, are nearly unreadable today. Tasso himself is far more moving in his shorter works than in his masterpiece.

The return to outdated medieval romance betrayed from the beginning the new uncertainty of a people that had suddenly grown afraid of its own voice. Within a few years, the work of Giambattista Marino set a pattern for the gilded, essentially vacant decorativeness that ended the great generations of Italian verse.

In the interval between Pulci and Tasso, other good work appeared: the *Arcadia* of Jacopo Sannazaro, the criticism of Pietro Bembo, and the professional lyricism of Giovanni Battista Guarini. But only the sonnets of the artist Michelangelo reached the old intellectual and spiritual heights.

As in France, originality fared better in prose. The most unique work, the notebooks of Leonardo da Vinci, is more document than creation. With the so-called "Madrid Codices," only recovered late in the 20th century, they offer a close portrait of an irreplaceable mind.

The writing of history produced two great exemplars. Niccolò Machiavelli (1469–1527), famous for *The Prince,* a realistic guide to cutthroat politics, is much more himself in his *Discourses on Livy* and his *History of Florence.* He is republican in sympathy and well ahead of his time both in methods and perspective. Francesco Guicciardini (1483–1540), author of a classic account of Italian history during his own time—the disastrous first three decades of the century—outdoes even his model, Machiavelli, in his sober analysis of the process of national growth and decline. Both men had seen flourishing careers as statesmen taken from them by events and understood the changes Italy now was to undergo.

Lesser but significant works were *The Courtier* of Baldassare Castiglione (1528), which set standards for aristocratic behavior throughout the literate West, and the *Lives of the Artists* of Giorgio Vasari, the major anecdotal and biographical source on the makers of one of the world's greatest creative periods of art. Within the same field, the *Treatise on Painting,* a practical and theoretical work by da Vinci, and the *Autobiography* of Benvenuto Cellini, an extraordinary adventure piece as well as a self-portrait of the artist-egotist, are memorable.

Fiction achieved high color, if not a high level, in the short stories of such as Matteo Bandello, Antonio Grazzini, and Agnolo Firenzuola. Probably more important were the modest fairy tales in Neapolitan dialect of the folklorist Giambattista Basile (1575–1632). Late in the period the best prose came from a new quarter entirely: the scientific writing of the physicist and astronomer Galileo, who kept away from the "classical" Tuscan dialect and became a fresh model for clarity and cogency for a later age.

The tyranny of the national will, however, showed plainly in the fates assigned to Italy's scientist philosophers: Giordano Bruno, whose understanding of relative location clearly anticipated today's cosmology, was burned at the stake in 1600; Tommaso Campanella, an early advocate of the primacy of experimental method, was imprisoned from 1599 to 1626; and Galileo was forced to recant in 1633 and was consigned to house arrest or rural isolation until his death.

Spain's Golden Age

Spain and England, the nations at the southern and western extremes of Europe, are connected by many historical ties over the centuries. The greatest of these is also the simplest: the gold of the New World. Imported by Spain, it fueled a boom-and-bust period of religious and political crusades that effectively stunted that country's development until modern times. The same gold, essentially stolen from the Spanish by British piracy and commerce, became in England an investment stock for many centuries of expansion and economic growth. For Spain, the period began with the discoveries of Columbus and, simultaneously, the final recovery of a unified Spain from Islam. The only warning of decline to come lay in the age of intolerance (the Spanish Inquisition, 1478–1810) begun at the same time.

Extensive contacts with Italy (where Naples was from the mid-1400's under effective Spanish control) brought the full influence of Renaissance learning and creativity. From the beginning, the Spanish made the Renaissance an original force, with experiences from New World explorations adding a powerful element. The greatest area of Spanish work was in the theater, where other countries (except Protestant Britain) had made only the most timid of starts.

The first strides date from the late 1400's. Juan del Encina, his follower, the Portuguese Gil Vicente, and the later Bartolomé de Torres Naharro of Naples, broke from the tradition of modest religious drama and staged performances of appropriate courtly material for their noble audiences. In the late 1500's, the touring Lope de Rueda found that a marketplace audience would respond to half-improvised comic interludes. The later Juan de Cueva extended his audiences and his material even further with stories from the national "epics," the old ballads of romance.

At the turn into the 1600's, a veteran of the ill-fated Spanish Armada, Lope de Vega (1562–1635) created a new form, the play of social circumstance, loosely termed *comedia* but encompassing every area of myth, legend, and contemporary material. In such works as *The King, the Greatest Alcade, El Castigo sin Venganza,* and *Peribáñez,* Lope deliberately flouted the Aristotelian rules to win popular success, and opened the door to a great theatrical age.

Tirso de Molina (*The Love Rogue,* 1630, the first formal appearance of the legend of Don Juan) and Juan Ruiz de Alarcón introduced new elements in characterization and depth of conflict. The latter, born in Mexico, was among the first of the Americans who would one day return the Spanish language to greatness.

Reaching slightly beyond the limits of the period, the work of Calderón de la Barca (1600–1681) ended the great creative age. His philosophical plays (*Life Is a Dream* is the most famous) or almost any of the one-act religious plays that occupied his last years, bring up issues of belief and intellectual conviction that still occupy the Spanish mind today.

Within this 150-year span of theatrical vitality, many other literary forms saw high achievement. In poetry, Garcilaso de la Vega (1503–1536) adapted the Renaissance forms to Spanish use, especially with the invention of the rhythmically freer form called the *silva.* Publication of his verse in 1543 set a standard of serious accomplishment for years to come. The Portuguese poet Luiz de Camões wrote the *Os Lusíadas,* a remarkable modern historic epic combining the age of global discovery with Portuguese antiquity. His lyric poems, too, rank him as Portugal's finest poet.

In religious writings, a mixture of intellectual seriousness and lyrical intensity reappeared with the mystic St. John of the Cross (1542–1591), whose poems were influenced by the brilliant Catholic visionary leader, and author of a noted spiritual autobiography, St. Theresa of Avila.

Something of Spanish temperament may be found, too, in the "last" poet of the age, Luis de Góngora (1561–1627). But his taste sought an academically approved immortality, and the end of fresh genius dates from Góngora's success.

In prose, the strongest historical writing sprang from an utterly new source, the reports of veterans of the great explorations and American conquests. Columbus, Cortés, and others enlarged literature by simply introducing it to a new reality. The great monuments of these firsthand accounts by Bernal Díaz and Bartolomé de las Casas command new readers still. Both their works date from the later 1500's.

In fiction, the vogue of the pastoral, imitated from an earlier Portuguese model, was perfected in *Diana Enamorada* by Jorge de Montemayor. The picaresque, commencing with *Lazarillo de Tormes* (author unknown), provided "realistic" escapism to a colorful if not always believable underworld.

The enduring genius of Spanish literature, however, was Miguel de Cervantes Saavedra (1547–1616), whose *Don Quixote* appeared before 1620.

CERVANTES, *creator of the great character and story* Don Quixote.

Cervantes belonged, like Rabelais, to no school other than that of his own bitterly ironic but always hopeful mind. Designed as a parody of chivalric literature, *Don Quixote* matured in the writing and became a parable of the whole of human existence. As with the works of Dante and Shakespeare, modern man has built it into the center of his spirit.

Finally, Spain produced in Francisco de Quevedo an exponent of that brilliant satire in which Catholic humanism was to find much of its best expression in the succeeding ages. His *Los Sueños* (1607) is a prose piece of savage force. A poet and novelist as well, Quevedo used the language with a natural power that contrasted sharply with Gongorism, the triumphant school of academic style, which he hated.

Quevedo's younger associate in the war of "ideas" against "mere words," Baltasar (Lorenzo) Gracián, won only exile and disgrace for his satiric allegory, *El Criticón.* Nevertheless, its near-existentialist view of death had great impact on the thinking of rationalist and metaphysical writers of the 18th and 19th centuries.

England Reawakens

English literature, in deep hibernation from the time of Chaucer, emerged with startling suddenness at the beginning of the 1500's. The preceding century had seen the culmination of the long religious tradition of the miracle play, preserved in several separate but related collections, and the introduction of the vice-and-virtue homilies of the morality play (as in *Everyman*).

In 1485, the year of the accession of the first Tudor king, the pioneering printer William Caxton published *Morte d'Arthur* by Sir Thomas Malory. Though little is known of the author, he set the chivalry, violence, and adulterous loves of the Arthurian legend in the realistic light of a man who has known similar experiences firsthand. The swift prose rendering has great grace and delicacy, and yet remains plainspoken throughout. It was on the person of the next king, however, that the English Renaissance was centered. Henry VIII fought the battles of political liberty and religious conscience cognizant only of his need for heirs. Eventually, Henry would establish an English church dependent on the state rather than on Rome and set a new course for English freedom.

John Skelton, Henry's boyhood tutor, was England's first lyric poet in an age. He took a strong stand on the issue of personal and sexual integrity, both in his verse and his life. From Skelton's time on, the issue cost lives.

The great poet of Henry's maturity, Sir Thomas Wyatt, had been a lover of Anne Boleyn, the woman for whom Henry abandoned the Roman Catholic Church. Boleyn, Wyatt's own son, and Wyatt's friend, the Earl of Surrey, all were to die under separate circumstances connected with the violent politics of the time. Surrey collaborated with the elder Wyatt on the first English sonnets and himself introduced the blank verse (unrhymed pentameter) that would come to full flower in the plays of Marlowe and Shakespeare.

A greater writer still was William Tyndale. His translations of the Bible, made under a ban, greatly influenced the later King James Version (1611). Yet Tyndale was to die at the stake in Europe, apparently betrayed for expressing his displeasure at the king's divorce.

The statesman who most wanted Tyndale silenced, and yet the leading humanist of his age, Sir Thomas More, found himself, like his friend Erasmus, unable to break with the Catholicism of his childhood. He in turn paid for his conscience with his life.

The education of the English and their creative growth proceeded almost simultaneously. Sir Thomas More's circle, which included John Colet, Thomas Linacre, Desiderius Erasmus, and Sir Thomas Elyot, was responsible for important translations from Greek, Latin, and Italian, as well as for the establishment of new principles of education. In mid-century, Castiglione's *Courtier* and Plutarch's *Lives* appeared in English translation, the latter in the version by Sir Thomas North echoed so often by Shakespeare. The *Metamorphoses* of Ovid, translated by Arthur Golding (1567), had a similar seminal effect.

Later in the century, the accounts of explorers, firsthand or summarized, had an even more rousing effect on the freethinking English than on the Spanish. News of the lands westward had their impact as early as More's speculative *Utopia*. Full accounts of voyages by Drake, Hawkins, Raleigh, the Cabots and others took on the character of national epics in the making, collected most notably by Richard Hakluyt in *Principall Navigations, Voiages, and Discoveries of the English Nation* (1598–1600), a work later extended by Samuel Purchas.

Similarly, the English sense of national identity was fed by historical chronicles. Raphael Holinshed's *The Chronicles of England, Scotland and Ireland* (1577) became an important source for Shakespeare's plays.

Religious writing culminated in the sermons of Lancelot Andrewes—chief among translators of the King James Bible (1611). In a different vein, a masterpiece of the English rational but believing temperament was Richard Hooker's *Laws of Ecclesiastical Polity* (published in part, 1594).

BRITISH MUSEUM

THE TYNDALE BIBLE, *published in 1525. This is the first page of the New Testament as it appeared in the first edition.*

The *Essays* of Francis Bacon (1597 and later) expressed an early literary excitement about the possibilities of science. Thomas Harriot combined exploration, mathematical skill, and association with the "atheist" idealist poets Marlowe and Chapman, in a single lucid personality.

All of these strands—scholarly, adventurous, religious, and controversial—contributed to the astonishing fullness of this first English maturity. But the finest flower of the age was its lyric and dramatic poetry. Of the many who took part, the amateur Sir Philip Sidney (1554–1586) wrote from a life that sought to fulfill every aristocratic ideal; and the professional Edmund Spenser (1552–1599) saw poetry as a way to preferment. Others fell somewhere between these two extremes.

Sidney's pastoral *Arcadia* (1590) and sonnet sequence, *Astrophel and Stella* (1591), reveal a personality of major dimension, perhaps more important to later literature than the Italian models Sidney followed. Spenser, perhaps most himself in the amazing youthful work *The Shepheardes Calendar* (1579), created in an unfinished allegorical epic, *Faerie Queene,* whose first three books (1590) established his career, a gorgeous monstrosity that other poets (Shakespeare, Milton, and Keats among them) have imitated and admired ever since.

Among the gentleman poets of lasting brilliance were Sir Walter Raleigh, Sir Fulke Greville, and Sir John Davies. Those who depended on patronage included George Chapman (first translator of Homer), Samuel Daniel, and Michael Drayton. Somewhere between were Thomas Campion, and the Catholic skeptic turned Protestant cleric, John Donne.

These writers generally occupied the "high," or aristocratic side of literary activity. The playwrights had the great luck of a theater that almost accidentally made its life from a wider, more heterogeneous audience, leaving court performances for special occasions. Even during its greatest period (1590–1614), the theater never won the academic respectability of poetry, but it could earn a living for a playwright and afford him the scope and response necessary for greatness.

The middle 1500's had seen the first native English comedies and tragedies. In 1586, the year of Sir Philip Sidney's death, Thomas Kyd's *The Spanish Tragedy* appeared. Based on the Roman Seneca's work, its themes of revenge, betrayal, and madness struck something deep in the Elizabethan experience. Christopher Marlowe's *Tamburlaine the Great,* the next year, introduced a marvelous melodic lilt to the iambic pentameter line, together with a theme of heroism based on personal ambition rather than on public service. *Doctor Faustus,* probably written in the year of his death by murder (1593), places Marlowe with Shakespeare among those who have given the West its most basic prototypes of character and conscience.

NEW YORK PUBLIC LIBRARY

SHAKESPEARE

The greatest poet in the language used blank verse—unrhymed lines of ten syllables. Here, in the late play *The Tempest,* the speech of Prospero seems to be the poet's farewell and may even allude to the Globe Theater shown above.

You do look, my son, in a movéd sort,
As if you were dismayed. Be cheerful, sir.
Our revels now are ended. These our actors,
As I foretold you, were all spirits, and
Are melted into air, into thin air.
And, like the baseless fabric of this vision,
The cloud-capped towers, the gorgeous palaces,
The solemn temples, the great globe itself—
Yea, all which it inherit—shall dissolve
And, like this insubstantial pageant faded,
Leave not a rack behind. We are such stuff
As dreams are made on, and our little life
Is rounded with a sleep. Sir, I am vexed.
Bear with my weakness, my old brain is troubled.
Be not disturbed with my infirmity. . . .

Shakespeare. William Shakespeare, born in 1564 (the year of Michelangelo's death), died in 1616, the same year as Cervantes. He stands alone among English writers, and indeed among writers of the world. His masterpieces are not single plays, but, whether by intention or not, cycles—the magical comedies of the 1590's, notably *Midsummer Night's Dream*; the historical plays later in the same decade, most fully realized in *Henry IV, Part I*; the great tragedies of the early 1600's, *Hamlet, King Lear, Othello,* and *Macbeth*; and finally the romances of the last years, especially *The Tempest.*

Throughout, Shakespeare worked with the simplest of principles, writing at the mind's own speed, using everything he read, but reworking it first, and depending for character upon the defining trait or flaw. A favorite character illustrates his range. Falstaff, the fictional drinking companion of the young Prince Hal, was based on an actual early friend, the valiant, principled Sir John Fastolfe, whom the mature Henry later had executed. Shakespeare made him a drunk, a lecher, a glutton, something of a coward, and the wittiest man in England; he eventually had to change Fastolfe's name and leave out the religious issues that brought his execution. When Prince Hal (now Henry V) rejects (rather than executes) him, Falstaff, by this time the most popular character on the English stage, dies of a broken heart. His death scene curiously echoes that of Socrates' in the *Dialogues.* Shakespeare, unable to speak openly of the religious wars that were still driving friend from friend, brother from brother, found a way to show the treachery of a king, and yet continue to glorify that king's "necessary" mark upon the English patriotic scene. This is myth-making on an Homeric level, yet with a realism that is thoroughly familiar to the modern temperament. The last plays grow steadily richer poetically but lose something of their dramatic fire, showing instead a moving spirit of acceptance and reconciliation.

Aside from the plays, many of which were published only after his death, Shakespeare wrote two long poems early in his career: a beautiful, mysterious lyric, *The Phoenix and the Turtle,* and a collection of sonnets of highly concentrated power that rank among the great "private" poems of the world.

In addition to Shakespeare and Marlowe, the English theater boasted other dramatists capable of moments of great force: Thomas Dekker and Philip Massinger in comedy; the collaborators Francis Beaumont and John Fletcher in comedy and tragedy; and the accomplished but nightmarishly bloodthirsty Cyril Tourneur, Thomas Middleton, John Ford, and John Webster in tragedy. Webster's *The Duchess of Malfi* (1616) stands as the masterpiece among the later plays.

The other unique figure of the age was Ben Jonson (1572–1637). Unlike Shakespeare, he was a classicist at heart, preferring emotional reserve and a controlled, allusive wit derived from the structure of the Latin epigram. He led drama out of the open air and back into the schoolroom with courage and imagination. His plays, notably *Volpone* (1606) and *Bartholomew Fair* (1614) are still performed, and his use of rhymed couplets greatly influenced the neoclassicists of the late 1600's.

The Age of Reason and Conscience 1600–1789

After 1600, society was looking for a less spontaneous, more ordered universe. It sought to deny parts of Renaissance thought and to freeze the rest into a new classicism. But the revolution had already taken place. The conservative impulse—which sought to preserve not only old forms and ideas but old hereditary privilege—still had to deal with the rising new class that was gaining economic and social influence in spite of all opposition. The class of businessmen, professionals, and civil servants would seek to emulate the old nobility in some respects, but it would also seek to recreate the literary world in its own lively but determinedly middle-class image. The literature of the age, though outwardly sober and conservative, mirrors these changes throughout.

Italy and Spain

The countries of the Catholic Mediterranean, Italy, Spain, and Portugal, suffered through the 17th and 18th centuries. They were victims of economic decline and dynastic warfare, as well as the continuing conservatism of a threatened church. In the three countries, over a span of 150 years, only the tradition of humanist scholarly inquiry produced consistently solid work.

The research of the Italian archival historian Ludovico Muratori spilled over into literary history, eventually leading to a form of literary criticism that could challenge the prevailing orthodoxy. Muratori, the dramatist Francesco Maffei, the literary historian Girolamo Tiraboschi, and the historical philosopher Giovanni Battista Vico played varying roles in this. Vico's *Scienza Nuova* (1725) was a "rational" study of history concentrating on the lifespan of an entire culture, its "personality," and the circumstances of its life and death. Modern historians have learned to use this approach, making mythic sense of many otherwise intractable bits of information.

In Spain, where scholarship had just recovered its earliest literary heritage, a Benedictine monk, Benito Fijóo y Montenegro, introduced the cool, clear rationalist side of the Enlightenment, setting a point of view that would deeply influence Spanish literature through a century or more.

Beyond these few, other writers of the age were more important to their own time than to the future of literature. Italy appreciated satire (Alessandro Tassoni, Giuseppe Parini), journalism (Gasparo Gozzi, Giuseppe Baretti, and Pietro Verri), and the theater (Metastasio, Carlo Goldoni, Vittorio Alfieri, and Lorenzo da Ponte, the librettist of Mozart's *Don Giovanni* [1787]). The Spanish Enlightenment extended into the time but not the spirit of the 1800's. In Portugal, the national taste for writing in Spanish reduced the literary output in Portuguese. Only the poet Francisco Rodrigues Lobo and the wide-ranging prose stylist, Francisco Manuel de Melo, achieved lasting reputations, both in the 1600's. After that, a strain of sincere religious writing produced the love letters of a nun, Marianna Alcoforado (first published in French in 1669), which the Portuguese have identified as a unique example of the national consciousness ever since.

France

The state of orthodoxy in the Mediterranean area did not hold in France. For nearly 100 years, beginning in the late 1500's, France enjoyed at least nominal religious toleration. During this period the active contention of several beliefs, including that of the strongly reformist Catholic Jansenists, contributed to the keenest intellectual atmosphere in Europe.

René Descartes, born before the turn of the century, announced the brilliance of the age. His *Discourse on Method,* a collection of essays (1637), opened up the question of belief, and of meaning itself, to the logical processes implicit in mathematical thought. Blaise Pascal, a generation younger, widened the area of discussion when he seemed to suggest in his incomplete and posthumously published *Pensées* (1670) that nothing could be certainly known. His deep sense of the limits of human understanding contrasted with Descartes' greater optimism. Ironically, both men also sought to justify the Catholic faith. Pascal was persecuted for his Jansenist sympathies.

A key to the swift appreciation of these very complicated men lies in the beauty, clarity, and cogency of their very different but highly polished styles. France was a society in the making. The rights of the landed aristocracy contended with the new power of men in business, the professions, and the civil service. Style was the delicate link that held these antagonistic groups together.

Drama. The emphasis on a "pure," elevated style found its most famous expression in the rhetorical verse of the French theater. In 1637 this theater produced *Le Cid* by Pierre Corneille. *Le Cid* announced a new high style and standard of action that conformed with the aspirations of the nation about to become the most powerful in Europe. Corneille's later plays and those of Jean Racine (*Andromaque,* 1667; *Britannicus,* 1669; *Phèdre,* 1677, among others) spoke the language of Senecan classicism and conformed strictly to the unities of Aristotle, in which the action of each play took place on a single day in a single place and was of a serious nature. Yet the authentic vitality of the new French national consciousness gave these works a depth their Senecan models had lacked. Their style has typified expression of the highest French aspirations ever since.

Between Corneille and Racine in age, the great comic playwright Molière wrote on the delicate line between belief and fraud in masterpieces such as *Le Tartuffe* (1664), *Le Misanthrope* (1666), and *Le Bourgeois Gentilhomme* (1670). His mockery of society usually finds a better reception with English-speaking audiences than the tragedies of Corneille and Racine.

In a different vein, the extraordinary *Fables* of Jean de la Fontaine (1668–1694) achieved an immediacy of impact. They were simple enough to be read by children, yet they were sophisticated satire to the adults who understood the contemporary references and context.

JEAN RACINE, *the great French dramatist of the age of Louis XIV.*

NEW YORK PUBLIC LIBRARY

Criticism. The 1600's were also a great period for literary criticism. The establishment of the French Academy in the 1630's gave France the first "official" court of usage and literary taste. The academy fixed both the language and literary forms, insisting on the virtue of "correctness." The better critics, such as Nicolas Boileau-Despréaux (1636–1711) recognized, however, that the genius of each great work was its power to define correctness anew.

Outside of "official" literary creation, several works of the late 1600's became literary models. *La Princesse de Cleves,* by Marie de la Vergne, Comtesse de la Fayette, was the first intimate piece of fiction in modern Europe. The posthumously published letters of the comtesse's friend, Madame de Sévigné, popularized epistolary collections. The worldly, often cynical epigrams of Francois de la Rochefoucauld became a model for succeeding generations.

On another level, the sermons and religious controversy of a gifted set of divines, notably Jacques Bénigne Bossuet and Francois de la Mothe Fénelon, pointed to the sharp yet civilized argument that would dominate controversial writing in the 1700's.

Thus, by 1700, the academician's emphasis on purity of speech and clarity of expression had been turned, through the pressures of a thriving society, into a search for the truth that lay under the expression, and for a logic of reform.

STORM, SHIPWRECK, EARTHQUAKE, AND WHAT HAPPENED TO DR. PANGLOSS, TO CANDIDE AND THE ANABAPTIST JACQUES

CHAPTER V

HALF the enfeebled passengers, suffering from that inconceivable anguish which the rolling of a ship causes in the nerves and in all the humours of bodies shaken in contrary directions, did not retain strength enough even to trouble about the danger. The other half screamed and prayed; the sails were torn, the masts broken, the vessel leaking. Those worked who could, no one co-operated, no one commanded. The Anabaptist tried to help the crew a little; he was on the main-deck; a furious sailor struck him violently and stretched him on the deck; but the blow he delivered gave him so violent a shock that he fell head-first out of the ship. He remained hanging and clinging to part of the broken mast. The good Jacques ran to his aid, helped him to climb back, and from the effort he

RANDOM HOUSE

CANDIDE, *Voltaire's moral but amusing tale, has been a favorite of illustrators. It is shown here in an edition by the American artist Rockwell Kent.*

The Enlightenment. Before his 35th year, Voltaire (Francois Marie Arouet, 1694–1778), a self-made millionaire, had been imprisoned, brutally beaten, and imprisoned again, all unjustly and all in the name of preserving the prerogatives of the aristocratic estate. Yet he became one of the principal heroes of the movement called the Enlightenment—a sort of common man's codification of the Renaissance. Together with his associates, Voltaire came to be known as a *philosophe,* a humble teacher of wisdom, but one whose teachings led toward revolutionary self-assertion.

Voltaire's endless curiosity and irreverence was to undermine the system with its own weapons: irony and information. In *Letters Concerning the English Nation* (1733), *Éléments de la Philosophie de Newton* (1736), and *Dictionnaire Philosophique* (1764) Voltaire showed his great enthusiasm for engaging the minds of his readers.

He was a contributor to the great collective project of the age as well. The *Encyclopédie* was brought into being principally by Denis Diderot; it used not only Voltaire but a host of other talented thinkers and writers, including Montesquieu and Rousseau. This first great rationalist collection of earthly knowledge was soon perceived by the monarchy to be subversive. The first installment was published openly in 1751, but the last, in 1772, had to be secretly printed and distributed. The *Encyclopédie* was a declaration of intellectual independence for men of every class throughout Europe, allowing the curious to learn without relying on either nobleman or priest.

This strong nonfiction informational interest left its mark on other works as well. Charles de Secondat Montesquieu towers above all historians of his day with a comparative study of governments and the circumstances that mold them, *L'Esprit des Lois* (1748). His doctrines of the separation of powers and the importance of individual liberty influenced the framers of the American Constitution. The reformist political economist Anne Robert Turgot and the mathematician Marie Jean Condorcet first considered human behavior as the result of needs, rather than as blind destiny or heroic example. Voltaire's *Charles XII* headed a copious production of narrative and biographical histories, as the Duc de Saint-Simon's *Mémoires* did of personal reminiscences.

The philosophes and encyclopedists were not dry-as-dust scholars, however, as their fiction proved. Diderot's stories were perhaps his most ingratiating work. Voltaire's *Candide,* the story of an innocent who trustingly believes the philosopher's maxim that this is the best of all possible worlds, is a masterpiece, both comic and oddly tragic at the same time.

The outstanding novelist, however, was Jean Jacques Rousseau (1712–1778). He was both the least characteristic thinker of his age and its purest product. The *Nouvelle Héloïse* and *Émile,* together with the late *Confessions,* make a new connection, that between the writer's inward state (his psychology) and his contribution to the public good. For Rousseau, the spiritual journey of Christian literature remained, but he interpreted the journey in wholly personal and wholly secular terms. Man was to make his own salvation.

For Rousseau, and for most of the writers in the succeeding two centuries, a man was valuable or good not because of his station at birth or his title or his education; rather, value was to be sought inside—in the man's emotional core. This led Rousseau to speculate on the inequalities of his own society and to reconsider the very basis of society itself. Though he was no political activist, his thoughts were deeply subversive to the old French regime, suggesting the psychological basis for the revolution that would come only after Rousseau's death. He was also a prophet of an artistic and literary revolution, the great movement called Romanticism that was about to sweep Europe.

England

The religious and philosophical issues of the 1600's led to spirited discussion and uneasy tolerance in France. In England, they led to a bitter civil war, the violent overthrow of the monarchy (Charles I was beheaded in 1649), and an austere interregnum during which literature concerned itself with controversy or (as with the theater) was simply outlawed. Only after the restoration of the monarchy in 1660 did the political situation become more stable and the social climate more permissive.

1600–1660. The poetry of the early 1600's was restrained and often intentionally crabbed. The exuberance of the age of Elizabeth had soured, leaving a polished but often cynical kind of "cavalier" poetry and an inward religious poetry we know as "metaphysical." Some poets worked in both styles or in some amalgam of the two. Two poets produced great poems, though small in scale: the uncommon religious poet, George Herbert (1593–1633), and Robert Herrick (1591–1674), whose work unexpectedly swims out of repetitively worked conceits to an occasional freshness and sincerity. The great favorite of the 20th century has been the eccentric Andrew Marvell (1621–1678), whose private combination of the cavalier and the metaphysical helped him reflect on the losses and achievements of his violent times.

In prose, the *Anatomy of Melancholy* (1621) of Robert Burton set out to be a psychological and physiological treatise. *Religio Medici* (1635) and *Hydriotaphia: Urne-Buriall* (1658) by the physician, Sir Thomas Browne, sought to reconcile science, personal faith, and the certainty of mortality. In effect, however, those books became portraits of the authors' minds, and mirrors for the speculations of their readers. With the works of Thomas Hobbes, particularly the *Leviathan* (1651), another sort of philosophical literature was born. Hobbes questioned the organization of society itself, gave little quarter to mankind, reflecting that most human lives are "nasty, brutish and short."

Hobbes's reduction of philosophy to simple and observable principles pointed forward to the great philosophical treatises of John Locke (1632–1704) and his successors, George Berkeley (1685–1753) and David Hume (1711–1776). Though not intended as pure literature, these works helped develop a precise yet idiomatic prose for "practical" use. It would gradually be reflected in more literary works through the 1700's.

History had a special appeal to those who were witnessing it and were often its victims. The Earl of Clarendon (Edward Hyde), an adviser to kings and an opponent of the Puritan forces of Oliver Cromwell, wrote a *History of the Rebellion* (posthumously published, 1702–1704), an important source for modern historians, but also a distinguished example of the literary polemics of the age. Thus, summing up the rebellion leader Oliver Cromwell, Clarendon writes:

> In a word, as he had all the wickednesses against which damnation is denounced and for which hellfire is prepared, so he had some virtues which have caused the memory of some men in all ages to be celebrated; and he will be looked upon by posterity as a brave, bad man.

Perhaps more important to contemporaries were the sermons and meditations of the famous preachers. The warfare of the century centered around issues of religious belief and practice, challenging the conscience of every man and woman. The meditations of John Donne stirred his listeners in the early 1600's, still echoing the exuberance of the previous age. Jeremy Taylor, a Church of England minister imprisoned and later reduced to teaching school during Cromwell's reign, published *Holy Living* (1650) and *Holy Dying* (1651), devotional books of great warmth and conviction. One of Taylor's early works, *Liberty of Prophesying,* dealt somewhat ahead of its time with the hope of religious toleration, a hope realized only after the death of thousands on both sides of the war between Episcopalian and Puritan parties.

Milton. The greatest English writer of the century was identified with the Puritan cause. John Milton (1608–1674) produced a few brilliant early poems (such as "Lycidas") before the civil war. He made vigorous efforts for the cause that eventually became Cromwell's, contributing his ability as a writer and his learning, and advising the government on both domestic and foreign affairs. Milton had enormous talents, but he had an equally passionate sense of personal responsibility for his ideas and beliefs. His prose pamphlets in favor of divorce, and against prior censorship of the press *(Areopagitica),* dared the prevailing ideas even of his own party.

The restoration of the monarchy (1660) ended Milton's government service. He had become blind and without property or financial resources. During the next few years he wrote the one great epic in modern English, *Paradise Lost* (1667). It retells the story of Adam and Eve and of their temptation by Satan and fall from God's favor.

The story of Satan's rebellion can be read in the light of the actual rebellion in which Milton had taken part. In fact, generations of readers have found Satan the most attractive and sympathetic character in the great poem.

MILTON

In the Middle Ages, romantic love had been a passion that occurred outside of marriage. John Milton's description of the devotion of Adam and Eve in *Paradise Lost* brings love and marriage together, preparing the way for scores of modern explorations of the ideal of love within marriage. In the opening lines, Adam and Eve are addressing God.

"But Thou has promised from us two a race
To fill the Earth, who shall with us extol
Thy goodness infinite, both when we wake,
And when we seek, as now, thy gift of sleep."
    This said unanimous, and other rites
Observing none, but adoration pure
Which God likes best, into their inmost bower
Handed they went; and eased the putting off
These troublesome disguises which we wear,
Straight side by side were laid, nor turned, I ween,
Adam from his fair spouse, nor Eve the rites
Mysterious of connubial love refused . . . .
These, lulled by nightingales, embracing slept,
And on their naked limbs the flowery roof
Showered roses, which the morn repaired.
    Sleep on,
Blest pair; and O yet happiest if ye seek
No happier state, and know to know no more.

THE

Pilgrims Progreſs:

In the ſimilitude of a

DREAM.

AS I walk'd through the wildterneſs of this world, I lighted on a certain place, where was a Denn; And I laid me down in that place to ſleep: And as I ſlept I dreamed a Dream. I dreamed, and behold *I ſaw a Man* * *cloathed with Raggs, ſtanding in a certain place, with his face from his own Houſe, a Book in his hand, and a great burden upon his back.* I looked, and ſaw him open the Book, and Read therein; and as he Read, he wept and trembled: and not being able longer to contain,

* Iſa.64. 6. Lu. 14.33 Pſ. 38. 4. Hab. 2. 2. Aċt.16. 31.

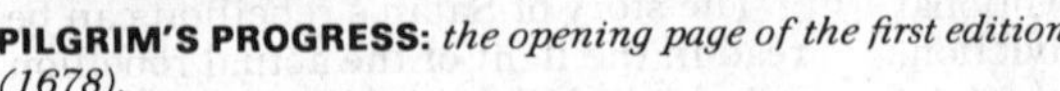

PILGRIM'S PROGRESS: *the opening page of the first edition (1678).*

CULVER PICTURES

MY UNCLE TOBY'S ROMANCE *with the Widow is a long, amusing tale in* Tristram Shandy, *the innovative and digressive masterpiece by Sterne.*

In many ways *Paradise Lost* is the culmination of the Renaissance tradition of producing new classics by imitating the old. It relies heavily on Homer, Vergil, Dante, Spenser, and, of course, the Bible; but most especially it relies on the blank verse paragraphs invented by Milton's secular predecessor, Shakespeare.

In other respects, however, the great poem is strikingly modern. Milton's descriptions borrow not only from the classical languages but from the new science of his own time. His emphasis on the importance of individual conscience and choice rings true—perhaps more true to modern readers than to Milton's contemporaries.

Paradise Lost is nowhere more forward-looking than in its treatment of the relationship between Adam and Eve. For the first time in our literature, we encounter husband and wife as a unit, neither more important than the other, sharing both joys and sorrows. Eve has none of the idealized qualities of Dante's Beatrice; nor is Adam the solitary seeker, yearning both for God and for his earthly love. This new equality of the sexes—and the new marriage relationship it allows—will be a major subject for serious writers from Milton's time to the present (see box on previous page).

The only achievement of the 1600's comparable to *Paradise Lost* was of quite a different order, though not a dissimilar message. *The Pilgrim's Progress,* by John Bunyan (in two parts, 1678–1684), told in spare, everyday prose of Christian's travels toward salvation. His trials and temptations and his final success offered comfort and hope to common readers who felt themselves to be on the same journey. The places in the imaginary landscape—the Slough of Despond, for example, and Vanity Fair—became part of the English language. *The Pilgrim's Progress* was the most popular book in the American colonies (after the Bible) through the 1700's and well into the 1800's, rivaled only by *Robinson Crusoe* (see below).

1660–1700. Meanwhile, at the court of the restored king, Charles II, literature of quite a different character was in fashion, particularly in the theater. The playwrights Sir George Etherege, William Wycherly, and William Congreve wrote dialogue unmatched for quickness till the present day; but their cynicism—sometimes appearing to be a rejection of all conventional moral values—makes them seem brittle and "unserious" to modern tastes.

The great literary figure in the generation after Milton's was John Dryden (1631–1700). In many ways he bridged the gap between the high seriousness of the Puritan cause and the frivolousness of the court. He first came to attention as a dramatist, specializing not in brittle comedy, but in the type of bombastic tragedy popular at the time. He admired Milton and even (with Milton's permission) put *Paradise Lost* into rhyming couplets for theatrical presentation.

Dryden was a man of public affairs, and in the 1680's he assisted the government by writing political propaganda. Among these pieces, the mock epics *Absalom and Achitophel* (1681–1682) and *MacFlecknoe* (1682) rank with the greatest satires in the language. Yet, like Milton, Dryden was a man of "tender conscience." His own religious odyssey led him to the Roman Catholic Church. This choice eventually disqualified him from government service or favor.

In his later years, Dryden did much of the work he is remembered for today. He translated Vergil's *Aeneid* into mellow and beautiful English verse, and he became the first great English literary critic. His *Essay of Dramatic Poesy* (1668) defines the English dramatic tradition in a way that is still persuasive today. Not until Samuel Johnson nearly a hundred years later would English have a critic of such broad and generous tastes.

In an extraordinarily beautiful fragment, *The Secular Masque,* Dryden, near the end of his life, marked the century's turning with what might have been the age's epitaph:

> All, all, of a piece throughout;
> Thy Chase had a Beast in view;
> Thy Wars brought nothing about;
> Thy Lovers were all untrue.
> 'Tis well an Old Age is out,
> And time to begin a New.

The novel. As if in direct response, a bankrupt businessman, Daniel Defoe (1659?–1731), made the first literary stir with a brace of poems that won him, alternately, royal favor and jail. He followed with an intense career in journalism in which nearly everything in his *Review* was written by himself. Finally, in *Robinson Crusoe* (1719), *Moll Flanders* (1721), and *The Journal of the Plague Year* (1721) he turned, as many a journalist has before and since, to simulated fact without bothering to inform the public of his technique. Defoe's racy and essentially nonliterary efforts stand as one of the major building blocks of the English novel.

This new form, seemingly light-years away from Milton's epic or Dryden's criticism, signaled the growth of an important, if less cultivated reading public. *Robinson Crusoe,* the story of a man stranded on a desert island and forced to self-reliance, struck a deep chord in the new readers. It was perhaps the most read and most durable book written in the 1700's. The novel's other building blocks included Samuel Richardson's *Pamela* (1740), a story composed of letters from an attractive young woman beset by suitors with questionable motives. Richardson's "sentimental psychology" became a major element of later fiction. In answer to Pamela came Henry Fielding's *Joseph Andrews* (1742), which brought an element of satire to the novel. Fielding parodied not only the sentimental style of Richardson, but also the classical epic, making both seem faintly ridiculous by mixing them. Finally, Tobias Smollett's *The Adventures of Roderick Random* (1748) established the picaresque, which featured a lovable but inept hero whose misfortunes made him a kind of negative everyman. Eventually the novel would become a solid literary form in its own right. But these early efforts flew in the face of established literary standards. Their authors were conscious of being a kind of literary underground.

Beginning about mid-century with the publication of Fielding's *Tom Jones,* a sophisticated mock epic, the novel began to gain some status in the literary world. *Tom Jones* was followed by *Tristram Shandy* (1759–1767) by Laurence Sterne, a comic masterpiece in which the intended story never gets told, being constantly interrupted by the narrator's free associations. The hero is not even born until a third of the way through the book. Sterne's methods—and his "sentiment"—made him a kind of celebrity. His books were admired and laughed at in France and Germany as well as in England. With Rousseau, he was a prophet of the new sensibility that would be called Romanticism.

Among other important novels are Oliver Goldsmith's *The Vicar of Wakefield* (1766), a gentle and less revolutionary novel of sentiment, and Horace Walpole's *The Castle of Otranto* (1764), the first of the "gothic" novels, relying on an exotic or mysterious setting and on the demonic or evil possibilities of the characters. Before the turn of the century, a new master, Jane Austen, had written her first three novels, though they were not published for many years.

The Augustans. Novelists were not the only writers to turn in new directions. Early in the century there developed a new and gentlemanly kind of literary journalism—weekly papers with informal essays on literature, politics, and other topical concerns of the day. Joseph Addison and Richard Steele produced the most famous of these papers, the *Tatler* and the *Spectator* (1709–1712), whose issues make engaging reading even today. The *Spectator* had many imitators in succeeding years. Only the *Rambler* by Samuel Johnson and, later, Goldsmith's *The Citizen of the World* are much remembered, however.

Both novelists and journalists were members of a new class: writers who could make their living with their pen alone. John Dryden was perhaps the first to succeed at this, offering the public his translations by subscription and sharing the proceeds with his printer. Other poets and men of letters followed his lead. Alexander Pope made a small fortune selling his translations of Homer, and later in the century, Samuel Johnson made both his reputation and income from the sale of his great dictionary.

Alexander Pope (1688–1744) was without doubt the most admired poet of the 1700's. He took the heroic couplet of Dryden and refined it to a fine, witty point. Later poets despaired of imitating him—perhaps no English poet has had so sure and exact a sense of the language. Yet Pope's verses are cold, appealing more to the head than to the heart. Later generations have questioned his subject matter but have never been able to deny his immense talent.

Perhaps the most sympathetic strain in Pope in his capacity for moral outrage. He parodies the inconsequential concerns of the coquette by placing her in a mock epic in *The Rape of the Lock* (1712). Later, he takes apart the venal and greedy literary underworld of his time in the *Dunciad* (1728, 1742). In a more relaxed vein, his *Imitations of Horace* (1733–1739) suggest something of the feeling of Horace's Rome, akin to Pope's London. In fact, the early 1700's have come to be known as England's "Augustan Age."

For a few short years, Pope was closely associated with the other literary giant of the day, Jonathan Swift (1667–1745). Swift was no poet; rather he was a man driven by a fierce sense of moral outrage. Cruelty and false principle enraged him, and he gained his "revenge" in writing the

POPE

The heroic couplet—lines of the same length as blank verse, but rhymed one to the next—was mastered by Alexander Pope. Here, in "Epistle to Dr. Arbuthnot," he uses it to heap scorn on an evil man.

Let *Sporus* tremble—'What? that Thing of silk?
Sporus, that mere white Curd of Ass's milk?
Satire or Sense alas! can *Sporus* feel?
Who breaks a Butterfly upon a Wheel?'
Yet let me flap this Bug with gilded wings,
This painted Child of Dirt that stinks and stings;
Whose Buzz the Witty and the Fair annoys,
Yet Wit ne'er tastes, and Beauty ne'er enjoys.
So well-bred Spaniels civilly delight
In mumbling of the Game they dare not bite.
Eternal Smiles his Emptiness betray,
As shallow streams run dimpling all the way.
Whether in florid Impotence he speaks,
And, as the Prompter breathes, the Puppet squeaks;
Or, at the Ear of Eve, familiar Toad,
Half Froth, half Venom, spits himself abroad,
In Puns, of Politicks, of Tales, or Lyes,
Or Spite, or Smut, or Rymes, or Blasphemies.
His wit all see-saw between *that* and *this,*
Now high, now low, now Master up, now Miss,
And he himself one vile Antithesis. . . .

most pointed and scathing satire ever produced in English. Swift served with Pope in the government of Queen Anne from 1710 to 1714. But when the queen died, Swift fled in disgrace to Ireland (where he had been born to Anglo-Irish parents). He served the rest of his life as the dean of the Anglican cathedral in Dublin.

Ironically, the one work of Swift's that remains a classic is *Gulliver's Travels* (1726). Swift wrote it as a parody of travel books and an indictment of mankind; it is revered as a charming children's story. The style of the book, a parody of low journalistic style, has been praised as a model for modern English. Meanwhile, the ironies Swift intended to be recognized—the small-mindedness of the tiny Lilliputians, the physical and moral monstrosity of the giant Brobdingnagians, and the perfect debasement of the filthy manlike Yahoos (far inferior to the placid horses they work for)—are often ignored or dismissed.

Three years after *Gulliver's Travels,* Swift published "A Modest Proposal," a brief and devastating suggestion in "scientific" language that the Irish, having no other means of earning a living, be encouraged to raise their own children as food for gentlemen's tables. The horrifying detail of the proposal suggests indirectly the deep sympathy Swift had for the Irish and the contempt he had for their English overlords.

Among others who associated with Pope and Swift was John Gay, a minor poet whose one great success was a "ballad opera." *The Beggar's Opera* (1728) used old English tunes to help tell the story of MacHeath, an amorous highwayman. It has never been off the stage long since it opened, and in an adaptation by German Bertolt Brecht it became *The Threepenny Opera,* a 20th-century classic with music by Kurt Weill. Even MacHeath survives in the modern adaptation as Mack the Knife in the song of that title.

THE RAKE'S PROGRESS, *a series of pointed engravings by William Hogarth, resembles Pope's pointed poetic satire. Hogarth was a friend of novelist Henry Fielding.*

The Johnson circle. A long generation further on, another distinguished circle centered around Dr. Samuel Johnson (1709–1784). Johnson was a literary journalist and informal scholar who made his reputation by compiling the first great dictionary of English (1755). He accomplished (with a handful of Scottish assistants) what the French Academy took 30 years to do. The dictionary, boasting hundreds of examples of usage from English poetry, was the standard for over a century and also served as the basis for Noah Webster's American dictionaries.

Johnson's other works include a few poems, a moral fable, the essays in his weekly *Rambler,* and an edition of Shakespeare whose preface is justly famous. His great importance, however, was as a critic, and his *Lives of the Poets* (1781) redefines English poetry. Although his judgments often differed from those of later critics, Johnson's sympathies were extremely broad and generous.

Johnson's interest in biography came to its fruition in the monumental story of his own life by the younger James Boswell. Boswell's *Life of Samuel Johnson,* filled as no previous biography had been with anecdotes, conversations, and everyday details, made a larger-than-life celebrity of Johnson, nearly eclipsing his own works altogether. Boswell had more in common with Rousseau or Sterne than with Johnson, and his own psyche—at once hero-worshipping and rebellious—is an essential ingredient of his great biography.

The rest of Johnson's circle was equally remarkable. Oliver Goldsmith, shy, self-deprecating, and clumsy, managed to produce classics in three different genres: the comic play *She Stoops to Conquer* (1773), the poem "The Deserted Village" (1770), and the sentimental novel *The Vicar of Wakefield.*

Edmund Burke (1729–1797) was a member of Parliament and the most distinguished political orator of his day. He opposed the war with the American colonies and fought corruption in colonial India for decades. Ironically, he is best remembered not for these "liberal" campaigns but for his *Reflections on the French Revolution* (1790). In it, he defended England's slow evolutionary process of political reform against the radical reformers who sought to bring the French Revolution to England. Burke's early essay "On the Sublime" was an important contribution to the changing ideas of art and beauty.

Among others in the Johnsonian circle were Sir Joshua Reynolds, one of the great painters of the age; David Garrick, the great actor and theatrical entrepreneur (a boyhood friend of Johnson's); and the economist Adam Smith.

At the edges of the circle were still other distinguished men, among them David Hume, whose skeptical writings set philosophy on a new course, and whose *History of England* (1754–1762) set a new standard for historiography. The magisterial history of Edward Gibbon, *The Decline and Fall of the Roman Empire,* argues sardonically that Christianity played a central role in Rome's collapse. Finally, Richard Brinsley Sheridan warmed the Restoration style in *The Rivals* (1775) and *The School for Scandal* (1777), two enduring classics of the English theater.

New directions. Meanwhile, poetry seemed to have come to a dead end. The mild Thomas Gray and milder but lovelier William Collins tried to put new poetic substance in outworn neoclassic forms. But the true poetic impetus lay elsewhere. A group of amateur antiquarians was busy digging out England's ancient poetic past. They collected ancient ballads, studied

Old English, and hunted for old manuscripts. The most influential of these "finds" proved to be forgeries: the works of Ossian translated by James Macpherson, and the "Rowley" poems of Thomas Chatterton. Authenticity aside, both seemed somehow to find a new root or starting place for future poetry. They caused great excitement in Germany as well as England. Another new sign lay in the genius of the "mad" Christopher Smart, author of the unforgettable "Song to David" (1763). It seemed that true lyric was so removed from the neoclassic tradition that one had to be fraudulent or insane to dare to write it.

As the century came near its end, this new sensibility was to transform poetry and literature, but that story properly belongs to the next age.

Romanticism and Nationalism

Some of the changes were external. In 1776 Britain's American colonies declared their independence, proclaiming a new set of political principles. Thirteen years later, the French rose up, first against their monarchy, then against their revolutionary leaders, finally in support of a crusade for world conquest. Other nations—the Germans, the Poles, the Scots, and the Irish—were rediscovering their national inheritances, seeking intellectual if not political independence.

At the same time, many of the changes were psychological. The late 1700's produced men that made no distinction between their public and private lives. In contrast to the decorous poets and critics of an earlier age, Rousseau, Sterne, Boswell and others were self-involved, alert first to their own feelings and emotions and only afterward to the demands of the public. None of these new writers would be likely to serve in government or accomplish great works of scholarship. They saw their role as custodians of their own and their readers' imaginations or souls, not of their bodies or minds.

This new sensibility, with its emphasis on the individual and his identity we know as the Romantic movement. It did not begin in a particular day or in a particular place, and many of those deeply involved in it did not consider themselves part of a movement at all. In retrospect, however, we can pick a year—1774—for convenience. And to characterize the great change, we turn to a new country and a new voice: the Germany of Johann Wolfgang von Goethe.

Germany

The great age of earlier German creativity was the Reformation of the 1500's. During the 1600's, the whole region was decimated by the Thirty Years War. Animosities between the many German states persisted for decades, and only in the 1700's did the German-speaking peoples begin a vigorous secular literature.

Perhaps the first sign of awakening was the career of Gottfried Wilhelm von Leibniz (1646–1716), a man of genius whose contributions to mathematics and philosophy were immense. Leibniz's talent for speculation and abstract thought revealed a particular trait in the German character—one seldom shared by the Germans' cousins in England.

The literary life of Germany still simmered on low at Leibniz's death, but a young organist named Johann Sebastian Bach (1685–1742) was already composing works that would be a summation of 300 years of European music and an anthology of ideas for the centuries to come.

Lessing. By mid-century, Germany was bursting with life, economic, political, and literary. The philosopher Gotthold Ephraim Lessing was constructing a theory of literature based on the model of the ancient Greeks rather than that of the Bourbon French. Lessing's classicism sought more than the ancient forms. He wanted a return to the spirit of the Athenian period. His admiration for Greek civilization has carried on in Germany to the present day. Lessing's landmark play, *Nathan the Wise* (1779), introduced a German blank verse modeled after another of his favorites, Shakespeare. His critical classic, *Laokoon* (1766), explored the differences between the visual and verbal imaginations, drawing on the discoveries of the great art historian J. J. Winckelmann. Shakespeare was brought to the national attention not only by the passionate advocacy of Lessing, but also by the translations of the talented Christoph Martin Wieland.

The philosopher Immanuel Kant (1724–1804) built on the works of Liebniz as well as on those of the Englishman David Hume. Kant, whose work was of incalculable importance to later philosophers and writers, concentrated on human powers of reason

FAUST, *the archetype of the Romantic hero, is tempted by Mephistopheles in an illustration for the play of Wolfgang von Goethe.*

NEW YORK PUBLIC LIBRARY

and intuition. Kant's interest in natural rather than "artificial" intellect inspired the critic Johann Gottfried von Herder (1744–1803) to suggest that artistic intuition had little to do with education or intellectual refinement. Like the language itself, Herder said, poetry rises from the collective consciousness of a people. Herder collected and edited German folk songs and encouraged others to examine the "popular" arts of the past as the English were doing at the same time.

Goethe. Herder also collaborated with Goethe and others in a pamphlet, *Von deutscher Art und Kunst,* that became the handbook of a movement termed *Sturm und Drang* (storm and stress). The movement's emphasis on the personal crises of an individual was inspired in part by Rousseau and by the new cult of "sentiment" in England. Its major result was the early work of Goethe himself. *The Sorrows of Young Werther* (1774) set Germany and all of Europe to writing novels about suicide. If German literature had ended at this point it would already have contributed a new note to the Romantic movement. But Goethe, Friedrich von Schiller, and Friedrich Hölderlin extended beyond the *Sturm und Drang* philosophy to a new lyric and drama that established the golden age of German literature.

Goethe towered over his associates. His *Faust* (in two parts, 1808 and 1832) is the greatest of all German works; a giant dramatic poem that seemed the epitome of its age. The novel of character growth, *Wilhelm Meister's Apprenticeship* (1795–1796), extended Goethe's influence on fiction. He also contributed to science, studying the morphology of living things.

But Goethe's greatest gifts remained always with the lyric: he could achieve a scene, an insight, or a passion with both perfect form and unparalleled emotional intimacy. The anthology of love lyrics *Westöstlicher Diwan* (1819) contains some of the most beautiful lyrics in any language.

Schiller. Friedrich von Schiller stands second to his friend in the German pantheon. He was an extraordinary dramatist, often taking aim at political injustice, as in the passionately liberal *Die Räuber* (1781). Among his later plays are *Wallenstein* (a trilogy, 1798–1799), *Mary Stuart* (1800), and *William Tell* (1804).

Schiller also wrote an extensive history of the Thirty Years War and a considerable body of lyric. His "Ode to Joy" is set in the last movement of Beethoven's Choral Symphony.

After these two giants, the single novel, fragment of a play, and body of Hellenic verse produced by Friedrich Hölderlin seem a small accomplishment. Yet Hölderlin strikes true to the ears of German speakers especially, and has a kind of abstract perfection that is very much his own.

Between 1800 and Goethe's death in 1832, Romanticism swept Europe. In Germany, the emphasis shifted to prose. Jean Paul Friedrich Richter wrote sentimental, charming novels of everyday life that gained wide popularity. Friedrich von Hardenberg, who called himself Novalis, left an unfinished novel, *Heinrich von Ofterdingen* (1802), at the time of his early death, as well as a group of religious elegies, the only major lyric of his generation. At the same time, Ludwig Tieck opened the vein of the macabre and supernatural, perhaps most successfully in the later *Phantasus* (1812–1816). In the hands of the musician and novelist, E. T. A. Hoffmann, this became the gothic tale. One of the remarkable scholarly accomplishments of the age was the collection of household tales (*hausmärchen*) by the brothers Jakob and Wilhelm Grimm. The Grimms traveled the German countryside listening to old storytellers and taking the tales down word for word, thus preserving an oral tradition that may be centuries old. The Grimms were also the founders of modern philology, the study of the development of language. Their discoveries helped explain not only archaic German but also Old and Middle English.

Germany after Goethe. After the defeat of Napoleon, the impulse for German unification was enormous. The region was fast becoming the most advanced industrial society of Europe. At the same time, however, the mid-1800's marked the beginning of substantial emigration to the United States—people who had grown dissatisfied with religious, political, or economic disadvantage left their homeland.

The great poet of the new age, Heinrich Heine (*Book of Songs,* 1827), left Germany in 1831 to avoid political repression and lived out his life in Paris as an advocate of liberal and radical ideas. Heine's fellow leader of the outlawed movement, Young Germany, the journalist Ludwig Börne, set both a new German prose style and a rallying point for liberals in his *Briefe aus Paris* (1830–1833). A poet of substantial talent, Georg Herwegh (*Gedichte eines Lebendigen,* 1841), retreated to exile after 1848; so, too, did the talented Ferdinand Freiligrath (*Ein Glaubensbekenntnis,* 1844).

Many novels through the late 1800's found enthusiastic readers in Germany, but none achieved the international appeal of Balzac or Dickens. In the theater, however, the developments were more significant. Early in the century, the work of Heinrich von Kleist (*The Prince of Homburg,* 1821) pointed the way toward the emotional violence of the later period. Franz Grillparzer (*A Dream Is Life,* 1817–1834; *The Jewess of Toledo,* 1855), Georg Büchner (*Danton's Death,* 1835; *Woyzek,* a fragment, published posthumously, 1850), and Friedrich Hebbel (*Judith,* 1840; *Die Nibelungen,* 1862), were all writers of significant influence. The mix of personal emotion, naturalism, and something between daydream and nightmare vision culminated in such later dramatists as Hermann Sudermann (*Die Ehre,* 1889; *Morituri,* 1897) and Gerhart Hauptmann (*The Weavers,* 1892). This theater of alienation juxtaposed outraged decency and triumphant vice in an atmosphere of social or psychological corruption.

The parallel development in music lay in the career of Richard Wagner, whose works (for example, *Der Ring des Nibelungen,* 1853–1874; *Tristan und Isolde,* 1857–1859) mirrored in myth the social agony of the times. Wagner, who wrote his own librettos, had nearly as much influence among writers as among later musicians. His marriage of structural complexity and a half-cranky, half-brilliant sexual egotism served as one of the great building blocks of 20th-century consciousness. Other writers outside the literary fold whose influence was great include Georg Hegel, who set out a philosophical system explaining cultural and national development; Karl Marx, whose reverse Hegelianism gave birth to a radical new social philosophy; Friedrich Nietzsche, whose philosophy of the *Übermensch* (superman) was the ultimate result of Romantic individualism; and pychologist Sigmund Freud, whose studies of the subconscious mind turned later writers inward in still another way.

The societies of Germany and Austria rode a rising economic tide but a declining social one. The generation of writers that would endure the period of world wars (1914–1945) seem often to have abandoned all hope. Frank Wedekind anticipated the tone of elevated self-loathing, usually with a negative sexual component that a certain kind of modernism frequently displays. His plays *Earth Spirit* (1895) and *Pandora's Box* (1903) were later used by the composer Alban Berg for his opera, *Lulu* (1934).

The work of Germany's two major modern lyricists, Stefan George (1868–1933) and Rainer Maria Rilke (*Neue Gedichte* [new poems], 1907–1908; *Duinese Elegies,* 1911–1922), shared a similar background in German, French and classical learning. Rilke seemed to achieve a directness of expression denied anyone else of his time.

As World War I drew near, the tense emotions of its age gave birth to the violent new style called expressionism. By the first year of fighting, three avant-garde expressionists, the poets Ernst Stadler, Georg Trakl, and Georg Heym, had already lost their lives, two in the trenches.

WORDSWORTH

These lines from Wordsworth's long poem *The Prelude* show the broad spacious quality of his verse, so new to readers accustomed to the couplets and worldly criticism of the preceding generations.

There was a Boy: ye knew him well, ye cliffs
And islands of Winander!—many a time
At evening, when the earliest stars began
To move along the edges of the hills,
Rising or setting, would he stand alone
Beneath the trees or by the glittering lake.
And there, with fingers interwoven, both hands
Pressed closely palm to palm, and to his mouth
Uplifted, he, as through an instrument,
Blew mimic hootings to the silent owls,
That they might answer him; and they would shout
Across the watery vale, and shout again,
Responsive to his call, with quivering peals,
And long haloos and screams, and echoes loud,
Redoubled and redoubled, concourse wild
Of jocund din; and, when a lengthened pause
Of silence came and baffled his best skill,
Then sometimes, in that silence while he hung
Listening, a gentle shock of mild surprise
Has carried far into his heart the voice
Of mountain torrents; or the visible scene
Would enter unawares into his mind,
With all its solemn imagery, its rocks,
Its woods, and that uncertain heaven, received
Into the bosom of the steady lake.
This Boy was taken from his mates, and died
In childhood, ere he was full twelve years old . . . .

England

The early German Romantics learned from the English. In the late years of the 1700's they repaid the debt. The works of Lessing, Goethe, and Schiller struck a sympathetic chord in England, helping to free aspiring poets from the restrictions of the still-admired rules of neoclassicism.

At the same time, much of the impetus for the English Romantic movement came from within the British Isles.

Poetry. The first near Romantic, the poet Robert Burns (1759–1796), spoke as a voice of reviving nationalism (*Poems, Chiefly in the Scottish Dialect,* 1786). Burns drew from the Scots' traditions and folklore and proved that a Scot need no longer be Anglicized to write great poetry in English.

Blake. The works of William Blake (1757–1827), whose *Songs of Innocence* appeared in 1789, contained a special kind of visionary independence. Its roots were partly in a tradition of religious mysticism of a deeply individual kind. Blake's later *Prophetic Books* (1793–1804) anticipated the mixture of politics, religion, and individualism that make up much of modern literature. His "high" lyric style had not been heard in England since the age of Milton. But Blake remained all but unheard in his lifetime.

Wordsworth and Coleridge. The real beginning of English Romanticism was the publication of the *Lyrical Ballads* (1798) by William Wordsworth (1770–1850) and Samuel Taylor Coleridge (1772–1834). Wordsworth, the greatest poet of the age, combined a Miltonic dignity with the plain speech and direct feeling of the English countryfolk among whom he had grown up. Coleridge's more polite and more inhibited poems often provided the trigger to Wordsworth's deeper, but slower response.

Byron. George Gordon (Lord) Byron (1788–1824), whose popularity, political involvement, and frequent lapses of taste made him the chief literary celebrity of his day, is perhaps best known for his *Don Juan* (1819–1824), a brilliant comic assertion of wit, sexuality, and physical self-confidence. Byron showed in *The Vision of Judgment* (1822) and a half-dozen lyrics even more concentrated instances of a prodigious and prodigal talent.

Keats and Shelley. John Keats (1795–1821) is probably the best loved lyric poet in the language. The great poems of the end of his life (among them, "Ode to a Nightingale," "Ode on a Grecian Urn," "To Autumn," and "La Belle Dame sans Merci") show a faith in the imagination far in advance of the symbolists. His best poems, along with those of Wordsworth, Byron, and Blake are with Chaucer, Shakespeare, Milton, and Pope the center of English literary achievement.

Percy Bysshe Shelley (1792–1822) is a possible addition to the other four Romantic masters. Other writers continue to rediscover him, admiring his heroic intellectual conceptions and his mastery of propulsive rhythmic force.

Almost as swiftly as the Romantic movement began, it ended. With the death of Keats, the high lyric style disappeared. Lesser writers were not of the same inspiration, and the succeeding generation seemed to hear other voices, abandoning the lyric or writing it without conviction.

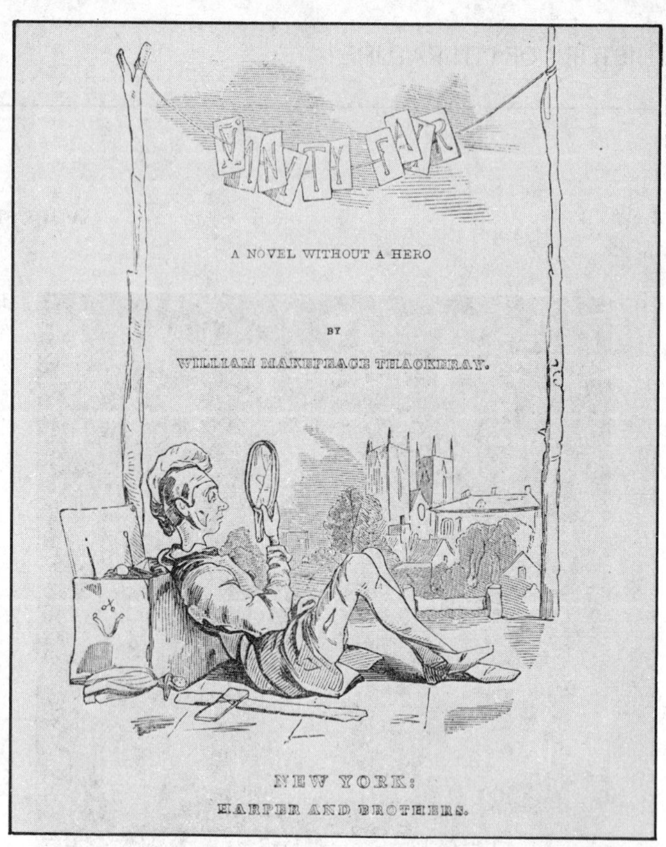

THE NOVEL *was the major form of the Victorian era. English novelist Charles Dickens wrote about members of the lower middle class, like Bob Crachit and Tiny Tim in* A Christmas Carol (left). *William Thackeray's* Vanity Fair *featured a drawing by the author on the title page.*

The novel. Meanwhile, a new age of novelists was approaching. Jane Austen wrote three of her novels in the 1790's but published only after 1810 (*Pride and Prejudice,* 1813; *Mansfield Park,* 1814; *Emma,* 1816). She went to Keats's imaginative church of the open heart but sat at the pew of keen observation and careful structure.

Sir Walter Scott, a Scotsman, became a model for intelligent commercial success all over Europe (*Waverley,* 1814; *Ivanhoe,* 1820). Mary Shelley (*Frankenstein,* 1818) and Maria Edgeworth (*Castle Rackrent,* 1800) extended the daring of women in literature to the portrayal of psychological and social nightmares. In mid-century, an extraordinary trio, Charlotte and Emily Bronte and Elizabeth Gaskell, widened this range still further. George Eliot (Mary Ann Evans) also became a major English novelist (*The Mill on the Floss,* 1860; *Middlemarch,* 1871–1872).

There were to be no English moral giants on the scale of the great French and Russian novelists. Charles Dickens, however (*The Posthumous Papers of the Pickwick Club,* 1836–1837; *David Copperfield,* 1850; *Bleak House,* 1853; *Our Mutual Friend,* 1865; among many others), attained to something at least as great. He wrote, like the early Wordsworth, with the courage of the decent lower middle class, though of city rather than country folk. Every writer in Europe learned from his broad sympathies, skillful characterizations, and shrewd sense of pace. If he lacked philosophic vision, he made up for it with a stage nearly as broad and all-encompassing as Shakespeare's.

William Makepeace Thackeray, Dickens' contemporary, continued the tradition of 18th-century social satire with a new vitality and a deft hand at well turned and swift moving prose (*Vanity Fair,* 1848; *Henry Esmond,* 1852).

As the century progressed, English writers of fiction who worked at a very high level include George Meredith (*The Ordeal of Richard Feverel,* 1859), Anthony Trollope (the "Barsetshire" novels, 1855–1867), Samuel Butler (*The Way of All Flesh,* 1903), and the remarkable Thomas Hardy (*Tess of the D'Urbervilles,* 1891; *Jude the Obscure,* 1896), also recognized as among the most enduring of English poets.

Victorian poetry. Poetry underwent a difficult time after the death of Keats. The large voices among the Victorians belonged to Alfred Tennyson (*Poems,* 1832; *In Memoriam,* 1851; *Idylls of the King,* 1859–1885) and Robert Browning (*Men and Women,* 1855; *The Ring and the Book,* 1868). Both were so preoccupied with the responsibilities of national greatness that their considerable gifts were ultimately betrayed. Tennyson's saving grace is his occasional flight of sober lyric; Browning's is his delight in the sheer variety of life's ironies.

Other interesting, intelligent poets seemed unable to find a sense of identity. They include Matthew Arnold and the gifted friend whose premature elegy he was to write, Arthur Hugh Clough; and the "pre-Raphaelites," a group seeking a supposed medieval spiritual unity; the group included Dante Gabriel Rossetti, William Morris, and Coventry Patmore. Even a few of great promise seemed somehow blocked from fully realizing their gifts. These include Elizabeth Barrett Browning (*Sonnets from the Portuguese,* 1850) and Christina Rossetti (*Goblin Market,* 1862; *A Pageant,*

ELIZABETH BARRETT BROWNING, *wife of Robert, was a talented poet in her own right.*

1881), and the novelist George Meredith (*Modern Love,* 1862).

A. C. Swinburne stands apart from the rest (*Poems and Ballads,* 1866; *Tristram of Lyonesse,* 1882). With him stands Nobel laureate (1907) Rudyard Kipling. Both are too talented to ignore, but impossible, in this age, to take altogether seriously.

Three very private lyricists, however, wrote poems that deeply impressed later generations: the novelist Thomas Hardy (*Wessex Poems,* 1898; and three other collections, to 1928), A. E. Housman (*A Shropshire Lad,* 1896), and the astonishing, and endlessly moving Gerard Manley Hopkins, whose *Poems* was not published until 1918. These three would be "adopted" by other literary "outsiders"—Irishmen, Americans, and others—after 1914.

AUTOBIOGRAPHY

A newly popular form in the 1800's was the introspective account of one's own life. Two prominent Englishmen—the priest John Henry Newman and the philosopher John Stuart Mill—wrote extensively about themselves. These short excerpts are descriptions of major life crises.

NEWMAN

If I looked in the mirror and did not see my face, I should have the sort of feeling which actually comes upon me, when I look into this living busy world, and see no reflexion of its Creator . . . What shall be said to this heart-piercing, bewildering fact? I can only answer, that either there is no Creator, or this living society of men is in a true sense discarded from His presence.

MILL

It occurred to me to put the question directly to myself. 'Suppose that all your objects in life were realized, that all the changes in institutions and opinions which you are looking forward to, could be completely effected at this very instant: would this be a great joy and happiness to you?' And an irrepressible self-consciousness distinctly answered, 'No!' At this my heart sank within me: the whole foundation on which my life was constructed fell down.

Nonfiction. Developments in poetry and fiction were paralleled in the prose of ideas. The critics and essayists of Wordsworth's age—Coleridge (*Biographia Literaria,* 1817), William Hazlitt (*Table Talk,* 1821–1822), Charles Lamb (*Essays of Elia,* 1823–1833), Thomas De Quincey (*Confessions of an English Opium Eater,* 1821)—introduced a new Rousseauesque point of view and a corresponding psychology of literature.

Class consciousness, and the fears of its consequences, played a part in the prose of the later works of Thomas Carlyle (*Sartor Resartus,* 1833–1834), John Ruskin (*The Stones of Venice,* 1851–1853), and Walter Pater (*Studies in the History of the Renaissance,* 1873; *Marius the Epicurean,* a novel, 1885). These writers did much to advance the historical awareness of the age, but they wrote with such preciosity as to be all but unbearable to many modern readers.

Two other writers, however, the economist and philosopher John Stuart Mill (*On Liberty,* 1859; *Autobiography,* 1873), and the churchman John Henry Newman (*Apologia Pro Vita Sua,* 1864), discovered a remarkable new directness. It is as if each writer had assimilated the Romantic experience to his own purposes. Each, in fact, underwent a substantial crisis of the soul and wrote of it (see box).

The problem of doubt lay very much at the center of the age, and spiritual journeys led to uncertainty rather than to knowledge. Nowhere was this more evident than in the theory of evolution, developed independently by Alfred Russel Wallace and Charles Darwin (*Origin of Species,* 1869). Even Darwin himself might rather have clung to the old certainties rather than accept man's relationship to the animal kingdom.

Matthew Arnold shared the age's sense of uncertainty. In fact, his vision of the sea of faith ebbing while on the shore "ignorant armies clash by night" ("Dover Beach") exemplifies the pessimism of a civilization past its prime. Yet Arnold did succeed in grasping several conditional articles of faith; even as he doubted, he expressed many of the age's certainties as well. Arnold was also the most perceptive literary critic of the age. His essays provide a summing up for the 1800's, much as Johnson's writings did for his age and Dryden's for his.

The United States

From the mid-1800's on, English literature found itself unexpectedly "twinned"—impressed with, yet confounded by, works from its former colonies in America. The colonies had always had writers, and after 1850, even the "mother country" could not afford to ignore them any more.

As early as 1662, the American poet Michael Wigglesworth was writing that God made man of great potential but that the stubborn creature refused to live up to it. This theme of mixed self-assertion and inadequacy would sound again and again in American letters. James Russell Lowell characterized it in 1848 as "a moral and physical stoop in the shoulders."

Religion, its ordering and its rewards, were the subject of early writings: Anne Bradstreet (c 1612–1672) and Edward Taylor (1642–1729) wrote religious verse in which a certain homeliness of conceit announced the native strain. Roger Williams (*The Bloudy Tenent of Persecution for Cause of Conscience,* 1644) stood out amid the quarrels and chronicles of the first settlers for his wholesale dedication to tolerance and his outrage at its violation.

Substantial writing began with the activities of the Founding Fathers. The works of Thomas Jefferson, Benjamin Franklin, John Adams, and Alexander Hamilton were worthy of note. The universal republican (born an Englishman) Thomas Paine (*Common Sense,* 1776; *The Rights of Man,* 1791–1792; *The Age of Reason,* 1794–1795) was prosecuted in England, imprisoned in France, and abhorred in America for his radical hatred of tyranny. Like Blake, he has always stood for an eloquent but sometimes incoherent individualism.

The Federalist Papers (1786–1788), principally by Hamilton and James Madison, brilliantly worked out a more conservative but equally rugged vision of constitutional, republican government. Thomas Jefferson, whose *A Summary View of the Rights of British America* (1774) established the intellectual grounds for American freedom of political choice, is primarily responsible for the language of the Declaration of Independence. Benjamin Franklin's famous journal, *Poor Richard's Almanack* (1732–1757), like his later *Autobiography,* demonstrates the wide range of interests and penetrating good sense that made Franklin the first of the Americans to win substantial attention abroad. The correspondence of the first years of independence is also fundamental. *The Adams-Jefferson Letters,* for example, include personal letters by Abigail Adams, a testimony to the independent women the brilliant French critic de Tocqueville would soon call America's chief asset.

AMERICAN FICTION *in the early 1800's produced memorable characters, from the shy Ichabod Crane in Irving's "The Legend of Sleepy Hollow" to the heroic Natty Bumppo in Cooper's* Deerslayer *novels.*

1800–1860. Formal literature first reached a high level with the generation of Washington Irving ("Rip Van Winkle," "The Legend of Sleepy Hollow," in *The Sketch Book of Geoffrey Crayon, Gent.,* 1802–1803) and James Fenimore Cooper (*Leatherstocking Tales,* 1823–1841, which includes *The Last of the Mohicans* and *The Deerslayer*). Irving told fanciful versions of legends that originated with the Dutch and English settlers in New York City and the Hudson River valley. Cooper's stories, which were greatly admired in Europe, were early tales of frontiersmen and the mysterious American Indian. The Massachusetts writers espoused a kind of decency resembling England's Victorian values. Among those associated with this "native" school of poetry were William Cullen Bryant, Henry Wadsworth Longfellow, James Russell Lowell, and John Greenleaf Whittier. All had genuine talent, but their work seems diminished by their choice of bland subjects and decorous styles.

A renegade from this school was Ralph Waldo Emerson, the transcendentalist philosopher who led a group of moral and social reformers. They included Henry David Thoreau, the feminist Margaret Fuller, and the educational theorist Bronson Alcott.

Emerson's *Essays* of 1831 and 1844 earned him popularity and authority. But his greatness lies in his poems ("Ode," "Hamatreya," "The Apology," "Threnody," "Concord Hymn"). Clumsy, over- and under-written at the same time, both agnostic and neck-deep in nonconformist religion, and choked full of beauty, they uncannily prefigure the elements that have distinguished nearly every major American poet since.

Thoreau's *Walden* (1854) is an account of his "retirement" to the wilderness to "test his self-reliance and to meditate. It, too, prefigures a whole school of modern writing in support of simple and natural living. Thoreau's earlier essay, "Civil Disobedience," became important to generations of American dissenters.

The 1850's also saw a flowering of genius in fiction. Edgar Allan Poe's eerie stories of crime and the supernatural were perhaps the first American works to have a serious influence on European literature. The novelists Nathaniel Hawthorne (*The Scarlet Letter,* 1850) and Herman Melville (*Moby-Dick,* 1851) produced works of great strangeness and considerable imaginative scope.

In poetry one man has come to stand above all others of his generation. In 1855 Walt Whitman published the first edition of *Leaves of Grass.* This collection, considered strange at the time for its free verse forms and most undecorous sexual exuberance, was reissued with additions during the rest of the poet's life. The depth and power of its greatest poems has only grown with time. Among the most famous are "Song of Myself," "Crossing Brooklyn Ferry," "When Lilacs Last in the Dooryard Bloom'd"(an elegy for Abraham Lincoln), and "I Saw in Louisiana a Live-Oak Growing."

In these same years Emily Dickinson (1830–1886) was writing poems of great insight and beauty that would not be published until after her death. Her gifts of metaphor and feeling place her near the very top rank of the world's lyric poets.

1860–1914. The Civil War (1861–1865) demonstrated one more high talent in the deepest speeches of Abraham Lincoln. But the violent conflict also seemed to silence this first great wave of literary inspiration. Not even the inexhaustible Whitman attained his former level afterward.

Certain continuities, however, remained. Americans had always seen themselves first through humor. Early humorous writers often worked by overstatement and broad parody, as seemed to fit the expansive new country. They portrayed sharp New Englanders and drawling frontiersmen for an army of readers who had known few of either at firsthand. During and after the war, this tradition was taken a step further: "Artemus Ward" (Charles F. Browne) and "Petroleum V. Nasby" (David R. Locke) were slick but not unpointed comics.

Another school of writers provided more authentic local color, beginning to characterize the regional differences of the American continent. Bret Harte and Jack London portrayed California and the West; Joel Chandler Harris retold the fables and legends of the black people of the South. Later, Edgar Lee Masters and Sherwood Anderson colored in the Midwest and Willa Cather the Great Plains states.

Still another strain was that of

moral outrage and reform. It began before the war in the crusade for the abolition of slavery led by William Lloyd Garrison, Wendell Phillips, John Greenleaf Whittier, Harriet Beecher Stowe (*Uncle Tom's Cabin,* 1852), and Julia Ward Howe ("Battle Hymn of the Republic," 1862).

In the so-called Gilded Age (the 1870's and '80's), as corrupt an era as America has ever known, this movement began as polite dismay, then grew to almost violent reformism in the work of Ida Tarbell, Lincoln Steffens, Upton Sinclair, and others, to whom President Teddy Roosevelt gave the name "muckrakers."

Mark Twain. All of these elements combined in the work of Mark Twain (Samuel Langhorne Clemens, 1835–1910). His comic sense was sure, his ear for American speech (especially that of his native Missouri) was nearly perfect, and his eye for fraud and moral posturing was uncanny. Twain was an adventurer, and he wrote eloquent accounts of his work on a steamboat (*Life on the Mississippi,* 1883), and as a traveler to the still-desolate West (*Roughing It,* 1872). His first great success in fiction was *The Adventures of Tom Sawyer* (1876), still a classic account of growing up mischievous in a small town. The sequel to *Sawyer,* however, became a more universal classic. *Huckleberry Finn,* the barefoot independent son of the town drunk, is one of the great characters in any literature. He runs away down the Mississippi in the company of Jim, a runaway slave, the two completely interdependent, and the whole panorama of a fast-changing America unfolding before them. Huck Finn's emotional self-reliance and his special blend of knowing and innocence appear in American fiction down to the present day.

MARK TWAIN, *shown here in old age, was the greatest of America's comic writers.*

William Dean Howells became something of a teacher to Twain's generation. His own novels showed a genuine but polite realism. But perhaps his influence was greatest through the effects of his personal friendship and conversation. Among those in his circle were Hamlin Garland; Stephen Crane (*Maggie: A Girl of the Streets,* 1893; *The Red Badge of Courage,* 1895); the economist and social theorist, Thorstein Veblen (*The Theory of the Leisure Class,* 1899); and Twain himself.

Howells' realism was taken to a new level by Theodore Dreiser (*Sister Carrie,* 1900; *An American Tragedy,* 1925), who seemed barely able to write English, yet modulated it beautifully. Dreiser was among the first to write of the underside of the American experience: of the price paid for success and the costs of failure. For all his commitment to a sociological view, however, he wrote from the heart and with astonishing perceptiveness.

At the top of the social order, Henry Adams (descendant of Presidents John and John Quincy Adams) looked with shock and disappointment at the politics of the Gilded Age and looked back with longing at the supposed ideal of the Middle Ages. His emotional shell-shock and perceptive insight anticipated a mood often expressed by later American intellectuals.

WHITMAN

Walt Whitman's poetry breaks out of rhyme and metric pattern to become a vehicle for free—yet oddly disciplined—expression.

I saw in Louisiana a live-oak growing,
All alone stood it and the moss hung down from the branches,
Without any companion it grew there uttering joyous leaves
of dark green,
And its look, rude, unbending, lusty, made me think of myself,
But I wondered how it could utter joyous leaves standing alone
there without its friend near, for I knew I could not.
And I broke off a twig with a certain number of leaves upon it
and twined it around a little moss,
And brought it away, and I have placed it in sight in my room,
It is not needed to remind me of my own dear friends,
(For I believe lately I think of little else than of them,)
Yet it remains to me a curious token, it makes me think of
manly love;
For all that, and though the live-oak glistens there in Louisiana
solitary in a wide flat space,
Uttering joyous leaves all its life without a friend a lover near,
I know very well I could not.

English Internationalism

Swift, Goldsmith, Sheridan, and Burke were Irishmen who had made their mark in English literature. Yet to make such a mark, they had, by necessity, to Anglicize themselves, making England their cultural (if not emotional) home.

In the last quarter of the 1800's, however, Irish nationalism brought the development of a new Irish literature in English. One of the foundations of the new literary movement was the Abbey Theatre, founded by the talented Lady Augusta Gregory. Among the dramatists encouraged by the Abbey were John Millington Synge, whose *Riders to the Sea* (1904) may be the finest one-act play in the language; and Sean O'Casey, whose *Juno and the Paycock* (1924) is a classic study of the greatness and tragedy of the Irish character. Also associated with the Abbey group were the poet A.E. (George Russell) and William Butler Yeats (1865–1939), who was to become the greatest English poet of the century.

Meanwhile, in London a reawakening theater bore two thoroughly Anglicized but basically Irish playwrights: Oscar Wilde (*Lady Windermere's Fan,* 1892; *The Importance of Being Earnest,* 1895) and George Bernard Shaw (*Candida,* 1893; *Major Barbara,* 1905; *Pygmalion,* 1913; *Saint Joan* (1923). Both Wilde and Shaw were literary sensations in London, in part because of their Irish irreverence in an otherwise decorous literary world. Shaw was undoubtedly the driest wit and one of the great geniuses in the language. He was an important figure, too, for his music and literary criticism and for his successful advocacy of political and social causes in his plays and essays.

Gradually, the literature of the Irish, Americans, and English, began to blend into a new international English tradition. This had begun as early as 1876, when the American-born novelist Henry James (*The Portrait of a Lady,* 1881; *The Bostonians,* 1886; *What Maisie Knew,* 1897; *The Ambassadors,* 1903) settled permanently in London and wrote of a "Eur-America" that was a single interacting society. Polish-born novelist Joseph Conrad (*Heart of Darkness,* 1902; *Nostromo,* 1904; *The Secret Agent,* 1907) became an early example of the writer who excels in a language other than his own mother tongue.

Among the writers of this new internationalism were the American Ezra Pound, whose first book of lyrics, *Personae,* was published in 1909, and who would spend a large part of his life in Europe; T.S. Eliot, born in St. Louis and educated at Harvard, but choosing to live the rest of his life in England (*Prufrock and Other Observations,* poems, 1917); and the English novelist D.H. Lawrence (*Sons and Lovers,* 1913), who would live for years in America. These and later internationalists (W.H. Auden, Vladimir Nabokov) properly belong to the modern period, yet the trend toward one English-speaking tradition was well under way before the modern era began in 1914–1918.

Russia

If American literature was one major new force in the 1800's, Russian literature was the other. The Russians, half European and half Asian, had always stood at the outer edge of the European tradition. Their established church was orthodox, related to the Byzantine and Greek rather than to the Roman Catholic. But two great rulers of the 1700's, Peter and Catherine, had brought the Russian state closer to the European powers. The French language and taste were especially influential—and yet there remained something unique and powerful about the Russian character, a freshness that would be widely recognized and admired by the end of the 1800's.

Early Russian literature lay in the oral tradition of *byliny*: poetic legends mixing heroic figures of the Middle Ages with elements of magic and exotic trapings from Islamic and Mongol sources. Early writings in church Slavonic dealt primarily with religious matters, but included some translations of Western works.

Over the next centuries, westernizers sought to bring Russia into the European mainstream, but some of the best work came from the anti-Europeans. In the autobiography of an outstanding dissenter, the *Life of the Archpriest Avvakum* (1672–1673), the first use of colloquial Russian prose appears. "God pays no attention to fine speech, but keeps his eye on His business," wrote this old believer, who was burned at the stake for his frankness.

The beginnings of a Russian theater and a poetry modeled on the French appeared in the 1600's. Later, as Enlightenment ideas spread at the court of the czars, the more natural verse of Mikhail V. Lomonosov (1711–1765), a scientist, historian, and humanist, and the realistic satire of the plays of Denis I. Fonvizin (*The Minor,* 1782), brought work of high achievement.

The poet Gavriil R. Derzhavin (1743–1816) wrote elaborately on a classical model. Nikolai M. Karamzin (1766–1826), author of a classic history of Russia, also had great influence through stories and travel letters written in the then-current English "sentimental" form. More prophetically, the same model in the hands of Aleksandr Radishchev (*Journey from St. Petersburg to Moscow,* 1790) earned its author a term in Siberia for its outspoken advocacy of emancipation of the serfs. Ivan A. Krylov (*Fables,* 1809) was a Russian La Fontaine who found in peasant wisdom an escape from the moral and practical restraints imposed by the czarist government.

THE INSPECTOR-GENERAL *in Gogol's play of that name shouts at the peasants, accusing them of dishonesty, even though he is the dishonest one.*

BETTMANN ARCHIVE

Pushkin. The event that brought Russia into the European fold once and for all was the invasion and ultimate defeat of Napoleon's armies in 1811–1812. Within a few years, Aleksandr Pushkin (1799–1837) wrote and published works that would become the basis of a modern Russian literature. His major works include the Shakespearean-type tragedy, *Boris Godunov*; the novel *The Captain's Daughter*; a history of a peasant rebellion; and short stories such as the famous "Queen of Spades." Towering above the rest, however, is the verse novel *Eugene Onegin* (1825–1831), the great poetic masterpiece of Russian literature. Pushkin's combination of deep seriousness and lively vitality have been the envy of Russian writers ever since.

The other poets of Pushkin's generation—notably Mikhail Lermontov, Evgeny Baratynsky, Nikolai Yazykov, and Fëdor Tyutchev—also exerted great influence.

A slightly later group of writers explored the possibilities of realism, drawing especially on the experiences of the peasants. This group included Aleksei Tolstoy, Nikolai Nekrasov, and Ivan Nitkin.

In prose, the time was one of intense critical squabbling between westernizers, who favored European forms and attitudes, and "Slavophiles," who stuck to the forms and values of old Russia. The vigorous and original criticism, both social and literary, of Vissarion Grigoryevich Belinsky and Aleksandr Herzen helped turn Russian thought toward the material and moral welfare of all human beings, a social awareness that would deeply influence the 20th century.

The novel. The Russian novel reflected these social concerns. Nikolai Vasilyevich Gogol (1809–1852) began with affectionate and romantic pieces about peasant and Cossack life. But with the play *The Inspector-General* (1836) and a series of stories including "The Overcoat," he turned his attention to an almost scientific approach to social hypocrisy and poverty. Gogol never accepted easy answers. In *Dead Souls* (1842), his most unforgettable work, the behavior of the sharp operator, Chicherin—who buys lists of dead serfs from unscrupulous landowners, then uses this "property" to gain mortgages from banks—is symbolic at once of greed and of the indomitable human ability to scavenge life from death itself. Gogol was a part of a great movement to reform Russia, particularly to abolish serfdom. The medieval institution of serfdom was finally ended by the czar in 1860, the year before the beginning of America's Civil War.

Among other reformist works were *Oblomov* (1858) by Ivan Goncharov, portraying the emptiness of the outdated but change-resistant aristocracy. *A Sportsman's Sketches* (1852), by Ivan Turgenev, had great effect in dramatizing the issue of serfdom.

Turgenev of all Russians worked most in the contemporary European manner and spent much of his time abroad. His novel *Fathers and Sons* (1861) is a prototype of the novel of the cultivated but socially alienated man that would dominate European fiction to the present day.

Tolstoy and Dostoevski. The next 20 years saw the publication of works of supreme genius by Fëdor Dostoevski (*Crime and Punishment*; *The Idiot*; *The Possessed*; and *The Brothers Karamazov*); and by Leo Tolstoy *(War and Peace*; *Anna Karenina)*. They stand with the efforts of Dickens, Balzac, and a very few others as the major works of modern literature. Each writer developed an extensive moral philosophy. Tolstoy's matured into the nonviolence later preached by Gandhi. Dostoevski's views contributed to 20th-century existentialist thought.

These novels even surpass the writers' abilities to understand themselves. In *War and Peace,* Tolstoy set out with a deeply conservative idea, but wrote of the lives of extraordinary individuals, almost universally in conflict with the spirit of their times. In *The Brothers Karamazov,* Dostoevski intended to write about loss of faith and to follow it with a second novel about its recovery. The sequel never appeared; yet *The Brothers Karamazov* suggests its own kind of faith, even when confronted with every betrayal the world is capable of. The only affirmation is a touching of hands and an impulsive burst of tears at the conclusion. No one who has read this scene has ever forgotten it.

The succeeding generation included the poets of that strange self-criticizing lyric called symbolism. Vladimir Soloviev seems to herald the new movement; its most significant members included Andrei Bely and Aleksandr Blok.

Short fiction and drama.

In short fiction and the drama, the new generation included Maxim Gorky and Mikhail Artzybashev. The one true inheritor of the vision of Tolstoy and Dostoevski, however, was named Anton Chekhov.

Chekhov. Chekhov was a writer of restrained yet immensely suggestive and evocative short stories and "small" plays. A doctor, he seemed almost scientific in his dissection of the Russian malaise, yet laughter and a kind of joy in human nature keep breaking in. Among his greatest works for the stage are *Uncle Vanya* (1899) and *The Cherry Orchard* (1904).

Chekhov lived at the edge of a new era in Russia. In 1905, the reformers staged an unsuccessful revolt against the czar. In 1917 and 1918, a revolution succeeded, hastened by the stresses of World War I. The next generation, including Anna Akhmatova, Osip Mandelstam, and Boris Pasternak, would carry on the tradition of literary greatness through the years of trial and repression. But their history belongs properly to the age of the moderns.

Eastern Europe

A world of languages and peoples exists between Russia and the West. The literary growth of Czechoslovakia, Poland, and Hungary typifies that of the whole area.

Both Poland and the states that would become Czechoslovakia played major roles in medieval and Renaissance times. Poland's early literature, however, relied on Latin; while Czechoslovakia (then the states of Bohemia and Moravia) developed a vernacular tradition by the 1300's. By the mid-1500's, a vernacular tradition in Polish had at last taken hold.

These early years had been prosperous and powerful for Eastern Europe. But the Thirty Years War in the 1600's decimated the Protestant Czechs, and power politics steadily gnawed at Poland's boundaries and independence. Bohemia substantially lost its identity and its literature. But the Czech language began to revive in the 1700's. Hungarian began to emerge from the shadow of Latin at the same time. Only in the 1900's did the Slovak leader L'udovít Štúr finally provide his people with its own unified literary tongue.

Poland.

Of the three nations, Poland had by far the strongest sense of identity. The early 19th century, with its romanticism and nationalism, produced a fervent response from young Polish writers. Four of them, writing chiefly from exile in France, were later to be thought of as fathers of a new Polish literature: the poets Adam Mickiewicz, Juliusz Slowacki, Zygmunt Krasinski; and, though hardly known till after his death, the gifted Cyprian Norwid.

As the century wore on, the first fire waned. A practical, "positivist" approach took over in Warsaw, and Poland produced fine, if less emotional works, from the novelists Bolesław Prus and Henryk Sienkiewicz (Nobel Prize in Literature, 1905), and the playwright Gabryela Zapolska. Finally, as World War I approached, violent emotion returned, but now in the name of modernism. The dramatist Stanislaw Wyspiánski, the poets Kasimierz Tetmajer and Jan Kasprowicz, and the novelist Władysław Reymont (Nobel Prize for Literature, 1924), all spoke for a free, original, and deeply patriotic literary tradition.

Czechoslovakia.

The same years had seen similar advances in the Czech and Slovak tongues. The early 1800's produced the Czech poets Karel Hyneck Mácha and Jan Kollar. Mácha wrote in an international, high literary style of deep melancholy, but Kollar sought something else. A passionate spokesman for pan-Slavism, he became the spiritual father of poetry in the Slovak tongue. Each had followers in the next generation.

The years before World War I saw both a thoroughly modern and a thoroughly heroic literature in the two cousin languages, soon to be combined in one nation by the results of war.

Hungary.

In Hungary, stimulated by the remarkable cultural and economic growth of Budapest, the 1800's saw an even more rapid development. Three poets successively dominated the 19th century: Mihǎly Vörösmarty, Sándor Petöfi, and János Arany. There were several novelists, including the talented Mór Jókai. As World War I approached, a vigorous popular theater produced the internationally successful writers of sophisticated comedy, Ferenc Molnar and Ferenc Herczeg. On another level was the deeply modernist, often intellectual poetry of the literary journals, one of whose representatives, Endre Ady, won a wide European following.

The very fragmentation and competition among the peoples of East Europe seemed in the 1800's to encourage a kind of provincialism. But in the 1900's, under the pressures of war and political repression, the Eastern Europeans would help define their countries' cultural identity and yet produce works of international appeal and influence.

Scandinavia

The tradition of the Scandinavian tongues looked back to such medieval figures as the Danish historian Saxo Grammaticus (c 1150–c 1220) and the Swedish religious visionary, St. Bridget (c 1300–1373). Only in the 1700's did true national literatures begin to emerge. Among the pioneers were Norway's Ludvig Holberg (1684–1754), Sweden's Olof von Dalin (1708–1763) and Carl Michael Bellman (1740–

1795), and Denmark's Johannes Ewald (1743–1781) and Adam Oehlenschlager (1779–1850). The task that these men had was nothing less than to establish a literary tradition despite the indifference of the cultivated intelligentsia, who looked for literature in French—and later, in the German—language.

The development of a tradition was assisted by two important nonliterary writers. Swedish scientist Emanuel Swedenborg (1688–1772) wrote on subjects ranging from engineering to physiology and psychology. Later he became a philosophical mystic whose speculations have had wide appeal. Carolus Linnaeus (1707–1778) was a botanist and founder of the modern system of taxonomy; he wrote in a vivid, translucent style.

With the Romantic movement, a new spirit of nationalism encouraged writers in the vernacular. In Norway, newly freed from Danish domination, folk literature studies built the national consciousness (notably in great collections by Jørgen Moe and Peter Christian Asbjørnsen). In Sweden, similar research produced the work of Arvid Afzelius. Denmark produced the most significant figure of all, the educator and writer Nikolai Grundtvig (1783–1872), whose *Northern Mythology* (1808) echoed through all three countries.

A fourth Scandinavian literature, that of Finland, was also awakening. Important works appeared both in the Swedish language and in native Finnish. The most notable were the legend-based epic, *King Fjalar* (1844), written in Swedish by Johan Ludvig Runeberg; and the *Kalevala,* in Finnish, a folk epic dating from the Middle Ages, but only assembled and given formal structure in the mid-1800's, written by two physicians.

From these beginnings, writers of the later 1800's entered the mainstream of European literature. In Denmark, early Romanticism gave way to a sober, reflective period, typified in the verse of Paul Møller and S.S. Blicher. The dominant author and critic of the day, Johan Heiberg (1791–1860), was perhaps most important as the inspiration for new talent. Two of his protégés attained world importance. The philosopher Søren Kierkegaard (1813–1855) defined the passionate relationship of the soul to its belief, influencing what later came to be called existentialism. Hans Christian Andersen (1805–1875), famous as a writer of fairy tales ("The Fir-Tree," "The Ugly Duckling," "The Emperor's Nightingale"), was one of the first to understand the potential of the imagination as a subtle, independent force.

As the turn of the century approached, in common with the rest of Europe, Denmark found itself moving toward to a new aesthetic of realism, led by the famous critic Georg Brandes

DOUBLEDAY

AMERICAN SWEDISH NEWS EXCHANGE

IBSEN AND STRINDBERG, *Scandinavian giants of the modern theater, agreed only on their dark, pessimistic view of life.*

(*Main Currents in Nineteenth-Century Literature,* 1872–1890). In the new atmosphere, major novelists included Jens Jacobsen and Henrik Pontoppidan (*The Promised Land,* 1891–1895; *Kingdom of the Dead,* 1912–1916), the poet Holger Drachmann, the later proletarian novelist Martin Andersen Nexø, and the productive and imaginative Johannes Jensen.

In Norway, an equivalent tradition of realistic self-analysis was anticipated in *The Governor's Daughters* (1854–1855), by Camilla Collett, whose publication shocked the decorous Norwegian public. This tradition culminated in the work of Nobel Prize winners Knut Hamsun (1859–1952) and Sigrid Undset (1882–1949).

Ibsen and Strindberg. Of greatest world impact, however, were the dramas of Björnstjerne Björnson and Henrik Ibsen. A fine novelist and poet, Björnson began with epic drama but reached his peak in works that dealt with the problems of a slowly modernizing Norway (*Beyond Our Power,* a drama in two parts, 1883–1895). He was a Nobel Prize winner in 1903.

Henrik Ibsen (1828–1906) stands, with Chekhov and Shaw, among the greatest of modern playwrights. From romantic drama (*Brand,* 1866; *Peer Gynt,* 1867), through the most innovative realism (*A Doll's House,* 1879; *The Wild Duck,* 1884; *Hedda Gabler,* 1890), to a deep symbolism (*When We Dead Awaken,* 1900), he showed a rare gift for the expression of universal concerns. Ibsen had a special feeling, too, for the problems of women. At the same time, he felt little identity with his countrymen, and spent most of his time abroad.

In Sweden, after a first fine burst of Romantic poets (such as Erik Geijer and Esaias Tegnér), writing turned to issues and problems. Women's rights were covered in the work of novelist and journalist Frederika Bremer. A surprising backlash of misogyny appeared in the work of talented Carl Almquist. And an iconoclastic attack on Christian orthodoxy was apparent in the writings of Abraham Rydberg.

With the coming of Johan August Strindberg (1849–1912), however, Sweden found something rather more urgent. This unpleasant but unmistakable genius was master of the entire sequence of styles from realism to expressionism. The novel *The Red Room* (1879), and such plays as *The Father* (1887), *Miss Julie* (1888), *The Dream Play* (1902), and *The Ghost Sonata* (1907), have a sweep and force that is utterly convincing.

After Strindberg, Sweden saw a literature of individuals, not movements. The poets Verner von Heidenstam (Nobel Prize, 1916), Gustaf Fröding, and Erik A. Karlfeldt (Nobel Prize, 1931), and the novelists Selma Lagerlöf (the first woman to receive the Nobel Prize, 1909) and Hjalmar Söderberg, especially stand out.

Something of the vigor of this period was communicated, too, to the former possession, Finland. Writing in Swedish, the popular novelist Zachris Topelius, the politically radical Arvid Mörne, and the poet Jarl Hemmer especially distinguished the century since Finnish independence. The free-verse poet Edith Södergran and the prose writer Runar Schildt lent a special modernity to the decade after World War I. In Finnish, the 19th century's leading writers were the novelist Alexis Kivi (Stenvall) (*The Seven Brothers,* 1870) and the feminist playwright, Minna Canth. In modern times Finland produced Nobel Prize winner F.E. Sillanpää (*Fallen Asleep While Young,* 1931), the poet Eino Leino, and the mid-20th century novelists Mika Waltari and Väinö Linna.

France

The development of French literature after the French Revolution followed a singular path. The early Romanticism of Germany and England were not picked up by the French, who were caught in the turmoil of revolution (1789), the Reign of Terror (1793–1794), and the imperial exertions of Napoleon (ending in 1815). A literary reawakening was delayed, but when it came, after 1815, it was to have great impact.

The novel. The post-Napoleonic age was one of titans in French fiction. By mid-century France had produced four of the world's great novelists—Victor Hugo (1802–1885), Honoré de Balzac (1799–1850), Stendhal (1783–1842), and Gustave Flaubert (1821–1880).

Hugo began with poetry and drama. His genius for heroic and sentimental verse is difficult to appreciate today, though Americans hear a similar note in the poetry of Walt Whitman. His play *Hernani* (1830) was one of the great landmarks of the century—and a scandal to its first audience, announcing as it did the end of the classic restraints on French drama. His great novel, *Les Misérables* (1862), was written in the romantic mode of Sir Walter Scott and of Alexandre Dumas *pere* (*The Three Musketeers,* 1844), but extends and broadens it.

Balzac's great interlinked series of novels and short stories, under the overall title *La Comedie Humaine,* "jump-cuts" characters and events. Balzac catches the moral dilemma of his materialistic society by exposing its double standards mercilessly. The occasional roughness of his technique becomes a part of the overall surface, like the graininess of a very high speed photograph.

Stendhal (*The Red and the Black,* 1831), and Flaubert (*Madame Bovary,* 1856), use a slower film, but with extremely daring subjects—adultery, female sexuality, frustrated ambitions, murder—with a seriousness that anticipates the fiction of the present century.

Drama. After Hugo's *Hernani,* the theater held much of the early excitement of Romanticism, but poetry claimed the larger talents. Hugo's own lyrics stand alone. But a host of others, including Alfred de Musset, Auguste Barbier, Alfred de Vigny, Gerard de Nerval, and Théophile Gautier brought lyricism in French poetry back to exuberant life.

By mid-century, the theater turned from serious subjects to farce, situation plays, and sentimental romance. These remain models for popular theater and films to the present day. The plays of the younger Dumas (*La Dame aux Camélias,* 1852), and Edmond Rostand (*Cyrano de Bergerac,* 1897) reveal the sentimental at its most popular.

Poetry. Poetry alone refused to give up its deep emotion and high seriousness. Charles Baudelaire (*Les Fleurs du Mal,* 1857) introduced a new ethic for the poet, working for the sake of ultimate truth—or beauty—alone, without reference to social concerns or conventions. Many others followed his example, attracted by the moral freedom his stand seemed to offer. The poems are often beautiful, but the cost of producing them was high. Arthur Rimbaud, the most prodigiously gifted of his generation (*Le Bateau Ivre, Les Illuminations*), found the emotional strains unbearable and lapsed into silence. Others who felt the strains were Paul Verlaine, Rimbaud's destroying and self-destructive friend; Stéphane Mallarmé, whose verbal ingenuity points the way to the Joyce of *Finnegans Wake;* Jules Laforgue, self-effacing in his best work nearly to the point of invisibility; and Charles Péguy, as stubborn in virtue as the others in diffidence or vice. To these men, the contrary roles of sinner and saint were somehow at one in the poet, who became a hero of sorts in the battle for men's souls.

Later novels. Novels, too, changed their style and path over the years, though to a greater extent than poetry, they kept their central role as public entertainment first, public statement second. George Sand (1804–1876), a woman of great influence on her age, progressed to a fiercely feminist concern with social problems of every description (*The Haunted Pool,* 1846; *Les Maitres Sonneurs,* 1853). Alphonse Daudet, the brothers Edmond and Jules Goncourt, and the extremely influential Émile Zola (whose major work was a 20-novel study of a family's dissolution) together developed what Zola called a "scientific" naturalism. Successors included the very successful Guy de Maupassant.

The lifting of naturalism to the level of high art, however, was left to Marcel Proust (1871–1922). At the beginning of *À la Recherche du Temps Perdu* (literally, "in search of lost time," but translated as *Remembrance of Things Past*), written largely before World War I, a vast flow of feelings and reminiscences begins with the remembered taste of a *madeleine,* a kind of polite macaroon, in childhood. The book ends with an elaborate but joyless party, symbolic of a society that has left its best days behind. Between beginning and end, Proust creates a world of simple sense experience that somehow comes to exemplify nearly all knowledge and feeling, including the reader's own.

Criticism. Among the many major critics of the century, Charles Sainte-Beuve (1804–1869), and the later Hippolyte Taine (1828–1893), exhibited, though in different ways, a characteristically French mode of thinking. Both sought explanations for events—and literary works—in the conditioning that produced the man or the nation. One of the early studies of a national personality was that of Alexis de Tocqueville (1805–1859), whose observations on America and Americans in *Democracy in America* (1835) seem still valid 150 years later.

Spain and Spanish-America

Spanish literature began to stir after 1833, when a turn toward political liberalism made possible the return of exiles who knew European Romanticism at first hand. Early expressions included sharp sketches by Mariano José de Larra and the poetry of José de Espronceda.

A wakening in the theater began with *Don Álvaro* (1835) by Ángel de Saavedra, and continued for about a decade. A generation later, major poets appeared, including Gustavo Bécquer and the remarkable Rosalía de Castro.

Beginning in the last quarter of the 1800's, Spanish novelists slowly developed a kind of realism. Notable examples include Pedro Antonio de Alarcón's *The Three-Cornered Hat* (1874), Armando Palacio Valdés's *The Joy of Captain Ribot* (1889) and *La aldea perdida* (*The Lost Village,* 1911), and Vicente Blasco Ibáñez's uncharacteristic, but world-famous war novel, *The Four Horsemen of the Apocalypse* (1916). The period produced a Nobel Prize winner in the occasionally inspired playwright José Echegaray. The energetic novelist Benito Pérez Galdós (1843–1920) wrote vast sequences of popular history, attempting to wake his people to some sense of their own past.

Like England, Spain also faced the pleasures and pains of dealing with its younger literary "twin"—Spanish America. Hispanic Americans had been writing since the gifted lyrics of the Mexican nun and feminist intellectual, Juana Inés de la Cruz (1651–1695). But true Latin American literary identity did not begin until the revolutionary ferment of the 1800's.

The experience of Andrés Bello, tutor to the great liberator of South

America, Simón Bolívar, was in many ways typical of the life of Latin-American writers to this day. He spent years traveling back and forth between Europe and his native Venezuela, and eventually made a career as an educator in Chile. His poetry was based on European models, but its life stemmed from the new continent it described (*Silva a la Agricultura de la Zona Torrida,* 1826). Writers of the next generation often traveled as exiles, avoiding unstable (and often dangerous) political upheavals. The exiled Cuban poet José María Heredia, for example, published in New York and lived out his years in Mexico. The poet Esteban Echeverría and the novelist José Mármol (*Amalia,* 1851–1855), were both exiles to Uruguay from Argentina. Still later, the poet and novelist Jorge Isaacs (*María,* 1867) was driven from his Colombian plantation by civil war.

From the beginning, politics, personality, and regionalism were inextricably mixed. At mid-century, Domingo Sarmiento, in exile from Argentina (but later to become its president), wrote a classic study of tyranny by charisma, *Facundo* (1845). Others who made major careers out of the politics of reform were Ecuador's Juan Montalvo, Puerto Rico's Eugenio María de Hostos, and Peru's Manuel González Prada. Regional writing explored the worlds of the Argentine gaucho (notably, the epic *Martin Fierro,* 1872–1879, by José Hernández), and of the Peruvian past in the half-fictional historical "anecdotes" of Ricardo Palma. A rising sense of class consciousness began what would become a great literary exploration of the differences between native and European, rich and poor. Representative works are a bitter novel about Chile's ruling class, *Martin Rivas* (1862), by Alberto Blest Gana, and *Cumandá* (1871), by Juan León Mera, about the Ecuadorian Indians.

Modernismo. Late in the 1800's, a new lyric voice was heard in the Americas. The hero of the cause of Cuban independence, José Martí, whose exile took him not only to Spain, but to New York City as well, wrote a substantial body of lyric (*Ismaelillo,* 1882). Once and for all, Martí broke completely with the stilted Spanish "classical" style, proving as much a literary as a political revolutionary. At the same time, many others were making the break, including Julian del Casal (Cuba), Salvador Díaz Mirón (Mexico), the remarkable José Asunción Silva (Colombia), and Manuel Nájera Gutiérrez (Mexico). The revolution was completed with the first book by a precocious poetic genius, the Nicaraguan Rubén Darío (*Azul,* 1888). Darío drew from the French of Baudelaire and Verlaine, but also owed much to the North Americans Whitman and Poe. The new style was called *modernismo,* and the word would echo through the first half of the 1900's.

The new writers' self-assertion ended forever Latin America's inferiority complex before the older European work. Darío excited the writers in Spain as deeply as he did those in the Americas.

A decade later, the United States humiliatingly defeated Spain in the Spanish-American War. This provided a sharper break between the mother country and her former colonies. The Latin Americans continued to follow *modernismo.* Spain claimed Darío too, but as the source of quite a different movement. Later called "The Generation of '98," it included Spain's most celebrated minds of the time—the social thinker Ángel Ganivet; critic and moral philosopher Miguel de Unamuno (*The Tragic Sense of Life in Men and Nations,* 1913); novelist and playwright Ramon del Valle Inclán; outspoken novelist of poverty and political action, Pío Baroja (*La Lucha por la Vida,* a trilogy, 1904); essayist José Martínez Ruiz (known as "Azorin"); and playwright and Nobel Prize winner Jacinto Benavente y Martínez (*Bonds of Interest,* 1907; *The Passion Flower,* 1913). Darío himself, whether in European or American persona, continued to grow in achievement until his death in 1916.

In Latin America after Darío's death, the next movement, called *Criollismo,* sought Latin American solidarity in its unique racial mix: native Indian, European, and African.

The American Spain, with its growing population, vigor, and potential wealth, now had uniquely original literary quality. The European parent drew from this discovery a sense of new life. In the 1900's, the revival would produce, in both Spains, work in the forefront of world literature.

Modern World Literature

The literature of the modern era was deeply influenced not only by literary fashion but by world events. Among these, two were of incalculable importance. One was the awakening of the East. The European world order that had been established in 1815 at the end of the Napoleonic wars had remained in place through the 1800's. But in the early years of the 1900's, it was made obsolete by the growing power and influence of countries outside its plan. The most important of these in the beginning was Japan, though as the century progressed, the shadow of China, a state composed of nearly a quarter of mankind, loomed larger and larger.

The second world development that deeply influenced literature was the establishment of modern totalitarian states. The growth of Hitler's Nazi Party in Germany and its eventual attempt to obliterate whole segments of the population—Slavs, gypsies, Jews—reminded all men of goodwill of the thin line between civilization and savagery. In the very same years, the Stalinist terror in the Soviet Union, often aimed at writers and intellectuals, duplicated the Nazi evil under a different creed. The apparatus of modern tyranny—secret police, torture, concentration camps, forced labor—was later adopted in many parts of the developing world, particularly in South America, parts of Africa, and Southeast Asia.

Writers responded to the physical and emotional violence of the century with a new voice. The Victorian age had replaced religious faith with scientific certainty. Now that prop—and faith in man's ability to act reasonably—had also failed. Twentieth-century writers were often grim and disillusioned. At the same time, their works became symbols of the human impulse to resist, to subvert, and to survive even the most unspeakable evils.

In countries less touched by violent change, the winds of modernism continued to blow strong. With its emphasis on the interior life of the individual—and the potential there for violence as well as pleasure—modernism seemed to reflect many of the same attitudes expressed by the dissenting writers under totalitarianism. For many modernism offered a necessary sanctuary from the horrors of world affairs—an interior, personal space where life could go on even in the midst of violence and repression.

Asia

The beginning of a new relationship between East and West begins with the victory of Japan in the Russo-Japanese War (1905) and with the establishment of the first Chinese republic in 1912. The roots of these developments lie in the late 1800's, however.

Japan. After a long period of isolation, Japan was opened once again to the outside world by an American naval officer, Matthew C. Perry, in 1854; in 1868 the Meiji restoration signaled Japan's reawakening. In literature, this meant an acceleration of translations and imitations of Western dramatic and fictional forms. The ancient literary form of the language was replaced by the vernacular at the urging of critic Shoyo Tsubouchi. The first major novel to follow this innovation was *Ukigumo* (1887–1889) by Shimei Futabatei.

Traditional Japanese fiction had had erotic (even pornographic) elements and portrayed the picaresque adventures of underworld characters. The Western works most admired by the Japanese encouraged the continuation of these elements. But the Western models also introduced a new sense of individualism and encouraged a questioning of social and political establishments.

Important writers prior to World War II included the poet Tōson Shimazaki and the novelists Sōsecki Natsume and Junichiro Tanizaki. Perhaps the best-known work in the West was *Rashomon,* a story told from several points of view, by novelist Ryūnosuke Akutagawa.

After the defeat of the Japanese in World War II, a new generation of writers came to world attention. They included the Nobel Prize-winning novelist Yasunari Kawabata (1899–1972), his close friend Yukio Mishima (1925–1970), and Kōbō Abe (*Woman in the Dunes,* 1964). All three attempted to deal with Japan's sudden emergence into the modern world and the destruction of its older traditions. They seemed disillusioned with modern Japan and reflected the tensions of the earth-shaking changes that the Japanese nation was experiencing. Both Kawabata and Mishima committed suicide.

The same sense of disillusionment was reflected in more recent novels. *Nights of a Fool* (1979) by So Aono, for example, is a tale of failed youthful rebellion involving both drugs and sex. It is familiar to Western readers, yet has particular poignance in its Japanese setting, where old traditions die hard.

China. There are fewer works known to the West from Chinese writers in this century, yet China's literature, too, is entering the international mainstream. The adoption of a vernacular and revitalization of intellectual life was begun with the May Fourth Movement in 1919. The philosopher Hu Shih, who was educated in the United States, played a major role in the movement.

Among the writers of stature in the first half of the century were Lu Hsün (1881–1936) and Ch'ien Chung-shu, author of the complex and appealing novel *Fortress Besieged* (1946).

Throughout Chinese history, literature had been enlisted in the working of political and social ends. With the victory of Chinese Communism, it retained this role, focusing much of the controversy during the Cultural Revolution of the 1970's.

Even in propagandist works, however, the marks of modern sensibilities have begun to appear. The technique, the acceptance of internal psychological development, and the emphasis on the development of character all owe something to Western influence (as does the Marxism of China's political leaders). Among the works reflecting these modern preoccupations are *Mountain Swallow* (1977) by Yang Ta-ch'un and *A Place for Love* (1979) by Liu Hsin-Wu.

The interchange between China and the rest of the world seems destined to increase in the coming years, and will likely have great influence both on the East and the West.

Islam. At the other geographic end of Asia (and extending through the Arabian Peninsula and North Africa), the Islamic nations seem to be nearing a period of renewed flowering and international influence. Dominated in the early century by Western nations searching for oil and other commodities, the Muslims reacted with an intense cultural conservatism. Yet they have been deeply influenced by world events, experiencing both the violence of war and the displacement, and a sudden prosperity and feeling of cultural identity.

Important writers of the early 1900's included Persia's poet of emancipation, Iradj, who contributed to the establishment of the modern nation of Iran and even advocated the emancipation of women; the novelist Sadegh Hedayet, also Iranian; the Egyptians Ahmad Shawqi and Hafiz Ibrahim; and the Turkish short story writer Mahmud Tymur.

In the second half of the century, one of the major events in the Islamic consciousness was the permanent establishment of the state of Israel, which displaced the Muslim Palestinians. The modern Palestinian poet 'Aqi expressed his wistful sense of loss in "On One Single Night." In this poem he personified his own and his people's experiences in the memory of a woman's face and the voices of children far away. Other Palestinians gave voice to more militant sentiments. Mahmud Darwish, for example, wrote that hammers in the hands of workers and guns in the hands of fighters are the only roses he wants to see.

Other important Muslim writers, reflecting in varying degrees the old traditions of Islam and the new sensibilities of this century, are the novelist of Egypt's national aspirations, Najib Mafuz; and the Algerian novelist Khateb Yassin, who brings to Arabic the influence of modern French symbolism.

The Islamic literatures have made little impression on the modern West, but the increasing importance of Islamic countries to the world economy seems certain to bring them greater influence in the years to come.

Literatures of Judaism

The story of the Jews has a peculiar place in the history of the 20th century. It is a story filled with contradictions and tragedy.

From the destruction of the Temple at Jerusalem by the Romans in 70 A.D., the Jews were dispersed to many parts of the world. In the Middle Ages, communities could be found in Christian Europe, in Islamic North Africa and Spain, and as far away as India.

The Jews stubbornly retained their separate identity wherever they settled, thanks in part to the preservation of Hebrew, the language of their Scriptures. At the same time, however, they made major contributions to the learning and literatures of other peoples. In Islamic Spain, for example, Jewish intellectuals wrote poetry in Hebrew and Spanish and philosophy in Arabic. The philosopher Maimonides (*Guide for the Perplexed,* 1190) served as a spokesman for his entire age.

At the end of the Middle Ages, a period or persecution dispersed the Jews once again, and they turned inward. Where they found tolerance, they continued to contribute to the secular tradition. But where persecution continued, as in Eastern Europe, religious orthodoxy and a new Jewish mysticism absorbed the energy of writers and philosophers. One of the mystical reactions to orthodoxy resulted in the birth of Hasidism, an emotional and joyful but intensely separatist movement that survives to the present day.

A new secularism among the Jews in Germany is of more interest in a literary sense. The German humanist Moses Mendelssohn (1729–1786) had an important influence on early German Romanticism. At the same time, he was a major figure in the Haskalah, the Jewish Enlightenment that produced both the religious tradition of Reform Judaism, which is more open to developments in the secular and non-Jewish worlds, and the beginning of a secular literature both in Hebrew and in Yiddish, the vernacular of Eastern European Jews. Although linguistically related to German, Yiddish was written in traditional Hebrew characters. Israel Axenfeld, I.M. Dick, and I.B. Levinson were among those who began traditions of fiction and drama in Yiddish during the early 1800's.

Major writers in Hebrew during the century included the Italian "Jewish supremacist" S.D. Luzzatto, and a host of poets and novelists in Russia, including Judah Leon Gordon, famous for the purity and beauty of his language, and the novelist Mendele mocher sforim (S.Y. Abramovich). Like many Jewish writers, Mendele wrote both in Hebrew and Yiddish and often translated his stories from one language to the other.

Later in the century, in Poland, the Polish poet and novelist Isaac Loeb Peretz developed a major Yiddish tradition of stories about small local Jewish communities (*Stories and Pictures,* 1900–1901). His contemporary, Sholom Aleichem, eventually emigrated to the United States, and gradually won audiences in every major language. His novel *Tevye's Daughters* (translated 1949) became the basis of the Broadway musical *Fiddler on the Roof.*

The 1900's brought immense changes to the world community of Jews. Early in the century, an unprecedented wave of immigration made New York City a capital of world Judaism, thanks in part to the persecution of Jews in Eastern Europe. With the birth of Nazism in Germany in the 1920's and 1930's, the persecutions of earlier decades seemed pale by comparison. One of every three Jews alive at the time died at the hands of the Nazis between 1938 and 1945. Millions of others were driven from Europe, settling in North America, South America, and eventually in the newly established state of Israel.

Long before Israel was established, Jews had begun to return to their historic homeland. The social philosopher Asher Ginzberg (1856–1927) and the poet Hayyim Nahman Bialik (1873–1934) established themselves in Palestine and helped create a modern Hebrew language and style.

Among other early writers in the new Israel were Saul Tchernihovsky, a poet of great gifts, and Rachel (Rachel Blovstein), a lyric poet of uncommon simplicity and grace. The next younger generation included Abraham Shlonsky, Leah Goldberg, and others. Shmuel Y. Agnon won the Nobel Prize for Literature in 1966. Writers of the 1960's and '70's included Moshe Shamir, Amos Oz, A. Appelfeld, and S. Yizhar.

In Yiddish, important works were produced both in Israel and in the United States. The 1978 Nobel laureate was Isaac Bashevis Singer, an American whose stories first appeared in a Yiddish newspaper in New York; they were eventually translated into English and other languages. The stories were mainly about Singer's early life in the ghetto communities of Poland, but others took place in New York, Florida, Argentina, and Israel, reflecting the new dispersion—and internationalism—of the Jewish community. Other novelists, short story writers, and poets continued to write in Yiddish, although most were less prominent outside their own language.

One vital tradition of modern Jewish literature has been in the accumulation of personal histories from the Holocaust—the attempted eradication of the Jews by the Nazis. Thousands of personal accounts and analyses have appeared, yet the documentation continues to grow—a record unique in world literature in its attempt to comprehend catastrophic events through the most minute details of individual experience.

Literature of Dissent

The Soviet Union. The revolution struck at a moment of great literary ferment. Among writers, many welcomed the change, but some would soon recoil in horror as the new system hardened into tyranny; others fled Russia and lived out their lives in obscurity, cut off from their mother tongue and countrymen.

Among the émigrés were poets Konstantin Balmont, V.I. Ivanov, and Ivan A. Bunin, a master of Russian prose who won the Nobel Prize in 1933. (Another in this group was Vladimir Nabokov, who would one day win fame as a writer in English.)

Those who stayed faced years of great uncertainty. Novelist and dramatist Maxim Gorky (1868–1936) prospered during the excitement of the early 1920's; but as the party line on literary style hardened, he was forced into the narrow mold of "social-ist realism" and squandered his great talent.

The poets Sergei Yesenin and Vladimir Mayakovsky both won great fame as supporters of the new regime of Lenin. But within a few years, they rejected the terrifying excesses of the new system. Marina Tsvetayeva, an astonishingly pure lyric talent, emigrated at the beginning of the revolution, but returned, unable to bear the loneliness of exile. The life of Stalinist Russia proved to be no more tolerable. She—and both Yesenin and Mayakovsky—were suicides.

Perhaps the greatest poet of the period was Osip Mandelstam, an intellectual whose lyrics look back to Pushkin and forward to the modern poets of Europe. Along with Isaac Babel, who celebrated the early revolutionary times with a mixture of Jewish humor and Cossack adventure, Mandelstam died in a labor camp. Both were victims of one of Stalin's many purges, which especially singled out writers of Jewish descent.

This tragic list of defections, suicides, and labor camp deaths is also a list of some of the century's greatest literary talents. The two finest writers who survived did so by remaining officially silent. The poet and novelist Boris Pasternak devoted most of his official time to translation. He and his gifted friend, Anna Akhmatova, continued to write privately, however, and to share their work with a small circle of trusted friends. Pasternak's novel *Doctor Zhivago* was smuggled out of the Soviet Union and published in Paris in 1957. He was awarded the Nobel Prize, but his government would not allow him to accept it.

Other writers survived after a fashion by choosing noncontroversial subjects for their novels and poetry. Stories of war (*Armored Train 14–69,* V.V. Ivanov, 1923) or revolution (*The Silent Don,* Mikhail Sholokhov, 1928–1940) were especially popular.

During the 1930's, the period of Stalin's mass purges, writers were subjected to particularly stringent

THE LOWER DEPTHS *by Maxim Gorky starred the great actor and theorist Constantin Stanislavsky at its first performance in Moscow.*

NEW YORK PUBLIC LIBRARY

controls, and it seemed that the vitality of Russian literature might be snuffed out once and for all by death and intimidation. After World War II, however, a new period of creativity began.

Memories of the heroic Soviet effort during the recent war served some writers with material for a lifetime (for example, *Days and Nights* by Konstantin Simonov, 1945, an epic of the defense of Stalingrad). Then the death of Stalin in 1953 brought a relaxation of the state's standards for writers, and a tenuous alliance was formed between established literary personalities (Ilya Ehrenburg and Alexandr Tvardovsky, editor of an official literary magazine), young writers ambitious to extend the role of literature (Yevgeny Yevtushenko, Andrei Voznesensky, and others), and older critics of the Soviet system who had not dared speak in Stalinist times.

The most notable among this last group was Alexander Solzhenitsyn. After serving as an officer in World War II, Solzhenitsyn was arrested by the secret police. He served a term in the Soviet labor camps, and survived a bout with an often fatal type of cancer. The major achievement of "the thaw" in Soviet literary censorship was the publication of Solzhenitsyn's *One Day in the Life of Ivan Denisovich* (1962), thanks in part to the support of Tvardovsky. The book is a factual yet ironic account of a prisoner's day in a labor camp, and it brought the subject to the attention of Russian readers for the first time.

The thaw was short-lived, however. None of Solzhenitsyn's other major works was ever published officially in the Soviet Union. The novels *The First Circle* (1964) and *Cancer Ward* (1966), and the long nonfiction documentary of the labor camp system, *The Gulag Archipelago* (1973–1976), were circulated secretly in typescript and finally smuggled to the West, where they were published both in Russian and in translation. Publication of the first volumes of *Gulag* earned Solzhenitsyn both a Nobel Prize and exile from his native land. He settled—not altogether happily—in the United States.

Solzhenitsyn's daring was followed by an extraordinary group of dissenters who risked imprisonment or exile to publish according to their own lights, most often in *samizdat* (literally "self-publishing," meaning that the works were read only secretly in typescript). Among those whose works found their way to publication in the West were the remarkable poet Joseph Brodsky, critic Andrei Sinyavsky, satirist Aleksandr Zinoviev (*The Yawning Heights,* 1979), and the recorder of prison camp life (and inspiration of Solzhenitsyn's *Gulag*) Varlam Shalamov (*Kolyma Tales,* 1978).

Eastern Europe. The experience of writers in the countries of Eastern Europe came to resemble that of the Soviets after World War II, but their earlier histories depend on their own national fortunes.

Poland. Poland regained its independence in the treaty ending World War I, and its writers embarked on a vigorous literary revival that owed much to the modernist ideas of Western Europe. Outstanding among the new Polish writers were members of the Skamander group, led by poets Kasimierz Wierzyński and Julian Tuwim. Wierzyński's career followed the fortunes of the nation well into modern times. During the Great Depression of the 1930's, he turned to social criticism. In 1944, he wrote a moving narrative of his wartime experience (the Poles were invaded by Germany in 1939 and were occupied throughout the war). After the takeover of Poland by a Communist government controlled by the Soviet Union, Wierzynski emigrated, but continued to write with conviction from abroad.

IVAN DENISOVICH, *the labor camp prisoner of Solzhenitsyn's novel, was played by Tom Courtenay in the film version.*

CULVER PICTURES

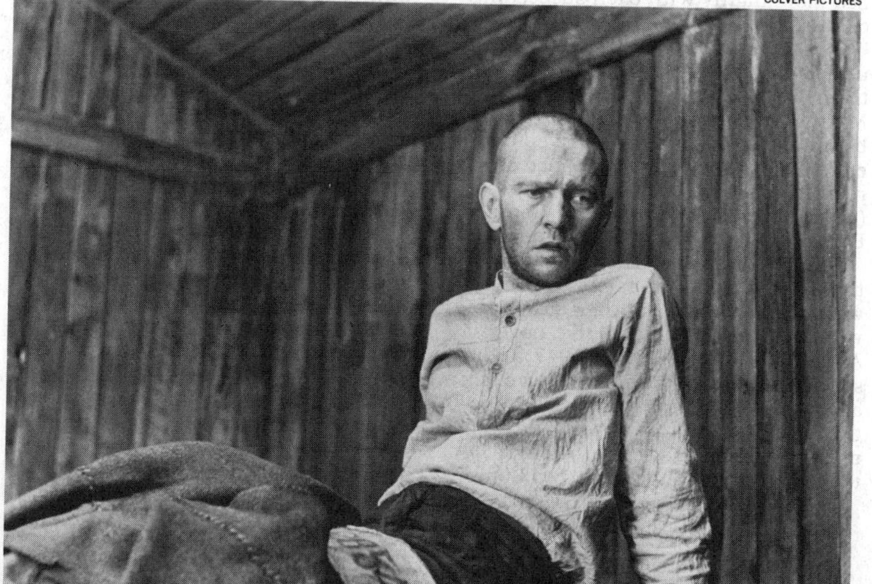

In the years after the war, Polish writers faced many of the moral challenges and physical dangers shared by writers in the Soviet Union. Among the works of particular distinction were the short stories of Tadeusz Borowski, who had survived a stay at the concentration camp at Auschwitz, and the novel *Ashes and Diamonds* (1948) by Jerzy Andrzejewski, which marked the beginning of a distinguished and morally independent career.

After the Soviet repression of neighboring Czechoslovakia in 1968, many Polish writers chose to emigrate. Others stayed, preferring to press for the relaxation of literary control or to wait for a change in political conditions. Among those who stayed and those who left, a remarkably high standard was maintained, and hope persisted that one day the groups would be reunited. During the political crises of 1981, in which the Poles again reached for more independence, the great exiled poet Czeslaw Milosz (Nobel Prize, 1981) returned for the first time since 1953. He found that unofficial publication of his work made it familiar to Polish readers, just as he was familiar by similar means with the younger poets working in Poland.

Czechoslovakia and Hungary. These countries were in a sense formed by the Treaty of Versailles after World War I. In a brief period of independence between the wars, both established literatures of international stature.

In Czechoslovakia, the plays and novels of Karel Capek (*R.U.R.,* 1920, a futuristic play in which he coined the word "robot") were performed; they soon received international attention through translation. The novel *The Good Soldier Schweik* (1920–1923) by Jaroslav Hašek was a wry portrait of the new nation's character.

Most remarkable of all was the work of Franz Kafka. Born in Prague of German Jewish parents, Kafka wrote in German about the frightening moral deracination of his time (*The Trial,* 1925; *The Castle,* 1926). His nightmarelike stories exerted wide influence on European letters, catching the mood of frustration and helplessness that gripped much of the war-torn Continent.

In Hungary, major figures included the poets Attila József, Miklós Radnóti (who died in a Nazi concentration camp), and Gyula Illyés; the novelists Pál Szabó and Lajos Zihaly; and the dramatist Lászlo Németh.

In the period since the establishment of Communist regimes controlled by the Soviet Union, neither Czechoslovakia nor Hungary have been as successful as Poland in maintaining an atmosphere conducive to literature. Revolts were put down violently by the Soviets in Hungary in 1956 and in Czechoslovakia in 1968. Important books may be printed only unofficially or abroad, and writers continue to risk great danger if their views are not officially accepted.

Among the leading writers of recent years are the Czech novelists Ludvik Vaculik (*The Guinea Pigs,* 1973), Milan Kundera (in exile), B. Hrabal, and Ivan Klima; the dramatists Pavel Kohout (in exile) and Vaclav Havel (jailed for "subversion" in 1979); and the poets Miroslav Holub and Jan Skacel. Among the Hungarians are novelists George Konrad, Miklos Meszoly, and Gyula Hernadi; and the poet Sandor Weöres.

Modernism

If the literature of dissent in the Soviet Union and Eastern Europe concentrated on the outward oppression of tyranny, the literatures of Western Europe concentrated on the inward—often on the oppressiveness of the writer's own mind and being.

This approach, which came to be known as "modernism," began in the late 1800's with the French poets Baudelaire, Rimbaud, and Mallarmé. The very title of Baudelaire's great work, *Les Fleurs du Mal* (The Flowers of Evil), suggests the mood that was beginning to settle on poetry even before the turn of the century. Baudelaire's poem "Le Voyage" ends with setting sail for something, but what it is is completely in doubt: "Heaven or Hell, what's the difference?"

In one of Rimbaud's poems, "Le Bateau Ivre," the journey is purely imaginary, taking place in the mind of a child while he is lying in the bottom of a rowboat tied up at the river's edge. And in a late, lonely sonnet of Mallarmé, the journey is stillborn: a swan is stuck in the ice, unable to muster the will or energy to break the ice with its wing before it utterly freezes over.

Uncertainty had arrived in many other disciplines as well. The new study of psychology, tied as it was to the subconscious, was ambiguous and dark by definition. Philosophers limited their scope of inquiry to small questions dealing with the meanings of words, having abandoned metaphysical speculations and questions of man's behavior to man. The new physics and non-Euclidean geometry called even mathematical "truth" into question. Perhaps worst of all, studies of society were suggesting that all governments were inherently irrational and unjust, yet they seemed ever more firmly in control, even as the prospect of war came closer with each passing day.

Yet literature during this time experienced one of its greatest rebirths. In the West, writers built on the inheritance of the French symbolists, returning to childhood, and to a simpler, if intellectually demanding, "mythic" way of explaining the real world. They searched the past myths from Greece and Rome, and from the Celtic and Germanic stories of the Middle Ages for parallels and patterns in which to set their own words. This new myth differed from the old in that it sought to explain not the fate of nations and peoples, but of individuals—it was subjective, rather than objective. But writers from many different backgrounds came to agree on the value of common mythological references as a way of bridging the huge gap between one human mind and another.

By its very nature, this new style of writing in the purest form made its first appeal to a cultured few. James Joyce's *Ulysses* (and even more, his later *Finnegans Wake*) required more previous knowledge in the reader than any influential piece of writing since the Renaissance. Yet gradually the use of symbol and myth filtered down into more popular works, until even unsophisticated readers came to understand and expect it. Gradually, a new "modern" sensibility was developed that today influences the beginning poet or short story writer as well as the scholarly professional. It is in this sense that the following pages take the word "modernism."

France

World War I sounded the death knell for French dreams of international glory. The shock of this experience can be seen in the career of the novelist Romain Rolland, whose *Jean Christophe* (1904–1912) is a confident masterpiece, but whose work over the next 40 years never dared so much again.

Among those whose careers spanned the pre- and postwar eras, the works of Colette (*The Innocent Wife,* 1903; *Cheri,* 1920; *Gigi,* 1945) seem more likely to last than those of Rolland. Confined to the intimate world of feelings and personal relations, her works reveal a talent that the world has valued more highly with each succeeding decade.

One group of French writers continued to seek for great meaning. Among them were Jules Romains and Roger Martin Du Gard (Nobel Prize, 1937), both authors of extraordinary epic cycles. Others sought significance in a revived Catholicism. Nobel laureate (1952) Francois Mauriac and Georges Bernanos were the most prominent.

France's reputation as a leader of the European avant-garde, however, was advanced by another group of writers. These included the novelist André Gide (Nobel Prize, 1947), who specialized in explorations of his characters' psychological states; Jean Cocteau (1889–1963), a writer (and film maker) of genuine grace, though he tended often to the bizarre; and Louis-Ferdinand Céline, who extended the tradition of self-loathing to new heights.

In the theater, Jean Giraudoux brought both innovations of style and a quixotic humanism. After 1945, the French developed the new theater of the absurd. The leading figure in this was Samuel Beckett, a transplanted Irishman whose *Waiting for Godot* (1952) became a classic of modern drama. Beckett received the Nobel Prize in 1969. Among other figures in the absurdist movement were Jean Anouilh, Jean Genet, and Eugéne Ionesco.

Another strand in French writing was the cult of action. It is prefigured in the works of André Malraux (*La Condition Humaine,* 1933), but the experience of writers who served in the French Resistance during the German occupation in World War II made something more of it. Jean-Paul Sartre built a philosophy on the importance of action to defining one's existence in a meaningless world. In addition to philosophical works, his philosophical novels (*Nausea,* 1938) and plays were greatly admired. Sartre's associate Albert Camus gave further expression to the existentialist philosophy, notably in his novels *The Stranger* (1942) and *The Plague* (1947).

French poetry produced no master after World War I to match the great symbolists. Paul Valéry dominated the period between the wars, writing in the symbolist tradition. Alexis Saint-Leger Leger, writing as St. John Perse, wrote outside the main tradition, yet the quality of his verse won him the Nobel Prize in 1960. Other poets—including Paul Éluard, René Char, Louis Aragon, and André Breton—concerned themselves with the movements called surrealism and dada.

After 1950, the French popular novel retained great vitality, producing among others the polished detective stories of Georges Simenon. At the same time, serious literature seemed to languish. As always, the French excelled in criticism, however. The works of Roland Barthes, Michel Foucault, and others developed new approaches to the study of both literature and society.

The new criticism did bring one new movement to literature—an extraordinarily circumstantial style pioneered by Alain Robbe-Grillet and Marguerite Duras, and mastered by Egyptian-born Edmond Jabès in *The Book of Questions* (1963–1965).

Throughout the latter part of the century, some of the liveliest writing in French has come from outside the mother country. In parts of Africa and the Americas formerly controlled by France, a movement stressing native sources grew up, providing such poets as Léopold Senghor (Senegal), Léon Damas (French Guiana), and Aimé Césaire (Martinique), who may be the best French-language poet of the age.

At the same time, there was an explosion of talent among the writers of French-speaking Canada. These include poets Alain Grandbois, Claude Gauvreau, Anne Hébert, and many others; and such novelists as Gabrielle Roy, André Langevin, Marie-Claire Blais, and Madeleine Gagnon.

Italy

Through the 1800's, the Italian writers of international appeal could have been fit into a single room—a terrible fate for the people who introduced the West to civilization. Among the few were the great novelist Alessandro Manzoni (*The Betrothed,* 1827) and the remarkable poet Giacomo Leopardi (*Canti,* written 1816–1836). Later in the century, the novels of Giovanni Verga became models for realist writers of the 1900's.

Much of the literary activity of the 1800's was involved with the struggle for Italian unification. The great creative efforts of the new nation went into the grand opera, which helped to form a sense of national identity. In Verdi's *Otello* (1887) and *Falstaff* (1893), the authentic Italian voice may be heard as it had not rung out in centuries (though ironically, both stories came from Shakespeare).

In the first decades of the 1900's, the rhetorical poet Gabriele D'Annunzio won great international celebrity. But it was the dramatist Luigi Pirandello who brought a genuine modernism to Italy. His *Six Characters in Search of an Author* (1921) and *Henry IV* (1922) became classics of the European theater and had great influence on later dramatists.

The period of Fascism and Italy's eventual defeat in World War II read like a play even more bitter than Pirandello dared to write. Yet literary production continued. Under Fascism, the poets Giuseppe Ungaretti, Eugenio Montale, and Salvatore Quasimodo (the last two Nobel Prize winners) developed a deliberately obscure style in order to write honestly without being silenced by the Fascist state. After World War II, their style became more accessible, but their deep human concerns remained.

Novelists included the early modernist Italo Svevo and Alberto Moravia, whose long career seemed to mirror the history and moods of the country itself. In the 1940's, novelists awakened to a new realism, and for nearly 20 years, Italian fiction was filled with a passionate and reformist spirit. Among the writers of this era were Cesare Pavese, Elio Vittorini, Carlo Levi (*Christ Stopped at Eboli,* 1945), Ignazio Silone, and Italo Calvino.

New writers have continued to appear, many from outside traditional literary circles, and writers like Calvino continued to prosper. The contemporary style most admired, however, concerns itself most often with European intellectualism rather than with the realities of Italian life.

EDWARD ROONEY

SIX CHARACTERS *find the author and tell him what to write in Pirandello's absurdist play.*

Spain and Portugal

World War I did not have the same earth-shaking effects in Spain and Portugal as in France. The Spanish had already lost their hopes for world importance. At the same time, they were approaching a cataclysm of their own—the Spanish Civil War (1936–1939), in which the authoritarian forces of Francisco Franco overcame the socialist and reformist Republicans.

Before the Civil War, such earlier prodigies as Unamuno, Pío Baroja, and Valle Inclán were still active. Among the younger generation were novelists Ramón Pérez de Ayala and Gabriel Miró Ferrer. The brilliant critic and cultural commentator José Ortega y Gasset came to acceptance as Unamuno's successor.

But it was in lyric poetry that this generation stood out. Using the style of *modernismo* learned from South America, Juan Ramón Jiménez earned a Nobel Prize (1956), and the brothers Manuel and Antonio Machado gained international recognition.

Some 20 years younger, a new generation was even more remarkable. It included Jorge Guillén, Vicente Aleixandre (Nobel Prize, 1977), Luis Cernuda, and the great dramatist and lyric poet Federico García Lorca (*Blood Wedding,* 1933; *The House of Bernardo Alba,* 1936). Together, these poets brought Spain to the forefront of European literature, but their success was short-lived.

The Civil War sent most of the leading writers into exile, and Antonio Machado and García Lorca were killed during the fighting. The long rule of Francisco Franco was not friendly to experiment or to political comment, and many poets stayed away for the rest of their lives.

It was not until the death of Franco in the 1970's that the Spanish poets were welcomed back to their own land. By this time major new writers had appeared. It seemed that the latter decades of the century might bring still another flowering of Spanish literary genius.

Meanwhile, in neighboring Portugal, an authoritarian regime also encouraged conservative literary styles. Only the poems of Fernando Pessoa (*Mensagem,* 1934) and the powerful realistic novel about Brazil, *A Selva* (1930) by J.M. Ferreira de Castro, stand out in the period between the wars. In the 1950's, the psychological novel *Sibila* by Agustina Bessa Luís attracted admiring attention.

Only in the 1970's, during a period of political reform, did Portugal's literature reawaken. The musings of three Portuguese women published in 1974, and modeled on the *Letters of a Portuguese Nun* written centuries earlier, shocked the reading public and became one of the symbols of the movement that restored democracy to the country that same year. The voice of feminism and of frankly sexual material from a woman's point of view seemed to bring centuries of male-centered literature into question.

Since the revolution of 1974, many other new and serious works have appeared, including the frank love poems of Vitorino Nemésio, and the novel *Sinais de Fogo* by Jorge de Sena.

Latin America. The great excitement of 20th-century literature in Spanish and Portuguese continued to be in South America, however. That continent (and the Spanish-speaking countries of Central America and the Caribbean) boasted a booming economy untouched by the great wars of the century and a continuing spirit of optimism despite grave social and political problems.

In the generation born near the turn of the century, many gained international fame. Among these were poets César Vallejo of Peru, Pablo Neruda of Chile (Nobel Prize, 1971), and Octavio Paz of Mexico; and the great fiction writers Jorge Luis Borges of Argentina (*The Aleph,* 1949) and Miguel Angel Asturias of Guatemala (Nobel Prize, 1967). Others who achieved a high level on a smaller scale were the poets Gabriela Mistral of Chile and Juana de Ibarbourou of Uruguay.

After mid-century, the older writers continued to produce, while a younger generation often equaled or surpassed them. Among the younger generation, Gabriel García Márquez of Colombia (*One Hundred Years of Solitude,* 1967) brought a truly mythical scope to the novel, and was read both in Spanish and in translation throughout the world. Other major world novelists included Carlos Fuentes of Mexico (*The Death of Artemio Cruz,* 1964) and Mario Vargas Llosa of Peru. These and other important writers (Cuba's Alejo Carpentier, Chile's José Donoso) often lived and wrote in exile as repressive regimes—both of the right and the left—came and went in their home countries. In the 1970's, many lived in or frequently visited Spain.

In Brazil, where Portuguese rather than Spanish is spoken, awakening to the new modernism arrived late through the efforts of the black poet Mario de Andrade and others. In the 1930's, the important scholarly work of sociologist Gilberto Freyre pointed toward the development of the realistic novel. Yet Brazilian writers, like their brothers in Latin America, developed a unique mix of realism and free fantasy. This mixture is exemplified in the work of Brazil's major novelist, Jorge Amado (*The Violent Land,* 1942; *Gabriela, Clove and Cinnamon,* 1958; *Tieta do Agreste,* 1977).

Among other Brazilian writers, José Lins do Rêgo was the first to write about the impoverished wilderness of the northeast. Younger writers with international followings include the poet Jorge de Lima and the novelist Clarice Lispector.

CULVER PICTURES

MARAT/SADE: *The crazed asylum inmates shocked audiences of Peter Weiss's play.*

Germany

Germany stood at the center of the terrible whirlwind that consumed large parts of Europe between 1914 and 1945. Her defeat in World War I and the terms of the Versailles Treaty brought nothing but despair and foreboding. To the great cultural historian Oswald Spengler, the war itself was but one symptom of *The Decline of the West* (1918–1922). In a sense, he took the suicide of Goethe's hero Werther and applied its example to all of Europe. The bleakness of his vision matched the bleakness of the time.

The same myth of decay is evident in the novels of the great Thomas Mann (Nobel Prize, 1929), but Mann finds some solace in myth. *The Magic Mountain* (1924) is one of the monuments of modern literature, and Mann's output continued through still another world war.

Austria was demoted by the Versailles settlement from a superpower (with control over much of Hungary and Czechoslovakia) to a mini-state. The modernist and often bitterly ironic works of Austria's authors—including Robert Musil, Karl Kraus, and Hermann Broch—reflect the sudden change in the country's status.

The 1920's were a period of intense experimentation in Germany itself. The ruin of war and Germany's dire financial crisis hung over the era and gave it an element of cynicism, yet there was also an attitude of heedless gaiety.

The mixture of lyricism, fantasy, and nighmare that had characterized the later works of Strindberg and Wedekind dominated the theater under the name expressionism. Perhaps the most enduring production of the period was the work of a young dramatist named Bertolt Brecht. His *The Threepenny Opera* (performed in 1928), an adaptation of John Gay's *Beggar's Opera* (performed in England in 1728), with music by Kurt Weill, seemed to catch the mood of the age; it has often been produced in the years since. Its mordant songs ("Mack the Knife") are familiar in several languages. Brecht himself became a major figure in later drama as an exile in New York in the 1930's and '40's and later as a resident of East Germany. But none of his influential "epic theater" pieces (*Mother Courage and Her Children,* 1941) was successful with American audiences.

World War I itself was the subject of perhaps the most famous novel in German written during the 1920's. *All Quiet on the Western Front* (1929) by Erich Maria Remarque is a classic of realistic war narrative and antiwar feeling. In a different vein, the novels of Hermann Hesse, turning to mysticism rather than realism or nightmare, have received constant attention in the years since their publication. His best known works include *Steppenwolf* (1927) and *Death and the Lover* (1933). He won the Nobel Prize in 1946.

With the rise of Adolf Hitler to power in the 1930's, many German writers went into exile and German literature went into eclipse. Among those who recorded the terrible time of persecution and war was the German-Jewish poet Nelly Sachs (*O, The Chimneys,* 1967). She won the Nobel Prize in 1966.

After the defeat of the Nazi forces, Germany was in ruins. Yet within a few years Germany rediscovered its literary voice. In the theater, fierce dramatists of justice called the nation to account for the terrors of its past, following in the stylistic footsteps of Brecht. Rolf Hochhuth (*The Deputy,* 1963) and Peter Weiss (*The Persecution and Assassination of Jean Paul Marat as Performed by the Inmates of the Asylum of Charenton under the Direction of the Marquis de Sade,* 1964) demonstrated the ability of the theater to question and shock. Among other dramatists of worldwide influence were the Swiss writers Max Frisch and Friedrich Dürrenmatt.

Among novelists, the major voices included Günter Grass, whose *The Tin Drum* (1959) was a sardonic review of German attitudes during the Nazi period; and Heinrich Böll, recipient of the Nobel Prize in 1972.

Germany after the war was a divided nation. While West Germany received all the benefits and hazards of rapid economic growth and contact with other Western nations, East Germany, under the control of the Soviet Union, languished. Writers there were required, as in the rest of Eastern Europe, to select topics and attitudes sympathetic to the state. Yet beginning in the late 1960's, the Eastern writers became more daring and the regime somewhat more yielding. As individuals, German writers, both East and West, continued to contribute to the larger world of literature.

Scandinavia

The Scandinavian countries offered no writers of the stature of Ibsen or Strindberg in the years after 1914, yet their separate literary traditions, influenced by the international style of modernism, continued.

In Sweden, which remained neutral through both world wars and gradually erected a prosperous democratic socialist state, the major writer of the early 1900's was Pär Lagerkvist, who combined a true modernist sensibility with the characteristic reserve of his native land. Among his most important works are *The Dwarf* (1944) and *Barabbas* (1950). He was awarded a Nobel Prize in 1951.

Among other significant writers are Vilhelm Moberg, who spent considerable time in the United States and chronicled the story of Swedish immigrants to the United States in *The Emigrants* (1949), *Unto a Good Land* (1952), and *The Settlers* (1956). Novelist Harry Martinson and poet Eyvind Johnson were self-educated men who spoke for the workingman at home and who were awarded Nobel Prizes in 1974 for their advocacy.

In Norway, the modern period began with the novels of Johan Bojer (1872–1959), which sometimes approached the mythic in their sense of Norse identity. A generation younger, Sigrid Undset wrote a long trilogy about medieval Norway under the collective title *Kristin Lavransdatter* (1920–1922); it combined historical sensitivity with a very modern understanding of psychology. Undset received a Nobel Prize in 1928.

The most famous writer from Denmark in the 1900's was Baroness Karen Blixen, who wrote under the pen name Isak Dinesen both in Danish and in English. Many of her stories are set in East Africa, where she lived from 1914 to 1931. Her *Seven Gothic Tales* (1934), mysterious and understated, brought her world fame.

Two talented and original dramatists flourished in Denmark in the years between the world wars—Kaj Munk and Kjeld Abell. Munk's satirical plays showed a deep moral concern, and during the German occupation of Denmark in World War II he was put to death. Ironically, German dramatists after the war learned from him.

In recent years, leading Scandinavian writers have included the Swedish novelist Ivar Lo-Johansson, Norwegians Odd Bang-Hansen and Halldis Vesaas, and Danes Tage Skou-Hansen and Aage Dons. Although they write in languages read by only a few million, their concerns and their methods are those of the rest of Europe and of the world.

Greece

Greece only regained its political independence from the Muslim Turks after a prolonged war in the 1820's. Its literature had been held back until then by the insistence of academics on using the ancient (and by then, unspoken) form. Through the inspiration of the great poet Dionysios Solomos (1798–1857) and the crusading of later literary reformers, the poems and stories of the modern Greeks began to appear in the modern vernacular or demotic Greek, rather than in the classic language.

It was not until the 1890's, however, that writers appeared who would fully realize the promise of the new literary freedom. These men, contemporaries of France's Paul Valéry and Ireland's W.B. Yeats, produced a poetry that rivaled that of any language in the world. The most influential in this early group was Kostes Palamas. A generation later, Angelos Sikilianos began to explore the rich possibilities in Greece's mingled heritage of Christian and pagan symbols. Konstantin Kafavis has gained an international following since his death in 1933 because the lonely and pessimistic tone of his verse seemed to echo feelings in the rest of the world. In a characteristic poem, he writes, "No use to seek escape to another city. You will be a ruined man there as you are here. The city you live in follows you wherever you go."

Some poets of the next generation shared the same pessimism in the wake of Greece's involvement in both world wars. Yet an epic strain seemed still to grow even amid the pessimism. Nikos Kazantzakis wrote *The Odyssey: A Modern Sequel* (1938), a giant poem of some 33,000 lines, and later won a huge following with his novel *Zorba the Greek* (1946).

The poet George Seferis worked in another direction. His compelling mixture of intense symbolism and inventiveness made him the most influential poet from Greece in centuries. Odysseus Elytis combined modernist abstraction and characteristic Greek themes. Both Seferis and Elytis have received the Nobel Prize for Literature.

Greece has developed other forms of modern literature, from the psychological novel and play to works of Marxist advocacy. But the extraordinary success of its poets suggests wider implications for modern literature. Even as these poets become more and more Greek in their expression, they become more recognizable to the world literary scene. Like writers in Eastern Europe and Scandinavia, they contribute at once to the vitality of numerically small languages and to the creation of an international literary community.

Modern Literature in English

English was the dominant language of the 1900's, both in number of speakers and in literary achievement. The greater part of this mastery was attained in the first half of the century. The Irish supplied two masters of great importance; the Americans experienced a wave of fresh creativity as their literature came to worldwide attention; and the rest of the English-speaking world—from Great Britain, Australia, Canada, and both white and black Africa—supplying a wide range of talent.

Britain and Ireland

The first of the great world wars left Britain not defeated or destroyed, but bled white. Although it seemed the strongest nation on Earth in 1918, the rest of the century would be one long retreat from world power.

At home, the very meaning of the term British became vague. London was filling up with the residents of colonies and former colonies, acting more as a world capital for the English-speaking than as a capital for England. In fact, much of the most interesting literary activity, while centered on London, was carried on by non-Englishmen. James Joyce wrote in Switzerland and published in Paris (for largely English readers). W.B. Yeats belonged to Dublin. Ezra Pound and T.S. Eliot were Americans, one of whom circled around England, the other of whom made it his permanent home.

James Joyce. The great innovator in English in the 1900's was without doubt James Joyce. An Irishman in exile, Joyce redefined modernism for the English speakers' peculiar sensibilities. For Joyce (and for many who followed him) the story itself became a "symbol." By using the substructure of an older (and usually familiar) story, Joyce found a way of giving mythic significance to the most prosaic stuff of daily life. In *Ulysses* (1922), he used the story of Homer's *Odyssey,* yet not in the logical way that would suggest a retelling. He does not say "this is what Ulysses (Odysseus) would be like if he returned." He suggests rather that the elements of the story have quite literally repeated themselves in the lives of contemporary characters. Other tales of the past also reappear: the life of the great central character, Leopold Bloom, is a partial echo of the life of William Shakespeare.

In one sense, little about *Ulysses* is logical. First-time readers have a hard time following the "story," and Joyce's reliance on a stream-of-consciousness narrative seems to put things frequently out of order. Yet in another sense, the narrative is relentlessly logical. The parts are all carefully related not only to other parts but to their "originals" in the *Odyssey* or in other sources alluded to.

The technique of *Ulysses* has immense disadvantages. It could not, for example, tell a story with a complex plot. But for relating a simple action or emotion and giving it a global significance, the technique is unrivaled. In an important way, it is a new approach to writing, and the resulting work is a new form, neither exactly a novel, a play, or a poem, but a kind of amalgam of the three.

Yeats, Pound, and Eliot.

Other strains of modernism in English were developed by the Irish William Butler Yeats and by the transplanted Americans Ezra Pound and T.S. Eliot. Yeats began as a leader of the Irish renaissance and a founder of Dublin's Abbey Theatre. Yet in the second half of his life he exerted a different influence—more on the modernist poets of English than on his own Irish countrymen. Among his collections of poetry are *The Wild Swans at Coole* (1917), *The Tower* (1928), and *Last Poems* (1940).

Ezra Pound, some 20 years younger than Yeats, brought a characteristically ornery American style to a broad range of modern poetry. He was a great literary propagandist, an early student both of oriental and of Italian Renaissance poetry, and a founder of the imagist school of poetry. His later years were darkened by his support of the Italian Fascist government during World War II. Ironically, his greatest poetry was written after the war, when he was captured by American troops, tried, imprisoned, and finally confined to a mental hospital in the United States. Readers of Pound's *Pisan Cantos* and his free translation of the Confucian *Book of Odes* will find a man slowly awakening to the enormity of his own self-betrayal and will also find some of the most beautiful American writing since Emerson.

T.S. Eliot, a protégé of Pound's, was born in St. Louis and studied at Harvard. Shortly after leaving Harvard, he went to England and lived there the rest of his life. His long poem *The Waste Land* (1922) was perhaps the most important poem in English during the 1920's. A somber work incorporating medieval myth, yet remaining resolutely in common—even prosaic—language, it set the tone for a whole generation of poets. Eliot later became a convert to Anglo-Catholicism and expressed conservative political beliefs when many other writers were liberal. Yet his poetry and his measured criticism seem sure to keep him in the top rank of poets in English.

Others who were associated with this modern school centered on London were the American poet Robert Frost, and to a lesser extent D.H. Lawrence (whose novels overshadowed his work as a poet), W.H. Auden, and the American William Carlos Williams.

The end of this creative ferment can be placed at the year 1939. Yeats died in that year, an old man; the second great war broke out in Europe; and James Joyce published his last work, *Finnegan's Wake.* This book carried the logic of modernism to its extreme, invading even the sanctity of word meanings and coherence of phrase, creating multiple layers of meaning, and reinterpreting history as a self-centered dream. Many critics have been unable or unwilling to grant its success, yet its sales have continued to grow year after year, perhaps because, meaning or no meaning, it is one of the funniest books in the world and one of the most touching.

The Bloomsbury group.

Meanwhile, a group of British writers had founded a circle nicknamed by its neighborhood, Bloomsbury. Virginia Woolf, a novelist of great gifts (*Mrs. Dalloway,* 1925; *To the Lighthouse,*

HOLT, RINEHART AND WINSTON

FROST

Among American poets in the 20th century, Robert Frost was one who appealed both to serious students of poetry and to a wider audience. He brought the modernist spirit to the New England countryside, creating poems that were at once sophisticated and homespun. Below is "The Need of Being Versed in Country Things," about a house destroyed by fire.

The house had gone to bring again
To the midnight sky a sunset glow.
Now the chimney was all of the house that stood,
Like a pistil after the petals go.

The barn opposed across the way,
That would have joined the house in flame
Had it been the will of the wind, was left
To bear forsaken the place's name.

No more it opened with all one end
For teams that came by the stony road
To drum on the floor with scurrying hoofs
And brush the mow with the summer load.

The birds that came to it through the air
At broken windows flew out and in,
Their murmur more like the sigh we sigh
From too much dwelling on what has been.

Yet for them the lilac renewed its leaf,
And the aged elm, though touched with fire;
And the dry pump flung up an awkward arm;
And the fence post carried a strand of wire.

For them there was really nothing sad.
But though they rejoiced in the nest they kept,
One had to be versed in country things
Not to believe the phoebes wept.

1927), was at its center. She had been influenced by the school of Yeats, Pound, and Joyce, yet her use of modernist effects had a distinctly English flavor. Others in the Bloomsbury group included the biographer Lytton Strachey (*Eminent Victorians,* 1918), the novelist E.M. Forster (*Howard's End,* 1910; *A Passage to India,* 1924), and the economist John Maynard Keynes. The breadth of the group's membership and interest reminds one of the earlier circle that gathered around Samuel Johnson in the late 1700's.

The English accomplished important things in the field of analysis and criticism, beginning with Keynes's *Economic Consequences of the Peace* (1919). Among other monumental works of this kind must be numbered the thoroughly individual history of World War II by former Prime Minister Winston Churchill, whose wartime speeches enriched the language as had none since the previous century. Another critic of note was the essayist and novelist George Orwell, whose *Animal Farm* (1945), an angry fable of Stalinism, has become a standard description of totalitarian government.

After the 1920's, however, the excitement in English letters diminished, and the field was left to more conservative writers, including novelists W. Somerset Maugham and Graham Greene, playwright Noel Coward, and poet Robert Graves. Young writers in the 1930's—W.H. Auden, Stephen Spender, and Christopher Isherwood—looked optimistically to socialism for new hope, but the disaster of the Spanish Civil War and the treaty signed between the Communist Soviet Union and Nazi Germany withered their enthusiasm within a few years.

After 1945. World War II shattered the power of Britain as World War I had shattered France's. Postwar literature has a kind of elegiac quality, looking backward nostalgically and forward uncertainly. A trilogy of novels by Anglo-Irish writer Joyce Cary *(Herself Surprised, To Be a Pilgrim, The Horse's Mouth)* follows a housekeeper, the old man she works for, and the visionary artist whose model and mistress she had been from 1900 to the end of World War II. The decline of the characters' fortunes is redeemed only by their stubbornness and faith. The parallel decline of Britain itself is not difficult to draw.

In a different vein, *Under the Volcano* (1947), a novel by expatriate Englishman Malcolm Lowry, tells in vivid modernist style of a talented man's alcoholic dissolution in Mexico. The protagonist considers himself an honorary British consul in the small resort community where he lives. Even as he hopes for some world-restoring success, he drags down everyone and everything important to him. The novel was unsuccessfully published in New York and only gained a wide audience after the author's death in 1958.

New life and energy came to the British theater in the 1950's from the so-called "angry young men," writers from the working classes in England angry at the disabilities imposed on them by England's rigid class structure. The group took its name from John Osborne's play *Look Back in Anger* (1956). The plays and novels of these writers introduced a new vocabulary and new concerns to the English literary scene.

A younger generation of dramatists used the advances of the earlier group to somewhat different purposes. By mixing anger, lower- and middle-class settings, and the techniques of the theater of the absurd, such writers as Tom Stoppard and Harold Pinter created a whole new type of play. Pinter especially manages to communicate in some fashion through plays in which nothing—including the air itself—seems to move (*The Birthday Party,* 1958; *Old Times,* 1970).

Among the British writers of fiction, the older ones produced extended cycles concerning the nature of upper-class life in the 1900's (C.P. Snow, Anthony Powell, Richard Hughes). A younger contingent, including Alan Sillitoe, Kingsley Amis, and D.M. Thomas, had something in common with the theater's angry young men. Finally, there was a remarkable group of women writers following in the footsteps of Ivy Compton-Burnett (1892–1969). They included Iris Murdoch, Doris Lessing (*The Golden Notebook,* 1962), and Muriel Spark (*The Prime of Miss Jean Brodie,* 1961; *Loitering with Intent,* 1981).

The British Commonwealth

By the second half of the century, important writers in English were appearing in every corner of the globe. Although Britain had long since given up its colonial holdings, most of these outland writers were from Commonwealth countries and continued to feel some cultural ties with Britain itself.

Most notable among this group are Nobel laureate (1973) Patrick White of Australia (*The Eye of the Storm,* 1974); the fine short story writer of the 1920's Katherine Mansfield, and the later novelist Janet Frame, of New Zealand; and novelists Hugh MacLennan (*Two Solitudes,* 1945), Brian Moore, Margaret Laurence, and Margaret Atwood of Canada.

The racial and social agonies of South Africa were movingly portrayed by Alan Paton (*Cry, the Beloved Country,* 1948) and Nadine Gordimer (*July's People,* 1981), and by dramatist Athol Fugard.

The strongest new voices, however, belonged to the writers of the black experience in Nigeria, South Africa, and the Caribbean. Among the best known are South Africa's Ezekiel Mphahlele (*Down Second Avenue,* 1959) and Nigeria's Wole Soyinka (*Kongi's Harvest,* 1966). They have spearheaded a movement that now includes a wide range of distinct talents: among others, the Caribbean poet Derek Walcott and the novelist Samuel Selvon; the Nigerians Amos Tutuola, Chinua Achebe, and Gabriel Okara; the South Africans Alex La Guma, Lewis Nkosi, and Peter Abrahams; and Gambia's Lenrie Peters. The experience of the so-called Third World is also evoked by the East Indian V.S. Naipaul, who sees both the old and new worlds sympathetically, but always, through force of circumstance, from the outside.

The United States

1910–1940. In the decade beginning in 1910, the American literary scene was suddenly crowded with new life and energy. In London, the American T.S. Eliot published "The Love Song of J. Alfred Prufrock," his first substantial poem. Robert Frost published *A Boy's Will* and *North of Boston,* his first collections. Vachel Lindsay published three collections. A very young F. Scott Fitzgerald was hailed for his first novel, *This Side of Paradise.* And in the Middle West, there were major books of poetry (*Chicago Poems* by Carl Sandburg) and fiction (*Winesburg, Ohio* by Sherwood Anderson and *Main Street* by Sinclair Lewis). At the same time, a new dramatist named Eugene O'Neill was establishing himself as America's first great writer for the stage, and the older Theodore Dreiser was at the height of his considerable powers.

During the 1920's and '30's, these young men came to maturity and were joined by still others: novelists Ernest Hemingway (*The Sun Also Rises,* 1926), William Faulkner (*The Sound and the Fury,* 1929), John Dos Passos (*U.S.A.,* 1930–1936), Thomas Wolfe (*Look Homeward, Angel,* 1929), and John Steinbeck (*Tortilla Flat,* 1935). Major new voices in poetry included Wallace Stevens, William Carlos Williams, the extraordinarily gifted E.E. Cummings, and Hart Crane.

Of these writers, no fewer than six would receive the Nobel Prize: Lewis (1930), O'Neill (1936), Eliot (1948), Faulkner (1949), Hemingway (1954), and Steinbeck (1962). The awards suggest not only the quality of the work these writers produced, but also (and perhaps more accurately) how international their influence was.

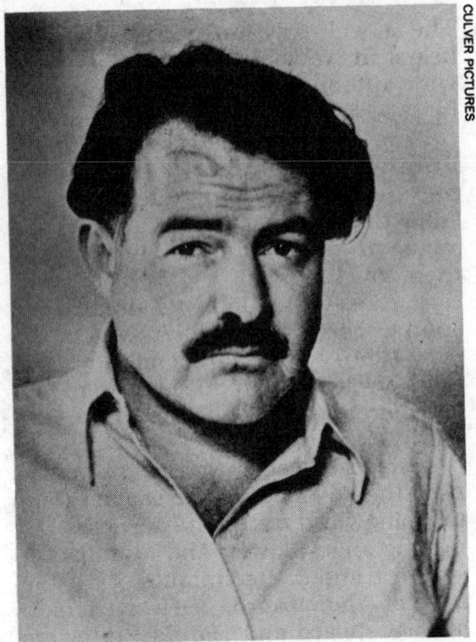

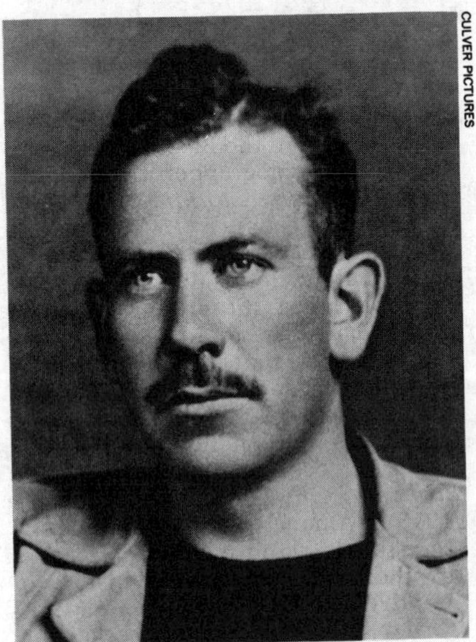

MODERN MASTERS *of American literature include F. Scott Fitzgerald* (left), *Ernest Hemingway* (center), *and John Steinbeck* (right). *Despite their many differences, they shared many typically American values and beliefs.*

To round out the picture of a 30-year period of remarkable creativity, it remains only to mention a few writers whose influence was not as immediately felt. These include Ezra Pound, whose personal influence and poetic example outlasted both long exile and suspicion of treason; Henry Miller, an American novelist working chiefly in Paris, who found a new excitement in portraying sex and whose books were consequently banned; the Russian émigré Vladimir Nabokov, whose modernist sensibility went somewhat against the American grain but whose influence on other writers was great; and finally, Edmund Wilson, with T.S. Eliot among the first great American literary critics, who did much to inform American readers about the currents of modern literature and culture.

American characteristics.

Taken together, these writers—of such widely varying backgrounds, tastes, and appeals—made American literature from 1910 to 1940 the most serious and influential in the world. Despite their great differences, some generalizations will help explain what they brought to world literature.

They maintained a deceptive air of natural speech in their writing, whether taking it from the American backwoods, small towns, or big cities. Even the most sophisticated, Eliot and Pound, reached their greatest heights with ordinary diction that deliberately avoided poeticisms.

Beneath this natural surface, however, something more complex was usually at work. *The Great Gatsby* by Fitzgerald, *The Sun Also Rises* by Hemingway, and *The Grapes of Wrath* by Steinbeck are all social novels on the surface—the first the story of a bootlegger's lost ideals, the second of a generation wasted by World War I, the third of the disaster of the Great Depression. Yet all three are consciously crafted to recall classical myth. Gatsby and Hemingway's heroes are all ruined "knights" resembling those in the stories of the search for the Holy Grail. *Grapes of Wrath* is a retelling of the book of Exodus—one family's odyssey across a continent in search of a promised land. (Steinbeck's later *East of Eden* uses the biblical story of the loss of paradise and the murder of Abel by Cain.)

The American writers used their mythic material with an interesting twist, however. The traditional stories usually assume that the hero has done something wrong and deserves the tragedy he lives through. But American writers tend to identify wth the lawbreaker and the unfortunate and to blame "society" for tragedy. Fitzgerald's Nick Carraway says to Jay Gatsby, "You're worth more than the lot of them"—the seemingly upstanding and law-abiding citizens. Steinbeck clearly feels something similar for the victimized Joad family. And Hemingway spent the rest of his life trying to find heroes as worthwhile as the doomed Lady Brett Ashley and the accursed Robert Cohn.

This identification with the loser seemed even to carry over into the writers' lives. Where writers of the Soviet Union, Eastern Europe, and Third World countries often risked destruction at the hands of the state, the American writers seemed to seek to destroy themselves.

The years of the 1930's, though darkened by the Great Depression, were still years of hope and excitement in American literature. In addition to Thomas Wolfe and Steinbeck, new writers included William Saroyan (*The Daring Young Man on the Flying Trapeze,* 1934); and a great new popular theater was evident. The increased concern with social and economic issues was shown by dramatists like Clifford Odets (*Waiting for Lefty,* 1935), but their earnestness was balanced by the wit and lightheartedness of such comic writers as George S. Kaufman and Moss Hart, collaborators on *You Can't Take It With You* (1936) and *The Man Who Came to Dinner* (1939). The period also saw the heyday of sophisticated musical comedies and film comedies, a new form that attracted many writers to Hollywood. During World War II (1941–1945), many writers worked for the U.S. government writing propaganda for the war effort.

The 1940's. In a sense, the 1930's ended with the two great plays of the 1940's. In *The Glass Menagerie* (1944), the young Tennessee Williams deepened the domestic play, bringing to it a Chekhovian humor and an ear for the poetry of Southern speech. In *Death of a Salesman* (1949) Arthur Miller had an equal impact, enriching the play of social concern with a feeling for the complexities of family life. In the same decade, Eugene O'Neill, long out of fashion, returned to the theater with *The Iceman Cometh* (1946). *Long Day's Journey into Night,* his last and perhaps his best play, was not produced until 1956, three years after O'Neill's death.

The new generation of writers looked to a new kind of realism. Building on the precedent of James T. Farrell, whose trilogy *Studs Lonigan* (1932–1935) had shocked the previous decade, Norman Mailer (*The Naked and the Dead,* 1948), Nelson Algren (*The Man With the Golden Arm,* 1949), and James Jones (*From Here to Eternity,* 1951) used language and explicit descriptions centering around the violence of war and sex that would have been unthinkable 20 years earlier. The first and third of these books are the two principal war novels to come from the American experience in World War II; the other is about near-wartime conditions in the big city drug trade. The latter two reached millions who might otherwise not have known about them through popular (and considerably laundered) movie versions.

At the same time, the courts of the land were reducing censorship. One of the principal battles had been fought in the 1930's over allowing the distribution of James Joyce's *Ulysses.* Later, favorable decisions allowed the sale of D.H. Lawrence's *Lady Chatterley's Lover* (1928), and finally the works of Henry Miller (*Tropic of Cancer* and *Tropic of Capricorn*).

CULVER PICTURES

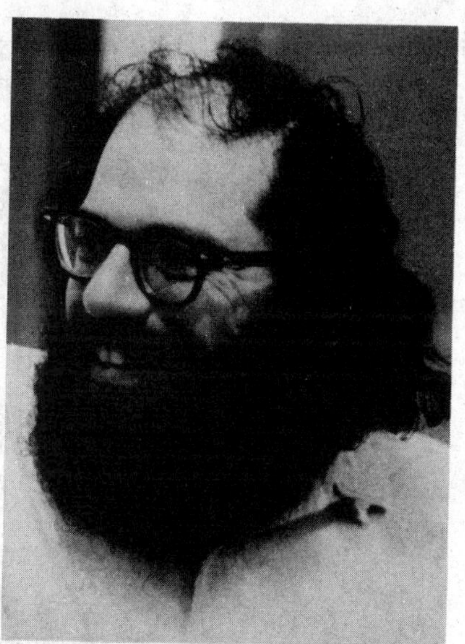

UPI

POETRY *from outside the establishment came from* Langston Hughes (left), *a leader of the Harlem renaissance of the 1930's, and from* Allen Ginsberg *of the 1950's beat generation.*

Humor and satire. In a thoroughly different vein, the traditions of American humor continued to find literary expression. Not long after the turn of the century, newspaperman Don Marquis created archy the cockroach, who wrote a daily column in supposed blank verse, providing an insect's jaundiced views on the human race. Sportswriter Ring Lardner turned to ironic stories about baseball players and other small-town characters. Lardner's ear for flat midwestern speech—and his sense for the moral foibles of his characters—was unmatched.

In the late 1920's, a younger group of writers centered around a new magazine, *The New Yorker.* On its early staff were James Thurber and E.B. White. Beginning with reminiscences of his boyhood in Ohio, Thurber became a skilled and appealing writer in his chosen area. The surface simplicity and humor of his stories and sketches often hid a complex and sometimes bitter moralist. E.B. White often used his humor for more serious purposes. In addition to parodies, brief sketches, and light verse, he wrote polished yet informal essays on a wide variety of topics, and his children's book *Charlotte's Web* became a classic.

Among other writers in a humorous vein whom *The New Yorker* published were Wolcott Gibbs, Dorothy Parker, S.J. Perelman, and Woody Allen.

Alone among large circulation magazines, *The New Yorker* also continued to publish serious fiction. It printed many stories by writers who also wrote novels: John O'Hara (*Appointment in Samarra,* 1934), J.D. Salinger (*The Catcher in the Rye,* 1951), and Truman Capote (*Breakfast at Tiffany's,* 1958). In the 1950's and '60's, the stories of John Cheever (*The Wapshot Chronicle,* 1957), an anatomist of suburban life and types, and of John Updike (*Rabbit, Run,* 1961) were particularly prominent. Most of these writers straddled the vague line between "commercial" and "quality" fiction; they were not highly experimental, and their range was somewhat limited, but they were among the most prolific and interesting writers of the period.

After 1950. The only strong literary movement after mid-century was that of the "beat generation." The poet Allen Ginsberg, together with novelists Jack Kerouac (*On the Road,* 1957) and the somewhat older William Burroughs (*Junkie,* 1953; *Naked Lunch,* 1959), wrote graphically of a freer way of life that conceded nothing to the politics and social mores of the day. Their acceptance of a place outside of established society and their almost obsessive search for new experience set the stage for the great youth rebellion of the 1960's.

Until the 1960's, American poetry was dominated by the aging generation born before 1914: Cummings and Stevens, Frost and Eliot, William Carols Williams, and the still green memory of Hart Crane.

The outspoken emotionalism and equally aggressive intelligence of Allen Ginsberg's "Howl" (1956) and "Kaddish" (1961) seemed to stir something in poets who until then had remained merely academic. Among the major works were Robert Lowell's *Life Studies* (1959) and *Notebook* (1969), and John Berryman's *77 Dream Songs* (1964) and *His Toy, His Dream, His Rest* (1968). Among other important poets of the 1950's and '60's were Theodore Roethke, Robert Creeley, Richard Wilbur, and Sylvia Plath.

Although poetry seemed about to fall asleep again in the 1970's, poets including Denise Levertov, Gary Snyder, John Hollander, Charles Olson, and A.R. Ammons gave hope for continuing achievement.

Literary minorities. America's two literary minorities—blacks and women—seemed to look forward to different futures. American women writers from the time of Edith Wharton and Willa Cather have written freely and with passion. Many of the major figures in the Southern reawakening of the 1940's were women: Flannery O'Connor, Eudora Welty, Carson McCullers. Again in the so-called cosmopolitan style of the 1950's, Jean Stafford, Mary McCarthy, and Hortense Calisher had important places. In addition, women traditionally made up a fair proportion of the writers of popular and mass market fiction—books that make up in readership what they lack in "serious" literary value.

Gradually, however, women writers were coming to view themselves specifically as women. Many of those listed above showed the way for a fuller appreciation of women's joys and sorrows, but younger women, including novelists Anne Beattie and Mary Gordon (*Final Payments,* 1979) promised to go even further in their exploration of the subject. Women were also gaining new footholds in literary and cultural criticism (Susan Sontag, Gloria Steinem).

The story of black writers in America goes back into the 1800's, when Frederick Douglass won admiration as an orator and Booker T. Washington (*Up From Slavery,* 1901) used his influence to improve economic and educational conditions among blacks.

The first black poets of serious note were Countee Cullen (1903–1946) and Langston Hughes (1902–1967). Together they helped set off the Harlem renaissance of the 1920's and '30's.

In the 1940's and '50's, black writing took a more serious and prosaic turn. Richard Wright's *Native Son* (1940) was an early attempt to tell

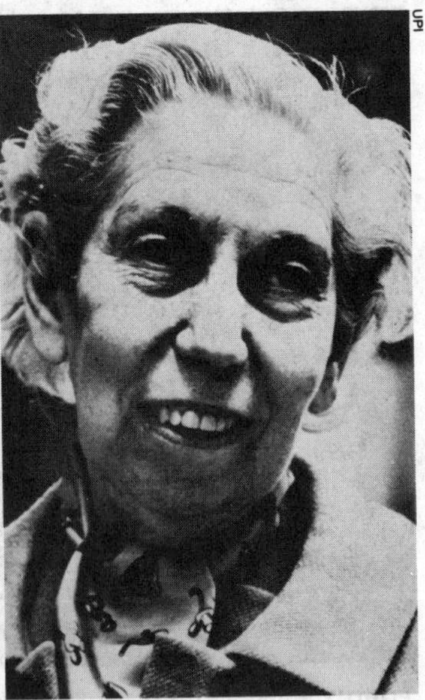

CONTEMPORARY WRITERS *of great influence include poet Sylvia Plath* (top left), *Southern novelist Eudora Welty* (top right), *and Nobel Prize winners Isaac Bashevis Singer* (bottom left) *and Saul Bellow* (bottom right).

both white and black readers what it felt like to be a black man in America. Other books in a similar vein were Ralph Ellison's *The Invisible Man* (1952) and *Go Tell It on the Mountain* (1953) by James Baldwin, who would write several novels in the coming decades (*Another Country,* 1962).

In the 1960's seriousness turned often to anger, and books such as *The Autobiography of Malcolm X* and *Soul on Ice* by Eldridge Cleaver gained wide attention for their unvarnished accounts of black life and their inflated rhetoric.

In the 1970's, serious black writers had difficulty finding publishers—and readers—for their books. Novelists Ishmael Reed, Toni Morrison, and David Bradley were promising but not fully realized talents. The future of the black writer seemed uncertain.

Perhaps the most significant event affecting black literature was the remarkable success of *Roots,* a long television narrative based on the book by Alex Haley. Although the book was not of high literary quality, it struck a nerve in its predominantly white audience, making a part of the black man's experience clear as if for the first time.

The contribution of black writers to American literature has not approached the immense contribution of black musicians and composers to American music. Yet the great popular success of *Roots* suggests that perhaps the stage for a great black American writer has been set.

In a sense, every literary production in America is the product of some minority: it is Irish-Catholic or big-city ethnic, western, midwestern, or southern, written by a woman, etc. Even the old Protestant writer thinks and functions today as a member of a minority.

Among the most prominent of these groups in the 1960's and '70's were the writers of Jewish heritage who were dealing with Jewish concerns. Their novels were often quintessentially American, yet this very fact seemed often to trouble them, to take attention away from their Jewishness.

Perhaps the most well known of the products of these writers was *Portnoy's Complaint* (1969) by Philip Roth, a bawdy and funny account of a Jewish boyhood and young adulthood in New Jersey and New York City, meretricious and irrepressible by turns. Roth's later novels (*Zuckerman Unbound,* 1981) sometimes aimed higher but rarely accomplished as much.

A special contribution of the Jewish-American writers to American literature is their unique and affecting sense of humor. *Catch-22* (1961), a novel about the insanity of the wartime armed services, by Joseph Heller, was perhaps the most successful comedy novel of the era. Among other important writers to whom their Jewishness is a significant concern are Bernard Malamud (*The Fixer,* 1966) and the Canadian Mordecai Richler. In addition, Isaac Bashevis Singer, a Nobel laureate whose stories were written originally in Yiddish, has gained a wide audience in translation.

Perhaps foremost among serious American novelists—and incidentally among novelists of Jewish descent—is Saul Bellow, winner of the Nobel Prize in 1976. From his early *Henderson the Rain King* (1959) to *Humboldt's Gift* (1976), Bellow sought answers to some longstanding American questions about the importance of personal heritage, the need for being at once a member of a group and an independent individual, and the need for intellectual and physical striving and yet for stillness and meditation.

The future. James Joyce believed that literature is a way of obliterating the gap between past, present, and future. Remembering, recording, and prophesying are not so different from each other, because every man's personal odyssey continues to be repeated somewhere in some form each day. Literature introduces us to the swing of life: from perplexity to reassurance and back to perplexity again. No question is ever answered but another riddle of equal magnitude takes its place.

Yet writers and readers do find a kind of solace in literature, if only in its reminder to seek the permanent and the good. *Choose something like a star,* writes Robert Frost, speaking not only of literature but of vision itself, *To stay our minds on and be stayed.*

—Robert LaGuardia and Lawrence Lorimer

LITERATURE GLOSSARY

A

Abdiel: in Milton's *Paradise Lost,* the only one of Satan's angels who would not join the revolt against heaven.

Absurd, Literature of the: modern type of literature in which the author flouts the conventions of his chosen literary form (usually drama or novel) and uses character and situation to emphasize the meaninglessness and absurdity of his characters' lives. The ancestor of the movement is considered to be Alfred Jarry's play *Ubu Roi* (1896), and its ideas were carried forward in Franz Kafka's novels. The major absurdists—Albert Camus, Jean-Paul Sartre, Jean Genet, Eugène Ionesco, and Samuel Beckett—emerged during or after World War II. Later writers in the tradition include Edward Albee and Harold Pinter.

Academy: school of philosophy near Athens in ancient Greece, started by Plato about 387 B.C. It was named for Academia (Akademeia), the area in which it was located. The Academy continued to exist until 529 A.D., when it was closed by Emperor Justinian. Subsequently, the term "academy" was applied to a school of higher or special education, or to an organization made up of learned persons. Among the latter are the Royal Academy, a select British society of artists; the French Academy, a select French society of literary persons whose duties include maintaining and revising the prime dictionary of the French language; and the Swedish Academy, which serves much the same function as the French and in additon awards the annual Nobel Prize in Literature.

Achates: in Vergil's *Aeneid,* a Trojan, faithful friend of Aeneas. After the fall of Troy he followed Aeneas through all his wanderings and hardships with such fidelity that his name has been used as the synonym for a loyal friend.

Acheron, GM: River of Woe, one of the four rivers of Hades. In the *Odyssey* it was the principal or boundary river of Hades over which Charon ferried the souls of the dead on their journey from the upper to the lower world. It also is used to mean the region of Hades itself.

Achilles, GM: hero of the *Iliad* and the bravest of the Greeks in the Trojan War. He was the son of Peleus, king of Thessaly, and Thetis, a sea nymph. When he was born, Thetis plunged him in the river Styx to make his body invulnerable, but neglected to protect the heel by which she held him. To save him from death in the Trojan War, she sent him to the court of King Lycomedes, where he was dressed as a girl and played with the princesses. But Troy could not be taken, and Odysseus, in the guise of a merchant, went to find him. Odysseus offered to sell jewels and weapons to the girls, and the one who chose arms he knew was Achilles; the youth gladly went off with him to war, where he was killed by Paris, who shot him with an arrow in his only vulnerable spot—the heel. See also *Iliad.*

Acrostic: any piece of writing, usually verse, in which sets of letters taken in a certain order spell a word or words. Sometimes a series, composed of the first letter in each line, spells the word or words; sometimes the final letter of each line is used; occasionally letters from the middle of the lines are chosen. If only one set of letters spells a word, the verse is a simple acrostic. If the verse contains more than one hidden series, it is called a double acrostic. The 119th Psalm is a famous acrostic (in Hebrew), and the entire book of Lamentations is a series of acrostics. However, acrostics in Hebrew in the Bible lose their distinctive form when translated. Acrostics have also been used in the making of literary puzzles.

Actaeon, GM: famous hunter who offended Artemis. One story is that he came upon her bathing, another that he boasted of being a better hunter than she. For punishment she changed him into a stag, and he was killed by his own dogs.

Adam Bede: novel by English writer George Eliot, published in 1859. It tells of the love of Adam Bede, a carpenter, for Hetty Sorrel, a pretty dairymaid, who does not love him. She is seduced and abandoned by Arthur Donnithorne, the local squire. Bede marries Dinah Morris, a Methodist preacher, who befriends Hetty.

Adonais: elegy on the death of John Keats by English poet Percy Bysshe Shelley, published in 1821. It mourns the death of Keats, condemns the critics whose reviews were thought to have hastened his death, and ends on a joyous note, hailing Keats into the company of the immortals.

Adonis, GM: beautiful youth beloved by Aphrodite. When he was killed by a wild boar, Aphrodite put him in the care of Persephone, queen of Hades, who wanted to keep him herself; Zeus then decreed that Adonis should spend six months of the year on Earth and six in the underworld. His death and return symbolize winter and summer, and his worship embodied a midsummer festival. Shakespeare's poem, "Venus and Adonis," tells the love story of the youth and the goddess.

AN ACROSTIC

The first letters of each line in this poem (by a father for his children's birthdays) spell the names of the children.

Pulled by the years, he grows away from us
And upward toward manhood's might.
Under it all, we know the boy he is,
Light and worryless, the world still
all aright.

Joining her brother, she too grows away.
Undaunted by the future's wild embrace,
Day by day she strives toward womanhood.
Yet we hold still the girl, her light and
careless grace.

Please also consult the guide to the Bible for more complete information on entries dealing with biblical themes. The symbols used in this guide are as follows: G-*Greek;* R-*Roman;* N-*Norse;* M-*myth;* L-*legend.*

Aegisthus: See *House of Atreus.*

Aeneas, GRM: son of Anchises and Aphrodite, and one of the heroes of the Trojan War described in Homer's *Iliad.* He married Creusa, daughter of Priam, king of Troy. When Troy was taken and in flames, Aeneas departed, bearing his old father on his shoulders and leading his little son Ascanius by the hand. The wanderings of Aeneas from this point on are celebrated in Vergil's great Latin epic, the *Aeneid.* See also *Aeneid.*

Aeneid: Latin epic poem by the Roman poet Vergil, left incomplete at his death in 19 B.C.; it is a classic work telling of the founding of Rome by the Trojan hero Aeneas. It narrates Aeneas's wanderings before he reaches the seven hills of Rome. Seeking a new home, he sails from Troy with a fleet of 20 ships. He is shipwrecked on the coast of Africa, where Dido, queen of Carthage, begs him to remain. She falls deeply in love with him and takes her own life in grief when the gods command him to take up his travels again. Aeneas meets her ghost when he descends into Hell to speak to his father's spirit. After seven years of adventure and hardship, Aeneas comes to the river Tiber. Here he kills his rival, Turnus, marries Lavinia, daughter of Latinus, king of Latium, and founds the city of Lavinium. Aeneas is the legendary ancestor of the city of Rome, for his son founded Alba Longa where Romulus and Remus were born and which was superseded by Rome itself. John Dryden's famous translation of the collected writings of Vergil, including the *Aeneid,* appeared in 1697.

Aeolus, GRM: god of the winds who lived on an island where he kept the winds in a cave. One day Odysseus in his wanderings came to this place, and the kindly Aeolus gave him the four winds tied up in a leather bag with a command to the fair winds to blow the wanderers home. But one night while Odysseus slept, his sailors decided they too must share the treasure in the mysterious leather bag. They untied the string; the fierce winds rushed out and drove the ships back to Aeolus. He was so disgusted at this stupidity that he would not help them further.

Aesir, NM: race of gods that included most of the major deities: Odin, Tyr, Thor, Frigga, Balder, and Loki. The Aesir warred with the other race of gods, the Vanir (of whom the chief deities were Frey and Freya), but eventually made peace with them. Their home was Asgard.

Aesop's Fables: collection of very short stories in which animal characters behave and speak like human beings, showing the weaknesses and foibles of human nature. Each fable ends with a moral. They are attributed to Aesop, a deformed Phrygian slave who lived about 620–560 B.C. He was freed by his master and is said to have won fame for his wisdom at the court of Croesus, king of Lydia. There is a legend that Aesop saved the throne for Peisistratus, king of Athens, by telling his fable of "King Log and King Stork" to the discontented mob that was threatening to dethrone him.

AESOP: *a 19th-century illustration of "The Sick Lion and the Fox."*

Some of the stories themselves are centuries older than Aesop and are of Oriental origin. Babrius in the first century B.C. put them into Greek verse, and Phaedrus in the first century A.D. translated them into Latin. In the 14th century, Maximus Planudes, a monk, collected 144 fables, and from these all the later collections known as Aesop's have been taken. La Fontaine translated them into French verse in the 17th century.

Agamemnon: See *House of Atreus.*

Ahab: See *Moby-Dick.*

Ajax (the Greater), GM: one of the Greek heroes of the Trojan War. On the death of Achilles, Ajax and Odysseus were rivals for the arms of the dead hero. They fell to Odysseus, and Ajax, maddened by jealousy, killed himself. Another account of the story is found in Sophocles' tragedy *Ajax,* which tells how Ajax, blinded with insane disappointment, mistook a flock of sheep for the sons of Atreus and slew them all. When his reason returned, he was so ashamed of his deed that he killed himself with his sword.

Ajax (the Less), GM: one of the Greek heroes in the siege of Troy. Except for Achilles, none was swifter than he. He was skilled with the spear, but he was a great boaster. On his way home he was shipwrecked, but Poseidon cast him on a great rock. Instead of giving thanks, he bragged that he had saved himself. So Poseidon split the rock, and Ajax was drowned.

Aladdin: in *The Arabian Nights' Entertainments,* the son of a poor tailor, who finds a magic lamp and ring. Two jinn, servants of the lamp and ring, come to do the bidding of the new owner. Aladdin gains great wealth, marries the sultan's daughter, and builds a marvelous palace.

Albion: ancient poetic name for the island of Britain.

Alcestis, GM: wife of Admetus. Apollo had secured the promise of the gods that Admetus need never die, but on condition that when his death day came, another should offer to die in his place. Alcestis willingly gave her life for her husband. But the grief of Admetus was so great that Hercules brought her back from the lower world. Her story is the subject of Euripides' play *Alcestis,* and Chaucer included her in his *Legend of Good Women.*

Alchemist, The: comedy of humours by English playwright Ben Jonson, performed in 1616. Face, a butler, invites Subtle, posing as an alchemist, and the strumpet Doll Common to use his master's house to trick numerous hypocritical townsmen out of their money. The play is an example of Jonson's use of characters dominated by "humours" (see also *Humours*). It also uses type-names, such as Tribulation Wholesome for an unctuous Puritan minister. Jonson treats the rogues Face and Subtle more sympathetically than their victims.

Alexandrian Age: period of learning and literary activity in Egypt from about 300 B.C. to 30 B.C., when Alexandria was the cultural center of the world. The great Alexandrian Library, containing the largest collection of manuscripts (400,000, it is said) of ancient times, was founded during the reign of Ptolemy Soter of Egypt (323–283 B.C.) and enlarged by his successors.

The Alexandrian period was distguished by great scientists and mathematicians, such as Euclid, Archimedes, and Diophantus, and the last of the Greek poets, Callimachus, Theocritus, and Apollonius Rhodius.

Alexandria Quartet, The: four novels—*Justine* (1957), *Balthazar* (1958), *Mountolive* (1958), and *Clea* (1961)—by Anglo-Irish writer Lawrence Durrell. Together they tell a story of love as it exists in the atmosphere of relativity that dominates 20th-century life. Each book portrays the same characters from a different point of view, raising questions as to the nature of truth. The background is the exotic Middle Eastern city, Alexandria.

Alexandrine: See *Stanza.*

Ali Baba: in *The Arabian Nights' Entertainments* story of "Ali Baba and the Forty Thieves," a poor woodcutter who one day overhears the magic words by which the Forty Thieves enter their treasure cave. "Open Sesame," says Ali Baba when the thieves are gone; and he enters, loads his donkey with gold, and goes home. His brother also goes to the cave. But he forgets the words and cannot get out. When the thieves find him, they kill him. At last the robber captain discovers who it is that knows their secret. He hides his men in jars that he brings to Ali Baba's house, intending to jump out and kill him while he sleeps. But Morgana, the little servant girl, kills them all with boiling oil.

Alice's Adventures in Wonderland: classic fantasy by British mathematician Charles Lutwidge Dodgson (who wrote under the pseudonym Lewis Carroll), published in 1865. Alice falls into a rabbit hole but preserves her indestructible common sense in spite of the topsy-turvy world she discovers underground. The story has levels of satire that are appreciated by adults. However, attempts to identify Alice's queer companions, such as the March Hare, the Mad Hatter, or the Mock Turtle, with public figures in Victorian England have not been verified. As far as anyone knows, they are simply delightful nonsense creatures, originally invented by Carroll to amuse a young friend, Alice Liddell, while on a boat trip up the Thames. *Through the Looking-Glass,* a sequel, appeared in 1872; the two books, with the classic illustrations by John Tenniel, are usually published as one.

Allegory: story with a literal meaning that suggests a deeper, figurative meaning. The characters often personify ideas or qualities, a type of person, or even a nation. The actions symbolize other more significant actions. An allegory is far more than a metaphor; it calls for greater length of figurative expression and a more sustained imagination on the part of both author and reader. Fables and parables are simple allegories with but one idea or moral to be put over. The long allegory can be narration or description, poetry, or drama. John Bunyan's *Pilgrim's Progress* is the most famous

ALICE: *John Tenniel's illustration of the popular heroine meeting the Dodo bird.*

allegory in English—the story of Christian's trials and troubles as he seeks the Celestial City.

Alliteration: beginning two or more consecutive words, or words near together, with the same letter or sound. "Now or never," "time and tide," "spick and span" are instances of alliteration in everyday phrases.

Alliteration was the base of ancient German and Old English versification. Each line broke into two halves, with most of the accented syllables beginning with the same sound. Although no longer used as a structural base, alliteration is a common and effective device in poetry.

All Quiet on the Western Front: antiwar novel by the German writer Erich Maria Remarque, published in 1929. It shocked the world because it dealt with the everyday horrors in the trenches in a cool, matter-of-fact, realistic style known in Germany as "the new objectivity." Without heroism, patriotism, or high-sounding words, its hero, a 19-year-old conscript, endures the attrition of the war and is killed just before the armistice.

All's Well that Ends Well: one of Shakespeare's "dark comedies," first performed in 1602. Helena, daughter of a physician, claims the hand of Bertram, count of Rousillon, as her reward for having cured the king of France. He reluctantly marries her, then leaves for a war in Florence, declaring that he will have nothing to do with her until she can show him both his ring and her child by him. She follows him, disguises herself, and tricks him into giving her both; he at last accepts her.

All the King's Men: Pulitzer Prize-winning novel by U. S. author Robert Penn Warren, first published in 1946. Based on the career of Louisiana politician Huey Long, the novel relates the rise of a demagogue named Willie Stark and its effect on the narrator, his press agent, Jack Burden.

Almanach de Gotha: social register of royal and noble European families.

Amazons, GM: race of warlike women who lived in Pontus near the Euxine Sea. No men were allowed to live among them, and all the boys who were born were either killed or sent to a neighboring country to live with their fathers. In Vergil's *Aeneid,* the Amazons fought against the Greeks in the Trojan War, and their queen was killed by Achilles. One of the Twelve Labors of Hercules was to steal the girdle of their queen, Hippolyte.

Ambassadors, The: late novel by Anglo-American writer Henry James, published in 1903, in which he returns to his favorite "international theme" of contrasting European and American values. Middle-aged Lambert Strether is sent to Paris by his wealthy fiancée, the widowed Mrs. Newsome, to bring home her son Chad, who is involved with a French woman. But Strether discovers that under the tutelage of his French mistress, Chad has grown in refinement and depth. Awakened to possibilities of life that are unknown in his Massachusetts hometown, Strether betrays his trust to Mrs. Newsome, knowing he will never be forgiven, and advises Chad to stay in Paris.

Ambrosia: food of the Greek gods. Together with their drink, nectar, it made them immortal.

American Language, The: scholarly work, first published in 1919, by U.S. journalist H. L. Mencken. In it he discusses the development of the American as opposed to the English language, studying in particular the unique expressions and idioms of American English. Substantial supplements were added in 1945 and 1948.

American Tragedy, An: novel by U.S. writer Theodore Dreiser, published in 1925. Its central character, Clyde Griffiths, has a secret affair with Roberta, a fellow factory worker. Clyde is obsessed with his chances for future advancement with the company. When he meets the wealthy local belle Sondra, she becomes the symbol of his aspirations. Roberta becomes pregnant and Clyde takes her to a secluded lake, planning to drown her. Although he loses his nerve, the boat overturns, and Roberta is drowned. Clyde is executed for murder. The story was based on an actual murder case; the motive—the insidiousness of the American dream of success—was supplied by Dreiser.

Anabasis, The: history by the Greek general Xenophon, first transcribed in the fourth century B.C. It deals with an unsuccessful expedition of 10,000 Greeks to aid the Persian king Cyrus. The Greeks are cut off and make a forced retreat, a "march upcountry," through hostile territory. Xenophon, one of the leaders of the Greeks, gives a lively account of the deprivations and narrow escapes they endure before they at last reach the sea.

Anapest: See *Foot.*

Anatomy of Melancholy, The: medical treatise by the English scholar Robert Burton, first published in 1621. Burton writes about "melancholy," which for him includes all states of mind from pessimism to insanity, and gives many quotes from ancient and contemporary authors. Thanks to Burton's wit, learning, and interest in curious facts, the book has long outlived its medical usefulness.

And Quiet Flows the Don: See *Silent Don, The.*

Androclus or **Androcles,** RL: runaway slave who hid in a lion's cave in Africa. Without fear he pulled a painful thorn from the lion's paw. In later years, Androclus was captured and thrown to the lions in the arena. But instead of attacking him, one old lion fawned upon him and caressed him. Androclus and his lion were set free. G. B. Shaw based his play, *Androcles and the Lion,* on this story.

Andromache, GM: wife of the Trojan hero Hector. After the capture of Troy and the death of Hector, the Greeks threw her little son Astyanax from the walls of the city, and she was taken captive by Neoptolemus, son of Achilles. Later Andromache became the wife of Helenus, brother of Hector. She is the subject of a tragedy by Racine, based on the *Andromache* by Euripides.

Andromeda, GM: princess of Ethiopia. Her mother, Cassiopeia, boasted that she was more beautiful than the daughters of Poseidon. In wrath Poseidon sent a sea monster to lay waste the land. Andromeda was chained to a rock in the sea as a sacrifice to be devoured by the creature. Perseus, flying home from his victory over the Gorgon Medusa, saw the beautiful maiden and saved her life. He had with him the head of Medusa; one look at it turned the monster into stone. Andromeda then married Perseus. The story is the basis of Corneille's classical drama *Andromède.*

Anglo-Saxon Chronicle: history of England up to 1154 A.D., the first prose work in Old English. The chronicle of England to the year 892 was collected from different local sources by order of Alfred the Great, who himself may have dictated the parts relating to his own time. The work was subsequently continued in various manuscripts, seven of which are still in existence.

Angry young men: group of British writers of the 1950's and 1960's, largely of working-class origin, who attacked contemporary social values in novels and plays. The prime example is John Osborne, whose play *Look Back in Anger* (1956) made the movement famous on both sides of the Atlantic. Other writers associated with the movement are Kingsley Amis and Alan Sillitoe.

Animal Farm: anti-Utopian novel, written in the form of a beast fable, by British author George Orwell, published in 1945. A group of farm animals overthrow their human masters and set up a communal society. But the pigs gradually take over, and the commune becomes a dictatorship. While universally applicable, the fable has a particular similarity to Orwell's view of events in the Soviet Union after the Bolshevik Revolution.

Anna Karenina: major novel by Russian writer Leo Tolstoy, published in 1873–1876. Anna, a warm and beautiful woman, leaves her husband, a cold bureaucrat, for her lover, Count Vronsky. Deprived of seeing her son and snubbed by her former friends, she is reduced to abject dependency on Vronsky. At last, having persuaded herself that Vronsky loves another, she throws herself in front of a moving train. The novel is a brilliant picture of aristocratic Russian society and contains the autobiographical character Levin, whose life is based on truer values than those of society.

Antaeus, GM: one of the giant sons of Poseidon and Gaea (earth). He could not be beaten as long as he touched the earth, for he received new strength from his mother. Hercules discovered the secret of his strength, lifted the giant into the air, and strangled him.

Anthology: literally, a collection of flowers; used metaphorically for a collection of beautiful or representative passages from literature. The most famous one was *The Greek Anthology,* a collection of 4500 short Greek elegiac poems and epigrams begun by Meleager about 60 B.C.; continued by Philippus of Thessalonica, who first applied the word *anthologia* to the collection; and enlarged until about 1320 A.D.

The numerous anthologies available today include anthologies of many authors' writings on a single subject, like love; of many authors' writings of a certain type, like the narrative essay; of several different works by one author; of children's literature; and of golden thoughts and sage sayings.

Antigone: tragedy by Greek dramatist Sophocles, performed in 440 B.C.; the final play of the *Oedipus* trilogy. It concerns the conflict between individual conscience and the authority of

ANIMAL FARM: *the dominant pigs work at their office in the 1955 animated cartoon of the novel-length fable by George Orwell.*

CULVER PICTURES

ANTIGONE: *Greek actress Irene Papas seeks to bury her brother in film version.*

CULVER PICTURES

the state. Antigone, the daughter of Oedipus, piously buries the body of her brother Polynices in defiance of King Creon's decree that his body remain unburied because of his treachery. Creon orders Antigone to be buried alive. She and her intended husband Haemon, Creon's son, commit suicide, as does Creon's wife when she learns of Haemon's death.

Antony and Cleopatra: tragedy by William Shakespeare, first presented about 1607; taken from Plutarch's *Lives.* Antony, who has been living with Cleopatra in Egypt, returns to Rome and renews his ties with Octavius, marrying his sister Octavia. When Antony then returns to Cleopatra, Octavius uses this insult to his sister as an excuse for invading Egypt. He defeats Antony at sea and pursues him to Egypt. Antony, defeated and believing that Cleopatra has killed herself, runs on his sword. He finds too late that the rumor is false, but lives long enough to kiss her goodnight. Cleopatra, learning that Octavius will exhibit her in Rome as a captive, kills herself by allowing herself to be bitten by an asp.

Aphorism: short sentence stating a truth or principle. An aphorism is formulated by one author, and differs from a maxim, or saying, which is folk wisdom. The term was first used by the Greek physician Hippocrates for his collection of medical principles.

Aphrodite, GM: goddess of love, beauty, and fertility. Hesiod says she was born of the foam of the sea; but in the *Iliad* she is the daughter of Zeus and Dione. In the *Odyssey* Hephaestus is her husband, and Ares her lover. She was the mother of Eros and of Aeneas by Anchises. She is identified with the Semitic fertility goddess Ishtar, called Ashtaroth in the Bible, and with the Roman goddess Venus.

Apollo, GM: god of youth and manly beauty, son of Zeus and Leto; also called Phoebus. He was the god of poetry and music; the grasshopper was sacred to him as the symbol of song. Orpheus was his son. Apollo was also the god of healing and could avert sickness or evil; Asclepius, god of medicine, was another son. In Homer, Apollo is the god of prophecy; his oracles were unerring and were honored everywhere. The one at Delphi was the most famous. Apollo was later identified with Helios, the sun god; Artemis, his twin, was goddess of the moon. The Romans took over the worship of Apollo from the Greeks.

Apollonian: See *Birth of Tragedy.*

Apology (or *apologia*): in literature, a term borrowed from the law courts of ancient Athens, where an apology was a speech for the defense in a trial. Socrates' speeches in his defense at his

CULVER PICTURES

AROUND THE WORLD: *Passepartout and Phileas Fogg in the popular film.*

trial, published by Plato, are known as *The Apology of Socrates.* Other authors have used the term as a title; at first it denoted an autobiography, but later "apology" was used for books that present the author's justification of his life.

Arabian Nights' Entertainments, The (or *The Thousand and One Nights*): famous collection of Indian, Persian, and Arabic folk tales and romances. Originally in the oral tradition, they were gathered in their present form in the 15th century and unified by the frame-story of Princess Scheherazade. Having married an embittered king who has the habit of killing his wives after his wedding night, the clever princess saves her life by starting to tell a tale each night but leaving it unfinished until the next day. After a thousand such tales, the king decides to spare her. The work became known in Europe in the 18th century. Among its best-known tales are "Ali Baba and the Forty Thieves" and "Aladdin, or the Wonderful Lamp."

Arachne, GM: Lydian maiden of great skill as a weaver. So beautiful was her work that she challenged Athena to a contest. Arachne wove a tapestry showing stories of the loves of the gods—Leda and the swan, Europa and the bull, Danae in her tower. The work was beautiful, but Athena ripped it into shreds to punish the maiden for her impiety and for daring to challenge her. Arachne then hanged herself, and Athena changed her into a spider, hanging by a thread from her own web and forever spinning. The biological name for spiders, *arachnids,* is derived from her name.

Arcadia: inland plateau of central Greece, shut in by mountains. The ancient inhabitants were shepherds and simple mountain folk. It is celebrated in the literature of many languages as a place of pastoral pleasure, contentment, and rest, and has come to symbolize the ideal country of lost or unattainable happiness.

Ares, GM: god of war; son of Zeus and Hera. In Homer's *Odyssey,* Ares is the lover of Aphrodite, whose husband Hephaestus catches them together in a net and holds them up to be laughed at by the gods. The story is typical of the low esteem in which Ares is held in Greek legend. The Romans identified Ares with their war-god Mars, for whom the month March is named.

Argonauts, GM: band of adventurers who sailed with Jason in the ship *Argo* to find the Golden Fleece. Jason, son of Aeson, king of Iolcus in Thessaly, demanded his kingdom back from his uncle Pelias, the usurper; Pelias agreed to give it up if Jason would bring back the Golden Fleece. Jason gathered a company of heroes, including Hercules, Castor and Pollux, and Theseus, and sailed to Colchis, where the fleece was guarded by a never-sleeping dragon.

Jason and the Argonauts arrived in Colchis after many adventures, but Aeetes, king of Colchis, would not give up the fleece until Jason performed several impossible tasks. Aeetes' daughter Medea, the enchantress, fell in love with Jason and helped him perform his tasks. Jason took the fleece and sailed home again on the *Argo,* taking Medea with him as his wife.

Argus, GM: monster with a hundred eyes; Hera set it to watch Io, one of Zeus's lovers. Zeus ordered Hermes to kill Argus; so Hermes played upon the lyre until all the hundred eyes were closed, then cut off the monster's head. Hera put the eyes of Argus in the tail of the peacock, her sacred bird.

Argus was also the name of the Greek shipwright who built the *Argo* (see *Argonauts*) and of Odysseus's faithful dog, the first to recognize Odysseus when he returned home ten years after the end of the Trojan War.

Ariadne, GM: daughter of Minos, king of Crete. She fell in love with Theseus, who had arranged to be sent from Athens as a sacrifice to be devoured by the Minotaur, intending to slay the monster instead. Before he entered the labyrinth, Ariadne gave him a spool of thread to unwind so he could find his way out. Theseus slew the Minotaur and returned to her, following the thread. She fled with him away from Crete, but he either abandoned her on the island of Naxos or was unwillingly blown away from the port. One story says Ariadne died of grief, another that Dionysus found her sleeping there and made her his wife.

Ariel: See *Tempest, The.*

Around the World in 80 Days: novel by French writer Jules Verne, published serially in *Le Temps,* 1871–1872. Phileas Fogg, a precise, dignified English gentleman, wagers that he can travel around the world in 80 days (then an unthinkable feat); as he sets out with his intrepid French valet Passepartout on a fabulous journey by ship, balloon, camel, elephant, and train, he is mistaken for a bank robber by Detective Fix, who pursues the two through the resulting series of adventures. Fogg wins his bet by a hair's breadth.

Artemis, GM: goddess of the hunt, of nature, and of chastity. The oldest conception of Artemis was probably as a harvest goddess. When Oenus of Calydon did not present her with a harvest offering, she sent the terrible Calydonian boar to ravage his fields. She was the goddess of nature, especially the wilderness, and her festivals were celebrated with all kinds of animals and fruits. The bear especially was associated with her, and the hind was also sacred to her. She was the protector of women and children and goddess of childbirth.

To the ancient Greeks, Artemis was daughter of Zeus and Leto and the twin of Apollo. As Apollo became known as the sun god, Artemis became goddess of the moon. The Romans identified her with their own goddess Diana.

Art for art's sake: poetic principle stating that a work of art should exist for its own sake rather than for a certain purpose, such as educating or morally uplifting the reader. The term was popularized by the French symbolist poets. Edgar Allan Poe in *The Poetic Principle* (1850) writes of "the poem written solely for the poem's sake."

Arthurian legend: cycle of verse and prose tales concerning the mythical King Arthur of Britain and his knights of the Round Table. The legend provided one of the principal themes of medieval romance throughout Europe. The Arthur of romance was of marvelous birth, conceived by Queen Igraine while his father Uther Pendragon was magically disguised as Igraine's husband. Arthur was marked for kingship as a young boy when he proved to be the only one who could remove the sword Excalibur from the stone in which it was imbedded. This was interpreted as a sign of the true king. (In a common variant, Arthur received Excalibur from the mysterious Lady of the Lake, also called Vivian or Nimue, who handed it up to him through the water.) Arthur married Guinevere and established his court at Camelot, where he was advised by the wizard Merlin, and where he gathered at his Round Table the flower of knighthood. It is the adventures and love affairs of the various knights that constitute the bulk of the legend. The adulterous love of Arthur's favorite knight, Lancelot, and his queen, Guinevere, led to the disintegration of the fellowship of the Round Table and Arthur's treacherous nephew Mordred attempted to usurp his throne. Though Arthur killed Mordred in battle, he was himself severely wounded. In some versions of the legend he died and was buried at Glastonbury, England. In others, Sir Bedivere threw Excalibur into the lake. The Lady's hand reached out to receive it. A barge appeared and carried Arthur to the isle of Avalon, from which he was expected to return some day, healed of his wounds.

There is some evidence that Arthur was a historical figure, a Celtic chieftain of the sixth century. The earliest stories about Arthur are Welsh. The chronicler Geoffrey of Monmouth describes Arthur's deeds in his largely fictitious *History of the Kings of Britain,* written in Latin in the twelfth century. The Norman-French poet Wace translated Geoffrey's history into a verse epic, *Brut,* adding the story of the Round Table. The first Arthurian poem in English was a translation of Wace's *Brut* by Layamon. The legend received its first sophisticated treatment in the romances of the French poet Chrétien de Troyes. In the 15th century the English prose *Morte d'Arthur* by Sir Thomas Malory fixed the legend in its traditional form. Modern versions include Wagner's operas *Tristan und Isolde* and *Parsifal,* Alfred Tennyson's poems *Idylls of the King* (1859–1885), and T. H. White's novel *The Once and Future King* (1958). See also *Holy Grail; Knights of the Round Table; Gawain; Lancelot; Percival; Morgan le Fay; Merlin;* and *Morte d'Arthur.*

CULVER PICTURES

ARTHUR: *the legendary king and his knights are portrayed in this 19th-century engraving as they discuss the founding of the "table round."*

Art of Love, The: poem by Roman poet Ovid (Publius Ovidius Naso), written in 1 B.C. It mocks the prevailing Roman tradition of didactic poetry by providing a handbook on the art of seduction down to the minutest details.

Art of Poetry, The: treatise on the art of writing poetry by the Roman poet Horace. The title was borrowed by Boileau for his book *L'Art poetique* (1674), which set forth literary principles that were carefully followed by authors of the French classical period.

Asclepius: See *Apollo.*

Asgard, NM: abode of the gods, reachable only over the rainbow bridge Bifrost.

Assonance: repetition of similar, closely juxtaposed vowel sounds in a poetic passage, often used as an alternative to rhyme. For example, consider the italicized vowels in a line by W.B. Yeats: 'They will not h*u*sh, the leaves afl*u*tter round me, the b*ee*ch l*ea*ves old."

As You Like It: comedy by Shakespeare, first produced about 1599. The principal characters are the exiled Duke; his usurper brother Frederick; Frederick's daughter Celia; the Duke's daughter Rosalind; her lover Orlando; his cruel older brother Oliver; and the comic characters Audrey, Touchstone the jester, and the melancholy Jacques. The complicated plot is set in the Forest of Arden, where the exiled Duke is living and whither the other characters either flee or pursue each other. Being a good comedy, *As You Like It* ends with not one but four marriages, as well as the restoration of the Duke.

Atalanta, GM: beautiful girl who challenged all her suitors to a foot race. If she lost, she would marry the winner; if she won, the loser would be put to death. A man whose name is given in legend as either Hippomenes or Milanion eventually won her because Aphrodite had given him three of the Golden Apples of the Hesperides; he threw them in front of Atalanta as they ran, and she stopped to pick them up, thus losing the race.

Athena, GM: goddess of wisdom, industry, and war; often called Pallas Athena. She was the daughter of Zeus and Metis, and was born full grown and fully armed from the brain of Zeus. Depicted on the west pediment of her temple in Athens, the Parthenon, was the contest between her and Poseidon for the position of patron of the city. Poseidon's gift to the city was a spring (or, in some versions, the horse); Athena's was the olive tree. The people selected her, and the city was named Athens in her honor. She was also the patroness of arts and crafts and the helper and protector of the Greeks in war. The Romans identified her with Minerva.

Atlantis: fabled island in the Atlantic Ocean, west of the Pillars of Hercules. Plato and Pliny both mention it. Plato in "Timaeus" says that it was larger than Asia Minor and Libya, and was a once-ideal state that became corrupt and militaristic and used its great power to try to conquer the world. It was destroyed by earthquakes and sank into the sea. That such an island ever existed is doubtful, yet the question was still debated in the 1600's and 1700's by such notable writers as Montaigne and Voltaire. The idea of an advanced civilization where learning and scientific research were encouraged appealed to Western rationalists who tried to identify the lost land with America and the Canary Islands. Sir Francis Bacon entitled his essay on such a utopia of learning *The New Atlantis* (1626). Atlantis's rediscovery occurs in Jules Verne's *20,000 Leagues Under the Sea* (1870), where science, in the shape of a submarine, fulfills its promise of answers to questions such as the one regarding Atlantis's existence. In contemporary science fiction, the corrupt or ruined aspect of Atlantis is emphasized, corresponding to the modern pessimistic outlook on scientific progress.

Atlas, GM: one of the Titans, who rebelled against the gods and lost. Atlas's punishment was to stand forever, holding up the heavens. His one respite came when Hercules shouldered the sky so that Atlas could fetch him some of the Golden Apples of the Hesperides. Atlas returned with the apples but refused to resume his burden; Hercules tricked him by asking him to take it for a moment while Hercules made a pad for his shoulders. Later Perseus turned Atlas to stone by showing him the Gorgon's head, and Atlas became the Atlas Mountains in North Africa. Atlas was the father of the Pleiades.

The Flemish cartographer Mercator in the 1500's used a picture of Atlas holding up the world on the title page of his books of maps, and such books have since been called atlases.

CULVER PICTURES

ATLAS: *the Greek god whose rebellion brought the punishment of holding up the heavens.*

Atreus: See *House of Atreus.*

Augean Stables: See *Hercules.*

Augustan Age: reign of Augustus Caesar (27 B.C.–14 A.D.), a time when Latin literature reached its highest development under the patronage of Augustus and his minister Maecenas. The great writers of the period were Vergil, Horace, Ovid, and Livy.

The reign of Queen Anne (1702–1714) is called the Augustan Age of English literature, a period notable for the writings of Steele, Swift, Pope, and Addison.

In France the term is applied to the reign of Louis XIV (1643–1715), when Corneille, Racine, and Molière wrote their brilliant plays.

Aurora: See *Eos.*

Autobiography: self-written life history of a person. *The Confessions of St. Augustine* (late fourth and early fifth centuries) is considered the earliest autobiography in Western literature. Cellini's *Autobiography of Benvenuto Cellini* is a vivid picture of the Italian Renaissance and some of its outstanding personages, as well as of the artist himself. Rousseau's *Confessions,* published in 1782, was the first great introspective autobiography. Novels can masquerade as autobiographies, like Defoe's *Moll Flanders,* or autobiographies as novels, like Joyce's *Portrait of the Artist as a Young Man.* Among the most famous modern autobiographies are: Benjamin Franklin's *Autobiography* (first published in full, 1868); Booker T. Washington's *Up from Slavery* (1901); *The Education of Henry Adams* (1906); André Gide's *If It Die* (1926); *The Autobiography of Lincoln Steffens* (1931); Charles Lindbergh's *The Spirit of St. Louis* (1954); and Claude Brown's *Manchild in the Promised Land* (1965).

Autobiography of Alice B. Toklas, The: written by U.S. expatriate Gertrude Stein as if her secretary and companion Alice Toklas wrote it about herself. The experimental work, published in 1933, actually relates the story of Stein's life. In addition to describing her intellectual development and her attempt to develop a literary cubism to match her friend Picasso's visual style, she has Ms. Toklas's persona say that she knew three geniuses in her life—Pablo Picasso, Alfred North Whitehead, and Gertrude Stein.

Autocrat of the Breakfast Table: familiar essays by U.S. physician and writer Oliver Wendell Holmes, published in the first twelve issues of the *Atlantic Monthly,* 1857–1858, and shortly after as a book. The setting is a boarding-house breakfast table. The table talk—usually a monologue delivered by the Autocrat (Holmes)—rambles informally over a variety of subjects.

Avalon: See *Arthurian legend.*

B

Babbitt: novel by U.S. writer Sinclair Lewis, published in 1922. Its hero George Babbitt, a small-town businessman and town booster whose horizons are limited to Zenith (the "greatest little city in the world"), gave his name to an emergent social type. Although Babbitt eventually comes to the vague realization that Zenith and his own ideas are narrow-minded and provincial, he lacks the strength to leave or change.

Babi Yar: prison camp for Jews in Russia during World War II; the subject of two works by Soviet authors: a poem by Yevgeny Yevtushenko (1961) and a novel by Anatoly P. Kuznetsov (1966–1967).

Yevtushenko's poem decries anti-Semitism and inhumanity both in the Soviet Union and in the world. Kuznetsov recounts his eyewitness impressions of the Nazi extermination of Kiev's entire Jewish population and censures Soviet authorities for their tacit approval and attempts to cover up the incident.

Bacchus: See *Dionysus.*

Balder, NM: god of light, son of Odin and Frigga. Frigga exacted a vow from all creation never to harm Balder, but she neglected to ask the insignificant mistletoe. Arrows, stones, spears, or battle-axes could not injure him. But Loki, the mischief-maker, cut off a twig of the mistletoe and made a dart of it. He gave it to the blind Hoder and directed his aim. Balder was pierced by the dart and fell dead. Hel (death) agreed to let Balder return to life if all things in the world would weep for him. All things on Earth wept except Loki; Balder never returned, but Loki was later punished.

Ballad: traditionally, a narrative poem in simple stanza form and of unknown folk authorship. Ballads deal with folk legends, heroes, supernatural stories, unhappy love, murders, and disasters. The grim and tragic stories bear testimony to their primitive origin, for the true ballads were handed down orally from generation to generation. There were almost no written ballads before the 15th century, but the ballads themselves are centuries older.

The typical ballad stanza is the simplest of verse forms. It has four lines, of which the first and third are unrhymed and have four accents each; the second and fourth are rhymed and contain three accents each.

In the 1700's, literary scholars began to take an interest in ballads. They had enormous influence on the English and German Romantic movements. Coleridge's "Rime of the Ancient Mariner" is an "art ballad," a literary adaptation of the folk ballad.

American ballads are of two kinds: those descended from the old Scottish or English ballads, which immigrated with the early settlers; and those that have sprung up spontaneously among mountaineers, cowboys, lumberjacks, and miners. Many of these, like the Scottish border ballads, deal with outlaws and violent death. Some, like "The Streets of Laredo," are native variants of older ballads.

Ballad of the Sad Cafe, The: novella by U.S. writer Carson McCullers, published in 1951, later dramatized by playwright Edward Albee (1963). Set in a dreary Southern small town, the action concerns the strange relationship, beginning in love and ending in violence, of three loners: a six-foot woman, her ex-convict former husband, and a tiny hunchback. Through them, the story explores the mystery and pain of loving and being loved.

Banquo: in Shakespeare's *Macbeth,* a thane (lord) murdered by Macbeth. Banquo's ghost returned to torment Macbeth.

Barabbas: novel by Swedish author Pär Lagerkvist, published in 1950. It describes the fate, after the Crucifixion, of the prisoner chosen to be saved instead of Jesus.

Barbara Frietchie: poem by U.S. poet John Greenleaf Whittier, published in 1864. It recounts an incident supposed to have occurred at Frederick, Maryland, during the Civil War. Barbara was a patriotic old woman who refused to lower the Union flag from her home when the Confederates under General Jackson entered the town; challenged by her courage, he did not permit his troops to molest her.

Barchester Towers: entertaining satire by English author Anthony Trollope, published in 1857. It relates the gossip about, and the ambitions of, the characters in an English diocese. The wife of the new bishop, Dr. Proudie, maneuvers to change church services, dictates who should marry whom, and assigns additional duties to disliked clergy. She and Obadiah Slope, the bishop's chaplain, are rivals for control of Barchester Towers. When Slope's hypocrisy and plotting are exposed, his hopes of a promotion are dashed, and he is banished from the town.

Battle Hymn of the Republic: poem by U.S. writer Julia Ward Howe, published in the *Atlantic Monthly* in 1862. Sung to the tune of "John Brown's Body," it became a favorite with Union soldiers in the Civil War and has remained one of the most popular of patriotic songs.

Baucis and Philemon, GM: very poor aged couple who lived in Phrygia. Zeus and Hermes, traveling in disguise, were welcomed and fed in their cottage. Not until the pitcher returned to the table miraculously filled did Baucis and Philemon realize they were entertaining gods. The old couple's prayer to die together was granted; their cottage was changed into a temple, and they were changed into trees that grew at the gate of the temple.

Bay Psalm Book: book of psalms translated from the Bible by Thomas Welde, John Eliot, Richard Mather, and other ministers of the Massachusetts Bay Colony; published in Cambridge, Massachusetts, in 1640. It is one of the first two books printed in English in the American colonies.

Beat generation: term applied to a group of cultural nonconformists in the late 1950's in the United States. "Beatniks," as they were known, were particularly associated with poetry, jazz, and the rejection of U.S. cultural values. They constituted a major Bohemian artistic movement. Chief among Beat writers were Allen Ginsberg, Jack Kerouac, Gregory Corso, and Lawrence Ferlinghetti.

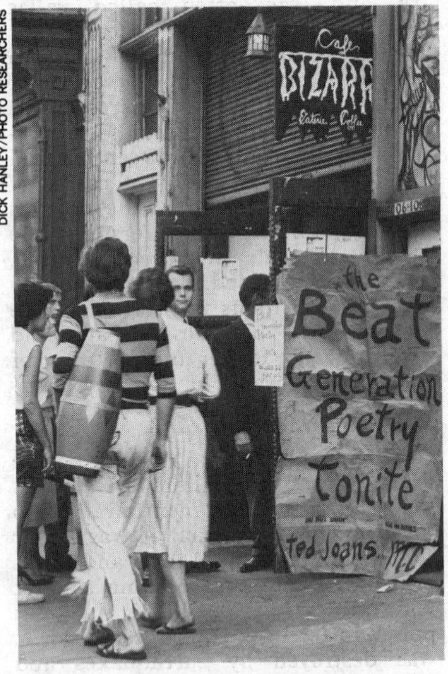

DICK HANLEY/PHOTO RESEARCHERS

BEAT POETS *rejected established values but brought back live poetry reading.*

Beauty and the Beast: fairy tale, first published in French *("La Belle et la Bête")* in 1757 but probably much older. Beauty's father, having picked a rose in the Beast's garden, is forced to send her to the Beast. She goes to live in the Beast's enchanted palace, and each day she refuses his offer of marriage. But when she finds the kind Beast wounded, she embraces and kisses him, and he turns into a handsome prince.

Becket, or the Honor of God: drama by French playwright Jean Anouilh, presented in 1959. It concerns the friendship and estrangement of King Henry II of England and Thomas à Becket, his archbishop of Canterbury, who finds his honor in the honor of God. Becket is killed by Henry's barons because he has angered the king. T. S. Eliot's *Murder in the Cathedral,* deals with the same story.

Becky Sharp: See *Vanity Fair*.

Bedivere: See *Arthurian legend*.

Beggar's Opera: ballad opera by British writer John Gay, performed in 1728. It was recognized by contemporaries as a threefold satire: (1) of the corrupt Walpole administration; (2) of contemporary Italian opera; (3) of conventional English romantic comedy, since it drew its characters from the underworld. The leading figures are the Peacham family, dealers in stolen goods; the love interest is between their daughter Polly and the gallant Captain MacHeath, a robber, bigamist, and murderer. German dramatist Bertolt Brecht adapted Gay's play for his satire on capitalism *The Threepenny Opera,* performed in 1928, with music by Kurt Weill.

CULVER PICTURES

BEGGAR'S OPERA: *Captain MacHeath is visited in jail by Polly Peacham* (right). *In Brecht's* Threepenny Opera, *MacHeath became Mack the Knife.*

Bellerophon, GM: son of Glaucus, king of Corinth. He committed murder and fled to Proetus, king of Argos, for protection. Antaea, Proetus's wife, fell in love with Bellerophon, and when he rejected her advances, she accused him to the king. Proetus sent him to Iobates, king of Lycia, with a secret message asking that he be put to death. Iobates sent him to kill the terrible monster Chimera, sure he would meet his death. But Bellerophon had tamed the winged horse Pegasus, and on his back he was able to approach the Chimera and kill it. After other trials, in which he was successful, Iobates saw his worth and gave him his daughter in marriage. As Euripides tells it, Bellerophon's pride led him to try flying to Mount Olympus, but Pegasus threw him and he was killed.

Belles-lettres (French for "beautiful literature"): artistic, esthetic, or imaginative literature as art, contrasted with practical, informational, or scientific writings. The term now refers especially to light essays of appreciation, prose poems, or impressionistic sketches that do not fall into any definite category.

Beowulf: Old English (Anglo-Saxon) epic poem in alliterative verse, written perhaps in the 700's A.D., based on a mixture of legendary and historical events that took place in sixth-century Scandinavia. It is the oldest epic in a European vernacular.

For twelve years the monster Grendel has walked into the Danish King Hrothgar's great mead hall Heorot and devoured as many as 30 warriors in one night. The young hero Beowulf, a prince of the Geats of southern Sweden, arrives to aid Hrothgar, wrestles with Grendel, and tears off his arm. Grendel flees to his den to die. The next night his mother, the water-hag, comes to avenge her son and devours another warrior. Beowulf follows her to the bottom of the sea and, after a terrible underwater fight, kills her and cuts off the head of Grendel's corpse. The Danes celebrate their delivery with great rejoicing in the mead hall and with speeches recalling heroic deeds of the past. Beowulf returns to his own people, laden with rich gifts.

Years later Beowulf becomes king of the Geats and rules for 50 years until a fearful dragon comes to lay waste his land. Beowulf and eleven companions set out to destroy it. At sight of the fire-breathing monster, his companions, except for the loyal Wiglaf, flee. With Wiglaf's aid, the aged Beowulf kills the dragon, but he receives his own death wound in the combat. His grieving people place his body on a great funeral pyre and bury the dragon's treasure with his ashes.

Bestiary: form of medieval literature in which the supposed natural habits of animals were used as examples for teaching Christian doctrine. A well known example used was the pelican, which was said to feed her young with her own blood; her action was said to reflect Christ's redemption of man. The writers of bestiaries gleaned their information from ancient authors, from legends, and from imagination, but their books were accepted as natural histories, perpetrating belief in fabulous beasts like the unicorn, the phoenix, and the hippogriff.

Betrothed, The: novel by Italian author Alessandro Manzoni, first published in 1827; often called the greatest of modern Italian novels. The plot centers on the trials endured in 17th-century Italy by two separated lovers, Renzo and Lucia, before their eventual reunion; their adventures bring them into contact with members of almost every class in Italian society. Manzoni's characters and descriptions are famous, and the book is comparable to *Don Quixote* in its evocation of national character.

BEOWULF: *the aged hero wrestles with a fire-breathing monster.*

CULVER PICTURES

Bhagavad-Gita: See *Mahabharata.*

Biblical influence on literature: with its striking imagery, poetic wisdom, religious concepts and terms, the Bible has exerted a profound influence over many languages and cultures. In cases where no written language existed, its translation became the occasion for developing an alphabet (for example, the Cyrillic alphabet, developed c 863, is still used by Eastern Church Slavs). World literature and art have been inspired by its stories and themes. Its proverbs and turns of phrase have become such integral parts of the European languages that speakers often do not realize the origin of derivative figures of speech (as in "grapes of wrath," "handwriting on the wall," "balm of Gilead," "thorn in the flesh").

Parts of the Bible were translated into the European languages in the 1300's and 1400's. These were, for the most part, word-for-word renderings, but even these clumsy translations were a major influence on the developing languages.

In the 1500's, the Reformation encouraged more ambitious translation projects. Martin Luther in Germany and the early English translators followed Humanist principles: to translate for sense rather than literally, and to translate from the original languages, Hebrew and Greek, rather than from the Vulgate Bible, itself a Latin translation.

Luther's work, completed in 1534, was a major landmark in the establishment of German as a literary language; it is still used by German Protestants today. It influenced all translations, biblical and secular, that followed.

Among the early English translators, the most influential was William Tyndale. His incomplete translation (about 1525) formed a basis for the "Great Bible" (1539) and influenced the Authorized (or King James) Bible (1611). This translation remained the standard English version for 300 years, and is still admired for its literary power. Its style influenced many generations of poets and prose writers.

The new translations and the spread of printing made the Bible available to the common people. In many homes it would be the only book. It was read privately and in groups, for inspiration, education, and entertainment. Its poetic images and syntax so influenced the imagination, phraseology, and literary taste of European writers that it is impossible to fully appreciate European and American literature without familiarity with it.

Bibliography: list of books and articles on a special subject or a certain author. For instance, a complete bibliography of Sir Walter Scott includes the titles of everything that Scott wrote, with dates of publication, all editions and formats, and every book about Scott or any of his works, as well as all magazine articles and monographs about him.

In a more general sense, bibliography is the serious study or descriptive history of all manuscripts, books, and their making, including references to authors and editions, the materials used in their makeup, and the dates and styles of their printing.

Billy Budd: late, short novel by U.S. writer Herman Melville, completed in 1891–1892 and published in 1925; a parable of the eternal conflict between good and evil and the limits of human justice. Unjustly accused of mutiny by his evil superior officer Claggart, the sailor Billy Budd, a model of natural innocence, kills Claggart and accepts his punishment—death. The story was the basis for an opera by Benjamin Britten.

Biography: written history of the life of a person. In early times biography was often written for political or moral purposes. In the first century A.D. Plutarch wrote his *Parallel Lives,* comparing the careers of a score of Romans with the same number of Greeks, pair by pair; countless later writers (Shakespeare among them) drew on this work for facts and characterization. Tacitus, the Roman historian, wrote a life of his father-in-law Agricola that is a classic; and Suetonius's *Lives of the Caesars* (written about 120 A.D.) is gossipy and full of scandal. These are samples of what is called "antique biography," written to emphasize certain moral qualities or to teach a political lesson.

Biography in English begins in the 1500's with William Roper's *Life of Sir Thomas More* and George Cavendish's *Life of Cardinal Wolsey.* In the 1600's Izaak Walton wrote *Lives* of Donne, Hooker, Herbert, and others that are the forerunners of modern personal biography. James Boswell's *Life of Samuel Johnson* (1791), considered one of the great biographies of all time, was based on Boswell's first-hand records of Johnson's sayings, habits, and most inconsequential everyday activities. Johnson himself wrote a critically important series of *Lives of the English Poets* (see entry).

In modern biography, the English writer Lytton Strachey initiated the "debunking" tradition of taking public figures down from their pedestals. In *Eminent Victorians* (1918) and *Queen Victoria* (1921), he portrayed the real person behind the popular public image, although many critics think he went out of his way to emphasize negative traits.

Although biography is an important literary form, not all biographies are or claim to be literature. Biographies may be written by historians as part of their historical studies, by family members to preserve the memory of an ancestor, or by journalists to inform readers about current personalities.

Birds, The: comedy by Greek playwright Aristophanes, first performed in 414 B.C.; generally considered the best of all ancient Greek comedies. Two Athenians, escaping from their city's courts and taxes, persuade all the birds to build a city in the air, called Cloud-Cuckooland. There they gain control of the food supplies of both men and gods, becoming rulers of the world and creating a utopia.

Birth of Tragedy from the Spirit of Music, The: essay by German philosopher Friedrich Nietzsche, published in 1872, in which the author defines two opposing dynamic cultural forces in ancient Greece. These two forces, which Nietzsche terms Dionysiac and Apollonian, are the dark, ecstatic side and the bright, rational side of man's nature; Nietzsche states that Greek tragedy was originally Dionysiac but eventually became too Apollonian, and he foresees a rebirth of "true" (that is, more Dionysiac) tragedy stemming from the work of German composer Richard Wagner.

Blank verse: unrhymed iambic pentameter, the most common metrical form in English dramatic and epic poetry. Shakespeare's plays, for example,

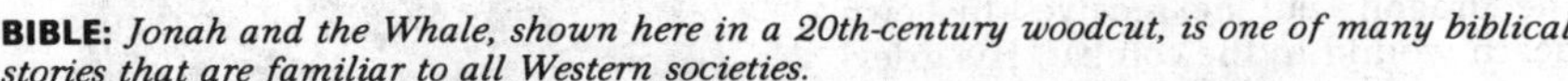

BIBLE: *Jonah and the Whale, shown here in a 20th-century woodcut, is one of many biblical stories that are familiar to all Western societies.*

are written in blank verse. It was first used by Henry Howard, Earl of Surrey, in his translations from the *Aeneid* in the 16th century. The first English drama written in blank verse was Sackville and Norton's tragedy *Gorboduc* in 1562. Christopher Marlowe made masterly use of it in his tragedy *Tamburlaine,* written in 1587. Shakespeare adopted and perfected it.

Bleak House: novel by English writer Charles Dickens, published serially, 1852–1853. It satirizes the injustice of delay in court proceedings.

Blood Wedding: drama by Spanish poet and playwright Federico García Lorca, first produced in 1933, a somber "rural tragedy" of violent passions. A timid bride runs away from her wedding feast with a former suitor, but she soon changes her mind again and wants to return. The bridegroom, who has caught up with the two, fights with the former suitor, and the two men kill each other.

Bloom, Leopold: See *Ulysses.*

Bloomsbury group: coterie of talented, elitist English intellectuals who began meeting in 1906, in the Bloomsbury district of London, to discuss philosophy and the arts and to gossip. Among others they included novelist Virginia Woolf; Fabian writer Leonard Woolf; economist John Maynard Keynes; biographer Lytton Strachey; artist Vanessa Bell; art critic Clive Bell; novelist E.M. Forster; painter Duncan Grant; and art critic/painter Roger Fry.

BLOOMSBURY GROUP'S REPRESENTATIVE WORKS

VIRGINIA WOOLF
Mrs. Dalloway (1925)
To the Lighthouse (1927)
A Room of One's Own (1929)
The Waves (1931)

LYTTON STRACHEY
Eminent Victorians (1918)
Queen Victoria (1921)

JOHN MAYNARD KEYNES
The Economic Consequences of the Peace (1919)
The General Theory of Employment, Interest and Money (1936)

CLIVE BELL
Civilization (1928)
Proust (1929)

E.M. FORSTER
Where Angels Fear to Tread (1905)
A Room with a View (1908)
A Passage to India (1924)

ROGER FRY
Vision and Design (1920)
Transformations (1926)
Cezanne (1927)

NEW YORK PUBLIC LIBRARY/ASTOR, LENOX & TILDEN FOUNDATIONS

BLUEBEARD: *the monstrous husband gives Fatima the key to the forbidden door.*

Bluebeard: fairy tale villain who murders his wives, one after the other, and hides them in a locked room. The story is built around the forbidden door (or forbidden chest) motif, one of the worldwide motifs of folklore. As a story, "Bluebeard" was first published as one of French author Charles Perrault's fairy tales. The original character is sometimes identified as the medieval French blackguard Gilles de Retz.

After murdering six wives, Bluebeard marries a seventh, named Fatima. Soon after the wedding Bluebeard goes off on a journey, leaving her all the keys of the castle but forbidding her to unlock one mysterious door. She unlocks the door and discovers the bodies of Bluebeard's dead wives. Overcome with terror, she drops the key, which becomes stained with blood and betrays her disobedience to Bluebeard on his return. She is rescued by her brothers, who kill Bluebeard. The Bluebeard story was the basis for Béla Bartók's opera *Bluebeard's Castle.*

Bohemian: originally, a native of Bohemia, a former kingdom in what is now Czechoslovakia. The word eventually came to mean a gypsy, then any person—especially an artist or writer—who lives outside the rules of bourgeois society. The term gained currency after the publication of French author Henri Murger's *Scenes de la vie de Bohème* (1848; *Scenes from Bohemian Life*) about life in the artists' quarter in Paris; the book formed the basis for Puccini's opera *La Bohème* (1896) and established a romanticized picture of the bohemian artist's life. See also *Beat generation.*

Boreas, GM: north wind; called Aquilo in Roman mythology.

Boris Godunov: history play by Russian poet Aleksandr Pushkin, published in 1831. It is the story of the

rise of Boris, his usurpation of the throne by murdering the true Tsarevich, the rise of the pretender Dmitri, Boris's death, and the overthrow of his son by the same kind of political treachery that brought Boris to the throne. An opera of that name by Modest Mussorgsky, derived from the play, was first performed in 1874.

Bors, Sir: See *Holy Grail.*

Bottom, Nick: weaver in Shakespeare's *Midsummer Night's Dream.* During a rehearsal for *Pyramus and Thisbe,* Puck puts an ass's head on Bottom; the fairy queen Titania falls in love with him because Oberon has put love drops on her eyes.

Bourgeois Gentilhomme, Le: See *Would-Be Gentleman, The.*

Brave New World: novel by British writer Aldous Huxley, published in 1932. Taking place in the year A.F. 632 ("after Ford" or "anno Fordi"), the novel satirizes 20th-century scientism and technocracy by portraying a society in which all social problems have been solved and life is virtually painless but meaningless. Human beings are born from test tubes and classified for life according to intelligence—from Alphas, who are brilliant and creative, to Epsilons, whose stupidity fits them for the lowest menial jobs. People constantly pacify themselves with a tranquilizer drug called *soma.* The story is concerned with two misfits—John Savage, an Indian who has retained some of his own culture, and Bernard Marx, an Alpha who thinks too much—and their failure to adjust to the society.

Breakfast at Tiffany's: short novel by U.S. writer Truman Capote, published in 1958; a seriocomic story about the transient life of Holly Golightly, a New York playgirl.

Bridge, The: long poem by U.S. author Hart Crane, published in 1930. This mystical work explores modern American consciousness through images of the subway, the airplane and, most importantly, the Brooklyn Bridge. Historical and legendary characters, such as Rip Van Winkle and Walt Whitman, are united in this effort to understand and express a national, democratic spirit.

Brobdingnag: See *Gulliver's Travels.*

Bronze Age: See *Golden Age.*

Brook Farm Institute of Agriculture and Education: community of 160 acres, organized in West Roxbury (now in Boston), Mass., in 1841 and abandoned in 1847. It was one of numerous experiments in communal living that took place in the decades before the Civil War in the United

States. Because of the distinguished names associated with it—including Nathaniel Hawthorne, Charles A. Dana, Ralph Waldo Emerson, and Amos Bronson Alcott—it has a secure place in the nation's social history.

The principal organizer and director of the community was George Ripley, who had been a Unitarian minister and an editor of *The Dial,* a literary magazine. He was also a leader of the transcendentalists. The aim of the community was to combine the roles of worker and intellectual, to contribute to intellectual freedom, and to foster a society of cultivated people.

Among residents of Brook Farm were teachers, shoemakers, printers, and carpenters. One dollar per day was paid for work. Housing, fuel, food, and clothing were provided nearly at cost. The community thrived for a while, but eventually interest waned.

Blithedale Romance (1852), by Nathaniel Hawthorne, is a fictionalized account of Brook Farm life. Hawthorne spent about six months at the farm but found the atmosphere not conducive to writing.

Brothers Karamazov, The: major work, often considered the masterpiece, of the Russian novelist Feodor Dostoevski, published in 1879–1880. It deals with the murder of a dissolute landowner, Feodor Karamazov, and the consequent reactions of his three sons. The eldest, Dmitri, a wild, impulsive, hard-drinking ex-soldier, a rival of his father for the favors of the fair Grushenka, is unjustly accused of the crime. The second son, Ivan, a proud and cold intellectual incapable of love, feels guilty of the intellectual crime of despising his father and wishing him dead. The youngest son, Alyosha, is a figure of saintlike innocence, capable of undivided love. In addition to being a suspenseful story of crime and mystery, the novel is Dostoevski's vehicle for exploring his religious and social ideas. The atheism and despair of Ivan are weighed against the faith of Alyosha, but there is no easy choice between them.

Dostoevski's original aim was to write a sequel to *The Brothers Karamazov* in which faith would be restored, but he never produced such a work. Instead, *The Brothers Karamazov* introduces a multitude of characters who between them express the deep divisions in Dostoevski's mind. At the same time, they demonstrate his remarkable ability to sense their psychological heights and depths.

Brunhild: See *Nibelungenlied.*

Buddenbrooks: novel by German author Thomas Mann, first published in 1901. It is a so-called dynastic novel, recounting the decline of a North German merchant family through four generations, from bourgeois respectability to artistic frailty.

C

Caesura (Latin for "cutting"): pause or break in the middle of a line of verse, indicated by double verticals, ‖. In English verse, both old and modern, the caesura comes about the middle of a line, usually where the sense causes a natural rhetorical pause. Examples of the caesura are as follows:

> I will speak out aloude ‖ I care not who heare it.
>
> (From Udall's *Ralph Roister Doister.*)
>
> Hanging so light ‖ and hanging so high
>
> On the topmost twig ‖ that looks up at the sky.
>
> (From Coleridge's "Christabel.")

Caliban: See *Tempest, The.*

CULVER PICTURES

CALL OF THE WILD: *author Jack London, famous for his tales of adventure.*

Call of the Wild, The: story of the Alaska goldfields by U.S. writer Jack London, published in 1903. A dog named Buck is stolen as a pup from his home, shipped to Alaska, and trained as a sled dog. When his master is murdered, Buck runs away into the forest to live with the wolves and adapts successfully. The story celebrates London's belief in the strength of primitive instincts and in the survival of the fittest.

Calydonian boar, GM: terrible boar sent by Artemis to ravage the fields of Calydon as a punishment to Oenus, king of Calydon, for failing to honor her with a harvest offering. A band of heroes hunted the boar, which was at last slain by Meleager.

Calypso: See *Odyssey.*

Camelot: See *Arthurian legend.*

Camille: work by the French writer Alexandre Dumas *fils;* first written as a novel (1848), then as a play (1852). The story centers on Marguerite Gauthier ("Camille"), a Parisian courtesan, who takes a young lover, Armand Duval, but is persuaded by his family to give him up. In the end, just before Marguerite's death from consumption, the two are reunited. The play provided a basis for Verdi's opera *La Traviata* (1853).

Candide: satirical novel by the French author Voltaire, published in 1759, directed against the notion that "everything happens for the best in this best of all possible worlds." The plot, thick with farcical misadventures (most of the incidents, however, having some precedent in history), is concerned with the sometimes divided fortunes of Candide, his beloved Cunegonde, and his tutor Dr. Pangloss, the very embodiment of optimism (a satire on the German philosopher Leibniz). In the end, somewhat reluctantly married to Cunegonde, Candide settles down to cultivate his garden.

Canterbury Tales, The: collection of tales, mostly in verse, by Geoffrey Chaucer; it is his masterpiece and one of the great works in English literature. The tales were written between about 1387 and 1400, the year of Chaucer's death. They tell of the poet joining a company of pilgrims on their way to Canterbury to visit the shrine of St. Thomas à Becket. To while away the journey, their host suggests that each pilgrim tell two stories going, two coming back: the pilgrim judged to have told the best tale is to get a free dinner. Chaucer only completed 24 of the tales, but these range from chivalric romance to folk tale to sermon to bawdy fable. The pilgrims, who come from all walks of life, are vividly described by Chaucer and, within the framework of the pilgrimage, he brilliantly develops their personalities. The work was influential in establishing the East Midlands dialect of English as the basis for Modern English.

Cantos: incomplete epic poem by U.S.-born poet Ezra Pound, the first parts of which were published in 1917 and the last in 1969. For the part published in 1948 *(The Pisan Cantos),* which were written while Pound was held for treason in an American military prison in Italy, the author was awarded the Bollingen Prize in Poetry for 1949. The entire work displays Pound's wide knowledge of world literature, Western and Oriental. One of the most important themes reflects the author's conviction that a capitalist system of economics is basically corrupt.

Carbonek: See *Holy Grail.*

Caretaker, The: play by British playwright Harold Pinter, first performed in 1960, about the barriers to communication between human beings in contemporary society. The plot explores a relationship between three characters: Davies, an opportunistic old tramp, is baited by a younger man, Mick, into revealing his antipathy for Aston, a former mental patient. The play uses techniques associated with the theater of the absurd.

Cassandra, GM: daughter of Priam, king of Troy, and Hecuba. Apollo gave her the gift of prophecy, but when she refused his love, he ordained that no one should believe her prophecies. Cassandra warned the Trojans to send Helen home to Greece; she warned them against the Wooden Horse; but nobody would heed her warnings. Upon the capture of Troy she fell to the lot of Agamemnon, returned to Greece with him, predicted his death and her own, and was killed by Clytemnestra. The name Cassandra has come to mean a prophet of doom.

Cassiopeia: See *Andromeda.*

Castle, The: novel by the Czech-born, German-Jewish writer Franz Kafka, left unfinished at his death and published posthumously in 1926. A man known only as K. tries to gain entrance to a mysterious castle, but his efforts are always blocked by bureaucrats. As an allegory, the novel has been interpreted in various ways, including man's search for God.

Castor and Pollux, GM: twin brothers, also called the Dioscuri, that is, sons of Zeus. (Pollux is the Roman form; the original Greek name was Polydeuces.) They took part in the voyage of the Argonauts and thus became the patrons of sailors and navigation. Castor was famous for his skill in managing horses and Pollux for his boxing. The gods rewarded their fidelity to each other by placing them together in the heavens. Their constellation is called Gemini, the Twins.

Catch-22: black comedic novel about World War II, written by U.S. author Joseph Heller, published in 1961. Yossarian, a bombardier, thinks everyone, friend or foe, is out to kill him. All he wants is to go home, but the number of missions he has to fly keeps going up. He can get out of flying more missions if he is crazy, but there's a catch: he has to tell the doctor he is crazy in order to be sent home; as soon as he does, he demonstrates the rational mind of someone who doesn't want to die; therefore he cannot be crazy. The book satirizes the military and the ideals of war and is remarkable for its vivid comic characters and situations.

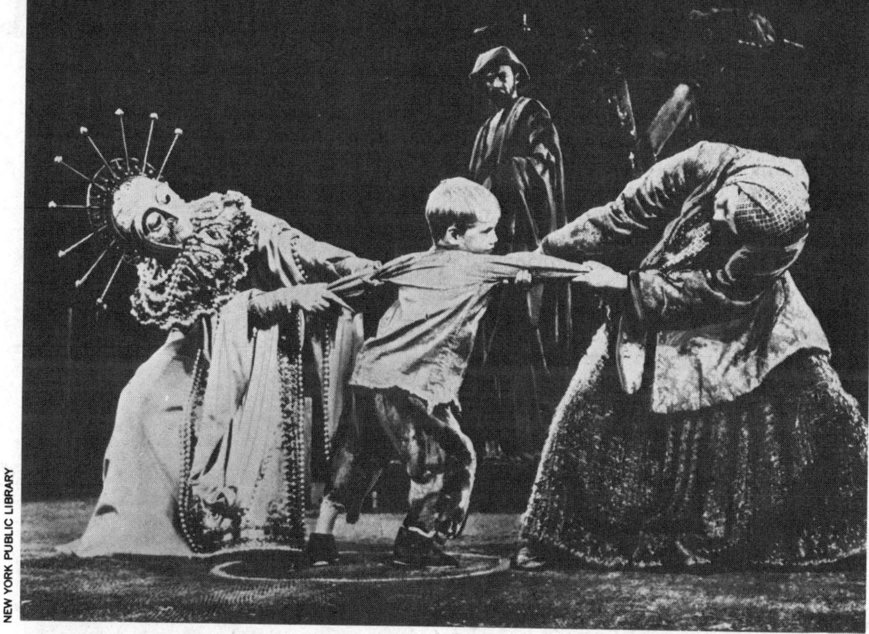

CAUCASIAN CHALK CIRCLE: *two women struggle for a child, a common theme in world legend and literature.*

Catcher in the Rye, The: novel by U.S. author J. D. Salinger, published in 1951, about youth's disenchantment with a hostile adult world. It is cast as a long, colloquial monologue spoken by Holden Caulfield, who has run away from his prep school, preferring to head for New York rather than go home. In spite of his external sophistication, Holden maintains an incorruptible innocence during a weekend of disillusioning experiences.

Catharsis: See *Poetics, The.*

Caucasian Chalk Circle, The: play by German dramatist Bertolt Brecht, presented in 1948. In it two women contest their right to a baby they both profess to love. Brecht took his story from a classical Chinese play, "The Chalk Circle"; a similar tale is the biblical story of the judgment of Solomon (I Kings 3).

Cavalier poets: group of English courtiers who were leading Cavaliers (supporters of King Charles I of England in his struggle with Parliament). Their poems are polished and elegant and often about the trials of romantic love. Those of note are Richard Lovelace, Sir John Suckling, and Thomas Carew; Robert Herrick is usually numbered among them, though he was a clergyman rather than a courtier.

Centaurs, GM: race of half-horse, half-man beings. They lived in the mountains of Thessaly. The famous battle of the Centaurs with the Lapithae arose from a quarrel at the marriage feast of Hippodamia and Pirithous, king of the Lapithae. The Centaurs were driven out of the country. For the story of a famous Centaur, see *Chiron.*

Cerberus, GM: three-headed dog that guarded the entrance to Hades. He prevented the living from entering the lower world and the dead from leaving. The few mortals who got by him either lulled him to sleep with music, like Orpheus, or pacified him with a drugged cake, like the Sibyl who guided Aeneas to Hades. Hercules simply overpowered Cerberus and carried him out of Hades, one of his twelve labors; he later brought him back. See also *Hercules.*

Ceres: See *Demeter; Persephone.*

Changeling: in British folklore, a child of the fairies or elves left in place of a stolen human baby. This superstition was especially prevalent in the Scottish Highlands, where a newborn child was carefully watched till the day of its baptism. After that it could not be stolen by the fairies. A deformed, sickly, or idiot child was often thought to be a changeling and was cruelly treated so that the fairies would come and take it back, returning the human child they supposedly stole.

Chanson de geste (French for "song of great deeds"): any epic poem in Old French, written in the eleventh to the 15th centuries. Most of them are of unknown authorship. They deal with the emperor Charlemagne and his twelve noble peers, or paladins, emphasizing the herioc deeds of the paladins as defenders of Christianity in legendary battles against the Saracens. Others deal with the wars of the barons among themselves or against the strong, just Charlemagne. The later *chansons* graded into romance, and love or marvelous, magical adventures replaced heroism as their principal theme. The oldest, most famous, and finest is the *Chanson de Roland.* Others are *Ogier the Dane, The Pilgrimage to Jerusalem, Bertha Greatfoot,* and *Huon de Bordeaux.* See also *Ganelon; Ogier the Dane; Roland.*

Chanson de Roland *(The Song of Roland)*: Old French *chanson de geste.* It recounts the fight of Roland, the most famous of Charlemagne's paladins, against the Saracens in 778. See also *Roland.*

Chanticleer (meaning "sing clear"): name of the cock in *Reynard the Fox* and other medieval beast fables. Chanticleer figures in Chaucer's "Nun's Priest's Tale." He is the hero of Edmond Rostand's drama *Chanticleer.* See also *Reynard the Fox.*

Chaos, GM: primeval formless void that existed before the creation of the world. According to Hesiod, from Chaos sprang Gaea (earth), Erebus (darkness), and Night.

Charge of the Light Brigade, The: poem by English poet Alfred Tennyson, immortalizing an incident of the Battle of Balaclava in the Crimean War. Because of an error in transmitting orders, a brigade of English cavalrymen was sent on a charge against Russian guns that could result only in their slaughter. All obeyed, evoking the poet's famous line, "Theirs not to reason why, theirs but to do or die. . . ."

Charis: in Homer's *Iliad,* the wife of Hephaestus, the god of the forge. Later the name was applied to any one of the three Graces, or Charites.

Charlemagne: king of the Franks (768–814) and emperor of the West (800–814). Charlemagne, his splendid court, and his twelve peers, or paladins, are the center of a vast cycle of romance and legend. The various *chansons de geste* celebrate the wars against the Saxons, wars in Italy and in Spain, wars with Charlemagne's own vassals and against the Saracens, his pilgrimage to Jerusalem, the false accusation against his innocent wife Blanchefleur, and the defeat of his rear guard at Roncesvalles, August 15, 778. See also *Chanson de geste.*

Charlotte's Web: children's story by U.S. writer E. B. White, published in 1952; a touching and sensitive story expressing appreciation for all forms of life. Charlotte, a spider, saves her friend Wilbur, a pig, from slaughter by weaving a web with the words "Some pig" on it, an event which, along with Charlotte's later variations, causes Wilbur's owners to think that a supernatural agent is protecting him.

CHARLOTTE'S WEB: *the spider makes a second special web for her friend Wilbur.*

Charon, GM: boatman who ferried the souls of the dead across the river Styx or the river Acheron. The fare was a small coin called an obol; it was the custom to place one in the mouth of a dead person to pay his way to Hades.

Charterhouse of Parma, The: novel by French author Stendhal, published in 1839. Set in the post-Napoleonic era, the story chronicles the adventures of the profligate Fabrizio del Dongo, which culminate in the death of his mistress and their child and his own retirement to a monastery. The work is notable for its sociopolitical examination of the times, and for its analysis of the Romantic movement.

Charybdis, GM: greedy and thieving woman who stole the oxen of Hercules and, as punishment, was turned into a terrible gulf and whirlpool by Zeus. She was placed opposite the monster Scylla in the strait between Italy and Sicily. There she remained a menace to mariners and sucked down several of the ships of Odysseus. See also *Scylla.*

Cherry Orchard, The: play in four acts by the Russian playwright Anton Chekhov, presented in 1904. The play mirrors Russian society at the end of the 19th century, when a long-established feudal system was giving way to social and economic changes. The cherry orchard on the estates of the once wealthy Ranevskis, representing all that was idyllic in the past, must now be sold. The Ranevskis are too inert to do much to help themselves, and in this they are contrasted with the practical Lopakhin, son of a former serf on the estate, who buys the cherry orchard, planning to cut down the trees and build houses.

Cheshire cat: appears in an old English phrase, "grin like a Cheshire cat," a similie for a broad, toothy smile. Nobody knows the origin of the comparison. In Lewis Carroll's *Alice's Adventures in Wonderland,* the Cheshire Cat vanishes by degrees until there is no cat left—just the grin.

Children's Hour, The: poem by U.S. author Henry Wadsworth Longfellow, first published in 1860. The poem is a reflection on the poet's love for his three little daughters, Alice, Allegra, and Edith. The title was used by U.S. playwright Lillian Hellman for her first staged play (1934), in which a neurotic girl wrecks a school and the lives of the two women who run it by falsely accusing them of lesbianism.

Child's Christmas in Wales, A: brief reminiscence by the Welsh poet Dylan Thomas of his boyhood Christmastime adventures, published in 1954.

Child's Garden of Verses, A: collection of poems by British author Robert Louis Stevenson, published in 1885. Among the poems, which all reflect the sense of wonder with which children explore their world, are such favorites as "My Shadow" and "The Lamplighter."

Chimera, GM: female monster with a lion's head, a goat's body, and a dragon's tail, who perpetually breathed fire. It was killed by Bellerophon riding the winged horse Pegasus. The term has come to be used for any fantastic notion or idea.

Chiron, GM: wise Centaur, skilled in medicine, who taught Asclepius the art of herbal healing. Many of the heroes of Greece were his pupils. Chiron was accidentally wounded by Hercules and placed in the heavens by Zeus as the constellation Sagittarius.

Christmas Carol, A: story by English writer Charles Dickens, published in 1843. Old Ebenezer Scrooge, a "clutching, covetous old sinner," and Tiny Tim, the crippled child of Bob Cratchit, Scrooge's downtrodden clerk, are two of the main characters. It is the story of Scrooge's regeneration: fantastic visitations by three spirits of Christmas—the ghosts of Christmas Past, Christmas Present, and Christmas Yet to Come—change him from an unfeeling money-lover to a benevolent human being who, along with other good deeds, sends a turkey to the Cratchit family to make their Christmas merry.

Chronicles of Narnia, The: collection of seven books by the literary scholar and medievalist C.S. Lewis. On one level, they are children's novels; but they can also be read as religious allegory concerning the war between good and evil. The titles are *The Lion, the Witch and the Wardrobe* (1950); *Prince Caspian: the Return to Narnia* (1951); *The Voyage of the "Dawn Treader"* (1952); *The Silver Chair* (1953); *The Horse and His Boy* (1954); *The Magician's Nephew* (1955); and *The Last Battle* (1956).

Cid, Song of the: twelfth-century heroic poem considered the first masterpiece of Spanish literature. It celebrates El Cid, Ruy (or Rodrigo) Díaz de Vivar, the great national hero of Spain of the eleventh century; he was a historical figure to whom the poem and later ballads gave almost legendary stature. *Le Cid* (1637), by French classical playwright Pierre Corneille, is the first great tragedy in modern French.

Cinderella: in world folklore, a little household drudge, cruelly treated, who attains wealth and marries a prince with the aid of a supernatural guardian. The story exists in more than 500 variants from Alaska to South Africa. The most familiar version is from the French of Charles Perrault, first translated into English about 1729.

Circe: in the *Odyssey,* a sorceress who lured travelers to her island of Aiaie and turned them into beasts by magic. When Odysseus landed there, his comrades were changed into swine. Circe could not harm Odysseus, for he was protected by the herb moly, which Hermes had given him. He compelled her to restore his companions to human form and dwelt with her for a year.

Classicism: principles and qualities ascribed to Greek and Roman literature and art, especially when used as a standard for later works. These qualities are simplicity, economy, balance, harmony, restraint, and objectivity. Classical art emphasizes overall form rather than detail, and represents general rather than particular types. Literary classicism adheres to established literary forms and fits expression to the form, rather than the form to the expression. It aims for pure, correct language, simple but elegant style, and orderliness of thought. During the late 1600's and early 1700's, classicism (or neoclassicism, as it was also called) was the dominant movement in French and English literature, as seen in the work of writers like Racine and Corneille, Dryden and Pope. Since the beginning of the 19th century, Romanticism has opposed classicism by emphasizing individuality, irrationality, and self-expression—all things that classicism excluded.

Classics: in literature, productions of surpassing excellence. They represent the highest standards in literature. In a narrower sense, the classics are the works of the ancient Greek and Roman writers. In general, the classics are those works that are read and enjoyed by successive generations.

NEW YORK PUBLIC LIBRARY

CINDERELLA: *the heroine's fairy godmother prepares to make a coach and four out of a pumpkin and a group of small household animals.*

Clytemnestra: See *House of Atreus.*

Come Back, Little Sheba: play by the U.S. dramatist William Inge, presented in 1950, exploring a theme of the dependent nature of love. It depicts a crisis in the life of Doc Delaney, an alcoholic struggling to overcome his illness, and Lola, his slovenly, once-pretty wife, who still dreams about the past, her baby who died, and her lost dog, Sheba.

Comedy: play written in an entertaining manner and having a happy ending. The form originated in ancient Greece and originally signified a bawdy masque, probably a representation of the older Dionysian orgiastic rites, since plays were presented as a part of the festival of Dionysus. There are several different types of comedy: comedy of situation, like Shakespeare's *Comedy of Errors;* comedy of manners (or "high comedy"), in which the comedy is based on the mores of high society, as in the plays of William Congreve, Richard Brinsley Sheridan, Oscar Wilde, and Noel Coward; low comedy, a forthright exhibition of man's cruder instincts; farce, in which the situation and plot complications border on the preposterous; satire, as in the plays of Aristophanes and Molière; and slapstick, or pie-in-the-face. In Shakespeare's so-called dark comedies, such as *Measure for Measure,* tragic situations are resolved by means that traditionally belong to comedy. In modern plays, comical treatment of horrible or frightening situations is "black humor."

Especially during the Middle Ages, the term *comedy* was applied to nondramatic literary works that treat life seriously but do not leave the reader with a sense of tragedy, such as Dante's *Divine Comedy.* See also *Commedia dell'arte.*

Commedia dell'arte: improvised comedy originating in Italy in the 1500's, based on a sketchily outlined stock plot called a scenario, embellished by farce, clowning, mime, music, and rapid patter. The *commedia* actors, often a group of professional strolling players, achieved a high degree of artistry and created a classic repertory of

COMMEDIA DELL'ARTE: *Scaramouche, the braggart soldier.*

NEW YORK PUBLIC LIBRARY

stock characters—Harlequin, Punchinello, Pantaloon, Pierrot, Columbine—with distinctive costumes and mannerisms. Although the names of the characters changed over the years, some of them, such as the braggart soldier Scaramuccia (or Il Capitano), go back as far as the Miles Gloriosus of Roman comedy. Others extend into the future; Beaumarchais' Figaro and Mozart's Leporello in *Don Giovanni* are descendants of the *zanni* (impudent servants), indispensable to *commedia* plays.

The *commedia* was superseded in the later 1600's in the cities by comedies with more individual characters, such as those by Molière; but the *commedia* remained popular in the small towns until the 1800's, thanks in part to the outstanding innovations of Carlo Gozzi. See also Volume 20, PERFORMING ARTS: *Drama*.

Common Sense: political pamphlet by the English-born American writer and revolutionist Thomas Paine, published in 1776, calling for the immediate separation from England of the American colonies. In attacking British rule Paine wrote: "Government, even in its best state, is a necessary evil; in its worst state, an intolerable one." The pamphlet, which was an immediate success, was widely read throughout the colonies and helped bring public opinion to support the Declaration of Independence.

Compleat Angler, The: dialogue on the superiority of the contemplative sport of fishing as against the active sport of hunting, by English author Izaak Walton, published in 1653, with additions by Charles Cotton in 1676. Although its practical importance has passed, its descriptions of natural beauty and its message of brotherly love have made it an enduring work.

Conceit: an elaborate metaphor in poetry. When a poet compares his lover's eyes to jewels, her hair to gold, he is using Petrarchan conceits. Shakespeare satirized such decorative conventions in his famous 130th sonnet, which begins, "My mistress' eyes are nothing like the sun." A metaphysical conceit is more complicated, working on several levels as it compares two images that seem to have nothing in common. For example, John Donne used the image of compass legs in "A Valediction: Forbidding Mourning" to represent the souls of two lovers who, though separated, are still joined.

Confessions: autobiography, posthumously published 1781–1788, by the Swiss-born French philosopher Jean-Jacques Rousseau. Romantic and self-justifying in tone, it gives a frank account of his life, loves, and intellectual voyagings, setting a fashion for such literature, especially in France.

Confessions of a Mask: autobiographical novel by the Japanese writer Yukio Mishima, published in 1960. It deals with the sexual awakening of the author and the extreme unhappiness his homosexuality causes him.

Confessions of an English Opium Eater: English writer Thomas De Quincey's account of his own experience, published as a book in 1822. It tells how much opium he could take in a day, what the effects were, how various trivial events of his life—glorified and distorted by the influence of the drug—became the material of his dreams, and how in fear of death he gradually reduced his dosage and almost overcame the habit. This book, first published without his name, brought De Quincey a market for his writings and assured his future literary career.

Confessions of Nat Turner: novel by U.S. author William Styron, published in 1966; it involved Styron in controversy even as it brought him fame because of his attempt, as a white man, to represent the consciousness of Nat Turner, the black leader of the slave insurrection that took place in 1831 in Virginia. Little is known about the historical preacher; Styron in effect created his personality from his own views on slavery, racism, and the need for violence in achieving freedom.

Connecticut Yankee in King Arthur's Court, A: satirical novel by U.S. author and humorist Mark Twain, published in 1889. Hank Morgan, a brash, hardheaded, ingenious Yankee is hit on the head in a fight and is transported back to the Middle Ages—to Camelot in the year 528. Twain used the device to air his contempt for and prejudices toward Europe, the church, and monarchy.

Consolation of Philosophy, The: dialogue by the Roman statesman Boethius, written while he was in prison awaiting execution (522–524 A.D.). Boethius and his philosophic muse discuss his troubles and expound a Neoplatonic philosophy of good and evil, happiness and free will. The work was very popular for over a thousand years; it was translated into English by King Alfred, Chaucer, and Queen Elizabeth I, among others.

Consonance: repetition of identical consonant sounds in a poetic passage, with changes in the intervening vowels. Example: *bake, book, bike, back.* It is similar to alliteration, in which identical consonant sounds are also used. But, while the initial sounds of alliterative words are more important than the intervening consonants, for words in consonance it is the final consonant sound that is most significant. *Block* and *cake* are in consonance; *lamp* and *light* are alliterative.

Count of Monte Cristo, The: romantic novel by the French author Alexandre Dumas *père,* published in 1845, telling a tale of intrigue and encompassing love, hate, greed, courage, and revenge. Falsely accused of a political crime, the hero, Edmond Dantès, who is shortly to be married, is imprisoned in the Chateau d'If in the harbor of Marseilles. Managing to escape to the island of Monte Cristo, he there becomes a man of mystery, rich and powerful, before returning to take his revenge on his enemies.

Couplet: two consecutive rhyming lines of verse. The last two lines of a Shakespearean sonnet are a couplet. The most usual type is the heroic couplet, ten syllables to a line, in imabic pentameter; it was used first by Chaucer and brilliantly perfected by Pope and Dryden.

A perfect judge will read each work of wit
With the same spirit that its author writ.
(From Pope's "Essay on Criticism.")

Courtier, The: book by Italian Renaissance author Baldassare Castiglione, of a type called a *courtesy book:* that is, a book in which the proper attributes and behavior of a courtier and gentleman are defined. These precepts are presented in the form of a dialogue among a group of Italian gentlemen and ladies. *The Courtier* was published in Italy in 1528 and soon was translated into other languages of Europe, where it had great influence.

Courtly love: conception of love that arose from the medieval code of chivalry and from the attitude toward high-born women fostered by the cult of the Blessed Virgin Mary. A knight or courtier was expected to court a wise, lovely, virtuous woman who remained aloof. For her he was to write songs and poems and to do great deeds; the suffering his unrequited love inspired supposedly ennobled him. Needless to say, courtly love and marriage were incompatible. The notion was developed by the French troubadours, popularized by the court of Eleanor of Aquitaine in the 1100's, and persisted into the Elizabethan era. Its conventions are important in medieval romances, especially the Arthurian legends.

Coverley, Sir Roger de: fictional old gentleman of Worcestershire, presented by both Joseph Addison and Sir Richard Steele in many of their *Spectator* papers. Addison described him as "a gentleman that is very singular in his behavior, but his singularities proceed from his good sense."

Crane, Ichabod: See *Legend of Sleepy Hollow, The.*

Creusa: See *Medea.*

Crime and Punishment: masterly novel by the Russian writer Feodor Dostoevski, published in 1866, on the theme of redemption through suffering. The penniless student Raskolnikov believes that his natural superiority places him above the moral law of common men. He finds good reasons for committing two brutal murders, and the novel furnishes an examination of these reasons, which, one by one, are proved to be insupportable. Conscience will not permit Raskolnikov to use the money obtained through his crime, and his anguish slowly leads him to confess and embrace the consequent punishment—hard labor in Siberia—which is the gateway to his redemption.

Crisis, The: series of revolutionary pamphlets written for the American colonists by Thomas Paine from 1776 to 1783. The first, beginning "These are the times that try men's souls," was written to rally Revolutionary troops.

Criticism: the art of judging and pointing out the perfections and imperfections of works of art. Appreciation is as much a part of criticism as is detection of flaws. A good critic must have knowledge, taste, sympathy, and facility of expression. The chief objects of literary criticism are to judge, to interpret, and to give personal impressions of books.

Crito: dialogue by the Greek philosopher Plato. Socrates' friend Crito comes to the prison where Socrates is awaiting execution and outlines a plan of escape; Socrates considers whether he should escape and decides that it would be unjust, since he has lived under the laws of Athens and has no right to flout them even though he has been unjustly accused.

Croesus: sixth-century king of Lydia, who was reputed throughout the ancient world to be the richest man on Earth. He is the subject of various tales and legends told by the Greeks, most of them moral lessons concerning the fate of those who are excessively proud and prosperous.

Cronus, GM: son of Uranus (heaven) and Gaea (earth). His wife was Rhea. He was warned that a child of his would overthrow him, so he swallowed his children as soon as they were born, first Hestia, then Demeter, Hera, Hades, and Poseidon. But Rhea saved the infant Zeus by giving Cronus a swaddled stone to swallow instead. When Zeus grew up, he made Cronus vomit forth his brothers and sisters, then dethroned him.

Cry, the Beloved Country: moving novel by the South African writer Alan Paton, published in 1948, about the tragedies, both personal and national, that flow from racial persecution. The central character, Stephen Kumalo, a Zulu clergyman, finds that in Johannesburg his sister has been forced to become a prostitute and his son has become a murderer.

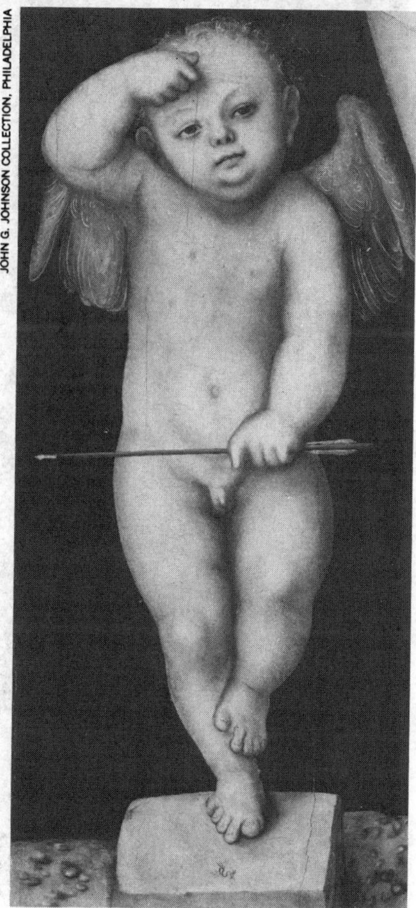

JOHN G. JOHNSON COLLECTION, PHILADELPHIA

CUPID: *the god of love removes his blindfold in the painting by Lucas Cranach the elder.*

Cuchulain: hero of the Ulster (or Ulaid) cycle of old Irish legend. He was the son of Lug, the sun god, nephew of Conchobor, king of Ulster, and the foremost hero among the Knights of the Red Branch. He is believed to have lived in the first century A.D. At the age of twelve he guarded the possessions of Culain, the smith of Ulster, to make up to him for having killed his hound; he thereby received his name: Cu (hound) + Culain (of Culain). He married Emer, the daughter of a druid. In *The Cattle Raid of Cooley,* the most ambitious saga of the Ulster cycle, Cuchulain defends Ulster single-handedly against the forces of Connaught.

Cupid, RM: god of love; son of Venus. He is pictured as a winged, naked boy with bow and arrows. A dart from his bow would create love in the breast of whatever god or mortal it wounded. The story of Cupid and Psyche begins with his wounding himself with one of his own arrows. In this story Cupid is a youth, as was his Greek original, Eros (see also *Psyche).* But usually he is personified as a little child. The chubby little cupids commonly seen in classical and Renaissance art are called *putti* ("little boys").

Cybele: See *Great Mother.*

Cycle: all the poems, romances, and narratives dealing with a certain hero, his followers, and deeds. There are extensive cycles concerning the exploits of King Arthur and his knights, and Charlemagne and his paladins. The tales of Siegfried make up another cycle, as do those about the Ulster cycle hero Cuchulain. See also *Arthurian legend; Chanson de geste; Nibelungenlied; Ulster cycle.*

Cyclopes, GM: race of one-eyed giants who dwelt in Sicily. The word is Greek for round-eyed; Cyclops is the singular form. In the *Odyssey,* they were huge man-eating shepherds. Traditionally, they labored for Hephaestus inside Mount Etna, helping to forge the thunderbolts of Zeus. See also *Polyphemus.*

Cyrano de Bergerac: romantic drama by French playwright Edmond Rostand, first performed in 1897. Loosely based on a historical Cyrano, the hero is a poet, lover, and swordsman who is disfigured by a long nose. Though he secretly loves the same woman as his best friend, he supplies his friend with the romantic speeches to woo her. As Cyrano dies at the end, she realizes that it was his words that won her heart.

D

Dactyl: See *Foot.*

Daedalus, GM: skilled Athenian architect and sculptor. The Greek word means "cunning craftsman." Daedalus's nephew was his apprentice and bid fair to outshine his master; in jealousy Daedalus killed his nephew and fled with his son Icarus to Crete. There he built the labyrinth for King Minos (see *Minotaur*); later he and his son were shut up in the labyrinth for an offense to Minos. Daedalus made wings of feathers and wax for them both, whereby they escaped. But Icarus flew too near the sun; the wax of his wings melted, and he fell into the sea, therafter named the Icarian Sea. Daedalus reached Sicily in safety.

Daisy Miller: short novel by U.S. expatriate writer Henry James, published in 1878. An American girl from Schenectady is traveling in Europe with her mother. Without realizing the difference between European and small-town American conventions, the mother allows her daughter the same freedom she had at home, but Daisy's ways are misjudged in the light of a more ancient, artificial code.

Danae, GM: daughter of Acrisius, king of Argos. To prevent the fulfillment of an old prophecy that he would die at the hand of Danae's son, Acrisius shut her up in a brazen tower. But Zeus fell in love with her and visited her there concealed in a shower of gold; their son was Perseus. Acrisius set the mother and child adrift in the sea in a large chest, but they were carried safely to an island. Perseus later did kill Acrisius accidentally, fulfilling the prophecy.

Dance of Death, The: medieval allegory of the mortality of earthly things, a popular theme for mortality plays and for pictures in which a figure of death leads a line dance, as in woodcuts by Holbein and in the final scene of Ingmar Bergman's movie *The Seventh Seal. Dance of Death* has been used by a number of authors as a title; best known is a play by Swedish playwright August Strindberg, first presented in 1901, in which an aging married couple torment each other.

D'Artagnan: See *Three Musketeers, The.*

David Copperfield: semi-autobiographical novel by Charles Dickens, published 1849–1850; a sentimental story of an orphan's struggles. It deals with the sufferings of young David after his mother's death, through the cruel treatment of his stepfather, schoolmasters, and employers. Uriah Heep, a deliberately "humble" person whose hypocrisy is exceeded only by his treachery, is one of the book's many memorable characters. David finds friends, too—his aunt Betsy Trotwood, the penniless but always optimistic Mr. Micawber, and the kite-flying Mr. Dick—and matures through their kindness to become a successful writer.

Dead Souls: novel by Russian author Nikolai Gogol, first published in 1842. Pavel I. Chichikov, a swindler, works out a scheme to buy up serfs who have died but who have not yet been taken off the census rolls, then mortgage these "dead souls" to buy land. Gogol wrote a second part, in which Chichikov reforms, but he destroyed most of the manuscript just before he died.

Death in the Family, A: novel by U.S. writer and critic James Agee, published posthumously in 1957 and winner of a Pulitzer Prize. Partly autobiographical, the novel is a sensitive description of the effects of his father's death on a young Southern boy. The stage adaptation, *All the Way Home* (1960), by Tad Mosel, also won a Pulitzer Prize and other awards.

Death in Venice: novella by German writer Thomas Mann, published in 1912; a symbolic tale of youth and age, art and life, love and suffering. An ailing middle-aged artist, Gustav von Aschenbach, visiting Venice to regain his strength, conceives a hopeless passion for Tadzio, a young Polish boy.

CULVER PICTURES

DEATH OF A SALESMAN: *the defeated Willy Loman, played in the original production by Lee J. Cobb, is quizzed by his troubled sons.*

Though he never speaks to the boy, Aschenbach's fascination with his beauty is so great that he is unable to tear himself away from cholera-infested Venice and willingly pays the price of his life.

Death of Artemio Cruz, The: novel by Mexican author Carlos Fuentes, published in 1962. It relates the reflections of Artemio Cruz as he lies on his deathbed. His history parallels that of modern Mexico, which, in Fuentes' eyes, grows corrupt as it becomes more powerful. Starting out as the illegitimate son of a peasant and a landowner, Cruz changes from a revolutionary soldier to a rich, powerful industrialist by betraying his idealism. There is an effective change of narrative voice, from first to second to third person, a form of experimentation prevalent in much modern Latin American literature.

Death of a Salesman: play by U.S. writer Arthur Miller, first performed in 1949; a modern tragedy of an ordinary man, Willie Loman, who is an aging traveling salesman. Faced with the loss of his livelihood and the failure of his sons, whom he has inculcated with his values of achieving success through being "well-liked," Willie is bewildered by his fate. Unable to understand why this familiar American dream worked for others but not for himself, Willie commits suicide in a final, pathetic effort to rescue his family through his insurance money.

Decameron, The: collection of 100 short tales by Italian writer Giovanni Boccaccio, written about 1350, containing stories ranging from tragedy and romance to popular farce. The stories are placed in a frame in which ten Florentines, fleeing the plague of 1348, take refuge in a country villa for ten days; each tells a daily story. Boccaccio took his tales from many sources and told them in a language and a form that influenced European prose writers for centuries.

Decline and Fall of the Roman Empire, The History of the: by English historian Edward Gibbon, published 1776–1788. This classic work in six volumes considers the fall of Rome and traces the dissolution of the empire over more than a thousand years. Gibbon attributes the decline of Rome primarily to the corruption of classical Greco-Roman rational ideals by the emotional appeal of Christianity and other Eastern religions.

Deianira: See *Hercules.*

Delphic oracle: shrine of Apollo at Delphi in Greece. In ancient times it was believed that Apollo communicated with mortals at Delphi through his priestess, the Sibyl, or Pythia, who was reputed to have special prophetic powers. Her sayings were usually uttered in obscure terms, subject to different interpretations.

Demeter, GM: goddess of agriculture, fertility, and marriage. She was the mother of Persephone, whom Pluto carried off to the underworld. The Romans identified Demeter with Ceres. See also *Persephone.*

Democracy in America: political analysis by French historian Alexis de Tocqueville, published in four volumes (two in 1835 and two in 1840); one of the early observations of the effects of democratic principles on society. Using the United States as his laboratory, Tocqueville was impressed by the disappearance of class distinctions, but expressed the fear that the danger of democracies lay in the tyranny of majority opinions over minority views.

Desdemona: See *Othello.*

Devil: personification of evil in religion, treated at times scornfully, humorously, or sympathetically in literature. Medieval morality plays tend to make the Devil an object of derision, a satyrlike buffoon. But in Dante's *Divine Comedy,* Lucifer is a gigantic brooding outcast at the center of the funnel-like Hell created by his fall. Milton's Satan, whose name before his fall was Lucifer, earns our begrudging admiration in *Paradise Lost*

NEW YORK PUBLIC LIBRARY

DEVIL: *a portrayal of Lucifer from a Czech manuscript, c 1500.*

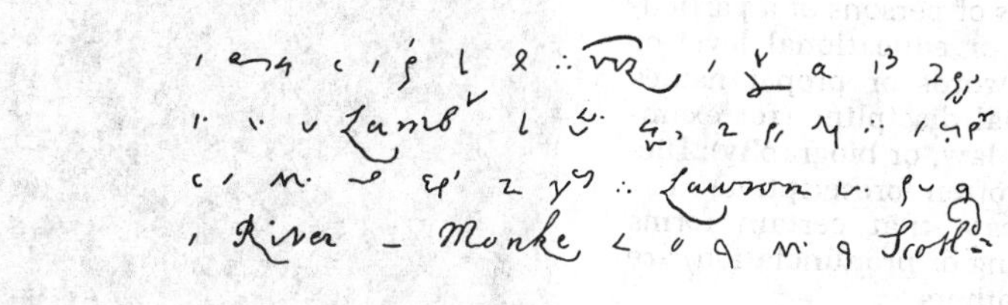

The condition of the State was thus - viz. The Rump after being disturbed by my Lord Lambert, was lately returned to sit again. The Officers of the Army all forced to yield — Lanson, lies still in the River, & Monk is with his Army in Scotland.

CULVER PICTURES

DIARY OF SAMUEL PEPYS: *the original was kept in code* (above), *which was not deciphered* (below) *until nearly 150 years after Pepys's death.*

when he declares that he would rather "reign in Hell than serve in Heaven" (Book I:263).

In addition to being the prince of evil, the Devil is the tempter of humanity. Mephistopheles, the Devil of the Faust legend, is the elegant, horned-and-tailed gentleman we have come to associate with the character. He barters with Faust for his soul and they make an infernal pact. Marlowe's Mephistopheles is himself a tragic figure, a proud, fallen angel whose despair gains our reluctant sympathy even as he plots Faust's damnation. Goethe's Mephistopheles, however, is cold, cynical, and witty. When Faust slips through his hands, we rejoice in his return to being an object of scorn such as he was in morality plays (see also *Faust*). The defeated and therefore ridiculous Devil also appears in Stephen Vincent Benét's *The Devil and Daniel Webster* (see entry). See also Volume 22, RELIGION AND PHILOSOPHY: *Biblical Glossary.*

Devil and Daniel Webster, The: short story by U.S. writer Stephen Vincent Benét, written in 1936; a humorous combination of history and folklore. Through his legendary oratorical skill, Daniel Webster wins an acquittal in the Devil's own court for Jabez Stone, a Yankee farmer who traded his soul to the Devil for wealth and power. It later became the basis for a play and an opera.

Devil's Dictionary, The (originally titled *The Cynic's Word Book*): collection of witty definitions, written in 1906, by U.S. writer Ambrose Bierce. The entries, which originally appeared in periodicals for which Bierce wrote from 1881 to 1906, demonstrate his flair for concision and irony as well as his cynical outlook.

Dialogue: literary form in which the author uses two or more characters discussing a subject. The most famous writer of the form was the philosopher Plato, in whose dialogues his mentor Socrates discusses philosophical problems with friends. See also *Crito; Phaedo; Republic; Symposium.*

Diana: See *Artemis.*

Diary: daily record, usually a description of personal, informal activities. The diaries of historical figures are helpful to historians in reconstructing past events and often provide intimate details of motives and manners that are not found in official records. Some are also good reading, such as the most famous diary in the English language, that of Samuel Pepys (1633–1703).

Perhaps the most famous diary of modern times is that of Anne Frank (1929–1945), a Dutch-Jewish girl who spent many months in hiding from the Nazis occupying Amsterdam.

Diary of Samuel Pepys: journal of daily events kept for the years 1660–1669 by Samuel Pepys, a British public official who was administrative head of the British navy and a friend of King Charles II. Pepys wrote in his own shorthand, which was first decoded in 1825. His accounts of the Stuart Restoration, the Great Fire of London, and many public figures and scholars of the period make it an invaluable historical document. In addition, his lively style and winning personality make the work a classic.

Dictionary: book consisting of word lists, usually arranged alphabetically. Dictionaries are of many different types, but customarily they provide information about the meaning, pronunciation, inflection, and etymology of each word listed. A dictionary may serve the needs of persons of a particular age group or educational level or include only words or proper names within a special discipline (for example, medicine, law, or biography). Dictionaries are often prescriptive; that is, they indicate that certain forms (such as spelling or pronunciation) are preferable to others.

The first distinguished and influential dictionary of English was Samuel Johnson's *A Dictionary of the English Language* (1755). The first great American lexicographer was Noah Webster, who published his *Compendious Dictionary of the English Language* (1806) and *An American Dictionary of the English Language* (1828).

The great modern historical dictionary of the English language is the *Oxford English Dictionary* (1933), a work consisting of twelve volumes and a supplement.

Dido or **Elissa:** princess of Tyre and the legendary founder of Carthage. Her husband was murdered by her brother for his wealth, but Dido fled from Tyre with the treasure. She landed in Africa and bargained for as much land as the hide of a bull would cover. She had the hide cut into thin strips and with them enclosed enough ground to erect her citadel. A neighboring king named Iarbas coveted the city, demanded her hand in marriage, and threatened war should she refuse. Rather than marry him, she built her funeral pyre and killed herself.

In the *Aeneid,* the legendary history of the Roman people, the author, Vergil, defies accepted chronology and makes Dido a contemporary of the wandering Aeneas; she kills herself in sorrow at Aeneas's leaving her.

Dime novel: novel with a sensational adventurous story line that was originated by Edward Zane Carroll Judson under the pseudonym Ned Buntline. The first such work appeared about 1850 and originally sold for ten cents. Themes of the very popular novels often dealt with the American Revolution, the Civil War, or the Western frontier. Their popularity declined in the 1890's, when comic strips and pulp magazines gradually replaced them.

Dionysiac: See *Birth of Tragedy.*

Dionysus, GM: god of an ecstatic religion, whose cult had, by classical times, been considerably tamed. His orgiastic rites were reduced to drunken revelry, and from being a god of fruits and fertility, he became primarily the god of grapes and wine. He was called Bacchus by the Romans. According to later mythology, he was the son of Zeus and Semele, who was burned to death when she foolishly persisted in her demand to see Zeus in his full glory. Dionysus was brought up in secret by the nymphs to save him from the jealous malice of Hera. When he grew up, he traveled through the world teaching men the arts of civilization, especially the cultivation of the grape. The wild, orgiastic aspects of his cult were strongly resisted in many places. Many stories depict the sad fate of those who opposed him; those who favored him received the gift of the vine; that is, the making and use of wine. He often took on the form of a panther, tiger, goat, bull, snake, ass, or lion.

DIVINE COMEDY: *Dante took great pleasure in finding suitable punishment for evil men in "The Inferno," but imagining the agonies, he also felt pity for the damned.*

Dioscuri: See *Castor and Pollux.*

Divine Comedy, The: long allegorical poem by the Italian poet Dante Alighieri, written about 1307–1321. It expresses the poet's vision of the divine plan for justice in this world and the next. Dante originally called it *The Comedy* because it begins in sorrow and ends happily, and also because it was written in the Italian vernacular at a time when serious works were written in Latin. "Divine" was added to the title in the 16th century.

In the first book, *Inferno,* the Roman poet Vergil (the highest representative of human reason and pagan ethics) guides Dante out of a dark wood by a roundabout journey through the Afterlife. On Good Friday in the year 1300, they enter Hell, descending through nine circles, each reserved for a certain type of sin, in which the sinners become increasingly more infamous and their torments more hideous. There Dante sees well known historical figures, princes, popes, and personal enemies, all vividly characterized. The lowest circle is reserved for traitors such as Judas Iscariot, Cassius, and Brutus.

In the second book, *Purgatorio,* Vergil leads Dante through Purgatory, where he sees those who are undergoing purification and is himself purged of his sins. The gates of Paradise are as far as human reason can go, so Vergil leaves. Dante's idealized beloved, Beatrice, guides him through the nine ascending circles of Paradise, which is described in the third book, *Paradiso.* In the tenth circle, St. Bernard becomes his guide and Dante briefly experiences a vision of the Eternal Light, Divine Wisdom, or God.

The number three, symbolizing the Trinity, is used throughout as a structural principle. Thus, the work is divided into three books, each having 33 cantos. The cantos are written in *terza rima,* a three-line verse form with the rhyme scheme a-b-a b-c-b c-d-c.

Doctor Faustus: See *Faust.*

Doctor Zhivago: novel by the Russian poet Boris Pasternak, which describes life in Russia from 1900 to the late 1920's, concentrating on the conflict between the forces of pure principle and the forces of humanity and individualism. The hero, a doctor and a poet, is a passive victim of his times. Banned in Russia, the book appeared first in Italian translation in 1957 and in English in 1958. Pasternak, whose work had not been published for many years, became the symbol of the courageous, uncompromising artist. He was awarded the Nobel Prize in 1958, but did not accept it because of official Soviet disapproval.

Doll's House, A: play by Norwegian dramatist Henrik Ibsen, performed in 1879. The central figure is Nora Helmer, a pampered, spoiled housewife, who babies her children and wheedles and coaxes her husband Torvald for whatever she wants. Suddenly something ugly enters this idyllic world: Nora is blackmailed by the discredited Krogstad, from whom she had borrowed money for a trip to save Torvald's health, thoughtlessly forging her father's signature on the note. Using her usual kittenish tactics, she begs Torvald not to fire Krogstad from his bank. The attempt fails; Torvald learns the truth, characteristically vents his sanctimonious moral outrage at her deception, and vows to separate her from the children. A repentant note from Krogstad softens him up, but Nora suddenly sees Torvald clearly and realizes she can no longer tolerate a marriage that casts her as a "doll" rather than as a responsible person. She walks out and, as the play ends, closes the door behind her.

Don Carlos: historical tragedy by German poet Friedrich Schiller, presented in 1787; a romanticized account of the Spanish king Philip II's ill-fated son Don Carlos, who died mysteriously in prison after his father had him confined for conspiracy. In this play, Don Carlos and the elder statesman, the Marquis de Posa, are portrayed as champions of liberty, opposed to Philip's cruel rule in the Spanish Netherlands. Their plotting is discovered and Philip has them both executed. The play was the basis for Verdi's opera *Don Carlo.*

Don Juan: character originally from medieval Spanish ballad tradition, who has come to symbolize the attractive and reckless seducer. His literary history begins with *The Rake of Seville,* a tragedy by Spanish writer Tirso de Molina, first performed in 1630, which established the basic core of the legend. Don Juan seduces several honorable women and kills the father of one of them in a duel. At a later date, while planning a dinner party and a fresh seduction in the presence of a memorial statue of the man he has murdered, he arrogantly invites the statue to dinner. The "stone guest" arrives at the banquet and Don Juan is swallowed into Hell.

Other versions include *The Stone Banquet* (1665) by the French dramatist Molière, a satire rather than a tragedy, and *Don Juan Tenorio* (1844), a play by Spanish writer José Zorilla y Moral that depicts a repentant rogue who, after 30 years of knavery, is saved from Hell at the last moment by a virtuous woman. The work that is most likely to ensure Don Juan's immortality is Mozart's opera *Don Giovanni,* written to a libretto by Lorenzo da Ponte and first performed in 1787. This superb work combines the reckless gaiety of the incorrigible Don and the comic arias of his valet Leporello, with an ominous musical undertone of impending doom.

Don Juan (pronounced Ju' an in this work), an incomplete epic by the English poet Lord Byron, published intermittently from 1819 to 1824, contains the requisite sexual escapades, but little else of the original legend. The Byronic hero is an iconoclast, leveling satiric tirades on hypocrisy in general and England in particular. George Bernard Shaw's play *Man and Superman* (1903) contains a dream interlude, *Don Juan in Hell,* that is often performed as an independent work.

Don Quixote de la Mancha: picaresque in prose, published in two parts in 1605 and 1615, by the Spanish writer Miguel de Cervantes. It began as a satire of the romances of chivalry popular in Cervante's day.

An impoverished old gentleman, Alonzo Quixano, infatuated with knight-errantry, changes his name to Don Quixote de la Mancha, and with an uncouth peasant, Sancho Panza, as his squire, embarks on a series of misadventures. His valorous deeds, such as tilting at windmills that he believes to be giants, are inspired by a peasant girl whom he reveres as the Lady Dulcinea. Ironically, he dies thinking he has been a failure, although in his pursuit of his illusory ideals he has shown far greater nobility than his sane, materialistic contemporaries.

Don Quixote has had a lasting influence on Western literature, and Sancho Panza ranks with the great comic characters of all time; Quixote and Sancho are often said to represent the two facets of the Spanish character. It is the greatest prose work of Spanish literature, and its episodic structure influenced the form of the novel in the 18th and 19th centuries.

DON QUIXOTE: *the wayward hero and his companion set out on their adventures.*

CULVER PICTURES

Dover Beach: prophetic poem by the English writer Matthew Arnold, published in 1851. It reflects the negative side of Victorian self-confidence and belief in progress. It begins serenely: "The sea is calm to-night." But as the poet watches the ebbing tide, he has a vision of the "sea of faith" withdrawing from the world and exposing its naked reality of tragedy and pain. The poem ends with the image of the world as a "darkling plain . . . Where ignorant armies clash by night."

Dracula: novel by British writer Bram Stoker, published in 1897. This Gothic horror story became the model for innumerable stories on "the matter of Transylvania." Based on Slavic folk legends, they deal with vampires and werewolves. Stoker's Dracula was a charming and cultured Transylvanian count who assumed the form of a bat at night and sucked the blood of sleeping maidens.

Dragon: fabulous monster, pictured usually as a winged, fire-breathing serpent. Its literary function is to symbolize the forces of evil a hero must overcome. Often guardian of a rich hoard, as are Beowulf's Grendel and Sigurd's Fafnir, the dragon may in fact be a mythic representation of the conquering people's enemy—an opposing tribe perhaps in possession of desirable woods or precious metals. The dragon is often associated with water (as is the Hydra slain by Hercules and the biblical Leviathan) or with fire (as is the Chimera killed by Bellerophon); it therefore can symbolize the destructive forces in nature as well.

Because of its fearsome quality, the dragon was used as an emblem in war. It appears on the shields of Agamemnon, Norse and Roman soldiers, and on royal Anglo-Saxon banners. Medieval romances recount numerous tales of dragon-slayers, such as Arthur, Tristan, and Lancelot. Other dragon-killing heroes are Hercules, Apollo, Perseus, Bellerophon, Sigurd, and Beowulf. In Christian legend, the dragon, symbolizing Satan, was overcome by the archangel Michael. Many saints, the most famous being St. George, are pictured standing upon a dragon, a symbol of their having conquered evil.

Drama: literary composition in prose or verse, representing life and character through action and dialogue; it is usually intended for performance on a stage. Many great poets were dramatists, but not all drama is literature. Because of the presence of an audience, a successful drama must entertain. But financial success of a play is not in itself a just criterion for rating its literary merits. Many Broadway hits become dated or fade into oblivion, having nothing more to recommend them than fashionable ideas and, perhaps, witty dialogue.

Certain plays never become outdated, however, and these may be considered literature. Shakespeare's plays, in particular *Hamlet, Macbeth, A Midsummer Night's Dream,* and *Julius Caesar,* never cease to excite audiences; they are often performed. Molière's plays, too, are frequently revived. *Tartuffe, the Misanthrope, The Would-Be Gentleman,* and others are considered masterpieces of comic literature. People often mistakenly believe that only serious dramas, not comedy, can gain literary value. But since Aristophanes there have been comedies that rate that distinction. There are also many popular tragedies that are remembered, if at all, with embarrassment.

Of all drama, the classic Greek tragedies are perhaps the most durable, having endured for thousands of years without becoming stale. Society and religion have changed greatly since the time of Sophocles, Aeschylus, and Euripides, but their themes and poetry still have the power to move us.

In addition to plays that are meant to be performed, poets sometimes write "closet" dramas. Although the poet's ideas are expressed in dialogue, the play is intended to be read, not viewed. Milton's *Samson Agonistes* is an example. Shelley and Tennyson also wrote closet dramas.

See also Volume 20, PERFORMING ARTS: *Drama.*

Dramatic monologue: form of dramatic poetry in which the story is told through the voice of a single person to an imaginary audience. The writer does not intrude to offer his comments, but allows the reader to decide what value to place on the speaker's words. Robert Browning was the master of the form in "My Last Duchess" and "Fra Lippo Lippi."

Dramatic Poetry, Essay of: critical work by English writer John Dryden, published in 1668, during the Restoration, when the theaters were reopened. In the form of a dialogue between four friends, Dryden discusses the comparative merits of ancient, French, and English drama. Dryden sought to prove the greatness of English drama, both old and new. Through the voice of one of his characters, he shows a deep appreciation of Shakespeare and other English playwrights. He also makes a case for simplicity in writing to replace the learned and complicated metaphors that bogged down metaphysical poetry.

Dream Play, A: play by Swedish author August Strindberg, first presented in 1907. *A Dream Play* is a seminal work in avant-garde theater. Strindberg reproduced the jumpy continuity of a dream, in which characters appear, disappear, and reappear without apparent reason, and symbol is more important than substance. Indra's Daughter descends to Earth to experience human life and finds it painful. At the end of the play, having taken part in the disjointed lives and dreams of the other characters as well as her own, she promises to bring their lamentations to the throne of God.

Dr. Jekyll and Mr. Hyde: dual central character in English author Robert Louis Stevenson's *The Strange Case of Dr. Jekyll and Mr. Hyde* (1886). The doctor, a gentle, well-trusted physician engaging in chemical research, concocts a potion with which he changes himself into a mad criminal, Mr. Hyde. Jekyll finds himself helpless against the potion's effects, which eventually destroy him.

Drury Lane: street and district in London. It was named for Sir William Drury, who built a residence there during the early 1500's. It is the site of the Drury Lane Theatre, built in 1663 and rebuilt (most recently in 1812) several times after fires. The oldest English theater still in use, Drury Lane was the home of some of the greatest triumphs in the history of the English theater, most notably those of the actor David Garrick, its manager from 1747 to 1775.

Dryads, GM: wood nymphs, also called hamadryads. Unlike other nymphs, who were immortal, they lived and died with the trees in which they dwelt.

Dubliners: collection of short stories by James Joyce, published in 1914, in which Joyce portrays the middle-class world he knew in Dublin; several characters reappear in his *Ulysses.*

Duncan: See *Macbeth.*

Dunciad, The: satire in heroic couplets by English poet Alexander Pope, first published in 1728 and reissued several times in revised and extended versions. Pope directs his venom against various contemporary literary figures, chiefly ignorant critics and, in the later versions, Colley Cibber, an English actor who was appointed poet laureate in 1730.

Dutchman: short play by U.S. writer Imamu Amiri Baraka (LeRoi Jones), his first professional production, done in 1964. It brought him recognition as an important writer and spokesman for the black nationalist movement. The two characters—a 30-year-old white woman, Lula, and a 20-year-old black man, Clay—meet on a train. Their conversation alternates between flirtation and confrontation as Clay realizes his identity as a black man in a white world.

Dwarf: in folklore, a small, supernatural man living in the mountains or in the depths of the earth. Dwarfs are often represented as old men with long white beards. Sometimes helpful, sometimes malicious, they were believed to possess great knowledge; they were guardians of the earth's wealth and were skilled miners and metalworkers. The armor and swords they forged often had magical properties in legends.

In the households of kings and noblemen, real human dwarfs were often kept as entertainers or court fools. In literature, they appear in such roles to comment on the action of normal society, from which they were ex-

DR. JEKYLL AND MR. HYDE: *the gentle doctor and his grotesque second self were played in the film of the 1930's by Fredric March.*

CULVER PICTURES

CULVER PICTURES

CULVER PICTURES

DWARF: *an evil dwarf in a wild natural setting.*

cluded. Oskar, the narrator of Günter Grass's novel *The Tin Drum* (see entry), uses his willfully stunted growth to distance himself from the wartime Germany around him. This affords him the opportunity to observe with the mind of a man and the viewpoint of a child.

Dwarfs are frequently used in literature to symbolize evil human urges. The dwarf Quilp in Dickens' *The Old Curiosity Shop* represents lechery; Swift transfers the pettiness of society to the diminutive world of the Lilliputians in order to satirize his contemporaries. Benevolent dwarfs appear in Tolkien's *Lord of the Rings* as Hobbits and in Frank Baum's *Wizard of Oz* as Munchkins. In fairy tales, the dual literary function of dwarfs comes across in the character of Rumpelstiltskin, the little man who first saves the heroine only to become, in his demands for an odious payment, the villain from whom the heroine must in turn be saved. The dwarfs who trick Rip Van Winkle in Washington Irving's story (see entry) are neither good nor evil, but merely mischievous.

Dybbuk: in Jewish folklore, an evil demon or soul of a dead man that takes over the body of a living person. *The Dybbuk* is a well known play by Russian-Yiddish author S. Ansky (pen name of Solomon Rapoport), first presented in 1920. Paddy Chayefsky rewrote it as *The Tenth Man* (1960).

E

East of Eden: novel by U.S. author John Steinbeck, published in 1952. The story is based on the biblical conflict between Cain and Abel and is set in the Salinas valley of central California about the time of World War I. Violent fraternal conflict occurs first in the lives of Adam Trask and his brother Charles and then becomes evident again as Adam's twin sons, Cal and Aron, grow up. Their mother, Cathy, who deserts the twins to become a prostitute, is a key figure in the drama, as is the philosophical Chinese servant Lee.

Echo, GM: nymph who kept Hera occupied with her chatter while Zeus chased the other nymphs. Discovering the ruse, Hera in fury changed her voice to an echo. Echo fell in love with Narcissus but, being able only to repeat the last word of what he said, could never tell him of her love.

Eclogue: short pastoral poem. The word orginally meant "selection," but Vergil's pastorals *(Bucolia),* imitating those of the Greek poet Theocritus, were published as *Eclogae,* and the word acquired a special meaning.

Edda: two ancient works in Old Norse or Icelandic. The first, the Poetic or Elder Edda, is a collection of Old Norse poems explaining the creation of the world and celebrating gods and heroes. It is the main source of our knowledge of Norse mythology. Most of the poems were probably composed between the tenth and 13th centuries, though some are versions of tales hundreds of years older, such as the tales of Sigurd. The Younger or Prose Edda was written by Snorri Sturluson, an Icelandic historian and statesman of the early 13th century. It is a book of Norse poetics and poetic mythology, in which many examples of the poetry of the skalds (minstrels) are preserved, along with commentary by Snorri.

Eden: paradise where all living things exist in harmony. An Eden differs from a utopia in being a "natural" state rather than a perfect society. In Wells's *The Time Machine,* the Eloi may be said to be living in an Eden until the truth about their destiny becomes clear.

The notion of man's original, "natural" state, free from sin and want, had a powerful effect on Western civilization. During the 18th and 19th centuries, it was popular in Europe to view American Indians as having lived in this state before the coming of the white man, a view fostered by Rousseau's doctrine of the "noble savage."

Elaine: See *Lancelot.*

El Dorado (Spanish for "the golden one"): originally, the name given to a mythical South American Indian chief; later the name of a legendary treasure-filled city. The chief was said to cover himself with gold dust at religious festivals. Spanish explorers searched but did not find him. The name came to mean a region where treasure and riches are to be had for the taking.

Electra: See *House of Atreus.*

Elegy: serious, meditative poem, usually containing the poet's reflections on death. A modern example of this type of poetry is Gray's "Elegy Written in a Country Churchyard." Elegy in the modern sense is usually a lament for the dead, most often a dead friend of the poet. Among the greatest elegies of this type in the English language are Milton's "Lycidas," Shelley's "Adonais" (on the death of Keats), Tennyson's "In Memoriam," Matthew Arnold's "Thyrsis," and Walt Whitman's "O Captain! My Captain!" (on the death of Lincoln).

Elegy Written in a Country Churchyard: reflective poem by English poet Thomas Gray, published in 1751. The churchyard mentioned is Stoke Poges in Buckinghamshire, England. The poem reflects upon fleeting fame and inevitable death: "The paths of glory lead but to the grave." The poem is sometimes considered an early work of the English Romantic movement.

Elizabethan Age: period roughly covered by the reign of Queen Elizabeth I in England (1558–1603) and the years directly following. A time of exploration and discovery for England, it was marked by great literary output and brilliant achievement, especially in poetry and drama. Shakespeare is the brightest name of the age. Francis Bacon, a philosopher and a lawyer for the queen, wrote brilliant essays. *The Faerie Queene,* one of the great poems in English, was written in her honor by Edmund Spenser. Sir Philip Sidney, Michael Drayton, Christopher Marlowe, Ben Jonson, John Donne, and many others helped to make the Elizabethan Age one of the most brilliant periods in English literature.

Elmer Gantry: satirical novel by U.S. writer Sinclair Lewis, published in 1927. Lewis paints a devastating portrait of the hard-drinking, woman-chasing Gantry, who turns his gift for oratory into a successful career as an evangelistic preacher, a "Professional Good Man." Lewis used the character to satirize hypocrisy and sham in U.S. religion, particularly in revivalism.

Elysium, GM: also called the Islands of the Blest and the Elysian Fields; the abode of the good after death. Homer locates the islands somewhere in the Western ocean. Men favored by the gods went to Elysium, a land ruled by Rhadamanthus, where the sun always shines. In Vergil's *Aeneid,* the abode of the blessed is a part of the underworld, but it is a pleasant place.

Emperor's New Clothes, The: children's story by Danish writer Hans Christian Andersen. The emperor's new clothes, woven by a pair of swindlers, are supposedly made of a cloth invisible to anyone who is stupid or incompetent. When he wears them in procession, no one but a child will point out that he has no clothes on. Only then do the emperor and his people realize they have been duped. The story has been called "the truest allegory of politics."

Encyclopedia: reference work that gives information either in all general fields of knowledge or in a specific field, such as technology, sports, or music. The earliest known writer to compile information in an encyclopedic manner was a Roman, Marcus Terentius Varro; the oldest extant encyclopedia is the *Natural History* of Pliny the Elder, a work consisting of 37 books, published in 77 A.D. Pliny's work was a principal authority until after the Renaissance.

In the early 1700's, several encyclopedialike works were published in England. But the first great encyclopedia in the modern sense was the French *Encyclopédie* of Denis Diderot, published in 28 volumes, 1751–1772. Contributors included Montesquieu, Rousseau, Voltaire, d'Alembert, and other leading thinkers of the day, collectively known as the Encyclopedists, or *philosophes.* The encyclopedia contributed both to the spread of learning and to the consequent social discontent that helped bring on the French Revolution.

Perhaps the greatest encyclopedia published in English was the eleventh edition of the *Encyclopaedia Britannica,* published in 1912, a voluminous summary of progress in all scholarly fields. Since 1912, scores of encyclopedic works have been published for many different audiences and in many special fields.

Endgame: one-act play by Irish-born French dramatist Samuel Beckett, presented in 1957. *Endgame* is a symbolic, plotless drama in the absurdist tradition; little happens, and the four characters spend the play in exchanging cryptic, allusive, and wounding remarks. The main character, Hamm, is a blind invalid; the others are his servant Clov and his aged parents, who spend the entire play in two ashcans.

Enlightenment, The: intellectual movement that swept through Europe during the 1700's. Its ideas were taken from the scientists and philosophers of the 1600's, notably Isaac Newton, René Descartes, and John Locke, and its perceived intent was to enlighten, or educate, society about man's reason and perfectibility, thus ridding man of prejudice and irrationality. The chief figures of the Enlightenment in France, known as the *philosophes,* included Voltaire, Rousseau, Montesquieu, and Diderot. Many of them collaborated on Diderot's *Encyclopédie.* The Enlightenment had a profound effect on politics, particularly the American and French revolutions. See also *Encyclopedia; Philosophes.*

Eos, GM: goddess of the dawn, daughter of Hyperion and Thea; known to the Romans as Aurora. Every morning she drove her chariot into the sky to announce the rising sun. Homer usually calls her "rosy-fingered Dawn." She had a penchant for carrying off good-looking young mortal men.

Epic: long narrative poem celebrating the deeds of historical or legendary heroes. The ancient Greek *Iliad* and *Odyssey* of Homer typify the ancient epic. Vergil's *Aeneid* is called the first full-length literary epic by a single author, since Homer (if there was a Homer) composed in the oral tradition. The Old English *Beowulf* stands out as the most important epic in Germanic literature, although the German *Nibelungenlied* is as well known. Like the Homeric epics, these two were composed in the oral tradition and written down later, as were the French epic *The Song of Roland* and the Spanish *Song of The Cid.* The two great literary epics of European literature are Dante's *Divine Comedy* and Milton's *Paradise Lost.* None written since then has been adjudged equal to these, but epics are still being written; Nikos Kazantzakis's *The Odyssey, A Modern Sequel* (1938) is an outstanding 20th-century example.

Epigram: in ancient Greece, an inscription (usually in verse) on a monument; hence, a short poem expressing one pointed thought. From Roman times on, the epigram was often satirical and usually ended with a witticism or a surprise. The epigrams of Martial (c 40–104 A.D.), a Roman poet, became a model for many later writers.

An epigram is also any thought tersely and pointedly expressed in prose or verse, usually in one sentence, that sometimes seems contradictory: "Where ignorance is bliss, 'tis folly to be wise."

Epithalamium: among the ancient Greeks, a wedding poem, originally sung in chorus at the door of the bridal chamber. The Greek poet Theocritus wrote a marriage song honoring Helen and Menelaus, and the Roman poet Catullus composed a well known epithalamium. Edmund Spenser's *Epithalamion* (1595), honoring his own marriage, is the most famous in English literature; John Donne also wrote several.

Erewhon: satirical Utopian novel by English writer Samuel Butler, published in 1872. The title is an anagram of Nowhere, the literal translation of "Utopia." The book is a satire on hypocrisy, the church, parental tyranny, and the unintelligence of society in general.

Erin: ancient name of Ireland.

Erinyes: See *Furies.*

Eris, GM: goddess of discord, sister of Ares. She was not invited to the wedding of Peleus and Thetis, and out of spite threw a golden apple among the guests, marked "To the fairest." Hera, Athena, and Aphrodite each claimed it and appealed to Zeus to decide. He sent them to young Paris, a shepherd on Mt. Ida. Each one made a great promise to win his favor, but when Aphrodite promised him the fairest of all women for his wife, Paris gave the prize to her. Thus Eris with her apple caused even greater strife, for when Paris saw Helen, the wife of Menelaus, he fell in love with her and carried her off to Troy; this elopement was the cause of the Trojan War.

Erl-king: in Teutonic folklore, the king of the elves, who steals away human children. In later German legend, his home is the Black Forest. Goethe wrote his famous ballad "Erlkönig" on this subject; it was set to music by Franz Schubert (1816) and translated into English by Sir Walter Scott.

Eros: See *Cupid.*

Essay: short literary composition, usually in prose, telling the writer's thoughts and reflections on a subject. There are three kinds of essay: the formal, polished essay on a specific subject; the technical or scientific exposition; and the personal essay.

The term "essay" was first used by the French writer Michel de Montaigne in 1571; he chose the word *essais* to designate his writings as attempts, trials, or experiments. The first of Montaigne's *Essays* came out in 1580. They were a new kind of writing, dealing with any subject or idea that came to the author's mind. They were brief or rambling, full of interruptions, personal moods, and opinions, formless and yet unified by the personality of the author.

Francis Bacon was the first of the English essayists; he put out a volume of ten essays in 1597. The *Tatler* and the *Spectator* papers (1709–1714) of Addison and Steele are witty informal essays. The *Essays of Elia* (1820–1833) by Charles Lamb are examples of the leisurely personal essay; Macaulay's essays, in contrast, are impersonal and informative. Later important English essayists include Mathew Arnold, John Ruskin, Thomas Carlyle, Virginia Woolf, Alice Meynell, G. K. Chesterton, and George Orwell.

The essay is uniquely suited to expressing the writer's personal view of life, as shown in the writings of Emerson and Thoreau. Other U.S. essayists have written gently humorous or satirical pieces, like those of James Thurber or E. B. White, or have written about science and nature from a personal viewpoint, like Rachel Carson, Joseph Wood Krutch, and Loren Eiseley.

Essay on Man, An: essay in rhymed couplets by English poet Alexander Pope, published in 1733–1734. It attempts to explain the nature of man, his place in the universe, and his relation to mankind and to God. The style is epigrammatic, and many of its lines have become familiar quotations.

Eteocles: See *Seven Against Thebes.*

Ethan Frome: short novel by U.S. writer Edith Wharton, published in 1911. Ethan and his wife's cousin Mattie are driven together by the jealousy of his invalid wife Zenobia and by the long, dark Vermont winter. They attempt suicide but fail. At the end, they are all left together but miserable.

Eugene Onegin: novel in verse by Russian poet Aleksandr Pushkin, first published in 1831. Eugene, a shallow society gentleman, arouses the love of the innocent young Tatiana while on a visit to the country, but he scorns her. Years later, when she is married to a prince and has become a leading figure in the society of St. Petersburg, he falls in love with her, but she is too honorable to countenance adultery. The book was made into an opera by Tchaikovsky (1879).

Eumaeus: See *Odyssey.*

Eumenides: See *Furies.*

Euphemism: See *Figures of speech.*

Europa, GM: daughter of Agenor, king of Phoenicia. Zeus fell in love with her and took on the shape of a beautiful bull and mingled with the cattle of Agenor. Europa noticed and caressed him. When she climbed upon his back, he plunged into the sea and swam off with her to Crete. She became the mother of Minos, Sarpedon, and Rhadamanthus. Subsequently, she married the king of Crete. The continent of Europe was named for her, but the derivation is obscure.

Eurydice: See *Orpheus.*

Eurystheus: See *Hercules.*

Everyman: English morality play, first presented about 1500 A.D. As in other morality plays, the characters are personified abstractions and the play, didactic in purpose, is intended to encourage virtue. Death has summoned Everyman, who seeks company on his journey; but his friends Beauty, Worldly Goods, and others will not come. Only Good Deeds will accompany him, though weak from neglect until Confession and Knowledge revive him. Austrian playwright Hugo von Hofmannsthal adapted *Everyman* to the problems of modern man in his *Jedermann* (1911). See also *Morality plays.*

Excalibur: See *Arthurian legend.*

F

Fable: short tale told to illustrate a truth or moral. The most common type is the beast fable, in which animals take on human characteristics. The moral is often stated at the end of the fable, but it may not be stated at all, being implicit. A fable may be made up to illustrate a proverb, or the fable may itself be reduced to a proverbial phrase ("sour grapes"; "cry wolf"). In ancient times, fables were routinely ascribed to Aesop (see also *Aesop's Fables*). After Aesop, the foremost fabulists were the 17th-century French author Jean de La Fontaine, much admired for his literary style, and the 18th–19th-century Russian author Ivan Krylov, many of whose fables are original rather than retold. More recently, James Thurber wrote a series of *Fables for Our Times* (1940), and George Orwell's *Animal Farm* (1945) is an extended beast fable. See also *Reynard the Fox.*

Faerie Queene, The: long allegorical poem by English poet Edmund Spenser. Books I to III of the projected twelve books were published in 1589; books IV to VI in 1596; and the fragmentary seventh book, the "Mutability Cantos," in 1609. *The Faerie Queene* is an epic allegory, in conscious imitation of the language of Chaucer, telling of Arthur's search for Gloriana, the Faerie Queene. Each book tells of an adventure of one of Arthur's knights, each of whom embodies a personal virtue. A moral and spiritual allegory, the poem is also an allegory of Elizabethan politics, in which Gloriana represents Queen Elizabeth. Spenser invented a unique stanza form for the work. See also *Stanza.*

Fafnir: See *Nibelungenlied; Volsunga Saga.*

Fagin: See *Oliver Twist.*

Fairies: in world folklore, a race of supernatural beings with magical powers. They are usually pictured as resembling humans, though many have the power to assume strange animal shapes. In modern children's stories fairies are usually beautiful and good, but in ancient folk belief they were dreaded, and encounters with them were dangerous. Shakespeare

FREE LIBRARY OF PHILADELPHIA/RICHARD GIMBEL COLLECTION

FALL OF THE HOUSE OF USHER: *Poe wrote many stories of suspense and terror.*

chievous spirits in *A Midsummer-Night's Dream.* They are also a common device in romances.

Fairy tales: popular term for short fictional stories like "Cinderella," "Hansel and Gretel," or "Rumpelstiltskin" that are the traditional heritage of people all over the world. Although they often contain supernatural beings or elements such as witches, talking animals, or magic wands, they are not necessarily about fairies. The heroes and heroines are often children mistreated by adults, or ordinary people subject to the whims of lords and kings. A number of universal motifs borrowed from mythology recur in fairy stories, chiefly the magic aid (whether it be a ring of power or a fairy godmother) and the transformation, in which a person is changed into someone or something else. Some scholars define fairy tales, in fact, as the result of ordinary people dreaming the fulfillment of their wishes through some means remembered from myth.

The German word for fairy stories is *Märchen,* and it is used universally by folklorists. Among the many who have collected and written down or retold fairy tales, the foremost are, in France, Charles Perrault; in Germany, the Brothers Grimm; and in England, Andrew Lang. Among authors famous for their original fairy tales, the foremost is Hans Christian Andersen.

Fall of the House of Usher, The: Gothic horror story by U.S. writer Edgar Allan Poe, published in 1839, notable for its ominous atmosphere and mounting tension. Roderick Usher, the main character, is consumed by a sense of doom that is based on a mysterious hereditary trait. At the end, the collapse of his ancestral home symbolizes the collapse of his mind.

Falstaff, Sir John: See *Henry IV; Merry Wives of Windsor, The.*

Farce: See *Comedy.*

Farewell to Arms, A: novel by U.S. writer Ernest Hemingway, published in 1929. Against the background of World War I on the Italian front, Frederick Henry, an American lieutenant and ambulance driver, and Catherine Barkley, an English nurse, fall in love. The horror and senselessness of war is one of the themes in this work, which put Hemingway's reputation as a novelist on firm ground.

Far from the Madding Crowd: novel by British writer Thomas Hardy, published in 1874. The title is taken from a line of Gray's "Elegy." The central character is Bathsheba Everdene, a haughty and capricious young woman whose romantic adventures end in disillusionment.

Fata Morgana: See *Morgan le Fay.*

Fates, GRM: female spirits that presided over the destinies of both gods and men. The Greeks called them Moirai; the Romans, Parcae. They were sisters, the daughters of Zeus: Clotho, who spun out the thread of human life; Lachesis, who measured its length, and Atropos, who cut it. Aeschylus attributed to the Fates power over men and gods alike. In Norse mythology, they were the Norns, whose names were Urd, Verdandi, and Skuld; the three Weird Sisters in Shakespeare's *Macbeth* are an echo of this myth.

Fathers and Sons: novel by Russian author Ivan Turgenev, published in 1862, memorable for the character Bazarov, who became the representative type of the new generation of "nihilists" (cultural and political anarchists). A careful description of Russian society on the eve of the emancipation of the serfs, the work focuses on the contrasting values of Nikolai Petrovich Kirsanov, an aristocratic landowner, his son Arkady, a liberal freethinker, and Arkady's radical friend Bazarov.

FATES: *the three grim women engraved after a drawing of Michelangelo.*

Faun, RM: creatures of nature, half man, half goat. Faunus, identified with the Greek god Pan, was the Roman rural god of the fields. See also *Pan; Satyrs.*

Faust: figure in many legends and literary works, loosely based on a 16th-century German magician, Georg Faust. Generally, Faust is archetypical of the overreacher, one with an insatiable desire for power and knowledge.

The Tragical History of Doctor Faustus, a play by English dramatist Christopher Marlowe, first presented in 1588, is one of the two most famous dramatizations of the legend. The play is in the morality tradition and antipapist. Faustus, a good and learned man, sells his soul to Mephistopheles, the Devil, practices necromancy, and plays tricks on the pope. When payment is due, he despairs and is taken to Hell.

Faust, a poetic drama by German author Johann Wolfgang von Goethe (published in two parts, 1808 and 1832) is the other famous version of the legend. Faust is tempted by the Devil and, although he sins seriously, he remains aware of truth and goodness; he is saved by divine intervention. Faust also comes to love, but later abandons, Gretchen.

Other works derived from the Faust legend include Thomas Mann's novel *Doktor Faustus* and several operas, notably Gounod's *Faust,* Boito's *Mefistofele,* and Berlioz's *The Damnation of Faust.*

Fenris Wolf or **Fenir,** NM: monster son of Loki. The gods kept him bound with the magic chain Gleipnir. In order to lure him into allowing himself to be chained, Thor placed his hand in the Wolf's mouth as a pledge; finding himself trapped, the Wolf bit Thor's hand off. It was told that the Wolf would escape at Ragnarök, swallow Odin, and be killed by Odin's son Vitharr. See also *Ragnarök.*

Ficciones (*Fictions*): Pulitzer Prize-winning collection of short pieces, published in 1944, by the Argentine writer Jorge Luis Borges. The term *ficción,* coined by the author, represents a new genre—the story disguised as essay (including footnotes). Historical and imaginary characters, their works, and events are discussed in such a way that the reader no longer knows what is historically verifiable. Each enigmatic *ficción* serves not only as a vehicle for Borges's philosophical ideas, but also as a metaphor for a universe in which we never know what is real and what we have imagined.

Fiction: all imaginative literature in narrative or dramatic form. The term embraces drama, short stories, novels, and romances (see separate entries); it is often used as a synonym for novel. Even in historical novels the plot is imaginative. Many narrative and dramatic poems are fiction, but the term usually refers to prose.

Figures of speech: words, phrases, or statements used for expressive purposes and not meant to be taken literally. They are a part of everyday speech and are basic to slang, literature, and poetry. Common figures are:

Simile, an explicit comparison of two unrelated objects indicated by the words *like* or *as*: "The road curved like a snake."

Metaphor, a more subtle figure in which the resemblance or comparison is implied rather than spelled out: "You are an angel." "The road snaked around curves."

Personification, the attribution of human qualities to a nonhuman being or object: "The sun smiled down." Many myths represent ancient personifications of natural forces or objects.

Metonymy, in which one word is exchanged for another with which it is closely associated: "You can't fight City Hall" (that is, the powers that be). *Synecdoche* is a related figure in which a part is substituted for the whole, as in the use of the expression "to count noses" for counting people.

Hyperbole, an intentionally extravagant statement: "I looked in a hundred stores to find this." Its opposite is *understatement,* which represents something as less than it actually is. One form of understatement is *litotes,* in which an idea is expressed as the negative of its opposite: "He's not a bad writer." "That's not a bad idea."

Euphemism, the substitution of a more acceptable or more tactful expression for an unpleasant reality: "senior citizens" for old people; "police action" for war.

Oxymoron, the use of two or more words seemingly in contradiction to each other but harmonious in some deeper sense. Milton's description of Hell, "No light, but rather darkness visible" (Paradise Lost I:63), is a famous example.

Finnegan's Wake: novel by Irish-born writer James Joyce, published in 1939. It is a stream-of-consciousness experiment in form and meaning. Drawing on 17 languages, it attempts to give coherence to all human experience and, through the dreams of Humphrey Chimpden Earwicker, to find the universal myth.

Fixer, The: novel by U.S. author Bernard Malamud, published in 1966, based on a true case in czarist Russia during a period of anti-Semitism. Yakov Bok, an insignificant Jewish handyman, finds himself accused of the ritual murder of a Christian boy in Kiev; in defying this injustice and enduring his imprisonment, he attains heroic status.

Fleurs du Mal, Les *(The Flowers of Evil)*: collection of poems by French poet Charles Baudelaire that embraces his entire poetic output. First published in 1857 with little success, it became one of the most influential works of modern poetry. The poems are so arranged as to constitute a symbolic, spiritual autobiography that, in theme and form, is one of the first instances of modernism. Baudelaire substitutes the terms *idéal* and *spleen* for the traditional dichotomies of good and evil. Spleen is inertia, self-involvement, pettiness, debasement. The conflict between the poet's efforts to free himself for a better life and his constant relapse into the closed, hellish world of the self provide the dynamics of the poems.

Folklore: collectively, the myths, legends, folk tales, proverbs, riddles, and verse that are orally transmitted within a culture. Superstitions, children's games, and customs associated with festivals or rites of passage are also regarded as folklore, and sometimes the term includes more highly developed popular arts, crafts, songs, and dances. The term "folklore" was coined in 1846 by William J. Thomas of England to describe literary and artistic survivals of an earlier age. Such relics were formerly called "popular antiquities."

Fool: in literature, two types of character: God's Fool, and the jester. God's Fool is the man of absolute purity of heart, knowing nothing of the ways of the world, who succeeds because of his purity; the prime example is Sir Perceval in the Arthurian legends. Dostoevski's Prince Myshkin in *The Idiot* is a more modern rendition of the type. The jester was a man retained by a ruler or noble to entertain him; the jester often had far more latitude in what he could say than any other person around a ruler, and he thus had the opportunity to serve as the ruler's conscience. A well known literary example is the fool in Shakespeare's *King Lear*.

Foot: in versification, the basic unit of meter. A foot consists of a group of two or three syllables, of which one is accented. The principal feet used in English poetry are:

iambus, unaccented plus accented, as in the word ăgree′.

trochee, accented plus unaccented, as in the word dai′ lў̆.

dactyl, accented plus two unaccented, as in the word des′ pĕrăte.

anapest, two unaccented plus one accented, as in the word ĭnsĭncere′.

spondee, two accented syllables, as in the word thir′ teen′.

See also *Meter*.

Forsyte Saga, The: series of novels by English writer John Galsworthy, including *The Man of Property* (1906), *In Chancery* (1920), and *To Let* (1921), published together as *The Forsyte Saga* in 1922. The history of the Forsyte family was continued in *The White Monkey* (1924), *The Silver Spoon* (1926), and *Swan Song* (1928), which were collected in *A Modern Comedy* (1929).

This social chronicle depicts the changes in manners and morals from Victorian England to the post-World War I period. According to the author, the underlying theme is the conflict beauty creates in men's lives.

For Whom the Bell Tolls: novel by U.S. writer Ernest Hemingway, published in 1940. Its hero, Robert Jordan, is an American volunteer in the Spanish Civil War, who joins a band of Spanish guerrillas in the mountains and organizes their sortie to blow up a strategic bridge. He falls in love with one of the partisans, a young girl named Maria, and in the course of the book develops an awareness of the larger purpose of the war and a compassion for oppressed people everywhere.

FOOL: *a jester is arguing with an image of himself. Jesters are often used to suggest that nonsense is sometimes wisdom and that good sense is often foolishness.*

CULVER PICTURES

Frankenstein: novel by English writer Mary Wollstonecraft Shelley, wife of the English Romantic poet. Published in 1818, before the author was 20, the novel is a sympathetic portrayal of a creature that a scientist named Frankenstein assembles from parts of corpses and then brings to life—but her creature, unlike his malevolent counterparts in later horror films, is gentle and kind, a victim of society. Only the fact that people shun him for his monstrous appearance turns him at last against humanity; he flees to Arctic regions to escape this rejection and ultimately destroys his creator. The creature in the novel was given no name, but the name of his creator, Frankenstein, eventually was applied to him also.

CULVER PICTURES

FRANKENSTEIN: *the monster as played by Boris Karloff in the 1931 film.*

Free verse: verse that is rhythmical without formal meter, stanza, or rhyme. The term *vers libre* ("free verse"), coined by the 19th-century French symbolists, was adopted by a modern school of poets in Europe and the U.S. who sought to liberate poetry from conventional metrical rules. Among the early exponents of the school were Amy Lowell, Carl Sandburg, Ezra Pound, and T. S. Eliot, but it has since become the characteristic poetic idiom of the 20th century.

Free verse is not exactly new and it is not exactly free. The Psalms of the King James Bible and Walt Whitman's

Leaves of Grass are early and influential examples of free verse in English. Modern poets prefer free verse because it allows them to use the natural rhythms of speech.

Frey or **Freyr,** NM: god of fertility, crops and peace. He was one of the gods called Vanir and brother of Freya. His marriage with Gerth (or Gerda), the frozen earth, symbolized the coming of spring.

Freya, NM: beautiful goddess of love, music, and spring; often called the Venus of the North. She was one of the Vanir and sister of Frey. In the stories of the gods and giants, Freya was forever being promised to one giant or another in exchange for some favor. In Wagner's opera *Das Rheingold,* Alberich's cursed magic ring was offered to the giants as a substitute for Freya.

Friar Tuck: in English legend, a fat short-frocked friar or priest who traveled with Robin Hood. In his first meeting with the famous outlaw, the friar displayed both his strength and his shrewdness, besting the hero in a contest of wills and proving his equal with swords. The friar later joins Robin Hood's band and becomes his confessor.

Frigga, NM: queen of the heavens, goddess of marriage, and wife of Odin; sometimes confused with Freya. With Odin she ruled heaven and earth. She was the mother of Balder. Friday was named for Frigga.

Frogs, The: play by Greek comic dramatist Aristophanes, presented in 405 B.C. Dionysus goes to Hades to fetch back a tragedian for Athens, which had none worthy of the name since the recent death of Sophocles, the last surviving of the three great writers of tragedy. He arrives in time to witness and judge a contest in tragedies between Aeschylus and Euripides. The two authors criticize each other (and Aristophanes parodies them both); in the end, Aeschylus wins. The Frogs of the title are a chorus, whose famous croaking refrain is: *Brekekekex ko-ax ko-ax.*

Furies or **Erinyes,** GM: avenging spirits who tormented wrongdoers. They were often personified as three ruthless women, daughters of earth and darkness; they are sometimes interpreted as representations of a guilty conscience. In Aeschylus's play *Eumenides,* they mercilessly pursue Orestes for his murder of his mother. The term "Eumenides" (meaning "well disposed") is a euphemism for these dreaded haunters; Aeschylus explains the name by having them renounce their lust for the blood of the guilty at the end of the play.

G

Gabriela, Clove and Cinnamon: novel by Brazilian author Jorge Amado, published in 1958. It explores the mysteries of love through the story of Gabriela, an extremely desirable and sensual mulatto.

Gaea or **Ge,** GM: earth goddess, both mother and wife of Uranus, and mother of the Titans: Cyclopes, Furies, Giants, and Cronus.

Galahad: chaste and perfect knight who, in later versions of Arthurian legend, achieved the quest of the Holy Grail. See also *Holy Grail; Lancelot.*

Galatea: See *Pygmalion.*

Gallic Wars, Commentaries on the: military history by Roman general and politician Julius Caesar, first published in 51 B.C. It is a terse account of his military campaigns in Gaul and Britain, important as a historical document for its account of the culture of the conquered people, and often used as a Latin textbook because of its direct, simple style.

Ganelon: in the Charlemagne romances, the count of Mayence, a sly and treacherous knight who was responsible for Roland's death. See also *Roland.*

Gareth: See *Gawain.*

Gargantua and Pantagruel: comic masterpiece by the French humanist author, François Rabelais. It appeared in 1532–1564, and tells the story of the giant Gargantua, his son Pantagruel, and their companions, especially the rascally Panurge. Their adventures, recounted in five books (the fifth being of doubtful authenticity), ridicule contemporary follies and superstitions and satirize religion, politics, the law, and 16th-century French society.

Gawain: in Arthurian legend, one of the knights of the Round Table, nephew of King Arthur. Known as "the Courteous," he is the chief hero of the earlier legends and the model for young knights, though his importance declines in later legends. He was the older brother of Gareth, who was accidentally killed by Lancelot at the rescue of Guinevere from the stake. Gareth's death resulted in the breakup of the Round Table. Gawain battled Lancelot in revenge and received a fatal wound from him.

The 14th-century English poem *Sir Gawain and the Green Knight,* an anonymous epic in alliterative verse, is the most famous single Arthurian tale in English. See also *Sir Gawain and the Green Knight.*

Gemini: See *Castor and Pollux.*

Genie: See *Jinni.*

George, Saint: originally a Christian saint and martyr of the Eastern Church, who became famous for having slain a dragon and rescued a princess from it. The English soldiers of the First Crusade gave him credit for helping them to take Antioch in 1098; he became a popular saint in England and was declared the country's patron saint by Edward III in the 1300's. His flag, a red cross on a white background, was incorporated in the British flag. In medieval legend and art St. George was primarily the dragon-slayer, and his victory was a common allegory for the victory of good over evil.

Geryon: See *Hercules.*

Ghost: in folk belief, an apparition, usually the disembodied spirit of a dead person not at rest. In literature, ghosts are used to create an eerie mood, to inform the other characters that all is not well, and/or to haunt a guilty conscience. Hamlet's father's ghost appears to verify Hamlet's suspicions about his mother and uncle and to demand revenge. Shakespeare uses Banquo's ghost in *Macbeth* to harass the guilt-ridden murderers. Ghosts may appear to request proper burial, as in Matthew Gregory Lewis's *The Monk,* or to forecast doom, as the demonic apparition of a raven in Edgar Allen Poe's poem seems to with his cry of "Nevermore." Poe's masterly use of ghosts in his poems and stories centers on the psychology of the haunted flesh-and-blood narrator. In many of his stories, and in Emily Bronte's *Wuthering Heights,* the ghost acts as a symbol of love's endurance beyond the grave. That mourning disturbs the sleep of the dead is a theme that occurs in folk ballads and ghost tales, and the ghost's return may be met with horror or delight by the mourner. In Dickens' *A Christmas Carol,* the ghost comes to convey a warning to Scrooge of what lies in store for him if he doesn't mend his ways.

Ghost Sonata, The: play by Swedish author August Strindberg, first presented in 1908. The best known of Strindberg's so-called chamber plays, it had considerable influence on European theater during the early part of the 20th century, chiefly on account of its masterful blending of the dreamlike and the naturalistic in this eerie tale of the tragic love of the Student and the Hyacinth Girl, Adèle.

Ghoul: in Eastern folklore, an evil spirit that opens graves and eats corpses.

Giants: in mythology and folklore, monstrous, manlike beings of superhuman strength and powers, but with ungodlike chracteristics. The Greek mythological giants, the Titans, warred against the Olympian gods and were conquered and confined under Tartarus (see also *Titans*). The giants of Norse mythology were the Jotunns who are supposed to fight against the gods at Ragnarök. In Celtic mythology, the gods vanquished the Fomors, or sea giants. Giants appear in many other legends. Famous giants in literature, include Rabelais' Gargantua in *Gargantua and Pantagruel* and Swift's race of Brobdingnag in *Gulliver's Travels*.

Gift of the Magi, The: story by U.S. writer O. Henry, who published his most famous New York stories from 1902 to 1910. O. Henry was master of the surprise-twist ending that relies on coincidence, and this story displays his talent. It tells of newlyweds who cannot afford to buy each other Christmas presents. She sells her prize possession, her beautiful long hair, to buy him a chain for his gold watch; he sells his watch in order to buy her a comb set for her hair.

Gilgamesh, The Epic of: epic poem recounting the adventures of Gilgamesh, the great hero of Sumerian legend. The tale exists in various fragmentary versions, dating from different times between 2000 B.C. and the 600's B.C. The epic tells the adventures and deeds of Gilgamesh and his friend Enkidu; it contains legends that have parallels in other cultures and religions, such as a great flood, the killing of a sacred bull, and a number of deeds reminiscent of those of Hercules, culminating with Gilgamesh's journey in search of Enkidu after his friend's death.

Glass Menagerie, The: drama by U.S. playwright Tennessee Williams, presented in 1944. Invited to dinner at the home of a friend from work, Jim O'Connor unwittingly becomes the center of the family's hopes—a possible escape from home for his friend Tom Wingfield, a chance for love for Tom's withdrawn sister Laura, and the "gentleman caller" of their mother Amanda's romantic dreams. Jim gently encourages Laura and admires her beloved collection of fragile glass animals, but reveals that he is engaged, shattering their hopes. Tom, seeing his last chance vanish, at last breaks away.

Golden Age, GRM: first era of the world, when Saturn reigned and truth, innocence, and ideal happiness prevailed. There was no law, nor need for any; there were no weapons, no wars. The Romans commemorated this era every year in the festival of the Saturnalia. The Golden Age was followed by the Silver Age and Bronze Age; in every age, men and their conditions were a little worse than before. The Heroic Age followed, during which the Trojan War was fought. The classical Greeks and Romans called their own period the Iron Age and thought that things were getting worse all the time.

Golden Ass, The: Latin romance in eleven books by Roman author Apuleius, written in the second century A.D. It is written in the form of an autobiography by one Lucius, who by mistaken enchantment is changed into an ass. He recounts his travels in search of a charm to restore him to human shape, during the course of which he sees and hears many strange things. His stories are a remarkable blend of humor and realism, everyday events and fantasy; best known is the tale of Cupid and Psyche.

Golden Bough, The: classic study, by English scholar Sir James Frazer, of comparative religion and mythology, published in twelve volumes, 1890–1915. It has been an important source for many later writers, including T. S. Eliot, who acknowledged his indebtedness to Frazer for certain parts of *The Waste Land*. Many of the author's inferences and conclusions have been proved wrong, but the book remains important in its field. The "Golden Bough" was a tree branch that Aeneas broke off and took to the underworld as a protective charm.

Golden Bowl, The: novel by U.S. author Henry James, published in 1904, in which James examines a delicate and complicated marital tangle. Maggie Verver, a young American girl, marries an Italian prince, with whom her friend Charlotte had an affair; Charlotte marries Maggie's millionaire father but resumes her liaison with the prince. James was particularly concerned with the characters' illusions and deceptions, since everyone knows what is going on but no one chooses to admit it.

Golden Fleece: See *Argonauts*.

Gone with the Wind: phenomenally successful novel by U.S. writer Margaret Mitchell, published in 1936; an epic of the South during and after the Civil War. Scarlett O'Hara, a vivacious, spoiled Southern belle, grows and changes as the South of her girlhood is defeated and forced to change.

Good Earth, The: Pulitzer Prize-winning novel by U.S. writer Pearl

GLASS MENAGERIE: *the fragile Laura Wingfield and her "gentleman caller" in the wistful play by Tennessee Williams.*

DAVID MINK, MARTHA GALPHIN: © VORIES FISHER/GOODMAN THEATRE/ART INSTITUTE OF CHICAGO

GONE WITH THE WIND: *Clark Gable (Rhett Butler) and Vivien Leigh (Scarlett O'Hara) starred in the 1939 film.*

CULVER PICTURES

Buck, published in 1931. Based on the author's observations during nearly 40 years in China, this story of a Chinese peasant family's struggles for survival became the most famous of the author's many works on that country.

Gordian knot, GL: knot tied by Gordias, king of Phrygia, so intricate and complicated that no one could untie it. An oracle prophesied that whoever should master it would rule all Asia. Alexander the Great cut it with one stroke of his sword. To "cut the Gordian knot" means to solve any problem with bold, unconventional action.

Gorgons: See *Medusa.*

Gothic novel: type of melodramatic novel, so named because the setting is often a decayed Gothic castle. Other characteristics are a terrified heroine, a lonely landscape, secret passageways, and old family secrets (usually dreadful). The first of the genre was *The Castle of Otranto* (1764), by the noted 18th-century English gossip Horace Walpole, in which the wicked Manfred, who rules unlawfully in Otranto, schemes to keep his throne but is at last destroyed by the ghost of the murdered rightful ruler. Among Walpole's many successors were the English writers Ann Radcliffe, whose *Mysteries of Udolpho* (1794) made her the most popular writer of the day, and "Monk" M.G. Lewis, nicknamed for his novel *The Monk* (1795), a catalogue of horrors about an abbot who is led astray by the Devil and commits numerous crimes. Perhaps the foremost writer of Gothic tales was Edgar Allen Poe; there are also elements of Gothic atmosphere in the Brontës, Hawthorne, and other Romantic writers. Later writers in the genre include Isak Dinesen.

The term Gothic has also come to be used for contemporary "formula" novels that include some of the traditional elements.

Graces, GRM: three beautiful daughters of Zeus, called Charites in Greek and Gratiae in Latin. They were Aglaia (Brilliance), Euphrosyne (Joy), and Thalia (Bloom). They accompanied the Muses and often Aphrodite, Eros, or Dionysus.

Grapes of Wrath, The: novel by U.S. author John Steinbeck, published in 1939, the moving story of a family of farmers, the Joads, forced to leave their homestead in the Oklahoma dustbowl region and head for California in search of work on the fruit farms. Beset by problems on the journey and harassed on their arrival in California, they are utterly defeated by the end of the book, though still courageous. The novel's fierce criticism of migrant workers' social and economic plight aroused the nation's conscience on its first publication.

Great Expectations: novel by English author Charles Dickens, published in 1861. Pip, a village boy brought up by the kind blacksmith Joe Gargery, meets the half-demented, jilted spinster Miss Havisham, falls in love with her ward Estella, then longs to become a gentleman. He suddenly receives wealth from an anonymous source, goes to London, and, thanks to a series of misfortunes, finally realizes that Joe Gargery's life of honest labor makes more sense than his own empty "great expectations."

Great Gatsby, The: novel by U.S. author F. Scott Fitzgerald, published in 1925, generally regarded as his greatest work. Set in New York, it is an exposure of the boredom and spiritual bankruptcy of the "jazz age," and of the thoughtless cruelty of great wealth. Its plot is concerned with the efforts of Jay Gatsby, a wealthy racketeer who poses as a playboy, to win his idealized love, the spoiled and wealthy Daisy, who is a cousin of Nick Carraway, the story's narrator. Not only does Gatsby fail, but he dies alone and deserted even by the hangers-on who had flocked to his lavish parties.

Great Mother: important deity of prehistoric origin. The Mother was originally the deity of agricultural societies; she was the earth, great and fruitful. The year was her lover, strong in the summer but dying in the autumn, only to be reborn at the winter solstice. This cycle was personified in the society's queen, who was also chief priestess; each year a new king was chosen and the old one sacrificed. The Mother was the chief deity of ancient Near Eastern and Mediterranean matriarchal societies. When these were supplanted by male-oriented societies, the Mother goddess was reduced to the position of mother of the gods.

Ancient writers identified practically every pre-Olympian goddess with the Great Mother, who for them represented an idea rather than a specific deity. Thus Rhea, Gaea, and Ops were all vaguely linked with the Mother and with each other. In the classical period, when piety for the Olympian gods had weakened, the cult of the Mother revived; she became known as Cybele. Her suitor was Attis, whom she drove mad so that he castrated or killed himself—an echo of the old rites. A corrupted form of the legend is the story of Venus and Adonis.

Grendel: in the Old English epic poem *Beowulf,* the night-stalking, man-eating monster from whom Beowulf delivered the Danes (see also *Beowulf*). An interesting modern novel, *Grendel,* written by John Gardner and published in 1971, retells the Beowulf story from the monster's point of view.

Griffin: also spelled griffon and gryphon; a fabulous monster with a lion's body and wings and the head of an eagle. It was believed by the Greeks to guard the gold of Scythia. The Greeks may have taken their notion from the statues of winged lions in Assyrian palaces and temples.

GRIFFIN: *the monster is half eagle and half lion.*

Grimm's Fairy Tales: popular name for a collection of folk tales (collected 1812–1815) by the brothers Jakob and Wilhelm Grimm of Germany, distinguished scholars and philologists. They were originally published as *Kinder und Hausmärchen* (*Children's and Household Tales*). The stories were transcribed from oral recitations of peasants and other members of the vanishing class of illiterate storytellers. The work is the first example of modern folk tale scholarship. The collection contains the familiar stories of "Hansel and Gretel," "The Goose Girl," "Rumpelstiltskin," "The Frog Prince," "Snow White," and many others.

Gudrun: See *Volsunga Saga.*

Guinevere: See *Arthurian legend.*

Gulag Archipelago, The: work by Nobel Prize-winning Russian novelist Alexander Solzhenitsyn, published outside of Russia between 1973 and 1976. This work caused an international furor on its publication, partly because of its content—a description of conditions in Soviet labor camps between 1918 and 1956, based on the author's and other prisoners' experiences—and partly because the Soviet government stepped up its harassment of Solzhenitsyn and his family, finally exiling him to the West in February, 1974.

"Gulag" is a Russian acronym for Chief Administration of Corrective Labor Camps. The work is written in a colloquial but highly emotional style and is filled with Solzhenitsyn's sense of outrage at the inhumanity of the labor camp system.

Gulliver's Travels: satire by Irish writer Jonathan Swift, published in 1726. In four parts it tells of Lemuel Gulliver's voyages to imaginary lands: Book I, to the island of Lilliput, where he finds himself a giant prisoner of a race of people six inches tall but every bit as vain and pompous as the people

GULLIVER'S TRAVELS: *Gulliver is tied to a primitive wagon and is being transported to the capital of Lilliput by his captors.*

of his homeland; Book II, to Brobdingnag, the land of the giants, where he suffers the indignities of being swallowed and burped up by a squalling infant and being carried away by a puppy; Book III, to various countries, chief of which is the floating island of Laputa, the Cloud Cuckooland of eccentric scholars; and Book IV, to the country of the Houyhnhnms, a land where horses with an intelligence superior to that of mankind carry on an ideal government, despite the fact that they share their island with the Yahoos, a filthy and stupid race resembling humans.

Gunnar: See *Volsunga Saga.*

Gunther: See *Nibelungenlied.*

Gutenberg Bible: edition of the Vulgate Bible; the first book to be printed with movable type, published in 1456. The inventor of the type and the printing press was Johann Gutenberg, a German printer.

H

Hades, GM: god of the lower world; in later myth called Pluto and other names, it being dangerous to speak his true name. The same name was applied to the dim and gloomy underworld, abode of the dead. It was surrounded by several rivers: the Styx, over which Charon ferried the shades of those duly buried; the Acheron, or river of woe; Phlegethon, the river of fire; Cocytus, the stream of lamentation; and, in later myth, Lethe, the waters of forgetfulness. Cerberus, the three-headed dog, guarded the entrance. Tartarus was the section in which the wicked suffered torment; below Tartarus the Titans were chained. The land of the blessed, where Aeneas meets the dead heroes of Troy in the sixth book of the *Aeneid,* is a part of the underworld, but this is a later myth; for earlier authors such as Homer, all of the underworld was gloomy.

Hagen: See *Nibelungenlied.*

Hamlet: tragedy by William Shakespeare, first published in 1603. Hamlet, prince of Denmark, comes home to discover that his father is dead and his uncle, Claudius, now married to his mother, has become king. The ghost of his father reveals that Claudius murdered him, and the dead king demands vengeance. Hamlet defers action and indulges in melancholy indecision. He confronts Claudius with the truth by having the murder reenacted in a court play, breaks his relationship with the fair Ophelia, kills her father by mistake instead of Claudius, and is sent to England by the king to be put to death. But he is captured by pirates and returned to Denmark. There he finds that Ophelia, mad with grief, has drowned herself. Hamlet is killed by a poisoned sword in a fencing match with Ophelia's brother, Laertes, but stabs the king before he dies and thus finally avenges his father.

Though the plot of *Hamlet* is similar to other Elizabethan revenge tragedies, it differs in focusing its interest on Hamlet's indecision. The problem of the irresolute hero has fascinated critics and made this one of Shakespeare's most studied and analyzed plays.

Hansel and Gretel: popular folk tale first published by the Brothers Grimm in 1812. Hansel and Gretel are abandoned children who rescue themselves from a wicked witch by pushing her into the red-hot oven she has prepared to cook them. The story is an example of the common folk-tale motif of a stupid ogre who is tricked by his intended victim. It was adapted by the German composer Engelbert Humperdinck as a children's opera in 1893.

Harlequin: character in the *commedia dell'arte,* called Arlecchino in the Italian, often the lover of Columbine. Harlequin has a bald head and pointed cap, a mask, and a wooden sword. His typical costume is of a multicolored diamond pattern.

Harpies, GRM: ugly, foul, winged monsters with the faces of women and bodies of vultures. The word "harpy" comes from a Greek word which means to snatch; the Harpies were be-

Please also consult the guide to the Bible for more complete information on entries dealing with biblical themes. The symbols used in this guide are as follows: G-*Greek;* R-*Roman;* N-*Norse;* M-*myth;* L-*legend.*

lieved to snatch away missing persons, plunder travelers of their goods, and carry off or defile the food of offenders against the gods.

Heart Is a Lonely Hunter, The: first novel by U.S. writer Carson McCullers, published in 1940. Set in a small Georgia town, it is a poignant study of loneliness and the delusion of communication. The central image is Mr. Singer, a deaf mute. To him the principal characters—Mick, a tomboyish adolescent girl; Biff, the owner of a seamy cafe; Jake, an alcoholic drifter; and Copeland, a black doctor—pour out their dreams, longings, and anger.

Heart of Darkness: long short story by Polish-born English author Joseph Conrad, published in 1902. The narrator, Marlow, travels to the "heart of darkness"—the jungle of cruelly exploited colonial Africa—to find in the dying Kurtz another sort of darkness and evil.

Heathcliff: See *Wuthering Heights.*

Hecate, GM: obscure goddess with great power but no clearly defined province. She later became associated with magic and sorcery, and was known as the protector of witches.

Hector: son of King Priam of Troy and his wife Hecuba; husband of Andromache and father of Astyanax. See also *Iliad.*

Hecuba, GM: principal wife of King Priam of Troy and the mother of Hector, Paris, Polyxena, Cassandra, and many other children. The Trojan War made her a tragic figure: Hector and Paris were killed; Priam was murdered after Troy fell; Polyxena was sacrificed on the tomb of Achilles; and Cassandra, who fell to the lot of Agamemnon, was murdered by Clytemnestra. Hecuba herself became the property of Odysseus. She appears in Euripides' *Trojan Women;* in his *Hecuba,* she avenges the death of her youngest son, Polydorus, in Thrace.

Hedda Gabler: late play by the Norwegian dramatist Henrik Ibsen, written in 1890. Hedda, disgusted with her didactic husband Tesman, seizes an opportunity to manipulate her former lover Løvborg, who is now involved with her schoolmate Thea; she destroys the brilliant manuscript on which his future depends and brings about his accidental death. When this crime brings her under the control of the manipulative Judge Brack, Hedda falls into deeper despair and shoots herself. One of Ibsen's most complicated heroines, Hedda has been variously interpreted as wicked and neurotic or as the heroic victim of social constraints.

Heep, Uriah: See *David Copperfield.*

Heidi: children's book by Swiss writer Joanna Spyri, published in 1880. The orphaned Heidi is sent to live with her stern grandfather high in the Alps; she lives for a time in Frankfurt, where she becomes a friend of the invalid Klara, and finally returns to her beloved Alps.

Hel or **Hela,** NM: goddess of the underworld or death. She was the daughter of Loki. In her kingdom of death, Niflheim, she ruled over nine worlds, to which she allotted the dead. All those who died of sickness or old age were sent to her, but those who died in battle were sent to Valhalla.

Helen of Troy, GM: most beautiful of all women; the cause of the Trojan War. She was the daughter of Zeus and Leda, the sister of Castor and Pollux. See also *Eris; Trojan War.*

Helios, GM: sun god, later identified with Apollo. He was the father of Phaethon. Each day Helios drove his flaming chariot (the sun) drawn by four horses across the sky.

Hell: in worldwide belief, the abode of the dead, usually conceived of as a place of torment for the wicked. It has intrigued Western imagination at least since the time of the Greeks, who believed tortures were devised in Tartarus for the eternal torment of those who offended the gods (see also *Sisyphus; House of Atreus; Tantalus*). Hell is described in Vergil's *Aeneid,* Book IV, as a place of mourning rather than torment. Those whose bones lie unburied beg the ferryman Charon to carry them across the river Styx, but a century must pass before he will oblige; suicides wander in this gloomy place, eternally longing for the above world sorrows they killed themselves in order to escape.

Two of the greatest evocations of Hell in Western literature are found in Dante's *Divine Comedy (Inferno)* and Milton's *Paradise Lost.* In Dante's Hell, punishments suit the sins of the damned and show the justice of the divine plan. Despite biblical references to the contrary, Dante depicts Hell as a region of cold, symbolizing the plight of the soul cut off from God: the lowest depth of Hell is a great frozen lake, over which a great winged Satan broods.

In Milton's epic, Hell is described as "A dungeon horrible, on all sides

HENRY IV: *the old soldier Falstaff steals the limelight from the young hero-king in Shakespeare's play. Falstaff is one of the great comic characters in English literature.*

FOLGER SHAKESPEARE LIBRARY

round,/ As one great furnace flamed; yet from those flames/ No light, but rather darkness visible/ Served only to discover sights of woe,..." (Book I: 60–64). It is an ironic tribute to these poets that readers much prefer their powerful visions of damnation to Dante's evocation of blessedness in *Paradiso* and to Milton's descriptions of Heaven and God in *Paradise Lost*.

Hellen: legendary founder of Greece. The story of Hellen is believed to have originated about the eighth century B.C. as part of a nationalist movement. According to the legend, his three sons, Dorus, Xuthus, and Aeolus, were the forefathers of the Dorian, Ionian, and Achaean Greeks (the latter two through their sons Ion and Achaeus). The Greeks in general are called Hellenes, and their culture Hellenic.

Henry IV: two-part history play by William Shakespeare, based on historical accounts of Henry's defense of the throne he had usurped from Richard II. Part I was presented in 1596, Part II in 1597.

A rebellion against Henry is led by the young Welsh rebel Hotspur, who is contrasted with Henry's own son Prince Hal, a wayward, idle youth who is less interested in affairs of state than in his drinking companions. Among them is Falstaff, one of the great comic characters of all literature—a fat old knight with enough shrewd wit to get out of all scrapes, derived ultimately from the braggart soldier of *commedia dell'arte*. At the end of Part I, Prince Hal reforms and kills Hotspur in battle. In Part II, King Henry dies and Hal rejects his disreputable cronies to assume the serious burden of kingship as Henry V.

Henry V: history play by William Shakespeare, first performed in 1599. It is a chauvinistic but stirring representation of Henry V's victory over the French at Agincourt in 1415, portraying him as a vital young warrior king. At the close, Henry seeks to unite the two kingdoms by his marriage to the French princess Katharine.

Hephaestus, GM: god of fire and the forge, master smith of the gods, and patron of mortal metalworkers. He was the son of Zeus and Hera. For taking his mother's part in a quarrel Zeus hurled him down from Mt. Olympus, and after that he limped, having hurt his leg in the fall. In the *Iliad,* his wife is Charis; in the *Odyssey,* Aphrodite. His forges were believed to be under the world's volcanoes, particularly under Mt. Etna. Hephaestus created Pandora, the first woman, and made the armor of Achilles. He was identified with the Roman Vulcan.

Hera, GM: sister and wife of Zeus and queen of the gods. She was the mother of Ares, Hebe, and Hephaestus, as well as the goddess of women and marriage. Story after story pictures her as a jealous wife, taking out her resentment on the other loves of Zeus and on their children. She became identified with the Roman Juno, for whom the month June is named.

Hercules or **Heracles,** GM: celebrated and popular Greek hero, who had miraculous strength and prowess. Some stories make him the son of Zeus and Alcmene, and trace many of his troubles to Hera's jealousy: she sent two huge serpents to kill him when he was a baby but he crushed them in his cradle; she also sent a fit of madness, which caused him to kill his sons. For this misdeed, the Delphic Oracle commanded him to do penance in obedience to Eurystheus, king of Argos, who imposed on him a series of almost impossible tasks, his famous Twelve Labors (see table).

There are many stories of Hercules's other feats. He freed Prometheus; killed a sea monster for Laomedon, the treacherous king of Troy who afterward refused to pay; and accompanied the Argonauts. He killed his friend Iphitus in a fit of insanity and was punished for it by being enslaved to Omphale, who set him to women's work. He died from the poison of Nessus's cloak, given him by his wife Deianira, who believed it a love charm. But he was made immortal and was married in heaven to Hebe. Hercules is usually pictured with a lion's skin cloak, a club, and a marvelous bow, which he was supposed to have willed to Philoctetes.

THE TWELVE LABORS OF HERCULES

THE NEMEAN LION. Hercules strangled this monstrous man-eating lion, then skinned it.

THE HYDRA OF LERNA. Destruction of this nine-headed water snake was difficult. Since two heads grew back for each severed one, and one head was immortal, Hercules, helped by Iolaus, seared the stumps as he cut the heads off, then buried the immortal head under a great rock.

THE ERYMANTHIAN BOAR. In order to bring the boar in alive, Hercules chased it into a snowfield and tired it out.

THE ARCADIAN STAG. To capture this golden-antlered stag, Hercules chased it on foot for a year, then wounded it with an arrow.

THE STYMPHALIAN BIRDS. Hercules destroyed these man-eating birds by flushing them out with a bronze rattle and shooting them with arrows.

THE AUGEAN STABLES. Ordered to clean in one day the filthy stables of King Augeus, who had thousands of cattle, Hercules diverted the rivers Alpheus and Peneus.

THE CRETAN BULL. Herucles captured this monstrous bull, a gift of Poseidon to King Minos, then brought it to Greece and turned it loose.

THE HORSES OF DIOMEDES. Diomedes, king of Thrace, fed his mares on human flesh; Hercules tamed them by killing Diomedes and feeding him to them.

THE GIRDLE OF HIPPOLYTE. Hercules fought the Amazons, then either killed their queen Hippolyte to obtain her girdle or made it the price of her ransom.

THE CATTLE OF GERYON. Hercules journeyed to an island in the western ocean, killed the three-headed, three-trunked monster Geryon, and either brought back his cattle in a magical golden vessel given him by Helios or drove them through all of Europe to Greece.

CERBERUS. Hercules went down to Hades, seized its three-headed watchdog Cerberus, brought him up to the mortal world, then returned him to Hades.

THE GOLDEN APPLES OF THE HESPERIDES. Hercules secured the apples, Gaea's wedding present to Hera, by persuading Atlas to fetch them while he shouldered Atlas's task of holding up the sky; he then tricked Atlas into taking the burden back.

Hermaphroditus, GM: son of Hermes and Aphrodite, a beautiful man with whom the nymph Salmacis fell in love. When she prayed that she might be united with him forever, the gods merged the two into one body. In biology the term *hermaphrodite* applies to plants or animals (such as the earthworm) in which one individual is both male and female.

Hermes, GM: son of Zeus and Maia, messenger and herald of the gods. He conducted the dead to Hades. He was the god of science and invention, and invented the lyre by fastening strings across a tortoise shell. He was the guardian of travelers, roads, and commerce, was gifted with trickery, and was the protector of thieves. He stole the cattle of Admetus from under the nose of Apollo and tricked away Aphrodite's girdle. He is represented wearing a winged cap and winged sandals, and carrying the winged caduceus. The Romans identified him with Mercury.

Hero, GM: beautiful priestess of Aphrodite in the temple at Sestos on the European side of the Hellespont. She was dearly beloved by Leander, a youth on the opposite shore, who used to swim across to her every night. One night in a storm he was drowned, and Hero in despair threw herself into the waters and perished also. Christopher Marlowe's poem, "Hero and Leander," is based on this story.

Herzog: novel by U.S. writer Saul Bellow, published in 1961; a seriocomic story of alienation in modern life. Moses Herzog, an absent-minded history professor, achieves a temporary truce in the ongoing conflict between the worlds of the isolated imagination, the cultural heritage of the past, and the brutal private and public experiences of his generation by writing imaginary letters arguing his views with personal friends and public figures, both living and dead.

Hesperides, GM: daughters of Atlas and Hesperis. They were beautiful nymphs appointed to guard the Golden Apples given by Gaea to Hera on her wedding day. The wonderful garden of the Hesperides beyond the sea was guarded by a dragon that never slept. To secure some of the Golden Apples was one of the Twelve Labors of Hercules. He succeeded with the help of Atlas, according to one story; by killing the dragon, according to another.

Hestia: See *Vesta.*

Hexameter: see *Meter.*

Hiawatha: poem by U.S. poet Henry Wadsworth Longfellow, published in 1855, written in an eight-syllabled trochaic verse imitating the Finnish epic *Kalevala.* It embodies many legends and much of the culture of the North American Indians in the life of Hiawatha, son of Wenonah. He is reared by his grandmother, "daughter of the moon, Nokomis," marries Minnehaha, and becomes a hero of his people.

Hippolyte, GM: queen of the Amazons (also called Antiope). To steal her girdle was one of the Twelve Labors of Hercules. Hippolyte married the hero Theseus; their son was Hippolytus.

Hippolytus, GM: son of Theseus and Hippolyte. His stepmother, Phaedra, fell in love with him and hanged herself in shame and despair when he repulsed her. She left a note for Theseus accusing Hippolytus of trying to seduce her; Theseus cursed his son. Hippolytus fled from his father's wrath to the shore, where his horses took fright at the sea monster sent by Poseidon to destroy him. Hippolytus was dashed to death among the rocks. Euripides' *Hippolytus* (428 B.C.) is based on this version of the story, as is Jean Racine's masterpiece *Phèdre* (1677).

History of Plymouth Plantation, A: journal account of Pilgrim life from 1620–1647, written by William Bradford, the English-born governor of the Plymouth colony in colonial America. It was published posthumously in 1856, and provides information about the day-to-day lives of the Pilgrims.

History of Rome: massive work written by Roman historian Titus Livius (c59B.C.–17A.D.), better known as Livy, from around 26 B.C. to the time of his death. Of the 142 books covering Roman history from the legendary arrival of Aeneas in Italy to the death of the emperor Tiberius's brother in 9 B.C., only 35 volumes survive. The work describes the rise of the Roman state and foreshadows its fall.

Hobbit, The: fantasy by English philologist J. R. R. Tolkien, published in 1937. The author was a scholar specializing in Old English and Old Norse, and many of the monsters, dwarfs, and trolls that appear in his stories are drawn from old legends. The Hobbits are a good-natured, peaceable race of small people who dwell in Middle-earth in the uncertain past. One of the Hobbits, Bilbo Baggins, goes off on an adventure with a wizard and several dwarfs to slay a bothersome dragon. In the course of many adventures, Bilbo finds a ring that makes its wearer invisible. This ring is the subject of a subsequent trilogy, *The Lord of the Rings.* See also *Lord of the Rings.*

Holinshed's Chronicles: properly titled *The Chronicles of England, Scotland, and Ireland,* a history by English author Raphael Holinshed, published in 1578; used by Shakespeare as the chief historical source for his history plays.

Holy Grail: also called the Sangreal, the platter or cup used by Christ at the Last Supper, in which Joseph of Arimathea miraculously preserved the blood from the wounds of Christ. According to legend, Joseph brought it to Britain where it was guarded for generations. It fed or healed those who saw it, but vanished at the approach of an impure person. It disappeared when its keepers became sinful, and thereafter became the quest of many a knight. It could be found only by the chaste and perfect knight. Only Perceval, Bors, and Galahad were worthy to achieve the quest, discovering it in Carbonek Castle. In late Arthurian legend, Galahad became the one perfect and successful quester. In the older Grail cycle, however, two romances name Gawain as the quester and winner; seven name Perceval; and only one Galahad.

Hopscotch: antinovel by Argentine writer Julio Cortázar, who lived in Paris after 1951. This deliberately difficult work made him an international literary figure when it was published in 1963 because of its experimental style. In disjointed scenes and in voices that switch from first person to third, it tells the story of Horatio Oliveira, an Argentine expatriate living in Paris, and his mistress Maga, with whom he has an agreement to meet only by chance. The chapters are interchangeable, and Cortázar suggests at least two orders in which the book can be read; he invites the reader to devise others.

Horatian Ode: See *Ode.*

Hornblower, Horatio: brilliant, sensitive British naval officer, hero of a series of novels by English author C. S. Forester, of which the first and perhaps best known is *Captain Horatio Hornblower* (three volumes, 1937–1939). Forester's tales eventually take Hornblower through his entire naval career, from midshipman to admiral, during and after the Napoleonic Wars. The Hornblower stories are noted for their historical accuracy and their rousing adventures; the central theme of all the tales is the loneliness of command.

Hostage, The: play by Irish author Brendan Behan, first presented in 1958. *The Hostage* is a farce; the plot is not taken seriously, and the action is often interrupted for a comic song. The hostage of the title is a British soldier, being held by members of the Irish Republican Army (IRA), in a Dublin lodging house as a hostage for the life of an IRA man captured and condemned to death by the British. Leslie, the hostage, and the maid Teresa fall in love amidst the antics of the lodgers.

House of Atreus: royal house of Greece whose descendants were doomed because of ancestral crimes of murder, incest, and cannibalism. The founder of the line was Tantalus, father of Pelops and Niobe. He was punished for serving the flesh of Pelops to the gods. Tantalus's punishment after death was to be surrounded forever by food and water that he could not reach.

Pelops's two sons were Atreus, king of Mycenae, and Thyestes. After Thyestes seduced Atreus's wife, Atreus killed his brother's children and served their flesh to him at a royal banquet. Atreus's sons were Agamemnon, who became king of Mycenae, and Menelaus, king of Sparta, both Greek leaders of the Trojan War, which was fought over the abduction of Menelaus's wife Helen. Thyestes' son was Aegisthus. Perhaps the most famous version of the legend is the *Oresteia,* a trilogy of dramas by the Greek tragic poet Aeschylus, performed in 458 B.C.

The first play, *Agamemnon,* deals with the triumphant return of the king from the Trojan War, only to meet his death at the hands of Clytemnestra, his wife, and Aegisthus, who had become her lover. Clytemnestra, who was Helen's sister, murders her husband in revenge for his past murder of their daughter, Iphigenia, whom he had sacrificed to Artemis in order to pacify the goddess and to attain good weather for the trip to Troy.

COURTESY OF HOUSE OF THE SEVEN GABLES, SALEM, MASS.

HOUSE OF SEVEN GABLES: *The house in Salem, Massachusetts, is the setting for Hawthorne's novel. It is still standing.*

In other versions of Iphigenia's story, most notably Euripides' *Iphigenia in Tauris,* Artemis saves her; the father, unknown to anyone but Iphigenia and the goddess, offers a deer in her place. She becomes a priestess of Artemis and later saves her brother Orestes from sacrifice.

In the second play, *Libation-Bearers* (Greek: *Choephoroe*), Agamemnon's children Orestes and Electra revenge their father's murder by killing their mother and Aegisthus. In the third play, *The Eumenides,* Orestes, who actually committed the matricide, is pursued by the Furies. The play takes place in the realm of divine beings, where Orestes is brought to trial. He is acquitted by the persuasive arguments of Apollo.

Electra, by the Greek playwright Euripides, is another well known tragedy based on this legend, performed in 423 B.C. It is a psychological study of Orestes' accomplice, his sister, in which she plays a much more forceful role in the murder of her mother than she does in Aeschylus's play. Sophocles also used her as the central character of his tragedy, *Electra,* written between 430 and 415 B.C. Eugene O'Neill's *Mourning Becomes Electra* is a modern reworking of the same theme.

House of the Seven Gables, The: novel by U.S. author Nathaniel Hawthorne, published in 1851. The story is set in Salem, Massachusetts, and deals with a family descended from a witch-burning ancestor. Aging Hepzibah Pyncheon, who lives in the house of seven gables, has had to open a shop because of her poverty. Her old brother Clifford arrives home, his mind weakened by 30 years of unjust imprisonment. Judge Pyncheon, his cousin, who engineered Clifford's arrest, continues to persecute the old man. But the malicious judge, the last family representative of Puritan hypocrisy, dies of apoplexy in time for old Hepzibah and Clifford to have a few years of peace; the witches' curse that has doomed the family is lifted.

Howl and Other Poems: collection of poems, published in 1956, that brought recognition to "Beat" poet Allen Ginsberg; it made him a spokesman for the generation of dropouts in the 1950's and 1960's who found themselves alienated from American society.

Huckleberry Finn, The Adventures of: novel by U.S. writer Mark Twain, published in 1884; generally considered his masterpiece and one of the masterpieces of American literature. The story, told in the vivid vernacular of Huck, a true child of nature, deals with his daring act of helping Jim, a runaway slave, to escape. In an epic voyage, Huck and Jim, floating down the Mississippi on a raft, enjoy a peace, freedom, and mutual respect that is a sharp contrast to the meanness of society in the river towns where they stop. Twain uses the irony of Huck's innocent view of life to criticize the barbarity of "sivilization." The novel contains many famous comic scenes, notably those with the Duke and the Dauphin, two traveling confidence men.

Human Comedy, The: collective name given to the body of novels by the French writer Honoré de Balzac. Balzac intended to portray the private dramas of all aspects of French life—Paris and the provinces; the worlds of peasants, soldiers, businessmen, and fashionable society. The first of the series, *Les Chouans,* a historical novel, appeared in 1830. The last two works, *Cousin Bette* and *Cousin Pons,* appeared in 1847–1848 and are numbered among his masterpieces. Though Balzac did not live to complete his ambitious project, he covered an enormous range of subjects and environments. His description and psychology were realistic. He was fascinated by money, success, and failure and their effects on character.

One of the best-known works is *Eugénie Grandet* (1833), the story of the daughter of a miser, who lives the penurious life of a household drudge until middle age when her father's death makes her an heiress and she gives her money to the poor. Perhaps the most famous is *Père Goriot* (1835), the story of a bourgeois father who sacrifices his fortune and his life for the pretensions of his two snobbish daughters.

Humours: four fluids found in the human body, the proportions of which were believed by medieval and Renaissance philosophers to determine temperament. An excess of yellow bile produced a hot temper. Too much black bile gave one a melancholy outlook. Blood produced a genial disposition, and phlegm, a slow and passive one. Ben Jonson used the theory of humours in creating characters for his comedies (see also *The Alchemist*), and Robert Burton, in *Anatomy of Melancholy,* discussed the concept from the 17th-century medical point of view.

Hunchback of Notre Dame, The: melodramatic romance by French writer Victor Hugo, published in 1831,

HUNCHBACK OF NOTRE DAME: *the gentle monster as played by Lon Chaney in film.*

CULVER PICTURES

THE ICEMAN COMETH: *Hickey* (left foreground) *visits Harry Hope's saloon, where he will challenge the illusions of the other patrons.*

set in the Middle Ages. Quasimodo, a mistreated hunchback who is bell-ringer at the cathedral of Notre Dame, secretly adores the dancer Esmeralda. When a hypocritical clergyman, Frollo, falsely condemns Esmeralda as a witch, Quasimodo hides her in the belfry. Esmeralda is discovered and put to death, but the hunchback has his revenge by hurling Frollo to his death from the bell tower.

Hydra: See *Hercules.*

Hyperbole: See *Figures of speech.*

I

Iago: See *Othello.*

Iamb or **iambus:** See *Foot.*

Icarus: See *Daedalus.*

Iceman Cometh, The: tragedy by U.S. playwright Eugene O'Neill, presented in 1946 and often considered his greatest work. Hickey, the charismatic and previously well liked traveling salesman, disrupts the lives of the inmates of the back room of Harry Hope's saloon by trying to make them give up their pipe dreams, presenting his own reformation as an example. In the end he admits that he killed his wife because he could not bear her love and forgiveness; and all but two of his cronies return to their own illusions, convinced that they saw through Hickey all the time.

Idiot, The: novel by Russian author Feodor Dostoevski, first published in 1868. In its hero, Prince Myshkin, the author intended to portray a truly good man and his effect on society; Myshkin, who is trusting, passionless, and rather simple-minded, unwittingly wrecks the lives of several persons with whom he becomes involved.

Idyll: short poetic description of pastoral or rustic life. Idylls take their name especially from the *Idylls* of the Greek poet Theocritus of the third century B.C. *Idyll* is sometimes used in the titles of longer narrative poems—for example, Tennyson's *Idylls of the King.*

Idylls of the King, The: long series of poems by English poet Alfred Lord Tennyson, published in twelve parts from 1859 to 1885. An allegory of the passing of an old order, based on the Arthurian legends, the work traces the life of King Arthur from his rise to the kingship with Merlin's help, through his conflict with Lancelot and Guinevere, to his death.

Igraine: See *Arthurian legend.*

Iliad: Greek epic poem by Homer. A recitative poem in the ancient bardic tradition, it was composed orally in about the ninth century B.C. and first transcribed in the sixth century B.C. The *Iliad* is a tale of the Trojan War, but it does not tell the whole story, only the tale known as "The Wrath of Achilles," with flashbacks to previous events of the war. The Greek hero Achilles, deprived of a slave girl by the Greeks' leader Agamemnon, sulks in his tent. When the war goes against the Greeks, he is persuaded to allow his friend Patroclus to fight in his armor. The Trojan hero Hector kills Patroclus, and Achilles in wrath goes out to battle, kills Hector, and drags his body in the dirt around the walls of Troy. Late at night Hector's father Priam, king of Troy, comes to Achilles and moves him to give Hector's body back for burial.

Generally considered among the greatest literary works of Western civilization, the *Iliad* is the starting point for the *Odyssey* and the *Aeneid,* and, with them, has served as a model for every later epic in the classical tradition. See also *Trojan War.*

Ilium: Greek name for the city of Troy. See also *Troy.*

Imaginary Invalid, The: play by the French dramatist Molière, performed in 1673. Argan, a hypochondriac, wants a doctor for a son-in-law and tries to force his daughter to marry the preposterous Dr. Diafoirus. But Angélique loves another, and Argan finally contents himself with becoming his own doctor in a ceremonial ballet that pokes fun at the scientific jargon and pretensions of the medical profession. This play was Molière's last work; he died while playing the role of Argan.

Imagism: 20th-century Anglo-American poetry movement that stressed direct sensory impressions and realistic images rather than abstract language and conceits. It is related to French symbolism.

The movement dates from about 1910 to 1918. Its principles were formulated by Ezra Pound in 1913. Other imagists include H.D. (Hilda Doolittle), Richard Aldington, and F.S. Flint. Forerunners of the movement were T.E. Hulme and Ford Madox Ford. When the name was adopted by Amy Lowell and her colleagues, Pound referred to his poetry as "vorticism."

Importance of Being Earnest, The: comedy by Irish-born playwright and poet Oscar Wilde, presented in 1895. This witty and farcical masterpiece of satire pokes fun at the Victorian manners and attitudes of the upper class and clergy. The madcap plot hinges on the efforts of Jack Worthing (who has a second life in town as "Ernest") to produce a background more respectable than his real one—being found in a handbag in the cloakroom of Victoria Station—and thus satisfy Lady Bracknell, mother of the girl he loves.

Inferno: See *Divine Comedy, The.*

In Memoriam (Latin for "in memory [of]"): series of poems by English poet Alfred Tennyson, published in 1850 but written at intervals from 1833 on. They were inspired by grief for his intimate friend Arthur Hallam, who died in 1833. The poems constitute one of the major elegies in English; they record the poet's sense of loss and the meditations it evokes as he passes through varying moods.

In Praise of Folly: satire on human nature by Dutch scholar and humanist Desiderius Erasmus, first published in 1509. Though Erasmus wrote it in a week, it has always been his most popular work. The book is dedicated to Sir Thomas More, and the Latin title is a pun on his name.

Inspector General, The: comedy by Russian author Nikolai Gogol, first presented in 1836. The citizens of a small provincial town, hearing that the inspector general is coming from the capital, mistake Chlestakov, a minor civil servant, for the inspector. He takes advantage of the situation, exposes their shams and corruption, and skips town just as the real inspector general arrives.

Intimations of Immortality (in full, "Ode: Intimations of Immortality from Recollections of Early Childhood"): poem by English Romantic author William Wordsworth, published in 1807. Its argument for immortality rests on the poet's belief that our childhood is filled with memories of pre-existence that fade as we grow old: "Our birth is but a sleep and a forgetting." Yet these memories persist as intuitions or "intimations" and do not vanish altogether, even in "the light of common day."

Invictus (Latin for "unconquered"): well known poem by English writer and editor William Ernest Henley, written in 1875 while he was in a tuberculosis hospital. The much-quoted poem ends with the famous lines:

> I am the master of my fate.
> I am the captain of my soul.

Invisible Man, The: title of two novels. In English author H. G. Wells's novel, published in 1897, a scientist discovers a formula that makes him invisible but also turns him into a megalomaniac. U.S. author Ralph Ellison's classic novel, published in 1952, is a chronicle of the destruction of a young black man's faith in people and society, as he gradually realizes that his individuality is invisible to everyone, black and white, with whom he deals.

Iphigenia, GL: subject of the plays *Iphigenia in Aulis,* by Euripides and by Racine; and *Iphigenia in Tauris,* by Euripides and by Goethe; and of two operas by Gluck. See also *House of Atreus.*

I Promessi Sposi: See *Betrothed, The.*

Irish renaissance: literary movement in Ireland around the turn of the 20th century. It sought to establish an Irish national consciousness based on their culture, literature, and folklore. The movement gained its greatest strength after the Irish failed to secure home rule from England. Associated with the movement were the authors William Butler Yeats, John Millington Synge, Sean O'Faolain, Liam O'Flaherty, Frank O'Connor, Sean O'Casey, and James Joyce, though he refused to consider himself a part of it. Also associated with the movement is the Abbey Theatre in Dublin, organized by Yeats and Lady Gregory, where the plays of Yeats, Synge, O'Casey, and other Irish renaissance dramatists were given their first performances.

Iseult: See *Tristan and Iseult.*

Ishmael: narrator of Melville's *Moby Dick,* who emphasizes his separateness from the events of the book by introducing himself in the very first line with "Call me Ishmael," the name of the biblical outcast. See also *Moby Dick.*

Isis: chief female goddess of Egyptian mythology; the sister and wife of Osiris and the mother of Horus. She was credited with magical powers to bring the dead back to life, which she used to resurrect Osiris after Set murdered him. The worship of Isis became popular in Greece about the fourth century B.C. and was later adopted by the Romans; it lasted in Europe until the sixth century A.D. See also *Osiris.*

Ithaca: one of the Ionian islands off the west coast of Greece, ruled in ancient times by the Greek epic hero Odysseus.

Ivanhoe: novel by English writer Sir Walter Scott, published in 1819; a romantic, action-filled tale of chivalry set in medieval England during the reign of Richard the Lion-Hearted and focusing on the rivalry between Norman and Saxon.

J

Jabberwock: imaginary monster in Lewis Carroll's *Through the Looking-Glass;* the creature is the subject of the famous poem "Jabberwocky" found by Alice in a Looking-Glass book. The poem contains many imaginative coined words, and the first four lines (explained by Humpty Dumpty in the Sixth Square) are famous:

> 'Twas brillig, and the slithy toves
> Did gyre and gimble in the wabe:
> All mimsy were the borogoves,
> And the mome raths outgrabe.

Jack and the Beanstalk: title of a nursery tale based on a world myth. Jack and his widowed mother are so poor that she sends him to sell their cow for food. Instead, he trades the cow for a handful of beans. His mother, angry at the foolish trade, tosses the beans out the window, where they sprout into a great stalk. The lad climbs the stalk to a giant's house where there is great wealth, outwits the giant, and returns to his mother with riches so they may both live happily ever after. This story is known among the North American Indians and South African natives.

Jack the Giant-killer: title of an old English nursery tale based on a British story first translated by Geoffrey of Monmouth. Jack, a farmer boy of Arthurian times, kills the giant of Cornwall by tricking him into a deep pit. With the help of a cloak that makes him invisible, seven-league boots of marvelous speed, and a magic sword, he kills all the giants in the land.

Jane Eyre: novel by British writer Charlotte Brontë, published in 1847. It is the strange love story of a modest and plain but intelligent governess and her ill-tempered, discourteous employer, Rochester. The impediment to their love and the cause of Rochester's moodiness is an insane wife whom he has kept hidden in the house. When Jane learns of her existence, she leaves. Later when the wife is killed and Rochester is blinded in a fire, the lovers are reunited.

Janus, RM: god of doorways, gates, and entrances; the patron of all beginnings. Janus is represented with two heads facing in opposite directions, evidently symbolizing the two faces of a door.

Jason: See *Argonauts.*

Jekyll and Hyde: See *Dr. Jekyll and Mr. Hyde.*

Jerusalem Delivered: epic poem on events of the First Crusade, written by

Italian poet Torquato Tasso, published about 1580. The poem relates in 20 cantos the capture of Jerusalem by Godfrey of Bouillon and his Crusaders at the end of the eleventh century.

Jester: See *Fool.*

Jinni or **genie:** in Arabian folklore, a demon inhabiting wild and desolate places, representing the hostile elements. In Muslim literature, jinn are supernatural beings, both good and evil, constituted of fire and able to assume all manner of shapes. They are obliged to serve those who possess a magic ring, lamp, or other object.

Jocasta: See *Oedipus.*

John Brown's Body: modern epic poem for which the U.S. writer Stephen Vincent Benét won a Pulitzer Prize in 1929. This book-length narrative of Civil War days tells not only the historical events but also the moods and emotions of the war.

John Henry: in American folklore, the famous black steel driver, buried in Big Bend Tunnel, West Virginia, with his twelve-pound hammer in his hand. John Henry was the strongest and fastest of the gang at work on the Allegheny tunnel. So fast did he work that a boy had to stand by with a pail of cold water to keep his hammer cool. His boss bragged to a steam drill salesman that he needed no such modern contraption, because one of his workmen could beat a steam drill any day. A bet was laid and John Henry rose to the boast. He burst a blood vessel beating the steam drill through the rock.

Johnny Appleseed: in American folklore, a kindly, eccentric figure who traveled through the frontier territories planting apple trees. The legend is based on the activities of John Chapman, who was known as Johnny Appleseed during his lifetime (1774–1845).

Joseph and His Brothers: tetralogy of novels by German author Thomas Mann; a retelling of the Old Testament story of Joseph. The four novels are *The Stories of Jacob* (1933), *Young Joseph* 1934), *Joseph in Egypt* (1936), and *Joseph the Provider* (1943).

Joseph Andrews: novel by English novelist Henry Fielding, published in 1742. It tells the story of a virtuous servingman, Joseph Andrews. The book was begun as a parody of Richardson's *Pamela* (the story of a virtuous, long-suffering maidservant); Fielding makes his hero Pamela's brother.

Jove: See *Zeus.*

Julius Caesar: history play by Shakespeare, presented around 1599; it is about the betrayal and death of Caesar. Though warned by a soothsayer, Caesar goes to the Senate, where he is stabbed to death by Brutus, Cassius, and their fellow conspirators. Mark Antony rouses the people against the conspirators in his famous funeral oration ("Friends, Romans, countrymen . . ."), they flee Rome, and civil war ensues. The armies of Brutus and Cassius are defeated at Philippi, and both men commit suicide.

Jungle Books, The: two volumes of short stories published in 1894 and 1895 by Indian-born English writer Rudyard Kipling. Their hero is Mowgli, a boy brought up by a wolf pack, who learns from the wolves and other animals—Bagheera, the black panther; Kaa, the python; Baloo, the bear—the wisdom of survival in the jungle. Mowgli later joins the world of men.

Jungle, The: muckraking novel by U.S. author Upton Sinclair, published in 1916; it was instrumental in bringing about the pure-food laws as a result of its exposé of the conditions of Chicago's meat-packing industry. It relates the experiences of Jurgis Rudkis, a Lithuanian immigrant who comes to the United States in hopes of making a better life. He finds work in the stockyards, where he is cheated and exploited. He and his family descend into poverty, sickness, death, and crime. Disillusioned and alone, Rudkis hears a socialist speech and realizes that the only way workers can achieve their goal is through socialism. See also *Muckrakers.*

Juno: See *Hera.*

Juno and the Paycock: play by Irish author Sean O'Casey, first presented in 1924. Juno Boyle, an Irish mother, struggles amid war, poverty, and the drunkenness of her comic husband Jack, the "Paycock," to maintain her family. Eventually Jack's legacy, on which the family's fortunes depended, comes to naught; Juno's son is killed by the Irish Republican Army, her pregnant daughter is abandoned, and Juno and her daughter leave the pixilated Paycock.

Jupiter: See *Zeus.*

K

Kabuki: type of Japanese drama, developed from the formal, classical Nō drama in the 1600's, and still very popular. Kabuki is played only by male actors, who wear stylistically exaggerated makeup and act with extravagant manner. Japanese artists of the late 1800's portrayed many noted kabuki actors with characteristically ferocious expressions.

Kalevala (literally, "land of heroes"): Finnish national epic. It comprises the mythological ballads, chants, and poems of Finland handed down by the bards; it was collected by Zacharias Topelius in 1822 and again by Elias Lönnrot in 1835. Lönnrot enlarged his collection for the second book in 1849.

The poems tell myths and hero tales; they date back to very ancient times. The collection is named for the three sons of Kaleva, a Finnish giant: Vainamoinen, a seer, god of music and inventor of the harp; Ilmarinen, the smith; and the hero Lemminkainen.

Kidnapped: novel by English author Robert Louis Stevenson, published in 1886. The hero of the book, young David Balfour, is sent to sea by a treacherous and cruel uncle; while at sea he meets Alan Breck, a spirited and hard-fighting Jacobite. After landing in Scotland, the two make their way through the Highlands, avoiding the English soldiers, until David returns to his home and receives his rightful inheritance.

King Arthur: See *Arthurian legend.*

King Cole: legendary king of Britain of the third century. He is mentioned, as King Coel, in Geoffrey of Monmouth's *History of the Kings of Britain*; he is also the subject of John Masefield's poem "King Cole" and is the "merry old soul" of the nursery rhyme.

King Lear: tragedy by William Shakespeare, presented in 1606, based on folklore (retold in Holinshed) about a semilegendary King Leir of Britain. Lear demands that his three daughters declare their love for him. Hurt when Cordelia, the only honest one, doubts that she can feelingly respond to such a command, he banishes her and bestows his kingdom on his two wicked daughters, Goneril and Regan, who soon humiliate him and turn him out. Lear goes mad at the realization of his daughters' cruelty and the loss of his kingdom, and wanders through a violent storm accompanied by his Fool. All those loyal to Lear suffer. Cordelia returns with her husband, the king of France, and is reunited with her father, but the villainous Edmund, victorious over the French, has her executed, and Lear dies of grief.

Knickerbocker, Diedrich: name under which Washington Irving wrote his farcical history of New York (1809). The surname Knickerbocker, an old Dutch name, was at first applied to the original Dutch colonists of New York; later the term came to mean simply "New Yorker."

Knighthood: in medieval times, soldiers pledged to the service of a liege lord. Knights were pledged also to certain codes of honor and chivalry.

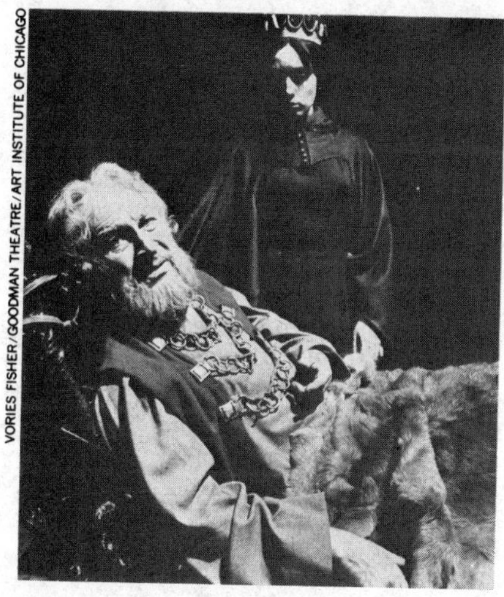

KINGS: *from legend (King Arthur) to nursery rhyme (King Cole) to tragedy (King Lear), royalty plays a large part in traditional literature.*

In the Middle Ages, boys chosen for knighthood began their training early. At seven or eight a candidate left home and went into the service of a nobleman, where he served as a page. At 14 the boy was promoted to the office of squire. Under the tutelage of a knight, he became proficient in the use of medieval weapons—the sword, shield, mace, lance, and battle-ax. At 21 the young man was received into knighthood in an elaborate ceremony—partly religious and partly a celebration. The night before the ceremony his armor was placed before an altar where he kept an all-night prayer vigil. After a religious service and solemn vows in the morning, he was dubbed a knight.

When English longbows proved their ability to pierce French armor at the battle of Agincourt in 1415, knights became obsolete as troops. The rising central power of European kings tended to curb the feudal power of barons and orders of knighthood. The feudal system died out, and the designation of "knight" became an honorary title. Today in England, knighthood, with the title of "Sir," is conferred by the ruling sovereign upon outstanding men in various fields—science, civil service, scholarship, and many others. The equivalent title for women is "Dame."

Knights of the Round Table: in Arthurian legend, the select body of knights who sat with King Arthur at a huge round table. The traditional number of knights was 150. Of these the best known are Lancelot, Gawain, and Tristram (Tristan), all representatives of the highest ideals of worldly chivalry; the older stalwarts Bedivere and Kay; and the younger knights Gareth, Galahad, and Perceval. See also *Arthurian legend; Gawain; Holy Grail; Lancelot; Perceval;* and *Siege Perilous.*

Koran or **Quran:** sacred book of Islam, written in Arabic. Islamic peoples consider it the Word of God, revealed to Muhammad.

The Koran was the first book to be written in Arabic, and as such it had an enormous influence on Arabic writing and thought. An authoritative version was compiled under the Caliph Othman in the 650's A.D.; today the Cairo edition of 1919 is the standard.

Kriemhild: See *Nibelungenlied.*

Kristin Lavransdatter: trilogy of historical novels by Norwegian author Sigrid Undset, depicting a woman's life in medieval Norway. The three novels are *The Bridal Wreath* (1920), *The Mistress of Husaby* (1921), and *The Cross* (1922).

Kubla Khan: poem fragment by English Romantic poet Samuel Taylor Coleridge, published in 1816 and subtitled "A Vision in a Dream." Coleridge wrote it in 1797 under the influence of laudanum (a form of opium to which he eventually became addicted). He fell asleep over a book describing Kubla Khan. When he awoke three hours later, he realized he had composed a poem in his sleep, and managed to write down 55 lines of it before he was interrupted. The result is a haunting poem that begins:

In Xanadu did Kubla Khan
A stately pleasure-dome decree:
Where Alph, the sacred river, ran
Through caverns measureless to man
Down to a sunless sea.

L

La Belle Dame sans Merci: ballad written in an archaic medieval style by English poet John Keats, published in 1820. It tells the story of a noble knight, destroyed by his love for a supernatural being who is beautiful but merciless. The symptoms she causes in the poet resemble those of tuberculosis, from which Keats was dying.

Labyrinth, GM: great mazelike building in Crete, built by Daedalus for King Minos to confine the Minotaur (see also entries). The word is now used for any complex and puzzling system of passageways or alleys. *Labyrinths* is also the title of an anthology of short *ficciones* selected from two story collections by Jorge Luis Borges, published in 1962. See also *Ficciones.*

Lady Chatterley's Lover: novel by the English writer D. H. Lawrence, published in 1928. Lady Chatterley's husband, Sir Clifford, is impotent. She finds fulfillment as a woman in an affair with her gamekeeper, Mellors, a man who knows no sexual restraints. This was Lawrence's last novel and the one that focuses most directly on the author's mystique of the regenerative powers of freely expressed sexuality. The work was banned in the U. S. until 1959 and in England until 1960.

Lady of the Lake or **Vivian** or **Nimue:** See *Arthurian legend.*

Laertes: See *Hamlet; Odysseus.*

Laius: See *Oedipus.*

Lake poets: three English Romantic poets—Coleridge, Wordsworth, and Southey—so called because they lived in England's Lake District, a region of hills and lakes in Cumberland, Westmoreland, and Lancashire. The term *Lake school* was first applied to them in ridicule in the *Edinburgh Review* in 1817.

L'allegro (Italian for "the cheerful one"): short, joyous poem by English poet John Milton, written in 1632. The poem is an idyll in praise of the delights of life in country and town and is a companion piece to the melancholy "Il Penseroso." Some well known expressions, such as "to trip the light fantastic," derive from this poem.

Lancelot: favorite knight of King Arthur, and the lover of Queen Guinevere. His adulterous love finally led to a break with his king and divided the loyalties of the Knights of the Round

Table. Lancelot fled to Brittany. When Arthur was battling Mordred for his kingdom, Lancelot returned to help him, but Arthur had died. He spent his remaining years as a penitent hermit and Guinevere entered a nunnery.

Lancelot was the father of Galahad by the Princess Elaine. Another Elaine, "the lily maid of Astolat," died for love of him, This legend is treated in Tennyson's poems "Lancelot and Elaine" and "The Lady of Shalott."

The earliest Lancelot legends portray him as the kidnapped son of King Ban de Benoic. He is educated for knighthood by the mysterious Lady of the Lake.

Laocoön, GM: Trojan priest who, with his two sons, was strangled by sea serpents. According to some sources, this punishment was visited on him for warning the Trojans not to accept the Wooden Horse of the Greeks. The agony of Laocoön and his sons, told in Vergil's *Aeneid,* is the subject of a famous classical sculptural group. This sculpture inspired "Laokoon" (1766), a classic essay on art by the German critic G. E. Lessing.

Last of the Mohicans: See *Leatherstocking Tales.*

Latinus: legendary king of ancient Latium, ancestor of the Latins. In Vergil's *Aeneid,* he was the king who welcomed Aeneas at the mouth of the river Tiber; Aeneas married his daughter Lavinia.

Laura: idealized beloved of the 14th-century Italian Renaissance poet Petrarch, to whom he addressed over 300 sonnets and many other lyrics. Dates of their first meeting and of Laura's death, as well as the many poems written after her death, suggest that she was a real woman rather than a poetic creation, but she has never been satisfactorily identified. These love poems constitute the poet's spiritual autobiography and were a formative influence on the development of lyric poetry, particularly in England.

Lazarillo de Tormes, The Life of: first picaresque novel, published in 1554 by an unknown Spanish author. It inaugurated the vogue throughout Europe for the novel of the road in which the rogue hero encounters a cast of villains and thieves not only in the underworld but also in the palace, the manor, and the church.

Leander: See *Hero.*

Leatherstocking Tales: novels of early frontier life by U.S. author James Fenimore Cooper. Their hero is the white scout Natty Bumppo, known under various nicknames in the novels; he combines the Indian's knowledge of the woods with Yankee ingenuity. The series contains: *The Pioneers* (1823), *The Last of the Mohicans* (1826), *The Prairie* (1827), *The Pathfinder* (1840), and *The Deerslayer* (1841). These books were widely translated and remained popular throughout Europe long after their reputation declined in the United States.

Leaves of Grass: only collection of poems by U.S. writer Walt Whitman. First published in 1855, it was expanded and revised throughout Whitman's life. Its present form was established in 1892. In this work Whitman assumes the stance of a national bard. He celebrates himself ("Song of Myself") and his country.

CULVER PICTURES

LEAVES OF GRASS: *Walt Whitman revised this collection throughout his lifetime.*

He celebrates democracy, fellowship, the love of men, and the love of men and women. He celebrates the eternal cycle of birth and death ("Out of the Cradle Endlessly Rocking"). When he mourns personal loss through death ("When Lilacs Last in the Dooryard Bloom'd"), all nature mourns with him. Readers were originally shocked by the poet's conceit, his prophetic tone, and his egalitarian acceptance of all aspects of life. His irregular verse form, the forerunner of free verse, was also considered unpoetic. Today this work is considered the embodiment of American Romantic nationalism.

Leda, GM: wife of Tyndareus. Zeus saw her bathing in a river and took the shape of a swan in order to make love to her. The story inspired several works of art, notably the poem "Leda and the Swan" by W. B. Yeats. Although sources vary, Leda's children, Helen of Troy, Castor, and sometimes Pollux, are assumed to have been fathered by Zeus. Clytemnestra was her daughter by Tyndareus.

Legend: popular story that, though rooted in historical fact, cannot be verified in all its details. Many outstanding historical figures—for example, the Frankish king Charlemagne, the Celtic chieftain Arthur, the English outlaw Robin Hood, and the Spanish soldier El Cid—have, with their followers, been subjects of many legends in which the embellishments of imagination obviously outweigh historical accuracy. On the other hand, some heroes of legend, such as the Swiss William Tell, may not have existed at all, although some circumstances or persons in the tales built around them have a historical basis.

Legend of Sleepy Hollow, The: tale by U.S. writer Washington Irving, published in *The Sketch Book* in 1820. While returning late from paying court to Katrina Van Tassel, Ichabod Crane—an ungainly and timorous schoolmaster—encounters a spectral headless horseman. After a wild race with the fearful apparition, Ichabod disappears from the community. Katrina marries the daredevil horseman Brom Bones, who looks "exceedingly knowing" whenever Ichabod and his disappearance is mentioned.

Lethe, GM: one of the rivers of Hades. To drink of its waters brought forgetfulness of the past to the souls of the dead. The word means oblivion.

Let Us Now Praise Famous Men: landmark in literary journalism, published in 1941 by the U.S. poet and novelist James Agee, accompanied by photographs by Walker Evans. The work grew out of a routine magazine assignment that required Agee to live for a time among the white sharecroppers of Alabama during the Depression years. His involvement with their personal histories and their hopeless economic cycle resulted in an angry book of protest that was also a highly subjective revelation of the author's own feelings of guilt as an observer—one of the privileged living among the wretched of the earth.

Leviathan: highly influential political treatise by British philosopher Thomas Hobbes, published in 1651. Its pessimistic realism is surpassed only by the political doctrines of Machiavelli. Unlike many philosophers who thought man's natural goodness was corrupted by society, Hobbes believed that the life of man in the state of nature was "solitary, poor, nasty, brutish, and short." He advocated a strong authoritarian government as the only means of controlling the "war of everyone against everyone."

Life Is a Dream: play by the Spanish dramatist Pedro Calderón de la Barca,

CULVER PICTURES

LET US NOW PRAISE FAMOUS MEN *combined a moving report on poor men's lives with eloquent photographs of the subjects by Walker Evans, like the one above.*

performed in 1635. Segismundo, the son of King Basilio of Poland, is thought to have died in infancy but actually has been imprisoned in a tower by his father. His father has a change of heart and has the young man drugged, dressed like a prince, and brought to the palace. Segismundo awakes, but believes he is dreaming. His father, alarmed at the prince's uncouth behavior, sends him back to prison. The people revolt and thrust kingship on the prince, who has realized that since life is as transient as a dream, only noble behavior gives it meaning.

Life of Samuel Johnson: biography of English man of letters Samuel Johnson, by James Boswell, published in 1791; perhaps the most famous biography in the English language. Boswell began to make notes and collect material for the *Life* when he first met Dr. Johnson in 1763, continuing until Johnson's death in 1784. Boswell's own fame rests almost entirely on this biography of his friend; Johnson's fame is also dependent on this book, since his conversations are of as much interest as his writings.

Life on the Mississippi: autobiographical account by U.S. author Mark Twain, published in full in 1883, giving a vivid picture of his days as a Mississippi River pilot before the Civil War. The rugged apprenticeship of the river pilot, the excitement on the river levees, the steamboat races, the gambling on board the ships, and a wealth of human incident make this a classic account of river life.

Lilith: in Jewish folklore, a female demon of the night who was believed to prey on children. In medieval rabbinical literature, Lilith was Adam's first wife, displaced by Eve, on whom she worked vengeance by threatening her children. In Goethe's *Faust,* Lilith figures as a witch in the Walpurgis Night scene.

Lilliput: See *Gulliver's Travels.*

Limerick: five-line jingle, usually nonsensical. The meter is anapestic. The first, second, and fifth lines each contain three feet and rhyme with one another. Lines three and four each contain two feet and rhyme with each other. The name is thought to come from an old custom of singing extempore nonsense verses at parties to which the chorus was always the same: "Will you come up to Limerick?" Edward Lear's *Book of Nonsense* (1846) contains many limericks. Often the limerick has a place name in the first line. Example:

There was a young lady from Niger
Who smiled as she rode on a tiger;
They came back from the ride
With the lady inside,
And the smile on the face of the tiger.

Little Foxes, The: family melodrama by U.S. playwright Lillian Hellman, presented in 1939. The play is a study of greed and evil, personified in the various members of a Southern family, the Hubbards, who viciously and eagerly set out to exploit each other and the working people of their town in order to make their enterprises rich and profitable.

Little John: devoted companion of Robin Hood; a skilled bowman whom Robin defeated in a joust; he then became second in command of the merry band. He was nicknamed Little John because of his great height.

Little Mermaid, The: fairy tale by the 19th-century Danish author Hans Christian Andersen about a mermaid who falls in love with a mortal prince. She sacrifices her voice and her mermaid's tail, enduring agonizing pain in her efforts to win his love—and an immortal soul—but fails and dies. Her suffering earns her a place with the daughters of the air, who can gain a soul through their good deeds.

Little Prince, The: children's story and parable for adults by the French aviator Antoine de Saint-Exupéry, published in 1943. The prince comes from a tiny planet where he takes care of one lovely rose. On Earth he discovers many beautiful roses. A fox teaches him that all men, foxes, and roses look alike, until love invested in one makes it different from the others.

Little Red Riding Hood: in European folklore, a little girl who goes to visit her grandmother and is eaten by a wolf disguised as her grandmother. In the version best known today, the child is rescued at the crucial moment by a passing woodcutter, and her grandmother, whom the wolf had previously eaten, is restored from the wolf's stomach. The story is known in English translations from the French of Charles Perrault and the German of the Grimm brothers.

Little Women: story by the U.S. author Louisa May Alcott, published in 1868. It is about four New England sisters, Jo, Meg, Beth, and Amy March, and was based largely on the author's own family. Two sequels, *Little Men* (1871) and *Jo's Boys* (1886), continue the family story after the sisters are grown up and married.

Lives of the English Poets: collection of biographical and critical essays by Samuel Johnson, published in two parts in 1779 and 1781. Among the 52 writers discussed are John Milton, Alexander Pope, John Dryden, and Joseph Addison.

Lohengrin: in Germanic legend, the swan knight, a son of Parsifal, who appeared mysteriously in Antwerp in a boat drawn by swans. He rescued Princess Elsa of Brabant and married her on condition that she never ask his name. When she broke the pact, the swanboat returned on the Rhine and carried him away. The name taboo is a common motif in folk tales. This legend was the basis of Wagner's opera *Lohengrin* (composed 1847).

Loki, NM: god of evil and fire, the trickster and mischief-maker. Hel, Jormungandr the Midgard serpent, and the Fenris Wolf were his offspring. He tricked the blind god Hoder into killing Balder and refused to weep to ensure Balder's release from Hel, goddess of death. For this, he and his offspring were put in chains, but at the end of the world (Ragnarök) they will break loose, and they and the good gods will destroy each other.

Lolita: novel by Russian-born author Vladimir Nabokov, published in 1955; a subtle, absurdist history of the infatuation of a sophisticated middle-aged professor, Humbert Humbert, for a bubble-gum-chewing, twelve-year-old American girl. It was the first of Nabokov's works in English to reach a wide popular audience.

Loneliness of the Long-Distance Runner, The: short story by the English writer Alan Sillitoe, published in 1959, in which a Borstal (reform school) boy evens his score with the system by losing a race against another school.

Long Day's Journey into Night: domestic tragedy by the U.S. dramatist Eugene O'Neill, the most personal and intimate of all his works. Written about 1941, it was not performed until 1956, after the author's death. The play embodies all the bitterness and ambivalence of the author's feelings toward his family. It is set in a country house in the year 1912. The characters—the four members of the Tyrone family—are patterned on O'Neill's family. The father is a matinee actor who regrets prostituting his talent; the mother is a drug addict who lives on memories of her innocent Catholic girlhood. The elder son is an alcoholic, and the younger son (O'Neill), while struggling to break away to a new life, learns he is stricken with tuberculosis, then an incurable disease.

Look Back in Anger: play by English writer John Osborne, performed in 1956, and considered the representative work of Britain's "angry young men." Jimmy Porter, an educated young man of working-class background, finds himself between two worlds and unable to fit into either. He vents his frustration on his middle-class wife.

Look Homeward, Angel: first novel by U.S. writer Thomas Wolfe, published in 1929. It is of the type called in Germany a *Kunstlerroman,* a novel of an artist's development. Its autobiographical hero Eugene Gant, a physical giant and precocious genius, loves and hates his home town of Altamont (Asheville, N.C.), struggles against the limited horizons of his family, receives vague intimations of immortality from a few sympathetic people, and finally sets out on a quest for fame and fortune as a writer.

Lord Jim: major novel by Polish-born writer Joseph Conrad, written in 1900, dealing with a young English seaman who impulsively abandons his sinking ship carrying Islamic pilgrims. Unable to understand or to reconcile this ignoble act with his own self-image, Jim cannot face returning home. He lives out his life among the South Sea island natives, whose love and admiration for him are expressed in their nickname *Tuan* (Lord) Jim. But luck is against Jim. Unwittingly he betrays his native friends and meets death at their hands, a fate that finally resolves his guilt.

Lord of the Flies: novel by the English writer William Golding, published in 1954, in which a group of English schoolboys, stranded on an island, seem to reenact the Fall of Man. Their attempts to establish order, parliamentary rule, and rational priorities are defeated by mysterious forces that they all sense but cannot understand. The author suggests that these forces of evil are within man.

Lord of the Rings: trilogy of fantasy novels with allegorical overtones, written by the English scholar J. R. R. Tolkien. It consists of *The Fellowship of the Ring* (1954), *The Two Towers* (1954), and *The Return of the King* (1955). It deals with the long, often grim and terrible quest of the Hobbits to destroy the magic ring they possess in order to keep it from falling into the hands of evil powers. See also *Hobbit.*

Lorelei: beautiful siren whose song lures boatmen to their death. She is said to haunt a certain rock in the Rhine, which today bears her name. Her story, often considered a folk legend, was invented by the German Romantic poet Clemens Brentano in 1800. A well known German poem by Heinrich Heine, "Die Lorelei," recounts the legend.

Lost Generation: generation whose coming of age coincided with World War I, a traumatic experience that led to an abrupt break with the traditions of the past. Works of the U.S. writers of this period constitute the second great flowering of American literature. (The first was the New England renaissance.) Representative writers of the lost generation include Ernest Hemingway, F. Scott Fitzgerald, William Faulkner, John Dos Passos, James T. Farrell, Archibald MacLeish, E. E. Cummings, and Hart Crane.

Lottery, The: haunting short story by the U.S. writer Shirley Jackson, published in 1949, in which some ordinary townspeople carry out, in an everyday fashion, a primitive magical rite of human sacrifice.

Lotus-Eaters or **Lotophagi:** in the *Odyssey,* a race of people visited by Odysseus in his wanderings. They ate only the fruit of the lotus, which caused a state of forgetfulness, languor, and contentment. Those of Odysseus's crew who tasted the lotus while they were ashore had to be bound and dragged home. Tennyson's poem, "The Lotus-Eaters," is one description of the experience.

Love Song of J. Alfred Prufrock, The: poem by the Anglo-American poet T. S. Eliot, published in *Poetry* magazine in 1915. The poem is a dramatic monologue that records the thoughts and perceptions of its narrator, Prufrock, a thoughtful, sensitive, middle-aged man who longs to express

LORD OF THE FLIES: *this story of the return of a group of schoolboys to primitive savagery was filmed by director Peter Brook.*

CULVER PICTURES

his real thoughts and emotions to his sophisticated companions but is paralyzed by insecurity. The poem is an ironic commentary on the crippling power of social convention and the unheroic quality of modern man.

Lower Depths, The: play by the Russian writer Maxim Gorki, performed in 1902. It deals with some derelicts—a thief, a prostitute, an impoverished baron, an alcoholic actor—who inhabit the sleazy lodgings of a brutal slumlord. A gentle hobo-philosopher, Luka, joins them briefly and stirs their hopes for a better life. Luka leaves and they revert to their misery.

Lucifer: See *Devil.*

Lusiads, The: epic poem by Luís Vaz de Camões, published in 1572, and considered the outstanding epic of the Portuguese people. The principal concern of the poem is an account of Vasco da Gama's discovery of the sea route to India, but the action is interlaced with many accounts of the glorious history and achievements of the Portuguese. Venus, protectress of Portugal, and other mythological figures play important parts.

Lyrical Ballads: collection of poems by the English poets William Wordsworth and Samuel Taylor Coleridge, published in 1798. It is now regarded as the official opening of the English Romantic movement. It included, among many well known poems, Coleridge's "Rime of the Ancient Mariner" and Wordsworth's "Tintern Abbey." Wordsworth's preface to the second edition (1800) is the classic statement of Romantic poetic principles.

Lyric poetry: most emotional and musical of the three divisions of poetry, the others being dramatic and epic (or narrative) poetry. A lyric expresses subjective feeling, the personal hopes, joys, sorrows, and fantasies of the author. It is usually intense and comparatively short. Sonnets, odes, hymns, and elegies are lyrics.

The word *lyric* comes from the Greek *lyra,* an ancient musical instrument of the harp type; lyrics were originally intended to be sung to the accompaniment of the lyre. The word *lyrics* still is used to mean the words of a song.

Lysistrata: comedy by the Greek poet Aristophanes, performed 411 B.C. During the war between Athens and Sparta, the women of all the Greek states, led by Lysistrata, decide to refuse to make love with their men unless they conclude the war. In spite of lapses on both sides, their bargaining is finally successful.

CULVER PICTURES

MACBETH: *Lady Macbeth is tortured by guilt after helping to murder the king.*

M

Macbeth: tragedy by Shakespeare, performed c 1606. When the Scottish noble Macbeth, thane of Cawdor, meets three witches who hail him as king of Scotland, his latent ambitions are triggered. Spurred on by his strong-willed wife, he murders King Duncan and usurps the throne. But the couple are haunted by their bloody deed. Lady Macbeth goes mad and dies. Macbeth, tormented by ghosts, is slain by the noble Macduff, and the throne is restored to Duncan's son Malcolm. The play was based on Holinshed's *Chronicles.* Macbeth was an actual historical figure.

Madame Bovary: novel by French writer Gustave Flaubert, published in 1857. It ruthlessly censures Romanticism in its portrayal of a provincial wife, Emma Bovary, who finds life married to a dull country doctor a great disappointment. Emma magnifies routine flirtations with neighboring men into grand passions, neglects her home, and spends money recklessly on affairs. Rejected by her young lover, she commits suicide. Her unsuspecting husband dies of grief, and their only child goes to the workhouse.

Madrigal: in poetry, usually a brief love lyric or pastoral poem. In music, a madrigal is also a song for several voice parts. It evolved during the Renaissance and was especially popular in Italy and England.

Magician of Lublin, The: novel by the Yiddish writer Isaac Bashevis Singer, published in 1960. This story of 19th-century Poland has a picaresque quality. The hero Yasha Mazur is a charismatic actor-magician who, in his travels through Poland, is loved by many women and is faithless to all. Seeing the hand of God in a series of misfortunes that befall him, the feckless Yasha becomes a penitent and retires to a solitary cell, attracting many pilgrims by his saintliness.

Magic Mountain, The: novel by the German writer Thomas Mann, published in 1924. It was set in a tuberculosis sanatorium in Davos, Switzerland, on the eve of World War I, where patients from all over Europe are gathered. Young Hans Castorp comes there to visit a relative. He is beguiled by the mountain's rarefied atmosphere and dreamlike sense of timelessness, and after a small lung defect is discovered, he stays on as if spellbound, for seven years.

Mahabharata: long heroic epic of ancient India, written in Sanskrit between 350 and 600 B.C. The heroes are the Pandava brothers, who struggle to win a kingdom, then abandon it to go on a spiritual quest. The work is a compendium of Indian lore. It contains the celebrated *Bhagavad-gita* ("Song of God"), a dialogue between one of the Pandavas and the god Krishna, expressing the essence of Hindu philosophy.

Maid Marian: May Queen of English folk May Day games and morris dances in which Robin Hood also figures. In the late Robin Hood ballads and legends, she is his companion and sweetheart in Sherwood Forest.

Main Street: novel published in 1920; it established the literary reputation of U.S. author Sinclair Lewis. It satirizes life in a typical small midwestern town, Gopher Prairie, seen through the eyes of sophisticated, college-educated Carol Kennicott, who comes there as the wife of a doctor.

Major Barbara: comedy by the Irish playwright George Bernard Shaw, performed in 1907. Barbara Undershaft, in rebellion against her wealthy father, a munitions maker, becomes a major in the Salvation Army and devotes her life to saving the souls of the poor. In time she discovers that the poor are more interested in soup than salvation, and realizes that her father helped them more by creating jobs and wealth than she has by joining them. Shaw's argument is that the servants of God and Mammon should unite for the benefit of all.

Malade Imaginaire, La: See *Imaginary Invalid, The.*

Malaprop, Mrs: character in English author Richard Brinsley Sheridan's comedy *The Rivals*; she constantly misuses similar-sounding words (that is, *progeny* for *prodigy; illiterate* for *obliterate*). Such mistakes are now termed "malapropisms."

Maltese Falcon, The: classic detective novel by the U.S. writer Dashiell Hammett, published in 1930. The work was influential in removing the mystery story from the genteel country house to a realistic underworld setting; Hammett's detective, Sam Spade, is the prototype of the hard-boiled private eye. The story concerns a mysterious black statue that is so desired by the large cast of mysterious characters that they are willing to commit murder to get possession of it.

Man and Superman: philosophical comedy by Irish playwright George Bernard Shaw, published in 1903. John Tanner is a social revolutionist, utterly opposed to society's conventions and, above all, determined not to be enmeshed in love and marriage. But Ann Whitefield changes all that. The play contains a dream sequence, *Don Juan in Hell*, that is often performed separately. In it the principal characters appear as Don Juan, Doña Ana, The Statue (Stone Guest), and the Devil. As Don Juan in his dream, Tanner is a superman, but as John Tanner, he is merely a man.

Manchild in the Promised Land: autobiographical novel by U.S. author Claude Brown, published in 1965; a vivid story of a black boy growing up in New York's Harlem—the "Promised Land" its residents, Southern sharecroppers, dreamed of before migrating north. Sonny, the hero, is an accomplished thief and truant at eight; a veteran of juvenile court and reform schools; shot in the stomach while stealing at 13. He eventually escapes street life, but most of his friends end in prison or die by violence or drug overdoses.

Mandragola, La (*The Mandrake*): play by Niccolò Machiavelli, written in 1520; considered the first modern Italian comedy. Callimaco steals Lucrezia from her aged husband through a clever strategem.

Manfred: dramatic poem by the English Romantic poet George Gordon, Lord Byron, published in 1817. Set in a lonely Gothic castle in the Alps, the poem describes the last days of the proud, tormented Manfred, who has transcended human limitations by his own study and diligence, but who is haunted by the memory of an incestuous love.

Mansfield Park: novel by English author Jane Austen, published in 1814. Fanny Price, a poor girl, is sent to live at Mansfield Park with her wealthy relatives, the Bertrams. Her spoiled cousins prove themselves ill-equipped for adult responsibilities, but Fanny falls in love with and helps redeem one of them.

Man Without a Country, The: short story by U.S. clergyman and author Edward Everett Hale, published in 1863. A naval officer, Philip Nolan, blurts out at his court-martial that he wishes never to hear of the United States again. For punishment he is compelled to live out his life on shipboard, never touching port. He dies brokenhearted, a fervent patriot.

Marco Polo, Book of: autobiographical account, written between 1300 and 1324, of the adventures of Marco Polo, a Venetian merchant traveling through Asia who became an official in China under Kubla Khan. His book greatly influenced European ideas about the world. Its concrete facts regarding the geography, history, and customs of a largely unknown continent were read with a mixture of disbelief and wonder. Maps were drawn that relied on the information in his book, making the age of exploration possible. Western eyes had been opened and a certain wanderlust took hold of Europe. Nearly two centuries later, Columbus made notes in the margins of his Latin copy of Marco Polo's adventures as he undertook his own journey to what he hoped would be Asia.

Mark: See *Tristan and Iseult*.

Marriage of Figaro, The: popular comedy by the French writer Pierre Augustine Caron de Beaumarchais, presented in 1784. It reflects the climate of opinion that paved the way for the French Revolution. Its hero is the clever and resourceful Figaro, who, in the author's earlier play, *The Barber of Seville*, helped his master Count Almaviva win the lovely Rosine for a wife. In this play Figaro is the count's rival, for Almaviva is tired of his wife and enamored of her maid Suzanne, Figaro's fiancée. Figaro outwits the count's attempts to seduce Suzanne. The play was not allowed on the public stage for three years because of its candid criticism of the nobility. When it was at last released, Figaro's change from friendly accomplice to bitter rival was not lost on French audiences, who were to overthrow their own masters five years afterward. The play was the basis of Mozart's opera *Le nozze di Figaro* (1786).

Mars: See *Ares*.

Mary Poppins: modern children's classic, written in 1934 by British actress and writer Pamela L. Travers. Mary Poppins is a whimsical and magical nanny of the Edwardian era in London, who uses her magical powers to entertain the children and often to solve their problems.

Masque or **mask:** early form of drama in which the actors wore enlarged figures of heads to identify the characters and magnify the voices. Dance, dumb show, and costume were emphasized over plot or character portrayal. The characters were usually mythological or allegorical. Masques were extremely popular in England in the early 1600's and found their greatest exponent in Ben Johnson.

Measure for Measure: late comedy by Shakespeare, presented in 1603. The Duke of Vienna appoints Angelo to reform the loose conduct of his subjects. Angelo institutes a harsh, puritanical rule, sentencing a young gentleman, Claudio, to death because his fiancée is pregnant. Claudio's sister, Isabella, pleads for him and Angelo agrees to release Claudio in return for Isabella's favors. The duke discovers this and arranges the exposure of his reformer's hypocrisy. He restores justice and a normal amount of sinfulness to his city.

Medea, GM: enchantress who was daughter of the king of Colchis. She fell in love with Jason when he came seeking the Golden Fleece and used her magic to help him secure it. She married and returned home with Jason. When he left her to marry Creusa, she murdered her children by him and killed her rival with a poisoned robe. Her story is told in Euripides' tragedy, *Medea,* and has been the subject of subsequent dramas and operas.

Medusa, GM: most famous of the Gorgons, who were three dreadful sisters with serpents for hair. The sight of her turned men to stone. She was beheaded by Perseus, who escaped this fate by looking only at her mirror image in a shield given him by Athena.

Meistersinger: See *Minnesinger*.

Melodrama: originally a play with some music and singing and a highly sensational plot. Now a melodrama is any play with striking, exaggerated incidents and violent emotion; in effect, an operatic plot without music. The

MEDUSA: *the sight of her turned men to stone. She was killed by Perseus.*

CULVER PICTURES

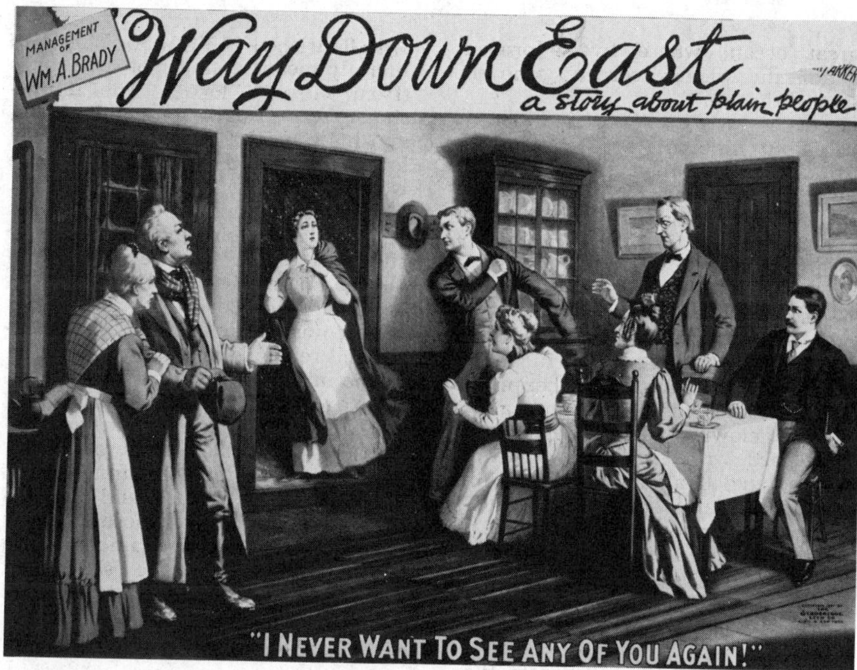

CULVER PICTURES

MELODRAMA: *the poster for this 1890's play suggests the exaggerated situations and emotions in melodrama, a form that survives in radio and television soap operas.*

19th century was the heyday of melodrama.

Menelaus: See *House of Atreus.*

Mentor: in the *Odyssey,* the faithful friend and counselor to whom Odysseus entrusted his household and the education of his son Telemachus when he left for Troy. The term is now applied to anyone who guides or influences another's ideas.

Mephistopheles: in medieval European demonology, one of the seven lords of Hell. He was the Devil to whom Faust sold his soul in exchange for knowledge and power. See also *Devil.*

Merchant of Venice, The: comedy by Shakespeare, completed c 1597. Antonio, the merchant of Venice, borrows money from Shylock, a Jewish moneylender, so that his friend Bassanio may marry Portia. As security he offers a pound of flesh, which Shylock demands when he defaults in payment. Portia, disguised as a lawyer, saves Antonio through a legal quibble: Shylock may have the flesh but may shed no blood in taking it. The expression "a pound of flesh" has come to be used for reprisal of any kind.

Mercury: See *Hermes.*

Merlin: in Arthurian legend, the magician and seer who aided King Arthur in many marvelous ways. At one time when Arthur was opposed by eleven kings and one duke, Merlin caused all the tents of the enemies to fall down, and in the panic that followed, Arthur conquered his foes. By his help, too, Arthur won Guinevere for wife. Merlin made the Round Table and led Arthur to the sword that he took from the marvelous hand and arm that rose out of the lake.

Mermaid or **merman:** in world folklore, a being of the sea or lakes with the upper body of a woman or man and a fish's tail. Mermaids and mermen are believed to have the power of prophecy; seeing or sometimes just hearing them can mean disaster for the observer. Similar to the birdlike sirens in this way, mermaids often lure sailors to shipwreck with their singing (see also *Sirens*). A mermaid can acquire a soul if she is loved by a human. Marriages resulting from such love often occur in fairy tales, but are usually short-lived. In Jean d'Arras's story "Chronique de la Princesse" (c 1387), the mermaid Mélusine leaves her human husband after he breaks his promise not to spy on her. The attempt of the little mermaid in Hans Christian Andersen's tale to live on land in order to be loved by a human prince results in her death. See also *Little Mermaid, The.*

Merry Wives of Windsor, The: one of Shakespeare's happiest comedies, performed in 1597, featuring his great comic character, Falstaff. Falstaff writes love letters to two married women, who compare notes and decide to teach him a lesson. Mistress Ford invites him to a rendezvous, but her husband comes home unexpectedly, and Falstaff is hidden in a clothes hamper, then dumped into the Thames. After the wives set other traps for the unwitting Falstaff, they expose his duplicity to all in a final scene. See also *Henry IV.*

Metamorphoses: collection of Greek and Roman myths retold in 15 volumes of verse by the Roman poet Ovid in the first century A.D. Among the well known stories are those of Daedalus, Jason and Medea, and Orpheus and Eurydice. Many later writers, including Chaucer and Shakespeare, drew on the *Metamorphoses.* This title was also used by the Roman satirist Apuleius for a romance that is now better known as *The Golden Ass (see also entry).*

Metamorphosis, The: story by Czech-born, German Jewish writer Franz Kafka, published in 1916; his best-known short work. The story's central character, Gregor, is forced to realize his unimportance when he awakes one morning to find he has turned into a large insect.

Metaphor: See *Figures of speech.*

Metaphysical poets: label first applied derogatorily by John Dryden to a group of 17th-century English poets whose work was characterized by intellectual complexity often expressed in *conceits* (see also entry). John Donne is perhaps the most famous; others are Andrew Marvell, Abraham Cowley, Richard Crashaw, George Herbert, and Henry Vaughan. A renewed appreciation of the metaphysicals occurred in the early 1900's, and many modern poets reflect their influence.

METAPHYSICAL POETS' REPRESENTATIVE WORKS

JOHN DONNE (1571–1631)
"Hymn to God the Father"
"Death, Be Not Proud"
"A Valediction: Forbidding Mourning"
"Good Friday, 1613"

GEORGE HERBERT (1593–1633)
"The Pearl"
"The Collar"

RICHARD CRASHAW (c 1613–1649)
"The Flaming Heart"
"I Am the Door"

HENRY VAUGHAN (1621–1695)
"The Retreat"
"The World"

THOMAS TRAHERNE (1637–1674)
"Wonder"

ANDREW MARVELL (1621–1678)
"To His Coy Mistress"

ABRAHAM COWLEY (1618–1667)
"The Wish"

Meter: systematic rhythm in poetry; the arrangement of syllables in a poem so that each line contains a certain number of accented syllables or metrical feet (see also *Foot*). The various meters, named for the number of feet in a line, are: monometer (one foot), dimeter (two), trimeter (three), tetrameter (four), pentameter (five), hexameter (six), heptameter (seven), and octameter (eight).

Metonymy: See *Figures of speech.*

Micawber, Mr. Wilkins: See *David Copperfield.*

Midas, GM: king of Phrygia to whom Dionysus granted that all he touched would turn to gold. Midas soon tired of the gift when he discovered that even food and drink were transformed when he touched them. To remove the gift Dionysus bade him wash in the river Pactolus. He did so and was cured, but the sands of the river were turned to gold. The expression "the Midas touch" refers to one who has a knack for moneymaking.

CULVER PICTURES

MIDDLEMARCH *was the masterpiece of George Eliot (real name: Mary Ann Evans).*

Middlemarch: novel by the English writer George Eliot, published in 1871–1872, considered by many her finest work. It captures the total social milieu of the provincial English town of Middlemarch. One of its principal characters is Dorothea Brooke, an idealistic young woman. She marries Edward Casaubon, a middle-aged scholar who has dedicated his life to producing a monumental work, but eventually she learns that he is a mere pedant, as empty of ideas as he is of feelings, and that his book will never be finished. After Casaubon's death, Dorothea marries his cousin, Will Ladislaw, a man more like herself. In a parallel subplot, the ambitious young Dr. Lydgate marries the shallow Rosamond Vincy, whose materialistic values keep him constantly in debt and unable to realize his plans for a new hospital.

Midgard: NM: middle earth, halfway between Heaven and Hell, the abode of humanity. It was surrounded by the great ocean, where lived Jormungandr, the Midgard serpent, who encircled the world.

Midnight Ride of Paul Revere, The (or "Paul Revere's Ride"): much-quoted ballad by U.S. poet Henry Wadsworth Longfellow, which appeared in his *Tales of a Wayside Inn* (1863–1874).

Midsummer-Night's Dream, A: comedy by Shakespeare, printed in 1600, in which courtiers mingle incongruously with the fairy king Oberon, his queen Titania, his helper Puck, and a group of clownish artisans. The plot is concerned with two pairs of lovers whose tangled affairs are first worsened but finally straightened out by fairy intervention. The clumsy attempts of the artisans to present a play, the pranks of Puck, and the songs and dances of the fairies combine to make a novel and delightful play.

Miles Gloriosus (*The Braggart Warrior*): comedy by the Roman playwright Plautus, written about 200 B.C. Its chief character, a stupid, swaggering soldier, became one of the stock comic characters of subsequent European theatrical history. In the Italian *commedia dell'arte* he was known as Il Capitano and later as Scaramouche.

Mill on the Floss, The: novel by English novelist George Eliot, published in 1860; it powerfully portrays the characters of Maggie and Tom Tulliver, children of a miller. Dark-haired, generous, impulsive Maggie is often an embarrassment to her manly, almost too-perfect brother Tom, who blocks her chance for happiness with a neighbor, Philip Wakem. Tom becomes the mainstay of the family after his father's death, then evicts Maggie because of her indiscreet adventure with Stephen Guest. The book ends with the flood of the Floss, Maggie's attempt to rescue Tom, and their reconciliation as they drown together.

Mimir, NM: giant who lived beside the root of the world tree, Yggdrasil. Here he drank from the spring that flowed from the root of the tree; its waters gave him wisdom and all knowledge of the past and the future. Odin traded one of his eyes for a drink from Mimir's spring.

Minerva: See *Athena.*

Miniver Cheevy: poem by U.S. poet Edwin Arlington Robinson, published in 1917; a brief biography of a man "born too late," who scorns the dreary, humdrum world he lives in. Drinking helps Miniver maintain his belief that if he had lived in a more heroic age, he would have been equal to it.

Minnesinger: one of the lyric poets, singers, and musicians of Germany who flourished 1150–1350. The word literally means a singer of love songs (from *minne*: "love"). The minnesinger was usually of noble birth, and his songs had to do with courtly love, the worship by a knight of some woman, often far above him in rank. The minnesingers wrote both words and music to their songs, which were sung in the courts before knights and ladies. Contests were often held. As the minnesong developed, the subject matter was expanded to include political and religious themes. The greatest of the minnesingers was Walther von der Vogelweide in the early 1200's.

The *meistersingers* of 14th- to 16th-century Germany considered themselves the heirs of the minnesingers, though both their music and their poetry were inferior to those of their predecessors. The most famous of the meistersingers was the shoemaker Hans Sachs, who plays an important role in Wagner's opera *Die Meistersinger* (1868).

Minos, GM: king of Crete, the son of Zeus and Europa. He was the founder of the Cretan laws and, according to the *Odyssey,* was made a judge in Hades after he died. In other legends he was the tyrant who exacted a yearly tribute from the Athenians of seven youths and seven maidens to feed the monster Minotaur. See also *Minotaur.*

Minotaur, GM: monster of Crete, half human, half bull. Its father was a beautiful white bull presented by Poseidon to King Minos, who spared its life instead of sacrificing it to the god. Minos's wife, Pasiphae, fell in love with the bull and conceived Asterius, the Minotaur, after a tryst encouraged by Poseidon. To imprison the monster, Minos ordered Daedalus to build a labyrinth. The Minotaur was killed by Theseus. See also *Ariadne; Labyrinth; Minos.*

Miracle plays: medieval dramas dealing with events from the lives of saints. Like the mystery plays, they were originally part of church services associated with particular feasts. Only a few fragmentary English miracle plays survived the Reformation, but many European examples exist. See also *Mystery plays.*

Misanthrope, Le: comedy of manners by French dramatist Molière, performed in 1666. It portrays a frivolous, fashionable world in which flattery and flirtation are the chief social graces. The hero, Alceste, is a misfit. He detests insincerity and offends everyone by speaking the truth. His only tie to society is his love for the flirt Célimène. When she refuses his offer to go off and live in seclusion with him, Alceste goes off alone.

Misérables, Les: novel by French author Victor Hugo, published in 1862.

The hero, Jean Valjean, is an ex-convict who was sentenced to the galleys for stealing a loaf of bread. He becomes a successful businessman and mayor of his town, but he is hounded by Javert, a fanatical detective. When his convict past threatens the happiness of his adopted daughter Cosette, Valjean disappears. Cosette and her husband Marius, learning of his self-sacrifice, find him as he is dying.

Miss Julie: one-act tragedy by the Swedish dramatist August Strindberg, performed in 1888. On Midsummer's Eve, Miss Julie, the daughter of a count, takes part in the servants' merrymaking. Frustrated by a broken engagement, Julie flirts boldly with the handsome valet Jean and finally provokes him to seduce her. When the count comes home and rings the bell for his valet, Jean's inbred servility comes to the fore. Unable to accept the comedown from being mistress of the house to being mistress of the valet, Julie commits suicide.

VORIES FISHER

MOTHER COURAGE: *the heroine of Brecht's play earned her living but lost her children as a result of the Thirty Years War.*

Miss Lonelyhearts: novel by the U.S. writer Nathanael West, published in 1933. Miss Lonelyhearts is a newspaperman who gives advice to the lovelorn. His daily mail from "Desperate," "Anxious," "Broken-hearted," or "Sick-of-it-all" drives him to self-destructive, drunken behavior. Written with a black humor far in advance of its time, the book conveys an overwhelming mood of hopelessness.

Mnemosyne, GM: Titaness who was the goddess of memory and the mother, by Zeus, of the nine Muses.

Moby-Dick; or The White Whale: novel by U.S. author Herman Melville (1851), considered by many the finest American novel ever written. This tale of Captain Ahab's voyage in search of the great white whale that has crippled him is rich in symbolism and philosophical overtones. At the same time, it is an exciting narrative and a precise description of the New England whaling industry of the time. The narrator, Ishmael, is the only survivor of Ahab's mad quest.

Modest Proposal, A: short title of a satire by Irish-born writer Jonathan Swift, published in 1729, proposing a remedy for Ireland's poverty that will benefit all. With a series of carefully reasoned arguments, he suggests that the children of the poor, properly cooked and seasoned, would make tasty dishes at a gentleman's table and at the same time be a source of profit rather than burden to their parents.

Moira: See *Fates.*

Moll Flanders: picaresque tale by English author Daniel Defoe, published in 1722, in which the rogue is a woman. Moll, born in prison, is left to fend for herself in England when her mother is transported to America. After she is seduced at fourteen, Moll has a series of lovers and five husbands. She later prospers as a thief, until arrested and sentenced to death. The sentence is commuted to transportation to America where, joined by one of her former husbands, a highwayman, Moll gives up her wicked ways and establishes a successful plantation.

Morality plays: medieval dramatic poems of the 15th and 16th centuries, which developed from the miracle and mystery plays. They differ from these plays, which dramatize events from Bible history or saints' lives, in that the characters are abstractions, personifications of Sin, Hate, Pride, Folly, Lust, and the like. The best-known, most imaginative, and poetic is *Everyman,* which has had successful modern production. See also *Everyman.*

Mordred: See *Arthurian legend.*

Morgan le Fay: fairy (*fay* in Middle English) who appears in Arthurian and Carolingian legend. In some Arthurian tales, she is the sister of King Arthur and one of the three queens who accompany him to Avalon to cure his wounds. Malory's *Morte d'Arthur* describes her as a malicious crone who plots to kill Arthur and her own husband, King Uriens. In some Carolingian legends, such as that of Ogier the Dane, she is celebrated for her curative powers; in others she is the Fata Morgana who gave her name to mirages in the Straits of Messina.

Morte d'Arthur: long prose narrative version of the whole Arthurian legend, written by Sir Thomas Malory, printed by William Caxton in 1485. It is through this version, rather than the numerous medieval romances, that the modern image of Arthurian legend was formed. Its emphasis is on the fellowship of the Round Table rather than courtly love. See also *Arthurian legend; Knights of the Round Table.*

Mother Courage and Her Children: play by the German playwright Bertolt Brecht, performed in 1941. It is set in the period of the Thirty Years' War. Mother Courage and her children follow the armies and sell supplies to the soldiers. But the war that brings her a living also brings death; her children Eilif, Swiss Cheese, and Kattrin are all killed. Despite her losses, Mother Courage moves on, left in the ambiguous position of being both war profiteer and victim.

Mother Goose's Melody or **Sonnets for the Cradle:** collection of nursery rhymes and stories published in England in about 1765 by John Newbery, the first publisher of children's books. It includes the familiar "Baa, Baa, Black Sheep"; "Little Boy Blue"; "Patty Cake, Patty Cake"; and countless others. Mother Goose herself is a mysterious, untraceable figure who probably comes out of French folklore. The title, but not the rhymes, was taken from Charles Perrault's *Tales of My Mother Goose,* a fairy-tale collection first translated into English in 1729.

Mrs. Dalloway: novel by the English writer Virginia Woolf, published in 1925. The action takes place one beautiful day when Clarissa Dalloway plans and gives a party for her privileged, sophisticated circle of friends. The interactions of the guests make it clear that some of them have experienced heights of passion and depths of suffering that Mrs. Dalloway has never experienced; being a gracious and charming hostess will be the pinnacle of her achievement.

Much Ado About Nothing: one of Shakespeare's darker comedies about love and intrigue, produced c 1598–1599. The clever woman-hater Benedick and the twice-as-clever man-hater Beatrice are finally united in a double-wedding ceremony along with the more conventional pair of lovers, Claudio and Hero.

Muckrakers: journalists and novelists of the early 20th century who devoted their energies to exposing social evils and unfair or dishonest practices in big business or government, both in fiction and in reportage. A representative work was Ida M. Tarbell's *History of the Standard Oil Company* (1904). Other works include Thomas W. Lawson's *Frenzied Finance* (1904–1905); Upton Sinclair's novel *The Jungle* (1906), dealing with the meat-packing industry; and Brand Whitlock's *The Turn of the Balance* (1907), on capital punishment. Though these writers were contemptuously dubbed "muckrakers" by President Theodore Roosevelt, some of their works stimulated reform legislation.

Murder in the Cathedral: verse drama by the Anglo-American poet T. S. Eliot, performed in 1935. It deals with the last days of St. Thomas à Becket, Archbishop of Canterbury, whose defiance of his former friend, King Henry II, results in his murder by the king's knights. The play, first performed at Canterbury Cathedral, is often staged in churches.

Murders in the Rue Morgue: short story by U.S. author Edgar Allan Poe, published in 1841 and considered the first modern detective story. It introduced the mastermind detective C. Auguste Dupin, a brilliant amateur who uncovers clues and solves the crime by his deductive skill, setting a pattern for most later detective story writers. Dupin also appeared in Poe's later stories of crime and detection.

Muse, GM: any one of the nine daughters of Zeus and Mnemosyne who were patrons and goddesses of the arts and sciences. They were: Clio (history), Euterpe (music), Thalia (comedy and pastoral poetry), Melpomene (tragedy), Terpsichore (dancing and choruses), Erato (lyric and love poetry), Polyhymnia (sacred song), Urania (astronomy), and Calliope (epic poetry).

My Antonia: novel by U.S. writer Willa Cather, published in 1918. The narrator, Jim Burden, meets Antonia Shimerda, a Bohemian immigrant, when they are both growing up in Nebraska. She works hard—first in the fields, later as a maid—but never loses her humor and integrity. Jim leaves for college. He returns 20 years later and finds Antonia a middle-aged farm wife with many children who still retains the strength of character that makes her representative of the American pioneer spirit.

Mycenae, GM: ancient city, supposedly founded by Perseus and ruled by Agamemnon, the leader of the Greeks during the Trojan War (c 1250 B.C.). Following Homer's description of its site, excavations were begun in 1840 by Heinrich Schliemann in a ravine in Argos; they have yielded rich finds that include palace ruins, city walls, graves, gold cups and ornaments, bronze weapons, painted vases, and sculpture. These artifacts, along with tablets inscribed in the Linear B script (earlier found on Crete), indicate that the distinctive civilization of the Greek mainland derived from Crete.

Myshkin, Prince: See *Idiot, The.*

Mystery plays: short medieval dramatic works representing events from the Old or New Testament, especially those dealing with the birth, death, or resurrection of Christ. They were an elaboration of the church liturgy, associated with particular feasts, and originally given as part of the service. Later, as robust humor and comic byplay were introduced into the religious stories, they were forbidden in church and moved out to the courtyard or were given at markets and fairs. Famous examples are *Abraham and Isaac* and *The Harrowing of Hell.* The actors were members of local guilds or trade unions.

The surviving English mystery plays are known by the towns in which they were produced: York, Wakefield, and Chester. A fourth group of plays, formerly erroneously assigned to Coventry, are now called N-town plays.

Mystery story: popular genre of fiction in which a crime is solved, involving the elements of suspense, fear, and mystification. Stories of detection have been known since seventh-century China; the modern detective story—the "whodunit"—is considered to have begun with Edgar Allan Poe's "Murders in the Rue Morgue" (1841), which introduced the clever amateur detective Dupin. The most famous detective of all time is Sir Arthur Conan Doyle's Sherlock Holmes, whose adventures were published between 1891 and 1927.

Among the best-known fictional detectives are Rex Stout's Nero Wolfe; Erle Stanley Gardner's lawyer-detective Perry Mason; Agatha Christie's Belgian detective Hercule Poirot and her elderly English sleuth Miss Marple; and Dorothy Sayers' aristocratic Lord Peter Wimsey. The "hard-boiled" detective, born in the United States in the 1930's, is typified by Raymond Chandler's Philip Marlowe and Dashiell Hammett's Sam Spade. Police detectives who solve crimes as part of everyday routine include Georges Simenon's Inspector Jules Maigret.

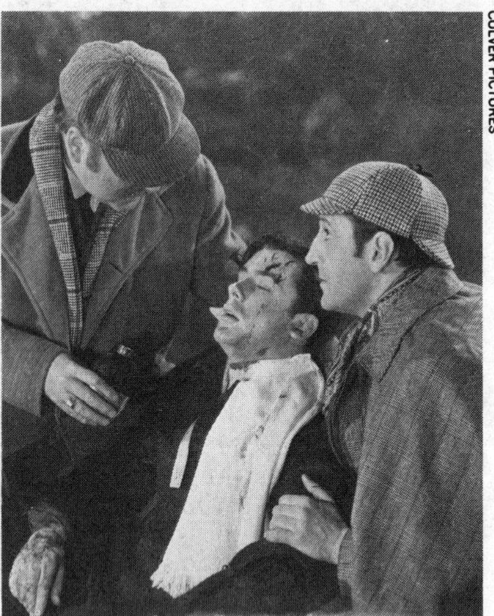
CULVER PICTURES

MYSTERY: *classic detective Sherlock Holmes helps the victim of a crime.*

Myth: traditional story that embodies elemental and deeply felt beliefs of a people, explaining the mysteries of existence by attributing them to the actions of supernatural beings. The actors in myths are deities, or semidivine beings; if they are not, the story is a folk tale.

Certain types of myth are universal; *creation myths,* which explain how the Earth and its people came to be; *nature myths,* which personify the elements, peopling the woods, fields, mountains, and sea with gods, nymphs, and other resident spirits and giving human attributes to natural forces like the sun, moon, stars, and winds; *culture myths,* which supply reasons for tribal customs and taboos and tell how a people acquired basic elements of their culture—corn or medicine or music.

GREEK AND ROMAN DEITIES

GREEK	ROMAN
Aphrodite	Venus
Apollon	Apollo
Athena	Minerva
Ares	Mars
Artemis	Diana
Cronus	Saturn
Demeter	Ceres
Dionysus	Bacchus
Eros	Cupid
Hades (Pluton)	Pluto
Hephaestus	Vulcan
Hera	Juno
Heracles	Hercules
Hermes	Mercury
Hestia	Vesta
Persephone	Proserpine
Poseidon	Neptune
Zeus	Jupiter

In Western culture the most familiar mythologies are those of the Greeks, the Romans, and the Norse. The Romans took much of their rich mythology from the earlier Greeks, and we know the stories more often in their Roman versions. For the equivalent names of Greek and Roman deities, see chart at right.

N

Naiads, GM: Greek nymphs who presided over springs and fountains, rivers, streams, and lakes.

Naked and the Dead, The: first novel by U.S. author Norman Mailer, published in 1948; generally considered one of the best American novels to come out of World War II. It deals with a representative group of U.S. officers and enlisted men invading a Japanese island. The author uses a device called the "Time Machine" to switch back into the past of each of the characters engaged in the action.

Nana: novel by the French writer Émile Zola, published in 1880. It is one of a long series of naturalistic novels that traces the tainted heredity of the Rougon-Macquart family. Nana, the daughter of alcoholic parents, becomes a prostitute, but because of her unusual beauty, she rises to become an "actress" and the mistress of important men. Zola does not glamorize Nana's role as the mistress of Paris. Her stupidity, fickleness, and improvidence bring ruin to her lovers and at last to herself.

Narcissus, GM: beautiful youth for whose love Echo died. He fell in love with his own reflection in a pool, pined away with longing for the unattainable image, and was changed into the flower that bears his name. Narcissism is excessive self-love. See also *Echo*.

Narrative poetry: poems that tell stories. There are three main classifications: epic, romance, and ballad. See also separate entries.

Nathan the Wise: verse drama by the German playwright Gotthold Ephraim Lessing, published in 1779. The setting is twelfth-century Jerusalem at the time of the Crusades. The story concerns a complicated web of obligation involving a Christian Knight Templar, the Muslim Sultan Saladin, and the respected Jewish merchant Nathan. It advances a concept of religious tolerance unusual for its time. The character of Nathan was based on Lessing's friend, the Jewish philosopher Moses Mendelssohn.

CULVER PICTURES

NARCISSUS: *the young man fell in love with his own image. His lover Echo could never tell him that she loved him, being able only to repeat his words back to him.*

Native Son: novel by Richard Wright, published in 1940; the first work by an American black to deal frankly and boldly with black-white relations. It tells the story of Bigger Thomas, a young black man who is employed as a chauffeur by the Daltons. Bigger is uneasy when Mary Dalton, a radical university student, befriends him. He helps Mary to her room when she is drunk and, to prevent her from disturbing the family, accidentally smothers her with a pillow. He then disposes of the body and engages in a series of bizarre acts to cover his deed. He is caught, tried, and sentenced to death. The mutual distrust of most black and white characters toward one another determines their behavior throughout the book.

NATIVE SON *by Richard Wright spoke frankly about black-white relations.*

CULVER PICTURES

Naturalism: movement of the late 19th century that adapted the theories of science and the objectivity of scientific method to literature and art. In France, Stendhal, Balzac, and Flaubert laid the groundwork for naturalism's leading exponents, Maupassant, Daudet, and especially Zola. The naturalistic novel was often a case history in which the character's heredity and environment, rather than his own will, determined his fate. The movement was important in late 19th-century German and English literature and had considerable effect on the work of 20th-century Italian neorealists such as Silone, Levi, and Moravia. Some examples in American fiction are Theodore Dreiser's *American Tragedy* (1925) and James T. Farrell's Studs Lonigan trilogy (1932–1935). In exploring the effects of environment on personality, the naturalists often chose extreme environments, such as slums or the underworld, and thus introduced new areas of subject matter to fiction.

Nausea: first novel of the French existentialist philosopher Jean-Paul Sartre, published in 1938. The hero, Antoine Roquentin, who lives the lonely life of a historical researcher, begins to have strange perceptions. He feels the chaos and unpredictability of the world around him and concludes that living is senseless in a world that so lacks meaning. He calls his feeling of malaise and self-disgust "nausea," and in the end decides that he can escape from the oppressiveness of life only in the realm of art.

Nausicaa: See *Odyssey*.

Nectar, GM: drink of the gods.

Nemesis, GM: goddess of vengeance and retribution who punished especially the proud and arrogant.

Neoclassicism: term applied to several post-Renaissance movements in art and literature when the classical forms and styles of Greece and Rome became the standard models. In literature its highest expression was perhaps in France during the late 1600's, in the dramas of Corneille and Racine, which adhered to classical principles with excessive rigidity. French neoclassicism influenced English literature from 1660 to the mid-1700's.

Neptune: See *Poseidon*.

Nestor: in the *Iliad,* an aged counselor of the Greeks at the time of the Trojan War, noted for wisdom and eloquence.

Newbery Medal: U.S. literary prize awarded annually since 1921 for the best juvenile book. Its name commemorates John Newbery (1713–1767), the first English publisher of children's books.

New Criticism: school of literary criticism developed in the 20th century. Its chief tenet is that a literary work stands on its intrinsic merit, regardless of its social, moral, historical, or political purpose. Its principal method is close reading—a painstaking word-for-word analysis of the text. By this method the "new critics" have revealed many subtleties and levels of meaning that were formerly overlooked in literary works. The term derives from the title of a work published in 1941 by the U.S. poet and critic John Crowe Ransom, but the method was advocated earlier by such critics as T. S. Eliot, William Empson, and I. A. Richards.

New England Renaissance or **American Renaissance:** the first flowering of a distinctive American literature that occurred between 1830 and 1870 and drew its inspiration from the European Romantic movement. One center of the burgeoning culture was Boston, where the aristocratic Harvard professors Henry Wadsworth Longfellow, Oliver Wendell Holmes, and James Russell Lowell were the literary elite. Another center was the small town of Concord, Massachusetts, where Ralph Waldo Emerson and Henry David Thoreau attracted an original and eccentric circle of transcendentalist thinkers and literary friends, among whom were two of America's greatest writers, Nathaniel Hawthorne and Herman Melville. A study of this period is Van Wyck Brooks's *The Flowering of New England.* See also *Transcendentalism.*

New Life, The: See *Vita Nuova, La.*

Nibelungenlied, also called *The Song of the Nibelungs*: Middle German epic, written about 1200 by an unknown author. It combines the earlier Germanic legends about the hero Siegfried, who slays the dragon Fafnir to get possession of a treasure, with legends about the destruction of the rival Burgundians. The stories are unified by focusing the tale on the Burgundian princess Kriemhild, sister of Gunther, one of three brother-kings of Burgundy.

After stealing the Nibelung treasure guarded by Alberich, Siegfried goes to woo Kriemhild. In order to marry her, he must help Gunther win the northern princess Brunhild, who will only marry a man who can surpass her in feats of strength. Gunther passes the test and wins Brunhild, although his acts are actually performed by Siegfried in a cloak of invisibility. Siegfried and Kriemhild marry, but one day in a quarrel, Kriemhild reveals the deception to Brunhild. Brunhild revenges herself on Siegfried by having him slain by Gunther's loyal vassal Hagen. Hagen robs Kriemhild of Siegfried's treasure and sinks it in the Rhine. The second part of the story deals with the change in Kriemhild from a sweet-natured maiden to a tragic woman bent on revenge. After long brooding she marries Etzel (the Hunnish king Attila). Years later she invites her brothers and Hagen to visit her and has them slain to the last man. She personally kills Hagen and is slain herself by a visiting warrior at Etzel's court.

Richard Wagner's four music dramas, *The Ring of the Nibelungs* (1853–1874; comprising *The Rhinegold, The Valkyrie, Siegfried,* and *The Twilight of the Gods*), are based on the legend, but rely more heavily on earlier, more highly supernatural Norse versions (particularly the *Völsunga Saga*). See also *Völsunga Saga.*

Nimue: See *Arthurian legend.*

Nineteen Eighty-Four: novel published in 1949 by the English satirist George Orwell; a prophetic forecast of the future under totalitarian rule. It is a terrifying projection of life in the superstate watched over by Big Brother, where the book's hero, Winston Smith, has a brief escape from absolute controls on his life through a love affair, is captured by the Thought Police and, after brainwashing, renounces all independent thought and "learns to love Big Brother."

Niobe, GM: proud mother, according to the *Iliad,* of seven sons and seven daughters. She bragged of her many children to Leto, the mother of two, Apollo and Artemis. To punish her, Apollo killed all her sons and Artemis killed all the girls. Niobe's grief was so great that in pity the gods changed her into a rock on Mt. Sipylus, from which her tears still flow when the snow above it melts.

Njals Saga (also called *The Story of Burnt Njall*): one of the greatest of the 13th-century Icelandic sagas; it demonstrates the ethics and manners of a society whose code of justice is the blood feud. Njall is a mature man and a respected judge, the head of a large family. He is a friend and father figure to the young hero Gunnar. But the quarrels and jealousies of their wives lead to a series of aggressive acts and retaliation between the two families. Njall's attempts to settle all scores justly are defeated by the rash reprisals of his sons. The feud culminates in Gunnar's death and the burning alive of Njall and his entire family.

Nō: highly stylized form of Japanese drama involving poetry, music, and dancing, developed in the 14th century by Kan-ami and his son Zeami Motokiyo. Most of the Nō plays still performed today were written by Zeami. They have two principal characters, the Shite and the Waki. The Shite sings and dances to the accompaniment of drums and flute (or a chorus

NŌ MASKS *show the highly stylized characters that are portrayed in the ancient Japanese form of drama.*

JAPAN NATIONAL TOURIST ORGANIZATION

sings his part while he dances), and the Waki explains the theme. Most plays deal with supernatural beings. Often the Shite plays the dual part of a character as he was in real life and as his ghost. The gestures, costumes, and masks are in themselves a meaningful language of exquisite refinement.

Nobel Prize for Literature: most prestigious of all literary prizes, awarded annually since 1921 by the Swedish Academy in Stockholm from a fund established by Alfred Nobel, the inventor of dynamite. The winners are chosen from throughout the world on the basis of the complete body of their work. U.S. writers who have won the award are: Sinclair Lewis, Eugene O'Neill, T. S. Eliot, William Faulkner, Ernest Hemingway, John Steinbeck, Saul Bellow, and Isaac Bashevis Singer.

Noble savage: term used in reference to the supposed innate goodness or moral superiority of the natural man, who is unspoiled by civilization. The concept became part of the back-to-nature philosophy of the Romantic movement and was popularized by the French writers Jean Jacques Rousseau and Chateaubriand. Some of the Indian characters in James Fenimore Cooper's *Leatherstocking Tales,* such as the wise Chingachgook and his brave son Uncas, are portrayed as noble savages having inborn virtue, grace, and delicacy of feeling.

No Exit: one-act play by the French writer Jean-Paul Sartre, produced in 1944. It deals with three characters, a man and two women, in Hell. Hell is a windowless drawing room with ugly furnishings. They soon learn that their punishment is suited to their crimes. Having sacrificed their true natures during life for the sake of their images in other people's eyes, they are doomed to live forever only in one another's eyes.

Notes from the Underground: novel by the Russian writer Feodor Dostoevski, published in 1864. The narrator, a petty clerk, has grandiose dreams of humiliating all his enemies for their fancied insults. Actually his intended victims are scarcely aware of his existence, and in their presence he succeeds only in humiliating himself. He ends by taking out his bitterness on a helpless prostitute.

Novel: sustained, fictional prose narrative of considerable length, traditionally containing a realistic portrayal of life, fully developed characters, and a point of view. The novel as we know it began in the 18th century with the publication of Samuel Richardson's *Pamela.* Unlike earlier prose fictions, *Pamela* concentrated minutely on the psychological development of its characters.

Among the world's most admired novelists are the English authors Henry Fielding, Jane Austen, Charles Dickens, and George Eliot; the French Honoré de Balzac and Gustave Flaubert; the Russians Feodor Dostoevski and Leo Tolstoy; the Irish James Joyce; the U.S. expatriate Henry James and writer Herman Melville. In the 20th century, the novel form has been greatly experimented with and expanded, and the merits of Latin American novelists such as Gabriel García Márquez and Jorge Amado have come to be recognized.

Nursery rhymes: verses, jingles, and poems of childhood passed on from generation to generation. Originally, some of these rhymes were adult comments on political leaders or social situations, disguised in catchy verse. Others were parts of courting songs or folk ballads. Riddles and counting-out rhymes also figure prominently in childhood poetry. Like fairy tales, nursery rhymes are often found in parallel versions in different countries. For example, "Billy Boy, Billy Boy," with slight variations, is common throughout Eastern European countries.

Nymphs, GRM: spirits of mountains, forests, trees, streams, the ocean, and springs. They were beautiful goddesses who often married human beings. Nymphs of the ocean were oceanids; nymphs of the sea, especially the Mediterranean, were nereids; nymphs of rivers, lakes, and springs were naiads; mountain nymphs were oreads; the nymphs of forests, groves, and trees were dryads.

Oberon: in medieval folklore, the king of the fairies or elves. He is the Alberich of German and French medieval romance, or his son. Unlike the sinister Alberich, the Oberon of Shakespeare's *Midsummer-Night's Dream* is an imperious mercurial being who masterminds the evening's madness.

Octopus, The: novel by the U.S. writer Frank Norris, published in 1901; intended as the first work in a trilogy dealing with the story of wheat. The octopus is the railroad whose encroachment spells impending doom for the California wheat farmers. A second volume, *The Pit* (1903), carries the story of wheat to the Chicago stock exchange and deals with the efforts of a broker to corner the market. A third volume was incomplete at the author's death.

Ode: in classical usage, a lyric poem designed to be chanted or sung. The most famous ancient odes are those written by the Greek poet Pindar (518–438 B.C.) in celebration of heroes of the Olympic Games. The form used by Pindar is virtually inimitable. The Latin poet Horace (65–8 B.C.) wrote odes that had little resemblance to Pindaric odes; the Horatian odes are graceful and polished but informal and conversational. They were imitated by Alexander Pope and many other poets of the early 1700's. In modern usage, an ode is a sustained lyric having a dignified subject and written in an elevated tone. Wordsworth's "Intimations of Immortality" is an example (see entry).

Ode on a Grecian Urn: poem by the English poet John Keats, written in 1819. In describing a pastoral scene of love pursuit on a Greek vase, the poet expresses wonder at the enduring freshness of art.

Odin, NM: supreme god; husband of Frigga and father of Balder, Thor, Bragi, Hoder, Tyr, Vali, Vidar, Hermod, and others of the Aesir. He was the god of war, but also the god of wisdom. To become so, he paid Mimir one eye for a drink from the spring of knowledge (Mimir's well) at the foot of the world tree Yggdrasil. Two ravens attended him, Hugin and Munin (thought and memory).

Odin learned the secret of the magic runes by hanging upside down from Yggdrasil, self-wounded by a spear. By this strange rite he acquired the powers of a wizard and a poet. He is the Woden of Germanic mythology; Wednesday is Woden's day.

Odysseus: son of Laertes; called Ulysseus by the Romans; in Homer's *Iliad* and *Odyssey,* a king of Ithaca and one of the foremost of the Greek chiefs in the Trojan War. He was a suitor of Helen of Troy but married Penelope; he was so unwilling to leave her when called to rescue Helen from the Trojans that he feigned madness by plowing the sands of his native shore to avoid going to war. His ruse was discovered when his infant son Telemachus was placed in his path and he veered out of the way; he was forced to go to Troy where he distinguished himself in valor and wisdom during the years of the siege. On the death of Achilles the arms of that hero were awarded to Odysseus. The Trojan Horse was Odysseus's idea. See also *Odyssey.*

Odyssey: epic by Homer; it describes the ten years of wandering and the hardships and adventures Odysseus encounters on his voyage home from the war. After dragging his crew away from the temptations of the Lotus-Eaters in Africa, he next escapes death from the one-eyed Cyclops, Polyphemus. He remains one year with Circe, the enchantress, and seven years with the ocean nymph Calypso on her island Ogygia, refusing the promise of immortality in order to return home.

THE ODYSSEY: *Odysseus and his crew are menaced by the one-eyed giant, the Cyclops, who is throwing huge boulders at their ship.*

He braves the dangers of Scylla and Charybdis, and has himself bound to the mast to escape the lure of the sirens' singing. Shipwrecked on the shores of Phaeacia, he is cared for by Nausicaa and her father, who gives him ships to continue his voyage home.

At last Odysseus reaches Ithaca, disguised as a beggar, and finds his wife Penelope surrounded by a host of insolent suitors, each coveting the kingdom. With the aid of his son Telemachus and his faithful herdsman Eumaeuas, he slays them all, reigning another good 16 years. Though the *Odyssey* lacks some of the dramatic freshness and heroic poignance of the *Iliad,* and contains many episodes from folklore and oriental romance, its superbly organized structure marks it as the work of Homer. See also *Charybdis; Circe; Lotus-Eaters; Penelope; Polyphemus; Scylla.*

Oedipus, GL: son of Laius and Jocasta, king and queen of Thebes. Having been warned that he would die by the hand of his son, Laius decided to destroy the newborn child and hung him by his heels on a tree in the forest. From this incident, probably, he was named Oedipus, meaning "swell foot." A passing herdsman found the infant and saved his life, and Oedipus was adopted and reared by the king of Corinth. In his young manhood he was told by the oracle at Delphi that he was destined to kill his father and wed his own mother. Horrified, he fled from Corinth, met Laius at a crossroad, and killed him in a quarrel over the right of way.

Finally Oedipus came to Thebes where the sphinx, a winged, woman-headed monster, was daily devouring the hapless people who could not answer her riddle. Oedipus answered instantly the famous question put to him, and the monster killed herself (see also *Sphinx*).

Creon, the king of Thebes, had promised the kingdom and his sister Jocasta for wife to whomever should free the city of this peril. Thus Oedipus unknowingly married his own mother and by her had two sons, Eteocles and Polynices, and two daughters, Antigone and Ismene. When the truth of their relationship was revealed to them, Jocasta hanged herself and Oedipus put out his own eyes, going into exile to Colonus in Attica, followed by his faithful daughter Antigone. This story is the basis of Sophocles' famous tragedy *Oedipus Rex.*

Of Human Bondage: semi-autobiographical novel by British writer W. Somerset Maugham, published in 1915; considered his finest work. It is the story of a sensitive young man's character development and growth to maturity. Philip Carey, a crippled orphan, raised by loveless relatives, becomes enslaved by a jealous passion for a Cockney waitress, Millie, who cruelly taunts him for his weaknesses. At last Philip frees himself from this emotional bondage, becomes a doctor, and marries an understanding woman.

Of Mice and Men: novel by U.S. writer John Steinbeck, published in 1937; a melodrama of the Depression years depicting the marginal existence of some outcasts of society. George Milton, a migrant worker, loves and protects his only friend, Lennie Small, a simple-minded giant who does not know his own strength. When Lennie unwittingly kills a flirtatious girl, George is forced to kill him to protect him from being lynched by a mob.

Ogier the Dane: one of Charlemagne's knights, also called Olger or, as a Danish national hero, Holger Danske. In early Charlemagne legends, he was a rebel who declared his intention to kill Charlemagne's son Charlot in a vendetta. Charlemagne had him imprisoned, but Archbishop Turpin protected him while pretending to starve him. The Saracens attacked and Turpin offered Charlemagne the aid of Ogier on condition that the knight might have his revenge on Charlot. Ogier satisfied himself by slapping Charlot in the face. He and Charlemagne were reconciled, and he became one of the twelve noble peers.

Ogre: in European fairy tales, a flesh-eating giant. The word was first used by the French writer Charles Perrault in his fairy tales and may have been invented by him.

Old Man and the Sea, The: late novel by U.S. author Ernest Hemingway, published in 1952. It deals with the struggles of an old Cuban fisherman to protect a huge fish, his first catch in 84 days, from sharks. The old man fights gallantly for two days but the sharks win in the end. The book's theme of the dignity and irony of primal struggle was a return of Hemingway's original, simple heroic code.

Oliver Twist: melodramatic novel of poverty and the London underworld by British writer Charles Dickens, published serially from 1837 to 1839. Oliver, an unknown waif, escapes from a workhouse only to fall into the hands of Fagin, the master of a den of young London thieves. Fagin forces Oliver to break into a house, where the boy is caught by his intended victims, who recognize at once that he is no common criminal. Through their kindly interest, Oliver discovers his true parentage; Fagin and his crew are brought before the law, and Oliver is adopted by a wealthy gentleman.

Olympus, Mount: highest mountain in the Olympus range and in Greece; considered by the ancient Greeks to be the abode of the gods.

One Day in the Life of Ivan Denisovich: novel by Russian writer Alexander Solzhenitsyn, published in 1962. It describes a typical "good" day in the life of a prisoner in a Soviet concentration camp in Siberia. Ivan counts the day good because he manages to conceal a little extra food for himself, because he incurs no unusual punishment for misconduct, and because he avoids the dreaded sentence to solitary confinement in a freezing cell that befalls one of his fellow prisoners. This was Solzhenitsyn's first novel, and the only one permitted publication in the U.S.S.R.

One Hundred Years of Solitude: novel by the Colombian writer Gabriel García Márquez, published in 1967. It

OLIVER TWIST: *in an illustration by the great 19th-century illustrator George Cruikshank, young Oliver asks the master of the workhouse for more food as his frightened friends watch.*

brought worldwide attention not only to its author but to the neglected literature of Latin America. The book chronicles the history of an imaginary isolated Colombian town, Maconda, through the stories of the members of its founding family, the Buendias, in a superb blend of myth and reality.

On Liberty: political-philosophical essay by British philosopher John Stuart Mill, published in 1859; a classic study of the problems of modern democracies. Mill argues that it is in the self-interest of the state to give its citizens the greatest amount of freedom. The state that enforces docility and discourages originality will eventually become the victim of its burdensome population of unproductive members.

Onomatopoeia: use of words to imitate natural sounds (for example, *achoo* tries to sound like a sneeze; *hahaha,* a laugh). In poetry, certain sounds or rhythms may be used to produce aural effects: a series of dactyls has the rhythm of a horse's gallop; the use of *z*-sounds has a buzzing quality. "Your life a sluice of sensation along your sides," writes D.H. Lawrence in a poem entitled "Fish," thus not only describing the fish but also creating the effect of it passing through water.

On the Road: novel by U.S. writer Jack Kerouac, published in 1957, regarded as the classic work of the Beat movement (see also *Beat generation*). A loosely structured book, written spontaneously in a few weeks, it deals with the cross-country jaunts of a group of young "Beats" in search of adventure, love, diversion, sex, enlightenment, and heightened experience. The Beat lifestyle and values—indifference to poverty; acceptance of all experience; and hunger for religious meaning—are reflected in the book.

Oracle, GRM: place where men might go to consult the gods in regard to the future and the conduct of human affairs. The answer was usually given through the voice of a priestess, after appropriate rituals had been performed and the priestess went into a trance. The message was couched in ambiguous, symbolic terms and could often be misinterpreted. The oracle of Apollo at Delphi was the most famous among the Greeks. See also *Delphic oracle.*

Oresteia: See *House of Atreus.*

Orestes: See *House of Atreus.*

Orion, GM: young and beautiful hunter, beloved by Eos and slain in jealousy by Artemis. Another story says that Artemis herself loved him and was tricked into shooting him by Apollo. After his death Orion became a major constellation in the heavens, where he appears wearing a belt studded with bright stars and carrying a club and sword.

Orlando Furioso: epic by Italian poet Ludovico Ariosto, published in 1516, enlarged in 1532. Its hero is the Roland of the Charlemagne legends, but in this version, romance takes precedence over heroic deeds. The poem's main story tells of Orlando's hopeless love for Angelica, the princess of Cathay, and his ensuing madness when Angelica elopes with a Moorish youth. Orlando's friend Astolfo makes a trip to the moon to find Orlando's wits and returns them to him.

Orpheus, GM: poet and musician of Thrace, son of Apollo and the muse Calliope. He received from Apollo the lyre, which he played so marvelously that he charmed the wild beasts and could make the trees and rocks move and the rivers stand still. When Eurydice, his wife, died from a serpent bite, Orpheus followed her to Hades and begged to be allowed to bring her back. Pluto was so moved by his music that he consented, but on condition that Eurydice follow behind and Orpheus never look back.

Orpheus promised; but just as they were leaving the world of gloom, he gave one backward look to see if she were really there. Eurydice vanished again to the realm of the dead, and Orpheus, inconsolable, returned home and vowed never more to associate with women. In revenge, the Maenads, women who celebrated the rites of Dionysus, wildly tore him to pieces, throwing his head and the lyre into the river Hebrus.

Several operas have been based on this theme, of which the most famous is the German composer Christoph Gluck's *Orfeo ed Euridice* (1762).

Osiris: ancient Egyptian god and judge of the dead. He was the brother and husband of Isis and the father of Horus. As ruler of Egypt he taught civilization to his subjects. He was killed by his brother Set (Typhon) but was resurrected by Isis and Horus, who defeated Set, establishing the worship of Osiris throughout Egypt.

Othello: tragedy by Shakespeare, produced in 1604. Othello, a Moor who has become a military hero in the service of Venice, is deceived by the lies and insinuations of the villain Iago, who bears Othello a grudge for promoting Cassio instead of him. He becomes enraged at his innocent wife Desdemona, the daughter of a Venetian senator, and strangles her. When he discovers he has wronged her, he commits suicide. Operas by Rossini (1816) and by Verdi (1887) were based on the play.

Ottava Rima: See *Stanza.*

Our Town: Pulitzer Prize-winning play by U.S. writer Thornton Wilder, first performed in 1938, dealing with the cycle of life in a New England town called Grovers Corners, but meant to be Everytown. A narrator comments on the town's activities and leading citizens; the action includes the courtship and marriage of a young couple, the death in childbirth of the young wife, and her burial. More important than the plot, perhaps, was the play's imaginative structure and manner of presentation.

Overcoat, The: short story by the Russian writer Nikolai Gogol, published in 1842. Akaki Akakyevich is a poor clerk whose great deed is to purchase a new overcoat, which makes him the center of attention at the office. When thieves steal his new coat, Akaki dies of grief and becomes a ghost who haunts St. Petersburg's citizens, particularly bureaucrats, to steal their coats. Akaki became a symbol to the Russians of the insulted and injured little man.

Oxymoron: See *Figures of speech.*

P

Paladins: twelve peers of Charlemagne, inmates of his palace, and his companions at arms. The word *paladin* at first meant palace dweller and then warrior. The names of the twelve differ in the *chansons de geste* that celebrate their deeds, but the most famous of the twelve were Roland and Oliver, Ganelon the traitor, Ferumbras, and Ogier the Dane.

Palladium, GM: famous statue of Pallas Athena possessed by the Trojans. No harm could befall the city so long as the statue remained within it, but Odysseus and Diomedes stole it for the Greeks, and Troy lost its protection.

Pamela, or Virtue Rewarded: first work of fiction by the pioneer English novelist Samuel Richardson, published in two parts, 1740–1741. It is also the first novel in letter form and, because this technique permits a direct and intimate revelation of the characters' thoughts and feelings, *Pamela* is regarded as the forerunner of the modern psychological novel. Pamela Andrews is a young servant girl whose letters to her anxious parents are vivid accounts of her efforts to ward off the dishonorable advances of her master, Mr. B. Even when she is kidnapped and held incommunicado by Mr. B., she manages to sneak out letters on her progress. Mr. B. at last proposes marriage, and Pamela becomes the very model of a virtuous wife, attempting to shame Mr. B. into fidelity.

Pan, GM: god of nature, forests, fields, and wildlife; the patron of flocks and shepherds; associated especially with the pastures of Arcadia. He is represented in human shape with the legs and horns of a goat. He invented the panpipe, or shepherd's pipe, a musical instrument made of reeds. He was fond of chasing nymphs and is a symbol of eroticism. He also frightened lonely travelers. Mysterious fear that comes from no obvious cause is called "panic" after him.

Pandarus: See *Troilus.*

ART MUSEUM, PRINCETON UNIVERSITY

PANDORA: *a watercolor by English artist and poet Dante Gabriel Rossetti.*

Pandora, GM: first woman; Zeus gave her a closed box, which he told her to give to her husband but never to open. In time Pandora became curious and opened the forbidden box. All the evils of humanity came crowding out and were let loose in the world; hope alone remained in the box, to comfort man in his afflictions.

Pantheon: temple for all the gods of a people or for their honored dead; also used to refer to all the gods. The Pantheon in Rome, built about 27 B.C. and rebuilt in the second century A.D., and the Panthéon in Paris, built between 1764 and 1781, are both marked by a great dome on top and contain the graves of many famous men.

Panza, Sancho: in Cervantes's novel *Don Quixote,* Quixote's squire, an earthbound, realistic peasant whose practical comments serve as a foil for Quixote's airy fantasies.

Paolo and Francesca: in Dante's *Inferno,* adulterous lovers who are among the most pitiable of all the sinners that Dante meets in Hell. They tell the poet how, as they were reading of Lancelot and Guinevere, their love was aroused and "That day we read no further." In real life Francesca was the young wife of one of the counts of Rimini. She fell in love with her brother-in-law, Paolo Malatesta. When her husband discovered them together, he had them put to death (1284).

Parable: short narrative in which everyday experiences are used to illustrate a moral theme. The teachings of Christ are often couched in parables in which he likens God or himself to a king, a shepherd, a sower, a father, or an employer.

Paradise Lost: epic poem in blank verse by English poet John Milton, published in 1667. Its purpose is "to justify the ways of God to man." It relates how some of the angels revolted against God and were cast out of Heaven into Hell. They decide to revenge themselves upon the Almighty by invading Earth and leading man to sin. Satan, chief of the fallen angels, corrupts Adam and Eve and brings about their expulsion from Paradise. *Paradise Lost* is regarded as the greatest epic in the English language. Milton wrote a sequel, *Paradise Regained* (1671), which deals with the theme of redemption.

Paradox: self-contradictory statement that nevertheless makes sense. An example is Oscar Wilde's remark, "There is only one thing in the world worse than being talked about, and that is not being talked about." Paradoxical situations, treated seriously or humorously, are often the basis for a plot.

Parallel Lives: See *Biography.*

Paris, GM: son of Priam, king of Troy. He was sought out to judge which of the three goddesses—Aphrodite, Hera, and Athena—was the fairest. Paris gave the prize to Aphrodite, who promised him the most beautiful woman in the world for his wife. She helped him win and carry off Helen, the wife of Menelaus of Sparta. Thus Paris caused the Trojan War and the destruction of Troy. He was killed by an arrow shot by Philoctetes the day the city was taken. See also *Eris.*

Parody: literary form in which a serious compostion, or the general manner of a serious author, is imitated in phraseology and style in order to point up the absurdities of the original. It is a particularly devastating form of criticism. Some parodies endure when their originals are forgotten.

Parzival: 13th-century German epic, written by Wolfram von Eschenbach, considered one of the greatest works of the Middle Ages. Its hero Parzival is the Arthurian knight Perceval, whose outstanding traits are innocence and simplicity. He stops at the castle of the Fisher King (Amfortas), the keeper of the Holy Grail. The Grail knights are under an enchantment and the Fisher King is dying of a wound that only a "stainless fool" can heal by proffering sympathy. Although Parzival is puzzled by the strange and wonderful things he sees there, such as the *graal,* a marvelous dish carried in a procession, and a bleeding spear, he is ashamed of calling attention to his ignorance and asks no questions. After a long spiritual quest, Parzival finds the Fisher King again and asks the question that heals the wound; he succeeds Amfortas as Grail Keeper. This story is the subject of Richard Wagner's last opera *Parsifal* (1882). See also *Holy Grail; Perceval.*

Passage to India, A: novel by British writer E. M. Forster, published in 1924. Set in colonial India, it explores the gulf of misunderstanding between the Indians and their British rulers. Mrs. Moore comes to India to visit her son, accompanied by his fiancée, Adela Quested. Both Englishwomen are eager to know "the real India." Mrs. Moore, who has an intuitive sympathy for Oriental thought, is able to bridge the gap between East and West in her delicate friendship with the young Indian, Dr. Aziz. But Adela is unable to rise above stereotyped reactions; while alone with Dr. Aziz in the Marabar caves, she imagines that he has assaulted her. Her accusations lead to a trial of Dr. Aziz that unleashes the repressed antagonisms of both races.

Pastoral: tradition in literature and art, invented by the Greek poet Theocritus in the third century B.C. It portrays idealized shepherds, milkmaids, or other rustics who live far from the bustle of civilized life in an idyllic never-never land (usually called Arcadia), where they engage in innocent plesures and amorous dalliance. Pastoral poetry developed strict conventions. Its tradition was revived in the Renaissance and was extremely popular in England. Edmund Spenser's *Shepheardes Calender,* Philip Sidney's *Arcadia,* and Christopher Marlowe's "The Passionate Shepherd to His Love" are examples. Pastoral painting was important in France before the Revolution; Beethoven's sixth symphony, describing country life, is called the "Pastoral."

Paterson: long poem by U.S. doctor/poet William Carlos Williams, published in four volumes from 1946 to 1951, with a postscript entitled "Book Five" added in 1958. Writing in a vernacular, structureless style about the town of Paterson, New Jersey, Williams is really, through the depiction of a semi-autobiographical character, exploring the role of man in modern America.

Patroclus: See *Iliad.*

Paul Bunyan: hero of lumber-camp folklore of the American timber country—from Michigan, Wisconsin, and Minnesota to the Pacific Northwest. The huge lumberjack became a symbol of American expansiveness and inventiveness; the tales of his incredible feats have been retold in different versions by many authors. Most say that Paul was born in Maine and rocked to sleep in a 20-foot boat off the coast. He later turned up in the midwestern forests and finally walked to Oregon because the trains were so slow. Some standard characters turn up in most Paul Bunyan tales: Johnny Inkslinger, his "businessman" partner; Hot Biscuit Slim, the fabulous lumber-camp cook; and of course, Babe, the Blue Ox, his most prized possession and companion. Babe was found in the Winter of the Blue Snow; he measured 42 ax handles and a plug of Star tobacco between the horns. Whenever Paul decided to move, he hitched the whole camp to Babe, and the huge ox would drag the bunkhouse, the kitchen, and all the buildings to the new spot.

Paul himself was the greatest logger of them all. Two cuts were all he ever made for one tree. Often he made one cut with the forward swing and cut the tree behind him on the back swing. One of the most famous of the tall tales relates how Paul and Babe straightened the narrow, crooked roads in upper Michigan. Some were so crooked that they doubled back, and the men would meet themselves coming from work. So Paul hitched Babe to one end of a road, yelled "Pull," and the ox pulled the whole thing straight. Paul found he had 14 miles of extra road left, so he rolled them up and sold them to Chicago for a street—Michigan Avenue, named for the state it came from.

Pecos Bill: hero of cowboy folklore of the American West. When his parents moved to west Texas, Bill fell out of the wagon when it was crossing the Pecos River. He grew up with the coyotes and thought he was a coyote himself. One day a cowboy came along and asked him why he was "running around naked with the varmints," and that was the first inkling he had that he was human.

Deciding to take up human ways, Pecos Bill became the greatest cowhand in the West. He raised his horse, Widow-Maker, on dynamite and nitroglycerin, and no one else could ride him. Bill, though, could ride anything; he once rode a cyclone across three states until, unable to throw him, it rained out from under him and made the Grand Canyon. He invented the lariat and cattle-roping, the six-shooter, and all the best "cuss" words; and he taught the bronco how to buck. Once he saved the cattle country from a Pacific tidal wave: when he heard it was coming, he quickly threw up a levee—which was later called the Rocky Mountains.

Bill married a famous rider named Slue-Foot Sue. After she died—and there are many different legends about her fate—he was so lonely that he took to drinking nitroglycerin, but it soon lost its kick and he started adding fish hooks and barbed wire. One night, they struck together, and that little spark was the end of Pecos Bill.

Peer Gynt: poetic drama by Norwegian author Henrik Ibsen, presented in 1867. Peer is a farm boy whose egotistical apetite for life and self-gratification is at once the pride and despair of his mother Ase and the gentle girl Solveig who loves him. Peer disgraces his family by abducting a girl on her wedding night and later deserting her. He flees to the mountain trolls and marries an elf-king's daughter. He then deserts her to travel the world, where he makes and loses fortunes, trafficking in slaves or Bibles. In middle age he realizes his life is worthless and returns to Norway where he is redeemed by Solveig's abiding love for him. The *Peer Gynt Suites* by the composer Edvard Grieg were originally written as incidental music for the play.

Pegasus, GM: swift and marvelous winged horse, born from the blood of Medusa at the moment Perseus cut off her head. Hippocrene, the fountain of poetic inspiration, gushed forth when his hoof struck a rock on the Muses' mountain; hence the winged horse is a symbol of poetry. Athena gave a golden bridle to the young hero Bellerophon, who tamed Pegasus with it and went on to wonderful adventures.

Pelias: See *Argonauts.*

Peloponnesian War, The: history written by Thucydides, an Athenian general who was an eyewitness to the disastrous war between Athens and Sparta (431–404 B.C.) that brought about the demise of the Greek city-states. Believing this to have been the largest-scale war in history, the author records it in minute and objective detail. He assesses its true cause to have been the threat of the ascendancy of Athens, a democratic and mercantile naval power, to the conservative agrarian-military power, Sparta.

Pelops: See *House of Atreus.*

Penelope: wife of Odysseus. During her husband's long absence she put off her horde of suitors with the excuse that she must finish the winding sheet she was weaving for her father-in-law. Each night she unraveled the work she had done that day. Penelope's Web is still an epithet given to any never-finished task.

Penseroso, Il: See *L'Allegro.*

Pentameter: See *Meter.*

Perceval: knight of the Round Table and the original seeker of the Holy Grail. The earliest stories about Perceval deal with the education of a simpleton and have their roots in folklore. At King Arthur's court, his many naive blunders are redeemed by his innocent charm. In later versions, Perceval became a hero in the long quest after the Holy Grail. See also *Holy Grail; Parzival.*

Père Goriot, Le: See *Human Comedy.*

Persephone, also called *Kore* (maiden), GM: daughter of Zeus and Demeter. She was carried off by Pluto to be his wife and queen of Hades. The prayers of Demeter moved Zeus to let Persephone return, but only if she had eaten nothing in the lower world. It was discovered that she had eaten seven pomegranate seeds and was therefore in bondage to Hades. She was allowed to spend part of the year with her mother but was compelled to return to Pluto for the other part. Her return to life symbolizes the growth of crops; her sojourn in the lower world, the planting of seed. In Roman versions, she is called Proserpine, daughter of Ceres.

Perseus, GM: son of Zeus and Danae. He founded the city of Mycenae, killed the dreadful Gorgon Medusa, and rescued Andromeda from the rock where she was chained as a sacrifice to a sea monster.

Personification: See *Figures of speech.*

Peter Pan: play for children by English author Sir James Barrie, performed in 1904. Peter is an elflike little personage who refuses to "grow up." He lures the Darling children to his home in Never-Never land where they meet the jealous fairy Tinker Bell and the terrible pirate Captain Hook.

Phaedo: dialogue by the Greek philosopher Plato, written in the fourth century B.C. It deals with the last day in the life of Socrates. In prison and condemned to death, the old philosopher discusses with his friends the immortality of the soul. At the appointed time, Socrates drinks the hemlock cheerfully, reproves his friends for their tears, and lies down to die; he dies reminding Crito that he owes a cock to Asclepius and asking him to pay the debt.

Phaedra: See *Hippolytus.*

Phaethon, GM: son of Helios, the sun god. He begged to be allowed to drive his father's great four-horse chariot across the sky. The boy soon lost control of the fiery horses; the chariot dipped too near the earth and scorched it, forming the Sahara desert, and the whole world would have been burned had not Zeus killed Phaethon with a thunderbolt.

Philemon: See *Baucis and Philemon.*

Philistines: Biblical enemy of the Israelites. In the 19th century the English critic Matthew Arnold took the term "philistine" from German student slang to refer to the prosperous members of the middle class who were indifferent to cultural and moral values.

Philoctetes, GM: hero who inherited the miraculous bow of Hercules. Because of an evil-smelling wound that would not heal, the Greeks on their way to Troy abandoned Philoctetes on the isle of Lemnos. When they learned that they needed Hercules's bow to win the war, Odysseus and Neoptolemus (or sometimes Diomedes) went to Lemnos to obtain it by treachery. Sophocles' play *Philoctetes* (409 B.C.) deals with young Neoptolemus's refusal to deceive or abandon the bitter, suffering hero. Philoctetes is brought back to Troy where his wound is healed and he slays Paris in battle. The 20th-century U.S. critic Edmund Wilson made Philoctetes the symbol of the artist in *The Wound and the Bow* (1941).

Philosophes: name applied to the French intellectual leaders of the 18th-century Enlightenment. Among them were scientists, philosophers, social critics, and writers, of whom the best-known were Denis Diderot, Voltaire, Baron de Montesquieu, Marquis de Condorcet, and Jean Jacques Rousseau, as well as the Scottish-born philosopher Davie Hume. Their great joint work was the compilation of a monumental *Encyclopédie* (1751–1772). Their skeptical attitudes toward religion, government, and social traditions are thought to have helped pave the way for the French Revolution. See also *Enlightenment.*

CULVER PICTURES

PHOENIX: *the mythical bird rises from the ashes of an old bird in a 1602 woodcut.*

Phoebe, GM: name for Artemis as moon goddess.

Phoebus, GM: name for Apollo as sun god, meaning "shining."

Phoenix: fabulous bird connected with Egyptian sun worship. It was large, very beautiful, and always male; there were never two in the world at once. It was believed to live for hundreds or thousands of years. At the end of that time it built a nest in which it burned itself alive. From the ashes rose the new, young phoenix.

Picaresque: fictional recounting of the life of a charming rogue; his or her adventures afford the writer the opportunity to satirize society as the hero encounters bigger knaves than himself in the high courts and in church positions. The picaresque originated in 16th-century Spain, with the anonymous *Lazarillo de Tormes* as its earliest example. In English, an early picaresque is Defoe's *Moll Flanders.*

Picaresques are often considered forerunners of the novel. Later works

PHILOSOPHE: *Voltaire was a leading light in the French Enlightenment of the 1700's.*

with picaresque qualities include Voltaire's *Candide* and the novel *Roderick Random* by Tobias Smollett.

Pickwick Papers, The (more correctly, *The Posthumous Papers of the Pickwick Club*): story by English author Charles Dickens, issued in parts in 1836–1837. It is made up of a series of adventures of Samuel Pickwick, Esq., founder and president of the Pickwick Club, his valet Sam Weller, and other companions. The work made Dickens famous at the age of 24.

Picture of Dorian Gray, The: novel by the Irish-born author Oscar Wilde, written in 1891. A strikingly beautiful youth, Dorian Gray, embarks on a vicious and depraved life. His deeds do not show in his appearance but only in a portrait of himself that hangs in an upper room, reflecting each new act of degeneracy and so mirroring his soul. In desperation Dorian murders the artist of the portrait, then stabs the picture. He is found dead, his body grotesquely revealing his state of corruption, his portrait once more that of a handsome, innocent youth.

CULVER PICTURES

PICTURE OF DORIAN GRAY: *the portrait reflects the degeneracy of its young subject.*

Pied Piper of Hamelin, The: narrative poem by the English poet Robert Browning, published in 1842, telling a moral tale from German folklore about a magician who offered—for a fee—to rid the town of Hamelin, on the River Weser, of a plague of rats. Taking his pipe, he played the rats a tune that had them swarming after him and into the river, where they drowned. The town corporation, however, refused to pay the piper, who once more took his pipe but this time lured the town children away and into a hillside, from which they never returned.

Pierrot ("little Peter"): gentle, lovesick clown, a stock character in early French and English pantomime who replaced the earlier Italian Arlecchino (Harlequin) as the lover of Columbine.

Piers Plowman (full title, *The Vision of William Concerning Piers the Plowman*): Middle English satirical and allegorical poem of the 14th century, ascribed to William Langland. It was first printed in 1550. The form is the familiar medieval dream allegory. The poet on a May morning falls asleep upon the Malvern hills and in his dream encounters representative types of the society of his day. Piers, a simple farmer (an allegorical figure for Christ), offers to guide them to the Tower of Truth if they will first help him cultivate his field. But only a few are willing to help, that is, work for salvation.

Pilgrim's Progress, The: allegory by the English preacher John Bunyan, written during his imprisonment for Nonconformist views and issued in two parts, 1678 and 1684. It describes the adventures of its hero, Christian, on his way from the City of Destruction to the Celestial City. He passes through the Slough of Despond, fights with the evil Apollyon, looks on Vanity Fair, passes the castle of the Giant Despair and, after these and many other trials, arrives at the Delectable Mountains and crosses the Black River to the Shining Gate. The book's plain, direct Anglo-Saxon style made it a great popular favorite, and for many years it occupied a place second only to the Bible in English homes.

Pillars of Hercules: two headlands opposite each other at the Strait of Gibraltar, supposed to have been raised up by Hercules in his travels to find the cattle of Geryon. They were Calpe (Gibraltar in Europe) and Abila (Sierra Bullones in Africa).

Pinocchio, The Adventures of: enduring children's story by the Italian writer Carlo Lorenzini, who published it in 1883 under the pseudonym "Collodi." Pinocchio, a puppet who comes to life, has several adventures whose outcome is designed to teach young readers the difference between right and wrong: for example, whenever Pinocchio tells a lie his nose grows long; when he tells the truth, it reduces to its normal size again.

Pit and the Pendulum, The: short story by U.S. author Edgar Allan Poe, published in 1842, in which a prisoner of the Inquisition describes the harrowing tortures to which he was subjected in the dungeons of Toledo.

Pixie or **pixy:** in English folklore, a fairy or sprite who mischievously leads people astray, rattles pans, knocks over buckets, and kisses girls in the dark.

Plague, The: novel by the French existentialist philosopher Albert Camus, published in 1947. On his daily rounds in the Algerian city of Oran, the novel's doctor-hero, Bernard Rieux, notices a dead rat. More and more dead rats appear in the city, then the first human cases come, and Oran is in the grip of an epidemic of bubonic plague. Although Rieux sees the ultimate futility of his efforts, he does all he can to relieve the suffering around him. On the surface, the book is a vivid chronicle of a calamity, but it also may be seen as an allegory for the Nazi occupation of France and for the human condition itself; Rieux's humanistic response to a hopeless situation represents Camus' solution to man's dilemma in an absurd world.

Platonic love: generally understood as a nonsexual attachment between a man and a woman based on intellectual affinities and mutual admiration. It is not derived directly from the philosopher Plato, who believed that sexual attraction for a beautiful youth led to a love of beauty itself, which, in turn, led to a love of the Good. The modern idea of platonic love stems from the Neoplatonists of the Italian Renaissance, who popularized the concept. The poems of the sculptor Michelangelo addressed to the virtuous widow Vittoria Colonna are an expression of platonic love.

Playboy of the Western World, The: play by the Irish dramatist John Millington Synge, performed in 1907, about a young country lad, Christie

PINOCCHIO: *an early illustration of the puppet come to life.*

NEW YORK PUBLIC LIBRARY

Mahon, who thinks he has killed his father and, horrified, flees his home. But he is received in a nearby town (where men are scarce) as though he were a hero, bold and brave, and the flattering attentions bring about a complete change in his naturally timid personality. Christie's moment of glory is over when his father turns up alive. The play opened at Dublin's Abbey Theatre and is considered one of the masterpieces of the Irish literary renaissance. But it originally offended Irish sensitivities, and its early performances caused riots in Dublin, New York, and Philadelphia.

Pleiades, GM: seven daughters of Atlas. They were raised to a constellation in the heavens after their deaths.

Plough and the Stars, The: tragicomedy by the Irish playwright Sean O'Casey, performed in 1926. It portrays some quarrelsome, gossiping, heavy-drinking occupants of a Dublin tenement during the week of the Easter Rising against the British in 1916. When the shooting starts, these brawling slum-dwellers are magically transformed. The gallantry of this rebellion against odds seems to rub off even on those who are opposed to the Irish resistance. Without denying his characters their sordid or comic moments, O'Casey conveys a picture of what the poet Yeats called the "terrible beauty" born of this event.

Plutarch's Lives: See *Biography.*

Pluto or **Pluton,** GM: most commonly used name for Hades, the god of the lower world, associating him with the god Plutus.

Plutus, GM: god of the earth's abundance and of wealth. He was the son of Demeter and was blinded by Zeus, according to some accounts, so he would bestow wealth impartially to all. Aristophanes' comedy *Plutus* (388 B.C.) deals with the restoration of his sight.

Poems, Chiefly in the Scottish Dialect: first book of poems by Scottish poet Robert Burns, published in 1786, in Kilmarnock, Scotland. (It is also known as the Kilmarnock volume.) It includes such Scottish favorites as "To a Mouse" and "To a Louse," as well as poems written in standard English, such as "The Cotter's Saturday Night." At the time that they were written, the English poems were more highly appreciated than those in the Scottish dialect, and they brought the young poet immediate fame. Later critics have favored the dialect poems.

Poetics, The: influential treatise on literary criticism, written by the Greek thinker Aristotle c 335–322 B.C. In this work, Aristotle urges the superiority of tragedy over other literary forms. He arrives at his critical principles empirically through close analysis of the tragedies that he finds most successful. Tragedy is defined by him as an "imitation of an action," in which a man of noble stature, through some "tragic flaw" *(hamartia),* rather than vice, falls from a high estate to catastrophe. Pride *(hubris),* which causes heroes to disregard laws or warnings, is a common tragic flaw. The purpose of tragedy, Aristotle believes, is to evoke terror and pity, and effect in the spectators a purgation *(catharsis)* of these emotions. Some of his observations on the limits of action and time in drama gave rise to rigid formulations—the "unities" of action, place, and time—which governed neoclassical drama in the 1600's.

Poet laureate: lifetime salaried appointment held by the official poet of the British court. The official laureateship began with the appointment of John Dryden in 1668. At one time it was considered proper for the poet laureate to commemorate national events and royal birthdays with a poem, but since 1843, no duties have been attached to the office.

Poetry: earliest and most characteristic type of literature. It seeks to express action, feeling, or thought in an imaginative way through the use of condensed, arresting, and emotive language that follows a metrical or rhythmic pattern. From the most primitive to the most sophisticated societies, poetry is regarded as having an almost magical value. Poetry is often divided into three types: lyric, narrative, and dramatic.

Point Counter Point: novel by the English writer Aldous Huxley, published in 1928. It deals with a set of sophisticated intellectuals who are unable to realize their expectations or to find wholeness and satisfaction in either their love or work. The novel is a *roman à clef;* that is, some of the characters are thought to be based on actual literary figures such as Katherine Mansfield, and D. H. Lawrence.

Polynices: See *Seven Against Thebes.*

Polyphemus: in the *Odyssey,* a Cyclops. When Odysseus and twelve of his men trespassed in his cave, Polyphemus kept them prisoner and began devouring them. Odysseus and his remaining men escaped by getting the giant drunk, putting out his eye with a burning stake, and then concealing themselves beneath the sheep as the flocks left the cave to graze. Polyphemus prayed to his father, the sea god Poseidon, that Odysseus would reach home "late . . . in evil case, with the loss of all his company, in the ship of strangers. . . ." The further misfortunes that befell Odysseus were arranged by Poseidon in answer to the Cyclops's prayer. See also *Cyclopes.*

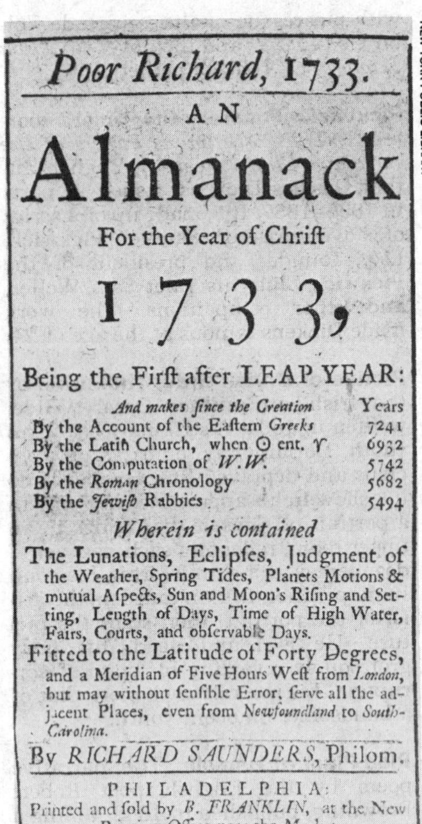

Poor Richard, 1733.

AN

Almanack

For the Year of Chriſt

1733,

Being the Firſt after LEAP YEAR:

And makes ſince the Creation	Years
By the Account of the Eaſtern *Greeks*	7241
By the Latin Church, when ☉ ent. ♈	6932
By the Computation of *W.W.*	5742
By the *Roman* Chronology	5682
By the *Jewiſh* Rabbies	5494

Wherein is contained

The Lunations, Eclipſes, Judgment of the Weather, Spring Tides, Planets Motions & mutual Aſpects, Sun and Moon's Riſing and Setting, Length of Days, Time of High Water, Fairs, Courts, and obſervable Days.

Fitted to the Latitude of Forty Degrees, and a Meridian of Five Hours Weſt from *London,* but may without ſenſible Error, ſerve all the adjacent Places, even from *Newfoundland* to *South-Carolina.*

By *RICHARD SAUNDERS,* Philom.

PHILADELPHIA:
Printed and ſold by *B. FRANKLIN,* at the New Printing-Office near the Market.

POOR RICHARD'S ALMANACK: *the title page of the only known copy of its first issue.*

Poor Richard's Almanack: series of almanacs by American statesman and author Benjamin Franklin, published regularly from 1732 to 1757, supposedly the work of a fictitious Richard Saunders. Many of the best-known American proverbs, such as "Early to bed and early to rise, makes a man healthy, wealthy, and wise," are from this source. Some of Poor Richard's sayings are actually of ancient origin, but Franklin often gave them an American slant. Richard's maxims on thrift were collected into a single issue, "The Way to Wealth," which enjoyed international popularity.

Porgy: novel by U.S. author DuBose Heyward, published in 1925. The story concerns Porgy, a lonely black cripple, and his love for Bess. Porgy kills Bess's former lover, Crown. While he is being questioned, Bess deserts him. The story is the basis for the folk opera *Porgy and Bess* (1935), composed in blues and jazz style by George Gershwin.

Portrait of a Lady, The: novel by U.S. expatriate author Henry James, published in 1881. It is the story of an idealistic and independent American girl, Isabel Archer, whose naiveté make her a prey of sophisticated Europeans. Isabel comes to realize her failure but proudly accepts it.

Portrait of the Artist as a Young Man, A: largely autobiographical novel by the Irish author James Joyce, published in 1916. Set in Dublin, it depicts Stephen Dedalus, its central character, through childhood, youth, and early manhood. It is about Stephen's awakening sense of himself as an artist and as an individual. The book uses "stream-of-consciousness," which presents a character's thoughts and feelings without authorial comment. Stephen breaks with his social, national, family, and religious inheritance. Stephen Dedalus is also a leading character in *Ulysses* (1922).

Poseidon, GM: god of the sea and all waters. He was a son of Cronus and Rhea, and brother to Zeus and Pluto. He created the first horse and was worshiped as a god of horses. He was also the "earth-shaker," the god of earthquakes, and of bulls. He was often pictured with a trident and holding a dolphin or fish. The Romans identified him with their Neptune.

Power and the Glory, The: novel by the English writer Graham Greene, published in 1940. It is set in a certain Mexican state during a time of revolution, when religion is suppressed. The hero, Father Montez, although an alcoholic and a sinner, refuses to renounce his calling; he lives as a fugitive performing his priestly services wherever needed. When he is at last captured and shot, another priest secretly arrives to replace him.

Pre-Raphaelite Brotherhood: group of English artists and writers formed under the leadership of the poet and painter Dante Gabriel Rossetti in 1848. They chose their name to show their opposition to conventional academic painting, which they believed stemmed from the style of the Italian Renaissance painter Raphael. The Pre-Raphaelites intended to use their art as an uplifting moral device, drawing on nature for subjects; Rossetti in particular was influenced by medieval subjects and style. Although the movement was specifically directed toward painting, it attracted writers and critics, including Rossetti's brother William and sister Christina, as well as John Ruskin. Rossetti also brought together a group of younger artists, including Edward Burne-Jones and William Morris, the nucleus of the aesthetic movement of the later 1800's.

Priam: in the *Iliad,* the last of the Trojan kings. He had 50 sons, including Hector and Paris, and twelve daughters, among them Cassandra and Polyxena. He was killed by Neoptolemus, the son of Achilles, when Troy was taken. See also *Hecuba.*

Pride and Prejudice: novel by English author Jane Austen, written under the title *First Impressions* in 1796 (when she was 21) and published after considerable revision in 1813. The scene is laid in the English countryside and the plot concerns the Bennett family's attempts to find suitable husbands for three daughters. The intimate drawing of the book's middle-class characters is done with humor and charm. Prejudice is represented by Elizabeth Bennett; pride, by Mr. Darcy, her wealthy suitor. As Darcy overcomes his pride, Elizabeth overcomes her prejudice, and the two are happily married at last.

Prince, The: political treatise by the Italian statesman-philosopher Niccolò Machiavelli, written in 1513 and dedicated to a younger member of the Medici family. Concerned with statecraft, it drew on the past for lessons as to how a prince ought to behave, pointing to Cesare Borgia—who combined personal charisma, brute force, and political cunning in upholding his authority—as the ideal prince. *The Prince* was influential throughout Renaissance Europe, where it earned Machiavelli a reputation for diabolical cunning, and was used as a practical manual of tyranny.

Procrustes, GM: brigand who shortened or stretched out his victims until they fit his bed. He was killed in the same manner by the hero Theseus. The term "Procrustean bed" has come to mean something that one must conform to against one's nature.

Prometheus, GM: son of the Titan Iapetus; brother of Atlas and Epimetheus. His name is thought to mean "the forethinker." Prometheus has come to symbolize the struggle of human intellect and aspiration against an indifferent or hostile cosmos. In some stories, he was the creator of mankind; in all stories, he was the great hero of culture, the founder of civilization. Defying Zeus, he stole fire from heaven in a hollow fennel stalk and gave it to man, teaching him its many uses. To punish him for this act—and possibly also for his refusal to divulge the secret of Zeus's final overthrow—Zeus had him chained to a rock, where an eagle fed perpetually on his liver, which was regenerated each night only to be devoured again each day. Though this punishment was to be eternal, Prometheus was at last freed by Hercules.

Prometheus's torture and defiance are celebrated by Aeschylus in the tragedy *Prometheus Bound* (written c 478 B.C.), the only extant play of a Prometheus trilogy; the story of his triumph and liberation is told in Shelley's poetic drama *Prometheus Unbound* (1820).

Prose: speech or writing that is distinguished from poetry chiefly by its lack of regular metrical pattern. Prose literature developed much later than poetry. Although prose is today generally considered more suitable for practical, expository, or narrative purposes, in ancient times, even histories and scientific or philosophical treatises were written in verse. In post-classical Europe, the Icelandic sagas (c twelfth century) are the earliest examples of a highly developed prose litera-

PRIDE AND PREJUDICE: *the main characters, Elizabeth Bennett and Mr. Darcy, each overcome a vice to bring their romance to a happy conclusion.*

CULVER PICTURES

ture. In English literature, although prose was written earlier, it was not until the emergence of the great 18th-century prose stylists—Addison, Swift, Johnson, and Burke—that prose acquired full prestige. Later, as the novel developed as an art form, differences between prose and poetry became less distinct. Free verse is often rhythmic prose, and novelists use imagery, symbols, rhythm, and emotive language in much the same ways as they are used by poets.

Proserpina: See *Persephone*.

Proteus, GM: lesser sea god, herder of the flocks of Poseidon. He had great wisdom and could foretell the future, but would not answer questions unless compelled to. If seized, he would rapidly change from one terrifying shape to another, but if the questioner held him fast, he would finally resume his own shape and give the true answers. The word *protean,* meaning changeable, comes from his name.

Proverb: brief saying that presents in epigrammatic form a bit of traditional wisdom. Proverbs form part of the heritage of peoples throughout the world, and there is a version of most well known proverbs in almost all languages. "Curiosity killed the cat" and "A rolling stone gathers no moss" are typical.

Pseudonym or **nom de plume** ("pen name"): fictitious name used by a writer either to conceal his identity or simply because he prefers it. Women writers have often used masculine pen names because they did not think their work would be judged seriously if their sex were known. Some famous writers who used pseudonyms are listed below.

Psyche: heroine of a tale that is probably of Greek origin, but is known through the Latin classic *The Golden Ass* by Apuleius. Psyche is so beautiful that she incites the jealousy of the goddess Venus, who sends her son Cupid to misguide Psyche in love. But Cupid falls in love with her himself. He visits her only at night on the condition that she does not try to behold him. One night Psyche tries to observe him with a lamp while he sleeps. Trembling at his beauty, she spills a drop of oil on him, and Cupid wakes and flees. Psyche, after performing many impossible tasks imposed on her by Venus, is at last granted immortality and reunited with Cupid.

Puck: in English folklore, a hobgoblin, usually of evil intent. In medieval times he became merely a mischievous fairy, often called Robin Goodfellow. The Puck of Shakespeare's *Midsummer Night's Dream* is a mischievous servant of Oberon.

Pun: play on words involving similar- or identical-sounding words with different meanings (one:won). Although the poet Oliver Wendell Holmes called it "the lowest form of wit" and Joseph Addison termed it "false wit," puns have a long tradition.

In early Greek and Hebrew literature, puns on names were believed to have magical properties. Since names determined fate, one could curse the enemy by finding an ominous pun in his name. Shakespeare was fond of puns, both serious and humorous, using them frequently in his plays. A famous pun appears in *Romeo and Juliet,* when Mercutio says, as he is dying, "Ask for me tomorrow and you shall find me a grave man."

The metaphysical poets also made serious use of puns. John Donne, addressing God in "Hymn to God the Father," uses the refrain, "When Thou has done, Thou hast not done . . . ." The phrase can mean either, "When you are finished (forgiving sins), you have not finished," or "When you think you have me (Donne), you still don't have me."

In the 20th century, James Joyce and his followers have continued to make extensive use of puns and other wordplay.

Punch and Judy: puppet show in which the leading characters are Punch, a humpbacked, hook-nosed fellow who does outrageous and tragic things with the utmost nonchalance; his wife Judy, whom he beats to death; and his baby, whom he throws out the window. The origin of Punch is to be found in the clown Punchinello of the old *commedia dell'arte.*

Puss in Boots: folk tale about an animal helper that is known in many versions throughout the world. The best-known version is Charles Perrault's "Le Chat booté" (1697), in which a resourceful cat brings his poor master great wealth and a king's daughter for a wife.

Pygmalion, GM: sculptor who fell in love with a statue of his own creation. Venus intervened, and the statue, Galatea, came to life. The story inspired several literary works, notably George Bernard Shaw's play *Pygmalion* (1913). Shaw's Pygmalion is Henry Higgins, an English speech expert who bets that he can pass off the vulgar Cockney flower girl Eliza Doolittle as an aristocrat by teaching her to speak proper English. He succeeds brilliantly, but is astonished to find that Eliza has acquired her own power over him. This play was the basis for the musical *My Fair Lady* (1956).

Pyramus and Thisbe: story told in Ovid's *Metamorphoses* of two lovers in Babylonia who can only meet and speak through the wall between their houses. On the night they agree to run away together, Thisbe is frightened by

PSEUDONYM	REAL NAME
Sholom Aleichem	Solomon Rabinowitz
Guillaume Apollinaire	Wilhelm Apollinaris de Kostrowitzky
Nicholas Blake	C. Day Lewis
Lewis Carroll	Charles Lutwidge Dodgson
Joseph Conrad	Józef Teodor Konrad Korzeniowski
Isak Dinesen	Karen Blixen
George Eliot	Mary Ann Evans
Anatole France	Jacques Anatole François Thibault
Maxim Gorki	Aleksei Maksimovich Peshkov
O. Henry	William Sydney Porter
John LeCarré	Davis J.M. Carnwell
Katherine Mansfield	Kathleen Mansfield Beauchamp
André Maurois	Émile Herzog
Molière	Jean-Baptiste Poquelin
Frank O'Connor	Michael O'Conovan
George Orwell	Eric Arthur Blair
Ellery Queen	Frederic Dannay and Manfred B. Lee
George Sand	Amandine A.L. Dupin Dudevant
Stendhal	Marie-Henri Beyle
Mark Twain	Samuel L. Clemens
Voltaire	François Marie Arouet

PUNCH AND JUDY: *a 19th-century view of the traditional puppet show characters who turn family violence into laughter.*

a lion and runs away from the meeting place. Pyramus, arriving late, finds her scarf bloodied by the lion, believes she has been killed, and falls upon his sword. Finding him dead, Thisbe also kills herself.

A riotous parody of the story is played by Bottom and his companions in Shakespeare's *Midsummer-Night's Dream.*

Q

Quatrain: See *Stanza.*

R

Ragnarök, N M: the "doom of the gods" and the end of the world. It is described in the visionary poem "Völuspá" (Sibyl's Prophecy) in the Icelandic Poetic Edda. The poem foretells a great battle between the Aesir (a race of good gods) and the forces of evil, led by Hel and Loki. The Fenris Wolf kills Odin and is in turn slain by Vitharr, Odin's son. Thor and the Midgard serpent fight to the death, as do Tyr and Garm (Hel's watchdog), Loki and Heimdall (rainbow bridge watchman). The sun and the earth fall into the sea and the sky is consumed by fire. Later the slain god Balder returns from the dead, and a new and happier cycle of life begins.

Ramayana: 24,000-stanza epic poem of India, probably dating from about the beginning of the Christian Era, and attributed to a poet called Valmiki. It relates the deeds of Rama, a mythological hero, particularly his winning of the beautiful Sita for a wife, the abduction of Sita by a demon king, and his rescue of her.

Rape of the Lock, The: mock-heroic epic by English poet Alexander Pope, published in two cantos in 1712, and in five in 1714. The poem uses all the conventions of the heroic epic—an invocation to the muse; supernatural intervention; and a descent to the underworld—to embellish the story of Lord Petre's theft of a lock of hair from the fashionable belle Belinda.

Raskolnikov, Rodion: See *Crime and Punishment.*

Rasselas: romance by the English man of letters Samuel Johnson, published in 1759. In describing Prince Rasselas's fruitless wanderings in search of happiness, Johnson was leveling an attack against the optimism and simplistic formulas for achieving satisfaction that were prevalent in the 18th century. The work has often been likened to Voltaire's *Candide,* which appeared about the same time.

LE ROUGE
ET LE NOIR
CHRONIQUE DU XIXe SIÈCLE,
PAR M. DE STENDHAL.
TOME PREMIER.
PARIS.
A. LEVAVASSEUR, LIBRAIRE, PALAIS-ROYAL.
1831.

THE RED AND THE BLACK: *an early title page showing the hero Julien Sorel at right.*

Raven, The: poem by U.S. author Edgar Allan Poe, published in 1845. At midnight in his chamber, the poet is visited by an ominous black bird who answers all his questions with a remorseless, "Nevermore."

Realism: in literature, the accurate representation of actual life. A reaction to the excesses of Romanticism, realism appeared, particularly in the novel, in the later part of the 19th century. Realists tended to emphasize character and its effect on motive and action, to write natural-sounding dialogue, and to dwell on details of everyday life. They abandoned such devices as unlikely coincidences, dramatic recognitions, and surprise endings, thus creating novels that were richer in texture, slower in movement, and more logical in development. Among the early masters of realism are the French writers Balzac and Flaubert; the English writers George Eliot, Samuel Butler, and Arnold Bennett; the Russian writers Gogol, Goncharov, Tolstoy, and Chekhov; the U.S. writers William Dean Howells and Mark Twain; and the U.S. expatriate writer Henry James.

Red and the Black, The: novel by the French writer Stendhal, published in 1830. It is a psychological portrait of a social outsider, Julien Sorel, who chooses to rise from his humble origins through a career in the church (the "black" as opposed to the army "red"). Ambitious, romantic, and sensitive, Julien heralded a new type of fictional hero. He ends as a condemned murderer.

Red Badge of Courage, The: novel by U.S. author Stephen Crane, published in 1895, when the author was in his mid 20's. Henry Fleming, a raw country boy, enlists at the outset of the Civil War; the book describes his mental states as he waits for action, his panic under fire, and his final conquest of cowardice through identification with his comrades. It is one of the first books to treat battle realistically rather than as a theater for displays of gallantry; Crane, however, had never been in a war.

Reliques of Ancient English Poetry: collection of traditional ballads, songs, and romances, published in 1765 by the English bishop Thomas Percy. Issued at a time when folk ballads were regarded as crude doggerel, the *Reliques* (or relics) drew the attention of the literary world to their power and artistry. The revival of interest in such folk materials was one of the mainsprings of the 19th-century Romantic movement.

Remembrance of Things Past: series of seven novels by the French writer Marcel Proust, published between 1913 and 1927. The novels are an autobiographical attempt to recapture the past in all its sensory reality. The narrator, beginning with his earliest memory (in *Swann's Way*), moves through free association to the recreation of the sights, scenes, smells, and the vivid personalities that dominated his childhood. He recaptures the novelty of his first love affairs, first ventures into society, social errors, and social successes. In doing so, he creates a portrait of the snobbish, fashionable world of his day and its less elegant underside. The work is a monumental achievement both as an inner portrait of an individual's growth and change, and as an outer portrait of a society in flux. The English titles of the individual novels are *Swann's Way, Within a Budding Grove, The Guermantes Way, Cities of the Plain, The Captive, The Sweet Cheat Gone,* and *The Past Recaptured.*

Remus: See *Romulus and Remus.*

Renascence: poem by U.S. poet Edna St. Vincent Millay, written when she was about 17, and published in 1912 in *The Lyric Year,* a collection of prize-winning poems. The poet begins with a lyrical description of her home on the Maine coast, where she is suddenly overwhelmed by an intense, painful knowledge of the suffering in the world; in death, she remembers the beauty of the living world and is reborn with a deeper love and understanding of life.

Republic, The: major dialogue by the Greek philosopher Plato; an inquiry into the nature of justice. Seeking to define justice, Socrates proposes the analogy of a perfect society in which justice prevails, thus providing the first literary description of utopia (a term coined later by Sir Thomas More). He describes in detail the education of the guardians (or ruling class), and proposes, among other things, equality of the sexes, eugenic breeding, and children held in common. The dialogue contains the famous parable of the cave, in which chained prisoners attempt to interpret passing shadows. The image is a metaphor for the phenomenal world we inhabit, a mere shadow of the real world.

Restoration: period of English history beginning in 1660 when Charles II was reestablished on the throne. After the 20-year Puritan revolution, literature and drama came back into favor, and the light spirit of comedy replaced the solemnity preferred by the Puritan rulers. Among the comic dramatists of the age were William Congreve and William Wycherly, whose polished, somewhat cynical comedies of manners have remained in the English theatrical repertoire for 300 years.

The greatest literary name of the era was John Dryden. He, too, was an active dramatist, but he is best remembered for his literary criticism ("Essay on Dramatic Poetry") and his accomplished verse translations (the works of Vergil). Dryden's broad and generous appreciation of the literature of the past set the stage for the neoclassical age of Pope and Swift.

Return of the Native, The: sixth novel of English author Thomas Hardy, published in 1878. Clym Yeobright, who has been in Paris, returns to the Wessex village in which he was born, planning to open a school and improve local conditions. His decision disappoints his mother's hopes, and she is alarmed when he falls in love with Eustacia Vye, an exotic, restless, and dissatisfied girl. An aura of fateful tragedy broods over their relationship. Clym's mother meets an accidental death, Eustacia drowns herself, and Clym, his sight impaired, finds his vocation as an itinerant preacher and lecturer.

Reynard the Fox: hero of a series of fables about beasts, widely told in France, Germany, Holland, and England during the Middle Ages. The animals behave like men and are often intended as satirical portraits of knights, clergy, or nobles. The characters include Reynard the Fox, Bruin the Bear, Noble the Lion, Baldwin the Ass, Tibert the Cat, Isengrim the Wolf, Grimbert the Badger, Chanticleer the Cock, Partlet the Hen, and various others. In all the versions, Reynard is a trickster, representing the triumph of brains over brawn.

RIME OF THE ANCIENT MARINER: *Gustave Doré's 19th-century view of the cursed ship in Coleridge's great Romantic poem.*

Rhinegold or **Rheingold:** in Germanic legend, the cursed treasure of the Nibelungs. See also *Nibelungenlied.*

Rhinoceros: play by the Rumanian-born French dramatist, Eugène Ionesco. Performed in 1960, it is a work in the tradition of the theater of the absurd. At first it seems strange when some characters in the play turn into rhinoceroses, but in time it becomes the thing to do. The main character, Bèranger, becomes an outcast because he does not conform.

Rhyme: correspondence in sound between two accented syllables, as in the words *believe/ deceive.* In poetry, the usual rhyme is end-rhyme, a correspondence between the final feet of two or more lines, but internal rhyme (rhyme within the line) is also common, as in the Tennyson line, "The splendor falls on castle walls."

Rhyme royal: See *Stanza.*

Rhythm: in prosody, the cadence of verse, dependent upon a succession of long and short syllables. See also *Foot; Meter.*

Richard II: historical tragedy by Shakespeare, dated 1595. The drama centers on the conflict between the young, spoiled, irresponsible King Richard and his forceful, ambitious cousin Henry Bolingbroke. After the death of Bolingbroke's father, John of Gaunt, Richard confiscates the family lands; Bolingbroke invades England while Richard is away, imprisons him on his return, and assumes the throne as Henry IV. Richard is then murdered by one of Henry's followers. Shakespeare's source for the play was Holinshed's *Chronicles.*

Richard III: historical tragedy by Shakespeare, written about 1594. It deals with the hunchbacked Richard of York, who ensures his succession to the throne by murder, marriage, and political intrigue. After the death of Edward IV, Richard imprisons and later orders the murders of Edward's two young sons (the "little princes in the Tower"), whose guardian he is supposed to be. Meanwhile the rival House of Lancaster has gathered adherents, and the earl of Richmond (Henry Tudor) leads the invading army. Richard, vainly seeking a horse, is killed at the battle of Bosworth Field by Richmond (the future Henry VII, first Tudor king of England).

Shakespeare's portrayal of Richard as a villian whose character is as twisted as his back was immensely popular in Tudor England; it gave Richard a reputation for evil that cannot be wholly sustained by historical fact.

Riders to the Sea: one-act play by John Millington Synge, first performed in Dublin in 1904; one of the finest achievements of the Irish literary renaissance. A starkly tragic play, it pictures a day in an Aran Island fishing village. The old woman Maurya, who has lost four sons at sea, sees her youngest son Bartley brought home drowned.

Right You Are If You Think You Are: play by Italian dramatist Luigi Pirandello, performed in 1917. Signor Ponza and his mother-in-law Signora Frola give their accounts of the marriage of Ponza to Signora Frola's daughter. The audience is teased by conflicting stories throughout the play and left bewildered at the end.

Rime of the Ancient Mariner, The: ballad in archaic style by English Romantic poet Samuel Taylor Coleridge, published in his and Wordsworth's *Lyrical Ballads* (1798). A hoary-headed old mariner detains a wedding guest with his grisly tale of a ship blown off course to the South Pole, then saved by an albatross that brings good luck and a south wind. But the mariner shoots the albatross, dooming the ship, and the bird is hung around his neck as a punishment. The ship drifts into a blazing sea around the equator; all die but the ancient mariner, who belongs to Life-in-Death. The mariner's torture finally ends, and the albatross falls into the sea, when he inadvertently blesses the water creatures. He is finally rescued, but his experience compels him to wander and tell his tale.

Ring and the Book, The: dramatic poem by English poet Robert Browning; the longest of his works, it was published in twelve books in 1868–1869. It deals with an actual murder trial in 17th-century Rome. The events of the tragedy are explained in the poem from many different points of view. The condemned man has his last words, but the reader does not know which of the many versions is the truth.

Ring of the Nibelung: See *Nibelungenlied.*

Rip Van Winkle: short story by U.S. author Washington Irving, published in seven parts in his *Sketch Book of Geoffrey Crayon,* 1819–1820. Rip, a good-natured likable ne'er-do-well, goes hunting one day and meets a strange, dwarfish man who leads him into the Catskills, where a group of little men are playing ninepins. Rip drinks the liquor they offer him and falls asleep; he wakes 20 years later to find himself an old man with a long white beard. Back in his village, he discovers that his wife is dead, his daughter has married, and a republic has been established.

Rise of Silas Lapham, The: novel by the U.S. realist William Dean Howells, published in 1885. Silas Lapham, a wealthy paint manufacturer, is a self-made man who attempts to provide advantages for his daughters by building a new house in Boston's exclusive Back Bay area. But the family meets with a cold reception from proper Bostonians, and their discomfort is increased by Lapham's social errors. Though the book ends with the loss of his fortune, Lapham has risen in the sense that he has learned to maintain complete integrity in business.

Rivals, The: lively comedy by English dramatist Richard Brinsley Sheridan, produced in 1775, when its author was 24. In order to satisfy the romantic expectations of Lydia Languish, Captain Jack Absolute woos her in the guise of a penniless Ensign Beverley. When Lydia learns that Beverley is actually the wealthy suitor that her aunt, Mrs. Malaprop, has chosen for her, she spurns him. Meanwhile, Bob Acres, also in love with Lydia, has challenged Ensign Beverley to a duel. When he reaches the field of honor and discovers the ensign to be his friend Jack Absolute, he renounces all claims to Lydia. Absolute's willingness to fight a duel over Lydia satisfies her romantic notions and she agrees to marry him. The brisk action and clever dialogue of this play have brought it continued popularity.

Robbers, The: tragedy by the German poet Friedrich Schiller, performed in 1782. It is a product of the *Sturm und Drang* period and considered the greatest success of the German Romantic theater. It deals with two brothers: Franz von Moor, who usurps his brother's inheritance and fiancée, and Karl von Moor, who becomes the outlaw leader of a robber band. In the end, Franz commits suicide and Karl surrenders to the authorities.

Robin Hood: romantic outlaw of English ballad and legend who lived with his merry companions—Little John, Friar Tuck, Will Scarlet, Allan-a-Dale, Will Stutly, and Maid Marian— in the greenery of Sherwood Forest in Nottinghamshire. Robin and his men were robbers with a difference: they waylaid rich travelers and distributed the bounty among the poor; they particularly delighted in outwitting their chief adversary, the sheriff of Nottingham. Robin himself was renowned for courage, generosity, chivalry, and marvelous skill in archery. There was probably a historical Robin Hood, perhaps in the twelfth century, but attempts to identify him with various individuals are not conclusive.

Robinson Crusoe: fictional narrative by the English journalist Daniel Defoe, published in 1719; one of the most famous adventure stories ever written. Robinson Crusoe, sole survivor of a shipwreck, is cast away upon a deserted island, with only his native wits and the gifts of fortune to save him from starvation. He first rescues from the wrecked vessel tools and provisions; next he organizes his time and energy, builds a home, plants crops, and tames wild creatures. At last Crusoe sees the print of a human foot on the sand. The footprint is that of a savage whom Crusoe names Friday and adopts as a servant. The island is invaded by savages and later by European sailors; all of Crusoe's resourcefulness is needed to save his life, but he eventually masters the situation and sails back to England in prosperity.

Rochester, Edward Fairfax: See *Jane Eyre.*

Roderick Random, The Adventures of: picaresque by English author Tobias Smollett, published in 1748; im-

ROBINSON CRUSOE: *an early illustration from a Dutch edition of this world classic.*

CULVER PICTURES

portant for its descriptions of 18th-century British navy life as it relates to the adventures of the penniless Roderick Random, who makes his fortune, aided and thwarted by surprising coincidences common to the genre. See also *Picaresque.*

Roland: nephew of Charlemagne and the most famous of his paladins. The *Chanson de Roland* is the greatest of French heroic epics. It celebrates Roland's friendship with Oliver, whom he first meets as an adversary in battle. The two are so equal in arms that neither can defeat the other, and in mutual admiration they become brothers and companions. In Charlemagne's expedition into Spain against the Saracens (778), Roland distinguishes himself as a champion of Christianity. When the army is returning through the Pyrenees, Ganelon, the traitor, has Roland put in charge of the rear guard. In the pass at Roncesvalles they are outnumbered by a horde of Saracens. The main army is already far in advance, but not beyond the sound of Roland's magic horn, called Oliphant. Oliver begs him three times to sound the horn for help, but Roland is too proud; when he at last consents to call for help, it is too late. Charlemagne hears the horn and hastens back to find his favorite warriors dead. He falls with wrath upon the Saracen army and destroys it to a man. Ganelon is examined and, discovered in his treacherous scheme, he is put to death.

Roman à clef (literally, "novel with a key"): work that portrays actual, well known people in the disguise of fictional characters. It may be read simply as a story by those who do not have the "key," but it has an additional dimension of interest for those who do. For an example, see entry on *Point Counter Point.* Many best-selling popular novels, especially those about the worlds of show business and politics are considered *romans à clef.*

Romance: form of vernacular story, originally in verse but later in prose, that developed first in France in the twelfth century and spread through Europe. (The word *romance* originally meant vernacular.) Medieval romances dealt with knights, deeds of chivalry, and courtly love; they differed from earlier epics in their lack of moral grandeur and seriousness, their episodic, digressive structure, and their subjectivity. Romances are often replete with magical events, fairies, dragons, wizards, and enchantment. The three main subjects or "matters" (*matières*) of romance are the "matter of France" (tales of Charlemagne and his twelve noble peers); the "matter of Britain" (King Arthur and his knights); and the "matter of Rome" (all ancient tales, whether Greek or Roman).

In modern fiction, novels that freely idealize and are little concerned with realism are called romances.

Romanticism: in the arts, a movement that swept Europe in the late 18th and early 19th centuries, in revolt against the rational ideals of the Enlightenment. The characteristics of the Romantic movement were many and often contradictory; no one artist or work of art embodies all of them. In general, Romanticism celebrated the intuitive, the irrational, the spontaneous, and the free. Romantic poets abandoned the formal rules demanded by the classical genres to express themselves in simple lyricism. They sought inspiration in nature and in native folk songs, but most of all in themselves. Thus, the cult of the artist and the individual was born.

The movement had its origins in Germany and England, where the hold of rigidly classical French culture was less tenacious. As its influence spread, its emphasis on freedom and individuality was extended to social and political causes. Nations, like individuals, discovered and developed their distinctive personalities. The literatures of many emergent nations, including Russia and the United States, were first developed under the impact of Romanticism.

The chief writers associated with early Romantic literature are Goethe and Schiller (Germany); Wordsworth, Coleridge, Shelley, Byron, Keats, and Scott (England); Chateaubriand and Hugo (France); and Poe, Emerson, Hawthorne, Melville, and Whitman (U.S.).

ROMEO AND JULIET: *Juliet prepares to kill herself in the 1968 film version of the play. She has discovered that Romeo, having mistaken her unconscious body for dead, has killed himself in grief.*

Romeo and Juliet: tragedy by Shakespeare, dated 1595–1596. Set in medieval Verona, it deals with a pair of "star-crossed lovers" who become the victims of an ancient and deadly feud between their families, the Montagues and the Capulets. Their secret marriage and plans to run away end in tragic misunderstanding, and both commit suicide. The shock causes their grief-stricken families to make a tardy peace.

Romulus and Remus: legendary founders of Rome; Romulus was supposed to have been its first king. They were twin sons of Mars and Rhea Silvia (Ilia). As infants, they were cast into the river Tiber by Amulius, Rhea's uncle, who had usurped her father's throne. The twins were found suckled by a she-wolf, then fostered by hill shepherds. In later years, they found their grandfather and restored him to his throne after killing Amulius. They decided to found a new city on the spot where the she-wolf had found them; Romulus, whom prophecies named as first king, began building a wall on the site. Remus, ridiculing him, leaped over the first stones, and Romulus killed him.

Rosinante: in *Don Quixote,* the tired, old, swaybacked, raw-boned horse on which the hero rode out to his adventures.

Rubáiyát, The ("the quatrains"): verses by Omar Khayyám, a Persian philosopher and poet of the late eleventh and early twelfth centuries A.D. The verses record melancholy reflections upon life in vivid and simple figures, likening existence to a day's rest in a journey, or man to a clay pot. The prevailing reflection is that since life is brief and the future uncertain, one should enjoy the present with feast and song. The quatrains are known in the West through a very free translation (1859) by the English poet Edward FitzGerald.

Rumpelstiltskin: dwarf in a folk tale known in many European stories under a variety of names. For helping the heroine spin flax into gold, he demands her firstborn child, but he agrees to let her keep it if she can guess his name within three days. When the heroine manages to discover his name, he destroys himself in a temper tantrum. The version best known is from *Grimm's Fairy Tales.*

Runes: alphabet used to write Germanic languages before the Latin alphabet was adapted for that purpose. Gothic tribes in Germany used runes for writing as early as 300 A.D., but they were most widely used during Viking times in Scandinavia, where many stones for monuments with runic inscriptions are still standing. In England, a modified runic alphabet was used by the Anglo-Saxons before the Norman conquest.

S

Sabines: early Italian tribe chiefly remembered for an event in Roman legendary history known as "the rape of the Sabines." In order to provide wives for his followers, Romulus, the legendary founder of Rome, invited his Sabine neighbors to a festival, during which his men kidnapped their women. The Sabines were, in fact, conquered and assimilated by the Romans in the early third century B.C.

Saga: strictly, an Icelandic prose narrative written between the twelfth and 15th centuries. Some sagas deal with the histories of Norwegian kings or the adventures of legendary heroes, but the most distinctive kind are the Family or Icelanders' sagas, which trace the histories of the early settlers of Iceland in the tenth and eleventh centuries. These artistically structured narratives are remarkable for their realism and vivid characterization. The word *saga* is now loosely applied to other long prose works, but particularly to family chronicles, such as Galsworthy's *Forsyte Saga.*

Saint Joan: play by the Anglo-Irish writer George Bernard Shaw, presented in 1923. Shaw portrays the 18-year-old Maid of Orleans as an early nationalist, a military genius on the order of Napoleon, and a feminist who demands the right to play a man's role. He views her execution as the inevitable fate of the truly superior person who, except in critical times, cannot be assimilated into society.

Samson Agonistes: play by the English poet John Milton, published in 1671. It is modeled on the Greek tragedies and intended for reading rather than performance. It focuses on the spiritual agony that Samson endures on finding himself "Eyeless in Gaza at the mill with slaves." Its climax is the return of Samson's physical and spiritual strength, and his destruction of the Philistines as they are mocking him in their temple.

Satan: See *Devil.*

Satire: in literature, any composition—whether verse, prose, or drama—that uses irony and wit in a sustained and systematic manner to criticize human and social weaknesses. Satire ranges from urbane and polite mockery to extremely bitter indictments of human morality, such as those for which the Roman poet Juvenal (c 60–130 A.D.) is famous. Jonathan Swift's *Gulliver's Travels* and George Orwell's *Animal Farm* are other powerful social satires.

Saturn, RM: ancient Italian god of the planting season and agriculture for who Saturday is named. He became identified with the Greek Cronus as father of the gods, and was supposed to have reigned benevolently in Italy during the Golden Age. His festival, the Saturnalia, celebrated in December, was a feast of liberation from business, social obligation, and moral restraints. Its spirit lingers on in the celebrations of pre-Lenten carnivals and New Year's Eve.

Satyrs, GM: minor woodland gods, having human forms but the horns and legs of goats or, sometimes the tails and ears of horses. Renowned for lechery, satyrs were descendants of Silenus and companions of Dionysus. At the great dramatic festival celebrated in Athens in honor of Dionysus, a satyr play, apparently a coarse farce, was presented by a tragic poet after a trilogy of tragedies. Only one of these plays, Euripides' *Cyclops,* survives in its entirety. See also *Faun; Pan.*

Scarlet Letter: novel by U.S. author Nathaniel Hawthorne, published in 1850, considered the first great American novel. Set in the Puritan era of 17th-century Boston, it deals with the scarlet *A* that the heroine, Hester Prynne, is forced to wear as a mark of her adultery. Though she and her illegitimate daughter Pearl live as outcasts, Hester refuses to name the child's father. Hester's husband suspects the earnest minister Arthur Dimmesdale and, through a game of cat and mouse, finally breaks him down; Dimmesdale publicly confesses his guilt and bares his chest to reveal a scarlet *A* imprinted on it.

SCARLET LETTER: *Hester Prynne is subjected to public exposure for her adultery.*

Scarlett O'Hara: See *Gone with the Wind.*

School for Scandal, The: play by the Anglo-Irish dramatist Richard Brinsley Sheridan, performed in 1777. Its satire is essentially moral, directed against hypocrisy and pretense. Its complicated plot, played out against a background of gossip and fashionable tittle-tattle, exposes Joseph Surface's duplicity in trying to win the considerable fortune of Maria, ward to Sir Peter Teazle, by making advances to Sir Peter's much younger, inexperienced wife. In the end, Joseph is found out; his generous cousin Charles is rewarded with Maria's hand; and Lady Teazle, having learned a lesson about life's real values, is reconciled with her husband. The play, one of the most popular in the English language, is often revived.

Scrooge: See *Christmas Carol, A.*

Scylla, GM: monster who lived in a rock in the strait between Italy and Sicily, opposite the dreaded whirlpool Charybdis. Scylla originally was a nymph loved by the sea god Glaucus, who begged the enchantress Circe for a charm to melt her indifference. But Circe, herself in love with Glaucus, poisoned Scylla's bath with herbs, transforming her into a monster with six heads (each with triple rows of teeth) and twelve feet. In despair, Scylla hurled herself into the sea and settled opposite Charybdis. The strait between them became a deadly passage for mariners such as Odysseus, one of the few who managed a safe passage through it. Choosing "between Scylla and Charybdis," therefore, means choosing between two equally dangerous hazards.

Seagull, The: play by the Russian writer Anton Chekhov, presented in 1896. It introduced a new style of understated, undramatic realism to the theater. Its theme is the mystery of art.

Arkadina, a celebrated actress, needs, above everything else, to keep her beauty and the center of the stage. Her lover, the novelist Trigorin, lives his life in order to write about it. Her young son Konstantin, struggling to become a writer, is bombarded with foolish advice; and Nina, the girl he loves, longs to experience life in order to become a great actress. Nina falls in love with Trigorin and becomes his mistress, providing him some new material. When he abandons her, she perseveres in her art, acting with a shoddy touring company, but Konstantin, despite his success as a writer, kills himself in grief over Nina's fate.

Season in Hell, A: prose poem by the French poet Arthur Rimbaud, published in 1873. In this tortured, allegorical autobiography, the 19-year-old poet celebrates himself as an outcast and one of the damned. After writing it, he burned the rest of his manuscripts and abandoned poetry.

Self-Reliance: essay by U.S. transcendentalist philosopher Ralph Waldo Emerson, published in 1841; his most popular and representative work. Its theme is the Romantic credo of individuality: "Trust thyself." Its message is that each person must trust his own instincts, even (perhaps especially) when they do not conform to the common opinion of society, "Else tomorrow a stranger will say with masterly good sense precisely what we have thought. . . ." The work contains many of Emerson's most quoted aphorisms, such as ". . . consistency is the hobgoblin of little minds. . . ."

Semele: See *Dionysus.*

Sense and Sensibility: novel by English author Jane Austen, published in 1811. Here, as in her other books, Austen paints with incomparable fidelity the middle-class English life she knew. The story reveals the nice distinction between sense and sensibility (or sentimentality) in the characters of the sisters Elinor and Marianne Dashwood. Although both are disappointed in love, Elinor keeps her balance while Marianne's emotionalism lands her in an embarrassing position. Both eventually find happiness, but Elinor manages it without even losing her dignity temporarily.

Sentimental Education, A: novel by French realist Gustave Flaubert, published in 1869. A young man from the provinces, Frédéric Moreau, supported by a wealthy and adoring mother, comes to Paris to prepare for a distinguished career. He falls in love with Mme. Arnoux, the virtuous wife of an unscrupulous art dealer. While waiting for something to come of this, Frédéric fails his examinations, drifts into casual affairs, and starts projects that he forgets to finish. Great events occur; a revolution takes place and the monarchy topples; but Frédéric's mind is elsewhere. When Mme. Arnoux finally turns to him, he is repelled by the realization that she is by then a woman of 50. Like Flaubert's *Madame Bovary,* this novel depicts the painful contrast between subjective life and objective reality.

Sentimental Journey Through France and Italy, A: fanciful sketches of continental wanderings by the pioneer English novelist Laurence Sterne, published in 1768, just before his death. The hero of the work is the whimsical Parson Yorick, who appeared in *Tristram Shandy,* Sterne's earlier novel. The book was influential in establishing the fashion for the sentimental novel and the cult of sensibility throughout Europe.

Separate Peace, A: novel by the U.S. writer John Knowles, published in 1959; it deals with the competitive friendship of two adolescent boys in a prep school. The narrator, Gene, though intelligent and able, envies the natural grace and reckless courage of his friend, Finny. As his envy deepens into suspicion that Finny's inspired zaniness is actually calculated to bring about his downfall, their relationship assumes the aspect of a deadly contest that only one of them can survive.

Seven Against Thebes: tragedy by the Greek dramatist Aeschylus, dating from 467 B.C. It is about the fratricidal struggle of Polynices and Eteocles, the sons of Oedipus, for possession of their father's throne at Thebes. Eteocles is ruling Thebes, after having usurped the throne that he and his brother were to have shared. Argive supporters of Polynices lead an attack against each of the gates of Thebes, one after another and, one by one, they are repulsed. But at the seventh gate the attacker is Polynices, whom Eteocles meets in a combat that is fatal to both but that preserves the city.

Sherlock Holmes: most famous detective in literature, created by English physician and writer Sir Arthur Conan Doyle, whose stories about Holmes appeared from 1887 to 1927. To his admirers, Holmes in his lodgings at 221-B Baker Street, London, was as real as any contemporary celebrity—with his dressing gown, his deerstalker cap, his moody violin playing and cocaine habit, and his admiring companion Dr. Watson, who recorded his exploits. Some of the best known of his adventures, are "A Study in Scarlet" (1887), "A Scandal in Bohemia," and "The Hound of the Baskervilles" (1902).

Sherwood Forest: ancient forest in Nottinghamshire, England, famous as the hideout of the legendary robber Robin Hood and his merry men. It was once a royal forest, but much of the area is now heathland.

She Stoops to Conquer: comedy by English dramatist Oliver Goldsmith, presented in 1773. Marlow, a bashful young man, is on his way to the estate of Mr. Hardcastle to examine Hardcastle's daughter as a potential wife. In jest, Tony Lumpkin, the squire's son, tells him that the estate is an inn, and he therefore proceeds to treat Hardcastle as an innkeeper and his daughter Kate as a barmaid. Kate, sensing that Marlow likes her that way, allows the deception to continue; thus "she stoops to conquer" and gains a husband.

Short story: brief, fictional prose composition, usually involving a limited number of characters in a single illuminating incident, or creating a single intense effect or mood through the ac-

SHORT STORY: *O. Henry was one of the most successful short story writers.*

cumulation of impressions. The Romantic movement brought early examples of the form with the stories of E.T.A. Hoffmann and J. L. Tieck in Germany, and Poe and Hawthorne in the United States. The modern realistic short story, dealing with representative characters and incidents from everyday life, was perfected by the French writer Guy de Maupassant. Russian writer Anton Chekhov freed the story from self-containment and plot. In deceptively formless sketches, he was able to create stories that suggested a great deal more than they said, and whose characters seemed to have a continuing life beyond the confines of the pages.

In the United States at the turn of the century, short stories by Mark Twain, Bret Harte, and Jack London were still reminiscent of the plot-centered tale. The surpise-ending stories of O. Henry depended exclusively on plot. The stories of Hamlin Garland, Stephen Crane, Henry James, and Sherwood Anderson aimed for different kinds of realism. Since then, many major U.S. writers, including Hemingway, Faulkner, and Fitzgerald, have written distinguished short stories. U.S. writers who have made the short story a major form of expression include J.D. Salinger, John Updike, Katherine Anne Porter, Flannery O'Connor, Eudora Welty, John Cheever, and John O'Hara.

Shropshire Lad, A: first book of poems by the English poet A. E. Housman, published in 1896. These lyrics, in their simplicity of form and spareness of phrasing, introduced a new speech to English poetry. Their tone is overwhelmingly nostalgic and elegiac; they deal with the passing of youth, and the transience of love and glory.

Shylock: See *Merchant of Venice.*

Sibyls, GRM: inspired prophetesses. Of ten sibyls, the Cumaean, the Delphian, and the Erythraean were the most famous. The Sibylline Books, containing prophetic sayings written by the sibyls, were kept in the temple of Jupiter at Rome and consulted in times of national danger. They were lost when the capital burned in 82 B.C.

Siege Perilous: seat at Arthur's Round Table in which it was perilous for any knight to sit except the one destined to achieve the quest of the Holy Grail. When Galahad arrived at Arthur's court, he was able to take his place unharmed in the Siege Perilous.

Siegfried: See *Nibelungenlied.*

Sigurd: See *Völsunga Saga.*

Silas Marner: novel by English author George Eliot, published in 1861. Silas is a lonely weaver, an outcast of society, whose only pleasure is counting his money until one day, after it has been stolen, he finds an infant girl in the snow. He raises Eppie as his daughter and his benumbed natural feelings come alive. Many years later, the mystery of the theft and the secret of Eppie's parentage are revealed. Though she is the daughter of the village squire, she refuses to leave Silas to join her natural father.

Silent Don, The: historical chronicle by Soviet writer Mikhail Sholokhov, in which the Don River follows its natural course, but the people who live on its banks are caught in the upheaval of sweeping events. It tells of the Don Cossacks, and of one in particular, Gregor Melekhov, during World War I, the Russian Revolution, and the ensuing civil war. *The Silent Don* (also translated as *The Quiet Don*) was originally published in four volumes between 1928 and 1940, and was translated into English as two volumes, *And Quiet Flows the Don* (1934) and *The Don Flows Home to the Sea* (1940).

Silver Age: See *Golden Age.*

Simile: See *Figures of speech.*

Sindbad (or **Sinbad**) **the Sailor:** merchant of Baghdad whose adventures are related in *The Arabian Nights' Entertainments.* Sindbad embarks on seven voyages and, like Odysseus, encounters many marvels, including the Roc, a gigantic bird; the furry Old Man of the Sea; and a valley where huge black snakes guard rocks of diamond. In each voyage he risks a grave danger for a great reward and returns home triumphantly with his riches.

Sirens, GM: group of sea nymphs whose singing was so sweet that sailors, hearing it, leapt into the sea and were drowned. Homer says there were two sirens; later writers mention three and sometimes describe them as women with the bodies of birds. Odysseus, warned against them by Circe, plugged the ears of his sailors with wax and had himself lasted to the mast with orders to his men not to free him, no matter how desperate his signals. Thus Odysseus and his companions sailed safely by. The Argonauts escaped the sirens only because Orpheus was on board and played sweeter and more magical music than theirs. After these failures, the sirens drowned themselves.

Sir Gawain and the Green Knight: Middle English verse romance known from a 14th-century manuscript that is ascribed to "The Pearl poet." It is regarded as the gem of romance literature. The mysterious Green Knight offers to let Gawain behead him on condition that he be allowed to behead Gawain in return. Gawain accepts this challenge, and cuts off the Green Knight's head. But the Green Knight picks up his head and puts it back on, making an appointment to meet Gawain the following year. Gawain keeps his bargain and, for having passed this test of courage, his life is spared.

Sirius, GM: dog of the hunter Orion, set in the sky as the constellation Canis Major. Sirius, also called the Dog Star, is the brightest star in the heavens. The period during July and August when Sirius rises at the same time as the sun was called the "dog days" by the ancients, who reckoned this period to be the hottest and unhealthiest of the year.

Sister Carrie: novel by U.S. author Theodore Dreiser, published in 1900; a naturalitstic story of Carrie Meeber, who comes to Chicago from a Wisconsin farm. After a short stint as a wage slave, she is easily persuaded to become the mistress of a salesman, Drouet, and enjoys the modest comfort and finery he provides. Drouet is soon replaced by Hurstwood, a respectable man who deserts his wife and family to take Carrie to New York. Hurstwood's attempt to reestablish himself in business does not succeed and, while Carrie finds a career on stage, he steadily deteriorates and commits suicide. Because Dreiser presented the story without moral condemnation of its characters, the novel caused such an outcry that it was withdrawn by its original publisher.

Sisyphus, GM: wily king of Corinth. For his general wickedness and, according to some sources, an offense against Zeus, his punishment in Hades was to roll a huge rock to the top of a hill; just before he reached the top, the rock would roll down again, and he would have to begin anew.

In *The Myth of Sisyphus* (1942) by French existentialist philosopher Albert Camus, this legend becomes a metaphor for modern man, whose tasks are equally futile or absurd. The essay examines suicide as a logical way out of a hopeless and meaningless existence, but finds a justification for living in the struggle itself.

Six Characters in Search of an Author: experimental play by the Italian dramatist Luigi Pirandello, presented in 1921. It becomes a dramatization of the act of creating a play. While rehearsing in a theater, a director is interrupted by six characters who have never been put into a story. They demand to act out their life histories. Their complicated affairs and inconsistent actions prove too unwieldy for the director to manage, and he dismissess them, but not with complete success.

Sketch Book of Geoffrey Crayon, Gent., The: collection of sketches and tales by the U.S. writer Washington Irving, published in 1819–1820. For its best-known stories, see *Rip Van Winkle* and *Legend of Sleepy Hollow.*

Slaughterhouse-Five, subtitled "The Children's Crusade": novel by the U.S. writer Kurt Vonnegut, Jr., published in 1969. Billy Pilgrim, a prisoner of war in Dresden and witness to the city's destruction by firebombing in World War II, tells a story that is both a war novel and a work of science fiction. Pilgrim describes the destruction and moves back and forth in time, connecting it to his life before and after.

Sleeping Beauty: folk tale that involves a slighted fairy who condemns a newborn princess to a long sleep that will begin with a prick of her finger. She can be awakened only by the kiss of a prince. The best-known versions are the Brothers Grimm's "Little Briar Rose" and Charles Perrault's *La Belle au bois dormant."* It is the subject of a popular ballet by Tchaikovsky.

Snow Country: best-known novel of the Nobel Prize-winning Japanese author Kawabata Yasunari, published in 1947. It is a slight story about the relationship of a rather cold, intellectual city gentleman with a naive geisha girl whom he meets at a remote hot springs resort. In a series of indelible scenes that have the quality of Japanese brush stokes, their meeting and parting is portrayed against a background world of snow and hot springs.

Socialist realism: officially approved style for art and literature in the Soviet Union and its satellites since 1932, except for a brief period of relaxation, the Thaw, that occured after the death of Stalin. According to this doctrine, a work of art or literature must reflect socialist ideals and convince the people to become better Communists. Some excellent writers—such as Maxim Gorki, Mikhail Sholokhov, Yevgeny Yevtushenko, and the East German Bertolt Brecht—have been considered socialist realists, but even their work, in some respects, falls outside its bounds. Most officially approved writers have been mediocre. The Soviet government has frequently battled with gifted writers who have been unable or unwilling to adhere to socialist realism.

Songs of Innocence and of Experience: two companion series of poems by English writer, artist, and mystic William Blake, notable for their imagery, symbolism, and lyrical beauty. They first appeared together in 1794, with illuminated engravings by Blake and the subtitle "Shewing the Two Contrary States of the Human Soul"; the poems in the two series contrast the joyful, innocent view of a child with a mature view of the realities of human experience and pain.

SONGS OF INNOCENCE: *a page with Blake's own illustration.*

METROPOLITAN MUSEUM OF ART, ROGERS FUND, 1917

PETRARCHAN SONNET

To one who has been long in city pent
'Tis very sweet to look into the fair
And open face of heaven—to breathe a prayer
Full in the smile of the blue firmament.
Who is more happy, when, with heart's content,
Fatigued he sinks into some pleasant lair
Of wavy grass, and reads a debonair
And gentle tale of love and languishment?

Returning home at evening, with an ear
Catching the notes of Philomel—an eye
Watching the sailing cloudlet's bright career,
He mourns that day so soon has glided by:
E'en like the passage of an angel's tear
That falls through the ether silently.

John Keats

SHAKESPEAREAN SONNET

When to the sessions of sweet silent thought
I summon up remembrance of things past,
I sigh the lack of many a thing I sought,
And with old woes new wail my dear time's waste.
Then can I drown an eye, unused to flow,
For precious friends hid in death's dateless night,
And weep afresh love's long since canceled woe,
And moan the expense of many a vanished sight.
Then can I grieve at grievances foregone,
And heavily from woe to woe tell o'er
The sad account of fore-bemoanéd moan,
Which I new pay as if not paid before.

But if the while I think on thee, dear friend,
All losses are restored and sorrows end.

Wm. Shakespeare

Sonnet: poem of 14 lines (customarily in iambic pentameter), arranged in accordance with a prescribed rhyming scheme. There are two standard forms, the Italian (or Petrarchan) and the Shakespearean (or English). They differ chiefly in that the Italian sonnet uses the first eight lines (the octet) to expose the theme, and the six remaining lines (the sestet) to resolve it, while the Shakespearean sonnet is often divided into three quatrains and ends with a summary rhymed couplet.

Sonnets from the Portuguese: sonnet sequences by English poet Elizabeth Barrett Browning, published in 1850; the artistic expression of her love for Robert Browning prior to their marriage. It contains the famous sonnet, "How do I love thee? Let me count the ways."

Sons and Lovers: autobiographical novel by English writer D. H. Lawrence, published in 1913, and considered by many his finest work. The hero, Paul Morel, is the son of a coal miner and a remarkable woman who, disappointed in her marriage, transfers her affections to her son and encourages his artistic gifts. Paul grows up and becomes involved with two women, but neither of them satisfies the expectations from love that have been created by his mother. When his mother suffers agony from cancer, Paul gives her an overdose of morphine. After her death he contemplates suicide, but eventually discovers the will to live without her.

Sorrows of Young Werther, The: novel by the German author Johann Wolfgang von Goethe, first published in 1774. The work represents Goethe's initial Romantic phase, which he later repudiated; it expressed the yearnings of young German Romantics and inspired numerous similar works and even some imitative suicides. Werther, an artistic youth, falls in love with Charlotte (Lotte), a rather conventional girl who is engaged to Albert, a decent but complacent young man. Werther's attempts to renounce Lotte, even after her marriage to Albert, prove futile. Their settled, bourgeois marriage enrages him, and his melancholy moods make the newlyweds so uncomfortable that they suggest that he cease his visits. After borrowing a pistol from Albert on the pretext of a journey, Werther shoots himself.

Sound and the Fury, The: novel by U.S. author William Faulkner, published in 1929. It is the story of the last stages in the decline of a once-proud Southern family, the Compsons. The story is told in an involved fashion that skips back and forth in time through the complex interior monologues of the three Compson brothers: Benjy, an idiot, protected by his brother Quentin and sister Caddy; Quentin, overbred and oversensitive, who loves his sister too well and commits suicide; and the "practical" Jason, free from the family's self-destructive notions of honor and gallantry, who survives disaster to lead a respectable, money-grubbing life. Caddy, the sister, is central in the thoughts of her brothers; she has left town in disgrace, leaving her illegitimate daughter, also named Quentin, behind. Another central figure in the monologues and in the final narrative section of the book is the black cook Dilsey.

Spectator: 18th-century London journal, written chiefly by Joseph Addison and Richard Steele, with a few other contributors. The *Spectator* appeared from 1711 to 1712 and in 1714, following in the wake of the *Tatler,* which had a successful run from 1709 to 1711, and which was also chiefly written by Addison and Steele. The *Spectator* offered witty commentary on daily life through such fictional characters as Sir Roger de Coverley, who represented the best values of the country gentleman. He and the other characters claimed to be members of "Mr. Spectator's Club." From this stance, they commented on literature and morality. These sketches of contemporary life and problems enjoyed great popularity and were imitated all over Europe. The *Spectator* and the *Tatler* were influential in establishing the 18th-century periodical essay, which, with its informal prose style, greatly affected English journalism.

Spenserian stanza: See *Stanza.*

Sphinx, GM: winged, woman-headed monster who preyed on the citizens of Thebes with the riddle "What creature walks on four legs in the morning, two at noon, and three in the evening?" If they could not answer it, she devoured them. When Oedipus answered the riddle "Man," explaining that a baby creeps, a grown man walks upright, and an old man uses a cane, the Sphinx dashed her head against a stone and died, and Oedipus became king of Thebes. The sphinx was originally a Near Eastern art motif, with a human head and a lion's body.

Spondee: See *Foot.*

Spoon River Anthology: book of verse by U.S. poet Edgar Lee Masters, issued in book form in 1915. Inspired by the Greek Anthology, it is a series of epitaphs in the form of dramatic monologues. A succession of the departed inhabitants of an Illinois small town speak from the quiet in which "all, all are sleeping on the hill"; thus they draw vignette portraits of themselves and their former neighbors. The work was part of a movement to debunk the myth of idyllic life in rural and small-town America.

Sportsman's Sketches, A: collection of short stories by the Russian writer Ivan Turgenev, published in 1852. The narrator, a country gentleman, describes his casual encounters with neighbors and peasants while he roams the countryside. The common theme of these stories, though often quietly understated, is the endless and cruel injustices that are the byproduct of serfdom. The book was a powerful influence in arousing public support for emancipation.

Stanza: unit of a poem, usually consisting of a recurring number of lines. The *quatrain* is the most common, consisting of four lines in which the rhyme pattern can be a-b-a-b or a-b-c-b. Ballad stanzas are quatrains.

Rhyme royal is a seven-line stanza in iambic pentameter in which the rhyme scheme is a-b-a-b-b-c-c. It is also called the Chaucerian stanza because of Chaucer's early use of it. *Ottava rima* is a similar stanza form, having eight lines instead of seven, and rhyming a-b-a-b-a-b-c-c. Sir Thomas Wyatt introduced it into English verse from the Italian. Byron made use of it in *Don Juan.*

The Spenserian stanza, invented by Edmund Spenser for use in *the Faerie Queen,* consists of nine iambic lines, rhyming a-b-a-b-b-c-b-c-c. The first eight lines are pentameter but the last, called an alexandrine, is hexameter.

The sonnet was originally a stanza, but is now an independent lyric. See also *Ballad; Couplet; Sonnet.*

Steppenwolf: novel by the German author Hermann Hesse, published in 1927. The story is told mainly through the bizarre journals left by the mysterious Harry Haller before his disappearance. The journals tell of his conviction that he has a dual nature—part domesticated human, part "wolf of the Steppes" *(Steppenwolf)*—and is a wild outsider who despises human life, activities, and values. The fantastic ending finds Harry in the Magic Theater "for madmen only," where he glimpses the meaning of life and decides to bear it.

Stopping by Woods on a Snowy Evening: deceptively simple, short lyric poem, written by Robert Frost in 1923, one of his best-known works. The poet, on a journey home, stops impulsively in the woods for a moment's contemplation. The seductive mystery of the deep snow, dark night, and solitude exert a powerful fascination over him that he reluctantly resists because he has "promises to keep,/ And miles to go before I sleep."

Stranger, The: novel by the French existentialist philosopher Albert Camus, published in 1942 and set in Algiers. From its opening sentences "Mother died today. Or, maybe yesterday; I can't be sure"—the reader is shocked into recognition that the narrator, Meursault (he has no first name), represents a new breed of modern man who is estranged from the deepest realities of life, even the instinct for self-preservation. Meursault adapts uncomplainingly to his absurd existence—a routine job, casual acquaintances, and aimless recreation. Nothing upsets him very much. Faced with death, however, he discovers a reason for living.

Stratford-on-Avon: English borough northwest of London on the Avon River, known for its associations with William Shakespeare, who was born there and lived there in retirement.

Stream of consciousness: phrase first applied by U.S. psychologist William James to the sum of external and internal stimuli that invade the periphery of consciousness at a given moment. Attempts to mirror this stream of images, thoughts, and impressions in literature have been made by 20th-century novelists, notably James Joyce and Virginia Woolf.

Streetcar Named Desire: play by the U.S. author Tennessee Williams, presented in 1947 and awarded a Pulitzer Prize. Blanche Dubois, an aging, unstable Southern belle, comes to stay with her sister, Stella. Her refined behavior and coquettish manner provoke a tragic conflict with her earthy brother-in-law, Stanley Kowalski.

Studs Lonigan: trilogy of naturalistic novels by U.S. writer James T. Farrell, published between 1932 and 1935. The novels faithfully record a lower middle-class Irish environment in Chicago in the 1920's and 1930's. In boyhood, the hero, Studs, is the admired leader of the neighborhood gang. This proves to be the peak achievement of his life. As he grows older the social and cultural limitations of his milieu, the repetition of often sordid and brutal pleasures, and the dull routine of menial occupations deaden whatever spark of natural superiority he had long before his death at an early age. Although the book documents the meanness of his life in great detail, it makes Studs a figure of lyrical poignancy.

Sturm und Drang ("Storm and Stress"): period in German literature in the late 1700's that sowed the seeds of the German Romantic movement. This short-lived revolt against the Enlightenment was strongly influenced by the poetry of the Gaelic bard Ossian and the discovery of Shakespeare. Its most notable productions were dramas, characteristically tragic, turbulent, and unrestrained. Among them were the youthful Goethe's *Götz von Berlichingen* and Schiller's *Die Räuber (The Robbers).*

Styx, GM: principal river of Hades, believed to encircle the lower world seven times. Over this river Charon ferried the souls of the dead. It was held in such terror and reverence that even the gods swore their irrevocable oaths by its name.

Sun Also Rises, The: novel by U.S. writer Ernest Hemingway, published in 1926. It deals with a group of young expatriates in Paris who drink too much and make love indiscriminately, but who seek and sometimes find purification in ritual acts—fishing in a trout stream or attending a bullfight—that suggest that they are searching for a dimly remembered innocence and honor. The work expressed the feelings of the "lost generation" of the 1920's.

Superman: concept of German philosopher Friedrich Nietzsche of the superior being: the man who overcomes and transcends himself and the limitations of his times. The idea, although variously understood, has fascinated many writers, and literary versions of the superman (usually seen negatively) were portrayed even before he was described by Nietzsche. Raskolnikov in Dostoevski's *Crime and Punishment* and Wolf Larsen in Jack London's *Sea Wolf* are both criminal supermen; those seen from a more admiring point of view include Bazarov in Turgenev's *Fathers and Sons* and architect Howard Roark in Ayn Rand's *Fountainhead.*

The Nazis in Germany derived their philosophy of the superman from Nietzsche, but it is clear in *Thus Spake Zarathustra* that Nietzsche is talking about a super-individual, not a super-state or a "master race." As Zarathustra says, there is no "way" to become a superman; the way is different for each person.

Surrealism: movement in literature and art that began in 1924, in Paris, with the poet André Breton's first surrealist manifesto. Surrealists seek to explore and express the subconscious. Dreams and hallucinations are often a source of ideas, giving surreal works their characteristic quality of fantasy. Among the most famous surrealist writers are Eugene Ionesco, Jean Genet, and Samuel Beckett.

Symbolism: widespread revolt, occurring in the late 19th century, against realism and naturalism in the arts. In essence, artists and writers turned away from representations of objective reality to symbolic representations of their inner lives. As the Norwegian painter Edvard Munch put it: "I paint not what I see, but what I saw."

In a restricted sense, the term is associated with a group of French writers, followers of Charles Baudelaire, Stéphane Mallarmé, and Paul Verlaine, who, in a manifesto written by Jean Moréas in 1886, gave the movement its name.

TALE OF TWO CITIES: *Sidney Carton is led to the guillotine in 1930's film version.*

CULVER PICTURES

Symposium (Greek for "banquet"): dialogue by the ancient Greek philosopher Plato, in which his mentor Socrates and his friends, including Aristophanes, Phaedrus, Agathon (the host), and Pausanias, meet at dinner and discuss the nature of love; a latecomer, Alcibiades, makes a speech honoring Socrates. Another dialogue of the same name was written by Xenophon; it also features Socrates.

Synecdoche: See *Figures of speech.*

T

Tale of Genji, The: greatest classic of Japanese literature, written around the year 1005 by Murasaki Shikibu, a court lady. Often considered the oldest novel in the world, it portrays aristocratic life in the Heian period, an age of exquisite refinement in which an elegant society occupied itself with writing poems, painting, and viewing nature. The story is long and episodic and deals with the romantic adventures of Prince Genji, whose mistresses are sensitively and sympathetically portrayed.

Tale of Two Cities, A: novel by English writer Charles Dickens, published in 1859, set in Paris and London at the time of the French Revolution. The symbol of the revolution is Mme. DeFarge, who sits before her wine shop, knitting a scroll that records the names and crimes of the nobility.

The chief characters are Dr. Manette, whose 18-year imprisonment in the Bastille has broken his health; Lucie Manette, his daughter, who rescues him and takes him to London; Charles Darnay, a French nobleman who disavows his aristocratic family, changes his name, and goes to London; and Sydney Carton, an unconventional, alcoholic barrister. Carton and Darnay both fall in love with Lucie, but she chooses Darnay. During the terror, Darnay returns to Paris to rescue a family servant, but he is arrested and sentenced to death; for Lucie's sake, Carton takes his place and dies in his stead.

Taming of the Shrew, The: comedy by Shakespeare dated 1593–1594. The plot, given in a play, concerns Katharina, a beautiful but harsh-tongued and obstinate girl whom no one wishes to marry. Petruchio of Verona marries and tames her, mostly by inhuman treatment. Katharina becomes a wife who appears to be so loving and meek that Petruchio wins a wager from friends when she behaves docilely toward him in public.

Tam O'Shanter: narrative poem by Scottish poet Robert Burns, published in 1791, based on a local legend. It is a story about Tam, who gets drunk on market day and, with his mare Maggie, makes a spooky midnight journey home, encountering a party of dancing witches and warlocks. Unlike any other poem in Burns's repertory, this is a virtuoso's showpiece, in which the poet exhibits his bag of dazzling magic tricks and demonstrates the full range of his gifts for humor, satire, tragic insight, and elegant parody.

Tannhäuser: in German legend, a knight and minnesinger of the 13th century who entered a cave in a mountain (Venusberg) where he was to live with Venus in her court of pleasure for seven years. At length he repented and made a pilgrimage to Rome to seek forgiveness for his sins. But Pope Urban told him that he could no more be forgiven than the staff in his hand could sprout leaves. In despair, Tannhäuser turned away, discarded his staff, and returned to Venus. In a few days the dry staff miraculously bloomed, and the pope sent messengers far and wide seeking Tannhäuser, but he was never found. The story is the basis for the opera *Tannhäuser* by Richard Wagner, first performed in 1845.

Tantalus: See *House of Atreus.*

Tartuffe: satiric comedy by the French dramatist Molière, first presented in three acts in 1664, then expanded to five acts in 1669. The public was outraged by what it viewed as a mockery of piety. Tartuffe is a religious hypocrite who insinuates himself into the good graces of the wealthy Orgon. He convinces Orgon to disinherit his son, give Tartuffe his daughter's hand in marriage, and turn over his large estate to him. Elmire, Orgon's wife, arranges for him to overhear Tartuffe making love to her, but even then Orgon believes Tartuffe's defense. Orgon is finally turned out of his house and recognizes Tartuffe's treachery. At the last minute, the king intervenes and restores daughter and property to Orgon.

Telemachus: See *Odysseus; Odyssey.*

Tempest, The: late comedy by Shakespeare, usually dated 1612–1613. It tells the story of Prospero, an exiled magician, once duke of Milan, who causes a ship to founder on the enchanted isle where he and his daughter Miranda live. Aboard the ship are his enemies: his brother Antonio, usurper of the dukedom; the king of Naples; and his son, Ferdinand. With the help of his magic sprite Ariel, Prospero teases, beguiles, and frightens, but finally forgives his enemies, teaching them a lesson in magnanimity. Miranda and Ferdinand fall in love, and the old magician renounces his magic

CULVER PICTURES

THE THREE MUSKETEERS: *early film star Douglas Fairbanks plays D'Artagnan battling a host of enemies in a tavern.*

to return to the sober responsibilities of his dukedom. A striking minor character is Caliban, the deformed, bestial slave of Prospero.

Tender Is the Night: novel by U.S. author F. Scott Fitzgerald, published in 1934, which tells of the marriage of a young psychiatrist, Dick Diver, to one of his mental patients, Nicole. Supported by Nicole's money, they are popular members of a restless, fashionable international set. But Dick's loss of meaningful work and the burden of being caretaker to Nicole makes him seek refuge in drink. As Nicole gains emotional strength, their marriage dissolves, and Dick drifts into obscurity and alcoholism.

Tess of the D'Urbervilles: novel by English author Thomas Hardy, published in 1891. Tess Durbeyfield, a beautiful English village girl, is a lineal descendant of the aristocratic d'Urbervilles. Alec, a son of that family, pursues and seduces Tess, then abandons her. A child is born, whom she names Sorrow, but he soon dies. Some years later the idealistic Angel Clare marries Tess, but he leaves her when, on the wedding day, she tells him of her past. He experiences a change of heart and tries again to win her love, but Alec seeks to claim her and prevent any reconciliation. Tess kills Alec, and she and Clare flee, hoping to escape from the country. They are overtaken at Stonehenge and Tess is imprisoned and sentenced to death.

Tevye the Dairyman: collection of tragicomic stories written by the Yiddish author Sholom Aleichem between 1894 and 1916. Taking place during the last years of czarist Russia, the stories purport to be monologues told to the author by Tevye as, over the years, they accidentally meet. *Tevye's Daughters,* a collection of later stories that deal with the fates of the dairyman's seven children, was published in English translation in 1949. Three of the stories became the basis of the 1960's hit musical *Fiddler on the Roof.* In the face of the unhappy destinies of his family, his people, and himself, Tevye never loses his faith in God, which is, in fact, made stronger by his trials.

Thanatopsis (Greek for "a vision of death"): reflective poem by the U.S. poet William Cullen Bryant, begun when he was only 16 and published in 1817. The poem belongs to the tradition of the English "graveyard school" of poetry, and conveys a majestic image of the immortality of the soul.

Theseus, GM: principal hero of the Athenians; he was a son of Aegeus, king of Athens, and Aethra. When he was a child, his father left a sword and sandals under a heavy rock, instructing Aethra to allow Theseus to come to him in Athens when he was big enough to move the rock. This Theseus did, taking the dangerous overland route because of his ambition to equal the fame of Hercules. He killed all the highwaymen along the way (see also *Procrustes*), and arrived in Athens already famous. He made himself known to Aegeus and volunteered to free Athens from the yearly tribute of youths and maidens sent to feed the Minotaur in Crete. With the help of Ariadne, daughter of the Cretan king, Minos, he found his way in and out of the labyrinth, where he killed the Minotaur; he then carried Ariadne away with him. He later was either separated from her or deserted her (see also *Ariadne*).

After Theseus became king of Athens, he married the Amazon queen Hippolyte, by whom he had a son, Hippolytus. After her death he married Ariadne's sister Phaedra.

Thisbe: see *Pyramus and Thisbe.*

This Side of Paradise: first novel by the U.S. writer F. Scott Fitzgerald, published in 1920. It brought him sensational fame and made him the spokesman for the jazz age generation. It deals with the boyhood and young manhood of Amory Blaine. From a midwestern background, Amory sets out to capture wealth, fame, and beautiful women, but he fails to make the grade at Princeton, achieves only a mediocre success in advertising, and loses, for lack of money, the girl he loves.

Thor, NM: god of thunder, a son of Odin. He was the god of strength and a defender in time of war, a friend of humanity. The sound of thunder was supposed to be from the rolling wheels of his chariot; the thunderbolt was his hammer, which always returned to his hand after being hurled. Thursday is named for Thor.

Thrace: name the ancient Greeks gave to the territory lying between Macedonia and the Black Sea, extending north to the Danube and south beyond the Hellespont. The ancient Greeks thought of the Thracians as savages. The chief city of Thrace was Byzantium. The territory today is divided among Turkey, Bulgaria, and Greece.

Three Musketeers, The: cloak-and-sword romance by the French writer Alexandre Dumas *père,* published in 1844. It deals with events in the 17th century; its hero, D'Artagnan, a gay and reckless guardsman in the service of Louis XIII, is based on an actual historical character. His three loyal friends—the musketeers—are the bravest and most resourceful soldiers of the age. Each has a distinctive personality: the gigantic, comic Porthos is a tower of strength and dependability; Athos is reflective and clever; Aramis is dour and pessimistic.

Threepenny Opera, The: See *Beggar's Opera.*

Three Sisters, The: play by the Russian dramatist Anton Chekhov, presented in 1901. It deals with three young women who live on dreams of escaping their dull provincial town and going to Moscow. They pin their hopes for escape on their brother Andrei, but he marries a stupid girl who moves into their home and tyrannizes both him and his sisters. The sisters' lives are briefly enlivened by romances with officers of the local military garrison, but these, too, end in disappointment when the regiment leaves.

Thule: name given by the Greeks and Romans to the northernmost inhabited place in the world, possibly Iceland or Norway. Described as a cold and eerie place by the Greek explorer Pytheas, who visited there around 300 B.C. after a six-day voyage north from Britain, the region captured the literary imagination. Writers often use Vergil's phrase "ultima Thule" to describe the farthest regions. An actual Thule was founded in Greenland in 1910 by Danish explorer Knud Rasmussen.

Thus Spake Zarathustra: philosophic essay by the German philosopher Friedrich Nietzsche, written from 1883 to 1885. The work is in the form of a narrative in which the ancient Persian prophet Zoroaster (Zarathustra) is the spokesman for the author. The prophet's message is that if man is to survive he must surpass his present limitations and become a superman; his will is his most important asset. Zarathustra reviles Christianity as a religion for the protection of weaklings and a crippling hindrance to the strong individual's will to power. He celebrates a life of independence, boldness, courage, danger, and action. See also *Superman.*

Time Machine, The: science fiction fantasy by the British novelist H. G. Wells, published in 1895. The hero invents a time machine that permits him to journey into the future, where he meets a future race, the Eloi. They are charming, gentle, and dainty creatures who do no work, read no books, and eat only vegetables since animals are extinct. He then discovers, to his horror, that they share the planet with a race of underground workers, the apelike Morlocks, carnivorous creatures who exist by feeding on the Eloi.

Tin Drum, The: first novel by the German writer Günter Grass, published in 1959. The hero, Oskar Matzerath, is determined to thwart his father's plan to make him a grocer; he stops growing at the age of three and remains an obnoxious child, beating a tin drum throughout the rise and fall of Nazi Germany. After the war, when the survivors of the family move to West Germany, he decides to become an adult and participates, as a cabaret drummer, in the postwar life. But he conceives the delusion that he is Jesus and is confined in a mental hospital from which he tells his story.

TOM JONES, *title character in Richardson's 18th century classic, was played by Albert Finney. The legendary Tom Thumb, a diminutive figure, originated in King Arthur's time.*

CULVER PICTURES

The Hiſtory of *Tom Thumbe*, the *Little*, for his ſmall ſtature ſurnamed, *King* ARTHVRS *Dwarfe*:

Whoſe Life and aduentures containe many ſtrange and wonderfull accidents, publiſhed for *the delight of merry Time-ſpenders.*

Imprinted at London for *Tho: Langley.* 1621.

NY PUBLIC LIBRARY

Tintern Abbey: short title for an early masterpiece of the English poet William Wordsworth, included in his and Coleridge's first collection, *Lyrical Ballads* (1798). It deals with his characteristic theme, the mystery of the recurrence and withdrawal of grace and inspiration. The poet revisits a scene of his youth, where he had once experienced an almost mystical identification with nature, to draw spiritual sustenance from it again.

Tiresias, GM: blind prophet of Thebes whose life spanned several generations. He appears in Sophocles' *Oedipus Rex* and *Antigone,* in the *Odyssey,* and in many Greek legends. At one time he found two snakes copulating and killed the female. As a punishment, he was turned into a woman; later he was turned back into a man, but thereafter he possessed the knowledge and insight of both men and women.

Titans, GM: children of Uranus (heaven) and Gaea (earth). The sons were Oceanus, Coeus, Creus, Hyperion, Iapetus, and Cronus. The daughters were Theia, Rhea, Themis, Mnemosyne, Phoebe, and Tethys. The children of Cronus and Rhea were Zeus and the Olympian gods. Cronus dethroned Uranus, and Zeus in turn dethroned Cronus. In this struggle the Titans fought against the gods, were defeated, and confined under Tartarus, the deepest part of Hades.

Tom Jones (full title: *The History of Tom Jones, a Foundling*): comic novel by the pioneer English novelist Henry Fielding, published in 1749. It relates the adventures of high-spirited, impulsive, and generous Tom, who, despite many discreditable escapades, at last wins the confidence of his foster father, Squire Allworthy, and the love of beautiful Sophia Western. The novel is remarkable for its vitality and its sweeping picture of 18th-century London and country life.

Tom Sawyer, The Adventures of: classic novel of small-town American boyhood, written by U.S. author Mark Twain in 1876. It was based on his memories of growing up in Hannibal, Missouri. Tom, an imaginative boy who is fond of adventure stories, finds himself involved in a real life adventure when he and his friend Huck Finn witness a murder committed by Injun Joe. The terrified boys run away, but return in time to prevent an innocent man from being condemned for the crime. The book is a perennial favorite among children. Its sequel, *Huckleberry Finn,* is an American classic.

Tom Thumb: in English legend, the inch-high son of a plowman in the time of King Arthur. His adventures range from being swallowed by mistake to a climactic fall into the sea, where he is eaten by a fish that is then caught and taken to King Arthur's cook. The cook saves Tom's life. Tom is then presented to the king and knighted. He ends up being killed by a spider.

To the Lighthouse: novel by English writer Virginia Woolf, published in 1927. Stream-of-consciousness techniques and symbolism create the emotional atmosphere for a seaside house party. The book is dominated by the symbol of the lighthouse offshore. The people at the house party, directed by the cold, rational Mr. Ramsay, an eminent scholar troubled by self-doubt, are seen primarily through the eyes of two women: Mrs. Ramsay, a warm, beautiful woman, mother of many children, who gives of herself and her concern to the point of exhaustion; and Lily Briscoe, an artist who is troubled by conflicts between other people's expectations of her as a woman and her own view of herself as an artist. The novel covers a period of years, and not until the final scene do any of the characters reach the lighthouse.

Tragedy: form of drama in which a solemn theme is set forth in action, usually proceeding to a fatal outcome. The language, whether verse or prose, is of an elevated quality. The term is now applied to novels, other literary works, and to real events that are terrible or fatal. See also *Poetics.*

Tragic flaw: See *Poetics.*

Transcendentalism or **New England transcendentalism:** philosophical and literary movement centered in Concord, Massachusetts, in the early 19th century. It was an influential part of the general intellectual ferment now called the American renaissance or the "flowering of New England." New England transcendentalism was an aspect of the general Romantic revolt against the rationalism of the Enlightenment and the narrowness of organized religion.

The Concord group investigated Eastern and mystical philosophies but, above all, they sought inspiration in nature and placed their faith in intuition. Their chief spokesman was Ralph Waldo Emerson. In essays such as "Self-Reliance," he repeatedly advocated trust in hunches, instincts, feelings, and other subjective touchstones. Thus, his friend Henry David Thoreau took to the woods to learn what life was about by living, a gesture that has had a powerful impact on the American imagination.

Other prominent transcendentalists were Bronson Alcott, Margaret Fuller, George Ripley, and Orestes Brownson. Although they were all fiercely individualistic, their ideas led them to champion social reforms and to found the idealistic, experimental communes of Brook Farm and Fruitlands. See also *Brook Farm.*

Treasure Island: adventure story by English writer Robert Louis Stevenson, published in 1883. Its boy hero, Jim Hawkins, gets possession of a map of an island where pirate treasure is buried. Some friends outfit a vessel to set out to search for it. But the crew of the *Hispaniola* is made up of pirates and desperadoes who are seeking the treasure themselves. The chief villain is the fascinating one-legged pirate, Long John Silver. Jim and his friends overcome the pirates and finally find the treasure.

Trial, The: novel written in German, in 1915, by the Jewish Czech writer Franz Kafka, published posthumously in 1925. A bank clerk, Joseph K., is suddenly accused of a crime by a bureaucratic official. He can never discover the exact nature of the crime, and though he devotes his life up to his execution to seeking clarification and demanding justice, all his efforts are futile. The book conveys an overwhelmingly fatalistic feeling that no man is innocent, and that there is no cure or acquittal for inner guilt. Like all Kafka's allegorical tales, it has many interpretations.

Tristan and Iseult: in Celtic legend, a pair of tragic lovers. Tristan, a nephew of King Mark of Cornwall, was escorting the beautiful Iseult to her wedding with the king. On the way, they accidentally drank a love potion intended for Mark and Iseult. Thereafter, they were committed to love each other forever. They made a death pact and died in each other's arms. Wagner's music drama *Tristan und Isolde* is a powerful expression of this love story. Tristan also appears in Malory's *Morte d'Arthur* as a knight of King Arthur's Round Table.

Tristram Shandy, The Life and Opinions of: novel by the English clergyman Laurence Sterne, published in nine volumes between 1760 and 1767. Though one of the earliest English novels, it is remarkable for its technique of free association. Tristram begins the story of his life from his conception, but as one digression leads to another, he does not actually get around to being born until Volume IV. The digressions range from bawdy anecdotes and sentimental portraits of his father and his Uncle Toby to discussions of topical problems of the day. The work was enormously popular and helped to establish the literary vogue known as the "cult of sensibility" (or sentimentality) in Europe.

Trochee: See *Foot.*

Troilus: young son of Priam, king of Troy, and Hecuba. He was killed in the Trojan war by Achilles. The legend of his love for the faithless Cressida is not a classical myth but a romance developed in the Middle Ages. Its finest expression is the poem *Troilus and Criseyde,* written in 1385 by Geoffrey Chaucer; it is also the subject of a rather cynical tragedy by Shakespeare, dated 1602–1603. The usual story is that Troilus falls in love with Cressida, the daughter of the pro-Greek Trojan priest Calchas. Pandarus arranges their meetings, and they become lovers. During a truce, Cressida is sent to the Greek camp in exchange for prisoners. Though the lovers vow fidelity, Cressida almost immediately becomes the mistress of Diomedes, plunging bewildered Troilus into jealous torments.

CULVER PICTURES

TROJAN HORSE: *this "gift" was filled with Greek warriors who destroyed the city.*

Trojan horse: hollow wooden horse, used during the Trojan War as a strategy by the Greeks to gain entrance to the city of Troy. Pretending to abandon the siege, the Greeks sailed away, leaving before the city gates the gigantic wooden horse with a number of men hidden inside it. Though they were warned by both Cassandra and Laocoön ("Whatever it is, I fear Greeks even when they bring gifts"), the Trojans were deceived into believing that the horse was an offering to Athena and would protect the city; they brought it inside the city walls. During the night, the Greek warriors crept out and opened the gates for their fellow Greeks, who sacked and burned the city. The story is told in the *Odyssey* and in the *Aeneid.*

Trojan War: struggle between the kingdom of Troy and an alliance of Greek kingdoms. According to legend, the war began when Paris, son of the Trojan king, Priam, carried off the beautiful Helen, wife of Menelaus, king of Sparta. Menelaus called on all the other Greek chieftains, who were bound by oath to avenge any injury done to the Spartan royal family. Under the leadershp of his brother, Agamemnon, king of Mycenae, the Greek heroes Achilles, Patroclus, Odysseus, Diomedes, Nestor, and the two Ajaxes sailed across the Aegean Sea to besiege Troy.

The Trojans, led by one of Priam's sons, Hector, struggled many years to overcome their Greeks foes. Victory was capricious, going from one side to the other. The gods of Olympus took sides and often interfered on behalf of their favorites.

Homer's great epic, the *Iliad,* opens in the tenth year of the war. It deals with Achilles' bitter quarrels with his leader Agamemnon, and his refusal to fight, which brings disaster to the Greeks. Some of the highlights of the *Iliad* are the death of Achilles' friend Patroclus and the funeral games held in his honor; Achilles' return to battle; his slaying of Hector and defiling of Hector's body; and the scene in which Achilles undergoes a change of heart and returns Hector's body to Priam for burial.

Tropic of Cancer: novel written by the U.S. bohemian writer Henry Miller, describing the highs and lows of his years of poverty in Paris during the Depression. It ranges from lyrical affirmations of the joy of life to scatological descriptions of the most sordid experiences. The book was first published in Paris in 1934, but its sexual frankness caused it to be banned in the United States until 1961. Its sequel, *Tropic of Capricorn,* dealing with Miller's earlier New York years, appeared in 1962.

Troubadours: poet-musicians who flourished in Europe between the late 1000's and 1200's. The troubadours composed their poetry in the language of Provence in southern France. They invented many forms of the lyric, and were instrumental in developing the concept of courtly love and in making the courts of Europe centers of culture. King Richard I (Richard the Lion-Hearted) of England was a troubadour himself. Others were William, duke of Aquitaine and count of Poitiers, the founder of the school; and Bertrand de Born and Arnaut Daniel, both mentioned in Dante's *Divine Comedy.* See also *Courtly love; Minnesinger; Trouvères.*

Trouvères: poet-musicians who wrote in the language of northern France during a period extending from the eleventh century to the 14th. They

CULVER PICTURES

20,000 LEAGUES UNDER THE SEA: *men in the* Nautilus *view a giant octopus.*

flourished after the decline of the southern troubadours, whose influence is paramount in their work. Among the best known are Thibaut IV, king of Navarre, Adam de la Halle, Colin Muset, and Rutebeuf. See also *Minnesinger; Troubadours.*

Troy: prehistoric city, background of Homer's great epic, the *Iliad.* Said to be located in northwestern Asia Minor on the southern shore of the Hellespont, Troy was a strategic port as well as the center of a prosperous farming area. On the basis of Homer's description of the region, German archaeologist Heinrich Schliemann began excavations in the Turkish mound Hisarlik from 1870 to 1890. The nine settlements that he unearthed on the site strongly indicate that the storied city really did exist. Homer's Troy is believed to be the seventh of these cities and to have flourished about 1200 B.C. See also *Iliad; Trojan War.*

Turn of the Screw, The: novel-length ghost story by U.S. expatriate writer Henry James, published in 1898. A young governess goes to an isolated country house to take care of two charming children, Miles and Flora. She sometimes sees a strange man and woman on the grounds whose descriptions match those of the former valet and governess, who are both dead. She gradually realizes that the children, though outwardly angelic, are possessed by these evil ghosts. Her attempts to free them end in tragedy.

Twelfth Night or **What You Will:** comedy by Shakespeare, presented c 1600. Viola and her twin brother, Sebastian, are shipwrecked. Viola is rescued and arrives in Illyria where, disguised as a boy, she becomes a page of Duke Orsino and soon falls in love with him. The duke sends his clever page to woo Countess Olivia on his behalf; Olivia becomes enamored of the page. The situation is resolved when Sebastian, Viola's twin, arrives. He marries Olivia and Viola marries Orsino. The play is enlivened by the comic character Sir Toby Belch.

Twenty Thousand Leagues under the Sea: one of French science fiction writer Jules Verne's extraordinary voyages, published in 1870. In this tale a group of scientists become the prisoners of the fascinating Captain Nemo, who carries them off in the *Nautilus,* a strange craft of his own invention that travels underwater. The work anticipates the invention of the submarine.

Tyr or **Tiu,** NM: war god; a son of Odin. Tuesday is named for him.

U

Ubu Roi (*King Ubu*): play by the French writer Alfred Jarry, presented in 1896. Ubu, who makes himself king of Poland, is greedy, brutal, coy, and vulgar; he was first intended as a caricature of a hated schoolmaster of Jarry's youth. The play is dominated by Ubu and by other characters who look and behave like outsize puppets. Their actions embody stupidity-on-the-rampage so powerfully, that the play does not have to make any sense. *Ubu Roi* shocked audiences and closed after two performances, but it is now considered the ancestor of the theater of the absurd.

Ugly Duckling, The: fairy tale by the 19th-century Danish writer Hans Christian Andersen. It deals with the loneliness of a little "duck" who is rejected by the flock because he is different. As he grows up into a beautiful swan, he realizes that being different may mean being superior. Andersen was himself a homely and ungainly youth, and this story, like many of his others, has a strongly autobiographical theme.

Ulster (or **Ulaid**) **Cycle:** body of ancient Irish prose tales, written in the eighth century, dealing with King Conchobar and his knights of the Red Branch, of whom the chief hero is Cuchulain. The stories concerning these boastful, jealous, quarrelsome, chariot-riding warriors are often comic and grim, and sometimes, as in the legend of the beloved Irish heroine Deirdre, sorrowful and beautiful. The most important story is "The Cattle Raid of Cooley," in which Cuchulain, all alone, battles the forces of Connaught. See also *Cuchulain.*

Ulysses: Latin form of Odysseus. Also, a novel by the Irish writer James Joyce, published in 1922, a landmark of 20th-century fiction. The story takes place in Dublin in one day, June 16,

UNCLE TOM'S CABIN: *the slave Eliza (scarcely seeming black in this 19th-century picture) escapes across thin ice from the wicked overseer Simon Legree.*

1904. The ordinary events of that day, as experienced by the leading characters—the autobiographical Stephen Dedalus; Leopold Bloom, a Jewish advertising salesman; his wife Molly Bloom, the eternal daughter of Eve—are carefully recorded. Intermingled are all the stimuli that touch their consciousnesses, all their bodily functions, and all their subjective mental processes, which, in the course of a day's wanderings, take them back and forth in their own lives and in the history of the human race. Joyce uses free association, interior monologue, and sometimes interpolates brilliant literary parodies. The book was banned in the United States until 1933.

Uncle Remus: chief character in several collections of tales by the U.S. writer Joel Chandler Harris, published between 1880 and 1906. The tales, told in dialect by a kindly old black man, Uncle Remus, to a little white boy on a plantation, are actually reworkings of authentic African folk tales. They offer evidence of the extensive African culture brought to the New World by slaves. Most of them deal with the animal tricksters Br'er Rabbit and Br'er Fox. The best-known story is "Tar-Baby," in which a tar doll is placed in Br'er Fox's path. Angered when the doll does not move or speak to him, Br'er Fox hits it and sticks to the doll. "Sticky figure" stories are common in both African and American Indian folklore.

Uncle Tom's Cabin or **Life Among the Lowly:** novel written in 1852 by the New England abolitionist Harriet Beecher Stowe. It had tremendous influence in arousing antislavery sentiment, and is considered one of the most effective propaganda novels of all time. Miss Stowe tried to be fair to both sides. The Southern plantation owners, the St. Clares, are presented as gentle and cultured people, and their old black slave Uncle Tom is devoted to them. The villain, Simon Legree, is an overseer who whips the slaves to get more work out of them. His brutality causes Tom's death. Other major characters are the St. Clares' daughter Little Eva and her black playmate Topsy, and the young black couple Eliza and George. Eliza's escape with her baby across the ice is the book's most suspenseful event.

Uncle Vanya: play by the Russian dramatist Anton Chekhov, presented in 1897. Vanya, an intelligent and sensitive man, manages the estate of his dead sister to provide for her scholarly husband Serebryakov and her daughter Sonya. When Serebryakov visits the estate with his new young wife Yelena, Vanya falls in love with her. He also realizes that his brother-in-law is spoiled, selfish, and ungrateful, and his scholarly work is bogus. The final outrage occurs when Serebryakov announces his intention to sell the estate. The enraged Vanya attempts to shoot him but misses. The visitors depart, leaving Vanya and Sonya to their life of humdrum work and the realization that their goodness, patience, and sincerity will never be rewarded.

Under Milk Wood: radio play for voices by Welsh poet Dylan Thomas. It was published in 1954. In this outpouring of soaring song and verse, Thomas depicts the folk of a Welsh village on a spring day. Whether they are unhappy, exotic, or a bit mad, he portrays them in lyrical terms.

Under the Volcano: novel by English writer Malcolm Lowry, published in 1947. Through effective experimental techniques, Lowry describes the despair, alcoholism, and final disintegration of Geoffrey Firmin, a former British consul living in Mexico.

Unicorn: fabulous beast resembling a horse, with a long, slender horn projecting from its forehead. Unicorns were described by Aristotle and Pliny. Their horns were traditionally a sure antidote to poison, and medieval rulers valued a cup made from a unicorn's horn or a potion made from ground horn. Supposedly, the unicorn could be tamed and caught only by a virgin, in whose lap he would at once gently lay his head.

Unities: term used in drama criticism for the unities of action, time, and place that were to be observed in a play. According to these rules, a play was to deal with a single, logically connected action, performed in a single place within a single day. Aristotle mentioned the unities of action and time in the *Poetics;* his later interpreters added unity of place and insisted on the rigid application of all three. The unities were taken most seriously by the classical French dramatists of the 17th century, such as Racine and Corneille.

Up from Slavery: autobiography by U.S. educator Booker T. Washington (1856–1915), published in 1901. The son of a slave and a white man, Washington managed to get an education and, at age 25, he became president of Alabama's Tuskegee Normal and Industrial Institute for Negroes. In his book Washington stressed the importance of better education and better jobs for blacks.

UNCLE VANYA: *Vanya and Yelena do not notice Yelena's hypocritical husband.*

WALTER ABEL, GENEVA BUGBEE, DAN BLY: © VORIES FISHER/GOODMAN THEATRE OF THE ART INSTITUTE OF CHICAGO

Uranus, GM: personification of the sky or heaven wedded to his mother Gaea (earth). Uranus was the father of the Cyclopes, Furies, and Titans. He was dethroned by his son Cronus.

U.S.A.: trilogy of novels by U.S. writer John Dos Passos, whose three volumes—*The 42nd Parallel* (1930); *1919* (1932); and *The Big Money* (1936)—cover American life from the eve of World War I to the early Depression years. Using a variety of expressionist techniques, the author presents episodic narratives of fictional characters from a range of regional and social milieus. Interspersed throughout are the devices of the Newsreel (snatches of actual news stories, headlines, popular songs), the Biography (lives of celebrities of the period), and the Camera Eye (subjective reminiscences). The overall effect is a portrait of a nation, colored by the author's pessimistic belief that the times are out of joint. Nobody wins in this work, neither the apparent darlings of society—film stars, public relations men, advertisers—nor the lonely outsiders.

Uther Pendragon: See *Arthurian legend.*

Utopia: humanistic treatise in two parts, written in Latin by English statesman Sir Thomas More and published in 1516. It presents a critique of contemporary social and political ills, and offers a solution to them by the description of Utopia, an ideal island society where reason governs and no one grasps for power. The island has given its name (literally meaning "no place") to all such ideal societies.

V

Valhalla, NM: great hall of Odin in Asgard, where the souls of heroes slain in battle were received with rejoicing and honor (the word means "hall of the slain"). There they feasted and fought each other for sport.

Valkyries, NM: beautiful war maidens, messengers of Odin. They rode through the air above the scene of battle, selecting the warriors worthy to be slain, and carrying them to Valhalla. The name probably meant "choosers of the slain." Brunhild appears as a Valkyrie in the *Völsunga Saga* and in Wagner's opera cycle *Der Ring des Nibelungen.*

Vampire: in folklore, an "undead" person who sleeps in his grave or a coffin filled with his native earth by day but who preys on human victims to drink their blood at night. Usually the victim of a curse himself, the vampire is a sympathetic monster in literature, like the werewolf. The erotic undertones of his lust for blood and subsequent possession of virgins make him a romantic character as well. Belief in vampires is worldwide, but the most familiar vampire lore is of Slavic origin. It became popularly known through Bram Stoker's horror novel *Dracula* (1897).

Vanity Fair: novel by English writer William Makepeace Thackeray, published in 1847–1848, subtitled "A Novel Without a Hero." It satirizes social customs in early 19th-century England (the period of the Napoleonic Wars) through the contrasting histories of the fortunes of two young women—Becky Sharp, an unprincipled, opportunistic charmer, and Amelia Sedley, a passive, modest, softhearted girl, whom life soon crushes under its weight. A well known description of Napoleon—"He is as great as a man can be without virtue"—could well be applied to Becky Sharp. Though she may not engage the reader's sympathy, her vitality and spirit command his fascinated attention.

Venus: See *Aphrodite.*

Verse: in general, metrical composition as differentiated from prose; specifically, one metrical line composed of a number of feet. The word "verse" is also often used to mean "stanza." The term usually refers to compositions of a superficial nature (as in "light verse") that make no pretense at being poetry.

Vesta or **Hestia,** RM: virgin goddess of the fire and hearth, not only for the home but for the state. The fire in her temple was never allowed to go out and was tended by the six Vestal Virgins, chosen for their beauty and lineage. They were sworn to 30 years of chastity and were buried alive if they broke their vows.

Vicar of Wakefield, The: novel by English author Oliver Goldsmith, set in 18th-century rural England. First published in 1766, it describes a kindly English vicar's noble reaction to the loss of his fortune and to succeeding mishaps that affect his five growing children.

Victorian era: in English literature, the period defined by the reign of Queen Victoria (1837–1901), an era of progress, reform, and national expansion, in which pragmatic philosophies, utilitarianism, and laissez-faire economics became dominant. The age is notable for literary productivity of all kinds, but its most typical product is the leisurely, realistic middle-class novel, such as was written in mid-century by Dickens, Thackeray, George Eliot, and Anthony Trollope; and later on by Thomas Hardy and Joseph Conrad. Representative Victorian poets are Tennyson, Browning, and Matthew Arnold. In a narrow sense, the term *Victorian* connotes prudishness and complacency, but the great Victorian writers were all critical of their age. Dickens wrote more about poverty than about prosperity; Arnold called his contemporaries "philistines" and saw the "naked shingles of the world" beneath the calm facade of Dover Beach; and the historian Thomas Carlyle tried to tell his generation that man's destiny was not happiness but work.

Vita Nuova, La (*The New Life*): collection of sonnets, completed in 1292, and other poems, addressed by the Italian Renaissance poet Dante to his beloved Beatrice, whom he first saw at the age of nine. The poems are interspersed throughout a prose commentary that follows the development of his love for Beatrice up to and after her death.

Vivian: See *Arthurian legend.*

Völsunga Saga: 13th-century Icelandic saga, a prose narrative that draws on heroic tales recounted in the eddas. A slightly different version is given in the *Nibelungenlied*; the German names of the characters appear in parentheses here.

Sigurd (Siegfried) is the last of the Völsungs, who were named after Sigurd's grandfather, Völsung, the grandson of the god Odin. Sigurd kills the dragon and acquires its cursed treasure. He awakens the Valkyrie maiden Brunhild from her sleep and marries her, but soon goes on a journey to the land of the Nibelungs. There a potion makes him forget Brunhild, and he marries Gudrun (Kriemhild), sister of King Gunnar (Gunther). In disguise, he woos and wins Brunhild for Gunnar. She learns of the deception, has Sigurd killed, and kills herself. Gunnar and his brothers sink the treasure in the Rhine. Gudrun marries Atli (Etzel: based on the historical Attila the Hun), who kills her brothers in an effort to get the treasure; Gudrun then kills Atli and her two sons by him. Richard Wagner's four music dramas comprising *The Ring of the Nibelungs,* are largely based on these legends. See also *Nibelungenlied.*

Vulcan: See *Hephaestus.*

W

Waiting for Godot: play by the Irish-born French writer Samuel Beckett, published in 1952 and performed in 1953, a classic of the theater of the absurd. The characters Vladimir (Didi) and Estragon (Gogo) are two tramps who are waiting in a static landscape for a Mr. Godot. Other characters come and go, senseless (but unquestioned) beatings occur, farcical attempts at suicide fail. At times a messenger appears to tell them that Mr. Godot is not coming, will be delayed, or will come tomorrow. It is not clear, or meant to be clear, who or what Godot is—God? Salvation? Grace? Death? It is only clear that waiting (the condition of life) is boring, intolerable, and absurd.

Waiting for Lefty: one-act proletarian play by the U.S. dramatist Clifford Odets, presented in 1935. The scene is a meeting of desperate taxicab drivers in the Depression era. Their cynical union boss, Fatt, has advised them not to strike; without their leader, Lefty, they are confused. While they argue, the scene switches rapidly to vignettes showing their home life and the fate of other workers facing the same dilemma. When news comes to the hall that Lefty has been killed, one of the men asks what they are to do. Actors planted in the audience, and members of the aroused audience as well, give them the answer: "Strike! Strike! Strike!"

Walden: book of essays published in 1854 by the U.S. philosopher-writer Henry David Thoreau. It describes the author's experiment in living alone in the woods for two years (1845–1847) in a house he built on the shores of Walden Pond. In describing the natural life and seasonal changes at the pond, Thoreau provides a reflective critical commentary on the false "playing at life" that most civilized societies mistake for living. In addition to its literary value, *Walden* has a symbolic value: it is a paean to independence and a warning to the reader to test his own values, lest he die without ever having lived.

Walpurgis Night: in German folklore, the eve of May 1st (May Day), when the Devil and the witches were believed to hold a riotous festival on the Brocken, a peak in the Harz Mountains. Goethe's *Faust* contains a scene describing Walpurgis Night.

War and Peace: epic novel by the Russian writer Leo Tolstoy, published in 1864–1869, one of the great novels of all time. It presents a panoramic view of Russian aristocratic society in the early 19th century before, during, and after Napoleon's invasion of Russia. Its numerous characters are all vividly realized, from the old aristocrat Count Bolkonsky through the young and idealistic Petya Rostov. Soldiers, peasants, princesses, simple workmen, and even Napoleon himself are portrayed. Perhaps the most memorable characters are the hero Pierre Bezukhov, a fat, awkward, impractical idealist, whose eccentric reflections provide a commentary on his age, and the high-spirited beauty Natasha Rostov, whom he has loved since her childhood and eventually marries.

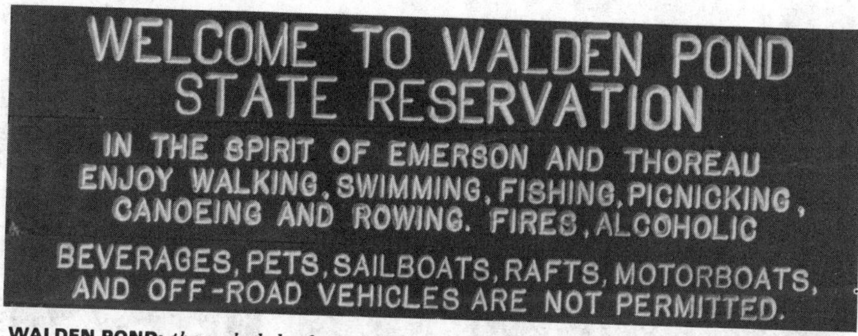

WELCOME TO WALDEN POND
STATE RESERVATION
IN THE SPIRIT OF EMERSON AND THOREAU
ENJOY WALKING, SWIMMING, FISHING, PICNICKING,
CANOEING AND ROWING. FIRES, ALCOHOLIC
BEVERAGES, PETS, SAILBOATS, RAFTS, MOTORBOATS,
AND OFF-ROAD VEHICLES ARE NOT PERMITTED.

PHILIP JON BAILEY/TAURUS PHOTOS

WALDEN POND: *the secluded refuge of Henry David Thoreau has become a state park, a turn of events Thoreau would doubtless have deplored.*

War of the Worlds: science fiction novel by English writer H. G. Wells, published in 1898. It simulates the horror of a Martian invasion that fails only because the invaders cannot tolerate Earth's bacteria. A radio version in 1938 by Orson Welles and the Mercury Theatre players caused a great panic among listeners who thought the play was an actual news broadcast.

Waste Land, The: poem by the Anglo-American poet T. S. Eliot, published in 1922. Both stylistically and thematically it is one of the major works in modern English poetry. Its theme is that of a culture in distress, presented in a series of disjointed images and scenes drawn from commonplace upper- and lower-class daily life as well as from ancient, obscure fertility rituals. Its title and controlling imagery are taken from the Grail legend. The progress of the poem suggests the sick Fisher King's search through the wasteland of modern life—the Unreal City—for a cure for his illness. The poem integrates words, phrases, and images from other literary works so that the traditions of the past form a contrapuntal echo to the modern dilemma. The poem was published with several pages of notes explaining its allusions.

Waverley Novels: collective title given to the historical romances of English author Sir Walter Scott. *Waverley,* published anonymously in 1814, was the first of the series. The others, until 1827, were signed "by the author of *Waverley.*" *Waverley* has the distinction of being the first historical novel. In it and in other works dealing with Scotland's heroic and colorful past, Scott touched off the springs of Romantic nationalism and became the most popular, most widely imitated novelist in Europe. His historical novels includes *Guy Mannering, The Antiquary, Old Mortality, The Heart of Midlothian, Rob Roy, The Bride of Lammermoor, Ivanhoe, Quentin Durward,* and *Kenilworth*

Way of all Flesh, The: novel by the English writer Samuel Butler, published posthumously in 1903. It cruelly dissects the relationships of three generations of a Victorian family. In his bitter rejection of the hypocritical piety of his clergyman father, Butler's autobiographical hero Ernest Pontifex also rejects the religion and bourgeois values that his parents represent.

Way of the World, The: play by the English dramatist William Congreve, presented in 1700, considered the outstanding comedy of the Restoration period. Like most plays of the period, its plot is fantastically complicated. Its high point is the famous bargaining scene between the lovers Mirabell and Mrs. Millamant, in which they each state their conditions for marriage. This is not the expected witty duel of the sexes; it is, instead, a frank expression of deeper values by two people who are each too intelligent to be satisfied with the "way of the world."

Werewolf: in worldwide folklore, a human being who turns into a wolf and preys on other humans. Lycanthropy, or the temporary transformation of a human being into animal form, was long assumed to be the power of witches. But in fairy tales the transformation is often caused by a curse rather than an act of will, as in "Beauty and the Beast" and "The Frog Prince." Ovid relates the tale of Lycaon, a Greek king who was transformed into a wolf by Jupiter as a punishment for serving the god human flesh. However, in R. L. Stevenson's *The Strange Case of Dr. Jekyll and Mr. Hyde,* the metamorphosis is caused by the doctor's experiments and, as such, is a result of his will. When Jekyll loses control over the transformation, he fits the pattern of the victims of the curse, who are romantic, sympathetic figures. The werewolf as benevolent savior occurs in *William of Palerne,* a 14th-century English romance in which the beast aids the hero and is at last returned to human form.

Who's Afraid of Virginia Woolf?: play by the U.S. dramatist Edward Albee, first performed in 1962. A young married couple, Nick and Honey, new in the academic community, visit

WHO'S AFRAID OF VIRGINIA WOOLF?: *the wife of the young professor challenges George, an older professor, in the film version of Edward Albee's vitriolic yet moving play.*

George and Martha, a middle-aged professor and his wife, for a drink and an evening of "fun and games." But the games played by George and Martha are deadly. They lacerate each other's egos, seduce and humiliate Nick, and attempt to destroy Honey. The games are designed to strip away illusions until all four are drunken, sobbing wrecks. One suspects, however, that George and Martha will pull themselves together to play the games the following evening.

Wild Duck, The: symbolic drama by Norwegian playwright Henrik Ibsen, first performed in 1885. The play is a study of the illusions that sustain people in everyday life. As one character says, "Take away the life-lie from the average man and straight away you take away his happiness."

Wilhelm Meister's Apprenticeship: symbolic novel by German author Johann Wolfgang von Goethe, published in 1795–1796. It is considered the model for the apprenticeship-to-life novel, called in German *Bildungsroman,* in which a youthful hero matures. Wilhelm, the son of a merchant, is an artistic, stagestruck youth who joins a troup of traveling players. He is disciplined into manhood by art. A sequel published in 1829, *Wilhelm Meister's Travels,* shows Wilhelm and his young son Felix setting out on a new voyage of experience and self-discovery. It apparently indicates that the apprenticeship to life is never over; that there is always more to learn. In this second novel, science and philosophy play a greater role than art.

William Tell: legendary Swiss patriot of the early 1300's, when Switzerland was ruled by Austria. Tell refused to acknowledge the Austrian governor, Gessler by bowing to Gessler's hat, which had been set on a pole in the town square of Altdorf. As punishment, Gessler ordered Tell to show his skill with the crossbow by shooting an apple off his son's head. Tell succeeded, then warned the governor that, had he missed, he would have shot Gessler too. Tell was seized but he escaped, and later did shoot Gessler, inciting the Swiss to revolt against Austrian rule.

Tell is the subject of a famous drama by Schiller (1804), from which Rossini derived his opera *William Tell* (1829).

Wind in the Willows, The: classic children's book by the English writer Kenneth Grahame, published in 1908. It is about a group of river animals—Mole, a fussy bachelor; Rat, a romantic poet; and Badger, a crabbed philosopher—and the troubles they incur because of their incorrigible young friend Toad, "the king of the Road," who has a passion for cars and reckless driving. After the conceited Toad has been imprisoned for stealing a car, and the stoats and the weasels have taken over Toad Hall, his friends help him recover his mansion, and finally succeed in reforming him.

Winesburg, Ohio: collection of poetic short stories, the masterpiece of U.S. writer Sherwood Anderson, published in 1919. The stories are linked in theme and by the central figure of George Willard, a dreamy adolescent who aspires to be a writer. As the people of the town reveal to George their loneliness, frustration, delusions, and dreams, the inarticulate soul of Winesburg comes to life. In the final story, "Departure," George is on the train that will carry him to the city, looking back on the village of Winesburg until it disappears.

Wings of the Dove: novel by U.S. expatriate author Henry James, published in 1902. It is a novel of grand manners, for all the characters are playing a delicate game for very high stakes. Milly Theale (the dove), an American heiress in Europe, gallantly ignores the fact that she has a fatal disease. Her friend Kate Croy, who cannot marry Merton Densher for lack of money, proposes that Densher marry Milly to inherit her wealth; he shrinks from the deception, until Kate seals the bargain by becoming his mistress. Milly responds to Densher's courtship, but when she learns of his relationship with Kate, she gives up her fight for life. After her death, a letter comes to Densher; both he and Kate know it is from Milly, offering money so they can marry. But they can no longer accept the money or one another and throw the letter unopened into the fire.

Winnie-the-Pooh: children's book written by English author A. A. Milne, first published in 1926. It relates the adventures of Christopher Robin, patterned on Milne's son; his stuffed bear, named Winnie-*Ther*-Pooh; and their friends Piglet, Owl, Rabbit, Eeyore, Kanga, and Roo in a whimsical landscape where there are heffalumps but no adults. In a later book, *The House at Pooh Corner* (1928), a new friend, Tigger, was introduced. Milne's books were illustrated by Ernest H. Shepard.

WINNIE-THE-POOH, *a stuffed bear, confers with his friend Christopher Robin.*

Witch: in worldwide belief, a person with supernatural knowledge and powers, usually acquired from the Devil in exchange for his or her soul. Witches are believed to be able to change shape, transform others, cause illness and death, concoct charms, and tell the future. In literature, their prophecies never lie, but they do mislead. Shakespeare's Three Weird Sisters in *Macbeth* are the most famous witches in literature. They serve to set the ominous mood in the first scene as well as to deceive Macbeth into a false security. The convention of three cackling crones originates with the sister Fates (see also *Fates*).

In literature, witches tend to be female. Although fairy-tale witches are commonly conceived of as hags, in poetic usage the witch is often seductive. In the *Odyssey,* Circe is an amorous witch who transforms Odysseus's men into swine (see also *Circe*). In Coleridge's "Christabel," an evil spirit assumes the form of a beautiful girl. Keats's "La Belle Dame Sans Merci" is also a lovely enchantress who saps a young man's vitality.

Witches often play the temptress in order to acquire a soul for the Devil. The Witches' Sabbaths in Goethe's *Faust* and Hawthorne's "Young Goodman Brown" both employ beautiful witches to seduce the hero. Marlowe's Helen of Troy in *Doctor Faustus* is another instance of the Devil using sexuality to steal a soul. In M.G. Lewis's *The Monk,* a Gothic novel, the villainous lecher, at one time a respected monk, is seduced into evil by a sorceress who looks like the Madonna. Shelley, in his poem "The Witch of Atlas," expands the convention to include a witch who is both beautiful and kind.

Witches are vengeful and tend to hold grudges against following generations, as in Hawthorne's *The House of Seven Gables.* Many Gothic tales are built around undying curses falling on the heads of innocent descendants.

Wizard of Oz, The: children's story by U.S. author L. Frank Baum, first published in 1900 and titled *The Wonderful Wizard of Oz.* Baum's tale of the adventures of Dorothy and Toto, the Scarecrow, the Tin Woodman, and the Cowardly Lion was so well received that Baum continued to write books about the land of Oz until his death. The first Oz book was illustrated by W. W. Denslow; the succeeding ones by John R. Neill.

Woden: See *Odin.*

Would-Be Gentleman, The: play by French dramatist Molière, performed in 1670, a satire on hypocrisy. M. Jourdain, a tradesman, aspires to be a gentleman by taking strenuous training in superficial courtesies. Fortunately, his inherent but more genuinely appealing vulgarity makes him impervious to the transformation.

Woyzeck: play by the German writer Georg Büchner, published in 1879, far in advance of its time in its modern style and psychological realism. Woyzeck is a poor conscript who supports his mistress Marie and their little boy by performing services for a captain and a doctor. The doctor uses him for medical experiments—literally as a guinea pig—but he is equally a guinea pig for the captain, who delights in taxing Woyzeck's simple mind with difficult questions. They also find amusement in teasing Woyzeck with stories of Marie's infidelities that Woyzeck at last realizes are true. He begins to behave strangely and to have violent dreams. One night he stabs Marie to death at a lonely pond, then dances madly at the inn, frightening everyone by his bloodstained hands and wild talk. Returning to the woods to retrieve his knife, Woyzeck drowns in the pond. The story is the basis of a modern opera, *Wozzeck,* by the German composer Alban Berg.

Wuthering Heights: novel by English writer Emily Bronte, published in 1847. Wuthering Heights is the Earnshaw estate set in the moors of northern England. Here the kindly Mr. Earnshaw brings a dark, ragged slum boy, Heathcliff, to be raised with his children Catherine and Hindley. Hindley hates the intruder and, on his father's death, reduces him to a servant. But Cathy and Heathcliff, both rebels, have already formed the intense relationship that is the core of the novel. Cathy makes a conventional marriage to genteel Edgar Linton, but cannot forget the wild Heathcliff, and he cannot forgive her betrayal. After Cathy's death, he takes revenge by marrying and mistreating Linton's weak-willed sister, acquiring the family properties, and ruining Hindley. He finds peace only by joining Cathy in death.

X

Xanadu: See *Kubla Khan.*

Y

Yahoo: See *Gulliver's Travels.*

Yearling, The: novel by U.S. writer Marjorie Kinnan Rawlings, published in 1938. Its subject is the turning point from boyhood to manhood in the life of twelve-year-old Jody Baxter, a child of the impoverished Florida scrub country. During a period when his father is ill and the family resources are depleted, Jody finds a fawn that he raises and shares his food with. When the fawn grows up and regularly devours the family crops, his mother shoots it. Jody runs away from home, but returns to face his family with forgiveness and understanding.

Yggdrasil, NM: great world tree, an ash tree, binding together heaven, earth, and the underworld. Rooted in the underworld, where a dragon was believed

THE WIZARD OF OZ: *Dorothy, played by Judy Garland, comforts the Cowardly Lion (Bert Lahr) in the musical film version of the children's classic.*

CULVER PICTURES

Please also consult the guide to the Bible for more complete information on entries dealing with biblical themes. The symbols used in this guide are as follows: G-*Greek;* R-*Roman;* N-*Norse;* M-*myth;* L-*legend.*

to forever gnaw at the roots, its trunk supported the world, and its top reached beyond heaven. Yggdrasil was the tree of life, and also the tree of knowledge, for Mimir's well of wisdom had its source beneath its roots. It was the tree of fate as well, for beneath it sat the Norns who presided over human destiny. An eagle sat in the top, and the squirrel Ratatook ran up and down it, carrying strife.

You Know Me, Al: novel in letter form by the U.S. writer Ring Lardner, published in 1916. The letters are written by Jack Keefe, a rookie pitcher with the Chicago White Sox, to his old bush-league pal, Al. They tell Al how Keefe is the sole mainstay of his ball club, how he is pursued by beautiful women, and admired by his teammates and coaches. Subsequent letters reveal gradually that Keefe is really a second-stringer whose conceit is undamaged by reality.

Yseult: See *Tristan and Iseult.*

Zephyrus, GM: god personifying the gentle west wind (the "zephyr"); called Favonius by the Romans.

Zeus, GM: supreme god identified with the Roman Jupiter. Zeus was the youngest son of Cronus and Rhea. When he was grown, Zeus overthrew his father, establishing the Olympian gods who were his brothers and sisters (see also *Cronus*). He married his sister Hera and also loved many mortal women.

Zeus was primarily king of the gods and heaven, the sky god and, especially, the thunder god. The thunderbolt was his weapon, and he was worshiped on mountain tops. His worship later took on moral and social aspects, and eventually embodied legal and political ideas as well. Zeus also was god and protector of the state and the god of personal and public oaths; murder was abhorrent to him. He was regarded in many stories as father of the world.

Zorba the Greek: novel by the Greek writer Nikos Kazantzakis, first published as *Alexis Zorba* in 1946, translated into English in 1952. It presents a rascally old Greek workman, capable of great feats of physical strength. Zorba is shown handling a mine on Crete for a bookish Briton—singing, dancing, relating amorous adventures, and even mishandling the Briton's funds. But under the impact of Zorba's uninhibited zest for life, his strait-laced employer is reeducated and becomes a freer person.

For Further Reference

General

Buchanan-Brown, John, editor. *Cassell's Encyclopedia of World Literature* (Revised Ed.). 3 volumes. William Morrow, 1973.

Di Yanni, Robert. *Introduction to Literature.* Random House, 1986.

Downs, Robert Bingham. *Books That Changed the World.* American Library Association, 1978.

Holman, C. Hugh, and William Harmon. *A Handbook to Literature* (5th Ed.). Macmillan, 1986.

Priestley, J. B. *Literature and Western Man.* Harper & Row, 1960.

Ancient

Duff, John Wight. *A Literary History of Rome.* Barnes & Noble, 1960–1964.

Else, Gerald F. *The Origin and Early Form of Greek Tragedy.* W.W. Norton, 1972.

Harvey, Sir Paul. *The Oxford Companion to Classical Literature.* Oxford University Press, 1937.

Highet, Gilbert. *The Classical Tradition.* Oxford University Press, 1949.

Wilkie, Brian, and James Hurt. *Literature of the Western World: The Ancient World Through the Renaissance* (2nd Ed.). Macmillian, 1988.

Eastern

Giles, Herbert A. *The Classical History of Chinese Literature.* 3 volumes. Gloucester Art, 1985.

Keene, Donald, editor. *Anthology of Japanese Literature from the Earliest Era to the Mid-Nineteenth Century.* Grove Press, 1955.

Keene, Donald. *Japanese Literature: An Introduction for Western Readers.* Grove Press, 1955.

Kritzeck, James, editor. *Anthology of Islamic Literature: From the Rise of Islam to Modern Times.* New American Library, 1975.

Kritzeck, James. *Modern Islamic Literature: From Eighteen Hundred to the Present.* New American Library, 1972.

Liu, Wu-chi. *An Introduction to Chinese Literature.* Indiana University Press, 1966.

MacDonell, Arthur A. *History of Sanskrit Literature.* Haskell Booksellers, 1969.

Majumdar, R.C., and A.D. Pusalker, editors. *The History and Culture of the Indian People.* 10 volumes. Macmillan, 1951–1955.

Winternitz, Moriz. *A History of Indian Literature.* 3 volumes. International Publications Service, 1978.

European

Butler, Kathleen. *A History of French Literature.* 2 volumes. Russell and Russell, 1966.

Chadwick, H.M. *The Heroic Age.* Cambridge University Press, 1967.

Chandler, Richard E., and Kessel Schwartz. *A New History of Spanish Literature.* Louisiana State University Press, 1961.

Fowlie, Wallace. *French Literature: Its History and Meaning.* Prentice-Hall, 1973.

Friederich, Werner P., et al. *An Outline of German Literature* (Revised Ed.). Barnes & Noble, 1961.

Jackson, W.T.H. *The Literature of the Middle Ages.* Columbia University Press, 1960.

Laborde, E.D. *History of Spanish Literature.* Folcroft Library Editions, 1973.

Nitze, William A., and Preston E. Dargan. *A History of French Literature: From Earliest Times to the Present.* Darby Books, 1985.

Northup, George T. *An Introduction to Spanish Literature* (3rd Ed.). University of Chicago Press, 1960.

Robertson, John G. *A History of German Literature* (5th Ed.). Dufour Editions, 1970.

Salmon, Paul. *Literature in Medieval Germany.* Cresset Press, 1967.

Stade, George, editor. *European Writers: The Romantic Century.* Scribner's, 1985.

English

Abrams, M.H., et al. *Norton Anthology of English Literature.* 2 volumes. W.W. Norton, 1979.

Baugh, Albert C., editor. *A Literary History of England* (2nd Ed.). Appleton-Century-Crofts, 1967.

The Cambridge History of English Literature. 15 volumes. Cambridge University Press, 1907–1916, 1932.

Harvey, Sir Paul, editor. *The Oxford Companion to English Literature.* Oxford University Press, 1967.

Sampson, George, editor. *The Concise Cambridge History of English Literature* (3rd Ed.). Cambridge University Press, 1970.

American

Gottesman, Ronald, et al. *Norton Anthology of American Literature.* 2 volumes. W.W. Norton, 1979.

Hart, James D. *Oxford Companion to American Literature* (4th Ed.). Oxford University Press, 1965.

Spiller, Robert E., et al. *Literary History of the United States.* 2 volumes. Macmillan, 1963.

Trent, W. P., et al. *Cambridge History of American Literature.* Macmillan, 1943.

VOLUME 17

Mathematics

U.S. WEIGHTS AND MEASURES For metric equivalents, see pages 1416, 1418, and 1419.

	Unit (abbreviation)	Equivalents
Length	mile (*mi*)	5,280 feet, 320 rods, 1,760 yards
	furlong (*fur*)	0.125 mile, 40 rods, 660 feet
	rod (*rd*)	5.50 yards, 16.5 feet
	yard (*yd*)	3 feet, 36 inches
	foot (*ft or* ′)	12 inches, 0.333 yard
	inch (*in or* ″)	0.083 foot, 0.027 yard
Area	square mile (*sq mi or* m^2)	640 acres, 102,400 square rods
	acre (*a or ac*)	4,840 square yards, 43,560 square feet
	square rod (*sq rd or* rd^2)	30.25 square yards, 0.006 acre
	square yard (*sq yd or* yd^2)	1,296 square inches, 9 square feet
	square foot (*sq ft or* ft^2)	144 square inches, 0.111 square yard
	square inch (*sq in or* in^2)	0.007 square foot
Volume	cubic yard (*cu yd or* yd^3)	27 cubic feet, 46,656 cubic inches
	cubic foot (*cu ft or* ft^3)	1,728 cubic inches, 0.0370 cubic yard
	cubic inch (*cu in or* in^3)	0.00058 cubic foot, 0.000021 cubic yard
Capacity Liquid Measure	gallon (*gal*)	4 quarts (231 cubic inches)
	quart (*qt*)	2 pints (57.75 cubic inches)
	pint (*pt*)	4 gills (28.875 cubic inches)
	gill (*gi*)	4 fluidounces (7.218 cubic inches)
	fluidounce (*fl oz or f*℥)	8 fluidrams (1.804 cubic inches)
	fluidram (*fl dr or f*ʒ)	60 minims (0.225 cubic inch)
	minim (*min or m*χ)	1/60 fluidram (0.003759 cubic inch)
Dry Measure	bushel (*bu*)	4 pecks (2,150.42 cubic inches)
	peck (*pk*)	8 quarts (537.605 cubic inches)
	quart (*qt*)	2 pints (67.200 cubic inches)
	pint (*pt*)	1/2 quart (33.600 cubic inches)

	Unit (abbreviation)	Equivalents
Weight Avoirdupois	short ton	20 short hundredweight, 2000 pounds
	long ton	20 long hundredweight, 2240 pounds
	short hundredweight (*cwt*)	100 pounds, 0.05 short ton
	long hundredweight (*cwt*)	112 pounds, 0.05 long ton
	pound (*lb or lb av or #*)	16 ounces, 7000 grains
	ounce (*oz or oz av*)	16 drams, 437.5 grains
	dram (*dr or dr av*)	27.343 grains, 0.0625 ounce
	grain (*gr*)	0.036 dram, 0.002285 ounce
Troy	pound (*lb t*)	12 ounces, 240 pennyweight, 5760 grains
	ounce (*oz t*)	20 pennyweight, 48 grains
	pennyweight (*dwt or pwt*)	24 grains, 0.05 ounce
	grain (*gr*)	0.042 pennyweight, 0.002083 ounce
Apothecaries	pound (*lb ap*)	12 ounces, 5760 grains
	ounce (*oz ap or* ℥)	8 drams, 480 grains
	dram (*dr ap or* ʒ)	3 scruples, 60 grains
	scruple (*s ap or* ℈)	20 grains, 0.333 dram
	grain (*gr*)	0.05 scruple, 0.002083 ounce, 0.0166 dram

LEARNING ARITHMETIC: JEFFRY W. MYERS/ALPHA PHOTO ASSOCIATES

VOLUME **17**

Mathematics

FUNDAMENTAL PHOTOS · SID GREENBERG/DPI · UPI · CULVER PICTURES · MOBIL OIL · SHARP

Mathematics plays an important part in our lives. Everyone can count, and most people do simple arithmetic. But about 40 percent of the people in the United States use mathematics beyond arithmetic. Carpenters use geometry. Machinists use trigonometry. Many businessmen and most scientists need algebra. Almost all scientists, including social scientists, need statistics. People working in the pure sciences and engineers use calculus and more advanced mathematics.

Indirectly, we are even more affected by mathematics. Computers, even the small computers built into appliances and automobiles, are based on mathematics. Automobiles and airplanes are designed using mathematics. So are roads, bridges, and skyscrapers.

How to use this volume. The contents have been specifically designed to help you review the mathematics you once studied but have now forgotten. For example, if you have forgotten a formula, you will find the ones most commonly used in easy-to-use tables.

If you are a parent helping a child, or if you want to learn more about mathematics, you can both teach and learn by using this volume. Unlike a textbook, this volume makes it easy for you by including the reasons behind the mathematical operations. Another helpful feature is the special emphasis given to problem solving—the kind of mathematics that occurs in everyday life.

The mathematics in this volume is broken into subjects in just the way that mathematics is divided in most schools.

Arithmetic. This section includes everything that is generally taught in the first eight grades in the United States. The essence of arithmetic is adding, subtracting, multiplying, and dividing whole numbers, decimals, and fractions. Knowledge of ratio, proportion, and percent also are required by anyone who wants to understand gasoline mileage or taxation. The arithmetic section emphasizes solving problems involving percents in business, banking, and taxation.

This section on arithmetic is concerned also with squares, square roots, cubes, cube roots, and exponents, including an introduction to exponents presented in the form of logarithms.

Algebra. Algebra deals with sentences about at least one *unknown* or *variable,* represented by a letter, such as x. These sentences can be *equations* or *inequalities.* A solution to a sentence involves finding the number or numbers that make the sentence true. When there are very many solutions, they are often shown on graphs, especially when the solutions are pairs of numbers. Many problems that would be difficult to solve using just arithmetic can be solved easily using algebra.

Geometry. Geometry is concerned with shapes and logical relations between shapes. It starts with simple ideas about points and lines. The rest of geometry is proved from these ideas. Each major relationship is called a *theorem.* Geometry progresses by using previous theorems to prove new ones.

Trigonometry. Trigonometry began as a numerical way to describe relationships in triangles. It is used to measure distances or angles indirectly, and is important in both astronomy and surveying. Trigonometry is used by many other branches of mathematics as well, often where triangles are not even involved.

Calculus. Calculus was invented to solve problems that deal with motion or with the areas or volumes of irregular shapes. It is based on the concept of a *limit,* which is a point or a number to which a sequence converges. Today calculus has become the most important branch of mathematics, used for solving problems in all areas of science and engineering and in the social sciences, such as economics and sociology, as well.

ARITHMETIC

Arithmetic and reading are probably the most necessary skills taught in school. Most people think that reading and writing came first in history, with counting developing later. But counting was first. This is known because bones that are thousands of years older than examples of the first writing contain marks for numbers. Trade between regions hundreds of miles apart, which requires skills beyond counting, such as addition and subtraction, started before writing. In the Middle East, it seems likely that writing words developed as a consequence of writing numbers.

The earliest arithmetic was counting. People marked scratches on a bone to show how many days between full moons or how many arrowheads were traded. The same idea is used when people count on their fingers or keep track of numbers with tallies. A tally is just a mark for each item counted. If votes at a club election were being counted, tallies could be used:

Jim ~~||||~~ ||

Sally ~~||||~~ ||||

Every fifth tally is put across a group of four. That makes it easier to see the total.

The tallies show that Jim has seven, or 7, votes and that Sally has nine, or 9, votes. "Seven" and "7" are names for the same number of tallies. Any set, or group, that has the same number of members as Jim's tallies has seven members. Matching each member of a set with exactly one of Jim's tallies would show that the set has seven members. If you match fingers with the tallies, the fingers of one hand and the thumb and index finger of the other match—seven fingers.

Arranging in order all the names for sets with different numbers of members enables us to *count.* The counting names are *one, two, three,* and so on. Think of a member of the set you are counting. Match it with the first number name, and think or say *one.* Then think of another member, and match it with *two.* When you have thought of all the members of the set, you have counted the set. The last number you match is the number of members in the set.

Counting is the easiest operation in arithmetic. The next easiest operations are addition, subtraction, multiplication, and division of counting numbers. Then arithmetic goes beyond the counting numbers to numbers that are shown as decimals or fractions.

For the arithmetic of the counting numbers, the following is addressed to people who are learning to add, subtract, multiply, and divide.

Numeration

Most languages use different names for the first ten or twenty numbers. Afterward, these names are combined with a few other names. *Two* is hidden in *twelve* and *twenty,* but easy to spot in *twenty-two* and *two hundred.* When we write numbers, however, we usually use a *numeration system.* In our numeration system, it is easy to see that only a few number names are combined to show all numbers. A number name, or any combination of number names, is also called a *numeral.*

Our numeration system was invented by people in India called Hindus, but spread by Arabs. It is called the Hindu-Arabic system, or just the Arabic system.

The Hindu-Arabic system uses the symbols 1, 2, 3, 4, 5, 6, 7, 8, and 9 for the first nine counting numbers. It also has a symbol for a number that is not a counting number, 0 (zero). The Hindus were the first people to see that zero is a number.

The ten Hindu-Arabic symbols are called *digits.* All numbers greater than nine are shown by combining digits.

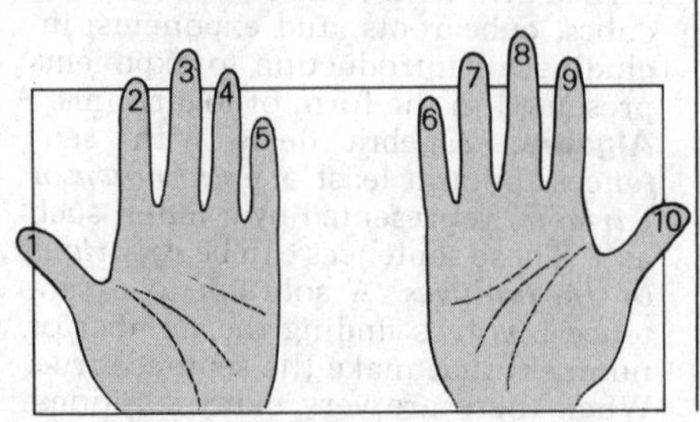

WHOLE NUMBERS *are called* digits, *from the Latin word for finger.*

Each digit in a combination has a meaning that comes from its place in the numeral. Therefore, the Hindu-Arabic system is called a *place-value* system.

Arabs read from right to left, so Hindu-Arabic numerals are read from right to left. Each place in a number is worth ten times as much as the place to its right. The place at the farthest right is the ones place. A digit in that place tells how many ones. The next place to the left is the tens place, where each digit is worth ten. So the number after 9 is written as 10, meaning one ten and zero ones. The numeral 23 means two tens and three ones.

The places are often shown in a table. Please turn to box on next page.

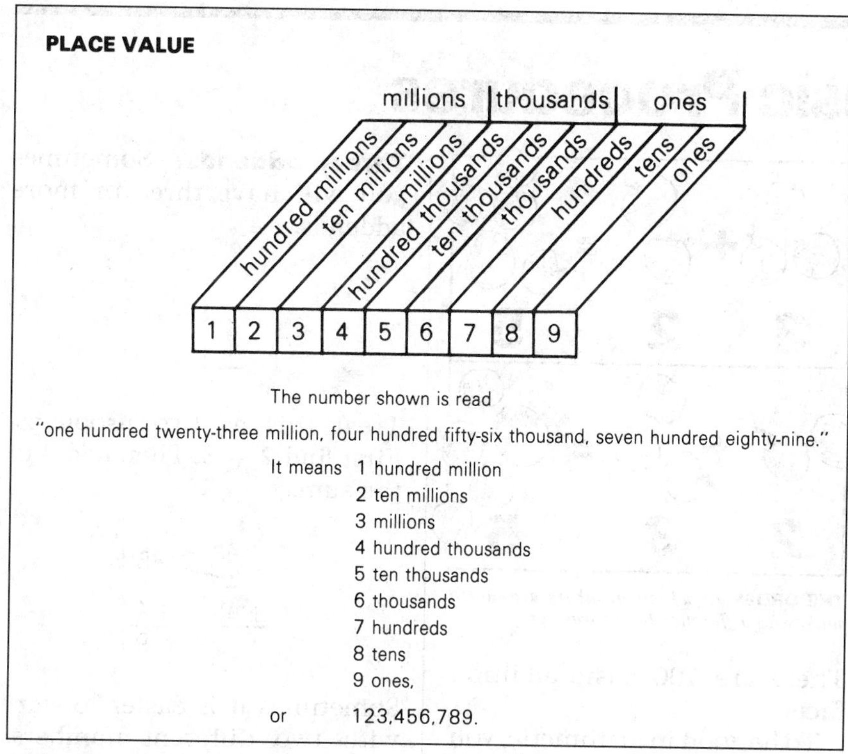

PLACE VALUE
millions
thousands
ones
hundred millions
ten millions
millions
hundred thousands
ten thousands
thousands
hundreds
tens
ones
1 2 3 4 5 6 7 8 9
The number shown is read
"one hundred twenty-three million, four hundred fifty-six thousand, seven hundred eighty-nine."
It means 1 hundred million
2 ten millions
3 millions
4 hundred thousands
5 ten thousands
6 thousands
7 hundreds
8 tens
9 ones,
or 123,456,789.

Comparing numbers. If one number has a leftmost place that is greater than the leftmost place in another number, the first number is greater than the second number. For example, 542 is greater than 97 because the leftmost place in 542 is hundreds, greater than the leftmost place in 97, which is tens. We write

$$542 > 97$$

where the symbol > means "is greater than." We can also write

$$97 < 542$$

where < means "is less than."

If the leftmost place in two numbers is the same, look from left to right until you find a place where the digits are different. Then the number with the greater digit is the greater number. For example, 783,492 is less than 783,621. The first digit that is different in the two numerals is in the hundreds place, where 6 is greater than 4.

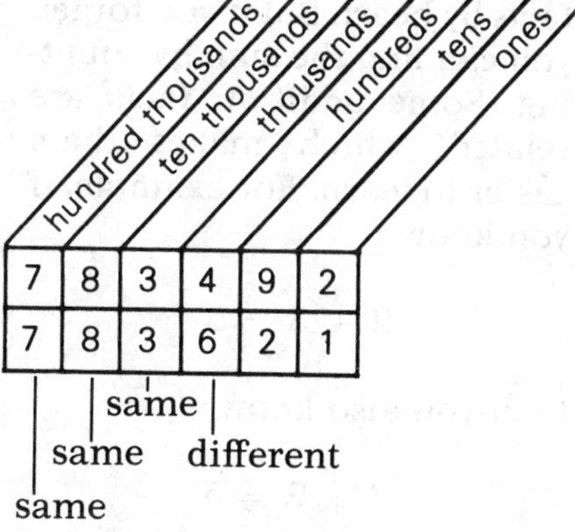

Rounding numbers. Often it is easier to use numbers that are not exact. The most common of such numbers and the easiest to use are called *rounded numbers.* The part of the number that most tells its size is kept. The rest of the number is replaced with zeros.

Choose how much of the number you want to keep. Perhaps you wish to round 3621 to hundreds: 3600. Or you might round 3621 to thousands: 4000; or to tens: 3620. Notice that sometimes the rounded number uses a digit that is one more than a digit in the original numeral.

When you want to change a digit when rounding, first decide which place you will round to. Look one place to the right. If the digit in that place is less than five, replace it and any digits to the right with zeros. If the digit in that place is five or greater, increase the digit in the place you are rounding to by one. Then change the digits to the right to zeros.

For example, to round 8427 to hundreds, look at the digit in the tens place. Tens is one place to the right of hundreds. The tens-place digit is two, which is less than five. So 8427 rounded to hundreds is 8400.

This can be shown in the following diagram.

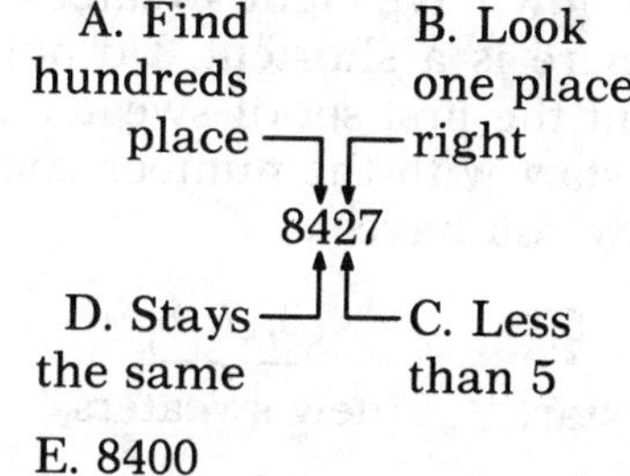

To round 65,822 to thousands, look at the hundreds place. You see that eight is greater than five, so the rounded number is 66,000.

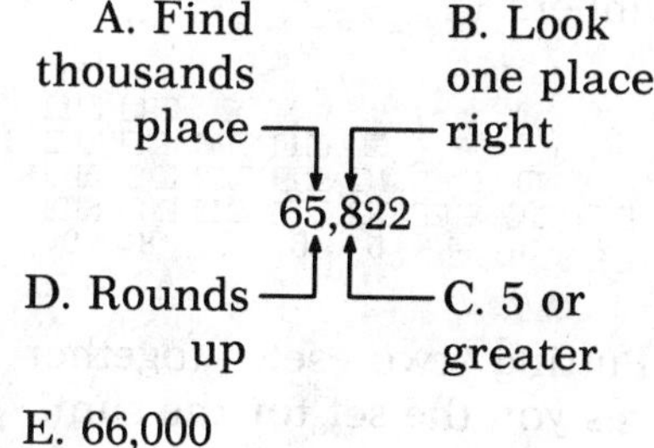

ROUNDING *the cat's weight to the nearest whole number gives an answer of 12.*

Basic Procedures

Addition

Addition is an extension of counting. Suppose you have five sweaters. On your birthday you get three more. You can use counting to find out how many you have in all.

$$5 + 3 = ?$$

Count the five sweaters. Then keep counting and count the new sweaters.

$$\underbrace{1, 2, 3, 4, 5,}_{\text{old sweaters}} \quad \underbrace{6, 7, 8}_{\text{new sweaters}}$$

You now have eight sweaters.

There is a shortcut. Do not count the first set of sweaters, but start with the number you know you have.

$$\underset{\text{start}}{\overset{\uparrow}{5,}} \quad \underbrace{6, 7, 8}_{\text{new sweaters}}$$

The number 8, which is the number of sweaters in all, or 5 + 3, is called the *sum.*

You can also add without counting. Every number stands for a set of objects. Here are sets for the first nine counting numbers.

1 2 3 4 5 6 7 8 9

Putting two sets together gives you the set for the sum.

5 + 3 = 8

Basic facts. Numbers that you add are called *addends.* If two addends are both digits, the statement showing their sum is called a *basic fact.*

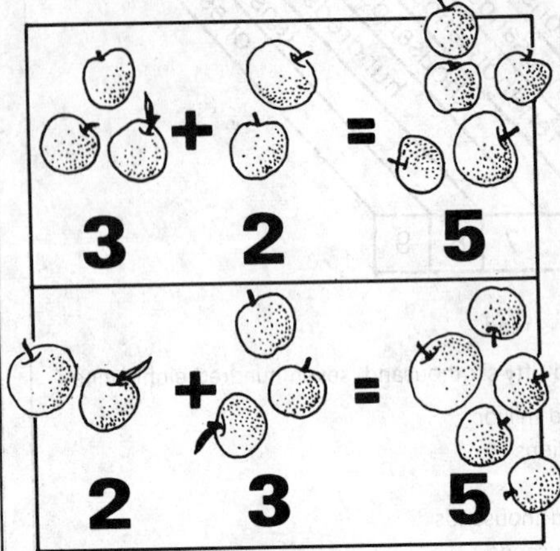

THE ORDER *in which numbers are added makes no difference to the answer.*

There are 100 basic addition facts.

To be good in arithmetic, you need to learn the basic addition facts by heart. But if you forget, you can find the sum by counting. Some addition facts are related, which makes them easier to learn. For example, if you know

$$2 + 3 = 5$$

then you also know

$$3 + 2 = 5$$

The order of the addends does not change the sum.

Addition can also be shown another way:

$$\begin{array}{r} 5 \\ +4 \\ \hline 9 \end{array} \quad \text{means the same as } 5 + 4 = 9$$

LEARNING BASIC FACTS *well is important to success in math.*

Three addends. Sometimes you will have three or more addends.

$$\begin{array}{r} 2 \\ 3 \\ +4 \\ \hline \end{array}$$

Treat this as two problems. First find 2 + 3. Then add 4 to the sum.

$$\begin{array}{r} 2 \\ 3 \\ +4 \\ \hline \end{array} \quad \begin{array}{r} 5 \\ +4 \\ \hline 9 \end{array}$$

Sometimes it is easier to start with two different numbers. You get the same answer.

$$\begin{array}{r} 2 \\ 3 \\ +4 \\ \hline \end{array} \quad \begin{array}{r} 2 \\ +7 \\ \hline 9 \end{array}$$

Beyond basic facts. Larger numbers are added in two stages. In the first stage, only the basic facts are needed with sums less than ten. One column is added at a time. The only new trick is to learn to start with the column on the right and move to the left. For numbers with three digits, add the ones first, then the tens, and then the hundreds. (Remember that Arabs read right to left.)

In the second stage, sums in a column can be more than ten. When that happens, *renaming* must take place. Renaming is the modern word for *carrying.*

To add with renaming, first add the ones. If the sum is ten or greater, write a small 1 at the top of the tens column for the tens in the sum. Write the ones in the ones column. Then add the tens, including the one shown by the small numeral 1.

It is easy to see why this method works if you use squares for the ones and sticks of ten squares for the tens. When you add 47 to 25, show 25 as two sticks five squares and 47 as four sticks seven squares.

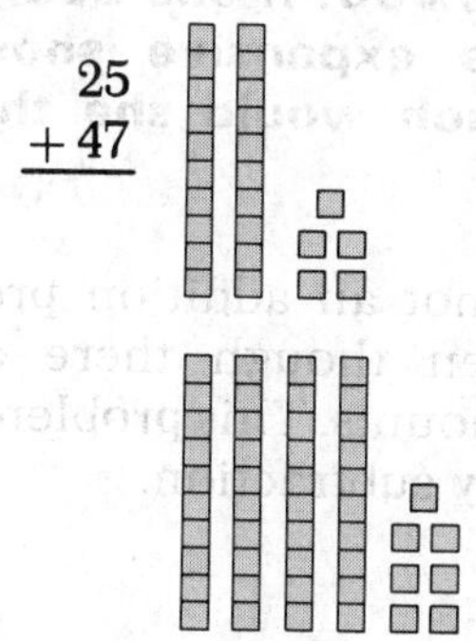

Take the five squares and the seven squares to make one stick and have two squares left over.

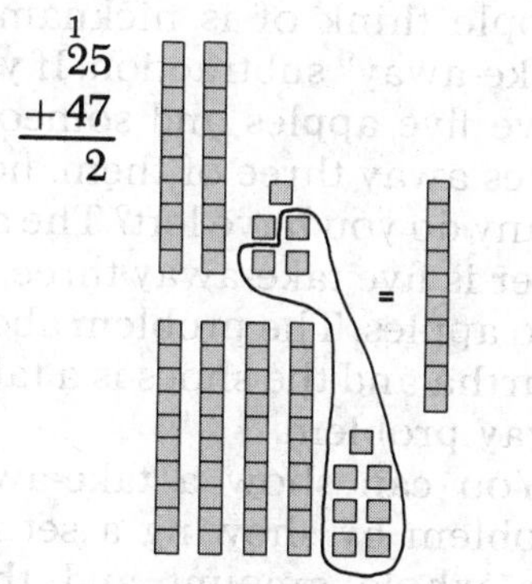

When the sticks and squares are counted, the sum is 72.

$$\begin{array}{r} {}^{1} \\ 25 \\ +47 \\ \hline 72 \end{array}$$

This same idea works for larger numbers. Tens are renamed as hundreds. Hundreds are renamed as thousands. And so on.

Here is an example:

$$\begin{array}{r} 4576 \\ +7928 \\ \hline \end{array} \quad \begin{array}{l} 6 + 8 = 14 \text{ (ones)} \\ 14 \text{ ones} = 1 \text{ ten } 4 \text{ ones} \end{array}$$

$$\begin{array}{r} {}^{1} \\ 4576 \\ +7928 \\ \hline 4 \end{array}$$

$$\begin{array}{r} {}^{1} \\ 4576 \\ +7928 \\ \hline 4 \end{array} \quad \begin{array}{l} 1 + 7 + 2 = 10 \text{ (tens)} \\ 10 \text{ tens} = 1 \text{ hundred} \\ \quad 0 \text{ ones} \end{array}$$

$$\begin{array}{r} {}^{11} \\ 4576 \\ +7928 \\ \hline 04 \end{array}$$

$$\begin{array}{r} {}^{11} \\ 4576 \\ +7928 \\ \hline 04 \end{array} \quad \begin{array}{l} 1 + 5 + 9 = 15 \text{ (hundreds)} \\ 15 \text{ hundreds} = \\ \quad 1 \text{ thousand } 5 \text{ hundreds} \end{array}$$

$$\begin{array}{r} {}^{111} \\ 4576 \\ +7928 \\ \hline 504 \end{array}$$

$$\begin{array}{r} {}^{111} \\ 4576 \\ +7928 \\ \hline 12504 \end{array} \quad \begin{array}{l} 1 + 4 + 7 = \\ \quad 12 \text{ (thousands)} \end{array}$$

When you add a column of numbers, sometimes the sum in a column is greater than 19. In that case, the small numeral you write at the top of the column to the left is 2 or greater.

For example:

$$\begin{array}{r} {}^{2} \\ 38 \\ 96 \\ 47 \\ +62 \\ \hline 3 \end{array} \quad \begin{array}{l} 8 + 6 + 7 + 2 = 23 \text{ (ones)} \\ 23 \text{ ones} = 2 \text{ tens } 3 \text{ ones} \end{array}$$

$$\begin{array}{r} {}^{22} \\ 38 \\ 96 \\ 47 \\ +62 \\ \hline 243 \end{array} \quad \begin{array}{l} 2 + 3 + 9 + 4 + 6 = 24 \text{ (tens)} \\ 24 \text{ tens} = 2 \text{ hundreds } 4 \text{ tens} \end{array}$$

Estimating. Sometimes you do not need an exact sum. For example, when you are shopping, you can estimate the cost of two or more items to see if you have enough money to buy them.

Estimate by rounding the addends. If the addends all have the same number of places, you can get a fairly good estimate just by rounding to that place. For example, if the numbers are 5432 + 2783 + 4597, the easiest estimate is

$$\begin{array}{rcr} 5432 & \text{rounds to} & 5000 \\ 2783 & \text{rounds to} & 3000 \\ +4597 & \text{rounds to} & +5000 \\ \hline & & 13000. \end{array}$$

In this case, the actual answer is 12,812, so 13,000 is a good estimate.

When the number of places is different, round to a place that gives you a reasonable estimate. For example, if most of the addends are hundreds,

BASIC ADDITION FACTS

0 + 0 = 0	1 + 0 = 1	2 + 0 = 2	3 + 0 = 3	4 + 0 = 4	5 + 0 = 5	6 + 0 = 6	7 + 0 = 7	8 + 0 = 8	9 + 0 = 9
0 + 1 = 1	1 + 1 = 2	2 + 1 = 3	3 + 1 = 4	4 + 1 = 5	5 + 1 = 6	6 + 1 = 7	7 + 1 = 8	8 + 1 = 9	9 + 1 = 10
0 + 2 = 2	1 + 2 = 3	2 + 2 = 4	3 + 2 = 5	4 + 2 = 6	5 + 2 = 7	6 + 2 = 8	7 + 2 = 9	8 + 2 = 10	9 + 2 = 11
0 + 3 = 3	1 + 3 = 4	2 + 3 = 5	3 + 3 = 6	4 + 3 = 7	5 + 3 = 8	6 + 3 = 9	7 + 3 = 10	8 + 3 = 11	9 + 3 = 12
0 + 4 = 4	1 + 4 = 5	2 + 4 = 6	3 + 4 = 7	4 + 4 = 8	5 + 4 = 9	6 + 4 = 10	7 + 4 = 11	8 + 4 = 12	9 + 4 = 13
0 + 5 = 5	1 + 5 = 6	2 + 5 = 7	3 + 5 = 8	4 + 5 = 9	5 + 5 = 10	6 + 5 = 11	7 + 5 = 12	8 + 5 = 13	9 + 5 = 14
0 + 6 = 6	1 + 6 = 7	2 + 6 = 8	3 + 6 = 9	4 + 6 = 10	5 + 6 = 11	6 + 6 = 12	7 + 6 = 13	8 + 6 = 14	9 + 6 = 15
0 + 7 = 7	1 + 7 = 8	2 + 7 = 9	3 + 7 = 10	4 + 7 = 11	5 + 7 = 12	6 + 7 = 13	7 + 7 = 14	8 + 7 = 15	9 + 7 = 16
0 + 8 = 8	1 + 8 = 9	2 + 8 = 10	3 + 8 = 11	4 + 8 = 12	5 + 8 = 13	6 + 8 = 14	7 + 8 = 15	8 + 8 = 16	9 + 8 = 17
0 + 9 = 9	1 + 9 = 10	2 + 9 = 11	3 + 9 = 12	4 + 9 = 13	5 + 9 = 14	6 + 9 = 15	7 + 9 = 16	8 + 9 = 17	9 + 9 = 18

round to hundreds. To add 354 + 52 + 1087 + 6 + 248, round to hundreds because there are two hundreds and only one thousand, one ten, and one number in the ones.

354	rounds to	400
52	rounds to	100
1087	rounds to	1100
6	rounds to	0
+ 248	rounds to	+ 200
		1800

The rounded sum of 1800 is close to the actual sum, which is 1747.

Another way to estimate in addition is to add from left to right. For the same problem, you would look at the leftmost column. It only contains the numeral 1 in the thousands place. The first estimate would be 1000. This is not a very good estimate, but it is easy. If you go to the second place, the sum is 3 + 2, or 5 (hundreds). This is 500, so a closer estimate would be 1500, keeping the 1000 from the first estimate and adding in the hundreds. The sum in the tens column is 5 + 5 + 8 + 4, or 22 (tens). This is 220. Adding that to the 1500 gives 1720, a very good estimate. With this method, you get a better estimate with each additional place.

PROBLEM SOLVING. Most addition problems are easy to recognize. One clue is that they often have the words "in all" or "altogether" in the problem, as in

Jed has 16 baseball cards and his brother has 12. How many cards do they have in all?

The "in all" tells you to add. The sum will be 16 + 12, or 28 baseball cards. Addition is the most common operation that uses more than two numbers at a time. If more than two numbers are to be combined, the problem often can be solved by addition.

On Friday 423 people came to the show. On Saturday there were 561. And on Sunday afternoon another 397 people came. How many people saw the show that weekend?

That kind of problem is solved by addition.

$$\begin{array}{r} {\scriptstyle 1\,1} \\ 423 \\ 561 \\ +397 \\ \hline 1381 \end{array}$$

The number of people who saw the show was 1381.

Sometimes, however, there are more than two numbers in a problem, but not all are to be combined by addition.

Martha had $45.30. She saw one pair of shoes she liked for $35.50, while another pair was $50. If she bought the less expensive shoes, how much would she then have?

This is not an addition problem, even though there are three amounts. This problem is solved by subtraction.

Subtraction

There are two different kinds of problems that can be solved by subtraction. The one most people think of is nicknamed "take-away" subtraction. If you have five apples and someone takes away three of them, how many do you have left? The answer is five take-away three, or two apples. The problem about Martha and the shoes is a take-away problem.

You can show a take-away problem by showing a set for the whole amount and then crossing out the part that is taken away. The part that is left is the answer, which is called the *difference*.

5 − 3 = 2

Not all subtraction is of the take-away type. For example, suppose you have $3 and you want to buy something that costs $5. Although the answer is still 5 − 3 = 2, nothing is taken away. A similar problem would be:

Mark is 5 feet tall. His baby sister is 3 feet tall. How much taller is Mark than his sister?

CALCULATOR TIPS

Estimation is especially important if you are using a calculator. If you punch a wrong button or make another mistake, the "answer" can be far from the actual sum.

You have less chance of making an error on a calculator if you punch in fewer digits. One way to do that is to do as much mentally as you can, and just punch in partial sums.

For example, you can group a problem like this:

You see	*You record*
$ 20.32, 100.00	120.32
25.00, 75.00	100.
179.63	179.63
51.20, 10.00	61.2
+ 5.00	+ 5.
	$466.15.

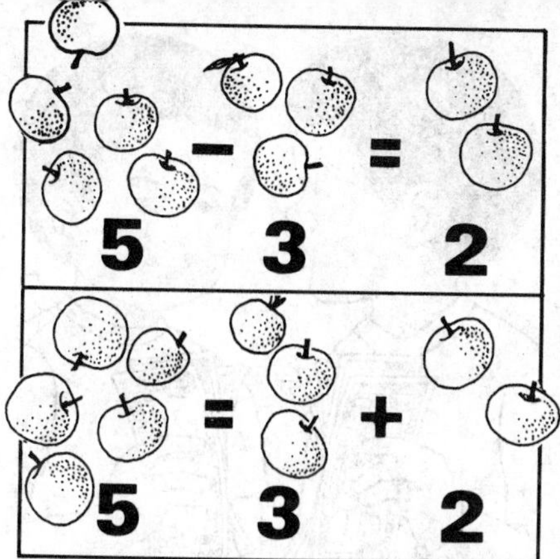

SUBTRACTION AND ADDITION *are closely related. The amount you are subtracting and the amount you have left always add up to the number you started with.*

Again, the answer is 5 − 3 = 2, but still nothing is taken away. This second kind of subtraction is called *comparison* subtraction. Two amounts are compared by subtracting one from the other. You do not take one amount from the other, as in take-away subtraction.

Notice that addition and subtraction are related in both subtraction types. You can tell that 5 − 3 = 2 is true if you know that 3 + 2 = 5 is true. This is easiest to see in the comparison model. If you had $2 more or if Mark's sister grew 2 feet, then you would have $5 or Mark's sister would be as tall as he is.

Basic facts. Like addition, subtraction has 100 basic facts. Often it is easier to learn the subtraction facts at the same time as you learn the addition facts.

$$\begin{array}{r}3\\+2\\\hline 5\end{array}\text{ and }\begin{array}{r}5\\-3\\\hline 2\end{array}\qquad\begin{array}{r}6\\+8\\\hline 14\end{array}\text{ and }\begin{array}{r}14\\-6\\\hline 8\end{array}$$

Notice that the basic subtraction facts can include numbers greater than nine. The top number, the one you subtract from, can be as great as 18, since it is the same as the sum in addition. In subtraction, it is called the *minuend.* The bottom number is called the *subtrahend.* The basic subtraction facts are problems in which the subtrahend and the difference are both digits.

Beyond basic facts. You subtract from right to left, in just the same way that you add. For example, to subtract 361 from 493, use the basic facts to subtract in each column.

$$\begin{array}{r}493\\-361\\\hline 2\end{array}\qquad\begin{array}{r}493\\-361\\\hline 32\end{array}\qquad\begin{array}{r}493\\-361\\\hline 132\end{array}$$

Sometimes, however, the top digit is smaller than the bottom one. In that case, rename. An old name for renaming in subtraction is *borrowing.* This can be shown with squares and sticks of ten squares.

Consider the problem 57 − 28. Starting with the right column, you need to subtract 8 from 7. Since you cannot do this, you rename 57 from 5 tens 7 ones into 4 tens 17 ones.

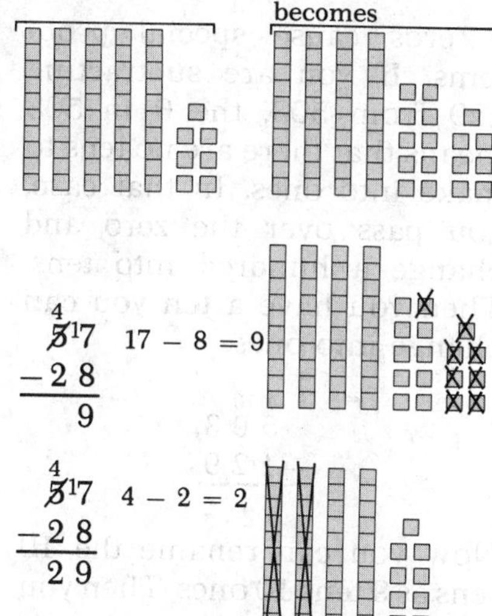

The small "helping numerals" and the crossing out of digits remind you of what you are doing. When you have learned subtraction well, you do not have to use them.

BASIC SUBTRACTION FACTS

0 − 0 = 0									
1 − 0 = 1	1 − 1 = 0								
2 − 0 = 2	2 − 1 = 1	2 − 2 = 0							
3 − 0 = 3	3 − 1 = 2	3 − 2 = 1	3 − 3 = 0						
4 − 0 = 4	4 − 1 = 3	4 − 2 = 2	4 − 3 = 1	4 − 4 = 0					
5 − 0 = 5	5 − 1 = 4	5 − 2 = 3	5 − 3 = 2	5 − 4 = 1	5 − 5 = 0				
6 − 0 = 6	6 − 1 = 5	6 − 2 = 4	6 − 3 = 3	6 − 4 = 2	6 − 5 = 1	6 − 6 = 0			
7 − 0 = 7	7 − 1 = 6	7 − 2 = 5	7 − 3 = 4	7 − 4 = 3	7 − 5 = 2	7 − 6 = 1	7 − 7 = 0		
8 − 0 = 8	8 − 1 = 7	8 − 2 = 6	8 − 3 = 5	8 − 4 = 4	8 − 5 = 3	8 − 6 = 2	8 − 7 = 1	8 − 8 = 0	
9 − 0 = 9	9 − 1 = 8	9 − 2 = 7	9 − 3 = 6	9 − 4 = 5	9 − 5 = 4	9 − 6 = 3	9 − 7 = 2	9 − 8 = 1	9 − 9 = 0
	10 − 1 = 9	10 − 2 = 8	10 − 3 = 7	10 − 4 = 6	10 − 5 = 5	10 − 6 = 4	10 − 7 = 3	10 − 8 = 2	10 − 9 = 1
		11 − 2 = 9	11 − 3 = 8	11 − 4 = 7	11 − 5 = 6	11 − 6 = 5	11 − 7 = 4	11 − 8 = 3	11 − 9 = 2
			12 − 3 = 9	12 − 4 = 8	12 − 5 = 7	12 − 6 = 6	12 − 7 = 5	12 − 8 = 4	12 − 9 = 3
				13 − 4 = 9	13 − 5 = 8	13 − 6 = 7	13 − 7 = 6	13 − 8 = 5	13 − 9 = 4
					14 − 5 = 9	14 − 6 = 8	14 − 7 = 7	14 − 8 = 6	14 − 9 = 5
						15 − 6 = 9	15 − 7 = 8	15 − 8 = 7	15 − 9 = 6
							16 − 7 = 9	16 − 8 = 8	16 − 9 = 7
								17 − 8 = 9	17 − 9 = 8
									18 − 9 = 9

Larger numbers may require more renaming. Instead of just renaming tens as ones, you may have to rename hundreds as tens, thousands as hundreds, and so on. You might have a problem that looks like this (with all the helping numerals shown):

```
 4 13 12
 5 4 3 ¹2
-1 6 7 8
 3 7 5 4.
```

Zeros cause special problems. If you are subtracting 129 from 503, the 0 in 503 means that there are no tens to make into ones. In that case, you pass over the zero and change a hundred into tens. Then you have a ten you can change into ones.

```
 4 10
 5 0 3
-1 2 9
```

Now you can rename the 10 tens as 9 tens 10 ones. Then you can subtract the ones.

```
    9
 4 10
 5 0 ¹3
-1 2 9
     4
```

You can finish the problem in the ordinary way.

```
    9
 4 10
 5 0 ¹3
-1 2 9
 3 7 4
```

Sometimes there is more than one zero that causes the problem. The same ideas can be used to solve the problem. As a shortcut, you can think of each zero as a ten; but you must remember when you reach the first nonzero digit, it must be changed to the next lower digit.

```
 599
 6000
-3257
 2743
```

Estimating. You can use the same ideas to estimate in a subtraction problem as you would use in addition. If all the numbers have the same place, you can round to that place. If the places are different in the numbers, you want to round to a sensible place. Since subtraction problems always involve only two numbers at a time, choosing the place to round to is easier than for addition. Always round both numbers to the highest place *in the number being subtracted.*

For example, to subtract 3706 from 74,298, you round both numbers to thousands because thousands is the highest place in 3706:

```
 74,298              74,000
- 3,706  becomes   - 4,000
                    70,000.
```

The estimate is 70,000. The actual answer is 70,592.

PROBLEM SOLVING. Clues to look for in subtraction problems are expressions such as "how much is left," "how much less," "how much more," and "how many are not." It may seem strange that both "how much less" and "how much more" are both clues indicating that a problem involves subtraction. But consider these two problems.

SUBTRACTION FACTS *can be used to discover how much more money Will has than Adam.*

Will has $5. Adam has $3. How much less does Adam have?

Will has $5. Adam has $3. How much more does Will have?

You can see that the mathematical problem is the same either way you say it. The answer is $5 – $3 = $2 in each case.

Also, it helps to remember the two types of subtraction. When something is taken away, or when two things are compared, the problem usually can be solved by subtraction. But some comparison problems use a different kind of comparison. They use comparison by multiplication.

CALCULATOR TIPS

Estimating is a useful check for subtraction with a calculator just as it is for addition. Estimating will eliminate many incorrect answers.

But there is a more important check you can use, either on a calculator or with paper and pencil. Since subtraction and addition are closely related, you can check subtraction by addition.

For example, to check

```
 4978
-3465
 1513
```

simply add the difference to the number being subtracted. If the result is the number you are subtracting from, the difference is correct.

```
 1513
+3465
 4978
```

Multiplication

Multiplication, like subtraction, can be related to addition. Consider this problem:

A touchdown in football is worth 6 points. Lyle scored 3 touchdowns today. How many points did he make?

You can solve the problem by addition

$$\begin{array}{r} 6 \\ 6 \\ +6 \\ \hline 18 \end{array}$$

or you can multiply

$$\begin{array}{r} 6 \\ \times 3 \\ \hline 18. \end{array}$$

In either case, the answer is the same.

When you look at multiplication this way, it is just repeated addition.

□□ + □□ + □□ = 18

6 { □□ □□ □□ = 18
3 groups

The answer in multiplication is called the *product* and the two numbers being multiplied are called *factors.* The bottom diagram shows that when the factors are 3 and 6, the product is 18.

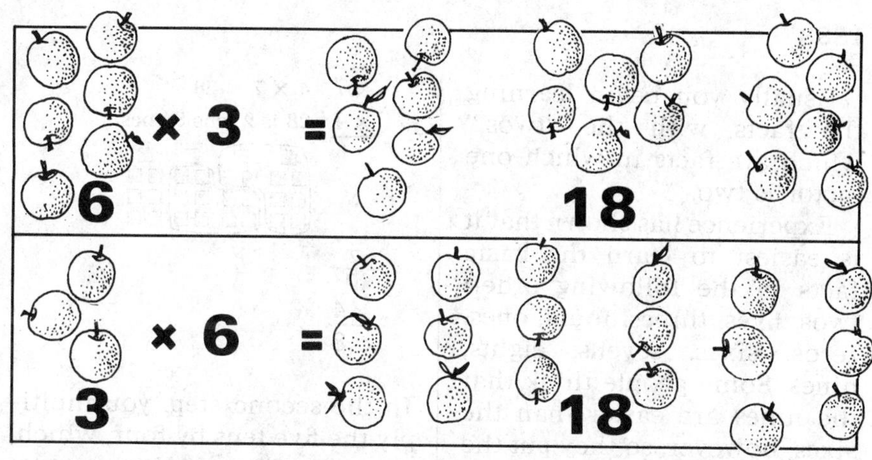

THE ORDER OF FACTORS *in multiplication makes no difference to the answer. Three groups of 6 apples and six groups of 3 apples both have 18 apples in all.*

There is also another way to think about multiplication. Line up your squares like marchers. Four sets of five squares look like this:

$4 \times 5 = 20$

This way of looking at multiplication suggests an important idea about multiplication. If the "marchers" were told "Right face," the diagram would show 5 × 4 instead of 4 × 5. But the number of marchers would not change. Changing the order of factors does not change the product. In this way, multiplication is like addition, but different from subtraction.

$5 \times 4 = 20$

Basic facts. The basic facts in multiplication have factors that are each single digits, such as 3 × 6 = 18. Basic multiplication facts are generally more difficult to learn than basic addition facts. Generally, you learn facts more easily by keeping one factor the same.

As in subtraction, there are separate names for each of the numbers in multiplication. The second number (in horizontal form) or the top number (in vertical form) is called the *multiplicand;* the other factor is called the *multiplier.* Generally, you keep the multiplicand the same when you are learning basic facts. Therefore the twos begin

$$1 \times 2 = 2$$
$$2 \times 2 = 4$$
$$3 \times 2 = 6$$

or in vertical form.

$$\begin{array}{r} 2 \\ \times 1 \\ \hline 2 \end{array} \quad \begin{array}{r} 2 \\ \times 2 \\ \hline 4 \end{array} \quad \begin{array}{r} 2 \\ \times 3 \\ \hline 6 \end{array}$$

BASIC MULTIPLICATION FACTS

zeros	0×0=0	1×0=0	2×0= 0	3×0= 0	4×0= 0	5×0= 0	6×0= 0	7×0= 0	8×0= 0	9×0= 0
ones	0×1=0	1×1=1	2×1= 2	3×1= 3	4×1= 4	5×1= 5	6×1= 6	7×1= 7	8×1= 8	9×1= 9
twos	0×2=0	1×2=2	2×2= 4	3×2= 6	4×2= 8	5×2=10	6×2=12	7×2=14	8×2=16	9×2=18
threes	0×3=0	1×3=3	2×3= 6	3×3= 9	4×3=12	5×3=15	6×3=18	7×3=21	8×3=24	9×3=27
fours	0×4=0	1×4=4	2×4= 8	3×4=12	4×4=16	5×4=20	6×4=24	7×4=28	8×4=32	9×4=36
fives	0×5=0	1×5=5	2×5=10	3×5=15	4×5=20	5×5=25	6×5=30	7×5=35	8×5=40	9×5=45
sixes	0×6=0	1×6=6	2×6=12	3×6=18	4×6=24	5×6=30	6×6=36	7×6=42	8×6=48	9×6=54
sevens	0×7=0	1×7=7	2×7=14	3×7=21	4×7=28	5×7=35	6×7=42	7×7=49	8×7=56	9×7=63
eights	0×8=0	1×8=8	2×8=16	3×8=24	4×8=32	5×8=40	6×8=48	7×8=56	8×8=64	9×8=72
nines	0×9=0	1×9=9	2×9=18	3×9=27	4×9=36	5×9=45	6×9=54	7×9=63	8×9=72	9×9=81

Usually you begin learning the facts with the "twos," which are facts in which one factor is two.

Experience has shown that it is easiest to learn the basic facts in the following order: twos, fives, threes, fours, ones, zeros, sixes, sevens, eights, nines. Some people think that the nines are easier than the sixes, however, so they put the nines right after the zeros.

Because the order of the factors does not change the product, you are actually learning part of other basic facts with each group you learn. For example, when you learn $4 \times 2 = 8$ (learning the twos), you are also learning $2 \times 4 = 8$, one of the fours. If you follow the recommended order, by the time you get to the nines, there is only one new fact to learn, $9 \times 9 = 81$.

Beyond basic facts. After you learn the basic multiplication facts, you can learn how to multiply when one factor has more than one digit. As with addition and subtraction, you work from right to left. If you do not have to rename, that is all you need to know.

$$\begin{array}{r}432\\ \times 3\\ \hline 6\end{array} \qquad \begin{array}{r}432\\ \times 3\\ \hline 96\end{array} \qquad \begin{array}{r}432\\ \times 3\\ \hline 1296\end{array}$$

Renaming in multiplication is like renaming in addition. You "carry" the digits you do not have a place for to the next column. After you have multiplied the ones, for example, you show any tens as a small digit over the tens column. Suppose you are multiplying 4×57. The first product is $4 \times 7 = 28$. You rename the 28 ones as two tens eight ones and write 8 in the ones column and a small 2 at the top of the tens column.

$$\begin{array}{r}57\\ \times 4\\ \hline\end{array} \quad \begin{array}{l}4 \times 7 = 28\\ \text{28 is 2 tens 8 ones}\end{array}$$

$$\begin{array}{r}{}^{2}\\ 57\\ \times 4\\ \hline 8\end{array}$$

In the second step, you multiply the five tens by four, which gives you 20 tens. You need to add the two tens from the first step as well. The total is 22 tens.

$$\begin{array}{r}{}^{2}\\ 57\\ \times 4\\ \hline 228\end{array} \quad \begin{array}{r}4 \times 5\ \text{(tens)} = 20\ \text{(tens)}\\ +\,2\ \text{(tens)}\\ \hline 22\ \text{(tens)}\end{array}$$

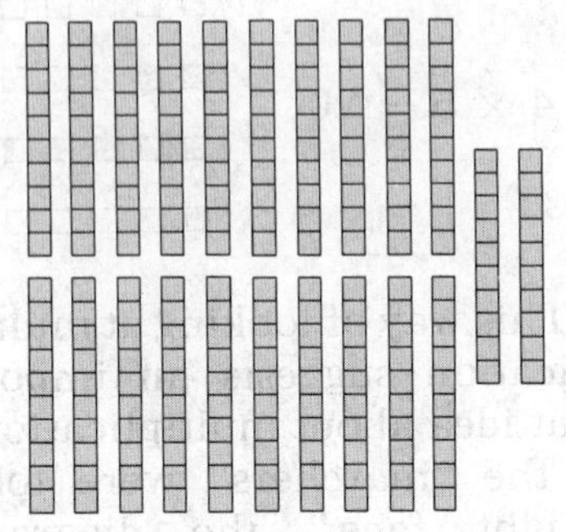

The same method can be used when there are more digits in the problem.

$$\begin{array}{r}{}^{2}\\ 384\\ \times 5\\ \hline 0\end{array} \qquad \begin{array}{r}{}^{4\,2}\\ 384\\ \times 5\\ \hline 20\end{array} \qquad \begin{array}{r}{}^{4\,2}\\ 384\\ \times 5\\ \hline 1920\end{array}$$

The separate steps that you do in your head look like this when they are written:

$5 \times 4 = 20$
$5 \times 8 = 40;\ 40 + 2 = 42$
$5 \times 3 = 15;\ 15 + 4 = 19.$

If both factors have more than one digit, multiplication involves one new step. After multiplying by the digit in the last place (the one farthest to the left), add the products formed by multiplying each place.

In $\begin{array}{r}359\\ \times 47\\ \hline\end{array}$ multiply first by 7, then by 40, to reach 47.

In $\begin{array}{r}359\\ \times 647\\ \hline\end{array}$ multiply first by 7, next by 40, then by 600 to reach 647. Then to get the final product, add the *partial products*.

$$\begin{array}{r}{}^{4\,6}\\ 359\\ \times 47\\ \hline 2513\end{array} \qquad \begin{array}{r}{}^{2\,3}\\ {}^{\not 4\,\not 6}\\ 359\\ \times 47\\ \hline 2513\\ 14360\\ \hline\end{array} \qquad \begin{array}{r}{}^{2\,3}\\ {}^{\not 4\,\not 6}\\ 359\\ \times 47\\ \hline 2513\\ 14360\\ \hline 16873\end{array}$$

If you write the small helping numerals, remember to cross out the first set before you continue multiplying. Even better, learn to keep them in your head.

You can also learn not to write the final zeros that appear when you multiply by tens, hundreds, or greater places.

$$\begin{array}{r}748\\ \times 263\\ \hline 2244\\ 44880\\ 149600\\ \hline\end{array} \quad \text{becomes} \quad \begin{array}{r}748\\ \times 263\\ \hline 2244\\ 4488\\ 1496\\ \hline 196724\end{array}$$

AUTOMATIC MULTIPLIER: *a gas pump automatically multiplies the amount of gas it pumps by the rate per gallon to give the total sale price.*

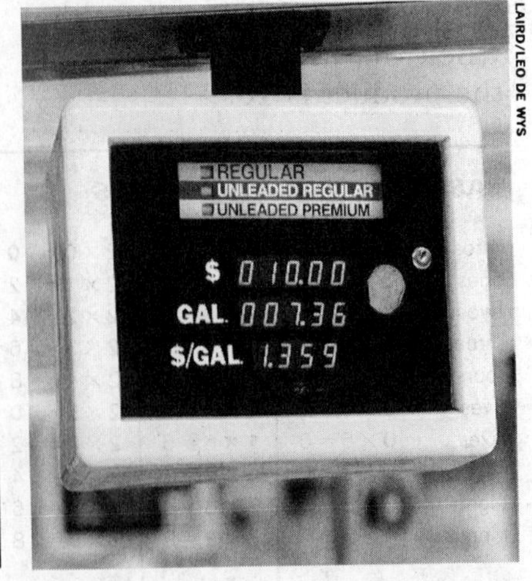

LAIRD/LEO DE WYS

If there is a zero in one of the places you are multiplying by, omit a whole partial product. When doing that, be careful about not dropping zeros at the end. It appears that you move over two places between partial products, not just one.

```
   6137                6137
 × 504    becomes    × 504
  24548               24548
  0000               30685
30685               3093048
```

Sometimes you multiply factors that have one or more zeros at their ends. There is an easy way to simplify such a problem. Write what the product would be if the factors had no zeros at the end. Add the number of zeros at the end of each factor, and write as many zeros as that sum. For the product of 490,000 and 3600, begin by multiplying 36 × 49.

```
  49
× 36
1764
```

There are four zeros in 490,000 and two zeros in 3600. The sum of 4 and 2 is 6, so write 6 zeros after 1764. The product is 1,764,000,000.

Estimating. The first, or leading, digits in the factors determine approximately how great the product will be. Therefore, a fairly good estimate can be obtained by rounding both factors to their leading digits.

To estimate 437 × 5637, begin by rounding 437 to hundreds and 5637 to thousands.

```
 5637                 6000
× 437    becomes    × 400
                 2,400,000
```

The true product of 5637 and 437 is 2,463,369.

PROBLEM SOLVING. Many students think they have spotted a multiplication problem when they see one number is much greater than the other. This is not always a reliable clue.

It is better to look for situations in which the same amount is involved several times. For example:

Robert walks 3 miles every day. How far does he walk in a week?

There are 27 cartons of a dozen eggs each to be sold. How many eggs will be sold in all?

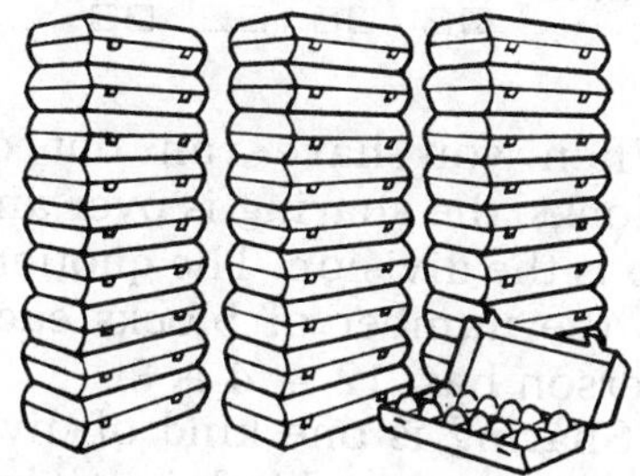

Notice that in both problems, it is hard to compare the size of two numbers, since only one number is given. You need to know how many days in a week or how many items in a dozen to solve the problem.

CALCULATOR TIPS

Sometimes a problem requires both multiplication and addition or both multiplication and subtraction to solve. This kind of problem can often be solved more easily if you use the property that combines the two operations, called the *distributive property.* For addition, the distributive property can be stated: The sum of two products with the same factor is the same as that factor times the sum of the other factors.
For example:

```
(3 × 2) + (3 × 5) = 3 × (2 + 5)
   6    +   15    = 3 ×    7
           21 = 21
```

The same property relates multiplication and subtraction. The difference of products with the same factor is equal to the product of that factor and the difference of the other factors.

```
(4 × 6) − (4 × 1) = 4 × (6 − 1)
  24    −    4    = 4 ×    5
           20 = 20
```

Remembering the distributive property often makes it easier to solve problems, especially with a calculator. Suppose you buy five packs of gum at 45¢ each and two rolls of mints at 45¢ each. You could multiply 5 × .45 to get the cost of the gum, $2.25, then multiply 2 × .45 to get the cost of the mints, 90¢.

But it is much easier to first add 5 + 2 = 7, which you can do in your head, then multiply 7 × .45 to get at the total cost of $3.15. Notice that

```
  5 × .45 =  2.25
+ 2 × .45 = + .90
  7 × .45 =  3.15
```

The same is true if you have any number of addends. If you run 3 miles each day, and during the four weeks of February 4 days, 2 days, 6 days, and 5 days, think:

```
     3 × (4 + 2 + 6 + 5) = 3 × 17 = 51,
not  3 × 4 =   12
     3 × 2 =    6
     3 × 6 =   18
     3 × 5 = + 15
               51
```

Both ways give the same result. But when you work with a calculator the first way is much better for two reasons. It can take more than twice as many keystrokes when you multiply first as it takes if you add each one and then multiply. The fewer keystrokes, the less likely that you will make a mistake.

Division

If you have twelve blocks that you want to share among four people, you can find the answer by division. One way to find the answer, or *quotient,* is to give each person a block.

Then give each person another block.

Now give each person another block.

When you have run out of blocks, the sharing is over and so is the division. The quotient is the number of blocks each person has, 12 ÷ 4 is 3.

Sharing is one kind of division. Another kind is giving division.

You want to play a game for which each person playing needs four blocks. You have twelve blocks. How many people can play the game?

Line up the possible players. Give the first one four blocks.

Give the next one four blocks.

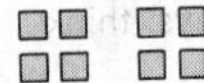

Now give the next one four blocks.

You have run out of blocks. This also means that 12 ÷ 4 is 3. Giving division produces the same answer as sharing division. The picture in your mind is different, however.

Notice that giving division is like multiplication backward. If the players each gave you their four blocks and there were three players, you would have twelve blocks. That is multiplication.

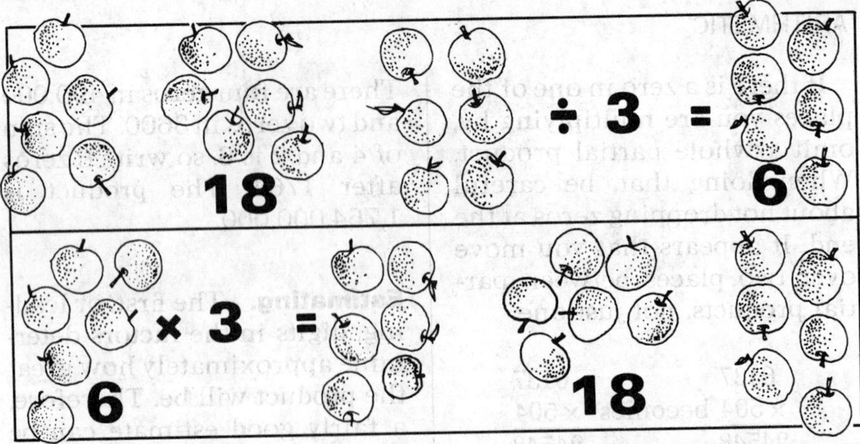

DIVISION AND MULTIPLICATION *are closely related. If 18 divided by 3 is 6, then 6 times 3 must be 18.*

Another way to show the relationship between division and multiplication is to show the blocks lined up in rows and columns as if for a parade.

column

row

4 × 5 = 20

If you know the total number in the parade and the total number in each row, you can use division to find the number in a column.

5

20 ÷ 5 = ?

?

Or you might know the number in a column and want to find the number in a row.

?

20 ÷ 4 = ?

4

Since multiplication is repeated addition, division must be repeated subtraction. That is especially easy to see for giving division.

You have 18 apples. You can put 6 in each box. How many boxes do you need?

You are giving each box six apples.

18
− 6 The first box
12
− 6 The second box
6
− 6 The third box
0

You are out of apples. You need three boxes, and 18 ÷ 6 = 3, where ÷ means "divided by."

Basic facts. As with the other operations with whole numbers, you start to learn division by learning the basic division facts. The number being divided is called the *dividend.* The number you divide by is called the *divisor.* The result is called the *quotient.* A basic division fact has a single-digit divisor and also a single-digit quotient.

Since there are 100 each of the basic addition, subtraction, and multiplication facts, you might think that there are 100 basic division facts. But there are only 90. This is because division by zero is not allowed, thus eliminating what would otherwise be ten division facts.

If you could divide by zero, sharing division would mean handing each person zero blocks each time you share blocks. Not very many blocks would be shared. Giving division would mean handing out zero blocks as well. You would never get rid of any blocks.

A good way to learn the basic division facts is at the same time as you are learning the basic multiplication facts. At the same time you learn

$$\begin{array}{r}7\\ \times 7\\ \hline 49\end{array} \quad \begin{array}{r}7\\ \times 8\\ \hline 56\end{array} \quad \begin{array}{r}7\\ \times 9\\ \hline 63\end{array}$$

you can also learn

$$7\overline{)49}\ (7) \quad 7\overline{)56}\ (8) \quad 7\overline{)63}\ (9).$$

You can do even better by using the idea that the order of the factors does not change the product. That way you can learn four facts at once, two multiplication and two division. This is called a "fact family."

$$\begin{array}{r}8\\ \times 9\\ \hline 72\end{array} \quad \begin{array}{r}9\\ \times 8\\ \hline 72\end{array} \quad 8\overline{)72}\ (9) \quad 9\overline{)72}\ (8)$$

Some families are only half that size, however.

$$\begin{array}{r}8\\ \times 8\\ \hline 64\end{array} \quad 8\overline{)64}\ (8)$$

Since division is closely related to multiplication, it is not surprising that division is distributive over addition and subtraction. The sum or difference of two problems with the same divisor can be found by dividing the sum or difference of the dividends by that divisor.

THE REMAINDER *is the number of flowers left after the rest are divided into equal groups.*

For example,

$$(10 \div 2) + (8 \div 2) = (10+8) \div 2$$
$$5 \quad + \quad 4 \quad = \quad 18 \quad \div 2$$
$$9 = 9$$

Beyond basic facts. Sometimes a division problem does not come out even. Suppose you were sharing 14 blocks among 4 people. After you had shared the first 12, you would have 2 blocks left over. That means the division has a *remainder* of 2.

$$4\overline{)14}\ \ (3 \text{ r } 2)$$

If a division problem has a single-digit divisor, a single-digit quotient, and a remainder that is not zero, it is a *near fact.* To find a near fact, start with the greatest fact whose quotient is less than the dividend. It is easier to think of multiplication facts than division facts, however, so you really think of the greatest multiplication fact with the divisor as a factor that has a product less than the dividend. To find 34 ÷ 4, you think: 4 × what number is almost 34? The answer is 8. So you write

$$4\overline{)34}.\ \ (8)$$

Then you subtract the product, 4 × 8 = 32 from the dividend.

$$\begin{array}{r}8\\ 4\overline{)34}\\ 32\\ \hline 2\end{array}$$

The 2 is the remainder. To complete the problem, you write the 2 as a remainder.

$$\begin{array}{r}8 \text{ r } 2\\ 4\overline{)34}\\ 32\\ \hline 2\end{array}$$

If the division problem is not a fact or a near fact, it can be solved by a method known as *long division.* Long division is just an extension of the method used for the near facts. You try to find a product that is less than part of the dividend. Then subtract that product from the part of the dividend. The division is "long" because these steps are repeated several times.

BASIC DIVISION FACTS

ones	0 ÷ 1 = 0	1 ÷ 1 = 1	2 ÷ 1 = 2	3 ÷ 1 = 3	4 ÷ 1 = 4	5 ÷ 1 = 5	6 ÷ 1 = 6	7 ÷ 1 = 7	8 ÷ 1 = 8	9 ÷ 1 = 9
twos	0 ÷ 2 = 0	2 ÷ 2 = 1	4 ÷ 2 = 2	6 ÷ 2 = 3	8 ÷ 2 = 4	10 ÷ 2 = 5	12 ÷ 2 = 6	14 ÷ 2 = 7	16 ÷ 2 = 8	18 ÷ 2 = 9
threes	0 ÷ 3 = 0	3 ÷ 3 = 1	6 ÷ 3 = 2	9 ÷ 3 = 3	12 ÷ 3 = 4	15 ÷ 3 = 5	18 ÷ 3 = 6	21 ÷ 3 = 7	24 ÷ 3 = 8	27 ÷ 3 = 9
fours	0 ÷ 4 = 0	4 ÷ 4 = 1	8 ÷ 4 = 2	12 ÷ 4 = 3	16 ÷ 4 = 4	20 ÷ 4 = 5	24 ÷ 4 = 6	28 ÷ 4 = 7	32 ÷ 4 = 8	36 ÷ 4 = 9
fives	0 ÷ 5 = 0	5 ÷ 5 = 1	10 ÷ 5 = 2	15 ÷ 5 = 3	20 ÷ 5 = 4	25 ÷ 5 = 5	30 ÷ 5 = 6	35 ÷ 5 = 7	40 ÷ 5 = 8	45 ÷ 5 = 9
sixes	0 ÷ 6 = 0	6 ÷ 6 = 1	12 ÷ 6 = 2	18 ÷ 6 = 3	24 ÷ 6 = 4	30 ÷ 6 = 5	36 ÷ 6 = 6	42 ÷ 6 = 7	48 ÷ 6 = 8	54 ÷ 6 = 9
sevens	0 ÷ 7 = 0	7 ÷ 7 = 1	14 ÷ 7 = 2	21 ÷ 7 = 3	28 ÷ 7 = 4	35 ÷ 7 = 5	42 ÷ 7 = 6	49 ÷ 7 = 7	56 ÷ 7 = 8	63 ÷ 7 = 9
eights	0 ÷ 8 = 0	8 ÷ 8 = 1	16 ÷ 8 = 2	24 ÷ 8 = 3	32 ÷ 8 = 4	40 ÷ 8 = 5	48 ÷ 8 = 6	56 ÷ 8 = 7	64 ÷ 8 = 8	72 ÷ 8 = 9
nines	0 ÷ 9 = 0	9 ÷ 9 = 1	18 ÷ 9 = 2	27 ÷ 9 = 3	36 ÷ 9 = 4	45 ÷ 9 = 5	54 ÷ 9 = 6	63 ÷ 9 = 7	72 ÷ 9 = 8	81 ÷ 9 = 9

Here is an example showing how long division works. Start by dividing 78 by 5 using blocks and then progress to long division.

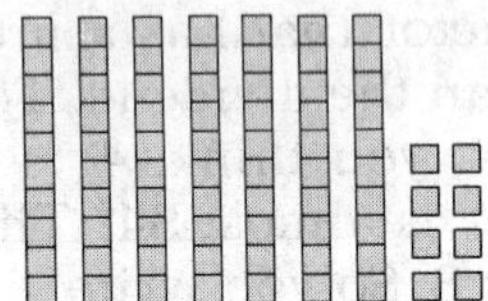

To divide by five, first divide the seven tens by five. This gives a partial answer of 14, since (70 ÷ 5) is 14. Then divide the eight ones by five, obtaining one with a remainder of three.

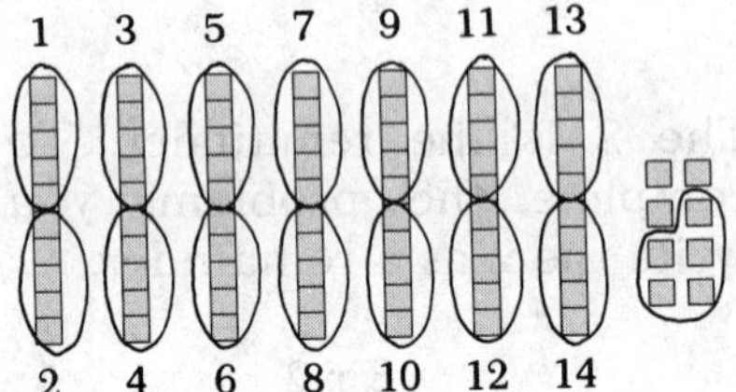

Add the two partial quotients: 14 + 1 r 3 is 15 r 3. The answer is 15 r 3.

When you use long division, you take advantage of the place-value system to break the problem into a series of easy steps. (You might want to reread the section on **Numeration** above.) Instead of finding all 14 of the fives in 70, begin by finding that there are at least ten fives in 70. Think of this and write it using place value, so that it looks like 7 ÷ 5 is 1 with some left over instead of 70 ÷ 5 is at least 10.

```
   1
5)78
```

Since 10 × 5 is 50, you can write the next step in place-value form also.

```
   1
5)78
  5
```

Subtracting the 50 from 78 gives you an easier problem to work with.

```
   1
5)78
  5
  28
```

Now you need to divide 28 by 5. This is a near fact. You look for the greatest fact that has 5 as a factor and a product less than 28. It is 5 × 5 = 25. Now your partial answer looks like this:

```
   15
5)78
  5
  28
  25.
```

To complete the long division, subtract 25 from 28 to find the remainder.

```
   15 r 3
5)78
  5
  28
  25
   3
```

Notice that long division gives the same answer as the concrete method using blocks.

When you use long division, it is easier to forget about place value and let the method take care of it for you. To divide 382 by 7, for example, look at the first *two* digits in the dividend and think 38 ÷ 7 is at least 5, since 7 × 5 = 35.

```
   5
7)382
```

Write the 35 under 38. Subtract 35 from 38 and bring down the 3.

```
   5
7)382
  35
   32
```

Now complete the solution by dividing 32 by 7 and finding the remainder.

```
   54 r 4
7)382
  35
   32
   28
    4
```

Each time you get another part of the quotient, go through the same basic steps: divide, multiply, subtract, and bring down. The same four steps are repeated each time.

When you have more than a single digit in the divisor, division is more difficult. You need to use estimates, since you cannot use basic facts. As a result, the digit you place in the quotient is called a *trial quotient.*

The method of estimation that produces the fewest incorrect estimates is based on rounding. There is one difference, however, from ordinary rounding. When the number you are rounding is exactly between rounding up and rounding down, you round down. Thus, you would round 35 to 30 (not to 40) to make your best estimate.

To divide 4827 by 27, first round 27 to 30 in your mind, and use 4 ÷ 3 to estimate your first trial quotient. You should write the 1 above the 8 in the dividend instead of above the 4, however, since you are really estimating 48 ÷ 30 instead of 4 ÷ 3. (You have to keep that in mind if place value is to work properly.)

```
     1
27)4827
```

You multiply 27 × 1, however, not the rounded figure.

```
     1
27)4827
   27
   212
```

Your second estimate is based on 21 ÷ 3 = 7. Again, you multiply 27 × 7 = 189.

Proceed to estimate the last trial quotient by thinking of 23 ÷ 3, which is also 7.

```
       177
  27)4827
     27
     212
     189
      237
      189
       48
```

At this point you should know that something is wrong. A remainder cannot be greater than the divisor. The last estimate of 7 was too low. You need to increase the trial quotient by one. Just cross out the incorrect estimate and work based on it.

```
         8
       177 r 21   (last 7 crossed out)
  27)4827
     27
     212
     189
      237
      189   (crossed out)
       48   (crossed out)
      216
       21
```

If you are dividing 7396 by 450, begin by rounding *down,* since 450 is halfway between 400 and 500. The first estimate is based on 7 ÷ 4, so it is 1. But remember to place the 1 above the 9 in the dividend, since the estimate is really 739 ÷ 400. Now multiply 450 × 1, subtract, and bring down.

```
          1
  450)7396
      450
      2896
```

Your second estimate is based upon 28 ÷ 4, so use 7 as the second trial quotient.

```
         17
  450)7396
      450
      2896
      3150
```

This time the number you are supposed to subtract is greater than the number you are supposed to subtract from. Reduce the trial quotient by one and try again.

```
          6
         17 r 196   (7 crossed out)
  450)7396
      450
      2896
      3150   (crossed out)
      2700
       196
```

In a few cases your estimate can be off by more than one, so that you have to cross out two trial quotients before you get one that works.

Estimating. A good reason for estimating the complete quotient in long division is to make sure that your first trial quotient is in the right place. Estimating a complete quotient for a division problem is done with rounded numbers. Round the divisor in the ordinary way to its first place, just as you would for estimating a product. Then look at the dividend. Round it to the first place. Is the first digit of the rounded divisor smaller than the first digit of the rounded dividend? If so, proceed with the estimate. If not, round the dividend to the second place and complete the estimate.

For example, to estimate 8391 ÷ 58, first round 58 to 60 and 8391 to 8000. Since 6 is smaller than 8, the estimate is

```
   about  100
       60)8000.
```

This is not a very close estimate (the correct quotient is 144 r 39), but it is good enough to make sure that the first trial quotient is in the correct place.

To estimate 6234 ÷ 73, start by rounding to 6000 ÷ 70. But 7 is greater than 6, so you round 6234 to 6200.

```
   about   80
       70)6200
```

Again the estimate is not very close, but it is close enough to the real quotient of 85 r 29 to make sure that your first trial quotient is in the right place.

PROBLEM SOLVING. There are four main situations in which you divide. The first two correspond to sharing and giving division.

CALCULATOR TIPS

When you divide on a calculator, you do not get a quotient and a remainder. Unless the remainder is 0, you get an answer that is a decimal fraction. The next section deals with decimals.

If you need a remainder, you can get one using a calculator. First divide in the ordinary way. If there is a remainder, the quotient will have a whole-number part and a part after the decimal point. The whole number part is the quotient not counting the remainder. Remember or write down the whole number part. Now multiply that number by the divisor. You should get a number that is smaller than the dividend. Subtract the dividend from the product. The answer will be shown as a negative number, but the amount will be the correct remainder.

For example, to find the quotient and remainder for 235,988 ÷ 4397, first divide on the calculator. You will get an answer of 53.670230 if your calculator shows eight places. The quotient is 53. Multiply 4397 × 53, which gives 233,041. Subtract 235,988 and you get −2947, so the remainder is 2947.

1\. Divide to find how many items when each of a known number of sets is to be equal.

Edna has picked 52 flowers. If she puts the same number in each of 4 vases, how many will go in a vase?

Divide 52 by 4. Thirteen flowers go in each vase.

2\. If you know how many items are in each group, divide to find the number of groups.

George has 123 eggs to pack in boxes of a dozen. How many boxes will he need?

Divide 123 by 12. He needs ten boxes and has three eggs left.

3\. Divide to find how many times one amount is when compared with another.

A turtle crawls 30 feet an hour, but a person easily walks 4 miles an hour. A person travels how many times as fast as a turtle?

First get the same units of measure for a turtle and a person. One mile is 5280 feet, so 4 miles is 21,120 feet. Divide 21,120 by 30 to get the answer: A person travels 704 times as fast as a turtle.

4\. Divide to find the average of a set of numbers.

Jill's house is four blocks from Karen's, Nancy's house is six blocks away, and Jennifer's house is eight blocks away. What is the average distance Karen needs to go to visit her friends?

To find the average, first add all of the numbers in the set, then divide by the number of numbers in the set: $4 + 6 + 8 = 18$. Now divide to find the average: $18 \div 3 = 6$. The average is six blocks.

Decimals

Whole numbers are very useful, but in some applications of arithmetic, they aren't adequate. For example, if you are measuring something, its length may be in between two units, say between 14 and 15 inches. How can you express a number that is in between?

Perhaps the most useful way to express such numbers is with decimals. A dot (the *decimal point*) is written just to the right of the ones place. With whole numbers, each place to the *left* of the ones is worth *ten times* as much as the place before it. In the same way, each place to the *right* of the decimal point is worth *one-tenth* as much as the place to its left. Thus, in the numeral 14.6 the decimal point marks the 4 as being in the ones place. The 6 after the decimal point is in the *tenths* place. One way to picture this is with a kind of ruler on which the numbers in between the whole numbers are shown.

Notice that there are nine numbers in the tenths shown equally spaced between 84 and 85. By including 84.0, which is the same amount as 84, there are ten tenths for each unit, one for each digit in the system.

The system can be extended indefinitely to smaller and smaller numbers. The next smaller place after the tenths is the *hundredths*. Ten hundredths make up one tenth, just as ten tenths make up one one. To show the places to the right of the decimal point, we can use the same kind of chart as was used for the places to the left. The number 987.6543 shown on the place-value chart is read "nine hundred eighty-seven and six thousand five hundred forty-three ten-thousandths." Note that the decimal point is read as *and*. Often, also, people read decimal numbers in another way: "Nine hundred eighty-seven point six five four three."

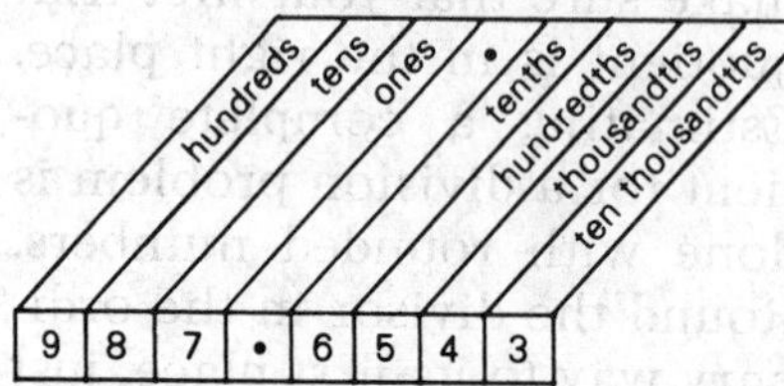

Any number shown with a decimal point in the numeral is called a *decimal*. Thus, 85.0 is a decimal, although it has the same value as 85. Decimals for numbers smaller than 1 are sometimes called *decimal fractions*. When working with decimals, it is common to write a 0 in the ones place if a decimal is smaller than 1. For example, five tenths is written 0.5. Although this is not necessary, it is a good precaution, for the decimal point is small and may be overlooked. The 0 in the ones place helps make the decimal point stand out.

One of the main advantages of the decimal system is that the algorithms developed for whole numbers also work for decimals—provided you watch carefully where you put the decimal point in the answer. For example, to add or subtract decimals, you write the problem in vertical form, lining up the decimal points. Then the decimal point in the answer is just below the decimal points in the problem. Regrouping is handled exactly the same as for whole numbers. In addition, tenths are regrouped as ones, hundredths are regrouped as tenths, and so forth. In subtraction, you go the other way, with ones regrouped as tenths, tenths regrouped as hundredths, etc.

Here are the steps for addition:

A. Line up the decimal points vertically.

B. Add as if the decimals were whole numbers.

C. Put the decimal point in the answer in line with the decimal points in the problem.

To add 34.53 + 1.8 + 0.09

A.	B.	C.
34.53	1 1 34.53	1 1 34.53
1.8	1.8	1.8
+0.09	+0.09	+0.09
	36 42	36.42

Some people find that it is easier to keep the decimal points in line if they write 0's in any decimal places at the right that are not filled. In the problem above, since some of the numbers are given to hundredths, but 1.8 is given only to tenths, they would write 1.8 as 1.80. Then the right-hand margin of the problem lines up as well as the decimal points:

34.53
1.80
+0.09

84 | 84.1 | 84.2 | 84.3 | 84.4 | 84.5 | 84.6 | 84.7 | 84.8 | 84.9 | 85

This practice may be helpful, but in scientific work the number of decimal places given is one way to indicate the precision of a measurement. Thus, 1.80 would mean a quantity measured to hundredths, while 1.8 would mean a quantity measured to tenths. Writing in extra zeros in such cases means a loss in the total information carried by the number.

For subtraction, the steps are similar to those for addition:

A. Line up the decimal points vertically. You may wish to make the number of decimal places the same by writing in 0's.
B. Subtract as with whole numbers.
C. Put the decimal point in your answer in line with the decimal points in the problem.

To subtract 58.2 − 6.73:

A.	B.	C.
58.20	7 11 58.20	7 11 58.20
−6.73	−6.73	−6.73
	51 47	51.47

In subtraction it is particularly helpful to write in the extra 0's.

Multiplication of decimals also uses the same algorithm as multiplication of whole numbers except for the placement of the decimal point in the product. The rules for placing the decimal point are a little trickier than they are for addition and subtraction.

First consider multiplication of a decimal by a whole number. To find 3 × 0.5,

think	5 tenths	or	0.5
	×3		×3
	15 tenths		1.5

since 15 tenths is 1 one and 5 tenths. Similarly, 3 × 0.05 is 15 hundredths, or 0.15. The number of decimal places in the product is the same as the number of decimal places in the factors. A whole number has 0 decimal places.

One way to see how this rule extends when both factors are decimals is to use estimation. Suppose you need to multiply 3.1 × 4.25. Since decimal algorithms are just like whole-number algorithms except for the placement of the decimal point, you can begin by finding 31 × 425, which is 13,175. However, 3.1 is close to 3 and 4.25 is close to 4, so the answer to 3.1 × 4.25 should be close to 3 × 4, or 12. Placing a decimal point in 13175 to get a number close to 12 gives 13.175, so 3.1 × 4.25 = 13.175. There is 1 decimal place in 3.1 and there are 2 decimal places in 4.25, so there are 3 decimal places in the product. If you try this with several examples, you will find that the rule is that the number of decimal places in the product is the same as the total number of decimal places in the factors.

A. Multiply as you do with whole numbers.
B. Count the decimal places in the factors.
C. Place the decimal point in the product so that the number of decimal places equals the total number of decimal places in the factors.

To find 0.49 × 3.275:

A.
```
   3.275
   ×0.49
   29475
 1 3100
 1.60475
```

B. 3.275 has 3 decimal places.
0.49 has 2 decimal places.

C. The product has 5 decimal places.

Notice that you do not need to line up the decimal points, since this device is not used in finding the product. Also, as a check, you should notice that 0.49 is about 0.5 and 3.275 is about 3, so the answer should be about 0.5 × 3, or 1.5 (which it is).

Sometimes, when multiplying decimals, there are more decimal places required in the product than there are digits. Consider 0.02 × 0.03. The product of 2 and 3 is 6, but you need 4 decimal places in the answer. So you must write in additional 0's to make the answer come out right:

```
  0.03
  0.02
0.0006
```

Decimals make it very easy to multiply by 10, 100, 1000, or any number that is also a place in the place-value system. Look at the following examples:

1.2345	1.2345	1.2345
×10	×100	×1000
12.345	123.45	1234.5

To multiply a decimal by a number such as 10, 100, or 1000:

A. Count the zeros in the whole number.
B. The product is a decimal that has a decimal point as many places to the right as there are zeros in the whole number.

Sometimes this is called "moving the decimal point," and is shown as follows:

$$100 \times 43.89 = 4389.$$

Division of a decimal by a whole number is quite easy. For example, to divide 4.2 by 6, you know that the answer must be 0.7 because 6 × 0.7 = 4.2. In general, to divide a decimal by a whole number:

A. Write the problem in the ⟌ form and divide as with whole numbers.
B. Put the decimal point in the quotient directly above the decimal point in the dividend.

DECIMAL COINS. *U.S. coins have decimal value. A dime is .10 dollars, a quarter is .25, etc.*

To divide 96.6 by 23:

A.
```
      4 2
23 ) 96.6
     92
      4 6
      4 6
```

B.
```
      4.2
23 ) 96.6
     92
      4 6
      4 6
```

Remainders do not have the same meaning in decimal division as in whole-number division. Instead of using remainders, the decimal division algorithm is continued either until the remainder is zero or until we have gone one place beyond the number of places desired. In the latter case, the quotient is then rounded (the same way whole numbers are rounded) to the place desired. This procedure can be used for whole-number division also, instead of expressing the answer as a quotient and a remainder. For example:

1.5 ÷ 8

```
  0.1875
8)1.5000
  8
   70
   64
    60
    56
     40
     40
```

3.2 ÷ 7, round to hundredths

```
  0.457
7)3.200
  2 8
    40
    35
     50
     49
      1
```

0.457 is 0.46 rounded to hundredths.

In the case of 1.5 ÷ 8, 0's were written in until the division came out even. For 3.2 ÷ 7, 0's were written in until the division went one place beyond hundredths, to thousandths.

Many division problems will not come out even, no matter how many places they are extended. In particular, if you find the same remainder occurring more than once (after you have started bringing down the written-in 0's), the same pattern of digits will repeat over and over. This phenomenon is discussed in more detail in the section on fractions.

Division of a decimal by a decimal is generally accomplished by first converting the problem to division of a decimal by a whole number. In this way the placement of the decimal point in the quotient is much simplified. Recall that if both the divisor and dividend are multiplied by the same number, the quotient is unchanged. Even better, since remainders are not used in division of decimals, the whole decimal quotient stays the same. (Whole-number remainders change when the divisor and dividend are multiplied by the same number.)

The usual way to convert a decimal division problem to division by a whole number is to multiply both dividend and divisor by 10, 100, 1000, or any number that is a place in the place-value system. By using the method of "moving the decimal point," the problem does not even need to be rewritten.

A. Multiply the divisor by "moving the decimal point" to the right of the rightmost digit.

B. Multiply the dividend by "moving the decimal point" as many places as in A. (You may need to write in some 0's.)

C. Divide.

To divide 1.27 by 0.453 (round quotient to hundredths):

```
A. 0.453)1.27      B. 0.453)1.270

C.          2.803
   0.453)1.270 000
          906
          364 0
          362 4
            1 600
            1 359
              241
```

The quotient, rounded to hundredths, is 2.80.

Estimation is a good way to check computation with decimals, particularly computation on a calculator. Often the decimal part of the problem will be small enough that you can estimate by rounding to whole numbers. In other cases, however, especially when the decimals involved are smaller than 1, more complicated means of estimation can be used. In general, the methods used with whole numbers can be used with small modifications.

To estimate addition or subtraction of decimals, round all numbers in the problem to the greatest place in the smallest number that has more than one nonzero digit.

```
 28.45               28
  9.206  rounds to    9
+87.4               +87
                    124

 0.6974              0.7000
-0.0358  rounds to  -0.0400
                     0.6600
```

To estimate multiplication or division of decimals, round all numbers except the dividend so that there is only one nonzero digit. The dividend should have either one or two nonzero digits so that it will "divide."

```
  2.9375               3
×0.0452  rounds to  ×0.05
                     0.15

                       about 0.4
3.29)1.3486  rounds to  3)1.3
```

Fractions

When something whole is divided into parts, each part is a *fraction* of the whole (from the Latin word meaning "to break"). In arithmetic, fractions are used to deal with *equal* parts. Parts are equal if they have the same size.

If a pizza is divided into two equal parts, each part is half of the whole pizza.

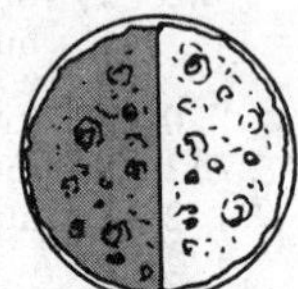

One-half is written $\frac{1}{2}$. The top numeral, 1, is called the *numerator* and tells the number of equal parts being counted. The bottom numeral, 2, is called the *denominator* and tells the number of equal parts in all. If a pizza is divided in three equal parts, then the number for one of those parts is one-third, written $\frac{1}{3}$. The number that represents the two equal parts that are shaded below is $\frac{2}{3}$.

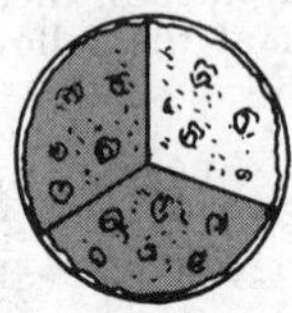

The shape of the whole does not matter. Here is a rectangle divided into fourths. The shaded region represents $\frac{3}{4}$.

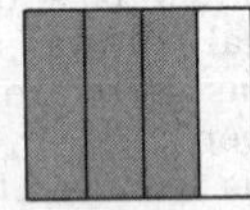

Here is a square divided into eighths. The shaded region represents $\frac{5}{8}$.

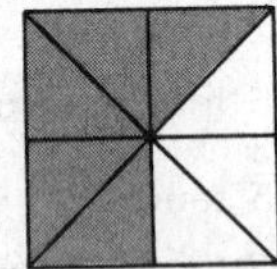

Sometimes the whole is not a single object but is, instead, a set of objects. For example, if two persons were sharing two oranges, the fraction for one-half would be shown as

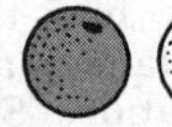

Similarly, $\frac{4}{6}$ of six oranges could be shown as

    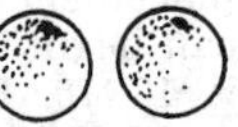

When we use the word fraction we usually mean a part smaller than the whole. But there are also fractions larger than the whole. If a hungry customer eats two and a half pizzas, a picture to illustrate this would be

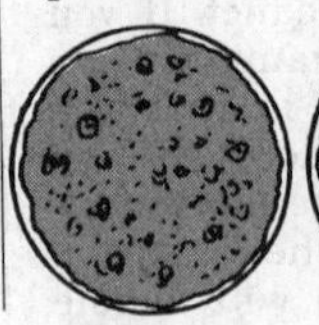 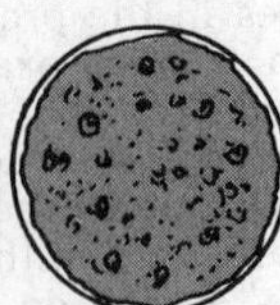 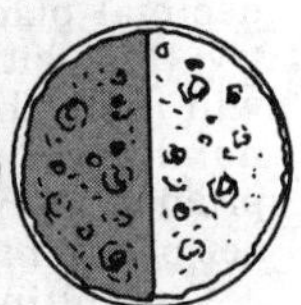

A FRACTION IS A PIECE OF A WHOLE. *This candy bar is broken into two equal pieces or halves. The bar has a total of 18 small squares, 9 in each half; so 9/18 is the same as ½.*

BARRY FEIG

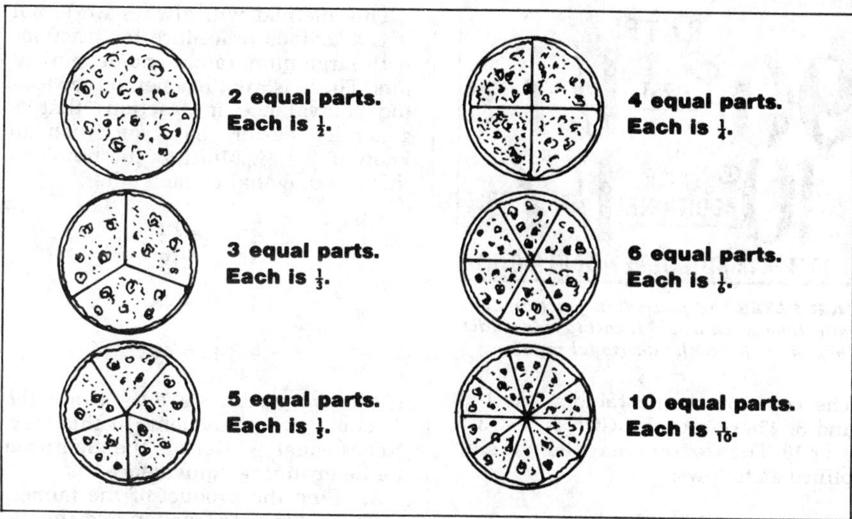

This means 2 wholes + 1 half. It may be written $2\frac{1}{2}$. A whole number followed by a fraction has several names. The most common name is *mixed number,* but it is also called mixed numeral or mixed form.

If the person ate the pizzas one-half a pizza at a time, there is another way that could be used to picture a fraction greater than one whole.

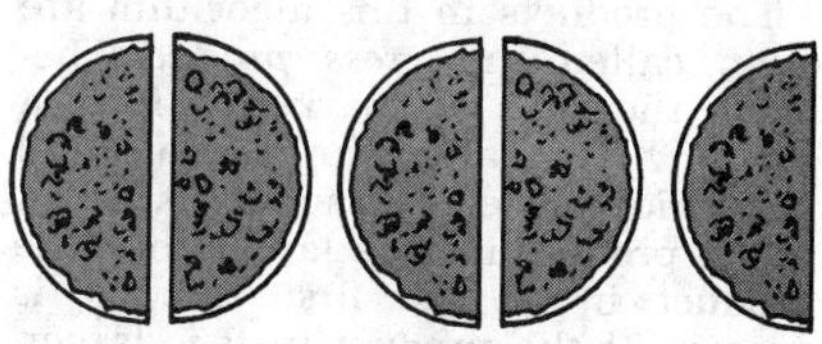

Since there are five half pizzas shown, the amount can be described with a fraction that has 5 for the numerator (number of equal parts counted) and 2 for the denominator (number of equal parts of one whole). This numeral, $\frac{5}{2}$, is called an *improper fraction.* The fraction is "improper" because the numerator is greater than the denominator. Fractions whose numerator is less than the denominator are sometimes called *proper fractions.*

You are likely to encounter fractions in measurement. A fraction of a length is just an equal part of a unit. Here is $\frac{5}{8}$ of an inch, for example.

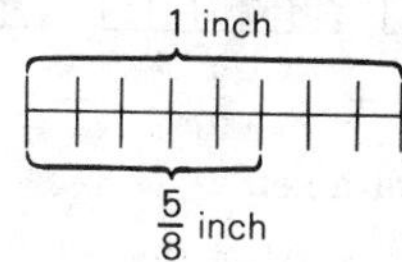

Mixed numbers occur often in measurement, as in $2\frac{5}{8}$ inches, or $12\frac{1}{2}$ miles. Improper fractions are not generally used in measurement—or anywhere else. But they have important uses in computation.

Just as we may speak of a fraction of a whole or a fraction of a set of objects, we can also speak of a fraction of a number. For example, $\frac{4}{6}$ of a set of 6 oranges is 4 oranges. So $\frac{4}{6}$ of 6 is 4.

There may be more than one fraction that describes a particular division of parts or objects or numbers. For example, consider this set of 6 oranges.

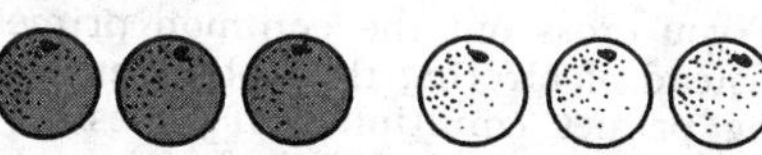

Three of the six oranges have been shaded, so $\frac{3}{6}$ of the oranges are shaded. But the set has also been divided into two equal parts, so we can say that $\frac{1}{2}$ of the oranges are shaded. We can conclude that $\frac{1}{2}$ of 6 oranges is 3.

Finding a Fraction of a Number

You can use the drawings above to see that $\frac{1}{2}$ of 2 = 1, $\frac{1}{2}$ of 4 = 2, $\frac{1}{2}$ of 6 = 3, and so forth. In general,

To find one-half of any number, divide the number by 2.

Now consider $\frac{1}{3}$. The set of 6 oranges can also be separated into three equal parts.

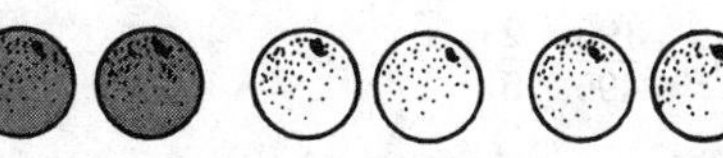

One of the parts is $\frac{1}{3}$ of the set, and one part is 2 oranges; so, $\frac{1}{3}$ of 6 = 2. Again, the rule is easy to determine:

To find one-third of any number, divide the number by 3.

This can be generalized into a set of steps for finding a part of any number:

To find one equal part of any number, divide the number by the size of the part you are finding. The quotient is the answer.

For example, to find one-fourth of 12, $\frac{1}{4}$ of 12 is the same as $12 \div 4$. $12 \div 4 = 3$.

Simplifying

Now consider fractions whose numerator is not 1.

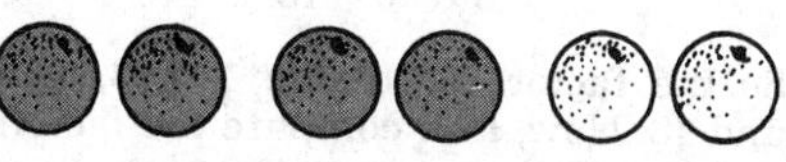

The drawing indicates that $\frac{2}{3}$ of 6 is 4. But we have already shown that $\frac{4}{6}$ of 6 is 4. There must be something about $\frac{2}{3}$ and $\frac{4}{6}$ that is the same.

In fact, $\frac{2}{3}$ of any number is the same as $\frac{4}{6}$ of the same number. In arithmetic $\frac{2}{3}$ and $\frac{4}{6}$ are called *equivalent fractions.* The word *equivalent* means that the fractions have equal values, even though they are made up of different numerals. In other words, $\frac{2}{3}$ and $\frac{4}{6}$ are equivalent because they represent the same number.

We usually write that number as $\frac{2}{3}$. This is because $\frac{2}{3}$ is the *simplest form* that represents the number. Other forms that represent the number, such as $\frac{4}{6}$, $\frac{6}{9}$, and $\frac{8}{12}$, all involve greater numbers than 2 and 3, so they are not so simple.

Notice that $\frac{4}{6}$ is the same as $\frac{2}{3} \times \frac{2}{2}$ and $\frac{6}{9}$ is the same as $\frac{2}{3} \times \frac{3}{3}$. In general,

If you multiply the numerator and denominator of a fraction by the same number, you get an equivalent fraction.

Thus, $\frac{3}{4}$ is equivalent to $\frac{9}{12}$ because $\frac{3}{4} \times \frac{3}{3} = \frac{9}{12}$.

Since multiplication and division are closely related, you can turn this rule around. The number shown by $\frac{9}{12}$ is equivalent to $\frac{3}{4}$ because $\frac{9}{12} \div \frac{3}{3} = \frac{3}{4}$.

If you divide the numerator and denominator of a fraction by the same number, you get an equivalent fraction.

Clearly you can use this second form of the rule to find a fraction in simplest form. For example, to find the simplest form of $\frac{4}{6}$, you divide the numerator and denominator by 2 to get $\frac{2}{3}$. It is not always easy, however, to tell what number will divide both the numerator and the denominator evenly. If you were asked to find the simplest form of $\frac{85}{119}$, you might have to try several numbers before you could find the divisor that would give you the simplest form.

Mathematicians have developed methods that can be used to handle this kind of problem. One method finds the *greatest common factor (GCF)* of the numerator and denominator.

Factors are the numbers that are multiplied to find a product. For example, $3 \times 4 = 12$; thus we can say that 3 and 4 are *factors* of 12. Similarly, $2 \times 6 = 12$; so 2 and 6 are factors of 12. There is no whole number that can be multiplied by 5 to equal 12. So 5 is not a factor of 12. In fact, the only whole-number factors of 12 are 1, 2, 3, 4, 6, and 12.

Similarly, we can find the factors of 18:

$$1 \times 18 = 18$$
$$2 \times 9 = 18$$
$$3 \times 6 = 18$$

So the factors of 18 are 1, 2, 3, 6, 9, and 18. Now, let's compare the factors of 12 with the factors of 18:

12: 1 2 3 4 6 12
18: 1 2 3 6 9 18.

You can see that 1, 2, 3, and 6 are factors of both 12 and 18. These are called the *common factors* of 12 and 18. The *greatest common factor (GCF)* of 12 and 18 is 6. We can use the GCF to simplify a fraction containing 12 and 18.

When both the numerator and the denominator of a fraction are divided by their greatest common factor, the resulting fraction is in simplest form.

Thus, to find the simplest form of $\frac{12}{18}$ you would divide 12 and 18 each by 6.

$$\frac{12 \div 6}{18 \div 6} = \frac{2}{3}$$

The simplest form of $\frac{12}{18}$ is $\frac{2}{3}$.

There is another way to look for the greatest common factor that is often useful. Any number whose only factors are 1 and itself is a *prime number.* For example, 2, 3, 5, 7, 11, 13, 17, 19, and 23 are all prime numbers. All other numbers, below 27 except for 1, are *composite numbers.* A rule known as the fundamental theorem of arithmetic says:

Any whole number has exactly one set of prime factors.

The product of the prime factors (often with some repeated) is the number. For example, the factors of 12 are 1, 2, 3, 4, 6, and 12. Of these, only 2 and 3 are prime numbers. We can multiply these numbers to get 12. Therefore,

$$2 \times 2 \times 3 = 12$$

is the *prime factorization* of 12. The prime factorization of 18 is $2 \times 3 \times 3$.

The prime factorizations of two numbers may be used to find their greatest common factor. The GCF is the product of the prime numbers that are common to both prime factorizations. Taking 12 and 18 once again:

$$12 = \boxed{2} \times 2 \times \boxed{3}$$
$$18 = \boxed{2} \qquad \times \boxed{3} \times 3$$

The common prime factors are 2 and 3. Therefore the GCF of 12 and 18 is 2×3, or 6.

This procedure works for large numbers, too. For $\frac{54}{252}$ the prime factorizations are

$$\frac{54}{252} = \frac{\boxed{2} \times \boxed{3} \times \boxed{3} \times 3}{\boxed{2} \times 2 \times \boxed{3} \times \boxed{3} \times 7}$$

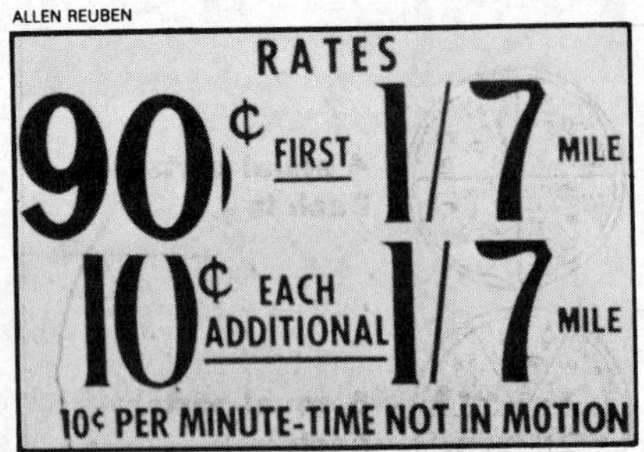

TAXI RATES *are figured in fractions of a mile. How much would it cost to ride a mile? How much for each additional mile?*

The common prime factors are 2, 3, and 3. Therefore, the GCF is $2 \times 3 \times 3$, or 18. The fraction may then be simplified as follows:

$$\frac{54 \div 18}{252 \div 18} = \frac{3}{14}$$

You may notice, however, that in the list of prime factors, the numbers uncircled are

$$\frac{54}{252} = \frac{3}{2 \times 7}$$

If you cross out the common primes instead of circling them, the remaining primes (multiplied if necessary) will be the simplified fraction. In many cases, this is the easiest way to simplify a fraction containing large numbers. The algorithm for this method is:

A. Factor both the numerator and denominator into primes.
B. Cross out any factors that are common to both numerator and denominator.
C. Multiply the factors left in the numerator and those left in the denominator. The result is the fraction in simplest form.

To find the simplest form of $\frac{198}{495}$

A. $$\frac{198}{495} = \frac{2 \times 3 \times 3 \times 11}{3 \times 3 \times 5 \times 11}$$

B. $$\frac{198}{495} = \frac{2 \times \not{3} \times \not{3} \times \not{11}}{\not{3} \times \not{3} \times 5 \times \not{11}}$$

C. $$\frac{198}{495} = \frac{2}{5}$$

Equivalence

When presented with two fractions such as $\frac{84}{88}$ and $\frac{252}{264}$, you may need to know whether or not they are equivalent. One way to find this out is to reduce both fractions to simplest form.

$$\frac{84}{88} = \frac{\not{2} \times \not{2} \times 3 \times 7}{\not{2} \times \not{2} \times 2 \times 11} = \frac{21}{22}$$

$$\frac{252}{264} = \frac{\not{2} \times \not{2} \times \not{3} \times 3 \times 7}{\not{2} \times \not{2} \times 2 \times \not{3} \times 11} = \frac{21}{22}$$

This method will always work, but it is a tedious procedure for fractions with large numerators and denominators. There is another method for testing equivalence in fractions that is generally easier. Say you wish to know if $\frac{3}{4} = \frac{12}{16}$. Multiply the numbers that are diagonal to each other:

$$\frac{3}{4} \times \frac{12}{16}$$

$$3 \times 16 = 48$$

$$4 \times 12 = 48$$

If the two products are the same, the fractions are equivalent. In this case, $\frac{3}{4}$ does equal $\frac{12}{16}$. Here is the algorithm for determining equivalence:

A. Find the product of the numerator of the first fraction and the denominator of the second fraction.
B. Find the product of the denominator of the first fraction and the numerator of the second fraction.
C. If the products in A and B are the same, the fractions are equivalent. Otherwise, they are not.

Is $\frac{2}{3}$ equivalent to $\frac{9}{12}$?
A. $2 \times 12 = 24$
B. $3 \times 9 = 27$
C. $\frac{2}{3}$ is not equivalent to $\frac{9}{12}$.

The products in this algorithm are often called the *cross products* because they can be marked to form a sort of X. The algorithm can also tell you which of the two fractions is larger. If the product in A is larger than the product in B, the first fraction is greater. If the product in B is larger, the second fraction is greater. In the example above, the product in B is greater than the product in A, so $\frac{9}{12}$ is greater than $\frac{2}{3}$.

Addition

Intuitively, it is easy to see what the sum of two fractions that have the same denominator would be in each of the models. For parts of a whole:

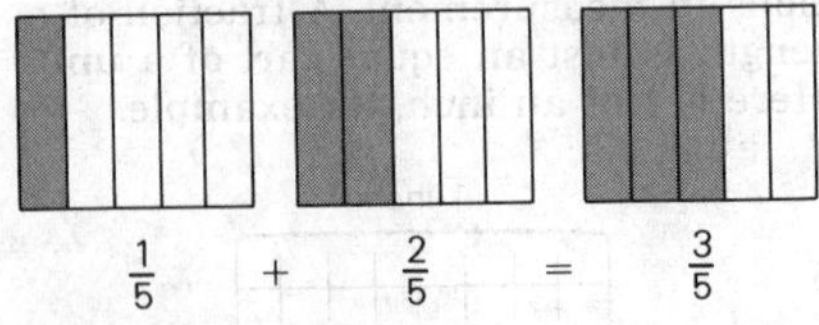

For parts of a set:

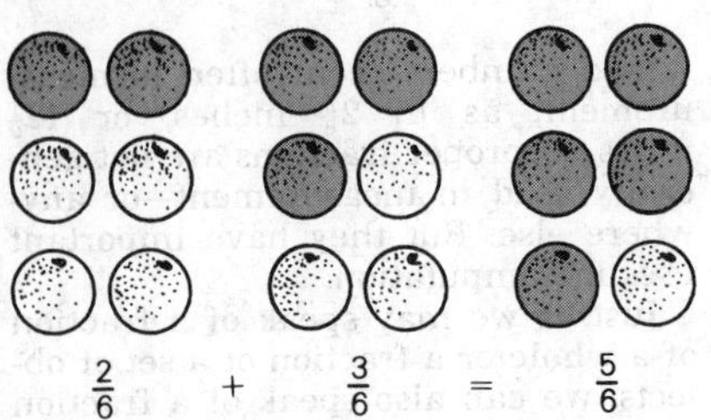

$$\frac{2}{6} \quad + \quad \frac{3}{6} \quad = \quad \frac{5}{6}$$

Using the measurement model:

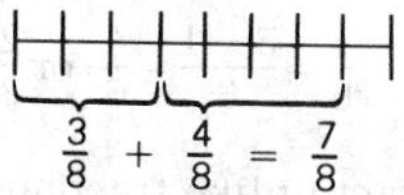

$\frac{3}{8} + \frac{4}{8} = \frac{7}{8}$

Fractions that have the same denominator are called *like fractions.* Here are the steps for adding like fractions:

A. Add the numerators.

B. Put the sum from A over the common denominator. The result is the sum of the fractions.

Here are the steps for $\frac{2}{7} + \frac{3}{7}$.

A. $\frac{2}{7}+\frac{3}{7}=\frac{2+3}{7}=\frac{5}{7}$

B. $\frac{2}{7}+\frac{3}{7}=\frac{5}{7}$

Common denominator. In many cases, the fractions that you are required to add are not like fractions. To add fractions that have different denominators, you must first change them to like fractions.

The diagrams below do not help you very much in finding the sum of $\frac{1}{4}$ and $\frac{1}{2}$.

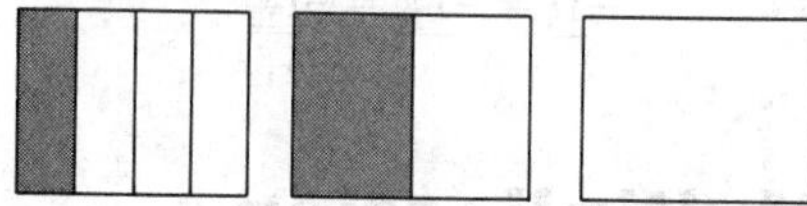

But you can change the number with the smaller denominator to fourths. Then the answer is easy to see.

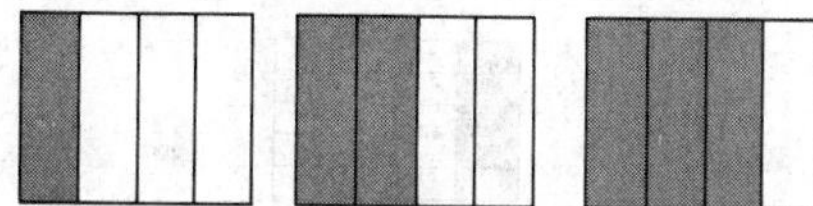

Another way to solve this problem is to use the rule for finding equivalent fractions. You can multiply both the numerator and denominator of $\frac{1}{2}$ by the same number to get an equivalent fraction that has 4 as a denominator.

$$\frac{1}{4}+\frac{1}{2}$$

$$=\frac{1}{4}+\frac{1\times 2}{2\times 2}$$

$$=\frac{1}{4}+\frac{2}{4}$$

Then you can follow the steps for adding like fractions.

$$\frac{1}{4}+\frac{2}{4}=\frac{3}{4}$$

Here is another example.

$$\frac{2}{3}+\frac{1}{6}$$

$$=\frac{2\times 2}{3\times 2}+\frac{1}{6}$$

$$=\frac{4}{6}+\frac{1}{6}=\frac{5}{6}$$

Sometimes it is necessary to find equivalent fractions for both addends. There is no whole number you can multiply by 3 to get 4. (While the equivalence rules work for *any* numbers, it is not practical to use multipliers that are not whole numbers in arithmetic.) You can, however, find a number to multiply by 3 that will give the same number as the product of 4 and another number. In this case, the product you are looking for is 12.

$$3\times 4=12$$
$$4\times 3=12$$

Then, you can add $\frac{1}{4} + \frac{1}{3}$ as follows.

$$\frac{1}{4}+\frac{1}{3}$$

$$=\frac{1\times 3}{4\times 3}+\frac{1\times 4}{3\times 4}$$

$$=\frac{3}{12}+\frac{4}{12}=\frac{7}{12}$$

This suggests one very simple procedure for adding fractions:

A. Multiply the numerator and denominator of the first fraction by the denominator of the second fraction.

B. Multiply the numerator and denominator of the second fraction by the denominator of the first fraction.

C. Add the like fractions that result.

Here is this procedure for $\frac{4}{5} + \frac{5}{7}$.

A. $\frac{4}{5}=\frac{4\times 7}{5\times 7}=\frac{28}{35}$

B. $\frac{5}{7}=\frac{5\times 5}{7\times 5}=\frac{25}{35}$

C. $\frac{4}{5}+\frac{5}{7}=\frac{28}{35}+\frac{25}{35}=\frac{53}{35}$

The answer is $\frac{53}{35}$. However, $\frac{53}{35}$ is an improper fraction, and should be changed to a mixed number because mixed numbers (a whole number and a fraction) are easier to understand.

$$\frac{53}{35}=1\tfrac{18}{35}$$

This is just slightly more than $1\frac{1}{2}$.

When you are changing an improper fraction to a mixed number, you want to find out how many times the denominator can be subtracted from the numerator and what number will be left over. 35 can be subtracted from 53 once, with a remainder of 18. But this is just the definition of whole-number division with a remainder. So, the steps for converting an improper fraction to a mixed number are:

A. Divide the numerator by the denominator.

B. The quotient is the whole-number part of the mixed number. The remainder is the numerator of the fraction part. (The denominator is the same as for the improper fraction.)

Then, to find $\frac{109}{4}$ as a mixed number,

A. $4\overline{)109}$ = 27 r 1

B. $\frac{109}{4}=27\frac{1}{4}$

Often you will encounter problems in which the addends occur as mixed numbers. One way to solve these problems is to convert the mixed numbers to improper fractions. To convert a mixed number to an improper fraction,

A. Multiply the whole-number part of the mixed number by the denominator of the fraction part.

B. Add the product from A to the numerator of the fraction part of the mixed number.

C. Put the sum from B over the denominator of the fraction part. The resulting improper fraction is the answer.

To find an improper fraction that is equivalent to $3\frac{2}{5}$

A. $5 \times 3 = 15$

B. $15 + 2 = 17$

C. The answer is $\frac{17}{5}$.

You can use this method of conversion to solve problems given in mixed numbers.

$$2\tfrac{3}{4}+5\tfrac{7}{8}$$

$$=\tfrac{11}{4}+\tfrac{47}{8}$$

$$=\tfrac{22}{8}+\tfrac{47}{8}$$

$$=\tfrac{69}{8}=8\tfrac{5}{8}$$

A second method of adding mixed numbers uses the mixed numbers directly, so it does not involve the double conversion (from mixed number to improper fraction and then back to mixed number).

To add mixed numbers without converting them to improper fractions,

A. Write the problem in vertical form.

B. Add the whole number part.

C. Add the fraction part.

D. The answer is the mixed number formed by combining the sums or differences from B and C. Improper fractions should be rewritten as mixed numbers and the whole numbers combined by addition.

Here are some examples:

$$\begin{aligned} 2\tfrac{1}{4} &= 2\tfrac{3}{12} \\ +7\tfrac{2}{3} &= +7\tfrac{8}{12} \\ & \quad 9\tfrac{11}{12} \end{aligned}$$

$$\begin{aligned} 3\tfrac{7}{8} &= 3\tfrac{35}{40} \\ +4\tfrac{2}{5} &= +4\tfrac{16}{40} \end{aligned}$$

$$7\tfrac{51}{40} = 7 + 1\tfrac{11}{40} = 8\tfrac{11}{40}$$

Least common denominator. Using the products of the denominators as a common denominator for addition always works, but it is often cumbersome in simplifying. For example:

$$\frac{1}{6}+\frac{2}{9}=\frac{9}{54}+\frac{12}{54}=\frac{21}{54}$$

This fraction must then be simplified to $\frac{7}{18}$.

This problem can be made less cumbersome if you find the smallest denominator that can be used. This is called the *least common denominator (LCD).* Sometimes it is easy to find the least common denominator. For example, it is not very hard to notice that 18 is the LCD of $\frac{1}{6}$ and $\frac{2}{9}$. If you multiply $\frac{1}{6}$ by $\frac{3}{3}$ and $\frac{2}{9}$ by $\frac{2}{2}$, you get

$$\frac{3}{18}+\frac{4}{18}=\frac{7}{18}$$

Other times it seems difficult to find the least common denominator. As with the greatest common factor, the most reliable way to find the least common denominator is to begin with a prime factorization of the denominators. Look at a relatively tough problem.

$$\frac{11}{30}+\frac{9}{14}$$

The prime factors of 30 and 14 are

$$\begin{aligned} 30 &= 2\times 3\times 5 \\ 14 &= 2\times \quad\quad 7 \end{aligned}$$

The number we are looking for, the least common denominator, is also the least common multiple of 14 and 30. You could make a list of the multiples of both numbers until you found one the same. But making out such lists is too much work just to find the least common denominator of the fractions.

From the fundamental theorem of arithmetic, however, you can show that the least common multiple must have all of the prime factors of each number in the pair—and no other. Looking back at the prime factorization, circle each prime factor:

$$\begin{aligned} 30 &= ②\times ③\times ⑤ \\ 14 &= 2\times \quad\quad ⑦ \end{aligned}$$

The least common multiple is the product of these numbers:

$$2\times 3\times 5\times 7 = 210$$

Note that any prime factor of both numbers, in this case 2, is used only once in the least common multiple. So the least common denominator in our problem is also 210. Next, you must multiply the numerators of the fraction by the number that will make them equivalent to the original. You'll discover that the proper number in each case will be the factor or factors *not* part of the prime factorization of the original denominator.

$$\frac{11}{30}=\frac{11\times 7}{210}=\frac{77}{210}$$

$$\frac{9}{14}=\frac{9\times 3\times 5}{210}=\frac{9\times 15}{210}=\frac{135}{210}$$

The factor not part of the prime factorization of 30 is 7. The factors not part of the prime factorization of 14 are 3 and 5. Note that since 2 is part of both factorizations, it is not used.

Now we can do the addition:

$$\frac{11}{30}+\frac{9}{14}$$

$$=\frac{77}{210}+\frac{135}{210}$$

$$=\frac{212}{210}=1\frac{2}{210}=1\frac{1}{105}$$

Here are the steps for adding unlike fractions using the prime factorization method of finding the least common denominator:

A. Factor both denominators into primes.
B. List each factor that appears in the prime factorizations (using common factors only once). The product of these factors is the least common denominator.
C. Multiply the numerators by the primes in the LCD that are not in the original denominator.
D. Add the like fractions.

Here is how this algorithm works with $\frac{7}{24}+\frac{8}{21}$:

A. $24 = 2\times 2\times 2\times 3$
$\quad 21 = \qquad\qquad 3\times 7$

B. $2\times 2\times 2\times 3\times 7 = 168$, the LCD.

C. $\dfrac{7\times 7}{168}+\dfrac{8\times(2\times 2\times 2)}{168}=\dfrac{49}{168}+\dfrac{64}{168}$

D. $\dfrac{49}{168}+\dfrac{64}{168}=\dfrac{113}{168}$

Subtraction

Subtraction is closely related to addition. In fact, the algorithms that are used for subtraction are just like the ones used for addition. To subtract like fractions:

A. Subtract the numerators.
B. Put the difference from A over the common denominator of the original fractions.

For example,

$$\frac{5}{6}-\frac{1}{6}=\frac{5-1}{6}=\frac{4}{6}\text{, or }\frac{2}{3}$$

To subtract unlike fractions:

A. Change the fractions to equivalent fractions with the same (least common) denominator.
B. Subtract the resulting like fractions.

For example,

$$\frac{7}{8}-\frac{5}{6}$$

$$=\left(\frac{7}{8}\times\frac{3}{3}\right)-\left(\frac{5}{6}\times\frac{4}{4}\right)$$

$$=\frac{21}{24}-\frac{20}{24}=\frac{1}{24}$$

The same algorithms for finding the LCD apply.

When subtracting mixed numbers, you may either convert both to improper fractions, or you may subtract fraction from fraction and whole number from whole number. In the second method, you may have to regroup, as in the following example:

$$\begin{aligned} 6\tfrac{1}{4} &= 6\tfrac{3}{12} = 5\tfrac{15}{12} \\ -1\tfrac{2}{3} &= -1\tfrac{8}{12} = -1\tfrac{8}{12} \\ &\qquad\qquad\quad 4\tfrac{7}{12} \end{aligned}$$

Multiplication

After the complexities of adding and subtracting fractions, multiplication of fractions is actually easy. Here is a diagram for $\frac{1}{4}\times\frac{3}{8}$.

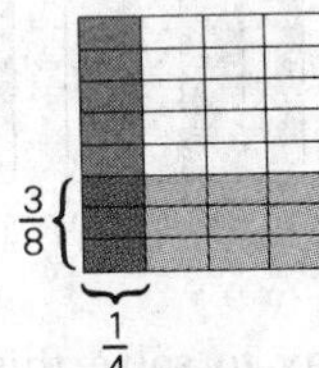

The regions for $\frac{1}{4}$ and for $\frac{3}{8}$ are shaded differently. The region that has both shadings is the product $\frac{1}{4}\times\frac{3}{8}$. Notice that the horizontal and vertical line segments separate the whole into 32 equal parts. One of the equal parts is $\frac{1}{32}$ of the whole. Since there are 3 of the equal parts in the region that represents $\frac{1}{4}\times\frac{3}{8}$, the product is $\frac{3}{32}$.

$$\frac{1}{4}\times\frac{3}{8}=\frac{3}{32}$$

From the formula for the area of a rectangle, you can see that the number of equal parts in this kind of diagram will always be the product of the denominators of the factors. Similarly, the number of equal parts in the product will be the product of the numerators of the factors. Therefore, to multiply two fractions,

A. Multiply the numerators.
B. Multiply the denominators.
C. Simplify the answer if necessary.

It is easy to see that if two proper fractions are multiplied, their product will *always* be *less* than either of the factors. This may seem confusing because the product of two whole numbers greater than 1 is always greater than the factors. It may be useful when multiplying proper fractions to use the word "of" instead of "times." In the example above, the problem can be stated as:

$$\frac{1}{4} \text{ of } \frac{3}{8}$$

By stating the problem this way, we can see why the product will be smaller. In effect, we are dividing $\frac{3}{8}$ into four equal parts. One of these parts will have the value $\frac{3}{32}$.

We can turn the problem around as a check. If $\frac{3}{32}$ is $\frac{1}{4}$ of $\frac{3}{8}$, then $4 \times \frac{3}{32}$ should equal $\frac{3}{8}$:

$$\frac{4}{1} \times \frac{3}{32} = \frac{12}{32} = \frac{3}{8}$$

There is a shortcut for multiplying that often simplifies a problem. Consider

$$\frac{2}{3} \times \frac{3}{8} = \frac{2 \times 3}{3 \times 8} = \frac{6}{24} = \frac{1}{4}$$

In the second step, you already have the product expressed in factored form.

$$\frac{2 \times 3}{3 \times 8}$$

You can put that fraction into simpler form by dividing both numerator and denominator by 3. You show this by crossing out the 3's in the numerator and denominator and writing a small 1 (since 3 ÷ 3 = 1) above or below each crossed-out 3.

$$\frac{2 \times \overset{1}{\cancel{3}}}{\underset{1}{\cancel{3}} \times 8}$$

The resulting fraction represents a factored form of $\frac{2}{8}$. But both the numerator and denominator of $\frac{2}{8}$ can be divided by 2. You show this by crossing out the 2 and the 8. You write a small 1 above the 2 (2 ÷ 2 = 1) and a small 4 below the 8 (8 ÷ 2 = 4). The whole thing looks like this.

$$\frac{\overset{1}{\cancel{2}} \times \overset{1}{\cancel{3}}}{\underset{1}{\cancel{3}} \times \underset{4}{\cancel{8}}}$$

When you have crossed out all of the common factors of the numerator and denominator, you multiply the numbers represented by the small numerals. The answer, directly this time, is $\frac{1}{4}$. This method is called *canceling.*

In practice, it is not necessary to rewrite the original multiplication problem. You start canceling when the problem is still shown as the product of two fractions. Here is the way $\frac{3}{10} \times \frac{5}{9}$ looks using canceling.

$$\frac{\overset{1}{\cancel{3}}}{\underset{2}{\cancel{10}}} \times \frac{\overset{1}{\cancel{5}}}{\underset{3}{\cancel{9}}} = \frac{1}{6}$$

Without canceling, the problem would look like this:

$$\frac{3}{10} \times \frac{5}{9} = \frac{15}{90} = \frac{1}{6}$$

This solution is more difficult, since a fraction with large numbers must be simplified. Both methods work, however, and you should use the one you are comfortable with.

Multiplying mixed numbers is not as easy as multiplying fractions. The easiest way to handle mixed numbers in multiplication is to convert them to improper fractions. Then you can multiply by the usual algorithm, either with or without canceling.

Multiplying two mixed numbers without converting them to improper fractions is so complicated that it is not worth learning. But it is useful to know how to multiply a whole number by a mixed number without converting to improper fractions.

A. Write the problem in vertical form. Multipy the fraction part of the mixed number by the whole number and write the answer as a partial product.
B. Multiply the whole-number part of the mixed number by the whole number and write the answer as a partial product.
C. Add the partial products.

Here is $6 \times 2\frac{5}{8}$ by this method.

$$\begin{array}{r} 2\frac{5}{8} \\ \times 6 \\ \hline 3\frac{3}{4} \\ 12 \\ \hline 15\frac{3}{4} \end{array} \qquad \left(\frac{6}{1} \times \frac{5}{8} = \frac{30}{8} = 3\frac{3}{4}\right)$$

Notice that when a whole number and a fraction are multiplied, it is usual to rewrite the whole number as a fraction with 1 as a denominator. This becomes more important in division of fractions.

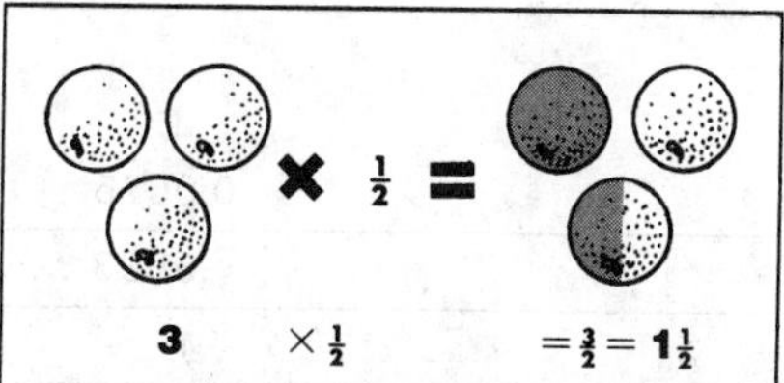

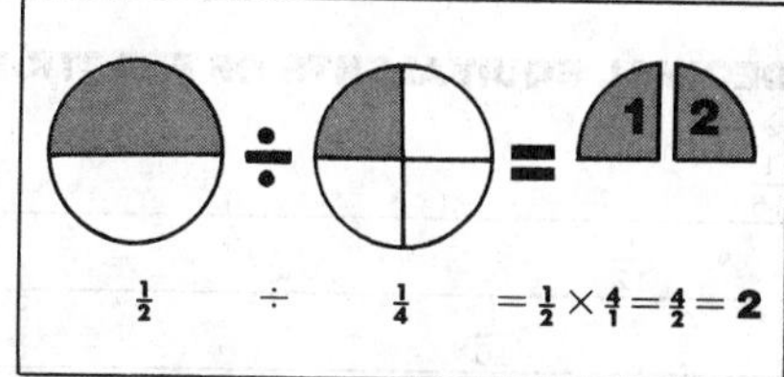

MULTIPLYING AND DIVIDING BY A FRACTION *give surprising results. Multiplication gives an answer* smaller *than the multiplicand. Division gives an answer* larger *than the dividend.*

Division

Division of fractions involves one more step than multiplication of fractions. The basic idea behind this step is to turn a division problem into a multiplication problem. You may recall the rules stated in the introduction to fractions: To find half of a number, divide by 2, etc. This rule turned a problem of multiplying by a fraction into a problem involving division by a whole number. Now, consider a problem of dividing by a fraction, and see how it can be changed into a problem involving multiplication by a whole number.

A bank teller is asked for $75 in quarters by a storekeeper. He wants to know how many quarters are in $75.

The problem can be stated mathematically as follows:

$$75 \div \frac{1}{4} = ?$$

If you were doing the problem in your head, however, you would probably say, "There are 4 quarters in one dollar; therefore in $75, there are 4 × 75 quarters." You could write it

$$75 \times 4 = 300$$

You can see that dividing 75 by $\frac{1}{4}$ is the same as multiplying 75 by 4. Since 4 means $\frac{4}{1}$, we have *inverted* the fraction—turned it upside down—and multiplied.

The inverted form of a number is called its *reciprocal.* Any number multiplied by its reciprocal equals 1:

$$\frac{1}{4} \times \frac{4}{1} = \frac{4}{4} = 1 \qquad \frac{5}{6} \times \frac{6}{5} = \frac{30}{30} = 1$$

To divide fractions, follow this algorithm: Multiply the dividend (the number to be divided) by the reciprocal of the divisor (the number you are dividing by).

Here is an example:

$$\frac{2}{3} \div \frac{3}{4} = \frac{2}{3} \times \frac{4}{3} = \frac{8}{9}$$

You can see from the examples above that when you are dividing by a proper fraction, the quotient will be *larger* than the dividend. 300 is larger than 75, and $\frac{8}{9}$ is larger than $\frac{2}{3}$. This may seem confusing because in division by a whole number greater than 1, the quotient is always *smaller* than the dividend.

DECIMAL EQUIVALENTS OF FRACTIONS

$\frac{1}{16}$	0.0625
$\frac{1}{12}$	.0833 . . .
$\frac{1}{10}$	.1
$\frac{1}{9}$	.1111 . . .
$\frac{2}{16}$ $\frac{1}{8}$	.125
$\frac{1}{7}$	.1428 . . .
$\frac{2}{12}$ $\frac{1}{6}$	.1666 . . .
$\frac{3}{16}$	.1875
$\frac{2}{10}$ $\frac{1}{5}$	.2
$\frac{2}{9}$	.2222 . . .
$\frac{4}{16}$ $\frac{3}{12}$ $\frac{2}{8}$ $\frac{1}{4}$	.25
$\frac{2}{7}$	.2857 . . .
$\frac{3}{10}$	.3
$\frac{5}{16}$	.3125
$\frac{4}{12}$ $\frac{3}{9}$ $\frac{2}{6}$ $\frac{1}{3}$	.3333 . . .
$\frac{6}{16}$ $\frac{3}{8}$	.375
$\frac{4}{10}$ $\frac{2}{5}$	.4
$\frac{5}{12}$	.4166 . . .
$\frac{3}{7}$	.4285 . . .
$\frac{7}{16}$	.4375
$\frac{4}{9}$	.4444 . . .
$\frac{8}{16}$ $\frac{6}{12}$ $\frac{5}{10}$ $\frac{4}{8}$ $\frac{3}{6}$ $\frac{2}{4}$ $\frac{1}{2}$	.5
$\frac{5}{9}$	.5555 . . .
$\frac{9}{16}$	.5625
$\frac{4}{7}$	.5714 . . .
$\frac{7}{12}$	.5833 . . .
$\frac{6}{10}$ $\frac{3}{5}$	.6
$\frac{10}{16}$ $\frac{5}{8}$	.625
$\frac{8}{12}$ $\frac{6}{9}$ $\frac{4}{6}$ $\frac{2}{3}$	.6666 . . .
$\frac{11}{16}$	.6875
$\frac{7}{10}$	.7
$\frac{5}{7}$	.7142 . . .
$\frac{12}{16}$ $\frac{9}{12}$ $\frac{6}{8}$ $\frac{3}{4}$	.75
$\frac{7}{9}$	.7777 . . .
$\frac{8}{10}$ $\frac{4}{5}$	.8
$\frac{13}{16}$	.8125
$\frac{10}{12}$ $\frac{5}{6}$	.8333 . . .
$\frac{6}{7}$	.8571 . . .
$\frac{14}{16}$ $\frac{7}{8}$	.875
$\frac{8}{9}$	.8888 . . .
$\frac{9}{10}$	.9
$\frac{11}{12}$	.9166 . . .
$\frac{15}{16}$	.9375

To understand what division by a fraction really means, consider the example of the bank teller once again. He wanted to know how many units smaller than 1 were in 75. Clearly there will be more than 75. Consider the following:

How many \$5 bills are in \$75?
$75 \div 5 = 15$
How many \$1 bills are in \$75?
$75 \div 1 = 75$
How many half-dollars are in \$75?
$75 \div \frac{1}{2} = 75 \times \frac{2}{1} = 150$
How many quarters are in \$75?
$75 \div \frac{1}{4} = 75 \times \frac{4}{1} = 300$
How many dimes are in \$75?
$75 \div \frac{1}{10} = 75 \times \frac{10}{1} = 750$

The smaller the fraction used as a divisor, the larger the quotient will be.

To divide two mixed numbers, it is easiest to convert both of them to improper fractions and proceed as with division of proper fractions.

Calculators and Fractions

Calculating machines are not designed to work with fractions. If you have a problem involving fractions, you need to convert it to one with decimals. There are several ways to do this. One of the handiest things to do is to memorize the decimal equivalents of the fractions that are used most. A table of decimal equivalents appears on this page.

The equivalents with three dots after them are not exact; in fact, there are no exact decimal equivalents. To use the decimals in the table, round off to the thousandths place.

Even if you know many decimal equivalents, there will come a time when you need a decimal equivalent that you have not memorized. You can convert any fraction to a decimal by dividing the numerator by the denominator. This procedure is simple and quick on a calculator. If you are doing the division by hand, simply write the numerator with a decimal point and as many 0's as needed. To change $\frac{5}{16}$ to a decimal, think

$$16\overline{)5.0000}\quad = 0.3125$$

Sometimes it simplifies your thinking, when working with a calculator, if you (mentally) convert any problem with fractions to a problem with whole numbers and decimals. For example, if you know the decimal equivalents, $\frac{2}{3} + \frac{3}{4}$ becomes 0.667 + 0.75, or approximately 1.417. The exact answer is $1\frac{5}{12}$, but the decimal approximation is close enough for most purposes.

Ratio and Proportion

Suppose that your car goes 20 miles for each gallon of gasoline you put in the gas tank. That is an example of a *rate:* 20 miles per gallon.

Gallons	1	2	3	4	5
Miles	20	40	60	80	100

The table shows the rate in another way. The same idea can be expressed as a *ratio.* The ratio of gallons to miles is 1 to 20.

In general, a ratio is used to express a relationship between two quantities. If the two quantities change with each other, as the miles and gasoline do, then a ratio is exactly like a rate. If the two quantities do not change, then a ratio is exactly like a fraction. For example, you could say that the ratio of boys to girls at a party is 2 to 1. That ratio applies to a particular party, so it is not a rate. However, saying that the ratio is 2 to 1 is the same as saying there are half as many girls as boys.

Ratios are shown in several ways in mathematics. A ratio of 3 to 5 is sometimes shown with a colon, as 3:5. Because of the ease in computation, however, the most common way to show a ratio of 3 to 5 is as a fraction, as $\frac{3}{5}$. The fraction form is used whether the ratio represents a rate or a fraction. You have to determine from the specific situation what the meaning of the fraction is.

Ratios are not what we ordinarily think of as numbers. For example, it makes no sense to add, subtract, multiply, or divide ratios. But they have some properties that are like numbers. For example, you can define equality:

Two ratios are equal if the fractions that represent them are equivalent.

Equal ratios are quite useful. They are used often enough to have a special name. A statement that two ratios are equal is a *proportion.* When the colon notation is used, there is a special symbol for a proportion. To write that the ratio of 3 to 5 is equal to the ratio of 6 to 10, you would write

$$3{:}5{::}6{:}10$$

This system is not used very much any more because it is easier to work with the fraction form:

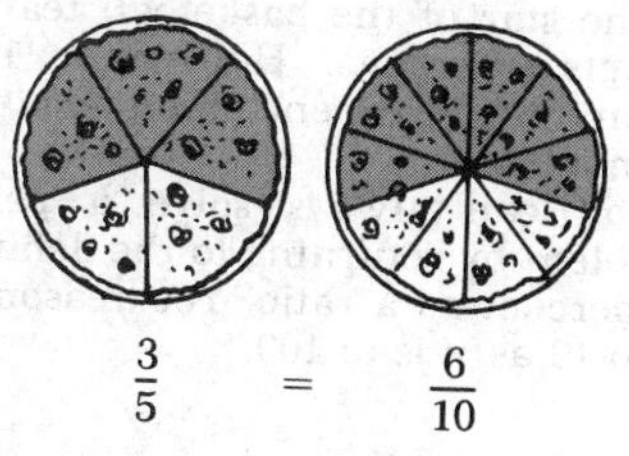

$$\frac{3}{5} = \frac{6}{10}$$

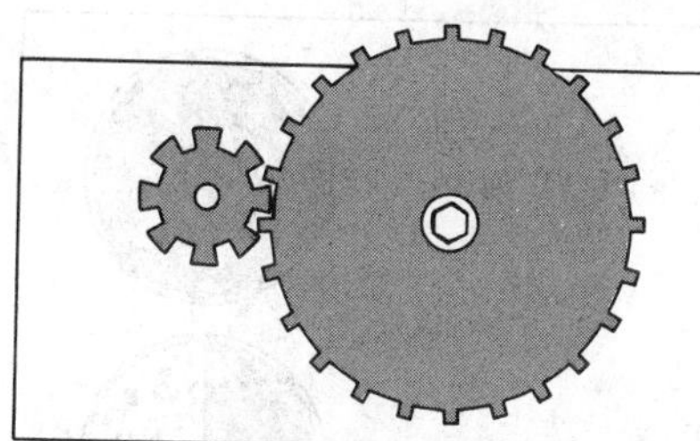

GEAR SYSTEMS *can be described by ratios. These gears are related in a ratio of 1:3 (the gear on the right has 3 times as many teeth) or 3:1 (the gear on the left turns 3 times for 1 turn of the right one).*

Because equality for ratios is the same as equivalence for fractions, the cross-products may be used to determine whether or not a statement that two ratios are equal is really a proportion:

A. Multiply the numerator of the first ratio by the denominator of the second.

B. Multiply the denominator of the first ratio by the numerator of the second.

C. If the products found in A and B are equal, then the statement is a proportion.

Remember that the numbers you multiply are those diagonal to each other:

$$\frac{3}{5} = \frac{6}{10}$$

Since $3 \times 10 = 30$ and $5 \times 6 = 30$, the statement is a proportion.

Often, problems involving proportions give you three of the four numbers. The other number is missing. By using the cross-products, you can find the missing number. According to traditional terminology, the top left and bottom right numbers in a proportion are called the *extreme terms.* The bottom left and top right are called the *mean terms.* (This may be easier to remember if you know that extreme means "outside" and mean means "inside.") As you read a proportion, "three is to five as six is to ten," the extremes are the first and last numbers you say, and the means are the two middle numbers.

Using this language, the cross-product rule is:

The product of the mean is equal to the product of the extremes.

There are four cases in which a proportion with one term missing can occur. Here n represents the missing term.

$$\frac{n}{4} = \frac{3}{12} \qquad \frac{2}{n} = \frac{4}{14} \qquad \frac{3}{9} = \frac{n}{36} \qquad \frac{5}{2} = \frac{15}{n}$$

While the above examples are easy ones, which you may be able to solve mentally, it is useful to see how each can be solved using the cross-product rule.

$\frac{n}{4} = \frac{3}{12}$ is a proportion if and only if $n \times 12 = 4 \times 3$, or $n \times 12 = 12$. You know that this is true if n is 1, so the proportion is $\frac{1}{4} = \frac{3}{12}$.

$\frac{2}{n} = \frac{4}{14}$ is a proportion if and only if $2 \times 14 = n \times 4$. For most people, it is more comfortable to rewrite this as $n \times 4 = 28$. You can divide the parts on both sides of the equal sign by 4.

$$\frac{n \times \cancel{4}}{\cancel{4}} = \frac{28}{4}$$

The fours cancel on the left side, so

$$n = \frac{28}{4} = 7$$

The other problems can be solved in similar fashion.

The proportions here have all been designed to use whole numbers and to give whole-number answers. In applications this may not be the case. For example, suppose that you are baking cupcakes, using a recipe for 12 cupcakes. But you want to make 10 because that is all that will fit in your cupcake pan. The recipe calls for 2 cups of flour. How much should you use?

In setting up a proportion, the important thing is to keep the terms in the right order. For example, you can think "12 cupcakes is to 10 cupcakes as 2 cups of flour is to n cups of flour."

$$\frac{12}{10} = \frac{2}{n}$$

$$12 \times n = 10 \times 2$$

$$12 \times n = 20$$

$$n = \frac{20}{12} = 1\frac{2}{3}$$

You need $1\frac{2}{3}$ cups of flour for 10 cupcakes. (Remember to reduce the other ingredients in proportion.) Notice that there is no single right way to set up the proportion. The numerators and denominators might be reversed, or you might reason, "2 cups of flour is to 12 cupcakes as n cups of flour is to 10 cupcakes":

$$\frac{10}{12} = \frac{n}{2} \text{ or } \frac{2}{12} = \frac{n}{10}$$

In either case, the answer will be the same. There *are* wrong ways to write a proportion, however, so it is a good idea to write out the proportion to be sure your reasoning is straight. Here is a simplified algorithm to solve any proportion.

A. Find the product of the known numerator and denominator pair.

B. Divide by the other known term.

For example, in $\frac{n}{37} = \frac{53}{61}$, the known numerator and denominator pair is 53 and 37. So $n = (53 \times 37) \div 61$.

Percent

There is a special case of ratio that is very much used in business, in education (particularly in testing), and in some branches of science. It is *percent.* In Latin, percent means "for each hundred" or "per hundred." It is a ratio in which the second term (or denominator) is 100, but it is written as a whole number followed by a special sign, %. Thus, 25% means the ratio of 25 to 100, or $\frac{25}{100}$.

Percent computations are closely related to decimals since, for example 25% = 0.25. In fact, we often convert percents to decimals for some computations. It is important to remember, however, that a percent is a ratio, and, like other ratios, it is not subject to all procedures of arithmetic. In most situations, for example, multiplication or division of one percent by another makes no mathematical sense. Translating percents to decimals often helps us understand that they are fractions—parts of a whole.

To change a percent, such as 37%, to a decimal, divide the percent by 100 and drop the % sign. In practice, this means moving the decimal point two places to the left. So, 37% is equal to 0.37. The procedure works even when the percent has a decimal place. 12.5% is equivalent to .125.

Sometimes, after completing a problem, you may wish to express the result as a percent. To express a decimal as a percent, multiply by 100 and add the % sign. In practice, this means moving the decimal point two places to the right. Thus, 0.6125 is written as 61.25%.

Percents can be greater than 100%. 100% is the same as the ratio $\frac{100}{100}$, or 1. So, 100% of something is all of it. Similarly, 200% of something is twice as much. The same rules for changing from decimals to percents and back apply to percents greater than 100%. So, 107% is equal to 1.07, and 3.56 is equal to 356%.

Since percents are just ratios, you may wonder why there is any need for them at all. Here are some reasons why percents are more useful than ratios. Although ratios are not numbers, they share with numbers the property of being able to be compared. For example, the ratio of 2 to 3 is greater than the ratio of 3 to 5. This may not be immediately obvious. When given as percents, however, the ratio of 2 to 3 is $66\frac{2}{3}$% and the ratio of 3 to 5 is 60%. It is easy to see that $66\frac{2}{3}$% is greater than 60%.

Sometimes it is necessary to specify a very small ratio. For example, interest rates on credit cards are usually expressed on a daily basis as something like 0.03287% per day. This is easier to think about than $\frac{3287}{10,000,000}$, although both ratios are the same.

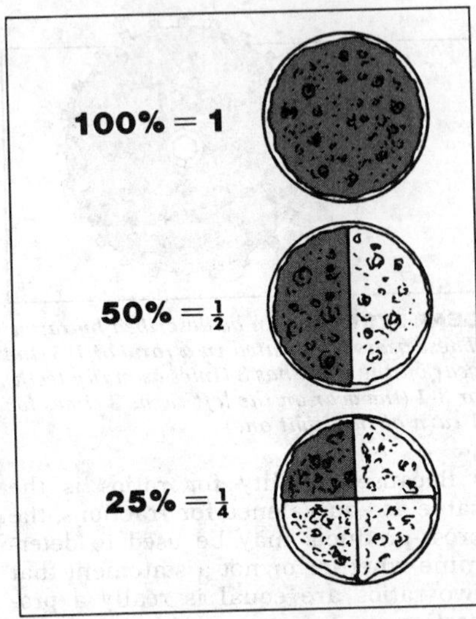

Finally, because percents and decimals convert so easily from one to another, computation with percents is easier than computation with ratios expressed as fractions.

Percentage Problems

Typically, you will encounter three different situations in percent problems.

1. You need to find a percent of a number.
2. You need to find what percent one number is of another.
3. You know a percent of a number and you want to find the number.

Finding a percent of a number. Suppose you read that 5% of the 827 businesses in your town lost money. How many lost money?

One way to solve all percent problems is to go back to the basic definition of a percent as a ratio. Then the problem can be solved with the same methods used for solving proportions. Your reasoning may be, "5 is to 100 as n is to 827." Note that $\frac{5}{100}$ is the fractional equivalent of 5%.

$$\frac{5}{100} = \frac{n}{827}$$

Multiply the cross-products:

$$5 \times 827 = 100 \times n$$
$$100 \times n = 4135$$

Divide both sides by 100 to get the value of n:

$$n = 41.35$$

Since 0.35 of a business cannot lose money, the number should be rounded to the whole number 41.

A second way to solve the problem is to convert the percent to a decimal. To find a percent of a number using decimals:

A. Change the percent to a decimal.
B. Multiply the number by the decimal.

For the example above:

A. 5% = 0.05

B.
$$\begin{array}{r} 827 \\ \times 0.05 \\ \hline 41.35 \end{array}$$

A third way to find a percentage of a number is to use a formula. A *formula* is a sentence involving one or more letters for which you substitute numbers appropriate to the specific situation. For the percent formula, the letter r is used to represent the percent expressed as a decimal (it stands for *rate*). The letter b represents the number (it stands for *base*). And the letter p is used for the percent of the number (it stands for *percentage,* which means a percent of a number). The steps for finding a percent of a number, or percentage, are to rewrite the percent as a decimal, which gives r, and to multiply the decimal by the number, or base. The result is the percentage. In formula form, this is

$$\text{percentage} = \text{base} \times \text{rate or } p = b \times r$$

To use the formula, you substitute the numbers you are given for the letters in the formula. For the example above, $b = 827$ and $r = 0.05$, so

$$p = b \times r$$
$$41.35 = 827 \times 0.05$$

Finding what percent one number is of another. Now consider a problem in which you know two numbers and you want to find out what percent one is of another.

The star of the basketball team attempts 19 shots. He makes 11 of them. What percent of his shots has he made?

You can always solve a percent problem by returning to the definition of percent as a ratio. You reason, "11 is to 19 as n is to 100."

$$\frac{11}{19} = \frac{n}{100}$$
$$11 \times 100 = 19 \times n$$
$$19 \times n = 1100$$
$$n = 57.89\ldots$$

Rounded to the nearest percent, he has made 58% of his shots.

Using decimals, you would follow these steps.

A. Divide the percentage by the base.
B. Change the resulting decimal to a percent.

The base is the number of shots the player has taken, or 19. The percentage is the number of shots he has made, or 11.

A. $19\overline{)11.0000}$ = 0.5789 . . .

B. 0.58 = 58%

In order to use the formula, we can rearrange it to solve for the rate. If

$$\text{base} \times \text{rate} = \text{percentage}$$

we can divide the parts on both sides of the equal sign by the base:

$$\frac{\cancel{\text{base}} \times \text{rate}}{\cancel{\text{base}}} = \frac{\text{percentage}}{\text{base}}$$

The bases on the left side cancel, leaving us with a new formula:

$$\text{rate} = \frac{\text{percentage}}{\text{base}} \quad \text{or} \quad r = \frac{p}{b}$$

In the above example,

$$r = \frac{11}{19}$$
$$r = .5789$$
$$r = 58\%$$

Finding a number when another number is a certain percent of it. Sometimes you have information about a percentage and a rate, but do not know the base.

A commercial tells you that 62% of all cassette makers use Smith tape. Later it says 5000 cassette makers use Smith tape. If both statements are true, how many cassette makers are there?

First let us look at how you can use proportions to solve the problem. You can reason that "62 is to 100 as 5000 is to n." This gives you a proportion which you can solve in the regular way.

$$\frac{62}{100} = \frac{5000}{n}$$
$$62 \times n = 100 \times 5000$$
$$62 \times n = 500{,}000$$
$$n = 500{,}000 \div 62$$
$$n = 8064.5\ldots$$

Since there are no partial cassette makers, you should round your answer to 8065.

FORMULAS FOR SOLVING PERCENT PROBLEMS

Where b = **base** (the number equivalent to 100%)
r = **rate** (the percent expressed as a decimal)
and p = **percentage** (the number equivalent to the rate),
use the following formulas:

1. **To find what number is a certain percent of another number.** (The number you know is b, the percent is r; solve for p.) $$p = b \times r$$

2. **To find what percent one number is of another.** (The number equal to 100% is b, the number whose percent you are trying to find is p; solve for r.) $$r = \frac{p}{b}$$

3. **To find a number when another number is a certain percent of it.** (The number you know is p, the percent it is of the other number is r; solve for b.) $$b = \frac{p}{r}$$

Using decimals, you would follow these steps.

A. Change the percent to a decimal.
B. Divide the percentage by the decimal. The percentage in our example is 5000. So:

A. 62% = 0.62

B. $0.62\overline{)5000.00.0}$ = 80 64.5 . . .

To use the formula, we can rearrange it to solve for the base. If

$$\text{base} \times \text{rate} = \text{percentage}$$

then we can divide both sides by the rate

$$\frac{\text{base} \times \cancel{\text{rate}}}{\cancel{\text{rate}}} = \frac{\text{percentage}}{\text{rate}}$$

The rates on the left side cancel, leaving us with a new formula:

$$\text{base} = \frac{\text{percentage}}{\text{rate}} \quad \text{or} \quad b = \frac{p}{r}$$

In the example above,

$$b = \frac{5000}{0.62}$$
$$b = 8064.5$$

It is useful to know all three ways of attacking a percent problem, but most textbooks use a single method and stick to it. If you are helping someone understand a percent problem, you should try to work with the method that person normally uses.

Special Uses of Percents

There are many situations where percent problems occur in newspapers, magazines, or television or in daily life. Here are a few situations you will probably encounter.

BATTING AVERAGE *represents the ratio of a player's hits to his times at bat. Darryl Strawberry has 622 hits in 2342 at-bats; 622 ÷ 2342 = .266, Strawberry's batting average.*

topps® 710 DARRYL STRAWBERRY ✦ OF

HT: 6'6" WT: 190 BATS: LEFT THROWS: LEFT DRFT: METS #1-JUNE, 1980
ACQ: VIA DRAFT BORN: 3-12-62, LOS ANGELES, CALIFORNIA HOME: LOS ANGELES, CALIF.

COMPLETE MAJOR LEAGUE BATTING RECORD

YR CLUB	G	AB	R	H	2B	3B	HR	RBI	SB	SLG	BB	SO	AVG
83 METS	122	420	63	108	15	7	26	74	19	.512	47	128	.257
84 METS	147	522	75	131	27	4	26	97	27	.467	75	131	.251
85 METS	111	393	78	109	15	4	29	79	26	.557	73	96	.277
86 METS	136	475	76	123	27	5	27	93	28	.507	72	141	.259
87 METS	154	532	108	151	32	5	39	104	36	.583	97	122	.284
MAJ. LEA. TOTALS	670	2342	400	622	116	25	147	447	136	.525	364	618	.266

GW-RBI (1987): 5 GW-RBI (CAREER): 47

Darryl led Texas League with 34 HR, 100 Bases on Balls and .602 Slugging Pct. at Jackson in 1982.

THIS WAY TO THE CLUBHOUSE . . . *Darryl signed as a 1st round Draft selection with the Mets, July 11, 1980 by Scout Roger Jongewaard.*

TOPPS CHEWING GUM CO.

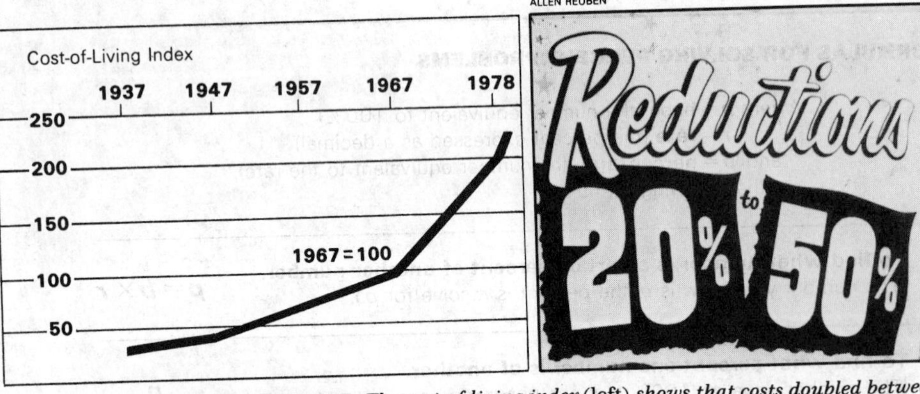

INCREASE AND DECREASE. *The cost-of-living index* (left) *shows that costs doubled between 1967 and 1978, going from 100 to 200. The sale sign* (right) *announces a decrease in prices.*

Increase and decrease. You learn that the cost of living has gone up 11% since last year. This is called a *percent of increase.* The statement means that the cost of living now is 11% more than it was a year ago. Another way to look at this is to say that the cost of living now is 111% of what it was a year ago. Both statements mean the same thing.

Say that the cost of living a year ago was figured at $120 per week. Using the 11% rate of increase, what is the cost of living now?

One way: Find 11% of $120. It is $13.20. Now add.

$$\begin{array}{r} \$120.00 \\ +\$13.20 \\ \hline \$133.20 \end{array}$$

The cost of living now is $133.20.

Another way: Find 111% of $120. It is found in the same way you find a percentage when the percent is less than 100%.

$$\begin{array}{r} \$1\,20 \\ \times 1.11 \\ \hline 1\,20 \\ 12\,0 \\ 120 \\ \hline \$133.20 \end{array}$$

The second way is usually easier.

Now suppose that the cost of living has gone *down* 9% over the year. If it was figured at $120 a week a year ago, what is it today?

This situation is termed a *percent of decrease*—that is, 9% is a percent of decrease. You can think of it either as 9% less than the original amount or as 91% of the original amount. Either way can be used to find the current amount.

One way: First find 9% of $120. It is $10.80. Then subtract $10.80 from $120 to get the cost of living now, which is $109.20.

Another way: Find 91% of $120. It is $109.20.

It should be clear than an increase of n% is the same as $(100 + n)$%; and a decrease of n% is the same as $(100 - n)$%. While percents do not add or subtract, the definition of percent of increase or decrease is the percentage that is to be added or subtracted from the base.

It may seem that if the cost of living increased 10% one year and decreased 10% the next year, the new cost of living would be the original number. This is not the case, as you can easily show:

Original cost of living: $100.
Cost of living after year 1:

$$100 \times 1.10 = \$110$$

Cost of living after year 2:

$$110 \times .90 = \$99$$

As you can see, the percentages are calculated for different bases. 10% of $100 is $10; but 10% of $110 is $11. Equal percents of different bases yield different amounts.

Discounts. One of the uses of percent that you will frequently encounter is a discount that a store is giving. A discount is actually a percent of decrease. If the store advertises "20% discount," what will an item priced at $20 cost?

Since a discount is a percent of decrease, you can calculate the amount of discount and subtract it from the price; or you can subtract the discount from 100%, and multiply this new rate times the price. Using the first method, you find 20% of $20, which is $4. Then you subtract this discount from the original price. The item will cost $16. Using the second method, you subtract 20% from 100% to get 80%. Then you find 80% of $20 and get the new price directly.

Sometimes you will encounter a double discount. Say an item is originally marked 15% off. Then there is a storewide sale—everything in the store 10% off. If an item originally cost $50, what is the price after the double discount?

You may think that the answer is to subtract 25% of $50, but that would not give the correct answer. Remember that percents of different bases do not add or subtract. You must first find the price after the first discount, then subtract the second discount from this new price.

15% of $50 = $7.50
$50.00 − $7.50 = $42.50
10% of $42.50 = $4.25
$42.50 − $4.25 = $38.25

The new price is $38.25. Note that a straight 25% discount would have brought the price to $37.50.

Interest. Another area in which you will frequently run into percent is interest. *Interest* is a percent of increase that is paid on money saved or borrowed. Interest is always stated on a yearly basis unless another term of measurement is given. Frequently stores and credit cards add "carrying charges" to unpaid bills. These are also a form of interest.

First consider interest on savings. If you saved $100 at 5% simple interest for a year, you would have $105 at the end of the year.

Most banks, however, offer compound interest. *Compound interest* is interest that is paid both on the money originally saved (called the *principal*) and on the interest that has accumulated in your account. Say that the interest is compounded quarterly. This means that every three months (four times a year, or once each quarter), the bank pays interest. That interest, however, stays in the bank. It gets interest, also. At the end of the first quarter, $100 gets $\frac{1}{4}$ of the annual rate of 5% interest. This means you have earned 1.25% of $100, or $1.25. There is now $101.25 in the account.

During the next three months, another $1.25 interest accumulates on the $100. But 5% interest is also paid on the $1.25 earned in the first quarter. While this is not very much (only $0.015625), at the end of the second three months there is $102.515625 in the account. At the end of another three months there is $103.79706 (with some rounding taking place). Then, after a full year, there will be $105.09452 in the account.

In this example, quarterly compounding yields only $.09 more than simple interest in the first year. Over several years, however, it begins to make a great difference. At the end of the second year, it would yield $110.44858, that is, $.44 over the $110 that would have been earned through simple interest. By the end of the third year, the difference would be over a dollar.

In the example, quarterly compounding was used. Many banks offer daily compounding of interest, which produces an even greater gain.

The effects of compound interest are such that any amount of money in-

ACCOUNT SUMMARY	PREVIOUS BALANCE	PAYMENTS	DEBIT AND CREDIT (–) ADJUSTMENTS	NEW PURCHASES AND CASH ADVANCES NO.		FINANCE CHARGE AT PERIODIC RATE	FINANCE CHARGE ITEM CHARGES	TOTAL NEW BALANCE*	MINIMUM PAYMENT
PURCHASES	108 69	50 00				96		59 65	5 00
CASH ADVANCES	00							00	00
TOTAL	108 69	50 00				96		59 65	5 00

*If payment of your New Balance is received on or before the Payment Date, New Purchases posted during the Period and appearing on this Statement will not be subject to an additional **FINANCE CHARGE**. The **FINANCE CHARGE** for Cash Advances, however, will continue to accrue and will appear on your next statement.

TO PAY YOUR NEW BALANCE IN FULL REMIT THIS AMOUNT

TO PAY IN INSTALLMENTS REMIT THIS AMOUNT OR MORE

AMOUNT PAST DUE	00
TOTAL MINIMUM PAYMENT DUE	5 00

CREDIT LIMIT $1,000.00 CREDIT AVAILABLE $940.00

PURCHASE BALANCES SUBJECT TO FINANCE CHARGE AND PERIODIC RATES		
PURCHASE AVERAGE DAILY BALANCE	FIRST $ 500	OVER $ 500
	63 87	
MONTHLY PERIODIC RATE	.0150000	.0100000
ANNUAL PERCENTAGE RATE	18.00%	12.00 %

CASH ADVANCE BALANCES SUBJECT TO FINANCE CHARGE AND PERIODIC RATES	
SUM OF DAILY CASH ADVANCE BALANCES	ALL
DAILY PERIODIC RATE	.0003287
ANNUAL PERCENTAGE RATE	12.00%

PAYMENT OF EITHER TOTAL NEW BALANCE OR YOUR TOTAL MINIMUM PAYMENT MUST REACH US BY:

IF YOU HAVE ANY QUESTIONS SEE ITEM #7 ON REVERSE SIDE OR CALL OUR CUSTOMER SERVICE DEPARTMENT AT:

FINANCE CHARGE *is a form of interest. This charge card customer was charged 1.5% (.0150000) of $63.87, which came to $.96.*

vested at 5% interest compounded quarterly will double in 14 years. If the interest were not compounded, the money would not double until 20 years had passed.

When you borrow money from a bank, you have to pay interest. Generally speaking, the interest you pay will be higher than the interest the bank pays you on your savings. That is one of the ways that banks make money. They pay you one rate for the use of your money, then loan that money to someone else who pays them a higher rate.

Interest paid on loans is a special form of percent of increase. There are many variations from bank to bank and from loan to loan. Here are a few of the kinds most frequently encountered.

Simple interest on the total amount: You borrow $1000 at 9% interest for six months. At the end of half a year you pay back $1045. Since the interest is stated on a yearly basis, interest for half a year will be $\frac{1}{2} \times$ 9% or 4.5%.

Simple interest discounted: You ask for a loan of $1000 at 9% for 6 months. The bank gives you $955, since they have taken out (or "discounted") the interest in advance. At the end of 6 months you pay the bank $1000. The true rate of interest on the loan is higher than 9%, since the borrower did not have the use of the full $1000. In fact, the true rate of interest is about 9.4%.

Interest on a declining balance: Most people prefer to pay back loans a little bit at a time. Say you borrow $1000 at 9% interest and agree to pay it back monthly over a 6-month period (usually the period is longer, but this allows comparison with the two previous examples). Say you agree to pay $175 per month and adjust the last payment to come out even. The first month you would have $1000. After making the first payment, your loan would only be $825. After the second payment, it would be $650. So your interest should be for one month on $1000, two months on $825, three months on $650, and so forth. You can calculate this as

$$\begin{aligned}
\$1000 \times 0.09 \times \tfrac{1}{12} &= \$\ 7.50 \\
\$825 \times 0.09 \times \tfrac{1}{6} &= \$12.375 \\
\$650 \times 0.09 \times \tfrac{1}{4} &= \$14.625 \\
\$475 \times 0.09 \times \tfrac{1}{3} &= \$14.25 \\
\$300 \times 0.09 \times \tfrac{5}{12} &= \$11.25 \\
\$125 \times 0.09 \times \tfrac{1}{2} &= \$\ 5.625 \\
\text{Total interest} &\quad \$65.625
\end{aligned}$$

In practice, the total interest would be added to the payment schedule and the amount of the payment would be adjusted, so the actual figures would differ somewhat. Banks have tables prepared to give them the amount of payment required. Also, there are many ways of calculating declining interest. This is the simplest one, but not necessarily what your bank would use. Note that the true rate of interest, using the method shown here, is more than 13.1%, even though the stated rate is 9%.

Most credit card or "instant money" loans are based on a declining balance with stated rates of 12% or 18%. Consequently, the true rate of interest, which varies with the method of calculation and the time taken to repay, can be very high.

Commissions. Another application of percent that you will sometimes encounter is the commission. A *commission* is a payment made to a salesperson that is based on the dollar amount of the sales that person has made. In the simplest case, a straight commission would be, say, 6% of sales. A salesperson who sold $200,000 worth of goods during the year would receive $12,000.

Often a commission plan is more complicated. For example, a salesperson may receive a base salary plus a commission of 2% on sales over $100,000, 4% on sales over $200,000, and 6% on sales over $300,000. A salesperson who sold $350,000 worth of goods and who had a base salary of $12,000 a year would receive

$$\begin{aligned}
& \$12{,}000 \text{ salary} \\
0.02 \times \$100{,}000 = {} & \quad 2{,}000 \\
0.04 \times \$100{,}000 = {} & \quad 4{,}000 \\
0.06 \times \ \$50{,}000 = {} & \quad 3{,}000 \\
\text{Total} & \ \$21{,}000
\end{aligned}$$

Taxes. One place where everyone eventually encounters percent is in taxes. Most taxes are based on percent in one way or another.

The simplest kind of tax is the *sales tax.* In most states, people are charged a percent of the purchase price of certain items. At a rate of 5%, you are charged $.05 on each dollar.

Social security taxes are also figured on a straight percentage basis. Such taxes are usually withheld from an employee's pay under the label FICA (which stands for Federal Insurance Contributions Act). The rate of FICA tax changes from time to time, but for any year, it is figured as a straight percentage of salary. For example, if you earn $15,000, and the FICA rate is 8%, $1,200 will be withheld from your pay. (Incidentally, this is only half of the full tax; your employer is required to contribute an equal amount.)

There is a maximum amount of FICA tax any one person must pay in a given year. For example, in a given year the maximum may be $2,000. If the rate is 8%, this means that the tax will be withheld from your pay until your salary reaches $25,000 for the year. Then no more tax will be withheld until the beginning of the next year.

We call this kind of tax *regressive,* because as your income increases, you pay at a lower rate. For example:

Employee A earns $25,000.
He paid $2,000 in FICA tax.
He was taxed at a rate of 8%.
Employee B earns $50,000.
She paid $2,000 in FICA tax.
She was taxed at a rate of 4%.

By contrast, *federal income taxes* are *progressive.* As your income increases, you pay at a higher rate. Consider the following table (the rates are for illustration only—actual tax rates change from year to year):

On income *between and*	*Tax Rate*
0– 4,000	0
4,001– 8,000	8%
8,001–12,000	12%
12,001–16,000	16%
16,001–20,000	20%
20,001–24,000	24%
24,001–28,000	28%

If, after taking the deductions and exemptions allowed by law, Mr. A's taxable income is $14,000, his tax can be figured as follows:

Tax on the first	$ 4000 =	$ 0
Tax on the next	4000 =	320
Tax on the next	4000 =	480
Tax on the next	2000 =	320
Total on $14,000 =		$1,120

For his whole income, the effective rate of tax is 1,120 ÷ 14,000, or 8%.

Mr. B, on the other hand, has taxable income of $28,000. His tax will be:

Tax on the first	$ 4000 =	$ 0
Tax on the next	4000 =	320
Tax on the next	4000 =	480
Tax on the next	4000 =	640
Tax on the next	4000 =	800
Tax on the next	4000 =	960
Tax on the next	4000 =	1,120
Total on $28,000 =		$4,320

His effective rate of tax is 4,320 ÷ 28,000, or 15.4%.

Mr. B's taxable income is twice as large as Mr. A's, but he pays at twice the effective rate and in dollars his tax bill is nearly four times as large. A progressive tax falls most heavily on those with higher incomes.

Most taxpayers need not compute their own taxes from tables like the one above, but income taxes are computed on this principle.

Percents on a Calculator

Many (although not all) calculators have a percent key on them. This is a convenience in keeping track of the decimal point, as the percent key automatically changes the percent to a decimal before multiplying. Thus, you would find 17% of 6978 by entering 6978, pushing the × button, entering 17, and pushing the % button. There is no need to convert 17% to 0.17. (If you have no percent key, you have to convert and multiply in the ordinary way.)

With a calculator, you can definitely save time and make fewer errors by using the second method for any percents of increase or decrease. For example, to find the price of a $78 item after a 15% discount (with the percent key), you would enter 78, push the × button, enter 85, and push the % button.

Formulas

We have already met some formulas in our discussion of percents. A formula is a mathematical sentence that uses one or more letters. You replace the letters with numbers appropriate to the particular situation and find the missing quantity.

Some of the simpler formulas deal with the properties of simple figures (squares, rectangles, etc.) on a plane surface. These formulas are easy to learn because they can be checked by simple measuring, and many are useful throughout a person's life.

Perimeter

Formulas dealing with perimeter are based on addition. The *perimeter* is the distance around a figure. To find the perimeter of a polygon (a closed figure with three or more straight sides), we add the lengths of the sides.

Rectangle. A *rectangle* is a figure with 4 straight sides and 4 right angles. The sides that are opposite each other have the same length, as shown in the diagram. The longer sides are usually labeled l (for length) and the shorter sides w (for width). Thus, one formula for the perimeter, P, of a rectangle is

$$P = l + w + l + w.$$

The numbers represented by the l's can be added, to make $2 \times l$. Similarly, the w's can be combined to make $2 \times w$. So, another formula for the perimeter of a rectangle is

$$P = (2 \times l) + (2 \times w).$$

In writing mathematical formulas the multiplication sign (×) is usually left out. When a number is written directly beside a letter, with no operation sign between them, the operation is multiplication. The expression $2l$ means $2 \times l$; similarly, $2w$ means $2 \times w$. So, another way to write the formula for the perimeter of a rectangle is

$$P = 2l + 2w.$$

Square. The *square* is a special kind of rectangle in which all the sides are equal in length. The length of any one side is usually designated as s. The formula for the perimeter of a square is

$$P = s + s + s + s \quad \text{or} \quad P = 4s.$$

Other polygons. In general, the lengths of the sides of any polygon can be called a, b, c, and so forth. Thus, the formula for the perimeter of any polygon is just $P =$ the sum of the lengths of as many sides as the polygon has. For a triangle

$$P = a + b + c.$$

For a general polygon with seven sides the formula would be

$$P = a + b + c + d + e + f + g.$$

If some of the sides are known to be equal, they can be combined as in the formulas for the perimeter of a rectangle.

Circle. A special perimeter problem is finding the *circumference* (or distance around) a circle. A *circle* is a plane figure whose boundary is equally distant from a single point called the center. The distance from the center to the circle is called the *radius* of the circle. A line that extends from one point on the circle to another point and passes through the center is called the *diameter* of the circle. The diameter is always exactly twice the length of the radius. This is expressed in the formula

$$d = 2r.$$

All circles with the same diameter have the same circumference. Early mathematicians carefully measured hundreds of circles and found that the circumference of a circle was always 3.1416 . . . times the diameter. (The number cannot be exactly expressed as a decimal.) This number is a *constant:* it never changes for any circle. Instead of writing out 3.1416 . . . each time they used it, early

PERIMETER

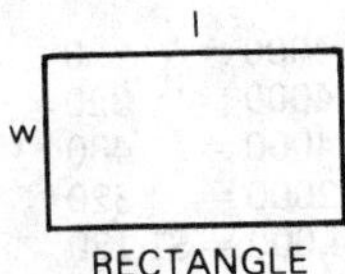

RECTANGLE
P = 2l + 2w

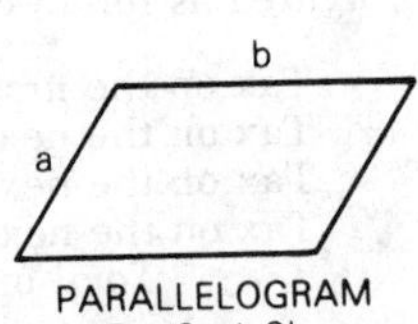

PARALLELOGRAM
P = 2a + 2b

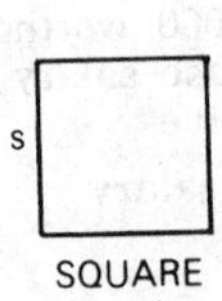

SQUARE
P = 4s

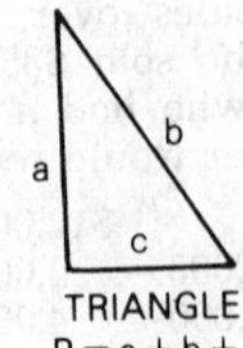

TRIANGLE
P = a + b + c

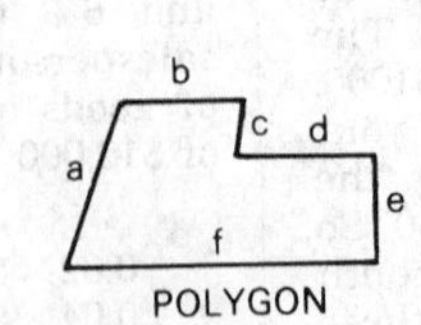

POLYGON
P = a + b + c + d + e + f

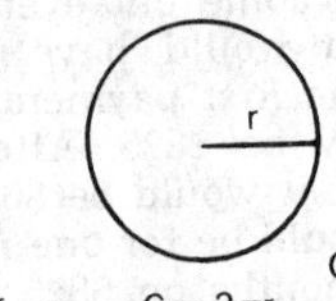

C = 2πr

CIRCLE

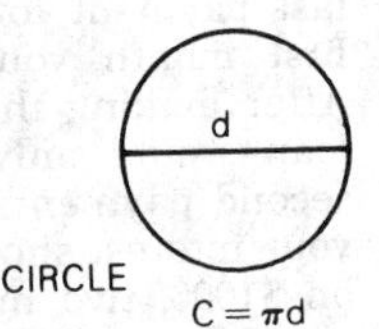

C = πd

mathematicians gave this number a special symbol, the Greek letter *pi*, which looks like this:

$$\pi.$$

Using this symbol, we can write a formula for the circumference of a circle:

$$C=\pi d$$

Since $d = 2r$, another formula is

$$C=\pi 2r$$

or (since the order of multiplication makes no difference to the answer)

$$C=2\pi r.$$

LAND MEASUREMENT *still uses geometrical principles. This farmer of the early 1900s is using surveying equipment to make his calculations of acreage more accurate.*

Area

The *area* of a plane figure is the number of units of area that the figure contains. The standard form for a unit of area is a square 1 unit on a side: a square inch, a square centimeter, a square mile, etc. In starting out, it is best to take a figure that has a whole number of square regions.

Rectangle. A rectangle is a four-sided figure. Its sides meet at a right (or square) angle, and as we have learned, its opposite sides are of equal length. The rectangle above has 12 equal square regions. You can note that the length is 4 units and the width is 3 units. Since $4 \times 3 = 12$, the area of this rectangle is the product of the length and width. Experimenting with other rectangles will show that this is always the case when the rectangle can be divided into unit squares. Mathematicians have shown that it is also the case when there are bits and pieces left over. If we call the area *A*, the length *l*, and the width *w*, the formula for the area of any rectangle is

$$A=lw$$

where *lw* means the same as $l \times w$.

Square. A square is a special case of rectangle. Since all four sides of a square are the same length, the area is $s \times s$. Instead of writing *ss* or $s \times s$, people write s^2. The small 2 is an *exponent*. It is read "squared." The number 3^2 is "three squared" and it means 3×3, or 9. So the formula for the area of a square is written

$$A=s^2.$$

Parallelogram. A *parallelogram* is like a rectangle. It has four sides, and the opposite sides are parallel and equal in length. (Sides are *parallel* if the distance between them is the same at any point.) However, a parallelogram need not have 4 right angles (when it does, it becomes a rectangle).

The area of a parallelogram cannot be found by multiplying the lengths of two sides. But a parallelogram can be "made into" a rectangle. If you draw a line from D to E so that the line is at right angles to line AB, you have created a triangle with corners at A, D, and E.

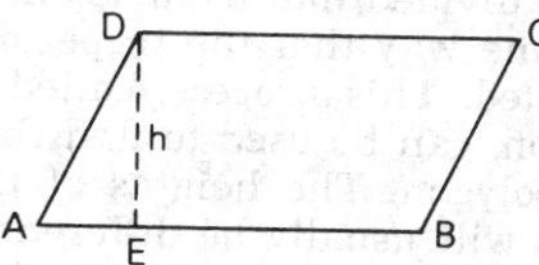

If you "tear off" the triangle and move it to the other side of the figure, you form a rectangle. The area of the rectangle will be the same as the area of the original parallelogram.

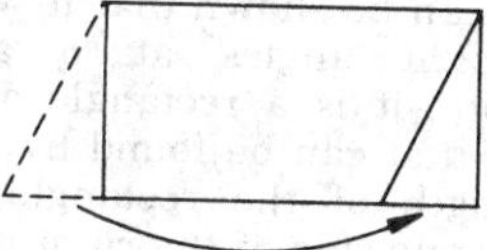

The formula for finding the area of the rectangle is

$$A=lw.$$

l is equal to the length of the bottom side of the parallelogram. *w* is equal to the new line DE that we drew above.

We call the length of the bottom side *b* (for base) and the length of the new line DE *h* (for height). The measurement of *h* must be at right angles to the base *b*. So the formula for finding the area of a parallelogram is

$$A=bh.$$

Triangle. Just as the area of a parallelogram can be worked out by comparing the parallelogram with a rectangle, the area of a triangle can be found by comparing the triangle with a parallelogram. The procedure is easier to picture with triangle one of whose angles is square (a right triangle). Then you can deal with any triangle.

AREA

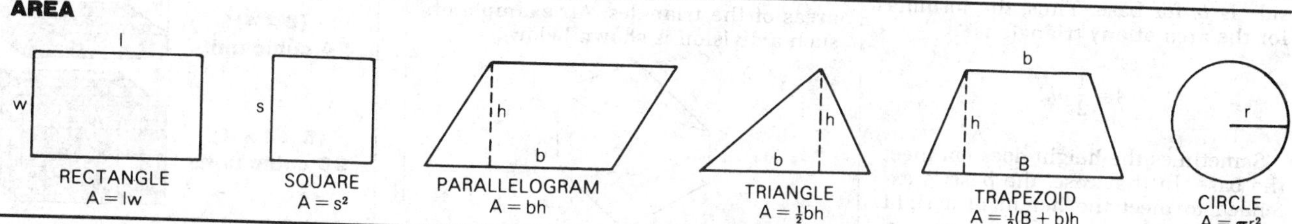

Consider the right triangle *ABC* (which means the triangle with corners, called *vertex points,* named *A, B,* and *C*). It has a right angle at point *A.*

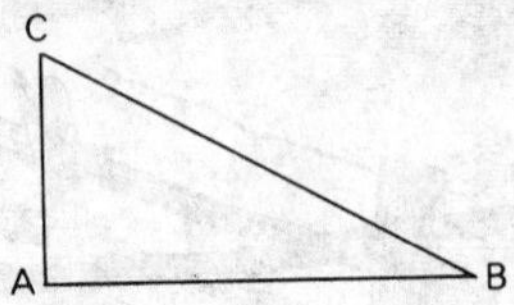

If you make a copy of the triangle that has the same size and shape and call it triangle *abc,* you can place it so that point *b* is matched with point *C,* point *c* is matched with point *B,* and point *a* is opposite point *A.*

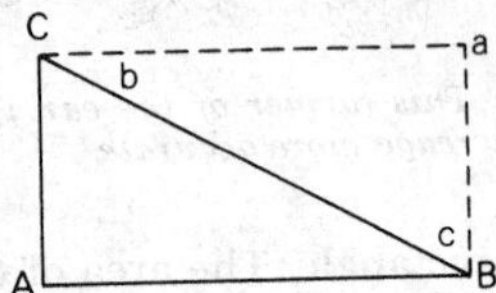

You know that the resulting figure has right angles at *A* and at the copy of *A.* It can be shown that it will also have right angles at *B* and *C.* Therefore, it is a rectangle and has an area that can be found by $A = lw$. The length of the rectangle is the same as one side of the right triangle, and the width is the same as another side of the right triangle. If we call one side *b* (for base) and the other *h* (for height), the area of the rectangle is *bh.* Since this is also the area of two identical triangles, the area of one triangle is one-half the area of the rectangle, or $\frac{1}{2}bh$. The same procedure could be followed for any right triangle, so the formula for the area of a right triangle is

$$A = \frac{1}{2}\,bh.$$

If you use the same technique with a triangle that is not a right triangle, you get a parallelogram instead of a rectangle.

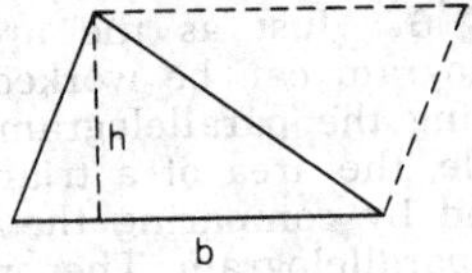

In this case the height, *h,* is not one of the sides of the triangle. It is the length of a line from one vertex of the triangle that is at right angles to another side. The length of the other side is *b,* for base. Thus, the formula for the area of any triangle is

$$A = \frac{1}{2}\,bh.$$

Sometimes the height does not meet the base. In that case, the base is extended to meet the height at a right angle.

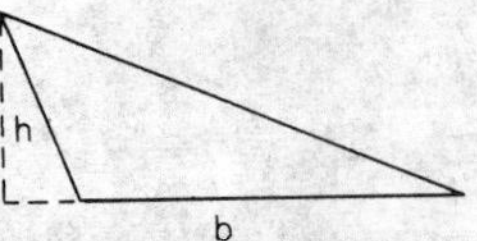

Only the part of the base line that is part of the triangle is counted as the base in the formula. The extension is used merely to determine the length of the height line.

Trapezoid. Another polygon is the trapezoid. A *trapezoid* is a four-sided figure that has two parallel sides. To determine the area of a trapezoid, you draw a line that divides it into two triangles.

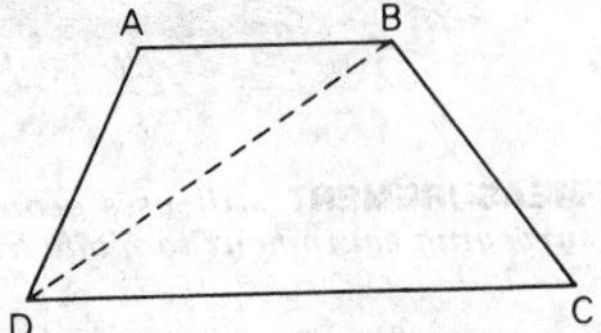

The trapezoid can be called *ABCD.* It is separated into triangle *ABD* and triangle *BCD.* Since sides *AB* and *DC* are parallel (which is what makes *ABCD* a trapezoid), the height dropped from *B* to side *DC* is the same as the height from *D* to the extension of *AB.*

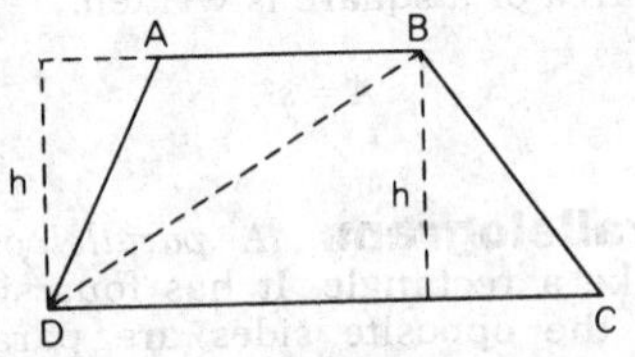

Call the base *AB* by the letter *b* and the base *DC* by the letter *B.* Then the area of triangle $ABD = \frac{1}{2}bh$ and the area of triangle $BDC = \frac{1}{2}Bh$. The area of the trapezoid is the sum of the areas of the triangles, or $A = \frac{1}{2}Bh + \frac{1}{2}bh$. The two products can be combined by algebraic techniques to give the familiar form for the area of a trapezoid.

$$A = \frac{1}{2}\,(B + b)h$$

Other polygons. Any polygon can be divided into triangles in much the same way that the trapezoid was separated. This process, called triangulation, can be used to find the area of a polygon. The heights of the triangles will usually be different, however, so there is no single formula that can be used. If you need to determine the area of an irregular polygonal region, however, it is handy to separate it into triangles and sum the areas of the triangles. An example of such a division is shown below.

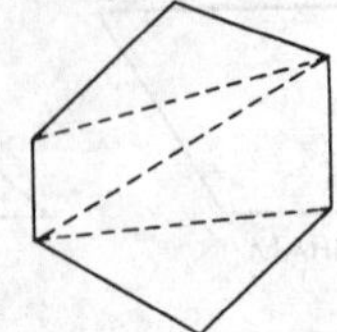

Circle. A circle can be divided into a number of pie-shaped pieces that are almost triangles.

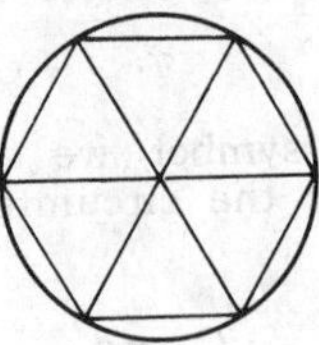

As the number of pie-shaped pieces gets larger, the sum of the areas of the triangles gets closer to the area of the circle. By this kind of analysis and by other mathematical techniques, the area of a circle has been determined to be

$$A = \pi r^2$$

where π is 3.1416. . . .

Volume

Finding the volume of a solid object is like finding the area of a plane figure. First a figure is studied that can be filled with standard units of volume, which are cubes 1 unit on a side—cubic inches, cubic centimeters, etc. Then that figure is used to derive the volumes of the other figures.

Rectangular prism. The best place to start is with the rectangular prism (also known as the rectangular parallelopiped). A *rectangular prism* is a box; it has six sides, each of which is parallel to its opposite side. The angles at the corners are all right angles, so the sides, called *faces,* are all rectangles. Opposite sides have the same dimensions.

If you fill the bottom layer of such a box with unit cubes (and the box has whole-number dimensions), the number of unit cubes will be the same as the area of the bottom of the box. You can fit in as many layers as the height of the box.

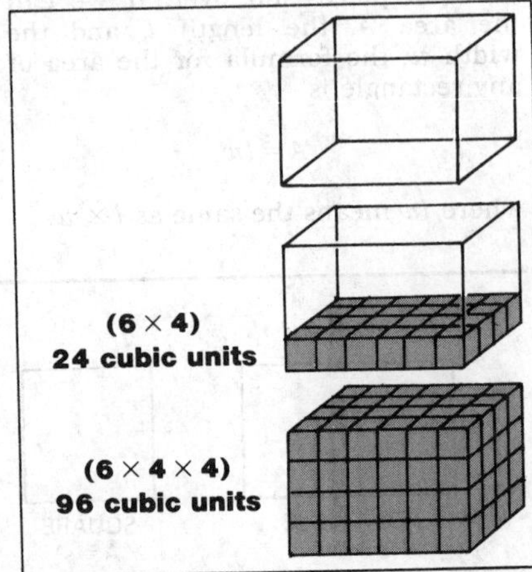

If the dimensions of the bottom of the box are l and w and the height of the box is h, then the volume, V, of the rectangular prism is

$$V = lwh.$$

Sometimes the area of the bottom of the box is figured as B (for base). Since $B = lw$, the volume of a rectangular prism can also be given by the formula

$$V = Bh.$$

Cube. Just as a square is a special kind of rectangle, a cube is a special kind of rectangular prism. A *cube* is a rectangular prism in which all of the faces have the same dimensions, and every *edge* has the same length. Any edge, e, is used in the formula instead of l, w, or h. Then the volume of a cube is

$$V = e \times e \times e$$

which is usually written as

$$V = e^3$$

The small raised 3 is an exponent. It is read "cubed," and means that the number it is written by is to be multiplied by itself twice. For example, $5^3 = 5 \times 5 \times 5 = 125$.

Other prisms. The same ideas that were used to determine the volume of a rectangular prism can be used to find the volume of other figures that are similar. A *prism* is a solid figure that has two opposite sides that are polygons of the same size and shape. The faces joining the corresponding sides of the polygons are rectangles or parallelograms. First consider the case where the faces joining the two polygons, which are called *bases* of the prism, are triangles.

Once again, begin by finding the area of a base (B). In the case of the triangular prism, you know that this area will be $\frac{1}{2}bh$, where b equals one side of the triangle and h equals its height at right angles. One layer of cubic units will have the same number as the area of the base (B). There will be as many layers as the height of the prism. So, if B represents the area of the base and h the height of

MOBIL OIL CO.

CYLINDRICAL STORAGE TANKS *are an example of the many geometrical solids visible in everyday life.*

the prism (which is the length of an edge that connects corresponding points of the two bases), the volume is

$$V = Bh.$$

This formula should look familiar to you, since it is one version of the formula for the volume of a rectangular prism. In fact, the same formula can be used for any prism. If the bases are parallelograms or trapezoids, the same general formula can be used. Only the formula for finding the area of the base will differ.

If the faces connecting the bases of a prism are parallelograms instead of rectangles, the prism appears to be tilted.

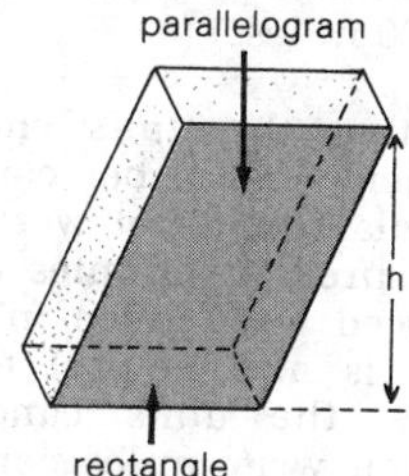

The bases are parallel, however, so the distance between the bases is the same everywhere. In this case the distance between the bases is *not* the length of an edge. Instead, it is the distance between the bases measured at right angles. The formula stays the same:

$$V = Bh$$

Cylinder. A *cylinder* is like a prism except that the bases are circles that have the same radius and there is a curved surface instead of faces.

You can still picture stacking layers of cubic units (and bits and pieces) to fill the cylinder, so the formula for the volume of a cylinder is also

$$V = Bh$$

where B is the area of the circular base and h is the distance between bases.

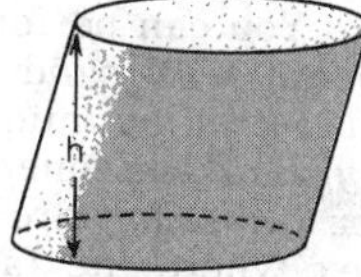

This formula also applies if the cylinder does not have the bases directly opposite one another. h must be measured at right angles.

The remaining solid figures are more difficult to understand without higher mathematics, although the formulas are in the realm of arithmetic. In particular, it is generally considered useful to teach the volume of the cone, pyramid, and sphere.

Cone. The *cone* has a circular base and a curved surface which rises to a point.

If you have a cone and a cylinder

VOLUME

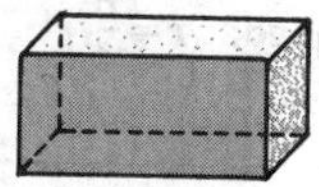

RECTANGULAR PRISM
$V = lwh$
$V = Bh$

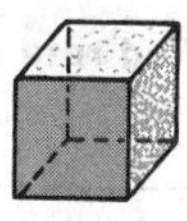

CUBE
$V = e^3$

PRISM
$V = Bh$

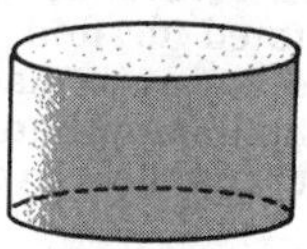
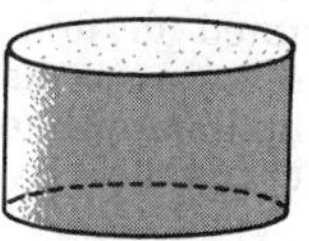

CYLINDER
$V = Bh$

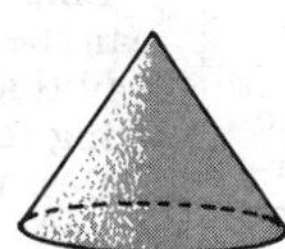

CONE
$V = \frac{1}{3}Bh$

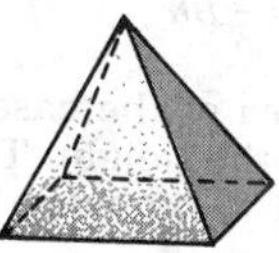

PYRAMID
$V = \frac{1}{3}Bh$

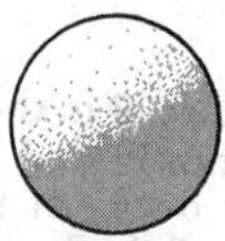

SPHERE
$V = \frac{4}{3}\pi r^3$

that have the same base and the same height, and if they are open at the base, you can experiment with their comparative volumes. (A conical paper cup and a matching can are ideal for this experiment.) Fill the cone with sand or water. Use the cone to fill the matching cylinder. If you are careful, it should take exactly 3 cone-fuls of sand or water to fill the cylinder.

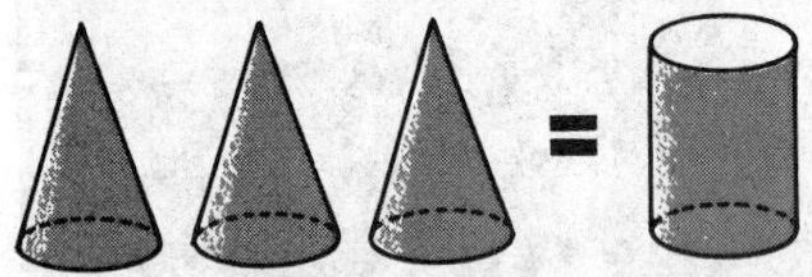

Therefore, the formula for the volume of a cone is

$$V=\frac{1}{3}Bh$$

where B is the area of the base and h is the height. This formula even works if the sharp point of the cone (called the *vertex*) is not directly over the center of the circle, as long as the measurement of h is at right angles to the base.

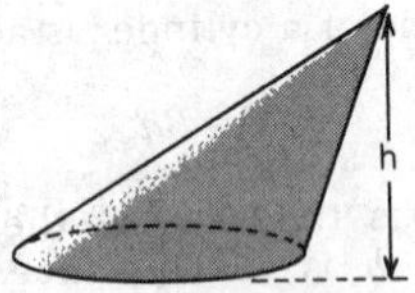

Pyramid. You can perform a similar experiment with sand or water, this time using a pyramid to fill a prism. A *pyramid* has one base that is a polygon, faces that are triangles, and a vertex where the faces meet. Here is a square pyramid—one whose base is a square.

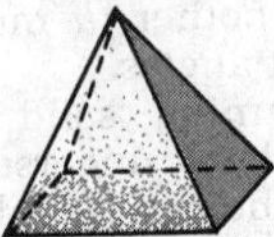

Pyramids can have any polygon as a base, however. There are triangular pyramids, rectangular pyramids, and so forth.

If a pyramid and a prism have the same height and have a base that is the same size and shape, it will take 3 pyramids of sand or water to fill the prism. So the formula for the volume of a pyramid is

$$V=\frac{1}{3}Bh$$

where B is the area of the base of the pyramid and h is the height. The vertex does not need to be over the center of the base.

Sphere. A *sphere* is a solid figure that corresponds to a circle. Any point on its surface is equally distant from a point called the center. In other words, a sphere is a ball. There is no easy way to establish the formula for the volume of a sphere, but it is

$$V=\frac{4}{3}\pi r^3$$

where r is the radius (the distance from the center of the sphere to a point on its surface) and π is 3.1428 . . . (the ratio of a circle's circumference to its diameter).

Distance-Rate-Time

There are hundreds of thousands of formulas used in mathematics and the sciences, but only a very few used in arithmetic. Besides the formulas for perimeter, area, and volume, one that often occurs is the formula for distance-rate-time.

To understand the distance-rate-time formula, it is helpful to consider a practical problem. The K family is driving across the country. Their car can average 50 miles per hour. How far can they travel in 8 hours of driving? The formula is

$$d=rt$$

where d is the distance to be traveled, r is the rate of speed, and t is the time traveled.

In the example,

$$d=50 \text{ miles per hour} \times 8 \text{ hours}$$
$$d=400 \text{ miles.}$$

Notice that the units chosen for measurement must be compatible. The formula would not work if time were measured in minutes or if the rate of speed were given in feet per second. It is also helpful to understand how the units cancel each other. If you write miles per hour as

$$50\,\frac{\text{miles}}{\text{hour}}$$

the hours in the example cancel each other, leaving distance in miles:

$$d=50\,\frac{\text{miles}}{\cancel{\text{hour}}}\times 8\,\cancel{\text{hours}}$$
$$d=400 \text{ miles.}$$

Like other formulas, this formula can be restated to find other units. Say that the K family had been traveling for 6 hours and had covered 240 miles. What was their average rate of speed?

Beginning with the original formula (turned around for convenience):

$$rt=d$$

If you divide both sides of the equal sign by t, you restate the formula:

$$\frac{r\cancel{t}}{\cancel{t}}=\frac{d}{t} \qquad r=\frac{d}{t} \text{ or } d\div t$$

In words, "rate equals distance divided by time." Substituting the values from the example,

$$r=\frac{240 \text{ miles}}{6 \text{ hours}} \qquad r=40\,\frac{\text{miles}}{\text{hour}}$$

The K family was averaging 40 miles per hour.

Similarly, the K family could use the formula to find out how long it would take to travel 600 miles at 50 miles per hour. This time, we restate the formula as follows:

$$rt=d \qquad \frac{\cancel{r}t}{\cancel{r}}=\frac{d}{r} \qquad t=\frac{d}{r} \text{ or } d\div t$$

Substituting the values, we get

$$t=\frac{600 \text{ miles}}{50\,\frac{\text{miles}}{\text{hour}}}$$

$$t=12 \text{ hours.}$$

To see how miles cancel out in the problem, use the rule for dividing fractions, inverting the $\frac{\text{miles}}{\text{hour}}$ fraction and multiplying:

$$t=600 \text{ miles}\div 50\,\frac{\text{miles}}{\text{hour}}$$

$$t=600\,\cancel{\text{miles}}\times\frac{1 \text{ hour}}{50\,\cancel{\text{miles}}}$$

$$t=12 \text{ hours}$$

The restating of the formula relies on simple rules of algebra. If you don't understand how the restatements work, however, you can memorize the three variations of the formula and use them to find distance, rate, or time. They are summarized in the box on this page.

DISTANCE, RATE, AND TIME

Where d = distance
r = rate of speed
t = time

To find distance:	$d=rt$
To find rate of speed:	$r=\frac{d}{t}$
or	$r=d\div t$
To find time:	$t=\frac{d}{r}$
or	$t=d\div r$

Measurement

Mathematics has two roots in history. The first is counting. The second is measuring. While counting led to the whole numbers, which were later extended to other number systems, measurement led to fractions and geometry. The interaction of counting and measurement over the centuries has created mathematics.

Length

Early people had ways of measuring length. Even today, primitive people all over the world have a concept of length. The distance from one campground to another might be expressed as "three days' walk." We use similar measurements when we say that a nearby town is "twenty minutes away" by car.

Parts of the body were used for measuring shorter lengths. The length of a stride, called a *pace,* was one way to measure. Others were the width of a palm, called a *hand,* or the length of a joint in the thumb, called an *inch.* A *cubit* was variously defined, based on the length of an arm. A *fathom* was the distance between two outstretched arms. Other handy items for measuring shorter distances were seeds of grain, such as barley seeds.

All these measures were useful, but they suffered from the same flaw. People (and seeds) come in different sizes. My inch might be longer than your inch. So the governments began to set *standard measures.* The king's body would be used as a standard, for example. The length of the king's arm was a cubit, the length of the king's foot was a standard foot. Other standard measures involved relationships: an inch was the same length as seven barley seeds.

While this brought some improvement, it did not solve all of the problems. Kings changed from time to time. Although very similar, not all barley seeds are alike. Nations and towns began to measure length by standard measures marked on metal bars. Although this helped solve the problem in those places, trade between one place and another was often confusing. (Even today, Canada and the United States do not use the same measure for a gallon.)

Customary units. It was out of this long history that the customary units used in the United States developed. They are based on units that the early colonists brought from England, but they have been standardized by the Federal Government.

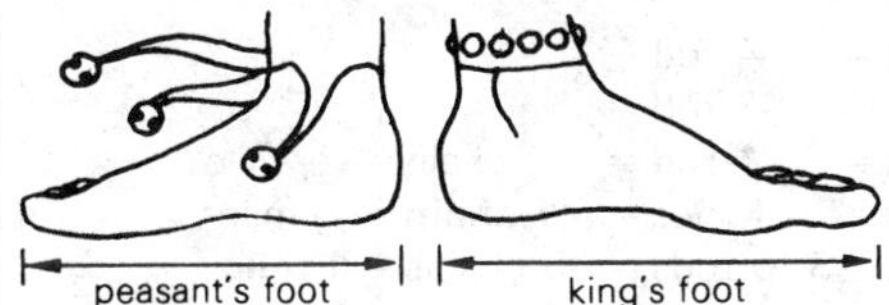

BIG FOOT OR LITTLE? *If measure were based on our own feet, each person would be measuring by a different standard.*

To begin learning how to measure length, it helps to use nonstandard units. The paper clip is often used.

This line is less than 2 paper clips long.

One may also measure the length of a room in paces or the length of a desk in book-lengths.

In the customary system, the first unit studied is the standard *inch.* Here is the same line that you measured in paper clips, now measured in inches.

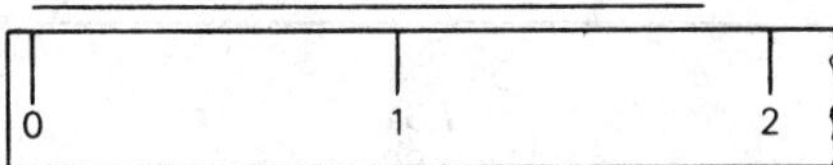

It is about 2 inches (sometimes written 2″) long.

Notice that there is not exactly a whole number of inches. This is true in nearly all measurement situations. Therefore, with an inch ruler (a stick marked into inches only, with no fractions of inches marked), you can measure only *to the nearest inch.* To get a more precise measurement, you must introduce fractions of inches. In a learning situation, these are introduced one at a time. The largest units are introduced first. Here is the same line measured to the nearest half inch.

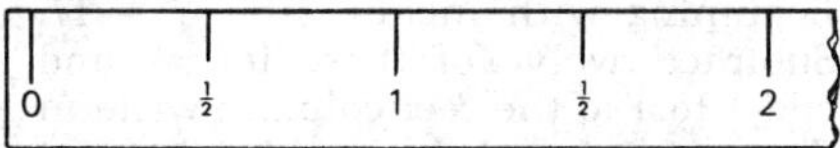

The line still measures closer to 2 inches than to $1\frac{1}{2}$ inches. Now let us measure the line to the nearest quarter inch.

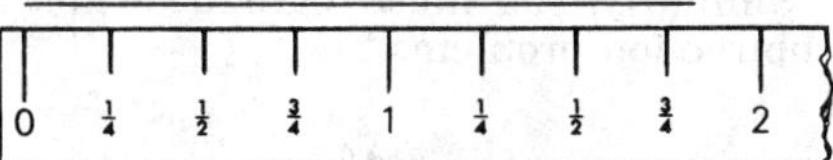

The line is $1\frac{3}{4}$ inches long to the nearest quarter inch.

You can see the connection between measurement and the concept of fractions.

The inch and fractions of an inch are useful in measuring short lengths (although not good for *very* small lengths, such as the length of a bacterium). Other units are more useful for larger lengths. You would not want to think that your car got 1,267,200 inches to a gallon of gasoline, for example.

The next larger customary unit that is used is the foot. A *foot* is defined as having the same length as 12 inches. Feet are used (along with inches) by carpenters in building houses and in many other common measurements, including the height of a person.

For many other measurements it is more common to use a yard. A *yard* is defined as having the same length as 3 feet. Cloth is measured in yards, and a football field is marked off in lengths of 5 yards.

The next larger measure that is in common use is the mile. A *mile* is the same length as 5,280 feet or 1,760 yards. Distances from point to point on the earth's surface, especially if they are longer than 1,000 yards, are usually measured in miles.

Very large and small. Most people have little occasion to use measures longer than the mile. Astronomers, however, must measure distances so great that they need a set of measures all their own. Astronomical measures are neither U.S. customary nor international metric, but can be interpreted in either system. Here are the customary-measure interpretations.

An *Astronomical Unit* (A.U.) is the average distance from the sun to the earth. It is about 93,000,000 miles. This measure is too short to be very useful outside the solar system. Larger distances are measured in light-years, the distance that light travels in one year. A *light-year* is 5,880,000,000,000 miles (to the nearest ten billion miles). Even the light-year is not the longest measure used. Because of the way that astronomers measure distances between stars, they find it convenient to use a measure called the *parsec,* which is the same length as 19,160,000,000,000 miles.

Other scientists need very small measures to describe the size of atoms or the width of light waves. One *Angstrom unit* (A or A.U.) is equal to $\frac{4}{1,000,000,000}$ of an inch, for example. Ten A.U.'s is equal to one *nanometer* (nm) in the metric system.

One way of dealing with very large

LENGTH (DISTANCE)

CUSTOMARY UNITS

1 inch =	$\frac{1}{12}$ foot =	$\frac{1}{36}$ yard			
12 inches =	**1 foot** =	$\frac{1}{3}$ yard =	$\frac{2}{33}$ rod		
36 inches =	3 feet =	**1 yard** =	$\frac{2}{11}$ rod		
	$16\frac{1}{2}$ feet =	$5\frac{1}{2}$ yards =	**1 rod** =	$\frac{1}{4}$ chain =	$\frac{1}{320}$ mile
	66 feet =	22 yards =	4 rods =	**1 chain** =	$\frac{1}{80}$ mile
	5,280 feet =	1,760 yards =	320 rods =	80 chains =	**1 mile**

METRIC-CUSTOMARY EQUIVALENTS

Metric to Customary

1 centimeter (cm) =	0.3937 inch			
1 decimeter (10 cm) =	3.937 inches =	0.328 foot		
1 meter (m) =	39.37 inches =	3.28 feet =	1.09 yards	
1 dekameter (10 m) =	393.7 inches =	32.8 feet =	10.9 yards	
1 hectometer (100 m) =		328 feet =	109.4 yards	
1 kilometer (km) =		3,281 feet =	1094 yards =	.62 miles
10 kilometers =			10,940 yards =	6.21 miles

Customary to Metric

1 inch =	2.54 cm	
1 foot =	30.48 cm	
1 yard =	91.44 cm =	0.914 m
1 rod =		5.03 m
1 chain =		20.12 m
1 mile =	1609 m =	1.61 km
10 miles =		16.1 km

inches 1 2
cm 1 2 3 4 5

feet/yards 1 2
meters 1 2

miles 1 2
km 1 2 3

and very small measurements is to use scientific notation (*see* Exponents below).

Conversions. As you can see, relationships between the units in the U.S. customary system follow no particular pattern. It is therefore useful to learn these relationships by heart. The table above can be used for that purpose. Some of the measures of length are not often used and may be unfamiliar.

In using this table of equivalents to convert measurements from one unit to another, find the unit your measurement is in now in bold type. Then look to the right or left of it to find the desired unit and multiply by the figure found there.

For example, if you know that a field is 25 yards long, and you want to find the length in rods, you would locate *yards* in the box. To the right, you find "$\frac{2}{11}$ rods." Multiply 25 by $\frac{2}{11}$.

$$\frac{2}{11} \times 25 = \frac{50}{11} = 4\frac{6}{11}$$

The field is $4\frac{6}{11}$ rods long.

Similarly, if you know that a fence is 7.54 chains long, and you want to know how many feet that is, you find *chain* in the box. To the left, you find "66 feet." Multiply 7.54 by 66.

$$\begin{array}{r} 7.54 \\ \times 66 \\ \hline 497.64 \end{array}$$

The fence is 497.64 feet long (about 497 feet, 8 inches).

Other problems with customary measure involve performing basic arithmetic procedures on mixed quantities. For example, in the following addition and subtraction problems, you must learn new ways to regroup.

$$\begin{array}{rrr} \overset{1}{5} \text{ yards} & \overset{1}{2} \text{ feet} & 10 \text{ inches} \\ +2 \text{ yards} & 2 \text{ feet} & 7 \text{ inches} \\ \hline 8 \text{ yards} & 2 \text{ feet} & 5 \text{ inches} \end{array}$$

Beginning with inches, 10 + 7 = 17. Subtract twelve of these inches and add 1 foot to the feet column; write in the remaining 5 inches. In the feet column, 2 + 2 + 1 = 5. Subtract 3 feet and add 1 yard to the yards column; enter the remaining 2 feet. Add the yards.

Similarly, you must regroup in this subtraction problem.

$$\begin{array}{rr} \overset{4}{\cancel{5}} \text{ miles} & \overset{2640}{\cancel{880}} \text{ yards} \\ -3 \text{ miles} & 1320 \text{ yards} \\ \hline 1 \text{ mile} & 1320 \text{ yards} \end{array}$$

Since you can't subtract 1320 from 880, you must regroup one mile, making it 1760 yards. Adding 1760 to 880 gives 2640. Then you can subtract the yards and the miles.

It is easier, whenever possible, to convert to decimals. For example, if you know that 880 yards is exactly half a mile and that 1320 yards is $\frac{3}{4}$ mile, you could rewrite the problem above as

$$\begin{array}{r} 5.50 \text{ miles} \\ -3.75 \text{ miles} \\ \hline 1.75 \text{ miles} \end{array}$$

Fortunately, there are fewer occasions to multiply or divide mixed units. If you should need to do so, there are two ways to simplify:

1. Before multiplying or dividing, convert the mixed units to a small unit. For example, 2 yards 2 feet 7 inches is equal to 72 + 24 + 7 inches, or 103 inches.
2. Before multiplying or dividing, convert quantities to mixed whole numbers and decimals, if convenient.

Metric units. In the customary system, conversions from one unit to another and basic arithmetic procedures are often difficult. In the international metric system, things are much simpler.

The original metric system was conceived at the end of the eighteenth century in France. Some supporters of the French Revolution insisted that a new "rational" system of measurement be adopted.

The basic measure of length, the meter, was originally defined as one ten-millionth of the distance along an imaginary line from the North Pole to the equator, passing through Paris. Other units of length were then defined on the basis of the meter.

France adopted the metric system in 1837 and other countries gradually followed suit. Today, the United States is the only major country in the world that does not use the metric system as its major system of measurement.

The precise standards for metric measure have been refined since 1837. A unit based on the size of the earth turned out to be too imprecise.

NORTH POLE TO EQUATOR: *the meter was originally defined as one ten-millionth of this distance on a line through Paris.*

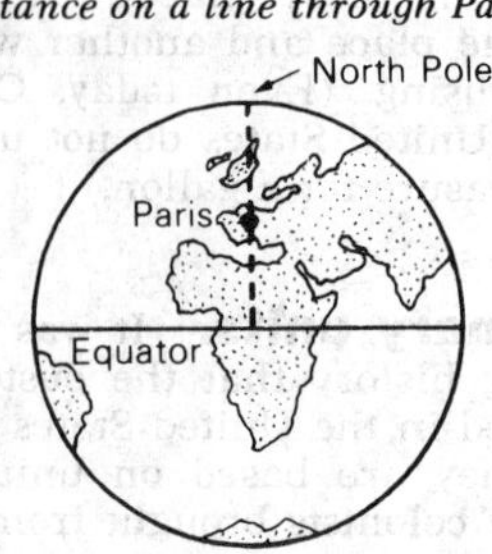

CULVER PICTURES

LONG DISTANCE: *stars are often hundreds or thousands of light years away. A single light year is about 6.9 trillion miles.*

For a while, the distance between two very carefully drawn marks on a metal bar in France was used as the standard meter, but this was not sufficiently precise for scientific purposes either. In 1960 the meter was defined in terms of a certain wavelength of light produced by the element krypton.

The metric system has changed very little, however. It is based on 10, just like the decimal system. Each unit is 10 times or 1000 times larger than the next smaller unit, and the relation between units is designated by standard prefixes. Since metric measure is the system used by science (even in the U.S.), the system has been extended from the very small to the very large. Currently, the smallest prefix used is *atto-*. An attometer is 0.000 000 000 000 000 001 of a meter. (In the metric system, spaces rather than commas are used to make numerals easier to read.) The largest prefix used is *tera-*. A terameter is 1 000 000 000 000 times as long as a meter. Here is a list of all the standard prefixes with their numerical meaning.

atto-	0.000 000 000 000 000 001
femto-	0.000 000 000 000 001
pico-	0.000 000 000 001
nano-	0.000 000 001
micro-	0.000 001
milli-	0.001
centi-	0.01
deci-	0.1
deka-	10
hecto-	100
kilo-	1 000
mega-	1 000 000
giga-	1 000 000 000
tera-	1 000 000 000 000

For nonscientific work, only three metric length units are in common use. These are the centimeter (cm), meter (m), and kilometer (km). They correspond roughly to the inch, yard, and mile in the U.S. customary system. The basic unit, the meter, on which all other units of length are based, is a little more than 3 inches longer than a yard. A centimeter is .01 meter and is a little less than .4 inch. The kilometer, equal to 1,000 meters, is about 1,100 yards or .62 mile.

Children learn the metric system very quickly and need not be concerned with the equivalents between the metric and customary systems. It is no more difficult to measure a book or a desk in centimeters than in inches, and the length of a soccer field (100 meters) differs little from the length of an American football field (100 yards). For convenience, however, a table of length equivalents is given on the preceding page.

Area and Volume

Units of area and volume are based on the units of length. For example, a square inch is the area of the region shown below.

1 sq. in.

The relationship between square units is different from the relationship between measures of length. Each relating number is squared. For example, since there are 3 feet in a yard, there are 3 × 3, or 9, square feet in a square yard. Similarly, there are 12 × 12, or 144, square inches in a square foot.

In the metric system, the same concepts are used. Here is a region with an area of 1 square centimeter. The exponent ^{2} is often used as an abbreviation for *square* in the metric system: cm^2 is read "square centimeters."

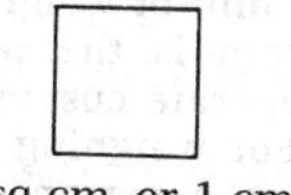
1 sq cm, or 1 cm^2

Since there are 100 centimeters in a meter, there are 100 × 100, or 10 000, square centimeters in a square meter.

In both the customary and metric systems there are special units that are used for measuring large areas, such as the area of a farm or a nation. The customary measure is the *acre*, which is 4,840 square yards, or 43,560 square feet. The corresponding metric measure is the *hectare* (100 ares), which is 10 000 square meters. The relationship between the customary and metric measures is

1 acre = 0.4 hectare
1 hectare = 2.47 acres

Volume is measured in much the same way as area. A cube 1 unit on a side contains 1 unit of volume. The relationships are also cubed. There are 3 × 3 × 3, or 27, *cubic feet* in a *cubic yard;* 12 × 12 × 12, or 1728, *cubic inches* in a cubic foot; and 100 × 100 × 100, or 1 000 000, *cubic centimeters* in a *cubic meter.* In the metric system the exponent ^{3} is often used as the abbreviation for *cubic;* for example, cubic meter can be abbreviated as cu m, or as m^3, which is read "cubic meters."

Oddly, there is an entirely separate system for measuring volume in both the customary and metric systems. This system is the capacity system. *Capacity* is the same as volume, but the term is usually applied to liquids, whereas *volume* is usually applied to solids. Both capacity and volume are used to measure empty spaces (such as the space inside a box). Finally, to make matters even more complicated, the customary system uses a different set of measures for capacity of "dry" items (usually small items in bulk, such as apples or wheat) than it does for "wet" items and very small "dry" items, such as a collection of grains of flour or crystals of sugar.

The basic "wet" measures of capacity in the customary system are the *ounce* (properly, *fluid ounce* or fluid-ounce), *cup, pint, quart,* and *gallon.* A fluid ounce is the same as 1.8 cubic inches. The table on the next page shows relationships between these units.

In the "dry" system, there are also pints and quarts, but they are not the same volume as in the "wet" system. For example, a liquid pint is the same as 28.875 cubic inches, but a dry pint is the same as 33.6 cubic inches. The relationships between dry measures are similar to those between liquid measures, but the size of the units is different. The two systems are shown in the table on the next page.

While capacity in the metric system does not separate into "wet" and "dry" branches, it is treated as a separate system from volume. The basic unit of capacity is the liter, which is the same as 1 cubic decimeter or

VOLUME

CUSTOMARY UNITS

1 cubic inch (cu. in.)		
1,728 cu. in.	= **1 cubic foot (cu. ft.)**	
46,656 cu. in.	= 27 cu. ft.	= **1 cubic yard**

METRIC UNITS

1 cubic millimeter (mm³)		
1,000 mm³	= **1 cubic centimeter (cm³)**	
	1,000,000 cm³	= **1 cubic meter (m³)**

Conversions

1 cu. in. = 16.387 cm³	1 mm³ = 0.000061 cu. in.
1 cu. ft. = 28,316 cm³	1 cm³ = 0.061 cu. in.
= 0.028 m³	1 m³ = 61,024 cu. in.
1 cu. yd. = 0.765 m³	= 35.53 cu. ft.
	= 1.31 cu. yd.

CAPACITY

CUSTOMARY UNITS, LIQUID (1 fluid ounce capacity = 0.902 cu. in. volume)

fluid ounce (fl. oz.) = $\frac{1}{8}$ cup				
8 fl. oz. =	**cup**	= $\frac{1}{2}$ pt.		
16 fl. oz. =	2 cups =	**pint (pt.)** = $\frac{1}{2}$ qt.		
32 fl. oz. =	4 cups =	2 pt.	= **quart (qt.)** = $\frac{1}{4}$ gal.	
128 fl. oz. =	16 cups =	8 pt.	= 4 qt.	= **gallon (gal.)**

METRIC UNITS (1 centiliter capacity = 1 cc³ volume)

1 milliliter (ml)			
10 ml	= **1 centiliter (cl)**		
1,000 ml	=	100 cl = **1 liter (l)**	
	100,000 cl =	1,000 l = **1 kiloliter (kl)**	

Conversions

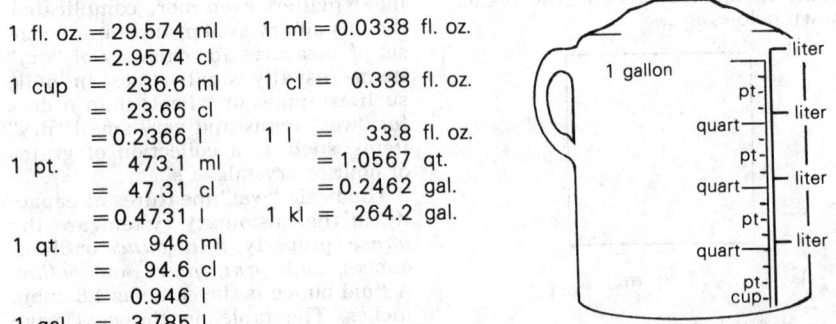

1 fl. oz. = 29.574 ml	1 ml = 0.0338 fl. oz.
= 2.9574 cl	
1 cup = 236.6 ml	1 cl = 0.338 fl. oz.
= 23.66 cl	
= 0.2366 l	1 l = 33.8 fl. oz.
1 pt. = 473.1 ml	= 1.0567 qt.
= 47.31 cl	= 0.2462 gal.
= 0.4731 l	1 kl = 264.2 gal.
1 qt. = 946 ml	
= 94.6 cl	
= 0.946	
1 gal. = 3.785 l	

1000 cubic centimeters. The system of prefixes is then applied to the basic unit, the liter. Thus, a centiliter is 0.01 liter, or the same as 10 cubic centimeters. A kiloliter is 1 000 liters, or the same as 1 cubic meter.

In relation to the customary system, a liter is 1.06 quarts (liquid) and a liquid quart is 0.95 liter.

Weight and Mass

In the customary system, there is an entirely separate system for measuring weight. Weight is the force that attracts a material object to the center of Earth. For any particular object, the weight varies (slightly) with the location of that object on Earth. If the object is not on Earth, the variation can be great. On the moon, weight is defined as the force that attracts an object to the center of the moon. This is about one-sixth the force that the same object encounters on the surface of the Earth. Thus, astronauts on the moon weigh much less than they do on Earth.

The basic unit of weight in the customary system is the pound. There are three separate customary systems of weight. For weighing common objects (such as a person or a head of cabbage), the *avoirdupois* system is used. For weighing precious metals, the *troy* system is used. Finally, for weighing drugs, the *apothecaries'* system is used. Let us consider the common, or avoirdupois, system first.

The most common units of weight are the *ounce, pound,* and *ton.* The ton, however, can be either a short ton or a long ton. In the United States, the short ton is regularly used. The relationships are shown in the table on the next page. Notice that the ounce used in weight is not the same as the (fluid) ounce used in capacity.

Both the troy and apothecaries' pounds are somewhat lighter than the avoirdupois pound. There are only 12 ounces in a troy or apothecaries' pound, but each ounce is slightly larger than an avoirdupois ounce.

In the metric system, while there is a unit of weight, it is more common to measure mass than weight. *Mass* is the unchanging quality a material object has that gives it weight. Since two objects of the same mass weigh the same when they are in the same location, mass and weight are the same in many common situations. The distinction between mass and weight is often not considered in elementary grades.

The basic unit of mass in the metric system is the gram. A *gram* is the mass of a cubic centimeter of pure water under standard conditions of temperature and pressure. The commonly used measures are the *milligram* (0.001 gram), the gram, the *kilogram* (1 000 grams), and the *metric ton* (1 000 000 grams, or 1 000 kilograms). A gram is about 0.04 ounce (avoirdupois). It works out that a metric ton is just 1.1 (short) tons or 2,200 pounds.

The kilogram is the unit used most in everyday life and is equal to about 2.2 pounds. The table on the next page of weights (and measures of mass) shows the relationships in detail.

Time

There is one system of measures that is the same in both the customary and metric systems: measures of time.

1 second (sec. or s)	$\frac{1}{60}$ minute
1 minute (min. or m)	60 seconds
1 hour (hr. or h)	60 minutes
1 day (no abbrev.)	24 hours
1 week (wk. or w)	7 days
1 year (yr. or y)	365 days

The year is the time it takes Earth to orbit the sun. While we think of a year as 365 days, it is actually close to $365\frac{1}{4}$ days. Therefore, every fourth year is declared a "leap year," with 366 days. The extra day is added as February 29.

WEIGHT/MASS

CUSTOMARY UNITS (WEIGHT)

1 ounce (oz.)
16 oz. = **1 pound (lb.)**
2,000 lb. = **1 ton**

METRIC UNITS (MASS)

1 milligram (mg)
1,000 mg = **1 gram (g)**
1,000 g = **1 kilogram (kg)**

Conversions

1 oz.	= 28,350 mg		1 mg	= 0.000035 oz.
	= 28.35 g		1 g	= 0.0353 oz.
1 lb.	= 453.6 g		1 kg	= 35.27 oz.
	= 0.4536 kg			= 2.205 lb.
1 ton	= 907.2 kg		1 ton (metric)	= 2,205 lb.
	= .9072 ton (metric)			= 1.1 ton (customary)

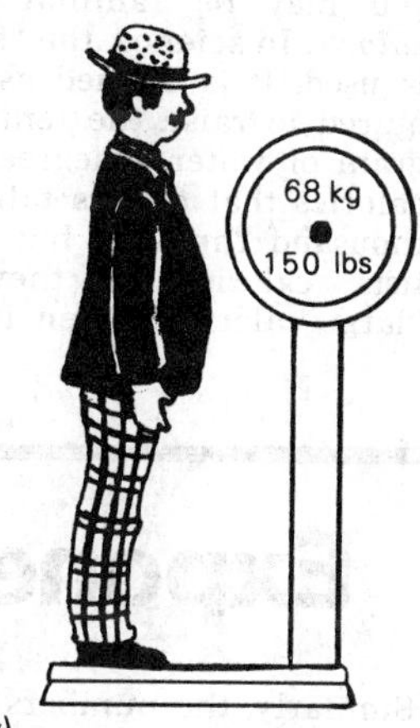

Temperature

Although metric and customary are the same for time, they are not for temperature. The customary measure of temperature is the *Fahrenheit* scale, named after the person who developed it. On this scale, water freezes at 32 degrees (written 32°) (under standard conditions) and boils at 212°. This scale was one of several developed by Gabriel Fahrenheit and published in 1724. Another scale, published by Anders Celsius in 1742, was adopted, in modified form, as the metric method of measuring temperature. In its present form the *Celsius* (formerly *centigrade*) scale sets the freezing point of water (under standard conditions) at 0° and the boiling point at 100°. Thus, to convert from Fahrenheit to Celsius, you use the formula

$$C = \frac{5}{9}(F - 32)$$

and to convert from Fahrenheit to Celsius

$$F = \frac{9}{5}C + 32$$

In scientific work another scale is often used. It is called the *Kelvin* scale or the Absolute scale. Scientists have established that the coldest temperature possible is −273.16° below zero. Setting −273.16°C at 0° Kelvin and using degrees of the same size as Celsius degrees gives a Kelvin temperature of 273.16°K for the freezing point of water and 373.16°K for the boiling point.

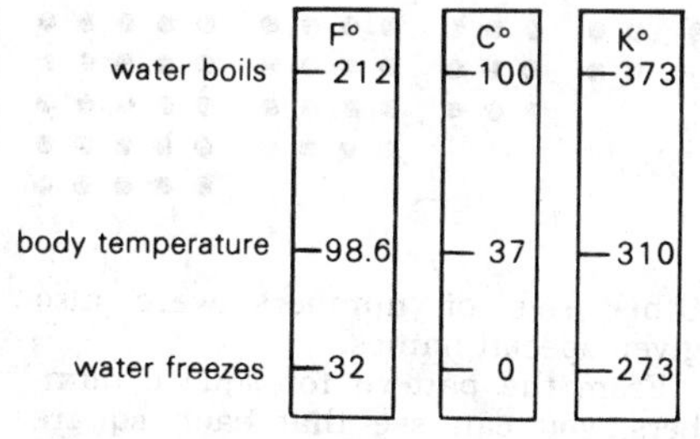

Measuring Angles

Several methods of measuring angles are in common use. None of them are particularly identified with either the metric or customary systems. The most commonly used measure for angles is the degree system. A right angle is set at 90°. Here are a few angles with their degree measure marked.

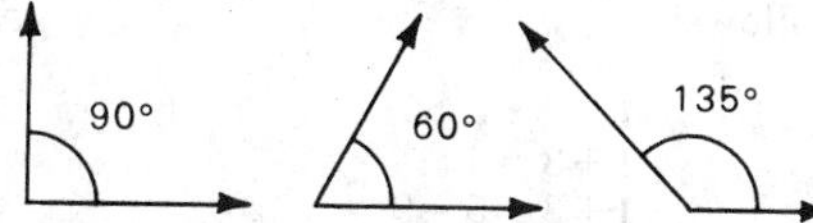

The degree system can also be used for measuring parts of a circle, called arcs. The number of degrees in an arc is the same as the number of degrees in the angle that has its vertex at the center of the circle and whose sides intercept that arc. Both arcs and angles can be any number of degrees.

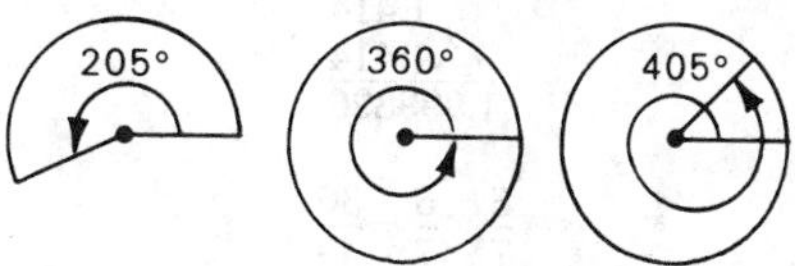

In the degree system there are measures for angles smaller than a degree. These units have the same name as units of time, although there is no relationship.

1 second (sec. or ″)	$\frac{1}{60}$ minute
1 minute (min. or ′)	60 seconds
1 degree (deg. or °)	60 minutes

You may encounter another system of measures for angles and arcs: the radian system. Radians emerge as a natural measure in parts of higher mathematics. All the other units discussed so far have been arbitrary—people decided to call such and such an amount an inch or a gram. The radian results from the properties of angles and circles; no other unit will do for certain problems.

A *radian* is the angle measure or arc measure defined so that the arc measured by the angle is the same length as the radius of the circle the arc is part of. In the diagram, CB and CA each have the same length as AB, so angle *C* measures 1 radian. One radian is equal to about 57.3°.

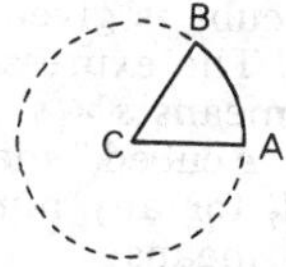

Since π radians ($\pi = 3.1416\cdots$) is 180°, radian measures often are expressed as multiples of π. For example, the radian measure of a right angle is $\frac{1}{2}\pi$.

Compound Measures

The measures discussed so far are generally independent measures. Some, such as area, volume, and ca-

METRIC SPEED LIMIT: *if 48 km per hour is the same as 30 mph, what is the metric equivalent of 55 mph?*

UPI

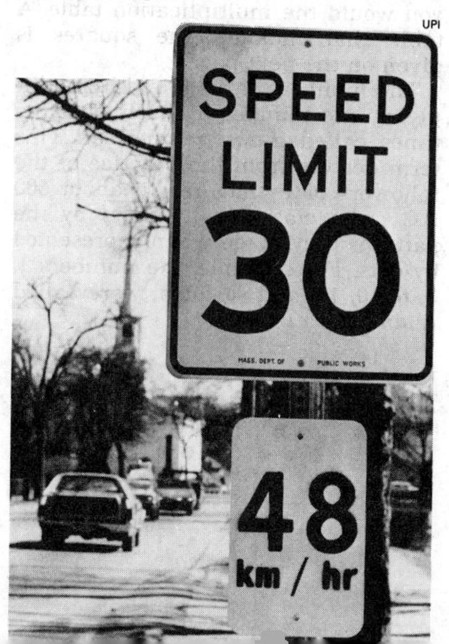

pacity, are more complicated, combining two or more measures. The measures discussed next are still more complex.

Measures of length are often combined with measures of time. The measures of velocity (or rate of speed) used with cars are good examples. Another combination you may encounter is a measure of weight with a measure of area—pounds per square inch. In each case, the word *per* means "for each." As we have seen, the "*per*" combinations can be written as fractions:

$$\frac{\text{mile}}{\text{hour}} \quad \frac{\text{kilometer}}{\text{hour}} \quad \frac{\text{pound}}{\text{square inch}}$$

Another kind of combination is expressed in English with a hyphen. One example is man-hours. The expression 12 man-hours means that it will take 12 persons one hour to do a task that one person could do in 12 hours.

Another combination measure that you may be familiar with is the *calorie.* In science, the "small calorie" is used. It is defined as the heat required to raise the temperature of 1 gram of water 1 degree Celsius. The calories that dieters talk about are a thousand times as big as the scientists' calories, so they are called "large calories" when it is necessary to distinguish them.

Calories, small or large, are a measure of heat in the metric system. Another measure of heat that is often used is the British Thermal Unit, commonly referred to by the initials B.T.U. One B.T.U. is the amount of heat required to raise the temperature of 1 pound of water 1 degree Fahrenheit. Since a pound is a measure of weight, and a gram, used in defining the calorie, is a measure of mass, the B.T.U. and the calorie do not actually measure the same thing—but people use them both as measures of heat.

Exponents

In working with measurement and formulas, you encountered exponents. For example, the area of a square is given by the formula $A = s^2$ and the volume of a cube is given by the formula $V = e^3$. The expression s^2, read "*s* squared," means $s \times s$. The expression e^3, read "*e* cubed," means $e \times e \times e$. In general, for any number *b*, the expression b^n means

$$\underbrace{b \times b \times b \times \cdots \times b}_{n \text{ times}}$$

The number *b* is called the *base,* and the number *n* is called the *exponent.*

Squares

The exponent you will encounter most often is ^{2}. Not only do squared numbers occur in the formulas for areas, but they also occur in many other formulas that are not treated in this article. As a result, it is convenient to memorize the first few just as you would the multiplication table. A table that includes the squares is given on the next page.

The number that is found by multiplying one number by itself is sometimes called a *square number.* This term derives from the practice of the followers of Pythagoras in about 500 B.C., who classified numbers by the patterns they made when represented by dots. For example, the numbers 1, 3, 6, 10, 15, and so forth, were called *triangular numbers.*

Similarly, the numbers 1, 4, 9, 16, 25, and so forth were called *square numbers.*

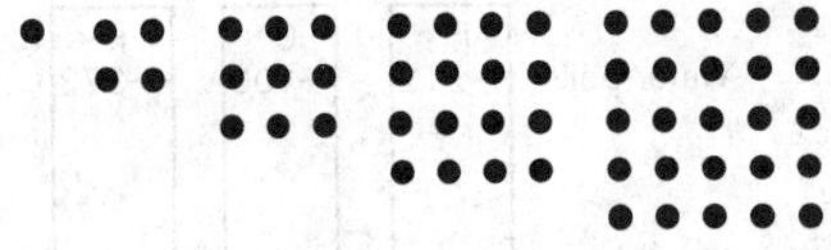

Other sets of numbers were also given special names.

From the pattern for square numbers, you can see that each square number can be formed by adding each successive odd number. The left column and the bottom row of each square add up to an odd number (except for 1, which stands alone).

1 $\quad 1+3=4 \quad 1+3+5=9$

So square numbers can be found as follows:

$$\begin{aligned} &1 \\ &1+3=4 \\ &1+3+5=9 \\ &1+3+5+7=16 \\ &1+3+5+7+9=25 \end{aligned}$$

and so forth.

It is easy to see that every number has a square number associated with it. A decimal or a fraction can be squared as easily as a whole number.

$$\begin{array}{r} 1.414 \\ \times 1.414 \\ \hline 1.999396 \end{array}$$

$$\frac{6}{7} \times \frac{6}{7} = \frac{36}{49}$$

Square Roots

By the same token, there is a positive number that can be squared to produce the given number. Any number that, when squared, produces a second number, is called a *square root* of the second number. Thus, 5 is a square root of 25. There is a special sign used to indicate the square root of a number. It is $\sqrt{\ }$. Thus,

$$\sqrt{25} = 5.$$

If you know that the area of a square is 144 cm² (that is, 144 square centimeters), then the length of one side is $\sqrt{144}$ centimeters, which you probably recognize as 12 centimeters. Suppose that you know, however, that the area of a square is 2 cm². Then the length of a side is $\sqrt{2}$, but what is the common name for that number? Note that earlier you saw

$$\begin{array}{r} 1.414 \\ \times 1.414 \\ \hline 1.999396 \end{array}$$

so $\sqrt{2}$ is very close to 1.414. You could get closer by finding a digit for the ten thousandths place that would give a number closer to 2 than 1.999396. For example, $1.4142^2 = 1.9999616$. It can be shown, however, that there is no terminating or repeating decimal that is exactly equal to $\sqrt{2}$. In fact, unless the square root of a number is a whole number, there is no terminating or repeating decimal that can exactly represent the square root. There is also no fraction that can exactly represent the square root of a whole number that does not have a whole-number square root. For example, $\frac{10}{7}$ is close to $\sqrt{2}$, but

$$\frac{10}{7} \times \frac{10}{7} = \frac{100}{49} = 2\frac{2}{49}$$

The only exact way to represent square roots that are not whole numbers is with the square-root sign. Otherwise you must use an approximation.

For most purposes an approximation to thousandths is sufficient. People frequently use tables to find the approximate square roots of numbers. Usually, such tables are combined with the squares of the whole numbers (and may include other numbers as well). The table on this page gives the squares and square roots for the whole numbers from 1 to 100. It is often convenient to know by heart the squares from 1 through 15 and the square roots of 2, 3, and 5.

If you do not have a table of square roots handy, or if you are looking for a number that is not in the table, the following method can be used.

The method that is usually taught in schools today, especially in upper-level arithmetic or first-level algebra classes, is the method of *iteration*. To iterate is to repeat. In mathematics, the word iteration refers to a process in which you repeat the same steps over and over. Here are the steps for finding a square root by iteration.

A. Make an estimate of the square root.

B. Divide the estimate into the number whose square root you are seeking.

C. Average the quotient you got from B with your estimate from A.

D. Use the average from C as a new estimate and repeat steps B, C, and D, going one decimal place farther each time, until the estimate and quotient are the same for one more decimal place than you want.

E. Round the quotient to the decimal place you want. It will be the appropriate approximation of the square root.

To find the square root of 132 to the nearest thousandth:

A. Since 12^2 is 144, use 11 as your first estimate.

B. $11\overline{)132}$ = 12

C. $(11 + 12) \div 2 = 11.5$

D. $11.5\overline{)132}$ = 11.47

$(11.47 + 11.5) \div 2 = 11.485$

$11.49\overline{)132}$ = 11.488

$(11.488 + 11.49) \div 2 = 11.489$

$11.489\overline{)132}$ = 11.4893

E. The square root of 132 to the nearest thousandth is 11.489.

TABLE OF SQUARES AND SQUARE ROOTS

No.	Square	Square root	No.	Square	Square root
1	1	1	**51**	2,601	7.141
2	4	1.414	**52**	2,704	7.211
3	9	1.732	**53**	2,809	7.280
4	16	2	**54**	2,916	7.348
5	25	2.236	**55**	3,025	7.416
6	36	2.449	**56**	3,136	7.483
7	49	2.646	**57**	3,249	7.550
8	64	2.828	**58**	3,364	7.616
9	81	3	**59**	3,481	7.681
10	100	3.162	**60**	3,600	7.746
11	121	3.317	**61**	3,742	7.810
12	144	3.464	**62**	3,844	7.874
13	169	3.606	**63**	3,969	7.937
14	196	3.742	**64**	4,096	8
15	225	3.873	**65**	4,225	8.062
16	256	4	**66**	4,356	8.124
17	289	4.123	**67**	4,489	8.185
18	324	4.243	**68**	4,624	8.246
19	361	4.359	**69**	4,761	8.307
20	400	4.472	**70**	4,900	8.367
21	441	4.583	**71**	5,041	8.426
22	484	4.690	**72**	5,184	8.485
23	529	4.796	**73**	5,329	8.544
24	576	4.899	**74**	5,476	8.602
25	625	5	**75**	5,625	8.660
26	676	5.099	**76**	5,776	8.718
27	729	5.196	**77**	5,929	8.775
28	784	5.292	**78**	6,084	8.832
29	841	5.385	**79**	6,241	8.888
30	900	5.477	**80**	6,400	8.944
31	961	5.568	**81**	6,561	9
32	1,024	5.657	**82**	6,724	9.055
33	1,089	5.745	**83**	6,889	9.110
34	1,156	5.831	**84**	7,056	9.165
35	1,225	5.916	**85**	7,225	9.220
36	1,296	6	**86**	7,396	9.274
37	1,369	6.083	**87**	7,569	9.327
38	1,444	6.164	**88**	7,744	9.381
39	1,521	6.245	**89**	7,921	9.434
40	1,600	6.325	**90**	8,100	9.487
41	1,681	6.403	**91**	8,281	9.539
42	1,764	6.481	**92**	8,464	9.592
43	1,849	6.557	**93**	8,649	9.644
44	1,936	6.633	**94**	8,836	9.695
45	2,025	6.708	**95**	9,025	9.747
46	2,116	6.782	**96**	9,216	9.798
47	2,209	6.856	**97**	9,409	9.849
48	2,304	6.928	**98**	9,604	9.899
49	2,401	7	**99**	9,801	9.950
50	2,500	7.071	**100**	10,000	10

Cubes

The other common exponent, the cube, occurs in the formulas for the volume of a cube and a sphere. Multiplying a number by itself 3 times gives the cube of the original number. Thus, the cube of 3 is $3 \times 3 \times 3$, or 27. This is written as $3^3 = 27$. It is generally useful to know the cubes of the numbers 1 through 10 (see the table that follows).

Just as the base of a squared number is the square root of the number, the base of a cubed number is the cube root. The symbol for the cube root is $\sqrt[3]{\ }$. Therefore, $\sqrt[3]{64} = 4$.

In general, it is too difficult to find cube roots by hand, so most people use a table. Here is a table of the cubes and roots from 1 through 10.

TABLE OF CUBES AND CUBE ROOTS

No.	Cube	Cube root
1	1	1
2	8	1.260
3	27	1.442
4	64	1.587
5	125	1.710
6	216	1.817
7	343	1.913
8	512	2
9	729	2.080
10	1,000	2.154

Other Powers

Exponents can be any number whatsoever. The number 3^4 is $3 \times 3 \times 3 \times 3$, or 81. This is read as "three to the fourth power." The number 2^5, or two to the fifth power, is $2 \times 2 \times 2 \times 2 \times 2$, or 32. The square of a number is also called the number to the second power. Likewise, the cube is the third power. The number alone (for example, 2) is the first power, also written 2^1.

Sometimes you want to multiply or divide two powers of the same number—for example, $2^3 \times 2^2$. This means

$$(2 \times 2 \times 2) \times (2 \times 2)$$

or

$$2 \times 2 \times 2 \times 2 \times 2.$$

So,

$$2^3 \times 2^2 = 2^5$$

Similarly, you can show that

$$3^4 \times 3^5 = 3^9.$$

In general, for any number a raised to the mth and nth powers,

$$a^m \times a^n = a^{(m+n)}$$

This property makes a multiplication problem a matter of adding exponents.

Now look at division. As you know, division of two numbers is essentially the same as finding a fraction, so $2^3 \div 2^2$ is the same as

$$\frac{2 \times 2 \times 2}{2 \times 2}$$

You can use cancellation to find the answer.

$$\frac{\cancel{2} \times \cancel{2} \times 2}{\cancel{2} \times \cancel{2}} = 2 \quad \text{or} \quad 2^3 \div 2^2 = 2^1$$

Similarly, you may show that $3^5 \div 3^2$ is equal to $3^{(5-2)}$, or 3^3. In general, for any number a raised to the mth and nth powers,

$$a^m \div a^n = a^{(m-n)}$$

What happens to this last formula if n is greater than m? Look at an example worked out. For $3^2 \div 3^5$ you have

$$\frac{3 \times 3}{3 \times 3 \times 3 \times 3 \times 3}$$

Using cancellation, this becomes

$$\frac{\cancel{3} \times \cancel{3}}{\cancel{3} \times \cancel{3} \times 3 \times 3 \times 3} = \frac{1}{3 \times 3 \times 3} = \frac{1}{3^3}$$

For exponents, this is indicated with a negative sign. In other words, 3^{-3} means $\frac{1}{3^3}$. You may know that when you subtract a larger number from a smaller one, the same convention is used. The difference is indicated by a negative sign. If you have \$10 in the bank, and you write a check for \$15, then you have −\$5 dollars in the bank (and you had better make a deposit fast!). With this convention, the rule

$$a^m \div a^n = a^{(m-n)}$$

is true when m is either greater than or less than n. Notice that with this rule you can divide by subtracting exponents.

Scientific Notation

Scientists often use a method based upon exponents to record numbers. This method is called scientific notation. Scientific notation is based upon the notion that it is easier to read exponents than it is to count zeros. For example, the number 100 has 2 zeros and it is equal to 10^2. The number 1,000,000 has 6 zeros, and it is equal to 10^6. Scientists sometimes talk about a large number called the *googol*, which is 10^{100}. This is much easier to read than 1 followed by 100 zeros.

For example, suppose that you measured the diameter of the planet Mercury to the nearest 10 kilometers and determined that it was 4,880 kilometers. In scientific notation you would report that measurement as 4.88×10^3 kilometers. Since $10^3 = 1000$, the measurement indicates 4,880. A measurement of 4.880×10^3 would mean a measurement of 4,880 to the nearest kilometer.

With negative exponents, scientific notation can be used to designate numbers smaller than 1. For example, a report of 2.34×10^{-2} centimeters means 0.0234 centimeters.

As you probably have noticed, in scientific notation each number is represented as a number of ones times a power of 10. In this way, it is easy to keep track of the zeros. If a number is a power of 10 already, just the power of 10 is reported; for example, you write 10^{27} instead of 1×10^{27}.

Logarithms

If $10^0 = 1$ and $10^1 = 10$, can the numbers between 1 and 10 be expressed as fractional exponents? The answer is yes, and the fractional exponents are called *logarithms.*

In the system of logarithms, or logs, as they are often called, the exponents are written as whole numbers in the following form:

$$\log 10 = 1$$

The following table gives the logarithms for whole numbers between 1 and 10:

log	
1	0
2	0.3010
3	0.4771
4	0.6021
5	0.6990
6	0.7782
7	0.8451
8	0.9031
9	0.9542
10	1

The logs given here are decimal approximations. More detailed tables give logs to 6 or more decimal places and may also give logs for numbers to the hundredths place—for 1.00, 1.01, 1.02, etc.

With a detailed table of logs for numbers from 1.00 to 9.99, it is possible to express any number from 1 to 1000. Logs resemble scientific notation in the way they express numbers. For example:

$$621 = 6.21 \times 10^2$$
$$\log 621 = 2 + \log 6.21 = \text{about } 2.7900$$

Notice that the exponent in scientific notation becomes the whole number in the logarithm. A whole number (an exponent of 10) plus a decimal fraction (the exponent of a number between 1 and 10) form the log for any number.

Operations with logs. We have learned that to multiply like numbers that have exponents, we can simply add the exponents:

$$6^2 \times 6^3 = 6^5$$

Logarithms make it possible to extend this idea to numbers without exponents, since logs give every number its own exponent. Using the table above, some simple examples will illustrate. If $3 \times 3 = 9$, then

$$\log 3 + \log 3 = \log (3 \times 3)$$
$$.4771 + .4771 = .9542$$

Had we not known the answer, we could have used the log table to convert the log 0.9542 back into a number. It is the log of 9.

The system works for larger numbers as well. Consider 4000×50:

$$4000 = 4 \times 10^3$$
so $$\log 4000 = .6021 + 3 = 3.6021$$
$$50 = 5 \times 10^1$$
so $$\log 50 = .6990 + 1 = 1.6990$$

Now the multiplication problem is a simple matter of adding the logs of the two numbers and converting the result.

$$\begin{array}{lr} \log 4000 & 3.6021 \\ +\log \quad 50 & 1.6990 \\ \hline \log (4000 \times 50) & 5.3011 \end{array}$$

Looking in the table, we find that .3011 is the log of 2 (approximately).

So $$5.3011 = 2 \times 10^5 = 200{,}000$$

Logarithms may also be used for division. For example, we know that

$$8 \div 2 = 4$$

We also know that division of like numbers with exponents can be accomplished by subtracting exponents. The problem above can be written

$$2^3 \div 2^1 = 2^2$$

In the log system,

$$\log 8 - \log 2 = \log (8 \div 2)$$
$$.9031 - .3010 = .6021$$

And we find that .6021 is the log of 4.

For such simple problems, of course, logarithms are not practical. But for more elaborate problems, logs can save time and reduce the chance for error. They are used in many fields of advanced mathematics.

—*Bryan H. Bunch*

ALGEBRA

Sixteen centuries ago (275 A.D.) a man named Diophantus lived in Alexandria, Egypt. Little is known about him, as most of his writings were lost. Enough is known, however, from the few books he left, to give him the name "Father of Algebra." He solved many difficult problems and extended the subject beyond what is taught in high schools today. But his contribution was nearly forgotten.

More than five centuries later, in the year 825, Muhammad ibn-Mūsa of Khwarazm (now Khiva in southern U.S.S.R.) wrote a book called *Al-jabr wal-mugābalah.* In Arabic, the word *al-jabr* means reduction, reunion, or bone setting; the other phrase in the title of the book means comparison. Reducing a problem to its essentials is a general characteristic of mathematics, but it is most clearly evident in algebra.

Algebra is often defined as generalized arithmetic, and it does use the same basic operations. But it goes further than arithmetic in studying the nature of numbers themselves. It relies strictly on the logic inherent in the number system. Students of arithmetic may be surprised by the similarities between the two fields and also by their differences. A secure understanding of arithmetic is necessary to an understanding of algebra.

Number Systems

Arithmetic begins with the study of *natural numbers.* These are the everyday counting numbers 1, 2, 3, and so on. The natural numbers are *ordered:* it is always possible to determine that one natural number is greater than, equal to, or less than another. In adding and multiplying natural numbers, the result is always a natural number. For example:

$$6+7=13$$
$$6\times 7=42$$

But subtraction of natural numbers raises a problem that can be solved only by creating a new kind of number. If 8 is subtracted from 5, no natural number can express the result. Hence, *negative numbers* are added to the system. Negative numbers make subtraction possible for all numbers. For example:

$$5-8=-3$$

The result is read, "negative 3." Positive numbers may be written with a positive sign (+), but if a numeral appears without a sign, it is assumed to be positive. Zero, which is neither positive nor negative, has no sign.

Whether negative numbers are useful depends on the particular problem. For example, if you are solving a problem that involves measures of length or area, a negative answer seems nonsensical. In fact, it took people many centuries to see the use of negative numbers in any problem.

We are familiar, however, with several everyday situations where negative numbers are useful. One is in measurement of temperature. On a cold day the temperature may be *below zero.* Another situation is in computing the balance in a bank account. Consider the statement below.

Banks do not like a person's balance to be in negative numbers. But without them, it would be very difficult to keep track of the situation where debits (checks written) exceed credits (deposits made).

The system of numbers including both the natural numbers and negative numbers is called the set of *integers* or *signed numbers.*

In order to complete this system, one very important addition must be made. What happens if a person with $8 in a bank account writes a check for $8? When a number is subtracted from itself, the answer is "zero." In a system with negative and positive numbers, "zero" (written 0) is different from "nothing." Now it is a point midway between +1 and −1, a point where there is no positive or negative value. When 0 is joined to the signed numbers, the set of *whole numbers* is formed.

Division, however, presents a problem that even the whole numbers cannot always handle. Sometimes division of two whole numbers results in another whole number:

$$6\div 2=3$$

But many division problems do not result in a whole number. For example:

$$5\div 2=?$$

In order to answer this problem, fractions must be used. Fractions make it possible to divide any whole number by another:

$$5\div 2=\tfrac{5}{2}=2\tfrac{1}{2}$$

The system including positive and negative whole numbers and fractions is called the set of *rational numbers.* Later, we will have to expand the system again.

Bank Statement	CREDITS	DEBITS	BALANCE
	$100.		+ $100.
		$40.	+ 60.
		25.	+ 35.
	50.		+ 85.
		97.	− 12.
		13.	− 25.
	150.		+ 125.

The Number Line

The rational numbers can be placed on a line to make a scale. Such a line is called a *number line.*

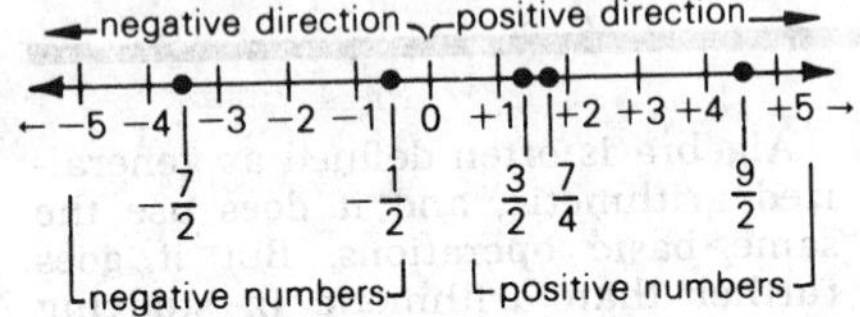

The positive numbers are to the right of zero and the negative numbers are to the left of zero. Notice that on the number line, a point can be located that corresponds to each rational number. For example, the point corresponding to $\frac{3}{2}$ is the midpoint between 1 and 2. The point midway between $\frac{3}{2}$ and 2 is the point corresponding to $\frac{7}{4}$.

The following is a summary of the types of numbers discussed so far:

Natural numbers	N = 1, 2, 3, 4, . . .
Whole numbers	W = 0, 1, 2, 3, . . .
Integers	I = . . . −3, −2, −1, 0, 1, 2, 3, . . .
Rational numbers	R = numbers that can be named in the form $\frac{a}{b}$, where *a* and *b* are integers and $b \neq 0$.

The following diagram shows the relationships among these numbers.

Each of these sets of numbers can be matched with certain points on a number line. The number associated with each point is called the *coordinate* of the point.

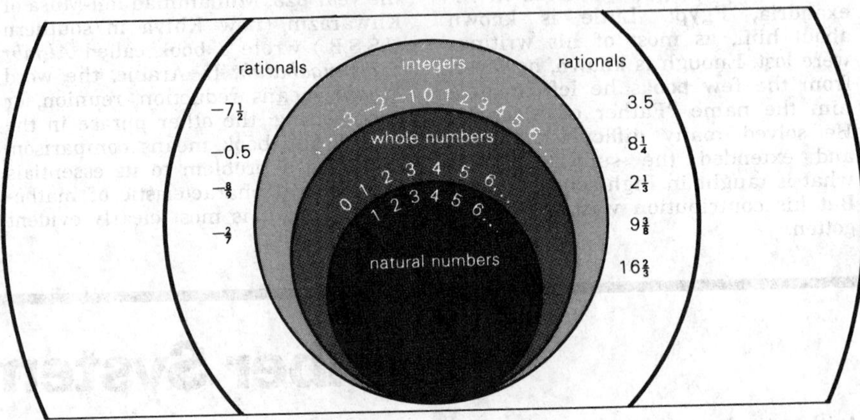

The Rational Numbers

Basic Properties

In algebra, as in other branches of mathematics, certain basic statements are assumed to be true about numbers and the relationships among them. These basic statements are called *properties,* or *axioms* of the system.

In combining rational numbers, the basic properties of addition and multiplication of natural numbers are assumed to hold true. These properties make it possible to determine the meaning of sums, differences, products, and quotients of rational numbers, since they govern the ways in which numbers can be combined.

The *commutative property for addition* states that the order in which two numbers are added does not change their sum. That is,

$$a + b = b + a$$

where *a* and *b* represent any rational numbers.

The *associative property for addition* states that the way in which three or more numbers are grouped for addition does not change their sum. That is, $(a + b) + c = a + (b + c)$. For example:

$$(3+4)+5 = 3+(4+5)$$
$$7+5 = 3+9$$
$$12 = 12$$

(Parentheses are used as a symbol of grouping; the parentheses around $a + b$ in the statement above signify that the sum of *a* and *b* is to be treated as a whole.)

The *commutative property for multiplication* states that the order in which two numbers are multiplied does not change their product; that is, *ab* is equal to *ba*. For example:

$$6 \cdot 4 = 4 \cdot 6$$
$$24 = 24$$

(In algebra the multiplication of two letters, or of a letter and a number, is indicated by writing them adjacent to each other without a sign between them: *xy* means "*x* times *y*," and 5*c* means "5 times *c*." The multiplication of two numbers is signified by a dot; the multiplication sign (×) could too easily be mistaken for the letter *x*, which is often used to signify an unknown quantity.)

The *associative property for multiplication* states that the way in which three or more numbers are grouped for multiplication does not change their product. Thus it is always true that $a \cdot (bc) = (ab) \cdot c$. For example:

$$3 \cdot (4 \cdot 5) = (3 \cdot 4) \cdot 5$$
$$3 \cdot 20 = 12 \cdot 5$$
$$60 = 60$$

Another important property required in algebra is the *distributive property,* which interprets multiplication in terms of addition. It states that if two numbers are to be multiplied by a third number, the result will be the same if the sum of the two numbers is multiplied by the third. Where *a, b,* and *c* are rational numbers,

$$ac + bc = (a + b)c.$$

For example:

$$2 \cdot 4 + 3 \cdot 4 = (2+3) \cdot 4$$
$$8 + 12 = 5 \cdot 4$$
$$20 = 20$$

PROPERTIES OF ADDITION AND MULTIPLICATION

$$a + b = b + a$$
$$(a + b) + c = a + (b + c)$$
$$ab = ba$$
$$a \cdot (bc) = (ab) \cdot c$$
$$ac + bc = (a + b) \cdot c$$

Operations

Each of the four basic operations of arithmetic can be performed on the rational numbers in such a way that the five properties above will hold true.

Addition. The expression (+3) + (+2) means positive 3 plus positive 2. This may be done on the number line. A positive number is added by starting with the first number and moving to the right a number of spaces equivalent to the second number. The distance of this point from 0 is the sum. Thus, to add +2 to +3, start at +3 and move two spaces to the right arriving at +5. Therefore, (+3) + (+2) = +5.

$$(+3)+(+2)=5$$

−5 −4 −3 −2 −1 0 +1 +2 +3 +4 +5

When adding a negative number, move to the left from the first number. Thus, (+3) + (−2) = +1. Reversing the order of the addends does not change the sum. Thus, (−2) + (+3) also = +1, and this can be confirmed on the number line.

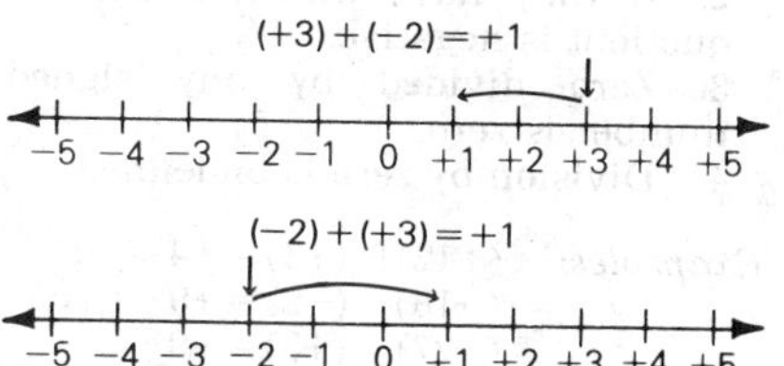

Three or more numbers may be added on the number line in any order and the sum will be the same. Thus, both the commutative and associative properties of addition hold for signed numbers.

It is possible, of course, to add signed numbers without using the number line. To do so requires the use of the concept of the *absolute value* of a number. The absolute value of a number is its *distance* from zero on the number line without regarding the positive or negative direction from 0. The absolute value is designated symbolically by the use of two vertical bars. Thus,

$|-3|=3$ The number −3 is 3 units from 0.

$|3|=3$ The number 3 is also 3 units from 0.

The absolute value of a number is never negative, since it is the undirected distance that the number is from 0. Using the concept of absolute value, add two signed numbers as follows:

A. If the two numbers have the same sign, add their absolute values and use the common sign.

$$(+3)+(+2)=+5$$
$$(-3)+(-2)=-5$$

B. If the two numbers have different signs, find the *difference* of their absolute values and use the sign of the number having the larger absolute value.

$$(+3)+(-2)=+1$$
$$(-3)+(+2)=-1$$

The sum of any rational number a and 0 equals a: $a+0=a$. The number 0 is called the *additive identity.*

Subtraction. Subtraction is the *inverse* operation to addition.

If $(+5)+(+3)=+8,$
then $(+8)-(+5)=+3.$

To subtract positive numbers on the number line, begin with the subtrahend and measure off the distance to the minuend. For example:

$$(+8)-(+5)=+3$$

−1 0 +1 +2 +3 +4 +5 +6 +7 +8 +9

The distance from +5 to +8 is 3. Or, to describe the operation in terms of addition, +3 is the number that, added to +5, gives +8. Similarly,

$$(+4)-(+7)=-3.$$

−1 0 +1 +2 +3 +4 +5 +6 +7 +8 +9

The distance from +7 to +4 is −3, or three spaces in the negative direction. In terms of addition, −3 is the number that, added to +7, gives +4.

The procedure is the same for negative numbers. For example, if the temperature in the morning is −8 degrees and is −1 degree at noon, what change has occurred?

$$(-1)-(-8)=?$$

The temperature has gone up (in the positive direction) 7 degrees, and this can be verified on the number line.

$$(-1)-(-8)=+7$$

−9 −8 −7 −6 −5 −4 −3 −2 −1 0 +1

The distance from −8 to −1 is +7. Or, +7 is the number that, added to −8, gives −1.

To subtract signed numbers without referring to the number line, we must consider the *additive inverse* of a number, that is, the number with the same absolute value but opposite sign. Thus, the additive inverse of +3 is −3, and that of −8 is +8. The principle for subtracting signed numbers is: *To subtract a number from another, add its additive inverse.* In practical terms this means: *Change the sign of the second number and add.* Consider the examples below:

$$(+8)-(+5)=(+8)+(-5)=+3$$
$$(+4)-(+7)=(+4)+(-7)=-3$$
$$(-1)-(-8)=(-1)+(+8)=+7$$

ADDING AND SUBTRACTING SIGNED NUMBERS

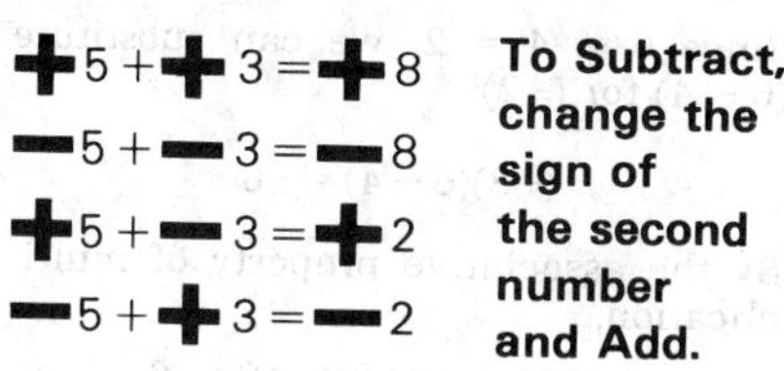

In algebra, the plus sign and the minus sign are used in two ways. A minus sign may indicate the operation of subtraction, as in (+3) − (+5), or it may indicate a negative number, as in −3. Similarly, the plus sign is used to indicate a positive number and the operation of addition. To avoid confusion, it is customary in algebra to think of

$$5-3$$

as meaning "positive 5 combined with (added to) negative 3," the sum being equal to positive 2. The value of the expression is the same whether it means

$$(+5)-(+3)$$

or

$$(+5)+(-3),$$

but thinking of it the second way is helpful in many algebraic situations. The same understanding can also be useful in practical situations. For example, the bank statement shown above uses positive numbers (credits) to show money coming into an account and negative numbers (debits) to show money going out. The balance of the account is the *algebraic sum* of these positive and negative numbers.

Multiplication. To find the product of two signed numbers, it is necessary to have rules that are consistent with the rules for the multiplication of natural numbers in arithmetic. The expression (+3)(+4) represents the product of positive 3 and positive 4 and is evaluated as +12. The product can be interpreted as the *sum* of three positive fours: (+4) + (+4) + (+4), or +12. Similarly, (+3)(−4) can be interpreted as the sum of three negative fours, (−4) + (−4) + (−4), or −12.

On the other hand, (−3)(−4) cannot be assigned a value using the interpretation of multiplication as repeated addition, as was done in the previous examples, because both factors are negative. The product of one positive and one negative number is a negative number. We can see that the product of −3 and −4 must be |12|, but what is the sign? The following steps give the answer.

We know that

$$(-3)(+2)=-6.$$

Since $6-4=2$, we can substitute $(6-4)$ for $(+2)$:

$$(-3)(6-4)=-6$$

By the associative property of multiplication,

$$(-3)(+6)+(-3)(-4)=-6$$
$$-18+(-3)(-4)=-6.$$

The only value for $(-3)(-4)$ that makes this statement true is $+12$.

$$(-18)+(+12)=-6$$

so, $$(-3)(-4)=+12.$$

The product of any two negative rational numbers is a positive number.

Here is a summary of the rules for multiplying signed numbers.

To find the product of two signed numbers, multiply the absolute values of the numbers. Then:
1. If the factors have *like signs,* the product is positive.
2. If the factors have *unlike signs,* the product is negative.
3. If one of the factors is 0, the product is 0.

To find the sign of the product of three or more signed numbers, multiply the absolute values of the numbers. Then:
1. If the *number of negative signs is even,* the product is positive.
2. If the *number of negative signs is odd,* the product is negative.
3. If one of the factors is 0, the product is 0.

Examples:
$$(-2)(-2)=+4$$
$$(-2)(-2)(-2)=-8$$
$$(3)(-2)(-2)=+12$$
$$(3)(2)(-2)=-12$$

Division. Division is the inverse operation to multiplication. We learned in arithmetic that

$$8\div 2=4$$
$$8\times \tfrac{1}{2}=4.$$

Thus, we could change a division problem into multiplication.

We call $\frac{1}{2}$ the reciprocal of 2. The reciprocal, or *multiplicative inverse,* of a number is the value that will give a product of 1 when multiplied by that number. In the following examples, each of the numbers to the left of the equal sign is the multiplicative inverse of the other:

$$2\times \tfrac{1}{2}=1$$
$$3\times \tfrac{1}{3}=1$$
$$\tfrac{7}{4}\times \tfrac{4}{7}=1$$

Since a division problem may be changed into a multiplication problem, the method of obtaining the sign of the answer in division (quotient) must be the same as that used in multiplication.

To find the quotient of two signed numbers, find the quotient of the absolute values of the numbers. Then:
1. If the dividend and divisor have *like signs,* the quotient is positive.
2. If they have *unlike signs,* the quotient is negative.
3. Zero divided by any signed number is zero.
4. Division by zero is undefined.

Examples:
$$(+12)\div(+3)=+4$$
$$(-18)\div(-2)=+9$$
$$(-27)\div(+3)=-9$$
$$(+15)\div(-30)=-\tfrac{1}{2}$$
$$(0)\div(2)=0$$
$$2\div 0=\text{undefined}$$

MULTIPLYING AND DIVIDING SIGNED NUMBERS

- $+\cdot+=+$
- $-\cdot-=+$
- $+\cdot-=-$
- $-\cdot+=-$

- $+\div+=+$
- $-\div-=+$
- $+\div-=-$
- $-\div+=-$

Numerical Evaluation

A collection of algebraic symbols holding a place for a number is called an *algebraic expression.* If you find the numerical value of an algebraic expression when values are assigned to various letters, then you have *evaluated the expression.* This process is particularly useful in evaluating formulas. For example, at an average rate r, in time t an automobile will travel a distance d, as expressed by the formula

$$d=rt.$$

If $r=80$ km/h and $t=4$h,

then $d=(80)(4)=320$ km.

Letters such as those in the formula above are used to represent unspecified numbers and are called *variables.*

Many formulas also have *constants,* which are expressed by numbers or special symbols. For example, in the formula for finding the circumference of a circle,

$$C=2\pi r,$$

"2" and π are constants; r and C are variables.

If you substitute numbers for the variables, the expression may be evaluated. In the expression

$$b+7=?$$

when $b=1$, the answer is 8; when $b=2$, the answer is 9; and so on.

To evaluate $2a+3b$ when $a=4$ and $b=-2$, replace a by 4 and b by -2.

$$2a+3b=?$$
$$2(4)+3(-2)=?$$
$$8\;\;6=2$$

Recall that writing two letters or a number and a letter together without any sign means that they are to be multiplied together. Thus xy means x is to be multiplied by y, and $3x$ means x is to be multiplied by 3.

When a number represented by a symbol is to be multiplied by itself, it is customary to write x^2 instead of xx. Similarly, x^3 stands for xxx, y^7 stands for the product of seven y's, and 3^2 means 3(3), or 9. When a number is multiplied by itself, the product is called a power of that number. Thus, x^2 is called the second power of x, or x squared; x^3 is the third power of x, or x cubed; x^4 is the fourth power of x; x^5 is the fifth power of x, and so on. The number that is multiplied by itself is the *base,* and the superscript, which indicates the power, is called the *exponent.*

An exponent applies only to the base that precedes it. Thus, xy^2 means xyy, and $2x^3y$ means $2xxxy$. If two or more bases are to be raised to the same power, they are placed in parentheses, and the superscript is placed outside. Thus, $a(bc)^2$ means $a(bc)(bc)$, or ab^2c^2.

$$a^2=a\cdot a$$
$$ab^2=a\cdot b\cdot b$$
$$(ab)^2=a\cdot b\cdot a\cdot b=a^2b^2$$

Examples: To evaluate $8a^2$ when $a = -3$, replace a by -3:

$$8(-3)^2 = 8(9) = 72$$

To evaluate $-2a^3b$ when $a = -1$ and $b = 3$, replace a by -1 and b by 3:

$$-2(-1)^3(3) = -2(-1)(3) = 6$$

To evaluate $5x(yz)^2$ when $x = -2$, $y = 4$ and $z = 2$, replace x by -2, y by 4, and z by 2:

$$\begin{aligned} &5(-2)(4 \times 2)^2 \\ &= 5(-2)(8)^2 \\ &= 5(-2)(64) \\ &= -640 \end{aligned}$$

Order of Operations

In the expression $7 + 3 \times 4$, no grouping symbols are present. Therefore the expression could be interpreted in more than one way. It might mean

$$(7+3) \times 4 = 10 \times 4 = 40$$

or $$7 + (3 \times 4) = 7 + 12 = 19.$$

This ambiguity is clearly undesirable. To prevent any confusion when evaluating expressions, always use the following order in performing operations:

1. Perform operations included within signs of grouping, such as parentheses or fraction lines, first.
2. Compute all indicated powers.
3. Compute all other multiplication operations and any division operations in the order they occur, from left to right.
4. Perform additions and subtractions last, in any order.

Following this order in evaluating $3a^2$ when $a = 5$, the power (25) is evaluated first and then multiplied by 3, producing the result, 75. In evaluating $a + 2b$ when $a = 5$ and $b = 6$, the multiplication of 2 by 6 is performed before adding the 5, producing 17.

Example: To evaluate $2\pi r(r + h) + 3h$, when $\pi = \frac{22}{7}$, $r = 7$, and $h = 2$, substitute the numbers for the letters:

$$2(\tfrac{22}{7})(7)(7+2) + 3(2)$$

Perform the operations in parentheses first:

$$2(\tfrac{22}{7})(7)(9) + 3(2)$$

Multiply and divide next:

$$396 + 6$$

Finally, add or subtract. The result is 402.

Algebraic Expressions

A *term* is an algebraic expression whose parts are not separated by + or − signs. For example, $3x$, abc, $2x^2$, and -10 are called terms. An expression containing one term, such as

$$xy,\ y,\ 2x,\ 5x^2y^3, \text{ or } -17x^2b,$$

is called a *monomial.* An expression containing two terms, such as

$$2x + 1,\ 3a + 5b, \text{ or } a^2 + b^2,$$

is called a *binomial.* An expression containing three terms, such as

$$a + b + c, \text{ or } y^2 + 4x - 3,$$

is called a *trinomial.*

An algebraic expression that is formed by two or more terms is called a *polynomial.* Thus, the above binomials and trinomials are also polynomials.

The numbers that are multiplied together to form a term are called the *factors.* The factors of the term $7x^2y$ are 7, x^2, y. Other factors are $7x$, $7x^2$, xy, x^2y, $7y$, and so on. (Any factor may be considered as an exact divisor of the total value of the expression.)

The numerical factor of a term is called the *numerical coefficient* of that term. In $-7x^2y$, -7 is the numerical coefficient. In c^3d^2, the numerical coefficient is not written but is understood to be 1.

The factors of a term that consist of letters form the *literal factors* of the term. In $-7x^2y$, x^2y is the literal factor.

Like terms are terms that have the same literal (letter) factors. Thus, $5x^2y$, $-3x^2y$, and $+\frac{1}{2}x^2y$ are like terms.

Unlike terms are terms that do not have the same literal factors. Thus, $-2a$, $5b$, 5, $7x^2$, $6x$, $2x^2y$, and $2xy^2$ are unlike terms. Note that literal factors are unlike unless both the letters and the exponents associated with each of them are exactly the same.

Addition. Like terms may be combined by making use of the properties for operations on numbers. For example,

$$-3xy + 5xy$$

can, by the associative property of multiplication, be changed to

$$(-3 + 5)xy$$

Thus, $$-3xy + 5xy = 2xy$$

Like terms may be combined by combining their numerical coefficients and multiplying the result by their common literal factor.

Examples:

$$\begin{array}{r} +\ a \\ (+)-7a \\ \hline -6a \end{array} \qquad \begin{array}{r} +7x^2y \\ -2x^2y \\ (+)-3x^2y \\ \hline 2x^2y \end{array} \qquad \begin{array}{r} -4c^2 \\ +7c^2 \\ (+)-2c^2 \\ \hline c^2 \end{array}$$

Since like terms can be combined, two or more polynomials can be added by arranging them so that their like terms are in vertical columns; the like terms in each column can then be combined.

Example: To add the polynomials $3x^2 - 2xy + 4y^2$, $5y^2 - x^2$, and $-5xy + 3x^2 + 3$, arrange like terms in vertical columns and add:

$$\begin{array}{rrrr} 3x^2 & -2xy & +4y^2 & \\ -x^2 & & +5y^2 & \\ +3x^2 & -5xy & & +3 \\ \hline 5x^2 & -7xy & +9y^2 & +3 \end{array}$$

Subtraction. Subtracting a quantity is equivalent to adding the additive inverse of that quantity. Thus, polynomials may be subtracted by arranging them so that like terms are in vertical columns, changing the signs of the terms in the polynomial to be subtracted (thus obtaining its additive inverse), and then combining like terms.

Example: To subtract $-5b + 2a + 4c$ from $3a + 7b$, arrange like terms in columns:

$$\begin{array}{r} 3a + 7b \\ \underline{(-)2a - 5b + 4c} \end{array}$$

Then write the additive inverse of the expression to be subtracted (change its signs) and add:

$$\begin{array}{rrr} 3a & +\ 7b & \\ -2a & +\ 5b & -4c \\ \hline a & +12b & -4c \end{array}$$

These expressions may also be written in horizontal form, as follows:

$$(3a + 7b) - (+2a - 5b + 4c)$$

The parentheses are used to make it easy to see which terms are being subtracted.

$$\begin{aligned} &(3a + 7b) - (+2a - 5b + 4c) \\ &= (3a + 7b) - 2a + 5b - 4c \\ &= 3a - 2a + 7b + 5b - 4c \\ &= a + 12b - 4c \end{aligned}$$

Notice that the parentheses were removed before the solution could be reached. This requires further discussion. *If an expression inside a parentheses that is preceded by a "−" sign contains more than one term, the sign of each term is changed when the expression is written without the parentheses.*

Thus, $-(a + b - c) = -a - b + c$

In effect, the whole expression is being multiplied by -1.

Sometimes one set of grouping symbols occurs within another. When this happens, remove the grouping symbols, one set at a time, beginning with the innermost set.

$$\begin{aligned}-[-2n-(n-4)] &= -[-2n-n+4]\\ &= +2n+n-4\\ &= +3n-4\end{aligned}$$

Multiplication. To multiply $+13a$ by $-2b$, the expression may be rewritten as $(+13)(-2)(ab)$ by the application of the commutative and associative properties for multiplication. Hence, the product is $-26ab$.

Comparing the last result with the original factors shows that a short way to obtain the product of two monomials is to multiply their coefficients and then multiply this product by the product of their literal factors.

Thus, $(-3x^2)(-2y) = +6x^2y$.

Sometimes the two monomials to be multiplied contain powers of the same base, as in the case of $(3a^2)(5a^4)$. Since $(3a^2)(5a^4)$ means $(3aa)(5aaaa)$, which is $15aaaaaa$, or $15a^6$, it can be seen that powers of the same base can be multiplied by adding the exponents. If a literal term has no exponent, the exponent is understood to be 1.

Thus, $(x^3)(x) = x^4$

Examples:

$$(+2a^3b^2)(-7a^2b^7) = -14a^5b^9$$

$$c^3(5c^2d) = 5c^5d$$

$$3xy^3(-4x^2y^2) = -12x^3y^5$$

Repeated multiplication of monomials may occur when raising a monomial to a power. Thus,

$$\begin{aligned}(2x^2)^4 &= (2x^2)(2x^2)(2x^2)(2x^2)\\ &= 16x^8\end{aligned}$$

Note that when taking a power of a power, the exponents are multiplied.

To multiply a polynomial by a monomial, as in $2x(3x^2 - y + 5)$, the distributive property requires that each term of the polynomial be multiplied by the monomial. The product is the sum for all the resulting terms. For example:

$$\begin{aligned}&2x(3x^2-y+5)\\ &6x^3-2xy+10x\end{aligned}$$

Another illustration:

$$\begin{aligned}&-2a^2(2+4ab+7b^2)\\ &-4a^2-8a^3b-14a^2b^2\end{aligned}$$

The distributive property is also used to multiply two binomials. For example:

$$\begin{aligned}&(3x-5y)(2x+3y)\\ &= 3x(2x+3y)-5y(2x+3y)\\ &= (3x)(2x)+(3x)(3y)-(5y)(2x)\\ &\qquad -(5y)(3y)\\ &= 6x^2+9xy-10xy-15y^2\\ &= 6x^2-xy-15y^2\end{aligned}$$

In general, to multiply two polynomials, multiply each term of the one polynomial by each term of the other polynomial and add the resulting terms.

In practice, this operation may be carried out by arranging the two expressions vertically and carrying out operations as you would with large numbers in arithmetic. Procedures may be carried out from left to right, as here, or from right to left. Like terms in the partial products should be lined up under each other.

$$\begin{array}{r}5a-3b\\ \underline{2a-4b}\\ 10a^2-6ab\qquad\\ \underline{-20ab+12b^2}\\ 10a^2-26ab+12b^2\end{array}$$

A simpler way to arrange for multiplication of binomials is to note that the first and third term of our product above are products of the first terms and second terms of the factors. The middle term of the product is the sum of the *cross-products:*

$$(5a-3b)(2a-4b)$$

$$-6ab$$

$$-20ab$$

$$10a^2-26ab+12b^2$$

Division. Division may be seen as simplifying a fraction. To simplify

$$\frac{-16a^5}{2a^3}$$

note that $-16 \div 2 = -8$. Also, $a^5 \div a^3 = a^2$.

So, $$\frac{-16a^5}{2a^3} = -8a^2$$

The numerical procedure is the same if the problem is considered as a conventional division problem. To do

$$-16a^5 \div 2a^3$$

change $2a^3$ to its multiplicative inverse, $\frac{1}{2a^3}$, and multiply:

$$-16a^5 \times \frac{1}{2a^3} = \frac{-16a^5}{2a^3} = -8a^2$$

PROVING AN ALGEBRA FORMULA WITH GEOMETRY

We have learned that

$$(a+b)^2 = a^2 + 2ab + b^2$$

and learned the algebraic procedure for multiplying binomials algebraically. We can see what is happening if we imagine a square whose side measures a + b.

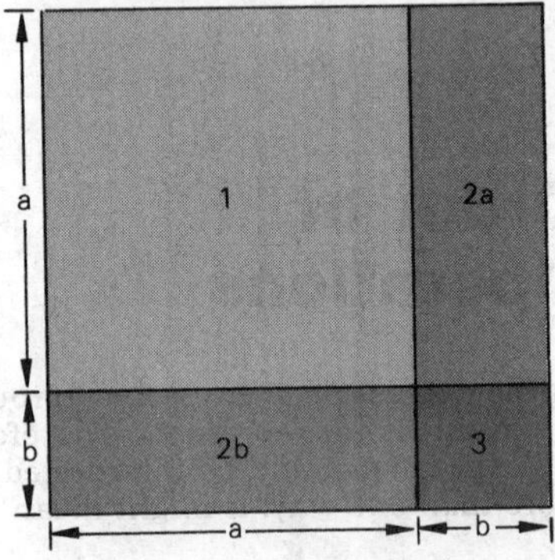

The formula for finding the area of the square, is

$$A = s^2$$

In our case, this is the same as

$$A = (a+b)^2$$

But we can also see that the area could be measured if we knew the sum of the areas of the four smaller quadrilaterals marked off by the dotted lines and numbered. The region marked 1 is a square with sides of a. So

$$A_1 = a^2$$

The regions marked 2a and 2b are rectangles with the same measurement-length of a and width of b. The area of one rectangle equals ab, and the two together equal 2(ab). So

$$A_2 = 2ab$$

The region marked 3 is a square with sides of b, so

$$A_3 = b^2$$

Altogether the area of the large square $(a + b)$ must be equal to $A_1 + A_2 + A_3$. Combining these, we get

$$A = a^2 + 2ab + b^2$$

So $(a + b)^2 = a^2 + 2ab + b^2$

Note that when a term with an exponent is divided by a like term with an exponent, the exponents are subtracted. In the example above,

$$a^5 \div a^3 = a^{5-3} = a^2$$

The same procedure is followed when dividing a polynomial by a monomial, except that each term of the polynomial must be divided separately. For example:

$$\frac{5x^3 - 10x^2 - 15x}{5x}$$

$$= x^2 - 2x - 3$$

The result of each problem may be checked by multiplying the quotient and the divisor. The product should be equal to the dividend. To check the example above,

$$(5x)(x^2 - 2x - 3)$$
$$= 5x^3 - 10x^2 - 15x$$

A polynomial may also be divided by another polynomial in a manner similar to that used in long division in arithmetic, as shown:

$$\begin{array}{r} x+2 \\ 2x-1\overline{)2x^2+3x-3} \\ \underline{2x^2-x} \\ 4x-3 \\ \underline{4x-2} \\ -1 \end{array}$$

1. Divide $2x^2$ by x.
2. Write x in the quotient.
3. Multiply x by $2x-1$.
4. Write the product under the dividend.
5. Subtract (signs change).
6. Repeat the process.

As in arithmetic, there is often a remainder. The remainder may be expressed as the numerator of a fraction in which the divisor is the denominator. In the example above, the full quotient can be expressed as

$$x + 2 + \frac{-1}{2x-1}$$

or $$x + 2 - \frac{1}{2x-1}$$

Before dividing two polynomials, both must be in descending powers of the variable, and no powers from the highest power down to the constant term can be skipped. For example,

$$\frac{x^3 + 4 + 4x}{x+2}$$

must be written and solved as follows:

$$\begin{array}{r} x^2-2x+8 \\ x+2\overline{)x^3+0x^2+4x+4} \\ \underline{x^3+2x^2} \\ -2x^2+4x \\ \underline{-2x^2-4x} \\ 8x+4 \\ \underline{8x+16} \\ -12 \end{array}$$

Factoring Polynomials

It is often useful in algebra to be able to break an expression into its factors. For example, expressions with exponents are difficult to evaluate; often the evaluation is simpler if the expression is rewritten as a group of factors with lower exponents.

$$x^2 + 4x + 3$$

is equal to the product of

$$(x+1)(x+3)$$

Breaking expressions down in this way is called *factoring*. The procedures are similar to those dealing with fractions in arithmetic.

One method of factoring is called the ***greatest common factor*** method. The greatest common factor (GCF) of two or more monomials is the common factor with the greatest numerical factor and the greatest degree. For example, to factor $10x^2$, $6x$, and $4x^3$, proceed as in arithmetic.

$$\begin{aligned} 10x^2 &= \boxed{2} \cdot 5 \cdot \boxed{x} \cdot x \\ 6x &= \boxed{2} \cdot 3 \cdot \boxed{x} \\ 4x^3 &= \boxed{2} \cdot 2 \cdot \boxed{x} \cdot x \cdot x \end{aligned}$$

The common factors are circled. Their product is $2x$, which is the GCF.

This procedure, along with the distributive property, is useful when finding the factors of binomials and trinomials. For example, to write $12x^2 + 8x$ in factored form, use the distributive property in the form $ab + ac = a(b + c)$. Then use the GCF as one of the factors. The remaining expression (in this case, a binomial) is the other factor.

$$12x^2 + 8x = 4x(3x) + 4x(2)$$
$$= 4x(3x + 2)$$

We have already seen how to multiply binomials by multiplying their first and second terms and using the sums of the cross-products as the middle term:

$$(x+1)(x+3)$$

x

$3x$

$$x^2 + 4x + 3$$

The resulting trinomial in this example is *quadratic;* it has one term in the second power and none in a higher power.

To factor a quadratic trinomial, the procedure is reversed. For example, to find the factors of

$$x^2 + 5x - 24$$

look for two binomial factors such that the product of their first term is x^2.

$$(x \quad)(x \quad)$$

The product of the last terms of the binomial must equal −24. But −24 has many factors:

3 and −8	2 and −12
−3 and 8	−2 and 12
4 and −6	1 and −24
−4 and 6	−1 and 24

The factors that will satisfy this situation must *add* to +5 so that the cross-products will add to $+5x$, the middle term of the trinomial. A look at the table above shows that −3 and 8 will do this.

So the factors of the trinomial are $(x-3)$ and $(x+8)$. To check, multiply these binomials; the result should be the original quadratic trinomial.

$$(x-3)(x+8)$$
$$= x^2 + 5x - 24$$

If the squared term of a trinomial is negative and the constant is positive, the expression may be arranged in ascending order, although it is possible to factor if they are arranged in descending order. For example, to factor

$$56 - b^2 - b,$$

rearrange in ascending order of exponents.

$$56 - b - b^2$$
$$= (8 + b)(7 - b)$$

The trinomial *must* be in ascending or descending order, however.

Sometimes a quadratic trinomial has two equal factors:

$$x^2 - 6x + 9$$
$$= (x-3)(x-3)$$

This may also be written as $(x-3)^2$.

Not all quadratic trinomials are factorable by this method. For example, $x^2 + 4x + 2$ cannot be factored to give two factors with coefficients that are whole numbers. The first term, x^2, requires that x be the first term of each binomial. The last term, 2, can be written only as the product of 2 and 1. But $(x+2)(x+1)$ does not equal $x^2 + 4x + 2$, since its middle term is $3x$ instead of $4x$. (The factors involve fractions, so the solution cannot be found by sight.)

Products of sums and differences. If the binomials $(x+3)$ and $(x-3)$, which represent the sum and difference, respectively, of the terms x and 3, are multiplied together, a quadratic without a middle term results because the cross-products add to zero:

$$(x+3)(x-3)$$

$+3x$

$-3x$

$$x^2-9$$

The resulting quadratic is the difference of the squares of the two original terms. *When binomials representing the sum and difference of two terms are multiplied, the product is always the difference of their squares.*

Examples:

$$(x-5)(x+5)=x^2-25$$

$$(2x+3y)(2x-3y)=4x^2-9y^2$$

$$(2-x)(2+x)=4-x^2$$

Since multiplication of the sum and difference of two terms will produce an expression that is the difference of their squares, factoring an expression that is the difference of two squares should change it back to the product of two binomials that are the sum and difference of the squared terms. For example:

$$x^2-9=(x+3)(x-3)$$

$$4y^2-1=(2y+1)(2y-1)$$

$$49a^2-36b^2=(7a+6b)(7a-6b)$$

In the previous examples, trinomials like $x^2-12x-45$ and $a^2+2a-35$ all had coefficients of the x^2 term equal to 1.

Consider $16x^2-11x-5$. The coefficient of x^2 is not 1. To factor $16x^2-11x-5$, it is necessary to consider factors of both 16 and −5.

Factors of 16	*Factors of −5*
$2\cdot 8$	$1\cdot(-5)$
$4\cdot 4$	$-1\cdot(5)$
$16\cdot 1$	

The possible factors are as follows:

Possible factors	*Sums of cross-products*
$(2x+1)(8x-5)$	$-10x+8x=-2x$
$(4x+1)(4x-5)$	$-20x+4x=-16x$
$(x+1)(16x-5)$	$-5x+16x=11x$
$(2x-1)(8x+5)$	$10x-8x=2x$
$(4x-1)(4x+5)$	$20x-4x=16x$
$(x-1)(16x+5)$	$5x-16x=-11x$

Only the last possibility produces the correct middle term, $-11x$. So

$$16x^2-11x-5$$
$$=(x-1)(16x+5)$$

Here is a summary of the steps for factoring trinomials:

1. List all combinations of factors of the first term in the trinomial.
2. List all combinations of factors of the last term of the trinomial. These factors must be arranged in all possible combinations with the first terms.
3. Select combination(s) in which the sum of the cross-products will give the second term of the trinomial.
4. Insert proper signs.
5. Check by multiplying the factors.

Complete factoring. In factoring an expression, the highest common monomial factor should be removed first. The resulting factor may be a factorable quadratic trinomial or a difference of two squares. If it is one of these, it may be replaced by two binomial factors by factoring again. In other words, factoring should be continued until prime factors (factors that cannot be factored further) are obtained.

In factoring $12x^2+14x-10$, the highest common monomial factor is 2, giving $2(6x^2+7x-5)$. But $6x^2+7x-5$ is also factorable, giving $(3x+5)$ and $(2x-1)$. So the factors of the original expression are 2, $(3x+5)$, and $(2x-1)$.

To factor $4a^3+48a-28a^2$, rearrange in descending order of exponents, factor the highest common monomial, and then factor the quadratic trinomial as follows:

$$4a^3-28a^2+48a$$
$$=4a(a^2-7a+12)$$
$$=4a(a-4)(a-3)$$

First-Degree Equations

One of the most powerful tools of mathematics is the *equation.* Equations are often used in solving problems in daily life. To translate a situation in real life into an equation, begin by choosing a variable and giving it meaning.

A plane is flying from San Francisco to Los Angeles. Normal flight time is 45 minutes. If the plane is 21 minutes from San Francisco, how many minutes is it from Los Angeles?

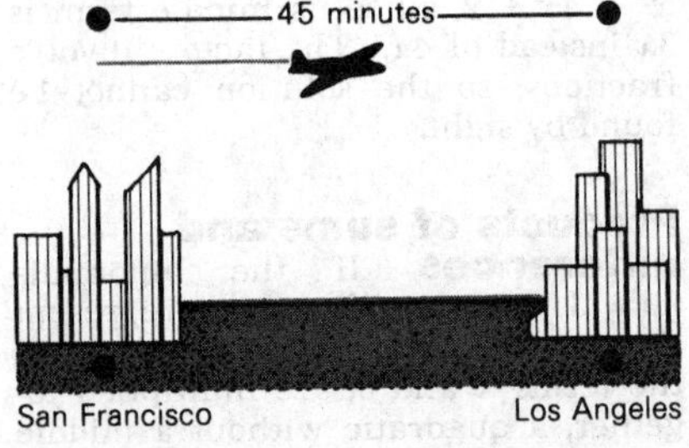

This problem is easy enough to solve by simple arithmetic. But putting it in algebraic language helps to clarify it. Let x be the number of minutes from Los Angeles. Then $x+21$ is the total flight time. Thus,

$$x+21=45$$

is a mathematical representation of the problem. You might also reason that if x is the time left to fly, $x=45-21$. Either way, the answer is that the plane is 24 minutes from Los Angeles. Statements such as $x+21=45$ are called *equations.* An equation is a kind of sentence in which the symbols to the left of the equal sign are equal to the symbols to the right of it.

An equation can be thought of as a sentence in which the equal sign is a verb. Just as sentences in English may be true or false, so can sentences in algebra. It is usually not difficult to decide whether a sentence dealing with numbers is true or false.

$$7\times 2=14$$
$$7+2=9$$
$$7\div 2=3\tfrac{1}{2}$$
$$7-2=4$$

The first, second, and third sentences are true and the fourth sentence is false. The symbol ≠ (read "is not equal to") can be used to make the fourth sentence true.

$$7-2\neq 4$$

The expression $x+21=45$ is called an *open sentence.* It is neither true nor false until we know what value x is holding. The quantity x is often referred to as an unknown. When the number is found that makes $x+21=45$ a true statement, the equation is solved.

The number 24 is called the *solution set.* The most important thing about an equation is its solution set. Thus, the following definition is necessary in order to classify all equations with the same solution set.

Definition. *Two equations that have the same solution are equivalent equations.*

This definition is very useful. If we begin with a true equation, we may find many ways to modify both sides of the equation in order to put it in a form in which we can easily solve it.

Properties of Equations

There are two basic properties of equations.

1. *An equation remains equal if equal quantities are added to or subtracted from both sides.*

If $a = b$

then $a + c = b + c$

Also, if $a = b$

then $a - c = b - c$

It happens that we can use this property to solve the equation

$$x + 21 = 45$$

If we subtract 21 from (add −21 to) both sides of the equation, we get

$$x + 21 - 21 = 45 - 21$$
$$x = 24$$

This new equation has the same solution as the earlier one. The two equations are different ways of saying the same thing.

This property of equations—that equal quantities may be added or subtracted—is called the *addition property of equality.* The property can be used more than once. For example, to solve for x in

$$10x - 2 - 7x = 4 + 2x$$

first combine like terms:

$$3x - 2 = 4 + 2x$$

Then subtract $2x$ from both sides (this will make x disappear from the right side of the equation):

$$3x - 2x - 2 = 4 + 2x - 2x$$
$$x - 2 = 4$$

Add 2 to each side to obtain the solution:

$$x - 2 + 2 = 4 + 2$$
$$x = 6$$

In order to check your solution, substitute it in the original equation:

$$10x - 2 - 7x = 4 + 2x$$
$$10(6) - 2 - 7(6) = 4 + 2(6)$$
$$60 - 2 - 42 = 4 + 12$$
$$16 = 16$$

The equation is true where $x = 6$. This may not be the only solution, however. Certain equations may have a few or even a great number of solutions.

2. *An equation remains equal if both sides are divided or multiplied by an equal quantity.*

If $a = b$

then $\frac{a}{c} = \frac{b}{c}$

This property has one important exception. It is not true where $c = 0$. (Division by 0 is undefined.)

Consider the equation

$$2x = 12$$

It can be solved by dividing both sides by 2:

$$\frac{2x}{2} = \frac{12}{2}$$

$$x = 6$$

Since we wanted x alone, it was necessary to divide both sides of the equation by 2. To check, substitute the solution in the original equation:

$$2x = 12$$
$$2(6) = 12$$
$$12 = 12$$

Applying this second property to multiplication,

if $a = b$

then $ac = bc$

Consider the equation

$$\frac{a}{4} = 5$$

It can be solved by multiplying both sides of the equation by 4:

$$4 \cdot \frac{a}{4} = 4 \cdot 5$$

$$a = 20$$

To check, substitute the solution in the original equation:

$$\frac{20}{4} = 5$$

$$5 = 5$$

These properties of equations make it possible to solve equations with one unknown when the unknown is not raised to a power. Equations of this kind are called *first-degree equations.*

To solve a given equation, any one of the following steps may be appropriate. There is no specific order in which they are to be applied.

Step 1. Use the distributive property to separate the terms, if needed, and simplify both sides of the equation as much as possible.

Step 2. Use the addition property of equality to get all terms containing the variable on one side and all constant terms on the other.

Step 3. Combine like terms in each member.

Step 4. Use the multiplication or division properties for equations to get the unknown by itself on one side.

Step 5. Check by substituting the solution for the unknown.

The following are examples of equations requiring more than one step.

$$8x - 4 = 12$$

Add 4 to each side:

$$8x - 4 + 4 = 12 + 4$$
$$8x = 16$$

Divide each side by 8:

$$\frac{8x}{8} = \frac{16}{8}$$

$$x = 2$$

Check:
$$8(2) - 4 = 12$$
$$16 - 4 = 12$$
$$12 = 12$$

In the next example, the unknown appears on both sides of the equation.

$$6x = 18 - 3x$$

Since it is best to have the unknown appear on only one side, add $3x$ to each side:

$$6x + 3x = 18 - 3x + 3x$$
$$9x = 18$$

Divide both sides by 9:

$$\frac{9x}{9} = \frac{18}{9}$$

$$x = 2$$

The last example requires simplification before the equation properties can be used.

$$4(x - 3) = 2(x + 1)$$

Multiply on both sides:

$$4x - 12 = 2x + 2$$

Subtract $2x$ from both sides and add 12 to both sides:

$$4x - 2x - 12 + 12 = 2x - 2x + 2 + 12$$
$$2x = 14$$

Divide both sides by 2:

$$\frac{2x}{2} = \frac{14}{2}$$

$$x = 7$$

PROBLEM SOLVING. In order to solve problems algebraically, it is first necessary to translate or change English words and phrases into mathematical expressions. In spoken or written language there are many ways to say the same thing, but mathematical language must be very precise. Here are some common English words and their mathematical translations.

English	Algebra
A number	x
A number plus 2 A number increased by 2 2 more than a number	$x + 2$
A number minus 2 A number decreased by 2 A number less 2 2 less than a number	$x - 2$
The sum of x and y	$x + y$
The difference of x and y	$x - y$
The quotient of x and y	$\frac{x}{y}$
The product of x and y	$x \cdot y$ or xy
of	· (multiply)
is	= (equals)
2 times a number A number multiplied by 2 The product of 2 and a number	$2x$
A number divided by 2 One-half of a number The quotient of a number and 2	$\frac{x}{2}$

Here are some examples of English-to-algebra translations.

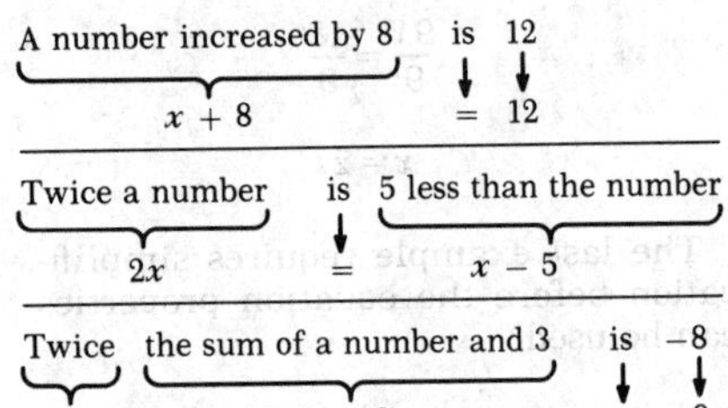

While the examples above all use x as the variable, it often helps in problem solving to use a letter for the variable that reminds you of the nature of the amount. For example, you may use n for number.

For a problem about a rectangle whose length is 3 meters more than its width, write the length as $w + 3$. Similarly, if the problem involves a time that is twice as many hours as an unknown time, the two times are t and $2t$.

Yvonne lost 12 pounds since she started her diet. Now she weighs 113 pounds. How much did she weigh before the diet?

Choose a variable to represent the single unknown number in the problem—the weight before Yvonne started the diet. Since this unknown is weight, w is a good choice. Then w is the unknown weight in pounds.

The first condition tells you how much Yvonne weighs now compared with how much she weighed before the diet. Her weight now is 12 pounds less than it was at the beginning of the diet. The new weight, according to the first condition, is $w - 12$ pounds.

The second condition is that her weight is now 113 pounds. The two ways of writing her weight in pounds after the diet are $w - 12$ and 113. These two different expressions represent the same number, so they are equal.

$$w - 12 = 113$$

Solving this equation gives the unknown number, w.

$$w = 113 + 12$$
$$w = 125$$

Therefore, Yvonne weighed 125 pounds before she started her diet.

Check: The first condition was that "Yvonne lost 12 pounds since she started her diet." If her original weight was 125 and her weight after the diet was 113, then this condition checks if $125 - 113 = 12$. Since it does, the first condition checks.

The second condition, that her weight is now 113 pounds, checks if $125 - 12 = 113$. Since $125 - 12$ *does* equal 113, that condition checks also.

This problem was very easy. You could probably solve it without using algebra at all. But it illustrates a method that can be used to solve much more difficult problems.

Here is another problem.

Larry paid $3.56 for two steaks at the supermarket. One steak cost 74¢ more than the other. How much did he pay for each?

For money problems, it is often easier to work with cents than with dollars. One condition in the problem is "one steak cost 74¢ more than the other." The second condition, which is stated first in this problem, is "Larry paid 356¢ for two steaks."

Call the cost in cents of the less expensive steak c. Then the first condition tells that the more expensive steak cost $c + 74$ cents.

The second condition could be reworded as "the cost of the less expensive steak plus the cost of the more expensive steak is 356¢." This condition gives an equation:

$$c + (c + 74) = 356.$$

Solving this equation gives the cost of the less expensive steak.

$$\begin{aligned} c + c + 74 &= 356 \\ 2c + 74 &= 356 \\ 2c &= 356 - 74 \\ 2c &= 282 \\ c &= 141 \end{aligned}$$

Thus, the less expensive steak cost $1.41. The more expensive steak was 74 cents more, or $2.15.

Check: From the first condition, one steak cost 74¢ more than the other. $1.41 + 74¢ = $2.15, so that condition checks.

The second condition is that the sum of the two costs is $3.56. Since $1.41 + $2.15 = $3.56, that condition is also fulfilled.

Measurement problems.

Measurement problems often involve the perimeter of a geometric figure, such as a rectangle or triangle. Remember that the perimeter is the sum of the sides. For a rectangle, the opposite sides are equal, so the perimeter is twice the length plus twice the width:

$$P = 2l + 2w$$

The length of a rectangle is 4 more inches than its width. The perimeter of the rectangle is 20 inches. What are the sides of the rectangle?

P = 20 in.   w

l = w + 4

WORD PROBLEMS

The following is a general procedure to use when solving word problems.

STEP 1. Read the problem carefully and determine what number or numbers need to be found.

STEP 2. Represent one unknown number by a suitable variable.

STEP 3. Use one condition stated in the problem to write an expression for a second number.

STEP 4. Use a second condition to find two expressions that are equal. Then write these two expressions algebraically and connect them with an equals sign.

STEP 5. Solve the equation.

STEP 6. Check to see if the resulting solution matches the conditions stated in the problem.

Use w for the width of the rectangle in inches. Then the condition that "the length of a rectangle is 4 more inches than its width" means that the length is $w + 4$.

The other condition is that the perimeter is 20 inches. From the formula, the perimeter is twice the length plus twice the width. Combining the conditions gives

$$20 = 2(w + 4) + 2w$$

which is more commonly written with the left and right sides reversed:

$$2(w + 4) + 2w = 20.$$

Solve the equation for w, the number of inches in the width.

$$\begin{aligned} 2(w + 4) + 2w &= 20 \\ 2w + 8 + 2w &= 20 \\ 4w + 8 &= 20 \\ 4w &= 20 - 8 \\ 4w &= 12 \\ w &= 3 \end{aligned}$$

Since $w = 3$, the width is 3 inches. The length is $w + 4$, or $3 + 4 = 7$ inches.

Check: The first condition is that "the length of a rectangle is 4 inches more than its width." Since 7 is 4 more than 3, that part of the problem checks.

The second condition is "the perimeter of the rectangle is 20 inches." From the formula,

$$\begin{aligned} P &= 2(7) + 2(3) \\ &= 14 + 6 \\ &= 20. \end{aligned}$$

The length of a rectangle is 8 more than twice the width. The perimeter is 88 feet. Find the length and width.

Let w be the width of the rectangle in feet. One condition from the problem tells you that the length of the rectangle is 8 more than twice w. This length is $2w + 8$. The second condition in the problem is that the perimeter is 88 feet. The perimeter equals twice the length plus twice the width, so both conditions can be expressed in an equation.

$$\begin{aligned} 2(2w + 8) + 2w &= 88 \\ 4w + 16 + 2w &= 88 \\ 6w + 16 &= 88 \\ 6w &= 88 - 16 \\ 6w &= 72 \\ w &= 12 \end{aligned}$$

Width of the rectangle: $w = 12$ feet.
Length of the rectangle:

$$\begin{aligned} 2w + 8 &= 2(12) + 8 \\ &= 24 + 8 \\ &= 32 \text{ feet.} \end{aligned}$$

Check: The first condition was "the length of a rectangle is 8 more than twice the width." Is 32 feet 8 more than twice 12 feet, or 8 more than 24? Yes, so that part checks.

The second condition is that "the perimeter is 88 feet." A rectangle whose length is 32 feet and whose width is 12 feet has a perimeter

$$\begin{aligned} P &= 2(32) + 2(12) \\ &= 64 + 24 \\ &= 88 \end{aligned}$$

One angle of a triangle is twice the smallest angle. The third angle is 30° more than the first angle. What are the sizes of the angles?

First, it is necessary to know an important fact about triangles: the sum of the three angles in any triangle is 180°.

This problem has three conditions. The first is that one angle is twice another. Call the number of degrees in the smaller angle d. Then the larger angle measures $2d$ degrees.

The second condition is that the third angle is 30° more than the first angle. Notice that the first angle referred to is identified in the problem as "one angle of a triangle." This is the *larger* of the first two angles and it measures $2d$ degrees. Therefore, the second condition tells that the third angle has a measure of $2d + 30°$.

The third condition is the hidden one: The sum of the angles is 180°. Putting the three conditions together means that one side of the equation shows the sum of the degree measures of the three angles, while the other side is 180.

$$\begin{aligned} d + 2d + (2d + 30) &= 180 \\ d + 2d + 2d + 30 &= 180 \\ 5d + 30 &= 180 \\ 5d &= 180 - 30 \\ 5d &= 150 \\ d &= 30 \end{aligned}$$

The solution of the equation tells that the smallest angle is 30°. Then the first angle is 2(30) degrees, or 60°. Finally, the third angle measures 60° + 30°, or 90°.

Check:
Condition 1: $2(30) = 60$.
Condition 2: $60 + 30 = 90$.
Condition 3: $30 + 60 + 90 = 180$.

Lever problems.

A lever is a simple machine that can be used to reduce a force by increasing a distance. Essentially, a lever is a long bar that is rotated about a point called the *fulcrum.* Long ago, Archimedes worked out the rule by which a lever works: When a lever is in balance, the product of the distance from the fulcrum to where the force is applied is the same for both sides of the lever. A seesaw is a type of lever. The point where the seesaw is suspended is the fulcrum.

The law of the lever can be written as an equation. The force can be thought of as a weight in pounds, a commonly used force in any case. Capitals are used for the weight and distance on one side of the fulcrum and lower-case letters are used for the weight and distance on the other side.

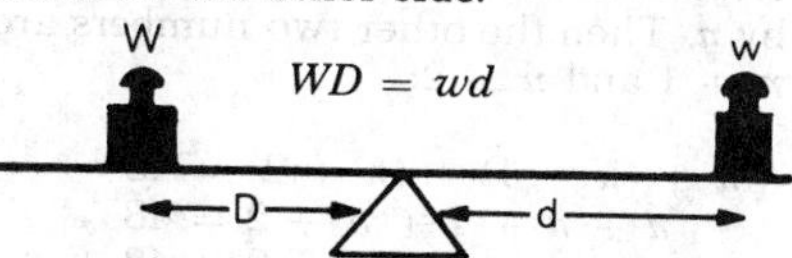

Fred, who weighs 70 pounds, is sitting 4 feet from the fulcrum on a seesaw. Kathy, who weighs 50 pounds, is on the other side. How far from the fulcrum should Kathy sit to balance Fred?

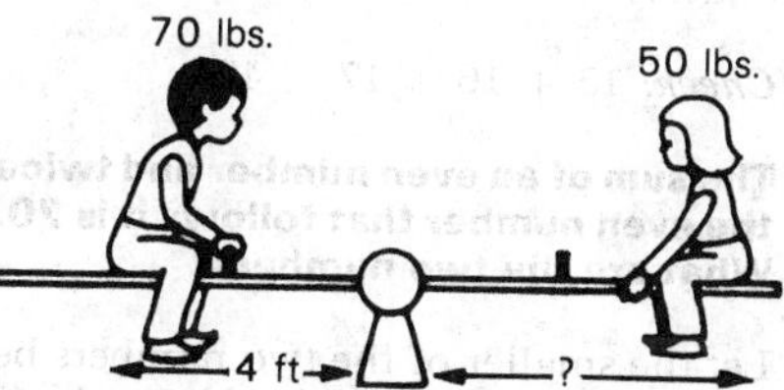

From the law of the lever, we know that the product of Fred's weight and distance from the fulcrum equals the product of Kathy's weight and distance. We know Fred's weight and distance, but we only know Kathy's weight. Substituting into the equation for the law of the lever gives

$$\begin{aligned} 70(4) &= 50d \\ 280 &= 50d \\ 5.6 &= d. \end{aligned}$$

Kathy should be 5.6 feet from the fulcrum to balance the seesaw.

Check: $70 \cdot 4 = 50 \cdot 5.6$
$280 = 280.$

Number problems.

Many problems involve the relationship between two numbers.

One of two numbers is three times as large as the other. Their sum is 16. What are the two numbers?

The two conditions are easy to spot. Let n be the smaller number. Then the larger number is $3n$. From the other conditions, the sum is 16, so the equation is

$$\begin{aligned} n + 3n &= 16 \\ 4n &= 16 \\ n &= 4. \end{aligned}$$

The smaller number is 4 and the larger is 12.

Check: $4 + 12 = 16.$

Often number problems involve successive (also called consecutive) numbers or successive odd or even numbers. Successive numbers are counting numbers that come one right after the other, such as 4, 5, and 6 or 109, 110, 111.

Three successive numbers have a sum of 48. What are the numbers?

Represent the smallest of the numbers by n. Then the other two numbers are $n + 1$ and $n + 2$.

$$n + (n + 1) + (n + 2) = 48$$
$$n + n + 1 + n + 2 = 48$$
$$3n + 3 = 48$$
$$3n = 48 - 3$$
$$3n = 45$$
$$n = 15$$

The smallest of the three successive numbers is 15, so the other two are 16 and 17.

Check: $15 + 16 + 17 = 48$.

The sum of an even number and twice the even number that follows it is 70. What are the two numbers?

Let the smaller of the two numbers be n. Even numbers (and odd numbers, too) are two units apart, not just one, so the even number that follows n is $n + 2$. Twice this number is $2(n + 2)$.

$$n + 2(n + 2) = 70$$
$$n + 2n + 4 = 70$$
$$3n + 4 = 70$$
$$3n = 70 - 4$$
$$3n = 66$$
$$n = 22$$

The smaller number is 22, so the next even number is 24.

Check: $22 + 2(24) = 22 + 48 = 70$.

Age problems.

Age problems are puzzles that would be difficult to solve without algebra.

Sally's mother is four times as old as Sally. In four years Sally's mother will only be three times as old as Sally. What are their ages now?

It is usually a good idea to choose the smallest number in a problem as the variable, so let s be Sally's age. Her mother's age now is $4s$. In four years, Sally's age will be $s + 4$, while her mother's age will be $4s + 4$. The other condition of the problem says that after four years Sally's mother will be three times as old as Sally. The equation represents the situation then.

$$4s + 4 = 3(s + 4)$$
$$4s + 4 = 3s + 12$$
$$4s = 3s + 12 - 4$$
$$4s = 3s + 8$$
$$4s - 3s = 8$$
$$s = 8$$

Sally is 8 and her mother 32 at the beginning of the problem. Four years later, Sally is 12 and her mother is 36.

Check: $36 = 3(12)$.

Coin and stamp problems.

Problems that involve coins usually require that you know the common values of the coins. Often the problem is given in numbers of different kinds of coins. To solve the problem, write an equation in terms of the monetary values involved instead of the numbers of coins. Stamp problems are similar.

? quarters + ? dimes = $9.90

Emma had four times as many quarters as dimes. She had $9.90 in all. How many quarters and how many dimes did she have?

It is easiest in algebraic expressions to work in whole numbers, so translate $9.90 to 990¢. The value of a dime is 10¢, so the value of n dimes in cents is $10n$.

A quarter is worth 25¢. There are four times as many quarters as dimes in this problem. If there are n dimes, there are $4n$ quarters. So the value of all the quarters in cents is $25(4n)$.

	dimes	quarters
number	n	$4n$
value	$10n$	$25(4n)$

The sum of the two values is 990 in cents, so the following equation expresses the problem:

$$10n + 25(4n) = 990.$$

Solving the equation for n will give the number of dimes.

$$10n + 25(4n) = 990$$
$$10n + 100n = 990$$
$$110n = 990$$
$$n = \frac{990}{110}$$
$$n = 9$$

Number of dimes: $n = 9$.
Number of quarters: $4n = 4(9) = 36$.

Check: "Emma had four times as many quarters as dimes." According to the solution, Emma had 36 quarters and 9 dimes. Is 36 the same as 4 times 9? Yes, so the first part of the problem checks.

"She had $9.90 in all." According to the solution, Emma had 9 dimes, or 90¢. She had 36 quarters, which is 36 × 25, or 900, cents. In terms of dollars, she had 90¢ in dimes and $9 in quarters. Adding, 90¢ + $9 = $9.90 The second part of the problem also checks.

Capacity problems.

Problems that involve two different-sized containers are called "capacity problems," although they may use different weights or some other measure.

A truck that can haul 5 tons at a time and one that can haul 10 tons at a time are used to move ore from a mine to a smelter. The smaller truck can make three trips for every two that the larger one makes. How many trips in all will it take the two trucks working together to move 70 tons of ore?

In each trip, the smaller truck moves 5 tons, so the amount of ore it moves in n trips can be represented by $5n$. One trip by the larger truck, then, moves $10n$ of ore in n trips. For every three trips by the smaller truck, the larger one makes two, so the larger truck makes only two-thirds as many trips in a given amount of time. To move 70 tons of ore, then

$$5n + 10(\tfrac{2}{3}n) = 70.$$

Multiply both sides by 3 to clear the fraction.

$$15n + 10(2n) = 210$$
$$15n + 20n = 210$$
$$35n = 210$$
$$n = 6$$

The smaller truck makes six trips, while the larger one makes $\frac{2}{3}(6)$, or four, trips.

Check: In six trips the smaller truck carries 6(5) or 30 tons of ore. In four trips, the larger truck carries 4(10) of 40 tons of ore. Together they carry 30 + 40 = 70 tons.

Mixture problems.

These problems typically involve two substances that have different prices or different amounts of some nutrient. The problem is to mix the two substances in the right proportions.

A grocer has two kinds of candy, one selling for $1.20 a pound and the other selling for $1.80 a pound. He wants to sell a mixture of the two for $1.60 a pound. How much of each kind should he use to make 60 pounds of the mixture?

Start by assigning the value of the necessary number of pounds, n, of the cheaper candy at $120n$ cents. The number of pounds of the more expensive candy must be $60 - n$. Therefore, the value of the more expensive candy in cents is $180(60 - n)$. The total value of the mixture in cents is to be $160(60)$.

$$120n + 180(60 - n) = 160(60)$$
$$120n + 10{,}800 - 180n = 9600$$

You can simplify your arithmetic by dividing each term of the equation by 10.

$$\begin{aligned} 12n + 1080 - 18n &= 960 \\ 12n - 18n &= 960 - 1080 \\ -6n &= -120 \\ n &= 20 \end{aligned}$$

This means that you need 20 pounds of the cheaper candy and 60 − 20, or 40, pounds of the more expensive candy.

Check: The cost of 20 pounds of the cheaper candy is \$24. The cost of 40 pounds of the more expensive candy is \$72. Therefore, the total cost of the mixture is \$96. If 60 pounds of the mixture cost \$96, then it is selling for \$1.60 —\$96 divided by 60—a pound.

Time-rate-distance problems. Often these problems are the most difficult for a beginner in algebra to solve. Yet, they are not really much more difficult than the other problems. The key is usually recognizing that the *time* is the same for both moving bodies in the problem.

Two cars that are 630 miles apart travel toward each other at different rates. One travels 55 miles an hour, while the other travels 50 miles an hour. If they both leave at noon, when will they meet?

As noted, the key to solving this is to recognize that although the cars will travel different distances, when they meet they will have traveled the same amount of time, which can be called t hours. In t hours, the faster car will travel $55t$ miles while the slower car will travel $50t$ miles. The total distance that both cars will travel is 630 miles. Therefore,

$$\begin{aligned} 55t + 50t &= 630 \\ 105t &= 630 \\ t &= 6 \text{ hours.} \end{aligned}$$

Since each car will travel for 6 hours, they will meet at 6:00 P.M.

Check: The faster car travels 330 miles and the slower car travels 300 miles. 330 + 300 = 630.

Linear Inequalities

A statement like $x > 5$ is called an inequality. Inequalities use the following signs:

$>$ = is greater than
$\geq$ = is equal to or greater than
$<$ = is less than
$\leq$ = is equal to or less than

Inequalities are solved by a method similar to the one used in solving equations. The only real difference between the methods is in the multiplication property for inequalities and in graphing the solution set.

Many different numerals could replace x in $x > 5$. Actually, any one of a set of numbers could be used. It would be the set of all real numbers greater than 5. In symbols, this is stated as $\{x \mid x > 5\}$, or the set of all x such that x is greater than 5. This set may be graphed on the number line. To graph this set, simply draw a number line and extend an arrow beginning at 5 and pointing to the right.

−2 −1 0 +1 +2 +3 +4 +5 +6 +7

Notice that an open circle must be drawn at 5, since it is not included in the solution set.

Consider the graph for the solution set of $x \leq 3$.

The solution set of $x \leq 3$ is an infinite set.

$\{x \mid \; x \leq 3\}$

−5 −4 −3 −2 −1 0 +1 +2 +3 +4 +5

Any number that is less than or equal to 3 makes $x \leq 3$ true. Thus, the graph includes 3 and all points to the left. Notice that the circle has been shaded to show that 3 is included in the solution set. Open circles are always used on graphs of solution sets with < or > and closed (shaded) circles are used on the graphs of solution sets with ≤ or ≥.

The inequality $2 < 5$ is a true statement. If −3 is added to both sides of the inequality, the following result is obtained:

$$\begin{aligned} (-3) + 2 &< 5 + (-3) \\ -1 &< 2 \end{aligned}$$

which is also a true statement. This example suggests the following *addition property for inequalities,* which is the same as that for equations: *Adding (subtracting) the same quantity to both sides of an inequality never changes the solution set.*

Another property used in solving inequalities is the *multiplicative property for inequalities multiplying both sides of an inequality by a positive quantity never changes the solution set.*

Notice the difference from the multiplicative property of equations. An equation may be multiplied by any number, positive or negative. In inequalities, however, *when multiplying both sides by a negative number,* you must change the direction of the inequality sign.

In symbolic form, this property may be stated as follows:

Let a, b, and c represent any numbers. If $a > b$ then $ac > bc$ if c is positive and $ac < bc$ if c is negative.

For example:
$$\begin{aligned} 4 + 3 &< 9 \\ 5(4+3) &< 5 \cdot 9 \\ 20 + 15 &< 45 \\ 35 &< 45 \end{aligned}$$

but
$$\begin{aligned} 4 + 3 &< 9 \\ -5(4+3) &> -5 \cdot 9 \\ -20 - 15 &> -45 \\ -35 &> -45 \end{aligned}$$

This procedure is true of algebraic expressions as well as numbers.

Fractions

In arithmetic, fractions are simplified by making use of the principle that the numerator and denominator of a fraction may be divided by any nonzero quantity without changing the value of the fraction.

Algebraic fractions are reduced by making use of the same principle. The value of any algebraic fraction is unchanged if the numerator and denominator are both divided by the same nonzero quantity; in order to divide, the quantity must be a factor of both numerator and denominator. For example:

To simplify $\dfrac{-4xy^3}{10xy^2}$

divide numerator and denominator by $2xy^2$. Find the common factors:

$$\begin{aligned} -4xy^3 &= \textcircled{2} \; -2 \; \textcircled{x} \; \textcircled{y} \; \textcircled{y} \; y \\ 10xy^2 &= \textcircled{2} \; 5 \; \textcircled{x} \; \textcircled{y} \; \textcircled{y} \end{aligned}$$

The product of the common factors, $2xy^2$, becomes the divisor:

$$\frac{-4xy^2 \div 2xy^2}{10xy^2 \div 2xy^2} = \frac{-2y}{5}$$

An easier procedure is to identify the uncircled factors in the table above.

Division by zero is undefined, but the above solution need not be qualified by adding that $x \neq 0$ and $y \neq 0$. Since the original fraction contains x

and y as factors of its denominator, we may assume they do not equal zero.

If the numerator or denominator of an algebraic fraction is a polynomial, it is usually necessary to factor it first and then determine what factors may be divided into both numerator and denominator. For example:

To simplify $\dfrac{3x-6}{9x-18}$

factor numerator and denominator

$$\frac{3(x-2)}{9(x-2)}$$

and divide both numerator and denominator by 3 and $(x-2)$. The result, in simplest form, is $\frac{1}{3}$. Notice that x cannot equal 2, since this would result in division by 0; $x \neq 2$, because the original fraction would be undefined if it did.

To simplify $\dfrac{x^2+2x}{x^2-3x-10}$

factor numerator and denominator

$$\frac{x(x+2)}{(x-5)(x+2)}$$

Divide numerator and denominator by $(x+2)$:

$$\frac{x}{x-5}$$

Signs of Fractions

Every fraction may be considered to have three signs: the sign of the numerator, the sign of the denominator, and the sign of the fraction itself. The possible combinations of these signs can be divided into two categories.

Zero or two (−) signs	**One or three (−) signs**
$+\frac{+a}{+b}=+\left(+\frac{a}{b}\right)=\frac{a}{b}$	$+\frac{-a}{+b}=+\left(-\frac{a}{b}\right)=-\frac{a}{b}$
$+\frac{-a}{-b}=+\left(+\frac{a}{b}\right)=\frac{a}{b}$	$+\frac{+a}{-b}=+\left(-\frac{a}{b}\right)=-\frac{a}{b}$
$-\frac{-a}{+b}=-\left(-\frac{a}{b}\right)=\frac{a}{b}$	$-\frac{+a}{+b}=-\left(+\frac{a}{b}\right)=-\frac{a}{b}$
$-\frac{+a}{-b}=-\left(-\frac{a}{b}\right)=\frac{a}{b}$	$-\frac{-a}{-b}=-\left(+\frac{a}{b}\right)=-\frac{a}{b}$

These fractions illustrate the principle that *any two of the signs of a fraction may be changed without changing the value of the fraction.*

It is sometimes necessary to employ the above principle to change the signs of a fraction in order to facilitate reducing the fraction or performing other operations with it.

Accordingly, in simplifying the expression

$$\frac{25-5x}{x^2-25}$$

factoring produces the form

$$\frac{5(5-x)}{(x-5)(x+5)}$$

In this form, there is no common factor to divide both numerator and denominator. By changing two signs, such as the signs of the fraction and of its numerator, this fraction becomes

$$-\frac{5(x-5)}{(x-5)(x+5)}$$

which can be simplified to

$$-\frac{5}{x+5}$$

It should be emphasized at this point that in a case such as

$$\frac{3(x+2)}{2(2+x)}$$

it is not necessary to make any sign changes in order to reduce to $\frac{3}{2}$, since $x+2$ and $2+x$ are the same except for the fact that their terms happen to be written down in different order. They are equal by the commutative property for addition.

Operations on Fractions

Multiplication. In arithmetic, fractions are multiplied by multiplying their numerators together to form the numerator of the product and multiplying their denominators together to form the denominator of the product. For example:

$$\frac{2}{5}\cdot\frac{3}{7}=\frac{6}{35}$$

Algebraic fractions are multiplied in exactly the same way. As in arithmetic, like factors in the numerators and denominators may be "canceled," that is, divided out by applying the principle that the numerator and denominator may be divided by the same nonzero number without changing the value of the fraction.

Example: To multiply

$$\frac{10x^2y}{3}\cdot\frac{2y}{5x}$$

divide numerator and denominator by $5x$, with the result:

$$\frac{2xy}{3}\cdot\frac{2y}{1}$$

Multiply numerators together and denominators together for the answer:

$$\frac{4xy^2}{3}$$

If an integral expression is to be multiplied by a fraction, it is helpful to think of it as having the denominator 1.

Example: To multiply

$$2x\cdot\frac{3y}{x^2}$$

write $2x$ with the denominator 1:

$$\frac{2x}{1}\cdot\frac{3y}{x^2}$$

Divide numerator and denominator by x:

$$\frac{2}{1}\cdot\frac{3y}{x}$$

Multiply numerators together and denominators together, with the result:

$$\frac{6y}{x}$$

If, in fractions to be multiplied, the numerator or denominator or both are polynomials, it is advisable to factor them first. This makes it easy to simplify by dividing numerator and denominator by the factors that appear in both.

Example: To multiply

$$\frac{x^2-16}{x}\cdot\frac{2x}{3x-12}$$

factor: $\dfrac{(x-4)(x+4)}{x}\cdot\dfrac{2x}{3(x-4)}$

Divide numerator and denominator by x and by $(x-4)$:

$$\frac{x+4}{1}\cdot\frac{2}{3}$$

Multiply numerators together and denominators together:

$$\frac{2(x+4)}{3} \text{ or } \frac{2x+8}{3}$$

Division. In arithmetic, the division example $\frac{3}{4}\div\frac{7}{5}$ is performed by changing the divisor to its multiplicative inverse and then multiplying.

Thus $\frac{3}{4} \div \frac{7}{5}$ becomes $\frac{3}{4} \cdot \frac{5}{7}$, or $\frac{15}{28}$. The multiplicative inverse, or reciprocal, of a number is formed by inverting the number.

Algebraic fractions can also be divided by multiplying by the multiplicative inverse, or reciprocal, of the fraction that is the divisor.

Example: To divide

$$\frac{3x^3}{6} \div \frac{x^2}{9}$$

change to multiplication by replacing the divisor with its multiplicative inverse:

$$\frac{3x^3}{6} \cdot \frac{9}{x^2}$$

Divide numerator and denominator by 3 and x^2:

$$\frac{x}{2} \cdot \frac{9}{1}$$

Multiply numerators together and denominators together:

$$\frac{9x}{2}$$

Numerators and denominators that are polynomials should be factored to make it possible to reduce the answer.

Example: To divide

$$\frac{x^2-4x-21}{3x+6} \div \frac{x-3}{x+2}$$

factor and change to multiplication by replacing the divisor with its multiplicative inverse:

$$\frac{(x-7)(x+3)}{3(x+2)} \cdot \frac{x+2}{x-3}$$

Divide numerator and denominator by $(x + 2)$:

$$\frac{(x-7)(x+3)}{3} \cdot \frac{1}{x-3}$$

Write the products of numerators and denominators to give the respective numerator and denominator of the answer:

$$\frac{(x-7)(x+3)}{3(x-3)}$$

Addition and subtraction. In arithmetic, if fractions have the same denominator, they are added or subtracted by adding or subtracting their numerators and placing the result over their common denominator. Thus, $\frac{2}{5} + \frac{1}{5} = \frac{3}{5}$.

Algebraic fractions that have the same denominator are added and subtracted (combined) in the same way.

Example: To combine

$$\frac{2}{x-2} + \frac{1}{x-2} - \frac{5x}{x-2}$$

add and subtract the numerators and place the sum over the common denominator:

$$\frac{2+1-5x}{x-2}$$

Combine like terms:

$$\frac{3-5x}{x-2}$$

In arithmetic, when fractions do not have the same denominators, they must first be changed to equivalent fractions having the same denominators before they can be added or subtracted. Such equivalent fractions are obtained by multiplying the numerator and denominator of each fraction by some nonzero number so selected that the multiplication will produce the common denominator in each.

Algebraic fractions can also be added or subtracted by converting them to equivalent fractions with a common denominator that is divisible by each of the original denominators.

Example: To combine

$$\frac{5}{2x^2y} - \frac{2}{3xy} + \frac{4}{x^2}$$

the common denominator must be divisible by $2x^2y$, $3xy$, and x^2. The lowest common denominator is $6x^2y$. Note that each literal factor appears in the lowest common denominator raised to the highest power to which it appears in any individual denominator. The denominator of the first fraction, $2x^2y$, must be multiplied by 3 to convert it to the common denominator, $6x^2y$. Therefore, its numerator, 5, must also be multiplied by 3 to keep the value of the fraction unchanged. Similarly, the second fraction must be multiplied by $2x/2x$, and the third by $6y/6y$. Thus, the example becomes

$$\frac{5(3)}{2x^2y(3)} - \frac{2(2x)}{3xy(2x)} + \frac{4(6y)}{x^2(6y)}$$

Then, after multiplying

$$\frac{15}{6x^2y} - \frac{4x}{6x^2y} + \frac{24y}{6x^2y}$$

and combining the numerators over the common denominator, we obtain

$$\frac{15-4x+24y}{6x^2y}$$

It is sometimes necessary to change two of the signs in one fraction to convert it to a form with the same denominator as another.

Example: To combine

$$\frac{2}{x-2} + \frac{3}{2-x}$$

change the sign of the second fraction and the sign of its denominator:

$$\frac{2}{x-2} - \frac{3}{-2+x} \quad \text{or} \quad \frac{2}{x-2} - \frac{3}{x-2}$$

Combine the numerators over the common denominator:

$$\frac{2-3}{x-2}$$

Combine like terms:

$$\frac{-1}{x-2}$$

This answer may also be written as

$$\frac{1}{2-x}$$

by changing the signs of the numerator and denominator; this form has the advantage of having fewer minus signs.

In combining fractions with polynomial denominators, it is necessary to factor the denominators in order to discover the lowest common denominator.

Example: To combine

$$\frac{3}{y^2+7y+10} - \frac{2}{y^2-25}$$

first factor the denominators:

$$\frac{3}{(y+5)(y+2)} - \frac{2}{(y+5)(y-5)}$$

Since the lowest common denominator must be divisible by each of the original denominators, it must contain as factors all the factors in any one of the original denominators. In this case the lowest common denominator is $(y + 5)(y - 5)(y + 2)$. Therefore, change each fraction to an equivalent fraction with the common denominator:

$$\frac{3(y-5)}{(y+5)(y+2)(y-5)} - \frac{2(y+2)}{(y+5)(y-5)(y+2)}$$

Multiply in the numerators:

$$\frac{3y-15}{(y+5)(y+2)(y-5)} - \frac{2y+4}{(y+5)(y-5)(y+2)}$$

Combine the numerators over the common denominator:

$$\frac{3y-15-(2y+4)}{(y+5)(y-5)(y+2)}$$

Note how the parentheses preceded by the minus sign are used to ensure that the second fraction is subtracted from the first. To complete the operation, remove the parentheses:

$$\frac{3y-15-2y-4}{(y+5)(y-5)(y+2)}$$

Combine like terms:

$$\frac{y-19}{(y+5)(y-5)(y+2)}$$

Fractions with Equations

Sometimes equations contain algebraic fractions. When solving equations of this type, it is usually desirable to find first an equivalent equation that is free of fractions. This is done by multiplying each member of the equation by the lowest common denominator (LDC) of the fraction.

For example, $\frac{1}{2}$ and $\frac{1}{5}$ of a certain number equals 28. What is the number?

Let $x=$ the number

$\frac{x}{2}=\frac{1}{2}$ the number

$\frac{x}{5}=\frac{1}{5}$ the number

then, $\frac{x}{2}+\frac{x}{5}=28$

This is an example of an equation that must be cleared of fractions. To clear it, we multiply both sides of the equation by the LCD, in this case, 10:

$$10\left(\frac{x}{2}+\frac{x}{5}\right)=(28)\ 10$$

$$\frac{10x}{2}+\frac{10x}{5}=280$$

Simplify each fraction and solve for x:

$$5x+2x=280$$
$$7x=280$$
$$x=40$$

Check: $\frac{1}{2}$ of $40=20$
$\frac{1}{5}$ of $40=8$
Sum $=28$

If any fraction is multiplied by a number that contains the denominator of the fraction as a factor, the product will be integral. That is,

$$ab\cdot\frac{c}{b}=ac$$

This is the reason behind the rule that any equation may be cleared of fractions by multiplying by a common multiple of the denominators.

Notice how parentheses are used to show the multiplication. They are usually retained until the multiplication is completed.

Solve: $\frac{2x}{3}-\frac{5}{6}=\frac{x}{2}$

The LCD of all denominators is 6. So, multiply each member of the equation by 6:

$$6\left(\frac{2x}{3}-\frac{5}{6}\right)=\left(\frac{x}{2}\right)6$$

$$6\left(\frac{2x}{3}\right)+6\left(-\frac{5}{6}\right)=\left(\frac{x}{2}\right)6$$

Use the distributive property:

$$2(2x)+1(-5)=(x)3$$
$$4x-5=3x$$
$$x=5$$

Check: Substitute in original equation.

$$\frac{2(5)}{3}-\frac{5}{6}\overset{?}{=}\frac{(5)}{2}$$

$$\frac{10}{3}-\frac{5}{6}\overset{?}{=}\frac{5}{2}$$

$$\frac{20}{6}-\frac{5}{6}\overset{?}{=}\frac{15}{6}$$

$$\frac{15}{6}=\frac{15}{6}$$

Equations with polynomials in the numerator and/or denominator can be solved the same way. However, fractional equations cannot have denominators of 0. Therefore, all solutions should be checked when both sides of an equation are multiplied by an expression containing the variable.

Solve: $\frac{4}{m-3}-\frac{1}{m}=\frac{6}{m}$

Multiply each member by $m(m-3)$, the LCD:

$$m(m-3)\left(\frac{4}{m-3}\right)-m(m-3)\left(\frac{1}{m}\right)=m(m-3)\left(\frac{6}{m}\right)$$

$$\frac{m(m-3)(4)}{(m-3)}+\frac{-m(m-3)}{m}=\frac{m(m-3)(6)}{m}$$

Divide out like terms:

$$4m-(m-3)=6(m-3)$$
$$4m-m+3=6m-18$$
$$21=3m$$
$$7=m$$

Check: Substitute in original equation.

$$\frac{4}{7-3}-\frac{1}{7}\overset{?}{=}\frac{6}{7}$$

$$\frac{4}{4}-\frac{1}{7}\overset{?}{=}\frac{6}{7}$$

$$\frac{28}{28}-\frac{4}{28}\overset{?}{=}\frac{24}{28}$$

$$\frac{24}{28}=\frac{24}{28}$$

First-Degree Equations in Two Variables

The open sentence $2x+y=7$ contains two variables, x and y, each of which may be regarded as having a set of possible replacements, or a *domain.* The open sentence will be true or false when a pair of numbers—one for x and one for y—is substituted in the equation. Thus, if

$$x=2,\ y=3$$
$$2(2)+3=7$$

If

$$x=5,\ y=-3$$
$$2(5)-3=7$$

There are an infinite number of pairs of values of x and y that will make the sentence true. However, not all pairs of values of x and y make it true. If $x=2$ and $y=1$, for example, $2x+y\neq 7$.

When an open sentence contains two variables, a solution consists of a pair of numbers—one number for each variable. Furthermore, the pair of numbers causes the sentence to be true only if the numbers are substituted for the correct variables. For example, the pair $x=2$ and $y=3$ makes $2x+y=7$ a true sentence, but $x=3$ and $y=2$ does not. The pair of numbers in which $x=2$ and $y=3$ is represented by the notation (2,3), with the number representing x listed before that representing y. (Note that they are in alphabetical order.) Such number pairs as (2,3) are said to be *ordered pairs,* since any pair is different from the pair consisting of the same numbers with their order reversed. For example, (–5,2) represents the ordered pair in which $x=-5$ and $y=2$, whereas (2,–5) represents the ordered pair in which $x=2$ and $y=-5$.

The solution set of an open sentence

in two variables is a set of ordered pairs of numbers. Thus, in $2x + y = 7$, some of the ordered pairs in the solution set are (2,3), (1,5), (5,−3), ($2\frac{1}{2}$,2).

Finding Number Pairs

A good way to obtain some of the ordered pairs included in the solution set of an equation in two variables is to solve the equation for one variable in terms of the other. Then, by substituting arbitrarily selected values for the other variable, the corresponding values of the one solved for can be discovered. Thus, to get some of the ordered pairs in the solution set for $3x + y = 5$, transform the equation into $y = -3x + 5$ by subtracting $3x$ from each member. In this form, y is expressed in terms of x. Arbitrarily picking a value of x, say $x = 2$, gives $y = -3(2) + 5$, or $y = -1$, as the corresponding y value that will make the sentence true. If $x = 3$, $y = -3(3) + 5$, or $y = -4$. Therefore, (3,−4) is another ordered pair in the solution set of $3x + y = 5$. For convenience, the ordered pairs are often arranged in a table:

x	2	3	4	5
y	−1	−4	−7	−10

A more difficult example might involve more than one step in solving for one variable in terms of the other. To get ordered pairs for the solution set of

$$5x - 2y = 3$$

add $2y$ to each member:

$$5x = 2y + 3$$

Then add −3:

$$5x - 3 = 2y$$

Finally, divide both sides by 2

$$\frac{5x-3}{2} = y$$

The equation is now transformed so that it is solved for y in terms of x. Substituting arbitrarily selected values of x, the corresponding values of y are:

x	0	1	2	−7
y	$-\frac{3}{2}$	1	$\frac{7}{2}$	−19

Graphs of Ordered Pairs

The solution sets of sentences in two variables consist of ordered number pairs. These cannot be pictured on the number line, since the number line can show only numbers, and not number pairs.

In order to picture, or graph, ordered number pairs, we can represent them by points on a plane, such as the surface of a page of this book, instead of by points along a line. Each point of a plane representing a number pair is located with reference to two axes perpendicular to each other.

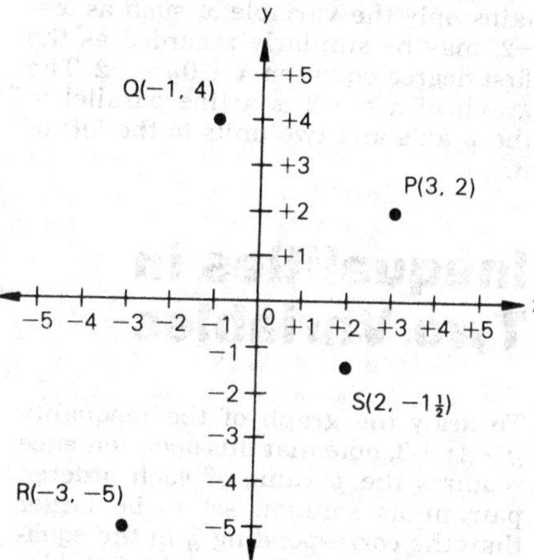

The horizontal axis—the x-axis—is a number line used to locate the first number in a number pair. The vertical axis—the y-axis—is another number line that is used to locate the second number in the number pair. The two axes, or number lines, intersect at their zero points, and this point of intersection, therefore, represents the point (0,0), which is called the *origin*. To locate a point representing some number pair, such as (3,2), count three units along the x-axis to the right of the origin (the positive direction for x), then up two units in a direction parallel to the y-axis (the positive direction for y). In the figure above, P is the point (3,2).

Negative values of x are counted off along the x-axis to the left of the origin and negative values of y are counted off in the descending direction parallel to the y-axis. Q is the point (−1,4), while R is the point (−3,−5), and S is the point (2,−$1\frac{1}{2}$).

The procedure for locating a point that represents an ordered number pair is similar to the method of locating a street corner by giving the number of the avenue and the number of the street that intersect there. It may also be compared to the method a navigator uses for locating a position by giving the longitude and latitude of that position.

Every ordered number pair represents one, and only one, point in the plane, and every point in the plane has one, and only one, ordered number pair corresponding to it. The pair of numbers that corresponds to a point are known as the *coordinates of the point*. Thus, (3,2) are the coordinates of P in the figure above. The x coordinate is called the *abscissa* of the point; the y coordinate is its *ordinate*. Hence, the abscissa of P is 3 and the ordinate is 2.

The method explained here for setting up a correspondence between ordered number pairs and the points in a plane is known as the *rectangular coordinate system* (because the axes are at right angles to each other). It is also called the *Cartesian coordinate system* in honor of the French mathematician René Descartes (1596–1650), who invented it. Other coordinate systems are used in more advanced mathematics.

Graphing First-Degree Equations

The solution set of the equation $y = 2x + 3$ is a set of ordered pairs. Some of them are shown in the following table:

x	−2	0	3
y	−1	3	9

If the points corresponding to these number pairs are located on a rectangular coordinate system, they will lie in a straight line.

In advanced mathematics it is proved that the points representing the solution set of any first-degree equation in two variables must lie in a straight line. Furthermore, all the points along the line will represent the ordered number pairs in the solution set. The graph of the solution set of $y = 2x + 3$ is the line in the graph below that passes through the three points whose coordinates are shown in the table.

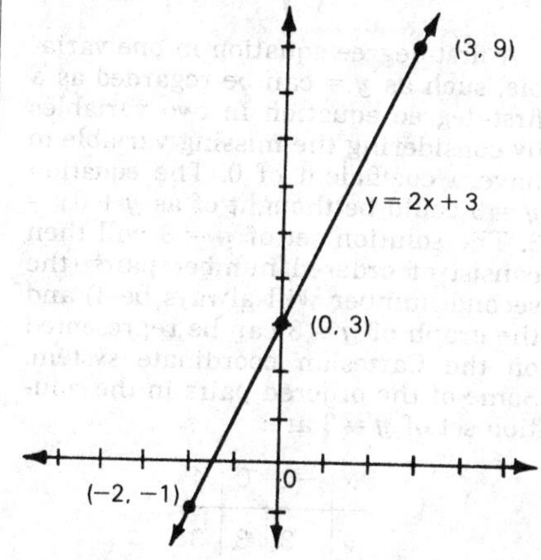

The graph includes all the points on the line—each representing an ordered pair in the solution set.

If any point whatsoever is now taken on the line, say $(\frac{1}{2},4)$, its coordinates will make the open sentence true: $4 = 2(\frac{1}{2}) + 3$.

To draw the graph of a first-degree equation, it is customary to plot at least three points on the Cartesian coordinate system. Two points will enable the line to be drawn, and the third point serves as a check on the accuracy of the first two. Accuracy in drawing the graph is improved if the points are not taken too close together. The coordinates of the three needed points are most easily obtained by solving the equation for one variable in terms of the other and then choosing arbitrary values for that other variable.

Example: For the graph of $4y - 3x + 4 = 0$, solve for y in terms of x:

$$4y = 3x - 4$$

$$y = \frac{3x}{4} - 1$$

Then let x take the arbitrary values -4, 0, and 4. The corresponding values for y are:

x	−4	0	4
y	−4	−1	2

Plotting these points and drawing the straight line determined by them gives the graph of this equation.

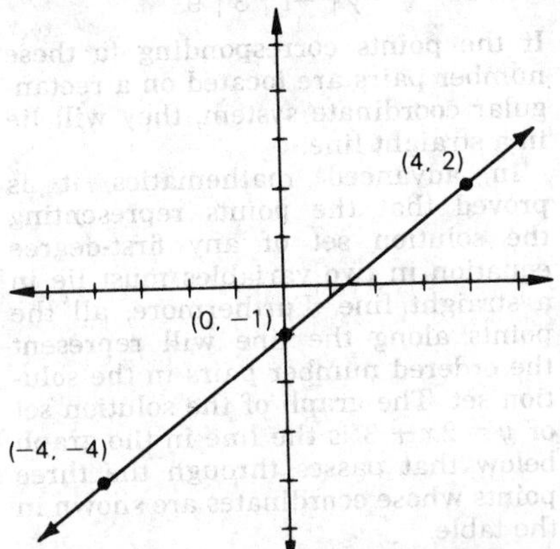

A first-degree equation in one variable, such as $y =$ can be regarded as a first-degree equation in two variables by considering the missing variable to have a coefficient of 0. The equation $y = 3$ could be thought of as $y + 0x = 3$. The solution set of $y = 3$ will then consist of ordered number pairs (the second number will always be 3) and the graph of $y = 3$ can be represented on the Cartesian coordinate system. Some of the ordered pairs in the solution set of $y = 3$ are:

x	−2	0	4
y	3	3	3

What this really means is that $y = 3$ no matter what value x assumes; hence the graph is a line parallel to the x-axis and three units above it.

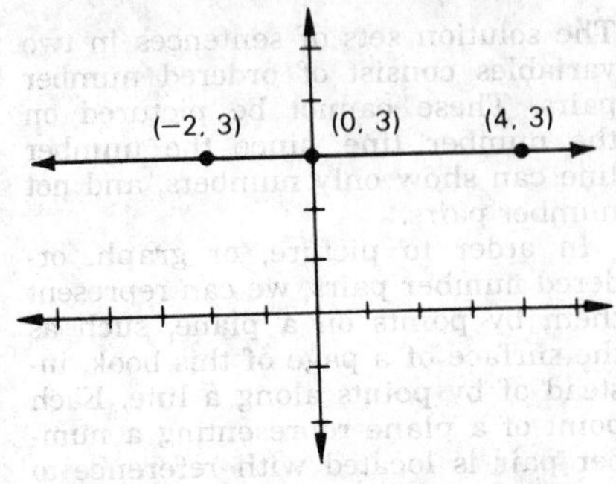

A first-degree equation that contains only the variable x, such as $x = -2$, may be similarly regarded as the first-degree equation $x + 0y = -2$. The graph of $x = -2$ is a line parallel to the y-axis and two units to the left of it.

Inequalities in Two Variables

To draw the graph of the inequality $y > 2x + 3$, note that this open sentence requires the y value of each ordered pair in its solution set to be larger than the corresponding y in the equation $y = 2x + 3$. The graph of the inequality $y > 2x + 3$, therefore, consists of all points in the plane above the line that represents the graph of $y = 2x + 3$. These points are shown in the shaded area below which is referred to as a *half-plane* since it extends indefinitely upward and to the left.

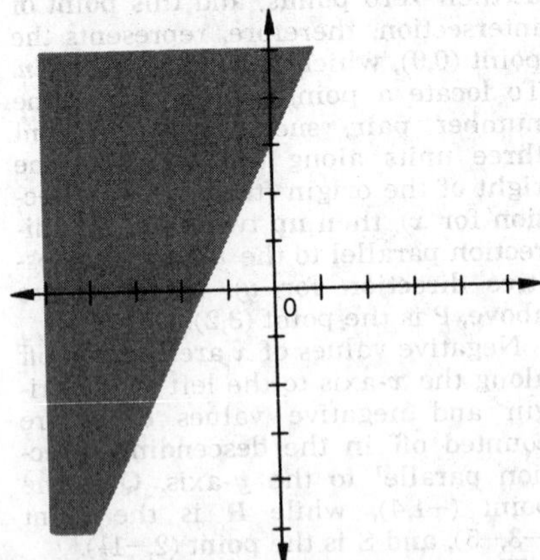

Systems of Equations

A group of two equations in which unknowns may be equal is called a *system of equations*. The equations in such a system are said to be *simultaneous*. The solution to a system of equations is an ordered pair that makes both equations true. One way to solve a system of equations is to graph both equations and find the coordinate of the point of intersection. For example, the graphs of $3x - y = 3$ and $x + y = 5$ are shown below.

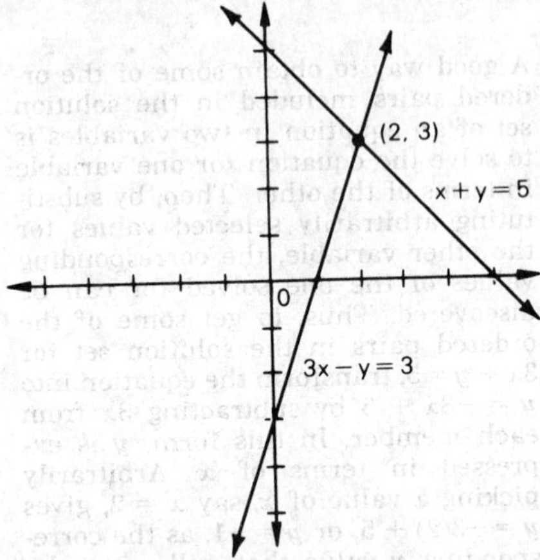

Notice that the graphs intersect at (2,3). Since this point lies on the graph of each equation, it is clear that (2,3) satisfies both $3x - y = 3$ and $x + y = 5$.

Graphical solutions of systems of equations are only approximate. Therefore, this method of solving systems of equations is practical only for integer solutions. We also solve systems of equations algebraically. The solutions obtained by such a method will not be approximations.

Solving by addition. Solving a system of equations by addition is one way solutions may be obtained algebraically. By the additive property of equations, one true equation may be added to another and the resulting equation will also be true. If the adding can be done so that one of the variables is eliminated, we can easily solve for the other. For example, in the system

$$3x + y = 5$$
$$x - y = 7$$

add the equations, like terms to like terms. The y's drop out, and the new equation is

$$4x = 12$$
$$x = 3$$

Now substitute this value of x in either of the two original equations (in this case the second, $x - y$, is easier to use):

$$3 - y = 7$$
$$-y = 7 - 3$$
$$y = -4$$

The common solution is $x = 3$, $y = -4$, or the number pair $(3,-4)$.

To check this solution, the number pair must be substituted in both original equations, since the fact that it checks in one does not guarantee that it will also check in the other.

Check:

$$3x+y=5 \qquad x-y=7$$
$$3(3)-4=5 \qquad 3-(-4)=7$$
$$9-4=5 \qquad 3+4=7$$
$$5=5 \qquad 7=7$$

The method of solving simultaneous equations by addition depends on eliminating one of the variables through adding. Adding two equations will eliminate one variable when the coefficients of that variable are additive inverses of one another; that is, are equal in absolute value but opposite in sign, as in the above equations ($+y$ and $-y$).

In the system

$$2a+b=3$$
$$2a-3b=-41$$

neither variable has coefficients in the two equations that are additive inverses of each other. However, this situation can be achieved by multiplying both members of the second equation by -1 and then adding the two equations:

$$2a+b=3$$
$$\underline{-2a+3b=41}$$
$$4b=44$$

Divide both members by 4:

$$b=11$$

Substitute 11 for b in the first equation and solve for a:

$$2a+11=3$$
$$2a=3-11$$
$$2a=-8$$
$$a=-4$$
$$a=-4 \qquad b=11$$

Check:

$$2a+b=3 \qquad 2a-3b=-41$$
$$2(-4)+11=3 \qquad 2(-4)-3(11)=-41$$
$$-8+11=3 \qquad -8-33=-41$$
$$3=3 \qquad -41=-41$$

In the system

$$3x+4y=18$$
$$5x-y=7$$

adding will not eliminate either variable. However, if the second equation is first multiplied by 4, adding will eliminate y, since its coefficients will then be additive inverses of each other: $+4y$ and $-4y$.

Multiply both members of the second equation by 4 and add:

$$3x+4y=18$$
$$\underline{20x-4y=28}$$
$$23x \quad =46$$

Divide both members by 23:

$$x=2$$

Substitute 2 for x in the second equation and solve for y:

$$5x-y=7$$
$$5(2)-y=7$$
$$10-y=7$$
$$-y=7-10$$
$$-y=-3$$
$$y=3$$
$$x=2 \qquad y=3$$

Check:

$$3x+4y=18 \qquad 5x-y=7$$
$$3(2)+4(3)=18 \qquad 5(2)-3=7$$
$$6+12=18 \qquad 10-3=7$$
$$18=18 \qquad 7=7$$

At times it is convenient to multiply both equations in a system by different nonzero constants in order to get the coefficient of one variable to be the additive inverse of the other. For example, the system

$$2x-3y=2$$
$$5x+4y=51$$

can be solved by multiplying the first equation by 4 and the second by 3 to make it possible to eliminate y by adding. Or the first equation can be multiplied by 5 and the second by -2 to cause the elimination of x by adding.

Before adding the equations in a system, you should transform them so that the terms containing the variables are on one side and the constant terms are on the other side. For example, to solve

$$5x=5-2y$$
$$3y=15-9x$$

change the equations to:

$$5x+2y=5$$
$$9x+3y=15$$

and proceed as before.

Solving by substitution.

In the system

$$x+3y=9$$
$$4x+5y=22$$

it is very easy to transform the first equation in order to have one variable—x in this case—expressed in terms of the other. By subtracting $3y$ from each side of the first equation, we obtain

$$x=9-3y$$

If this expression for x is substituted for x in the other equation, the resulting equation will contain only the variable y and will have in its solution set the ordered number pairs common to the solution sets of both original equations:

$$4x+5y=22$$
$$4(9-3y)+5y=22$$
$$36-12y+5y=22$$
$$-7y=22-36$$
$$-7y=-14$$
$$y=2$$

Now substitute 2 for y in the first equation and solve x as follows:

$$x=9-3y$$
$$x=9-3(2)$$
$$x=3$$
$$x=3 \qquad y=2$$

Check:

$$x+3y=9 \qquad 4x+5y=22$$
$$3+3(2)=9 \qquad 4(3)+5(2)=22$$
$$3+6=9 \qquad 12+10=22$$
$$9=9 \qquad 22=22$$

This method of solving a system of simultaneous equations is known as the method of substitution, because one variable was eliminated by substituting for it an expression in terms of the other variable.

The method of substitution may be used on any pair of simultaneous first-degree equations, but it is particularly convenient to use when one of the equations is in a form that expresses one variable in terms of the others. For example, in the system

$$a-14=2b$$
$$b=4a$$

the second equation gives b in terms of a. Substituting this expression for b in the first equation gives an easy solution for a.

PROBLEM SOLVING.

There are many problems that involve two unknown quantities. A single equation with two variables generally has an infinite number of solutions, with each solution a pair of numbers. Often, as in the algebra problems earlier in this section, one variable can easily be related to another, for example, when a rectangle is 3 units longer (l) than it is wide (w), you can write both amounts in terms of one variable, w. But it is often much easier to use one set of conditions to write one equation in both variables and another set of conditions to write a second equation in the same two variables.

If a problem has a single solution, the two equations, solved as a system, will reveal it. For example, if both equations are graphed on the same plane, the graphs will intersect in one point that is the single solution. Solving the system by addition or by substitution will also produce the solution.

Some examples of the different kinds of problems that can be solved using two variables start on the next page.

A plane travels 1080 miles in 6 hours when flying with the wind. On a return trip the same day, it travels 600 miles in 5 hours flying against the wind. Find the speed of the plane in still air and the speed of the wind.

Let x equal the speed of the plane in miles per hour when flying in still air and y equal the speed of the wind in miles per hour. The speed of the plane flying with the wind will be $x + y$, and the speed of the plane flying against the wind will be $x - y$.

	rate × *time* = *distance*
	(*mph*) (*h*) (*m*)
with wind	$(x + y) \times 6 = 1080$
against wind	$(x - y) \times 5 = 600$

Removing parentheses gives:

$$6x + 6y = 1080$$
$$5x - 5y = 600.$$

It is convenient to solve this system by dividing both members of the first equation by 6 and both members of the second equation by 5. The resulting equations show how far the plane flies in one hour with the wind and against the wind.

$$x + y = 180$$
$$x - y = 120$$

We can then add the equations and solve for x:

$$2x = 300$$
$$x = 150.$$

Substitute 150 for x and solve for y:

$$x + y = 180$$
$$150 + y = 180$$
$$y = 30$$

$x = 150$ $y = 30$
plane speed = 150 mph
wind speed = 30 mph.

Tickets to the concert sold for $1 for high-school students and $2.50 for adults. The total amount collected was $297.50. If 140 tickets were sold, how many students attended the concert?

One condition refers to the money involved, while the other condition is about the number of people attending. Let s be the number of students and a be the number of adults.

For the condition involving money, you can write the equation

$$100s + 250a = 29{,}750.$$

where the money amounts have all been changed to a number of cents.

For the condition involving numbers of people, the equation is

$$s + a = 140$$

so the system of equations is

$$100s + 250a = 29{,}750$$
$$s + a = 140.$$

This system can be simplified by dividing the terms of the first equation by 50. After dividing each term by 50, the system becomes

$$2s + 5a = 595$$
$$s + a = 140.$$

When there is a variable in one equation that has a coefficient of one, it is usually easier to solve by substitution. The problem asks for the number of students. Therefore, solve the second equation for a and substitute for a in the first equation.

$$a = 140 - s$$

Substituting gives

$$2s + 5(140 - s) = 595$$
$$2s + 700 - 5s = 595$$
$$2s - 5s = 595 - 700$$
$$-3s = -105$$
$$s = 35.$$

The solution is that 35 students attended the play.

Check: If 35 students attended, then 105 adults must have bought tickets. The 105 adults paid $262.50, while the 35 students paid $35.

$$\begin{array}{r} \$262.50 \\ +\ 35.00 \\ \hline \$297.50 \end{array}$$

Tanya was supposed to use five tins of punch concentrate and seven bottles of seltzer to make 87 cups of punch, but she made a mistake and used five bottles of seltzer and seven tins of concentrate. If she got 69 cups of punch, how many ounces are in a bottle of seltzer? (A punch cup holds 3 ounces.)

In this problem, you need to change cups to ounces, since the problem asks for a solution in ounces: 87 cups is 261 ounces, and 69 cups is 207 ounces.

Let c represent a tin of concentrate and s represent a bottle of seltzer. The correct mixture gives a condition that can be described by the equation

$$5c + 7s = 261.$$

Similarly, the second condition yields the equation

$$7c + 5s = 207.$$

The system, then, is

$$5c + 7s = 261$$
$$7c + 5s = 207.$$

To solve such a system, first multiply both equations by suitable numbers, that is, numbers chosen so that one variable can be eliminated by addition. For example, multiply the first equation by 7 and the second by −5.

$$35c + 49s = 1827$$
$$-35c - 25s = -1035$$

Adding the two equations in the new system gives

$$24s = 792.$$

Divide by 24.

$$s = 33$$

One bottle of seltzer contains 33 ounces.

Check: You need to know the size of a tin of concentrate to check. Return to one of the original equations to find out how many ounces there are in a tin of concentrate. Substitute 33 for the variable s.

$$7c + 5(33) = 207$$
$$7c + 165 = 207$$
$$7c = 207 - 165$$
$$7c = 42$$
$$c = 6$$

A tin of concentrate has 6 ounces. Now use the other equation as a check.

$$5c + 7s = 261$$
$$5(6) + 7(33) = 261$$
$$30 + 231 = 261$$
$$261 = 261$$

One kind of puzzle that can be solved with a system of equations is called a *digit problem.* Digit problems refer directly to the relationship between the digits in a numeral and the number represented by the numeral.

A two-digit number is formed from consecutive digits. The number itself is five times the sum of its digits. What is the number?

Since o looks rather like 0, to avoid confusion call the ones place the units place and use u for the variable for that place, with t as the variable for the tens place.

Remember that a digit in the tens place is worth ten times as much as one in the units place, so any two-digit number can be written as

$$10t + u$$

The first condition is that the number is formed from consecutive digits, so $u = t + 1$. The second condition is that the number is five times the sum of its digits, so

$$10t + u = 5(t + u).$$

Together these two equations form a system:

$$u = t + 1$$
$$10t + u = 5(t + u).$$

Completing the multiplication in the second equation gives

$$10t + u = 5t + 5u$$

or

$$5t - 4u = 0.$$

Substituting $u = t + 1$ into $5t - 4u = 0$ gives

$$5t - 4(t + 1) = 0$$
$$5t - 4t - 4 = 0$$
$$t = 4.$$

Therefore, one part of the solution is that the tens digit of the numeral is 4. Since the two digits are consecutive, the units digit must be 5, so the numeral is 45.

Check: The other condition is that the number is five times the sum of its digits. The sum of the digits is 9, and $5(9) = 45$.

Similar techniques can be used to solve equations with more than two variables.

Quadratic Equations

A *quadratic equation* is an equation that in simplest form contains the second power of the variable. Such an equation is also called a *second-degree equation.* The degree of a term is determined by the sum of the highest exponents of each variable in that term. For example, the degree of the equation $x + y = 4$ is 1; of $6x^3y^2 = 10$ it is 5; of $2x^2 + 5x = 8$ it is 2.

A quadratic equation such as

$$x^2 + 2x - 8 = 0$$

cannot be solved solely by the properties for first-degree equations. These properties provide no means for disposing of the x^2 term so that an equivalent equation with a single x on one side and a single number on the other can be obtained.

Solution by Factoring

The quadratic equation $x^2 + 2x - 8 = 0$ is in a form that suggests factoring the left member: $(x + 4)(x - 2) = 0$. In factored form, the equation represents a situation in which the product of two numbers is equal to zero. The product of two numbers can be zero if, and only if, one or both of the two numbers is zero. Thus, if $(x + 4)(x - 2) = 0$, either the factor $x + 4$ must equal 0, or the factor $x - 2$ must equal 0, or both must equal 0.

Thus, if the first factor, $x + 4$, equals 0, we have a first-degree equation $x + 4 = 0$, whose solution is $x = -4$. Setting the second factor, $x - 2$, equal to 0 gives another first-degree equation, $x - 2 = 0$, whose solution is $x = 2$. It happens that in this case both factors cannot equal 0 at the same time. Thus, the solution set of the original quadratic equation is (−4, 2). The equation, then, should be true where x equals either of the two solutions. The solutions of a quadratic equation are called its *roots.*

The complete solution and check for $x^2 + 2x - 8 = 0$ would be as follows:

$$x^2 + 2x - 8 = 0$$

Factor: $(x + 4)(x - 2) = 0$

Set each factor equal to 0:

$$x + 4 = 0 \qquad x - 2 = 0$$

Solve the resulting first-degree equations:

$$x = -4 \qquad x = +2$$

Check: For $x = -4$:

$$x^2 + 2x - 8 = 0$$
$$(-4)^2 + 2(-4) - 8 = 0$$
$$16 - 8 - 8 = 0$$
$$0 = 0$$

For $x = 2$:

$$x^2 + 2x - 8 = 0$$
$$(2)^2 + 2(2) - 8 = 0$$
$$4 + 4 - 8 = 0$$
$$0 = 0$$

Solving quadratic equations by factoring hinges on the fact that the product of the factors is zero. If the product of the factors is not zero, it is impossible to reach any conclusion concerning the value of the individual factors. For example, if the product of two factors is +12, one factor may be +6 and the other +2; one may be −6 and the other −2; or they may be 4 and 3, 12 and 1, 24 and ½, 36 and ⅓, or 18 and ⅔, and so on. For this reason, *all the nonzero terms of a quadratic equation must be brought together on one side of the equation.* For example, to solve $2x^2 + 5x = 3$, subtract 3 from both members:

$$2x^2 + 5x - 3 = 0$$

Factor: $(2x - 1)(x + 3) = 0$

Set each factor equal to 0:

$$2x - 1 = 0 \quad x + 3 = 0$$

Then solve the resulting first-degree equations:

$$2x = 1$$
$$x = \tfrac{1}{2} \qquad x = -3$$

Check: For $x = \frac{1}{2}$:

$$2x^2 + 5x = 3$$
$$2(\tfrac{1}{2})^2 + 5(\tfrac{1}{2}) = 3$$
$$\frac{1}{2} + \frac{5}{2} = 3$$
$$3 = 3$$

For $x = -3$:

$$2x^2 + 5x = 3$$
$$2(-3)^2 + 5(-3) = 3$$
$$2(9) + 5(-3) = 3$$
$$18 - 15 = 3$$
$$3 = 3$$

The procedure for solving a quadratic equation by factoring may make use of any one of the types of factoring. It may be necessary, for example, to factor the difference of two squares in order to solve. To solve $x^2 = 64$, subtract 64 from both members:

$$x^2 - 64 = 0$$

Factor: $(x - 8)(x + 8) = 0$

Set each factor equal to 0:

$$x - 8 = 0 \qquad x + 8 = 0$$

Solve these two equations:

$$x = 8 \qquad x = -8$$

Check: For $x = 8$: For $x = -8$:

$$x^2 = 64 \qquad x^2 = 64$$
$$(8)^2 = 64 \qquad (-8)^2 = 64$$
$$64 = 64 \qquad 64 = 64$$

It may be necessary to take out the highest common monomial factor.

Example: To solve $2y^2 - y = 0$, factor: $y(2y - 1) = 0$

Set each factor equal to 0:

$$y = 0 \quad 2y - 1 = 0$$

Solve:

$$2y = 1$$
$$y = 0 \qquad y = \tfrac{1}{2}$$

Check: For $y = 0$: For $y = \frac{1}{2}$:

$$2y^2 - y = 0 \qquad 2y^2 - y = 0$$
$$2(0)^2 - 0 = 0 \qquad 2(\tfrac{1}{2})^2 - \tfrac{1}{2} = 0$$
$$0 - 0 = 0 \qquad 2(\tfrac{1}{4}) - \tfrac{1}{2} = 0$$
$$0 = 0 \qquad \tfrac{1}{2} - \tfrac{1}{2} = 0$$
$$0 = 0$$

An equation of this type is often incorrectly solved because of a misapplication of one of the properties concerning equivalent equations. It would be incorrect to change

$$2y^2 - y = 0$$

to

$$2y - 1 = 0$$

by dividing both members by y. The postulate governing division of both members of an equation by a number states that an equivalent equation is produced only when the division is by a nonzero number. Since the variable y may possibly equal 0, it cannot be used as a divisor. The equation $2y - 1 = 0$ is not equivalent to the original equation, $2y^2 - y = 0$, because $2y - 1 = 0$ has only one root, $\frac{1}{2}$, while $2y^2 - y = 0$ has two roots, 0 and $\frac{1}{2}$.

In general, one may not divide by an expression containing the variable without considering the possibility that the expression may equal zero for some value or values of the variable. Note, on the other hand, that in the equation $2y - 2 = 0$, it is perfectly correct to divide both members by 2, yielding the equivalent equation $y - 1 = 0$; in this case, the division is by a nonzero number, as required by the postulate. The equations $2y - 2 = 0$ and $y - 1 = 0$ are equivalent; both have the root 1 as their only solution.

It is sometimes advantageous to divide both members of a quadratic equation by a nonzero number even before factoring, in order to simplify the solution of the equation. For example, to solve $15x^2 + 30 = 45x$, subtract $45x$ from each member:

$$15x^2 - 45x + 30 = 0$$

Divide all members by 15:

$$x^2 - 3x + 2 = 0$$

Factor: $(x-2)(x-1) = 0$

Set each factor equal to 0:

$$x - 2 = 0 \qquad x - 1 = 0$$

Then solve these two equations:

$$x = 2 \qquad x = 1$$

Check: For $x = 2$:

$$\begin{aligned} 15x^2 + 30 &= 45x \\ 15(2)^2 + 30 &= 45(2) \\ 15(4) + 30 &= 45(2) \\ 60 + 30 &= 90 \\ 90 &= 90 \end{aligned}$$

For $x = 1$:

$$\begin{aligned} 15x^2 + 30 &= 45x \\ 15(1)^2 + 30 &= 45(1) \\ 15 + 30 &= 45 \\ 45 &= 45 \end{aligned}$$

In all the quadratic equations solved so far, two roots have been obtained. It is true, in general, that quadratic equations have two roots. These roots, however, may be equal to each other.

Example: To solve $x^2 = 6x - 9$, subtract $6x$ from each member and add 9 to each member:

$$x^2 - 6x + 9 = 0$$

Factor: $(x-3)(x-3) = 0$

Set each factor equal to 0:

$$x - 3 = 0 \qquad x - 3 = 0$$
$$x = 3 \qquad x = 3$$

Check: For $x = 3$:

$$\begin{aligned} x^2 &= 6x - 9 \\ (3)^2 &= 6(3) - 9 \\ 9 &= 18 - 9 \\ 9 &= 9 \end{aligned}$$

This equation is considered to have two roots, although both roots are 3. Mathematicians prefer to establish general statements that have as few exceptions as possible. In higher mathematics, it is shown that an equation of the nth degree, where n is a positive integer whose members are polynomials, has exactly n roots, although some or all of these roots may be equal. Thus, a first-degree equation has exactly one root, a second-degree equation has exactly two roots; a third-degree equation has exactly three roots, and so on. When the graphs of second-degree equations are studied, other reasons also appear for considering them to have two roots, even though these roots may be equal.

Incomplete Quadratic Equations

Any quadratic equation can be put in the form $ax^2 + bx + c = 0$, where $a \neq 0$. When $b = 0$, the equation is a special case of the quadratic of the form $ax^2 + c = 0$ and is known as an *incomplete quadratic equation.* For example, $6x^2 - 24 = 0$ is an incomplete quadratic equation. It may be solved by dividing both members by 6 to yield $x^2 - 4 = 0$. This can be factored into $(x - 2)(x + 2) = 0$; when each factor is set equal to 0, two roots, +2 and −2, are obtained.

However, $6x^2 - 24 = 0$, like other incomplete quadratic equations, can also be solved by a method that depends on transforming it so that the square of the variable is equal to a number: $6x^2 = 24$, $x^2 = 4$, so $x = +2$ or $x = -2$. Finding the number whose square is the given number is called finding the square root of the given number. The square root of 4 was found to be +2 or −2. The equation $x^2 = 4$ was really solved by taking the square root of both members and assuming that the square roots of equal quantities are equal. To solve $x^2 = 36$, the square roots of both members can be taken, obtaining $x = +6$ and $x = -6$ (this result is usually written in the shorter form, $x = \pm 6$).

The method for solving an incomplete quadratic equation without factoring is illustrated below. To solve $3x^2 - 75 = 0$, divide both members by 3:

$$x^2 - 25 = 0$$

Add 25 to both members:

$$x^2 = 25$$

Then take the square roots of both members:

$$\sqrt{x^2} = \sqrt{25}$$
$$x = \pm 5$$

Check: For $x = +5$:

$$\begin{aligned} 3x^2 - 75 &= 0 \\ 3(5)^2 - 75 &= 0 \\ 3(25) - 75 &= 0 \\ 75 - 75 &= 0 \\ 0 &= 0 \end{aligned}$$

For $x = -5$:

$$\begin{aligned} 3x^2 - 75 &= 0 \\ 3(-5)^2 - 75 &= 0 \\ 3(25) - 75 &= 0 \\ 75 - 75 &= 0 \\ 0 &= 0 \end{aligned}$$

Square Roots

In solving $x^2 = 4$, it was pointed out that this open sentence speaks of a number whose square is 4. A number whose square is a given number is said to be a *square root* of the given number. In other words, the square root of a number is one of the two equal factors of the number.

Every perfect square has two square roots, which are opposite in sign. The positive one is called the *principal* square root of the number. By conventional notation, the symbol $\sqrt{\ }$ (called a *radical sign*) is used to stand for the principal square root only. Thus $\sqrt{25} = 5$, $\sqrt{100} = 10$, $\sqrt{36} = 6$. Note that $(\sqrt{2})(\sqrt{2}) = 2$. The negative square root is denoted by placing a minus sign before the radical sign: $-\sqrt{9} = -3$.

Irrational and real numbers. The discussion of square roots makes it necessary to return to a discussion of the number system. In defining rational numbers, we said that any rational number could be defined as the quotient of two integers:

$$R = \frac{a}{b}$$

where a and b are integers and $b \neq 0$.

Some square roots have perfect integer solutions. For example:

$$\sqrt{64} = \pm 8$$

But many square roots do not have solutions that can be expressed as an integer *or* as the quotient of any two integers. That is, they cannot be expressed by any common fraction or by a precise decimal. They are *irrational numbers.*

Other important mathematical quantities are also irrational. For example, π, the ratio of the diameter of a circle to its circumference, is *approximately* $\frac{22}{7}$. In decimals it is

$$3.141592654\ldots$$

to the nearest billionth. But no matter how far calculations are extended, no decimal can express the value of π exactly. Thus it too is irrational.

The set of all rational and irrational numbers is called the set of *real numbers.* The real numbers are in one-to-one correspondence with the points on the number line; that is, every real number can be associated with one and only one point on the line. Also, every point on the line can be associated with only one real number. Together, the two statements above are called the *completeness property* of the set of real numbers. The number line is complete.

Often, we cannot locate exactly the point for an irrational number. We can only get closer and closer approximations for the locations. For example, in trying to locate $\sqrt{3}$ on a number line:

$$1.7 < \sqrt{3} < 1.8$$
$$1.73 < \sqrt{3} < 1.74$$
$$1.732 < \sqrt{3} < 1.733$$

Since we do not wish to continue the process of estimating the point for $\sqrt{3}$ forever, it seems reasonable to assume that there is exactly one point corresponding to $\sqrt{3}$.

The properties for the basic operations of rational numbers also hold for the basic operations of real numbers.

To summarize, the set of real numbers (R) includes all the numbers discussed so far. The following diagram shows some of the important relationships between these numbers.

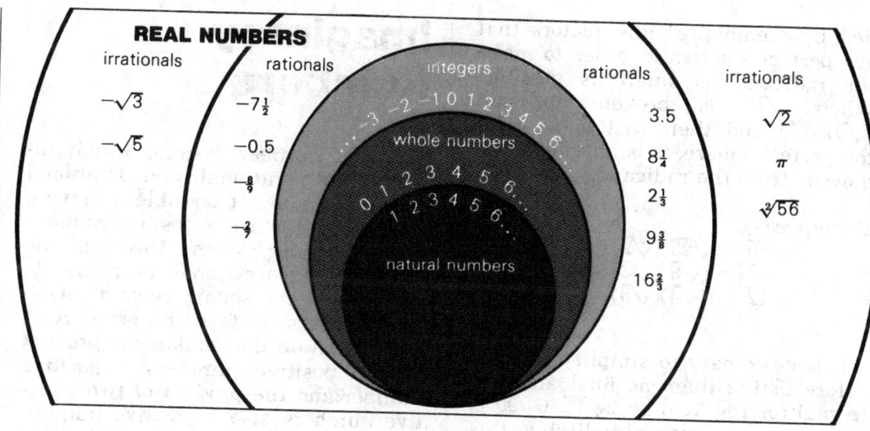

Computing square roots.

The square root of a number may not be obvious by inspection. However, the square root of such numbers can be approximated closely using arithmetic. A method for finding square roots by approximation was given in Arithmetic—Exponents above.

Often the steps can be reduced by factoring before beginning the approximation. If a and b represent counting numbers,

$$\sqrt{ab} = \sqrt{(a)(b)} = \sqrt{a}\,\sqrt{b}$$

For example:

$$\sqrt{160} = \sqrt{(16)(10)} = \sqrt{16}\,\sqrt{10} = 4\sqrt{10}$$

Notice that we chose for the first factor, 16, a counting number whose square root is a counting number, 4. The second factor is irrational and the square root must be approximated. A good estimate for $\sqrt{10}$ is 3.162. So, $4\sqrt{10} \approx 4(3.162) \approx 12.648$. (The symbol $\approx$ means "is approximately equal to.")

Operations on Radicals

Irrational numbers involving radical signs, such as $2\sqrt{5}$, are called radicals. Since they are numbers, it can be assumed that the results of adding, subtracting, multiplying, and dividing them must be consistent with the postulates that have been assumed to govern these operations on the other sets of numbers, such as the integers and fractions.

Every radical has an *index.* The index of $\sqrt[3]{\ }$ is three and is read "cube root of." The index of $\sqrt{\ }$ is two ("square root of"), even though no number appears at its left. *Operations on radicals must be made on radicals with the same index.*

Multiplication. Suppose it is desired to multiply two radicals with the same index, such as $\sqrt{25}$ and $\sqrt{4}$. The product, $(\sqrt{25})(\sqrt{4})$, is the same as (5)(2), the answer to which is 10. The same answer would result if the numbers under the radical sign, called the *radicands,* were multiplied together to form the radicand of the product. For example,

$$(\sqrt{25})(\sqrt{4}) = 5 \cdot 2 = 10$$

but

$$(\sqrt{25})(\sqrt{4})$$

also

$$= \sqrt{100} = 10$$

If the radicands are not perfect squares, as they are in the above example, consideration of their decimal approximations will show that this is a suitable procedure for producing their product, provided they have the same index. Thus,

$$(\sqrt{3})(\sqrt{7}) = \sqrt{21}$$

and

$$(\sqrt[3]{4})(\sqrt[3]{5}) = \sqrt[3]{20}$$

If the radicals to be multiplied have numerical coefficients, say $2\sqrt{5}$ and $3\sqrt{6}$, they may be multiplied by multiplying the coefficients and making this product the coefficient of the answer. By the commutative and associative postulates for multiplication,

$$(2\sqrt{5})(3\sqrt{6}) = (2)(3)(\sqrt{5})(\sqrt{6}) = 6\sqrt{30}$$

Division. Since division is the inverse of multiplication, solving $21\sqrt{18} \div 3\sqrt{6}$ is equivalent to asking the question, "By what number must $3\sqrt{6}$ be multiplied to give $21\sqrt{18}$?" The answer, $7\sqrt{3}$, shows that division of radicals of the same index may be performed by dividing their coefficients to form the coefficient of the answer and then dividing their radicands to form the radicand of the answer. Often, it is easiest to view the division as simplifying a fraction:

$$\frac{28\sqrt{30}}{7\sqrt{10}} = 4\sqrt{3}$$

Simplification. Since $(\sqrt{4})(\sqrt{3}) = \sqrt{12}$, in turn $\sqrt{12}$ can be transformed into $(\sqrt{4})(\sqrt{3})$. But $\sqrt{4} = 2$, and therefore $\sqrt{12} = 2\sqrt{3}$. The form $2\sqrt{3}$ is considered simpler than $\sqrt{12}$ because its radicand is a smaller number. Radicals that are square roots are simplified by "removing" any factors that are perfect squares in order to make the radicand as small as possible. When $\sqrt{18}$ is broken up into $(\sqrt{9})(\sqrt{2})$ and then written as $3\sqrt{2}$, the perfect square, 9, is, in effect, "removed" from the radicand.

Examples:

$$\sqrt{50} = (\sqrt{25})(\sqrt{2}) = 5\sqrt{2}$$
$$\sqrt{27} = (\sqrt{9})(\sqrt{3}) = 3\sqrt{3}$$
$$3\sqrt{12} = 3(\sqrt{4})(\sqrt{3}) = (3)(2)\sqrt{3} = 6\sqrt{3}$$

It is customary to simplify radicals before listing them as final answers. In multiplying $3\sqrt{6}$ by $2\sqrt{15}$, $6\sqrt{90}$ is first obtained. Upon simplifying, this becomes $(6\sqrt{9})(\sqrt{10})$, or $(6)(3)\sqrt{10}$; hence $18\sqrt{10}$.

In simplifying a radical, it is not necessary to remove the largest perfect square factor as long as the process is continued until there are no more perfect square factors to be removed. Thus, in simplifying $\sqrt{72}$, if one had noticed that $\sqrt{72} = (\sqrt{36})(\sqrt{2})$, one would have obtained $6\sqrt{2}$ by removing the 36. Yet one might have written $\sqrt{72}$ as $(\sqrt{9})(\sqrt{8})$ instead, and gotten $3\sqrt{8}$, which, in turn, is $(3\sqrt{4})(\sqrt{2})$, or $(3)(2)\sqrt{2}$, and finally $6\sqrt{2}$.

Addition and subtraction.

Just as $5x - 3x + 7x$ can be combined into one term, $9x$, by the application of the distributive postulate, so the same postulate requires that $5\sqrt{3} - 3\sqrt{3} + 7\sqrt{3}$ become $9\sqrt{3}$ when combined. Just as $2x + 3y$ cannot be combined into one term, neither can $2\sqrt{5} + 3\sqrt{7}$ be combined. Radicands must be the same in order to combine radicals. But $5\sqrt[3]{7} + 2\sqrt{7}$ cannot be combined into one term even though both radicands are the same, for in order to combine radicals their indices must be the same as well as their radicands. Radicals having the same index and same radicand may be combined by algebraically combining their coefficients and writing the sum before their common radical factor.

Examples:

$$7\sqrt{2} - 4\sqrt{2} + 9\sqrt{2} = 12\sqrt{2}$$
$$8\sqrt{7} - 18\sqrt{7} = -10\sqrt{7}$$
$$9\sqrt[3]{5} - 8\sqrt[3]{5} = \sqrt[3]{5}$$

Radicals cannot be combined into a single term if their radicands differ. It is sometimes possible, however, to change a radicand by simplifying it to make it the same as that in another radical to which it is to be added.

Example: To combine $7\sqrt{50} - 4\sqrt{98}$, simplify as follows:

$$(7)(\sqrt{25})(\sqrt{2}) - (4)(\sqrt{49})(\sqrt{2})$$
$$= (7)(5)\sqrt{2} - (4)(7)\sqrt{2}$$
$$= 35\sqrt{2} - 28\sqrt{2}$$
$$= 7\sqrt{2}$$

Imaginary Numbers

The real number system, which includes both rational and irrational numbers, makes it possible to have a square root for every positive number in the number system. However, the rational and irrational numbers do not include the square roots of negative numbers. In fact, the property of multiplication that makes the product of two positive numbers a positive number and the product of two negative numbers also a positive number makes it impossible to get a negative number by squaring any of the real numbers.

To compute the square roots of negative numbers, the number system is extended to include the *imaginary numbers,* those whose squares are negative. The symbol i is used for the number which is $\sqrt{-1}$. It was chosen to represent this number because it is the first letter of the word "imaginary."

Notice that $i^2 = -1$. Since $\sqrt{-4}$ can be simplified as $(\sqrt{4})(\sqrt{-1})$, or $2\sqrt{-1}$, $\sqrt{-4}$ is $2i$; $\sqrt{-49}$ would be $7i$, and so on. It is possible to simplify $\sqrt{-3}$ as $(\sqrt{3})(\sqrt{-1})$; therefore, $\sqrt{-3}$ is $i\sqrt{3}$. If $2i$ is squared, it equals $4i^2$, which in turn is $4(-1)$, or -4.

If $-3i$ is squared, $(-3i)^2$, it equals $9i^2$, which, in turn, is $9(-1)$, or -9. The square of an imaginary number is a negative real number.

Complex numbers. The imaginary numbers, when combined with the real numbers, form an extended number system called the *complex number system.* Complex numbers include all the real numbers, such as the rational numbers 5 and $\frac{2}{5}$; all the irrational numbers, such as $\sqrt{2}$ or $\sqrt[3]{73}$; all the imaginary numbers, such as $-2i$ and $i\sqrt{5}$; and combinations of both real and imaginary terms, such as $2 - 3i$ or $\sqrt{2} + 7i$. The complex numbers obey the commutative and associative postulates for addition and multiplication and the distributive postulate. But most important, any first-degree or second-degree equation whose coefficients are complex numbers will have solutions that are also complex numbers.

Other Solutions for Quadratic Equations

Completing the square.

Since factoring is restricted to the use of integral coefficients, a quadratic equation whose roots are irrational cannot be solved by factoring. A method for solving a quadratic equation, called *completing the square,* does permit solutions whether the roots are rational or irrational.

The method of completing the square requires transforming the equation into a form in which the square root of both members can be taken, as in the method for solving an incomplete quadratic equation. In order to take the square root, a perfect-square trinomial is needed on the side containing the variable. Therefore, a method is required for getting a perfect square there.

Examination of quadratic trinomials that are perfect squares, such as $x^2 + 6x + 9$, which is $(x + 3)^2$, or $x^2 - 8x + 16$, which is $(x - 4)^2$, shows that the constant term (9 in the first example) must be the square of one–half the middle term's coefficient (in the first example, one–half of 6 is 3). In the method of solving a quadratic equation by completing the square, this fact is used to create, or "complete," a perfect square on one side. To solve

$$x^2 + 4x - 21 = 0$$

add 21 to both members:

$$x^2 + 4x = 21$$

Complete the square by adding to both members the number found by taking one–half of 4 and squaring it ($4 \div 2 = 2$ and $2^2 = 4$):

$$x^2 + 4x + 4 = 21 + 4$$

Factor: $(x + 2)^2 = 25$

Take the square root of both members:

$$x + 2 = \pm 5$$

Subtract 2 from both members:

$$x = \pm 5 - 2$$

Combine and solve:

$$x = 3 \qquad x = -7$$

This example illustrates the use of the method of completing the square in an equation whose roots are rational. This equation could have been solved by factoring. The next example illustrates the use of the method of completing the square in an equation whose roots are irrational and which, therefore, cannot be solved by factoring. To solve

$$x^2 + 6x - 4 = 0$$

add 4 to both members:

$$x^2 + 6x = 4$$

Complete the square by taking one–

half of 6, squaring it, and adding the result to both members:

$$x^2+6x+9=4+9$$

Factor: $(x+3)^2=13$

Take the square root of both members:

$$x+3=\pm\sqrt{13}$$

Then subtract 3 from both members:

$$x=-3+\sqrt{13}$$
$$x=-3-\sqrt{13}$$

Irrational roots may be checked by substitution in the original equation, just as rational roots are checked. The next example illustrates this procedure by checking one root in this equation.

Check: For $x = -3 + \sqrt{13}$:

$$x^2+6x-4=0$$
$$(-3+\sqrt{13})^2+6(-3+\sqrt{13})-4\stackrel{?}{=}0$$
$$9-6\sqrt{13}+13-18+6\sqrt{13}-4\stackrel{?}{=}0$$
$$0=0$$

Quadratic formula. Any quadratic equation in one variable may be put into the form $ax^2 + bx + c = 0$, where a, b, and c stand for the coefficients of x^2, x, and the constant term, respectively, and $a \neq 0$. By solving this equation, which stands for any quadratic equation, mathematicians evolved a formula that gives the roots of any quadratic equation when the particular values of a, b, and c for that equation are substituted in it. The method of completing the square was used. Starting with

$$ax^2+bx+c=0$$

divide both members by a:

$$x^2+\frac{b}{a}x+\frac{c}{a}=0$$

Subtract $\frac{c}{a}$ from both members:

$$x^2+\frac{b}{a}x=-\frac{c}{a}$$

Complete the square $\left(\text{one-half of } \frac{b}{a} \text{ is } \frac{b}{2a}\text{, and squaring gives } \frac{b^2}{4a^2}\right)$:

$$x^2+\frac{b}{a}x+\frac{b^2}{4a^2}=-\frac{c}{a}+\frac{b^2}{4a^2}$$

Factor the left side and add the fractions on the right after finding the common denominator:

$$\left(x+\frac{b}{2a}\right)^2=\frac{-4ac}{4a^2}+\frac{b^2}{4a^2}$$

$$\left(x+\frac{b}{2a}\right)^2=\frac{b^2-4ac}{4a^2}$$

Take the square roots of both members:

$$x+\frac{b}{2a}=\frac{\pm\sqrt{b^2-4ac}}{2a}$$

Subtract $\frac{b}{2a}$ from both sides to solve for x:

$$x=\frac{-b\pm\sqrt{b^2-4ac}}{2a}$$

Since $ax^2 + bx + c = 0$ represents any quadratic equation, its solution is a formula for the roots of any quadratic equation.

The use of the formula is illustrated below in solving a quadratic equation that has rational roots. To solve

$$x^2=10-3x$$

put the equation in $ax^2 + bx + c = 0$ form:

$$x^2+3x-10=0$$

Identify a, b, and c:

$$a=1 \quad b=3 \quad c=-10$$

Use the formula:

$$x=\frac{-b\pm\sqrt{b^2-4ac}}{2a}$$

Substitute values of a, b, and c:

$$x=\frac{-3\pm\sqrt{9-4(1)(-10)}}{2(1)}$$

Simplify:

$$x=\frac{-3\pm\sqrt{9+40}}{2}$$

$$x=\frac{-3\pm\sqrt{49}}{2}$$

$$x=\frac{-3\pm7}{2}$$

$$x=2 \qquad x=-5$$

The quadratic formula is most useful to obtain irrational roots where other methods of solution are not possible. To solve

$$4x^2-3x-2=0$$

identify a, b, and c:

$$a=4 \quad b=-3 \quad c=-2$$

Use the formula:

$$x=\frac{-b\pm\sqrt{b^2-4ac}}{2a}$$

Substitute

$$x=\frac{3\pm\sqrt{(-3)^2-4(4)(-2)}}{2(4)}$$

Simplify:

$$x=\frac{3\pm\sqrt{9+32}}{8}$$

$$x=\frac{3\pm\sqrt{41}}{8}$$

$$x=\frac{3+\sqrt{41}}{8} \qquad x=\frac{3-\sqrt{41}}{8}$$

PROBLEM SOLVING. The steps in solving a problem that results in a quadratic equation are exactly the same as shown in the box at the bottom of page 1430.

There are many practical problems that can be solved with quadratic equations. Here is a simple example.

A = 52 sq. ft. x

3x + 1

The length of a rectangular plot of ground exceeds three times its width by 1 foot. Its area is 52 square feet. Find its length and width.

Let x equal the number of feet in width, $3x + 1$ the length. As the area of a rectangle is width times length, the area is $x(3x + 1) = 52$. Remove parentheses:

$$3x^2+x=52$$

Subtract 52 from both members:

$$3x^2+x-52=0$$

Factor:

$$(3x+13)(x-4)=0$$

Set each factor equal to 0:

$$3x+13=0 \qquad x-4=0$$

$$3x=-13$$

$$x=\frac{-13}{3} \qquad x=4$$

The root $-13/3$ must be rejected as an answer to the problem, since the domain of the variable, x, must be restricted to positive numbers if it is to represent the number of feet in the width of a rectangle. If $x = 4$, $3x + 1 = 13$. Thus the plot is 4 feet wide and 13 feet long.

Check: For length: For area:

$$\begin{array}{r} 4 \\ \times\ 3 \\ \hline 12 \\ +\ 1 \\ \hline 13 \end{array} \qquad \begin{array}{r} 13 \\ \times\ 4 \\ \hline 52 \end{array}$$

Many simple number problems require quadratic equations for their solution, especially when multiplication is involved.

The product of a number and ten more than the number is 39. What is the number?

Call the unknown number n. Then you know that the product of n and $n + 10$ is 39, or

$$n(n + 10) = 39.$$

When you carry out the multiplication, this can be recognized as the quadratic

$$n^2 + 10n = 39$$

or $$n^2 + 10n - 39 = 0.$$

You can factor this equation as

$$(n + 13)(n - 3) = 0.$$

Set each factor equal to 0:

$$n + 13 = 0 \qquad n - 3 = 0$$
$$n = -13 \qquad n = 3.$$

There are two numbers that meet the conditions of the problem: -13 and 3.

Check: $-13(-3) = 39$
$3(13) = 39.$

A man wanted to make a brace that was a right triangle with the longest side an inch longer than the next longest, and the shortest side 8 inches shorter than the longest side. What dimensions should he use for the triangle?

This problem requires use of a relation from geometry, one with which you are probably familiar—the Pythagorean theorem. If c is the longest side of a right triangle and a and b are the other two sides, then it is always true that

$$a^2 + b^2 = c^2.$$

If you use c for the longest side, the conditions of the problem allow you to write the other two sides in terms of c.

$$a = c - 1$$
$$b = c - 8$$

Then the Pythagorean theorem becomes

$$(c - 1)^2 + (c - 8)^2 = c^2.$$

This is a quadratic formula in c. First you need to square all the parts in parentheses.

$$c^2 - 2c + 1 + c^2 - 16c + 64 = c^2$$

Collect like terms.

$$c^2 - 18c + 65 = 0$$

This is easily factored if you remember that 65 is 13 times 5.

$$(c - 13)(c - 5) = 0$$

$$c - 13 = 0 \qquad c - 5 = 0$$
$$c = 13 \qquad c = 5$$

Therefore the longest side of the triangle is 13 inches or 5 inches.

Check: One answer cannot be true. For 13, you get

$$a = 13 - 1 = 12$$
$$b = 13 - 8 = 5$$
$$c = 13$$
$$12^2 + 5^2 = 13^2$$
$$144 + 25 = 169.$$

This answer is correct. But for 5 you get

$$a = 5 - 1 = 4$$
$$b = 5 - 8 = -3$$
$$c = 5.$$

Even though these values satisfy the Pythagorean theorem, they have to be rejected because b cannot be negative. No real triangle has a side with a negative length!

"Working alone," Phil said, "I can bale this hay in three hours less than you can." But Phil and Dale worked together and got the hay baled in 5 hours. How long would it have taken each of them working alone if Phil's original statement were correct?

Call the time it would take Phil to bale the hay by himself t hours. Then the time that Dale would have taken would be $t + 3$ hours. Suppose the amount of hay to be baled is A acres.

In one hour, Phil would bale $\frac{A}{t}$ acres of hay. Check this by noting that this means that in t hours he would bale $t\frac{A}{t}$ acres, or A acres.

Similarly, in one hour Dale would bale $\frac{A}{t+3}$ acres of hay. But in 5 hours they would bale the whole field, or A acres of hay. This yields the equation

$$5\left(\frac{A}{t} + \frac{A}{t+3}\right) = A.$$

At first glance, this does not help solve the problem, since there is one equation in two variables. Completing the multiplication, however, reveals that A appears in every term.

$$\frac{5A}{t} + \frac{5A}{t+3} = A$$

Since A is not zero (or it would not take 5 hours to bale the hay), you can divide both sides of the equation by A, leaving only the single variable t.

$$\frac{5}{t} + \frac{5}{t+3} = 1$$

The lowest common denominator of the two fractions is $t(t + 3)$. Multiplying both sides of the equations by this expression gets rid of the fractions.

$$5(t + 3) + 5t = t(t + 3)$$
$$5t + 15 + 5t = t^2 + 3t$$
$$10t + 15 = t^2 + 3t$$
$$0 = t^2 - 7t - 15$$

or the quadratic equation

$$t^2 - 7t - 15 = 0.$$

Since the factors of 15 are either 5 and 3 or 15 and 1, this equation cannot be solved by factoring ($3 - 5 = -2$; $1 - 15 = -14$). Therefore, use the method of completing the square to solve the equation.

$$t^2 - 7t - 15 = 0$$
$$t^2 - 7t = 15$$

One-half of the coefficient of t is $\frac{7}{2}$. The square of $\frac{7}{2}$ is $\frac{49}{4}$, which must be added to both sides of the equation.

$$t^2 - 7t + \frac{49}{4} = 15 + \frac{49}{4}$$
$$t^2 - 7t + \frac{49}{4} = \frac{60}{4} + \frac{49}{4}$$
$$(t - \frac{7}{2})^2 = \frac{109}{4}$$

Now take the square root of each side.

$$t - \frac{7}{2} = \pm\sqrt{\frac{109}{4}} = \pm\frac{\sqrt{109}}{2}$$

If you use a calculator or look up $\sqrt{109}$ in a table, you will find that it is equal to 10.440 (to three decimal places). Or simply estimate that $\sqrt{109}$ is just a little more than $\sqrt{100}$, or 10. Using the more exact value, $\frac{\sqrt{109}}{2}$ is about 5.22. The fraction $\frac{7}{2}$ in decimals is 3.5, and the sign $\approx$ means "is approximately equal to."

$$t - 3.5 \approx \pm 5.22$$
$$t \approx 3.5 \pm 5.22$$

$$t \approx 8.72 \text{ or } t \approx -1.72$$

Clearly the negative answer must be rejected, so to the nearest tenth of an hour Phil can bale the hay in 8.7 hours working alone. This means that Dale would take 11.7 hours working alone.

Check: This kind of problem is difficult to check. You can check the numerical answer in the first equation that only involves t, but be sure that the equation was correct. Common sense provides a good check. You would expect the time taken for the two together to be something like half the average time for the two. The average of 8.7 and 11.7 is 10.2, and half of that is 5.1, close to the 5 hours stated in the problem.

—Everett T. Draper
Bryan H. Bunch

GEOMETRY

Geometry is a branch of mathematics that plays a major role in our daily lives. The study of points, lines, planes, and solid figures influences architecture, automobile and airplane design, landscaping, and almost everything that is made or built by man. Many shapes studied in geometry occur naturally in our environment. Snowflakes, sea shells, plants, and even the orbits of planets have specific geometric shapes.

The word geometry means "measure of the earth." The Babylonians and the Egyptians employed basic geometrical properties to measure land boundaries as early as 2000 B.C. Today's geometry has its roots in ancient times, but it has become more complex and has been divided into many different branches.

The Babylonians knew how to find the area of rectangles, right triangles, and isosceles triangles. The Pythagorean theorem, named for the Greek mathematician Pythagoras, was known to the Babylonians, although they offered no proof for it. The Babylonians may also have been the first to divide the circle into 360 equal parts.

The Babylonians and Egyptians seemed to be satisfied with the practical aspects of geometry. The Greeks, on the other hand, began questioning the reasoning behind the practical applications. Thales, a Greek philosopher from Miletus, born about 640 B.C., is given credit for the beginnings of demonstrative geometry as we know it today. The full history of Greek geometry written by Eudemus has been lost. Parts of it have been restored by combining information from later literature. Because many records of geometrical discoveries were lost or transmitted only orally, it is difficult to accurately attribute specific theorems and proofs to their originators. For example, Pythagoras, born about 540 B.C., founded a mathematical fraternity that developed many geometrical principles. The principle that bears his name, stating that in a right triangle the square of the hypotenuse is equal to the sum of the squares of the legs, was certainly not discovered by him, and he may not have found the first proof.

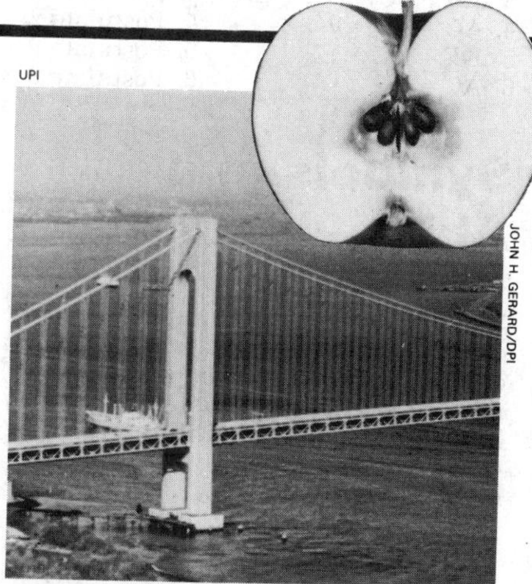
UPI

JOHN H. GERARD/DPI

SYMMETRICAL CURVES *appear both in nature and in manmade objects.*

The bulk of Greek geometry was set down in a logical fashion by Euclid in about 300 B.C. He wrote 13 books called "Euclid's Elements." Number theory and elementary algebra as well as geometry are discussed in them. The systematic approach of "Elements" has had a tremendous influence on modern scientific thinking. The books provide the basic foundation for elementary geometry as it is studied today.

Euclidean geometry is not the only possible geometry, however. Modern geometricians have shown that the geometry of Euclid depends on the unprovable postulate that parallel lines never meet no matter how far they are extended. If this postulate is changed, other whole geometrical systems can be developed. Nikolai Lobachevski (1793–1856), János Bolyai (1802–1860), Karl Gauss (1777–1855), and G. F. B. Riemann (1826–1866), all developed non–Euclidean geometries. In addition to having mathematical interest, these geometries have practical application in astronomy, physics, and other fields (*see* Glossary).

In many ways, however, Euclidean geometry will never be outdated. Its basic understandings of space and shape are used every day in architecture, engineering, and design.

Plane Geometry

Plane geometry is concerned with the study of figures that can be drawn on a flat surface (or plane). Such figures include triangles, rectangles, and circles.

Language of Geometry

There are many ways to solve a problem in geometry. Early geometry used a method called *inductive reasoning,* in which experiments are performed to find the answer to a particular problem. The results of the experiments suggest an answer, and finally a conclusion is drawn. Later, however, the Greeks turned the procedure around. They wanted to know *why* these relationships worked. So they began with certain general statements, or facts, called *premises.* Using these premises, they drew conclusions. If the premises are true and the reasoning is logical, then the conclusion drawn is valid. This is called *deductive reasoning* and it is the basic method of demonstrative geometry.

Geometric terms are carefully defined, and the relationships between various figures are carefully studied. But the meaning of certain basic terms must be left undefined. Among the basic terms in plane geometry are *point, line,* and *plane.* A *point* can be represented by a dot on a piece of paper. Technically it has no length or width. A *line* may be either straight or curved, but in this discussion the word refers to a straight line. A line is endless and has length but no width. A *plane* is a flat surface that extends indefinitely in all directions and has two dimensions: length and width.

As in other branches of mathematics, certain other statements must be accepted without proof. Such statements are called *postulates.*

Definition 1. A *postulate* is a statement accepted without proof.

Some geometries have two kinds of statements accepted without proof: postulates and axioms. Axioms define basic mathematical properties and postulates define geometric relationships. The word postulate will be used in this discussion for any statement accepted without proof.

The following are basic mathematical postulates:

Postulate 1. A quantity is equal to itself. This is called the principle of *identity.*

Postulate 2. The whole is equal to the sum of all its parts.

Postulate 3. Quantities equal to the same quantity, or to equal quantities, are equal to each other.

Postulate 4. A quantity may be substituted for its equal in an equation. This is called the principle of *substitution.*

Postulate 5. If equals are added to equals, the sums are equal.

Postulate 6. If equals are subtracted from equals, the differences are equal.

A statement that can be proven by deductive reasoning is called a *theorem.*

A theorem consists of two parts: the hypothesis (or given information) and the conclusion (or part to be proven). When a theorem is stated in an "if-then" form, the statement following the "if" is the hypothesis (given), and the statement following the "then" is the conclusion (to be proven). To prove the conclusion, the given information, postulates, definitions, and any previously proven theorems may be used.

Definition 2. A *theorem* is a statement that can be proven by reasoning from postulates, definitions, and previously proven theorems.

The following steps outline a logical method for doing a geometric proof:

1. Draw a diagram labeling all necessary parts.
2. State the hypothesis specifically in terms of the diagram.
3. State the conclusion specifically in terms of the diagram.
4. Prove the conclusion using deductive reasoning.

In writing out the logical reasoning in step 4, it is convenient to use a two-column method. The left column lists the statements used to reach the conclusion, and the right column lists the reasons that allow you to make each statement (given information, postulate, definition, and previously proven theorem).

Example: Given the diagram below, prove that if AB = EF and BC = DE, then AC = DF.

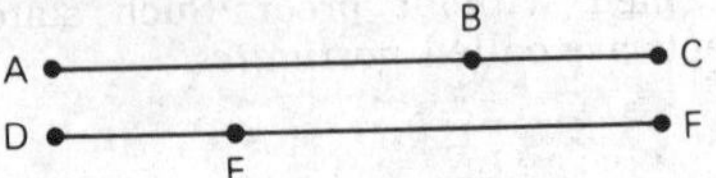

Given: AB = EF, BC = DE
To prove: AC = DF

Proof:

Statements	Reasons
1. AB = EF	1. Given
2. BC = DE	2. Given
3. AB + BC = DE + EF	3. Postulate 5
4. AC = AB + BC	4. Postulate 2
5. DF = DE + EF	5. Postulate 2
6. AC = DF	6. Postulate 3

Symbols and Abbreviations

When writing out definitions, proofs, or explanations, it is simpler and quicker to abbreviate many commonly used terms. This can be done by the use of a symbol to represent a word. The following is a list of commonly used symbols.

SYMBOLS

- + plus
- − minus
- × times, or multiplied by
- = equals
- ≅ congruent, is congruent to
- ~ similar, is similar to
- > is greater than
- < is less than
- ∠ angle
- ∠s angles
- △ triangle
- △s triangles
- ⊥ perpendicular, is perpendicular to
- ∥ parallel, is parallel to
- ▱ parallelogram
- ○ circle
- ⌒ arc

Lines

As we have learned, the term *line* refers to a straight line unless otherwise specified. A line extends indefinitely in two directions and contains an infinite number of points. It is designated by a small letter and drawn with an arrow at each end to show that it extends indefinitely in both directions.

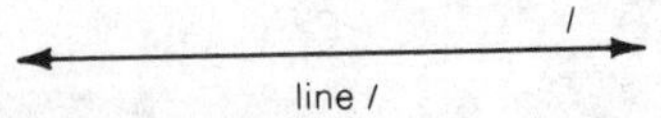

Postulate 7. Given any two points in a plane, only one line can be drawn connecting them.

Definition 3. *Collinear points* are points on the same line.

Definition 4. A *line segment* is the finite part of a line bounded by two points on the line.

A line segment is designated by the capital letters used for the two points.

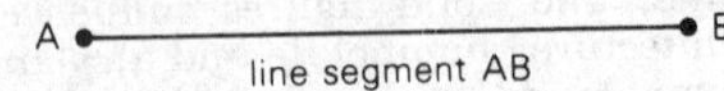

Definition 5. The *length of a line segment* is the distance between its endpoints.

If A and B are distinct points, the length is a positive number. If A and B are the same point, the length is zero.

Definition 6. The *midpoint* of a line segment is the point on that line segment that divides it into two equal parts.

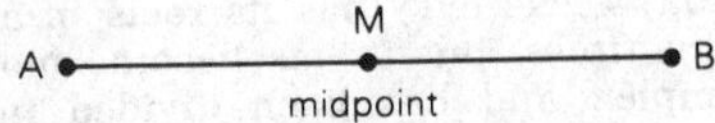

Definition 7. To *bisect* a line is to divide it into two equal parts.

Definition 8. A *ray* is a line segment extended endlessly from one endpoint.

Definition 9. A *transversal* is a line that intersects two or more lines.

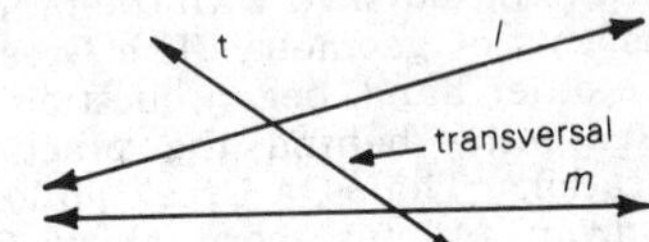

Definition 10. Two *lines are parallel* if they lie in the same plane but never meet (intersect).

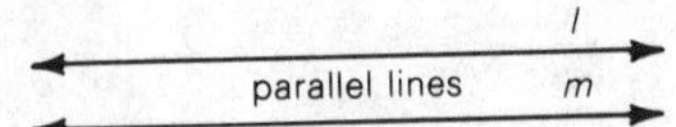

Postulate 8. Through a given point, only one line can be drawn parallel to a given line.

Postulate 8 is called the *parallel postulate.* A good way of picturing parallel lines is to think of straight railroad tracks.

LAND MEASURE *was the practical problem these early Egyptians solved with geometry.*

CULVER PICTURES

Angles

Everywhere you look, angles stare back at you. The floor and wall form an angle, the back of a chair forms an angle with the seat, and two pens with their points touching form an angle.

Definition 11. An *angle* is a figure formed by a pair of rays with a common endpoint.

That endpoint is called the *vertex* of the angle.

An angle can be designated in different ways. Three capital letters can be used, the vertex always being assigned the middle letter. A number can be used. If the angle is part of a figure, and no ambiguity exists, the letter at the vertex can be used.

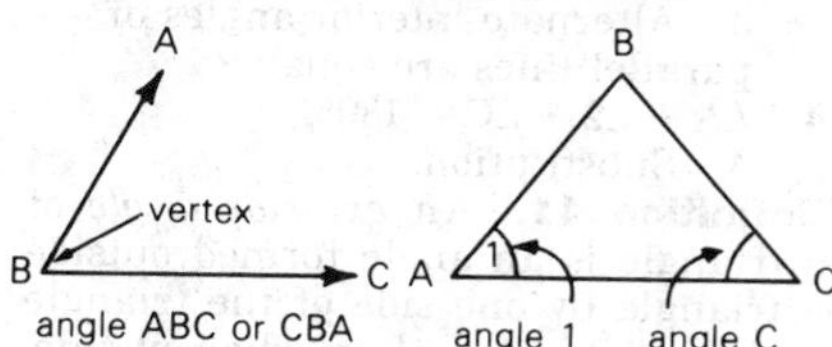

To measure an angle, an instrument called a protractor is used. Angles are measured in degrees. There are two scales going in opposite directions on the protractor. Each one starts at 0° and ends at 180°. To measure an angle using a protractor, follow these steps:

1. Place the center point located on the bottom of the protractor on the vertex of the angle.
2. Make sure the bottom of the protractor is even with one side of the angle.
3. To determine the measure of the angle, use the scale whose zero lies on a side of the angle.
4. The measure of the angle is the number of degrees intercepted on the arc of the protractor.

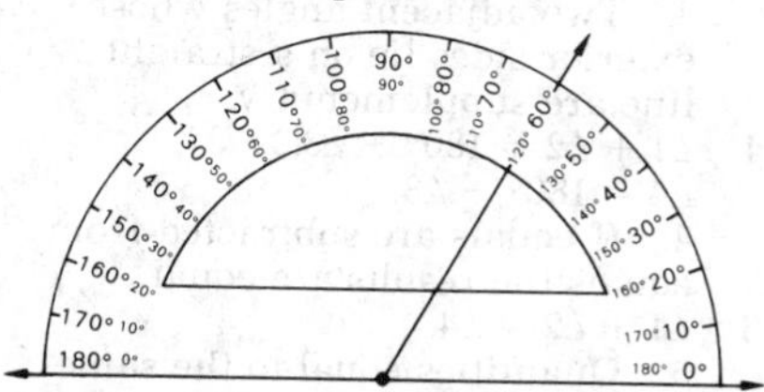

Angles are classified by their measures.

Definition 12. A *right angle* is an angle whose measure is 90°.

Definition 13. An *acute angle* is an angle whose measure is less than 90°.

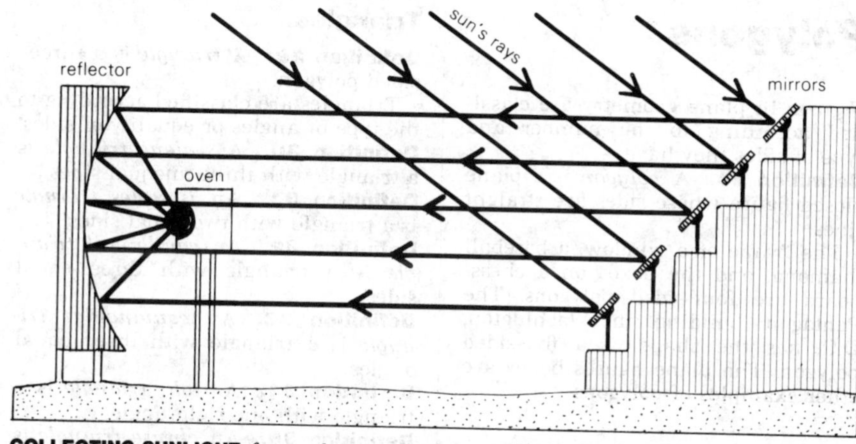

COLLECTING SUNLIGHT *for a solar generator requires a knowledge of angles. The angle at which the sunlight strikes the reflector is the same as the angle at which it glances off.*

Definition 14. An *obtuse angle* is an angle whose measure is more than 90° but less than 180°.

Definition 15. A *straight angle* is an angle whose measure is 180°.

Definition 16. A *reflex angle* is an angle whose measure is greater than 180° but less than 360°.

Definition 17. Two *angles are equal* if they have the same measure.

Definition 18. *Perpendicular lines* are intersecting lines that form right angles.

Definition 19. A *bisector of an angle* is a ray that divides an angle into two parts of equal measure.

Postulate 9. Every angle has a bisector.

Definition 20. Two *angles are adjacent* if they have a common vertex and a common side between them.

Definition 21. *Vertical angles* are the opposite angles formed when two lines intersect.

Definition 22. *Complementary angles* are two angles the sum of whose measure is 90°.

Definition 23. *Supplementary angles* are two angles the sum of whose measure is 180°.

Postulate 10. When two adjacent angles have their exterior sides on the same line, they are supplementary.

Theorem 1. If two angles are complementary (supplementary) to the same or equal angles, they are equal to each other.

The proof follows from the definition of complementary (supplementary) angles and postulates 3 and 6.

Theorem 2. If two angles are equal, their complements (supplements) are equal.

Theorem 3. Vertical angles are equal.

The proof follows from postulate 10 and theorem 1.

When two lines are cut by a transversal, many angles are formed. If the two lines are parallel, the angles formed have many interesting relationships.

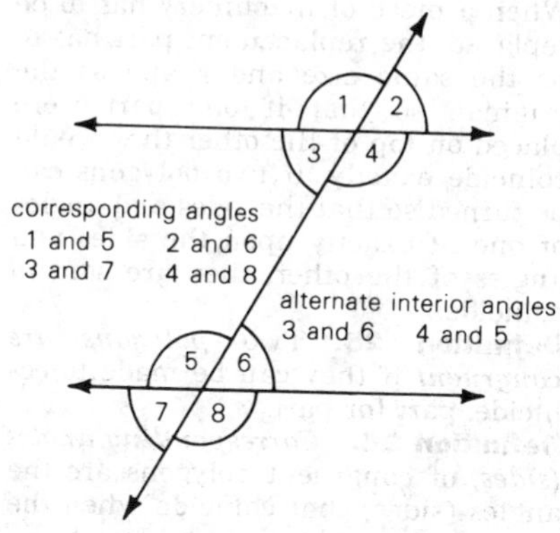

Postulate 11. If two lines are cut by a transversal so that alternate interior angles are equal, the lines are parallel.

Theorem 4. If two lines are cut by a transversal so that corresponding angles are equal, the lines are parallel.

The proof follows from the definition of vertical angles, theorem 3, and postulate 11.

Theorem 5. When two parallel lines are cut by a transversal, the alternate interior (corresponding) angles are equal.

ANGLES

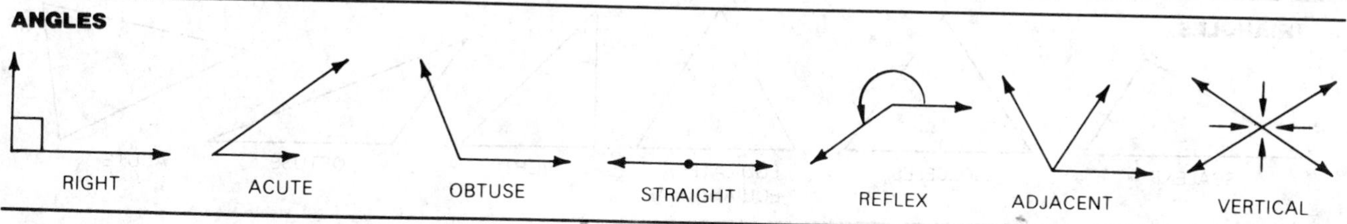

Polygons

Figures in plane geometry are classified according to the number and type of sides they have.

Definition 24. A *polygon* is a plane closed figure whose sides are straight lines.

The frame of a window, a baseball diamond, and the boxes on a chessboard are four-sided polygons. The Pentagon building in Washington, D.C. has the shape of a five-sided polygon. The plane figures below are other examples of polygons.

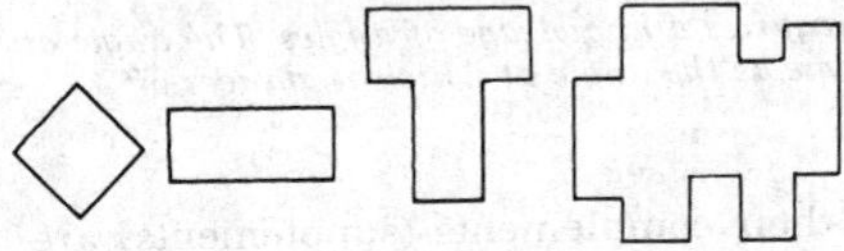

A polygon is designated by capital letters, one at each vertex.

Congruent polygons. Some things are unique and some are made by mass production so that there are hundreds or thousands exactly alike. When a piece of machinery has to be replaced, the replacement part has to be the same size and shape as the original, so that if one part were placed on top of the other they would coincide exactly. If two polygons can be turned so that the sides and angles of one fit exactly upon the sides and angles of the other, they are said to coincide.

Definition 25. Two *polygons are congruent* if they can be made to coincide, part for part.

Definition 26. *Corresponding angles (sides)* of congruent polygons are the angles (sides) that coincide when the polygons coincide.

Postulate 12. Corresponding angles (sides) of congruent polygons are equal.

The symbol for congruence is ≅. The ~ part of the symbol means "same shape" and the = part means "same size."

Definition 27. *Consecutive vertices* of a polygon are endpoints of one side of the polygon.

Definition 28. *Consecutive angles* of a polygon are angles whose vertices are consecutive.

Triangles.

Definition 29. A *triangle* is a three-sided polygon.

Triangles are classified according to the type of angles or equality of sides.

Definition 30. A *scalene triangle* is a triangle with three unequal sides.

Definition 31. An *isosceles triangle* is a triangle with two equal sides.

Definition 32. An *equilateral triangle* is a triangle with three equal sides.

Definition 33. An *equiangular triangle* is a triangle with three equal angles.

Definition 34. A *right triangle* is a triangle with one right angle.

Definition 35. An *obtuse triangle* is a triangle with one obtuse angle.

Definition 36. An *acute triangle* is a triangle with three acute angles.

Starting from any vertex of a triangle, a line can be drawn to a point on the opposite side.

Definition 37. An *angle bisector* of a triangle is a line segment that bisects one angle and is extended to the opposite side.

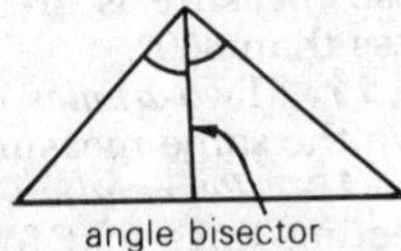

angle bisector

Definition 38. A *median* of a triangle is a line segment drawn from a vertex to the midpoint of the opposite side.

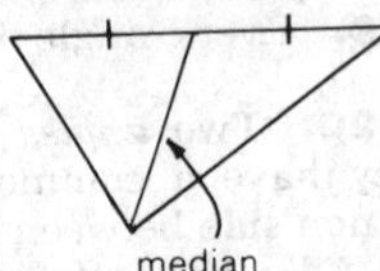

median

Definition 39. An *altitude* of a triangle is a line segment drawn from a vertex to the opposite side and perpendicular to that side.

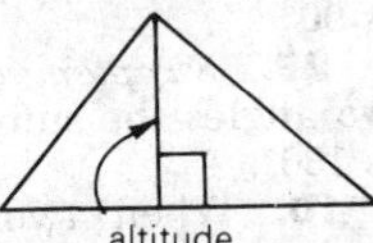

altitude

Definition 40. A *perpendicular bisector* of a side of a triangle is a line segment drawn perpendicular to the side and bisecting it.

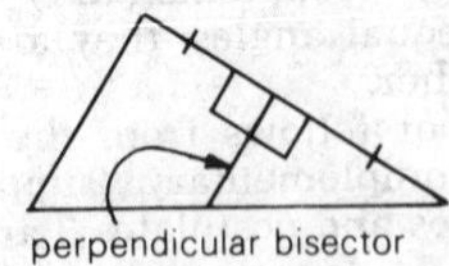

perpendicular bisector

Theorem 6. The sum of the angles of a triangle is 180°.

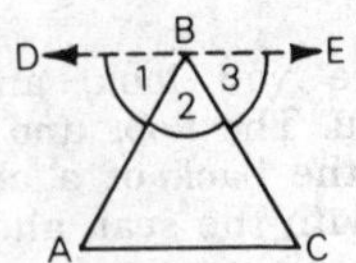

Given: △ABC

To prove: $\angle A + \angle 2 + \angle C = 180°$

Proof:

1. Through B draw DE ∥ AC.
   1. Through a given external point, a line may be drawn parallel to a given line.
2. $\angle 1 + \angle 2 + \angle 3 = 180°$ (straight angle).
   2. The whole is equal to the sum of its parts.
3. $\angle 1 = \angle A$, $\angle 3 = \angle C$.
   3. Alternate interior angles of parallel lines are equal.
4. $\angle A + \angle 2 + \angle C = 180°$.
   4. Substitution.

Definition 41. An *exterior angle* of a triangle is an angle formed outside a triangle by one side of the triangle and the extension of an adjacent side.

Theorem 7. The measure of an exterior angle of a triangle is equal to the sum of the measures of the two nonadjacent (remote) interior angles.

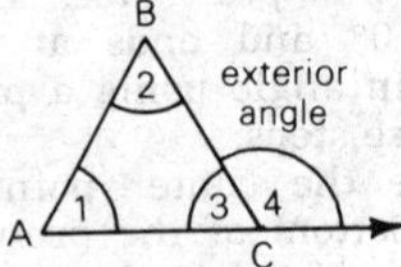

Given: △ABC, ext. ∠4

To prove: $\angle 1 + \angle 2 = \angle 4$

Proof:

1. △ABC, exterior angle 4.
   1. Given.
2. $\angle 1 + \angle 2 + \angle 3 = 180°$.
   2. Theorem 6.
3. $\angle 3 + \angle 4 = 180°$.
   3. Two adjacent angles whose exterior sides lie on a straight line are supplementary.
4. $\angle 1 + \angle 2 = 180° - \angle 3$, $\angle 4 = 180° - \angle 3$.
   4. If equals are subtracted from equals the results are equal.
5. $\angle 1 + \angle 2 = \angle 4$.
   5. Quantities equal to the same quantity are equal to each other.

Congruent Triangles

Definition 42. Two *triangles are congruent* if they can be made to coincide part for part.

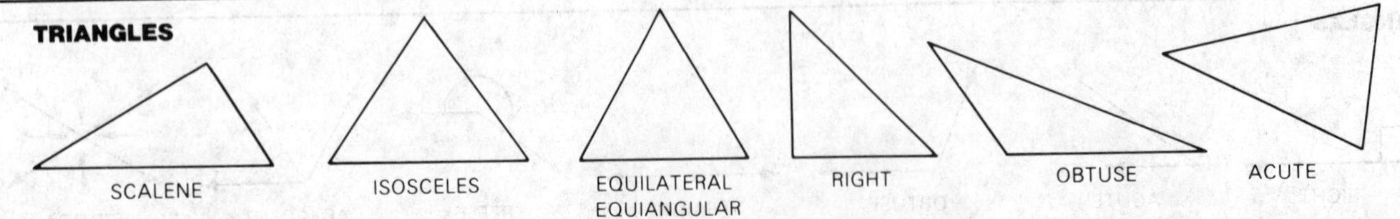

Postulate 13. Corresponding parts of congruent triangles are equal.

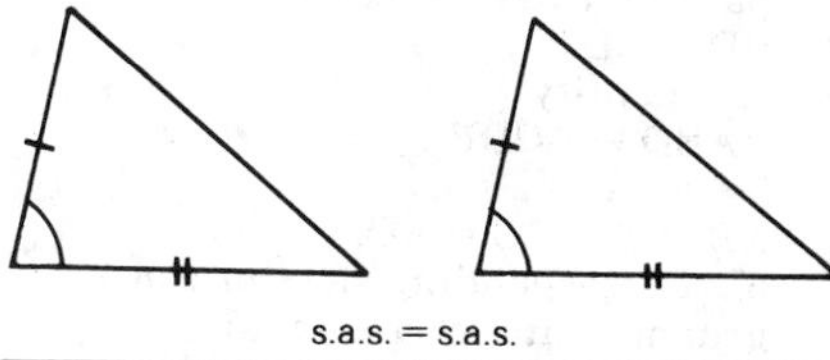

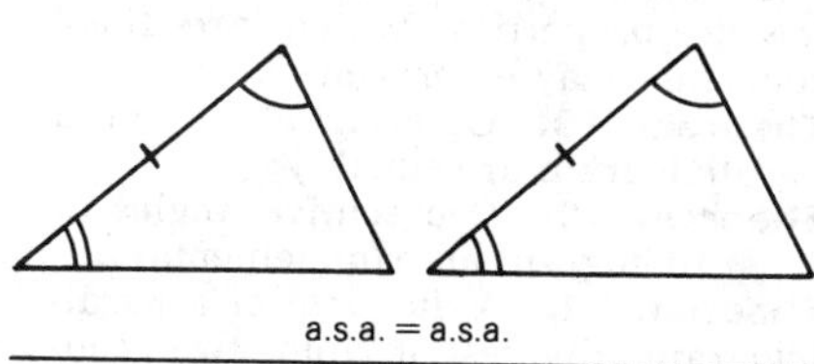

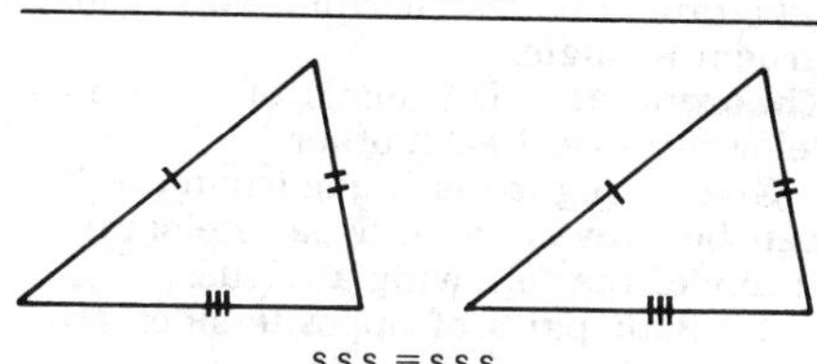

Postulate 14. Two triangles are congruent if two sides and the included angle of one are equal to the corresponding parts of the other (*s.a.s. = s.a.s.*).

Postulate 15. Two triangles are congruent if two angles and the included side of one are equal to the corresponding parts of the other (*a.s.a. = a.s.a.*).

Postulate 16. Two triangles are congruent if the three sides of one triangle are equal to the corresponding sides of the other (*s.s.s. = s.s.s.*).

Theorem 8. Two triangles are congruent if two angles and a side opposite one of them are equal to the corresponding parts of the other (*a.a.s. = a.a.s.*).

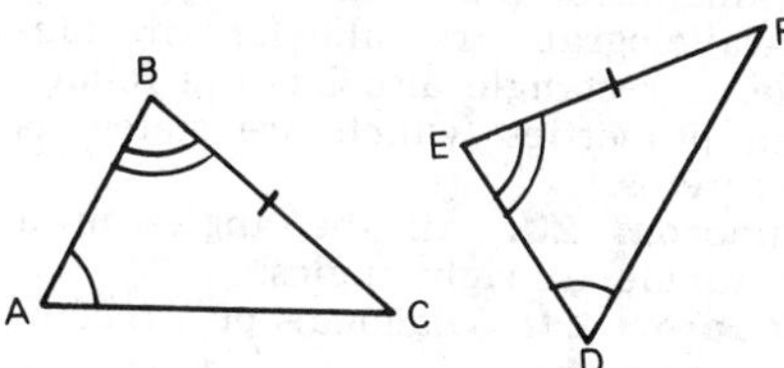

Given: △ABC, △DEF, ∠A = ∠D, ∠B = ∠E, BC = EF
To prove: △ABC ≅ △DEF

Proof:
1. ∠A = ∠D, ∠B = ∠E, BC = EF.
   1. Given
2. ∠C = ∠F.
   2. If two angles of one triangle are equal to two angles of another triangle, the third angles are equal.
3. △ABC ≅ △DEF.
   3. *a.s.a. = a.s.a.*

Are two triangles congruent if two sides and a nonincluded angle of one are equal to corresponding parts of the other? What if three angles of one triangle are equal to the corresponding angles of a second triangle? In order to show that a relationship is not true for a group of figures, all that is necessary is to find one example where the relationship does not work. Below are examples of two noncongruent triangles that have two equal sides and an equal nonincluded angle, and of two noncongruent triangles with equal angles.

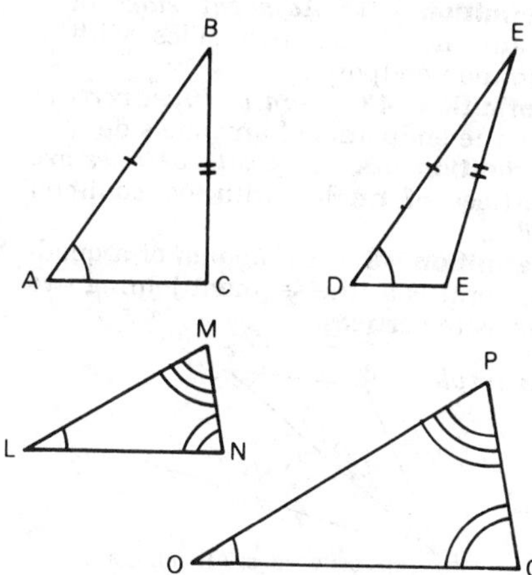

Therefore, if *a.a.a. = a.a.a.* or *s.s.a. = s.s.a.*, two triangles are not necessarily congruent.

Theorem 9. If two sides of a triangle are equal, the angles opposite them are equal. (Base angles of an isosceles triangle are equal.)

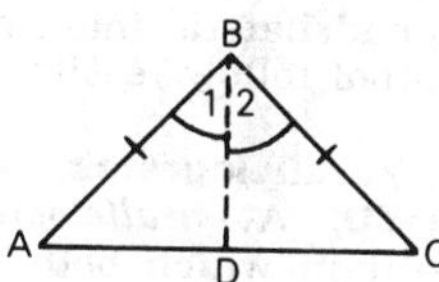

Given: △ABC, AB = BC
To prove: ∠A = ∠C

Proof:
1. AB = BC.
   1. Given.
2. Draw BD so it bisects ∠B and meets AC at D.
   2. Every angle has a bisector.
3. ∠1 = ∠2.
   3. An angle bisector divides an angle into two equal parts.
4. BD = BD.
   4. Identity.
5. △ABD ≅ △BCD.
   5. *s.a.s. = s.a.s.*
6. ∠A = ∠C.
   6. Corresponding angles of congruent triangles are equal.

Theorem 10. If two angles of a triangle are equal, the sides opposite are equal.

A corollary is a theorem that can be easily deduced from a postulate or another theorem.

Theorem 11 (corollary). If a triangle is equiangular, it is equilateral.

The proof follows directly from theorem 10.

The postulates and theorems for proving triangles congruent can be applied in proving parts of overlapping triangles equal.

UPI

THE TRIANGLE *is important for its structural strength in this geodesic playground piece.*

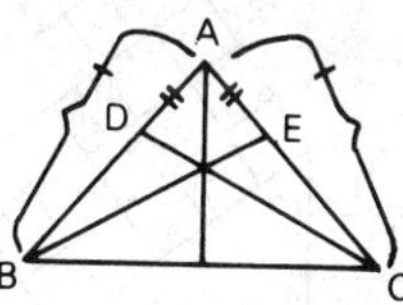

Given: Isosceles △ABC, AB = AC, AD = AE
To prove: BE = DC

Proof:
1. AB = AC, AD = AE.
   1. Given.
2. ∠A = ∠A.
   2. Identity.
3. △ABE ≅ △ADC.
   3. *s.a.s. = s.a.s.*
4. BE = DC.
   4. Corresponding parts of congruent triangles are equal.

Right Triangles

To prove two right triangles congruent, it is possible to use any of the congruence postulates or theorems already stated. The following two theorems provide a more convenient method for proving right triangles congruent.

Theorem 12. Two right triangles are congruent if the legs of one of them are equal to the corresponding parts of the other.

This theorem is a corollary of postulate 14.

Theorem 13. Two right triangles are congruent if the hypotenuse and leg of one of them are equal to the corresponding parts of the other (*h.l. = h.l.*).

A Greek mathematician, Pythagoras, born *circa* 540 B.C., is credited with a famous theorem applicable only to right triangles.

Theorem 14 (Pythagorean Theorem). The square of the hypotenuse of a right triangle is equal to the sum of the square of the legs.

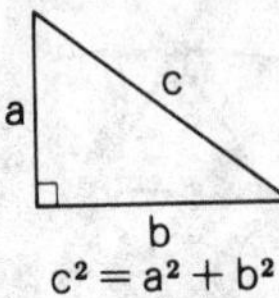

$c^2 = a^2 + b^2$

Theorem 15. If the square of one side of a triangle is equal to the sum of the squares of the other two sides, then the triangle is a right triangle.

Definition 43. A *Pythagorean triple* is any group of three integers such that the sum of the squares of two of them is equal to the square of the third.

One example of a Pythagorean triple is 3,4,5, since $3^2 + 4^2 = 5^2$. The following illustrates a simple "proof" that if the lengths of the legs of a right triangle are 3 and 4 and the hypotenuse is 5, then the Pythagorean Theorem holds.

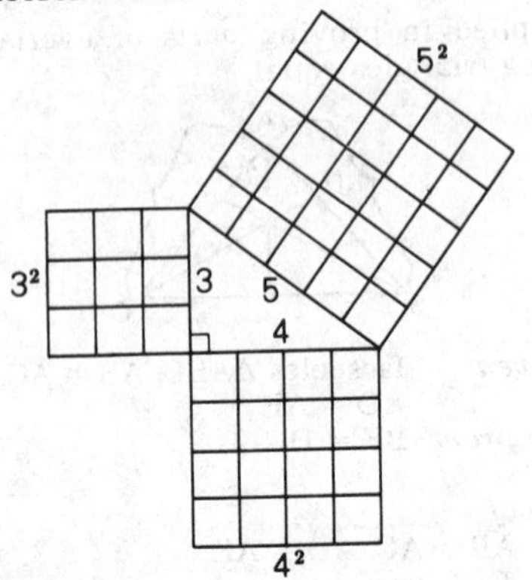

Theorem 16. If *a,b,c* is a Pythagorean triple, then any integral multiple is also a Pythagorean triple. For example, if 3,4,5 is a Pythagorean triple, so is 6,8,10.

Other Pythagorean triples are 5, 12,13 and any integral multiple, or 8,15,17 and any integral multiple.

Two special right triangles are an isosceles right triangle and a 30°, 60°, 90° right triangle. Given the length of the hypotenuse is *h*, then the lengths of the legs are determined as shown in the diagram below.

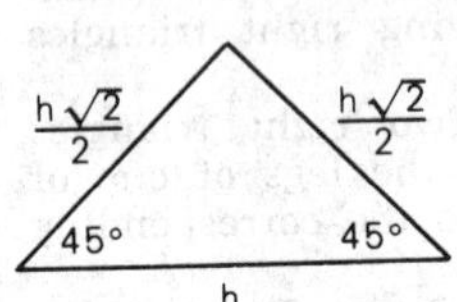

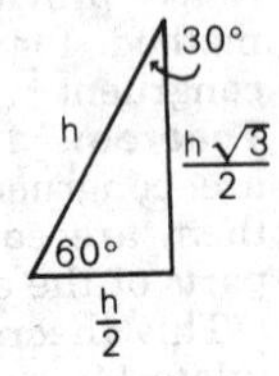

Quadrilaterals.

Definition 44. A *quadrilateral* is a four-sided polygon.

A quadrilateral is designated by four capital letters, one at each vertex.

Definition 45. *Opposite sides* of a quadrilateral are two sides with no common endpoint.

Definition 46. *Adjacent sides* of a quadrilateral are two sides with a common endpoint.

Definition 47. *Consecutive vertices* are the endpoints of any one side.

Definition 48. *Opposite vertices* are vertices of angles with no common sides.

Definition 49. A *diagonal* of a quadrilateral is a line segment joining two opposite vertices.

Example:

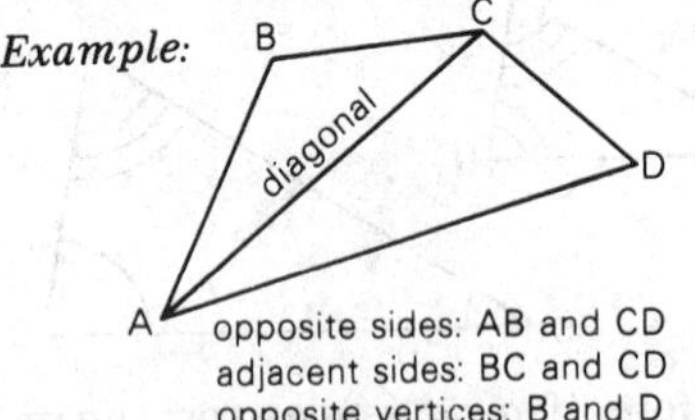

Theorem 17. The sum of the angles of a quadrilateral is 360°.

This theorem is a corollary of the theorem that the sum of the angles of a triangle is 180°. Draw any diagonal of the quadrilateral. The diagonal divides the quadrilateral into two triangles. The proof follows easily.

Parallelograms

Definition 50. A *parallelogram* is a quadrilateral in which both pairs of opposite sides are parallel.

Parallelograms have many special properties.

Theorem 18. Opposite sides of a parallelogram are equal.

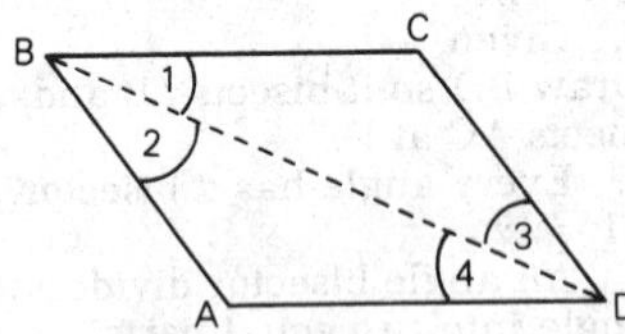

Given: ABCD is a ▱
To prove: AB = CD, BC = AD

Proof:

1. ABCD is a parallelogram.
   1. Given.
2. AB ∥ CD, BC ∥ AD.
   2. Opposite sides of a parallelogram are parallel.
3. ∠1 = ∠4, ∠2 = ∠3.
   3. Alternate interior angles of parallel lines are equal.
4. BD = BD.
   4. Identity.
5. △ABD ≅ △CDB.
   5. a.s.a. = a.s.a.
6. AB = CD, BC = AD.
   6. Corresponding sides of congruent triangles are equal.

A parallelogram also has the following properties, which are theorems and may be proven.

Theorem 19. Opposite angles of a parallelogram are equal.

Theorem 20. Consecutive angles of a parallelogram are supplementary.

Theorem 21. A diagonal of a parallelogram divides it into two congruent triangles.

Theorem 22. Diagonals of a parallelogram bisect each other.

Given a figure is a quadrilateral, it can be proven to be a parallelogram if any of the following are true:

1. Both pairs of opposite sides are parallel.
2. Both pairs of opposite sides are equal.
3. Two opposite sides are both equal and parallel.
4. The diagonals bisect each other.
5. Both pairs of opposite angles are equal.

To find the area of a parallelogram, call one side the base. Then the opposite side is also a base. The perpendicular distance between the bases is the height (altitude) of the parallelogram. The area is equal to the base times the height.

Rectangles

Definition 51. A *rectangle* is a parallelogram one of whose angles is a right angle.

Since a rectangle is a parallelogram, all the theorems that apply to a parallelogram are valid for a rectangle. A rectangle also has the following properties, which are stated as theorems.

Theorem 23. All the angles of a rectangle are right angles.

Theorem 24. Diagonals of a rectangle are equal.

To find the area of a rectangle, choose any side as a base. The opposite side is also a base. Either of the other sides is the perpendicular distance between the bases. Therefore, the area is the product of the lengths of two adjacent sides.

Rhombuses

Definition 52. A *rhombus* is a par-

QUADRILATERALS

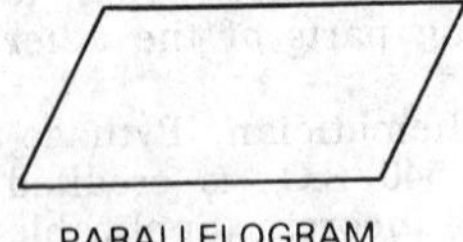
PARALLELOGRAM

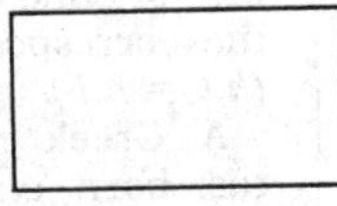
RECTANGLE

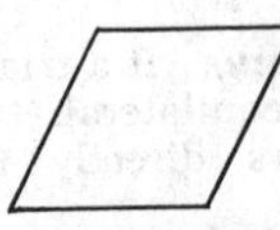
RHOMBUS

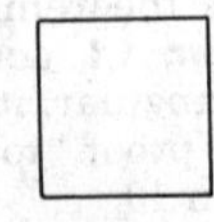
SQUARE

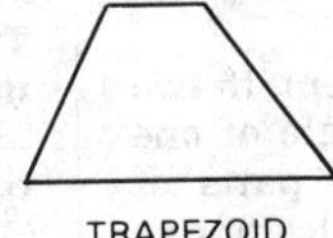
TRAPEZOID

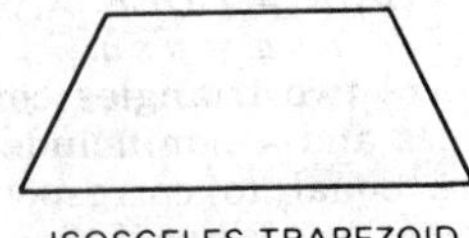
ISOSCELES TRAPEZOID

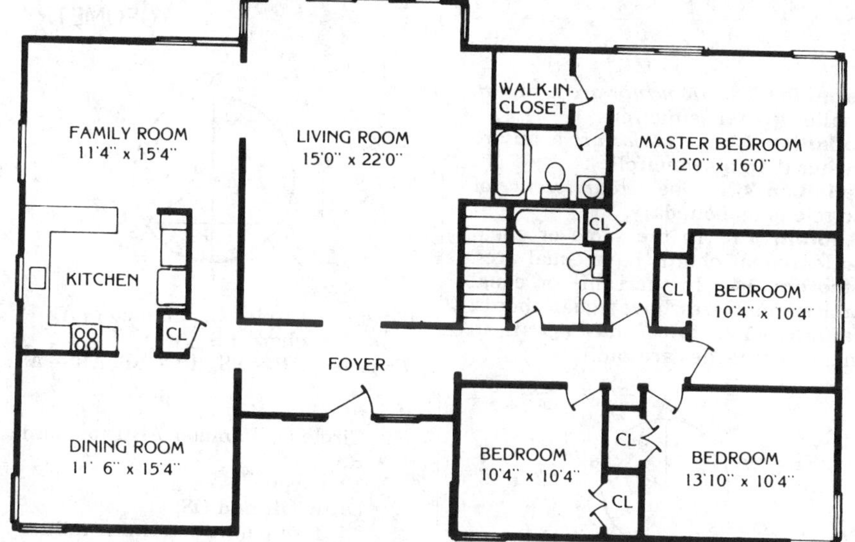

THE RECTANGLE *is nearly always the shape of our living spaces as this floorplan shows.*

allelogram having two adjacent sides equal.

Since a rhombus is a parallelogram, all the theorems that apply to a parallelogram are valid for a rhombus. A rhombus also has the following properties, which are stated as theorems.

Theorem 25. All the sides of a rhombus are equal.

Theorem 26. The diagonals of a rhombus are perpendicular to each other.

Theorem 27. The diagonals of a rhombus bisect the angles.

Squares

Definition 53. A *square* is a rectangle having two adjacent sides equal.

A square has all the properties of a rectangle and a rhombus. The area of a square is the product of the lengths of any two sides.

Trapezoids

Definition 54. A *trapezoid* is a quadrilateral with exactly two sides parallel.

Definition 55. An *isosceles trapezoid* is a trapezoid in which the nonparallel sides are equal.

The parallel sides are called the bases. The nonparallel sides are called the legs.

The following properties, stated as theorems, are valid for isosceles trapezoids.

Theorem 28. Base angles of an isosceles trapezoid are equal.

Theorem 29. Diagonals of an isosceles trapezoid are equal.

The area of a trapezoid is one-half the product of the height and the sum of the bases.

More polygons. Triangles, squares, and rectangles are very commonly used and known polygons, but many others exist and are used extensively in art and design. For example, the border on the Susan B. Anthony dollar is an eleven-sided polygon.

Definition 56. A *pentagon* is a five-sided polygon.

Definition 57. A *hexagon* is a six-sided polygon.

Definition 58. A *heptagon* is a seven-sided polygon.

Definition 59. An *octagon* is an eight-sided polygon.

Definition 60. A *nonagon* is a nine-sided polygon.

Definition 61. A *decagon* is a ten-sided polygon.

Definition 62. A *convex polygon* is a polygon in which each angle measures less than 180°.

Definition 63. A *concave polygon* is a polygon in which at least one angle measures more than 180°.

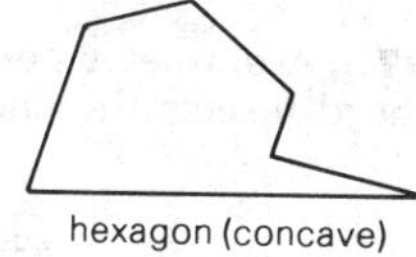

hexagon (concave)

Although the hexagon above fits its definitions, it is not the common conception of what a hexagon looks like. Both of these polygons are concave. The more commonly encountered and used polygons are convex. Often their sides are of equal length and their angles of equal measure.

Definition 64. A *regular polygon* is a polygon that is equilateral and equiangular.

The following table lists the sum of the interior angles of polygons starting with triangles and ending with decagons:

Number of Sides (n)	*Sum of Interior Angles*
3	180° = 180° × 1
4	360° = 180° × 2
5	540° = 180° × 3
6	720° = 180° × 4
7	900° = 180° × 5
8	1080° = 180° × 6
9	1260° = 180° × 7
10	1440° = 180° × 8

Theorem 30. The sum of the interior angles of a polygon is $180°(n - 2)$, where n is the number of sides.

Although no formal proof is offered, the formula can be generalized from the information in the table.

Theorem 31. The measure of any interior angle of a regular polygon is equal to $\frac{180°(n-2)}{n}$, where n is the number of sides.

This theorem is a corollary of theorem 30 and the definition of a regular polygon.

Definition 65. An exterior angle of a polygon is the angle formed by one side of the polygon and the extension of the adjacent side.

Theorem 32. The sum of the exterior angles of a polygon of any number of sides is 360°.

The proof follows from theorem 30 and the postulate that two adjacent angles whose exterior sides lie on a straight line are supplementary.

Polygons may have any number of sides. As the number of sides of a convex polygon gets larger and larger, the shape appears more and more like a circle.

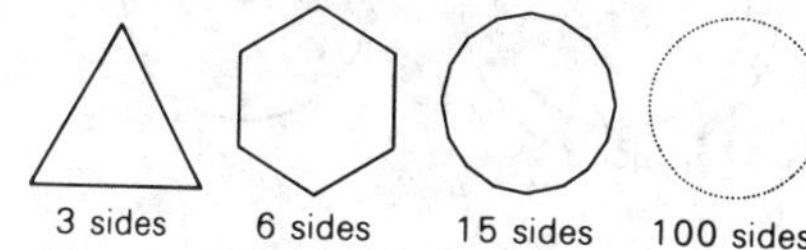

REGULAR POLYGONS

PENTAGON HEXAGON HEPTAGON OCTAGON NONAGON DECAGON

Circles

Definition 66. A *circle* is the set of all points at a given distance from a given point.

The given point is called the *center* of the circle. If a capital letter is placed at the center point, the circle is designated by that letter.

Definition 67. A *radius* is a line segment from the center to any point on the circle.

Definition 68. A *chord* is a line segment joining any two points on a circle.

Definition 69. A *diameter* is a chord that passes through the center of the circle.

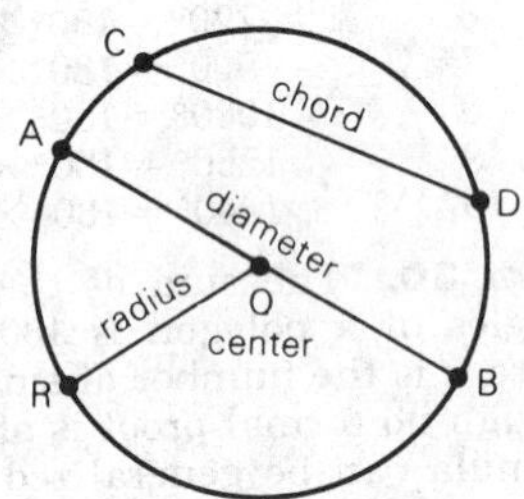

Postulate 17. Radii (diameters) of the same or equal circles are equal.

Postulate 18. The length of the diameter of a circle is equal to two times the length of the radius.

Definition 70. An *arc* is the part of the circle between any two points on the circle.

An arc is designated by the capital letters at its endpoints with an arc (⌒) sign over them.

The endpoints of a diameter divide the circle into two equal arcs called *semicircles.* If two points, A and B, not the endpoints of a diameter, are chosen on a circle, they divide the circle into a major and minor arc.

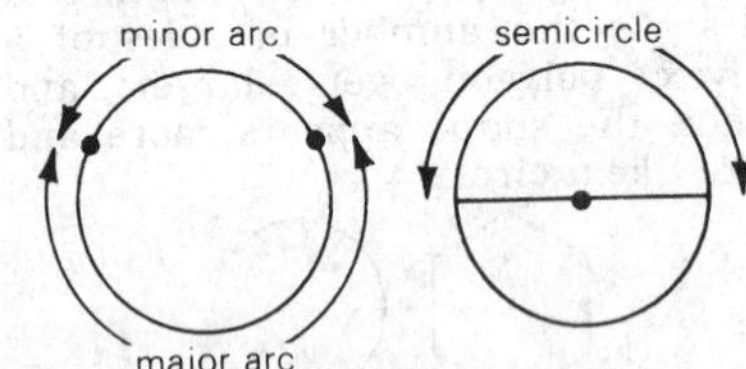

Definition 71. A *minor arc* is an arc smaller than a semicircle.

Definition 72. A *major arc* is an arc greater than a semicircle.

Definition 73. The *circumference* of a circle is its boundary.

Theorem 33. In the same or equal circles, equal chords have equal arcs.

Theorem 34. In the same or equal circles equal arcs have equal chords.

Definition 74. A *central angle* is an angle whose sides are radii.

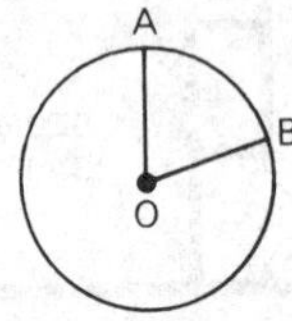

central angle AOB

Theorem 35. In the same or equal circles, equal central angles have equal arcs.

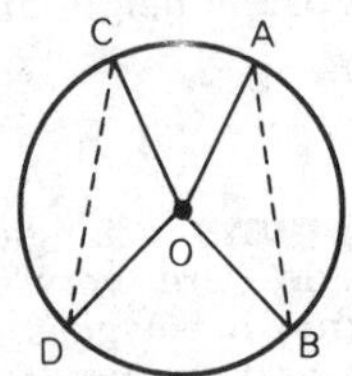

Given: Circle O, central $\angle AOB$ = central $\angle COD$

To prove: $\widehat{AB} = \widehat{CD}$

Proof:

1. Circle O, central $\angle AOB$ = central $\angle COD$.
   1. Given.
2. Draw CD and AB.
   2. Two points determine a line.
3. AO = CO, DO = BO.
   3. Postulate 17.
4. $\triangle AOB \cong \triangle COD$.
   4. *s.a.s.* = *s.a.s.*
5. AB = CD.
   5. Corresponding parts of congruent triangles are equal.
6. $\widehat{AB} = \widehat{CD}$.
   6. Theorem 33.

Theorem 36. In the same or equal circles, equal arcs have equal central angles.

Theorem 37. A diameter perpendicular to a chord bisects the chord and its arcs.

MADISON SQUARE GARDEN, *shown under construction, is a circular structure.*

UPI

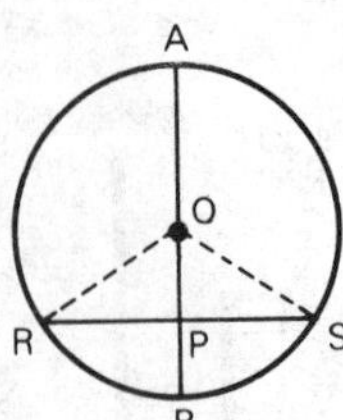

Given: Circle O, diameter AB ⊥ chord RS

To prove: RP = PS, $\widehat{RB} = \widehat{SB}$, $\widehat{AR} = \widehat{AS}$

Proof:

1. Circle O, diameter AB ⊥ to chord RS.
   1. Given.
2. Draw OR and OS.
   2. Two points determine a line.
3. $\angle OPR$ and $\angle OPS$ are right angles.
   3. Perpendicular lines form right angles.
4. OP = OP.
   4. Identity.
5. OR = OS.
   5. Postulate 17.
6. $\triangle OPR \cong \triangle OPS$.
   6. *h.l.* = *h.l.*
7. RP = PS, $\angle ROP = \angle POS$.
   7. Corresponding parts of congruent triangles are equal.
8. $\widehat{RB} = \widehat{SB}$.
   8. Theorem 35.
9. $\widehat{ARB} = \widehat{ASB}$.
   9. A diameter divides a circle into two equal arcs.
10. $\widehat{AR} = \widehat{AS}$.
    10. Equals subtracted from equals are equal.

Theorem 38. A perpendicular drawn from the center of a circle to a chord bisects the chord.

This is a corollary of theorem 37.

Theorem 39. In the same or equal circles, equal chords are equidistant from the center.

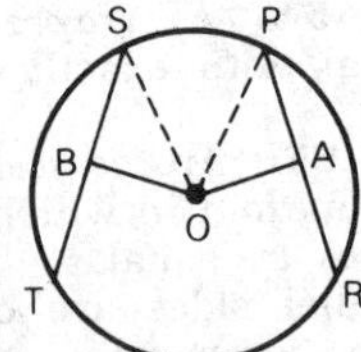

Given: Circle O, chords PR and ST, PR = ST, OA ⊥ PR, OB ⊥ ST

To prove: OB = OA

Proof:

1. Circle O, chord PR = chord ST.
   1. Given.
2. Draw radii OP and OS.
   2. Two points determine a line.
3. OP = OS.
   3. Postulate 17.
4. $\angle PAO$ and $\angle SBO$ are right angles.
   4. Perpendiculars form right angles.
5. PA = $\frac{1}{2}$PR, SB = $\frac{1}{2}$ST.
   5. Theorem 38.
6. PA = SB.
   6. Halves of equals are equal.

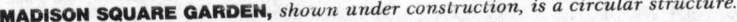

7. ΔBSO ≅ ΔPAO.
   7. *h.l.* = *h.l.*
8. OB = OA.
   8. Corresponding parts of congruent triangles are equal.

Theorem 40. In the same or equal circles, chords that are equidistant from the center are equal to each other.

The proof is similar to the one for theorem 39.

Definition 75. A *tangent* to a circle is a line that touches the circle at one and only one point, no matter how far it is extended.

Theorem 41. A tangent is perpendicular to the radius drawn to the point of tangency.

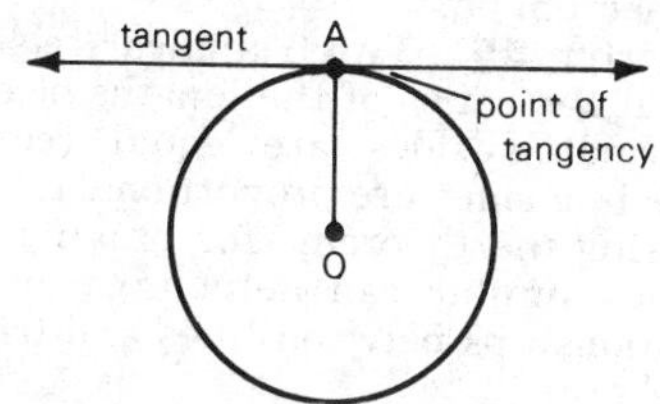

Definition 76. The length of a tangent drawn from a given external point is the length of the line segment whose endpoints are the given external point and the point of tangency.

Theorem 42. The lengths of tangents drawn to a circle from a common external point are equal.

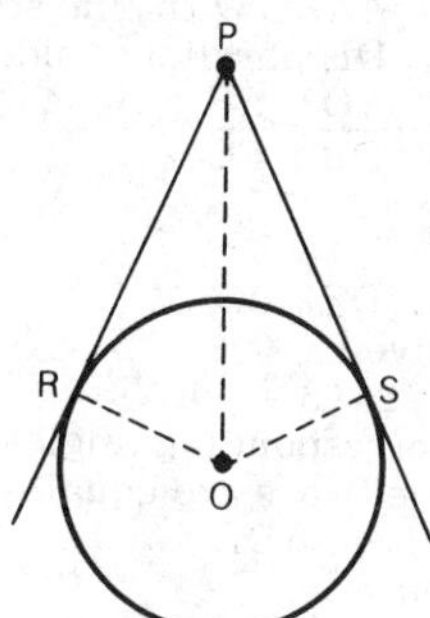

Given: Circle O, PR tangent at R, PS tangent at S
To prove: PR = PS

Proof:
1. Circle O, PR tangent at R, PS tangent at S.
   1. Given.
2. Draw OP, OR, and OS.
   2. Two points determine a line.
3. OR = OS.
   3. Postulate 17.
4. OP = OP.
   4. Identity.
5. OR ⊥ RP, OS ⊥ PS.
   5. Theorem 41.
6. PRO and PSO are right angles.
   6. Perpendiculars form right angles.
7. ΔPRO ≅ ΔPOS.
   7. *h.l.* = *h.l.*
8. PR = PS.
   8. Corresponding parts of congruent triangles are equal.

Definition 77. A *secant* is a line that is drawn from an external point and intersects a circle in two points.

Arc and angle measurement.

Definition 78. The *measure (m) of a circle* is 360°.

Definition 79. The *measure of a semicircle* is 180°.

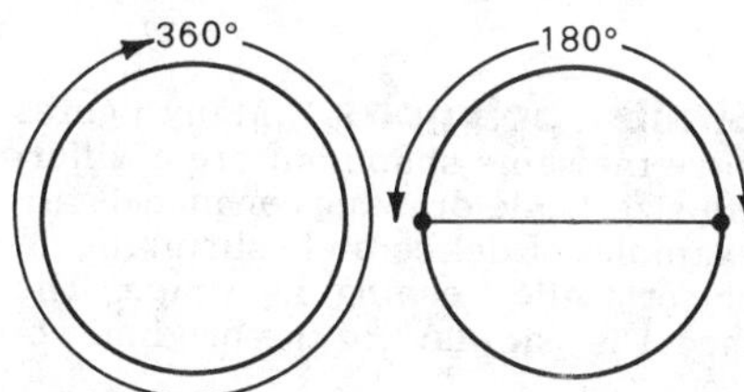

Definition 80. The *measure of a minor arc* is the measure of the central angle that intercepts the arc.

Definition 81. The *measure of a major arc* is 360° minus the measure of the minor arc that has the same endpoints.

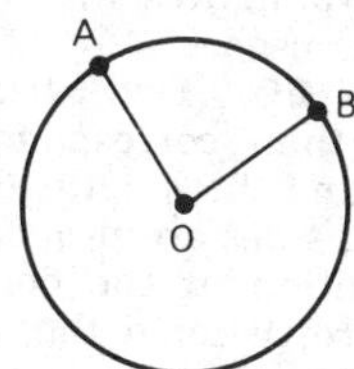

$m\ \widehat{AB}$ (minor) = $m\angle AOB$

$m\ \widehat{AB}$ (major) = $360° - m\angle AOB$

Definition 82. An *inscribed angle* of a circle is an angle whose vertex is on the circle and whose sides are chords of the circle.

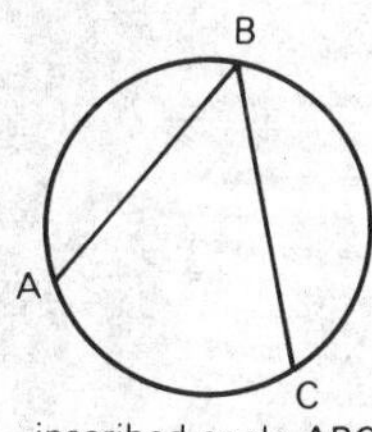

inscribed angle ABC

Definition 83. A central angle is measured by its intercepted arc.

Theorem 43. An inscribed angle is measured by one-half its intercepted arc.

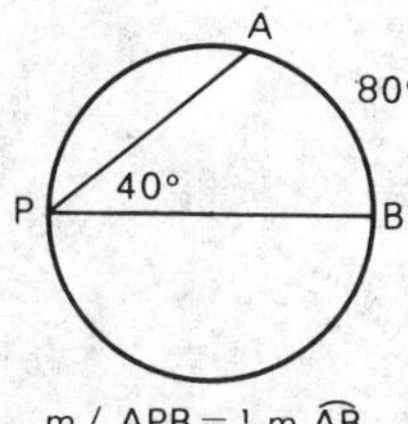

$m\angle APB = \frac{1}{2}\ m\ \widehat{AB}$

Theorem 44. An angle formed by a tangent and a chord is measured by one-half its intercepted arc.

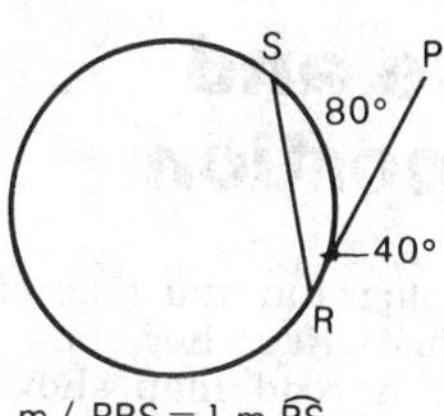

$m\angle PRS = \frac{1}{2}\ m\ \widehat{RS}$

Theorem 45. An angle formed by two chords intersecting within a circle is measured by one-half the sum of the opposite intercepted arcs.

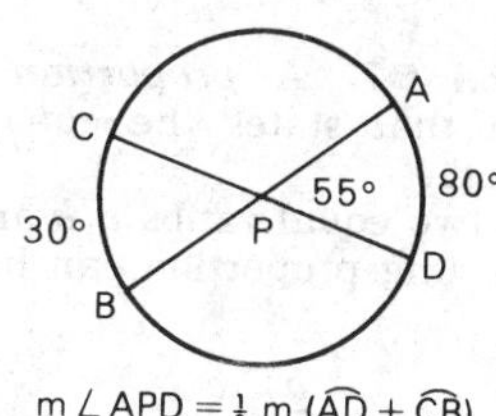

$m\angle APD = \frac{1}{2}\ m\ (\widehat{AD} + \widehat{CB})$

Theorem 46. An angle formed by two secants, two tangents, or a tangent and a secant intersecting outside a circle is measured by one-half the difference of the two intercepted arcs.

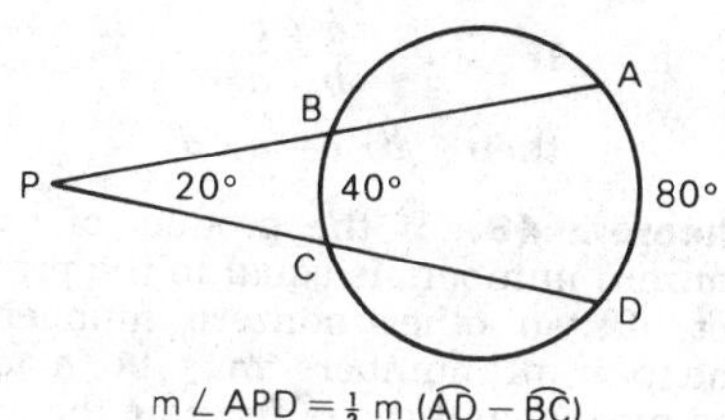

$m\angle APD = \frac{1}{2}\ m\ (\widehat{AD} - \widehat{BC})$

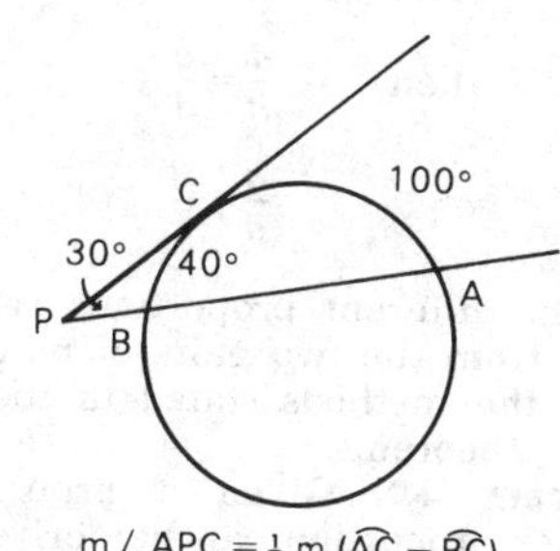

$m\angle APC = \frac{1}{2}\ m\ (\widehat{AC} - \widehat{BC})$

Definition 84. A circle circumscribed about a polygon is a circle that passes through each vertex of the polygon.

Definition 85. A circle is inscribed in a polygon when all the sides of the polygon are tangent to the circle.

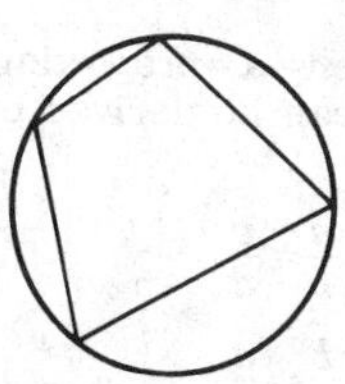
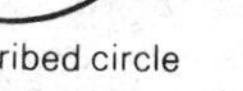
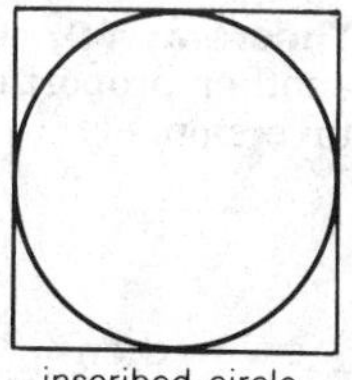

circumscribed circle inscribed circle

Ratio and Proportion

The photograph you take of a friend looks just like her but is much smaller. A road map shows relative distances, not actual distances. These are examples of ratio and proportion being put to use.

Definition 86. The *ratio* of two quantities a and b is

$$\frac{a}{b},\ b \neq 0$$

Definition 87. A *proportion* is an equation that states the equality of two ratios.

Given two equal ratios a/b and c/d, the following proportion can be written:

$$\frac{a}{b}=\frac{c}{d}$$

Then a and d are called the extremes of the proportion and b and c the means.

Theorem 47. In a proportion, the product of the means is equal to the product of the extremes.

If $\frac{a}{b}=\frac{c}{d}$,

then $b \cdot c = a \cdot d$

Theorem 48. If the product of two nonzero numbers is equal to the product of two other nonzero numbers, one pair of numbers may be made the means, and the other pair the extremes of a proportion.

If $a \cdot d = b \cdot c$,

then $\frac{a}{b}=\frac{c}{d}$

or $\frac{b}{a}=\frac{d}{c}$

Eight different proportions can be made from the two pairs of numbers using the methods stated in the following theorems.

Theorem 49. Given a proportion, another proportion can be derived by alternating the means or the extremes.

If $\frac{a}{b}=\frac{c}{d}$,

then $\frac{a}{c}=\frac{b}{d}$

and $\frac{d}{b}=\frac{c}{a}$

Theorem 50. Given a proportion, another proportion can be derived by inversion.

If $\frac{a}{b}=\frac{c}{d}$,

then $\frac{b}{a}=\frac{d}{c}$

Theorem 51. Given a proportion, another proportion can be derived by addition or subtraction.

If $\frac{a}{b}=\frac{c}{d}$,

then $\frac{a+b}{b}=\frac{c+d}{d}$

or $\frac{a-b}{b}=\frac{c-d}{d}$

Similar polygons. Many figures have the same shape but are a different size. Scale drawings or models are examples of deliberately shrinking an object while keeping its shape. The model is "similar" to the original object.

Definition 88. Two *polygons are similar* if

1. they have the same number of sides and angles
2. all corresponding angles are equal, and
3. the lengths of the corresponding sides are proportional.

When two figures are similar, the symbol ~ is used.

Definition 89. Two *triangles are similar* if their corresponding angles are equal and the lengths of their corresponding sides are proportional.

By definition, if the corresponding sides are proportional, the ratio of their lengths is equal.

A SCALE MODEL *is built in proportion to the object it represents. The scale of this model is about one inch to eight feet.*

UPI

Theorem 52. Two triangles are similar if three angles of one triangle are equal to the three corresponding angles of the other *(a.a.a. = a.a.a.)*.

Theorem 53. Two triangles are similar if two angles of one triangle are equal to the two corresponding angles of the other *(a.a. = a.a.)*.

Theorem 53 is a corollary of theorem 52 and the postulate that if two angles of one triangle are equal to two angles of another, the third angles are equal.

Theorem 54. Two right triangles are similar if a second angle of one is equal to the corresponding second angle of the other.

This theorem is a direct corollary of theorem 53.

Theorem 55. Two triangles are similar if the ratios of the lengths of corresponding sides are equal (corresponding sides are proportional).

Using the theorems for proving triangles similar can help prove many relationships between lines and triangles.

Theorem 56. A line segment parallel to one side of a triangle divides the other two sides into proportional segments.

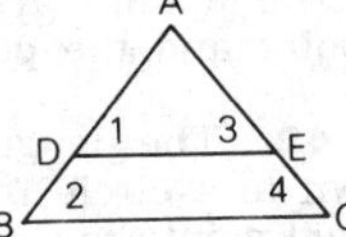

Given: △ABC with line segment DE parallel to side BC

To prove: $\frac{AD}{DB}=\frac{AE}{EC}$

Proof:

1. △ABC, DE ∥ BC.
   1. Given.
2. ∠1 = ∠2, ∠3 = ∠4.
   2. Corresponding angles of parallel lines are equal.
3. △ABC ~ △ADE.
   3. *a.a. = a.a.*
4. $\frac{AB}{AD}=\frac{AC}{AE}$
   4. Corresponding sides of similar triangles are proportional.
5. $\frac{AB-AD}{AD}=\frac{AC-AE}{AE}$
   5. Theorem 51.
6. $\frac{DB}{AD}=\frac{EC}{AE}$
   6. Substitution.
7. $\frac{AD}{DB}=\frac{AE}{EC}$
   7. Theorem 50.

Theorem 57. An angle bisector of a triangle divides the opposite side into segments proportional to the adjacent sides.

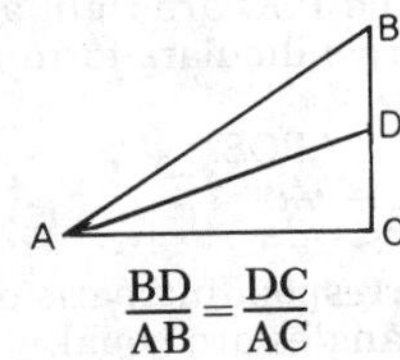

$$\frac{BD}{AB}=\frac{DC}{AC}$$

Theorem 58. Corresponding altitudes of similar triangles have the same ratio as any two corresponding sides.

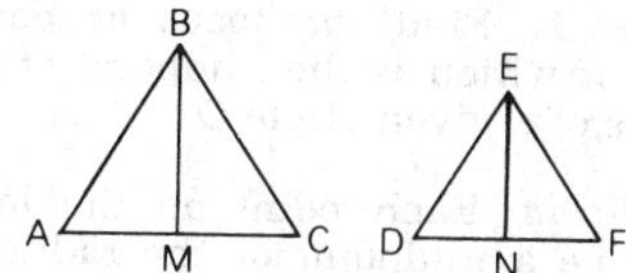

Given: △ABC ~ △DEF, with sides AB and DE, AC and DF, BC and EF corresponding, altitude BM drawn to side AC, altitude EN drawn to side DF

To prove: $\frac{AB}{ED} = \frac{BM}{EN}$

Proof:

1. △ABC ~ △DEF, sides corresponding and altitudes drawn as above.
   1. Given.
2. ∠1 and ∠2 are right angles.
   2. Perpendiculars form right angles.
3. △ABM and △DEN are right triangles.
   3. A right triangle is a triangle with one right angle.
4. ∠A = ∠D.
   4. Definition 89.
5. △ABM ~ △DEN.
   5. Theorem 54.
6. $\frac{AB}{ED} = \frac{BM}{EN}$
   6. Definition 89.

Theorem 59. If two chords intersect in a circle, the product of the segments of one equals the product of the segments of the other.

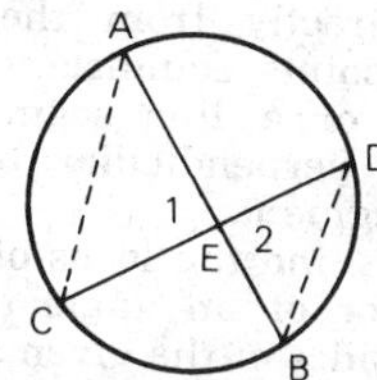

Given: Circle O, chords AB and CD intersecting at E

To prove: AE · EB = CE · ED

Proof:

1. Circle O, chords AB and CD intersecting at E.
   1. Given.
2. Draw AC and DB.
   2. Two points determine a line.
3. ∠1 = ∠2.
   3. Vertical angles are equal.
4. $m\angle C = \frac{1}{2}\, m\text{AD}$, $m\angle B = \frac{1}{2} m\text{AD}$.
   4. An inscribed angle is measured by one-half its intercepted arc.
5. ∠C = ∠B.
   5. Quantities equal to the same quantity are equal to each other.
6. △ACE ~ △DBE.
   6. a.a. = a.a.
7. $\frac{AE}{ED} = \frac{CE}{EB}$
   7. Definition 89.
8. AE · EB = CE · ED.
   8. Theorem 47.

Constructions

Euclidean geometric constructions permit only the use of an unmarked straightedge and a compass. The straightedge is used to draw a line or line segment and the compass to draw an arc or to mark off (measure) a line segment.

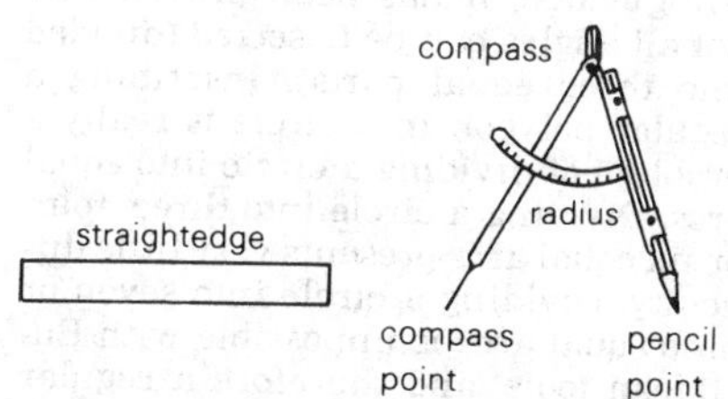

Construction 1. To construct a line segment equal in length to a given line segment.

Given: Line segment AB

To construct: A line segment equal in length to line segment AB

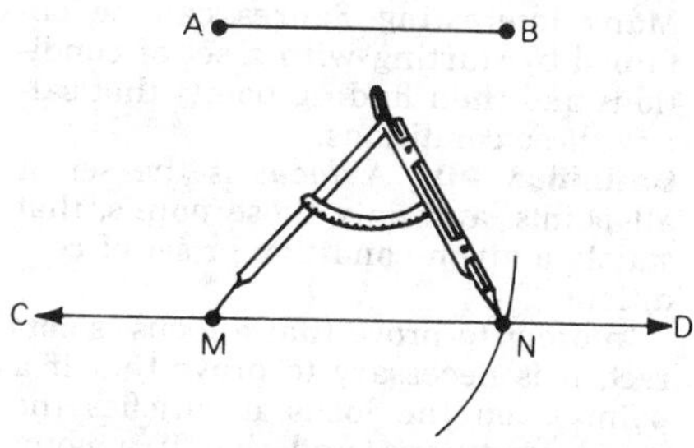

1. Using the straightedge, draw any line CD and mark a point M on it.
2. Open the compass to a radius equal to the length of AB.
3. Keeping this radius, place the compass point on M and mark off an arc that intersects CD at a point N.
4. MN = AB.

The proof for the equality of line segments AB and MN rests on the fact that they are radii of equal circles and therefore equal to each other.

Construction 2. To construct an angle equal to a given angle.

Given: ∠ABC and point E

To construct: An angle with vertex E equal in measure to ∠ABC

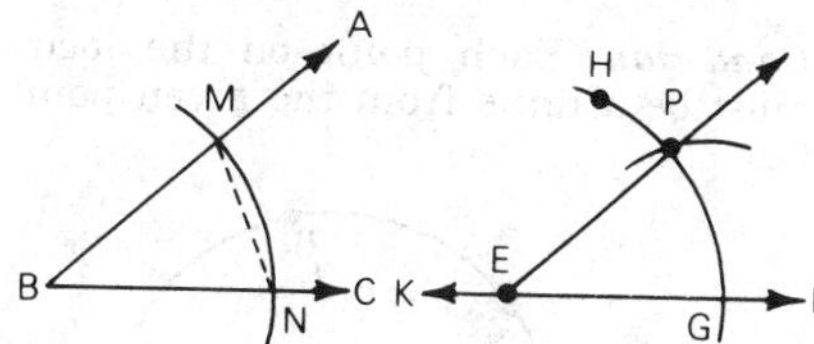

1. Through point E, draw any line KL.
2. Place the compass point at B and, using any convenient radius, draw an arc intersecting AB at M and BC at N.
3. Keeping the same radius, place the compass point at E and draw an arc intersecting KL at G. Call it arc GH.
4. Draw MN.
5. Open the compass to a radius equal to the length of MN. Place the compass point at G and mark off an arc that intersects arc GH at P.
6. Draw EP.
7. ∠ABC = ∠PEG.

MN and PG are equal chords in equal circles and therefore intercept equal arcs. Then central angles ABC and PEG are equal.

Construction 3. To bisect a given line segment.

Given: Line segment AB

To construct: The bisector of AB

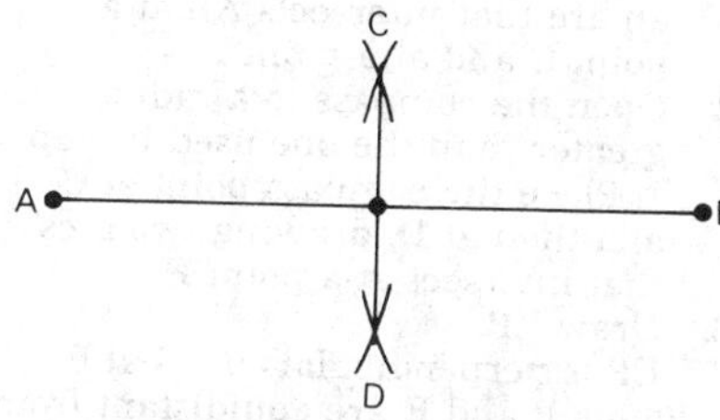

1. Make the radius of the compass any convenient length greater than half the length of AB.
2. Place the compass point at A and mark off one arc above AB and one below AB.
3. Keeping the same radius, place the compass point at B and mark off one arc above AB and one below AB so that they intersect the arcs drawn in step 2 at points C and D respectively.
4. Draw CD.
5. CD is the perpendicular bisector of AB.

The proof depends on the following theorem.

Theorem 60. If two points are equidistant from the endpoints of a line segment, they determine the perpendicular bisector of the line segment.

Construction 4. To bisect a given angle.

Given: ∠ABC

To construct: The bisector of ∠ABC

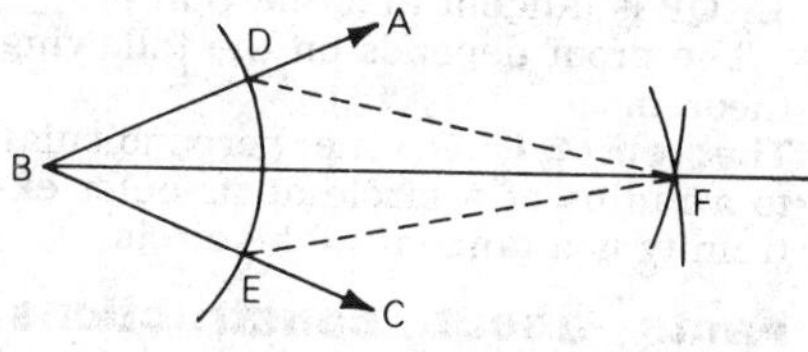

1. Place the compass point at B and, using a convenient radius, draw an arc that intersects AB at a point D and BC at a point E.
2. Place the compass point at E and then at D, using a radius of sufficient length to mark off two arcs that intersect at a point F.
3. Draw BF.
4. BF is the angle bisector of ∠ABC.

Triangle DBF is congruent to triangle EBF. Then angles ABF and FBC are equal corresponding angles.

Construction 5. To construct a line perpendicular to a given line through a given point on the line.

Given: Point P on line AB
To construct: A line through P ⊥ AB

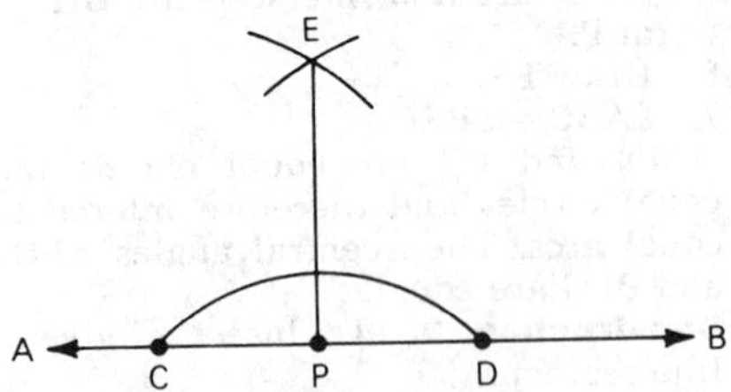

1. Place the compass point at P and, using a convenient radius, draw an arc that intersects AB at a point C and at a point D.
2. Open the compass to a radius greater than the one used in step 1. Place the compass point at C and then at D, drawing two arcs that intersect at a point E.
3. Draw EP.
4. EP is perpendicular to AB at P.

Points P and E are equidistant from the endpoints of line segment CD. By theorem 60, EP is the perpendicular bisector of CD and therefore perpendicular to AB.

Construction 6. To construct a line tangent to a given circle through a point on the circle.

Given: Circle O with point P on it
To construct: A tangent to circle O at point P

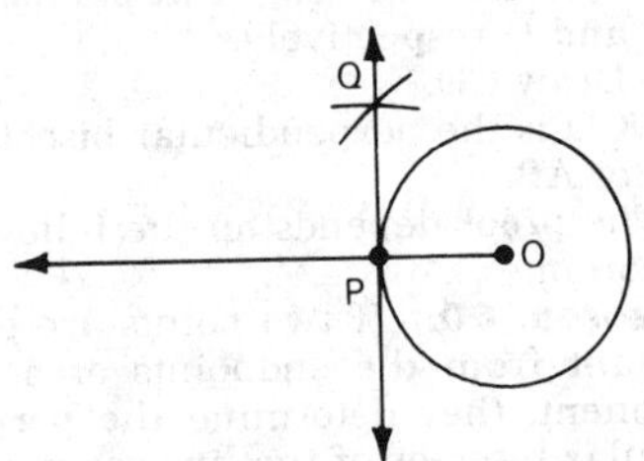

1. Draw radius OP and extend it outside the circle.
2. At P, construct PQ ⊥ OP. (Use construction 5.)
3. QP is tangent to circle O at P.

The proof depends on the following theorem.

Theorem 61. A line perpendicular to a radius of a circle at its outer extremity is a tangent to the circle.

Facts about constructions.

More than one approach can be used to perform a particular Euclidean construction. In the early 1900's, a mathematician named Lemoine developed a quantitative method for comparing different approaches to solving a construction problem. The science built on his work is called *geometrography.*

Other mathematicians have concerned themselves with different aspects of Euclidean constructions. In the 1700's, Mascheroni discovered that Euclidean constructions could be done with only a compass, using points to determine a line. Other mathematicians showed that, given a circle and its center, Euclidean constructions could be done with just a straightedge.

Some constructions are not solvable. For example, using a compass and a straightedge, it has been proven that not all angles can be trisected (divided into three equal parts). Inscribing a regular polygon in a circle is really a problem of dividing a circle into equal arcs. Dividing a circle into three, four, or six equal arcs presents very little difficulty. Dividing a circle into seven or nine equal arcs is impossible with Euclidean tools, and therefore a regular heptagon and a regular nonagon are impossible to inscribe in a circle.

Locus (Loci)

Many interesting figures can be obtained by starting with a set of conditions and then finding points that satisfy these conditions.

Definition 90. A *locus* is the set of all points, and only those points, that satisfy a given condition or set of conditions.

In order to prove that a locus is correct, it is necessary to prove that if a point is on the locus it satisfies the given conditions, and that if a point satisfies the given conditions it is on the locus.

To draw a locus is to draw the path made up of all the points. The following procedure provides a logical method of finding a locus.

1. State the condition or conditions the points have to meet.
2. Draw a diagram of any given points or lines.
3. Find a number of points satisfying the condition or conditions.
4. Draw the path made by the points.
5. Describe the locus.

This method does not guarantee that the locus drawn is the correct one. A proof is still necessary.

Locus 1. Find the locus of points *a* units from a given point O.

Condition: Each point on the locus must be *a* units from the given point O.

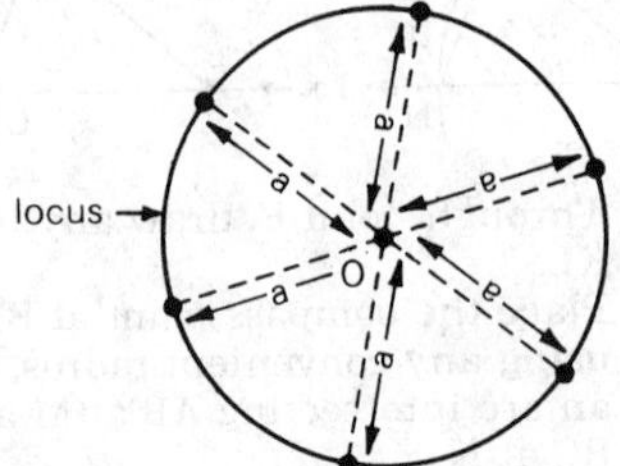

The locus is a circle with center O and radius of length *a* units. The proof follows directly from the definition of a circle.

Locus 2. Find the locus of points each of which is the midpoint of the radius of a given circle O.

Condition: Each point on the locus must be a midpoint of the radius of the given circle.

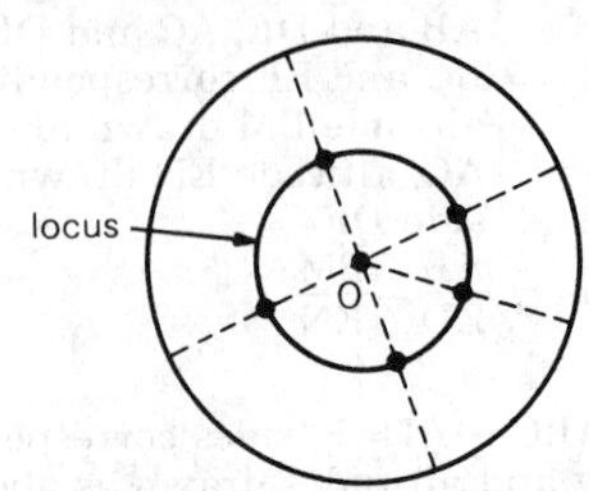

The locus is a circle with center O and radius half of the length of the radius of circle O. These two circles are called concentric circles (having the same center).

Locus 3. Find the locus of points equidistant from the endpoints of a given line segment.

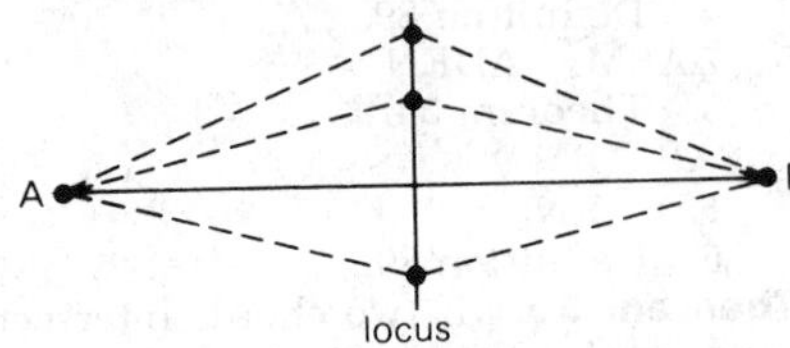

The locus is the perpendicular bisector of the line segment AB. This follows directly from the theorem that two points equidistant from the endpoints of a line segment determine the perpendicular bisector of the line segment.

Locus 4. Find the locus of points in the interior of an angle equidistant from the sides of the given angle.

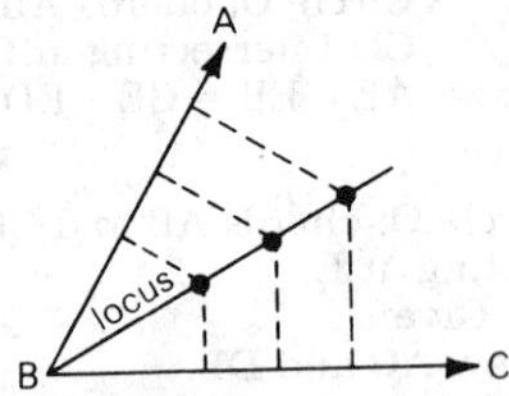

The locus is the angle bisector of angle ABC.

Locus 5. Find the locus of points equidistant from two parallel lines.

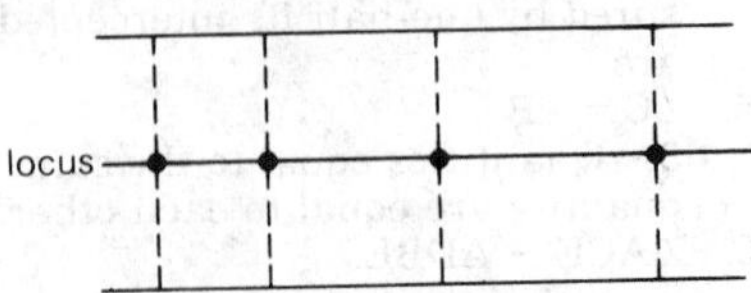

The locus is one line parallel to and equidistant from each of the given lines.

Locus 6. Find the locus of points within a given angle that are equidistant from its sides, and at a given distance d from its vertex.

Conditions: (1) Points are within a given angle. (2) Points are equidistant from the sides of the angle. (3) Points are at a given distance d from the vertex.

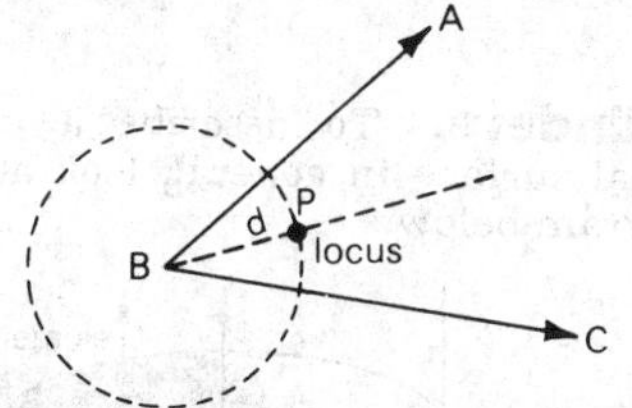

The locus of all points satisfying condition 2 is the angle bisector of the given angle. The locus of all points satisfying condition 3 is a circle with center at the vertex and radius of length d. Therefore, the locus satisfying all three conditions is a point P on the intersection of the angle bisector and the circle with center at the vertex and radius of length d.

Inequalities

Geometry makes use of the basic mathematical principles described in the following postulates.

Postulate 19. The whole is greater than any of its parts.

Postulate 20. (Substitution) A quantity may be substituted for its equal in an inequality.

Postulate 21. (Trichotomy) Given any two quantities, exactly one of the following is true:

1. The first quantity is less than the second.
2. The first quantity is equal to the second.
3. The first quantity is greater than the second.

Postulate 22. (Transitivity) If the first of three quantities is greater than the second, and the second is greater than the third, then the first is greater than the third.

If $a > b$ and $b > c$, then $a > c$

Postulate 23. The shortest distance between two points is a straight line.

Theorem 62. The measure of an exterior angle of a triangle is greater than the measure of either remote interior angle.

An exterior angle of a triangle is equal to the sum of the two remote interior angles. Then, by postulate 19, the exterior angle must be greater than either of the remote interior angles.

Theorem 63. The sum of the lengths of any two sides of a triangle is greater than the length of the third side.

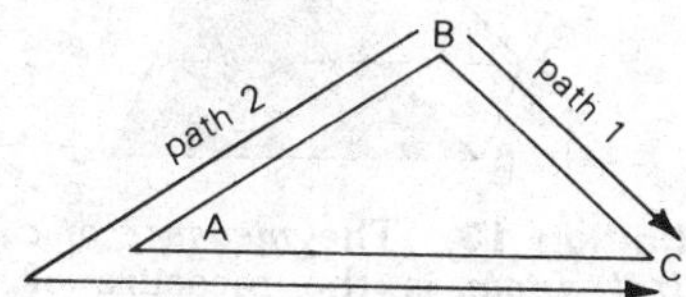

Informal proof: Either of two paths can be followed to get from point B to point C. By postulate 23, the length of path 2 > the length of path 1, and AB + AC > BC, by substitution.

Line Symmetry

Definition 91. A figure is symmetric about a given line if each point on one side of the line has a matching point on the other side of the line at the same distance from the line.

The line is called a *line of symmetry,* and if the figure were to be folded on this line of symmetry the two halves would coincide. In the illustrations below, the face is symmetric to a vertical line l. The curve is symmetric to a horizontal line x (the x axis). A butterfly's wings are also perfectly symmetrical.

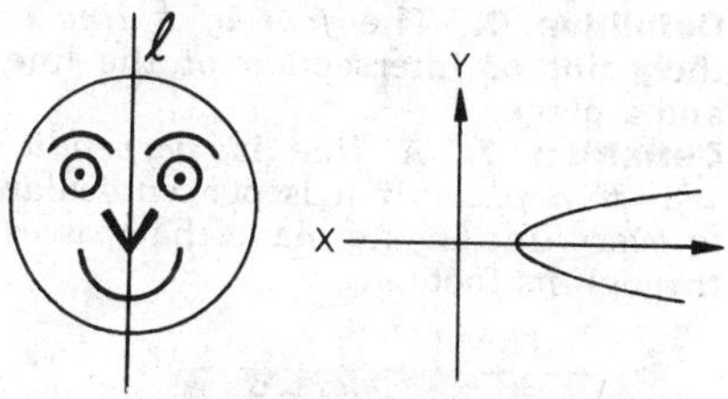

JOHN H. GERARD/DPI

Solid Geometry

CULVER PICTURES

THE GREAT PYRAMIDS *of Egypt show the Egyptians' grasp of practical geometry and architecture. Just how the huge stones were moved into place is still a mystery.*

Looking at the objects that surround us, we find that most of them have not two but three dimensions: length, width, and depth (thickness). When two-dimensional or plane geometry is extended to three dimensions, a square becomes a cube, a triangle becomes a cone or pyramid, and a circle becomes a sphere or cylinder. Much of the food we eat comes packed in cylindrical cans or rectangular boxes. We eat ice cream out of cone shapes, play tennis with a spherical ball, live in rectangular solids called skyscrapers, and operate the engines of cars with the help of cylindrical pistons.

Definitions

In order to study solid geometry in a systematic fashion, basic terms must be agreed upon. As in plane geometry, point, line, and plane are undefined terms. A plane is usually represented by a parallelogram and designated by a capital letter. A line is designated by a small letter and a point by a capital letter.

Definition 1. *Collinear points* are two points that lie on the same line.

Definition 2. *Coplanar lines* are lines that lie in the same plane.

Definition 3. *Skew lines* are lines that do not lie in the same plane.

Definition 4. The *intersection of a line and a plane* is the set of points that lie both on the line and in the plane.

For example, the intersection of plane A and line *l* below is one point P. The intersection of plane B and line *k* is all the points on line *k*.

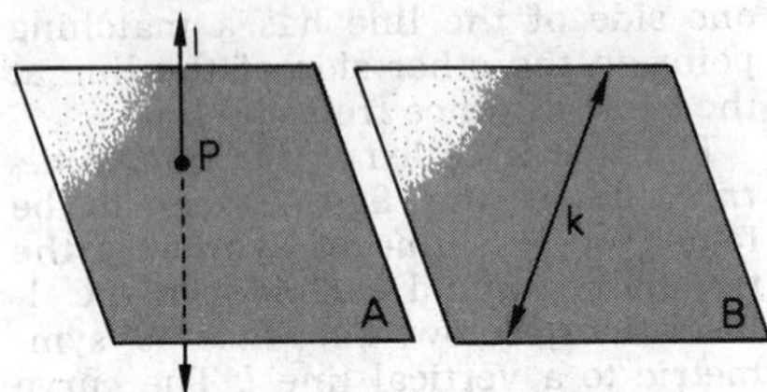

Definition 5. The *intersection of two planes* is the set of points that lie in both planes.
Definition 6. The *foot of a line* is the point of intersection of the line and a plane.
Definition 7. A *line is perpendicular to a plane* if it is perpendicular to every line in the plane that passes through its foot.

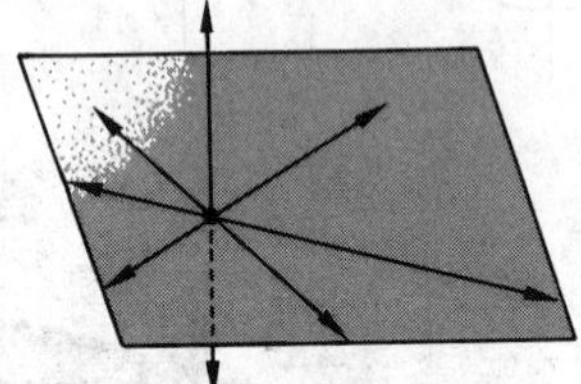

Postulate 1. If a line passes through two points in a plane, it lies entirely in the plane.
Postulate 2. A plane and a line that does not lie in the plane can intersect in one and only one point.
Postulate 3. If two planes intersect, their intersection is one and only one line.
Postulate 4. A plane is determined by three points that are not collinear.
Theorem 1. A plane is determined by a line and a point not on that line.
Theorem 2. A plane is determined by two parallel lines.

Theorems 1 and 2 are corollaries of postulate 4.
Definition 8. *Parallel planes* are two planes that do not intersect, no matter how far they are extended.
Theorem 3. If two parallel planes are cut by a third plane, the lines of intersection are parallel.

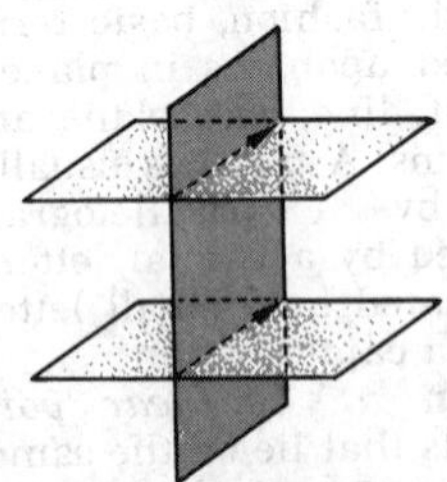

Definition 9. The *distance from a point to a plane* is the length of the perpendicular from the point to the plane.
Definition 10. The *distance between two parallel planes* is the perpendicular distance between them.

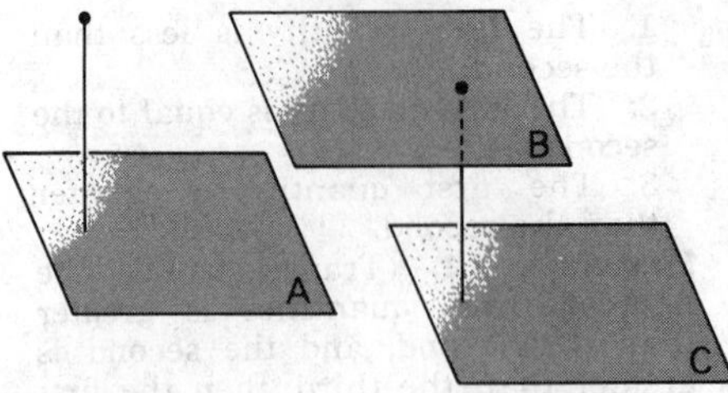

An angle in three-dimensional or solid geometry is called a dihedral angle.
Definition 11. A *dihedral angle* is a figure formed by two planes meeting in a common line.

For simplicity, a dihedral angle can be designated by the two capital letters of its edge.
Definition 12. The *plane angle of a dihedral angle* is the angle formed by two lines, one in each face, each perpendicular to the edge of the dihedral angle at the same point.

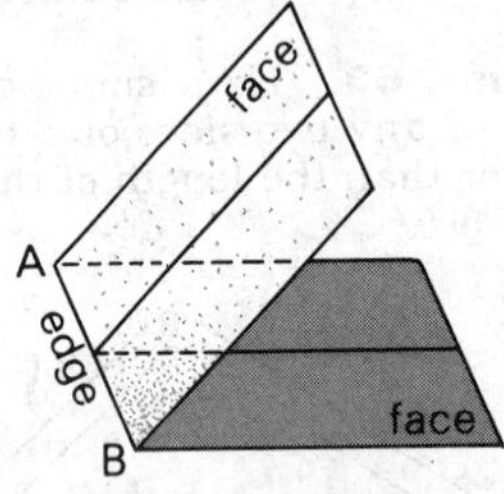

Definition 13. The *measure of a dihedral angle* is the measure of its plane angle.
Definition 14. Two *dihedral angles are equal* if their plane angles are equal.
Definition 15. Two *dihedral angles are complementary (supplementary)* if their plane angles are complementary (supplementary).
Definition 16. A *dihedral angle is acute, right, or obtuse* if its plane angle is acute, right, or obtuse.

Solid Figures

Definition 17. A *geometric solid* is a surface completely enclosing a portion of space.

Some of the most commonly met geometric solids are the box, which can be a rectangular solid or a cube, and the sphere.

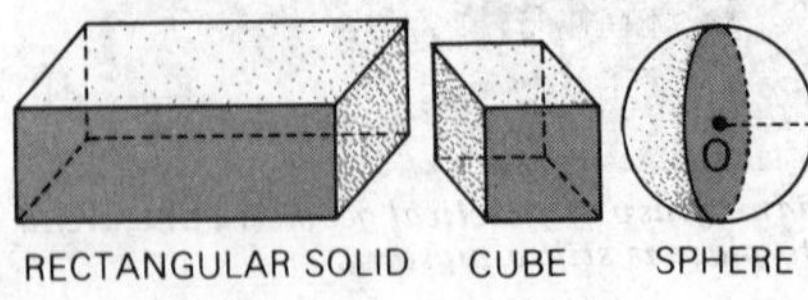

Area and volume.

The area of a plane figure is the total number of square units needed to cover the figure.
Definition 18. The *surface area of a geometric solid* is the sum of the areas of the plane figures that bound it.

Volume refers to the amount of space enclosed by the geometric solid. One cubic unit is the amount of space enclosed by a cube with a side of one unit.
Definition 19. The *volume of a geometric solid* is the total number of cubic units enclosed by its boundaries.

Cylinders.

To describe a cylindrical surface in general, look at the diagram below.

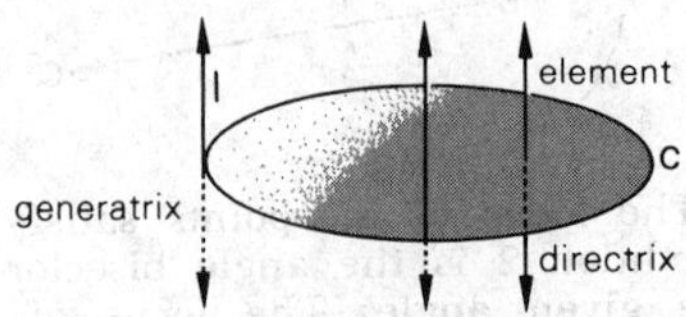

Let *c* be any plane curve. Let *l* be any straight line touching *c* but not coplanar with *c*. Let *l* move so that it is always in contact with *c* but still parallel to its original position. The surface traced is a cylindrical surface. Line *l* is the *generatrix* of the surface, and curve *c* is the *directrix*. Line *l* in any one of its positions is called an element of the cylindrical surface.
Definition 20. A *cylinder* is the geometric solid formed by two parallel planes cutting all the elements of a cylindrical surface.

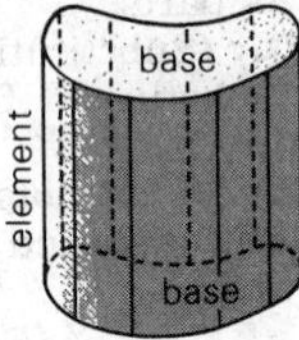

Definition 21. A *right circular cylinder* is a cylinder whose bases are parallel circles perpendicular to the elements.
Definition 22. An *oblique circular cylinder* is a cylinder whose bases are parallel circles not perpendicular to the elements.

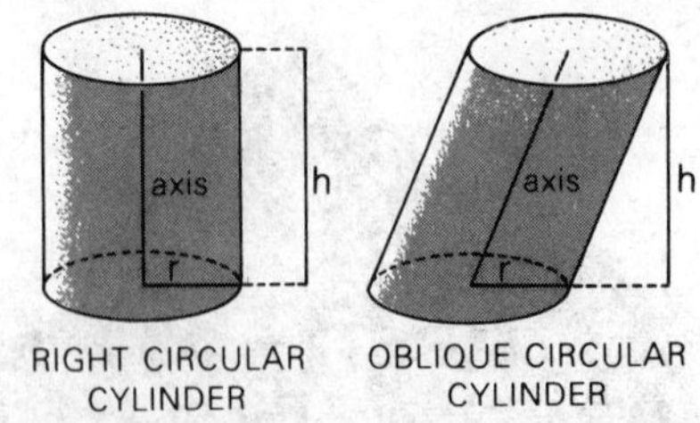

A right circular cylinder is also called a cylinder of revolution, because it can be generated by revolving a rectangle about one of its sides as an axis.

Many common items, such as canned vegetables and tennis balls, come packed in right circular cylinder packages.
Postulate 5. The surface area of a right or oblique circular cylinder is the area of the curved cylindrical surface plus the area of the bases.

$$SA = 2\pi rh + 2\pi r^2$$

Postulate 6. The volume of a circular cylinder is equal to the product of the area of its base and the measure of the altitude.

$$V = \pi r^2 h$$

Cones.

To describe a conical surface in general, look at the diagram below.

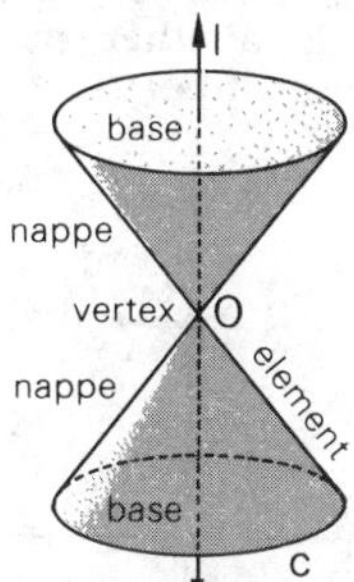

Let c be any plane curve. Let l be any line passing through point O and touching c but not coplanar with c. Let l move so that it is always in contact with c and passing through point O. The surface traced is a conical surface composed of two sections called nappes separated by the vertex of the surface.

Definition 23. A *cone* is the solid formed by one nappe of a conical surface and a plane cutting all the elements.

Definition 24. A *circular cone* is a cone whose base is a circle.

Definition 25. A *right circular cone* is a circular cone whose axis is perpendicular to the base.

Definition 26. An *oblique circular cone* is a circular cone whose axis is not perpendicular to the base.

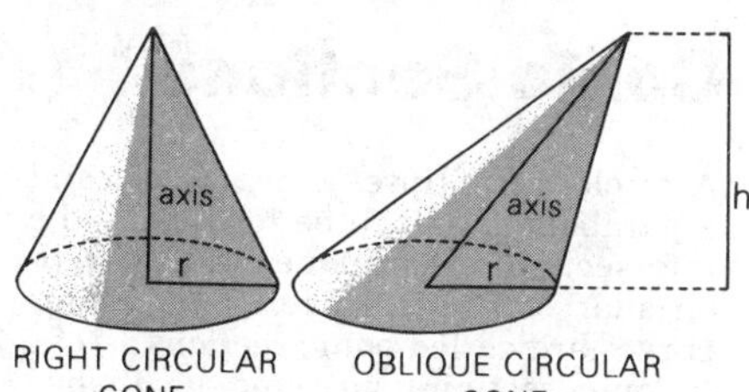

A right circular cone is also called a cone of revolution, because it can be generated by revolving a right triangle about one of its legs as an axis.

Rockets going into space use cones as shapes for their noses or heads. Volcanoes found in nature are shaped like cones.

Definition 27. The *slant height* of a right circular cone is the length of one of the elements.

Postulate 7. The surface area of a right circular cone is equal to the area of the curved surface plus the area of the base.

$$SA = \pi rl + \pi r^2 \quad \text{or} \quad \pi r(l + r)$$

NATURAL GEOMETRIC SOLIDS: *the earth is a nearly perfect sphere. Quartz crystals form a complex rectangular solid.*

Postulate 8. The volume of a circular cone is equal to one-third the product of the area of its base and altitude.

$$V = \frac{1}{3}\pi r^2 h$$

Spheres.

To describe a spherical surface, look at the diagram below.

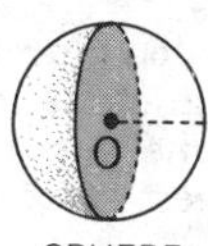

SPHERE

Let O be any point in space. Then a spherical surface with center O is a closed surface all of whose points are equidistant from O.

Definition 28. A *sphere* is a geometric solid bounded by a spherical surface.

Postulate 9. The surface area of a sphere is

$$SA = 4\pi r^2$$

Postulate 10. The volume of a sphere is

$$V = \frac{4}{3}\pi r^3$$

Polyhedrons.

The great pyramids of Egypt, Indian tepees, and the crystals formed when water freezes have geometrical properties in common. All three are specific examples of solid figures called polyhedrons.

Definition 29. A *polyhedron* is a geometric solid enclosed by polygons.

Definition 30. A *pyramid* is a polyhedron whose base is a polygon of any number of sides and whose lateral (side) faces are triangles having a common vertex.

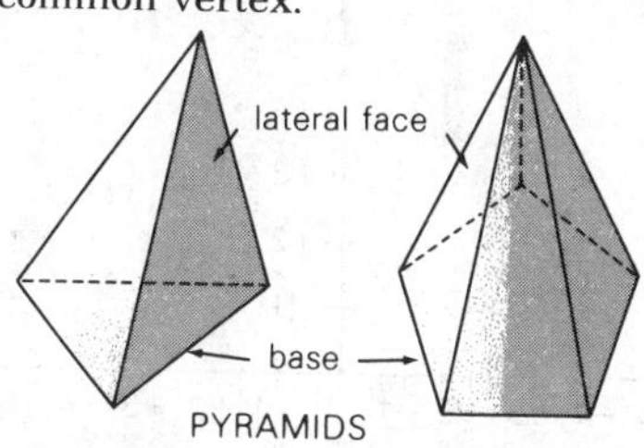

PYRAMIDS

Definition 31. A *prism* is a polyhedron with congruent polygonal bases and lateral faces that are all parallelograms.

Definition 32. A *right prism* is a prism whose lateral faces are perpendicular to the bases.

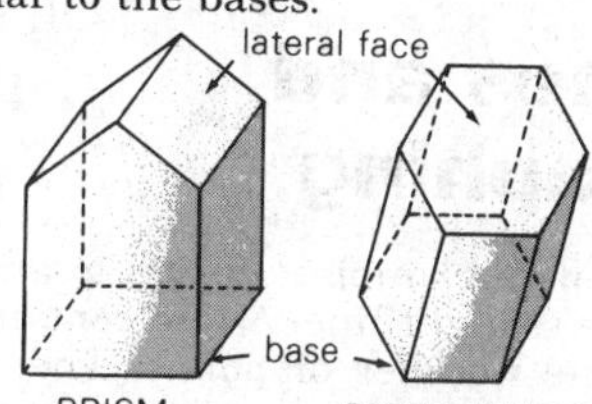

PRISM RIGHT PRISM

Definition 33. A *regular polyhedron* is a polyhedron whose lateral faces and bases are congruent regular polygons and which has the same number of faces intersecting at each vertex.

Theorem 4. There cannot be more than five different types of regular polyhedrons.

REGULAR POLYHEDRONS

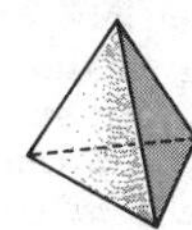

TETRAHEDRON

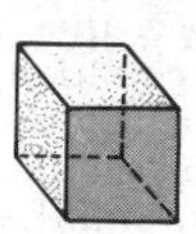

HEXAHEDRON (CUBE)

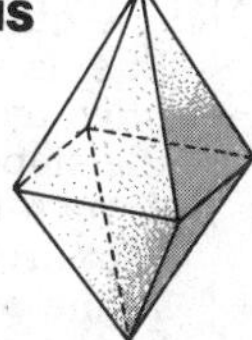

OCTAHEDRON

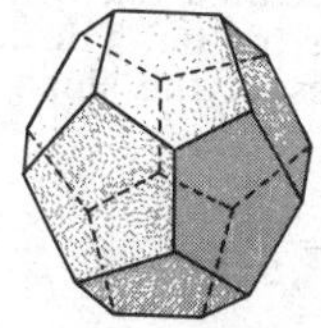

DODECAHEDRON

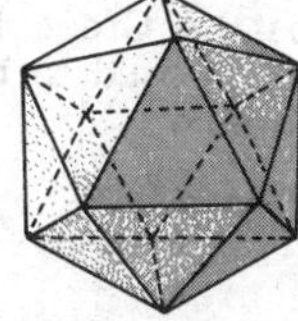

ICOSAHEDRON

Analytic Geometry

Analytic geometry is an extension of the study of algebra and geometry. Algebraic principles and methods are used to analyze geometric figures. For example, the path a ball follows when thrown or the orbit of the moon can be graphically illustrated with the use of analytic geometry.

Given an algebraic representation of a curve, it is helpful to the analysis to draw a diagram. A frame of reference is necessary to convert the algebraic expression into a graph. The frame of reference most commonly used is a set of rectangular coordinate axes, called x and y. The axes are marked in equal unit spaces, and points are plotted by locating their position relative to both axes.

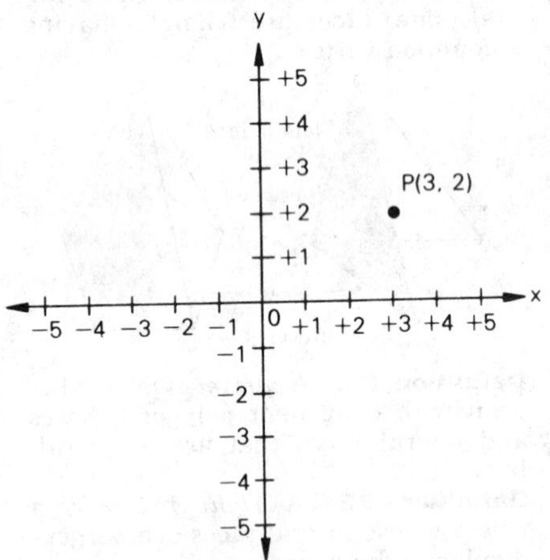

Lines and Graphing

One of the simplest curves to analyze is the straight line. A line contains an infinite number of points. The equation of a line can be written in many forms. One useful form is called the *slope-intercept* form,

$$y = mx + b$$

where m is the slope and b is the y intercept.

Definition 1. The *slope of a line* is the ratio of the change in y to the change in x.

The change in y is called Δy, and the change in x is called Δx, where Δ is the Greek letter 'delta.' The letter m is used to represent the slope of a line:

$$m = \frac{\Delta y}{\Delta x}$$

Definition 2. The *y intercept of a line* is the point where the line crosses the y axis.

The x coordinate of the y intercept is always zero.

If a line slopes up toward the right, it has a positive slope. If it is parallel to the x axis, it has a zero slope. If it slopes down toward the right, it has a negative slope. If the line is parallel to the y axis, the slope is undefined.

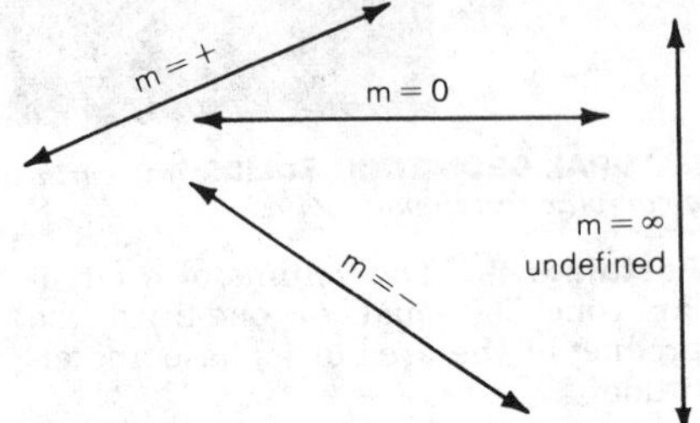

Much of the work done in analytic geometry is concerned with graphing curves. One method of graphing any curve, including a straight line, is to use a table of values. The following is a procedure to follow for constructing a table of values.

1. Make a two-column table, one column for x and one for y.
2. Choose some positive and some negative values of x and zero, if possible.
3. Substitute each value of x in the equation to find the corresponding value of y.
4. Plot each point (x,y).
5. Connect the points with a smooth curve.

Example: Graph $y = 2x + 1$

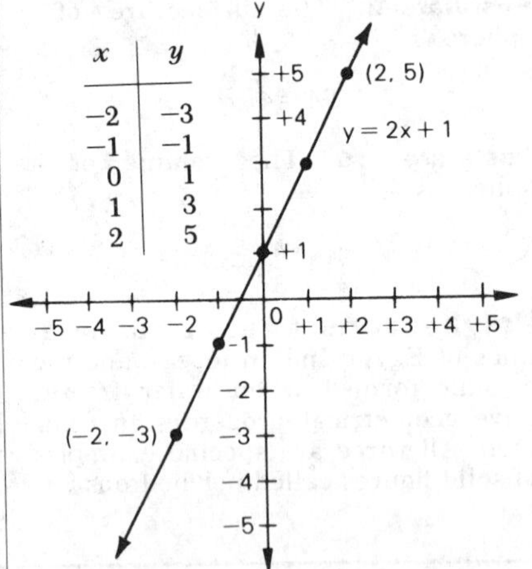

x	y
−2	−3
−1	−1
0	1
1	3
2	5

A quicker way to graph a straight line is to use the information supplied by the equation when written in the slope-intercept form. If $y = mx + b$, then the coordinates of the y intercept are $(0,b)$ and the slope is m. $(0,b)$ is one point on the line. To find a second point, start at the y intercept and use the information the slope gives you. Two points determine a line.

Example: Graph $y = 2x + 1$

1. Plot the y intercept (0,1).
2. The slope is equal to $\frac{\Delta y}{\Delta x} = \frac{2}{1} = 2$.

Start at (0,1) and go up two units on the y axis and over one unit on the x axis. This is another point on the line. Draw the line using a straightedge.

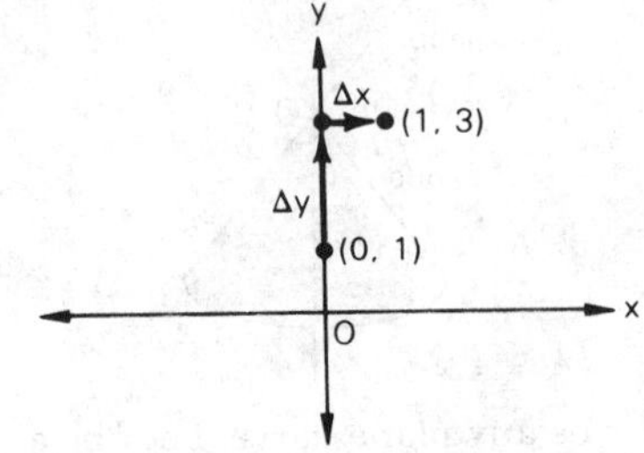

Given the y intercept and the slope of a line, an equation of the line can be written.

Example: A line passes through the point (0,4) and has a slope of −3. Write an equation of the line.

Substituting in the slope-intercept form, we get

$$y = -3x + 4$$

as the equation of this line.

There are many other forms of an equation of a line. Most equations can be transformed into the slope-intercept form by solving for y. One exception is a line parallel to the y axis. These lines have the form $x = c$, where c is a constant.

Conic Sections

A circle, an ellipse, a hyperbola, and a parabola can each be formed by the intersection of a plane and a right circular conic surface. These four curves are called conic sections.

Conic sections surround us in our environment. The shock wave of a sonic boom forms a hyperbola; the moon has an elliptical orbit around Earth. A baseball thrown from one player to another follows a path the shape of a parabola.

Apollonius, born c. 262 B.C., wrote a famous treatise called "Conic Sections." It consisted of eight books. He is credited with naming the ellipse, parabola, and hyperbola. Hypatia, the first woman mathematician to be recognized in the history of mathematics, wrote a commentary on Apollonius's "Conic Sections." In the 17th century, Pierre de Fermat published papers that discussed the conic sections in relation to analytic geometry.

CULVER PICTURES

THE GUGGENHEIM MUSEUM *in New York resembles an inverted cone. Modern architecture often uses less common geometric shapes.*

Today conic sections are used in the design of many modern inventions.

Each conic section may also be described in terms of plane geometry for purposes of analysis. The following sections take up each of the four conic sections in turn.

Circles

Definition 3. A *circle* is the set of all points at a given distance from a given point.

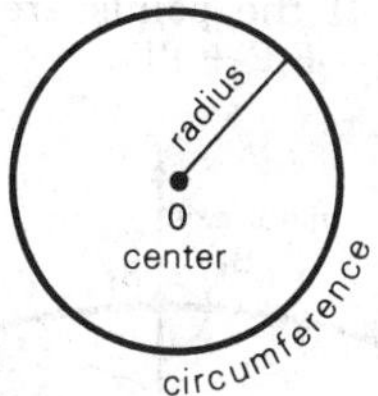

Definition 4. The *center of a circle* is the given point.

Definition 5. A *radius of a circle* is any line drawn from the center of the circle to the edge.

Definition 6. The *circumference of a circle* is its boundary.

Using the distance formula,

$$d = \sqrt{(x_2 - x_1)^2 + (y_2 - y_1)^2}$$

where x_1 and y_1 are the coordinates of the center of the circle, and x_2 and y_2 are a point on its circumference,

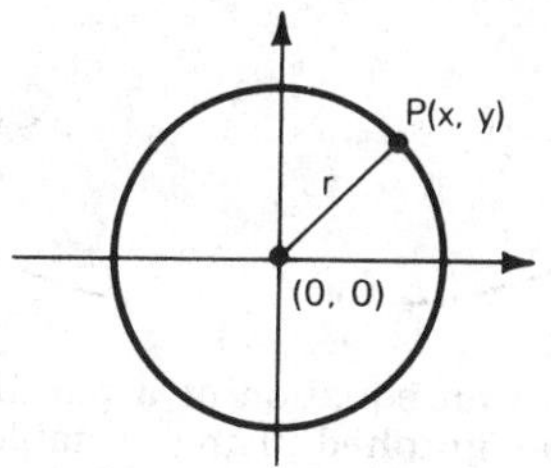

we can solve for d, which will be the radius of the circle, or r.

Given the center of the circle is at $(y_1 = 0, x_1 = 0)$ and the length of the radius is r, choose any point $P(x_2, y_2)$ on the circumference. Then by the distance formula:

$$r = \sqrt{(x-0)^2 + (y-0)^2}$$

$$r = \sqrt{x^2 + y^2}$$

$$r^2 = x^2 + y^2$$

This is the standard form of an equation of a circle with center (0,0) and radius of length r.

Given an equation of a circle, the graph can be drawn by making a table and following the procedure outlined on the previous page. An easier method, which provides a fairly accurate sketch, is to use the information supplied by the equation of a circle in standard form.

Example: Graph $x^2 + y^2 = 25$

This is the equation of a circle in standard form with center at (0,0) and radius of length $\sqrt{25}$, or 5. Therefore, every point on the circumference is 5 units from the center. The circle will pass through the points (0,5), (5,0), (0,–5), (–5,0).

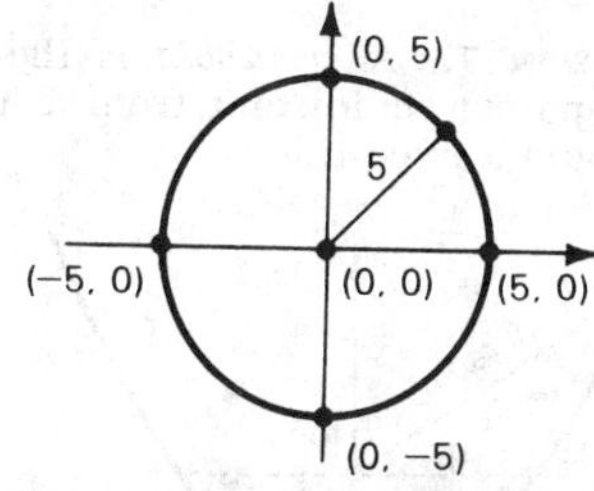

If the center of the circle is moved from (0,0) to another point in the plane (h,k), the standard equation of a circle becomes

$$(x-h)^2 + (y-k)^2 = r^2,$$

center (h,k), radius $= r$.

To graph an equation of a circle, use the information that the standard form of the equation tells you.

CONIC SECTIONS

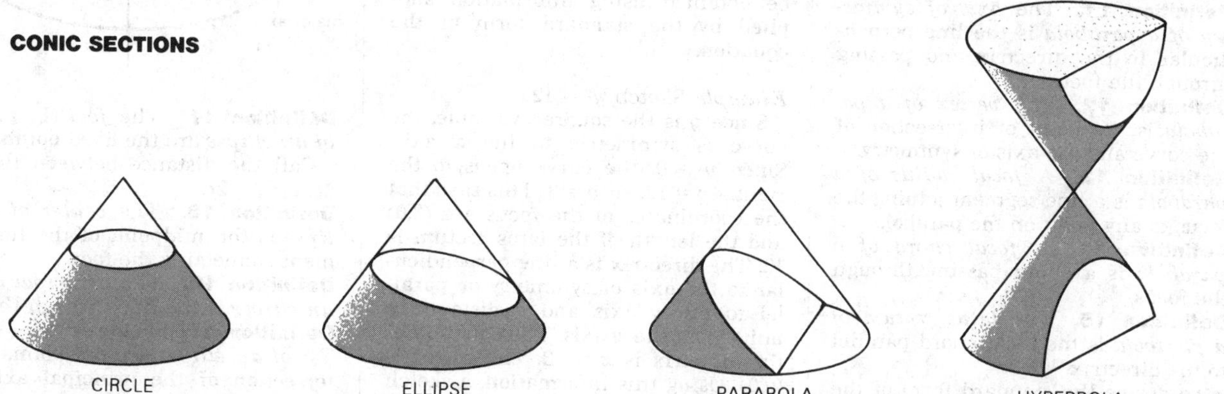

Example: Graph
$(x-3)^2 + (y-2)^2 = 16$

This equation says the circle has center (3,2) and a radius of length 4. Therefore, every point on the circumference is 4 units from the center. The circle will pass through the points (3,6), (7,2), (3,–2), and (–1,2).

The standard equation of a circle can be constructed from information about the circle.

Example: Given that the center of a circle is at (4,1) and that it passes through the point (1,5), write an equation of the circle.

First find the length of the radius by using the distance formula

$$r = \sqrt{(4-1)^2 + (1-5)^2}$$
$$= \sqrt{9+16}$$
$$= 5$$

Then the equation of the circle is

$$(x-4)^2 + (y-1)^2 = 25$$

Parabolas

Definition 7. A *parabola* is the set of all points equidistant from a fixed point and a fixed line.

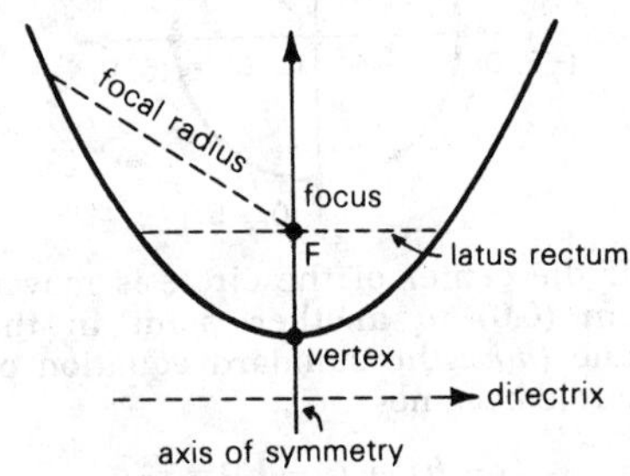

Definition 8. The *focus (F) of a parabola* is the fixed point.
Definition 9. The *directrix (l) of a parabola* is the fixed line.
Definition 10. The *axis of symmetry of a curve* is the line about which the curve is symmetric.
Definition 11. The *axis of symmetry of a parabola* is the line perpendicular to the directrix and passing through the focus.
Definition 12. The *vertex of a parabola* is the point of intersection of the curve and the axis of symmetry.
Definition 13. A *focal radius of a parabola* is a line segment joining the focus to any point on the parabola.
Definition 14. A *focal chord of a parabola* is a chord passing through the focus.
Definition 15. The *latus rectum of a parabola* is the focal chord parallel to the directrix.

To derive the standard form of the equation of a parabola with vertex at (0,0) and the y axis the axis of symmetry, use Definition 7. Let $(0,p)$ be the fixed point, $y = -p$ the fixed line, and $P(x,y)$ any point on the curve.

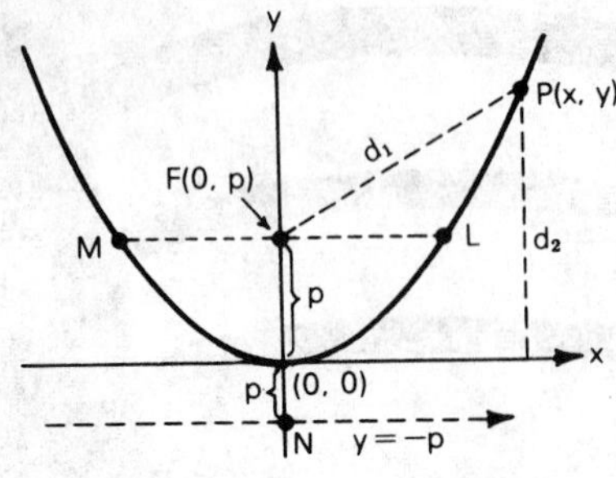

By definition of a parabola, if the focus is $(0,p)$ then $FN = 2p = FL$. The length of the latus rectum $= ML = 2FL = 4p$. Length is measured as a positive quantity, so the absolute value, $|4p|$, is used. The following are standard forms of an equation of a parabola.

Vertex (0,0), y axis the axis of symmetry

$$x^2 = 4py$$

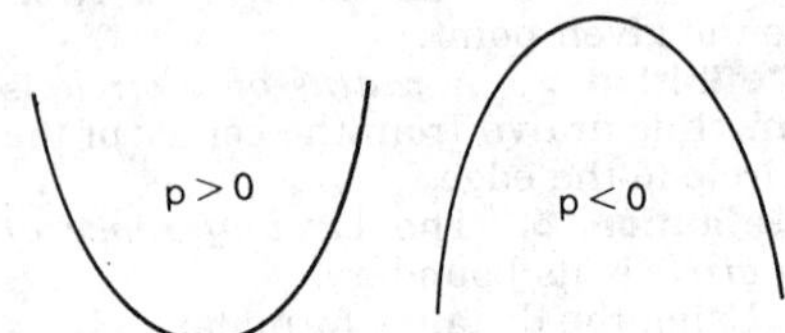

Vertex (0,0), x axis the axis of symmetry

$$y^2 = 4px$$

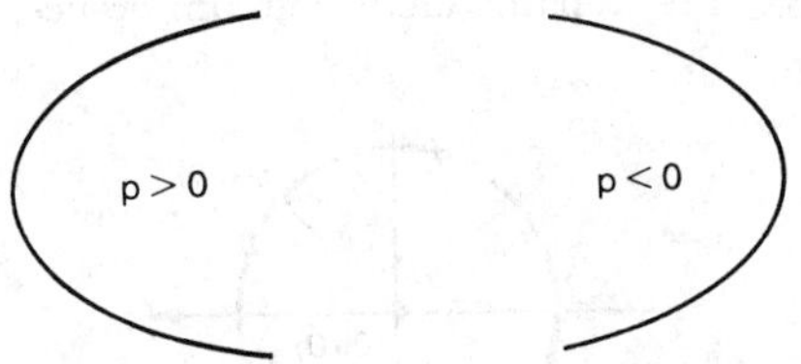

Given an equation of a parabola, it can be graphed using a table. For most purposes a sketch of the curve will suffice. A quick sketch can easily be obtained using information supplied by the standard form of the equation.

Example: Sketch $y^2 = 12x$

Since y is the squared variable, the curve is symmetric to the x axis. Since $p > 0$, the curve opens to the right. $4p = 12$, so $p = 3$. This says that the coordinates of the focus are (3,0) and the length of the latus rectum is 12. The directrix is a line perpendicular to the axis of symmetry or parallel to the y axis and a distance p units from the y axis. The equation of the directrix is $x = -3$. The vertex is (0,0). Using this information, a sketch can be drawn.

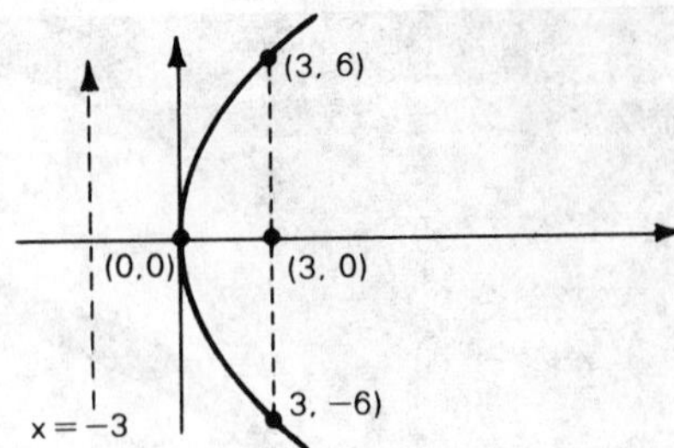

If the vertex of a parabola is at any point (h,k) in the plane, the following are standard equations.

Vertex (h,k), $x = h$ axis of symmetry

$$(x-h)^2 = 4p(y-k)\begin{cases} p>0 \text{ opens up} \\ p<0 \text{ opens down}\end{cases}$$

Vertex (h,k), $y = k$ axis of symmetry

$$(y-k)^2 = 4p(x-h)\begin{cases} p>0 \text{ opens to right} \\ p<0 \text{ opens to left}\end{cases}$$

Example: Given a parabola symmetric to the line $y = 2$ with vertex (4,2) and latus rectum of length 6, write an equation.

$$2p = 6,\ p = 3$$
$$(y-2)^2 = 12(x-4)$$

Ellipses

Definition 16. An *ellipse* is the set of all points such that for any point the sum of its distances from two fixed points is a constant.

Call the sum of the distances of any point on the ellipse from the fixed points $2a$. If the points are called F_1 and F_2, $2a = F_1P + PF_2$.

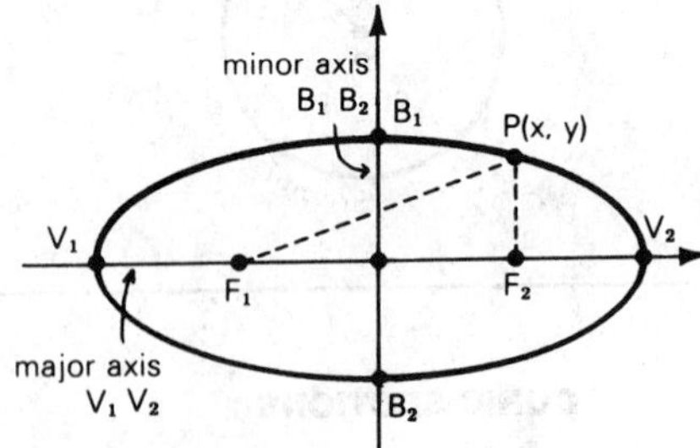

Definition 17. The *foci* (F_1 and F_2) *of an ellipse* are the fixed points.

Call the distance between the foci $2c$. $F_1F_2 = 2c$.
Definition 18. The *center of an ellipse* is the midpoint of the line segment connecting the foci.
Definition 19. The *principal axis of an ellipse* is the line through the foci.
Definition 20. The *vertices* (V_1 and V_2) *of an ellipse* are the points of intersection of the principal axis and the ellipse.

Definition 21. The *major axis of an ellipse* is the line segment whose endpoints are the vertices of the ellipse.
Definition 22. The *minor axis of an ellipse* is a line segment through the center, perpendicular to the major axis and bounded by the ellipse.

The standard equations of an ellipse, which can be derived from Definition 16, are as follows:

Center (0,0), foci ($\pm c$,0), x axis the principal axis

$$\frac{x^2}{a^2}+\frac{y^2}{b^2}=1,\ a>b$$

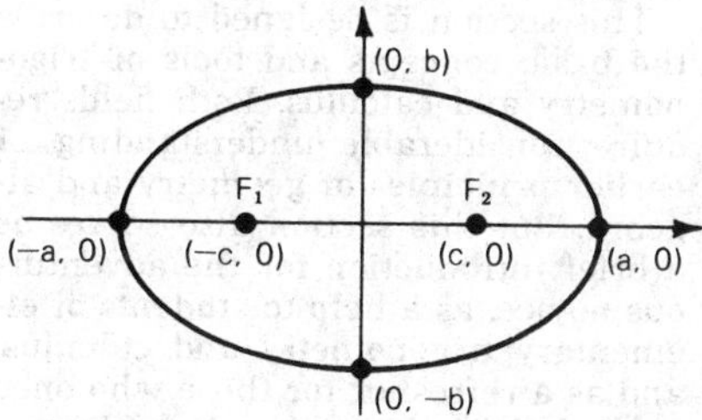

Center (0,0), foci (0,$\pm c$), y axis the major axis

$$\frac{y^2}{a^2}+\frac{x^2}{b^2}=1,\ a>b$$

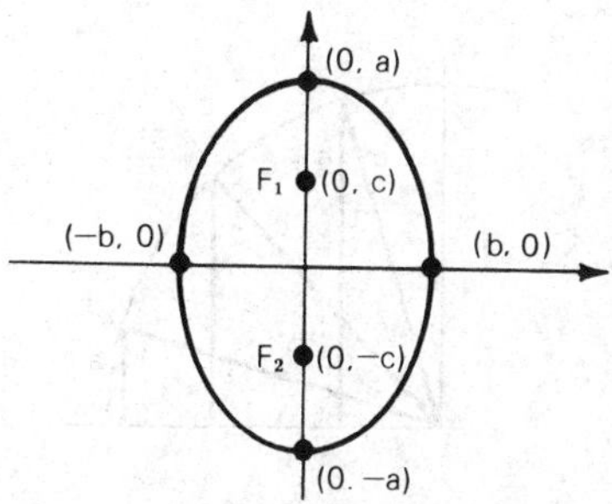

By definition of an ellipse, if $2a$ is the sum of the distances of any point from the foci, then:

1. a is $\frac{1}{2}$ the length of the major axis.
2. b is $\frac{1}{2}$ the length of the minor axis.
3. c is the distance from the center to either focus.
4. $a^2=b^2+c^2$.

An easy way to sketch an ellipse is to use the information supplied by the standard equation.

Example: Sketch $\frac{x^2}{25}+\frac{y^2}{16}=1$

$$a=5,\ b=4,\ a>b$$
$$a^2=b^2+c^2,$$
$$25=16+c^2$$
$$c=3$$

Vertices (± 5,0), foci (± 3,0), endpoints of minor axis (0,± 4)

If the center of the ellipse occurs at any point (h,k) in the plane, the standard equations of an ellipse become:

$$\frac{(x-h)^2}{a^2}+\frac{(y-k)^2}{b^2}=1,$$
$a>b$, principal axis $y=k$

$$\frac{(y-k)^2}{a^2}+\frac{(x-h)^2}{b^2}=1,$$
$a>b$, principal axis $x=h$

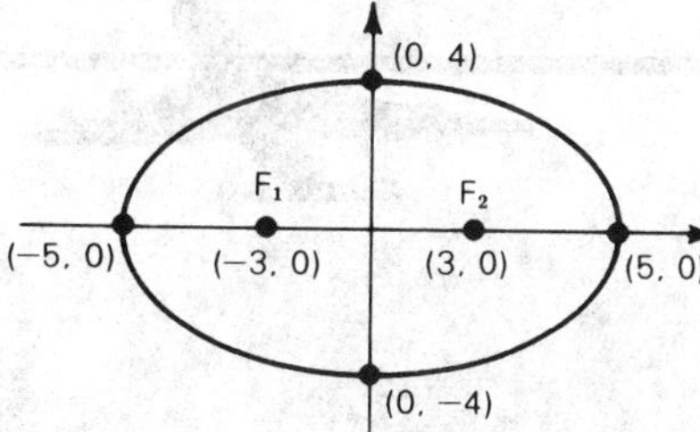

It is interesting to note that if the length of the major axis and the length of the minor axis are equal, the equation of an ellipse becomes

$$\frac{x^2}{a^2}+\frac{y^2}{a^2}=1$$
or $$x^2+y^2=a^2,$$

which is the standard equation of a circle with radius of length a. The circle is a limiting form of an ellipse.

Hyperbolas

Definition 23. A *hyperbola* is the set of all points such that for any point the difference of its distances from two fixed points is a constant.

Call the difference of the distances of any point on the hyperbola from the fixed points $2a$.

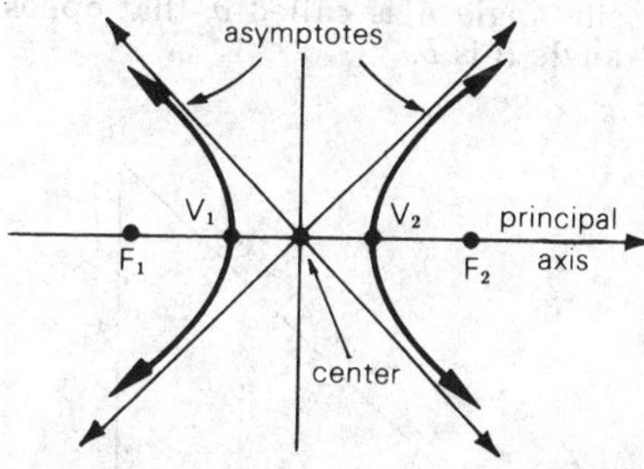

Definition 24. The *foci* (F_1 and F_2) *of a hyperbola* are the fixed points.

Call the distance between the foci $2c$.

Definition 25. The *principal axis of a hyperbola* is the line passing through the two foci.
Definition 26. The *center of a hyperbola* is the midpoint of the line segment connecting the foci.
Definition 27. An *asymptote of a hyperbola* is a line that the curve approaches but never intersects.

The standard equations of a hyperbola, which can be derived from Definition 23, are as follows:

Center (0,0), foci ($\pm c$,0), x axis the principal axis

$$\frac{x^2}{a^2}-\frac{y^2}{b^2}=1$$

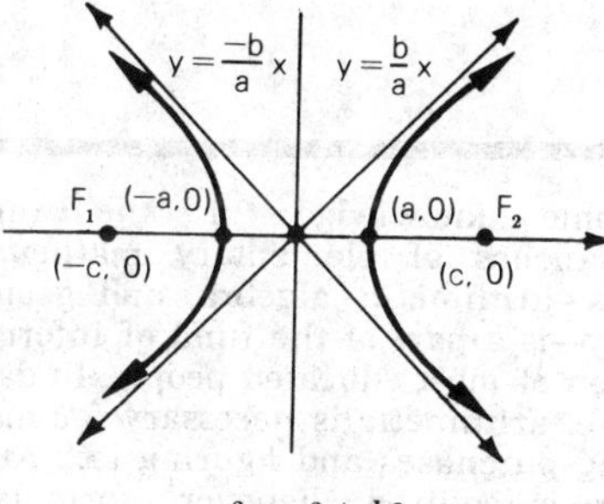

$$c^2=a^2+b^2$$

Equations of the asymptotes $y=\pm\frac{b}{a}x$

Center (0,0), foci (0,$\pm c$), y axis the principal axis

$$\frac{y^2}{a^2}-\frac{x^2}{b^2}=1$$

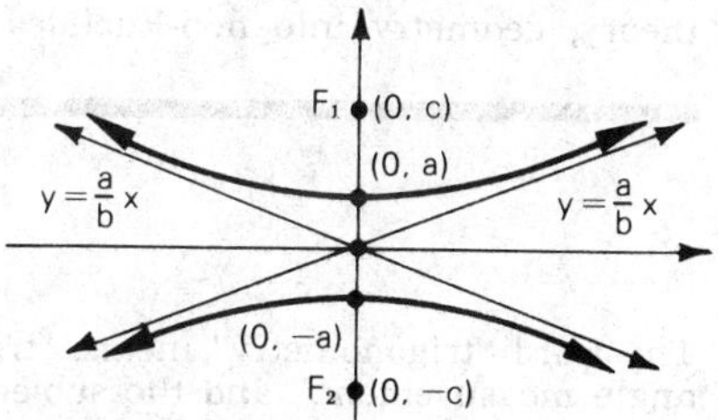

$$c^2=a^2+b^2$$

Equations of the asymptotes $y=\pm\frac{a}{b}x$

If the center of a hyperbola is a point (h,k) in the plane, the standard equations are as follows:

$$\frac{(x-h)^2}{a^2}-\frac{(y-k)^2}{b^2}=1,$$
Principal axis $y=k$

$$\frac{(y-k)^2}{a^2}-\frac{(x-h)^2}{b^2}=1,$$
Principal axis $x=h$

Example: Given the center of a hyperbola is (2,1), the x axis the principal axis, the distance between the foci is 26, and the difference of the distances from any point on the hyperbola to the foci is 24, write the equation.

$$2c=26 \qquad 2a=24$$
$$c=13 \qquad a=12$$
$$c^2=169 \qquad a^2=144$$

$$c^2=a^2+b^2$$
$$169=144+b^2$$
$$b^2=25$$

$$\frac{(x-2)^2}{144}-\frac{(y-1)^2}{25}=1$$

—*Mona Fabricant*

TRIGONOMETRY AND CALCULUS

Some knowledge of the three branches of elementary mathematics—arithmetic, algebra, and geometry—is a part of the fund of information of most educated people. In daily life, arithmetic is necessary for making purchases and figuring tax. Algebra is required whenever a formula is to be used, and geometry can help solve many practical problems such as how much siding or paneling or carpet to buy.

All of these mathematical fields lead to studies unfamiliar to non-mathematicians. Arithmetic moves into the theory of numbers, elementary algebra into linear algebra and group theory, geometry into non-Euclidean geometries and geometries of four dimensions. Most of the mathematical discoveries of the last hundred years are beyond the understanding of even university mathematics students.

CHRIS REEBERG/DPI

CALCULATIONS *of a plane's speed, acceleration and heading require advanced math.*

The first steps toward advanced mathematics, however, are slightly closer to the familiar. They usually consist of the studies of trigonometry and calculus.

This section is designed to describe the basic concepts and tools of trigonometry and calculus. Both fields require considerable understanding of earlier principles of geometry and algebra. But this section also serves as a brief introduction for the adventurous novice, as a help to students of elementary trigonometry and calculus, and as a refresher for those who once studied the subjects but have forgotten them.

Trigonometry

The word "trigonometry" means "triangle measurement," and the subject began in antiquity as a device to aid in solving problems with right triangles—problems of the kind that still arise in surveying and navigation. In modern times, trigonometry has been developed to deal with every kind of triangle, including spherical ones, and also with quantities that rise and fall such as vibrations, alternating current, and business cycles.

Any three points define a triangle, whether on a plane, on Earth, or out in space. Furthermore, any triangle can be split into two right-angled triangles. All we have to do is drop a perpendicular from one point of the triangle to the opposite side, as we do in these triangles. In the first two, the sum of triangles ACD and BCD makes triangle ABC; in the third, the difference between ACD and BCD makes triangle ABC. In this way, problems about triangles in general can be converted into problems about right triangles.

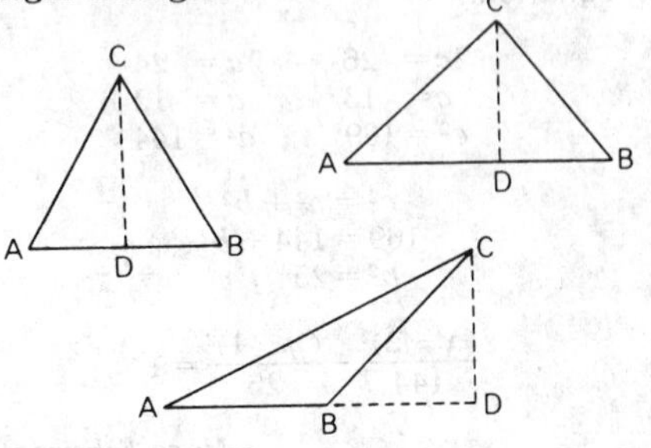

Trigonometric Ratios

Right triangles. In any right triangle, the side opposite the right angle is called the *hypotenuse.* If the right angle is labeled C, the hypotenuse can be called *c.* The side opposite angle A is called *a;* that opposite angle B is *b.*

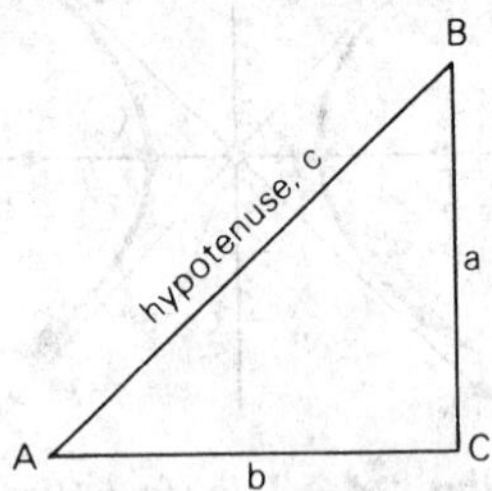

Let us now consider the ratio of side *a* to side *c*, that is, the ratio *a/c.* To do so, we put vertex A at the center of a circle of radius *c.* If A is small, as in triangle 1, then *a* will be small compared to *c*, and *a/c* will be small. As A increases, as in triangles 2 and 3, *a* will increase, and, since *c* stays the same, the ratio *a/c* will increase. As A gets closer and closer to being a right angle, side *a* will get closer to *c*, in position and in length, so that the ratio *a/c* will become closer and closer to 1.

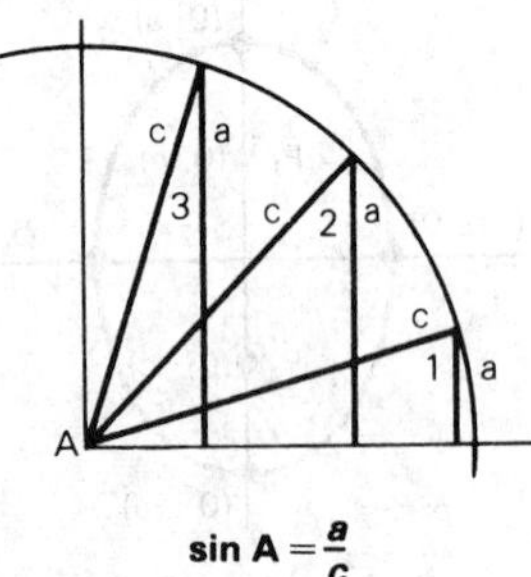

$$\sin A = \frac{a}{c}$$

The same thing happens in triangles of any size. In the two right triangles below,

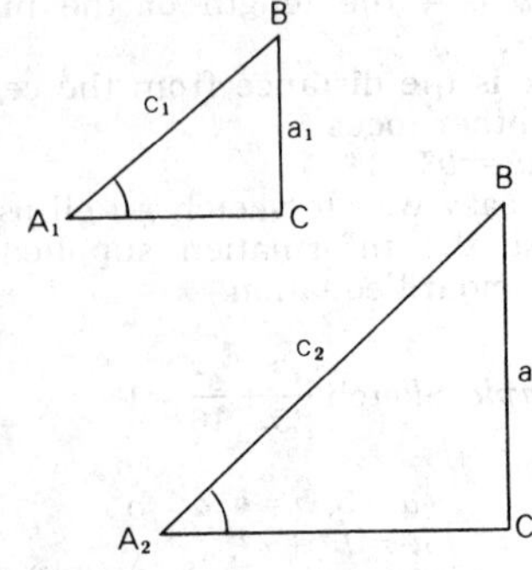

if $\angle A_1 = \angle A_2$, the triangles are similar, and we know from geometry that their corresponding sides are proportional. So

$$\frac{a_1}{c_1} = \frac{a_2}{c_2}$$

Sine, cosine, tangent. The ratio a/c depends on the measure of angle A, and not at all on the individual lengths of a and c. As A changes, a/c changes, so the ratio a/c is a *function* of angle A; it is called the *sine of A,* written sin A.

Angle B in triangle ABC also has a sine; it is b/c. It can be shown, however, that b/c is also dependent on the measure of angle A.

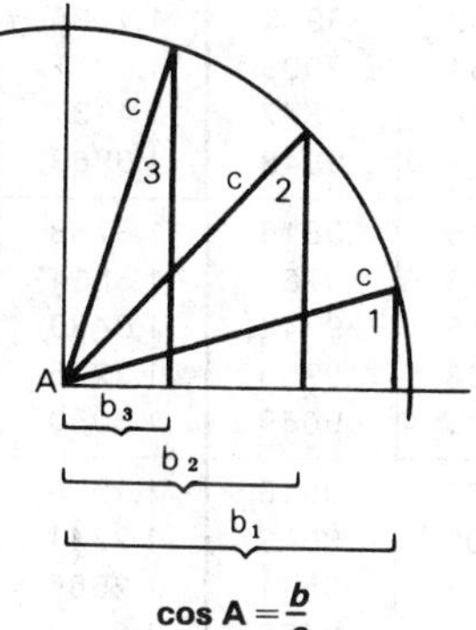

$\cos A = \frac{b}{c}$

If A is small, b is nearly as long as c, and the ratio b/c approaches 1. As the measure of A increases, the length of b decreases, and b/c approaches zero. This ratio is called *cosine A,* written cos A. The value of cos A is inverse to that of sin A, increasing when sin A decreases, and vice versa.

The word "sine" comes from a Latin mistranslation of the Arabic transliteration of the Hindi word for "chord." The word "cosine" is an abbreviation of "complement's sine of A." Another trigonometric ratio that takes its name from geometry is the tangent. In our triangle ABC, the tangent of A, written tan A, is a/b.

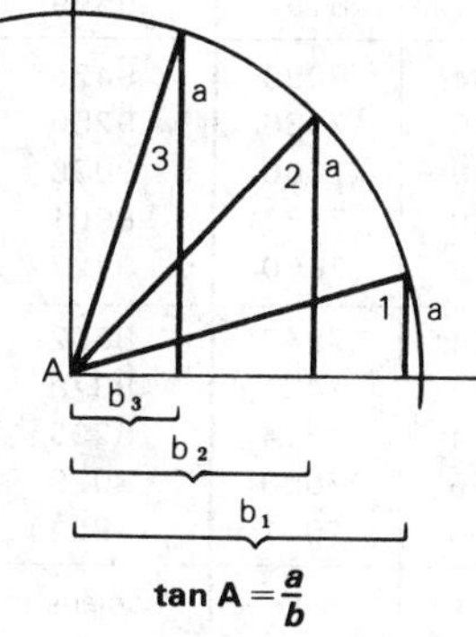

$\tan A = \frac{a}{b}$

When A is small, tan A is small. At 45°, a and b are the same length, so tan A is 1. As A approaches 90°, tan A increases faster and faster.

It is sometimes helpful to give names, not just letters, to the three sides of the triangle, and to state the ratios in terms of these names. The side opposite the right angle is, of course, the hypotenuse. When considering the two legs in relation to angle A, it is usual to call a the *opposite* and b the *adjacent.*

The three ratios, then, are:

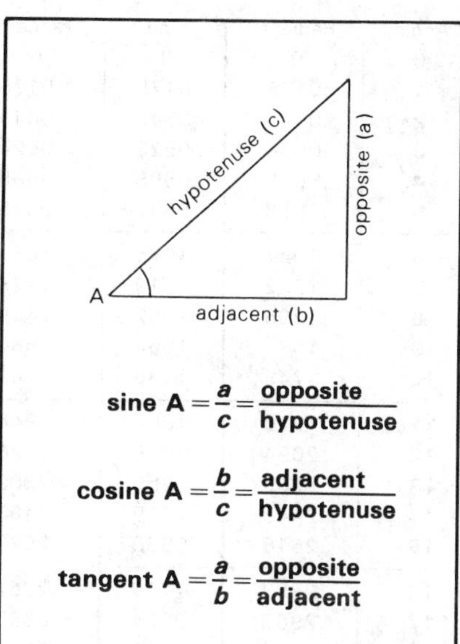

$$\text{sine } A = \frac{a}{c} = \frac{\text{opposite}}{\text{hypotenuse}}$$

$$\text{cosine } A = \frac{b}{c} = \frac{\text{adjacent}}{\text{hypotenuse}}$$

$$\text{tangent } A = \frac{a}{b} = \frac{\text{opposite}}{\text{adjacent}}$$

This leads to a mnemonic: sin = O/H, cos = A/H, and tan = O/A. More briefly, SOH-CAH-TOA.

Cosecant, secant, cotangent. Three more ratios are used in trigonometry, although somewhat less frequently than those we have met. These are the reciprocal functions, so called because each is the reciprocal of one of the first three. They are the cosecant (written csc), secant (sec), and cotangent (cot), defined as follows:

$$\csc A = \frac{\text{hypotenuse}}{\text{opposite}} = \frac{c}{a} = \frac{1}{\sin A}$$

$$\sec A = \frac{\text{hypotenuse}}{\text{adjacent}} = \frac{c}{b} = \frac{1}{\cos A}$$

$$\cot A = \frac{\text{adjacent}}{\text{opposite}} = \frac{b}{a} = \frac{1}{\tan A}$$

Arc sin, arc cos, arc tan. If $x = \sin A$, then we write $A = \text{arc sin } x$ to mean "A is the angle whose sine is x." This is also sometimes written $A = \sin^{-1} x$, not to be confused with $(\sin x)^{-1}$, which is sin x raised to a power of -1. Arc sin, arc cos, etc., are called inverse functions and will be dealt with in more detail in a later section.

Values of the ratios. We can readily calculate the values of the ratios for some special triangles. The 30°–60°–90° triangle is one of these. The best place to start is with an equilateral triangle, such as ABC, and we can choose our measuring units so that each side is 2 units long.

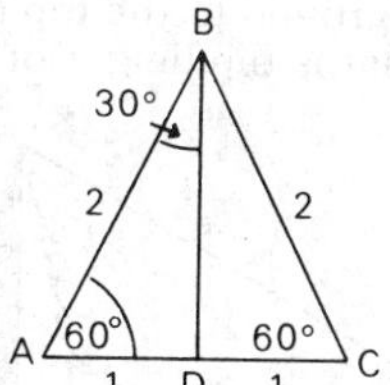

Bisect angle B, and let the bisector intersect AC at D. Since the two triangles ABD and CBD are congruent, D is a right angle, and AD = CD = 1. Angle A, as one of the angles of an equilateral triangle, measures 60°, so triangle ABD is a 30°–60°–90° triangle.

The length of BD is given by the Pythagorean theorem.

$$AB^2 = BD^2 + AD^2$$
$$4 = BD^2 + 1$$
$$BD^2 = 3, \; BD = \sqrt{3}$$

The values of the ratios may now be calculated:

$\sin 60° = \frac{\sqrt{3}}{2}$ $\qquad \csc 60° = \frac{2}{\sqrt{3}}$

$\cos 60° = \frac{1}{2}$ $\qquad \sec 60° = 2$

$\tan 60° = \sqrt{3}$ $\qquad \cot 60° = \frac{1}{\sqrt{3}} = \frac{\sqrt{3}}{3}$

$\sin 30° = \frac{1}{2}$ $\qquad \csc 30° = 2$

$\cos 30° = \frac{\sqrt{3}}{2}$ $\qquad \sec 30° = \frac{2}{\sqrt{3}}$

$\tan 30° = \frac{1}{\sqrt{3}} = \frac{\sqrt{3}}{3}$ $\qquad \cot 30° = \sqrt{3}$

Another special triangle has angles of 45°, 45°, and 90°. This is the isosceles right triangle. If each leg is one unit long, the hypotenuse is obtained from the Pythagorean theorem.

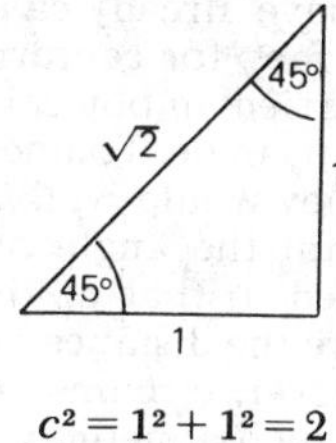

$$c^2 = 1^2 + 1^2 = 2$$
$$c = \sqrt{2}$$

The values of the ratios, then, are:

$\sin 45° = \frac{1}{\sqrt{2}} = \frac{\sqrt{2}}{2}$ $\qquad \csc 45° = \sqrt{2}$

$\cos 45° = \frac{1}{\sqrt{2}} = \frac{\sqrt{2}}{2}$ $\qquad \sec 45° = \sqrt{2}$

$\tan 45° = \frac{1}{1} = 1$ $\qquad \cot 45° = 1$

Application. This example is typical of the use to which trigonometry has been put since antiquity. At a distance of 60 feet from a tree, a surveyor finds that the angle of elevation from the ground to the top of the tree is 30°. What is the height of the tree?

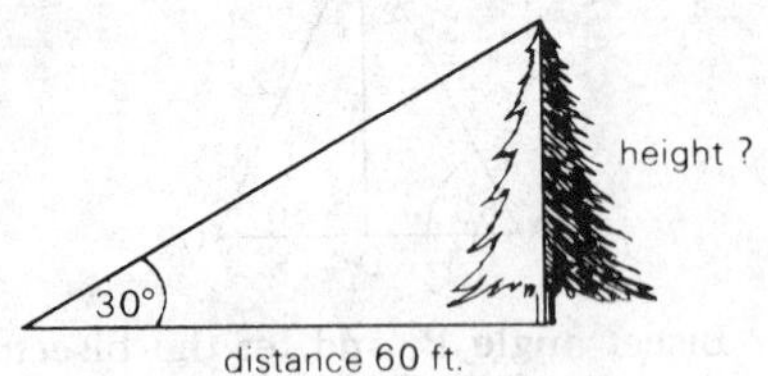

Assuming that the tree is growing at right angles to the ground, the ratio of the tree's height to its distance from the surveyor is equal to tan A, the side opposite the angle over the side adjacent to it. Since we know that the angle at A is 30° and we also know tan 30°, we can write an equation that can be solved for the tree's height. Let h be the unknown height. Then the equation is

$$\tan 30^\circ = \frac{h}{60}$$

or

$$\frac{\sqrt{3}}{3} = \frac{h}{60}$$

so

$$\frac{\sqrt{3}}{3}(60) = h.$$

Since the trigonometric functions of 30°, 45°, and 60° involve $\sqrt{2}$ and $\sqrt{3}$, it is wise to memorize approximate values for these roots, which are $\sqrt{2} \approx 1.41$ and $\sqrt{3} \approx 1.73$. With that in mind, you know that

$$h \approx \frac{1.73}{3}(60) = 34.6.$$

The tree is about 34.6 feet tall.

Trigonometric tables. The tree problem contained an angle of 30°, for which we have already calculated the tangent. In fact, for centuries, surveyors have carried an object shaped like a 30-60-90° triangle. To find the height of a tree, they would walk away from the tree until the angle of elevation corresponded to that of the triangle, and measure the distance accordingly. Often, however, circumstances get in the way of such a method. In order to find the height of the tree, given any angle of elevation, tables of the trigonometric functions have been calculated. The earliest known table is on a Babylonian cuneiform tablet. The one we show gives the values of the ratios for each degree of angle from 0° to 90°. Others are available that give values for subdivisions of a degree. Today, many pocket calculators can also give the sine, cosine, and tangent.

To use the table to find sin 28°, locate the column headed "Sine" and go down it until you are opposite 28 in the "Angle" column on the left. Sin 28° is .4695. The cosine and tangent of angles from 0° to 45° are read in the same way: cos 28° = .8829, and tan 28° = .5317.

TRIGONOMETRIC FUNCTIONS

Angle	Radians	Sine	Tangent	Cotan.	Cosine		
0°	0	0	0	∞	1	1.5708	**90°**
1	.0175	.0175	.0175	57.2900	.9998	1.5533	**89**
2	.0349	.0349	.0349	28.6363	.9994	1.5359	**88**
3	.0524	.0523	.0524	19.0811	.9986	1.5184	**87**
4	.0698	.0698	.0699	14.3007	.9976	1.5010	**86**
5	.0873	.0872	.0875	11.4301	.9962	1.4835	**85**
6	.1047	.1045	.1051	9.5144	.9945	1.4661	**84**
7	.1222	.1219	.1228	8.1443	.9925	1.4486	**83**
8	.1396	.1392	.1405	7.1154	.9903	1.4312	**82**
9	.1571	.1564	.1584	6.3138	.9877	1.4137	**81**
10	.1745	.1736	.1763	5.6713	.9848	1.3963	**80**
11	.1920	.1908	.1944	5.1446	.9816	1.3788	**79**
12	.2094	.2079	.2126	4.7046	.9781	1.3614	**78**
13	.2269	.2250	.2309	4.3315	.9744	1.3439	**77**
14	.2443	.2419	.2493	4.0108	.9703	1.3265	**76**
15	.2618	.2588	.2679	3.7321	.9659	1.3090	**75**
16	.2793	.2756	.2867	3.4874	.9613	1.2915	**74**
17	.2967	.2924	.3057	3.2709	.9563	1.2741	**73**
18	.3142	.3090	.3249	3.0777	.9511	1.2566	**72**
19	.3316	.3256	.3443	2.9042	.9455	1.2392	**71**
20	.3491	.3420	.3640	2.7475	.9397	1.2217	**70**
21	.3665	.3584	.3839	2.6051	.9336	1.2043	**69**
22	.3840	.3746	.4040	2.4751	.9272	1.1868	**68**
23	.4014	.3907	.4245	2.3559	.9205	1.1694	**67**
24	.4189	.4067	.4452	2.2460	.9135	1.1519	**66**
25	.4363	.4226	.4663	2.1445	.9063	1.1345	**65**
26	.4538	.4384	.4877	2.0503	.8988	1.1170	**64**
27	.4712	.4540	.5095	1.9626	.8910	1.0996	**63**
28	.4887	.4695	.5317	1.8807	.8829	1.0821	**62**
29	.5061	.4848	.5543	1.8040	.8746	1.0647	**61**
30	.5236	.5000	.5774	1.7321	.8660	1.0472	**60**
31	.5411	.5150	.6009	1.6643	.8572	1.0297	**59**
32	.5585	.5299	.6249	1.6003	.8480	1.0123	**58**
33	.5760	.5446	.6494	1.5399	.8387	.9948	**57**
34	.5934	.5592	.6745	1.4826	.8290	.9774	**56**
35	.6109	.5736	.7002	1.4281	.8192	.9599	**55**
36	.6283	.5878	.7265	1.3764	.8090	.9425	**54**
37	.6458	.6018	.7536	1.3270	.7986	.9250	**53**
38	.6632	.6157	.7813	1.2799	.7880	.9076	**52**
39	.6807	.6293	.8098	1.2349	.7771	.8901	**51**
40	.6981	.6428	.8391	1.1918	.7660	.8727	**50**
41	.7156	.6561	.8693	1.1504	.7547	.8552	**49**
42	.7330	.6691	.9004	1.1106	.7431	.8378	**48**
43	.7505	.6820	.9325	1.0724	.7314	.8203	**47**
44	.7679	.6947	.9657	1.0355	.7093	.8029	**46**
45°	.7854	.7071	1.0000	1.0000	.7071	.7854	**45°**
		Cosine	Cotan	Tangent	Sine	Radians	Angle

For angles from 45° to 90°, enter the table at the bottom, using the column labels at the bottom and the angle column at the far right. Thus, sin 72° = .9511, cos 72° = .3090, and tan 72° = 3.0777.

Care is needed because each entry in the table does double duty: the number that is the sine of 10° is the same number that is the cosine of 80°. (We have already seen that this is so.) To read a table like this one correctly, one must remember to go "left down, right up."

When an angle does not measure an exact number of degrees, linear interpolation provides a close approximation. For example, to find the sine of 20°30′, first convert the minutes to a fraction of a degree by dividing by 60 (since 60′ = 1°).

$$30' = \frac{30}{60} = \frac{1}{2}^\circ$$

Since 20°30′ is between 20° and 21°, we look in the table for the sines of those two angles, subtract the smaller from the larger, and divide the result by 2. Add the result to the sine of 20°.

sin 21°	.3584
sin 20°	−.3420
difference	.0164
$\frac{1}{2}$ difference	.0082
sin 20°	+.3420
sin 20°30′	.3502

The same kind of interpolation may be used to find an angle's measure when you are given one of its trigonometric functions.

For example, to find the angle whose cosine is 0.4035, look in the cosine column for the value closest to it. Looking up the cosine column from the bottom, you find the value for cos 66° is .4067, and for cos 67° it is .3907. The angle we want must be between these two.

cos 66°	.4067
cos x	.4035
cos 67°	.3907

To find how far above 66° the unknown angle is, find how far it is from cos 66° to cos x and how far it is from cos 66° to cos 67°.

$$\cos 66° - \cos x = .0032$$
$$\cos 66° - \cos 67° = .0160$$

Assume that x will be as far between 66° and 67° as its cosine is between cos 66° and cos 67°. In other words,

$$x = 66° + \frac{.0032}{.0160}$$
$$x = 66.2° \text{ or } 66°12'.$$

PROBLEM SOLVING. With the aid of a trigonometric function table and interpolation, or with a good calculator, you can solve many problems. The key idea is that if you know two useful parts of a right triangle, then you can find the other parts. Most often, you know an angle and a side.

A bracing wire from the top of a cable-television pole meets the ground at an angle of 59°. The place where it meets the ground is 15 feet from the base of the pole. How tall is the pole?

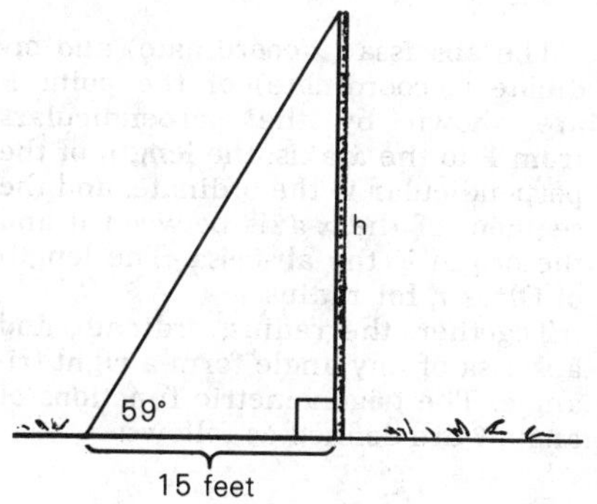

In this case, you know the side adjacent to the angle and the angle. You wish to determine the side opposite the angle. This suggests that you should use the tangent, since it is the ratio of the side opposite to the side adjacent.

$$\tan 59° = \frac{h}{15}$$

From the table, tan 59° = 1.6643 so

$$1.6643 \approx \frac{h}{15}$$
$$h \approx 15(1.6643)$$
$$h \approx 24.9645.$$

The pole is about 25 feet high.

You have a ladder that is 36 feet long. The instructions that came with the ladder tell you that it is not safe to use it at an angle of less than 85° from the ground. How high can the ladder reach on the side of your house?

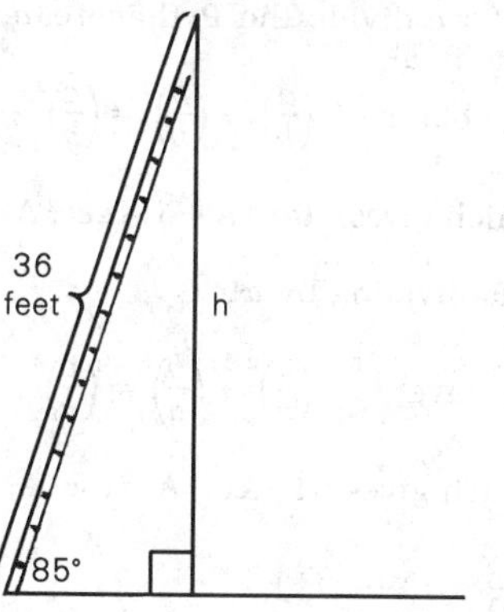

In this case you know the hypotenuse of a right triangle and an angle. The side of the triangle that you wish to locate is the side opposite the angle, so you think of the sine function, since it is defined as the side opposite over the hypotenuse.

$$\sin 85° = \frac{h}{36}$$

From the table, the sine of 85° is about 0.9962, so

$$0.9962 \approx \frac{h}{36}$$
$$36(0.9962) \approx h$$
$$h \approx 35.8632.$$

The ladder will reach almost 36 feet up the side of the house.

A plane's altimeter reports that it is 37,428 feet above ground. Its radar shows that the airport is at an angle of 32° 15′. How far is the airplane from the airport?

This problem as stated does not make it clear which distance is required: the distance along the ground from a point just below the airplane (the ground distance) or the direct-line distance the airplane must travel through in landing (the travel distance). Either of these can be calculated; if you know one side and one acute angle of a right triangle, you can use trigonometry to find the other two sides.

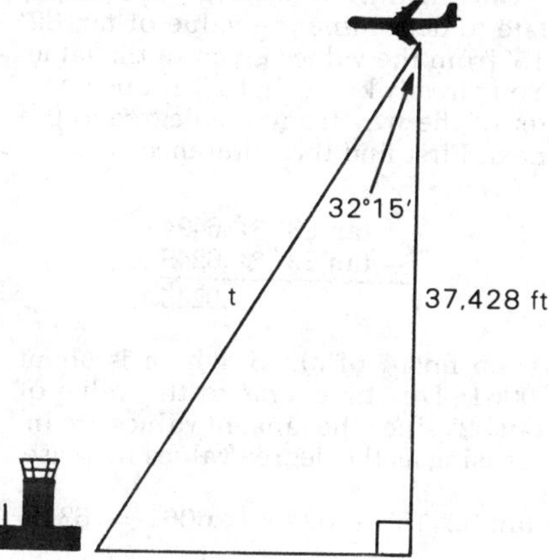

Assume that the problem is to find how far the plane must travel to reach the airport, which is the hypotenuse. You know the adjacent side to the known angle, making the cosine function the easiest to use. Use t for the travel distance to the airport.

$$\cos 32°\,15' = 37{,}428/t$$

Interpolate to find the value of cos 32° 15′. Notice that the value of the cosine function is going down between 0° and 90°. Since $\frac{15}{60}$ is $\frac{1}{4}$, subtract $\frac{1}{4}$ of the difference between cos 32° and cos 33° from cos 32° to get the approximate cosine of 32° 15′.

$$\begin{array}{r} \cos 32° \approx 0.8480 \\ -\cos 33° \approx 0.8387 \\ \hline 0.0093 \end{array}$$

One-fourth of 0.0093 is about 0.0023.

$$\begin{array}{r} 0.8480 \\ -\ 0.0023 \\ \hline 0.8457 \end{array}$$

Therefore,

$$0.8457 \approx 37{,}428/t$$
$$0.8457t \approx 37{,}428$$
$$t \approx 44{,}257.$$

The travel distance from the plane to the airport is about 44,257 feet or about 8.4 miles.

Now use the same information to find the ground distance to the airport. It is better to go back to the original information rather than base a further calculation on the value found for the travel distance. First, the travel distance is known to be an approximation. Second, there is always the chance that the travel distance has been calculated indirectly. In the original data, you know an angle and the side adjacent to that angle. You want to find the length of the side opposite the angle, so the appropriate trigonometric function is the tangent. Use g for the ground distance.

$$\tan 32° \, 15' = g/37{,}428$$

Once again, it is necessary to interpolate to determine the value of tan 32° 15′ from the values given in the table. You already know that 15′ is one-quarter of the way from one degree to the next. First find the difference

$$\begin{array}{r} \tan 33° \approx .6494 \\ -\ \tan 32° \approx .6249 \\ \hline .0245. \end{array}$$

Then find $\frac{1}{4}$ of .0245, which is about .0061. This time, *add* to the value of tan 32°, since the tangent values are increasing as the degree values increase.

$$\tan 32° \, 15' \approx .6249 + .0061 = .6310$$

Therefore,

$$g/37{,}428 \approx .631$$

or $g \approx 23{,}617.$

The ground distance is 23,617 feet or approximately 4.5 miles.

Relations Among the Functions

Co-functions. When two angles are complementary (the sum of their measures is 90°), the sine of one is equal to the cosine of the other. The definitions of the other functions lead immediately to the fact that the tangent of an angle is the cotangent of its complement, and the secant of an angle is the cosecant of its complement. The pairs are called co-functions.

$\sin A = \cos (90° - A)$ $\cos A = \sin (90° - A)$

$\tan A = \cot (90° - A)$ $\cot A = \tan (90° - A)$

$\sec A = \csc (90° - A)$ $\csc A = \sec (90° - A)$

Reciprocal functions. By definition, cosecant, secant, and cotangent are the reciprocals of sine, cosine, and tangent, respectively. The product of each pair of these reciprocal functions is therefore unity:

$$\sin A = \frac{1}{\csc A}, \text{ so } \sin A \csc A = 1$$

$$\cos A = \frac{1}{\sec A}, \text{ so } \cos A \sec A = 1$$

$$\tan A = \frac{1}{\cot A}, \text{ so } \tan A \cot A = 1$$

Quotient identities. From their definitions,

$$\frac{\sin A}{\cos A} = \frac{a/c}{b/c} = \frac{a}{b} = \tan A.$$

By taking reciprocals of both sides,

$$\frac{\cos A}{\sin A} = \cot A.$$

Pythagorean identities. In a right triangle,

$$a^2 + b^2 = c^2.$$

If we divide this equation through by c^2,

we have $\left(\frac{a}{c}\right)^2 + \left(\frac{b}{c}\right)^2 = \left(\frac{c}{c}\right)^2$

which gives $\sin^2 A + \cos^2 A = 1.$

Note that $\sin^2 A$ is the usual way of writing $(\sin A)^2$ or $(\sin A)(\sin A)$.

If we divide the Pythagorean equation by b^2,

we obtain $\left(\frac{a}{b}\right)^2 + \left(\frac{b}{b}\right)^2 = \left(\frac{c}{b}\right)^2$

which gives $\tan^2 A + 1 = \sec^2 A.$

And dividing by a^2,

we have $\left(\frac{a}{a}\right)^2 + \left(\frac{b}{a}\right)^2 = \left(\frac{c}{a}\right)^2$

which gives $1 + \cot^2 A = \csc^2 A.$

The General Angle

Until now, we have been concerned only with the angles of a right triangle, that is, with angles whose measures are between 0° and 90°. By placing angles within a coordinate system, we can extend the definitions of the ratios to cover angles of any size whatsoever.

We take a rectangular system, familiar from coordinate geometry, in which x-coordinates range horizontally, increasing to the right, and y-coordinates increase vertically upward. The point where $x = 0$ and $y = 0$ is called the origin. Left of the origin, x is negative; below the origin, y is negative.

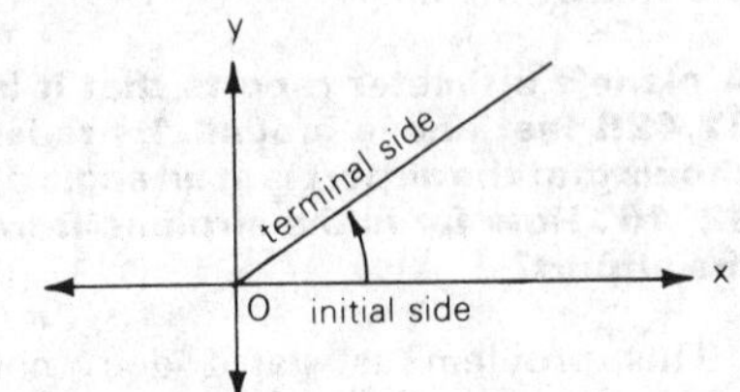

When an angle has its vertex at the origin and one side—the initial side—along the x-axis, it is said to be in standard position.

The other side of the angle—the terminal side—is reached by a rotation from the initial side. If the rotation is in the counterclockwise direction, it is called positive; if clockwise, negative. The following figure shows angles of 60°, 200°, and −40° in standard position.

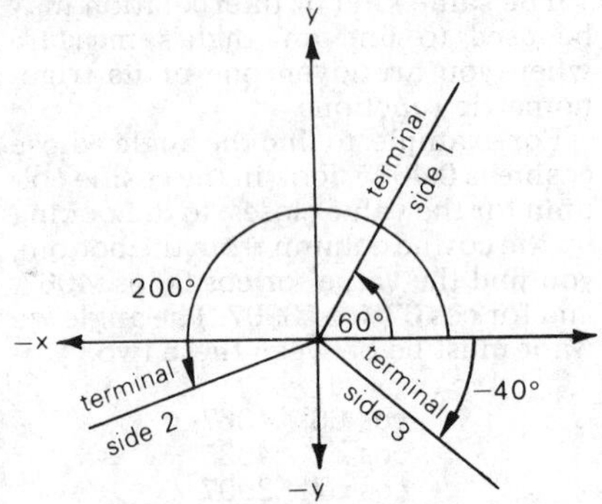

A rotation of 360° would be a complete circle, so an angle of 360° would have its terminal side coincident with its initial side, exactly like an angle of 0°. Terminal side 1 in the figure above could be reached after a rotation of 60°, or of 360° + 60°, which is 420°, or even of 720° + 60°, which is 780°. Terminal side 2 could also be the terminal side of an angle of −160°. And terminal side 3 could be that of an angle of 320°.

The functions defined. Any angle in standard position can be specified by the location of its terminal side. The following figure shows two terminal sides OP, one specifying the acute angle θ (Greek letter theta), the other specifying the reflex angle, which we are also calling θ.

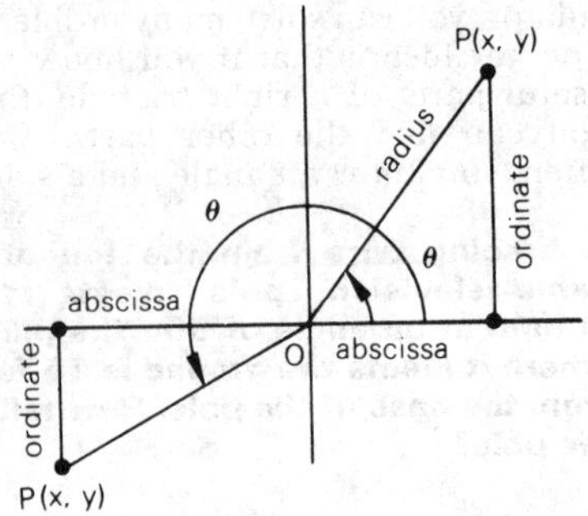

The abscissa (x-coordinate) and ordinate (y-coordinate) of the point P are shown by the perpendiculars from P to the x-axis: the length of the perpendicular is the ordinate, and the segment of the x-axis between it and the origin is the abscissa. The length of OP is r, for radius.

Together, the radius, ordinate, and abscissa of any angle form a right triangle. The trigonometric functions of angle θ are defined as follows:

$$\sin\theta = \frac{\text{ordinate}}{\text{radius}}$$

$$\cos\theta = \frac{\text{abscissa}}{\text{radius}}$$

$$\tan\theta = \frac{\text{ordinate}}{\text{abscissa}}$$

The reciprocals of these functions are csc θ, sec θ, and cot θ, as before.

The four quadrants. The x and y axes divide the plane into four quadrants, whose standard notation is I, II, III, and IV, labeled counterclockwise.

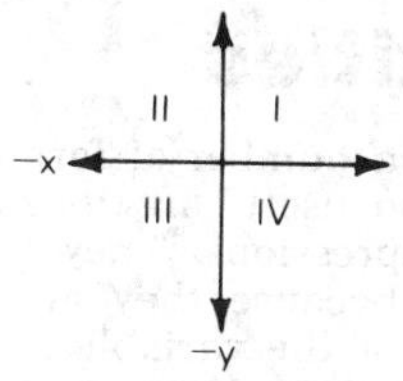

Below, the four quadrants are shown separately.

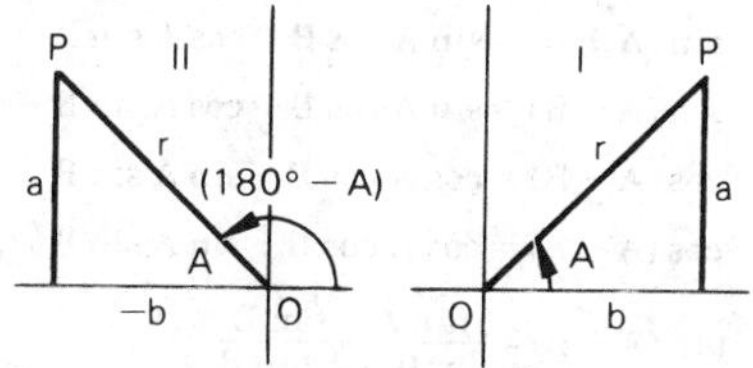

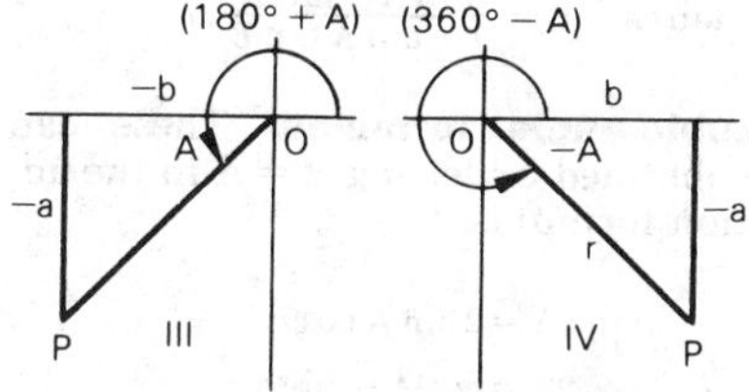

A right triangle has been drawn in each. Each triangle contains an acute angle A with vertex at the origin and hypotenuse OP = r. The triangles are therefore congruent, with corresponding legs of the same length.

From Quad. I, $\sin A = a/r$
Quad. II, $\sin(180° - A) = a/r$
Quad. III, $\sin(180° + A) = -a/r$
Quad. IV, $\sin(360° - A) = -a/r$
$\sin(-A) = -a/r$

So, $\sin A = \sin(180° - A)$
$= -\sin(180° + A)$
$= -\sin(360° - A) = -\sin(-A)$

We can investigate cosine in the same way.

From Quad. I, $\cos A = b/r$
Quad. II, $\cos(180° - A) = -b/r$
Quad. III, $\cos(180° + A) = -b/r$
Quad. IV, $\cos(360° - A) = b/r$
$\cos(-A) = -b/r$

So, $\cos A = -\cos(180° - A)$
$= -\cos(180° + A)$
$= \cos(360° - A) = \cos(-A)$

And we can do the same for tangent.

From Quad. I, $\tan A = a/b$
Quad. II, $\tan(180° - A) = -a/b$
Quad. III, $\tan(180° + A) = -a/b$
Quad. IV, $\tan(360° - A) = a/b$
$\tan(-A) = a/b$

So, $\tan A = -\tan(180° - A)$
$= -\tan(180° + A)$
$= \tan(360° - A) = \tan(-A)$

Any angle can thus be related to an angle in the first quadrant; each trigonometric function of the angle will be numerically equal to that of the reference angle, but the sign (positive or negative) may change, according to the quadrant and function concerned.

In Quad. I, sin, cos, and tan are all positive; in II, only sin is positive; in III, only tan is positive; and in IV, only cos. In brief, the functions that are positive in I, II, III, and IV are A, S, T, C; a mnemonic for this is All Seniors Take Calculus (which is helpful, even though untrue!).

Since the reciprocal of a number has the same sign as the number, in every quadrant cosecant will have the same sign as sine, secant the same as cosine, and cotangent the same as tangent.

This analysis will help find the function of angles in any quadrant. For example, to find the values of the functions of 210°:

Since 210° = 180° + 30°, it is in Quad. III, where sin and cos are negative and tan is positive.

$$\sin 210° = -\sin 30° = -\frac{1}{2}$$

$$\cos 210° = -\cos 30° = -\frac{1}{2}\sqrt{3}$$

$$\tan 210° = \tan 30° = \frac{1}{\sqrt{3}}$$

$$\csc 210° = -2$$

$$\sec 210° = \frac{-2}{\sqrt{3}}$$

$$\cot 210° = \sqrt{3}$$

Quadrantal angles. When the terminal side of an angle in standard position lies along one of the axes, the angle completely fills one or more quadrants and is called a quadrantal angle. These are the right and straight angles, 0°, 90°, 180°, 270° (or −90°), 360°, 360° + 90°, and so on.

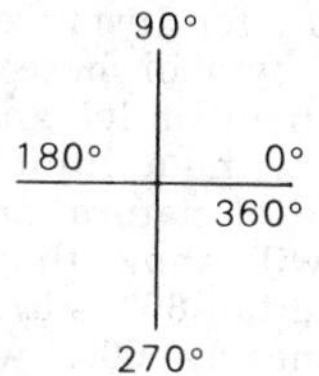

For an angle of 0° (or 360°, etc.), the terminal side lies along the x-axis, with $x = r$ and $y = 0$, so that

$$\sin 0° = \frac{0}{r} = 0$$

$$\cos 0° = \frac{r}{r} = 1$$

$$\tan 0° = \frac{0}{r} = 0.$$

For an angle of 90°, $x = 0$ and $y = r$, so

$$\sin 90° = \frac{r}{r} = 0$$

$$\cos 90° = \frac{0}{r} = 0$$

$$\tan 90° = \frac{r}{0} = \text{undefined.}$$

For 180°, $x = -r$ and $y = 0$, sin 180° and tan 180° are both equal to zero; but $\cos 180° = -r/r = -1$.

For 270°, $x = 0$ and $y = -r$; $\sin 270° = -r/r = -1$; $\cos 270° = 0/r = 0$; and tan 270° is $-r/0$, which again is undefined.

FUNCTIONS OF SPECIAL ANGLES

Angle A Deg	Rad	Sin A	Cos A	Tan A	Csc A	Cot A
0	0	0	1	0	∞	∞
30	$\frac{\pi}{6}$	$\frac{1}{2}$	$\frac{\sqrt{3}}{2}$	$\frac{\sqrt{3}}{3}$	2	$\sqrt{3}$
45	$\frac{\pi}{4}$	$\frac{\sqrt{2}}{2}$	$\frac{\sqrt{2}}{2}$	1	$\sqrt{2}$	1
60	$\frac{\pi}{3}$	$\frac{\sqrt{3}}{2}$	$\frac{1}{2}$	$\sqrt{3}$	$\frac{2\sqrt{3}}{3}$	$\frac{\sqrt{3}}{3}$
90	$\frac{\pi}{2}$	1	0	∞	1	0
120	$\frac{2\pi}{3}$	$\frac{\sqrt{3}}{2}$	$-\frac{1}{2}$	$-\sqrt{3}$	$\frac{2\sqrt{3}}{3}$	$\frac{-\sqrt{3}}{3}$
180	π	0	−1	0	∞	∞
225	$\frac{5\pi}{4}$	$\frac{-\sqrt{2}}{2}$	$\frac{-\sqrt{2}}{2}$	1	$-\sqrt{2}$	1
270	$\frac{3\pi}{2}$	−1	0	∞	−1	0
330	$\frac{11\pi}{6}$	$-\frac{1}{2}$	$\frac{\sqrt{3}}{2}$	$\frac{-\sqrt{3}}{3}$	−2	$\sqrt{3}$
360	2π	0	1	0	∞	∞

These values, and those of the reciprocal functions, are collected in the table shown. Instead of the word "undefined," the symbol for infinity, ∞, is used there. This is not to say that tan 90°, for instance, equals infinity. The symbol here means "increases without limit," and $-\infty$ means "decreases without limit." Reference to the table of natural trigonometric functions will show that tan 87° is over 19, and tan 89° is 57. In fact, tan 89°54′ is nearly 600, while values above one million—or any other number we choose—can be obtained by taking the angle close enough to 90°. This meaning for the ∞ sign also applies to csc 0°, and to all its appearances in the table of functions of quadrantal angles.

Solving Oblique Triangles

Now that we can find the sine and cosine of any angle, we are ready to use two formulas that relate the sides to the angles of triangles that are oblique, that is, triangles that do not contain a right angle. They may be acute-angled, or contain an obtuse angle.

Cosine law. Take a triangle ABC with C at the origin; B on the x-axis a distance a from C, so that B is the point $(a, 0)$ and A any point (x, y). Both triangles below satisfy these requirements.

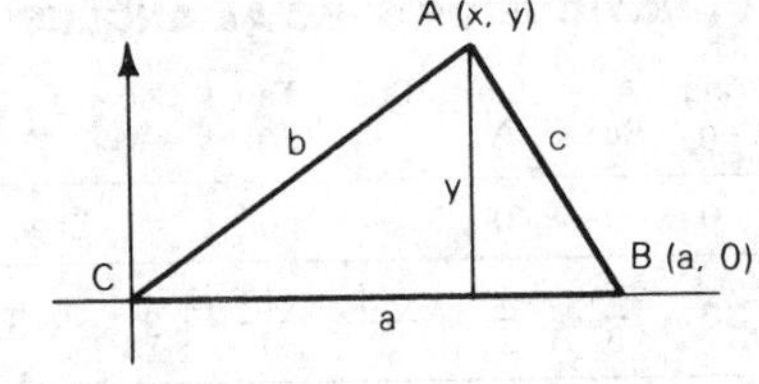

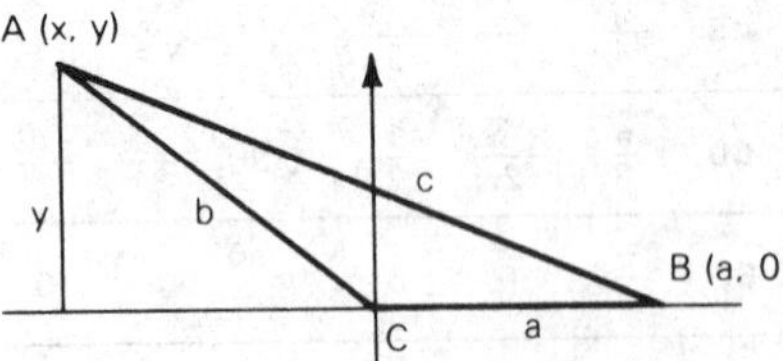

The distance from A to B is given by

$$c^2 = (x-a)^2 + (y-0)^2$$
$$= x^2 - 2ax + a^2 + y^2$$
$$= a^2 + (x^2 + y^2) - 2ax.$$

But $x^2 + y^2 = b^2$, and $x/b = \cos C$, so, substituting for $(x^2 + y^2)$ and for x, we have

$$c^2 = a^2 + b^2 - 2ab \cos C.$$

If we placed vertex A at the origin, or vertex B, we would obtain

$$a^2 = b^2 + c^2 - 2bc \cos A$$
$$b^2 = c^2 + a^2 - 2ca \cos B.$$

These are three forms of the cosine law. It can be used to obtain the cosine of any angle in any triangle whose sides are known, or the third side when two sides and the included angle are known.

Example. Two sides of a triangle are 15 units and 35 units long, and the included angle is 110°. What is the length of the third side, to the nearest tenth?
Solution. We will use the cosine law, noting that $\cos 110° = -\cos 70°$.

$$x^2 = 15^2 + 35^2 - 2(15)(35)(-.3420)$$
$$= 225 + 1225 + 359.1 = 1809, \text{ approx.}$$
$$x = 42.5$$

Sine law. Taking the same triangles,

$$\sin C = \frac{y}{b}, \text{ so } y = b \sin C$$

$$\sin B = \frac{y}{c}, \text{ so } y = c \sin B.$$

Therefore, $b \sin C = c \sin B$

$$\frac{b}{\sin B} = \frac{c}{\sin C}$$

Placing vertex A at the origin, we have

$$\frac{a}{\sin A} = \frac{c}{\sin C}$$

Combining these results, we have the sine law:

$$\frac{a}{\sin A} = \frac{b}{\sin B} = \frac{c}{\sin C}$$

PROBLEM SOLVING. Both the law of cosines and the law of sines can be used to solve oblique triangles, although in some cases there are two possible solutions when you use the law of sines. Note that either the law of cosines or the law of sines must be used, but it is not your choice—if one can be used to solve the problem, the other cannot.

To determine the length of a tunnel, you measure the distance from a point where both ends of the tunnel can be seen. It is 135 meters to one end of the tunnel and 197 meters to the other end. The angle between the lines from your outside point to the two ends is 43°. How long will the completed tunnel be?

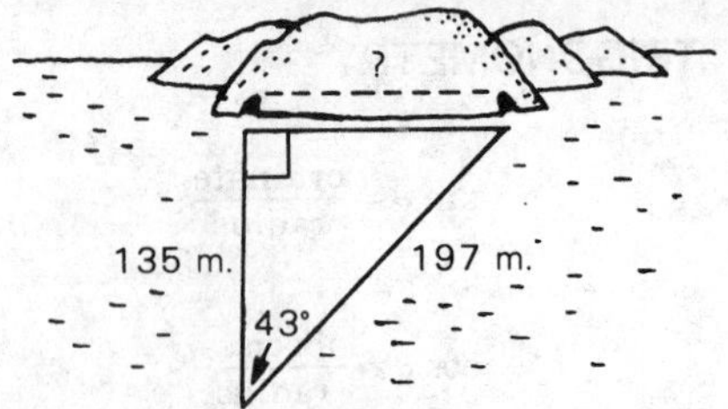

In this case you know two sides and the included angle, so the law of cosines will work and the law of sines will not. If you call the length of the tunnel x, then

$$x^2 = 135^2 + 197^2 - 2(135)(197)\cos 43°$$
$$x^2 \approx 18{,}225 + 38{,}809 - 53{,}190(0.7314)$$
$$x^2 \approx 18{,}131.$$

To two decimal places, the square root of 18,131 is 134.65, so the finished tunnel will be 134.65 meters long.

Trigonometric Identities

There are a number of formulas that prove to be useful in the manipulation of expressions. They are called *identities* because they are true for all values of the variables, except, of course, for those that make denominators zero. They are given here, without proof.

Addition formulas.

$$\sin(A+B) = \sin A \cos B + \cos A \sin B$$
$$\sin(A-B) = \sin A \cos B - \cos A \sin B$$
$$\cos(A+B) = \cos A \cos B - \sin A \sin B$$
$$\cos(A-B) = \cos A \cos B + \sin A \sin B$$
$$\tan(A+B) = \frac{\tan A + \tan B}{1 - \tan A \tan B}$$
$$\tan(A-B) = \frac{\tan A - \tan B}{1 + \tan A \tan B}$$

Double-angle formulas. These can be obtained by letting B = A in the addition formulas.

$$\sin 2A = 2 \sin A \cos A$$
$$\cos 2A = \cos^2 A - \sin^2 A$$
$$= 2\cos^2 A - 1$$
$$= 1 - 2\sin^2 A$$
$$\tan 2A = \frac{2 \tan A}{1 - \tan^2 A}$$

Half-angle formulas. Since the formulas above are true for all values of A, we can substitute $\frac{1}{2}$A for A in them, and, of course, A for 2A. Doing this in the alternatives for cos 2A, we have

$$2 \sin^2 \tfrac{1}{2} = 1 - \cos A$$

$$2 \cos^2 \tfrac{1}{2}A = 1 + \cos A.$$

So,

$$\sin \tfrac{1}{2}A = \pm\sqrt{\tfrac{1}{2}(1 - \cos A)}$$

$$\cos \tfrac{1}{2}A = \pm\sqrt{\tfrac{1}{2}(1 + \cos A)}.$$

Product formulas.

$$\sin A \sin B = \tfrac{1}{2}\cos(A-B) - \tfrac{1}{2}\cos(A+B)$$

$$\sin A \cos B = \tfrac{1}{2}\sin(A-B) + \tfrac{1}{2}\sin(A+B)$$

$$\cos A \cos B = \tfrac{1}{2}\cos(A-B) + \tfrac{1}{2}\cos(A+B)$$

Function-addition formulas.

$$\sin A + \sin B = 2\sin\tfrac{1}{2}(A+B)\cos\tfrac{1}{2}(A-B)$$

$$\sin A - \sin B = 2\cos\tfrac{1}{2}(A+B)\sin\tfrac{1}{2}(A-B)$$

$$\cos A + \cos B = 2\cos\tfrac{1}{2}(A+B)\cos\tfrac{1}{2}(A-B)$$

$$\cos A - \cos B = -2\sin\tfrac{1}{2}(A+B)\sin\tfrac{1}{2}(A-B)$$

$$\sin A + \cos B = 2\sin[\tfrac{1}{2}(A-B)+45°] \times \cos[\tfrac{1}{2}(A+B)+45°]$$

$$\sin A - \cos B = 2\cos[\tfrac{1}{2}(A-B)+45°] \times \sin[\tfrac{1}{2}(A-B)+45°]$$

Tangent formulas. This identity is called the tangent law:

$$\frac{\tan\frac{1}{2}(A-B)}{\tan\frac{1}{2}(A+B)} = \frac{a-b}{a+b}$$

Three substitutions that can be useful in calculus are obtained from the double-angle formula, by putting $\tan \frac{1}{2}A = t$. Then,

$$\tan A = \frac{2t}{1-t^2}$$

$$\sin A = \frac{2t}{1+t^2}$$

$$\cos A = \frac{1-t^2}{1+t^2}$$

Analytic Trigonometry

Trigonometry is much more than a study of the ratios of the sides of a triangle. Sine and cosine can be functions of numbers such as 2, $\sqrt{3}$, and π, retaining all the relations established by referring to ratios and angles.

Circular measure. Suppose a circle with radius r is centered at the origin. A radius line starting at the x-axis would sweep out angles as it wraps around the circle, intersecting succeeding points on the circle. At the end of one complete revolution, it would have traveled around the complete circumference of the circle, a distance of $2\pi r$: it would also have swept out an angle of 360°.

Unit circle. The radius of the circle can just as well be 1 unit as r; any unit will do, whether it be an inch or a centimeter, or your height. The circumference of a circle with a radius of 1 unit is 2π, corresponding to a rotation of 360°. Halfway around the circle, π corresponds to 180°; a quarter-way around, $\frac{1}{2}\pi$ corresponds to 90°.

In a circle of radius r, a certain angle at the center intercepts an arc of length r on the circumference. Exactly the same angle intercepts an arc of length 1 on the unit circle. The measure of this angle is called 1 radian; its symbol is *rad* in the international metric system.

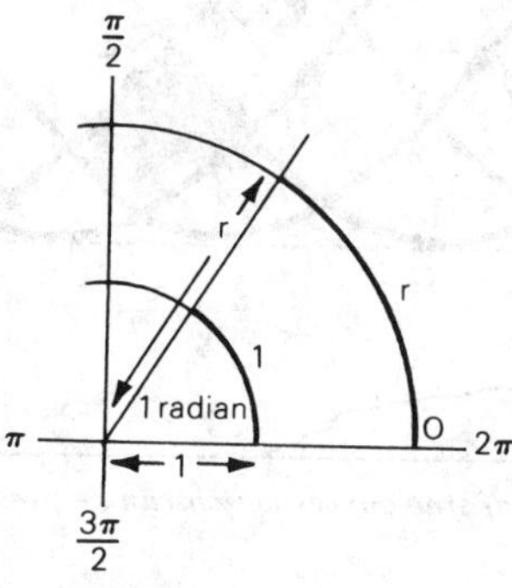

Since a complete revolution is 2π radians, or 360°, an angle of 1 radian may be found as follows:

$$2\pi\ (\text{rad}) = 360°$$

$$1\ \text{rad} = \frac{360°}{2\pi} = \frac{180°}{\pi} = 57°.2958\ldots$$

For conversion,

$$\text{degrees} = \text{radians} \times \frac{180}{\pi}$$

$$\text{radians} = \text{degrees} \times \frac{\pi}{180}$$

We have seen that the values of the sine function repeat themselves after A has completed a revolution of 360°. Thus, sin 1° = sin 361°, and so on. The *period* of the sine function, therefore, is 360°. Using radians for angle measurement, the period of the sine function is 2π (radians). Thus,

$$\sin A = \sin A + 2\pi = \sin A + 4\pi,$$

and so on. The cosine function repeats in the same way.

The sine of a number is the sine of the angle that has that number of radians. The sine of the number $\frac{1}{4}\pi$, for example, is

$$\sin \tfrac{1}{4}\pi\ (\text{rad}) = \sin 45° = \tfrac{1}{2}\sqrt{2}$$

Graphing the functions. Graphs of sin x, cos x, tan x are shown above. The graphs of sin x and cos x are clearly continuous and similar to each other, whereas the graph of tan x contains jumps, or discontinuities.

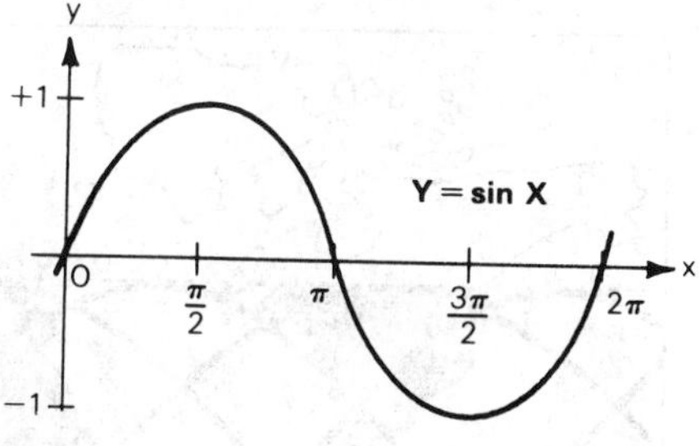

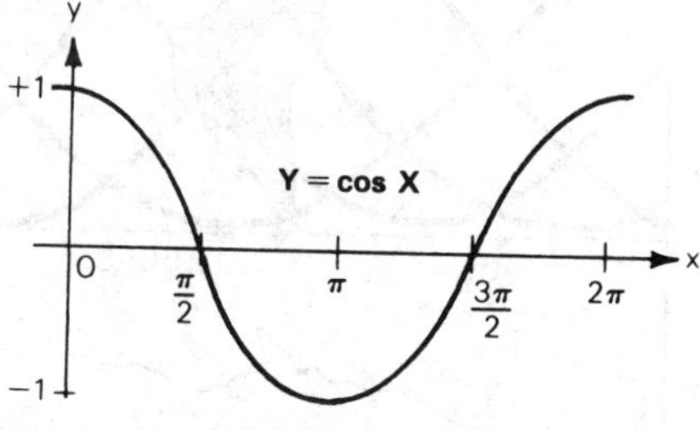

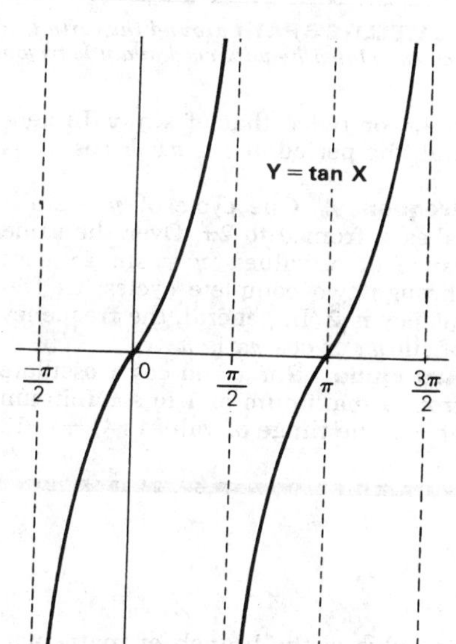

As x approaches $\frac{1}{2}\pi$, the absolute value of tan x increases without limit. If x is slightly less than $\frac{1}{2}\pi$, then x is positive; if slightly more, then x is negative. Lines such as $x = \frac{1}{2}\pi$ that the tangent curve approaches are called *asymptotes*.

Period. As we have seen, the period of sin x and cos x is 2π radians. The period of tan x is π radians, or 180°.

The following graph shows sin $2x$, 2 sin x, and sin $\frac{1}{2}x$.

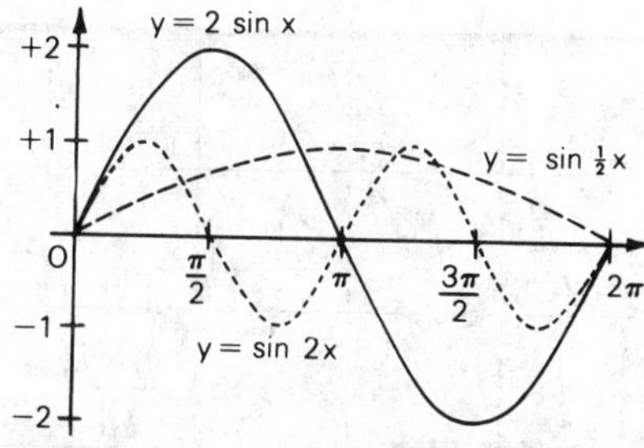

The period of sin $2x$ is π, or half the period of sin x. The period of sin $\frac{1}{2}x$

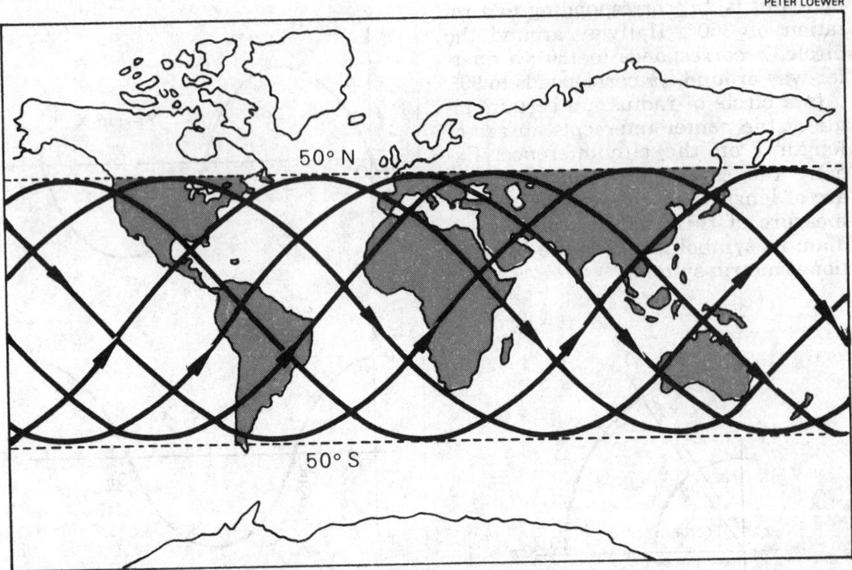

A SATELLITE'S PATH *around the earth traces a series of sine curves which can be predicted and calculated by advanced analytic trigonometry.*

is 4π, or twice that of sin x. In general, the period of sin nx or cos nx is $1/n$.

Frequency. One cycle of $y = \sin x$ takes x from 0 to 2π. Over the same range of x values, $y = \sin 2x$ goes through two complete cycles; its frequency is 2. In general, the frequency of sin nx or cos nx is n.

Amplitude. Sin x and cos x oscillate from a maximum of 1 to a minimum of -1. The range of values is $1 - (-1)$, or 2, and half this range, 1, is called the amplitude. Since tan x has no maxima or minima, it does not have an amplitude. The amplitude of 2 sin x is 2; of n sin x, is n.

Series expansions. When a function is the sum or difference of two trigonometric functions, its graph may be obtained by adding or subtracting the ordinates of the two original functions.

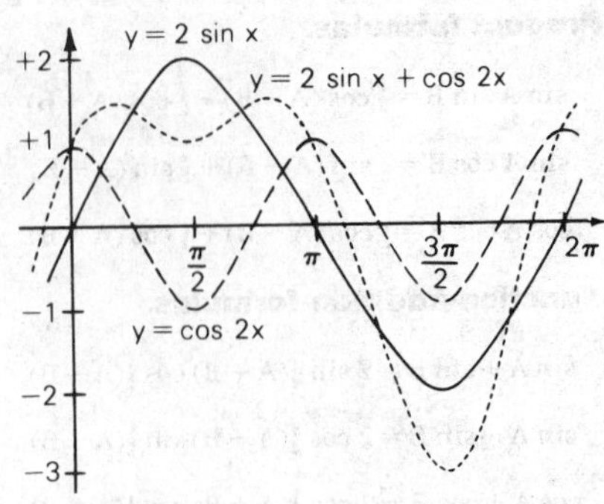

In the figure, cos $2x$ and 2 sin x are both plotted, along with their sum, $y = 2 \sin x + \cos 2x$. The shape of the sum does not look like a sine or a cosine curve. The addition of more sine or cosine functions produces a tremendous variety of periodic functions. There is a method by which an infinite series of sine and cosine functions can be found that has a sum equal to almost any given periodic function, including ones as unlikely as the shape of the teeth of a saw, or as asymmetric as a facial profile. Such a series is called a *Fourier series.*

Fourier series provide the numerical means of calculating various quantities such as π. Others can be used to analyze the cycles of economics, sleep patterns and heart rhythms, sunspots, tides, and the sound of violins.

Calculus

Calculus is the branch of mathematics that deals with quantities that change. If a moving object increases its distance from its starting place at a constant rate, we can calculate its rate of speed by simple arithmetic procedures. But if it is accelerating or decelerating or if it changes direction, arithmetic cannot tell us the object's speed at any moment or its distance from the starting point. Calculus is the advanced mathematical study that can solve this kind of problem.

The electrical resistance of a wire changes in a complicated way as its temperature changes; calculus will enable an engineer to calculate the resistance in any temperature range. Isaac Newton knew that the gravitational force of the sun on a planet was continually changing with the distance between the two bodies. In order to calculate the orbits of planets, Newton used his new calculus (a similar system was invented by Leibnitz at about the same time).

These examples show that calculus may be used when there is a continually shifting relationship between quantities. Given such a relationship—from the sciences, from engineering, economics, or another field—calculus can help discover the situation at any given point in time or space.

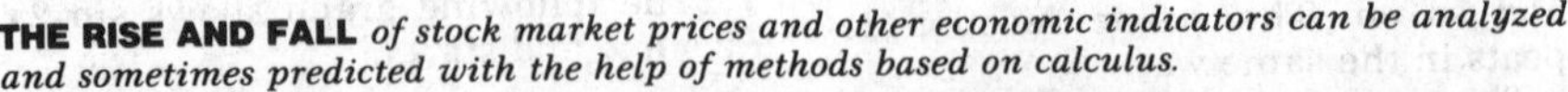

THE RISE AND FALL *of stock market prices and other economic indicators can be analyzed and sometimes predicted with the help of methods based on calculus.*

The concept of limit. The fundamental concept in calculus is that of a *limit.* To explain this concept, we can use the physics of a falling object. By gravitation theory, a ball falling freely will fall 16 feet $\times\ t^2$ in t seconds:

$$s = 16 \text{ ft} \times t^2$$

Suppose we want to know the speed of a ball after it has been falling for 3 seconds. Since its distance, s, equals

$16t^2$, we can calculate that in 3 seconds it will have fallen $16(3)^2$ or 144 feet. Its average velocity during this fall was $144 \div 3$ or 48 feet per second. But this is not the velocity it will have at the 3-second point. By 4 seconds after the start, it will have fallen $16(4)^2$ or 256 feet, so that in the second after the 3-second moment, it will fall 256 minus 144 feet, or 112 feet, for an average velocity of 112 feet per second. But this, too, is not the velocity at the instant of 3 seconds.

In the following table, the time and distance fallen from the start are shown for a succession of moments. The two left columns show the time and distance fallen from the start. The center column shows smaller and smaller increments of time following the 3-second point, and the two right columns show the distance fallen and the velocity of the ball during these increments. Between 3 and 3.5 seconds, the velocity is 104 feet per second. Between 3 and 3.1 seconds, it is 97.6 feet per second; between 3 and 3.01 seconds it is 96.16; between 3 and 3.001, it is 96.016; and so on. As the time interval gets smaller, the velocity gets closer to 96 feet per second. By taking as small intervals as necessary, we can calculate the velocity to be as close to 96 as we wish. We say that, in the limit, the velocity at the instant of 3 seconds is 96 feet per second.

The graph of $s = 16t^2$ gives some picture of what we have been doing. The second of the two figures exaggerates the curve between the 3-second point and the 4-second point.

Between 3 and 4 seconds, the velocity is 112 feet per second, which is also the slope of a line *(a)* joining the 3-second point (144) to the 4-second point (256). (The slope of a line between two points is the difference of their y-coordinates divided by the difference of their x-coordinates.) The straight line connecting 3 and 3.5 seconds is closer to the curve, just as the velocity of the ball is closer to that at 3 seconds. As the time interval comes closer to zero, the line joining the two points gets closer to being the tangent of the curve at 3 seconds. The velocity at that point will be equal to the slope of the tangent. This is a geometrical interpretation of a rate-of-change problem that can be solved by the *differential calculus.*

An example of a different kind was given by Newton himself in his great work *Principia.* He considered the problem of finding the area under a curve such as the one in the following figure.

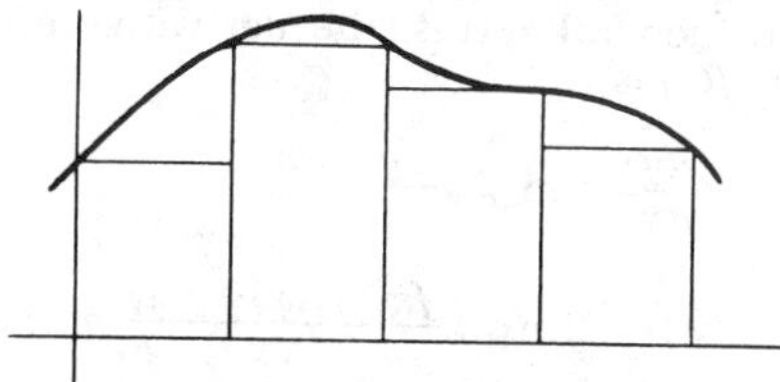

If you fill the space with a set of rectangles of the same width, the sum of the areas of the rectangles will approximate the area under the curve. There will be space left over, showing that the area of the rectangles is

THE FALL OF A BALL

Fallen from start		Fallen after 3 seconds		
time, t (sec)	distance, s (feet)	$t-3$ Δt	$s-144$ Δs	velocity $\frac{\Delta s}{\Delta t}$
4	256	1	112	112
3.5	196	.5	52	104
3.1	153.76	.1	9.76	97.6
3.01	144.9616	.01	.9616	96.16
3.001	144.096016	.001	.096016	96.016
3	144	0	0	?

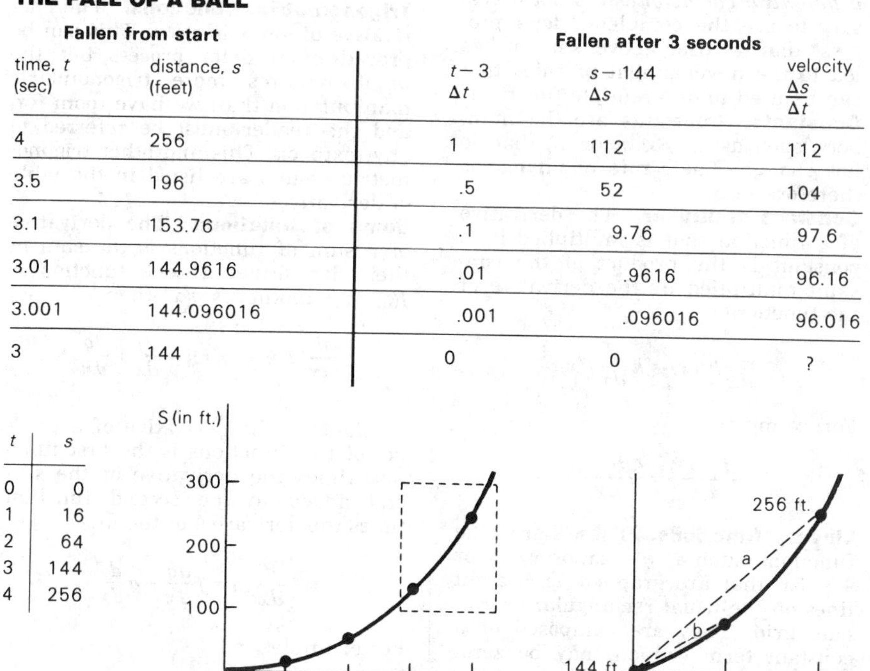

less than that under the curve. To find a closer approximation, use thinner rectangles.

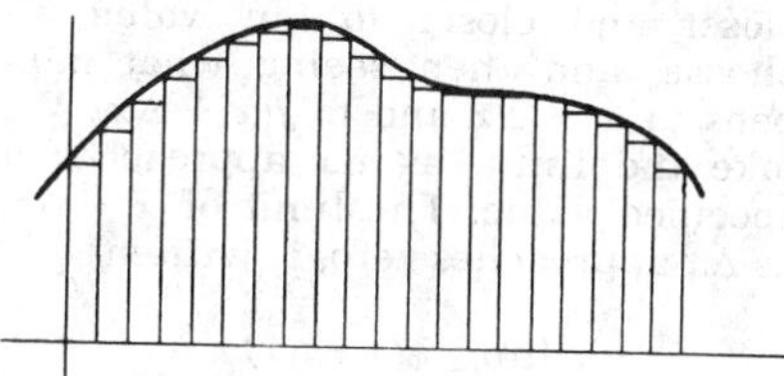

The sum of the areas of these rectangles will still be smaller than that under the curve, but it will be closer. As the width of the rectangles approaches zero, their total area will come closer and closer to the area under the curve. In the limit the areas will be equal.

The *integral calculus* uses this kind of reasoning to find areas and volumes. It also reverses the differential calculus, finding the equation of the curve from that of its tangent.

Differential Calculus

Relationships are expressed mathematically by equations. The relation between Fahrenheit and Celsius temperatures is $F = \frac{9}{5}C + 32$. Simple interest accrues by the formula $I = PRT$. For the falling ball, $s = 16t^2$. When C changes in the temperature equation, F will change; as T changes in the interest equation, I will change. Thus, F will depend on C; F is called a function of C. Similarly, I is a function of T. If y depends on x, then we write $y = f(x)$, which is read "f of x," to mean that y is a function of x. In this case, y is called the dependent variable, and x is the independent variable. This means that as x (the independent variable) changes, y (the dependent variable) must change, too.

If y is a function of x, then x must also be a function of y. Thus, $x = f(y)$. In calculus, however, the usual form is $y = f(x)$.

Since calculus is concerned particularly with changes in variables, it has a special notation for such a change: the Greek capital letter delta. A change in x is written Δx, which is read "delta x." A change in y is Δy. (Note that the symbol Δ has no value of its own.)

If $y = f(x)$ and x increases by Δx causing y to increase by Δy, then

$$y + \Delta y = f(x + \Delta x).$$

This is a symbolic way of saying that wherever x occurs in the original function, it must be replaced by $x + \Delta x$. For example,

if $\quad y = x^2 + 3x,$
then $y + \Delta y = (x + \Delta x)^2 + 3(x + \Delta x).$

The size of the change in x is not specified by the symbol Δx. We control the size of it, allowing Δx to get closer and closer to any value we choose, and then seeing what happens to $x + \Delta x$ and to $f(x + \Delta x)$. We take the limit, as Δx approaches a specified value. The limit of $x + \Delta x$, as Δx approaches zero, is written

$$\lim_{\Delta x \to 0}(x + \Delta x).$$

It is intuitively obvious that as Δx approaches zero, $x + \Delta x$ must approach x.

$$\lim_{\Delta x \to 0}(x + \Delta x) = x$$

Another example is

$$\lim_{x \to 3} x^2 = 9$$

which means that as x gets closer and closer to 3 (from either direction), its square gets closer and closer to 9.

The limit of a sum of functions is the sum of the individual limits; the limit of a product or quotient is the product or quotient of the limits (always provided that there is no denominator of zero).

The derivative. The rate at which a function is changing at any given moment is called the *derivative* of that function. Finding derivatives is the main concern of the differential calculus.

The general method is to find the rate of change over an interval, and then let that interval approach zero, so that, in the limit, the rate of change will be the instantaneous one. This is what we did, at some length, in our investigation of the falling ball. We will now see how it can be done for any function.

We will follow the method through with a specific example,

$$y = x^2 + 3x + 1.$$

If x changes by an amount Δx, and y by Δy,

$$\begin{aligned} y + \Delta y &\\ &= (x + \Delta x)^2 + 3(x + \Delta x) + 1 \\ &= x^2 + 2x\,\Delta x + \Delta x^2 + 3x + 3\,\Delta x + 1 \\ &= (x^2 + 3x + 1) + 2x\,\Delta x + \Delta x^2 + 3\,\Delta x \end{aligned}$$

(Note that Δx^2 means the square of Δx.) Now, subtracting y from the left and the equivalent $(x^2 + 3x + 1)$ from the right, we have

$$\Delta y = 2x\,\Delta x + \Delta x^2 + 3\,\Delta x.$$

This is the actual change in y over a certain interval. To find the rate of that change (that is, the amount y changes as x changes), we divide by Δx:

$$\frac{\Delta y}{\Delta x} = \frac{2x\,\Delta x + \Delta x^2 + 3\Delta x}{\Delta x}$$

$$= 2x + \Delta x + 3$$

This is the rate of y's change for any value of Δx. In particular, we want the instantaneous rate of change when Δx approaches zero, and so we take the limit, which is the derivative:

$$\frac{dy}{dx} = \lim_{\Delta x \to 0} 2x + \Delta x + 3$$

The symbol dy/dx means the derivative of y with respect to x; that is, the instantaneous rate of change of y when x changes. (Like delta, the d has no value of its own.)

All that remains is to determine what the limit is. Obviously, the Δx becomes zero, while the $2x$ and the 3 are unchanged, so that

$$\frac{dy}{dx} = 2x + 3.$$

In general terms, the derivative of $y = f(x)$ is

$$\frac{dy}{dx} = \lim_{\Delta x \to 0} \frac{\Delta y}{\Delta x}$$

$$= \lim_{\Delta x \to 0} \frac{f(x + \Delta x) - f(x)}{\Delta x}$$

Instead of dy/dx, the symbol $f'(x)$ is sometimes used for the derivative. This is read "*f* prime of *x*."

Differentiating functions.

The process of finding the derivative is called *differentiating*, and the derivative is also known as the *differential coefficient*. It is not necessary to use the complete "delta process" that we used above, since it has led to the development of rules that can be used to differentiate functions.

Constants. Constants are the numbers, such as 2, $\sqrt{3}$, π, or $4i$, that do not change. Their rate of change is therefore zero.

Constant multiplier. The derivative of a function that is multiplied by a constant is the product of the constant multiplied by the derivative of the function:

$$\frac{d}{dx} kf(x) = k\frac{d}{dx} f(x)$$

For example:

$$\frac{d(4x^2)}{dx} = \frac{4d(x^2)}{dx}$$

Linear functions. These are the functions, such as $y = 2x$, or $x + 3$, or $4 - 5x$, that are graphed as straight lines on the usual rectangular coordinate grid. They are composed of a constant term (which may be zero) and a linear term in which the variable is multiplied by a constant (which may be 1). For example:

$$\begin{aligned} y &= mx + b \\ y + \Delta y &= m(x + \Delta x) + b \\ \Delta y &= m\,\Delta x \\ \frac{\Delta y}{\Delta x} &= m \end{aligned}$$

and in the limit when $\Delta x \to 0$,

$$\frac{dy}{dx} = m.$$

The equation $y = mx + b$ is the standard form for an equation of a straight line, m being its slope. This confirms that the derivative of a linear function is the slope of the corresponding line. When $y = x$, the derivative $dy/dx = 1$.

Functions of higher order. Carrying out a delta process for $y = x^2$, we have:

$$\begin{aligned} y + \Delta y &= (x + \Delta x)^2 \\ y + \Delta y &= x^2 + 2x\,\Delta x + \Delta x^2 \\ \Delta y &= 2x\Delta x + \Delta x^2 \end{aligned}$$

$$\frac{\Delta y}{\Delta x} = \frac{2x\Delta x + \Delta x^2}{\Delta x}$$

$$\frac{\Delta y}{\Delta x} = 2x + \Delta x$$

$$\frac{dy}{dx} = 2x$$

The derivative of x^3, by a similar process, is $3x^2$; that of x^4 is $4x^3$; and in general,

$$\frac{d}{dx} x^n = nx^{n-1}$$

Trigonometric functions. The derivative of sin x is cos x. This can be proved by a delta process but the proof requires more trigonometric manipulation than we have room for, and the reader must be referred to any textbook. This and other trigonometric results are listed in the table of derivatives.

Sums of functions. The derivative of a sum of functions is the sum of their derivatives. If one function is $f(x)$ and another is $g(x)$, then

$$\frac{d}{dx}[f(x) + g(x)] = \frac{df}{dx} + \frac{dg}{dx}$$

Products. The derivative of a product of two functions is the first function times the derivative of the second added to the second function times the derivative of the first:

$$\frac{d}{dx} fg = f\frac{dg}{dx} + g\frac{df}{dx}$$

For example:

$$\frac{d}{dx} x^2 \sin x = x^2 \cos x + 2x \sin x$$

TABLE OF DERIVATIVES

Function, f	Derivative, $\frac{df}{dx}$
c	0
x	1
kx	k
x^n	nx^{n-1}
$k[g(x)]$	$k\,g'(x)$
$\frac{1}{x}$	$\frac{-1}{x^2}$
$\frac{1}{x^n}$	$\frac{-n}{x^{n+1}}$
$\sqrt{x}$	$\frac{1}{2\sqrt{x}}$
$u+v$	$u'+v'$
uv	$uv'+vu'$
$\frac{u}{v}$	$\frac{(vu'-uv')}{v^2}$
$f[u(x)]$	$\frac{df}{du}\cdot\frac{du}{dx}$
$\sin x$	$\cos x$
$\cos x$	$-\sin x$
$\tan x$	$\sec^2 x$
$\cot x$	$-\csc^2 x$
$\sec x$	$\sec x \tan x$
$\csc x$	$-\csc x \cot x$
arc $\sin x$	$\frac{1}{\sqrt{1-x^2}}$
arc $\cos x$	$\frac{-1}{\sqrt{1-x^2}}$
arc $\tan x$	$\frac{1}{(1+x^2)}$
arc $\cot x$	$\frac{-1}{(1+x^2)}$
arc $\sec x$	$\frac{1}{x\sqrt{x^2-1}}$
arc $\csc x$	$\frac{-1}{x\sqrt{x^2-1}}$
e^x	e^x
a^x	$a^x \ln a$
$\ln x$	$\frac{1}{x}$
$\log_a x$	$\frac{1}{x \ln a}$

Quotients. The rule for differentiating a quotient may be derived from the rule for products. It is:

$$\frac{d}{dx}\frac{f}{g}=\frac{g(df/dx)-f(dg/dx)}{g^2}$$

Thus,

$$\frac{d}{dx}\frac{x^2}{\sin x}=\frac{(2x\sin x-x^2\cos x)}{\sin^2 x}$$

Chain rule. If y is a function of a variable u, and u is a function of x, then

$$\frac{dy}{dx}=\frac{dy}{du}\cdot\frac{du}{dx}$$

This very important rule allows derivatives of quite complicated functions to be found readily. Suppose $y=(x^2+3)^5$. Instead of having to multiply out the fifth power of a binomial, we set

$$u=x^2+3$$

so $$\frac{du}{dx}=2x.$$

Since $$y=u^5$$ $$\frac{dy}{du}=5u^4.$$

Then, by the chain rule,

$$\frac{dy}{dx}=\frac{dy}{du}\cdot\frac{du}{dx}=5u^4\cdot 2x=10x(x^2+3)^4.$$

For functions of functions of functions, the rule can continue chaining. For example,

if $$y=\sin^2 x^4$$

then $$u=x^4,\quad\text{and}\ \frac{du}{dx}=4x^3$$

$$v=\sin u,\quad \frac{dv}{du}=\cos u$$

$$y=v^2,\quad \frac{dy}{dv}=2v$$

$$\frac{dy}{dx}=\frac{dy}{dv}\cdot\frac{dv}{du}\cdot\frac{du}{dx}$$
$$=2v\cos u\,4x^3$$
$$=8x^3\sin x^4\cos x^4$$

Applications.

The problem of the falling ball can now be solved, using the power of the calculus. When $s=16t^2$, the velocity at any instant is the derivative at that instant:

$$v=\frac{ds}{dt}=16(2t)=32t\,(\text{ft/sec})$$

For any particular instant, we substitute the appropriate value of t. When $t=3$,

$$v=32(3)=96\ \text{ft/sec}$$

which is the answer we obtained in discussing the limit concept.

Acceleration is the rate at which the velocity is changing, so we can find the acceleration at any moment by differentiating the velocity function, $v=32t$:

$$\text{acc.}=\frac{dv}{dt}=\frac{d(32t)}{dt}=32\ \text{ft/sec}$$

This is the well-known acceleration due to gravity. Being a constant, it obviously has the same value at any time.

Acceleration is found by differentiating again the derivative of the distance function with respect to time. The derivative of a derivative is called the second derivative and is written d^2y/dx^2, which is read "D2Y by DX squared." It can also be written $f''(x)$, which is read "f double prime of x."

$$\frac{d}{dx}\cdot\frac{dy}{dx}=\frac{d^2y}{dx^2}$$

$$\text{Acceleration}=\frac{dv}{dt}=\frac{d}{dt}\cdot\frac{ds}{dt}=\frac{d^2s}{dt^2}$$

Maxima and minima. The functional relations that have been mentioned so far have all moved in one direction. As time increased, the ball fell down; it didn't turn and go back up again. As the distance between a planet and the sun decreases, the gravitational force of the sun continues to increase. Many functions, however, do have turning points. The ball may be thrown up, rise to a maximum height, and then fall. The graph of a vibration rises and falls, as does that of any periodic function, which is described by sines and cosines. In such cases, the critical points where the turns occur are of particular interest.

The graph of $y=x^3-3x+1$ shows two critical points.

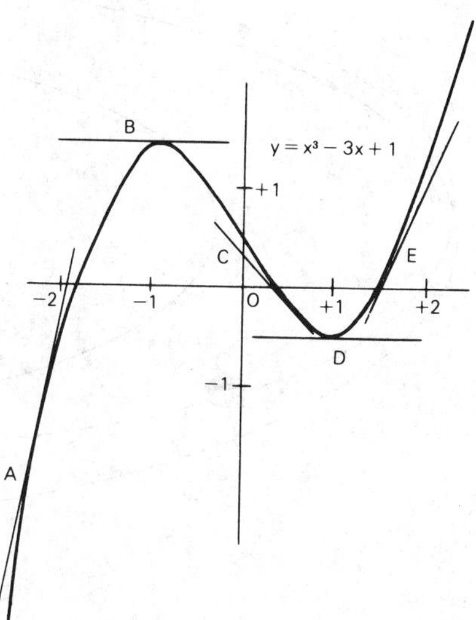

In one, the curve rises to a maximum, then falls; in the other, it falls to a minimum, then rises. The value of y at the maximum need not be the greatest value over the entire curve, but is a value that is greater than that of the neighboring points. Similarly, the minimum is lower than its neighbors.

Before (to the left of) the maximum, the slope of the tangent at any point, A, is positive; at the maximum, B, it is zero; and after the maximum, at C, the slope is negative. Before the minimum, the slope is negative; at the minimum, D, it is zero; and after it, at E, the slope is positive.

Since the slopes of the tangents are zero at the critical points, the derivatives must also be zero. To find those points, then, we differentiate the function and find where that derivative is zero:

$$y = x^3 - 3x + 1$$

$$\frac{dy}{dx} = 3x^2 - 3$$

Setting $dy/dx = 0$,

$$0 = 3(x^2 - 1) = 3(x - 1)(x + 1).$$

Therefore, $x = 1$ or -1
and $y = -1$ or 3

The critical points are therefore $(1, -1)$ and $(-1, 3)$.

We also want to be able to tell which is the maximum, which the minimum, without having first drawn the graph. From B to C, the slope changes from zero to negative, that is, it decreases. The derivative of the slope reflects this change by being negative. After the minimum, the slope increases from zero to a positive value; its derivative is positive. Since the slope is the derivative of the function, the derivative of the slope is the second derivative of the function. In this example,

$$\frac{d^2y}{dx^2} = 6x.$$

This is negative when $x = -1$, indicating a maximum; it is positive when $x = 1$, showing a minimum there.

Example: Of all the rectangles that have a perimeter of 48 units, which has the largest area?

Solution: If the two sides are x and y, the perimeter is $2x + 2y$, so that

$$x + y = 24$$

and $y = 24 - x.$

The area, A, is:

$$A = xy = x(24 - x) = 24x - x^2.$$

Finding the derivative and equating it to zero,

$$\frac{dA}{dx} = 24 - 2x = 0$$

Thus, $x = 12$, and $y = 12$

$$\frac{d^2A}{dx^2} = -2: \text{ maximum.}$$

The rectangle with largest area is the square with side 12.

Integral calculus

An integral is the reverse of a derivative. If a function has an integral I, then the derivative of I is the original function. The symbol used for an integral is an old-time long S; if the integration is with respect to x, then the function is followed by dx. For example,

$$\frac{dx^2}{dx} = 2x, \quad \text{so} \quad \int 2x\,dx = x^2.$$

The derivative of a constant is zero, so the derivative of $x^2 + c$, where c is any constant, is also $2x$. The integral of $2x$ is thus $2x + c$, where c is any constant (including zero). When applied to problems, the constant of integration, c, must be evaluated from other information, for instance, the initial conditions of the problem.

Integration. The process of finding an integral is generally more difficult than that of differentiating, but there are a few helpful rules.

Constant multiplier. The integral of a constant multiplied by a function is the constant multiplied by the integral of the function:

$$\int k\,f(x)\,dx = k\int f(x)\,dx$$

Sum of functions. The integral of a sum is the sum of the integrals:

$$\int (f + g)\,dx = \int f\,dx + \int g\,dx$$

THE FLIGHT PATH *of the Pioneer space shot to Venus, more than 8 million miles long, was calculated with complex mathematical formulas on high-speed computers.* NASA

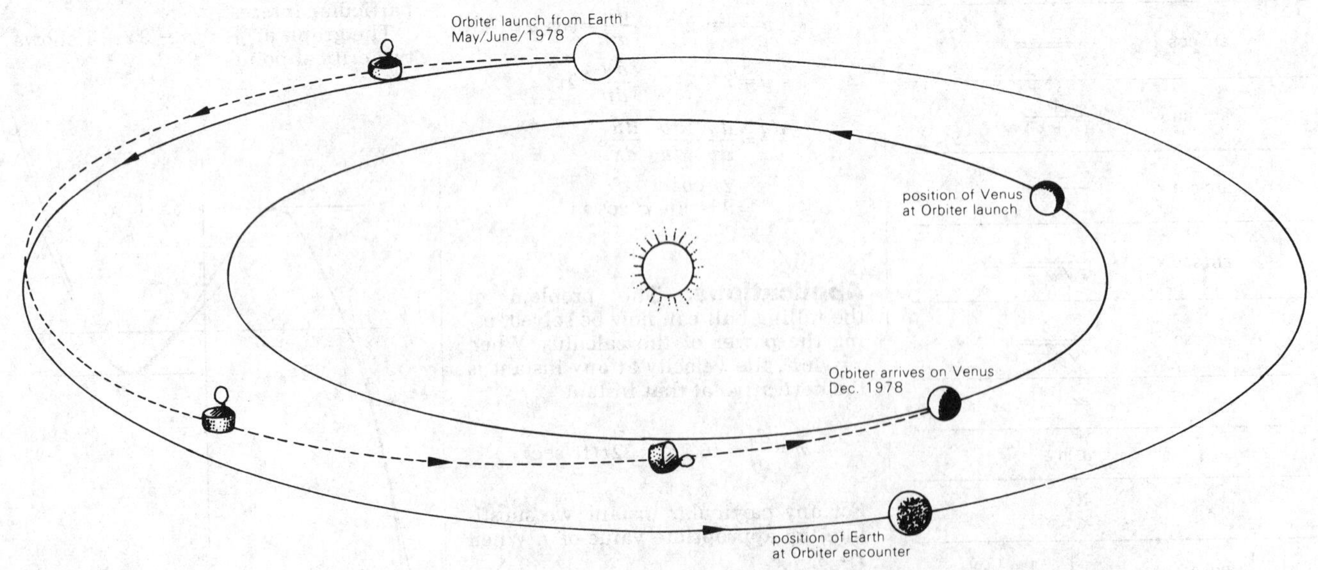

TABLE OF INTEGRALS

Function, f	Integral, $\int f\,dx$	
k	kx	
$k\,f(x)$	$k\int f(x)\,dx$	
x	$\frac{1}{2}x^2$	
x^n	$\frac{x^{n+1}}{(n+1)}$	$(n \neq -1)$
$\frac{1}{x}$	$\ln x$	
$\frac{1}{x^n}$	$\frac{-1}{(n-1)x^{n-1}}$	$(n \neq 1)$
$\sqrt{x}$	$(\frac{2}{3})x^{3/2}$	
$\frac{1}{\sqrt{x}}$	$2\sqrt{x}$	
$x^{n/r}$	$\frac{rx^{(n/r)+1}}{(r+n)}$	
$x^{-n/r}$	$\frac{r}{(r-n)x^{(n/r)-1}}$	
e^x	e^x	
$\ln x$	$x\ln x - x$	
$\sin x$	$-\cos x$	
$\cos x$	$\sin x$	
$\tan x$	$\ln \sec x$	
$\cot x$	$\ln \sin x$	
$\sec x$	$\ln(\tan x + \sec x)$	
$\csc x$	$\ln(\csc x - \cot x)$	
$\sin^2 x$	$\frac{1}{2}x - \frac{1}{2}\sin x \cos x$	
$\sec^2 x$	$\tan x$	
$\csc^2 x$	$-\cot x$	
$\sec x \tan x$	$\sec x$	
$\csc x \cot x$	$-\csc x$	
$\frac{1}{(ax+b)}$	$\left(\frac{1}{a}\right)\ln(ax+b)$	
$\frac{1}{(x^2+a^2)}$	$\left(\frac{1}{a}\right)\arctan\left(\frac{x}{a}\right)$	
$\frac{1}{(x^2-a^2)}$	$\left(\frac{1}{2a}\right)\ln\frac{(x-a)}{(x+a)}$	
$\frac{1}{\sqrt{(a^2-x^2)}}$	$\arcsin\left(\frac{x}{a}\right)$	
$\frac{1}{\sqrt{(x^2 \pm a^2)}}$	$\ln(x+\sqrt{(x^2 \pm a^2)})$	

There are no elementary formulas for the integral of a product or quotient of functions.

Power rule. This basic formula for integration is obtained from the one for differentiation:

$$\frac{d}{dx}x^{n+1} = (n+1)x^n$$

$$\int x^n\,dx = \frac{x^{n+1}}{(n+1)} + c$$

This holds except when $n = -1$, which would make the denominator zero. In that case:

$$\int x^{-1}\,dx = \int \frac{1}{x}dx = \ln x + c$$

where $\ln x$ is the natural logarithm of x (to the base e).

Example: $\int\left(4x^3 + x - 5 + \frac{1}{x^3}\right)dx$

$$= 4\int x^3 dx + \int x dx - 5\int dx + \int x^{-3} dx$$

$$= \frac{4x^4}{4} + \frac{x^2}{2} - 5x + \frac{x^{-2}}{-2} + c$$

$$= x^4 + \tfrac{1}{2}x^2 - 5x - \frac{1}{2x^2}$$

Substitution. Some expressions can be integrated with the help of a substitution. To integrate $(4x + 1)^9$, first set u equal to $(4x + 1)$. We must also substitute for dx so that we can integrate with respect to u:

$$\frac{du}{dx} = 4, \quad \text{so} \quad dx = \tfrac{1}{4}du$$

$$\int(4x+1)^9\,dx = \int u^9 \tfrac{1}{4}\,du$$

$$= \frac{\frac{1}{4}u^{10}}{10}$$

$$= \frac{1}{40}(4x+1)^{10} + c$$

The definite integral. Any given value of x can be substituted into $f(x)$ to obtain the value of the function at that particular point. If $x = 3$, then $5x^2 = 45$. We can find the difference in values of the function over a particular domain by substituting again and subtracting. Thus, if $x = 1$, then $5x^2 = 5$. The difference between this value and the one at $x = 3$, is $45 - 5 = 40$. This can be written:

$$5x^2\Big]_1^3 = 45 - 5 = 40$$

or, in general,

$$f(x)\Big]_a^b = f(b) - f(a).$$

When such a substitution is to occur after an integration, the limits a and b are attached to the integral sign:

$$\int_a^b 10x\,dx = (5x^2 + c)\Big]_a^b$$
$$= (45 + c) - (5 + c) = 40$$

The integration constant disappears, and this type of integral is called a *definite integral.* Integrals discussed earlier have no limits of integration and so have an indefinite constant.

Basic properties.

$$\int_a^b k\,f(x)\,dx = k\int_a^b f(x)\,dx$$

$$\int_a^b (f+g)dx = \int_a^b f dx + \int_a^b g dx$$

$$\int_a^a f(x)\,dx = 0$$

The integral over an interval is the sum of the integrals over its parts:

$$\int_a^b f dx = \int_a^c f dx + \int_c^d f dx + \int_d^b f dx$$

Areas by integration. The following figure shows a curve. As we have learned, to find the area under the curve, we must divide it into rectangles of equal width whose heights are equal to that of the curve at a given point. The height of the first rectangle is y_1, of the second, y_2, and so on to the last one, y_n. Their width is Δx.

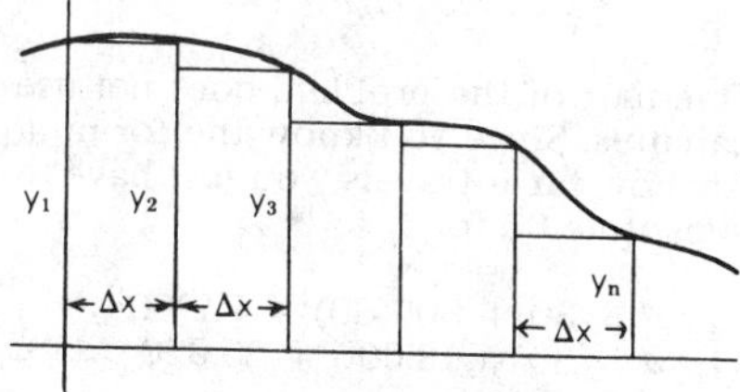

The sum of the areas is therefore:

$$y_1\Delta x + y_2\Delta x + y_3\Delta x + \ldots + y_n\Delta x$$
or $f(x_1)\Delta x + f(x_2)\Delta x + \ldots + f(x_n)\Delta x.$

To approximate the area better, use more rectangles of smaller width. As the number of rectangles approaches infinity, their width approaches zero. In the limit, the sum of the areas of the rectangles will equal the area under the curve.

The fundamental theorem of the integral calculus states that, if an interval of $f(x)$ from $x = a$ to $x = b$ is divided into n equal subintervals of width Δx, then

$$\int_a^b f(x)\,dx = \lim_{n\to\infty}\Big[f(x_1)\Delta x + f(x_2)\Delta x + \ldots + f(x_n)\Delta x\Big]$$

Example: Find the area under the parabola $y = x^2$ from $x = 2$ to $x = 4$.

$$\int_2^4 x^2\,dx = \frac{x^3}{3}\Big]_2^4 = \frac{64}{3} - \frac{8}{3} = \frac{56}{3}$$

—*Barbara Sheridan*

PROBLEM SOLVING. The calculus was invented to solve many specific problems that could not be easily solved with algebra or geometry. Here are a few examples.

For a given rocket, you know that it will travel $30 + 300t + 7.2t^2$ meters after it is fired, where t is the time in seconds it has been in operation. How fast will it be going and how far will it have traveled after 60 seconds?

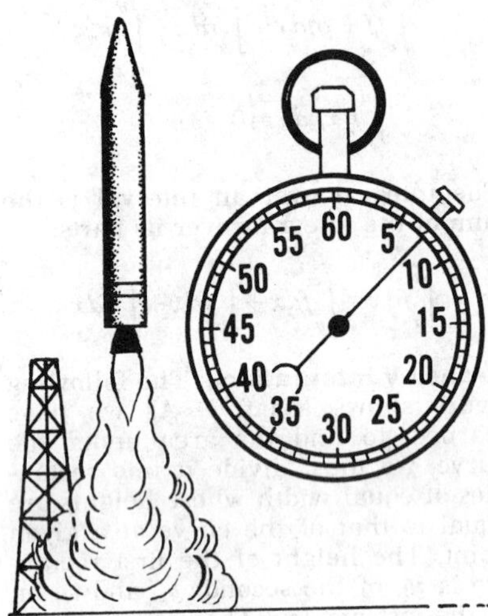

One part of the problem does not use calculus. Since you know the formula for how far it travels, you just have to substitute 60 for t.

$$d = 30 + 300(60) + 7.2(60^2)$$
$$d = 30 + 18{,}000 + 25{,}920$$
$$d = 43{,}950$$

In 60 seconds, the rocket will reach a height of 43,950 feet.

To find how fast it is traveling, however, you need to differentiate the function. The derivative of $30 + 300t + 7.2t^2$ is $0 + 300 + 2(7.2t) = 300 + 14.4t$. Therefore, the speed at 43,950 feet is $300 + 14.4(60)$ or 1164 feet per second.

Water is being drained from a spherical storage tower at a constant rate of 50 cubic feet a minute. The storage tank has a radius of 25 feet. How fast is the water level going down when the depth of water in the tank reaches 10 feet?

You know that the change in the volume of the water, V, with respect to time, t, is -50 cubic feet a minute, or $\frac{dV}{dt} = -50$.

As the water is drained, the partial water remaining has a shape called a segment of a sphere. The formula for the volume of such a segment is $V = \frac{1}{6}\pi h(3h + h^2)$, or $\frac{1}{2}\pi h^2 + \frac{1}{6}\pi h^3$, where h is the height of the water.

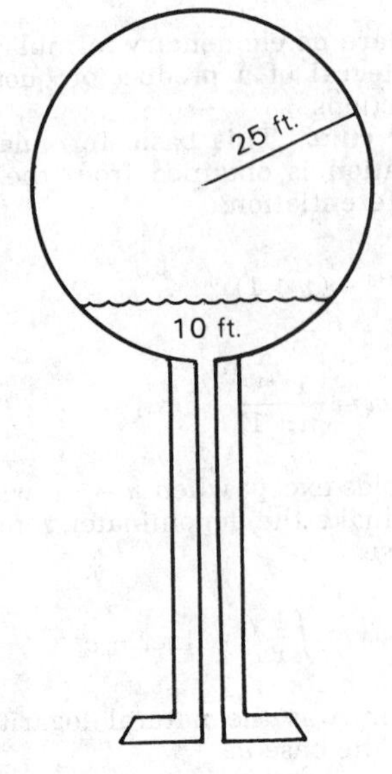

Use implicit differentiation with respect to t to get a different formula for $\frac{dV}{dt}$.

$$\frac{dV}{dt} = \pi h\left(\frac{dh}{dt}\right) + \frac{1}{2}\pi h^2\left(\frac{dh}{dt}\right)$$

Therefore, substituting -50 for $\frac{dV}{dt}$ and 10 for h, you get

$$-50 = 10\pi\left(\frac{dh}{dt}\right) + 50\pi\left(\frac{dh}{dt}\right).$$

Solve for $\frac{dh}{dt}$.

$$-50 = 60\pi\left(\frac{dh}{dt}\right)$$
$$\frac{dh}{dt} = \frac{-5}{6\pi}$$

Using $\frac{22}{7}$ for π gives an approximate value of $\frac{-110}{42} = -\frac{55}{21}$, or about 2.6 feet per minute.

Find the amount of paint needed to paint a region that is the shape of a parabola 15 feet tall with a base of 10 feet if 1 quart of paint covers 80 square feet.

To determine the area of this section of the parabola, first find its equation.

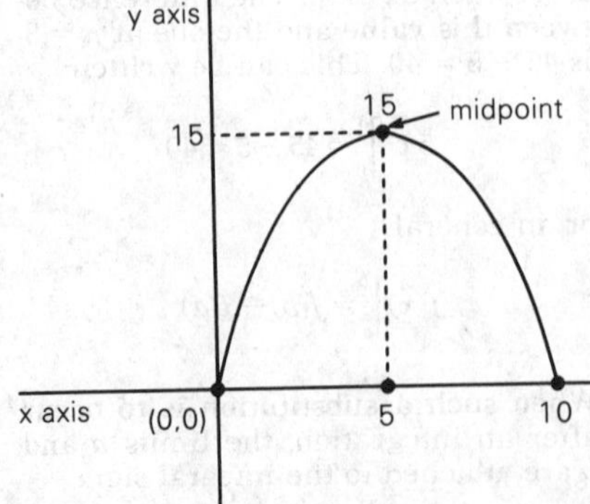

Assume that the left part of the curve goes through the origin. Then you know three points on the parabola: (0, 0), (5, 15), and (10, 0). The general equation of a parabola whose maximum is the point (h, k) is

$$y = a(x - h)^2 + k$$

so for this parabola, using (5, 15) as the maximum, you have

$$y = a(x - 5)^2 + 15.$$

But you also know that the parabola passes through (0, 0), so you can substitute 0 for both x and y to obtain the value of a.

$$0 = a(0 - 5)^2 + 15$$
$$-15 = 25a$$
$$a = \frac{-3}{5}$$

Substitute this value of a into the previous equation to obtain the equation of the parabola.

$$y = \frac{-3}{5}(x - 5)^2 + 15$$
$$y = \frac{-3}{5}(x^2 - 10x + 25) + 15$$
$$y = \frac{-3x^2}{5} + 6x$$

Check: It is worth it to stop at this point and make sure you have the right equation. Substitute the known values of (0, 0), (5, 15), and (10, 0) into the equation to make certain it is correct.

$$0 = 0 + 0$$
$$15 = -15 + 30 = 15$$
$$0 = -60 + 60$$

Now the area under the curve is the definite integral between 0 and 10 of the function

$$y = f(x) = \frac{-3x^2}{5} + 6x, \text{ or}$$

$$\int_0^{10}\left(\frac{-3x^2}{5} + 6x\right)dx.$$

The function $F(x)$ that represents the indefinite integral is

$$F(x) = \frac{-3x^3}{15} + 3x^2 + C$$

so the definite integral is

$$F(10) - F(0) = \frac{-3(1000)}{15} + 3(100)$$
$$= -200 + 300$$
$$= 100.$$

Therefore, the area under the curve is 100 square feet. Since a quart of paint covers 80 square feet, you need $1\frac{1}{4}$ quarts of paint.

MATHEMATICS GLOSSARY

Archimedes (287?–212 BC). The son of an astronomer, Archimedes was born in Syracuse, Sicily, then an important city in the Greek empire. He visited Alexandria in Egypt where he met the leading scholars of the day, but then returned home to Syracuse. His writing consisted of a number of short books, each a masterpiece of order and clarity. Many covered geometric topics, such as the measurement of the area and volume of solids. One of these stated that the volume of a sphere is two-thirds of the volume of a cylinder around it. Archimedes asked that the diagram of this discovery be put on his tombstone. He also found the value of π to lie between 3.1409 and 3.1429 (it is actually 3.14159 . . .).

Archimedes studied spirals, and found a way to express very large numbers in the deficient system of letters that the Greeks used. His work on mechanics included his famous method of finding the specific gravity of a body by water displacement.

When Syracuse was attacked by Rome, Archimedes invented the catapult, concave mirrors to focus sunlight and thus set fire to wooden ships, and other ingenious devices. Legend has it that when the Romans invaded Syracuse, Archimedes was sitting on the ground studying a diagram. He shouted to a Roman soldier not to step on it, and the Roman killed him.

Bernoulli Family (1623–1807). In three generations this Swiss family produced eight mathematicians, three of whom were very important to the development and application of calculus. All of them started out by studying something other than math, two being physicians, and three lawyers. The oldest of the dynasty was Jakob (Jacques), who became a professor at Basel in 1687. His youngest brother, Johann (Jean), later held the same position.

The brothers corresponded with Leibnitz and discovered much of what is now in beginning texts on calculus. Johann became involved in the dispute about who discovered calculus, Leibnitz or Newton (*see* Leibnitz). Johann hated Newton and championed Leibnitz. When his son, Daniel, won a prize that Johann had expected to receive, he threw Daniel out of the house.

Daniel was the third great Bernoulli. He became a professor at St. Petersburg in Russia, then returned to Basel to the professorship his father and uncle had held. His work extended from mathematics to astronomy and hydrodynamics. Daniel Bernoulli is regarded as the founder of mathematical physics.

Binomial Theorem. A general rule for predicting how a binomial (two-term) expression will expand as it is multiplied by itself. Elementary algebra shows how a simple binomial behaves:

$$(1+x)^1 = 1 + x$$
$$(1+x)^2 = 1 + 2x + x^2$$
$$(1+x)^3 = 1 + 3x + 3x^2 + x^3$$

Following this pattern, we could write the expansion of $(1 + x)^4$ if we knew the coefficients.

The pattern of coefficients in such a series was referred to in a Chinese work around 1100 A.D., and was known to Arab mathematicians in the 1400's. The coefficients of the series are embodied in Pascal's Triangle (*see* Pascal's Triangle).

Isaac Newton extended the theorem to negative and fractional exponents. These require a formula for the calculation of coefficients, and Newton used his new discovery, calculus, to help compute the series. A century later Euler and Gauss completed the study by producing a rigorous proof of the theorem.

The general form of the binomial theorem for the power n, is:

$$(1+x)^n = 1 + nx + \frac{n(n-1)}{2}x^2$$
$$+ \frac{n(n-1)(n-2)}{3 \cdot 2}x^3 + \ldots$$
$$\frac{n(n-1)(n-2)\ldots(1)}{n\ldots 3 \cdot 2}x^n$$

Computer Number System. A system of numeration that can be electronically stored and manipulated. The terminal of a computer has keys labeled with all the digits. One can ask it to multiply 8 × 7, but the computer cannot handle the number 8 or the number 7 in its calculations. It must translate these numbers into a system that it can use. Then, at the end of its calculations, it translates the answer, 56, back into the system that the user of the computer understands.

The decimal system that we normally use has 10 digits (from 0 to 9). When we have more than 9 items to count, we put 1 in the tens place and start over with the 0 to 9 digits in the units place. After 19, we make it 2 (for two tens) in the tens column, and again start over in the units place. This takes us to 99. When we get to 100, which is 10 times 10, we have to put 1 in the hundreds column. In this way, we can express any number, no matter how large, with only 10 different digits.

A computer has to work with *current ON* or *current OFF*—only two different "digits." We can write 1 for ON and 0 for OFF, and with them build the system that the computer uses. It is called the *binary system.*

In decimal notation, the digit on the far right tells how many units there are; the next one, how many tens; then hundreds (ten^2); thousands (ten^3); and so on. Each place represents a number ten times as large as the place before. The system is called base ten numeration. Binary is a base two system. The digit on the far right tells how many units there are; the next, how many twos; the next, fours

ARCHIMEDES *was one of the first to apply mathematics to weaponry. This print shows cannon trajectories.*

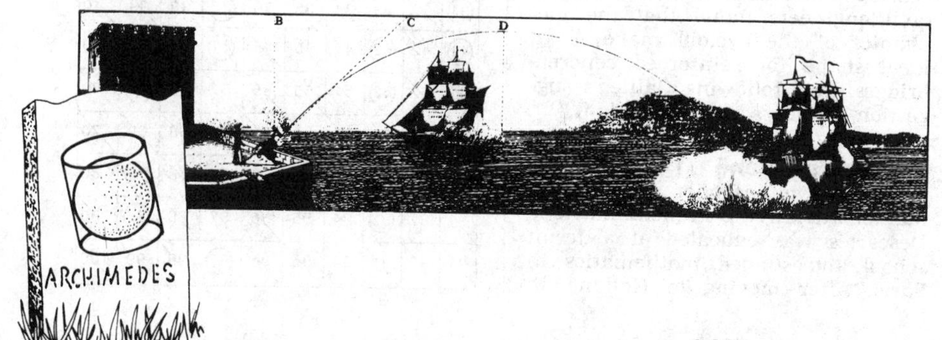

WIDE WORLD

THIS MICROCHIP, *shown magnified many times to show its circuitry, is the essential part of pocket calculators, computers, and other monitoring and computing devices.*

(since four is two times two); the next, eights (two^3); then sixteens; thirty-twos; and so on. Each place represents a number two times as large as the place before.

So for one, we write 1; for two we go into the twos column and write 10 (read one-oh, or one-zero; it is not ten); for three, which is two and one, we write 11 (one-one); for four, we go into the fours column with 100 (one-oh-oh, or one-zero-zero). The first 16 numerals are shown in the table below.

Decimal	Binary	Decimal	Binary
1	1	9	1001
2	10	10	1010
3	11	11	1011
4	100	12	1100
5	101	13	1101
6	110	14	1110
7	111	15	1111
8	1000	16	10000

There is no end to the system, though. Any number can be written as a binary numeral. For instance,

$$\begin{aligned} &53.75 \text{ (in base ten)} \\ &= 32+16+4+1+\tfrac{1}{2}+\tfrac{1}{4} \\ &= 1(32)+1(16)+0(8)+1(4)+0(2) \\ &\quad +1(1)+1(\tfrac{1}{2})+1(\tfrac{1}{4}) \\ &= 110101.11 \text{ (in base two)} \end{aligned}$$

Binary numbers can be shown with light bulbs; for 1101 (the number 13 in base ten), the lights would be *on-on-off-on.* They can be sent down a wire by having a current go *blip! blip! pause blip!* They can be stored on tape by magnetizing it, *north north south north.* Each digit—or the physical form used for it—is called a bit, for *BI*nary digi*T.*

Numbers are usually stored in computer memory in base two but they may also be stored in the related base sixteen (hexadecimal). Base sixteen requires 16 different digits. When written in ordinary print, letters a-f are used for the digits from 10 to 15. Sixteen is 10, and two hundred fifty-six, the square of the base, is 100. Since four binary digits can represent every number from 0 to 15, each four-bit sequence can represent a hexadecimal digit. Eighteen, as one sixteen plus two ones, would be (0001)(0010).

Feeding data into a computer does not require knowledge of binary or hexadecimal notation, but in designing programs, one should understand the computer's own language.

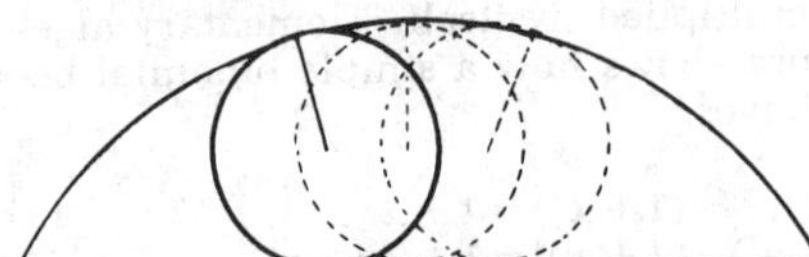

Cycloid. A cycloid is the curve traced out by a fixed point on a circle when the circle rolls along a straight line. Galileo studied the curve and suggested it could be used as the arch of a bridge. Sir Christopher Wren, the architect who redesigned London after the great fire of 1666, calculated the length of an arc of a cycloid and the position of its center of gravity. Christiaan Huygens proved that if tiny spheres or beads are placed in a cycloid-shaped bowl and allowed to slide down under the pull of gravity, then no matter where they are placed, they take the same time to reach the bottom. In the 20th century, civil engineers found that the mechanics of the cycloid make it an ideal shape for reinforced concrete bridges, thus following Galileo's suggestion 300 years after he made it.

Descartes, René (1596–1650). A soldier and philosopher as well as a mathematician, the Frenchman René Descartes was educated at a Jesuit school and studied mathematics in Paris. After moving to Holland in 1628, he spent 21 years with no fixed address, using the address of a school friend, who became a priest, for his mail.

Descartes' first written work was to be a philosophical treatise on the physical world. In it he used the Copernican system, which shows that the sun is the center of the solar system. This view had not yet been accepted by the Church, however. When Descartes heard that the Church was persecuting Galileo for similar beliefs, he was frightened. He put his paper away and it was not published until after his death.

In 1637, Descartes' *Discourse on Method* established him as a leading philosopher. One of the papers appended to this work was on geometry. In it he developed the method of graphing algebraic functions. The coordinate system of locating a point by its distance from two axes is sometimes called the *Cartesian system* in Descartes' honor. The important field of analytic geometry would not exist without this system.

Descartes' principal mathematical interest was in solving classical problems of Euclidean geometry. Such problems are of little interest today, but the tools Descartes used in trying to solve them have become an essential part of modern mathematics.

Eratosthenes' Sieve. A method of finding prime numbers (whole numbers that cannot be divided by numbers other than themselves and one without leaving a remainder). To implement this method, write out the numbers in order, as far as you want to go. Ignore 1, as it is neither prime nor multiple. Circle 2, then cross out every second number, which will be every number divisible by 2. Circle 3, then cross out every third number, which is every number divisible by 3. Circle 5 (noting that 4 has been crossed out), and cross out every fifth number. Continue in this way until every number that is divisible has been crossed out, and the prime numbers are all circled.

1	(2)	(3)	4	(5)	6	(7)	8	9	10
(11)	12	(13)	14	15	16	(17)	18	(19)	20
21	22	(23)	24	25	26	27	28	(29)	30
(31)	32	33	34	35	36	(37)	38	39	40
(41)	42	(43)	44	45	46	(47)	48	49	50
51	52	(53)	54	55	56	57	58	(59)	60
(61)	62	63	64	65	66	(67)	68	69	70
(71)	72	(73)	74	75	76	77	78	(79)	80
81	82	(83)	84	85	86	87	88	(89)	90
91	92	93	94	95	96	(97)	98	99	100

Eratosthenes of Cyrene (276–194 BC), whose method this was, also calculated from the shadow of the sun at noon that the circumference of Earth is about 25,000 miles, which is correct.

Euclid (fl. 300 BC). Little is known about the life of the author of the world's best-selling textbook, *Elements,* on which the teaching of elementary geometry is still based. Eu-

CULVER PICTURES

clid was probably educated in Athens, at the academy founded by Plato in the previous century. When the great institute in Alexandria was formed, Euclid was one of its galaxy of scientists, poets, historians, and artists. King Ptolemy is said to have asked Euclid for an easy introduction to his subject, to which Euclid replied "There is no royal road to geometry."

Elements contains all of geometry known to the ancient world, put by Euclid into strictly logical order. Unproved common notions and postulates are placed at the beginning. But then every theorem is proved from what went before. Many of the theorems may have been discovered before Euclid's time, but he may have originated some of the theorems and many of the proofs. Euclid also wrote works on optics, astronomy, music, and mechanics.

See also Non-Euclidean Geometry.

Euler, Leonhard (1707–1783). The most prolific of all mathematicians, Euler (pronounced oiler) produced enough work to fill 80 volumes. In his last 17 years he was totally blind, but his mathematical productivity actually increased.

Born the son of a Swiss pastor, Euler was sent to a university to study theology, but he also studied mathematics with Johann Bernoulli, whose sons became his friends. The Bernoullis finally persuaded Euler's father that Euler should be a mathematician. His first post was in St. Petersburg. He married there and in the ensuing years fathered 13 children.

Euler was able to work amid all his children, and the outpouring of mathematical papers never stopped. He also wrote textbooks for the Russian schools, and helped reform the country's weights and measures. As he finished a paper, he put it on top of a stack, from which the printer took it. This meant that papers at the bottom of the stack might wait for years for publication.

In 1740, Frederick the Great invited Euler to join the Berlin Academy. Tired of the conditions at the Russian court, Euler accepted. Yet Russia continued to pay Euler part of his salary. And when, during the Russian invasion of Berlin in 1760, Euler's farm was damaged, the army, and then the Empress, each paid Euler more than the damage was worth.

During his first stay in Russia, Euler lost an eye. In 1766 he returned to the court of Catherine the Great. Aware that he was losing the sight in his remaining eye because of a cataract, Euler had a desk made with a slate top, and practiced writing equations on it in chalk without looking. When blindness came, he dictated to his sons, chalking formulas on the table for them. Not having to concern himself with proofreading and other matters, his output increased. When he was 76, he chalked his last words on the table: "I die."

Much of the notation of modern mathematics began with Euler. He used A, B, C for the angles of a triangle, and *a, b, c* for the sides opposite them, $f(x)$ for a function of x, i for $\sqrt{-1}$, e for the base of natural logarithms, π for the ratio of circumference to diameter. He also discovered the relationship

$$e^{i\pi}+1=0$$

Euler's work touched every branch of pure mathematics and mathematical physics, including algebra, number theory, the calculus of variations, topology (which he helped to found), magnetism, and astronomy.

Fermat's Last Theorem. An unproved conjecture posed in 1637 by the Frenchman Pierre de Fermat (1601–1665). While the theorem seems to be true, it has never been proved. Search for the proof has led major and minor mathematicians alike into the theory of numbers and the development of new concepts.

Fermat stated his conjecture in the margin of a book that asked for whole-number solutions to the equation $x^2 + y^2 = a^2$. There are many such solutions, such as $3^2 + 4^2 = 5^2$. But there are no whole numbers that satisfy the equation $x^3 + y^3 = a^3$ or $x^4 + y^4 = a^4$. As Fermat stated it, "It is impossible to separate a cube into two cubes, a fourth power into two fourth powers, or generally, any power above the second into two powers of the same degree. I have found a truly marvelous proof of this, which this margin is too narrow to contain."

We now state this as: $x^n + y^n = z^n$ has no integral solutions for $n > 2$. Proofs have been found for many specific cases. Euler proved it for $n = 3$; that is, there are no whole numbers for which $x^3 + y^3 = z^3$. It is fairly easy to prove it true for $n = 4$ and to show that only cases where n is a prime number need be considered. About 1825, it was proved for $n = 5$; 15 years later for $n = 7$. Before World War I, a prize of 100,000 marks was offered for a general proof. Many tried, but no proof for all n appeared. Modern computer methods have pushed the proof to include primes into the hundreds of millions. But still there is no general proof. The theorem remains easy to understand and yet still not fully proved.

Fibonacci Series. A series of numbers that gives the answer to the following problem: How many pairs of rabbits can be produced from a single pair in a year, if a) each pair begets a new pair every month; b) the new rabbits become productive in their second month; and c) there are no deaths?

The problem was published in 1202 by Leonardo Pisano, nicknamed Fibonacci (son of Bonacci, or "son of good nature"). He gave the answer: In the first and second month, there are the original pair only; in the third month there is a new pair, making 2; in the fourth, the parents have another pair, making 3; in the fifth, the parents and the first pair each have another pair, making 5; and so on. The pairs in each month of the first year are: 1, 1, 2, 3, 5, 8, 13, 21, 34, 55, 89, 144.

Four centuries later, Kepler referred to the series, mentioning that each number is the sum of the two immediately before it ($1 + 1 = 2$; $1 + 2 = 3$; $2 + 3 = 5$; etc.).

Fibonacci numbers show up in nature as well as in hypothetical problems. In elm and basswood trees, one leaf is halfway around the twig from

THE FIBONACCI SERIES *describes the idealized pattern of rabbit offspring.*

month	rabbit pairs	Fibonacci number
1		1
2		1
3		2
4		3
5		5
6		8
7		13

the next leaf. In beech and hazel trees, one leaf is $\frac{2}{3}$ of a screw turn from the next. In oak and apricot, one is $\frac{3}{5}$ of a turn from the next; in poplar and pear, $\frac{5}{8}$; willow and almond $\frac{8}{13}$. The amount of turn in each case is given by dividing one Fibonacci number by the next. Related arrangements can be found in the whorls on a pineapple, the scales on a fir cone, and the florets of a sunflower.

See also Golden Section and Pascal's Triangle.

Galois, Evariste (1811–1832). Galois was both a victim of incredible misfortune and a creator of brilliant mathematical ideas, in a life that ended when he was 20. Bored and frustrated by a classical education in a repressive French high school, Galois was held back for a year. He discovered mathematics through reading research papers when he was 14. He produced his own original work in algebra at 16.

At 17, Galois tried to enter the École Polytechnique in Paris, but his habit of working out complicated mathematics in his head rather than on the blackboard, where his examiner could see it, led to his rejection. That same year his first paper was published, on continued fractions, and a second one was sent to the Academy of Sciences. It was received—and forgotten.

At 18, he again tried for the École Polytechnique, but the examiner was unable to understand ideas that were at the forefront of algebra, and in frustration Galois threw a blackboard eraser at him. A second paper was sent to the Academy. The secretary took it home to read—and died. The paper was lost. A third paper was returned because it could not be understood.

Bitterly frustrated, Galois joined a group of political activists who wanted an end to France's monarchy and a return to the republic. He was arrested and released. A month later he was arrested again, and jailed for six months—for wearing the uniform of a disbanded National Guard unit.

Days after his release, political enemies picked a fight with him over a girl, and challenged him to a duel. He knew that he would be killed. The night before the duel, he desperately wrote his will—all the mathematics he could dash down on paper. He begged his friends "preserve my memory since fate has not given me life enough for my country to know my name." He did die, but the Galois theory of equations, Galois groups, and Galois fields have kept mathematicians busy ever since.

Gauss, Karl Friedrich (1777–1855). Gauss was the greatest mathematician of the early 19th century. The son of a German laborer, Gauss taught himself to read and to add before he was three years old. When he was ten, the teacher at the local school gave out a problem asking the children to add a long series of large numbers. The teacher knew a formula that gave a quick answer, but the boys did not. Gauss, however, wrote the answer on his slate the moment the problem was presented, having immediately spotted the nature of the series, and having derived the formula for himself. Fortunately, the teacher's young assistant in the school loved mathematics and shared his own studies with the boy genius.

The Duke of Brunswick heard of Gauss, and paid his college tuition, later giving him a pension. One of Gauss's studies was of the theory of numbers. Euler and Legendre had both been unable to prove a particular conjecture concerning the divisibility of numbers. Gauss proved it while in college. He had already invented the method of least squares, which is still important in determining how well experimental observations fit a theoretical law. Gauss's interest in statistics also led him to formulate the bell-shaped normal or Gaussian curve.

CULVER PICTURES

In 1801, the first asteroid was observed. From very little information, Gauss determined the best way of calculating its orbit; years later the asteroid returned to sight and proved his calculations to be right. From astronomy, Gauss turned to geodesy and mapping, then to other branches of mathematical physics, such as electricity and magnetism (the gauss is now the unit of magnetic flux). In 1833, Gauss invented the electric telegraph. Toward the end of his life, he returned to more abstract analysis.

In 1807, the Duke of Brunswick died, and Gauss needed a source of income. He was offered the position of director of the Göttingen observatory, and he accepted.

A perfectionist, Gauss would not publish a paper until he was completely satisfied with it. After his death, other mathematicians studied his unpublished notes for many years. They found that he had anticipated many of the mathematical advances during the remainder of the 19th century.

Gödel's Proof. The proof that a system cannot establish the logical consistency of its own axioms is called Godel's proof. Euclid's geometry is a system in which logical conclusions are drawn from a set of "common notions" and "self-evident axioms." Mathematicians wanted to set arithmetic, algebra and other branches of mathematics on a similar axiomatic basis. To do so, they needed a way to be certain that the axioms chosen were self-consistent; that is, that they would not lead to contradictions. In 1931, Kurt Gödel, then 25 years old, showed that even ordinary arithmetic cannot become completely axiomatic.

Goldbach's Conjecture. This is the hypothesis that any even number can be expressed as the sum of two primes. A prime is a whole number that cannot be divided (without remainder) by any numbers except itself and 1. The first seven are 2, 3, 5, 7, 11, 13, and 17. Examples of the conjecture are

$$28 = 11 + 17$$
$$30 = 13 + 17$$
$$32 = 3 + 29$$
$$= 13 + 19$$

It is obviously true that for any two primes other than 2, which is the only even prime, their sum is an even number. It is not obvious that every even number can be the sum of two primes.

The hypothesis was first raised in a letter from Christian Goldbach (1690–1764) to Euler. It was published in England in 1770, but has never been proved. Computer methods have proved it true for every even number up to 10,000, and for some beyond that, but there is still no proof that it is always true. The search for its proof has helped develop the theory of numbers.

Golden Section. A proportion between two parts of a line or two sides of a rectangle that the ancient Greeks considered to be more pleasing than any other is termed a golden section. When a golden section divides a line segment into two parts, the ratio of the whole to the larger part is the same as that of the larger part to the smaller:

A C B

$$\frac{AB}{AC} = \frac{AC}{CB}$$

In a golden rectangle, the same proportion holds. Its length = AB and its width = AC. The Parthenon in Athens and some of Le Corbusier's buildings reflect the golden section. The proportions of a standard postcard and legal size paper are close, and many of the design elements of great paintings display the golden ratio.

To construct a golden rectangle, start with a square, ABCD, and find the midpoint E of side AD.

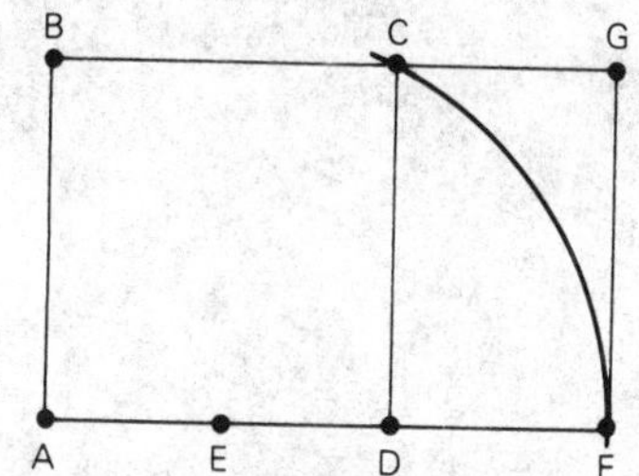

With radius EC, center E, draw an arc that intersects an extension of line AD at F. Then ABGF is a golden rectangle. If the square is taken away, what is left, DCGF, is also a golden rectangle.

The actual dimensions of the golden section can be calculated from the construction as follows. If the line AB has a length of one unit and it is divided into two parts, the length of the parts can be called g and $1 - g$. By the golden proportion

$$\frac{AB}{AC}=\frac{AC}{CB}$$

$$\frac{1}{g}=\frac{g}{1-g}$$

$$1-g=g^2$$

$$g^2+g-1=0$$

$$g=\frac{\sqrt{5}-1}{2}$$

$$g=0.618\ldots$$

The ratio is thus 1 to .618, which is the same as 1.618 to 1.

The golden section is related to the Fibonacci series. If each Fibonacci number is divided by the one preceding it, the results come closer and closer to the golden ratio:

$8 \div 5 = 1.6$
$144 \div 89 = 1.617$
$1597 \div 987 = 1.618034$

Khwarizmi, al-, Muhammad ibn-Mûsa (780–?850 AD). Khwarizmi was an Iranian (Persian) scholar, one of many brought by the Caliph of Baghdad to his court. Khwarizmi wrote books on arithmetic, algebra, and the astrolabe and sundial, and provided astronomical tables. One of his books gave full details of the Hindu base ten system of numerals. This book was translated into Latin at the time of the Crusades, the book taught the superior Hindu system to Europe. Until then, Europeans had done arithmetic with cumbersome Roman numerals or Greek letters.

The Latinization of Khwarizmi's name gave us the word *algorithm,* which now means a routine for performing a calculation. The title of Khwarizmi's book on equations included the Arabic word *al-jabr,* which gave us the word *algebra* for the entire subject.

Lagrange, Joseph Louis (1736–1813). A professor of mathematics before he was 20, Lagrange taught in Turin (now a city in Italy), where he was born. His interest in mathematics had been fired by an essay on calculus. He had never been interested in geometry. Calculus gave him a method by which many problems could be treated analytically without diagrams. Even Newton had given all his proofs in the form of Euclidean geometry, but Lagrange made a complete break with this tradition, attacking problems of vibrating strings and the moon's motion entirely with calculus.

In 1795, Lagrange became a professor at the newly founded École Polytechnique in Paris. When France was seeking to establish a more rational system of measurement, Lagrange helped choose the base ten system over base twelve. The result was the metric system now universally used in the sciences.

Laplace, Pierre Simon de (1749–1827). Born of peasant stock in a small French town, Laplace learned mathematics at a local military academy. When he was 18, he left for Paris and tried to see D'Alembert, the secretary of the French Academy. D'Alembert refused to be bothered. Laplace, undaunted, wrote him a letter about the principles of mechanics and D'Alembert was so impressed that he immediately found Laplace a position as professor of mathematics at the Military Academy in Paris. Twenty years later, one of Laplace's students there was Napoleon Bonaparte. When Napoleon came to power, he heaped honors on his old professor.

Laplace wrote two great works, one on the theory of probability and the other on celestial mechanics. The latter concerns the problems of how planetary orbits are perturbed by other planets; his contributions were so great that he has been called "the Newton of France."

Leibnitz (also Leibniz), **Gottfried Wilhelm von** (1646–1716). A lawyer, diplomat, historian, philosopher, and theologian, Leibnitz did not consider mathematics to be his major interest. Yet he invented calculus in much the same form that we use it today.

Leibnitz took his bachelor's degree at the age of 17, and his doctorate in law at 20. He then entered the service of the German dukes, which was to become a lifelong profession. As a young man, Leibnitz invented a calculating machine that could perform the four arithmetic operations and also extract square roots. His interest in advanced mathematics, however, was sparked in 1672 when he met the Dutch physicist Christiaan Huygens. The next year, while on a diplomatic assignment in London, Leibnitz attended meetings of the Royal Society, where he displayed his calculator. Mathematics became one of the subjects on which he worked in his spare time.

In 1682, he published his first paper on calculus, "A new method for maxima and minima and tangents." It contained our symbols *dy* and *dx,* and our equals and times signs. Four years later, his paper on integral calculus introduced our integral sign.

CULVER PICTURES

The Bernoullis then joined Leibnitz in discovering most of what is now studied in the first two years of calculus. Later, Euler, Lagrange, and Laplace applied Leibnitz's form of calculus to Newton's mechanics.

Newton invented the method of fluxions, his form of the calculus, in 1666, a few years before Leibnitz. Newton wrote letters about his method and lectured on it, but he did not publish its essentials until 1693. Leibnitz wrote about his own calculus in his notebooks in 1675, in a letter to Newton in 1677, and in print in 1684.

At the end of the century, a minor Swiss mathematician suggested in print that Leibnitz had taken the idea of calculus from Newton. Then, in 1704, an anonymous review of one of Newton's papers implied that Newton had borrowed his ideas from Leibnitz. These suggestions caused great furor. British mathematicians rose to attack Leibnitz; the Bernoullis defended him. The controversy raged for decades.

It is now generally agreed that Leibnitz's and Newton's works were independent. Both drew on the same mathematical base, of course, and both were working in the same direction.

Later developments in mathematics have shown Leibnitz's system to be more useful. Newton's fluxional calculus was suitable for physics, but limited; Leibnitz's differential calculus was flexible and far superior.

Napier, John (1550–1617), and **Briggs, Henry** (1561–1631). Before the 17th century, arithmetic had to be carried out in longhand, without any mechanical aids. Constructing trigonometric and astronomical tables required years of tedious computation. Napier, a wealthy Scottish landowner who entertained himself with mathematics, attacked this problem in two ways. He had the multiplication tables engraved on sticks in such a way that by sliding the sticks up and down and adding the numbers, multiples of fairly large numbers could be obtained. The device, known as Napier's bones, was a kind of multiplying toy.

Napier's more substantial contribution, however, was the system of logarithms. With this system, multiplication could be carried out by addition, division by subtraction, and the arduous task of finding powers and roots by simple multiplication and division.

At first, Napier's system was rather clumsy, and it was considerably improved during his correspondence with Briggs, who held Britain's first professorship of mathematics, at London University. Napier and Briggs had so much admiration for each other's work that when they at last met, a quarter of an hour is reported to have passed before either spoke a word. Briggs calculated and, in 1625, published the first tables of logarithms. These tables were welcomed by mathematicians and astronomers. One of the first to use them was the great astronomer and mathematician Johannes Kepler.

Newton, Isaac (1642–1727). Newton spent his childhood on a farm in England and was expected to become a farmer. In school he was more interested in making mechanical toys than in studying. When he left school, he showed more interest in books than in farming. He was sent to Trinity College, Cambridge, in 1661, where he intended to study chemistry. In his first month at college, realizing that he knew no geometry, he bought a copy of Euclid's work, which he found obvious. He then mastered Descartes on his own, though with difficulty, and attended lectures on mathematics.

After Newton took his degree, he stayed in college, but fear of the plague, from 1665–1666, sent him home for safety. In those two years he worked out his invention of calculus, developed the generalized form of the binomial theorem, demonstrated that white light

NAPIER'S BONES

Napier's bones took advantage of the following principle: If two 3-digit numbers are to be multiplied, they can be laid out as follows:

469 × 672:

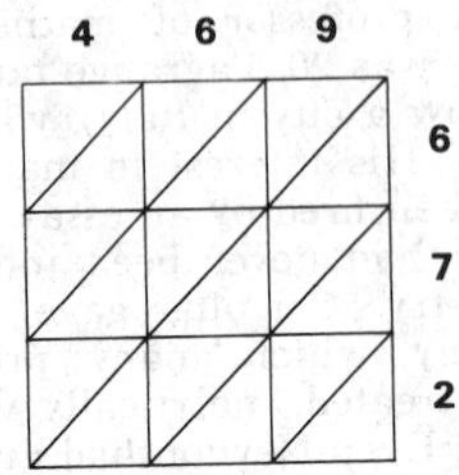

Draw diagonals through the boxes and do each individual multiplication of single digits, placing the digits as shown

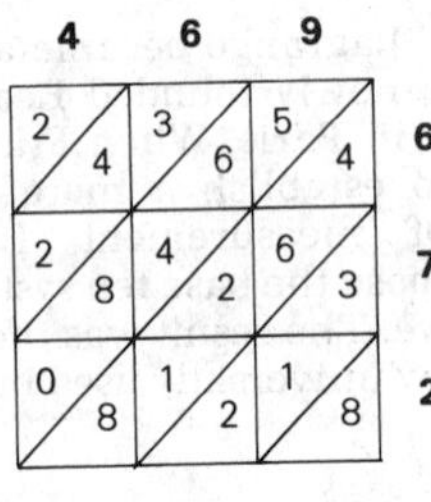

$4 \times 6 = {}^{2}{}_{4}$, etc.

Starting in the lower right-hand corner, add the sums of each diagonal column, putting its number directly below or to the left. The sum of the first column is 8; the sum of the second is 3 + 1 + 2 = 6. If the sum is more than 9, carry the tens to the next column

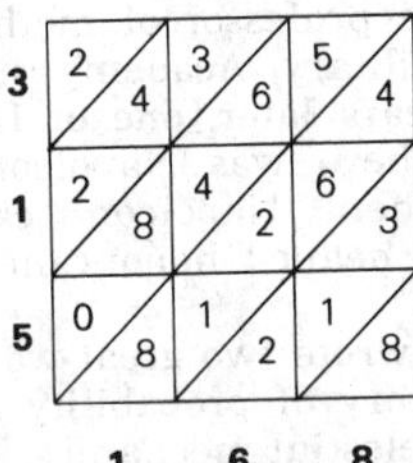

The answer reads from top left to bottom right:

469 × 672 = 315,168

Napier's bones were strips (or sticks) with the multiplication facts for each digit. By placing them in the right relation to each other, one could copy off the facts and add the diagonal columns as above.

CULVER PICTURES

THE NATURE OF LIGHT *was one of the mysteries that Isaac Newton explored.*

is made up of all other colors, and discovered the law of gravitation. When Newton returned to Cambridge, he was given a faculty position, which he kept until the end of the century. His work in mathematics was in algebra and the theory of equations, as well as in calculus.

Absent-minded, occupied with his own thoughts, and slovenly of dress, Newton delayed publishing his results, communicating them, instead, in letters, lectures, or circulated manuscripts. In 1684, Edmund Halley went to Newton to ask for help. The greatest astronomers of the time had been unable to calculate what the orbit of a planet would be if the law of gravitation were true. Newton replied that the orbit was an ellipse—as he had determined five years before. Halley persuaded him to publish this finding, which he did in his great work *Principia* in 1687.

Newton's later years were spent as Master of the Mint, in writing on theology, and in a dispute with Leibnitz over who first discovered calculus. Newton kept his health until he was over 80, and died in his sleep.

Non-Euclidean Geometry. Geometry that differs from Euclid's axioms, especially the parallel postulate, is non-Euclidean geometry. Euclid wrote: When a straight line intersects two straight lines, if the interior angles on the same side are together less than two right angles, then the two straight lines, if extended, will meet on that side. From this postulate it follows that through a point not on a given line there is only one line parallel to the given line.

This postulate seems far less self-evident than Euclid's other postulates, and Euclid himself seems to have

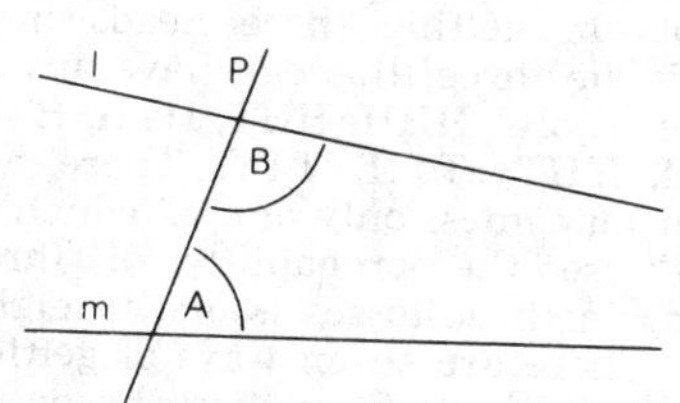

PARALLEL POSTULATE
Where A + B < 180° lines l and m will meet on the angle side of line p.

tried to prove it from his other axioms. Mathematicians continued trying to prove it until 1829. Then **Nikolai Ivanovich Lobachevski** (1793–1856), of Kazan University in Russia, convinced that the postulate could not be proved, published a geometry specifically denying it. He assumed that through a point not on a given line, there can be drawn more than one line that does not meet the given line. This is equivalent to the assumption that although the interior angles are less than two right angles, the lines never meet. Lobachevski's geometry contained no logical contradictions, but seemed so contrary to common sense that Lobachevski himself called it imaginary geometry.

So it remained until the work of **Georg Friedrich Bernhard Riemann** (1826–1866) at Göttingen University in Germany. In 1854, Riemann substituted the third possibility, that if the interior angles are two right angles, the two lines meet if extended far enough. This is equivalent to the statement that through a point not on a line, no parallels can be drawn.

Riemann saw that his geometry applied, in fact, to the surface of a sphere. The shortest distance between two points on Earth is a geodesic, a part of a great circle, and all great circles intersect, as is shown by the meeting of the meridians at the North and South Pole. We may restate Riemann's assumption as follows: given a geodesic and a point outside it, there is no geodesic through the point that does not meet the given one. For a spherical surface, this is perfectly acceptable—perhaps even self-evident. To restrict the intersection of geodesics to only one point, a hemisphere is an even better model. Riemann's "elliptic" geometry thus becomes a generalization of Euclid's geometry to curved space. Riemann further realized that the generalizations he was making made a valid system quite apart from intuitive ideas of shapes in space.

In 1868, a model was found for Lobachevski's "hyperbolic" geometry. Called a pseudosphere, it is the shape of the bells of two trumpets blowing into each other. Interesting comparisons can be made between Euclidean,

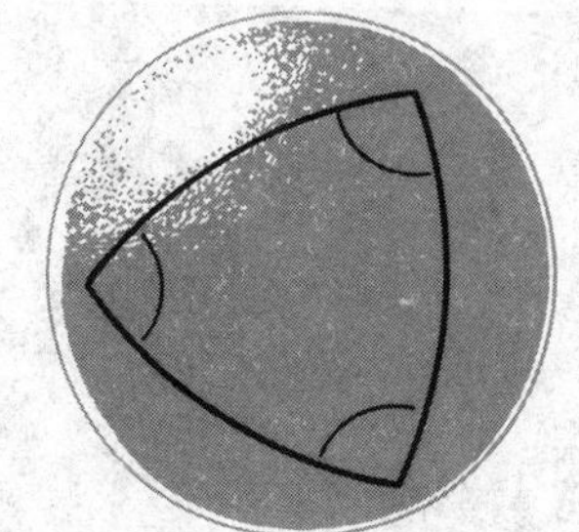

A TRIANGLE ON A SPHERE *has angles whose sum is more than 180° as Riemann showed.*

Lobachevskian, and Riemannian geometries. In Euclidean, the sum of the measures of the angles of a triangle is equal to two right angles; in Lobachevskian, it is less than two right angles; in Riemannian, it is more. In Euclidean, an angle inscribed in a semicircle is a right angle; in Lobachevskian it is acute; in Riemannian, obtuse.

Number Personalities. Numbers can be thought of as having personalities. Ancient Greek mathematicians classified numbers as *perfect, abundant,* and *deficient.*

To determine a number's "personality," you must first find all the proper divisors of a number—those numbers that divide into it evenly, including 1, but excluding the number itself. This chart gives some examples.

Number	Proper Divisors
3	1
24	1,2,3,4,6,8,12
50	1,2,5,10,25
96	1,2,3,4,6,8,12,16,24,48

When the sum of a number's proper divisors equals the number itself, the number is said to be a perfect number. Very few numbers are perfect.

The number 6 is perfect. The proper divisors of 6 are 1, 2, and 3. When you add $1+2+3$ the sum is 6. The number 28 is also perfect. The divisors are 1,2,4,7, and 14; their sum is 28. The next larger perfect number is 496. The divisors are 1,2,4,8,16,31,62,124, and 248; their sum is 496. The next larger perfect number is 8,128. This is followed by 33,550,336; 8,589,869,056; and 137,438,691,328. After this, perfect numbers get very large, having, in turn, 19, 37, 54, 65, and 77 digits.

There is a formula for finding perfect numbers. When n equals a prime number (a number whose only divisors are 1 and the number itself), then $(2^{n-1})(2^n-1)$ results in a perfect number, provided (2^n-1) is also prime.

Perfect numbers have some odd properties. For example, except for 6, the final sum of their digits is one.

$$496: 4+9+6=19, \quad 1+9=10, \quad 1+0=1$$

$$8128: 8+1+2+8=19, \quad 1+9=10, \quad 1+0=1$$

Except for 6 again, a perfect number is the sum of the cubes of consecutive odd numbers.

$$28 = 1^3+3^3$$
$$496 = 1^3+3^3+5^3+7^3$$
$$8128 = 1^3+3^3+5^3+7^3+9^3+11^3+13^3+15^3$$

When the sum of a number's proper divisors is greater than the number itself, the number is said to be abundant. The chart below shows some abundant numbers.

Abundant Number	Proper Divisors	Sum of Proper Divisors
12	1,2,3,4,6	16
48	1,2,3,4,6,8,12,16,24	76
100	1,2,5,10,20,25,50	113

When the sum of a number's proper divisors is less than the number itself, the number is said to be deficient, The chart below shows some deficient numbers.

Deficient Number	Proper Divisors	Sum of Proper Divisors
15	1,3,5	9
39	1,3,13	17
125	1,5,25	31

Listing all the numbers from 2 to 100 and classifying them as perfect, abundant, or deficient numbers is a good way to get familiar with the "personalities" that numbers have.

Pascal, Blaise (1623–1662). Pascal was important enough as a mathematician to have given his name to the arithmetic triangle, a geometric theorem, a law of hydrostatic pressure, and the metric unit of pressure.

When he was twelve, Pascal's father taught him the basics of geometry; without receiving any hint, Pascal then realized—and proved—that the sum of the angles of a triangle is equal to two right angles. At 16, he produced a theorem that began the study of projective (or descriptive) geometry. His "Essay on Conics" used his theorem to deduce 400 others, including classical ones. Descartes at first refused to believe the essay was the work of a boy.

Pascal also invented the first calculating device in history. He had these manufactured and sold about 50. They can still be seen in museums and have been copied commercially; plastic versions are still made for elementary schools.

Pascal suggested experiments with the barometer, and from these experiments discovered the fundamentals of atmospheric pressure. The experiments included taking a barometer up a mountain to see the decrease in atmospheric pressure.

Pascal engaged in a correspondence with Pierre de Fermat on gambling with dice, and from this the modern theory of probability developed. Studying the ancient arithmetic triangle, Pascal realized the relation between the entries in a row and the number of ways of choosing items from a set (*see* Pascal's Triangle).

As a young man, Pascal had been influenced by Jansenism, an anti-Jesuit Christian doctrine. Putting mathematics aside, he wrote a series of religious *Provincial Letters* and the philosophical *Thoughts,* which was published after his death and for which he is most famous outside of mathematics.

CULVER PICTURES

BLAISE PASCAL, *mathematician and philosopher.*

Pascal's Triangle. An arrangement of numbers that displays the coefficients of the binomial theorem and the number of ways of choosing items from a set.

1 1
1 2 1
1 3 3 1
1 4 6 4 1
1 5 10 10 5 1
1 6 15 20 15 6 1
1 7 21 35 35 21 7 1
1 8 28 56 70 56 28 8 1

Each number is the sum of the two above it. For example, in the fourth row, $4 = 1 + 3$ and $6 = 3 + 3$. The 1 at the beginning and end of each row can be thought of as the one above plus an invisible zero.

The series has some remarkable properties. The first diagonal in either direction consists entirely of ones. The second diagonal gives the natural numbers in order. The third gives triangular numbers—the numbers of dots that can be arranged in triangles. The sums of the numbers in each row are the powers of two: 2, 4, 8, 16, etc. The sums of the numbers along slant lines are the Fibonacci series.

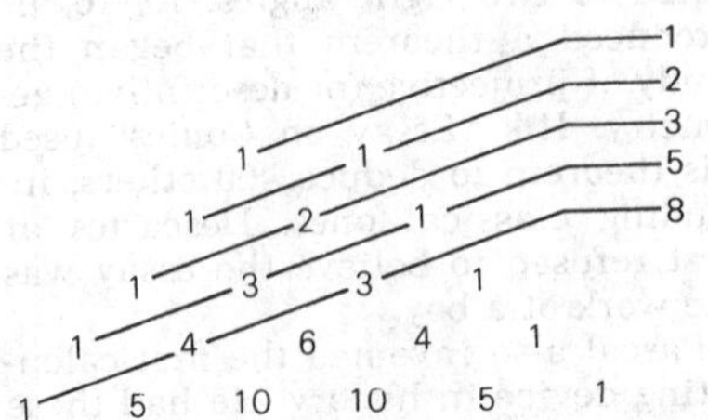

The entries in each row give the number of ways of choosing groups of items from a set. For example, there is only one way of choosing no items from a set of three; there are three ways of choosing one item from three (A,B, and C); three ways of choosing items two at a time (AB, BC, and CA); and one way of choosing three at a time (ABC). The entries in the third row are 1, 3, 3, 1. To find the number of ways of choosing three items from a set of five, find the fourth entry (since zero is the first) of row five. It is 10, and the 10 combinations of three things chosen from five are ABC, ABD, ABE, ACD, ACE, ADE, BCD, BCE, BDE, and CDE.

The binomial theorem expands $(1 + x)^n$ as a series. For example, $(1 + x)^2 = 1 + 2x + x^2$. The individual coefficients of the terms are 1, 2, 1, which are the numbers on the second row of the triangle. For $(1 + x)^4$, the coefficients are on the fourth row, and the series is $1 + 4x + 6x^2 + 4x^3 + x^4$.

The triangle is given the name of Pascal, who studied it in relation to probability theory. However, its first European appearance was in 1527, on the title page of an arithmetic book, and it appeared in Chinese texts centuries before that.

Probability. Probability is the likelihood of an event happening. An event that is completely impossible, such as a cat giving birth to a chicken, is assigned a probability of zero; one that is absolutely certain, such as the sun rising tomorrow, is given a probability of one. Every event that is neither certain nor impossible has a probability that is a fraction between one and zero. Determining what that fraction is for any event, and how it relates to the probabilities of other events, is the function of probability theory.

In flipping a coin, there are only two possible outcomes, heads or tails. In one flip, either can happen, but in a very large number of tosses, we expect about half to be heads and the other half tails. The probability of getting heads is therefore $\frac{1}{2}$, the same as it is for a tails. But if a coin is flipped three times, what is the probability of getting three heads in a row? The three flips can have any of these results: HHH, HHT, HTH, HTT, THH, THT, TTH, TTT. There are eight outcomes, only one of which is HHH, so the probability of three heads in three tosses is one in eight, or $\frac{1}{8}$. There are seven ways of getting results different from three heads, so the probability of not getting three heads is $\frac{7}{8}$, and the odds against three heads are seven to one.

If two heads have already been tossed, what are the chances of getting a third head? Since the overall probability of three heads is $\frac{1}{8}$, one feels that the probability of getting that third head is different from the probability of getting the first head. But it isn't. The probability of getting one head in one toss is $\frac{1}{2}$, no matter what went before.

The eight possible results of flipping the coin three times can be sorted into groups, each containing the same number of heads. For three heads, there is only HHH; for two heads there are three possibilities: HHT, HTH, and THH; for one head there are also three possibilities: HTT, THT, TTH; and for no heads, there is only TTT. The number of ways that each number of heads can come up is 1, 3, 3, 1. These are the numbers in the third row of Pascal's triangle (*see* Pascal's triangle). If there were four tosses, then four heads could come up in one way; three heads in four ways; two heads in six ways; one head in four ways; and no heads in one way. The numbers 1, 4, 6, 4, 1 are the numbers along the fourth row of Pascal's triangle.

Probability is also concerned with the number of ways of arranging items. In how many ways, for instance, can three people stand in a line? One can have ABC, ACB, BAC, BCA, CAB, or CBA. With only three items, the different permutations can be listed. But for a larger number of items they must be calculated. In the case of three items, the first item is chosen from three, so there are three ways of choosing it. Two items remain, so for each of the three first choices, we have two choices for the second item. This will leave only one item left, which can be chosen in only one way. The total ways of arranging or permuting three items, then, is $3 \times 2 \times 1$, or six ways, and this is written 3! (read three factorial). The number of ways of permuting five items is 5!, which equals 120.

Turning to a seemingly different set of random events, we might ask how many different five-card hands can be dealt from a 52-card deck. The first card can be drawn in 52 ways. There are now 51 left, which is the number of ways the second card can be drawn. For the third, there are 50; for the fourth and fifth, 49 and 48. The total number of possible drawings of cards is therefore 52 × 51 × 50 × 49 × 48. However, these include all the various permutations of each hand: JQKA2 as well as KAJ2Q, 2KJAQ, and so on. As we have seen, each set of five items can be arranged in 120 ways, so the number of possible drawings must be divided by 120 to give the number of different five-card hands:

$$\frac{52 \times 51 \times 50 \times 49 \times 48}{5 \times 4 \times 3 \times 2 \times 1} = 2{,}598{,}960$$

Just four of all these are royal flushes. So the probability of getting a royal flush is four in 2,598,960 or one in 649,740.

Games of chance are only one area where probability theory is important. It also provides a theoretical basis for many disciplines including atomic theory, genetics, insurance, sampling techniques, and the statistical analysis of data.

Pythagoras (died ca. 500 BC). The most famous theorem of geometry—that the square of the hypotenuse of a right-angled triangle is the sum of the squares of the other two sides—is named for Pythagoras, although it had been known (if not proved) for hundreds of years before his birth.

Pythagoras was born on the Greek island of Samos, studied in Egypt and Babylon, and eventually settled in Croton, a Greek colony in southern Italy. He gathered a "school" of like-minded pupils who concerned themselves not only with mathematics but with a mystical or religious philosophy and a stern discipline for daily life. The Pythagoreans were vegetarians, not even wearing wool; they went barefoot, and believed that earthly life is a kind of exile. Pythagoras taught them arithmetic, geometry, astronomy, and the harmonic proportions of music. The contributions of Pythagoras himself to mathematics are shrouded in legend. He may have discovered the theorem that the angles of a triangle are equal to two right angles. He was interested in the number of counters required to make patterns such as a square. These are numbers like 4 and 9, which we still call squares. The Pythagoreans saw esthetic and philosophical significance in numbers. For example, the triangular number ten, which is 1 + 2 + 3 + 4, was thought to represent the universe.

Statistics. In everyday language, statistics are a collection of numerical data. In mathematics, statistics is the study of methods of obtaining and analyzing such data.

The best known way of representing a set of values is by their *average,* or *arithmetic mean.* This is found by adding up the values and dividing the sum by the number of values involved. The mean of 5, 9, and 10 is $(5 + 9 + 10) \div 3$, which is $24 \div 3$ or 8.

The mean is the commonest statistical measure, but it can be misleading. Consider a group of five people whose average age is 20. One probably thinks of five college students, but they could also be four children, aged 3, 4, 5, and 8, and their 80-year-old great-grandfather. In a similar way, the average income in a city or country may be skewed by a very small number of people with very high incomes. Other ways of classifying the data are therefore required.

The *median* is the value in the middle of the population, with as many values above the median as below. In the set of five people above, the median age is five, since two are younger and two are older than five. The third measure of central tendency is the *mode,* the value that occurs most often. In the family group above, there is no mode, since no age appears more than once. But in a larger group of numbers, the mode may be more informative than the mean or the median.

Some sets of data show a greater variability than others. Our group of five people varied in age much more than a group whose ages are 18, 19, 20, 21, and 22, even though this group has the same average age. To test for these differences, statistics has developed a measure of variability called the *standard deviation,* or root-mean-square deviation. To calculate this, first subtract each value from the mean and square each difference; add the squares and divide by the number of values to get the variance. The square root of the variance gives the standard deviation.

In our group of five aged 18, 19, 20, 21, and 22, the differences of each age from the mean are 2, 1, 0, 1, and 2. The squares of these numbers are 4, 1, 0, 1, and 4. The variance is $10 \div 5$, or 2; and the standard deviation is $\sqrt{2}$, or 1.4. By contrast, the group aged 3, 4, 5, 8, and 80 has a standard deviation of 30—very large for a mean of 20.

From formulas involving mean, variance, and standard deviation, a pollster with a small sample can tell if the sample is reasonably representative of the larger population; an agriculturist can compare the effect of different fertilizers on crop yields; a manufacturer can keep better control of the quality of the product; and a scientist can decide whether his experiments confirm his hypothesis.

PROBABILITY *is a study useful to scientists, social scientists—and cardplayers. The probability is high that the center player's aces (seen in the mirror) will win.*

CULVER PICTURES

Topology. Topology is the study of the structure of surfaces and spaces without regard to size or even to shape; it is also called projective or rubber-sheet geometry. In Euclidean geometry, two shapes are considered equivalent if their corresponding parts are all of the same size, as in congruent triangles. In projective geometry, two shapes are equivalent if one could be drawn on a slide and the other become the projection on a screen. If the screen is at an angle to the slide, a triangle on the slide will project into a differently shaped triangle on the screen, but both will still be triangles.

In topology, shapes are equivalent if one can be transformed into the other by a continuous deformation. A rubber band can be stretched to the shape of a circle, a larger circle, a square, or a triangle. Thus, a circle is equivalent to a larger circle, to a

ALLEN REUBEN

CULVER PICTURES

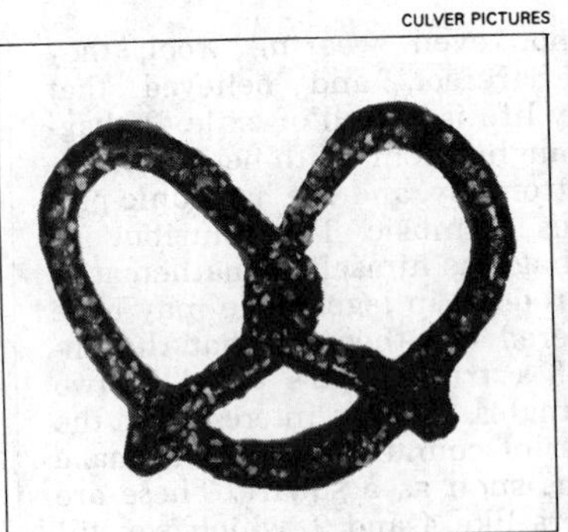

FUNDAMENTAL PHOTOGRAPHS

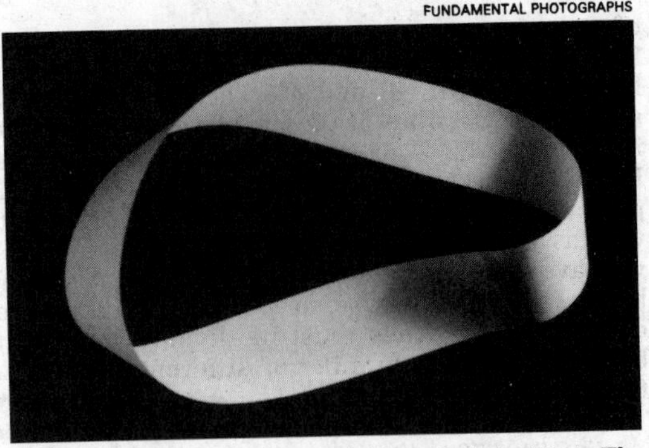

COFFEE CUP AND DOUGHNUT *are examples of a torus, a shape in which there is a hole. The pretzel at center is a 3-holed object. The Möbius strip* (right) *is a topological curiosity with a single unbroken surface twice as long as the sheet it was made of.*

square, or to a triangle. A circle is not equivalent to a line segment, however, since that would involve a discontinuity—cutting the rubber band. Nor is a circle equivalent to a figure eight, since that deformation would require sticking points together, which is another discontinuity.

When surfaces are considered, that of a sphere, a cube, a pyramid, and a prism are all equivalent. The same balloon could be inflated to fit tight inside a spherical container, a cubical one, a pyramid, or a long, closed cylinder. But a torus (the shape of a doughnut or inner tube) is not equivalent to these. To deform a torus into a sphere, one would first have to cut it to get rid of the hole, and cutting introduces a discontinuity.

A cup with an ordinary handle is, topologically, a torus, as is a spool of thread, and a kitchen spoon with a hang-up hole. All of these can be continuously deformed into each other. However, a championship cup with two handles is another type, belonging with every other two-holer. Topology, then, classifies surfaces by the number of holes in them.

In the mid-19th century, Augustus Ferdinand Möbius revealed an entirely new kind of surface. If we take a strip of paper and tape the ends together, we get a simple loop or cylinder. If we draw a line along it, starting at any point inside the loop, the line will go once around the inside surface. If we now take another strip and give it a twist of half a revolution before joining the ends together, the result is no longer simple. If we draw a line starting at a point "inside," we soon find ourselves outside. By the time the line gets back to its starting point, it has traveled the full length of both "sides" of the strip. There is no inside or outside surface; the Möbius strip has only one continuous surface. Cutting the Möbius strip along its median line, the result is *not* two connected loops as one might expect; it is a single loop with two twists. —*Barbara Sheridan*

For Further Reference

Arithmetic

Asimov, Isaac. *Realm of Numbers.* Fawcett, 1977.

Devi, Shakuntala. *Figuring: The Joy of Numbers.* Harper & Row, 1977.

Froman, Robert. *Arithmetic for Human Beings.* Simon & Schuster, 1974.

Willerding, M. F. *Elementary Mathematics: Its Structure and Concepts.* Wiley, 1970.

Algebra

Asimov, Isaac. *Realm of Algebra.* Fawcett, 1982.

Jacobs, Harold R. *Elementary Algebra.* W. H. Freeman, 1979.

Geometry

Berger, M. *Geometry I.* Springer-Verlag, 1987.

Berger, M. *Geometry II.* Springer-Verlag, 1987.

Coxeter, H. S. M. *Introduction to Geometry* (2nd Ed.). Wiley, 1969.

Moise, Edwin E. *Elementary Geometry from an Advanced Standpoint.* Addison-Wesley, 1974.

Polya, G. *How to Solve It.* Princeton University Press, 1971.

Advanced Mathematics

Courant, Richard, and Fritz John. *Introduction to Calculus and Analysis, Volume One.* Interscience, 1975.

Courant, Richard, and Herbert Robbins. *What Is Mathematics? An Elementary Approach to Ideas and Methods.* Oxford University Press, 1979.

Feller, William. *An Introduction to Probability Theory and Its Applications, Volume One.* Wiley, 1968.

Sawyer, W. W. *What Is Calculus About?* Mathematics Association, 1975.

Recreational Mathematics

Gardner, Martin. *The Incredible Dr. Matrix.* Scribner's, 1977.

Gardner, Martin. *Mathematical Carnival: A New Round-Up of Tantalizers and Puzzles from "Scientific American."* Random House, 1977.

Loyd, Sam. *Best Mathematical Puzzles of Sam Loyd.* Dover, 1959.

Steinhaus, Hugo. *Mathematical Snapshots* (3rd Ed.). Oxford University Press, 1969.

General

Fadiman, Clifton. *Fantasia Mathematica.* Simon & Schuster, 1958.

Glenn, William, and Donavan Johnson. *Invitation to Mathematics.* Dover, 1973.

Jacobs, Harold R. *Mathematics, A Human Endeavor.* W. H. Freeman, 1970.

Kasner, Edward, and James R. Newman. *Mathematics and the Imagination.* Simon & Schuster, 1940.

Lieber, Lillian R., and Hugh G. Lieber. *The Education of T. C. Mits.* W.W. Norton, 1978.

Newman, James R. *The World of Mathematics.* Simon & Schuster, 1960.

Rapport, Samuel, and Helen Wright. *Mathematics.* New York University Press, 1963.

Sawyer, Walter W. *Mathematician's Delight.* Penguin, 1950.

Stein, Sherman K. *Mathematics—The Man-Made Universe* (3rd Ed.). W. H. Freeman, 1976.

Tietze, Heinrich. *Famous Problems in Mathematics.* Graylock Press, 1965.

History

Bell, E. T. *Men of Mathematics.* Simon & Schuster, 1986.

Cajori, Florian. *A History of Mathematics* (4th Ed.). Chelsea Publishing, 1985.

Reference

Gellert, W., et al. *The VNR Concise Encyclopedia of Mathematics.* Van Nostrand Reinhold, 1977.

James, Glenn, and Robert C. James. *Mathematics Dictionary* (3rd Ed.). Van Nostrand Reinhold, 1968.

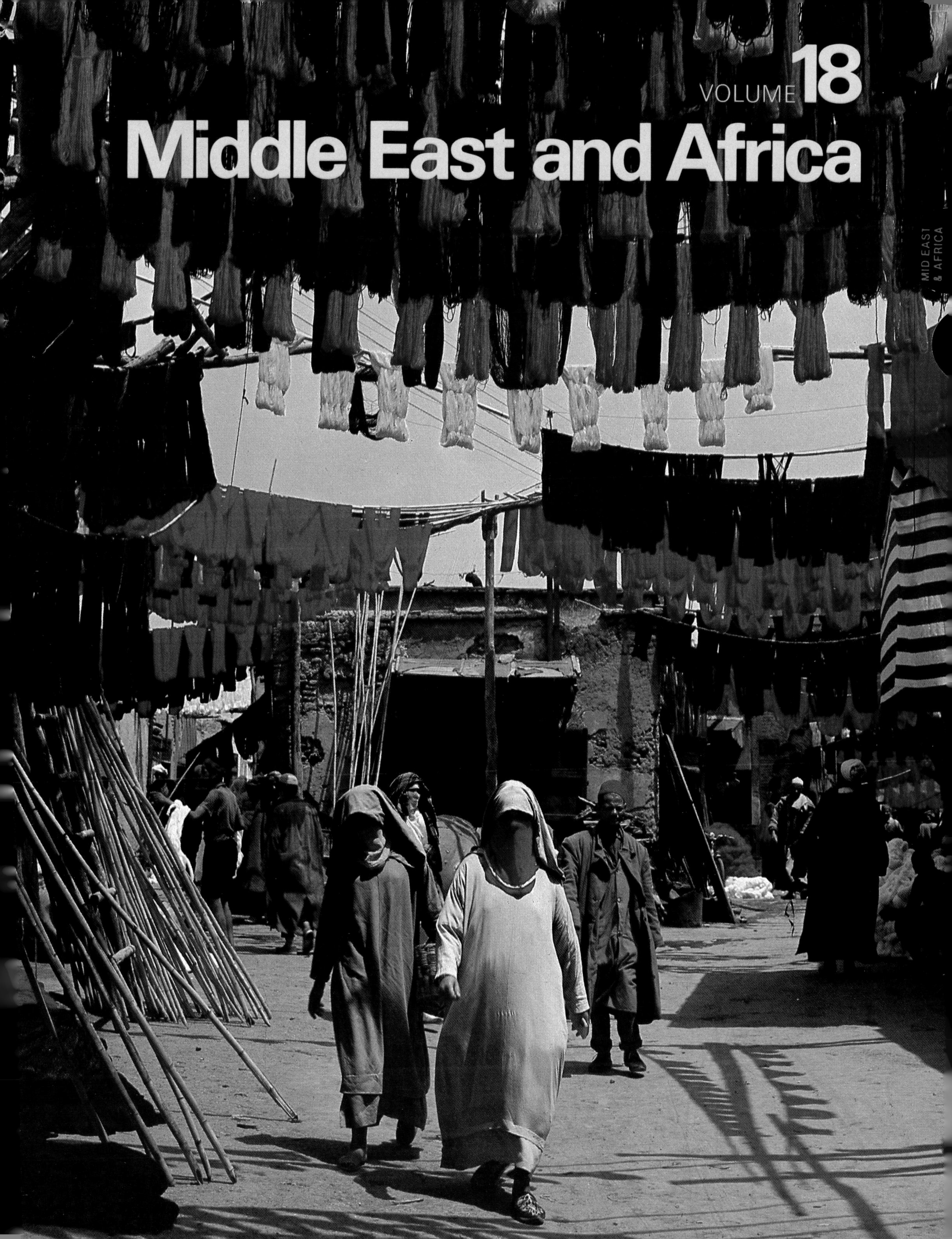
VOLUME 18
Middle East and Africa
MID EAST
& AFRICA

For national flags see VOLUME 12: GOVERNMENT AND LAW.

BRITISH MUSEUM

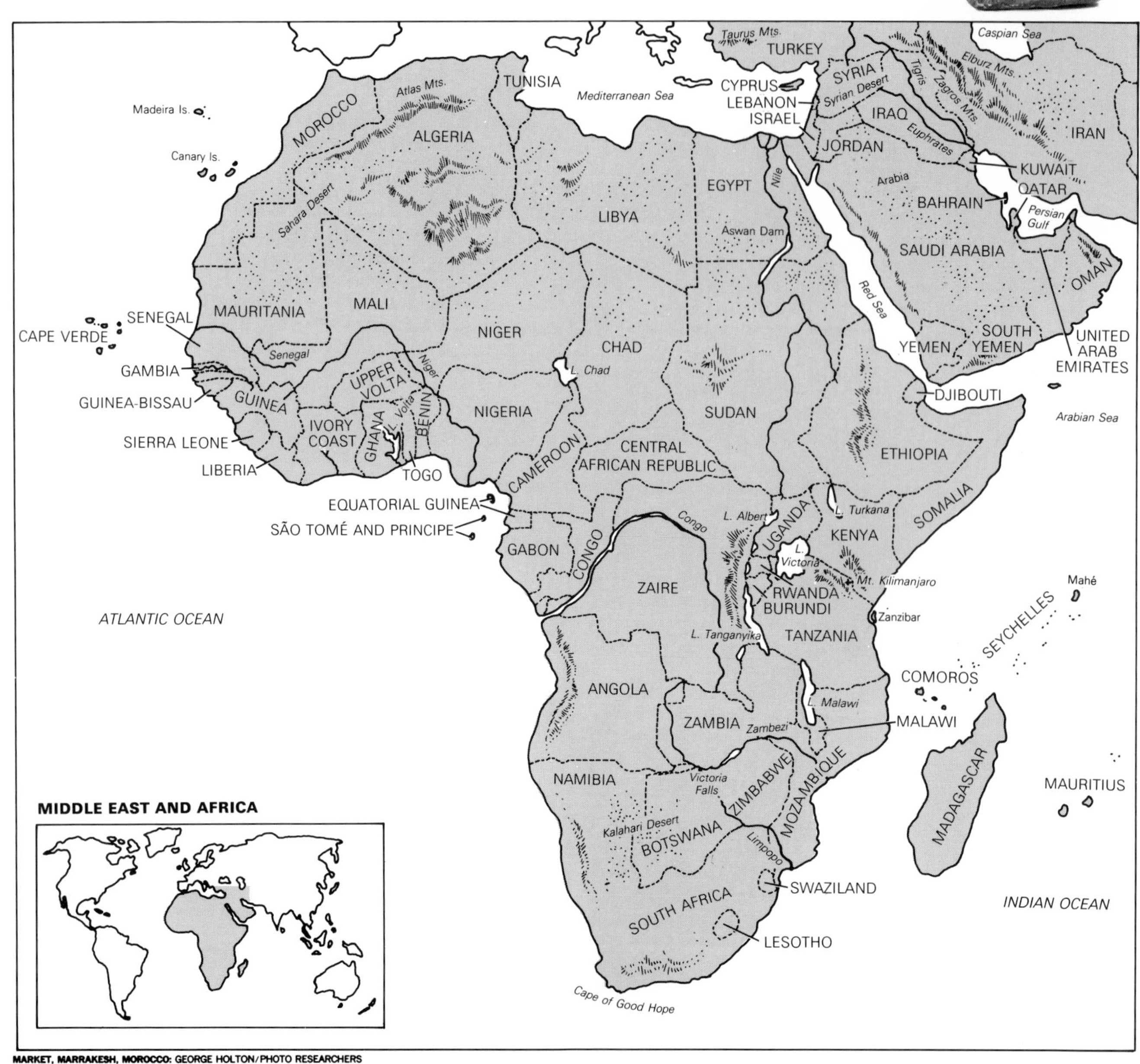

MARKET, MARRAKESH, MOROCCO: GEORGE HOLTON/PHOTO RESEARCHERS

VOLUME 18

Middle East and Africa

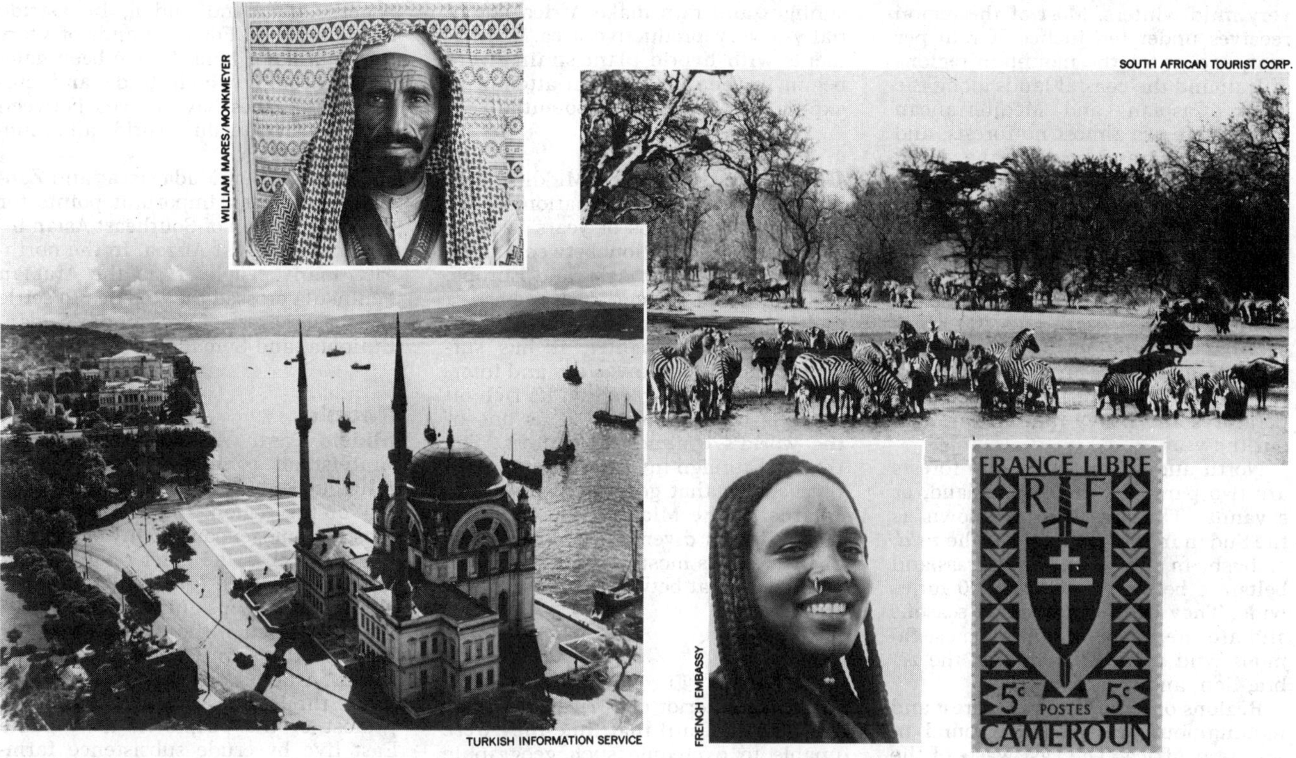

WILLIAM MARES/MONKMEYER

SOUTH AFRICAN TOURIST CORP.

TURKISH INFORMATION SERVICE

FRENCH EMBASSY

The area of the Middle East depends on exactly what boundaries one uses in defining the region. For instance, northwestern Africa, often called the Maghreb, includes the nations of Morocco, Algeria, Tunisia, and Libya, while Egypt occupies northeastern Africa. These countries, all lying north of the great deserts of Africa, are part of the Islamic world and their histories are closely interwoven with the histories of the great civilizations that developed in the Middle East.

For our purposes, the Middle East does not include any part of Africa (including Egypt). It does, however, include all of Turkey, Cyprus, and the entire Sinai and Arabian peninsulas. It extends as far east as Iran's eastern border with Pakistan, Afghanistan, and the Soviet Union; as far north as the Turkish and Iranian borders with the Soviet Union, Bulgaria, Greece, and the Black and Caspian seas; as far west as the easternmost waters of the Aegean and Mediterranean seas, and the border between the Sinai Peninsula and Egypt; and as far south as the Red and Arabian seas. The population of the region, so defined, is over 150 million.

Africa, with an area of about 11.6 million square miles, is the world's second largest continent. Its population, more than 650 million in 1990, represents some 10 percent of the world's total.

Africa south of the Sahara (also called sub-Saharan Africa and black Africa) can be roughly defined as that part of the continent south of latitude 20°N. Included in this definition are the islands off the coast of West Africa, such as Bioko in the Gulf of Guinea, and the islands near the coast of East Africa, including Madagascar and Zanzibar.

The land. The Middle East, comprised largely of the Arabian Peninsula, contains the vast central plateau of the Arabian desert, rising gradually from sea level along the Persian Gulf, westward to the highland regions that dominate the Red Sea coast. Northward lies the Syrian desert. Much of Turkey consists of the highland areas of the Pontic and Taurus mountains. The Zagros dominate western Iran, as does the Elburz range in northern Iran.

The Bosporus and Dardanelles straits off the coast of western Turkey connect the Black and Mediterranean seas. The Persian Gulf, off the eastern coast of the Arabian Peninsula, is important as the chief waterway for the Middle East's rich oil traffic.

Africa can be described as an immense block of rock that rises from the west, where the average elevation is about 1000 feet, to the east, where the average elevation is about 6000 feet.

There are few good harbors along the smooth coastline. Cliffs or steep slopes separate narrow coastal plains from level interior plateaus, which are also called tablelands.

Rivers. The Middle East contains only one great river system—the Tigris-Euphrates—which rises in Turkey and flows through Iraq, eventually draining into the Persian Gulf. There is a general shortage of water, badly needed for irrigation in this region.

There are four major river systems in Africa—the Congo in central Africa, the Niger in West Africa, the Nile in the northeast, and the Zambezi in the southeast. The main rivers are generally navigable on the interior plateaus, but there are rapids and waterfalls where they enter the coastal plains, thus restricting access to the interior by boat.

Rift valleys. The rift valleys are the outstanding natural features of Africa. They are two great parallel trenches, or faults, extending from the Middle East southward through East Africa to the mouth of the Zambezi River in southeastern Africa.

The rift valleys contain Africa's great extinct volcanoes, including Mt. Kenya and Mt. Kilimanjaro. The rift valleys also contain many of Africa's major lakes, including Victoria, Albert, Tanganyika, and Nyasa.

Climate and vegetation. The climate of the Middle East is generally dry, with extremely hot summers and very mild winters. Most of the region receives under ten inches of rain per year, except for the mountain regions of Iran and the coastal lands along the Black, Caspian, and Mediterranean seas. There are almost no forests, and shrubs and grasslands are the dominant vegetation, where there is any.

Africa is divided by the equator into roughly balanced geographical halves. Equatorial, or tropical, rain forests stretch across central Africa to the lakes region in a belt that extends about 400 miles north and 400 miles south of the equator. Rain forests also extend along the south coast of West Africa. The rain forests have high temperatures and heavy rainfall throughout the year.

North and south of the rain forests are two parallel belts of grassland, or savanna. The grassland is known as the Sudan in the north and as the *veld,* or bush, in the south. Both grassland belts are between 500 and 700 miles wide. They have wet and dry seasons and are the home of Africa's most famous wild animals, including the zebra, lion, and rhinoceros.

Regions of temperate rain forest and mountainous grassland are found in southern Africa. The vast waste of the Sahara in northern Africa, the largest desert in the world, is balanced by the smaller Namib and Kalahari deserts in southwestern Africa.

The climates of Africa vary greatly. Desert regions are hot and dry, rain forest regions are hot and wet, and the grassland areas receive irregular amounts of rainfall. In spite of these extremes in climate, the amount of sunlight and rain make Africa potentially a very productive area. Experiments with hybrid plant strains were begun in the 1960's in an attempt to exploit this agricultural potential.

Crossroads.

The Middle East has been a focus of international commerce for thousands of years because of its central location between three continents—Africa, Asia, and Europe. For the same reason, it has been a melting pot of religious and cultural exchange; consequently, it has suffered from foreign invasions and internal warfare. Most recently, its rich oil deposits have reinstated it as one of the world's commercial centers. The threat of foreign invasion accompanies the benefits that go with this wealth. Internally, the Middle East's cultural and religious diversity has led to one of the world's most recent and heated conflicts—that between the Arabs and Israelis.

Isolation.

Europeans knew little about the interior of Africa before the late 1800's. Until that time they were unable to overcome such geographic barriers as the Sahara in the north, the rift valleys in the east, and the lack of good harbors and navigable rivers. Tropical diseases, particularly malaria, also helped greatly to bar the Europeans.

The geography of Africa did not isolate its peoples from other parts of the world or from each other, however. Five African states, Mauritania, Mali, Niger, Chad, and Sudan, lie astride latitude 20°N. For thousands of years these "linking lands" have been gateways through which trade and cultural influences have moved between the Mediterranean world and sub-Saharan Africa.

The islands of Madagascar and Zanzibar have been important points for the introduction of Southeast Asian influences into East Africa. In the northeast, many peoples from the Arabian Peninsula crossed the Red Sea to settle the coastal areas of present-day Sudan, Ethiopia, and Somalia.

PEACEFUL SCENE ON THE VAAL, *in South Africa's Transvaal. Formerly the independent Boer South African Republic, the province is one of the world's richest in gold and diamonds.*

SOUTH AFRICAN TOURIST CORP.

People.

Middle East. Although the current Arab-Israeli conflict underscores the religious, ethnic, and cultural diversity of the region, the Middle East is mostly homogeneous. Many of the people are Arabs. The chief religion is Islam. The Israeli Jews and the Turks are the only significant minority groups, although there are also Copts, Kurds, Greeks (in Cyprus), and Armenians. Arabic is the major language, while the Israelis speak Hebrew.

Most of the people in the Middle East live by crude subsistence farming. They use outdated techniques and get along without most of the comforts and innovations of the modern world. Nomads herd livestock in the deserts or grasslands, as they have done for thousands of years. Most people live in rural villages, with the rest in crowded seacoast urban areas.

Africa. Africa is a continent of great human diversity. In addition to European languages, for example, over 800 indigenous languages are spoken by Africa's people.

Although many millions of Africans are of mixed origins, the population includes five major physical types: Negroid, Pygmoid, Bushmanoid, Caucasoid, Mongoloid.

South of the Sahara, the population is predominantly Negroid. There is wide variation in physical characteristics among Africa's approximately 200 million Negroids, but most have dark skin, kinky hair, and broad noses. Negroid population density is greatest in southern West Africa and throughout the lakes region of East Africa.

Nilotes, in East Africa, are a Negroid subgroup. They are extremely tall, sometimes exceeding seven feet in height.

Negroids speak languages belonging to the Niger-Congo language family, which is the largest in Africa. This language family includes nearly 100

Bantu languages, of which Swahili is the most common.

Pygmoids, found in the forest regions of central and South-West Africa (Namibia), are very short, averaging less than five feet in height.

Bushmanoids live mainly in and around the Kalahari Desert in central and southwestern Africa. Hottentots, a significant subgroup of Bushmanoids, live in South-West Africa (Namibia) and southern Africa.

Caucasoids occupy the northern and northeastern regions of Africa, including the Sahara. They are characterized by narrow noses and curly or wavy hair. Caucasoids include peoples who speak Arabic and Berber languages and who are a part of the Semitic and Hamitic ethnic groups. European and Asian Caucasoid minorities also exist.

Mongoloids migrated from Southeast Asia to Madagascar in large numbers many centuries ago. Their descendants are short, with yellowish-brown skin, broad noses, and straight hair.

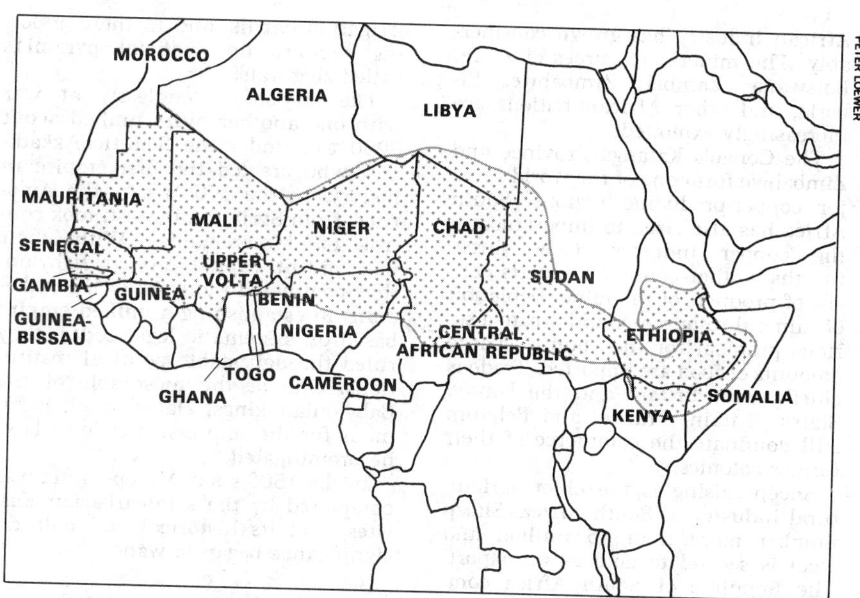

THE FAMINE BELT, *a huge east-west slice of Africa just south of the mighty Sahara, as it was in 1974, a bad year. Man is still at the mercy of nature in much of Africa.*

Economy.

Middle East. While the Middle Eastern economy has been revolutionized by the vast wealth accumulated from the working oil fields, which lie mainly along the Persian Gulf, agriculture is still the region's main economic activity.

Wheat is the most important crop grown, but other cereal crops, as well as fruits and nuts, are also significant. Less than ten percent of the land is cultivated and methods are crude. There are serious water shortages in many regions because of scant rainfall and few rivers.

Industry, mostly related to oil production, has increased since World War II, but it is still largely undeveloped and includes a substantial amount of handcraft manufacturing. Textile and construction materials manufacturing, along with food processing, are other important industries. Israel has the most diversified industrial development, while Lebanon, although plagued by civil war, remains the banking and commercial center of the Middle East.

Mining is the most prosperous economic activity in the region. Over half of the world's known oil reserves are located here, mostly along the Persian Gulf coasts. Japan, Western Europe, and the United States are the chief markets for oil exports. The revenues from this trade have been used to benefit the exporting countries by improving educational and transportation facilities, as well as by greatly modernizing and developing the agricultural and industrial sectors of the economy. The revenues are also used to purchase armaments.

Africa. Africa, second to Asia in size, is cut by the equator about halfway in its length from north to south. In the northwest, an extension of the European Alpine system forms the Atlas Mountains. The rest of the continent is a plateau, separated from the ocean by a narrow coastal plain. This plateau consists of ancient rock, minerals from which supply the major portion of the commercial wealth of the continent.

Internal trade and communication are difficult, with one-third of the continent having no outlet to the sea. The rivers, although navigable for long distances, are treacherous because of rapids and waterfalls. The Congo River in south-central Africa is an unsatisfactory waterway because the seasonal fluctuations in depth are so great. These conditions, however, give rise to vast potential waterpower—more than in any other continent.

Africa may be divided into three major climatic regions, and its natural resources are determined by the differences between these regions. The north is dominated by the Sahara, greatest of the trade-wind deserts, an arid area contributing oil and natural gas to the economic importance of the continent.

Egypt, in northeastern Africa and a part of the Sahara, differs from the desert only because it has an irrigated valley as a result of the Nile floods. The people live only on the delta and banks of the river. Cotton is the chief crop, its long fiber commanding a high price. Cotton constitutes a large share of the country's exports. Its biggest customer today, replacing Britain, is the Soviet Union. The bulk of Egyptian foreign trade is controlled by and moved through the port of Alexandria.

The second natural division is the equatorial region, characterized by dense rain forests. The vegetation of Africa shades out gradually from this thickly treed area. In spite of its million or more square miles of forests, Africa as a whole exports little timber. Nearly half the forest area lies in the equatorial zone, and the other half lies farther south, particularly in the Republic of the Congo, Zaire, and Zimbabwe. South Africa itself lacks sufficient timber and must import large quantities of wood.

The timber wealth of Africa lies in the mahogany, ebony, rosewood and other cabinet woods of the equatorial zone, although they have been very little developed. Timber is produced despite the serious disadvantages of high production and transport costs.

Rail charges are high on bulky commodities, and valuable timber stands are far from the coast. The cost of logging is great, especially because there are so many different species of trees to the acre; it is difficult to get trees out of the jungle. In addition, the tropical hardwoods, in which Africa is most wealthy, represent a negligible part of the world's trade in timber. To date, the economic importance of Africa's forests has been in byproducts such as palm oil, rubber, cork, gums, and dyes.

The equatorial zone harbors the cacao tree and is one of the important commercial sources of cocoa, producing about half of the world's supply. At one time the bulk of the world's rubber came from the Congo basin and from the equatorial forests of the Amazon basin, but this production was rendered less valuable by the development of plantation rubber in Southeast Asia and by the production of synthetic rubber.

Of the major world commodities, Africa leads in the production of very few. Gold, diamonds, and exotic items such as ostrich feathers are the exceptions. South Africa is the leading producer of gold and diamonds. Since World War I and World War II, South

African industry has grown considerably. The mineral resources of Zaire, Botswana, Zambia, Zimbabwe, Liberia, and other African nations are increasingly exploited.

The Congo's Katanga Province and Zimbabwe form one of the world's major copper-producing regions. South Africa has also risen to importance in the copper industry. Over three-fourths of that country's exports consist of products of the mine. Depletion of mineral resources could create a serious problem for the country. Large amounts of food are imported. Trade is chiefly with Britain and the United States. Britain, France, and Belgium still dominate the commerce of their former colonies.

Sheep raising is the chief agricultural industry of South Africa. Sheep number more than 45 million and wool is second to gold as an export. The Republic of South Africa comprises a territory wealthy in a few minerals, with areas of fertile soil and an almost ideal climate. Man has generally found it an agreeable place to live.

History of the Middle East

The earliest epoch of world history begins with the appearance of civilization and the accompanying written records in the Tigris-Euphrates valley in Mesopotamia (modern Iraq) around 3000 B.C., and in the Nile Valley of Egypt a little later. Mesopotamia, the heart of the Middle East, is often called the cradle of civilization. Its history begins with the states of Sumer, in the southern part of the Tigris-Euphrates valley, where the institutions and ways of life that set the pattern for all of ancient Near Eastern civilization were created.

Sumer. The Sumerians, organized in independent city-states, were ruled by a strong king in each city. The king's leadership was derived from the local patron god. The king was also commander of the army, and royal successions were often accomplished through violent political upheavals.

The priests of the local gods also had significant political and economic power. They were large landowners and temple estate administrators; the temple estate was the center of urban economic life. Agriculture was the basis of the economy in general.

The Sumerians developed impressive and advanced codes of law that have been preserved and that furnish considerable insight into their ancient culture. They also made important pioneering achievements in literature, mathematics, and astronomy. Engineering was highly advanced, as is seen in the Sumerians' construction of irrigation canals, and in their imposing temples on artificial pyramids called ziggurats.

The city-states, endlessly at war with one another, were unified about 2250 B.C. under the Semitic Akkadians, who created the first empire in history. In the 1700's B.C., the Amorites, from Syria to the west, took control of Mesopotamia. With their magnificent capital city at Babylon, they completed the work of the Akkadians in establishing a unified empire based on systematic legal codes; they ruled through stable political institutions. One of the most able of the Babylonian kings, Hammurabi, is famous for the impressive code of laws he promulgated.

In the 1500's B.C. Mesopotamia was conquered by the semibarbarian Kassites, and its historical and cultural significance began to wane.

Other ancient powers. After the 1200's B.C. the invaders of Mesopotamia introduced a new "iron age," in which widely available iron (used for tools and weapons) replaced copper, which had been obtained mostly from the Sinai Peninsula and Cyprus. The resulting economic and political changes brought about a decline of the great Mesopotamian empires. They were replaced by new powers.

After 1400 B.C. the Phoenicians (Canaanites) and Hebrews on the Mediterranean coast and inland made major contributions to the region's culture. The Hebrews, by developing the first ethical monotheism, set the stage for the appearance of Christianity. The Phoenicians introduced the alphabet, which led to most Western writing systems. The Phoenicians also created a great trading empire with a major colony, Carthage, on the coast of North Africa, as well as another at Cadiz in Spain. The maritime activities that made this commerce possible also promoted a general spread of culture throughout the Mediterranean world.

The Assyrians returned Mesopotamia to imperial rule from about 900 B.C. until the fall of their empire in 612 B.C. At its height, the Assyrian empire was larger than any of its predecessors and included both Syria and Egypt.

In the 540's B.C. the Persian empire was founded by Cyrus the Great. The enormous empire was efficiently ruled through able administrators, with good communications at their command, under a benevolent type of federalism. The empire finally fell in 330 B.C. to the Macedonian conqueror, Alexander the Great. Zoroastrianism became an influential world religion during the Persian imperial era.

During the period that the great powers ruled Mesopotamia, another distinctive civilization appeared in the northwest, beginning in the early part of the second millennium B.C. The Hittites created an empire about 1650 B.C., with its capital at Hattusas in central Asia Minor (modern-day Turkey). They conquered Syria and, briefly, Babylonia, but fell short of subduing Egypt. Politically, the Hittite empire was a loosely constructed confederation of city-states. The Hittite empire fell to a barbarian invasion about 1200 B.C., though some Neo-Hittite city-states lingered on in Syria until the 700's B.C.

Foreign rule. After 330 B.C. the Middle East and Egypt came under the rule of the Greek, or Hellenistic, kings, who divided up Alexander's empire. Beginning around 30 B.C., Rome conquered most of that area, which it would control for about five centuries. During the Greek and Roman periods, the Middle East became important commercially and underwent a period of relative peace and stability. The artistic and cultural achievements of the Mediterranean were diffused throughout the Middle East.

The late Roman Empire was divided between the western, Roman portion, and the eastern part, later the Byzantine Empire, administered from its capital at Constantinople (modern-day Istanbul, in Turkey). This east-west split brought increasing diversity in the political and cultural development of the two areas.

Arab conquest. Early in the 600's A.D., the Muslims, followers of the Prophet Muhammad's new Islamic faith, emerged from the Arabian Peninsula to create a great empire that included all of the Middle East and Egypt. Under the first Islamic, or Umayyad dynasty the armies of the Arabs, fired by religious zeal, reached as far west as Spain and as far east as the borders of India.

In 749 A.D. the Abbasid dynasty took control of this huge empire. With their capital at Baghdad (in modern–day Iraq), the Abbasids inspired a great era of Muslim learning and cultural achievement. But by the 1000's A.D. the Arab world was torn by power struggles between the local states of North Africa and Egypt and the Abbasid caliphate, which in the 1000's and 1100's was reinvigorated by various invading Turkish groups. Chief among these were the Seljuks, who spread their power over most of the Middle East.

The Turks. As the Seljuk Turks fought their way into Asia Minor, dealing the Byzantine Empire a crushing blow at Manzikert in 1071 A.D., Christian European armies prepared for the First Crusade (1096–1099), which advanced into the Middle East and captured Jerusalem.

In the 1200's Mongols under Genghis Khan burst out of central Asia to create a brief empire that stretched from China to Syria, and as far west as Poland and Hungary. Baghdad was sacked in 1258, ending the Abbasid dynasty and generally reversing the great cultural achievements of the Abbasid era. In the 1300's, the Mongol invasions were repeated, this time under Tamerlane.

By the 1300's, the Ottoman Turks had replaced the Seljuks and had pushed farther west into Asia Minor, completing the Byzantine conquest in 1453 with the capture of Constantinople. By the 1500's the Ottomans controlled most of the Middle East (except Persia), Egypt, the Balkans, and northern Africa; but by the 1700's political dissension and warfare had reduced and weakened their empire.

Nationalism. During the 1800's the new European national states, especially France, had begun to penetrate North Africa. The Middle East, more isolated from European influence, became increasingly divided into small powerless kingdoms or states. During the same period the Ottoman Empire lost most of its European possessions. After its defeat in World War I, the empire was broken up by the victorious powers. In the general settlement, Syria and Lebanon were mandated to France, while Britain took over Palestine and Iraq. But the settlement was not to last. The people of the Middle East demanded independence, and in the 1920's the modern states of Turkey and Saudi Arabia were established. Other countries, however, had to wait until the 1930's and 1940's, and some even later, before gaining independence.

The Middle East today. After World War II British-mandated Palestine, claimed by both Arabs and Jews, was to be divided, according to a UN proposal of 1947, into an Arab state and a Jewish state. With the British mandate at an end, the Jews established the state of Israel in 1948 with their portion of the allotted territory. The Palestinians, however, rejected the plan. This led to the first Arab-Israeli war, in 1948–1949, which left the issue unresolved. War broke out again in 1967 and again in 1973 as the Arab states, led by Egypt, tried to regain Israeli-occupied territories.

An active Palestinian terrorist movement, aimed at destroying the Israeli nation, has caused further violence and political disruption in the Middle East since the 1960's. The Palestine Liberation Organization (PLO), which has engineered these terrorist attacks, continues to insist on the annihilation of Israel and a return of Israeli-occupied areas to Palestinian rule.

The postwar Arab-Israeli conflict has made the Middle East one of the world's most troublesome regions. The Arab states, unable to unite except in their opposition to Israel, have tried to enforce an economic boycott of Israel, but Western nations have supported the new country with economic and military aid and trading privileges.

In an attempt to end the strife between Arabs and Jews, Egypt's president, Anwar el-Sadat, signed a peace treaty with Israel in 1979. Inevitably, widespread protests came from the Arab world. Although a large part of the Sinai Peninsula had already been returned to Egypt, the execution of the peace agreement itself was delayed in 1981 over technical disputes, including Israel's insistence on control of the occupied Gaza Strip and the West Bank of the Jordan River, and on holding all of Jerusalem rather than share it with the Arabs.

The Arab-Israeli dispute has especially broad international implications. The Arab states have used their great deposits of oil as a political tool to enforce anti-Israeli policies. Raising oil prices or reducing supplies has several times demonstrated the Arabs' dangerous power over the industrialized nations of both East and West.

While the Middle East is increasingly developing a wealthy and educated upper class, most of its people still live in the traditional backward conditions. Plagued by poverty, corruption, and poor administration, the states of the Middle East are unified only in their Islamic faith, which has dominated their region since the teachings of Muhammad were first formulated. Indeed, after the violent Iranian Islamic revolution of 1979, Islam itself promises to become a potent vehicle for renewed nationalistic aspirations throughout the Middle East.

MIDDLE EAST PEACE MOVES: *Menachem Begin of Israel and the late Anwar el-Sadat of Egypt confer in Jerusalem in 1977. Yasir Arafat* (inset) *heads the disaffected Palestinian Arabs who are agitating for an Arab state of their own in Palestine.*

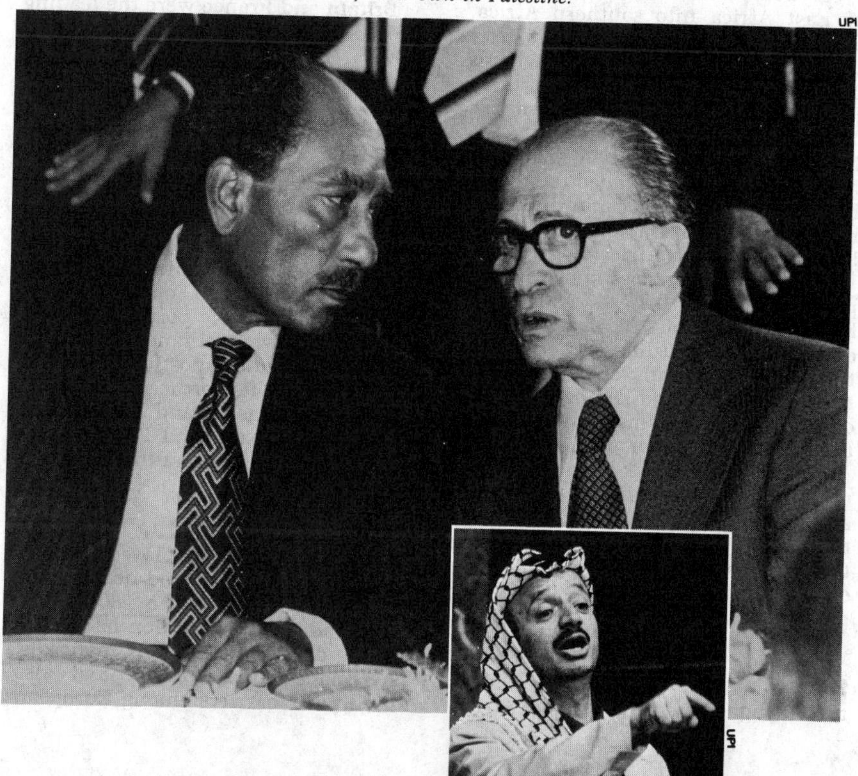

UPI

History of Africa

Africa is perhaps man's earliest home. Evidence has been found of a tool-making primate who lived almost 2 million years ago in present-day Tanzania, in east Africa.

Caucasoid peoples appeared in the lower Nile Valley by about 4000 B.C., and Negroid peoples appeared on the grasslands of West Africa after about 2000 B.C. Bantu-speaking Negroid peoples migrated southward and eastward from West Africa over the next three millennia, and as they invaded new regions, Pygmies in central Africa and Bushmen in southern Africa were either exterminated or driven into isolated areas.

Egypt. In the northeast of Africa, Egyptian civilization began shortly after that of Sumer, after 3000 B.C. In contrast to Mesopotamia's turbulent history of warfare, invasion, conquest, and cultural assimilation, Egypt's history is one of stability and stately regularity. Egyptian civilization, which grew up along the mighty Nile River, was unified by a strong ruler (a pharaoh) who was worshipped as a god and who personally owned all of Egypt.

The pharaoh gave large land grants to two social classes—priests and high government officials—that came to hold considerable power and influence. The priests of Amon at Thebes, for example, became so powerful that one pharaoh, Amenhotep IV (ruled 1375–1357 B.C.), felt compelled to reject Amon and his priests and insist on the worship of Aton. He moved the traditional capital from Thebes to Aketaten (modern-day Tel-el-Amarna) and proceeded to reestablish the pharaoh's political and economic, as well as religious, supremacy over the priesthood of Amon. Following Amenhotep's death, a restoration to Amon-worship was effected and later a dynasty of the high priests of Amon was established.

Egypt, which had been ruled once before (c 1800–1600 B.C.) by a foreign Semitic group—the Hyksos—saw its empire crumble after 1000 B.C. A succession of foreign rulers, beginning with the Libyans, included the Persians, Greeks, and Romans.

Mediterranean North Africa. Phoenician sailors from the Middle East were the first recorded explorers of the coast of northern Africa. From the founding of Phoenician colonies after the 1100's B.C. until the 600's A.D., when Arabs conquered Africa north of the Sahara, North Africa was part of Mediterranean civilization.

During the 500's and 400's B.C. the Phoenician city of Carthage, on the coast of modern-day Tunisia, was a commercial and maritime center of the western Mediterranean world. By the mid-200's B.C., however, its leadership had been usurped by Rome. The Romans established rich colonies in North Africa and commercial activity between Africa and the Mediterranean world reached its height.

African kingdoms. Strong, centralized Negroid monarchies first appeared in Kush and Axum, south of Egypt. This pattern spread throughout West Africa and from the lakes region of East Africa into southern Africa. For more than a thousand years after their first appearance, black kingdoms of this kind rose and fell, most of them leaving behind few material remains.

In North Africa, Mediterranean civilization was permanently displaced by Muslim Arabs who invaded the region in the 600's. Islam became the dominant religion and Arabic the dominant language of North Africa.

The Arabs did not establish lasting political control. Instead, native Berber-speaking peoples formed their own empires. Two Muslim Berber dynasties, the Almoravids and the Almohads, had direct and lasting influence on the black kingdoms of West Africa through holy wars, or jihads.

Following the breakdown of Roman rule in North Africa in the 400's A.D., and the first Muslim Arab conquest of the region, which began in the 600's, the people of Western Europe were cut off from the people of sub-Saharan Africa for about 1000 years.

Slave trade. In the early 1400's the Portuguese began to explore Africa by sea. Later in the same century they established trading settlements on the African coasts. Other European nations had appeared by the mid-1500's, and they began to develop a prosperous trade in slaves. By the mid-1600's the Dutch had established a trading port at the Cape of Good Hope, now South Africa's city of Cape Town.

By the mid-1600's the British had taken the lead in establishing trading posts in Africa. The most prosperous aspect of this commercial activity was the "triangular trade" by which Africans were captured and sold as slaves to meet the labor needs of colonial plantations in America.

The slave trade flourished in the 1700's, but by the early 1800's most European nations had made attempts to abolish it. Freed blacks were resettled in Africa, notably in Freetown (Sierra Leone, established in 1787) and Liberia (established in 1822).

Colonialism. European efforts to reach the interior of Africa were undertaken in the mid-1800's, but by 1875 European rule was still limited to less than one-tenth of the continent.

After 1875, though, many European nations joined in a massive carving up of the continent. The Berlin Conference (1884–1885) tried to set standards for the colonization of Africa to prevent violent struggles among the European powers. However, African territorial boundaries, established at the conference, were drawn up strictly for the convenience of the European nations, and their disregard for African political, economic, or ethnic unity was one of the factors leading to instability among present-day African nations.

Britain and France were the leading powers on the continent by the early 1900's. Britain, following victory in the Boer War of 1899–1902, established the gold-rich Union of South Africa by combining the Afrikaner, or Boer, states of Transvaal and the Orange Free State with Cape Colony and Natal. Germany lost its African possessions after its defeat in World War I. Under the postwar League of Nations mandate system, Britain held a vast empire from Egypt to South Africa, including considerable portions of western Africa, while France controlled extensive colonies, mostly in West Africa, as well as its northern possessions of Morocco, Algeria, and Tunisia. Belgium, Italy, Spain, and Portugal also held African colonies at this time.

Economic aspects. European governments first employed charter companies to exploit and develop the wealth of Africa. By the 1800's, Europe's industrial revolution had led to increased demands for raw materials. The industrial revolution had also raised tariff barriers among European nations. African colonies could supply the raw materials and provide markets for manufactured goods from the mother country.

In central and southern Africa, mining companies came to dominate colonial economies. Iron ore, lead ore, manganese, gems, and other minerals continue to be mined extensively throughout these regions.

By the late 1960's, Zambia and the Congo (now Zaire) were leading producers of copper and cobalt; the Congo and Nigeria led in tin ore production; Guinea and Ghana in bauxite; Nigeria in columbite; South Africa in gold and platinum; South Africa and the Congo in uranium; and the Congo in industrial diamonds.

Mining was supported by a network of roads, railroads, and ports. Other companies established plantations that produced palm oil, rubber, cacao, and coffee. Mines and plantations alike used African labor.

Both mining and plantation farming called for large capital investments. In South Africa, where immense deposits of gold and diamonds had been discovered in the 1870's and 1880's, progress was rapid. By the 1930's, South Africa had become considerably urbanized and industrialized.

The colonial impact. Colonialism changed the way of life of many Africans. Modernization and urbanization were introduced at the expense of tribal life and values, which were largely destroyed. Economies were transformed from primitive exchange systems to monetary ones. Education, administered mainly by Christian missionaries, had the effect of establishing a small, elite class of skilled black workers who could profit from the modern economy. Most Africans, however, were denied access to the prosperity enjoyed by the Europeans, who owned and operated the immensely profitable industrial, mining, and agricultural enterprises they had imposed on the land. The best the masses could hope for under this system was to obtain menial and low-paying employment in white-owned businesses. Most Africans remained subsistence farmers, with few political or human rights.

Nationalism. More contacts with the outside world and exposure to Western influences during World War II intensified the desire of Africans for freedom and progress. African nationalists paid great attention to Asia, where many nations became independent from colonial rule immediately after World War II. The nonviolent campaign of Mohandas Gandhi in India was particularly appealing to African leaders.

The newly formed United Nations soon became a forum for advocates of

African independence. The growing Cold War between the Soviet Union and the United States often brought African leaders backing in their efforts to win freedom for their countries.

Independence. France, Britain, and Belgium allowed their empires to fade away slowly as nation after nation gained independence in Africa, beginning in the mid-1950's. France, in particular, continued to maintain close ties with several former African colonies. It offered economic and technical assistance and still has considerable cultural, economic, and political influence on most of its former possessions. Portugal held tenaciously to its colonies, with the result that they gained independence only after bloody military revolutions.

White rule became the method employed by white settlers in South Africa and Rhodesia (modern-day Zimbabwe). The settlers hoped to gain independence from Europe while retaining control over the economies and politics of their respective states. Most black African nations are today joined in an economic boycott of white-ruled South Africa, which still employs "apartheid," a policy of rigid racial separation. The boycott has been ineffective, however, because of South Africa's dominant economic position on the continent.

Modern era.

The newly independent nations of Africa were confronted by many difficulties of all kinds—economic, social, and political.

Economic. Progress in agriculture was limited by poor soil, too much or too little water, overgrazing and overfarming, land ownership problems, the small size of most farms, and widespread dependence on a few "cash crops." The crops were often prey to diseases and brought low prices on the world market.

On the other hand, many thousands of African farmers were being trained in soil conservation and crop rotation, and the formation of farm cooperatives was being encouraged. The new nations of Africa received agricultural aid from many countries and organizations, including the United States and the United Nations.

Industrial development was slowed by a lack of capital for investment, trained labor, and adequate transportation facilities. Half of the continent's railroads were in the Republic of South Africa, and the remaining track linked inland mining and commercial agricultural regions with ports on the coasts, but there were few interior connections. Roads were generally poor and unsuited to the economical operation of vehicles. Air transport had developed considerably, but remained too expensive for large-scale use.

Social. Literacy was a major problem in the new nations of Africa. Only

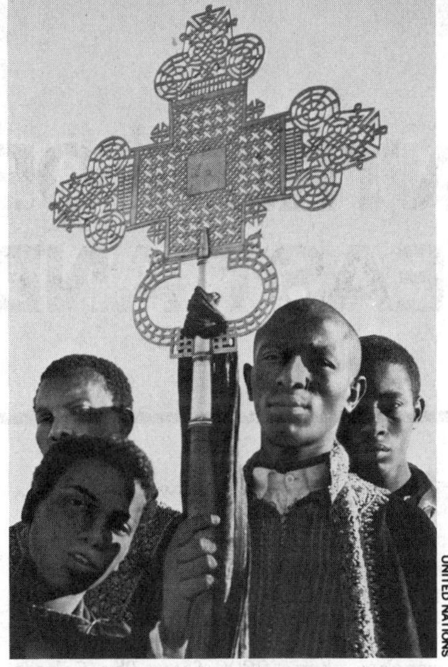

UNITED NATIONS

YOUNG CHRISTIAN PRIESTS *in Ethiopia belong to the very ancient Coptic Church.*

about ten percent of adult Africans were literate, and less than 40 percent of school-age children attended elementary school. African nations devoted a large part of their budgets and foreign aid to education, and many Africans were awarded scholarships for higher education in Europe and the United States.

Africa, excluding the Republic of South Africa, had very few doctors and hospitals. Although modern medicines and improved sanitation had lowered the death rate in most regions, some of these areas were soon threatened by widespread malnutrition.

Political. Most independent African nations were organized along Western political lines. But initial efforts to establish multiparty democratic systems gave way to domination by a single political party. One-party rule came to be advocated by such figures as Julius Nyerere, president of Tanzania, and Kwame Nkrumah, leader of Ghana from 1957 to 1966.

Cooperation. The new nations of Africa have readily joined regional and international organizations in order to speed social and economic development. The ideal of "pan-Africanism," or the unity of all African peoples, found expression in the Organization of African Unity (OAU), which was founded in May, 1963, by 30 African nations at a conference in Addis Ababa, Ethiopia.

Various other groupings and alliances were formed, each with its own interpretation of the future course of Pan-Africanism, but all serving as forums where matters of common interest could be discussed. The only major organization, other than the OAU, that seems likely to survive is the African-Malagasy-Mauritius Common Organization (OCAM), an economic association, founded in 1964, of ten French-speaking African nations.

United Nations. The United Nations has played a major role in bringing independence to Africa. Every state that gained independence has eventually won membership in the UN, and has become active in the General Assembly, where the fight continues against white minority rule in South Africa. African states wield considerable voting power in the UN General Assembly, where they make up nearly one-third of the membership. Most of the new nations of Africa view the UN as the key instrument of future advance in such areas as health and education.

Africa today.

Africa's primary problems are still internal disunion and economic underdevelopment. Having achieved political independence, many African nations discovered that they were being indirectly controlled by the economic actions of more developed nations, a policy called neocolonialism. Two solutions to the problem of neocolonialism were presented by President Houphouet-Boigny of the Ivory Coast and by Presidents Nyerere and Touré of Tanzania and Guinea. Houphouet encouraged economic development by attracting foreign investment, even though this allowed foreign influence on the Ivory Coast's governmental policies. Nyerere and Touré preferred to maintain entire independence, even though this created a degree of poverty and slowed development.

Most African governments considered themselves African socialists although they owed little to European socialism. They were characterized by centralized economic planning and attempts to engage their people in political activity and developmental projects.

Since independence, almost all African nations have followed a nonaligned foreign policy, accepting aid from both the Western and Soviet blocs. By the 1970's many African nations were also accepting aid from China and Japan. Through the UN and the OAU, Africa has tried to be a third force in international relations.

Through the economic and political turmoil that has enveloped most of Africa, an African intellectual community has emerged. This grouping of professional people, politicians, artists, and scholars has taken ideas and techniques from outside systems and adapted them to the needs of their own societies. Some fresh concepts and novel insights have developed in each country and have contributed to the culture of the continent as a whole.

This notable advance has taken place behind the publicized scenes of military coups, tribal conflicts, and economic failures. It has made possible establishment of educational structures based on European models, the growth of trade languages (or lingua francas), immense improvement in communications systems, and expansion of Islam and Christianity.

COUNTRIES OF THE MIDDLE EAST AND AFRICA

Algeria

Official name: *Democratic and Popular Republic of Algeria*
Area: *919,595 sq. mi., 2,381,740 sq. km.*
Population: *(1990 est.) 25,714,000*
Capital: *Algiers (Pop., 1989, 2,400,000)*
Language: *Arabic, French*
Religion: *Islam*
Currency unit: *Dinar*
National holiday: *Nov. 1*

Algeria, a republic in northern Africa, is bounded on the north by the Mediterranean Sea, on the east by Tunisia and Libya, on the south by Niger and Mali, and on the west by Mauritania, Spanish Sahara, and Morocco. Algeria became independent in 1962 after more than a century of French rule.

The land. Most of Algeria is part of the vast desert waste of the Sahara. A narrow northern zone, where the bulk of the people live, is dominated by two parallel east-west mountain chains—the Tell Atlas and the Saharan Atlas. Both are part of the massive Atlas Mountains, which stretch across northern Africa. The Tell Atlas is a series of coastal mountains and valleys parallel to the Mediterranean Sea. The Saharan Atlas lies about 200 miles inland. Between the two ranges is a plateau area.

Most of the desert surface of southern Algeria is composed of rock and gravel, but there are some large sand areas. In the southeast are the Ahaggar Mountains, a volcanic rock mass that reaches above 9600 feet. The Sahara region is sparsely populated.

In Algeria's coastal region, the winters are mild and rainy and the summers are hot and dry. The plateau region receives little rain. The Sahara is hot and dry and receives less than four inches of rain a year.

The people. Most of Algeria's rapidly growing population is Muslim of Arab-Berber stock. More than 1 million people of European origin left Algeria after independence was won in 1962. This loss deprived the new nation of badly needed skilled technical and administrative personnel.

Algeria has a high literacy rate compared with other African nations. The population is over 50 percent urban, although nearly two-thirds of the labor force is absorbed by agriculture.

Economy. Algeria has traditionally been an agricultural country, although there is relatively little good farmland. The bulk of its produce, which consists of wheat and barley and a variety of vegetables and fruits, comes from the region between the Tell Atlas and the Mediterranean.

Industry and mining have increased significantly in recent years, and now account for nearly half of the gross national product, compared with under ten percent from agricultural products. Oil has become an important resource, and about 60 million metric tons are produced annually.

In 1986 Algeria's imports cost $7.9 billion and its exports earned $8.1 billion. The most valuable Algerian export for many years was wine. The major exports today are petroleum and natural gas from rich fields discovered in the Sahara in the 1950's.

Western Europe and the United States are Algeria's most important trading partners.

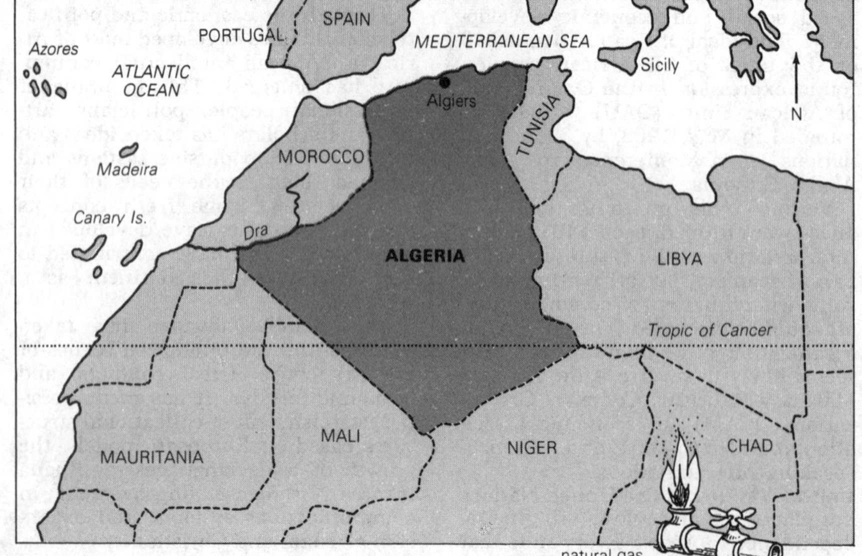

Government. Algeria is governed according to its constitution of 1976, which provides for a one-party socialist assembly as well as an elected president.

Algeria is a member of the United Nations, the Organization of Petroleum Exporting Countries (OPEC), the Arab League, and the Organization of African Unity.

History. The territory of present-day Algeria was invaded many times and dominated by many peoples before the country won its independence in 1962. Until the modern era, Algeria was often included in larger units that included parts of present-day Morocco and Tunisia.

The earliest known settlers were Berber-speaking peoples. The Phoenicians, who arrived in about 1200 B.C., established control over part of North Africa. Their rule ended in 146 B.C. with the fall of Carthage to Rome.

Roman domination ended with invasions by the Vandals in the 400's A.D. In the 500's the region came under Byzantine rule. In the 600's the Arabs began to sweep through North Africa, and Algeria became part of the Arab-dominated Muslim world that stretched from Spain to Arabia.

Ottoman era. In the early 1500's the Spanish, crusading against the Muslims who had withdrawn from Spain to North Africa, captured several Algerian cities. The inhabitants of Algeria appealed for help to a Muslim commander, Khayr-ad-Din, who drove the Spanish from Algiers in 1519. He offered allegiance to the Ottoman Empire in return for men and supplies. With Turkish aid, the Spanish were driven out of Algeria.

Algeria remained formally part of the Ottoman Empire until 1830. As an Ottoman province, its boundaries came to be roughly those of the modern Algerian state. Because of its great distance from Istanbul, Algeria became a Turkish regency in name only, and a Turkish *dey*, or governor, ruled the country almost as an independent state. The Turks held control of the coastal region, but the interior remained largely under traditional tribal rule.

French rule. The French occupation of Algeria began in 1830. The Turkish dey quickly capitulated, but native Algeria, led by Abd-al-Qadir (Abd-al-Kader), resisted. Not until 1847, when Abd-al-Qadir was captured, did France secure control over most of the country.

Large numbers of French and other Europeans settled in Algeria soon after the defeat of Abd-al-Qadir, and by 1900 Europeans made up 14 percent of Algeria's total population. The new settlers built up the Algerian economy, developing commercial agriculture for the French market. But the development basically served the needs of only the French Algerians, who gradually gained control of most of the best land.

By the early 1900's, the lack of economic opportunities and political inequalities created growing unrest within the Muslim majority. France attempted piecemeal reforms, but none succeeded in meeting the needs of the people.

Algerian desire for self-determination grew following World War II. In 1954 an armed rebellion against the French was begun by the National Liberation Front (FLN). The FLN slowly won the allegiance of most of the non-European Algerian population during a bitter struggle against the French in the years that followed.

Finally, in 1960, after a military effort that brought 500,000 French troops to Algeria and resulted in a series of French domestic political crises, French President de Gaulle agreed to negotiate with the FLN.

The two countries reached agreement only after months of bargaining. During that period part of the French army based in Algeria attempted a military coup against de Gaulle; also a last-ditch terrorist campaign against French withdrawal was waged by the Secret Army Organization (OAS) in Europe. On July 3, 1962, after 132 years of French rule, Algeria became independent.

Independence. The fruits of victory were almost lost in a near civil war that erupted immediately after independence was granted. Ahmed Ben Bella, a leader of the FLN who had been imprisoned in France since 1956, made a successful bid for power with the support of the FLN army.

By the end of 1962 Ben Bella had been elected premier by a newly formed national assembly, and he appeared to be securely in power. In June, 1965, however, Ben Bella was deposed in a bloodless coup led by the army, and Houari Boumedienne, a military leader of the independence struggle, emerged as head of the new regime.

Boumedienne's military regime declared war on Israel in 1967, subsequently breaking off relations with the United States (reestablished in 1974) and allying itself more closely with the Soviet Union group of states.

A semidemocratic constitution was granted in 1976, and in the elections of 1977 Boumedienne was elected president. He died the following year and Chadli Benjedid was elected president.

In response to severe rioting and protesting in 1988, Algeria adopted a new constitution in 1989. It permits the formation of political parties and guarantees freedom of expression and the right to strike.

Angola

Official name: *People's Republic of Angola*
Area: *481,350 sq. mi., 1,246,700 sq. km.*
Population: *(1990 est.) 8,802,000*
Capital: *Luanda (Pop., 1989, 1,300,000)*
Language: *Portuguese, African languages*
Religion: *Roman Catholic, Protestant, Animist*
Currency unit: *Kwanza*
National holiday: *Independence Day, Nov. 11*

Angola, on the southwestern coast of Africa, consists of two sections: Angola proper and Cabinda. Angola proper is bounded on the north by Zaire, on the east by Zaire and Zambia, on the south by South-West Africa (Namibia), and on the west by the Atlantic Ocean.

The smaller Cabinda region, about 2800 square miles in area, is an enclave separated from Angola proper by Zaire. It is bounded on the north by the People's Republic of the Congo and on the west by the Atlantic Ocean.

The land. Most of Angola lies on a deeply dissected plateau with an average elevation of 4000 feet. A narrow

BOMBARDMENT OF ALGIERS *by the French in 1830, after the Dey of Algiers slapped the French consul and refused to apologize. By 1847 the French had occupied all of Algeria.*

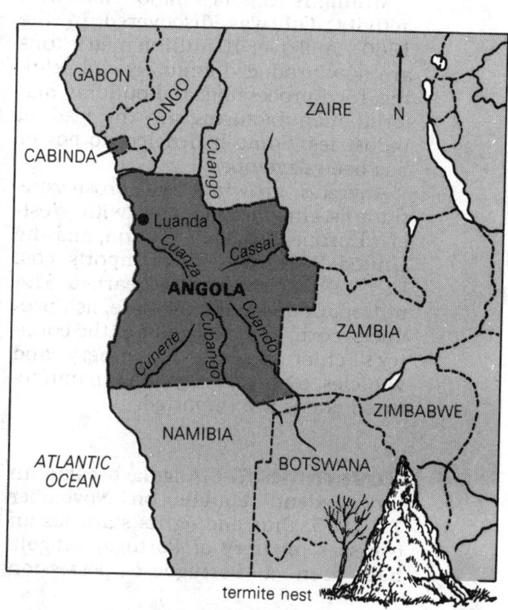

coastal plain skirts the plateau on the west, and in the east a higher plateau rises to 7000 feet. Low-lying Cabinda is covered by dense tropical jungle.

Much of the interior of Angola is heavily forested. Some portions of the east are swampy; the Moçâmedes Desert lies in the southwest. Many rivers rush down from the plateau toward the borders.

Angola's climate is varied. Cabinda and the coastal and northern regions are tropical, with high heat and humidity. The south and southeast are generally drier. The lower areas are hot, and the higher regions cool.

LOOK

SCHOOLCHILDREN IN ANGOLA, *a new country impoverished by incessant guerrilla warfare since 1961.*

The people. The overwhelming majority of the people are Bantu-speaking Africans of many tribal groups, including the Bakongo, Kimbundu, Ovimbundu, and Chokwe. About one percent of the population is European, and there is a small group of mixed African and European origin.

The official language is Portuguese, but a number of African languages are spoken. The illiteracy rate is extremely high, as in most African nations. Catholicism is the religion of over 60 percent of the population, although animism is still practiced and considered traditional. The very sparse population is only 18 percent urban.

Economy. Angola is a rich land. There are diamonds, oil, copper, manganese, iron, gold, and other minerals, and the hydroelectric potential is considerable. Farming is the chief economic activity of most of the people, however.

The basic food crops are manioc, corn, rice, and vegetables. Coffee, cotton, sisal, and sugar cane are the major cash crops, and they are raised on plantations. The country's forests yield palm products and timber, and there is fishing off the coasts.

Mining is Angola's major industrial activity. Oil was discovered in the 1960's, and over 10 million metric tons are now produced annually. Oil refining, food processing, and building material manufacturing are the leading industries. Some hydroelectric power has been developed.

Angola's growing and prosperous trade is chiefly conducted with Western Europe, the Soviet Union, and the United States. In 1986 imports cost $1.1 billion and exports earned $1.4 billion. Coffee, gold, iron ore, fish products, corn, sisal, and oil are the country's chief exports. Machinery and vehicles, textiles, drugs, and manufactured goods are imported.

Government. Angola became an independent republic on November 11, 1975, thus ending its status as an overseas territory of Portugal. Angola had been a Portuguese possession since the middle of the 17th century.

The head of the Angolan government is its president, who is aided by a prime minister and a cabinet. The Communist Party's Central Committee and Political Bureau select the president and act as Angola's legislative body.

Angola is a member of the United Nations and the Organization of African Unity.

History. Angola was part of the large, advanced Bantu-speaking kingdom of the Congo when it was visited in 1482 by the Portuguese explorer Diogo Cão. Friendly relations were established, and Portugal sent missionaries, traders, and settlers to the territory in the 1500's. Portions of the territory later came under direct Portuguese administration, but when the Congo kindgom began to disintegrate, Portugal did little to develop or exploit the region's resources.

During the 1600's the Portuguese defeated Dutch attempts to win control of Angola, and in the 1700's and 1800's Angola was a major source of slaves for Portugal's Brazil colony. In 1878 slaving was prohibited and replaced by a system of contract labor. Under the contract system, men over 18 who were employed fewer than six months a year could be forced to work. Women and young children were frequently drafted to meet labor needs as well.

Portugal's title to Angola was affirmed and the colony's boundaries set in 1885 and 1886. Colonial development was largely in private hands until the 1930's, when the government encouraged the Portuguese to settle there.

The government initiated full exploitation of the area's resources and imposed centralized control by breaking the power of local chiefs. Portugal's official policy was to incorporate Angola into the culture, society, and economy of European Portugal.

Nationalism. Although some political participation was permitted Angolans after 1951, when Angola was declared an overseas province, the government failed to meet the education, health, and welfare needs of the majority of the people. This neglect spurred the growth of a nationalist movement, and in 1961 an insurrection broke out in Cabinda and northern Angola.

Portugal moved to suppress the revolt by military force, but guerrilla warfare continued in the north and nationalist leaders established a government in exile that demanded independence.

The United Nations urged Portugal to liberate its prized and profitable colony, but instead Portugal attempted to improve Angola's economic, social, and educational conditions. It initiated programs of industrialization and oil production to modernize the economy. But guerrilla warfare continued up to 1974, as the United States, South Africa, the Soviet Union, and Zaire competed for influence in the colony.

After years of bloody warfare and economic decline, caused largely by massive Portuguese emigration, the guerrillas, helped by Soviet-aided Cuban troops, established an independent Marxist regime in 1975. South African troops staged an unsuccessful attack on the new regime in 1978.

In December, 1988, Cuba signed an accord agreeing to the removal of all its troops by July, 1991. The Angolan government and antigovernment guerrilla forces declared a cease-fire in June, 1989, ending a 14-year civil war.

Bahrain

Official name: *State of Bahrain*
Area: *231 sq. mi., 600 sq. km.*
Population: *(1990 est.) 512,000*
Capital: *Manama*
(Pop., 1989, 150,000)
Language: *Arabic*
Religion: *Islam*
Currency unit: *Dinar*

Bahrain is a tiny, oil-rich island nation in the Gulf of Bahrain, an inlet of the Persian Gulf between the Qatar peninsula and the Saudi Arabian coast. The country's major islands are Bahrain, the largest, Sitra, Al Muharraq, Umm an Nasan, Jidda, and Hawar.

The land and people. All of the islands are deserts with extremely hot and humid climates. Almost no rain falls on them, and their only water comes from a few underground springs. Cities developed around these springs, and about two-thirds of Bahrain's people live in two major cities, Manama, on Bahrain Island, and Muharraq. Bahrain is one of the most densely populated countries in the world, with over 1300 people per square mile. Ninety percent of the labor force is engaged in mining and industry.

Native Bahrainis are Muslim Arabs, and they constitute about 80 percent of the population. There are also Arabs from other countries, Iranians, Indians, and European oil workers.

Economy. Oil is the small country's principal natural resource and chief export. Reserves are being rapidly depleted, though, and annual production has dropped from nearly 4 million metric tons in the early 1970's to 2.5 million in the early 1980's. Additional income is derived from the processing of Saudi Arabian crude oil. The oil business in general continues to dominate the economy. Since 1975 Bahrain's gas industry has been totally nationalized, as has 60 percent of its oil industry.

Dates, grain, vegetables, and citrus fruits are raised in the islands' oases. Trade passing through Manama, one of the best ports in the Persian Gulf, is an important source of income.

Bahrain's imports, mostly machinery, chemicals, and food, cost an estimated $3.1 billion in 1985. Its exports were estimated at $2.8 billion. Trade is largely with Britain, Saudi Arabia, the United States, and Japan.

Government. The nation's first Parliament was created in 1973, but it was dissolved in 1975. It is now a constitutional monarchy in theory, but the emir has absolute authority.

Bahrain is a member of the United Nations, the Organization of Arab Oil Petroleum Exporting Countries, and the Arab League.

History. Bahrain's islands may have been inhabited as early as 3000 B.C., and they were known to the ancient Greeks. Their strategic location for trade and rich beds of pearl oysters attracted several conquerors. In 1507 Portugal occupied the islands and held them until 1602, when the Persians conquered them.

In 1782 Arab tribes seized power and founded the Khalifa dynasty. In 1820 Bahrain entered into treaty relations with Britain, and in 1861 the two countries concluded a treaty for the protection of Bahrain.

The discovery of oil in 1931 brought Bahrain sudden international importance and radically changed the islanders' traditional way of life. Iran laid claim to the islands and protested the British presence there.

In the mid-1950's and mid-1960's Bahraini pan-Arab nationalists incited anti-British riots and called for union with other Arab states. The Khalifa dynasty maintained its control, however, and Bahrain remained under British protection until independence in 1971.

Bahrain is making vigorous attempts to diversify its industry in the light of diminishing oil reserves. Aluminum smelting has become one of its newer enterprises.

Benin

Official name: *People's Republic of Benin*
Area: *43,484 sq. mi., 112,622 sq. km.*
Population: *(1990 est.) 4,840,000*
Capital: *Porto-Novo (Pop., 1989, 150,000)*
Language: *French, African languages*
Religion: *Christian, Islam, traditional religions*
Currency unit: *Franc CFA (African Financial Community)*
National holiday: *Establishment of the People's Republic, Nov. 30*

Dahomey, renamed Benin in 1975, is a republic in west Africa, bounded on the east by Nigeria, on the south by the Atlantic Ocean, on the west by Togo, and on the north by Upper Volta and Niger. Dahomey received its independence from France in 1960.

The land. Most of Benin lies at an elevation of less than 1000 feet above sea level. Benin has a narrow, sandy coastline. Behind the coast are marshes and lagoons. The mainland begins in a low-lying clay plain that is intensively cultivated. There are grasslands in the north.

A low dividing ridge crosses the country at its greatest width. Rivers south of the ridge drain into the sea. To the north they are tributaries of the Volta and Niger rivers.

The climate in the coastal region is hot and wet. In the north it is dry from November to June, and rainy from June to November.

The people. The population of Benin includes many ethnic groups. The Fons live in the southern part of the country. The Nagots live in western Benin and in the districts of Porto-Novo and Abomey. The Baribas live in

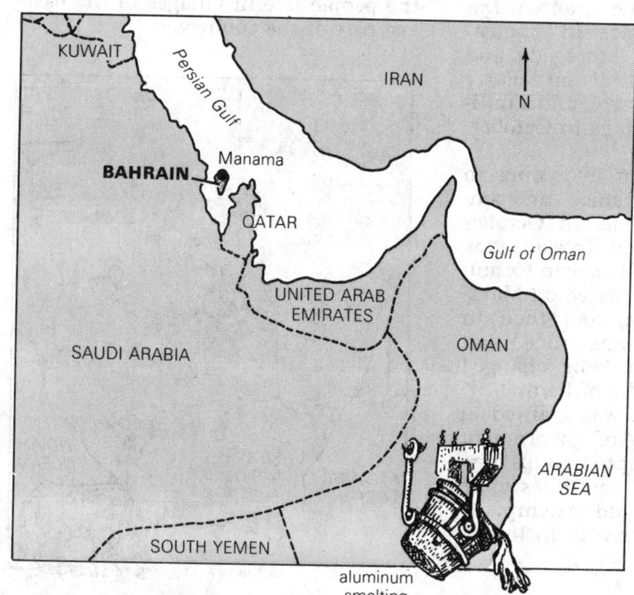

aluminum smelting

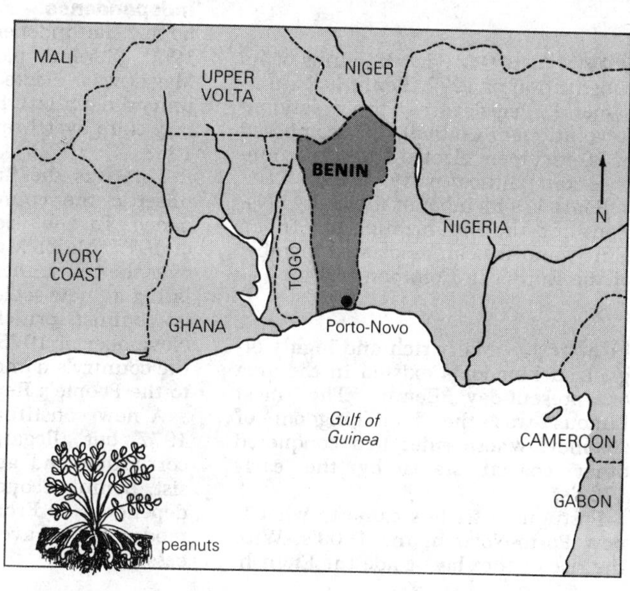

peanuts

A VOODOO CEREMONY *in Benin. Tribal leaders whiten their faces to frighten evil spirits.*

the north. Other ethnic groups are the Peuls, the Sanbas, the Azios, and the Adjas. There is a small European population.

Animism is followed by two-thirds of the population, Christianity by 20 percent, and Islam by 15 percent. Most people live in rural areas and 72 percent of the labor force is agricultural.

The port of Cotonou is Benin's largest city and economic center. Porto-Novo, the capital, is the second largest city.

Economy. Benin's economy depends on agriculture, while fishing and livestock raising contribute additional income. Corn, coffee, peanuts, and millet are the main crops. Mineral deposits of iron, gold, and chromite are largely unexploited. Industry is insignificant, but the processing of agricultural products is one of the goals for developing the economy and for establishing an export trade.

Trade consists almost exclusively of importing food and manufactured goods from France.

Government. By the terms of its constitution of 1977, Benin has a unicameral legislature, the National Revolutionary Council. It is composed of 79 members elected from the country's sole political party.

Benin is a member of the United Nations and the Organization of African Unity, and it is an associated member of the European Common Market.

History. Many rich and highly organized kingdoms existed in the area of present-day Benin. The most famous was the Fon kingdom of Abomey, whose ruler had conquered other coastal states by the early 1700's.

Portuguese traders came to what is now Porto-Novo in the 1600's. With the rise of the slave trade the English, Dutch, Spanish, and French also came to the area. European slave companies dealt largely with the foreign minister of the kingdom of Abomey.

French rule. In 1851 the French established themselves at Cotonou, and in 1890 hostilities broke out between France and Abomey. France established a protectorate over the area and exiled the king, although France continued to use tribal chiefs in administering the region. The boundaries of Dahomey were defined by 1898, and in 1904 Dahomey became part of the Federation of French West Africa.

Local conflicts dominated Dahomey's politics after World War II. In 1947 France introduced a territorial assembly, and Sourou-Migan Apithy, a southern leader, and Hubert Maga, a northerner, were elected to the French National Assembly. But regional movements did not solidify into a single national organization.

France granted Dahomey internal autonomy in 1957, and Apithy was elected prime minister. In 1958 Dahomey voted to become a member of the French Community.

Independence. France granted Dahomey its independence in August, 1960. Several parties merged, and Maga was elected president. Party unity did not last, however, and a military coup overthrew Maga in October, 1963.

This was the first of five coups to unsettle the country since independence. In the fifth one, in October of 1972, Major Mathieu Kerekou took over the government. He began formulating a "new society" based on Marxist-Leninist principles, and then in November of 1975 he announced that the country's name was being changed to the People's Republic of Benin.

A new constitution was granted in 1977, but allegations of government corruption and attempted coups persist. Benin's economy continues to be dependent on French aid. Attempts to modernize it have met with little success so far.

Botswana

Official name: *Republic of Botswana*
Area: *231,805 sq. mi., 600,372 sq. km.*
Population: *(1990 est.) 1,276,000*
Capital: *Gaborone (Pop., 1989, 175,000)*
Language: *English, Setswana*
Religion: *Traditional religions, Christian*
Currency unit: *Pula*
National holiday: *Independence Day, Sept. 30*

Botswana, a republic in southern Africa, is bordered on the northeast by Zimbabwe, on the east and south by South Africa, and on the west and north by South-West Africa. A large, sparsely populated country, Botswana was the British protectorate of Bechuanaland before receiving its independence in 1966.

The land. The Kalahari Desert occupies most of central and western Botswana. This dry region, covered with sand, grass, and thorn bush, has no rivers. The land in eastern Botswana is well watered and fertile. The Okavango River flows into northern Botswana and forms an area of swamps and marshes. The Molopo and Limpopo rivers run along the southern border.

Northern Botswana has a tropical climate. Farther south, the climate is generally hot and dry. The north receives an average of 27 inches of rain a year, but the south receives less than 9 inches.

The people. Most of Botswana's people are Bantu-speaking Africans. There are eight principal tribes in Botswana, each with its own traditional tribal area. The Bamangwato is the largest tribal group. Eighty percent of the people live in villages in the eastern part of the country.

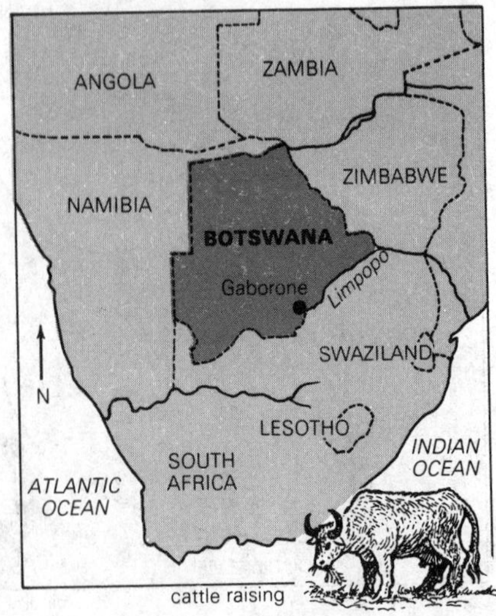

Economy. Cattle are the basis of Botswana's traditional economic life. Most of the people are herdsmen, but the mining of diamonds, copper, and nickel has been the most significant factor in the country's vast economic improvement since 1966. The basic food crops of Botswana include corn, sorghum, and peanuts.

Botswana's economy is closely linked with South Africa's. The two are joined in a customs union and many Botswanian workers migrate into South Africa.

Government. The head of state and chief executive of Botswana is the president, who is elected along with the legislature, the National Assembly. Assembly candidates must indicate their choice for president, and the presidential candidate with the greatest number of supporters elected to the assembly becomes president. A House of Chiefs, composed of members of the eight dominant tribes, serves as an advisory body to the National Assembly.

Botswana is a member of the United Nations, the Organization of African Unity, and the Commonwealth of Nations, and it is an associated state of the European Common Market.

History. Botswana's dry, thorn bush grassland attracted few immigrants until the early 1800's, when Tswana-speaking people entered the area. The Tswana were driven from the Transvaal, in present-day South Africa, by invading Zulus. In the years following, there were tribal wars and conflicts with Boer pioneers from the Transvaal.

British rule. In 1885 the British placed present-day Botswana under their protection. They viewed the area as economically useless, but strategically important because it served as an access route to the north, which was then unoccupied by whites. The land served also as a wedge between the Germans, then in South-West Africa, and their Boer allies, in the Transvaal.

In 1895 the British government incorporated the land south of the Molopo River into the Cape Colony, later a part of South Africa. The British instituted indirect rule in the protectorate, allowing the Botswana chiefs to retain their authority under the protection of the British Crown. The protectorate soon became economically dependent upon South Africa, into which the British had long assumed Bechuanaland would eventually be incorporated.

The protectorate progressed slowly until after World War II, when political change became rapid, spurred by the development of nationalism in other parts of Africa. A serious issue arose in 1948, when Seretse Khama, chief of the Bamangwato tribe, married a white Englishwoman. Although a tribal council had approved the marriage, the British refused to allow him to return to the country until 1956, after he surrendered his claim to the chieftaincy.

Independence. Botswana achieved domestic self-rule in 1960 and Seretse Khama became the country's elected president. An advocate of moderation, he founded the Bechuanaland Democratic Party. Britain granted the country its independence on September 30, 1966.

Seretse Khama ruled a democratic, nonracial government that clashed with the racist regimes in South Africa and Rhodesia (now Zimbabwe). Violence erupted in 1978 over the issue of Rhodesian forces in Botswana. Khama died in 1980 and was succeeded by Dr. Quett K. J. Masire.

Burkina Faso

See Upper Volta

Burundi

Official name: *Republic of Burundi*
Area: *10,747 sq. mi., 27,834 sq. km.*
Population: *(1990 est.) 5,474,000*
Capital: *Bujumbura (Pop., 1986, 272,600)*
Language: *Kirundi, French*
Religion: *Roman Catholic*
Currency unit: *Franc*
National holiday: *Independence Day, July 1*

Burundi, a small densely populated highland country in central Africa, is bordered on the north by Rwanda, on the east and south by Tanzania, on the southwest by Lake Tanganyika, and on the west by Zaire. Burundi was united with present-day Rwanda as the then Belgian-administered United Nations trust territory of Ruanda-Urundi until 1962, when it became independent.

The land. Plateaus, lying at elevations of between 2500 and 3500 feet, cover most of Burundi. The Great Rift Valley, which stretches along Burundi's western boundary, is bordered by peaks above 7000 feet. The country's land surface is badly eroded, and soil erosion is a basic problem. The climate is temperate.

The people. Two tribal groups are dominant in Burundi, the Hutu and the Tusi, or Watusi. The Hutu, constituting about 85 percent of the population, are mostly farmers. The Tusi, who make up about 15 percent of the total, are traditionally herdsmen and warriors. The Tusi long dominated the Hutu and provided the country's ruling group.

Economy. Burundi is chiefly an agricultural country, and coffee is the main export. Cotton and rice are also grown.

Government. Burundi's republic is ruled by a military government with no legislature. The president is responsible to a 31-member Military Committee for National Salvation.

History. The Tusi, who probably came south from the area of Ethiopia, overran Burundi and Rwanda in the 1500's. A Tusi aristocracy headed by a *mwami,* or king, established its rule, and the Hutu became a subject people.

In 1890 Germany seized the area of present-day Burundi and Rwanda, which became known as Ruanda-Urundi. Belgium occupied the region in 1916 during World War I, and after the war Ruanda-Urundi became a Belgian mandate under the League of Nations. Ruanda-Urundi became a UN trust territory in 1946.

Burundi became independent on July 1, 1962. Moderate Tusi and Hutu formed the National Union and Progress Party, which then became the majority party in Burundi. Mwami Mwambutsa IV, who had come to the throne in 1915, became chief of state.

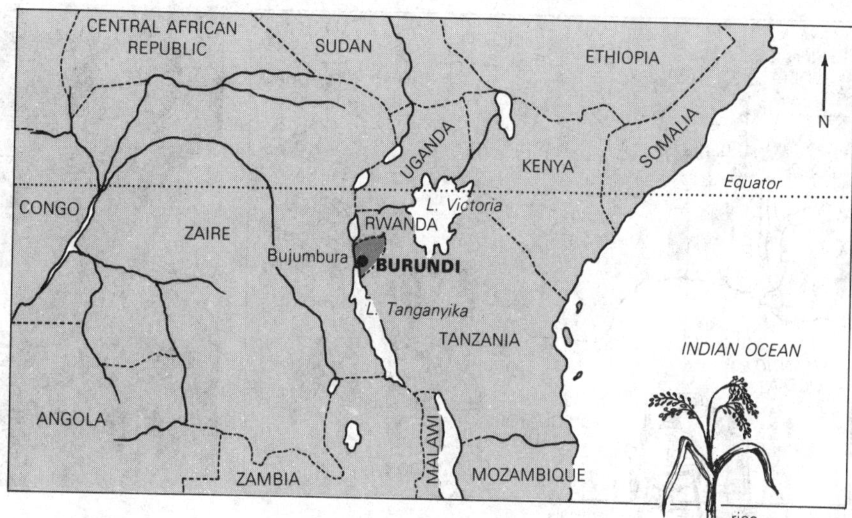

In 1966 the monarchy was overthrown and a republic was established. Rivalry between the elite Tusi and the discontented Hutu erupted into open and bloody civil war in 1972–1973. Mass executions followed. The Supreme Military Council under Jean-Baptiste Bagaza came to power in 1976, but it was overthrown in 1987 by Pierre Buyoya. Buyoya and the Military Committee for National Salvation have restored religious freedom and freed political prisoners.

In August, 1988, a bloody skirmish occurred between the Hutu and Tutsi tribes, exhibiting the bitter rivalry that still exists between them. Thousands of Hutu refugees fled to neighboring Rwanda.

Cameroon

Official name: *Federal Republic of Cameroon*
Area: *183,568 sq. mi., 475,442 sq. km.*
Population: *(1990 est.) 11,109,000*
Capital: *Yaoundé (Pop., 1989, 800,000)*
Language: *French, English, African languages*
Religion: *Christian, Islam, traditional religions*
Currency unit: *Franc CFA (African Financial Community)*
National holiday: *Independence Day, May 20*

Cameroon, a federal republic in western Africa, is bordered on the northeast by Chad, on the east by the Central African Republic, on the southeast by the Congo Republic, on the south by Gabon and Equatorial Guinea (Río Muni), and on the west by the Atlantic Ocean and Nigeria. Cameroon is a federation of two former United Nations trust territories—one French-administered, now East Cameroon, and the other under British control, West Cameroon.

The land. Cameroon has a varied landscape. In the north are broad grasslands. In the center of the country is the Adamawa Plateau, with elevations of between 2600 and 5000 feet above sea level. In the south is a densely forested plateau averaging 2000 feet in elevation. The volcanic Mt. Cameroon, which rises over 13,300 feet, is near the coast. The coastal region is forested and marshy.

The climate throughout the country is hot and humid. Some regions in the south receive as much as 180 inches of rain each year.

The people. Many quite different tribes live in Cameroon. Bamileke, Kirdi, and Fulani peoples live in central and northern Cameroon. Bantu-speaking people inhabit parts of southern Cameroon. Some pygmies live in the forests of the south. Cameroon's largest cities include Yaoundé, the capital, and Douala, the major port.

Economy. Cameroon has a variety of resources and products. Cacao, coffee, cotton, and bananas are grown. Rubber and timber are also important products.

Oil production began in 1978 and new deposits of gas and oil were discovered in 1979. One-third of the gross national product comes from agricultural products, and one-quarter from industrial products that include aluminum, paper, and chemicals. There is little hydroelectric power for the developing industries.

In 1986 imports cost $1.5 billion and exports earned $1.11 billion. The chief exports are cacao and coffee. Cameroon's imports include manufactured goods, machinery, transportation equipment, chemicals, and petroleum products.

Cameroon has close economic relations with France, and it has a customs union with some of its neighbors.

Government. The federal government of Cameroon is headed by a president who has strong executive powers and is popularly elected to a five-year term. Legislative powers rest with the Federal National Assembly. The assembly has 180 members elected to five-year terms by universal suffrage.

Cameroon belongs to the United Nations and the Organization of African Unity, and is an associated state of the European Common Market.

History. Cameroon was the original home of the agricultural Bantu-speaking people, who swept westward across central Africa in prehistoric times. Between the 1600's and 1800's, the Portuguese and British established trading posts in the area. In 1884 Germany established the Kamerun protectorate, which covered about the same area as the present-day republic.

After World War I the German protectorate was divided into separate French and British mandates under the League of Nations. The two mandates later became UN trust territories. France acquired the larger share of the former German territory. Britain acquired two disconnected land areas. The one in the north was inhabited by Muslim Fulani, who had a feudal system closely allied to that of northern Nigeria. The part in the southwest was a humid forest area with Bantu-speaking inhabitants.

France administered its territory as part of the Federation of French Equatorial Africa. East Cameroon received internal autonomy from France in 1958, and full independence in 1960 under Ahmadou Ahidjo. Britain administered its territory with Nigeria, using local chiefs and permitting some representation in Nigerian assemblies.

In 1961 the northern region expressed the desire to remain with Nigeria, but the southern region voted to join the Republic of Cameroon. A federal republic was formed on October 1.

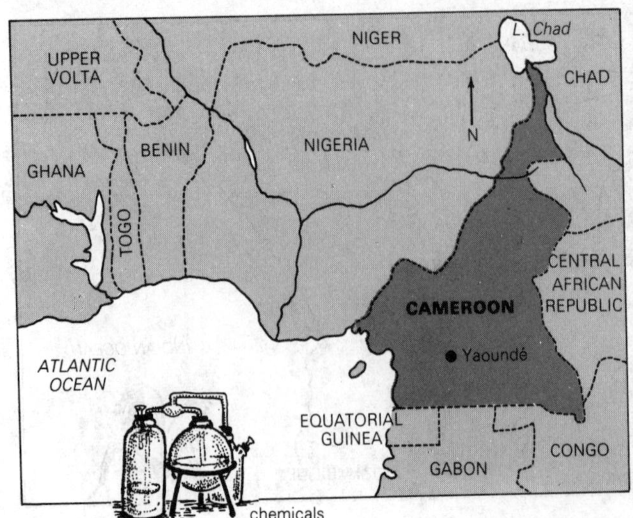

AN OLD MAN *of northern Cameroon. The pipe is typical of the region. Despite its diverse origins, Cameroon is a stable country.*

In 1972 East and West Cameroon were joined into a united republic by popular referendum. Ahidjo was president of Cameroon from 1961 until his resignation in 1982. He was replaced by Paul Biya, his prime minister.

In 1986 a toxic volcanic gas eruption from Lake Nios killed over 1500 people. International aid and scientific teams helped deal with the situation.

Cape Verde

Official name: *Republic of Cape Verde*
Area: *1,557 sq. mi., 4,033 sq. km.*
Population: *(1990 est.) 375,000*
Capital: *Praia (Pop., 1989, 25,000)*
Language: *Portuguese, Crioulo*
Religion: *Roman Catholic*
Currency unit: *Escudo*

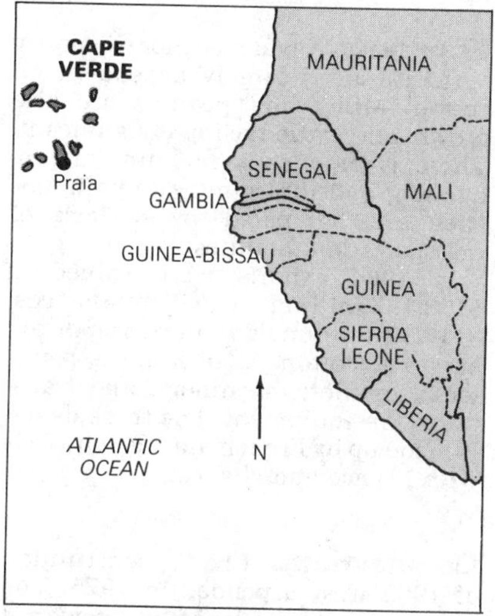

The country of Cape Verde consists of a group of islands lying in the central Atlantic Ocean some 300 miles west of Senegal on the western coast of Africa. There are ten islands and several islets in the group.

The land and people. The islands are volcanic in origin and are mountainous, rocky, and barren. The climate is extremely hot and dry. The majority of the population is of mixed African and Portuguese descent. About one-third is African, and a very small proportion is European. Portuguese is the official language, but a Creole dialect of Portuguese and other languages is widely spoken. Roman Catholicism is the predominant religion.

Two-thirds of the labor force is agricultural and 80 percent of the people live in rural areas. The population's density and illiteracy are both high.

Economy. The islands have no exploitable mineral resources, and their soil is generally too dry and poor to support vegetation. Bananas, coffee, nuts, oil seeds, and corn are raised, and some salt is produced. Fish are abundant off the coasts and some livestock is grazed. The islands have several good ports, and the refueling of ships is the main economic activity.

Trade is limited. In 1981 imports cost $104 million and exports earned $6 million. Coffee, fish, bananas, and nuts are exported, and foodstuffs, textiles, and building materials are imported. Most trade is with mainland Portugal.

Government. The Cape Verde Islands became independent of Portugal on July 5, 1975. The constitution, approved in 1981, provides for a president elected by the 86-member People's National Assembly. The sole legal party is the African Party for the Independence of Cape Verde.

Cape Verde is a member of the United Nations and the Organization of African Unity.

History. The Cape Verde Islands were uninhabited when they were discovered in 1456 by the Portuguese. The Portuguese began to settle the islands in the late 1400's and early 1500's, and African slaves began to be imported. In 1587 a governor was appointed for the colony, and in the 1600's and 1700's settlers from Spain, Italy, and Britain joined the Portuguese on the islands. The colony thrived on plantation agriculture and trading.

In 1951 the colony was made an overseas province of Portugal, and in 1961 the islanders received full Portuguese citizenship.

Since independence, Cape Verde has been severely plagued with devastating droughts and famines, especially in 1978. The banana crop, the nation's most significant cash crop, has suffered considerably during this period.

Central African Republic

Official name: *Central African Republic*
Area: *240,535 sq. mi., 622,980 sq. km.*
Population: *(1990 est.) 2,879,000*
Capital: *Bangui (Pop., 1989 est., 300,000)*
Language: *French, Sangho and other African languages*
Religion: *Protestant, Catholic, traditional*
Currency unit: *Franc CFA (African Financial Community)*
National holiday: *Independence Day, Dec. 1*

The Central African Republic, a landlocked country in central Africa, is bounded on the north by Chad, on the east by Sudan, on the south by the People's Republic of the Congo and by Zaire, and on the west by Cameroon. Before its independence from France, the territory was known as Ubangi-Shari because of its location near the Ubangi and Shari (Chari) rivers.

The land. The Central African Republic lies on a plateau with an average elevation of 2000 feet above sea level. In the east are mountains with heights ranging up to almost 4600 feet. There are forests in the south, but savanna woodlands and grasslands cover most of the country. Tributaries of the Shari River in the north, and of the Ubangi River to the south, flow through the country.

Because of the altitude, the climate is quite mild. Temperatures average between 70°F and 80°F.

The people. The Central African Republic is a sparsely populated country inhabited by peoples of the Mandjia-Baya, Banda, M'Baka, and Zande tribes. The people are mostly farmers.

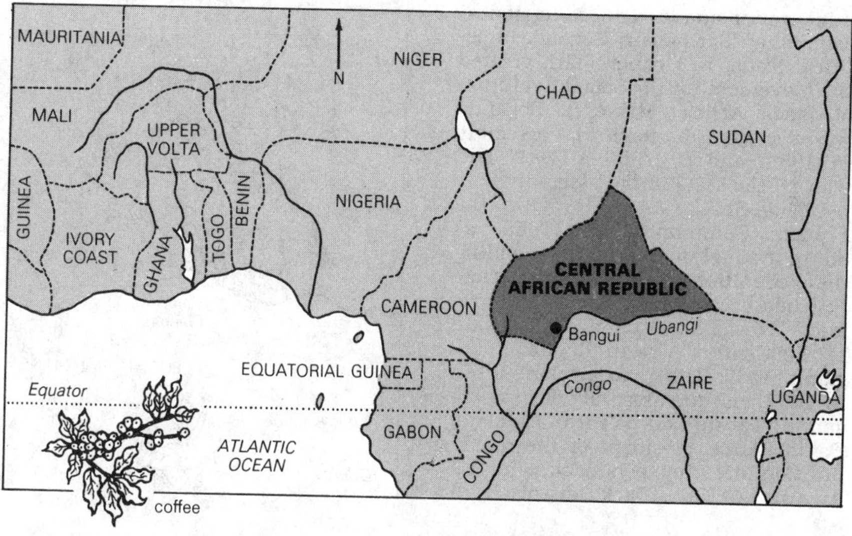

A few thousand Europeans live in Bangui and in other smaller towns.

Economy. The Central African Republic traditionally has been an agricultural country. The economy is sluggish, but recent increases in cotton production have highlighted the nation's hopes for immediate improvement. Coffee is also an important crop.

Timber and mineral resources are largely unexploited, with the exception of diamonds. Diamonds were mined extensively, beginning in the early 1960's. They added greatly to the country's wealth, but within ten years deposits were nearly exhausted.

In 1984 imports cost $139.6 million and exports earned $145.2 million. The Central African Republic is a member of a customs union that includes Cameroon, Chad, the Congo (Brazzaville), and Gabon.

Government. The Central African Republic is presently headed by a Military Committee of National Redress, which, in 1981, suspended a newly approved constitution.

The nation is a member of the United Nations and the Organization of African Unity, and it is an associated state of the European Common Market.

History. Little is known of the early history of the present-day Central African Republic. The French entered the region in the mid-1800's and gave it the name Ubangi-Shari. They met with little opposition from the tribesmen who lived there.

In 1899 France permitted private companies to develop the region. Company abuses led to loss of life from forced labor and disease, and loss of capital because of inefficient management. In 1910 France united Ubangi-Shari with present-day Chad, the Congo (Brazzaville), and Gabon in the Federation of French Equatorial Africa.

In 1946 France reorganized the administration and introduced territorial assemblies. Barthelemy Boganda, a political leader in Ubangi-Shari, created the Movement for the Social Evolution of Black Africa (MESAN). Boganda was elected to the territorial assembly in 1952, and by 1956 MESAN had won all the seats in the assembly.

Ubangi-Shari voted to join the French Community in 1958 as an individual member, thus ending the Federation of Equatorial Africa. Boganda became the nation's first premier. Ubangi-Shari changed its name to the Central African Republic. Boganda was killed in an airplane crash in 1959, and the assembly elected Boganda's cousin and political associate, David Dacko, president of the republic. Complete independence came on August 13, 1960. Dacko dissolved all opposition parties in 1962.

In 1965 Colonel Jean Bedel Bokassa, deposed Dacko and assumed the position of chief of state. In 1976 he proclaimed the country to be a monarchy, the Central African Empire with himself as emperor.

Bokassa ruled the country harshly and tyrannically from 1976 to 1979. A French-aided coup in 1979 restored the republic with Dacko as president. Another coup in 1981 removed Dacko and instituted a military government.

Chad

Official name: *Republic of Chad*
Area: *495,800 sq. mi., 1,284,000 sq. km.*
Population: *(1990 est.) 5,053,000*
Capital: *Ndjamena (Pop., 1989, 551,700)*
Language: *French, Arabic, Sara*
Religion: *Islam, traditional religions*
Currency unit: *Franc CFA (African Financial Community)*
National holiday: *Independence Day, Jan. 11*

Chad, a large, landlocked republic in central Africa, is bounded on the north by Libya, on the east by Sudan, on the south by the Central African Republic and Cameroon, and on the west by Nigeria and Niger. The country derives its name from Lake Chad, which is located on its western border.

The land. Most of Chad is a vast plain. The northern region of the country forms part of the Sahara. Grasslands cover central and southern Chad. The country's lowest point is the dry Bodele Depression, in north-central Chad. In the extreme north is the Tibasti Massif, with elevations of about 11,000 feet. The country's most important rivers are the Shari and the Logone.

Northern Chad is hot and dry and receives less than ten inches of rain a year. The climate in the south is more tropical, and rainfall averages about 40 inches a year.

The people. Chad is a sparsely populated country. The composition of Chad's population differs in each part of the country. Arabs and Hamitic people live in the north. People of the Sara tribe, the largest tribal group in Chad, live in the south.

Most of the people are illiterate, and 90 percent of the labor force is absorbed by agriculture and herding. Chad's major cities are Ndjamena, the capital, Sarh, and Moundou.

Economy. Chad's economy, mostly agricultural, is largely dependent on cotton. Millet and peanuts are also grown, and cattle raising is significant. There is practically no mineral production, and the country's few industries are hampered by a lack of transportation facilities.

In 1984 exports were valued at $113.15 million and imports cost $114.38 million. The most important export is cotton. Chad imports petroleum, textiles, machinery, and transportation equipment. The trade deficit is made up by French aid. Most trade is with France and Nigeria.

Government. Chad's constitution of 1962 was suspended in 1975. The country is now governed by a powerful president who heads a military regime without a legislative body.

Chad is a member of the United Na-

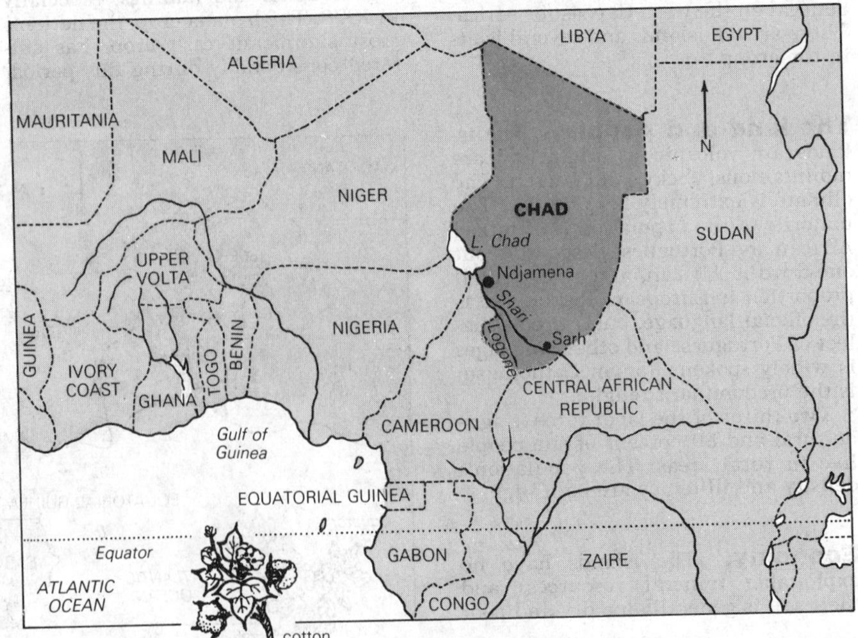

JACQUES JANOUX/PETER ARNOLD

MUD VILLAGE (above) *of Chad's Massa tribe. Independent in 1960—the anniversary is celebrated in Abeche* (below)*—Chad has been victim of a civil war between north and south.*

CARL FRANK/PHOTO RESEARCHERS

tions and the Organization of African Unity, and it is an associated state of the European Common Market.

History. The area that is now Chad was for many centuries an important crossroads. From about 200 B.C. to 1000 A.D. its inhabitants maintained close contact with the people of the Nile Valley, with whom they shared a fairly similar culture.

Christianity flourished in central Chad in about 300 A.D. Later, nomadic peoples from Darfur, in Sudan, overran Chad, dispersed the indigenous inhabitants, and created an empire known as Kanem in the region near Lake Chad. In the 1000's Islam penetrated the area. From that time on the peoples of Chad strengthened their commercial ties with the peoples of the Mediterranean coast.

In the period from about 1000 to 1600 many internal and foreign wars occurred. As a result, the Kanem empire moved its center to Bornu, on the southwestern side of Lake Chad in what is now northern Nigeria.

Both the sultanate of Bagirmi and the Wadai empire became powerful in Chad. They maintained their control until the late 1800's. At that time Rabih, a warlord and slave trader from Sudan, gained control of Chad.

The French, who had established themselves in Chad in the 1890's, defeated Rabih in 1900 and proceeded to conquer all of Chad. The present boundaries of Chad were established in 1913. In 1920 Chad became a member of the Federation of French Equatorial Africa.

During World War II Chad supported Free France and contained important Allied bases. Postwar politics were at first largely controlled by the French. After 1958, however, African leaders rapidly gained prominence. France gave Chad its independence in August, 1960, and François Tombalbaye became the country's first president. Tombalbaye was assassinated in the coup of 1975.

Libyan-backed northern Muslims have waged guerrilla warfare against the Bantu-dominated governments of Chad since 1966. They staged an ill-fated major offensive in 1979.

A coup in 1979, backed by Nigeria, ousted the military government. The country became the scene of a bloody civil war from 1979 to 1982, as opposing factions fought for control of the government. Considerable tension still exists in Chad. The country is currently ruled by another military government.

Libyan-backed supporters of former President Goukouni invaded Chad in 1983 and were able to occupy the northern third of the country. President Hissen Habré was supported by France and the United States and succeeded in removing most of the Libyan influence in 1987.

Comoros

Official name: *Federal and Islamic Republic of the Comoros*
Area: *719 sq. mi., 1,862 sq. km.*
Population: *(1990 est.) 460,000*
Capital: *Moroni (Pop., 1989, 18,000)*
Language: *Malagasy, French*
Religion: *Islam*
Currency unit: *Franc CFA (African Financial Community)*

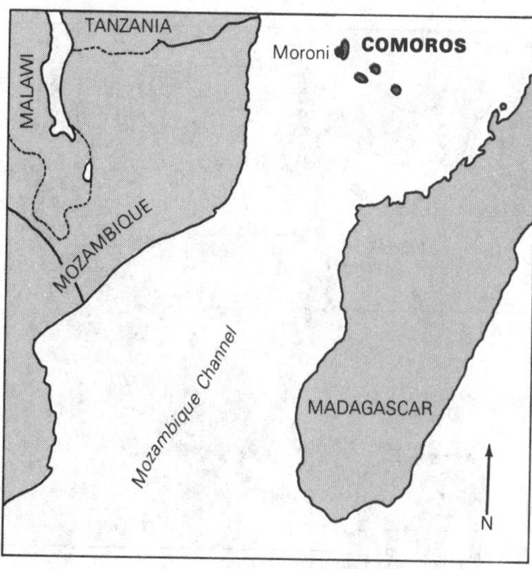

Comoros lies in the Mozambique Channel between the eastern coast of Africa and the island of Madagascar. The territory consists of three main islands—Anjouan is 164 square miles, Mohéli is 112 square miles, and Grande Comore, the northernmost, and on which the capital, Moroni, is located, is 443 square miles.

The land and people. The islands are of volcanic origin and consist of mountainous or deeply dissected plateau cores ringed by narrow coastal plains. Coral reefs surround the islands. The climate is tropical.

Most of the people of Comoros are a mixture of Arab and African stocks, but there are Arabs, Indians, and Europeans. They are mostly Muslims. The country has high rates of population density and illiteracy. Most of the national labor force is agricultural.

Economy. The islands have almost no mineral resources, but their soil is very rich, and agriculture is the mainstay of the economy. Rice, corn, vegetables, and fruits are raised for local consumption. The chief commercial crops are vanilla, spices, coffee, sisal, and coconuts. Industry is limited to the processing of the agricultural products of the islands.

About one-third of the country's land is owned by Europeans, who exploit it and deprive Comoros of the income derived from it. French economic aid is vital to the economy.

Trade, carried on chiefly with France and the United States, is quite insignificant.

Government. Comoros's constitution of 1978 provides for a 38-member unicameral legislature, the Federal Assembly. The president, head of the government, appoints governors to each of the islands.

Comoros is a member of the United Nations.

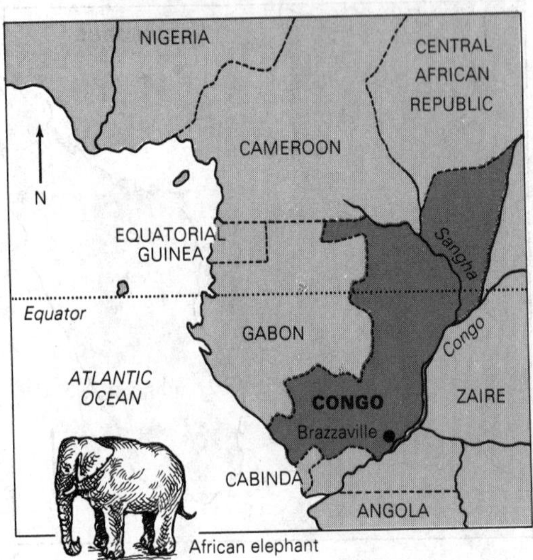

African elephant

History. The Comoro Islands have been known since ancient times. They were conquered by Arabs in the 600's. In the 1500's they were visited by the Portuguese, French, and Dutch, and the French established a settlement. In the 1800's the Arab kingdoms on the islands were attacked by Malagasy armies from Madagascar, and years of warfare followed. By the 1900's the rulers of the islands had ceded authority to France.

The French expanded agricultural production by opening plantations. In 1912 the islands were joined with Madagascar into a single French colony. In 1946 their status was changed to that of an overseas territory, and they were granted internal autonomy.

On July 6, 1976, the islands declared their final independence from French rule. The island of Mayotte opposed independence and chose to maintain its ties with France. (The inhabitants of Mayotte are mainly Christian, while most of the Comoros population is Muslim.) The separation of Mayotte and the French domination of the economy of Comoros continue to be sources of international and domestic tension.

Congo

Official name: *People's Republic of the Congo*
Area: *132,000 sq. mi., 342,000 sq. km.*
Population: *(1990 est.) 2,305,000*
Capital: *Brazzaville (Pop., 1989, 600,000)*
Language: *French, African languages*
Religion: *Christian, traditional religions*
Currency unit: *Franc CFA (African Financial Community)*
National holiday: *National Day, Aug. 15*

The People's Republic of the Congo, in central Africa on the equator, is bordered on the north by the Central African Republic, on the east and southeast by Zaire, on the southwest by the Cabinda region of Angola and the Atlantic Ocean, on the west by Gabon, and on the northwest by Cameroon. The Congo, formerly a territory in French Equatorial Africa, received its independence from France in 1960.

The land. The Congo has a varied geography. Along the coast is a relatively cool and practically treeless plain. Farther inland is the wet and forested Mayombé Escarpment, which is cut by the Kouilou River. The Niari Basin, a region of woodlands and grassy plains, lies east of the escarpment; north of it are the grassy Batéké plateaus. The Congo and Ubangi rivers form the eastern border. The country has a hot, tropical climate.

The people. There are many different ethnic groups in the Congo. The Bacongo people make up almost half the population, and the Bateke make up another 20 percent. About half the people are Christian, half are animists, and there is a small Muslim minority.

Most of the people live in rural areas. The country's major cities include Brazzaville, the capital and major river port, and Pointe Noire, a port city on the Atlantic Ocean.

Economy. The economy of the Congo is based largely on agriculture, and about 80 percent of the laborers are farmers. Bananas, manioc, peanuts, rice, tropical fruits, and corn are grown for local consumption. Forestry is becoming very important to the Congo's economy.

The Congo has a well developed transportation system. The Congo-Ocean railroad links Brazzaville and Pointe Noire, and the Congo and Ubangi rivers provide excellent water routes for the Congo and neighboring countries.

The largest source of income is from mining. Rich potash deposits were depleted by 1977, but offshore oil was discovered in 1973 and its production and refining have prospered since then. There are also rich deposits of unexploited iron ore. Some industrial development has resulted. In 1977 most industry was nationalized.

The Congo's balance of trade has greatly improved; its main trading partner is France. Imports cost the Congo $630 million in 1986, while exports earned $650 million. The Congo imports machinery and consumer goods, and its exports include timber, diamonds, and petroleum.

Government. According to the Congo's socialist constitution of 1979, the country is governed by a president and a prime minister. Legislative authority rests with the 153-member National People's Assembly, elected from a single political party.

The Congo is a member of the United Nations and the Organization of African Unity, and it is an associated state of the European Common Market.

History. The Balali people, an offshoot of the Bacongo kingdom centered in nearby Angola, overran the M'Bochi and Vili people living in the present-day Congo many centuries ago. Portuguese explorers had begun trading with these people in the 1400's. The original trade in gold and ivory was replaced by the slave trade. British, Dutch, and French companies joined the trade until slaving was abolished in the 1800's.

French rule. The French explorer Pierre Savorgnan de Brazza reached the area in 1873, and signed an agreement with the Batéké king. The French obtained European recognition of their influence over the region of the present-day Congo at the Berlin Conference on African Affairs in 1884.

The French called the area Middle Congo. In 1910 France joined the Middle Congo with present-day Gabon, Chad, and the Central African Republic to form the Federation of French Equatorial Africa.

France gave private companies control over developing the country, but company rule was harsh. Africans were deprived of legal rights, and in the 1920's African political dissatisfaction was expressed in the rise of various local religious sects. The most important sect was the Matswa movement among the Bacongo.

The Middle Congo supported Free France during World War II. In 1944, in gratitude for its support, France held a conference to discuss colonial reforms in Brazzaville. Shortly after, the Middle Congo became an overseas territory within the French Union, and many political parties developed, largely along tribal lines.

Independence. In the mid-1950's Fulbert Youlou became the dominant political figure in the country. Youlou, a Bacongo and a Roman Catholic priest, had gained the support of the Matswa movement. In 1958 the Middle Congo agreed to join the French Community and change its name to People's Republic of the Congo. In 1959 Youlou became the first president; the Republic of Congo became independent on August 15, 1960.

Since the military coup of 1963, the Congo has come increasingly under the influence of the communist nations, especially China and the Soviet Union. The Congolese Worker's Party is the dominant political force in the country now. Nonetheless, French influence, especially on economics, remains very strong.

Cyprus

Official name: *Republic of Cyprus*
Area: *3,572 sq. mi., 9,251 sq. km.*
Population: *(1990 est.) 708,000*
Capital: *Nicosia (Pop., 1986 est., 163,700)*
Language: *Greek, Turkish*
Religion: *Orthodox Christian, Islam*
Currency unit: *Pound*
National holiday: *Independence Day, Aug. 16*

Cyprus, an independent island republic in the eastern part of the Mediterranean Sea, lies about 40 miles south of Turkey.

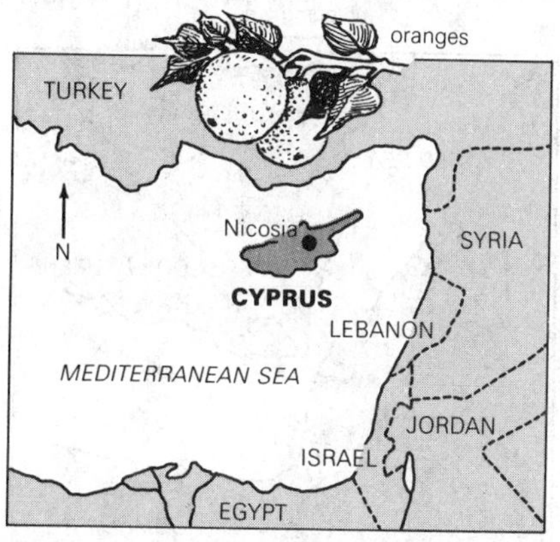

The land.

The island of Cyprus is mountainous. Two ranges rim the coasts—the Kyrenia Mountains in the north and the Olympus Mountains in the south. A wide, fertile plain occupies the center of the island. Summers are hot and dry, and winters are cool with occasional rain.

The people.

About four-fifths of the Cypriots are Greek Christians, and about one-fifth are Turkish Muslims. The island's population is concentrated in the central plains, especially around Nicosia, and along the southern coast, in the port cities of Limassol and Famagusta.

Cyprus is densely populated, with about 175 people per square mile; over half live in rural areas. Just less than half of the labor force is employed in manufacturing, while about one-third is agricultural.

Economy.

Copper, asbestos, and iron mined in the Olympus Mountains are among Cyprus's principal exports. Vegetables, oranges, and wines produced for the European market are also important. Wheat, olives, and carobs (a cattle fodder) are grown. The island has not developed any heavy industry, but there are many light manufacturing plants. Tourism is an important source of income.

Cyprus has a strong economy, but its balance of trade is unfavorable. In 1985 imports cost $1.13 billion while exports earned only $418.9 million. Most trade is with Britain and other Western European nations.

Government.

The Republic of Cyprus was politically separated in 1975 from the northern Turkish-controlled part of the island, seized in 1974. The Turkish Cypriot state, created by referendum, also has a republican form of government. Both are governed by separate presidents and elected legislative assemblies.

Cyprus is a member of the United Nations, the Commonwealth of Nations, and the Council of Europe.

History.

People have lived on Cyprus since before 4000 B.C. The ancient Greeks traded with Cyprus and established colonies on the island. From about 800 B.C. to modern times, Cyprus was ruled by whatever nation dominated the adjacent seas. Phoenicians, Assyrians, Persians, Romans, Byzantines, Arabs, Crusaders, and Venetians all occupied the island.

In 1571 the Ottoman Turks conquered Cyprus and held it until 1878, when Britain took control. During the period of Ottoman rule a Turkish-speaking Muslim minority developed alongside the original Greek-speaking Christian majority. In 1914, at the beginning of World War I, Britain formally annexed Cyprus from the Ottoman Empire, an ally of Germany. In 1925 the island became a British Crown colony.

During the years of Venetian and Ottoman government, the island underwent an economic and cultural decline, but as a British colony it experienced a revival. With this revival came an awakening of national consciousness and a rising demand on the part of Greek Cypriots for union with Greece, *enosis*, a demand that Turkish Cypriots opposed. In 1955 Greek Cypriots began a guerrilla war against the British.

Independence. In 1959, after years of bloody fighting, an agreement signed by Britain, Greece, and Turkey granted Cyprus independence with strict safeguards for the rights of the Turkish minority.

MISSION OF CYPRUS TO THE UN

LEADER OF THE GREEKS *on Cyprus, Archbishop Makarios was president until 1977.*

Archbishop Makarios, head of the Cypriot Orthodox Church and leader of the Greek community, became president, with a Turkish Cypriot leader as vice president. Friction between the Greek and Turkish communities paralyzed the new government.

In December of 1963, Makarios proposed constitutional changes that the Turkish minority felt would reduce their rights. This disagreement led to an armed conflict between Greek and Turkish Cypriots; Greece and Turkey intervened. A UN peacekeeping force finally mediated a cease-fire, but a satisfactory solution to the problem was not reached.

Makarios was temporarily deposed in a 1974 coup, and Turkey invaded the island. The Turkish Cypriot state was created in 1975, declared itself a republic in 1983, and adopted a constitution and held elections in 1985. Since Makarios's death in 1977, there have been renewed attempts to reunify the two sectors of Cyprus.

Djibouti

Official name: *Republic of Djibouti*
Area: *8,996 sq. mi., 23,300 sq. km.*
Population: *(1988 est.) 500,000*
Capital: *Djibouti (Pop., 1989, 200,000)*
Language: *French, Somali, Afar, Arabic*
Religion: *Muslim*
Currency unit: *Franc*

The country of Djibouti, formerly the French Territory of Afars and Issas, is bordered on the north by Ethiopia and the Red Sea; on the east by the Bab al Mandeb Strait, the Gulf of Tadjoura (an inlet of the Gulf of Aden), and the Somali Republic; and on the south and west by Ethiopia.

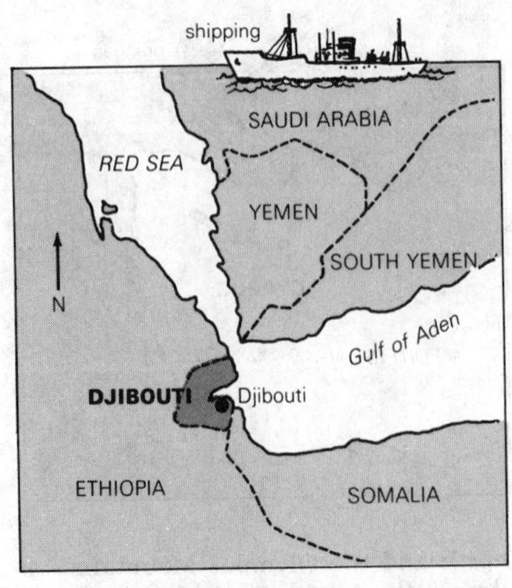

The land. Most of the country is desert. The interior is a low, rolling desert basin. North of the Gulf of Tadjoura, the Mabla and Gouda mountains rise to a peak of just under 6000 feet. Their slopes hold the territory's only forests. The coastline is low and flat except along the southern shore of the Tadjoura gulf, which is steep. The climate is hot and dry.

The people. The original inhabitants of the region are the Issa Somalis and the Hamitic Afar people. There are now large minorities of Arabs and Europeans. Almost all the people are Muslim, and they speak French, Afar, Arabic, and Somali. Most of the Issas and Afars are seminomadic, and the principal cities of the country are along the coast.

Only 20 percent of the population is literate; 80 percent is unemployed. One-third of the labor force is employed in commerce, and two-thirds of the people live in urban areas.

Economy. The country's strategic location at the mouth of the Red Sea insures its economic importance. Its only known mineral resource is salt, which is largely unexploited. Herding, especially of goats, is the chief activity of the people. Some farming is possible with irrigation near the coast. Vegetables, melons, and dates are the main crops. Shipbuilding and construction are the only industries.

Trade is the mainstay of the economy. A modern port at Djibouti, the capital, is an important refueling, storage, and distribution point for Red Sea and Indian Ocean commerce. Most of the country's own small trade consists of the importing of necessities from France.

Government. After 115 years of French rule, Afars and Issas became the independent nation of Djibouti on June 27, 1977.

The republic is ruled by a president aided by a prime minister and a cabinet. There is a unicameral legislative Parliament, with 65 elected members equally representing Afars and Issas.

Djibouti is a member of the United Nations, the Organization of African Unity, and the Arab League.

History. The region has been inhabited for many years by the seminomadic Issas and Afars. In 1862 Afar chiefs ceded power to the French government; by 1869 several French trading settlements and ports that had been established on the coast were prosperous.

Treaties signed in the 1880's with the Afars and the Issas extended French authority, and in 1896 the territory became known as the colony of French Somaliland. Djibouti rapidly became an important port and refueling station; in the early 1900's a railroad was built between it and the capital of Ethiopia.

In 1946 the colony was made an overseas territory, and in 1956 it was granted internal self-government. In the 1950's and 1960's France initiated programs to improve education and welfare in the territory and to broaden its economy. In 1967, acting on a request by the territorial assembly, the French National Assembly changed the name French Somaliland to the more accurate French Territory of Afars and Issas. In a 1967 referendum the people voted to remain under French control.

Ethiopia, ethnically related to the Afars, and Somalia, ethnically related to the Issas, clashed over territorial disputes, as well as over the fairness of the vote that deprived both of the possibility of absorbing the colony. In 1976 and 1978 there were more hostilities, with Ethiopia and Somalia charging each other with interference in Djibouti's internal affairs. In 1978 Ethiopia drew on Soviet aid and Cuban troops, while Somalia was assisted by North and South Yemen. As Ethiopia and Somalia waged war, Djibouti accepted large numbers of refugees and immigrants fleeing the confrontation. It welcomed French and U.S. military protection.

French troops are currently stationed in Djibouti. France also gives extensive financial aid to insure the new country's economic stability until the crisis is over and it is no longer threatened.

NATIVE TRANSPORT *passing along the Rue de Paris in Djibouti. Independent since 1977, the territory had been a French colony since the 1860's and is still sustained by France.*

PAT MILLER/MONKMEYER

Egypt

Official name: *Arab Republic of Egypt*
Area: *386,661 sq. mi., 1,001,450 sq. km.*
Population: *(1990 est.) 56,219,000*
Capital: *Cairo (Pop., 1986, 6,325,000)*
Language: *Arabic*
Religion: *Islam*
Currency unit: *Pound*
National holiday: *National Day, Oct. 6*

Egypt is an independent country in northern Africa. In 1958 Egypt and Syria joined to form the United Arab Republic. Syria withdrew from the union in 1961, but Egypt continued to use the name until September of 1971, when a new constitution was adopted. The country is a major center of Arab culture and a leading force in the movement for unity in the Arab world.

Egypt is bordered on the north by the Mediterranean Sea; on the east by Israel and the Red Sea; on the south by Sudan; and on the west by Libya. In 1967, during the Arab-Israeli war, Israel occupied the Gaza Strip and almost all of the Sinai region of Egypt.

The Sinai was returned to Egypt in 1982. Taba, a small disputed beach area located in the Sinai, was returned in 1989.

The land. Egypt consists of two principal regions that are divided by the Suez Canal. East of the canal is the Sinai Peninsula, a rugged desert country with only a few oases. The region west of the canal is mainly desert.

The Nile River flows northward through the western region. The fertile valley formed by the river is between two and ten miles wide. In the north the valley widens into a delta through which the Nile reaches the Mediterranean Sea. The desert begins at the edge of the valley. The flow of the Nile is regulated by several large dams that provide maximum water for irrigation.

Summers in Egypt are very hot and dry, and winters are warm and dry. A little winter rain falls in the area of Alexandria, in the north.

The people. The population of Egypt is concentrated in the Nile valley and its delta. The country has a high rate of population growth, about 2.3 percent a year during the 1970's. The government employs an active birth control program. Over half of the people live in rural areas, but almost 99 percent of the people live in less than four percent of the total area. Half of the labor force is agricultural. Egypt has a relatively high literacy rate of nearly 50 percent.

Most Egyptians are descended from Hamitic-speaking peoples who inhabited the Nile valley in ancient times. There is some mixture of Arab stock from the time of the Muslim conquest in the 600's. Over 90 percent of the people are Muslim and Arabic-speaking. Most of the remaining people are Copts (Egyptian Christians). Nomadic herdsmen, or Bedouin, roam the desert regions in search of food and water for their livestock.

The major cities are Cairo, the capital, near the junction of the Nile valley and the delta, Alexandria, the main port, Port Said, Tanta, and Aswan on the Lower Nile.

Economy. Egypt's economy, traditionally based on agriculture, is industrializing rapidly to counter unemployment created partly by rapid increases in population growth. Nonetheless, agriculture still accounts for one-third of the national product and nearly 80 percent of all exports.

Cotton is the major crop, followed by sugar, rice, and corn. The Nile River and its Aswan Dam provide abundant irrigation as well as hydroelectric power.

The main industries process the cotton grown in the country. Modern textile and chemical plants have been established in many towns, especially in and near Tanta, near the Mediterranean Sea. Armament industries have also been founded. Tourism provides additional income.

Egypt's revenues from the operation of the Suez Canal were halted in 1967 when the Arab-Israeli war broke out. The canal did not regain its former significance again until the late 1970's, when it became a major oil-shipment route connecting the Persian Gulf with the West.

Most Egyptian energy needs are supplied by its own oil. In 1987, 45 million metric tons of crude oil were produced. Coal was discovered in the late 1960's, as was uranium in the late 1970's. Iron ore is mined and converted into steel.

Large-scale nationalization of industry took place in the 1950's and 1960's, but it was largely reversed after the war with Israel in 1973 in the hopes of attracting foreign investment.

In 1986 imports cost $11.4 billion while exports earned only $3.3 billion. Imports include cereals, machinery, and raw materials. The main exports are cotton and textiles. Most trade is conducted with the Soviet Union, the United States, and Western Europe. Egypt receives extensive economic aid from many of these same nations, including the Soviet Union and the United States.

Government. The Arab Republic of Egypt has a presidential system of government. The president is nominated by the legislature and approved by popular vote. He is elected to a six-year term. The president appoints a cabinet, headed by a prime minister, which is responsible to the legislature.

Legislative power is vested in a unicameral, 458-member People's Assembly. The Shura Council is a 210-member consultative body.

Egypt is a member of the United Nations, the Organization of African Unity, the Organization of Arab Petroleum Exporting Countries, and the Arab League.

History. Civilization has existed in Egypt for over 5000 years. Successive Egyptian dynasties ruled until foreign invaders overran the country. The first of these invasions occurred in 945 B.C., when a Libyan prince, Sheshonk, seized control of Egypt. Libyans ruled Egypt until the late 700's B.C., when an Ethiopian dynasty took power. In about 670 B.C. Assyrians took over the country, only to be conquered by Persians in 525 B.C.

THE PEOPLE OF EGYPT *live in a narrow fertile strip along the Nile, as they have for some 5000 years. The rest of Egypt is desert. To the right is Anubis, a god of ancient Egypt.*

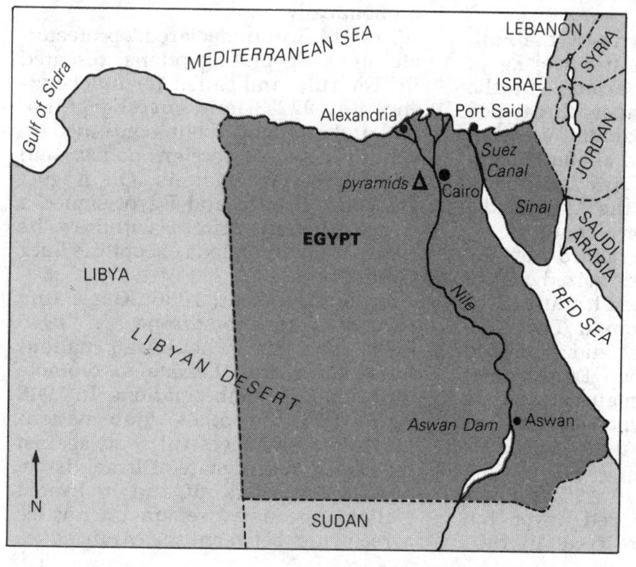

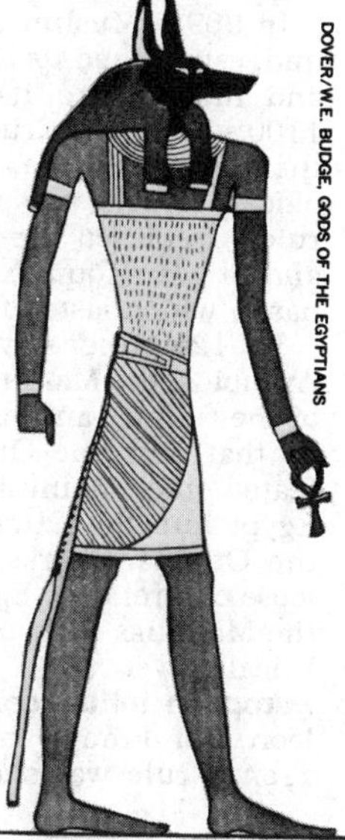

DOVER/W.E. BUDGE, GODS OF THE EGYPTIANS

CULVER PICTURES

THE SUEZ CANAL *in its first year. Built by the French Suez Canal Company, it was opened with much pomp in 1869. By 1882 Egypt, with the canal, had fallen into British hands.*

In 332 B.C. Alexander the Great of Macedonia conquered Egypt and brought the country into his empire. At Alexander's death in 323 B.C., one of his generals, Ptolemy, took control of Egypt and founded the Ptolemaic dynasty. Egyptian culture and politics became infused with the Greek tradition, or Hellenized. Egypt prospered under the Ptolemies—academies were built and trade was encouraged.

In 30 B.C. Egypt, weakened by internal conflicts, fell to the powerful forces of Rome. During the Roman occupation, probably in about the 300's A.D., Christianity spread to Egypt, and the Coptic Church, the church of the Christian Egyptians, was established.

Islam. Egypt remained under Roman authority until 639 A.D. In that year, Arab-speaking Muslims conquered Egypt. Since that time, Egypt has been closely identified with the Islamic world. The Muslims converted most of the Egyptian people, and Egypt became a major part of the early Muslim empires.

In 969 a Muslim dynasty, the Fatimid, established its control over Egypt and made Cairo its capital. In the 1100's Christian Crusaders threatened the Muslim empire. Saladin, a Syrian officer, came to the aid of the Muslim rulers, repulsed the Christian troops, and in 1169 founded the Ayyubid dynasty, which lasted for a century.

In 1250 the slave guards of the Ayyubids, the Mamluks, seized control of the country and ruled it until 1517. In that year the Ottoman Turks defeated the Mamluks and absorbed Egypt into the Ottoman Empire. But the Ottoman Turks maintained only loose control over Egypt, and they left the Mamluks most of their former political power.

European influence. In 1798 Napoleon I of France invaded Egypt, but French rule was short-lived. In 1801 British and Ottoman forces expelled the French. In 1805 an Albanian Muslim soldier, Muhammad Ali (Mehemet Ali) seized power and established a dynasty that lasted until 1952. Although Muhammad Ali and his successors did much to westernize Egypt, their attempts were only partially successful.

In 1869 the Suez Canal was opened. The canal, built by the French Suez Canal Company, which obtained operations rights for 99 years, shortened the routes between Europe and the East, and increased Britain's interest in Egypt.

In 1876 Egypt, near bankruptcy from enormous expenditures from efforts to westernize the country, was forced to accept French and English financial advisers. In 1882, after a brief Egyptian nationalist uprising led by Ahmad Arabi, British troops occupied Egypt. Between 1883 and 1907 Sir Evelyn Baring (Lord Cromer) exercised chief responsibility for Egypt, and did much to develop the country economically.

In 1914 Britain declared a protectorate over Egypt. Egyptians resented British rule and called for independence. In 1922 Britain gave Egypt limited independence, but continued to control defense, foreign policy, and other important matters. On August 26, 1936, Britain and Egypt signed a treaty whereby Britain withdrew its troops from all regions except the Suez Canal zone.

In the same year, 1936, King Faruq succeeded to the throne. In 1945 Egypt and six other Arab nations formed the Arab League to promote unity among member nations. In 1948 Egypt and the other Arab nations fought an unsuccessful war against the newly created state of Israel. Israel drove the invaders out, and the United Nations negotiated separate armistice agreements between the Arab states and Israel, but no final peace treaty was signed. Egypt obtained control of the Gaza Strip, a small area on the Mediterranean Sea that had once been part of Palestine.

Republic. After the 1948 Arab-Israeli clash, Egypt, troubled by failure in the war, a corrupt regime, and social unrest, fell into political turmoil. In 1952 an army group called the Free Officers seized control of the government and forced the king to abdicate.

General Muhammad Najib (Naguib) became prime minister. In June, 1953, Egypt became a republic, and Najib became president. In 1954 Lieutenant Colonel Gamal Abdel Nasser, a leader of the military revolt, ousted Najib and assumed the position of president.

In 1956 the United States withdrew offers of a loan for the building of a high dam at Aswan. Because of the withdrawal of the loan offer, Nasser nationalized the Suez Canal and announced his intention to use canal revenues to build the dam. Nasser also accepted large-scale Soviet aid for the project. A dispute over free access to the canal arose after nationalization, and a new conflict erupted. British, French, and Israeli forces attacked in October, 1956, and after a brief but intensive struggle, both sides accepted a UN cease-fire.

U.A.R. On February 1, 1958, Egypt, in an effort to build Arab unity, joined with Syria to form the United Arab Republic (U.A.R.). The following month, the U.A.R. joined with the Kingdom of Yemen to form the United Arab States. In September, 1961, Syria withdrew from the U.A.R., and three months later Egypt ended its ties with Yemen. In 1962 the U.A.R. supported republican forces fighting against Yemeni royalist forces.

In 1967 the U.A.R. blockaded the Gulf of Aqaba, bringing about a brief war in which Israeli forces were victorious and during which they occupied some Egyptian territory, including the Sinai Peninsula. A UN-arranged cease-fire ended the fighting, with Israel still holding the occupied territory. In

JIHAN EL-SADAT, *the former president's widow, a strong advocate of women's rights.*

WIDE WORLD

1973 Egypt tried to regain the occupied areas but was thwarted by Israel.

Contemporary Egypt. The increasingly unpopular Nasser regime ended when Nasser died in 1970. Anwar el-Sadat, who replaced him, promulgated a new constitution in 1971 and permitted political parties to develop. As opposition to his role as peacemaker with Israel rose in 1979, he was forced to dissolve Parliament and to create the new National Democrat Party as the supreme political entity in Egypt.

Sadat severed relations with the Soviet Union during the 1970's, and in 1977 entered into peace talks with Israel's president, Menachem Begin. A peace treaty was signed in 1979, and the agreed-upon Israeli withdrawal from the Sinai was completed in 1982.

Sadat's conciliatory policies toward Israel and the United States have somewhat alienated Egypt from the other Arab states.

Sadat was assassinated in 1981 by Muslim extremists. He was succeeded by his vice president, Hosni Mubarak, who has largely continued his policies.

Equatorial Guinea

Official name: *Republic of Equatorial Guinea*
Area: *10,831 sq. mi., 28,051 sq. km.*
Population: *(1990 est.) 360,000*
Capital: *Malabo on Bioko (Pop., 1988 est., 38,000)*
Language: *Spanish, Fang, Bubi*
Religion: *Roman Catholic, Animist*
Currency unit: *Ekuele*

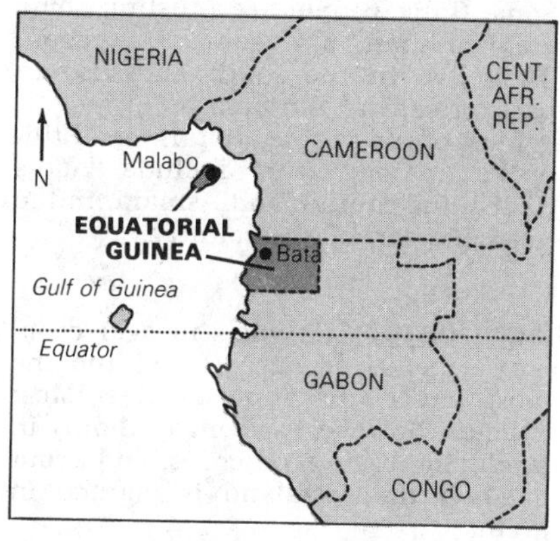

Equatorial Guinea, formerly known as Spanish Guinea, consists of two provinces—Río Muni and Bioko. Río Muni, on the west African mainland and adjacent islands, is bounded on the north by Cameroon, on the east and south by Gabon, and on the west by the Gulf of Guinea, an arm of the Atlantic Ocean. Bioko occupies two islands and several islets in the Gulf of Guinea. Bioko Island, the larger island, is about 20 miles northwest of Río Muni; Pagalu, the smaller, is some 370 miles southwest of the mainland province.

The land. In Río Muni, a coastal plain gives way some twelve miles inland to a higher, rolling plateau, which rises in the east to a hilly region. Bioko consists of two volcanoes separated by a narrow valley. Its coastline is steep, except in the southwest, where there is an excellent harbor at San Carlos. Pagalu is also volcanic in origin, and has a rugged terrain.

The climate of the territory is tropical, with very high heat and humidity throughout the year.

The people. Most of the people of Bioko are descended from the islands' native people, the Bubes. There are also Europeans and other Africans. Most of Río Muni's population is part of the Fang people. There are people of other African tribal groups and a small number of Europeans. Río Muni's population is nearly triple that of Bioko.

Equatorial Guinea is sparsely populated, with only 15 percent of the population living in urban areas and over 90 percent of the labor force employed in agriculture.

Catholicism is the predominant religion, although there are some Protestants, Muslims, and people who have held to traditional religions. Spanish is the official language, but a number of African languages are spoken.

Economy. Equatorial Guinea's economy is chiefly agricultural, and its mineral resources remain largely unexplored and unexploited. The main products are cacao, grown on Bioko plantations, and coffee, timber, and forest products from Río Muni. There is little manufacturing.

Most of Equatorial Guinea's products are exported to Spain, which furnishes needed imports.

Government. Since 1979 the Supreme Military Council has ruled the country. A 1982 constitution allows for presidential elections and a 60-member House of Representatives.

Equatorial Guinea is a member of the United Nations and the Organization of African Unity, and it is an associated state of the European Common Market.

History. Little is known of the history of the region before it was visited by Europeans. The islands of Fernando Póo (now Bioko) and the nearby mainland were discovered in the 1470's by the Portuguese, and they remained Portuguese until 1778, when they were ceded to Spain. Possession of the mainland was disputed until 1900, when the Treaty of Paris granted Río Muni to Spain. Spanish settlers established plantations using African laborers.

In the 1950's and 1960's Spain's goal was the improvement of the welfare of the people, the expansion of the economy, and the incorporation of the territory into the Spanish nation.

Equatorial Guinea was granted internal self-government in 1963, and in 1968 was granted independence.

President Nguema Biyoto Masie, having assumed dictatorial power by 1969, led a bloody reign of terror for eleven years. In attempting to establish Río Muni's predominance, he reestablished slavery and deprived the people of their human and civil rights.

Masie was executed following a coup in 1979 that established a military regime. A new constitution, approved in 1982, prepares the way for a return to civilian government. Equatorial Guinea receives extensive aid from Spain, and increasing assistance from the Soviet Union, Cuba, and China.

Ethiopia

Official name: *People's Democratic Republic of Ethiopia*
Area: *471,776 sq. mi., 1,221,900 sq. km.*
Population: *(1990 est.) 51,375,000*
Capital: *Addis Ababa (Pop., 1989 est., 2,000,000)*
Language: *Amharic, English*
Religion: *Coptic Christian, Islam*
Currency unit: *Birr*

Ethiopia, an ancient kingdom in east Africa, is bordered on the north by the Red Sea, on the east by the Strait Bab al Mandeb, and by Djibouti and the Somali Republic, on the south by Kenya, and on the west by Sudan. The former Italian colony of Eritrea was incorporated into Ethiopia in 1962.

The land. Most of Ethiopia is occupied by the Ethiopian Highlands, a region formed of a tremendous thickness of volcanic lava split by deep

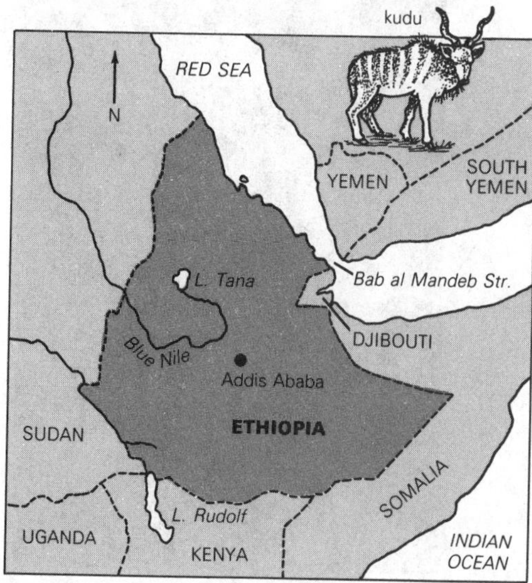

gorges and canyons. The Great Rift Valley divides the highlands along a line running southwest from the east-central part of the country.

A large mountain mass northwest of the Great Rift Valley rises more than 15,000 feet. There is a plateau in the southeast with elevations above 10,000 feet. In the northern part of the country, close to the Red Sea, is a low-lying desert region, the Danakil Depression.

There are many rivers and lakes in Ethiopia. At the western end of the Rift Valley is the Omo River, which drains into Lake Rudolf, along the border with Kenya. Lake Tana, near the center of the Ethiopian Highlands, is the source of the Blue Nile. The Takkaze River, another Nile tributary, originates near the eastern slope of the highlands. The Awash River in the eastern end of the Rift Valley flows northeast through a dry plain to its final destination in Lake Abbe.

Ethiopians distinguish three major natural regions—the Kolla, the Woina Dega, and the Dega. The Kolla is a zone of desert plants, dry shrubs, and savanna grasslands with elevations up to 6000 feet. The Woina Dega reaches elevations between 6000 and 8000 feet and is well cultivated. The Dega is a region of mountain grasslands lying above 8000 feet.

The people. There are many ethnic groups in Ethiopia. Among the most important are the Amhara, Tigrean, and Galla peoples. The Amhara people live in the central highlands, and the Tigrean people live in the northern part of the country.

Both the Amhara and Tigrean peoples are Coptic Christians, and they form the ruling groups in Ethiopia. Some Galla people are Muslim, some are Christian, and some are pagan. They live in the south and also in parts of central Ethiopia.

Most of the people are farmers. Ethiopia's major cities include Addis Ababa, the capital, and Asmara, in the northern part of the country.

Economy. Ethiopia's meager economy depends on agriculture, and the most important crop is coffee. Most farmers, however, are engaged only in producing basic food crops, and about one-half the farmland is planted in grains.

Although Ethiopia has deposits of gold, platinum, and other minerals, mining is poorly developed, partly due to the high costs of overland transportation. Industrial production greatly increased in the 1960's, and the country has textile and food processing plants. Ethiopia's many rivers provide a potential source for hydroelectric power, a shortage of which, along with a shortage of advanced technology, limits further industrialization. Foreign investment has been instrumental in Ethiopia's development.

The textile industry, especially, has undergone rapid growth in recent years, and even more rapid industrial growth is planned by the government. Nonetheless, only five percent of the gross national product is contributed by industry, while over half is contributed by agriculture, despite its lagging technological progress. Since 1975, much industry and most agriculture has been nationalized.

In 1986 imports cost $976.6 million and exports earned $487.6 million. Coffee is the main export item, while petroleum products and machinery are the chief imports. Exports go mainly to the United States, while imports come from Saudi Arabia, Japan, and West Germany.

TROUBLED ETHIOPIA. *A starving child* (below) *in 1974, the year when Emperor Haile Selassie* (right) *was deposed. Wars, a radical regime, and more famine have since plagued Ethiopia.*

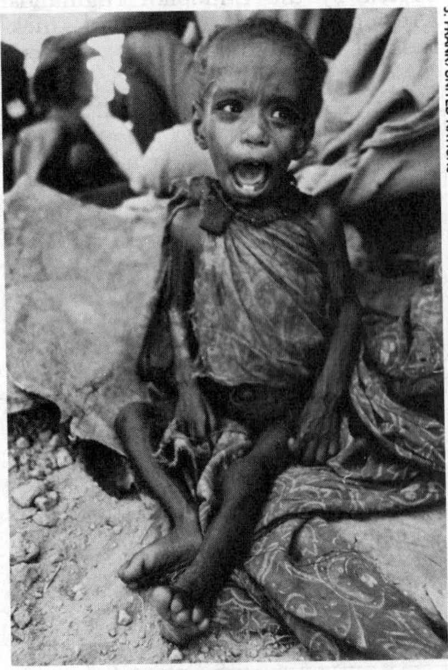

J. FRANK/UNITED NATIONS

U.S. DEPT. OF STATE

Government. Ethiopia's 1987 constitution provides for an executive branch of government consisting of a president, vice president, council of state, and council of ministers. The legislative branch, called the Shengo, consists of 835 members. Ideally, governmental power and decision making would be distributed throughout the different branches of government, however, the dictator remains the supreme authority.

History. Ethiopia is one of the world's oldest kingdoms, and the historical and archaeological records of Ethiopian culture go back to about 500 B.C. The present-day rulers claim descent from the queen of Sheba, whose descendents ruled over the ancient Semitic-speaking Sabaean people, whose origins are in southern Arabia.

Ethiopia was under Semitic influence until 324 A.D., when the emperor Azana was converted to Christianity. Muslims invaded Ethiopia in the 600's. The Muslims converted the Galla people and pushed the Amhara people to the highlands, where they remained cut off from the rest of the world until the early 1500's.

In the 1400's Portugal sent an expedition to Ethiopia. In 1527 Muslims overran Ethiopia, but with the aid of Portugal, Ethiopia expelled the Muslim sultan in 1541. Portuguese Jesuits came to Ethiopia and tried to bring the Ethiopian Christians into the Roman Catholic Church. In 1632 the emperor, Fasilidas, expelled the Jesuits.

Political unrest, poor relations with Britain, and religious wars marked the period until 1887. At that time Italy attempted to gain territory in Ethiopia. Italy proclaimed Ethiopia a protectorate in 1889, and in 1895 the Italian army invaded Ethiopia. Italy was defeated at the Battle of Adua in 1896, but retained the coastal region of Eritrea.

Modern Ethiopia. In 1916 Ras Taffari became the regent for the empress Zauditu. He succeeded to the throne at her death in 1930, and took the name Haile Selassie I.

In 1935 Italy, then under the rule of Benito Mussolini, renewed its claims on Ethiopia and invaded the country. The emperor unsuccessfully appealed to the League of Nations for help. In 1936 Italy united Ethiopia, Eritrea, and Italian Somaliland to form Italian East Africa.

In 1941 English and Ethiopian troops defeated the Italian occupation forces, and Haile Selassie returned to the throne. In 1962, Eritrea was federated with Ethiopia, but the Eritrean Liberation Front has led repeated attempts since 1970 to effect secession. Fighting recurs in sporadic border disputes with Somalia over control of the Ogaden region. Somalia has also lent support to the Eritrean rebels.

Strikes, student protests, and army rebellion led to the deposition of Haile Selassie in 1974; he died a year later.

The new military government began a socialist restructuring of the society and economy, but it was troubled by renewed warfare against Somalia and by the Eritrean rebels. Several bloody coups ensued until 1977, when Mengistu Haile Mariam, a ruthless dictator, assumed leadership of the nation and its socialist revolution.

Mengistu has eliminated Chinese influence over Ethiopia, while increasing ties to Cuba and the Soviet Union.

Several years of severe drought in Ethiopia and neighboring countries resulted in the mid-1980's in widespread famine. The drought abated in 1987, but resumed in 1988, causing widespread famine once again.

Gabon

Official name: *Gabonese Republic*
Area: *103,346 sq. mi., 267,667 sq. km.*
Population: *(1990 est.) 1,069,000*
Capital: *Libreville (Pop., 1989, 210,000)*
Language: *French, African languages*
Religion: *Christianity, Islam, traditional religions*
Currency unit: *Franc CFA (African Financial Community)*
National holiday: *Independence Day, Aug. 17*

Gabon, a republic in West Africa, is bordered on the north by Equatorial Guinea and Cameroon, on the east and south by the People's Republic of the Congo, and on the west by the Atlantic Ocean. Gabon was a French territory until 1960, when it received its independence.

The land. Most of Gabon is covered by wet tropical forests. Inland from a coastal plain is the edge of the African Plateau, called the Crystal Mountains in the north and the Mayombé Mountains in the south. In the southeast are the Batéké plateaus, comprised of grasslands. Gabon's principal river is the Ogooué. The climate throughout the country is hot and humid.

The people. There are many different tribal groups in Gabon, most of which are Bantu-speaking. The Fang, who migrated from the north in the 1800's, form the largest group. There are also peoples of the Eschira, Okande, and Adouma tribes.

Gabon is about half Christian (especially Roman Catholic) and half animist. There is a small minority of Muslims. Gabon has a literacy rate of 40 percent, which is high compared with other African nations.

SOTHEBY PARKE-BERNET/EPA

RELIQUARY *of wood and brass from Gabon, a remarkably wealthy and stable country.*

Gabon is thinly populated. Most of the people live in rural areas. The major city is the capital, Libreville. Port Gentil is Gabon's major port.

Economy. The economy of Gabon is based largely on mining and forestry, although most of the people are engaged in subsistence farming. Manioc, corn, and bananas are the country's main crops.

Gabon is one of the richest of the black African nations because of its mining, which accounts for one-third of the gross national product, and its lumbering, which accounts for one-third of the exports. Both enterprises are largely foreign owned. Gabon has some of the world's largest deposits of manganese and iron ore. Offshore oil deposits have been exploited, and about 10 million metric tons, accounting for nearly half of the nation's export revenues, are produced annually. Uranium and gold are also produced.

In 1986 exports earned an estimated \$1 billion while imports were estimated at \$970 million. Gabon exports petroleum and wood products, and it imports foodstuffs and manufactured goods. Most of its trade is with France.

Government. Gabon has a presidential system of government. Executive power is vested in a president popularly elected to a seven-year term. Legislative power rests with a unicameral National Assembly. The assembly has 111 members elected by universal suffrage and nine members appointed to five-year terms. There has been only one state-approved political party since 1968.

Gabon is a member of the United Nations, the Organization of African Unity, and the Organization of Petroleum Exporting Countries (OPEC), and it is an associated state of the European Common Market.

History. Little is known of the early history of the Gabon area. In the 1400's Portuguese explorers established trade relations with the Loango kingdom. The original trade in gold dust, ivory, palm oil, and wood soon gave way to slaving. Several European countries joined in the slave trade, but France became predominant.

French rule. Slave trading was abolished in the early 1800's, and in 1849 France established a center for freed slaves at Libreville. In 1899 France began granting concessions to private companies to develop the region. Company abuses led to depopulation, depletion of resources, and loss of capital. In 1910 Gabon became part of French Equatorial Africa.

Political activities before World War II were confined mainly to groups in Libreville, religious cults, and Fang tribal societies. After the war, France liberalized its colonial system, and in 1946 created the French Union. Gabon was permitted to establish territorial assemblies and to elect deputies to the French National Assembly. Jean-Hilaire Aubame, representing the northern Fang people, was elected to the French assembly.

Self-rule. France granted Gabon internal self-government in 1957. Leon M'Ba, representing the southern Fang and other groups in his party, the Gabonese Democratic Bloc (BDG), became prime minister of a coalition government that included Aubame's party.

Gabon became a member of the French Community in 1958, but broke its ties with French Equatorial Africa, from which it had long desired to secede because of its own wealth.

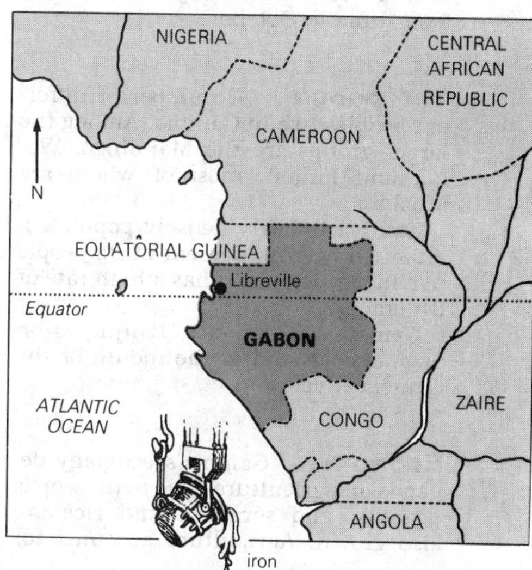

Gabon became independent on August 17, 1960, and M'Ba was elected president. Early in 1964 a military coup threatened the regime, but the French intervened in support of M'Ba. In 1964 M'Ba's party won a majority of seats in the National Assembly, and M'Ba continued as president until his death in 1967. He was succeeded by Albert Bongo. In 1968 the BDG became the Gabon Democratic Party. Bongo was elected to a seven-year term in 1973, and reelected in 1980.

France still has great influence on Gabon's economy and French troops are stationed in the country. Bongo has sought to establish closer ties with other Common Market nations.

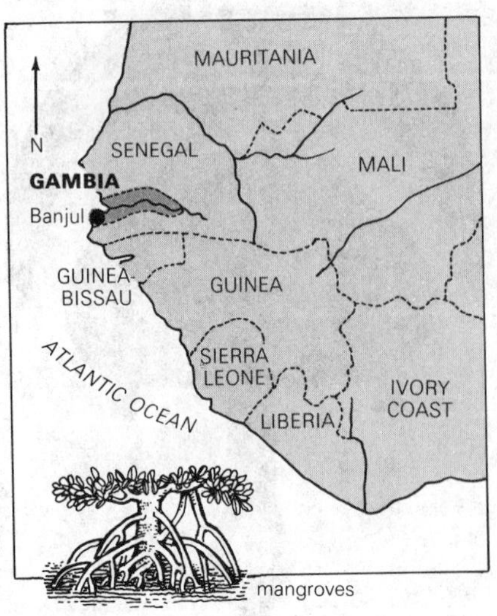

Gambia

Official name: *Republic of the Gambia*
Area: *4,361 sq. mi., 11,295 sq. km.*
Population: *(1990 est.) 820,000*
Capital: *Banjul (Pop., 1989, 45,000)*
Language: *English, African languages*
Religion: *Islam, traditional religions*
Currency unit: *Dalasi*
National holiday: *Independence Day, Feb. 18*

Gambia, a small independent nation in West Africa, is bordered on the north, east, and south by Senegal, and on the west by the Atlantic Ocean. Gambia received its independence in 1965 after a century and a half of British control.

The land. Gambia is dominated by the Gambia River, which flows through the narrow country from east to west for a distance of over 200 miles. Mangrove swamps line the river for about 150 miles inland from the ocean. Beyond the swamps the land is grassy with patches of sandy soil. Sandstone plateaus cover the region farthest from the river.

Gambia receives about 40 inches of rain a year. The rainy season lasts from June to October.

The people. A number of different peoples live in Gambia. Among the larger groups are the Mandingo, Wolof, and Fulani, most of whom are Muslims.

Gambia is fairly densely populated, although over 90 percent of its people live in rural areas. It has a high rate of illiteracy.

Gambia's major city, Banjul, is on St. Mary's Island at the mouth of the Gambia River.

Economy. Gambia's economy depends on agriculture. The main crop is peanuts, and sorghum and rice are also grown. Agriculture accounts for nearly 60 percent of the gross national product and employs 70 percent of the nation's labor force. Tourism is increasing in importance. There are few mineral deposits and little industry in the country.

In 1985 Gambia's imports cost $104 million and its exports earned $32 million. Peanuts accounted for about 95 percent of the value of exports. Gambia imports rice, wheat, sugar, petroleum products, motor vehicles, and manufactured goods.

Government. Gambia has a parliamentary system of government. Legislative power rests with the House of Representatives, which has 50 members, 35 of whom are elected. The head of state is the president, who is the leader of the majority party in the House.

Gambia is a member of the United Nations, the Organization of African Unity, and the Commonwealth of Nations, and it is an associated state of the European Common Market.

History. Little is known about the early history of Gambia. A Carthaginian, Hanno, may have sailed up the Gambia River in the 500's B.C. During the 900's A.D., the Gambia region was probably a distant outpost of the empires of Ghana and Mali.

In the 1400's the Portuguese explored the Gambia region and traded with the people there, as did Dutch, English, and French merchants in the following years. Between the 1500's and the 1700's, slaves from the area were transported to America.

By the 1700's the British and French had established trading posts and forts at the mouth of the Gambia River. British and French merchants competed vigorously throughout the 1700's for control of trade with Gambia, but in 1783 Gambia was awarded to Britain by treaty.

British rule. Throughout the 1800's British merchants trading on the Gambia River resisted proposals that Gambia should become part of French-controlled Senegal. Gambia was ruled from the British Crown colony of Sierra Leone until 1843, when Gambia was made a Crown colony. The two colonies once again were administered jointly for a brief period, from 1866 to 1888, but after 1888 Gambia remained a separate entity.

In 1889 Britain and France agreed on the present boundaries of Gambia, which Britain had been acquiring piece by piece from tribal chiefs since the early 1800's.

After World War II Britain faced the problem of Senegalese demands for Gambia. Senegal wanted Gambia in order to round out its own boundaries and to eliminate smuggling between the two countries. Gambians had mixed feelings about union with Senegal. They realized that their country could not be economically successful, but there were significant differences in language and culture between the two countries.

POLITICS IN GAMBIA: *President Dawda Jawara addresses local village authorities. The country is one of the few functioning democracies in Africa.*

UNITED NATIONS

Self-rule. Out of the differences of opinion created by possible unification with Senegal, Dawda Jawara formed the Progressive People's Party, which won elections held in 1960 and 1962.

In 1963 Gambia became self-governing with Jawara as prime minister. He led Gambia to independence in February, 1965. Gambia became a republic in 1970, and Jawara was elected president. He was reelected in 1977.

In 1982 Gambia and Senegal became confederated states, agreeing to integrate their security forces and monetary systems, while maintaining national independence.

Ghana

Official name: *Republic of Ghana*
Area: *92,099 sq. mi., 238,540 sq. km.*
Population: *(1990 est.) 15,234,000*
Capital: *Accra (Pop., 1989, 1,450,000)*
Language: *English, African languages*
Religion: *Christian, Islam, traditional religions*
Currency unit: *Cedi*
National holiday: *Independence Day, Mar. 6*

Ghana, a republic in western Africa, is bordered on the north by Upper Volta, on the east by Togo, on the south by the Gulf of Guinea, an arm of the Atlantic Ocean, and on the west by the Ivory Coast and Upper Volta. Ghana was formed in 1957 by the union of the former British colonies of the Gold Coast and Ashanti, the British protectorate of the Northern Territories, and British Togoland.

The land. Grasslands and forests occupy much of Ghana's land. The Volta River and its principal tributaries, the Black Volta, White Volta, and Oti, drain all of northern Ghana and about half of the south. Extensive grassy plains and isolated hills are typical of the Volta basin landscape. The south and west of Ghana is hilly and forested.

In the southeast the Volta River flows between the Akwapim Hills and the Togo Mountains. At that point there is a large dam and power plant, at Akosombo. The climate throughout the country is tropical.

The people. Many Ghanaians are Akan-speaking people, mainly Fanti along the coast and Ashanti farther inland. The Ga people, who are related by culture and language to the Ashanti, live around the city of Accra. In the north are the Moshi-Dagomba people.

One-third of Ghana's population is literate and over two-thirds lives in rural areas.

Most Ghanaians are farmers. Ghana's major cities include the capital, Accra; Kumasi; and the ports of Tema and Takoradi.

Economy. Ghana's economy progressed rapidly after the 1950's, but its growth has now leveled off. Nearly half of the gross national product comes from agricultural products, and about 15 percent from manufacturing and mining.

Ghana is the world's top cacao producer, and yams, rice, and grains are basic food crops. Lumbering is a significant economic activity.

Ghana is rich in mineral deposits, especially diamonds, manganese, gold, and bauxite. Industrial growth has been gradual, although Tema's aluminum production and hydroelectric power from the Volta River Project have improved prospects for increased growth. Accra is also an industrial center.

In 1983 Ghana's imports cost $577 million and its exports earned $440 million. The major exports are cacao, gold, diamonds, manganese, timber, and aluminum. Ghana imports manufactured goods, machinery, food, and chemicals. The country's major trading partners are Britain, the United States, and Western Europe.

Government. Military coups in 1966, 1972, 1979, and 1981 resulted in the formation of successive new governments. Although Ghana received a new constitution in 1979, it was suspended following the 1981 coup. The country is now ruled by a military-backed civilian cabinet.

Ghana is a member of the United Nations, the Organization of African Unity, the Economic Community of West African States, and the Commonwealth of Nations. It is also an associated state of the European Common Market.

History. Ghana is named after a medieval empire in western Africa. In 1471 Portuguese explorers encountered the Fanti people, who were then migrating southward. In the years that followed several European countries engaged in trade for gold, ivory, and slaves supplied by the Ashanti through Fanti middlemen.

British rule. The British and the Ashanti waged wars throughout the 1800's. In 1874 the British finally achieved victory and formed the coastal area of Ghana into the Gold Coast colony. In 1896 Britain exiled the Ashanti king, Prempeh I, and in 1901 the British established the colony of Ashanti, which included the interior north of the Gold Coast colony.

In the same year, 1901, the Northern Territories, the region north of Ashanti, became a British protectorate. The German colony of Western Togoland became a British mandate under the League of Nations after World War I, and was administered together with the Gold Coast.

TRADITIONAL AFRICA: *a Ghanaian chief, surrounded by his family and tribal entourage, attends the installation of another chief. The clothes and ornaments display his wealth.*

UNITED NATIONS

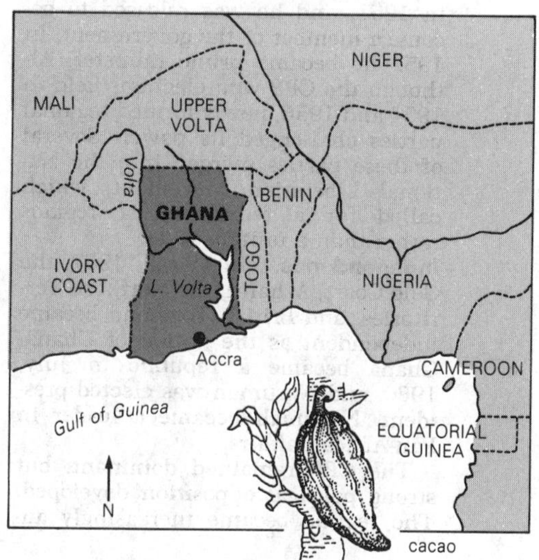

KWAME NKRUMAH, *Ghana's founder and later dictator, on Independence Day, 1957.*

In the 1920's railroads were built and cacao became an important export. A new class of educated Africans formed trade unions, professional associations, and cultural groups, and began to contest the power of traditional chiefs, through whom Britain administered the country.

After World War II, Ashanti representatives were given seats in the colony's legislative council, which had been established at the beginning of colonial rule, and in 1946 the council acquired an African majority.

In 1947 Dr. J. B. Danquah organized a nationalist movement, the United Gold Coast Convention (UGCC). Kwame Nkrumah broke away from UGCC in 1949 and founded the Convention People's Party (CPP). Riots broke out in 1950 in support of Ghanaian independence, and Nkrumah was arrested for his conspicuous role in the disturbances.

Nkrumah's party won elections held in 1951, and he was released to become a member of the government. In 1952 he became prime minister. Although the CPP won elections held in 1954 and 1956, newly formed regional parties challenged its power. Several of these parties merged into the National Liberation Movement, which called for a federation of regions rather than a unitary state.

Independence. In March, 1957, the Gold Coast, Ashanti, the Northern Territories, and British Togoland became independent as the nation of Ghana. Ghana became a republic in July, 1960, and Nkrumah was elected president. Nkrumah became a leader in Pan-African affairs.

The CPP remained dominant, but strong political opposition developed. The regime became increasingly authoritarian, and its opponents resorted to plotting and an attempted assassination of the president.

In 1964 Nkrumah acquired dictatorial powers. He ran the country into debt, and his regime was accused of corruption. Nkrumah was deposed following a 1966 military coup. There was another bloodless military coup in 1972. Civil constitutional rule was restored following the 1978 coup, but charges of ineffectiveness led to yet another coup in 1981.

The government seeks increased economic diversity and self-reliance, but lack of political stability hinders these attempts.

Guinea

Official name: *Republic of Guinea*
Area: *94,926 sq. mi., 245,857 sq. km.*
Population: *(1990 est.) 7,269,000*
Capital: *Conakry (Pop., 1989, 600,000)*
Language: *French, African languages*
Religion: *Islam, traditional religions*
Currency unit: *Syli*
National holiday: *Independence Day, Oct. 2*

Guinea, a republic in western Africa, is bounded on the north by Guinea-Bissau, Senegal, and Mali, on the east by Mali and the Ivory Coast, on the south by Liberia and Sierra Leone, and on the west by the Atlantic Ocean. Guinea had been a territory of France for many years until 1958, when it declared its independence.

The land. The countryside of Guinea is quite varied. There is a wide, rainy coastal plain, but farther inland the land is drier and has elevations of more than 3000 feet above sea level. In the central part of the country is the mountain region of Fouta Djallon. From the mountains the land descends to the east into the drainage basins of the Senegal and Niger rivers. There are grasslands and forests in the east.

Temperatures vary throughout the country. In the coastal region temperatures average about 80°F. The Fouta Djallon is relatively cool. Temperatures range over 80°F in the region north and east of the Fouta Djallon.

The people. There are many different ethnic groups in Guinea. The larger groups are the Fulani, Malinke, and Susu. A majority of the people are Muslim, and most of the rest animist.

Most of the people live in rural areas. Guinea's largest city is the capital, Conakry, situated on Tombo Island off the mainland of Guinea. Conakry is also Guinea's major port. Nearly 85 percent of the labor force is agricultural and 65 percent of the population is illiterate.

Economy. Two-fifths of the gross national product is derived from agriculture, one-fifth from mining, and about 14 percent from manufacturing. Cash crops include bananas, coffee, palm products, and peanuts. Manioc, fruits, millet, and rice are basic food crops.

Guinea has the richest bauxite deposits in the world. Iron ore, diamonds, and gold are also mined. The country has abundant hydroelectric power.

In 1983 Guinea's imports cost $350 million and its exports earned $465 million. Guinea trades mainly with the United States, the Soviet Union, and Western Europe. Its main imports are petroleum products, machinery, and foodstuffs. The chief exports are bauxite and alumina, pineapples, coffee, bananas, and palm kernels.

Government. Guinea is a republic but it is presently operating without a constitution. The Military Committee for National Redressment (CMRN) took over the government in 1984.

Power is vested in the 17-member CMRN and in 16 civilian ministers. The government rules primarily by decree. The president is chief of state.

Guinea is a member of the United Nations and the Organization of African Unity, and it is an associated state of the European Common Market.

History. Little is known of the early history of Guinea. Beginning in the 1400's the peoples of Guinea were in regular commercial contact with European sailors and merchants. They had also been trading across the Sahara.

Islam penetrated what is now Guinea, and many of the Fulani of upper Guinea became Muslims. In the

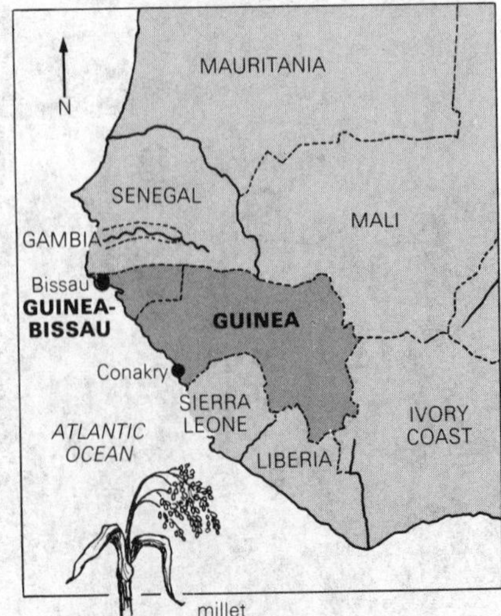

early 1700's Muslims in the Fouta Djallon region revolted against their pagan rulers and created a state of their own.

The French began to acquire portions of Guinea in the 1800's. The indigenous peoples fought against these acquisitions, but they were largely unsuccessful. Samori ibn Ture, a warrior who assembled his own army and ruled much of upper Guinea, fought a frequently victorious guerrilla war against the French in the 1880's and 1890's. By 1898, however, French armies had forced Samori into exile.

French rule. In 1895 Guinea became a part of French West Africa, and was subject to direct rule from France. In the Muslim area of Fouta Djallon, however, France initiated a system of indirect rule. Schools and hospitals were provided in both the coastal and interior areas.

The peoples of the coastal region, particularly those of Conakry, became thoroughly acquainted with French culture. A railroad was built that linked Conakry to Kankan, in upper Guinea, by 1925, thus making possible the export of tropical products.

In 1946 Guinea became a territory within the French Union, but Guinea was the only French territory that refused to join the newly formed French Community in 1958. In October, 1958, under the leadership of Sékou Touré, Guinea became independent.

Independence. At the time of independence, France withdrew financial and administrative help, causing a serious crisis in Guinea. France resumed ties in 1963.

Since 1958 Guinea has experienced economic difficulties and the loss of civil and human rights under the dictatorial and Communistic rule of President Touré.

After Touré's death in 1984, the Guinean military staged a bloodless coup; they now rule the country.

Guinea-Bissau

Official name: *Republic of Guinea-Bissau*
Area: *13,944 sq. mi., 36,155 sq. km.*
Population: *(1990 est.) 998,000*
Capital: *Bissau (Pop., 1988 est., 125,000)*
Language: *Portuguese, Crioulo*
Religion: *Animist, Islam, Roman Catholic*
Currency unit: *Escudo*

Guinea-Bissau lies on the western coast of Africa. It is bounded on the north by Senegal, on the east and south by Guinea, and on the west by the Atlantic Ocean.

The land. Guinea-Bissau consists of a mainland, with a deeply indented coast, and a number of offshore islands, including those of the Bijagos archipelago. Most of the country consists of low coastal plain, much of which is swampy. In the east is a higher, drier savanna region.

There are many rivers and streams, and the Cacheu, Mansoa, Geba, and Crubal rivers have large deltas. The climate is characterized by high temperatures and extreme humidity.

The people. Most of the population is African, and there are small groups of Portuguese and mulattoes, people of mixed African and European origin. The Africans are members of many tribal groups, including the Balante, Mandyako, and Malinke.

Many languages are spoken, including Portuguese and African languages, but a Creole patois is the most commonly understood tongue. Over two-thirds of the people are animists, one-third are Muslims, and 5 percent are Roman Catholic.

Most of the people in the sparsely settled country live in rural areas. Only 19 percent are literate, and nearly 90 percent are subsistence farmers.

Economy. Guinea-Bissau has little mining but potentially large bauxite deposits may someday help to diversify its economy. Meanwhile, Guinea-Bissau remains basically an agricultural land, and its standard of living is very low. The country's forests are exploited for their timber. The main commercial crops are palm kernels and peanuts raised on European-owned plantations. Basic food crops include rice, millet, coconuts, manioc, beans, and bananas. There is little industry.

Almost all of the country's limited trade is with Portugal. Peanuts and palm kernels are the chief exports, and machinery and consumer goods are imported.

Government. In 1984 the provisional government, led by a president and the Revolutionary Council, was dissolved. The new 1984 constitution called for the reinstatement of the 150-member National Assembly. The president is elected and is assisted by the vice president of the Council of State and a council of ministers.

Guinea-Bissau is a member of the United Nations and the Organization of African Unity, and it is an associated state of the European Common Market.

History. Portuguese sailors were the first Europeans to visit present-day Guinea-Bissau, in 1446. Portugal established trading posts and ports at the mouth of the rivers and on the Bijagos islands. In the late 1400's the region was made a dependency of the nearby Portuguese colony of Cape Verde Islands. From the late 1500's through the mid-1800's the colony, like the whole of West Africa, prospered from the slave trade.

Portugal occupied only coastal portions of the territory, and sent very few permanent settlers. In the 1800's Portuguese claims to the region were disputed by Britain and France. In the late 1800's agreement was reached on the division of west-central Africa among the European powers, and Portuguese control of the area was formally recognized.

Portuguese attempts to control the interior led to rebellions among the Africans, angered by Portugal's participation in the slave trade. The rebellions were put down by 1915, and Portuguese settlers expanded their plantations in the colony. In the 1930's colonial administration was centralized.

PORTUGUESE GUINEA, *like other Portuguese colonies, was lost only after bitter fighting.*

In 1951 the colony was made an overseas province. Portugal did little to develop the economy and virtually ignored the education, health, and general welfare needs of the African population. Forced labor, under the "contract labor" system, remained the rule. In 1961 Portugal did, however, formally grant full Portuguese citizenship to African Guineans.

With encouragement from neighboring African states, a national liberation movement developed in the early 1960's. In 1961 a rebellion for independence began. By the mid-1960's the rebel leaders had claimed control over most of the country and its people, and the Portuguese armed forces had been unable to quell the uprising.

By 1970 the rebel forces controlled two-thirds of the country. A constitution was granted in 1973, and on September 10, 1974, Guinea-Bissau became the first Portuguese territory in Africa to win independence.

Portugal, having been the first of the European nations to colonize Africa, was among the last to relinquish its colonies. The resources of a small impoverished nation like Portugal were inadequate to maintain colonies.

Dissatisfaction with a proposed merger of Guinea-Bissau with Cape Verde brought about the overthrow of the government in a coup on November 14, 1980.

Iran

Official name: *Islamic Republic of Iran*
Area: *636,296 sq. mi., 1,648,000 sq. km.*
Population: *(1990 est.) 55,249,000*
Capital: *Teheran (Pop., 1986, 8,719,480)*
Language: *Persian*
Religion: *Islam*
Currency unit: *Rial*

Iran, an oil-rich nation in the Middle East, is bounded on the north by the Soviet Union, on the east by Afghanistan and Pakistan, on the west by Iraq and Turkey, and on the south by the Gulf of Oman and the Persian Gulf.

REVOLUTION IN IRAN: *a young girl and her mother wear the traditional feminine chador, symbol of the Islamic revolution in 1979. Among liberated women, the chador is disliked.*

The land.

Central Iran lies on a great plateau that has an average elevation of 4000 feet above sea level. It contains two barren, salty deserts—the Dasht-i-Kavir and the Dasht-i-Lut. West and south of the plateau are the rugged Zagros Mountains, and to the north the Elburz range rises to over 18,000 feet above sea level. Narrow, fertile lowlands skirt the country's seacoasts.

Iran's climate varies from region to region. Rainfall averages only twelve inches a year for the country as a whole, but the plateau receives less than five inches and the mountains and northern coasts may receive as much as 40 inches annually. In the central deserts summer temperatures rise above 115°F, but the mountain areas are cooler both in summer and in winter.

The people.

Population is concentrated on the lower mountain slopes and in the coastal regions. Ancient Iran was settled by tribes that migrated into the region from Europe. The country's population also includes Arabs, Jews, Armenians, and nomadic Kurds, Baluchi, Turkoman, and Bakhtiari, highly independent minorities.

Most of the people are Muslims, over 90 percent of whom are Shiite, the remainder being Sunni. Half the people live in rural areas, half in urban areas.

Economy.

The wealth of Iran is derived from oil, but farming and herding are the occupations of most Iranians. The bulk of the cultivated land is in the moist northwest, where wheat and barley are the leading crops. Corn, rice, sugar beets, tea, tobacco, and fruits are also raised. Cotton thrives on the edges of the plateau, and goats, sheep, and camels are grazed in semidesert areas. Fishing prospers on the Caspian coast.

Industry has increased since 1950 and it now accounts for nearly one-fifth of the gross national product, while oil production and agriculture each account for one-quarter. Iran has ten percent of the world's oil resources, but annual production dropped from 260 to 145 million metric tons between 1978 and 1979, at the time of the revolution, and it has dropped even more since then. The oil industry was nationalized in 1951, but several international companies are still involved in the ownership and operation of various Iranian petroleum enterprises. Revenues from oil production and refining constitute the largest single portion of Iran's national income.

Most of Iran's industries process agricultural products, producing cotton and wool textiles, dried fruits, cigarettes, vegetable oils, and leather. Carpet weaving is an ancient craft that is still important.

Iranian imports cost $10.5 billion in 1986 while its exports earned $13.3 billion. West Germany, Japan, and North Korea are its major trading partners.

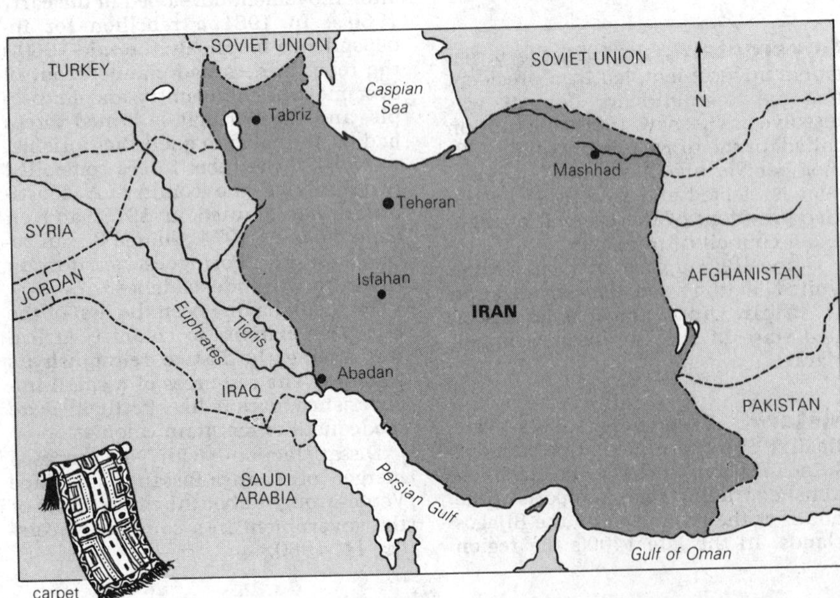

Government.

Iran's constitutional monarchy was overthrown in 1979. A revolutionary government now rules under the political and religious leadership of Ali Khamenei, who has nearly absolute authority. A president and prime minister are under his control, as is the 270-member unicameral *Majlis.*

Iran is a member of the United Nations, the Organization of Petroleum Exporting Countries (OPEC), and the Colombo Plan.

History.

The modern history of the Middle East began in Iran in 1908, when the region's first oil was found there. In ancient times, too, Iran—or Persia—was important as the core of the great Persian Empire, which ruled the entire Near East in the 500's and 400's B.C. Alexander the Great conquered the empire in the 300's B.C., and his successors were defeated by Parthians in the 200's B.C. It was not until the 200's A.D. that Persians regained control of their land, under the Sasanian dynasty.

Sasanians ruled until 641, when they were overthrown by Arab armies that converted the Persians to Islam. Seljuk Turks replaced the Arabs as rulers in the 1000's, and they in turn were overthrown by the Mongols in the 1200's. When the Mongol empire disintegrated in the 1500's, Persians again took control and rebuilt and reunited the country.

Under Shah Nadir, who ruled in the 1700's, the Persians drove out invading Afghans and went on to conquer Afghanistan and part of India. Civil war followed Nadir's death in 1747 and caused the loss of all the newly conquered territory. The Qajar faction emerged dominant from the civil wars and founded a dynasty that ruled until the 1920's.

Although Persia remained sovereign during the 1800's and early 1900's, it was subject to the competing economic and political influences of Russia and Britain. In 1905 a rebellion broke out among Persians who objected to the weak shah's dependence on these foreign states, and in 1906 the shah yielded to the rebel's demands for a constitution and an elected assembly.

Riza Shah. Foreign interference increased after the discovery of oil in 1908, however, and in 1921 Riza Pahlevi, an army officer, led a coup that drove the pro-British shah into exile. In 1923 Pahlavi became prime minister, and in 1925 the Majlis proclaimed him shah.

Shah Riza began the modernization

PHILIPPE LEDRU/SYGMA

SHAH OF IRAN *celebrates his 59th birthday in 1978, a few months before his fall.*

of Persia. During his reign, communications, education, and industry were expanded and the judiciary, military, and all of society began to be reordered on a Western pattern. Britain retained its influence only as operator of the Iranian oil fields.

During World War II Iran declared itself neutral, but Britain and Russia occupied the country. In 1941 the Allies forced Riza Shah to yield the throne to his son, Muhammad Riza.

Contemporary Iran. After the war a strong Iranian nationalist movement developed, with the ending of foreign control as its primary goal. Muhammad Mossadegh, a leader of the nationalists, became prime minister in 1951 and ruled as a dictator.

During Mossadegh's ministry the British-owned oil fields were nationalized. Iran was unable to market the oil without foreign help, however, and the country faced financial ruin. In 1953 the shah removed Mossadegh from office and had him arrested.

Oil production began again in 1954 under the direction of British, U.S., French, and Dutch companies that shared the profits with Iran. Oil revenues were spent on programs of social and economic reform as industrialization and modernization were rapidly increased.

Shah Muhammad Riza Pahlevi, crowned in 1967, eventually established strict martial law to control his rivals, which included Islamic fundamentalists and political conservatives. Labor strikes and riots spurred further military reaction as production dropped. The shah's U.S.–aided military adventures in neighboring lands further undermined his popularity; he was finally deposed by militant revolutionaries in February, 1979. Militants seized the U.S. embassy in Teheran on November 4, 1979, and held 53 Americans hostage until January, 1981, seriously damaging U.S.-Iranian relations.

In September, 1980, Iran and Iraq began a sporadic bloody war brought on by border disputes. As the war dragged on, other Persian Gulf nations began to feel threatened by Iran's success in the war. In 1987 an increased naval presence by the United States and other countries, in order to protect shipping in the Gulf, created a tense and volatile situation. In July, 1988, a cease-fire was declared between Iran and Iraq.

IRAN'S LONG HISTORY: (left) *Darius's fifth-century B.C. palace of Persepolis, ceremonial center of the ancient Persian empire, and* (center right) *the fanatical Khomeini, the Islamic leader of the revolution.*

HERMAN GANTNER/MONKMEYER

EPA

Iraq

Official name: *Republic of Iraq*
Area: *167,925 sq. mi., 434,924 sq. km.*
Population: *(1990 est.) 18,868,000*
Capital: *Baghdad*
(Pop., 1986, 3,800,000)
Language: *Arabic*
Religion: *Islam*
Currency unit: *Dinar*
National holiday: *Anniversary of the revolution and establishment of the republic, July 14*

Iraq, an Arab republic in the Middle East, lies in the valleys of the Tigris and Euphrates rivers. It is bordered on the north by Turkey, on the east by Iran, on the south by Kuwait, Saudi Arabia, and a neutral zone jointly administered with Saudi Arabia, and on the west by Syria and Jordan.

The land. The high Zagros Mountains rim Iraq on the north and east. The western and southwestern regions are desert. Central Iraq consists of a "lower plain," in the southern part of the Tigris-Euphrates valley, and an "upper plain," a rolling, hilly region in the northeast of the country.

About five inches of rain fall yearly on the lower plain; the upper plain receives about 15 inches of rain a year. The rest of the country is quite dry. Summer temperatures in Iraq's desert areas often climb above 120°F, but averages for the country as a whole range from about 50°F in winter to 95°F in summer.

The people. The population is concentrated in the river valleys. Most Iraqis are Arab, but the population also includes a large Kurdish minority in the northeast. Bedouin tribes live in the southwest.

Nearly three-quarters of the population is literate and two-thirds live in urban areas. Almost half the labor force is engaged in agriculture.

Economy. Oil is the most important part of Iraq's economy, and has contributed to the country's gradually improving standard of living. Oil accounts for half the gross national product; 101.2 million metric tons were produced in 1987. The richest fields are at Kirkuk, Mosul, and Basra. The government has been nationalizing the oil industry since 1950, but the largest firms are still internationally owned and pay royalty fees to Iraq.

Iraq has some light industries that produce chiefly building materials, textiles, carpets, cigarettes, dried fruits, and leather goods.

Agriculture is also important to the economy. Farmers in the fertile central plain grow barley, wheat, rice, tobacco, cotton, and dates. Sheep are raised on the upper plain and on the fringes of the desert. Large-scale irrigation and flood control programs were undertaken in the 1950's and 1960's to create more farm land.

The country's chief export is oil, which accounted for all but a small portion of the $10.7 billion earned by exports in 1984. Barley, dates, wool, and cotton are also exported. Imports, which cost $12.3 billion in 1984, include foodstuffs, machinery, iron, and steel. Western Europe and Japan are Iraq's chief trading partners.

Government. According to its 1970 constitution, Iraq is ruled by the socialistic Revolutionary Command Council, which elects the president and appoints a council of ministers. The legislative body is the 250-member unicameral National Assembly. Elections to the legislature were held in 1980, for the first time since 1958. There is one political party.

Iraq is a member of the United Nations, the Organization of Petroleum Exporting Countries (OPEC), and the Arab League.

History. Modern Iraq is the site of ancient Mesopotamia, "the land between the rivers," where the oldest known civilization—that of the Sumerians—flourished in about 3000 B.C. Other great empires—Babylonia, Assyria, and Persia—followed Sumer in the fertile lowlands between the Tigris and the Euphrates rivers.

In 750 A.D., Arab Muslims conquered the region and converted the people to Islam. Arab rule continued until 1258, when Mongol armies devastated the country. Iraq made little recovery under the Ottoman Turks, who took power in 1638 and ruled the area until World War I.

After the war Britain received a League of Nations mandate over Iraq. In 1921 Iraqis chose as king Emir Faisal of the Arabian province of Hejaz, and in 1924 the country was proclaimed a constitutional monarchy.

Independence. In 1932 the League of Nations recognized Iraq's sovereignty by admitting it as a full member. Faisal died in 1933 and was succeeded by his son Ghazi, who reigned until his death in 1939. Ghazi's young son and heir, Faisal II, was a minor, and a regent ruled in his name.

Iraq's modern history has been turbulent. During the 1930's minority groups rebelled against the new government, and nationalists fought against the presence of British personnel and troops. During 1941 a pro-Nazi group briefly controlled the government, but it was overthrown, and Iraq supported the Allies in World War II.

Faisal II came of age in 1953, but in 1958 army officers led by General Abdel Karim Qasim overthrew the gov-

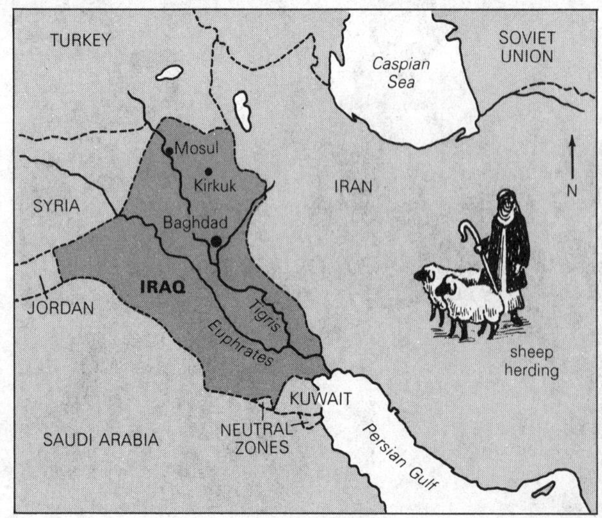

HENRI BUREAU/SYGMA

WAR IN THE MIDDLE EAST. *The Iranian oil refinery at Abadan on the Persian Gulf burns after an Iraqi attack in the war begun in 1980.*

ernment, assassinated King Faisal, and proclaimed Iraq a republic. Qasim became premier, but was killed in February 1963 during another coup, in which Abdel Salaam Arif took power.

Contemporary Iraq. After the unsuccessful attempt to form a federation with the United Arab Republic (U.A.R.) and Syria, Arif, in November, 1963, split with the pan-Arab leaders in the U.A.R. and Syria. In the following year a new constitution took effect that favored a close alliance, but not a merger, with the U.A.R.

Arif died in an accident in 1966, and his brother, Abdel Rahman Arif, became president. Several attempted coups in 1965 and 1966 resulted in a long series of governmental reorganizations, and then in 1968 Abdel Arif was ousted. A Revolutionary Command Council took power, and it has ruled since.

A major domestic problem began in 1961 when rebel Kurds demanded the establishment of an independent Kurdish state. Some Kurdish autonomy was granted in 1966 and again in 1974, but fighting, especially heavy in 1974, 1975, and 1979, continues. Iraqi bombings of Kurdish villages in Iran worsened relations between those two countries.

As border conflicts increased and Iran fell into revolution, a major Iranian-Iraqi war broke out in 1980. The brutal war left some 300,000 Iraqis dead before a cease-fire was declared in July, 1988. Peace negotiations began later that year.

Iraq also participated in the 1948-1949, 1967, and 1973 Arab wars against Israel. It led the united Arab protest against the Israeli-Egyptian peace accords of 1978–1979.

Iraqi-Soviet relations were strong until the mid-1970's, when tensions were created by Iraq's increasing trade with Western nations, its armed conflict with the Soviet-backed Palestine Liberation Organization (PLO), and its 1978 purges of the Iraqi Communist Party.

Israel

Official name: *State of Israel*
Area: *7,992 sq. mi., 20,700 sq. km.*
Population: *(1990 est.) 4,445,000*
Capital: *Jerusalem*
(Pop., 1987, 468,000)
Language: *Hebrew and Arabic*
Religion: *Jewish, Christian, Islam*
Currency unit: *Shekel*
National holiday: *Independence Day, May 15*

Israel, a Jewish republic established in 1948 in the land of ancient Palestine, lies on the eastern coast of the Mediterranean Sea. A bitter war between Israel and the Arab states of the Middle East accompanied the proclamation of the State of Israel in 1948.

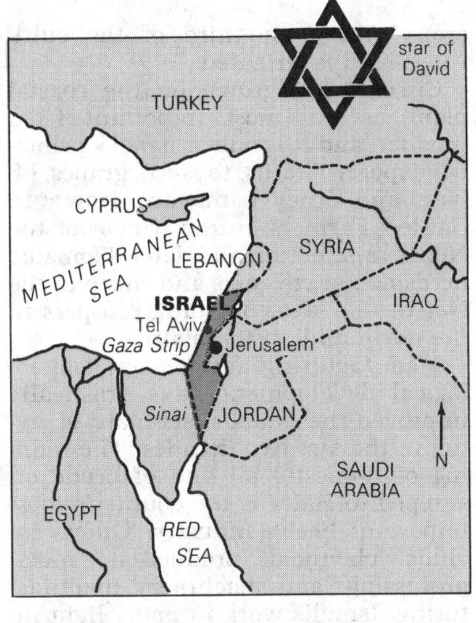

The boundaries set in 1948–1949 by truce agreements left the new state bordered on the north by Lebanon, on the east by Syria and Jordan, on the south by the Gulf of Aqaba, on the southwest by the Sinai region of Egypt, and on the west by the Mediterranean Sea and the Gaza Strip, a small area once part of Palestine, under Arab administration.

Israel's 1948–1949 boundaries were disputed by the Arab states and defended by Israel until 1967, when a new Arab-Israeli war erupted. In the 1967 campaign Israeli forces occupied the Sinai Peninsula and the Gaza Strip, the Syrian border area, and that part of Jordan lying west of the Jordan River, including all of the ancient city of Jerusalem, which had been divided between Israel and Jordan. The Sinai region was returned to Egypt in 1982, as a condition of the 1979 peace treaty between the two countries.

The land. Israel is a small, irregularly shaped country with a varied landscape. A narrow, fertile plain borders the Mediterranean. In central Israel, the hilly Judaean plateau rises east of the coastal plain. In the north rise the highlands of Galilee, a region of rolling hills and rich valleys. Near Israel's eastern border the land drops sharply into the valley of the Jordan River. The wedge-shaped, barren Negev desert, in the south, occupies more than half of Israel's land area.

The Jordan, Israel's principal river, flows along the northeastern border into Israel's largest freshwater lake, the Sea of Galilee, and on into the Dead Sea. Smaller streams run through the northern and central portions of the country, but in the southern regions only dry river beds are found.

The southern desert receives almost no rain, but rainfall in the northern and central areas averages 20 inches a year, most of it falling during the winter and spring. In the desert, average summer daytime temperatures climb to about 100°F; winter temperatures average 65°F. Temperatures along the coast and in the hills average 80°F in summer and 45°F in winter.

The people. Since 1948, when Israel became a state, over 1 million Jews from many parts of the world have poured into the area. Most Arabs fled Israel during the 1948–1949 Arab-Israeli war. Today, 85 percent of the population is Jewish, eleven percent is Muslim, and only three percent is Christian.

Israel is the most literate country in the Middle East. Six percent of its labor force is agricultural, while 25 percent is industrial. With nearly 500 people per square mile, Israel is

CHILDREN IN KIBBUTZ HAZIRIM, *in Israel's Negev. These third graders are eager to learn.*

SHEILA R. TURNER/MONKMEYER

densely populated and overwhelmingly urban.

Population is concentrated in the more fertile and temperate northern and central regions of Israel. The two largest cities, Haifa and Tel Aviv-Jaffa, are on the coast. Jerusalem, the capital, lies in the center of the Judaean Hills.

Economy. The people of Israel have worked hard to meet the challenge of a harsh land. In an area that a few decades ago had only a subsistence agriculture, Israelis have developed manufacturing industries and have increased agricultural production to feed an expanding population and to export their products.

Israel's desert lands hold a great variety of mineral resources. Potash and salts are obtained from the Dead Sea, copper is mined in the southern Negev, and stone is quarried in the center of the country. Israel has some oil and natural gas, but not enough to meet its needs. Diamonds account for one-third of the total export revenues.

Israel's economy is basically self-sufficient, despite its dependence on highly inflated oil imports, the tremendous expense of its military establishment, and an Arab boycott designed to isolate it economically. Part of the reason for the success of Israel's economy is the extensive international aid it has received, particularly from the United States.

Nearly one-third of Israel's gross national product is derived from manufacturing, while agriculture contributes seven percent. Israel's land is intensively cultivated. In areas that once were swamps or deserts, farmers use every available piece of land and every drop of water to raise their crops. About one-third of the cultivated land is irrigated.

Citrus fruit, grown on the coastal plain, is the most important farm product, and it is one of Israel's principal exports. Grains, tobacco, grapes, olives, and other fruits are grown in Galilee. Farmers on the fringes of the Negev raise cotton and dates. Nomadic herdsmen graze goats and sheep in the Negev, and dairy farming prospers in the north and on the plain.

Manufacturing and general technological development have drastically improved the Israelis' standard of living in the last two decades. The refining of domestic oil and of crude oil shipped to Haifa is the country's most important heavy industry. Others include chemical production, metal processing, and machinery manufacturing. Israelis work in many light industries, including diamond polishing, textile weaving, glass making, food processing, and wine making.

Many industries and farms are operated as cooperatives or collectives. Most of Israel's factory, farm, and office workers belong to *Histradrut,* the leading national labor union, which provides a wide variety of social and economic services.

Imports cost $9.6 billion in 1986 while exports earned $6.1 billion. Diamonds are the most important export; citrus fruits and manufactured goods are also significant. Imports are mostly oil and machinery.

Most of Israel's trade is with the United States and Western Europe. Grants as well as loans from the United States, reparations payments from West Germany, technical aid from the United Nations, and contributions from private groups and individuals around the world help to support the Israeli economy.

TWO LEADERS: *David Ben-Gurion, Israel's first prime minister, with Golda Meir.*

WIDE WORLD

Government. Israel is a parliamentary democracy. The chief of state is a president, who is elected every five years by the Parliament, or *knesset.* With the advice of the *knesset,* the president appoints a prime minister to act as chief executive. The prime minister and the cabinet he chooses are responsible to the Parliament.

Members (120) of the *knesset,* which has one house, are popularly elected to a normal term of four years. Participation in government is open to all Israeli citizens, including non-Jews.

Israel has a membership in the United Nations.

History. Although the state of Israel is new, the land is ancient. In about 2000 B.C. wandering tribes of Hebrews appeared in "Canaan," later called Palestine. Perhaps 500 years later a group of Hebrews was conquered and enslaved by the Egyptians.

After 1200 B.C., Hebrews once again inhabited Palestine and developed a society based on herding and agriculture. Over the next 1000 years there developed the Hebrew culture and religion that produced the Hebrew Bible, the Old Testament; gave root to Christianity; and contributed its part to the foundation of Western civilization.

Despite the strength and importance of their culture, the Jews were never powerful militarily or politically. In the 900's B.C. the Hebrew kingdom split in two—the kingdom of Israel in the north and the kingdom of Judah (the source of the word Jew) in the south. By 586 B.C. both kingdoms had been conquered and most Jews were in exile in Babylonia. Fifty years later Babylon fell and the Jews were permitted to return to Palestine.

Those who returned settled in southern Palestine and rebuilt Jerusalem. They were free from foreign domination only briefly, however. Palestine became in turn a province of Persia (538–332 B.C.), of Alexander (332–323 B.C.), of Egypt (323–198 B.C.), and of the Syrian Seleucid dynasty (198–168 B.C.).

The Jews were able to maintain their own society and culture, however, and it was during the period after the Babylonian captivity that the Hebrew Bible was compiled from earlier and contemporary writings.

In 168 B.C. the Jews successfully rebelled against the Seleucids, only to be subjugated in 63 B.C. by the Romans. In 70 A.D. the Jews tried to throw off Roman rule, but they were crushed and their capital city, Jerusalem, was destroyed.

The diaspora. Many Jews left Palestine and scattered throughout the world in what was called the *diaspora,* or the dispersion. Palestine remained in the hands of the Romans and their successors, the Byzantines, until the 600's. Then the armies of a new religion, Islam, made Palestine part of a vast Arab empire.

Four hundred years later, the Seljuk Turks conquered Palestine, but they were soon challenged by the Christian crusaders, who penetrated the country. Finally, Egypt drove out the crusaders and held Palestine until it became a part of the Ottoman Turkish Empire in the 1500's. Palestine remained Turkish until the end of World War I.

Many of the dispersed Jews had never been completely accepted into the societies in which they had settled. Often they were victims of prejudice and persecution, but they maintained their religion, their culture, and the hope that they would one day return to Palestine, or "Zion."

Zionism. During the 1800's a Zionist, or nationalist, movement arose, and small groups of Jews returned to Palestine as pioneers. The first Zionist Congress was held in 1897 at Basel, Switzerland, under the leadership of Theodore Herzl, an Austrian Jew.

The congress greatly strengthened

ISRAEL'S WAR GAINS *by 1973* (right), *and female soldiers training in the same year. All of Sinai has since been returned to Egypt.*

the efforts of the early idealistic pioneers and formulated the Basel Program, which called for the settlement of Jews in Palestine and the creation of a homeland there for the Jewish people. Zionism as an international mass movement included both religious idealists and political nationalists, and it won the support of many non-Jews.

The Zionists tried to persuade Turkey to allow the mass settlement of Jews in Palestine, but the request was refused. In 1917, during World War I, Britain's foreign secretary, Arthur Balfour, publicly announced Britain's support for the Zionist program.

This "Balfour Declaration" pledged to facilitate "the establishment in Palestine of a national home for the Jewish people" without injuring the non-Jewish population already living there. Britain occupied Palestine during the war. In 1922 the League of Nations gave Britain a mandate over Palestine—then including both present-day Israel and Jordan—that obliged it to fulfill the Balfour pledge.

British mandate. The Zionists were well organized. They established organizations to encourage immigration, handle finances, set up political structures, and plan extensive agricultural and industrial development. The Jewish community developed alongside the traditional Arab society, but Jewish immigration and land purchases and the pioneer spirit of the Jews encountered Arab resistance.

The British sought to appease the Arabs by restricting Jewish activity. Finally, in 1939–1940, they drastically limited Jewish immigration and land purchases to keep Jews a minority in Palestine. The Arabs were not satisfied, however.

During World War II the Palestinian Arab leader, the mufti of Jerusalem, cooperated with the Germans. The Jews supported the British in the war, and a Jewish brigade fought in the Middle East and in Europe.

Jews did defy the British effort to close Palestine to refugees from Nazi countries, and many Jews entered Palestine despite British opposition. Opinion in the non-Arab world began to turn against Britain. By the end of the war the deadlock over Palestine was complete. Britain, unable to find a solution satisfactory to all sides, submitted the dilemma to the United Nations in February, 1947.

Statehood. In November, 1947, the United Nations voted to terminate the British mandate and to partition Palestine into an Arab state, a Jewish state, and a multinational enclave around Jerusalem. The British left Palestine by May 15, 1948, and an Israeli government took power. It was recognized by most non-Arab states.

Sporadic fighting had broken out in Palestine immediately after the UN partition resolution. On the heels of the British withdrawal, the Arab states of the Middle East, united in the Arab League, invaded Israel. The Israelis drove the invaders out, and in 1949 the United Nations negotiated separate armistice agreements between Israel and the Arab states. But no final peace treaty was signed, and a formal state of war continued.

The Arabs refused to recognize Israel and employed tactics of encirclement, noncommunication, economic boycott, and border harassment. When Egypt began a military buildup on Israel's frontier in 1956, Israel invaded Egyptian territory. Shortly the United Nations arranged a cease-fire.

After several years of uneasy peace, local clashes broke out along the Israeli-Syrian border in 1967, and Egypt massed troops on Israel's border. Israel struck out at Egypt and at Jordan, which had joined the conflict, occupying the Gaza Strip, the Sinai Peninsula, western Jordan, and the heights east of the Sea of Galilee. A cease-fire was established after about four months, and it remained more or less in effect until October of 1973, when Egypt launched an attack across the Suez Canal and Syrian forces struck the Golan Heights. In 18 days the United Nations worked out a cease-fire. A disengagement agreement was agreed to by Egypt and Israel in December of 1973, and by Syria and Israel in May of 1974.

Prime Minister Menachem Begin, elected in 1977, and Egypt's President Anwar el-Sadat, signed a peace treaty in 1979. The treaty called for Israel's withdrawal from the Arab territory it had annexed.

Attempts for a peaceful resolution of the conflict between Israel and the Arab states have been greatly hindered by the terrorist anti-Israeli policies of the Palestine Liberation Organization (PLO), led by Yasir Arafat. Israeli-PLO tension led to a limited war between Lebanon and Israel in 1978, and an Israeli invasion of Lebanon in 1982, which forced the withdrawal of the PLO from that country.

Menachem Begin resigned in 1983, and was succeeded by Yitzhak Shamir, his foreign minister.

In December, 1987, a Palestinian uprising, called the intifada, erupted on the West Bank and in the Gaza Strip, in protest against occupation of the territories by Israel.

In November, 1988, the PLO declared an independent Palestinian state in the occupied territories, but the new state was not accorded much international recognition. Later, in an attempt to gain additional diplomatic recognition, the PLO recognized the right of Israel to exist.

Ivory Coast

Official name: *Republic of Ivory Coast*
Area: *124,504 sq. mi., 322,463 sq. km.*
Population: *(1990 est.) 12,070,000*
Capital: *Abidjan (Pop., 1989, 2,100,000)*
Language: *French, African languages*
Religion: *Traditional religions, Islam, Christian*
Currency unit: *Franc CFA (African Financial Community)*
National holiday: *Independence Day, Aug. 7*

The Ivory Coast, a republic in western Africa, is bordered on the north by Mali and Upper Volta, on the east by Ghana, on the south by the Atlantic Ocean, and on the west by Liberia and Guinea. The Ivory Coast was a territory of France until 1960, when it received its independence.

CACAO BEANS, *the origin of chocolate and hot cocoa, one of Ivory Coast's chief products, being dried by villagers for export.*

The land. The surface of the Ivory Coast is relatively flat. There are plantations along the eastern part of the country's coast, beyond which are tropical rain forests. There are forests along the western part of the coast. North of the forest is a savanna region. There are mountains in the west and northwest with elevations above 5000 feet.

Three almost parallel rivers flow from north to south—the Sassandra in the west, the Bandama, and the Comoé in the east. The Cavalla River flows along part of the Ivory Coast's western border.

The Ivory Coast has a hot, tropical climate. The coastal region receives an average of about 80 inches of rain each year, and the northern part of the country receives an average of about 50 inches yearly.

The people. There are many ethnic groups in the Ivory Coast. The most important are the Baule, Senufo, Agni, and Kru. Most of the people are farmers. The Ivory Coast's largest city and major port is Abidjan, the country's capital.

Economy. The Ivory Coast's economic life depends heavily on agriculture. The country's most important crops are coffee, cacao, pineapples, and bananas. Although most of the Ivory Coast's land is undeveloped, it is one of the world's leading producers of both coffee and cacao. Once grown on large European-owned plantations, both are now raised mainly on small African-owned farms. The basic food crops are yams, manioc, and rice. Fishing is also important to the economy.

Although the Ivory Coast is only lightly industrialized, its agricultural diversification, aided by significant foreign investments and increases in mining and industry, have made it the most prosperous and self-sufficient state of former French West Africa. Its industries include food processing, textiles, and oil refining. Lumbering is very prosperous, as is the mining of diamonds and manganese. Possible oil and iron ore deposits are now being explored.

The Ivory Coast's trade volume has risen sharply since 1960. In 1985 imports cost $1.72 billion, while exports earned $2.94 billion. France is the most significant trading partner. The Ivory Coast's major imports are machinery, petroleum products, and consumer goods. Exports include coffee, cacao, bananas, timber, and pineapple. The Ivory Coast joined with Dahomey, Upper Volta, and Niger in 1959, and with Togo in 1966, for mutual economic cooperation.

Government. The Ivory Coast has a presidential system of government. Executive powers are vested in a president, who is popularly elected to a five-year term. Legislative power is held by a 175-member National Assembly. Assembly members are elected by universal suffrage to five-year terms. There is only one political party.

The Ivory Coast is a member of the United Nations and the Organization of African Unity, and it is an associated state of the European Common Market.

History. The important Muslim city of Kong in the north of the present-day Ivory Coast dates from the 1000's as a caravan trade center. African kingdoms in the southeast of the country date from the time of the expansion of the Ashanti people from present-day Ghana in the 1700's and 1800's.

French rule. France had contacts with the Ivory Coast in the 1600's and 1700's. In 1893 France established the Ivory Coast colony, and in 1904 the colony was made a part of the Federation of French West Africa. But the total conquest of the area was not completed until the end of World War I.

There was little freedom of political expression for Africans until after World War II. At that time Felix Houphouët-Boigny founded the Ivory Coast Democratic Party (PDCI), a local section of the African Democratic Rally. The PDCI grew rapidly and became the dominant political force in the country.

In 1946 the colony became a territory within the French Union. With support from French Communists and the French administration, Houphouët-Boigny was elected to the French National Assembly.

He gained fame in the assembly for his law abolishing forced labor. France then attempted to suppress the PDCI, and as a result many regional parties sprang up. In 1950 Houphouët-Boigny broke with the Communists and adopted a pro-French policy. He rebuilt his party, benefiting from prosperity created by a coffee boom.

Independence. From 1956 to 1959 Houphouët-Boigny was a member of successive French administrations. In 1958 his country voted overwhelmingly to become an autonomous member of the French Community.

The Ivory Coast became independent on August 7, 1960, and Houphouët-Boigny was unanimously elected president of the republic. All opposition parties were silenced, and the PDCI became the country's sole legal political party, a status it still enjoys.

The Ivory Coast has become a leader of African pro-Western sentiments under the long, peaceful, and prosperous rule of Houphouët-Boigny, who is still in power. Its economy has rapidly developed, averaging a growth rate of ten percent each year since 1960, and the country has become a model of successful transition from a European-operated to an African-operated economy. The people of the Ivory Coast enjoy a high standard of living.

Jordan

Official name: *Hashemite Kingdom of Jordan*
Area: *37,737 sq. mi., 97,740 sq. km.*
Population: *(1990 est.) 3,065,000*
Capital: *Amman (Pop., 1988 est., 800,000)*
Language: *Arabic*
Religion: *Islam*
Currency unit: *Dinar*
National holiday: *Independence Day, May 25*

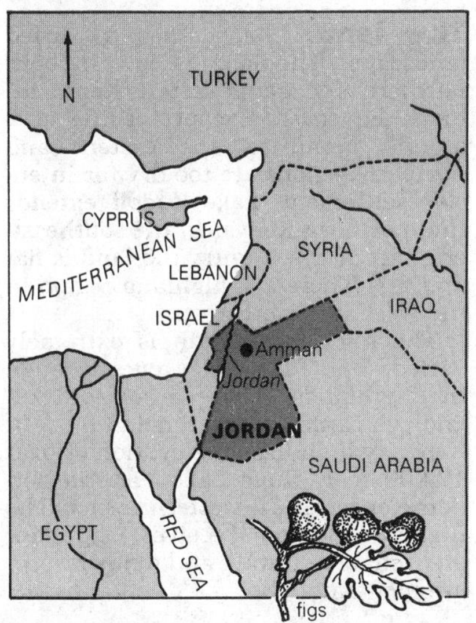

The Hashemite Kingdom of Jordan is bordered on the north by Syria and Iraq, on the east and south by Saudi Arabia, and on the west by Israel. Jordan has a short coastline on the Gulf of Aqaba.

The land. Most of Jordan is barren land. Almost the entire eastern half of the country is desert, partly covered by salt or lava. In the west a hilly region separates the desert from a wide, deep gorge that runs the length of the country. The Jordan River flows through the northern part of this gorge, from the Sea of Galilee into the salty Dead Sea.

South of the Dead Sea the gorge is a dry river bed, the Wadi al Araba. West of the Jordan River lies the fertile Judaean Hill region, which was seized from Palestine in 1948 and occupied by Israel in 1967.

In the western uplands, Jordan's climate is mild, with average temperatures of from 45°F to 76°F and from 15 to 25 inches of rainfall a year. Almost no rain falls in the desert, where summer temperatures rise above 120°F.

The people. Most of the people are Arabs, many having immigrated from Palestine during the 1948–1949 Arab-Israeli war. Sunni Muslims make up 95 percent of the population, and Christians only 5 percent. The majority of the people of the occupied West Bank are Palestinians. They are frequently at odds with the Bedouins of eastern Jordan.

The population, slightly more rural than urban, is densest in the northwestern hills and valleys. The labor force is 80 percent agricultural and 20 percent industrial.

Economy. Jordan is a very poor, arid country, with little surface water, infertile soil and few exploitable resources. Potash and phosphates, mined around the Dead Sea, are Jordan's most important minerals. Some marble, gypsum, manganese, and ceramic clays are also mined, and there are untapped reserves of copper, iron, sulfur, and silicon.

Only about ten percent of Jordan's land is suitable for cultivation, and only part of that is farmed. Agriculture contributes one-tenth of the gross national product, and one-quarter of Jordan's food demands must be met by imports. The best growing regions are in the moist northwest, but even there some irrigation is necessary. Barley and wheat are the main crops. Beans, tobacco, and citrus and other fruits grow in the Jordan valley, and grapes, dates, figs, olives, and nuts are raised in the drier areas. Goats, sheep, camels, and horses are raised.

One-quarter of the gross national product is contributed by industry, mainly handicraft manufacture.

Natural phosphates, vegetables, and fruits are the most important of Jordan's exports, which were valued at $732 million in 1986. The country imported $2.4 billion worth of goods in 1986, primarily foodstuffs, petroleum, pharmaceuticals, textiles, and machinery. Most trade is with the United States, Britain, West Germany, and the Arab states.

TYPICAL OUTDOOR CAFE *in Amman, Jordan, where the men, many of them exiled Palestinians, play games, smoke their water pipes, and talk hour after hour. Women are never allowed in cafes.*

WILLEM VAN DE POLL/MONKMEYER

Government. Jordan is a constitutional monarchy. The hereditary head of state is a king who wields great authority over all branches of government. He appoints the prime minister and other members of the cabinet and may dismiss them at will.

The ministers are also responsible to the lower house of the National Assembly, the House of Representatives, which is elected every four years by universal suffrage. Members of the upper house, the Senate, are appointed by the king.

Jordan is a member of the United Nations and the Arab League.

History. The area of Jordan is believed to have been inhabited since prehistoric times, and it was part of the land of the ancient Hebrews. As a part of Syria, the region was occupied by a succession of Middle Eastern empires. The last was the Ottoman Empire, which controlled the country from the 1500's into the 1900's.

After World War I Jordan became part of a new Syrian kingdom, which came under French control. In 1922 the League of Nations gave Britain a mandate over Palestine and Transjordan, as the territory between the Jordan River and Saudi Arabia was called. In 1923 Transjordan gained semi-independent status within the mandate area.

Emir Abdullah ibn Husayn, an Arabian ruler, governed with British advice. He was the first of the *Hashemite* ("of Hashem," or "Husayn") dynasty. For the next 20 years the country moved toward independence with British assistance. Transjordanian troops aided the Allies in World War II, and a treaty signed in 1946 with Britain established Transjordan's sovereignty. Britain retained great influence, however.

In 1948–1949 Transjordan participated in the Arab war against the newly proclaimed state of Israel. Abdullah annexed a portion of Palestine just west of the Jordan River and changed the country's name from Transjordan, "across the Jordan," to Jordan.

Contemporary Jordan. King Abdullah was assassinated in 1951, and his son and heir, Talal, was judged incompetent. Talal's son, Hussein, came to the throne in 1952. Hussein sought British aid in meeting the country's pressing economic and social problems. But the presence in the country of a large number of Palestinian refugees demanding renewed war with Israel led to political instability.

Anti-Western riots in 1955 and 1956 forced the departure from the country of all British personnel and an end to British assistance. In 1957 and 1958 King Hussein himself barely avoided being deposed during a government upheaval.

The territory that Jordan annexed from Israel in 1948, the West Bank of Jordan and Jerusalem, was regained by Israel in the June, 1967, war.

Palestinian guerrillas based in Jordan continued raids on Israel. Jordanian troops tried, unsuccessfully, to squelch these raids. Other Arab states supported the Palestinians, and, in 1974, at an Arab summit meeting, the Palestine Liberation Organization was designated as the sole representative of the Arabs on the West Bank. The Jordanian government accepted this, although it heightened tensions between Jordan's Bedouin population and the Palestinians. Hussein subsequently dissolved Parliament to reduce its Palestinian representation.

Hussein has led Jordan and other Arab states in their condemnation of Egypt for its 1979 peace treaty with Israel. He replaced Jordan's pro-Western policy with political nonalignment.

Jordan's economy has suffered from the persistent warfare and Palestinian terrorism that has been carried on in the region for years. Its unemployment problems were seriously heightened when Israel reoccupied the West Bank in 1967, thus forcing large-scale Palestinian emigration into Jordan. Meanwhile, the fertile agricultural lands and irrigation water supplies of the West Bank were lost. Jordan's ailing economy receives heavy aid from the Arab oil states, but the United States has continued its support as well.

DOME OF THE ROCK, *ancient mosque on the Temple Mount in Jerusalem, belonged, with the old city, to Jordan until 1967. Then Israel captured the West Bank and all Jerusalem.*

PAN AMERICAN AIRWAYS

Kenya

Official name: *Republic of Kenya*
Area: *224,960 sq. mi., 582,645 sq. km.*
Population: *(1990 est.) 25,393,000*
Capital: *Nairobi (Pop., 1989, 1,100,000)*
Language: *English, Swahili, other African languages*
Religion: *Traditional religions, Christian, Islam*
Currency unit: *Shilling*
National holiday: *Independence Day, Dec. 12*

Kenya, a republic in eastern Africa, is bordered on the north by Sudan and Ethiopia, on the east by the Somali Republic and the Indian Ocean, on the south by Tanzania, and on the west by Uganda.

Kenya received its independence from Britain in 1963.

The land. Kenya has a varied landscape. The land is low in both northern Kenya and eastern Kenya behind the coast. Except for the area around Mombasa, the eastern and northern regions are too dry for intensive settlement. Lake Rudolf extends into northern Kenya. In the southeastern part of the country the land is flat and dry. There is a highland region in the west and southwest.

The highland terrain is extremely varied. The Rift Valley cuts through the highlands. There are also lakes and volcanic peaks, including Mt. Kenya, which has an elevation of over 17,000 feet. Huge Lake Victoria borders Kenya's southwestern corner. The highland region receives abundant and reliable rainfall, and temperatures are moderate.

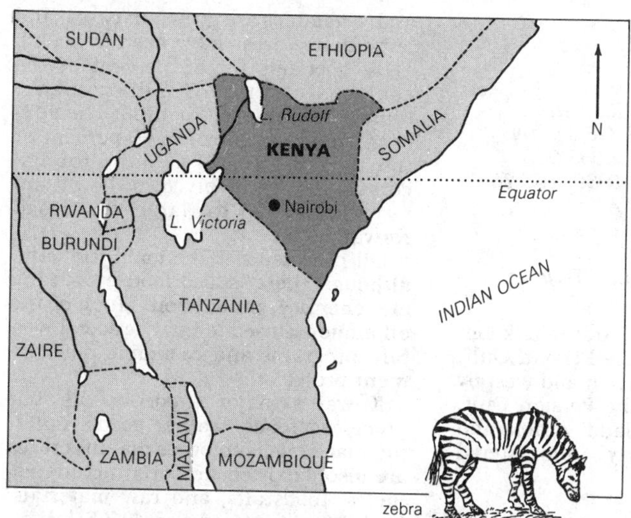

FAMOUS FOR BIG GAME *and photographic safaris, Kenya's huge tourist industry has made it one of the most familiar African countries.*

The people. Africans make up about 97 percent of Kenya's large population, and Europeans, Asians, and Arabs account for the remaining three percent. Kenya's people belong to many different tribes. The largest tribes are the Kikuyu, Luo, Baluhya, Masai, and Kamba. The Kikuyu people have played an important role in Kenya's political history.

Kenya's largest city is its capital, Nairobi. Mombasa, on the Indian Ocean, is the country's major port. Kenya's population is 90 percent rural, and almost three-fourths of the labor force is agricultural.

Economy. Kenya's steadily growing economy is largely based on private African enterprise supported by the government. Agriculture is the foundation of the economy, with the highlands as its mainstay. Many crops are grown on European-owned plantations, including coffee, tea, and sisal. While coffee and tea are its most important crops, Kenya is the world's largest producer of pyrethrum, a vegetable ingredient used in certain insecticides. The staples of the country, produced by Africans and Europeans, include corn, wheat, vegetables, dairy products, and meat.

Although Kenya is apparently not well endowed with mineral resources, the country is a major producer of soda ash. The Kenyan government has made efforts to develop the country's industry and has encouraged tourism, largely safaris from Nairobi to see the country's varied wildlife.

In 1988 imports cost $1.7 billion and exports earned $1.2 billion. Kenya's main imports are machinery, chemicals, food, and fabrics. Exports include coffee, tea, sisal, pyrethrum, and petroleum products. The country's main trading partners are Britain, the United States, West Germany, the Netherlands, and Japan.

With a well built seaport at Mombasa with connecting railroads and roads, Kenya is the principal handler of Uganda's trade. Kenya, Uganda, and Tanzania cooperate closely in communications, technical services, trade, and economic development.

Government. Kenya has a presidential system of government. Executive power is held by a president, who is popularly elected to a five-year term. Legislative power is vested in a 175-member House of Representatives. House members are popularly elected to five-year terms.

Kenya is a member of the United Nations, the Organization of African Unity, and the Commonwealth of Nations, and it is an associated state of the European Common Market.

History. Starting in the 700's the people of present-day Kenya traded with the Arabs, mainly for slaves. By the 1600's Turks and Portuguese had joined the trade, but in the early 1800's Britain outlawed the slave trade.

British rule. In 1887 the sultan of Zanzibar, who had nominal control of the region, granted the British East African Company control over all of present-day Kenya in return for a fixed sum of money. Britain declared the area a protectorate in 1895. In the same year Britain began building a railroad from Mombasa to Uganda with the aid of Indian laborers.

To make the railroad pay for itself by transporting agricultural products, the British government encouraged Europeans to settle and farm in Kenya by offering long-term land leases in

THE OLD LION OF KENYA. *Jomo Kenyatta, Kenya's first president and before that leader of the Mau Mau terrorists, joins native dancers with Dr. Tubman of Liberia. Both are now dead.*

the highlands. Britain set up reserves of land for Africans displaced by European settlers outside the highlands.

Britain established a legislative council in the region in 1907. In 1920 all but the coastal area became a Crown colony. The coastal region became the Kenya Protectorate.

Nationalism. In 1938 the highland region, which became known as the "white highlands," was officially closed for settlement to all but Europeans. The European community came to dominate political affairs. Meanwhile, the African population, especially the numerous Kikuyu people, was increasing and crowding the reserves. Many Africans were forced to seek work in the new cities. Although an African was nominated to the legislative council in 1944, power remained in the hands of the white settlers and unrest grew among the Africans. Kikuyu, such as Harry Thuku and Jomo Kenyatta, created political organizations in the 1940's.

Starting in 1952 the Mau Mau, militant Kikuyu trying to gain independence for Kenya, terrorized the country. Thousands of Africans and some whites were killed before the uprising ended in 1956. Thereafter, Britain made steady concessions to the Africans, and on December 12, 1963, Kenya became independent.

Independence. In 1964 Kenya became a republic with Jomo Kenyatta (1891–1978) as its first president. Kenyatta's regime gave Kenya a peaceful and relatively stable beginning, although charges of government corruption were made in 1974–1975, and there was an attempted coup in 1982.

Relations with Uganda and Tanzania have been poor since 1976. In 1980 military and economic aid was accepted from the United States, which, in return, gained access to Kenya's military bases.

Kuwait

Official name: *State of Kuwait*
Area: *6,880 sq. mi., 17,818 sq. km.*
Population: *(1990 est.) 2,083,000*
Capital: *Kuwait (Pop., 1989, 167,768)*
Language: *Arabic*
Religion: *Islam*
Currency unit: *Dinar*
National holiday: *National Day, Feb. 25*

Kuwait is an oil-rich Arab sheikdom on the west coast of the Persian Gulf. It is bordered on the north and west by Iraq, on the east by the Persian Gulf, and on the south by Saudi Arabia and a neutral zone jointly administered with Saudi Arabia.

The land and people. Kuwait's surface is level desert broken only by a single ridge of hills and a few small oases. The climate is extremely hot, and almost no rain falls.

Native Kuwaitis are Arabs but there are large minorities of Indians, Iranians, and non-Kuwaiti Arabs, as well as European and U.S. oil workers. Three-quarters of the labor force is comprised of foreign workers, largely Palestinians employed in either government work or in the oil industry. Almost all Kuwaitis live in urban areas, and most are Sunni Muslims. The largest cities are Kuwait, the capital, and Al Ahmadi, the oil port.

Economy. Oil is Kuwait's only important natural resource. An estimated one-fifth of the world's proved oil reserves lie beneath Kuwait's land and off its coasts. Water, however, is scarce. Water is imported and seawater is desalinated. Most of the land is not suitable for cultivation, but fruits and vegetables are grown in oases, and large desert areas have been irrigated.

Oil accounts for 85 percent of the country's exports; 73 million metric tons were produced in 1988. The government took control of 60 percent of the industry in 1974. Many foreign companies are involved in the oil enterprise and they pay large royalties to Kuwait.

Oil processing is the main industry, although there is also food processing and chemical production. Much of the oil money is used to finance social welfare programs and economic development projects.

Kuwait's major export is oil, but processed foods, leather goods, building materials, and other manufactures are also exported. Imports include vehicles, foodstuffs, and raw materials. In 1978 exports earned $17.6 billion while imports cost only $4.6 billion. Kuwait's chief trading partners are Japan, the United States, and the United Kingdom.

Government. Kuwait is a constitutional monarchy in which the ruler, an emir, exercises great power. The emir is assisted by a prime minister and a council of ministers. The legislative body is the National Assembly, made up of 50 elected members.

Kuwait is a member of the United Nations, the Arab League, and the Organization of Petroleum Exporting Countries (OPEC).

History. Kuwait was first settled in the early 1700's by Arab people from the interior of Arabia. It grew prosperous as a trading center and a pearl fishery. Attacks from South Arabia in the late 1700's impoverished the country, but by the end of the 1800's the economy had recovered.

In 1899, after attempts by the Otto-

THE EMIR OF KUWAIT *alights from a Kuwait Airways jet. He belongs to the al-Sabah dynasty, which has ruled Kuwait since 1759.*

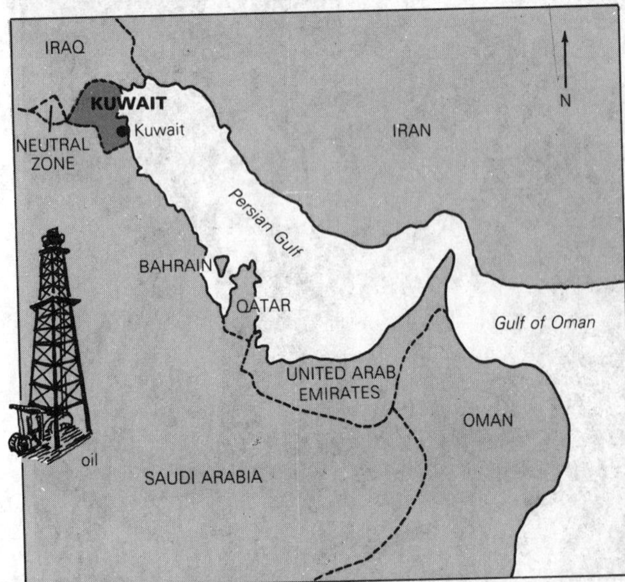

man Empire to annex Kuwait, the country signed a treaty of protection with Britain. By that treaty and a later agreement, Britain assumed responsibility for Kuwait's foreign affairs and defense.

The beginnings of full-scale oil production in 1946 radically changed the way of life of the people of Kuwait. Within 20 years the country had become a wealthy welfare state.

Kuwait gained full independence in June, 1961, when the 1899 protective treaty with Britain was canceled and replaced by a treaty of friendship. Within the month, Iraq announced its intention of annexing Kuwait, which it claimed as Iraqi territory. British troops were sent to protect Kuwait, and later an international force of the Arab League replaced the British troops. Arab League forces remained in Kuwait until the threat from Iraq ended in 1962. The dispute was not finally settled until 1963, however, when new leaders seized power in Iraq.

Since 1962 the Kuwait Fund for Arab Economic Development has been a major source of funds for development projects in other Arab lands. In 1967, after renewed Arab-Israeli hostilities caused severe economic problems in many Arab states, Kuwait increased its aid to these Arab lands.

As part of the Arab bloc, Kuwait fought Israel in the Arab-Israeli war in 1973 and opposed the 1979 Egyptian-Israeli peace treaty. The large Palestinian element in Kuwait's population has been influential in the country's anti-Israeli policies.

Lebanon

Official name: *Republic of Lebanon*
Area: *4,015 sq. mi., 10,400 sq. km.*
Population: *(1990 est.) 3,392,000*
Capital: *Beirut (Pop., 1980, 702,000)*
Language: *Arabic*
Religion: *Christian, Islam*
Currency unit: *Pound*
National holiday: *Independence Day, Nov. 22*

Lebanon is an independent republic at the eastern end of the Mediterranean Sea. It is bordered on the north and the east by Syria, on the south by Israel, and on the west by the Mediterranean Sea.

The land. Mountains cover more than half of Lebanon. The Lebanon Mountains run through the center of the country, and the Sharqi, or Anti-Lebanon, chain extends along the eastern border. A narrow, fertile plain lies between the coast and the Lebanon Mountains, and the Bekaa, a fertile plateau, lies between the Lebanon and the Sharqi ranges. Lebanon's major river, the Litani, flows through the Bekaa.

Lebanon's climate is mild and moist. Average temperatures range from 50°F in winter to 80°F in summer, and yearly rainfall averages between 30 and 50 inches.

The people. The Lebanese people are largely Arab. Approximately half the population is Christian and half is Muslim. There are many separate sects within each community. The largest are the Maronite Christians and the Sunni Muslims.

The population is concentrated in port cities along the coast, especially Beirut, Tripoli, and Sidon. Heavy emigration, primarily to North and South America, has characterized the Lebanese population since the 1860's, and there are almost as many Lebanese living abroad as in Lebanon. Many emigrants maintain economic and social ties with Lebanon and contribute to the country's economic and cultural life.

Lebanon is very densely populated, with nearly 800 people per square mile. Its population is 60 percent urban. Three-quarters of the people are literate.

Economy. Lebanon's economy is more diversified than that of many other Middle Eastern nations. Agriculture, industry, and trade are all important. The country has no major exploitable mineral resources except for some deposits of iron ore.

Agriculture occupies almost 20 percent of the labor force and contributes 9 percent of the gross national product. The leading crops are grains, tobacco, olives, and citrus and other fruits. Sheep, pastured in the mountains, and timber forests, in central Lebanon, are also of economic importance.

The availability of a well educated and skilled labor force and the development of the country's great hydroelectric resources enabled Lebanon's industry to expand rapidly after 1960. Lumber and food processing, textile weaving, oil refining, and cement production are the leading industries. Income from tourism is also important.

International trade and finance are vital to the Lebanese economy. Lebanon is a leading banking center, and Lebanese ports handle a large share of the trade passing through the eastern Mediterranean. Services and trade contribute over half of the gross national product and occupy 75 percent of the labor force.

Most Lebanese exports, worth an estimated $221.4 million in 1986, go to Saudi Arabia; imports, estimated at $390.6 million in 1986, come from Western Europe and the United States. The main exports are agricultural products, and the major imports include machinery, textiles, and manufactured consumer goods.

Government. Lebanon is a republic in which power is divided between Christians and Muslims. A Christian president, elected by a unicameral Parliamant, is head of state. A prime minister, who is a Muslim, and a cabinet are responsible to Parliament. Members of Parliament are popularly elected under a system by which each religious group elects a number of representatives in proportion to its membership.

Lebanon is a member of the United Nations and the Arab League.

History. Lebanon is an ancient land. In its forests grew the Cedars of Lebanon mentioned in the Old Testament. Its excellent ports have made it a vital trading center since ancient times. Before 2000 B.C. the area was the home of the Canaanites, later the Phoenicians, who were the leading traders of the ancient world. In the 800's B.C. it was conquered by the Assyrians.

Lebanon's history has been closely associated with that of Syria, but Lebanon was set apart by the strong influence of Christianity. Because of its proximity to Palestine, Phoenicia was the site of some of the earliest Christian communities, and by the 300's A.D. it was entirely Christian. A small group of Lebanese Christians escaped Muslim armies that conquered and converted most of Syria-Lebanon in the 600's A.D. Their descendants became the Maronites—Arab Christians affiliated with the Roman Catholic Church.

Ottoman era. In the 1500's the Ottoman Empire conquered both Lebanon and Syria, but Lebanon was allowed a great deal of autonomy. This relative freedom and the country's commercial importance placed Lebanon in an advantageous position that it maintained through the 1800's. In addition, the presence of a large number of British and French missionary schools and colleges made it a center for Arab intellectual development in the 1800's. Here many of the early leaders of the modern Middle East were educated in Western ways and learning.

During the period of Ottoman rule, Lebanese Christian and Muslim communities expanded, and the two occasionally came into conflict. In 1860 a revolt by Christian peasants against Muslim overlords touched off widespread religious strife, eventually leading to civil war. Britain and France intervened and forced Turkey to give Lebanon an autonomous government that divided power between the Christians and the Muslims, a system that has again broken down.

Independence. After the defeat of the Ottoman Empire in World War I, France received a League of Nations mandate over Lebanon. In 1926 the French created a republican government, but the Lebanese demanded complete independence. In 1941, following Germany's defeat of France in World War II, a free Lebanese government proclaimed the country's independence of the German-controlled Vichy French administration.

A treaty recognizing Lebanon's sovereignty was signed in 1943 by Lebanon and the Free French government. In 1945 Lebanon was admitted to the United Nations; it also joined the Arab League. All foreign troops had left the country by 1946, and in 1947 elections were held.

During the 1950's and 1960's Lebanon strengthened its economy and expanded social welfare and development programs.

Civil war flared again from 1975 to 1976, with Palestinians and leftist Muslims teamed against Christian Maronite factions of the army and Israeli-backed Christians. UN troops temporarily reestablished peace.

The use of southern Lebanon by the PLO (Palestine Liberation Organization) as a base from which to conduct terrorist attacks against Israel, led, in 1982, to the invasion of Lebanon by Israel. The defeat of the Palestinian forces led to the withdrawal of the PLO from part of Lebanon.

Since the beginning of the civil war in 1975, several attempts have been made by foreign countries to restore order in Lebanon. In 1983 multinational peacekeeping forces were installed in Beirut to support the elected government. After attacks on the U.S. embassy, and on the headquarters of the U.S. and French units, the forces were withdrawn. More recently, in 1986, Syrian troops moved into Beirut to oversee a cease-fire agreement, but fighting broke out between Lebanese factions anyway.

Owing to the constant battling between factions, Lebanon suffers terribly from political instability. It has so far proved impossible to form a government that can hold the support of enough of the factions to be effective.

Lesotho

Official name: *Kingdom of Lesotho*
Area: *11,716 sq. mi., 30,355 sq. km.*
Population: *(1990 est.) 1,757,000*
Capital: *Maseru (Pop., 1986, 109,382)*
Language: *English, Sesotho*
Religion: *Christian, traditional religions*
Currency unit: *Maloti*
National holiday: *Independence Day, Oct. 4*

Lesotho, a republic in southern Africa, lies entirely within the borders of the Republic of South Africa. Lesotho, formerly known as Basutoland, received its independence from Britain in 1966.

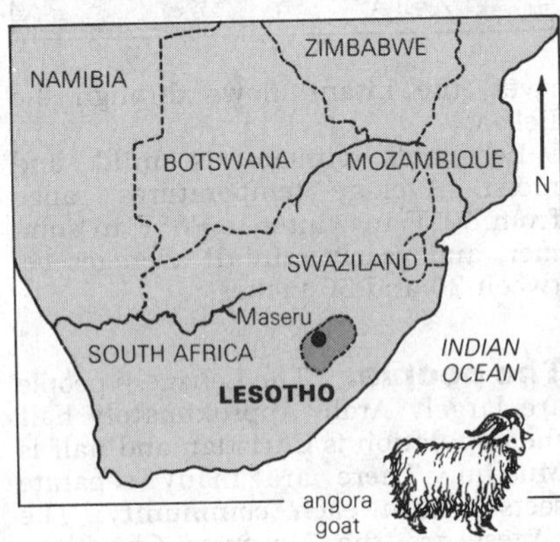

The land.

The Drakensberg Mountains dominate most of Lesotho. The mountains reach elevations of about 11,000 feet above sea level, but they have areas of grassland and alpine pasture. Lowlands, in the west, occupy about one-quarter of Lesotho. The Orange River and its tributaries flow through the country. Rainfall averages about 28 inches a year.

The people.

Almost the entire population is made up of Africans of the Basuto tribe. Most of the people live in the lowlands. About 70 percent of the people are Christian. Many thousands of Basutos are employed in the Republic of South Africa because Lesotho cannot support its population. Lesotho's major city is its capital, Maseru. Almost all of Lesotho's people live in rural areas, and 87 percent of the labor force is engaged in subsistence agriculture.

Economy.

Lesotho is a poverty-stricken nation. Its economy is based on subsistence agriculture, livestock raising, and the earnings of workers employed in South Africa. The chief crops are corn, beans, sorghum, peas, and wheat. Cattle, sheep, and goats are raised throughout the country, and hides, wool, and mohair are produced.

There are only a few small industries in the country. Mineral deposits, except for diamonds, have not been discovered. Diamond mining is important to the economy.

In 1985 imports cost $284 million while exports earned only $18 million. Lesotho imports food, machinery, vehicles, manufactured goods, and petroleum products. Exports include wool and mohair, diamonds, and livestock. Most of Lesotho's trade is with the Republic of South Africa, with which Lesotho has a customs union. Lesotho receives financial aid from Britain.

Government.

In 1986 a military coup led by officers of the Royal Lesotho Defense Force overthrew Prime Minister Leabua Jonathan. A military council was formed consisting of self-appointed officers and civilians. The king is chief of state and exercises executive and legislative power under the advice of the military council.

History.

The Basuto tribal grouping emerged in the early 1800's from the union of Sotho and other Bantu-speaking peoples under the leadership of a northern chief, Moshesh. Moshesh had successfully defended these peoples from raiding Zulu and Matebele bands.

The newly organized nation ran into conflict with the Boers, Dutch farmers migrating northward from the Orange Free State. The conflicts led Moshesh to sign a treaty of friendship with the British governor of Cape Colony. In 1868 Britain declared a protectorate over present-day Lesotho to prevent seizure of the country by the neighboring Orange Free State.

British rule. In 1871, a year after the death of Moshesh, the British gave control of Basutoland to Cape Colony. Between 1880 and 1882 Cape Colony troops waged the Gun Wars, a series of military campaigns, to disarm Basutoland's inhabitants who had rebelled against Cape Colony rule. The effort failed, and Cape Colony abandoned the territory. In 1884 Basutoland became a British High Commission Territory.

The British administered the territory through a resident commissioner who rarely acted contrary to the wishes of the paramount chief. Basuto traditional law survived under British rule.

Basutoland's economic affairs were tied to South Africa, and until 1948 Britain assumed that South Africa would eventually incorporate Basutoland. Union with South Africa was unacceptable to Basutoland, however, because of South Africa's policy of apartheid, or rigid separation of the races.

Nationalism. In the 1950's the Basutoland African Congress, an African nationalist organization, campaigned for Basutoland's independence. The congress also sought support from

Britain and the United Nations to lessen Basutoland's economic dependence on South Africa.

In 1964 Britain abolished the High Commission, and appointed a representative to Basutoland. On October 4, 1966, Basutoland became an independent member of the Commonwealth. The new nation, renamed Lesotho, was led by the Basuto paramount chief, Moshoeshoe II. In 1967 the king accepted the role of a constitutional monarch.

In 1970 Prime Minister Leabua Jonathan seized control of the government. A military coup overthrew Jonathan in 1986 and reinstated King Moshoeshoe II as chief of state.

Relations with South Africa have sometimes been strained. In 1985 South Africa accused Lesotho of harboring anti-apartheid guerrillas.

Liberia

Official name: *Republic of Liberia*
Area: *43,000 sq. mi., 111,370 sq. km.*
Population: *(1990 est.) 2,628,000*
Capital: *Monrovia (Pop., 1989, 400,000)*
Language: *English, African languages*
Religion: *Christian, Islam, traditional religions*
Currency unit: *Dollar*
National holiday: *Independence Day, July 26*

Liberia, a republic in western Africa, is bordered on the north by Guinea, on the east by the Ivory Coast, on the south by the Atlantic Ocean, and on the west by Sierra Leone. Liberia declared itself a sovereign nation in 1847.

The land. Most of Liberia is occupied by hills and low uplands. The country has a rocky coastline, beyond which are swampy plains. In the north, along the border with Guinea, are the grass-covered Nimba Mountains, with elevations of about 4500 feet. The Lofa, St. Paul, St. John, and Cess rivers flow through the country.

Liberia is one of the rainiest areas in western Africa. The rainy season extends from May through October. Rainfall averages more than 140 inches a year in the coastal region and over 100 inches a year in the interior of the country.

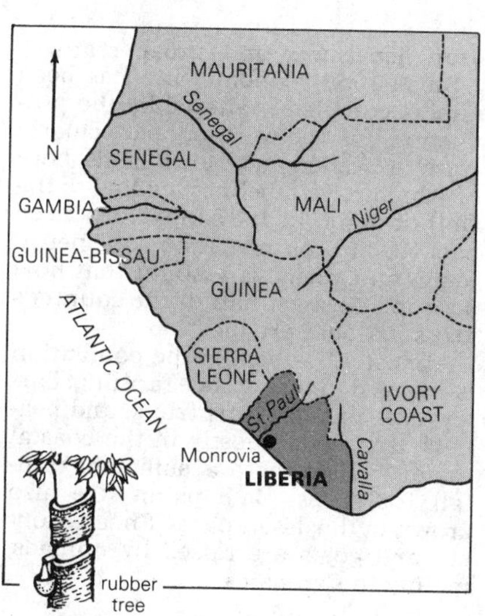

The people. There are two distinct population groups in Liberia—the Americo-Liberians, descended from blacks brought to Liberia from the United States during the 1800's, and the tribal peoples, who form the majority of Liberia's people. Liberia's indigenous tribes include the Kru, Mandingo, Gola, Vai, and Kissi.

The major cities of Liberia are Monrovia, Harbel, and Buchanan.

Economy. Liberia's economy is based on subsistence agriculture, mining, and rubber growing. The people raise cassava, rice, palm fruit, and bananas for local consumption.

Liberia exported only palm oil products, coffee, and cassava until 1926, when the Firestone Rubber Company established rubber plantations in Liberia and lent the government capital for development. In the 1960's other private companies established rubber plantations in Liberia, and in 1981, over 279 million pounds were produced, mostly by foreign companies.

One-third of Liberia's national product comes from mining. The nation is one of the world's top iron ore producers. Diamonds are also important.

In 1984 imports cost $360 million while exports earned $450 million. Liberia's main imports are food, fuel, and machinery. The main exports are iron ore and natural rubber. Most trade is conducted with the United States, West Germany, Britain, and Italy. Liberia receives economic assistance from the United States.

Government. Liberia is a civilian republic. Executive power rests with an elected president, a vice president, and a presidentially appointed cabinet. Legislative power is distributed between a 26-member Senate and a 62-member House of Representatives.

History. Europeans began establishing trading posts in Liberia in the 1400's. In 1822 the American Colonization Society began to settle freed slaves from the United States in Liberia. Malaria killed most of the original colonizers, but several new groups followed. They negotiated treaties with the native tribes, until consolidation of the land was completed in 1838.

Agents of the American Colonization Society administered the region until July 26, 1847, when Liberia declared its independence. Most world powers quickly recognized the new nation's independence, but the United States withheld recognition until 1862.

In the early 1900's Liberia was faced with a financial crisis when the world market price for its coffee dropped. Liberia sought the aid of foreign countries. In 1926 the Firestone Rubber Company leased large land areas from Liberia, providing an important source of revenue. In the 1930's a League of Nations study of labor conditions uncovered widespread forced labor. This resulted in the resignation of Liberia's president, Charles D. B. King.

During World War II U.S. soldiers built the first roads into the interior, and in 1948 a modern port opened at Monrovia, built with U.S. money.

William V. S. Tubman was president of Liberia from 1944 to 1971. He ended the Firestone company's monopoly by inaugurating an open-door policy of international investment, thus beginning the development of the country's rich resources of iron ore. Tubman died in 1971 and was succeeded by William R. Tolbert who attempted to reform the government but met with growing discontent over the minority (Americo-Liberian) rule. As he turned to oppressive forms of control, riots broke out in 1979. In a military coup by tribal people in 1980, Tolbert and many of his top aides were killed.

The military government, led by Samuel K. Doe, suspended the constitution but promised to return the government to civilian rule. A new constitution was drafted and elections were held in 1985. Doe was elected president and inaugurated in 1986.

MOTHER AND CHILD *in Liberia attend a UNICEF children's clinic.*

UNITED NATIONS

Libya

Official name: *Socialist People's Libyan Arab Jamahiriya*
Area: *679,362 sq. mi., 1,759, 540 sq. km.*
Population: *(1990 est.) 4,206,000*
Capital: *Tripoli (Pop., 1981, 858,000)*
Language: *Arabic*
Religion: *Islam*
Currency unit: *Dinar*
National holiday: *Independence Day, Dec. 24*

Libya, a country in north central Africa, is bordered on the north by the Mediterranean Sea and the Gulf of Sidra, on the east by Egypt and Sudan, on the south by Chad and Niger, and on the west by Algeria and Tunisia. Libya is made up of three historic regions—Tripolitania in the northwest, Cyrenaica in the northeast, and the Fezzan in the southwest.

HOLDING BACK THE DESERT, *once covered by olive trees, in Libya's Tripolitania. The sand, creeping in from the south, is anchored with tough grasses, then planted with trees.*

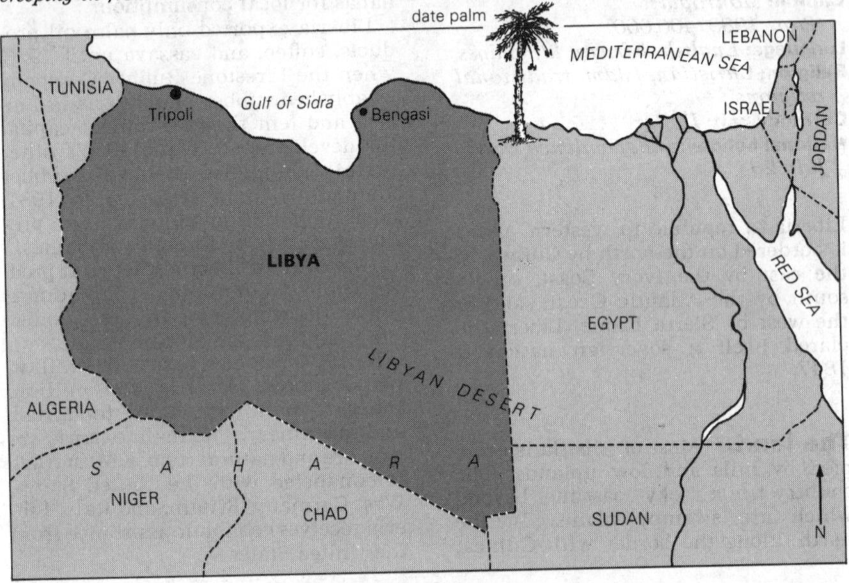

The land. Libya is almost entirely desert. Less than two percent of the land is cultivated, and less than one percent is forested.

The Gulf of Sidra (Sirte) divides Libya's Mediterranean coast into two major segments, northern Tripolitania in the west and northern Cyrenaica in the east. There are oases in the coastal region separated from each other by sand dunes and salt marshes. There are highlands beyond the coast, including the Jabal Nafusah in Tripolitania and the Al Jabal al Akhdar in Cyrenaica.

The Sahara has many landscapes, three of which are important in Libya—upland bare rock surfaces, as in the Hammadah al Hamra in southern Tripolitania; gravel-covered plains, as in the Sarir Tibasti in the south; and areas of extensive sand dunes, as in the Idehan Marzug in the Fezzan and the Sand Sea of Calanscio of northeastern Cyrenaica.

There are few oases in southern and eastern Libya. Oases are more common in the southwestern Fezzan, where they are usually formed by springs and wells in valleys and at the foot of escarpments.

Libya does not have any year-round rivers, but there are dry water routes in many parts of the country. There are deep, salty lakes in Libya, the largest of which is Arrashia, in Cyrenaica. Rainfall averages about 14 inches a year along the Mediterranean coast. There is virtually no rainfall in the desert regions.

The people. Most of the people in Libya are Arabic-speaking Sunni Muslims of mixed Arab and Berber origin. There are also some Berber-speaking peoples in northern Libya and in the desert region. Italians form the largest European community in Libya. Half of the labor force is foreign.

Libya is one of Africa's least densely populated countries. Only at oases in the Sahara and near the borders of the Mediterranean Sea is permanent human habitation possible. Many of the people are nomads, who must move about in the desert in search of grazing land for their flocks. Most of the cities and towns are concentrated in the coastal region. Libya's largest cities are Tripoli and Bengasi.

Economy. The modern economy of Libya is based on oil production. The traditional economy is based on dates and other produce of the coast and oases, flocks and herds raised by the nomads, the catch of Mediterranean fishermen, and urban crafts.

Since 1959 economic life has been almost completely altered by the production of petroleum, particularly from the Zelten and Dahra fields, both of which have pipelines leading to the Gulf of Sidra. In 1987 Libya produced over 46 million metric tons of petroleum, an enormous amount that now accounts for over half of the country's gross national product.

Almost 20 percent of the population is engaged in subsistence farming. Barley, date palms, citrus fruits, and peanuts are grown, mostly in the coastal region, where there is sufficient rainfall for crops. Date palms are also grown in the desert oases. Sheep, camels, and goats are raised by nomads, mainly in Cyrenaica.

CULVER PICTURES

THE BURNING OF THE PHILADELPHIA *in Tripoli harbor in 1804. Captured by the enemy in the Tripolitan War, the American frigate was burned by her own captain in a daring raid.*

Libya's industry centers on the production and processing of its oil and its agricultural products. There are canneries in Tripolitania that process fish caught in the coastal waters.

In 1984 Libya's imports cost $8.2 billion and exports earned $11 billion. The country's main imports are chemicals, manufactured goods, textiles, iron and steel, and machinery. Although Libya's chief export is petroleum, hides and skins, peanuts, and fruits are also important exports. Most of Libya's trade is conducted with France, West Germany, Italy, the Netherlands, and Great Britain.

Government. Libya was a constitutional monarchy until a coup of 1969 when the monarchy was overthrown and a twelve-man Revolutionary Command Council took power. The council appoints a prime minister as head of government. The council, through its leader, also controls the unicameral legislative body, the General People's Congress.

Libya is a member of the United Nations, the Organization of African Unity, the Organization of Petroleum Exporting Countries (OPEC), and the Arab League.

History. Libya's three main regions have had a separate existence for most of the country's history. Even after the Arab conquest of the region in the mid-600's, Cyrenaica was administered for the most part from Egypt, and Tripolitania was administered by dynasties in northwestern Africa. The Fezzan has also had its own distinctive history. Regional differences are still important in modern-day Libya.

Ottoman era. Libya came under the rule of the Ottoman Turks in the 1500's. For over a century, from 1711 to 1835, a local dynasty, the Qaramanli, controlled Tripoli. In the early 1800's the United States fought against the bey, or governor, of Tripoli, whose pirates were raiding U.S. ships.

European nations united to eliminate piracy in the Barbary States—Tripoli in Libya plus Algiers and Tunis to the west—thus cutting off one of the major sources of government revenue. The Qaramanli regime declined, and the Ottoman government reestablished direct control of Tripoli in 1835.

Italian rule. In the mid-1800's a Muslim, Muhammad ibn Ali, known as the Great Sanusi, created the Sanusian religious brotherhood, which became the most important social and political force in Cyrenaica and the Fezzan. In 1911 Italy wrested control of Libya from the Ottoman Empire after a short war, and the Sanusiya served as the focal point of resistance to Italian colonialism.

During World War II major battles were fought in Libya. The North African campaigns virtually wiped out the Italian colonial settlements, and after the war a defeated Italy was stripped of its colonies. A deadlock over which major power should assume trusteeship for Libya led to the decision to give the former colony complete independence.

Independence. Libya became a unified state in 1963, and the Sanusian chief, Idris, became king. Greatly increased oil revenues were channeled into low-cost housing, education, and roads. This policy continues under Colonel Muammar el-Qaddafi, who took power in 1969 and was elected revolutionary leader of the council in 1977. The council advocates the unity of all Arab countries and has taken firm steps to rid the country of foreign investors, and to close down the British and U.S. military installations.

Qaddafi has led Libya into socialism and Muslim traditionalism. Since 1975 Soviet political ties have been strengthened, but Libya, while actively supporting communism as an international ideal, clearly makes its own domestic and external decisions. It engaged in border clashes with both Egypt and Chad in 1977, and in 1979 aided Uganda against a rebellion in that country.

Qaddafi has become increasingly dictatorial and a virtual police state now exists under his extreme rule. Relations with the United States were severed in 1980 and Libyan exiles have been threatened for their refusal to return to their homeland. In 1981 the Libyan mission to the United States was expelled because of Libyan support for international terrorism.

Madagascar

Official name: *Democratic Republic of Madagascar*
Area: *226,658 sq. mi., 587,041 sq. km.*
Population: *(1990 est.) 11,802,000*
Capital: *Tananarive or Antananarivo (Pop., 1986, 703,000)*
Language: *Malagasy, French*
Religion: *Christian, traditional religions*
Currency unit: *Franc CFA (African Financial Community)*
National holiday: *Proclamation of the republic, Oct. 14*

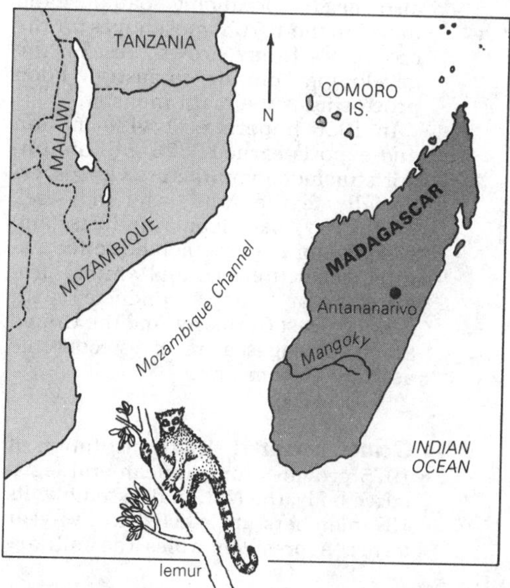

The republic of Madagascar is an island nation in the Indian Ocean, some 240 miles off the southeastern coast of Africa. Its territory consists of the large island of Madagascar and several small, adjacent islands. Madagascar received its independence in 1960.

The land. Madagascar is about 1000 miles long and 360 miles at its greatest width. Most of the island is dominated by a great interior highland, which has an average elevation of about 4000 feet above sea level.

The highlands contain deep canyons and volcanic mountains, with elevations as high as about 9400 feet. Steep cliffs border the highlands, especially in the east. The major rivers are the Mangoky, Betsiboka, and Mania.

Easterly winds, which blow all the year on the eastern cliffs, bring heavy rains to eastern Madagascar, but it is dry to the west of the cliffs and in the south.

The people. Madagascar's indigenous population is made up of 18 different ethnic groups. The largest is the Hova, or Merina, who live mainly in the central highlands and are important in the political life of the country. The Betsileo people also live in the central highlands. The country's largest city is its capital, Tananarive, which is situated in the highlands.

The population is predominantly rural and the labor force is 85 percent agricultural. Fifty-five percent of the people are animists, 40 percent are Christian, 5 percent Muslim.

Economy. The economy of the island nation has suffered because of its isolation. Madagascar's economy is based on agriculture. Coffee, vanilla, rice, sugar, and cloves are the principal crops. Although mineral resources are not well developed, Madagascar is a major producer of graphite. The island also began producing bauxite and nickel in the 1970's; most hopes for the economy's future growth rest on the developing mining industry. Food processing is the main industry.

In 1986 imports cost $438 million and exports earned $326 million. Imports include manufactured goods, especially textiles and iron and steel, machinery, petroleum products, and food. Major exports include coffee, vanilla, sugar, tobacco and animal products. Most trade is conducted with France, West Germany, and the United States. Madagascar receives economic assistance from France.

Government. The constitution of 1975 provides for a unicameral legislative body, the National Assembly. Its 137 members are elected to five-year terms. A president rules the military government and is popularly elected to a seven-year term. The president heads the Supreme Revolutionary Council and appoints its members. This council deals mainly with policy-making. An appointed prime minister and a 28-member cabinet deal with the daily management of the government.

History. Arab traders established small, feudal principalities along the Madagascar coast as early as the 1000's or 1100's. In the 1500's and 1600's Dutch, French, and British merchants established trading and supply posts on the island as part of their routes to India. Buccaneers established a short-lived republic on the island in the 1700's.

During the 1500's and 1600's the indigenous peoples were involved in civil wars. Confederations and military commands were established on the island, but most collapsed because of internal strains or the rebellion of subjugated peoples. In the central plateau, however, the Hova people slowly expanded their area.

In the early 1800's a Hova king, Radama I, brought European advisers to his court, welcomed missionaries, and instituted education in the Malagasy language. Later rulers played the British and the French off one another. In 1890 French claims to Madagascar were recognized by Britain, and in 1896 it became a French colony. France abolished the Hova monarchy and exiled the queen. By 1904 the French controlled the island.

Modern Madagascar. Short-lived local nationalist movements emerged briefly during World War I and again in the 1920's. In 1947 discontent over land confiscation and the periodic imposition of involuntary labor led to a serious revolt. France suppressed the revolt and took steps to develop Madagascar's economy, but at the same time it prohibited political activity.

In 1956 France changed its policy and permitted political activity in all French African colonies. Of the several political parties that emerged in Madagascar, the nationalist Social Democratic Party (PSD) won power.

In October, 1958, under the leadership of the PSD headed by Philibert Tsiranana, Madagascar became an autonomous republic within the French Community. In June, 1960, the country became the "Malagasy Republic" (later changed back to Madagascar), an independent republic with a presidential system of government. Discontent over European control of the economy led to civil unrest and culminated in military coups in 1972 and 1975. Massive Chinese aid was accepted and French-owned plantations were nationalized. Political and civil disturbances have continued, however, and President Didier Ratsiraka (in office since 1975) has resorted to stern military rule to maintain order.

Malawi

Official name: *Republic of Malawi*
Area: *45,747 sq. mi., 118,484 sq. km.*
Population: *(1990 est.) 8,198,000*
Capital: *Lilongwe (Pop., 1989, 175,000)*
Language: *English, African languages*
Religion: *Christian, Islam*
Currency unit: *Kwacha*
National holiday: *Independence Day, July 6*

Malawi, a small, landlocked republic in southern Africa, is bordered on the north and northeast by Tanzania, on the southeast, southwest, and south by Mozambique, and on the west by Zambia. Malawi, formerly called Nyasaland, received its independence from Britain in 1964.

The land. Most of Malawi is occupied by mountains and plateaus. Because of its rugged terrain, Malawi has been described as "Switzerland without snow." The Great Rift Valley runs through Malawi in a north-south line. Lake Nyasa, or Malawi, which stretches along the eastern border, lies in the valley. The Shire River, the lake's outlet, flows southward into Mozambique.

West of the lake the land climbs steeply to a plateau with elevations between 4000 and 7000 feet. The Shire Highlands are south of Lake Malawi. East of the Shire River is Mt. Mlanje, which has an elevation of about 9800 feet.

The lake region of Malawi has a generally hot, humid climate. Temperatures throughout the rest of the country vary with differences in altitude.

The people. Most of Malawi's people are Bantu-speaking. The largest groups, the Nyanja and Yao, live mainly near Lake Malawi. The Nyanja are descendants of early inhabitants of Malawi. There are also communities of Europeans and Asians.

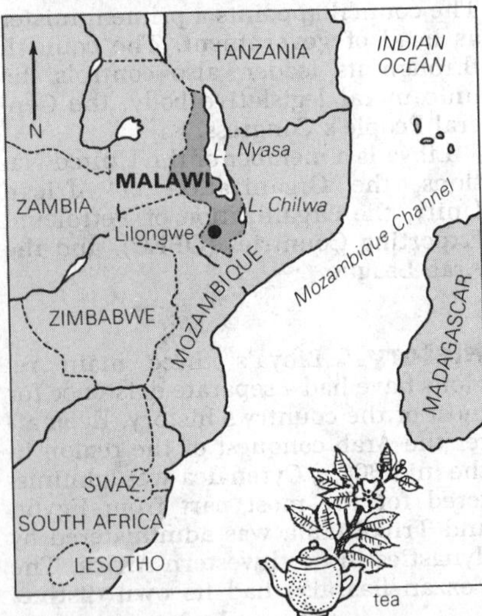

Lilongwe and Blantyre, in central Malawi, and Zomba, in the southern part of the country, are Malawi's largest cities.

Most of the people are subsistence farmers who live in rural areas. The country is fairly densely populated.

Economy. The economy of Malawi is based on agriculture. Malawi's resources cannot support its population, and many workers find employment in nearby countries. Basic food crops include corn, millet, cassava, peanuts, and rice. Commercial crops include cotton, tobacco, and tea.

There is no mining or manufacturing of any significance in the country, but heavy South African aid is helping to reverse this. Industry now contributes 13 percent of the gross national product, compared with 50 percent contributed by agriculture. Tourism is also increasing in importance, but Malawi's landlocked position and its limited transportation system have slowed economic development.

In 1986 Malawi's imports cost $258 million and its exports earned $245 million. The country's major imports are manufactured goods, especially textiles and iron and steel, chemicals, petroleum products, and machinery. Exports include cotton, tobacco, tea, and peanuts. Most of Malawi's trade is with Britain, the Soviet Union, and South Africa.

Government. Malawi is ruled by a president who controls the unicameral National Assembly and its 118 members.

Malawi is a member of the United Nations, the Organization of African Unity, and the Commonwealth of Nations, and it is an associated state of the European Common Market.

History. Malawi owes its name to the Malawi, or Maravi, people who entered the area in the 1500's. Portuguese explorers in the mid-1500's believed them to be the rulers of a vast empire. The western shore of Lake Malawi became a popular route for Bantu-speaking immigrants entering central Africa from the north, and by the 1800's the area's dense population made it a favorite target for Arab slave-raiders.

European interest in present-day Malawi originated in the1870's, after the explorations of David Livingstone and other Scottish missionaries who were anxious to put an end to the slave trade. In 1889 missionary pressure for governmental action against the Arab slave traders and the threat of Portuguese occupation led Britain to declare the area the British Central Africa Protectorate.

Cecil Rhodes's British South Africa Company financed the region's administration in the early years of the protectorate, but a dispute over political control led the British government to accept complete responsibility for the territory. In 1907 the name of the area was changed to Nyasaland.

DR. LIVINGSTONE, *famous Scottish explorer of the region now called Malawi.*

Nationalism. African nationalistic movements developed early in Nyasaland, organized by politically conscious laborers returning from work in the mines of the Rhodesias (now Zambia and Zimbabwe) and South Africa. Because of resentment of British colonial policies and fear of federation with both the Rhodesias, nationalists formed the Nyasaland African Congress in 1944.

THE MALAWI AREA *was called British Nyasaland from 1907 until independence.*

In 1951 the leadership of the congress demanded self-government for Nyasaland. Two years later, however, against African sentiment, Britain joined the two Rhodesias and Nyasaland into the Federation of Rhodesia and Nyasaland.

The nationalists, under the leadership of Dr. Hastings Banda, attracted wide support in denouncing the federation. Britain finally agreed to an African elected majority in the Nyasaland legislative council, and in elections held in 1961 Dr. Banda's Malawi Congress Party won an impressive victory.

Independence. Britain formally dissolved the federation in 1963, and on July 6, 1964, the country became independent, with Banda as its prime minister.

In 1966 Malawi became a republic, and Banda became the first president. In 1967 Malawi signed a trade agreement with South Africa, despite South Africa's policy of apartheid and the opposition of other African countries. The two countries remain at odds over the apartheid issue, but are close economically. Malawi has a pro-Western foreign policy.

Dr. Banda was declared president for life in 1970, and his control has become increasingly dictatorial since then. He dismissed his cabinet in 1977.

Mali

Official name: *Republic of Mali*
Area: *479,000 sq. mi., 1,240,000 sq. km.*
Population: *(1990 est.) 9,182,000*
Capital: *Bamako*
(Pop., 1986 est., 862,600)
Language: *French, African languages*
Religion: *Islam*
Currency unit: *Franc*
National holiday: *Independence Day, Sept. 22*

Mali, a landlocked republic in western Africa, is bordered on the north by Algeria, on the east by Niger, on the southeast by Upper Volta, on the south by the Ivory Coast and Guinea, and on the west by Senegal and Mauritania. Mali, long a French territory known as the Soudan, was joined with Senegal from 1959 until 1960 as the Mali Federation. It declared its independence in 1960.

The land. Most of Mali is flat, with areas of low plateaus. The vast desert wasteland of the Sahara occupies the northern third of the country. In the northeast is a mountain region.

The Niger River flows through southern Mali, and the Senegal River flows from southwestern Mali. The desert region is hot and dry, but the southern part of the country is cooler.

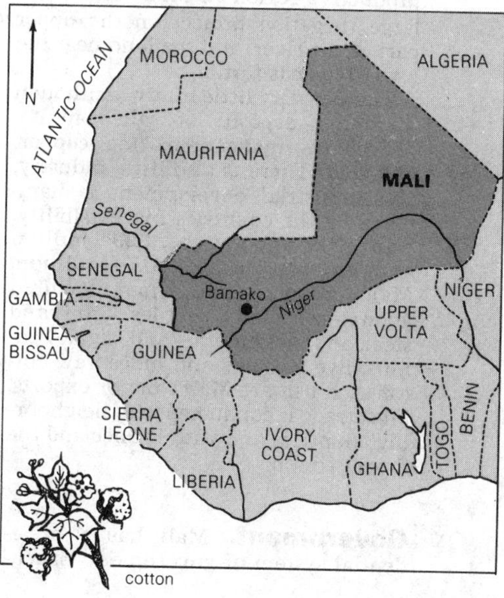

MOSQUE IN MALI, *a huge empty country dominated by the Sahara. Mali, with its Niger River valley, has always formed a bridge between Islamic North Africa and the south.*

The people. There are many different ethnic groups in Mali. The largest are the Mande, followed by the Fulani and over 20 others. Most of Mali's people are Muslims, and only five percent are literate.

Mali is very sparsely populated and 80 percent of its labor force farms.

The country's largest cities are Bamako, Mopti, Ségou, and Tombouctou (Timbuktu). All are near the Niger River or its tributaries.

Economy. The economy of Mali is based on agriculture. Millet, rice, and corn are the basic food crops. The principal commercial crops are peanuts and cotton. Fish from the Niger River are an important export. Cattle, sheep, and goats are raised, mainly in central and northern Mali.

The Niger River valley is the most productive region in Mali. There is a large irrigation project on the upper part of the river, and the land near the lower Niger is fertile.

There is very little mining, although there are deposits of salt, bauxite, phosphates, manganese, zinc, copper, and gold. There is also little industry, and industrial development is hampered by the country's inaccessibility.

In 1985 imports cost $294 million and exports earned $174 million. Major imports include manufactured goods—especially textiles, iron and steel, and machinery—and sugar. Peanuts, live animals and hides, raw cotton, and fish are Mali's major exports. Most trade is conducted with neighboring countries and with France and the Soviet Union.

Government. Mali has a presidential system of government. Executive power is vested in a president, who is elected to a six-year term. Legislative power is held by the National Assembly. The 137 members of the assembly are elected by universal suffrage to three-year terms. There is only one political party.

Mali is a member of the United Nations and the Organization of African Unity, and it is an associated state of the European Common Market.

History. In the early 1200's A.D. Sundiata, a powerful leader of a group of Mandingo people, defeated Sumanguru, ruler of the Susu people, and created the Mali empire. By the 1300's this empire stretched from the Gambia River to what is now the northwestern border of Nigeria. The people of Mali traded gold from the upper Niger and Senegal River regions for the salt of the Sahara and luxury goods from northwestern Africa.

In the early 1300's, Mali's most illustrious ruler, Mansu Musa (1312–1337), extended the empire from Niger to the southern Sahara. In the late 1400's the then ruler of Mali was overthrown by the king of the new state of Songhai. The Songhai kings governed the vast area once loyal to Musa until 1591, when a Moroccan army crossed the Sahara and defeated the Songhai. The Moroccan army was not strong enough to control the entire empire, and the territory broke up into smaller city-states.

During the 1800's two Muslim reformers, Ahmadu Lobo and Al-hajj Umar, created Islamic theocracies in the region. The creation of the Islamic states was one phase of a wave of religious revivalism that swept tropical Africa south of the Sahara.

French rule. France at that time was extending its colonial rule southward from northern Africa, and Al-hajj Umar's state clashed with French forces. By 1880 France had emerged victorious, and in 1895 France formed the colony of the Soudan, which it administered as part of French West Africa. In 1946 this area became a territory, and in 1958 the territory became an autonomous member of the French Community.

In 1959 France joined the Soudan with Senegal to form the Mali Federation, and in June, 1960, the federation became an autonomous member of the French Community. Two months later Senegal withdrew from the federation, and on September 22, 1960, the former Soudan withdrew from the French Community and proclaimed itself the Republic of Mali.

Independence. Modibo Keita became the first president of the new republic in 1960. He was ousted in 1968 in a bloodless coup led by army officers; Moussa Traoré took over the presidency. Traoré was elected as president in 1979 when Mali's new constitution came into effect.

Under Keita, Mali, aided by China, had turned to socialism. Traoré quickly dissolved the agricultural collectives and encouraged private enterprise, so that exports and agricultural production, especially of cotton, improved significantly, though the economy suffered at the same time from severe droughts and famines. Mali receives economic aid from many countries, especially France.

Mauritania

Official name: *Islamic Republic of Mauritania*
Area: *397,955 sq. mi., 1,030,700 sq. km.*
Population: *(1990 est.) 2,038,000*
Capital: *Nouakchott (Pop., 1989, 400,000)*
Language: *Arabic, French*
Religion: *Islam*
Currency unit: *Ouguiya*
National holiday: *Independence Day, Nov. 28.*

Mauritania, a republic in western Africa, is bounded on the north by Algeria, on the east by Mali, on the south by Senegal, and on the west by the Atlantic Ocean and Morocco. Mauritania received its independence from France in 1960.

The land. About two-thirds of Mauritania is desert. In the west long lines of sand dunes are separated by broad lowlands. In the north and east rocky desert surfaces are common. There is cultivated land in the southwest, near the Senegal River, which flows along the country's southwestern border. The climate of Mauritania is generally hot and dry.

The people. Most Mauritanians are nomadic Moors, people of mixed Berber and Arab stock. Black Muslims live in southern Mauritania, mainly near the Senegal River, and Taureg people live in the central part of the country. Mauritania's largest cities are Kaédi, Port Étienne, and Nouakchott, the capital.

Nearly all of the people are Muslims and only 17 percent of the population is literate. Mauritania is lightly populated, and 47 percent of the labor force is employed in agriculture.

Economy. Following its independence, Mauritania developed mining enterprises, but it remains a poor country with a small gross national product.

Its gross national product is now about 20 percent agricultural and 20 percent industrial. Agriculture is based on livestock breeding. Sheep, cattle, goats, and camels are raised, mainly in central and northern Mauritania. The only considerable area of cultivated land is in the Chemanna, the Mauritanian part of the Senegal River valley.

The basic food crops are millet, dates, rice, and corn. Acacia trees, the source of gum arabic, are grown in the central part of the country. Fish from the Senegal River also provide an important source of income.

The country's mining wealth is based on its iron ore deposits, mainly at Fderik. Gypsum is also important and copper contributed to the nation's wealth before its deposits were depleted in 1978.

In 1985 imports cost $358.4 million and exports earned an estimated $296 million. Major imports are manufactured goods, machinery, and foodstuffs. Major exports include live animals, fish, iron ore, copper, and gum arabic. Most trade is conducted with France, the Congo, the United States, and West Germany.

Government. Mauritania has been governed since 1978 by the Military Committee of National Salvation. Its constitution and legislature were both suspended at that time.

Mauritania is a member of the United Nations, the Arab League, and the Organization of African Unity, and it is an associated member of the European Common Market.

History. In about the 800's a confederation of nomadic Berbers entered Mauritania from the north and forced the existing black population southward. The Berbers adopted Islam in the 900's, but retained many of their traditional beliefs. In the 1000's they united to form the Almoravids, which quickly became a powerful religious and political force.

The Almoravids overran Morocco, western Algeria, and Muslim Spain. Their leaders founded the famous city of Marrakesh, in Morocco, and established a dynasty that lasted almost 100 years. A branch of the Almoravids went south and conquered the empire of Ghana in 1076. Starting in the 1300's nomadic Arabs migrated into Mauritania.

In the 1800's the French established their control over areas to the north, Morocco and Algeria, and Senegal and present-day Mali to the south. In the early 1900's, France began to occupy Mauritania. In 1903 it became a French protectorate, and in 1920 a colony, part of French West Africa. But effective French control over the entire country was not achieved until 1934.

In 1946 Mauritania became a territory in the newly formed French Union, and in 1958 an autonomous member of the French Community. On November 28, 1960, France granted the country its independence. In 1961 Mokhtar Ould Daddah became Mauritania's first president. Under his leadership, the country was modernized somewhat, but he was ousted in the military coup of 1978.

In 1976 Mauritania annexed the southern portion of former Spanish Sahara, but this action was met with Saharan guerrilla reprisal attacks staged from 1976 to 1980 by the Algerian-backed Polisario Front. Mauritania's ruling military government renounced its claim to the territory in 1980 and Morocco promptly annexed it. Relations with Algeria have improved since then.

Mauritius

Official name: *Mauritius*
Area: *790 sq. mi., 2,045 sq. km.*
Population: *(1990 est.) 1,141,000*
Capital: *Port Louis (Pop., 1986, 138,482)*
Language: *English, French, Creole*
Religion: *Hindu, Islam, Christian*
Currency unit: *Rupee*
National holiday: *Independence Day, Mar. 12*

Mauritius is an island nation in the Indian Ocean, about 500 miles east of the island of Madagascar. The country's territory includes the island of Mauritius, Rodrigues Island, and the smaller islands of the Agalega and Cargados Carajos archipelagos.

The land. The islands of Mauritius are volcanic in origin, and Rodrigues rises sharply from the sea. On Mauritius, a 2200-foot central plateau is rimmed by rocky mountains. Many rivers and streams flow down from the mountains. Rodrigues is mountainous and barren except for some fertile valleys. The Agalega islands are low and fertile, and the Cargados Carajos islands are little more than rocky reefs.

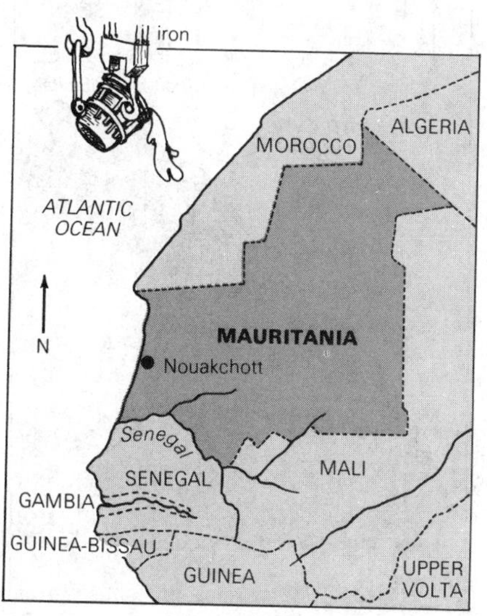

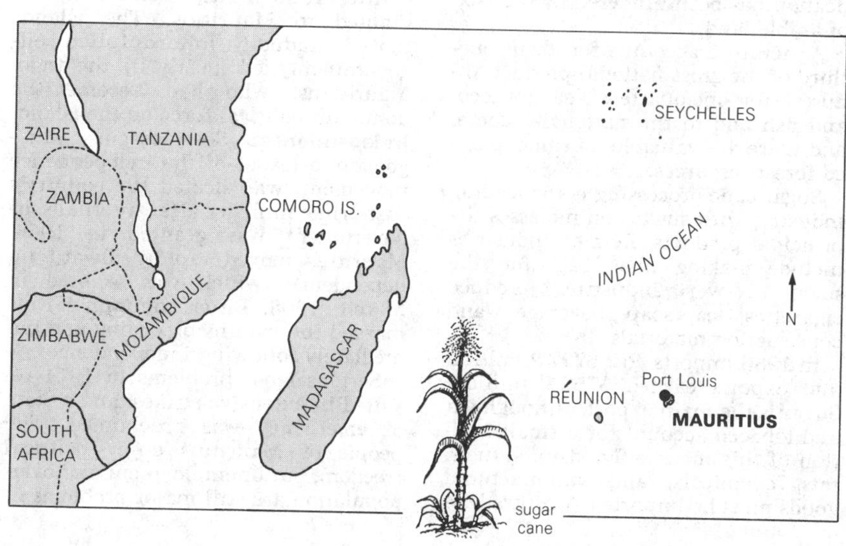

The country's climate is semitropical, with hot summers, cool winters, and extremely high humidity. Rainfall is heavy—from 50 to 200 inches a year on all the islands. Cyclones are a frequent danger, especially between December and April.

The people. The population density of Mauritius is very high—almost 1200 persons per square mile. The annual growth rate averaged about three percent during the 1950's and 1960's (following the elimination of malaria), but fell to half of that during the 1970's. The decrease in growth was due largely to government population control programs, which are opposed by the country's main religions. The high growth rate poses an economic problem by swelling the ranks of the labor force, 20 percent of which is employed in agriculture.

Mauritius has a high literacy rate, about 94 percent.

The people of Mauritius are of varied origins, and the population is rather sharply divided along ethnic lines. Between 65 and 70 percent of the population is Indo-Mauritian, of Indian background; under 5 percent is Sino-Mauritian, of Chinese descent; and about 30 percent, called the "general population," is of European, African, and mixed origins.

English is the official language, but Creole, a French dialect, is the common tongue. Chinese, Hindi, French, and Arabic are also spoken. Slightly less than half the population is Hindu, about 30 percent is Christian, and some 15 percent is Muslim.

Economy. Mauritius depends almost completely on sugar. During the early 1960's efforts were undertaken to diversify the economy, but 90 percent of the gross national product is still derived from sugar production. Decreases in sugar prices and recurring cyclones that damage the sugar crops have hurt the economy. Diversification has been hindered by the lack of arable land.

Agriculture accounts for about one-third of the gross national product, industry for one-quarter. Tea, tobacco, and fish add to the national income, and there are valuable, but unexploited forest resources.

Sugar cane processing is the leading industry, with sugar and molasses the principal products. Related industries include making fiber bags for the sugar. Newer industries produce cigarettes, tea, soap, beverages, and construction materials.

In 1986 imports cost $727.2 million and exports earned $752.1 million. Sugar is the main export, although tea and tobacco account for a small fraction of this income. Foodstuffs, fuels, fats, chemicals, and manufactured goods must be imported. Most trade is with Britain, which also supplies economic assistance.

Government. Mauritius has a parliamentary form of government. Executive power is held by a prime minister and cabinet responsible to a popularly elected legislature.

Mauritius is a member of the Commonwealth of Nations and the United Nations, and it is an associated state of the European Common Market.

History. Mauritius has been known for many centuries to Arab and Malay sailors, who probably first used it for shelter before 1000. Portuguese sailors landed on the island in the 1500's, but they did not establish settlements. The Dutch, who named the island Mauritius for their ruler, Prince Maurice, attempted to establish a colony but failed.

No successful settlement was made until 1715, when the French East India Company claimed the island for France and renamed it Ile de France. The French began sugar cultivation, using slave labor, and the colony grew prosperous.

In 1767 the French government took control from the company and made the island a naval base for use in France's struggle with Britain for control of India. Britain captured the island in 1810, and in 1814 the Treaty of Paris awarded the island to Britain.

British rule. The island, renamed Mauritius, was Britain's main source of sugar during the 1800's. Few Britons settled there, however, and French cultural influence remained strong. In 1833 Britain abolished slavery on Mauritius, and indentured workers, mostly from India, were brought to work the sugar plantations.

The economy grew increasingly dependent on sugar, which was subject to damage by cyclones and drought and to sharp fluctuations in world market prices.

After 1886 limited home rule was granted to Mauritius. The islands moved gradually toward fuller self-government, led mostly by the Indo-Mauritians, who had become the dominant political force on the island.

Independence. Seewoosagur Ramgoolam, a leader of the independence movement, was elected the country's first prime minister after internal self-government was granted in 1964. Mauritius moved rapidly toward independence, which was granted in March, 1968. Bitter communal riots marked the months preceding and immediately following independence.

Serious labor problems in 1971 resulted in extensive strikes, and a state of emergency was proclaimed. The people of Mauritius enjoy political freedom, but unemployment and overpopulation are still major problems.

Morocco

Official name: *Kingdom of Morocco*
Area: *171,834 sq. mi., 445,050 sq. km.*
Population: *(1990 est.) 26,249,000*
Capital: *Rabat (Pop., 1989, 591,000)*
Language: *Arabic*
Religion: *Islam*
Currency unit: *Dirham*
National holiday: *Independence Day, Mar. 3*

Morocco, a kingdom in northern Africa, is bounded on the north by the Mediterranean Sea, on the east by Algeria, on the west by the Atlantic Ocean, and on the south by Mauritania. Between 1912 and 1956 Morocco was divided into a French zone, two Spanish zones, and the international zone of Tangier.

The land. The western end of the Atlas Mountain system dominates Morocco. In the north the Rif Atlas runs parallel to the Mediterranean Sea. The Middle Atlas, which has elevations of over 10,900 feet, and the Grand Atlas, which has elevations of over 13,600 feet, run through central Morocco. The Anti-Atlas, in the southwest, borders the desert region of the Sahara, which stretches along eastern and southern Morocco.

The Moroccan Meseta, or plateau, lies on the Atlantic side of the Grand Atlas and Middle Atlas. It is irrigated in places, as at Marrakesh, and is crossed by rivers leading into lowland plains. The Moulouya River and valley are east of the Middle Atlas.

The Grand Atlas and Middle Atlas intercept rain-bearing winds, which bring moisture to the north and west, and cause hot, desert conditions in the south and near-desert conditions in the east.

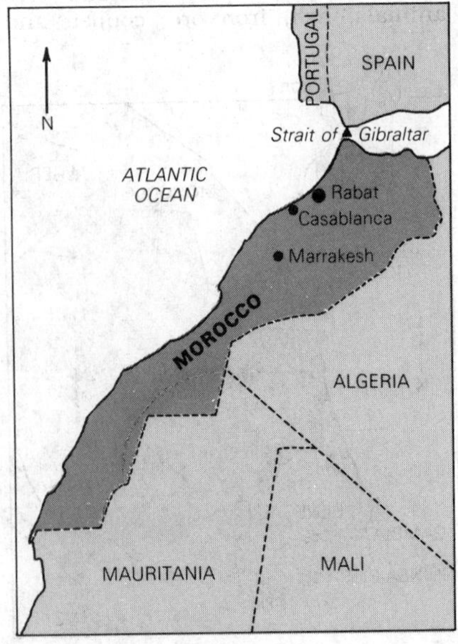

EUGENE GORDON/TAURUS PHOTOS

COPPERSMITH IN MARRAKESH *with his apprentice son. Throughout the Middle East, the time-honored crafts still flourish, producing fine handmade objects in traditional forms.*

The people. The Moroccans are descended from Berber-speaking peoples, possibly the original inhabitants of the area, and from later Arab settlers. Most of the people are Sunni Muslim. There is a small Jewish population in the country, and there are small communities of Europeans, mainly French and Spanish.

Morocco's major cities include Rabat, the capital; Casablanca, an industrial and commercial center and port; Fez; Marrakesh; and Tangier.

The country's recent rapid rise in population—about three percent each year—contributes to its high rates of unemployment and emigration to Western Europe. Two-thirds of the people live in rural areas, and half the labor force works in agriculture, compared with one-fifth in industry.

Economy. The economy of Morocco is based primarily on agriculture. The basic food crops are wheat and barley, wine grapes, citrus fruits, and vegetables. With the aid of foreign capital, particularly from France, Morocco has become an important source of seasonal fruits and vegetables for Western Europe. Large irrigation projects have been developed to increase agricultural production. Sheep and goats are raised in the mountains.

Morocco has deposits of several minerals. Phosphate rock, used in the production of fertilizers, is the most important, and Morocco is a world leader in its production. Iron ore, manganese, cobalt, and zinc are also mined. There are a number of small industries in the country. Cement, superphosphates, Moroccan leather, flour, sugar, and other products are produced. Tourism has become an important industry, and overseas Moroccan workers return a significant portion of their incomes to their native land.

In 1983 imports cost $3.8 billion while exports earned $2.2 billion. The major imports are petroleum products, food, manufactured goods, especially iron and steel and textiles, and machinery. Morocco's exports include live animals, fish, fruit, vegetables, phosphates and fertilizers, iron ore, and leather. Most trade is conducted with France, West Germany, the United States, and Spain.

Government. Morocco's 1972 constitution provides for a constitutional monarchy. The prime minister has considerable authority. The legislature is the unicameral parliament, with 306 members, each elected to a six-year term.

Morocco is a member of the United Nations, the Organization of African Unity, and the Arab League.

History. The earliest known inhabitants of present-day Morocco were Berber-speaking peoples. In the 600's B.C. Phoenicians landed on the Moroccan coast and established trading posts in the region. In the 100's A.D. Rome established a province in northwestern Morocco. Roman domination came to an end in the 400's with the invasion of the Vandals.

In the early 700's Muslim armies invaded Morocco, and the Berber-speaking peoples gradually adopted Islam. In the late 700's most of the country united under Idris, a member of the Alid family. His son founded the city of Fez.

In 1056 A.D. Berber-speaking tribes formed a powerful religious and political force, the Almoravids. They founded the city of Marrakesh in 1062 and established a dynasty that ruled until 1147. The Almohads, another Berber confederation, defeated the Almoravids and established a dynasty that lasted until 1269. The Marinid dynasty succeeded the Almohads.

In 1544 Morocco came under the rule of another Alid dynasty, the Sa'dis, and in 1664 yet another branch of the Alid, the Filalis, or Alawites, assumed control.

European control. Although only about seven miles from Europe, Morocco did not come under European rule until the 1900's. In the early 1900's Britain, Spain, France, and Germany competed for control of Morocco. In 1912 the Moroccan sultan was forced to sign the Treaty of Fez with France, and most of Morocco became a French protectorate. In the same year Spain obtained control of a region in the north and one in the south. In 1923 the city of Tangier became an international zone.

In 1921 a leader in the Rif Mountains, Abd al-Krim, led a rising against the Spanish, and then fought a combined Spanish and French force. He was defeated in 1926. After 1925 the government of French Morocco was more centralized and the European population in Morocco began steadily to increase.

Nationalism. Moroccan nationalism began to develop in the late 1920's. In 1927 France placed Muhammad bin Yusuf (Muhammad V) on the throne, believing he would act favorably to France. The French assumption appeared valid when in 1930 Muhammad signed the Berber *Dahir,* which downgraded the importance of Islamic law. After that, however, Muhammad responded to the appeals of the nationalists, to France's alarm.

By the time of World War II he was cautiously cooperating with the nationalists while maintaining favorable relations with France. In 1953 France forced Muhammad to abdicate in order to end his nationalist activity. He went into exile, but as a result nationalist disturbances intensified. In 1955 France accepted the necessity of dealing with Muhammad, and he returned to Morocco in triumph.

Independence. Negotiations quickly led to independence for French Morocco, achieved on March 2, 1956. By agreements in April, 1956, and April, 1958, the Spanish zones were granted independence, and in October, 1956, Tangier was incorporated into Morocco. In 1969 Ifni, a former Spanish enclave was ceded to Morocco.

Morocco claimed all of Spanish Sahara, but in 1975 Mauritania was granted the region's southern portion. The Algerian-backed Polisario Front (Saharan liberation army) fought to establish an independent Western Sahara, but by 1980 Morocco, aided by the United States, had annexed the entire region. Mauritania had renounced its claim to the southern portion a year earlier.

King Hassan II ascended to the throne in 1961, and a year later he made Morocco a constitutional monarchy. His own authority was greatly restricted by a new constitution in 1972. After 1973 Hassan, pressured by public opinion, began a broad program of the "Moroccanization" of the nation's economy. Foreign-owned farms were nationalized. Morocco has its own form of socialism, which permits considerable private enterprise.

Mozambique

Official name: *People's Republic of Mozambique*
Area: *302,330 sq. mi., 783,031 sq. km.*
Population: *(1990 est.) 15,830,000*
Capital: *Maputo (Pop., 1986, 882,800)*
Language: *Portuguese, African languages*
Religion: *Christian, Islam, traditional religions*
Currency unit: *Escudo*
National holiday: *Independence Day, June 25*

Mozambique, on the eastern coast of Africa, is bounded on the north by Tanzania, on the east by the Mozambique Channel and the Indian Ocean, on the south by Swaziland and South Africa, and on the west by Zimbabwe, Zambia, and Malawi.

The land. Most of the long, irregularly shaped land consists of a flat or rolling plateau, ranging from 800 to 2000 feet in elevation. In the east a narrow lowland skirts a coast, and in the west a zone of high plateaus and mountains reaches a peak of nearly 8000 feet. The most important of the country's many rivers are the Zambezi, which crosses central Mozambique, and the Limpopo, in the south.

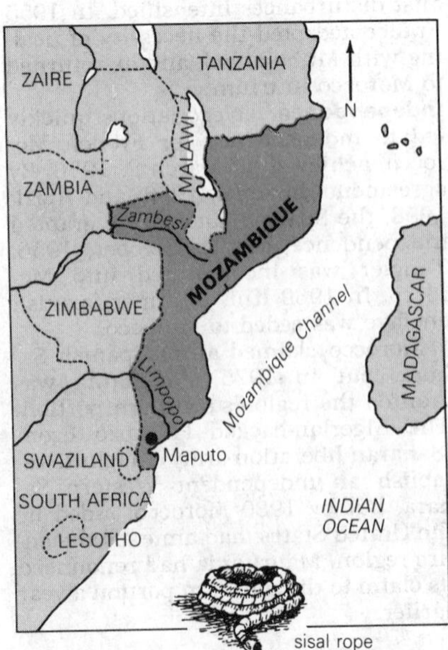

sisal rope

The climate is hot and humid along the coast, especially in the north. Temperatures are moderate in the interior, which is also drier.

The people. About 98 percent of Mozambique's population is African. Europeans constitute about one and a half percent, and the remainder is of Chinese, Indian, Pakistani, and mixed backgrounds. Most of the Africans belong to a variety of Bantu-speaking tribes.

Portuguese is the official language, but many African languages are more commonly spoken. Most of the people follow traditional religions, but there are large numbers of Muslims and Roman Catholics. About 80 percent of the labor force consists of subsistence farmers.

Economy. Mozambique is a very poor land, with a primarily agricultural economy. Its mineral resources have not been fully exploited, although some coal, bismuth, bauxite, and copper are mined. Mining and industry are increasing gradually as hydroelectric power becomes available. Most of the country's forests still stand uncut.

Farming is especially productive in the river valleys and in the north, where sugar cane, cotton, corn, copra, tea, sisal, manioc, fruits, and vegetables are raised. Most farms have been collectivized and many industries have been nationalized since 1975.

Industry is limited to the processing of agricultural products, the milling of cotton textiles, and the manufacture of such items as rope, soap, cement, and leather goods. An important contribution to the economy is made by money earned by Mozambique laborers hired to work in the mines of neighboring Zimbabwe and of South Africa.

Mozambique has a rather poor balance of trade. In 1983 imports cost $636 million and exports earned only $132 million. Nuts, cotton, sisal, sugar, and copra are among the leading exports, and machinery, vehicles, fuels, and industrial raw materials are among the imports. The bulk of the country's trade is with South Africa, the United States, and with Western Europe.

Government. By the terms of its constitution of 1975, Mozambique is ruled by a president who is the head of the Frelimo (Front for the Liberation of Mozambique) Party, which led the struggle for independence. Executive power is vested in the president and a council of ministers led by the prime minister. The legislature is the 250-member People's Assembly. Mozambique is a one-party state.

History. Mozambique has been inhabited for many centuries by Bantu-speaking peoples. Between the 900's and 1300's sophisticated city-states, such as Sofala, developed on the basis of iron and gold exports to Asia and the Arab world. When the Portuguese, the first Europeans to reach the region, arrived in the early 1500's, Arab trading colonies had been established along the coast. In the 1530's the Portuguese sacked the coastal trading cities and broke the trade network established with Africa and India. The Portuguese then established a monopoly over sea trade and began to explore the interior.

Unsuccessful in their search for gold and silver, the Portuguese turned to the slave trade for revenue. The slave trade had been carried on before the arrival of the Europeans, but the Portuguese expanded it, and it soon became the colony's most profitable enterprise.

Soldier-settlers, called *prazeros,* established petty chieftainships in the interior. They seized African villages, which they converted into peasant colonies, and ruled independently of Portuguese authority. Slavery was legally abolished in 1878, but the labor situation scarcely changed. *Prazeros* kept their slaves, but referred to them as "contractual laborers." Local officials cooperated with the *prazeros* by declaring unemployed Africans vagrants and thus eligible to be forced into contracts requiring them to work for the Europeans.

In the 1930's Portugal tightened its control over its colonies. The government took over the exploitation of the colonies' resources.

In 1951 Mozambique's status was changed to that of an overseas province, and in 1961 Portugal granted its African inhabitants full Portuguese citizenship. Although some reforms were initiated in 1961 to improve the welfare and education of the Africans, little progress was made. Forced labor continued in many places, and African political rights were limited.

In the 1960's, the United Nations and many countries, and some groups within Mozambique, increased pressure on Portugal to improve conditions in the colony and at least to grant Mozambique self-determination. In the 1960's, with support from other African states, a Mozambique nationalist liberation organization developed. In 1964 it began a rebellion against Portugal. Guerrilla warfare, concentrated in the north, continued through the 1960's despite an increase in Portuguese military strength in Mozambique to counter it.

Since its independence on June 25, 1975, Mozambique has been torn apart by a civil war between guerrillas of the Mozambique National Resistance (Renamo) and supporters of the Marxist-socialist government. Renamo was originally supported by South Africa and Rhodesia. In 1984 South Africa and Mozambique signed a nonaggression accord, but South Africa is still being accused of supporting Renamo.

During the 1980's Renamo closed down about a third of Mozambique's health clinics and schools. Renamo continues to be better equipped than the government and that, in addition to the government's political and economic problems, has led to Mozambique's economic devastation.

Starvation worsened in the late 1980's because of periods of drought and flooding. Relief efforts were only partially successful because of guerrilla interference with refugee camps receiving food and medicine.

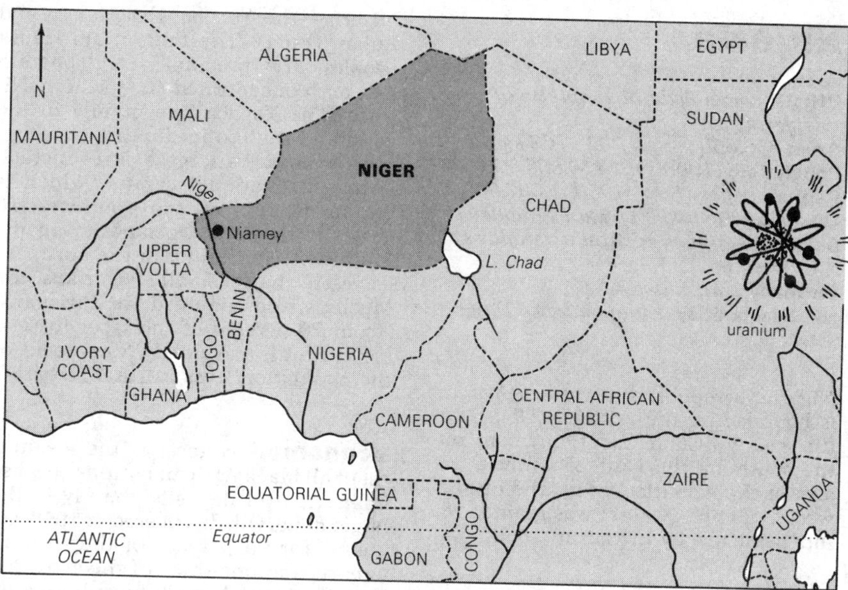

Namibia

See South Africa.

Niger

Official name: *Republic of Niger*
Area: *489,200 sq. mi., 1,267,000 sq. km.*
Population: *(1990 est.) 7,691,000*
Capital: *Niamey (Pop., 1989, 450,000)*
Language: *French, African languages*
Religion: *Islam, traditional religions*
Currency unit: *Franc CFA (African Financial Community)*
National holiday: *Independence Day, Aug. 3*

Niger, a republic in western Africa, is bounded on the north by Algeria and Libya, on the east by Chad, on the south by Nigeria and Benin, and on the west by Upper Volta and Mali. Niger was granted its independence from France in 1960.

The land. Most of Niger is flat. In the north there is desert and in the east there are scrubby and grassy lowlands. In north-central Niger a great mass of volcanic mountains known as the Aïr (Azbine) rise to elevations of almost 6000 feet. Lake Chad lies at the southeastern corner of Niger. The Niger River flows through southwestern Niger.

Niger's climate is hot and dry. Half of Niger receives less than four inches of rain each year. Rainfall averages about 20 inches a year near the border with Nigeria.

The people. There are four main ethnic groups in Niger—the Hausa, Dyerma, Fulani (Fula), and Tuareg. The southern part of the country is heavily populated, especially near the Niger River. Most of the people are Muslim. Niger's largest cities are Niamey, the capital, and Zinder.

Over 90 percent of the people live in rural areas in this sparsely populated country. Most of the labor force is agricultural.

Economy. Rich uranium deposits, recently discovered in the northern desert, now contribute about two-thirds of the nation's exports. Tin and tungsten are also mined. The country's industry is poorly developed.

Agriculture, the economic mainstay before uranium's discovery, is still important. The basic food crops are millet, sorghum, rice, beans, and wheat, and the main commercial crops are peanuts, cotton, and tobacco. Most of the cultivated land is near the border with Nigeria. Cattle, sheep, and goats are raised in most parts of the country.

In 1985 imports were estimated at $354 million while exports earned an estimated $251 million. The main imports are manufactured goods, machinery, and petroleum products. Uranium is the major export, and peanuts, livestock, and vegetables are also significant. France, Nigeria, and the Netherlands are Niger's chief trading partners.

Government. The Supreme Military Council has ruled Niger since the 1974 military coup, when both the legislature and the constitution were summarily suspended.

Niger is a member of the United Nations and the Organization of African Unity, and it is an associated state of the European Common Market.

History. Much of what is now western Niger was part of the Songhai Empire, which flourished from the 1400's to the late 1500's, when it was conquered by a Moroccan army. During the same period, the city-states of the Hausa people in southern Niger maintained their independence from foreign domination. In the north the nomadic Tuareg roamed the arid fringe of the Sahara. All of these peoples traded with North Africa, and the city of Zinder was a center for trade caravans.

In the early 1800's the Hausa region was engulfed in revolution. Usuman dan Fodio, a Fulani Muslim cleric, led a holy war or *jihad* against the Hausa ruling class of Gobia, one of the more important city-states. He voiced long-existing religious and social complaints of the subjects of the Hausa rulers.

The war lasted from 1804 to 1810, by which time nearly all the Hausa states had come under Fulani rule. In time, all of southern Niger and northern Nigeria owed allegiance to Fulani overlords.

French rule. The power of the Fulani rulers, and of the Tuareg, was broken by the French, whose army conquered what is now Niger between 1890 and 1914. Beginning in 1895 Niger was administered as part of French West Africa. After World War II Niger became a territory within the French Union.

In 1958 the Niger Progressive Party, led by Hamani Diori, won an overwhelming majority of seats in the territorial assembly. In that year Niger became an autonomous member of the French Community. The assembly soon dissolved all opposition parties.

Independence. On August 3, 1960, Niger became independent and Diori became president. He was ousted in the 1974 military coup.

Niger suffered greatly from drought and famine between 1968 and 1975. Massive UN and U.S. aid was supplied during the crisis.

Niger's economy is hampered by a poorly developed transportation system as well as its landlocked location. It relies heavily on French aid.

Nigeria

Official name: *Federal Republic of Nigeria*
Area: *356,669 sq. mi., 923,768 sq. km.*
Population: *(1990 est.) 118,865,000*
Capital: *Lagos (Pop., 1983, 1,097,000)*
Language: *English, African languages*
Religion: *Islam, traditional religions, Christian*
Currency unit: *Naira*
National holiday: *Independence Day, Oct. 1*

Nigeria, a republic in western Africa, is bounded on the north by Niger, on the east by Chad and Cameroon, on the south by the Gulf of Guinea, an arm of the Atlantic Ocean, and on the west by Benin. Nigeria was granted its independence by Britain in 1960.

The land. Most of Nigeria is occupied by plains or low rolling hills. There are tropical forests and mangrove swamps along the coast. The Niger River, which flows through south-central Nigeria, forms a large delta where it reaches the ocean.

There are grassy savannas in central Nigeria, north of the junction of the Niger and Benue rivers. In the north-central part of the country is the Bauchi Plateau, which has an elevation of almost 6000 feet above sea level. There is grassland and desert in the far north. The Adamawa Mountains are in the southwest.

The climate of Nigeria is hot and humid. Some areas in the south receive as much as 150 inches of rain each year.

The people. Nigeria is one of the most populous countries in Africa. It has one-fifth of all the blacks in Africa. There are four main ethnic groups in Nigeria—the Yoruba, Ibo, Hausa, and Fulani (Fula). The Fulani and Hausa peoples are predominantly Muslim and are concentrated in northern Nigeria. The Yoruba live mainly in the west, and the Ibo in the east.

The country's largest cities include Lagos, the national capital, which is on an island off the southwestern coast; Ibadan and Ogbomosho, in the southwest; and Kano, in the north.

Nearly half of all Nigerians are Muslims, and one-third are Christians. About 70 percent of the labor force is agricultural, and nearly 80 percent of the population lives in rural areas.

Economy. Nigeria is the wealthiest of all black African nations because of its rich oil deposits, mainly in the Niger delta. Oil, discovered in 1958, accounts for 95 percent of the nation's exports and one-third of the gross national product. Sixty-four million metric tons of oil were produced in 1987. Gas, coal, tin, and columbite are other natural resources.

Nigerian industry, supported by abundant hydroelectric power reserves from the Niger River, accounts for seven percent of the gross national product. Textiles, cement, wood products, and automobiles are the principal manufactures.

Nigeria's agriculture, the mainstay of the economy before 1960, is based on the production of peanuts, oil palm products, cacao, cotton, and rubber. The country's basic food crops include yams and corn. Nigeria has rich forest resources, and timber is exported. Fish from the Niger River provide an additional source of food. Cattle are raised mainly in the northern part of the country.

In 1986 exports, mostly oil, earned $6.8 billion. Imports, mostly food, chemicals, machinery, and iron and steel, cost $5.3 billion. Most trade is with Western Europe and the United States.

Government. Nigeria was returned to civilian rule in 1979 for the first time since 1966. According to its constitution of 1979, it is ruled by an elected president and a bicameral National Assembly comprised of a 95-member Senate and a 449-member House of Representatives. Members of both houses are elected to four-year terms.

In 1983 the military overthrew the civilian government. The Armed Forces Ruling Council is a 28-member governing body led by the president. A national council of ministers serves as a cabinet. The government will be returned to civilian rule in 1992.

History. The many peoples of Nigeria have a rich heritage. In about the 1100's the Yoruba people settled in western Nigeria, and in the north Hausa people established agricultural states. In southern Nigeria the early states of Ife and Benin produced sculpture that is now world famous. In the 1200's the Hausa in the north were converted to Islam by the Fulani people, who came from eastern Africa. In the early 1800's a Fulani leader, Usuman dan Fodio, conquered the Hausa city-states and replaced the Hausa dynasties with Fulani emirs.

Portuguese traders came to Nigeria in 1472, and Portugal and other European countries shared in the lucrative slave trade that developed. The British penetrated the area beginning in 1807

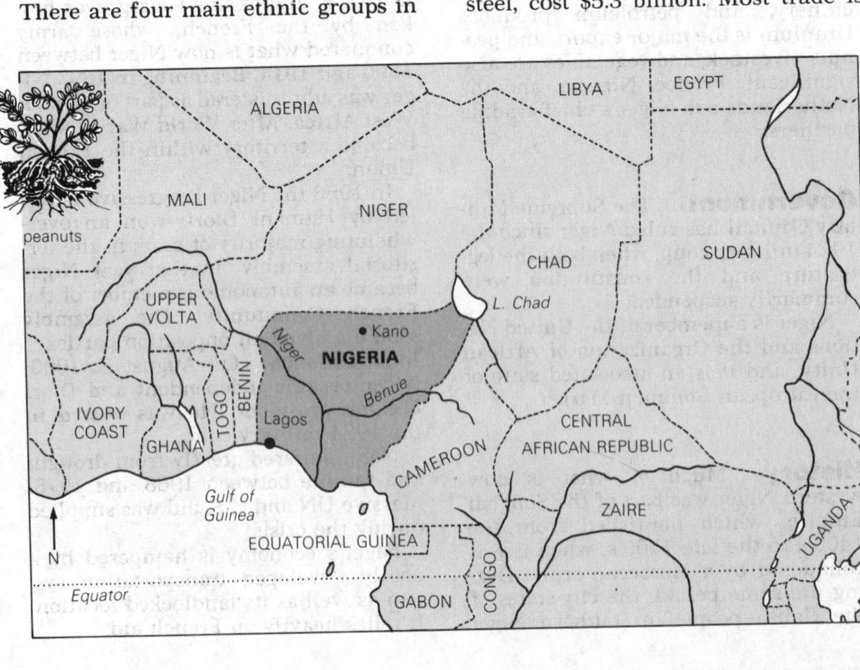

YORUBA SCULPTURE *from Ife, Nigeria: a superb head dating from about the 1300's.*

CIVIL WAR IN NIGERIA. *Biafran recruits in training. The eastern region, calling itself Biafra, seceded in 1967. Before it was defeated, there were over 1 million casualties.*

to halt the slave trade. Lagos was occupied by Britain in 1861, and the United Africa Company, later known as the Royal Niger Company, opened the Niger valley to trade. In 1885 the Oil Rivers Protectorate was set up in the coastal region.

British rule. The British government took over direct administration of the protectorate in 1891, and by 1893, with the addition of a region beyond the coast, formed the Niger Coast Protectorate. In 1900 it became the Protectorate of Southern Nigeria. In the same year the territory of the Royal Niger Company became the Protectorate of Northern Nigeria. In 1903 the emirates of the north came under British control.

The protectorates were united in 1914, and after World War I the former German colony of Cameroon was added as a mandate under the League of Nations. In 1939 southern Nigeria was divided into the Eastern and Western provinces.

Nigerians had begun to seek greater freedom before World War I, but nationalist movements tended to be regional. Most prominent were the Northern Peoples' Congress (NPC) led by Sir Ahmadu Bello, the Action Group in the Western region led by Chief Obafemi Awolowo, and the National Council of Nigeria and Cameroons (NCNC) led by Dr. Nnamdi Azikiwe. After World War II regional legislatures and elections were introduced throughout the country.

In 1954 the first national elections were held, and the NPC and NCNC obtained the most votes. Eastern and Western Nigeria became self-governing in 1957, but the north, which was less developed, did not achieve self-government until 1959.

Independence. On October 1, 1960, Nigeria became an independent nation. In 1961 a UN plebiscite was held in the British Cameroons, and the Northern Cameroons voted to become part of Nigeria, which then consisted of three regions—Eastern, Western, and Northern Nigeria. On October 1, 1963, Nigeria became a republic. In 1966 two successive coups resulted in the establishment of a military regime. A year later, the Ibos, frustrated by the northern Muslims' apparent monopoly on political power and oil revenues, proclaimed the independent Republic of Biafra. After a bloody civil war, the Ibos were defeated, but the republic was badly weakened. The severe droughts and famines that persisted between 1968 and 1974 further wracked the politically torn country.

In 1979, civilian rule was restored in Nigeria, but the government was ousted in a coup in 1983. Another coup in 1985 installed Ibrahim Babangida, who moved quickly to institute austerity measures in an effort to rescue the country's troubled economy.

Oman

Official name: *Sultanate of Oman*
Area: *82,030 sq. mi., 212, 457 sq. km.*
Population: *(1990 est.) 1,345,000*
Capital: *Muscat (Pop., 1981 est., 70,000)*
Language: *Arabic*
Religion: *Islam*
Currency unit: *Omani rial*
National holiday: *Nov. 18*

Oman, known as Muscat and Oman until 1970, is an Arab sultanate in the southeastern corner of Arabia, occupying a strategic position at the mouth of the Persian Gulf. The country is bordered on the northwest by the United Arab Emirates, on the north by the Gulf of Oman, on the east and south by the Arabian Sea, on the southwest by the People's Democratic Republic of Yemen, and on the west by Saudi Arabia. The borders of Oman are largely undefined, and some continue to be disputed.

The land. A narrow plain skirts the country's 1000-mile coastline. The northwestern portion of the plain, the Batinah, is quite fertile. Rugged mountains rise sharply to nearly 10,000 feet above the plain. In the interior is a low, barren plateau, the eastern end of the vast Rub al Khali, or "Empty Quarter," of the Arabian Peninsula. The climate throughout the country is hot and dry.

The people. The native people are Arab, but there are Indian, Iranian, and black minorities. Population is concentrated in three main regions—Muscat, on the northeast; Oman, in the mountains; and Dhofar, on the Arabian Sea coast.

Half the people are Ibadi Muslims and one-quarter are Sunni Muslims. Oman is very sparsely populated and almost all of its people live in rural areas. The labor force is one-third foreign, 80 percent agricultural.

Economy. Oman's major product and resource is oil, which was first produced in 1967. In 1987, 28.2 million metric tons were produced, and oil accounted for almost 95 percent of the nation's exports.

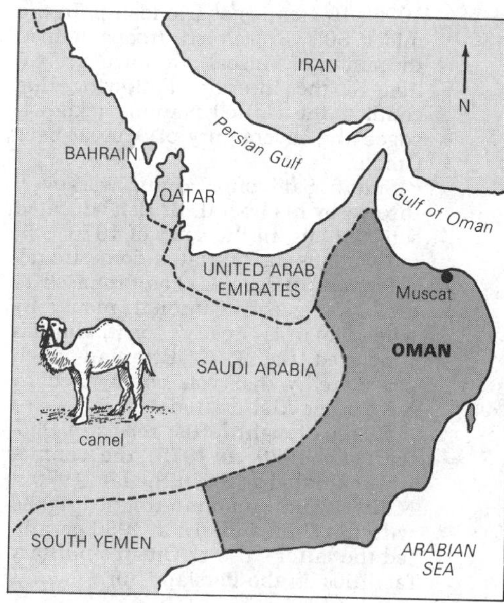

Dates are the leading agricultural product, and coconuts, cereals, and citrus fruits are also grown. Large herds of camels are raised in the interior, and there is good fishing off the coast. There is little industry other than oil processing.

Trade is very prosperous. Exports, mainly oil, earned $4.4 billion in 1984 while imports, mostly food, consumer, and manufactured items, cost $2.9 billion. Britain, India, and Pakistan are the chief trading partners.

Government. The sultan of Oman is still an absolute monarch who rules with the aid of his ministers. The sultanate has no constitution, legislature, or legal political parties.

Oman is a member of the United Nations and the Arab League.

History. Arab peoples have inhabited Muscat and Oman for many centuries. Because of its strategic position at the mouth of the Persian Gulf, the land attracted conquerors seeking control of the gulf. In 1508 the Portuguese occupied Muscat, and during the following century they competed for control with the Ottoman Turks, who had captured several areas.

By 1650 the native Arabs had driven out both the Portuguese and the Turks. Arab control was not secure, however, until 1737, when Ahmad ibn Said fought off a Persian invasion.

During the 1700's and 1800's the sultanate extended its control over parts of southern Iran and eastern Africa. In the later 1800's, however, internal political disputes divided the region between coastal Muscat and interior Oman. The power of both declined, and foreign territories were lost.

In 1891 Muscat granted special privileges to Britain in return for British protection. Close ties with Britain were reaffirmed several times in the 1900's by treaties of friendship. In the mid-1950's British-led troops helped the sultan of Muscat put down a rebellion in the interior. Following this conflict, the United Nations acknowledged the sovereignty of Muscat over Oman.

Sultan Said bin Taimur was overthrown by his liberal, British-educated son, Quabus, in the coup of 1970. Sultan Quabus has initiated domestic development programs, has promised to establish a constitutional monarchy when Oman is "ready" for it, and has supported the 1979 Egyptian-Israeli peace treaty that was condemned by most other Arab nations.

Quabus fought leftist rebels in Dhofar from 1970 to 1975; the conflict was rekindled again in the late 1970's. Military and economic treaties signed with the United States in 1980 permitted the latter's use of Oman's military facilities on the Persian Gulf.

Qatar

Official name: *State of Qatar*
Area: *4,250 sq. mi., 11,000 sq. km.*
Population: *(1990 est.) 353,000*
Capital: *Doha*
(Pop., 1989 est., 215,000)
Language: *Arabic*
Religion: *Islam*
Currency unit: *Riyal*

Qatar, an oil-rich Arab sheikdom, occupies the Qatar peninsula on the southern shore of the Persian Gulf, which borders the country on the north, east, and west. Qatar is bordered on the south by Saudi Arabia and the United Arab Emirates.

The land and people. The Qatar Peninsula is a low plain, thinly covered with sand. The climate is hot and dry, and rainfall is less than four inches a year. The people of Qatar are of Arab stock but also include Iranians and Pakistanis. Over 80 percent of both the population and the labor force is comprised of foreigners. Most of the people are Sunni Muslims.

Economy. Qatar lacks skilled native labor, but it is one of the richest nations in the world. Oil is its only natural resource, and the country has almost no cultivable land. Fishing, pearl diving, and the herding of goats and camels were the main means of livelihood before the discovery of oil; they continue to contribute to the economy of Qatar.

Oil production, begun in 1949, is the country's only significant industry and it accounts for most of the gross national product. Qatar produced 15 million metric tons of oil in 1987. In 1977 all gas and oil reserves were nationalized. Foreign oil companies pay large royalty fees to Qatar's sheik.

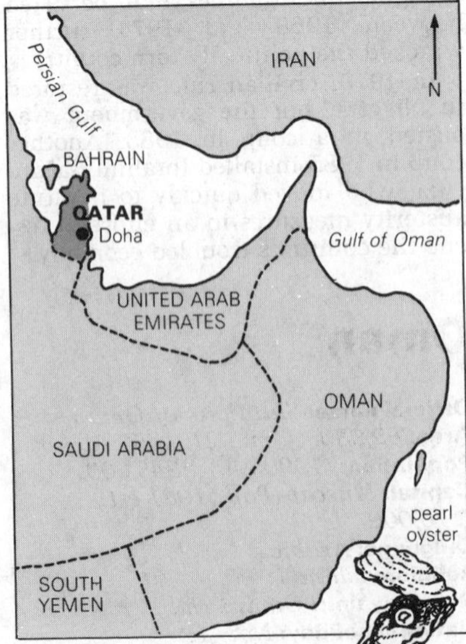

In 1985 imports cost $1.2 billion, and exports earned $3.1 billion. Oil and pearls are Qatar's main exports, while food, machinery, and raw materials are its chief imports. Most trade is with Japan, Western Europe, and the United States.

Government. Qatar is under the absolute rule of a hereditary sheik, who is assisted by a 30-member advisory council.

Qatar is a member of the United Nations, the Organization of Petroleum Exporting Countries (OPEC), and the Arab League.

History. Qatar has been inhabited by Arab peoples for many centuries. The sheiks of Qatar were compelled to pay tribute to the sheiks of Bahrain for protection and support until 1872. In 1868 Qatar entered into the first of a series of treaties with Britain, which was then building a strong position in the Persian Gulf. Between 1872 and 1914, however, the Ottoman Turks maintained a fort in Qatar and controlled the country.

In a treaty signed in 1916 Qatar's sheiks granted Britain special diplomatic and commercial rights in return for protection. The discovery of oil in 1939 brought wealth and international importance to the sheikdom. In 1971 Britain terminated its treaty relationships with the Persian Gulf sheikdoms and withdrew. On September 3, 1971, Qatar declared itself to be a fully independent state.

In 1972 a bloodless palace coup was staged by Emir Khalifa ibn Hamad.

Rhodesia

See Zimbabwe.

Rwanda

Official name: *Republic of Rwanda*
Area: *10,169 sq. mi., 26,338 sq. km.*
Population: *(1990 est.) 7,603,000*
Capital: *Kigali (Pop., 1981, 156,650)*
Language: *Kinyarwanda, French*
Religion: *Roman Catholic, traditional religions*
Currency unit: *Franc*
National holiday: *Independence Day, July 1*

Rwanda, a landlocked republic in eastern Africa, is bordered on the north by Uganda, on the east by Tanzania, on the south by Burundi, and on the west by Lake Kivu and Zaire. Rwanda was joined with present day Burundi as Ruanda-Urundi until 1962, when it received its independence from Belgium, along with Burundi.

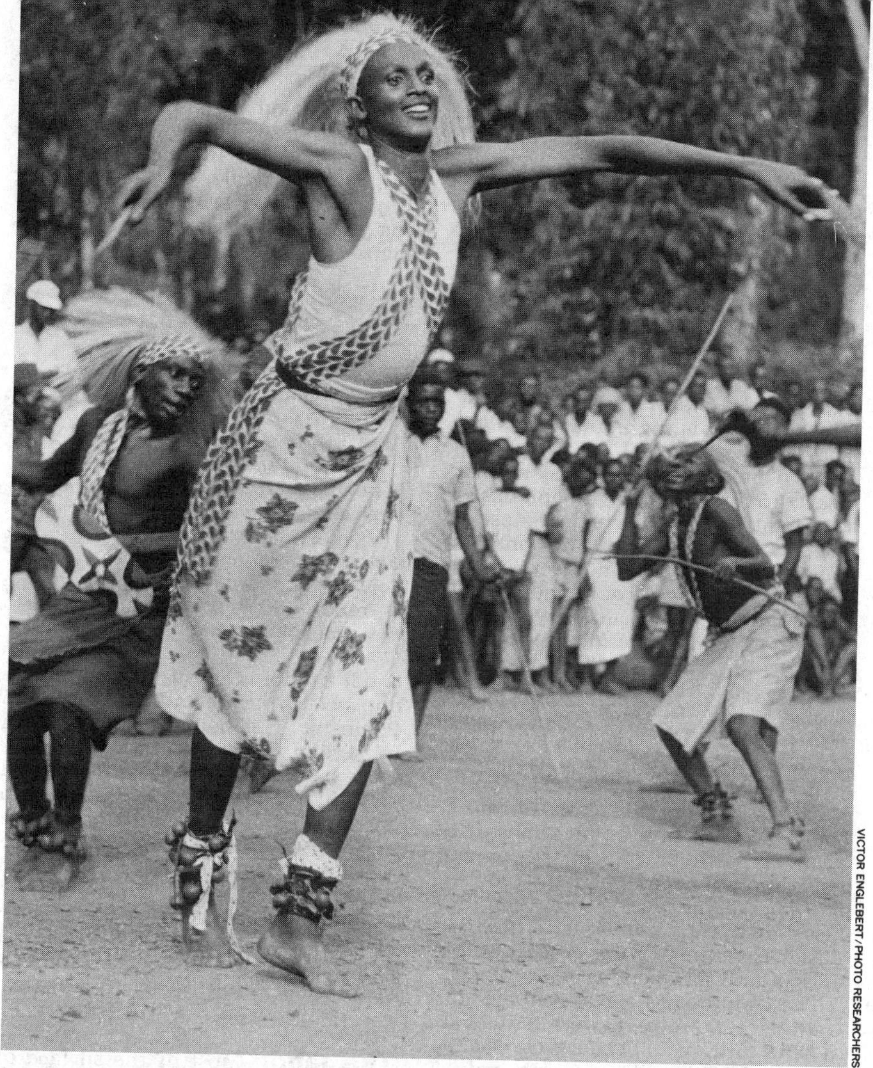

SHEER JOY OF THE DANCE. *A Tusi of Rwanda mimes a bird. The Tusi, tall invaders, dominated the short Hutu majority until 1959, when a civil war ended Tusi rule; many fled.*

The land. Rwanda is composed mainly of hills and uplands. A continuous chain of mountains with elevations above 6500 feet runs along Rwanda's western border. An eroded plateau slopes eastward from the mountains. In the north there are active volcanoes in the Virunga Mountains, which reach an elevation of over 14,700 feet. The Kagera River drains Rwanda's plateau. Lake Kivu is in western Rwanda.

There are two wet and two dry seasons each year. In most places between 40 and 60 inches of rain falls during the wet seasons.

The people. There are three ethnic groups in Rwanda—the Hutu, the Tusi ("Watusi"), and the Twa. About 86 percent of the people are Hutu, 13 percent are Tusi, and about one percent are Twa. Until recently the Hutu, traditionally farmers, were dominated by the Tusi under a feudal system. The Twa people, pygmy forest-dwellers, are probably descendants of Rwanda's original inhabitants.

Rwanda has a population density of nearly 500 people per square mile, and the annual increase is three percent. Almost all the people are subsistence farmers living in rural areas. The population density results in high emigration rates.

Over half the people are Christians, most of these being Roman Catholic. Kigali is the largest urban center.

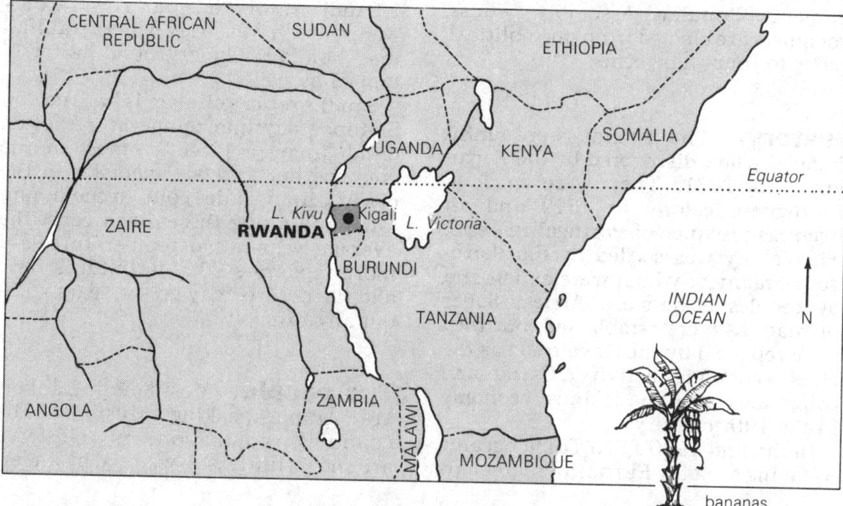

Economy. About two-thirds of Rwanda's gross national product is derived from agriculture. The basic food crops are beans, corn, and sweet potatoes, and the basic cash crop is coffee. Cattle are numerous and are a symbol of both wealth and social position.

Soil erosion and drought are constant problems throughout the country. Belgium instituted a ten-year economic development plan in 1952, and new drought-resistant crops were introduced.

Although Rwanda has deposits of cassiterite, tungsten, and other minerals, the country's resources have not been fully developed, and there is little industry.

In 1987 exports earned about $113.2 million and imports cost $354.2 million. Rwanda's principal exports are coffee, tin, and tungsten. Imports include foodstuffs, textiles, machinery, chemicals, and petroleum products. Most trade is with Kenya and Western Europe.

Government. Rwanda has a presidential system of government. The president is assisted by a 17-member presidentially appointed cabinet of ministers. The 1978 constitution vests legislative power in a unicameral National Development Council comprised of 70 members. The president and legislature are elected by universal suffrage.

History. The Tusi people, who probably came from Ethiopia, invaded Rwanda in the 1500's. They established themselves as a ruling aristocracy, headed by a mwami, or king, over the agricultural Hutu people.

In 1894 the first European, Graf von Goetzen, a German, reached the kingdom, and in 1899 Germany established a protectorate over the region. Germany administered the area as part of German East Africa until World War I. After the war the former protectorate became a mandate of Belgium under the League of Nations.

Belgium was to administer the region jointly with present-day Burundi as Ruanda-Urundi. In 1946 the area became a UN trust territory.

Belgium permitted little African political activity, and until the 1950's supported traditional Tusi rule over the Hutu majority. At that time Africans organized political parties along ethnic lines, and the tribal Party of the Hutu Emancipation Movement (PARMEHUTU), composed mainly of Hutu people, opposed the Tusi-dominated National Rwandan Union (UNAR). Tension between the Hutu and the Tusi led to civil war in 1959. The Hutu ended Tusi dominance, and large numbers of Tusi fled to neighboring countries.

In elections held in 1961 PARMEHUTU won an overwhelming victory. The Belgium trusteeship was ended on June 28, 1962, and Rwanda was declared an independent republic on July 1, 1962. Grégoire Kayibanda of PARMEHUTU became president.

Kayibanda initiated a policy of reconciliation and appointed Tusi ministers to his cabinet. But in 1963 fighting again broke out between the Tusi and the Hutu. In July of 1973 Kayibanda was deposed in a bloodless military coup.

Rwanda is joined in an economic community with Burundi and Zaire.

São Tomé and Principe

Official name: *Democratic Republic of São Tomé and Principe*
Area: *372 sq. mi., 964 sq. km.*
Population: *(1990 est.) 125,000*
Capital: *São Tomé (Pop., 1984, 34,997)*
Language: *Portuguese*
Religion: *Roman Catholic*
Currency unit: *Dobra*

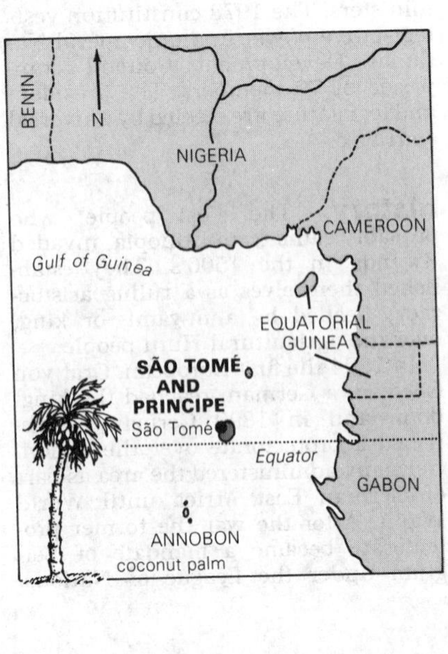

The islands of São Tomé and Principe and their offshore islets lie some 125 miles off the western coast of Africa in the Gulf of Guinea, just north of the equator and west of Gabon and Equatorial Guinea.

The land and people. The islands are volcanic in origin and consist of a hilly, forested interior ringed by a wide, flat, coastal plain. São Tomé and Principe's climate is extremely hot. The humidity is high, and rainfall is heavy.

São Tomé, the southern island, has nearly 15 times as many inhabitants as the slightly smaller Principe. Most of the population is black. Many laborers have been imported in recent years from Angola and Mozambique. They work on plantations run by white settlers on which local residents refuse to work.

Economy. The island nation's economy has steadily declined owing to price decreases in its major crop, cacao, and nationalization of more than 50 percent of the plantations. The economy is still based primarily on the cultivation of cacao but copra, coffee, coconuts, palm oil, and cinchona are also important commercial crops. Industry is limited to the processing of agricultural products.

The country has a poor balance of trade. In 1986 imports were estimated at $25.6 million and exports earned an estimated $9.3 million. Cacao, palm, coconut products, and coffee are exported. Food, textiles, and other necessities are imported. Portugal is the country's chief trading partner; the United States, Britain, and the Netherlands take some of the exports.

Government. On July 12, 1975, the islands were granted independence by Portugal. According to the constitution, the country is ruled by a president who appoints a prime minister to assist him in executive decision making. Legislative power is vested in a unicameral Popular Assembly whose members are elected from one political party to four-year terms.

History. The islands were uninhabited when discovered by the Portuguese in 1471. They were made a Portuguese colony in 1522 and an overseas province of Portugal in 1951. The colony was settled by the Portuguese, many of whom were exiles, and by peoples of western Africa. Sugar plantations were established, but they were replaced by the slave trade as the chief economic activity. Cacao and coffee took over the islands' economy in the 19th century.

In the mid 1960's São Tomé became a staging area for European mercenaries hired to subdue uprisings for independence in the Portuguese territories on the African mainland.

In an effort to revive the faltering economy, the government is encouraging private enterprise to stimulate foreign investment in the islands.

Saudi Arabia

Official name: *Kingdom of Saudi Arabia*
Area: *927,000 sq. mi., 2,400,000 sq. km.*
Population: *(1990 est.) 16,758,000*
Capital: *Riyadh (Pop., 1989 est., 1,500,000)*
Language: *Arabic*
Religion: *Islam*
Currency unit: *Rial*
National holiday: *Sept. 23*

Saudi Arabia is an oil-rich Arab kingdom occupying the bulk of the Arabian Peninsula. It is bounded on the north by Jordan, Iraq, and Kuwait. (Agreement has been reached with Iraq and Kuwait on the partitioning of two "neutral zones" formerly along the northern border.) It is bordered on the east by the Persian Gulf, United Arab Emirates, Qatar, and Oman; on the south by Oman and the two Yemens; and on the west by the Gulf of Aqaba and the Red Sea. Many of the boundaries are not demarcated.

The land. Most of the surface of Saudi Arabia is barren. A narrow, infertile plain, the Tihama, lies along the western coast. To its east the Hejaz Mountains, in the north, and the Asir Mountains, in the south, rise sharply to 11,000 feet. These treeless, sandstone and lava mountains slope into an interior plateau, which consists of two desert regions—An Nafud, in the north, and the Rub al-Khali, in the south.

The interior plain occupies about 90 percent of the country's area and is largely uninhabited. Along the eastern border, rolling coastal plains slope into the Persian Gulf.

Saudi Arabia has no rivers—only wadis, dry river beds where rainfall may run off. Underground water is tapped by wells.

Saudi Arabia's climate is hot and dry. Summer daytime temperatures often climb to over 125°F in most of the country, but nights, especially in the desert, can be quite cold. In the mountains and along the eastern coast the average year-round temperature is a more moderate 80°F. Rainfall is rare, and the deserts may go for years without any rain.

The people. Most Saudi Arabians are Arabic-speaking Muslims. The country's population is clustered around its few oases, watered by under-

YOUNG GIRLS *in neat school uniforms study biology in their school at Jidda, port city for Mecca. The fine equipment of the school reflects wealth from Saudi Arabia's abundant oil.*

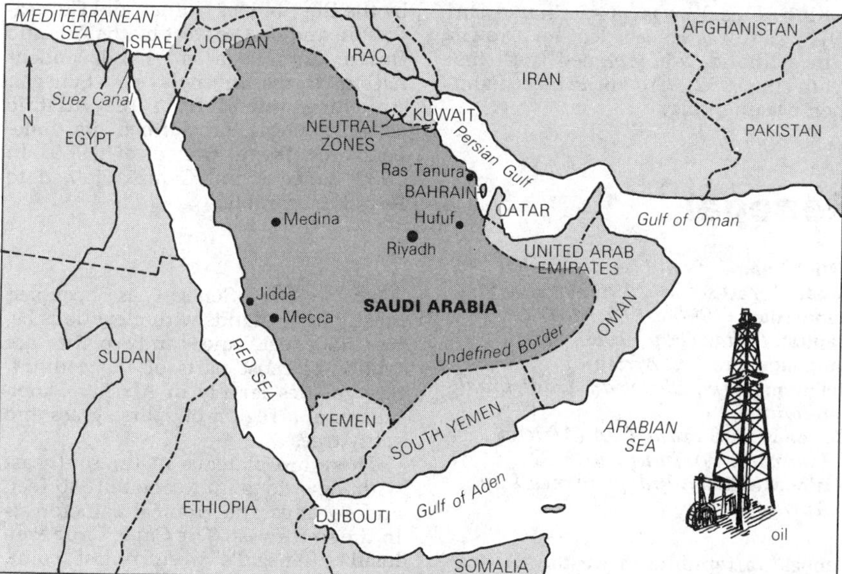

IBN SAUD (above), *founder of Saudi Arabia, a country that curiously combines modern technology and comforts with traditional ways and strict Islam, as suggested by these workers praying close to oil tanks in Jidda.*

ground springs, where such towns as Mecca, Jidda, Riyadh, Hufuf, and Medina developed.

Nomadic Bedouin tribesmen have long roamed the deserts. Government programs have been settling the nomads in areas where irrigation can make sedentary life possible.

Almost 50 percent of the population is composed of foreigners who fill the gap created by Saudi Arabia's lack of skilled labor. The national literacy rate is 52 percent, and one-quarter of the labor force is agricultural.

Economy. Over 60 percent of Saudi Arabia's gross national product comes from mining and industry, compared with four percent from agriculture. The country has the world's second highest production rate of oil, with 209.5 million metric tons of crude oil produced in 1987. Aramco (Arabian American Oil Company), the world's single most productive oil company, was nationalized by Saudi Arabia in 1979. The principal refinery is on the east coast, at Ras Tanura.

Oil revenues are used to provide free education and health care for Saudi Arabians, government funding, and domestic improvements, including industrialization and agricultural expansion and modernization.

Most of the people in Saudi Arabia live as farmers or herders. The country's only major crops are grains, citrus fruits, and dates, which are grown in oases. Sheep, goats, and camels graze in Saudi Arabia's vast deserts. There is some pearl diving and fishing along the coasts. Money spent in the country by Muslim pilgrims to the holy cities of Mecca and Medina is the second most important source of Saudi Arabia's income.

Saudi Arabia's prosperous international trade is based on oil. In 1985 imports cost $24 billion and exports earned $30.2 billion. Foodstuffs, textiles, clothing, machinery, and transportation equipment are imported. Saudi Arabia sells oil throughout the world, but Western Europe is its largest customer. The United States, Western Europe, and other Middle Eastern states are the kingdom's main sources of imports.

Government. Saudi Arabia is an absolute monarchy with a king who serves as the political and religious leader of the country. The king appoints a Council of Ministers, but there is no legislature or constitution.

Saudi Arabia is a member of the United Nations, the Organization of Petroleum Exporting Countries (OPEC), and the Arab League.

History. Saudi Arabia became a nation in 1926, but Arabia has been inhabited since ancient times by Arab herdsmen and traders, and it was the site of several ancient kingdoms. Muhammad the prophet was born in the trading city of Mecca in 570 A.D., and the city became an important center of the Muslim religion.

During the century following Muhammad's death in 632, Muslim armies conquered North Africa and the entire Middle East and Muslim power extended into Spain. Religious disputes and competition for power soon brought disorder to Arabia, however. It was divided into two major sheikdoms—Nejd in the interior of the peninsula and the Hejaz in the west—and many petty states.

Parts of Saudi Arabia were conquered in the 1200's by the Egyptians and in the 1500's by the Ottoman Turks. The conquerors were most interested in the Hejaz because of the importance of controlling the Muslim holy city of Mecca, its capital.

Wahhabis. In Nejd in the 1700's a Muslim sect whose goal was to reform and purify Islam was founded by Muhammad Ibn Abd al-Wahhab. His followers, the Wahhabis, allied with Muhammad ibn Saud, a ruler of part of Nejd.

Saud's successors carried Wahhabism to the Persian Gulf, and by 1806 they had conquered the Hejaz from the Sharifs, the rulers of Mecca who controlled the Hejaz. But Saud's Wahhabis were driven back into the interior of Nejd by Turkish and Egyptian troops. In Nejd they lost power to the rival sheikdom of al-Rashid.

Nearly 100 years later, in 1902, Saud's direct descendant, Abd-al-Aziz ibn Saud, conquered Nejd's capital, Riyadh, from the Rashids. By 1913 he had defeated the Rashids and had driven the Ottomans from most of central Arabia.

In 1916 Saud's rival for power, Sharif Husayn of Mecca, led a pan-Arab revolt against the Turks that carried his sons to the thrones of the new Arab states of Iraq and Transjordan (present-day Jordan). After World War I uneasy relations between the Husayns and the Saudis led to warfare in 1924. The Saudis captured the Hejaz and forced out the Husayns.

In 1926 Abd-al-Aziz united Nejd and the Hejaz and two small dependencies, Asir and Hasa, into a Wahhabist state. He proclaimed himself king of the entire region, which he named Saudi Arabia in 1932.

Modern Saudi Arabia. Under Abd-al-Aziz the modernization of Arabia began, and the discovery of oil in 1938 greatly speeded up the process by providing a source of income for the government. Large-scale oil production began in 1945, after World War II. Oil revenues made possible social changes that promised to affect radically Saudi Arabian life, but the country somehow maintained internal political and social stability.

Abd-al-Aziz's son, Saud, succeeded him in 1953, but in 1964 he was replaced by his half-brother, Faisal.

Saudi Arabia has supported conservative Arabian societies, and it aided both Yemen and Oman when those countries faced political revolts or invasions. It refused to help Egypt, a country leaning toward radical social change, during the 1967 Arab-Israeli war, but it did support the Arab cause during the 1948–1949 and the 1973 Arab-Israeli wars.

Saudi Arabia works hard to moderate Arab conflicts and affairs. It buys armaments from the West, and redistributes them to Arab nations at its discretion. It was a leader of the Arab oil boycott of 1973–1974 designed to force the formulation of anti–Israeli policies by Western nations, and it rebuked Egypt for its role in the 1979 Egypt-Israeli peace treaty.

King Faisal was assassinated in 1975 and was succeeded by Crown Prince Khalid, who reigned until his death in 1982. Crown Prince Fahd then became king.

Senegal

Official name: *Republic of Senegal*
Area: *75,750 sq. mi., 196,192 sq. km.*
Population: *(1990 est.) 7,740,000*
Capital: *Dakar (Pop., 1989, 850,000)*
Language: *French, African languages*
Religion: *Islam, Christian, traditional religions*
Currency unit: *Franc CFA (African Financial Community)*
National holiday: *Independence Day, April 4*

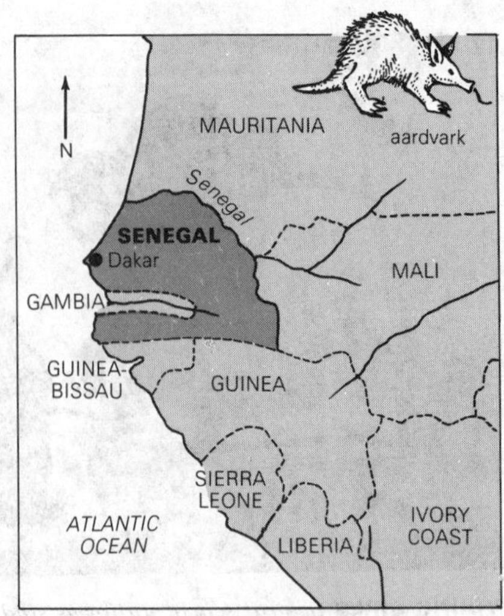

Senegal, a republic in western Africa, is bordered on the north by Mauritania, on the east by Mali, on the south by the Republic of Guinea and Guinea-Bissau, and on the west by the Atlantic Ocean. Gambia, a small independent nation, forms an enclave in Senegal, stretching inland from the Atlantic coast. Senegal proclaimed its independence from France in 1960. In 1982 Senegal and Gambia joined to form Senegambia.

The land.

Senegal is occupied mostly by lowlands with elevations below 650 feet, and sandy plains are typical of most parts of the country. Senegal lies largely in Africa's Sahelian zone, a region of sparse grass and spiny trees.

There are plateaus in the southeast with elevations up to about 1640 feet, and swamps and tropical rain forests in the southwest. The Cape Verde Peninsula, Senegal's westernmost point, protrudes into the Atlantic Ocean.

MARKET IN DAKAR *reveals the relative prosperity of Senegal, a well developed country.*

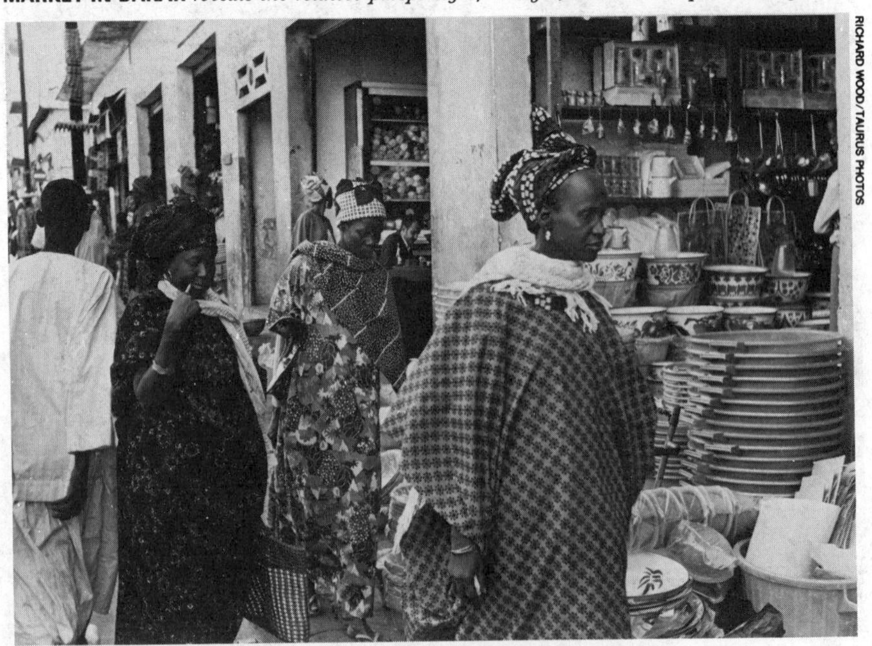

RICHARD WOOD/TAURUS PHOTOS

Four major rivers flow through the country—the Senegal in the north, the Gambia and Saloum in central Senegal, and the Casamance in the south.

Temperatures are moderate in most parts of the country. Some regions in southern Senegal receive as much as 60 inches of rain each year. The peninsula receives about 24 inches a year.

The people. There are many tribal groups in Senegal. The largest groups are the Wolof; the Fula, or Peul; the Serer; the Mandingo; and the Tukulor. Most of the people are Muslims. There is a small number of non-Africans; they are mainly Europeans, Syrians, and Lebanese.

Dakar, located on the peninsula, is Senegal's largest city. Other large cities are Kaolack, Saint Louis, Thiès.

Two-thirds of the nation's people live in rural areas, and 70 percent of the labor force is agricultural.

Economy. About 30 percent of Senegal's gross national product is derived from agriculture, and 20 percent from industry. The basic food crops are millet, sorghum, and rice. Peanuts are the main commercial crop. Fishing is also important in the Senegalese economy.

Senegal has rich phosphate deposits. Industry is centered in Dakar and is well developed. Peanuts, phosphates, and fish are processed for export.

In 1982 imports cost $713 million and exports earned $476.5 million. The main imports are textiles, machinery, and foodstuffs. The principal exports are peanuts, peanut oil, and phosphates. Most trade is conducted with France. Senegal receives economic aid from France.

Government. Senegal has a presidential system of government. Executive power is held by a president who is popularly elected to a five-year term. Legislative power is held by a 120-member National Assembly. Assembly members are popularly elected to five-year terms.

Senegal is a member of the United Nations and the Organization of African Unity, and it is an associated state of the European Common Market.

History. Between about the 400's and 200's B.C. the peoples of what is now Senegal traded by sea with the Carthaginians. During the next millennium they traded with the merchants of ancient Ghana and Mali.

Portuguese sailors visited the shores of Senegal during the 1400's, and beginning in the 1500's French, Dutch, and British merchants came to the region. In the late 1600's the French established settlements at Saint Louis and on Gorée Island, near the Cape Verde Peninsula.

Under a succession of energetic colonial governors, the French tried to transform Senegal into a profitable outpost of their empire. But few Frenchmen could be induced to settle there, and wars with Britain over control of the area were costly. Britain conquered Senegal in the 1750's and administered the area in union with Gambia as the Crown colony of Senegambia.

French rule. By the 1800's France had gradually reestablished its control over most of the country. Only at that time did the French alter the indigenous way of life. From 1854 to 1865, under the aggressive governor Louis Léon César Faidherbe, the French subjugated the people living between Saint Louis and Gorée Island, and successfully asserted their authority over the peoples living on both banks of the Senegal River.

The Senegalese opposed the French at every turn. Muslims along the Senegal River, many of whom had become subject to a Fulani-ruled empire in the 1700's, unsuccessfully fought the French. In the interior, al-hajj 'Umar, a Muslim reformer who had created Islamic states in the region in the 1800's, temporarily halted the French advance.

In 1904 Dakar became the capital of French West Africa. The more important schools and hospitals of French West Africa were located there, and Senegal's coastal region became the most westernized part of French West Africa.

In 1946 Senegal became a territory within the French Union. In elections held in 1951 and 1957 Léopold Senghor, a French-educated poet, led the Senegalese Progressive Union to victory. In 1958 Senegal became an autonomous member of the French Community.

Independence. In 1959 France joined Senegal with present-day Mali to form the Mali Federation. On August 20, 1960, Senegal withdrew from the federation and proclaimed its independence. Senghor became Senegal's first president and he was reelected in 1978.

During Senghor's long and stable rule, Senegal normalized relations with Mali (1963) and improved its relations with the Arab states. In the mid-1970's Senghor allowed the establishment of political parties and free elections, making Senegal one of the most democratic nations in Africa.

There have been attempts to improve the lagging economy through diversification, but Senegal remains largely dependent on French aid.

In 1982 Senegal and Gambia formed a confederation, called Senegambia, in which they maintained their independence, but integrated various governmental responsibilities.

Seychelles

Official name: *Republic of the Seychelles*
Area: *145 sq. mi., 376 sq. km.*
Population: *(1990 est.) 71,000*
Capital: *Victoria (Pop., 1989, 30,000)*
Language: *Creole, English*
Religion: *Roman Catholic*
Currency unit: *Rupee*

The Seychelles Archipelago consists of about 90 islands and islets in the Indian Ocean, some 1000 miles east of Kenya. The largest island is Mahé. Others include Silhouette, Praslin, La Digue, and Curieuse.

The land. Most of the smaller islands are coral, barren and uninhabitable. The large ones consist of a mountainous, forested interior ringed by a low, flat coastal plain. The climate is warm, with heavy rainfall.

The people. Population density is uneven, with four-fifths of the people living on Mahé. Most of the inhabitants are descendants of early French

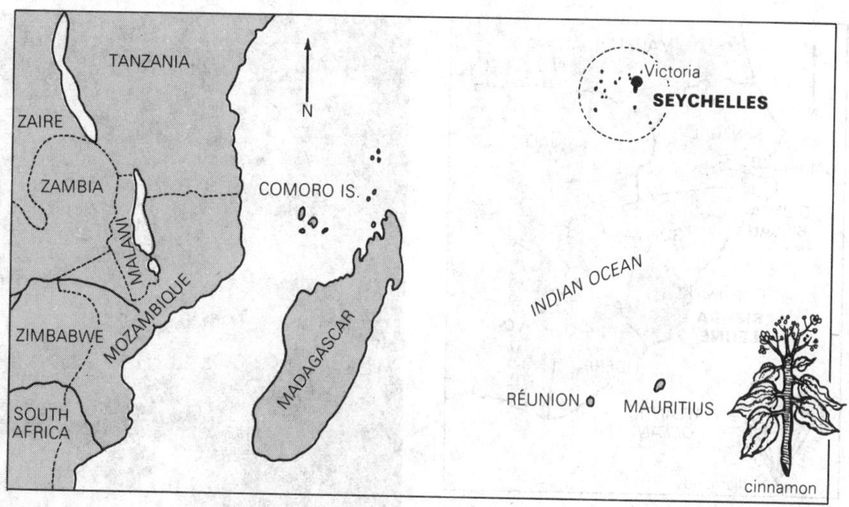

settlers and their African slaves. About one-quarter of the workers are engaged in agriculture, and over one-half work in manufacturing and industry. The country's literacy rate is 80 percent.

Economy. The islands are poor, but a rapidly developing tourism industry has created virtually full employment and has helped the economy greatly since the 1971 opening of the first commercial airport. Most of the islanders subsist by farming small plots and fishing. Projects have been undertaken to diversify agriculture and to expand fishing into a commercial activity.

Large plantations produce coconuts, palms, and spices, especially cinnamon; the country's industries process these products. Seychelles lacks natural resources and has no mining industries. Its trade is virtually nonexistent. Copra and cinnamon products are the main exports, but they are far outweighed by consumer imports.

Britain, neighboring African states, and Pakistan are the nation's chief trading partners.

Government. According to the nation's 1979 constitution, the People's Progressive Party is the only party in Seychelles, and it dominates the islands' political processes. The president rules with assistance from the unicameral, 25-member National Assembly.

The country is a member of the United Nations, the Organization of African Unity, and the Commonwealth of Nations. It is also an associated state of the European Common Market.

History. The Seychelles were uninhabited when discovered by the Portuguese in the early 1500's. They were not settled until the mid-1700's, when the French established communities on the islands and claimed them for France.

Britain received the islands in 1814 by the Treaty of Paris and administered them with the Mauritius colony until 1888, when the two were separated. In 1903 Seychelles became a Crown colony.

Seychelles became an independent nation on June 28, 1976, ending nearly 160 years of British colonial rule. It had a pro-Western foreign policy, but in a military coup in 1977 a socialist regime took control of the government.

Sierra Leone

Official name: *Republic of Sierra Leone*
Area: *27,699 sq. mi., 71,740 sq. km.*
Population: *(1990 est.) 4,168,000*
Capital: *Freetown (Pop., 1989, 470,000)*
Language: *English, African languages*
Religion: *Traditional religions, Islam, Christian*
Currency unit: *Leone*
National holiday: *Independence Day, April 27*

Sierra Leone, a republic in western Africa, is bordered on the north by Guinea, on the east by Liberia, and on the south and west by the Atlantic Ocean. Sierra Leone received its independence from Britain in 1961.

The land. Sierra Leone has a varied landscape. In the northwest a mountainous peninsula extends into the Atlantic Ocean. Inland from the peninsula and in other places along the coast there are swampy plains. Further inland there are plateaus.

There are forests and grasslands in the north and east. In the northeast are the Loma Mountains, with a peak elevation of over 6390 feet. Many rivers flow through the country, including the Rokel and the Moa.

Sierra Leone has a tropical climate, and the peninsula is one of the rainiest parts of western Africa, receiving about 145 inches of rain each year.

The people. There are some 20 tribal groups in Sierra Leone, the largest of which are the Mende and the Temne. The Mende live mainly in the south and the Temne live in the north. There are also several thousand Creoles, descendants of freed slaves who came to Sierra Leone in the 1700's and 1800's.

The Creoles live mainly in and near Freetown, the country's capital and largest city. Bo, Kenema, and Makeni are also major urban centers.

Islam is followed by 60 percent of the people, animism by 30 percent, and Christianity by 10 percent. The people are predominantly illiterate and are subsistence farmers.

Economy. The economy of Sierra Leone is based on agriculture. The basic food crops are rice and cassava. Palm kernels, cacao, kola nuts, ginger, and coffee are important commercial crops. Fishing is also an important source of income for the people along the coast.

Sierra Leone has rich mineral resources, and the country is one of the world's major producers of diamonds. It also has the world's greatest deposits of rutile (used in paint manufacture), first commercially mined here in 1979. Bauxite, along with diamonds, account for nearly three-quarters of the nation's exports; iron ore is also important. In 1985 Sierra Leone's total exports, which also included coffee, earned $111.9 million. Imports, mainly

PANNING FOR ALLUVIAL DIAMONDS *in a Sierra Leone river. Diamonds are one of the country's chief exports; they are also smuggled out. Sierra Leone was founded as a refuge for freed slaves from Britain; neighboring Liberia was a later refuge for freed U.S. slaves.*

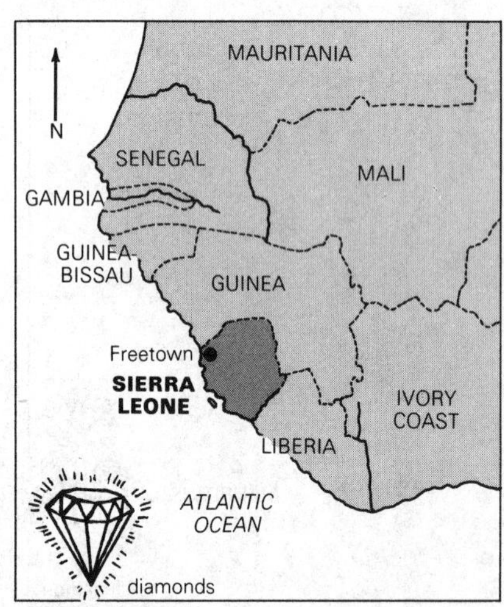

UNITED NATIONS

food, textiles, machinery, and petroleum products, cost $135.9 million. Most trade is carried on with Britain and the United States.

Government. According to its 1978 constitution, Sierra Leone is ruled by a president who is elected to a seven-year term. The legislature is a 124-member unicameral parliament. Members of parliament, the majority of whom are elected, serve five-year terms.

Sierra Leone is a member of the United Nations, the Organization of African Unity, and the Commonwealth of Nations. It is also an associated state of the European Common Market.

History. The Portuguese explorer Pedro da Cintra visited Sierra Leone in 1462 and gave the area its name, which means Lion Mountain. The course of Sierra Leone's modern history was affected by the proclamation in 1772 by Britain's Lord Chief Justice William Mansfield that slavery was never acknowledged by law; consequently, slaves held in England were set free.

In London and in other British cities freed slaves found it difficult to obtain employment, and they constituted a source of embarrassment to the British government. The government gave its support to a plan of a private company, the Society for the Abolition of Slavery, to ship the freed slaves to Africa.

In 1788 the first shipload of freed slaves settled in present-day Sierra Leone. First by purchase and later by force, they acquired land and built villages near what later became Freetown. In 1791 the Sierra Leone Company began administering the settlement. New groups of freed slaves came to Sierra Leone from Nova Scotia and Jamaica.

British rule. In 1808 the coastal area became a British Crown colony. The colony grew in wealth and importance, new settlements were made along the coast, and the settlers began to increase their trade contacts with the tribes of the interior. The settlers also took more and more tribal land. In the early 1800's the number of settlers was increased by the addition of slaves freed at sea by a British patrol stationed in Freetown.

In 1896, in a move to prevent French territorial expansion, the British government established a protectorate over the interior. The two regions—the colony and the protectorate—were administered separately until 1924. British administrative policy during the 1930's and 1940's helped to integrate the peoples of the protectorate with those of the colony. It also worked to eliminate the antagonism between the descendants of the settlers, the Creoles, and the Africans.

At first the peoples of the coast felt superior because of their higher educational level, but the growth of indigenous political movements reversed this. In 1951 Milton Margai, a Mende physician from the protectorate, led the Sierra Leone People's Party to an important electoral victory over the combined opposition of the parties loyal to two Creoles, Dr. H. C. Bankole-Bright and I. T. A. Wallace-Johnson.

Independence. When Sierra Leone became independent on April 27, 1961, Margai became the country's first prime minister.

The All People's Congress took control of the government in 1969, and by popular referendum an official one-party state was established in 1978. Political turmoil has ensued since the nation's independence, including several military coups, disputed elections in 1967, and the attempted overthrow and assassination of President Siaka Stevens in 1971. A republic was proclaimed on April 19, 1971, and Stevens was reelected in 1978.

Economic development has been slowed by political unrest, and British aid has been important to the country.

Somalia

Official name: *Somali Democratic Republic*
Area: *246,201 sq. mi., 637,657 sq. km.*
Population: *(1990 est.) 8,415,000*
Capital: *Mogadishu (Pop., 1989, 1,000,000)*
Language: *Somali*
Religion: *Islam*
Currency unit: *Shilling*
National holiday: *Foundation of the Republic Day, July 1*

The Somali Republic, an independent country in eastern Africa, is bordered on the north by Djibouti and the Gulf of Aden, on the east by the Indian Ocean, on the south by Kenya, and on the west by Ethiopia. The Somali Republic was formed in July, 1960, by a union of the former Italian Somalia Protectorate and British Somaliland.

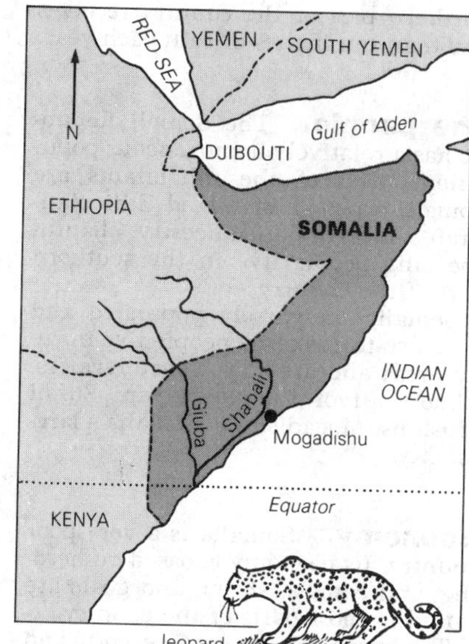

The land. Most of the Somali Republic is occupied by a featureless, high plain. In some places, especially in the north, high limestone cliffs border the plain. Near the eastern coast the plain is sandy, and gives way inland to low hills and ridges.

In the northeastern part of the country, the Somali Peninsula juts into the Indian Ocean. Near the peninsula are the Carcar Mountains, which have an average elevation of 3000 feet. The country's main rivers are the Giuba (Juba) and the Shabali (Scebeli).

Although the southwestern part of the country receives about 20 inches of rain each year, semi-arid and arid conditions prevail in most parts. The

NOMADIC WOMEN OF SOMALIA *move in search of greener pastures. Camels bear portable huts. The barren landscape is typical of Somalia.*

UPI

northern part of the country receives less than ten inches of rain each year.

The people. The Somali Republic has a relatively homogeneous population. Most of the inhabitants are Somali, a people of mixed Ethiopian, Arab, and Indian ancestry. Bantu-speaking people live in the southern part of the country.

Somalia is sparsely populated and over two-thirds of its people live in rural areas and are subsistence farmers. Almost all of the people are Sunni Muslims. Mogadishu is Somalia's largest city.

Economy. Somalia is a very poor country. Its economy is based on herding, and camels, sheep, and goats are raised in most parts of the country.

The basic food crops are corn and sorghum, and the main cash crop is bananas, which are grown mainly on irrigated plantations in the southern part of the country. Sugar cane and a variety of fruits are also grown.

Although there are small canneries and leather tanneries, industry is poorly developed. The Somali Republic has deposits of iron ore, gypsum, beryl, and columbite, but mineral deposits have not been fully exploited.

In 1985 imports cost about $470 million and exports earned about $110 million. The main imports are rice, petroleum products, textiles, and machinery. The main exports are bananas, live animals, and hides and skins. Most trade is conducted with Italy, Kenya, Saudi Arabia, and the Soviet Union.

Government. According to its 1979 constitution, Somalia is ruled by a president, who is elected to a seven-year term, and a 177-member unicameral People's Assembly. The assembly's members are elected to five-year terms.

Somalia is a member of the United Nations, the Organization of African Unity, and the Arab League. It is also an associated state of the European Common Market.

History. In about the 900's the Galla people, who were originally from Ethiopia, migrated into what is now the Somali Republic and pushed the indigenous agricultural Bantu-speaking peoples southward. Between the 1200's and 1300's the Somali peoples displaced the Galla.

Arabs and Persians made settlements on the northern coast between the 800's and 1500's, and helped make Islam the dominant religion. In the early 1800's the sultan of Zanzibar obtained control of the southern part of the country.

The protectorates. Egyptians occupied the area of the Somali Republic between 1874 and 1885. The Egyptian occupation was ended when Britian established a protectorate over the northern part of the country. Under the terms of an agreement made with the sultan of Zanzibar, Italy established the Protectorate of Somalia in the south in 1889.

Between 1900 and 1920 both the British and the Italians fought a rebellion led by a Muslim religious leader, Sayyid Muhammad Abdulla Hassan, whom they called the "Mad Mullah."

In the 1920's and 1930's the fascist government of Italy maintained firm control of the south and encouraged settlement by Italian colonists. Italy used the region as a staging base to attack Ethiopia in 1934. After World War II broke out, Britain took over the administration of the Italian protectorate in 1941.

Postwar politics centered on reuniting the Somali people. Haja Muhammad Hussein, leader of the Somali Youth League (SYL), a nationalist movement he had founded in 1943, called for unification of the Italian and British protectorates under a single UN trusteeship.

In 1949, however, the UN General Assembly voted to return southern Somalia to Italy as a trusteeship for a ten-year period so that Italy could prepare the region for independence. In 1956 elections were held and Abdullah Issa of the SYL became the first prime minister of Somalia.

In 1954 a British-Ethiopian agreement granted the Haud area of Ogaden in the western part of the country to Ethiopia, but the Somali people retained the right to graze their cattle on the land. A legislative council was created in British Somaliland in 1957, and on June 26, 1960, Britain granted Somaliland its independence.

Independence. On July 1, 1960, after the Italian trusteeship had ended, the Italian and British regions were united to form the Somali Republic.

At the time of independence Ethiopia withdrew the rights of the Somali to graze cattle in Ogaden. Both the Somali Republic and Ethiopia claimed the area, and fighting broke out in 1963. Fighting also broke out with Kenya over disputed land.

Members of all political parties united in the Somali National Congress to deal with the territorial claims of the Somali Republic to land in Ethiopia, northern Kenya, and French Somaliland (present-day Djibouti). In 1977–1978 war in Ogaden broke out against Ethiopia. Somalia, which had established close ties with the Soviet Union, ordered Soviet troops out of its country because of Soviet assistance to Ethiopia. Soviet-armed Cuban troops helped Ethiopia push Somalia out of Ogaden, but tensions persisted. In 1988 a peace agreement was reached between Somalia and Ethiopia about fighting in Ogaden.

Following the 1969 military coup, Somalia's businesses were partly nationalized. After 1975 the collectivization of farms was the result of a newly formed one-party socialist state.

Somalia has a firm anti-Western foreign policy, but its refugees from Ogaden (following the war) received extensive aid from the West, as well as from the Arab states. The massive immigration of refugees, which began in 1977, added to the problems caused by the droughts and famines of the mid-1970's, especially 1975, in overtaxing Somalia's economy.

South Africa

Official name: *Republic of South Africa*
Area: *472,359 sq. mi., 1,223,404 sq. km.*
Population: *(1990 est.) 36,696,000*
Capitals: *Cape Town—legislative (Pop., 1980, 213,830); Pretoria—administrative (Pop., 1980, 528,407); Bloemfontein—judicial (Pop., 1980, 230,688)*
Language: *English, Afrikaans, Bantu languages*
Religion: *Protestant, Roman Catholic, traditional religions*
Currency unit: *Rand*
National holiday: *Republic Day, May 31*

The Republic of South Africa, an independent country in southernmost Africa, is bordered on the north and northeast by Mozambique, Swaziland, Botswana, Zimbabwe and Angola; on the east and south by the Indian Ocean; and on the west by the Atlantic Ocean. Lesotho lies completely within the borders of South Africa.

Between 1910 and 1961 South Africa was a union of four provinces—Cape Province in the west, Orange Free State in the central part, Transvaal in the northeast, and Natal in the east. On May 13, 1961, South Africa withdrew from the British Commonwealth because its policy of apartheid, the rigid separation of the races, was unacceptable to other Commonwealth countries. On May 31, 1961, South Africa became a republic.

The land. Most of South Africa is occupied by a plateau that slopes inward from its rim. The most striking feature of the landscape is the Great Escarpment, which borders the plateau in an almost unbroken line running southward from the northeastern corner of the country, rounding the southern coast, and continuing northward on the western side of the country. The upper edge of the escarpment is over 5000 feet above sea level.

South Africa's highest point is in the east, where the Drakensberg, a mountainous region, reaches an elevation of over 11,400 feet above sea level.

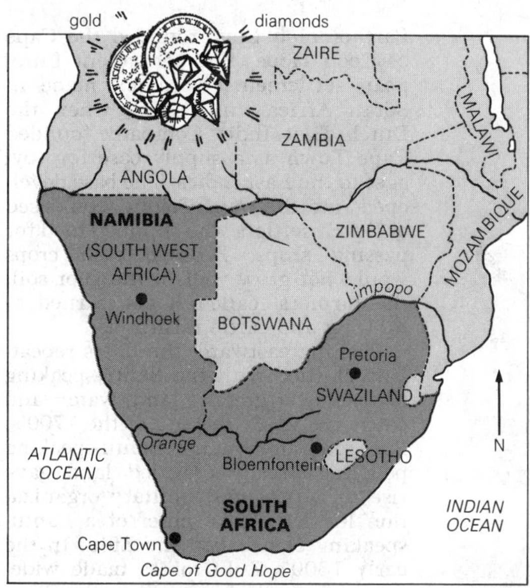

APARTHEID CONTROL IN SOUTH AFRICA. *Blacks, though 70% of the population, must carry identification cards and are otherwise penalized. Apartheid regulations are elaborate and govern most aspects of South African life.*

Between the oceans and the foot of the Great Escarpment is a coastal zone about 100 miles wide. This region consists of greatly eroded, steplike land cut by streams and valleys, especially in the wetter, eastern side of the country. In the south these steps give way to long, low mountains known as the Cape Ranges, some of which reach the sea in peninsulas.

Cape Agulhas, the southernmost point of Africa, separates the Atlantic Ocean on its west from the Indian Ocean on its east. The most famous point on the Atlantic coast is the Cape of Good Hope.

Most of the plateau is drained by the Orange River and its principal tributary, the Vaal. Both rivers flow westward from the Great Escarpment. The Augrabies Falls are at the head of a deep canyon leading to the Atlantic Ocean at the point where the Orange River leaves the surface of the plateau. The northern half of the Transvaal is drained by the Limpopo River, which forms the border with Zimbabwe.

Climate. Rainfall in South Africa is much heavier on the east coast and on some parts of the Cape Ranges than on the plateau surface. Half of the country receives less than 20 inches of rain a year, and water-supply problems are common, particularly in the west.

The climate is moderate in most parts of the country. Northern and eastern Transvaal are tropically hot, but most of South Africa has cool winters with occasional frost.

The people.

The South African population is legally divided into four distinct groups—Bantu, or Negro (black); white; Colored, those of mixed origins; and Asian. Bantus make up about 70 percent of the population; whites, 17; Coloreds, nine; and Asians, three percent.

Most of the people are Christians. Over one-quarter of the labor force is occupied by agriculture, while over ten percent is engaged in manufacturing of various kinds.

Most of the Negro Africans are Bantu-speaking peoples. Among the main tribal groups are the Xhosa, Zulu, and Sotho. About two-thirds of the Negro Africans live either on farms owned by whites or on reserves established by the government.

A majority of the whites are Afrikaners, Afrikaans-speaking people descended from Dutch, German, and French Huguenot settlers. Most of the remainder of the whites are of British descent. The Coloreds are descended largely from the indigenous Hottentots, Malays, and white settlers. The Asians are largely of Indian origin.

The major cities of South Africa include Johannesburg, in the Transvaal, a major commercial center and industrial city; Cape Town, in Cape Province, South Africa's legislative capital and major port; Durban, in Natal, the Indian Ocean outlet for the Transvaal and the center of the English-speaking and Indian business communities; Pretoria, in the Transvaal, South Africa's administrative capital and major industrial center; and Port Elizabeth, in Cape Province, an industrial city and port.

Economy.

South Africa has the most highly developed industrial economy of any African country. Economic development has been made possible largely by South Africa's rich mineral resources, especially diamonds and gold.

Black African labor plays an essential part in South Africa's growing economy. Although black Africans form the bulk of unskilled labor in industry, agriculture, and mining, they are generally barred from the skilled labor force. The whites are the most economically prosperous group in South Africa. Although Coloreds and Asians are economically better off than the black Africans, they are not as prosperous as the whites.

Agriculture. Under ten percent of the gross national product comes from agricultural production. Most farming is done on large, white-owned farms. Agriculture employs a considerable proportion of Afrikaners and most black Africans. Crop production, however, is restricted by limited rainfall and ungrateful soil in most parts of the country.

The basic food crop of the black African population is corn. Fruits, especially citrus and grapes, are the most important commercial crops. They are grown mainly in the region inland from Cape Town. Cattle and sheep are raised, and wool and hides are important exports.

Mining and manufacturing. Manufacturing developed rapidly after World War II, and now, combined with mining, it accounts for two-fifths of the gross national product. The government owns many industries, but it encourages private enterprise. Foreign investments are considerable.

Mining provides the capital and supports the markets required for economic growth. Iron, steel, cement, machinery, and a great variety of consumer goods are produced.

South Africa has rich mineral resources, and it is one of the world's largest producers of diamonds and gold. In 1986 over 10 million metric carats of diamonds were produced. South Africa is one of the world's leading producers of gold. Gold comes from mines in the Witwatersrand, in the northern part of the country, and from Odendaalsrus, in central South Africa. Waste materials at the gold

CULVER PICTURES

BANTU WARRIORS *of the kind that strongly opposed both Boer and English expansion in southern Africa. Fiercest of them all were the Zulu, who developed a powerful military machine.*

mines are reprocessed to yield uranium. South Africa also has vast resources of coal and iron ore.

Trade. Most of South Africa's trade is with Britain, the United States, West Germany, and Japan. Its unpopular apartheid policy has hindered trade with the rest of Africa, although it has joined Botswana, Lesotho, and Swaziland in a customs union.

In 1983 South Africa's imports cost only $14.4 billion and exports earned $18.2 billion. Iron and steel, copper, diamonds, fruit, and wool are important exports. Imports include machinery, petroleum, transportation equipment, and consumer items.

Government.

South Africa was ruled solely by a white minority until 1984 when Coloreds, people of mixed race, and Asians were allowed limited representation in the government.

Blacks remain unrepresented in the government because they are not considered South African citizens. Tribal groups were assigned homelands that were granted nominal independence and blacks are considered citizens of the homelands rather than of South Africa. Although the homelands have their own governments, they are still heavily influenced by the South African government and remain economically tied to South Africa. South Africa is the only country that recognizes the homelands' autonomy.

South Africa is a republic. According to the 1984 constitution, executive power is held by a president who is elected to a five-year term by an electoral college comprised of representatives from each of the three houses The president is advised by a cabinet and ministers' councils.

Legislative power is held by a tricameral parliament with different chambers for different racial groups; blacks are excluded. The House of Assembly consists of 178 members and represents whites. The House of Representatives represents the Colored population, and has 85 members. Indians are represented in the House of Delegates, which consists of 45 members. Members of the three houses serve five-year terms.

History.

Bantu-speaking peoples from northern Africa came to South Africa in the 1400's or 1500's, destroying or intermarrying with the indigenous Hottentots.

In the 1480's a Portuguese explorer, Bartholomeu Dias, rounded the Cape of Good Hope. But permanent European settlements were not made in South Africa until 1652, when the Dutch East India Company founded Cape Town as a supply base for voyages to the East Indies. The base developed into the Cape Colony, composed of Dutch settlers who supplied food for passing ships. Because cash crops would not grow well in the poor soil, the farmers, called Boers, turned to hunting and cattle raising.

Pushing eastward, the Boers repeatedly clashed with the Bantu-speaking peoples over grazing land, water, and cattle thefts. By the end of the 1700's, Boer pressure on the Bantu-speaking peoples' already crowded land gave rise to a powerful military organization led by Chaka, chief of a Bantu-speaking clan called the Zulu. In the early 1800's Zulu forces made widespread destructive attacks on the Europeans and on other African peoples in southern Africa.

British-Boer conflict. The British seized control of the colony in 1795. They stimulated the economy and extended the government to the frontier. Britain abolished slavery in 1834, and in 1836 it returned to the Bantu-speaking peoples territory captured from them by the Boers.

The Boers, irritated by the liberal racial policies and the new legal institutions of the British, undertook a mass migration to the east known as the Great Trek. During the migration, the Boers destroyed the Zulu forces.

To deny the Boers access to the sea, the British annexed the seaport city of Natal in 1844. The Boers then journeyed to the north and founded the republics of the Transvaal and the Orange Free State, which Britain recognized as independent states in the 1850's.

The discovery of diamonds in 1867 and gold in 1886 in the two republics attracted many English-speaking immigrants. British and Afrikaner businessmen cooperated in Cape Colony, but the discovery of gold only strained

THE SIEGE OF KIMBERLEY *by Boers near the beginning of the Boer War. English civilians were forced to take shelter in dugouts. The siege was lifted in February of 1900.*

CULVER PICTURES

relations between Britain and the Transvaal. The Transvaal refused to enter into any political or economic union with Britain's colonies.

In 1895 the Cape Colony's prime minister, Cecil Rhodes, supported the Jameson Raid, an attempt to overthrow the Transvaal's president, Paul Kruger, and install an English-speaking government. The raid turned the political conflict into an ethnic conflict between Afrikaners and Englishmen. In 1899 the dispute erupted into the Boer—or South African—War, which the British won.

By 1902 Britain had conquered the Afrikaner republics, but granted them self-government in 1906. On May 31, 1910, the British colonies of Cape Colony and Natal were united with the former republics to form an independent Union of South Africa. At that time reserves of land were marked off for occupation by the Bantu-speaking peoples.

The union. During World War I South Africa fought with Britain against Germany. Led by two Afrikaners, Jan Christiaan Smuts and Louis Botha, South African forces captured the German colony of South-West Africa. In 1919 Smuts became South Africa's first prime minister.

After World War I a steady price for gold and cheap labor encouraged the country to industrialize. Taxes, drought, and overcrowding on government-created reserves had driven many young black Africans off the land in search of jobs. Racial segregation was extended into industry and labor agitation became a punishable crime.

In the 1920's the National Party, formed by conservative Afrikaners, came to power. The party extended racial segregation beyond the industrial color bar. Apartheid legislation came to include residential segregation, prohibitions against individual ownership of land by black Africans, restriction of movement, segregated churches, separate and unequal educational facilities, and denial of the vote to black Africans.

In 1952 the African National Congress, an African association formed in 1912 to protest racial discrimination, organized boycotts and demonstrations to protest the racial laws. The government retaliated by jailing some 10,000 participants and by enacting a severe law declaring government critics "subversive."

In 1960 South African police fired into a crowd of nonwhites demonstrating against racial policies in Sharpeville, some 30 miles south of Johannesburg. World opinion rallied against South Africa, but the government turned a deaf ear. In 1961 Albert Luthuli, a Zulu chief, received the Nobel Peace Prize for advocating peaceful methods for resolving South Africa's racial problems.

The republic. On May 31, 1961, South Africa withdrew from the British Commonwealth and became a republic. In 1962 South Africa withdrew its delegation to the United Nations when the General Assembly voted economic sanctions against it because of its racial policies. But heavy British and U.S. investments in South Africa blocked the effective application of sanctions.

In 1963 South Africa created the Transkei, an all-African Bantustan, or homeland, with a government separate from, but not independent of, the republic. In 1976 it was declared an independent homeland, as was Bophuthatswana in 1977, Venda in 1979, and Ciskei in 1981.

South Africa's determined and strictly enforced policies of apartheid have led to great racial strife, often culminating in violence. In 1976, during racial rioting, about 600 people, mostly Bantus, were killed. Black discontent has continued with recent rises in unemployment. The United States and other Western nations have joined African nations in a call for black majority rule. South Africa has virtually no foreign relations with black Africa, Asia, or communist nations.

Namibia (South-West Africa), at the strong urging of the United Nations, was scheduled to gain independence from South Africa in 1978. When South Africa backed out of the deal at the last moment, guerrilla warfare began and in 1980 the United Nations sent troops into a newly created demilitarized zone as a cease-fire was effected. In 1989 a constituent assembly in Namibia approved a draft constitution allowing for a democratic form of government with an executive president, elections for the members of parliament, and an independent judiciary. A declaration of fundamental rights called for freedom of movement, speech, and the press. Namibia's complete independence is expected in 1990.

South Yemen

Official name: *People's Democratic Republic of Yemen*
Area: *111,075 sq. mi., 287,683 km.*
Population: *(1990 est.) 2,585,000*
Capital: *Aden (Pop., 1989, 250,000)*
Language: *Arabic*
Religion: *Islam*
Currency unit: *Dinar*

The People's Democratic Republic of Yemen is an Arab state in the southwestern Arabian Peninsula. It was created in 1967 from the former British colony of Aden and the protectorates of South Arabia, a group of 20 sheikdoms and sultanates, most of which had been united in the British-protected Federation of South Arabia between 1959 and 1967.

The People's Democratic Republic

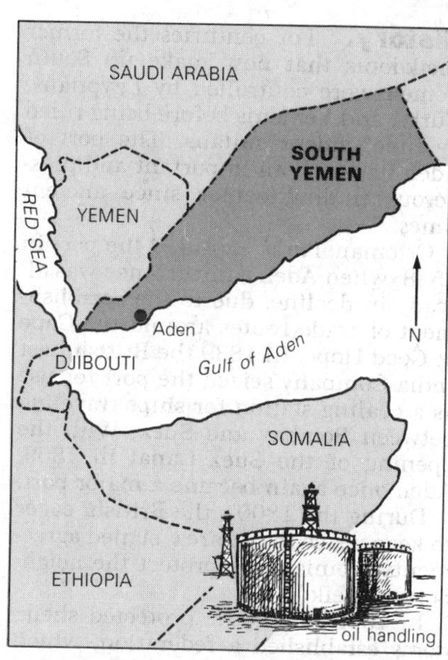

of Yemen is bordered on the north and west by Yemen and the Rub al Khali desert of Saudi Arabia; on the east by the sultanate of Oman; and on the south by the Gulf of Aden and the Indian Ocean. Socotra, an island in the Indian Ocean, is part of Yemen, as are the islands of Perim and Kamaran.

The land and people. Rugged mountains rise in west South Yemen, but most of the region is a high rolling desert plateau on which almost no rain falls.

The country's population, composed almost entirely of Sunni Muslim Arabs, is concentrated along the coast, especially in Aden, the largest city.

Economy. Herding and farming are the principal occupations of the Yemeni people. Cotton, grains, and fruits are raised, and sheep and goats are grazed on the fringes of the desert. There is some fishing along the coast. Soap and cigarette manufacturing, oilseed production, and salt refining are important.

The port city of Aden is the principal commercial center for the lower Arabian Peninsula. It has a large oil refinery and oil storage facilities, and is a major Arabian port for oil exporting and ship refueling. Income from this transit trade is vital to the economy of South Yemen. Trade in South Yemen's own goods is small.

Government. According to its 1970 constitution, South Yemen is ruled by the chairman of the Supreme People's Council, the unicameral legislature. The council is comprised of 111 elected members. A prime minister assists the chairman.

South Yemen is a member of the United Nations and the Arab League.

History. For centuries the former sheikdoms that now make up South Yemen were controlled by Egyptians, Turks, and Yemenis before being ruled by independent sultans. The port of Aden has been an important and prosperous trading center since ancient times.

Ottoman Turks captured the port in 1538, when Aden's importance was already in decline, due to the establishment of trade routes around the Cape of Good Hope. In 1839 the British East India Company seized the port for use as a coaling station for ships traveling between Bombay and Suez. With the opening of the Suez Canal in 1869, Aden once again became a major port.

During the 1800's the British, eager to keep peace in the area, signed agreements promising to protect the neighboring sheikdoms.

In 1959 six of the protected sheikdoms established a federation, which by 1965 included 16 sheikdoms and Aden. Yemen's independence was in part achieved by the efforts of Arab nationalist groups that were active in the area, particularly, the National Liberation Front (NLF). Independence was granted in 1967.

The left-wing NLF seized control of the government in 1969 and proclaimed a socialist republic in 1970. Massive nationalization and repressive rule ensued. Relations were broken with the United States, while the Soviet Union became a close ally.

As the two Yemens prepared to merge in 1978, bloody coups took place in both countries and the Yemens remained separate. The United States and Saudi Arabia aided Yemen's successful defeat of a 1979 South Yemen invasion. A cease-fire was established as the Yemens continue to explore the possibility of unification.

Sudan

Official name: *Democratic Republic of Sudan*
Area: *967,499 sq. mi., 2,505,813 sq. km.*
Population: *(1990 est.) 25,037,000*
Capital: *Khartoum (Pop., 1983, 476,218)*
Language: *Arabic, African languages*
Religion: *Islam, Christian, traditional religions*
Currency unit: *Pound*
National holiday: *Independence Day, Jan. 1*

Sudan, a republic in northern Africa, is bordered on the north by Egypt; on the east by the Red Sea and Ethiopia; on the south by Kenya, Uganda, and Zaire; and on the west by the Central African Republic, Chad, and Libya. From 1899 to 1953 Sudan was ruled jointly by Britain and Egypt as a condominium. From 1954 to 1956, Sudan was self-governing, and on January 1, 1956, it became independent.

The land. Sudan, the largest country in extent in Africa, has a varied landscape. Most of northern Sudan is occupied by the desert region of the Sahara. The Nile River flows north through central Sudan, creating a fertile region. The river's two main branches, the Blue Nile and the White Nile, meet at Khartoum, and then the great, single river flows northward into Egypt.

In west-central Sudan the Marra Mountains reach elevations well above 10,000 feet. East of the Marra Mountains is the Kordofan Plateau. In central Sudan the Nuba Mountains reach elevations of over 4300 feet. South of Khartoum, in the east-central Sudan, there are tropical savanna lands.

In the south there are tropical rain forests, and in the extreme southern part of the country the White Nile overflows to create a swampy region called the *Sudd*. The Atbara River, a tributary of the Nile, flows through eastern Sudan.

Rainfall averages only about four inches a year in east-central Sudan, and the Red Sea coast is arid and hot. It is relatively rainy in the western mountain region, and the south has a hot and humid tropical climate.

The people. There are two distinct groups of people in Sudan: Muslims in the northern provinces of Kassala, Khartoum, Blue Nile, Kordofan, Darfur, and Northern; and Negro (black) tribes in the southern provinces of Upper Nile, Bahr el Ghazal, and Equatoria.

Most of the Muslims, who make up the majority of Sudan's population, are Arabic-speaking. They are divided into great tribal groups including the Jaaliin, Shaiqiyya, and Kababish. The more important non-Arabic speaking peoples in northern Sudan are the Beja, who live near the Red Sea; the Nubians, living along the Nile from Dongola to the Egyptian border; the Negroid Nuba, in southern Kordofan; and the Negroid Fur in Darfur.

Most of the southern tribes are pagan or Christian. They make up about one third of the population. The major tribes include the Dinka, Shilluk, Nuer, and Azande.

Economy. The economy of Sudan is based on agriculture. The main food crops are millet, sesame seeds, peanuts, castor beans, and dates. The major cash crop, grown primarily in the Gezira flat between the Blue and White Nile, is cotton. Sudan is, for the most part, self-sufficient in food and almost 80 percent of its workers are farmers.

Gum arabic is produced for export, and camels and sheep are raised in many parts of the country.

Sudan's industry is concerned primarily with processing agricultural products. Although Sudan extracts iron ore, chromite, and other minerals, its mining is underdeveloped. Transportation and irrigation systems have been improving in recent years.

Between 1983 and 1984 imports cost $1.388 billion and exports earned $732 million. The major imports are petroleum products, textiles, machinery, and foodstuffs. The major exports are cotton, sesame seed, and gum arabic. Most trade is conducted with Britain, West Germany, and Italy.

Government. According to its 1973 constitution, Sudan is governed

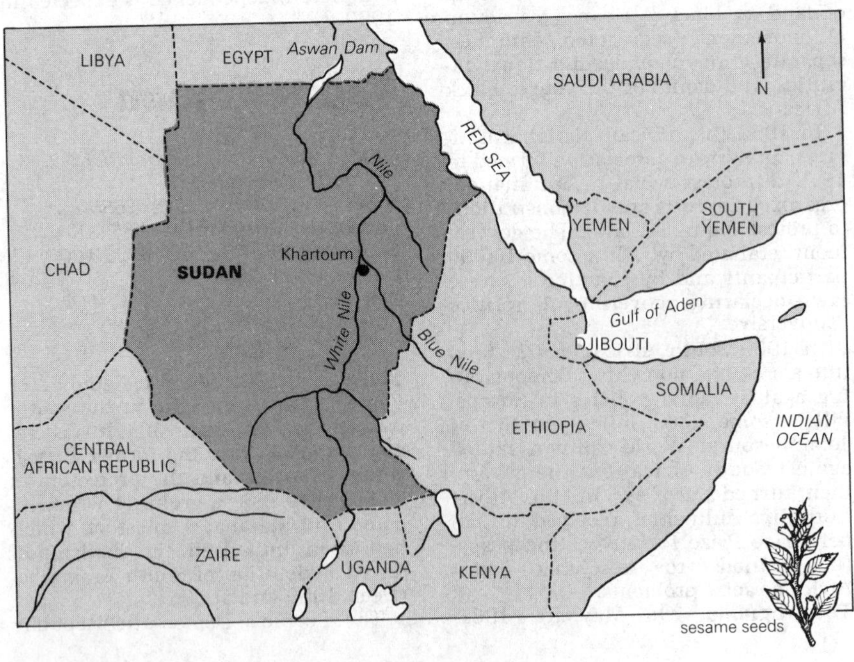

by a powerful president and a unicameral, 301-member National Assembly. Most of the legislators are elected.

Sudan is a member of the United Nations, the Organization of Arab Unity, and the Arab League. It is also an associated state of the European Common Market.

History. Sudan's history has always been closely linked with that of Egypt. In about 3000 B.C. the pharaohs of ancient Egypt sent expeditions into Sudan to raid for slaves, and by about 2000 B.C. Egypt had extended its rule into Sudan. The region of present-day Sudan came to be called Kush. The power of Egypt began to decline after about 2000 B.C.

A Nubian leader from Napata, in north-central Sudan, proclaimed himself king of Kush in 750 B.C. He gained control of Egypt and established a Sudanese dynasty that lasted until 661 B.C., when the Assyrians conquered Egypt. After that time, Egyptian civilization in Sudan declined.

The kingdom of Kush reestablished itself as an independent state and survived until about 350 A.D., at which time it was destroyed by the kingdom of Axum, in northern Ethiopia. After that, black peoples from the south began to migrate into northern Sudan. Beginning in the 500's the peoples of Northern Sudan became Christians, and two Christian dynasties, Maqurra and Alwa, were established.

In the late 1200's the Mamluks, a Muslim dynasty in Egypt, destroyed Maqurra. Arabs began migrating into northern Sudan, and many of the people were converted to Islam. Alwa survived until the early 1500's, at which time a black tribe called the Funj established the powerful Muslim state of Sennar. Until its decline some 300 years later, the Funj dynasty provided Sudan with unity and security.

Egyptian conquest of Sudan began in 1820, and Sennar was overrun by Egyptian armies. At the junction of the White and Blue Niles, Egypt created a military and administrative center, Khartoum, which became the capital of Egyptian Sudan. Egyptian rule lasted until 1885. In that year a Sudanese, Muhammad Ahmad al-Mahdi, captured Khartoum after a four-year religious and political struggle against Egyptian rule.

Condominium. Sudan remained under the firm control of Muhammad Ahmad's successor until an Anglo-Egyptian military force conquered Sudan in 1896–1898. Sudan became a condominium ruled jointly by Britain and Egypt in 1899, but in fact Britain controlled Sudan. The period of British rule was considered by many a model of the best colonial administration, achieving security and economic development.

Although nationalist movements emerged in the 1920's, they became important only during World War II. The local nationalist movement was strongly marked by rivalry between two major Muslim religious brotherhoods, the Khatmiya and the Ansar. The Khatmiya, led by Sayyid Ali al-Mirghani, favored union with Egypt. The Ansar, led by Sayyid Abd al-Rahman al-Mahdi, a son of Muhammad Ahmad al-Mahdi, took a more pro-British stand and favored complete independence.

In 1953 Egypt and Britain signed an agreement granting Sudan self-government, and soon all sides were able to agree on complete independence for Sudan. A parliament was established in January, 1954, and the National Unionist Party, which represented a more secular policy than the brotherhoods, formed the first cabinet. On January 1, 1956, Sudan became an independent republic.

Independence. The Umma Party, mainly the Ansar, and the People's Democratic Party, largely the Khatmiya, formed a coalition, and in July, 1956, the National Unionist Party was forced from power. Political instability ensued and, following a 1969 military coup, General Gaafar al-Nimeiry took control of the newly formed socialist state. Several attempted coups were designed to depose Nimeiry, but by 1972 he had outlawed the Communist Party and established the Sudanese Socialist Union Party as the only party in Sudan.

In spite of some student unrest, considerable stability was achieved. The southern provinces had gone into rebellion against the north in 1963 and were granted regional autonomy in 1975.

Nimeiry has led Sudan out of favor with the Soviet Union, a strong ally before the 1972 purges of the Communist Party. Sudan has since then become more friendly with the West.

In 1985, Nimeiry was overthrown in a military coup led by his defense minister Abdel Rahman el-Dahab.

Swaziland

Official name: *Kingdom of Swaziland*
Area: *6,704 sq. mi., 17,363 sq. km.*
Population: *(1990 est.) 779,000*
Capital: *Mbabane (Pop., 1989, 40,000)*
Language: *Siswati (Swazi), English*
Religion: *Traditional religions, Christian*
Currency unit: *Lilangeni*
National holiday: *Independence Day, Sept. 6*

Swaziland, a country in southeastern Africa, is bordered on the north, south, and west by the Republic of South Africa, and on the east by Mozambique. Britain granted Swaziland internal self-government in 1967 and full independence in 1968.

The land. Swaziland possesses three well defined veld, or grassland, regions—the highveld, middleveld, and lowveld. The highveld, in western Swaziland, is mountainous and has an average elevation of 3500 feet. To the east is the middleveld, with an average elevation of 2000 feet. The lowveld, in eastern Swaziland, has average elevations of 1000 feet. The Lebombo, a plateau region, is in the extreme eastern part of the country.

The Great Escarpment, a geological feature of southern Africa that rises some 6000 feet above the plain and rims the great South African plateau, runs through Swaziland.

The highveld is humid and receives between 40 and 90 inches of rain each year. The climate in the middleveld and Lebombo plateau is subtropical and drier, receiving between 30 and 45 inches of rain each year. The lowveld receives between 20 and 30 inches of rain each year. As a whole, Swaziland is a very wet country.

The people. Most of the people of Swaziland belong to the Bantu-speaking Swazi tribe. The Swazi have traditionally been a pastoral people. There is also a small number of Bantu-speaking people of the Zulu group in southern Swaziland.

About 2.5 percent of the people are of European origin, mainly Afrikaans-speaking in southern Swaziland and English or Afrikaans-speaking in the north. There is a small community of people of mixed European and African descent that controls a great deal of the economy.

Nearly two-thirds of the people are Christians, and most of the labor force is occupied in agriculture.

There are only two large cities in Swaziland—Mbabane, the capital, and Manzini, formerly known as Bremersdorp, the country's commercial center and a lively market town for the nation's varied economy.

Economy. Nearly 30 percent of Swaziland's gross national product is contributed by agriculture, and nearly 40 percent by mining and industry combined. The economy is more diversified than most others in Africa,

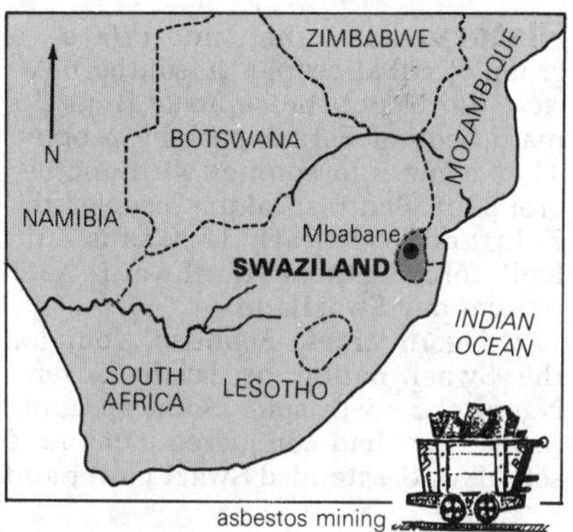

asbestos mining

owing largely to the country's fertile soil, rich forests, abundant water supply, and gambling casino at the Royal Swazi Hotel, which contributes extensive government revenues.

In recent years the Swazi have become successful farmers. The basic food crops are corn and sorghum. The chief cash crops are cotton and tobacco. Sugar cane, citrus, rice, and other fruits and vegetables are grown in irrigated areas.

Cattle are raised in most parts of the country. The Swazi have traditionally valued cattle as a symbol of social status; only in recent years have cattle acquired economic importance. Forestry, mainly in the highveld, is of growing importance to the economy.

Swaziland's mineral resources include large deposits of iron ore and asbestos. There are also deposits of coal, gold, tin, barytes, and pyrophyllite. Iron ore mined at Ngwenya, in western Swaziland is carried by rail to the port of Lourenço Marques, in Mozambique, for export. There is little manufacturing apart from the processing of minerals and agricultural products.

Swaziland's main imports are textiles, machinery, and petroleum products. The leading exports are iron ore, asbestos, and sugar. Most trade is conducted with South Africa, Britain, and Japan.

Swaziland has close economic ties with South Africa, and many Swazis find work in South Africa. Customs duties for Swaziland are collected by South Africa, and Swaziland receives a fixed percentage of South Africa's customs revenue each year. Swaziland also uses South African currency.

Government. Swaziland has a parliamentary system of government. The constitution of 1978 provides for a bicameral Parliament (Liblandla) led by a prime minister. The king chooses ten of the 20 Senate members and ten of the 50 House of Assembly members. Parliament functions chiefly as the king's advisory council.

Swaziland is a member of the United Nations, the Organization of African Unity, the Commonwealth of Nations, and is an associated state of the European Common Market.

History. In the mid-1700's a group of tribal peoples in southern Africa, the Ngoni, broke away from the main body of Bantu-speaking peoples. They came into conflict with another group of Bantu-speaking people, the Zulu, and by the early 1800's the Zulu had forced them northward into present-day Swaziland.

A Ngoni chief, Sobhuza, founded the Swazi nation by fusing several Ngoni clans wth some Sotho-speaking people they had conquered. Sobhuza's son Mswati extended Swazi power and prestige among neighboring peoples.

European influence. Europeans began to settle in the area in the 1800's, and the Swazi ruler granted them many land concessions. Both the British colony of Natal, in present-day South Africa, and the Afrikaner, or Boer, Republic of the Transvaal, also in present-day South Africa, claimed Swaziland. In 1890 a compromise was reached, and a provisional government was established composed of representatives of the Swazi, the British, and the Transvaal Afrikaners.

To appease the Afrikaners, the British ceded administration of Swaziland to the Transvaal in 1894, despite Swazi protests. In the Boer, or South African, War (1899–1902) the British conquered the Transvaal and assumed control of Swaziland. In 1907 the British High Commissioner for South Africa took over the administration.

The rise of nationalism in the 1940's and 1950's threatened the Swazi aristocracy and the white community, both of whom feared the loss of power and privilege. In 1960 these groups requested Britain to grant a constitution that would preserve the status quo. A British-sponsored constitution promulgated in 1964 was not satisfactory.

Independence. Traditionalist forces, led by the Swazi chief Sobhuza II, formed the Imbokodvo Party, which won a majority of seats in the legislative council in Swaziland's first elections in 1964. In April, 1967, Britain granted Swaziland self-government; independence was gained on September 6, 1968.

In 1973 King Sobhuza II repealed the constitution; he replaced it in 1978, making the king the chief of state. Sobhuza II died in 1982 and was replaced by two different queen regents until Mswati III became King in 1986.

Syria

Official name: *Syrian Arab Republic*
Area: *71,498 sq. mi., 185,180 sq. km.*
Population: *(1990 est.) 12,471,000*
Capital: *Damascus (Pop., 1988 est., 2,800,000)*
Language: *Arabic*
Religion: *Islam*
Currency unit: *Pound*
National holiday: *Independence Day, April 17*

The Syrian Arab Republic, a Middle Eastern state, is bounded by Turkey on the north, Iraq on the east, Jordan on the south, and Lebanon, Israel, and the Mediterranean Sea on the west. The present country of Syria was created after World War I out of a larger, historical region that included present-day Jordan, Lebanon, and Israel.

The land. A narrow, fertile plain follows Syria's Mediterranean coast.

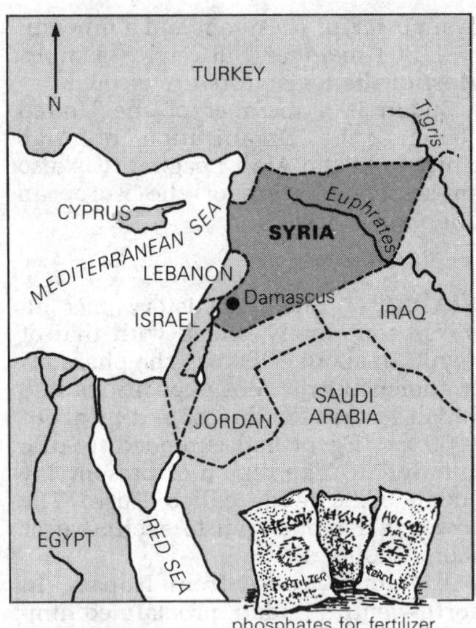

phosphates for fertilizer

To its east the rugged Alawite and Anti-Lebanon mountains rise to over 9000 feet on the northwestern border.

The Orontes River waters a fertile valley east of the mountains, and in northern and northeastern Syria are the rolling plains and rich valley of the Euphrates River. In central Syria, arid, rolling hills give way to the barren Syrian desert, which occupies the southeastern corner of the country.

Syria's coastal climate is mild and rather moist, with about 30 inches of rain each year along the coast. Central and eastern Syria are quite dry, with the extremely hot summers and cold winters of the desert.

The people. Most Syrians are Muslim Arabs, but the population also includes Kurds, Druze, and Armenians. Population is densest in the temperate, fertile western part of the country. Damascus, the capital and largest city, lies in the southwest near the Lebanese border.

Almost three-quarters of the people are Sunni Muslims, about 15 percent are other types of Muslims, and 13 percent are Christians. Half the population lives in urban areas, and one-third of the labor force is agricultural.

Economy. About one-quarter of Syria's gross national product is derived from industry; one-fifth is from commerce, and slightly less is from agriculture. The country's main natural resource is oil, 12 million metric tons of which was produced in 1987. Oil accounts for four-fifths of Syria's exports.

Agriculture. About one-third of the country's land is cultivated, and one-third is suitable for pasturage. Most farmland is in the west and north, and much of it requires irrigation. A land redistribution program in the 1950's and 1960's created many small farms from large estates.

The leading farm crops are cotton, wheat, and barley. Corn and other grains, dates, olives, sugar beets, and tobacco are also raised, and wool and silk are important commodities. Large herds of goats and sheep are grazed on the central plains.

Industry. Textiles account for two-fifths of Syria's manufacturing output, and food processing is the most important industry. Leather products, dried fruits, and wines are the leading manufactures. Gypsum and asphalt are processed. Many industrial, commercial, and financial enterprises were nationalized in the 1960's.

Trade. International trade is important in the Syrian economy, and the country's chief port, Latakia, is a major Middle Eastern commercial center. Syria collects fees and taxes on oil from Iraq carried to the Mediterranean by pipeline across Syria. In 1984 exports earned $1.3 billion while imports cost $3 billion. Oil, cotton, tobacco and grains are the chief exports, and machinery, industrial raw materials, clothing, foodstuffs, and other consumer items are imported.

Most trading activity is controlled by the government. Lebanon, France, the Soviet Union, the United States, and West Germany are Syria's leading trading partners.

Government.

According to a 1973 constitution, Syria is ruled by a president who is elected to a seven-year term. The prime minister is head of the Council of Ministers, which shares executive power with the president. The legislature is the unicameral People's Council, whose 195 members are elected.

History.

The modern nation of Syria has its roots in the ancient region of Syria, which was the site of some of the earliest civilizations. Syria was the center of the trade routes used by the great nations of the ancient world.

Located between the Tigris-Euphrates Valley and the Nile Valley, it was often the object of rivalry between the powerful nations that grew up in both valleys. Trade and war between the civilizations to the north and south of Syria brought many different peoples and cultures to the area.

Between 2000 B.C. and 333 B.C., the Akkadians, the Sumerians, the Amorites, the Hittites, the Egyptians, the Assyrians, and the Persians successively occupied parts of the Syrian region. During that time three groups, the Hebrews, the Aramaeans, and the Canaanites, made permanent settlements in the land.

In 333 B.C. Alexander the Great conquered Syria from the Persian Empire. After his death, Syria went to one of his generals, Seleucus, who founded the Seleucid dynasty that ruled Syria (including modern Israel, Lebanon, and Jordan) until the Romans conquered the region in 64 B.C.

Syria was one of the first Roman provinces to have had Christianity, in the first century A.D., and Syria's language, Aramaic, was the language of most early Christians, many of whom lived within what was then western Syria.

In the 630's Muslim Arab armies conquered the region. Islam replaced Christianity, Arabic replaced Aramaic, and Syria became an Arab country. The city of Damascus became the center of a great Arab empire and Syria's prosperity increased.

As the Arab empire weakened, however, Syria entered a decline. Ruled by outsiders, it suffered neglect. The Christian Crusades against the Muslim Middle East in the 1000's, 1100's, and 1200's did great damage to Syria and its economy, and the invasions of Mongols and Tatars from the north and east in the 1200's and 1300's left Syria weak and impoverished.

Ottoman rule. In 1516 the Ottoman Turks conquered Syria and made it part of their empire. Under the Ottoman Turks Syria remained peaceful, but neglect and poor government caused the economy and cultural life to decline further, especially in the 1700's, when the disintegration of the empire brought anarchy to Syria.

The opening of the Suez Canal in 1869 also hurt the country by taking away much of the trade between the Mediterranean and the Indian Ocean that had previously passed overland through Syria. Some economic improvements were made in the later 1800's, but the country remained largely undeveloped.

Nationalism. In the late 1800's Syria began to feel the impact of the spirit of nationalism that had been growing in Europe. Syria became a center for an Arab cultural revival and for Arab nationalism, and Syrians demanded self-government.

When the Ottoman Empire entered World War I on the side of Germany, Syria cooperated with the Allies. In return, Britain supported Syrian Arab nationalism and aided a successful 1916 Arab uprising against the Ottoman government.

At the end of the war in 1918 French troops tried to occupy the country, but Faisal ibn-Husayn, a leader of the nationalist rebellion, proclaimed Syria's sovereignty. A Syrian National Congress was called, and in 1920 Faisal was proclaimed king. France, which had received a League of Nations mandate over Syria, deposed Faisal later in 1920 and set up its own government.

Syrian discontent with French rule led in 1925 to a two-year rebellion, which the French put down harshly. Discontent grew. In 1930 the French proposed a constitution that would have made the country a republic but would not have granted complete independence. The Syrians rejected it.

Independence. In 1941, during World War II, the Vichy French government of Syria was driven out by British and Free French forces. Syria was formally declared an independent republic, although British and French troops did not withdraw until after the war, in 1946.

In 1943 Shukri al-Kuwatly was elected the first president of the republic, and in 1945 Syria entered the United Nations and joined other Arab states in forming the Arab League.

Turmoil marked the first two decades of the republic, and the military became the dominant factor in political life. In 1949 an army officer, Husni al-Zaim, ousted the civilian government. More coups followed, and from 1949 to 1954 the government was dominated by Colonel Adib Shishakly, who ruled behind the official presidency of Hashim al-Atasi. In 1954 Shishakly was forced into exile, and the next year al-Kuwatly again became president.

In 1958 Syria merged with Egypt to create the United Arab Republic (U.A.R.), with Egypt's Gamal Abdel

DAMASCUS, CAPITAL OF SYRIA, *is an ancient oasis city, here set against the mountains with the Syrian desert on the east. It is also a modern commercial and industrial center.*

ANDANSON/SYGMA

Nasser as president. In 1961 the Cairo government imposed an unpopular socialist program on the Syrian part of the U.A.R., and Syria withdrew from the union.

Contemporary Syria. Political instability increased. In March, 1963, a military coup overthrew the government and a new cabinet was appointed. The new cabinet was dominated by Baathists, members of the pan-Arab Baath Party, advocating a socialist and pan-Arab program.

Following a 1970 military coup, a socialist state was established under the strong and stabilizing presidency of Hafez al-Assad. The socialist Baath Party became the only legal party in Syria. As a leader of pro-PLO (Palestine Liberation Organization) and pan-Arabian politics, Syria has received massive Soviet military and economic aid. The Soviets, however, were somewhat alienated by Syria's intervention in 1976 in Lebanon's civil war involving Palestinian guerrillas, and by Syria's ousting of its national Communist Party.

Syria's Golan Heights on its border have been occupied by Israel since the 1967 Arab-Israeli war, and Syria has been a leader of the Arab opposition to the 1979 Egyptian-Israeli peace treaty. Serious internal dissension has been created since the late 1970's by increasing violence between the privileged ruling Alawite sect, to which Assad belongs, and the Sunni Muslims. Moreover, Syrian-Iraqi relations have seriously deteriorated. In 1982, Syrian and Israeli forces clashed during the Israeli invasion of Lebanon.

Tanzania

Official name: *United Republic of Tanzania*
Area: *364,900 sq. mi., 945,100 sq. km.*
Population: *(1990 est.) 25,994,000*
Capital: *Dodoma (Pop., 1989, 160,000)*
Language: *Kiswahili, English*
Religion: *Traditional religions, Islam, Christian*
Currency unit: *Shilling*
National holiday: *Union Day, April 26*

Tanzania, a republic in eastern Africa, was formed in 1964 by the merger of the mainland nation of Tanganyika and the offshore island nation of Zanzibar. Britain had granted independence to Tanganyika in 1961 and to Zanzibar in 1963.

Mainland Tanzania is bordered on the north by Uganda and Kenya; on the east by the Indian Ocean; on the south by Mozambique, Malawi, and Zambia; and on the west by Zaire, Burundi, Rwanda, and Lake Tanganyika. The Indian Ocean islands of Zanzibar and Pemba, the former republic of Zanzibar, lie some 20 miles east of the mainland.

The land. Tanganyika is by far the larger part of the republic, with an area of some 361,800 square miles. Zanzibar, which includes Zanzibar and Pemba islands, has an area of 1020 square miles.

Tanganyika is occupied mainly by a high, semi-arid plateau, with mountain masses in the northeast and southwest. Mt. Kilimanjaro, the highest point, is near the Kenya border, and Lake Victoria is part of the northern lowland. The coastal plain is humid and the Rufiji River flows through central Tanganyika.

Zanzibar and Pemba are low-lying coral islands with many inlets. There are mangrove swamps on the islands. The islands' temperatures are high from December to March and lower between June and October. Heavy rains fall in April and May, and there are light rains in November and December.

The people. Over 96 percent of Tanzania's population lives on the mainland, and the country's largest city, Dar es Salaam, is in Tanganyika. Christianity, Islam, and animism each account for about one-third of the nation's religious following. About 90 percent of the labor force is occupied by subsistence farming.

Tanganyika's people include members of some 120 tribes, most of which are Bantu-speaking. The largest tribe is the Sukuma. There are also groups of Arabs, Europeans, and people of Indian and Pakistani origin.

Zanzibar and Pemba also have many different peoples, including Shirazis, descendants of ancient Persians, Africans from the mainland, Arabs, Asians, and people from the Comoro Islands.

Economy. The economy of Tanzania is based on agriculture. The basic food crops are rice, corn, and sorghum.

In Tanganyika, cotton, coffee, and sisal, a fiber used in rope, are the most important commercial crops.

Sisal and coffee are generally grown on mountain slopes, and cotton is produced mainly in the lowlands near Lake Victoria. Most of the plantations are owned by Europeans, but Africans also grow coffee on small plots. Cattle are currently raised in most parts of the mainland.

Large quantities of cloves are grown on plantations in Zanzibar and Pemba. Coconuts are also an important commercial crop. Fishing is significant in the islands' economy.

Industry in Tanzania consists mainly of food processing. Mineral resources are considerable on the mainland, but they are widely distributed and transportation costs are high. Diamonds are mined, and there are also deposits of lead, gold, and iron ore.

Agriculture, which accounts for over half of the gross national product, is largely collectivized. Industry, which contributes less than ten percent of the gross national product, has become increasingly nationalized since 1967.

In 1983 imports cost $799 million while exports earned $359 million. The major imports are petroleum products, textiles, and machinery. The major exports are sisal, coffee, cotton, and cloves. Most trade is with Britain and other West European nations.

Government. Tanzania has been ruled since 1977 by its Revolutionary Party. The president is elected to a five-year term. The president is assisted by

SLAVE MARKET *on Zanzibar island in the 19th century. The Arabs were great slave traders, even before the Western nations. Arab slave trading was hard to wipe out.*

NEW YORK PUBLIC LIBRARY

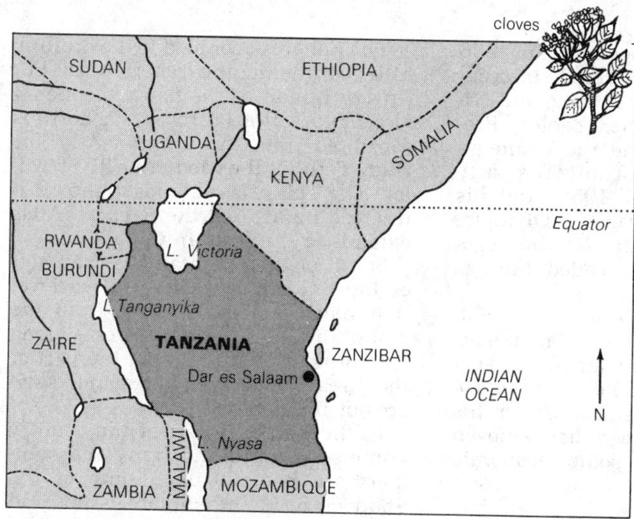

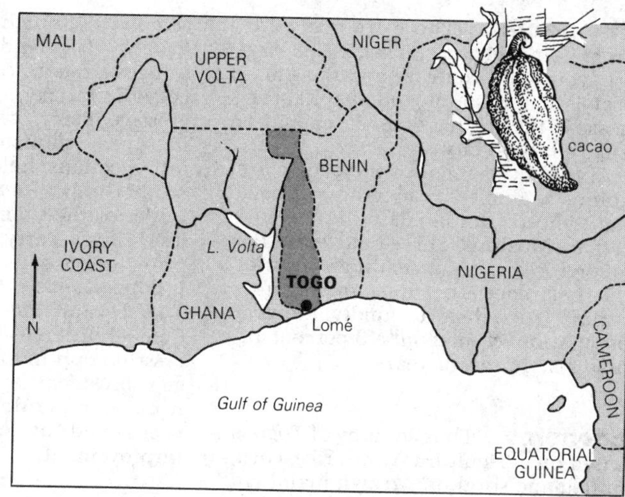

two vice presidents; one serves as the prime minister and the other is the president of Zanzibar. Legislative power is held by a 244-member National Assembly.

Zanzibar, given a separate constitution and legislature in 1979, is also controlled by the Revolutionary Party.

Tanzania is a member of the United Nations, the Organization of African Unity, and the Commonwealth of Nations. It is also an associated state of the European Common Market.

History. The 1964 union of Tanganyika and Zanzibar merged the histories of two separate regions in eastern Africa.

Zanzibar. Arabs began colonizing Zanzibar in the 700's. Portuguese arrived in the late 1500's and brought the area under Portuguese rule. Arabs from Oman broke Portugal's control of the islands in about 1700, and established a sultanate. The Arabs developed a prosperous slave market and they encouraged clove plantations.

In the 1800's Britain gained control of the islands and ended the slave trade. In 1890 Britain formally established a protectorate over Zanzibar. The sultan remained as nominal ruler, however, and until 1956 the islands were ruled primarily by Arabs under British supervision.

Two political parties were formed in the 1950's—the Zanzibar Nationalist Party (ZNP), representing the Arabs, and the Afro-Shirazi Party (ASP), representing mainly the African population and some Shirazi. In 1957 the ASP split, and the Zanzibar and Pemba Peoples' Party (ZPPP) was formed.

On June 24, 1963, Zanzibar became self-governing, and elections were held in July. Although the African-dominated ASP won the largest number of the votes, the government was controlled by a coalition of the ZNP and ZPPP.

Zanzibar received its independence on December 9, 1963, and Sheik Muhammad Shamte became prime minister of the coalition government. The opposition, consisting largely of Africans, staged a bloody coup against Arab rule on January 12, 1964. The sultan was overthrown and a republic proclaimed. Sheik Adeid Amani Karume, leader of the ASP, became president.

Tanganyika. In the 700's Arabs also established settlements in the coastal region of Tanganyika. The Portuguese settled in the region in the late 1400's. The Arabs developed a prosperous slave trade in the interior, which flourished until the 1800's, when it was checked by Christian missionaries led by David Livingstone.

Germany began colonizing the area in 1884, and in 1890 the region became part of German East Africa. After World War I Tanganyika became a British mandate under the League of Nations, and in 1946 it became a UN trust territory. Nationalism grew in the 1950's, and in 1954 Julius Nyerere formed a nationalist political party, the Tanganyika African National Union (TANU). The candidates of TANU were victorious in the first elections for a legislative council held in 1958.

In 1959 Britain took steps to establish self-government for Tanganyika, which became fully independent on December 9, 1961. A republic was proclaimed in 1962, and Tanzania was created in 1964 by the merger of Tanganyika and Zanzibar.

United Republic. Nyerere, president of Tanganyika since 1961, became the president of the United Republic of Tanzania in 1964.

In the 1960's and 1970's Nyerere introduced a form of socialism in which there was communal farming, the goal of national self-reliance for workers, and the nationalization of many privately owned businesses.

The revolutionary army that was responsible for the 1964 overthrow of the sultan of Zanzibar joined with revolutionary forces in Tanzania in the successful execution of the 1977 military coup there. The Revolutionary Party now in power is repressive and socialistic.

In 1979 the Tanzanian army was welcomed as Uganda's liberator when it marched into that country on a retaliatory mission. Tanzanian forces ended up deposing Uganda's ruthless despot, Idi Amin.

A new national capital to replace Dar es Salaam was developed at Dodoma, in central Tanzania.

Togo

Official name: *Republic of Togo*
Area: *21,600 sq. mi., 56,000 sq. km.*
Population: *(1990 est.) 3,566,000*
Capital: *Lomé (Pop., 1989, 400,000)*
Language: *French, African languages*
Religion: *Traditional religions, Christian*
Currency unit: *Franc CFA (African Financial Community)*
National holiday: *Independence Day, April 27*

Togo, a republic in western Africa, is bordered on the north by Upper Volta; on the east by Benin; on the south by the Gulf of Guinea, an arm of the Atlantic Ocean; and on the west by Ghana.

After World War I Togo was divided by Britain and France into separate League of Nations mandates, and after 1946 they were administered as separate UN trust territories. In 1957 the British territory became part of Ghana, and in 1960 the French territory received its independence.

The land. Grasslands occupy most of Togo. There is a sandy coast, behind which are lagoons. Inland from the lagoons is the Terre de Barre, a low, clay plain that rises to a sandy plateau. The Togo Atakora Mountains cross the center of the country. The Mono and Ogou rivers flow through Togo. The climate is hot and humid.

The people. There are many different ethnic groups in Togo. The largest groups are the Ewe and the Adja–Watyi in the south and the Kabrai–Losso in the north. Lomé, the capital, is Togo's largest city.

Almost 60 percent of the people are animists, about 25 percent are Christians (mostly Roman Catholic), and the rest are Muslims. Three-quarters of the labor force is in agriculture; most of the remainder is occupied in manufacturing. Togo has a rapidly growing population, with about a 3 percent annual rise in recent years.

Economy. The economy of Togo is based on agriculture. Yams, rice, corn, millet, and sorghum, grown mainly in the interior, are the main food crops. Cacao and coffee are the leading commercial crops. Palm products, such as copra and palm oil, are important, and the peoples near the coast and the lagoons prepare copra and coconut oil.

Togo has rich phosphate deposits; approximately 3 million tons are shipped annually. Mining and industry are relatively undeveloped, though, and account for only about one-quarter of the country's gross national product, while agriculture accounts for nearly one-half.

In 1985 imports cost $262.3 million and exports earned $242.3 million. The main imports are machinery, foodstuffs, consumer goods, and fuels. The major exports are phosphate, coffee, and cacao. Most trade is conducted with France, the Netherlands, West Germany, and Britain.

Government. According to the 1979 constitution, executive power is held by a president who appoints and is aided by a Council of Ministers. Legislative power is vested in a unicameral National Assembly that has 77 members. Both the president and members of the legislature are elected to seven-year terms. The Assembly of the Togolese People is the sole political party.

History. Between about the 1200's and the 1800's many African tribal kingdoms established their rule over the area of present-day Togo. In the 1400's Portugal developed trade relations with the Ewe. By the mid-1890's Germany had established a protectorate over Togo. After World War I the German protectorate was divided into separate British and French mandates under the League of Nations. In 1946 the mandates became trust territories under the UN.

Britain administered its trust territory along with the Gold Coast colony. In 1956 British Togoland voted to join the Gold Coast, which became the independent nation of Ghana in 1957.

After World War II France established a locally elected territorial assembly in French Togoland. In 1956 French Togoland obtained internal self-government from France, and Nicolas Grunitzky, of the Togolese Progressive Party, became the country's first prime minister. Grunitzky's party lost elections held in 1958, and his brother-in-law, Sylvanus Olympio, leader of the Committee for the Togolese Unity Party, succeeded him as prime minister.

Independence. On April 27, 1960, Togo became independent. Lieutenant Colonel Etienne Eyadema led a successful coup in 1967; he has been Togo's president ever since. Under his firm, stable rule, Togo has enjoyed peace and at least some economic improvement.

Tunisia

Official name: *Republic of Tunisia*
Area: *63,170 sq. mi., 163,610 sq. km.*
Population: *(1990 est.) 8,095,000*
Capital: *Tunis (Pop., 1989, 1,700,000)*
Language: *Arabic*
Religion: *Islam*
Currency unit: *Dinar*
National holiday: *Independence Day, June 1*

Tunisia, a republic in northern Africa, is bounded on the north and east by the Mediterranean Sea, on the south by Libya, and on the west by Algeria. Tunisia received its independence from France in 1956.

The land. Tunisia has four contrasting geographical regions—the Sahel, or plains, along the east coast; a steppe region inland from the coast; the Atlas mountain system in the north; and a low-lying desert region, part of the Sahara, in the south.

The Sahel is occupied by low rolling hills. Paralleling the eastern coast, but further inland, is the flatter steppe region. The Tell Atlas in the far north is separated from the Saharan Atlas, or High Tell, by the Medjerda River valley. The Tell Atlas extends to the coast in Cape Blanc, and the Saharan Atlas extends to the coast in Cape Bon.

South of the mountains is the Shott el Jerid, a salt lake close to sea level that receives some streams from the mountains. In the southwest, along the boundary with Algeria, lies part of the Great Eastern Erg, a major sand area of the Sahara.

In the northern part of the country winters are mild and rainy and summers are hot and dry. South of the Shott el Jerid the climate is hot and dry with less than four inches of rain a year.

The people. Most of Tunisia's people are Muslim, and are descended from indigenous Berber-speaking peoples and later Arab immigrants. There are small communities of Jews and Europeans, mainly French, Italian, and Maltese. There are nomadic Berber tribes in the desert region.

Tunis, the capital, is the country's largest city and principal port. Bizerte, Sfax, Sousse, and Gabès are also important seaports. Qairouan is an historic Muslim holy city.

Tunisia's population, almost half urban, has grown at a rapid rate of about two and a half percent a year over the last decade. Literacy has also increased over that period, owing to aggressive government educational programs. The increases in growth and literacy have created a surplus of skilled labor, 30 percent of whom are occupied by farming; while another 30 percent are distributed among manufacturing, construction, and mining.

DANCER AND MUSICIANS IN TUNIS. *Long a civilized region, Tunisia today is stable and prosperous, and its large urban population lives in a sophisticated Arab-French environment.*

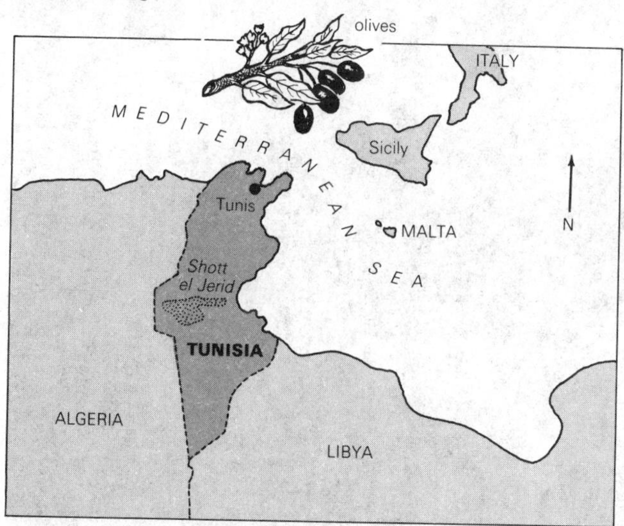

BERBER WOMAN AND DAUGHTER *making flour with grindstones in the ancient way. The Berbers are the native people of North Africa.*

Economy.

Industry and mining combined account for nearly 30 percent of Tunisia's gross national product, while commerce and banking account for just under 25 percent, and agriculture for about 20 percent. The diversified economy is largely state-controlled, but private enterprise is encouraged.

Tunisia has rich phosphate, iron ore, and oil deposits that account for most of its mining and industry. Food processing is also significant.

Tunisia is one of the world's leading producers of olive oil, and wheat, barley, and olives are the main crops. Figs, citrus fruits, and wine grapes are also grown, and livestock raising is the major occupation of the nomads.

In 1985 imports cost $2.7 billion while exports earned $1.8 billion. The major imports are food, lumber, textiles, and machinery. The major exports are oil, phosphates, olive oil, and fruits. Most trade is conducted with France, Italy, and other Western European nations.

Government.

Tunisia has a presidential system of government. Executive power is vested in a president, who is popularly elected to a five-year term. Legislative power is held by the National Assembly, which is also popularly elected every five years.

Tunisia is a member of the United Nations, the Arab League, and the Organization of African Unity.

History.

In 814 B.C. the Phoenicians founded the city of Carthage, near the site of present-day Tunis. In 146 B.C. Rome destroyed Carthage and Tunisia came under Roman domination. Roman rule ended in the 400's A.D. with invasions by the Vandals. In the 500's the region came under Byzantine rule.

A decisive break in Tunisian history occurred with the arrival of Muslim Arabs in the mid-600's. Although the native Berber-speaking people were the most Romanized and Christianized people of northwestern Africa, Tunisia became part of the Arab-Muslim world.

Tunisia shared the fortunes of the dynasties that arose in northern Africa and Spain. In the early 800's the Aghlabids gained control of Tunisia. The Fatimids controlled much of Tunisia in the 900's, and in the 1100's a Morocco-based dynasty, the Almohad, gained control. In 1228 the Almohads were succeeded by the Hafsids, who controlled Tunisia until the early 1500's, when the Ottoman Turks began a series of invasions.

By 1574 Tunisia had become part of the Ottoman Empire, but it was soon able to achieve a considerable measure of self-rule. In 1705 an Ottoman Turkish ruler of Tunisia, owing allegiance to the sultan, established the Husaynid dynasty, which lasted until the monarchy was abolished in 1957.

The local Tunisian government attempted internal reforms and westernization early in the 1800's. But Tunisia soon fell victim to foreign indebtedness and increasing European interference. In 1881, after a brief military campaign, France established a protectorate over Tunisia.

French administration. Although large numbers of French and other Europeans settled in the country, native institutions were left largely intact. Tunisians learned technical skills from the French and benefited from the country's economic growth without being overwhelmed in the process.

THE PHOENICIANS *invented our alphabet. Carthage, near Tunis, was their colony.*

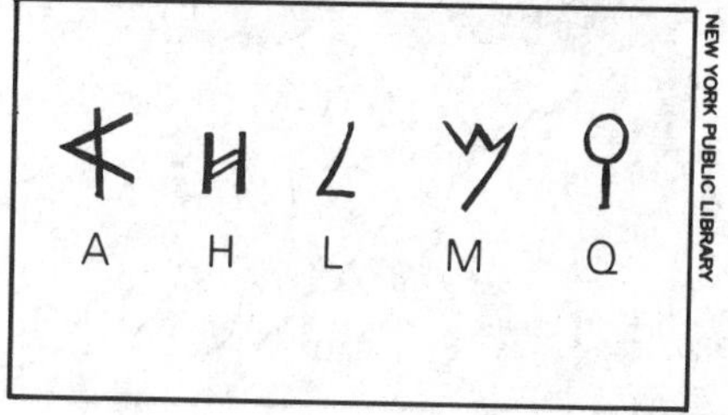

Nationalism developed rapidly after World War I, and the Tunisian struggle for independence came to be personified by Habib Bourguiba, who organized the nationalist Neo-Destour Party in 1934. The Neo-Destour itself grew out of an earlier, more traditional party, the Destour, or Constitution Party.

After a long period of intermittent negotiations and armed struggle, France agreed to grant Tunisia internal self-government in 1954. On March 20, 1956, France granted Tunisia complete independence, and in 1957 Tunisia become a republic with Bourguiba as president.

Independence. Tunisia, since its independence, has made impressive domestic improvements in education and in economic development. Diplomatically, the period from 1956 until neighboring Algeria won its independence from France in 1962 placed Tunisia in the delicate position of attempting to maintain necessary relations with France while supporting the Algerian independence movement.

Fighting erupted in Tunisia between the French and the Tunisian supporters of the Algerians. Relations between the two worsened. In 1964 the government nationalized French holdings in Tunisia, and France ended its technical and economic assistance.

Under Bourguiba's rule, Tunisia restored relations with France, but lost favor with the Arab states for its support of Egyptian-Israeli peace moves. Tension with Libya increased after the two nations failed to carry through with a proposed merger in 1974. In 1980 Libya attacked Gafsa in Tunisia.

Bourguiba was elected president for life in 1974. Labor riots in 1978 became widespread as many political opponents of the president denounced his autocratic rule. Bourguiba has been a liberal autocrat, respecting human rights and allowing the economy to prosper. In 1983 Bourguiba legalized two opposition political parties.

In November, 1987, Prime Minister Zine al-Abidine Ben Ali declared Bourguiba senile, and replaced him as president. Ben Ali was elected president in April, 1989.

EPA

PEASANT WOMEN *in Turkey gathering dried juice from poppies on a government farm. The juice is used to make opium. Some is legally grown, but there is also a large smuggling trade.*

Turkey

Official name: *Republic of Turkey*
Area: *301,382 sq. mi., 780,576 sq. km.*
Population: *(1990 est.) 56,549,000*
Capital: *Ankara*
(Pop., 1989, 3,300,000)
Language: *Turkish*
Religion: *Islam*
Currency unit: *Lira*
National holiday: *Republic Day, Oct. 29*

Turkey is a republic located both in Asia and in Europe. Most of the country lies in Asia Minor, or Anatolia. The small European portion of Turkey, called Thrace, is on the Balkan peninsula. The republic was formed in 1923 from the Turkish region that had long been the core of the Ottoman Empire.

Turkey is bordered on the north by Bulgaria, the Black Sea, and the Soviet Union; on the east by Iran; on the south by Iraq, Syria, and the Mediterranean Sea; and on the west by the Aegean Sea and Greece.

The land. Thrace consists of rolling plains bounded by uplands in the north and a mountainous coastline in the south. It is separated from Anatolia by a small sea—the Sea of Marmara—and two straits—the Bosporus in the east and the Dardanelles in the west.

In Asian Turkey the Pontic Mountains, rising over 11,000 feet, follow the shores of the Black Sea. The Taurus mountain range on the southern coast rises to a peak of over 11,500 feet above the Mediterranean. Narrow, fertile plains separate both ranges from the sea.

Between the mountain ranges is the Anatolian Plateau, with an average elevation of 3000 feet. Toward the west the plain breaks into a series of fertile river valleys separated by low ridges. In the east the plateau merges with the Pontic and Taurus mountains in the rugged highland of Armenia, where Mt. Ararat, Turkey's highest point, rises to 16,946 feet. Turkey's largest lakes—Van, in the east and Tuzi, in the west—are salt water lakes.

Many rivers flow from Turkey's highlands toward the long coastline. The longest is the Kizil, which rises in the eastern highlands and flows west and north to empty into the Black Sea. Other important rivers are the Firat, or Euphrates, which rises in Turkey and flows south, the Ceyhan in central Anatolia, and the Sakarya in the northwest.

Climate. Thrace and coastal Anatolia have a mild, moist climate. Temperatures range from 40° to 80°F, and rainfall averages 20 to 40 inches annually. Most rain falls in the winter.

In the dry Anatolian Plateau only ten to 20 inches of rain falls a year, and temperatures are hotter in summer and colder in winter than on the coasts. The inland mountains have a colder climate and are often snow-covered.

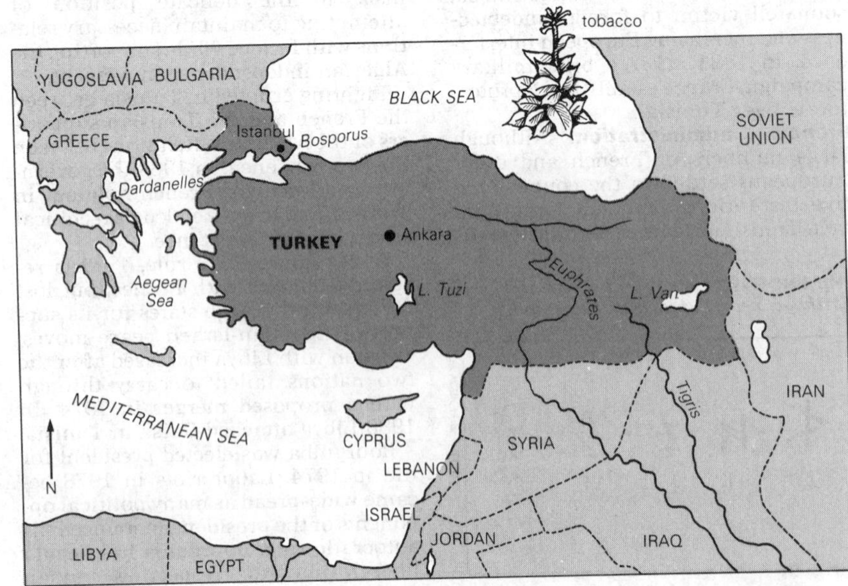

The people. Most Turks are Turkish—related to peoples of Central Asia. They speak Turkish. Over 98 percent of the population is Muslim. The largest minority group is the Kurds, a seminomadic people who inhabit the eastern highlands. There are also small Greek and Armenian minorities.

Most Turks live in small towns encircling the Anatolian Plateau. The interior of the plateau is quite sparsely settled. The densest population is in northwestern Anatolia and eastern Thrace, where Istanbul, the country's largest city, is located. The capital, Ankara, is in central Anatolia.

Economy. Throughout its history the area that is now Turkey has been famous for its agricultural and mineral products. Turkey's economy is still based heavily on agriculture, but industrialization began in the 1950's.

Turkey's wide variety of known minerals include rich deposits of coal and chrome and fairly large reserves of oil, zinc, copper, iron, and lead. Turkey

LOUIS GOLDMAN/PHOTO RESEARCHERS

SULEYMANIYE MOSQUE, *one of the Ottoman treasures of Istanbul, or Constantinople, built in the 16th century. It was inspired by the Byzantine church of Hagia Sophia (537 A.D.).*

also has abundant waterpower and an electrical power capacity (three-quarters of which is thermal) that has helped the rapid growth of its industries. About 20 percent of the gross national product is now contributed by agriculture, and about 30 percent by industry. The Turkish government operates about one-fifth of the entire economy.

Agriculture. Over half of the labor force is occupied by farming and herding. Some one-third of the land area is cultivated, and over one-third is used for pasture. Sheep, goats, cattle, and other livestock are grazed on the Anatolian plain and in the eastern highlands.

Cereals, especially wheat, are the major farm crops. Cotton and sugar beets are also important, and legumes, citrus and other fruits, and nuts are raised. Tobacco is the most important commercial crop. Most farms are small, and agricultural methods are generally outmoded and inefficient. Evergreen forests cover some 13 percent of the country's area, and forestry is important. There is some fishing off the coasts.

Industry. Oil refining has become important recently, but otherwise Turkey's industry, which has expanded greatly since 1950, consists primarily of the processing of agricultural products. Textile weaving is the leading industry. Refined sugar, flour, paper, tobacco products, dried fruits, oils, canned foods, cement, and iron and steel and chrome products are among Turkey's most important manufactured products.

Trade. Turkey has a generally unfavorable balance of trade. In 1986 exports earned only $7.4 billion while imports cost $11.1 billion. The chief exports are agricultural products, especially grain, tobacco, cotton, and sugar. Metal ores are also exported. Machinery and motor vehicles, fuels, manufactured consumer goods, as well as industrial raw materials, are the main imports.

Most Turkish trade is carried on with Western Europe.

Government.

A new constitution was promulgated in 1982. It provided for a strong presidency with a term of seven years. The only legislative body is the 450-member parliament.

Turkey is a member of the United Nations, also of the Organization for Economic Cooperation and Development (OECD), the North Atlantic Treaty Organization (NATO), and the Council of Europe.

History.

Although the Turks did not appear there until the Middle Ages, the region called Turkey has been inhabited since ancient times. The history of the land extends back nearly 4000 years to the civilization of the Hittites and earlier.

After conquests by Persians, Greeks, and Romans, Turkey became, in the 200's A.D., the core of the eastern half of the Roman Empire. In 330 A.D. Byzantium (then named Constantinople, the modern Istanbul) became the capital of the Byzantine Empire, the successor to the Roman Empire.

In the 900's the first Turks, the Seljuks, migrated into Asia Minor from central Asia. In the 1000's they conquered territory in Anatolia, adopted Islam, and established a kingdom ruled from central Turkey. The Byzantine emperors, with the aid of Christian Crusaders, successfully defended western Anatolia and the rest of the empire from the Seljuks, who were overwhelmed by the Mongols in the 1200's.

Ottomans. A second group of Turks renewed the attack on the Byzantine Empire in the late 1200's. These were the Ottomans named after their leader, Osman. The Ottomans, after 200 years, succeeded in conquering the empire. In 1453 they captured the capital, Constantinople.

From Constantinople the Ottomans ruled a mighty empire which, at its height under Sulayman the Magnificent, who ruled from 1520 to 1566, was probably the most powerful in the world. It stretched from Austria in Europe in the north to the Indian Ocean in the south, and from Persia (Iran) in the east to Algeria in the west.

The Ottoman Empire in the 1500's was not only the largest and the most powerful state in the world, but the most efficiently governed as well. Its society was ordered along a feudalistic pattern, and its leaders combined political power with religious influence. The Ottoman Empire had an administrative bureaucracy, a court system, taxation methods, and an army and navy that were excellent even by modern standards.

Decline. The 300 years following Sulayman's reign, however, witnessed an almost uninterrupted decline. A disastrous defeat by the armies of the Holy Roman Empire in 1571 ended Ottoman military supremacy and put the bold, once-conquering Turkish armies on the defensive. Governmental administration collapsed under weak sultans and bureaucratic corruption, and military discipline crumbled.

Local authorities gradually assumed power, and by the 1800's many provinces were independent in fact, if not in name. In addition, France, Britain, Austria, and Russia conquered parts of the empire, and the Balkan provinces rebelled, leaving Turkey only Thrace of its once considerable European possessions. The Ottoman Empire in the 1800's had become the "Sick Man of Europe."

Toward the end of the 1800's progress was made in reforming the government and restoring order. The era also saw the beginning of a cultural and literary revival. In 1876 Abd-al-Hamid II took the throne and a liberal constitution was proclaimed.

The sultan soon ended the reform efforts, however. He revoked the constitution, abused his subjects, especially the minority nationalities, and took Turkey into wars that resulted in disastrous losses.

Young Turks. In the discontent caused by his failures and abuses, a revolutionary party was formed, the Committee of Union and Progress, or the "Young Turks." The party hoped to restore Turkish power by westernizing the country and by expanding Turkish territory.

In 1908, with the support of the army, the Young Turks forced Abd-al-Hamid to grant a new constitution and parliamentary government. In

1909 he was deposed and replaced by his brother.

Soon, however, the Young Turks divided into factions. Moreover, in trying to regain lost territories they lost still more. As each of their projects failed, their government grew more despotic. By 1913 a military wing of the party assumed power by a coup d'etat.

Under this government Turkey entered World War I on the side of Germany and suffered terrible losses. When the war ended in 1918, the country was occupied by troops from many Allied countries and was threatened with partition among the Allied states. All that remained of the Ottoman Empire was Anatolia and Thrace, and the Young Turk government fled into exile.

In 1920 a nationalist party organized an unofficial Turkish government under Mustafa Kemal to drive out the Allied occupation forces. Kemal, with the support of the majority of Turks, organized an army and by 1923 had forced the Allies to leave and to recognize Turkey's sovereignty over Asia Minor and eastern Thrace in the Treaty of Lausanne.

The republic. In October, 1923, Turkey was proclaimed a republic, with an elected legislature and with Kemal as president. The political and religious authority of the old sultanate and the caliphate were abolished.

Kemal, who was later given the surname "Atatürk," or "father of the Turks," radically reformed Turkish government, economy, and society, turning its medieval Islamic social and political structure into that of a modern, Western-style nation. At Atatürk's death in 1938 his prime minister, Ismet Inönü, became the president and continued the country's westernization program.

Turkey did not participate in World War II, but it favored the Allies. After the war it pursued a pro-Western policy, joining the North Atlantic Treaty Organization. Turkey was aided in its fight against expanding communist influence by U.S. economic aid under the Truman Doctrine and Marshall Plan.

In 1950 the Democratic Party took power from Inönü's Republican People's Party government. The Democratic government faced rising discontent at home. Economic expansion and modernization had proceeded rapidly, and in 1950 severe inflation threatened the economy. The government responded with unpopular financial restrictions. Unrest was met with repression, which the people, especially Turkey's new educated class, resented.

Contemporary Turkey. In 1960 a military group seized power. They established a second republic by 1961. Inönü became prime minister and initiated ambitious economic development programs that were designed to develop natural resources, modernize agriculture, and expand industry at a moderate pace. Inönü's government fell in 1965.

Prolonged political and economic unrest resulted in civil riots and subsequent changes in government in the next decade. As ethnic and religious tensions mounted in the mid-1970's, they were accompanied by extensive terrorist activity. As the republic was on the verge of crumbling, owing to increased violence and incipient civil war, martial law was proclaimed. The government was taken over by the military in 1980.

Economic difficulties persist, provoked by the extreme differences between the affluent cities and the backward, poor rural areas. Huge trading deficits and mounting inflation have added to the difficulties.

Turkey's foreign relations have been complicated by its proximity to the Soviet Union and its friendship with Israel. Turkey invaded Cyprus in 1974, helping the minority Turkish Cypriots to occupy the northern part of the island nation. The invasion has strained Turkish-United States and Turkish-Greek relations.

Uganda

Official name: *Republic of Uganda*
Area: *91,134 sq. mi., 236,036 sq. km.*
Population: *(1990 est.) 17,593,000*
Capital: *Kampala (Pop., 1986, 592,200)*
Language: *English, Luganda, Swahili, other African languages*
Religion: *Christian, Islam, traditional religions*
Currency unit: *Shilling*
National holiday: *Independence Day, Oct. 9*

Uganda, a republic in eastern Africa, is bounded on the north by Sudan; on the east by Kenya; on the south by Tanzania and Rwanda; on the west by the Republic of Zaire. Uganda gained independence from Britain in 1962.

The land.

Most of Uganda is occupied by a plateau with elevations between 3000 and 6000 feet above sea level. The Ruwenzori Mountains run along the western border, reaching an elevation of more than 16,760 feet in the Margherita Peak. In the east Mt. Elgon reaches an elevation of almost 14,180 feet.

Lake Victoria is at the southeastern corner of Uganda. Lakes Edward and Albert are in western Uganda, and Lake Kyoga is in central Uganda. The Albert Nile and the Victoria Nile are among the many rivers flowing through Uganda.

Uganda has a tropical climate. In the northeast rainfall averages about 20 inches a year, but in the southwest and west it averages between 50 and 60 inches a year.

The people.

There are many tribal groups in Uganda, most of which are Bantu-speaking. The largest Bantu–speaking tribe is the Baganda. Other large groups include the Iteso, the Banyankole, and the Basoga. There are also peoples of Nilotic and Nilo–Hamitic stock, and small communities of Asians and Europeans.

Uganda's largest cities include Kampala, the capital; Entebbe; and Jinja. All three are near Lake Victoria.

Half the people are Christians, ten percent are Muslims, and the rest are animists. About 90 percent of the labor force is occupied by agriculture, and over 90 percent of the people live in rural areas.

Economy.

Uganda's economy expanded greatly in the 1960's, but growth was stunted by political turmoil in the 1970's. The aggressive nationalization of business, beginning in 1969, resulted in considerable losses of European capital.

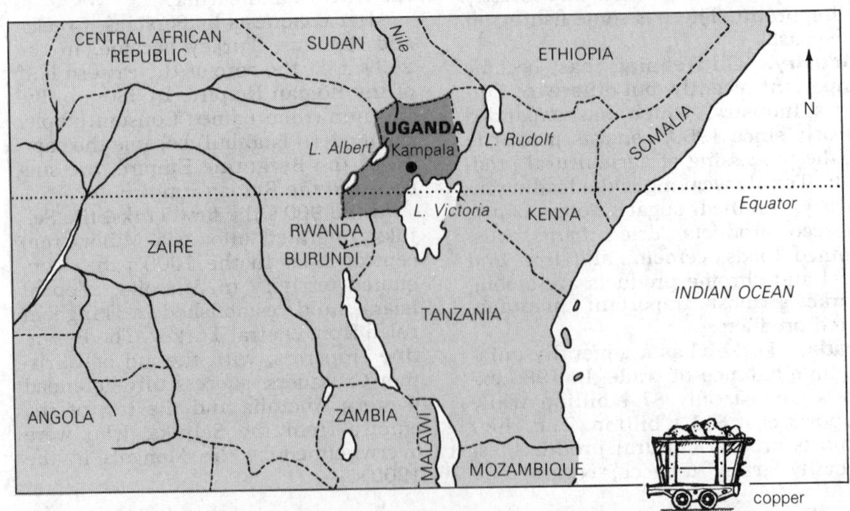

Uganda's economy is based on agriculture. The basic food crops are corn, beans, and cassava, and the main cash crops are cotton and coffee. Tobacco, sugar cane, and tea are also grown. Cattle are raised in many parts of the country, and fish from Uganda's lakes are important to the economy.

Uganda has rich copper deposits, as well as deposits of apatite, beryl, and bismuth.

Most industry is engaged in the processing of Uganda's mineral and agricultural products. The Owen Falls hydroelectric plant, near Lake Victoria, supplies most of the country's electricity, and industry is concentrated in the Owen Falls region.

In 1985 imports cost $390 million and exports earned $380 million. The major imports are textiles, petroleum products, iron and steel, and machinery. The principal exports are coffee, cotton, and copper. Most trade is conducted with Britain, the United States, Belgium, and Luxembourg. Uganda has close economic ties with Kenya and Tanzania.

Government. In January, 1986, the National Resistance Council seized the government. The 80-member unicameral legislative council is led by a president and a prime minister.

Uganda is a member of the United Nations, the Organization of African Unity, and the Commonwealth of Nations. It is also an associated state of the European Common Market.

History. Between the 1400's and 1600's various peoples established kingdoms in present-day Uganda. In the 1600's the Buganda kingdom became powerful and conquered many of the existing states.

James Augustus Grant and John Hanning Speke explored the source of the Nile in 1862 and established trade relations between Britain and Mutesa I, the *kabaka*, or king, of Buganda. Protestant and Roman Catholic missionaries followed, as well as Muslims, who were in contact with neighboring regions. In the 1880's, Mutesa's successor, Mwanga, attempted to stop the spread of Christianity in the area, and many Christians were killed under widespread persecution.

British rule. In the year 1888 the Imperial British East Africa Company concluded a treaty with Buganda, and the kingdom came under the company's administration. The company withdrew from Uganda because of economic difficulties, and in 1894 Britain established a protectorate over the region. By 1896 the protectorate included all of present-day Uganda.

In 1900 the Buganda regent signed the Uganda Agreement with Britain, which established administrative arrangements that were to endure until Uganda achieved self-government in

UPI

IDI AMIN, *brutal dictator of Uganda, when in power. He was ousted in 1978.*

1962. The kabaka, or king, with his *lukiko*, or assembly, was recognized as the ruler of Uganda as long as he cooperated with Britain. Four regions were marked out—the Eastern, Western, Northern, and Buganda regions. The Buganda region occupied south-central Uganda.

Britain established a legislative council following World War I, and African members were appointed to the council after World War II. In 1953 Buganda demanded independence from the rest of Uganda. It feared being forced into federation with the British protectorate of Kenya and Tanganyika, and thereby coming under the control of Kenya's white settler community. In the same year, Kabaka Edward Mutesa II was exiled after refusing to nominate Bugandan members to the legislative council.

Independence. In March of 1962, Uganda was granted self-rule. Milton Obote, prime minister, led a coalition party that was able to incorporate Buganda peacefully. On October 9, 1962, Uganda became independent, with Obote as prime minister and the king of Buganda, Edward Mutesa II, as president.

In 1966 Obote took full control of the government, suspended the constitution, and ousted President Mutesa. Obote assumed the position of president. In January of 1971 Obote was overthrown by troops led by General Idi Amin, who then named himself president.

Amin, a Muslim traditionalist, became president for life, expelled most Asians from the country in 1972, abolished the Parliament, and opened virtual warfare against the Christian tribes. Amin's harsh and repressive tactics, as well as his avid attempts to Africanize the economy, led to shortages of skilled labor, a depression in exports, excessive inflation, and hostile relations with Western Europe and the United States. When Amin ordered an invasion of Tanzania in 1978, Tanzanian troops marched into Uganda and were welcomed as its liberators. Amin was ousted.

Political anarchy ensued until 1980 when Obote returned to rule. He restored good relations with the West, and although he promised to respect human rights and provide a liberal administration, the going was slow.

Obote was overthrown in a military coup in 1985.

United Arab Emirates

Official name: *United Arab Emirates*
Area: *32,280 sq. mi., 83,600 sq. km.*
Population: *(1990 est.) 2,250,000*
Capital: *Abu Dhabi*
(Pop., 1987 est., 420,000)
Language: *Arabic, English*
Religion: *Islam*
Currency unit: *Dirham*

The United Arab Emirates, formerly called Trucial Oman and the Trucial States, is a union of seven Arab sheikdoms on the southern coast of the Persian Gulf. The United Arab Emirates is bordered on the north by Qatar; on the east by the Gulf of Oman; on the south by Oman and Saudi Arabia; and on the west by Saudi Arabia.

Abu Dhabi, Dubai, Sharjah, Ajman, Umm al Qaiwain, Ras al Khaimah, and Fujairah make up the union. When Britain ended its protective treaty relations with the sheikdoms they formed a union and became an independent nation.

The land and people. Flat, hot, and dry, except for the humid coast, the region is mainly barren desert dotted with a few oases. Rainfall averages only three inches a year.

The native Arabs account for only a quarter of the total population. In all, about 40 percent of the people are

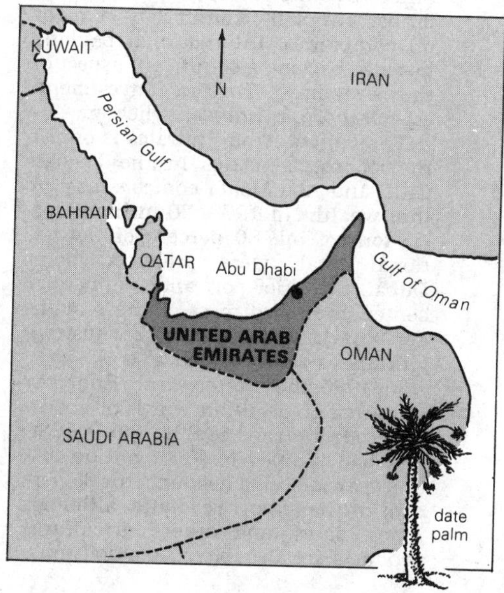

C.R. RICHARDSON/TAURUS

PROSPERITY *from oil revenues is shown in Abu Dhabi's buildings and banking.*

Arabs, and about 50 percent are Iranians, Pakistanis, and Indians. Foreigners, working mostly in the oil industry, account for nearly 90 percent of the labor force.

Most of the country's people are Sunni Muslims, and 90 percent live in urban areas. Arabic is the official language, but English is commonly used. Dubai, capital of Dubai state, is the major port and the principal city.

Economy. Nomadic grazing of livestock, pearl diving, fishing, trading and date farming, were once the only means of livelihood in the states. They became of secondary importance after 1958, when the production of oil became the mainstay of the economy. Since 1976 the government has owned 60 percent of the country's two major oil companies. International banking has also become a significant aspect of the economy. Foreign investment, especially from France, is heavy.

The United Arab Emirates is one of the richest countries in the Persian Gulf, and Abu Dhabi controls most of that wealth. In 1979, 70 million metric tons of oil, 80 percent of the national total, were produced here. Dubai, the chief port and commercial center, produced most of the remainder. Sharjah oil resources are just beginning to be developed.

In 1986 the United Arab Emirates imported $6.6 billion worth of goods. Its exports earned $9.8 billion in 1986 and had jumped to $13.4 billion just one year later. Oil accounts for 95 percent of the export revenues, although hides, dates, and other agricultural products are also exported. Foodstuffs, machinery, and consumer items are the main imports. Britain, Japan, and India are the country's chief trading partners.

Government. The United Arab Emirates, a federation formed on December 2, 1971, is ruled by an elected sheik and a Supreme Council of Ministers composed of seven rulers from each state. The Supreme Council is the de facto legislative body. The unicameral National Council, with 40 members appointed by the Supreme Council, serves as an advisory body.

The United Arab Emirates is a member of the United Nations, as well as of the Organization of Petroleum Exporting Countries (OPEC), and of the Arab League.

History. For centuries the sheiks of the region known as the Trucial Oman battled for control of the territory. In the 1500's, when Portugal controlled the Persian Gulf, the sheiks turned to piracy and the slave trade. By the 1700's their ships ranged over the entire Persian Gulf and into the Arabian Sea. They waged undeclared war against the English East India Company, the principal trader in the area.

At the beginning of the 1800's the company and Britain suppressed the piracy, and in 1820 they signed a treaty of peace with the sheikdoms. By later agreements the sheiks promised to abandon slaving and piracy, turned control of their foreign affairs and defense over to Britain, and granted the British exclusive trading privileges.

Until the 1950's the sheikdoms experienced little internal or external strife. The discovery of oil in the 1950's, however, and the wealth and influx of foreigners that oil production brought to the states, disrupted the traditional society. In the 1960's programs were initiated to use oil revenues for health care, education, and technological improvements.

In the 1950's and 1960's border disputes with neighboring states were frequent. In 1971, after Britain withdrew from the area, six of the sheikdoms entered into a union and the seventh joined in 1972. Qatar and Bahrain were offered membership in the union, but both declined. In 1979 the United Arab Emirates severed diplomatic relations with Egypt to show its disapproval of the Egyptian-Israeli peace treaty signed in that year.

Upper Volta

Official name: *Burkina Faso*
Area: *105,870 sq. mi., 274,200 sq. km.*
Population: *(1990 est.) 8,941,000*
Capital: *Ouagadougou (Pop., 1989, 300,000)*
Language: *French, African languages*
Religion: *Traditional religions, Islam, Christian*
Currency unit: *Franc CFA (African Financial Community)*
National holiday: *Republic Day, Dec. 11*

Upper Volta, a republic in western Africa, is bounded on the north and west by Mali; on the east by Niger; and on the south by Benin, Togo, Ghana, and the Ivory Coast. Upper Volta received its independence from France in 1960.

The land. Most of Upper Volta is occupied by sandy plains. In the east, along the border with Niger, is a region of swamps. The Volta Noire, or Black Volta, the Volta Rouge, or Red Volta, and the Volta Blanche, or White Volta, flow through the country. The climate in most of Upper Volta is hot and dry.

The people. There are many different tribal groups in Upper Volta. Almost half of the population is of the Mossi tribe. Other large tribal groups include the Bobo, the Gurunsi, the Samo, and the Marka. There is a small French population.

The largest cities are Ouagadougou, the capital, and Bobo Dioulasso.

Almost three-quarters of the people are animists, 25 percent are Muslims, and 10 percent are Christians. Over 90 percent of the people live in rural areas and almost 85 percent of the laborers are subsistence farmers. Less than 10 percent of the people are literate.

Economy. Upper Volta, hindered by a lack of water resources, by poor soil, and by its landlocked situation, is a poor country. Only 17 percent of its gross national product is derived from industry, while over two-fifths of it comes from agriculture.

The basic food crops are millet and sorghum. Peanuts and cotton are also grown. Cattle, sheep, and goats are raised in most parts of the country.

Industry is poorly developed. There are deposits of manganese, bauxite, and gold, but mining is basically undeveloped. Many of the people work outside the country, mostly in Ghana and the Ivory Coast. A railroad connects Ouagadougou with the Ivory Coast port of Abidjan.

In 1983 imports cost $279.5 million and exports earned $55.3 million. The main imports are foodstuffs, textiles, and machinery. The major exports are live animals and hides and skins. Most trade is conducted with Ghana, the Ivory Coast, and France. Upper Volta is a member of an economic union with Benin, the Ivory Coast, Niger, and Togo.

Government. Following the coup of 1980, the constitution was suspended and the National Assembly was dissolved. The country is now ruled by the Military Committee of Reform for National Progress.

Upper Volta is a member of the United Nations and the Organization of African Unity, and it is an associated state of the European Common Market.

History. In about 1000 A.D. the Mossi people migrated into Upper Volta and established there two principal kingdoms—Ouagadougou and Yatenga. The kingdoms competed with the Dagomba and Mamprussi peoples to the south for primacy in the area. In about 1300 the Mossi came into conflict with the warriors of the ancient empires of Mali and Songhai.

In the 1400's and 1500's Mossi armies raided areas beyond Timbuktu, in present-day Mali. They later raided areas in what is now Benin and Nigeria. The Mossi successfully guarded the northern approach routes to Upper Volta until the 1800's, when the French began to conquer the area.

French rule. France gained control over most of the region in 1896, and in 1904 the area became part of the colony of Upper Senegal and Niger. In 1919 a separate colony of Upper Volta was created. In 1932 Upper Volta was divided among Niger, the Ivory Coast, and French Sudan (present-day Mali), but the territory was reestablished as a single unit in 1947.

During the 1950's politics in Upper Volta largely reflected African, rather than exclusively national, considerations. At that time a local branch of the African Democratic Rally (RDA), an African regional organization with headquarters in the Ivory Coast, had many followers in Upper Volta. In the late 1950's, however, the Upper Volta branch of the RDA began to take up national issues and joined with a smaller reform group to form the Voltaic Democratic Union (VDU).

Independence. In August, 1960, Upper Volta became an independent country. In 1966 Lieutenant Colonel Sangoulé Lamizana led a successful military coup, suspended the constitution, and established a provisional government. Civilian rule was restored in 1978, but it lasted only two years. Coups in 1980 and 1983 both installed military governments.

Since the severe droughts and famines of the early 1970's, the country has sought self-sufficiency in food. Agriculture and transportation have improved, with French aid.

Yemen

Official name: *Yemen Arab Republic*
Area: *75,300 sq. mi., 195,000 sq. km.*
Population: *(1990 est.) 7,162,000*
Capital: *Sana (Pop., 1987 est., 510,000)*
Language: *Arabic*
Religion: *Islam*
Currency unit: *Riyal*
National holiday: *Proclamation of the republic, Sept. 26*

Yemen lies in the southwestern corner of the Arabian peninsula on the coast of the Red Sea. It is bordered on the north and east by Saudi Arabia; on the south by South Yemen; and on the west by the Red Sea. The eastern desert boundary is undefined.

The land. East of a narrow coastal plain, rugged mountains rise to over 12,000 feet, towering above a high central plateau. The eastern border is also mountainous, and desert land lies at the northern border.

In the desert and along the coastal plain less than ten inches of rain fall a year, and temperatures rise to over 130°F. A more temperate climate prevails in the mountains and the central plateau, where an average of twelve inches of rain fall a year and average temperatures range from 60°F to 80°F.

The people. The Yemeni are Arab Muslims of the Sunni and the Shia sects. Population is concentrated on the coast and on the temperate central plateau, where the capital, Sana, is located.

Almost two-thirds of the labor force is occupied in agriculture. Many people work abroad and provide a major source of revenue for Yemen.

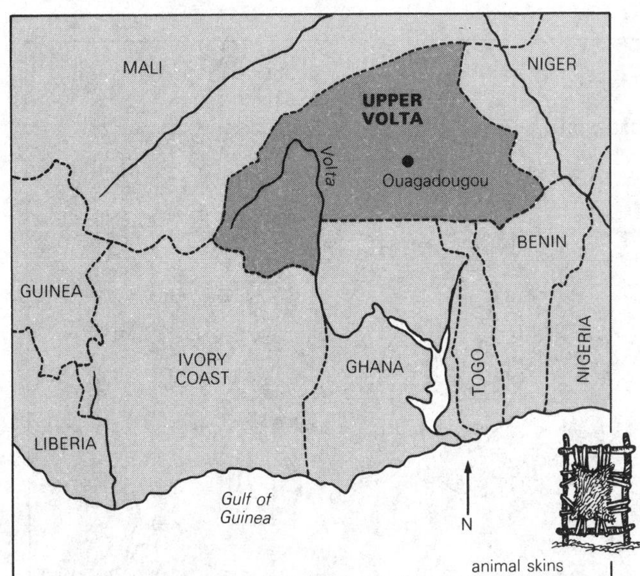

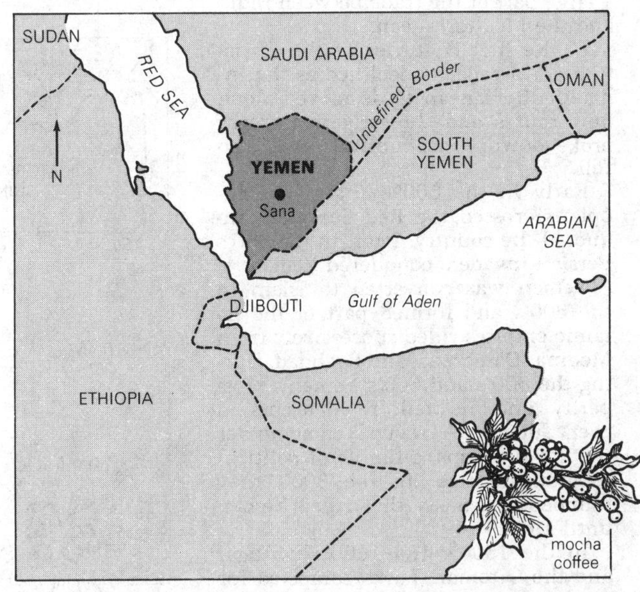

Economy. Yemen is one of the poorest countries in the world and it receives extensive aid from the oil-rich Arabian states and from communist nations. Yemen has no known important mineral resources, and its industry is limited to the manufacture of handcrafts.

Trade was important in Yemen before the civil war of the mid-1960's, and Al Hudaydah was an active port. Since that time, however, commercial activity has nearly ceased; in 1986 exports earned an estimated $10 million while imports were estimated at $1.2 billion.

Yemen's economy is based on agriculture. Coffee was traditionally the main cash crop until the 1970's, when irrigation projects resulted in high yields of cotton, now the country's leading export. Qat, a mild narcotic shrub, cotton, and coffee are the most important crops. Yemeni farmers also raise grains, citrus fruits, vegetables, and tobacco. Herders graze sheep, goats, camels, and horses in the more barren regions.

Government. The constitution was suspended in 1974. The president is assisted by a 15-member appointed advisory council of ministers. Legislative power is vested in a 159-member Consultative Assembly.

Yemen is a member of the United Nations and the Arab League.

History. During the first 1000 years before our era, several states, of which the best known was the Sabean, or Sheban, developed in Yemen. A high degree of economic prosperity earned the country the name of *Arabia Felix* among the Greeks and Romans.

Yemen's prosperity was based on an elaborate system of irrigation and the export of frankincense, precious jewels, and spices. Yemen also controlled a large part of the trade between India and the Mediterranean.

In the first centuries of the Christian era prosperity declined as the India-Mediterranean trade moved along new routes and the irrigation works broke down. The cultural level also fell.

Early in the 500's Christian Ethiopians crossed the Red Sea and conquered the country. Later in the 500's Persian invaders conquered Yemen.

Yemen was converted to Islam in the 600's and formed part of the Islamic empires ruled successively from Medina, Damascus, and Baghdad. During the 500's and 600's Yemen's prosperity and its culture deteriorated even further. A revival came under the Zaydi imams, a family of political religious leaders. In the 800's they founded a dynasty that ruled Yemen until 1962.

In the 1500's and 1600's Portugal and the Ottoman Turks competed for control of Yemen, but their invading forces were driven off. During the next 200 years the country suffered a cultural and economic relapse caused by its isolation from the new trade routes.

In 1872 the Ottoman Turks succeeded in making Yemen part of their empire, but Yemeni resistance continued in the highlands until World War I. The Ottomans were forced to withdraw in 1918, at the end of World War I, leaving Yemen an independent nation under the Zaydi ruler.

The imam closed the country to outsiders, and although Yemen joined the Arab League in 1945 and the United Nations in 1947, it had almost no contact with the rest of the world. In 1948 Yahya was killed during an attempted revolution, and his son, Ahmad, succeeded him.

Ahmad gradually allowed foreign diplomats into Yemen. In 1958 Yemen and the United Arab Republic (U.A.R.) formed a federation, the United Arab States. By early 1962 the union had been abolished, however.

A republic was declared following the military coup of 1962, after which a civil war raged between the royalist forces of the deposed imam and republican army troops. The war involved the rest of the Middle East. Egypt sent arms and troops to aid the republicans, and Jordan and Saudi Arabia provided the royalists with arms and money.

The civil war finally ended with the establishment of a leftist socialist state in 1969, but there were continued coups and violence.

As a merger of Yemen and South Yemen was nearing implementation in 1978, the presidents of both countries were assassinated and the merger was called off.

The aborted merger resulted in war between the Yemens in 1979. South Yemen received massive Soviet aid and Yemen was supported by Saudi Arabia and the United States. A cease-fire was arranged later that year.

Zaire

Official name: *Republic of Zaire*
Area: *905,562 sq. mi., 2,345,408 sq. km.*
Population: *(1990 est.) 35,330,000*
Capital: *Kinshasa (Pop., 1985 est., 3,000,000)*
Language: *French; Lingala, Kingwana, Kikongo, Tshiluba, other African languages*
Religion: *Christian, Islam, traditional religions*
Currency unit: *Zaire*
National holiday: *Independence Day, June 30*

Congo (Kinshasa), renamed Zaire in 1971, is a country in central Africa bordered on the north by the Central African Republic and Sudan; on the east by Uganda, Rwanda, Burundi, and Tanzania; on the south by Zambia and Angola; and on the west by the Congo and the Cabinda region of Angola. The country was a colony of Belgium until 1960, when it received its independence.

The land. Tropical grasslands and forests are typical of most of Zaire's landscape. The interior of the country is a vast plain with swamps in some places. There are highlands along the eastern border, including Mount Ruwenzori, which has an elevation of about 16,800 feet. There are also highlands in the south.

There are many lakes along Zaire's eastern border, including lakes Albert, Edward, Kivu, Tanganyika, and Mweru.

The Congo River flows through part of northeastern Zaire and along the western border. The wide, navigable lower part of the river drops nearly 1000 feet between the city of Kinshasa and the sea. The Ubangi and Kasai riv-

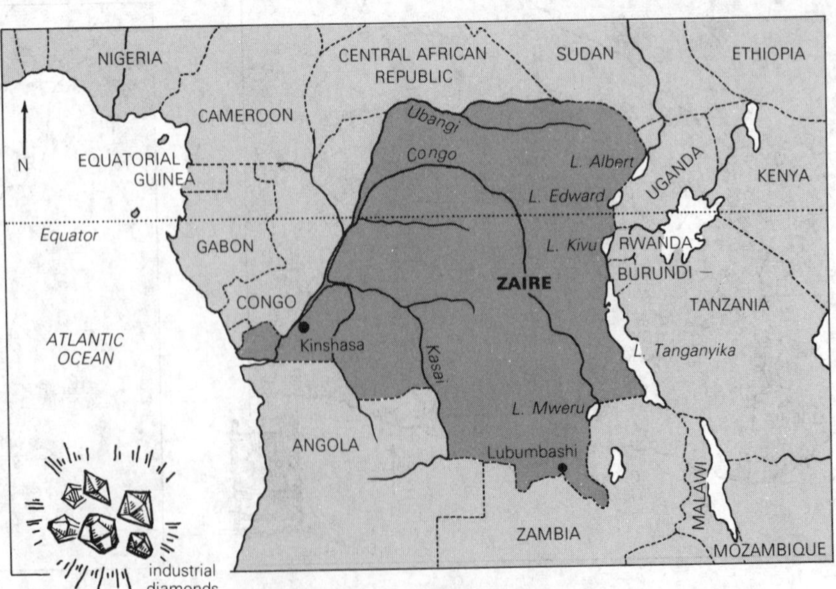

ers are the main tributaries flowing into the middle Congo River. The climate throughout the country is tropical.

The people. Most of Zaire's indigenous population is Bantu-speaking. Many different groups of people, including the Bacongo, Lulua, and the pygmies, live in Zaire. About two-thirds of the people are Christian, a small number are Muslim, and most of the remainder follow traditional tribal religions.

In 1966 Zaire renamed its cities that had Belgian names. Léopoldville, the capital, became Kinshasa, and the important city of Elisabethville was renamed Lubumbashi. Stanleyville became Kisangani.

Economy. Since independence in 1960, the economy of Zaire has been seriously disrupted by political instability and civil wars. The Belgians had developed the country's rich mineral resources and had built railroads to complement river navigation. Most of the technically trained Belgians left during the political disorder following independence.

The mineral riches include copper, which accounts for half of the country's export revenues, and cobalt and industrial diamonds, of which Zaire is the world's largest producer. What little industry there is is engaged chiefly in mineral and agricultural processing, although Zaire manufactures half of the consumer goods required. There are great potential, but so far unexploited, reserves of water, oil, and gas.

Nearly three-quarters of the labor force is occupied by agriculture. Corn, millet and sorghum, peanuts, coffee, and fruits are the main crops.

In 1986 imports cost $872 million while exports earned $1 billion. Western Europe and the United States are Zaire's chief trading partners. The main exports include copper, cobalt, diamonds, tin, palm oil, and coffee. The main imports are foodstuffs, petroleum products, transportation equipment, and textiles.

Government. A constitution promulgated in 1978 provides for a powerful president who is the head of the Political Bureau of the Popular Revolutionary Movement (MPR). He is assisted by a premier. Legislative power is held by the unicameral National Legislative Council, whose 310 members are elected to five-year terms.

Zaire is a member of the United Nations and the Organization of African Unity, and it is an associated state of the European Common Market.

History. Many different tribal peoples have lived in the vast region of the present-day Zaire. Among the earliest inhabitants were the pygmies and the Bacongo peoples. Portuguese sailors reached the region in 1482, but the area remained largely unknown until the late 1800's. Between 1874 and 1877 the British explorer Henry Stanley explored the area. In 1884 Belgium's King Leopold II obtained European recognition of a Congo Free State at the Berlin Conference on African Affairs.

TOM PIX/PETER ARNOLD

COPPER MINE *in Lubumbashi, Katanga (Shaba) province. Katanga tried to secede from Zaire in 1960 but lost the civil war.*

Colonial rule. Between 1885 and 1908 Leopold's agents used unscrupulous methods to secure labor to exploit the Congo's rubber and ivory resources. Mistreatment of the people created an international scandal, and in 1908 Leopold turned over control of the area to the Belgian Parliament.

From then until 1960, large companies controlled the economy, Roman Catholic missionaries with government subsidies controlled education, and Belgian administrators ran the government.

Under Belgian rule there was economic advancement, and a high literacy rate was achieved. But there was little secondary education and no higher education until the founding of Lovanium University in 1954.

The administration encouraged vocational training and the breaking of tribal ties, but would not allow the inhabitants to gain political experience. Early African political expression took the form of national religious sects. After World War II, however, Belgium slowly liberalized its colonial rule.

In 1954 the Bacongo people, led by Joseph Kasavubu, demanded political rights and autonomy from the rest of the country. From then on the tempo of political change greatly accelerated. In 1955 Belgium discussed a plan for citizenship, but in response to growing African pressure, Belgium announced in January, 1960, that independence would be granted June 30.

Independence. The country held elections in the midst of turmoil. Patrice Lumumba, leader of the National Congolese Movement, became the prime minister, and Kasavubu won the next highest position of president.

Lumumba's government faced both a mutiny in the army and the flight of most of the country's European technicians and administrators. The Congo's richest province, Katanga, under the leadership of Moise Tshombe, seceded from the new republic in July, 1960.

Lumumba was overthrown in September, 1960, and by 1963 UN forces had ended Katanga's secession. In 1964 Tshombe, a friend of the United States and Europe, became prime minister despite the objections of many African states, which saw him as a tool of European mining interests.

Joseph Mobutu became president and head of state following a 1965 military coup. Political stability and some economic progress was finally achieved under his long rule, which continues. His attempt in 1974 to "Africanize" the economy left Zaire with a scarcity of capital and skilled labor, and since 1977 a renewal of European participation in the economy has been courted. Recent drops in copper prices have hurt the economy considerably.

In the mid-1970's Zaire tried to help Angolan forces prevent a Soviet–backed leftist takeover of that government. However, leftist forces finally won, and since 1977 the new Angolan government has aided Katanga (now called Shaba) Province rebels in their renewed secession movement. The province is important because of its rich copper fields.

Zambia

Official name: *Republic of Zambia*
Area: *290,586 sq. mi., 752,614 sq. km.*
Population: *(1990 est.) 8,112,000*
Capital: *Lusaka (Pop., 1980, 538,469)*
Language: *English, African languages*
Religion: *Traditional religions, Christian*
Currency unit: *Kwacha*
National holiday: *Independence Day, Oct. 24*

Zambia, in southern Africa, is bordered on the north by Zaire and Tanzania; on the east by Malawi; on the south by Mozambique, Zimbabwe, Botswana, and South-West Africa (Namibia); and on the west by Angola. In 1964 Zambia became independent.

The land. Most of Zambia is occupied by a high plain, with elevations between 3000 and 4000 feet above sea level. In the east are the Muchinga Mountains, with a peak of over 6000 feet. The Abercorn Highlands are in the far north of the country.

The Zambezi River flows along the border with Zimbabwe, and the Luangwa and Kafue rivers, tributaries of the Zambezi, flow through Zambia. Along the Zambezi River is Victoria Falls, where the river plunges more than 300 feet into a deep canyon. Kàriba Lake, formed by the Kariba Dam on the Zambezi River, is one of the largest manmade lakes in the world.

In the northeast is the Chambeshi River, which flows into a swampy region near Lake Bangweulu. Lakes Mweru and Tanganyika lie along the northern border.

Zambia has a subtropical climate. The country receives between 25 and 30 inches of rain a year.

The people. Most of the people in Zambia are Bantu-speaking Africans. About one percent of the population is European. Most Europeans live in the north-central part of the country. There are also some Asians and people of mixed origins.

Economy. Mining accounts for half of the gross national product, while agriculture and manufacturing contribute about ten percent each. About 90 percent of all export revenues come from copper production. North-central Zambia is known as the "Copper Belt." Over half of the country's energy demands (mostly from mining) are met by its abundant domestic waterpower reserves. There is also an oil pipeline from Tanzania. Zinc, lead, and cobalt are mined along with copper.

Zambia's basic food crops are corn, cassava, and millet. Tobacco, peanuts, and cotton are also grown.

Most of Zambia's farms and industries were nationalized by 1975 in an effort to close the gap between white minority prosperity and black majority destitution and poverty; however, the problem continues.

In 1986 imports cost $714 million and exports earned $431 million. The main imports are textiles, petroleum products, iron and steel, and machinery. The major exports are copper, zinc, and tobacco. Most trade is conducted with Britain, West Germany, South Africa, and Japan.

Government. Zambia has a presidential system of government. Executive power is vested in a president who is popularly elected to a five year term. The president appoints a vice president. Legislative power rests with the 135-member National Assembly. Assembly members are popularly elected (except for ten who are appointed to five-year terms).

Zambia is a member of the United Nations, the Organization of African Unity, and the Commonwealth of Nations. It is also an associated state of the European Common Market.

History. Little is known of the early history of Zambia. In the early 1800's, Mulambwa, chief of one Bantu-speaking tribe, the Lozi, built a powerful state in Barotseland, in the northwestern part of the country.

In the 1830's the Lozi state crumbled before the Kololo, a military band composed of different Bantu-speaking clans. In the 1860's, however, the Lozi reestablished their dominance in Barotseland. By the late 1800's, under the Lozi ruler Lewanika, Lozi authority in the region was acknowledged by neighboring peoples.

In the mid-1800's Europeans began to settle in present-day Zambia, and in 1890 Cecil Rhodes's British South Africa Company obtained a monopoly over rights from Lewanika. In 1891 Rhodes divided the region north of the Zambezi River into three protectorates—Nyasaland, Northeastern Rhodesia, and Northwestern Rhodesia (which included Barotseland). In 1911 the company joined Northeastern and Northwestern Rhodesia to form Northern Rhodesia.

Control of the region by the British South Africa Company ended in 1923, and the British government took over the administration of Northern Rhodesia. Southern Rhodesia, however, became self-governing, and white settler governments came to power there. Thus when representatives of the Southern Rhodesian government and the white settlers of Northern Rhodesia, at a meeting in Victoria Falls in 1936, decided to work for the union of the two countries, the Africans of Northern Rhodesia were outraged. Nonetheless, in 1953 Britain established the Federation of Rhodesia and Nyasaland.

Opposition from African nationalists in Northern Rhodesia and Nyasaland led Britain to dissolve the federation in December, 1963. In parliamentary elections held in Rhodesia in January, 1964, the United National Independence Party led by Kenneth Kaunda won a majority of the seats. On October 24, 1964, Northern Rhodesia became the independent nation of Zambia. Kaunda became the first president. He was reelected in 1968, 1973, and 1978.

Kaunda leads black African opposition to white minority rule and the South African apartheid policy of separate societies. He has aligned Zambia, economically, with Tanzania, while accepting aid from communist and democratic nations in order to reduce his economic dependence on South Africa and Zimbabwe (before its 1980 independence). In 1979 there were border clashes with Zimbabwe (formerly Rhodesia).

Kaunda is the leader of a one–party state, but his socialist policies have humanistic overtones and he has made a sincere effort to improve the lives of black Zambians.

Zimbabwe

Official name: *Republic of Zimbabwe*
Area: *150,819 sq. mi., 390,620 sq. km.*
Population: *(1990 est.) 10,482,000*
Capital: *Harare (Salisbury) (Pop., 1989, 700,000)*
Language: *English, African languages*
Religion: *Anglican, Presbyterian, Roman Catholic, traditional religions*
Currency unit: *Pound*
National holiday: *Independence Day, Nov. 11*

Zimbabwe, formerly Rhodesia, had its independence (self-declared in 1965) officially recognized by Britain on April 18, 1980. Zimbabwe is bordered on the north by Zambia; on the east by Mozambique; on the south by South Africa; and on the west by Botswana and South-West Africa (Namibia).

The land. Most of Zimbabwe is occupied by a level plateau that has an elevation of over 3000 feet above sea level. The higher portions of the plateau are in the east. In east-central Zimbabwe are the Inyanga Highlands, with elevations of about 8500 feet.

The only extensive lowlands are in the southeast, near the Limpopo River and its principal tributary, the Shashi. The Zambezi River flows along part of the northern border, and many other rivers flow through the country. Kariba Lake borders northwestern Zimbabwe.

The lowlands are hot and dry, but temperatures on the plateau above 3500 feet are moderate. Rainfall is confined to the period from October to April.

The people. About 95 percent of the people are of African origin, and about five percent are of European background. Most of the Europeans are of British or South African origin.

The Africans are mostly Bantu-speaking, and mainly of the Shona (Mashona) tribe in the east and the Ndebele (Matabele) in the southwest. The Ndebele are related to the Zulu people of South Africa. Many of the Africans are Christians.

The major cities are Harare, the capital, and Bulawayo.

Economy. Zimbabwe's economy is dominated by its white minority. Most natives, living outside the commercial economy, are subsistence farmers. Whites own most farms, businesses, industries, and mines, though many have left since independence.

Despite serious water shortages, Zimbabwe has important agricultural production. The basic crops are corn and grains. The major commercial crops are tobacco and sugar, which are grown mainly on European-owned farms. Cattle and sheep are raised in most parts of the country.

Zimbabwe has rich mineral resources, particularly gold, asbestos, and chronium ore. Nickel has become important in recent years. Oil is in short supply, but industry is more highly developed in Zimbabwe than in most African countries. Consumer goods are the most significant industrial products.

Between 1965 and 1980 Britain, supported by a United Nations request, called for economic sanctions against Rhodesia (now Zimbabwe) because of its illegally declared independence. The embargo seriously damaged the nation's commerce. Tobacco and minerals are Zimbabwe's main exports, while machinery, iron and steel products, and textiles are its main imports.

Government. According to its constitution of 1980, Zimbabwe is ruled by a prime minister. There is also an elected president and a bicameral Parliament. The 100-member House of Assembly has 80 blacks and 20 whites, all elected to five-year terms. The 40 members of the Senate are elected by representative factions.

History. In about 1000 A.D. Bantu–speaking tribes from central Africa drove off the aboriginal Bushmen living in the region of present-day Zimbabwe. They established trade relations with Arabs of the eastern coast of Africa and, through them, with Indian sea traders.

The Bantu-speaking people founded the Zimbabwe civilization, which left imposing stone ruins. In the 1400's another Bantu-speaking people, the Shona, expelled or absorbed their predecessors and built the Monomotapa empire, which was based on gold mining.

In the 1600's Portuguese from Mozambique ravaged the African states in the Zambezi valley, and the Monomotapa empire collapsed. The Portuguese imposed their overlordship on the Shona, and destroyed the trade between Africa and India. By the 1800's the power of the Portuguese had declined, and in the early 1800's the Matabele subjugated the Shona.

British control. Matabeleland lay in the path of British expansion northward from Cape Colony in South Africa, and in 1888 the Matabele king accepted British protection over the area. He also granted to Cecil Rhodes, for whom Rhodesia was named, a monopoly over mining rights for his British South Africa Company. Rhodes then organized the white occupation of the territory. The Matabele rebelled in 1893 but were defeated.

The company administered Southern Rhodesia until 1923, when the white settlers voted for autonomy under British rule and Southern Rhodesia became a Crown colony.

In 1953 Britain established the Federation of Rhodesia and Nyasaland, but on December 31, 1963, the federation was dissolved. Northern Rhodesia and Nyasaland became independent, and Southern Rhodesia remained under British control as the self-governing colony of Rhodesia.

Independence. The Rhodesian government pressed for independence, but Britain refused, insisting on assurances of adequate representation for the country's African majority. Despite Britain's position, Prime Minister Ian Smith declared Rhodesia independent on November 11, 1965. Britain responded by leading an international economic embargo against the country. The discord led to a civil war with guerrilla activity (aided by Mozambique and Zambia) aimed at overthrowing Smith's government and establishing a nationalist and multiracial one in its place.

Elections to a new government, under the aegis of Britain, were finally held in 1979, and the radical nationalist advocate, Robert Mugabe, was elected prime minister. He promised that his regime would work to mend old wounds and would promote equitable representation of all races.

Britain accepted Zimbabwe's independence in 1980 and the new nation is now trying to normalize economic, international, and domestic affairs.

BIRTH OF A NEW NATION. *Prime Minister Muzorewa of Zimbabwe's transitional government* (left), *and Ian Smith, white supremacy leader.*

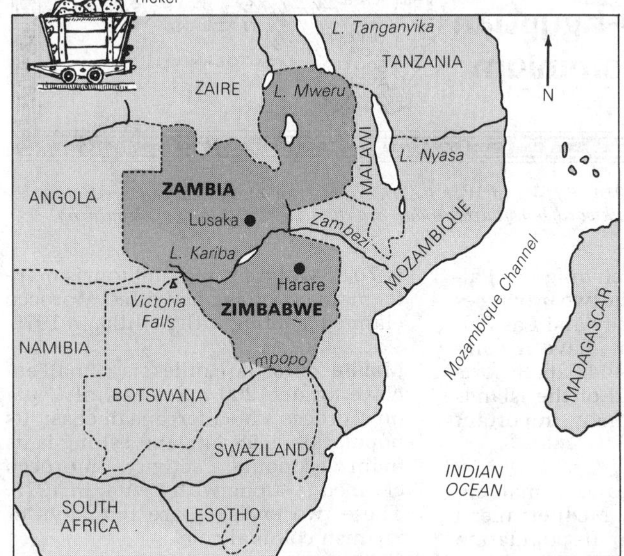

UPI

DEPENDENCIES IN AFRICA

French Dependency

Mayotte (144 square miles), a tiny island that was formerly part of the Comoros, has a population of 57,363. Located just northwest of Madagascar, it chose (by popular referendum) to become a department of France in 1976, when the rest of the Comoros became independent.

Norwegian Dependency

Bouvet Island (23 square miles), an uninhabited volcanic island in the South Atlantic Ocean, lies between the southern tip of South Africa and Antarctica. There is some seal hunting here.

Portuguese Dependency

The Madeira Islands (307 square miles) are located 360 miles northwest of Morocco, in the Atlantic Ocean. They consist of two island groups, which have a total population of 270,000. The Madeiras were offered autonomy in 1976, but they are still a Portuguese dependency, though the islands have their own political and administrative organization and a Regional Assembly. The economy is largely based on banana cultivation, and on the production of sugar and wine. The fishing and tourist industries are also important.

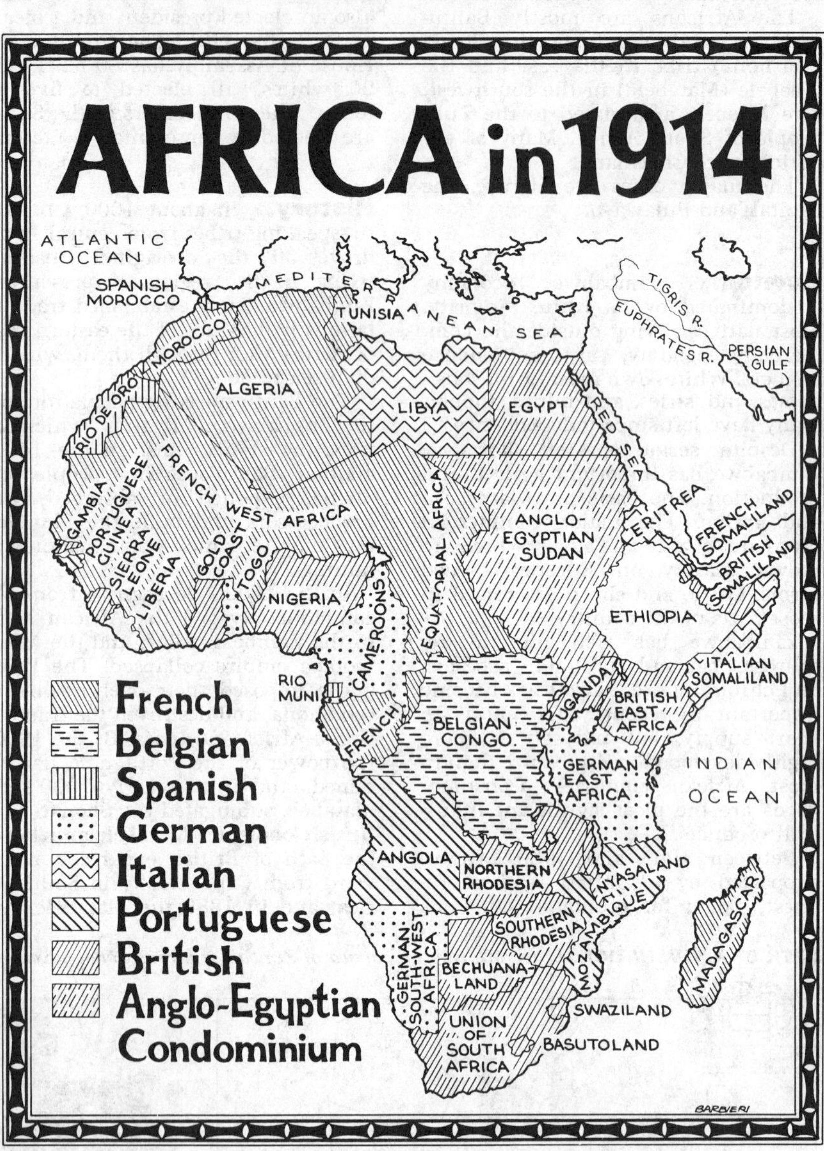

COLONIAL AFRICA *in 1914. By World War I Africa had been mostly carved up among the colonial powers. Many awkward boundaries today are the result of colonial bargaining.*

Spanish Dependencies

The Canary Islands (2,807 square miles), in the Atlantic Ocean off the west coast of Morocco, form two provinces of Spain. Tenerife is the most important of this group of islands. There are several significant commercial ports on the islands including Las Palmas and Santa Cruz. The two provinces —Santa Cruz de Tenerife and Las Palmas de Gran Canaria—have a combined population of 1,444,626. Resorts and tourism on several of the islands are becoming increasingly important to the economy.

Ceuta (7.5 square miles) is a small enclave on Morocco's Mediterranean coast opposite Gibraltar. Its population is 70,864, and fishing and tourism are its main economic activities. Morocco claimed it, along with Melilla, in 1975.

Melilla (4.8 square miles) is a small enclave located 200 miles east of Ceuta on Morocco's Mediterranean coast. Its population is 58,449, and fishing is its main economic activity. Morocco claimed it, along with Ceuta, in 1975. These two enclaves are remnants of Spanish colonial rule.

CITIES OF THE MIDDLE EAST AND AFRICA

Abadan, in southwestern Iran, situated on the northern end of Abadan Island at the head of the Persian Gulf. Abadan is a major oil refining and shipping center of the Middle East. Pipelines link the city with oil fields to the north. Pop., 296,081.

Abidjan, the capital of the Ivory Coast. The city is located on the Ebrie Lagoon, which is connected to the Gulf of Guinea by the Vridi Canal. Abidjan has modern port facilities and is the terminus of a highway network and a railroad from Ouagadougou, in neighboring Upper Volta. Pop., 2,100,000.

Abu Dhabi, city on the Persian Gulf, temporary capital of the United Arab Emirates. Oil production is its chief industry. Pop., 420,000.

Accra, the capital of Ghana. The city lies on the Gulf of Guinea and is a seaport. Accra has an international airport and is linked by railroad to the agricultural districts of Ghana's interior. The University of Ghana is in Accra. Pop., 1,450,000.

Addis Ababa, the capital and largest city of Ethiopia. It is situated in a hilly region in the central part of the country. Addis Ababa is the country's chief commercial, industrial, and educational center. Its industries produce cement, textiles, food, processed tobacco, beverages, and footwear. Ethiopia's first university, the National University, was founded at Addis Ababa in 1961. Pop., 2,000,000.

Aden, the capital and chief port of the Democratic Republic of Yemen, located on the Gulf of Aden. Situated along the important shipping lane between the Mediterranean Sea and the Indian Ocean, Aden is a major trading center. Light industries produce textiles, cigarettes, soap, and metal utensils. Pop., 250,000.

Aleppo, in northwestern Syria, an important trading center that is connected by rail with major cities in Turkey and Iraq. There is some light manufacturing; local factories produce cement, carpets, textiles, and vegetable oils. Pop., 639,428.

Alexandria, situated west of the Rosetta mouth of the Nile River on the Mediterranean Sea, the principal seaport and second largest city of Egypt. The city has an eastern and a western harbor, but the western harbor is deeper and handles most maritime traffic. Raw cotton and farm produce are the main exports.

Alexandria was founded by Alexander the Great in 332 B.C. It became an important port and intellectual center, and was famous for its lighthouse, which was one of the seven wonders of the ancient world, its library, and its school of medicine. Pop., 2,259,000.

Algiers, the capital of Algeria, the major Mediterranean port on the northwest coast of Africa. The city's port handles such exports as wool, fruit and vegetables, and wine, most of which are sent to France. Local industries produce cement, metal products, chemicals, and paper. Tourism is also important. Pop., metro. area, 2,400,000.

Amman, the capital of Jordan, in the northwestern part of the country, about 25 miles (40 km.) northeast of the Dead Sea. Amman is Jordan's chief industrial and commercial center and the hub of a rail and highway network. Industries include food processing and the manufacture of textiles, leather goods, cement, and tiles. Pop., 800,000.

Ankara, the capital and second largest city of Turkey, located on the central Anatolian plateau on the Ankara River. The city is an important commercial and industrial center.

Ankara markets and processes agricultural products of the surrounding region and is famous for the production of Angora goat wool, or mohair. Other manufactures include cement, textiles, leather goods, and tile. Pop., 3,300,000.

Antananarivo, formerly Tananarive, the capital of Madagascar, situated on the east-central part of Madagascar Island. The city is an administrative, agricultural, and commercial center; its industries include food products, textiles, and cigarettes. Pop., 703,000.

Aswan, the capital of Aswan Governorate in Egypt, located on the east bank of the Nile River, about 550 miles (886 km.) south of Cairo. The city is the site of the Aswan and Aswan High dams. Aswan's dry, mild climate makes it a popular tourist resort during the winter months. New industries include a fertilizer plant and copper and steel mills. Pop., 246,000.

Baghdad, the capital and largest city of Iraq, located on both banks of the Tigris River, in the east-central part of the country. The city is the intellectual, commercial, and industrial center of Iraq. The chief industry is oil refining, but factories manufacture a variety of products, including shoes, clothing, and cement. Pop., 3,800,000.

Bamako, the capital of Mali, situated on the Niger River, in the southwestern part of the country. It serves as the trade center for the surrounding area and exports peanuts, cotton, and tobacco. Bamako is connected to Dakar in Senegal by rail and has an international airport. Pop., 862,600.

Bangui, the capital of the Central African Republic, located on the Ubangi River, near the Zaire border. The city is the country's major port and handles almost all its foreign trade. Bangui is linked by road with Chad, Cameroon, and Sudan, and has an international airport. Local industry consists of food processing and the manufacture of textiles, shoes, and soap. Pop., 300,000.

Banjul, formerly Bathurst, seaport and capital of Gambia, located on St. Mary's Island at the mouth of the Gambia River. It is the commercial and transportation center of Gambia, and exports peanuts, beeswax, and hides. Peanut processing is the chief industry. Pop., 45,604.

Beirut, the capital of Lebanon, located on the eastern shore of the Mediterranean Sea, at the foot of the Lebanon Mountains. Long an important center for east-west trade, Beirut is a busy port and transportation center. It lies on the Cairo-Istanbul-Baghdad railway, is the hub of a good road network, and has an international airport. Beirut is also a banking and educational center. Pop., 702,000.

Bengasi, or Benghazi, a seaport of Libya, situated on the shore of the Gulf of Sidra on the Mediterranean Sea. The city is a transportation and administrative center. Local industries include brewing, food processing, and the manufacture of bricks and cement. Pop., 282,192.

Bethlehem, in western Jordan, located about five miles (eight km.) southwest of Jerusalem. It is part of the West Bank, which has been occupied by Israel since 1967. Bethlehem was the birthplace of Jesus and is mentioned often in the Bible. The Church of the Nativity, built by Emperor Constantine in 330 A.D., occupies the reputed site of the stable where Jesus was born. The major business in Bethlehem is the sale of souvenirs to tourists and pilgrims. Pop., 27,000.

Bissau, on the west coast of Africa, the capital and chief port of Guinea-Bissau. The major exports are peanuts and copra. The city is linked by rivers to communities in the interior and has an airport. Pop., 125,000.

Brazzaville, the capital and largest city of the Congo, on the Zaire River directly opposite Kinshasa. Brazzaville is an important river port and the country's commercial and educational center. Major industries include food processing and the manufacture of textiles, construction materials, and matches. Pop., 600,000.

Bujumbura, the capital of Burundi, in east-central Africa, located at the northern end of Lake Tanganyika. The city, which was formerly called Usumbura, is an important lake port and trade center for agricultural produce from the surrounding region. Pop., 272,600.

Cairo, the capital of Egypt and the largest city in Africa, on the Nile River, at the head of the Nile Delta. It is an important transportation, commercial, and industrial center. Manufactures include metals, plastics, food products, textiles, and chemicals. Al-Ahzar University, founded in 970 A.D., is the world's oldest and largest center of Islamic scholarship. Cairo has many museums, mosques, and universities. Pop., 6,325,000.

Cape Town, the legislative capital of the Republic of South Africa and the capital of Cape Province. Cape Town is located on the southwestern shore of Table Bay, near the southern tip of Africa. It is an important manufacturing center whose industries include textiles, chemicals, oil refining, fertilizers, food processing, and ship repair. It is a very busy port. Exports include diamonds, fruit, gold, and other minerals. Pop., 213,830.

Casablanca, the largest city in Morocco, on the Atlantic coast of North Africa. Possessing one of the world's largest artificial ports, Casablanca handles most of Morocco's passenger traffic and foreign trade. Phosphates are the city's chief export. Industries include textiles, cement, and glass manufacture. Pop., 1,506,373.

Conakry, the capital of Guinea, on the island of Tombo. Conakry is Guinea's largest city, chief port, and commercial and industrial center. Its deep-water harbor is one of West Africa's finest. Exports include bauxite and iron ore. Pop., 600,000.

Dakar, the capital and chief seaport of Senegal, located on the Cape Verde Peninsula on Africa's west coast. The city, which has a strategic location and an excellent harbor, is a transportation center with important air, rail, and shipping facilities.

Dakar's diversified industries produce canned fish, refined sugar, chocolate, peanut oil, and textiles. The city is the seat of the University of Dakar, the Pasteur Institute, and also the Institut Francais d'Afrique Noire. Pop., 850,000.

DRAMATIC SCENERY OF CAPE TOWN *in South Africa, the legislative capital of the country.*

RUSSELL A. THOMPSON/TAURUS PHOTOS

Damascus, the capital and largest city of Syria, situated in the southwestern part of the country on the Barada River. The city is in an oasis that has been continuously inhabited since prehistoric times. Modern Damascus is a major Middle Eastern administrative, communications, commercial, and industrial center. Its products include cement, glass, textiles, and sugar.

Damascus was a noted marketplace on caravan routes during ancient and medieval times. The city retains its ancient citadel, bazaars, Roman gates, and historic churches. It is the home of the University of Damascus. Pop., 2,800,000.

Dar es Salaam, the former capital of Tanzania, a major seaport of East Africa. Its harbor is on a bay, linked by a narrow channel to the Indian Ocean. The city is an administrative, transportation, and economic center. Among its exports are coffee, sisal, cotton, gold, diamonds, and tin. Dar es Salaam's industries produce textiles, cement, pharmaceuticals, and processed foods. Pop., 870,020.

Djibouti, the capital of Djibouti and an East African port, located on the Gulf of Tadjoura. Djibouti is the terminal of a railroad that originates in Addis Ababa, Ethiopia; its exports are mainly Ethiopian products. They include coffee, hides and skins, and oilseeds. Pop., 200,000.

Doha, the capital and chief port of Qatar, located on the east side of the Qatar peninsula on the Persian Gulf. Since the discovery of oil in Qatar in the 1940's, Doha has become an important commercial center. Oil is its chief export. Pop., 215,000.

Durban, a major seaport and tourist resort on the east coast of South Africa. The city, which lies on Natal Bay in the Indian Ocean, has a subtropical climate and excellent beaches. Its chief exports are coal, manganese, and other minerals. Durban's industries produce machinery, furniture, textiles, glass, paper, and processed foods. Pop., 843,327.

Freetown, the capital and chief port of Sierra Leone. It is located on the estuary of the Sierra Leone River and has an excellent natural harbor. Freetown is the transportation and commercial center of Sierra Leone. Exports include palm oil and palm kernels, cocoa, coffee, and ginger. Pop., 470,000.

Gaborone, the capital of Botswana, primarily an administrative and cultural center. It has a national museum and art gallery. Pop., 175,000.

Giza, or Al Jizah, on the west bank of the Nile, near Cairo, Egypt. The city is a trade and manufacturing center. Its manufactures include cotton textiles, footwear, and cigarettes. It is also a resort center, and the great pyramids and the Sphinx lie five miles (eight km.) to the west. It is the seat of Egypt's motion-picture industry and of Cairo University. Pop., 1,246,713.

Haifa, Israel's major port and an important industrial center. The city is situated in northern Israel, at the foot of Mt. Carmel, on the Bay of Haifa in the Mediterranean Sea. Among its many industries are flour and textile mills, foundries, cement works, and an oil refinery. The Haifa Institute of Technology is located in the city. Pop., 227,800.

Isfahan, a city in central Iran, about 200 miles (320 km.) south of Teheran, located on the Zaindeh River. The city is famous for its magnificent architecture, particularly its mosques, which are decorated with brilliantly colored tile. Most of the city's finest buildings were constructed during the reign of Shah Abbas the Great (1586–1628). Isfahan is the center of the Iranian textile industry and is known for its metalwork. Pop., 671,825.

Istanbul, the largest city in Turkey, located on the western, or European bank of the Bosporus, near its entrance to the Sea of Marmara. One of the Mediterranean's busiest ports, Istanbul is Turkey's principal transportation, commercial, and industrial center. Its manufactures include processed foods, tobacco, leather goods, cement, glass, and soap.

The city was the capital of the Byzantine and Ottoman empires and has many historic buildings. The most famous of these is Hagia Sophia, a sixth-century church that is now a museum, whose dome dominates the city. The city was formerly called Constantinople and, in ancient times, Byzantium. Pop., 2,132,407.

Izmir, a seaport in western Turkey, located at the southern end of the Gulf of Izmir on the Aegean Sea. Formerly called Smyrna, the city is Turkey's second largest port and a principal transportation center. Izmir's industries concentrate on processing the agricultural products shipped from its port. Pop., 520,838.

Jerusalem, one of the great religious centers of the world, a holy city of Jews, Christians, and Muslims, and the capital of Israel. Jerusalem is located in the Judean Hills of central Palestine, about 35 miles (56 km.) from the Mediterranean Sea and about 13 miles (21 km.) west of the north end of the Dead Sea.

The Old City of Jerusalem, which was occupied by Jordan in 1948, contains most of the holy places, while the New City is the religious, economic, and administrative center of the State of Israel. During the brief Arab–Israeli war of June, 1967, Israeli troops captured the Old City, which has been integrated with the Israeli sector. Pop., 468,000.

Jidda, or Juddah in Saudi Arabia, a port on the Red Sea about 45 miles (72 km.) west of Mecca. Jidda, a walled city, is an import center and the chief port for pilgrims to Mecca. Pop., 561,104.

Johannesburg, the largest city in the Republic of South Africa, in southern Transvaal Province, about 30 miles (48 km.) southwest of Pretoria. Johannesburg is situated on a plateau 5750 feet (1753 m) above sea level. It is the industrial and commercial center of South Africa. Gold mining is the chief industry; manufactures include cut diamonds, chemicals, plastics, and paper products. Pop., 1,432,643.

Kampala, the capital of Uganda, situated in east-central Africa, near the equator. The city is a trade and transportation center for the surrounding region, which produces coffee, tea, sugar cane, cotton, tobacco, and livestock. The city also has small industries. It is the seat of Makerere University. Pop., 592,200.

Khartoum, the capital of Sudan, in northern Africa, situated near the junction of the White Nile and the Blue Nile. Khartoum is the communications, commercial, financial, and educational center of Sudan. It contains modern stores and boulevards, as well as a bazaar and several mosques and churches. Pop., 476,218.

Kigali, the capital of Rwanda, situated about 135 miles (218 km.) south of the equator in central Africa. It lies in a poor agricultural area; iron and tin are mined nearby. Pop., 156,650.

Kimberley, a city in central South Africa, one of the major diamond centers of the world. Founded after the discovery of diamonds in 1870, the city's industries include mining, cutting, and polishing diamonds. It is a commercial and industrial center. Pop., 103,789.

Kinshasa, formerly Léopoldville, the capital and largest city of Zaire, situated in west-central Africa on the Zaire (Congo) River. Kinshasa is the cultural, administrative, financial, commercial, and transportation center of the country. Its industries manufacture chemicals, textiles, processed foods, mineral oils, and cement. It is the seat of Lovanium University. Pop., 3,000,000.

Kirkuk, in northeastern Iraq, 145 miles (230 km.) north of Baghdad. The city is the oil center of the country and a market for grain, fruit, cotton, and sheep raised in the surrounding area. Kirkuk is connected by oil pipeline with Baniyas, Syria, and Tripoli, Lebanon. Pop., 290,000.

Kuwait, the capital of Kuwait and a port, located at the northwestern end of the Persian Gulf. The main export is oil. Pearls and hides are also exported. Pop., 78,116.

Lagos, the capital and major port of Nigeria, located on the mainland and

MODERN CITY OF JIDDA. *Saudi Arabia's Red Sea port and entrance city to inland Mecca.*

ALAIN NOGUES/SYGMA

on islands in Lagos Lagoon, off the Gulf of Guinea. Its modern harbor handles much trade. Its manufactures include textiles, chemicals, metal products, and furniture. Lagos is connected by road and rail to other Nigerian cities and is served by an international airport. Pop. 1,097,000.

Libreville, capital of Gabon, located 30 miles (48 km.) north of the equator on the Atlantic Ocean. It is Gabon's largest city and a major port. Hardwoods are exported. Pop., 210,000.

Lilongwe, capital of Malawi, situated 50 miles (80 km.) west of Lake Nyasa, in southeast Africa. It lies in a fertile agricultural area and is an administrative and commercial center. Pop., 175,000.

Lomé, the capital and major seaport of Togo, located on the Gulf of Guinea. The city is the commercial and industrial center of the country. It exports phosphate, cacao, coffee, copra, timber, and palm oil. Lomé is connected by rail with the cities of the interior. Pop., 400,000.

Luanda, a seaport on the west-central coast of Africa, capital of Angola. The city is Angola's major industrial center. It produces soap, tobacco, and plastics. There is also a large oil refinery. Luanda's chief exports are coffee, sugar, cotton, fish, and manganese. It is linked to Malange and Casengo in the interior by rail and is served by an airport. Pop., 1,300,000.

Lusaka, the capital of Zambia, located in the south-central part of the country. The city lies in an agricultural region and is an administrative and commercial center. Lusaka is the hub of a road and rail network that links it to Zaire, Tanzania, and Malawi. Pop., 538,469.

Malabo, formerly Santa Isabel, the capital of Equatorial Guinea, located on the island of Bioko (Macias Nguema) off the west-central coast of Africa. It is a seaport that exports cacao and coffee raised on local plantations. Pop., 38,000.

Manama, the capital and principal city of the sheikdom of Bahrain, situated on the northern coast of Bahrain Island, on the Persian Gulf. Refining and exporting petroleum are the port city's main industries; there is also some boat building and fishing. Pop., 150,000.

Maputo, formerly Lourenço Marques, the capital and largest city of Mozambique, located on an inlet of the Indian Ocean, near the country's southern border. It is the country's administrative, communications, and commercial center. Its modern port exports coal, cotton, ores, sugar, and hardwoods. Its chief manufactures are cement, pottery, food products, shoes, and rubber. Pop., 882,800.

Marrakesh, in west-central Morocco, on the western slopes of the Grand Atlas Mountains in North Africa. Marrakesh is one of the largest cities of Morocco and a major Muslim religious center. Manufactures include wool, flour, carpets and leather goods. Pop., 1978, 330,400.

Maseru, the capital of Lesotho, in southern Africa. The city is located near the western border with the Republic of South Africa. Maseru is the nation's transportation and commercial center. Pop., 109,382.

Mashhad, or Meshed, in northeastern Iran, near the border with the Soviet Union, about 440 miles (708 km.) east of Teheran, the capital. Mashhad is an important holy city, with a Shiite shrine. It is also a leading commercial and transportation center. Manufactures include cotton, wool, carpets, processed foods, pharmaceuticals, and leather. Pop., 670,180.

Mbabane, the capital and chief town of Swaziland, a former British protectorate in southeastern Africa. Mbabane is located about 95 miles (153 km.) southwest of Maputo, capital of Mozambique, with which it is linked by rail. Exports from Mbabane include iron ore and asbestos. Pop., 40,000.

Mecca, the chief holy city of the Muslim world. It is located in a valley in west-central Saudi Arabia, east of Jidda, its port on the Red Sea. Mecca is the birthplace of Muhammad. It contains the Kaaba, chief shrine of Islam, which is visited by many thousands of pilgrims each year. The city is also the capital of the province of Hejaz and a commercial center. Pop., 366,801.

Medina, in west-central Saudi Arabia, about 100 miles (160 km.) from the Red Sea coast. It is second only to Mecca as a Muslim holy city. The Great Mosque in Medina contains the tomb of Muhammad; it is visited annually by many thousands of pilgrims. The city is located in a fertile oasis and is a market center for agricultural products. Pop., 198,186.

Mogadishu, the capital and chief port of Somalia, in eastern Africa. It lies on the Indian Ocean, about 700 miles (1130 km.) southeast of Addis Ababa, the capital of Ethiopia. Mogadishu exports bananas and also hides. Pop., 1,000,000.

Mombasa, the chief port of Kenya, off the coast of eastern Africa. Mombasa is located on a small island in the Indian Ocean and is linked to the mainland by a causeway, a bridge, and ferries. The city exports coffee, cotton, tea, sugar, and other agricultural products. Pop., 340,000.

RUSSELL A. THOMPSON/TAURUS PHOTOS

NAIROBI, *prosperous capital of Kenya, a modern city of over 800,000 people.*

Monrovia, the capital, largest city, and chief port of Liberia in West Africa. Monrovia is located on Cape Montserrado, near the mouth of the Saint Paul River, on the Atlantic Ocean. The city is the commercial, educational, and cultural center of Liberia. Exports include rubber, iron ore, gold, and coffee. The city was named for U.S. President James Monroe. Pop., 400,000.

Moroni, the capital of the Comoros Islands, at the north entrance to the Mozambique Channel. Moroni is located on the east coast of Grande Comore Island. It is on the largest of the islands and is the chief port. Pop., 18,000.

Mosul, in Iraq, on the west bank of the Tigris River, about 220 miles (350 km.) northwest of Baghdad, the capital. Mosul is situated in an oil-producing region. The ruins of ancient Nineveh, the capital of Assyria, are across the river. Pop., 508,500.

Muscat, capital of Oman, a country in the southeastern part of the Arabian Peninsula. The city is located on Muscat Bay, an arm of the Gulf of Oman, at the entrance to the Persian Gulf. Pop., 70,000.

Nairobi, the capital and largest city of Kenya. It is the focus of several rail lines that carry coffee, cotton, tea, and sisal from parts of Kenya and Uganda to the Indian Ocean port of Mombasa. Principal industries include meat packing, flour milling, and the manufacture of furniture, soap, chemicals, foodstuffs, and paper products. Pop., 1,100,000.

Nazareth, an ancient town of northern Israel, southwest of the Sea of Galilee. It was the home of Mary and Joseph during the boyhood of Jesus. Tourism is the major industry, but Nazareth is also a trade center for an agricultural region. Pop., 34,000.

Ndjamena, formerly Fort-Lamy, the capital of Chad, located about 70 miles (112 km.) south of Lake Chad. It is the largest city and chief transportation, industrial and commercial center of Chad. Pop., 551,700.

Niamey, the capital of Niger. An inland port on the Niger River, it is a market center for the agricultural products of the region. Pop., 450,000.

Nicosia, the capital of Cyprus, an island in the eastern Mediterranean Sea near Turkey. It is a commercial center of the Messaori Plain, which produces wheat, wine, olive oil, almonds, citrus fruits, and livestock. Textiles, leather, machine tools, and cigarettes are manufactured there. Pop., 163,700.

Nouakchott, capital of Mauritania. Lying four miles from the Atlantic Ocean, it is a market center with limited port facilities. Pop., 400,000.

Ouagadougou, the capital and leading city of Upper Volta. It is connected by rail with Abidjan, an Atlantic port on the Ivory Coast. Ouagadougou is the trade center for the surrounding agricultural region. Its main exports are peanuts, cotton, and handicrafts. Pop., 300,000.

Port Louis, the capital and chief port of Mauritius, an island in the Indian Ocean about 500 miles (800 km.) east of Madagascar. Sugar, the main crop and export of Mauritius, is shipped from Port Louis. Pop., 138,482.

Porto-Novo, the capital of Benin, situated on the southern coast of western Africa, on the Gulf of Guinea. Porto-Novo is a seaport that exports palm products and cotton. Pop., 150,000.

Port Said, a port in northeastern Egypt, situated at the northern end of the Suez Canal. It lies on a narrow strip of land between the Mediterranean Sea and Lake Manzala. Port Said is primarily a fueling stop for ships passing through the canal, although there is some industry. Pop., 342,000.

Praia, the capital of Cape Verde, a group of islands that lie in the Atlantic Ocean, about 500 miles (800 km.) west of Africa. Praia, situated on São Tiago Island, is a seaport that exports citrus fruits, sugar cane, coffee, and castor beans. Pop., 25,000.

Pretoria, the administrative capital of South Africa and the capital of Transvaal Province, situated on the Apies River about 34 miles (55 km.) northeast of Johannesburg. Pretoria is a transportation, industrial, and political center, and the seat of two universities. Its manufactures include steel, chemicals, ceramics, glassware, processed foods, and tobacco. Pop., 528,407.

Qom, or Qum, in north-central Iran, 75 miles (120 km.) southwest of Teheran. It is a transportation and industrial center, and its manufactures include textiles, pottery, glass, and footwear. The city has many mosques and is a major Shiite religious center that attracts thousands of pilgrims. Pop., 246,831.

Rabat, the capital of Morocco, situated on the south bank of the Bou Regneg, near its mouth on the Atlantic Ocean. Local handicraft industries produce leather goods, baskets, tapestries, and embroidered cloth. The city is the site of Mohammed V University. Pop., 591,000.

Riyadh, the capital of Saudi Arabia, located in the east-central part of the country on the Nejd Plateau. Riyadh is the commercial and educational center of the kingdom and serves as a trade center for the dates, vegetables, and grain produced in the surrounding area. After the discovery of huge deposits of oil, the city was rapidly expanded and modernized. Pop., 1,500,000.

Salisbury, or Harare, the capital of Zimbabwe, located in the northeastern part of the country. Surrounded by a rich gold-mining region, it is a transportation and commercial center for southeastern Africa. It has steel and textile mills, and tobacco processing is a major industry. Pop., 700,000.

Sana, the capital of the Yemen Arab Republic, located in a high mountain valley in southwestern Arabia. It lies in the center of a rich, irrigated, agricultural region that produces fruits and coffee. It is also the cultural and commercial center for the area. Pop., 510,000.

São Tomé, capital and port city of São Tomé and Principe. It lies on the island of São Tomé in the Gulf of Guinea. It processes and exports cacao, coffee, and coconuts raised on the island. Pop., 34,997.

Shiraz, capital of Fars Province, in southwestern Iran. It is a commercial center for fruits, silk, and tobacco grown in the surrounding region, and it produces chemicals, cement, carpets, and textiles. Founded in the 600's, it served as the country's capital several times before the 1900's. It was a center for Persian culture and learning. Pop., 414,408.

Suez, a seaport in northeastern Egypt, situated at the southern end of the Suez Canal, at the head of the Gulf of Suez. The port is a refueling station with extensive port facilities and a center for petroleum trade. The city has a large oil refinery and paper and fertilizer plants. Pop., 368,000.

Tabriz, a city in northwestern Iran, situated near the border with the Soviet Union. Tabriz is a commercial center for an area that produces rice, tobacco, and fruits. Its manufactures include rugs, leather goods, and cotton thread. Pop., 598,576.

Teheran, or Tehran, the capital of Iran, formerly called Persia, situated in the north, about 70 miles (110 km.) from the Caspian Sea. The city is the cultural, industrial, and transportation center of Iran. Manufactures include cotton, glass, metal products, construction materials, and automobile parts. Pop., 8,719,480.

Tel Aviv-Jaffa, a port in Israel, situated on the Mediterranean Sea. The city which includes the ancient port of Yafo (Jaffa), is Israel's industrial and commercial center. Its industries include woodworking, textile milling, food processing, and the manufacture of chemicals and tobacco products. Tel Aviv supports several theaters, an orchestra, and a university. Pop., 348,100.

Tripoli, the capital of Libya, situated in northwestern Libya on the Mediterranean Sea. The city is a transportation and trading center for an agricultural region. Its industries produce textiles, tobacco products, and salt. Pop., 858,000.

Tunis, the capital of Tunisia, situated in the northeastern part of the country on the Lake of Tunis. Tunis is connected to the Mediterranean Sea by a canal that ends at the subsidiary port, Halq al Wadi. The city is the major commercial, industrial, and transportation center of the country. Its products include processed foods, textiles, carpets, and olive oil. Pop., 1,700,000.

Victoria, seaport and capital of Seychelles, on an archipelago in the Indian Ocean. The city lies on Mahe Island and exports the island's cinnamon, fish, and coconut products. Pop., 30,000.

Windhoek, the capital of Namibia, or South-West Africa. It is located about 250 miles (400 km.) east of Walvis Bay. Windhoek is Namibia's administrative, economic, and transportation center and is linked by railroad to South Africa. It ships Persian lamb skins and produces meat, clothing, and bone meal. Pop., 61,260.

Yaoundé, the capital of Cameroon in western Africa. It is located in the west-central part of the country, about 130 miles (210 km.) east of Dauala, its port on the Atlantic Ocean. Yaoundé is Cameroon's commercial and educational center. It is also a transportation center and market for the region's coffee, cacao, copra, and sugar cane. Pop., 800,000.

GLOSSARY OF THE MIDDLE EAST AND AFRICA

Abbasids, the second and most renowned Islamic dynasty (750–1258 A.D.). Islamic civilization reached its zenith during the first 300 years of Abbasid rule, when there was a cultural and scientific renaissance.

In 1055 the Seljuk Turks captured Baghdad—the Abbasid capital. The final destruction of the Abbasid dynasty in Baghdad occurred in 1258, when Mongol forces sacked the city and murdered the last Abbasid caliph.

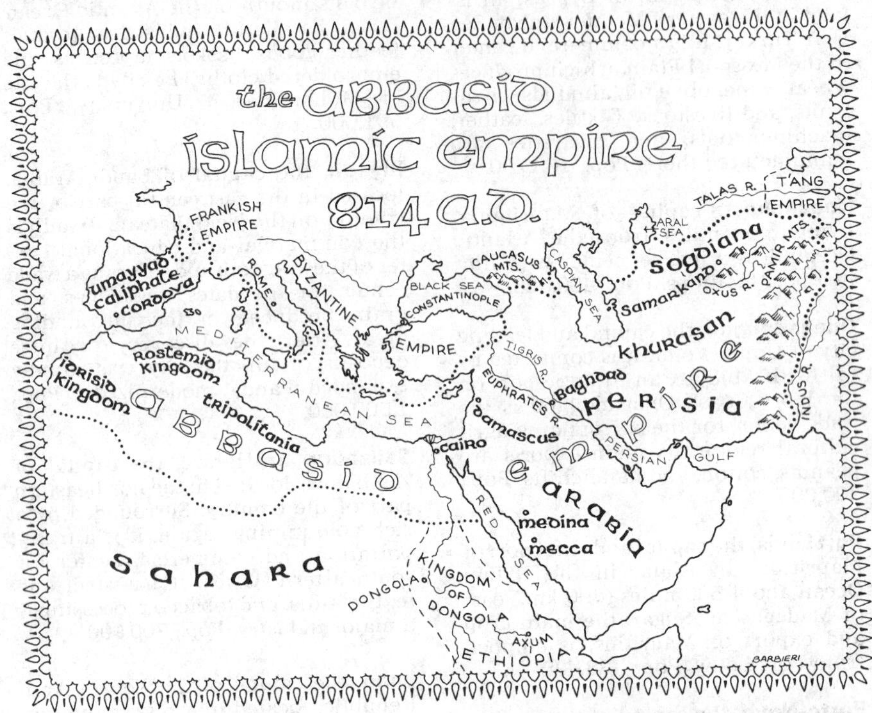

Aden, Gulf of, an arm of the Indian Ocean, bounded on the north by Arabia and on the south by Africa's Somali coast. The gulf is 500 miles (885 km.) long and connects with the Red Sea to the west through the Bab al Mandeb Strait.

Apartheid, an Afrikaans word meaning "apartness" or "separateness." It is used to describe the South African government's policy of rigid separation of the races and plans for their separate development.

The policy has been enacted into a series of far-reaching laws governing the social, economic, political, and educational affairs of South Africa's people. The laws recognize four groups: the whites; the "Bantu", or black Africans; the "Coloreds," of mixed racial origin; and the Asians, predominantly of Indian origin.

Foes of apartheid charge that the policy is meant to ensure the continued domination of South Africa's white minority over the country's nonwhite population. Apartheid has been bitterly attacked throughout the world, and in 1961 South Africa withdrew from the Commonwealth of Nations as a consequence of such attacks.

SOUTH AFRICAN APARTHEID *is dramatized by the racial signs in a local railway station.*

Aqaba, Gulf of, an extension of the Red Sea lying between the Sinai Peninsula and the Arabian Peninsula. The gulf is 110 miles (177 km.) long and from five to 17 miles (eight to 27 km.) wide.

Arabia, a large peninsula in southwestern Asia, separated from the bulk of the continent in the northeast by the Persian Gulf and the Gulf of Oman. High mountains along the western and southern boundaries are separated from the Red Sea on the west and the Gulf of Aden on the south by narrow coastal plains. The central Arabian Plateau slopes gently eastward into the Persian Gulf basin. It is about 1200 miles (1930 km.) long with a maximum breadth of 1300 miles (2090 km.). Its area is about 1 million square miles (2.6 million sq. km.) in all.

Arabian Sea, an arm of the Indian Ocean lying between the Indian subcontinent and the Arabian Peninsula.

Arab League, officially the League of Arab States. An organization of Arab nations in northern Africa and the Middle East formed March 22, 1945. Membership in 1981 included Algeria, Bahrain, Djibouti, Egypt, Iraq, Jordan, Kuwait, Lebanon, Libya, Mauritania, Morocco, Oman, the Palestine Liberation Organization, Qatar, Saudi Arabia, Somalia, Sudan, Syria, Tunisia, the United Arab Emirates, the People's Democratic Republic of Yemen, and the Yemen Arab Republic.

The league was organized to promote the common social, economic, and cultural interests of the Arab peoples. The members attempt to work together in the fields of foreign policy, law, education, finance, and trade. In April, 1964, Iraq, Jordan, Syria, and the United Arab Republic (Egypt) formed the Arab Common Market, which came into effect on January 1, 1965, and which is open to all members of the Arab League.

Most of the members have signed the Joint Defense and Economic Cooperation Treaty, which affirms their desire for the peaceful settlement of international disputes and provides for military cooperation.

Ashanti Kingdom, a black empire of West Africa. In about 1697 the Ashanti tribes formed the Ashanti Confederacy, a state that grew in power and extent during the 1700's. Ashanti prosperity was based on the state's control of coastal slave trading.

During the 1800's the Ashanti fought a series of wars against the British. The Ashanti lost their sovereignty in 1874, and in 1901 the area was annexed to Britain's Gold Coast colony.

Asia Minor, a peninsula of southwestern Asia, lying west of an indefinite line between the Gulf of Iskenderun and the Black Sea. It is bounded on the west by the Aegean Sea and on the south by the Mediterranean. Its former name, Anatolia, is used for the Asian part of modern Turkey.

Aswan High Dam, a dam across the Nile at Aswan, Egypt. It is 364 feet (111 m) high and 12,565 feet (3,830 m) long and impounds the water of Lake Nasser to irrigate land and generate electric power.

Atlas Mountains, a 1500-mile-long (2415 km.) mountain system of North Africa, extending from the southwest coast of Morocco westward to Cape Bon on the northeast coast of Tunisia. The Atlas system includes the Anti–Atlas in the southwest; the Grand, or High, Atlas in central Morocco; and the Saharan Atlas stretching across northern Algeria. The Grand Atlas includes Toubkal, 13,661 feet (4167 m), the highest peak in the Atlas system.

Barbary States, four North African countries known today as Morocco, Algeria, Tunisia, and Libya. From the 1600's to the 1800's the region was a stronghold for pirates and adventurers who raided shipping on the Mediterranean Sea and exacted tribute from maritime nations.

Caliph, literally "he who follows behind" or "successor," the title assumed by the religious and political leaders of the Muslim community who were recognized as the successors of Muhammad (570–632), the Arabian prophet and founder of Islam. On Muhammad's death, four of his companions succeeded him in turn. They are known as the "orthodox caliphs."

Carthage, an ancient city-state that, according to tradition, was founded in 814 B.C. by Phoenician colonists. Carthage was located on the northern coast of Africa, bordering the Mediterranean Sea, near the present-day city of Tunis, in Tunisia. With a large harbor and fertile surrounding territory, Carthage became one of the greatest maritime and commercial powers of the ancient world and the political rival of Rome.

In the 200's B.C. Rome challenged Carthage in three wars—the Punic Wars. It was finally destroyed by the Romans in 146 B.C.

Chad, a lake in north-central Africa, located at the junction of the boundaries of Chad, Niger, Cameroon, and Nigeria. Lake Chad is fed by the Chari and Logone rivers and, while it has no outlet, it remains fresh. Its area fluctuates between 3800 and 10,000 square miles (9840 to 25,900 sq. km.).

Congo River, See Zaire River.

Dead Sea, a salt lake, about 400 square miles (1036 sq. km.) in area, on the Israel-Jordan border, into which the Jordan River flows. Lying 1296 feet (395 m) below sea level, its shores and surface are at the lowest known point of land on Earth. It is saltier than seawater and contains many other minerals as well.

Elburz Mountains, a mountain range in northern Iran separating the Caspian Sea from the Iranian Plateau. It is a crescent-shaped chain whose summits often reach above 13,000 feet (3965 m). Mt. Damavand, 18,934 feet (5775 m), is the highest peak.

Ethiopian Mountains, an extensive upland region of eastern Africa, lying mainly in Ethiopia. It rises sharply from surrounding lowlands and has many peaks between 7000 and 13,000 feet (2135 to 3965 m). The highest peak of the area, Ras Dashen, is 15,158 feet (4623 m).

Euphrates, a river in southwest Asia that rises in eastern Turkey. It flows southeast for 1700 miles (2737 km) through Syria and Iraq to the Persian Gulf. The river is formed by two headstreams, the Kara and the Murat. At about 120 miles (193 km) from the Persian Gulf, the Euphrates joins the Tigris River to form the Shatt al-Arab.

Syria and Iraq depend on the Euphrates for water for irrigation. Ancient peoples built a complex system of canals that allowed the Tigris and Euphrates plain to support the civilizations of Babylonia, Assyria, and later of Persia.

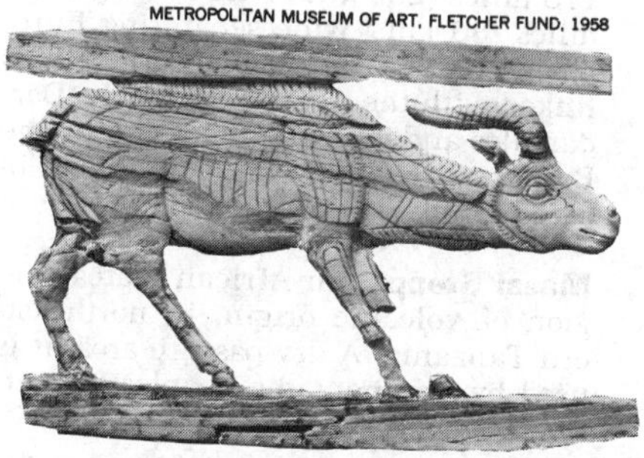

IVORY PLAQUE, *from the Assyrian Empire, centered on the Tigris and Euphrates area.*

Galilee, Sea of, or Lake Tiberias, a freshwater lake in northeastern Israel at the border with Syria. It is about 690 feet (210 m) below sea level and is fed and drained by the Jordan. Its area is 65 square miles (168 sq. km.).

Ghana, an early Negro empire in West Africa, founded in the 200's or 300's A.D. along the upper waters of the Niger River, at the southern edge of the Sahara. Ghana, which controlled the southern end of trans-Saharan caravan routes, flourished from the 700's until its destruction in 1076 by the Almoravids, Berber-speaking peoples who embraced Islam and launched a holy war.

Good Hope, Cape of, a point of land at the southwestern tip of Africa, on the Atlantic.

Guinea, Gulf of, a great inlet of the Atlantic Ocean in west central Africa. Generally accepted as extending from Senegal to Angola, it includes the bights of Benin and Biafra. The adjacent mainland is known as the Guinea Coast.

Jordan, a river in the Middle East that rises in four headstreams in the Anti–Lebanon Mountains of Syria. It flows south for some 200 miles (320 km.) in

Israel and Jordan through the Sea of Galilee and into the Dead Sea. The Yarmuk River is the principal tributary of the Jordan, whose course lies in the Great Rift Valley.

Kalahari, a desert of southern Africa, with an area of more than 100,000 square miles (260,000 sq. km.). It extends southward from Lake Ngami through central Botswana into northern South Africa as far as the Orange River and westward from Botswana into Namibia (South-West Africa).

Kilimanjaro, the highest mountain in Africa, located on the border of Kenya and Tanzania. Kibo, the site of relatively recent volcanic activity, is the highest peak at 19,340 feet (5,895 m). It is covered by glaciers. Mawenzi, the other main peak, is 17,564 feet (5,354 m) and has no glaciers.

Marmara, Sea of, an inland sea, some 175 miles (280 km.) long and up to 50 miles (80 km.) wide separating European Turkey from Asian Turkey. It is linked with the Aegean Sea by the Dardanelles and with the Black Sea by the Bosporus. The city of Istanbul is located on its northeastern shore.

Masai Steppe, an African plateau region of volcanic origin, in northeastern Tanzania. A dry pasture area, it is used by seminomadic peoples for cattle grazing.

Negev, a semidesert region in southern Israel. The Negev contains copper, potash, phosphate, and oil deposits. Limited agriculture is carried on with water brought by pipeline from the north.

Niger, a major river in West Africa, rising in southeastern Guinea and flowing northeast into Mali and then southeast through Niger and Nigeria. The river flows for about 2,600 miles (4,200 km.) and empties into the Gulf of Guinea. About 80 miles (130 km.) from its mouth, the Niger forms an extensive delta.

Nile, the longest river in Africa and in the world. Its course can be traced from the Kagera River headwaters in northern Tanzania to the Mediterranean Sea, a distance of 4145 miles (6673 km.).

The Nile proper is formed by the joining of the White Nile and the Blue Nile at Khartoum, in Sudan. The White Nile flows north from Tanzania into Uganda and Sudan, where it is joined by its major tributaries, the Ghazal and the Sobat, before joining the Blue Nile. The Nile proper continues north through Egypt and forms an extensive delta north of Cairo.

Nubian Desert, a desert area in northeastern Sudan, lying between the Nile River and the Red Sea.

Nyasa, the third largest lake in Africa, located on the borders of Tanzania, Malawi, and Mozambique. The lake has a surface area of 11,430 square miles (29,604 sq. km.) and a mountainous shoreline. Its only outlet is the Shire River, a tributary of the Zambezi River.

Olduvai Gorge, a deep canyon in northern Tanzania, about 150 miles (240 km.) northwest of Mt. Kilimanjaro, that is the site of rich fossil beds.

Oman, Gulf of, an arm of the Arabian Sea between Oman and Iran. It is linked with the Persian Gulf by the Strait of Hormuz.

Orontes, a 246-mile long (396 km.) river in western Syria. It rises in northeastern Lebanon and flows north to the Turkish border, where it turns and flows west to the Mediterranean Sea.

Persian Gulf, a shallow extension of the Arabian Sea, bounded by the United Arab Emirates, Qatar, Saudi Arabia, Kuwait, Iraq, and Iran. It is some 550 miles (885 km.) long and is connected with the Gulf of Oman to the southeast.

Red Sea, an inland sea between northeastern Africa and the Arabian Peninsula, part of the Great Rift Valley system. It is about 1300 miles (2100 km.) long and between 130 to 250 miles (210 to 400 km.) wide.

The sea is connected to the Mediterranean by the Suez Canal and to the gulf of Aden through the strait of Bab al Mandeb.

Sahara, a desert region of North Africa extending about 3000 miles (4800 km.) from west to east and 1000 miles (1600 km.) from north to south. It is the world's largest desert, and its relief is extremely varied.

The Sahara includes high, deeply dissected plateaus, such as the Tibesti, Ahaggar, and Aïr; depressions such as the Qattara; and plains 600 to 1200 feet (180 to 360 m) above sea level. The landscape includes only 20 percent sandy desert, or erg, and extensive stony desert, or reg.

Rainfall averages less than ten inches a year, and the only permanent rivers are the Nile and Niger. Inhabited largely by nomadic people, the desert has rich mineral deposits.

Sasanids, an Iranian (Persian) dynasty that ruled from 227 to 642 A.D.

The Sasanian period saw the restoration of the Achaemenid, or old Persian, culture that had existed in Iran before Alexander the Great's conquest in the 300's B.C. The Sasanids were engaged in almost continual war with Rome and later, with the Byzantine Empire.

Sinai, a triangular peninsula that forms the easternmost portion of Egypt. It extends southward from a 150-mile-long (240 km.) Mediterranean coast for over 200 miles (320 km.) to the northern tip of the Red Sea. Two extensions of the Red Sea—the Gulf of Suez and the Gulf of Aqaba—form the western and eastern boundaries of the peninsula.

The extensive central plateau of Al-Tih rises to the south and culminates in Mt. Catherina, 8652 feet (2637 m) high. Nearby is Musa Mountain, thought by many to be the Mount Sinai of the Old Testament.

Songhai, the largest of the early Negro empires of West Africa. The state was founded on the middle Niger River in about 700 A.D. Islam was introduced into Songhai during the 1000's and

NILE EXCURSION BOAT *docks at Abu Simbel on the upper river. Nile trips, primarily to see the many ruins from ancient Egypt, are becoming increasingly popular with tourists.*

PETER ARNOLD

MONKMEYER

FORGOTTEN PEOPLE, *the Dogons live near the bend of the Niger River. Their ancestors took refuge here in the 12th century, when the Mali Empire, predecessor to Songhai, was formed.*

adopted by both rulers and people.

The Songhai kingdom was conquered by Mali in the late 1200's or early 1300's. Under Sonni Ali, who ruled from about 1464 to 1492, Songhai won its independence from Mali. In 1468 it captured Tombouctou, or Timbuktu, one of West Africa's leading trade centers.

Songhai reached its greatest heights in the 1500's under Askia Muhammad I. A power struggle after his death weakened the empire, which was destroyed in 1591 by an invading Moroccan army.

Suez, Gulf of, an arm of the Red Sea extending northwest to the Suez Canal. It is 180 miles (290 km.) long.

Tanganyika, an African lake on the border of Tanganyika and Zaire. It is 420 miles (676 km.) long and has an area of 12,700 square miles (32,893 sq. km.). Its depth of 4710 feet (1436 m) makes it the world's second deepest lake.

Umayyads, the first great Islamic dynasty. The name was derived from Umayyah, a clan related to that of the prophet Muhammad.

The governor of Syria, Muawiya, an Umayyad, rebelled against Ali, son-in-law of the prophet and the last of the four "orthodox" caliphs. Muawiya was hailed as caliph at Jerusalem in 660. The next year Ali was assassinated and Muawiya, in complete control, moved the capital to Damascus.

Between 685 and 715 the Islamic Empire reached its greatest extent. In 698 the Byzantines were driven from Carthage and the Islamic Empire encompassed all of North Africa westward to the Atlantic Ocean. In 711 a Muslim army landed on Gibraltar, and ultimately conquered Spain. Other Muslim armies pushed east into India and north into the present-day Soviet Union.

There was growing discontent throughout the empire, however. Opposition centered in Iraq with the Abbasids; they finally overcame the Umayyads in 750. The Abbasids hunted down and killed all Umayyads, except for Abd ar Rahman, who escaped to Spain in 756.

Despite geographical difficulties, the Umayyads established central control of the peninsula; they were based in Córdoba and Seville. A large portion of the population was converted to Islam, although a substantial number remained Christian.

Early in the 1000's, the dynasty declined. Local dissension disrupted the state. After 1031 the Umayyads disappeared and Spain entered a period of political fragmentation.

Victoria, a lake in east-central Africa, the world's second largest freshwater lake. Lake Victoria lies mainly in Uğanda and Tanzania, but borders on Kenya. The lake, which is about 250 miles (400 km.) long and 200 miles (320 km.) wide, is the major source of the Nile River.

Victoria Falls, a waterfall in southern Africa on the Zambezi River between Zambia and Zimbabwe. The falls are 5580 feet (1700 m) wide and drop 355 feet (108 m).

Volta, a river system of Ghana, about 1000 miles (1600 km.) long. The Volta, which empties into the Gulf of Guinea, is formed by the joining of the Black Volta and the White Volta, both of which rise in Upper Volta.

Witwatersrand, a region in southern Transvaal, northeastern South Africa, vital to its economy, that consists of a 62-mile-long (100 km.) ridge of gold-

VICTORIA FALLS, *on the Zambia-Zimbabwe border, plunge 335 feet and are over 5500 feet wide; they form one of the world's great natural wonders.*

TOM PIX/PETER ARNOLD

bearing rock. It has exceptionally rich gold deposits and also yields manganese and uranium.

Zagros Mountains, a mountain range in southwestern Iran that forms the western and southern borders of the Iranian plateau. The range is about 600 miles (965 km.) long and rises to a height of 15,000 feet (4570 m).

Zaire, or Congo, a river in central Africa. With its tributaries, it is one of the world's longest river systems, draining about 1.4 million square miles (3.6 million sq. km.). The Lualaba, its headstream, rises on the Katanga plateau in Zaire and flows north to join the Luapula and Lukuga rivers.

Before turning to the west at Kisangani, where it becomes the Zaire proper, the river crosses the 60-mile (96 km.) stretch of the Boyoma (Stanley) Falls. About 350 miles (564 km.) from its mouth, it widens to form Malebo (Stanley) Pool, where Brazzaville and Kinshasa are located, at the end of the inland navigation route. The Zaire then falls some 850 feet (260 m) over a series of waterfalls, which lead into the river's estuary.

For Further Reference

Middle East

Armajani, Yahya, and Thomas Ricks. *The Middle East: Past and Present* (2nd Ed.). Prentice-Hall, 1986.

Askari, Hossein, and John T. Cummings. *Middle East Economies in the 1970s.* Frederick A. Praeger, 1976.

Avi-Yonah, Michael, editor. *The Encyclopedia of Archaeological Excavations in the Holy Land. Volume 2.* Prentice-Hall, 1975.

Borthwick, Bruce M. *Comparative Politics of the Middle East: An Introduction.* Prentice-Hall, 1980.

Bowman, David H. *Conflict & Community: A Guide to the Middle East Mosaic.* Friend Press, 1979.

Burney, C. A. *The Ancient Near East.* Cornell University Press, 1977.

Carleton, Patrick. *Buried Empires: The Earliest Civilizations of the Middle East.* Hyperion Press, 1979.

Churba, Joseph. *Politics of Defeat: America's Decline in the Middle East.* Cyrco Press, 1978.

Costello, V. F. *Urbanization in the Middle East.* Cambridge University Press, 1979.

Coulson, N. J. *A History of Islamic Law.* Edinburgh University Press, 1964.

Ellis, Howard S. *Private Enterprise & Socialism in the Middle East.* American Enterprise, 1970.

Glassman, Jon D. *Arms for the Arabs: The Soviet Union and War in the Middle East.* Johns Hopkins University Press, 1976.

Gordon, Murray. *Conflict in the Persian Gulf.* Checkmark, 1981.

Harden, Donald. *The Phoenicians.* Frederick A. Praeger, 1962.

Hay, Rupert. *Persian Gulf States.* Middle East Institute, 1959.

Hitti, Philip K. *History of the Arabs* (8th Ed.). St. Martin's, 1963.

Hourani, Albert. *Emergence of the Modern Middle East.* University of California Press, 1980.

Janowsky, Oscar I. *Foundations of Israel.* Van Nostrand, 1959.

Kramer, Samuel N. *The Sumerians.* University of Chicago Press, 1963.

Lewis, Bernard. *The Arabs in History.* Hillary House, 1966.

Mansfield, Peter. *The Middle East: A Political & Economic Survey.* Oxford University Press, 1980.

Morton, H. V. *In Search of the Holy Land.* Dodd, Mead, 1979.

Nicholson, R. A. *Literary History of the Arabs.* Cambridge University Press, 1930.

Olmstead, Albert. *History of the Persian Empire.* University of Chicago Press, 1948.

Olson, Robert, editor. *Islamic and Middle Eastern Societies.* Amana Books, 1987.

Oppenheim, A. Leo. *Ancient Mesopotamia.* University of Chicago Press, 1964.

Orlinsky, Harry M. *Ancient Israel.* Cornell University Press, 1954.

Thompson, Jack H., and Reischauer, Robert D. *Modernization of the Arab World.* Van Nostrand Reinhold, 1966.

Von Piuka, Otto. *Armies of the Middle East.* Mayflower Books, 1979.

Warriner, Doreen. *Land & Poverty in the Middle East.* Hyperion Press, 1980.

Whetten, L. L. *The Canal War: Four-Power Conflict in the Middle East.* MIT Press, 1974.

Zartman, I. William, editor. *Elites in the Middle East.* Frederick A. Praeger, 1980.

Africa

Bailey, Richard. *Africa's Industrial Future.* Westview, 1977.

Baker, Samuel W. *In the Heart of Africa.* Negro University Press, 1884.

Balandier, Georges. *Daily Life in the Kingdom of the Kongo: from the Sixteenth to the Eighteenth Century.* Pantheon Books, 1968.

Barbour, Neville, editor. *A Survey of North West Africa (The Maghrib).* Oxford University Press, 1959.

Bohannan, Paul, and Philip Curtin. *Africa and Africans* (3rd Ed.). Waveland Press, 1988.

Crummel, Alexander. *Africa & America: Addresses and Discourses.* Scholarly, 1977.

Damachi, Ukandi G. *Leadership Ideology in Africa: Attitudes Toward Socioeconomic Development.* Frederick A. Praeger, 1976.

Davenport, T. H. *South Africa: A Modern History* (3rd Ed.). University of Toronto Press, 1987.

De Kiewiet, C. W. *A History of South Africa.* Oxford University Press, 1967.

Fage, J. D. *An Atlas of African History.* Edwin Arnold, 1966.

Hance, William A., editor. *Southern Africa and the United States.* Columbia University Press, 1968.

Hepple, Alex. *South Africa.* Frederick A. Praeger, 1966.

Hutchison, Alan. *China's African Revolution.* Westview, 1976.

Johnston, H. A. S. *The Fulani Empire of Sokoto.* Oxford University Press, 1967.

Johnston, Harry H. *History of the Colonization of Africa by Alien Races.* Cooper Square, 1966.

Kajubi, W. S., et al. *African Encyclopedia.* Oxford University Press, 1974.

Lloyd, Peter C. *Slums of Hope? Shanty Towns of the Third World.* St. Martin's, 1979.

Mair, Lucy. *African Kingdoms.* Oxford University Press, 1977.

Mazrui, A. *The African Condition.* Cambridge University Press, 1980.

Moore, Clark D., and Ann Dunbar, editors. *Africa Yesterday and Today.* Bantam Books, 1968.

Obichere, Boniface I., editor. *African States and the Military: Past and Present.* Biblio Distribution Center, 1986.

O'Brien, Rita C. *White Society in Black Africa.* Merrimack Book Service, 1972.

Oliver, Roland, editor. *The Dawn of African History.* Oxford University Press, 1968.

Oliver, Roland, editor. *The Middle Age of African History.* Oxford University Press, 1967.

Oliver, Roland, and J. D. Fage. *A Short History of Africa.* New York University Press, 1963.

Ranger, T. O. *Aspects of Central African History.* Northwestern University Press, 1968.

Roberts, S. *Law and the Family in Africa.* Mouton, 1977.

Rotberg, Robert I. *A Political History of Tropical Africa.* Harcourt, Brace & World, 1965.

Ward, W. E. F. *A History of Africa.* 2 volumes. Allen & Unwin, 1966.

Wills, A. J. *An Introduction to the History of Central Africa* (3rd Ed.). Oxford University Press, 1973.

Wilson, John A. *The Culture of Ancient Egypt.* University of Chicago Press, 1956.

VOLUME 19

People

PEOPLE

WIDE WORLD

SIGNERS OF THE U.S. DECLARATION OF INDEPENDENCE
as adopted by Congress, July 4, 1776

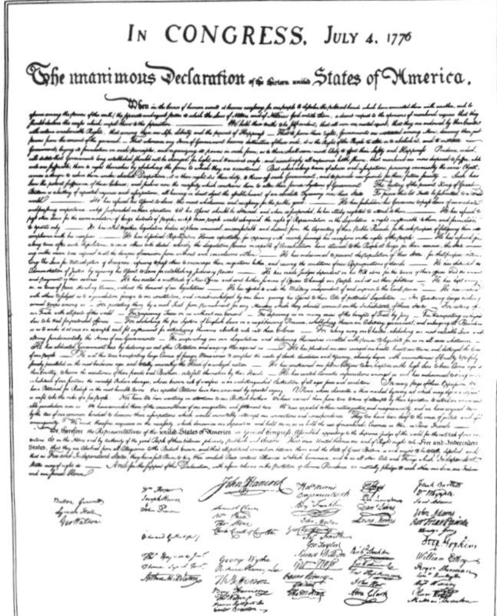

IN CONGRESS. JULY 4, 1776

The unanimous Declaration of the thirteen united States of America.

THE BETTMANN ARCHIVE

Name	Delegate From
Adams, John	Massachusetts
Adams, Samuel	Massachusetts
Bartlett, Josiah	New Hampshire
Braxton, Carter	Virginia
Carroll, Charles, of Carrollton	Maryland
Chase, Samuel	Maryland
Clark, Abraham	New Jersey
Clymer, George	Pennsylvania
Ellery, William	Rhode Island
Floyd, William	New York
Franklin, Benjamin	Pennsylvania
Gerry, Elbridge	Massachusetts
Gwinnett, Button	Georgia
Hall, Lyman	Georgia
Hancock, John	Massachusetts
Harrison, Benjamin	Virginia
Hart, John	New Jersey
Hewes, Joseph	North Carolina
Heyward, Thomas, Jr.	South Carolina
Hooper, William	North Carolina
Hopkins, Stephen	Rhode Island
Hopkinson, Francis	New Jersey
Huntington, Samuel	Connecticut
Jefferson, Thomas	Virginia
Lee, Francis Lightfoot	Virginia
Lee, Richard Henry	Virginia
Lewis, Francis	New York
Livingston, Philip	New York

Name	Delegate From
Lynch, Thomas, Jr.	South Carolina
McKean, Thomas	Delaware
Middleton, Arthur	South Carolina
Morris, Lewis	New York
Morris, Robert	Pennsylvania
Morton, John	Pennsylvania
Nelson, Thomas, Jr.	Virginia
Paca, William	Maryland
Paine, Robert Treat	Massachusetts
Penn, John	North Carolina
Read, George	Delaware
Rodney, Caesar	Delaware
Ross, George	Pennsylvania
Rush, Benjamin	Pennsylvania
Rutledge, Edward	South Carolina
Sherman, Roger	Connecticut
Smith, James	Pennsylvania
Stockton, Richard	New Jersey
Stone, Thomas	Maryland
Taylor, George	Pennsylvania
Thornton, Matthew	New Hampshire
Walton, George	Georgia
Whipple, William	New Hampshire
Williams, William	Connecticut
Wilson, James	Pennsylvania
Witherspoon, John	New Jersey
Wolcott, Oliver	Connecticut
Wythe, George	Virginia

MOTHER TERESA: J.P. LAFFONTE/SYGMA

VOLUME 19
People

UPI

SPRINGER/BETTMANN FILM ARCHIVE

ATLAN/SYGMA

EWING GALLOWAY

THE BETTMANN ARCHIVE

LOOK

This volume contains information about the people, past and present, who have made important contributions to the development of modern civilization. Each person cited—statesman, soldier, religious leader, scientist, writer, or social activist—helped make the world what it is today. The volume is organized in four sections that, used separately or in combination, provide a wealth of biographical information.

Timeline of People. The timeline is divided into four rows. The first three rows are organized by subject and present in chronological order the names, birth dates, and death dates of all the people whose biographies appear in the remaining three sections.

People whose contributions were in the fields of government, the military, crime, law, and social reform are listed in row one.

People whose contributions were in the fields of science, exploration, philosophy, religion, medicine, education, business, architecture, entertainment, and sports are listed in row two.

Row three lists important figures in the fields of literature, the arts, and music.

The fourth row presents a chronological key that marks major historical events from ancient times to the present. The reader can easily identify the period of history in which any given figure lived by locating that person's name and birth and death dates in the appropriate row and then scanning down to the fourth row.

By reading along any of the first three rows, the reader can see when the major figures in a particular field of endeavor lived, who their predecessors were, and who followed them. By reading down the rows, the reader can see which important people in all fields of human activity were living during a particular period in world history, and which major events were occurring during their lifetimes.

The timeline thus provides a structure for a sound understanding of the flow of human history. It is designed to be used in conjunction with the other three sections of this volume.

Biographies of Famous Men and Women. This section is arranged alphabetically and contains short biographical sketches of famous men and women, living and dead. Artists, emperors, generals, saints, writers, painters, inventors—all have exerted a profound influence in their fields. Each biography outlines the major accomplishments of its subject and explains the importance of those contributions. Many of these biographies identify their subjects as leading figures in historical epochs or movements—such as the Industrial Revolution or the Romantic movement. These events are treated in depth in other sections of *The Volume Library.*

Nobel Prize winners. The third section, also arranged alphabetically, contains biographical sketches of Nobel Prize winners. Here the reader will find a wealth of information about the recipients of the Nobel Prize. Special emphasis is placed on the contributions for which they were awarded a Nobel Prize. This is especially useful in the sciences. It is one thing to know that a person won the Nobel Prize in Chemistry. It is another thing entirely to know *why* he or she was so honored.

Men and Women of the 1980's. The final section contains biographical sketches of men and women whose works, activities, and ideas are as fresh as today's newspaper. While many of their names are familiar, and some are not so well known, they are all still at work in their respective fields. Their biographies are included because their contributions are likely to withstand the test of time or because their activities have been especially noteworthy. Their lives and works are important to our understanding of the complex tapestry that is modern life.

PEOPLE 2600 B.C.

Key: fl.=flourished c =circa d.=died r. =reigned

Government, Military, Crime, Social Reform, Law

Khufu (Cheops) fl. c 2600 BC Egyptian Pharaoh.
Hammurabi fl. c 1800 BC King of Babylon. Wrote code of civil laws.
Ikhnaton d. c 1354 BC Egyptian Pharaoh. Changed religious practices.
Tutankhamen fl. c 1350 BC Pharaoh of Egypt, called King Tut.
Ashurbanipal r. 669–626 BC Last great king of Assyria.
Nebuchadnezzar II d. 562 BC King of Babylon.
Croesus r. 560–546 BC King of Lydia. Known for legendary wealth.
Cyrus the Great c 600–529 BC Founder of Persian empire.
Darius I c 558–486 BC King of Persia.
Leonidas d. 480 BC King of Sparta. Fought at Thermopylae.
Xerxes the Great c 519–465 BC King of Persia. Invaded Greece.
Themistocles c 527–c 462 BC Athenian statesman, victor at Salamis.
Pericles c 495–429 BC Greek statesman. Founded Delian League.
Alcibiades c 450–404 BC Athenian general and statesman.
Lysander d. 395 BC Spartan admiral. Defeated Athenians.
Alexander the Great 356–323 BC King of Macedonia.
Demosthenes c 385–322 BC Athenian orator and statesman.
Seleucus I c 358–280 BC Macedonian general, founder of Seleucid dynasty.
Shih Huang Ti 259–210 BC First emperor of China.
Hannibal 247–183 BC Carthaginian general. Fought against Rome.
Mattathias Maccabeus d. 166 BC Jewish priest. Founded dynasty.
Judas Maccabeus d. 160 BC Jewish patriot. Fought Syrians.
Marcus Porcius Cato (the Elder) 234–149 BC Roman statesman.
Spartacus d. 71 BC Roman slave and revolutionary.
Catiline 108–62 BC Roman politician and conspirator.
Pompey the Great 106–48 BC Roman general and statesman.
Marcus Porcius Cato (the Younger) 95–46 BC Roman statesman.
Gaius Julius Caesar 100–44 BC Roman general and statesman.
Marcus Tullius Cicero 106–43 BC Roman orator and statesman.
Herod Antipater d. 43 BC Arab procurator of Judea.
Marcus Junius Brutus c 85–42 BC Roman politician and assassin.
Mark Antony c 83–30 BC Roman soldier and politician.
Cleopatra VII 69–30 BC Queen of Egypt.
Herod the Great c 73–4 BC King of Judea.
Augustus 63 BC–14 AD First emperor of Rome.

Science, Invention, Philosophy, Education, Religion, Exploration, Business, Medicine, Architecture, Entertainment, Sports

Anaximander 611–547 BC Greek natural philosopher.
Lao-tze c 604–531 BC Chinese philosopher. Founded Taoism.
Pythagoras fl. 500's BC Greek philosopher and mathematician.
Zoroaster fl. 500's BC Persian religious leader.
Buddha c 563–c 483 BC Indian philosopher, founder of Buddhism.
Confucius c 551–479 BC Chinese teacher and philosopher.
Socrates c 470–399 BC Athenian philosopher and teacher.
Hippocrates c 460–c 377 BC Greek physician.
Democritus c 460–c 370 BC Greek philosopher.
Plato c 427–347 BC Greek philosopher and author.
Aristotle 384–322 BC Greek philosopher.
Euclid fl. c 300 BC Greek mathematician.
Epicurus 341–270 BC Greek philosopher.
Archimedes c 287–212 BC Greek mathematician and inventor.
Hipparchus fl. c 160–c 126 BC Greek astronomer, mathematician.
Jesus c 4 BC–c 29 AD Central figure of Christian religion.

ARCHIMEDES

THE BETTMANN ARCHIVE

Literature, Art, Music

Homer c 8th century BC Greek epic poet.
Sappho fl. c 600 BC Greek lyric poet of Lesbos.
Aeschylus 525–456 BC Greek tragic poet and dramatist.
Pindar c 522–c 443 BC Greek lyric poet of Thebes.
Phidias c 500–c 432 BC Greek sculptor.
Euripides c 485–406 BC Greek tragic dramatist.
Sophocles c 496–406 BC Greek tragic dramatist.
Thucydides c 471–400 BC Greek historian.
Herodotus fl. 400's BC Greek historian and traveler.
Aristophanes 450–380 BC Greek comic poet.
Xenophon c 434–c 355 BC Greek historian and soldier.
Praxiteles c 400–330 BC Greek sculptor.
Lysippus fl. late 300's BC Greek naturalistic sculptor.
Gaius Valerius Catullus c 84–54 BC Roman lyric poet.
Vergil 70–19 BC Roman epic poet of the *Aeneid*.
Horace 65–8 BC Roman lyric poet.
Ovid 43 BC–c 17 AD Roman poet.

Events

c 2580 B.C. Great Pyramid of Cheops built in Egypt.
c 1193 B.C. Mycenaeaen Greeks destroy Troy.
776 B.C. First recorded Olympic Games held in Greece.
586 B.C. Jews in exile in Babylon.
490 B.C. Greeks defeat Persians at Battle of Marathon.
431–404 B.C. Peloponnesian War. Sparta defeats Athens.
221 B.C. Shih Huang Ti completes unification of China.
146 B.C. Third Punic War ends. Rome destroys Carthage.
58 B.C. Julius Caesar begins Roman conquest of Gaul.
27 B.C. Augustus becomes first Roman emperor.
c 30 A.D. Jesus is crucified.

1330 A.D.

NATIONAL GALLERIES OF SCOTLAND

ROBERT BRUCE

Pontius Pilate d. c 36 AD Roman governor of Judea.
Herod Antipas d. c 40 AD Judean tetrarch of Galilee.
Caligula 12–41 AD Emperor of Rome, said to be insane.
Claudius I 10 BC–54 AD Roman emperor and historian.
Lucius Annaeus Seneca c 4 BC–65 AD Roman statesman and stoic.
Nero 37–68 AD Roman emperor, noted for brutality.
Vespasian 9–79 AD First Flavian emperor of Rome.
Pliny the Younger c 61–c 112 Roman public official and author.
Trajan c 53–117 Roman emperor, conqueror of Dacia.
Hadrian 76–138 Roman emperor. Built Hadrian's Wall.
Diocletian 245–313 Roman emperor. Divided Roman Empire.
Constantine I c 280–337 First Christian emperor of Rome.
Attila c 406–453 King of the Huns. Invaded Gaul and northern Italy.
Leo I c 390–461 Roman pope, called St. Leo the Great.
Arthur fl. 6th century Legendary king of Britain.
Justinian I the Great 483–565 Byzantine emperor. Preserved Roman law.
Charles Martel c 688–741 Leader of the Franks.
Charlemagne 742–814 King of the Franks. Founded empire.
Alfred the Great 849–899 King of Wessex. Codified laws.
Otto I the Great 912–973 German king and Holy Roman Emperor.
Brian Boru 926–1014 Irish king and national hero.
Macbeth d. 1057 King of the Scots. Inspired Shakespeare play.
William I (the Conqueror) 1027–1087 First Norman king of England.
El Cid Campeador c 1043–1099 Spanish soldier. Conquered Valencia.
Geoffrey of Monmouth c 1100–c 1155 English bishop and historian.
Thomas à Becket 1118–1170 English archbishop of Canterbury.
Henry II 1133–1189 King of England. First Plantagenet ruler.
Saladin 1138–1193 Muslim military leader. Captured Jerusalem.
Richard I 1157–1199 King of England, called the Lion-Hearted.
Minamoto Yoritomo 1147–1199 First Japanese shogun.
Eleanor of Aquitaine 1122–1204 Queen of France and England.
John c 1167–1216 King of England. Signed Magna Carta.
Philip II 1165–1223 King of France. Increased French territory.
Genghis Khan 1162–1227 Leader of the conquering Mongol hordes.
Alexander Nevski c 1220–1263 Russian ruler and national hero.
Kublai Khan 1215–1294 Mongol ruler. Founded Yuan dynasty, China.
Robert Bruce 1274–1329 King and liberator of the Scots.

Saint Paul d. c 67 AD Christian missionary, theologian.
Pliny the Elder 23 AD–79 Roman scholar and naturalist.
Ptolemy fl. 2nd century AD Egyptian astronomer and mathematician.
Galen c 130–c 200 Greek physician and writer.
Plotinus c 205–270 Roman Neoplatonic philosopher.
Saint Anthony 250–355 Egyptian Christian hermit and monk.
Saint Augustine 354–430 Numidian Christian theologian.
Saint Patrick c 385–c 461 Patron saint of Ireland.
Anicius Boëthius c 480–524 Roman statesman, philosopher.
Saint Benedict of Nursia c 480–c 543 Italian Benedictine monk.
Saint Gregory I the Great c 540–604 Roman pope.
Muhammad 570–632 Arabian prophet, founder of Islam.
Eric the Red fl. 980–1000 Norwegian explorer and hero.
Leif Ericson fl. c 1000 Norwegian explorer.
Pierre Abélard 1079–1142 French philosopher.
Averroës 1126–1198 Moorish philosopher and writer.
Maimonides 1135–1204 Spanish-Hebrew philosopher and physician.
Saint Francis of Assisi 1182–1226 Italian friar.
Saint Thomas Aquinas c 1225–1274 Italian Christian philosopher.
Saint Albertus Magnus c 1200–1280 German philosopher and teacher.
Roger Bacon c 1214–1294 English scholar and reformer.
Marco Polo c 1254–c 1324 Italian explorer.

THE BETTMANN ARCHIVE

SAINT FRANCIS OF ASSISI

Cornelius Tacitus c 55 AD–c 120 AD Roman historian and orator.
Plutarch c 46 AD–c 120 Greek writer of biographies.
Bede or **Baeda** 673–735 English historian and monk.
Li Po c 700–762 Chinese lyric poet of T'ang dynasty.
Lady Shikibu Murasaki c 978–c 1026 Japanese novelist.
Omar Khayyam d. c 1123 Persian astronomer and poet.
Chrétien de Troyes d. c 1190 French medieval court poet.
Snorri Sturluson 1179–1241 Icelandic poet and historian.
Niccolò Pisano c 1220–c 1283 Italian sculptor.
Giovanni Cimabue c 1240–c 1302 Florentine painter.
Dante Alighieri 1265–1321 Italian medieval poet.
Giotto di Bondone c 1266–c 1337 Italian painter, architect.

Emperor Vespasian orders construction of Colosseum in Rome. — 75
Earliest form of magnetic compass in use in China. — 271
Constantine makes Christianity state religion of Roman Empire. — 313
Roman Empire ends in West; Emperor Romulus Augustulus deposed by Odoacer, a German chieftain. — 476
Muhammad flees Mecca to Medina; Hegira begins Muslim lunar calendar. — 622
Charles Martel halts Arab invasion of Europe at Battle of Tours. — 732
Normans conquer England. — 1066
First Crusade captures Jerusalem. — 1099
Construction of west facade of Chartres Cathedral begins. — 1137
King John of England signs Magna Carta, limiting royal power. — 1215
Hundred Years' War between England and France begins. — 1337

PEOPLE *(continued)*

1340

Government / Military / Crime / Social Reform / Law

Tamerlane c 1336–1405 Mongol conqueror. Founded Timurid dynasty.
Henry V 1387–1422 English king. Victor at Agincourt.
Giovanni di Bicci de' Medici 1360–1429. Florentine banker.
Saint Joan of Arc 1412–1431 French heroine of Orleans battle.
Charles VII 1403–1461 King of France. Drove English from France.
Cosimo de' Medici 1389–1464 Florentine administrator.
Lorenzo de' Medici 1449–1492 Florentine patron of the arts.
Rodrigo Borgia 1431–1503 Became Pope Alexander VI.
Piero de' Medici 1472–1503 Florentine successor to Lorenzo.
Isabella I 1451–1504 Spanish queen. Financed Columbus voyages.
Ivan III, the Great 1440–1505 Czar of Russia.
Cesare Borgia 1476–1507 Spanish duke of Valentinois.
Julius II 1445–1513 Italian pope. Patron of the arts.
Ferdinand II 1452–1516 Spanish king of Castile and Aragon.
Lucrezia Borgia 1480–1519 Spanish duchess. Patron of the arts.
Montezuma II 1466–1520 Last Aztec emperor of Mexico.
Leo X 1475–1521 Italian pope. Reigned during Reformation.
Niccolò Machiavelli 1469–1527 Italian statesman and writer.
Thomas Wolsey 1473–1530 English cardinal and statesman.
Atahualpa 1502–1533 Last Inca king of Peru.
Giulio de' Medici 1478–1534 Florentine who became Pope Clement VII.
Thomas More 1478–1535 English statesman, author, saint.
Anne Boleyn 1507–1536 English queen. Second wife of Henry VIII.
Alessandro de' Medici 1511–1537 Hereditary ruler of Florence.
Thomas Cromwell 1485–1540 English statesman, church reformer.
Pedro de Alvarado 1485–1541 Spanish conquistador.
Francis I 1494–1547 King of France.
Henry VIII 1491–1547 King of England.

Science / Invention / Philosophy / Education / Religion / Exploration / Business / Medicine / Architecture / Entertainment / Sports

John Wycliffe c 1330–1384 English religious reformer.
John Huss c 1370–1415 Bohemian religious reformer.
Filippo Brunelleschi 1377–1446 Florentine architect.
Henry the Navigator 1394–1460 Prince of Portugal.
Johann Gutenberg 1400–1468 German inventor of printing.
Thomas à Kempis 1380–1471 German priest and writer.
William Caxton 1422–1491 First English printer.
Giovanni Pico della Mirandola 1463–1494 Italian scholar.
Girolamo Savonarola 1452–1498 Italian religious reformer.
Tomás de Torquemada c 1420–1498 Spanish monk. Led Inquisition.
John Cabot 1450–1499 Italian explorer for England.
Christopher Columbus 1451–1506 Italian discoverer of Americas.
Amerigo Vespucci 1454–1512 Italian navigator.
Bramante 1444–1514 Italian Renaissance architect.
Vasco de Balboa 1475–1519 Spanish discoverer of Pacific Ocean.
Ferdinand Magellan c 1480–1521 Portuguese navigator.
Juan Ponce de León 1460–1521 Spanish discoverer of Florida.
Vasco da Gama 1460–1524 Portuguese explorer.
Huldreich Zwingli 1484–1531 Swiss religious reformer.
Desiderius Erasmus 1466–1536 Dutch humanist and scholar.
William Tyndale c 1494–1536 Translated Bible into English.
Paracelsus c 1490–1541 Swiss physician and alchemist.
Francisco Pizarro c 1470–1541 Spanish conqueror of Peru.
Hernando de Soto 1500–1542 Spanish explorer.
Nicolaus Copernicus 1473–1543 Polish astronomer.
Martin Luther 1483–1546 German religious reformer.
Hernán Cortés 1485–1547 Spanish conqueror of Mexico.
Paul III 1468–1549 Italian pope, religious reformer.

ERASMUS

Literature / Art / Music

Petrarch 1304–1374 Italian poet, known for love sonnets.
Giovanni Boccaccio 1313–1375 Italian poet and humanist.
Geoffrey Chaucer 1344–1400 English medieval poet.
Thomas Malory fl. c 1400 English writer of Arthurian legends.
William Langland 1330–1400 English poet and satirist.
Jean Froissart 1337–1410 French historian.
Hubert Van Eyck c 1366–1426 Flemish painter.
Masaccio 1401–1428 Florentine Renaissance painter.
Jan Van Eyck c 1370–c 1440 Flemish court painter.
Giovanni da Fiesole 1387–1455 Italian painter.
Lorenzo Ghiberti 1378–1455 Italian sculptor, goldsmith.
François Villon 1431–c 1463 French lyric poet.
Rogier van der Weyden 1400–1464 Flemish painter.
Donatello 1386–1466 Italian Renaissance sculptor.
Fra Filippo Lippi c 1406–1469 Italian painter and monk.
Paolo Uccello 1397–1475 Florentine painter.
Luca della Robbia c 1400–1482 Italian sculptor, ceramicist.
Andrea del Verrocchio c 1435–1488 Italian painter, sculptor.
Andrea Mantegna 1431–1506 Italian Renaissance artist.
Sandro Botticelli 1444–1510 Florentine painter.
Giovanni Bellini 1430–1516 Venetian painter.
Hieronymus Bosch 1450–1516 Flemish painter of grotesques.
Leonardo da Vinci 1452–1519 Italian artist and scientist.
Raphael 1483–1520 Italian Renaissance artist.
Albrecht Dürer 1471–1528 German painter, engraver.
Matthias Grünewald 1460–1528 German Gothic painter.
Andrea del Sarto 1486–1530 Florentine painter.
Lucas van Leyden 1494–1533 Dutch painter, engraver.
Antonio Allegri da Correggio 1494–1534 Italian painter.
Hans Holbein 1497–1543 German painter and engraver.

Events

1348 Bubonic plague reaches Europe, millions die.
1418 Portuguese expeditions begin to explore west coast of Africa.
1453 Constantinople falls to Turks, marking end of Byzantine empire.
1455 Johann Gutenberg completes first Bible printed with movable type.
1492 Columbus makes first voyage of discovery to New World.
1517 Martin Luther posts his 95 Theses, launching Reformation.
1521 Spanish conquistadors overthrow Aztec empire in Mexico.
1543 Copernicus's theory that Earth revolves around sun is published.
1545 Council of Trent meets to define Catholic theology in response to Reformation.

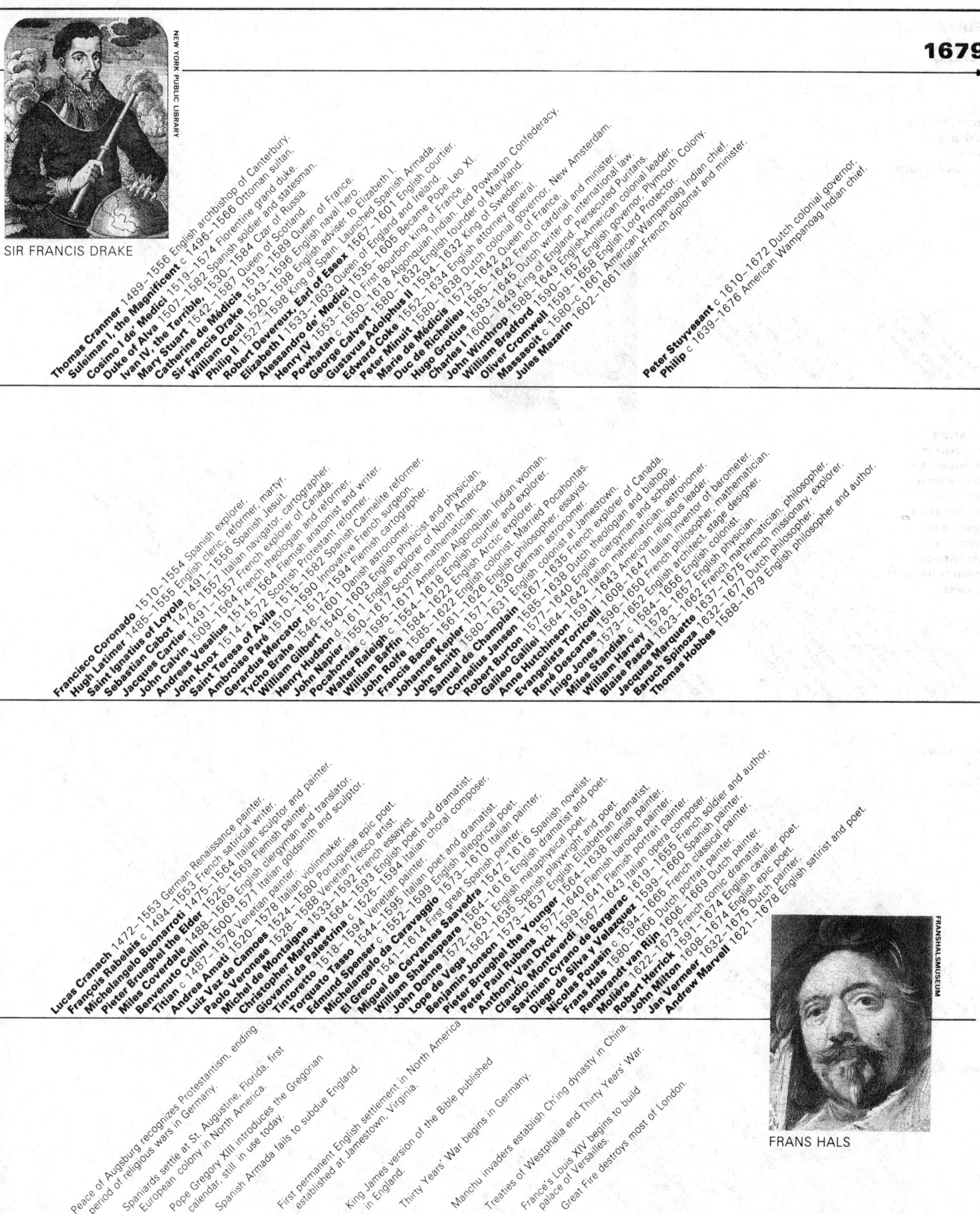
1679
Thomas Cranmer 1489–1556 English archbishop of Canterbury.
Suleiman I, the Magnificent c 1496–1566 Ottoman sultan.
Cosimo I de' Medici 1519–1574 Florentine grand duke.
Duke of Alva 1507–1582 Spanish soldier and statesman.
Ivan IV, the Terrible, 1530–1584 Czar of Russia.
Mary Stuart 1542–1587 Queen of Scotland.
Catherine de Médicis 1519–1589 Queen of France.
Sir Francis Drake 1543–1596 English naval hero.
William Cecil 1520–1598 English adviser to Elizabeth I.
Philip II 1527–1598 King of Spain. Launched Spanish Armada.
Robert Devereux, Earl of Essex 1567–1601 English courtier.
Elizabeth I 1533–1603 Queen of England and Ireland.
Alessandro de' Medici 1535–1605 Became Pope Leo XI.
Henry IV 1553–1610 First Bourbon king of France.
Powhatan c 1550–1618 Algonquian Indian. Led Powhatan Confederacy.
George Calvert 1580–1632 English founder of Maryland.
Gustavus Adolphus II 1594–1632 King of Sweden.
Edward Coke 1552–1634 English attorney general.
Peter Minuit 1580–1638 Dutch colonial governor. New Amsterdam.
Marie de Médicis 1573–1642 Queen of France.
Duc de Richelieu 1585–1642 French cardinal and minister.
Hugo Grotius 1583–1645 Dutch writer on international law.
Charles I 1600–1649 King of England. Persecuted Puritans.
John Winthrop 1588–1649 English-American colonial leader.
William Bradford 1590–1657 English governor. Plymouth Colony.
Oliver Cromwell 1599–1658 English Lord Protector.
Massasoit c 1580–c 1661 American Wampanoag Indian chief.
Jules Mazarin 1602–1661 Italian-French diplomat and minister.
Peter Stuyvesant c 1610–1672 Dutch colonial governor.
Philip c 1639–1676 American Wampanoag Indian chief.
Francisco Coronado 1510–1554 Spanish explorer.
Hugh Latimer 1485–1555 English cleric, reformer, martyr.
Saint Ignatius of Loyola 1491–1556 Spanish Jesuit.
Sebastian Cabot 1476–1557 Italian navigator, cartographer.
Jacques Cartier 1491–1557 French explorer of Canada.
John Calvin 1509–1564 French theologian and reformer.
Andreas Vesalius 1514–1564 Flemish anatomist and writer.
John Knox 1514–1572 Scottish Protestant reformer.
Saint Teresa of Avila 1515–1582 Spanish Carmelite reformer.
Ambroise Paré 1510–1590 Innovative French surgeon.
Gerardus Mercator 1512–1594 Flemish cartographer.
Tycho Brahe 1546–1601 Danish astronomer.
William Gilbert 1540–1603 English physicist and physician.
Henry Hudson d. 1611 English explorer of North America.
John Napier 1550–1617 Scottish mathematician.
Pocahontas c 1595–1617 American Algonquian Indian woman.
Walter Raleigh c 1554–1618 English courtier and explorer.
William Baffin 1584–1622 English Arctic explorer.
John Rolfe 1585–1622 English colonist. Married Pocahontas.
Francis Bacon 1561–1626 English philosopher, essayist.
Johannes Kepler 1571–1630 German astronomer.
John Smith 1580–1631 English colonist at Jamestown.
Samuel de Champlain 1567–1635 French explorer of Canada.
Cornelius Jansen 1585–1638 Dutch theologian and bishop.
Robert Burton 1577–1640 English clergyman and scholar.
Galileo Galilei 1564–1642 Italian mathematician, astronomer.
Anne Hutchinson 1591–1643 American religious leader.
Evangelista Torricelli 1608–1647 Italian inventor of barometer.
René Descartes 1596–1650 French philosopher, mathematician.
Inigo Jones 1573–1652 English architect, stage designer.
Miles Standish c 1584–1656 English colonist.
William Harvey 1578–1657 English physician.
Blaise Pascal 1623–1662 French mathematician, philosopher.
Jacques Marquette 1637–1675 French missionary, explorer.
Baruch Spinoza 1632–1677 Dutch philosopher.
Thomas Hobbes 1588–1679 English philosopher and author.
Lucas Cranach 1472–1553 German Renaissance painter.
François Rabelais c 1494–1553 French satirical writer.
Michelangelo Buonarroti 1475–1564 Italian sculptor and painter.
Pieter Brueghel the Elder 1525–1569 Flemish painter.
Miles Coverdale 1488–1569 English clergyman and translator.
Benvenuto Cellini 1500–1571 Italian goldsmith and sculptor.
Titian c 1487–1576 Venetian painter.
Andrea Amati 1520–1578 Italian violinmaker.
Luiz Vaz de Camoes 1524–1580 Portuguese epic poet.
Paolo Veronese 1528–1588 Venetian fresco artist.
Michel de Montaigne 1533–1592 French essayist.
Christopher Marlowe 1564–1593 English poet and dramatist.
Giovanni da Palestrina c 1525–1594 Italian choral composer.
Tintoretto 1518–1594 Venetian painter.
Torquato Tasso 1544–1595 Italian poet and dramatist.
Edmund Spenser c 1552–1599 English allegorical poet.
Michelangelo da Caravaggio 1573–1610 Italian painter.
El Greco 1541–1614 First great Spanish painter.
Miguel de Cervantes Saavedra 1547–1616 Spanish novelist.
William Shakespeare 1564–1616 English dramatist and poet.
John Donne 1572–1631 English metaphysical poet.
Lope de Vega 1562–1635 Spanish playwright and poet.
Benjamin Jonson 1573–1637 English Elizabethan dramatist.
Pieter Brueghel the Younger 1564–1638 Flemish painter.
Peter Paul Rubens 1577–1640 Flemish baroque painter.
Anthony Van Dyck 1599–1641 Flemish portrait painter.
Claudio Monteverdi 1567–1643 Italian opera composer.
Savinien Cyrano de Bergerac 1619–1655 French soldier and author.
Diego de Silva y Velazquez 1599–1660 Spanish painter.
Nicolas Poussin c 1594–1665 French classical painter.
Frans Hals 1580–1666 Dutch portrait painter.
Rembrandt van Rijn 1606–1669 Dutch painter.
Molière 1622–1673 French comic dramatist.
Robert Herrick 1591–1674 English cavalier poet.
John Milton 1608–1674 English epic poet.
Jan Vermeer 1632–1675 Dutch painter.
Andrew Marvell 1621–1678 English satirist and poet.
1555 Peace of Augsburg recognizes Protestantism, ending period of religious wars in Germany.
1565 Spaniards settle at St. Augustine, Florida, first European colony in North America.
1582 Pope Gregory XIII introduces the Gregorian calendar, still in use today.
1588 Spanish Armada fails to subdue England.
1607 First permanent English settlement in North America established at Jamestown, Virginia.
1611 King James version of the Bible published in England.
1618 Thirty Years' War begins in Germany.
1644 Manchu invaders establish Ch'ing dynasty in China.
1648 Treaties of Westphalia end Thirty Years' War.
1661 France's Louis XIV begins to build palace of Versailles.
1666 Great Fire destroys most of London.

NEW YORK PUBLIC LIBRARY

SIR FRANCIS DRAKE

FRANSHALSMUSEUM

FRANS HALS

PEOPLE *(continued)*

1680

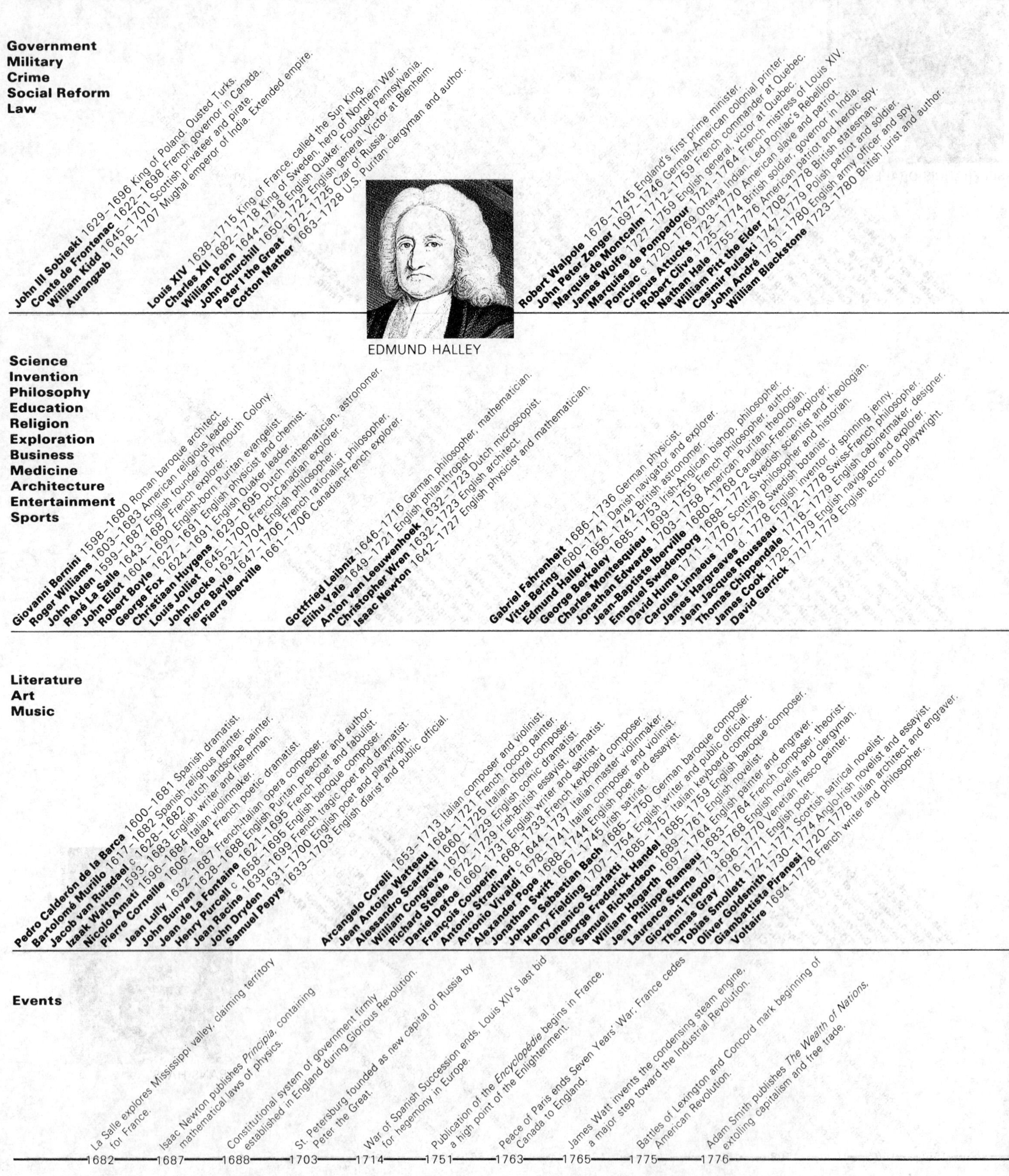

Government Military Crime Social Reform Law

John III Sobieski 1629–1696 King of Poland. Ousted Turks.
Comte de Frontenac 1622–1698 French governor in Canada.
William Kidd 1645–1701 Scottish privateer and pirate.
Aurangzeb 1618–1707 Mughal emperor of India. Extended empire.
Louis XIV 1638–1715 King of France, called the Sun King.
Charles XII 1682–1718 King of Sweden, hero of Northern War.
William Penn 1644–1718 English Quaker. Founded Pennsylvania.
John Churchill 1650–1722 English general. Victor at Blenheim.
Peter I the Great 1672–1725 Czar of Russia.
Cotton Mather 1663–1728 U.S. Puritan clergyman and author.
Robert Walpole 1676–1745 England's first prime minister.
John Peter Zenger 1697–1746 German-American colonial printer.
Marquis de Montcalm 1712–1759 French commander at Quebec.
James Wolfe 1727–1759 English general, victor at Quebec.
Marquise de Pompadour 1721–1764 French mistress of Louis XIV.
Pontiac c 1720–1769 Ottawa Indian. Led Pontiac's Rebellion.
Crispus Attucks 1723–1770 American slave and patriot.
Robert Clive 1725–1774 British soldier, governor in India.
Nathan Hale 1755–1776 American patriot and heroic spy.
William Pitt the Elder 1708–1778 British statesman.
Casimir Pulaski 1747–1779 Polish patriot and soldier.
John André 1751–1780 English army officer and spy.
William Blackstone 1723–1780 British jurist and author.

EDMUND HALLEY

Science Invention Philosophy Education Religion Exploration Business Medicine Architecture Entertainment Sports

Giovanni Bernini 1598–1680 Roman baroque architect.
Roger Williams 1603–1683 American religious leader.
John Alden 1599–1687 English founder of Plymouth Colony.
René La Salle 1643–1687 French explorer.
John Eliot 1604–1690 English-born Puritan evangelist.
Robert Boyle 1627–1691 English physicist and chemist.
George Fox 1624–1691 English Quaker leader.
Christiaan Huygens 1629–1695 Dutch mathematician, astronomer.
Louis Jolliet 1645–1700 French-Canadian explorer.
John Locke 1632–1704 English philosopher.
Pierre Bayle 1647–1706 French rationalist philosopher.
Pierre Iberville 1661–1706 Canadian-French explorer.
Gottfried Leibniz 1646–1716 German philosopher, mathematician.
Elihu Yale 1649–1721 English philanthropist.
Anton van Leeuwenhoek 1632–1723 Dutch microscopist.
Christopher Wren 1632–1723 English architect.
Isaac Newton 1642–1727 English physicist and mathematician.
Gabriel Fahrenheit 1686–1736 German physicist.
Vitus Bering 1680–1741 Danish navigator and explorer.
Edmund Halley 1656–1742 British astronomer.
George Berkeley 1685–1753 Irish-Anglican bishop, philosopher.
Charles Montesquieu 1689–1755 French philosopher, author.
Jonathan Edwards 1703–1758 American Puritan theologian.
Jean-Baptiste Iberville 1680–1768 Canadian-French explorer.
Emanuel Swedenborg 1688–1772 Swedish scientist and theologian.
David Hume 1711–1776 Scottish philosopher and historian.
Carolus Linnaeus 1707–1778 Swedish botanist.
James Hargreaves d. 1778 English inventor of spinning jenny.
Jean Jacques Rousseau 1712–1778 Swiss-French philosopher.
Thomas Chippendale 1718–1779 English cabinetmaker, designer.
James Cook 1728–1779 English navigator and explorer.
David Garrick 1717–1779 English actor and playwright.

Literature Art Music

Pedro Calderón de la Barca 1600–1681 Spanish dramatist.
Bartolomé Murillo 1617–1682 Spanish religious painter.
Jacob van Ruisdael c 1628–1682 Dutch landscape painter.
Izaak Walton 1593–1683 English writer and fisherman.
Nicolo Amati 1596–1684 Italian violinmaker.
Pierre Corneille 1606–1684 French poetic dramatist.
Jean Lully 1632–1687 French-Italian opera composer.
John Bunyan 1628–1688 English Puritan preacher and author.
Jean de La Fontaine 1621–1695 French poet and fabulist.
Henry Purcell c 1658–1695 English baroque composer.
Jean Racine 1639–1699 French tragic poet and dramatist.
John Dryden 1631–1700 English poet and playwright.
Samuel Pepys 1633–1703 English diarist and public official.
Arcangelo Corelli 1653–1713 Italian composer and violinist.
Jean Antoine Watteau 1684–1721 French rococo painter.
Alessandro Scarlatti 1660–1725 Italian choral composer.
William Congreve 1670–1729 English comic dramatist.
Richard Steele 1672–1729 Irish-British essayist, dramatist.
Daniel Defoe 1660–1731 English writer and satirist.
François Couperin 1668–1733 French keyboard composer.
Antonio Stradivari c 1644–1737 Italian master violinmaker.
Antonio Vivaldi 1678–1741 Italian composer and violinist.
Alexander Pope 1688–1744 English poet and essayist.
Jonathan Swift 1667–1745 Irish satirist.
Johann Sebastian Bach 1685–1750 German baroque composer.
Henry Fielding 1707–1754 English writer and public official.
Domenico Scarlatti 1685–1757 Italian keyboard composer.
George Frederick Handel 1685–1759 English baroque composer.
Samuel Richardson 1689–1761 English novelist.
William Hogarth 1697–1764 English painter and engraver.
Jean Philippe Rameau 1683–1764 French composer, theorist.
Laurence Sterne 1713–1768 English novelist and clergyman.
Giovanni Tiepolo 1696–1770 Venetian fresco painter.
Thomas Gray 1716–1771 English poet.
Tobias Smollett 1721–1771 Scottish satirical novelist.
Oliver Goldsmith 1730–1774 Anglo-Irish novelist and essayist.
Giambattista Piranesi 1720–1778 Italian architect and engraver.
Voltaire 1694–1778 French writer and philosopher.

Events

1682 La Salle explores Mississippi valley, claiming territory for France.
1687 Isaac Newton publishes *Principia*, containing mathematical laws of physics.
1688 Constitutional system of government firmly established in England during Glorious Revolution.
1703 St. Petersburg founded as new capital of Russia by Peter the Great.
1714 War of Spanish Succession ends. Louis XIV's last bid for hegemony in Europe.
1751 Publication of the *Encyclopédie* begins in France, a high point of the Enlightenment.
1763 Peace of Paris ends Seven Years' War. France cedes Canada to England.
1765 James Watt invents the condensing steam engine, a major step toward the Industrial Revolution.
1775 Battles of Lexington and Concord mark beginning of American Revolution.
1776 Adam Smith publishes *The Wealth of Nations*, extolling capitalism and free trade.

1807
James Oglethorpe 1696–1785 British founder of Georgia.
Frederick II the Great 1712–1786 King of Prussia.
Charles Stuart 1720–1788 English "Bonnie Prince Charlie."
Ethan Allen 1738–1789 American who led Green Mountain Boys.
Benjamin Franklin 1706–1790 American statesman and scientist.
Honoré Mirabeau 1749–1791 French statesman.
John Burgoyne 1722–1792 English army general at Saratoga.
John Paul Jones 1747–1792 American Revolutionary naval hero.
Charlotte Corday 1768–1793 French revolutionary patriot.
John Hancock 1737–1793 American Revolutionary leader.
Louis XVI 1754–1793 King of France during French Revolution.
Jean Paul Marat 1743–1793 French revolutionary leader.
Marie Antoinette 1755–1793 Queen of France.
Georges Danton 1759–1794 French revolutionary leader.
Richard Henry Lee 1732–1794 American statesman.
Maximilien de Robespierre 1758–1794 French revolutionary leader.
Friedrich von Steuben 1730–1794 Prussian army officer.
Francis Marion 1732–1795 American Revolutionary commander.
Catherine II the Great 1729–1796 Empress of Russia.
Edmund Burke 1729–1797 English statesman and orator.
Francis Lightfoot Lee 1734–1797 American statesman.
Mary Wollstonecraft 1759–1797 English feminist author.
Patrick Henry 1736–1799 American Revolutionary leader.
George Washington 1732–1799 First President of the U.S.
Benedict Arnold 1741–1801 American army officer and traitor.
Samuel Adams 1722–1803 American patriot and statesman.
Robert Emmet 1778–1803 Irish revolutionary hero.
Toussaint L'Ouverture 1743–1803 Haitian soldier, liberator.
Alexander Hamilton 1755–1804 American founding father.
Philip Schuyler 1733–1804 American Revolutionary leader.
Charles Cornwallis 1738–1805 English general.
Horatio Nelson 1758–1805 British naval hero of Trafalgar.
Charles Fox 1749–1806 British statesman, abolitionist.
William Pitt the Younger 1759–1806 British statesman.
Joseph Brant 1742–1807 American Mohawk Indian chief.
Oliver Ellsworth 1745–1807 Chief justice of the U.S.
Leonhard Euler 1707–1783 Swiss mathematician.
Junipero Serra 1713–1784 Spanish Franciscan missionary.
Henry Mühlenberg 1711–1787 German-American clergyman.
Charles Wesley 1707–1788 English Methodist preacher.
Adam Smith 1723–1790 Scottish economist and philosopher.
John Wesley 1703–1791 English Methodist leader.
Antoine Lavoisier 1743–1794 French chemist.
Josiah Wedgwood 1730–1795 English potter and inventor.
Luigi Galvani 1737–1798 Italian physiologist.
CULVER PICTURES, INC.
Johann von Herder 1744–1803 German philosopher and critic.
Immanuel Kant 1724–1804 German philosopher.
Joseph Priestley 1733–1804 English clergyman and chemist.
Charles de Coulomb 1736–1806 French physicist.
Robert Morris 1734–1806 American financier and senator.
Gotthold Lessing 1729–1781 German critic and dramatist.
Denis Diderot 1713–1784 French writer and editor.
Phyllis Wheatley 1753–1784 African-born U.S. poet.
Samuel Johnson 1709–1784 English writer, lexicographer.
Christoph von Gluck 1714–1787 German opera composer.
Thomas Gainsborough 1727–1788 English painter.
Wolfgang Amadeus Mozart 1756–1791 Austrian composer.
Joshua Reynolds 1723–1792 English portrait painter.
Edward Gibbon 1737–1794 English historian.
James Boswell 1740–1795 Scottish diarist and biographer.
Robert Burns 1759–1796 Scottish national poet.
Horace Walpole 1717–1797 English man of letters.
Pierre de Beaumarchais 1732–1799 French dramatist.
CULVER PICTURES, INC.
Luigi Boccherini 1743–1805 Italian composer and cellist.
Johann von Schiller 1759–1805 German poet and dramatist.
Jean Fragonard 1732–1806 French rococo painter.
American Revolution ends as Britain recognizes American independence.
First steam-powered cotton mill opens in England, heralding Industrial Revolution.
Constitution of United States signed by delegates in Philadelphia.
French Revolution begins.
King Louis XVI executed during Reign of Terror in France.
U.S. acquires Louisiana Territory from France for $15 million.
Napoleon crowns himself emperor of France.
1783
1785
1787
1789
1793
1803
1804

CATHERINE II (THE GREAT)

IMMANUEL KANT

PEOPLE *(continued)*

1809

Government
Military
Crime
Social Reform
Law

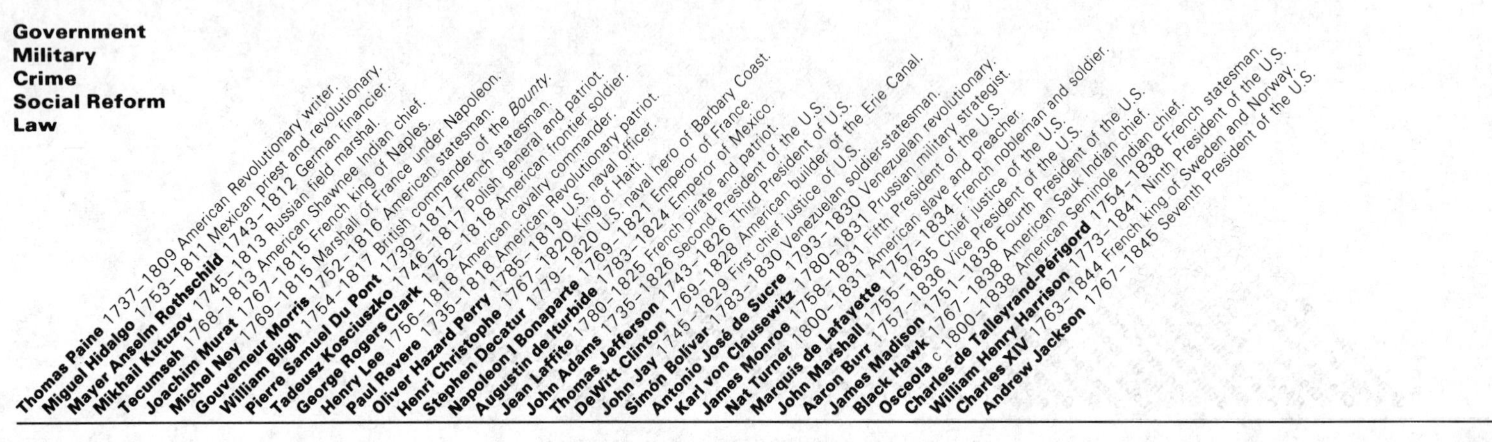
Thomas Paine 1737–1809 American Revolutionary writer.
Miguel Hidalgo 1753–1811 Mexican priest and revolutionary.
Mayer Anselm Rothschild 1743–1812 German financier.
Mikhail Kutuzov 1745–1813 Russian field marshal.
Tecumseh 1768–1813 American Shawnee Indian chief.
Joachim Murat 1767–1815 French king of Naples.
Michel Ney 1769–1815 Marshal of France under Napoleon.
Gouverneur Morris 1752–1816 American statesman.
William Bligh 1754–1817 British commander of the *Bounty*.
Pierre Samuel Du Pont 1739–1817 French statesman.
Tadeusz Kosciuszko 1746–1817 Polish general and patriot.
George Rogers Clark 1752–1818 American frontier soldier.
Henry Lee 1756–1818 American cavalry commander.
Paul Revere 1735–1818 American Revolutionary patriot.
Oliver Hazard Perry 1785–1819 U.S. naval officer.
Henri Christophe 1767–1820 King of Haiti.
Stephen Decatur 1779–1820 U.S. naval hero of Barbary Coast.
Napoleon I Bonaparte 1769–1821 Emperor of France.
Augustín de Iturbide 1783–1824 Emperor of Mexico.
Jean Laffite 1780–1825 French pirate and patriot.
John Adams 1735–1826 Second President of the U.S.
Thomas Jefferson 1743–1826 Third President of the U.S.
DeWitt Clinton 1769–1828 American builder of the Erie Canal.
John Jay 1745–1829 First chief justice of U.S.
Simón Bolívar 1783–1830 Venezuelan soldier-statesman.
Antonio José de Sucre 1793–1830 Venezuelan revolutionary.
Karl von Clausewitz 1780–1831 Prussian military strategist.
James Monroe 1758–1831 Fifth President of the U.S.
Nat Turner 1800–1831 American slave and preacher.
Marquis de Lafayette 1757–1834 French nobleman and soldier.
John Marshall 1755–1835 Chief justice of the U.S.
Aaron Burr 1757–1836 Vice President of the U.S.
James Madison 1751–1836 Fourth President of the U.S.
Black Hawk 1767–1838 American Sauk Indian chief.
Osceola c 1800–1838 American Seminole Indian chief.
Charles de Talleyrand-Périgord 1754–1838 French statesman.
William Henry Harrison 1773–1841 Ninth President of the U.S.
Charles XIV 1763–1844 French king of Sweden and Norway.
Andrew Jackson 1767–1845 Seventh President of the U.S.

Science
Invention
Philosophy
Education
Religion
Exploration
Business
Medicine
Architecture
Entertainment
Sports

Meriwether Lewis 1774–1809 American expedition leader.
Sacagawea c 1787–1812 American Shoshone Indian interpreter.
Giambattista Bodoni 1740–1813 Italian printer, designer.
Zebulon Pike 1779–1813 American explorer and Army officer.
Benjamin Rush 1745–1813 American physician and statesman.
Robert Fulton 1765–1815 U.S. steamboat engineer.
James Watt 1736–1819 Scottish engineer and inventor.
Daniel Boone 1734–1820 U.S. pioneer, hunter, explorer.
Benjamin Henry Latrobe 1764–1820 U.S. architect, engineer.
Elizabeth Ann Seton 1774–1821 First native-born American saint.
William Herschel 1738–1822 German-British astronomer.
Edmund Cartwright 1743–1823 English clergyman and inventor.
Edward Jenner 1749–1823 English naturalist and physician.
Pierre L'Enfant 1754–1825 French architect, city planner.
Eli Whitney 1765–1825 U.S. inventor of cotton gin.
Pierre Laplace 1749–1827 French astronomer, mathematician.
Alessandro Volta 1745–1827 Italian physicist.
Humphry Davy 1778–1829 English experimental chemist.
Jean Lamarck 1744–1829 French naturalist.
Georg Hegel 1770–1831 German philospher and teacher.
Sarah Siddons 1755–1831 English tragic actress.
Jeremy Bentham 1748–1832 English utilitarianist philosopher.
Nicolas Carnot 1796–1832 French physicist.
Baron Georges Cuvier 1769–1832 French naturalist.
Eleuthère Du Pont 1771–1834 French chemist, entrepreneur.
Thomas Malthus 1766–1834 British economist.
Wilhelm von Humboldt 1767–1835 German philologist, diplomat.
André Ampère 1775–1836 French mathematician and physicist.
Davy Crockett 1786–1836 U.S. frontiersman and politician.
Nathaniel Bowditch 1773–1838 U.S. mathematician, astronomer.
William Clark 1770–1838 American expedition leader.
John Dalton 1766–1844 English chemist and physicist.
Joseph Smith 1805–1844 U.S. Mormon leader.
John Chapman 1774–1845 U.S. folk hero, called Johnny Appleseed.

THE BETTMANN ARCHIVE
PIERRE L'ENFANT

Literature
Art
Music

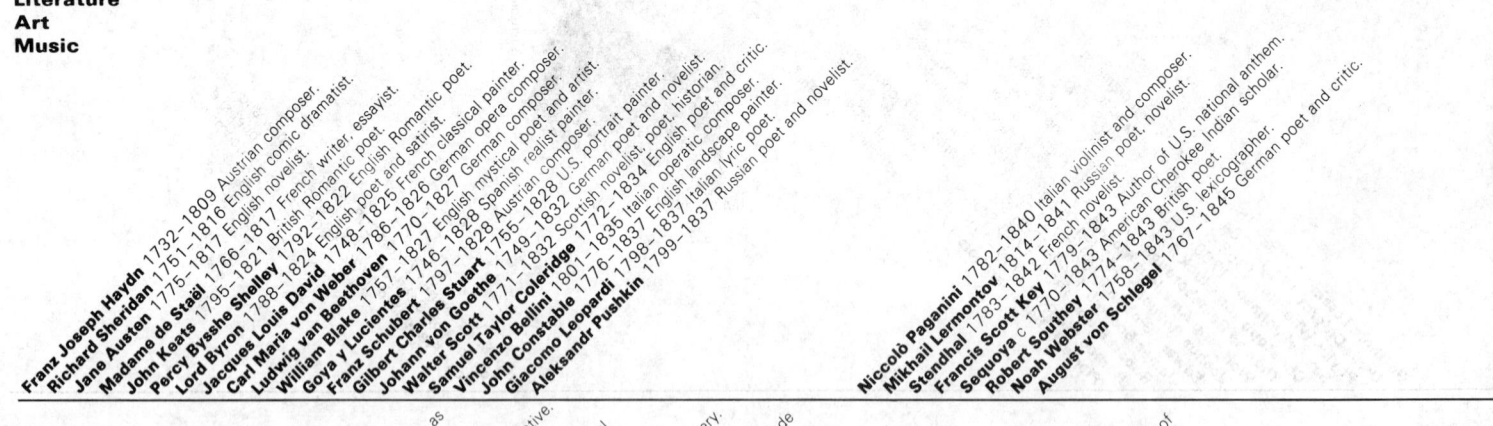

Franz Joseph Haydn 1732–1809 Austrian composer.
Richard Sheridan 1751–1816 English comic dramatist.
Jane Austen 1775–1817 English novelist.
Madame de Staël 1766–1817 French writer, essayist.
John Keats 1795–1821 British Romantic poet.
Percy Bysshe Shelley 1792–1822 English Romantic poet.
Lord Byron 1788–1824 English poet and satirist.
Jacques Louis David 1748–1825 French classical painter.
Carl Maria von Weber 1786–1826 German opera composer.
Ludwig van Beethoven 1770–1827 German composer.
William Blake 1757–1827 English mystical poet and artist.
Goya y Lucientes 1746–1828 Spanish realist painter.
Franz Schubert 1797–1828 Austrian composer.
Gilbert Charles Stuart 1755–1828 U.S. portrait painter.
Johann von Goethe 1749–1832 German poet and novelist.
Walter Scott 1771–1832 Scottish novelist, poet, historian.
Samuel Taylor Coleridge 1772–1834 English poet and critic.
Vincenzo Bellini 1801–1835 Italian operatic composer.
John Constable 1776–1837 English landscape painter.
Giacomo Leopardi 1798–1837 Italian lyric poet.
Aleksandr Pushkin 1799–1837 Russian poet and novelist.
Niccolò Paganini 1782–1840 Italian violinist and composer.
Mikhail Lermontov 1814–1841 Russian poet, novelist.
Stendhal 1783–1842 French novelist.
Francis Scott Key 1779–1843 Author of U.S. national anthem.
Sequoya c 1770–1843 American Cherokee Indian scholar.
Robert Southey 1774–1843 British poet.
Noah Webster 1758–1843 U.S. lexicographer.
August von Schlegel 1767–1845 German poet and critic.

Events

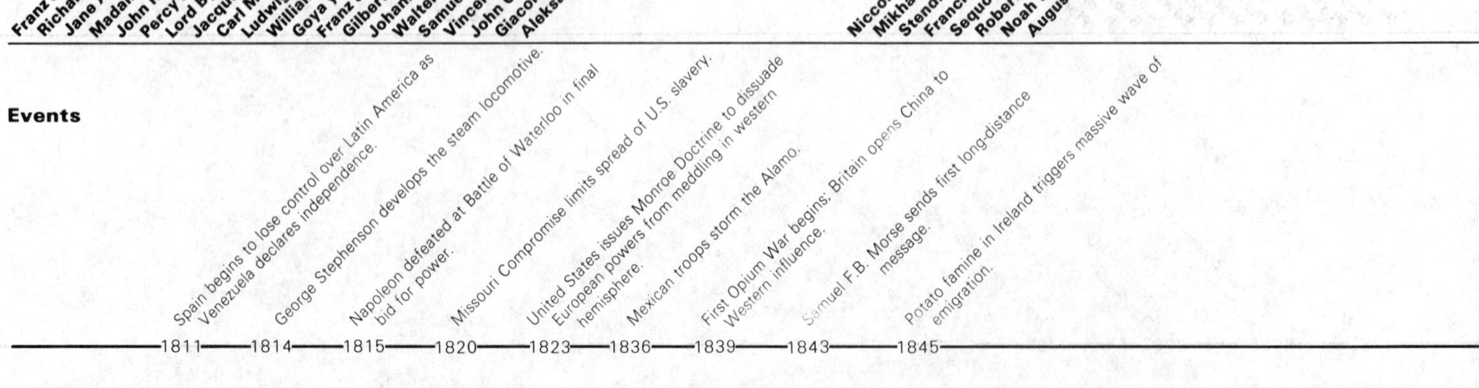
1811 Spain begins to lose control over Latin America as Venezuela declares independence.
1814 George Stephenson develops the steam locomotive.
1815 Napoleon defeated at Battle of Waterloo in final bid for power.
1820 Missouri Compromise limits spread of U.S. slavery.
1823 United States issues Monroe Doctrine to dissuade European powers from meddling in western hemisphere.
1836 Mexican troops storm the Alamo.
1839 First Opium War begins; Britain opens China to Western influence.
1843 Samuel F.B. Morse sends first long-distance message.
1845 Potato famine in Ireland triggers massive wave of emigration.

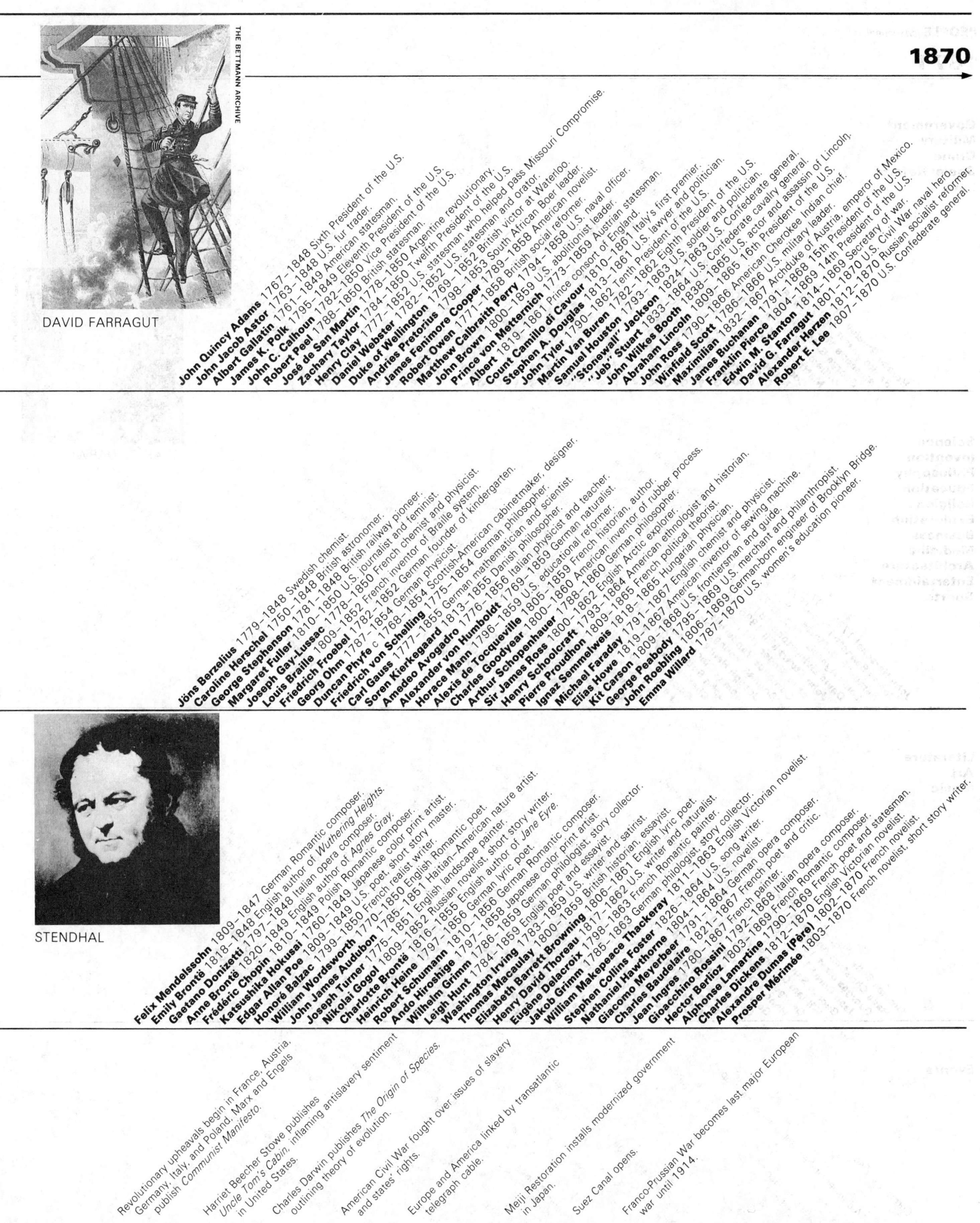

1870

DAVID FARRAGUT

John Quincy Adams 1767–1848 Sixth President of the U.S.
John Jacob Astor 1763–1848 U.S. fur trader.
Albert Gallatin 1761–1849 American statesman.
James K. Polk 1795–1849 Eleventh President of the U.S.
John C. Calhoun 1782–1850 Vice President of the U.S.
Robert Peel 1788–1850 British statesman.
José de San Martín 1778–1850 Argentine revolutionary.
Zachary Taylor 1784–1850 Twelfth President of the U.S.
Henry Clay 1777–1852 U.S. statesman who helped pass Missouri Compromise.
Daniel Webster 1782–1852 U.S. statesman and orator.
Duke of Wellington 1769–1852 British victor at Waterloo.
Andries Pretorius 1798–1853 South African Boer leader.
James Fenimore Cooper 1789–1858 American novelist.
Robert Owen 1771–1858 British social reformer.
Matthew Calbraith Perry 1794–1858 U.S. naval officer.
John Brown 1800–1859 U.S. abolitionist leader.
Prince von Metternich 1773–1859 Austrian statesman.
Albert 1819–1861 Prince consort of England.
Count Camillo di Cavour 1810–1861 Italy's first premier.
Stephen A. Douglas 1813–1861 U.S. lawyer and politician.
John Tyler 1790–1862 Tenth President of the U.S.
Martin Van Buren 1782–1862 Eighth President of the U.S.
Samuel Houston 1793–1863 U.S. soldier and politician.
"Stonewall" Jackson 1824–1863 U.S. Confederate general.
"Jeb" Stuart 1833–1864 U.S. Confederate cavalry general.
John Wilkes Booth 1838–1865 U.S. actor and assassin of Lincoln.
Abraham Lincoln 1809–1865 16th President of the U.S.
John Ross 1790–1866 American Cherokee Indian chief.
Winfield Scott 1786–1866 U.S. military leader.
Maximilian 1832–1867 Archduke of Austria, emperor of Mexico.
James Buchanan 1791–1868 15th President of the U.S.
Franklin Pierce 1804–1869 14th President of the U.S.
Edwin M. Stanton 1814–1869 Secretary of war.
David G. Farragut 1801–1870 U.S. Civil War naval hero.
Alexander Herzen 1812–1870 Russian socialist reformer.
Robert E. Lee 1807–1870 U.S. Confederate general.

Jöns Berzelius 1779–1848 Swedish chemist.
Caroline Herschel 1750–1848 British astronomer.
George Stephenson 1781–1848 British railway pioneer.
Margaret Fuller 1810–1850 U.S. journalist and feminist.
Joseph Gay-Lussac 1778–1850 French chemist and physicist.
Louis Braille 1809–1852 French inventor of Braille system.
Friedrich Froebel 1782–1852 German founder of kindergarten.
Georg Ohm 1787–1854 German physicist.
Duncan Phyfe c 1768–1854 Scottish-American cabinetmaker, designer.
Friedrich von Schelling 1775–1854 German philosopher.
Carl Gauss 1777–1855 German mathematician and scientist.
Soren Kierkegaard 1813–1855 Danish philosopher.
Amedeo Avogadro 1776–1856 Italian physicist and scientist.
Alexander von Humboldt 1769–1859 German naturalist.
Horace Mann 1796–1859 U.S. educational reformer.
Alexis de Tocqueville 1805–1859 French historian, author.
Charles Goodyear 1800–1860 American inventor of rubber process.
Arthur Schopenhauer 1788–1860 German philosopher.
Sir James Ross 1800–1862 English Arctic explorer.
Henry Schoolcraft 1793–1864 American ethnologist and historian.
Pierre Proudhon 1809–1865 French political theorist.
Ignaz Semmelweis 1818–1865 Hungarian physician.
Michael Faraday 1791–1867 English chemist and physicist.
Elias Howe 1819–1867 American inventor of sewing machine.
Kit Carson 1809–1868 U.S. frontiersman and guide.
George Peabody 1795–1869 U.S. merchant and philanthropist.
John Roebling 1806–1869 German-born engineer of Brooklyn Bridge.
Emma Willard 1787–1870 U.S. women's education pioneer.

STENDHAL

Felix Mendelssohn 1809–1847 German Romantic composer.
Emily Brontë 1818–1848 English author of *Wuthering Heights*.
Gaetano Donizetti 1797–1848 Italian opera composer.
Anne Brontë 1820–1849 English author of *Agnes Gray*.
Frédéric Chopin 1810–1849 Polish Romantic composer.
Katsushika Hokusai 1760–1849 Japanese color print artist.
Edgar Allan Poe 1809–1849 U.S. poet, short story master.
Honoré Balzac 1799–1850 French realist writer.
William Wordsworth 1770–1850 English Romantic poet.
John James Audubon 1785–1851 Haitian–American nature artist.
Joseph Turner 1775–1851 English landscape painter.
Nikolai Gogol 1809–1852 Russian novelist, short story writer.
Charlotte Brontë 1816–1855 English author of *Jane Eyre*.
Heinrich Heine 1797–1856 German lyric poet.
Robert Schumann 1810–1856 German Romantic composer.
Ando Hiroshige 1797–1858 Japanese color print artist.
Wilhelm Grimm 1786–1859 German philologist, story collector.
Leigh Hunt 1784–1859 English poet and essayist.
Washington Irving 1783–1859 U.S. writer and satirist.
Thomas Macaulay 1800–1859 British historian, essayist.
Elizabeth Barrett Browning 1806–1861 English lyric poet.
Henry David Thoreau 1817–1862 U.S. writer and naturalist.
Eugène Delacroix 1798–1863 French Romantic painter.
Jakob Grimm 1785–1863 German philologist, story collector.
William Makepeace Thackeray 1811–1863 English Victorian novelist.
Stephen Collins Foster 1826–1864 U.S. song writer.
Nathaniel Hawthorne 1804–1864 U.S. novelist.
Giacomo Meyerbeer 1791–1864 German opera composer.
Charles Baudelaire 1821–1867 French poet and critic.
Jean Ingres 1780–1867 French painter.
Gioacchino Rossini 1792–1868 Italian opera composer.
Hector Berlioz 1803–1869 French Romantic composer.
Alphonse Lamartine 1790–1869 French poet and statesman.
Charles Dickens 1812–1870 English Victorian novelist.
Alexandre Dumas (Père) 1802–1870 French novelist.
Prosper Mérimée 1803–1870 French novelist, short story writer.

1848 Revolutionary upheavals begin in France, Austria, Germany, Italy, and Poland. Marx and Engels publish *Communist Manifesto*.
1851 Harriet Beecher Stowe publishes *Uncle Tom's Cabin*, inflaming antislavery sentiment in United States.
1859 Charles Darwin publishes *The Origin of Species*, outlining theory of evolution.
1861 American Civil War fought over issues of slavery and states' rights.
1866 Europe and America linked by transatlantic telegraph cable.
1868 Meiji Restoration installs modernized government in Japan.
1869 Suez Canal opens.
1870 Franco-Prussian War becomes last major European war until 1914.

PEOPLE *(continued)*

1871

Government / Military / Crime / Social Reform / Law

Horace Greeley 1811–1872 U.S. editor, newspaper founder.
Benito Juarez 1806–1872 President of Mexico.
Giuseppe Mazzini 1805–1872 Italian national hero.
George G. Meade 1815–1872 U.S. general, victor at Gettysburg.
William H. Seward 1801–1872 U.S. secretary of state.
Matthew F. Maury 1806–1873 U.S. naval officer, scientist.
Cochise 1825–1874 American Apache Indian chief.
Millard Fillmore 1800–1874 13th President of the U.S.
Charles Sumner 1811–1874 U.S. statesman and abolitionist.
Andrew Johnson 1808–1875 17th President of the U.S.
Mikhail Bakunin 1814–1876 Russian revolutionary.
George Armstrong Custer 1839–1876 U.S. Army officer.
Antonio de Santa Anna 1794–1876 Mexican soldier and statesman.
Crazy Horse 1844–1877 American Sioux Indian chief.
Louis Thiers 1797–1877 French president, Third Republic.
William Marcy "Boss" Tweed 1823–1878 U.S. politician.
Victor Emmanuel II 1820–1878 First king of modern Italy.
William Lloyd Garrison 1805–1879 U.S. abolitionist leader.
Benjamin Disraeli 1804–1881 British prime minister, author.
James A. Garfield 1831–1881 20th President of the U.S.
Giuseppe Garibaldi 1807–1882 Italian patriot.
Jesse James 1847–1882 U.S. outlaw.
Wendell Phillips 1811–1884 U.S. orator and abolitionist.
Allan Pinkerton 1819–1884 U.S. detective.
Charles Gordon 1833–1885 British soldier and hero.
Ulysses S. Grant 1822–1885 18th President of the U.S.
Louis Riel 1844–1885 French-Canadian revolutionist.
Chester A. Arthur 1830–1886 21st President of the U.S.
Samuel J. Tilden 1814–1886 U.S. political leader.
Philip H. Sheridan 1831–1888 U.S. cavalry general.
Morrison R. Waite 1816–1888 Chief justice of the U.S.
Jefferson Davis 1808–1889 U.S. president, Confederate States.
Sitting Bull c 1831–1890 American Sioux Indian chief.
John A. Macdonald 1815–1891 Canadian prime minister.
Charles Parnell 1846–1891 Irish political leader.
William T. Sherman 1820–1891 U.S. Civil War general.

THE BETTMANN ARCHIVE

CHARLES DARWIN

Science / Invention / Philosophy / Education / Religion / Exploration / Business / Medicine / Architecture / Entertainment / Sports

John Herschel 1792–1871 British astronomer.
James Bennett 1795–1872 Scottish-American journalist, publisher.
Samuel F. B. Morse 1791–1872 U.S. inventor and painter.
Louis Agassiz 1807–1873 Swiss-American naturalist and teacher.
David Livingstone 1813–1873 Scottish missionary and explorer.
John Stuart Mill 1806–1873 British philosopher, economist.
Isaac Singer 1811–1875 U.S. inventor and manufacturer.
Cornelius Vanderbilt 1794–1877 U.S. industrialist.
Brigham Young 1801–1877 U.S. Mormon leader.
Joseph Henry 1797–1878 U.S. physicist, meteorologist.
James Clerk Maxwell 1831–1879 British physicist and author.
John Sutter 1803–1880 U.S. pioneer of California gold rush.
Charles Darwin 1809–1882 British naturalist and author.
Ralph Waldo Emerson 1803–1882 U.S. philosopher, essayist.
Peter Cooper 1791–1883 U.S. manufacturer, philanthropist.
Karl Marx 1818–1883 German economist and philosopher.
Cyrus McCormick 1809–1884 U.S. businessman. Patented reaper.
Gregor Mendel 1822–1884 Austrian monk and botanist.
Richard Hoe 1812–1886 U.S. inventor of rotary press.
Henry Ward Beecher 1813–1887 U.S. abolitionist clergyman.
James Eads 1820–1887 U.S. innovator in bridge building.
A. Bronson Alcott 1799–1888 U.S. philosopher and educator.
Asa Gray 1810–1888 U.S. botanist. Wrote classic text.
John Ericsson 1803–1889 Swedish inventor. Designed warships.
James Joule 1818–1889 Self-taught English physicist.
Maria Mitchell 1818–1889 U.S. astronomer and teacher.
John C. Frémont 1813–1890 U.S. explorer, soldier, senator.
Heinrich Schliemann 1822–1890 German archaeologist.
P. T. Barnum 1810–1891 U.S. circus impresario.

Literature / Art / Music

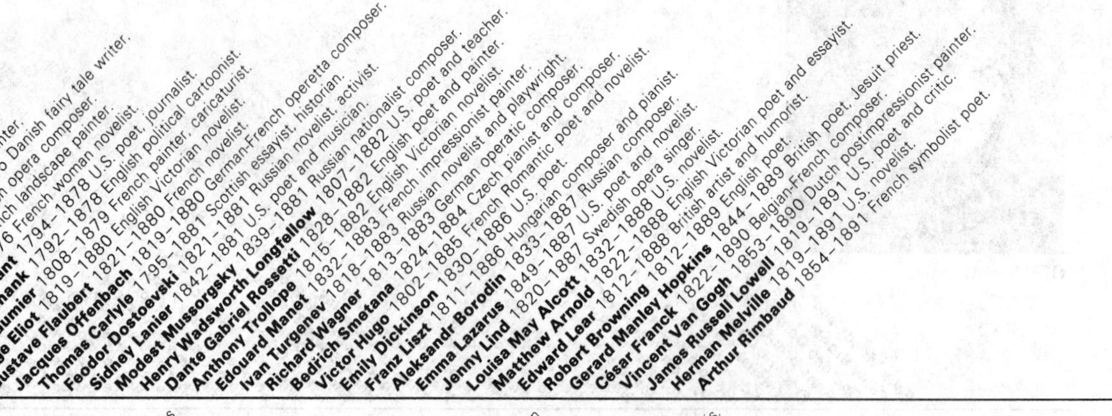

Thomas Sully 1783–1872 U.S. portrait painter.
Hans Christian Andersen 1805–1875 Danish fairy tale writer.
Georges Bizet 1838–1875 French opera composer.
Jean Corot 1796–1875 French landscape painter.
George Sand 1804–1876 French woman novelist.
William Cullen Bryant 1794–1878 U.S. poet, journalist.
George Cruikshank 1792–1878 English political cartoonist.
Honoré Daumier 1808–1879 French painter, caricaturist.
George Eliot 1819–1880 English Victorian novelist.
Gustave Flaubert 1821–1880 French novelist.
Jacques Offenbach 1819–1880 German-French operetta composer.
Thomas Carlyle 1795–1881 Scottish essayist, historian.
Feodor Dostoevski 1821–1881 Russian novelist, activist.
Sidney Lanier 1842–1881 U.S. poet and musician.
Modest Mussorgsky 1839–1881 Russian nationalist composer.
Henry Wadsworth Longfellow 1807–1882 U.S. poet and teacher.
Dante Gabriel Rossetti 1828–1882 English poet and painter.
Anthony Trollope 1815–1882 English Victorian novelist.
Edouard Manet 1832–1883 French impressionist painter.
Ivan Turgenev 1818–1883 Russian novelist and playwright.
Richard Wagner 1813–1883 German operatic composer.
Bedrich Smetana 1824–1884 Czech pianist and composer.
Victor Hugo 1802–1885 French Romantic poet and novelist.
Emily Dickinson 1830–1886 U.S. poet.
Franz Liszt 1811–1886 Hungarian composer and pianist.
Aleksandr Borodin 1833–1887 Russian composer.
Emma Lazarus 1849–1887 U.S. poet and novelist.
Jenny Lind 1820–1887 Swedish opera singer.
Louisa May Alcott 1832–1888 U.S. novelist.
Matthew Arnold 1822–1888 English Victorian poet and essayist.
Edward Lear 1812–1888 British artist and humorist.
Robert Browning 1812–1889 English poet.
Gerard Manley Hopkins 1844–1889 British poet, Jesuit priest.
César Franck 1822–1890 Belgian-French composer.
Vincent Van Gogh 1853–1890 Dutch postimpressionist painter.
James Russell Lowell 1819–1891 U.S. poet and critic.
Herman Melville 1819–1891 U.S. novelist.
Arthur Rimbaud 1854–1891 French symbolist poet.

Events

1871 Germany unified.
1876 Alexander Graham Bell patents the telephone.
1876 General George A. Custer defeated by Sioux Indians at Little Bighorn.
1881 American Federation of Labor founded.
1885 Berlin Conference partitions Africa among European powers, marking zenith of European imperialism.
1886 Statue of Liberty erected in New York harbor.
1889 Eiffel Tower built for International Exhibition in Paris.
1890 U.S. Congress passes Sherman Antitrust Act to check rising power of big business.

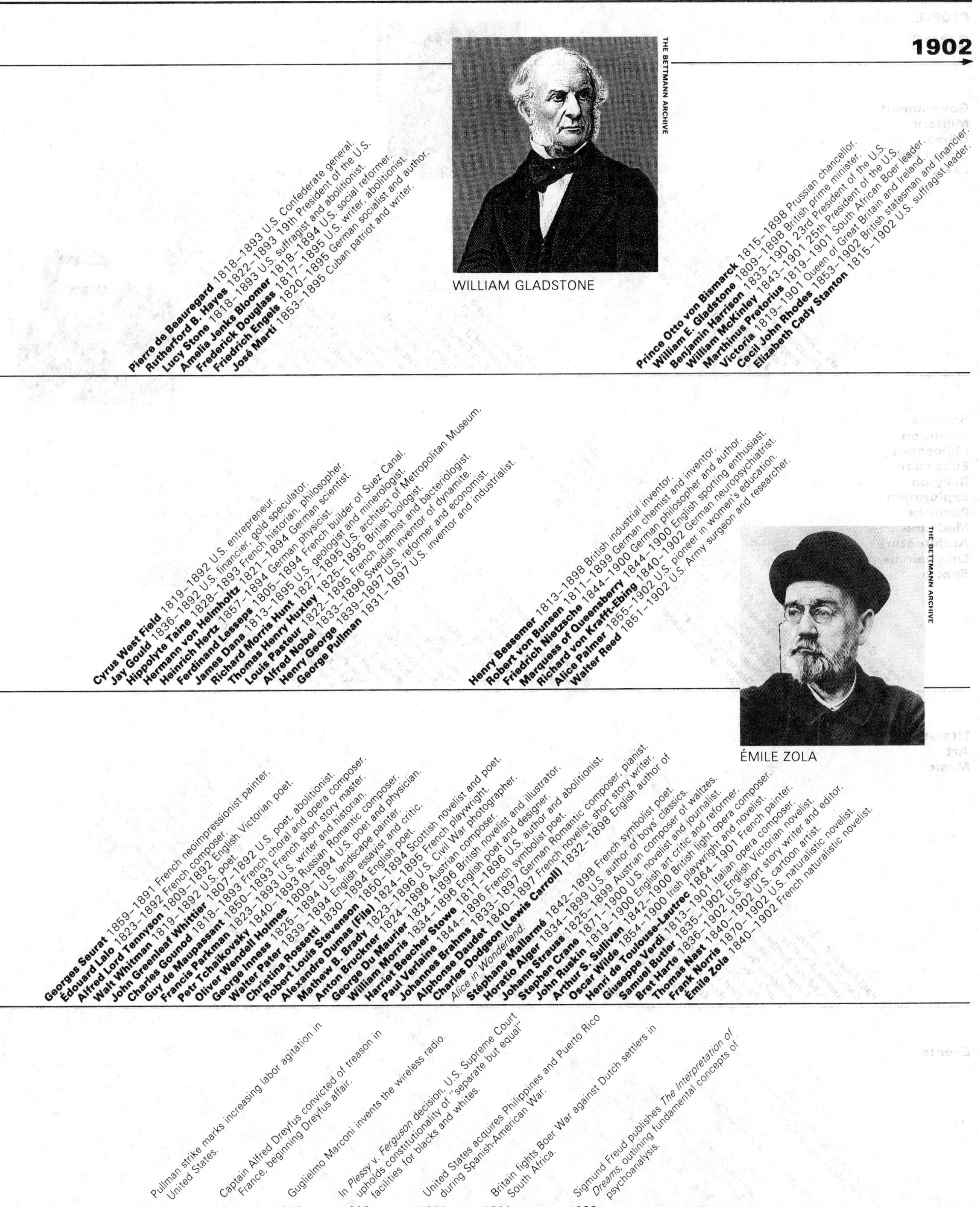

1902

Pierre de Beauregard 1818–1893 U.S. Confederate general.
Rutherford B. Hayes 1822–1893 19th President of the U.S.
Lucy Stone 1818–1893 U.S. suffragist and abolitionist.
Amelia Jenks Bloomer 1818–1894 U.S. social reformer.
Frederick Douglass 1817–1895 U.S. writer, abolitionist.
Friedrich Engels 1820–1895 German socialist and author.
José Martí 1853–1895 Cuban patriot and writer.

THE BETTMANN ARCHIVE

WILLIAM GLADSTONE

Prince Otto von Bismarck 1815–1898 Prussian chancellor.
William E. Gladstone 1809–1898 British prime minister.
Benjamin Harrison 1833–1901 23rd President of the U.S.
William McKinley 1843–1901 25th President of the U.S.
Marthinus Pretorius 1819–1901 South African Boer leader.
Victoria 1819–1901 Queen of Great Britain and Ireland.
Cecil John Rhodes 1853–1902 British statesman and financier.
Elizabeth Cady Stanton 1815–1902 U.S. suffragist leader.

Cyrus West Field 1819–1892 U.S. entrepreneur.
Jay Gould 1836–1892 U.S. financier, gold speculator.
Hippolyte Taine 1828–1893 French historian, philosopher.
Hermann von Helmholtz 1821–1894 German scientist.
Heinrich Hertz 1857–1894 German physicist.
Ferdinand Lesseps 1805–1894 French builder of Suez Canal.
James Dana 1813–1895 U.S. geologist and mineralogist.
Richard Morris Hunt 1827–1895 U.S. architect of Metropolitan Museum.
Thomas Henry Huxley 1825–1895 British biologist.
Louis Pasteur 1822–1895 French chemist and bacteriologist.
Alfred Nobel 1833–1896 Swedish inventor of dynamite.
Henry George 1839–1897 U.S. reformer and economist.
George Pullman 1831–1897 U.S. inventor and industrialist.

Henry Bessemer 1813–1898 British industrial inventor.
Robert von Bunsen 1811–1899 German chemist and inventor.
Friedrich Nietzsche 1844–1900 German philosopher and author.
Marquess of Queensberry 1844–1900 English sporting enthusiast.
Richard von Krafft-Ebing 1840–1902 German neuropsychiatrist.
Alice Palmer 1855–1902 U.S. pioneer in women's education.
Walter Reed 1851–1902 U.S. Army surgeon and researcher.

THE BETTMANN ARCHIVE

ÉMILE ZOLA

Georges Seurat 1859–1891 French neoimpressionist painter.
Édouard Lalo 1823–1892 French composer.
Alfred Lord Tennyson 1809–1892 English Victorian poet.
Walt Whitman 1819–1892 U.S. poet.
John Greenleaf Whittier 1807–1892 U.S. poet, abolitionist.
Charles Gounod 1818–1893 French choral and opera composer.
Guy de Maupassant 1850–1893 French short story master.
Francis Parkman 1823–1893 U.S. writer and historian.
Petr Tchaikovsky 1840–1893 Russian Romantic composer.
Oliver Wendell Holmes 1809–1894 U.S. poet and physician.
George Inness 1825–1894 U.S. landscape painter.
Walter Pater 1839–1894 English essayist and critic.
Christina Rossetti 1830–1894 English poet.
Robert Louis Stevenson 1850–1894 Scottish novelist and poet.
Alexandre Dumas (Fils) 1824–1895 French playwright.
Mathew B. Brady 1823–1896 U.S. Civil War photographer.
Anton Bruckner 1824–1896 Austrian composer.
George Du Maurier 1834–1896 British novelist and illustrator.
William Morris 1834–1896 English poet and designer.
Harriet Beecher Stowe 1811–1896 U.S. author and abolitionist.
Paul Verlaine 1844–1896 French symbolist poet.
Johannes Brahms 1833–1897 German Romantic composer, pianist.
Alphonse Daudet 1840–1897 French novelist, short story writer.
Charles Dodgson (Lewis Carroll) 1832–1898 English author of *Alice in Wonderland*
Stéphane Mallarmé 1842–1898 French symbolist poet.
Horatio Alger 1834–1899 U.S. author of boys' classics.
Johann Strauss 1825–1899 Austrian composer of waltzes.
Stephen Crane 1871–1900 U.S. novelist and journalist.
John Ruskin 1819–1900 English art critic and reformer.
Arthur S. Sullivan 1842–1900 British light opera composer.
Oscar Wilde 1854–1900 Irish playwright and novelist.
Henri de Toulouse-Lautrec 1864–1901 French painter.
Giuseppe Verdi 1813–1901 Italian opera composer.
Samuel Butler 1835–1902 English Victorian novelist.
Bret Harte 1836–1902 U.S. short story writer and editor.
Thomas Nast 1840–1902 U.S. cartoon artist.
Frank Norris 1870–1902 U.S. naturalistic novelist.
Émile Zola 1840–1902 French naturalistic novelist.

1894 — Pullman strike marks increasing labor agitation in United States.
1894 — Captain Alfred Dreyfus convicted of treason in France, beginning Dreyfus affair.
1895 — Guglielmo Marconi invents the wireless radio.
1896 — In *Plessy v. Ferguson* decision, U.S. Supreme Court upholds constitutionality of "separate but equal" facilities for blacks and whites.
1898 — United States acquires Philippines and Puerto Rico during Spanish-American War.
1899 — Britain fights Boer War against Dutch settlers in South Africa.
1900 — Sigmund Freud publishes *The Interpretation of Dreams*, outlining fundamental concepts of psychoanalysis.

PEOPLE *(continued)*

1903

Government, Military, Crime, Social Reform, Law

Mark Hanna 1837–1904 U.S. politician, entrepreneur.
Theodor Herzl 1860–1904 Hungarian-Jewish Zionist leader.
Joseph 1840–1904 American Indian chief, Nez Percé tribe.
Paul Kruger 1825–1904 South African Boer leader.
James Longstreet 1821–1904 U.S. Confederate general.
Susan B. Anthony 1820–1906 U.S. women's rights pioneer.

THE BETTMANN ARCHIVE

GERONIMO

Grover Cleveland 1837–1908 Twice President of the U.S.
Geronimo 1829–1909 American Apache Indian chief.
Leopold II 1835–1909 King of the Belgians.
Red Cloud 1822–1909 American Oglala Indian chief.
Edward VII 1841–1910 King of Great Britain and Ireland.
Carry Nation 1846–1911 U.S. temperance leader.
William Booth 1829–1912 British founder of Salvation Army.
Mutsuhito 1852–1912 Emperor of Japan, known as Meiji.
August Bebel 1840–1913 German socialist labor leader.
Harriet Tubman c 1820–1913 U.S. abolitionist.
Adlai E. Stevenson 1835–1914 U.S. Vice President.
Porfirio Diaz 1830–1915 President of Mexico.
Sergei Yulievich Witte 1849–1915 Russian statesman.
Franz Josef I 1830–1916 Emperor of Austria-Hungary.
Horatio Herbert Kitchener 1850–1916 British general.
Grigori Rasputin c 1872–1916 Russian religious mystic.
Yüan Shih-K'ai 1859–1916 First president, Republic of China.

THE BETTMANN ARCHIVE

PORFIRIO DIAZ

Science, Invention, Philosophy, Education, Religion, Exploration, Business, Medicine, Architecture, Entertainment, Sports

Josiah Gibbs 1839–1903 U.S. mathematical physicist.
Frederick Olmsted 1822–1903 U.S. landscape architect. Designed Central Park.
Herbert Spencer 1820–1903 British philosopher.
Henry Morton Stanley 1841–1904 British explorer, journalist.
Meyer Guggenheim 1828–1905 Swiss-American smelting magnate.
Samuel Langley 1834–1906 U.S. astronomer, aviation pioneer.
Stanford White 1853–1906 U.S. neo-Renaissance architect.
William Kelvin 1824–1907 British physicist, mathematician.
Dmitri Mendeleev 1834–1907 Russian chemist. Classified elements.
Antoine Becquerel 1852–1908 French physicist.
Elizabeth Blackwell 1821–1910 First U.S. woman physician.
Jean Dunant 1828–1910 Swiss founder of Red Cross.
Mary Baker Eddy 1821–1910 U.S. founder of Christian Science.
William James 1842–1910 U.S. pragmatic philosopher.
Robert Koch 1843–1910 German bacteriologist.
Florence Nightingale 1820–1910 British hospital reformer.
Alfred Binet 1857–1911 French developer of IQ testing.
Joseph Pulitzer 1847–1911 U.S. editor and publisher.
Clara Barton 1821–1912 U.S. nurse, Red Cross leader.
Joseph Lister 1827–1912 English inventor of antiseptic surgery.
Robert Scott 1868–1912 British Antarctic explorer.
Wilbur Wright 1867–1912 U.S. aviation pioneer.
Rudolf Diesel 1858–1913 German automotive engineer.
John Pierpont Morgan 1837–1913 U.S. financier.
John Muir 1838–1914 U.S. naturalist and conservationist.
George Westinghouse 1846–1914 U.S. inventor, manufacturer.
Paul Ehrlich 1854–1915 German bacteriologist.
Henry Moseley 1887–1915 British physicist.
Booker T. Washington 1856–1915 U.S. educator and black leader.
Percival Lowell 1855–1916 U.S. astronomer.

Literature, Art, Music

Paul Gauguin 1848–1903 French postimpressionist painter.
Camille Pissarro 1830–1903 French impressionist painter.
James Whistler 1834–1903 U.S. painter and etcher.
Frédéric Bartholdi 1834–1904 French sculptor.
Anton Chekhov 1860–1904 Russian playwright, short story writer.
Antonin Dvorak 1841–1904 Czech composer.
Jules Verne 1828–1905 French science fiction writer.
Paul Cézanne 1839–1906 French painter.
Paul Lawrence Dunbar 1872–1906 U.S. poet.
Henrik Ibsen 1828–1906 Norwegian playwright.
Edward Grieg 1843–1907 Norwegian Romantic composer.
Augustus Saint-Gaudens 1848–1907 Irish-American sculptor.
Edward MacDowell 1861–1908 U.S. composer.
Nikolai Rimski-Korsakov 1844–1908 Russian composer.
Edward Everett Hale 1822–1909 U.S. author, clergyman.
George Meredith 1828–1909 British Victorian novelist, poet.
Frederic Remington 1861–1909 U.S. Western artist.
Algernon Charles Swinburne 1837–1909 English lyric poet.
John Millington Synge 1870–1909 Irish dramatist.
Samuel Clemens (Mark Twain) 1835–1910 U.S. novelist.
Winslow Homer 1836–1910 U.S. painter.
Julia Ward Howe 1819–1910 U.S. author, poet, reformer.
Marius Petipa 1819–1910 French ballet dancer, choreographer.
William Sidney Porter (O. Henry) 1862–1910 U.S. short story writer.
Henri Rousseau 1844–1910 French primitivist painter.
Leo Tolstoy 1828–1910 Russian novelist.
Sir William Gilbert 1836–1911 British author, librettist.
Gustav Mahler 1860–1911 Austrian composer and conductor.
Jules Massenet 1842–1912 French lyric opera composer.
Johann Strindberg 1849–1912 Swedish dramatist.
Ambrose Bierce 1842–1914 U.S. journalist and satirist.
Frédéric Mistral 1830–1914 French Provençal poet.
Jacob Riis 1849–1914 Danish-American social reformer.
John Tenniel 1820–1914 English illustrator, satirist.
Alexander Scriabin 1872–1915 Russian composer, pianist.
Thomas Eakins 1844–1916 U.S. painter.
Henry James 1843–1916 U.S. author and critic.
Jack London 1876–1916 U.S. writer of adventure stories.

Events

1903 — Orville and Wilbur Wright test first airplane at Kitty Hawk, North Carolina.
1904 — Construction of Panama Canal begins.
1904 — Japan emerges as a major power in Russo-Japanese War.
1905 — Albert Einstein develops theory of relativity.
1909 — American explorer Robert E. Peary reaches North Pole.
1911 — Revolution in China overthrows Ch'ing dynasty, establishes republic.
1912 — *Titanic* sinks in North Atlantic; over 1500 die.
1913 — Henry Ford introduces first industrial assembly line.
1914 — World War I begins.

1930

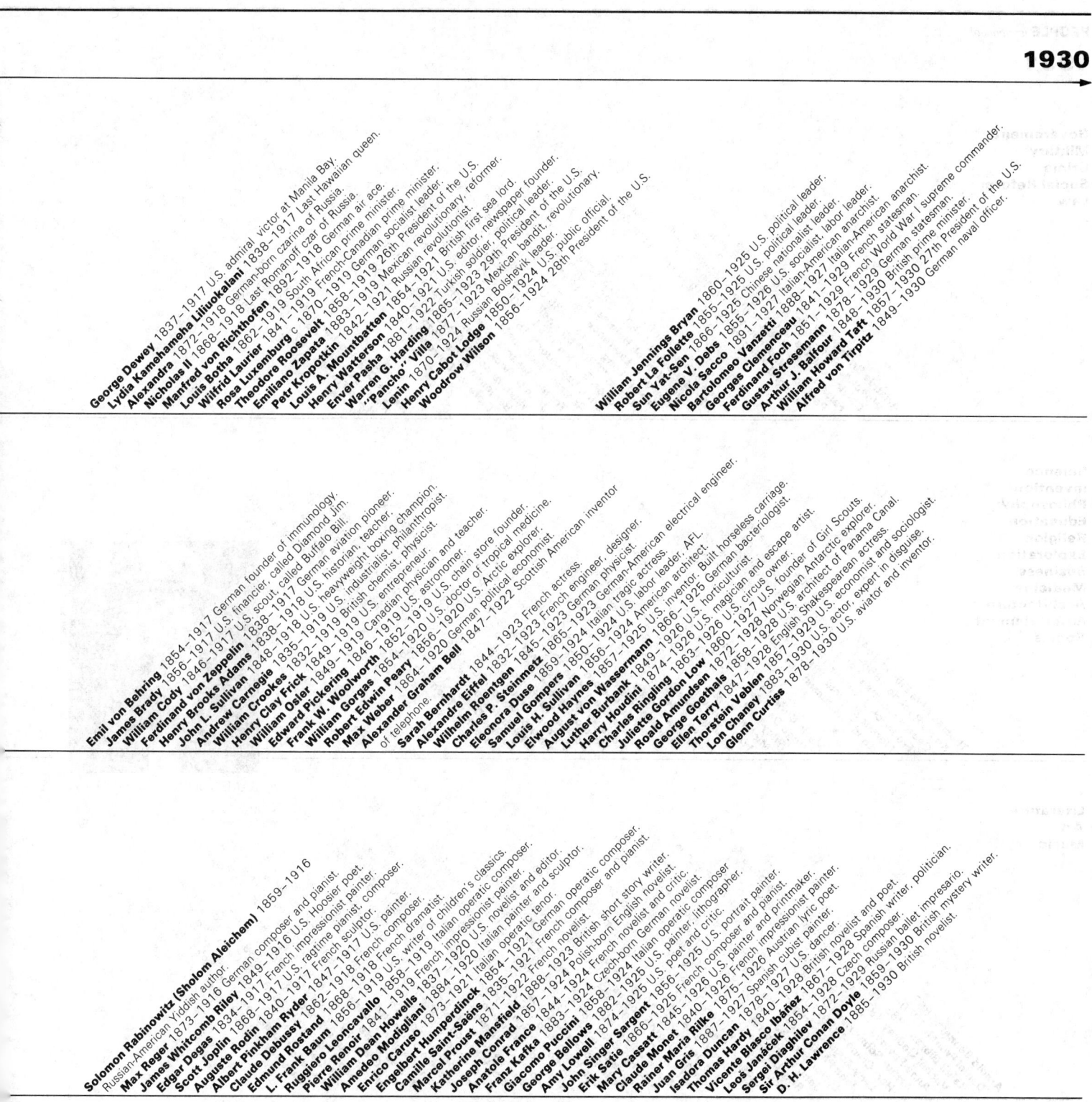

George Dewey 1837–1917 U.S. admiral, victor at Manila Bay.
Lydia Kamehameha Liliuokalani 1838–1917 Last Hawaiian queen.
Alexandra 1872–1918 German-born czarina of Russia.
Nicholas II 1868–1918 Last Romanoff czar of Russia.
Manfred von Richthofen 1892–1918 German air ace.
Louis Botha 1862–1919 South African prime minister.
Wilfrid Laurier 1841–1919 French-Canadian prime minister.
Rosa Luxemburg c. 1870–1919 German socialist leader.
Theodore Roosevelt 1858–1919 26th President of the U.S.
Emiliano Zapata 1883–1919 Mexican revolutionist.
Petr Kropotkin 1842–1921 Russian revolutionary, reformer.
Louis A. Mountbatten 1854–1921 British first sea lord.
Henry Watterson 1840–1921 U.S. editor, newspaper founder.
Enver Pasha 1881–1922 Turkish soldier, political leader.
Warren G. Harding 1865–1923 29th President of the U.S.
"Pancho" Villa 1877–1923 Mexican bandit, revolutionary.
Lenin 1870–1924 Russian Bolshevik leader.
Henry Cabot Lodge 1850–1924 U.S. public official.
Woodrow Wilson 1856–1924 28th President of the U.S.
William Jennings Bryan 1860–1925 U.S. political leader.
Robert La Follette 1855–1925 U.S. political leader.
Sun Yat-Sen 1866–1925 Chinese nationalist leader.
Eugene V. Debs 1855–1926 U.S. socialist, labor leader.
Nicola Sacco 1891–1927 Italian-American anarchist.
Bartolomeo Vanzetti 1888–1927 Italian-American anarchist.
Georges Clemenceau 1841–1929 French statesman.
Ferdinand Foch 1851–1929 French World War I supreme commander.
Gustav Stresemann 1878–1929 German statesman.
Arthur J. Balfour 1848–1930 British prime minister.
William Howard Taft 1857–1930 27th President of the U.S.
Alfred von Tirpitz 1849–1930 German naval officer.

Emil von Behring 1854–1917 German founder of immunology.
James Brady 1856–1917 U.S. financier, called Diamond Jim.
William Cody 1846–1917 U.S. scout, called Buffalo Bill.
Ferdinand von Zeppelin 1838–1917 German aviation pioneer.
Henry Brooks Adams 1838–1918 U.S. historian, teacher.
John L. Sullivan 1858–1918 U.S. heavyweight boxing champion.
Andrew Carnegie 1835–1919 U.S. industrialist, philanthropist.
William Crookes 1832–1919 British chemist, physicist.
Henry Clay Frick 1849–1919 U.S. entrepreneur.
William Osler 1849–1919 Canadian physician and teacher.
Edward Pickering 1846–1919 U.S. astronomer.
Frank W. Woolworth 1852–1919 U.S. chain store founder.
William Gorgas 1854–1920 U.S. doctor of tropical medicine.
Robert Edwin Peary 1856–1920 U.S. Arctic explorer.
Max Weber 1864–1920 German political economist.
Alexander Graham Bell 1847–1922 Scottish American inventor of telephone.
Sarah Bernhardt 1844–1923 French actress.
Alexandre Eiffel 1832–1923 French engineer, designer.
Wilhelm Roentgen 1845–1923 German physicist.
Charles P. Steinmetz 1865–1923 German-American electrical engineer.
Eleonora Duse 1859–1924 Italian tragic actress.
Samuel Gompers 1850–1924 U.S. labor leader, AFL.
Louis H. Sullivan 1856–1924 American architect.
Elwood Haynes 1857–1925 U.S. inventor. Built horseless carriage.
August von Wassermann 1866–1925 German bacteriologist.
Luther Burbank 1849–1926 U.S. horticulturist.
Harry Houdini 1874–1926 U.S. magician and escape artist.
Charles Ringling 1863–1926 U.S. circus owner.
Juliette Gordon Low 1860–1927 U.S. founder of Girl Scouts.
Roald Amundsen 1872–1928 Norwegian Antarctic explorer.
George Goethals 1858–1928 U.S. architect of Panama Canal.
Ellen Terry 1847–1928 English Shakespearean actress.
Thorstein Veblen 1857–1929 U.S. economist and sociologist.
Lon Chaney 1883–1930 U.S. actor, expert in disguise.
Glenn Curtiss 1878–1930 U.S. aviator and inventor.

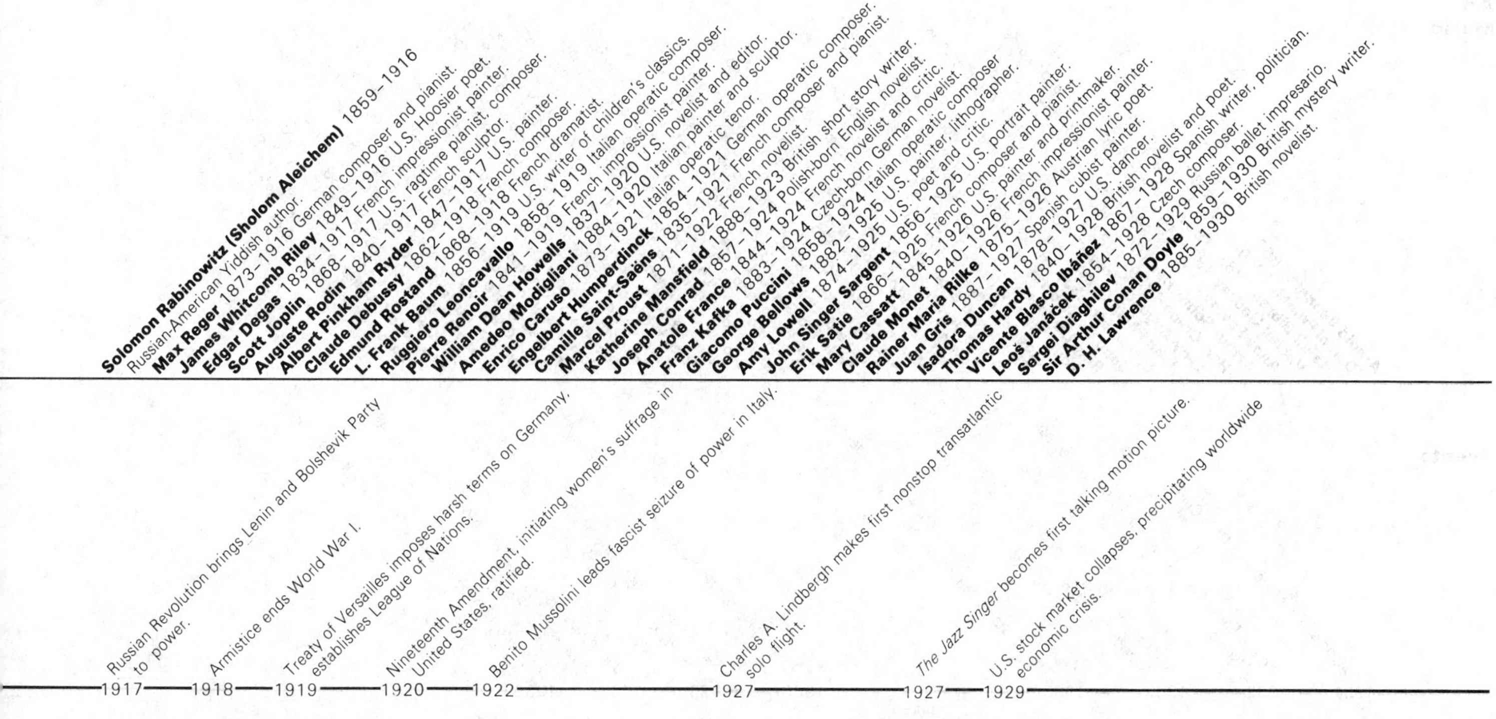

Solomon Rabinowitz (Sholom Aleichem) 1859–1916 Russian-American Yiddish author.
Max Reger 1873–1916 German composer and pianist.
James Whitcomb Riley 1849–1916 U.S. Hoosier poet.
Edgar Degas 1834–1917 French impressionist painter.
Scott Joplin 1868–1917 U.S. ragtime pianist, composer.
Auguste Rodin 1840–1917 French sculptor.
Albert Pinkham Ryder 1847–1917 U.S. painter.
Claude Debussy 1862–1918 French composer.
Edmund Rostand 1868–1918 French dramatist.
L. Frank Baum 1856–1919 U.S. writer of children's classics.
Ruggiero Leoncavallo 1858–1919 Italian operatic composer.
Pierre Renoir 1841–1919 French impressionist painter.
William Dean Howells 1837–1920 U.S. novelist and editor.
Amedeo Modigliani 1884–1920 Italian painter and sculptor.
Enrico Caruso 1873–1921 Italian operatic tenor.
Engelbert Humperdinck 1854–1921 German operatic composer.
Camille Saint-Saëns 1835–1921 French composer and pianist.
Marcel Proust 1871–1922 French novelist.
Katherine Mansfield 1888–1923 British short story writer.
Joseph Conrad 1857–1924 Polish-born English novelist.
Anatole France 1844–1924 French novelist and critic.
Franz Kafka 1883–1924 Czech-born German novelist.
Giacomo Puccini 1858–1924 Italian operatic composer
George Bellows 1882–1925 U.S. painter, lithographer.
Amy Lowell 1874–1925 U.S. poet and critic.
John Singer Sargent 1856–1925 U.S. portrait painter.
Erik Satie 1866–1925 French composer and pianist.
Mary Cassatt 1845–1926 U.S. painter and printmaker.
Claude Monet 1840–1926 French impressionist painter.
Rainer Maria Rilke 1875–1926 Austrian lyric poet.
Juan Gris 1887–1927 Spanish cubist painter.
Isadora Duncan 1878–1927 U.S. dancer.
Thomas Hardy 1840–1928 British novelist and poet.
Vicente Blasco Ibáñez 1867–1928 Spanish writer, politician.
Leoš Janáček 1854–1928 Czech composer.
Sergei Diaghilev 1872–1929 Russian ballet impresario.
Sir Arthur Conan Doyle 1859–1930 British mystery writer.
D. H. Lawrence 1885–1930 British novelist.

1917 Russian Revolution brings Lenin and Bolshevik Party to power.
1918 Armistice ends World War I.
1919 Treaty of Versailles imposes harsh terms on Germany, establishes League of Nations.
1920 Nineteenth Amendment, initiating women's suffrage in United States, ratified.
1922 Benito Mussolini leads fascist seizure of power in Italy.
1927 Charles A. Lindbergh makes first nonstop transatlantic solo flight.
1927 *The Jazz Singer* becomes first talking motion picture.
1929 U.S. stock market collapses, precipitating worldwide economic crisis.

PEOPLE *(continued)*

1931

Government
Military
Crime
Social Reform
Law

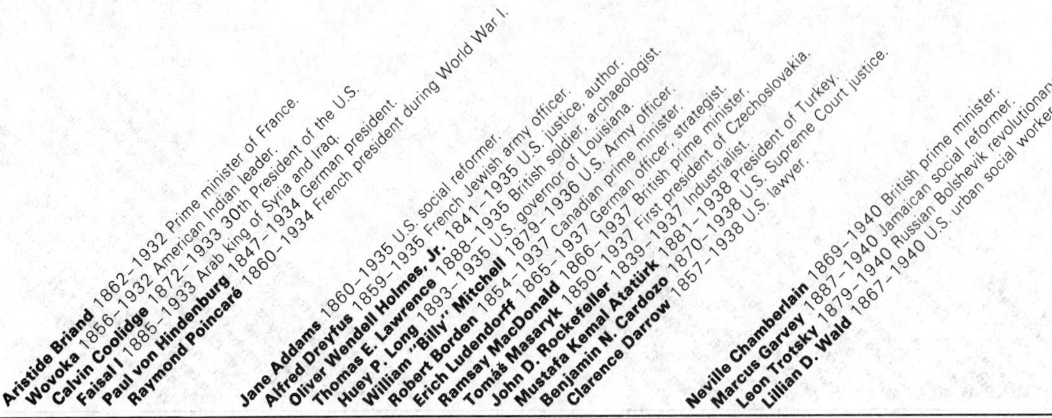

Aristide Briand 1862–1932 Prime minister of France.
Wovoka 1856–1932 American Indian leader.
Calvin Coolidge 1872–1933 30th President of the U.S.
Faisal I 1885–1933 Arab king of Syria and Iraq.
Paul von Hindenburg 1847–1934 German president.
Raymond Poincaré 1860–1934 French president during World War I.
Jane Addams 1860–1935 U.S. social reformer.
Alfred Dreyfus 1859–1935 French Jewish army officer.
Oliver Wendell Holmes, Jr. 1841–1935 U.S. justice, author.
Thomas E. Lawrence 1888–1935 British soldier, archaeologist.
Huey P. Long 1893–1935 U.S. governor of Louisiana.
William "Billy" Mitchell 1879–1936 U.S. Army officer.
Robert Borden 1854–1937 Canadian prime minister.
Erich Ludendorff 1865–1937 German officer, strategist.
Ramsay MacDonald 1866–1937 British prime minister.
Tomáš Masaryk 1850–1937 First president of Czechoslovakia.
John D. Rockefeller 1839–1937 Industrialist.
Mustafa Kemal Atatürk 1881–1938 President of Turkey.
Benjamin N. Cardozo 1870–1938 U.S. Supreme Court justice.
Clarence Darrow 1857–1938 U.S. lawyer.
Neville Chamberlain 1869–1940 British prime minister.
Marcus Garvey 1887–1940 Jamaican social reformer.
Leon Trotsky 1879–1940 Russian Bolshevik revolutionary.
Lillian D. Wald 1867–1940 U.S. urban social worker.

Science
Invention
Philosophy
Education
Religion
Exploration
Business
Medicine
Architecture
Entertainment
Sports

Thomas Alva Edison 1847–1931 Versatile U.S. inventor.
Knute Rockne 1888–1931 Norwegian-American football coach.
George Eastman 1854–1932 U.S. photographic inventor.
Frederick J. Turner 1861–1932 U.S. frontier historian.
Florenz Ziegfeld 1869–1932 U.S. theatrical producer.
Knud Rasmussen 1879–1933 Danish polar explorer. Studied Eskimos.
Marie Curie 1867–1934 Polish-French discoverer of radium.
Hugo De Vries 1848–1935 Dutch botanist.
Wiley Post 1899–1935 U.S. aviation pioneer.
Michael Pupin 1858–1935 Yugoslav-American physicist.
Ivan Pavlov 1849–1936 Russian experimental psychologist.
Oswald Spengler 1880–1936 German philosopher, historian.
Alfred Adler 1870–1937 Austrian psychiatrist.
Amelia Earhart 1898–1937 U.S. transoceanic flier.
Guglielmo Marconi 1874–1937 Italian pioneer in radio.
Ernest Rutherford 1871–1937 British physical chemist.
George Ellery Hale 1868–1938 U.S. astronomer.
Konstantin Stanislavski 1863–1938 Russian actor, producer.
Havelock Ellis 1859–1939 British scientist and author.
Douglas Fairbanks 1883–1939 U.S. film actor.
Sigmund Freud 1856–1939 Austrian founder of psychoanalysis.
Charles Mayo 1865–1939 American co-founder of Mayo Clinic.
William Mayo 1861–1939 American co-founder of Mayo Clinic.
Eugène Dubois 1858–1940 Dutch geologist, anatomist.
Joseph J. Thomson 1856–1940 English discoverer of electron.

JAMES JOYCE

Literature
Art
Music

Arnold Bennett 1867–1931 English novelist.
Daniel French 1850–1931 U.S. sculptor.
Kahlil Gibran 1883–1931 Lebanese-American poet and artist.
Vachel Lindsay 1879–1931 U.S. poet and lecturer.
Anna Pavlova 1881–1931 Russian ballet dancer.
Arthur Schnitzler 1862–1931 Austrian author and physician.
Hart Crane 1899–1932 U.S. poet.
Lady Augusta Gregory 1852–1932 Irish dramatist.
John Philip Sousa 1854–1932 U.S. composer and bandmaster.
Lytton Strachey 1880–1932 British writer of biographies.
John Galsworthy 1867–1933 British novelist, playwright.
Ring Lardner 1885–1933 U.S. author and sportswriter.
Louis Tiffany 1848–1933 U.S. glass designer, painter.
Frederick Delius 1862–1934 British composer.
Sir Edward Elgar 1857–1934 English late Romantic composer.
Alban Berg 1885–1935 Austrian composer.
Edwin Arlington Robinson 1869–1935 New England poet.
Will Rogers 1879–1935 U.S. humorist, actor, columnist.
Maxim Gorki 1868–1936 Russian social realist writer.
A. E. Housman 1859–1936 English poet, classical scholar.
Rudyard Kipling 1865–1936 English author and journalist.
Federico García Lorca 1899–1936 Spanish poet, dramatist.
Luigi Pirandello 1867–1936 Italian author and dramatist.
Ottorino Respighi 1879–1936 Italian symphonic composer.
Miguel de Unamuno 1864–1936 Spanish writer and philosopher.
George Gershwin 1898–1937 U.S. composer.
Maurice Ravel 1875–1937 French composer.
Edith Wharton 1862–1937 U.S. novelist, short story writer.
Karel Capek 1890–1938 Czech dramatist and essayist.
Feodor Chaliapin 1873–1938 Russian operatic bass.
Gabriele D'Annunzio 1863–1938 Italian poet, political figure.
James Weldon Johnson 1871–1938 U.S. poet and diplomat.
Thomas Wolfe 1900–1938 U.S. novelist.
Zane Grey 1875–1939 U.S. Western writer.
William Butler Yeats 1865–1939 Irish poet and dramatist.
F. Scott Fitzgerald 1896–1940 U.S. novelist.
Paul Klee 1879–1940 Swiss painter and graphic artist.
Sherwood Anderson 1876–1941 U.S. author.
James Joyce 1882–1941 Irish author of *Ulysses*.

Events

1931 — Japan seizes Manchuria from China.
1932 — Amelia Earhart is first woman to fly solo across the Atlantic.
1933 — Adolf Hitler becomes chancellor of Germany; sets up Nazi dictatorship.
1933 — Franklin D. Roosevelt takes office as President of United States; launches New Deal.
1936 — Josef Stalin purges Russian Communist Party.
1936 — German troops reoccupy the Rhineland as Hitler begins to pursue expansionist policy.
1937 — Japan invades China; World War II begins in Asia.
1939 — Germany invades Poland; World War II begins in Europe.

1949

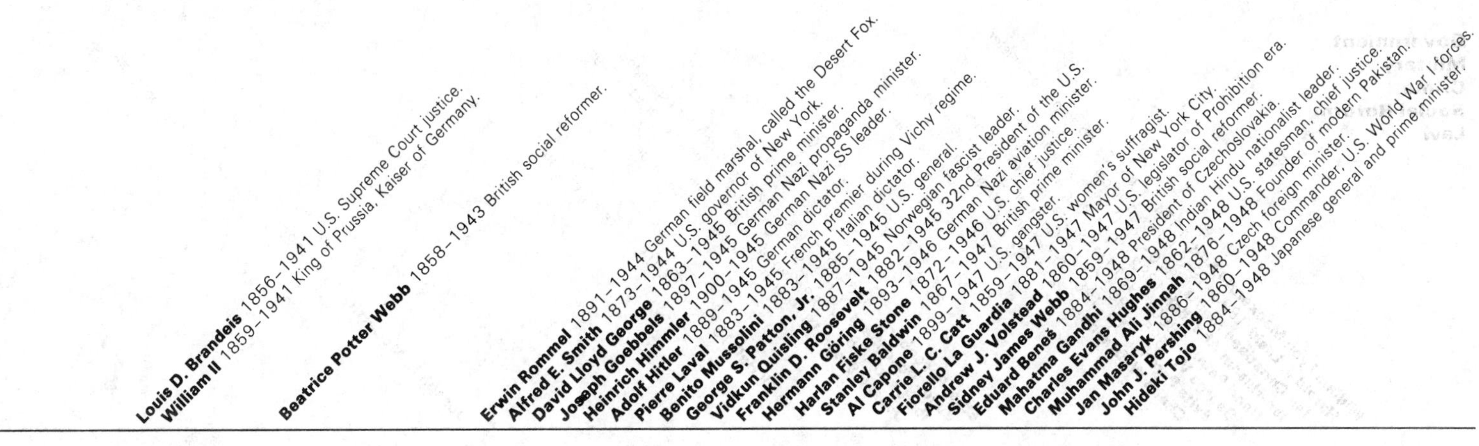

Louis D. Brandeis 1856–1941 U.S. Supreme Court justice.
William II 1859–1941 King of Prussia, Kaiser of Germany.
Beatrice Potter Webb 1858–1943 British social reformer.
Erwin Rommel 1891–1944 German field marshal, called the Desert Fox.
Alfred E. Smith 1873–1944 U.S. governor of New York.
David Lloyd George 1863–1945 British prime minister.
Joseph Goebbels 1897–1945 German Nazi propaganda minister.
Heinrich Himmler 1900–1945 German Nazi SS leader.
Adolf Hitler 1889–1945 German dictator.
Pierre Laval 1883–1945 French premier during Vichy regime.
Benito Mussolini 1883–1945 Italian dictator.
George S. Patton, Jr. 1885–1945 U.S. general.
Vidkun Quisling 1887–1945 Norwegian fascist leader.
Franklin D. Roosevelt 1882–1945 32nd President of the U.S.
Hermann Göring 1893–1946 German Nazi aviation minister.
Harlan Fiske Stone 1872–1946 U.S. chief justice.
Stanley Baldwin 1867–1947 British prime minister.
Al Capone 1899–1947 U.S. gangster.
Carrie L. C. Catt 1859–1947 U.S. women's suffragist.
Fiorello La Guardia 1881–1947 Mayor of New York City.
Andrew J. Volstead 1860–1947 U.S. legislator of Prohibition era.
Sidney James Webb 1859–1947 British social reformer.
Eduard Beneš 1884–1948 President of Czechoslovakia.
Mahatma Gandhi 1869–1948 Indian Hindu nationalist leader.
Charles Evans Hughes 1862–1948 U.S. statesman, chief justice.
Muhammad Ali Jinnah 1876–1948 Founder of modern Pakistan.
Jan Masaryk 1886–1948 Czech foreign minister.
John J. Pershing 1860–1948 Commander, U.S. World War I forces.
Hideki Tojo 1884–1948 Japanese general and prime minister.

Frederick Banting 1891–1941 Canadian research physician.
Henri Bergson 1859–1941 French philosopher and writer.
Lou Gehrig 1903–1941 U.S. baseball hero.
Franz Boas 1858–1942 German-American anthropologist, author.
George Washington Carver 1864–1943 U.S. botanist.
John Pierpont Morgan, Jr. 1867–1943 U.S. financier.
Max Reinhardt 1873–1943 Austrian theater manager.
Nikola Tesla 1856–1943 Yugoslav-American inventor.
Alexis Carrel 1873–1944 French surgeon.
Arthur Eddington 1882–1944 English astronomer.
Robert Goddard 1882–1945 U.S. physicist, rocket pioneer.
W.C. Fields 1880–1946 U.S. comic film star.
James Jeans 1877–1946 British physicist, astronomer.
Jack Johnson 1878–1946 U.S. heavyweight boxing champion.
Walter Johnson 1887–1946 U.S. baseball player.
John Maynard Keynes 1883–1946 British economist.
Henry Ford 1863–1947 U.S. automotive pioneer.
Max Planck 1858–1947 German physicist.
Alfred N. Whitehead 1861–1947 British mathematician.
Charles Austin Beard 1874–1948 U.S. historian.
Ruth Fulton Benedict 1887–1948 U.S. anthropologist, author.
Sergei Eisenstein 1898–1948 Soviet film director.
D. W. Griffith 1875–1948 U.S. silent film director.
Jean Lumiere 1864–1948 French chemist and inventor.
"Babe" Ruth 1895–1948 U.S. baseball hero.
Orville Wright 1871–1948 U.S. aviation pioneer.
Solomon Guggenheim 1861–1949 U.S. industrialist.
Edward Thorndike 1874–1949 U.S. educational psychologist.
Stephen Wise 1874–1949 U.S. Zionist leader and rabbi.

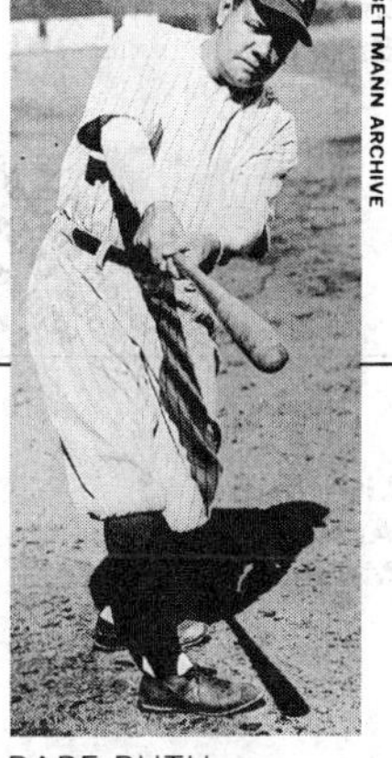

BABE RUTH

Ignace Jan Paderewski 1860–1941 Polish pianist and statesman.
Rabindranath Tagore 1861–1941 Indian author and mystic.
Virginia Woolf 1882–1941 English novelist and essayist.
George M. Cohan 1878–1942 U.S. entertainer, writer, producer.
Grant Wood 1892–1942 U.S. midwestern painter.
Stephen Vincent Benét 1898–1943 U.S. poet.
Sergei Rachmaninoff 1873–1943 Russian composer and pianist.
Vassily Kandinsky 1866–1944 Russian painter, theoretician.
Aristide Maillol 1861–1944 French sculptor.
Piet Mondrian 1872–1944 Dutch nonobjective painter.
Edvard Munch 1863–1944 Norwegian expressionist artist.
Romain Rolland 1866–1944 French writer and scholar.
Antoine de Saint-Exupéry 1900–1944 French aviator, writer.
Ida M. Tarbell 1857–1944 U.S. author and editor.
William Allen White 1868–1944 U.S. author and editor.
Béla Bartók 1881–1945 Hungarian composer.
Robert Benchley 1889–1945 U.S. humorist, critic, actor.
Theodore Dreiser 1871–1945 U.S. editor and novelist.
Jerome Kern 1885–1945 U.S. song writer.
Paul Valéry 1871–1945 French poet and essayist.
Countee Cullen 1903–1946 U.S. poet.
Manuel de Falla 1876–1946 Spanish composer.
László Moholy-Nagy 1895–1946 Hungarian painter, designer.
Gertrude Stein 1874–1946 U.S. avant-garde writer.
Alfred Stieglitz 1864–1946 U.S. pioneer photographer.
H. G. Wells 1866–1946 English writer of fantasy.
Pierre Bonnard 1867–1947 French painter and lithographer.
Willa Cather 1873–1947 U.S. midwestern novelist.
Franz Lehár 1870–1948 Hungarian operetta composer.
James Ensor 1860–1949 Belgian artist of the fantastic.
Maurice Maeterlinck 1862–1949 Belgian writer, naturalist.
José Clemente Orozco 1883–1949 Mexican muralist.
Richard Strauss 1864–1949 German Romantic composer.
Sigrid Undset 1882–1949 Norwegian historical novelist.

1941 Japanese attack on Pearl Harbor brings United States into World War II.
1943 German defeat at Stalingrad becomes major turning point in World War II.
1945 Germany and Japan surrender; U.S. atomic bombs destroy Hiroshima and Nagasaki.
1947 United States launches Marshall Plan to rebuild war-ravaged nations of Europe.
1947 India and Pakistan gain independence from Britain.
1948 State of Israel established.
1949 Berlin blockade marks increasing Cold War tensions between Communist bloc and the free world.
1949 Communists win Chinese civil war, establish People's Republic of China.

PEOPLE *(continued)*

1950

Government, Military, Crime, Social Reform, Law

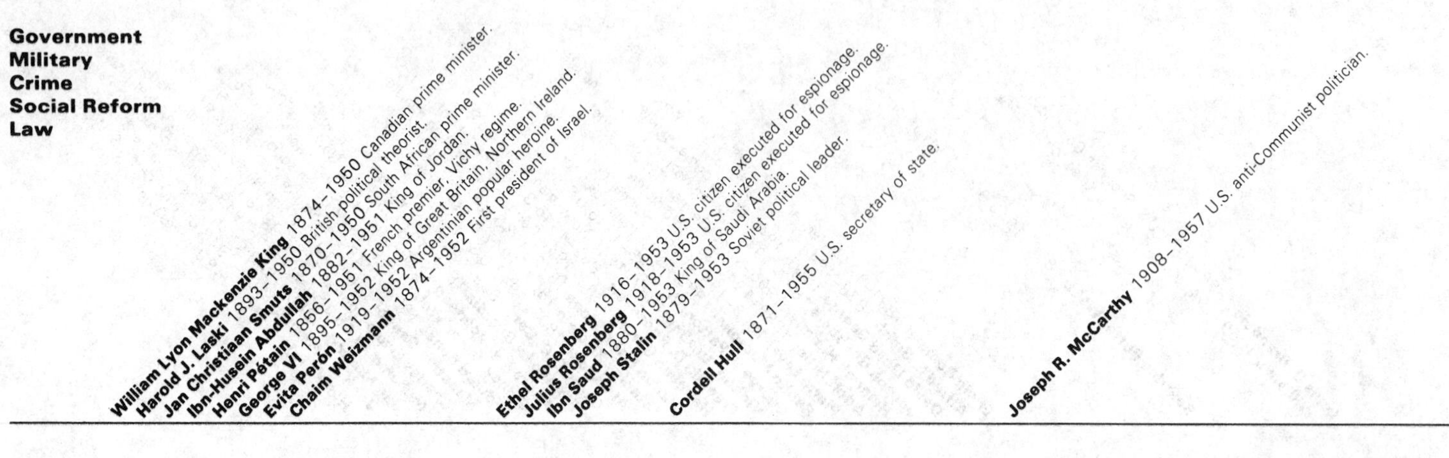

William Lyon Mackenzie King 1874–1950 Canadian prime minister.
Harold J. Laski 1893–1950 British political theorist.
Jan Christiaan Smuts 1870–1950 South African prime minister.
Ibn-Hussein Abdullah 1882–1951 King of Jordan.
Henri Pétain 1856–1951 French premier, Vichy regime.
George VI 1895–1952 King of Great Britain, Northern Ireland.
Evita Perón 1919–1952 Argentinian popular heroine.
Chaim Weizmann 1874–1952 First president of Israel.
Ethel Rosenberg 1916–1953 U.S. citizen executed for espionage.
Julius Rosenberg 1918–1953 U.S. citizen executed for espionage.
Ibn Saud 1880–1953 King of Saudi Arabia.
Joseph Stalin 1879–1953 Soviet political leader.
Cordell Hull 1871–1955 U.S. secretary of state.
Joseph R. McCarthy 1908–1957 U.S. anti-Communist politician.

Science, Invention, Philosophy, Education, Religion, Exploration, Business, Medicine, Architecture, Entertainment, Sports

Eliel Saarinen 1873–1950 Finnish-American architect.
Lincoln Ellsworth 1880–1951 U.S. explorer and aviator.
Robert Flaherty 1884–1951 U.S. filmmaker and explorer.
William Randolph Hearst 1863–1951 U.S. publishing magnate.
Benedetto Croce 1866–1952 Italian philosopher.
John Dewey 1859–1952 U.S. philosopher, educational reformer.
Elizabeth Kenny 1886–1952 Australian nurse.
Maria Montessori 1870–1952 Italian physician and educator.
Philip Murray 1886–1952 U.S. labor leader, CIO.
George Santayana 1863–1952 Spanish-American poet, philosopher.
Robert A. Millikan 1868–1953 U.S. physicist.
Jim Thorpe 1888–1953 American Indian Olympic athlete.
William Tilden, Jr. 1893–1953 U.S. tennis champion.
Lionel Barrymore 1878–1954 U.S. character actor.
Enrico Fermi 1901–1954 Italian-American nuclear physicist.
August Lumière 1862–1954 French chemist and inventor.
Mary McLeod Bethune 1875–1955 U.S. educator.
Pierre Teilhard de Chardin 1881–1955 French Jesuit scientist.
James Dean 1931–1955 U.S. film actor, cult figure.
Albert Einstein 1879–1955 German-American theoretical physicist.
Alexander Fleming 1881–1955 British bacteriologist.
José Ortega y Gasset 1883–1955 Spanish philosopher.
"Babe" Didrikson 1914–1956 U.S. track star and golfer.
Irene Joliot-Curie 1897–1956 French physicist.
Alfred C. Kinsey 1894–1956 U.S. biologist, sex researcher.
Connie Mack 1862–1956 U.S. baseball player and manager.
Humphrey Bogart 1899–1957 U.S. stage and film actor.
Richard E. Byrd 1888–1957 U.S. aviator and explorer.

THE BETTMANN ARCHIVE

SHOLEM ASCH

Literature, Art, Music

Edgar Lee Masters 1869–1950 U.S. poet and novelist.
Edna St. Vincent Millay 1892–1950 U.S. poet, dramatist.
Vaslav Nijinsky 1890–1950 Russian ballet dancer.
George Orwell 1903–1950 British author, social commentator.
George Bernard Shaw 1856–1950 Irish dramatist and critic.
Kurt Weill 1900–1950 German composer for theater.
André Gide 1869–1951 French novelist and essayist.
Serge Koussevitzky 1874–1951 Russian-American conductor.
Huddie Ledbetter 1888–1951 U.S. folk and blues singer.
Sinclair Lewis 1885–1951 U.S. journalist and novelist.
Arnold Schoenberg 1874–1951 Austrian-American composer.
Knut Hamsun 1859–1952 Norwegian novelist.
Ferenc Molnár 1878–1952 Hungarian playwright.
Raoul Dufy 1877–1953 French Fauvist painter, designer.
John Marin 1872–1953 U.S. marine watercolor artist.
Eugene O'Neill 1888–1953 U.S. playwright.
Sergei Prokofiev 1891–1953 Soviet composer.
Dylan Thomas 1914–1953 Welsh poet and lecturer.
Sidonie Colette 1873–1954 French novelist.
Charles Ives 1874–1954 U.S. composer and businessman.
Reginald Marsh 1898–1954 U.S. painter.
Henri Matisse 1869–1954 French artist.
James Agee 1909–1955 U.S. film critic, script writer, novelist.
Arthur Honegger 1892–1955 French-Swiss composer.
Fernand Léger 1881–1955 French cubist painter.
Thomas Mann 1875–1955 German author.
Robert Sherwood 1896–1955 U.S. author and playwright.
Wallace Stevens 1879–1955 U.S. poet.
Maurice Utrillo 1883–1955 French painter.
Max Beerbohm 1872–1956 British essayist, caricaturist.
Bertolt Brecht 1898–1956 German poet and playwright.
Lyonel Feininger 1871–1956 U.S. painter.
H. L. Mencken 1880–1956 U.S. editor, writer, social critic.
A. A. Milne 1882–1956 British writer of children's stories.
Jackson Pollock 1912–1956 U.S. abstract expressionist painter.
Sholem Asch 1880–1957 Polish-born Yiddish author.
Constantin Brancusi 1876–1957 Rumanian sculptor.

Events

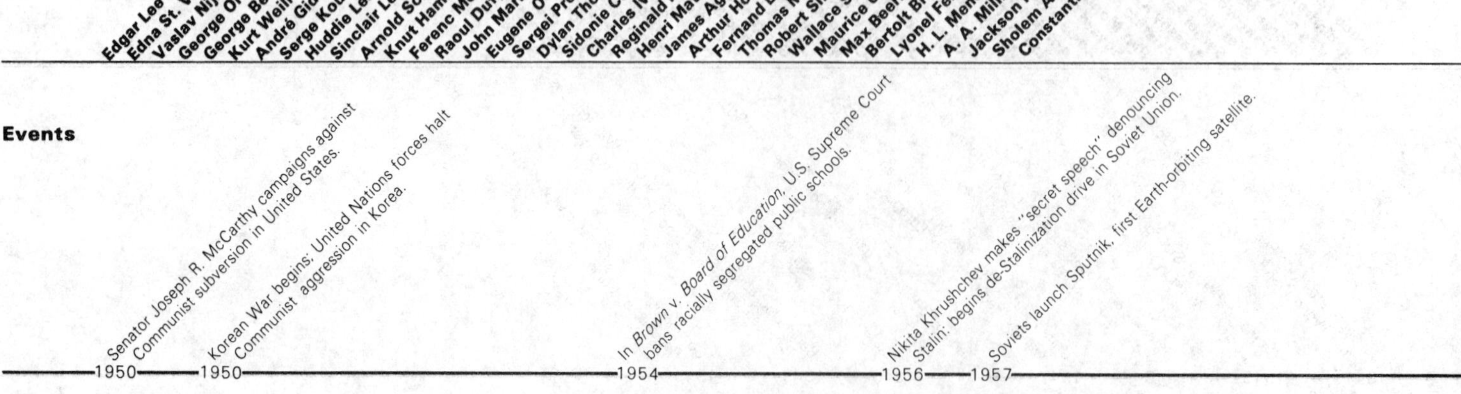

1950 Senator Joseph R. McCarthy campaigns against Communist subversion in United States.
1950 Korean War begins; United Nations forces halt Communist aggression in Korea.
1954 In *Brown v. Board of Education*, U.S. Supreme Court bans racially segregated public schools.
1956 Nikita Khrushchev makes "secret speech" denouncing Stalin; begins de-Stalinization drive in Soviet Union.
1957 Soviets launch Sputnik, first Earth-orbiting satellite.

1963

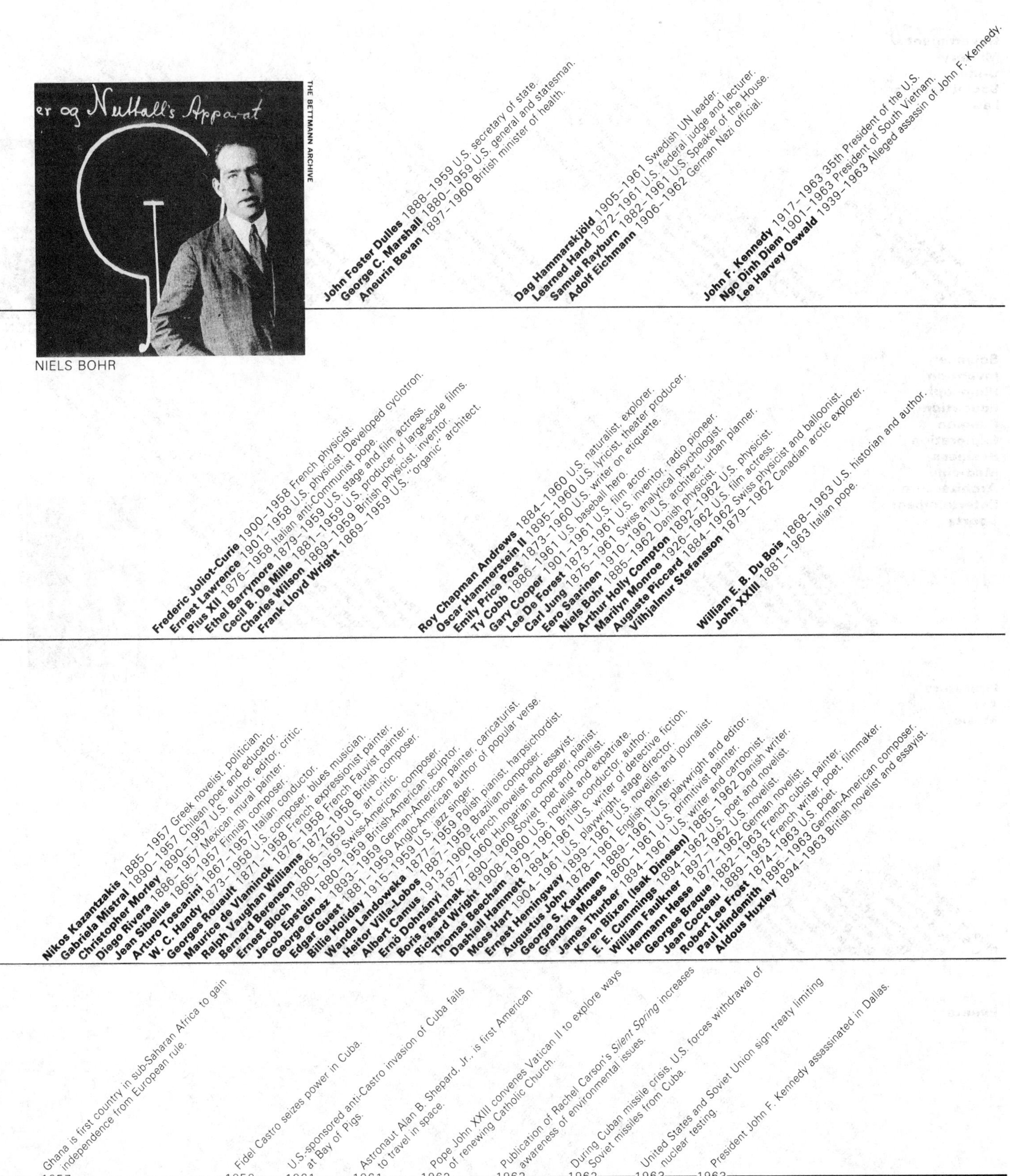

THE BETTMANN ARCHIVE

NIELS BOHR

John Foster Dulles 1888–1959 U.S. secretary of state.
George C. Marshall 1880–1959 U.S. general and statesman.
Aneurin Bevan 1897–1960 British minister of health.

Dag Hammarskjöld 1905–1961 Swedish UN leader.
Learned Hand 1872–1961 U.S. federal judge and lecturer.
Samuel Rayburn 1882–1961 U.S. Speaker of the House.
Adolf Eichmann 1906–1962 German Nazi official.

John F. Kennedy 1917–1963 35th President of the U.S.
Ngo Dinh Diem 1901–1963 President of South Vietnam.
Lee Harvey Oswald 1939–1963 Alleged assassin of John F. Kennedy.

Frederic Joliot-Curie 1900–1958 French physicist.
Ernest Lawrence 1901–1958 U.S. physicist. Developed cyclotron.
Pius XII 1876–1958 Italian anti-Communist pope.
Ethel Barrymore 1879–1959 U.S. stage and film actress.
Cecil B. De Mille 1881–1959 U.S. producer of large-scale films.
Charles Wilson 1869–1959 British physicist, inventor.
Frank Lloyd Wright 1869–1959 U.S. "organic" architect.

Roy Chapman Andrews 1884–1960 U.S. naturalist, explorer.
Oscar Hammerstein II 1895–1960 U.S. lyricist, theater producer.
Emily Price Post 1873–1960 U.S. writer on etiquette.
Ty Cobb 1886–1961 U.S. baseball hero.
Gary Cooper 1901–1961 U.S. film actor.
Lee De Forest 1873–1961 U.S. inventor, radio pioneer.
Carl Jung 1875–1961 Swiss analytical psychologist.
Eero Saarinen 1910–1961 U.S. architect, urban planner.
Niels Bohr 1885–1962 Danish physicist.
Arthur Holly Compton 1892–1962 U.S. physicist.
Marilyn Monroe 1926–1962 U.S. film actress.
Auguste Piccard 1884–1962 Swiss physicist and balloonist.
Vilhjalmur Stefansson 1879–1962 Canadian arctic explorer.

William E. B. Du Bois 1868–1963 U.S. historian and author.
John XXIII 1881–1963 Italian pope.

Nikos Kazantzakis 1885–1957 Greek novelist, politician.
Gabriela Mistral 1890–1957 Chilean poet and educator.
Christopher Morley 1890–1957 U.S. author, editor, critic.
Diego Rivera 1886–1957 Mexican mural painter.
Jean Sibelius 1865–1957 Finnish composer.
Arturo Toscanini 1867–1957 Italian conductor.
W. C. Handy 1873–1958 U.S. composer, blues musician.
Georges Rouault 1871–1958 French expressionist painter.
Maurice de Vlaminck 1876–1958 French Fauvist painter.
Ralph Vaughan Williams 1872–1958 British composer.
Bernard Berenson 1865–1959 U.S. art critic.
Ernest Bloch 1880–1959 Swiss-American composer.
Jacob Epstein 1880–1959 British-American sculptor.
George Grosz 1893–1959 German-American painter, caricaturist.
Edgar Guest 1881–1959 Anglo-American author of popular verse.
Billie Holiday 1915–1959 U.S. jazz singer.
Wanda Landowska 1877–1959 Polish pianist, harpsichordist.
Heitor Villa-Lobos 1887–1959 Brazilian composer.
Albert Camus 1913–1960 French novelist and essayist.
Ernö Dohnányi 1877–1960 Hungarian composer, pianist.
Boris Pasternak 1890–1960 Soviet poet and novelist.
Richard Wright 1908–1960 U.S. novelist and expatriate.
Thomas Beecham 1879–1961 British conductor, author.
Dashiell Hammett 1894–1961 U.S. writer of detective fiction.
Moss Hart 1904–1961 U.S. playwright, stage director.
Ernest Hemingway 1899–1961 U.S. novelist and journalist.
Augustus John 1878–1961 English painter.
George S. Kaufman 1889–1961 U.S. playwright and editor.
Grandma Moses 1860–1961 U.S. primitivist painter.
James Thurber 1894–1961 U.S. writer and cartoonist.
Karen Blixen (Isak Dinesen) 1885–1962 Danish writer.
E. E. Cummings 1894–1962 U.S. poet and novelist.
William Faulkner 1897–1962 U.S. novelist.
Hermann Hesse 1877–1962 German novelist.
Georges Braque 1882–1963 French cubist painter.
Jean Cocteau 1889–1963 French writer, poet, filmmaker.
Robert Lee Frost 1874–1963 U.S. poet.
Paul Hindemith 1895–1963 German-American composer.
Aldous Huxley 1894–1963 British novelist and essayist.

1957 Ghana is first country in sub-Saharan Africa to gain independence from European rule.
1959 Fidel Castro seizes power in Cuba.
1961 U.S.-sponsored anti-Castro invasion of Cuba fails at Bay of Pigs.
1961 Astronaut Alan B. Shepard, Jr., is first American to travel in space.
1962 Pope John XXIII convenes Vatican II to explore ways of renewing Catholic Church.
1962 Publication of Rachel Carson's *Silent Spring* increases awareness of environmental issues.
1962 During Cuban missile crisis, U.S. forces withdrawal of Soviet missiles from Cuba.
1963 United States and Soviet Union sign treaty limiting nuclear testing.
1963 President John F. Kennedy assassinated in Dallas.

PEOPLE *(continued)*

1964

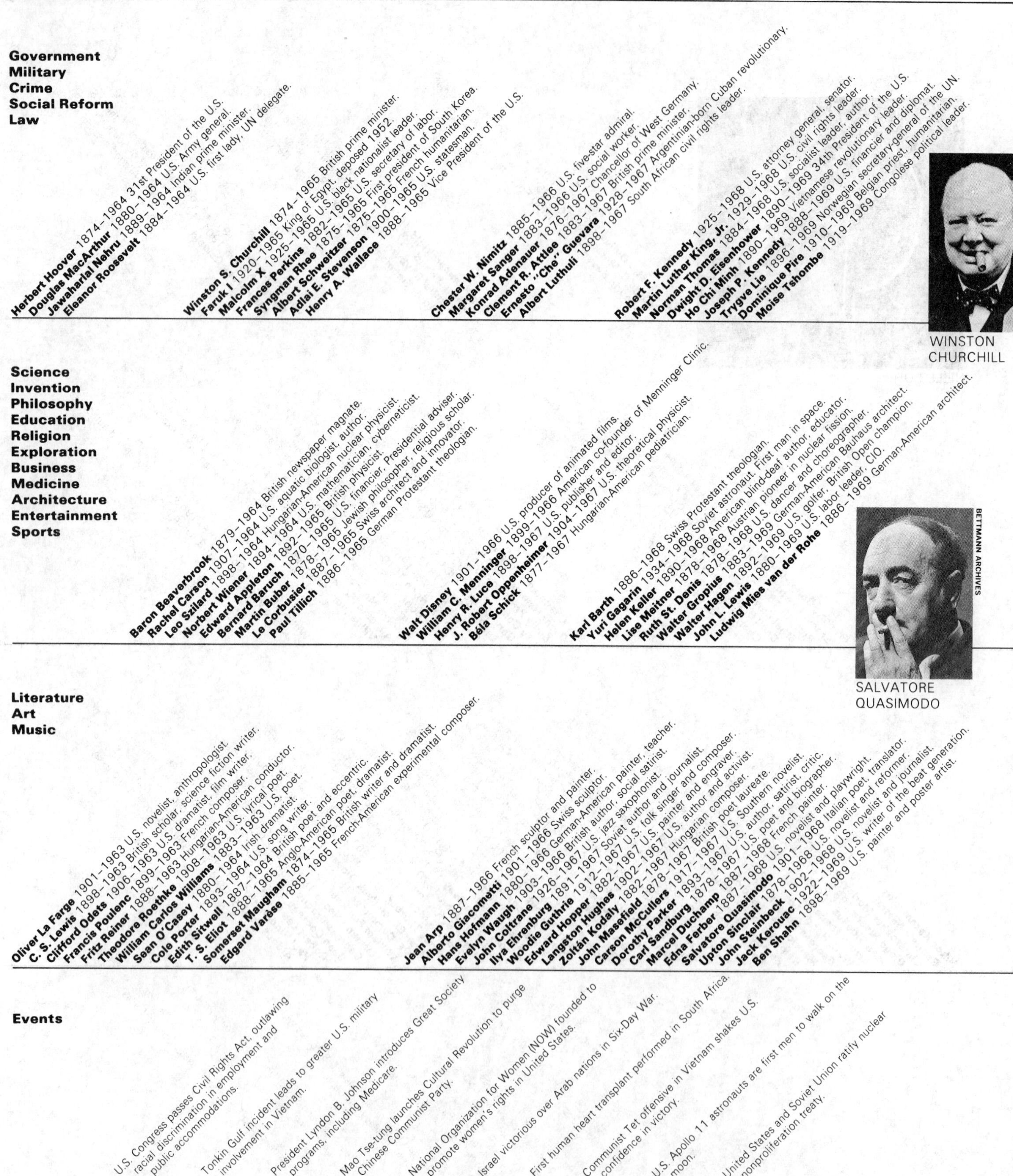

Government / Military / Crime / Social Reform / Law

- **Herbert Hoover** 1874–1964 31st President of the U.S.
- **Douglas MacArthur** 1880–1964 U.S. Army general.
- **Jawaharlal Nehru** 1889–1964 Indian prime minister.
- **Eleanor Roosevelt** 1884–1964 U.S. first lady, UN delegate.
- **Winston S. Churchill** 1874–1965 British prime minister.
- **Faruk I** 1920–1965 King of Egypt, deposed 1952.
- **Malcolm X** 1925–1965 U.S. black nationalist leader.
- **Frances Perkins** 1882–1965 U.S. secretary of labor.
- **Syngman Rhee** 1875–1965 First president of South Korea.
- **Albert Schweitzer** 1875–1965 French humanitarian.
- **Adlai E. Stevenson** 1900–1965 U.S. statesman.
- **Henry A. Wallace** 1888–1965 Vice President of the U.S.
- **Chester W. Nimitz** 1885–1966 U.S. five-star admiral.
- **Margaret Sanger** 1883–1966 U.S. social worker.
- **Konrad Adenauer** 1876–1967 Chancellor of West Germany.
- **Clement R. Attlee** 1883–1967 British prime minister.
- **Ernesto "Che" Guevara** 1928–1967 Argentinian-born Cuban revolutionary.
- **Albert Luthuli** 1898–1967 South African civil rights leader.
- **Robert F. Kennedy** 1925–1968 U.S. attorney general, senator.
- **Martin Luther King, Jr.** 1929–1968 U.S. civil rights leader.
- **Norman Thomas** 1884–1968 U.S. socialist leader, author.
- **Dwight D. Eisenhower** 1890–1969 34th President of the U.S.
- **Ho Chi Minh** 1890–1969 Vietnamese revolutionary leader.
- **Joseph P. Kennedy** 1888–1969 U.S. financier and diplomat.
- **Trygve Lie** 1896–1969 Norwegian secretary-general of the UN.
- **Dominique Pire** 1910–1969 Belgian priest, humanitarian.
- **Moise Tshombe** 1919–1969 Congolese political leader.

WINSTON CHURCHILL

Science / Invention / Philosophy / Education / Religion / Exploration / Business / Medicine / Architecture / Entertainment / Sports

- **Baron Beaverbrook** 1879–1964 British newspaper magnate.
- **Rachel Carson** 1907–1964 U.S. aquatic biologist, author.
- **Leo Szilard** 1898–1964 Hungarian-American nuclear physicist.
- **Norbert Wiener** 1894–1964 U.S. mathematician, cyberneticist.
- **Edward Appleton** 1892–1965 British physicist.
- **Bernard Baruch** 1870–1965 U.S. financier, Presidential adviser.
- **Martin Buber** 1878–1965 Jewish philosopher, religious scholar.
- **Le Corbusier** 1887–1965 Swiss architect and innovator.
- **Paul Tillich** 1886–1965 German Protestant theologian.
- **Walt Disney** 1901–1966 U.S. producer of animated films.
- **William C. Menninger** 1899–1966 American co-founder of Menninger Clinic.
- **Henry R. Luce** 1898–1967 U.S. publisher and editor.
- **J. Robert Oppenheimer** 1904–1967 U.S. theoretical physicist.
- **Béla Schick** 1877–1967 Hungarian-American pediatrician.
- **Karl Barth** 1886–1968 Swiss Protestant theologian.
- **Yuri Gagarin** 1934–1968 Soviet astronaut. First man in space.
- **Helen Keller** 1880–1968 American blind-deaf author, educator.
- **Lise Meitner** 1878–1968 Austrian pioneer in nuclear fission.
- **Ruth St. Denis** 1878–1968 U.S. dancer and choreographer.
- **Walter Gropius** 1883–1969 German-American Bauhaus architect.
- **Walter Hagen** 1892–1969 U.S. golfer, British Open champion.
- **John L. Lewis** 1880–1969 U.S. labor leader, CIO.
- **Ludwig Mies van der Rohe** 1886–1969 German-American architect.

BETTMANN ARCHIVES

SALVATORE QUASIMODO

Literature / Art / Music

- **Oliver La Farge** 1901–1963 U.S. novelist, anthropologist.
- **C. S. Lewis** 1898–1963 British scholar, science fiction writer.
- **Clifford Odets** 1906–1963 U.S. dramatist, film writer.
- **Francis Poulenc** 1899–1963 French composer.
- **Fritz Reiner** 1888–1963 Hungarian-American conductor.
- **Theodore Roethke** 1908–1963 U.S. lyrical poet.
- **William Carlos Williams** 1883–1963 U.S. poet.
- **Sean O'Casey** 1880–1964 Irish dramatist.
- **Cole Porter** 1893–1964 U.S. song writer.
- **Edith Sitwell** 1887–1964 British poet and eccentric.
- **T. S. Eliot** 1888–1965 Anglo-American poet, dramatist.
- **Somerset Maugham** 1874–1965 British writer and dramatist.
- **Edgard Varèse** 1885–1965 French-American experimental composer.
- **Jean Arp** 1887–1966 French sculptor and painter.
- **Alberto Giacometti** 1901–1966 Swiss sculptor.
- **Hans Hofmann** 1880–1966 German-American painter, teacher.
- **Evelyn Waugh** 1903–1966 British author, social satirist.
- **John Coltrane** 1926–1967 U.S. jazz saxophonist.
- **Ilya Ehrenburg** 1891–1967 Soviet author and journalist.
- **Woodie Guthrie** 1912–1967 U.S. folk singer and composer.
- **Edward Hopper** 1882–1967 U.S. painter and engraver.
- **Langston Hughes** 1902–1967 U.S. author and activist.
- **Zoltán Kodály** 1882–1967 Hungarian composer.
- **John Masefield** 1878–1967 British poet laureate.
- **Carson McCullers** 1917–1967 U.S. Southern novelist.
- **Dorothy Parker** 1893–1967 U.S. author, satirist, critic.
- **Carl Sandburg** 1878–1967 U.S. poet and biographer.
- **Marcel Duchamp** 1887–1968 French painter.
- **Edna Ferber** 1887–1968 U.S. novelist and playwright.
- **Salvatore Quasimodo** 1901–1968 Italian poet, translator.
- **Upton Sinclair** 1878–1968 U.S. novelist and reformer.
- **John Steinbeck** 1902–1968 U.S. novelist and journalist.
- **Jack Kerouac** 1922–1969 U.S. writer of the beat generation.
- **Ben Shahn** 1898–1969 U.S. painter and poster artist.

Events

- 1964 — U.S. Congress passes Civil Rights Act, outlawing racial discrimination in employment and public accommodations.
- 1964 — Tonkin Gulf incident leads to greater U.S. military involvement in Vietnam.
- 1965 — President Lyndon B. Johnson introduces Great Society programs, including Medicare.
- 1966 — Mao Tse-tung launches Cultural Revolution to purge Chinese Communist Party.
- 1966 — National Organization for Women (NOW) founded to promote women's rights in United States.
- 1967 — Israel victorious over Arab nations in Six-Day War.
- 1967 — First human heart transplant performed in South Africa.
- 1968 — Communist Tet offensive in Vietnam shakes U.S. confidence in victory.
- 1969 — U.S. Apollo 11 astronauts are first men to walk on the moon.
- 1969 — United States and Soviet Union ratify nuclear nonproliferation treaty.

1975

- **Charles de Gaulle** 1890–1970 President of France.
- **Alexander Kerensky** 1881–1970 Russian political leader.
- **Gamal Abdel Nasser** 1918–1970 President of Egypt.
- **Antonio Salazar** 1889–1970 Dictator of Portugal.
- **Sukarno** 1901–1970 First president of Indonesian Republic.
- **Dean Acheson** 1893–1971 U.S. secretary of state.
- **Hugo Black** 1886–1971 U.S. Supreme Court justice.
- **Ralph Bunche** 1904–1971 U.S. diplomat, political scientist.
- **François Duvalier** 1907–1971 Dictator of Haiti.
- **John M. Harlan** 1899–1971 U.S. Supreme Court justice.
- **Nikita Khrushchev** 1894–1971 Soviet chief of state.
- **Lin Piao** 1908–1971 Chinese minister of defense.
- **Whitney M. Young, Jr.** 1921–1971 U.S. civil rights leader.
- **J. Edgar Hoover** 1895–1972 U.S. director of F.B.I.
- **Kwame Nkrumah** 1909–1972 First president of Ghana.
- **Lester B. Pearson** 1897–1972 Canadian prime minister.
- **Harry S. Truman** 1884–1972 33rd President of the U.S.
- **Duke of Windsor** 1894–1972 King of Great Britain and Ireland who abdicated.
- **David Ben-Gurion** 1886–1973 Prime minister of Israel.
- **Lyndon B. Johnson** 1908–1973 36th President of the U.S.
- **Jeannette Rankin** 1880–1973 U.S. legislator and pacifist.
- **Eddie Rickenbacker** 1890–1973 U.S. air ace of World War I.
- **Winthrop Rockefeller** 1912–1973 U.S. public official.
- **Juan Perón** 1895–1974 President of Argentina.
- **Earl Warren** 1891–1974 U.S. chief justice.
- **Georgi Zhukov** 1895–1974 Soviet military commander.
- **Chiang Kai-shek** 1886–1975 Chinese nationalist leader.
- **Eamon de Valera** 1882–1975 Prime minister of the Republic of Ireland.
- **Francisco Franco** 1892–1975 Spanish soldier and dictator.
- **Haile Selassie** 1892–1975 Emperor of Ethiopia.

- **Max Born** 1882–1970 German-British theoretical physicist.
- **Oscar Lewis** 1914–1970 U.S. anthropologist and author.
- **Chandrasekhara Raman** 1888–1970 Indian physicist.
- **Walter Reuther** 1907–1970 U.S. labor leader, UAW.
- **Bertrand Russell** 1872–1970 British philosopher, mathematician.
- **Bobby Jones** 1902–1971 U.S. golf champion.
- **Richard Neutra** 1892–1971 Austrian-American architect.
- **Reinhold Niebuhr** 1892–1971 German-American liberal theologian.
- **Louis Leakey** 1903–1972 British archaeologist.
- **Maria Mayer** 1906–1972 Polish-American theoretical physicist.
- **Jackie Robinson** 1919–1972 U.S. baseball star.
- **Igor Sikorsky** 1889–1972 Russian-American helicopter designer.
- **Noel Coward** 1899–1973 British playwright and composer.
- **John Ford** 1895–1973 Irish-American film director.
- **Jacques Maritain** 1882–1973 French philosopher, author.
- **Selman Waksman** 1888–1973 Russian-American microbiologist.
- **Patrick Blackett** 1897–1974 English nuclear physicist.
- **Samuel Goldwyn** 1882–1974 U.S. film producer.
- **Charles A. Lindbergh** 1902–1974 U.S. pioneer aviator.
- **Vittorio de Sica** 1901–1974 Italian realistic film director.
- **Julian Huxley** 1887–1975 British scientist and educator.
- **Edward L. Tatum** 1909–1975 U.S. geneticist.
- **Arnold Toynbee** 1889–1975 English historian and author.

SMITHSONIAN INSTITUTION

CHARLES LINDBERGH

- **E. M. Forster** 1879–1970 British novelist, critic, librettist.
- **François Mauriac** 1885–1970 French novelist and essayist.
- **John O'Hara** 1905–1970 U.S. realist writer.
- **John Dos Passos** 1896–1970 U.S. novelist.
- **Mark Rothko** 1903–1970 Russian-American abstract painter.
- **Nelly Sachs** 1891–1970 German-Swiss poet and dramatist.
- **Louis Armstrong** 1900–1971 U.S. jazz trumpeter, bandleader.
- **Rockwell Kent** 1882–1971 U.S. woodcut artist, author.
- **Ogden Nash** 1902–1971 U.S. poet and humorist.
- **Igor Stravinsky** 1882–1971 Russian-American composer.
- **Rufino Tamayo** 1899–1971 Mexican artist.
- **Yukio Mishima** 1925–1972 Japanese novelist and activist.
- **Marianne Moore** 1887–1972 U.S. poet.
- **Ezra Pound** 1885–1972 U.S. poet, translator, critic.
- **C. P. Snow** 1905–1972 British writer and physicist.
- **Edmund Wilson** 1895–1972 U.S. author, literary critic.
- **Conrad Aiken** 1889–1973 U.S. poet, man of letters.
- **W. H. Auden** 1907–1973 Anglo-American poet, playwright.
- **Elizabeth Bowen** 1899–1973 Anglo-Irish novelist.
- **Pablo Casals** 1876–1973 Spanish cellist and conductor.
- **William Inge** 1913–1973 U.S. dramatist, screenwriter.
- **Jacques Lipchitz** 1891–1973 Lithuanian-American sculptor.
- **Pablo Neruda** 1904–1973 Chilean poet and diplomat.
- **Pablo Picasso** 1881–1973 Spanish artist.
- **J. R. R. Tolkien** 1892–1973 British fantasy novelist.
- **Miguel Angel Asturias** 1899–1974 Guatemalan novelist, poet.
- **Duke Ellington** 1899–1974 U.S. jazz musician, composer.
- **Walter Lippmann** 1889–1974 U.S. author and editor.
- **Darius Milhaud** 1892–1974 French composer.
- **David Oistrakh** 1908–1974 Soviet violinist and teacher.
- **Thomas Hart Benton** 1889–1975 U.S. midwestern painter.
- **Barbara Hepworth** 1903–1975 British sculptor.
- **Dmitri Shostakovich** 1906–1975 Soviet composer.
- **Rex Stout** 1886–1975 U.S. writer of detective fiction.
- **Thornton Wilder** 1897–1975 U.S. playwright and novelist.
- **P. G. Wodehouse** 1881–1975 Anglo-American humorist writer.

- 1970 — U.S. incursion into Cambodia provokes widespread antiwar demonstrations.
- 1971 — President Richard Nixon imposes wage and price controls to check inflation in United States.
- 1972 — Nixon visits China and Soviet Union initiating period of detente with Communist superpowers.
- 1973 — Israel fights Yom Kippur War against Egypt and Syria.
- 1973 — Embargo by Arab oil producers leads to massive increase in oil prices.
- 1974 — Implicated in Watergate cover-up, Richard Nixon becomes first U.S. President to resign from office.
- 1975 — Vietnam War ends as North Vietnamese army captures Saigon.

PEOPLE *(continued)*

1976

Government, Military, Crime, Social Reform, Law

- **Chou En-lai** 1898–1976 Chinese Communist prime minister.
- **Chu Teh** 1886–1976 Chinese Communist general.
- **Mao Tse-tung** 1893–1976 Chinese Communist statesman.
- **Bernard Law Montgomery** 1887–1976 British field marshal.
- **Anthony Eden** 1897–1977 British prime minister.
- **Ludwig Erhard** 1897–1977 German chancellor.
- **Hubert Horatio Humphrey** 1911–1978 U.S. Vice President.
- **Jomo Kenyatta** 1889–1978 President of Kenya.
- **Golda Meir** 1898–1978 Prime minister of Israel.
- **Louis Mountbatten** 1900–1979 British naval commander.
- **Nelson A. Rockefeller** 1908–1979 Vice President of the U.S.
- **William O. Douglas** 1898–1980 U.S. Supreme Court justice.
- **Alexei Kosygin** 1904–1980 Soviet premier.
- **Muhammed Reza Shah Pahlevi** 1919–1980 Shah of Iran.
- **Tito** 1892–1980 Yugoslavian Communist leader.
- **Moshe Dayan** 1915–1981 Israeli military leader and minister.
- **Anwar el-Sadat** 1918–1981 President of Egypt.
- **Roy Wilkins** 1901–1981 U.S. civil rights leader.
- **Leonid Brezhnev** 1906–1982 Soviet chief of state.
- **Indira Gandhi** 1917–1984 Prime minister of India.
- **Sékou Touré** 1922–1984 First president, Republic of Guinea.

THE BETTMANN ARCHIVE

CHOU EN-LAI

Science, Invention, Philosophy, Education, Religion, Exploration, Business, Medicine, Architecture, Entertainment, Sports

- **Alvar Aalto** 1898–1976 Finnish architect, furniture designer.
- **Martin Heidegger** 1889–1976 German philosopher and teacher.
- **Samuel Eliot Morison** 1887–1976 U.S. nautical historian.
- **Charles Chaplin** 1889–1977 British filmmaker and actor.
- **Alfred Lunt** 1892–1977 U.S. stage actor.
- **Roberto Rosselini** 1906–1977 Italian film and operatic director.
- **Wernher Von Braun** 1912–1977 German-American rocket engineer.
- **Margaret Mead** 1901–1978 U.S. author.
- **Jean Monnet** 1888–1979 French political economist.
- **Pier Luigi Nervi** 1891–1979 Italian architect.
- **Jean Renoir** 1894–1979 French filmmaker and director.
- **Erich Fromm** 1900–1980 German-American psychoanalyst and author.
- **Alfred Hitchcock** 1899–1980 British-American film director.
- **George Meany** 1894–1980 U.S. labor leader, AFL-CIO.
- **Jean Piaget** 1896–1980 Swiss child psychologist.
- **Jean-Paul Sartre** 1905–1980 French existentialist philosopher.
- **Max Delbrück** 1906–1981 German-American genetic biochemist.
- **Sir Hans Krebs** 1900–1981 German-British biochemist.
- **Joe Louis** 1914–1981 U.S. heavyweight boxing champion.
- **Harold Urey** 1893–1981 U.S. chemist. Discovered deuterium.
- **Luis Buñuel** 1900–1983 Spanish film director and writer.
- **Jack Dempsey** 1895–1983 U.S. heavyweight boxer.
- **Buckminster Fuller** 1895–1983 U.S. architect, philosopher.
- **Count Basie** 1904–1984 U.S. jazz pianist, bandleader.
- **François Truffaut** 1932–1984 French "new wave" film director.

THE BETTMANN ARCHIVE

ALFRED HITCHCOCK

Literature, Art, Music

- **Benjamin Britten** 1913–1976 British composer.
- **Alexander Calder** 1898–1976 U.S. sculptor and illustrator.
- **Agatha Christie** 1891–1976 British mystery writer.
- **Max Ernst** 1891–1976 German-American painter, collage artist.
- **André Malraux** 1901–1976 French novelist and statesman.
- **Walter Piston** 1894–1976 U.S. composer.
- **Man Ray** 1890–1976 U.S. artist and photographer.
- **Paul Robeson** 1898–1976 U.S. actor and singer.
- **Maria Callas** 1923–1977 U.S. operatic soprano.
- **Robert Lowell** 1917–1977 U.S. poet.
- **Vladimir Nabokov** 1899–1977 Russian-American novelist.
- **Elvis Presley** 1935–1977 U.S. popular singer.
- **Giorgio de Chirico** 1888–1978 Italian painter, designer.
- **Norman Rockwell** 1894–1978 U.S. illustrator.
- **Ignazio Silone** 1900–1978 Italian antifascist writer.
- **James T. Farrell** 1904–1979 U.S. novelist and essayist.
- **Richard Rodgers** 1902–1979 U.S. musical comedy composer.
- **Oskar Kokoschka** 1886–1980 Austrian-British painter, writer.
- **John Lennon** 1940–1980 English rock musician, song writer.
- **Marshall McLuhan** 1911–1980 Canadian author, commentator.
- **Henry Miller** 1891–1980 U.S. author and expatriate.
- **Katherine Anne Porter** 1890–1980 U.S. short story writer.
- **Samuel Barber** 1910–1981 U.S. composer.
- **William Saroyan** 1908–1981 U.S. novelist and playwright.
- **Archibald MacLeish** 1892–1982 U.S. poet, public official.
- **Carl Orff** 1895–1982 German composer and educator.
- **Artur Rubinstein** 1889–1982 Polish-American pianist.
- **George Balanchine** 1904–1983 Russian-American choreographer.
- **Arthur Koestler** 1905–1983 Hungarian author, journalist.
- **Joan Miró** 1893–1983 Spanish surrealist painter.
- **William Walton** 1902–1983 English composer.
- **Rebecca West** 1892–1983 Irish-British writer.
- **Tennessee Williams** 1914–1983 U.S. Southern playwright.
- **Truman Capote** 1924–1984 U.S. Southern novelist.
- **Lillian Hellman** 1905–1984 U.S. dramatist.
- **Liam O'Flaherty** 1896–1984 Irish novelist.
- **Mikhail Sholokhov** 1905–1984 Soviet epic novelist.

Events

- 1977 — Egyptian President Anwar el-Sadat makes surprise trip to Jerusalem.
- 1979 — Ayatollah Ruhollah Khomeini sets up Islamic republic in Iran; militants storm U.S. embassy and hold diplomats hostage.
- 1979 — Israel and Egypt sign peace treaty.
- 1980 — Soviet Union invades Afghanistan.
- 1980 — Iran-Iraq war begins.
- 1981 — U.S. space shuttle *Columbia*, world's first reusable spacecraft, is launched.
- 1981 — Polish government declares martial law and outlaws Solidarity, first independent labor union in communist world.
- 1982 — Britain and Argentina clash over control of Falkland Islands.
- 1983 — Space shuttle *Challenger* launched; Sally Ride is first American woman to travel in space.
- 1983 — Terrorist bombing in Beirut kills 237 U.S. Marines.
- 1983 — U.S. troops topple Marxist regime in Grenada.
- 1984 — Poison gas leak at Bhopal, India, kills 2500 in worst industrial accident on record.

present

- **Enver Hoxha** 1908–1985 Premier of Albania.
- **Harold Macmillan** 1894–1986 British prime minister.
- **Vyacheslav Molotov** 1890–1986 Soviet premier.
- **Sven Palme** 1927–1986 Swedish prime minister.
- **Hyman G. Rickover** 1900–1986 U.S. admiral.
- **Rudolf Hess** 1894–1987 German Nazi political figure.
- **Maxwell D. Taylor** 1901–1987 U.S. general and statesman.

- **Ayatollah Khomeini** 1900– Iranian religious leader.
- **Hirohito** 1901– Emperor of Japan.
- **Habib Bourguiba** 1903– President of Tunisia.
- **Deng Xiaoping** 1904– Premier, People's Republic of China.
- **James W. Fulbright** 1905– U.S. statesman.
- **William J. Brennan, Jr.** 1906– U.S. Supreme Court justice.
- **Léopold Senghor** 1906– First president of Senegal.
- **Robert C. Weaver** 1907– U.S. economist, Cabinet member.
- **Harry Blackmun** 1908– U.S. Supreme Court justice.
- **Thurgood Marshall** 1908– U.S. Supreme Court justice.
- **Barry Goldwater** 1909– U.S. conservative political figure.
- **Andrei Gromyko** 1909– Soviet economist, foreign minister.
- **Dean Rusk** 1909– U.S. secretary of state.
- **Ronald W. Reagan** 1911– 40th President of the U.S.

UNIVERSITY OF CHICAGO

SUBRAHMANYAN CHANDRASEKHAR

- **Dian Fossey** 1932–1985 U.S. naturalist and author.
- **Orson Welles** 1915–1985 U.S. film producer, director, actor.
- **Cary Grant** 1904–1986 U.S. film actor.
- **Christa McAuliffe** 1948–1986 U.S. civilian astronaut.
- **Fred Astaire** 1899–1987 U.S. dancer, choreographer.
- **Gunnar Myrdal** 1898–1987 Swedish social, political economist.
- **I. I. Rabi** 1898–1988 Austrian-American nuclear physicist.

- **Karl A. Menninger** 1893– American co-founder of Menninger Clinic.
- **Martha Graham** 1894– U.S. dancer and choreographer.

- **Helen Hayes** 1900– U.S. stage and film actress.
- **Linus Pauling** 1901– U.S. biochemist and peace activist.
- **Henry Steele Commager** 1902– U.S. historian, educator.
- **Bruno Bettelheim** 1903– Austrian-American child psychologist.
- **Konrad Lorenz** 1903– Austrian naturalist and ethologist.
- **Benjamin Spock** 1903– U.S. pediatrician, political activist.
- **Ernest Walton** 1903– Irish pioneer in atomic fission.
- **John Gielgud** 1904– British Shakespearean actor.
- **B. F. Skinner** 1904– U.S. behavioral psychologist.
- **Agnes De Mille** 1905– U.S. dancer and choreographer.
- **Ashley Montagu** 1905– Anglo-American anthropologist.
- **John Huston** 1906–1987 U.S. film writer, director, actor.
- **Albert Sabin** 1906– Polish-American developer of polio vaccine.
- **Laurence Olivier** 1907– British actor, director, producer.
- **Michael De Bakey** 1908– U.S. heart transplant surgeon.
- **Edward Teller** 1908– Hungarian-American physicist.
- **Douglas Fairbanks, Jr.** 1909– U.S. actor, businessman.
- **Edwin H. Land** 1909– U.S. physicist and inventor.
- **Subrahmanyan Chandrasekhar** 1910– U.S. astrophysicist.
- **Mother Teresa of Calcutta** 1910– Albanian humanitarian.
- **Luis Alvarez** 1911– U.S. nuclear physicist.
- **Alec Guinness** 1914– British classical and comic actor.
- **Thor Heyerdahl** 1914– Norwegian anthropologist and mariner.
- **Ingmar Bergman** 1918– Swedish filmmaker.
- **Akira Kurosawa** 1910– Japanese film director.
- **Jacques-Yves Cousteau** 1910– French oceanographer and author.
- **Michelangelo Antonioni** 1912– Italian film director.
- **Glenn T. Seaborg** 1912– U.S. chemist.

UPI/BETTMANN NEWSPHOTOS

JAMES BALDWIN

- **Marc Chagall** 1887–1985 Russian-born painter.
- **Robert Graves** 1895–1985 British poet, novelist, critic.
- **Eugene Ormandy** 1899–1985 Hungarian-American conductor.
- **Simone de Beauvoir** 1908–1986 French existentialist writer.
- **Jorge Luis Borges** 1899–1986 Argentine author and critic.
- **Jean Genet** 1910–1986 French playwright and poet.
- **Bernard Malamud** 1914–1986 U.S. novelist, short story writer.
- **Henry Moore** 1898–1986 English sculptor.
- **Georgia O'Keeffe** 1887–1986 U.S. painter.
- **Jean Anouilh** 1910–1987 French dramatist.
- **Jascha Heifetz** 1901–1987 Russian-American violinist.
- **Andrés Segovia** 1893–1987 Spanish classical guitarist.
- **Andy Warhol** 1931–1987 U.S. pop artist and filmmaker.
- **James Baldwin** 1924–1987 U.S. novelist and playwright.
- **Alan Paton** 1903–1988 South African novelist, political figure.
- **Irving Berlin** 1888– Russian-American song writer.
- **Virgil Thomson** 1896– U.S. composer and critic.
- **Aaron Copland** 1900– U.S. composer.
- **Séan O'Faoláin** 1900– Irish novelist and essayist.
- **Marian Anderson** 1902– U.S. concert singer, public official.
- **Rudolf Serkin** 1903– Czech-American concert pianist.
- **Salvador Dali** 1904– Spanish surrealist painter.
- **William de Kooning** 1904– Dutch-American abstract painter.
- **Geisel, Theodore Seuss (Dr. Seuss)** 1904– U.S. artist, writer of children's books.
- **Graham Greene** 1904– British novelist.
- **Vladimir Horowitz** 1904– Russian-American concert pianist.
- **Isaac Bashevis Singer** 1904– Polish-American Yiddish author.
- **Elias Canetti** 1905– Bulgarian-born German writer.
- **Robert Penn Warren** 1905– U.S. poet, novelist, critic.
- **Samuel Beckett** 1906– Irish-born novelist, playwright.
- **James A. Michener** 1907– U.S. novelist.
- **Alberto Moravia** 1907– Italian novelist.
- **Herbert von Karajan** 1908– Austrian conductor.
- **Francis Bacon** 1909– English painter.
- **William H. Schuman** 1910– U.S. composer.
- **John Cage** 1912– U.S. experimental composer.
- **Eugene Ionesco** 1912– Rumanian-French dramatist.
- **Mary McCarthy** 1912– U.S. critic and novelist.

- 1985 Mikhail Gorbachev becomes Soviet leader; introduces reform program.
- 1986 Space shuttle *Challenger* explodes on takeoff, presenting major setback for U.S. space program.
- 1986 U.S. warplanes bomb Libya, striking important blow in struggle against international terrorism.
- 1986 Explosion at Chernobyl reactor in Soviet Union is world's worst nuclear accident.
- 1987 Largest-ever decline in U.S. stock prices causes panic in world financial markets.
- 1987 U.S. surgeons perform first five-organ transplant.
- 1987 United States and Soviets negotiate first agreement to reduce their nuclear arsenals by eliminating medium- and short-range missiles.
- 1988 Iran and Iraq agree to a cease-fire in their war, which began in 1980.
- 1988 Major revision of Soviet political system is approved, transferring some power from the Communist Party to popularly elected legislatures.
- 1988 The space shuttle *Discovery* makes first American manned space flight since the *Challenger* blew up 32 months before.

PEOPLE *(continued)*

present

Government
Military
Crime
Social Reform
Law

Menachem Begin 1913– Israeli prime minister.
Willy Brandt 1913– Chancellor of West Germany.
Gerald R. Ford 1913– 38th President of the U.S.
Richard M. Nixon 1913– 37th President of the U.S.
Edmund S. Muskie 1914– U.S. secretary of state.
Pieter Willem Botha 1916– South African political leader.
Robert McNamara 1916– U.S. secretary of defense.
François Mitterand 1916– President of France.
Harold Wilson 1916– British prime minister.
Nelson Mandela 1918– South African nationalist leader.
Yasuhiro Nakasone 1918– Japanese prime minister.
Helmut Schmidt 1918– Chancellor of West Germany.
Kurt Waldheim 1918– President of Austria.
Pierre Trudeau 1919– Canadian prime minister.
Zhao Ziyang 1919– Chinese chief of state.
Javier Perez de Cuellar 1920– Peruvian diplomat.
Elliott Richardson 1920– U.S. public official.
George P. Shultz 1920– U.S. secretary of state.
John P. Stevens 1920– U.S. Supreme Court justice.
Lloyd Bentsen 1921– U.S. Vice Presidential candidate.
Alexander Dubcek 1921– Czech Communist premier.
Julius Nyerere 1922– President of Tanzania.
Jim Wright 1922– Speaker of the U.S. House of Representatives.
Henry A. Kissinger 1923– U.S. secretary of state.
George H. Bush 1924– 41st President of the U.S.
James E. Carter, Jr. 1924– 39th President of the U.S.
Alexander M. Haig 1924– U.S. NATO commander, statesman.
William H. Rehnquist 1924– U.S. chief justice.
Noboru Takeshita 1924– Japanese prime minister.
Margaret Thatcher 1925– British prime minister.
Fidel Castro 1926– Cuban revolutionary, prime minister.
Valéry Giscard d'Estaing 1926– President of France.
Elizabeth II 1926– Queen, Great Britain, Northern Ireland.
Cesar Chavez 1927– U.S. farm labor leader.
Yasir Arafat 1929– Palestinian commando leader.
Mikhail S. Gorbachev 1929– Soviet chief of state.
John Turner 1929– Canadian prime minister.
Sandra Day O'Connor 1930– U.S. Supreme Court justice.

UPI/BETTMANN NEWSPHOTOS

SANDRA DAY O'CONNOR

Science
Invention
Philosophy
Education
Religion
Exploration
Business
Medicine
Architecture
Entertainment
Sports

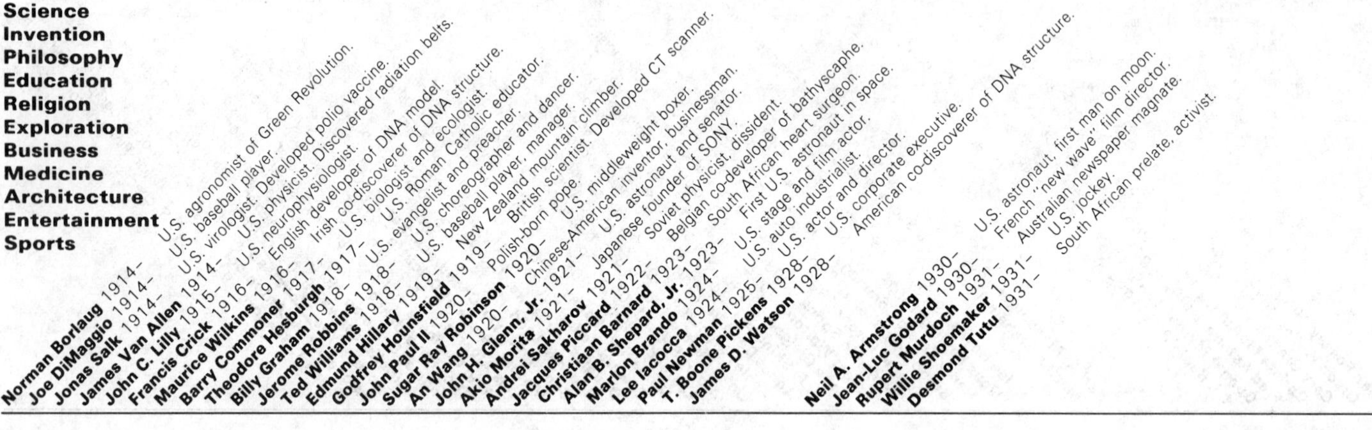

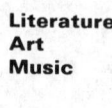

Norman Borlaug 1914– U.S. agronomist of Green Revolution.
Joe DiMaggio 1914– U.S. baseball player.
Jonas Salk 1914– U.S. virologist. Developed polio vaccine.
James Van Allen 1914– U.S. physicist. Discovered radiation belts.
John C. Lilly 1915– U.S. neurophysiologist.
Francis Crick 1916– English developer of DNA model.
Maurice Wilkins 1916– Irish co-discoverer of DNA structure.
Barry Commoner 1917– U.S. biologist and ecologist.
Theodore Hesburgh 1917– U.S. Roman Catholic educator.
Billy Graham 1918– U.S. evangelist and preacher.
Jerome Robbins 1918– U.S. choreographer and dancer.
Ted Williams 1918– U.S. baseball player, manager.
Edmund Hillary 1919– New Zealand mountain climber.
Godfrey Hounsfield 1919– British scientist. Developed CT scanner.
John Paul II 1920– Polish-born pope.
Sugar Ray Robinson 1920– U.S. middleweight boxer.
An Wang 1920– Chinese-American inventor, businessman.
John H. Glenn, Jr. 1921– U.S. astronaut and senator.
Akio Morita 1921– Japanese founder of SONY.
Andrei Sakharov 1921– Soviet physicist, dissident.
Jacques Piccard 1922– Belgian co-developer of bathyscaphe.
Christiaan Barnard 1923– South African heart surgeon.
Alan B. Shepard, Jr. 1923– First U.S. astronaut in space.
Marlon Brando 1924– U.S. stage and film actor.
Lee Iacocca 1924– U.S. auto industrialist.
Paul Newman 1925– U.S. actor and director.
T. Boone Pickens 1928– U.S. corporate executive.
James D. Watson 1928– American co-discoverer of DNA structure.
Neil A. Armstrong 1930– U.S. astronaut, first man on moon.
Jean-Luc Godard 1930– French "new wave" film director.
Rupert Murdoch 1931– Australian newspaper magnate.
Willie Shoemaker 1931– U.S. jockey.
Desmond Tutu 1931– South African prelate, activist.

Literature
Art
Music

John Hersey 1914– U.S. author.
Saul Bellow 1915– Canadian-American novelist.
Arthur Miller 1915– U.S. playwright.
Robert Motherwell 1915– U.S. abstract painter.
Yehudi Menuhin 1916– U.S. concert violinist and conductor.
Gwendolyn Brooks 1917– U.S. poet and novelist.
Andrew Wyeth 1917– U.S. realist painter.
Leonard Bernstein 1918– U.S. conductor, pianist, composer.
Alexander Solzhenitsyn 1918– Soviet author and dissident.
Margot Fonteyn 1919– English ballerina.
J. D. Salinger 1919– U.S. author.
Pete Seeger 1919– U.S. folk singer, political activist.
Isaac Asimov 1920– U.S. science writer, novelist.
Ray Bradbury 1920– U.S. science fiction writer.
Federico Fellini 1920– Italian film director.
Ravi Shankar 1920– Indian sitar player, composer.
Kurt Vonnegut 1922– U.S. novelist.
Nadine Gordimer 1923– South African writer.
Norman Mailer 1923– U.S. novelist and journalist.
Luciano Berio 1925– Italian avant-garde composer.
William Styron 1925– U.S. novelist and essayist.
Allen Ginsberg 1926– U.S. avant-garde poet.
Joan Sutherland 1926– Australian operatic soprano.
Leontyne Price 1927– U.S. operatic soprano.
Mstislav Rostropovich 1927– Soviet cellist, conductor.
Neil Simon 1927– U.S. comic playwright.
Edward Albee 1928– U.S. dramatist.
Gabriel García Márquez 1928– Colombian novelist.
George Crumb 1929– U.S. composer.
Claes Oldenburg 1929– U.S. pop artist.
Beverly Sills 1929– U.S. operatic soprano.
Harold Pinter 1930– British playwright.

SPRINGER/BETTMANN FILM ARCHIVE

EDWARD ALBEE

present

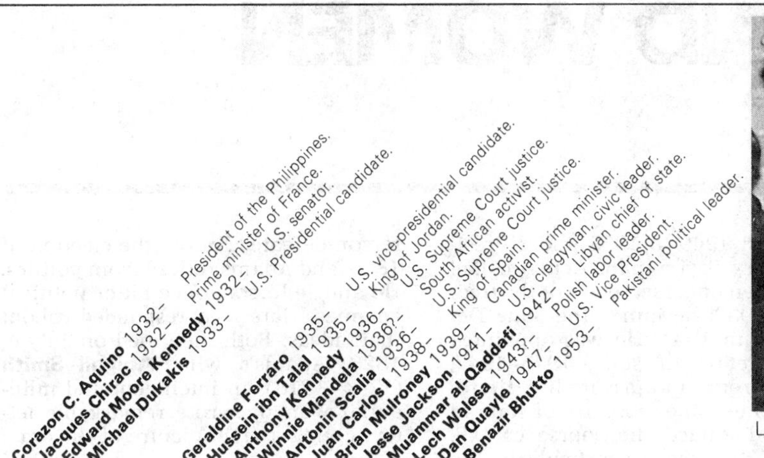

Corazon C. Aquino 1932– President of the Philippines.
Jacques Chirac 1932– Prime minister of France.
Edward Moore Kennedy 1932– U.S. senator.
Michael Dukakis 1933– U.S. Presidential candidate.

Geraldine Ferraro 1935– U.S. vice-presidential candidate.
Hussein ibn Talal 1935– King of Jordan.
Anthony Kennedy 1936– U.S. Supreme Court justice.
Winnie Mandela 1936?– South African activist.
Antonin Scalia 1936– U.S. Supreme Court justice.
Juan Carlos I 1938– King of Spain.
Brian Mulroney 1939– Canadian prime minister.
Jesse Jackson 1941– U.S. clergyman, civic leader.
Muammar al-Qaddafi 1942– Libyan chief of state.
Lech Walesa 1943?– Polish labor leader.
Dan Quayle 1947– U.S. Vice President.
Benazir Bhutto 1953– Pakistani political leader.

LECH WALESA

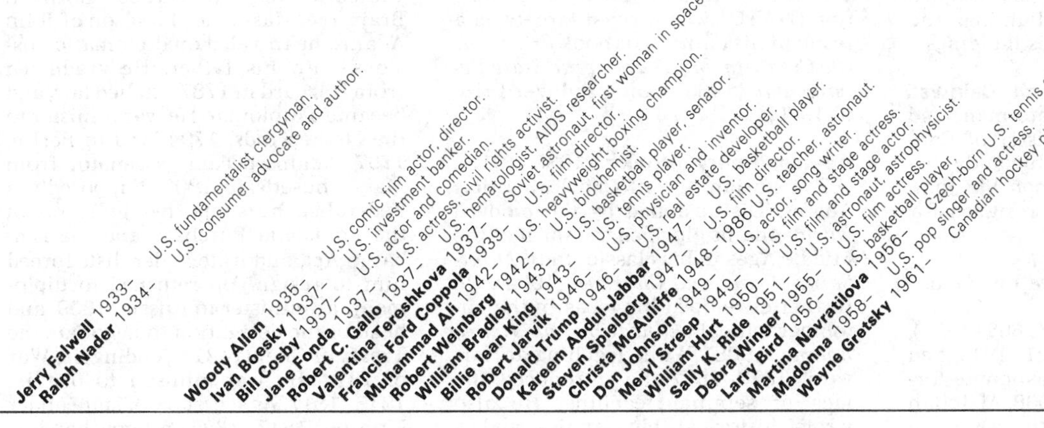

Jerry Falwell 1933– U.S. fundamentalist clergyman.
Ralph Nader 1934– U.S. consumer advocate and author.

Woody Allen 1935– U.S. comic film actor, director.
Ivan Boesky 1937– U.S. investment banker.
Bill Cosby 1937– U.S. actor and comedian.
Jane Fonda 1937– U.S. actress, civil rights activist.
Robert C. Gallo 1937– U.S. hematologist, AIDS researcher.
Valentina Tereshkova 1937– Soviet astronaut, first woman in space.
Francis Ford Coppola 1939– U.S. film director.
Muhammad Ali 1942– U.S. heavyweight boxing champion.
Robert Weinberg 1942– U.S. biochemist.
William Bradley 1943– U.S. basketball player, senator.
Billie Jean King 1943– U.S. tennis player.
Robert Jarvik 1946– U.S. physician and inventor.
Donald Trump 1946– U.S. real estate developer.
Kareem Abdul-Jabbar 1947– U.S. basketball player.
Steven Spielberg 1947– U.S. film director.
Christa McAuliffe 1948–1986 U.S. teacher, astronaut.
Don Johnson 1949– U.S. actor, song writer.
Meryl Streep 1949– U.S. film and stage actress.
William Hurt 1950– U.S. film and stage actor.
Sally K. Ride 1951– U.S. astronaut, astrophysicist.
Debra Winger 1955– U.S. film actress.
Larry Bird 1956– U.S. basketball player.
Martina Navratilova 1956– Czech-born U.S. tennis star.
Madonna 1958– U.S. pop singer and actress.
Wayne Gretsky 1961– Canadian hockey player.

KAREEM ABDUL-JABBAR

John Le Carré 1931– British novelist.
V.S. Naipaul 1932– West Indian novelist and essayist.
John Updike 1932– U.S. novelist, poet, and critic.
Krzysztof Penderecki 1933– Polish composer.
Philip Roth 1933– U.S. novelist.
Yevgeny Yevtushenko 1933– Soviet poet.
Leroi Jones (Amiri Baraka) 1934– U.S. playwright, social activist.
Luciano Pavarotti 1935– Italian operatic tenor.
Rudolph Nureyev 1938– Soviet ballet dancer, choreographer.
Joyce Carol Oates 1938– U.S. novelist, poet, playwright.
Margaret Atwood 1939– Canadian poet and novelist.
Joseph Brodsky 1940– Soviet-American poet.
Bob Dylan 1941– U.S. folk-rock singer and composer.
Alice M. Walker 1944– U.S. writer, social activist.
Michael Jackson 1958– U.S. pop singer and performer.
Wynton Marsalis 1961– U.S. trumpet virtuoso.

BIOGRAPHIES OF FAMOUS MEN AND WOMEN

A

Aalto, (Hugo) Alvar (Henrik) (1898–1976), Finnish architect and furniture designer. Aalto used natural materials—brick and timber—and open space in imaginative ways to create buildings that were personal and warm. He planned and built apartments, factories, hospitals, and other public buildings in Finland, Germany, Denmark, and the United States. He also designed harmonizing furniture, lighting, and interior decoration for his buildings.

Abbott, Sir John Joseph Caldwell (1821–1893), lawyer, statesman, and Conservative prime minister of Canada, 1891–1892. He reluctantly became prime minister when Sir John Macdonald died. Abbott resigned for health reasons.

Abd-al-Aziz ibn-Saud: *See* Ibn Saud.

Abdullah ibn-Husein (1882–1951), emir of Transjordan, 1921–1946, and first king of the state of Hashemite Jordan, 1946–1951. From 1908, Abdullah represented Mecca in the Ottoman Turkish chamber of deputies. He led the Arabs in revolt against Turkey during World War I. Abdullah became head of Transjordan in 1921 and established his army, the Arab Legion. He was assassinated in 1951.

Abélard, Peter (or **Pierre**) (1079–1142), French philosopher who tried to establish logical foundations for medieval Christian thought. Abélard set up his own school of logic outside Paris about 1100, then moved to Paris. There he fell in love with his pupil Héloise, niece of a canon of Notre Dame. She bore his son, and they were secretly married. In revenge, her uncle had Abélard attacked and castrated. Héloise entered a convent, and Abélard became a Benedictine monk about 1118. His rationalist philosophies often conflicted with church doctrine and were considered heretical. He lived in many different monasteries, and founded a community of the Paraclete, which he gave to Héloise and her nuns. Condemned by the pope for heresy in 1140, he died on the way to Rome.

Acheson, Dean Gooderham (1893–1971), U.S. statesman, secretary of state from 1949 to 1953 under President Harry S. Truman. Acheson had briefly been undersecretary of the treasury in 1933; he joined the State Department in 1941. He was appointed undersecretary of state, 1945–1947, and then retired to private life. He returned to become secretary of state in 1949 and guided the course of U.S. postwar diplomacy, particularly the policy of containing communist expansion through the use of foreign aid. The North Atlantic Treaty Organization (NATO) was formed largely as a result of his efforts. His book *Present at the Creation: My Years in the State Department* (1969) won a Pulitzer Prize in 1970.

Adams, Henry Brooks (1838–1918), U.S. historian, son of Charles Francis Adams. Disillusioned by the modern world, Adams glorified the spirit of the Middle Ages in his classic study, *Mont-Saint-Michel and Chartres* (1904). He further developed his ideas in the autobiographical *Education of Henry Adams* (1906). While teaching at Harvard, 1870–1877, he introduced the idea of seminar teaching. He also wrote historical biographies and a nine-volume *History of the United States from 1801–1817* (1889–1891).

Adams, John (1735–1826), U.S. lawyer and diplomat, second President of the United States, 1797–1801. Graduating from Harvard in 1755, he taught school and studied law. His public career began with his work toward American independence, protesting British colonial policies and serving in the Continental Congresses (1774, 1775). He signed and supported the Declaration of Independence. Adams went to France in 1778 and became minister to Holland in 1780. He secretly negotiated the peace treaty with Britain and obtained diplomatic recognition and a loan from Holland, 1782. He then served as minister to Britain, 1785–1788. In the first U.S. Presidential election, Adams became Vice President and served two terms, 1789–1797. He became a leader of the Federalists and was elected President in 1796. Adams took office opposed by both the followers of Thomas Jefferson and the members of his own party who followed Hamilton and urged war with the new government in France. Adams secured peace with France in 1800, but lost Federalist support. Jefferson defeated him in the election of 1800, and Adams retired from politics. He and Jefferson, once bitter political enemies, later corresponded about their ideas. Both men died on July 4, 1826. Adams's wife, **Abigail Smith** (1744–1818), an intelligent and influential woman, wrote remarkable letters giving a vivid picture of the era.

Adams, John Quincy (1767–1848), U.S. statesman, sixth President of the United States, 1825–1829. Born in Braintree, Mass., the eldest son of John Adams, he traveled on diplomatic missions with his father. He graduated from Harvard in 1787, studied law, and became a diplomat. He was minister to the Netherlands, 1794, and to Berlin, 1797. Adams became a senator from Massachusetts in 1803. Supposedly a Federalist, he supported Jefferson in the Louisiana Purchase and the Embargo Act, and irate Federalists forced him to resign. He returned to diplomacy, as minister to Russia, 1809, and head of the delegation to negotiate the Treaty of Ghent (1814), ending the War of 1812. He was minister to Britain, 1815–1817. As secretary of state under Monroe, 1817–1825, Adams handled the negotiations for the acquisition of Florida and played an important part in formulating the Monroe Doctrine (1823). In 1824 Adams ran for President against Henry Clay, Andrew Jackson, and William H. Crawford, all southerners. No candidate received a majority, but Adams, with Clay's support, won the vote in the House of Representatives. He made Clay his secretary of state, arousing accusations of a political deal. Congress, led by the defeated Jackson and his supporters, refused to pass any of the legislation the President supported. In the elections of 1828, Adams lost to Jackson. He returned to Congress as representative from Massachusetts, 1831–1848.

Adams, Samuel (1722–1803), U.S. patriot and statesman, one of the chief instigators of the American Revolution. Adams became a fierce and articulate political agitator. He organized public protest against the Stamp Act (1765) and the Boston Massacre (1770), formed the Boston Committee of Correspondence in 1772, and organized the Boston Tea Party of 1773. He repeatedly attacked Britain in newspapers and pamphlets. Adams was a delegate to both Continental Congresses

(1774, 1775), and a signer of the Declaration of Independence. He served in Congress until 1781 and was governor of Massachusetts, 1794–1797.

Addams, Jane (1860–1935), U.S. social reformer and leader in the international peace movement. For more than 40 years she worked at Hull House, the Chicago settlement house that she and Ellen Gates Starr had founded in 1889. She described her work in *Twenty Years at Hull House* (1910) and other books. She was a leader also in women's suffrage, labor and welfare reform, and the pacifist movement. She was president of the Women's International League for Peace and Freedom (founded in 1915) and shared the 1931 Nobel Peace Prize. She was elected to the Hall of Fame in 1965.

Adenauer, Konrad (1876–1967), German statesman. As the first chancellor of West Germany after World War II, he was responsible for its postwar recovery. Adenauer served as mayor of Cologne, 1917–1933, and as speaker of the Prussian *Landtag*, 1928–1933. The Nazis forced him to retire and arrested him in 1933 and again in 1944. After the war, Adenauer led the newly formed Christian Democratic Union Party and was chancellor from 1949 until his retirement in 1963. Under him, West Germany regained sovereignty and chose to ally with the West.

Adler, Alfred (1870–1937), Austrian psychiatrist and founder of individual psychology. He graduated from the University of Vienna medical school in 1895 and joined Sigmund Freud in 1902. He disagreed, however, with Freud's stress on sex as the basis for mental illness, believing that feelings of inferiority were primarily responsible. He broke with Freud in 1911 to found his own school of psychiatry. Adler's books include the classic *Understanding Human Nature* (1927) and *The Practice and Theory of Individual Psychology* (1920; translated 1927).

Aeschylus (525–456 B.C.), Greek tragic poet, the first great tragic dramatist. Aeschylus introduced a second actor on stage, making true dramatic action and dialogue possible for the first time. Born at Eleusis, he probably served in the Athenian army during the Persian wars and was at the battles of Marathon (490) and Salamis (480). He entered the Athens competitions for tragedy in 499, and won prizes in 484, in 472 with a trilogy (of which *The Persians* survives), and in 458 with the *Oresteia*. Aeschylus wrote about 90 plays in all, but only seven tragedies survive: *The Persians; Seven Against Thebes; The Suppliants; Prometheus Bound* (part of a lost Prometheus trilogy); and *Agamemnon, The Libation Bearers,* and *The Eumenides* (the *Oresteia* trilogy).

THE BETTMANN ARCHIVE

JANE ADDAMS

THE BETTMANN ARCHIVE

AESCHYLUS

Aga Khan, hereditary title (meaning honorable chief) of the spiritual leaders of the Ismailian Muslim community. **Aga Khan I** (Hasan Ali Shah; 1800–1881) was governor-general of Kerman province in Persia, but later went to India, where he aided the British government.

His work was carried on by his son, **Aga Khan II** (Ali Shah; d. 1885), who was succeeded by his son **Aga Khan III** (Muhammad Shah; 1877–1957). A leader in the establishment of the All-India Muslim League in 1906, and its first president, he worked for Indian independence. Immensely wealthy, he founded the Muslim university at Aligarh. In 1947 the Aga Khans became identified with the newly formed Muslim country of Pakistan.

Aga Khan IV (Karim al-Hussaini Shah; 1936–) succeeded Aga Khan III in 1957.

Agassiz, (Jean) Louis (Rodolphe) (1807–1873), Swiss-born U.S. naturalist, known for his studies of glaciers and zoology and for his revolutionary influence on teaching methods in natural history, especially his emphasis on field work. As a result of his observations of glaciers in Switzerland, Agassiz proposed the idea of the ice ages (*Études sur les glaciers,* 1840). His zoological studies included both fossils and the many modern species he observed in his expeditions all over the world. While teaching at Harvard University, 1848–1873, he founded the museum of comparative zoology there. He was elected to the Hall of Fame in 1915.

Agee, James (1909–1955), U.S. film critic, script writer, and novelist. With photographer Walker Evans, he created a moving study of the life of Alabama sharecroppers, *Let Us Now Praise Famous Men* (1941). He wrote a number of film scripts, among them *The African Queen* (1951). Agee's novels were *The Morning Watch* (1951) and *A Death in the Family* (1957), which won a Pulitzer Prize in 1958. His perceptive film reviews and articles were collected in two volumes, *Agee on Film* (1958–1960).

Aiken, Conrad Potter (1889–1973), U.S. poet and man of letters. Aiken's varied styles of poetry cannot easily be characterized; one critic has said, "everything he touches turns to verse." He received the Pulitzer Prize for *Selected Poems* (1929), the National Book Award for his *Collected Poems* (1953), and the National Medal for Literature, 1969. He also wrote *A Letter from Li Po* (1955), the novel *Blue Voyage* (1927), and *A Reviewer's ABC: Collected Criticism* (1958).

Albee, Edward Franklin III (1928–), U.S. playwright, the foremost U.S. dramatist of the 1960's, noted for his sense of drama and dialogue. His plays were widely performed and praised. They include *The Zoo Story* (1960), *The Death of Bessie Smith* (1961), *The American Dream* (1961), *Who's Afraid of Virginia Woolf?* (1962; film version, 1966), *Tiny Alice* (1965), *A Delicate Balance* (1966), *Seascape* (1975), and *The Man Who Had Three Arms* (1983).

Albert (1819–1861), prince consort of England (after 1857) and husband of Queen Victoria, a son of the German duke of Saxe-Coburg-Gotha. As Victoria's confidential adviser, he counseled her on foreign and domestic policy and helped to maintain the Crown's influence within the constitutional monarchy. Albert promoted the arts and sciences; he organized the Great Exhibition of 1851.

Albertus Magnus, Saint (or **Albert the Great**) (c. 1200–1280), German scholastic philosopher and scientist, called by Roger Bacon "the most noted of Christian scholars." Born in Swabia, he became a Dominican and taught at

Paris, Cologne, and other great universities of Europe. Albertus taught the scientific methods of Aristotle and himself made notable studies in botany and metallurgy. His influence made the works of Aristotle the prime authority on natural science and philosophy throughout medieval Europe.

Alcibiades (c 450–404 B.C.), Athenian general and statesman, nephew of Pericles and friend of Socrates. Alcibiades was Athens's best-loved, yet most mistrusted citizen. He was an influential member of the war party in Athens during the Peloponnesian War. While leading an expedition against Syracuse, 415–413, he was recalled to Athens to stand trial for sacrilege. He fled to Sparta and aided the Spartans against Athens. The Spartans also mistrusted him, however, and he went on to Persia. After a political upheaval in Athens in 411, Alcibiades returned there to command the army and navy in 407. Following a Spartan victory at Notium in 406, he left Athens and lived from then on in exile. He was murdered in Phrygia.

ALEXANDER THE GREAT

THE BETTMANN ARCHIVE

Alcott, Louisa May (1832–1888), U.S. author whose book *Little Women* (1868–1869) is a classic of children's literature. She drew on her own family's experiences for it and her other popular books: *An Old-Fashioned Girl* (1870), *Little Men* (1871), *Eight Cousins* (1875), and *Jo's Boys* (1886). An earlier book, *Hospital Sketches* (1863), told of her experiences as a Civil War nurse. Her father, **Amos Bronson Alcott** (1799–1888), was a brilliant educator and philosopher, a member of the Concord, Mass., circle of Thoreau and Emerson.

Alden, John (c 1599–1687), one of the founders of Plymouth Colony. Born in England, he came to America on the *Mayflower* in 1620 and was a signer of the Mayflower Compact. Alden is best remembered as the hero of Longfellow's poem *The Courtship of Miles Standish.* Although the story is fictional, Alden, who settled in Duxbury, Mass., did marry Priscilla Mullens.

Aleichem, Sholom: *See* Rabinowitz, Solomon.

Alexander VI, Pope: *See* Borgia.

Alexander the Great (356–323 B.C.), king of Macedonia, son of Philip II. By his widespread conquests, Alexander spread the language and culture of Greece over great expanses of the ancient world. As a young man, Alexander was tutored by Aristotle, 342–335. When he came to the throne in 336, he immediately suppressed the rebellions that had broken out in Greece after his father's murder. He then went to war with Persia, winning famous victories at Granicus and Issus, 333, and conquering Syria and Egypt. In 331 he founded the city of Alexandria. His armies moved eastward, and by 325 Macedonia ruled from Egypt to India. To unify the empire, Alexander encouraged intermarriage with conquered peoples; he married Roxana, a Bactrian princess. He gave administrative offices to foreigners as well as Greeks and established colonies along the trade routes. He died in Babylon, on his way home to Macedonia.

Alexander Nevski (c 1220–1263), Russian ruler and national hero. The son of Grand Duke Jaroslav of Novgorod, Alexander defended Russia's western frontiers against invaders. His most famous victories were in 1240 over the Swedes at the Neva River, for which he earned the surname Nevski; and in 1242 over the Teutonic Knights on the ice of Lake Peipus. In 1252 he became grand duke of Vladimir. He was canonized by the Russian Orthodox Church.

Alfred the Great (849–899), king of Wessex, 871–899, and overlord of several other English kingdoms, one of the greatest English kings. The youngest son of Ethelwulf, he inherited a realm that had been continually harried by Viking invasions. Finally, Alfred forced the Danes to accept the Treaty of Wedmore (878), which gave them limited lands (the Danelaw) in England. To rebuild the country, Alfred had to establish his power firmly. He codified the laws, created a navy, revised the government, and encouraged a revival of culture and learning. He invited scholars to translate great Latin works into Old English, the language of the West Saxons. Alfred, himself an excellent scholar, translated several works. He also ordered scholars to begin the compilation of *The Anglo-Saxon Chronicle,* a history of early England.

Alger, Horatio (1834–1899), U.S. author of books for boys, known especially for his rags to riches stories of poor boys who became rich and successful. Alger wrote more than 100 popular books, including *Ragged Dick* (1867), *Luck and Pluck* (1869), and *Tattered Tom* (1871).

Ali, Muhammad (1942–   ), U.S. boxer (born Cassius Marcellus Clay), one of the most colorful and exciting fighters in the history of boxing, famed for his speed, agility, and boastfulness. In 1964 he defeated Sonny Liston for the heavyweight championship. He then joined the Black Muslims and changed his name. He was stripped of his title after refusing induction into the U.S. armed forces on religious grounds; his license to box was restored in 1970. In 1974 he regained the championship and defended it successfully several times, often for purses over $1 million. In 1978 he lost the title in the ring, but won it back the same year, becoming the only heavyweight to win the title three times. He then retired.

Allen, Ethan (1738–1789), American Revolutionary War soldier, leader of the Green Mountain Boys, a group of Vermont settlers seeking independent control of their lands. Less than a month after the Revolution began, on May 10, 1775, Allen and his men, along with Benedict Arnold, led a successful surprise attack on the British at Fort Ticonderoga, N.Y. Allen later was captured and imprisoned by the British, but was released in 1778.

Alva, Duke of; Fernando Álvarez de Toledo (1507–1582), Spanish soldier and statesman. He is best remembered for his bloody suppression of Protestantism and rebellion in the Spanish Netherlands between 1567 and 1573. Failing to subdue the Netherlands, he fell from the king's favor, and not even his conquest of Portugal, 1580–1581, restored him.

Alvarado, Pedro de (c 1485–1541), Spanish conquistador, one of the conquerors of Mexico and Central America. He sailed to Yucatán in 1518 and was chief lieutenant under Hernán Cortés in the conquest of Mexico in 1519. Alvarado marched south and conquered the Indians of Guatemala, 1523–1527, then went on to El Salvador and Ecuador. He returned to Spain in 1536, then set out to seek the Seven Cities of Cíbola.

Alvarez, Luis Walter (1911–1988), U.S. physicist who did important research in nuclear physics, radar, and cosmic rays. He led a group that built the first proton linear accelerator, 1945–1947. In the early 1960's, using the hydrogen bubble chamber and special computer programs, he developed a technique for detecting high-energy states of subatomic particles. For this work he was given the 1968 Nobel Prize in Physics. Later Alvarez used cosmic-ray detectors in an attempt to locate hidden burial chambers in ancient Egyptian pyramids.

Amati, a famous family of violinmakers of Cremona, Italy, during the 16th and 17th centuries. **Andrea Amati** (c 1520–c 1578) founded the school and developed the shape and style of violin for which the family became famous. His work was carried on by his sons **Antonio** (c 1550–1638) and **Girolamo** (1551–1635).

The greatest Amati was **Nicolo** (1596–1684), Antonio's son. He taught both Antonio Stradivari and Andrea Guarnieri, founders of the other great violinmaking families. The last great Amati craftsman was Nicolo's son **Girolamo** (1649–1740).

Ampère, André Marie (1775–1836), French mathematician and physicist. Ampère's research in electricity and magnetism laid the foundations for the study of electromagnetism. His name is perpetuated in the word *ampere,* a measure of electric current.

Amundsen, Roald (1872–1928), Norwegian explorer who led the first expedition, in 1911, to reach the South Pole. Sailing in the sloop *Gjöa* with a crew of six, he also determined the position of the North Magnetic Pole and navigated a Northwest Passage, 1903–1906. With explorers Lincoln Ellsworth and Umberto Nobile, he flew over the North Pole in a dirigible in 1926. Among his books was *My Life as an Explorer* (1927).

Anaximander (c 611–c 547 B.C.), Greek natural philosopher, associate of Thales. Anaximander developed the first known systematic theory explaining the natural order of things. His theory was that the world derived from a single substance he called "the unlimited," from which opposite characteristics (hot-cold, wet-dry) separated. He is also credited with introducing the sundial into Greece and with making a map of the known world.

Andersen, Hans Christian (1805–1875), Danish author, known around the world for his stories and fairy tales, which include "The Ugly Duckling," "The Emperor's New Clothes," and "The Little Mermaid." Andersen was a tall, gawky, simple man whose moods alternated between joy and melancholy. The son of a cobbler in the village of Odense, he went to Copenhagen in 1819 to work in the Royal Theater; the directors rejected his plays but sent him through school. He began publishing his stories in 1835. Though he had many friends (including the king of Denmark), he was unlucky in love and never married.

Anderson, Marian (1902–), U.S. concert singer, known for her rich contralto voice. She placed first in a competition for young singers sponsored by the New York Philharmonic in 1925, but found few roles available to her in the United States. She established her reputation in Europe, and then returned to the U.S. concert stage. In 1955 she became the first black American to sing with the Metropolitan Opera, playing in *A Masked Ball.* She was named a UN delegate in 1958, and was given the Kennedy Center Honor for a lifetime of achievement in 1978.

Anderson, Sherwood (1876–1941), U.S. writer, best known for the sketches and stories in *Winesburg, Ohio* (1919). These studies of the frustrated lives of people in a small midwestern town influenced many later short story writers. Anderson came from the small town of Camden, Ohio. He wrote other story collections (*The Triumph of the Egg,* 1921); his novels were not as successful.

André, John (1751–1780), English army officer, a major in the British army in America during the American Revolution. He conducted negotiations with Benedict Arnold for the betrayal of West Point, but was discovered in civilian clothes, arrested, and hanged as a spy.

Andrea del Sarto: *See* Sarto, Andrea del.

Andrews, Roy Chapman (1884–1960), U.S. naturalist, explorer, and writer. In 1916 he led the American Museum of Natural History's first expedition to study prehistoric life in central Asia. In later expeditions to Asia, 1927–1928, his finds included fossil dinosaur eggs and parts of the skeleton of *Baluchitherium,* the largest known land animal. Andrews's books include *Ends of the Earth* (1929), *This Amazing Planet* (1940), and *In the Days of the Dinosaurs* (1959).

Angelico, Fra: *See* Fiesole, Giovanni da.

Annunzio, Gabriele d': *See* D'Annunzio, Gabriele.

Anouilh, Jean Marie Lucien Pierre (1910–1987), French dramatist whose many plays, both light and serious, mixed wit and charm with bitter cynicism. *Antigone* (1944) made his work popular in France. Several other plays were translated into English, often as films or TV plays. Among the best known are *Waltz of the Toreadors* (1956), *Thieves' Carnival* (*Le bal des voleurs,* 1938), *The Lark* (*L'Alouette,* 1953), and *Becket* (1959).

Anthony, Saint (c 250–c 355), founder of Christian monasticism. The heir of a wealthy Egyptian family, he gave up all his property in about 270 and retired to the desert to live as a hermit. In 305 he came out to organize a community of other hermits, considered the first monastery. He then returned to solitude, occasionally emerging to teach and to preach against heresies.

Anthony, Susan Brownell (1820–1906), U.S. reformer and pioneer for women's rights, born into a Quaker, abolitionist family. She began to work for the temperance movement in 1852 and the American Antislavery Society in 1856. In 1869, with Elizabeth Cady Stanton, she organized the National Woman Suffrage Association. For more than 30 years, she worked in various suffrage groups, writing and giving lectures. Claiming her civil rights under the Constitution, she voted in an election in 1872. She was arrested and fined, but she refused to pay. She was president of the National American Woman Suffrage Association, 1892–1900, and helped compile *The History of Woman Suffrage* (4 volumes, 1881–1902).

Antonioni, Michelangelo (1912–), Italian film director, distinguished for his innovative camera technique, his use of color, and his themes of boredom and alienation in modern society. Antonioni received wide critical acclaim for his trilogy of films, *L'Avventura, La Notte,* and *Eclipse* (1960–1963). His later films include *The Red Desert* (1964); *Blow-Up* (1966), which aroused much controversy among critics; and *The Passenger* (1975).

Antony, Mark (c 83–30 B.C.), Roman soldier and politician. A supporter of Julius Caesar during the first civil war (49–45), Antony roused the Roman people and seized power when Caesar was murdered in 44. The power struggle that followed between Antony and Caesar's heir Octavian (later the emperor Augustus) destroyed the last of the Roman Republic. After he and Octavian had joined to defeat the republicans at Philippi (42), Antony took control of Rome's eastern provinces. There he fell in love with Cleopatra. In the final struggle with Octavian, Antony's and Cleopatra's forces were defeated at sea off Actium in 31. Octavian invaded Egypt in 30, and Antony committed suicide.

Appleseed, Johnny: *See* Chapman, John.

Appleton, Sir Edward Victor (1892–1965), British physicist. He did research on the ionosphere and discovered in it an upper layer of free electrons, now named the Appleton layer, that reflects radio waves. He won the 1947 Nobel Prize for Physics.

Aquinas, Saint Thomas (c 1225–1274), Italian theologian, the foremost Christian philosopher of the Middle Ages. His *Summa Theologica* (1266–1273) was one of the most influential documents of scholastic philosophy. He taught at Paris, then returned to Italy and lectured at the papal court, 1259–1268. He then returned to Paris to dispute the interpretation of Aristotle. Aquinas contributed to the liturgy (*Mass for Corpus Christi,* 1264) and wrote commentaries on Aristotle. His numerous writings include the

THE BETTMANN ARCHIVE

ARISTOTLE

Summa contra gentiles (1259–1264), written to persuade unbelievers; and a commentary (1254–1256) on Peter Lombard's *Sentences,* the standard textbook of medieval theology.

Archimedes (c 287–212 B.C.), Greek mathematician and inventor. He is credited with inventing various mechanical devices, including the Archimedean screw. He himself was far prouder of his mathematical studies, particularly in geometry. He supposedly discovered his famous principle ("a body immersed in a fluid loses as much in weight as the weight of the fluid it displaces") when his bath overflowed as he sat down in it.

Aristophanes (c 450–c 380 B.C.), Greek comic poet, one of the world's great writers of comedy. He was a contemporary of Socrates and other eminent Athenians, whom he ridiculed in his popular plays. He satirized contemporary politics, philosophy, literature, and educational ideas, particularly the war policies and the Athenian leaders. Of his eleven surviving plays, many of which are still performed, the most famous are *The Clouds* (423), *The Birds* (414), *Lysistrata* (411), and *The Frogs* (405).

Aristotle (384–322 B.C.), Greek philosopher, one of history's most influential thinkers. At 17, he left his birthplace in Macedonia for the center of Greek culture, Athens, where he became Plato's pupil and associate. When Plato died in 347, Aristotle joined several other Platonists in forming a school in Asia Minor. In 342 he accepted an invitation from the king of Macedonia to return to his homeland as tutor to the prince, Alexander. When Alexander became king in 336, Aristotle returned to Athens and founded a new school. Aristotle was one of the great geniuses of history. His ideas are woven into the very fabric of Western thought, reaching us not only through his own works

THE BETTMANN ARCHIVE

NEIL ARMSTRONG

but also through the countless works he influenced. His study of logic, the *Organon,* shaped European education for a thousand years. His other works, among them the *Physics,* the *Metaphysics,* the *Politics,* and the *Poetics,* left an indelible stamp on Christian thought through the overriding influence they exerted on medieval philosophers and theologians.

Armstrong, Louis Daniel (1900–1971), nicknamed Satchmo (short for "satchelmouth"), influential U.S. jazz musician of the 1920's and best known of all time. Born in New Orleans, he learned to play the trumpet with the early jazz bands. After playing with King Oliver and other famous groups, he formed his own bands from 1926 on. He had a distinctive hoarse singing voice and an irresistible smile. In later years, he made many world tours.

Armstrong, Neil Alden (1930–), U.S. astronaut, commander of the *Apollo 11* space flight and the first man to set foot on the moon (July 20, 1969). His words as he stepped onto the moon were, "That's one small step for a man, one giant leap for mankind." Armstrong, a research pilot, was the first civilian to command a U.S. spacecraft (*Gemini 8,* 1962). His fellow astronauts on *Apollo 11* were Edwin Aldrin, Jr., and Michael Collins.

Arnold, Benedict (1741–1801), American Revolutionary army officer who later became a traitor. He served heroically in the first years of the Revolution, notably at Saratoga (1777). Many reasons have been suggested for Arnold's treason: he married into a Loyalist family, needed money, and felt he had been unfairly denied promotion. He negotiated with the British for the betrayal of West Point. The plan was revealed when John André was captured and Arnold fled to British lines. He spent the rest of his life in Canada and England.

Arnold, Matthew (1822–1888), English poet, essayist, and critic, a leading literary figure of the Victorian age. Most of his poetry, which tends to be serious and reflective, was written before he was 30. "Dover Beach," "Thyrsis," and "The Scholar-Gipsy" are among the best known. His critical essays on literature, education, and religion were published in *Essays in Criticism* (1865, 1888) and other books. Son of a famous headmaster of Rugby, he was also a distinguished educator, serving as government inspector of schools, 1851–1853, and as professor of poetry at Oxford, 1857–1867.

Arp, Jean (or **Hans)** (1887–1966), French sculptor and painter, a central figure in the development of Dadaism and surrealism in art, and a pioneer in organic abstract sculpture. Arp was a member of The Blue Rider, a group of Europe's leading artists in the period before World War I. His sculpture is based on rounded natural forms such as the human body and eggs.

Arthur, legendary king of Britain. The historical Arthur seems to have lived around 500 A.D. and to have led the Britons in war against the Saxons. According to legend, Arthur was the son of King Uther Pendragon and a great leader. Bards and poets combined his story with other legends about Merlin, Lancelot, Tristram, and the Holy Grail to form the Arthurian cycle of legends about Camelot and the Knights of the Round Table. The two main sources for the Arthurian cycle are Geoffrey of Monmouth and Sir Thomas Malory.

Arthur, Chester Alan (1830–1886), U.S. lawyer who became 21st President of the United States, 1881–1885, after the assassination of James A. Garfield. Born in Fairfield, Vt., Arthur graduated from Union College in 1848, studied law, and began a successful practice in New York. He opposed slavery and won several legal victories in civil rights cases. In politics, Arthur was active in building the New York Republican Party. In 1871 he became collector of the port of New York, a federal post controlled by the state political machine. He was removed from office in 1878 by President Hayes, who had forbidden federal officials to take part in party politics. In 1880 the Republicans nominated Garfield and, to conciliate the pro-patronage "Stalwart" faction, chose Arthur as their Vice Presidential candidate. Arthur became President on September 19, 1881, after Garfield was shot. During his administration, much Republican legislation was passed, including high tariffs and the Civil Service Act (1883). The dominant wing of the party, however, blocked Arthur's renomination in 1884.

Asch, Sholem (1880–1957), Polish-born Yiddish author; he later lived in the United States, then in Israel. Through his well-known novels on biblical subjects, Asch became a highly controversial writer. His books include *The Nazarene* (1939), *The Apostle* (1943), *East River* (1946), *Mary* (1949), and a collection of short stories, *Tales of My People* (1948).

THE BETTMANN ARCHIVE
SHOLEM ASCH

Ashurbanipal (or **Assurbanipal)**, last great king of Assyria, reigning from 669 to 626 B.C. Under Ashurbanipal, the empire encompassed Assyria, Babylonia, Egypt, Syria, Palestine, and, later, Elam. He took great interest in arts and culture and collected extensive libraries of cuneiform tablets in his palace at Nineveh. The inscriptions found there are the basis for most studies of ancient Assyria.

Asimov, Isaac (1920–), Russian-born U.S. scientist and author. Acclaimed for his science fiction works such as the *Foundation* trilogy (1951–1953) and *The Caves of Steel* (1954), he also wrote popular introductions to science, including *Wellsprings of Life* (1960), a summary of evolutionary theory, *Inside the Atom* (1961), *Our World in Space* (1974), and *Views of the Universe* (1981).

Asoka (d. c 232 B.C.), emperor of India, c 273–c 232. After fighting to expand the huge empire created by his grandfather Chandragupta, he renounced violence and became a devout Buddhist and a benevolent ruler. Inscriptions (in the ancient Indo-Aryan language) on rocks and pillars throughout his empire record his legal reforms, his public works, his moral zeal, and his encouragement of Buddhist missionary work.

Assisi, Saint Francis of: *See* Francis of Assisi, Saint.

Astaire, Fred (1899–1987), U.S. dancer, singer, and actor, born Frederick Austerlitz, celebrated for his effortless grace, inventiveness, and high standards. As the most elegant song-and-dance man in motion picture musical comedy, he made many films with such stars as Ginger Rogers, Rita Hayworth, and Cyd Charisse, and developed ballroom and tap dancing into stylish and disciplined art.

Astor, John Jacob (1763–1848), German-born U.S. fur trader, founder of the Astor fortune. His first fur-trading posts were in upper New York State and in Canada. After the Louisiana Purchase (1803), he built trading posts farther west, and soon his American Fur Company extended to the Pacific coast. Astor acquired extensive property in Manhattan that became extremely valuable. When he retired in 1834, he was reputed to be the richest man in America, with a $20 million fortune.

Asturias, Miguel Ángel (1899–1974), Guatemalan writer and diplomat, best known for his novels. *The President* (translated 1963) is a study of dictatorship; *The Eyes of the Interred* (translated 1973) centers on the Caribbean banana trade; *The Bejeweled Boy* (translated 1972) is based on Guatemalan folklore. Asturias was awarded the Nobel Prize in Literature in 1967.

Atahualpa (c 1502–1533), last Inca ruler of Peru. After the death of his father Huayna Capac in 1525, Atahualpa defeated his half brother Huascar and became sole ruler. The Incas met the Spanish conquistadors hospitably, but in 1532 Pizarro and his soldiers treacherously captured Atahualpa and killed hundreds of Incas in a surprise attack. A vast ransom—often described as a roomful of gold and silver—was collected for Atahualpa. Pizarro took the ransom, but accused Atahualpa of various crimes and had him strangled.

Attila (d. 453), king of the Huns, who led his barbarian horde from eastern Europe in a series of invasions of the later Roman Empire and earned a lasting name for ferocity. After devastating large parts of the eastern empire in two campaigns (441–443, 447), Attila invaded Gaul in 451. The Roman general Aetius and the Visigothic king Theodoric combined to defeat him in the great battle of Maurica. Attila withdrew and invaded northern Italy the following year. He died on the eve of another campaign in the east.

Attlee, Clement, 1st Earl Attlee (1883–1967), British statesman and Labour Party leader. In 1942 he became deputy prime minister in Churchill's wartime coalition cabinet. With the Labour victory in 1945, he became prime minister. National health and insurance schemes were put into effect, and independence was granted to India. Labour was defeated in 1951; Attlee resigned as party leader in 1955 and was then made an earl.

Attucks, Crispus (c 1723–1770), American patriot, one of the men killed by British troops in the Boston Massacre, March 5, 1770. Traditionally, Attucks is described as a runaway slave who had become a sailor, and the first black American patriot. Other accounts say that he was an Indian, or half black, half Indian.

Auden, Wystan Hugh (1907–1973), Anglo-American poet and playwright. In the 1930's he led a circle of socially involved writers that included Stephen Spender and Christopher Isherwood. He came to the United States in 1939, exerting a strong influence on U.S. poetry in the 1940's. His early work includes *The Dance of Death* (1933), *Journey to a War* (1939), and several plays with Isherwood, including *The Ascent of F. 6* (1936). Auden's philosophical *Age of Anxiety* (1947) won the Pulitzer Prize; *The Shield of Achilles* (1956) was given the National Book Award. He wrote the libretto for Stravinsky's opera *The Rake's Progress* (1953). He was awarded the National Medal for Literature in 1967.

Audubon, John James (1785–1851), Haitian-born U.S. nature artist, a pioneer in the study of American bird life. Audubon came to the United States about 1804 and traveled widely, studying and drawing birds. Seeking a publisher for his collection of drawings, he went to England in 1826. There, many of his best-known collections were published: *The Birds of America* (4 volumes, 1827–1838), with hand-colored plates made from his drawings; and *Ornithological Biography* (5 volumes, 1831–1839). His last major project was *Viviparous Quadrupeds of North America* (1845–1854). Audubon's work interested the public in ornithology and conservation and inspired the founding of the Audubon Societies.

JOHN JAMES AUDUBON

THE BETTMANN ARCHIVE

RULERS OF THE ROMAN EMPIRE

27 B.C.–14 A.D.	Augustus (Octavianus)*
14 A.D.–37 A.D.	Tiberius
37–41	Caligula*
41–54	Claudius I*
54–68	Nero*
68–69	Galba
69	Otho
69	Vitellius
69–79	Vespasian*
79–81	Titus
81–96	Domitian
96–98	Nerva
98–117	Trajan*
117–138	Hadrian*
138–161	Antoninus Pius
161–180	Marcus Aurelius
161–169	Lucius Aurelius Verus
180–192	Commodus
193	Pertinax
193	Didius Julianus
193–211	Septimius Severus
211–217	Caracalla
211–212	Geta
217–218	Macrinus
218–222	Heliogabalus or Elagabalus
222–235	Alexander Severus
235–238	Maximinus
238	Gordianus I
238	Gordianus II
238	Balbinus and Pupienus
238–244	Gordianus III
244–249	Philip the Arabian
249–251	Decius
251	Hostilian
251–253	Gallus
253	Aemilianus
253–259	Valerian
259–268	Gallienus
268–270	Claudius II
270	Quintillus
270–275	Aurelian
275–276	Tacitus
276	Florian
276–282	Probus
282–283	Carus
283–284	Numerianus
283–285	Carinus
284–305	Diocletian
286–305	Maximian
305–306	Constantius I
305–311	Galerius
306–337	Constantine I (the Great)*
337–340	Constantine II
337–350	Constans
337–361	Constantius II
361–363	Julian the Apostate
363–364	Jovian
364–375	Valentinian I (West)
364–378	Valens (East)
375–383	Gratian (West)
375–392	Valentinian II (West)
379–394	Theodosius the Great (East)
383–388	Maximus (West)
392–394	Eugenius (West)
394–395	Theodosius (sole emperor)

*See main biography.

Augustine, Saint (354–430), early Christian theologian and one of the great Latin doctors of the church. His works, especially the *Confessions* (397) and *The City of God (De civitate dei),* are among the most influential documents of church thought and doctrine. Augustine (Aurelius Augustinus) was born in North Africa, the son of a pagan, Patricius, and a Christian, Monica. He taught in Carthage, Rome, and Milan, where, influenced by Neoplatonism and by the sermons of Bishop Ambrose, he underwent a startling conversion to orthodox Christianity in 387. He turned to a life of study and contemplation, but in 396, he was made bishop of Hippo (in Roman Africa). He vigorously defended orthodoxy against the Manichaean, Donatist, and Pelagian heresies. His rigorous doctrine, still considered radical, emphasized predestination and the need for divine grace.

Augustus (63 B.C.–14 A.D.), born Gaius Octavius (in English, Octavian), first emperor of Rome. Octavian, the adopted son of his great-uncle Julius Caesar, fought with Mark Antony for control of Rome after Caesar's murder in 44 B.C. The two later joined to defeat the republican forces led by Caesar's assassins at Philippi in 42 B.C. The victors then resumed their struggle for power, and Antony was defeated at the Battle of Actium (31 B.C.), leaving Octavian master of the Roman armies. With them, he controlled the entire Mediterranean area as well as most of Europe. Octavian did not intend to usurp the ruling power of the Senate. However, the government of the republic was so tattered by civil war that the Senate and people gradually conferred on him most of the governing power. The Senate gave him the title "Augustus" in 27 B.C. Under Augustus's rule, Rome became a great center of culture and learning. Art, literature (Vergil, Horace, Ovid), and architecture flourished. Newly conquered lands were settled, and the stable political foundations of the Roman Empire were laid.

Aurangzeb (1618–1707), last of the great Mughal emperors of India. After imprisoning his father, Shah Jahan, and disposing of his brothers, he took the throne in 1658, calling himself Conqueror of the World. With a series of aggressive military campaigns, Aurangzeb extended the Mughal empire to nearly the size of present-day India. But the long wars ravaged the land, exhausted the treasury, and weakened his position as leader. A devout Muslim, he also alienated and persecuted the Hindus. Unrest and rebellion spread, and when he died, the empire had begun its decline.

Austen, Jane (1775–1817), English novelist, author of witty, gently satirical domestic novels of provincial English life. *Pride and Prejudice* (1813) is her best-loved book; the others are *Sense and Sensibility* (1811), *Mansfield Park* (1814), *Emma* (1816), and *Northanger Abbey* and *Persuasion,* both published posthumously in 1818.

Averroës (1126–1198), Latin name of Abu'l-Walid Muhammad ibn-Ahmad ibn-Rushd, Moorish philosopher, known as the Commentator for his exhaustive commentaries on the works of Aristotle. He also wrote books on law, grammar, and astronomy, and a standard text on medicine. Averroës asserted that philosophy and religion explain the truth in different ways. His European followers took this to mean that philosophy was superior to religion, and the arguments over Averroism eventually led to a separation of the two fields.

Avogadro, Amedeo, Conte di Quaregna e di Ceretto (1776–1856), Italian physicist and professor at Turin. He discovered (and gave his name to) one of the fundamental laws of modern chemistry. Avogadro's law (published 1811) stated that equal volumes of gases at the same temperature and pressure contain equal numbers of molecules. The principle was not widely accepted until 1860.

B

Bach, pious and respectable North German family of musicians and composers. Its foremost member was **Johann Sebastian Bach** (1685–1750), whom many consider the world's greatest composer. J. S. Bach's music represents the height of the German baroque style. In 1708 Bach became organist of the Ducal Chapel in Weimar, where he composed organ works. In 1717 he moved to the court of Prince Leopold at Cöthen, where he composed instrumental works (Brandenburg concertos, 1721) and developed the modern method of tuning keyboard instruments (*Well-tempered Clavier,* 1722). From 1723 to his death, Bach was in charge of music for the churches of Leipzig. During this period he wrote his religious works: chorales, oratorios and motets, the *Passions* (St. John, St. Matthew), and the Mass in B minor (1733).

Of J.S. Bach's sons, the two most notable are **Carl Philip Emanuel Bach** (1714–1788), who wrote sonatas and symphonies and was Haydn's mentor; and **Johann Christian Bach** (1735–1782), who wrote church music and operas and influenced Mozart.

Bacon, Sir Francis (1561–1626), English statesman, philosopher, and essayist. Bacon's collected *Essays,* published in 1625, are noted for a lofty style and a highly practical attitude. His scientific and philosophical studies, *Novum Organum* (1620) and *De augmentis scientiarum* (1623; an expanded version of his *Advancement of Learning,* 1605), led later scholars to observe and work from facts rather than rely on theories derived from ancient and medieval philosophy. His only known experiment—stuffing a chicken with snow to see whether cold would halt decay—brought on a chill that caused his death.

Bacon, Francis (1909–), English painter, influenced by both cubism and surrealism, whose work is distinctive for its images of horror and anguish. His paintings are often based on photographs or works of the past, such as his *Studies After Velasquez' Portrait of Pope Innocent X* (1951–1953) and *Studies for a Portrait of Van Gogh* (1956–1957).

Bacon, Roger (c 1214–1294), English scholar and Franciscan friar. Bacon was master of the traditional branches of medieval learning, but he despised the scholars of his time for their reliance on authority as the ultimate basis of knowledge. His aggressive advocacy of a more experimental approach to scholarship—as well as his interest in astrology and alchemy—brought him the disfavor of his superiors. Between two periods of confinement, 1257–1267 and 1278–1292, he had the support of Pope Clement IV, for whom he wrote *Opus majus* (1268), delineating his plan for the reform of scholarly methods.

Baffin, William (c 1584–1622), English explorer and navigator. Baffin explored much of the northwest coast of Canada. He explored Hudson Strait, made records of tides and navigational information, and, by sailing north of the Arctic Circle, discovered the bay and island named after him. He sailed to India from 1617 to 1619, making navigational surveys of the Red Sea and the Persian Gulf. He is also credited with being the first to measure longitude at sea by lunar observation.

Bakunin, Mikhail Aleksandrovich (1814–1876), Russian revolutionary, a leading advocate of 19th-century anarchism. Bakunin traveled widely in Europe, becoming increasingly active in revolutionary causes. He was eventually arrested in 1849 in Germany and handed over to the Austrian and later the Russian police. After seven years in prison, he was moved to a penal colony in Siberia, but he escaped to London in 1861. He joined the International Workingmen's Association (the "First International"), where he led a faction bitterly opposed to Karl Marx and finally was expelled. Opposed to state socialism, Bakunin advocated peasant revolts and the destruction of all forms of government. His followers included many Russian revolutionaries as well as strong anarchist groups in Spain and Italy.

Balanchine, George (1904–1983), Russian-born U.S. choreographer whose works, mostly neoclassical in style, greatly influenced American dance. Balanchine was trained as a dancer at the Imperial St. Petersburg Theater Ballet School. He left Russia in 1924, joined the Diaghilev troupe, and worked in Europe until 1934. Between 1934 and 1948, Balanchine, with Lincoln Kirstein, organized several ballet companies in the United States, ultimately forming the New York City Ballet, for which Balanchine became artistic director, 1948–1982. Among Balanchine's many ballets are *Serenade* (1934), *Concerto Barocco* (1941), *Symphony in C* (1948), *Don Quixote* (1965), and the *Davidsbündlertänze* (1980), to music of Robert Schumann. He frequently worked with composer Igor Stravinsky, producing such ballets as *The Nightingale* (1925), *Orpheus* (1948), *Agon* (1958), and a restaging of *Firebird* (1970).

Balboa, Vasco Núñez de (c 1475–1517), Spanish explorer who discovered the Pacific Ocean. In 1510 he traveled to San Sebastián (now Colombia), then to Darién (in modern Panama), where he established a settlement. Searching for gold the Indians said would be found on the "other coast" of Panama, Balboa crossed the isthmus in 1513 and became the first European in the New World to see the Pacific. The governor of the settlement he had founded later accused Balboa, falsely, of treason and had him beheaded.

Baldwin, James Arthur (1924–1987), U.S. writer, noted for his perceptive

SIR FRANCIS BACON

THE BETTMANN ARCHIVE

portrayal of the black experience in America. Baldwin's first book was *Go Tell It on the Mountain* (1953), a semiautobiographical novel. Among his other novels are *Giovanni's Room* (1956) and *Another Country* (1962), which show similarities in society's persecution of blacks and homosexuals; and *Tell Me How Long the Train's Been Gone* (1968). His essays were collected in *Notes of a Native Son* (1955), *Nobody Knows My Name* (1961), and *The Fire Next Time* (1963). He also wrote a play, *Blues for Mr. Charlie* (1964), and *The Price of the Ticket* (1985).

Baldwin, Stanley, 1st Earl Baldwin of Bewdley (1867–1947), British statesman and Conservative Party leader. Baldwin entered Parliament in 1908 and held several government posts during World War I. He served three times as prime minister, 1923, 1924–1929, 1935–1937. In this post, he handled the national crises caused by the general strike of 1926 and by Edward VIII's abdication in 1936.

Balfour, Arthur James, 1st Earl Balfour (1848–1930), British statesman and Conservative Party leader. He succeeded his uncle, Lord Salisbury, as leader of the Conservatives, 1891–1911, and then as prime minister, 1902–1906. In 1917, while Balfour was foreign secretary (1916–1919), he issued the Balfour Declaration, which gave a degree of British support to a Jewish national home in Palestine, but both Zionists and Arabs found support for their positions in this policy statement.

Baltimore, Lord: *See* Calvert, George.

Balzac, Honoré de (1799–1850), French novelist, considered the founder of the realistic French novel. Balzac is remembered for *The Human Comedy (La Comédie humaine),* a monumental series of novels giving a panoramic view of French life and society of the early 1800's. Balzac gave the stories unity by building them around a central cast of characters. Among the best known of the books are *Eugénie Grandet* (1833) and *Le Père Goriot* (1835).

Banting, Sir Frederick Grant (1891–1941), Canadian research physician who shared the 1923 Nobel Prize for Physiology and Medicine with J. J. R. Macleod (1876–1935). In 1921, working with Charles H. Best under the direction of Macleod, Banting isolated insulin. Later Macleod and J. P. Collip purified it for human use. Banting shared his prize with Best, and Macleod shared his with Collip.

Baraka, Imamu Amiri (1934–), U.S. poet and playwright (originally Le Roi Jones). He dealt with racial tensions in a straightforward way that made many people uncomfortable in such plays as *Dutchman, The Toilet,* and *The Slave* (all 1964). His poetry includes *Preface to a Twenty-Volume Suicide Note* (1961), *The Dead Lecturer* (1964), *The System of Dante's Hell* (1965), and *Black Magic* (1969).

Barber, Samuel (1910–1981), U.S. composer noted for his romantic, lyrical compositions. Barber's opera *Vanessa* won the Pulitzer Prize in 1958. Among his other vocal pieces are *Knoxville, Summer of 1915* (1947) and the cantata *Prayers of Kierkegaard* (1954). He wrote works for strings, including the *Adagio for Strings* (1936), and concertos for violin and cello. His Piano Concerto no. 1 (1963) won a Pulitzer Prize, and his opera *Antony and Cleopatra* was performed at the opening of the new Metropolitan Opera House, Lincoln Center, 1966.

Barnard, Christiaan (1922–), South African surgeon who performed the world's first human heart transplant. Barnard headed a team of doctors that replaced the heart of Louis Washkansky at Groote Schuur Hospital (Capetown, S. Africa) in December, 1967. Washkansky survived only 18 days, but the operation was a milestone in medical history. In 1971 Barnard performed one of the first complete heart-lung transplants. He headed the cardiac unit at Groote Schuur until his retirement in 1983.

JOHN BARRYMORE

THE BETTMANN ARCHIVE

Barnum, Phineas Taylor (1810–1891), U.S. impresario. In 1842 he opened the American Museum in New York City, where he exhibited freaks, rare animals, and other sensational acts. Barnum introduced and made famous the dwarf "General Tom Thumb," the Swedish opera singer Jenny Lind, and the elephant Jumbo. In 1871 Barnum formed his own circus, which he called "The Greatest Show on Earth." Ten years later, he joined forces with his chief rival, James Anthony Bailey, to form the Barnum and Bailey Circus. Barnum is often considered the inventor of modern publicity techniques. One of his famous quips was "There's a sucker born every minute."

Barrymore, a family of U.S. actors, descendants of Irish-American actors John Drew (1827–1862) and Louisa Lane Drew (1820–1897). Their daughter Georgiana married English actor Maurice Barrymore (1848–1905), whose real name was Blythe. Their children were:

Lionel (1878–1954), a noted character actor in stage and film roles and later on radio (in "Dr. Kildare"). He won an Academy Award for *A Free Soul* (1931).

Ethel (1879–1959), who was for years known as "first lady of the American theater." On stage, she starred in Ibsen's *A Doll's House* (1905) and *The Corn Is Green* (1940–1943). She also acted in many films, winning a 1944

Academy Award for *None But the Lonely Heart*.

John (1882–1942), a handsome, romantic hero of many plays and films. He was particularly admired as Hamlet and in other Shakespearean roles.

Barth, Karl (1886–1968), Swiss theologian who tried to direct Protestant theology back to a scriptural, God-centered discipline. In his *Epistle to the Romans* (1919; translated 1930), Barth portrays man as sinful and in need of grace. Barth's *Church Dogmatics* (12 volumes, 1932–1962) examines the Christian message through interpretation of Scripture.

Bartholdi, Frédéric Auguste (1834–1904), French sculptor who used a total of 300 giant copper sheets to create the Statue of Liberty as a gift from France to the United States commemorating the Franco-American alliance of 1778. It was unveiled in Paris in 1884, dismantled, and reassembled in New York harbor in 1886. The *Lion of Belfort* (1888), considered Bartholdi's greatest work, was carved from a red sandstone hill above Belfort, France.

Bartók, Béla (1881–1945), Hungarian composer. Strongly influenced by Slavic folk music, he expanded ethnic melodies and rhythms through the use of dissonant chord combinations and chromatic structure. Among his most frequently performed works are the opera *Duke Bluebeard's Castle* (1911), the ballet *The Miraculous Mandarin* (1918–1919), the collection of piano pieces *Mikrokosmos* (1926–1937), and the Concerto for Orchestra (1943). Bartók moved to the United States in 1940.

Barton, Clara (1821–1912), in full, Clarissa Harlowe Barton, U.S. nurse who founded the American Red Cross (1881). Barton worked with wounded soldiers during the Civil War and set up a bureau to help find soldiers reported missing in action. At the time of the Franco-Prussian War, she worked from 1869 to 1873 in Europe with the International Red Cross, which later asked her to organize the movement in the United States. After her vigorous campaign to overcome American isolationist feeling, the United States signed the 1864 Geneva convention, establishing the American branch; she was its first president (1882–1904).

Baruch, Bernard Mannes (1870–1965), U.S. financier and philanthropist, adviser to U.S. Presidents from Wilson to Truman. After amassing a fortune, he was in 1914 appointed adviser on war mobilization by President Wilson. As chairman of the War Industries Board, 1918–1919, he supervised all U.S. industrial output. Later he was economic consultant for the Versailles Treaty. For the next 30 years, Baruch advised virtually every President. Most notable was his advice on economic mobilization during World War II. As first U.S. representative on the UN Atomic Energy Committee, 1946, he proposed the Baruch Plan to control atomic weapons.

Basie, William (Count) (1904–1984), U.S. jazz musician, known for his emphasis on strong rhythm based on a four-beat measure. His style was known as the "jump style" or "Kansas City jazz." Basie, also a pianist and composer, was a popular bandleader in Chicago and New York in the big band era of the 1930's and 1940's.

Battenberg: *See* Mountbatten.

Baudelaire, Charles Pierre (1821–1867), French poet and critic. His collection of poems, *Les fleurs du mal (Flowers of Evil),* had a lasting impact on the development of modern poetry, particularly on the French symbolists, on modern imagery, and on poets such as T.S. Eliot. The first edition of *Les fleurs du mal* (1857) caused Baudelaire to be brought to trial for immorality; in the second edition (1861), six poems were suppressed, but many new and brilliant poems were added.

Baum, Lyman Frank (1856–1919), U.S. writer, author of the children's classic *The Wonderful Wizard of Oz* (1900). The first Oz book, an enormous success, was made into a musical comedy (1901) and later became a movie classic (1939). Baum wrote 14 more books about the land of Oz and its fantastical inhabitants. His other books for children include *Father Goose: His Book* (1899) and *The Magical Monarch of Mo* (1903).

Bayle, Pierre (1647–1706), French rationalist philosopher and critic. As professor of philosophy and history at Rotterdam (from 1681), he opposed superstition, defended freedom of thought, and urged religious tolerance. He was dismissed for his views in 1693. His most important work, *Historical and Critical Dictionary* (1697; second edition, 1702), is a comprehensive, seemingly orthodox, treatment of philosophy, theology, and biography, with comments and criticism in footnotes. These annotations cleverly reflect Bayle's skepticism, which influenced many writers of the Enlightenment.

Beard, Charles Austin (1874–1948), U.S. historian known for his original, often controversial, approach to history. Beard analyzed history in terms of the factors—such as economic motives and military influence—that affected it. Among his many books on the United States is *The Economic Origins of Jeffersonian Democracy* (1915). *American Foreign Policy in the Making* (1946) showed his later tendencies toward isolationism. He wrote many books with his wife, **Mary R. Beard** (1876–1958), notably *The Rise of American Civilization* (2 volumes, 1927), *America in Mid-Passage* (1939), and *The American Spirit* (1942).

Beaumarchais, Pierre Augustin Caron de (1732–1799), leading French dramatist of the 18th century. During a crowded and colorful career, he was a watchmaker, a music master to Louis XV's daughters, a secret agent, and a strong supporter of the American Revolution. His two most famous and popular plays, *The Barber of Seville* (1775) and *The Marriage of Figaro* (1784), provoked much controversy by mocking the nobility. Both became famous operas—Mozart's *The Marriage of Figaro* (1786) and Rossini's *The Barber of Seville* (1816).

Beauregard, Pierre Gustave Toutant de (1818–1893), U.S. Army officer and Confederate general. A career soldier, he was named superintendent of West Point in 1860, but resigned almost immediately when Louisiana, his home state, seceded from the Union. Joining the Confederacy as a brigadier general, Beauregard ordered the firing on Fort Sumter (April, 1861). He headed the troops at Bull Run (Manassas) and at Shiloh and led the defense of Charleston (1862–1864). His military career ended with his surrender in April, 1865.

Beauvoir, Simone de (1908–1986), French writer who influenced the course of contemporary intellectual French thought, particularly through her existentialist concept of involvement. Her most famous book is *The Second Sex* (1949), a brilliant historical study of women's suppression and secondary position to men. Other well-known works are the novels *The Blood of Others* (1945), *The Mandarins* (1954), and three novellas collected in *The Woman Destroyed* (1969); the autobiographical works *Memoirs of a Dutiful Daughter* (1958) and *The Force of Circumstances* (1963); and a condemnation of society's indifference to the aged, *The Coming of Age* (1972).

Beaverbrook, 1st Baron; William Maxwell Aitken (1879–1964), Canadian-born British newspaper publisher and statesman. As a financier, he amassed a fortune by consolidating the Canadian cement industry. Moving to England, he secured control of the London *Daily Express* in 1916 and eventually built the largest newspaper chain in Britain. He became a peer in 1916 and held important government posts in World Wars I and II.

Bebel, August (1840–1913), German socialist labor leader and author. He and Wilhelm Liebknecht founded the German Social Democratic Party in 1869. He led his party in the German parliament, but spent several years in prison on political charges. One of his books, *The Woman and Socialism* (1883), is a classic socialist work; it has been called the workingman's bible.

Becket, Thomas à (1118–1170), English prelate and saint. Thomas entered the world of courtly affairs in his thirties, joining the household of Theobald, the powerful archbishop of Canterbury. In 1155, on Theobald's recommendation, Henry II appointed Thomas chancellor of England. Thomas and Henry became good friends, and the king's influence assured Thomas's election as archbishop of Canterbury in 1162. To Henry's disappointment, however, Thomas resigned the chancellorship and soon the two were battling over civil encroachment on the church's authority. Their controversy grew increasingly bitter until at last the king became so enraged that four knights, acting on what they took to be his wishes, murdered Thomas in Canterbury cathedral, December 29, 1170. The martyr quickly became the center of a cult of veneration and within three years was canonized. Thomas's martyrdom is the subject of literary works by Alfred Tennyson, T. S. Eliot, Jean Anouilh, and others.

Beckett, Samuel Barclay (1906–1989), Irish-born writer whose play *Waiting for Godot* (1952) founded a new genre, the theater of the absurd. Beckett settled in Paris in 1937. His first works were written in English, but he later wrote in French. He won critical recognition with his first novel in French, *Molloy* (1951), which was followed by two similar novels of comic futility, *Malone Dies* (1951) and *The Unnameable* (1953). Beckett's other plays include *Endgame* (1958), *Krapp's Last Tape* (1958), and *Not I* (1973). He won the Nobel Prize for Literature in 1969.

Becquerel, Antoine Henri (1852–1908), French physicist who discovered radioactivity. In 1896 he found that the element uranium emitted an invisible radiation, similar to x-rays, that could pass through metal and darken a photographic plate. He shared the 1903 Nobel Prize for Physics with the Curies.

Bede (or **Baeda)** (c 673–735), called the Venerable Bede, English historian and monk. He is remembered for his masterly *Ecclesiastical History of the English Nation* (written in Latin), completed in 731, the major source for English history from the Roman invasion (55 B.C.) to 731. Bede spent his life quietly in a monastery in County Durham, studying and writing on grammar, science, and theology. He was canonized in 1899.

Beecham, Sir Thomas (1879–1961), British conductor, a leader in the revival of opera in England. He introduced the works of Richard Strauss, as well as Frederick Delius and Igor Stravinsky to British audiences. After World War I, Beecham founded several opera companies, the London Philharmonic Orchestra in 1932, and the Royal Philharmonic Orchestra in 1947. Thereafter, he devoted himself to orchestral music. He wrote his autobiography, *A Mingled Chime* (1949), and a biography of Delius (1958).

Beecher, Henry Ward (1813–1887), U.S. Congregational clergyman, son of evangelist Lyman Beecher (1775–1863) and brother of Harriet Beecher Stowe. In 1847 he settled in Brooklyn, N.Y., where his moving oratory drew huge weekly crowds. From the pulpit he opposed slavery and supported women's suffrage. Preaching in England during the Civil War, he convincingly presented the Northern view.

Beerbohm, Sir Max (1872–1956), in full, Henry Maximilian Beerbohm, English essayist, critic, and caricaturist, nicknamed the incomparable Max. His sophisticated drawings and essays satirized the society of his time. He contributed to the *Yellow Book* and succeeded Shaw as drama critic of the *Saturday Review* (1898). His books include *A Christmas Garland* (1912), parodies of Hardy, Conrad, and other writers; *Zuleika Dobson* (1911), a comic novel; and several books of caricatures.

Beethoven, Ludwig van (1770–1827), German composer, one of the most powerful and original musicians of all time. As a child, Beethoven showed unusual talent for the violin and piano, and his father, court musician at Bonn, determined to make him known as a child prodigy. He was playing at the court by the time he was twelve and was court organist until 1792, when he moved to Vienna. The music Beethoven wrote from about 1795 on had the classical precision of 18th-century music, as in the First Symphony (1799). After about 1803, his music became more strongly emotional, with more innovations in style. During these intensely creative years he produced six symphonies, concertos for violin and for piano (including the *Emperor,* 1809), the opera *Fidelio* (1805–1806), and numerous sonatas and chamber works. By about 1810, when he was 39, however, Beethoven had become totally deaf. Despite this tragedy, during his last period of writing he produced the Ninth Symphony *(Choral),* the *Missa Solemnis* (1818–1823), and some of his finest quartets.

Begin, Menachem (1913–), prime minister of Israel (1977–1983). Begin was born in Poland, escaped to Lithuania in 1939, was arrested by the Russians, and served time in a labor camp. He reached Palestine in 1942 and was soon in command of a paramilitary force. A Zionist from his youth, Begin fought the British with guerrilla tactics until Israel became independent in 1948. He was elected to parliament in 1949. His political group, the Likud bloc of the Labor Party, was on the ballot for the first time in 1973. In the May, 1977, election, it secured the largest number of seats in parliament of any party. In September, 1978, with President Carter as the mediator, Begin and President Sadat of Egypt agreed on terms for peace between the two countries and for the return of the Sinai to Egypt. In 1982 his authorization of the Israeli invasion of Lebanon, aimed at destroying the Palestine Liberation Organization's military bases, caused one of the worst crises in Israeli history.

Behring, Emil Adolf von (1854–1917), German bacteriologist, founder of the science of immunology. In 1889 he became one of Robert Koch's laboratory assistants in Berlin. There Behring did research on infectious diseases and developed antitoxin immunization against diphtheria (1890) and tetanus (1892). He was awarded the first Nobel Prize for Physiology and Medicine in 1901.

Bell, Alexander Graham (1847–1922), Scottish-born U.S. inventor and teacher of the deaf who developed the telephone. Experimenting with speech transmission as early as 1865, Bell had become interested in the mechanical production of sound across wires. He was one of several to patent the telephone in 1876. After a legal battle, his patent was established. He was the first to speak in a conversation between Boston and New York, in 1877. Among Bell's other inventions was an improved wax recording cylinder for the phonograph invented by Edison.

ALEXANDER GRAHAM BELL

THE BETTMANN ARCHIVE

Bellini, a famous Italian family of Renaissance painters, founders of the Venetian school of painting.

Jacopo (c 1400–c 1470) was taught by Gentile da Fabriano. Few of his works survive, the most notable being his sketchbooks, which show new scientific techniques of painting, especially perspective. They were used to teach his sons:

Gentile (c 1429–1507), famous in his time for his portraits (*Mohammed II,* painted in Constantinople, 1479–1481). His processions and panoramic views are his main contributions to the school.

Giovanni (c 1430–1516), who defined the Venetian school. At first influenced by the classical style of his brother-in-law Andrea Mantegna, he later developed a technique of subtle light and color with concern for form rather than line. Primarily a painter of religious subjects, he is best known for his large altarpieces (*Madonna with Saints,* 1488) and smaller madonnas (*Madonna of the Trees,* 1487). He taught Giorgione and Titian.

Bellini, Vincenzo (1801–1835), Italian operatic composer noted for his writing of dramatic *bel canto* roles. His first successful opera, *Il Pirata (The Pirate),* was produced at La Scala in 1827. His other operas include *La Sonnambula* (*The Sleepwalker,* 1831); his masterpiece, *Norma* (1831); and *I Puritani* (*The Puritans,* 1835).

Bellow, Saul (1915–), Canadian-born U.S. author, one of the leading American novelists of the mid-20th century. In *Herzog* (1961) Bellow described with irony and humor the plight of the intellectual alienated from his society. *Herzog* won the National Book Award, as did *The Adventures of Augie March* (1953) and *Mr. Sammler's Planet* (1970). Among his other works are *Henderson the Rain King* (1959), *Humboldt's Gift* (1975), *The Dean's December* (1982), and *More Die of Heartbreak* (1987). He won the Nobel Prize for Literature in 1976.

Bellows, George Wesley (1882–1925), U.S. painter and lithographer who showed realistic action in his bold paintings of sports scenes. He was also noted for portraits and cityscapes. Bellows captured the ruggedness of prizefighting in *Stag at Sharkey's* (1907). He was one of the organizers of the famous Armory Show in 1913.

Benchley, Robert Charles (1889–1945), U.S. humorist, critic, and actor. He was drama critic for *Life,* 1921–1929, and for the *New Yorker,* 1929–1940. Benchley's humorous essays were collected in many popular books, including *My Ten Years in a Quandary* (1936) and *Benchley Beside Himself* (1943). He was best known to the public for the comic "scientific" lectures he delivered in short films.

Benedict, Ruth Fulton (1887–1948), U.S. anthropologist known for her concept of the interdependence of culture and personality. Her best-known book is *Patterns of Culture* (1934). She studied American Indian folklore and religion (*Zuni Mythology,* 1935), race relations (*Race: Science and Politics,* 1940), and contemporary cultures (*The Chrysanthemum and the Sword,* 1946). Benedict also wrote poetry under the pseudonym Anne Singleton.

Benedict of Nursia, Saint (c 480–c 543), Italian monk and founder of the Benedictine Order. Studying in Rome, he was repelled by the debauchery he saw there and retired to a cave at Subiaco for three years. About 529 he established a monastery at Monte Cassino, where he wrote his *Holy Rule,* describing the regulations and duties of his order. The work became the basis for Western monastic life.

Beneš, Eduard (1884–1948), Czech statesman, president of Czechoslovakia, 1935–1938 and 1940–1948. During World War I he joined Tomáš Masaryk (see separate article) in working to free the Czechs and Slovaks from the Austro-Hungarian empire. When an independent Czechoslovakia was proclaimed in 1918, he became foreign minister. He became prime minister in 1921 and succeeded Masaryk as president in 1935. Under Nazi pressure, Beneš resigned in 1938 and fled to England. He resumed the presidency in 1945 but resigned in 1948.

Benét, family of U.S. writers and poets of whom the best known is **Stephen Vincent Benét** (1898–1943). He won two Pulitzer prizes, one for his dramatic epic poem on the Civil War, *John Brown's Body* (1928), and one for an epic poem on American history, *Western Star* (1943). Benét also wrote the well-known short story "The Devil and Daniel Webster" (1936).

His brother **William Rose Benét** (1886–1950) was an editor for various literary magazines. He won a Pulitzer Prize for his autobiographical poem *The Dust Which Is God* (1941).

Ben-Gurion, David (1886–1973), born David Grien, Polish-born Israeli statesman and Israel's first prime minister. He became interested in Zionism as a child and went to Palestine in 1906. He helped organize defense units that protected Jewish settlers against Arab raids. Exiled in 1915 by the Ottoman Turkish government, which then ruled Palestine, he went to the United States where he organized the Jewish Legion that fought in World War I. In 1918 he returned to Palestine, became head of the Labor Party, and helped organize an underground army. Ben-Gurion's goal of establishing a Jewish state in Palestine was achieved in 1948 with the proclamation of the state of Israel. He became prime minister and minister of defense and served until 1953, retired for two years, and then returned to office until 1963.

THE BETTMANN ARCHIVE
DAVID BEN-GURION

Bennett, (Enoch) Arnold (1867–1931), English novelist. In his "Five Towns" books, considered his best work, he describes life in the sordid pottery-making towns of Staffordshire, where he lived as a boy. A prolific writer, Bennett shows the influence of French naturalism. Most notable are *The Old Wives' Tale* (1908), *Clayhanger* (1910), *Riceyman Steps* (1923), and (with Edward Knoblock) the play *Milestones* (1912).

Bennett, James Gordon (1795–1872), Scottish-born U.S. journalist and newspaper publisher, founder of the most successful "penny paper," the New York *Herald* in 1835. To compete with the other popular one-cent papers, Bennett played up lively, sensational news coverage, emphasizing crime, scandal, and society news. By 1860 the *Herald* had the largest circulation of any American newspaper.

His son, **James Gordon Bennett, Jr.** (1841–1918), took over the *Herald* and continued its success with journalistic stunts. In 1869 he sent reporter Henry M. Stanley to search for Dr. David Livingstone, who had disappeared in Africa.

Bennett, Viscount Richard Bedford (1870–1947), lawyer, statesman, Conservative prime minister of Canada, 1930–1935. He brought some economic relief to Canada, although his major plan for economic and social reform during the Depression was unsuccessful owing to organizational problems.

Bentham, Jeremy (1748–1832), English philosopher, jurist, and social reformer, founder of Utilitarianism. As described in his *Introduction to the Principles of Morals and Legislation* (1789), Utilitarianism equates good with happiness and makes maximum happiness (or pleasure) an ethical goal; all legislation should assure the "greatest happiness of the greatest number." Bentham effected many reforms and his philosophy spread throughout Europe.

Benton, Thomas Hart (1889–1975), U.S. painter, one of the foremost regionalist artists, grandnephew of Senator Thomas Hart Benton. He became famous after World War I, particularly in the 1930's, for his strong, realistic paintings and murals of midwestern farm life. Among them are *Louisiana Rice Field* (1939) and *July Hay* (1943). His mural *The Arts of Life in America* is in the Whitney Museum in New York.

Berenson, Bernard (1865–1959), U.S. art critic, recognized as an expert on Renaissance art. Among Berenson's many books are *Italian Painters of the Renaissance* (1930) and *Aesthetics and History of the Visual Arts* (1949). Selections from his diaries were published in 1960 under the title *The Passionate Sightseer.*

Berg, Alban (1885–1935), Austrian composer whose mature works combine the twelve-tone system of Arnold Schoenberg with traditional musical style. He became famous in 1925 with the first production of his opera *Wozzeck,* a work so dissonant that it shocked its audience. In later years, *Wozzeck* and Berg's other opera, *Lulu* (unfinished at his death), were performed frequently. He also wrote instrumental works, including pieces for string quartet and chamber orchestra.

Bergman, Ingmar (1918–), Swedish filmmaker. Bergman is known for somber, highly personal films in which lonely people struggle with faith, love, sex, guilt, and other basic problems. He also made urbane comedies, such as *Smiles of a Summer Night* (1955). His many world-famous films include *The Seventh Seal* (1956), *Wild Strawberries* (1957), *The Virgin Spring* (1959), *Persona* (1967), *Shame* (1968), *Cries and Whispers* (1972), and *Fanny and Alexander* (1983). He has also directed stage plays and was head of the Royal Dramatic Theater in Stockholm, 1963–1966 and 1978 to the present.

Bergson, Henri (1859–1941), French philosopher, one of the most influential thinkers of the early 20th century. Bergson stressed the importance of the life force, or *élan vital,* an intuitive movement toward purpose and creativity. For Bergson, existence meant not only being, but also continuing through change and movement. His masterpiece is *Two Sources of Morality and Religion* (1932). Earlier works in translation include *Time and Free Will* (1889), *Matter and Memory* (1896), *Laughter* (1901), and *Creative Evolution* (1907). A lucid and imaginative writer, Bergson won the 1927 Nobel Prize for Literature.

Bering, Vitus (1680–1741), Danish navigator and explorer. On a voyage that started in 1728 from the Kamchatka peninsula, he found that Asia and North America are separated by a strait. It was later named after him, as were Bering Island and Bering Sea. Peter the Great of Russia sent him to explore the north coast of Siberia in 1725. In 1741 he discovered Mount Saint Elias in the Yukon. He died of scurvy on the return voyage.

Berio, Luciano (1925–), Italian composer. Berio's compositions employ a wide range of sounds, techniques, and effects. His most acclaimed work is *Sinfonia* (1968), a musical collage for orchestra and vocal group, in which word sounds and even stage effects and lighting are as important as the music. Other works include *Passagio* (1963), a dramatic piece, *Opera* (1970), and *Coro* (1976), scored for 40 instruments and 40 voices.

Berkeley, George (1685–1753), Irish Anglican bishop, remembered as a philosopher. His most famous doctrine is that a thing exists because it is perceived by the senses. In 1724 he was appointed dean of Derry. He lived in Rhode Island from 1728 to 1731 and then returned to Ireland to become bishop of Cloyne, 1734. His works include *An Essay Toward a New Theory of Vision* (1709), *Treatise Concerning the Principles of Human Knowledge* (1710), and *Alciphron* (1732).

Berlin, Irving (1888–1989), Russian-born U.S. composer of hundreds of popular songs and show tunes, including the favorites "White Christmas," "Blue Skies," and "God Bless America." An immigrant to New York (his real name was Israel Baline), Berlin was for a time a singing waiter. During his long career, he wrote many musical comedies, including *Top Hat* (1935), *Call Me Madam* (1950), and *Mr. President* (1962).

Berlioz, (Louis) Hector (1803–1869), French Romantic composer, known for the variety and intense dramatic quality of his work. The *Symphonie Fantastique* (1830), a classic of 19th-century music, was his first completed score. The symphonies *Harold in Italy* (1834) and *Romeo and Juliet* (1839) followed. A Requiem, *Grande Messe des Mortes,* appeared in 1837 and the opera *Benvenuto Cellini* in 1838. The oratorios *Damnation of Faust* and *L'Enfance du Christ* were published in 1846 and 1854. He wrote the massive opera *The Trojans* from 1855 to 1858.

Bernadotte, Jean Baptiste: *See* Charles XIV.

Bernhardt, Sarah (1844–1923), stage name of Henriette Rosine Bernard, one of the most famous actresses in theater history. Born in Paris, she made her stage debut in 1862 in Racine's *Iphigénie in Aulide.* In the next few years, her appearances at the Comédie Française and other Paris theaters established

THE BETTMANN ARCHIVE

SARAH BERNHARDT

THE BETTMANN ARCHIVE

PRINCE OTTO VON BISMARCK

BLACK HAWK

THE BETTMANN ARCHIVE

her reputation as "the divine Sarah." After her debut in England, in 1879, she toured Europe, the United States, and Canada. Besides performing the plays of Racine, Hugo, and Shakespeare (including the title role in *Hamlet*), Bernhardt was also popular in contemporary dramas. Her greatest successes were *Fédora* (1882), *Théodora* (1884), and *La Tosca* (1887), all melodramas by Victorien Sardou. She starred in several films, among them *La Dame aux Camélias* (1910) and *Queen Elizabeth* (1912). Although one of her legs was amputated in 1915, she continued to act till 1922.

Bernini, Giovanni Lorenzo (1598-1680), Italian architect and sculptor whose work epitomizes the Roman baroque style. He, more than any other artist, is responsible for the appearance of modern Rome. Working under the patronage of Pope Urban VIII and others, Bernini designed the square in front of St. Peter's, the pope's palace, and many churches, fountains, and memorials. For more than a century, his sculpture influenced art throughout Europe. His best-known pieces include *Apollo and Daphne* (1622-1624), *David* (1623), and the Roman fountain *Four River Gods* (1648-1651).

Bernstein, Leonard (1918-), U.S. conductor, pianist, and composer. In 1943 he was appointed assistant conductor of the New York Philharmonic and in 1958 he became its first American-born permanent conductor, serving as musical director until 1971. Bernstein wrote, for orchestra, such works as the *Jeremiah Symphony* (1942) and *The Age of Anxiety* (1949). He also composed the scores for the musicals *On the Town* (1944), *Candide* (1956), and *West Side Story* (1957). Bernstein's *Mass* (1971) opened the Kennedy Center for the Performing Arts. He is the author of *The Joy of Music* (1959) and *The Infinite Variety of Music* (1966).

Berzelius, Jöns Jacob (1779-1848), Swedish chemist who made many major experimental contributions to modern chemistry. To discover their exact nature and chemical composition, he analyzed several thousand compounds, 1807-1817. Later, in 1826, he published a table of proportions and atomic weights. Berzelius introduced the present system of abbreviations for the elements and the method for writing chemical formulas. He also proposed an electrochemical basis for the formation of compounds in 1814. He discovered several new elements (thorium and selenium) and isolated others (strontium, barium).

Bessemer, Sir Henry (1813-1898), British engineer and inventor. From 1856 to 1858 he developed a process for removing carbon from molten pig iron, thus enabling industry to produce inexpensive steel in large quantities.

Bethune, Mary McLeod (1875-1955), U.S. educator who worked to improve opportunities for black students. In 1904 she founded a school for girls in Daytona Beach, Fla. It was merged in 1923 with Cookman Institute to form Bethune-Cookman College. She served as president of the college for more than 20 years, as director of the Division of Negro Affairs of the National Youth Administration, 1936-1944, and as a government and presidential adviser.

Bettelheim, Bruno (1903-), Austrian-born U.S. psychologist known for his studies of child development. He wrote *Love Is Not Enough: The Treatment of Emotionally Disturbed Children* (1950), *Children of the Dream* (1969), about life in an Israeli kibbutz, *The Uses of Enchantment* (1976), a study of fairy tales and their relation to child development, and *A Good Enough Parent* (1987).

Bevan, Aneurin (1897-1960), British statesman who, as minister of health, 1945-1951, introduced the British national health service. Bevan, a coal miner, became a trade unionist and was elected to Parliament in 1929. He was minister of health in Clement Attlee's Labour government but resigned in 1951 in a dispute over free medical service. He led the left wing of the Labour Party, advocating socialist policies and nuclear disarmament.

Bierce, Ambrose Gwinett (1842-c 1914), U.S. journalist and satirist noted for his misanthropic views and bitter cynicism. The best expression of Bierce's outlook is *The Devil's Dictionary* (1911, a revision of *The Cynic's Word Book*, 1906), a collection of sardonic definitions. His short stories, such as those collected in *Tales of Soldiers and Civilians* (1891, 1895), are based on the themes of death and horror and are notable for their sudden twists of fate and surprise endings. He disappeared in Mexico in 1914.

Binet, Alfred (1857-1911), French psychologist who originated the first methods for IQ (intelligence quotient) testing. While director of the psychology laboratory at the Sorbonne, Paris, Binet in 1905 devised an objective test for measuring children's intelligence. He administered his test to the schoolchildren of Paris and used the results to establish intelligence norms for different age groups.

Bismarck, Prince Otto von (1815-1898), Prussian statesman and first chancellor of the German empire, 1871-1890, known as the Iron Chancellor. Extremely conservative, Bismarck worked to make Prussia predominant among the German states. In 1862 William I of Prussia appointed him minister president, the head of the Prussian government. He instigated war with Denmark in 1864 and then with Austria. Prussia defeated Austria in 1866 and assumed leadership of the North German confederation. Bismarck next provoked the Franco-Prussian War (1870-1871) and dictated the peace terms after Prussia's victory. In 1871 William I was proclaimed emperor of Germany, and Bismarck was created a prince and named chancellor. To weaken the position of the liberals and socialists, he carried out major domestic social and economic reforms. In foreign affairs, he presided over the Berlin Congress (1878) and concluded the Triple Alliance with Italy and Austria-Hungary (1882). He resigned the chancellorship in 1890 after disagreements with the new Kaiser, William II.

Bizet, Georges (1838-1875), French composer whose colorful and melodic *Carmen* (1875) is one of the most popular of operas. Bizet's other operas include *The Pearl Fishers* (*Les Pêcheurs de perles,* 1863) and *The Fair Maid of Perth* (*La jolie fille de Perth,* 1867). His popular works for orchestra include incidental music for Daudet's play *L'Arlésienne* and his Symphony in C (written at age 17).

Black, Hugo La Fayette (1886-1971), justice of the U.S. Supreme Court for 34 years, 1937-1971. From 1926 to 1937 he served in the U.S. Senate. When President Franklin D. Roosevelt appointed him to the Supreme Court, controversy arose over his membership in the Ku Klux Klan. However, he became one of the most liberal justices, particularly in civil rights matters.

Blackett, Patrick Maynard Stuart (1897-1974), English physicist whose research in nuclear physics and cosmic rays won him the 1948 Nobel Prize for Physics. After developing an improved version of the Wilson cloud chamber, he made the first photographs of nuclear disintegration and a cosmic ray shower. During World War II, he led Britain's research in antisubmarine strategy.

Black Hawk (1767-1838), in Indian named "Ma-ka-tae-me-she-kia-kiak," or "Black Sparrow Hawk," chief of a Sauk Indian tribe in Illinois. He aided the British during the War of 1812 and, with British help, tried to ally the tribes against settlers moving west in the 1820's. Keokuk, a rival chief, had moved the tribe into Iowa, in accord with an 1804 treaty ceding Sauk and Fox land east of the Mississippi River. But in 1832, Black Hawk, disputing the treaty, led his people back to Illinois. The governor of Illinois called for federal troops, thus starting what came to be called the Black Hawk War. The Sauk, unaided by other tribes, fled north through the Rock River valley and were massacred at the Battle of the Bad Axe River in Wisconsin, in August, 1832. Black Hawk was captured, but later was freed in Keokuk's custody.

Blackstone, Sir William (1723–1780), British jurist. In 1758, already famous for his lectures on the law, he became a professor at Oxford. He was appointed King's Counsel in 1761, and solicitor general to the queen in 1763. He then published his great book, *Commentaries on the Laws of England* (4 volumes, 1765–1769), which has been a guide to legal practice in Britain and the United States ever since.

Blackwell, Elizabeth (1821–1910), English-born U.S. physician, the first woman in the United States to receive the degree of doctor of medicine. After being refused admission to several medical schools, she finally entered the Geneva (N.Y.) Medical School, receiving her degree in 1849. Four years later, after medical studies in Europe, she and her sister Emily (1826–1910), against great opposition, opened a private dispensary in New York. Staffed entirely by women, it was incorporated in 1857 as the New York Infirmary and College for Women. In 1869 Dr. Blackwell returned to England, where she was professor of gynecology at the London School of Medicine for Women from 1875 to 1907.

Blake, William (1757–1827), English lyric and mystical poet and artist. Among his best-known works are *Songs of Innocence* (1789), *Songs of Experience* (1794), and *The Marriage of Heaven and Hell* (1793). As an artist, Blake pioneered in new engraving techniques, reproducing both text and art work from hand-lettered, etched copperplates, then adding color or gold. This "illuminated printing" was used to illustrate his own books, including his great symbolic poems *Milton* (1808) and *Jerusalem* (1808–1818), as well as editions of other works. He did the *Illustrations for the Book of Job* (1826) and was illustrating Dante's *Divine Comedy* when he died.

Blasco Ibáñez, Vicente (1867–1928), Spanish writer and politician, famous for his World War I novels *The Four Horsemen of the Apocalypse* (1916) and *Mare Nostrum* (1918). Many critics think these works are inferior to his novels about his native Catalan countryside, particularly *Reeds and Mud* (*Cañas y Barro,* 1902) and *The Cabin* (*La Barraca,* 1899). As a liberal republican, Blasco Ibáñez was often exiled or imprisoned.

Bligh, William (1754–1817), English naval officer who commanded H.M.S. *Bounty* during the famous mutiny in 1789. After the ship left Tahiti en route to the West Indies, Fletcher Christian, chief mate, and several crew members took command of the ship and set Bligh and 18 men adrift in the open sea. Navigating nearly 4000 miles in an open boat, Bligh and his crew reached the East Indies and eventually returned to England. A warship dispatched to Tahiti captured some of the mutineers and took them back to England for trial. Charles Nordhoff and James N. Hall's popular book *Mutiny on the Bounty* (1932) and its sequels gave Captain Bligh a reputation for unusual cruelty. However, his naval career continued successfully after the mutineers' trial. In 1805 he became a colonial governor in New South Wales (where he faced another mutiny), and in 1814 a vice admiral.

Blixen, Karen Dinesen (Isak Dinesen) (1885–1962), Danish writer of eerie, enigmatic tales. She married a cousin in 1914 and moved to a coffee plantation in present-day Kenya, in East Africa, about which she wrote *Out of Africa* (1937) and *Shadows on the Grass* (1961). In 1931 she returned to Denmark and dedicated herself to writing. Her collected stories appear in *Seven Gothic Tales* (1934), *Winter's Tales* (1942), and *Last Tales* (1957).

ELIZABETH BLACKWELL

THE BETTMANN ARCHIVE

KAREN DINESEN BLIXEN

THE BETTMANN ARCHIVE

Bloch, Ernest (1880–1959), Swiss-born U.S. composer. Many of Bloch's compositions, though modern in style, were based on traditional Hebrew themes, notably *Schelomo* (1916), *Israel* (1917), and the Sacred Service (*"Avodath Hakodesh,"* 1934). He also wrote the opera *Macbeth* (1903), chamber music, and orchestral works.

Bloomer, Amelia Jenks (1818–1894), U.S. social reformer. One of the earliest women journalists, in 1849 she founded *The Lily,* a popular monthly journal in which she championed women's suffrage and temperance. Also a lecturer, she became best known (sometimes through ridicule) for the "Bloomer costume," an attempt at reforming women's dress. It consisted of a short skirt worn over loose trousers tied at the ankles.

Boas, Franz (1858–1942), German-born U.S. anthropologist. He emphasized field study, not theory, in his studies of the Indians of North America (particularly the Pacific Northwest), Mexico, and Puerto Rico between 1886 and 1931. He taught at Columbia University from 1896 to 1937, establishing a well-known anthropology department there. His many works include *The Mind of Primitive Man* (1911) and *Race, Language and Culture* (1940).

Boccaccio, Giovanni (1313–1375), Italian poet, writer, and humanist, called the father of classic Italian prose. Sent from his home in Florence to study in Naples, Boccaccio fell in love with a young woman, supposedly the "Fiammetta" of his early works: *Il Filocolo* (c 1336), *Il Filostrato* (c 1338), and *La Teseida* (c 1340–1341). About 1340, disappointed in love and beset by financial problems, he returned to Florence. About ten years later he met the poet Petrarch, and their friendship influenced both his own career and the future of humanist scholarship. At the same time, he was creating his masterpiece, *The Decameron* (c 1349–1351), a collection of 100 prose tales remarkable for their realistic treatment of human themes and emotions.

Boccherini, Luigi (1743–1805), Italian composer and cellist, best known for his elegant chamber music. Serving as court composer in Madrid and later in Berlin, he wrote more than 200 works in this genre, as well as sacred music, symphonies, and concertos.

Bodoni, Giambattista (1740–1813), Italian printer and type designer, creator of "modern" type styles, including a popular type face bearing his name. In 1768 he became head of the printing house of the duke of Parma, and made it one of the most famous in Europe. In 1818, after his death, the *Manual of Typography (Manuale Tipografico)* appeared, containing specimens of typefaces he designed.

Boëthius, Anicius Manlius Severinus (c 476–524), statesman of the later Roman Empire and philosopher. During the Middle Ages, his works were the chief source of knowledge about ancient Greek and Roman culture. In about 510 Boëthius served as a minister of the emperor Theodoric, who later came to suspect him of subversion and magic. Boëthius was imprisoned in 522 and executed. While in prison, he wrote his most famous book, *De Consolatione Philosophiae (The Consolation of Philosophy).*

Bogart, Humphrey DeForest (1899–1957), U.S. stage and screen actor, famed for his style of playing "tough guy" roles. Bogart played gangsters (*The Petrified Forest:* stage version, 1934; film, 1936); private detectives (*The Maltese Falcon,* 1942; *The Big Sleep,* 1946); and loners and outcasts (*Casablanca,* 1942; *Treasure of the Sierra Madre,* 1948; *The African Queen,* 1952, for which he received an Academy Award).

Bohr, Niels Henrik David (1885–1962), Danish physicist. His theory of atomic structure, formulated in 1913, was a fundamental contribution to the development of nuclear physics. He won the 1922 Nobel Prize for Physics. Bohr was founder and a director of the Copenhagen Institute of Theoretical Physics. He became an advocate of international atomic control and, in 1957, was given the first Atoms for Peace Award.

Boleyn, Anne (c 1507–1536), queen of England, 1533–1536, second wife of Henry VIII, and mother of Elizabeth I. Anne came to the royal court about 1522 and was admired for her beauty. When Henry and his first wife, Catherine, separated about 1531, Anne became the king's mistress. They were secretly married in January, 1533, and in May the marriage was declared valid. Anne's daughter Elizabeth was born in September, 1533. She had no son (a baby boy was born dead in 1536) and soon became unpopular with both the court and the king. She was accused of adultery, condemned by the Privy Council, and beheaded.

Bolingbroke, Henry: *See* Henry IV.

Bolívar, Simón (1783–1830), Venezuelan soldier-statesman known as the Great Liberator for his role in freeing Colombia, Venezuela, Ecuador, Peru, and Bolivia from Spanish rule. Educated in Europe, he was influenced by the 18th-century rationalists Rousseau, Montesquieu, and Voltaire. He also admired Napoleon as an example of individual achievement and glory. The Latin American independence movement began in 1808, at a time when Spain was weakened by Napoleon's invasion. Bolívar's native Venezuela declared its independence in 1811, but Spain immediately moved to regain control. In the next eight years, Bolívar won a series of minor victories, followed by defeat or counterrevolution. Often in exile, he issued manifestos calling for unity among the colonies and outlining his political theories. In 1819 Bolívar marched his troops in a trek over the Andes to crush the Spanish troops at Boyacá, liberating Colombia. The final liberation of Venezuela came in 1821, followed by Ecuador, 1822; Peru, 1824; and Bolivia, formerly Upper Peru, 1825, the last two with the help of Antonio José de Sucre, leader of a second liberation army.

Bonnard, Pierre (1867–1947), French painter, illustrator, and lithographer. His best-known paintings are landscapes and still lifes, characterized by bright, warm colors, as in his *Fishing Boats* (1929) and *The Breakfast* (1943). Among those who influenced his work were Gauguin and Vuillard, his associate in the "Nabis" group of painters reacting from impressionism.

Boone, Daniel (1734–1820), U.S. pioneer, explorer, hunter, and Indian fighter. As a young man, Boone tried farming in North Carolina, but preferred the life of a hunter and guide. In 1775 he led a group of settlers through the Cumberland Gap to Kentucky. There, in a place later called Boonesborough, he built a fort and established a frontier settlement. He later lost his holdings in a legal dispute, and moved to Missouri about 1799. A legendary figure even during his lifetime, Boone was a great leader in the settlement, expansion, and defense of the frontier.

Booth, John Wilkes (1838–1865), U.S. actor, remembered as the assassin of Abraham Lincoln. The brother of actor Edwin Booth, he also was well known as a Shakespearean actor. During the Civil War, he sympathized with the South and joined a conspiracy to murder the President and several Cabinet officers. On April 14, 1865, Booth shot and fatally wounded Lincoln during a performance at Ford's Theater in Washington, D.C. Booth escaped after leaping to the stage and shouting, *"Sic semper tyrannis!* The South is avenged!" He was killed while being captured twelve days later.

Booth, William (1829–1912), British evangelist, founder and first general of the Salvation Army. Ordained a Methodist minister, he sought converts among the poorer sections of London, but the church's neglect of poverty caused him to resign in 1865 and organize his followers into the Christian Mission. In 1878 it was renamed the Salvation Army. Booth's social service plan for aid to prisoners, alcoholics, and the poor was published in 1890 as *In Darkest England and the Way Out.*

Borden, Sir Robert Laird (1854–1937), Canadian statesman, prime minister of Canada, 1911–1920. He was first elected to parliament in 1896 and became leader of the Conservative Party in 1901. As prime minister, Borden directed Canada's participation in World War I, pushing through a military conscription law in 1917. He was chief Canadian delegate at the Paris Peace Conference in 1919 and represented Canada at the Washington Disarmament Conference in 1921.

Borges, Jorge Luis (1899–1986), Argentine author, scholar, and critic. Borges initially wrote poetry and essays, but began writing stories in which essay and narrative are blended. These pieces are his most characteristic writings. A number of Borges's collected pieces were translated into English as *Labyrinths* (1962). Other works in English are *Dreamtigers* (1964; poems from the collection *El Hacedor,* 1960), *Aleph & Other Stories* (1970), and the poetry collection *The Gold of the Tigers* (translated 1977).

Borgia (originally Spanish Borja), an Italian Renaissance family prominent in church and political affairs, and notorious for their intrigues.

Rodrigo Borgia (c 1431–1503), a Spanish cardinal, became Pope Alexander VI in 1492. He is known as the most wicked of the Renaissance popes because of his mistresses and his political ruthlessness in scheming with his son **Cesare Borgia** (c 1476–1507) to form a new state out of the several principalities of central Italy. As part of his plan to found a papal dynasty, Alexander made Cesare a cardinal, but Cesare renounced the office to become the duke of Valentinois (in France). He subdued the central Italian states by war and political murder, but his father's death in 1503 ruined his plans. Cesare was idealized as a model ruler in Machiavelli's *The Prince.*

Lucrezia Borgia (1480–1519) gained an evil reputation that properly belongs to her father, Pope Alexander, and brother. To further his ambitions, her father made three marriages for her. The first was annulled. Her second husband was murdered, apparently by order of Cesare. After marriage to Alfonso d'Este, duke of Ferrara, and Alexander's death, her family's schemes collapsed. She became a patroness of the arts.

Borlaug, Norman Ernest (1914–), U.S. agronomist, called the father of the "Green Revolution." He won the 1970 Nobel Prize for Peace for his work in developing new cereals for use in nations threatened by famine.

Through genetic engineering, he developed new wheat and rice strains that increase crop yield enormously.

Born, Max (1882–1970), German-born British theoretical physicist who made fundamental contributions in quantum mechanics and shared the 1954 Nobel Prize for Physics. Born did work in relativity, optics, and quantum and wave mechanics, developing the statistical interpretation of wave phenomena in subatomic particles. As a teacher, Born attracted many students in Germany and Britain (where he fled in 1933). After he retired, he wrote and spoke about scientists' responsibilities for the use of nuclear energy in war and peace. His books include *Atomic Physics* (1935), *The Restless Universe* (1935), and *Natural Philosophy of Cause and Chance* (1949).

Borodin, Aleksandr (Porfirevich) (1833–1887), Russian composer, one of "the Five" who encouraged the use of Russian themes. Borodin wrote symphonies; string quartets; a symphonic tone poem, *In the Steppes of Central Asia* (1880); and several songs. His colorful opera *Prince Igor* was completed after his death by Rimski-Korsakov and Glazunov.

Bosch, Hieronymus (c 1450–c 1516), Flemish painter. His paintings show a fascination with sin and hell. Their symbolism includes grotesque nightmare forms and visions, as in the *Garden of Earthly Delights* and the *Temptation of St. Anthony.* Similarities have been drawn between his work and that of the surrealists of the 20th century.

Boswell, James (1740–1795), Scottish lawyer, diarist, and biographer. Boswell met the celebrated essayist and wit, Dr. Samuel Johnson, in 1763. He kept voluminous records of their friendship and published his *Life of Johnson* in 1791. Boswell also wrote a *Journal of a Tour to the Hebrides* (1785). His entertaining London and Continental journals were found in the 1920's and later published.

Botha, Louis (1862–1919), first prime minister of the Union of South Africa. In 1900, during the Boer War, he became commander in chief of the Boer army. As the first prime minister of the colony of Transvaal, he advocated cooperation between the Boers and the British South Africans. When the union of former colonies was created in 1910, he became its first prime minister. During World War I, he suppressed the revolt of pro-German South African factions and led the conquest of German South West Africa.

Botticelli, Sandro (1444–1510) originally Alessandro di Mariano Filipepi, Italian Florentine painter. His patrons were the great families of Florence, especially the Medicis, who commissioned him to paint two mythological subjects, *Primavera* (c 1475) and *Birth of Venus* (c 1482). Two of his best-known works, they show the lyrical line and rich ornamentation that made him famous. Later Botticelli was influenced by the fanatical religious leader Girolamo Savonarola.

Bourbon, a European royal house that ruled France between 1589 and 1848 except between 1792 and 1814, the period of the first French republic; Bourbons also ruled Spain, Naples, and Sicily. In 1589 the Capetian-Valois line became extinct and Henry of Navarre became the first Bourbon ruler of France as Henry IV.

Bourbon rule in Spain began in 1700, when Philip, duke of Anjou, a grandson of King Louis XIV of France, succeeded to the Spanish throne. It ended with the revolution of 1931, when Alfonso XIII fled Spain.

Bourbon rule in Naples and Sicily began in 1735, when Charles, the son of Philip of Spain, became king of Naples and Sicily. The reigns of the Bourbon kings are listed below.

Bourguiba, Habib (1903–), Tunisian nationalist leader, first president of the republic of Tunisia. Bourguiba founded a nationalist Tunisian newspaper and headed nationalist political groups during the 1930's. He was imprisoned several times by the French. After World War II, he traveled to many countries, publicizing the Tunisian cause. Bourguiba became premier of a newly independent Tunisia in 1956 and was elected president in 1957. Under him, Tunisia became progressive and politically stable. He was ousted in a bloodless coup in 1987.

Bowditch, Nathaniel (1773–1838), U.S. mathematician and astronomer, author of the "seaman's bible" of navigation. Correcting and revising the book then used by sailors, Bowditch produced *The New American Practical Navigator* (1802), which became a standard astronomical reference for generations of sea navigators. Bowditch also translated (1829–1839) Laplace's *Celestial Mechanics.*

Bowell, Sir Mackenzie (1823–1917), editor, businessman, statesman, and Conservative prime minister of Canada, 1894–1896. Religious and cultural controversies caused problems within the Conservative Party and discontent with his leadership caused him to resign.

Bowen, Elizabeth Dorothea Cole (1899–1973), Anglo-Irish novelist noted for her sensitive portrayals of well-to-do cosmopolitan women. Her novels include *The Hotel* (1927), *To the North* (1932), *The Death of the Heart* (1939), *The Heat of the Day* (1949), *A World of Love* (1955), *A Time in Rome* (1960), and *Eva Trout* (1968). She also wrote criticism and stories, including *The Demon Lover* (1945).

Boyle, Robert (1627–1691), English scientist, one of the first great modern chemists. He made many important discoveries in the physics of sound, in optics, and in other fields, but was even more devoted to his studies in chemistry, particularly the chemistry of combustion and of respiration. He formulated Boyle's law for gases in 1662. He was leader of a group of scientists (the "Invisible College") who in 1663 became the Royal Society of London, a leading force in the scientific revolution of the 17th century.

Bradbury, Ray (1920–), U.S. writer of stories and novels of fantasy and space travel. His most famous books are *The Martian Chronicles* (1950), *Fahrenheit 451* (1953), *Dandelion Wine* (1957), and *Something Wicked This Way Comes* (1962). His poetry includes *When Elephants Last in the Dooryard Bloomed* (1972) and *Where Robot Mice and Robot Men Run Round in Robot Towns* (1977).

Bradford, William (1590–1657), English-born Pilgrim leader. He sailed from Holland on the *Mayflower* and in 1621 was elected governor of Plymouth Colony. Reelected 30 times between 1622 and 1656, he governed wisely and helped the settlement to survive. His *A History of Plimmoth Plantation, 1620–1647* (1856) is a detailed account of Pilgrim life.

Brady, James Buchanan (1856–1917), U.S. financier, known as Diamond Jim because of the jewels he wore. Rising from an obscure background, he amassed a fortune as a financier and became a famous café society figure. In 1912 he endowed the Brady Urological Institute at Johns Hopkins University.

Brady, Mathew B. (c 1823–1896), U.S. photographer, famous for his Civil War photographs. He made many portrait photographs of the great, and published his *Gallery of Illustrious Americans* in 1850. During the Civil War, Brady accompanied the Union forces with a wagon full of equipment. Although the venture ruined him financially, his *National Photographic Collection of War Views* (1870) is an invaluable pictorial record of the war.

Brahe, Tycho (1546–1601), Danish astronomer who, in 1572, discovered "Tycho's star" in the constellation Cassiopeia. In 1576 he was commissioned by the king of Denmark to build Uraniborg ("castle of the sky"), one of the first modern observatories, on an island near Copenhagen. In 1599, out of favor with the new king, Brahe settled in Prague, where he was joined by Johannes Kepler. His principal work,

Astronomiae instauratae Progymnasmata (1602–1603), was edited by Kepler. In it Brahe stated that Earth is immobile, but other planets revolve around the sun, which annually moves around Earth.

Brahms, Johannes (1833–1897), German Romantic composer and pianist who created world-renowned classics in every 19th-century style except opera. Brahms was especially skillful in the use of rhythm, rich harmony, and counterpoint. Like Beethoven, with whom he was often compared, he was a master of the symphony form. Brahms's compositions include four symphonies (1877, 1878, 1884, 1886), concertos for piano, violin, and violin and cello, the Variations on a Theme by Haydn (1873), and four books of Hungarian dances (1869, 1880), as well as songs and chamber works. *The German Requiem (Ein Deutsches Requiem)* appeared in 1868.

Braille, Louis (1809–1852), French teacher of the blind and inventor of the Braille system, enabling the blind to read. At the age of three he was accidentally blinded. Sent to a school for the blind in Paris, he developed a system of dots, embossed on thin cardboard, that corresponded to the alphabet and could be differentiated by touch. The system also was used to teach music and mathematics. Braille himself became a master organist and cellist.

Bramante (c 1444–1514), real name Donato d'Agnolo or d'Angelo, leading Italian architect of the High Renaissance. After living in Milan, where he designed several churches (Sta. Maria della Grazie, c 1488–1499), he settled in Rome in 1499. His study of the ancient ruins increased the symmetry and classicism of his own style. Bramante designed much of the construction in the Vatican for popes Julius II and Alexander VI. He made the original plan for St. Peter's Basilica, but died before it was completed.

Brancusi, Constantin (1876–1957), Rumanian abstract sculptor, a leading influence in modern art. He lived in Paris, at first producing traditional work. However, his sculpture became more abstract as he reduced natural forms to simple, streamlined, geometric shapes in bronze, marble, or wood. *Bird in Space* (1919) is his most famous work.

Brandeis, Louis Dembitz (1856–1941), justice of the U.S. Supreme Court, 1916–1939. As an attorney in Boston, 1878–1916, he was known as the "people's attorney" because of his work on behalf of reforms to benefit the public. Brandeis was named to the Supreme Court by President Wilson and soon became known for his frequent minority opinions in favor of liberal causes.

THE BETTMANN ARCHIVE

MARLON BRANDO

Brando, Marlon (1924–), U.S. actor, whose intense, controlled dramatic style and manner of speaking set a new mode of Hollywood film acting in the 1950's. Brando's first success was as the brutal Stanley Kowalski in *A Streetcar Named Desire,* whom he played on Broadway in 1947 and on film in 1951. His other films include *Viva Zapata!* (1952); *The Wild One* (1954); *On the Waterfront* (1954), for which he won an Academy Award; *One-Eyed Jacks* (1960), which he also directed; *The Godfather* (1972); *Last Tango in Paris* (1973); and *Apocalypse Now* (1979).

Brandt, Willy (1913–), German politician, born Herbert Frahm. With the rise of Nazi power, Frahm fled to Scandinavia, where he lived from 1933 to 1945. Writing as "Willy Brandt," he became known for his articles attacking the Nazi regime. After the war he became a leader of the Social Democrats and served as mayor of West Berlin from 1957 to 1966. Elected chancellor of West Germany in 1969, he began a new policy of accommodation with Eastern Europe, for which he was awarded the 1971 Nobel Peace Prize. In 1974, taking the blame for a government espionage scandal, Brandt resigned.

Brant, Joseph (1742–1807), Indian name Thayendanegea, chief of the Mohawk Indian tribe. He aided the British in the French and Indian War and, in 1774, became secretary to the superintendent of Indian affairs. During the American Revolution, he remained loyal to the British and led raids on American settlements, including the massacre at Cherry Valley, N.Y. (1778). After the war, he worked for a peaceful frontier and eventually settled in Canada. There he did missionary work for the Episcopal Church and translated the prayer book into Mohawk (1787).

Braque, Georges (1882–1963), French painter who, with Pablo Picasso, founded the cubist school about 1908. Braque's paintings are mostly still lifes and portraits, broken up into the series of angular planes that are characteristic of cubism. He also originated the collage, in which cutouts from newspapers and other sources are pasted on canvas. His later work was less angular and geometric, and more colorful, but still cubist in inspiration. *Still Life with Playing Cards* (1913), *Guitar, Fruit and Pitcher* (1927), and *Woman with a Mandolin* (1937) are among his important works.

Brecht, Bertolt (1898–1956), German poet and playwright, noted for his stark dramas on social themes. In prewar Berlin, his greatest success was the satirical *Threepenny Opera* (*Die Dreigroschenoper,* 1928), written with composer Kurt Weill. Unpopular with the Nazis because of his openly Marxist sympathies and antimilitarism, Brecht left Germany in 1933, living in Scandinavia and the United States until after World War II. His most typical plays were written in this period, including *The Life of Galileo* (1937–

MATHEW B. BRADY

THE BETTMANN ARCHIVE

1939), *Mother Courage and Her Children* (1941), and *The Caucasian Chalk Circle* (1948). In 1948 he moved to East Berlin, where he founded and directed the Berliner Ensemble.

Breughel, Pieter: *See* Brueghel.

Brezhnev, Leonid Ilyich (1906–1982), Soviet political leader who replaced Nikita Khrushchev as first secretary of the central committee of the Communist Party of the Soviet Union. Brezhnev was a political officer in the Red Army during World War II. After holding a series of government posts, he became chief of state in 1960 and first secretary in 1964. In this post, he apparently was responsible for the 1968 Soviet invasion of Czechoslovakia. In 1970 he announced the "Brezhnev doctrine," which allowed the Soviet Union to interfere in the internal affairs of other communist states. The Soviet invasion of Afghanistan, 1979, caused a sharp decline in U.S.-Soviet relations in the last years of his leadership.

Brian Boru (926–1014), also called Brian Boroimhe or Borumha, Irish king and national hero who liberated the Irish from Scandinavian domination. After liberating his native Munster, about 978, he conquered other parts of Ireland, crowning himself king in 1002. Brian was murdered on the day of his final victory over the Danes at Clontarf.

Briand, Aristide (1862–1932), French statesman. He served eleven times as premier of France. After World War I, Briand, as foreign minister, negotiated the Locarno Pact (1925) and signed, with the United States, the Kellogg-Briand Pact (1928) renouncing war. He shared the 1926 Nobel Prize for Peace.

Britten, (Edward) Benjamin, Baron Britten of Aldeburgh (1913–1976), English composer. Many of Britten's song cycles and choral pieces drew on traditional English themes, folk songs, and harmonies. They include *A Ceremony of Carols* (1942), *Hymn to St. Cecilia* (1942), and *War Requiem* (1963). Britten's operas are notable for their dramatic psychological characterization, as in *Peter Grimes* (1945) and *Billy Budd* (1951). Others are *The Rape of Lucretia* (1946) and *The Turn of the Screw* (1954). His orchestral works include *The Young Person's Guide to the Orchestra* (1946).

Brodsky, Joseph (Alexandrovich) (1940–), Soviet-born poet and essayist. Born into a Jewish family in Leningrad, he was imprisoned in a labor camp for "social parasitism" before being expelled from the Soviet Union in 1972. He now lives in the United States. Among his books are *Elegy to John Donne* (1967), *Song Without Music* (1969), and *History of the Twentieth Century* (1986). Widely regarded as the best living Russian poet, Brodsky won the Nobel Prize for Literature in 1987.

Brontë, English family that produced three 19th century authors. The Brontës settled in 1820 at Haworth, in the Yorkshire moors that provided the setting for some of their books. Tutored by their father, the four young Brontës spent much of their time alone.

Charlotte (1816–1855) wrote quite frankly about a woman's emotions in her famous *Jane Eyre* (1847). She also wrote *Shirley* (1849), an early regional novel, and *Villette* (1853), perhaps her best book.

(Patrick) Branwell (1817–1848), a literary and artistic failure, turned to opium and alcohol, dying at age 31.

Emily Jane (1818–1848) wrote the intense, dramatic *Wuthering Heights* (1847), creating the memorable character Heathcliff.

Anne (1820–1849) wrote the realistic *Agnes Gray* (1847) and the outspoken *The Tenant of Wildfell Hall* (1848).

Brooks, Gwendolyn (1917–), U.S. writer and poet. She won the 1950 Pulitzer Prize for poetry for *Annie Allen* (1949). Her other books of poetry include *A Street in Bronzeville* (1945), *The Bean Eaters* (1960), and *Selected Poems* (1963). A novel, *Maud Martha*, appeared in 1953. In 1968 she published *In the Mecca*, a long poem describing ghetto life through the device of a search for a lost child.

Brown, John (1800–1859), U.S. abolitionist leader, famous for his fanatic hatred of slavery. Brown began his personal crusade to free the slaves as early as 1839, becoming active in antislavery movements and aiding fugitive slaves. Shortly after he and his sons settled in Kansas in 1855, they killed five neighboring proslavery men. In 1859, in an attempt to acquire arms for escaping slaves, Brown led his followers in a raid on the federal arsenal at Harpers Ferry, Va. The attack failed, and Brown was captured, tried for treason, and hanged. He became a martyr to abolitionists, and the hero of the Civil War song, "John Brown's Body."

JOHN BROWN

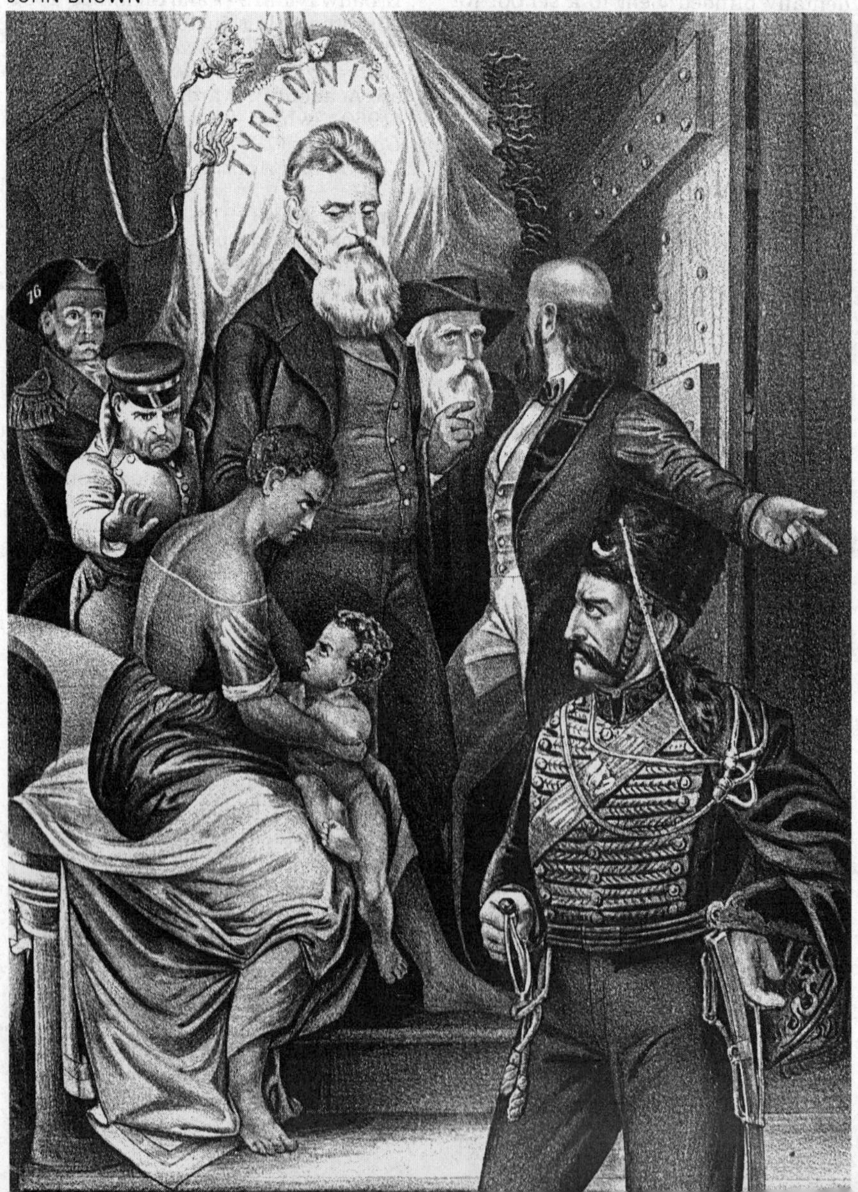

LIBRARY OF CONGRESS

Browning, Elizabeth Barrett (1806–1861), English poet remembered for her romantic love lyrics. A lifelong invalid, she became an established poet with *The Seraphim and Other Poems* (1838) and *Poems* (1844). The poet Robert Browning fell in love first with her verse, and then with her. After a lengthy correspondence, they were married in 1846, despite her father's vigorous protests and her ill health. Mrs. Browning immortalized her love in *Sonnets from the Portuguese* (1850), her most famous work, published after she and her husband had moved to Italy. She also wrote *Aurora Leigh* (1856), a novel in verse, and *Poems Before Congress* (1860).

Browning, Robert (1812–1889), a 19th-century English poet. His first notable publication was *Bells and Pomegranates* (1841–1846), comprising several verse plays, including *Pippa Passes* and such well-known poems as "My Last Duchess" and "The Pied Piper of Hamelin." Browning married Elizabeth Barrett in 1846 and they lived happily in Italy until her death in 1861. He returned to England with their son and, soon afterward, published *The Ring and the Book* (1868–1869), considered his finest work.

Broz, Josip: *See* Tito.

Bruce, Robert (1274–1329), liberator of the Scots, later Robert I, king of Scotland. Though at first loyal to Edward I of England, he eventually joined forces with those seeking Scottish independence. After killing John Comyn, a regent of Scotland, he declared himself king in 1306. To defend his crown, he gathered an army, but was defeated and fled to Ireland. Returning to Scotland the next year, Bruce again gathered support to confront the English king, this time the weaker Edward II. At the Battle of Bannock Burn (1314), he won a decisive victory and was recognized as king of the Scots by both England and France.

Bruckner, Anton (1824–1896), Austrian composer. His music is somber and mystical, influenced by both Richard Wagner and the classical Viennese melodic tradition. Bruckner is best known for his nine symphonies, large-scale works emphasizing the brasses of the orchestra. He wrote several choral works and several masses.

Brueghel (or **Bruegel**), Renowned Flemish family of painters of the 16th and 17th centuries.

The principal member was **Pieter Brueghel the Elder** (c 1525–1569). Though several of his masterpieces, such as *The Procession to Calvary,* are on religious subjects, he is best known for his colorful, precise paintings of Flemish peasant scenes. Among the best known are *Wedding Dance* and *Hunters in the Snow.*

His son **Pieter Brueghel the Younger** (1564–1638), also called "Hell" Brueghel, painted in his father's style with a preference for scenes of hell.

Another son, **Jan** (1568–1625), also called "Velvet" Brueghel, was fond of painting his portrait subjects dressed in velvet. His landscapes and still lifes were considered the greatest of his age. He collaborated with Peter Paul Rubens on several paintings; Jan painted the scene and Rubens the figures.

Brunelleschi, Filippo (1377–1446), Italian architect, often called the founder of Renaissance architecture because he added new concepts of sculptured form in space to the revived Roman classicism. Deeply interested in perspective, he made it a science in his perfectly proportioned buildings. He lived and worked primarily in Florence. His masterpiece there is the dome of Santa Maria dei Fiore, built 1420 to 1434. Other buildings include the church of San Lorenzo, the Pazzi Chapel, and the Pitti Palace.

Brutus, Marcus Junius (c 85–42 B.C.), Roman politician. He supported the Roman general Pompey in his wars against Julius Caesar. When Caesar was victorious, he pardoned Brutus and, in 46, made him governor of Cisalpine Gaul. When Caesar's power continued to grow, threatening the existence of the Roman Republic, Brutus joined a conspiracy against him. He was one of those who assassinated Caesar in 44. Brutus and his followers fled to Athens and raised an army of Greeks and Macedonians, but they were pursued and defeated at Philippi in 42 by the united forces of Mark Antony and Octavian. Following the defeat, Brutus committed suicide.

Bryan, William Jennings (1860–1925), U.S. political leader, memorable for his dramatic oratory and popular appeal. An active Democrat, he was elected to Congress in 1890 and 1892. At the 1896 Democratic convention in Chicago, Bryan made his famous "Cross of Gold" speech advocating free silver (a challenge to the use of gold as a monetary standard). The speech so excited the convention that he was nominated for the Presidency. Bryan was defeated by William McKinley. In 1900 and again in 1908, Bryan won the nomination for President, but each time he was defeated. He came to be identified with the farmers and with fundamentalist religion. In 1912 he helped to get the nomination for Woodrow Wilson, and then became Wilson's secretary of state. He resigned in 1915 because he disagreed with Wilson's stand on neutrality during World War I. Bryan's last public appearance was in 1925 as a prosecutor at the trial of John T. Scopes, a Tennessee teacher accused of teaching evolution. Bryan volunteered to testify personally and was mercilessly cross-examined on his fundamentalist beliefs by Clarence Darrow, the attorney for the defense. Apparently weakened by the strain of the trial, Bryan died suddenly a few days later.

Bryant, William Cullen (1794–1878), U.S. poet and journalist, known for his lyrical nature poems. His most famous poems are "Thanatopsis" (1817) and "To a Waterfowl" (in *Poems,* 1821). He entered newspaper work and, from 1829 until his death, was editor in chief of the New York *Evening Post,* a leading liberal, antislavery journal.

Buber, Martin (1878–1965), Jewish philosopher and religious scholar, born in Austria. He is best known for his poetic *I and Thou* (1923), an exploration of communication between person and person, or persons and God. Buber was also a translator of the Bible and a scholar of the Hasidic tradition, contributing such works as *The Tales of the Hasidim* (1950) and *Hasidim and Modern Man* (1960). He settled in Jerusalem in 1938.

Buchanan, James (1791–1868), 15th President of the United States, 1857–1861. Born near Mercersburg, Pa., he graduated from Dickinson College in 1809 and studied law. Successful as a lawyer, he entered politics and served in Congress, 1821–1831. Buchanan was minister to Russia, 1832–1833, and a senator from Pennsylvania, 1834–1845. He became secretary of state under President James K. Polk, 1845–1849, and then minister to Britain. As the Presidential campaign of 1856 approached, Buchanan became the Democrats' compromise candidate. After his election, he attempted to steer a middle course between Northern and Southern factions and to pacify the South, but he was unable to stop the movement toward civil war.

Buddha (c 563–483 B.C.), original name Siddhartha, Indian philosopher whose name is given to Buddhism. He was born into a noble family, the Gautama, and his early life was one of luxury. He married his cousin Yasodhara, and they had a son, Rahula. According to tradition, at 29, Buddha saw an old man, a sick man, a corpse, and a religious beggar, becoming aware for the first time of old age, illness, death, and serenity. He then left his wife and son and set out to seek the truth, wandering for six years through northern India. Finally, at Gaya, he learned to resist temptation and overcome suffering. He had found *nirvana,* a state of total detachment that ends pain. Buddha spent the rest of his life teaching in the Ganges valley.

Buffalo Bill: *See* Cody, William F.

Bunche, Ralph Johnson (1904–1971), U.S. diplomat and political scientist. For his role as UN mediator in the dis-

UNITED NATIONS

RALPH JOHNSON BUNCHE

pute between Israel and the Arab states in 1948–1949, he won the 1950 Nobel Peace Prize. In 1945 he became the first black division head in the State Department. Beginning in 1946, he served the United Nations in various capacities, directing work with trusteeships from 1946 to 1954. From then until 1967, Bunche was undersecretary for special political affairs; he then served as undersecretary-general, from 1968 to 1971.

Bunsen, Robert Wilhelm von (1811–1899), German chemist, a pioneer in spectrum analysis and the inventor of the carbon-zinc electric cell (1841), a photometer (1844), calorimeters, and a fuel pump. He made improvements in the burner named after him, but probably did not create the basic design. In 1860 Bunsen and his assistant Gustav Kirchhoff invented spectroscopy and with it discovered the elements cesium and rubidium.

Buñuel, Luis (1900–1983), Spanish film writer and director noted for using both stark realism and surrealism to expose the hypocrisy of conventional morality and to shock audiences into social consciousness. *Un Chien Andalou* (1928) and *L'Age d'or* (1930) are surrealist classics, precursors of the underground film movement. Buñuel later won wider audiences with *Los Olvidados* (1950), *Viridiana* (1961), *Belle de Jour* (1967), and *The Discreet Charm of the Bourgeoisie* (1973).

Bunyan, John (1628–1688), English Puritan preacher and author, remembered for *Pilgrim's Progress,* an allegory of a common man struggling to reach heaven. Bunyan served from 1644 to 1647 in the parliamentary army in the English Civil War. There he encountered Puritan beliefs and became a convert. After the Restoration (1660), he was imprisoned for breaking a law that forbade unlicensed preaching. He was released in 1672. He wrote several books in prison, including his autobiography, *Grace Abounding to the Chief of Sinners* (1666). In prison briefly a second time, Bunyan wrote the first part of *Pilgrim's Progress* (1678; second part, 1684), which soon became a classic and, until the late 19th century, could be found, with the Bible, in nearly every home.

Burbank, Luther (1849–1926), U.S. horticulturist, famed for producing more than 800 new hybrid varieties of plants. Having little formal education, he learned about plants from books and from farming in Massachusetts. In 1873 he developed his first new species, the Burbank potato. He moved to Santa Rosa, Calif., in 1875 and established a nursery. There he developed more than 100 varieties of plum, many kinds of berry, and such flowers as the Burbank rose and Shasta daisy.

Burghley (Burleigh), 1st Baron: *See* Cecil, William.

Burgoyne, Sir John (1722–1792), English army general who, during the American Revolution, led the British in the critical Battle of Saratoga. Marching south from Canada, he gained several minor victories, but was defeated at Saratoga, N.Y., October 17, 1777. Burgoyne, nicknamed Gentleman Johnny, returned to England, resigned his post, and wrote a successful comedy, *The Heiress* (1786).

Burke, Edmund (1729–1797), Irish-born English statesman, orator, writer, and political theorist. He entered Parliament in 1765. Advocating compromise in the quarrel with the American colonies, he made several famous speeches there, including "On American Taxation" (1774) and "On Conciliation with America" (1775). When the French Revolution began, Burke attacked its ideals of violence and the overthrow of tradition (*Reflections on the French Revolution,* 1790). His unpopular views lost him Whig support, and he retired from Parliament in 1794.

Burns, Robert (1759–1796), national poet of Scotland. His first success was *Poems, Chiefly in the Scottish Dialect* (1786). With James Johnson, an Edinburgh printer and song collector, Burns began to collect, edit, and write lyrics for old Scottish folk tunes. Many of these were collected in *Scots Musical Museum* (5 volumes, 1787–1797), including "Auld Lang Syne" and "Flow Gently, Sweet Afton."

Burr, Aaron (1757–1836), Vice President of the United States under Jefferson, 1801–1805. He was an officer during the American Revolution and then a senator from New York, 1791–1797. Burr was a bitter political opponent of Alexander Hamilton. Their feud eventually ended in a duel, in 1804, in which Hamilton was killed. His political career destroyed, Burr joined a conspiracy to seize Spanish territory in the Southwest and create a new empire. He was arrested for treason in 1807, but was acquitted.

Burton, Robert (1577–1640), English clergyman and scholar, chiefly remembered as the author of *The Anatomy of Melancholy* (1621). Supposedly a medical treatise, it is actually a treasury of information from classical, biblical, and contemporary sources.

Bush, George Herbert Walker (1924–), 41st President of the United States (1989–). Son of a senator and a veteran of World War II, he was active in Republican politics in the early 1960's. He won a seat in the House of Representatives in 1966 and was named to the Ways and Means Committee. Despite the support of President Nixon, his bid for the Senate in 1970 was unsuccessful. He became U.S. permanent representative to the UN in 1970 and chairman of the Republican National Commission in 1973. Bush was appointed by President Ford in 1975 to head the Central Intelligence Agency. He challenged Ronald Reagan for the Republican Presidential nomination in 1980, accepting the role of running mate after Reagan's stunning victory in the Texas primary. During the long primary campaign for the 1988 Republican Presidental nomination he prevailed over five other candidates, stressing his many years of public service in high government offices. He then went on to defeat the Democratic nominee, Michael Dukakis, by 54 percent of the popular vote, winning in 40 states.

Butler, Samuel (1835–1902), English novelist. He made his reputation with *Erewhon* (1872), a satirical treatment of a utopia resembling Victorian England. His semiautobiographical novel, *The Way of All Flesh* (written 1873–1885; published 1903), is remembered as a witty attack on Victorian education, customs, and morals.

Byrd, Richard Evelyn (1888–1957), U.S. naval officer, aviator, and explorer who made pioneer flights over the North Pole, 1926, and the South Pole, 1929, as well as a transatlantic crossing in 1927. He also led several expeditions to Antarctica, exploring new territory and establishing the base "Little America." Byrd spent the winter of 1934 alone in a tiny hut, narrowly surviving to become the first to inhabit the interior of Antarctica. He wrote *Discovery* (1935) and *Alone* (1938).

Byron, George Gordon, 6th Baron Byron (1788–1824), English poet and satirist, considered one of the most romantic figures in literary history. His major works contain many elements drawn from his colorful life. *Childe Harold's Pilgrimage* (1812), a long poem written after Byron's travels in Spain and Greece, brought him immediate recognition. The Oriental tales followed, including *The Giaour* and *The Bride of Abydos* (1813), and the gloomy *The Corsair* and *Lara* (1814), all reflecting the agitation and melancholy of two of Byron's love affairs. In the poetic drama *Manfred* (1817), the mock heroic *Beppo* (c 1818), and, most of all, the satirical *Don Juan* (1818–1824), Byron expressed his disillusionment with life and society. In 1823 Lord Byron joined the Greek struggle for independence, but died at Missolonghi the next year.

C

Cabot (in Italian, Caboto), family of Italian-born explorers of the Americas.

John, or Giovanni (c 1450–1499), was the first explorer in the service of England to visit the New World. He landed at Cape Breton Island in 1497, thinking it was Asia. In 1498 he explored the coasts of Greenland, Baffin Island, and Newfoundland.

Sebastian (c 1476–1557), navigator and cartographer, son of John, is credited with a 1509 voyage in search of a northwest passage to the Indies. From 1526 to 1530, again seeking the Orient, he explored several areas of South America. He was mapmaker to King Ferdinand II of Spain and published an engraved map of the world in 1544.

Caesar, Gaius Julius (traditionally 100–44 B.C., probably 102–44 B.C.), Roman general and statesman who brought the Roman Republic to an end. Caesar was one of the most influential and controversial men in history; his intents and motives are still disputed. As a young man holding office in Rome, Caesar went deep into debt to win the people's favor with shows and circuses. In 60 he made a private pact with the two most powerful men in Rome, Pompey and Crassus, forming with them the First Triumvirate. Caesar was given command of the provinces of Gaul; he spent the next nine years conquering the Gallic tribes and southern Britain. He described the campaign in his *Commentaries on the Gallic War,* which for centuries served as a model of clear Latin prose. In 49 the Senate, influenced by a jealous Pompey, ordered Caesar to resign his command. Caesar refused; when he crossed the river Rubicon into Italy with his army, Pompey fled to Greece and Caesar became Roman dictator. He pursued Pompey to Greece in 48 and defeated him at Pharsalus. He then followed Pompey into Egypt, where he restored the queen Cleopatra to her throne. By 45 Caesar had defeated or forgiven all of Pompey's former followers and was the master of the Roman world. In Rome he used his power to restore order and stability. On the Ides of March (March 15) in 44, a group of Caesar's enemies and disgruntled republicans assassinated him at a Senate meeting.

Cage, John Milton, Jr. (1912–), U.S. experimental composer whose musical ideas strongly influenced many modern composers and other artists, especially dancers. Rejecting the idea of the composer as sole creator of a piece, Cage developed "aleatory" music, in which the final performance depends as much on chance as on the composer. In some of his piano works, he scatters the sheets of music, then picks them up and plays them in the resulting random order. His best-known pieces include *Imaginary Landscape No. 4* (1951), for twelve randomly tuned radios, and *Telephones and Birds* (1977).

Calder, Alexander Stirling (1898–1976), U.S. sculptor and illustrator who first designed the mobile—a movable sculpture created from pieces of metal delicately balanced by wires so that they move with air currents. Fine examples of these are *A Universe* (1934) and *Mobile* (1958, at the UNESCO building, Paris).

Calderón de la Barca, Pedro (1600–1681), Spanish playwright, the last great dramatist of the Golden Age of Spanish literature. Calderón combined the careers of playwright and occasional soldier until 1651, when he became a priest. In 1666 he was appointed honorary chaplain to Philip IV. He continued to write plays for the court and *autos sacramentales* (short religious dramas), such as his *El gran teatro del mundo (The Great Theater of the World).* His best-known play is *La vida es sueño (Life Is a Dream),* a verse drama about dream and reality.

Calhoun, John Caldwell (1782–1850), Vice President of the United States, 1825–1832, and chief spokesman for states' rights in the pre-Civil War South. An eloquent speaker and writer, he helped draft a South Carolina constitution (1810) based on sectional agreement rather than majority rule. When he entered national politics, tariffs on Southern goods and restrictions on slavery led Calhoun to take the position that a state could nullify a federal law it deemed unconstitutional. When South Carolina nullified the Tariff Act of 1832, President Jackson threatened Calhoun, his own Vice President, with arrest. Calhoun resigned and began a 17-year battle in the Senate against compromise bills, arguing that they failed to face the basic issue of states' rights and balance between North and South. During the debates on the Compromise of 1850, he predicted that sectional disputes would tear the Union apart.

Caligula (12–41 A.D.), real name Gaius Caesar Germanicus, Roman emperor, 37–41. His nickname Caligula ("Little Boot") was given him as a boy by his father's soldiers because he wore military boots. Shortly after becoming emperor, Caligula had a severe illness, which may have weakened his mind. Later Roman historians report that he ruled with great cruelty and extravagance; some say he was insane, citing such stories as the one that he appointed his horse consul of Rome. He was assassinated in 41.

Callas, Maria (1923–1977), U.S. opera singer, born in New York of Greek parents. Callas, the most versatile soprano of her day, initiated a revival of interest in the *bel canto* operas of Bellini (*Norma*), Donizetti, and Rossini. She was also distinguished for the dramatic intensity of her performances.

Calvert, George, 1st Baron Baltimore (c 1580–1632), English statesman and colonizer, considered the founder of Maryland. A member of Parliament and secretary of state until his conversion to Roman Catholicism, Calvert retired from public life and secured a royal charter, hoping to establish a colony for members of his faith as well as for business purposes. His agent sailed to Newfoundland in 1621, and in 1623 the settlement of Avalon was chartered. Baltimore settled there briefly in 1627, but finding the climate too severe, he petitioned the king for a land grant near the settlements in Virginia. The official charter was granted in 1632 after his death to his son **Cecil, 2nd Baron Baltimore** (c 1605–1675).

MARIA CALLAS

THE BETTMANN ARCHIVE

Calvin, John (1509–1564), in French, Jean Cauvin or Chauvin, French theologian and reformer. Educated in Paris as a Catholic, Calvin gradually converted to Protestant views; from 1534 on he became more and more a leader of reform. In the same year, he moved to Basel to avoid religious persecution. There he published the first edition of his great work, *Institutes of the Christian Religion* (1536). In 1541 he organized the Reformed Church in Geneva with a new hierarchy and a new service. Calvin soon established a theocratic government in Geneva, and the city became the center of Calvinism. His final edition of the *Institutes,* summarizing evangelical teaching, was published in 1559. Calvin considered the Bible the only source of knowledge on questions of faith. His doctrines included the superiority of faith to good works, salvation by God's grace, and divine predestination for the elect. Calvin is considered to have been the father of the Reformed Huguenot Church in France, the Dutch Reformed Church, and the Scottish Presbyterian Church. He also influenced the English Puritans.

Camões (Camoëns), Luiz Vaz de (c 1524–1580), Portuguese epic poet, considered Portugal's greatest poet. *Os Lusíadas* ("The Men of Portugal," 1572), his greatest work, is a long lyric poem in the classical mode, celebrating the exploits of Portugal's explorers and conquerors, set in a background of classical mythology. He drew on his own adventurous life and his travels in Africa and India. Camões is also remembered for his exquisite love sonnets, based on a tragic love affair, and several dramatic works.

Camus, Albert (1913–1960), French novelist and essayist, a leading existentialist best known for his "philosophy of the absurd," a concept of reality as the conflict between nature's chaos and the human need for order. Camus' major works are the novels *The Stranger* (1942), *The Plague* (1947), and *The Fall* (1956), and the philosophical essays *The Myth of Sisyphus* (1942) and *The Rebel* (1951). He won the 1957 Nobel Prize for Literature.

Canetti, Elias (1905–), Bulgarian-born German writer and winner of the 1981 Nobel Prize in Literature who has lived mostly in England since 1938. He is best known for his nightmarish novel *Auto-da-Fe* (1935), an indirect condemnation of the fascist mentality, and for *Crowds and Power* (1960), an analysis of mass behavior. Canetti is remarkable for his ability to combine the comic and the horrifying, and for his nonchalant and anecdotal treatment of bizarre material.

Čapek, Karel (1890–1938), Czech author, a leading innovator in the European theater. Čapek's best-known play is *R. U. R.* (1920), a satirical drama in which robots—a term he coined—take over the world. He also wrote several excellent novels, among them *Krakatit* (1925), *An Ordinary Life* (1935), and *War with the Newts* (1937).

Capone, Alphonse (1899–1947), Italian-born U.S. gangster. The scar of a razor slash gave him the nickname Scarface. Capone grew up in Brooklyn, then moved to Chicago, where he organized a gang of gunmen to corner the market in bootleg liquor, gambling, and other vices. The resulting gang wars reached their peak in the St. Valentine's Day Massacre of 1929, in which seven members of a rival gang were lined up against a garage wall and shot. Capone went to prison, 1931–1939, for income tax evasion. He died in retirement.

Capote, Truman (1924–1984), U.S. author noted for his depiction of eccentric characters and for his authentic recreation of speech and lifestyles. His novels include *Other Voices, Other Rooms* (1948), *The Grass Harp* (1951), and *Breakfast at Tiffany's* (1958; film, 1961). Capote wrote several film and television scripts (*A Christmas Memory,* published as a story, 1956; television version, 1966). He combined fictional and journalistic techniques in *In Cold Blood* (1965; film, 1967), an account of a mass murder. *Music for Chameleons* (1980) is a collection of both fiction and nonfiction.

Caravaggio, Michelangelo Merisi da (1573–1610), an Italian naturalistic painter known for the emotional intensity of his work and his striking use of light and shadow. Among his best-known works are *Conversion of St. Paul* (1601) and *Death of the Virgin* (1605–1606). His personal life was turbulent. Police records show many arrests, and in 1606 he was banished from Rome for committing a murder. In 1608 he was attacked and disfigured by enemies in Naples.

ALBERT CAMUS

THE BETTMANN ARCHIVE

Cardozo, Benjamin Nathan (1870–1938), justice of the U.S. Supreme Court. From 1914 to 1932 he served on the New York Court of Appeals, becoming chief justice in 1926. In this position, he did much to reshape legal doctrine by defining the judicial role in the creation of the law. As a member of the liberal wing of the Supreme Court, 1932–1938, he supported decisions affecting the economy, upholding the passage of Social Security and other New Deal legislation. Cardozo wrote four respected volumes of essays, among them the classic *Nature of the Judicial Process* (1921).

Carlyle, Thomas (1795–1881), Scottish essayist and historian. *Sartor Resartus* ("The Tailor Retailored," 1833–1834), a long satirical essay, made him known as a writer. His interpretive history *French Revolution* (1837) set forth, in dramatic style, his theory that the revolution was a judgment on the weak leaders of the French aristocracy. Carlyle's deep admiration of strong leadership was most evident in *Heroes, Hero Worship, and the Heroic in History* (1841), in which he saw history as the record of the deeds of great men. Carlyle's heroes were such men as Luther, Cromwell, and Frederick the Great.

Carnegie, Andrew (1835–1919), Scottish-born U.S. industrial magnate, known for his phenomenal accumulation of wealth in the iron and steel business and for his philanthropy. He introduced the sleeping car to American railways, began the use of iron in bridge building, and founded the Carnegie Steel Company (which became, in 1901, part of U.S. Steel). From the 1880's on, he endowed hundreds of Carnegie libraries in English-speaking countries and established foundations for education and peace. After retiring in 1901, he spent about $300 million on philanthropy.

Carnot, Nicolas Léonard Sadi (1796–1832), French physicist whose discoveries laid the groundwork for the science of thermodynamics. His principle regarding the changing of heat into energy was published in 1824 ("On the Motive Power of Heat"); it is a basis of the second law of thermodynamics. His conclusions on the conservation of energy are fundamental to the first law of thermodynamics.

Carrel, Alexis (1873–1944), French surgeon who developed a method for suturing blood vessels that made blood transfusion safe. He also laid the basis for artery and organ transplants. For this work he received the 1912 Nobel Prize in Physiology and Medicine. During World War I Carrel helped devise a fluid method of treating wounds. In his later years, he espoused improving mankind under the guidance of a racially restricted group. At the end of World War II, he was accused of collaboration with the Nazis. He died while the charges were being investigated.

Carroll, Lewis: *See* Dodgson, Charles Lutwidge.

Carson, Christopher (Kit) (1809–1868), U.S. frontiersman, a legendary hero of the West. As a guide for John C. Frémont's expeditions to California, 1842–1845, Carson acquired a national reputation. Still more stories were told of his heroism in the Mexican War (1846–1847). Serving as Indian agent at Taos, N.M., he resigned when the Civil War began, becoming an officer in the First New Mexican Volunteer Infantry.

Carson, Rachel Louise (1907–1964), U.S. aquatic biologist and writer. Her book *Silent Spring* (1962) exposed the fact that overuse of pesticides was endangering the balance of life on Earth; it was a pioneer work in arousing public concern about the environment, pollution, and human ecology. She also wrote several books on the sea and the life it supports, notably *The Sea Around Us* (1951).

Carter, James Earl, Jr. (Jimmy) (1924–), 39th President of the United States (1977–1981). He was born in Plains, Ga., and graduated from the U.S. Naval Academy in 1946. After seven years in the Navy, Carter resigned and entered his family's peanut farming business. He entered politics in 1962, when he was elected to the Georgia State Senate. Eight years later he was elected governor of Georgia. Carter was an early entrant in the campaign for the Presidential nomination in 1976. Campaigning on a promise to bring the government back to the people, he narrowly defeated President Ford by a vote of 297 to 240 in the electoral college. One of Carter's first acts in office was to pardon most Vietnam War draft evaders. In most matters, he found it difficult to get Congress to follow his lead. A Department of Energy was established, but other parts of Carter's energy program were rejected. Among Carter's achievements were a peace agreement between Israel and Egypt; Senate ratification of treaties giving Panama possession of the Panama Canal at the end of 1999; and resumption of full diplomatic relations with China. However, the Senate did not ratify the arms treaty, SALT II. From November, 1979, until the last day of his administration, Carter was preoccupied with the problem of the Americans held hostage in the embassy in Teheran, Iran. An attempt to free them by force in April, 1980, failed, but negotiations finally led to their release on January 20, 1981. Carter won renomination for the Presidency in 1980, but he was badly defeated in the election by Ronald Reagan, the Republican candidate.

Cartier, Jacques (1491–1557), French navigator and explorer who discovered the St. Lawrence River. In 1534 he reached the Gulf of St. Lawrence and claimed for France the land that is now Quebec Province. From the Indians Cartier learned of wealth in Saguenay and searched for it on his second trip in 1535. He sailed up the St. Lawrence River to an island he named Mount Royal (or Montréal). Still in search of treasure, in 1541 he undertook a third expedition. Finding unfriendly Indians and no gold, Cartier returned to France in 1542.

Cartwright, Edmond (1743–1823), English country clergyman, inventor of the power loom that revolutionized the English textile industry. In 1785 he patented his first loom and set up a weaving mill. He also patented a wool-carding machine and a rope-making machine, and experimented with a steam engine. None of his inventions ever brought him financial success, but in 1809 Parliament granted him £10,000, on which he retired.

Caruso, Enrico (1873–1921), Italian operatic tenor, memorable for his powerful voice and his wide repertoire. He sang at La Scala, Milan, in 1899 and made his Metropolitan Opera debut in 1903. Among his most popular roles were the duke in Verdi's *Rigoletto* and the clown Canio in *Pagliacci*. He was the Met's leading tenor for nearly 20 years.

Carver, George Washington (c 1864–1943), U.S. botanist and educator, remembered for his practical agricultural research. He went to agriculture school at Iowa State College, becoming the first black to graduate from the school (1896). He joined Tuskegee Institute in Alabama, where he started an agricultural research center devoted to helping impoverished Southern farmers. Where the soil had been ruined by cotton farming, Carver taught the farmers to rotate their crops with peanuts and sweet potatoes. He developed hundreds of uses for byproducts of these crops, such as shampoo, soap, and dye.

Casals, Pablo (1876–1973), Spanish cellist and conductor, considered the greatest cello interpreter of his time. When Franco took over as dictator of Spain in 1939, Casals refused to play in public for several years in protest. He finally left Spain. After World War II he organized annual festivals of chamber music in Prades, France, and in Puerto Rico.

Cassatt, Mary (1845–1926), U.S. painter and printmaker noted for her impressionistic portraits of mothers and children. In 1874 she settled in Paris, where she became a close friend of Edgar Degas. Her style combines the line of Correggio and the design of the Japanese printmakers, as shown in *La Loge* (c 1882), *Lady at the Tea Table* (1885), and *Mère et enfant* (1905).

THE BETTMANN ARCHIVE

FIDEL CASTRO

Castro, Fidel (1926–), Cuban revolutionary who became premier of Cuba in 1959 after overthrowing the government of dictator Fulgencio Batista. On July 26, 1953, he led an abortive attack on the Moncada barracks in Santiago. At his trial Castro delivered the famous "History will absolve me" speech, indicting the Batista regime. Granted amnesty in 1955, he launched a guerrilla war, gained the support of the people, and finally forced Batista to flee in 1959. As leader of Cuba, backed by his brother Raúl and Che Guevara, Castro allied himself with communist and revolutionary movements around the world. He nationalized American-owned property in Cuba, and in 1961 Cuba and the United States broke diplomatic relations. Castro set up totalitarian rule and suppressed the Cuban press. However, outside efforts to unseat him (notably the U.S.-backed invasion in 1961) found no support among Cubans. Under a new constitution adopted in 1976, he became president of the Republic of Cuba.

Cather, Willa Sibert (1873–1947), U.S. novelist. She used her own experience of prairie life in *O Pioneers!* (1913) and *My Ántonia* (1918). *One of Ours* (1922) won a Pulitzer Prize. Her novels of French Catholicism—*Death Comes for the Archbishop* (1927), set in New Mexico, and *Shadows on the Rock* (1931), set in Quebec—emphasize her faith in traditional values.

Catherine II, the Great (1729–1796), empress of Russia, 1762–1796. The daughter of a German prince, she married Prince Peter of Russia in 1745. Catherine despised her backward husband and when he became czar in 1762, almost immediately arranged a coup d'état to remove him from the throne. She was acclaimed empress, and Peter died soon after. A strong-willed, intellectual, and enlightened woman, Catherine worked zealously to reform Russia's provincial administration, education, and medical facilities. She annexed parts of Poland and Turkey, extending the empire to the Black Sea. But, while she brought to the nobility European culture and learning, she depended on their goodwill and allowed them many privileges and harsh new powers over their serfs.

Catiline (c 108–62 B.C.), full name Lucius Sergius Catilina, Roman politician who, after being defeated for the consulship by Cicero in 64, conspired to overthrow the Roman government. Cicero exposed the conspiracy in 63 in the famous "Catline orations," and Catiline fled. The conspirators in Rome were executed, and Catiline and his band were cut down by the Roman army the next year.

Cato, Marcus Porcius (234–149 B.C.), called Cato the Elder and Cato the Censor, Roman orator and statesman, also an early author of Latin prose. A vociferous advocate of virtue and simplicity, Cato denounced the luxury and immorality of the wealthy Romans of his day. During a mission to Carthage, Cato became convinced that the city was becoming a threat. Thereafter, whenever he spoke in the Senate, even to vote on a bill, he would add the opinion that "Carthage must be destroyed." He at last persuaded Rome to annihilate Carthage in the Third Punic War (149–146).

Cato, Marcus Porcius (95–46 B.C.), called Cato the Younger or Cato of Utica, Roman statesman, the great-grandson of Cato the Elder. He was renowned by later Romans for his integrity. In the Senate, Cato tried to defend the traditions of the republic against the power of Pompey and the innovations of Caesar. During the civil war, Cato supported Pompey, believing him to be the lesser evil. When opposition to Caesar collapsed, Cato killed himself.

Catt, Carrie Lane Chapman (1859–1947), U.S. leader in the women's suffrage movement. As organizer of the National American Woman Suffrage Association, she gathered 2 million women to campaign for suffrage. She was the group's president, 1900–1904 and 1915–1920. In 1920 the 19th Amendment was ratified, granting women the right to vote. Catt subsequently reorganized the powerful suffrage association into the League of Women Voters, dedicated to the political education of women.

Catullus, Gaius Valerius (c 84–c 54 B.C.), Roman poet, one of the greatest lyric poets of antiquity. Whether light or passionate, his poetry is simple and evocative. His best-known poems reflect his long affair with Clodia, sister of Cicero's enemy Clodius.

Cavour, Count Camillo Benso di (1810–1861), Italian statesman and leader in the struggle to unify Italy, often called Italy's first premier. In 1847 he founded a newspaper, *Il Risorgimento,* urging the king to form a constitutional government and advocating war against Austria, which dominated Italy. Elected to the Piedmont parliament in 1848, Cavour became prime minister in 1852. An 1858 alliance with Napoleon III of France against Austria ended disastrously when Napoleon signed a private peace with Austria in 1859. Italy gained nothing, and Cavour resigned. In 1860 he returned to office, supporting the troops of Giuseppe Garibaldi. He then maneuvered all the factions until Italy, except for Venetia and Rome, was unified under King Victor Emmanuel II, in 1861.

Caxton, William (c 1422–1491), the first English printer. He set up his first press in Bruges, Flanders, and in 1475 printed his own translation of *The Recuyell of the Historyes of Troye,* the first book printed in the English language. In 1476 Caxton returned to England and set up his press near London. An "Indulgence" is the first known piece of printing in England. The first dated book printed by Caxton was *Dictes and Sayenges of the Phylosophers* (1477). He also printed the first illustrated book, an encyclopedia called *The Myrrour of the World* (1481), as well as books by Malory and Chaucer.

Cecil, William, 1st Baron Burghley (or **Burleigh)** (1520–1598), English statesman, chief adviser to Queen Elizabeth I. In 1558 the new queen appointed him secretary of state; they formed a remarkable ruling partnership that lasted for 40 years. Cecil and Elizabeth agreed on all major issues, seeking peace and security for England. He was made a baron in 1571 and lord treasurer in 1572, taking charge of finances. Cecil's greatest concern was the extreme religious factions, both Catholic and Puritan, that threatened the throne. He justified the repression of the Catholic rebels who, with French and Spanish aid, supported Mary Stuart's claim to the throne. He took responsibility for ordering Mary's execution for treason in 1587.

His son, **Robert Cecil** (1563–1612), succeeded him as Elizabeth's adviser and was named secretary of state in 1596. Cecil won a struggle for power with the earl of Essex in 1598, and served both the queen and her successor, James I, who named him earl of Salisbury.

Cellini, Benvenuto (1500–1571), Italian goldsmith and sculptor who described his unruly life in his famous *Autobiography* (written 1558–1562; first printed, 1728). This colorful work contains valuable insights into life in 16th-century Rome, Florence, and France. The most celebrated example of Renaissance goldsmith work is the enamel and gold saltcellar Cellini made for Francis I of France. Much of Cellini's other gold work has been lost, but his bronzes, *Nymph of Fontainebleau* (1543–1544) and *Perseus with the Head of Medusa* (1554), are fine examples of his sculpture.

Cervantes Saavedra, Miguel de (1547–1616), Spanish poet and novelist, creator of *Don Quixote,* considered by many the first modern novel. *Don Quixote* (*Don Quijote de la Mancha,* published in two parts, 1605, 1615) is not only an attack on the absurd romances of chivalry so popular in Cervantes's time, but also a true romantic novel whose characters undergo change and growth, unlike the static characters of earlier literature. Some of his other works are *Exemplary Novels* (*Novelas exemplares,* 1613), a series of stories; and *Voyage to Parnassus* (*Viaje del Parnaso,* 1614). Cervantes himself lived an eventful life. In 1569, having wounded a schoolmate in a brawl, he was sentenced to ten years of exile. Escaping, he fought in the Battle of Lepanto in 1571, permanently injuring his left hand. Another battle between Spain and Turkey in 1575 ended with Cervantes the prisoner of Turkish pirates. He was finally ransomed in 1580, but similar scrapes and misfortunes dogged him to the end of his life.

Cézanne, Paul (1839–1906), French painter of still life and landscape who had a revolutionary influence on the development of abstract art. In 1861 he went to Paris, where he met many impressionists, including Pissarro, from whom he learned techniques of observing nature and colors. To this he added his own concepts of solid form and design made by breaking natural structure into planes of color. Though Cézanne achieved very little recognition during his lifetime, he had a significant influence on later artists, especially the cubists. His works include *L'Estaque* (1883–1885), *The Card Players* (1890–1892), *Still Life with Apples* (1895), and *Mont Sainte-Victoire* (1904).

Chagall, Marc (1887–1985), Russian-born painter known for his individualistic use of color, fantasy, and symbolism. Examples of his early work are *I and the Village* (1911), *To*

Donkeys and Others (1911), and *Pregnant Woman* (1912–1913). He illustrated several books, notably Gogol's *Dead Souls* (1923–1927) and La Fontaine's *Fables* (1927–1930). He designed stained glass windows, "The Twelve Tribes of Israel," for a hospital near Jerusalem (1960–1961), and a series of windows for the cathedral of Metz (1958–1960).

Chain, Ernst Boris: *See* Fleming, Sir Alexander.

Chaliapin, Feodor Ivanovich (1873–1938), Russian operatic basso whose interpretation of the title role in Mussorgsky's *Boris Godunov* is one of the legends of opera. After his debut in St. Petersburg in 1894, he sang leading basso roles throughout Europe and in 1922 made a sensational debut at the Metropolitan Opera. Chaliapin's vivid acting and resonant voice also brought him fame in his roles in *Faust* and *Mefistofele.*

Chamberlain, (Arthur) Neville (1869–1940), British statesman, prime minister from 1937 to 1940. He followed an unsuccessful "policy of appeasement" toward the fascist powers. His Munich agreement with Hitler (1938), which he claimed would bring "peace in our time," encouraged Hitler to occupy all of Czechoslovakia. When Germany invaded Poland in 1939, Chamberlain declared war, but early British defeats forced his resignation in 1940.

Champlain, Samuel de (c 1567–1635), French explorer, often called the father of Canada. In 1603 Champlain made the first of many voyages to North America, exploring the St. Lawrence River as far as Montreal. He charted the coast of what is now New England and helped found a settlement at Port Royal, Nova Scotia. In 1608 Champlain obtained permission to establish a year-round trading post at Quebec, the first permanent French colony in North America. In 1609 he discovered Lake Champlain, and in 1611 he built a trading post at Montreal. In 1612 he was made acting governor of New France. He settled in Quebec as head of the colony. When the English captured Quebec in 1629, Champlain was taken prisoner to England, but he returned to Quebec in 1633.

MARC CHAGALL

THE BETTMANN ARCHIVE

THE BETTMANN ARCHIVE

CHARLIE CHAPLIN

Chaney, Lon (1883–1930), U.S. film actor, known as "the man of a thousand faces" because of his talent with disguise and makeup. Chaney's best-remembered film roles include *The Penalty* (1920), *The Hunchback of Notre Dame* (1923), *The Unholy Three* (1925), and *The Phantom of the Opera* (1925).

Lon Chaney, Jr. (1912–), his son, won an Academy Award for his role as Lenny in *Of Mice and Men* (1939). Thereafter, he played mainly in monster movies, notably *The Wolf Man* (1940).

Chaplin, Charles Spencer (1889–1977), British filmmaker of international fame, usually identified with his best-known characterization, "the little fellow," a hapless but spunky tramp. He first appeared in Mack Sennett's Keystone comedies and then, with other stars, formed United Artists and began to produce his own films. In *The Tramp* (1915), he developed "the little fellow's" character more fully. Chaplin went on to play him in *Easy Street* (1917), *The Gold Rush* (1925), and *Modern Times* (1936). *The Great Dictator* (1940) was his first talking film. Chaplin left Hollywood and the United States during the McCarthy era, when his politics were attacked as subversive. *A King in New York,* a satire on U.S. congressional investigations, appeared in Britain in 1957. Chaplin was knighted by Queen Elizabeth in 1975.

Chapman, John (1774–1845), better known as Johnny Appleseed, U.S. frontier hero who planted and tended orchards from western Pennsylvania to Illinois. He began his mission around 1800, planting seeds from the cider mills of Pennsylvania throughout the Ohio valley. He walked barefoot, wore a tin pan for a hat, and read the Bible to the settlers who took him in. His peaceful courage and kindly ways made him a legendary figure even before he died.

Chardin, Pierre Teilhard de: *See* Teilhard de Chardin, Pierre.

RULERS OF FRANCE

Carolingian Line	747–768	Pepin the Short
	768–814	Charlemagne, or Charles the Great (Holy Roman* Emperor, 800–814)
	814–840	Louis I the Pious (le Débonnaire)
	840–877	Charles I the Bald (Holy Roman Emperor as Charles II)
	877–879	Louis II
	879–882	Louis III
	879–884	Carloman
	884–887	Charles II the Fat (Holy Roman Emperor as Charles III)
	888–898	Odo, count of Paris
	893–923	Charles III the Simple
	922–923	Robert I
	923–936	Rudolf, duke of Burgundy
	936–954	Louis IV
	954–986	Lothair
	986–987	Louis V
Kingdom of France Capetian Line	987–996	Hugh Capet
	996–1031	Robert II
	1031–1060	Henry I
	1060–1108	Philip I
	1108–1137	Louis VI
	1137–1180	Louis VII
	1180–1223	Philip II, or Philip Augustus*
	1223–1226	Louis VIII
	1226–1270	Louis IX (Saint Louis)
	1270–1285	Philip III
	1285–1314	Philip IV
	1314–1316	Louis X
	1316	John I (*Fr.* Jean)
	1316–1322	Philip V
	1322–1328	Charles IV
House of Valois	1328–1350	Philip VI
	1350–1364	John II
	1364–1380	Charles V
	1380–1422	Charles VI
	1422–1461	Charles VII*
	1461–1483	Louis XI
	1483–1498	Charles VIII
	1498–1515	Louis XII
	1515–1547	Francis I*
	1547–1559	Henry II
	1559–1560	Francis II
	1560–1574	Charles IX
	1574–1589	Henry III
House of Bourbon	1589–1610	Henry IV*
	1610–1643	Louis XIII
	1643–1715	Louis XIV*
	1715–1774	Louis XV
	1774–1792	Louis XVI (executed 1793)*
	1793–1795	Louis XVII (nominal king only)
The Republic	Sept. 20, 1792–Oct. 26, 1795	National Convention,
	Oct. 27, 1795–Nov. 9, 1799	The Directory (*Fr.* Directoire)
The Consulate (Fr. Consulate)	1799–1804	Napoleon Bonaparte, First Consul
First Empire	1804–1814	Napoleon I, Bonaparte,* emperor of the French
The Restoration	1814–1824	Louis XVIII
	1824–1830	Charles X
	1830–1848	Louis Philippe
The Second Republic	1848–1852	Louis Napoleon, president*
The Second Empire	1852–1870	Napoleon III (Louis Napoleon),* emperor
The Third Republic (Presidents)	1871–1873	Louis Adolphe Thiers*
	1873–1879	Marshal MacMahon
	1879–1887	Jules Grévy
	1887–1894	Marie François Sadi-Carnot
	1894–1895	Jean Casimir-Périer
	1895–1899	François Félix Faure
	1899–1906	Émile Loubet
	1906–1913	Armand Fallières
	1913–1920	Raymond Poincaré*
	1920	Paul Deschanel
	1920–1924	Alexandre Millerand
	1924–1931	Gaston Doumergue
	1931–1932	Paul Doumer
	1932–1940	Albert Lebrun
Vichy Government	1940–1944	Marshal Henri Philippe Pétain,* chief of the state
	1942–1944	Pierre Laval, chief of government*
Provisional Government (Presidents)	1944–1946	Charles de Gaulle
	1946	Félix Gouin (Jan. 23)
	1946	Georges Bidault (June 19)
	1946	Léon Blum (Dec. 12)
The Fourth Republic (Presidents)	1947–1954	Vincent Auriol
	1954–1959	René Coty
The Fifth Republic (Presidents)	1959–1969	Charles de Gaulle*
	1969–1974	Georges Pompidou
	1974–1981	Valéry Giscard d'Estaing*
	1981–	François Mitterrand*

*See main biography.

THE BETTMANN ARCHIVE

CHARLEMAGNE

Charlemagne (or **Charles the Great**) (c 742–814), king of the Franks, 768–814, who founded a great empire in western Europe. He was the elder son of Pepin the Short, the first Frankish king of the Carolingian dynasty. In a brilliant career, Charlemagne extended his domain from the Atlantic to the Adriatic, from the North Sea to the Pyrenees. He imposed Christianity on his subjects throughout the empire. In 778 he crossed the Pyrenees into Spain to make war on the Moors, but was forced to withdraw. The last stand of his rear guard during the retreat into France was celebrated in the medieval epic *The Song of Roland.* On Christmas Day, 800, Charlemagne was crowned emperor of the Western Roman Empire by Pope Leo III. He regarded himself as the successor to the emperors of Rome, but later ages saw him as the founder of a new European empire, and both the Holy Roman and the Napoleonic empires were patterned on Charlemagne's empire. Charlemagne tried to set up a strong central government and to encourage art and learning in his empire, but his dominion soon disintegrated into feudalism after he died.

Charles I (1600–1649), king of England, Scotland, and Ireland, 1625–1649, the son of James I. When he came to the throne, England was at

CHARLES I

war with Spain. The largely Puritan Parliament, which controlled the king's income, was not only opposed to the costly wars, but also to his avowed Anglican beliefs. In the Petition of Right (1628), the House of Commons denounced the power of the king to levy taxes. Charles, believing in the divine right of kings, dissolved his uncooperative Parliament in 1629 and ruled for eleven years without a legislature. In those years, Charles supported persecutions of the Puritans and offended his subjects by his taxes and levies to raise money. In 1640 an insurrection in Scotland forced him to summon a new Parliament to obtain funds. He dissolved the assembly in three weeks and called another Parliament the same year. It remained in session and forced the king to halt the persecutions. The conflict between Charles and Parliament grew worse. In 1642 he tried to arrest five leaders of Parliament, and the Londoners rioted. The king fled the city, and civil war began. After several defeats by the parliamentary army, Charles sought refuge in Scotland and tried to negotiate with various factions. He was eventually handed over to parliamentary commissioners and brought to trial by the extremists under Oliver Cromwell. In 1649 he was beheaded, and rule by Parliament replaced the monarchy in England.

Charles II (1630–1685), called the Merrie Monarch, king of England, Scotland, and Ireland, 1660–1685. The son of Charles I, executed in 1649, he grew up in exile. He invaded England in 1651, but the royalist army was crushed, and he narrowly escaped to France. After Cromwell died in 1658, Charles was invited to return to England and was crowned in 1660. The king's personality—shrewd, amusing, unscrupulous, and pleasure-loving—set the tone for Restoration England. His court was gay and often licentious. Charles had no children by the queen, but many illegitimate children by his mistresses. His favorite was Nell Gwynn, who had been an orange seller in a theater. Despite the disasters of the Great Plague in 1665 and the Great Fire of London in 1666, art, literature, and science flourished under Charles. Charles did not try to claim absolute power, but controlled Parliament by political maneuvers. Parliament, in turn, subdued him by keeping his income low. For more money, the king accepted subsidies from France for waging war against the Dutch. His religious policy, by an agreement signed in 1660, was one of toleration, though nonconformists were nonetheless persecuted. Late in his reign there was parliamentary opposition to the succession of his Catholic brother James.

Charles V (1500–1558), Holy Roman Emperor, 1519–1556, and king of Spain (as Charles I), 1516–1556. Heir to both the Spanish and German Hapsburg empires, Charles controlled Spain, the Netherlands, Austria, and much of Italy and Germany. As a sincere and zealous defender of the Catholic faith, Charles tried to stem the Protestant Reformation begun by Luther in 1517. He tried to control the rebellious German Protestant princes with edicts and armies, but in 1555 he was forced to sign the Peace of Augsburg, which granted religious freedom to the Protestant princes. Charles's empire had no central administration and was held together only by his position as ruler of the scattered domain. In 1556, worn out by the burden of empire, Charles retired to a monastery, relinquishing the Spanish crown to his son Philip II and the German Hapsburg possessions to his younger brother Ferdinand.

Charles VII (1403–1461), king of France, 1422–1461, who drove the English out of France, ending the Hundred Years' War. In 1422 young Charles was crowned king at Poitiers. The English, who held northern France, besieged Charles at Orléans in 1428, but he was saved by the help of Joan of Arc. After he was crowned king at Reims, Charles formed powerful alliances, chose bold leaders, retook Paris in 1437, and eventually recaptured all of France.

Charles XII (1682–1718), king of Sweden, 1697–1718, Sweden's greatest warrior king and dashing hero, who almost conquered all of northeastern Europe. When Swedish dominion in the Baltic was challenged by Denmark, Poland, and Russia, Charles began a brilliant, daring campaign known as the Northern War. He forced the Danes out of the war, routed the Russians at Narva (1700), then overran Poland. He invaded Russia in 1708, but almost his whole army was killed or captured at Poltava in 1709. Failing to induce the Turks to pursue war against Russia, Charles returned to Sweden in 1714. He gathered another army and invaded Norway, where he was killed during a siege in 1718. His wars bled Sweden dry of men and money and reduced it to the ranks of lesser powers.

Charles XIV (Charles John) (1763–1844), born Jean Baptiste Jules Bernadotte, marshal of Napoleon's empire, later king of Sweden and Norway, 1818–1844. In 1809 the Swedes, having no heir to the throne, invited him to become crown prince. He accepted and was adopted with the name Charles John (Swedish, Carl Johan) by the old king, Charles XIII. As crown prince, Charles John led Sweden into the coalition against Napoleon. After fighting in the Battle of Leipzig (1813), he marched into Denmark and forced the Danes to relinquish Norway, which united with Sweden in 1815. He and his wife Désirée founded the current Swedish dynasty.

Charles Martel (c 688–741), whose name means Charles the hammer, leader of the Franks and founder of the Carolingian line of kings of France. In a civil war within the Frankish kingdom, Charles took over the ruling office of mayor of the palace in 717; by 725 he had defeated his rivals. He is most famous for his victory over the Muslim forces at Tours (732), which drove back the last Arab forces to invade western Europe. Charles's sons, Pepin the Short (father of Charlemagne) and Carloman, divided the kingdom after his death.

Chaucer, Geoffrey (c 1344–1400), greatest English poet of the medieval era, considered the father of English poetry. He was the first to fashion a rhyme and metrical scheme out of Middle English, which was still in a transition period and marked by uncertain accents. *The Canterbury Tales* (c 1387), his most popular work, is a masterpiece of human character study, comprising tales told by a group of pilgrims on their way to Canterbury. It provides brilliant characterizations of the pilgrims, who range from the bawdy to the pious. The *Tales* embody all of the major medieval literary forms: romance, lay, beast-fable, folk tale, allegory, and sermon. Not as popular but considered of equal literary worth is *Troilus and Criseyde* (c 1385), Chaucer's retelling of the ancient myth of tragic young love. Other works are *Book of the Duchess* (1369), *Parliament of Fowls* (c 1380), and *Legend of Good Women* (c 1386).

Chekhov, Anton Pavlovich (1860–1904), Russian playwright and short story writer. Chekhov wrote an astounding number of short stories, some comic, others philosophical. Among his masterpieces are "A Daughter of Albion" (1883), "Misery" (1886), "The Duel" (1891), and "Ward No. 6" (1892). Late in his career, Chekhov introduced the play of "indirect action," for which he is most famous.

The major dramatic events occur offstage, and the drama lies in the characters' responses to them. His first play of this kind was *The Seagull* (1896), followed by *Uncle Vanya* (1897), *The Three Sisters* (1901), and *The Cherry Orchard* (1904).

Cheops: *See* Khufu.

Chiang Kai-shek (1886–1975), real name, Chiang Chung-cheng, Chinese statesman and general, leader of the Kuomintang (Nationalist Chinese) army, 1925–1949, and thereafter head of the Nationalist Chinese government on Taiwan. From 1911, Chiang fought with other revolutionary forces, under Sun Yat-sen, to overthrow the Manchu dynasty. Later he struggled against local warlords who dominated China. But when the Chinese Communists began fighting for more widespread changes, Chiang allied himself with the warlords and established in 1927 a government in Nanking, which he headed until 1949. In the 1930's he allied briefly with the Communists to fight the Japanese, but civil war began again about 1941 and continued throughout World War II, breaking into open war after the defeat of Japan. In 1949, after the Communist victory, Chiang fled to the island of Taiwan.

Chippendale, Thomas (c 1718–1779), English cabinetmaker. Chippendale's reputation was based not only on the excellent pieces made in his workshop, but on his catalog of furniture design, *The Gentleman and Cabinet Maker's Director* (1754). Borrowing motifs from French (rococo), Chinese, and Gothic styles, his designs are characterized by lightness and grace of line. They dominated 18th-century furniture-making throughout Europe and America.

Chirico, Giorgio de (1888–1978), Italian painter and theatrical designer. He originated "metaphysical" painting, art that captures the feeling of a dream in its portrayal of deserted landscapes and puzzling objects. Some of his well-known paintings are *Enigma of an Afternoon, Jewish Angel,* and *Toys of a Prince.* Chirico rejected modern and surrealist art after 1930, producing instead more technically complex and detailed work.

Chopin, Frédéric François (1810–1849), Polish-born composer and pianist, the foremost Romantic composer of music for solo piano. His charm and virtuosity made him a favorite of the Polish nobility and, later, of Parisian society. Dismayed by Russia's seizure of Poland, he settled in France in 1831. Chopin's music for piano is still popular, particularly his sonatas, études, preludes, waltzes, and concertos in F minor (1829) and E minor (1830). His mazurkas and polonaises are based on Slavic themes and rhythms.

Chou En-lai (1898–1976), Chinese Communist revolutionary who helped to establish and lead the People's Republic of China. Chou was allied first with Sun Yat-sen, leader of the revolutionary Kuomintang (Nationalist) Party, and then with Sun's successor, Chiang Kai-shek. In 1927 the Shanghai workers' uprising, directed by Chou, caused Chiang to break with the Communists and begin a purge of their leaders. Chou was condemned to death but escaped to become political commissar in Chu Teh's People's Army. There he first became associated with Mao Tse-tung. In 1936 Chou began building a united front within China to fight Japan, effecting an uneasy truce with the Kuomintang until 1941, when the civil war resumed. After the Communist victory in 1949, Chou became prime minister. He was also the foreign minister, 1949–1958, and chief architect of China's foreign policy. He is generally given credit for bringing about rapprochement with the United States.

Chrétien de Troyes (d. c 1190), French medieval court poet who wrote several early Arthurian romances. Chrétien introduced such figures as Lancelot and Parsifal, as well as the story of the Holy Grail, in *Le Chevalier de la Charrette, Le Conte du Graal,* and other poems. Little is known about Chrétien except through references in his work.

Christ, Jesus: *See* Jesus.

Christie, Dame Agatha Mary Clarissa (1891–1976), British novelist known for her constant output of ingeniously plotted murder mysteries. Her egotistic Belgian detective Hercule Poirot is known to readers throughout the world. Among Christie's over 100 works are *The Murder of Roger Ackroyd* (1926), *Murder in the Calais Coach* (1934), and *And Then There Were None* (1940); and the plays *Witness for the Prosecution* (1953; film, 1957) and *The Mousetrap,* which in 1963 became the longest running stage production in London.

Christophe, Henri (1767–1820), king of Haiti, 1811–1820. A former slave, Christophe was active in the struggle led by Dessalines to win Haitian independence from France in 1804. Civil war followed Dessalines' assassination in 1806, and Christophe emerged as ruler of the north of Haiti. In 1811 he proclaimed himself King Henri I and instituted military rule over the whole island. His harsh government eventually caused another revolt. He committed suicide in 1820.

Churchill, John: *See* Marlborough, Duke of.

Churchill, Sir Winston Leonard Spencer (1874–1965), English statesman and author. Churchill was acclaimed on his 80th birthday by the British nation as "the greatest living Briton." He served in the army in India and the Sudan and was a correspondent in the Boer War. He was elected to Parliament in 1900 as a Conservative but later joined the Liberal Party. As first lord of the admiralty, 1911–1915, he prepared the British fleet for World War I. He resigned after the failure of the Gallipoli campaign, commanded a battalion in France, then was made minister of munitions. After the war, he returned to the Conservative Party and was Chancellor of the Exchequer, 1924–1929. Churchill became prime minister in May, 1940, during the early months of World War II. His leadership for five difficult years was an immeasurable contribution to victory. The stirring speeches he made during the war are among the finest rhetoric of modern times. From 1951 to 1955, Churchill served once again as prime minister. In 1963 he was made an honorary citizen of the United States by special act of Congress. Churchill's published works include *The Second World War* (6 volumes, 1948–1953) and *A History of the English-Speaking Peoples* (4 volumes, 1956–1958). In 1953 he was awarded the Nobel Prize for Literature.

Chu Teh (1886–1976), Chinese Communist revolutionary and general, often called the father of the Chinese Red Army. He fought together with Mao Tse-tung, 1927–1949, and led the Long March of 1934–1935, when the Communists were forced into northwest China. After the revolution, Chu kept command of the People's Liberation Army until 1954. In 1959 he became chairman of the National People's Congress, China's major legislative body.

Cicero, Marcus Tullius (106–43 B.C.), Roman orator, statesman, and writer. Cicero became consul in 63 and made his reputation as a patriot with a sensational attack in the Senate on Catiline's conspiracy against the state. However, he was later charged with executing the conspirators without due process, and was forced into exile for a year. Cicero later sided with Pompey and the republicans against the growing power of Julius Caesar. After Caesar's assassination in 44, he tried to rouse the Senate and people against Antony and restore the republic, but Antony had him killed in 43. Cicero was, until the 20th century, the most studied and imitated writer in the Western world. His essays, his orations, and his letters display his elegant mastery of Latin prose.

El Cid (Campeador) (c 1043–1099), name given to Ruy (or Rodrigo) Díaz de Bivar, Spanish soldier. The twelfth-century epic poem, *Poema del Cid,* made him a national hero of Spain. Raised at the court of Ferdinand I, king of Castile and Leon, Díaz fought the

ANGUS McBEAN (LONDON) COURTESY DODD MEAD

DAME AGATHA CHRISTIE

SAMUEL CLEMENS

Moors for Ferdinand and for his son Sancho. Exiled by Sancho's successor Alfonso in 1081, he entered the service of the Moorish kings of Saragossa and campaigned against the Christians in Aragon and Catalonia. He captured Valencia in 1094 and ruled it until his death.

Cimabue, Giovanni (Cenni di Peppi or **Pepo)** (c 1240–c 1302), Italian painter of the Florentine school, often credited with the movement toward realism that marked the transition from Byzantine to Renaissance art. The fresco *Crucifixion,* in the Church of St. Francis in Assisi, is his masterpiece.

Clark, Charles Joseph (1939–), professor, statesman, Progressive Conservative prime minister of Canada, 1979–1980. Clark's ideas on the importance of private companies, energy conservation, and arms control earned him support as prime minister. However, opposition to Clark's proposed budget caused him to resign.

Clark, George Rogers (1752–1818), American frontier soldier. During the Revolution, he raised a militia to protect the Kentucky frontier. In 1778 he captured Fort Kaskaskia and Cahokia on the Mississippi River, and in 1779 he took Vincennes on the Wabash. These conquests helped the Americans gain the Northwest Territory.

Clark, William (1770–1838), U.S. soldier and explorer, a leader of the Lewis and Clark expedition. He was a brother of frontiersman George Rogers Clark. In 1803 Thomas Jefferson appointed Meriwether Lewis and William Clark to explore the West and establish a land route to the Pacific. They left in 1804 from near St. Louis, Mo. Following the Missouri River and crossing the Rockies, they reached the Pacific Ocean. They returned in 1806 with maps and descriptions of the region. Clark was made governor of the Missouri Territory, 1812–1821, and served as superintendent of Indian affairs.

Claudius I (10 B.C.–54 A.D.), full name Tiberius Claudius Drusus Nero Germanicus, Roman emperor from 41 A.D. to 54. He was proclaimed emperor after Caligula's assassination. He wrote histories, now lost, of the Etruscans and the Carthaginians. Claudius built a moderately liberal administration around freedmen, rather than the upper classes. He ordered the invasion of Britain, established new colonies, and built aqueducts, roads, and a new harbor on the Tiber. According to legend, he was poisoned by his fourth wife, Agrippina.

Clausewitz, Karl von (1780–1831), Prussian general whose theories on land warfare influenced modern war strategy. In 1818 he was made a general and director of the Prussian war college. During the next few years he wrote his major work, *Vom Kriege (On War),* in which he asserted that war is a political measure, not an end in itself.

Clay, Henry (1777–1852), U.S. statesman remembered chiefly as the "Great Compromiser" or the "Great Pacificator." Clay was congressman and senator from Kentucky, Speaker of the House, and secretary of state. He first earned his reputation as an arbitrator in 1820, by helping to formulate the Missouri Compromise: To balance Missouri's admission to the Union as a slave state, Maine would be admitted as a free state. In 1849 he became involved in contention over slavery in the new states. The Compromise of 1850 was based on Clay's "Omnibus Bill," which provided for California's entrance as a free state but reserved the right of other Southwest territories to be slave or free.

Clemenceau, Georges (1841–1929), French statesman who led France during World War I. He was elected to the Chamber of Deputies in 1876 and led the extreme left. He served in the Senate, 1902–1906, and then as premier, 1906–1909. In 1917, when wartime morale was at its lowest, he formed the famous Victory Cabinet. Known as "the Tiger" for his fierce spirit of resistance, his bold program carried France to victory. He was hailed as "Father Victory," but was later criticized for the terms of the peace treaty.

Clemens, Samuel Langhorne (1835–1910), pen name **Mark Twain**, U.S. journalist, novelist, and lecturer, America's greatest humorist and a leading U.S. literary figure. His boyhood escapades are reflected in *The Adventures of Tom Sawyer* (1876). Life in a small Missouri town also provided the setting, the backwoods vernacular, and the pre-Civil War attitudes found in the classic *Huckleberry Finn* (1884). *Life on the Mississippi* (1883) chronicles Twain's early life as a riverboat pilot. He became a journalist in Virginia City, Nev., where his day-to-day reporting gave him experience in descriptive writing, character study, and recreation of regional dialect and humor. The title tall tale of *The Celebrated Jumping Frog of Calaveras County, and Other Sketches* (1867) brought him his first national fame. Accounts of his travels in the United States and abroad appear in *Innocents Abroad* (1869), *Roughing It* (1872), and *Following the Equator* (1897). His later works, such as *Pudd'nhead Wilson* (1894), *A Connecticut Yankee in King Arthur's Court* (1889), and *The Mysterious Stranger* (published 1916), concern themselves with injustice and cruelty. Other writings condemn the treacheries of nations, as in "The United States of Lyncherdom" (1901) and "The Czar's Soliloquy" (1905). He was elected to the Hall of Fame in 1920.

Cleopatra VII (69–30 B.C.), queen of Egypt, descendant of the Macedonian general Ptolemy and famous as one of the most captivating women in history. In a conflict with her brother Ptolemy XII, her co-ruler and rival, she enlisted the aid of Julius Caesar, who restored her to her throne. She had a son, Ptolemy Caesar or Caesarion, by Caesar, and they lived in Rome from 46 until Caesar's assassination in 44. She then returned to Egypt and made Caesarion her co-ruler. Cleopatra met Mark Antony in 41 and so charmed him that he soon settled with her in Alexandria, her capital. She bore him three children and became his wife, although he was already married to Octavian's sister. Octavian declared war on Cleopatra in 32. At Actium (31), her desertion of Antony ensured Octavian's victory. When Octavian took Alexandria (30), a rumor of Cleopatra's death caused Antony to take his life. Learning that Octavian planned to exhibit her in Rome as a captive, Cleopatra killed herself by the bite of an asp, or Egyptian cobra.

Cleveland, (Stephen) Grover (1837–1908), twice President of the United States, 1885–1889 and 1893–1897. Cleveland, son of a Presbyterian minister, was born in Caldwell, N.J. He was elected mayor of Buffalo in 1881 and reformed the city government. His integrity and efficiency won him election as governor of New York in 1882, despite the enmity of party bosses. In 1884 the Democrats nominated Cleveland for President on a platform of liberal reform. After one of the most vicious campaigns in the nation's history, Cleveland, in spite of accusations of immorality, was elected over James G. Blaine. He thus became the first Democratic President since the Civil War. Cleveland married Frances Folsom in the first White House wedding, 1886. He pushed for lower tariffs in 1887 and, as a result, lost the backing of his party. Though he had a plurality of the popular vote in 1888, the electoral college chose Benjamin Harrison. Cleveland was reelected in 1892, inheriting the financial problems left by the Harrison administration. As a result, he was blamed for the Panic of 1893. He sent federal troops to guard the mails in the Pullman strike of 1894; the troops broke the strike and he was branded as antilabor. He again fell out with his party over fiscal policy and was not renominated in 1896. He retired to Princeton, N.J. At his death he was remembered as an honest reformer and servant of the public.

Clinton, DeWitt (1769–1828), U.S. public official, builder of the Erie Canal. As mayor of New York intermittently for twelve years, 1803–1815, Clinton introduced liberal reforms, including the city's first public school system. He ran for the Presidency in 1812 but was defeated by Madison. He spent the years 1811–1816 securing approval to build a canal through New York State from the Hudson River to Lake Ontario. As governor of New York, 1817–1823, he saw the project completed and was reelected in 1825.

Clive, Robert, Baron Clive of Plassey (1725–1774), British soldier and statesman who secured British control over India. As a young man he went to India as a clerk in the British East India Company, became an army officer, and led a number of campaigns, driving the French out of India. In 1757 he conquered Bengal, southern India's main province, at the Battle of Plassey. Clive's later governorship of Bengal, 1765–1767, was spent in reforming the administration. After he returned to England, he was accused of encouraging graft and corruption. After an inquiry in Parliament in 1772, he took to opium and later committed suicide.

Cobb, Tyrus Raymond (Ty) (1886–1961), U.S. baseball player nicknamed the Georgia Peach. He joined the major leagues in 1905 as an outfielder for the Detroit Tigers and stayed with the team for 22 years. When he retired in 1928, he was a member of the Philadelphia Athletics. Cobb held records for playing in 3033 games, scoring 2244 runs, making 4191 hits, and stealing 892 bases—96 in 1915. His record lifetime batting average was .367. In 1936 he became the first member of the Baseball Hall of Fame.

Cochise (c 1825–1874), Apache Indian leader, often called the Apache Napoleon, chief of the Chiricahua Apaches during their resistance to white settlement in the Southwest. In 1860, unjustly blamed for a kidnaping, he was captured by soldiers; when he escaped, six of his fellow Chiricahua were hanged. Enraged by this and by other white actions, including the selling of captured Apaches into slavery, Cochise went to war. In the next ten years he almost drove white soldiers and settlers from Arizona, but he finally surrendered in 1872.

Cockcroft, Sir John Douglas: *See* Walton, Ernest Thomas Sinton.

Cocteau, Jean (1889–1963), French writer, poet, and filmmaker. Cocteau wrote volumes of poetry and poetic novels (*Les Enfants terribles,* 1929; filmed by Cocteau, 1950). His plays include *The Infernal Machine* (1934) and *Les Parents terribles* (1938; translated as *Intimate Relations*). Cocteau also experimented with films (*Beauty and the Beast,* 1946), produced ballets, and wrote essays.

Cody, William Frederick (Buffalo Bill) (1846–1917), U.S. frontiersman and showman. Cody earned his nickname by shooting 4280 buffalo (by his own count) to feed railroad construction crews. During and after the Civil War, he established a reputation as a U.S. Army scout, partly because of the hundreds of "dime novels" that made him a popular hero. Cody turned to acting in 1872 in a play based on tales of his adventures. In 1883 he began successful tours of the United States and Europe with his Wild West show, which he ran until 1916. The cast included the sharpshooter Annie Oakley and, for a time, Chief Sitting Bull.

Cohan, George Michael (1878–1942), U.S. entertainer, the most famous American theater personality of his generation. In a long, illustrious career, Cohan wrote, starred in, and produced many Broadway shows. He is best remembered for such songs as "Yankee Doodle Dandy" and "Give My Regards to Broadway." The World War

TY COBB

NATIONAL BASEBALL LIBRARY, COOPERSTOWN, N.Y.

I song "Over There" won him a congressional medal.

Coke, Sir Edward (1552–1634), English jurist and statesman, a defender of the common law against royal power. As attorney general under Queen Elizabeth and James I, he prosecuted such famous cases as those of the earl of Essex (1601) and the members of the Gunpowder Plot (1605). When King James I tried to lessen the power of the common law, Coke, then chief justice of the Common Pleas court, ruled that the common law is supreme and a royal proclamation cannot change it. The enraged king demoted him in 1613 to chief justice of the King's Bench and in 1616 dismissed him. Coke entered Parliament in 1620 and became a spokesman for parliamentary rights. He helped draft the Petition of Right (1628), stating Parliament's position against the divine right of kings. His treatises are among the greatest in English law.

Coleridge, Samuel Taylor (1772–1834), English poet and critic, best remembered for the imaginative poems "Kubla Khan" and "The Rime of the Ancient Mariner." Coleridge's life was a constant conflict between his poetic ambitions and practical considerations—his financial problems, his unhappy domestic life, and his lifelong ill health, which led him to long periods of taking opium. He became a close friend of William Wordsworth, and in 1798 they published *Lyrical Ballads,* one of the most influential books of the Romantic period. The first edition contained his "Ancient Mariner" as well as Wordsworth's "Tintern Abbey." To escape his unhappy home life, Coleridge traveled widely. From about 1806 to 1816 he wrote little poetry, but was a journalist, dramatist, and lecturer. He settled at Highgate in 1816 and began another period of intense creativity, completing his critical study *Biographia Literaria* (1817). With this and other critical works stressing the role of the reader's imagination, Coleridge strongly influenced modern criticism.

Colette, Sidonie Gabrielle (1873–1954), French novelist. She was known for her warm, sensitive studies of human character and her understanding of nature, recalled from her childhood in Burgundy. Her earliest works, the *Claudine* series (1900–1903), were written with her first husband and published under his pen name, Willy. After their divorce, Colette gradually built her own successful writing career. Her novels include *La Vagabonde* (1910), *Chéri* (1920), *Sido* (1929), *La Chatte* (1933), and *Gigi* (1944; stage version, 1951; film, 1958).

Coltrane, John (1926–1967), U.S. jazz musician and theorist, a virtuoso of the tenor and soprano saxophone. He played in the bands of Dizzy Gillespie, Miles Davis, and Thelonius Monk, and later became identified with the sophisticated style known as "new black music." His playing was enriched by the study of African and Asian music.

Columbus, Christopher (c 1451–1506), in Spanish, Cristóbal Colón, Italian navigator and explorer, known as the discoverer of the Americas. Around 1480 Columbus formulated a plan to reach Asia by sailing west. In 1492 Ferdinand V and Isabella I of Spain accepted his proposals and financed his expedition. On August 3, 1492, he set sail with about 90 men on the caravels *Niña* and *Pinta* and his flagship *Santa María.* On October 12, having put down a mutiny en route, he reached an island in the Bahamas (probably Watlings) and named it San Salvador. Believing he had reached India, he set out for Japan and China; he visited Cuba and Hispaniola, where he built a fort of timbers from the *Santa María,* which had run aground. He returned to Spain on March 15, 1493. Columbus made three more journeys to the New World, 1493–1496, 1498–1500, and 1502–1504, financed by the Spanish sovereigns. He discovered and explored various islands in the Caribbean and along the Central and South American coasts. His brothers Diego and Bartolomé helped him establish a colony on Hispaniola in 1493, but their misrule caused the colony to revolt and Columbus was relieved of his governorship in 1500. On his fourth voyage, his ships foundered on the coast of Jamaica, and he and his men were marooned for a year before they were rescued. He died a rich man at Valladolid, Spain.

Commager, Henry Steele (1902–), U.S. historian and educator, a prolific writer on American history. His books include *The Growth of the American Republic* (with Samuel Eliot Morison, 1931–1942), *The Blue and the Gray* (1950), *The Nature and Problems of History* (1965), and *The Empire of Reason* (1977).

Commoner, Barry (1917–), U.S. biologist, a leading spokesman for the view that technology and pollution by synthetic materials are the main dangers to human ecology. Commoner researched the dangers of radioactive fallout in the mid-1950's, then studied a wide range of ecological problems. In 1966 he became director of the Center for the Biology of Natural Systems (St. Louis, Mo.). He wrote *Science and Survival* (1966), *The Closing Circle* (1971), and *The Poverty of Power* (1976).

Compton, Arthur Holly (1892–1962), U.S. physicist, known for his discovery in 1923 of the Compton effect: the change in wavelengths of x-rays when scattered by matter. His contribution, which gave further proof of quantum theory, consisted in verifying the effect's existence experimentally as well as suggesting reasons for it. He shared the 1927 Nobel Prize for Physics. During World War II, he was director of the group that produced the first self-sustained atomic chain reaction.

THE BETTMANN ARCHIVE

CONFUCIUS

Conan Doyle, Sir Arthur: *See* Doyle, Sir Arthur Conan.

Confucius (c 551–479 B.C.), in Chinese K'ung Fu-tzu ("Master K'ung"), Chinese teacher and philosopher whose ideas deeply influenced the cultures of Asia. Confucius was an official in Shantung until 517, when he began to teach, attracting many disciples. He trained them for government service, hoping they would apply his principles. He came to hold the highest position allowed to commoners, but ultimately went into exile in order to express his ideas on reforms. After his death, many of his sayings were published as the *Analects.* Central to his philosophy is the principle of *jen,* benevolent love or virtue. He also stressed proper conduct, self-improvement, and the need for rulers to be upright and righteous. Though his ideas were influential, they must be distinguished from Confucianism, the ethical philosophy that evolved from them.

Congreve, William (1670–1729), English playwright, the master of Restoration comedy. In witty dialogue, Congreve ridiculed the manners and morals of his audience. His greatest successes were *The Old Bachelor* (1693) and *Love for Love* (1695). His last play, *The Way of the World* (1700), although not well received in his day, is now considered his masterpiece and often revived.

Conrad, Joseph (1857–1924), real name Józef Tecdor Konrad Korzeniowski, Polish-born English novelist, a master of English prose style though he spoke no English till he was 20. He served in the English and French merchant marine, 1874–1886, and used his sea experience with ships and the tropics in some of his best-known works, including the novels *The Nigger of the "Narcissus"* (1897), *Lord Jim* (1900), and *Nostromo* (1904), and the short story "The Secret Sharer" (1912). His major themes were the loneliness of the human soul and man's struggle with nature, with other men, and with guilt.

Constable, John (1776–1837), English painter considered the father of modern landscape painting. Departing from the brownish landscapes of the Dutch painters, he flooded his canvas with color, producing the atmospheric effects for which his work is known. His paintings include *The Hay Wain* (1821) and *Dedham Mill* (1820).

Constantine I (Constantine the Great) (c 280–337), in full, Flavius Valerius Aurelius Constantinus, the first Roman emperor to become a Christian. Constantine adopted Christianity in 312, after defeating Maxentius, his rival for the throne of the Western empire. In 313 Constantine and Licinius, emperor of the East, issued the Edict of Milan, granting full religious toleration. Thereafter, the two emperors fell out. Licinius was defeated and executed in 325, leaving Constantine ruler of the empire. Constantine became a great patron of Christianity. In 325 he called the Council of Nicaea, at which he banned the Arian heresy. He rebuilt Byzantium, renamed it Constantinople, and settled his court there in 330.

Cook, James (Captain Cook) (1728–1779), English navigator and explorer. Between 1768 and 1779 Cook made three great voyages of exploration and discovery in the Pacific, charting New Zealand, the east coast of Australia, the Pacific coast of North America, and most of the South Pacific islands. He was killed in a fight with natives in the Hawaiian Islands during the third voyage. His example of scientific navigating and chartmaking and the health measures he devised for seamen on long voyages greatly encouraged English maritime exploration and trade. His *Journals* were edited and published after his death.

Coolidge, (John) Calvin (1872–1933), 30th President of the United States, 1923–1929, born on a farm near Plymouth, Vt. After graduating from Amherst College, 1895, he studied law and began practice in Northampton, Mass. After holding a number of local and state offices, he became governor of Massachusetts in 1919. His handling of a policemen's strike in Boston in 1919 brought him into national prominence. At the Republican convention of 1920, after losing the Presidential nomination to Warren G. Harding, Coolidge was nominated for the Vice Presidency by acclamation. Harding died on August 2, 1923, and Coolidge, visiting in Vermont, was sworn in by his father, a notary public. In office, Coolidge advocated economy in government and minimal regulation of business and industry. In 1924 Coolidge was reelected, with Charles G. Dawes as Vice President. Business and the stock market flourished, prosperity spread, and foreign affairs were negligible. In the summer of 1927, Coolidge, famous for saying as little as possible, announced, "I do not choose to run for President in 1928." He reopened his law office in Northampton and wrote occasional newspaper and magazine articles.

Cooper, Gary (1901–1961), real name Frank James Cooper, U.S. film actor. In 35 years and 88 films, Cooper came to personify the honest, simple man who becomes a hero when circumstances demand it. His movies include *The Virginian* (1929); *Mr. Deeds Goes to Town* (1936); and *Sergeant York* (1941) and *High Noon* (1952), for which he won Academy Awards. His most familiar line of dialogue was "Yup."

Cooper, James Fenimore (1789–1858), U.S. novelist, remembered for his frontier adventure stories, which made him the most popular author of his time in both America and Europe. His Leatherstocking tales, about the Pathfinder Natty Bumppo, established an American romantic tradition of brave frontiersmen and noble savages. Among them are *The Last of the Mohicans* (1826), *The Pathfinder* (1840), and *The Deerslayer* (1841). Cooper was also a social critic and moralist, and defended his idea of the American dream in such books as *The American Democrat* (1838).

Cooper, Peter (1791–1883), U.S. inventor, manufacturer, and philanthropist who, in 1859, after a varied and successful business career, founded Cooper Union in New York. It provided free public education for adults, particularly for working people. Cooper's fortune came mainly from an iron works, where he built the "Tom Thumb," the first U.S. steam locomotive, in 1830, and introduced the Bessemer process into U.S. steelmaking in 1856.

Copernicus, Nicolaus (1473–1543), in Polish, Mikolaj Kopernik, Polish astronomer who published the theory on which modern astronomy is based. He put forth his first ideas of a sun-centered universe about 1512, then proceeded to make observations of the planets. His findings were compiled in his great work *De revolutionibus orbium coelestium* (*On the Revolutions of Heavenly Bodies,* in six books, 1543). The first book sets forth the basic Copernican universe: an Earth that rotates daily and moves about the sun yearly. He explained the seasons, equinoxes, sunrise, and sunset. The other five books give theories, computations, and observations of planetary motion.

Copland, Aaron (1900–), U.S. composer, known particularly for his use of American folk song themes in serious compositions. In his early works, such as *Music for the Theater* (1925), he also showed the influence of jazz rhythms and contemporary French music. Among his works with American folk themes are the ballet scores *Billy the Kid* (1938), *Rodeo* (1942), and *Appalachian Spring* (1944), for which he won a Pulitzer Prize. Copland wrote music for films (*The Red Pony,* 1948) and the opera (*The Tender Land,* 1954). His later orchestral works include *Music for a Great City* (1967). A lecturer and critic, he published several books, including *Copland on Music* (1960).

Corbusier, Le: *See* Le Corbusier.

Corday, Charlotte (1768–1793), full name Marie Anne Charlotte Corday d'Armont, French revolutionary patriot, assassin of Jean Paul Marat. A provincial, romantic girl of noble family, she determined to become a heroine in the Girondist cause and in 1793 went to Paris. There she became convinced that Marat was an evil influence and must be killed. Pretending to have a list of the Girondists in her home town, she gained entrance to Marat's house and stabbed him while he sat in his bath. She was guillotined four days later.

Corelli, Arcangelo (1653–1713), Italian composer and violionist. His distinctive style of playing, which still influences contemporary violinists, was modeled on an imitation of vocal style. Corelli was a master of the preclassical sonata and concerto. He is credited with developing the *concerto grosso,* and his most famous works are in this form.

Corneille, Pierre (1606–1684), French dramatist, creator of the classical French tragedy. After writing a number of comedies, he produced his first great success, the tragicomedy *Le Cid,* about 1637. For nearly 40 years, Corneille produced elegant dramas, formal in style, that were popular with the French court and the audiences of Paris. They included three masterpieces of French tragedy—*Horace* (1640), *Cinna* (1641), and *Polyeucte* (1643).

Cornwallis, Charles, 1st Marquess Cornwallis (1738–1805), English general. After several victories, Cornwallis and his army of 7500 invaded Virginia in the spring of 1781. His base at Yorktown was besieged by some 16,000

French and American troops and by French ships in the York River. He surrendered his entire army to George Washington on October 18, 1781, ending British hopes for victory. The loss had little effect on his career, and he later served with distinction as governor-general of India, 1786–1793.

Coronado, Francisco Vásquez de (1510–1554), Spanish explorer who searched for treasure in the American Southwest. In 1540 Coronado was sent by the viceroy of Mexico to capture the rumored riches of Cíbola near what is now Zuñi, N.M. Coronado and his men conquered the Zuñi pueblos, but found no treasure. The expedition then split up. Some went to southern California; others discovered the Grand Canyon. Coronado and his group moved east and, in search of even richer lands called Gran Quivira, crossed Texas and Oklahoma into central Kansas. Again disappointed in his search for gold, Coronado returned to Mexico in 1542.

Corot, Jean Baptiste Camille (1796–1875), French classical landscape painter. He traveled widely and, like other artists of his day, made sketches and studies out of doors, later transferring these scenes to large canvases in his studio. Today these spontaneous sketches are considered his finest work. Of Corot's finished paintings, only his earlier oils have the firm structure and tranquil, dignified mood of *La Trinité des monts* (1826–1828) and *La Rochelle* (1851). His popular landscapes of the period 1850–1870 are done in gray, misty colors.

Correggio, Antonio Allegri da (c 1494–1534), a leading Italian Renaissance painter. His techniques for decorating domes—using foreshortening and perspective—were original and influential. Correggio lived quietly and worked mostly in Parma. There he created magnificent frescoes on the cupola of the Church of San Giovanni (*Ascension of Christ,* 1521–1524) and in the dome of the Parma cathedral *(Assumption of the Virgin),* where he worked from 1522 to 1530. His easel paintings include *Jupiter and Antiope* (1521–1522) and *Danae* (1532).

Cortés, Hernán (1485–1547), Spanish explorer and conqueror of Mexico. In 1519 Cortés and a large force sent by the governor of Cuba explored the Yucatán peninsula and other parts of the coast of Mexico. The Spaniards entered the wealthy Aztec capital of Tenochtitlán (later Mexico City) and were cordially received by the ruler, Montezuma, who thought Cortés the incarnation of a god. Montezuma became a puppet ruler. In 1520, while Cortés and many of his men were away, the Aztecs revolted. Montezuma was killed and the Spaniards were besieged. Cortés returned, and during the "Sad Night" the Spaniards managed to escape, but lost many men and much treasure. Cortés then reorganized his forces, recruiting many Indian allies, and recaptured the city in 1521. In 1523 Cortés was made governor of Mexico, but while he was away on a military campaign in Honduras, 1524–1526, his political enemies usurped his position. However, he did retain his title and a large estate in the valley of Oaxaca.

Coulomb, Charles Augustin de (1736–1806), French physicist who pioneered in research on electricity. In addition to doing important original work in the field of electricity and magnetism, he invented in 1777 the torsion balance, which he used to verify his theories about electric charges, later expressed in Coulomb's law. The coulomb, a unit of electrical charge, was named for him.

Couperin, François (1668–1733), French composer. He was organist of the Church of St. Gervais, Paris, from 1685 until his death. An admirer of Corelli and Lully, Couperin united the Italian and French musical styles in his famous suites for harpsichord, *Ordres* (1713, 1717, 1722, 1730), notable for their melodic beauty and clarity.

Cousteau, Jacques-Yves (1910–), French oceanographer. Cousteau invented the aqualung in 1943 and first became known for his scientific and archaeological studies underwater, reported in such books as *The Silent World* (1953) and *The Living Sea* (1963). He made many film and TV documentaries, including the award-winning film *The Silent World* (1956) and *World Without Sun* (1966). He made yearly expeditions on his ship *Calypso* and carried on experiments in which divers lived underwater for long periods of time.

METROMEDIA PRODUCERS CORP.
JACQUES-YVES COUSTEAU

Coverdale, Miles (c 1488–1569), English clergyman who translated the first printed English Bible. Coverdale was originally an Augustinian monk, but later converted to Lutheran doctrines. His translation was first published in Cologne in 1535. Coverdale's edition of the Great Bible (1539) was widely read in England. Its psalter was included in the Book of Common Prayer (1549). He became bishop of Exeter in 1551 but was later removed from office and imprisoned by Mary I. He was released by request of his admirer, King Christian III of Denmark, and lived abroad until after Elizabeth I's accession in 1558.

Coward, Sir Noel Pierce (1899–1973), British playwright, composer, and actor. In the 1920's he became known as the most versatile man in British and American theater. He wrote light, witty plays and revues, acted in many

HERNAN CORTES

THE BETTMANN ARCHIVE

of them, and produced some. He also produced many films. His stage successes include *Hay Fever* (1925), *Private Lives* (1930), *Design for Living* (1932), and *Blithe Spirit* (1941). His numerous songs include "Mad Dogs and Englishmen."

Cranach, Lucas (1472–1553), German painter of the Renaissance whose landscapes influenced the Danube school of painters. Cranach's earlier works are considered his finest: *Rest on the Flight into Egypt* (1504) is noted for its original combination of figure and landscape. Cranach painted many classical themes, often with humor (*Nymph of the Spring,* 1537, and *Venus,* 1532).

Crane, Harold (Hart) (1899–1932), U.S. poet. He is best known for his mystical epic poem *The Bridge* (1930), in which he tried to capture the essence of the American spirit in a series of poems with the Brooklyn Bridge as their central image. Crane was a follower of both Whitman and Rimbaud. His other work is a volume of poems, *White Buildings* (1926). After leading an increasingly dissolute life, he drowned himself by jumping off a ship.

Crane, Stephen (1871–1900), U.S. author who became famous at the age of 23 with the publication of *The Red Badge of Courage* (1895), a starkly realistic novel about a Civil War soldier. On the strength of this book, Crane, who had never seen a battle, was sought by newspapers as a war correspondent. He covered wars in Cuba and Greece before dying of tuberculosis. Crane also wrote *Black Riders* (1895), a book of intense poems; and *The Open Boat and Other Tales of Adventure* (1898).

Cranmer, Thomas (1489–1556), English clergyman who became the first archbishop of Canterbury in the Church of England. He worked for the church's establishment under the king's sovereignty. A university theologian, Cranmer first came to favor in 1529 by suggesting ways in which Henry VIII might obtain a divorce from Catherine of Aragon. He remained in the king's favor and was made archbishop of Canterbury in 1533. Cranmer immediately annulled Henry's first marriage, making his marriage with Anne Boleyn valid. When Queen Mary, a Catholic, came to the throne in 1553, Cranmer was accused of treason and heresy. He publicly recanted his Protestantism, but, when sent to be burned at the stake, reaffirmed his Protestant beliefs.

Crazy Horse (c 1844–1877), in Indian, Tashunca-Uitco, Oglala Sioux chief, military leader during the Sioux wars of 1875–1877, which included the famous Battle of the Little Bighorn. In 1874 gold was discovered in South Dakota's Black Hills, which had been granted to the Sioux nation in 1868. Miners and soldiers filled the region, and the government ordered the Sioux onto reservations and sent out the cavalry to enforce the order. In June, 1876, Crazy Horse and the Sioux wiped out General Custer and his cavalry regiment at the Little Bighorn. Crazy Horse surrendered in 1877 and was killed while a prisoner in an Army stockade, perhaps deliberately, perhaps while attempting to escape.

Crick, Francis Harry (1916–), English molecular biologist. Early in the 1950's, he and James D. Watson began to work toward finding the structural chemistry of DNA (deoxyribonucleic acid), the cell material that carries genetic information. In 1953, using data from research done by Maurice H.F. Wilkins, Crick and Watson suggested a model of the DNA molecule's structure —a double helix, or two coiled helical chains. This finding has been called the most important development in biology of the 20th century, and for it Crick, Watson, and Wilkins shared the 1962 Nobel Prize in Physiology and Medicine.

Croce, Benedetto (1866–1952), Italian philosopher, critic, and political leader, known for his ideas on aesthetics and the philosophy of history. Croce published many of his essays in the journal *La Critica,* which he founded in 1903 and published for more than 40 years as a forum for important European literary works. His philosophy appears in the four-volume *Filosofia dello spirito* (*Philosophy of the Spirit,* begun in 1902). A dedicated antifascist, Croce led the Italian intellectuals' resistance to Mussolini in the 1920's, remaining active in liberal politics till the late 1940's.

Crockett, David (Davy) (1786–1836), U.S. frontiersman and politician. Crockett served under Andrew Jackson in the Creek Indian War of 1813–1814. After two terms in the Tennessee legislature, he was elected to Congress in 1827, after a campaign in which he passed out free liquor during his opponent's speeches. At first a Jacksonian, he later joined the Whigs, who built up his legend as a boastful, outspoken frontier hero. Failing to win reelection for a fourth term in 1835, he went to Texas, where he died at the siege of the Alamo.

Croesus (r. 560–546 B.C.), the last king of Lydia in Asia Minor, a monarch of legendary wealth. Having been told by an oracle that he would destroy a great empire, he attacked the Persians under Cyrus the Great and was crushed—thus destroying his own empire.

Cromwell, Oliver (1599–1658), leader of the Puritans during the English Civil War and, as lord protector, sole ruler of

THE BETTMANN ARCHIVE

DAVY CROCKETT

England from 1653 to 1658. Cromwell, a gentleman farmer, did not become well known politically until Parliament, dissolved by King Charles I in 1629, was recalled in 1640. An intensely pious Calvinist, he then became the leading spokesman for the powerful Puritan faction in Parliament's struggles with the king. When war between Parliament and the king seemed inevitable, Cromwell organized and commanded a strong cavalry troop in the parliamentary army. Without any military experience, he soon proved to be a brilliant commander. He made the New Model Army of zealous Puritans into an efficient war machine, and it remained the base of his power. The "Roundheads" decisively defeated the king's forces at Marston Moor (1644) and Naseby (1645). The Independents, the extreme wing of the army under Cromwell, struggled for power with the more moderate parliamentary members who wished to negotiate with the king. At last Cromwell seized the king and sent soldiers to drive out members of Parliament who opposed him. With the consent of the few members remaining—the "Rump" Parliament—the king was tried and beheaded in 1649. For several years Cromwell, head of the ruling "council of state," and his army fought against Royalist uprisings in Scotland and England, and particularly in Ireland, where he ordered a brutal massacre. In 1653, having established peace, he decided that to restore order, strong rule was needed. He dissolved Parliament and became lord protector of the Commonwealth—a virtual dictator, remembered as tyrannical and intolerant, though efficient and zealous for reform. He died with the mood of England set for a return to monarchy.

Cromwell, Thomas (c 1485–1540), English statesman, adviser to Henry VIII and his principal agent in the reformation of the English church and the dissolution of the monasteries. Cromwell entered the service of Cardinal Wolsey about 1520, handling his business affairs. When Wolsey fell from favor in 1529, Cromwell gradually gained the king's confidence. An excellent administrator, he carried out plans to establish the English church under the king's rule. In 1539–1540 Cromwell arranged Henry's marriage with Anne of Cleves, a German Lutheran princess, but the move was a failure. Cromwell became earl of Essex in April, 1540, but quickly fell into disfavor, was convicted of treason, and executed that July.

Crookes, Sir William (1832–1919), English chemist and physicist. In 1861 he discovered the element thallium and, while studying its behavior in a vacuum, was led to invent the radiometer, which measures radiant energy. In 1878 he invented an improved vacuum tube, called the Crookes or cathode-ray tube.

Cruikshank, George (1792–1878), English artist and caricaturist, famed for his illustrations and political cartoons. His skillful etchings illustrated works by Dickens, Scott, and other famous authors of the time. He also did a series of well-known antialcohol pictures, including *The Drunkard's Children* (1848).

Cullen, Countee (1903–1946), U.S. poet, one of the first black Americans to win recognition as a major poet. His first volume, *Color* (1925), made his reputation. His other books include *Copper Sun* (1927), *Black Christ* (1934), a translation of Euripides' *Medea* (1935), and *On These I Stand* (1947).

Cummings, Edward Estlin (1894–1962), who signed his work "e e cummings," U.S. poet and artist. During World War I, Cummings served as an ambulance attendant in France, where he was mistakenly imprisoned as a spy. His experiences in the internment camp are recorded in his first book, *The Enormous Room* (1922). Cummings also made a name as a painter and a playwright (*him,* 1927), but he is best known for his poetry, which includes both acid satire and lyrical love poems. His many volumes of collected poetry include *Poems 1923–1954* (1954), *95 Poems* (1958), and *73 Poems* (1963), published posthumously.

Curie, Marie Sklodowska (1867–1934), Polish-born French physicist, discoverer of radium and twice winner of the Nobel Prize, in 1903 for physics and in 1911 for chemistry. She was assisted in her radium research by her husband, **Pierre Curie** (1859–1906). The Curies, working with Becquerel's findings on radioactivity, announced in 1898 their discovery of two new elements, polonium and radium. Marie Curie served as head of the physics laboratory at the Sorbonne and in 1906, succeeded her husband as professor of physics there. She published *Traité de radioactivité* in 1910. Her daughter Irène also became a scientist and Nobel Prize winner (*see* Joliot-Curie, Irene).

Curtiss, Glenn Hammond (1878–1930), U.S. pioneer aviator and inventor. Beginning in 1908 Curtiss won many U.S. and international flying competitions, often in planes of his own design. In 1911 he invented a flying boat; a later model, built for the Navy, made the first transatlantic crossing in 1919.

Custer, George Armstrong (1839–1876), U.S. Army officer, remembered chiefly for his disastrous and unexpected defeat by the Sioux Indians at Little Bighorn (June 25, 1876). After the Civil War, Custer led an expedition into the Black Hills of South Dakota—territory granted to the Sioux by treaty—and discovered gold. During the ensuing Sioux wars, he led the Seventh Cavalry. Either an error of judgment or egotism caused him to lead his outnumbered troops into the fatal Battle of the Little Bighorn.

Cuvier, Georges Léopold Chrétien Frédéric Dagobert, Baron (1769–1832), French naturalist, founder of the sciences of comparative anatomy and paleontology. Cuvier's method of classifying animals from fossil remains was based on relationships between various parts of the body. He believed that animal species do not change over time, but die out because of catastrophes.

Cyrano de Bergerac, Savinien (1619–1655), French soldier and author. He entered the army at the age of 17 but retired in 1640 because of war wounds. He then took up philosophy and writing. His fantastic travelogs, *Les États et empires de la Lune* and *Les États et empires du Soleil* (translated as *Voyages to the Moon and Sun*), were published posthumously in 1657 and 1662. The romantic verse play *Cyrano de Bergerac* (1897) by Edmond Rostand uses Cyrano's name but has little factual basis.

Cyrus the Great (c 600–530 B.C.), founder of the Persian empire. Cyrus, a vassal of the Median king Astyages, rebelled against his overlord in 553 and united the Persian tribes. In 550 he defeated Astyages, gaining the realm of the Medes and Persians. After conquering Croesus of Lydia and subduing the rest of western Asia, Cyrus captured the city of Babylon in 539. He is mentioned in the Old Testament for freeing the Jews from Babylonian captivity.

D

Dali, Salvador (1904–1989), Spanish artist and illustrator, one of the most colorful personalities in 20th-century art. Dali joined the surrealists in the late 1920's and soon became known for fantastic scenes of carefully detailed but distorted reality. His most famous painting is *The Persistence of Memory* (1931), showing limp watches in a dream landscape. With filmmaker Luis Buñuel, he produced the surrealist film *Un Chien Andalou;* he also designed

MARIE CURIE

THE BETTMANN ARCHIVE

for the ballet. His religious works include *Christ on the Cross* and illustrations for the Bible. He wrote several books, including *Diary of a Genius* (1965).

Dalton, John (1766–1844), English chemist and physicist who first propounded the modern atomic theory. A versatile scientist, Dalton first studied weather; he published *Meteorological Observations and Essays,* one of the earliest works on meteorology, in 1793. In 1794 he became the first to describe colorblindness, with which he was afflicted; it has since been called Daltonism. Dalton's interest in the properties of gases, a popular field of study for chemists at the time, resulted in his law of partial pressures (Dalton's law, 1801) and his law of multiple proportions (1803). From the latter he deduced the atomic theory; the idea and the name "atom" he took from Democritus, but his was a chemical rather than a philosophical theory. He also drew up a table of atomic weights for known elements (1808).

Dana, James Dwight (1813–1895), U.S. geologist and mineralogist. Several of his books—notably the *Manual of Mineralogy* (1848) and *Manual of Geology* (1862)—became classic texts and were still being used more than a hundred years later. Dana was geologist for the Wilkes expedition to Antarctica, 1838–1842. He taught natural history and geology at Yale, 1849–1892.

D'Annunzio, Gabriele (1863–1938), Italian poet, dramatist, and political figure, widely known for a personal life as colorful and intense as his writing. An ardent nationalist, he helped persuade Italy to enter World War I on the side of the Allies. A national hero after the war, he led a short-lived but popular occupation of Fiume (in present Yugoslavia), which he claimed for Italy. D'Annunzio wrote about his celebrated love affair with actress Eleonora Duse in his novel *Flame of Life* (1900). Some of his finest works are his first poems, *Primo vere* (1880) and *Canto nuovo* (1882), the novel *The Child of Pleasure* (1889), and the drama *The Daughter of Jorio* (1907).

Dante Alighieri (1265–1321), Italian poet. Dante is considered to be one of the world's greatest poets, chiefly because of his *Divine Comedy.* His first major poem was *Vita Nuova* (*New Life,* written around 1293). It told of his idealized love for Beatrice Portinari, with whom he had first fallen in love when he was nine years old and she eight. She died in 1290 but remained the inspiration of his life; she later became a symbol of human perfection in the *Divine Comedy.* Dante became a leading figure in Florentine politics but was exiled when a rival party came to power in 1301. For the rest of his life he lived and wrote in various cities throughout Italy. The *Divine Comedy,* begun about 1307, is an allegorical poem describing Dante's pilgrimage through Hell (the *Inferno*), Purgatory (the *Purgatorio*), and Paradise (the *Paradiso*). His other works include treatises on philosophy, politics, and the use of the Italian vernacular as a literary language.

UPI/BETTMANN NEWSPHOTOS

SALVADOR DALI

THE BETTMANN ARCHIVE

JAMES DEAN

Danton, Georges Jacques (1759–1794), French revolutionary leader. Danton, a Paris lawyer, came to power early in the French Revolution and gained immense popularity and influence. He became minister of justice in the government of 1792, and is often blamed for the September massacres. When the Committee of Public Safety was formed in 1793, he was its leading member, but after three months he was supplanted by Robespierre and the Reign of Terror. He opposed the terror, and the radical Jacobins countered with charges of graft. They had him guillotined.

Darius I (Darius the Great) (c 558–486 B.C.), king of Persia, 521–486, during whose reign the Greco-Persian wars began. Darius reorganized the administration of the empire, improved methods of taxation, built roads, and introduced a postal system. In 499 the Ionian Greek cities of Asia rebelled against the Persian empire. They received aid from Athens, and Darius sent an expedition to punish Athens in 490. His army was caught unawares and routed at the Battle of Marathon (490). Darius died while planning a new invasion of Greece.

Darrow, Clarence Seward (1857–1938), U.S. lawyer, defense counsel in many of the most famous trials in U.S. courtroom history. He practiced law in Ohio and Illinois and in 1894 became counsel for the Chicago and North Western Railway. When the railway union went on strike during the 1895 Pullman strike, Darrow resigned to defend union president Eugene Debs. He went on to counsel labor in other important cases, winning, in 1898, a union's right to strike without reprisals. In the Leopold-Loeb murder case, 1924, Darrow's clients were convicted, but in an unprecedented defense, he saved their lives by pleading society's responsibility for the creation of individual criminals. In the 1925 Scopes trial he challenged a law prohibiting the teaching of evolution.

Darwin, Charles Robert (1809–1882), British naturalist and author, originator of the theory of biological evolution. From 1831 to 1836 he sailed as a naturalist on H.M.S. *Beagle,* which explored South American coasts, the Galápagos Islands, Tahiti, and Australia. His research led to *The Structure and Distribution of Coral Reefs* (1842), a theory of reef formation still generally accepted. He also carefully observed the animals and birds of these lands and in 1837 began a notebook on "Transmutation of Species," recording differences between island and mainland forms and the breeds of domestic animals. The *Beagle* observations and his later research eventually appeared in *On the Origin of Species by Means of Natural Selection, or the Preservation of Favoured Races in the Struggle for Life* (1859). Its major thesis is that plant and animal species continue to exist according to how well they adapt to the environment. Those species that fail to adapt die out, leaving the "fittest" to survive. Though Darwin's theories, and his later works supporting them, caused a storm of controversy, he took no part in the debates, but lived quietly, studying and writing.

Daudet, Alphonse (1840–1897), a French novelist, short story writer, and dramatist. He lived mostly in the south of France, about which he wrote in *Tartarin de Tarascon* (1872), his best-known novel, and in *Lettres de mon moulin* (1869), a collection of tales and sketches first published in a Paris journal. His emotions about the Franco-Prussian War are reflected in the stories in *Contes du lundi* (1873), which include his most famous work, *"La derniere classe"* ("The Last Class").

Daumier, Honoré (1808–1879), a French caricaturist, lithographer, and painter, famous for his political and social satires. In 1832 he was imprisoned for depicting King Louis Philippe as Gargantua swallowing bags of gold extorted from the people. For the journals *La Caricature* and *Le Charivari,* he produced more than 4000 cartoons and became one of the most notable 19th-century caricaturists. Daumier's paintings done after 1848 were traditional and realistic. Almost unknown in his lifetime, they came to be considered works of genius.

David, Jacques Louis (1748–1825), French painter of the French Revolution and the Napoleonic era, founder of the modern French school of classicism. Through his painting, David encouraged patriotism in the heroic Roman style (*Oath of the Horatii,* 1784–1785). When the revolution finally broke out in 1789, he became a leading political figure and used his art to glorify the cause, as in the *Death of Marat* (1793), his tribute to a murdered hero. David became court painter to Napoleon, and went into exile when the monarchy was restored.

Davis, Jefferson (1808–1889), president of the Confederate States of America. Davis, a West Pointer, distinguished himself in the Mexican War, 1846–1847. Returning to Mississippi in 1847, he became a U.S. senator. As secretary of war under Franklin Pierce, 1853–1857, he expanded and improved the Army. In 1857 he returned to the Senate, where he worked to preserve both slavery and the Union. Even in 1861, after his home state seceded, he made a final speech in the Senate, urging peace. Davis was immediately chosen president of the Confederacy. Throughout the war Davis kept close control of military strategy and held the Confederacy together by his devotion to principle and strength of will. Davis was captured in 1865, one month after Lee's surrender at Appomattox. He was imprisoned in chains and charged with treason, but he was released two years later and the charges were dropped. Davis retired to his home, "Beauvoir," in Mississippi. True to his principles, he refused amnesty and never regained U.S. citizenship.

Davy, Sir Humphry (1778–1829), English experimental chemist. He taught chemistry at the Royal Institute in London, 1802–1812, and was president of the Royal Society, 1820–1827. He first applied the technique of electrolysis to chemicals, thereby discovering sodium, potassium, and other elements. He also showed that chlorine is an element. In 1815 he invented the Davy safety lamp, long used to protect miners from explosions.

Dayan, Moshe (1915–1981), chief strategist of Israel's wars with the Arab states. Appointed chief of staff in 1953, Dayan launched the Israeli attack that took the Sinai Peninsula and the Gaza Strip in 1956. In 1967, while directing the Six-Day War in which Israel took Jerusalem and the Suez, Dayan was made minister of defense. He left the cabinet in 1974, but rejoined it in 1977 as minister of foreign affairs under Premier Menachem Begin.

Dean, James (1931–1955), real name James Byron, U.S. actor. Dean made only a few movies before his death in an automobile crash, but the roles he played made him a powerful cult symbol of misunderstood youth. His films were *East of Eden* (1954), *Rebel Without a Cause* (1955), and *Giant* (1955).

De Bakey, Michael Ellis (1908–), U.S. surgeon who made advances in cardiovascular surgery. He originated operations for replacing blood vessels with synthetic tubing and invented the De Bakey heart pump, which relieves a weak heart of its main pumping effort during an operation. He was one of the first U.S. surgeons to do work with heart transplants.

Debs, Eugene Victor (1855–1926), U.S. labor leader and founder of the Socialist Party of America. A critic of craft unions, he helped form the American Railway Union in 1893 and was its first president. Debs's union supported the strike against the Pullman Car Company in 1894 by refusing to move Pullman cars. Unmoved by injunctions, federal troops, and local violence, Debs went to jail for his action. In jail he converted to socialism, establishing the Socialist Party of America in 1898. He ran for President in every election from 1900 to 1912. In 1920 he ran again and polled 920,000 votes, although in prison at the time for speaking against the 1918 Espionage Act. His prison experiences are described in *Walls and Bars* (1927).

Debussy, (Achille) Claude (1862–1918), French composer whose music reflects the direct influence of impressionist painting and symbolist poetry. A poem by the symbolist Mallarmé inspired his *Prelude to the Afternoon of a Faun* (*Prélude á l'après-midi d'un faune,* 1894). A play by Maeterlinck was the basis for his opera *Pelléas et Mélisande* (1902), a psychological music-drama that caused an uproar in Paris. Debussy's innovations in harmony and rhythm seemed revolutionary to his audiences, and he spent most of his life in poverty. His later works include the tone poem *La Mer* (1905), *Images* (1912), and *Jeux* (1913).

Decatur, Stephen (1779–1820), U.S. naval officer. He became famous for his exploits against the pirates of the Barbary Coast of North Africa (Algiers, Tunis, and Tripoli), who were seizing U.S. ships and sailors. In 1804 Decatur, commanding a schooner, took a small raiding party into the harbor of Tripoli and burned a captured ship, helping to end the war between the United States and the Barbary states. Decatur served in the War of 1812 and then returned to the Mediterranean in 1815 to enforce the peace treaties and stop the pirate raids.

Defoe, Daniel (1660–1731), English writer and satirist, author of *Robinson Crusoe.* Defoe was at first a merchant; he traveled extensively and was once captured by Algerian pirates. From 1683 on he became increasingly involved in politics, writing many critical and satirical pamphlets and becoming a confidant of King William III. In 1703 he was fined and pilloried for his pamphlet *The Shortest Way with the Dissenters,* in which he ridiculed church bigotry. He was a popular favorite, however, and London turned out to decorate his pillory and drink his health as he stood his punishment. Defoe spent the rest of his life writing and avoiding his creditors. *Robinson Crusoe* was published in 1719; his other works include *A Journal of the Plague Year* (1722) and the novel *Moll Flanders* (1722).

De Forest, Lee (1873–1961), U.S. inventor. For his invention in 1906 of the audion, the first radio tube, and of other electronic equipment, De Forest is often called the father of the radio. He patented more than 300 inventions, including the "phonofilm," an early development in talking motion pictures. He also pioneered in radio broadcasting, transmitting the voice of Caruso from the Metropolitan Opera in 1910 and giving the first news broadcast in 1916.

Degas, (Hilaire Germain) Edgar (1834–1917), French painter famous for his ability to capture the human figure in spontaneous motion. With an income provided by his wealthy family, Degas maintained a studio in Montmartre, Paris. In 1862 he became associated with the impressionists and adopted their style of painting contemporary scenes in bright colors. Degas' most typical subjects, which he did in oil and pastel, are scenes of horse racing (*At the Race Course,* 1869–1872), the theater and ballet (*The Dancing Class,* 1876), Parisian cafés (*Absinthe,* 1876), and graceful women bathing and dressing (*After the Bath,* 1885).

De Gaulle, Charles André Joseph Marie (1890–1970), French general, president of France from 1959 to 1969. De Gaulle, a career army officer, fought in World War I until wounded and captured at Verdun in 1916. After the war he taught military history, served as aide to Marshal Pétain, and wrote books advocating a mechanized professional army for defense instead of the Maginot Line. When the French government surrendered to the Germans in 1940, De Gaulle went to London. There he organized the Free French forces and became the symbol of French resistance. In 1944 he returned to France and entered liberated Paris in triumph. He led the provisional government of the new Fourth Republic and resigned in 1946 before the new constitution was adopted. Disappointed with the new government, De Gaulle formed a nationalist party that lasted until 1953. He then retired from public life. As a result of the 1958 Algerian crisis, he returned to become head of state, ushering in the Fifth Republic. Under him, France's former colonies, including Algeria, became independent; France withdrew from NATO and became an important independent force in world politics; and the economy became stable and prosperous. He retired in 1969.

De Kooning, Willem (1904–), Dutch-born U.S. artist, a leading figure in postwar abstract expressionism. He settled in the United States in 1926. De Kooning's paintings are marked by bold brush strokes and bright splashes of color. His best-known works are a series of paintings done in the 1950's on the theme of "Woman"; they were somewhat representational.

Delacroix, (Ferdinand Victor) Eugène (1798–1863), French painter who is distinguished by his portrayal of exotic scenes, rich fabrics, and violent action. Delacroix was trained in the neoclassic manner of David, but he soon adopted the turbulence, brilliant color, and emotion of Romantic art. He was politically liberal, and he sympathized with the oppressed and championed freedom (*Liberty Leading the People,* 1830). His travels in Spain and Morocco in 1832 brought his work an oriental flavor (*Oriental Lion Hunt,* 1834).

Delbrück, Max (1906–1981), German-born U.S. biologist, pioneer in the biochemistry of genetics. In the 1950's he discovered that bacteriophages (bacterial viruses) reproduce by mating and evolve by genetic mutation. He then developed a theory of the genetic processes in these viruses. He shared in the 1969 Nobel Prize in Physiology and Medicine.

Delius, Frederick (1862–1934), British composer whose distinctive lyrical music was significant in the 20th-century revival of English music. In 1884 he moved to Florida as an orange grower, writing the *Florida Suite.* He settled in Germany to study music, writing *Appalachia* (1902), *Sea Drift* (1903), several operas, and other works all heard first in Germany. He is best known for short orchestral pieces like *Brigg Fair* (1907) and *On Hearing the First Cuckoo in Spring* (1912).

Della Robbia: *See* Robbia, Luca della.

De Mille, Agnes George (1905–), U.S. dancer and choreographer, famous for her innovative use of American folk material and idioms. For the newly formed American Ballet Theater, she choreographed *Rodeo* (1942), which won her wide recognition. *Fall River Legend* (1948) also became a classic in modern ballet. Her work for the stage and films introduced dance to a larger audience, through such musicals as *Oklahoma!* (1943) and *Brigadoon* (1947). Her autobiography, *Dance to the Piper,* appeared in 1951.

De Mille, Cecil Blount (1881–1959), U.S. film producer and director, the creator of large-scale historical and religious films with spectacular settings, lavish costumes, and casts of thousands. His first film, *The Squaw Man* (1913), was produced in collaboration with Samuel Goldwyn and Jesse L. Lasky. De Mille's first religious epics were *The Ten Commandments* (1923) and *The King of Kings* (1927). In 1932 he produced his first talking picture, *The Sign of the Cross.* Later, De Mille's colorful circus picture, *The Greatest Show on Earth,* won an Academy Award as the best picture of 1953. His 70th film was a remake of *The Ten Commandments* (1956).

Democritus (c 460–c 370 B.C.), Greek philosopher. Little is known about his life; according to tradition, he was rich enough to travel and study in Egypt and other eastern countries. He developed Leucippus' theory that matter is composed of minute, indivisible particles called atoms. Democritus further held that all phenomena, even the soul, were material, though the atoms of the soul were of a special kind—round, smooth, and mobile, like those of fire. His explanations of the world in terms of matter and motion anticipated modern scientific thinking. He also developed a moral system based on moderation.

Demosthenes (c 384–322 B.C.), Athenian statesman and the greatest of ancient Greek orators. According to legend, Demosthenes taught himself to speak clearly by standing by the sea and shouting over the waves with pebbles in his mouth. Between 351 and 341, he delivered a series of *Philippics,* speeches warning the Athenians against the coming conquest by Philip of Macedon. On the death of Philip's son Alexander the Great (323), Demosthenes promoted a Greek uprising against Macedon; it failed, and he took poison. Demosthenes' speeches were admired and imitated by all later ancient orators. His well-known speech *On the Crown* (330) is a defense of his political career.

Dempsey, Jack (1895–1983), U.S. heavyweight fighter. Born William Harrison Dempsey in Manassa, Colo., he was nicknamed the Manassa Mauler. He won the world heavyweight championship in 1919 by defeating Jess Willard in a fierce bout. In the next seven years he defended his title successfully, notably in 1923 against Luis Firpo. He lost the title to Gene Tunney in 1926. Failing to win it back in a controversial rematch, Dempsey retired in 1927.

Deng Xiaoping (Teng Hsiao-p'ing) (1904–), political leader of the People's Republic of China (1977–1987). Deng was born in Szechwan Province and came from a family of landlords. At 16 he left China and studied in France until 1926, when he returned to China and became active in the Communist movement. He participated in the Long March (1934–1935), in which the Red Army, in its struggle with the Chiang Kai-shek government, fought its way from the southeastern to the northwestern part of the country. Deng rose rapidly in the Communist Party and the government, becoming general secretary of the party in 1956. However, he was purged from power in 1967 during the Cultural Revolution. Restored to authority in 1973, he again lost favor following the death of Chou En-lai in 1976, but he made another comeback after Mao Tse-tung died in 1976. Since 1977 Deng has been the most powerful figure in the government and the party; he was named leader of the Central Advisory Commission in 1982. He is known as a pragmatist who favors policies leading to economic growth and modernization.

Descartes, René (1596–1650), French philosopher and mathematician who devised analytic geometry and founded modern philosophy. In 1619 he had a dream in which he realized that all science could be expressed with mathematics. He moved to Holland in 1629 and spent the next 20 years developing the implications of his dream. In 1637 he published his first work, the *Discourse on Method,* containing his discovery of the Cartesian coordinate system for expressing algebraic equations by means of geometry. In this and his subsequent works, *Meditations* (1641) and *Principles of Philosophy* (1644), he expounded a philosophy using critical doubt as a method and making man's thoughts the point of origin for philosophical argument. These two ideas greatly influenced all later philosophers. Descartes doubted everything in order to test its validity; he based his proof on his famous axiom *"cogito, ergo sum"* ("I think; therefore, I exist"), and established a distinction between mind and matter (known as Cartesian dualism). His work enabled scientists of the next centuries, using the calculus made possible by his analytic geometry, to discover the laws of physics. In 1649 Descartes was persuaded to come to Sweden to tutor Queen Christina. His delicate health was strained by her insistence that he tutor her at five o'clock on winter mornings; within four months he was dead.

De Sica, Vittorio (1901–1974), Italian film director and actor whose *Shoeshine* (1946) and *The Bicycle Thief* (1948) are masterpieces of the realist genre and landmarks in the recovery of postwar Italian cinema. Together with *Miracle in Milan* (1950) and *Umberto D* (1951), they exemplify de Sica's use of film as a compassionate commentary on social issues. His later work includes *Two Women* (1960), *The Condemned of Altona* (1963), and *The Garden of the Finzi Continis* (1971).

De Soto, Hernando (c 1500–1542), Spanish explorer, the first to explore the southeastern part of the United States. In 1538 he led an expedition to Cuba, then to Florida. He and his soldiers, more than 500 men, explored as far north as the Carolinas. They then moved westward, discovering the Mississippi River in 1541 and reaching what is now Oklahoma and Texas. De Soto died in 1542, and his men buried him in the Mississippi.

De Valera, Eamon (1882–1975), Irish statesman. He was frequently imprisoned for his revolutionary activities, beginning with the 1916 Easter Rebellion. In 1921 he became leader of the *dáil éirann* (Irish legislature), but resigned in opposition to the treaty demanding an oath of allegiance to Britain. He then formed *Fianna Fáil,* a radical group outside the assembly. In 1927 he finally brought his party into the *dáil* to be a strong opposition force. De Valera was head of state from 1932, serving as prime minister of an independent Eire, 1937–1948, 1951–1954, and 1957–1959. He served as president from 1959 until 1973.

Devereux, Robert: *See* Essex, 2nd Earl of.

De Vries, Hugo (1848–1935), Dutch botanist who contributed to the theory of evolution by his studies of mutants. In 1900 he discovered the importance of Gregor Mendel's theories on genetics and did significant experiments with plant mutations, publishing *The Mutation Theory* (1901–1903). De Vries also studied the physiology of plant cells.

Dewey, George (1837–1917), U.S. naval officer, remembered for his victory at the Battle of Manila Bay. When war with Spain broke out in 1898, he was in command of the Asian squadron stationed near Hong Kong. Ordered to the Philippines, where the Spanish fleet was anchored, he sailed to Manila and destroyed the enemy squadron, May 1, 1898. He returned to the United States a national hero and received the special rank of admiral of the Navy.

THE BETTMANN ARCHIVE

CHARLES DICKENS

THE BETTMANN ARCHIVE

EMILY DICKINSON

Dewey, John (1859–1952), U.S. philosopher and educational reformer. Dewey's ideas form the basis for modern theories of education. His principal innovation was to replace learning by rote with learning that engages the child's interest and participation. He became professor of philosophy at Columbia University, where he remained until his retirement in 1930. Dewey expanded William James's pragmatic philosophy into what he called "instrumentalism," modeled on scientific investigation. His interest in education was in part a result of his faith in democracy and his belief that education is of the greatest importance to a democratic society. His many books include *The School and Society* (1899), *Democracy and Education* (1916), *Experience and Nature* (1925), and *Problems of Men* (1946).

Diaghilev, Sergei Pavlovich (1872–1929), Russian impresario who introduced modern ballet to Europe and initiated the 20th-century revival of interest in ballet. Diaghilev's genius as an impresario lay in his gift for recognizing artistic brilliance. He first presented Russian artists and singers (including Chaliapin) in Paris and there organized his own company, the Ballet Russe, in 1909. The original troupe included Pavlova, Nijinsky, and Tamara Karsavina, performing in ballets choreographed by Massine, Fokine, and Balanchine. Diaghilev's scene designers included such artists as Picasso, Bakst, Matisse, and Derain. Among those who wrote his scores were Stravinsky (*Firebird,* 1910; *Petrouchka,* 1911), Ravel, Poulenc, Milhaud, and Prokofiev. The Ballet Russe disbanded on Diaghilev's death, but his influence was felt throughout 20th-century art, music, and dance.

Díaz, (José de la Cruz) Porfirio (1830–1915), president of Mexico for more than 25 years. Díaz supported the Reform movement of Benito Juárez (1858–1861), but in 1871 he opposed the reelection of Juárez as president and in 1876 he led a successful revolt against his successor. Díaz then became president, serving 1877–1880 and 1884–1911. He ruled dictatorially, and, though he encouraged industrial development and suppressed banditry, he brought the peasants few benefits. In 1911 a revolution led by Francisco Madero forced him into exile.

Dickens, Charles John Huffam (1812–1870), English author, the most popular of English novelists. As a child Dickens worked in a factory, attended school for a few years, and became a newspaper reporter before he was 20. His first stories, published under the pen name Boz, were collected as *Sketches by Boz* in 1836. In the same year he began to publish the *Pickwick Papers,* which made him famous overnight. During the next 30 years Dickens published nearly 20 novels and collections of stories, most of which first appeared in newspapers or magazines. His best-known works include *Oliver Twist* (1838), *A Christmas Carol* (1843), and *David Copperfield* (1849–1850). He was known especially for his characters, his humor, and his pathos, but his descriptions of poverty and injustice spurred the growing social conscience of his public.

Dickinson, Emily Elizabeth (1830–1886), U.S. poet who, living a withdrawn and secluded life, produced some of the most imaginative American poetry of the 19th century. Among her best-known poems are "After great pain . . . ," "I never saw a moor . . . ," and "My life closed twice. . . ." Dickinson's innovations in style and structure were far ahead of her time. Discouraged by a critic to whom she sent four poems in 1862, she never again tried to publish. Shy and nervous, she formed a few intense friendships, but remained secluded in her home, dressed always in white. After her death thousands of poems were found locked away.

Diderot, Denis (1713–1784), French writer, philosopher, and editor of the *Encyclopédie* (1751–1772), a 28-volume encyclopedia on which he worked for 20 years. Originally a French translation of a British publication, it was expanded by Diderot, with the assistance of Jean LeRond d'Alembert, into an original work based on science and reason. With such contributors as Voltaire and Rousseau, the encyclopedia was one of the most influential works of the Enlightenment.

Didrikson (Zaharias), Mildred (Babe) (1913–1956), U.S. athlete, thought to be the greatest woman athlete of modern times. Outstanding in basketball, baseball, and track, she won the javelin and 80-meter hurdle events in the 1932 Olympic Games. As a professional golfer, she won the U.S. Open in 1948, 1950, and 1954.

Diefenbaker, John George (1895–1979), lawyer, statesman, and Progressive Conservative prime minister of Canada, 1957–1963. He introduced the Canadian Bill of Rights and agricultural and social reforms. Diefenbaker reneged on an agreement he had made with the United States to arm missiles in Canada with nuclear warheads because of controversy over whether Canada should adopt nuclear weapons.

Diesel, Rudolf (1858–1913), German engineer who invented the diesel engine, an internal combustion engine that is ignited by air compression and operates on unrefined fuels. He patented his idea in 1892; the first successful engine was built in 1897.

DiMaggio, Joseph Paul, Jr. (Joe) (1914–   ), U.S. baseball player, called "the greatest team player of all time." Di Maggio, also known as Joltin' Joe, the Yankee Clipper, and other nicknames, joined the outfield on the New York Yankees in 1936. During his career he batted .325 and was voted most valuable player three times.

Dinesen, Isak: *See* Blixen, Karen Dinesen.

Diocletian (c 245–c 313), full name Gaius Aurelius Valerius Diocletianus, Roman emperor, 284–305, who first divided the Roman Empire into eastern and western empires. Commander of Emperor Numerian's bodyguard, he was proclaimed emperor by the army on Numerian's death. To simplify the administration of the empire, he ruled the eastern half from Nicomedia and made his colleague Maximian ruler in the west. He ordered the last great Roman persecution of Christians, beginning in 303. Diocletian abdicated in 305 and retired to Spalato (now Split, Yugoslavia).

Disney, Walter Elias (1901–1966), U.S. film producer. He created the unforgettable Mickey Mouse for *Steamboat Willie* (1928). It was followed by the popular series *Silly Symphonies,* introducing Donald Duck and Pluto. In 1937 Disney produced the first feature-length cartoon, *Snow White and the Seven Dwarfs.* It was followed by more classics: *Fantasia* (1940), *Pinocchio* (1940), *Bambi* (1942), *Cinderella* (1950), *Peter Pan* (1953), and others. Disney also produced feature-length nature films (*Vanishing Prairie,* 1955), live features (*Mary Poppins,* 1964), and television programs. In 1955 he opened the Disneyland amusement park in Anaheim, Calif.

Disraeli, Benjamin, 1st Earl of Beaconsfield (1804–1881), British statesman and author, prime minister in 1868 and 1874–1880. Disraeli began his career as an author with the novel *Vivian Grey* (1826). Although Disraeli's family was Jewish, the children were baptized as Christians—a fortunate step, since Jews were excluded from Parliament until 1858. He was first elected to Parliament as a Conservative in 1837. He was Chancellor of the Exchequer in three cabinets and became prime minister in 1868. He lost the election that year but returned to the office in 1874. During his second administration, he sponsored humanitarian reforms, but his real advances were in foreign affairs. He bought enough shares in the Suez Canal Company to win control of it for Britain; passed a bill proclaiming Queen Victoria empress of India; prevented Russia from taking Constantinople after defeating Turkey in 1877; and acquired Cyprus. In 1880 his ministry was turned out of office and he returned to writing. His novels include *Henrietta Temple* (1837), *Lothair* (1870), and *Endymion* (1880).

Dodgson, Charles Lutwidge (1832–1898), pseudonym **Lewis Carroll**, English mathematician and author of *Alice in Wonderland.* Dodgson taught mathematics at Oxford, was ordained a deacon, and wrote books on mathematics and logic. Shy and stammering, he preferred the company of children and delighted in entertaining them. For one of them, Alice Liddell, he made up the stories of *Alice's Adventures in Wonderland* and *Through the Looking-Glass,* published in 1865 and 1872, with illustrations by Sir John Tenniel. Another work of note is *The Hunting of the Snark* (1876), a nonsense poem.

Dohnányi, Ernő (or Ernst von) (1877–1960), Hungarian composer and pianist. He was conductor of the Budapest Philharmonic Orchestra and director of works in the Hungarian Academy of Music, then taught in the United States after World War II. His compositions include suites, choral works, piano pieces, and many other forms; his Symphony in F is considered his best work.

Donatello (c 1386–1466), full name Donato di Niccolò di Betto Bardi, Italian sculptor. He introduced vitality and realism into his modeling of the human body. His early works in the cathedral of Florence include *St. Mark* (1411–1412) and *St. George* (1415–1420) and the famous *Lo Zuccone* (completed in 1436), also known as "pumpkin head." After his study of antiquity in Rome, he did a bronze *David* (after 1432), the first large, free-standing nude statue of the Renaissance. His nine-foot bronze equestrian statue *Gattamelata* (1446–1453) is a rare monumental work of the age. One of his last works is the *Repentant Magdalen,* carved in wood.

Donizetti, (Domenico) Gaetano Maria (1797–1848), Italian opera composer, known for his melodic but melodramatic operas. Of the 65 operas and operettas he wrote, his masterpiece is the tragic *Lucia de Lammermoor* (1835). The comedies *Don Pasquale* (1843) and *L'Elisir d'amore* (1832) are also widely performed. Many Donizetti works were written for the leading sopranos of his day and are often revived as showpieces, including *Anna Bolena* (1830), *Roberto Devereux* (1837), and *The Daughter of the Regiment* (1840).

Donne, John (1572–1631), English poet and Anglican priest, famous in his time as a preacher, but known today as an intense and powerful metaphysical poet. Donne's uneven meter, abrupt language, and startling metaphors greatly influenced 20th-century poetry. Raised a Roman Catholic, Donne studied for the law, but his career in government was destroyed by his secret marriage in 1601 to Anne More, a young relative of his employer. For the next 14 years, Donne supported his family by odd bits of writing and the favors of wealthy patrons. His early poetry, not published, included the love poems in *Songs and Sonnets* and the witty *Elegies* and *Satires.* It was his prose, particularly the anti-Catholic *Pseudo-Martyr* (1612), that brought Donne to the king's notice. Under pressure from the court, he took orders as an Anglican clergyman in 1615. Most of Donne's *Divine Poems* were written about this time, including "A Litany," "La Corona," and the "Holy Sonnets." He rapidly became the most famous preacher of his day, and his sermons were admired by the king and the court. From 1621 until his death he was dean of St. Paul's, London. He wrote little, though some sermons were published; his poetry was not published until 1633.

Dos Passos, John Roderigo (1896–1970), U.S. novelist who wrote panoramic studies of early 20th-century industrial American life. The best known of his works is *U.S.A.,* a trilogy including *The 42nd Parallel* (1930), *Nineteen-Nineteen* (1932), and *The Big Money* (1936). An ambulance corps driver in World War I, he used his experiences as a basis for *One Man's Initiation* (1919) and *Three Soldiers* (1921). He also wrote another trilogy, *District of Columbia* (1952). Dos Passos used innovative techniques in his fiction, such as montages of newspaper headlines and biographies integrated into the text.

Dostoevski, Feodor Mikhailovich (1821–1881), Russian novelist. As a young writer, he became involved in a group interested in social and political reform. In 1849 he was arrested, tried, and sentenced to death for conspiring against the government. At the last moment the sentence was commuted to four years of hard labor in Siberia. In 1859 he returned to St. Petersburg and began to write again. In his later years he became increasingly religious and reactionary. During this period he wrote his major novels: *Notes from the Underground* (1864), *Crime and Punishment* (1866), *The Idiot* (1868–1869), and *The Brothers Karamazov* (1879–1880). These novels reveal deep psychological insight as well as the problem of evil and redemption.

Douglas, Stephen Arnold (1813–1861), U.S. lawyer and politician. From 1847 until his death, Douglas was a senator from Illinois and a leader of the Democratic Party. His Kansas-Nebraska Act of 1854 introduced his principle of "popular sovereignty" and destroyed a series of earlier Senate compromises on slavery. Douglas and Abraham Lincoln held their famous debates during the 1858 Senate race in Illinois, won by Douglas. At the Democratic convention of 1860, when Douglas was nominated, the Southern delegations withdrew and nominated their own candidates.

Douglas, William Orville (1898–1980), associate justice of the U.S. Supreme Court. Douglas headed the Securities and Exchange Commission, 1936–1939. As a Supreme Court justice (from 1939), Douglas was often attacked by conservatives for his liberal interpretations of the law. He wrote books on problems of democracy, including the controversial *Points of Rebellion* (1970). He also wrote books on the wilderness and conservation (*Of Men and Mountains,* 1950). He retired from the Court in 1975 because of poor health.

Douglass, Frederick (1817–1895), U.S. writer and speaker, a leading voice of the abolitionist movement. His eloquent *Narrative of the Life of Frederick Douglass, an American Slave* (1845) is a classic. Born a slave (originally named Frederick Augustus Washington Bailey), Douglass learned to read and write from his owner's wife. In 1838 he escaped to New York and became a speaker for the Massachusetts Anti-Slavery Society. To avoid reenslavement when his *Narrative* was published, he went to England to lecture on slavery and women's rights. On his return he founded the antislavery weekly *North Star,* published until 1860. After the Civil War Douglass involved himself in the issues of Reconstruction and held federal office. In 1889 he was appointed minister to Haiti, but resigned in 1891 in a dispute over U.S. policies.

BETTMANN ARCHIVES

FREDERICK DOUGLASS

Doyle, Sir Arthur Conan (1859–1930), British author, creator of the brilliant detective Sherlock Holmes. Conan Doyle was a physician until 1891, when the success of his Holmes stories, beginning with *A Study in Scarlet* (1887), made him a full-time author. The stories, supposedly written by Holmes's companion Dr. Watson, include *The Adventures of Sherlock Holmes* (1891), *The Hound of the Baskervilles* (1902), and many others. Holmes became so popular that Doyle found him a nuisance and tried to kill him off, but an irate public demanded *The Return of Sherlock Holmes* (1904). Doyle himself preferred his historical novels, such as *The White Company* (1891).

Drake, Sir Francis (c 1543–1596), England's first great naval hero. Drake privateered against Spanish ships in the West Indies and set out on a voyage around the world in 1577. In his ship the *Golden Hind,* he raided Spanish ships and towns on the Pacific coast of South America, then sailed across the Pacific and returned to England in 1580, the first Englishman to circumnavigate the globe. He was knighted on board his ship by Queen Elizabeth I, who gave him command of a fleet. With it he once again plundered the Spanish colonies. Drake's raids on the Spanish Main (the Caribbean) induced Philip II of Spain to invade England. In 1588 Philip sent his fleet, the great Armada, to clear the English Channel. Drake led the English attack on the Armada in the Channel; his victory made England dominant on the seas. Drake died off Porto Bello, Panama, during another raid.

BRITISH INFORMATION SERVICES

SIR ARTHUR CONAN DOYLE

Dreiser, Theodore (1871–1945), U.S. novelist famous for his realistic portrayals of men and women trapped and destroyed by social forces. His first novel, *Sister Carrie* (1900), was suppressed immediately after publication, and Dreiser suffered a nervous collapse. *Jennie Gerhard* (1911) fared better, but *The Genius* (1915) also was suppressed, causing literary figures such as H.L. Mencken and Ezra Pound to support Dreiser in his fight against censorship. Dreiser's most famous work, *An American Tragedy,* appeared in 1925, became a successful play, and was filmed twice.

Drew, Charles Richard (1904–1950), black American physician. Drew developed techniques of blood preservation for use in transfusions. He resigned as director of the American Red Cross Blood Bank during World War II because the bank wanted to segregate blood by the donor's race. He died after an automobile accident, denied admittance to a nearby hospital because of his race.

Dreyfus, Alfred (1859–1935), French Jewish army officer whose trial for treason ushered in twelve years of political controversy that changed the course of the Third Republic, dividing France politically and emotionally. In 1894 Captain Dreyfus was court-martialed for selling military secrets to the Germans. The only evidence against him was the similarity between his handwriting and that on the questionable documents. Public opinion and the anti-Semitic faction of the press were eager for his conviction. Dreyfus was sentenced for life and sent to Devil's Island. In 1896 an army intelligence officer found evidence that the handwriting in question was that of another officer, Major Esterhazy. Although Dreyfus's family and friends demanded a new trial, neither the army nor the government took action. Soon the "Dreyfus affair" became a scandal used by the republicans and liberals, notably Émile Zola, Anatole France, and Georges Clemenceau, against the anti-Semitic faction, the military, and the right-wing nationalists. The case went before another military court in 1899. Dreyfus was declared guilty but was fully pardoned by the president of the republic. Not until 1906 was his name officially cleared by the French courts. He was then awarded the Legion of Honor and returned to his military career.

Dr. Seuss: *See* Seuss, Dr.

Dryden, John (1631–1700), English poet, critic, and playwright. Dryden developed the model for modern English prose style and set the tone for 18th-century English poetry. Supported by an inheritance, he lived in London society and, after the Restoration in 1660, enjoyed the favor of King Charles II. In 1668 he was named poet laureate, a post he held until the revolution of 1688. Of Dryden's poems, the best known are his heroic satire *Absalom and Achitophel* (1681) and the song *Alexander's Feast* (1697). Of his plays, *Marriage-à-la-Mode* (1672) and *All for Love* (1677) are considered the best. His most notable piece of criticism is his *Essay of Dramatick Poesie* (1668), written in the polished, controlled style that he developed. Also important are his *Fables* (1700) and his many excellent translations of classical authors.

Dubček, Alexander (1921–), Czechoslovak statesman. Dubček, a lifelong Communist Party worker, became a member of the Presidium in 1962. When elected premier in 1968, he relaxed press censorship and promised democratic reforms and a more independent foreign policy. His attempt ended when the Soviet Union sent troops to occupy the country. Dubček was given a diplomatic post, but in 1970 was recalled, expelled from the Communist Party, and dismissed from public life.

Dubois, (Marie) Eugène (François Thomas) (1858–1940), Dutch geologist and anatomist, discoverer of Java man. In 1890–1891 Dubois found the bones of an early manlike creature on Java and named his find *Pithecanthropus erectus,* believing the creature to be an intermediate between ape and man. Later finds showed that *Pithecanthropus* was a primitive man rather than an intermediate.

Du Bois, William Edward Burghardt (1868–1963), U.S. writer, scholar, and civil rights leader. He taught at Atlanta University, 1897–1910, heading the sociology department there, 1933–1944. In 1905 Du Bois helped found the Niagara movement, which in 1909 became part of the National Association for the Advancement of Colored People. He edited the NAACP journal, *Crisis,* from 1910 to 1932. Opposed to the compromise policies of Booker T. Washington, Du Bois and the NAACP demanded immediate enforcement of civil rights for blacks. In 1900 Du Bois called the first Pan-African Conference, demanding self-government for African colonies. When the fifth conference met in 1945, he was its co-chairman. In 1961 he joined the Communist Party and then emigrated to Ghana, where he died. Du Bois' lifetime position was that blacks should develop their own cultural values; his own scholarly contribution to this goal was enormous. Some of his best-known works are *The Philadelphia Negro* (1899), *The Souls of Black Folk* (1903), *Black Reconstruction* (1935), *Color and Democracy* (1945), and *The World and Africa* (1947).

Duchamp, Marcel (1887–1968), French artist best known for his "non-art," which anticipated the Dadaists, pop, and op art of the later 20th century. In 1913 Duchamp's cubist-futurist *Nude Descending the Staircase No. 2* caused a sensation at the Armory Show in New York. He also created the *Bicycle Wheel* (1913) and the sensational *Fountain* (1917).

Dufy, Raoul (1877–1953), French painter, illustrator, and textile designer. In 1900 he left his native Le Havre for Paris, where he was influenced by the impressionists (*Posters at Trouville,* 1906). In 1907 he joined the Fauves, led by Henri Matisse. Dufy's typical mature style includes rapid lines and bright color washes. In the 1920's and 1930's he painted many scenes of sailboats, horse races, and concerts, such as *Paddock at Deauville* (1930) and *Red Concert* (1946).

Dulles, John Foster (1888–1959), U.S. secretary of state, 1953–1959. Dulles was the U.S. delegate to the United Nations, 1946–1949. He became secretary of state under President Eisenhower. He initiated the Cold War policy of deterring communist aggression by the threat of U.S. military reprisal. To augment this threat, he developed controversial policies of "brinkmanship" and "massive retaliation."

Dumas, family name of two French authors. **Alexandre** (1802–1870), called Dumas *père,* was the author of several hundred enormously popular historical plays and adventure novels, notably *The Three Musketeers* (1844), its sequel *The Man in the Iron Mask* (1848–1850), and *The Count of Monte Cristo* (1845). The historical research and much of the writing for Dumas' novels were done by a team of writers directed by August Maquet (1813–1888); Dumas then rewrote, adding his master touch. Dumas' son **Alexandre** (1824–1895), called Dumas *fils,* wrote a number of successful plays, notably *La Dame aux camélias* (*Camille,* 1852), from his novel of the same name.

Du Maurier, Daphne (1907–1989), English author noted for her novels and stories utilizing the Gothic elements of suspense and horror. Her *Rebecca* (1938) is a 20th-century classic in the field of romantic novels; the film version (1940) also became a classic. Other works are *Jamaica Inn* (1936), *My Cousin Rachel* (1952), *The Scapegoat* (1957), and *The House on the Strand* (1970). Her short story "The Birds" (1952) became a successful film.

Du Maurier, George Louis Palmella Busson (1834–1896), French-born British novelist and artist known for his gentle social satire. At first a book illustrator, in 1864 he became a staff member of *Punch,* for which he drew successful satirical commentaries on Victorian life. Later he wrote and illustrated the popular novels *Peter Ibbetson* (1891) and *Trilby* (1894), sentimental recollections of his student days. He was the grandfather of novelist Daphne du Maurier.

Dunant, Jean Henri (1828–1910), Swiss founder of the International Red Cross and co-winner of the first Nobel Peace Prize, in 1901. After witnessing the bloody Battle of Solferino (1859) in Italy between the French and Austrians, Dunant directed all his efforts toward establishing an international organization to care for war victims. His activities led to the Geneva Conference of 1863 and Geneva Convention of 1864, by which the International Red Cross was founded.

Dunbar, Paul Lawrence (1872–1906), U.S. poet noted for his verse recreating black dialect. Dunbar, the son of former slaves, published his first volume of poems, *Oak and Ivy,* in 1893, followed by *Majors and Minors* (1895) and *Lyrics of Lowly Life* (1896). His poems express nostalgia for plantation life as well as the restlessness of emancipated blacks.

Duncan, Isadora (1878–1927), U.S. dancer who revolutionized dancing during the early 20th century and led in developing modern dance. She advocated dance that was a natural expression of the human body and adopted a loose Greek tunic and bare feet as the freest way to dance. Her autobiography, *My Life,* appeared in 1927.

Du Pont, a French family best known for founding one of the largest chemical companies in the world.

Pierre Samuel du Pont de Nemours (1739–1817), French statesman, economist, and royalist politician, emigrated to the United States during the French Revolution with his sons, Éleuthère and Victor. He went back to France in 1802, but in 1815, on Napoleon's return to power, he returned to the United States.

Éleuthère Irénée du Pont (1771–1834), his son, studied in Paris under chemist Antoine Lavoisier before emigrating in 1799. By 1804, with money from his father's land interests, he had established the original E. I. du Pont de Nemours gunpowder works on a farm in Wilmington, Del. Éleuthère's company was later expanded into one of the largest in the world.

Dürer, Albrecht (1471–1528), German Renaissance painter and engraver. His early works include many charcoal portraits, book illustrations, and the first landscapes to be drawn from nature north of the Alps (*Landscape with Houses,* 1494). It was through Dürer that the Italian Renaissance came to the north. Twice he visited Italy, and after 1505 his work combined the composition, proportion, and perspective of the Italian masters with Gothic detail and realism (*Adoration of the Magi,* 1511). His well-known works include a self-portrait (1498), *Four Apostles* (1526), and his cycle of woodcuts, the *Apocalypse* (1511). However, most critics agree that Dürer's greatest achievement is his engravings, including *Knight, Death, and the Devil* (1513).

Duse, Eleonora (1859–1924), Italian actress, most famous for her tragic roles. She began her career at 14 as Juliet and in 1879 firmly established her reputation in the title role of *Thérèse Requin* by Émile Zola. After touring all over the world, she gave one of her most brilliant performances in her Vienna debut in *La Dame aux camélias,* 1892. In 1897 Duse fell in love with Gabriele D'Annunzio and brought special intensity to her roles in his plays (*La Gioconda,* 1898). She was also famous for her performances in Ibsen's plays, as Nora in *A Doll's House,* Rebecca in *Rosmersholm,* and as Hedda Gabler.

Duvalier, François (Papa Doc) (1907–1971), Haitian dictator who ruled for 14 years with terror and voodoo. Promising reform, Duvalier, a country doctor, was elected president in 1957 and soon took full control of the government. His secret police, the Tontons Macoutes, terrorized or eliminated opponents and suppressed attempts to overthrow his regime. Duvalier intimated that his personal power derived from the voodoo spirit world. In 1964 he declared himself president for life.

He was succeeded in 1971 by his son **Jean-Claude Duvalier** (1951–), known as Baby Doc. The world's youngest president, Jean-Claude fled Haiti with his family in 1986 during a period of violent public turmoil.

Dvorak, Antonín (1841–1904), Czech composer. He developed the nationalist musical movement started by Smetana, combining universal elements with characteristically Czech melodies and rhythms. Dvorak taught in the United States from 1892 to 1895, writing his best-known symphony, No. 5 in E minor ("From the New World," 1893). His First (1880) and Fourth (1889) symphonies are more typical examples of his work. The Cello Concerto in B minor (1895) encouraged new interest in solo cello.

Dylan, Bob (1941–), U.S. folk singer and composer, born Robert Zimmerman. Influenced by Huddie Ledbetter and Woody Guthrie, he achieved fame in the 1960's as a semi-Western-style performer. His cynical and angry lyrics and reclusive life made him a cult figure among young people. Dylan's memorable songs of social protest include "Blowin' in the Wind" and "The Times They Are A-Changin'."

E

Eads, James Buchanan (1820–1887), U.S. civil engineer and inventor. In the late 1830's Eads invented a diving bell, which he used to salvage sunken steamboats. He later built gunboats for use in the Civil War. Eads then designed a steel arch bridge spanning the Mississippi River. Though his plans were condemned as impractical, the finished span (1867–1874) put Eads in the first rank of bridge engineers. His greatest feat was a system of jetties at the mouth of the Mississippi, diverting river deposits into the sea and leaving a deep channel for ship traffic.

Eakins, Thomas (1844–1916), U.S. artist. Eakins painted scenes from his native Philadelphia in an honest and realistic manner, with painstaking attention to perspective and anatomy. He did many famous portraits (*Walt Whitman,* 1887), sports scenes (*Max Schmidt in a Single Scull,* 1871), and scenes from theater (*The Concert Singer,* 1892). His interests in science and anatomy are shown in the famous medical paintings *The Gross Clinic* (1875) and *The Agnew Clinic* (1889).

Earhart, Amelia (1898–1937), U.S. flier, famed for two solo transoceanic flights, across the Atlantic in 1932 and the Pacific in 1935. She was the first woman to complete such flights. She established an altitude record in 1931 for the autogiro, a plane using both rotor and propeller. In July, 1937, she set out on an around-the-world flight accompanied by a navigator. The plane disappeared near Howland Island in the Pacific, and she was presumed dead. More than 30 years later, however, it was still rumored that she was alive.

Eastman, George (1854–1932), U.S. inventor, industrialist, and philanthropist. Eastman devised a process for making dry photographic plates and in 1880 began to manufacture them in Rochester, N.Y. He then devised the small "Kodak" camera and transparent roll film. In 1892 he organized the Eastman Kodak Company and, by 1927, had a virtual monopoly on U.S. photographic equipment. Eastman gave most of his fortune to the University of Rochester, where the Eastman School of Music was established.

Eddington, Sir Arthur Stanley (1882–1944), English astronomer. His early reputation was based on theories of star formation and motion. He pioneered in research on the internal makeup of stars, demonstrating that their interiors are gaseous and that mass and brightness are related (*The Internal Constitution of the Stars,* 1926). Eddington was an early exponent in Britain of Einstein's theories of relativity, interpreting them in *Space, Time, and Gravitation* (1920). He also wrote *The Nature of the Physical World* (1928) and *The Expanding Universe* (1933).

Eddy, Mary Baker (1821–1910), founder of the first Church of Christ, Scientist, in 1879. She suffered from a spinal illness during her younger years and so read widely on questions of health. In 1866 she suffered a near-fatal fall and later wrote that she had regained her health through reading the New Testament; from this dates her discovery of

AMELIA EARHART

U.S. COAST GUARD

Christian Science. She wrote down its principles in *Science and Health* (1875); a *Key to the Scriptures* was added later. In 1883 she founded the *Christian Science Journal;* in 1908 the *Christian Science Monitor.*

Eden, Sir (Robert) Anthony, 1st Earl of Avon (1897–1977), English statesman, a skillful diplomat who sought to preserve world peace. Eden was foreign minister from 1935 to 1938, when he resigned in protest against Prime Minister Chamberlain's conciliatory policies toward fascist Italy. During World War II and again from 1951 to 1955 under Prime Minister Churchill, Eden was foreign minister. After Churchill, Eden became prime minister in 1955. He resigned in 1957 after being criticized for instigating military action during the Suez crisis of 1956.

Edison, Thomas Alva (1847–1931), U.S. inventor called the Wizard of Menlo Park for his more than 1000 inventions, including the incandescent light. Edison patented his first invention, a vote recorder, in 1868. It was followed by such devices as the stock ticker and a transmitter and receiver for the telegraph. In 1876 he opened a laboratory at Menlo Park, N.J., where he invented the microphone and the phonograph (1877). In 1879 Edison succeeded in making the incandescent light bulb, and the age of electricity began. The first central electric power plant, built in New York City, was the Edison General Electric Company. In 1889 Edison was invited to the Paris Centennial Exposition as "the genius of the age." When World War I broke out, he invented substitutes for drugs, dyes, and other substances previously bought from Germany, as well as explosives and safety devices. He spent his final years working on improvements for the wireless, radio, movies, automobiles, and airplanes.

Edward VII (1841–1910), born Albert Edward, king of Great Britain and Ireland from 1901 to 1910. His mother, Queen Victoria, disapproved of her son's "wild behavior" and therefore did not consult with him on matters of state, even when he was an adult. Yet, both as prince of Wales and as king, Edward was immensely popular. His interest in sports and social life was welcomed by the British after 40 years of Victoria's somber widowhood. He was liberal in domestic politics and, in foreign affairs, had a gift for personal diplomacy that did much to strengthen Britain's position in Europe.

Edward VIII: *See* Windsor, Duke of.

Edwards, Jonathan (1703–1758), American Puritan theologian whose fiery preaching and emphasis on faith led to the Great Awakening of the 1740's. Edwards became pastor of Northampton Church in Massachusetts in 1727, where a series of sermons on faith brought about hundreds of conversions in 1734–1735. By the 1740's all New England was in the midst of a mass religious revival. His most famous sermon is the Calvinist classic *Sinners in the Hands of an Angry God* (1741).

Ehrenburg, Ilya Grigorievich (1891–1967), Russian author and journalist whose satires on the West made him a popular Soviet writer. Ehrenburg was imprisoned by the czarists in 1908, but escaped to France. His early novels, written in Belgium, include *A Street in Moscow* (1927) and *Out of Chaos* (1934). In the late 1930's he returned to Russia. He became known in the United States for a series of satirical articles written on a visit in 1946. His later works were *The Fall of Paris* (1941) and his memoirs (1964–1967).

Ehrlich, Paul (1854–1915), German bacteriologist, a pioneer in the use of chemistry in medical science, and winner of the Nobel Prize for Medicine in 1908. Ehrlich founded the modern science of hematology (the study of blood), and his work with toxins and antitoxins, particularly for diphtheria, led to present techniques of immunization. His discovery in 1909 of the arsenic compound known as Salvarsan, or "606," revolutionized the treatment of syphilis. He also did studies in histology and in chemotherapy, the use of chemicals in the control of disease.

Eichmann, Adolf (1906–1962), German Nazi official who, during World War II, was in charge of the Gestapo's Bureau of Jewish Affairs under Himmler and Heydrich. By Eichmann's own figures, more than 6 million Jews died in the ghettos and in slave-labor, concentration, and extermination camps under his administration. He escaped to Argentina after the war, but was captured in 1960 by Israeli agents. Tried by a special court in Israel, he was found guilty of war crimes and executed.

Eiffel, Alexandre Gustave (1832–1923), French engineer who designed and built the Eiffel Tower for the Paris Exposition of 1889, a notable example of 19th-century engineering skill. He made his reputation as a master bridge builder, having constructed several bridges in Europe, Africa, and Indochina. In 1885 he designed the inner structure for the Statue of Liberty.

Einstein, Albert (1879–1955), German-born U.S. theoretical physicist. Einstein held academic posts in Zurich, Prague, and Berlin before becoming professor of theoretical physics at the Institute for Advanced Study in Princeton, N.J., in 1933. He became a U.S. citizen in 1940. In 1905 Einstein published papers containing three of his greatest contributions: the photoelectric law, which was the first application to matter of Planck's quantum theory; a mathematical analysis of the Brownian motion; and the special theory of relativity, which introduced his famous equation $E=mc^2$, and ultimately changed man's concept of time and space. In 1916 he published his general theory of relativity, with a new concept of gravitation. Einstein won the Nobel Prize in Physics in 1921. He spent the rest of his life trying to develop a unified field theory and elaborating on quantum physics. Einstein was the best-known and most respected scientist of his era. Although a pacifist, in 1939 he urged construction of an atomic bomb before the Nazis developed one. One of the byproducts of the 1952 U.S. bomb test was the discovery of a new chemical element, which was named einsteinium. Einstein's books include *The Meaning of Relativity* (5th revised edition, 1956); *Why War?* (with Sigmund Freud, 1933); and *The World As I See It* (1949).

Eisenhower, Dwight David (1890–1969), 34th President of the United States, 1953–1961, and Allied commander in chief during World War II. Born in Denison, Tex., he was raised in Abilene, Kans. He graduated from West Point in 1915. Eisenhower distinguished himself in various command and staff assignments and was put in charge of war plans in 1941. He became commander of U.S. troops in Europe in 1942 and planned and directed the invasions of North Africa and Italy. In 1943 he was made supreme Allied commander in Europe. He planned and executed the invasion of France in 1944 and directed the Allied forces for the rest of World War II. In 1945 he was named U.S. Army chief of staff. In 1948 he became president of Columbia University, but resigned in 1950 to become head of the forces of the North Atlantic Treaty Organization. In 1952 and 1956 Eisenhower, running as a Republican, defeated Adlai Stevenson for the Presidency. During his tenure as President, he delegated much of his authority to his Cabinet and to Congress, preferring to remain above party politics. He visited heads of state all over the world; his personal diplomacy contributed to world peace and cooperation. He published war memoirs, *Crusade in Europe* (1948), and memoirs of his Presidency, *The White House Years* (3 volumes, 1963–1965).

Eisenstein, Sergei Milhailovich (1898–1948), Soviet film director. He originated the use of montage in film and pioneered in the casting of nonprofessionals as actors. Of his six completed films, *Strike* (1924), *Potemkin* (1925), *October (Ten Days That Shook the World)* (1927), and *Old and New* (1929) vividly commemorate Russian revolutionary events; *Alexander Nevsky* (1938) and *Ivan the Terrible*

(1942–1946) are epic treatments of Russian heroes. His books *Film Form* and *Film Sense* are considered classics of film theory.

Eleanor of Aquitaine (1122–1204), queen of France, 1137–1152, and of England, 1154–1189, the inspiration for much of the courtly literature and song of the twelfth century. Her marriage to Louis VII of France ended in 1152; later that year she married Henry Plantagenet (later Henry II). A strong-willed woman, Eleanor maintained her own court in Aquitaine and supported her sons in their rebellion against Henry in 1173; in retaliation he imprisoned her in various castles for ten years. Her son Richard I (the Lion Hearted) ordered her release after Henry's death, and she helped manage the affairs of state during his long absences. When Richard was captured during a crusade, Eleanor helped raise the ransom that was demanded. After Richard's death in 1199, Eleanor, nearing 80, rallied support for her son John's bid for the throne. She died at 82, having survived two husbands and eight of her ten children.

Elgar, Sir Edward William (1857–1934), English late Romantic composer. His works are strongly melodic and traditional; he was King Edward VII's favorite composer. His best-known orchestral works are the *Enigma Variations* (1899), the *Pomp and Circumstance* marches (1901, 1905), and *Falstaff* (1913).

Eliot, George: *See* Evans, Mary Ann.

Eliot, John (1604–1690), known as the apostle to the Indians, English-born Puritan evangelist. Settling in America in 1631, he became pastor at Roxbury, near Boston. He began his missionary work in 1646 and soon established a town of "praying Indians." It and other settlements of converts, numbering about 4000, were virtually wiped out during King Philip's War (1675), but the missionary work continued. Eliot taught and preached in the Indian language, translating and publishing the Bible in Indian (1661, 1663).

Eliot, Thomas Stearns (T. S.) (1888–1965), Anglo-American poet, critic, and dramatist. Eliot's poetry expresses emotion in a condensed, controlled form, using complex symbolism, allusions to many literatures and cultures, and a variety of styles from scholarly to conversational. Eliot, born in St. Louis, emigrated to England in 1915 and later became a British citizen. His earliest published poems are among his best known—"The Love Song of J. Alfred Prufrock," from *Prufrock, and Other Observations* (1917), and *The Waste Land* (1922), his most famous work. Eliot became an Anglican in the 1920's, calling himself "an Anglo-Catholic in religion, a classicist in literature, and a royalist in politics." This influence is most evident in *Ash-Wednesday* (1930) and in the *Four Quartets* (1940–1942). Eliot was also an incisive literary critic; his critical works include *The Sacred Wood* (1920) and *After Strange Gods* (1934). Of his verse dramas, *Murder in the Cathedral* (1935) became a classic, though Eliot himself preferred *The Family Reunion* (1939). Though his work was thought obscure in the 1920's, by the 1940's he was a dominant literary figure. He won the 1948 Nobel Prize for Literature.

Elizabeth I (1533–1603), queen of England and Ireland, 1558–1603, the daughter of Henry VIII and Anne Boleyn. Because of her Protestant connections, Elizabeth, third in line for the throne, was the center of many political and religious intrigues after her father's death. Her Catholic half-sister, Mary I, was fearful of Elizabeth's popularity, but only dared keep her imprisoned a short time. When she succeeded

RULERS OF ENGLAND

Anglo-Saxon kings	828–839	Egbert
	839–858	Ethelwulf
	858–860	Ethelbald
	860–866	Ethelbert
	866–871	Ethelred I
	871–899	Alfred (the Great)*
	899–925	Edward (the Elder)
	924–940	Athelstan
	940–946	Edmund I (the Deed-doer)
	946–955	Edred
	955–959	Edwy (the Fair)
	959–975	Edgar (the Peaceful)
	975–978	Edward (the Martyr)
	978–1016	Ethelred II (the Unready)
	1016	Edmund II (Ironside)
Danish kings	1016–1035	Canute (the Great)
	1035–1040	Harold I (Harefoot)
	1040–1042	Harthacanute (or Hardecanute)
Saxon kings	1042–1066	Edward (the Confessor)
	1066	Harold II
Norman kings	1066–1087	William I (the Conqueror)*
	1087–1100	William II (Rufus)
	1100–1135	Henry I (Beauclerck)
	1135–1154	Stephen of Blois
Plantagenets	1154–1189	Henry II*
	1189–1199	Richard I (the Lion-Hearted)*
	1199–1216	John (Lackland)*
	1216–1272	Henry III
	1272–1307	Edward I
	1307–1327	Edward II
	1327–1377	Edward III
	1377–1399	Richard II
House of Lancaster	1399–1413	Henry IV
	1413–1422	Henry V*
	1422–1461	Henry VI
	1470–1471	
House of York	1461–1470	Edward IV
	1471–1483	
	1483	Edward V
	1483–1485	Richard III
House of Tudor	1485–1509	Henry VII
	1509–1547	Henry VIII*
	1547–1553	Edward VI
	1553–1558	Mary I (Bloody Mary)
	1558–1603	Elizabeth I*
House of Stuart	1603–1625	James I
	1625–1649	Charles I*
Commonwealth or Protectorate	1649–1653	Council of State
	1653–1658	Oliver Cromwell*
	1658–1659	Richard Cromwell
Restoration of the monarchy. House of Stuart restored	1660–1685	Charles II*
	1685–1688	James II
	1689–1702	William III } joint rule
	1689–1694	Mary II } joint rule
	1702–1714	Anne
House of Hanover	1714–1727	George I
	1727–1760	George II
	1760–1820	George III
	1820–1830	George IV
	1830–1837	William IV
	1837–1901	Victoria*
House of Saxe-Coburg	1901–1910	Edward VII*
House of Windsor	1910–1936	George V
	1936	Edward VIII*
	1936–1952	George VI*
	1952–	Elizabeth II*

*See main biography.

THE BETTMANN ARCHIVE

ELIZABETH I

Mary in 1558, Elizabeth reestablished Protestantism. She tried to remain tolerant of Roman Catholics until numerous plots to replace her by her cousin Mary Stuart, queen of Scots, were discovered during the 1570's and 1580's. Thereafter, Catholicism was suppressed, and Mary Stuart was executed for treason in 1587. The Puritans were likewise suppressed, but only insofar as they, too, tried to interfere in politics. In foreign policy, Elizabeth was able to placate her European enemies or to play them off against each other for most of her reign. During this time the English navy developed into a fighting force strong enough to defeat the Spanish Armada in 1588 and lay the foundation of British naval supremacy. Elizabeth, the "Virgin Queen," had many suitors and favorites (notably the earls of Essex and Leicester), but was too independent of mind and jealous of her position ever to take a husband. She chose the wisest counselors, in particular William Cecil and his son Robert, but she ruled by her intuitive understanding of foreign and domestic politics and by the boundless love and admiration of her people. Her reign, the Elizabethan Age or English Renaissance, became a period of glory for England in war, commerce, and culture.

Elizabeth II (1926–), queen of Great Britain and Northern Ireland, and head of the Commonwealth. During World War II, as Princess Elizabeth, she broke royal tradition to serve in the Auxiliary Territorial Service, which later became the Woman's Royal Army Corps. In 1947 she married her third cousin, Philip Mountbatten, formerly prince of Greece, who was given the title duke of Edinburgh. Their first son, the heir apparent, Prince Charles, was born in 1948. Princess Anne was born in 1950, Prince Andrew in 1960, and Prince Edward in 1964. Elizabeth succeeded to the throne in 1952, after the death of her father, George VI. In 1953 and 1954, she made a round-the-world tour of the Commonwealth countries, the first reigning monarch to visit Australia and New Zealand. On a tour of North America in 1957, she became the first monarch to open the Canadian Parliament. In 1982 Elizabeth traveled to Canada to sign the Constitution Act, which gave Canada the right to change its constitution without approval from the British Parliament.

Ellington, Edward Kennedy (Duke) (1899–1974), U.S. jazz musician and composer. Ellington developed the big band jazz style of the 1930's, with emphasis on the ensemble rather than on soloists. He wrote many familiar tunes ("Mood Indigo," "Caravan") and several orchestral pieces (*Black, Brown, and Beige,* 1943; *Liberian Suite,* 1948), as well as scores for stage (*Beggar's Holiday,* 1946) and films (*Anatomy of a Murder,* 1959).

THE BETTMANN ARCHIVE

DUKE ELLINGTON

Ellis, (Henry) Havelock (1859–1939), British scientist and author, best known for his writings on sexual psychology. His works on sex were based on much original data, with a biological, rather than a clinical, interpretation. *Studies in the Psychology of Sex* was published in seven volumes from 1898 to 1928. The first volume scandalized England and was suppressed; the others were published in the United States. Ellis wrote essays and edited several collections in drama and science. He also wrote *The Criminal* (1899), the first English study of criminal psychology, and *The World of Dreams* (1911).

Ellsworth, Lincoln (1880–1951), U.S. explorer and aviator, the first person to cross both the Arctic and the Antarctic by air. In 1926 Ellsworth, Amundsen, and Nobile flew 3393 miles in the dirigible *Norge,* making the first crossing of the north polar basin. In 1935 Ellsworth made a 2300-mile flight across the Antarctic continent.

Ellsworth, Oliver (1745–1807), one of the framers of the U.S. Constitution, chief justice of the United States (1796). He represented Connecticut at the 1787 Constitutional Convention and, with Roger Sherman, drew up the plan for state representation in the two Houses of Congress. Ellsworth went to the Senate in 1789 and continued his work in planning the new government. He was chief author of the Federal Judiciary Act (1789), setting up the court system.

Emerson, Ralph Waldo (1803–1882), U.S. philosopher and essayist, leader of the transcendentalists and of the 19th-century New England intellectual revolution. Emerson prepared for the ministry and was briefly minister of the Second Church of Boston, 1829–1832, preaching sermons that rejected dogma and urged individual moral and ethical choice. He resigned abruptly and in 1834 settled in Concord, Mass., to write and lecture. The core of his beliefs was presented in *Nature* (1836), his first book. In two historic speeches, "The American Scholar" (1837) and the address to the Harvard Divinity School (1838), he offended orthodox beliefs by urging scholars to create a new American culture and by calling for reform of the ministry. His famous essay "Self-Reliance" (in *Essays, First Series,* 1841) was a rejection of traditional frameworks in favor of individual creativity. He published other essays and several volumes of poetry (1846, 1867) containing the famous "Snow Storm" and "Concord Hymn."

Emmet, Robert (1778–1803), Irish revolutionary hero. He became involved with the United Irishmen in 1798 and soon fled to avoid arrest. He planned insurrection from abroad, counting on both a French invasion of England and strong support in Ireland. In 1803 government spies discovered the rebels' arms cache, and Emmet moved quickly to start an uprising in Dublin. Spies and poor discipline made it a disaster. Emmet escaped, but when he returned to be near his fiancée, he was captured and hanged.

Engels, Friedrich (1820–1895), German socialist and economist, collaborator with Karl Marx in the formulation of the theory of communism. Prepared for a business career, he became involved with radical politics while working for his father's textile firm in England. In 1845 he published *The Condition of the Working Classes in England in 1844,* a condemnation of capitalism. He met Marx in Belgium in 1844, and the two prepared a statement known as the *Communist Manifesto* (1848). After the revolution of 1848 failed in Germany, Engels went to England. He shared his salary with the destitute Marx and after the latter's death edited several of his works. The best known of Engels' own works are *Socialism, Utopian and Scientific* (1878) and *The Origin of the Family, Private Property, and the State* (1884).

Ensor, James Sydney, Baron (1860–1949), Belgian artist noted for his fantastic, macabre paintings. Working in isolation in his home town, Ostend, he introduced his typical grotesque figures and carnival masks in the 1880's (*Self Portrait with Masks,* 1889). In 1888 he painted his famous *Entrance of Christ into Brussels.* It was shown for the first time in 1929, and Ensor was rewarded by being made a baron.

Enver Pasha (1881–1922), Turkish soldier and political leader of the Young Turks. He led in the revolutionary movements that deposed Sultan Abdul-Hamid II in 1909. In 1913 he led the coup that put the Young Turks in power. As war minister and army commander, he was one of the most powerful men in Turkey. Enver dreamed of a "Pan-Turkic" union of all the Turkic peoples of central Asia, and undertook daring but disastrous military campaigns against Russia in World War I. He fled to Germany after the war, but later joined another rising against Russia and was killed.

Epicurus (341–270 B.C.), Greek philosopher, founder of the Epicurean school of philosophy. Epicurus taught that pain should be avoided or quietly endured and that pleasure should be accepted; in this way, a person can attain serenity, the ultimate goal. His emphasis on pleasure was later distorted by the rival school of Stoics, and the Epicureans came to be falsely pictured as reveling in sensual pleasure.

Epstein, Sir Jacob (1880–1959), American-born British sculptor. His portraits, mostly rough, striking, impressionistic bronzes, include *Albert Einstein, Paul Robeson,* and *Somerset Maugham.* Of his large commissioned works, *Madonna and Child* (1951), *Christ in Majesty* (1957), and a bust of William Blake (1957) are well known. Epstein at first was criticized for his "distortions," and much of his religious work aroused controversy.

Erasmus, Desiderius (c 1466–1536), Dutch scholar and humanist whose critical attitude toward accepted teachings and beliefs of his time encouraged scholars to question the entire range of medieval thought. Erasmus entered a monastery as a young man but found the life irksome. He left the order and became a teacher and writer, living all over Europe. From 1500 on he published successively larger editions of his *Adagia,* a collection of ancient proverbs that earned him a name as the foremost scholar in northern Europe. He spent some time in England, where he taught Greek at Cambridge and befriended Thomas More. He opposed the Reformation, feeling that a revival of early Christian piety would be of greater benefit than a disruption of the church. His most influential work, a new edition of the New Testament in Greek and Latin, appeared in 1516 and became a model for critical scholarship. His most enduring work is *In Praise of Folly* (*Encomium moriae,* 1509), a witty satire on human nature.

Erhard, Ludwig (1897–1977), German economist, chancellor of West Germany, 1963–1966. Erhard, well known as an economist, was appointed director of the Institute of Economic Studies at Nuremberg in 1926. Following World War II, he was minister of economic affairs, 1949–1963, and successfully directed his country's economic redevelopment.

Eric the Red (or **Eric Thorvaldsson**) (fl. 980–1000), Norwegian explorer, founder of the first Scandinavian settlement on Greenland. The stories of Eric and his son Leif are told in the Icelandic sagas. In about 982, Eric, outlawed from Iceland for three years, sailed to explore a land he had seen to the west. He found green fields, suited for grazing cattle. Returning to Iceland in 985, he talked about "Greenland" and interested many settlers in following him there. About 350 colonists settled on farms on the coast, founding a colony that lasted about 400 years.

THE BETTMANN ARCHIVE

ERIC THE RED

Ericson, Leif (fl. c 1000), Norwegian explorer, son of Eric the Red, one of the first European discoverers of North America. According to the Icelandic sagas, Leif was sailing from Norway to his father's home in Greenland in about 1000, but missed the island and continued west to a land that he named Vinland because of the grapevines he found growing. Leif also named other parts of the coast—perhaps Labrador or New England—Helluland and Markland. At least two other Norse expeditions—one earlier, one later—are also recorded in the sagas. The Vinland Map, published in 1965, was the first modern evidence of these eleventh-century Norse expeditions.

Ericsson, John (1803–1889), Swedish-born U.S. naval engineer and inventor who designed the first modern warships. While living in England, Ericsson experimented with placing a ship's engine below the waterline and using a screw propeller instead of a paddle wheel. In 1839 he emigrated to the United States and built iron warships for the Navy, using his new propulsion system. In 1861 he designed the armored, steam-driven *Monitor,* which had guns mounted in a revolving tower. It defeated the Confederate ironclad *Merrimack* in 1862, and Ericsson became a popular hero.

Ernst, Max (1891–1976), German-born painter, among the first to experiment with the collage. In 1919 Ernst founded a Dadaist group in Cologne, and in 1922 he settled in Paris, where he joined the surrealist movement. Ernst lived in the United States, 1941–1956, painting miniature pictures ("microbes") of the Arizona landscape and, at the same time, creating massive cement statues of monsters. He then returned to France.

Essex, 2nd Earl of; Robert Devereux (1567–1601), English courtier and soldier. Though Essex was a particular favorite of Elizabeth I, she declined to give him the political power he demanded. He shared command of the expedition that captured Cádiz in 1596, but his other military ventures were not so successful. Sent to quell the Irish rebellion of 1599, he made a truce with the rebels instead. For his disobedience he was banished from court. He planned a coup against the court party in 1601; receiving no aid from Scotland or Ireland, he tried and failed to start an uprising in London. He was tried for treason, condemned, and beheaded.

Euclid (fl. c 300 B.C.), Greek mathematician whose textbook on geometry, the *Elements,* remained the authority for 2000 years. Euclid founded a school in Alexandria during the reign of Ptolemy I (306–283). One of his pupils was Ptolemy, who asked if there were not an easier way to learn; Euclid replied, "There is no royal road to geometry." The organizational system of the *Elements,* based on rigorous logic rather than on intuition, profoundly influenced all later mathematics.

Euler, Leonhard (1707–1783), Swiss mathematician, a founder of modern mathematical analysis. Even though he eventually went blind, Euler published a prodigious amount on mathematics, physics, astronomy, and other sciences. His principal works are the *Introduction to the Analysis of Infinities* (1748) and his textbooks on the calculus.

Euripides (c 485–406 B.C.), Greek dramatist, the youngest of the three classic Greek tragedians (the other two being Aeschylus and Sophocles). He saw tragedy as the result of human flaws rather than divine intervention. Euripides' plays were too unusual in his time to be generally appreciated; he wrote some 92 plays but won the prize for tragedy only five times. The later ancients preferred his plays, however, and twice as many of them have survived as those of any other Greek dramatist. The most familiar are *Medea, Hippolytus, Electra, Orestes, Alcestis, The Trojan Women, The Bacchae, Iphigenia at Aulis,* and *Iphigenia in Tauris.*

Evans, Mary Ann (or **Marian**) (1819–1880), pen name **George Eliot**, Victorian novelist noted for psychological insights into her characters. Her best-known books are *Adam Bede* (1859),

The Mill on the Floss (1860), *Silas Marner* (1861), and *Middlemarch* (1871–1872). She defied Victorian conventions and was ostracized by her family for her 25-year unwed but open union with George Henry Lewes (1817–1878), a liberal journalist and critic.

Eyck, Van: *See* Van Eyck.

F

Fahrenheit, Gabriel Daniel (1686–1736), German physicist who brought the mercury thermometer into general use and originated the thermometer scale that bears his name. He lived in England and Holland, where he developed and manufactured meteorological instruments.

Fairbanks, Douglas Elton (1883–1939), U.S. actor noted for his roles as a handsome, swashbuckling hero. He played in such films as *The Mark of Zorro* (1920), *The Three Musketeers* (1921), *Robin Hood* (1922), *The Thief of Bagdad* (1924), and *The Gaucho* (1927). Fairbanks and his wife, screen heroine Mary Pickford, were founders of United Artists.

His son, **Douglas Fairbanks, Jr.** (1909–), often played dashing, acrobatic heroes much like his father's roles, as in *The Prisoner of Zenda* (1937), as well as more sophisticated roles. He later became a British television producer and businessman.

Faisal I (Faisal ibn Husain) (1885–1933), founder and first king of Iraq. Raised with desert Arabs, he commanded rebel Arab troops in World War I and became army commander in chief. Proclaimed king of Syria in 1920, he differed with French authorities and was exiled. He was named king of Iraq in 1921 and from then on worked to strengthen the kingdom. Iraq achieved independence and League of Nations membership in 1932.

Falla, Manuel de (1876–1946), Spanish composer, a leader in 20th-century Spanish music, noted for his use of folk idiom. Falla's most famous compositions are *Nights in the Gardens of Spain* (1909–1916) for piano and orchestra, and the ballets *Love, the Magician* (*El amor gelico,* 1915) and *The Three-Cornered Hat* (*El sombrero de tres picos,* 1919).

Faraday, Michael (1791–1867), English chemist and physicist who discovered electromagnetic induction, introduced the concept of the magnetic field, discovered the basic laws of electrolysis, isolated benzene, and built the first dynamo. Faraday was unsurpassed in his ability to theorize, to see basic relationships in physics, to devise experiments for testing his theories, and to report his results clearly and simply. The series of science lectures and demonstrations he gave from 1826 became an institution. For him are named the *farad* (the unit of electrical capacitance), an effect, a constant, the laws of electrolysis, and numerous pieces of scientific equipment.

Farragut, David Glasgow (1801–1870), U.S. naval officer. Farragut joined the Navy as a midshipman at the age of nine and fought in the War of 1812. After the Civil War broke out, he was given command of a squadron and ordered to take New Orleans. He made a bold dash past the coastal defenses in the early morning hours and captured the city in April, 1862. His daring tactics served him equally well at Mobile Bay in 1864. Shouting "Damn the torpedoes, full speed ahead!" he sailed right through a minefield and went on to occupy the bay, closing the South's last Gulf port.

Farrell, James Thomas (1904–1979), U.S. writer known for his naturalistic portrayals of lower middle-class Irish life in Chicago, particularly in his Studs Lonigan trilogy. *Young Lonigan* (1932), *The Young Manhood of Studs Lonigan* (1934), and *Judgment Day* (1935) depict a way of life conditioned by poverty, hopelessness, and squalor. *A World I Never Made* (1936) was the first of a Danny O'Neill series (1936–1954) and *Invisible Swords* (1971) was the final novel of a tetralogy. Farrell also published many volumes of short stories and several books of essays.

DAVID FARRAGUT

THE BETTMANN ARCHIVE

Faruk I (1920–1965), king of Egypt, 1936–1952. Under his leadership Egypt retained close ties with Britain until the beginning of World War II. During the war Faruk was sympathetic to the Italians and Germans; not until 1945, under British pressure, did he declare war on the Axis. His popularity declined because of his extravagant living, which offended the largely Muslim population, and because of Egypt's defeat by Israel in 1948. He was deposed by a coup in 1952 and died in exile.

Faulkner, William (1897–1962), U.S. novelist and short story writer. Faulkner was a pilot in World War I and held various jobs in and around Oxford, Miss., before settling there to write fiction. For many years his reputation was clouded by the sensationalism of his brutal novel *Sanctuary* (1931). Many found his style, especially his "interior monologues," intricate and overly obscure. His most characteristic works, set in mythical Yoknapatawpha County, Miss., deal with the people of the South and the influence of the Southern past; they include *The Sound and the Fury* (1929), *As I Lay Dying* (1930), *Light in August* (1932), *Absalom, Absalom!* (1936), and the short story "The Bear" (1942). A remarkable trilogy, *The Hamlet* (1940), *The Town* (1957), and *The Mansion* (1959), chronicles the history of the Snopes family in Yoknapatawpha County. Faulkner was awarded the 1949 Nobel Prize for Literature; his acceptance speech on the writer's craft has become famous. His delightful novel *The Reivers* (1962) won a Pulitzer Prize.

Feininger, Lyonel (1871–1956), U.S. painter known for his structural use of planes of light and color in ocean scenes and cityscapes. From 1919 he taught at the Bauhaus, where he became associated with the Blue Rider group. Reflecting the Bauhaus approach, his early work used solid cubist structure *(The Church).* His later paintings, often in line and watercolor, were more abstract (*The Tug,* 1941).

Fellini, Federico (1920–), Italian director acclaimed for his highly personal, poetic film style and for extending the scope of contemporary film beyond neorealism. In *La Strada* (1954) he introduced tragicomic lyricism to the neorealist film; in *La Dolce Vita* (1959), *8½* (1963), and *Juliet of the Spirits* (1965) the individual's quest for identity is pursued through a complex reality blending past, present, dream, and fantasy. Later Fellini films include *Satyricon* (1969), the nostalgic *Amarcord* (1974), *Orchestra Rehearsal* (1979), and *City of Women* (1980).

Ferber, Edna (1887–1968), U.S. novelist and playwright. The settings for her novels, many of which were adapted for the stage and films, include the Mississippi River (*Show Boat,* 1926), early Oklahoma (*Cimarron,* 1929), the Texas oil country (*Giant,* 1952), and frontier Alaska (*Ice Palace,* 1958). *So Big* (1925) won a Pulitzer Prize. Her plays, written with George S. Kaufman, include *The Royal Family* (1927) and *Dinner at Eight* (1932).

Ferdinand II (1452–1516), king of Aragon, 1479–1516. By his marriage to Queen Isabella of Castile, Ferdinand also became king of Castile and León, reigning as Ferdinand V, 1474–1504 and 1506–1516. Ferdinand and Isabella, ruling the kingdoms jointly, were known as the *Reyes Católicos* ("Catholic sovereigns"). The union of their kingdoms was a major step in the founding of the Spanish nation. They led a campaign to drive the Moors out of Spain and captured Granada, the last Moorish stronghold, in 1492. The same year, they expelled the Jews from Spain and sent Columbus on his first voyage to the New World. After Isabella's death in 1504, Ferdinand was forced to relinquish Castile to his son-in-law Philip I of Hapsburg, husband of Joan the Mad (1479–1555). Philip died in 1506, Joan went mad, and Ferdinand resumed the crown. He was succeeded by Philip's son Charles (later Charles V, Holy Roman Emperor).

Ferdinand V (of Castile): *See* Ferdinand II.

Fermi, Enrico (1901–1954), Italian-born U.S. nuclear physicist. Fermi taught at the universities of Florence and Rome and conducted research in electrons and in radioactivity induced by neutrons. He won the Nobel Prize in Physics in 1938. In 1939 he came to the United States, where he taught at Columbia and Chicago. A small grant from President Roosevelt started the project which eventually, as part of the Manhattan Project, produced the first controlled chain reaction (Chicago, 1942).

Field, Cyrus West (1819–1892), U.S. entrepreneur who laid the first transatlantic cable. By the age of 33 Field had amassed a fortune. In 1854 he formed a company to lay a transoceanic cable. After three failures, he succeeded in 1858, laying a cable between Newfoundland and Ireland. The first message it carried was from Queen Victoria to President Buchanan. The cable broke three weeks later. Not until 1866 did Field establish a permanent system.

Fielding, Henry (1707–1754), English writer and public official whose lively and good-natured *Tom Jones* (1749) was one of the first modern English novels. Fielding began his career as a playwright, writing burlesques such as *Tom Thumb the Great* (1730) and political satires so biting that in 1737 Prime Minister Walpole imposed strict regulations on the London theater. Turning to fiction, Fielding showed his theater experience in clever plot situations, natural dialogue, and clear characterizations. His first major book, *Joseph Andrews* (1742), satirized Richardson's sentimental *Pamela.* His other novels are *Jonathon Wild* (1743) and *Amelia* (1751).

Fields, W. C. (1880–1946), real name William Claude Dukenfield, U.S. comic film star famous for his role as a crafty drunkard, cynical about traditional virtues and feelings, with a particular dislike for animals and children. His first film was *Sally of the Sawdust* (1925), followed by *Million Dollar Legs* (1932), *Tillie and Gus* (1934), *The Bank Dick* (1941), and *Never Give a Sucker an Even Break* (1941).

Fiesole, Giovanni da (Fra Angelico) (c 1387–1455), Italian painter. He was ordained a priest about 1423 and, because of his deep religious convictions, never painted nude figures or classical themes. His best-known early work is *Coronation of the Virgin* (1435), noted for its design and color. In 1436, commissioned by Cosimo de' Medici, he decorated the convent of San Marco in Florence with frescoes, the most famous of which is *The Annunciation* (1437).

Fillmore, Millard (1800–1874), 13th President of the United States, 1850–1852. Born in a log cabin in Locke, N.Y., Fillmore had almost no schooling, but was indentured to a clothmaker until he was 19. He then read law and opened his own practice in 1823. Entering politics as a state assemblyman, he soon became a leader of the Whigs in New York State. Narrowly defeated for the governorship in 1844, he became nationally known. The Whigs nominated him as Zachary Taylor's running mate in 1848. As President, Taylor firmly opposed the provisions of the Compromise of 1850, but when Fillmore took office after Taylor's death, he chose to support Clay's compromise measures as the only way to prevent the Union from splitting over the slavery question. He promised to use force if necessary to enforce the controversial Fugitive Slave Law. This decision led to the downfall of both the Whig Party and Fillmore's own political career. He lost the party nomination in 1852, but was chosen the candidate of the "Know-Nothing" Party in 1856. Overwhelmingly defeated, he never ran for office again.

Fitzgerald, Francis Scott Key (F. Scott) (1896–1940), U.S. author whose novels and short stories epitomize the spirit of the 1920's. His life mixed brilliant early success with later failure and despair as a Hollywood screenwriter. *The Great Gatsby* (1925), his study of success and failure, is usually considered his masterpiece. Fitzgerald's other novels are *This Side of Paradise* (1920), *The Beautiful and Damned* (1921), *Tender Is the Night* (1934), and *The Last Tycoon* (1941). Among his popular stories are "The Diamond as Big as the Ritz" and "Crazy Sunday." Selections from his essays, notebooks, and letters were collected in *The Crack Up* (1945). After a long struggle with alcoholism, he died at 44.

His wife **Zelda Sayre** (1900–1948), also a writer, was eclipsed by Fitzgerald and destroyed by her own mental instability. Her novel, *Save Me the Waltz* (1932), was reissued in 1967.

Flaherty, Robert Joseph (1884–1951), American filmmaker and explorer, called the father of the documentary film for his pioneering use of film to record the daily lives of Eskimos, South Sea islanders, and others. His *Nanook of the North* (1920–1922) and *Moana* (1926) set high standards for factual yet dramatic filming of real life. Other films include *Man of Aran* (1934), *Elephant Boy* (1937), and *Louisiana Story* (1948).

Flaubert, Gustave (1821–1880), the French novelist whose naturalistic style profoundly influenced the development of the modern novel. His most influential work is considered to be *Madame Bovary* (1857), which was censored after its first publication. His other notable works include *Salammbô* (1862), *Sentimental Education* (1869), and *Three Tales* (1877).

Fleming, Sir Alexander (1881–1955), British bacteriologist who discovered penicillin. In 1928 one of Fleming's bacteria cultures was accidentally contaminated and destroyed by a mold. Continued research on this mold, named *Penicillium notatum,* showed it prevented bacterial growth. By 1940, **Dr. Howard W. Florey** (1898–1968) and **Dr. Ernst B. Chain** (1906–1979) found a method to purify penicillin for use in injections. The three men shared the 1945 Nobel Prize for Medicine.

Foch, Ferdinand (1851–1929), French military commander who led the Allied forces to victory during World War I. Foch was commissioned in 1873, but saw little active fighting before the war. At the École de Guerre in 1895, he delivered a celebrated series of lectures on massive war offensives; in 1907 Clemenceau made him director of the school. During the war, Foch brilliantly displayed his strategy, taken in part from the German strategist Clausewitz, whom he admired. In 1918 he was put in charge of the Allied armies on the western front; that same year, he framed the armistice that ended the war.

Fonda, Jane (1937–), movie actress, daughter of the popular star Henry

Fonda. Born in New York City, she made her movie debut in 1960 in *Tall Story*. In her early movies she played pert and sexy parts. In later movies, such as *Klute* (1971) and *The China Syndrome* (1979), she demonstrated her ability as a dramatic actress. Fonda has also starred in *Barefoot in the Park* (1967), *They Shoot Horses Don't They?* (1969), *Coming Home* (1978), and *On Golden Pond* (1981). With her husband Tom Hayden, Fonda has been active in civil and women's rights movements. She was particularly prominent in opposition to the Vietnam War.

Fonteyn, Margot (1919–), in full, Dame Margot Fonteyn de Arias, English ballerina. A member of the Royal Ballet, she was well known for her portrayals of Giselle and of Aurora in *The Sleeping Beauty*. She also danced in revivals of *Petrouchka* and *Firebird*. In the 1960's Fonteyn and Rudolph Nureyev toured the world in a number of productions, including Prokofiev's *Romeo and Juliet*.

Ford, Gerald R. (1913–), 38th President of the United States, 1974–1977, born in Omaha, Neb. Ford was an outstanding football player in high school and at the University of Michigan, but he turned down the opportunity to become a professional and, instead, went to the Yale Law School, from which he was graduated in 1941. After serving with the Navy in World War II, he entered politics in 1946, when he was elected to the House of Representatives. He was reelected 13 straight times; in 1965 he became the House minority leader. Ford was appointed to the Vice Presidency after the resignation of Spiro Agnew in October, 1973. After only eight months in that office he became President on the resignation of Richard Nixon, August 9, 1974. About a month after his inauguration, he granted Nixon a pardon; this act was not a popular one and may have contributed to his failure to win election to a full term in 1976. In that contest, which was a close one, he lost to Jimmy Carter, getting 48 percent of the popular vote.

Ford, Henry (1863–1947), U.S. automotive pioneer who invented mass production and the assembly line. In 1903 he founded the Ford Motor Company in Dearborn, Mich. The famous Model T appeared in 1908; in black only, with a four-cylinder engine, it was the lowest-priced car on the market until it was replaced by the Model A in 1927. Ford's impact as a production expert was immeasurable. His goals were a cheap, efficient car available to millions and a wage policy permitting his employees to buy industrial products (including, of course, Ford cars). Ford the man was inconsistent. His $5 a day wage, announced in 1914, was nearly double the average wage, yet he treated workers paternalistically and fought the labor movement. An active pacifist, he nonetheless switched Ford production to war goods overnight upon U.S. involvement in world wars I and II.

Ford, John (1895–1973), originally Sean O'Fienne, Irish-American film director known especially for Westerns and stories centered on the American past and its traditions. Of Ford's nearly 200 films, the best known are *The Informer* (1935), *Stagecoach* (1939), *The Grapes of Wrath* (1940), *How Green Was My Valley* (1941), *The Fugitive* (1947), and *The Quiet Man* (1952). He directed the World War II series *Why We Fight*.

Forster, Edward Morgan (E. M.) (1879–1970), British writer. The best known of his novels are *A Room with a View* (1908), *Howard's End* (1910), and *A Passage to India* (1924), a sensitive, subtle examination of the conflict and lack of communication between British colonials and their Indian subjects. Forster also published a book of fantasy short stories, *The Celestial Omnibus* (1911), prepared the critical lectures in *Aspects of the Novel* (1927), and collaborated on the libretto for Benjamin Britten's opera *Billy Budd* (1951). His novel *Maurice*, written in 1913–1914, was published in 1971.

Foster, Stephen Collins (1826–1864), U.S. song writer famous for his ballads and songs of the American South—which he visited only once, in 1852. His most famous are "Old Folks at Home" ("Swanee River," 1851), "My Old Kentucky Home" (1853), "Old Black Joe" (1860), "Oh! Susannah" (1848), "Jeanie with the Light Brown Hair" (1854), and "Beautiful Dreamer" (1864).

Fox, Charles James (1749–1806), British statesman and orator. He entered Parliament at 19 and was soon known for his unrelenting opposition to the power of King George III. He supported independence for the American colonies and was sympathetic to the French Revolution. Although Fox was always influential in Parliament, he was almost always in opposition. His last and greatest triumph was to persuade Parliament to abolish the slave trade in 1806. In this and in his other measures, he showed a powerful love of liberty and equality that did much to guide the course of 19th-century liberalism after his death.

Fox, George (1624–1691), English founder of the Society of Friends, or Quakers, 1652. Fox, a shoemaker by trade, possessed a deep religious interest that was unsatisfied by established churches. In 1647 he started traveling, preaching informally, making converts, and often offending established church authority; by the end of his life, he had been imprisoned eight times. Fox extended his preaching to other European nations, America, and the West Indies.

THE BETTMANN ARCHIVE

GEORGE FOX

Fra Angelico: *See* Fiesole, Giovanni da.

Fragonard, Jean Honoré (1732–1806), French painter whose coy rococo art reflected the age of frivolity before the French Revolution. After about 1765, Fragonard abandoned serious painting for naughty pictures that appealed to court ladies, actresses, and Parisian bankers. His series called *The Progress of Love* was ordered by Madame du Barry. Fragonard fell into disfavor during the revolution and died poor.

France, Anatole (1844–1924), pen name of Jacques Anatole François Thibault, French critic, novelist, and poet known for the satire and humanism of his work and for his clarity of style. Of his many works, *The Crime of Sylvestre Bonnard* (1881), *Penguin Island* (1908), and *The Revolt of the Angels* (1914) are well known. His favorite objects of ridicule were church and state and the hypocritical morality of society. He won the Nobel Prize for Literature in 1921.

Francis I (1494–1547), king of France, 1515–1547, who brought the Renaissance to France. Francis succeeded his father-in-law, King Louis XII, and continued Louis' wars in Italy. Francis's meeting with Henry VIII of England in 1520 was marked by such splendor that it was called the Field of Cloth of Gold, but the kings made no alliance. Francis launched a series of costly and unsuccessful wars against Charles VI, the Holy Roman Emperor, in Italy, losing much French territory. As a result of the Italian campaigns, the Renaissance was brought to France. The king persuaded Leonardo da Vinci to settle at Amboise and also hired Benvenuto Cellini, who created for him a magnificent saltcellar. Many lesser artists were imported to decorate French palaces, such as Francis's château at Chambord, the finest example of early Renaissance architecture.

Francis II, Holy Roman Emperor: *See* Hapsburg (family).

Francis of Assisi, Saint (c 1182–1226), original name Giovanni Francesco Bernardone, Italian founder of the Franciscan Order. He is remembered as a pious, gentle friar who saw nature as a reflection of God and called all living creatures his brothers and sisters. A worldly young man, Francis was converted by several mystical experiences and renounced his property to live in poverty and imitate the life of Christ. By about 1210, his preaching had attracted many followers, and he established an order of friars. Frequently ill, he began to live a more secluded life about 1223. After his death, it was reported that Francis had suffered the stigmata. He was canonized in 1228.

Franck, César Auguste (1822–1890), Belgian-born French composer. Included among his greatest compositions are the oratorio *Les Béatitudes* (1879), the Symphony in D minor (1889), the Piano Quintet (1879), and the symphonic poem *Le Chasseur maudit* (1882).

Franco, Francisco (1892–1975), in full, Francisco Paulino Hermenegildo Teódulo Franco y Bahamonde, Spanish soldier and dictator. When the Spanish Civil War broke out in 1936, Franco became leader of the nationalist forces. He took Madrid in 1939, ending the war, and made himself chief of state, merging all the nationalist factions and repressing all opposition. He kept Spain nominally neutral in World War II, although his sympathies were with the Axis powers, who had sent him military aid during the Civil War. In 1947 a formal constitution proclaimed Spain a monarchy. It gave Franco life tenure as head of state and awarded him the right to choose his successor. He chose to restore the monarchy, vacant since 1931 when Alfonso XIII was deposed. Franco designated Juan Carlos, grandson of Alfonso, to succeed him, thereby returning the Borbón family to the Spanish throne.

Franklin, Benjamin (1706–1790), American statesman, scientist, and writer. After learning the printing trade and submitting himself to a rigorous self-education program, which lasted virtually all his life, Franklin opened a shop in Philadelphia in 1730. He published the *Pennsylvania Gazette,* a lively newspaper, and the popular *Poor Richard's Almanack.* By 1748, when he retired from business, Franklin had entered active politics and had promoted such enterprises as a library, a volunteer fire company, the American Philosophical Society, and an academy that later became the University of Pennsylvania. He also had invented the Franklin stove, bifocal eyeglasses, and a clock. In 1752 he conducted his famous kite experiments with electricity, which made him an internationally recognized scientist. In 1757 and again in 1762, Franklin was sent to England to represent the colonies. In 1775 he returned to America and immediately helped draft the Declaration of Independence. In 1776 Franklin went to France, where his charm and wit made him as popular with the government as with the ladies. He secured the military assistance the colonies needed in the Revolutionary War and, in the process, became a popular hero of France. Though nearly 80 when he returned home, he helped draft the U.S. Constitution in 1787. Franklin's versatility, practicality, and humorous cynicism—typical of the American spirit—are all apparent in his unfinished *Autobiography.*

Franz Josef I (or **Francis Joseph**) (1830–1916), emperor of Austria from 1848 and king of Hungary from 1867, the last major Hapsburg ruler of Austria-Hungary. Convinced of the rightness of absolute rule, Franz Josef depended on royal prestige, on the army, and on a strict police force to enforce his rule. Franz Josef's foreign wars were largely unsuccessful, as was his foreign policy, and Austria lost power to Prussia. His hopes for a lasting Hapsburg dynasty were ended by the execution of his brother Maximilian in Mexico, the suicide of his son the crown prince, and the assassinations of his wife in 1898 and of his heir, Francis Ferdinand, in 1914. Two years after Franz Josef's death, the monarchy fell.

BENJAMIN FRANKLIN

THE BETTMANN ARCHIVE

Frederick II (Frederick the Great) (1712–1786), king of Prussia, 1740–1786. Frederick was a friend of Voltaire and other leading intellectuals and an enlightened despot. He had no fear of risking the Prussian army. One of his first official acts was to invade Silesia, precipitating the War of the Austrian Succession (1740–1748). His military prestige reached its height in the Seven Years' War (1756–1763), from which Prussia emerged as a great power. Through his writings and his patronage of arts and sciences, Frederick was known to Europe as the philosopher king. An avid flute player, he engaged C.P.E. Bach as his accompanist for concerts at court. In his old age, Frederick, stooped and spare, became a memorable figure. Though he grew lonely and cynical, his people remembered him fondly as *"der alte Fritz"* (old Fred).

Frémont, John Charles (1813–1890), U.S. explorer and soldier. Frémont became a mapmaker for the Army and in 1842 mapped part of the Oregon Trail. In 1843–1844 he explored the Pacific Northwest and, in midwinter, crossed the Sierra Nevada into California. He was sent back to California in 1845 with instructions to seize the area if war with Mexico broke out. He supported the California settlers in the Bear Flag uprising in 1846 and, when the Mexican War began, secured the rest of California. For refusing to turn over the territory to General Stephen Kearny in 1847, he was court-martialed. He resigned from the Army in 1848, settling on his land in California, where gold was found the next year. Frémont became the state's first U.S. senator in 1850. A popular hero, in

1856 he was the Republican Party's first Presidential nominee, but he lost the election. He again served in the Army during the Civil War and was governor of Arizona Territory, 1878–1883.

French, Daniel (1850–1931), U.S. sculptor whose many monumental works include two of the most famous and popular sculptures in the United States. French's first commission was *The Minute Man* (1875), celebrating the 100th anniversary of the Battle of Concord (Mass.). This early success assured his career as a sculptor. Even more famous is the seated marble *Lincoln,* dedicated in 1922, in the Lincoln Memorial, Washington, D.C.

Freud, Sigmund (1856–1939), Austrian physician and founder of psychoanalysis. Though Freud is usually thought of as a medical man, he also had a wide knowledge of philosophy, sociology, and literature. He became a practicing neurologist in Vienna. From 1902 Freud was professor of neuropathology at the University of Vienna. Being of Jewish descent, he moved to England after the Nazi occupation of Austria in 1938. In treating patients for various emotional problems, Freud developed his original theories of neurosis and his psychoanalytic technique of free association. He then began to consider the significance of his patients' dreams and reported his findings in *The Interpretation of Dreams* (1900), which he considered his most important work. He also described the influence of the unconscious mind in normal persons (*The Psychopathology of Everyday Life,* 1904). Freud's libido theory was his most controversial; he later altered it to a theory of life instinct vs. death instinct (*Beyond the Pleasure Principle,* 1921). During his later life, Freud applied his thinking to culture, art, sociology, and religion, producing such provocative books as *Totem and Taboo* (1913), *On Creativity and the Unconscious* (1925), *Civilization and Its Discontents* (1930), and *Moses and Monotheism* (1939). His influence, and the influence of his ideas, on all facets of modern thought and culture are still considered to be enormous.

SIGMUND FREUD

THE BETTMANN ARCHIVE

Frick, Henry Clay (1849–1919), U.S. entrepreneur. Frick became a millionaire by the age of 30 by supplying Pittsburgh steel mills with coke. As chairman of Andrew Carnegie's steel company, 1889–1900, he broke the Homestead Strike of 1892 (during which he was shot and stabbed) and made the company the largest steel producer in the world. After breaking with Carnegie, he founded U.S. Steel, which bought out Carnegie in 1901. Frick left his townhouse and noteworthy art collection to New York City as a museum.

Froebel, Friedrich Wilhelm August (1782–1852), German educator. Froebel began teaching school, then worked with Pestalozzi in Switzerland. In 1816 he founded his first school. After developing his ideas, he opened the first kindergarten ("garden of children") in 1837. Froebel believed in the innate creativity of children and the use of many different materials (clay, paint, paper, blocks) to allow children to develop creatively through play.

Froissart, Jean (c 1337–c 1410), French historian remembered for his *Chronicles,* a history covering the first half of the Hundred Years' War. His broad travels and familiarity with court life, where he came to know such leaders as Edward the Black Prince, gave him considerable material. Although full of factual errors, the *Chronicles,* in four books written between about 1371 and 1404, provide vivid, detailed accounts of the customs of 14th-century nobility.

Fromm, Erich (1900–1980), German-born U.S. psychoanalyst whose theories emphasize the importance of cultural and economic factors in creating neuroses and psychoses rather than the libidinal factors stressed by orthodox Freudian theory. After settling in the United States in 1934, Fromm wrote many popular books, including *Escape from Freedom* (1941), *The Art of Loving* (1956), *The Sane Society* (1955), *May Man Prevail* (1961), and *Revolution of Hope* (1968).

Frontenac et Palluau, Comte de; Louis de Baude (1622–1698), French army officer and governor of New France (Canada). He extended French influence from Hudson Bay to the Gulf of Mexico, encouraging the expansion of the fur trade and the expeditions of La Salle (with whom he conspired in illegal fur trading). He conflicted with the authority of the church and in 1682 was recalled for misgovernment. Sent back to Canada in 1689, he successfully resisted attacks by the British and Iroquois.

Frost, Robert Lee (1874–1963), U.S. poet who used the simple language and images of rural New England to create poetry with deep meaning. As a young man, Frost tried teaching, factory work, and farming in New Hampshire, all with little success. In 1912 he took his family to England, where he published *A Boy's Will* (1913) and *North of Boston* (1914). British critics praised his poetry, and by the time he returned to the United States in 1915, his books were a success. Four of his books received Pulitzer prizes: *New Hampshire* (1923), *Collected Poems* (1930), *A Further Range* (1936), and *A Witness Tree* (1942). He also gave many public readings; at President John F. Kennedy's inauguration, he recited "The Gift Outright" (from *In the Clearing,* 1962).

Fulbright, James William (1905–), U.S. senator, sponsor of the Fulbright Act (1946), which provides stipends for U.S. scholars to study abroad. Fulbright was president of the University of Arkansas, 1939–1941, and was a senator from Arkansas from 1945 to 1975. As chairman of the Senate Foreign Relations Committee, he exerted a powerful influence on U.S. policies, particularly foreign aid and the Vietnam War.

Fuller, (Richard) Buckminster (1895–1983), U.S. architect, inventor, and philosopher known for his concepts of energy and architecture based on the "dymaxion" *(dynamic* plus *maximum)* theory of comprehensive design. His most famous invention was the geodesic dome, which utilizes the dymaxion concept in two ways: the shape encloses the most space with the least surface, and the structure provides the greatest stability with the least bulk. The domes came to be used worldwide. Fuller concerned himself constantly with creating organic and economic environments for people; he coined the term "spaceship earth." He wrote *No More Secondhand God* (1963) and other books.

Fuller, (Sarah) Margaret, Marchioness Ossoli (1810–1850), U.S. journalist. Taught at home because there were few schools for women, she loved learning, but her father's strenuous tutoring weakened her health. From 1839 to 1844 Fuller conducted "conversation" classes in Boston to enable women to gain knowledge in the arts, philosophy, and mythology. Her friendship with Emerson led to the editorship of the *Dial;* she later was literary critic for Greeley's *Tribune.* Her classic *Woman in the Nineteenth Century* (1845) urged the emotional and intellectual emancipation of women. Traveling in Europe in 1846, she was caught up in the Italian revolution. Secretly married to a liberal Italian nobleman, she kept an account of the revolution, which she considered her best manuscript. Returning to the United States in 1850, she, her husband, and her child perished, along with her manuscript, in a shipwreck off Fire Island.

Fulton, Robert (1765–1815), U.S. engineer and builder of the first commercially successful U.S. steamboat. In 1786 he went to Europe to study painting, but became more interested in canal engineering and new types of boats, launching a submarine in 1800. With Robert Livingston, then U.S. minister to France, Fulton tested a steamboat on the Seine in 1803. His designs were influenced by the steamboats he had seen operating in England and France. In 1806 he returned to the United States with an English steam engine and built another steamboat, which he launched on the Hudson River in 1807. The next year, Fulton and Livingston began a passenger service on the Hudson with their boat, which had been rebuilt and named the *Clermont.*

G

Gagarin, Yuri Alekseyevich (1934–1968), Soviet cosmonaut who made the first manned space flight. Gagarin orbited Earth in the *Vostok 1* on April 12, 1961. A carpenter's son, Gagarin grew up on a collective farm and became a military pilot in 1955. He died in a test flight of a new plane.

Gainsborough, Thomas (1727–1788), English painter of portraits and landscapes. At 25 years of age he began to paint portraits; his first clients were merchants and squires. In 1760 he moved to fashionable Bath, where his subjects were members of society and the nobility. There he developed his style of light, fast brush strokes and delicate colors. *The Blue Boy* (1779) and *Morning Walk* (1785) are typical Gainsborough portraits. He said that portraits provided his living, but that landscapes (such as *The Harvest Wagon,* 1784) gave him more pleasure.

Galen (c 130–c 200), Greek physician, founder of experimental physiology. Physician to many Greek and Roman officials, his views made him unpopular with his colleagues. Galen's writings on anatomy and physiology were remarkably complete and accurate. Translated into Latin in the 1500's, they provided the basis for the development of modern medicine.

Galileo Galilei (1564–1642), Italian mathematician, physicist, and astronomer. He was one of the first to emphasize use of scientific experiment and systematic observation rather than philosophical speculation in understanding the nature of the universe. Galileo was the inventor of several scientific instruments and the first to use a telescope in astronomy, observing the Milky Way and the moon's surface. His studies of gravity and motion laid the basis for Newton's laws. Supposedly, Galileo dropped large and small weights from the Tower of Pisa to prove that all bodies fall at the same speed. Like most thinkers of his day, Galileo worked under the scrutiny of the church. His inventions and discoveries won him fame, but his growing belief that the universe functions according to mathematical laws was too much for the theologians who guarded the Christian world against heresy. His observations with the telescope led him to believe that Earth revolves around the sun. In 1632 he published the *Dialogue Concerning the Two Chief World Systems,* in which he rejected the Ptolemaic (Earth-centered) view of the universe for the Copernican (sun-centered). He was brought to trial before the Inquisition in 1633, where he was forced to renounce the Copernican teachings and put under permanent house arrest. As Galileo left the court, he is said to have murmured, "And yet it moves," referring to Earth's movement around the sun.

Gallatin, (Abraham Alfonse) Albert (1761–1849), Swiss-born U.S. statesman and financier, secretary of the treasury, 1801–1814. An advocate of economy in government, Gallatin criticized Hamilton's tax policies. An early member of the Jeffersonian Democrats, he became Jefferson's secretary of the treasury in 1801. By his careful policies he greatly reduced the public debt. Serving as a diplomat after 1813, he negotiated the Treaty of Ghent that ended the War of 1812.

Galsworthy, John (1867–1933), English novelist and playwright, best known for his epic social chronicle of late Victorian and Edwardian England, *The Forsyte Saga.* His history of the Forsyte family includes *The Man of Property* (1906), *In Chancery* (1920), *To Let* (1921), and the novels collected in the trilogy *A Modern Comedy* (1929). Galsworthy wrote with compassion for oppressed people and concern for social justice, as in the plays *Strife* (1909) and *Loyalties* (1922). He was awarded the Nobel Prize for Literature in 1932.

Galvani, Luigi (or **Aloisio**) (1737–1798), Italian physiologist who first produced an electric current. A teacher of anatomy at the University of Bologna, he performed experiments in "animal electricity." Galvani made a device of copper and iron, placing a probe of one metal on a nerve of a recently killed frog, and a probe of the other on a muscle. He attributed the twitching of the frog's legs to electricity from the nerve itself ("galvanism"); in fact, the current was generated by the two metals, the frog's body acting merely as a conductor.

Gama, Vasco da (c 1460–1524), Portuguese explorer who discovered a sea route from western Europe to India by way of the Cape of Good Hope. In 1497 da Gama left Lisbon with four ships and a crew of 170; he rounded the cape discovered by Días a few years before and landed in Calicut on the Malabar coast in 1498. In 1502 da Gama returned to India, where he attacked Calicut and its fleet in revenge for the murder of Portuguese settlers in 1501. In 1524 he returned for a third time as viceroy of Portuguese India.

Gandhi, Indira Priyadarshini Nehru (1917–1984), prime minister of India (1966–1977, 1980–1984). The daughter of Jawaharlal Nehru, she grew up in the midst of the struggle for Indian independence. In 1942 she married a

INDIRA GANDHI

UPI

journalist, Feroze Gandhi, not related to Mohandas Gandhi. A member of the Congress Party, Gandhi worked and traveled with her father, India's first prime minister. She became party president in 1959 and, after her father's death in 1964, she was made a cabinet minister. She succeeded to the prime ministership in 1966 and won reelection in 1971. In an effort to carry out her reforms and to end what she called a conspiracy against her program, she imposed emergency rule in 1975 and suspended elections. When elections were finally held, she was defeated. She was charged with official corruption and jailed for a short time, but at the next election, in January, 1980, she won an overwhelming victory and returned to power. Gandhi was assassinated by Sikh extremist members of her own security guard.

Gandhi, Mohandas Karamchand (Mahatma) (1869–1948), great Hindu leader in the struggle for an independent India whose theory of nonviolent resistance had immeasurable impact on later social reform movements elsewhere. From 1893 Gandhi spent about 20 years in South Africa handling legal affairs of Indians unjustly treated by whites. There he developed his technique of nonviolence *(satyagraha).* In 1919 Gandhi became the leader of a strong nationalist movement in India. He led millions of Indians in campaigns of civil disobedience and organized boycotts of British goods, particularly cloth, using the hand spinning wheel as a symbol of freedom. After 1930 mass protests occurred frequently, embarrassing the British and enlisting world sympathy for Indian independence. Gandhi fasted and went to prison repeatedly, as did his wife Kasturbai; she died in jail in 1944; Gandhi, in poor health, was released. India became independent in 1947, but Gandhi could not prevent its being partitioned to form the separate Muslim state of Pakistan. Deeply regretting his failure to achieve Hindu-Muslim unity, he did not celebrate independence, but devoted his efforts to quieting riots and safeguarding the Muslim minority. He was assassinated by a Hindu fanatic.

García Lorca, Federico (1899–1936), Spanish poet and dramatist known for his plays of passion, violence, and tragedy, colored by the use of themes from Andalusian gypsy life. As co-director of La Barraca, a traveling theatrical group, he helped repopularize drama in Spain. García Lorca's best-known works are the plays *Blood Wedding* (*Bodas de sangre,* 1933), *The House of Bernarda Alba* (*La casa de Bernarda Alba,* 1936), and the gypsy poems in *Primer romancero gitano* (1928). In 1936 he was kidnaped and executed by Franco supporters in Granada.

Garfield, James Abram (1831–1881), 20th President of the United States for six months in 1881. Garfield was born in a log cabin in Orange, Ohio, and raised in poverty. After graduating from Williams College in 1856, he taught school, then became a state senator. During the Civil War, he formed and led a regiment of volunteers and was made a major general. He resigned from the Army in 1863 to become a congressman from Ohio, a post he held for the next 17 years. Garfield was elected a U.S. senator in 1880. Later that year his name was proposed as a dark-horse candidate to break a tie in the balloting for the Republican Presidential nomination. He was nominated and elected, with Chester A. Arthur as his running mate. On July 2, 1881, four months after he had taken office, he was shot by Charles J. Guiteau, a disgruntled lawyer who had failed to be appointed consul to France. Garfield died on September 19.

Garibaldi, Giuseppe (1807–1882), Italian patriot, a leader in the *Risorgimento,* the movement to unify Italy. Garibaldi, a member of Mazzini's revolutionary Young Italy movement, was forced to flee Italy in 1834. For several years he conducted guerrilla warfare in revolutions in South America. There he married his wife Anita, who later fought beside him in Italy. He returned to Italy in 1848, joined northern Italy's revolt against Austria, and led the heroic defense of Rome against the French. When Rome fell in 1849, he led a masterly retreat north, pursued by armies of Austria, France, Spain, and Naples. Anita died on the retreat, but Garibaldi escaped to America. He returned to Italy in 1854 and entered the service of King Victor Emmanuel II of Sardinia-Piedmont. In 1860 he and "the Thousand" *(i Mille),* his band of 1000 volunteers in their famous red shirts, sailed to Sicily. In six months they had taken Sicily and Naples for the king. In succeeding years Garibaldi grew disillusioned with the new government, founded by Cavour, which would not let him complete the conquest of Italy. He lived in retirement at his home on Caprera, except for an expedition in 1870 to aid the French in the Franco-Prussian War.

Garrick, David (1717–1779), English actor, playwright, and theatrical manager, the leading actor of his time in tragedy and comedy. In 1741 his portrayal of Shakespeare's Richard III astounded the London theater world, and his reputation as an actor continued undiminished until his death. As manager of the Drury Lane Theater, 1747–1776, he instituted reforms in acting, lighting, and administration. His original plays include the successful farce *The Lying Valet* (1741), but he is best remembered for his free adaptation and interpretation of Shakespeare.

Garrison, William Lloyd (1805–1879), U.S. abolitionist leader known for his

THE BETTMANN ARCHIVE

PAUL GAUGUIN

passion and eloquence in demanding an end to slavery. In 1831 Garrison founded the *Liberator,* the chief organ of the abolitionist movement. He considered abolition a moral crusade, differing with those who sought political solutions. He lost some support by insisting that women take an equal part in the movement. Because the U.S. Constitution permitted slavery, he called it "a covenant with death and an agreement with hell," and burned a copy publicly in 1854. Garrison was president of the American Anti-Slavery Society for more than 20 years. He also supported women's rights, pacifism, and better treatment of the American Indian.

Garvey, Marcus (1887–1940), Jamaican social reformer remembered for his "back to Africa" campaign in the United States urging American blacks to return to their "homeland." In 1914 he founded the Universal Negro Improvement Association, dedicated to promoting black business, cultural pride, and eventual resettlement in Liberia. He formed the Black Star Steamship Line and other black enterprises, but the Nigerian government in 1924 rejected his resettlement plans and the Black Star Line went bankrupt. Accused of fraud and eventually deported, Garvey continued to speak for black unity.

Gauguin, (Eugène Henri) Paul (1848–1903), able French postimpressionist painter, best known for his exotic, primitivist paintings of Tahiti. Gauguin, a successful Paris stockbroker, began to enjoy his artistic hobbies more than his job. He exhibited with the impressionists in 1880–1882 and then abandoned his old way of life in order to paint. A visit to Martinique inspired a love for the tropics; he also painted in Brittany and, briefly, at Arles with Van Gogh. Gauguin's "synthetic symbolism" was characterized by pure, bright colors and simple, flat forms (*The Yellow Christ,* 1889). After

1891 he lived in poverty in Tahiti and the Marquesas. There he produced such works as *Ia Orana Maria* (1891), *The Moon and the Earth* (1893), and *Golden Bodies* (1901).

Gaulle, Charles de: *See* De Gaulle, Charles.

Gauss, Carl Friedrich (1777–1855), German mathematician and scientist. A child prodigy, he began solving complex problems at age eight and made most of his fundamental discoveries before he was 18. At 19 he solved a geometric problem that had puzzled mathematicians since the time of Euclid. He also developed a non-Euclidean geometry that he never published because of its controversial nature. Gauss's work outlining modern number theory appeared in *Disquisitiones arithmeticæ* (1801), his chief publication. He spent the rest of his life chiefly working in astronomy, though he also did work in topology, mechanics, electricity, and numerous other fields.

Gay-Lussac, Joseph Louis (1778–1850), French chemist and physicist. In 1804 he made several ascents in a balloon to study terrestrial magnetism and analyze the air. His major discovery, published in 1809, was the general law governing the volumes of gases in chemical combination. Several important industrial processes were developed in his later research.

Gehrig, (Henry) Louis (1903–1941), U.S. baseball player known as the Iron Horse. Lou Gehrig signed as first baseman with the New York Yankees in 1925 and by his retirement in 1939 had compiled a batting record often surpassing that of his teammate Babe Ruth. His lifetime average was .341, and he played in more than 2000 consecutive major league games and seven World Series. A sclerosis disease caused his early retirement and death.

Genet, Jean (1910–1986), French writer whose life, like his writing, demonstrated his rebellion against society. Before becoming famous, he was frequently in prison for various crimes; many of his manuscripts were written in jail. Genet's books deliberately show the world as evil, as in *Our Lady of the Flowers* (1942, 1951). After 1949 he wrote only for the theater; *The Balcony* appeared in 1957, *The Blacks* in 1959.

Genghis Khan (c 1167–1227), title of Temujin, leader of the Mongols, whose cavalry hordes overran Asia from Peking to the Caspian Sea. His father, a tribal chief of the Mongols, was murdered by a rival tribe, the Tatars, and Temujin spent years fighting to survive and to regain his position. By 1206 he had mastered all Mongolia and was acclaimed *Khan,* or chief, with the title *Genghis,* which means "wide" or "extensive." He first conquered northern China, then turned west and swept over Turkestan and Persia as far as European Russia. A brilliant strategist, he ensured success by building his army's reputation for savage ferocity, especially if resisted.

Geoffrey of Monmouth (c 1100–c 1155), English chronicler. His *History of the Kings of Britain* (c 1135) was the prime source for the medieval legends of King Arthur. He also wrote a *Life of Merlin* in verse (c 1150). Geoffrey claimed that his *History* was derived from ancient sources, but scholars believe that much of it was his own invention. The *History,* one of the most popular books of the Middle Ages, makes Arthur's reign the high point of the history of Britain before the Saxon conquest.

George VI (1895–1952), king of Great Britain and Northern Ireland, 1936–1952, and emperor of India, 1936–1947. George became king on the abdication of his brother Edward VIII. As a prince, he had served on battleships during World War I; during World War II, he set an example of courage by visiting soldiers and civilians in dangerous areas. He and Churchill both wanted to accompany the invasion of Normandy but, each fearing the other's loss to the nation, they talked each other out of going.

George, David Lloyd: *See* Lloyd George, David.

George, Henry (1839–1897), U.S. reformer and economist who proposed and popularized the idea of a single tax. Observing the spectacular rise in land values as the West was settled, George came to believe that land belongs to the people, not to private owners who benefit from its increasing scarcity. He therefore proposed a single tax on the rent from land and the abolishment of all other taxes. To explain his ideas, George wrote *Progress and Poverty* (1879), which became popular worldwide.

Geronimo (c 1829–1909), Chiricahua Apache warrior, one of the most famous Indian leaders in the Southwest. For about 15 years he led campaigns against the Mexicans, who in 1858 had killed his entire family. Geronimo agreed in 1886 to surrender to the U.S. Army if he and his men could join relatives being held in Florida; on the subsequent trip he and his followers escaped. It took 5000 troops 18 months to apprehend Geronimo and his band of 35 men, eight children, and 100 women. He was finally put in military confinement at Fort Sill, Okla., where he dictated his memoirs.

Gershwin, George (1898–1937), original name Jakob Bruskin Gershvin, U.S. composer, an innovator in the composition of truly American music. His symphonic jazz work *Rhapsody in Blue* (1924) is performed more often than any other American composition. Gershwin first wrote songs and musical comedies, with lyrics by his brother Ira, including *Lady, Be Good* (1924) and *Of Thee I Sing* (1931); the shows contained such songs as "The Man I Love" and "I Got Rhythm." The Concerto in F for piano (1925) and *An American in Paris* (1928) followed the success of *Rhapsody.* In 1935 Gershwin produced *Porgy and Bess,* his most mature work, and America's best-known opera.

Ghiberti, Lorenzo (1378–1455), Italian sculptor and goldsmith, most famous for two sets of magnificent bronze doors made for the baptistery at Florence. In 1401 Ghiberti defeated the sculptor Brunelleschi in a competition to choose an artist. His first set of doors, modeled after an earlier pair made by Andrea Pisano, showed scenes from the life of Christ. The 28 panels were completed in 1424; the following year Ghiberti began work on the second set of doors. Completed in 1452, they comprised ten large panels of Old Testament scenes. Michelangelo called the Ghiberti doors worthy to be the "gates of Paradise."

Giacometti, Alberto (1901–1966), Swiss sculptor noted for his elongated, rough-edged sculptures of human figures, considered one of the most singular of contemporary sculptors. His figures communicate a sense of loneliness and isolation. Two of his well-known works, completed during his surrealist period, are *The Palace at 4 a.m.* (1933) and *Woman Walking* (1934). Other noted pieces are *City*

GEORGE GERSHWIN

BETTMANN/SPRINGER FILM ARCHIVE

Square (1948–1949) and *Man Pointing* (1947).

Gibbon, Edward (1737–1794), English historian known for his monumental *History of the Decline and Fall of the Roman Empire* (6 volumes, 1776–1788). The *Decline and Fall* was widely attacked, mostly for its skeptical presentation of Christianity, but it became a classic because of its graceful narrative and overall sense of the unity of Western civilization.

Gibbs, Josiah Willard (1839–1903), U.S. mathematical physicist, considered the founder of physical chemistry. Gibbs's studies and theories were far ahead of the science of his time. Though he taught at Yale for 32 years, his lectures were so advanced for his students that his main influence came from his writings on thermodynamics, optics, vector analysis, mechanics, and other fields.

Gibran, Kahlil (1883–1931), Lebanese-American poet and artist, born in Syria, famous for his book of mystical prose poems, *The Prophet* (1923). Emotional and sensual, the poems concern such timeless themes as love, good, and evil. Gibran's other books include *Jesus, the Son of Man* (1928) and *The Garden of the Prophet* (1933). His paintings and earlier plays, written in Arabic, were widely known in the Middle East.

Gide, André Paul Guillaume (1869–1951), French novelist and essayist whose works of self-exploration influenced modern world literature. His *Journal,* covering more than 50 years, is a humanist testament of great warmth and pure literary style. Gide's early works disregarded accepted moral conventions; later he attacked social problems. His many books include *The Fruits of the Earth* (1897), *The Immoralist* (1902), *Strait Is the Gate* (1909), *The Vatican Swindle* (1914), *The Counterfeiters* (1926), and his revealing autobiography *If It Die* (1926). Gide won the Nobel Prize for Literature in 1947.

Gielgud, Sir (Arthur) John (1904–), British actor, director, and producer, best known for his portrayals of Shakespearean characters, including Hamlet, Romeo, Macbeth, and King Lear, and for the Shakespearean recitation "The Ages of Man." He also appeared in Edward Albee's contemporary drama *Tiny Alice* (1964), in such films as *Becket* (1964) and *Sebastian* (1967), and in the television film series *Brideshead Revisited* (1981).

Gilbert, William (1540–1603), English physicist and physician, the foremost English scientist of the Elizabethan period. Though a leading London physician, doctor to Queen Elizabeth and James I, Gilbert is better known for his experiments in magnetism and electricity. He described Earth as a great magnet with magnetic poles; his *De Magnete, magneticisque corporibus* (1600) is considered the first great English scientific work.

Gilbert, Sir William Schwenck (1836–1911), British author, best known for his collaboration with Sir Arthur Sullivan on the famous Gilbert and Sullivan comic operas. These were produced by Richard D'Oyly Carte with such success that a new theater, the Savoy, was built to stage them. They include *H.M.S. Pinafore* (1878), *The Pirates of Penzance* (1879), and *The Mikado* (1885).

Ginsberg, Allen (1926–), U.S. poet and leading figure in avant-garde movements. Ginsberg first became known as a spokesman for the "beat generation," principally through reading his poem "Howl" (*Howl, and Other Poems,* 1956). In the long run, however, Ginsberg's personality had perhaps even more influence than his writing. An advocate of oriental religions, marijuana, peace, love, and "flower power," he exemplified and popularized the "hippie" style of the 1960's and 1970's.

Giotto di Bondone (c 1266–1337), Italian painter, architect, and sculptor, often called the first Renaissance painter. Giotto's most famous frescoes, painted about 1303–1305, in which he broke with tradition by portraying human emotion in a naturalistic fashion, are in the Arena Chapel at Padua: *Meeting of Joachim and Anna, The Nativity,* and *Flight into Egypt.* Other important works survive in Assisi and in Florence.

Giscard d'Estaing, Valéry (1926–), president of France, 1974–1981. A brilliant student in college, Giscard d'Estaing was elected to the national assembly when only 29. In 1959 he became a deputy cabinet minister under President de Gaulle, and in 1962 finance minister. Put out of office in 1966, he returned to the post in 1969 under President Pompidou. In 1974 Giscard d'Estaing was elected president, but in 1981 he lost a runoff election to François Mitterand. As president, he furthered European economic cooperation and closer ties with the United States.

Gladstone, William Ewart (1809–1898), one of the greatest statesmen and prime ministers of Britain. Energetic, sympathetic, and righteous, Gladstone entered Parliament in 1832 with strong conservative opinions. As he learned more of social and political conditions, his views became more liberal. At the end of his more than 60 years in Parliament, he was known as the Grand Old Man of Liberalism. He first became prime minister in 1868, replacing his famous rival Disraeli. Except for Disraeli's second cabinet, 1874–1880, Gladstone was prime minister almost continuously until 1894, despite Queen Victoria's increasing dislike for him. He secured many of the great liberal reforms of the period, notably universal education and voting rights. His political opinions were based on moral judgments, and on moral grounds he opposed many of Britain's foreign and imperial policies. His last effort was to grant home rule to Ireland; when it finally failed, he retired in 1894.

THE BETTMANN ARCHIVE

WILLIAM GLADSTONE

Glenn, John Herschel, Jr. (1921–), U.S. astronaut who made the first orbital flight of the U.S. space program, February 20, 1962. A Marine Corps officer, Glenn orbited Earth three times in *Friendship 6,* a Mercury-Atlas capsule. He left the space program in 1964 and was elected to the U.S. Senate from Ohio in 1974.

Gluck, Christoph Willibald von (1714–1787), German composer who changed 18th-century opera into its modern form. Working in Italy and Austria, he wrote many successful traditional operas in the 1740's and 1750's. Gluck introduced his changes in the "reform operas" *Orfeo ed Euridice* (1762) and *Alceste* (1767). He simplified the plot to convey a story and eliminated vocal display that added nothing to the drama. His operas in the new style included *Iphigénie en Aulide* (1772).

Godard, Jean-Luc (1930–), French film critic and pioneering director of the French "new wave" *(nouvelle vague)* cinema. In revolt against traditional filmmaking, he used the camera as a means of subjective expression, stressed film technique as an end in itself, and abandoned conventional sequence structure. His films include *Breathless* (1960), *A Woman Is a Woman* (1961), *La Chinoise* (1967), and *Every Man for Himself* (1980).

Goddard, Robert Hutchings (1882–1945), U.S. physicist and engineer, the foremost American rocket pioneer. Goddard's experiments, beginning about 1910, laid the groundwork for most later work in rocketry. His paper "A Method of Reaching Extreme Altitudes" (1919) first predicted the use of rockets to reach the moon. Though much of his early work was ridiculed, Goddard continued to develop new techniques; he experimented with liquid fuels in the 1920's and later with gyroscopic guidance systems.

Goebbels, (Paul) Joseph (1897–1945), German propaganda minister of the Third Reich. One of the early Nazi Party members, Goebbels was responsible for much of the pageantry and propaganda that made Nazism popular. He took control of all national media when Hitler came to power in 1932. He and his family committed suicide during the fall of Berlin in 1945.

Goethals, George Washington (1858–1928), U.S. Army engineer, chief architect of the Panama Canal. In 1907 President Theodore Roosevelt named Goethals to oversee the building of the canal. He tactfully managed to overcome civilian workers' prejudice against his Army rank and concerned himself with food, housing, and health measures for the more than 30,000 men working on the site. When the canal was completed in 1914, Goethals became the first civil governor of the Canal Zone.

Goethe, Johann Wolfgang von (1749–1832), German author and poet. Goethe's life spanned the change from rationalism to romanticism, a change he helped bring about. Influenced by Herder while a student in Strasbourg, he became a leader in the literary movement known as *Sturm und Drang.* His novel of this period, *The Sorrows of Young Werther* (1774), epitomized the antirational yearnings of his generation. He made numerous scientific studies through the years. A journey to Italy from 1786–1788 converted him to classical and humanistic ideals; from then on he grew from sufferer to sage. His view of life as development took form in *Wilhelm Meister,* a series of novels published between 1796 and 1829. The famous friendship between Goethe and Schiller provided poetic inspiration for both. Goethe resumed his work on the Faust theme and published Part I of *Faust* in 1808. He finished Part II in 1832. It was his masterpiece, an enigmatic and inexhaustible work. Many of his most moving works were his short lyrics, such as the well-known *"Erlkönig."*

Gogh, Vincent van: *See* Van Gogh, Vincent.

Gogol, Nikolai Vasilievich (1809–1852), Russian novelist and short story writer, founder of Russian realism and the first of the great 19th-century Russian novelists. From his childhood in the Ukraine he wrote the half-fantastic folk tales in *Evenings on a Farm near Dikanka* (1831–1832). His sharp powers of observation are shown notably in the short stories *The Nose* (1835) and *The Carriage* (1836), and in the play *The Inspector General* (1835). Gogol's masterpiece, *Dead Souls* (1842), satirizes greed and fortune hunting.

Goldsmith, Oliver (c 1730–1774), Anglo-Irish novelist, poet, playwright, and essayist. He first won recognition for his *Enquiry into the Present State of Polite Learning in Europe* (1759). *The Citizen of the World* (1762) established his reputation as a first-rank essayist. Goldsmith is probably best remembered for *The Vicar of Wakefield* (1766), a novel of rural life noted for its characterizations; the still popular comedy *She Stoops to Conquer* (1773); and the poem "The Deserted Village" (1770).

Goldwater, Barry Morris (1909–), U.S. political figure known for his staunch espousal of conservative political principles. As U.S. senator from Arizona, 1953–1964, he led the Republican conservative wing in opposition to expansion of federal authority and in support of national defense legislation. He was nominated for the Presidency in 1964 but was decisively defeated. Reelected to the Senate in 1968, he retired in 1986.

Goldwyn, Samuel (1882–1974), U.S. film producer, born in Poland. A pioneer in the movie industry, Goldwyn, with Jesse Lasky, in 1913 produced *The Squaw Man,* directed by C. B. deMille. He then founded his own film company and, after several mergers, became head of Metro-Goldwyn-Mayer in 1925. He introduced such stars as Valentino and Pola Negri and made such memorable films as *The Little Foxes* (1941) and *The Best Years of Our Lives* (1946). He was also known for "goldwynisms" like "Include me out."

Gompers, Samuel (1850–1924), U.S. labor leader, founder of the American Federation of Labor (AFL). He led his union from the Knights of Labor in 1886 to form the AFL. He served as its president until his death, except for the year 1895. A firm conservative, Gompers fought socialist and radical forces and firmly believed in unionism within capitalism; his goals were basically economic, involving wages, hours, and working conditions.

Goodyear, Charles (1800–1860), U.S. inventor of the vulcanization of rubber. In 1839 he accidentally discovered that a mixture of rubber and sulfur becomes elastic when heated and retains its elasticity under extreme temperature changes. After a long, costly legal battle, he finally won, in 1852, a patent for his process, the basis of the modern rubber industry. Ironically, Goodyear earned very little money from his discovery; he died in New York deeply in debt.

Gorbachev, Mikhail Sergeyevich (1931–), general secretary of the Communist Party of the Soviet Union. After joining the Communist Party in 1952, he was active in the Komsomol (Young Communist League). He became a member of the Central Committee in 1971, and was named agriculture secretary in 1978. When Yuri Andropov was elected general secretary in 1982, after the death of Leonid Brezhnev, Gorbachev helped him implement a broad series of reforms. As the successor to Konstantin Chernenko, 1985, he pledged himself to making the Soviet system of centralized planning more efficient and indicated a wish to maintain a course of peaceful coexistence with the West. The youngest Soviet leader in many years, Gorbachev has called for "glasnost" (openness) and "perestroika" (restructuring) in the modernization of Soviet society.

Gordon, Charles George (1833–1885), British soldier who became an almost legendary hero for his exploits in various outposts of the British empire. He led a band of Chinese volunteers in defense of Shanghai, 1863–1864, earning the nickname Chinese Gordon. He then served in Egypt, Ethiopia, and South Africa. In 1884 he was sent to Khartoum in the Sudan, where the Mahdi, a religious fanatic, was waging a "holy war" against the ruler of Egypt. Gordon evacuated the town but was besieged there from March, 1884, until January, 1885. The British government delayed in sending help; new troops arrived two days after Gordon had been killed.

Gorgas, William Crawford (1854–1920), U.S. physician known for his work in controlling yellow fever and malaria. He so successfully eradicated yellow fever in Cuba, by destroying mosquito breeding grounds, that in 1904 he was sent as chief sanitary officer on the Panama Canal project. There he virtually wiped out yellow fever and checked malaria. Gorgas later worked on tropical medicine in other countries.

Göring, Hermann Wilhelm (1893–1946), German Nazi official, second to Hitler in power in the Third Reich. He joined the National Socialist Party in 1922 and, when the 1923 Munich beer hall *putsch* failed, he fled to Sweden, where he was arrested for drug addiction. In 1926 he returned to Germany. When Hitler became chancellor, Göring was named his second in command, serving as minister of aviation and head of the German air force *(Luftwaffe),* 1935–1945, and as virtual economic dictator from 1936 on. Captured by American forces in 1945, he was indicted as a war criminal at Nuremberg and sentenced to death, but committed suicide several hours before his scheduled execution.

Gorki (or **Gorky**), **Maxim** (1868–1936), pen name of Aleksei Maksimovich Peshkov, probably the most influential Russian writer of social realism. His early works were very successful novels, short stories, and plays whose characters were social outcasts; the play *The Lower Depths* (1902) was the most famous. Gorki became a popular hero with his revolutionary poem "Song of the Stormy Petrel" (1901). His autobiographical trilogy, *Childhood* (1913), *In the World* (1915–1916), and *My Universities* (1923), secured his reputation as the leading Soviet writer of his time.

Gould, Jay (1836–1892), U.S. financier who acquired a huge personal fortune by stock and financial manipulations. With his partner James Fisk and the political help of "Boss" Tweed, Gould sold fraudulent Erie Railroad stock at great profit; his speculations in gold brought on the panic of Black Friday (September 24, 1869). Gould indulged in many other profitable schemes and by 1890 owned half the railroad mileage in the Southwest.

Gounod, Charles François (1818–1893), French composer of opera and sacred music, best known for his opera *Faust* (1860). A student of theology and church music, he first gained notice with a Mass in G (1851). Gounod's skill in vocal writing and orchestration was most effective in *Faust,* his only successful opera, and in his later oratorios and choral works (*La Redemption,* 1882).

Goya y Lucientes, Francisco José de (1746–1828), Spanish painter and engraver. Influenced by Velázquez and the Italian tradition, Goya, as court painter to Charles III from 1786, produced conventional, elegant court portraits. An illness in 1792 that left him deaf seemingly sharpened his perceptions and under Charles IV his portraits became more honest and revealing (*The Naked Maja,* c 1797; *Family of Charles IV,* 1800). In his own work he used new drawing techniques in the bitter *Caprichos* (1799), 80 etchings attacking social and political wrongs. Goya's later work grew more dramatic and realistic, graphically showing the horrors of the Napoleonic wars, notably in *Desastres de la guerra (Disasters of War).* Unable to live under the dictatorial rule of Ferdinand VII, he finally went into exile in 1824.

Graham, Martha (1894–), U.S. choreographer and dancer, for many years the leading figure in modern dance. Her personal style of movement was both angular and abrupt, conveying great emotion. Graham studied with Ruth St. Denis but soon began to develop her own style, often drawing on Mexican ritual, as in *Primitive Mysteries* (1931) and *El Penitente* (1940). She took themes from literature and Greek legend in the works *Deaths and Entrances* (1943), *Appalachian Spring* (1944), *Clytemnestra* (1958), and *Alcestis* (1960).

Graham, William Franklin (Billy) (1918–), U.S. evangelist. He was ordained a Southern Baptist minister in 1939. He began to travel and hold revival meetings in the 1940's, attracting huge crowds by his vigorous preaching. Graham transformed the old-fashioned "revival" into a powerful, up-to-date force, using television, film, and radio. He made many world tours and wrote several books, including *My Answer* (1960) and *The Jesus Generation* (1971).

Grant, Cary (1904–1986), British-born U.S. film actor, originally Alexander Archibald Leach, the epitome of casual sophistication and one of Hollywood's most memorable and romantic leading men. Although he never won an Academy Award, he remained a great box-office attraction for most of his 34-year career. Of his more than 72 films, the better known include *I'm No Angel* (1933), *Notorious* (1946), *Mr. Blandings Builds His Dream House* (1948), *To Catch a Thief* (1955), and *North by Northwest* (1959).

Grant, Ulysses Simpson (1822–1885), U.S. Civil War general and 18th President of the United States, 1869–1877. Born in Point Pleasant, Ohio, he was christened Hiram Ulysses, but the congressman who appointed him to West Point in 1839 mistakenly gave his name as Ulysses Simpson Grant. Though he thought it an unjust war, Grant served in the Mexican War. He was forced to resign from the Army in 1854 because of heavy drinking. (Grant's drinking was legendary, but he later became a teetotaler.) Grant then moved to St. Louis and worked a farm, which he named "Hardscrabble." He had given up the farm and was clerking in the family store in Galena, Ill., an apparent failure, when the Civil War broke out in 1861. He was made a colonel in an Illinois regiment and, after his first success, became a general. His bloody, plodding, stubborn campaigns in the western theater of the war impressed Lincoln, and Grant was made commander of the Union armies in 1864. He wore Lee's army down until Lee surrendered at Appomattox in 1865. The nation rewarded Grant by electing him President in 1868 and 1872. His second term was marred by government and business scandals. Grant was personally honest, but he showed great favoritism to friends and relatives and could never believe wrong of a friend. He left the White House in 1877. In 1881 he lent his name to a banking house, Grant & Ward, which went bankrupt in 1884 and proved to be a fraud. Penniless, Grant contracted to write his *Personal Memoirs,* which he finished a few days before he died of cancer. He was buried in New York City.

Graves, Robert Ranke (1895–1986), British poet, novelist, and critic. He is perhaps best known for his novels about the Roman emperor Claudius, *I, Claudius* (1934) and *Claudius the God* (1934), though he considered his poetry more important (*Collected Poems,* 1959). Graves's other books include *The White Goddess* (1948; revised 1952, 1961), a difficult but remarkable study of myth in poetry; *Goodbye to All That* (1929; revised 1957), an autobiography; and translations of Suetonius (1959), Terence (1962), and other classical writers.

Gray, Asa (1810–1888), U.S. botanist whose *Manual of the Botany of the Northern United States* (1848) is still considered, after a century, an indispensable text for American botany students. Gray obtained a medical degree in 1831 and then began his life's work, the systematization and classification of American flora. He also wrote several books aimed at developing popular interest in botany.

Gray, Thomas (1716–1771), English poet, author of one of the most famous and frequently quoted English poems, *Elegy Written in a Country Churchyard* (1751). This long, meditative poem made Gray very influential, particularly at Cambridge, where he spent much of his life as a student and tutor. He also wrote several odes based on Old Norse and Welsh poetry.

El Greco ("the Greek") (1541–1614), Spanish nickname of Domenikos Theotokopoulos, the first great Spanish painter, born in Crete. El Greco settled in Toledo, Spain. His paintings, characterized by their intense colors, their dramatic composition, and their elongated, emaciated, often tormented figures, captured the religious mysticism of the 16th-century Spanish church. His works include the masterpiece *Burial of Count Orgaz* (1586), *St. Martin and the Beggar* (1597–1599), the profoundly religious *Assumption* (1613), and many portraits. His dramatic *View of Toledo* (1610) was the first pure Spanish landscape.

Greeley, Horace (1811–1872), U.S. editor and journalist. He founded the New York *Tribune* in 1841. As its editor for 30 years, Greeley set high reporting and editorial standards, created columns for foreign news and public opinion, and included on his staff such journalists as William Dean

HORACE GREELEY (seated)

Howells and Margaret Fuller. He used the influential *Tribune* to crusade for the abolition of slavery, the Free Soil movement, labor unions, and utopian socialist movements. Greeley himself was both admired and scorned. He yearned for public office, but his uncompromising moral stands were not matched by political sophistication. As Liberal Republican candidate for President in 1872, he underwent intense abuse and a crushing defeat that supposedly caused his death. Though it did not originate with him, Greeley's quote "Go West, young man" was from a *Tribune* editorial urging homesteading in the West.

Greene, Graham (1904–), British novelist known both for his suspense thrillers and for his serious novels. Among the books Greene termed "entertainments" are *The Ministry of Fear* (1943), *The Third Man* (film script, 1949; novel, 1950), and *Our Man in Havana* (1958). His "Catholic novels," so called because of their themes of sin and redemption, include *Brighton Rock* (1938), *The Power and the Glory* (1940), and the *Heart of the Matter* (1948). Greene wrote plays and novels outside these categories (*A Burnt-Out Case,* 1961; *The Honorary Consul,* 1973); many of his novels were filmed. He published an autobiography, *A Sort of Life,* in 1971, and the sequel, *Ways of Escape,* in 1980.

Gregory I (Saint Gregory the Great) (c 540–604), Roman official and churchman, elected pope in 590. A fine administrator, Gregory established the papal authority that lasted through the Middle Ages. He extended its influence into western Europe, outside the domain of the Byzantine emperor. In 596 he sent a mission that successfully converted Britain. He also made reforms in the liturgy; the Gregorian chant is named for him.

Gregory, Lady (Isabella) Augusta Persse (1852–1932), Irish dramatist and theater director, a leader in the Irish literary renaissance. With Yeats, Lady Gregory organized the Irish Literary Theatre, later the famous Abbey Theatre. Her plays include the one-act comedies *Spreading the News* (1904), *The Rising of the Moon* (1907), and *The Workhouse Ward* (1908). She also wrote *Gods and Fighting Men* (1904), a romance based on Irish sagas.

Grey, Zane (1875–1939), U.S. writer who created a popular form with his romantic novels of the American West. His popularity was assured with *Riders of the Purple Sage* (1912), which sold over a million copies. He wrote nearly 60 volumes, influencing the public's view of the frontier and setting the pattern for the movie Westerns.

Grieg, Edvard Hagerup (1843–1907), Norwegian composer who developed a distinctly Nordic musical idiom using folk themes and Romantic harmonies. His finest pieces are the shorter works for piano, orchestra, and voice, such as the *Lyric Pieces* (1867–1901) for piano. Grieg's fame, however, comes from his popular Piano Concerto in A minor (1868); and the orchestral suite *Peer Gynt* (1876), commissioned by Ibsen to accompany his play. *Peer Gynt* contains the well-known "Anitra's Dance" and "In the Hall of the Mountain King."

Griffith, David Wark (D. W.) (1875–1948), U.S. silent film director. He directed more than 300 one-reel films for the Biograph Company before forming his own company. In 1915 he produced *Birth of a Nation,* one of the most famous and controversial films in history. It and *Intolerance* (1916) influenced filmmaking worldwide. Griffith's innovations, including vista shots, close-ups, fade-ins and fade-outs, and cross-cutting, all helped free film from stage conventions. His other well-known works are *Broken Blossoms* (1919), *Way Down East* (1920), and *Orphans of the Storm* (1922).

Grimm, family name of two German philologists, **Jakob Ludwig Carl** (1785–1863) and his brother **Wilhelm Carl** (1786–1859). Today they are best known as the collectors of the stories known as *Grimm's Fairy Tales,* first published in three volumes in 1812–1815. From 1841 they were both professors and members of the Academy at Berlin. Jakob's interests were more linguistic, Wilhelm's more literary. Jakob's work in German grammar and on sound shifts in Indo-European languages (Grimm's law, 1822) did much to make linguistics a scientific study. The brothers' last and greatest project was a German dictionary; the first volume was issued in 1854, but it was so exhaustive that it was not completed until 1960.

Gris, Juan (1887–1927), real name José Victoriano González, Spanish painter, a leader in the cubist movement. In the early 1900's he worked closely with Picasso and Braque, but soon developed a personal, rather severe, style of cubism. A well-known Gris still life is *Guitar and Flowers.*

Gromyko, Andrei Andreyevich (1909–1989), Soviet economist and diplomat, named foreign minister in 1957. He was Soviet ambassador to the United States, 1943–1946. After participating in several international meetings (Teheran, 1943; Yalta, 1945), he was appointed Soviet delegate to the United Nations. While he was on the UN Security Council, Gromyko's taciturn manner and frequent use of the veto became a symbol of Russian stubbornness. Entrusted with many important diplomatic missions during his long tenure as foreign minister, he served on the Politburo from 1973 and was president of the Soviet Union from 1985 to 1988.

Gropius, Walter Adolf (1883–1969), German-born U.S. architect, designer, and teacher, founder of the Bauhaus school of architecture and applied arts. In 1919 he formed the Bauhaus in Weimar, emphasizing artistic unity and the need for designer-craftsmen in industrial production. In 1925 the school moved to Dessau, into buildings designed by Gropius, and began to lead the international development of functional and industrial architecture. Gropius resigned in 1928 to design industrial and workers' housing. In 1934 he fled the Nazis, first to England and eventually to the United States. He headed the Harvard School of Architecture, 1938–1952, and founded the Architects' Collaborative.

Grosz, George (1893–1959), German-born U.S. caricaturist and painter, noted for his bitterly satirical portrayals of the German middle class, militarism, war profiteering, and Nazism. He was identified with the schools of expressionism and Dadaism, and was a founder of the New Objectivity, an art movement using extensive detail. In 1932 he emigrated to the United States.

Grotius, Hugo (1583–1645), in Dutch, Huig de Groot, Dutch jurist and statesman, known for his writings on international law. A distinguished lawyer in The Hague, he was internationally known as a man of wide learning. Grotius was serving in government when a religious schism in Holland sent him to prison in 1619; he escaped and eventually entered the diplomatic service in Sweden. His major work, *De jure belli ac pacis* (*On the Law of War and Peace,* 1625), describes not only international law, but all the forms of law governing mankind.

Grünewald, Matthias (c 1460–1528), German Gothic painter who for 300 years was known in art history by the wrong name. His real name was Mathis Gothardt Neithardt. Very little is known about most of his work or his life, except that he maintained a workshop in Seligenstadt near Frankfort, about 1501–1525. Grünewald's fame rests on a single masterpiece, the many paneled Isenheim altarpiece, finished about 1516 on commission for the archbishop of Mainz. His work is noted for its mystic vision and brilliant color.

Guest, Edgar Albert (1881–1959), U.S. poet born in England, known for his folksy, homespun verse. Many of Guest's simple, optimistic verses were collected in *A Heap o' Livin'* (1916), *Just Folks* (1917), and *Life's Highway* (1933).

Guevara, (Serna) Ernesto (Che) (1928–1967), Latin American Marxist political leader and revolutionary, known for his role in the Cuban revolution of 1959. As Castro's chief aide, he was instrumental in the nationalization of industry and agriculture during Cuba's transition to socialism. He was president of Cuba's national bank, 1959–1961, and minister of industry, 1961–1965. Guevara's *On Guerrilla Warfare* was published in 1960. While participating in a revolutionary movement in Bolivia, he was killed in 1967.

Guggenheim, a family of U.S. industrialists and philanthropists whose fortune was based on their worldwide mining interests.

The family founder was Swiss-born **Meyer Guggenheim** (1828–1905), who emigrated to the United States in 1847; by 1901 the Guggenheims virtually controlled the U.S. smelting industry.

Daniel (1856–1930), who made the family business international, established a school of aeronautics at New York University and a famous fund to promote aviation.

Solomon (1861–1949) endowed the Solomon R. Guggenheim Foundation of Art, which commissioned Frank Lloyd Wright to build the Guggenheim Museum in New York (opened 1959).

Simon (1867–1941) established fellowships for advanced study of arts and sciences.

JOHANN GUTENBERG

ROBIN CARSON/COURTESY OF WOODIE GUTHRIE PUBLICATIONS, INC

WOODIE GUTHRIE

Guinness, Sir Alec (1914–), British actor of classical drama and comedy, perhaps best known for his versatility in such films as *Kind Hearts and Coronets* (1949) and *The Lavender Hill Mob* (1951). He played at the Old Vic in London and in Canada's first Stratford Shakespeare Festival (1953). His other movie roles include *Oliver Twist* (1948), *The Horse's Mouth* (1959), *Lawrence of Arabia* (1962), and *The Bridge on the River Kwai* (1957), which won him an Academy Award. His characterization of George Smiley in the television films *Tinker, Tailor, Soldier, Spy* (1980) and *Smiley's People* (1982), both adapted from works by John Le Carré, has been highly praised.

Gustavus II Adolphus (1594–1632), king of Sweden, 1611–1632, the "Lion of the North" and champion of the Protestant cause during the Thirty Years' War (1618–1648). After introducing order and reform at home, he set out to secure Sweden's power in the Baltic. Leaving Swedish affairs to his capable chancellor Axel Oxenstierna, he entered the war in Germany in 1629 and won a series of brilliant victories. He was killed leading a cavalry charge at the Battle of Lützen. His military innovations determined the style of land warfare for the next 200 years.

Gutenberg, Johann (c 1400–1468), German goldsmith and printer, the European inventor of printing with movable type. As early as 1438 he had made a printing press, movable type forms, and, possibly, a typecasting mold. About 1450 he borrowed money and entered a partnership with Johann Fust to form a printing business. In a lawsuit in 1455, Fust persuaded one of Gutenberg's assistants, Peter Schoeffer, to testify against him, and so gained possession of Gutenberg's printing materials. The first printed Bible was issued in 1456 by Fust and Schoeffer, but historians give credit to Gutenberg for this work, since most of the setting and printing probably were completed before the lawsuit. Several other books printed in the 1450's and 1460's have been credited to him.

Guthrie, Woodie (1912–1967), in full, Woodrow Wilson Guthrie, U.S. folk singer and composer of more than 1000 songs, perhaps best known for "This Land Is Your Land." He worked and wrote songs for the union movement ("The Union Maid"). His songs, many for children and some in "talking blues" style, show a deep love for the land and people of the United States and a hatred of social injustice. Guthrie's life and songs helped inspire a generation of young activists in the 1960's.

H

Hadrian (76–138 A.D.), full name Publius Aelius Hadrianus, Roman emperor, 117–138. Hadrian was born in Spain and, as the emperor Trajan's closest living relative, succeeded him to the throne in 117. Instead of continuing Trajan's wars, Hadrian dedicated his reign to the welfare of the empire. He toured the provinces; in Britain, he built the wall named for him as a defense against the northern tribes. His other projects included his tomb in Rome, now called the Castel Sant' Angelo, and his sumptuous villa at Tivoli. He also built monuments, temples, and even a city in memory of his young favorite, Antinoüs, who drowned in the Nile in 130.

Hagen, Walter (1892–1969), U.S. professional golfer, the first American to win the British Open championship, in 1922 (he won again in 1924, 1928, and 1929). A self-taught player with an unorthodox style, he also won the U.S. Open twice.

Haig, Alexander Meigs, Jr. (1924–), U.S. military commander and secretary of state, 1981–1982. In 1969 Haig was named assistant to Henry Kissinger, national security adviser to the President. Appointed a full general in 1972, he became Army vice chief of staff. The next year Haig left the Army to become head of President Nixon's staff. He was a strong defender of Nixon during the Watergate scandal, but was himself comparatively unscathed by the unfolding events. He remained chief of the White House staff under President Ford, until he was appointed supreme commander of NATO, 1974–1979. He retired in 1979 and entered private business. President-elect Reagan appointed him secretary of state, but Haig held the post for only a year and a half before he resigned.

Haile Selassie (1892–1975), Ethiopian statesman, born Lij Tafari, who took the name Haile Selassie ("Might of the Trinity") when he was crowned emperor in 1930. His title "Lion of Judah" comes from his claim to being a direct descendant of Solomon and Sheba. He served as regent and virtual ruler, 1916–1930; when he became emperor he gave Ethiopia its first written constitution, organized a national legislature, and instituted domestic reforms. Driven into exile by the Italian invasion in 1935, he returned in 1941. In 1950 he annexed the Italian colony of Eritrea and sent Ethiopian troops to fight in Korea. A new constitution (1955) gave more powers to the legislature, but Haile Selassie dominated Ethiopia until a military coup early in 1974 ended his long reign.

Hale, Edward Everett (1822–1909), U.S. Unitarian clergyman and author, best known for his short story *The Man Without a Country* (1863). He was minister of the South Congregational Church in Boston, 1856–1901, and in 1903 became chaplain of the U.S. Senate. The author of more than 50 books, Hale advocated a liberal Christianity and the "social gospel" movement, working for education for blacks and for better housing.

Hale, George Ellery (1868–1938), U.S. astronomer who developed a method of photographing the stars and the sun and developed many large telescopes, including the 200-inch Hale telescope at Mount Palomar, Calif. Hale made outstanding contributions to the sciences of spectroscopy and astrophysics, invented the spectroheliograph for the study of solar phenomena, and wrote of island universes and outer space in *The Depths of the Universe* (1924) and *Beyond the Milky Way* (1926).

Hale, Nathan (1755–1776), American Revolutionary army officer. After the Americans were defeated on Long Island in 1776, Hale volunteered to spy for George Washington. Disguised as a Dutch schoolmaster (with his own Yale diploma for credentials), he crossed British lines and had nearly completed his mission when he was apprehended. Probably betrayed by his own Tory cousin Samuel Hale, he was convicted of spying. Before he was hanged, Hale is supposed to have said, "I only regret that I have but one life to give for my country."

Halley, Edmund (1656–1742), British astronomer known for proving that comets orbit the sun, and for correctly determining the length of these orbits. After financing the publication of Isaac Newton's *Principia,* Halley used Newton's theory as the basis for his own most famous accomplishment—the correct orbital calculation of the great comet of 1682, now known as Halley's comet; he predicted, correctly, that it would return in 1758. He also conducted research on eclipses and the motion of stars.

Hals, Frans (c 1580–1666), Dutch painter, famous for his spontaneous portraits and portrait groups of the sturdy citizens of 17th-century Holland. He painted portraits of people from all levels of society—*The Laughing Cavalier* (1624) and *A Man with a Beer Keg* (1635). Toward the end of his life, he received a pension from the town. To show his gratitude he painted two of his most famous portrait groups, the *Men Regents* and the *Women Regents of the Old Men's Home* (1664).

Hamilton, Alexander (1755–1804), American Founding Father, the first U.S. secretary of the treasury, 1789–1795. Born in the West Indies, he was sent by his family to study in New York. During the Revolutionary War he was George Washington's aide, 1777–1781. A delegate to the Constitutional Convention, 1787, he gained public notice when he published, with James Madison and John Jay, *The Federalist* (1787–1788), a series of essays urging state ratification of the new Constitution. As secretary of the treasury, Hamilton sought to build U.S. credit and strengthen the federal government. He levied heavy taxes, created a national bank, and urged strong tariffs. He considered himself Washington's prime minister and joined the militia to subdue resistance when his tax policies brought on the Whiskey Rebellion, 1794. Hamilton's policies often clashed with those of Thomas Jefferson. For a time the two men struggled bitterly to drive each other from the Cabinet. Ironically, because he hated Aaron Burr more, Hamilton was forced to support Jefferson for President in 1800. Charging slander, Burr challenged Hamilton to a duel. He accepted, was mortally wounded, and died the following day.

Hammarskjöld, Dag Hjalmar Agne Carl (1905–1961), Swedish statesman, secretary-general of the United Nations, 1953–1961. Hammarskjöld directed the establishment in 1956 of the UN Emergency Force for the Middle East and conducted peace missions to China and the Middle East. He was killed in a plane crash while on a peace mission to the strife-torn African Republic of the Congo. *Markings,* philosophical selections from his diaries, was published posthumously. Hammarskjöld was awarded the 1961 Nobel Prize for Peace.

Hammerstein, Oscar, II (1895–1960), U.S. lyricist and theater producer. With Rudolf Friml he wrote *Rose Marie* (1924); with Sigmund Romberg, *Desert Song* (1926) and *New Moon* (1927); with Jerome Kern, *Show Boat* (1927); and with Richard Rodgers, such successes as *Oklahoma!* (1943), *Carousel* (1945), *South Pacific* (1949), and *The Sound of Music* (1959). Many of his productions were innovative in their use of ballet, musical soliloquies, and dramatic plots in the musical comedy format. *South Pacific* won a Pulitzer Prize for drama.

Hammett, Dashiell (1894–1961), U.S. writer, first of the "hard-boiled" detective fiction school. He was a Pinkerton detective for several years, winning his first promotion for catching a thief who had stolen a Ferris wheel. Hammett's two best books, *The Maltese Falcon* (1930) and *The Thin Man* (1934), were made into well-known movies; their detectives, Sam Spade and Nick Charles, were heroes of radio shows.

Hammurabi (r. between 1900–1700 B.C.), the great king of the first dynasty of Babylon. He is celebrated as the originator of a code of civil laws that guaranteed justice for all and protected the poor against oppression by the rich. The Code of Hammurabi (found as an inscription on a column) regulated such matters as trade and property and established harsh but just penalties for theft and other crimes. Hammurabi united his kingdom and established the powerful, long-lived Babylonian empire, composed of subject city-states.

Hamsun, Knut (1859–1952), pen name of Knut Pedersen, Norwegian writer whose works portray individuals struggling with environmental forces. Typical novels are *Hunger* (1890) and *Growth of the Soil* (1917), for which he won the 1920 Nobel Prize for Literature. He later wrote *Vagabonds* (1927) and *The Woman at the Pump* (1928). Hamsun concentrated on the psychological reality of man versus nature and was impatient with social welfare and urban society.

Hancock, John (1737–1793), American Revolutionary leader, one of the first signers of the Declaration of Independence. In 1764 Hancock inherited a thriving mercantile business from his uncle. To avoid Stamp Act duties, he resorted to smuggling and so became popular with the radical patriots. He was elected to the Massachusetts General Court, 1769–1774, and was president of the two provincial congresses, 1774, 1775, and of the second Continental Congress, 1775–1777. He resigned when George Washington was elected chief of the continental army, a position he coveted. When Massachusetts became a state in 1780, Hancock was its first governor, serving 1780–1785 and 1787–1793.

Hand, (Billings) Learned (1872–1961), U.S. jurist whose opinions were so respected that he was called "the tenth man on the U.S. Supreme Court." In 1959 the Court honored him for 50 years of service as a federal judge. His notable decisions include a 1945 antitrust suit against the Aluminum Company of America and the upholding of the conviction of eleven Communists under the Smith Act in 1950. His papers and addresses appear in *The Spirit of Liberty* (1952) and his Holmes lectures at Harvard in *The Bill of Rights* (1958).

GEORGE HANDEL

THE BETTMANN ARCHIVE

Handel, George Frederick (1685–1759), German-born English composer of dramatic and sacred music of the baroque period. His oratorio *The Messiah* is one of the most often performed choral works. In 1709 he became *Kapellmeister* to the elector of Hanover, but spent much of his time in England. When the elector became George I of England, Handel, who preferred English life, became court composer. A frank and hearty man, Handel was also deeply devout. He went blind in 1753 but continued to play the organ and direct concerts until his death. Besides *The Messiah* (1742), he is known for the opera *Julius Caesar* (1742); many other oratorios, including *Israel in Egypt* (1739) and *Judas Maccabeus* (1747); and the instrumental "Water Music" (1715) and "Royal Fireworks" (1749).

Handy, William Christopher (1873–1958), U.S. composer and blues musician, whose most famous composition is "St. Louis Blues" (1914). Although both primitive and fully developed blues were popular before W. C. Handy's time, particularly in New Orleans, he augmented the style and made it widely known. He came to be called "Father of the Blues" (the title of his autobiography, 1941). He also wrote "Memphis Blues" (1912) and "Beale Street Blues" (1914).

Hanna, Marcus Alonzo (1837–1904), U.S. entrepreneur and political figure. Convinced that the success of business depended on proper government (which he saw embodied in the Republican Party), Mark Hanna sponsored several politicians. By using his own large fortune, which he amassed in the coal and iron business, he made William McKinley governor of Ohio in 1891 and 1893. Then, campaigning with money assessed from large corporations, he secured McKinley's election as President, 1896 and 1900. As a U.S. senator, appointed 1897, Hanna led the powerful Republican inner circle and was a close Presidential adviser.

Hannibal (247–183 B.C.), Carthaginian general, one of the greatest generals of antiquity. He became commander of the Carthaginian army at the age of 26 and brought on the Second Punic War with Rome in 218 by attacking Roman allies in Spain. Determined to carry the war to Italy, he left Spain with his army, which included a number of elephants, and marched through Gaul. Late in the year he made his famous crossing of the Alps and marched into Italy. Within two years he had annihilated Roman armies at Lake Trasimeno and at Cannae, but his army was so depleted that he could not take Rome. He remained in Italy until 203, when he was recalled to Carthage to defend the city against a Roman army under Scipio. He was defeated at Zama in 202. Thereafter he fought for other enemies of Rome; threatened with arrest by the Romans, he committed suicide.

Hapsburg (or **Habsburg**), one of the great ruling houses of Europe, identified mainly with Austria and Spain. In 1273 **Count Rudolf of Hapsburg** became German king, reigning 1273–1291. Various descendants ruled Austria, Hungary, and Bohemia. In 1440 **Frederick V** became German king and, in 1452, Holy Roman Emperor (as Frederick III). His son **Maximilian I** (given the title archduke) was able to consolidate all the hereditary family lands; he also was a master of the Hapsburg practice of acquiring land by marriage. Maximilian married **Mary of Burgundy**; his son and daughter married into the Spanish royal house. The combined territories were inherited by Holy Roman Emperor **Charles V**, his grandson. Charles abdicated in 1556, dividing the lands into Austrian and Spanish lines.

Charles's son **Philip II** of Spain, who reigned 1556–1598, inherited Spain, the Netherlands, and Spanish America. The Spanish line continued until 1700, when **Charles II** died without heirs, bringing on the War of the Spanish Succession.

The Austrian dynasty of Hapsburgs was continued by Charles's brother **Ferdinand I**, Holy Roman Emperor from 1556 to 1564 and also, by marriage, elective king of Hungary and Bohemia. The last male heir was **Charles VI**; on his death in 1740, a family agreement made his daughter **Maria Theresa** empress, but her accession led to the War of the Austrian Succession (1740–1748). Though Austria lost Silesia, Maria Theresa and her husband, **Francis of Lorraine**, managed to retain most of the family lands, which were passed down through the house of Hapsburg-Lorraine.

The Austrian Hapsburgs were Holy Roman emperors until 1806, when **Francis II** (1768–1835) dissolved the empire but ruled as "emperor of Austria," 1804–1835. Austria gradually lost preeminence to Prussia. World War I brought the final destruction of the Hapsburg dynasty. The last emperor, **Charles I**, abdicated in 1918, and Hapsburg family members who kept their titles were barred from Austria.

Harding, Warren Gamaliel (1865–1923), 29th President of the United States, 1921–1923. Born in Corsica (now Blooming Grove), Ohio, Harding worked as a journalist in Marion, then bought a local newspaper. He became a prominent booster and public speaker and was elected to the U.S. Senate in 1914. He was nominated as a dark-horse Presidential candidate at the 1920 Republican convention. Advocating a "return to normalcy" and rejection of President Wilson's postwar policies, he was elected. Among the men he appointed to his administration were some who proved to be unscrupulous. In 1923 the shock of learning about the Teapot Dome oil scandal apparently killed him. He was succeeded by his Vice President, Calvin Coolidge. Harding's reputation was blackened not only by the scandals of his administration, in which he had no part, but also by the disclosure of his long love affairs with Carrie Phillips, wife of one of his friends, and Nan Britton.

Hardy, Thomas (1840–1928), British novelist and poet whose works express the mood of the bleak countryside of Wessex. His first important novel was *Far from the Madding Crowd* (1874), followed by *The Return of the Native* (1878), *The Mayor of Casterbridge* (1886), *Tess of the D'Urbervilles* (1891), and *Jude the Obscure* (1896). Hardy often portrayed his characters as victims of a predestined fate. In later years he turned to poetry. His most ambitious verse is *The Dynasts* (1904–1908), an epic drama of the Napoleonic wars.

Hargreaves, James (d. 1778), English inventor of the spinning jenny, patented in 1770. Little is known of Hargreaves, a poor spinner who lived in Standhill, England. It is said that the idea of a many spindled machine occurred to him about 1764, when his daughter Jenny overturned his spinning wheel. He then developed the "jenny," which produced eight times the work of hand machines.

Harrison, Benjamin (1833–1901), 23rd President of the United States, 1889–1893. Born in North Bend, Ohio, he was a grandson of President William Henry Harrison. During the Civil War, he commanded a regiment under Sherman. A term in the U.S. Senate, 1881–1887, increased his national reputation, and in 1888 he received the Republican Presidential nomination and conducted the first "front-porch campaign." In the election, Grover Cleveland had more popular votes, but Harrison won in the electoral college. In the campaign of 1892, Harrison and Cleveland again were the nominees. Though Harrison's administration had been successful in foreign affairs, public opinion on domestic issues had turned against the Republicans, and Cleveland won the election. Because of his reputation, the government of Venezuela engaged him as chief counsel in the arbitration of its boundary dispute with Great Britain, 1898–1899.

Harrison, William Henry (1773–1841), ninth President of the United States, March–April 1841. Harrison joined the Army in 1791 and fought Indians in the Northwest Territory. He became secretary of the territory in 1798 and then its delegate to Congress, where he originated the first homestead law. While governor of Indiana Territory, 1800–1812, he fought a battle against the Indian followers of Tecumseh at Tippecanoe in 1811, which made him a national hero. During the War of 1812, he was given command of the Army in the Northwest. His victory at the Thames River in 1813 ended Tecumseh's War and the threat of British invasion. After the war, Harrison retired from the Army and went into politics. After serving in Congress and in the Senate, he became the Whig Presidential candidate in 1836. Defeated that year, in 1840 he was swept into the White House by the famous "log cabin" campaign, with its slogan "Tippecanoe and Tyler too!" Worn out by campaigning and besieged by office-seekers, Harrison caught pneumonia at the inauguration and died a month later.

Hart, Moss (1904–1961), U.S. playwright and stage director, co-author of many highly successful plays. He collaborated with Irving Berlin on *Face the Music* (1932) and with George S. Kaufman on the Pulitzer Prize winner *You Can't Take It With You* (1936) and *The Man Who Came to Dinner* (1939). Hart also wrote the musical *Lady in the Dark* (1941) and *Winged Victory* (1943). In 1955 he directed *My Fair Lady* and in 1960 both produced and directed *Camelot. Act One,* his story of his own theatrical career, appeared in 1959.

Harte, Bret (1836–1902), originally Francis Brett Harte, U.S. author, remembered for his colorful short stories about life in the mining country of early California. In 1868 Harte became first editor of the *Overland Monthly,* for which he wrote such sketches as "The Luck of Roaring Camp" and "The Outcasts of Poker Flat." Suddenly famous, he moved East, where he enjoyed a brief vogue in literary circles. After 1878 he lived in England and Europe, where he was still popular.

Harvey, William (1578–1657), English physician, the first to discover the workings of the circulation of the blood. In 1628 his book *Essay on the Motion of the Heart and the Blood* appeared. It excited great controversy, but Harvey lived to see its acceptance. He also did pioneer studies of animal and human reproduction, using as his laboratory the royal deer parks, which Charles I put at his disposal.

Hawthorne, Nathaniel (1804–1864), U.S. author who examined the Puritan conscience in novels and short stories. After his graduation from Bowdoin, he spent twelve isolated years writing, producing *Twice-Told Tales* (1837). In 1842 he married Sophia Peabody and in 1846 published the short stories *Mosses from an Old Manse. The Scarlet Letter* (1850), his masterpiece, deals with the psychological effects of sin in the context of Puritan morality. Three other well-known books followed: *The House of the Seven Gables* (1851), *Tanglewood Tales* (1853), and *The Marble Faun* (1860). In the same period he published the popular *Wonder-Book for Girls and Boys* (1852).

Haydn, Franz Joseph (1732–1809), Austrian composer, the first of the great composers in the Viennese classical style. As much as one person can be said to invent a musical form, Haydn invented the string quartet. He also combined earlier symphonic forms into the classical structure perfected by Mozart and Beethoven. Haydn served as court composer to the famous Hungarian house of Esterházy for over 45 years. Haydn's works include more than 100 symphonies and at least 75 string quartets. The Symphony No. 104 in D *(London)* is considered his most perfect instrumentally, but his "Surprise" Symphony in G is more famous. Of his oratorios, the best known are *The Creation* (1798) and *The Seasons* (1801). He also wrote many operas.

Hayes, Helen (1900–), original name Helen Hayes Brown, U.S. actress. In 1928 she married playwright Charles MacArthur. Her Broadway plays include *Dear Brutus* (1918), *Mrs. McThing* (1952), and the title role in *Victoria Regina* (1935). She received an Academy Award for her acting in the 1932 film *The Sin of Madelon Claudet;* she also appeared in *Anastasia*

HELEN HAYES (as Queen Victoria)

UPI/BETTMANN NEWSPHOTOS

(1956) and on television, and acted in *A Touch of the Poet* (1958) and *Long Day's Journey Into Night* (1971), both by Eugene O'Neill. In 1955 a New York theater was named the Helen Hayes.

Hayes, Rutherford Birchard (1822–1893), 19th President of the United States, 1877–1881. He was elected to Congress in 1864, during the Civil War, while he was still serving as a brigadier general in the Union Army. He was governor of Ohio, 1868–1872, and was persuaded by the Republicans to run again in 1875. His success drew national attention, and the following year he was nominated for President as a compromise candidate. In the famous Hayes-Tilden Presidential election of 1876, both parties claimed victory, and Hayes was finally declared the winner by a special electoral commission. He served one term, pushed through a few reforms, and, refusing to run again, retired to work on humanitarian and educational projects.

Haynes, Elwood (1857–1925), U.S. inventor who produced the first successful "horseless carriage" in the United States (1893), now on display at the Smithsonian Institution, Washington, D.C. Haynes also developed several metal alloys for making high-speed cutting tools and discovered a process for making stainless steel.

Hearst, William Randolph (1863–1951), U.S. publisher who built an empire on the tactics of sensationalism. In 1885 Hearst persuaded his father, who owned the San Francisco *Examiner,* to give him charge of the paper. In two years he built up the paper's circulation and increased profits. In 1895 he bought the New York *Morning Journal.* By 1927 he published 25 daily papers in 17 cities and owned several magazines. With glaring headlines, color sections, sensational crime articles, and a jingoist editorial policy, he built unheard-of circulation and amassed a personal fortune. Hearst prepared public opinion for the Spanish-American War, 1898, to such an extent that it was called "Hearst's War"; however, he opposed U.S. participation in both world wars. He at first supported Roosevelt's New Deal but then turned against it. At one time one of the world's richest men, Hearst owned several estates, including the famous San Simeon in California, which he filled with antiques and art treasures.

Hegel, Georg Wilhelm Friedrich (1770–1831), German philosopher. Though Hegel's writings are among the most obscure of philosophical works, his ideas had wide influence. He applied his "dialectical method" to the study of history, concluding that the Prussian state represented history's high point. The idea that history is a system of constant progress and improvement is due largely to Hegel; on the other hand, the

NY PUBLIC LIBRARY

GEORG HEGEL

COURTESY W.R. HEARST, JR.

WILLIAM RANDOLPH HEARST

Marxist idea of the supremacy of the state is also based on Hegel. Among his many works was an *Encyclopedia of the Philosophical Sciences* (1817); more of his thought was compiled from lecture notes by his followers after his death.

Heidegger, Martin (1889–1976), German philosopher who influenced greatly the development of existentialism, though he claimed not to be an existentialist himself. His major work, *Sein und Zeit* (*Being and Time,* 1927), considers the basic metaphysical question, "Why is there something, rather than nothing?" His philosophy, emphasizing fate and futility, is essentially atheistic. A professor of philosophy, Heidegger was the first Nazi rector of the University of Freiburg, 1933–1934; he was one of the German intellectuals who gave the early Nazi regime public support, though he soon became disillusioned, resigned his post, and returned to teaching. His work is often compared with that of Husserl and Kierkegaard.

Heifetz, Jascha (1901–1987), Russian-born U.S. violinist, considered the outstanding figure among modern string players. Celebrated for his extraordinary virtuosity at a very early age, Heifetz performed a wide range of music from Bach to Sibelius to Walton. He played chamber music with such artists as pianist Artur Rubenstein and cellist Gregor Piatigorsky.

Heine, Heinrich (1797–1856), German lyric poet. Heine's most familiar works are his early poems, published as *Buch der Lieder* (*Book of Songs,* 1827). Many of them were set to music by Schubert, Schumann, Hugo Wolf, and others. From 1831 on, Heine lived in Paris and wrote for French and German newspapers. His political opinions made him unwelcome in Prussia and Austria, especially after publication of his long political satire, *Deutschland: Ein Wintermarchen* (*Germany: A Winter's Tale,* 1844). Probably his best-known poem is *"Die Lorelei."*

Hellman, Lillian (1905–1984), U.S. playwright and writer. Her noted plays, usually indictments of selfishness and injustice, include *The Children's Hour* (1934), *The Little Foxes* (1939), *Watch on the Rhine* (1941), *Another Part of the Forest* (1946), and *Toys in the Attic* (1960). She also wrote the autobiographical *An Unfinished Woman* (1970), *Pentimento* (1974), and *Scoundrel Time* (1976).

Helmholtz, Hermann Ludwig Ferdinand von (1821–1894), German scientist, one of the discoverers of the principle of conservation of energy. Awarded a medical degree in 1842, he turned to the field of physics and published his classic *On the Conservation of Force* in 1847. As a professor of physiology, 1849–1871, he investigated nerve impulses, color vision, and optics, and invented the ophthalmoscope. In 1858 he published a theory of the physical bases of musical tones. His masterpiece in acoustics is *The Sensations of Tone* (1862).

Hemingway, Ernest Miller (1899–1961), U.S. novelist, short story writer, and journalist. After World War I, in which he was wounded, he became a foreign correspondent in Paris. There he became one of the expatriate writers of the "lost generation," influenced by such writers as Gertrude Stein and Ezra Pound. His first success was *The Sun Also Rises* (1926), followed by *A Farewell to Arms* (1929), *For Whom the Bell Tolls* (1940), and notable short stories, including "The Snows of Kilimanjaro" and "The Killers." He became known also as a daring sportsman and hunter (*Green Hills of Africa,* 1935), deliberately seeking out danger to prove his courage and masculinity. During World War II, Hemingway was a war correspondent. His most important postwar work was *The Old Man and the Sea* (1952), which won a Pulitzer Prize; soon afterward, he won the 1954 Nobel Prize for Literature. Works published after his death by suicide include *A Moveable Feast* (1964) and *Islands in the Stream* (1971).

Henry, Joseph (1797–1878), U.S. physicist, a pioneer in work with electromagnetism. Research in electromagnetism led to his invention of the short-coil magnet (1829), used in modern generators and electric motors, a telegraph, and the discovery (1832) of electromagnetic induction (discovered at the same time by Michael Faraday). Henry did research on transformers, radio waves, and solar energy. In 1846 he became first secretary of the Smithsonian Institution, where his meteorological study led to the creation of the U.S. Weather Bureau.

Henry, O.: *See* Porter, William Sidney.

Henry, Patrick (1736–1799), American Revolutionary leader and famous orator. A brilliant young lawyer, Henry demonstrated powerful oratory in the courtroom. In 1765 he was elected to the Virginia House of Burgesses, where he delivered a famous speech opposing the Stamp Act and affirming the colonies' right to self-government: "If this be treason, make the most of it." Henry was a member of the Virginia state committee of correspondence and a delegate to the Continental Congresses (1774, 1775). In 1775 he met with the revolutionary committee in Richmond, where, in another fiery speech ("Give me liberty or give me death"), he persuaded the assembly to organize the Virginia militia. After 1776 Henry was governor for several terms; he was a leader in the move to adopt a Bill of Rights.

Henry II (1133–1189), king of England, 1154–1189, first of the Plantagenet line. Henry was the son of Geoffrey Plantagenet, count of Anjou, and Matilda, daughter of Henry I of England. He succeeded Stephen of Blois, nephew of Henry I, after years of civil war. In addition to England, he ruled a vast French domain, acquired by inheritance and through his marriage to Eleanor of Aquitaine. He annexed Ireland in 1171. Henry established many of the forms and procedures of English law. Planning to assert his authority over the church, he made his chancellor, Thomas à Becket, archbishop of Canterbury, but Becket turned against him. Henry's long quarrel with his chancellor led to Becket's murder (1170). Henry's last years were taken up with the rebellions of his four sons, principally Richard (later Richard I) and John (later John I). The perfidy of his sons, combined with illness, killed him.

Henry IV (1553–1610), earlier Henry of Navarre, king of France, 1589–1610. The son of Anthony of Bourbon and Jeanne d'Albret, queen of Navarre, Henry was raised a Protestant. In 1572 he became king of Navarre and married Margaret of Valois, sister of Charles IX of France. A week later, the leading French Protestants, in Paris for the wedding, were slaughtered in the St. Bartholomew's Day Massacre. Henry renounced Protestantism to avoid persecution but was held prisoner at the court; in 1576 he escaped to Navarre, where he recruited and led the Huguenots and rebels against Henry III, Charles IX's successor. In 1589 he and King Henry III joined forces against the powerful duke of Guise and the Holy League. When the king was murdered that same year, Henry of Navarre became Henry IV, the first Bourbon king of France. He had reconquered most of France by 1593, except Paris; saying "Paris is well worth a Mass," he publicly converted to Catholicism and was admitted to Paris. Henry published the Edict of Nantes in 1598, granting the rights of the French Protestants. His main concern was the welfare of his subjects, and he apparently originated the phrase, "a chicken in every pot." He restored agriculture, commerce, and French power and influence in Europe. He divorced the childless Margaret in 1599 and in 1600 married Marie de Médicis; from this marriage came the Bourbon line.

Henry V (1387–1422), king of England, 1413–1422. Shakespeare called him "the mirror of all Christian Kings." He aided his father, Henry IV, in suppressing various rebellions, but seemed impatient to become king. When he succeeded his father, Henry began to plan his life's ambition, the conquest of France. He annihilated the French army in 1415 at Agincourt, a victory that made him the most respected and feared monarch in Europe. By the Treaty of Troyes (1420), Henry became heir to the French throne; he also married Catherine, the daughter of the French king. Worn out by his campaigns, Henry fell ill and died.

Henry VIII (1491–1547), king of England, 1509–1547. Henry, known as "bluff King Hal," was one of the most colorful rulers in English history. He married six times, and he separated the Church of England from the Roman Catholic Church. While the young Henry amused himself, his minister Cardinal Wolsey managed matters of state until the lack of a male heir became acute. Henry's marriage to his brother's widow, Catherine of Aragon, had produced one surviving daughter (later Mary I). Wolsey failed to get Henry a divorce, whereupon Henry arrested Wolsey, broke with Rome, made himself head of the Church of England, divorced Catherine, and married Anne Boleyn, in 1533. The second marriage also produced a girl (later Elizabeth I). Between 1536 and 1539 the monasteries were dissolved. Their wealth and property went to Henry, whose court was becoming more and more extravagant. In 1536 Henry had Anne Boleyn executed on charges of adultery and married Jane Seymour, who died giving birth to the future Edward VI in 1537. Henry made a political marriage to Anne of Cleves in 1540, but found her unattractive. When the European political situation shifted six months later, he had the marriage annulled. He soon married Catherine Howard, who was executed for adultery in 1542. He then married Catherine Parr, who soothed his last years and outlived him.

Henry the Navigator (1394–1460), Portuguese prince. After 1416 he organized numerous voyages; his captains found the Madeiras and the Azores in the Atlantic, negotiated Cape Bojador on the African coast, and discovered the Senegal and Geba rivers. Under Henry, the slave trade began; he encouraged it as a way of converting Africans and bringing his ships more profit. He also founded a famous school for mariners.

Hepworth, Dame Barbara (1903–1975), English abstract sculptor. Hepworth carved directly in wood or stone, typically using holes and tunnels in the form. Her *Pierced Form* (1931) is a famous early work. In the 1950's she experimented with metals and casting. Later works are *Empyrean* (1953–1954), *Winged Figure* (1962), and *Squares and Two Circles* (1967).

Herbert, Victor (1859–1924), Irish-born U.S. composer and conductor known for his melodic operettas. Of his more than 40 operettas, *Babes in Toyland* (1903), *The Red Mill* (1906), *Naughty Marietta* (1910), and *Sweethearts* (1913) are well known; they introduced many still popular melodies.

Herder, Johann Gottfried von (1744–1803), German critic and philosopher, the immediate source of inspiration for the German Romantic poets. Herder introduced Goethe and others to the works of Shakespeare and Ossian and developed or expounded on many of the philosophic ideas that recur in Romantic poetry. His best-known work is his collection of folk songs and poetry, *Volkslieder* (1778–1779), later renamed *Stimmen der Völker in Liedern* ("Voices of the People in Songs").

Herod, the name of a line of rulers in Judea during the first years of the Christian era. The founder of the family was **Antipater**, of Arab origin, who gained the favor of the conquering Romans and was made procurator of Judea in 47 B.C.

Herod the Great (c 73–4 B.C.), his son, was a friend of Mark Antony and of Julius Caesar. He first became governor of Galilee and by 37 B.C., with Roman help, was unchallenged king of Judea. He was king at the time of the birth of Christ and ordered the slaughter of infants in Bethlehem shortly before his death.

His son **Herod Antipas** (c 21 B.C.–39 A.D.), was tetrarch of Galilee at the time of the Crucifixion. He was succeeded by other Herods, but the line ended about 100 A.D.

Herodotus (fl. 400's B.C.), the first Greek (and European) historian, whose history of the Greco-Persian wars is still one of the most enjoyable of history books. His *History* consists of two parts: an account of the Persian empire and of the countries it included, and the story of the Persian wars. His entertaining narrative is concerned with events rather than with politics; he accurately described countries and customs and recounted good tales. He remains a principal source for ancient history.

Herrick, Robert (1591–1674), English Cavalier poet who revived the style of the classical love lyric. About 1200 of Herrick's poems are contained in his only book, *Hesperides* (1648) published with *His Noble Numbers,* a collection of about 200 sacred poems. His charming lyrics include "Cherry Ripe" and "Delight in Disorder."

Herschel, family of British astronomers who made notable discoveries about the stars and planets.

Sir William Herschel (1738–1822), originally named Friedrich Wilhelm, was born in Germany and emigrated to England as a musician. An amateur astronomer, he soon devoted all his time to his interest. Herschel constructed the longest telescopes of his time, noted and identified more than 2500 nebulas, and discovered double stars and infrared rays. In 1781 he discovered the planet Uranus and originally named it for King George II; the king named him court astronomer and knighted him.

Caroline Lucretia Herschel (1750–1848), Sir William's sister, also an astronomer, made calculations for Herschel's work, completed his catalog of stars, and discovered several comets and nebulas.

Herschel's son, **Sir John Frederick William Herschel** (1792–1871), chemist, mathematician, and astronomer, enlarged his father's catalog of northern nebulas and star clusters. With his improved reflecting telescope, he made a survey of the southern skies from an observatory at the Cape of Good Hope. He also contributed to mathematical analysis and to photography.

Hersey, John Richard (1914–), U.S. author noted for his documentary accounts of the human side of world events, notably *Hiroshima* (1946) and *The Wall* (1950). He worked as a correspondent and editor for such magazines as *Time, Life,* and *The New Yorker.* His other works include *A Bell for Adano* (1944), *A Single Pebble* (1956), *The Child Buyer* (1960), and *The Algiers Motel Incident* (1968).

Hertz, Heinrich Rudolf (1857–1894), German physicist who in 1888 demonstrated the existence of electromagnetic waves. He studied their velocity and length, showing that their properties of refraction, reflection, and polarization make them similar to light waves. High-frequency radio waves are often called Hertzian waves. Hertz later studied the photoelectric effect and also wrote *Principles of Mechanics* (1894).

Herzen (or **Gertsen**), **Alexander Ivanovich** (1812–1870), Russian writer and reformer, a founder of Russian socialism. In London he published essays and periodicals, notably *Kolokol* (*The Bell,* 1857–1865), which printed the first uncensored attack on the oppression of the czarist government. Herzen believed in a native Russian socialism based on the peasant communes. The next generation of reformers, more extreme, criticized him for not having a revolutionary program.

Herzl, Theodor (1860–1904), Hungarian-born Jewish leader who organized Zionism into an internationally recognized movement devoted to founding a Jewish state. In his widely read pamphlet *The Jewish State* (1896), he envisioned a land free of the "social disease" of anti-Semitism. From 1897 Herzl led the Zionist movement. His charisma attracted widespread Jewish support and impressed many statesmen. However, bitter controversy arose in 1903 over land grants for the new state. His health weakened, Herzl died the next year.

Hess, Rudolf (1894–1987), German Nazi political figure, a devoted associate of Adolf Hitler, whom he served as private secretary and cabinet minister. In 1939 Hitler named Hess second to Hermann Göring in line of succession to the dictatorship. In 1941 Hess captured the world's attention with a sensational flight to Scotland to negotiate peace with England. Imprisoned in England for the remainder of the war, he was sentenced to life imprisonment at the Nuremberg trials in 1946.

Hesse, Hermann (1877–1962), German-born novelist known for his sensitive exploration of psychological and philosophical themes. His best-known works include *Siddhartha* (1923), *Steppenwolf* (1927), *Narcissus and Goldmund* (1930), and *Magister Ludi* (*Das Glasperlenspiel,* 1943). Considered one of the most subtle and probing of modern novelists, he won the 1946 Nobel Prize for Literature.

Heyerdahl, Thor (1914–), Norwegian anthropologist, leader of the Kon-tiki, Aku-Aku, and Ra expeditions. Believing that the Indians of Peru had been the first settlers of Polynesia, Heyerdahl built and sailed *Kon-tiki,* a balsa raft, across the Pacific in 1947, showing that such a trip could be made. In 1955–1956 Heyerdahl's expedition to Easter Island showed that the island's first inhabitants probably had been Peruvian Indians. Noting the many similarities between ancient Near East and American Indian cultures, Heyerdahl then set out to demonstrate that ancient Near Eastern peoples could have crossed the Atlantic in boats made of papyrus reeds. His first attempt failed when *Ra I* foundered in mid-Atlantic in 1969, but *Ra II* made the trip from Morocco to Barbados in 1970. Heyerdahl's expeditions are described in his books *Kon-tiki* (1948), *Aku-Aku: The Secret of Easter Island* (1957), and *The Ra Expeditions* (1971).

THOR HEYERDAHL

DOUBLEDAY, INC.

Hidalgo y Costilla, Miguel (1753–1811), Mexican Catholic priest known as the father of Mexican independence. On September 16, 1810, in the village of Dolores (which in Spanish means "sorrows"), he issued the *grito de Dolores* ("cry of Dolores"), calling for racial equality, the end of Spanish rule, and the redistribution of land. Thousands of Indians and mestizos joined him, forming a revolutionary army under the banner of the Virgin of Guadalupe. Initially successful, his army was defeated in the Battle of Calderon, January, 1811, and Father Hidalgo was defrocked and shot. His name became a revolutionary symbol and the anniversary of his proclamation became Mexico's Independence Day.

Hillary, Sir Edmund (1919–), New Zealand explorer, first man to reach the summit of Mount Everest, the highest mountain in the world. Hillary and Tenzing Norkay, a Sherpa guide, reached the top of Everest on May 29, 1953. In 1957–1958 Hillary also led the first overland crossing of Antarctica, using cross-country tractors. He later led several more Everest expeditions, as well as one to Nepal in 1968.

Himmler, Heinrich (1900–1945), German Nazi leader. Head of the SS (*Schutzstaffel,* a Nazi elite military and police unit) from 1929, Himmler gained control of all German police in 1936, when the Gestapo merged with the SS. His special interest was the extermination of "non-Aryans"—Jews, Poles, and Russians—in the camps under his direction. In 1943 he became minister of the interior, with power second only to that of Hitler. On being arrested by British troops in 1945, Himmler poisoned himself.

Hindemith, Paul (1895–1963), German-born composer. He superimposed modern harmony on early counterpoint and baroque styles; much of his work is dissonant, but not atonal. In 1934 Hitler banned Hindemith's music and in 1940 he settled in the United States. His compositions include the opera and symphony *Mathis the Painter* (*Mathis der Maler,* 1934); the ballet *Nobelissima Visione* (1938); and *Symphonic Metamorphoses on Themes by Weber* (1943).

Hindenburg, Paul von (1847–1934), German war hero and last president of the Weimar Republic. After retiring as a general in 1911, after 45 years in the army, he was recalled when World War I began to command the German army on the Russian front. His success was phenomenal, and in 1916 he was made chief of the general staff. He and his subordinate Ludendorff became the virtual rulers of Germany until the armistice in 1918. In 1925 Hindenburg, then 78 years old, was again brought out of retirement to be elected president of the Weimar Republic. Believing that the Nazi Party could be kept under control, he appointed Hitler chancellor in 1933.

Hipparchus (fl. c 160–c 126 B.C.), Greek astronomer and mathematician. He discovered the precession of the equinoxes; compiled a catalog of about 800 stars showing the celestial latitude and longitude of each; and calculated the length of the solar year and the lunar month. He is also credited with inventing trigonometry.

Hippocrates (c 460–c 377 B.C.), Greek physician considered the father of medicine. Few verifiable facts are known about his life, though he supposedly studied on the island of Cos. The so-called Hippocratic collection of treatises was not compiled until long after his death. He emphasized diet, fresh air, and exercise, as well as the healing tendency of nature; he used and prescribed few drugs. The famous maxims "Art is long, life is short" and "One man's meat is another man's poison" are attributed to him. The Hippocratic oath, taken by all medical graduates, was probably not written before 200 A.D.

Hirohito (1901–1989), emperor of Japan from 1926. Dominated by the military leaders of Japan, he permitted the war with China, 1937–1945, and the aggression that led to Japan's entry into World War II in 1941. After Japan's defeat, Hirohito publicly repudiated the doctrine of the emperor's divinity; in 1947 a new constitution stripped him of policy-making authority. In 1971 he toured Europe, becoming the first reigning monarch in 2600 years to leave Japan.

Hiroshige, Ando (1797–1858), Japanese artist, the last great master of the color print *(ukiyo-e).* He produced more than 5000 prints, mainly landscapes, seascapes, and flowers and birds. His most successful series of prints was the *Fifty-Three Stages of the Tokaido* (1832), which depicted scenes at each of the 53 stages, or overnight stations, on the road between Tokyo and Kyoto.

Hitchcock, Alfred (1899–1980), British-born U.S. film and television director respected as an expert and daring craftsman, and widely famed as cinema's master of suspense and psychological melodrama. His films *Lifeboat* (1944) and *Rear Window* (1954) display his technical expertise; *The Trouble with Harry* (1955) his macabre humor; *Psycho* (1960) and *The Birds* (1963) his thematic originality.

Hitler, Adolf (1889–1945), Austrian-born German dictator, chancellor of Germany, 1933–1945, who led his country to defeat during World War II. While living in Vienna, 1907–1913, the young Hitler, a poverty-stricken, solitary art student dropout, adopted his political philosophy: Aryan "supermen" must master the world at the expense of non-Aryan "subhumans." During World War I, Hitler was twice wounded and twice decorated. After the armistice, he was assigned by the army to spy on the German Workers' Party in Munich. The tiny nationalistic group appealed to him; he joined and reorganized it into the National Socialist or Nazi Party, adopting the swastika symbol and "Heil" salute. After attempting a coup (the Munich *Putsch*) in 1923, Hitler served a short term in prison, where he dictated the successful *Mein Kampf* ("My Struggle"). With his new wealth, he purchased a villa in Berchtesgaden. Hitler took the legal way to power. Using his special talents for speech-making, he held emotional mass meetings throughout Germany, calling on the people to make Germany triumphant over all. By 1930 the Nazi Party was the second largest in the country. Appointed chancellor in 1933, within a year Hitler had assumed full dictatorial powers and the title *Führer* ("leader"). To consolidate his power, he outlawed all but Nazi-controlled organizations, used the secret police (the Gestapo) to spy, and concentration camps to punish. He purged the army, launched a rearmament program, and began to build his empire. Hitler absorbed Austria in 1938 and Czechoslovakia in 1939. He launched World War II by marching into Poland in 1939. Most of Western Europe then fell to the Führer, who had personal command of his troops. Germany invaded the Soviet Union in 1941, but Hitler, crazed with power, had lost his military judgment. His failure to capture Stalingrad, 1942–1943, was the turning point; unable to cope with defeat, he refused to recognize it or to negotiate for peace. As the tide of war turned against him, his mass annihilation of Jews, socialists, gypsies, and others was accelerated; by 1945 the Holocaust of the death camps had consumed more than 6 million victims. Hitler survived several assassination attempts by those who realized Germany's sure defeat. Early in 1945, ill and half mad, Hitler retreated to the bunker in the Berlin chancellery. There he was joined by his mistress Eva Braun, whom he married before they committed suicide, April 30, 1945.

Hobbes, Thomas (1588–1679), English philosopher whose most influential contribution was his thinking on the nature of man and the state. Hobbes's political thought antagonized both royalists and parliamentarians, and when the English Civil War broke out in 1640, he moved to Paris. There he tutored the exiled Prince Charles (later Charles II of England) and published *Leviathan* (1651), the most famous statement of his political philosophy. His views offended everyone, and he returned to England. After the Restoration, Hobbes became a favorite of Charles II, but again his opinions made him unpopular; he was accused of atheism and forbidden to publish in England. When almost 90 years of age, he was translating the *Iliad* and feuding with mathematicians over how to square a circle.

Ho Chi Minh (1890–1969), born Nguyen Tat Tan, Vietnamese revolutionary leader, president of the Democratic Republic of North Vietnam, 1946–1969, who waged a life-long struggle to rid Vietnam of foreign domination. Born during French rule of Vietnam, Ho left his country in 1910 and spent the next few years in Europe, joining the French Communist Party in 1920. In the 1920's and 1930's Ho recruited Vietnamese refugees in Southeast Asia for a liberation army, and was put under sentence of death by French authorities. In 1941, with General Nguyen Vo Giap, he formed the Viet Minh to fight the French and the Japanese, who had occupied Vietnam during World War II. In 1945 the Viet Minh forced the Japanese from Hanoi and proclaimed the Democratic Republic of Vietnam. Elected president in 1946, Ho called for resistance against the French, who refused to leave Vietnam. He also began a series of widespread national reforms. When the 1954 Geneva Conference, precipitated by the French defeat at Dien Bien Phu, divided Vietnam in half, Ho led the North, Ngo Dinh Diem the South. When the unification elections scheduled at Geneva were canceled by South Vietnam, widespread resistance by Ho's supporters led to the formation of the National Liberation Front in the South. Throughout the ensuing war and U.S. involvement with the Saigon government, he insisted on a unified Vietnam.

Hoe, Richard March (1812–1886), U.S. inventor. In 1830 he succeeded his father as manager of Hoe & Company, which manufactured printing presses. He made improvements in the flatbed press and then, to meet the needs of large-circulation newspapers, designed the first rotary press, used by the Philadelphia *Public Ledger,* 1847. Hoe later designed the web press (1871).

Hofmann, Hans (1880–1966), German-born painter and art teacher, a major figure in the development of abstract expressionism. In 1930 Hofmann closed his art school in Munich and settled in the United States, later becoming a citizen. By 1934 he had opened two influential schools of modern art; he taught that creative expression grows from internal feelings translated into pure form. Hofmann's paintings, characterized by brilliant color and cubist structure, include *Construction* (1948) and *Joy—Sparks of the Gods* (1964).

Hogarth, William (1697–1764), English painter and engraver who satirized the injustices and hardships of life in London. About 1729 he produced several small group portraits (*The Wollaston Family,* 1730), which established his reputation as a portrait painter. His later famous portraits include *Hogarth's Servants* (c 1750). To make his dramatic satirical commentaries, Hogarth revived the picture cycle, a series of paintings later engraved. *A Harlot's Progress* (c 1731) was so popular and so widely copied that he delayed publishing a second series, *A Rake's Progress,* until he had secured passage of the copyright act of 1735 (Hogarth's Act).

Hohenstaufen, medieval German ruling family of the 12th and 13th centuries. The first of the line was Count Frederick (d. 1105) of Staufen in Swabia, whose two sons, Frederick II of Swabia and Conrad of Rothenburg, were the nephews and closest heirs of the last Salian king of Germany, Henry V, who died in 1125. The electors, however, chose Lothair of the Welfs to be German king and Holy Roman Emperor, instituting a long power struggle between the Welfs, favored by the popes, and the Hohenstaufens. In 1138 Conrad finally was made king by a Hohenstaufen rebellion; on his death in 1152, his nephew Frederick Barbarossa became king and later Holy Roman Emperor. One of Barbarossa's sons became Henry VI, king of Germany, 1169–1197, Holy Roman Emperor, 1191–1197, and, by marriage, king of Sicily. Another son, Philip, then became German king, but was assassinated in a dispute with the Welf claimant to the throne. Henry VI's son Frederick became German king in 1212 and emperor in 1220; on his death in 1250 his son Conrad IV became the last Hohenstaufen emperor, 1250–1254.

Hohenzollern, German ruling family whose most important members came into prominence as, first, electors of Brandenburg, then kings in Prussia, and finally, emperors of Germany. The Hohenzollerns' dominance grew as Prussia came to dominate a united Germany. The first rulers in the Brandenburg line were descendants of one son of Frederick III of Zollern (d. c 1200). From Frederick's other son were descended numerous minor Hohenzollern princes and rulers. Frederick I, first elector of Brandenburg, reigned 1415–1440. By the 1600's, the small state, still under continuous Hohenzollern rule, had grown to include the duchy of Prussia and lands along the Rhine. The "Great Elector," Frederick William (r. 1640–1688), was succeeded by his son, who became first king of Prussia as Frederick I (r. 1701–1713). The most famous of the later Hohenzollern kings of Prussia was Frederick the Great (r. 1740–1786), his grandson. Prussia's steady growth was halted during the reign of Frederick William III (r. 1797–1840), who, by his indecisive behavior toward Napoleon, lost much of the Prussian lands by the Treaty of Tilsit, 1807. He joined France against Russia in 1812. Prussia guided by Bismarck came to dominate Germany in the reign of William I, who in 1871 took the title of Kaiser or emperor of Germany. His son William II was the last Kaiser and the last Hohenzollern ruler.

Hokusai, Katsushika (1760–1849), Japanese artist known for his wood engravings of landscapes and scenes of Japanese life; he was a master of the *ukiyo-e,* the Japanese color print. Hokusai's important works include his sketchbooks, the *Mangwa* (1814–1878); *Waterfalls of the Provinces* (before 1829), and *36 Views of Mount Fuji* (1834–1835); and many volumes of sketches showing Japanese life in vivid color.

Holbein, Hans (the Younger) (c 1497–1543), German painter and engraver. He studied under his father, Hans Holbein the Elder (c 1465–1524) of Augsburg, then wandered for several years before settling in Switzerland. In Basel he met the Dutch scholar Erasmus, of whom he painted a famous portrait in 1523. Before he left Switzerland, Holbein painted another masterpiece, *Family of the Artist* (1528). He then went to London with an introduction from Erasmus to Sir Thomas More, whose family portrait he painted about 1528. His work became popular with the court of Henry VIII; he painted *The Ambassadors* (1533), some of Henry's wives (*Anne of Cleves,* 1539–1540), members of the court, and the king himself.

Holiday, Billie (1915–1959), U.S. jazz singer, born Eleanora Fagan, often called Lady Day. A professional singer at age 15, she performed with the Benny Goodman band in 1933, appearing later with Teddy Wilson, Count Basie, Artie Shaw, and others. Her highly intense and personal style brought her a fine reputation among jazz musicians. Private tragedy and addiction to alcohol and narcotics interrupted her career and hastened her death.

Holmes, Oliver Wendell (1809–1894), U.S. poet, physician, and essayist. He received a medical degree at Harvard in 1835 and taught anatomy and physiology there, 1847–1882. Of his medical writings, an essay on childbed fever (1848) brought him both praise and abuse from other doctors. His first verse was published in 1836 *(Poems);* by 1857 Holmes was well known in New England for his witty poetry and lectures. His best-known work is *The Autocrat of the Breakfast-Table* (1858), a collection of conversational

UPI/BETTMANN NEWSPHOTOS
HO CHI MINH

MUSEES NATIONAUX/MUSEE GUIMET, PARIS
KATSUSHIKA HOKUSAI

OLIVER WENDELL HOLMES

NY PUBLIC LIBRARY

sketches that first appeared in the *Atlantic Monthly.* He is also remembered with affection by readers for the poems "The Chambered Nautilus" and "Old Ironsides."

Holmes, Oliver Wendell (1841–1935), son of poet-physician Oliver Wendell Holmes, U.S. jurist, one of the ablest justices to sit on the U.S. Supreme Court. A true skeptic, raised in the intellectual climate of 19th-century New England, he constantly probed for the roots of law rather than legal precedents. In his famous *The Common Law* (1881), he defined the language of law as experience, not logic. Holmes served 20 years on the Massachusetts Supreme Court, 1882–1902. As a U.S. Supreme Court justice, 1902–1932, he advocated judicial self-restraint, opposing the use of the Court's power either to force or oppose change. A frequent and eloquent dissenter, Holmes was the exemplification in his time of the liberal spirit.

Homer, author of the ancient Greek epic poems the *Iliad* and the *Odyssey.* Many scholars have wrangled over the so-called "Homeric question": the date, authorship, and sources of the poems. Though the epics as we know them may be solely the product of oral tradition, classical Greeks believed that the poems were the work of Homer, and they recorded stories and conjectures about him. He was supposedly blind. Many cities claimed him as a native. Proposed dates for him have ranged from the twelfth to the seventh centuries B.C. Much has since been learned about the poems, but in the matter of Homer himself, modern scholars know little more than the ancients.

Homer, Winslow (1836–1910), U.S. painter best remembered for his realistic scenes of the sea and the New England coast. In 1881 Homer settled at Prout's Neck, Maine, where he lived a secluded, eccentric life, though he had become internationally known. One of the paintings from this period is *The Lookout—"All's Well"* (1896). From his occasional travels to the Caribbean islands came *The Gulf Stream* (1899) and many watercolors.

Honegger, Arthur Oscar (1892–1955), French-born Swiss composer, one of "the Six," a group of postwar French composers including Milhaud and Poulenc. His music—operas, songs, chamber compositions, choral works—is characterized by polytonality and strong rhythms. Typical Honegger compositions are the oratorios *King David* (1921) and *Joan of Arc at the Stake* (1938), and the opera *Judith* (1926).

Hoover, Herbert Clark (1874–1964), 31st President of the United States, 1929–1933, whose term as President was only one episode in a 40-year career of public service. A mining engineer, he lived and worked all over the world. At the outbreak of World War I, he organized a volunteer agency to supply food, clothing, and medicine to civilians in the war zone. During the war, he served as U.S. food administrator, in charge of wartime controls and production. Afterward he became famous as director of relief in countries threatened with famine. He was secretary of commerce, 1921–1928, when he was nominated for President. He defeated the Democratic candidate, Alfred E. Smith. The stock market crash of 1929 was the first of several economic crises during Hoover's administration. He took measures to end the Depression that followed, but in the election of 1932, Hoover was defeated by Franklin D. Roosevelt, chiefly as a result of the country's economic difficulties. He retired until after World War II, when he once again directed European relief. He also headed the Hoover commissions (1947, 1953) to improve efficiency in the executive branch of government.

Hoover, J(ohn) Edgar (1895–1972), U.S. law enforcement official, head of the Federal Bureau of Investigation for more than 45 years. In 1924 Hoover became director of the newly formed Federal Bureau of Investigation. Under Hoover the FBI's domain came to include investigation of federal crimes, search for missing persons, national security, police training, and surveillance of national figures.

Hopkins, Gerard Manley (1844–1889), British poet and Jesuit priest whose work is noted for its sensory vividness and use of "sprung rhythm." This meter uses stress instead of syllables to scan the poetic line; it deeply influenced subsequent British and American poetry. Hopkins burned his first collection of poems in 1868 when he decided to become a Jesuit. His later writings include the famous "Wreck of the Deutschland" (1875) and the frequently quoted sonnet "The Windhover" (1878). His poems were first collected and published in 1918 by Robert Bridges.

Hopper, Edward (1882–1967), U.S. painter and engraver, best remembered for his scenes of the American city. Early in his career, Hopper came under the influence of the "ashcan" school, which advocated realism based on the American scene. With bright colors and sharp-edged contrast, he revealed the loneliness of urban life, as in *Early Sunday Morning* (1930), *New York Movie* (1939), and *Nighthawks* (1942).

Horace (65–8 B.C.), in full Quintus Horatius Flaccus, Roman poet, one of the great lyric poets. As a young man, he was introduced by his friend Vergil to Rome's greatest patron of the arts,

Maecenas, who provided for him and recommended him to the emperor Augustus. Horace's *Satires* are light poetic essays; the *Odes* and *Epodes* are his lyric masterpieces, with their complex structure and decorous, philosophical tone. One of his *Epistles,* the famous *Ars Poetica (Art of Poetry),* had a considerable influence on European literature, particularly classicism.

Horowitz, Vladimir (1904–1989), Russian-born U.S. pianist famous for the technical perfection and intensity of his playing. He is known particularly for his interpretations of Chopin and Scarlatti. Horowitz performed in Russia for several years and in 1928 made his American debut with the New York Philharmonic. After a lengthy career, illness forced him into retirement in 1953. He made a spectacular comeback in 1965 at New York's Carnegie Hall, performing again in 1974 and 1981 with enormous success.

Houdini, Harry (1874–1926), Ehrich Weiss, U.S. magician famous for his amazing escapes from locks, handcuffs, and sealed chests. In a typical feat he was bound, shackled, locked into a chest, and lowered into the water, freeing himself in 59 seconds. He credited his feats to technical power alone, scorning those who claimed to work with the supernatural.

HARRY HOUDINI

THE BETTMANN ARCHIVE

Housman, Alfred Edward (A.E.) (1859–1936), English poet and classical scholar. Though Housman made notable Latin translations, he is best remembered for two volumes of bittersweet verse, *A Shropshire Lad* (1896) and *Last Poems* (1922). The poems, mostly short lyrics, are noted for their simple language, melodious verse, and pessimistic tone. Their subject matter is friendship, the passing of youth, and human vanity. *More Poems* (1936) was published posthumously.

Houston, Samuel (1793–1863), U.S. soldier and politican who led the Texas war of independence against Mexico. Houston grew up with Cherokee Indians in Tennessee and fought under Andrew Jackson in the Creek Indian War of 1813. When war with Mexico broke out in 1835, Houston commanded the Texas volunteers; he captured the Mexican general Santa Anna at San Jacinto in 1836, ending the war. He was twice president of the Republic of Texas, and, after Texas joined the Union in 1845, he was its U.S. senator until 1859, when he became governor. He was deposed in 1861 for opposing secession and the Confederacy.

Howe, Elias (1819–1867), U.S. inventor of the sewing machine. He secured a patent on his invention in 1846, but it was violated by others, including Isaac Singer. Howe won a final lawsuit in 1854. His machine, which laid the basis for the mass production of cloth goods, won a gold medal at the 1867 Paris Exhibition.

Howe, Julia Ward (1819–1910), U.S. author and poet, best remembered as the author of "The Battle Hymn of the Republic" (1862). Howe and her husband edited the abolitionist paper *The Commonwealth.* She also campaigned for women's rights, prison reform, and international peace. Her works include *Modern Society* (1881) and *Margaret Fuller* (1883).

Howells, William Dean (1837–1920), U.S. novelist and editor. As a young man he wrote a campaign biography of Abraham Lincoln, who rewarded him with a consular post in Venice, 1861–1865. After returning to the United States in 1866, he joined the staff of the *Atlantic Monthly* and was its editor from 1871–1881; as an editor on *Harper's Magazine,* 1886–1891, he wrote memorable essays on the writer's craft. A pioneer in introducing realism to U.S. fiction, Howells was a close friend of Mark Twain and Henry James; he promoted acceptance of their work. His own major novels include *The Rise of Silas Lapham* (1885) and *A Hazard of New Fortunes* (1890).

Hoxha, Enver (1908–1985), Albanian statesman, first premier of Albania under a Communist regime, 1944–1954. He founded the Albanian Communist Party in 1941 and led the fight to free Albania from the Axis powers during World War II. Hoxha stepped down from the premier's post in 1954 and became first secretary of the central committee. He sided with China during the Sino-Soviet split.

Hudson, Henry (d. 1611?), English explorer. Hudson made four attempts to discover a northwest passage. During the first, in 1607, he sailed to Greenland and Spitsbergen for the Moscovy Company. He explored the Barents Sea in 1608; on a voyage in the *Half Moon* for the Dutch, 1609, he reached New York and sailed about 150 miles up the Hudson River. With the British ship *Discovery* in 1610, Hudson sailed through Hudson Strait into the bay and examined its eastern shore. The ship was frozen in for the winter. After the spring thaw, the crew mutinied because of scarce rations; Hudson and his son were set adrift in a small boat, and they vanished without a trace.

Hughes, Charles Evans (1862–1948), chief justice of the U.S. Supreme Court, 1930–1941. Hughes's early investigations into corrupt electric and insurance industries made him well known. He was elected governor of New York in 1906, defeating William Randolph Hearst. His two terms were marked by extensive reform. A term as a Supreme Court justice, 1910–1916, ended when he became the Republican and Progressive candidate for the Presidency; he narrowly lost to Wilson. As secretary of state, 1921–1925, Hughes reduced the naval arms race between the United States and Japan and maintained the Open Door Policy in China. Named chief justice in 1930, he supported civil rights legislation and was instrumental in defeating Roosevelt's 1937 attempt to pack the court with New Deal justices.

Hughes, (James) Langston (1902–1967), U.S. writer of verse, fiction, history, and drama, who with Countee Cullen initiated the Harlem Renaissance of the 1920's. Hughes spent his early life as a seaman; after attending Lincoln University on a scholarship granted for his poetry, he traveled to Russia and Spain. Active in social causes, he campaigned on behalf of the unjustly accused "Scottsboro boys" in the 1930's (*Scottsboro Limited,* 1932). Some of his best-known works are the poetry volumes *The Dream Keeper* (1932) and *Shakespeare in Harlem* (1942) and the autobiographical *I Wonder as I Wander* (1956). He also expressed black attitudes through his character Jesse B. Semple.

Hugo, Victor Marie (1802–1885), French poet and novelist, leader of the French Romantic movement. Hugo's career began early, and he was soon known for his drama and poetry. The preface to his play *Cromwell* (1827) contained the famous doctrine of romanticism, which called for a literature uniting elements of both tragedy and comedy. In 1831 *The Hunchback of Notre Dame* revealed his superb prose style. Hugo was elected to the French Academy in 1841 and named a peer of France in 1845. Disagreement with Louis Napoleon forced him into exile in 1851, where he produced some of his greatest poetry (*Les Châtiments,* 1853; *Les Contemplations,* 1856) and the masterpiece *Les Misérables* (1862). With the downfall of Napoleon in 1870, Hugo returned to Paris, where he lived and wrote until his death.

Hull, Cordell (1871–1955), U.S. statesman called the father of the United Nations by President Franklin D. Roosevelt, under whom he was secretary of state, 1933–1944. Convinced as a tax expert that open trade would ensure world peace, he won passage of the Trade Agreements Act (1934), which adjusted tariffs to stimulate trade with Latin America. He continued to promote peace at the Pan-American conferences and headed the Moscow Foreign Ministers Conference in 1943. Hull laid the groundwork for the 1945 San Francisco conference at which the UN was established; he received the Nobel Peace Prize that year.

Humboldt, (Friedrich Heinrich) Alexander, Baron von (1769–1859), German naturalist whose observations and studies of natural history in all parts of the world helped establish the sciences of physical geography, climatology, and meteorology. In particular, Humboldt was the first to study and describe the natural history of Latin America. His *The Cosmos: Outline of a Description of the Physical World* (1845–1862) was one of the most widely read books of its time.

His brother **Wilhelm, Baron von Humboldt** (1767–1835), a diplomat and linguist, was one of the founders of the science of comparative philology.

Hume, David (1711–1776), Scottish philosopher and historian. Hume left Scotland in 1734 to live in France, where he wrote his influential *Treatise of Human Nature,* setting forth his skeptical theories of knowledge and of morals. It was published in 1739–1740, after Hume had returned from France. He later rewrote the first part, which in its revised edition (1758) became known as *An Enquiry Concerning Human Understanding.* Hume's *History of England* (6 volumes, 1754–1762) made him famous and became the standard work for generations. From 1763 to 1766 he was at the British embassy in Paris, honored by society. On his return, he invited Rousseau to England; Rousseau came but soon fled back to France, believing himself persecuted. Hume retired in 1769 to Edinburgh, but continued to publish and revise. He finished his autobiography, *The Life of David Hume, Written by Himself,* shortly before he died.

DEMOCRATIC NATIONAL COMMITTEE

HUBERT HUMPHREY

Humperdinck, Engelbert (1854–1921), German composer known mainly for his children's opera *Hansel and Gretel* (1893). Greatly influenced by Richard Wagner, he helped prepare the score of Wagner's *Parsifal* for publication. He also wrote compositions for piano and string quartet, and incidental music for plays.

Humphrey, Hubert Horatio (1911–1978), U.S. politician. After helping to merge the Minnesota state Democratic and Farmer-Labor parties, he was elected mayor of Minneapolis as their candidate in 1945. From 1948 to 1965 he served in the U.S. Senate, where his greatest success was in securing passage of the 1964 civil rights bill. After an unsuccessful bid for the Presidential nomination in 1960, he was elected Vice President in 1964 under Lyndon Johnson. He ran for President in 1968. Narrowly defeated by Richard Nixon, he returned to the Senate in 1970.

Hunt, (James Henry) Leigh (1784–1859), English poet and essayist. A friend of Shelley, Keats, and Lamb, he championed their work in his essays. Hunt became editor of *The Examiner* in 1808; in 1813 he and his brother John were imprisoned for libeling the prince regent. Released in 1815, Hunt continued to advocate governmental reforms and abolition of the slave trade. He published several other political and literary periodicals, supporting the work of poets he personally enjoyed. Hunt's best-known poem is "Jenny Kissed Me"; he also wrote an interesting autobiography (1850).

Hunt, Richard Morris (1827–1895), U.S. architect whose notable buildings include the Metropolitan Museum and the Vanderbilt residence on Fifth Avenue, both in New York. Hunt studied at the École des Beaux Arts in Paris, then returned to New York to work with the firm making additions to the U.S. Capitol. He brought with him the styles popular in France and came to the attention of wealthy New Yorkers; he built homes such as the Vanderbilts' "Biltmore" in North Carolina and the palatial "cottages" at Newport, R.I.

Huss (or Hus), John (c 1370–1415), Bohemian religious reformer whose martyrdom caused the Hussite Wars, 1419–1434. Huss studied at Prague and later became lecturer, dean of philosophy, and rector. He became interested in some of the moderate teachings of the English reformer John Wycliffe, especially his proposals for reform of the corrupt and wealthy clergy, who held half the land in Bohemia and taxed it heavily. Eventually he became leader of the Hussite movement (named for him), opposing exploitation by the church. He was supported by the king and some church members, but in the confusion of the Great Schism, 1378–1417, he was accused of heresy and later excommunicated. In 1412 Huss took a position against the sale of indulgences and advocated disobedience to papal commands in conflict with Christ's law. He then went into hiding until 1414, when he agreed to defend his position at the Council of Constance if his safety were guaranteed. However, shortly after he arrived in Constance (Germany), he was imprisoned and burned at the stake.

Hussein ibn Talal (1935–), third Hashemite king of Jordan, who succeeded to the throne in 1952. Though Hussein was faithful to the Arab cause against Israel, his reign was marked by frequent revolutionary plots; most of the other Arab states opposed the existence of a monarchy in Jordan. In 1970 and 1971 Hussein fought a virtual civil war that drove out Palestinian guerrillas stationed in Jordan. He has since accepted the position that the Palestine Liberation Organization (PLO) is the sole representative of Palestinians.

Huston, John (1906–1987), U.S. film writer, director, and actor distinguished for his direction of action, masculine style, and sympathetic portrayal of well-developed characters. His films include *The Maltese Falcon* (1941), *The Treasure of Sierra Madre* (1948), *The African Queen* (1951), *Moby Dick* (1956), *A Walk with Love and Death* (1970), *The Man Who Would Be King* (1976), and *Prizzi's Honor* (1985).

Hutchinson, Anne Marbury (1591–1643), American religious leader, an early advocate of religious freedom. Born in England, she went to Boston with her family in 1634. A skilled nurse, she won the admiration of the Boston settlers and soon began to preach. Her doctrine of salvation by grace, not deeds, was counter to New England Calvinism, causing conflict with Governor Winthrop and the orthodox churchmen who feared her doctrine would lead to rejection of the clergy's rule of the colony. Hutchinson was tried and convicted of sedition and heresy in 1637. Banished from Massachusetts, she formed a settlement in the new colony of Rhode Island. After her husband's death in 1642, she went to Long Island, where she and her family were killed by Indians.

Huxley, Aldous Leonard (1894–1963), British novelist and essayist, the grandson of T. H. Huxley, who wrote the frightening novel of a mechanistic utopia, *Brave New World* (1932). In the late 1930's he settled in California. He was nearly blind for most of his life. Huxley's novels are often outrageously satirical (*Crome Yellow,* 1921; *Antic Hay,* 1923), although some are marked by deeper seriousness (*Those Barren Leaves,* 1925; *Point Counter Point,* 1928). His later works were influenced by Huxley's preoccupation with Hindu mysticism. Notable are the novels *Eyeless in Gaza* (1936) and *Ape and Essence* (1949); the histories *Grey Eminence* (1941) and *The Devils of Loudon* (1952); and an account of his experimentation with the drug mescaline, *The Doors of Perception* (1954). He was the brother of scientist Julian Huxley.

Huxley, Sir Julian Sorell (1887–1975), British scientist, author, and educator in the fields of biology, embryology, and evolution. The grandson of T.H. Huxley, he possessed a unique talent for relating science to religion and society. Huxley gained a wide reputation as a professor of zoology at Oxford, 1919–1925. After 1929 he traveled to Africa and the Soviet Union on behalf of groups seeking scientific exchange; he was head of UNESCO, 1946–1948. Huxley's many works include *The Individual in the Animal Kingdom* (1912), *Africa View* (1931), *A Scientist Among the Soviets* (1932), and *New Wine in Old Bottles* (1957). He was the brother of author Aldous Huxley.

THOMAS HUXLEY

THE BETTMANN ARCHIVE

Huxley, Thomas Henry (1825–1895), British biologist who popularized Darwinian evolution and first theorized that humans, too, had evolved (*Man's Place in Nature,* 1863). Educated in London, Huxley was assigned as surgeon to the H.M.S. *Rattlesnake,* 1845–1850. Without books or equipment, he conducted research on marine organisms that led to the classifications of sea squirts, squids, and jellyfish. When Darwin's *The Origin of Species* (1859) appeared, Huxley became its defender and engaged in many debates; his most famous was with the bishop of Oxford, in which Huxley declared science independent of theology. Huxley's position regarding religion was that the available scientific evidence led to neither an affirmation nor a denial of God; he coined the term "agnostic" to describe this position.

Huygens, Christiaan (1629–1695), Dutch mathematician, astronomer, and physicist whose notable achievements include the discovery of the rings of Saturn (1656), the invention of the pendulum clock (1656), and the development of the wave theory of light (1677). Historically placed between Galileo and Newton, Huygens' range was broader than either. His other studies were on optical research, improvements in the telescope, calculations about Earth's shape, and mathematical probability.

I

Ibáñez, Vicente Blasco: *See* Blasco Ibáñez, Vicente.

Iberville, Sieur d'; Pierre le Moyne (1661–1706), Canadian-born French soldier and explorer. With his brother **Jean-Baptiste le Moyne, Sieur de Bienville** (1680–1768), he founded the earliest permanent French colonies—called Louisiana—on the American Gulf Coast. With four ships and 200 colonists, he and his brother sailed from France to Mobile Bay, arriving in 1699. They established the colony on the site of Biloxi; returning the next year, they built a fort above the mouth of the Mississippi River. In 1702 a third settlement was made near the Mobile River. Iberville died in the West Indies on a naval mission. Bienville became colonial governor of Louisiana and founded New Orleans in 1718.

Ibn Saud (c 1880–1953), in full, Abd-al-Aziz ibn Abd-al-Rahman ibn Faisal al-Sa'ud, king of Saudi Arabia, 1932–1953, who founded the kingdom and made it important in world politics. The descendant of an old ruling family, he defeated his rivals, drove the Turks out of eastern Arabia, and by 1927 had gained control of most of the Arabian peninsula, which became the kingdom of Saudi Arabia in 1932. When oil was discovered in Saudi Arabia, he used the oil profits to modernize education, transportation, agriculture, and medical care. He helped found the Arab League in 1945.

Ibsen, Henrik Johan (1828–1906), Norwegian playwright considered the father of modern drama. His tightly structured problem plays moved drama from sentimental escapism to social-psychological realism. In 1848 Ibsen wrote his first play, *Catiline.* In 1857 he took charge of a theater in Oslo (then Christiania), where he wrote a series of plays, all unsuccessful. In 1858 he married and he soon began to live abroad, where his first successes, the dramatic poems *Brand* (1865) and *Peer Gynt* (1867), were written. Over the next 30 years his works changed the dramatic landscape forever. Ibsen's method of moving the dramatic action forward slowly, giving the characters time to explore the implications of their actions, became a standard technique of contemporary drama. Ibsen's plays concern the importance of individual integrity and the tragic effects of hypocrisy, both individual and social. His first social problem play was *Pillars of Society* (1877), followed by *A Doll's House* (1879), *Ghosts* (1881), *An Enemy of the People* (1882), *The Wild Duck* (1884), *Rosmersholm* (1886), *Hedda Gabler* (1890), *The Master Builder* (1892), and *When We Dead Awaken* (1899).

Ignatius of Loyola, Saint: *See* Loyola, Saint Ignatius of.

Ikhnaton (or Akhenaten) (fl. 14th century B.C.), name assumed by Egyptian Pharaoh Amenhotep IV (r. c 1379–1362 B.C.). He instituted a new state worship of a universal sun god, Aton. Resisted by the Theban nobility, he moved to Akhetaton (now Tell el-Amarna), where he initiated an artistic and religious revolution, attempting to destroy all trace of the old religion. Ikhnaton neglected his empire, whose provinces fell away or were conquered; his religion was abandoned after his death. Ikhnaton's queen was the beautiful Nefertiti; her head appears in much of the Amarna art, a new style that produced some of the world's masterpieces. Ikhnaton was succeeded by Tutankhamen.

Inge, William Motter (1913–1973), U.S. playwright whose works depict life in small-town America. His first play was *Farther Off From Heaven* (1947), followed by *Come Back, Little Sheba* (1950) and *Picnic* (1953), which won the Pulitzer Prize and the New York Drama Critics' Circle Award. *Bus Stop* (1955) and *The Dark at the Top of the Stairs* (1957), as well as his earlier plays, were made into successful films. Inge won an Academy Award for the screenplay *Splendor in the Grass* (1961).

Ingres, Jean Auguste Dominique (1780–1867), great French academic painter of the neoclassical school. In 1801 he won the *Prix de Rome* scholarship, with which he went to Italy, remaining there 1806–1824. Known in Paris for his portraits (*Mme. Rivière,* 1805), he made many pencil portraits of the French colony in Rome (*The Samaty Family,* 1818) that are notable for their exquisite draftsmanship. Returning to France in 1824, Ingres led the academic resistance to Romantic art, painting such neoclassical themes as *Apotheosis of Homer* (1827).

Inness, George (1825–1894), U.S. landscape painter. Inness's early work showed the romantic realism typical of the Hudson River school. About 1859, after he moved to Medfield, near Boston, his style matured into a freer, more personal interpretation of nature (*Harvest Time,* 1864; *Autumn Oaks,* 1875; *June,* 1882). Though he cared little for recognition or money, he acquired both late in life. He was more concerned about social problems and Swedenborgianism.

Ionesco, Eugene (1912–), noted Rumanian-born French playwright of the theater of the absurd. Initiating a new form of drama, he wrote short, symbolic "anti-plays" characterized by paradoxes and bizarre twists of reality. His works include *The Bald Soprano* (1950), *The Chairs* (1952), *Rhinoceros* (1960), *The King Dies* (1962), *A Stroll in the Air* (1963), and *Hunger and Thirst* (1966).

Irving, Washington (1783–1859), U.S. writer, a pioneer in American humorous literature and in the development of the short story. His first major comic work, *Salmagundi* (1807–1808), was a satirical periodical in the style of Addison's *Spectator.* In 1809 he published *Diedrich Knickerbocker's History of New York,* a parody of American colonial history. After several years away from writing, Irving brought out *The Sketch Book of Geoffrey Crayon, Gent.* (1820), containing the stories "Rip Van Winkle" and "The Legend of Sleepy Hollow." Its success made him America's leading literary figure. His later books include the still read *Tales of a Traveller* (1824) and *The Alhambra* (1832), his impressions gained from travels in Germany and a diplomatic post in Spain. Irving was the first

THE BETTMANN ARCHIVE

WASHINGTON IRVING

American writer to be internationally admired.

Isabella I (1451–1504), queen of Castile and León, 1474–1504. Isabella and her husband, Ferdinand of Aragon, succeeded her half brother Henry IV as joint rulers of Castile and León. After Ferdinand became king of Aragon in 1479, he made her co-ruler in 1481; they ruled the two kingdoms jointly from then on. Isabella, known as *La Católica* ("the Catholic") for her zealous faith, was the one responsible for the major events of the reign: the reconquest of the rest of Spain from the Moors, the expulsion of Moors and Jews from Spain, the establishment of the Spanish Inquisition, and the financing of the voyages of Columbus (for which, contrary to legend, she did not have to pawn her jewels). One of her daughters, Catherine, was the first wife of Henry VIII of England.

Iturbide, Agustín de (1783–1824), emperor of Mexico, 1822–1823. On the defeat of Mexican revolutionary forces under Hidalgo and Morelos, Iturbide, a wealthy landowner, formed a coalition of conservative and clerical opposition to Spanish rule and drew up the Plan of Iguala (1821), declaring Mexico independent. His plan unified anti-Spanish sentiment, and the Spanish viceroy yielded. However, Iturbide went on to declare himself emperor and to rule despotically. He was driven from Mexico in 1823 and, on his return in 1824, was captured and executed.

Ivan III Vasilievich (the Great) (1440–1505), grand duke of Moscow, 1462–1505. Although described as cautious, cowardly, and unwilling to take risks, he managed to increase Moscow's territorial boundaries immensely. He conquered the ancient free city of Novgorod (1478), annexed much of Lithuania, and ceased paying tribute to the Tatar chief. In 1472 Ivan married Sophia (also called Zoë), niece of the last Byzantine emperor. Byzantine court customs were introduced, and Moscow came to be considered the "third Rome," following Constantinople. Ivan began calling himself "czar," strengthened the central government, subdued feudal resistance, and issued a code of legal procedure for court use.

Ivan IV Vasilievich (the Terrible) (1530–1584), Russian czar. Crowned at age 17, Ivan and his advisers, under church influence, enacted governmental reforms for a time. Then, after a mock abdication in 1564, Ivan created a special realm, the *oprichnina;* from this private court, with its elite army, he started a reign of terror against the feudal boyars, whom he blamed for Russia's misfortunes. Ivan's military campaigns, which influenced much of his policy, opened Siberia to colonization, 1552–1556, but he was driven from the Baltic by the Poles and Swedes, 1577–1583. A man of extreme passions, he married seven times; though deeply religious, in a fit of rage he killed his son Ivan in 1580.

Ives, Charles Edward (1874–1954), U.S. composer. He worked in the insurance business most of his life; illness

RULERS OF RUSSIA

House of Rurik

1462–1505	Ivan III the Great*
1505–1533	Basil III
1533–1584	Ivan IV the Terrible*
1584–1598	Fëdor I
1598–1605	Boris Godunov
1605	Fëdor II
1605–1606	Dmitri (the Imposter)
1606–1610	Basil (IV) Shuiski
	(Interregnum, 1610–1613)

House of Romanov

1613–1645	Michael Romanov*
1645–1676	Alexis
1676–1682	Fëdor III
1682–1689	Ivan V and Peter I (the Great)
1689–1725	Peter I (the Great) (alone)*
1725–1727	Catherine I
1727–1730	Peter II
1730–1740	Anna
1740–1741	Ivan VI
1741–1762	Elizabeth
1762	Peter III
1762–1796	Catherine II (the Great)*
1796–1801	Paul I
1801–1825	Alexander I
1825–1855	Nicholas I
1855–1881	Alexander II
1881–1894	Alexander III
1894–1917	Nicholas II*

*See main biography

forced him to give up composing about 1915. Ives experimented with rhythm and harmony, producing works of extreme complexity. His best-known compositions include his Second Piano Sonata (1909–1915), also called *Concord, Mass., 1840–1860;* and his Third Symphony (1911), which belatedly won a Pulitzer Prize in 1947. Other works are *Fourth of July* (1913) and *Three Places in New England* (1903–1914).

J

Jackson, Andrew (1767–1845), seventh President of the United States, 1829–1837. During the War of 1812 he led the Tennessee militia to victories over the Creek Indians in 1813 and in January, 1815, repulsed a much larger British force at New Orleans. Jackson's victories made him a hero. In 1823 Jackson was elected to the U.S. Senate and ran for the Presidency. Though he was defeated in 1824, he won in 1828 and was reelected in 1832. As President, he relied on a few close friends who made up what was popularly called the Kitchen Cabinet. Jackson introduced the spoils system and was the first President to build up a political machine composed of party members. Such tactics earned him the nickname King Andrew. A tall, gaunt man with an unmistakable profile and a vicious temper, Jackson was one of the most controversial of Presidents. He was a hero to the people, especially of the South and West, but a boorish ogre to the landowners and bankers. The first populist President, he anticipated the people's will and left office more popular than ever. He retired to his home, the Hermitage, in Tennessee.

Jackson, Thomas Jonathan (Stonewall) (1824–1863), U.S. Army officer and Confederate general, a brilliant strategist and stern soldier, Lee's ablest commander. After Jackson left West Point, 1846, he distinguished himself in the Mexican War. He then taught military tactics and natural philosophy at Virginia Military Institute. At the outbreak of the Civil War, Jackson was ordered to bring his cadets to Richmond. At the Battle of Bull Run (Manassas), 1861, as the rest of the Confederate line broke under Union attack, an officer exclaimed, "There is Jackson standing like a stone wall." He then took command in the Shenandoah valley, where his 1862 campaign was a model of military tactics. More victories followed. Jackson and Robert E. Lee formed a superb fighting team, driving the Union Army back to the Potomac. At Chancellorsville in 1863, Jackson, though outnumbered, surprised Hooker's army and forced a retreat. Returning at twilight, he was shot accidentally by his own men and died eight days later.

James, Henry (1843–1916), U.S. author and critic. Brother of psychologist William James, he traveled and studied abroad and attended Harvard. By the late 1860's he was writing short stories for the *Nation* and the *Atlantic Monthly.* Resuming his European travels, he established friendships with Turgenev, with Flaubert and other French realists, and later with notable English literary figures. Settling in England in 1876, James lived there as an expatriate for the next 20 years. In this period he created his major "international" novels, in which American innocence is carefully balanced against European experience: *The American* (1876), *The Europeans* (1878), *Daisy Miller* (1878), *The Portrait of a Lady* (1881), and *Washington Square* (1881). His later novels, more subtle, complex, and psychologically probing, include *The Turn of the Screw* (1898), *The Wings of the Dove* (1902), *The Ambassadors* (1903), and *The Golden Bowl* (1904). His prefaces to his novels and his other critical essays set down his principles for the art of fiction.

James, Jesse Woodson (1847–1882), U.S. outlaw who in 1867 formed a gang of bank and train robbers that terrorized the Middle West, becoming the subject of songs and legends. James learned his deadly skills of daring and marksmanship while engaged in guerrilla warfare for the Confederates. After the war, he and his brother Frank (1843–1915) became outlaws. Eventually, Jesse was shot by two of his followers for a $10,000 reward; his brother retired to a Missouri farm.

James, William (1842–1910), U.S. philosopher and psychologist, a founder of the philosophy of pragmatism. Brother of novelist Henry James, he studied at Harvard and in 1865 accompanied Louis Agassiz on an Amazon expedition, gaining respect for first-hand observation. He returned to Harvard in 1872, having overcome several years of depression and illness; he taught there until 1907. He established the first laboratory for experimental psychology in the 1870's and published his monumental *The Principles of Psychology* in 1890. In his classic *Varieties of Religious Experience* (1902), he considered the states of mind produced by religious belief. *Pragmatism* (1907) elucidates the doctrine that the meaning of ideas is found in their practical consequences. James, a warm, humorous man, was a popular teacher.

Janáček, Leoš (1854–1928), the leading Czech composer of the early 20th century. His romantic compositions show Russian and Wagnerian influences but have a distinctly Czech flavor. His well-known operas include *Jenufa* (1904), *The Makropulos Affair* (1926), and *From the House of the Dead* (1930). Janáček directed the college of organists at Brno, 1881–1919, and was a student and collector of Czech folk music. *Taras Bulba* (1924) and *Sinfonietta* (1926) are his best-known orchestral works.

Jansen, Cornelius Otto (1585–1638), Dutch theologian, Roman Catholic bishop of Ypres from 1636. In his treatise *Augustinus,* published posthumously in 1640 and condemned by the pope, Jansen proposed a spiritual and intellectual reorientation of the church contrary to the prevailing scholasticism. The century-long controversy that followed concerned not only whether Jansenist doctrines should be condemned but whether these doctrines, as stated and condemned, were actually to be found in the *Augustinus.*

Jay, John (1745–1829), first chief justice of the United States, 1789–1794. A wealthy and conservative aristocrat, Jay at first opposed American independence, fearing revolution and popular democracy. After the Declaration was signed, however, he fought for its ratification; he was president of the Continental Congress in 1778. Several frustrating diplomatic missions and a term as secretary of foreign affairs, 1784–1790, convinced Jay of the need for a stronger central government. He enthusiastically supported the Constitution, writing several of the *Federalist* papers (1787–1788). Washington named him chief justice in 1789, and Jay organized and established the procedures of the new Supreme Court. In 1794 he negotiated the hated Jay Treaty, which, while it averted a second war with Britain, failed to resolve important grievances, enraged France, and caused Jay to be labeled a traitor by his political enemies. The treaty cost him a chance for the Presidency, though he later became governor of New York, 1795–1801.

Jeanne d'Arc: *See* Joan of Arc.

Jeanneret, Charles Édouard: *See* Le Corbusier.

Jeans, Sir James Hopwood (1877–1946), English physicist, mathematician, and astronomer, who developed an original tidal theory of the creation of the universe and theories concerning stars and stellar energy. His popular books, blending science and philosophy in a lucid style, include *The Universe Around Us* (1929), *The Mysterious Universe* (1930), and *The Stars in Their Courses* (1931).

Jefferson, Thomas (1743–1826), third President of the United States, 1801–1809. Jefferson was elected to the Virginia House of Burgesses in 1769 and in 1775 became a delegate to the Continental Congress, where he was appointed to a committee to draft a Declaration of Independence. Jefferson wrote the first draft, which was adopted with only minor revisions.

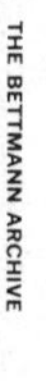

EDWARD JENNER

JOAN OF ARC

After two terms as governor of Virginia, in 1783 he took a seat in the Continental Congress. He then served as minister to France and became the first U.S. secretary of state. Fearing the possible tyranny of a strong federal government, he was in constant conflict with Alexander Hamilton, then secretary of the treasury and head of the Federalist Party. Jefferson helped organize the Democratic-Republican Party in opposition to the Federalists. Jefferson was Vice President under John Adams. In 1801 he tied in electoral votes with Aaron Burr and was elected President by the House of Representatives. Burr became Vice President. One of Jefferson's most important acts as President was the Louisiana Purchase in 1803. Jefferson was an exemplar of the Enlightenment: a scholar, author, farmer, natural scientist, and architect. He designed his home, Monticello, and founded and planned the University of Virginia. His library became the basis of the Library of Congress, and his later correspondence with John Adams is still studied by political philosophers.

Jenner, Edward (1749–1823), English naturalist and country physician who developed vaccination. When Jenner was a child, he was bled and half-starved, inoculated with smallpox, then locked up until the disease had run its course—the only method of immunization then known. Later, while studying medicine, he investigated the country belief that farmers who had had the animal disease cowpox were immune to smallpox. In 1796 he inoculated a young boy with cowpox; the child recovered and, when inoculated later with smallpox, remained well. Jenner published his results in 1798. The Royal Jennerian Society for vaccination was set up in 1803, and Jenner's work was eventually accepted and honored.

Jesus (c 4 B.C.–c 29 A.D.), also called Jesus of Nazareth and Jesus Christ, considered by Christians the son of God as well as the central figure of the Christian religion. The principal sources for the events in Jesus' life are the first four books of the New Testament, the Gospels as told by the evangelists Matthew, Mark, Luke, and John. Indirect references to his teachings and influence are found in contemporary Jewish and Roman histories. According to the Gospels, Jesus was born in Bethlehem, in Judea near the Jewish religious center of Jerusalem. He grew up in Nazareth, in the Judean province of Galilee, then under the rule of the Romans. In about 27 A.D., having been baptized by John the Baptist, Jesus began his ministry. He recruited twelve disciples and went about the countryside teaching in the synagogues, preaching to large crowds, and healing the sick. He proclaimed the coming of a "kingdom of God" and was believed by his followers to be the Messiah, the Savior foretold by the Hebrew prophets. Jesus became increasingly unpopular with Jewish religious leaders. In the third year of his ministry, when he was in Jerusalem for the Jewish feast of the Passover, Jesus was betrayed to hostile authorities by his disciple Judas Iscariot in the garden of Gethsemane. He was arrested, accused of blasphemy, tried, and convicted by the ecclesiastical court for calling himself the son of God. Pontius Pilate, the Roman procurator of Judea, yielded to popular pressure and passed the death sentence. Jesus was crucified on a hill called Calvary (or Golgotha), near Jerusalem and, according to Christian doctrine, rose from the dead on the third day.

Jinnah, Muhammad Ali (1876–1948), the founder of modern Pakistan and his country's first governor-general. Jinnah joined the Muslim League in 1913 and soon was its leader. For many years he hoped for Hindu-Muslim unity in India but, fearing the power of the Hindu majority, he came to believe that a separate Muslim state was needed. After 1940 he led the Muslim League in a fierce, often violent, struggle for the creation of the state of Pakistan. On India's becoming independent in 1947, Pakistan was formed, and Jinnah was named its head. He died a year later, but his ideas remained influential in the new state.

Joan of Arc, Saint (c 1412–1431), in French, Jeanne d'Arc, called the Maid of Orléans, a French peasant girl who led the army that defeated the English at Orléans in 1429, a turning point in the Hundred Years' War. According to her own testimony, Joan saw visions and heard voices from God. They told her she must help the dauphin Charles drive out the English and their allies, the Burgundians, who held nearly half of France. Joan, only 16, convinced Charles of her mission. Wearing white armor and carrying a white banner with the lilies of France and an image of Christ, she led 4000 men and defeated the 10,000 English troops besieging Orléans. She then persuaded Charles to go with her to Rheims, where she stood beside him as he was crowned Charles VII. Joan stayed with the army, but failed in an attack on Paris. At Compiègne she was wounded and later taken prisoner. Before an ecclesiastical court, the Maid was discredited before the French people and convicted of heresy and witchcraft. Unaided by Charles and refused an appeal to the pope, she was burned at the stake in 1431. The church annulled the charges in 1456.

John (c 1167–1216), king of England, 1199–1216. By the time of John's birth, his father, Henry II, had already apportioned his estates among John's older brothers, so John was nicknamed Lackland. He tried to usurp the throne twice; first from his father, then from his brother Richard I while Richard was on the Third Crusade. After succeeding Richard in 1199, John lost most of England's continental lands to France. John's dispute with the barons over his rights to levy taxes and dispense justice ended at Runnymede in 1215 when the barons forced him to sign the agreement known as Magna Carta.

John, Augustus Edwin (1878–1961), English painter of portraits and gypsy life. As a student in London he won a prize for his work *Moses and The Bronze Serpent* (1898). He later roamed through Wales and Ireland, where he lived in gypsy camps and painted their romantic life (*Encampment at Dartmoor,* 1906). His portraits are spontaneous and vivid; two of his best-known works are *The Smiling Woman* (1908) and *Dylan Thomas* (c 1936–1940).

John III Sobieski (1629–1696), soldier king of Poland, 1674–1696, hero of the wars against the Turks. Sobieski rose to prominence fighting brilliantly against the Cossacks, the Tatars, and the Swedes, becoming supreme commander by 1668. When the Turks invaded, Sobieski defended the Ukraine, even though the Polish king had already ceded it and other Polish lands in a humiliating treaty (1672). When the king died, Sobieski hurried to Warsaw with 6000 troops and was elected king. Though Leopold of Austria opposed John's ambitions for Poland, they became allies against the Turks. John, leading the Polish cavalry, was the hero of Vienna in 1683, breaking the Turks' siege and driving them out of central Europe. Poland gained little from the victory, and the end of John's reign was marked by intrigues and unrest.

John XXIII (1881–1963), born Angelo Giuseppe Roncalli, pope of the Roman Catholic Church from 1958 to 1963, one of the most respected and loved pontiffs of modern times. John, the son of a peasant farmer, received his doctorate in theology and was ordained in 1904; he served the Vatican as apostolic delegate and nuncio from 1921, and as a UNESCO observer from 1946, becoming a cardinal in 1953. Though 77 years old when elected pope, he soon proved himself to be energetic, imaginative, and liberal. He called the 21st ecumenical council (Vatican II) in 1962 to investigate ways to renew the church and unite Christendom; he also made changes in the Mass. He conferred with many world leaders and often visited local hospitals and prisons. *Pacem in terris* (1963) was perhaps his best-known encyclical.

John Paul II (1920–), pope of the Roman Catholic Church (1978–), born Karol Wojtyla in Poland. Ordained a priest in 1949, he taught theology for a time. In 1958 he was named bishop of Krakow, Poland, and in 1967 he was made a cardinal. When he was elected pope in October, 1978, he was the first non-Italian to hold the office in 456 years. Since assuming office he has traveled widely, visiting Latin America, Poland, the United States in 1979 and 1987, and the Far East in 1980, among other places. Conservative theologically, John Paul II strongly opposes abortion and the admission of women to the priesthood. The pope was seriously wounded by a gunman on May 13, 1981, as he rode through a throng in St. Peter's Square, Rome.

Johnson, Andrew (1808–1875), 17th President of the United States, 1865–1869, after Lincoln's assassination. Johnson became active in local politics and in 1843 began a ten-year term in Congress as spokesman for the small farmers and the mountaineers of eastern Tennessee. He became a Democratic senator in 1857, remaining in the Senate even after Tennessee seceded from the Union, the only Southern senator left. Johnson's credentials as a Democrat and border-state Union supporter made him a good running mate for Abraham Lincoln in the 1864 Presidential campaign; he became President on April 14, 1865, after Lincoln's death. Johnson tried to implement Lincoln's moderate plans for postwar reconstruction, but was stopped by Congress. Radical Republicans overrode most of his vetoes and passed several bills to restrict Presidential authority. Johnson disregarded the new Tenure of Office Act and in 1868 dismissed Edwin M. Stanton, secretary of war. Impeachment proceedings, involving a welter of irrelevant charges, were brought against him. He was tried before the Senate and, though acquitted by one vote, retired from office a bitter man. In 1875 he was again elected to the Senate, but he died a few months later.

Johnson, James Weldon (1871–1938), U.S. poet and diplomat whose *Autobiography of an Ex-Colored Man* (1912) became a classic novel of black literature. Johnson, a lawyer, wrote the well-known song "Lift Every Voice and Sing." His campaign for Theodore Roosevelt in 1904 led to his appointment as consul to Venezuela, 1906, and to Nicaragua, 1909. In 1916 he joined the NAACP as an organizer and later was a leader in the Harlem Renaissance, publishing *Book of American Negro Poetry* (1922) and *God's Trombones* (1927), black folk sermons in free verse.

Johnson, John Arthur (Jack) (1878–1946), U.S. heavyweight boxing champion, the first black to hold that title. Called the Galveston Giant, he learned to box in athletic clubs; in 1908 he broke the color bar by persuading champion Tommy Burns, whom he knocked out, to accept his challenge. James Jeffries, a retired champion, was persuaded to meet Johnson, and in 1910 Johnson defended his title in a decisive fight. In the next few years he amassed and spent a huge fortune, then lost his title to Jess Willard in 1915.

Johnson, Lyndon Baines (1908–1973), 36th President of the United States, 1963–1969. In 1934 Johnson married Claudia Alta (Lady Bird) Taylor, who became widely known for her support of conservation and beautification projects. Johnson was elected to Congress in 1937; in 1949 he entered the Senate. As Democratic majority leader, 1955–1961, he displayed unusual ability for compromise and political persuasion. He and his old friend Sam Rayburn, Speaker of the House, worked together to pass major legislation, including the first civil rights bills passed since 1875. Johnson made a bid for the 1960 Democratic Presidential nomination but was nominated for Vice President instead. Running with John F. Kennedy, he was elected. When Kennedy was assassinated in 1963, Johnson became President. Johnson began as one of the most popular Presidents in U.S. history and ended as one of the most reviled. His folksy public manner worked both for and against him. He was elected President in 1964 by a wide popular margin running against Senator Barry Goldwater, but then his domestic programs to build a Great Society began to give way to increasing military involvement in Southeast Asia. When the Vietnam War became nationally unpopular, Johnson declined to run in 1968. He retired to his LBJ Ranch near Johnson City, Texas (named for his grandfather), and published his memoirs, *The Vantage Point,* in 1971.

Johnson, Samuel (1709–1784), English writer, lexicographer, and literary arbiter. He studied briefly at Oxford, married, and in 1737 left his native Lichfield for London, where he worked at a wide variety of literary and journalistic projects. By 1755 he had finished his *Dictionary of the English Language,* which made him the supreme judge of English literary taste of his day. The dictionary was remarkable for its careful definitions and its numerous literary examples of usage. Johnson gained a wide following for his essays in his periodicals, *The Rambler* (1750–1752) and *The Idler* (1758–1760), and for his philosophical tale *Rasselas* (1759). In 1763 Johnson met a young admirer of literary genius, James Boswell. During the rest of his life he and Boswell were occasional companions, making a long tour of the Scottish isles in 1773, about which both wrote books. Johnson also prepared and edited an edition of Shakespeare's works (1765) and wrote poetry, political pamphlets, and *Lives of the English Poets* (1781), containing many of his best essays. In 1791, after Johnson's death, Boswell published his *Life of Samuel Johnson, LL.D.,* which made Johnson familiar to later generations as a conversationalist and personality. It is perhaps the best-known biography in English.

Johnson, Walter Perry (1887–1946), U.S. baseball figure, one of the sport's greatest pitchers, called the Big Train because of his blinding fast ball. Johnson played for the Washington Senators. In the years 1907–1927 he won 414 games, struck out nearly 3500 batters, and pitched 5923 innings with 113 shutouts. Johnson was one of the first five men elected to the Baseball Hall of Fame, in 1936.

Joliot-Curie, Irène (1897–1956), a French physicist, daughter of scientists Marie and Pierre Curie. She and her husband **Frédéric Joliot-Curie** (1900–1958; original surname Joliot) won the 1935 Nobel Prize in Chemistry for their work in producing radioactive isotopes artificially by bombarding elements with alpha particles. This method was later developed by Enrico Fermi to achieve nuclear fission.

Jolliet (or Joliet), Louis (1645–1700), French-Canadian explorer, a pioneer in opening up the Great Lakes region. A fur trapper, he went to Sault Ste. Marie in 1670 and met Father Jacques Marquette; he sailed back through the Great Lakes as far as Lake Erie. In 1672 Jolliet and Marquette were commissioned by Frontenac to find the "great Western river." They canoed down the Wisconsin River into the Mississippi, traveling as far as the Arkansas River, then turned north on the Illinois River and portaged near Chicago. On the way back to Quebec, Jolliet's canoe overturned, and all his journals of the expedition were lost.

Jones, Inigo (1573–1652), English architect and stage designer who introduced Italian Renaissance architecture in England. Returning from his first stay in Italy in 1605, he was employed by the royal court, primarily as a stage designer for the lavish court masques, often working with playwright Ben Jonson. During a second visit to Italy, 1613–1614, Jones was impressed by the classically styled architecture of Andrea Palladio. The Banqueting Hall in Whitehall (1619–1621), Jones's masterpiece, is in Palladian style. Other works include the Queen's Chapel at St. James.

Jones, John Paul (1747–1792), born John Paul, the only naval hero of the American Revolution. He was born in Scotland and went to sea as a boy; he settled in Virginia about 1774, adding "Jones" to his name to avoid British naval authorities. Commissioned in the Continental navy in 1775, he seized or sank many British vessels and even raided the British coasts. In 1779 he took command of an old French ship that he renamed the *Bonhomme Richard* in honor of Franklin's *Poor Richard's Almanack.* Later that year, he defeated the larger British ship *Serapis* in one of the most daring sea battles in history. During the battle, though his ship was almost a wreck, Jones declared, "I have not yet begun to fight." Instead of rewarding or promoting Jones, Congress only promised (but never gave) him better ships to command. After a year of similarly ill-rewarded service in the Russian navy for Catherine the Great, he settled in Paris and died in misery.

Jones, Le Roi: *See* Baraka, Imamu Amiri.

Jones, Robert Tyre, Jr. (Bobby) (1902–1971), U.S. golfer, considered the greatest in the sport's history. An amateur golf champion at age 14, he won his first professional trophy, the U.S. Open, in 1923. After several years of phenomenal tournament victories, in 1930 he won golfing's Grand Slam: both the British and the U.S. Amateur and Open championships. He was the first to win all four in the same year. He then retired from tournament golf.

Jonson, Benjamin (c 1573–1637), English Elizabethan dramatist. His satires on high and low London society entertained and instructed a large public while maintaining high artistic standards. Jonson's personality offended many; he was in and out of royal favor and occasionally imprisoned, but the quality of his work was never disputed. His epitaph reads "O rare Ben Jonson." Jonson's first comedy was *Every Man in His Humour* (1598); Shakespeare acted in the original cast. Jonson then became embroiled in the War of the Theatres, in which he and the playwrights Dekker and Marston viciously satirized one another in their works. In 1603 Jonson became court playwright to James I, for whom he produced some outstanding court masques. His most brilliant plays were written in the next few years: *Volpone* (1606), *Epicoene, or The Silent Woman* (1609), *The Alchemist* (1610), and *Bartholomew Fair* (1614). His last years were plagued by debt, but he was consoled by the admiration of the "Tribe of Ben," a group of young writers including Herrick.

Joplin, Scott (1868–1917), American ragtime pianist and composer of innovative piano rags. He learned to play the piano at home and at 17 moved to St. Louis, earning his living by playing in saloons. *The Maple Leaf Rag* (1899) was an immediate success, enabling him to devote himself entirely to composition. His ragtime opera *Treemonisha,* produced in New York in 1915 at his own expense, failed to arouse interest. Disappointed and ill, Joplin died in a state hospital. His music became immensely popular in the 1970's, particularly after its use in the film *The Sting* (1974).

Joseph (c 1840–1904), Indian name Hinmaton-Yalaktit ("thunder from the water"), Nez Percé chief remembered as a wise and able statesman. When gold was discovered in Oregon in 1860, other Nez Percé chiefs were tricked into signing a treaty ceding their land to the miners. Chief Joseph, who had not signed, refused to honor the treaty or to move his band from their lands. When the United States sent out troops in 1877, and fighting broke out, Joseph led his band in a 1500-mile retreat,

CHIEF JOSEPH

SMITHSONIAN INSTITUTION NATIONAL ANTHROPOLOGICAL ARCHIVES

fighting rear-guard battles all the way. Captured 30 miles from Canada, Joseph renounced armed resistance with the words, "From where the sun now stands, I will fight no more forever."

Joule, James Prescott (1818–1889), English physicist whose experiments helped to establish the first law of thermodynamics. His work with electrical, mechanical, and chemical effects led to his discovery of the mechanical equivalent of heat, indicating that various forms of energy can be converted into one another. His name is given to a unit of energy, the joule.

Joyce, James Augustine Aloysius (1882–1941), Irish writer whose experiments with language and stream of consciousness style affected nearly every major writer of the 20th century. After 1902 he spent most of his life abroad, in Paris, Trieste, and Zurich, but the mood and influence of Ireland permeated his writing. Admired but never financially successful, Joyce was often deep in debt and troubled by failing vision. His masterpiece, the novel *Ulysses* (1922), chronicles a day in Dublin as seen principally by his characters Leopold and Molly Bloom and Stephen Dedalus. It displays inventiveness of language and brilliant use of the interior monologue. Joyce also wrote *Dubliners* (1914), a short story collection; *Portrait of the Artist as a Young Man* (1916), a semiautobiographical novel; *Exiles* (1918), an Ibsenesque drama; and *Finnegan's Wake* (1939), which carries even further than *Ulysses* Joyce's experiments with sounds and associations of words.

Juan Carlos I (1938–), king of Spain (1975–). Grandson of Alfonso XIII, the Spanish king deposed in 1931, Juan Carlos was designated by Francisco Franco as his successor. Juan Carlos assumed the throne in 1975, on Franco's death. In 1978 a new constitution was enacted, establishing Spain as a constitutional monarchy. Juan Carlos has proved to be a strong force for democracy. In 1981 members of the military attempted a coup and held members of the government hostage. Juan Carlos, the only figure in power who was free, was able to get the leaders of the coup to surrender without bloodshed.

Juárez, Benito Pablo (1806–1872), Mexican president, 1861–1872. A Zapotec Indian, Juárez grew up amid military and church abuses directed against the Mexican people, particularly the Indians. A man of rare honesty, he governed Oaxaca, 1847–1852, while representing Indian legal interests. As secretary of state in Álvarez's cabinet, he drafted the liberal constitution of 1857. Civil war followed, and Juárez fled to Veracruz; when the war ended in 1861, he returned and was elected president.

THE BETTMANN ARCHIVE

BENITO JUAREZ

Bankrupt, the new government suspended foreign payments; its European creditors intervened. Juárez again fled, this time before a French invasion that set up Maximilian as Napoleon's puppet emperor. On the withdrawal of French troops Juárez regained support, brought about Maximilian's capture, and was reelected president in 1867.

Julius II (1445–1513), Italian Roman Catholic pope, born Giuliano della Rovere, memorable as a great Renaissance patron of the arts. Julius was a nephew of Pope Sixtus IV, who in 1471 made him a cardinal; in 1503 he became pope. A proficient soldier, Julius extended the papal states and attempted to drive out the French. To glorify the city of Rome, he commissioned such masterworks as Bramante's plan for a new St. Peter's, Raphael's frescoes in the Vatican, and Michelangelo's frescoes for the Sistine Chapel ceiling.

Julius Caesar: *See* Caesar, Gaius Julius.

Jung, Carl Gustav (1875–1961), Swiss psychiatrist, founder of the school known as analytical psychology. At the University of Zurich he met Sigmund Freud in 1907. The two worked together for a time, but major differences ended the collaboration in 1912, when Jung published *Symbols of Transformation,* which, with *Psychological Types* (1921), laid the foundations of analytical psychology. Jung's theory made several major contributions to modern psychology. He differentiated and named the two representative personality types, introvert and extrovert. He stressed immediate conflicts as more important causes of neuroses than the conflicts of childhood. Finally, he developed the idea of a collective unconscious, composed of universal symbols and archetypes from the cumulative experience of the human race. Among his other important books are *Modern Man in Search of a Soul* (1933) and *The Undiscovered Self* (1958).

Justinian I the Great (483–565), full name Flavius Petrus Sabbatius Justinianus, Byzantine emperor, 527–565. Justinian tried to restore the greatness of the Roman Empire by reconquering the West; he succeeded in taking North Africa and Italy. He also carried out a major building program, including aqueducts, fortresses, and the great church of Santa Sofia (now a mosque) in Constantinople. He had the laws, constitutions, and legal decisions of the empire collected into a great code, which became the model for later Western codes of law. Justinian was strictly orthodox in his Christian beliefs. Forbidding all pagans to teach, he had Plato's 900-year-old Academy closed in 529.

Kafka, Franz (1883–1924), Czech-born German novelist whose work has an intense, nightmarish quality. Kafka's central characters are invariably guilt-ridden and isolated; the world they live in is incomprehensible and terrifying. Kafka himself was sensitive in the extreme. Dominated by his father, he mistrusted his literary talents and often contemplated suicide. Of the works published before his death in a tuberculosis sanitorium, the best known are the stories "The Metamorphosis" (1916) and "In the Penal Colony" (1919). His novels *The Trial* (1925) and *The Castle* (1926) appeared posthumously.

Kandinsky, Vassily (1866–1944), Russian painter and art theoretician, a founder of abstract expressionism. In 1910 Kandinsky painted a watercolor that critics consider the first purely abstract painting. In the same year, he wrote the influential *Concerning the Spiritual in Art* (published in 1912), describing his theories of artistic nonobjectivity. He was also a leading exhibitor in the Munich avant-garde *Blaue Reiter* (Blue Rider) group. After living in Russia during World War I, Kandinsky returned to Munich, where he taught at the Bauhaus, 1922–1933. When Hitler closed the Bauhaus, he settled in France. His paintings include *On the White Edge* (1913) and *Pink Compensation* (1933).

Kant, Immanuel (1724–1804), German philosopher. Though he became famous, he lived all his life at Königsberg and never traveled. Short and frail, he maintained his health by leading a regulated life. His chief pleasures were a quiet social life and reading travel books. Kant's theory of knowledge, which combined and extended both the rationalist and the empiricist lines of philosophy current in his day, had a great influence on subsequent philosophers. He first propounded his theory in his famous *Critique of Pure Reason* (1781). In two supplemental works, *Critique of Practical Reason* (1788) and *Critique of Judgment* (1789–1790), he applied his theory to ethics, aesthetics, and teleology.

Kaufman, George Simon (1889–1961), U.S. playwright. Kaufman was drama editor of *The New York Times,* 1917–1930. His first success, written with Marc Connelly, was *Dulcy,* the hit of the 1921–1922 Broadway season. With Connelly he also wrote *Beggar on Horseback* (1924). With collaborators such as Moss Hart and George Gershwin, he wrote the Pulitzer Prize winners *Of Thee I Sing* (1931) and *You Can't Take It With You* (1936), as well as *The Man Who Came to Dinner* (1939) and *Silk Stockings* (1955). He wrote or directed at least one hit per year from 1921 to 1941.

Kazantzakis, Nikos (1885–1957), a Greek novelist best known for *Zorba the Greek* (1946), *The Greek Passion* (1948), and *The Last Temptation of Christ* (1951). Kazantzakis lived intensely, both politically and artistically. He took part in the stormy politics of Greece, serving in two national cabinets. A master of the modern Greek language, Kazantzakis produced superb translations of *Faust* and *The Divine Comedy,* and wrote a modern *Odyssey* (1938). His novels reflect the simplicity, spirituality, and passion of Greek peasant life. Religious and political pressures finally drove him from Greece.

Keats, John (1795–1821), English Romantic poet. Keats was apprenticed to a surgeon and studied medicine, but his friends, particularly critic Leigh Hunt, persuaded him to devote himself to writing poetry. His first publication, *Poems by John Keats* (1817), was indifferently received and *Endymion* (1818) was savagely criticized. His greatest poems, concerning beauty, time, and mortality, were written during the year 1819. Among these are the odes "On a Grecian Urn," "To a Nightingale," and "On Melancholy," as well as the ballad, "La Belle Dame sans Merci." Seriously ill with tuberculosis, Keats was sent to Italy for the winter in 1820; he died in Rome.

Keller, Helen Adams (1880–1968), U.S. blind and deaf author and educator. A severe illness in infancy left her blind, deaf, and mute. Anne Sullivan, herself partially blind, was engaged to work with Keller, who learned to recognize words from hand signals, to read and write Braille, and eventually to speak. After Keller graduated cum laude from Radcliffe in 1904, Sullivan accompanied her on numerous tours on behalf of education for the deaf and blind. Keller's books include *The Story of My Life* (1902) and *Teacher: Anne Sullivan Macy* (1955).

Kelvin, 1st Baron; William Thomson (1824–1907), Irish-born British mathematician and physicist who in 1848 devised the absolute temperature scale named after him. Lord Kelvin was professor of natural philosophy at the University of Glasgow, Scotland, from 1846 to 1904, when he became chancellor. He formulated the second law of thermodynamics, 1851–1854, then became interested in telegraphy and made a number of improvements and inventions that made the laying of submarine telegraph cables possible. He also improved the mariner's compass; invented equipment for use in physics, oceanography, and other branches of science; and made valuable studies of light, electricity, and magnetism.

Kemal Atatürk, Mustafa (1881–1938), Turkish army officer and first president of the independent Turkish republic, 1923–1938. In military school Mustafa earned the name "Kemal" ("perfection") for excellence in mathematics. Though he urged neutrality and resisted the alliance with Germany, he proved his military genius in World War I, especially at Gallipoli in 1915. After the war, he organized the nationalist movement and led the military campaign that drove out the Greeks, 1921–1922. After the sultan was deposed, Kemal became president of the new republic in 1923; he was reelected three times. Virtually a dictator, though beloved by the people, he did much to westernize Turkey. He planned for industrialization, campaigned against illiteracy, adopted the Latin alphabet, instituted equal rights for women, and reestablished Turkey's international position. When surnames were adopted in 1934, he became known as Atatürk ("father of the Turks").

Kempis, Thomas à: *See* Thomas à Kempis.

Kennedy, U.S. family prominent in business and politics.

Joseph Patrick Kennedy (1888–1969), a financier and founder of the family, was ambassador to Britain, 1938–1940, and active in other government posts. In 1914 he married **Rose Fitzgerald** (1890–), whose father, John Francis Fitzgerald, had been mayor of Boston.

The oldest of their nine children, **Joseph P. Kennedy, Jr.** (1917–1944), was killed during World War II. The other three sons, John, Robert, and Edward, all eventually entered politics. **Edward Moore Kennedy** (1932–) became senator from Massachusetts in 1962.

Kennedy, John Fitzgerald (1917–1963), 35th President of the United States, 1961–1963. Kennedy commanded a PT boat in the Pacific in World War II, and was decorated for his heroic rescue of the crew of his PT-109 after it was sunk. He entered politics in 1946, served three terms in the House, and became U.S. senator from Massachusetts in 1952. In 1960 he was nominated for the Presidency with Lyndon Johnson as his running mate. The theme of the Kennedy platform was established in his acceptance speech with the words, "We stand today on the edge of a new frontier." His election victory was due in part to the impression he made in his television debates with the Repbulican candidate, Richard Nixon. At the age of 43 he became the youngest man to be elected President, as well as the first Roman Catholic. In office, Kennedy was vastly popular, largely as a result of his homey yet intellectual style, his attractive family, and his courage and vision. As a result of the Cuban missile crisis in 1962 and the nuclear test ban treaty, he was admired all over the world as a firm but peaceful leader. His domestic programs were largely thwarted by Congress. On November 22, 1963, Kennedy was assassinated in Dallas, Tex., while riding in a motorcade. The Warren Commission investigation determined that his sole assassin was Lee Harvey Oswald. Of his family, the most prominent members were his wife, Jacqueline Bouvier Kennedy (1929–), and his brother Robert, his attorney general. Kennedy was the author of *Why England Slept*

HELEN KELLER

COURTESY AMERICAN FOUNDATION FOR THE BLIND, NEW YORK

(1940), a study of British appeasement of the Nazis written as a thesis at Harvard; and *Profiles in Courage* (1956), a Pulitzer Prize-winning historical study of eight U.S. senators.

Kennedy, Robert Francis (1925–1968), U.S. politician. During the 1950's he served as an attorney in the Justice Department and as Senate subcommittee counsel, first under Senator Joseph McCarthy and then during investigations of labor racketeering. He managed the successful Presidential campaign of his brother John F. Kennedy and served in the administration as attorney general, 1961–1964. He became U.S. senator from New York in 1964 and made a bid for the 1968 Democratic Presidential nomination. After a primary victory in California in June, 1968, Robert Kennedy was murdered by Sirhan Sirhan, a young man who claimed to be an Arab nationalist opposed to Kennedy's pro-Israel policies.

Kenny, Elizabeth (Sister Kenny) (1886–1952), Australian nurse who developed a revolutionary and controversial treatment for poliomyelitis. Working with polio patients in 1911, she rejected the traditional method of immobilizing patients in casts and advocated heat treatments and physical therapy. By the mid 1930's, "Kenny Clinics" had been set up throughout Queensland and New South Wales.

Kent, Rockwell (1882–1971), U.S. artist and author, known especially for his strong, dramatic woodcuts. Kent's varied life—he lived in Newfoundland, Alaska, and Greenland and worked as a Maine lobsterman—gave him subject matter for his paintings and illustrations (*Northern Light,* woodcut c 1928). He illustrated such literary classics as *Moby-Dick* (1930), as well as his own books, *N by E* (1930) and an autobiography, *It's Me O Lord* (1955).

Kenyatta, Jomo (c 1889–1978), first president of independent Kenya (1964–1978). In his youth he became involved in a movement to regain Kikuyu tribal lands; he visited England as a Kenyan spokesman. In 1938 he published *Facing Mount Kenya.* Soon he was a powerful force in Kenya, calling for abolition of the color bar and African political rights. In 1952 he was imprisoned for being a leader of the terrorist Mau Mau society. Widespread protest forced his full release in 1961, after which he led the fight for independence. Under his leadership Kenya followed a pro-Western course and became one of the most prosperous countries in black Africa.

Kepler, Johannes (1571–1630), German astronomer who formulated the laws of motion of the planets. In 1600 Kepler became Tycho Brahe's assistant at the observatory near Prague. Brahe died in 1601 and Kepler took his place as imperial court mathematician. Kepler's greatest work, *Astronomia Nova* (*New Astronomy,* 1609), contains the first two of his three laws regarding the elliptical orbits of the planets. Kepler's third law was published in 1619; at the same time, he proposed the idea of the "harmony of the spheres."

Kerensky, Alexander Feodorovich (1881–1970), Russian political leader, head of a moderate government in postrevolutionary Russia. Kerensky, a socialist, was a member of the last Russian *duma* (parliament). In March, 1917, the czar was overthrown and Kerensky took office in the new provisional government. A fine orator, he managed to effect a temporary coalition between extreme factions. He became premier in July, 1917. His middle-of-the-road tactics failed, and the government fell to a Bolshevik coup in November. Kerensky fled to England in 1918, then to France, and finally to the United States, where he taught and lectured, mainly at Stanford University. His books include *Prelude to Bolshevism* (1919) and *Russia and History's Turning Point* (1966).

Kern, Jerome David (1885–1945), U.S. composer of many popular musical comedies and songs. His first musical comedy was *Mr. Wix of Wickham* (1904). His more than 50 stage and film musicals include *Sunny* (1925), *Show Boat* (1927), *Sweet Adeline* (1929), and *Roberta* (1933). His famous songs include "Look for the Silver Lining," "Make Believe," "Ol' Man River," and "Smoke Gets in Your Eyes."

Kerouac, Jack (1922–1969), in full Jean-Louis Lebrid de Kerouac, U.S. writer, spokesman for the "beat" generation. Kerouac's novel *On the Road* (1957) has been called "the beatniks' bible." It is a loose narrative in which the characters travel restlessly, searching for new experiences. Kerouac's other novels include *The Subterraneans* (1958), *The Dharma Bums* (1958), and *Big Sur* (1962).

JOMO KENYATTA

UPI/BETTMANN ARCHIVE

Key, Francis Scott (1779–1843), U.S. lawyer who wrote "The Star-Spangled Banner" (1814). During the War of 1812, Key, sent to negotiate a prisoner release, was detained on board a British ship during the shelling of Fort McHenry, Md. Inspired by the sight of the U.S. flag, Key penned several exultant verses, which were soon being sung to the tune of an English drinking song. Because of its musical difficulty, the song did not become the national anthem until 1931. Key wrote little else; he became a U.S. district attorney in 1833.

Keynes, John Maynard, 1st Baron Keynes (1883–1946), British economist. As the British delegate to the Paris Peace Conference in 1919, Keynes argued unsuccessfully against the reparations clause of the Versailles Treaty; he resigned and published his protest in *The Economic Consequences of the Peace* (1919). During the 1930's he developed theories contrary to those being used to counter the worldwide Depression. Those theories were to form the basis of Keynesian economics. His most important work, *The General Theory of Employment, Interest, and Money* (1936), influenced the economic recovery program of President Franklin D. Roosevelt. During and after World War II, Keynes played a leading role in developing British and international economic policy. At the Bretton Woods, N.H., conference in 1944, he saw many of his ideas adopted, including the International Monetary Fund. His last service to the British government was to negotiate the Anglo-American loan of 1945. Keynesian economics still is considered influential today.

Khrushchev, Nikita Sergeyevich (1894–1971), premier of the Soviet Union, 1958–1964. He joined the Communist Party in 1918 and rose quickly within its ranks. By 1939 he was a full member of the powerful Politburo under Stalin. After Stalin died in 1953, he became first secretary of the Communist Party, a position he used to purge his political enemies and denounce Stalin. Despite opposition, he became premier in 1958. Khrushchev often operated on a double standard. He preached disarmament, but built the Berlin wall and threatened the United States with rockets in Cuba. Though he antagonized both the Chinese Communists and many of his own party, to the West he was a colorful leader who quoted Russian proverbs and pounded the table with his shoe during a United Nations address. He left office in 1964 and lived in near obscurity until his death.

Khufu (r. c 2600 B.C.), called Cheops by the ancient Greeks, second Pharaoh of the fourth dynasty of ancient Egypt. Little is known about his reign; the Greek historian Herodotus claims it was an evil one, but there is no other support for his claim. Khufu's tomb, the Great Pyramid at Giza, is the largest of the pyramids.

Kidd, William (Captain Kidd) (c 1645–1701), British privateer turned pirate. In 1691 Kidd was a respected New York landowner and a legitimate privateer against the French. A group of English noblemen hired him in 1695 to fight pirates in the Indian Ocean. He took treasure, several French ships, and the rich *Quedagh Merchant,* in which he sailed after scuttling his unseaworthy vessel. At Madagascar, he associated with several pirates and may have become a pirate himself. On returning to the New World, he learned that he had been officially denounced as a pirate—possibly by the noblemen who had originally hired him. On his way to New York to clear his name, Kidd was tricked into going ashore, arrested, tried in England, and hanged in 1701.

Kierkegaard, Søren Aabye (1813–1855), Danish philosopher and theologian, known as the father of existentialist philosophy. Kierkegaard trained for the ministry, but about 1841 he began to expound his thoughts on the individual and the choices available to each person, chief among them the choice between the secular world and God. Despising reason and systematic philosophy, he published under various pseudonyms, arguing against his own ideas. His works include *Either/Or* (1843) and *Fear and Trembling* (1843).

King, Billie Jean (1943–   ), U.S. tennis player and women's rights activist. An exceptional player from an early age, she won ten doubles and six singles titles at Wimbledon between 1961 and 1979. She also took the U.S. Open singles championship four times. King campaigned vigorously for women's rights and co-founded the magazine *Womensport* in 1974.

King, Martin Luther, Jr. (1929–1968), U.S. civil rights leader who headed the nonviolent struggle for racial equality during the 1950's and 1960's. A Baptist minister, King first made headlines by organizing a boycott against segregated buses in Montgomery, Ala., 1956. In 1957 he founded the Southern Christian Leadership Conference and led major campaigns against discrimination in all areas of society, including public facilities, interstate transportation, housing, and voter registration. He was spearheading a sanitation workers' strike in Memphis, Tenn., when he was assassinated in 1968. Although King's protests were nonviolent, he and his followers were jailed, stoned, and beaten. King was awarded the Nobel Peace Prize in 1964. His major books include *Stride Toward Freedom* (1958) and *Why We Can't Wait* (1964).

THE BETTMANN ARCHIVE

MARTIN LUTHER KING

King, William Lyon Mackenzie (1874–1950), Canadian statesman, prime minister of Canada, 1921–1930 and 1935–1948. After serving as minister of labor, he succeeded Wilfred Laurier as Liberal Party leader, 1919. During his second term as prime minister, he organized the Canadian war effort of World War II, and concluded joint defense agreements with the United States. King helped draft the United Nations Charter in 1945, and was a signer of the Washington declaration on atomic energy the same year.

Kinsey, Alfred Charles (1894–1956), U.S. biologist, known for his far-reaching studies of human sexuality. Kinsey's findings, including the results of more than 10,000 personal interviews, were published in *Sexual Behavior of the Human Male* (1948) and *Sexual Behavior of the Human Female* (1953). He founded Indiana University's Institute for Sex Research.

Kipling, (Joseph) Rudyard (1865–1936), English author. Born in India, he went to school in England, later writing *Stalky & Co.* (1899) about his school days. As a journalist in India, 1882–1889, he wrote verse and short stories that made him famous in England, where he published *Barrack-Room Ballads* in 1892. He and his American wife lived for a time in Vermont, where he wrote the two *Jungle Books* (1894–1895) and *Captains Courageous* (1897). He returned to England and lived in seclusion, refusing honors and writing increasingly subtle and complex short stories. His late works include *Kim* (1901), a novel of India, and *Just So Stories* (1902) for children. He won the 1907 Nobel Prize for Literature.

Kissinger, Henry Alfred (1923–   ), German-born U.S. secretary of state, 1973–1977. Kissinger's family left Germany for the United States in 1938. He studied at Harvard, held several teaching posts there, and by the 1950's was a recognized expert in foreign affairs. He was foreign policy adviser in the Eisenhower, Kennedy, and Johnson administrations. He served as head of the National Security Council under Presidents Nixon and Ford. As secretary of state, Kissinger played a major part in reshaping U.S. foreign policy, including the new attitude toward Red China and the ending of the Vietnam War. For the latter he shared the 1973 Nobel Peace Prize with North Vietnam's Le Duc Tho. President Reagan named him to lead a national commission on Central America in 1983.

Kitchener, Horatio Herbert, 1st Earl Kitchener of Khartoum and of Broome (1850–1916), Irish-born British general. Kitchener first became famous with the force that tried to rescue Gordon at Khartoum in the Sudan in 1885. He became commander of the Egyptian army in 1892 and fought to restore the Sudan to the British empire. After the Boer War began, he was placed in command in South Africa in 1900; in two years he had ruthlessly worn down Boer resistance. During World War I, Kitchener, by then a popular idol and a symbol of British military strength, was secretary of war. He died while on a mission to Russia when his ship struck a mine.

Klee, Paul (1879–1940), Swiss painter and graphic artist, one of the most original artists of the German expressionist school. Until 1914 he produced mainly woodcuts and lithographs in black and white (illustrations for *Candide,* 1911). One of the Blue Riders *(Blaue Reiter),* he taught at the Bauhaus, 1921–1931, and at Düsseldorf, 1931–1933, before the Nazis forced him to flee to Switzerland. He also exhibited, with Kandinsky and others, as the Blue Four. Klee's paintings include *Storm in Marc's Garden* (1915), *The Fruit* (1932), and *They Persuade the Child* (c 1940).

Knox, John (c 1514–1572), Scottish Protestant reformer, one of the chief organizers of the Presbyterian Church in Scotland. He studied for the priesthood, but adopted the Reformed faith about 1546. Knox went to England to work for the Reformation, but left when Mary I, a Roman Catholic, came to the throne in 1553. He was pastor of the English church at Geneva, Switzerland, 1555–1558, where he met and was strongly influenced by John Calvin. In 1559 he returned to Scotland and, after resisting French intervention, had already organized the Reformed Church of Scotland when Mary, Queen of Scots, returned from France in 1561. He successfully fought her bitter attempts to suppress both him and the Reformed Church. Before his death, Knox wrote *History of the Reformation in Scotland.*

Koch, Robert (1843–1910), German bacteriologist, winner of the 1905 Nobel Prize for Physiology and Medicine for his research on tuberculosis. Koch's studies of cattle anthrax, during which he developed methods of handling and growing cultures of bacteria, constitute the beginning of bacteriological research. He discovered and isolated the tuberculosis bacillus in 1882, the cholera bacillus in 1883, and tuberculin, used to diagnose tuberculosis, in 1890.

Kodály, Zoltán (1882–1967), Hungarian composer and folk music authority. With Bela Bartók, Kodály published anthologies of Hungarian folk songs (1906, 1921). His *Psalmus Hungaricus* (1923), celebrating the founding of Budapest, established his reputation; the comic opera *Háry János* (1926) secured it. Other works include *Te Deum* (1936), two sets of Hungarian dances (1930, 1933), and a symphony (1961).

Koestler, Arthur (1905–1983), Hungarian author and journalist best known for his novel *Darkness at Noon* (1941). Koestler was a foreign correspondent during the Spanish Civil War, where he was captured and sentenced to death by Franco's government. Later released, he published *Spanish Testament* (1938, U.S. title *Dialogue With Death*). His autobiographical works include *Scum of the Earth* (1941) and *Arrow in the Blue* (1952).

Kokoschka, Oskar (1886–1980), Austrian-born British artist of the German expressionist school. Kokoschka at first painted portraits (*Portrait of Auguste Forel,* 1910); he also wrote expressionist prose and poetry, as in *Columbus Enchained* (1913), illustrated with his own graphics. Later he became known for his landscapes and cityscapes. He moved to England in 1938, where he painted several large political allegorical works (*Prometheus-Saga,* 1950). After 1953 he taught at Salzburg.

NEW YORK PUBLIC LIBRARY

TADEUSZ KOSCIUSZKO

Kosciuszko, Tadeusz (1746–1817), Polish general and patriot, a hero in America and in Poland. With a passion for freedom, Kosciuszko fought brilliantly as a volunteer with the American colonists during the Revolutionary War. Congress rewarded him with citizenship and the rank of brigadier general. In 1784 he returned to Poland and joined the army to fight for Polish independence from Russia. While commanding the revolutionary forces in 1794 against a combined army of Russians and Prussians, he was wounded, captured, and taken prisoner to Russia. Released in 1796, he returned to the United States; then he moved to France and finally settled in Switzerland, where he still acted as a spokesman for Polish freedom.

Kosygin, Alexei Nikolaevich (1904–1980), premier of the Soviet Union, 1964–1980. He was mayor of Leningrad, 1938–1939, and soon became an important member of the Soviet government, serving first as minister of finance, then as minister of light industry. He was demoted after Stalin's death in 1953, but by 1960 he had become vice premier. He became premier after the ouster of Nikita Khrushchev in 1964.

Koussevitzky, Serge (1874–1951), Russian-born U.S. conductor. A virtuoso on the double bass, he gave concerts throughout Europe and in 1909 formed both a music publishing firm and an orchestra in Moscow. He left Russia in 1920 and in 1924 became conductor of the Boston Symphony. He introduced the music of such American composers as Copland and Piston, commissioned works by Stravinsky, Ravel, and Prokofiev, and set up a foundation in 1942 to encourage new music. He also began the Berkshire Festivals (Tanglewood, Mass.).

Krafft-Ebing, Baron Richard von (1840–1902), German neuropsychiatrist who became most famous for his studies of abnormal sexual behavior. Trained in psychology, he worked primarily in clinical psychiatry, also studying criminal psychology and genetic factors. His most famous work, *Psychopathia Sexualis* (1886), was translated into many languages.

Krebs, Sir Hans Adolf (1900–1981), German-born British biochemist. He shared the 1953 Nobel Prize for Physiology and Medicine for his description of the citric acid cycle (Krebs cycle), the chemical reactions by which carbohydrates, fats, and proteins are oxidized in living cells, and the chief source of metabolic energy. Krebs also did research on vitamin deficiency.

Kropotkin, Petr Alekseevich (1842–1921), Russian revolutionary and anarchist. Inspired by the Swiss craft guilds, Kropotkin advocated the destruction of governmental controls, free associations of individuals, and abolition of the wage system. He was arrested for sedition in 1874, escaped to Switzerland, and then lived in exile in France and London. Though highly critical of the Bolsheviks, he returned to Russia after the revolution. His kindly character and warmth made anarchism attractive to many followers who objected to the movement's earlier terrorism. His chief works are *Memoirs of a Revolutionist* (1899) and *Mutual Aid* (1902).

Kruger, Paul (1825–1904), born Stephanus Johannes Paulus Kruger, South African Boer statesman, leader in the Transvaal's fight for independence. Kruger and his family left Cape Colony and arrived in Transvaal about 1840. He diligently worked to unify the Transvaal, and, after it was annexed by the British, led a movement to restore its independence. He was active in the Boer rebellion of 1880, and became president of the restored Transvaal republic in 1883. Continuing conflict with the British culminated in the Boer War, 1899–1902, lost by the Boers at Pretoria. Kruger fled to Europe and died in exile.

Kublai Khan (1215–1294), Mongol khan, or ruler, and founder of the Yüan dynasty in China. A grandson of Genghis Khan, Kublai fought his brother Arik Böke for the throne and in 1264 became ruler of the Mongol empire. Considering himself the successor to the emperors of China, he built a new capital, called Tai-tu or Khanbalik (Cambaluc), at present-day Peking, and a summer residence at Shang-tu (Xanadu). During his reign, the Polos journeyed to his court; Marco Polo described its splendor in his *Travels.*

Kurosawa, Akira (1910–), Japanese director whose *Rashomon* (1950) introduced Western audiences to Japanese film, considered the most Western of Japanese filmmakers. His work reflects versatility in many genres: *Seven Samurai* (1954) is an action film; *The Hidden Fortress* (1958) and *Yojimbo* (1961) are Samurai "Westerns"; *Ikiru* (1952) deals with social commitment; *The Bad Sleep Well* (1960) is a melodrama; *The Idiot* (1951) and *The Lower Depths* (1957) are adaptations of Western works. Recent films include the historical epic *Kagemusha* (1980) and *Ran* (1985), based on Shakespeare's *King Lear.*

Kutuzov, Mikhail Ilarionovich Golenischev (1745–1813), commander of the Russian army during Napoleon's invasion of Russia in 1812. When Napoleon invaded Russia, Kutuzov retreated, fighting minor battles. The French followed him to Moscow; there, winter and the vulnerability of the long French supply and communications lines forced Napoleon to turn back. Kutuzov's men harassed the retreating French army until it was almost destroyed.

L

La Farge, Oliver Hazard Perry (1901–1963), U.S. writer and anthropologist who studied and wrote about American Indian life. He taught ethnology and later headed archaeological expeditions to Arizona, Mexico, and Guatemala. La Farge wrote *Laughing Boy* (1929), a novel of Navaho Indian life, for which he received a Pulitzer Prize. In addition to several other novels, he wrote the text for a *Pictorial History of the American Indian* (1956).

Lafayette (or **La Fayette**), **Marie Joseph Paul Yves Roch Gilbert du Motier, Marquis de** (1757–1834), French nobleman. In 1777 Lafayette, disregarding royal objections, went to America to fight with the colonists for independence. Barely 20 years old, he was virtually adopted by George Washington, whom he idolized and served with devotion. Among his many American military distinctions, he led the army that defeated Cornwallis at Yorktown in 1781. He then returned to France, "the hero of two worlds." During the French Revolution, Lafayette became for a time the most powerful man in France, as popular leader of the moderates and commander of the national guard, 1789–1791. A strong advocate of constitutional monarchy, he held several prominent political positions, wrote the Declaration of Rights, 1789, and helped shape the constitution, 1791. However, for favoring the monarchy and forcefully opposing the violent rioting in Paris, he was forced out of office by the extremists. While fleeing France, he was captured and imprisoned by the invading Austrians, 1792–1797. After the monarchy was restored, Lafayette again emerged as a liberal member of the chamber of deputies. His last important post was as commander of the national guard in the revolution of 1830.

Laffite (or **Lafitte**), **Jean** (c 1780–c 1825), notorious French pirate, patriot, and smuggler. With headquarters at Barataria Bay on the Gulf Coast, Laffite and his brother Pierre led a band of pirates who looted rich Spanish ships and smuggled goods into New Orleans. During the War of 1812, Laffite offered his services to General Andrew Jackson. For their brilliant fighting in the Battle of New Orleans (1815), the pirates received full pardon. However, Laffite soon set up new headquarters at Galveston, Tex., where he harbored nearly 1000 criminals. Threatened by the U.S. Navy for terrorizing Gulf traders, Laffite sailed away in 1821 and was never heard of again.

La Follette, Robert Marion (1855–1925), U.S. statesman and political leader known as Fighting Bob for his leadership of Republican insurgents. He supported direct primaries, just taxation, pacifism, and government control of railroad rates. La Follette served as a Republican in the House of Representatives, 1885–1891. During this period he attracted notice as a leader of those in revolt against the Republican political machine in Wisconsin. In 1900 he was elected governor on a platform of political reform. Twice reelected governor, La Follette resigned in 1906 to enter the U.S. Senate, remaining there until his death. Although his opposition to U.S. participation in World War I temporarily lost him much popular support, he was nominated for the Presidency by the Progressive Party in 1924.

La Fontaine, Jean de (1621–1695), French poet known for his *Fables* in verse. In 1667 La Fontaine began to compose his celebrated short tales about animal characters who behave like humans. Although their simplicity and ingenuous charm make stories like "The Fox and the Crow" appealing to children, they are essentially satires on French society of La Fontaine's time. The series, totaling about 240 fables, was collected in volumes that were published 1668–1694.

La Guardia, Fiorello Henry (1881–1947), U.S. public official, memorable as a colorful and respected mayor of New York City. Well known among the poor through the legal aid bureau he organized, La Guardia was elected a Republican congressman, serving 1917–1921 and 1923–1933. Called the chronic dissenter, he battled constantly for reforms, especially on behalf of labor. As mayor of New York, 1933–1945, he was both controversial and beloved. Without regard for party politics, he cleared slums, fought crime, built health clinics, and read the Sunday comics over the radio to the children of the city.

Lalo, Édouard Victor Antoine (1823–1892), French composer who helped develop 19th-century French chamber music. His works include the operas *Fiesque* (1866) and *Le Roi d'Ys* (1888); a ballet, *Namouna* (1882); and a romantic violin concerto, *Symphonie Espagnole* (1873), which to this day is a concert favorite.

Lamarck, Jean Baptiste Pierre Antoine de Monet, Chevalier de (1774–1829), French naturalist who advanced a theory of evolution stating that plants and animals develop organs and characteristics necessary for survival. As a part of his theory, he proposed the idea that the characteristics acquired in this way can be inherited; this controversial idea is called Lamarckism. He also distinguished between vertebrates and invertebrates, making detailed studies of the latter. His great work is *A Natural History of Invertebrate Animals* (7 volumes, 1815–1822).

Lamartine, Alphonse Marie Louis de Prat de (1790–1869), French poet, historian, and statesman best known for his *Méditations Poétiques* (1820), which significantly influenced the Romantic revival in France. In 1848 Lamartine became a member of the executive committee of the provisional government and served as minister of foreign affairs until Louis Napoleon's coup in 1849 ended his political career.

Land, Edwin Herbert (1909–), U.S. physicist and inventor who developed the first modern polarizers for light and, in 1947, invented the Polaroid Land camera, which takes and develops pictures in seconds. As president of the Polaroid Corporation, he continued to do research in color vision. Land also invented a viewing system for three-dimensional pictures and perfected ways to observe living cells in natural color.

Landowska, Wanda (1877–1959), Polish pianist and harpsichordist. A foremost interpreter of early keyboard music, she was chiefly responsible for the 20th-century revival of interest in the harpsichord. She founded the École de Musique Ancienne in Paris in 1925.

Langland, William (c 1330–c 1400), English poet, the presumed author of *The Vision of Piers Plowman,* a satire that presents a vivid picture of English life in the 1300's. Little is known about Langland except that he was probably a monk and, judging from *Piers Plowman,* highly educated and politically sophisticated.

Langley, Samuel Pierpont (1834–1906), U.S. astronomer and aviation pioneer, generally credited with making the first steam-driven airplane. He was secretary of the Smithsonian Institution in Washington, D.C., 1887–1906, and helped establish the Astrophysical Observatory and National Zoological Park. Langley studied air transportation and designed a pilotless, motor-driven plane that in 1896 performed successfully in the air, flying 4200 feet over the Potomac.

Lanier, Sidney (1842–1881), U.S. poet, critic, and musician. Lanier, captured and imprisoned while fighting for the Confederacy, contracted tuberculosis in prison and, realizing his health was ruined, abandoned a legal career for music and writing. Some of his short lyrics, like "Corn" and "The Marshes of Glynn," made him famous. He also worked professionally as a flutist. Some of his lectures were collected in *The English Novel* (1883). He was named to the Hall of Fame in 1945.

Lao-tze (or **Lao-tse**) **(Master Lao)** (c 600–531 B.C.), Chinese philosopher, traditionally considered the founder of Taoism, one of the three major Chinese religious systems. Accounts of his life are based almost entirely on legend. The precepts of Lao-tze are set out in the *Tao-te ching,* one of the sacred books of China. However, the book seems to have been compiled several centuries after his death.

Laplace, Pierre Simon, Marquis de (1749–1827), French mathematician and astronomer noted for his work on gravitation. A mathematical genius, he developed the theory of probabilities and did brilliant research in integral calculus. In astronomy he extended knowledge of the motions of Jupiter and Saturn, the theory of the tides, and the stability of the solar system. His two chief astronomical works are *Mécanique céleste* (*Celestial Mechanics,* 1799–1825) and *Exposition du système du monde* (*Exposition of the World System,* 1796).

Lardner, Ring (1885–1933), in full Ringgold Wilmer Lardner, U.S. writer, best remembered for his humorous short stories written in characteristic American vernacular. He began his career in 1905 as a reporter for the South Bend (Ind.) *Times* and was later a sportswriter for various Chicago newspapers. After 1919 he became a syndicated writer of sports articles. His books include *You Know Me, Al* (1916), *Gullible's Travels* (1917), *How to Write Short Stories* (1924), *The Love Nest and Other Stories* (1926), and *Round Up* (1929).

La Salle, Sieur de; René Robert Cavelier (1643–1687), French explorer in North America. In 1669 he started westward on a tour of exploration that took him to the junction of the Ohio and Mississippi rivers. In 1682 he descended the Mississippi to its mouth, claiming the great valley in the name of France and calling it Louisiana in honor of Louis XIV. Two years later he set out from France on a voyage to colonize Louisiana. The expedition was plagued by poor organization and missed Louisiana, landing in Texas. In an attempt to reach Canada to seek help, La Salle was murdered by his own men.

Laski, Harold Joseph (1893–1950), British political theorist noted for his role in the development of the British Labour Party. Laski taught in Canada and the United States before returning to England to teach at the London School of Economics. In 1926 he became professor of political science at the University of London. He served on the executive committee of the Labour Party, 1936–1949, and was its chairman in 1945. Among his influential books are *Authority in the Modern State* (1919), *A Grammar of Politics* (1925), *The State in Theory and Practice* (1935), and *The American Democracy* (1948).

Latimer, Hugh (c 1485–1555), English churchman, reformer, and martyr who popularized the Reformation in England by his eloquent and lively sermons. Being in favor of Henry VIII's divorce from Catherine of Aragon, Latimer was appointed royal chaplain and, in 1535, bishop of Worcester; he resigned in 1539 in a dispute over the Six Articles. After Henry's death, he again became a leading reformer. When Mary I came to the throne and reinstituted Roman Catholicism, he was tried at Oxford for heresy and burned at the stake along with reformer Nicholas Ridley. At his execution, he said to Ridley, "We shall this day light such a candle by God's grace in England as, I trust, shall never be put out." His words became a lasting inspiration to English Protestants.

Latrobe, Benjamin Henry (1764–1820), English-born U.S. architect and engineer who helped design the U.S. Capitol. He came to the United States in 1796 and designed buildings for the Bank of Pennsylvania and the Bank of the United States. As surveyor of public buildings in Washington under President Thomas Jefferson, he contributed to the design of the original Capitol and superintended its rebuilding after it was burned in 1814.

CANADIAN CONSULATE GENERAL

WILFRID LAURIER

Laurier, Sir Wilfrid (1841–1919), Canadian statesman, the first French Canadian to be prime minister, 1896–1911. In 1871 Laurier was elected as a Liberal to the Quebec assembly; he was elected to the federal assembly in 1874. He became Liberal Party leader and, when the Liberals won the general election of 1896, became prime minister. His policy was to maintain French-Canadian identity within the state and to increase Canada's autonomy within the British empire.

Laval, Pierre (1883–1945), French collaborationist. Before World War II, he served several terms as premier and as foreign minister. After the French surrender in 1940, he joined the Vichy regime. At first he thought full cooperation with Hitler to be in France's national interest, but later he felt France should take a more independent stance. Hated by both the Resistance and the collaborators, he was shot for treason after the liberation.

Lavoisier, Antoine Laurent (1743–1794), French scientist, one of the founders of modern chemistry and the first to use the quantitative method of solving chemical problems. He demonstrated by actual weighing that matter may be altered but is never destroyed. In studies of combustion he showed that the combustible substance combines with oxygen, which he named. Lavoisier also discovered that water is a compound of two elements, hydrogen and oxygen, paving the way for the modern classification of elements and compounds. A man of wide interests, he set up a model farm; improved the manufacture of gunpowder; introduced reforms in taxation and banking; and helped organize the metric system of weights and measures. During the French Revolution he was convicted of having aristocratic sympathies and was executed.

Lawrence, David Herbert (D. H.) (1885–1930), British writer. From the time of his first novel, *The White Peacock* (1911), till his death, Lawrence lived an intense, restless, wandering life, in Italy, Mexico, Australia, and Taos, N.M. These experiences are reflected in nearly all his books. His first major work, *The Rainbow* (1915), was charged with obscenity and banned; his frank descriptions of sexual relations caused similar controversies over nearly all his novels, the most famous case being that over *Lady Chatterley's Lover* (1928). Lawrence's other novels include *Sons and Lovers* (1913), *Women in Love* (1920), *The Plumed Serpent* (1926), and *The Virgin and the Gipsy* (1930). His short stories and travel sketches appear in many collections, including *The Lovely Lady* (1933) and *Etruscan Places* (1932).

Lawrence, Ernest Orlando (1901–1958), U.S. physicist, a pioneer in developing the cyclotron. He supervised the building of the first cyclotron in 1933, at the University of California. Lawrence won the 1939 Nobel Prize for Physics for his research on atomic structure and on the cyclotron.

Lawrence, Thomas Edward (Lawrence of Arabia) (1888–1935), British soldier and archaeologist. Lawrence went on several archaeological expeditions in the Near East before World War I. In 1916 he was appointed British liaison officer to Faisal ibn Husain (later king of Iraq) and became a member of his Arab army. Lawrence and Faisal worked out a guerrilla campaign that culminated in the capture of Damascus from the Turks, 1918. Lawrence described the campaign in his *Seven Pillars of Wisdom,* first published in 1926. After the war, Lawrence, shunning fame, enlisted in the Royal Air Force under an alias. His ruse was discovered; he changed his name to Shaw and reenlisted. He died after a motorcycle crash in 1935. By his request, *The Mint,* recounting his Royal Air Force experiences, was not published until 1955.

Lazarus, Emma (1849–1887), U.S. writer, best known for her poem "The New Colossus," the sonnet engraved on the Statue of Liberty in New York harbor. Its much quoted first lines are, "Give me your tired, your poor. . . ." Among her other writings are the novel *Alide* (1874) and the play *Dance to Death* (1882).

Leakey, Louis Seymour Bazett (1903–1972), British archaeologist who discovered remains of some of the earliest known ancestors of modern man. In Tanzania, working with his wife, Dr. Mary D. Leakey, he found fossil remains of a type of primitive man *(Zinjanthropus)* that had lived about 1,500,000 years ago. In 1961 they found fossils of a creature they named *Kenyapithecus;* though more than 14 million years old, it appeared more manlike than apelike. From these findings, Leakey concluded that human life began in Africa and that several humanlike species developed side by side.

Lear, Edward (1812–1888), British artist and humorist, remembered for his witty limericks. Although he was a successful painter of birds and landscapes, he is best known for his books of nonsense verse. These include *A Book of Nonsense* (1846), *Nonsense Songs, Stories, and Botany* (1871), and *More Nonsense Rhymes* (1872). He traveled widely and wrote *Journal of a Landscape Painter in Albania and Illyria* (1841).

Le Corbusier (1887–1965), real name Charles Édouard Jeanneret, Swiss architect. A pioneer in ferro-concrete frameworks, he introduced the idea of massive supporting stilts in his Swiss Pavilion (1932) at the Cité Universitaire in Paris. Another style was shown in his chapel at Ronchamp (1955). Le Corbusier was an advocate of functionalism. His influential book *Toward a New Architecture* (1923) includes some of his most significant statements on modern architecture.

Ledbetter, Huddie (Leadbelly) (1888–1951), U.S. folk and blues singer. As a young man, Leadbelly led a fast life; he was often sent to prison but just as often managed to sing his way to parole or pardon. The folk musicologists Alan and John Lomax obtained his release from prison in Texas in 1934, and he helped them collect songs all over the South. As a performer he became famous, singing and playing his twelve-string guitar and talking easily about his songs. He recorded for the Library of Congress and wrote or popularized several well-known songs, including "Goodnight Irene" and "The Midnight Special."

Lederberg, Joshua: *See* Tatum, E.L.

Lee, Virginia family of American statesmen and colonial patriots. During the American Revolution, there were two important members.

Richard Henry Lee (1732–1794), a leading member of the Continental Congress, introduced on June 7, 1776, the resolution declaring the colonies independent of England. He later signed the Declaration of Independence and was a member of Congress under the Articles of Confederation, 1784–1787, and under the new Constitution. Opposed to a strong central government as set up in the Constitution, he suggested some of the ideas that became the Bill of Rights.

One of Richard's brothers, **Francis Lightfoot Lee** (1734–1797), vigorously opposed England while he was in the Virginia House of Burgesses, 1758–1776. He, too, signed the Declaration; unlike his brother, he supported the Constitution unreservedly.

Lee, Ann (1736–1784), religious figure, head of the sect known as Shakers. Born in Manchester, England, she joined the Shaking Quakers, or Shakers, as they were called, in 1758. As the leader of the sect, she suffered imprisonment several times. In 1774 she emigrated to the United States, where she founded a colony near Albany, New York. Persecuted also in the United States, she was beaten and imprisoned frequently.

Lee, Henry (1756–1818), American Revolutionary army officer and U.S. public official, a dashing cavalry commander popularly known as Light-Horse Harry Lee. A cousin of Richard Henry Lee, he was the father of Robert E. Lee. During the Revolution, he led a troop of irregulars known as Lee's legion; they aided Greene's campaigns in the Carolinas, 1780–1781. The eulogy written by Lee after Washington's death contained the famous phrase "First in war, first in peace, and first in the hearts of his countrymen."

Lee, Robert Edward (1807–1870), U.S. Army officer and Confederate general. He graduated from West Point in 1829, served with great distinction in the

ROBERT E. LEE

THE BETTMANN ARCHIVE

Mexican War, and was superintendent of West Point, 1852–1855. He commanded the detachment that captured John Brown at Harpers Ferry in 1859. At the outbreak of the Civil War, Lincoln offered him command of the Union forces, but Lee refused. He was not in favor of secession, but his first loyalty was to his native Virginia. He resigned from the U.S. Army and joined the Confederates, taking command of the army of Northern Virginia in 1862. Lee as the strategist and Stonewall Jackson as his field commander made a formidable combination. But after Jackson was killed and the invasion of the North ended in failure at Gettysburg in 1863, Lee was doomed to fighting and losing a defensive war. His example of calm resignation after the surrender at Appomattox in 1865 made defeat easier for the South to bear. After the war, Lee accepted the presidency of Washington College; its name was later changed to Washington and Lee.

Leeuwenhoek, Anton van (1632–1723), Dutch naturalist and microscopist. As a youth he used lenses to examine cloth in a factory in Amsterdam. In later years he assembled microscopes of great strength, some of them magnifying objects 270 times. Leeuwenhoek examined red blood cells and gave the first complete description of blood. In addition, he studied the anatomy of many insects, demonstrating that they hatched from tiny eggs rather than being spontaneously generated.

Léger, Fernand (1881–1955), French painter, often identified with "machine art." Originally trained as an architect, he became one of the leading painters of the cubist movement and a popular teacher of painting in Paris and New York. Léger's works have the sharpness and precision of machines, and include *Three Women* (1921), *The Station* (1923), and *The Constructors* (1950).

Lehár, Franz (1870–1948), Hungarian operetta composer. Lehár's most popular operetta, *The Merry Widow* (1905), was presented in Vienna and had over 5000 performances. His other works include *The Count of Luxemburg* (1909), *Eva* (1911), and *Friederike* (1928).

Leibniz (or **Leibnitz), Gottfried Wilhelm, Baron von Leibniz** (1646–1716), German philosopher and mathematician who made valuable contributions to logic and metaphysics and developed the calculus. Leibniz entered the diplomatic service of the elector of Mainz and was sent to Paris in 1672, where he met and exchanged ideas with the leading French thinkers of the time. From 1676, Leibniz was ducal librarian at Hanover. In his spare moments he developed his philosophy and his version of the calculus, which he published in 1684. Three years later, Newton published a version, and there ensued an argument over who should have the credit. This acrimony prevented Leibniz from being invited to accompany the elector of Hanover to London when he became King George I of England in 1714. Leibniz died in utter neglect. His studies in logic lay undiscovered among his papers for many years and did not become influential until the end of the 19th century.

L'Enfant, Pierre Charles (1754–1825), French army engineer and architect, planner of the city of Washington, D.C. After serving with the French army, he came to America and joined the Continental army. L'Enfant rose to the rank of major, and was highly regarded by George Washington. When Congress decided to build a federal city as the new nation's capital, L'Enfant drew up the plans for it in 1791. He provided for wide avenues and large tracts for parks and gardens built on a radial plan.

Lenin (1870–1924), real name Vladimir Ilich Ulyanov, Russian Bolshevik leader. His brother was hanged in 1887 for plotting to assassinate Czar Alexander III, and he himself was exiled to Siberia, 1897–1900, for antigovernment agitation. While in exile he completed his first major work, *The Development of Capitalism in Russia* (1899). When his exile was over, he lived in Munich and London, where he edited a radical newspaper under the pseudonym N. Lenin (sometimes V. I. Lenin) and gathered the core of a Bolshevik party that would follow his interpretation of Marxist doctrine. Lenin was in Switzerland when the March revolution of 1917 overthrew the imperial government of Russia. He quickly returned to Russia, went into hiding after the abortive July uprising, and emerged for the November revolution, which placed him in power. He made peace with Germany and spent the rest of his life organizing the Soviet Union and clarifying Marxist-Leninist ideology. He died of a stroke.

Lennon, John (Winston) (1940–1980), English rock singer and composer, a founder of the innovative English rock group The Beatles. Lennon and his colleagues Paul McCartney, George Harrison, and Ringo Starr (Richard Starkey) dominated rock music in the 1960's and drove their audiences to a frenzy. Lennon's second wife, the artist Yoko Ono, collaborated with him on the popular album *Double Fantasy.* He was shot in front of his New York apartment, generating enormous outbursts of public grief.

Leo I (Leo the Great) (c 390–461), pope from 440 to 461. Leo upheld papal authority over the Roman church, emphasizing its unity and universal character. He also vigorously suppressed heresies. In 452, when Attila the Hun invaded Italy, Leo persuaded him not to sack Rome. He also helped save the city from destruction by the Vandals under Genseric in 455.

Leo X (1475–1521), born Giovanni de' Medici, during whose reign as pope, 1513–1521, the Reformation began. He at first drove the French out of Italy, but Francis I returned in 1515 and forced Leo to cede control of some of the northern Italian states. In 1520 Leo allied himself with Holy Roman Emperor Charles V, who defeated Francis and returned the states to Leo. Leo, the son of Lorenzo the Magnificent, patronized writers, printers, and artists, including Raphael, and continued rebuilding St. Peter's. His extravagance led him to raise money selling indulgences, a practice criticized by many—among them Martin Luther, whom Leo excommunicated in 1520.

Leonardo da Vinci (1452–1519), universal genius of the Renaissance. At age 14 he was apprenticed to the respected Andrea Verrocchio, whose paintings Leonardo often finished with superior skill. In 1482 he left Florence for Milan, where for 17 years he worked for Duke Lodovico Sforza. Leonardo completed very few works of art, only three in Milan, including the mural *Last Supper* (1495–1497). Instead he filled his notebooks with drawings and annotations (written in mirror handwriting) that show his unique observations of the structure of nature and that touch on every science of his day. More than 5000 pages still exist, crowded with anatomical drawings, sketches of birds and flowers, designs for flying machines and fortifications, studies in optics, and even a plan for an automobile. After 1499 Leonardo wandered throughout Italy, staying for a time in Florence, where he painted the *Mona Lisa* (1503). He died in France, in lodgings given to him by his last patron, Francis I.

Leoncavallo, Ruggiero (1858–1919), Italian operatic composer who is remembered for his one successful opera, *I Pagliacci,* which was performed at Milan in 1892. Like Mascagni, he also rebelled against the Romantic tradition and wrote in a realistic style *(Verismo).* His other operas include *La Boheme* (1897), which failed because Puccini's earlier version surpassed Leoncavallo's, and *Zazà* (1900).

Leonidas (d. 480 B.C.), king of Sparta, 487–480, leader of the Greeks who fought the Persian army at Thermopylae in 480. To delay the Persians from invading Greece, Leonidas and about 6000 men took a stand in a pass at Thermopylae, on the invasion route. They held the pass until a Greek traitor showed the Persians a secret path lead-

THE BETTMANN ARCHIVE

GOTTFRIED LEIBNIZ

WIDE WORLD PHOTOS

JOHN L. LEWIS

ing behind the Greeks' position. The Persians surrounded Leonidas and his men and cut them down.

Leopardi, Giacomo (1798–1837), Italian poet, one of the greatest of the lyric poets. His poems are characterized by intense patriotism, a romantic lyricism, and a profound pessimism. His most important collection of poems is *Canti* (1831). He also wrote poetic and prose satires and philological studies.

Leopold II (1835–1909), king of the Belgians, 1865–1909, who established and then ruthlessly exploited the Congo Free State. Hoping to share in European colonial expansion, Leopold organized the International African Association in 1876, ostensibly to promote the civilization of central Africa. As a cover for his venture, Leopold formed the International Association of the Congo, to which tribal chiefs promised their allegiance. It was recognized as a country and renamed Congo Free State; Leopold became its sole sovereign in 1885. His atrocious exploitation of the natives, publicized in 1904, prompted the Belgian parliament to annex the Congo in 1908.

Lermontov, Mikhail Yurievich (1814–1841), Russian Romantic poet and novelist. A military officer, he was moved by the death in a duel of Alexander Pushkin to write *On the Death of the Poet* (1837), a criticism of court life which he addressed to the czar. He was arrested, court-martialed, expelled from the guards, and exiled. Pardoned after a year, he returned to St. Petersburg; he was exiled again for his part in a duel. Lermontov was killed in a duel while in exile. Among his most important long poems are *The Demon* (1839) and *Mtsyri* (1840). His greatest single work is the novel *A Hero of Our Time* (1840).

Lesseps, Ferdinand Marie, Vicomte de (1805–1894), French engineer and diplomat, the builder of the Suez Canal. In 1854 Said Pasha, viceroy of Egypt, granted him a concession to build the waterway; Lesseps raised the money and designed and supervised construction of the canal, which was begun in 1859 and opened in 1869. Ten years later he undertook to build a canal across the Isthmus of Panama. He underestimated the difficulties of the project, which had to be abandoned in 1889. The Panama Canal Company went bankrupt, cries of corruption and misappropriation were raised, and Lesseps was prosecuted, but the scandal was a political matter and did no damage to his reputation.

Lessing, Gotthold Ephraim (1729–1781), German critic and dramatist, influential in turning German literature from French classical models toward a national style. He is best known for the journal he helped to found, *Briefe, die Neueste Litteratur Betreffend* (*Letters Concerning the Most Recent Literature,* 1759–1767) and a treatise on poetry and painting, *Laokoon* (1766). His dramatic works include *Minna von Barnhelm* (1767), regarded as his best play; *Emilia Galotti* (1772); and *Nathan der Weise* (*Nathan the Wise,* 1779).

Lewis, Clive Staples (C.S.) (1898–1963), English author whose best-known work is *The Screwtape Letters* (1942, revised 1961), a series of witty letters to a junior Devil from his uncle on how to catch a Christian soul. Lewis also wrote literary studies (*The Allegory of Love,* 1936), science fiction novels with religious overtones (*Out of the Silent Planet,* 1938), and children's books.

Lewis, John Llewellyn (1880–1969)), president of the United Mine Workers (UMW) for 40 years, 1920–1960. Lewis worked in the mines until 1909, when he became a union executive. He became nationally known at the American Federation of Labor (AFL) convention in 1935. Although the AFL was organized by trades, Lewis suggested that assembly line workers be organized by industries. The AFL expelled the UMW, and Lewis helped form the rival Committee (later Congress) for Industrial Organizations (CIO); in 1938 he was elected its first president. The CIO organized many nonunionized industries, such as steel and car manufacturing. Lewis also campaigned for mine safety laws and a miners' welfare fund.

Lewis, Meriwether (1774–1809), U.S. soldier and explorer, leader of the Lewis and Clark expedition that made the first overland trip to the Pacific Northwest, charting territory gained in the Louisiana Purchase. In 1803 Thomas Jefferson named him to command the expedition; though he shared the post with his friend William Clark, Lewis kept much of the actual authority. After the success of the two-year trip, 1804–1806, Lewis was named governor of Louisiana Territory. While traveling to Washington to seek support, he died mysteriously, possibly by his own hand.

Lewis, Oscar (1914–1970), U.S. anthropologist known for his vivid accounts of the "culture of poverty." His studies of Mexican and Puerto Rican urban and rural poor were the basis for such books as *Five Families* (1959), *The Children of Sánchez* (1961), and *La Vida* (1966), which won the National Book Award.

Lewis, Sinclair (1885–1951), U.S. journalist and novelist, best known for *Main Street* (1920), a satirical depiction of middle-class life in a small town in Minnesota, and *Babbitt* (1922), a devastating portrait of a midwestern businessman. His other novels include *Arrowsmith* (1925), *Elmer Gantry* (1927), *Dodsworth* (1929), *Cass Timberlane* (1945), and *Kingsblood Royal* (1947). Each one deals bitingly with a fault that Lewis found in American society. In 1930 he became the first U.S. writer to receive the Nobel Prize for Literature.

Lie, Trygve Halvdan (1896–1969), Norwegian diplomat, the first secretary-general of the United Nations. In 1940 Lie became prime minister of the Norwegian government in exile. He headed Norway's delegation to the UN General Assembly in 1946 and served as secretary-general, 1946–1953. His support of the UN action in Korea led to Soviet attempts to block his renomination in 1951. Although he was reelected, the Soviet Union refused to recognize his leadership, and he resigned in 1953.

Liliuokalani, Lydia Kamehameha (1838–1917), last queen of the Hawaiian Islands, 1891–1893, who succeeded her brother Kalakaua. She was deposed in 1893 and the monarchy replaced by a republican government until Hawaii's annexation in 1898.

After one attempt to regain the throne, she lived in exile in the United States. A talented musician and poet, Liliuokalani wrote the song "Aloha Oe."

Lilly, John Cunningham (1915–), U.S. neurophysiologist who did revealing studies on the intelligence of dolphins. In order to investigate whether dolphins can think and reason, Lilly built his Communication Research Institute on St. Thomas, Virgin Islands; he also attempted to find a means of communicating with dolphins. His studies are reported in *Man and Dolphin* (1961) and *The Mind of the Dolphin* (1967).

Lincoln, Abraham (1809–1865), 16th President of the United States, 1861–1865. Lincoln sailed with cargo boats to New Orleans, worked as a clerk in New Salem, Ill., and read every book he could borrow. He became a prairie lawyer, based in Springfield. In 1834 he was elected to the Illinois legislature for the first of four terms. He married Mary Todd in 1842. Lincoln served a term in the U.S. House of Representatives, 1847–1849, but lost his backing when he criticized the Mexican War. In the mid-1850's he became the Illinois leader of the newly founded Republican Party. He ran as the Republican candidate for the U.S. Senate in 1858, opposing Stephen A. Douglas, who was seeking reelection. The high point in the campaign was a series of debates to which Lincoln challenged Douglas. Although Douglas won the election, the debates made Lincoln a national figure; at the Republican National Convention in 1860, he was nominated for the Presidency. When he won the election, the Southern states, alarmed at the aggressive antislavery policy of many leading Republicans, began to secede from the Union. No President ever suffered more abuse and vilification than Lincoln, and none bore it as well as he. Tall and strong, but a bit unkempt and shambling, he was sustained by his sense of humor, his magnanimity, and his faith in the justice of his cause. His main concern was to preserve the Union but, when public zeal for the war was waning, he widened the cause to include antislavery, though his Emancipation Proclamation of 1863 was of doubtful legality. He was reelected in 1864, defeating Democratic candidate George B. McClellan. Five days after Appomattox, on Good Friday (April 14), he was shot by John Wilkes Booth in Ford's Theater in Washington, D.C. He died the next morning; the following day became known as Black Easter.

DAVID LIVINGSTONE

THE BETTMANN ARCHIVE

Lind, Jenny (1820–1887), originally Johanna Maria Lind, Swedish opera singer known as the Swedish Nightingale. Lind's natural and pure coloratura soprano reached to G above high C. She made her debut in 1838 and performed throughout Europe and England, often in roles written for her by such composers as Verdi and Meyerbeer *(Robert le Diable).* Though audiences loved her, she gave up opera in 1849 for the concert stage. She toured the United States, 1850–1852, under the auspices of P. T. Barnum.

Lindbergh, Charles Augustus (1902–1974), U.S. aviator. In 1927 Lindbergh, an airmail pilot flying a monoplane he christened *Spirit of St. Louis,* made the first nonstop solo flight between New York and Paris. He thereby won the $25,000 Orteig Prize, offered in 1919 for the feat. He became an overnight hero, honored with tickertape parades and even a hit song, "Lucky Lindy." In 1929 Lindbergh married **Anne Morrow** (1906–). Three years later, their two-year-old son was kidnaped for ransom and found murdered; this was the most famous crime of the 1930's. To escape further publicity, the Lindberghs moved to Europe. Lindbergh's decoration by the Nazi German government in 1938, followed by his 1939 speeches in favor of U.S. isolationism, led many to accuse him of favoring appeasement of the Nazis. During World War II he was a consultant for aircraft firms, then retired from public life until the beginning of the 1970's, when he became a leading spokesman for conservation and ecology. Lindbergh's books include *We* (1927), his story of the flight to Paris, and *The Spirit of St. Louis* (1953), his autobiography, which won a Pulitzer Prize. Anne Morrow Lindbergh's books include *Gift from the Sea* (1955) and *Earth Shine* (1969).

Lindsay, (Nicholas) Vachel (1879–1931), U.S. poet known for his rhythmic, visionary verse. From 1906 to 1912 he tramped through the South and the West, distributing verse and lecturing as a modern wandering minstrel. In 1920 he became the first American poet to lecture at Oxford University. His poetry used folk themes, and he experimented with primitive and jazz rhythms. His books include *General William Booth Enters into Heaven and Other Poems* (1913), *The Congo and Other Poems* (1914), *The Chinese Nightingale* (1917), and *Golden Whales of California* (1920).

Linnaeus, Carolus (1707–1778), in Swedish, Carl von Linné, Swedish naturalist, founder of scientific nomenclature. He introduced a system based on the number of stamens and pistils; the system is the foundation of the modern method of classification. He also devised the two-name method of naming plants and animals known as the Linnaean, or binomial, system, and simplified plant description. Among the more important of Linnaeus's many books are *Systema Naturae* (*Systems of Nature,* 1735), *Fundamenta Botanica* (*Fundamentals of Botany,* 1736), and *Species Plantarum* (*Species of Plants,* 1753).

Lin Piao (1908–1971), Chinese military leader. He was active in Chu Teh's People's Army during its battles with Chiang Kai-shek's Nationalists; he led one of the units on the Long March, 1934–1935, and gained a reputation for daring in the Sino-Japanese War, 1937–1945. In 1955 Lin became a Politburo member and, in 1959, minister of defense. His *Long Live the Victory of People's War* (1965) was a major policy statement. He died in a plane crash; later, his plans for a coup were revealed.

Lipchitz, Jacques (1891–1973), U.S. sculptor, born Chaim Jacob Lipschitz in Lithuania. He lived in France from 1909 to 1941, then fled Nazi occupation for the United States, where he became a citizen in 1958. His early work was traditional but he turned to cubist techniques in 1914; considering that form too austere, he developed his "transparents," in which solid forms were opened up with space and held together with grids. He changed direction to the baroque in the 1930's, producing monumental pieces with religious and mythical themes. In his later years he created "semiautomatics," forms begun by molding hot waxy material in cold water by touch.

Li Po (c 700–762), Chinese poet of the T'ang dynasty, one of the greatest of oriental lyricists. Li Po led a wandering life and, though famous at court, was eventually banished because of his implication in a plot against the emperor. He wrote nearly 2000 poems on love, nature, pleasure, and sorrow. According to legend, he was drowned when, after drinking too much wine, he tried to embrace the moon's reflection in the water.

Lippi, Fra Filippo (or Lippo) (c 1406–1469), Italian painter of the Tuscan school. He was a Carmelite monk who indulged in many romantic adventures and finally ran off with a novice. His paintings, noted for an exquisite blending of realism and spiritual beauty, include *Annunciation* (c 1438) and a fresco series of the lives of John the Baptist and St. Stephen in the cathedral at Prato (c 1452–1465).

Lippmann, Walter (1889–1974), U.S. author and editor, an influential writer on public affairs. He was associate editor of the *New Republic* before World War I, then became assistant to the secretary of war, and later, at Woodrow Wilson's request, an aide to the U.S. delegation at the Paris Peace Conference. Lippmann entered newspaper work and in 1931 became a columnist for the New York *Herald Tribune,* commenting on political and economic affairs. He twice won the Pulitzer Prize. His books include *A Preface to Politics* (1913), *Public Opinion* (1922), and *The Essential Lippmann* (1963).

Lister, Joseph (1827–1912), British surgeon and scientist who introduced antiseptic surgery. He treated wounds and infections with a solution of carbolic acid, greatly reducing the incidence of gangrene, amputation, and death.

Liszt, Franz (1811–1886), Hungarian composer and pianist of amazing virtuosity and showmanship. He studied in Vienna and Paris and was soon performing in London and other large cities to tremendous acclaim. Liszt composed or transcribed more than 1300 works, mostly for piano. His best-known compositions are the fiery *Hungarian Rhapsodies.* He also introduced the "symphonic poem," a form of program music.

Livingstone, David (1813–1873), Scottish medical missionary and explorer in Africa. He studied medicine at Glasgow and in 1840 sailed for Africa. He worked among the people of Bechuanaland (present-day Botswana). In 1849 he headed north to explore, discovering Lake Ngami, the Zambezi River, and Victoria Falls. In 1858 Livingstone was commissioned to explore eastern and central Africa. He discovered lakes Shirwa and Nyasa in 1859. He began his last journey to Africa late in 1865, to discover the source of the Nile and to suppress slavery. The expedition was marked by hardship and privation, and Livingstone could not get back to the coast. In 1871 he was rescued by New York *Herald* journalist Henry M. Stanley, who greeted him with the celebrated words, "Dr. Livingstone, I presume?" They explored together for a time; then Livingstone, determined to find the source of the Nile, set out on another trip, on which he died.

Lloyd George, David, 1st Earl Lloyd George of Dwyfor (1863–1945), British prime minister, 1916–1922. Lloyd George entered Parliament in 1890 and soon made a name as an orator and Welsh nationalist. He was Chancellor of the Exchequer in Asquith's Liberal cabinet of 1908 and, in 1909, presented his "people's budget," which heavily taxed the rich. He followed it with his national and unemployment insurance acts of 1911, the first welfare state legislation. In 1916, during World War I, Lloyd George became war minister in the coalition government, replacing Kitchener. Later that year, supported by the Conservatives, he supplanted Asquith as prime minister. He put new vigor and efficiency into the home war effort and, doubting the competence of the British general staff, did his best to thwart them. He resigned in 1922 and continued as a leader of the opposition but never regained his former prominence.

Locke, John (1632–1704), English philosopher. He disagreed with the government of Charles II, disputing the divine right of kings, and was forced to flee to Holland in 1683; he did not return until 1689, after the accession of William and Mary. Locke's famous *An Essay Concerning Human Understanding* appeared in 1690. In it he denied the existence of innate ideas, stating that all knowledge is the result of experience. The human mind, a blank page, or *tabula rasa,* at birth, is written upon by sensations and reflections, the ultimate source of all ideas. As a political philosopher, Locke believed that government gains its legitimacy from the consent of the governed. He urged toleration of differing religious and political views. His work influenced the leaders of the American Revolution.

Lodge, Henry Cabot (1850–1924), U.S. public official and historian, a powerful voice in foreign policy in the era of World War I. He represented Massachusetts in the House of Representatives, 1887–1893, and in the Senate from 1893 until his death. An influential conservative Republican, Lodge led the opposition to President Wilson's peace policies after World War I, particularly U.S. participation in the League of Nations. Called the scholar in politics, he published biographies of Webster, Hamilton, and Washington, and other studies.

London, Jack (John Griffith) (1876–1916), U.S. writer of frontier adventure novels and stories. London's fiction was often based on his own experiences: he went to sea at 17, joined the gold rush to the Klondike, hunted seals in the Bering Sea, tramped through the United States and Canada, and became a newspaper correspondent in the Russo-Japanese War. London's first novel, *The Son of the Wolf,* appeared in 1900. Others include *The Call of the Wild* (1903), *The Sea Wolf* (1904), *White Fang* (1906), *The Iron Heel* (1907), and *Martin Eden* (1909).

Long, Huey Pierce (1893–1935), U.S. political figure remembered for his demagogic rule. He was governor of Louisiana, 1928–1931, and a U.S. senator, 1931–1935. Known as the Kingfish, Long received his strongest support from Louisiana's rural districts. As governor he built roads and hospitals and provided schools with free textbooks, using the resulting popular support to establish a virtually dictatorial regime in the early years of the Depression. Long wrote *Every Man a King* (1933), a book advocating a share-the-wealth program. He was killed by an assassin.

Longfellow, Henry Wadsworth (1807–1882), U.S. poet. Among his best-known poems are "Psalm of Life" (1839) and "The Wreck of the Hesperus" (1841). He also published *Evangeline* (1847), *The Song of Hiawatha* (1855), *The Courtship of Miles Standish* (1858), and *Tales of a Wayside Inn* (1863). Longfellow was elected to the Hall of Fame in 1900.

Longstreet, James (1821–1904), U.S. Army officer and Confederate general. He graduated from West Point in 1842 and distinguished himself in the Mexican War, during which he was wounded. A South Carolinian, he

HENRY WADSWORTH LONGFELLOW

joined the Confederacy when the Civil War began in 1861. He took part in the battles of Bull Run, Fredericksburg, and Gettysburg, and commanded the attack that broke enemy lines at Chickamauga. He fought against Grant in the Wilderness, 1864, and was again wounded. With a paralyzed arm, he returned to active service that same year. After the war Longstreet held several government positions, including that of minister to Turkey.

Lope de Vega: *See* Vega, Lope de.

Lorenz, Konrad Zacharias (1903–1989), Austrian naturalist known for his systematic study of animal behavior. For this work he shared the 1973 Nobel Prize in Physiology. Lorenz observed and defined two major characteristics: imprinting, the tendency of an animal to identify with the species with which it is raised; and releasers, certain gestures that cause instinctive reactions in other animals of the same species. Lorenz's books include *King Solomon's Ring* (1949), the controversial *On Aggression* (1966), attributing aggression to instinct, and *Behind the Mirror: A Search for a Natural History of Human Knowledge* (1973).

Lorenzo the Magnificent: *See* Medici (family).

Louis, Joe (1914–1981), originally Joseph Louis Barrow, U.S. prizefighter and world heavyweight boxing champion. He won the 1934 Golden Gloves championship in the light heavyweight division and three years later took the heavyweight title from James Braddock, becoming the second black to hold the world championship. He successfully defended his title 25 times in twelve years, knocking out six world champions. He retired in 1949, but returned to the ring to challenge Ezzard Charles in 1950 and Rocky Marciano in 1951, losing both bouts.

Louis XIV (1638–1715), king of France, 1643–1715, known as Louis the Great and, for the splendor of his reign, the Sun King. He became king when he was five years old under the regency of his mother, Anne of Austria, but the real power in France during his youth was Cardinal Mazarin, who had been the chief minister of his father, Louis XIII. Mazarin died in 1661, and Louis began to reign personally; under his rule France became the leading state in Europe. Louis encouraged everything that could add to the glory of the king or of France. He patronized art, music, ballet, and literature, assembled a glittering court, and built magnificent palaces, particularly Versailles. The governing power of the country was so concentrated in his hands that he could truly say, *"L'état, c'est moi"* ("I am the state"). Louis' desire for glory, however, embroiled France in a series of ruinous wars. The first three gained France bits of European territory, but the fourth, the War of the Spanish Succession (1701–1714), proved disastrous. Although Louis won the throne of Spain for his grandson Philip V, the war lost France large territories in North America and left the army broken and the treasury bankrupt. Furthermore, Louis revoked the Edict of Nantes in 1685 and suppressed all Protestant rights, causing the emigration of thousands of France's most productive citizens. His splendid reign of 73 years, the longest in European history, had become an unbearable burden, and his people rejoiced at his death.

Louis XVI (1754–1793), king of France, 1774–1792, grandson and successor of Louis XV. In 1770 he married Marie Antoinette of Austria. At the onset of his reign he was faced with a huge public debt inherited from Louis XV, which was increased after 1778 by aid to the American colonies in their struggle for independence from Britain. Louis appointed a series of reform-minded finance ministers but dismissed them when they sought to tax the upper classes. He was persuaded by liberal members of the nobility to convene the Estates-General to approve a new tax system, a move that helped unleash the French Revolution. The convention was taken over by the Third Estate, or middle class, which established a constitutional monarchy. A mob attacked Versailles and carried the royal family to Paris, where they were imprisoned. In 1791 Louis and his family attempted to escape from France but were captured and brought back to Paris. In June, 1792, the Tuileries, where the king was being held, was attacked by an angry mob. In September the monarchy was abolished in favor of the republic. Louis was tried, condemned, and guillotined in January, 1793.

Low, Juliette Gordon (1860–1927), U.S. youth leader, founder of the Girl Scouts of America. While living in Britain, she became interested in the newly formed Boy Scout and Girl Guide movements. After working with a Girl Guide group in Scotland, she organized a similar movement in her native Georgia in 1912. The name was changed to Girl Scouts in 1913. Low was president of the U.S. organization until 1920.

Lowell, Amy (1874–1925), U.S. poet and critic. An imagist, Lowell wrote mostly free verse, which was strikingly original, as was her personality. Her poetry volumes include *A Dome of Many-Coloured Glass* (1912), *Sword Blades and Poppy Seed* (1914), and *Pictures of the Floating World* (1919). Her prose works include *Tendencies in Modern American Poetry* (1917) and a critical biography of John Keats (1925).

JULIETTE LOW

Lowell, James Russell (1819–1891), U.S. poet and critic. In 1843 he became editor of a periodical of criticism, *The Pioneer,* to which Edgar Allan Poe, Nathaniel Hawthorne, and John Greenleaf Whittier contributed. Lowell's rhymed satire, *The Biglow Papers* (1846), gave him a reputation for shrewd political perception. More poetry appeared in 1848—*The Vision of Sir Launfal* and *A Fable for Critics.* As associate editor of the *North American Review,* 1864–1872, Lowell wrote a series of masterly essays on Dante, Shakespeare, and Emerson, among others. In 1877 he went to Spain as ambassador, and in 1880 to Britain.

Lowell, Percival (1855–1916), U.S. astronomer who founded the Lowell Observatory in Flagstaff, Ariz., in 1894. He was the brother of Amy Lowell. Lowell became widely known for his studies of the canals of Mars. In 1905 he predicted from mathematical calculations that another planet existed; discovered in 1930, the planet was named Pluto.

Lowell, Robert (1917–1977), U.S. poet. Lowell's poetry, characterized by its complexity and symbolism, includes *Land of Unlikeliness* (1944); *Lord Weary's Castle* (1946), which won the Pulitzer Prize for poetry in 1947; *Life Studies* (1959), for which he won the 1960 National Book Award; *For the Union Dead* (1964); and *Near the Ocean* (1967).

Loyola, Ignatius of (1491–1556), born Iñigo de Oñez y Loyola, Spanish saint, founder of the Society of Jesus, whose members are commonly called Jesuits. Loyola in his youth was a page in the court of Ferdinand and Isabella, king and queen of Spain. He entered the army and was crippled for life in a war with the French. During a long convalescence he read books of devotion and lives of the saints, deciding in 1522 to dedicate himself to the service of the Roman Catholic Church. At about that time he wrote a book of devotion called

Spiritual Exercises, which was to become the guide for his order. He completed his theological training in Paris. In 1534 he and six others took vows of chastity and poverty that marked the foundation of the Society of Jesus, dedicated to the conversion of the heathen. In 1540 the order was recognized by Pope Paul III, and Loyola became its first superior. He was canonized in 1628.

Lucas van Leyden (1494–1533), real name Lucas Hugensz or Jacobsz, Dutch painter and engraver. Lucas was a child prodigy who produced more than 200 engravings, etchings, and woodcut designs during his brief life. He was influenced by Dürer, whom he met in 1521, though Lucas showed more interest in genre in his paintings *(Card Players)* and engravings *(The Adoration of the Magi).*

Luce, Henry Robinson (1898–1967), U.S. publisher and editor born in China, where his parents were missionaries. In 1921 he took a reporting job on the Chicago *Daily News.* Two years later he and Britton Hadden founded the weekly news magazine *Time.* The success of this venture led to the establishment of three more magazines—*Fortune* (1930), a business monthly; *Life* (1936), a weekly specializing in pictorial reporting; and *Sports Illustrated* (1954).

Ludendorff, Erich Friedrich Wilhelm (1865–1937), German army officer. Ludendorff directed the capture of Liège in 1914, the first step in German World War I strategy. He was then assigned to the eastern front as second in command to Hindenburg. The two generals eventually acquired full command of the German war effort. Ludendorff, as chief military strategist, planned the unsuccessful final offensive of 1918. During the 1920's, Ludendorff joined with Hitler in leading the 1923 *Putsch.* He supported the Nazis until he and Hitler fell out in the 1930's.

Lully, Jean Baptiste (1632–1687), in Italian Giovanni Battista Lulli, French-Italian composer of operas. While still a boy he went to Paris and entered the service of Louis XIV as a ballet dancer. In 1672 Lully became director of the Académie Royale de Musique (now the French National Opera), for which he composed operas including *Alceste* (1674), *Thésée* (1675), *Amadis de Gaule* (1684), and *Armide et Renaud* (1686).

Lumière, family of French chemists and manufacturers known particularly for their work in early photography. **Louis Jean Lumière** (1864–1948), with his brother **Auguste Lumière** (1862–1954), invented in 1895 the Cinématographe, a combined moving picture camera, projector, and printer. Cinématographe shows became popular throughout Europe; the first ones were shown in the United States in 1896. The Lumières also made new types of photographic film and developed a process for color photography.

Lunt, Alfred (1892–1977), U.S. actor who, with his wife, the actress **Lynn Fontanne** (c 1887–1983), had a long and popular stage career. The Lunts first worked together in 1919; they were married in 1922. The first play in which they co-starred was *The Guardsman* (1925–1929). They also played in *Design for Living* (1933), *There Shall Be No Night* (1939), *Quadrille* (1954), and *The Visit* (1958–1959).

Luther, Martin (1483–1546), German monk and priest who began the Protestant Reformation. After joining the Augustinians, he was sent on a mission to Rome in 1510 and returned indignant at the worldliness of the Roman Catholic Church. In 1511 he became professor of biblical theology at Wittenberg, a post he held until the end of his life. Luther's studies brought him to the conclusion that men are saved by faith rather then by good works. When papal indulgences were offered for sale, he attacked them and other practices in his *95 Theses,* which he wrote and nailed to the church door in Wittenberg in 1517. Copies were printed and discussed all over Europe. These were followed by his treatises of 1520, in which he attacked papal authority and other official church doctrines. In 1520 Pope Leo X issued a papal bull excommunicating Luther. Luther burned the document publicly in Wittenberg. He was then summoned to appear before Emperor Charles V at the Diet of Worms, in 1521. Luther made an eloquent defense and refused to recant; an edict was issued outlawing him. Protected by Frederick, elector of Saxony, Luther hid in the castle of Wartburg, where he remained for nearly a year. There he began to translate the Bible into German. The work, completed in 1534, was the first complete Bible in a modern vernacular tongue. It had a strong influence on the development of the German literary language. In 1525 Luther married Katharina von Bora, a former nun. From 1522 on he lived at Wittenberg, worked at organizing a Protestant church, and disputed with more radical reformers. He also wrote essays, sermons, catechisms, and hymns, including the most famous of Protestant hymns, *"Ein' feste Burg"* ("A Mighty Fortress Is Our God").

Luthuli, Albert John (1898–1967), South African civil rights leader. A Zulu chief, he advocated nonviolent resistance to South African racial apartheid. As head of the African National Congress, he organized a campaign of civil disobedience in 1952. He was arrested for high treason and forbidden to leave the country. When Luthuli received the 1960 Nobel Prize for Peace, the South African government denounced the award but allowed him to go to Norway to accept it. Luthuli's autobiography, *Let My People Go,* appeared in 1962.

Luxemburg, Rosa (c 1870–1919), known as Red Rosa, Polish-born German socialist. She began to work with the German Social Democratic Party in 1898, leading its radical left wing in advocating mass strikes as a political tactic. With Karl Liebknecht, she split from the group to form the Communist Spartacus League, which led the abortive uprising of 1918–1919. She was killed while being arrested after the uprising. Among her books is *The Crisis in German Social Democracy* (1916).

Lysander (d. 395 B.C.), Spartan admiral. As commander of the Spartan fleet in 405, Lysander defeated the Athenians at Aegospotami and blockaded Athens. In 404 the starving Athenians surrendered to him, ending the Peloponnesian War. In spite of Lysander's military brilliance, his arrogance and power-seeking soon made him unpopular. When Thebes, Corinth, and other Greek cities rose against Sparta, he led an army into Boeotia and was killed in battle.

Lysippus (fl. late 300's B.C.), Greek sculptor whose naturalistic style became the model for Hellenistic sculpture. Lysippus became court sculptor to Alexander the Great and was the only artist allowed to sculpt his portrait. In all, he is said to have done some 1500 bronze works, including gods, athletes, and satyrs, but none of the originals has survived. Among the copies of his works is the *Apoxyomenos,* a statue of a man scraping himself clean with a strigil.

M

MacArthur, Douglas (1880–1964), U.S. Army officer who commanded Allied forces in the Pacific during World War II. In 1941 Japan attacked the Philippines and MacArthur led the defense of the islands, until, overwhelmed by the Japanese, he withdrew to Australia. As commander of Allied forces in the Pacific, MacArthur led the retaking of the islands, including the Philippines, in 1944. In 1950 MacArthur was named commander of U.S. and UN forces in Korea. He opposed U.S. policy, and in 1951 President Truman removed him from command. In a farewell speech before Congress, MacArthur said, "Old soldiers never die; they just fade away."

Macaulay, Thomas Babington (1800–1859), British historian, politician, and essayist. The first volumes of his major work, *History of England from the Accession of James II,* appeared in 1848; two more volumes were published later. Macaulay's work is known for its range of knowledge and brilliant narrative; it has been criticized for its political and cultural bias. Macaulay also wrote poetry, including the volume *Lays of Ancient Rome* (1842), which includes the famous poem "Horatius at the Bridge."

Macbeth (d. 1057), king of the Scots, 1040–1057, and the title character of Shakespeare's drama *Macbeth.* As ruler of Moray province, Macbeth revolted against King Duncan in 1040 and killed him in battle. He then ruled Scotland until he was killed in battle by Malcolm, Duncan's son. Shakespeare's plot—not historically accurate—was taken from the story told in Holinshed's *Chronicles.*

Maccabees (second and first centuries B.C.), also called Hasmonaeans, a family of Jewish patriots who prevented the subordination of Judaism by Hellenism. The most famous Maccabee was **Judas Maccabeus** (Judah the Hammer), son of Mattathias, a priest who founded the dynasty. In 168 the Syrian king tried to impose Hellenism on Judea. Mattathias, with the *hasidim* (the pious), fled to the mountains. Upon his death in 166, Judas led the Israelites in a series of victories over Syria, restoring temple worship in 165. He led the struggle for political independence until his death in 160. Members of Judas's family ruled Judea until 37 B.C., when Antigonus was executed and Herod began his rule.

MacDonald, (James) Ramsay (1866–1937), British statesman, a founder of the British Labour Party, 1894, and first Labour prime minister. He was elected to Parliament in 1906, but his pacifist ideas during World War I caused his defeat in 1918. Returned to Parliament in 1922, he led the Labour Party and in January, 1924, became prime minister. He resigned in November of that year when the Conservatives gained control of Parliament; he became prime minister again in 1929. After a financial crisis in 1931, he joined with the Conservatives and Liberals to form a coalition government with himself as prime minister. In 1935 he resigned.

JUDAS MACCABEUS

THE BETTMANN ARCHIVE

Macdonald, John Alexander (1815–1891), lawyer, Canadian statesman, prime minister of Canada, 1867–1873 and 1878–1891. Born in Scotland, he came to Canada with his family as a child. He was elected to the Canadian legislative assembly in 1844 as a member of the Conservative Party. He was a leading architect of the confederation of Canada in 1867, when he became the first prime minister of the new Dominion. Macdonald supported a system of protective tariffs, fearing that free trade would lead to Canada's annexation by the United States.

MacDowell, Edward Alexander (1861–1908), U.S. composer. The American scene and American Indian rituals are mirrored in such works as *Indian Suite* (1892), *Sea Pieces* (1898), *Fireside Tales* (1902), and his most famous work, *Woodland Sketches* (1896). Following his death, his widow established the MacDowell Colony, a summer residence for American composers in Peterborough, N.H.

Machiavelli, Niccolò (1469–1527), Italian statesman and writer whose masterpiece, *The Prince* (1513), is a study of realism in politics. He held many diplomatic posts in Florence, but he was dismissed when the Florentine republic fell and the Medicis returned to power in 1512. In *The Prince,* Machiavelli attempted to show that a ruler is justified in taking any steps that will maintain his power, whether right or wrong. From this is derived the term "Machiavellian," meaning crafty or cunning in politics.

Mack, Connie (1862–1956), born Cornelius McGillicuddy, U.S. baseball player and manager. He became a big-league catcher in 1886 with the Washington ball club. From 1901 to 1950 he managed the Philadelphia Athletics, during which time they won nine pennants and five World Series victories.

Mackenzie, Alexander (1822–1892), editor, statesman, and first prime minister for the Liberal Party in Canada, 1873–1878. He introduced the secret ballot and single-day elections to Canada.

MacLeish, Archibald (1892–1982), U.S. poet and public official. He published several books of poetry during the 1920's, and gained renown in 1932 with *Conquistador,* the first volume of his poetry devoted to political and social issues. It was followed by *The Fall of the City* (1937) and *Air Raid* (1938), verse plays for radio, and *America Was Promises* (1939). MacLeish served as librarian of Congress, 1939–1944, director of the Office of War Information, 1942–1943, and assistant secretary of state, 1944–1945. *J.B.: A Play in Verse,* written in 1957, was produced successfully on Broadway and won the Pulitzer Prize for drama. MacLeish also won Pulitzer prizes for *Conquistador* and for *Collected Poems, 1917–1952.*

Macleod, John James Rickard: *See* Banting, Sir Frederick Grant.

Macmillan, (Maurice) Harold (1894–1986), British prime minister from 1957 to 1963. He served in Winston Churchill's wartime government, led the opposition, 1945–1951, and in 1957 was chosen prime minister of a Conservative government. He neutralized Labour opposition by following middle-of-the-road domestic programs. His foreign policy was based on close cooperation with the United States. He led support for entry into the European Common Market. Macmillan resigned because of growing ill health in October, 1963.

Madison, James (1751–1836), fourth President of the United States, 1809–1817, and a principal architect of the U.S. Constitution. In 1776 he served on the Virginia constitutional committee and in 1779 was elected to the Continental Congress. He was instrumental in the calling of the Constitutional Convention in 1787. Madison was the author of the Virginia Plan, which formed the basis for many sections of the federal Constitution drawn up by the convention. He also wrote many of the *Federalist* papers urging ratification of the Constitution. He was elected to the first House of Representatives as a Federalist and served throughout George Washington's administration. He gradually drew away from his party and became a leader of the Jeffersonian group, then called Republicans. In the House he was prominent in securing the adoption of the Bill of Rights. In 1801 Madison entered Jefferson's Cabinet as secretary of state; in 1808 he himself was elected President. During the War of 1812 he lost much popular support, but he was reelected for a second term.

Maeterlinck, Count Maurice Polydore Marie Bernard (1862–1949), Belgian symbolist writer who was awarded in 1911 the Nobel Prize for Literature. His plays and poems are marked by a mystical and fatalistic viewpoint. His best-known dramas are *Pelléas and Mélisande* (1892; adapted as an opera by Debussy, 1902) and *The Blue Bird* (1908). He was also a naturalist and wrote popular studies, such as *The Life of the Bee* (1901).

Magellan, Ferdinand (c 1480–1521), Portuguese navigator. In 1519, under the auspices of Charles I of Spain, Magellan sailed for the New World with a fleet of five ships and 265 men. They crossed the Atlantic Ocean and sailed down the east coast of South America. In 1520 they entered the Pacific through the strait at the southern tip of the continent (now the Straits of Magellan). Crossing the Pacific, they discovered the Philippine Islands, where Magellan was killed. One ship reached Spain in 1522, completing the first voyage around the world.

Magritte, René (1898–1967), Belgian painter, a leading exponent of surrealism. His dream world paintings present ordinary objects in realistic detail, set in unreal, obscure, or fantastic surroundings. This startling juxtaposition creates a sense of mystery and unease, typical of his work. *Madame Recamier* (1951) is an outstanding example of his art.

Mahler, Gustav (1860–1911), Austrian composer and conductor, the last of the great German Romantics. He directed the Imperial Opera in Vienna from 1897 to 1907, and later was conductor of the New York Philharmonic. In his symphonies and songs, Mahler extended the traditions of Romantic music, adding touches of modern dissonance and subtle musical effects. Mahler wrote ten symphonies, the last unfinished, and several song cycles, including *Das Lied von der Erde* (*The Song of the Earth,* 1908), which has become his best-known work.

Mailer, Norman (1923–   ), U.S. novelist, essayist, poet, and journalist. Mailer's first novel, *The Naked and the Dead* (1948), came out of his experiences in World War II. His other novels include *The Deer Park* (1955) and *An American Dream* (1965). His book on the 1967 antiwar demonstration at the Pentagon, *The Armies of the Night* (1968), written in a highly personal journalistic style, won both the National Book Award and a Pulitzer Prize. Other books include *Miami and the Siege of Chicago* (1968), *The Executioner's Song* (1979), a novel based on the life of a convicted murderer, and *Tough Guys Don't Dance* (1984), a mystery thriller. Mailer ran unsuccessfully for mayor of New York in 1968; he described his campaign in *Running Against the Machine* (1969).

Maillol, Aristide (1861–1944), French sculptor known for his studies of the nude figure. Influenced by early Greek tradition, he produced such works as *Flora* (1911) and the *Crouching Woman.* Maillol also produced terracotta statuettes. Toward the end of his life he did many book illustrations.

HORACE MANN

Maimonides (or **Rabbi Moses ben Maimon**) (1135–1204), a famed Spanish-Hebrew physician, philosopher, and commentator on the Scriptures. Born in Córdoba, he studied under the great Arab scholars of his time. In 1165 he settled in Cairo, where he eventually became a physician in the court of Saladin. He attempted to reconcile rabbinic Judaism with Aristotelian philosophy. His greatest work is *Guide of the Perplexed* (1190), which contains the essence of his philosophy. Maimonides also wrote commentaries on the Hebrew Scriptures and works on medicine, logic, and mathematics.

Malamud, Bernard (1914–1986), U.S. novelist and short story writer, distinguished for his haunting portrayals of Jewish-American life in New York. *The Assistant* (1957) is one of his noted works, as are *The Natural* (1952), *The Fixer* (1966), *The Tenants* (1971), *God's Grace* (1982), and two collections of short stories, *The Magic Barrel* (1958) and *Idiots First* (1963).

Malcolm X (1925–1965), born Malcolm Little, U.S. black nationalist leader who popularized, then repudiated, the doctrines of the Black Muslims. Malcolm X educated himself and became a Black Muslim while in prison. Released in 1952, he became top recruiter and spokesman for the Black Muslims. His growing power in the organization led to his dismissal in 1963. After his 1964 pilgrimage to Mecca, he took the name El-Hajj Malik El-Shabazz. He returned converted to an ideal of universal brotherhood and black nationalism. He was shot to death while speaking in New York.

Mallarmé, Stéphane (1842–1898), French poet, leader of the symbolist movement in the late 1900's. His *L'Après-midi d'un faune* (*The Afternoon of a Faun,* 1876) inspired Debussy's musical suite of the same name. His small body of work, including *Poesies* (1887–1913) and *"Un Coup de dés"* ("A Cast of the Die," 1897), had an immeasurable influence on his contemporaries, such as Gide, Claudel, and Manet, who considered him the ideal poet.

Malory, Thomas (fl. 1400's), English author whose *Morte Darthur* (or *Morte d'Arthur*) became the best-known collection in English of the legends of King Arthur and his knights of the Round Table. Malory's identity is not established. If he was the Sir Thomas Malory mentioned in records of the time, he was several times imprisoned for various felonies. He may have died in 1471. *Morte Darthur* was first published in 1485 by William Caxton.

Malraux, André (1901–1976), French novelist, critic, and statesman. He spent several years in Indonesia and was in China during the revolutions of the 1920's. From this came his famous novel, *La Condition humaine* (1933), published in English as *Man's Fate.* Malraux participated in the Spanish Civil War, 1936–1939, from which came *L'Espoir* (1937), or *Man's Hope.* In World War II, during the German occupation of France, he was a member of the Resistance. After the war, he became France's minister of information under Charles de Gaulle, 1945–1946. He returned to government to serve as minister of cultural affairs from 1958 to 1969. Malraux also wrote important books on art history, including *The Voices of Silence* (1951). His autobiography, *Anti-Memoirs,* was published in 1968.

Malthus, Thomas Robert (1766–1834), British economist. In 1798 he published his *Essay on the Principle of Population,* a pessimistic study warning that population growth, which is geometric, will eventually outstrip food production, which grows arithmetically. His theories influenced Darwin in the line of reasoning that led to his principle of natural selection and survival of the fittest.

Manet, Édouard (1832–1883), French painter, a leader of the impressionists. After studying in several European art centers, he settled in Paris, where his paintings, such as *Absinthe Drinker* (1859) and *Picnic on the Grass* (1862), aroused much controversy, chiefly because of their realism and unorthodox composition and use of color. Rejected in official circles, Manet and his followers organized their own exhibits. By the early 1880's, his work had won widespread acceptance.

Mann, Horace (1796–1859), U.S. educator. As a member of the Massachusetts legislature, 1827–1837, he attracted notice with his criticism of the state public school system. Mann was named secretary of the Massachusetts board of education in 1837. He launched school reforms, advocating free universal nonsectarian education.

THE BETTMANN ARCHIVE

JEAN MARAT

His ideas, strongly resisted at first, ultimately prevailed. Mann served in the U.S. Congress, 1848–1853, where he was active in the antislavery movement.

Mann, Thomas (1875–1955), German novelist, short story writer, and critic. Mann developed cultural and psychological themes with great subtlety and power in his fiction. He took a strong stand against Nazism, leaving Germany in 1933. Important works in translation include *Buddenbrooks* (1901, translated 1924); *Death in Venice* (1912, translated 1924); *The Magic Mountain* (1924, translated 1927); *Joseph and His Brothers* (1933–1943, translated 1934–1944), a biblical tetralogy; and *Confessions of Felix Krull, Confidence Man* (1954, translated 1955). He won the 1929 Nobel Prize for Literature.

Mansfield, Katherine: *See* Murry, Kathleen Beauchamp.

Mantegna, Andrea (1431–1506), Italian Renaissance artist, one of the great fresco painters of the 1400's. His chief works are in Padua, his native city; Mantua, where his patron was the duke of Mantua; and Rome, where he decorated the Belvedere Chapel in the Vatican for Pope Innocent VIII. Two of his great works are *The Crucifixion* and *Parnassus* (1497).

Mao Tse-tung (1893–1976), Chinese Communist statesman and political leader. The son of a peasant, Mao went to Peking in 1918, where he became interested in social reform and helped found the Chinese Communist Party in 1921. Mao organized peasants in his native province of Hunan and rose in the party leadership. Chiang Kai-shek took control of the nationalist Kuomintang movement in 1926, and in 1927 he broke with the Communists. Nationalist pressure forced the Communists from their strongholds, and in 1934 Mao led the Long March. Traveling on foot over difficult terrain and under almost constant attack, they covered some 5000 miles, establishing a new capital in Yenan, in northern China. There Mao consolidated his position and developed a dedicated force. In 1937 large-scale warfare broke out between China and Japan, and an uneasy alliance was formed by the Communists and the Kuomintang. Japan's defeat in 1945 was accompanied by a renewal of open civil war. Within four years Chiang and his forces had been driven from the mainland. In 1949 the Communists proclaimed the People's Republic of China with Mao at its head. Under his leadership, a strong national government was established and a new economic program was introduced. In 1959 Mao resigned as head of the government but remained at the head of the Communist Party. In the early 1960's a bitter struggle between Mao and the leaders of the Soviet Union split the world communist movement. Later in the 1960's a Cultural Revolution was launched in China in which devotion to the writings of Mao became the touchstone of patriotism. During this period he reasserted his leadership. His campaign against bourgeois revisionism lasted four years as he consolidated his position; he purged those national and provincial authorities who opposed his proletarian reforms. In 1970 Mao was named supreme commander of the nation and the army, emphasizing his stature as China's most powerful figure.

Marat, Jean Paul (1743–1793), Swiss-born French revolutionary leader. In 1777 he settled in Paris, where, in 1789, he began publishing a journal, *L'Ami du peuple* ("The Friend of the People"), denouncing all those he regarded as enemies. In 1792 Marat, a member of the militant Jacobin society, was elected to the revolutionary National Assembly. He engaged in a bitter struggle with the Girondists, the assembly's moderates, and condemned a number of them to death. Charlotte Corday, a Girondist sympathizer, assassinated him as he sat in his bath.

Marconi, Guglielmo (1874–1937), Italian physicist and inventor who developed the first practical method of radio communication. He gave his first public demonstrations in England in 1896; in 1901 he transmitted signals from Newfoundland to England. For his achievements, he shared in the 1909 Nobel Prize for Physics.

Marco Polo: *See* Polo, Marco.

Maria Theresa (1717–1780), empress of the Holy Roman Empire, who, in 1740, on the death of her father, Charles VI, Holy Roman Emperor, became queen of Hungary and Bohemia and archduchess of Austria. Her claims to her father's possessions were disputed by several nations, bringing on the War of the Austrian Succession. By the Peace of Aix-la-Chapelle (1748) Maria Theresa's titles were recognized, although she lost Silesia to Frederick II of Prussia. An enlightened despot, Maria Theresa instituted economic, social, and educational reforms, and a nationwide civil service.

Marie Antoinette (1755–1793), queen of France as wife of Louis XVI. The daughter of Holy Roman Emperor Francis I and Maria Theresa of Austria, she married Louis in 1770. Soon after his accession in 1774, stories were circulated about her extravagance, and she became unpopular with the people. In 1789 she was attacked by a crowd of infuriated women who stormed the Palace of Versailles during the opening days of the French Revolution. In June, 1791, realizing that further violence was imminent, she persuaded Louis to flee from France, but they were stopped at Varennes and returned to Paris. Louis was executed in January, 1793, and Marie was kept in solitary confinement until, after two escape attempts, she too was executed, October 16.

Marin, John Cheri (1872–1953), U.S. artist, best known for his dynamic watercolors, often of ships and the seacoast. In 1936 a retrospective showing of his work at the Museum of Modern Art in New York City established his reputation. A well-known work of Marin's is *Lower Manhattan from the River*.

Marion, Francis (1732–1795), American Revolutionary War officer, called the Swamp Fox by the British because of his elusive tactics. In 1780 he organized Marion's Brigade, a volunteer troop composed mainly of South Carolina mountaineers and hunters. They directed a series of daring guerrilla raids against the British, burning their boats and harassing them. Marion's tactics and speed enabled him to defeat British troops far outnumbering his own men.

Maritain, Jacques (1882–1973), French philosopher noted for his application of the principles of Thomas Aquinas to the fields of art, education, and politics. His chief work, *The Degrees of Knowledge* (1932), contrasts the mathematical approach to the study of nature with the ancient metaphysical approach. Other noted works are *Preface to Metaphysics* (1934), *The Range of Reason* (1952), and *On the Uses of Philosophy* (1961).

Marlborough, 1st Duke of; John Churchill (1650–1722), English soldier and general, the victor in several famous battles against the French during the War of the Spanish Succession. He supported the Protestant cause, serving both William of Orange and Queen Anne. Named commander of the English forces in Holland, Marlborough won the Battle of Blenheim in 1704, one of the most famous victories in history. He and his wife Sarah, Queen Anne's friend and confidante, were influential at court until the family fell into royal disfavor in 1711.

Marlowe, Christopher (1564–1593), English poet and dramatist. The first of his plays, *Tamburlaine the Great,* was produced about 1587. It was followed by *The Tragedy of Dr. Faustus* (c 1588), *The Jew of Malta* (c 1589), and *Edward II* (c 1592). Marlowe was the first to use blank verse; his poetry is noted for its power and beauty. His "Hero and Leander," written with George Chapman, was published after his death. His career was cut short when, at the age of 29, he was killed in a quarrel.

Marquette, Jacques (Père Marquette) (1637–1675), French explorer and Jesuit priest. In 1666 he went to Canada as a missionary to the Indians and in 1668 founded a mission at Sault Ste. Marie, on Lake Superior. In 1673 he made an expedition by canoe down the Mississippi River with Louis Jolliet, charting the region and keeping a valuable journal, published in 1681. After this expedition, he worked among the Indians living near the Great Lakes.

Marsh, Reginald (1898–1954), U.S. painter remembered for his many paintings of the people and street scenes of New York City. He followed the tradition of the "ashcan" school of the preceding generation. He was also a noted magazine illustrator. Two of his murals, *Sorting Mail* and *Transfer of Mail from Tugboat to Liner,* are in the U.S. Post Office Building, Washington, D.C.

Marshall, George Catlett (1880–1959), U.S. Army officer and statesman, author of the Marshall Plan for European economic aid. He served as Army chief of staff during World War II, training U.S. ground and air forces. As secretary of state, 1947–1949, under President Harry S. Truman, he implemented the Marshall Plan for postwar economic recovery in Europe. During the Korean War he served as secretary of defense. He was awarded the 1953 Nobel Prize for Peace.

Marshall, John (1755–1835), chief justice of the United States, 1801–1835. He fought in the Revolutionary War and in 1781 began practicing law in Virginia. During the next few years he served in the state legislature. Marshall was elected to Congress in 1799 and in 1800 was appointed secretary of state by President John Adams. In 1801 he began his 34-year career on the Supreme Court. In his most important decisions, he established the right of the judiciary to pass on the validity of congressional legislation and laid down the basic theory of the implied powers of the Constitution.

Martel, Charles: *See* Charles Martel.

Martí, José Julián (1853–1895), Cuban patriot and writer, Cuba's greatest national hero. As a young man he worked for Cuban independence from Spain and was first exiled at the age of 17. Returning to Cuba in 1878 and refusing to remain politically uninvolved, he was again exiled in 1879. From New York City he wrote about and helped plan for Cuban independence, returning to his country when the war for independence broke out in 1895. He was killed shortly afterward. As a Latin American distinguished man of letters, Martí's greatest achievements were his essays, which include *Juárez* (1884), *San Martín* (1891), and *Bolívar* (1893). One of his poems was "Guantanamera."

Marvell, Andrew (1621–1678), English metaphysical poet and political writer, the author of "To His Coy Mistress" (c 1653) and many pastoral poems, such as "The Garden" (c 1653). A staunch defender of Oliver Cromwell, he wrote many political satires against the Restoration government in England. For the last 18 years of his life, he was a member of the House of Commons.

Marx, Karl Heinrich (1818–1883), German economist and philosopher whose economic theory of history became one of the most important doctrines of modern times. His theories, known as Marxism, emphasize the importance of economic factors in history and in determining people's attitudes and behavior. Marx became editor of a radical newspaper in the Rhineland, but government censorship led him to move to France in 1843. In Paris he worked on a radical German-language journal. He also met Friedrich Engels, with whom he formed a lasting friendship. Many of Marx's works were written in collaboration with Engels. In 1845 Marx was expelled from France because of his criticism of the king of Prussia; he moved to Brussels. In 1848 Marx published his most famous work, *The Manifesto of the Communist Party,* often called the *Communist Manifesto.* In it he proclaimed that history is an account of the struggles between one social class and another. Existing governments, he said, reflect the domination of the property-owning class. He called on the workers, or proletariat, to unite in a revolutionary movement to overthrow the existing system and establish a classless society. Marx returned to the Rhineland to establish a new radical journal, but he was expelled in 1849 and finally moved to England, where he remained until his death. In 1864 Marx helped organize the First International Working Men's Association, usually called the First International. In 1867 the first volume of Marx's major work *Das Kapital (Capital)* was published. In it he described the economic and social forces that he believed shape society and determine historical development. The second and third volumes of *Das Kapital,* edited by Engels, appeared after Marx's death. Marx's writings became the official doctrine of the international communist movement.

Mary, Queen of Scots (Mary Stuart) (1542–1587), queen of Scotland, 1542–1567, queen of France, 1559–1560. Mary succeeded her father, James V, at the age of one week. She was raised at the French court by her mother's family, the Guises. She first tried to claim the English throne after the death of Mary I (1558). As a Roman Catholic, she denied the validity of Henry VIII's marriage to Anne Boleyn and asserted that their daughter, Mary's successor Elizabeth I, was illegitimate. Mary based her own claim on her descent from her great-grandfather, Henry VII. After the death of her first husband, Francis II of France (1560), she began to rule personally in Scotland and enlisted the support of France, Spain, and the papacy against Elizabeth and England. In 1565 Mary married her cousin Henry Stewart, Lord Darnley, by whom she had a son, the future James I of England. Darnley was murdered in 1567; suspicion fell on James Hepburn, earl of Bothwell, and on Mary when she married Bothwell three months later. The Scot nobles revolted and forced Mary to abdicate. She took refuge in England as the guest of her cousin Elizabeth I but continued to scheme to usurp the throne of England. Finally, she was tried and condemned for conspiring to murder Elizabeth and was beheaded.

Masaccio (1401–1428), real name Tommaso di Giovanni di Simone Guidi, one of the first Florentine Renaissance painters. By introducing perspective and depth in paintings such as *Expulsion from Paradise* (1427), a fresco in the Brancacci Chapel of the Carmine Church in Florence, Masaccio created a new style that greatly influenced such later masters as Raphael and Michelangelo.

Masaryk, Tomáš Garrigue (1850–1937), Czech scholar and statesman. He was an active Czech nationalist and a member of the Austrian parliament. When World War I broke out, Masaryk supported the Allies and, in exile, formed an alliance with leaders of Slovakia. In 1918 the Allies recognized an independent Czechoslovakia and Masaryk was elected president. He held office until 1935.

His son, **Jan Garrigue Masaryk** (1886–1948), became foreign minister of Czechoslovakia in 1940. As a member of the provisional Czechoslovak government in London, 1940–1945, he inspired his countrymen with broadcasts from exile and became a popular hero. He returned to Czechoslovakia as foreign minister to Eduard Beneš, 1945. Increasing difficulties with Moscow led to a Soviet coup against the Czech government in February, 1948. In March Masaryk either jumped or was pushed to his death from his room at the foreign office.

Masefield, John (1878–1967), British poet. His first work, *Salt Water Ballads* (1902), reflecting his experiences as a seaman, contains his most popular poem, "Sea Fever." He became famous after the publication in 1911 of the narrative poem *The Everlasting Mercy,* which was followed by *The Widow in the Bye Street* (1912), *The Daffodil Fields* (1913), and his World War I prose works *Gallipoli* (1916) and *The Old Front Line* (1917). He was appointed poet laureate in 1930.

Massasoit (c 1580–c 1661), American Indian, chief of the Wampanoag Indians in southern Massachusetts when the Pilgrims arrived. In 1621 the Indian Samoset arranged a meeting with his chief, Massasoit, and Plymouth governor John Carver. From this meeting was drawn a treaty of peace that lasted for half a century. Massasoit was succeeded by his son Metacomet, known as King Philip.

Massenet, Jules Émile Frédéric (1842–1912), French composer of lyric, melodic operas. He completed his first opera, *Le Grand' Tante,* at the age of 25. In *Manon* (1884), his masterpiece, Massenet best revealed his gift for writing delicate, sensuous music. Other operas include *Werther* (1892), *Thaïs* (1894), *Le Jongleur de Nôtre-Dame* (1902), and *Don Quichotte* (1910).

Masters, Edgar Lee (1869–1950), U.S. poet and novelist. The popular *Spoon River Anthology* (1915) is a collection of some 200 realistic, often cynical epitaphs in free verse monologues spoken from the grave by the inhabitants of the fictitious small town of Spoon River. The work was later successfully adapted for the stage.

Mather, Cotton (1663–1728), American clergyman. The son of **Increase Mather** (1639–1723), also an influential clergyman, he became his father's assistant at North Church, Boston, assuming full charge during his father's absence. Mather was known as a linguist; he published an enormous number of books. Among them are his *Witchcraft and Possessions* (1685), which helped bring on the Salem witchcraft trials, and *The Ecclesiastical History of New England* (1702).

Matisse, Henri Émile Benoît (1869–1954), French postimpressionist artist. After several years of conventional art study, Matisse adopted impressionism but then went beyond impressionism, becoming one of the Fauvists and taking his inspiration from African, Islamic, and early Italian art. He became known for his extraordinary use of color and his simple outlines. In addition to many paintings, he also produced lithographs, sculpture, and brilliant ecclesiastical vestments, tapestries, and stained glass windows. Among his many famous paintings are *The Red Studio, Egyptian Curtain,* and *Piano Lesson.*

Maugham, (William) Somerset (1874–1965), British writer and dramatist. He achieved his first literary success with the novel *Lisa of Lambeth* (1897). Turning for a time to playwriting, he produced *Jack Straw* (1908) and *Loaves and Fishes* (1911). In addition to *Of Human Bondage* (1915), his best-known work, Maugham's other novels are *The Moon and Sixpence* (1919) and *The Razor's Edge* (1944). He was a prolific short story writer, often compared with Maupassant; Maugham's "Rain" is one of the most familiar contemporary short stories. *The Summing Up* (1938) and *A Writer's Notebook* (1949) are collections of essays.

Maupassant, Guy de (1850–1893), French naturalist short story writer and novelist. He became famous in 1880 when his short story *"Boule de Suif,"* considered a masterpiece of the naturalist genre, appeared in an anthology. After that, he published many volumes of short stories, including *La Maison Tellier* (1881) and *Claire de lune* (1884), as well as several novels, including *Bel-Ami* (1885).

Mauriac, François (1885–1970), a French writer who dealt with the themes of sin and redemption in his novels. Works in English translation include *Therèse* (1926), *Viper's Tangle* (1932), *Woman of the Pharisees* (1941), and *The Mask of Innocence* (1953). Mauriac also wrote plays, essays, and biographies, including *Life of Jesus* (1937), a reinterpretation of the historical Christ. He won the 1952 Nobel Prize for Literature.

Maury, Matthew Fontaine (1806–1873), U.S. naval officer. In 1842 Maury appointed supervisor of charts and instruments in the Navy Department, where he aided in organizing the Naval Observatory and Hydrographic Office. He studied winds and currents, compiling charts of oceanographic data from his own research and from information given by seamen. Maury's *The Physical Geography of the Sea* (1855) is considered the first textbook in oceanography. He served in the Confederate navy, 1862–1865.

Maximilian (1832–1867), in full Ferdinand Maximilian Joseph, archduke of Austria and emperor of Mexico, 1864–1867. At the age of 25, he was made governor of Lombardy and Venetia by his brother, Emperor Franz Josef of Austria. That same year he married the beautiful Carlota (Princess Charlotte of Belgium, 1840–1927). In 1863 Napoleon III of France laid plans to conquer Mexico and set up an empire there. The throne was offered to Maximilian, who was crowned in 1864. Although not an unkind ruler by the standards of the day, he could not supplant the strong feelings for native rule represented by Juárez. When Napoleon withdrew his troops from Mexico, Maximilian was captured. Given a

HENRI MATISSE

THE BETTMANN ARCHIVE

chance to escape, he refused it and went before the firing squad on June 19, 1867. Although Carlota lost her sanity, she survived for another 60 years.

Maximilian I (1459–1519), Holy Roman Emperor from 1493 to 1519. By his own marriages and those he arranged for his children, Maximilian extended the power and influence of the Austrian Hapsburgs to much of Europe, including the Netherlands, Spain, Burgundy, and Italy. He consolidated the imperial power in a central administration, suppressing minor local wars. Sometimes called the last knight, he was a fine horseman, archer, and gunner. He also encouraged the arts, wrote books, and was the patron of many artists, including Dürer. Maximilian's grandson succeeded him as Emperor Charles V.

Maxwell, James Clerk (1831–1879), British physicist. He became professor of experimental physics in 1871 at Cambridge University, where he published his greatest book, *Electricity and Magnetism* (1873). Maxwell is noted for his theoretical demonstration that light waves are electromagnetic. This theory, together with his ideas about electromagnetism in general, led to the discovery of radio communication. Maxwell also contributed to the knowledge of heat, color perception, and gases.

Mayer, Maria Goeppert (1906–1972), Polish-born U.S. physicist. She shared the 1963 Nobel Prize for Physics with J. Hans D. Jensen for her discovery and explanation of the shell structure of the atomic nucleus. In such a structure, the protons and neutrons move in independent orbits. Mayer worked at Columbia University on the separation of radium isotopes and later taught at the University of California.

Mayo, family name of two brothers, **Charles Horace** (1865–1939) and **William James** (1861–1939), doctors who in 1889 founded the Mayo Clinic in Rochester, Minn., one of the leading medical centers in the United States. Their father, **William Worrall Mayo** (1819–1911), was also a well-known doctor. The brothers also established the Mayo Foundation for Medical Education and Research in 1915. In World War I the Mayos were chief consultants in surgery to the U.S. Army. In their long surgical partnership, Charles specialized in goiter and neurosurgery, William in surgery of the stomach.

Mazarin, Jules (1602–1661), Italian-born French diplomat, successor to Richelieu and chief minister to Louis XIII and Louis XIV. In 1634 he was sent by Pope Urban VIII on a diplomatic mission to Paris, where he attracted the attention of Cardinal Richelieu. After Richelieu's death in 1642, Mazarin was appointed minister to Louis XIII. He retained that position under Louis XIV, becoming the most powerful man in France. Mazarin became a French citizen and in 1641 was created a cardinal. He brought the Thirty Years' War to a successful conclusion with the Treaty of Westphalia in 1648. He outmaneuvered and outlasted the populist uprising known as the Fronde (1648–1653) and negotiated international treaties to ensure French power.

Mazzini, Giuseppe (1805–1872), Italian national hero, a leading figure in the movement for Italian unification. In the 1820's Mazzini joined the Carbonari, a secret, nationalist revolutionary organization. In 1830 he was arrested and exiled. In 1831 he formed a new organization, *Giovine Italia,* or Young Italy, to work for a united republican Italy. In 1848 liberal revolutions broke out throughout western Europe, and Mazzini helped establish a republic in Rome, then under papal rule. When the pope fled, Mazzini became the senior member of the triumvirate ruling Rome. His orderly leadership of the city before it fell to French troops did much to localize the movement for national unity in Rome.

McCarthy, Joseph Raymond (1908–1957), U.S. politician. McCarthy was elected a senator from Wisconsin in 1946 and began his campaign in 1950 by claiming that a number of "known Communists" were working for the State Department. In 1952 he became chairman of the Permanent Subcommittee on Investigations and accused many prominent government persons of being Communists, including President Eisenhower. In 1954 he began a televised investigation of the U.S. Army, known as the Army-McCarthy Subcommittee hearings. His indiscriminate and unsupported accusations and his reliance on smear tactics lost him the support and respect of many. He was censured by the Senate.

McCarthy, Mary Therese (1912–1989), U.S. critic and novelist. After gaining a solid reputation as a critic, she published her first novel, *The Oasis,* in 1949. Her other novels, marked by a detached, satirical approach to their subjects, include *The Groves of Academe* (1952), *The Group* (1963), *Birds of America* (1971), and *Cannibals and Missionaries* (1979). Her autobiographical *Memories of a Catholic Girlhood* appeared in 1957.

McCormick, Cyrus Hall (1809–1884), U.S. businessman credited with inventing the reaper. In fact, the reaper was developed by his father, Robert McCormick, over a 30-year period. Cyrus demonstrated it in 1831 and patented it in 1834. He established the McCormick Harvesting Machine Company (now International Harvester) in Chicago in 1847. The basic features of the modern reaper are practically unchanged from the patented design.

LOOK

MARY MCCARTHY

McCullers, Carson Smith (1917–1967), U.S. novelist. She won critical acclaim for her sensitive novels *The Heart Is a Lonely Hunter* (1940), *Reflections in a Golden Eye* (1941), and *The Ballad of the Sad Café* (1951). All three were adapted for the screen. Her novel *The Member of the Wedding* (1946) was adapted for the Broadway stage in 1950. A posthumous collection of her stories and essays, *The Mortgaged Heart,* was published in 1971.

McKinley, William (1843–1901), 25th President of the United States, 1897–1901. A teacher, he resigned at the outbreak of the Civil War in 1861 to join the Union Army. McKinley was elected to Congress from Ohio in 1876 and held office until 1891, except for one term. He reached national prominence with the passage of his tariff bill of 1890. In 1891 he was elected to the first of two terms as governor of Ohio. Partly as a result of the backing of Mark Hanna, McKinley was nominated for the Presidency at the Republican convention of 1896. He was elected over William Jennings Bryan in 1896 and again in 1900. In 1898 he tried to prevent the Spanish-American War, but popular opinion overruled him. On September 6, 1901, McKinley was shot by Leon Czolgosz, a professed anarchist.

McLuhan, (Herbert) Marshall (1911–1980), Canadian author, expert on the mass media, perhaps best known for his statement, "The medium is the message." For McLuhan, the medium of communication is as influential as the content of the communication. *Understanding Media: The Extensions of Man* (1964) discussed technology as extensions of man's central nervous system. He also published *The Gutenberg Galaxy* (1962) and *War and Peace in the Global Village* (1968).

McMillan, Edwin Mattison: *See* Seaborg, Glenn T.

McNamara, Robert (1916–), U.S. businessman and government official, secretary of defense, 1961–1968. In 1946 he joined the Ford Motor Company, and in 1960 became its president. He was named secretary of defense by President John F. Kennedy, and retained the post under President Lyndon B. Johnson. From 1968 to 1981 he was president of the World Bank.

Mead, Margaret (1901–1978), U.S. anthropologist known for her studies of sexual roles and temperaments in Pacific societies. Several of her books are considered classics: *Coming of Age in Samoa* (1928), *Growing Up in New Guinea* (1930), and *Male and Female* (1949). She spent extensive time in the societies she studied, and acquired a reputation for reliable, detailed field reporting. Much of this research is found in her book *Culture and Commitment: A Study of the Generation Gap* (1970). The memoirs of her earlier years, *Blackberry Winter,* were published in 1972.

Meade, George Gordon (1815–1872), U.S. Army officer. During the Civil War he became a major general. In 1863 he reluctantly accepted command of the Army of the Potomac and led Union forces to victory at Gettysburg, but allowed Lee's army to escape. Grant took command in 1864, and Meade served under him for the duration.

Meany, (William) George (1894–1980), U.S. labor leader, first president of the AFL-CIO. He became secretary-treasurer of the American Federation of Labor (AFL) in 1939, and in 1952 became its president. When the AFL and the Congress of Industrial Organizations (CIO) merged in 1955 to form the most powerful U.S. labor organization, he became the group's president.

Medici, a Florentine family important in the political and cultural history of northern Italy from the 1400's to the 1700's. Among the most prominent Medicis were two queens of France: **Catherine de Médicis** (1519–1589), wife of Henry II, mother of Francis II, Charles IX, and Henry III, and instigator of the St. Bartholomew's Day Massacre (1572); and **Marie de Médicis** (1573–1642), wife of Henry IV and mother of Louis XIII. There were also three Medici popes: **Leo X** (**Giovanni de' Medici**, 1475–1521); **Clement VII** (**Giulio de' Medici**, 1478–1534), pope from 1523 to 1534; and **Leo XI** (**Alessandro de' Medici**, 1535–1605), pope in 1605.

The first prominent Medici was **Giovanni di Bicci** (1360–1429), who built a fortune in banking. His son **Cosimo** (1389–1464) assumed control of the domestic and foreign affairs of Florence. He began the Medici tradition of supporting the arts. Cosimo's grandson **Lorenzo the Magnificent** (1449–1492), the typical Renaissance prince, brought peace to Florence, which long had been feuding with Naples and the papacy. Lorenzo was a poet and a patron of the arts.

Lorenzo was succeeded by his son **Piero** (1472–1503). In 1494 Piero surrendered to an invading army of Charles VIII of France and fled from Florence. The Medicis were restored to power in 1512 owing to the friendship of Pope Julius II and Giovanni de' Medici.

A republican revolt broke out in Florence in 1527, and the Medicis were expelled. In 1530 the republic was forced to surrender to Holy Roman Emperor Charles V, who appointed **Alessandro de' Medici** (1511–1537) hereditary ruler of Florence. Alessandro was assassinated in 1537 and a descendant of another branch of the Medici family became grand duke as **Cosimo I** (1519–1574). In 1569 Florence became the grand duchy of Tuscany, which was ruled by Cosimo's descendants until 1737, when the line died out.

Meighen, Arthur (1874–1960), lawyer, businessman, statesman, and Conservative prime minister of Canada, 1920–1921 and 1926. He earned a reputation for being an excellent speaker and debater, and successfully argued against renewal of the Anglo-Japanese treaty.

Meir, Golda (1898–1978), Israeli prime minister from 1969 to 1974. Born in the Ukraine, she lived in the United States, then emigrated to Palestine in 1921. In the 1930's she toured Europe and the United States on behalf of the Zionist movement. A member of David Ben-Gurion's faction during the struggle for Israeli nationhood, Meir was one of the signers of the Proclamation of Independence (1948). She became prime minister in 1969. She was criticized, along with Moshe Dayan, for Israel's unpreparedness for the 1973 Arab-Israeli War. She resigned in 1974, but remained a leader in the Labor Party until her death.

Meitner, Lise (1878–1968), Austrian physicist whose research suggested the possibility of splitting the uranium nucleus (fission), thus setting off an atomic chain reaction. This discovery provided the basis for the atomic reactor and for the atom bomb. Meitner fled Austria after the Nazi occupation in 1938 and continued her nuclear research in Sweden.

Melville, Herman (1819–1891), U.S. author. Melville went to sea on a whaling ship at 22. His first novels, *Typee* (1846) and *Omoo* (1847), are based on his experiences with cannibals,

THE BETTMANN ARCHIVE

CATHERINE DE MEDICIS

UPI/BETTMANN ARCHIVE

GOLDA MEIR

MICHELANGELO

THE BETTMANN ARCHIVE

missionaries, and whalers in the South Seas. The story of Captain Ahab's vengeful pursuit of the white whale, *Moby-Dick* (1851), is now recognized as one of the world's greatest novels. *Billy Budd, Foretopman,* a short novel Melville left among his papers, was first published in 1924. Melville's other works include *The Piazza Tales* (1856), short stories.

Mencken, Henry Louis (1880–1956), U.S. editor and writer, America's most devastating social critic for over 20 years. From 1908 tc 1924 he was associated with the magazine *Smart Set.* He also served on the staff of the Baltimore *Sun,* 1906–1941. He edited the *American Mercury,* which he helped found, from 1924 to 1933. Mencken ridiculed contemporary letters, politics, and customs, as well as organized religion and big business. His research into American English was gathered in *The American Language,* published with revisions and supplements between 1919 and 1948. His satirical essays are collected in many books, including *Prejudices* (1922).

Mendel, Gregor Johann (1822–1884), Austrian monk and botanist who discovered the basic laws of heredity on which the science of genetics is founded. Born in Silesia, he became abbot of a monastery at Brünn (now Brno) and in 1856 began his experiments in its garden. Mendel grew many generations of garden peas, crossing and hybridizing them and keeping careful records. He discovered that certain hereditary units, now called genes, are dominant, others recessive; and that, through statistical laws, he could predict the characteristics that would appear most often in successive generations.

Mendeleev, Dmitri Ivanovich (1834–1907), Russian chemist who developed the periodic table for chemical elements, which he arranged according to their atomic weights. He published his famous paper on the classification of elements in 1869. In 1871, on the basis of his table, he predicted three elements yet to be discovered—gallium, scandium, and germanium.

Mendelssohn, Felix (1809–1847), in full, Jacob Ludwig Felix Mendelssohn-Bartholdy, German composer. Among his major works are his incidental music for William Shakespeare's *A Midsummer Night's Dream* (composed when he was 17), the *Italian* (1833) and *Scotch* (1842) symphonies, the oratorio *Elijah* (1846), and the piano pieces *Songs Without Words* (1830–1845).

Menninger, last name of two noted U.S. psychiatrists, **Karl Augustus** (1893–) and **William Claire** (1899–1966). With their father, **Dr. Charles Frederick Menninger**, they founded the Menninger Clinic (1919) and the Menninger Foundation (1946) for the study and treatment of mental illness. The clinic has grown into the largest psychiatric training center in the world. Karl Menninger's books include *The Human Mind* (1930), *Man Against Himself* (1938), *Love Against Hate* (1942), and *The Crime of Punishment* (1968). Among William Menninger's books are *Psychiatry in a Troubled World* (1948) and *You and Psychiatry* (1948).

Menuhin, Yehudi (1916–), U.S. violinist. A child prodigy, he made his formal debut at age seven as soloist with the San Francisco Symphony. Menuhin introduced concertgoers to Schumann's "lost" violin concerto. His virtuosity inspired Béla Bartók's Sonata for Violin. He was also responsible for initiating a cultural exchange between the United States and the Soviet Union, beginning in 1955. In 1963 he founded the Yehudi Menuhin School of Music in Suffolk, England.

Mercator, Gerardus (1512–1594), Flemish geographer and cartographer who produced the finest examples of early mapmaking. His earliest known map, showing the Holy Land, appeared in 1537. In his celebrated map of the world (1569), he introduced a system of map projection (known as the Mercator projection), in which latitude and longitude lines are at right angles to each other at any point on the map and the true direction from one point to another can be shown by a straight line.

Meredith, George (1828–1909), British poet and novelist. Meredith's works are noted for their wit and elegance, among them *The Ordeal of Richard Feverel* (1859), *The Egoist* (1879), and *Diana of the Crossways* (1885). His verse is contained in the volumes *Modern Love* (1862) and *Poems and Lyrics of the Joy of Earth* (1883).

Mérimée, Prosper (1803–1870), a French writer noted for his naturalistic short stories and novels. Among his literary works are *Carmen* (1845), on which Georges Bizet based his opera, and the historical novel *La Chronique du règne de Charles IX* (1829). He was appointed inspector of archaeological monuments in 1831 and wrote authoritative works on the archaeology of France, including *Notes de voyage* (1835–1840).

Metternich, Prince Clemens Wenzel Nepomuk Lothar von (1773–1859), Austrian minister of foreign affairs from 1809 to 1848. By his diplomacy and his arrangement of a marriage between Napoleon and Marie Louise of Austria in 1810, he protected Austria from the worst effects of the Napoleonic wars. After Napoleon's defeat, he led the Congress of Vienna (1814–1815) and instituted the Metternich system of European politics, which relied on the balance of power. For this and for encouraging the suppression of all popular movements for the next 30 years, he became the symbol of reaction. In the popular revolutions of 1848, he was the first to be driven from office.

Meyerbeer, Giacomo (1791–1864), real name Jacob Liebmann Meyer Beer, German composer of spectacular Romantic operas. He enjoyed his first success after he moved to Paris in 1826. His fame rests on *Robert le Diable* (1831), *Les Huguenots* (1836), *Le Prophète* (1849), and *L'Africaine* (1865).

Michelangelo Buonarroti (1475–1564), Italian sculptor, painter, architect, and poet. A member of the minor Florentine nobility, he studied art for a time with the painter Ghirlandajo. He soon attracted the attention of Lorenzo de' Medici and entered the Medici household. Because of unrest in Florence, Michelangelo went to Rome about 1496; there he carved a *Pietà* that immediately made him famous. He returned home and in 1504 created another masterpiece, a colossal *David* for the city of Florence. The next year Pope Julius II called Michelangelo to Rome, intending to have him carve a memorial tomb. Julius and Michelangelo, both strong-willed, intense, and egotistical, soon disagreed. Michelangelo disappeared from Rome for a time, but by 1508 had returned to work on the ceiling of the Sistine Chapel. His tremendous fresco, depicting the Creation, covers the vault and upper walls. It took four years to complete; Michelangelo himself painted nearly all of it. Its force and intensity brought him recognition as the greatest artist of his day. Pope Julius died in 1513; though Michelangelo continued to work on the statues for his tomb, there were continual disputes over the completion of the monument. For the new pope, Leo X, a Medici, he planned several works, including the Medici Chapel, but political unrest in Florence interrupted the work. In 1534 Michelangelo, again in Rome, was commissioned by the next pope to paint the *Last Judgment* on the end wall of the Sistine Chapel (completed 1536–1541). Late in life, Michelangelo began to work on the design for the unfinished basilica of St. Peter's, Rome. He also wrote some of his finest poetry in those years.

Michener, James Albert (1907–), U.S. writer. His *Tales of the South Pacific* (1947) won a Pulitzer Prize and was made into the musical *South Pacific* (1949). His other books include *The Bridges at Toko-Ri* (1953), a novel of the Korean War; and the best-selling novels *Hawaii* (1959), *The Source* (1965), *Iberia* (1968), *Centennial*

(1974), *Chesapeake* (1978), *The Covenant* (1980), *Poland* (1983), *Texas* (1985), and *Alaska* (1988). Among his works of nonfiction is *Kent State: What Happened and Why* (1971).

Mies van der Rohe, Ludwig (1886–1969), German-born U.S. architect noted for his glass and steel structures. After working with Walter Gropius and Le Corbusier, and serving as director of the Bauhaus, 1930–1933, Mies came to the United States in 1938 and in 1944 became a citizen. He was made director of the Department of Architecture at Illinois Institute of Technology in Chicago; he designed the institute's campus and buildings. His first masterpiece was the German pavilion at the International Exposition in Barcelona, Spain; erected in 1929 and demolished after the exposition, it became an architectural legend. Mies is known also for the Barcelona chair (designed for the pavilion), for steel and glass apartment towers on the lakefront in Chicago, and for the Seagram Building in New York.

Milhaud, Darius (1892–1974), French composer. He was a member of The Six, a group of French composers who had considerable influence on music during the 1920's. His polytonal music enraged many who heard it; his suite *Protée* (1920) caused a riot when it was performed. His other works include the ballet *La Création du monde* (*The Creation of the World,* 1923), and the operas *Medée* (1939) and *David* (1954).

Mill, John Stuart (1806–1873), British philosopher and economist. Mill was a utilitarian, holding that public policy should be based on what will bring pleasure to the most people. As an economist, he explored the meaning of value and its relation to supply and demand. Mill wrote *Principles of Political Economy* (1848), *On Liberty* (1859), *Utilitarianism* (1863), and *The Subjection of Women* (1869). His *Autobiography* was published in 1873.

Millay, Edna St. Vincent (1892–1950), U.S. poet. Her first work, *Renascence and Other Poems* (1917), revealed her youthful romanticism and established her reputation. Succeeding volumes included *Second April* (1921), *The Buck in the Snow* (1928), and *Huntsman, What Quarry?* (1939). *The Harp Weaver* (1923) won a Pulitzer Prize and showed her exceptional talent as a sonnetteer. *Make Bright the Arrows* (1940) and *The Murder of Lidice* (1942) are concerned with political events. Millay also wrote the libretto to Deems Taylor's opera *The King's Henchman* (1927), and the plays *Aria da Capo* (1921) and *Two Slatterns and a King* (1921).

Miller, Arthur (1915–), U.S. playwright whose *Death of a Salesman*

NEW YORK PUBLIC LIBRARY

JOHN STUART MILL

(1949) is one of the best-known contemporary U.S. dramas. His first success, *All My Sons* (1947), dealt with wartime profiteering. In *The Crucible* (1953), Miller used a story of witchcraft hysteria in New England of the 1600's to comment on the political witchhunts of the 1950's. Other plays include *A View from the Bridge* (1955), *After the Fall* (1963), *The Price* (1968), and the television film *Playing For Time* (1980). Miller published an autobiography, *Timebends,* in 1987.

Miller, Henry (1891–1980), U.S. author, best known for his novels of outspoken sexuality, including *Tropic of Cancer* (1934) and *Tropic of Capricorn* (1938). During the 1930's he became a leading figure among U.S. writers living in Paris. Condemned as obscene, Miller's books were not published in the United States until the 1960's. His other works include *The Colossus of Maroussi* (1941), an account of travel in Greece, and the sharply criticized *The Air-Conditioned Nightmare* (1945), about life in the United States.

Millikan, Robert Andrews (1868–1953), U.S. physicist who studied cosmic rays and gave them their name. For his isolation and measurement of the electron and his exact photoelectric determination of the light quantum, he was awarded the 1923 Nobel Prize for Physics.

Milne, Alan Alexander (1882–1956), British writer of whimsical children's stories that made Pooh, Piglet, and Eeyore classic figures in the world of children's literature. During his early career as a writer, he was an assistant editor of the magazine *Punch* (1906–1914). His books for children, written especially for his son Christopher Robin, are *When We Were Very Young* (1924), *Winnie-the-Pooh* (1926), *Now We Are Six* (1927), and *The House at Pooh Corner* (1928). Milne also wrote numerous comic plays (*Mr. Pim Passes By,* 1919) and novels.

Milton, John (1608–1674), English poet. His early poems, "L'Allegro," "Il Penseroso," and "Lycidas," show the influence of his extensive learning in the classics. During the 1640's Milton's interests turned gradually toward theological and political affairs. He strongly supported the Puritan leaders who controlled Parliament in opposition to Charles I and the Church of England. He wrote tracts supporting the Puritan cause and individual liberties, including the famous *Areopagitica* (1644). In 1649 Milton became Latin secretary to Cromwell's Council of State. By 1652 Milton had lost his eyesight; with the restoration of the monarchy in 1660, he lost most of his estate and narrowly missed imprisonment. Blind and out of favor, Milton retired and began *Paradise Lost,* which he dictated to his daughters. It was published in 1667. This great epic, telling the story of how Satan was expelled from Heaven and of how he took revenge by securing the expulsion of Adam and Eve from Eden, is one of the greatest works in all literature. In 1671 Milton published *Paradise Regained,* an epic on Christ's temptation in the wilderness, and *Samson Agonistes,* a poem in the form of Greek drama telling the story of the blinded Old Testament hero.

Minamoto Yoritomo (1147–1199), Japanese warlord and first of the ruling shoguns, or high military commanders, of the imperial court. By the twelfth century the emperors no longer controlled Japan, and continual wars between the great families kept Japan in a state of chaos. Yoritomo subdued the other great nobles and, after a series of fierce wars, established a military bureaucracy that brought order to Japan. Rather than becoming emperor, he kept the title shogun and organized the political framework for Japan's long period of military feudalism, dominated by the samurai (warrior) class.

Minuit, Peter (c 1580–1638), Dutch colonial governor of New Amsterdam, founder of what is now New York City. In 1625 he was appointed director-general of the Dutch West India Company's settlements in North America. In the following year he purchased Manhattan Island from the Indians for goods and trinkets valued at 60 guilders (about $24).

Mirabeau, Count de; Honoré Gabriel Riqueti (1749–1791), French statesman, the leading political figure at the beginning of the French Revolution. In 1789 he was elected a delegate to the Estates-General. Becoming a secret adviser to the king, he tried to put the king at the head of the revolution by forming a new government patterned on Britain's constitutional monarchy. Neither the king nor the National Assembly understood or would agree to his plan, and his attempt to moderate the revolution failed. Nevertheless he was elected president of the National Assembly in 1791, but died shortly after.

Miró, Joan (1893–1983). Spanish painter associated with the surrealists. Miró's paintings are distinguished by their striking use of color and their enlarged, simple forms. They include *Dog Barking at the Moon* (1926), *Women and Kite Among the Constellations* (1939), and the tile murals *Sun and Moon* (1958) in the UNESCO building in Paris. Besides his painting, his works include sculpture, engraving, and book illustrations.

Mishima, Yukio (1925–1972), Japanese novelist and playwright, born Kimitake Hiroaka. A passionate devotee of physical fitness and the ancient samurai arts, he formed the Tatenokai (Shield Society) with a group of young followers. His novels are remarkable for their ironic humor and sensuous detail. They include the tetralogy *The Sea of Fertility* (translated 1972–1974) and *The Sailor Who Fell from Grace With the Sea* (translated 1965). After failing to arouse popular reaction against the impotence of the Japanese army under the constitution, Mishima committed ritual suicide.

Mistral, Frédéric (1830–1914), French poet, a leader in the Provençal literary renaissance, known for his long narrative poems and lyrics in the *langue d'oc.* His most famous poem is *Mirèio* (1859). In 1905 he shared the Nobel Prize for Literature.

Mistral, Gabriela (1890–1957), pen name of Lucila Godoy de Alcayaga, Chilean poet and educator, the first Latin American to win the Nobel Prize for Literature, 1945. Following this award, she wrote "Appeal for Children," which helped to establish UNICEF. She represented Chile at the League of Nations and at the United Nations. Major volumes of her poetry include *Desolación* (1922), *Tala* (1938), and *Lagar* (1954). A bilingual edition, *Selected Poems of Gabriela Mistral,* appeared in 1971.

Mitchell, Maria (1818–1889), U.S. astronomer. Her discovery of a new comet in 1847 was rewarded with a gold medal from the king of Denmark. In 1905 she was elected to the Hall of Fame.

Mitchell, William (Billy) (1879–1936), U.S. Army officer; advocate of strong air power and an independent air force. He organized and commanded the American Expeditionary Air Force in World War I and rose to the rank of brigadier general. After the war Mitchell publicly criticized the War and Navy departments for mishandling aviation forces. His charges led to a court-martial at which he was convicted of insubordination. Rather than serve the sentence of a five-year suspension from duty, he resigned (1926) from the Army. He spent the rest of his life lecturing and writing in support of his ideas.

Mitterand, François (1916–), president of France (1981–). After serving in the French Resistance during World War II, Mitterand entered parliament in 1946 and held various ministerial posts from 1947 until 1958. He became the head of a unified Socialist Party in 1971 and revived its fortunes. He lost the presidential election to Charles de Gaulle in 1965 and to Valéry Giscard d'Estaing in 1974. In 1981, however, he defeated Giscard d'Estaing and gave France a left-of-center government for the first time in 23 years. He nationalized banks and some key industries, and supports NATO and a strong defense.

Modigliani, Amedeo (1884–1920), Italian painter and sculptor, noted for his portraits characterized by elongated faces and torsos. In his short, poverty-stricken life, he created an unmistakable style of art, examples of which are *Gypsy Woman and Baby* and *Reclining Nude.* He died of tuberculosis in a charity hospital.

Mohammed: *See* Muhammad.

Moholy-Nagy, László (1895–1946), Hungarian painter and designer associated with the Bauhaus school, both in Europe and at his "New Bauhaus" in Chicago. He was best known for his theories of nonrepresentational art consisting of purely visual elements—light, space, and color. He pioneered in the techniques of photomontage and photograms.

Molière (1622–1673), pen name of Jean Baptiste Poquelin, French writer of comedies. He became a theatrical manager in Paris in 1643. In 1646 he joined a troupe of actors and toured the provinces. Louis XIV saw him act in Paris in 1658 and was so pleased that "the king's comedians," as the Molière players were called, enjoyed royal patronage for 15 years. The presentation of his *Les Précieuses ridicules (The Ridiculous Misses)* in 1669 began a new era of satire. His plays held up to ridicule the follies, affectations, and frailties of human nature, satirizing misers, bores, pedants, and hypocrites. Molière's most famous plays include *L'École des femmes* (*The School for Wives,* 1662), *The Misanthrope* (1666), *Le bourgeois gentilhomme* (*The Would-be Gentleman,* 1670), and *Le Malade imaginaire* (*The Imaginary Invalid,* 1673).

Molnár, Ferenc (1878–1952), Hungarian playwright, famed for his witty and sophisticated dialogue and his sense of irony. He became, for a time, Europe's most successful playwright with such dramas as *Liliom* (1909), *The Guardsman* (1910), *The Swan* (1920), and *The Red Mill* (1923). In 1940 he settled in New York, where he lived until his death. A musical version of *Liliom* was produced in New York in 1945 as *Carousel.*

Molotov, Vyacheslav Mikhailovich (1890–1986), premier of the Soviet Union, 1930–1941, known for his anti-Western views and rigid Stalinist position. During his youth he organized Bolshevik student groups and helped found the newspaper *Pravda.* He played a major role in the 1917 Bolshevik revolution and by 1930 had become head of the Soviet of Peoples' Commissars, a post equivalent to that of premier. He also became foreign minister in 1939. Replaced as premier by Stalin in 1941, Molotov remained foreign minister until 1949, attending major international conferences. In conflict with Khrushchev, he lost all his influential offices and retired from government in 1962.

Mondrian, Piet (1872–1944), originally Pieter Cornelis Mondriaan, Dutch painter of the nonobjective school, noted for his brightly colored arrangements of squares and straight lines. His best known works include *Broadway Boogie-Woogie* (1942–1943) and *Composition in White, Black, and Red.*

Monet, Claude (1840–1926), French painter, one of the founders of impressionism. Between 1863 and 1865 he began working in the open air, where he could study the subtle effects of light on the subject matter. An important work from this period is *Le Dejeuner sur l'herbe* ("The Picnic," 1865). In 1874 his painting *Impression* gave the name to the new school of art, which at first was attacked. From 1899 to 1926, gradually losing his eyesight, Monet painted his water lily masterpieces.

Monnet, Jean (1888–1979), French political economist, considered the father of the European Economic Community (the EEC, or Common Market). Monnet served on Allied war materials committees during both world wars. In 1945 he was asked to draw up a plan for the postwar economic rehabilitation of France; the Monnet Plan went into effect in 1947 and modernized the French economy. Monnet's next major effort was the forming of the European Coal and Steel Community (ECSC) in 1950. Out of the success of the ECSC, Monnet developed plans for a common market; it came into being in 1957 as the European Economic Community.

Monroe, James (1758–1831), fifth President of the United States, 1816–1824. Through the influence of Virginia governor Thomas Jefferson, with whom he studied law, Monroe was elected to the Virginia assembly in 1782, and then became a delegate to Congress. In 1788 he was sent to the state convention called to ratify the federal Constitution; a determined anti-Federalist, Monroe spoke vigorously against adoption. Elected to the U.S. Senate in 1790, Monroe continued his opposition to Federalist policies and became a leader in the party led by Jefferson (then called the Republicans). In 1794 Monroe went to France as U.S. minister; though he was not particularly successful in this or his later diplomatic posts, he did aid in arranging the Louisiana Purchase. He returned to state politics but in 1811 was appointed secretary of state. Monroe remained at the head of the State Department until his own election to the Presidency in 1816. In 1820 he was reelected without opposition. As President, Monroe is remembered for the Monroe Doctrine, 1823, which was based in large part on work by Monroe's secretary of state, John Quincy Adams. It warned that the United States would not tolerate European interference in the affairs of the western hemisphere. At the end of his second term, Monroe retired to private life. He was elected to the Hall of Fame in 1930.

Monroe, Marilyn (1926–1962), U.S. movie actress and sex symbol, one of the legendary Hollywood stars of the 1950's, born Norma Jean Baker. Her best-known films include *Bus Stop* (1956), *Some Like It Hot* (1959), which enabled her to display her considerable comic talents, and *The Misfits* (1960). Her personal life and her marriages to Joe DiMaggio and Arthur Miller were the subject of intense public interest. Monroe committed suicide.

HENRY MOORE

THE BETTMANN ARCHIVE

Montagu, (Montague Francis) Ashley (1905–), British-born U.S. anthropologist and writer, well known for his works repudiating racial and feminine inferiority. The 1949 UNESCO "Statement on Race," mainly Montagu's work, states that scientific study proves race to be a social creation and not a biological reality. This idea was developed further in *Man's Most Dangerous Myth: The Fallacy of Race* (1942). *The Natural Superiority of Women* (1953) destroyed some long-standing beliefs concerning male superiority.

Montaigne, Michel Eyquem de (1533–1592), French essayist. In 1571 he began to write the series of essays by which he is remembered today. Among the most well known are "On Experience," "On Books," and "On The Power of the Imagination." The first two books of essays appeared in 1580 and were republished, together with a third, in 1588. Montaigne's essays are notable for the grace and freshness of their style. Sentences and anecdotes from the ancients are mingled with the author's own remarks about himself and humanity in general.

Montcalm, Marquis de; Louis-Joseph de Montcalm-Gozon (1712–1759), French general remembered for his part in the Battle of Quebec. Montcalm was sent to North America in 1756 to command French forces against the British. He had several early victories at Fort Ontario (1756), Fort William Henry (1757), and particularly at Ticonderoga (1758). Forced to retreat to the citadel at Quebec because of French losses elsewhere, Montcalm was decisively defeated in September, 1759, by a British force led by General James Wolfe on the Plains of Abraham near Quebec. Both generals were wounded in the battle; Wolfe died almost immediately, Montcalm the next day.

Montesquieu, Baron de La Brède et de; Charles Louis de Secondat (1699–1755), French historian and philosopher. His first published work, *Persian Letters* (1721), is a daring and subtle satire on the follies of the day. In 1734 he published a history of Rome. The work on which his fame chiefly rests, *De l'Espirit des lois (The Spirit of Laws),* appeared in 1748. In it he showed a preference for the independent freedom enjoyed by the legislative, executive, and judicial powers in England during his time. Montesquieu's thinking greatly influenced the framers of the U.S. Constitution.

Montessori, Maria (1870–1952), Italian physician and educator. In 1894 she became the first woman in Italy to graduate from the University of Rome with a medical degree. Interested in the needs of retarded children, she developed a method of teaching based on giving the child a large amount of freedom within a carefully controlled environment. Her students achieved such good results that the Montessori methods were later applied to normal children. Among her works are *The Montessori Method* (1912), *The Secret of Childhood* (1936), and *The Discovery of the Child* (1948).

Monteverdi, Claudio (1567–1643), Italian composer, the first great composer of operas. From 1590 to 1613 he was a court musician in the service of the duke of Mantua. From 1613 until his death he was head conductor of the choir at St. Mark's Cathedral in Venice. His works include the well-known operas *Orfeo* (1607) and *Arianna* (1608), and several books of madrigals.

Montezuma II (c 1466–1520), the last Aztec emperor of Mexico. He took the throne in about 1502 and waged wars of conquest that added territory in present-day Honduras and Nicaragua to his realm. When the Spaniards under Hernán Cortés invaded Mexico in 1519, they were at first thought to be gods, fulfilling the tradition that Quetzalcoatl would return. The Aztecs did not at first resist, and Cortés's men marched to the capital and seized the emperor. When his brother at last led an Aztec uprising, Montezuma was fatally wounded during the Aztec attack.

Montgolfier, Joseph Michel (1740–1810), French inventor who, with his brother **Jacques Étienne** (1745–1799), invented the first passenger-carrying balloon. He began experiments on balloons in about 1782; the two men successfully demonstrated their balloon on June 5, 1783. Louis XVI granted the Montgolfiers 40,000 francs so that they could give all their attention to aeronautics. Joseph also invented a parachute and a hydraulic press.

Montgomery, Bernard Law, 1st Viscount Montgomery of Alamein (1887–1976), British field marshal. Montgomery entered military service in 1908 and fought in France during World War I. During World War II he commanded the third division, which was evacuated from Dunkirk in June, 1940. As commander of the British eighth army in 1943, he drew together troops shaken by numerous losses and went on to win stunning victories in Africa, defeating Rommel's Afrika Corps at El-Alamein, Egypt. During the Normandy invasion, 1944, he led the 21st army group, which received the German surrender on May 4, 1945. In 1951 Montgomery was appointed deputy supreme commander of North Atlantic Treaty Organization forces. In 1958 he retired from this post, publishing his *Memoirs* the same year.

Moore, Henry (1898–1986), English sculptor. Influenced chiefly by primitive art and by the surrealist art of contemporary France, Moore's usual subject was the human figure in a standing, sitting, or reclining position. His major works include *Three Standing Figures* (1947–1948), *Madonna and Child* (1949), and *Reclining Figure* (1957–1958) at the UNESCO building in Paris.

Moore, Marianne Craig (1887–1972), U.S. poet. Her first book, *Poems,* was published in England in 1915. Her first American volume, *Observations,* appeared in 1924. In 1951 her *Collected Poems* received the Pulitzer Prize and the National Book Award. Other works include a volume of essays, *Predilections* (1955), and the verse collections *Like a Bulwark* (1956) and *O To Be a Dragon* (1959). She also translated the *Fables of La Fontaine* (1954).

Moravia, Alberto (1907–), pseudonym of Alberto Pincherle, Italian novelist known for his themes of boredom, indifference, and loveless sexuality, particularly in marriage. He wrote primarily about upper middle-class Italian society, often in the environment of fascism, as in *The Time of Indifference* (1929), *The Garden Party* (1941), *The Conformist* (1951), and *Conjugal Love* (1951). Moravia also treated the psychology of youth, as in *Two Adolescents* (1944). Two volumes of brief, grimly realistic portraits of Italian life after World War II are *Roman Tales* (1954) and *New Roman Tales* (1959). Later works include the novel *The Empty Canvas* (translated 1962) and *The Voice of the Sea and Other Stories* (translated 1978).

More, Sir Thomas (1478–1535), English statesman, humanist, and scholar. More rose to a position of favor under Henry VIII, who entrusted him with confidential missions and in 1521 knighted him. In 1529 More succeeded Thomas Wolsey as lord chancellor, but resigned in 1532 in dispute with Henry's wish to become head of the church in England. In 1534 More was accused of high treason and imprisoned in the Tower of London. He steadfastly refused to condone Henry's divorce or to renounce the pope's authority, and in 1535 he was beheaded. More was beatified in 1886 and canonized in 1935. More's great book, *Utopia* (1516), describes an ideal state.

Morgan, John Pierpont (1837–1913), U.S. financier who founded the prosperous private banking house J. P. Morgan and Company in 1895. Morgan built up a railroad empire, largely by reorganizing bankrupt lines, and took part in many famous financial battles over control of railroads. He bought out Andrew Carnegie in 1901 and formed the great United States Steel Corporation.

His son, **John Pierpont Morgan, Jr.** (1867–1943), succeeded his father as head of the Morgan firm. He negotiated war munitions purchases during World War I and later negotiated loans to France and Russia.

Morison, Samuel Eliot (1887–1976), U.S. historian. Morison's studies combined historical research with personal observation; for his Pulitzer Prize-winning biography of Columbus, *Admiral of the Open Sea* (1942), Morison sailed Columbus's route across the Atlantic. Morison's other studies include *The History of U.S. Naval Operations in World War II* (15 volumes, 1947–1962), *The Oxford History of the American People* (1965), *John Paul Jones* (1959, also a Pulitzer Prize winner), and *The European Discovery of America* (2 volumes, 1971–1974).

Morley, Christopher Darlington (1890–1957), U.S. author, editor, and critic. A writer of light verse and essays, he wrote *Parnassus on Wheels* (1917) and *The Haunted Bookshop* (1919), excursions into the world of books and book selling; *The Trojan Horse* (1937), a modern version of the Troilus and Cressida story; and *Kitty Foyle* (1939). Morley edited several magazines and was for many years a columnist.

Morris, Gouverneur (1752–1816), U.S. statesman and diplomat, an early supporter of the American Revolution. As a member of the Continental Congress, in 1778 he presented the report calling on Britain to recognize the independence of the colonies as a prerequisite to peace negotiations. In 1787 Morris represented Pennsylvania in the Constitutional Convention and was a member of the committee that drew up the final draft of the Constitution.

Morris, Robert (1734–1806), American financier and signer of the Declaration of Independence. He went from England to Philadelphia at 13, became a clerk in a mercantile business, and in 1754 became a partner in the firm. He lent money to the government during the Revolutionary War and in 1782 organized the Bank of North America. Morris served as U.S. senator from Pennsylvania, 1789–1795.

Morris, William (1834–1896), English poet and designer. Morris was educated as an architect but later turned to the manufacture of furniture and household decorations. Advocating handcrafted materials, he opened an influential decorating firm in 1861. Later he founded the Kelmscott Press, a private printing house devoted to artistically produced books. As a poet, Morris was associated with the Pre-Raphaelites. He is best known for historical narratives in verse, including *The Life and Death of Jason* (1867), *Sigurd the Volsung* (1876), and *The Earthly Paradise* (1868–1870). He was a prolific writer in many fields and also wrote prose romances such as *The Well at the World's End* (1896).

Morse, Samuel Finley Breese (1791–1872), U.S. painter and inventor who developed the electric telegraph. Morse's famous words, "What hath God wrought?" ushered in the age of telegraphic communication. In 1835 Morse developed a working model of the electric telegraph, but it was not until 1843, after many discouragements, that he was given $30,000 by Congress for an experimental line between Washington and Baltimore. On May 24, 1844, the first public message was sent over the line. Morse also invented the code used in telegraphic messages, now used worldwide. Morse was one of the most accomplished American portraitists and helped found the National Academy of Design in 1826. He was elected to the Hall of Fame in 1900.

Moseley, Henry Gwyn-Jeffreys (1887–1915), British physicist whose research established the atomic numbers and the order of the elements. Moseley studied the number of electrons emitted during the disintegration of radium and later determined the number of positive charges in atoms of gold and other elements. Moseley's brilliant studies of the x-ray spectra of the elements contributed greatly to the knowledge of atomic structure. He enlisted in the army during World War I and died at Gallipoli.

Moses, Anna Mary Robertson (Grandma Moses) (1860–1961), U.S.

GRANDMA MOSES

LOOK

painter. In her late 70's, her hands crippled with arthritis, she began painting farm scenes and country landscapes in oil, using old Currier and Ives prints as guides. Lacking training and unfamiliar with modern art, she developed a style known as modern primitive.

Motherwell, Robert (Burns), (1915–), American painter, leading representative of the abstract expressionists, known particularly for his use of black and white and of bulky forms and shapes. Noted examples of his work are *The Little Spanish Prison* (1941), *Elegies to the Spanish Republic* (begun in 1943), and *Two Figures with Cerulean Blue Stripe* (1960). He was also a master of the collage and gave it serious and sensitive treatment as an art form.

Mountbatten, formerly **Battenberg**, a princely family of German extraction. English members of the family anglicized the name to Mountbatten during World War I.

Louis Alexander Mountbatten, 1st Marquess of Milford Haven (1854–1921), oldest son of Prince Alexander of Hesse and Countess von Haucke, was naturalized as a British subject, joined the navy, and became first sea lord in 1912.

Louis Mountbatten, 1st Earl Mountbatten of Burma (1900–1979), the younger son of Louis Alexander Mountbatten, was supreme Allied commander in Southeast Asia (1943–1946) and viceroy and governor-general of India. He later was named admiral of the fleet and first sea lord.

Mozart, Wolfgang Amadeus (1756–1791), Austrian composer. A child prodigy, Mozart learned to play the harpsichord at the age of three and was composing two years later. His father, his sister, and he toured Europe as concert musicians until he was 16. Thereafter he returned to his native Salzburg and sought employment. From 1782 on, his operas made him famous; he settled in Vienna and became a friend of Haydn. Mercurial and extravagant, he died deep in debt. At the time of his death, he was working on a Requiem Mass; his fear that he was writing it as his own requiem apparently hastened his death. Mozart was the foremost composer of the classical period and had enormous influence on 19th-century composers. His works include many keyboard pieces; concertos for most contemporary orchestral instruments; 41 symphonies; and many operas, including *The Marriage of Figaro* (1786), *Don Giovanni* (1787), *Così fan tutte* (1790), and *The Magic Flute* (1791), all modern repertory favorites.

Muhammad (c 570–632), Arabian prophet and founder of Islam, the Muslim religion. He was born in Mecca. Orphaned at an early age, he was raised by an uncle, learning Bedouin ways as a shepherd and camel driver. In 595 he married a wealthy widow and became a merchant. In about 610, after years of meditation, Muhammad felt called to be a prophet to his people and to teach a new faith. He had little success in Mecca, and in 622, with a handful of followers, he went to Yathrib, which later became Medina, or the city of the prophet. The Muslim calendar begins with the date of Muhammad's flight, or Hegira, from Mecca. Muhammad later returned victorious to Mecca and laid the basis for the expansion of Islam to all of Arabia.

Muhammad Ali: *See* Ali, Muhammad.

Muhammad Reza Shah Pahlevi (1919–1980), shah of Iran. He became ruler in 1941 after the eviction of his father (suspected of collaborating with the Germans) by Soviet and British troops. Iran's petroleum wealth enabled him to carry out extensive land and social reforms. Opposition from both orthodox Muslims and liberals, however, led to a revolution in 1978, and he fled the country. Pahlevi died in exile in Egypt.

Mühlenberg, Henry Melchior (1711–1787), German-born American colonial clergyman. In 1742 he came to Pennsylvania as a missionary to Lutheran congregations. Soon he was overseeing nearly all the Lutheran churches in the northern colonies. He organized the first Lutheran synod, in 1748. Mühlenberg and his sons were active patriots in the American Revolution. Many later members of the family were prominent in Lutheran education.

Muir, John (1838–1914), Scottish-born U.S. naturalist and explorer, an influential American conservationist. Muir was a pioneer in the conservation movement in the United States. It was partly through his efforts that Sequoia and Yosemite Valley were made national parks. His writings include *Our National Parks* (1901), *The Yosemite* (1912), and *Story of My Boyhood and Youth* (1913). The natural wonders named for him include Alaska's Muir Glacier and Muir Woods National Monument, a redwood forest near San Francisco.

Mulroney, (Martin) Brian (1939–), Canadian politician and businessman, prime minister of Canada since September, 1984. A lawyer and former mining company executive, he was elected leader of the Progressive Conservative Party in 1983. Mulroney became prime minister after the 1984 general election in which his party won the largest parliamentary majority in Canadian history.

Munch, Edvard (1863–1944), Norwegian expressionist artist. His distinctive style began to appear in the early 1890's, and is evident in *The Sick Child* (1886) and *Spring* (1889). Munch's mature paintings use strong colors to portray powerful emotions. In addition to his oils, he also achieved a reputation for woodcuts and lithographs.

Murasaki, Lady Shikibu (c 978–c 1026), Japanese writer known as the author of Japan's greatest literary work, *Genji Monagatari,* or *The Tale of Genji* (English translation 1935). Her real name is unknown; Murasaki is the heroine of the work. *The Tale of Genji* is considered one of the finest novels written anywhere in the world. It expresses keen sensitivity to human emotions and the sadness of life.

Murat, Joachim (1767–1815), king of Naples, 1808–1815, as Joachim I Napoleon. He served under Napoleon, whose sister Maria he married in 1800. For his service in Napoleon's Austrian campaigns, he was awarded the throne of Naples. After Napoleon's defeat in 1814, Murat allied himself with the Austrians. When, in 1815, Napoleon returned to power, Murat tried to rejoin him, but his troops revolted and the Austrians captured his kingdom. He was court-martialed and shot in 1815.

Murillo, Bartolomé Esteban (1617–1682), Spanish painter of religious themes. Born in Seville, he went to Madrid, where he was befriended by Diego Velázquez and learned much by copying old masters. By 1650 he was recognized as the leader of the Sevillian school of art. He left about 400 paintings, including *Immaculate Conception* (1652) and *The Vision of St. Anthony* (1656).

Murray, Philip (1886–1952), Scottish-born U.S. labor leader who helped found the Congress of Industrial Organizations (CIO). He served as international vice president of the United Mine Workers of America, 1920–1942. He helped to organize the CIO in 1935, serving as president, 1940–1952, and the United Steel Workers of America in 1942, as president until his death.

Murry, Kathleen Beauchamp (Katherine Mansfield) (1888–1923), British writer of stream of consciousness short stories. Among collections of her short stories are *Bliss* (1920), *The Garden Party* (1922), and *The Dove's Nest* (1923). Her short stories, which depend more on atmosphere than on plot, capture a few hours in her characters' lives and are distinguished by sensitive characterization and subtle insights.

Muskie, Edmund Sixtus (1914–), former U.S. senator and former secretary of state. A veteran of World War II and a Democrat from Maine, Muskie served in the state legislature from 1947 to 1951 and in 1955 was elected governor of Maine. Three years later he was elected U.S. senator and was reelected three times. Muskie was the Democratic candidate for Vice President in the 1968 election, which the Republicans won. A leading candidate for the Democratic Presidential nomination in 1972, he withdrew from campaigning when his candidacy lost momentum. A firm liberal, Muskie was an influential senator until April, 1980, when President Carter named him secretary of state to succeed Cyrus Vance. He served until January, 1981.

Mussolini, Benito (1883–1945), Italian dictator, 1922–1943, founder of the Italian Fascist Party. Before World War I, he edited the socialist newspaper *Avanti* in Milan. When the war began, he became a militant nationalist and urged Italy to back the Allies against Germany. During widespread social and political disorder after the war, Mussolini founded (1919) the first of his *Fasci di combattimento,* groups of black-shirted followers that attacked socialists and others on the political left. He was elected to parliament in 1921. In 1922 his followers marched on Rome, whereupon King Victor Emmanuel III asked Mussolini to become premier. Mussolini soon suppressed all opposition, and by 1928 Italy had become a fascist state. Conflict with the Roman Catholic Church was ended by the Lateran Treaty of 1929, which created Vatican City. In 1935 Mussolini attacked Ethiopia and in 1936 gave aid to the rebel forces of Francisco Franco in the Spanish Civil War. As the ally of Nazi Germany, Mussolini occupied Albania in 1939 and in 1940 entered World War II. In July, 1943, after defeats in Africa and Sicily, Mussolini was deposed and imprisoned. Rescued by the Germans, Mussolini returned to Italy in September as leader of a puppet government. Forced to flee in April, 1945, he was captured and shot by partisans, who displayed his corpse in a public square.

Mussorgsky, Modest Petrovich (1839–1881), Russian composer. Although he was famous for his orchestral pieces and songs, Mussorgsky is now best remembered for his opera *Boris Godunov* (1874), his piano suite *Pictures at an Exhibition* (1874), and the orchestral suite *Night on Bare Mountain* (1867), rearranged by Rimski-Korsakov as *Night on Bald Mountain.* He wrote three unfinished operas, including *Khovanshchina* (completed by his friend Rimski-Korsakov), and many songs.

Mutsuhito (Meiji) (1852–1912), emperor of Japan, 1867–1912. He succeeded his father, Osahito, in 1867 and in the following year assumed the name Meiji, meaning "year of enlightened peace." During his long reign as emperor, he created the basis for a modernized Japanese state and introduced many Western ideas. He abolished feudalism, moved his capital from Kyoto to Yeddo (now Tokyo), and agreed to a new constitution and a parliamentary government.

NAPOLEON BONAPARTE

THE BETTMANN ARCHIVE

Myrdal, (Karl) Gunnar (1898–1987), Swedish social and political economist, influential in the development of the social welfare program in Sweden. Myrdal particularly studied the related influences of economics, society, and institutions on government policy, and for this work shared the 1974 Nobel Prize in Economics. In 1938 Myrdal undertook a Carnegie Corporation study of the problems of blacks in American society, from which came his classic book, *An American Dilemma* (1944). His other books include *Beyond the Welfare State* (1960) and *The Challenge of World Poverty* (1970).

N

Nabokov, Vladimir (1899–1977), Russian-born U.S. novelist. His most famous novels in English are *Lolita* (1955) and *Pale Fire* (1962). Among his other noted works, originally in Russian, are *King, Queen, Knave* (1928) and *Invitation to a Beheading* (1938). His autobiography, *Speak, Memory,* appeared in 1966.

Nader, Ralph (1934–), U.S. lawyer known for his role as consumer advocate and for his continued attacks on governmental and corporate irresponsibility to the individual. His *Unsafe at Any Speed* (1965) blamed the Detroit auto industry for putting profit before safety. Automobile safety laws passed in 1967 were largely a result of his well-documented exposures of negligence. In 1967 Nader drew together full- and part-time workers to assist him. "Nader's Raiders" investigated such areas as unsafe gas pipelines, pollution, workers' safety legislation, and the use of dangerous herbicides. Among his writings are *Taming the Giant Corporation* (1976) and *Who's Poisoning America* (1981).

Napier, John (1550–1617), Scottish mathematician who invented the system of logarithms. In a treatise published in 1614, Napier showed the correspondence between arithmetic and geometric progressions and demonstrated the use of logarithms as a means of facilitating computations. He was among the first to use the present system of decimal notation. Napier also originated several formulas in trigonometry and invented mechanical devices similar to modern calculating machines.

Napoleon I (or Napoleon Bonaparte) (1769–1821), emperor of France, 1804–1815. He was born in Corsica and educated at military schools in France. A military officer, he reached the rank of brigadier general in 1794 during the French Revolution. In 1796 he married Josephine de Beauharnais. After campaigns in Italy and Egypt, he gained control of the French government, assuming almost absolute power as first consul in 1799. In 1802 he was elected first consul for life and in 1804 he was proclaimed emperor. At home, Napoleon centralized the administration of France and reformed the nation's educational, financial, and legal systems. Abroad, he conducted a series of brilliant military campaigns and by 1810 Napoleon dominated most of the European continent. In 1809 Napoleon divorced Josephine and in 1810 married Archduchess Marie Louise of Austria. She bore him a son the following year. During 1808–1814, in the Peninsular War, Napoleon fought Britain, Portugal, and guerrillas in Spain in the Iberian Peninsula. Although generally successful, the war was extremely costly. The turning point in Napoleon's fortunes, however, was a decision to invade Russia in 1812. Forced to retreat through a severe Russian winter, his army suffered terrible losses. In 1813, at Leipzig, he confronted an alliance of European powers and was defeated at the Battle of the Nations. Napoleon abdicated on April 11, 1814, and was exiled to the island of Elba in the Mediterranean. The European powers refused to accept Napoleon II as his successor. He escaped and returned to France on March 1, 1815. Beginning what came to be called the Hundred Days of his rule, he resumed the war against the European powers. He met final defeat in June, 1815, at Waterloo. He was deported to the island of St. Helena, where he died.

Napoleon III (or **Louis Napoleon**) (1808–1873), born Charles Louis Napoleon Bonaparte, emperor of France, 1852–1870. A nephew of Napoleon I and the son of Louis Bonaparte, king of Holland, he grew up in exile. He began his attempts to regain the French throne in the 1830's, calling on the people's memories of the splendor of Napoleon's reign contrasted with the dullness of the "citizen king," Louis Philippe. In 1840 he invaded France and was imprisoned, but he escaped in disguise. Finally the revolution of 1848 forced Louis Philippe to abdicate. Louis Napoleon was elected to the new National Assembly and then became president of the republic. He arranged a coup to enable him to stay in office, and in 1852 was elected emperor as Napoleon III, beginning the Second Empire. As emperor he sought to restore France's past glory without ruinous wars, but few of his foreign policy plans succeeded. His reign was ended by the Franco-Prussian War in 1870. He was defeated in the first battle and fled to England, where he died.

Nash, Ogden (1902–1971), U.S. poet and humorist noted for his use of outrageous grammar, spelling, and rhymes. His work appeared in magazines and was collected in such volumes as *I'm a Stranger Here Myself* (1938), *Good Intentions* (1942), and *Everyone But Thee and Me* (1962). He also collaborated on the book and lyrics of the Broadway hit *One Touch of Venus* (1943).

Nasser, Gamal Abdel (1918–1970), president of Egypt, 1956–1970. In 1952 he was a leader of a coup that ousted King Faruk I of Egypt. In 1954 Nasser became premier and, after becoming president, he nationalized the Suez Canal. In 1958 Egypt and Syria joined to form the United Arab Republic, of which Nasser became president. Syria later withdrew from the union. In domestic affairs, Nasser's major achievement was land reform. In foreign affairs he encouraged militant Arab opposition to Israel. Early in his rule he promoted development of a Third World made up of nations supporting neither the United States nor the Soviet Union.

Nast, Thomas (1840–1902), U.S. cartoonist, best known for his cartoons attacking Boss Tweed's political machine, Tammany Hall. His Civil War cartoons made him famous. In the 1870's he added to his reputation with a series of cartoons in *Harper's Weekly* that aided in breaking up the corrupt rule of the Tweed Ring in New York. Nast created the Democratic Party symbol, the donkey, the Republican elephant, and the Tammany tiger. His fat, jolly, bearded Santa Claus became the standard version of the Christmas figure.

Nation, Carry Amelia Moore (1846–1911), U.S. temperance leader. Her first husband died of alcoholism, and in 1900 she began a series of hatchet-wielding raids on saloons. She was often arrested and won national recognition for her temperance efforts. She later took up lecturing, warning of the evils of fraternal organizations, tobacco, corsets, and immodest dress.

Nebuchadnezzar (or **Nebuchadrezzar**) **II** (d. 562 B.C.), king of Babylon, 605–562. His most famous battle, described in the Old Testament, came in 597, when King Jehoiachin of Judea rebelled against him. Nebuchadnezzar conquered Jerusalem, and the king and 10,000 Jews were carried to Babylon as captives. In 589 Zedekiah, who had succeeded to the Judean throne, revolted. Nebuchadnezzar then destroyed Jerusalem, blinded the king, and carried nearly all Jews into captivity. In Babylon, Nebuchadnezzar built the terraced Hanging Gardens, one of the Seven Wonders of the World.

Nehru, Jawaharlal (1889–1964), the first prime minister of independent India. He worked with Mohandas Gandhi in the struggle for Indian independence from Britain and was five times elected president of the Indian National Congress, India's dominant

GAMAL NASSER

NEBUCHADNEZZAR

ISAAC NEWTON

political party. He spent many years in jail for participation in civil disobedience campaigns protesting British rule. Nehru became India's first prime minister in 1947, a position he held until his death. He was a neutralist in international affairs and a leader of the Afro-Asian bloc. Nehru advocated modern scientific technology and industrialization, hoping to transform India's primitive economy into a modern socialist state. His daughter, Indira Gandhi, later became prime minister.

Nelson, Horatio, Viscount Nelson (1758–1805), English admiral and naval hero. From 1793 until his death, he was almost continually at sea, fighting the French. He lost the sight in his right eye in 1794 during the Corsican operation and his right arm in an attempt to take Santa Cruz de Tenerife in 1797. In 1797 he was given the Mediterranean command; he defeated a French fleet at the battle of the Nile (1798). In 1801 Nelson attacked Copenhagen and siezed the Danish fleet. In 1805 he annihilated the combined French and Spanish fleets off Cape Trafalgar, ensuring England's naval supremacy for the next century. He was shot during the battle and died aboard his flagship, H.M.S. *Victory.* His private life was notable for his attachment to Lady Emma Hamilton, for whom he left his wife.

Nero (37–68 A.D.), in full Nero Claudius Caesar Drusus Germanicus, Roman emperor, 54–68. Nero was legendary for his ruthlessness and cruelty. He was responsible for the murder of Claudius's son and a daughter, his own mother, two of his wives, and many others whom he thought dangerous. During Nero's reign much of Rome was destroyed by fire. Public opinion blamed him; he tried to blame the Christians. Later he built a magnificent new city. In 68 his troops revolted. Nero fled Rome and committed suicide.

Neruda, Pablo (1904–1973), pen name of Ricardo Eliezer Neftali Reyes y Basoalto, Chilean poet and diplomat. He was awarded the 1971 Nobel Prize for Literature. Closely associated with the Allende regime in Chile, he died shortly after its collapse. His *Veinte poemas de amor y una cancion desesperada* (1924) became one of the most popular books of poetry in the Spanish language. It was translated into English as *Twenty Love Poems and a Song of Despair* (1970). Other works translated into English are *Elementary Odes* (*Odas elementales,* 1954–1957, translated 1961) and *The Heights of Macchu Picchu* (*Alturos de Macchu Picchu,* 1948; translated 1967).

Nervi, Pier Luigi (1891–1979), Italian architect and design engineer. Nervi used modern materials, particularly reinforced concrete, to create powerful, graceful public buildings in many countries. He emphasized the importance of structural design in buildings such as the Exhibition Hall in Turin, Italy (1948–1949). Working with other architects, Nervi also designed the buildings for the 1960 Olympic Games in Rome and (with Marcel Breuer) the Paris headquarters of UNESCO.

Neutra, Richard (1892–1971), Austrian-born U.S. architect, one of the leading American exponents of the international school of architectural design and a leader in architecture for social welfare (*Survival Through Design,* 1954). Much of his work was concerned with the design of schools and health centers. Of his private homes, the most famous are the Lowell House (1927–1929), the Joseph von Sternberg home (1936), and the Kaufman Desert House, (1946–1947).

Nevski, Alexander: *See* Alexander Nevski.

Newman, Paul (1925–), U.S. film actor and director, noted for his roles as a casual, humorous, and tough-minded antihero. His more than 40 films include *Cat On a Hot Tin Roof* (1959), *The Hustler* (1961), *Cool Hand Luke* (1967), *The Sting* (1973), and *The Color of Money* (1986), for which he won an Academy Award as best actor.

Newton, Sir Isaac (1642–1727), English physicist and mathematician. From 1665 until 1667, Newton, living in the country with his family, made his greatest discoveries. They include the binomial theorem; the calculus; the reflecting telescope; the nature of light and color; and the law of gravitation. His *Principia* (1687), explaining the law of gravitation, proved that the laws of physics and mechanics could be expressed in simple mathematical formulas; this discovery was one of the greatest steps in the advancement of science. During his last years, Newton feuded with Leibniz; Leibniz had also discovered the calculus, but Newton claimed Leibniz had plagiarized his work.

Ney, Michel (1769–1815), French military leader, Napoleon's most brilliant marshal. During the Napoleonic wars, Napoleon called Ney "the bravest of the brave." Ney became a marshal of France in 1804. As commander of the rear guard during Napoleon's disastrous retreat from Russia, in 1812–1813, he saved the remnants of the French army. When Napoleon was exiled to Elba, the new king made Ney a peer and sent him with an army to oppose Napoleon's return to France in 1815. Instead, Ney rejoined Napoleon and fought at Waterloo. Defeated, he was condemned for treason and shot.

Ngo Dinh Diem (1901–1963), president of South Vietnam, 1955–1963. He began his career in the French colonial civil service. During the guerrilla warfare against the French in the early 1950's, he was captured by Viet Minh (nationalist) forces, but was later released. At the end of the war against the French in 1954, Vietnam was divided. Diem returned from self-imposed exile to become prime minister of South Vietnam. In 1955 he became president, ruling with his brother, Ngo Dinh Nhu. In the early 1960's, Diem, a Catholic, was accused of severe persecutions against the Buddhists and of creating a dictatorship in South Vietnam. He and his brother were deposed and assassinated in November, 1963.

Nicholas II (1868–1918), last czar of Russia, 1894–1917, and the last of the Romanov dynasty. Though a believer in absolute rule, Nicholas lacked the forcefulness to be a strong ruler or to resist the changes of his time. Though the revolutions that followed Russia's defeat by Japan in 1905 forced him to grant a constitutional government, he gave it little power. Popular dissatisfaction continued to grow during World War I, as Russia faced military defeats and economic problems. In 1915 Nicholas left the court to lead the army, leaving the government in the hands of the empress **Alexandra** (1872–1918). Alexandra, a German princess and granddaughter of Queen Victoria, was unpopular with many Russians because of her German birth. This, combined with the influence of the corrupt monk Rasputin, weakened the monarchy further. Nicholas abdicated in 1917, but neither the monarchy nor the moderate Kerensky government could stand against revolution. In 1918 all the imperial family, unable to leave Russia, were killed by the Bolsheviks.

Niebuhr, Reinhold (1892–1971), German-born U.S. Protestant theologian. Ordained a minister of the Evangelical (German Lutheran) Church, he taught for more than 32 years at Union Theological Seminary, New York. Niebuhr spoke for idealism without illusion and realism without despair. He helped to found the politically liberal Americans for Democratic Action and the World Council of Churches. His many books include *The Nature and Destiny of Man* (1941–1943).

Nietzsche, Friedrich Wilhelm (1844–1900), German philosopher. His theories were widely interpreted and frequently misinterpreted. He is most famous for the notion of the superman (*Übermensch),* whom he contrasted with man as he is, with the "last man," and with God. He condemned Christianity as a refuge for weakness. Nietzsche taught at Basel, 1869–1879, and for a time was a close friend of Richard Wagner; they later quarreled bitterly. In 1889 he suffered a mental breakdown and was insane until his death; his works were little known until shortly before he died. The best known of his books are *The Birth of Tragedy from the Spirit of Music* (1872), *Beyond Good and Evil* (1886), and, the most famous, *Thus Spake Zarathustra* (1883–1885).

Nightingale, Florence (1820–1910), British nurse and hospital reformer, considered the founder of modern nursing. She received her training in 1851 and served as superintendent of a small hospital, totally reorganizing the nursing facilities. In 1854 she took 38 women to nurse the Crimean War wounded, effecting a revolution in sanitation and personal care and becoming a heroine to the soldiers. In 1860 she opened a training school for nurses.

Nijinsky, Vaslav (1890–1950), Russian ballet dancer. He made his debut in St. Petersburg with the Imperial Ballet in 1907. In 1909 he was taken by the impresario Diaghilev to Paris, where he danced the title role in the premiere of Stravinsky's ballet *Petrouchka.* In Paris, Nijinsky was acclaimed for his choreography and for his spectacular performances in *Afternoon of a Faun, Rite of Spring,* and *Spectre de la Rose.* In 1917 he became incurably insane.

Nimitz, Chester William (1885–1966), commander of the U.S. fleet in the Pacific during World War II. During World War I, he was chief of staff to the Atlantic Fleet submarine commander. From 1942 to 1945 the Pacific fleet was instrumental in defeating the Japanese. Nimitz represented the United States at the surrender aboard the USS *Missouri,* September 2, 1945. He was made a five-star fleet admiral in 1944, retired in 1947, and later headed a UN commission for India and Pakistan.

FLORENCE NIGHTINGALE

THE BETTMANN ARCHIVE

Nixon, Richard Milhous (1913–), 37th President of the United States, 1969–1974, the first President ever to resign from office. In an aggressive campaign, he was elected to the House of Representatives in 1946. He became an active member of the House Un-American Activities Committee and sponsored a 1948 bill to control communism in the U.S. He then served in the Senate, 1950–1952. Nixon was Vice-President under Eisenhower, 1953–1961. The Republican Presidential candidate in 1960, he lost to John F. Kennedy. Beaten again in the 1962 California gubernatorial race, he retired from politics, but came back in 1968 to defeat Hubert Humphrey for the Presidency. In his first term, he established detente with China and the Soviet Union, visiting both countries in early 1972. He carried on the war in Southeast Asia despite increasing public protest. In the 1972 elections, he was reelected by a landslide over George McGovern and, through the negotiations of Henry Kissinger, his secretary of state, ended the Vietnam War. However, an investigation of the 1972 break-in at Democratic headquarters in the Watergate complex and of the Nixon reelection committee's campaign practices grew into a scandal involving top White House aides. The question of Nixon's own knowledge of the Watergate affair led to impeachment hearings. In July, 1974, a House committee approved three articles of impeachment against him. On August 8, 1974, Nixon resigned.

Nkrumah, Kwame (1909–1972), African nationalist leader. He led the British colony of the Gold Coast in West Africa to independence in 1957; it became the nation of Ghana. Nkrumah served as its first prime minister and then as its first president. He was a strong advocate of Pan-Africanism, refused to take sides in the Cold War, and urged small nations to act through the United Nations. Nkrumah was ousted by military officers in 1966.

RUDOLPH NUREYEV

UPI/BETTMANN ARCHIVE

Nobel, Alfred Bernhard (1833–1896), Swedish industrialist and inventor. In 1866 he invented dynamite, which he manufactured along with synthetic rubber and other industrial products. Nobel's industrial holdings made him wealthy; he left most of his estate to establish a fund for the Nobel prizes.

Norris, Frank (1870–1902), born Benjamin Franklin Norris, U.S. naturalistic novelist. Norris's best-known works are *McTeague* (1899), which deals with San Francisco's lower classes; *The Octopus* (1901), a novel about the conflict between wheat farmers and the railroad industry; and *The Pit* (1903), about wheat speculation in a commodities exchange.

Nureyev, Rudolph (1938–), Russian ballet dancer and choreographer. With Dame Margot Fonteyn of the Royal Ballet, Nureyev danced internationally in such classic ballets as *Romeo and Juliet, Swan Lake,* and *Giselle,* as well as in modern works by Martha Graham and Paul Taylor. He defected to the West in 1961 while in Europe with a Soviet troupe. In 1983 he became director of the Paris Opera Ballet.

Nyerere, Julius Kambarage (1922–), African nationalist leader who led Tanganyika to independence in 1961. He served as its first prime minister and then as its first president. In 1964 Nyerere became president of Tanzania, formed when Tanganyika and Zanzibar united, serving until 1985. He helped form the Organization of African Unity, and promoted neutrality in foreign affairs.

O

O'Casey, Sean (1880–1964), Irish dramatist, a leading member of the Irish literary revival. His two most famous works, *Juno and the Paycock* (1924) and *The Plough and the Stars* (1926), were produced by Dublin's Abbey Theatre. Originally a strong nationalist, O'Casey later moved to a socialist position; the intensely nationalist Abbey Theatre rejected his play *The Silver Tassie* in 1928. O'Casey eventually moved to England, where he wrote a six-volume autobiography, *Mirror in My House* (1956).

Odets, Clifford (1906–1963), U.S. dramatist, one of the founders of the Group Theater, 1930. Odets's plays were acclaimed for their realism and for their criticism of social attitudes and policies in the United States.

Among his most successful plays were *Waiting for Lefty* (1935), *Awake and Sing* (1935), *Golden Boy* (1937), and *The Country Girl* (1950).

O'Faoláin, Seán (1900–), Irish novelist, essayist, and biographer, best known for his idyllic novel, *A Nest of Simple Folk* (1933) and for the biographies *Life Story of De Valera* (1933) and *King of the Beggars: A Life of Daniel O'Connell* (1938). *The Irish, A Character Study* (1949) established him as the finest contemporary interpreter of Irish life. His stories were collected in 1958; he later published *The Talking Trees* (1970).

Offenbach, Jacques (1819–1880), German-born French composer, creator of the operetta form. His most famous work is the grand opera *The Tales of Hoffman (Contes d'Hoffmann).* He wrote some hundred works for the stage; they are characterized by elegance, wit, and satire. Still well known today are *La Périchole, La Vie Parisienne,* and *La Belle Hélène. Tales of Hoffmann* was unfinished at Offenbach's death; Ernest Guiraud (1837–1892) orchestrated it and added the famous barcarolle.

O'Flaherty, Liam (1896–1984), Irish novelist. His first novel, *Thy Neighbor's Wife,* appeared in 1924. He published his most famous work, *The Informer,* in 1925. He also published several collections of short stories, including *The Wild Swan* (1932) and *Two Lovely Beasts* (1948), and the autobiographical *Shame the Devil* (1934).

Oglethorpe, James Edward (1696–1785), founder of the Georgia colony in North America. In 1729 Oglethorpe conceived the idea of establishing a colony in America for the poor and persecuted. In 1732 he obtained a charter to found such a colony. In the next year he arrived with the first colonists and founded the city of Savannah. Oglethorpe served as governor of Georgia from 1733 to 1743.

O'Hara, John Henry (1905–1970), U.S. writer. Born in Pottsville, Pa., which provided the setting for his realistic novels and short stories of upper class America, he published his first novel, *Appointment in Samarra,* in 1934. Among his later novels are *Butterfield 8* (1935), *Ten North Frederick* (1955), *From the Terrace* (1958), and *The Instrument* (1967). O'Hara also wrote short stories, including the well known Pal Joey stories.

O. Henry: *See* Porter, William Sidney.

Ohm, Georg Simon (1787–1854), German physicist. In 1827 he announced the principle of the relationship between the force of a current, the current's strength, and the resistance of a conductor, now known as Ohm's law. The ohm, a unit of electrical resistance, was named in his honor.

Oistrakh, David Feodorovich (1908–1974), Soviet violinist and teacher. In 1937 Oistrakh won first prize at an international competition in Brussels. He first toured the United States in 1955. In 1956 he introduced in Western Europe a new violin concerto by Shostakovich, dedicated to him by the composer. His son, **Igor Davidovich Oistrakh** (1931–), also a violinist, often played with and conducted his father in concerts and on recordings.

O'Keeffe, Georgia (1887–1986), U.S. painter of decorative abstracts and stark, detailed studies of organic forms, especially flowers. She first gained prominence in 1916 when Alfred Stieglitz included her drawings in his show at "291," his New York gallery. O'Keeffe and Stieglitz later were married. Among her well-known paintings are *Black Iris* (1926), *Black Cross* (1929), and *Poppies* (1950).

Oldenburg, Claes (1929–), U.S. pop sculptor whose work expresses American themes in the form of giant hamburgers, ice cream cones, and all varieties of store merchandise. He created "total environments," filling his exhibit *The Store* (1961) with his plaster creations and creating a theater for mixed media and happenings. Among his more recent works are *Clothespin* (1976) and *Batcolumn* (1977).

Olivier, Sir Laurence Kerr (1907–1989), British actor, director, and producer noted for his interpretations of Shakespeare. In 1922 he began his career at Stratford-upon-Avon and became famous with the Old Vic company. Olivier filmed four of Shakespeare's plays: *Hamlet,* which won him an Academy Award, *Henry V, Richard III,* and *Othello.* Among his non-Shakespearean productions, *Oedipus* and *Uncle Vanya* were outstanding. Olivier appeared in many other films, including *Wuthering Heights* (1939) and *The Entertainer* (1960), and won Emmy Awards for performances in the television films *Love Among the Ruins* (1973) and *Brideshead Revisited* (1982). He was made director of the National Theatre of England in 1963. He was knighted in 1947 and made a life peer in 1970.

Olmsted, Frederick Law (1822–1903), U.S. landscape architect who designed some of the best-known public parks in the United States. In 1857, in association with Calvert Vaux, he won first prize in a competition to design New York's Central Park. After directing this project, Olmsted designed parks in Chicago, Boston, and Montreal, as well as the Capitol grounds in Washington. A leading advocate of national parks, Olmsted was Yosemite's first park commissioner.

Omar Khayyám (d. c 1123), Persian astronomer and poet whose *Rubáiyát,* a collection of quatrains celebrating life and love, is one of the masterpieces of world literature. During his lifetime, Omar served as philosopher, mathematician, and astronomer to Sultan Malik Shah. Today his fame, especially in the Western world, rests upon the *Rubáiyát* as translated into English in 1859 by Edward FitzGerald.

O'Neill, Eugene Gladstone (1888–1953), U.S. playwright. O'Neill's plays realistically explore the dark side of human experience. They include *Beyond the Horizon* (1920), *Anna Christie* (1922), *Desure Under the Elms* (1924), *Strange Interlude* (1928), and *The Iceman Cometh* (1946). O'Neill experimented with new stage techniques and symbolism in such dramas as *The Emperor Jones* (1921), *The Hairy Ape* (1922), and *The Great God Brown* (1925). His attraction to Greek drama is revealed in *Mourning Becomes Electra* (1931), modeled on Aeschylus' *Oresteia.* The autobiographical *Long Day's Journey Into Night,* first produced on Broadway in 1956, won a posthumous Pulitzer Prize. O'Neill was awarded the 1936 Nobel Prize for Literature.

Oppenheimer, J. Robert (1904–1967), U.S. theoretical physicist, a leader in the development of the atomic bomb. From 1943 to 1945 he directed the atomic bomb laboratory at Los Alamos, N.M. In 1947 he was appointed director of the Institute for Advanced Study at Princeton, N.J., serving until 1966. He was chairman of the Atomic Energy Commission's general advisory committee, 1947–1952. In 1954 he was declared a security risk because of alleged leftist activities, but in 1963 he was cleared of the charges. In the same year he received the Fermi Award of the Atomic Energy Commission.

Orff, Carl (1895–1982), German composer. Orff's music tends to be austere, rhythmic, and sonorous. His most familiar work is *Carmina Burana* (1936), settings of medieval Latin songs. His *Music for Children* (1930–1935; revised 1950–1954), for kindergartens and primary schools, is used around the world. Also notable are his dramatic works *Antigone* (1943–1948) and *Oedipus* (1956–1959), settings of poems by Hölderlin.

Ormandy, Eugene (1899–1985), Hungarian-born U.S. conductor. After years of guest conducting, he became conductor of the Minneapolis Symphony in 1931. He was appointed conductor of the Philadelphia Orchestra in 1938 and later became its musical director.

Orozco, José Clemente (1883–1949), Mexican painter whose art reflects his strong social convictions. With Diego Rivera, he led the renaissance in Mexican art during the 1920's. In this period, he painted some of his most outstanding murals in government buildings in Mexico City. His well-known *Zapatistas,* in the Museum of Modern Art, N.Y., is typical of his strong, simple style, as are *Prometheus* (1930) and *The Dive Bomber* (1936–1939).

Ortega y Gasset, José (1883–1955), Spanish philosopher and humanist. During the Spanish Civil War, he taught in Argentina, Peru, and Portugal, not returning to Spain until 1945. In his writings, Ortega examined the basic structure of political and social institutions, relating them to contemporary literature and art. Among his many works, *The Modern Theme* (1923), *The Dehumanization of Art* (1925), and *The Revolt of the Masses* (1929) are best known.

Orwell, George (1903–1950), pen name of Eric Arthur Blair, British author. His best-known works are the novels *Animal Farm* (1945) and *Nineteen Eighty-four* (1949). Other works include accounts of Orwell's own experiences and reflections, such as *Homage to Catalonia* (1938), one of the best books on the Spanish Civil War; and books on social conditions, such as *The Road to Wigan Pier* (1937), about unemployment among British coal miners.

Osceola (c 1800–1838), Seminole Indian leader. Born in Georgia, he settled in Florida. In 1835 the U.S. government attempted to move the Seminoles west of the Mississippi. Osceola and his people declared war. After two years, Osceola accepted an invitation to peace negotiations. Walking into a trap, he was seized and imprisoned in St. Augustine, Fla. He was later sent to a prison in South Carolina, where he died.

Osler, Sir William (1849–1919), Canadian physician. Osler did research on spleen and blood diseases, heart infections, and malaria. He taught for more than 20 years in the United States; the methods he used in training medical students at Johns Hopkins were widely adopted. His classic book is *Principles and Practice of Medicine* (1891).

Oswald, Lee Harvey (1939–1963), presumed assassin of President John F. Kennedy. He served in the Marine Corps, 1956–1959, and was twice court-martialed. He went to the Soviet Union to become a citizen; dissatisfied, he returned to the United States in 1962. After Kennedy was shot in a motorcade in Dallas, Oswald was arrested. Two days later he was killed by Jack Ruby, a Dallas nightclub owner.

THE BETTMANN ARCHIVE

OVID

Otto I (Otto the Great) (912–973), German king who revived the idea of a European empire. Claiming to be successor to the Caesars, he was crowned Holy Roman Emperor in 962. The son of Henry I, he was crowned king of Germany in 936. He spent the early part of his reign subduing rebellious nobles and tightening control over the church. In 955 he won a decisive victory over the Magyars and ended the Hungarian threat to Germany. In 962, while in Italy quelling disturbances on behalf of the papacy, Otto was crowned emperor by Pope John XII. His actual dominions were Germany and Italy; the empire's prestige came mainly from the church's support.

Ovid (c 43 B.C.–18 A.D.), Latin name Publius Ovidius Naso, Roman poet. He became a favorite of the emperor Augustus, but in 8 A.D. he was banished, for unknown reasons, to Tomi on the Black Sea, where he spent the rest of his life. His masterpiece, *Metamorphoses,* a long poem with change and transformation as its main theme, retells the principal Greek and Roman myths. His *Ars Amatoria (The Art of Love),* a poem on the refinements of love and seduction, has been a perennial favorite.

Owen, Robert (1771–1858), British social reformer. He started to work when he was ten. By the age of 19 he was manager of a Manchester cotton mill; at 28 he was part owner. He exercised paternalistic rule over his employees, something unheard of in the British factory system, demanding that his workmen live temperate lives. In 1824 Owen came to the United States and tried to found a socialist community at New Harmony, Ind., but the scheme failed. In 1828 he returned to England, where his ideas helped stimulate the British cooperative movement. Owen wrote *A New View of Society* (1813).

P

Paderewski, Ignace Jan (1860–1941), Polish musician, composer, and statesman, one of the most successful concert pianists the world has known. He made his debut in Vienna in 1887 and soon became a virtuoso, famous for his highly personal interpretations. His most famous composition, the *Minuet in G* in the style of Mozart, was written to trick his friends, who believed no one could write music comparable to Mozart's. Paderewski was a lifelong supporter of Polish independence. He helped establish the Polish republic; in 1919 he served briefly as its first prime minister.

Paganini, Niccolò (1782–1840), Italian violinist and composer whose innovative techniques revolutionized violin playing. His recitals throughout Europe, especially in Vienna, Paris, and London, were so successful that he amassed a fortune before he retired in 1835. A romantic, flamboyant figure on the concert stage, he specialized in performing 24 original caprices so difficult to play that they demanded a new technique on the violin.

Pahlevi: *See* Muhammad Reza Shah Pahlevi.

Paine, Thomas (1737–1809), English-born American political writer whose stirring pamphlets spurred the drive for colonial independence. He came to America in 1774 and soon joined the staff of the *Pennsylvania Magazine* in Philadelphia. His first popular pamphlet, *Common Sense* (1776), demanded an immediate declaration of independence. He enlisted in the colonial army that year and also began a pamphlet series, *The Crisis.* In 1787 Paine visited France and England. On the appearance of Edmund Burke's hostile *Reflections on the French Revolution,* Paine wrote a fierce defense of the revolution, *The Rights of Man* (1791–1792), in which he called on the English to follow the example of the French and set up a constitutional republic. The British government outlawed Paine for treason, but he had fled to France where, as an honorary citizen, he became a member of the Convention. Paine remained in France, writing his *Age of Reason* (1794–1796) about his deist beliefs, which were interpreted as atheism. Although Paine returned to the United States in 1802, he lived in obscurity till his death. He was elected to the Hall of Fame in 1945.

Palestrina, Giovanni Pierluigi da (c 1525–1594), Italian composer of religious music whose style of counterpoint influenced later church composers. Palestrina held several church posts as chapel master. His many works include more than 250 motets, about 100 masses, and a large number of hymns, lamentations, and secular madrigals.

Palmer, Alice Freeman (1855–1902), U.S. educator who built Wellesley into a first-rate women's college. She went to the newly organized college in 1879 as head of the Department of History, and then served as president, 1881–1888. Palmer also served as dean of women at the University of Chicago, 1892–1895.

Paracelsus (c 1490–1541), real name Theophrastus Bombastus von Hohenheim, Swiss alchemist and physician who established the role of pharmaceutical chemistry in medicine. Paracelsus disproved many accepted medical theories, taught the use of specific remedies instead of indiscriminate bleeding and purging, and introduced many new medicines. However, much of his work was colored by his beliefs in magic and alchemy.

Paré, Ambroise (1510–1590), French doctor who introduced significant changes into Renaissance surgery. While serving as an army surgeon, he developed the practice of using a ligature to tie arteries instead of cauterization to control hemorrhage during amputations. He also turned surgeons away from treating wounds with boiling oil. The French kings Henry II, Francis II, Charles IX, and Henry III were all treated by him.

Parker, Dorothy Rothschild (1893–1967), U.S. writer known for her biting wit, satirical light verse, and sophisticated short stories. She began her literary career as drama critic for *Vanity Fair* and book reviewer for *The New Yorker.* Among her books of poetry are *Enough Rope* (1926), *Death and Taxes* (1931), and *Not So Deep as a Well* (1936). Collections of short stories include *Laments for the Living* (1930) and *Here Lies* (1939). She also wrote several plays, including *Ladies of the Corridor* (1954).

Parkman, Francis (1823–1893), U.S. historian. Fascinated by the wilderness, Parkman lived for some time among the Indians of the Rocky Mountains, gaining firsthand experience for such works as *The California and Oregon Trail* (1849) and *The Conspiracy of Pontiac* (1851). Parkman's masterpiece was a seven-volume history, *France and England in the New World,* published 1865–1892.

Parnell, Charles Stewart (1846–1891), Irish political leader who led the struggle for Irish self-government. He was elected as a home rule candidate to the House of Commons in 1875, where he drew attention to the Irish cause by obstructing parliamentary business. He allied himself with Prime Minister Gladstone until Gladstone's home rule bill failed and Gladstone resigned in 1886. In 1887 the London *Times* accused Parnell and his followers of crimes committed by Irish nationalists. His vindication on this charge added to his prestige. In 1890 he was named as corespondent in a divorce suit filed against his mistress, Mrs. O'Shea; the scandal destroyed his public career.

Pascal, Blaise (1623–1662), French mathematician, scientist, and philosopher. A child prodigy, Pascal wrote a work on conic sections before he was 17; at 18 he invented a calculating machine. He contributed a number of theories and methods to mathematics and aided in the development of differential calculus. In the physical sciences, he worked out the principle known as Pascal's law, which describes the transmission of pressure by an enclosed liquid. It is the basic principle of most hydraulic machinery. Pascal took great interest in the religious doctrines of the Jansenists, which he defended in his epistles *Les Provinciales* (1656–1657). His *Pensées,* a collection of thoughts on philosophical and religious themes, is his best-known work. After Pascal's death, it was published in several editions, appearing in its entirety in 1844.

Pasternak, Boris Leonidovich (1890–1960), Soviet poet and novelist, best known for his epic novel of the revolution, *Doctor Zhivago.* He wrote several volumes of poetry, including the brilliant collection *My Sister, Life* (1922). He also translated Keats, Shelley, Shakespeare, and Goethe into Russian. *Doctor Zhivago,* translated into Italian in 1957 and into English in 1958, became a best-selling novel and a popular film in the United States, but it was not published in the Soviet Union. Pasternak at first accepted the 1958 Nobel Prize for Literature but he later declined it under pressure from the Soviet government.

Pasteur, Louis (1822–1895), French chemist, the founder of the modern science of bacteriology. Pasteur discovered that the souring of wine was caused by living microorganisms, and he went on to study the whole subject of fermentation. Pasteur also studied and successfully combatted fowl cholera, anthrax, and the contagious silkworm disease. He learned to treat many diseases with vaccines and made an extensive study of rabies. In 1886 the Pasteur Institute was founded to put into practice his method of vaccination against rabies. Through Pasteur's work, prophylactic treatment of diphtheria, tubercular disease, yellow fever, cholera, and plague was made possible. Milk pasteurization, the heating of milk to kill disease-causing microorganisms, is based on his discoveries.

Pater, Walter Horatio (1839–1894), English critic Pater began his literary career with a series of articles contributed to various journals, later collected in *Studies in the History of the Renaissance* (1873). At Oxford, where he lived a quiet scholarly life devoted to aesthetics, he wrote many famous works, including *Marius the Epicurean* (1885), *Imaginary Portraits* (1887), and *Plato and Platonism* (1893).

Paton, Alan (Stewart) (1903–1988), South African novelist who is widely known for his outstanding work *Cry, the Beloved Country* (1948). *Too Late the Phalarope* (1953) and *Tales of a Troubled Land* (1961) further illuminated the troubling South African racial situation. Paton served as national president of the South African Liberal Party until 1968, when the party was declared illegal.

Patrick, Saint (c 385–c 461), original name Sucat, patron saint of Ireland, born in Britain. According to Patrick's two short surviving works, *Confessio* and *Epistola,* he was taken from England by Irish raiders when he was 16. He escaped after being enslaved for six years, but he could not forget the Irish and eventually returned to preach to them. Other facts about Patrick's life are obscure; some scholars even believe there were two missionaries of that name. One story is that he escaped from Ireland and studied for the priesthood in Gaul, returning to Ireland in 432 as a missionary bishop. For the next 30 years, he worked to convert the country.

Patton, George Smith, Jr. (1885–1945), U.S. Army officer, known to his troops as Old Blood and Guts. During World War I he formed and commanded the first U.S. tank unit. During World War II he and his tank corps fought in North Africa, Sicily, and Italy. After the Allied invasion of Europe in 1944, Patton led the Third Army in a drive across Europe, crossing the Rhine into Germany in 1945. He died in December, 1945, after an auto accident.

LOUIS PASTEUR

THE BETTMANN ARCHIVE

Paul, Saint (d. c 67 A.D.), early Christian missionary and theologian, born in Tarsus, southern Turkey. While on the way to Damascus, in Syria, Paul, a Jewish official, had a vision and was converted to Christianity. After a visit to Arabia, he made his first missionary trip to Asia Minor and Syria. At first he preached in the Jewish settlements but soon broadened his mission to include Gentiles, or non-Jews, as well. Paul's greatest influence was in his insistence that the Christian message belonged equally to Jew and Gentile. His preference for an inclusive church eventually won over those who insisted that strict observance of the Hebrew law was a prerequisite of Christians. Paul then set out on much longer trips: to Ephesus, the capital of the Roman province of Asia; to Philippi, the largest city in Macedonia; and to Corinth, the capital of the Greek state of Achaia. In each of these cities he established a church. In 58 or 59, Paul was arrested in Jerusalem for disturbing the peace and sent to Rome for trial. According to one tradition, he was released and once again visited his churches. According to another, he was executed in Rome no later than 67 A.D.

Paul III (1468–1549), born Alessandro Farnese, Italian Renaissance churchman and pope who initiated many church reforms. To check the Protestant Reformation, which had spread throughout all of northern Europe and threatened to destroy Catholicism, Pope Paul began the Counter Reformation. In 1545 he convened the Council of Trent in an effort to reform the church from within, especially in regard to abuses by the clergy. Paul was also a great patron of the arts. He commissioned Michelangelo to paint *The Last Judgment* in the Sistine Chapel and resumed work on St. Peter's Basilica.

ANNA PAVLOVA

THE BETTMANN ARCHIVE

Pauling, Linus Carl (1901–), U.S. biochemist and peace advocate, the only person to have won two unshared Nobel prizes, one for chemistry and one for peace. He was among the first to apply the laws of quantum mechanics to chemistry. For his research on molecular structures and chemical bonds, he was awarded the 1954 Nobel Prize for Chemistry. Pauling also helped lead a worldwide campaign against nuclear weapons tests in the atmosphere and was awarded the 1962 Nobel Peace Prize. In the early 1970's he did extensive and controversial research on Vitamin C as a cold cure.

Pavlov, Ivan Petrovich (1849–1936), Russian physiologist and experimental psychologist, most famous for his pioneering experiments with conditioned reflexes, especially those involving dogs' digestive reflexes. His earlier work in digestion and his methods of studying digestive secretions won him the 1904 Nobel Prize for Physiology and Medicine.

Pavlova, Anna (1881–1931), Russian ballerina. At age ten she entered the Imperial Ballet School in St. Petersburg; in 1906 she was named prima ballerina. In 1910 she visited London and New York, making a triumphant debut in *Coppélia.* She toured with Diaghilev and with her own troupe. Of Pavlova's many classical roles, the one most identified with her was *The Dying Swan.*

Peabody, George (1795–1869), U.S. merchant, financier, and philanthropist. After making a fortune in dry goods and as a banker and broker, he settled in England, in 1837, where he worked to restore confidence in American credit abroad. Among the institutions he founded and endowed were the Peabody Institute in Baltimore and the Peabody museums at Yale and Harvard. Peabody was named to the Hall of Fame in 1900.

Pearson, Lester Bowles (1897–1972), Canadian diplomat who was awarded the 1957 Nobel Peace Prize for his efforts to resolve the 1956 Suez Canal crisis. He held several diplomatic posts before serving as secretary of state, 1948–1957. Out of office, he led the Liberal opposition in the House of Commons. After a Liberal victory, he was prime minister of Canada, 1963–1968.

Peary, Robert Edwin (1856–1920), U.S. naval officer and Arctic explorer, the first man to reach the North Pole. Peary began a series of Arctic explorations that culminated in 1909 in his reaching the North Pole. He wrote several books about his expeditions, including *Northward Over the "Great Ice"* (1898), *Nearest to the Pole* (1907), *The North Pole* (1910), and *Secrets of Polar Travel* (1917).

Peel, Sir Robert (1788–1850), British statesman, best remembered for organizing the London police force, now nicknamed bobbies after him. He entered Parliament at the age of 21 and was secretary for Ireland, 1812–1818, during which time he organized the Irish police force (nicknamed the peelers). In 1822 he became home secretary and in that capacity formed the London Metropolitan police force, which united the local constabularies. In the 1830's he became leader of a faction within the Tory Party that eventually became the Conservative Party. In 1834 and in 1841 he was elected prime minister. He held office until 1846, when he resigned.

Penn, William (1644–1718), English Quaker, founder of the colony of Pennsylvania ("Penn's woods"). After his father died, Penn inherited a large fortune. By settling his father's claim against the English government, he acquired a tract of land in America. The land, soon known as Pennsylvania, was west of the Delaware River and north of Maryland. Penn resolved to form a commonwealth where there would be religious tolerance. He arrived at Delaware Bay in 1682 and signed a treaty with the Indians. In the next year he founded Philadelphia, intending it to be what its name means in Greek: city of brotherly love. In 1684 he returned to England, where he was again harassed for his religious views. He visited Pennsylvania again in 1699, but returned to England permanently in 1701. Penn was elected to the Hall of Fame in 1935.

Pepys, Samuel (1633–1703), English public official whose famous diaries provide a valuable record of England in the 1600's. Pepys sat in Parliament and held important government posts, notably in the admiralty, where he made several important reforms. After the Revolution of 1688, when James II was driven from England, Pepys was dismissed from his offices. Pepys's famous diary covers the years 1660 to 1669, during the Restoration. His detailed and entertaining description of his own daily life and of important events of the day is an important source of information for historians.

Pericles (c 495–429 B.C.), Greek statesman. So great was the influence of this first citizen of Athens that his time came to be known as the Age of Pericles. He became the leading political figure in about 460 and remained so until his death. Pericles ordered the construction of the Parthenon, the Propylaea, and other public buildings on the Acropolis. He encouraged art and literature and instituted government reforms to strengthen democracy. He also founded the Delian League and gradually turned it into an Athenian empire. Believing that a struggle with Sparta was inevitable,

Pericles fortified Athens and its port Piraeus and built up the Athenian navy. When the Peloponnesian War broke out in 431, he employed a strategy of maritime defense. In 430 the plague swept Athens. The people blamed Pericles for this and rejected his leadership. He was returned to power in 429 but died of the plague soon after.

Perkins, Frances (1882–1965), the first woman to serve as a U.S. Cabinet member. In 1929 Perkins was named labor commissioner of New York State by Governor Franklin D. Roosevelt. When Roosevelt became President in 1933, he appointed her secretary of labor. She resigned in 1945 and was appointed U.S. delegate to the International Labor Conference held in Paris in 1946. She was a member of the U.S. Civil Service Commission, 1946–1952, and later a lecturer on labor relations.

Perón, Juan Domingo (1895–1974), Argentinian dictator (1946–1955, 1973–1974). In 1943 he took part in a military coup that overthrew the Castillo government; he made sweeping social reforms and by 1946 was president. A constitutional change allowed him to succeed himself in 1952. He ruled the country as virtual dictator but had strong popular support; his wife **Evita** (1919–1952) was a heroine of the common people. A military coup in 1955 forced Perón into exile. Eighteen years later, in 1973, a Peronist candidate won the presidency. He stepped down shortly after, allowing Perón to return to power in Argentina.

Perry, family name of two brothers who were U.S. naval heroes.

Oliver Hazard Perry (1785–1819), a sailor from the age of 14, organized and commanded the forces that defeated the British on Lake Erie in 1813. Having regained control of the lake, he delivered the now-famous report: "We have met the enemy and they are ours. Two ships, two brigs, one schooner, and one sloop." He died while leading a mission to Venezuela.

Matthew Calbraith Perry (1794–1858) commanded an expedition to Japan to negotiate a treaty opening Japan to trade. Commodore Perry landed at Yedo Bay with a show of naval force; he delivered a letter from President Fillmore to the emperor's representatives, promising to return for an answer the following year. When Perry returned in 1854 with even more ships, the Japanese signed the first commercial treaty between the two countries and thus opened Japan to Western contact.

Pershing, John Joseph (1860–1948), commander of American troops during World War I, nicknamed Black Jack for his stern discipline. A career soldier, he fought against the Indians during the 1880's and 1890's, and

THE BETTMANN ARCHIVE

JOHN PERSHING

served in the Spanish-American War, in the Philippines, and in Mexico. When the United States entered World War I in 1917, Pershing was made a full general and appointed commander in chief of the American Expeditionary Force. During a general offensive in September, 1918, his troops crushed the opposing German forces within 47 days and brought the war to an end. Pershing returned to the United States as a hero. In 1919 Congress made him general of the armies, the highest ranking officer in U.S. Army history. He published *My Experiences in the Army* (1931), for which he won the 1932 Pulitzer Prize for history.

Pétain, Henri Philippe (1856–1951), French army officer. During World War I, in 1916, he became famous as the man who stopped the Germans at Verdun. In 1917 he was made commander in chief of the French armies under General Foch, the Allied commander. In 1918 he was created marshal of France. During the German occupation of France in World War II, Pétain became chief of state of a collaborationist regime set up at Vichy. After France had been liberated by Allied armies, Pétain was tried for treason by the French government. He was sentenced to death, but the sentence was later commuted to imprisonment for life.

Peter I (Peter the Great) (1672–1725), czar of Russia, 1682–1725. Peter's main interest was in modernizing Russia and making it a major power in Europe. He traveled incognito all over Europe, working in shipyards, workshops, and factories to learn Western techniques; he hired experts and technicians and brought them back to Russia. Peter's victory in the Northern War gave Russia access to the Baltic trade routes. In 1703 he built St. Petersburg (now Leningrad), a new capital and Russia's first Baltic port.

Petipa, Marius (1819–1910), French dancer and choreographer whose career at the Russian Imperial Theater spanned 60 years. Petipa's influence in modern classical Russian ballet was unmatched; his versions of *Swan Lake, Raymonda,* and *Giselle* became classics in the ballet repertoire. He was chief collaborator with Tchaikovsky on *The Nutcracker* and *The Sleeping Beauty.*

Petrarch (1304–1374), in Italian Francesco Petrarca, Italian poet. Born in Tuscany, he later settled at Avignon, France, where he fell in love with the beautiful Laura, in whose honor he wrote the elegant, formal sonnets and odes that made him famous. His epic poem *Africa* (1338–1342) was widely admired. In 1341 he became poet laureate of Italy. Petrarch wrote both in prose and in verse, but he is remembered principally for his lyrics and sonnets. He was one of the earliest humanists of the Renaissance.

Phidias (c 500–c 432 B.C.), Greek sculptor. He became famous in about 460 with a memorial to the Athenian victory at the Battle of Marathon. When Pericles came to power in Athens, he commissioned Phidias to beautify the city. Phidias supervised the building of the Parthenon and made the statue of Athena (dedicated 438) for the interior. He also created the statue of Zeus (about 435) for the temple at Olympia, one of the Seven Wonders of the ancient world.

Philip (King Philip) (c 1639–1676), born Metacomet, American Indian chief of the Wampanoag tribe of New England. The second son of Massasoit, he became chief of the tribe in 1662. For several years he remained outwardly friendly toward the white settlers, but their gradual encroachments embittered him. When three of his warriors were executed for the murder of an Indian informer, he started King Philip's War (1675–1676), in which hundreds of colonists were massacred. Philip was finally captured and killed in 1676.

Philip II (Philip Augustus) (1165–1223), king of France, 1180–1223, the greatest Capetian ruler. In 1190 he went on the Third Crusade with King Richard I of England, but quarreled with him and returned the following year. Taking advantage of the English princes' rivalry, Philip regained nearly all their lands in France by 1208. By the end of his reign, Philip had strengthened royal power and quadrupled French territory. In his capital in Paris, he built the Louvre and established the University of Paris.

Philip II (1527–1598), king of Spain, 1556–1598, the son of Holy Roman Emperor Charles V. Philip married four times; his second wife was Mary I of England. In 1556 he succeeded his father as king of Spain and ruler of a vast empire that included Sicily, Naples, Milan, the Netherlands, Spanish America, and the Philippines. Philip's domestic and foreign policies stemmed from his passionate dedication to the Spanish empire and the Roman Catholic Church. He intensified the Spanish Inquisition and sent the duke of Alva to crush the Protestant revolt in the Netherlands in 1567. He sent his half brother, Don John, to destroy the Turks at the naval battle of Lepanto, 1571, and tried unsuccessfully to prevent the Protestant Henry of Navarre from becoming king of France. After Elizabeth I of England had executed the Catholic Mary Stuart, queen of Scots, Philip sent his navy, the Invincible Armada, to prepare the way for an invasion of England in 1588. The Armada's defeat ensured Protestant supremacy in northern Europe.

Phillips, Wendell (1811–1884), U.S. orator and reformer. He was a disciple of William Lloyd Garrison and a brilliant spokesman for abolitionism. He succeeded Garrison as president of the Anti-Slavery Society, 1865. After the slaves were freed, he spoke throughout the country on behalf of such movements as woman suffrage, prison reform, and the prohibition of alcoholic beverages.

Phyfe, Duncan (c 1768–1854), Scottish-born U.S. cabinetmaker. In 1792 Phyfe settled in New York City and set up a furniture shop. His designs were very popular in his day and are prized by collectors. Before 1820 he did his best work, in the Sheraton style, with fine proportions and graceful curves. It was usually of mahogany, decorated with parallel rows of reeding and simple ornaments such as a lyre, acanthus, or oak leaf. His later, less popular, work was in the Empire tradition.

Piaget, Jean (1896–1980), Swiss child psychologist. The central conclusion of Piaget's research was that children progress through four basic learning stages and that the intellectual growth at each stage can be clearly discerned by observation and by dialogue with the children themselves. The results of Piaget's work are contained in several books, including *The Language and Thought of the Child* (1923) and *Judgment and Reasoning in the Child* (1924).

Picasso, Pablo Ruiz y (1881–1973), Spanish-born painter. He lived in both Paris and Barcelona in the early 1900's, settling in Paris in 1903. His early works showed circus performers and the families of the poor, with one color tone predominating. From the Blue Period (1901–1904) come such paintings as *Gourmet, The Guitarist,* and *The Frugal Repast;* The Rose Period (1904–1906) produced *Harlequin* and *Gertrude Stein.* Picasso's *Les Demoiselles d'Avignon* (1906–1907), considered the first cubist painting, marked the beginning of a style that he developed along with Braque and the Fauvists, altering the course of 20th-century art. Among his notable cubist works are *Three Musicians* and *Man Smoking a Pipe.* During the 1930's his work was less cubistic and more personal and original, as in *Young Girl at a Mirror.* A new sense of emotion, reflecting his horror at the Spanish Civil War, produced the powerful *Guernica* (1937) and other paintings similar in theme. In the 1940's Picasso settled on the French Riviera; at Vallauris he began to work in pottery. His work—painting, lithographs, ceramics, sculpture—continued to change and explore new methods of expression. His variations on Delacroix's *Women of Algeria* and on Velazquez's *Maids of Honor* were among the most interesting of his later works.

Piccard, Auguste (1884–1962), Swiss physicist who set world records for ascending to the highest altitude and making the deepest descent into the ocean. In 1913, with his twin brother **Jean Félix Piccard** (1884–1963), he made a pioneering balloon flight across France and Germany. In 1931 he set a world record when he and a co-worker ascended almost 52,000 feet in a balloon with a pressurized cabin. The following year he bettered this record, obtaining valuable data on cosmic rays in the stratosphere. In 1934 Jean Piccard, with his wife Jeannette, ascended even higher, 57,579 feet. With his son **Jacques Piccard** (1922–), Auguste developed a device for underwater exploration known as a bathyscaphe. The second model took both father and son to a depth of more than 10,000 feet.

Pickering, Edward Charles (1846–1919), U.S. astronomer noted for his measurements of the brightness of stars. In 1876 he was named director of the Harvard Observatory, where he introduced photometry and photography into astronomical observations. In 1891, with his brother **William Henry Pickering** (1858–1938), also an astronomer, he set up an observatory at Arequipa, Peru, to study stars of the southern hemisphere.

Pico della Mirandola, Giovanni (1463–1494), Italian humanist scholar, often considered the model Renaissance man of learning. In 1484 he went to Florence as a protégé of Lorenzo de Medici. He mastered 22 languages, and at the age of 24 composed 900 theses, called *On the Dignity of Man,* summarizing all the knowledge of his day. In 1487 he was branded a heretic by Pope Innocent VIII and forced to recant 13 of the theses. He fled to France but, at the request of the Medicis, returned to Florence, where he became associated with the Platonic Academy.

Pierce, Franklin (1804–1869), 14th President of the United States, 1853–1857. Pierce began his political career as a Democratic member of the New Hampshire state legislature. In 1833 he entered Congress, first as a representative and later, in 1837, as the youngest member in the Senate. He resigned in 1842 to resume his law practice and become U.S. district attorney. Pierce joined the Army at the outbreak of the Mexican War in 1846, and was rapidly promoted, becoming a brigadier general under General Winfield Scott. At the Democratic convention of 1852, Pierce, almost unknown, was nominated as a compromise candidate against General Scott, the Whig nominee. Elected President by a large margin, Pierce quickly lost support because of his inept handling of the question of slavery in the territories and his policy in Cuba. Ignored by the 1856 convention, he retired.

Pike, Zebulon Montgomery (1779–1813), U.S. soldier and explorer, discoverer of Pike's Peak. In 1805 he commanded an Army expedition that unsuccessfully sought the headwaters of the Mississippi. The next year he set out to follow the Arkansas River to its source. Reaching Colorado (near present-day Pueblo), he discovered the peak on a side trip and tried unsuccessfully to reach its summit. Pike died while leading a force against York (now Toronto), Canada, in the War of 1812.

Pilate, Pontius (d. c 36 A.D.), Roman governor of Judea, 26–36 A.D., who presided over the trial of Jesus. During his rule he kept peace in the region but handled the delicate problem of Roman-Jewish relations with little skill. The circumstances surrounding Jesus' trial are hazy. According to the Gospels, Pilate condemned Jesus to placate the Jewish high priests. Legend says he took his life after returning to Rome.

Pindar (c 518–c 438 B.C.), Greek poet of Thebes. He began writing verse at an early age, and soon his poetry was popular throughout Greece. His greatest works were triumphal odes written to honor the victors of the Greek games. Four volumes are preserved, arranged according to the four festivals—Olympian, Pythian, Nemean, and Isthmean. Pindar also wrote many poems, hymns, and dirges.

Pinkerton, Allan (1819–1884), Scottish-born U.S. detective. During the 1840's he settled in Chicago, where he was associated with the police force. In 1850 he resigned to open the Pinkerton

National Detective Agency. During the Civil War, Pinkerton operated a secret service organization for the Union Army. After the war his detective agency became famous for breaking up the Molly Maguires, an Irish terrorist organization prominent in Pennsylvania during labor disputes in the coal regions. Pinkerton's agency was notorious among labor groups for its strike-breaking and other antilabor activities. Pinkerton published several books, including *The Molly Maguires and the Detectives* (1877) and *Thirty Years a Detective* (1884).

Pinter, Harold (1930–), British playwright. In his plays Pinter recreated everyday dialogue that conveys the alienation and isolation of modern man. His best-known plays are *The Room* and *The Dumb Waiter* (1957), *The Birthday Party* (1958), *The Caretaker* (1960), and *The Homecoming* (1964). His dramatic style led to the phrase "comedy of menace." Among his screenplays are *The Servant* (1963) and *Accident* (1967).

Pirandello, Luigi (1867–1936), Italian author known outside Italy mainly for his plays. *Six Characters in Search of an Author* (1921), his first successful drama, made him world famous in the 1920's. His other dramas, all based on his convictions that the human personality is ever-changing and that truth is relative, include *Henry IV* (1922) and *Each in His Own Way* (1924). Pirandello also wrote six novels and about 300 short stories. He was awarded the 1934 Nobel Prize for Literature.

Piranesi, Giambattista (1720–1778), Italian architect and engraver noted for his prints of buildings in Rome. He spent most of his life in Rome, making copperplate engravings of the city's ancient and modern architecture. These provide an invaluable record of the various architectural styles up to his time. He produced more than 1000 etchings, noted for their accuracy and drama, including *Le Antichità Romane* (1756).

Pire, Dominique Georges Henri (1910–1969), Belgian Roman Catholic priest and humanitarian who was awarded the Nobel Peace Prize for aiding refugees after World War II. In 1949 he formed Aid to Displaced Persons, with branches in many European cities. He later established several "homes of welcome" for aged refugees and a series of "European villages" for displaced persons, all based on the principles of fraternity and self-help. In 1962 he started the Island of Peace project for the uprooted in Pakistan and India.

Pisano, Niccolò (c 1220–c 1283), also known as Niccolò da Pisa, Italian sculptor whose work represents a transition from Gothic to Renaissance art. He spent most of his life in Pisa, where his greatest work was the hexagonal marble pulpit in the Baptistery (completed 1259) depicting scenes from the life of Christ.

Pissarro, Camille (1830–1903), a French impressionist painter. Pissarro exhibited with Cézanne, Manet, Renoir, and others in the impressionist shows in the 1870's and 1880's. Many of his best paintings are landscapes, noted for their bright, spontaneous atmosphere, including *The Haystack* (1873), *Peasant Woman with a Wheelbarrow* (1874), and *L'Île Lacroix, Rouen* (1888).

Piston, Walter Hamor (1894–1976), U.S. composer noted for his neoclassical chamber music and symphonic works. His Third and Seventh symphonies won the Pulitzer Prize (1948 and 1961); another of his symphonic works is the *Lincoln Center Festival Overture* (1962). Piston wrote the ballet suite *The Incredible Flutist* (1938) and several music texts: *Harmony* (1941), *Counterpoint* (1947), and *Orchestration* (1955).

Pitt, William, 1st Earl of Chatham (1708–1778), called Pitt the Elder, British statesman noted for his desire to reconcile the American colonies with England. He entered Parliament in 1735 and became a member of the cabinet in 1746. He became secretary of state in 1757, with the duke of Newcastle as prime minister. The leadership of these two statesmen helped bring about many of England's victories in the Seven Years' War with France, 1756–1763. When George III came to the throne determined to end the war, Pitt resigned in opposition in 1761. In 1766, however, he was asked to head a ministry and was made an earl. Ill health forced him to resign in 1768, but he kept up an active interest in public affairs in the House of Lords. He opposed the government's harsh treatment of the American colonies but still did not favor a settlement granting independence.

Pitt, William (1759–1806), called Pitt the Younger, prime minister during the worst period of the Napoleonic wars. The son of William Pitt, 1st Earl of Chatham, he entered Parliament in 1781. At the age of 23 he became Chancellor of the Exchequer, and at 24 prime minister, the youngest by far in English history. In 1793 Pitt helped form the first European coalition against revolutionary France and prepared England for war. In 1801 he brought about union with Ireland. He had intended to free the Roman Catholic laity from all restrictions, but he was blocked by King George. Chagrined by this failure, Pitt resigned in 1801. He returned as prime minister in 1804, when fear of a Napoleonic invasion brought him support from all parties. As head of the government, he formed a new coalition with Austria and Russia against France. Always in poor health, Pitt died in 1806.

Pius XII (1876–1958), born Eugenio Maria Giuseppe Giovanni Pacelli, Italian Roman Catholic churchman and pope, 1939–1958. After his ordination in 1899, he rose from a minor position in the Vatican to be papal secretary of state in 1930. He was made a cardinal in 1929 and elected pope in 1939. During World War II the Vatican was a sanctuary for refugees from both sides, but Pius was later severely criticized for not being more outspoken against the atrocities in the German concentration camps. After the war his anticommunist views were reflected in his approach to world affairs; in 1949 he excommunicated all Catholics who belonged to the Communist Party.

Pizarro, Francisco (c 1470–1541), Spanish conquistador. In 1522 Pizarro joined Diego de Almagro and others to explore the west coast of South America. When the expedition returned, Pizarro and about 13 men stayed in spite of great peril to continue the search for gold. When they returned to Spain in 1527 with reports of the wealthy Peruvian empire, Charles V of Spain granted Pizarro permission to conquer Peru. Pizarro and his men landed in 1532 and were cordially received by the Inca prince Atahualpa, who was immediately taken prisoner for refusing Spanish sovereignty. Though a room full of gold was delivered for his ransom, he was slain. By

FRANCISCO PIZARRO

THE BETTMANN ARCHIVE

1533 Pizarro, Diego de Almagro, and others had gained control of the Peruvian government; in 1535 they founded the city of Lima. Pizarro was assassinated in 1541 in revenge for having executed Almagro in a struggle over territory.

Planck, Max Karl Ernst Ludwig (1858–1947), German theoretical physicist who formulated the quantum theory. This hypothesis assumes that radiant energy is not waves, but quanta, or discrete particles. Both Albert Einstein's theory of relativity and Niels Bohr's theory of atomic structure were based on Planck's quantum theory. He was awarded the 1918 Nobel Prize for Physics.

Plato (c 427–347 B.C.), Greek philosopher. Plato left his native city of Athens when his teacher, Socrates, was executed in 399. He traveled widely in the next twelve years, visiting Italy and the court of Dionysius I of Syracuse. Returning to Athens, Plato founded a school of philosophy, the Academy, where he taught for the next 40 years. Plato presented his ideas in the form of dialogues between philosophers, often including Socrates. Among the most famous are the *Republic,* summarizing Plato's conception of justice and the nature of government, and the *Timaeus,* summarizing his view of the system of the universe. For Plato, reality resides in perfect and unchanging universal forms (Ideas), not in the illusory, transitory world of material things. This position made Platonic idealism a natural philosophic basis for the development of early Christian thought. Platonism remained a strong second tradition within Christianity even after being supplanted by the moderate realism of the medieval scholastic philosophers.

Pliny the Elder (23–79 A.D.), full name Gaius Plinius Secundus, Roman scholar and naturalist. He wrote literary and military treatises, but his only surviving work is the celebrated *Historia Naturalis (Natural History),* published in 77. Representing vast scholarship, the work consists of 37 books and contains, as Pliny said, 20,000 important facts gleaned from 100 authors. As science, the book contains little of value today, but it has great historical interest. Pliny died in the eruption of Vesuvius that destroyed Pompeii in 79.

Pliny the Younger (c 61–c 112 A.D.), full name Gaius Plinius Caecilius Secundus, Roman official and author, the nephew and adopted son of Pliny the Elder. He entered politics and became consul in 100. He was governor of Bithynia in Asia Minor in about 112. Pliny's fame rests chiefly on his ten volumes of *Letters,* which have great stylistic merit and are a valuable source of information on the social and political life of his period. Also extant is his *Panegyricus,* a speech in praise of the emperor Trajan, contrasting him with his tyrannical predecessor Domitian.

Plotinus (c 205–270), Roman philosopher. He founded the Neoplatonic school of philosophy that deeply influenced later philosophers and Christian theologians. Plotinus was probably born in Egypt; it is known that he studied in Alexandria. After joining an expedition to Mesopotamia to learn something of Eastern philosophy, he settled in Rome, where he taught and wrote and won many followers. Plotinus revived Plato's doctrines, translating them into a kind of antimaterialist mysticism. After his death, his writings were collected by a disciple, Porphyry, and published in the *Enneads.*

Plutarch (c 46–c 120 A.D.), Greek writer known for his biographies of ancient Greeks and Romans. Plutarch held various magistracies in Chaeronea, where he was born, and became a priest of Apollo at Delphi. Nothing else is known of his life. Plutarch's great work is *Parallel Lives,* biographies of 50 eminent Greeks and Romans, arranged in pairs, whose characters are compared and contrasted. His biographies were for centuries the prime source for historians and authors. Plutarch also wrote the *Moralia (Morals),* essays on ethics, grammar, manners, and other subjects.

Pocahontas (c 1595–1617), real name Matoaka, the daughter of Powhatan, chief of the Algonquian Indians of Virginia. She married an English settler and was taken to England, where she was welcomed as a princess. According to legend, when the Indians captured Captain John Smith of the Jamestown colony in 1608, Pocahontas begged her father to spare his life. In 1613 she was captured by the Jamestown settlers and held as hostage for the safe return of colonists whom the Indians had captured. During her captivity she became a Christian and in 1614 married John Rolfe, a settler. She went with him to England, where she was honored at court and in society. She died of smallpox on the return voyage.

Poe, Edgar Allan (1809–1849), U.S. poet and short story writer. His best-known poems, considered masterpieces in American literature, include "The Raven," "Lenore," "To Helen," "Ulalume," and "The Bells." He was also a master of tales of the grotesque, such as "The Fall of the House of Usher," "The Pit and the Pendulum," and "The Cask of Amontillado." "The Gold Bug" and "Murders in the Rue Morgue" were the first modern detective stories.

Poincaré, Raymond (1860–1934), president of the French Republic, 1913–1920, during World War I. An ardent patriot, Poincaré encouraged and inspired his people throughout the war. As premier, 1922–1924, he tried to force reparations payments from defeated Germany by initiating a French invasion of the Ruhr region in 1923.

THE BETTMANN ARCHIVE

MAX PLANCK

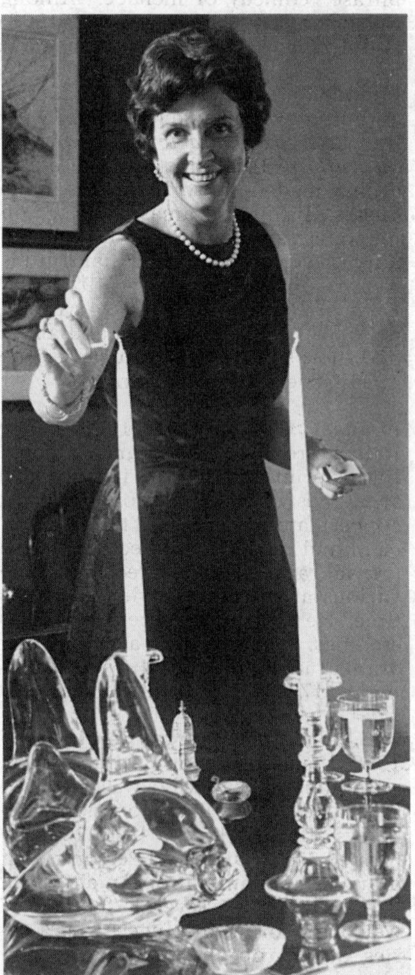
BARNES ASSOCIATES

EMILY POST

Reelected in 1926, he helped stabilize the failing French economy. Ill health forced his resignation in 1929.

Polk, James Knox (1795–1849), eleventh President of the United States, 1845–1849. In 1820 Polk was admitted to the Tennessee bar and rapidly became prominent in local politics. Backed by Andrew Jackson, Polk was elected to Congress in 1825 and became Speaker of the House in 1835. He was elected governor of Tennessee in 1839. At the Democratic convention of 1844, Polk, an advocate of expansionism, still backed by Jackson, was nominated as a dark-horse candidate. In an exciting campaign in which Texas and Oregon boundary disputes were major issues, he defeated Henry Clay. Polk carried out most of his plans for acquisition of land: the Oregon question was settled through a compromise with Britain, but the Texas boundary dispute led to a war with Mexico in 1846. The unpopular war ended in 1848, and the disputed territory was given to the United States, but Polk was not renominated. At the close of his term, Polk retired to Tennessee, where he died three months later.

Pollock, Jackson (1912–1956), U.S. painter, a leader of abstract expressionism. He studied under Thomas Hart Benton, 1921–1931, and his paintings of the 1930's were realistic in the Benton style. He later developed a highly abstract style, covering enormous canvases with a profusion of paint drippings. His paintings include *Cathedral* (1947) and *Drawing No. 132* (1951).

Polo, Marco (c 1254–c 1324), Italian traveler and adventurer. He recorded his extensive travels in *The Book of Marco Polo,* perhaps the greatest travel book of all time. Polo accompanied his father and uncle, wealthy Venetian merchants, on a journey to the Chinese court of the Mongol ruler, Kublai Khan, in 1271. In 1295, after an absence of 24 years, he returned to Venice. During a war against Genoa in 1298, Polo was captured. While in prison, he dictated to a fellow prisoner the story of his experiences in China. The narrative created a sensation in Europe and was for many years the only source of information on central Asia. Many believed Marco Polo's tales to be imaginary, but other travelers and later scholars verified most of his account.

Pompadour, Marquise de; Jeanne Antoinette Poisson (1721–1764), beautiful mistress of Louis XV of France. In 1745, at a masked ball at Versailles, she attracted the king, who in the same year made her his official mistress and gave her the title of marquise. Though she influenced the internal affairs of France, such as the appointment of some ministers, her political power has been greatly exaggerated. She was most prominent as a patron of the arts, especially of writers such as Voltaire and the encyclopedist Denis Diderot.

Pompey (Pompey the Great) (106–48 B.C.), full name Gnaeus Pompeius, Roman general and statesman. As a young man he allied himself with Sulla and helped to defeat the rebellion of Marius. In 71 he helped stamp out the slave insurrection of Spartacus in Rome. He formed a political alliance with the wealthy Marcus Crassus and secured the consulship for the year 70, although he was younger than the legal age. In 67 he was given extraordinary military powers by the Roman Senate to deal with Cilician pirates terrorizing the eastern Mediterranean. In 66 he defeated Mithridates, adding the province of Pontus to Rome's possessions. He then defeated the Armenians, annexed Syria, conquered Jerusalem, and made Judea a tributary of Rome. Pompey formed strong political ties with Julius Caesar in 60, when he, Caesar, and Crassus formed the First Triumvirate. But Caesar's influence increased and Pompey's declined. Civil war broke out between the two, and Pompey was decisively defeated at Pharsalus in 48. He fled to Egypt, where he was assassinated.

Ponce de León, Juan (1460–1521), Spanish explorer who, searching for the legendary fountain of youth, discovered Florida. He probably accompanied Columbus on his second voyage to the New World in 1493. Around 1508 he explored and colonized Puerto Rico, where he amassed a fortune; he also served as its first governor. He then went in search of an island called Bimini where, according to legend, there was a fountain whose water had curative properties—a "fountain of eternal youth." On Easter Sunday, 1513, he discovered and named the Florida peninsula. In 1521 he returned to Florida to establish a colony, but was killed by the Indians.

Pontiac (c 1720–1769), Ottawa Indian leader who brought together and led the most powerful tribal coalition in Indian history. In 1763 he organized disparate tribes from the Great Lakes to the Gulf of Mexico in an attempt to destroy British power west of the Alleghenies. Several campaigns were successful, but the planned capture of Detroit failed. In 1766 Pontiac signed a peace treaty with the British at Oswego, N.Y.

Pope, Alexander (1688–1744), English poet noted for his savage wit and polished style. With his *Essay on Criticism* (1711) and *The Rape of the Lock* (1712), he made his reputation. His translations of Homer's *Iliad* (1715–1720) and *Odyssey* (1725–1726) showed his skill in writing the heroic couplet and also made him wealthy. Pope achieved his greatest renown with the *Dunciad* (1728, revised in 1743), a satire directed against his critics and adversaries. His other important works include *An Essay on Man* (1733–1734), and a series called *Moral Essays,* which first appeared in 1731.

Porter, Cole (1893–1964), U.S. composer of popular songs. He wrote primarily for the Broadway theater. During a highly successful career, he produced the scores for such musicals as *Anything Goes* (1934), *Kiss Me, Kate* (1948), and *Can-Can* (1953). Among his many songs are such standards as "Night and Day," "Begin the Beguine," "In the Still of the Night," and "So in Love."

Porter, Katherine Anne (1890–1980), U.S. short story writer. Her first collection, *Flowering Judas* (1930), won immediate critical acclaim. Later collections include *Hacienda* (1934), *Pale Horse, Pale Rider* (1939), *The Leaning Tower* (1944), and *The Collected Stories of Katherine Anne Porter* (1965), which won the 1966 Pulitzer Prize and the National Book Award. Her novel *Ship of Fools* was published in 1962.

Porter, William Sidney (O. Henry) (1862–1910), U.S. short story writer known for his sketches about city life and his characteristically ironic surprise endings. In 1884 he settled in Austin, Texas, where he edited a humorous paper for a time and then became a bank teller. Convicted of embezzlement, he spent more than three years in prison, where he began writing stories. In 1902 Porter moved to New York. Adopting the pen name O. Henry, he wrote more than 200 stories, mostly about the lives of the people of New York. They appeared in such collections as *The Four Million* (1906), *The Voice of the City* (1908), and *Options* (1909).

Post, Emily Price (1873–1960), U.S. writer and authority on etiquette. The daughter of an eminent architect, she was educated in private New York schools and was a popular debutante. After writing several novels and magazine articles, she wrote *Etiquette* (1922), for many years the standard work on American social behavior. Her other books include *How to Behave Though a Debutante* (1928), *Children Are People* (1940), and *Motor Manners* (1950).

Post, Wiley (1899–1935), U.S. aviator who set several flying records during the early years of U.S. aviation. He made a record round-the-world flight with Harold Gatty in 1931. In 1933 Post made a solo flight around the world, breaking the previous record by more than a day, flying 15,596 miles in 7 days, 18 hours, and 49 minutes. In 1935 he was killed with Will Rogers, the well-known U.S. humorist, in a plane crash in Alaska.

Poulenc, Francis (1899–1963), French composer of urbane, elegant contemporary music. His operas *Les Dialogues des Carmélites* (1953–1956) and *La Voix humaine* (on a drama by Cocteau, 1959) were often performed in Europe and the United States. Poulenc was a member of the group called "the Six," which had considerable influence on European music in the 1920's and 1930's.

Pound, Ezra Loomis (1885–1972), U.S. poet and critic. He spent most of his life in Europe, where as editor and critic he encouraged the work of such writers as T. S. Eliot, Yeats, and James Joyce. At the same time, Pound was writing his own poetry (*Personae,* 1912) and making translations, mainly from Chinese and Japanese. In the early 1920's he began publishing his *Cantos,* a long, difficult, and influential set of poems on which he continued to work for 40 years. After World War II, the U.S. government indicted him for treason for pro-fascist radio broadcasts made from Italy. He was judged incompetent to stand trial and spent several years in a mental institution. Released in 1961, he returned to Italy.

Poussin, Nicolas (c 1594–1665), French artist, first of the French classical painters. After working in the Paris studios of several painters and sculptors, he left the city, which he hated, and settled in Rome, 1624. Influenced by ancient sculpture and Renaissance painting, he developed a personal classical style that marked the work of his mature years. Most of his paintings depict landscapes or historical events, as in *The Arcadian Shepherds* (1638–1639) and *The Funeral of Phocion* (1648).

Powhatan (c 1550–1618), born Wahunsonacock, American Indian chief who was head of an Algonquian confederacy that in the early 1600's included six tribes in eastern Virginia. He was initially hostile to the early white settlers, but when his daughter Pocahontas married the Englishman John Rolfe, Powhatan left the colonists in peace. However, after Powhatan's death, the Indians resumed their attacks on the settlers.

Praxiteles (c 400–330 B.C.), Athenian sculptor considered one of the greatest Greek artists by ancient writers, who praised his works for their sensuous grace. His only surviving work is a marble statue *Hermes and the Infant Dionysus,* but many Roman copies of other works exist, including statues of Aphrodite, Artemis, and Apollo.

Presley, Elvis (1935–1977), U.S. popular singer and guitarist, king of rock and roll for more than a decade. Successful as well in country-and-western and rhythm-and-blues styles, he captivated young audiences with his baritone voice and provocative delivery; his many recordings sold in the tens of millions. Among his best-known songs are "Hound Dog," "Love Me Tender," "Jailhouse Rock," and "Rock Around the Clock." His films include *Love Me Tender* (1956) and *Follow That Dream* (1962).

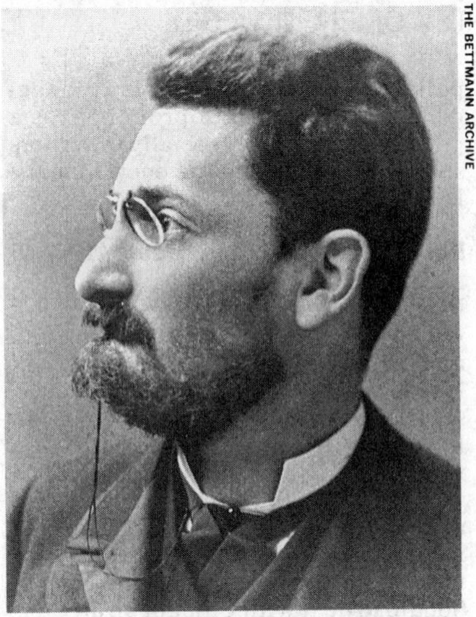
THE BETTMANN ARCHIVE

JOSEPH PULITZER

THE BETTMANN ARCHIVE

MARQUIS OF QUEENSBERRY

Pretorius, Andries Wilhelmus Jacobus (1798–1853), South African Dutch leader in the Boer struggle for independence. In 1835 he joined the Great Trek from Cape Colony to Natal, where in 1838 he was made commandant general of the Boer colonists. His defeat of a force of 10,000 Zulus made possible the organization of a Boer republic of Natalia. Pretorius then led the Boers in a second trek to the Vaal River, 1848, seeking independence from Britain. In 1852, after many battles with the English, the sovereignty of the South African Republic (the Transvaal) was acknowledged. In 1853 his eldest son, **Marthinus Wessels Pretorius** (1819–1901), succeeded him as commandant general and became the first president of the republic. The new capital city, Pretoria, was named in honor of his father.

Price, Leontyne (1927–   ), U.S. operatic soprano who first became known in the role of Bess in George Gershwin's *Porgy and Bess* in a company that toured Europe, 1952–1954. She performed regularly with the Metropolitan and other companies throughout the world. She sang the lead in Samuel Barber's opera *Antony and Cleopatra* at the opening of the Metropolitan Opera's new house in 1966.

Priestley, Joseph (1733–1804), English clergyman and chemist, best known as the discoverer of oxygen (1774). Priestley wrote more than 70 books on a wide variety of subjects. Among his other discoveries were the properties of nitrous oxide, ammonia, carbon monoxide, and sulfur dioxide. His work on gases led to Dalton's atomic theory. His philosophical and political views made many enemies. In 1794 he emigrated to America.

Prokofiev, Sergei Sergeevich (1891–1953), Russian composer. He studied privately under Reinhold Glière and then attended the St. Petersburg Conservatory, where one of his teachers was Rimski-Korsakov. He lived in Paris from 1923 to 1931 and in 1932 returned to the Soviet Union. Among his many works are six symphonies, including the Mozart-like *Classical Symphony;* the familiar *Peter and the Wolf* suite for children; the operas *War and Peace* and *The Love of Three Oranges;* and scores for the films *Lieutenant Kije* and *Alexander Nevsky.*

Proudhon, Pierre Joseph (1809–1865), French political theorist, usually regarded as the founder of anarchism. In 1840 he published *Qu'est-ce que la propriété?* ("What is property?"), to which his answer was, "Property is theft." He believed that private property should be widely dispersed among owner-producers, who would either operate as individuals or band together for mutual benefit. Proudhon settled in Paris in 1847 and became an active socialist during the revolution of 1848. He was imprisoned in 1849 for his violent attacks against the government. In 1858 he was forced to flee France for his revolutionary writing. Proudhon advocated cooperatives for small businesses, a monetary system based on productivity, the dissolution of giant business concerns, and the final abandonment of all forms of government.

Proust, Marcel (1871–1922), French novelist. He was prominent in Paris society until 1905, when the death of his mother and failing health led him to retire to the seclusion of a soundproof, cork-lined apartment. There he began writing the multivolume novel *À la recherche du temps perdu* (*Remem-*

brance of Things Past, 1913–1927), a study of the declining Parisian society of his youth. The first book, *Du coté de chez Swann (Swann's Way),* is the best known; the last parts were published after his death. In his writing, Proust experimented with time and memory in a startlingly original way.

Ptolemy (fl. 100's A.D.), in Latin, Claudius Ptolemaeus, Alexandrian astronomer, geographer, and mathematician. From 127 to 148 Ptolemy lived in Alexandria, Egypt, where he conducted astronomical observations; the dates of his work are calculated from the phenomena he observed and recorded. In a 13-volume series known as the *Almagest,* Ptolemy described Earth as the fixed center of the universe, with the sun, moon, planets, and stars revolving around it in separate zones from east to west. The Ptolemaic theory was generally accepted until the Copernican system supplanted it in the 1500's and 1600's. He also wrote the standard ancient geography text and invented trigonometry.

Puccini, Giacomo (1858–1924), Italian composer. He scored his first success with *Manon Lescaut* in 1893. This was followed by *La Bohème* (1896), *Tosca* (1900), and *Madame Butterfly* (1904). Puccini's other operas include *Girl of the Golden West* (*La Fanciulla del West,* 1910), the one-act opera *Gianni Schicchi* (1918), and *Turandot* (1926), unfinished at his death.

Pulaski, Casimir (1747–1779), Polish nobleman who fought in the American Revolution. In 1772 he was forced into exile for conspiring to capture the king of Poland. He met Benjamin Franklin in France and offered his services to the American army, which he joined in 1777. For distinguished service at the Battle of Brandywine, Pulaski was made a brigadier general of cavalry. He held this command during the winter campaign, 1777–1778. He then organized an independent cavalry unit, the Pulaski Legion. In the seige of Savannah, 1779, he was mortally wounded.

Pulitzer, Joseph (1847–1911), Hungarian-born U.S. editor and publisher who founded the Pulitzer prizes. In 1865 he arrived in St. Louis penniless. By 1878 he had purchased two St. Louis newspapers and combined them to form the St. Louis *Post-Dispatch.* In 1883 he bought the New York *World,* and in 1887 founded the New York *Evening World.* He gained national prominence with an aggressive editorial policy. Pulitzer endowed the School of Journalism at Columbia University and provided a fund for annual awards in U.S. journalism, letters, drama, and music, the Pulitzer prizes.

Pullman, George Mortimer (1831–1897), U.S. inventor and industrialist who designed the first Pullman sleeping car for railroads, making comfortable overnight travel possible. He formed a company to manufacture these cars in 1867 and in 1881 established Pullman City, a company-built town for employees near Chicago. Residents of this town began the Pullman strike of 1894, one of the most violent labor disputes in U.S. history.

Pupin, Michael Idvorsky (1858–1935), Yugoslav-born U.S. physicist who developed the Pupin coil, a device that extended the range of long-distance telephoning and telegraphing. He also did valuable research in x-ray technology and radio transmission. His autobiography, *From Immigrant to Inventor* (1923), won a Pulitzer Prize in 1924.

Purcell, Henry (c 1658–1695), English baroque composer. Among his many works, the opera *Dido and Aeneas* (1680) and *Te Deum and Jubilate,* created for Saint Cecilia's Day (1694), are considered his outstanding achievements. While organist at Westminster Abbey, Purcell wrote much church music; he also wrote incidental music for plays.

Pushkin, Aleksandr Sergeevich (1799–1837), Russian poet. A liberal aristocrat, he was exiled from Moscow in 1820 for writing revolutionary poetry. However, when Nicholas I became czar in 1825, he allowed Pushkin to return and resume his position at court, with time off to write. Among Pushkin's major works are the long poems *Ruslan and Ludmila* (1820) and *Evgeni Onegin* (1823–1831); the tragedy *Boris Godunov* (1825); the novel *The Captain's Daughter* (1836); and the novella *The Queen of Spades* (1834). In addition, Pushkin wrote some of the finest lyric poems in the Russian language.

Pythagoras (fl. 500's B.C.), Greek philosopher and mathematician. Though a native of Samos, in about 530 he established a school of philosophy at Crotona, Italy. He discovered that a tuned musical string has harmonic intervals that can be expressed with whole numbers; from this discovery derived both the scientific uses of mathematics and the philosophic concepts of harmony and balance. Pythagoras also taught transmigration of souls and demonstrated the so-called Pythagorean theorem, though it is not known certainly which proof he used.

Q

Quasimodo, Salvatore (1901–1968), Italian poet, teacher, and translator who received the 1959 Nobel Literature Prize for his poems about the horrors of war. His works, characterized by intense social and political awareness, include *Waters and Land* (1930) and *The Incomparable Earth* (1958). Quasimodo also did a number of sensitive translations of Shakespeare and Vergil.

Queensberry, 8th Marquess of; John Sholto Douglas (1844–1900), English nobleman and sporting enthusiast. In 1867 he sponsored the Queensberry rules for the sport of boxing. These rules emphasized skill and did not allow bare-knuckle fighting; they were adopted in England and the United States by the late 1800's.

Quisling, Vidkun Abraham Lauritz (1887–1945), Norwegian political leader whose name came to stand for any traitor who collaborates with the enemy. A founder of the Norwegian fascist political party, Quisling aided the German occupation of Norway in 1940 by declaring himself premier and failing to order Norwegian mobilization against the invaders. He was reduced to a puppet ruler by the Nazis and, after the liberation in 1945, was tried and executed for high treason.

R

Rabelais, François (c 1494–1553), French humanist remembered for his series of ribald satires, *Gargantua and Pantagruel.* He was a Franciscan and Benedictine monk before abandoning religious life to practice medicine. Despite opposition from the Sorbonne theological faculty and the French parliament, the first four parts of his masterpiece were published between 1532 and 1552; the final part appeared in 1562.

Rabi, Isidor Isaac (1898–1988), Austrian-born U.S. nuclear physicist who was awarded the 1944 Nobel Prize for Physics for research on radiofrequency spectra of atoms and molecules. After World War II, Rabi served as an adviser to the U.S. Atomic Energy Commission and to the U.S. Arms Control and Disarmament Agency.

Rabinowitz, Solomon (Sholom Aleichem) (1859–1916), Jewish author and humorist. Born in Russia, he received traditional Hebrew schooling. Early in his career he wrote poems and stories in Russian and Hebrew, but in 1883 he turned to Yiddish and raised its prestige as a literary language. He took up residence in the United States in 1914. By then he was known as "the Jewish Mark Twain." Through such beloved characters as Tevye the Dairyman (in *Tevye's Daughters,* English translation 1949; dramatized as *Fiddler on the Roof,* 1964) Sholom Aleichem recreated Jewish small-town life in Russia with great perceptiveness, warmth, and humor.

Rachmaninoff, Sergei Vassilievich (1873–1943), Russian composer, pianist, and conductor. He was conductor for the Moscow Imperial Theater, but after the Russian revolution of 1917, Rachmaninoff went to the United States. His Second Piano Concerto is among his most popular concert pieces; his *Preludes* for piano and his other symphonies and concertos are also frequently played.

Racine, Jean Baptiste (1639–1699), French tragic poet and dramatist. He went to Paris in 1663, where he was associated with Boileau, La Fontaine, and Molière. His first plays were produced by Molière's acting company. His most famous plays include *Andromaque* (1667), *Britannicus* (1669), *Bajazet* (1672), and *Phèdre* (1677).

Raleigh (or **Ralegh**), **Sir Walter** (c 1554–1618), English courtier, seaman, author, and explorer. After a number of military expeditions, he gained the favor of Queen Elizabeth I and became one of her greatest favorites. In 1584 he sent two ships to find a site for a colony in the New World, in what he called Virginia. In 1587 he sponsored a group of settlers who founded the ill-fated Roanoke colony. Elizabeth's successor, James I, was persuaded in 1603 to accuse Raleigh of plotting with Catholics and Spaniards, though Raleigh was known for his liberal religious attitudes and for his naval campaigns against Spain and its treasure ships. Raleigh was tried and sentenced to death, but the sentence was commuted to imprisonment in the Tower of London. After 13 years in the tower, Raleigh was released to search for gold in Guiana, on condition that he not attack the Spaniards. However, his second in command burned a Spanish border town, and Raleigh found no gold. When he returned to England, the king had him beheaded. Among Raleigh's writings are his *History of the World* (1614), written in prison, and a good deal of poetry, much of it for Queen Elizabeth.

Raman, Sir Chandrasekhara Venkata (1888–1970), Indian physicist who was awarded the 1930 Nobel Prize for Physics for his research on light diffusion and his discovery of the Raman effect, announced in 1928. He founded the *Indian Journal of Physics,* established the Indian Academy of Sciences, and trained hundreds of students for academic and scientific posts throughout India and Burma.

Rameau, Jean Philippe (1683–1764), French musician and composer. His *Traité de l'harmonie* (*Treatise on Harmony,* 1722) is considered the pioneer work in modern musical theory. A noted organist, Rameau wrote works for organ and harpsichord, ballets, and operas, of which the best was *Castor and Pollux* (1737). His operas, dramatic rather than lyric (the popular style at the time), were the models for French classic opera.

Rankin, Jeannette (1880–1973), U.S. legislator, pacifist, and women's rights advocate, the first woman to serve in Congress, elected for the first time in 1916. In addition to her leading role in the suffrage movement, she vigorously opposed the declaration of war on Germany in 1917. During a later term in Congress, 1941–1943, she was the only member to cast a vote against the declaration of war on Japan, later suggesting that President Roosevelt had provoked the attack on Pearl Harbor. In 1968 she led the Jeannette Rankin Brigade's march on Washington to oppose the Vietnam War.

Raphael (1483–1520), in Italian Raffaello Santi or Sanzio, Italian painter. Raphael painted many well-known madonnas (such as the famous *Sistine Madonna*) and portraits *(Pope Leo X with Cardinals).* His most mature and famous work is a series of frescoes in the Vatican known as the Vatican *Stanze* ("rooms"). It includes such panels as *The School of Athens* and *Disputà.* Raphael was later appointed to succeed Bramante as chief architect of St. Peter's.

Rasmussen, Knud Johan Victor (1879–1933), Danish polar explorer, born in Greenland, a leading authority on Eskimos. For 30 years, beginning in 1902, he explored the Arctic and made scientific studies of Eskimo culture, tracing their migration routes from Asia. In 1910 he set up a base in Thule and from this station carried out seven expeditions, including the longest dogsled journey ever made across the American arctic. Rasmussen's books include *Greenland by the Polar Sea* (1919) and *Across Arctic America* (1927).

Rasputin, Grigori Efimovich (c 1872–1916), Russian religious mystic, a corrupt but powerful influence in the court of Czar Nicholas II. He became a monk and, though given to debauchery, gained a reputation as a holy man through his magnetic personality and seemingly hypnotic powers. Rasputin moved to St. Petersburg in 1903 and won considerable influence over Alexandra, the wife of the czar. His power over the empress and the administration was considered by many a threat to Russia. He was assassinated by a group of nobles who hoped to save the monarchy, but it fell a few weeks later.

Ravel, Maurice Joseph (1875–1937), French composer best known for his symphonic work *Boléro* (1927). While still a student at the Paris Conservatory, he established his reputation with such piano compositions as *Pavane for a Dead Princess* (1899). He wrote chamber music, ballets, songs, symphonies, and several piano concertos, including one for the left hand (1931). Another of his popular works is the suite from the ballet *Daphnis et Chloé* (1912).

Ray, Man (1890–1976), U.S. artist and photographer, pioneer in Dadaism and surrealism. His important works include *Object to Be Destroyed* (1923) and *Observatory Time—The Lovers* (1932–1934). Ray was also a renowned photographer and an experimental filmmaker.

Rayburn, Samuel Taliaferro (1882–1961), U.S. statesman often called Mr. Democrat. He was elected to the Texas state legislature in 1907 and at the age of 29 became its youngest speaker. In 1912 Rayburn was elected to the U.S. House of Representatives. He established a record by serving there for more than 48 consecutive years. He was Speaker of the House for 17 years between 1940 and 1961, and was a trusted adviser to Presidents from Franklin Delano Roosevelt to John Fitzgerald Kennedy.

Reagan, Ronald (Wilson) (1911–), 40th President of the United States (1981–1989). A radio sports broadcaster and movie actor, Reagan was for six terms president of the Screen Actors' Guild (1947–1951, 1959). Originally a Democrat, Reagan became a Republican in 1962 and worked for conservative causes. He was elected governor of California in 1966 and reelected in 1970. He advocated cutting the cost of government, especially for welfare and educational services. Defeated for the Republican nomination for the Presidency in 1976 by President Ford, Reagan easily won it in 1980, then defeating the incumbent, Jimmy Carter. In office, he proposed large cuts in federal spending and an across-the-board income tax cut for three successive years, as well as less government regulation of business. On March 30, 1981, he was wounded in the left lung by a would-be assassin, but he recovered rapidly. He proposed the building of a controversial defense system known as the Strategic Defense Initiative, 1983, and in 1984 won reelection over Democrat Walter Mondale with 59 percent of the vote.

Red Cloud (1822–1909), in Indian, Mahpiua Luta, chief of the Oglala Sioux tribe, the only Indian chief to win a war against the United States. Fearing the loss of valuable hunting ground, Red Cloud staunchly refused to let settlers use the Bozeman Trail in Montana, despite offers of gifts from the U.S. government. He waged a two-year war that forced a government treaty and withdrawal from Sioux territory in 1868. Though Red Cloud kept peace after the treaty, he remained critical of deceitful Indian agents and the government.

Reed, Walter (1851–1902), U.S. Army surgeon famous for his research on yellow fever. In 1900 Reed headed a commission in Cuba seeking the cause of the yellow fever plaguing the Army camps. He found it was transmitted by a species of mosquito. His research made it possible to eradicate the disease in Cuba and elsewhere.

Reger, Maximilian (Max) (1873–1916), German composer and pianist whose works mark the transition between 19th- and 20th-century music. His revolutionary musical conceptions rejected all "program music" ideas and strove for absolute music. His compositions for organ, particularly the Fantasy and Fugue on the letters B-A-C-H, were his best known works.

Reiner, Fritz (1888–1963), Hungarian-born conductor. He conducted the Dresden Royal Opera from 1914 to 1922, when he moved to the United States; he led orchestras in Cincinnati and Pittsburgh and taught at the Curtis Institute. From 1953 until his death, he was musical director of the Chicago Symphony Orchestra.

Reinhardt, Max (1873–1943), original surname Goldmann, Austrian theater manager and producer known for spectacular staging and experimental theater design. He produced such varied works as *Faust, Oedipus Rex, Everyman,* and *Salome.* Moving to the United States in 1935, Reinhardt created the film *A Midsummer Night's Dream.*

Rembrandt Harmensz van Rijn (1606–1669), Dutch painter. As a young man, Rembrandt perfected the popular style of the period and was for many years a well-paid portrait painter. However, after the death of his wife in 1642, his style changed radically. His controversial *Night Watch* (1642) was highly criticized for its unflattering and honest portrayal of a fashionable shooting company. From then on his commissions were fewer, and he fell into debt, living in poverty on the outskirts of Amsterdam. Rembrandt's most famous paintings, notable for their rich colors, dramatic use of light and shadow, and depiction of character, include *The Anatomy Lesson of Dr. Tulp* (1632), *A Lady and Gentlemen in Black* (1633), *The Three Trees* (1643), *The Supper at Emmaus* (1648), *The Syndics of the Drapers' Guild* (1661–1662), and several self-portraits.

Remington, Frederic (1861–1909), U.S. artist, a painter of action-filled Western scenes. Remington painted and sketched the cowboys, Indians, soldiers, and animals that were part of frontier life. Among his works are the paintings *The Last Stand, Past All Surgery,* and *Conjuring the Buffalo Back,* and the bronze sculpture *Bronco Buster.*

THE BETTMANN ARCHIVE
WALTER REUTHER

Renoir, Pierre Auguste (1841–1919), French impressionist painter whose best-known paintings are of lovely women and children. Renoir introduced the rainbow palette, intense unmixed pigment (no black) applied in little spots or strokes. The result was the soft, vibrating color used by nearly all the impressionists. Renoir's works include *Little Girl with a Watering Can, The Luncheon of the Boating Party,* and sensuous nudes such as *Blue Nude* and *Two Bathers.*

His son **Jean Renoir** (1894–1979), French filmmaker and director, was noted for his films' humanist dimensions. Among his best-known films are *La Grande Illusion* (1937), *La Règle du Jeu* (*The Rules of the Game,* 1939), and *The River* (1951).

Respighi, Ottorino (1879–1936), Italian composer known for his colorful symphonic poems. He wrote the symphonic poems *The Fountains of Rome* (1916), *The Pines of Rome* (1924), and *Roman Festivals* (1929). He also made arrangements of old Italian music.

Reuther, Walter Philip (1907–1970), U.S. labor leader, head of the powerful United Auto Workers (UAW). As a young man, Reuther was fired as an apprentice tool-and-die maker for trying to organize other workers. In 1935 Reuther organized the UAW, becoming its president in 1946. When the Congress of Industrial Organizations (CIO), of which he was president, merged with the American Federation of Labor in 1955, Reuther became vice president of the combined union. He withdrew in 1968; the UAW later affiliated with the Teamsters. He died in a plane crash.

Revere, Paul (1735–1818), American patriot remembered for his ride on the night of April 18, 1775, from Charlestown (Boston) to Lexington to warn villagers that British troops were advancing. The resulting clash between the British and townsmen at Concord is usually considered the first battle of the American Revolution. Revere's feat was immortalized in Longfellow's poem "The Midnight Ride of Paul Revere." Revere was among the finest American silversmiths. He also operated a copper foundry and printed the first issue of Continental money during the American Revolution.

Reymont, Wladyslaw Stanislaw (1868–1925), Polish novelist remembered for his naturalistic studies of life among the lower classes. His best-known works are *The Promised Land* (1899), dealing with life in a factory town, and *The Peasants* (1902–1909), a tetralogy on the life of Polish peasants for which he was awarded the 1924 Nobel Prize for Literature.

Reynolds, Sir Joshua (1723–1792), English portrait painter. He was painter to King George III and was elected first president of the Royal Academy in 1768. For the next 20 years he dominated the academy and his famous *Discourses* became the expression of aesthetic principles for 18th-century England. His portraits include *Mrs. Siddons as the Tragic Muse, The Age of Innocence,* and *Dr. Johnson.* Reynolds, who preferred the company of men of letters, founded the famous Club, a London literary group that included Samuel Johnson, David Garrick, Oliver Goldsmith, and others.

Rhee, Syngman (1875–1965), first president of the Republic of Korea. He served a term in prison, 1897–1904, for his efforts to secure Korean independence, then went to the United States, becoming the first Korean to earn a U.S. doctoral degree. In 1919, after an uprising against Japanese rule in Korea, he was elected president of a Korean provisional government in exile in Shanghai. After Japan's defeat in 1945 and Korea's partition, Rhee was president of the newly established Republic of South Korea, 1948–1960.

Rhodes, Cecil John (1853–1902), South African statesman and financier, a leader of British colonial expansion in Africa. Born and raised in England, he went to South Africa in 1869 and gradually gained control of diamond fields around Kimberley. He returned to Britain a rich man and graduated from Oxford in 1881. He then returned to South Africa and served in various government positions. He made Bechuanaland (present-day Botswana) a British protectorate and in 1889 formed the British South Africa Company, which was given control over what later became Rhodesia. In 1890 Rhodes became prime minister and virtual dictator of South Africa. He was forced to resign in 1896 after he approved a raid on the Boer republic of the Transvaal. He died in 1902, willing part of his fortune to establish the Rhodes scholarships.

Richard I (Richard Coeur de Lion, or **Richard the Lion-Hearted)** (1157–1199), king of England, 1189–1199, son of Henry II and Eleanor of Aquitaine. During the 1170's and 1180's Richard waged war against his father and brothers to ensure his succession to the throne. He was crowned king in 1189. He spent less than a year of his reign in England. In 1190 he left for the Third Crusade. He conquered the island of Cyprus, then took Acre in 1191 and defeated Saladin, the Muslim leader, at Arsuf. Although Richard did not capture Jerusalem, his exploits became legendary throughout Europe. Learning that his brother John was plotting against him in England, Richard left Palestine for home in 1192. He was captured in Germany and held by the German emperor, but bought his freedom in 1194 with a ransom raised by taxation in England. After a short stay in England, he went to war against Philip II of France, who had intrigued with John against him. He died of a wound received in France.

Richardson, Elliott Lee (1920–), U.S. lawyer and public official. In the Nixon Cabinet, he became secretary of health, education, and welfare in 1970; after the 1972 elections, he was named secretary of defense. In 1973 he moved to the post of attorney general; later in 1973 he resigned rather than follow Nixon's orders to fire the special Watergate prosecutor. President Ford appointed him ambassador to Britain in January of 1975, but in February of 1976 Ford returned him to the Cabinet as secretary of commerce.

Richardson, Samuel (1689–1761), English novelist known as the originator of the English domestic novel. His first novel, *Pamela: or Virtue Rewarded* (1740), was a series of letters from a young girl whose employer tries to seduce her but fails. *Pamela* was followed by *Clarissa: or the History of a Young Lady* (1747–1748) and *The History of Sir Charles Grandison* (1753), all written in the form of letters.

Richelieu, Duc de; **Armand Jean du Plessis** (1585–1642), French cardinal and minister to Louis XIII, who strengthened the internal power and international prestige of the monarchy. Shortly after Richelieu was made bishop, he was elected to the Estates-General by the clergy of Poitou. He came to the attention of Marie de Medicis, the mother of Louis XIII, who brought him to court; in 1622 he was made a cardinal. He eventually became Louis' chief adviser and France's dominant power. Richelieu's great political aims were to suppress the Protestant Huguenots and to strengthen royal authority. To escape domination by the Austrian Hapsburgs, he involved France in the Thirty Years' War (1618–1648).

Richthofen, Baron Manfred von (the Red Baron) (1892–1918), German aviator, the most famous ace of World War I. He led the air combat group known as Richthofen's Flying Circus, in which Hermann Goering was a pilot. Richthofen himself was credited with downing 80 enemy planes.

Rickenbacker, Edward (Eddie) (1890–1973), the most famous U.S. fighter pilot of World War I. He shot down 26 German planes and was awarded the Congressional Medal of Honor. During World War II, Rickenbacker survived several weeks on a life raft after crashing in the Pacific.

Rickover, Hyman George (1900–), Russian-born U.S. naval officer who helped develop the world's first atomic-powered submarine. In 1947 Rickover began directing the Navy's nuclear propulsion program, which culminated in the launching of the U.S.S. *Nautilus* in 1954. Although he worked to advance nuclear power plant construction in the United States, 1956–1957, he later supported reduced military spending and the abolition of nuclear arms.

Ride, Sally Kristen (1951–), U.S. astronaut and astrophysicist, the first American woman to fly in space. While completing her dissertation at Stanford University, on the theoretical behavior of free electrons in a magnetic field, she was accepted into the National Aeronautics and Space Administration (NASA) program as a mission specialist. She began a period of intensive training, learning to fly a jet as well as logging hundreds of hours in facsimile spacecraft. Ride was chosen to be flight engineer on the seventh scheduled space shuttle mission (1983). In 1984 she flew on an eight-day mission. In 1986 she served on the Presidential Commission on the Space Shuttle Challenger Accident. In 1987 she left NASA for a science fellowship at Stanford University.

Riel, Louis (1844–1885), French-Canadian revolutionist and leader of the *métis,* the French-Indian inhabitants of the Canadian Northwest. Riel led the unsuccessful Red River Rebellion, 1869–1870, against the Dominion government to prevent it from taking over *métis* territory, previously controlled by Hudson's Bay Company. In 1885 he set up a provisional government and led a second revolt, which was also suppressed by Canadian forces. Riel was tried for treason and executed.

Riis, Jacob August (1849–1914), Danish-born U.S. journalist and social reformer known for his exposés of the horrors of slum conditions. He settled in the United States in 1870 and became a reporter on the New York *Tribune* and the *Evening Sun,* which published his first investigations of slum conditions. Riis also wrote several books, including *How the Other Half Lives* (1890), which brought about housing reforms.

THE BETTMANN ARCHIVE
PAUL ROBESON

Riley, James Whitcomb (1849–1916), U.S. poet who wrote in the folksy Hoosier dialect of southern Indiana. In 1877 he began to contribute poems to the Indianapolis *Journal,* signed with the pseudonym Benj. F. Johnson, of Boone. These were published in *The Old Swimmin' Hole and 'Leven More Poems* (1883). His well-known poems include "When the Frost Is on the Punkin" and "Little Orphant Annie."

Rilke, Rainer Maria (1875–1926), Austrian poet and writer. His writings contain elements of mysticism and were influenced by impressionist painting and symbolist poetry. His works include the novel *The Notebook of Malte Laurids Brigge* (1910); the cycle *Duino Elegies* (1922); and the poems *Sonnets to Orpheus* (1923).

Rimbaud, (Jean Nicholas) Arthur (1854–1891), French symbolist poet and adventurer. He began to write at age 15 and before he was 17 he had composed *Le Bateau ivre* (*The Drunken Boat,* 1871). After writing *Une Saison en enfer* (*A Season in Hell,* 1873) and *Illuminations* (published in 1887 but written much earlier), he abandoned writing and disappeared for a time, probably wandering in Europe. He finally settled in North Africa, where he was a trader, probably in firearms, ivory, and slaves, and contracted an incurable disease of which he died shortly after his return to France.

Rimski-Korsakov, Nikolai Andreevich (1844–1908), Russian composer and conductor best known for his colorful symphonic poem *Scheherazade* (1888). He was associated with a group called the Five, which included Balakirev and Borodin. He wrote 15 operas, including *The Maid of Pskov* (1873), *The Snow Maiden* (1882), and *Le Coq d'Or* (1907), as well as several symphonies. He also wrote the popular "Song of India" and "Flight of the Bumblebee."

Ringling, family name of five brothers who founded the largest circus in the United States. Under **Charles Ringling** (1863–1926), the brothers established an entertainment group, and then a circus in 1884. By 1900 it was the largest in America. In 1907 it was expanded by the acquisition of Barnum and Bailey Company. The last surviving brother, **John Ringling** (1866–1936), became head of the corporation that controlled Ringling holdings.

Rivera, Diego (1886–1957), Mexican mural painter, a leading figure in Mexican revolutionary art. His frescoes, painted in a folk-art style, reflect his strong proletarian sympathies. Typical of Rivera's paintings are such panels as *The Liberation of the Peon* (1931) and the huge *Nightmare of War and the Dream of Peace* (1952).

Robbia, Luca della (c 1400–1482), Italian Florentine sculptor. His first important work was his marble *Singing Gallery* (c 1431–1438) in the cathedral at Florence. He also worked in bronze before he developed a technique of enameling ceramic, which he used to produce several charming and colorful Madonna and child scenes.

Robbins, Jerome (1918–), U.S. dancer and choreographer noted for his use of American themes in his ballets and for distinctive choreography in a number of Broadway shows. Among Robbins's ballets are *Fancy Free* (1944) and *Age of Anxiety* (1950), both to music by Leonard Bernstein. He also did the choreography for *On the Town* (1944), *The King and I* (1951), *West Side Story* (1957), and *Fiddler on the Roof* (1964). He was ballet master and resident choreographer of the New York City Ballet, 1969–1983, before becoming co-director of the company with Peter Martins, a ballet dancer who went on to become a choreographer.

Robert I of Scotland: *See* Bruce, Robert.

Robeson, Paul (1898–1976), U.S. actor and concert singer best known for his recitals of black spirituals. Robeson attracted attention in 1923 in O'Neill's *The Emperor Jones.* He also played in the musical *Show Boat* (1927) and starred on stage as Othello. He made many concert appearances in the United States and Europe and played in many films. He left the United States in 1950 when denied a passport for refusing to state whether he had ever been a member of the Communist Party. He returned in 1963.

Robespierre, Maximilien François Marie Isidore de (1758–1794), French revolutionary leader considered responsible for the bloody Reign of Terror. He became a deputy to the Estates-General in 1789 and rose rapidly to power during the revolution. In 1792 he was elected to the National Convention, where he became leader of the radicals, or Montagnards. Robespierre voted for the execution of Louis XVI and attacked the Girondists' moderate polices. In 1793 Robespierre maneuvered to overthrow the Girondist Party. When disorders broke out, he was made head of the Committee of Public Safety, which was set up to preserve the peace. The committee instituted the Reign of Terror, a purge of all those thought to be enemies of the revolution. As Robespierre eliminated his enemies and gained power, he nearly succeeded in controlling the revolution. However, in 1794 his fellow committee members, in order to stop the terror, ordered his arrest and execution.

Robinson, Edwin Arlington (1869–1935), U.S. poet whose carefully crafted pessimistic verse about the inhabitants of Tilbury Town reflected his own New England background. Robinson was not well known until his *Collected Poems* (1921) won the Pulitzer Prize. His earlier books include *The Town Down the River* (1910) and *The Man Against the Sky* (1916). He later wrote a number of long blank-verse narrative poems based on the legends of King Arthur; one of these, *Tristram* (1927), was a popular success and also won a Pulitzer Prize.

Robinson, Jackie (1919–1972), U.S. baseball player, the first black player in the major leagues. He joined the Brooklyn Dodgers in 1946 and helped the team win six pennants. In 1949 his .342 batting average led the National League, and he was voted its most valuable player. His career average was .311. He retired from baseball in 1956.

Robinson, Sugar Ray (1920–1989), U.S. boxer, born Walker Smith. He won the welterweight crown, 1946, and the middleweight title, 1951, against Jake La Motta. After a three-year retirement, he regained the title, an unprecedented achievement. Celebrated for his speed and grace, Robinson lost only 19 out of 202 professional fights and was judged the best boxer, pound for pound, of his time.

Rockefeller, U.S. family of industrialists, politicians, and philanthropists.

John Davison Rockefeller (1839–1937) founded with his brother William (1841–1922) the Standard Oil Company and was its president from 1870 to 1911. By about 1900, Rockefeller had an estimated billion dollars. A noted philanthropist, he gave more than $500 million to charitable institutions. He set up the Rockefeller Foundation in 1913. His only son, **John D. Rockefeller, Jr.** (1874–1960), continued his father's business and philanthropic interests.

Nelson Aldrich Rockefeller (1908–1979), grandson of John D. Rockefeller, was coordinator of inter-American affairs during World War II and assistant secretary of state from 1944 to 1945. From 1959 to 1973 he was governor of New York. He was Vice President of the United States, 1974–1977, after being nominated by President Ford under terms of the 25th Amendment. His four brothers were **John Davison III** (1906–1978), head of the Rockefeller Foundation and chairman of Lincoln Center for the Performing Arts, 1961–1970; **Laurance S.** (1910–), director of Rockefeller Center; **Winthrop** (1912–1973), governor of Arkansas, 1967–1971; and **David** (1915–), head of the Chase Manhattan Bank, 1969–1981.

Rockne, Knute Kenneth (1888–1931), Norwegian-born U.S. football coach who perfected the use of the forward pass. He emigrated to the United States as a child and in 1910 entered Notre Dame University, where he became a track and football hero. He was head football coach there from 1918 until he was killed in a plane crash. His teams won 105 games, lost twelve, and tied five.

Rockwell, Norman Perceval (1894–1978), U.S. artist. During his long career as an illustrator, mainly for the *Saturday Evening Post,* Rockwell became the most familiar artist in the United States. His pictures were detailed, realistic everyday scenes, with the details telling a story. Besides his *Post* covers, his most famous paintings include the *Four Freedoms* series painted during World War II.

NORMAN ROCKWELL

SPRINGER/BETTMANN ARCHIVE

THE BETTMANN ARCHIVE

RICHARD RODGERS

FRENCH EMBASSY PRESS & INFORMATION DIVISION

AUGUSTE RODIN

UPI/BETTMANN NEWSPHOTOS

ELEANOR ROOSEVELT

Rodgers, Richard (1902–1979), U.S. composer who helped to create the modern American musical comedy. While at Columbia University, Rodgers began to work with lyricist Lorenz Hart; in 1927 they produced the musical *A Connecticut Yankee,* the first of many successes. After Hart's death in 1943, Rodgers joined with Oscar Hammerstein to produce the Pulitzer Prize-winning *Oklahoma!* (1943). Among the other popular shows written by Rodgers and Hammerstein are *Carousel* (1945), *South Pacific* (1949), *The King and I* (1951), and *The Sound of Music* (1959). Rodgers also wrote the score for the Navy documentary film, *Victory at Sea* (1952).

Rodin, (François) Auguste René (1840–1917), French sculptor. He lived and worked mostly in Paris, establishing his reputation with *The Age of Bronze,* exhibited in 1877; this work was so realistic that he was accused of casting the figure from a living man. One of the many commissions he received after this success was for a set of bronze doors *(The Gates of Hell),* on which he worked for the rest of his life. From this work came his masterpieces *The Thinker* and *The Kiss.* Other well-known Rodin pieces are *The Burghers of Calais,* the controversial *Balzac,* and other portraits.

Roebling, John Augustus (1806–1869), German-born U.S. civil engineer who designed and built the Brooklyn Bridge. He came to the United States in 1831 and soon became a manufacturer of steel cable and a pioneer builder of suspension bridges. His successful wire suspension bridge at Niagara Falls (finished in 1855) earned him his largest commission, the Brooklyn Bridge. While supervising the building of the tower structure, he was fatally injured. The bridge was completed under the direction of his son, Washington Augustus Roebling (1837–1926).

Roentgen, Wilhelm Conrad (1845–1923), German physicist who, in 1901, received the first Nobel Prize for Physics for his discovery of x-rays. Roentgen, director of the Physical Institute at the University of Würzburg, accidentally discovered that radiation passes through substances that are opaque to normal light.

Roethke, Theodore (1908–1963), U.S. poet. Roethke's highly regarded poetry, often based on his Michigan childhood, was tightly versified and rhymed. His most notable works are *The Waking* (1953), winner of the Pulitzer Prize, *Words for the Wind* (1958), and *The Far Field* (1964).

Rogers, Will (1879–1935), in full William Penn Adair Rogers, U.S. humorist and actor known for his satirical humor and folksy philosophy. He appeared in Wild West shows and vaudeville with his cowboy act, and while in New York introduced the humorous political satire for which he became famous. Rogers wrote a popular newspaper column and several books, and also appeared in films. He was killed in a plane crash.

Rolfe, John (1585–1622), English-born American colonist who in 1614 married Pocahontas, daughter of Chief Powhatan. He went to Virginia in 1610 and was the first colonist to cure tobacco, making it an exportable commodity. Rolfe and Pocahontas visited England in 1616; after her death he returned to Virginia and is thought to have been killed in an Indian raid.

Rolland, Romain (1866–1944), French writer and scholar best known for his epic works on music. He wrote several plays as well as biographies of Beethoven, Michelangelo, Tolstoy, and Gandhi. His masterpiece, *Jean Christophe* (1904–1912), is a ten-volume novel about a musical genius. Rolland was awarded the 1915 Nobel Prize for Literature.

Romanov, a Russian dynasty that ruled between 1613 and the Russian revolution of 1917. In 1613, after a nine-year period of civil war and foreign invasions, a national assembly elected Michael Romanov, grandnephew of Ivan IV, as czar. The Romanovs continued to rule Russia until 1917, when Nicholas II was forced to abdicate. The reigns of the Romanovs can be found on page 1687.

Rommel, Erwin (1891–1944), German field marshal. Rommel entered the army in 1910 and won the Iron Cross in World War I. In 1940, after commanding the SS troops in Nazi-occupied Europe, he took command in North Africa. There he won a series of brilliant victories against the British, earning the nickname the Desert Fox. He was finally defeated by Allied troops at El Alamein, Egypt, in 1942. Rommel then served in Italy and in France during the Allied landing at Normandy. He committed suicide in 1944 after learning he was implicated in a plot to assassinate Hitler.

Roosevelt, (Anna) Eleanor (1884–1964), U.S. writer, lecturer, and public servant, a constant support to her husband Franklin D. Roosevelt, especially after his crippling illness in 1921. While she was first lady, 1933–1945, she made many political trips and actively supported liberal legislation, especially in her syndicated newspaper column, "My Day." During World War II, she served in the Office of Civilian Defense. After her husband died, President Truman appointed her delegate to the United Nations, where she was chairman of the commission to draft the Universal Declaration of Human

Rights (adopted in 1948). During her later years, she traveled widely, lectured extensively, and wrote several books, including *On My Own,* (1958).

Roosevelt, Franklin Delano (1882–1945), 32nd President of the United States, 1933–1945. Roosevelt was elected as a Democrat to the New York Senate in 1910. In 1913 he became assistant secretary of the Navy. In 1920 he was nominated as Vice President, but was defeated. In 1921 his political career was temporarily halted by an attack of polio that left him handicapped for life. He nevertheless served as governor of New York, 1929–1932, and in 1932 ran successfully for the Presidency against Hoover, taking office in the midst of the Great Depression. Almost at once he closed all the banks in the country, declaring a bank holiday for a brief period. This was followed by the New Deal program, whose principles he explained to the nation by radio. Roosevelt was the first President to use the radio in this manner. He quickly acquired enormous power to combat the Depression. Appropriations amounting to $7 billion were placed at his disposal to restore buying power to the people and to put millions of idle men and women to work. He established many government agencies to meet the crisis. Some New Deal agencies were later declared unconstitutional by the U.S. Supreme Court. Roosevelt tried to pack the Court with new judges but failed. In 1936 Roosevelt was reelected by the greatest plurality any candidate had received. This vote he interpreted as a mandate to continue some of his more controversial programs. He was again reelected in 1940, the first U.S. President to be elected to a third term. The entry of the United States into World War II in 1941 turned Roosevelt's attention from domestic to foreign affairs. A vigorous war leader, he also promoted a postwar world organization, the United Nations. In 1944 Roosevelt won his fourth term as President, defeating Thomas A. Dewey. He died in 1945 shortly after his inauguration and a few days before Germany surrendered.

Roosevelt, Theodore (1858–1919), 26th President of the United States, 1901–1909. Roosevelt served in the New York legislature from 1882 to 1884 and spent the next two years as a cattle rancher in North Dakota. He was civil service commissioner from 1889 to 1895, when he resigned to become president of the board of police commissioners of New York City in a reform administration. In 1897 he was appointed assistant secretary of the Navy in President William McKinley's administration. Upon the outbreak of the Spanish-American War in 1898, he resigned to help organize the first U.S. volunteer cavalry—the Rough Riders—and saw action in Cuba. After the war he was elected governor of New York and two years later ran for Vice President on the Republican ticket. He succeeded to the Presidency on September 14, 1901, when McKinley was assassinated. He was reelected in 1904. One of the high points in his administration was a trust-busting campaign, an attempt to break up huge industrial combinations. His efforts to bring about peace between Japan and Russia in 1905 won him the Nobel Prize for Peace. At the end of his second term, Roosevelt led a scientific expedition to East Africa to collect big game specimens. When he returned, he again entered politics. Although there was strong Republican sentiment for his nomination, the convention renominated President Taft. Roosevelt entered the race as head of the Progressive Party, popularly known as the Bull Moose Party. This so split the Republican vote that the Democratic candidate, Woodrow Wilson, was elected President in 1912. Roosevelt then went on another trip, this time to the Amazon jungles of Brazil. On his return, he became a bitter critic of Wilson's administration. A prolific writer, Roosevelt wrote mainly about history and the outdoors. His books include *The Winning of the West* (1889–1896), *The Rough Riders* (1899), *Life of Oliver Cromwell* (1900), *The Strenuous Life* (1900), and *African Game Trails* (1910).

Rosenberg, Julius (1918–1953), the first U.S. civilian, along with his wife **Ethel Rosenberg** (1916–1953), to be executed for espionage. Julius and Ethel Rosenberg were indicted for conspiracy to deliver classified military information to the Soviet Union. At the trial, in 1951, the U.S. government charged the Rosenbergs with having persuaded David Greenglass (Ethel's brother) to steal top-secret data on nuclear arms from the Los Alamos atomic bomb project. Both defendants were found guilty. In spite of court appeals and a worldwide campaign for clemency in this highly controversial case, the Rosenbergs were put to death on June 19, 1953.

Ross, Sir James Clark (1800–1862), English admiral and explorer. In one of his six expeditions to the Arctic, 1819–1831, he determined the position of the magnetic North Pole. On an Antarctic expedition, 1839–1843, he reached the south magnetic pole in Victoria Land, which he discovered and named. He also discovered the sea there that is named for him.

Ross, John (1790–1866), Indian name Coowescoowe, chief of the eastern Cherokee Indians. The son of a Scottish father and Cherokee mother, Ross led the legal battle to keep the Cherokee from being evicted from their ancestral lands in Georgia. Although the Supreme Court under Chief Justice John Marshall sustained the Cherokees' right to remain on their lands, President Jackson did not enforce the ruling. From 1838 to 1839 the Army forced the Indians off their lands and across the South to Oklahoma. This march came to be called the Trail of Tears. Ross became chief of the new United Cherokee Nation, 1839–1866.

Rossellini, Roberto (1906–1977), Italian film and operatic director. His celebrated *Open City* (1945) marked the rebirth of European film after World War II and made Italian neorealist films known to the world. After *Paisan* (1946), his work took new directions, becoming noted for its passive objectivity and Catholic mysticism. Other films are *Stromboli* (1950), *Europa 51* (1951), *General della Rovere* (1959), and *Vanina Vanini* (1961).

Rossetti, family name of several English artists and writers.

Dante Gabriel Rossetti (1828–1882), poet and painter, was one of the leaders in establishing the Pre-Raphaelite Brotherhood, an aesthetic movement of the 19th century. Rossetti's works that reflect the Pre-Raphaelite interest in medieval symbolism and mysticism include the paintings *Annunciation, Beata Beatrix,* and *Dante's Dream* and the poem "The Blessed Damozel" (1850). *Ballads and Sonnets* (1881) contains some of his finest poems, including "House of Life."

Christina Georgina Rossetti (1830–1894), sister of Dante Gabriel, was a distinguished poet and a model for the Pre-Raphaelite painters. Her poems are collected in *Goblin Market* (1862), *The Prince's Progress* (1866), and *Sing-Song: A Nursery Rhyme Book* (1872), considered one of the finest children's books of the 19th century.

Rossini, Gioacchino Antonio (1792–1868), Italian composer best known for his brilliant, lively operas. Rossini wrote more than 40 operas, most of them before 1823. The best known today are *The Barber of Seville* (1816), *La Cenerentola* (1817), and *Semiramide* (1823). His overtures to such operas as *William Tell* and *La Gazza Ladra* remained popular after the operas were no longer performed. Rossini later wrote church music, including a *Stabat Mater* (1842).

Rostand, Edmond (1868–1918), the French dramatist best known for his *Cyrano de Bergerac* (1897), a romantic drama set in France during the reign of Louis XIII. Other plays include *L'Aiglon* (1900), a work about Napoleon's son, and *Chantecler* (1910), a largely autobiographical experimental work.

Roth, Philip (1933–), U.S. author known for his portrayal of Jewish life in mid-20th-century America. His works include *Goodbye, Columbus* (1959), which won the National Book

Award, *When She Was Good* (1967), *Portnoy's Complaint* (1969), and *Our Gang* (1971), as well as *My Life as a Man* (1974) and *Zuckerman Unbound* (1981).

Rothko, Mark (1903–1970), born Marcus Rothkovich, Russian-born U.S. painter, exponent of abstract expressionism in the years after World War II. His compositions are characterized by the frequent use of large rectangular bands of differing colors.

Rothschild, family of European Jewish bankers and financiers originally from Frankfurt, Germany.

Mayer Anselm Rothschild (1743–1812) was a German moneylender who became financial adviser to the count of Hesse-Cassel. Using the count's fortune, which he had preserved during the French Revolution, Rothschild founded his banking business. He then established branch banks throughout Europe, making his sons managers.

Anselm Mayer Rothschild (1773–1855) headed the family business in Frankfurt. Other concerns were operated by **Solomon Rothschild** (1774–1855) in Vienna; **Nathan Mayer Rothschild** (1777–1836) in London; **Karl Rothschild** (1788–1855) in Naples; and **James** (or **Jacob**) **Rothschild** (1792–1868) in Paris. All were made barons by the Austrian government in 1812. In 1885 the then head of the London house was made the 1st Baron Rothschild.

Rouault, Georges (1871–1958), the French expressionist painter known for his characteristic style of heavy black outlines, simplified forms, and rich vibrant colors. As a youth, Rouault worked with stained glass, which may have influenced his unusual technique. In 1905 he exhibited with the Fauvists. His canvases, ranging from religious scenes to portraits of clowns, include *La Sainte Face* (1933). He also produced several series of engravings.

Rousseau, Henri (1844–1910), French painter, nicknamed Le Douanier, known for his imaginative primitive art. His paintings, which include *The Sleeping Gipsy* (1897), *Village Street Scene* (1909), and *Jungle with a Lion* (1904–1906), had a profound influence on the surrealists.

Rousseau, Jean Jacques (1712–1778), Swiss-born French philosopher. Rousseau wrote articles for Diderot's *Encyclopédie* and in 1750 became famous for his *Discourses on the Arts and Sciences,* which extolled life in a primitive state, uncorrupted by civilization. Condemned for his antiroyalist views, Rousseau was forced to leave France for several years. His attacks on society as it is organized, his emphasis on the rights of man in the natural state, and his highly personal style made him popular with later Romantic writers. Among Rousseau's most important works are *The New Héloïse* (1761), an espistolary novel; *The Social Contract* (1762), a treatise on government and civilization; and *Émile* (1762), a novel about education, *Confessions,* an autobiography published after his death (Part I, 1781; Part II, 1788), revealed a depth of self-examination that has fascinated readers ever since.

ARTHUR RUBINSTEIN

Rubens, Peter Paul (1577–1640), Flemish baroque painter and diplomat. He studied painting in Antwerp and in 1600 went to Italy. There he was befriended by the duke of Mantua, who sent him on a diplomatic mission to the court of Spain, where he painted several portraits. He also spent much time in Venice and Rome. He returned to Antwerp in 1608 and was appointed court painter. Rubens's famous paintings are of allegorical, mythical, and religious subjects. They include *The Descent from the Cross, The Rape of the Sabines, Adoration of the Magi, The Assumption of the Virgin,* and *St. George.* In 1622 he painted the series *Life of Marie de Médicis* to decorate the Luxembourg Palace in Paris. Sent to London on another diplomatic mission, he did several paintings and was knighted by Charles I.

Rubinstein, Arthur (1889–1982), Polish-born U.S. pianist known particularly for his interpretations of Chopin and other Romantic composers. In 1906 he made his first concert tour of the United States, playing with the Philadelphia Orchestra. In later years, Rubinstein toured the world and was also seen on television.

Ruisdael (or **Ruysdael**) **Jacob van** (c 1628–1682), Dutch painter and etcher known for his landscapes. Ruisdael's paintings are mostly of rural scenes, with small figures set in large, somber landscapes. Among his many works are the masterpiece *The Windmill at Wijk* as well as *Jewish Cemetery* and *View of Haarlem.*

Rush, Benjamin (1745–1813), American statesman and physician. Rush made several important contributions to American medicine. In Philadelphia he established America's first free medical clinic, in 1786. He did pioneering work in mental disease, publishing *Diseases of the Mind* (1812). Rush also played an active role in the American Revolution. He signed the Declaration of Independence, served in the Army as a surgeon, and was treasurer of the U.S. mint from 1797 to 1813.

Rusk, Dean (1909–), U.S. public official, secretary of state from 1961 to 1969. He attended Oxford as a Rhodes scholar and then taught government at Mills College, 1934–1940. During World War II, he served in the Far East and, after holding various posts in the State Department, became undersecretary of Far Eastern affairs. Rusk was president of the Rockefeller Foundation, 1952–1960, before serving as secretary of state under Presidents Kennedy and Johnson.

Ruskin, John (1819–1900), English art critic and social reformer. Ruskin published the first of several volumes titled *Modern Painters* in 1843. He also wrote and lectured on architecture (*The Seven Lamps of Architecture,* 1849; *The Stones of Venice,* 1851–1853), advocating aesthetics based on moral and spiritual development. Turning to economics, he wrote several books urging social reform and greater sharing of wealth (*Sesame and Lilies,* 1865). Before he died, Ruskin dispersed his own inherited fortune, largely on philanthropic projects.

Russell, Bertrand Arthur William, 3rd Earl Russell (1872–1970), British philosopher, mathematician, essayist, and pacifist. Between 1910 and 1913, he and Alfred North Whitehead published the three volumes of their famous work on mathematical logic, *Principia Mathematica.* Russell acquired notoriety as a conscientious objector during World War I. In his later years, he supported the Campaign for Nuclear Disarmament and condemned U.S. involvement in Vietnam. His other works include *Introduction to Mathematical Philosophy* (1919), *History of Western Philosophy* (1945), and *Unpopular Essays* (1950). He was awarded the 1950 Nobel Prize for Literature.

Ruth, Babe (1895–1948), full name George Herman Ruth, U.S. baseball player whose lifetime total of 714 home runs made him one of the greatest batters in baseball history. Ruth began his major league career in 1914 with the Boston Red Sox and was the best left-handed pitcher in the American League. He joined the New York Yankees in 1920; in 1927 he hit 60 home runs in a single season, a record he held until 1961, when Roger Maris hit 61. His lifetime batting average was .342. He retired in 1935.

Rutherford, Ernest, 1st Baron Rutherford of Nelson (1871–1937), British physical chemist born in New Zealand. He established the existence of alpha and beta particles and developed a model of the atom with positive particles (which he later named protons) in the nucleus surrounded by moving electrons. With Frederick Soddy, he published in 1903 a general theory of radioactivity, for which he won the 1908 Nobel Prize in Chemistry. Rutherford did further research on radioactivity and transmutation of elements.

Ryder, Albert Pinkham (1847–1917), U.S. painter known for his mystical paintings of the sea, a part of his youth in New Bedford, Mass. In 1868 he moved with his family to New York City, where he studied art and lived as a recluse for the rest of his life. Ryder achieved glowing color by building up numerous layers of paint, a technique that caused his works to darken almost past recognition over the years. His paintings include *Toilers of the Sea, The Bridge,* and *The Race Track.*

S

Saarinen, Eero (1910–1961), U.S. architect, son of Eliel Saarinen. A leading modern architect, he often used aluminum and glass to achieve clean, precise effects. Among his buildings are an auditorium and chapel for the Massachusetts Institute of Technology; the General Motors Research Center at Warren, Mich.; the Trans World Airlines terminal at New York's Kennedy Airport; and the Vivian Beaumont Theater at Lincoln Center, New York.

Saarinen, (Gottlieb) Eliel (1873–1950), Finnish-born U.S. architect who fought classicism and advocated simplicity of design. Saarinen designed the League of Nations building in Geneva, Switzerland, and served as architectural director of the Cranbrook Foundation in Detroit. A specialist in urban planning, Saarinen wrote *The City: Its Growth, Its Decay, Its Future* (1943).

Sabin, Albert Bruce (1906–), Polish-born U.S. virologist who developed a live-virus oral vaccine against poliomyelitis. He also made invaluable studies of other viruses and virus diseases. His Sabin oral vaccine has been in general use since 1962.

Sacagawea (c 1787–1812), Shoshone Indian woman who accompanied the Lewis and Clark expedition to the Pacific, 1805–1806. The wife of Toussaint Charbonneau, the expedition's French-Canadian guide, she acted as interpreter.

Sacco, Nicola (1891–1927), Italian-born U.S. anarchist, defendant with **Bartolomeo Vanzetti** (1888–1927) in a famous murder trial in 1921. In spite of inconclusive evidence, Sacco and Vanzetti were convicted of killing two men in a payroll robbery in South Braintree, Mass., in 1920. They were executed in 1927. Many believed the two men to be victims of public sentiment against radical political views.

Sachs, Nelly (1891–1970), German-born poet and dramatist who became a Swedish subject. A personal appeal to Hitler by Swedish Nobel Prize-winner Selma Lagerlöf saved Sachs from a Nazi concentration camp in 1940. She shared the 1966 Nobel Prize for Literature for her lyric poetry and verse plays, written in German, depicting the persecution of the Jewish people. *O the Chimneys* (1950) is her best-known work. *And No One Knows Where to Go* (1957) and *Flight and Metamorphosis* (1959) are collections of her poetry.

Sadat, Anwar el- (1918–1981), second president of the Arab Republic of Egypt. Sadat was one of the original group of army officers who planned the overthrow of the Egyptian monarchy in 1952. Vice president at the time of Gamal Abdel Nasser's death in 1970, he was confirmed as president by the assembly. Although he led his country to attack Israel in 1973, he later severed Egypt's ties with the Soviet Union and made a dramatic visit to Israel. There he entered into negotiations with Menachem Begin that culminated in the 1979 Camp David accords. He shared the 1978 Nobel Peace Prize with Begin. Sadat was assassinated in Cairo by Muslim extremists.

EERO SAARINEN

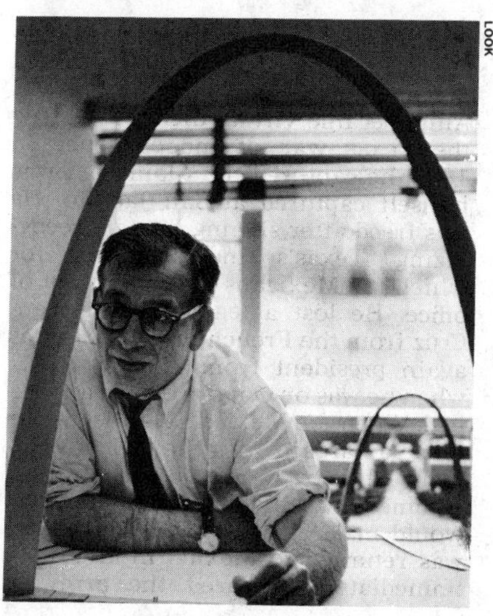
LOOK

St. Denis, Ruth (1878–1968), born Ruth Dennis, U.S. dancer and choreographer. Taking much from oriental dance, St. Denis created many original ballets in the early 1900's, two of which were *Rodha* and *Veil of Isis.* With Ted Shawn (1891–1972), her husband, she formed the influential Denishawn School of choreography, which trained such modern dancers as Martha Graham.

Saint-Exupéry, Antoine Marie Roger de (1900–1944), French aviator and author. His books, noted for their poetic style, include *Night Flight* (1932), *Terre des hommes* (translated as *Wind, Sand, and Stars,* 1939), and *Pilote de guerre* (translated as *Flight to Arras,* 1942). His *The Little Prince* (1943) became a classic of children's literature. Saint-Exupéry disappeared on a Mediterranean reconnaissance flight during World War II; it is thought that he was shot down by a German pilot who, in civilian life, was one of his admirers.

Saint-Gaudens, Augustus (1848–1907), Irish-born U.S. sculptor noted for his public monuments. Among his outstanding works are the Admiral Farragut Monument in New York, the statue of Abraham Lincoln in Chicago, and a memorial to Mrs. Henry Adams in Washington, D.C.

St. Laurent, Louis Stephen (1882–1973), lawyer, statesman, and Liberal prime minister of Canada, 1948–1957. As prime minister he helped to make Newfoundland a Canadian province, made the Supreme Court the court of final appeal, and introduced several social reforms.

Saint-Saëns, Charles Camille (1835–1921), French composer, pianist, and organist. Known throughout his career as a remarkable keyboard performer, Saint-Saëns was appointed organist of the Church of the Madeleine in 1857. He retired from that position in 1877 and gave recitals in Europe and America. His best-known compositions are the opera *Samson et Dalila* (1877), the symphonic poem *Danse macabre* (1847), the suite *The Carnival of the Animals* (1886), Symphony no. 3 in C minor (the Organ Symphony), and Sonata no. 1 in D minor for violin and piano.

Saladin (1138–1193), in full Salah-al-Din Yusuf ibn-Ayyub, Muslim military leader. In 1174 he became sultan of Egypt and subsequently conquered most of Syria. He then began a holy war to drive the Christians out of Palestine. In 1187 Saladin defeated the Christians at Tiberias and went on to capture the port of Acre, Jerusalem, and other towns. The news of Saladin's victories led the Christians of Europe to launch the Third Crusade in 1189. The Crusaders, led by Richard I of England and Philip II of France, retook Acre in 1191, but Saladin's military genius so discouraged them that many returned home. In 1192 Saladin accepted a three-year truce during which Christians were allowed access to Jerusalem.

Salazar, Antonio de Oliveira (1889–1970), Portuguese dictator, prime minister from 1932 to 1968. A professor of economics at Coimbra, in 1928 he was appointed minister of finance. In 1932 he was elected prime minister; in 1936 he also became minister of war and of foreign affairs, making him the virtual dictator of Portugal until 1968, when he was incapacitated by a stroke.

Salinger, Jerome David (1919–), U.S. author. Salinger's most famous book is the novel *The Catcher in the Rye* (1951). It contrasts the intensity of an adolescent boy and the phoniness of the adult world through which he wanders. Salinger also wrote *Nine Stories* (1953), *Franny and Zooey* (1961), and *Raise High the Roofbeams, Carpenter* (1963). His last published work was "Hapworth 16, 1924," a short story that appeared in *The New Yorker* on June 19, 1965.

Salk, Jonas Edward (1914–), U.S. physician and virologist who developed an effective vaccine for poliomyelitis. As a research fellow at the University of Michigan, he also helped develop a vaccine for influenza. In 1947 he became director of the virus research laboratory at the University of Pittsburgh, where in 1953–1954 he developed the polio vaccine; it was licensed for manufacture in 1955. He later founded the Salk Institute for Biological Studies.

Sand, George (1804–1876), pen name of Amandine Aurore Lucie Dupin Dudevant, French novelist. She is remembered for her personal life as well as her novels. An advocate of fewer restrictions on the conduct of women, she formed intimate relationships with her collaborator Jules Sandeau, the poet Alfred de Musset, and the composer Frédéric Chopin. She took the pen name George Sand for herself and wrote her first book, *Indiana,* in 1832. She wrote over 80 novels, producing her best work in such pastoral novels as *Jeanne* (1844) and *La Mare au Diable* (1846).

Sandburg, Carl (1878–1967), U.S. poet and biographer. Sandburg's first poetry was about the Midwest and the vigorous industrial cities of the early 1900's. His many volumes include *Cornhuskers* (1918), *Smoke and Steel* (1920), and *The People, Yes* (1936). His interest in the folklore of the Midwest and other parts of the United States was reflected in a huge collection of folk songs, *The American Songbag,* published in 1927. A student of the life of Abraham Lincoln, Sandburg won the 1940 Pulitzer Prize for history for *Abraham Lincoln: The War Years.* For his *Complete Poems,* he received the Pulitzer Prize in 1951.

Sanger, Margaret (1883–1966), U.S. social worker who founded the birth control movement in the United States. Educated as a nurse, Sanger was disturbed by the number of unwanted children born to low-income families. She began the American Birth Control League in 1917 and set up clinics in which she taught methods of birth control. Although such clinics were illegal in many states, she challenged these laws and won a series of favorable court decisions. She traveled all over the world, lectured, and wrote books and articles on birth control. Her books include *Woman Rebel* (1914), *What Every Girl Should Know* (1916), and *My Fight for Birth Control* (1931).

San Martín, José de (1778–1850), South American revolutionist, born in Argentina, who helped several countries achieve independence. Leading an army toward Upper Peru, a royalist stronghold, San Martín crossed the Andes into Chile. He defeated the Spanish at Chacabuco in 1817 and Maipú in 1818, freeing Chile from Spanish rule. He was offered control of the Chilean government but refused and continued on to Peru. There he met another revolutionist, Simón Bolívar, in 1822. Unable to work with Bolívar, San Martín resigned his command and retired to Europe, where he spent the remainder of his life.

Santa Anna, Antonio López de (1794–1876), president of Mexico. Elected president of Mexico in 1833, Santa Anna became virtual dictator. During the Texas war of independence in 1836, he captured the Alamo but was himself captured at San Jacinto. He was freed after signing a treaty recognizing Texas's independence, for which the Mexicans drove him out of office. He lost a leg defending Vera Cruz from the French in 1839. He was again president from 1841 to 1845, when he was once more ousted and exiled. When the Mexican War began, he made a bargain with the U.S. government whereby he would be helped to resume power in Mexico and in return would make peace on U.S. terms. He was returned to Mexico in 1846 and immediately prepared the army to

THE BETTMANN ARCHIVE

MARGARET SANGER

SAPPHO

UPI/BETTMANN ARCHIVE

JEAN-PAUL SARTRE

THE BETTMANN ARCHIVE

defend his country. After Mexico City fell in 1847, Santa Anna left Mexico. He returned in 1853, ruled another two years, and was overthrown and exiled again. He was allowed to return in 1875.

Santayana, George (1863–1952), Spanish-born U.S. philosopher and writer. Santayana took as his fields of interest knowledge, philosophy, and aesthetics. His most important philosophical work is in the four volumes of *Realms of Being* (1927–1940); he also wrote *The Sense of Beauty* (1896), *The Life of Reason* (1905–1906), and the novel *The Last Puritan* (1936).

Sappho (fl. c 610–580 B.C.), Greek lyric poetess, probably a native of Mytilene, in Lesbos. Only two of her compositions have survived in reasonably complete form, but there are many fragments. Her works include marriage hymns, lyrics with a folk song quality, and personal poems addressed to the young women of her salon.

Sargent, John Singer (1856–1925), U.S. painter, the leading American portrait painter of his time. Sargent was educated in Europe and spent much of his life in England. He is known for his murals in the Boston Public Library. Some of his famous portrait subjects were Ellen Terry, Mme. Gautreau *(Madame X),* Edwin Booth, Joseph Jefferson, and Woodrow Wilson.

Saroyan, William (1908–1981), U.S. novelist and playwright whose romantic works combined elements of the tragic and bittersweet with recollections of his Armenian family background. His short story collection, *The Daring Young Man on the Flying Trapeze,* appeared in 1934, followed by the dramas *My Heart's in the Highlands* (1939) and *The Time of Your Life* (1940). Other works include *My Name Is Aram* (1940) and *The Human Comedy* (1942).

Sarto, Andrea del (1486–1530), full name Andrea Domenico d'Agnolo di Francesco, Italian painter of the Florentine school. He is known as a colorist and a master of chiaroscuro (painting with dark and light contrasts for dramatic effect). His works include the fresco *Birth of the Virgin* and the paintings *Last Supper, Madonna of the Harpies,* and *Charity,* painted while he was at the court of Francis I of France.

Sartre, Jean-Paul (1905–1980), the French philosopher, novelist, and dramatist who led the post-World War II existentialist philosophical and literary movement. Its doctrine is set forth in such works as *Nausea* (1938), a novel; *No Exit* (1944), a play; and *Being and Nothingness* (1943), a philosophical treatise. His psychological study of Jean Genet, *Saint Genet, Actor and Martyr,* appeared in 1952. Sartre's autobiography, *The Words (Les Mots),* appeared in 1964. An independent man, he refused to accept the 1964 Nobel Prize for Literature.

Satie, (Alfred) Erik Leslie (1866–1925), French composer. Satie led the revolt in the early 1900's against the impressionistic style of Claude Debussy and Maurice Ravel and inspired a group called the Six, which included Darius Milhaud and Arthur Honegger. An accomplished pianist, Satie performed many of his own compositions, including *Three Gymnopédies* (1887) and *Three Pieces in the Form of a Pear* (1903).

Savonarola, Girolamo (1452–1498), Italian religious and political reformer. He joined the Dominican order in 1475 and began preaching on the sinfulness and corrupting influence of power in the wealthy city of Florence. In 1492, after the death of Lorenzo de' Medici, he and his followers ruled Florence as a Christian commonwealth, sternly opposing luxury and frivolity. Savonarola was accused of heresy and excommunicated in 1497. His political power began to wane, and the people of Florence, tired of his repressive regime, turned against him. Savonarola was hanged and burned at the stake.

Scarlatti, Italian family of baroque composers.

Alessandro Scarlatti (1660–1775) was a prolific composer and one of the founders of the Neapolitan school of opera. His best-known works are *La Rosaura* (1690) and *Il Tigrane* (1715). He composed hundreds of cantatas and oratorios.

His son **Domenico Scarlatti** (1685–1757) is considered the greatest keyboard composer of the 1700's. His harpsichord sonatas are among the most singular and brilliant ever written for that instrument; they are contained in the volume *Essercizi* (1738).

Schelling, Friedrich Wilhelm Joseph von (1775–1854), German philosopher. His idealist philosophy included a number of Romantic concepts, such as the supremacy of the artist and the parallel between genius and nature. In opposition to Hegel's philosophy, he developed late in life a metaphysic about man's knowledge of God that influenced existentialism.

Schick, Béla (1877–1967), Hungarian-born U.S. pediatrician who developed in 1913 the Schick test for diphtheria. His work laid the basis for modern pediatrics. His publication *The Serum Sickness* (1905) is a basic text in the medical science of allergies.

Schiller, Johann Christoph Friedrich von (1759–1805), German dramatist. Schiller wrote his first play, *Die Räuber* (*The Robbers,* 1781), while an army medical assistant. Under the influence of the *Sturm und Drang* literary movement, he constantly returned to the theme of freedom, as in *Don Carlos* (1787). In 1787 Schiller moved to Weimar, where he befriended Goethe. Their friendship proved an inspiration to both. With Goethe's help, Schiller became professor of history at Jena. His historical works include a *History of the Thirty Years' War* (1791–1793), from which he also derived his *Wallenstein* trilogy (1800), one of the world's greatest historical plays. Of similar merit are *Maria Stuart* (1800), *Die Jungfrau von Orleans* (*The Maid of Orleans,* 1801), and *Wilhelm Tell* (1804). Of his lyric poems, the best known is *"Das Lied von der Glocke"* ("Song of the Bell").

Schlegel, August Wilhelm von (1767–1845), German poet, translator, and critic, a leading figure in the German Romantic movement of the early 1800's. His influential book, *Lectures on Dramatic Art and Literature* (1815), based on lectures delivered in Vienna in 1808, was widely translated. Schlegel is best known for his translations into German of Shakespeare, Dante, and Cervantes and for his part in the influential critical journal, the *Atheneum,* which he and his brother Friedrich von Schlegel (1772–1829) edited.

Schliemann, Heinrich (1822–1890), German archaeologist whose faith in the historical truth of the *Iliad* led him to discover the ruins of Troy. Following clues in Homer, he found the site of ancient Troy at Hisarlik in Asia Minor. After excavating Troy, he dug at Mycenae and Orchomenos, unearthing the royal tombs there. His discoveries excited a widespread public interest in archaeology.

Schmidt, Helmut (1918–), chancellor of West Germany (1974–1982). He served as an officer in the German army in World War II, then entered politics as a member of the Social Democratic Party. Schmidt was elected to the Bundestag in 1953 and continued in it except for the period 1962 to 1965. From 1967 to 1969 he was his party's leader in the legislature; in 1968 he became vice chairman of the party. Schmidt then served as defense minister, 1969–1972, and finance minister, 1972–1973. He succeeded Willy Brandt as chancellor in May, 1974, when Brandt resigned as a result of a spy scandal. Schmidt was a firm supporter of the European Common Market and of NATO, although he has stressed the need for accommodation with the Soviet Union. Schmidt and French President Giscard d'Estaing, had a close working relationship. In addition, Schmidt has put great emphasis on keeping Germany strong economically. Helmut Kohl succeeded Schmidt in 1982 after Schmidt lost a vote of confidence in the lower house of parliament.

Schnitzler, Arthur (1862–1931), Austrian author and physician. A colleague of Sigmund Freud, Schnitzler wrote novels, short stories, and plays about the *fin-de-siecle* society of Vienna. His works are light and cynical, but with insight and sympathy for his characters. He is remembered chiefly for his plays, such as *The Affairs of Anatol* (1889), *The Games of Love* (1895), and *La Ronde* (1896).

Schoenberg, Arnold (1874–1951), Austrian-born U.S. composer. After his early compositions he abandoned the traditional concepts of tonality in music. From Schoenberg's atonal style evolved modern twelve-tone, or serial, music. He wrote *Verklärte Nacht* (*Transfigured Night,* 1899), the symphonic poem *Pelleas and Melisande* (1905), the melodrama *Pierrot Lunaire* (1912), and an opera, *Moses and Aaron* (1930–1932).

Schoolcraft, Henry Rowe (1793–1864), U.S. ethnologist, one of the earliest scientists to study American Indians. In 1822 he became the Indian agent for the tribes of the Lake Superior region. During his service he negotiated treaties by which the United States acquired 16 million acres of land from the Indians. In 1832 Schoolcraft headed an expedition that discovered the sources of the Mississippi. He wrote narratives of his travels and a six-volume history of American Indian tribes (1851–1857).

Schopenhauer, Arthur (1788–1860), German philosopher who propounded a mystical doctrine of the will in opposition to Hegel's rationalism. He published his major work, *The World as Will and Idea,* in 1819. A confirmed pessimist, Schopenhauer taught that reason is always subordinate to the irrational will. The suffering caused by this condition can be escaped only through art or Buddhist mysticism. His thought influenced philosophers such as Nietzsche and artists such as Wagner and Hesse.

Schubert, Franz Peter (1797–1828), Austrian Romantic composer who created the German *lied,* or art song, and was its greatest exponent. His most famous *lieder* include "The Wanderer," "Death and the Maiden," "Ave Maria," and "Who is Sylvia?" Schubert's melodic genius also extended to orchestral and chamber music, as in his Seventh Symphony (*Unfinished,* 1822), Ninth Symphony (*Great C-Major,* 1828), *Trout* Quintet (1819), and *Rosamunde* Overture (1823).

Schuman, William Howard (1910–), U.S. composer of symphonies, ballets, and chamber music. In 1943 he won the first Pulitzer Prize given in music for his *Secular Cantata No. 2, A Free Song.* His other works include ten symphonies; the ballets *Undertow* and *Judith;* the *American Festival Overture; The Mighty Casey,* an opera; and *This Is Our Time,* a cantata. From 1962 to 1969 he was director of the Lincoln Center for the Performing Arts in New York.

Schumann, Robert (1810–1856), German Romantic composer. He studied piano as a young man, but, overzealous at piano exercises, he crippled his right hand and turned to composition. His notable works are the First *(Spring)* and Third *(Rhenish)* symphonies (1841, 1850), the Piano Concerto in A (1845), numerous volumes of piano music *(Papillons, Albumblätter),* and *lieder.* His health deteriorated and he went insane shortly before his death.

His wife, **Clara Schumann** (1819–1896), was a concert pianist of great virtuosity; she also composed and taught music. After her marriage, Clara Schumann performed her husband's music, as well as that of Brahms, Beethoven, and Chopin. Her editing of Schumann's complete works following his death did much to secure his musical reputation.

Schuyler, Philip John (1733–1804), American Revolutionary soldier and political leader. He served in the French and Indian War, was a delegate to the Continental Congress (1775), and, as one of the four generals of the Continental army, was in command of Northern troops. Disagreements with his superiors forced him to resign in 1779; he then became Indian commissioner. He later served as U.S. senator from New York. With Alexander Hamilton (his son-in-law) and John Jay, he led New York's Federalist Party.

Schweitzer, Albert (1875–1965), Alsatian doctor, philosopher, biblical scholar, and musician. Before he was 35 years old, Schweitzer had established an international reputation as a biblical scholar and a musician. In 1903 he became head of the theology school at the University of Strasbourg. A distinguished organist, he published an authoritative biography of Johann Sebastian Bach in 1905 that was instrumental in reviving interest in the composer. In 1906 Schweitzer published *In Search of the Historical Jesus,* a pioneering work in textual analysis of the New Testament. Determining at the age of 30 to devote the remainder of his life to the service of mankind, Schweitzer entered medical school. In 1912 he sailed to French Equatorial Africa and founded a hospital at Lambaréné, in present-day Gabon, where he worked for the rest of his life. He kept up his interest in other disciplines, however, publishing a later book on the theology of St. Paul and making regular trips to Europe and North America to give lectures and organ recitals. Schweitzer received the 1952 Nobel Peace Prize.

Scott, Robert Falcon (1868–1912), British Antarctic explorer who died leading the second expedition to reach the South Pole. In command of the *Discovery* exploring the Antarctic regions, 1901–1904, he discovered and named King Edward VII Land. Scott began a second Antarctic journey in 1910. With four companions, he reached the South Pole in January of 1912, only to find that Roald Amundsen had reached it a month and four days earlier. Scott's entire party perished on the return journey. Scott's diary of the expedition tells of his party's heroic efforts.

Scott, Sir Walter (1771–1832), Scottish novelist, poet, historian, and biographer. As a youth, Scott was an insatiable reader of ballads and romances. While studying law at Edinburgh, he explored the Scottish countryside, collecting old songs and stories. Scott published a song collection, *Minstrelsy of the Scottish Border,* in 1802. It and the narrative poem *The Lay of the Last Minstrel* (1805) earned him wide popularity. He then started writing romances, notably *The Lady of the Lake* (1810). In 1814, *Waverly,* the first of a series of novels, was published anonymously; it was instantly successful. Many novels followed, including *Rob Roy* (1817) and *Ivanhoe* (1819).

Scott, Winfield (1786–1866), U.S. military leader who served as a general in three major American wars. During the War of 1812, he served at the Canadian front where he was decorated for heroism and was made a major general. In 1847 he commanded U.S. forces in the Mexican War and was made lieutenant general. Scott was the Whig candidate for President in 1852, but was defeated. When the Civil War broke out, he remained active in the Union Army until November, 1861, when he retired.

Scriabin, Alexander Nikolaevitch (1872–1915), Russian composer and pianist noted for his harmonic innovations. Among his orchestral works are three symphonies, the third of which is *The Divine Poem;* and the symphonic poems *Poem of Ecstasy* and *Prometheus,* which include a scheme for color projections during the performance.

Seaborg, Glenn Theodore (1912–), U.S. chemist noted for his work in transuranium elements. He shared the 1951 Nobel Prize for Chemistry with **Edwin M. McMillan** (1907–) for their discovery of the fissionable isotopes of uranium-233 and plutonium-239, artificial elements heavier than uranium. Seaborg and his co-workers discovered elements 93 through 98 and element 101.

STEVE KAGAN/PHOTO RESEARCHERS, INC.

PETE SEEGER

FRENCH EMBASSY PRESS AND INFORMATION SERVICE

LEOPOLD SENGHOR

Seeger, Pete (1919–), U.S. folk musician who sparked the folk music revival of the 1950's and 1960's. He sang for the union movement during the 1940's with the Almanac Singers. From 1948 to 1956 he sang with the Weavers ("Goodnight Irene"). Seeger also wrote several well-known songs, including "Where Have All the Flowers Gone" (1961). In the 1970's and 1980's he was active in efforts to stop pollution of the Hudson River, and participated in many environmental demonstrations.

Segovia, Andrés (1894–1987), Spanish concert guitarist who revived the classical guitar as a concert instrument. He edited many classical works written for guitar and arranged other compositions, particularly works by Bach, for his instrument. Guitar works were written for Segovia by such contemporary composers as De Falla, Villa-Lobos, and Castelnuovo-Tedesco.

Seleucus I (c 358–280 B.C.), surnamed Nicator ("conqueror"), Macedonian general who founded the Seleucid dynasty that ruled the Near East following the division of the empire of Alexander the Great. Civil war broke out among Alexander's generals after his death at Babylon in 323, but by 312 Seleucus had gained control of Babylon and began to expand his territory. His empire extended from Asia Minor to northern India. He founded Macedonian colonies and also built Antioch as his capital. He ruled from 312 until about 280, when he was assassinated.

Semmelweis, Ignaz Philipp (1818–1865), Hungarian physician who pioneered in the use of antiseptics. He proved that puerperal (childbed) fever was infectious and could be controlled by the use of antiseptics; he urged the washing of hands and instruments with soap or chlorinated lime.

Seneca, Lucius Annaeus (c 4 B.C.–65 A.D.), Roman philosopher, playwright, and statesman. He became tutor to the future emperor Nero and remained as an adviser after Nero's accession. Seneca was largely responsible for the sound government of Nero's early reign; when Nero's evil character began to affect affairs of state, Seneca retired. Soon after, Nero accused him of conspiracy and forced him to commit suicide. As a philosopher, Seneca was a Stoic. His *Dialogues* (moral essays) were studied by early Christians. As a playwright, he adapted his material from the Greeks, but his characters are less human and his style more rhetorical. Nevertheless, later ages considered him the greatest of Roman tragedians.

Senghor, Léopold Sédar (1906–), Senegalese national leader and poet. Educated in French schools in Senegal (then French West Africa), he later studied and taught in France. A poet as well as a political leader, he developed a philosophy of "negritude" that stressed the achievements of African art and called for the preservation and development of African artistic values. He published his *Selected Poems* (1964) and *Nocturnes.* In 1948 Senghor founded his own political party; it came to dominate Senegalese politics. After Senegal became an independent republic, 1960, he was elected president unanimously and remained in power until 1980.

Sequoya (c 1770–1843), Cherokee Indian, the only individual in history known to have developed an alphabet for a language with no written tradition. In about 1809 he began to formulate a written language for the Cherokee tongue, first experimenting with pictographs, and eventually using symbols for the syllables of the language. His completed syllabary contained 86 letters; with it Sequoya taught his tribe to read and write their language.

Serkin, Rudolf (1903–), Czech-born U.S. pianist. His European concert tours began in 1920; he made his U.S. debut in 1933. A prominent concert soloist, he was renowned for his performances of Mozart and Beethoven. Serkin was director of the Curtis Institute of Music in Philadelphia, 1968–1976, and helped establish a summer music school and festival in Marlboro, Vt.

Serra, Junipero (1713–1784), original name Miguel José Serra, Spanish Franciscan missionary. In 1767 he led a company of monks to California and in following years established 21 missions, including Mission Carmel (Monterey, 1771), San Luis Obispo (1772), and San Juan Capistrano (1776).

Seton, Saint Elizabeth Ann (1774–1821), Roman Catholic religious leader and educator. She was born in New York City as Elizabeth Ann Bayley; she married William Seton in 1794 and after his death in 1803 she converted to Roman Catholicism. In Emmitsburg, Md., in 1804, she opened a Catholic free school, considered the beginning of Roman Catholic parochial education in the United States. She also founded St. Joseph's College for women and formed a religious community for women, the Sisters of Charity, the first American religious society. She was the superior of the community and became known as Mother Seton. Upon her canonization in 1974 she became the first native-born American saint.

Seurat, Georges Pierre (1859–1891), French painter, the leader of the neo-impressionists. Seurat's style, called pointillism, is characterized by the breaking of color into dots that merge when viewed from a distance. His most famous canvas is *La Grande Jatte* (1884–1886), and his other works include *La Parade* (1887), and *Le Cirque* (1890).

Seuss, Dr. (1904–), pen name of Theodor Seuss Geisel, U.S. humorist and artist whose many illustrated books for children are populated with absurd and delightful animals and characters. Some lasting favorites are *And to Think That I Saw It on Mulberry Street* (1937), *The Cat in the Hat* (1957), and *Fox in Sox* (1965).

Seward, William Henry (1801–1872), U.S. statesman best remembered for his part in the purchase of Alaska from Russia, called Seward's Folly by those who thought the purchase ill-advised.

A lawyer with a large practice, he entered New York State politics in 1830, serving in the state senate and later as governor. In 1849 he was elected U.S. senator and fought against slavery. Seward became Abraham Lincoln's secretary of state in 1861 and served until 1869 in the Lincoln and Andrew Johnson administrations.

Shahn, Benjamin (1898–1969), U.S. artist known for his realistic murals, paintings, and posters depicting the lives of farm and factory workers, immigrants, and other personalities of the American scene. His storytelling art was often in support of liberal social and political causes. A famous series of paintings treats the trial of Sacco and Vanzetti in the 1920's, another the saga of the growth of the garment workers' union.

Shakespeare, William (1564–1616), English dramatist and poet who, for his dramatic skill, his creation of memorable characters, and his superb poetry, is considered the greatest writer in the English language. He was born in Stratford-upon-Avon, went to London in the late 1580's, after marrying Anne Hathaway, and by the late 1590's was well established and apparently prosperous. Shakespeare was a member of the Lord Chamberlain's Company, which became the King's Men after 1603. The company eventually owned their own theater and attracted the patronage of Queen Elizabeth and King James I. He remained in London until about 1612, when he retired to Stratford. Shakespeare's works consist of two long poems, *Venus and Adonis* and *The Rape of Lucrece,* written during his early years in London; a series of 154 sonnets published in 1609; a few miscellaneous poems; and the 37 plays for which he is most famous. Many of these plays were published in imperfect versions during his lifetime. They were collected and published together in 1623. Many of Shakespeare's early plays *(Henry VI, Richard II, Richard III, King John)* were based on English history. He also experimented with comedies *(Taming of the Shrew)* and formal tragedy. In the late 1590's he wrote *Romeo and Juliet,* a romantic tragedy. He also wrote a number of comedies, including *A Midsummer Night's Dream, Love's Labor Lost,* and *Much Ado About Nothing;* and continued the historical plays, both on the English kings *(Henry V)* and classical rulers *(Julius Caesar).* Between 1600 and 1606 he wrote four tragedies on which his outstanding reputation is most firmly based; they are *Hamlet, Othello, King Lear,* and *Macbeth.* During this same period he wrote the "dark comedies," such as *Measure for Measure,* so-called because of their somber mood. His late plays, such as *The Winter's Tale* and *The Tempest,* are allegorical romances, neither comic nor tragic.

Shankar, Ravi (1920–), Indian musician who introduced the sitar and the tradition of classical Indian music to Western audiences. Shankar wrote many compositions for radio broadcasts, the ballet score *Discovery of India,* and background music for such films as the *Pather Panchali* trilogy. His first Western concerts were given in 1956; his style of music later became popular with both classical and rock concert audiences.

Shaw, George Bernard (1856–1950), Irish dramatist whose plays are noted for their brilliant wit, social criticism, and sense of comedy. Among the most famous are *Man and Superman* (1903), *The Doctor's Dilemma* (1906), *Major Barbara* (1907), *Pygmalion* (1913), *Heartbreak House* (1919), *Back to Methuselah* (1921), and *Saint Joan* (1923). Shaw's prefaces to his plays contain much of his strongest prose in the form of stage directions. An unconventional, vigorous, highly original man, Shaw was known as a champion of spelling reform, vegetarianism, and Fabian socialism. He wrote *The Intelligent Woman's Guide to Socialism and Capitalism* (1928). He was awarded the 1925 Nobel Prize for Literature.

Shelley, Percy Bysshe (1792–1822), English Romantic poet. He was expelled from Oxford University for having co-authored an antireligious pamphlet, *The Necessity of Atheism* (1811). Shortly thereafter, he married Harriet Westbrook, but soon fell in love with Mary Wollstonecraft Godwin (who later wrote *Frankenstein*), the daughter of his friend William Godwin. They eloped to Europe and, after Harriet's suicide in 1816, were married. Shelley's poetry was pantheistic and idealistic. He experimented with many literary forms and also made translations from Greek, Latin, Italian, and German. His long poems include *Prometheus Unbound* (1820) and *Adonais* (1821), an elegy on the death of John Keats. A few of his short lyrics are "Ode to the West Wind," "The Cloud," and "To a Skylark."

PERCY SHELLEY

Shepard, Alan Bartlett, Jr. (1923–), U.S. astronaut, the first American in space. In the capsule *Freedom,* in 1961, he made a 15-minute suborbital flight and performed several maneuvers. In 1971 as commander of the Apollo 14 lunar landing mission, he was the fifth man to walk on the moon.

Sheridan, Philip Henry (1831–1888), U.S. Civil War cavalry general. At the outbreak of the Civil War in 1861, he was made quartermaster of the Department of Missouri in the Union Army. Before the end of 1863 he had distinguished himself in many battles. A spectacular victory at the Battle of Cedar Creek in 1864 won him promotion to major general. Sheridan was appointed commander in chief of the U.S. Army in 1883.

Sheridan, Richard Brinsley Butler (1751–1816), British politician and dramatist who excelled at writing comedies of manners. He created the humorous, word-twisting Mrs. Malaprop. *The Rivals,* the first of Sheridan's successful comedies, was produced in 1775. It was followed in 1777 by *The School for Scandal,* a satire on England's fashionable society. Both plays are still regularly performed. In 1776 Sheridan bought a part interest in Drury Lane Theatre, where he encouraged a revival of Restoration comedy and where *School for Scandal* was first performed. He served in Parliament as a Whig from 1780 to 1812.

Sherman, William Tecumseh (1820–1891), U.S. Civil War general. When the Civil War broke out in 1861, Sherman entered the Union Army as a colonel. After the Battle of Shiloh, 1862, he was promoted to general. He was made commander of the Department of Tennessee in 1863 and of the military division of the Mississippi in 1864. In May, 1864, Sherman left Chattanooga, Tenn., and marched through Georgia, taking Atlanta by September. On November 1 Sherman began his famous march to the sea, destroying everything in his path. He swept from Atlanta eastward to Savannah, taking the city December 21. He then moved northward along the coast through the Carolinas. Sherman served as commander of the Army, 1869–1883.

Sherwood, Robert Emmet (1896–1955), U.S. author and playwright. Sherwood became known as a dramatist with the production of *The Road to Rome* in 1927, followed by *The Petrified Forest* (1935). Sherwood was awarded four Pulitzer prizes: for the plays *Idiot's Delight* (1936), *Abe Lincoln in Illinois* (1938), and *There Shall Be No Night* (1940); and for the historical work *Roosevelt and Hopkins: An Intimate History* (1948).

Shih Huang Ti (259–210 B.C.), king of the Ch'in dynasty and first Chinese emperor, 221–210. Having unified the feudal provinces, Shih Huang Ti set up a strict, highly organized government. In 213 he ordered all classical books burned in an effort to destroy Confucianism, considered dangerous to his regime, and to ensure that Chinese history would begin with his reign. Scholars, however, preserved Chinese historical and philosophic traditions by hiding and memorizing the texts. He started building the Great Wall in 214 to protect China from the northern barbarians.

Shoemaker, Willie (William Lee) (1931–), U.S. jockey sometimes called the Shoe. He won his first race at age 18 and in 1953 broke the world's record for victories by a jockey in one calendar year, finishing the year with 485 wins. A rider of winning horses in three Kentucky Derbys and the most successful jockey in racing history, he rode his 8000th winning race in 1981 at age 49.

Sholokhov, Mikhail Aleksandrovich (1905–1984), Soviet novelist. He is best known for his epic novel *The Silent Don* (1928–1940) about the Don Cossacks during World War I, the Bolshevik revolution, and the subsequent civil war. The work became the most widely read novel in the Soviet Union. It was published in English in two volumes, *And Quiet Flows the Don* (1934) and *The Don Flows Home to the Sea* (1940). Sholokhov won the 1965 Nobel Prize for Literature.

Sholom Aleichem: *See* Rabinowitz, Solomon.

Shostakovich, Dmitri Dimitrievich (1906–1975), Soviet composer. His most notable works include his Fifth Symphony (1937), commemorating the 20th anniversary of the Russian revolution, and the Seventh Symphony (1942), composed during the siege of Leningrad. His Eleventh Symphony (1958) won the Lenin Prize and his Fifteenth Symphony was received enthusiastically at its premiere in 1972.

Sibelius, Jean (Johan Julius Christian) (1865–1957), Finnish composer whose work is filled with the spirit and folk tunes of Finland. Among his works are seven symphonies, instrumental works, the *Valse Triste* (1903), and the tone poems *The Swan of Tuonela* (1893), *Finlandia* (1899), and *Oceanides* (1914).

Siddons, Sarah Kemble (1755–1831), English actress. After touring with a family company, she starred unsuccessfully with Garrick in London in 1775. Soon, however, her beauty, intense acting, and rich voice made her the most popular actress of the time. She acted at Drury Lane, then at Covent Garden, where she gave her farewell performance as Lady Macbeth in 1812.

Sikorsky, Igor Ivan (1889–1972), Russian-born U.S. aeronautical engineer who designed the first practical helicopter. In 1913 Sikorsky built and flew the first multimotored airplane. During World War I he designed bombers for the Russian army. In 1919 Sikorsky went to the United States, where he developed the long-range passenger plane that initiated transoceanic air service. His helicopter design was introduced in 1939.

Sills, Beverly (1929–), originally Belle Silverman, U.S. coloratura soprano known for her expressive acting and singing. She began her career with several touring companies; in 1955 she joined the New York City Opera, singing in *Die Fledermaus.* Sills was noted for her *bel canto* roles in such operas as *Roberto Devereux* and *Lucia di Lammermoor* and for lyric and dramatic parts. She became director of the New York City Opera upon her retirement from singing in 1979.

Silone, Ignazio (1900–1978), Italian antifascist writer most known for his novel of peasant life under fascism, *Fontamara* (1930). Silone also wrote *Bread and Wine* (1937), *The Seed Beneath the Snow* (1942), *Secret of Luca* (1958), and *The Story of a Humble Christian* (1970). He became a member of the Italian Socialist Party in 1941 and lived in exile until 1944.

Simon, (Marvin) Neil (1927–), U.S. playwright whose comedies dominated the Broadway stage in the 1960's and 1970's. Simon wrote his first hit, *Come Blow Your Horn,* in 1961. Five years later, three of his plays—*Barefoot in the Park, The Odd Couple,* and *Star-Spangled Girl*—were running simultaneously on Broadway, along with his musical comedy *Sweet Charity.* Later comedies were *Plaza Suite* (1968), *The Prisoner of Second Avenue* (1971), *The Sunshine Boys* (1973), *Chapter Two* (1977), and *Brighton Beach Memoirs* (1983).

Sinclair, Upton Beall (1878–1968), U.S. writer whose novels describing social evils were a means of spurring reform. *The Jungle* (1906), which dealt with the meat-packing industry, prompted the passage of the first pure food laws. His other works include *Oil* (1927); *Boston* (1928), on the Sacco-Vanzetti case; and a series of eleven works featuring his fictional hero Lanny Budd, including *World's End* (1940) and *Dragon's Teeth* (1942).

Singer, Isaac Bashevis (1904–), Polish-born U.S. author. Singer wrote in both Hebrew and Yiddish; his books have been translated into several languages. Some of Singer's well-known works are *The Family Moskat* (1950), *Gimpel the Fool* (1957), *The Spinoza of Market Street* (1961), *The Manor* (1967), *A Crown of Feathers* (1973), which won a National Book Award, and *A Young Man in Search of Love* (1978). He was awarded the 1978 Nobel Prize for Literature.

Singer, Isaac Merrit (1811–1875), U.S. inventor who developed a practical sewing machine and manufactured it for general use. His invention, patented in 1851, resembled that of Elias Howe in many respects, and Howe won an infringement suit against Singer in 1854. Singer's company continued to prosper, however, and became the world's largest sewing machine manufacturer by 1860.

Sitting Bull (c 1831–1890), Hunkpapa Sioux Indian leader whose forces defeated Custer at Little Big Horn. In 1876 an Army expedition was sent to Sioux territory with orders to rid the gold-filled Black Hills of Indians. In the resulting battle, General George Custer and his men were wiped out by a united Indian force. Sitting Bull escaped to Canada but returned to surrender in 1881. He remained unreconciled to the white man's ways, consistently advising Sioux tribes not to sell their lands. When the Ghost Dance movement swept the plains, Sitting Bull was arrested by Indian police and, shortly after, killed.

Sitwell, Dame Edith (1887–1964), British poet. A book of poems, *Facade* (1922), for which William Walton

SITTING BULL

U.S. SIGNAL CORPS

wrote accompanying music, is representative of her earlier avant-garde romantic style. Her other books of poems include *Elegy for Dead Fashion* (1926), *Gold Coast Customs* (1929), and *Canticle of the Rose* (1949). A famous eccentric herself, she wrote *The English Eccentrics* (1933) and other prose works.

Skinner, Burrhus Frederic (B.F.) (1904–), U.S. behavioral psychologist. Skinner invented the teaching machine and programmed instruction, which attempt to apply positive reinforcement to learning. He is also known for the Skinner box, a device for observing and measuring changes in animal behavior. Skinner's *Walden Two* (1948), a novel about a utopian society, is based on behavioral science. He also wrote *Science and Human Behavior* (1953), *Beyond Freedom and Dignity* (1971), and *About Behaviorism* (1974).

Smetana, Bedřich (1824–1884), Czech pianist and composer, founder of the Czech national school of music. In 1856 he became an orchestra conductor in Göteborg, Sweden, and then conductor of the National Bohemian Theatre from 1866 until deafness caused his retirement. Among his works are the opera *The Bartered Bride* (1866) and the symphonic poem *Ma Vlast* (*My Country,* 1874–1879), containing "The Moldau."

Smith, Adam (1723–1790), Scottish economist and political philosopher. Smith's *Inquiry into the Nature and Causes of the Wealth of Nations* (1776), a treatise on the principles of political economy, recommended freedom of trade and circulation of gold as the bases of national prosperity. It was widely translated and influenced England and other countries in the development of commerce and industry.

Smith, Alfred Emanuel (1873–1944), U.S. political leader. Smith became a leader in the New York Democratic Party and was elected governor of New York in 1918, 1922, 1924, and 1926. In 1928 he became the Democratic Party's candidate for President, but he was defeated by Herbert Hoover in a campaign in which Smith's Roman Catholic religion was a major issue.

Smith, John (1580–1631), English colonist. After many adventures as a soldier of fortune in Europe, Asia, and Africa, he joined an expedition that sailed from England in 1606 to found a colony in Virginia. The expedition landed at Jamestown in 1607. According to his story, Smith was soon taken captive by the Indian chief Powhatan, but his life was saved by Pocahontas, the chief's daughter. Smith's published works include *A Description of New England* (1616) and *Generall Historie of Virginie* (1624).

Smith, Joseph (1805–1844), U.S. founder of the Church of Jesus Christ of Latter-day Saints (popularly known as the Mormon Church). Smith claimed to have been inspired by a vision and to have been told by an angel where to unearth a book written on golden plates; he translated it into English as the *Book of Mormon* (1830). In 1830 he organized his followers into a church. The most controversial teaching of the new church was Smith's revelation in 1843 that polygamy is lawful. The Mormons, constantly in conflict with their neighbors, moved from New York to Ohio to Missouri and then to Nauvoo, Ill., where from 1839 to 1844, Smith was head of the ruling group. In 1844 Smith and his brother Hyrum were jailed and then killed by a mob that feared the settlement. Most of Smith's followers went with Brigham Young to Utah.

Smollett, Tobias George (1721–1771), Scottish novelist best known for his satirical comic novels. In 1748 he published *The Adventures of Roderick Random,* about the adventures of a ship's surgeon. This was followed by *The Adventures of Peregrine Pickle* (1751) and *The Expedition of Humphrey Clinker* (1771).

Smuts, Jan Christian (1870–1950), twice prime minister of the Union of South Africa. In the Boer War, 1899–1902, he filled important positions in the Boer army and participated in the peace negotiations. He then helped form the Union of South Africa, holding several posts in the new government before serving as prime minister from 1919 to 1924 and from 1939 to 1948. He was defeated in 1948 by the Nationalist Party, which favored apartheid. He was a delegate to United Nations conferences in 1945.

Snorri Sturluson (1179–1241), Icelandic poet and historian, author of the *Younger Edda* (also called the *Prose Edda*), a prose work on Norse mythology and the rules of poetic composition. He also made a poetic collection of Norse sagas called the *Heimskringla (Ring of the World).* Snorri became chief judge of Iceland; however, his ambitions and intrigues led to his assassination.

Snow, Charles Percy (C.P.), Baron Snow (1905–1972), British author and physicist known for his attempt to unite the "two cultures"—science and the arts. In a series of novels, the first of which was *Strangers and Brothers* (1940), Snow considered several contemporary problems, among them the moral questions facing atomic-age scientists. Another in the series, *The Affair* (1960), masterfully depicts the place of power in the lives of men. Snow's famous lecture, *The Two Cultures and the Scientific Revolution,* was given at Cambridge in 1959.

Socrates (c 470–399 B.C.), Athenian philosopher. His life and teachings are known only from the writings of his contemporaries. Socrates was distinguished from other teachers in that he accepted no fees and asked questions instead of giving answers. Among his best-known pupils were Xenophon, Alcibiades, and Plato. His frank disregard for conventional ways and ideas brought him many enemies. He was accused of impiety in 399 and was condemned to death by poison. What is known of Socrates' teaching is recorded by Xenophon in his *Memorabilia* and Plato in his *Dialogues.* In many of the dialogues, Socrates is the chief speaker. Plato also recorded Socrates' defense plea at his trial in the *Apology.* Another view of Socrates was given by Aristophanes, who made him a character in *The Clouds.*

Solzhenitsyn, Alexander Isayevich (1918–), Soviet author widely known for his *One Day in the Life of Ivan Denisovich* (1962), which chronicles his own experiences in a Stalinist labor camp. In 1967 he attacked the silence of the Soviet Writers' Union in the face of increasing censorship; in 1969 he was expelled from the union. His novels *Cancer Ward* and *First Circle* (both 1968) were not published in the Soviet Union. He was awarded the 1970 Nobel Prize for Literature but did not leave the country to accept it. After publication of *The Gulag Archipelago,* a story of the labor camps, Solzhenitsyn was expelled from the Soviet Union early in 1974. Following a brief residence in Switzerland, during which time he undertook a documentary novel, *Lenin in Zurich: Chapters* (1976), he settled in the United States, where he formed a publishing company. His memoirs, *The Oak and the Calf,* were published in 1980.

Sophocles (c 496–406 B.C.), Athenian writer of tragedy. Sophocles was very popular during his lifetime, winning usually first, sometimes second, never third prize in the drama contests. Of his 120-odd plays, seven are extant: *Antigone, Electra, Trachinian Women, Oedipus Tyrannus* (or *Oedipus the King*), *Ajax, Philoctetes,* and *Oedipus at Colonus.* Sophocles modified the prevailing forms of drama by adding a third actor, by using painted scenery, and by reducing the role of the traditional chorus. His plays are tragedies of man versus the gods rather than tragedies of individual character.

Sousa, John Philip (1854–1932), U.S. bandmaster and composer of military marches, known as the March King. When he was 26, he became bandmaster of the U.S. Marine Corps. He left the post in 1892 to organize his own band, which he led on tours through the United States and most of Europe. His most popular marches include *Stars and Stripes Forever* (1897), *Washing-*

ton Post March (1889), and *Semper Fidelis* (1888).

Southey, Robert (1774–1843), British writer, one of the Lake poets. Southey's early fame came from his poetry, including *Joan of Arc* (1796), *The Curse of Kehama* (1810), and *Roderick* (1814). He became poet laureate in 1813. Today he is not thought of as a significant poet and is perhaps more appreciated for his *Life of Nelson* (1813), *History of Brazil* (1810–1819), and *History of the Peninsular War* (1823–1832).

Spartacus (d. 71 B.C.), Roman slave, leader of the gladiatorial war against Rome. He organized a band of rebellious gladiators and slaves that eventually numbered about 100,000. Several Roman armies were sent against the Spartacists, but they were able to hold out for two years (73–71). Spartacus was finally killed in the battle of Strongoli, and some 6000 of his followers were captured and crucified.

Spencer, Herbert (1820–1903), British philosopher who applied a form of evolutionary process to all phases of life, including sociology, psychology, ethics, and biology. His first work showing this broader application of evolutionary theories was *Principles of Psychology* (1855). With T.H. Huxley, he helped to bring about popular acceptance of Darwin's theory of evolution; he also had considerable influence on later psychology. His *System of Synthetic Philosophy* appeared in sections from 1862 to 1893.

Spengler, Oswald (1880–1936), German philosopher and historian. Spengler held that every civilization or culture passes through a cycle from youth through maturity and finally to death. His belief that Western civilization is approaching its end, to be superseded by Asia, is set forth in *The Decline of the West* (1918–1922; translated 1926–1928). Among his other works are *Man and Technics* (1931) and *The Hour of Decision* (1933).

Spenser, Edmund (c 1552–1599), English poet. Spenser's stature as a great poet has always rested on his *Faerie Queene* (1590; 1596), a lengthy allegorical poem that is difficult to read today. Spenser, who had already acquired some note as a poet with his *Shepherd's Calendar* (1579), worked at *The Faerie Queen* while in government service in Ireland, but finished only half of his intended plan of twelve books. Sir Walter Raleigh read part of it in 1589 and presented Spenser to Queen Elizabeth, to whom the poem was dedicated. Spenser was considered England's principal poet at the time of his death. The verse form he invented for *The Faerie Queen,* known as Spenserian stanza, was used by the Romantic poets.

THE BETTMANN ARCHIVE

EDMUND SPENSER

Spinoza, Baruch (or **Benedictus**) (1632–1677), Dutch philosopher. His first serious studies were of the Bible and the Talmud, but he could not accept their teachings fully. He was excommunicated from the Jewish synagogue in 1656 and, driven from Amsterdam, lived for a time near Leiden and afterward at The Hague. Although wholly devoted to philosophy, he earned a living by grinding lenses. Reacting to the philosophy of Descartes, whom he had studied, Spinoza tried to develop a complete metaphysical system that would explain all aspects of the world and at the same time inspire religious feeling. His ideas were published in several books, the main ones being *Tractatus theologico-politicus* (1670) and *Ethica* (1677).

Spock, Benjamin McLane (1903–), U.S. pediatrician and social activist. His book *The Common Sense Book of Baby and Child Care* (1946), one of the biggest selling books of all time, helped convince many American parents that children should be respected as human beings and treated with honesty. Beginning in the 1960's, Spock became very active in anti-Vietnam War and in antinuclear movements. He explained his antiwar views in *Dr. Spock on Vietnam* (1968).

Staël, Madame de (1766–1817), born Anne Louise Germaine Necker, French writer. Married briefly to Baron Eric de Staël-Holstein, she later formed liaisons with several of Europe's intellectual and political figures, including Talleyrand. Her political intrigues, however, forced her to leave France in 1793, during the French Revolution, and she was later banished from Paris by Napoleon. Among Mme. de Staël's important works are *Concerning the Influence of Passions on the Happiness of People and Nations* (1796) and *Thoughts on the Principal Events of the French Revolution* (1816).

Stalin, Joseph (1879–1953), born Iosif Vissarionovich Dzhugashvili, Russian dictator, general secretary of the Communist Party, 1922–1953, premier of the Soviet Union, 1941–1953. Stalin joined with Lenin and the Bolsheviks in 1912, adopted the name Stalin ("man of steel"), and became the first editor of *Pravda.* After the November revolution of 1917, he gradually gained control of the Russian Communist Party. On Lenin's death (1924), Stalin succeeded him as head of the party. Opposed by Leon Trotsky, he maneuvered Trotsky into exile to Siberia in 1929. Stalin speeded up the modernization of the Soviet Union with a series of five-year economic plans. To consolidate his power, he purged the Communist Party and the Russian army of opposition, 1936–1937. In August, 1939, he signed a nonaggression pact with Adolf Hitler. An accompanying secret protocol provided for the division of Poland and the Baltic states (Latvia, Estonia, Lithuania) between the two countries. Hitler invaded Poland in September, and Stalin annexed eastern Poland. In 1940 he added the Baltic states and Bessarabia, on the border with Rumania, to the Soviet Union. In June, 1941, despite the pact, Germany invaded the Soviet Union. As the war concluded, Stalin pressed his army westward into Germany. Consolidating his gains, Stalin dropped the so-called Iron Curtain dividing the new Soviet satellites from Western Europe. He relinquished control of the army in 1947 but remained prime minister. In 1953 he died of a cerebral hemorrhage.

Standish, Miles (or **Myles**) (c 1584–1656), English colonist in America. He joined the Pilgrims and came to America on the *Mayflower* in 1620. Chosen captain by the settlers, he handled negotiations with the Indians and had charge of defense. With John Alden he founded Duxbury, Mass., in 1631.

Stanislavski, Konstantin Sergeyevich Alekseyev (1863–1938), a Russian actor and producer, co-founder of the Moscow Art Theatre (1898). His concepts of character creation (known in the United States as the method) revolutionized 20th-century acting and directing. He rejected theatricality, declamation, and stereotypes in favor of a subjective style of acting based on the actor's own emotions. Stanislavski's theories are described in his *My Life in Art* (1924) and *An Actor Prepares* (1926). In New York City the Actors' Studio, under the direction of Lee Strasberg (1901–1982), followed Stanislavski's principles.

Stanley, Sir Henry Morton (1841–1904), original name John Rowlands, British explorer and journalist. He went to the United States as a boy, working for a New Orleans merchant named Stanley, whose name he took. In 1869 the New York *Herald* sent Stanley as a correspondent to find the English explorer David Livingstone, lost in central Africa. He reached Zanzibar in 1871 and found Livingstone, greeting him with the famous words, "Dr. Livingstone, I presume?" In 1874 Stanley set out on a second African expedition, during which he explored Lake Victoria and much of the Congo basin. He next became active in promoting the Congo Free State, 1879–1885, and then undertook an expedition to rescue Emin Pasha, the governor of the Equatorial Provinces. Stanley's writings include *How I Found Livingstone* (1872) and *In Darkest Africa* (2 volumes, 1890). He served in Parliament from 1895 to 1900.

Stanton, Edwin McMasters (1814–1869), U.S. secretary of war during the Civil War. He served as attorney general under Buchanan, 1860–1861, and was named secretary of war by Lincoln in 1862. During the Civil War, he ably discharged his duties, although his strong individualism often brought him into conflict with others. After Lincoln's assassination, he continued in office and clashed with President Andrew Johnson over Reconstruction policies. Johnson tried unsuccessfully to have Stanton removed from office; in retaliation, Johnson was impeached by the House of Representatives. The Senate upheld the President, and Stanton resigned in 1868.

Stanton, Elizabeth Cady (1815–1902), U.S. suffragist and reformer who in 1848 organized the first women's rights convention. She was the first president of the National Woman Suffrage Association, 1869–1890. At the convention she drew up a bill of rights for women, describing their inferior position in society and demanding redress. In 1850 she met Susan Anthony; the two collaborated for 40 years. They fought for women's voting rights, edited the newspaper *The Revolution,* and, with Matilda Gage, edited *The History of Woman Suffrage* (1881–1886).

EDWIN STANTON

ANSCO

Steele, Sir Richard (1672–1729), Irish-born British essayist and dramatist. In 1709 he and Joseph Addison founded a periodical called *The Tatler,* devoted to essays on manners and morality. Steele was the chief contributor, with Addison and others writing occasional pieces. In 1711 the two men founded *The Spectator,* to which Addison was the chief contributor. Steele next founded *The Guardian* and then *The Englishman,* a political journal reflecting his Whig sympathies. He later started several other journals as well as the famous *Plebeian* (1718), also outspokenly political. Steele was expelled from Parliament in 1714 for allegedly libeling the Tories in a pamphlet; however, when George I became king, he held several government posts.

Stefansson, Vilhjalmur (1879–1962), Arctic explorer, born in Canada of Icelandic parentage. Stefansson discovered large areas of the Canadian Arctic, lived with Eskimo peoples, and eventually became an expert on Eskimo culture. He wrote the books *My Life with the Eskimo* (1913) and *The Friendly Arctic* (1921).

Stein, Gertrude (1874–1946), U.S. author. After 1903 Stein spent most of her time in Paris, where her coterie included Pablo Picasso, Ernest Hemingway, F. Scott Fitzgerald, and many others whom she dubbed the lost generation. Stein's writings are difficult and obscure, but her experiments with language influenced a generation of modern writers. Among her best-known works are *Three Lives* (1910), *The Making of Americans* (1925), and *The Autobiography of Alice B. Toklas* (1933).

ADLAI STEVENSON II

ELEANOR ROOSEVELT MEMORIAL FOUNDATION

Steinbeck, John Ernest (1902–1968), U.S. novelist, journalist, and short story writer. Steinbeck's many works include *Tortilla Flat* (1935), *Of Mice and Men* (1937), *The Grapes of Wrath* (1939), *Cannery Row* (1945), and *East of Eden* (1952). He is known for his sympathetic treatment of the plight of the migratory workers (or Okies) during the Depression of the 1930's. His later writings include *The Winter of Our Discontent* (1961) and *Travels with Charley* (1962). Steinbeck was the recipient of the 1962 Nobel Prize for Literature.

Steinmetz, Charles Proteus (1865–1923), German-born U.S. electrical engineer. Steinmetz, who came to the United States in 1869, worked as a consulting engineer for the General Electric Company and patented more than 100 inventions. He was known especially for his work on the nature of alternating current and lightning. From 1902 to 1923 Steinmetz was also professor of electrical engineering and electrophysics at Union College.

Stendhal (1783–1842), pen name of Marie Henri Beyle, French writer of novels characterized by sharp psychological insights into complicated personalities. He is best known for the novels *The Red and the Black* (1831) and *The Charterhouse of Parma* (1839).

Stephens, Alexander Hamilton (1812–1883), U.S. legislator, later vice president of the Confederate States of America. He was a member of the U.S. House of Representatives, 1843–1859. As a member of the Georgia secession congress, he yielded to the majority, who favored the state's secession from the Union. Stephens served as vice president of the Confederate states from 1861 to 1865, but he was frequently at odds with President Jefferson Davis. After the war he served in Congress, 1873–1882.

Stephenson, George (1781–1848), British inventor and railway builder. In 1814 he built the first successful locomotive and in the next year equipped it with a steam blast. Stephenson then built several railroads, including one in a coal mine (opened 1822). He founded a locomotive factory at Newcastle in 1823. Under his supervision, the Liverpool and Manchester Railway opened in 1830 with his locomotive *Rocket.*

Sterne, Laurence (1713–1768), English novelist. Sterne created a sensation with the first two volumes of *The Life and Opinions of Tristram Shandy, Gent.* (1760). Their eccentric humor and lack of decorum made them so popular that new volumes appeared irregularly in succeeding years. The ninth and final volume appeared in 1767. His other writings include *A Sentimental Journey Through France and Italy* (1768).

Steuben, Baron Friedrich Wilhelm Ludolf Gerhard Augustin von (1730–1794), Prussian army officer and American Revolutionary general. He served in the Prussian army during the Seven Years' War 1756–1763, and at its close became grand marshal of a select group of army officers under Frederick the Great. Steuben went to America in 1777. The following year he joined the Continental army and directed the training of the troops, using Prussian drills that proved effective against the British in such battles as Monmouth and Yorktown.

Stevens, Wallace (1879–1955), U.S. poet. Stevens began his career as a poet in 1923 with the publication of *Harmonium.* This was followed by *The Man with the Blue Guitar* (1937) and *The Auroras of Autumn* (1950). His *Collected Poems* (1954) won the National Book Award and the Pulitzer Prize for poetry. Stevens's best-known poem is "Peter Quince at the Clavier."

Stevenson, U.S. family prominent in government and public service.

Adlai Ewing Stevenson (1835–1914), Vice President of the United States, 1893–1897, under Grover Cleveland. He ran again for Vice-President with Bryan in 1900; he also served in Congress.

Adlai Ewing Stevenson (1900–1965), statesman, lawyer, and political leader, grandson of the first Adlai Stevenson. He was active in the founding and organizing of the United Nations, 1946–1947. He was elected governor of Illinois in 1948 by a record margin. In 1952 and 1956 he was the unsuccessful Democratic candidate for President. Later he served as ambassador to the United Nations in the Kennedy and Johnson administrations.

Adlai Ewing Stevenson (1930–), politician, son of the second Adlai Stevenson. He served as U.S. senator from Illinois from 1970 to 1981.

Stevenson, Robert Louis Balfour (1850–1894), Scottish essayist, novelist, and poet whose many famous works include the children's classic *Treasure Island* (1883). A sickly child, Stevenson could not attend school regularly and was often left to his own devices; later, his illness demanded that he travel to warm climates such as the South Seas. From these experiences he became one of the most richly imaginative of writers. *Treasure Island* was followed in 1886 by the psychological thriller *The Strange Case of Dr. Jekyll and Mr. Hyde* and adventures such as *The Black Arrow* and *Kidnapped.* Stevenson's best-remembered poetry volume is *A Child's Garden of Verses* (1885). He died in Samoa and was buried there.

Stewart (or **Stuart), Charles Edward Louis Philip Casimir** (1720–1788), called Bonnie Prince Charlie, prince of England and Scotland, the "young pretender" to the throne. He became the leader of the English and Scottish sympathizers with the house of Stuart (called Jacobites), who hoped to place his father, James Francis Edward Stewart (1688–1766), son of King James II, on the throne. Charles landed in Scotland with an army in 1745. The Highland clans flocked to his support and he won early successes against the English, but his army was nearly destroyed at Culloden Moor in April, 1746. He went into hiding in Brittany but was expelled from France in 1748. Charles later alienated supporters by his dissolute life and vicious temper. He was never able to return to England and died in Rome.

Stewart, Potter (1915–1985), appointed an associate justice of the U.S. Supreme Court in 1958. Educated at Yale and at Cambridge University, England, Stewart practiced in New York City and Cincinnati, Ohio, and served as a judge on the U.S. Circuit Court of Appeals, 1954–1958.

Stieglitz, Alfred (1864–1946), U.S. photographer. He emphasized camera technique and intelligent composition at a time when much exhibition photography was the result of darkroom handiwork. He took the first successful pictures of snow (*Winter on Fifth Avenue,* 1893). Stieglitz also directed the Photo-Secession Gallery (called "291") in New York, 1905–1917.

Stone, Harlan Fiske (1872–1946), chief justice of the United States, 1941–1946. Stone was attorney general under Calvin Coolidge and was appointed to the Supreme Court in 1925. In his 21 years on the Court, he saw many of his dissenting views become majority opinions, including a 1943 decision that compulsory flag salute for schoolchildren is unconstitutional.

Stone, Lucy (1818–1893), U.S. woman suffragist and abolitionist. She put herself through Oberlin College by teaching because her father did not believe in education for women. In protest against taxation of women without representation at the polls, she attracted attention to the suffrage movement by selling her belongings for taxes in 1858. At her marriage to Henry Blackwell, the two read aloud a protest against current marriage laws that oppressed women; she continued to be known by her maiden name. She published the *Woman's Journal,* a women's suffrage weekly, for many years.

Stout, Rex Todhunter (1886–1975), U.S. writer, creator of the famous fictional detective Nero Wolfe. Beginning with *Fer-de-Lance* (1934), Stout published more than 40 books about the brilliant but immovable Wolfe and his urbane assistant Archie Goodwin. Among the best were *Too Many Cooks* (1938), *Black Orchids* (1942), *In the Best Families* (1950), and *The Doorbell Rang* (1965).

Stowe, Harriet Elizabeth Beecher (1811–1896), U.S. author. An ardent abolitionist, she wrote *Uncle Tom's Cabin, or Life Among the Lowly,* published first as a serial in an antislavery paper in Washington, D.C., and then as a book in 1852. The book aroused widespread emotion and helped to solidify sentiment against slavery in the Northern states. Stowe was elected to the Hall of Fame in 1910.

Strachey, Lytton (1880–1932), British biographer. Strachey's works, characterized by wit and a slightly ironic attitude toward his subjects, include *Eminent Victorians* (1918), *Queen Victoria* (1921), *Elizabeth and Essex* (1928), and *Portraits in Miniature* (1931).

Stradivari, Antonio (c 1644–1737), in Latin, Antonius Stradivarius, Italian violinmaker. His violins are unsurpassed in excellence of workmanship and beauty of tone. He was apprenticed to Nicolò Amati, one of a great family of violinmakers, and improved on his master's work. It is believed that Stradivari made 2000 violins during his lifetime. Today more than 500 are known to exist, as well as about a dozen violas and more than 50 cellos.

Strauss, Johann (1825–1899), called the Younger, Austrian composer known as the Waltz King. The son of a well-known musician, he took over his father's orchestra and toured successfully. After 1863 he devoted himself to composition and wrote more than 400 waltzes, including *The Blue Danube* and *Artist's Life* (both 1867), *Voices of Spring* (1882), and *The Emperor* (1888). Among his operettas were *Die Fledermaus* (1874) and *A Night in Venice* (1883).

Strauss, Richard (1864–1949), German composer and conductor. He began his career as conductor at Meiningen in 1885; in 1889 he went to Weimar as Kapellmeister. In 1894 he was appointed conductor at the Munich Opera House, and in 1898 at Berlin. His works include the operas *Salomé* (1905), *Elektra* (1909), and *Der Rosenkavalier* (1911); and richly orchestrated tone poems still performed widely: *Death and Transfiguration*

(1891), *Till Eulenspiegel's Merry Pranks* (1895), *Thus Spake Zarathustra* (1896), and *Don Quixote* (1898).

Stravinsky, Igor Fedorovich (1882–1971), Russian-born U.S. composer. In Paris he became famous for his compositions for the Diaghilev Ballet. These included *The Firebird* (1910) and *Petrouchka* (1911). Stravinsky's use of dissonance and changing rhythms caused a riot at the Paris premier of *Le Sacre du printemps (The Rite of Spring)* in 1913. He settled in the United States and became a citizen in 1945. Many of his later works were written on a twelve-tone scale, including *Agon* (1957) and *Threni* (1958). He wrote the opera *Rake's Progress* (1951) and other vocal works.

Stresemann, Gustav (1878–1929), German statesman. As minister of foreign affairs, 1923–1929, he negotiated the Locarno Pact, the admission of Germany to the League of Nations, and Germany's adoption of the Dawes and Young plans for the payment of war reparations. He shared the 1926 Nobel Peace Prize with Aristide Briand.

Strindberg, Johan August (1849–1912), Swedish playwright. His influential works range from naturalism to surrealism. Strindberg's first successful drama was *Master Olaf* (1872). It was followed by three plays bitterly attacking women, *The Father, Miss Julie,* and *Creditors,* all written about 1890. His later plays were mystical and surrealistic, notably *A Dream Play* (1902). In 1907 Strindberg founded an intimate theater in Stockholm and produced a series of chamber plays, the best known of which is *The Ghost Sonata* (1908).

Stuart, Charles Edward: *See* Stewart, Charles Edward.

Stuart, Gilbert Charles (1755–1828), U.S. painter of portraits. In 1776 he went to London, where he studied under Benjamin West. Stuart returned to the United States in 1792 and opened studios in New York, Washington, D.C., and Boston. He is best known for his portraits of George Washington, though he also painted Jefferson, Madison, and other American leaders.

Stuart, James Ewell Brown (Jeb) (1833–1864), Confederate general and cavalry commander. After graduating from West Point in 1854, he served in the U.S. Army but resigned at the outbreak of the Civil War to join the Confederacy. Stuart was an outstanding cavalryman and daring officer, as well as a romantic figure. He was mortally wounded near Richmond in May of 1864 during an attempt to halt the progress of Sheridan's cavalry.

Sturluson, Snorri: *See* Snorri Sturluson.

Stuyvesant, Peter (c 1610–1672), Dutch colonial governor of New York. He was sent to New Amsterdam (later New York City) to direct colonial affairs for the West India Company; he arrived in 1647. Stuyvesant expanded the territory of the Dutch colony, but his dictatorial methods made him unpopular. In 1664 he was forced to surrender his territory to the English.

Sucre, Antonio José de (1793–1830), Latin American revolutionary leader in the war for liberation from Spain, Bolívar's most trusted aide. A revolutionary since his teens, Sucre won the battle that freed Quito in 1822; two years later he won the Battle of Ayacucho, which marked the end of Spanish rule in Peru. He worked with Bolívar to organize the state of Bolivia and was its first president, 1826–1828. In 1830 Sucre led a congress to promote unity among the new states but he was assassinated on his way home to Quito.

Sukarno (1901–1970), first president of the Republic of Indonesia. Sukarno founded the Indonesian Nationalist Party in 1927. He was jailed by the Dutch for his nationalist activities, 1929–1932 and 1933–1942, but was released by occupying Japanese troops during World War II. At the end of the war, Sukarno and Muhammad Hatta declared Indonesia's independence. Sukarno became president and ruled until his effective powers were taken away in 1966 by a military coup. He first proposed in 1955 the idea of an uncommitted Afro-Asian Third World.

Suleiman I, the Magnificent (c 1496–1566), sultan of the Ottoman empire 1520–1566, known as a just and powerful ruler. Suleiman expanded the empire, capturing European land as far west as Budapest and Belgrade and taking Baghdad in the east. He improved the administration of his empire, setting down a code of government for which he is remembered in Turkey as "the law giver." He encouraged education and the arts. He was killed while invading Hungary.

Sullivan, Sir Arthur Seymour (1842–1900), British composer. Although he composed many serious choral and orchestral works, he is best remembered for his collaboration with W.S. Gilbert in the composition of light operas that include *H.M.S. Pinafore* (1878), *Pirates of Penzance* (1880), *The Mikado* (1885), *The Yeomen of the Guard* (1888), and *The Gondoliers* (1889). He also wrote hymns, including "Onward, Christian Soldiers" and many songs, including "The Lost Chord."

Sullivan, John Lawrence (1858–1918), U.S. heavyweight prizefighter, known as the great John L. He defeated Paddy Ryan for the heavyweight championship in 1882 but lost it to James J. Corbett in 1892.

THE BETTMANN ARCHIVE

LOUIS SULLIVAN

Sullivan, Louis Henri (1856–1924), U.S. architect. His buildings were original and experimental; his skyscrapers and office towers adapted good design to modern needs. In collaboration with Dankmar Adler, Sullivan designed in Chicago the Auditorium Building and the Stock Exchange. His other works include the Wainwright Building in St. Louis, Mo., and the Prudential Building in Buffalo, N.Y. Sullivan strongly influenced Frank Lloyd Wright and other later architects.

Sully, Thomas (1783–1872), U.S. portrait painter whose best-remembered work is *Washington Crossing the Delaware.* Among his over 2000 portraits are those of Queen Victoria, Presidents Jefferson and Madison, and Lafayette.

Sumner, Charles (1811–1874), U.S. senator who led the antislavery forces in Congress before and during the Civil War. He entered the U.S. Senate in 1851, retaining his seat until his death. He sought to repeal the Missouri Compromise and fought the introduction of slavery into Kansas. His impassioned speech, "The Crime Against Kansas," in 1856, incensed Representative Preston S. Brooks of South Carolina, who assaulted Sumner at his desk in the Senate chamber. Sumner never fully recovered from his injuries.

Sun Yat-sen (1866–1925), Chinese statesman, leader of the 1911 nationalist revolution. He practiced medicine for a short time but was forced to flee China after leading an abortive attempt at revolution in 1895. Sun spent 16 years in exile organizing a revolutionary party to overthrow China's Manchu dynasty. When a successful revolution took place in 1911, Sun returned to China as provisional president of the new Chinese republic. The following year he relinquished the presidency to General Yüan Shih-k'ai, after having organized the Kuomintang, a nationalist party. The despotic policies of Yüan caused Sun to break with him. During the chaos of warlord rule after Yüan's death in 1916, Sun formed a separate government in Canton. The Kuomintang and Communists allied against the warlords, but Sun died before China could be unified by the coalition.

Sutherland, Joan (1926–), Australian coloratura soprano. She became internationally known after starring in *Lucia di Lammermoor* at Covent Garden, 1959; she performed the same role at the Metropolitan Opera for her New York debut in 1961. Sutherland was also known for her roles in *Norma, I Puritani,* and *Semiramide.*

Sutter, John Augustus (1803–1880), U.S. pioneer born in Germany of Swiss parents. He arrived in California in 1839 and established a colony, New Helvetia, in the Sacramento Valley. The discovery of gold in 1848 on his property, Sutter's Mill, started a gold rush and brought an influx of squatters. The bonanza ruined Sutter's property and he went bankrupt in 1852. California later awarded him a small pension.

Swedenborg, Emanuel (1688–1772), Swedish philosopher. For the first 55 years of his life, he was an active and influential scientist, particularly in geology and mining. He also made revolutionary designs for airplanes and studied astronomy. In 1743 he turned his attention to religion. He felt his mission was to reveal spiritual meaning in certain books of the Bible. His theological works include *Heaven and Hell* (1758) and *The Apocalypse Revealed* (1766). After his death his English followers, known as Swedenborgians, formed the Church of the New Jerusalem, or New Church.

Swift, Jonathan (1667–1745), Irish author of the finest satires in the English language, principally *Gulliver's Travels.* In 1704, while vicar of a parish near Dublin, his *Tale of a Tub,* a satire on religion and learning of the time, appeared anonymously. Swift soon became known as the author. He was increasingly admired and popular in London, and in 1710 he settled there, becoming the chief political propagandist for the Tory government. When the Whigs came to power with George I's accession in 1714, Swift moved back to Ireland, where he was dean of St. Paul's Cathedral in Dublin until the end of his life. Many of his later writings, such as the *Drapier's Letters* (1724–1725), and the savage satire *A Modest Proposal* (1729), drew English attention to conditions in Ireland. Though *Gulliver's Travels* is now considered a children's book, when it appeared in 1726 it was understood as a brilliant satire on humanity and on conditions of the time.

Swinburne, Algernon Charles (1837–1909), English lyric poet. His *Poems and Ballads* (1866) was criticized for its sensuality. Other works are *Songs Before Sunrise* (1871), *Tristram of Lyonesse* (1882), and the drama *Atalanta in Calydon* (1865).

Synge, John Millington (1871–1909), Irish dramatist. After study in Germany, Italy, and France, he settled in Paris. There he translated poems by the French symbolist writers and wrote literary criticism. In the late 1890's, W.B. Yeats persuaded Synge to return to Ireland and write of the harsh life on the Aran Islands. His tragic one-act play *Riders to the Sea* (1904) is based on the life of Aran fisherman. In 1904 Synge became a director of Dublin's Abbey Theatre, along with Yeats and Lady Gregory. His other plays include *Playboy of the Western World* (1907) and *Deirdre of the Sorrows* (1910).

Szilard, Leo (1898–1964), Hungarian-born U.S. nuclear physicist, developer of the nuclear reactor and one of the developers of the atomic bomb. With Fermi, Szilard produced the first controlled nuclear reaction from an atomic pile in 1942. Opposed to the use of atomic weapons against civilian population centers, he led a successful fight for civilian control of atomic energy programs. In his later years he did research in molecular biology, sponsored the *Bulletin of Atomic Scientists,* and wrote the allegorical *Voice of the Dolphins* (1961).

T

Tacitus, Cornelius (c 55 A.D.–c 113 A.D.), Roman historian, lawyer, public official, and orator. His works include the *Dialogus,* a study of the decline of oratory; the *Agricola,* a life of his father-in-law Julius Agricola, describing Britain under Agricola's governorship (78–84 A.D.); the *Germania,* an account of the people, customs, and geography of Germany; and the *Annales* and *Historiae,* which together form a history of the Roman Empire from the death of Augustus to the death of Domitian (14–96 A.D.).

Taft, Robert Alfonso (1889–1953), U.S. political figure, son of President William Howard Taft and the principal exponent of conservative Republican politics in the 1940's and 1950's. He served in the Ohio legislature and then in the U.S. Senate, 1939–1953, as leader of the Senate Republicans. There he sponsored the controversial Taft-Hartley Labor Act of 1947 and carried out the legislative program of the Eisenhower administration.

Taft, William Howard (1857–1930), 27th President of the United States, 1909–1913. Taft was the only man ever to serve as both President and chief justice of the United States. He was a judge of the Ohio superior court from 1887 to 1890, when he was appointed solicitor general by President William Henry Harrison. He then became a federal circuit judge, 1892–1900. In 1900 he headed the Philippine Commission and was civil governor of the islands, 1901–1904. In 1904 he was appointed secretary of war and soon became President Theodore Roosevelt's most trusted adviser. In 1908 Taft was Roosevelt's choice as his successor; he was elected President on the Republican ticket. Progressive Republican support for Taft diminished when he signed the Payne-Aldrich Act of 1909, which maintained high tariffs. He soon came to be identified with the conservative wing of the Republican Party. In 1912, however, Taft was renominated as the Republican candidate for President. The Progressives then bolted the party, choosing Roosevelt as their candidate for President. With the Republican vote divided, the Democratic candidate, Woodrow Wilson, was elected. Taft became professor of law at Yale in 1912. In 1921 he was appointed chief justice of the Supreme Court, which he considered his greatest honor.

Tagore, Sir Rabindranath (1861–1941), Indian author and mystic who was awarded the 1913 Nobel Prize for Literature for his collection of poems *Gitanjali* ("Song Offering," 1910). Born into a wealthy family, he studied in England and then settled in Shileida, where he grew to love the Bengali countryside and the river Ganges. Among Tagore's hundreds of works are the poem collections *The Golden Boat* (1893) and *Dreams* (1900), the plays *Chitrā* and *King of the Dark Chamber,* and several novels.

TACITUS

THE BETTMANN ARCHIVE

Taine, Hippolyte Adolphe (1828–1893), French historian, philosopher, and critic, founder of a movement known as genetic criticism. Taine asserted that creative efforts are understood through the artist's heredity, environment, and time in history. He used this principle in studies into literary and political history. His works include *History of English Literature* (4 volumes, 1863–1864), *The Origins of Contemporary France* (1876–1893), on the French Revolution, and several volumes on the philosophy of art.

Takeshita, Noboru (1924–), Japanese politician, elected prime minister of Japan in November, 1987. Takeshita entered politics in 1951 and was first elected to the Diet (Japanese parliament) in 1958. He has held several cabinet posts, the most important as minister of finance in 1979 and from 1982 to 1986. In 1986–1987, he served as secretary-general of the ruling Liberal Democratic Party.

Talleyrand-Périgord, Charles Maurice de (1754–1838), French statesman noted for his ability to survive in politics despite changes of government. He was educated for the Roman Catholic clergy and in 1788 he became bishop of Autun. In 1789 he represented the clergy of his diocese in the Estates-General. After the outbreak of the French Revolution, he joined the third estate, or commons, which had proclaimed itself the National Assembly. He helped draft the Declaration of the Rights of Man. When the French monarchy was overthrown in 1792, Talleyrand went into exile. He returned to Paris in 1796 and served as foreign minister under the Directory, 1797–1799, and under Napoleon Bonaparte, 1799–1807. After Napoleon's defeat in 1814, Talleyrand helped bring about the restoration of the Bourbon monarchy. Louis XVIII made him foreign minister and he secured a number of advantages for France at the Congress of Vienna. Talleyrand resigned as foreign minister in 1815 and wrote his memoirs. After the revolution of 1830, he helped make Louis Philippe king and became his ambassador to Britain.

Tamayo, Rufino (1899–1971), Mexican painter known for his highly individualistic style combining ancient Mexican and modern European techniques. He was an outspoken critic of the Mexican revolutionary mural painters of the 1920's; although he established an international reputation, he was not popular in his native country. In 1938 he settled in the United States and in 1943 completed a famous mural at Smith College. Tamayo's later paintings are highly abstract.

Tamerlane (or Tamburlaine or Timur) (c 1336–1405), Mongol conqueror. Claiming descent from Genghis Khan, he founded the Timurid dynasty, which ruled Iran and southern Russia until 1500. Tamerlane came to power in about 1369 and by 1400 he controlled the land from the Tigris to India. By 1402 he had seized Syria and moved into Turkey. He died while planning to invade China.

Tarbell, Ida Minerva (1857–1944), U.S. author and editor known for her exposés of political and industrial corruption. She was an editor for *McClure's,* 1894–1906, and the *American Magazine,* 1906–1915. An early muckraker, she wrote the famous *History of the Standard Oil Company* (1904), in which she reported on the methods by which Standard Oil restricted free competition. Her other books include *The Business of Being a Woman* (1912) and *All in a Day's Work* (1939).

Tasso, Torquato (1544–1595), Italian poet whose masterpiece is the epic poem *Jerusalem Delivered.* Soon after it was completed in 1575, he became emotionally disturbed and extremely sensitive to criticism. He was confined in an institution in 1579 and, though released in 1586, never fully recovered. His other works include the romantic narrative *Rinaldo* (1562), the pastoral drama *Aminta* (1573), and the tragedy *Torrismondo* (1586).

Tatum, Edward Lawrie (1909–1975), U.S. geneticist who shared the 1958 Nobel Prize for Physiology and Medicine with Joshua Lederberg and George W. Beadle for establishing the role of genes in controlling certain chemical reactions in the cell affecting hereditary characteristics. The work was carried out on the common fruit fly *(Drosophila)* and on red bread mold *(Neurospora),* but the principles derived from the research were widely applicable in biology.

Taylor, Maxwell D. (1901–1987), U.S. Army general, chairman of the Joint Chiefs of Staff under President Kennedy. Commander of the 101st Airborne Division at the D-Day invasion of Normandy, 1944, and later commandant of the U.S. Military Academy (West Point), he became head of the American military government in postwar Berlin, 1949. He commanded the Eighth Army and United Nations forces during the Korean War, and was named Army chief of staff in 1955. A strong advocate of highly mobile forces capable of distant strikes, he frequently came in conflict with a military establishment that favored the use of nuclear weapons.

Taylor, Zachary (1784–1850), twelfth President of the United States, 1849–1850. Taylor was commissioned in the Army in 1808, served in the War of 1812, and became a colonel during the Black Hawk War, 1832. After serving against the Seminoles in Florida, where his troops gave him his nickname Old Rough and Ready, he was sent to the Southwest and in 1845 was ordered to Texas to defend the new state against a possible Mexican invasion. After the Mexican War began in 1846, Taylor's victories and eligibility as a popular Presidential choice led President Polk to reassign most of Taylor's troops to General Winfield Scott; Taylor nonetheless won the Battle of Buena Vista, 1847, although his men were outnumbered four to one. A national hero with no known political convictions, Taylor was nominated by the Whigs and elected President in 1848. He died 16 months later.

Tchaikovsky, Petr Ilich (1840–1893), Russian composer. His compositions contain highly original melodies, sudden shifts in mood and harmony, and frequent use of folk song material. His ballet scores for *Swan Lake* (1876), *The Sleeping Beauty* (1890), and *Nutcracker Suite* (1892) are world famous. He also composed six symphonies, of which the Fifth (1888) and Sixth (*Pathétique,* 1893) are best known. Among his other pieces are the Piano Concerto no. 1; the orchestral works *Romeo and Juliet, 1812 Overture, Marche Slav,* and *Capriccio Italien;* and the operas *Eugene Onegin* (1879) and *The Queen of Spades* (1890).

Tecumseh (1768–1813), American Indian chief of the Shawnees, a courageous warrior, humane leader, and great Indian statesman. With his brother Tenskwatawa, known as the Prophet, he organized a powerful and threatening Indian confederation of most of the tribes of the Northwest to fight against the whites. In 1811, while Tecumseh was away recruiting the support of tribes in the South, William Henry Harrison, governor of the Northwest Territory, defeated and dispersed the Shawnees at Tippecanoe. Tecumseh allied with the British in the War of 1812 and died in the Battle of the Thames in Canada.

Teilhard de Chardin, Pierre (1881–1955), French paleontologist and Jesuit theologian noted for his doctrine of cosmic evolution and for his lifelong attempt to reconcile Christian dogma with the findings of science. Teilhard wrote many scientific works, particularly on the paleontology of mammals. His notable philosophical books are *The Phenomenon of Man* (1938–1940) and *The Divine Milieu* (1926–1927). He was refused church permission to publish his later books during his lifetime.

Teller, Edward (1908–), Hungarian-born U.S. physicist, often called the father of the hydrogen bomb. In 1935 he emigrated to the United States (becoming a U.S. citizen in 1941) and worked on the atomic bomb at Los Alamos, N.M. In 1946, after several disagree-

THE BETTMANN ARCHIVE

JOHN TENNIEL

ments with the project's director Robert Oppenheimer, he left for a professorship at the University of Chicago. In 1950 he was appointed director of the U.S. hydrogen bomb development program. He worked on the bomb briefly at Los Alamos and then at the University of California at Livermore, where he was director of the Lawrence Radiation Laboratory, 1952–1960, and then professor of physics at large. He is the author of *The Legacy of Hiroshima* (1962) and *Energy from Heaven and Earth* (1979).

Tenniel, Sir John (1820–1914), English illustrator and satirist best known for his illustrations in Lewis Carroll's *Alice's Adventures in Wonderland* (1866). He spent most of his life as a staff member of the British magazine *Punch,* 1850–1901, for which he drew more than 2300 political cartoons.

Tennyson, Alfred, 1st Baron Tennyson (1809–1892), British poet. His first moderately successful collection appeared in 1832 and 1842; it contained such well-known poems as "The Lady of Shalott," "Ulysses," and "Locksley Hall." In 1850 *In Memoriam* (begun in 1833), commemorating the death of his friend Arthur Hallam, was an immediate success with the public and the critics. Queen Victoria befriended Tennyson, naming him poet laureate. His later works include *Maud* (1855), *The Idylls of the King* (1859), with later Arthurian poems in 1870; *Enoch Arden* (1864), and *Demeter and Other Poems* (1889). His most famous short poem is "Crossing the Bar."

Teresa of Ávila, Saint (1515–1582), Spanish nun and mystic who originated the Carmelite reform. After more than 25 years as a Carmelite nun, during which time she endured a bitter spiritual struggle, Teresa founded a convent in Ávila that was dedicated to the reform of her order. She spent the last years of her life establishing more reform convents (16 in all) throughout Spain. Her devotional writings include *Life, The Way of Perfection,* and *The Interior Castle,* all published after her death.

Tereshkova, Valentina Vladimirovna (1937–), Soviet cosmonaut, the first woman in space. A former textile worker, Tereshkova made a three-day orbital flight around the earth in 1963 in *Vostok 6.*

Terry, Dame Ellen Alicia (1847–1928), English Shakespearean actress. In 1878, when Henry Irving (1838–1905) took over management of the Lyceum Theatre, he chose Terry as his leading lady; their association lasted until 1902. She was especially well known for her role as Portia in *The Merchant of Venice,* but she also played Beatrice, Viola, Lady Macbeth, and Juliet with great charm. She carried on a famous long correspondence with George Bernard Shaw.

Tesla, Nikola (1856–1943), U.S. inventor born in Croatia (now Yugoslavia), known for his research on high-frequency alternating current. In 1884 he emigrated to the United States and for a time worked for Thomas Edison and George Westinghouse. He later established a research laboratory in New York. His inventions include an alternating-current (induction) motor and a transformer (Tesla coil).

Thackeray, William Makepeace (1811–1863), British author whose realistic novels of British society are famed for their portrayals of character, human nature, and manners and morals of the time. The serialization of his novel *Vanity Fair* (1847–1848) established his fame. His other major works include *Pendennis* (1848–1850), *Henry Esmond* (1852), and *The Rose and the Ring* (1854).

Thatcher, Margaret Hilda (1925–), born Margaret Hilda Roberts, the British prime minister from 1979 to date. Thatcher first won election to Parliament in 1959. Appointed minister of education in 1970, she replaced Edward Heath as leader of the Conservative Party in 1975. When the Conservatives won a majority in the parliamentary elections of 1979, the Labour government was ousted and Thatcher became Britain's first woman prime minister. In the early 1980's, support for her monetarist policies declined and she faced serious urban problems and mounting terrorist activity by the Irish Republican Army. Her decisive handling of the Falkland Islands conflict in 1982, however, helped ensure a Conservative victory in the 1983 general elections. The improvement in most sectors of the economy produced yet another Conservative victory in the elections of 1987.

Themistocles (c 528–462 B.C.), Athenian statesman. He believed that Athens should be a sea as well as a land power, and during the 480's he persuaded the Athenians to triple the size of their navy. His advice was vindicated in 480, when the Persian fleet threatened Athens; he tricked it into the narrows at Salamis and brought about a great Athenian naval victory. After Salamis, he rebuilt the fortifications of Athens and worked to counter Sparta's influence. He was ostracized about 471. Hounded by the Spartans, he went to Persia, where he became a provincial governor.

Theresa, Saint: *See* Teresa of Ávila, Saint.

Thiers, Louis Adolphe (1797–1877), French statesman and historian, an outstanding figure in French politics. In 1830 he was one of the founders of a liberal journal, *National,* which contributed to the fall of the reactionary Charles X. Under the succeeding king, Louis Philippe, he held several cabinet posts and was twice premier, 1836 and 1840. When Napoleon III became emperor in 1851, Thiers was exiled. He returned to Paris in 1853 and led the opposition against the imperial regime. After the fall of Napoleon in 1871, he was first president of the Third Republic, 1871–1873.

Thomas, Dylan Marlais (1914–1953), Welsh poet whose intense writing reflected his zest for life and his mastery of the rhythm and subtleties of the English language. Among Thomas's collections of poems are *The Map of Love* (1939), *Deaths and Entrances* (1946), and *Collected Poems* (1952). His prose work includes *Portrait of the Artist as a Young Dog* (1940), a collection of humorous autobiographical sketches; and *A Child's Christmas in Wales* (1954). He died in New York while rehearsing and revising his play *Under Milk Wood* (1954).

Thomas, Norman Mattoon (1884–1968), U.S. socialist leader who was six times a Presidential candidate of the U.S. Socialist Party, 1928–1948. He was a Presbyterian minister in New York until 1918, when he became a socialist; he then founded and edited *World Tomorrow,* 1918–1921. He also was associate editor of *The Nation,* 1921–1922. Thomas's books, which encourage democratic socialism and oppose military conscription, communism, and fascism, include *The Test of Freedom* (1954), *Mr. Chairman, Ladies and Gentlemen* (1955), and *Socialism Reexamined* (1963).

Thomas à Becket: *See* Becket, Thomas à.

Thomas à Kempis (c 1380–1471), born Thomas Hamerken, German priest and writer thought to be the author of *Imitation of Christ* (1486), a widely read devotional work. In 1407 he entered the Augustinian monastery of Agnetenberg, near Zwolle in the Netherlands. There he devoted his life to writing and copying manuscripts.

Thomas Aquinas: *See* Aquinas, Saint Thomas.

Thompson, Sir John Sparrow David (1845–1894), lawyer, statesman, Conservative prime minister of Canada, 1892–1894. He instituted the Canadian Criminal Code of 1892. He died shortly after being sworn in as a member of the Imperial Privy Council.

JIM THORPE

UPI/BETTMANN NEWSPHOTOS

Thomson, Sir Joseph John (1856–1940), English physicist. He discovered the electron, developed the mathematical theory of electricity and magnetism, and conducted research on positive ion beams. He won the 1906 Nobel Prize for work on the transmission of electricity through gases.

Thomson, Virgil Garnett (1896–1989), U.S. composer and critic. In 1925 he went to Paris, where he was influenced by the group of composers called the Six, including Erik Satie. Returning to New York, he became music critic on the New York *Herald Tribune,* 1940–1954. His works include the opera *Four Saints in Three Acts* (1934) with libretto by Gertrude Stein; scores for such films as *The Plow that Broke the Plains* (1936), *The River* (1937), and *Louisiana Story* (1948), which won the Pulitzer Prize for music in 1949; and a number of symphonies, chamber and choral works, and ballets.

Thoreau, Henry David (1817–1862), U.S. writer and naturalist. A member of the Concord circle, he was influenced by Emerson's transcendentalism. In 1845 he built a shanty near Walden Pond, where he lived for two years. His most famous book, *Walden, or Life in the Woods* (1854), is an account of his life there. He later spent a night in jail for refusing to pay a tax as a protest against the Mexican War, which his famous "On the Duty of Civil Disobedience" describes. His other works include *A Week on the Concord and Merrimack Rivers* (1849), *The Maine Woods* (1864), and *Cape Cod* (1865).

Thorndike, Edward Lee (1874–1949), U.S. educational psychologist. Working at Teachers College, Columbia University, Thorndike became known in the area of intelligence testing. He wrote or co-authored more than 500 books and articles, including *Educational Psychology* (1913–1914), *The Measurement of Intelligence* (1926), *Your City* (1939), and *Human Nature and the Social Order* (1940).

Thorpe, James Francis (1888–1953), Indian name Bright Path, U.S. athlete. Thorpe first played football for Carlisle (Pa.) Indian School. In 1911 and 1912 he was named an All-American. At the 1912 Olympics in Stockholm, Sweden, he became an international celebrity when he won both the decathlon and the pentathlon. He was later forced to return his gold medals for unknowingly violating the Olympic rules on amateur standing. In 1982 the medals were returned to him posthumously. Thorpe also played professional baseball and football. In 1950 an Associated Press survey named him the greatest male athlete of the first half of the 20th century.

Thucydides (d. c 400 B.C.), the greatest of Greek historians, born in Athens. In

THE THOREAU SOCIETY

HENRY DAVID THOREAU

424 Thucydides commanded an expedition to Amphipolis to save the city from the Spartans. The expedition failed and Thucydides was sent into exile, not returning to Athens until 404. During his exile, Thucydides began the *History of the Peloponnesian War,* which covers the war from its beginning in 431 to 411. The *History* is characterized by balance, objectivity, accuracy, and insight.

Thurber, James Grover (1894–1961), U.S. writer and artist whose sketches, stories, and cartoons made gentle fun of modern life. Thurber was for many years associated with *The New Yorker* magazine, where he worked from 1926 to 1933. In later years he was nearly blind. His works include *The Owl in the Attic* (1931); *The Seal in the Bedroom* (1932); *Fables for Our Time* (1940); *The Thurber Carnival* (1945); *The Thirteen Clocks* (1950), a children's story; and *Thurber Country* (1953). With E.B. White he wrote *Is Sex Necessary?* (1929), and with Elliott Nugent the play *The Male Animal* (1940).

Tiepolo, Giovanni Battista (1696–1770), Italian fresco painter of the Venetian school, known for his bright, rich colors. Tiepolo completed fresco cycles in Udine, Milan, and Bergamo, and decorated the Palazzo Labia in Venice in 1745. In 1750 he went to Würzburg, where he painted his masterpiece, the grand staircase in the prince archbishop's palace. He spent his last years in Spain working for Charles III.

Tiffany, Louis Comfort (1848–1933), U.S. artist internationally known for his *favrile* glass, used to make Tiffany lamps. He was the son of Charles Lewis Tiffany (1812–1902), founder of Tiffany and Company jewelers. Louis Tiffany, also a recognized painter and decorator, established the firm Tiffany Studios. He redecorated the reception rooms in the White House and designed interiors and stained glass windows for churches.

Tilden, Samuel Jones (1814–1886), U.S. political leader and lawyer. A Democrat, he was elected to the New York assembly in 1845 and supported such antislavery groups as the Barnburners and Free-Soilers. In 1866 he began a successful attack on William Tweed and the political corruption of the Tweed Ring in New York City. He was elected governor of New York in 1874. As the Democratic Presidential candidate in 1876, he won 250,000 more popular votes than Republican candidate Rutherford B. Hayes. However, Hayes won by one electoral vote.

Tilden, William Tatem, Jr. (1893–1953), U.S. tennis player, the first American to win the Wimbledon men's singles championship. With his cannonball serve, Tilden won the U.S. singles championship seven times in the 1920's and the Wimbledon title three times. He was on the U.S. Davis Cup team, 1920–1930.

Tillich, Paul Johannes (1886–1965), German-born Protestant theologian and philosopher who sought to interpret Christianity in modern terms. He taught theology at Berlin, Dresden, and Leipzig and became professor of philosophy at Frankfurt in 1929. Dismissed in 1933 by the Nazis, he emigrated to the United States and became a U.S. citizen. He taught at the Union Theological Seminary, Harvard, and the University of Chicago. His works include *Systematic Theology* (1951–1963), *The Courage To Be* (1952), and *The Eternal Now* (1963).

Tintoretto (1518–1594), born Jacopo Robusti, Italian painter, the last major artist of the Venetian school. Though he was an enemy of Titian (who had discharged Tintoretto from his studio), he admired his use of color, as well as the drawings of Michelangelo. Tintoretto's frescoes of the life of Christ for the Scuola di San Rocco, 1565–1567, are his masterpiece. His other works include *The Last Supper, Finding of St. Mark's Body,* and *Paradise* (in the doge's palace), the largest painting in the world.

Tirpitz, Alfred von (1849–1930), German naval officer who built up the German navy and who, through his influence with Kaiser Wilhelm II, helped prevent an accord between Germany and Britain before World War I. Entering the navy in 1865, he served as naval minister, 1897–1916, and became lord high admiral in 1911. He carried out unrestricted submarine warfare against enemy and neutral ships during World War I. After the sinking of the luxury liner *Lusitania* in 1915, his policy was abandoned and Tirpitz resigned.

Titian (c 1487–1576), born Tiziano Vecelli, foremost painter of the Venetian school. A superb colorist, Titian used a unique technique of applying pigment so as to model forms and create special textures. During his very long career, he produced both religious works like *Assumption of the Virgin, Entombment,* and *Trinity,* and mythological paintings, including *Sacred and Profane Love, Bacchus and Ariadne,* and *The Rape of Europa.* He was also a master portraitist and painted many versions of his patron, Holy Roman Emperor Charles V, as well as Pope Paul III and the writer Pietro Aretino.

Tito (1892–1980), name assumed by Josip Broz, president of the Federal People's Republic of Yugoslavia. He served in the Austro-Hungarian army in World War I and was captured by Russian troops in 1915. In 1917 he took part in the Bolshevik revolution in Russia; returning to Yugoslavia in 1920, he became a leader of the Yugoslav Communist movement. He was imprisoned several times for his revolutionary activities between 1928 and 1934. During World War II he led partisan guerrillas against Axis troops. When Yugoslavia was liberated in 1945, he became prime minister, minister of national defense, and virtual dictator. After 1953 he served as president of Yugoslavia. In 1948 a breach between Tito and Stalin, dictator of the Soviet Union, shook the communist world. Tito became a symbol of communist independence from Soviet domination.

Tocqueville, (Charles) Alexis (Henri Maurice Clérel) de (1805–1859), French historian. In 1831 he went to the United States to study U.S. penitentiaries. He later wrote *Democracy in America* (1835–1840), the first systematic study of a working democracy or of American institutions. Tocqueville entered French politics and became foreign minister after the 1848 revolution, but he proved to be better at analysis than at action. He retired to write a history of the French Revolution and its aftermath but only completed the first part, *The Ancien Regime* (1856), which became a classic. He also wrote *Recollections of 1848,* a personal account of the 1848 revolutions, which was not published until 1890.

Tojo, Hideki (1884–1948), Japanese general, prime minister of Japan, 1941–1944. As prime minister, Tojo secured the decision to attack Pearl Harbor in 1941 and to launch the Japanese offensive in the Far East. He resigned after the United States took Saipan in 1944. After the war, he was tried by the United States as a war criminal and executed in 1948.

Tolkien, John Ronald Reuel (1892–1973), English author best known as the creator of the world of Middle Earth, described in the fantasy trilogy *The Lord of the Rings.* The trilogy, introduced by the separate children's book, *The Hobbit* (1937), includes *The Fellowship of the Ring* (1954), *The Two Towers* (1954), and *The Return of the King* (1955).

Tolstoy, Leo (Count Lev Nikolaevich Tolstoy) (1828–1910), Russian novelist. He joined the army in 1852 and fought in the Crimean War. After traveling abroad, he spent his time happily supervising his estate, enjoying family life, and writing. To this period belong his two greatest novels: *War and Peace* (1864–1869), a panorama of Russian society during the Napoleonic wars, and *Anna Karenina* (1875–1877), a tragic novel of a love affair and its consequences. During the late 1870's he underwent a spiritual crisis during which he rejected orthodox Christianity and developed his own religion of love based on Christ's teachings. He turned his estate over to his family and tried to lead what he considered the simple, godly life of a peasant. His ideas made him famous as a sage but brought him into conflict with his wife and family. At 82, tired of family quarrels and eager to lead a more ascetic life, he left home for a monastery but died before he reached it. Tolstoy developed dozens of convincing characters in each of his novels and was equally a master of such epic scenes as marching armies and battlefield encounters. After 1880 Tolstoy wrote many religious and moral works, but he continued to write fiction as well. His late works include the short story "The Kreutzer Sonata" (1891) and two novels, *The Death of Ivan Ilich* (1886) and *Resurrection* (1899).

Torquemada, Tomás de (c 1420–1498), Spanish Dominican monk who

LEO TOLSTOY

THE BETTMANN ARCHIVE

organized and led the bloody Spanish Inquisition. To enforce religious and political orthodoxy in Spain, Pope Sixtus IV, at the request of the Spanish monarchs Ferdinand and Isabella, organized an inquisition to try those accused of heresy and punish offenders. Torquemada, formerly confessor to the queen, became first inquisitor-general in 1483 and held the post until his death. During Torquemada's term about 2000 "heretics" were burned at the stake. In 1492 he was influential in issuing an edict expelling all Jews from Spain. The government profited by taking over all abandoned estates but the country suffered from the loss of thousands of skilled workers and cultural and economic leaders.

Torricelli, Evangelista (1608–1647), Italian physicist and mathematician who in 1643 invented the barometer, often called the Torricellian tube. He was an assistant to Galileo, succeeding him as professor of mathematics and philosophy at the Florentine Academy. After he proved that air has weight, he devised the barometer to measure atmospheric pressure.

Toscanini, Arturo (1867–1957), Italian conductor. Noted for his uncompromising musical integrity, he strove to learn and follow a composer's intentions. Touring as cellist and assistant chorus master with an Italian opera company in 1886, he was asked to fill in as conductor for a performance of *Aida* in Rio de Janeiro. This he did from memory, thus beginning a 70-year career as a conductor. He was chief conductor at La Scala in Milan, 1898–1908 and 1921–1929; he led the Metropolitan Opera in New York, 1908–1915; and the New York Philharmonic, 1928–1936. During the 1930's he conducted at the Bayreuth, Salzburg, and Lucerne festivals. From 1937 to 1954 he led the NBC Symphony.

Toulouse-Lautrec (1864–1901), in full Henri Marie Raymond de Toulouse-Lautrec Monfa, French impressionist painter and lithographer. Lautrec was crippled as a result of two childhood accidents and his deformity greatly influenced the course of his life. He left the aristocratic environment of his family and in 1882 went to Paris, where he studied for a time and then set up his own studio in Montmartre. He frequented the brothels, cafés, theaters, and music halls of the district, and painted the people he knew there. Lautrec's paintings include *At the Moulin Rouge* (1892), *The Salon in the Rue des Moulins* (1894), and *Modiste* (1900). After 1891 he devoted much of his time to lithography. His famous designs for posters, such as *Aristide Bruant* and *Jane Avril,* greatly influenced modern advertising and graphic arts.

Touré, Sékou (1922–), first president of the African republic of Guinea, 1958–1984. After becoming a labor leader, Touré was elected as the Guinean deputy to the French National Assembly in 1956. He then was appointed head of the Guinean government under French rule. In 1958 he led his country in severing all ties with France. Though considered a Marxist, he kept Guinea neutral.

Toussaint L'Ouverture (1743–1803), real name François Dominique Toussaint, Haitian liberator and briefly president of Haiti, 1801–1802. A slave in the French-controlled colony, he joined a rebellion against white rule in 1791. By 1801 he had established his own administration. However, when Napoleon sent his forces to reconquer Haiti, after a valiant fight Toussaint was forced to surrender. Shortly thereafter, he was arrested and sent to France, where he died in prison.

Toynbee, Arnold Joseph (1889–1975), English historian best known for *A Study of History* (1934–1961), a twelve-volume work that comprehensively compares 21 civilizations, tracing patterns of growth, maturity, and decay in each. He also wrote *Hellenism: The History of a Civilization* (1959) and *Cities on the Move* (1970).

Trajan (c 53–117 A.D.), in full Marcus Ulpius Trajanus, Roman emperor, 98–117. Because of his popularity with his soldiers, Trajan was adopted by the emperor Nerva and succeeded him. Under Trajan's rule, the empire reached its greatest extent. In 106 he defeated the Dacians and made Dacia (now Rumania) a Roman province. He improved social conditions and built a number of public works, including roads and a new Roman forum. In 114 he began a campaign against the Armenians and Parthians, whom he defeated in 116.

Trollope, Anthony (1815–1882), British novelist who wrote of middle-class life in early Victorian England. His well-known works include *The Warden* (1855), *Barchester Towers* (1857), *Phineas Finn* (1869), and *The Eustace Diamonds* (1873). His *Autobiography* was published in 1883.

His mother, **Frances Milton Trollope** (1780–1863), supported the family for a time by her own writing. She wrote several novels but is most famous for *Domestic Manners of the Americans* (1832), which she wrote after touring the United States and which angered American readers.

Trotsky, Leon (1879–1940), name taken by Lev Davidovich Bronstein, one of the original leaders of the Soviet Communist revolution. Banished to Siberia in 1900 for revolutionary activities, he fled abroad and wrote for radical papers in Germany, France, Switzerland, and the United States. After the March, 1917, revolution in Russia, he returned there and, with Lenin, organized the Bolshevik seizure of power. As commissar for foreign affairs, he negotiated the treaty of Brest-Litovsk between Germany and Russia. He became commissar for war in 1918, formed the Red Army, and was largely responsible for the Bolshevik victory in the Russian civil war. Following Lenin's death, Trotsky lost a bitter contest for leadership to Joseph Stalin. He was expelled from the party and exiled in 1929. In 1940 he was assassinated in Mexico by Stalin's order. His books include a number of polemics and firsthand accounts, of which the most significant is his *History of the Russian Revolution* (3 volumes, 1932–1933).

Trudeau, Pierre Elliott (1919–), prime minister of Canada, 1968–1979, 1980–1984. A lawyer, he was first elected to Parliament in 1965. He became a cabinet minister in 1967 and leader of the Liberal Party the following year. Trudeau followed a policy stressing independence from American political and economic influence, but he was a supporter of NATO. He opposed moves for greater freedom for Quebec Province and became embroiled in a dispute with some of the provinces over the taxation of energy resources. His government established diplomatic relations with China in 1970. In 1980 he asked the British Parliament to give Canada full control over its constitution, supporting a controversial amendment regarding civil rights. His reform resolution was approved by the House of Commons in 1981. Canada's independence from the British Parliament was formally declared in 1982.

Truffaut, François (1932–1984), the French director who was one of the founders of Europe's new wave film movement. *The 400 Blows* (1959) was one of the first new wave feature films. *Jules et Jim* (1961) was typical of his sympathetic yet neutral portrayal of characters and his versatile camera technique. Other films include *Shoot the Piano Player* (1960), *Fahrenheit 451* (1966), *The Bride Wore Black* (1967), *Stolen Kisses* (1968), *Day for Night* (1973), *The Last Metro* (1980), and *Confidentially Yours* (1984).

Truman, Harry S. (1884–1972), 33rd President of the United States, 1945–1952. Truman distinguished himself in World War I as a captain in the field artillery. After the war he opened a men's store in Kansas City. When his business failed, rather than declare bankruptcy he spent ten years paying off his debts. In 1934 he was elected U.S. senator from Missouri. He became famous as chairman of a Senate committee to investigate waste in war production and in the military. In 1944 Truman was elected Vice President under Franklin D. Roosevelt. When

Roosevelt died in 1945, Truman succeeded him. In August, 1945, Truman gave his approval to the use of the atom bomb on Japanese cities, hastening the end of the war in the Pacific. After the war he established the Truman Doctrine and the Marshall Plan. He was reelected in 1948 in a surprise victory over Thomas E. Dewey. When South Korea was attacked in 1950, Truman came to its aid.

Tshombe, Moise-Kapenda (1919–1969), premier of the Congo, 1963–1965. When his country achieved independence in 1960, Tshombe headed a secessionist regime in Katanga Province aided by Belgian business interests. United Nations troops ended the revolt in 1963, but in six months Tshombe managed to become premier of a united Congo. He was ousted in 1965. Kidnaped in 1967, he died in Algeria in 1969.

Tubman, Harriet (c 1820–1913), U.S. abolitionist who operated one of the most famous and successful underground railroads (escape routes) to the North for slaves. She was born into slavery on a plantation in Maryland, but escaped in 1849. In the next ten years she made 19 trips to the South and brought more than 300 slaves to safety. During the Civil War she served as a scout and spy for the Union Army.

Tupper, Sir Charles (1821–1915), physician, statesman, and Conservative prime minister of Canada in 1896. Tupper's political career and ministerial portfolios earned him much respect. He resigned as prime minister after only ten weeks because of the defeat of a bill in parliament.

Turgenev, Ivan Sergeyevich (1818–1883), Russian author. His early work, the play *A Month in the Country* (1850) and the collection of stories called *Sportsman's Sketches* (1852), was concerned with the petty aristocracy in the provinces of Russia and their conflicts with the peasantry. Turgenev then wrote the novels *A Nest of Gentlefolk* (1858), again portraying the provincial aristocracy, and *On the Eve* (1860), the hero of which is a revolutionary. His most important novel, *Fathers and Sons,* was published in 1862. It deals with the ideological conflicts between the generations. Turgenev's political ideas were widely misunderstood. Discouraged by controversy, Turgenev left Russia in 1863 and lived in Germany and France until his death.

Turner, Frederick Jackson (1861–1932), U.S. historian. His essay "The Significance of the Frontier in American History" (1893) proposed that U.S. democracy is the product of the free land, resourcefulness, and individualism of the frontier. In 1933 he received the Pulitzer Prize for *The Significance of Sections in American History* (1932).

Turner, John Napier (1929–), politician, prime minister of Canada, June-September, 1984. Born in England and trained as a lawyer, he was first elected to parliament in 1962. He has served in the cabinet as solicitor general, minister of justice, attorney general, and minister of finance.

Turner, Joseph Mallord William (1775–1851), English painter known for his romantic landscapes. With watercolors, and later with oils, he was able to capture the effects of brilliant color and light. His works include *The Fighting Téméraire Tugged to Her Last Berth* and *Rain, Steam, and Speed.* His later works anticipated modern abstract painting.

Turner, Nat (1800–1831), black slave and preacher who was the leader of the Southampton insurrection. A religious fanatic and effective preacher, Turner felt he was called to lead the slaves against their masters. In 1831 Turner and a band of seven slaves murdered their master and his entire family. Joined by about 75 other slaves, the band killed 55 more white people before they were stopped. Turner was tried, condemned, and hanged along with 16 other members of the band.

Tutankhamen (c 1371–c 1352 B.C.), Pharaoh of Egypt from about 1361. "King Tut" is remembered because his splendid tomb, almost untouched by ancient grave robbers, gave modern historians much of their knowledge of the arts and burial customs of Egypt. Located in the Valley of the Tombs of the Kings, near Thebes, it was first explored in 1922. Tutankhamen married the daughter of Pharaoh Ikhnaton and Nefertiti. During his reign he moved the capital of Egypt from Akhetaton (Tell el-Amarna) back to Thebes and restored the old religion of Amen.

Twain, Mark: *See* Clemens, Samuel Langhorne.

Tweed, William Marcy (1823–1878), U.S. politician. In 1851 Tweed was elected alderman and rose in Tammany Hall, the Democratic Party organization of Manhattan. By 1863 he was virtually in control of New York politics. With a group of associates, the Tweed Ring, he was able to systematically rob the city treasury of well over $45 million. "Boss" Tweed's graft was exposed through the combined efforts of lawyer Samuel J. Tilden, the political cartoons of Thomas Nast in *Harper's Weekly,* and an editorial campaign in *The New York Times.* He was arrested in 1871 and convicted of embezzlement, but was released in 1875. Arrested again, he escaped to Spain, where he was apprehended. He died in New York's Ludlow Street jail.

Tyler, John (1790–1862), tenth President of the United States, 1841–1845. In 1825 he was elected governor of Virginia and in 1827 a U.S. senator as an anti-Jackson Democrat. In 1840 he was elected Vice President with William Henry Harrison on the Whig ticket. Tyler became the first Vice President to succeed to the Presidency when Harrison died a month after his inauguration. His term of office was marked by almost continual controversy with Congress, his party, and his Cabinet, all of whom resigned in 1841 with the exception of Daniel Webster, his secretary of state, who resigned in 1843. Much of the controversy concerned his refusal to sign his party's bill authorizing the establishment of a national bank. In 1861 Tyler came out of retirement to preside at the North-South peace conference in Washington, D.C. He was then elected to the Confederate Congress but died before it convened.

Tyndale, William (c 1494–1536), English religious reformer who first translated the Bible into English. Because he was not allowed to publish it in England, he went to Germany, met Martin Luther, and in 1525 began to print the translation in Cologne. He was soon expelled and fled to Worms, where the printing was finished later that year. In 1530 he published a translation of the first five books of the Old Testament. An advocate of the English Reformation, he was arrested as a heretic in Flanders, strangled, and burned. His translation became one source of the King James Bible (1611).

HARRIET TUBMAN

U

Uccello, Paolo (1397–1475), real name Paolo di Dono, Florentine painter who was among the first to experiment with foreshortening and linear perspective. His best-known works include a portrait of Sir John de Hawkwood in the cathedral at Florence; *Battle of San Romano;* and the Noah's ark frescoes in the church of Santa Maria Novella in Florence.

Unamuno y Jugo, Miguel de (1864–1936), Spanish philosopher, poet, and novelist who anticipated modern existentialism. Unamuno was exiled in 1924 but was reinstated in 1931 when Spain became a republic. His first novel *Paz en la guerra* (1897), is usually regarded as the first existentialist work. His longing for immortality was best expressed in his masterpiece *The Tragic Sense of Life in Man and in Peoples* (1913) and in his later novel *San Manuel Bueno, mártir* (1933).

Undset, Sigrid (1882–1949), Norwegian novelist born in Denmark who received the 1928 Nobel Prize for Literature for her historical novel of medieval Norway, *Kristin Lavransdatter* (3 volumes, 1920–1922). Other novels include *Jenny* (1911) and *Olav Audunsson* (4 volumes, 1925–1927; translated as *The Master of Hestviken*).

Updike, John Hoyer (1932–), U.S. novelist, short story writer, and poet. His most popular novels are *Rabbit, Run* (1960), *The Centaur* (1963), which won a National Book Award, *Couples* (1968), *Rabbit Redux* (1971), *The Coup* (1978), the Pulitzer Prize-winning *Rabbit Is Rich* (1981), and *The Witches of Eastwick* (1984). Some of his short stories were collected in *The Same Door* (1959) and *Pigeon Feathers and Other Stories* (1962).

Urey, Harold Clayton (1893–1981), U.S. chemist who did research on isotopes and was awarded the 1934 Nobel Prize for Chemistry for his discovery in 1931 of heavy hydrogen, or deuterium, an isotope of hydrogen. As part of the Manhatten Project during World War II, Urey directed research on separating fissionable uranium (U-235) from ordinary uranium (U-238) for use in the atomic bomb. He later worked on the chemical methods for determining the origin of the solar system.

Utrillo, Maurice (1883–1955), French painter. The illegitimate son of the painter Suzanne Valadon, he was adopted by the Spanish writer Miguel Utrillo. His works most often depict the streets of Paris in and around the old artists' quarter of Montmartre. Painted in light, bright colors, they are realistic in execution but emotional in conception. His paintings include *Rue de Mont Cenis* and *Sacre Coeur de Montmartre.*

V

Valera, Eamon de: *See* De Valera, Eamon.

Valéry, (Ambroise) Paul (Toussaint Jules) (1871–1945), French poet, essayist, and man of letters. He established a reputation as a symbolist poet, then gave up poetry for 20 years in favor of mathematics and the physical sciences. At the urging of André Gide, he began revising his earlier work in 1912, publishing *The Youngest of the Fates* in 1917. This work secured his literary reputation. A second volume, *Charmes* (1922), contains the famous "Graveyard by the Sea." Valéry's other works include writings on the dance, literature, and philosophy, and a massive study of the intellect, *Introduction to the Method of Leonardo da Vinci* (1895).

Van Allen, James Alfred (1914–), U.S. physicist. In 1958, after years of research on cosmic rays, he discovered the Van Allen radiation belt, a ring of electrically charged particles surrounding Earth. Van Allen supervised the testing of the first captured German V-2 rocket and was involved in many aspects of U.S. high-altitude research and rocket development.

Van Buren, Martin (1782–1862), eighth President of the United States, 1837–1841. In 1821 Van Buren entered the U.S. Senate as a Democratic-Republican. He resigned from the Senate to become governor of New York in 1828. His firm control of party politics enabled him to help secure the election of President Andrew Jackson, who made him secretary of state in 1829. In 1832 he was elected Vice President on the ticket with Jackson. In 1836 Van Buren was elected President with Jackson's support. In office he opposed the deposit of state funds in a national bank and the extension of slavery. He was unable to alleviate the severe business depression that began in 1837 and ran unsuccessfully for the Presidency as a Democrat in 1840 and as a member of the Free Soil Party in 1848.

Vanderbilt, Cornelius (1794–1877), often called Commodore, U.S. financier who founded a fortune with steamship and railroad lines. He began his business career at 16, when he purchased a sailboat and carried passengers between Staten Island and Manhattan. He continually expanded his enterprise and in 1850 made his fortune with a passenger steamship line that shortened travel time to California in the days of the gold rush. In the 1860's he sold his ships and built a lucrative railroad empire, the New York Central system, expanding his fortune to $100 million. A philanthropist, he founded Vanderbilt University.

THE BETTMANN ARCHIVE

CORNELIUS VANDERBILT

THE BETTMANN ARCHIVE

VINCENT VAN GOGH

Van Dyck (or Vandyke), Sir Anthony (1599–1641), Flemish painter who established the traditional style of the British portrait painters. In London Van Dyck ran a large workshop (or portrait factory), which was generously patronized by the aristocracy (*The Marchesa Grimaldi,* 1623). After 1623 he was official court painter to Charles I of England. He also painted religious works, including *Crucifixion, Elevation of the Cross,* and *The Betrayal of Christ.*

Van Eyck, family name of two brothers, the founders of the Flemish school of painting.

Hubert van Eyck (c 1366–1426) painted parts of a colossal altarpiece, *The Adoration of the Lamb,* in the Church of St. Bavon in Ghent, his only known work.

Jan van Eyck (c 1370–c 1440) was commissioned by John, duke of Holland, to paint decorations at The

Hague in 1422. In 1425 he became court painter to Philip the Good, duke of Burgundy. Among his many works are the triptych of the *Virgin and Child, Annunciation,* and several portraits, including the famous *Arnolfini and His Wife.*

Van Gogh, Vincent Willem (1853–1890), an outstanding Dutch postimpressionist painter. In 1885 he produced his first major work, *The Potato Eaters,* a drab, dark, and sympathetic portrait of a peasant family. In 1886 he joined his brother Theo, an art dealer, in Paris. There he met Gauguin, Seurat, and Toulouse-Lautrec. Van Gogh spent several years in the south of France, where he painted numerous brightly colored landscapes, still lifes, and figure studies. However, since he sold no paintings, he was forced to live in poverty. He suffered several nervous breakdowns; during one, he cut off his right ear after quarreling with Paul Gauguin. The last years of his life were spent in insane asylums. He committed suicide in 1890, after having produced, in the ten frantic years of his artistic career, more than 800 paintings, including the much-admired *Berceuse, The Bridge at Arles, Sunflowers,* and *Starry Night.*

Vanzetti, Bartolomeo: *See* Sacco, Nicola.

Varèse, Edgard (1883–1965), French composer noted for his use of new harmonies and rhythms and his experiments with electronic sound. His titles for compositions indicate his desire to create music unassociated with previous musical experience: *Hyperprism* (1922), *Ionization* (for percussion and two sirens, 1933), and *Density 21.5* (1935). He used new and unusual instruments, feeling that contemporary life was not represented by existing orchestral instruments.

Vaughan Williams, Ralph (1872–1958), British composer. Among his best-known works are *Fantasia on Greensleeves* and *Fantasia on a Theme by Tallis* (1910), the Mass in G minor (1923), and *Serenade to Music* (1938). He also composed two works based on the poetry of Walt Whitman, *Towards the Unknown Region* (1905) and *Sea Symphony* (1910), and the operas *Sir John in Love* (1929) and *Pilgrims' Progress* (1951).

Veblen, Thorstein Bunde (1857–1929), U.S. economist and sociologist. A severe critic of modern social and economic institutions, Veblen wrote *The Theory of the Leisure Class* (1899), *The Theory of Business Enterprise* (1904), *The Higher Learning in America* (1918), and *The Vested Interests and the State of Industrial Arts* (1919). He originated the phrase conspicuous consumption in describing the economic waste of the wealthy.

Vega, Lope de (1562–1635), in full Lope Félix de Vega Carpio, Spanish playwright and poet generally considered the founder of the Spanish drama. He is said to have written more than 1000 plays and 400 other works, including novels, epics, and poems. His works include the epic poems *The Beauty of Angelica* (1602) and *Jerusalem Conquered* (1608) and the prose masterpiece *Dorotea* (1632). His most famous plays include *Remedy in Misfortune* (1599), *The Dog in the Manger* (1613), *The Best Magistrate, the King* (1621), and *The Knight of Olmedo* (1622).

Velázquez, Diego Rodríguez de Silva y (1599–1660), Spanish painter known for his realism, silvery shadings, and the air of dignified reticence he gave to his portraits of royalty. In 1623, after painting a pleasing portrait of Philip IV, he was made court painter. His works include portraits of the king, the infantas Margarita and Maria, court jesters, beggars, and dwarfs; religious paintings such as *Adoration of the Magi* and *Crucifixion;* mythological works such as *Mercury and Argos;* genre paintings such as *The Spinning Women;* and the historical *Surrender of Breda.*

Verdi, Giuseppe (1813–1901), Italian composer. An early work, the comedy opera *King for a Day,* was hissed off the stage in Milan in 1840. Verdi's first success was *Nabucco* in 1842; from then on he continued to produce operatic masterpieces for more than 50 years. Among his 26 operas are *Ernani* (1844), *Rigoletto* (1851), *Il Trovatore* (1853), *La Traviata* (1853), *La Forza del Destino* (1862), *Don Carlo* (1867), *Aïda* (1871), *Otello* (1887), and *Falstaff* (1893). He also composed choral works, such as the Requiem Mass for the Italian patriot Alessandro Manzoni (1874).

Vergil (or Virgil) (70–19 B.C.), full name Publius Vergilius Maro, Roman poet of the classical period who composed the epic *Aeneid.* He went to Rome in about 40, where he enjoyed the patronage of the emperor Augustus. Vergil wrote in hexameter, or heroic verse. Besides the *Aeneid,* an epic of the history of the Roman people, he wrote the *Georgics,* a celebration of farm and rural life; and *Eclogues,* or *Bucolics,* a series of pastoral poems.

Verlaine, Paul Marie (1844–1896), French poet associated with the symbolist movement. His poetry is noted for its grace, delicacy, and lyricism. Verlaine's works include *Poèmes Saturniens* (1866), *Romances sans Paroles* (1874), and *Sagesse* (1880).

Vermeer, Jan (1632–1675), Dutch painter also known as Jan van der Meer van Delft. His portraits and scenes of the orderly, warm homes of the Dutch are brilliant studies of forms in light and shadow. They include *Young Woman with a Water Jug, The Lace Maker, The Painter's Studio,* and *Girl in a Red Hat.*

Verne, Jules (1828–1905), French novelist who made science fiction a popular literary form. He anticipated the submarine in *Twenty Thousand Leagues Under the Sea* (1870), pictured the flying machine and fast steamships in *Around the World in Eighty Days* (1873), and foretold space travel in *From the Earth to the Moon* (1865). His other imaginative works include *Five Weeks in a Balloon* (1863), *Voyage to the Center of the Earth* (1864), and *The Mysterious Island* (1875).

Veronese, Paolo (1528–1588), born Paoli Cagliari, Venetian artist born in Verona recognized for his frescoes depicting the high life of 16th-century Venetian society. His paintings contain scores of recognizable people of the time. They include *Supper at Emmaus* (c 1560), *The Rape of Europa* (1580), the frescoes in the doge's palace, and the *Triumph of Venice* (1578–1585), one of the world's finest painted ceilings. Veronese achieved spectacular effects in color, pattern, and composition, particularly in his painting of ceilings.

Verrocchio, Andrea del (c 1435–1488), real name Andrea di Michele di Francesco Cioni, Florentine painter and sculptor who was the master of Leonardo da Vinci. Little is known of Verrocchio's life, and only a few works can be ascribed to him. However, he did maintain one of the largest workshops in Florence and from it came such paintings as *The Madonna and Child with Two Angels.* Verrocchio is best known for his sculpture, especially the magnificent bronze equestrian statue of Bartolommeo Colleoni (Venice), the nude *David,* and *Boy with a Dolphin.*

Vesalius, Andreas (1514–1564), a Flemish anatomist who made the first comprehensive studies of human anatomy based on human dissection. Vesalius's principal work, *De Humani Corporis Fabrica* (*On the Structure of the Human Body,* 1543) was the first modern illustrated book on anatomy and a landmark in the history of science. It was the only major work on the human body since Galen, whose research was based on animal dissection.

Vespasian (9 A.D.–79 A.D.), in full Titus Flavius Sabinus Vespasianus, Roman emperor, 69–79, the first of the Flavian emperors. He became consul of Rome in 51 and proconsul of Africa in 63. In 67 he was sent to Judea by Nero to put down a revolt of the Jews. In 69, while still in Judea, Vespasian was declared emperor by his soldiers. He left his son Titus in command and returned to

Rome in 69. The following year the Judean war ended with the destruction of Jerusalem by Titus, and a revolt of the German tribe Batavi was suppressed. In 78 and 79 Roman armies extended their conquests in Britain. As emperor, Vespasian restored order to the government and its finances after the disastrous reign of Nero. He also ordered the construction of many public buildings, including the Colosseum.

Vespucci, Amerigo (1454–1512) Florentine navigator for whom the American continents were named. He made several voyages to the New World between 1497 and 1504 and, though the facts are obscure, he may have discovered the mainland of North America in 1498, before Columbus or the Cabots. He was the first to state that the land was not part of Asia, but a new continent. A German geographer, Martin Waldseemüller (1470–1518), suggested that the New World be named after Vespucci.

Victor Emmanuel II (1820–1878), last king of Sardinia and first king of modern Italy. He succeeded his father, Charles Albert, as king of Sardinia in 1849. In 1861 the kingdom of Italy was established with Victor Emmanuel II as constitutional monarch.

Victoria (1819–1901), queen of Great Britain and Ireland, 1837–1901, and empress of India, 1876–1901. She succeeded her uncle William IV on his death in 1837 and reigned longer than any other British monarch. In 1840 Victoria married a cousin, Prince Albert of Saxe-Coburg-Gotha, and became the mother of nine children. Her grandchildren included members of many European royal houses, including Kaiser William II of Germany and Alexandra, the last czarina of Russia. Prince Albert died in 1861 and Victoria remained in mourning for the rest of her life. Victoria had little political power since Parliament and the cabinet made almost all foreign and domestic policy. But her long reign and popularity made her a symbol of Britain in the 1800's. The word Victorian is used to describe the attitudes of her time.

Villa, Pancho (or Francisco) (1877–1923), born Doroteo Arango, Mexican bandit and revolutionary. When he was 16 he killed a man for molesting his sister, then fled to the mountains, changed his name, and lived as a cattle rustler and bandit. He later became one of the leaders of the Mexican Revolution of 1910 against President Diaz and of subsequent revolutionary outbreaks in 1914. He and other revolutionary leaders fought among themselves for control of the government. Villa's chief opponent was Venustiano Carranza, who finally drove him across the border into the United States. When Carranza was recognized as de facto

VICTORIA

president of Mexico by the U.S. government, Villa retaliated with a raid on Columbus, N.M., in which 16 U.S. citizens were killed. General John Pershing was sent to Mexico with U.S. troops to capture Villa, but Villa escaped. In 1920 he finally made peace with Carranza's successor.

Villa-Lobos, Heitor (1887–1959), Brazilian nationalist composer. Villa-Lobos was a prolific composer; his compositions number some 2000, though their quality is considered uneven. His most familiar works are the *Bachianas brasileiras* (1930–1945), in which he blended Brazilian rhythms and melodies with counterpoint in the style of Bach.

Villon, François (1431–after 1463), original name probably François de Montcorbier, French lyric poet known for his gay and tender ballades. He assumed the last name of Guillaume de Villon, who raised him and sent him to the Sorbonne. There he began drinking, brawling, and engaging in thievery, which eventually brought him imprisonment and exile from Paris. In 1463 Villon was sentenced to be hanged for attempted murder (ironically, a charge of which he was innocent), but the sentence was commuted to ten years of exile. He vanished, and nothing is known of his life beyond that point. His poetry collections include *Petit Testament* and his masterpiece *Grand Testament.* His best-known poems are "Ballad of Dead Ladies," "Prayer to Our Lady," and "Epitaph of Villon," written after he was sentenced to be hanged.

Vinci, Leonardo da: *See* Leonardo da Vinci.

Virgil: *See* Vergil.

Vivaldi, Antonio (1678–1741), Italian composer, one of the leading figures of early 18th-century music. A prolific composer and highly accomplished violinist, his instrumental compositions include over 400 concertos, among them the well-known *The Four Seasons,* and numerous operas. His *concerti grossi* led to the concerto form used by such composers as Beethoven and Mozart.

Vlaminck, Maurice de (1876–1958), French painter, one of the founders of the Fauvist school. At first, Vlaminck painted in his spare time while working as an actor, racing cyclist, and violinist. In 1895 he began art lessons and from 1901 shared a studio with André Derain on the island of Chatou. With Derain, Matisse, and others he participated in the first exhibit of the *fauves* ("wild beasts"). He, like other Fauvists, used vivid colors and free forms. Later he became a realist, painting many romantic landscapes and still lifes.

Volstead, Andrew Joseph (1860–1947), U.S. legislator. A member of the U.S. Congress from 1903 to 1923, he was the author of the Volstead Act (passed over the veto of President Woodrow Wilson in October, 1919), which provided for the enforcement of the 18th Amendment, prohibiting the manufacture, sale, and transportation of intoxicating liquors.

Volta, Count Alessandro (1745–1827), Italian physicist. He discovered constant/current electricity and invented the voltaic pile, the first primary (wet cell) battery. The volt was named for him.

Voltaire (1694–1778), pseudonym of François Marie Arouet, French writer and philosopher, a leading figure of the Enlightenment and author of one of the most widely read satires of all time, *Candide* (1759). Voltaire's voluminous works, which cover a huge variety of subjects, are written with wit and irony in a general protest against intolerance and complacency. His satirical writing and speech resulted in his arbitrary imprisonment in the Bastille in 1717 and in 1726. He lived in England from 1726 to 1729 and visited the court of Frederick the Great of Prussia from 1750 to 1753. His major works, include *Philosophical Letters* (1734), showing the wisdom of religious tolerance; the historical works *The History of Charles XII* (1731) and *The Age of Louis XIV* (1751); *Essay on Manners* (1756); the philosophical poems, *Poem on Natural Law* (1756) and *Poem on the Lisbon Disaster* (1756); the *Treatise on Tolerance* (1763); and the *Philosophical Dictionary* (1764).

Von Braun, Wernher (1912–1977), U.S. rocket engineer, born in Germany. He was technical director of German rocket research; as such he developed the V-2 long-range rocket. Von Braun came to the United States in 1945 where he worked for the government in developing guided missiles, ballistic missiles, and rockets for the manned lunar program. He became a U.S. citizen in 1955.

Vonnegut, Kurt, Jr. (1922–), U.S. novelist. Among his best-known works, memorable for their dark humor and fantastic plots, are *Slaughterhouse Five* (1969) and *Breakfast of Champions* (1973). Recent novels include *Jailbird* (1979) and *Deadeye Dick* (1982).

W

Wagner, (Wilhelm) Richard (1813–1883), German operatic composer. Wagner wrote many of his own librettos based on German folklore and mythology and developed the leitmotif, a melody used to express a recurring theme or personality. Among Wagner's best-known operas are *Tannhäuser* (1845), *Lohengrin* (1848), *Tristan und Isolde* (1865), *Die Meistersinger* (1868), and the four-work *Ring* cycle, *Das Rheingold* (1869), *Die Walküre* (1870), *Siegfried* (1876), and *Götterdämmerung* (1876). The *Ring* was first performed in August, 1876, at the Bayreuth Festspielhaus, a theater Wagner had built specially for his works.

Waite, Morrison Remick (1816–1888), chief justice of the United States, 1874–1888. In 1871 he represented the United States at the Geneva arbitration of the *Alabama* claims. In 1874 he was named chief justice by President Ulysses S. Grant. As chief justice, Waite clarified Reconstruction legislation and the constitutional amendments resulting from the Civil War. He also upheld the right of government to regulate business and industry in the public interest, enabling states to regulate railroads.

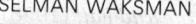

Waksman, Selman Abraham (1888–1973), Russian-born U.S. microbiologist. He was awarded the 1952 Nobel Prize for Physiology and Medicine for his discovery of streptomycin, an antibiotic effective against tuberculosis and various bacteria. He also isolated, identified, and synthesized other antibiotics, including actinomycin and candicidin.

Wald, Lillian D. (1867–1940), U.S. social worker. She founded the Henry Street Settlement in New York City in 1893. In 1902 she organized the first city school nursing service and, at her settlement house, began public health nursing. She was also instrumental in the establishment of the U.S. Children's Bureau, 1912, and the town and country nursing service of the Red Cross. She wrote *Windows on Henry Street* (1934) and was elected to the Hall of Fame in 1970.

Waldheim, Kurt (1918–) secretary-general of the United Nations, 1972–1981, president of Austria, 1986–. He served as Austria's permanent representative to the United Nations from 1965 to 1968, when he returned to Austria as foreign minister, 1968–1970. In 1971 he was appointed to his former position at the United Nations; in December of that year he was elected secretary-general to succeed the retiring U Thant. He won election to the Austrian presidency after a bitter dispute over the details of his service in the German army during World War II.

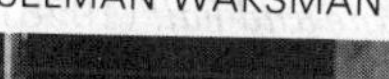

SELMAN WAKSMAN

UPI/BETTMANN NEWSPHOTOS

Wallace, Henry Agard (1888–1965), Vice President of the United States, 1941–1945. Wallace was secretary of agriculture, 1933–1940, before becoming Vice President under Franklin Roosevelt. In 1944, because of disagreements with the President, Wallace was not asked to run again. Appointed secretary of commerce in 1945, he became critical of administration policies toward the Soviet Union and was asked to resign. He was editor of the *New Republic*, 1946–1948, and was the unsuccessful Progressive Party candidate for the Presidency in 1948.

Walpole, Horace (Horatio), 4th Earl of Orford (1717–1797), English writer famous for his journals and letters. At his country estate, Strawberry Hill in Twickenham, he collected works of art and curios. His memoirs were published under the titles *The Memoirs of the Last Ten Years of the Reign of George II* (1822) and *Memoirs of the Reign of King George III* (1845). Among his other works are *Anecdotes of Painting in England* (1762–1771) and *The Castle of Otranto* (1764), one of the first Gothic romances. His fame as a writer rests, however, on his witty and gossipy correspondence. He was the fourth son of Robert Walpole.

Walpole, Sir Robert, 1st Earl of Orford (1676–1745), English statesman generally called England's first prime minister. Walpole began his 40-year career in Parliament in 1701 and soon became a Whig leader. He held several cabinet posts and brought the government through the South Sea Bubble/financial crisis in 1721. He was a master at political manipulation and became virtual ruler of England and Scotland after 1721. Walpole ruled in the name of George I and George II. He favored the commercial expansion of England and established the principle that the prime minister and the cabinet are responsible to Parliament for their actions and policies. After his death, his collection of paintings by old masters was sold to Catherine the Great of Russia; it became the basis for the collection in the Hermitage, Leningrad.

Walton, Ernest Thomas Sinton (1903–), Irish physicist. He shared the 1951 Nobel Prize for Physics with his colleague Sir **John D. Cockcroft** (1897–1967) for being the first to split atoms artificially. In 1932 they disintegrated a lithium atom into two helium atoms by bombardment with protons; they did this with the high-energy particle accelerator they built.

Walton, Izaak (1593–1683), English writer whose most famous work is *The*

Compleat Angler (1653), a book on fishing that presents the sport from a genial and philosophical point of view. Walton was also a skilled biographer, writing on John Donne, Richard Hooker, and George Herbert.

Walton, Sir William Turner (1902–), English composer. His *Façade* (1923), a setting of Edith Sitwell's poetry for chamber orchestra, won him instant recognition. Other frequently performed works are the oratorio *Belshazzar's Feast* (1931), *Symphony* (1934), a violin concerto (1939), and the opera *Troilus and Cressida* (1954). Walton composed music for the films *Henry V, Hamlet,* and *Major Barbara.*

Warhol, Andy (1931–1987), U.S. pop artist and experimental filmmaker noted for his creations based on mass-produced popular objects, such as soup cans, automobiles, and photographs of film stars. Warhol sought to illustrate the mechanization of life and art, carrying through this concept with his silk screen techniques, which could mass produce a picture; he named his studio The Factory. His movies exploited realism to the point of boredom: *Sleep* is a six-hour film of a man sleeping; *Chelsea Girls,* his most famous, is voyeuristic.

Warren, Earl (1891–1974), chief justice of the United States, 1953–1969. Under his leadership, the Supreme Court handed down some of the most far-reaching and socially minded decisions in its history. Warren became attorney general of California in 1939. He was elected governor of California as a Republican in 1942, 1944, and 1946. In 1948 he was the Republican Vice Presidential candidate. Appointed to the Court in 1953 by President Eisenhower, the following year Warren wrote the unanimous Supreme Court decision against racial segregation in public schools. In 1966 he delivered a controversial decision upholding the rights of suspects apprehended by the police *(Miranda* v. *Arizona).*

Warren, Robert Penn (1905–1989), U.S. poet, novelist, and critic best known for his Pulitzer Prize-winning novel *All the King's Men* (1946). A forceful, highly imaginative writer, Warren also wrote the novels *World Enough and Time* (1950), *Meet Me in the Green Glen* (1971), and *Selected Poems 1923–1943* (1944). Other volumes of poetry include *Promises* (1957) and *Now and Then* (1979), both Pulitzer Prize winners. His nonfiction includes the basic text *Understanding Poetry* (1938) and *Segregation: The Inner Conflict in the South* (1956). Warren helped found the *Southern Review* and edited it from 1935 to 1942.

Washington, Booker Taliaferro (1856–1915), U.S. educator and black leader. He was educated at the Hampton Institute, supporting himself by working as a janitor. In 1879 he became a teacher at Hampton and in 1881 was chosen to organize and direct Tuskegee Institute for the vocational and professional training of blacks. Washington urged blacks in the South to accept social segregation and to concentrate on acquiring more education and better jobs. He was opposed by other black leaders of his time who advocated political action for immediate civil rights. His autobiography, *Up from Slavery,* was published in 1901.

Washington, George (1732–1799), Revolutionary War general and first President of the United States, 1789–1797. Born in Westmoreland County, Va., the son of a Virginia planter, he received his education at home, worked briefly as a surveyor, and became a militia officer. He served in the French and Indian War and in 1755 rallied and led the retreat of the expedition under General Edward Braddock, which had been defeated near Fort Duquesne. He inherited the family estate, Mount Vernon, on the death of his half brother in 1752; he always liked farming best of all his roles, and Mount Vernon was his proudest possession. In 1759 he married Martha Custis, a wealthy widow. Washington was a member of the Virginia House of Burgesses, 1759–1774, and a member of the first and second Continental Congresses. Shortly after the outbreak of the American Revolution in 1775, he was appointed commander in chief of the American forces. He guided the American troops until the British troops surrendered at Yorktown in 1783. He then retired from the army. In 1787 Washington presided at the Constitutional Convention, held in Philadelphia. He was chosen as the first President of the newly formed United States and was inaugurated in New York on April 30, 1789. He was reluctantly persuaded to serve a second term. In 1796 he declined reelection and returned in the following year to Mount Vernon. Washington was a man of great dignity and gravity, with a supreme sense of duty and a firm faith.

Wassermann, August von (1866–1925), German bacteriologist who devised a blood-serum test for diagnosis of syphilis, the Wassermann test. Wassermann did research at the Robert Koch Institute for Infectious Diseases in Berlin and later at the Kaiser Wilhelm Institute in Berlin-Dahlem. He also studied diphtheria, typhoid, cholera, and tetanus.

Watson, James Dewey (1928–), U.S. biologist. He shared the 1962 Nobel Prize for Physiology and Medicine with Francis H.C. Crick and Maurice H.F. Wilkins for their work in determining the structure of the deoxyribonucleic acid (DNA) molecule. This work provided a basis for understanding how genetic material directs the growth of enzymes within cells, as well as the metabolism, and the differentiation of cells. Watson published *The Double Helix: Being a Personal Account of the Discovery of the Structure of DNA* in 1968.

Watt, James (1736–1819), Scottish engineer and inventor. While mathematical instrumentmaker to Glasgow University, he improved the steam engine of Thomas Newcomen by creating a separate condenser (1765). He continually improved steam engine designs and invented a double-acting engine. He also invented copying ink and discovered the chemical composition of water. Watt was the first to use the term horsepower. The watt, a unit of electrical power, is named for him.

Watteau, Jean Antoine (1684–1721), French painter widely regarded as the master of the rococo style. His pastoral scenes, filled with elegantly costumed figures, convey a mood of melancholy. Figures from Italian comedy appear frequently in his work, which is also characterized by fine drawing and delicate colors.

Watterson, Henry (1840–1921), called Marse Henry, U.S. journalist. He served in the Confederate army and later settled at Louisville, Ky., where he founded the *Courier-Journal* and became known as one of the foremost U.S. editors. He campaigned for civil rights for blacks and reconciliation between the North and South. He served in the U.S. Congress from 1876 to 1877.

Waugh, Evelyn Arthur St. John (1903–1966), English writer of bitter satires on contemporary society. His many novels include *Decline and Fall* (1928), *Vile Bodies* (1930), *Black Mischief* (1932), and *The Loved One* (1948), later made into a film. During World War II Waugh served in the British

JAMES D. WATSON

HARVARD UNIVERSITY

Royal Marines. His trilogy *Men at Arms* (1952), *Officers and Gentlemen* (1955), and *Unconditional Surrender* (1961) considers war as the struggle between civilization and barbarism.

Weaver, Robert Clifton (1907–), U.S. economist, government official, and educator, the first black to serve in a Presidential Cabinet. An authority on education, black labor, housing, and urban renewal, Weaver held a variety of government and teaching posts after 1934, when he became adviser on black affairs to the Department of the Interior. In 1961 Weaver was appointed administrator of the Housing and Home Finance Agency. The agency was superseded in 1965 by the Department of Housing and Urban Development (HUD), and Weaver was named secretary of the new department by President Lyndon Johnson. In November, 1968, Weaver resigned to become the president, 1969–1970, of Baruch College in New York City. He was professor of urban affairs at Hunter College from 1970 to 1978.

Webb, Sidney James, 1st Baron Passfield (1859–1947), British social and economic reformer who provided, with **Beatrice Potter Webb** (1858–1943), much of the basis for the Labour Party's socialist reforms. Among the founders of the socialist Fabian Society, the Webbs were married in 1892 and collaborated for over 40 years. They helped found the London School of Economics and Political Science in 1895, and the magazine *New Statesman* in 1913. They also wrote *The History of Trade Unionism* (1894) and *Soviet Communism: A New Civilization?"* (1935). In 1909 the Webbs issued a famous report challenging the basis of the poor-law system, an early social welfare program.

Weber, Carl Maria (Friedrich Ernst) von (1786–1826), German composer considered the founder of the German Romantic opera. His works, free of French or Italian influences, were rooted in German legend and tradition and written in German. Well known are his *Der Freischütz* (1820) and *Oberon* (1826).

Weber, Max (1864–1920), German sociologist and political economist whose best-known work is *The Protestant Ethic and the Spirit of Capitalism* (1904–1905). In this study Weber shows how certain Calvinist doctrines helped lead to the development of modern capitalism. He also wrote *The Theory of Social and Economic Organization* (1947) and *Basic Concepts of Sociology* (1962).

Webster, Daniel (1782–1852), U.S. statesman and orator, one of the leading members of the U.S. Senate before the Civil War. From New Hampshire, he served from 1813 to 1817 in the U.S. House of Representatives. He then established a law practice in Boston. In 1818–1819 he defended Dartmouth College against the attempts of state officials to dictate its policies. The Supreme Court, in a crucial decision, ruled in favor of Dartmouth, making Webster the leading lawyer of his day. During the 1820's Webster became famous for his oratory. In 1822 he was again elected to the U.S. House of Representatives from Massachusetts, and in 1827 he became U.S. senator. He attacked states' rights and defended the powers of the federal government. In 1836 Webster was an unsuccessful Whig candidate for the U.S. Presidency. He served as secretary of state under Presidents Harrison and Tyler from 1841 to 1843. He returned to the Senate from 1845 to 1850, where he opposed the Mexican War and the annexation of Texas and California for fear that the question of extending slavery to the territories would divide the Union. In 1850 he defended the compromise measures suggested by Senator Henry Clay of Kentucky to avert a civil war. Later in 1850 he was appointed secretary of state by President Millard Fillmore; he served until his death.

THE BETTMANN ARCHIVE

DANIEL WEBSTER

Webster, Noah (1758–1843), U.S. lexicographer. Dissatisfied with children's texts, which were based on British usage and grammar, he published in 1783 his *Grammatical Institute of the English Language* (Part 1, also called the *Blue-Backed Speller*). Millions of copies were sold before his death; the book was a standard school text for a century. A grammar (Part 2) was published in 1784, and a reader (Part 3) in 1785. Webster's *Compendious Dictionary of the English Language* appeared in 1806, and his major work, *The American Dictionary of the English Language,* in 1828. These volumes, along with the grammar series, were highly influential in standardizing American spelling and usage.

Wedgwood, Josiah (1730–1795), English potter and inventor of distinctive earthenware bearing raised designs. Wedgwood was especially noted for his tinted vases bearing white figures in relief and for his "jasperware." Wedgwood's perfected cream earthenware was called Queen's ware because of its patronage by Queen Charlotte.

Weill, Kurt (1900–1950), German theater composer of satirical operas and dramatic musical plays, the most famous being *Die Dreigroschenoper* (*The Threepenny Opera,* 1928), with libretto by Bertolt Brecht. Weill left Germany when the Nazi regime came to power; he settled in New York in 1935. There he composed the music for *Knickerbocker Holiday* (1938), *Lady in the Dark* (1941), and *One Touch of Venus* (1943). He also composed the music for *Street Scene* (1947) and *Lost in the Stars* (1949).

Weizmann, Chaim (1874–1952), Russian-born chemist, first president of Israel (1949–1952). He became a British subject in 1910 and served as chief of the British admiralty laboratories in London, where he discovered a process for synthesizing acetone. Weizmann became a leader in the Zionist movement, urging the acceptance of Britain's Balfour Declaration of 1917, which proclaimed Palestine a Jewish homeland. He was president of the World Zionist Organization, 1920–1946; and of the Jewish Agency for Palestine, 1929–1931, 1935–1946. He played an important role in the establishment of the state of Israel and headed its provisional government in 1948. In 1949 he was elected the first president of Israel.

Welles, (George) Orson (1915–1985), U.S. actor, director, writer, and producer whose controversial talents found their way into productions for stage, screen, and radio. In 1937 he founded the Mercury Theatre and presented a modern-dress version of Shakespeare's *Julius Caesar.* In 1938 his radio broadcast of H.G. Wells's *War of the Worlds* was so realistic that thousands of listeners panicked, fearing a Martian invasion. Among his film successes are *Citizen Kane* (1941), which introduced his revolutionary use of the camera, *The Magnificent Ambersons* (1942), *The Third Man* (1949), *The Trial* (1962), and *Falstaff* (1965).

Wellington, 1st Duke of; Arthur Wellesley (1769–1852), British soldier and statesman born in Ireland. He entered the army in 1787 and served in India, winning several campaigns. In 1808 Wellington was placed in command of the British army fighting against Napoleon in the Peninsular War in Portugal and Spain. He won the war in a series of brilliant campaigns, driving the French across the Pyrenees and pursuing them as far as Toulouse in 1814. Shortly afterward, Napoleon was exiled and peace was declared. Wellington became ambassador to France and representative to the Congress of Vienna. In 1815, during the Hundred Days of Napoleon's return, Wellington commanded the allied armies and brought about the emperor's final defeat at Waterloo, one of the great military victories of modern times. Wellington was commander in chief of the army of occupation in France, 1815–1818. After his return to Britain, he became a cabinet member in 1819 and prime minister in 1828. He was opposed to parliamentary reform and, when his policy on this issue was defeated, resigned in 1830. He later served under Sir Robert Peel as foreign secretary and commander in chief of the army.

Wells, Herbert George (1866–1946), English writer whose best-known works combine romantic fantasy with social philosophy. They include *The Time Machine* (1895), *The Island of Dr. Moreau* (1896), *The Invisible Man* (1897), *The War of the Worlds* (1898), and *The Sleeper Awakes* (1899). Among his other fiction works are the realistic comedies *Kipps* (1905) and *Tono-Bungay* (1909). His nonfiction best seller, *The Outline of History,* appeared in 1920.

Wesley, family name of two English brothers who founded Methodism.

Charles Wesley (1707–1788), while a student at Oxford, founded a religious club whose members were known derisively as methodists for their strict religious method—self-imposed rules for moral conduct. He was ordained in the Church of England in 1735. Charles was noted especially for his preaching and for his hymns. Of these he wrote nearly 9000, including "Jesus, Lover of My Soul," and "O for a Thousand Tongues."

John Wesley (1703–1791) was ordained in the Church of England in 1728 and became the leader of his brother's religious group at Oxford. In 1735 he went as an Anglican missionary to the new colony of Georgia, returning to England in 1738. At a religious meeting in London he experienced a religious conversion. In the next 50 years Wesley became the leader of a major religious revival in England. The emotional warmth of his preaching appealed especially to the poor, and he attracted many followers. When established churches would no longer allow his preaching, he began preaching in the open and attracted thousands at a time. He did not intend to form a separate denomination, but his organization of Methodist societies provided a nucleus for the new church. It became completely independent of the Church of England after his death.

West, Dame Rebecca (1892–1983), pseudonym of Cicly Isabel Fairfield, Irish-born English writer especially well known for works in which she raised journalism to a literary art. Her articles on the Nuremberg trials, collected in *The Meaning of Treason* (1947; revised as *The New Meaning of Treason,* 1964), were acclaimed for their insight and careful documentation. West's other works include the novels *The Thinking Reed* (1936) and *The Birds Fall Down* (1966), and a study of Yugoslavia, *Black Lamb and Grey Falcon* (1941).

Westinghouse, George (1846–1914), U.S. inventor and manufacturer who invented the air brake for trains and improved railway signaling devices. He also introduced the alternating current system to the United States. In the 1880's he organized the Westinghouse Electric Company.

Weyden, Rogier van der (c 1400–1464), Flemish painter, one of the leading painters of the early Netherlandish school. Included in his authenticated works are *Descent from the Cross, St. Luke Painting the Virgin, Crucifixion, Francesco d'Este,* and *Last Judgment.*

Wharton, Edith Newbold Jones (1862–1937), U.S. novelist and short story writer whose stories are set in a background of wealthy New York society of the early 1900's. Among her best-known novels are *The House of Mirth* (1905), *The Age of Innocence* (1920), for which she won a Pulitzer Prize, and *Hudson River Bracketed* (1929). Her shorter works include a novelette, *Ethan Frome* (1911), and the four tales that make up *Old New York* (1924). Her splendid autobiography, *A Backward Glance,* appeared in 1934.

THE BETTMANN ARCHIVE

REBECCA WEST

Wheatley, Phillis (c 1753–1784), U.S. poet. Born in Africa, she was brought to Boston as a slave when a child. At the age of 13 she began to write poetry. At 20 she was taken to England where she achieved great popularity. Her first book of verse, *Poems on Various Subjects, Religious and Moral* (1773), was dedicated to the countess of Huntington. In 1778 she was freed and married a free black, John Peters.

Whistler, James Abbott McNeill (1834–1903), U.S. artist whose most famous work is *Arrangement in Grey and Black,* popularly known as "Whistler's Mother." His paintings characteristically use soft, shaded colors without sharp light or shadow, as in *Thomas Carlyle* (another *Arrangement in Grey and Black*), *The White Girl,* and *Rosa Corder.* Whistler's etchings are considered masterpieces and include the *Thames Series* and the *Venice Series.* A self-assured, clever man known for his biting wit, Whistler wrote *The Gentle Art of Making Enemies* (1890).

White, Stanford (1853–1906), U.S. architect whose work represents the neo-Renaissance style. White designed several New York City landmarks—the Century Club, the *Herald* building, Madison Square Presbyterian Church, Washington Square Arch, and the old Madison Square Garden.

White, William Allen (1868–1944), U.S. journalist, a famous small-town newspaper editor. Born in Emporia, Kan., he worked on several Kansas newspapers, then bought the Emporia *Gazette* in 1895. In 1896 he wrote an editorial called "What's the Matter with Kansas?" for which he received nationwide attention. His books, which are warm and humorous, include *A Certain Rich Man* (1909), *In the Heart of a Fool* (1918), and *The Editor and His People* (1924). His autobiography was published in 1946. He won the 1923 Pulitzer Prize for editorial writing.

Whitehead, Alfred North (1861–1947), English mathematician and philosopher. His works include *Principia Mathematica,* with Bertrand Russell (3 volumes, 1910–1913); *An Enquiry Concerning the Principles of Natural Knowledge* (1919), a study of mathematical physics; and a trilogy, *Science and the Modern World* (1925), *Process and Reality* (1929), and *Adventures of Ideas* (1933), which brought him acclaim as a metaphysician.

Whitman, Walt (1819–1892), U.S. poet, the "good grey poet" whose *Leaves of Grass* is world famous. In 1855 Whitman published his free verse masterpiece *Leaves of Grass,* which he later revised and expanded several times. Dominant themes in these poems are freedom, the significance of the individual, and democratic society. Whitman's frequent references to himself and his frankness about sexual matters offended many people in his time. Among his best-known individual poems are "Song of Myself," "I Sing the Body Electric," "Song of the Open Road," "When Lilacs Last in the Dooryard Bloom'd," and "Out of the Cradle Endlessly Rocking."

Whitney, Eli (1765–1825), U.S. inventor of the cotton gin. His invention (1793) accelerated the slow process of separating cotton fibers from seeds. He was constantly involved in legal battles with those who copied the plans of his patented machine; the validity of his patent was not established until 1807. He later began manufacturing firearms. In his factory he introduced the concept of interchangeable parts, a step toward the modern industrial assembly line.

Whittier, John Greenleaf (1807–1892), U.S. poet and abolitionist. As editor and contributor to several newspapers, Whittier attacked slavery. His 1833 pamphlet *Justice and Expediency* was a forceful abolitionist tract. His narrative poems, describing many aspects of American life and frequently reflecting his Quaker background, include "Barbara Frietchie," "Maud Muller," "The Barefoot Boy," and "Snow-Bound." Among his books are *Legends of New England in Prose and Verse* (1831) and *Lays of My Home and Other Poems* (1843).

Wiener, Norbert (1894–1964), U.S. mathematician who developed the science of cybernetics, the study of control mechanisms and communications in animals and machines. Wiener's theories laid the background for automation. During World War II, he made a study of the handling of information by electronic devices. The results of Wiener's work are recorded in *Cybernetics* (1948). He also published *The Human Use of Human Beings* (1950) and *Cybernetics of the Nervous System* (1965).

NAACP

ROY WILKINS

Wilde, Oscar Fingal O'Flahertie Wills (1854–1900), Irish playwright, novelist, and poet remembered for the witty comedy *The Importance of Being Earnest* (1895). While a student at Trinity College, Dublin, he became known as an aesthete and wit, a reputation he carried throughout his life. Wilde's other works include a collection of fairy tales, *The Happy Prince and Other Tales* (1888); a novel, *The Picture of Dorian Gray* (1891); and the plays *Lady Windermere's Fan* and *Salome* (both 1893). His stirring poem *The Ballad of Reading Gaol* (1898) reflects his two-year imprisonment for immorality; his harsh treatment as a convict led to an early death. *De Profundis* (1905), written in prison, is a defense of Wilde's aesthetic and social beliefs.

Wilder, Thornton Niven (1897–1975), U.S. playwright and novelist. Wilder's first successful novel was *The Bridge of San Luis Rey,* for which he received a Pulitzer Prize in 1927. This was followed by several other novels, including *The Ides of March* (1948) and *The Eighth Day* (1967). His plays include *Our Town* (1938) and *The Skin of our Teeth* (1942), both of which won Pulitzer prizes, and *The Matchmaker* (1956), which was made into the popular musical *Hello, Dolly.*

Wilkins, Maurice Hugh Frederick (1916–), Irish biophysicist. He shared the 1962 Nobel Prize for Physiology and Medicine with Francis H. C. Crick and James D. Watson for their work in determining the molecular structure of the deoxyribonucleic acid (DNA). Wilkins's contribution lay in his x-ray studies of DNA, which showed a structure closely resembling the molecular model drawn up by Watson and Crick. Wilkins later turned his attention to the x-ray study of the structure of RNA (ribonucleic acid).

Wilkins, Roy (1901–1981), U.S. black civil rights leader. In 1931 he joined the staff of the National Association for the Advancement of Colored People (NAACP), becoming executive secretary in 1955 and serving as executive director from 1965 to 1977. In 1954 he was influential in bringing before the U.S. Supreme Court the case that resulted in the outlawing of racial segregation in the public schools. As chairman of the Leadership Conference on Civil Rights—a coordinating body for more than 100 national civil-rights, labor, and civic organizations—he helped bring about the passage of much civil rights legislation.

Willard, Emma Hart (1787–1870), U.S. educator who pioneered in higher education for women. In 1814 she opened the Middlebury (Vt.) Female Seminary in her home. In 1821 the school moved to Troy, N.Y., and Willard petitioned for and received state funds previously allotted only to men's schools. She was among the first to introduce the study of philosophy, mathematics, and foreign languages into women's education. She published several texts on geography, history, and astronomy, authored a theory of blood circulation, and wrote poetry, including "Rocked in the Cradle of the Deep."

William I (William the Conqueror) (1027–1087), the first Norman king of England, 1066–1087. On the death of his cousin Edward the Confessor, king of England, in 1066, William invaded England to claim the throne, although Harold, earl of Wessex, had already been elected king. William defeated Harold at the Battle of Hastings and was crowned king of England on Christmas Day. William replaced nearly all important officials in church

WILLIAM THE CONQUEROR

THE BETTMANN ARCHIVE

and state with his Norman followers. However, he retained Anglo-Saxon institutions and maintained a relatively well-ordered kingdom. He also carried out a complete survey of the English realm in 1086, recorded in the *Domesday Book.*

William II (1859–1941), full German name Friedrich Wilhelm Viktor Albert, king of Prussia and emperor (Kaiser) of Germany, 1888–1918. William in many ways set the stage for World War I. He alienated both Britain and Russia, preparing the way for an alliance of those nations against him; he pursued an expansionist policy in the Middle East; and he encouraged German reliance on militarism. When in 1914 the archduke of Austria was assassinated in Serbia, William supported the Austrian demands that precipitated the war. During the war, William's prestige and power declined. After Germany's defeat in 1918, he abdicated and fled to the Netherlands, where he lived in retirement. When he died in 1941, Hitler gave him a military funeral.

Williams, Roger (c 1603–1683), English-born American religious leader and founder of the Rhode Island colony. He came to the Massachusetts colony in 1631 and was a pastor in Salem. His tolerant religious views brought him into conflict with the civil authorities, and he was banished in 1635. With some followers, he founded Providence, the first American settlement based on religious toleration and the principle of the separation of church and state. In 1639 he founded the first Baptist church there. In 1643 he journeyed to England and secured from the king a charter for Rhode Island, then called the Providence Plantations in the Narragansett Bay. He served as governor several times, advocating democratic government.

Williams, Ted (Theodore Samuel) (1918–), U.S. baseball player known as the Splendid Splinter, considered one of the greatest natural hitters in baseball history. In his 21 years with the Boston Red Sox, interrupted by service in World War II and Korea, the left-handed outfielder led the American League four times in home runs and six times in batting. Williams's career batting average was .344; he hit 521 home runs. From 1969 to 1971 he managed the Washington Senators.

Williams, Tennessee (1914–1983), born Thomas Lanier Williams, U.S. playwright whose naturalistic works sympathetically and often shockingly portray the decay of life and culture in the South. Williams's first of a long series of Broadway successes was *The Glass Menagerie* (1944), followed by *A Streetcar Named Desire* (1947), *Cat on a Hot Tin Roof* (1955), *Suddenly Last Summer* (1958), and *Night of the Iguana* (1961). All were eventually made into films. Both *Streetcar* and *Cat on a Hot Tin Roof* won Pulitzer prizes.

Williams, William Carlos (1883–1963), U.S. writer whose poetry is characterized by the use of free verse, broken rhythms, and colloquial speech. He published numerous volumes of poems, but his major work is *Paterson* (1946–1958), a five-volume philosophical poem. His other works include *Sour Grapes* (1921); *Spring and All* (1922); a prose work, *In the American Grain* (1925); short stories; and an autobiography (1961).

Wilson, Charles Thomson Rees (1869–1959), British physicist, inventor of the Wilson cloud chamber, a device of great value in research on subatomic particles and cosmic rays. For developing the cloud chamber and the vapor-condensation method that made it useful in tracking the paths of particles, he shared the 1927 Nobel Prize for Physics.

Wilson, Edmund (1895–1972), U.S. writer and literary critic. He worked as a reporter for the New York *Evening Sun,* 1916–1917, and later became associate editor of the *New Republic,* 1926–1931. In 1944 Wilson began writing for *The New Yorker* magazine. His books of literary criticism include *Axel's Castle* (1931), *Triple Thinkers* (1938), and *The Wound and the Bow* (1941). His other works include *To the Finland Station* (1940), *Memoirs of Hecate County* (1946), *The Scrolls from the Dead Sea* (1955), and *Apologies to the Iroquois* (1960).

Wilson, Sir (James) Harold (1916–), British prime minister from 1964 to 1970 and from 1974 to 1976. Wilson entered Parliament in 1945. He became prime minister after the 1964 Labour victory. Under his leadership, a growing economic crisis was ended; the economy seemed to be recovering when Labour suffered an unexpected defeat in 1970. Four years later Labour was returned to power and Wilson again became prime minister. He resigned in 1976 and the party elected James Callaghan to succeed him.

Wilson, (Thomas) Woodrow (1856–1924), 28th President of the United States, 1913–1921. Wilson taught history at Bryn Mawr, Wesleyan, and Princeton. He was president of Princeton from 1902 to 1910, when he ran for governor of New Jersey. Elected on the Democratic ticket, he surprised both supporters and opponents by his liberal reforms. Nominated as the Democratic candidate for President in 1912, he defeated President Taft and Theodore Roosevelt, who split the Republican vote. In 1916 he was reelected on the slogan, "He kept us out of war," but in 1917 he led the United States into World War I, saying "the world must be made safe for democracy." In 1918 Wilson proposed a program, known as the Fourteen Points, on which a peace treaty at the end of World War I could be based. Wilson himself represented the United States at the peace conference in Paris, where he insisted on the establishment of a League of Nations as a basic provision of the treaty. Although the league was established, the U.S. Senate refused to ratify United States membership in it. Wilson toured the country speaking in favor of the League of Nations, but with little success. Already broken in health, he suffered a paralyzing stroke in October, 1919. For the rest of his term, he was an invalid protected by his wife, who, unknown to the country, took over his affairs and even helped him write his official signature.

JOHN WINTHROP

Windsor, Duke of (1894–1972), king of Great Britain and Ireland as Edward VIII from January 20 to December 11, 1936, eldest son of King George V. On the death of his father, on January 20, 1936, Edward became king. On December 11, still uncrowned, he abdicated to marry Wallis Warfield Simpson, an American who had been twice divorced and could not be the king's consort. Edward left England and was created duke of Windsor.

Winthrop, John (1588–1649), American colonial leader, the first governor of Massachusetts Bay Colony. He was chosen governor of the Massachusetts Bay Company in 1629 and sailed from England to America in 1630. Winthrop was elected governor twelve times in a period of 19 years, beginning in 1630. An autocratic ruler, he established the tradition of government by clergy. He left a voluminous journal, one of the most valuable sources of New England colonial history.

Wise, Stephen Samuel (1874–1949), U.S. rabbi, a foremost Zionist leader. In 1907 he founded the New York Free Synagogue and served as its rabbi until his death. He was one of the founders, in 1898, and later president, of the Zionist Organization of America. He was also a founder and president of the American Jewish Congress and of the World Jewish Congress.

Witte, Count Sergei Yulievich (1849–1915), Russian statesman. As minister of finance, 1892–1903, he instituted a program for improving and modernizing the Russian economy. In 1905 he negotiated the Treaty of Portsmouth, ending the Russo-Japanese War. When the czar granted representative government in hopes of quieting the 1905 revolution, Witte became prime minister. His moderate policies failed and he resigned.

Wodehouse, Sir Pelham Grenville (1881–1975), English humorist who created the comic figures Psmith, Jeeves, and Bertie Wooster. His best-known works are irreverent farces on British upper-class society. Among his many publications are *Leave It to Psmith* (1923), *The Inimitable Jeeves* (1924), *Blanding's Castle* (1935), *Mating Season* (1949), and *Author, Author* (1962). He became a U.S. citizen in 1955.

Wolfe, James (1727–1759), English general who defeated the French at Quebec. He served in Scotland during the Jacobite rebellion of 1745 and was sent to Canada during the French and Indian War. Wolfe distinguished himself at the siege of Louisburg in 1758 and led the British to victory over the French, led by Montcalm, on the Plains of Abraham near Quebec, September, 1759. Both generals were killed in the battle.

Wolfe, Thomas Clayton (1900–1938), U.S. novelist whose best-known work is the long and complex autobiographical novel *Look Homeward, Angel* (1929). His other works include *Of Time and the River* (1935) and the short stories collected in *From Death to Morning* (1935). *The Web and the Rock* (1939) and *You Can't Go Home Again* (1940) were published after his death.

Wollstonecraft, Mary (1759–1797), English author of *A Vindication of the Rights of Women* (1792), one of the earliest feminist writings, which argued compellingly for the emancipation of women through education. She married the writer and radical philosopher William Godwin (1756–1836), but died in childbirth shortly afterward. Their daughter, **Mary Wollstonecraft Godwin** (1797–1851), author of *Frankenstein,* married the poet Shelley.

Wolsey, Thomas (c 1473–1530), English cardinal and statesman whose flagrant misuse of the power of his office helped secure the success of the Reformation. Under Henry VIII he became lord chancellor, 1515; he was made a cardinal by Pope Leo X the same year. As Henry's chief minister, Wolsey strengthened both the royal power and his own influence. He demanded the privileges of the clergy while exerting great influence in state affairs. Though he claimed to need his great church powers for reform, he lived in lavish, worldly luxury. He angered the nobility by enforcing criminal laws against them and alienated the rest of the people by his heavy taxation to finance war with France. His downfall came after his failure to get papal sanction for a divorce for Henry from Catherine of Aragon. He was arrested in 1530 but died before coming to trial. Henry secured his divorce, took England out of the Roman Church, and began the Reformation.

Wood, Grant (1892–1942), U.S. painter. His paintings are characterized by clear, sharp, careful detail. They portray, often with a suggestion of irony, rural American life. Some of the best known are *John B. Turner, Pioneer* (1929), *American Gothic* (1930), and *Daughters of the American Revolution* (1932).

Woolf, Virginia (1882–1941), English novelist, essayist, and critic. In her novels she used the stream-of-consciousness technique to reveal character. Her works include *The Voyage Out* (1915), *Jacob's Room* (1922), *Mrs. Dalloway* (1925), *To the Lighthouse* (1927), *Orlando* (1928), and *Between the Acts* (1941). Her criticism appears in two series of *The Common Reader* (1925, 1932). Her classic essay on feminism, *A Room of One's Own,* appeared in 1929.

VIRGINIA WOOLF

BRITISH INFORMATION SERVICES LONDON/NATIONAL PORTRAIT GALLERY

Woolworth, Frank Winfield (1852–1919), U.S. merchant who developed the dime store. He began his business career with a five-cent store in Utica, N.Y., but it failed. In 1879 he moved to Lancaster, Pa., and opened a five-and-ten-cent store, which became very successful. Woolworth went on to open a chain of new stores, which at his death numbered more than 1000.

Wordsworth, William (1770–1850), English Romantic poet. In 1797 Wordsworth became a close friend of Samuel Taylor Coleridge, with whom he published *Lyrical Ballads* (1798). It includes "Lines Composed Above Tintern Abbey" and marks the beginning of the Romantic movement in England. "Tintern Abbey" was not well received; like all Wordsworth's best works, it uses language of such clarity and simplicity that it was criticized as being unpoetic. At about the same time he wrote the "Lucy" poems, including "She dwelt among the untrodden ways." In 1805 Wordsworth wrote "Ode: Intimations of Immortality." In 1813, with his wife Mary and sister Dorothy, he moved to Rydal Mount, where he lived for the rest of his life. There he finished his lengthy autobiographical poem, *The Prelude* (1850). In 1843 he was named England's poet laureate.

Wovoka (1856–1932), known also as Jack Wilson, American Indian of the Paiute tribe. He founded a messianic cult, his report of a revelation from the Great Spirit gaining credence among Indians throughout the West. Wovoka promised peace, a restoration of Indian property, and salvation through the performance of a sacred ghost dance. Wovoka was recognized as a messiah by many tribes, but the ghost dance movement was ruthlessly suppressed with such actions as the killing of Sitting Bull and the massacre of the Sioux band at Wounded Knee.

Wren, Sir Christopher (1632–1723), English architect. After the Great Fire of 1666, which destroyed much of London, Wren was put in charge of rebuilding the city. He planned the reconstruction of 52 London churches. His greatest work was the rebuilding of St. Paul's Cathedral, 1675–1711. For many years thereafter he continued to design important buildings, including the royal hospitals of Chelsea and Greenwich and Kensington Palace.

Wright, Frank Lloyd (1869–1959), U.S. architect, the creator and chief exponent of "organic" architecture, structures in harmony with people and the natural environment. Wright's designs for public and private buildings and his city-planning schemes, at first considered unconventional, had an important influence on U.S. and European architecture. In private residences, Wright frequently used patterned concrete blocks and cantilevered concrete construction. His famous buildings include the Imperial Hotel, Tokyo; Fallingwater, a home in Bear Run, Pa., built over a waterfall; buildings for S.C. Johnson & Son, Inc., in Racine, Wis.; the campus of Florida Southern College at Lakeland; the Guggenheim Museum in New York City; Taliesin East in Spring Green, Wis., and Taliesin West, near Phoenix, Ariz., the site of a school of architecture dedicated to his principles.

Wright, Orville (1871–1948), U.S. pioneer in aviation and aeronautics. In 1895, with his brother **Wilbur Wright** (1867–1912), he established a successful bicycle manufacturing business. After reading of glider experiments, the Wright brothers studied aeronautics and in 1900 built their first glider and took it to Kitty Hawk, N.C., for trial. They experimented for two years and made many glider flights. They eventually designed an engine and on December 17, 1903, made the first successful powered, man-carrying flight.

Wright, Richard (1908–1960), U.S. author whose novel *Native Son* (1940) made him the best-known black novelist of the mid-1900's. Wright was publishing short stories by age 16; his *Uncle Tom's Children* (1938) won the Federal Writers' Project prize. He continued to write while editing the Communist Party's *Daily Worker.* The autobiographical *Black Boy* appeared in 1945. He left the country after World War II in protest against the treatment of blacks. Settling in Paris, he published *The Outsider* (1953), *Black Power* (1954), and *White Man, Listen!* (1957).

Wycliffe, John (c 1320–1384), English scholar and religious reformer. He was educated at Oxford and taught there before becoming rector at Lutterworth, a post he held for most of his life. A moderate realist, he attacked the doctrine of transubstantiation, absolution, celibacy, and veneration of the saints. He also condemned the church's control of secular affairs and denied the validity of ecclesiastical authority when exercised by sinful clergy. In 1376 John of Gaunt summoned Wycliffe to London to preach against ecclesiastical abuse and opposition to government, which he did with great success. He eventually withdrew into relative seclusion and lived unmolested, perhaps because of the confusion surrounding the Great Papal Schism. With friends he translated the Bible into English and nurtured a sect known as the Lollards. His teachings profoundly influenced the great religious reformers Jan Hus and Martin Luther.

FRANK LLOYD WRIGHT

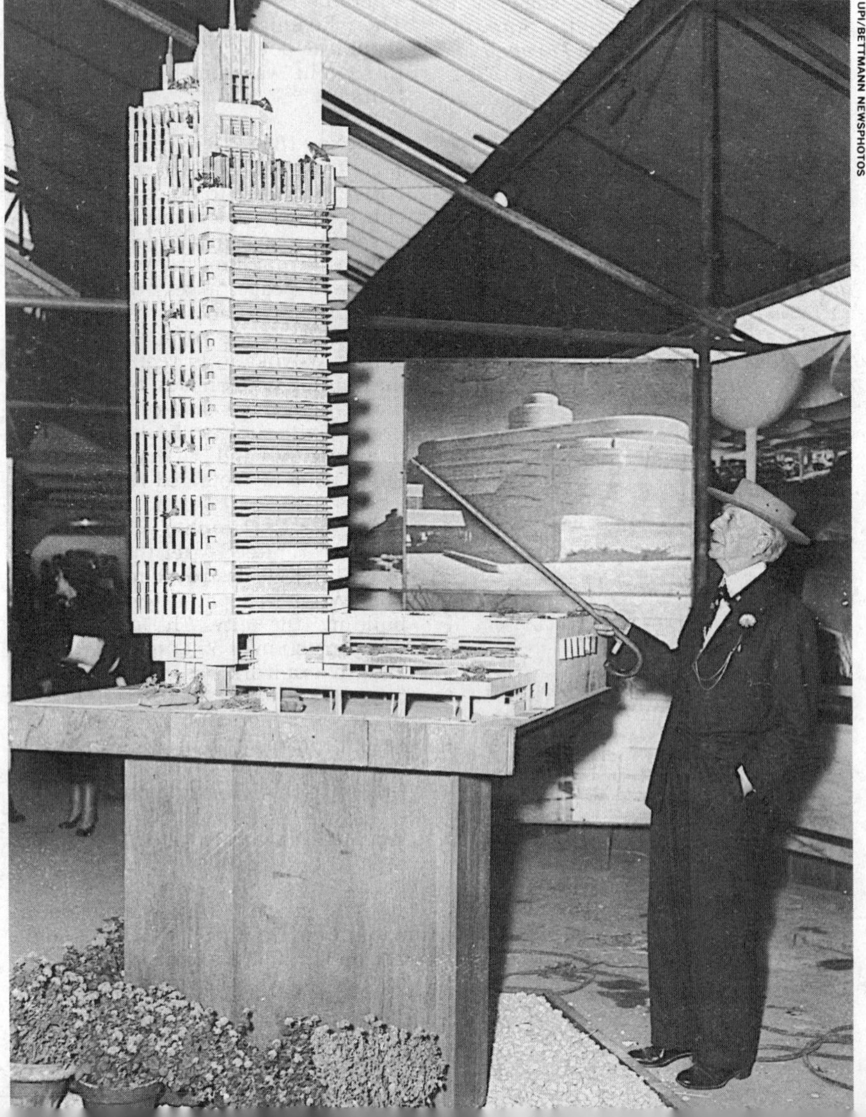
UPI/BETTMANN NEWSPHOTOS

Wyeth, Andrew Nelson (1917–), U.S. painter noted for his unique watercolors and temperas. Wyeth received technical training from his father, the well-known painter and illustrator **N.C. Wyeth**. Wyeth's scenes of country life show great psychological insight and realism. They include *Wind from the Sea* (1947), *Distant Thunder* (1961), and *Christina's World* (1948). In 1986 Wyeth revealed the existence of 240 drawings and paintings of exceptional intensity made over a period of 15 years, all but one depicting a woman named Helga.

Xenophon (c 434–c 355 B.C.), Greek historian and soldier. In 401 Xenophon joined an army of Greek mercenaries hired by Cyrus the Younger of Persia to dethrone his brother Artaxerxes. The story of the expedition and an account of the perilous return to Greece under Xenophon's leadership is given in the *Anabasis.* Xenophon also wrote the *Memorabilia,* a record of the life and teachings of his friend and former teacher Socrates; *Hellenica,* a history of Greece, 411–362; and the *Cyropaedia,* a biography of Cyrus the Great, which discusses particularly the Persian king's education.

Xerxes the Great (c 519–465 B.C.), king of Persia who mounted the last great expedition of the Persian wars against the Greeks. To revenge the defeated expeditions of his father, Darius, Xerxes launched a land and sea invasion in 480. His army, blocked by Leonidas and his troops in a pass at Thermopylae, massacred the Greeks, then invaded Attica and burned Athens. The Persian navy was destroyed by the Athenian navy under Themistocles at the Battle of Salamis, while Xerxes watched from his throne high on a bluff overlooking the bay. Xerxes returned to Persia, leaving his army, which the Greeks defeated in the spring of 479. Little is known of his later reign; he was assassinated in 465.

Yale, Elihu (1649–1721), English philanthropist in whose honor Yale University was named. Yale was born in

Massachusetts and as a child was taken to England, never to return to America. As head of the East India Company in Madras, from 1687, he amassed a fortune through trading and speculation. After returning to England in 1699, he became interested in the Collegiate School in Branford, Ct. He gave it substantial gifts of money and books. When the school was moved to New Haven, it was renamed Yale College.

Yeats, William Butler (1865–1939), Irish poet and dramatist, winner of the 1923 Nobel Prize for Literature. Yeats was a leader of the Irish literary renaissance and a founder of the Abbey Theatre (Dublin, 1904). His plays include *The Countess Cathleen* (1892) and *Kathleen ni Houlihan* (1902). His love for Irish lore is revealed in *Fairy and Folk Tales of the Irish Peasantry* (1886) and *The Secret Rose* (1897). Yeats combined his nationalist emotions with his love for the Irish revolutionary Maud Gonne in *The Wanderings of Oisin and Other Poems* (1889) and *The Wind Among the Reeds* (1899). His superb symbolism is seen in *A Vision* (1925), *The Cat and Moon* (1924), and *A Full Moon in March* (1935).

Yevtushenko, Yevgeny Alexandrovich (1933–), Soviet poet considered the leading spokesman for the post-World War II generation of Russian youth. A staunch Communist, his poetry nevertheless attacks injustices in Soviet society. Among his collections of poems published in English are *Red Cats* (1961) and *Other New Poems* (1967). *Babi Yar* (1961) recalls a Nazi massacre of Russian Jews in 1944 and indicts the Soviet state for its continuing anti-Semitism.

Young, Brigham (1801–1877), U.S. leader of the Mormon migration to Utah. He became a Mormon in 1832 and within a short time proved himself a vigorous religious leader. In 1844 he succeeded Joseph Smith as head of the church. To escape persecution, Young took its members to Utah, where they founded Salt Lake City. He was elected governor of the Mormon "State of Deseret" in 1849 and appointed governor of Utah territory by President Fillmore, a post he subsequently lost because of his practice of polygamy. Though harassed and finally indicted by the government, he continued to serve as leader of the Mormons until his death, at which time he had 17 wives.

Young, Whitney Moore, Jr. (1921–1971), U.S. social worker and civil rights leader. In 1961 he was made executive director of the National Urban League. Young served as adviser to many governmental agencies and wrote several books, including *Integration—The Role of Labor Education* (1959) and *To Be Equal* (1964).

Yüan Shih-k'ai (1859–1916), first president of the Chinese Republic. His diplomatic career began with service in Korea. In 1900 he became governor of Shantung. When the Manchu dynasty was overthrown he became president of the Chinese Republic in 1912, following the resignation of the Sun Yat-sen in the south. His government rapidly became dictatorial and at his death China was in a state of political turmoil.

Z

Zapata, Emiliano (c 1883–1919), Mexican revolutionist who led the most radical of the revolutionaries fighting against Porfirio Díaz, 1910, and whose name is synonymous with agrarian reform in Mexico. His plan demanded the return of large tracts of land to landless peasants. At the height of his success, Zapata and his followers controlled the whole of Morelos State and parts of other states; he was assassinated in 1919 but his example continued to inspire the peasants, known as *zapatistas.*

Zenger, John Peter (1697–1746), German born American colonial printer whose trial secured the first important victory for freedom of the press. For publishing the *New-York Weekly Journal* in opposition to the government press, he was brought to trial in 1735 for seditious libel. He was defended by a noted lawyer, Andrew Hamilton, who argued that published facts could not be libelous if true. Zenger was acquitted by the jury, setting a precedent for letting a jury decide whether writings are libelous.

Zeppelin, Count Ferdinand von (1838–1917), German inventor and aeronautical engineer. He retired from the army in 1891 and began experimenting with dirigible balloons. In 1900 the first successful flight was made. During World War I Germany used Zeppelins to bomb England.

Zhao Ziyang (1919–), Chinese government official, prime minister of the People's Republic of China since 1980. Zhao joined the Communist Party as a teenager and rose rapidly in the political hierarchy. While serving as leader of Sichuan Province in the late 1970's, he took the lead in introducing successful reforms in agriculture. As prime minister, he has continued to advocate economic reform. In 1987 Zhao became acting general secretary of the Communist Party while continuing to serve as prime minister.

Zhukov, Georgi Konstantinovich (1895–1974), chief Soviet military commander of World War II. Zhukov was a cavalry officer in the Red Army during the 1917 Russian revolution. By 1941 he had become chief of the general staff. He conducted the defense of Stalingrad, Leningrad, and Moscow; in 1945, he led the Russian advance on Berlin. Banished in 1946, he returned to power after Stalin's death in 1953. He became defense minister in 1955 and was elected to the presidium in 1957, but fell from power again that same year.

Ziegfeld, Florenz (1869–1932), U.S. theatrical producer who introduced the musical revue to the American stage with *The Follies of 1907.* For the next 20 years he produced new versions of the *Ziegfeld Follies,* introducing such stars as Eddie Cantor, Will Rogers, and Ed Wynn. During the 1920's Ziegfeld also produced the musicals *Sally, Rio Rita, Show Boat,* and *Bitter Sweet.*

Zola, Émile (1840–1902), French novelist. His most important work is a series of 20 novels, *Les Rougon-Macquart* (1871–1893), which traces the life of a single family through several generations. Among the best-known works in this series are *L'Assomoir,* which depicts life in a Parisian slum; *Germinal,* which describes a strike by coal miners; and *Nana,* about a prostitute. Zola's naturalistic technique is characterized by accurate and detailed descriptions, often of suffering and violence in the lower classes of society. He stressed the influence of the environment on the individual and in several works condemned the evils and injustices of society. In 1898 Zola came to the defense of a Jewish army officer accused of treason. Zola published an open letter, *J'accuse* ("I accuse"), to the president of France. Zola was tried for libel and sentenced to imprisonment but fled to England. In 1899 the Dreyfus case was reopened. Dreyfus's innocence was established and Zola's defense of him vindicated.

Zoroaster (or **Zarathustra)** (fl. 500's B.C.), founder of an ancient Iranian religion, Zoroastrianism. The religion sees life as a struggle between the spirit of good (Ahura Mazda) and that of evil (Ahriman). The religion's sacred book is the *Avesta.*

Zwingli, Huldreich (1484–1531), Swiss clergyman and reformer. Influenced by the writings of Martin Luther, Zwingli came to believe that the Bible is the only source of religious faith; that only Christ can mediate between man and God; and that predestination is the source of salvation. By 1523 he had established the Reformation of Zurich. He organized a new form of worship as well as a new system of church government. The theological reasons for his Reformed doctrines were set forth and explained in his *De Vera ac Falsa Religione* (*On the True and False Religion,* 1525).

THE NOBEL PRIZE WINNERS

Year	Peace	Physiology and Medicine
1901	**Jean Henri Dunant*** (1828–1910), Swiss founder of the International Red Cross and originator of the Geneva Convention; shared with **Frédéric Passy** (1822–1912), French, a founder of the International League of Peace and the Interparliamentary Peace Union.	**Emil Adolf von Behring*** (1854–1917), German bacteriologist, for his work on serum therapy, especially in relation to diphtheria.
1902	**Élie Ducommun** (1833–1906), Swiss organizer of the International Peace Bureau; shared with **Charles Albert Gobat** (1843–1914), Swiss president of International Peace Bureau and founder and secretary-general of Interparliamentary Peace Union.	**Sir Ronald Ross** (1857–1932), British physician, for determining the life cycle of the malaria parasite, which laid the foundation for later research that successfully combated the disease.
1903	**Sir William Randal Cremer** (1838–1908), British secretary of the Workman's Peace Association (later called the International Arbitration League) and a founder of the Interparliamentary Peace Union.	**Niels Ryberg Finsen** (1860–1904), Danish physician, for contributing to the treatment of skin diseases (especially Lupus vulgaris) by the use of concentrated rays of light.
1904	**Institute of International Law**, founded in 1873 at Ghent, Belgium (later in Geneva, Switz.), to codify international law and provide regulations for international arbitration.	**Ivan Petrovich Pavlov*** (1849–1936), Russian physiologist, for his research on the physiology of digestion.
1905	**Baroness Bertha von Suttner** (formerly **Countess von Kinsky**) (1843–1914), Austrian, founder and president of the Austrian Society of Friends of Peace.	**Robert Koch** (1843–1910), German physician, for his research on tuberculosis and the development of the science of bacteriology.
1906	**Theodore Roosevelt*** (1858–1919), U.S. President, responsible for the Treaty of Portsmouth ending the Russo-Japanese War.	**Camillo Golgi** (1844–1926), Italian physician, and **Santiago Ramón y Cajal** (1852–1934), Spanish histologist, for their work on the structure of the nervous system.
1907	**Ernesto Teodoro Moneta** (1833–1918), Italian president of the Lombard League for Peace, head of the Peace Congress at Milan, 1906; shared with **Jean Louis Renault** (1843–1918), French jurist, counselor to the Ministry of Foreign Affairs, France's representative at international conferences (including The Hague, 1907), and member of the Permanent Court of Arbitration.	**Charles Louis Alphonse Laveran** (1845–1922), French bacteriologist, for his research on protozoa-related diseases.
1908	**Klas Pontus Arnoldson** (1844–1916), Swedish founder of the Swedish Peace and Arbitration League and author of *Hope of the Centuries, a Book on World Peace;* shared with **Fredrik Bajer** (1837–1922), Danish founder of the Danish Peace Society and a founder and president of the International Peace Bureau.	**Élie Metchnikoff** (1845–1916), Russian zoologist and bacteriologist, and **Paul Ehrlich*** (1854–1915), German scientist and bacteriologist, for their separate research on immunity.
1909	**Auguste Marie François Beernaert** (1829–1912), Belgian president of the Interparliamentary Union and delegate to The Hague peace conferences; shared with **Paul H. Benjamin Balluet, Baron d'Estournelles de Constant de Rebecque** (1852–1924), French delegate to the 1907 Hague Peace Conference, founder and president of the League of International Conciliation.	**Emil Theodor Kocher** (1841–1917), Swiss surgeon, for his research on the physiology, pathology, and surgery of the thyroid gland.
1910	**International Peace Bureau**, founded by Ducommun to give continuity to peace congresses and the pacifist movement.	**Albrecht Kossel** (1853–1927), German physiological chemist, for his research on protein, including nucleic substances, which contributed to the knowledge of cellular chemistry.
1911	**Tobias Michael Carel Asser** (1838–1913), Dutch jurist, delegate to The Hague peace conferences, a founder of the Institute of International Law; shared with **Alfred Hermann Fried** (1864–1921), Austrian founder of the German Peace Society, editor of the peace publication *Die Friedenswarte.*	**Allvar Gullstrand** (1862–1930), Swedish ophthalmologist, for his research on ocular dioptrics (the refraction of light through the eye).
1912	**Elihu Root** (1845–1937), U.S. secretary of state, responsible for the arbitration of many international disputes, first president of the Carnegie Endowment for International Peace, representative to the Washington Disarmament Conference.	**Alexis Carrel*** (1873–1944), French surgeon and biologist, for his research on vascular suture and organ and blood vessel transplantation.
1913	**Henri Marie Lafontaine** (1854–1943), Belgian, president of the International Peace Bureau and authority on international law and arbitration.	**Charles Robert Richet** (1850–1935), French physiologist, for his research on anaphylaxis (drug or serum reaction).
1914	No award.	**Robert Bárány** (1876–1936), Austro-Hungarian physician, for his research on the physiology and pathology of the inner ear.
1915	No award.	No award.
1916	No award.	No award.
1917	**International Committee of the Red Cross**, founded by Dunant in 1863 to care for the victims of battle. (The Red Cross also received the award in 1944 and 1963.)	No award.
1918	No award.	No award.
1919	**Woodrow Wilson*** (1856–1924), U.S. President, author of the 14 Points treaty that ended World War I, advocate of the establishment of the League of Nations.	**Jules Bordet** (1870–1961), Belgian bacteriologist, for his discoveries in the field of immunity.
1920	**Léon Victor Auguste Bourgeois** (1851–1925), French, head of the French delegation at The Hague peace conferences and at the League of Nations, where he was chosen as first chairman.	**August Krogh** (1874–1949), Danish physiologist, for discovering the motor mechanism that regulates capillary action.

Nobel Prize winners who have individual biographies are indicated by an asterisk (*).

Physics	Chemistry	Literature
Wilhelm Conrad Roentgen* (1845–1923), German, for the discovery of x-rays (sometimes called Roentgen rays).	**Jacobus Hendricus van't Hoff** (1852–1911), Dutch, for developing laws of chemical dynamics and osmotic pressure.	**Sully Prudhomme**, pseudonym of René François Armand Prudhomme (1839–1907), French poet and literary critic.
Hendrik Antoon Lorentz (1853–1928) and **Pieter Zeeman** (1865–1943), Dutch physicists, for the discovery and explanation of the Zeeman effect, the influence of magnetism on radiation.	**Emil Hermann Fischer** (1852–1919), German, for synthesizing certain sugars and purines.	**Theodor Mommsen** (1817–1903), German classical scholar and historian.
Antoine Henri Becquerel* (1852–1908), French, for his discovery of radioactivity; shared with **Marie Sklodowska Curie*** (1867–1934), Polish-born French scientist, and **Pierre Curie** (1859–1906), French, for their research on the radiation phenomenon discovered by Becquerel.	**Svante August Arrhenius** (1859–1927), Swedish, for his theory of electrolytic dissociation.	**Björnstjerne Björnson** (1832–1910), Distinguished Norwegian poet, novelist, and dramatist.
John William Strutt, 3rd Baron Rayleigh, (1842–1919), British, for his discovery of argon and research on the density of gases.	**Sir William Ramsay** (1852–1916), British, for discovering helium, neon, xenon, and krypton and determining their places in the periodic table.	**Frédéric Mistral*** (1830–1914), French Provençal poet; shared with **José Echegaray y Eizaguirre** (1832–1916), Spanish dramatist.
Philipp Eduard Anton Lenard (1862–1947), Czech-born German, for his research on cathode rays.	**Adolf von Baeyer** (1835–1917), German, for his research on organic dyestuffs and hydroaromatic compounds.	**Henryk Sienkiewicz** (1846–1916), Polish novelist.
Sir Joseph John Thomson* (1856–1940), British, for research on electrical transmission through gases.	**Henri Moissan** (1852–1907), French, for isolating the element fluorine and for the development of the electric furnace that which bears his name.	**Giosuè Carducci** (1835–1907), Italian poet.
Albert Abraham Michelson (1852–1931), German-born American, for measuring the speed of light and inventing certain optical instruments.	**Eduard Buchner** (1860–1917), German, for discovering cell-free fermentation.	**Rudyard Kipling*** (1865–1936), British novelist and poet.
Gabriel Lippmann (1845–1921), Luxembourg-born French scientist, for inventing a process for color photography based on the phenomenon of interference.	**Ernest Rutherford,* 1st Baron Rutherford of Nelson** (1871–1937), British, for his investigations into the disintegration of elements and the chemistry of radioactive substances.	**Rudolf Christoph Eucken** (1846–1926), German philosopher.
Guglielmo Marconi* (1874–1937), Italian, and **Karl Ferdinand Braun** (1850–1918), German, for the development of a practical system of wireless telegraphy.	**Wilhelm Ostwald** (1853–1932), German, for his research on catalysis, chemical equilibrium, and the rate of chemical reactions.	**Selma Lagerlöf** (1858–1940), Swedish novelist and poet.
Johannes Diderik van der Waals (1837–1923), Dutch, for defining the relationship between liquids and gases.	**Otto Wallach** (1847–1931), German, for initiating research in the field of alicyclic substances.	**Paul von Heyse** (1830–1914), German novelist, playwright, and poet.
Wilhelm Wien (1864–1928), German, for the discovery of laws governing heat radiation.	**Marie Skiodowska Curie*** (1867–1934), Polish-born French scientist, for the discovery of the elements radium and polonium and the study of compounds composed of these elements (also co-winner of the 1903 physics prize).	**Count Maurice Maeterlinck*** (1862–1949), Belgian poet, dramatist, and essayist.
Nils Gustaf Dalén (1869–1937), Swedish, for the invention of valves used to regulate acetylene lights on coastal beacons and buoys.	**Victor Grignard** (1871–1935), French, for discovery of Grignard reagent, which helps in synthesis of organic compounds; shared with **Paul Sabatier** (1854–1941), French, for method of hydrogenating organic compounds in presence of finely divided metals.	**Gerhart Hauptmann** (1862–1946), German dramatist and novelist.
Heike Kamerlingh Onnes (1853–1926), Dutch, for investigating the properties of matter at low temperatures, which led to the liquefaction of helium.	**Alfred Werner** (1866–1919), German-born Swiss scientist, for research on the combining of atoms in molecules.	**Sir Rabindranath Tagore*** (1861–1941), Indian poet.
Max von Laue (1879–1960), German, for discovering that crystals cause the diffraction of x-rays.	**Theodore William Richards** (1868–1928), American, for determining the exact atomic weights of many chemical elements.	No award.
Sir William Henry Bragg (1862–1942) and **Sir (William) Lawrence Bragg** (1890–1971), British physicists, for using x-rays to analyze the structure of crystals.	**Richard Martin Willstätter** (1872–1942), German, for research on color pigments in plants, especially chlorophyll.	**Romain Rolland*** (1866–1944), French novelist and playwright.
No award.	No award.	**Verner von Heidenstam** (1859–1940), Swedish poet and prose writer.
Charles Glover Barkla (1877–1944), British, for the discovery of the x-radiation of elements.	No award.	**Karl Adolph Gjellerup** (1857–1919), Danish novelist; shared with **Henrik Pontoppidan** (1857–1943), Danish novelist.
Max Planck* (1858–1947), German, for formulating the quantum theory of light.	**Fritz Haber** (1868–1934), German, for the synthesis of the compound ammonia from the elements nitrogen and hydrogen.	No award.
Johannes Stark (1874–1957), German, for discovering the splitting of spectral lines in an electrical field (called the Stark effect) and the discovery of the Doppler effect in the canal rays produced by a cathode ray tube.	No award.	**Carl Friedrich Georg Spitteler** (1845–1924), Swiss poet.
Charles Édouard Guillaume (1861–1938), Swiss-born French scientist, for his discovery of invar, a steel-nickel alloy, and platinate, a nickel-iron alloy.	**Walther Hermann Nernst** (1864–1941), German, for his research on heat changes in chemical reactions.	**Knut Hamsun*** pseudonym of Knut Pedersen (1859–1952), Norwegian novelist.

THE NOBEL PRIZE WINNERS *(continued)*

Year	Peace	Physiology and Medicine
1921	**Karl Hjalmar Branting** (1860–1925), Swedish delegate to the League of Nations and member of the League Council, responsible for many social reforms in Sweden; shared with **Christian Louis Lange** (1869–1938), Norwegian representative at the second Hague Peace Conference and at the League of Nations, secretary-general of the Interparliamentary Peace Union.	No award.
1922	**Fridtjof Nansen** (1861–1930), Norwegian president of the Norwegian League of Nations Society, Norway's first delegate to the League of Nations, and the league's high commissioner for refugees (prize given for his famine relief work in Russia).	**Archibald Vivian Hill** (1886–1977), British physiologist, for discoveries related to the production of heat in muscles; shared with **Otto Fritz Meyerhof** (1884–1951), German physiologist, for discovering the fixed relationship between oxygen consumption and the amount of lactic acid in muscle.
1923	No award.	**Sir Frederick Grant Banting*** (1891–1941), Canadian physician, and **John James Rickard Macleod** (1876–1935), Scottish physiologist, for their discovery of insulin.
1924	No award.	**Willem Einthoven** (1860–1927), Dutch physiologist for the development of the electrocardiograph.
1925	**Sir (Joseph) Austen Chamberlain** (1863–1937), British foreign secretary who helped to negotiate the Locarno Pact (1925); shared with **Charles Gates Dawes** (1865–1951), U.S. Vice President, head of the committee that drafted the Dawes plan for payment of German World War I reparations.	No award.
1926	**Aristide Briand*** (1862–1932), French foreign minister, delegate at Locarno, co-author of the Kellogg-Briand Pact (a treaty to outlaw war); shared with **Gustav Stresemann*** (1878–1929), German minister of foreign affairs, who negotiated the Locarno Pact and secured Germany's admission to the League of Nations.	**Johannes A. G. Fibiger** (1867–1928), Danish pathologist, for his discovery that the parasite Spiroptera causes a type of skin cancer.
1927	**Ferdinand Édouard Buisson** (1841–1932), French educator, advocate of the League of Nations and founder-president of the League of Human Rights; shared with **Ludwig Quidde** (1858–1941), German pacifist author, president of the German Peace Society and of the German Peace Cartel.	**Julius Wagner von Jauregg** (1857–1940), Austrian neurologist and psychiatrist, for discovering the therapeutic value of malaria inoculation in the treatment of dementia paralytica (a kind of paralysis).
1928	No award.	**Charles Jean Henri Nicolle** (1866–1936), French physician and bacteriologist, for his research on typhus.
1929	**Frank Billings Kellogg** (1856–1937), U.S. secretary of state, co-author of the Kellogg-Briand Pact to outlaw war.	**Christiaan Eijkman** (1858–1930), Dutch hygienist, for his discovery of Vitamin B; shared with **Sir Frederick Gowland Hopkins** (1861–1947), British biochemist, for his discovery of Vitamin A.
1930	**Nathan Söderblom** (1866–1931), Lutheran archbishop of Sweden, organizer of the first Conference on Life and Work (1925), which later combined with Faith and Order conferences to become the World Council of Churches.	**Karl Landsteiner** (1868–1943), Austrian-born U.S. pathologist, for his discovery of the human blood groups.
1931	**Jane Addams*** (1860–1935), American founder of Hull House (a social settlement house), chairman of the International Congress of Women, and president of the Women's International League for Peace and Freedom; shared with **Nicholas Murray Butler** (1862–1947), U.S. educator, chairman of Lake Mohonk conferences on international arbitration and president of the Carnegie Endowment for International Peace.	**Otto Heinrich Warburg** (1883–1970), German physiologist, for his research on the respiratory enzyme.
1932	No award.	**Sir Charles S. Sherrington** (1857–1952) and **Edgar Douglas Adrian, 1st Baron Adrian of Cambridge** (1889–1977), British physiologists, for their research on neural function.
1933	**Sir Norman Angell** (1873–1967), British economist and author of *The Great Illusion*, influential in the founding of many peace organizations.	**Thomas Hunt Morgan** (1866–1945), U.S. zoologist, for his research on the function of chromosomes in heredity.
1934	**Arthur Henderson** (1863–1935), Scottish-born British Labour Party leader, president of the World Disarmament Conference at Geneva (1932–1934).	**George Hoyt Whipple** (1878–1976), **George Richards Minot** (1885–1950), and **William Parry Murphy** (1892–1987), U.S. physicians, for their development of a liver therapy to help correct anemias.
1935	**Carl von Ossietzky** (1888–1938), German author, editor of *Weltbühne*, a left-wing political newspaper, and staunch opponent of Hitler. (After this award, Hitler forbade Germans to accept any Nobel Prize in the future.)	**Hans Spemann** (1869–1941), German zoologist, for his discovery of the organizer effect in embryonic development.
1936	**Carlos Saavedra Lamas** (1880–1959), Argentine jurist, organizer of a conference in Buenos Aires that ended the Gran Chaco War (1935), president of the 1936 session of the League of Nations.	**Sir Henry Hallett Dale** (1875–1968), British physiologist, and **Otto Loewi** (1873–1961), German pharmacologist, for their discoveries relating to the chemical transmission of nerve impulses.
1937	**Edgar Algernon Robert Cecil, Viscount Cecil of Chelwood** (1864–1958), British assistant secretary of state for foreign affairs, an active participant in drafting the League of Nations covenant, president of the League of Nations Union.	**Albert von Szent-Györgyi** (1893–1986), Hungarian-born U.S. biochemist, for investigation of the biological combustion processes, especially with reference to Vitamin C and the catalysis of fumaric acid.
1938	**Nansen International Office for Refugees**, founded by the League of Nations in 1930 to give legal and social aid to refugees (named in honor of Fridtjof Nansen).	**Corneille Jean François Heymans** (1892–1968), Belgian physiologist, for discovering the role that the sinus and aortic mechanisms play in the regulation of respiration.
1939	No award.	**Gerhard Domagk** (1895–1964), German pathologist, for his discovery of the antibacterial effects of the sulfa drug prontosil (prize declined because of Nazi pressure).
1940	No award.	No award.
1941	No award.	No award.
1942	No award.	No award.

Nobel Prize winners who have individual biographies are indicated by an asterisk (*).

Physics	Chemistry	Literature
Albert Einstein* (1879–1955), German-born American, for his contribution to theoretical physics and for stating the law of the photoelectric effect.	**Frederick Soddy** (1877–1956), British, for research on the chemistry of radioactive substances and the origin and nature of isotopes.	**Anatole France***, pseudonym of Jacques Anatole François Thibault (1844–1924), French novelist, critic, poet, and playwright.
Niels Henrik David Bohr* (1885–1962), Danish, for his theories of atomic structure and radiation.	**Francis William Aston** (1877–1945), British, for discovering many isotopes with the technique of mass spectrography and for developing the whole-number rule of the weight and structure of atoms.	**Jacinto Benavente by Martinez** (1866–1954), Spanish dramatist.
Robert Andrews Millikan* (1868–1953), American, for his measurement of electron charges and his research on the photoelectric effect.	**Fritz Pregl** (1869–1930), Austrian, for developing a method of microanalyzing organic substances.	**William Butler Yeats*** (1865–1939), Irish poet and dramatist.
Karl Mann Georg Siegbahn (1886–1978), Swedish, for his research and discoveries in the field of X-ray spectroscopy.	No award.	**Wladyslaw Stanislaw Reymont** (1868–1925), Polish novelist.
James Franck (1882–1964) and **Gustav Hertz** (1887–1975), German physicists, for stating the laws governing the impact of an electron on an atom.	**Richard Zsigmondy** (1865–1929), Austrian-born German, for developing ways to study colloids.	**George Bernard Shaw*** (1856–1950), Irish dramatist, novelist, and critic.
Jean Baptiste Perrin (1870–1942), French, for research on the discontinuous structure of matter and the discovery of the equilibrium of sedimentation.	**Theodor Svedberg** (1884–1971), Swedish, for his research on disperse systems and colloid chemistry.	**Grazia Deledda** (1875–1936), Italian novelist.
Arthur Holly Compton* (1892–1962), American, for the discovery of the Compton effect, a wave-length charge in electron-scattered x-rays; shared with **Charles Thomson Rees Wilson*** (1869–1959), British, for developing the Wilson cloud chamber.	**Heinrich Otto Wieland** (1877–1957), German, for his research on bile acids and related substances.	**Henri Bergson*** (1859–1941), French philosopher.
Sir Owen Willans Richardson (1879–1959), British, for the discovery of Richardson's law, governing the motions of electrons emanating from hot bodies.	**Adolf Windaus** (1876–1959), German, for his research on the structure of sterols and their relationship to vitamins.	**Sigrid Undset*** (1882–1949), Danish-born Norwegian novelist.
Louis Victor de Broglie, duc de Broglie (1892–1987), French, for his discovery of the wave nature of electrons.	**Sir Arthur Harden** (1865–1940), British, and **Hans von Euler-Chelpin** (1873–1964), German-born Swedish scientist, for research on fermentation enzymes and fermentation of sugar.	**Thomas Mann*** (1875–1955), German-born U.S. novelist, playwright, and essayist.
Sir Chandrasekhara Venkata Raman* (1888–1970), Indian, for his research on light diffusion and the discovery of the Raman effect.	**Hans Fischer** (1881–1945), German, for the synthesis of hemin (a substance in hemoglobin), and for research on chlorophyll.	**Sinclair Lewis*** (1885–1951), U.S. novelist and playwright.
No award.	**Carl Bosch** (1874–1940) and **Friedrich Bergius** (1884–1949), German chemists, for developing methods of synthesizing ammonia and for liquefying coal.	**Erik Axel Karlfeldt** (1864–1931), Swedish lyric poet.
Werner Heisenberg (1901–1976), German, for founding quantum mechanics and for research that led to the discovery of allotropic forms of hydrogen.	**Irving Langmuir** (1881–1957), American, for his research on molecular films in surface chemistry.	**John Galsworthy*** (1867–1933), English novelist and playwright.
Paul Adrien Maurice Dirac (1902–1984), British, for his work in quantum mechanics; shared with **Erwin Schrödinger** (1887–1961), Austrian, for the Schrödinger equation, which describes the wavelike behavior of electrons.	No award.	**Ivan Alekseevich Bunin** (1870–1953), exiled Russian-born poet and novelist.
No award.	**Harold Clayton Urey*** (1893–1981), American, for discovering heavy hydrogen.	**Luigi Pirandello*** (1867–1936), Italian novelist and dramatist.
Sir James Chadwick (1891–1974), British, for his discovery of the neutron and the determination of its mass.	**Irène Joliot-Curie*** (1897–1956) and **Frédéric Joliot-Curie** (1900–1958), French chemists, for the synthesis of new radioactive elements.	No award.
Victor Francis Hess (1883–1964), Austrian-born American, for his discovery of cosmic radiation; shared with **Carl David Anderson** (1905–), American, for his discovery of the positron.	**Peter Joseph Wilhelm Debye** (1884–1966), Dutch-born American, for his research on dipole moments, defraction of x-rays, and electrons in gases.	**Eugene Gladstone O'Neill*** (1888–1953), U.S. dramatist.
Clinton Joseph Davisson (1881–1958), American, shared with **Sir George Paget Thomson** (1892–1975), British, for their separate discoveries of electron diffraction by crystals.	**Sir Walter Norman Haworth** (1883–1950), British, for his research on carbohydrates and Vitamin C; shared with **Paul Karrer** (1889–1971), Russian-born Swiss scientist, for his research on carotenoids, flavins, and vitamins A and B.	**Roger Martin du Gard** (1881–1958), French novelist.
Enrico Fermi* (1901–1954), Italian-born American, for discovery of new radioactive elements produced by neutron irradiation and for discovery of nuclear reactions initiated by slow neutrons.	**Richard Kuhn** (1900–1967), Austrian, for his research on carotenoids and vitamins.	**Pearl Sydenstricker Buck** (1892–1973), U.S. novelist.
Ernest Orlando Lawrence* (1901–1958), American, for his research on atomic structure and the invention of the cyclotron.	**Adolf Friedrich Johann Butenandt** (1903–), German, for his research on sex hormones; shared with **Leopold Ruzicka** (1887–1976), Yugoslavian-born Swiss scientist, for his research on polymethylenes and higher terpenes.	**Frans Eemil Sillanpää** (1888–1964), Finnish novelist and short story writer.
No award.	No award.	No award.
No award.	No award.	No award.
No award.	No award.	No award.

THE NOBEL PRIZE WINNERS *(continued)*

Year	Peace	Physiology and Medicine
1943	No award.	**C. P. Henrik Dam** (1895–1976), Danish biochemist, for his discovery of Vitamin K; shared with **Edward Adelbert Doisy** (1893–1987), U.S. biochemist, for his research on the chemical nature of Vitamin K.
1944	**International Committee of the Red Cross**, for administering relief to prisoners and disaster area victims during World War II.	**E. Joseph Erlanger** (1874–1965) and **Herbert Spencer Gasser** (1888–1963), U.S. physiologists, for their discoveries regarding the differentiated functions of single nerve fibers.
1945	**Cordell Hull*** (1871–1955), U.S. secretary of state, known as "the father of the United Nations," who improved U.S. relations with South America and negotiated the Declaration of Moscow (1943).	**Sir Alexander Fleming*** (1881–1955), Scottish bacteriologist; **Ernst Boris Chain** (1906–1979), German-born British biochemist; and **Howard Walter Florey, Baron Florey of Adelaide** (1898–1968), Australian pathologist, for the discovery of penicillin and its value as a cure for various infectious diseases.
1946	**John Raleigh Mott** (1865–1955), U.S. evangelist, president of the World's Alliance of the Young Men's Christian Association (YMCA); shared with **Emily Green Balch** (1867–1961), U.S. economist and sociologist, international secretary and honorary president of the Women's International League for Peace and Freedom.	**Hermann Joseph Muller** (1890–1967), U.S. geneticist, for discovering that x-ray irradiation can produce mutations.
1947	**American Friends Service Committee**, founded in 1917, and the **British Society of Friends**, founded in 1850, both organized by the Quakers to administer relief and to establish humanitarian and pacifistic programs and seminars.	**Bernardo Alberto Houssay** (1887–1971), Argentine physiologist, for discovering the role the pituitary hormone plays in the metabolism of sugar; shared with **Carl Ferdinand Cori** (1896–1984) and **Gerty Theresa (née Radnitz) Cori** (1896–1957), Czech-born U.S. biochemists, for discovering how glycogen is catalytically converted to lactic acid.
1948	No award.	**Paul Hermann Müller** (1899–1965), Swiss chemist, for discovering the effectiveness of DDT as a contact poison.
1949	**John Boyd Orr, 1st Baron Boyd Orr** (1880–1971), Scottish director-general of the United Nations Food and Agricultural Organization.	**Walter Rudolf Hess** (1881–1973), Swiss physiologist, for discovering how the brain serves as a coordinator for the internal organs; shared with **Antonio de Egas Moniz** (1874–1955), Portuguese neurologist, for discovering the value of prefrontal lobotomy in certain psychoses.
1950	**Ralph J. Bunche*** (1904–1971), U.S. director of the UN Department of Trusteeship, UN mediator in the Middle East, 1948–1949.	**Edward Calvin Kendall** (1886–1972), U.S. chemist; **Philip Showalter Hench** (1896–1965), U.S. physician; and **Tadeus Reichstein** (1897–), Polish-born Swiss chemist, for their discoveries concerning the structure and biological effects of the suprarenal cortex hormones in the brain.
1951	**Léon Jouhaux** (1879–1954), French labor leader; a founder of the International Confederation of Free Trade Unions.	**Max Theiler** (1899–1972), South African microbiologist, for developing the yellow fever vaccine.
1952	**Albert Schweitzer*** (1875–1965), French Protestant clergyman, philosopher, physician, and music scholar, founder of Lambaréné Hospital in French Equatorial Africa.	**Selman Abraham Waksman*** (1888–1973), Russian-born U.S. microbiologist, for his discovery of the antibiotic streptomycin.
1953	**George C. Marshall*** (1880–1959), U.S. Army general and secretary of state, author of the Marshall Plan for postwar European recovery.	**Sir Hans Adolf Krebs*** (1900–1981), German-born British biochemist, for his discovery of the citric acid cycle; shared with **Fritz Albert Lipmann** (1899–), German-born U.S. biochemist, for his discovery of coenzyme A.
1954	**United Nations High Commission for Refugees**, founded in 1951 to resettle refugees after World War II.	**John Franklin Enders** (1897–1985), U.S. bacteriologist; **Frederick Chapman Robbins** (1916–), U.S. pediatrician; and **Thomas Huckle Weller** (1915–), U.S. biologist, for developing a procedure to cultivate poliomyelitis viruses in tissue cultures.
1955	No award.	**Axel Hugo Theodor Theorell** (1903–1982), Swedish biochemist, for his research on the nature and action of oxidizing enzymes.
1956	No award.	**André Frédéric Cournand** (1895–1988), French-born U.S. physician and physiologist; **Werner Forssmann** (1904–1979), German surgeon; and **Dickinson Woodruff Richards** (1895–1973), U.S. physiologist, for the development of heart catheterization and research on pathological changes in the circulatory system.
1957	**Lester Bowles Pearson*** (1897–1972), Canadian secretary of state for external affairs and prime minister who proposed the United Nations Emergency Force (UNEF) to resolve the Suez crisis of 1956.	**Daniel Bovet** (1907–), Swiss-born Italian physiologist and pharmacologist, for developing synthetic muscle relaxants for use in surgery.
1958	**Father Dominique Georges Henri Pire*** (1910–1969), Belgian Dominican priest, founder of the Europe of the Hearts Movement for resettling displaced persons.	**George Wells Beadle** (1903–1989) and **Edward Lawrie Tatum*** (1909–1975), U.S. biologists, for discovering that genes regulate definite chemical processes; shared with **Joshua Lederberg** (1925–), U.S. geneticist, for research on genetic recombination and the organization of the genetic apparatus in bacteria.
1959	**Philip John Noel-Baker** (1889–1982), British delegate to the League of Nations, an author of the United Nations charter, delegate to the first UN General Assembly and advocate of international disarmament.	**Severo Ochoa** (1905–), Spanish-born U.S. biologist; and **Arthur Kornberg** (1918–), U.S. biochemist, for discovering the mechanisms by which ribonucleic acid (RNA) and deoxyribonucleic acid (DNA) are biologically synthesized.
1960	**Albert John Luthuli*** (1898–1967), South African tribal chief, president of the African National Congress, organizer of nonviolent political campaigns aimed against racial discrimination.	**Sir Frank Macfarlane Burnet** (1899–1985), Australian physician and virologist; and **Sir Peter Brian Medawar** (1915–), English biologist and zoologist, for their discovery of acquired immunological tolerance.
1961	**Dag Hammarskjöld*** (1905–1961), Swedish secretary-general of the UN, who directed the establishment of the 1956 UNEF in the Middle East and conducted peace missions to China and the Middle East.	**Georg von Békésy** (1899–1972), Hungarian-born U.S. biophysicist, for discovering the physical mechanisms by which the cochlea (a cavity in the inner ear) is stimulated.

Nobel Prize winners who have individual biographies are indicated by an asterisk (*).

Physics	Chemistry	Literature
Otto Stern (1888–1969), German-born American, for measurement of the magnetic moment of the proton and for developing the molecular ray method of studying the atom.	**George Charles de Hevesy** (1885–1966), Hungarian, for his research on using isotopes as tracer elements in chemistry.	No award.
Isidor Isaac Rabi* (1898–1988), Austrian-born American, for developing the resonance method of studying the magnetic properties of atomic nuclei.	**Otto Hahn** (1879–1968), German, for his discovery of the fission of heavy nuclei.	**Johannes Vilhelm Jensen** (1873–1950), Danish lyric poet and novelist.
Wolfgang Pauli (1900–1958), Austrian-born American, for the discovery of the Pauli principle of exclusion in quantum mechanics.	**Artturi Ilmari Virtanen** (1895–1973), Finnish, for developing new methods of agricultural and nutritive chemistry, especially for a method of fodder preservation.	**Gabriela Mistral***, pseudonym of Lucila Godoy de Alcayaga (1889–1957), Chilean poet and educator.
Percy Williams Bridgman (1882–1961), American, for his work on high-pressure phenomena in the field of thermodynamics.	**James Batcheller-Sumner** (1887–1955), American, for discovering that enzymes can be crystallized; shared with **John Howard Northrop** (1891–1987) and **Wendell Meredith Stanley** (1904–1971), U.S. chemists, for preparing enzymes and virus proteins in a pure form.	**Hermann Hesse*** (1877–1962), German-born Swiss novelist.
Sir Edward Victor Appleton* (1892–1965), British, for proving the existence of the ionosphere and of an atmospheric layer of free electrons (the Appleton layer).	**Sir Robert Robinson** (1886–1975), British, for research on biologically important plant products, particularly alkaloids.	**André Gide*** (1869–1951), French novelist.
Patrick Maynard Stuart Blackett* (1897–1974), British, for his discoveries in nuclear physics and cosmic radiation using the Wilson cloud chamber.	**Arne Wilhelm Kaurin Tiselius** (1902–1971), Swedish, for his research on electrophoresis and adsorption analysis, especially for his discoveries concerning the complex nature of serum proteins.	**Thomas Stearns Eliot*** (1888–1965), U.S.-born English poet and literary critic.
Hideki Yukawa (1907–1981), Japanese, for predicting the existence of the meson.	**William Francis Giauque** (1895–1982), Canadian-born American, for his research in the field of chemical thermodynamics, particularly the behavior of substances at extremely low temperatures.	**William Faulkner*** (1897–1962), U.S. novelist.
Cecil Frank Powell (1903–1969), British, for developing a technique of photographic high-speed particles and for his discovery of two types of mesons.	**Otto Paul Hermann Diels** (1876–1954) and **Kurt Alder** (1902–1958), German chemists, for the development of diene synthesis.	**Bertrand Arthur William Russell, 3rd Earl Russell*** (1872–1970), English philosopher and mathematician.
Sir John Douglas Cockcroft (1897–1967), British, and **E.T.S. Walton*** (1903–), Irish, for causing the transmutation of atomic nuclei by artificially accelerating atomic particles.	**Glenn Theodore Seaborg*** (1912–) and **Edwin Mattison McMillan** (1907–), U.S. chemists, for their discovery of plutonium and other transuranium elements.	**Pär Fabian Lagerkvist** (1891–1974), Swedish poet, dramatist, and novelist.
Felix Bloch (1905–1983), Swiss-born American, and **Edward Mills Purcell** (1912–), American, for independently developing nuclear resonance methods of measuring the magnetic fields of atomic nuclei.	**Archer John Porter Martin** (1910–), British, and **Richard Laurence Millington Synge** (1914–), British, for their discovery of partition chromatography.	**François Charles Mauriac*** (1885–1970), French novelist.
Frits Zernike (1888–1966), Dutch, for inventing the phase-contrast microscope.	**Hermann Staudinger** (1881–1965), German, for his research with macromolecular substances.	**Sir Winston Leonard Spencer Churchill*** (1874–1965), English statesman and author.
Max Born* (1882–1970), German-born British scientist, for basic research in quantum mechanics; shared with **Walther Bothe** (1891–1957), German, for developing the coincidence counting method, the principle of the Geiger counter.	**Linus Carl Pauling*** (1901–), American, for his research into the nature of chemical bonding (he also received the 1962 Nobel Prize for Peace).	**Ernest Hemingway*** (1899–1961), U.S. novelist and short story writer.
Willis E. Lamb, Jr. (1913–), American, for his discoveries concerning the structure of the hydrogen spectrum; shared with **Polykarp Kusch** (1911–), German-born American, for determining the magnetic moment of the electron.	**Vincent Du Vigneaud** (1901–1978), American, for his research on biologically important sulfur compounds and for synthesizing a polypeptidic hormone.	**Halldór Kiljan Laxness** (1902–), Icelandic novelist.
William Bradford Shockley (1910–), British-born American; **John Bardeen** (1908–), American; and **Walter Houser Brattain** (1902–), American, for development of the transistor.	**Sir Cyril Norman Hinshelwood** (1897–1967), British, and **Nikolai Nikolaevich Semyonov** (1896–1986), Russian, for their research on the mechanism of chemical chain reactions.	**Juan Ramón Jiménez** (1881–1958), Spanish lyric poet.
Tsung-dao Lee (1926–) and **Chen Ning Yang** (1922–), Chinese-born U.S. physicists, for disproving the law of conservation of parity.	**Alexander Robertus Todd, Baron Todd** (1907–), British, for his works on nucleotides and nucleotidic coenzymes (protein compounds found in cells).	**Albert Camus*** (1913–1960), French novelist.
Pavel A. Cherenkov (1904–), **Ilya Mikhailovich Frank** (1908–), and **Igor Y. Tamm** (1895–1971), Russian physicists, for discovery and interpretation of the Cherenkov effect, the emission of light when a charged particle passes through a medium faster than the speed of light in that medium.	**Frederick Sanger** (1918–), British, for his research on the structure of proteins, especially insulin.	**Boris Leonidovich Pasternak*** (1890–1960), Soviet novelist and poet (prize declined).
Emilio Gino Segrè (1905–1989), Italian-born American, and **Owen Chamberlain** (1920–), American, for demonstrating the existence of the antiproton (a proton carrying a negative charge).	**Jaroslav Heyrovsky** (1890–1967), Czech, for inventing and developing the polarographic method of analysis.	**Salvatore Quasimodo*** (1901–1968), Italian poet.
Donald Arthur Glaser (1926–), American, for the invention of the bubble chamber used for studying subatomic particles.	**Willard Frank Libby** (1908–1980), American, for developing radiocarbon dating techniques.	**Saint-John Perse** pseudonym of Alexis Saint-Léger Léger (1887–1971), French poet and diplomat.
Robert Hofstadter (1915–), American, for his research on nucleons; shared with **Rudolf Ludwig Mössbauer** (1929–), German, for developing a method of producing and measuring recoil-free gamma rays.	**Melvin Calvin** (1911–), American scientist, for his research on photosynthesis.	**Ivo Andrić** (1892–1975), Yugoslav novelist.

THE NOBEL PRIZE WINNERS

Year	Peace	Physiology and Medicine	Physics
1962	**Linus Carl Pauling*** (1901–), U.S. chemist, leader of a worldwide campaign against atmospheric nuclear testing culminating in the UN Test Ban Treaty.	**Francis Harry Compton Crick*** (1916–), British biologist; **James Dewey Watson*** (1928–), U.S. biologist; and **Maurice Hugh Frederick Wilkins*** (1916–), British molecular biologist, for discovering the molecular structure of DNA and the role it plays in transferring genetic information.	**Lev Davidovich Landau** (1908–1968), Russian, for his research on condensed gases, especially liquid helium.
1963	**International Committee of the Red Cross** (winner of the 1917 and 1944 Nobel awards) and the **League of Red Cross Societies** (the prize commemorated the 100th anniversary of the organization.)	**Sir John Carew Eccles** (1903–), Australian research physiologist; **Alan Lloyd Hodgkin** (1914–), British physiologist; and **Andrew Fielding Huxley** (1917–), British physiologist, for discovering the ionic mechanisms involved in the passage of electrical charges through nerve membranes.	**J. Hans D. Jensen** (1907–1973), German, and **Maria Goeppert Mayer*** (1906–1972), Polish-born American, for independently discovering that nuclear particles are arranged in layered shells; shared with **Eugene Paul Wigner** (1902–), Hungarian-born American, for his many contributions to nuclear physics.
1964	**Martin Luther King, Jr.*** (1929–1968), U.S. clergyman, founder and president of the Southern Christian Leadership Conference and advocate of nonviolent resistance to racial discrimination.	**Konrad E. Bloch** (1912–), German-born U.S. biochemist; and **Feodor Lynen** (1911–1979), German biochemist, for their discovery of the mechanism that regulates cholesterol and fatty acid metabolism.	**Charles H. Townes** (1915–), American, for fundamental work in quantum electronics leading to development of masers and lasers; shared with **Nikolai Gennadievich Basov** (1922–) and **Aleksandr Mikhailovich Prokhorov** (1916–), Russian physicists, for independent contributions to quantum electronics that made possible development of the laser.
1965	**United Nations Children's Fund (UNICEF),** founded in 1946 to alleviate the suffering of children throughout the world.	**François Jacob** (1920–), **André Michel Lwoff** (1902–), and **Jacques Lucien Monod** (1910–1976), French biologists, for their discovery that certain genes regulate the activity of other genes.	**Julian Seymour Schwinger** (1918–), American; **Richard Phillips Feynman** (1918–1988), American; and **Sin-itiro Tomonaga** (1906–1979), Japanese, for contributing to the theory of quantum electrodynamics.
1966	No award.	**Charles B. Huggins** (1901–), Canadian-born U.S. surgeon and cancer specialist, for discovering a hormonal treatment for prostate-gland cancer; shared with **Francis P. Rous** (1879–1970), U.S. pathologist, for demonstrating that some cancers are caused by viruses.	**Alfred Kastler** (1902–1984), French, for development of optical methods for studying the energy levels of atoms.
1967	No award.	**Haldan Keffer Hartline** (1903–1983), U.S. biophysicist; **George Wald** (1906–), U.S. biologist; and **Ragnar Arthur Granit** (1900–), Finnish-born Swedish physiologist, for their research on the physiological and chemical processes of the eye.	**Hans Albrecht Bethe** (1906–), Alsatian-born American, for his theory of how energy is produced in stars, namely by deuteron fusion and the carbon cycle.
1968	**René Cassin** (1887–1976), French jurist, an author of the Declaration of Human Rights and advocate of its adoption by the U.N.	**Robert William Holley** (1922–), U.S. biochemist; **Har Gobind Khorana** (1922–), Indian-born U.S. biochemist; and **Marshall Warren Nirenberg** (1927–), U.S. biochemist, for discovering that enzymes determine a cell's genetic function.	**Luis Walter Alvarez*** (1911–1988), American, for refining the bubble chamber technique for measuring high energy states of subatomic particles.
1969	**International Labor Organization** (ILO), founded in 1919 to promote the improvement of labor conditions throughout the world.	**Max Delbrück*** (1906–1981), German-born U.S. biologist; **Alfred D. Hershey** (1908–), U.S. biologist; and **Salvador Edward Luria** (1912–), Italian-born U.S. biologist, for discoveries concerning the replication mechanism and genetic structure of viruses.	**Murray Gell-Mann** (1929–), American, for proposing the "eightfold way," a system of unified classification for strongly interacting elementary particles.
1970	**Norman E. Borlaug*** (1914–), U.S. agronomist, director of the International Maize and Wheat Improvement Center of Mexico, an agricultural research organization dedicated to eliminating hunger and poverty.	**Sir Bernard Katz** (1911–), British biophysicist; **Ulf von Euler** (1905–1983), Swedish physiologist; and **Julius Axelrod** (1912–), U.S. pharmacologist, for their discoveries concerning hormonal transmitters at the nerve terminals and the mechanisms for their storage, release, and inactivation.	**Louis E. F. Néel** (1904–), French, for research on antiferromagnetism and ferromagnetism having important applications in solid state physics; shared with **Hannes O. G. Alfvén** (1908–), Swedish, for work in magnetohydrodynamics with application to plasma physics.
1971	**Willy Brandt*** (1913–), West German statesman who worked to ease East-West tensions over Berlin and the partition of Germany.	**Earl Wilbur Sutherland, Jr.** (1915–1974), U.S. biochemist, for his research on hormone function.	**Dennis Gabor** (1900–1979), Hungarian-born British scientist, for developing the holographic process.
1972	No award.	**Gerald M. Edelman** (1929–), U.S. biochemist, and **Dr. Rodney Porter** (1917–1985), British biochemist, for breaking down the chemical structure of antibodies.	**Dr. John Bardeen** (1908–), **Dr. Leon N. Cooper** (1930–), and **Dr. John Robert Schrieffer** (1931–), U.S. physicists, for development of a theory explaining superconductivity.
1973	**Henry A. Kissinger*** (1923–), German-born American, and **Le Duc Tho** (1911–), North Vietnamese, for negotiating the cease-fire in Vietnam.	**Karl Ritter von Frisch** (1885–1982) and **Konrad Lorenz*** (1903–1989), Austrian naturalists, and **Nikolaas Tinbergen** (1907–), Dutch zoologist, for founding the science of ethology, the systematic study of animal behavior patterns.	**Ivar Giaever** (1929–), Norwegian-born American, and **Leo Esaki** (1925–), Japanese, for their work on semi- and superconductors for miniature electronic devices; shared with Brian Josephson (1940–), British, for theoretical research on supercurrent.
1974	**Eisaku Sato** (1901–1975), former Japanese premier, for signing nuclear nonproliferation pact; shared with **Sean McBride** (1904–1988), Irish commissioner of the UN, for supervising efforts of South-West Africa to gain independent nation status.	**Albert Claude** (1898–1983), Luxembourg-born American; **Christian de Duve** (1917–), Belgian; and **George Emil Palade** (1912–), Rumanian-born American, cell biologists, for their studies of the workings of living cells.	**Sir Martin Ryle** (1918–1984) and **Anthony Hewish** (1924–), British radioastronomers, for their work in radioastrophysics, especially the discovery of pulsars.
1975	**Andrei D. Sakharov*** (1921–1989), Soviet scientist, for uncompromising work against violations of human dignity.	**David Baltimore** (1938–), American; **Howard M. Temin** (1934–), American; and **Renato Dulbecco** (1914–), Italian-born American, for discoveries of interaction between tumor virus and genetic cell material.	**James Rainwater** (1917–1986), U.S. physicist, and **Aage Bohr** (1922–) and **Ben Mottelson**, Danish physicists, for discoveries concerning the structure of the atomic nucleus.
1976	**Betty Williams** (1943–) and **Mairead Corrigan** (1944), Irish, for efforts to bring peace to Northern Ireland.	**Baruch Samuel Blumberg** (1925–) and **Daniel Carleton Gajdusek** (1923–), U.S. medical researchers, for discoveries concerning the origin and dissemination of infectious diseases.	**Burton Richter** (1931–), and **Samuel Chao Chung Ting** (1936–), U.S. physicists, for discovery, independently, of a revolutionary subatomic particle.

Nobel Prize winners who have individual biographies are indicated by an asterisk (*).

Chemistry	Literature	Economics
Max Ferdinand Perutz (1914–), Austrian-born British scientist, and **John Cowdery Kendrew** (1917–), British, for their discovery of the molecular structure of globular proteins, particularly hemoglobin and myoglobin.	**John Steinbeck*** (1902–1968), U.S. novelist.	
Giulio Natta* (1903–1979), Italian, and **Karl Ziegler** (1898–1973), German, for their research in forming macromolecular substances from simple hydrocarbons, important to the research of plastics.	**George Seferis**, pseudonym of Georgios Seferiadis (1900–1971), Greek poet, essayist, and diplomat.	
Dorothy Mary Crowfoot Hodgkin (1910–), British, for using x-rays to determine the molecular structure of biochemical compounds such as penicillin and Vitamin B_{12}.	**Jean Paul Sartre*** (1905–1980), French philosopher, playwright, and novelist.	
Robert Burns Woodward (1917–1979), American, for developing methods of totally synthesizing complex natural products, such as sterols, chlorophyll, and cholesterol.	**Mikhail Aleksandrovich Sholokhov*** (1905–1984), Soviet novelist.	
Robert Sanderson Mulliken (1896–1987), American, for his quantum mechanical theories of chemical bonding and the electrical structure of molecules.	**Shmuel Yosef Agnon**, formerly Czaczkes (1888–1970), Polish-born Israeli novelist and short story writer; shared with **Nelly Sachs*** (1891–1970), German-born Swedish poet.	
Manfred Eigen (1927–), German; **Ronald G. W. Norrish** (1897–1978), British; and **George Porter** (1920–), British, for their research on high-speed chemical reactions.	**Miguel Angel Asturias*** (1899–1974), Influential Guatemalan novelist, poet, and diplomat.	
Lars Onsager (1903–1976), Norwegian-born American, for discovering reciprocal relationships that are fundamental to certain kinds of thermodynamics, especially those in living cells.	**Yasunari Kawabata** (1899–1972), Japanese novelist.	
Odd Hassel (1897–1981), Norwegian, and **Derek Harold Richard Barton** (1918–), British, for their independent research in conformational analysis (how the three-dimensional shape of molecules relates to chemical reactions).	**Samuel Beckett*** (1906–1989), Irish novelist and playwright.	**Ragnar Frisch** (1895–1973), Norwegian, and **Jan Tinbergen** (1903–), Dutch, for the development of econometrics, the application of mathematical models to the analysis of economic processes.
Luis F. Leloir (1906–), French-born Argentine, for his discovery of sugar nucleotides and their role in the biosynthesis of carbohydrates.	**Alexander Isayevich Solzhenitsyn*** (1918–), Soviet novelist.	**Paul Anthony Samuelson** (1915–), American, for his many contributions to the field of economics, especially for raising the level of scientific analysis in economic theory.
Gerhard Herzberg (1904–), German-born Canadian, for his research on the spectra of radiation emitted by molecules and free radicals.	**Pablo Neruda***, pseudonym of Ricardo Eliezer Neftali Reyes y Basoalto (1904–1973), Chilean poet and diplomat.	**Simon Smith Kuznets** (1901–1985), Russian-born American, for contributions to the field of economics, especially for developing the concept of gross national product (GNP).
Christian Boehmer Anfinsen (1916–), **Stanford Moore** (1913–1982), and **William Howard Stein** (1911–1980), U.S. chemists, for research on the chemical structure of ribonuclease.	**Heinrich Böll** (1917–1985), German novelist and short story writer.	**Kenneth J. Arrow** (1921–), American, and **Sir John R. Hicks** (1904–1989), British, for their contributions to equilibrium and welfare theory.
Ernest Otto Fischer (1918–), German, and **Geoffrey Wilkinson** (1921–), British, for studies of organic and metallic atoms that could lead to eliminating lead, a major pollutant, from gasoline.	**Patrick White** (1912–), Australian novelist.	**Wassily Leontief** (1906–), Russian-born American, for creating the "input-output" technique to determine how various sectors of an economy interact.
Paul J. Flory (1910–1985), U.S. research chemist, for his work with macromolecules.	**Eyvind Johnson** (1900–1976), Swedish novelist and short story writer; shared with **Harry Edmund Martinson** (1904–1978), Swedish poet and novelist.	**Gunnar Myrdal*** (1898–1987), Swedish, and **Friedrich A. von Hayek** (1899–), English, for analysis of the interdependence of economic, social, and institutional phenomena.
John Warcup Cornforth (1917–), English chemist, and **Vladimir Prelog** (1906–), Swiss chemist, for studies of how properties of a chemical compound are affected by the arrangement of their atoms in three-dimensional space.	**Eugenio Montale** (1896–1981), Italian poet.	**Leonid V. Kantorovich** (1912–1986), Soviet, and **Tjalling C. Koopmans** (1910–1985), Dutch-born American, for contributing to the theory of optimum allocation of resources, which led to improved economic planning.
William Nunn Lipscomb, Jr. (1919–), American, for studies on the structure and bonding mechanism of boron-hydrogen compounds called boranes.	**Saul Bellow*** (1915–), U.S. novelist.	**Milton Friedman** (1912–), American, for achievements in consumption analysis, monetary history and theory, and for demonstrating the complexity of stabilization policy.

THE NOBEL PRIZE WINNERS *(continued)*

Year	Peace	Physiology and Medicine	Physics
1977	**Amnesty International**, founded in 1961, for its work on behalf of political prisoners.	**Rosalyn S. Yalow** (1921–), **Roger Guillemin** (1924–), born in France, and **Andrew V. Schally** (1926–), born in Poland, U.S. medical researchers, for discoveries concerning the functions of hormones in body chemistry.	**John H. Van Vleck** (1899–1980), American; **Philip W. Anderson** (1923–), American; and **Nevill F. Mott** (1905–), English, physicists, for research on the electronic structure of magnetic systems.
1978	**Anwar Sadat*** (1918–1981), Egyptian president, and **Menachem Begin*** (1913–), Israeli premier, for efforts to secure a Middle East accord.	**Werner Arber** (1929–), Swiss; **Daniel Nathans** (1928–) and **Hamilton O. Smith** (1931–), American microbiologists, for the discovery of enzymes that can break apart genetic material and isolate genes for study.	**Pëtr Kapitza** (1894–1984), Russian physicist, for work in low-temperature physics; **Arno A. Penzias** (1933–) and **Robert W. Wilson** (1936–), U.S. physicists, for discovery of cosmic microwave background radiation.
1979	**Mother Teresa*** (1910–), Yugoslav-born Indian Roman Catholic nun, for work among the lepers, the poor, and the orphans of Calcutta.	**Allan MacCleod Cormack** (1924–), U.S. physicist and **Godfrey Newbold Hounsfield*** (1919–), English medical researcher, for developing computer-assisted x-ray techniques.	**Sheldon L. Glashow** (1932–), American; **Steven Weinberg** (1933–), American, and **Abdus Salam** (1926–), Pakistani, physicists for theoretical work on forces that hold matter together.
1980	**Adolfo Pérez Esquivel** (1931–), Argentinian sculptor and architect, for his leadership of Paz y Justicia, an organization coordinating human rights activities in Latin America.	**Baruj Benacerraf** (1920–), U.S. immunologist, **George Snell** (1903–), U.S. geneticist, and **Jean Dausset** (1916–), French hematologist and immunologist, for discoveries explaining how cell structure relates to organ transplants and diseases.	**James W. Cronin** (1931–), American, and **Val L. Fitch** (1923–), American, for their work on the asymmetry of subatomic particles.
1981	**Office of the United Nations High Commissioner for Refugees**, for aiding the growing number of homeless and displaced people around the world.	**Roger W. Sperry** (1913–), U.S. neurobiologist, **David H. Hubel** (1926–), Canadian-born U.S. neurobiologist, and **Torsten N. Wiesel** (1924–), U.S. neurobiologist, for research vital to understanding the organization and functioning of the brain.	**Nicolaas Bloembergen** (1920–), Dutch-born American, **Arthur L. Schawlow** (1921–), American, and **Kai M. Siegbahn** (1918–), Swedish, for developing laser technology to analyze complex forms of matter.
1982	**Alfonso Garcia Robles** (1911–), Mexican diplomat, and **Alva Myrdal** (1902–1986), Swedish diplomat and author, for their work toward nuclear disarmament.	**Sune Bergstrom** (1916–) and **Bengt Samuelsson** (1934–), Swedish biochemists, and **John R. Vane** (1927–), British biochemist, for studies of workings of prostaglandins.	**Kenneth G. Wilson** (1936–), American, for analysis of continuous phase transistors.
1983	**Lech Walesa*** (?1943–), Polish founder of Solidarity labor union, for his nonviolent struggle for workers' rights.	**Barbara McClintock** (1902–), U.S. geneticist, for the discovery of mobile plant genes that affect heredity.	**Subrahmanyan Chandrasekhar*** (1910–), American, and **William A. Fowler** (1911–), American, for their contributions to understanding the evolution and devolution of stars.
1984	**Bishop Desmond Tutu*** (1931–), South African Anglican cleric, for his role in nonviolent opposition to apartheid.	**Cesar Milstein** (1927–), British-Argentinian immunologist, **Georges J.F. Köhler** (1946–), West German immunologist, and **Niels K. Jerne** (1911–), British-Danish immunologist, for the theory and development of a technique for producing monoclonal antibodies.	**Carlo Rubbia** (1934–), Italian, and **Simon van der Meer** (1925–), Dutch, for the discovery of subatomic particles W and Z, supporting the electroweak theory.
1985	**International Physicians for the Prevention of Nuclear War**, for their work in educating the public on the medical consequences of nuclear war.	**Michael S. Brown** (1941–) and **Joseph L. Goldstein** (1940–), U.S. molecular geneticists, for studies in cholesterol metabolism.	**Klaus von Klitzing** (1943–), West German, for the discovery of the quantized Hall effect, permitting exact measurements of electrical resistance.
1986	**Elie Wiesel** (1928–), Rumanian-born U.S. writer, in recognition of his life's work as an author, playwright, speaker, and witness to the Holocaust.	**Rita Levi-Montalcini** (1909–), U.S.-Italian developmental biologist, and **Stanley Cohen** (1922–), U.S. biochemist, for the discovery of chemical agents that help regulate cell growth.	**Ernst Ruska** (1906–1988), German, **Gerd Binnig** (1947–), German, and **Heinrich Rohrer** (1933–), Swiss, for pioneering work in electron microscope design.
1987	**Oscar Arias Sánchez** (1941–), Costa Rican president, for his efforts on behalf of a Central American peace plan.	**Susumu Tonegawa** (1939–), Japanese immunologist, for his discoveries in the area of antibody production.	**Karl Alex Müller** (1927–), Swiss, and **J. Georg Bednorz** (1950–), German, for their breakthrough work on superconductors.
1988	**United Nations peacekeeping forces** for their contribution to reducing tensions throughout the world.	**Gertrude B. Elion** (1918–) and **George C. Hitchings** (1905–), U.S. biochemists, and **Sir James Black** (1924–), British pharmacologist, for their discovery of principles important for drug treatment.	**Leon Max Lederman** (1922–), **Jack Steinberger** (1921–), and **Melvin Schwartz** (1932–), U.S. physicists, for subatomic particle discoveries.
1989	**Dalai Lama** (1935–), Tibetan exiled religious and political leader, for his persistent, nonviolent campaign to end China's domination of Tibet.	**J. Michael Bishop** (1936–) and **Harold E. Varmus** (1939–), U.S. medical researchers, for their work on cancer-causing genes.	**Norman F. Ramsey** (1915–), American, for development of the atomic clock; **Hans G. Dehmelt** (1922–), German-born American, and **Wolfgang Paul** (1913–), West German, for their work on methods of isolating atoms and subatomic particles for study.

Nobel Prize winners who have individual biographies are indicated by an asterisk (*).

ALBERT EINSTEIN
Physics 1921

THE BETTMANN ARCHIVE

SIGRID UNDSET
Literature 1928

NORWEGIAN EMBASSY INFORMATION SERVICE

Chemistry	Literature	Economics
Ilya Prigogine (1917–), Belgian, for studies expanding thermodynamic theory.	**Vicente Aleixandre** (1898–1984), Spanish poet.	**Bertil Ohlin** (1899–1979), Swedish, and **James Meade** (1907–), English, for contributions to the theory of international trade and international capital movements.
Peter Mitchell (1920–), English chemist, for work with the chemical processes responsible for the energy supply in living cells.	**Isaac Bashevis Singer*** (1904–), Polish-born U.S. novelist.	**Herbert A. Simon** (1916–), American, for research into the methods used by large, complex organizations in making business decisions.
Herbert C. Brown (1912–), English-born American, and **Georg Wittig** (1897–1987), German, chemists, for developing the use of boron- and phosphorous-containing compounds in organic synthesis.	**Odysseus Elytis**, pseudonym of Odysseus Alepoudhelis (1911–), Greek poet.	**Theodore W. Schultz** (1902–), U.S. agricultural economist and **Sir Arthur Lewis** (1915–), West Indian-born British political economist, for research into problems of developing countries.
Paul Berg (1926–), American, for the first preparation of a hybrid DNA, and **Walter Gilbert** (1932–), American, and **Frederick Sanger** (1918–), British, for the development of chemical and biological analyses of DNA structure.	**Czeslaw Milosz** (1911–), Lithuanian-born Polish-American poet, novelist, and educator.	**Lawrence R. Klein** (1920–), American, for the development and analysis of empirical models of business fluctuations.
Fukui Kenichi (1918–), Japanese, and **Roald Hoffmann** (1937–), Polish-born American, for the orbital symmetry interpretation of chemical reactions.	**Elias Canetti*** (1905–), Bulgarian-born German writer.	**James Tobin** (1918–), American, for analyses of financial markets and their influence and the spending and saving by families and businesses.
Aaron Klug (1926–), Lithuanian-born British scientist, for the determination of the structure of biological substances.	**Gabriel García Márquez*** (1928–), Colombian writer.	**George J. Stigler** (1911–), American, for studies of the economic effects of government regulation.
Henry Taube (1915–), Canadian-born American, for the study of electron transfer reactions.	**William Golding** (1911–), English author.	**Gerard Debreu** (1921–), American, for mathematical proof of the supply and demand theory.
Bruce Merrifield (1921–), American, for the development of a method of polypeptide synthesis.	**Jaroslav Seifert** (1902–1986), Czech author.	**Sir Richard Stone** (1913–), British, for the development of national income accounting systems.
Herbert A. Hauptman (1917–), American, and **Jerome Karle** (1918–), American, for the development of a way to map the chemical structures of small molecules.	**Claude Simon** (1913–), French novelist.	**Franco Modigliani** (1918–), Italian-born American, for analyses of household savings and of financial markets.
Yuan T. Lee (1936–), American, **Dudley R. Herschbach** (1932–), American, and **John C. Polanyi**, Canadian, for contributions to detailed understanding of chemical reactions.	**Wole Soyinka** (1934–), Nigerian poet.	**James M. Buchanan** (1919–), American, for methods of analyzing economic and political decision-making.
Jean-Marie Lehn (1939–), French, **Donald J. Cram** (1919–), American, and **Charles J. Pedersen** (1904–1989), American, for their work on producing synthetic molecules.	**Joseph Brodsky*** (1940–), Russian-born American poet and essayist.	**Robert M. Solow** (1924–), American, for contributions to the understanding of economic growth.
Johann Deisenhofer (1943–), **Hartmut Michel** (1948–), and **Robert Huber** (1937–), West German biochemists, for research on molecular structures.	**Naguib Mahfouz** (1911–), Egyptian novelist, playwright, and screenwriter.	**Maurice Allais** (1911–), French economist, for theories relating to monopolies and state-run enterprises.
Sidney Altman (1939–), Canadian-American, and **Thomas R. Cech** (1947–), American, for their work on the role of RNA as a catalyst.	**Camilio José Cela** (1916–), Spanish novelist.	**Trygve Haavelmo** (1911–), Norwegian, for his work on methods of testing economic theory.

DAG HAMMARSKJOLD
Peace 1961

UNITED NATIONS

ALEKSANDR SOLZHENITSYN
Literature 1970

HARPER & ROW

GODFREY HOUNSFIELD
Physiology and Medicine 1979

UPI/BETTMANN NEWSPHOTOS

U.N. PEACEKEEPING FORCES
Peace 1988

M. ATTAR/SYGMA

MEN AND WOMEN OF THE 1980'S

A

Abdul-Jabbar, Kareem (1947–), U.S. basketball player, born Lew Alcindor. He led UCLA to three national titles, 1967–1969, and won the Rookie of the Year Award, 1970, while playing for the Milwaukee Bucks of the National Basketball Association. Named the NBA's most valuable player six times between 1971 and 1980, Abdul-Jabbar was traded to the Los Angeles Lakers in 1975. Standing seven feet, three inches, he is one of the great scorers of basketball history.

Allen, Woody (1935–), U.S. film actor and director, born Allen Stewart Konigsberg. A former television writer and stand-up comic, he had a major success as author and star of the Broadway hit *Play It Again, Sam* in 1969. Some of his best-known films are *Bananas* (1971), *Love and Death* (1975), *Annie Hall* (1977, Academy Award), *Manhattan* (1979), and *Broadway Danny Rose* (1983). He received an Academy Award in 1987 for his screenplay *Hannah and Her Sisters.*.

Aquino, Corazon (Cojuangco) (1933–), president of the Philippines. Born into a wealthy and educated provincial family, she became a traditional wife and mother. Her life was dramatically altered by the political successes and ordeals of her husband, Benigno Aquino. As the man most likely to succeed the dictatorial president Ferdinand Marcos, Aquino was imprisoned under martial law and eventually murdered in 1983, allegedly by Marcos's soldiers. Mrs. Aquino led the opposition in demanding Marcos's resignation, at first only as a symbolic leader, then as a formal presidential candidate capable of winning unified support. After the election, both Aquino and Marcos claimed victory. Huge demonstrations, however, and a military rebellion caused Marcos to leave the country. Aquino was declared president on February 25, 1986.

Arafat, Yasir (1929–), Palestinian commando or *fedayeen* leader. As an officer in the Egyptian army, he fought against the French and British in 1956. He became head of the military arm of Al Fatah (Movement for the Liberation of Palestine), and in 1969 was named executive chairman of the Palestine Liberation Organization. A believer in armed conflict as the only solution to the Palestine question, Arafat and his *fedayeen* harassed Israel with small-scale acts of violence against both military and civilian targets. He was acclaimed by Arab leaders, 1974, as the only legitimate voice of the Palestinian people. In 1982, after the Israeli campaign in Lebanon and attacks on PLO military bases, Arafat and his guerrillas agreed to leave Lebanon, but they still play a pivotal role in Middle East politics.

Atwood, Margaret (1939–), Canadian poet and novelist. Educated at the University of Toronto and Radcliffe College in Cambridge, Mass., in 1966 she won Canada's highest literary prize for *The Circle Game,* her first book of poetry. Her novels include *The Edible Woman* (1969), *Surfacing* (1972), *Bodily Harm* (1982), and *The Handmaid's Tale* (1985). Atwood is noted for her clean, taut style and powerful introspection.

B

Bentsen, Lloyd M., Jr. (1921–), U.S. senator and Democratic Vice Presidential nominee, 1988. Born in Mission, Texas, he received a law degree from the University of Texas in 1942. He flew 50 missions as a bomber pilot in World War II and was shot down twice. After serving in the U.S. House of Representatives, 1949–1954, he returned to Texas and, backed by his father, a wealthy rancher and developer, he founded a successful insurance company. In 1970 Bentsen defeated George Bush for the U.S. Senate; he won reelection in 1976, 1982, and 1988. He served on the Finance Committee, becoming its chairman in 1986, and on the Intelligence and Environment and Public Works committees.

Bhutto, Benazir (1953–), Pakistani political leader, daughter of President Zulfikar Ali Bhutto, who was deposed by a military coup in 1977 and hanged two years later for conspiring to mur-

CORAZON AQUINO

REUTERS/BETTMANN NEWSPHOTOS

YASIR ARAFAT

UPI/BETTMANN NEWSPHOTOS

der a party colleague. She attended Radcliffe College in Cambridge, Mass., and Oxford University, where she became the first woman to be elected president of the Oxford Union (a debating society). Arrested in 1977 for protest activities against the new regime of General Zia ul-Haq, she frequently was held under house arrest until 1984, when she settled in London. She returned to Pakistan in 1986. After the death of General Zia in a plane crash in 1988, she emerged as one of the key figures in Pakistan's return to civilian government.

Bird, Larry Joe (1956–), U.S. basketball player, forward for the Boston Celtics since 1979. He accepted a scholarship to Indiana State University in 1974, and during his first season in the lineup averaged over 32 points a game. Considered the most complete team player in the National Basketball Association since Oscar Robertson, Bird is a formidable passer and shooter with an awesome sense of anticipation. He was voted the NBA's most valuable player in 1984, 1985, and 1986.

Blackmun, Harry Andrew (1908–), U.S. associate justice of the Supreme Court. He was graduated from Harvard Law School in 1932 and practiced law until 1959, when he became a federal circuit court judge. President Nixon appointed him to the Supreme Court in 1970. Blackmun is noted for his humanistic and liberal opinions on civil rights issues.

Boesky, Ivan Frederick (1937–), U.S. investment banker and central figure in a famous financial scandal. Son of a Russian immigrant, he studied law, turned to investment banking at age 30, and formed his own corporation in 1975. His goal, publicly expressed, was to control the largest amount of money in the world. As head of the biggest Wall Street arbitrage firm, in 1986 he agreed to pay a penalty of $100 million—half of it in fines to the Securities and Exchange Commission for violating insider trading rules, half to a fund to compensate wronged investors. He was sentenced to three years in prison and was barred from operating as a broker-dealer in the United States.

Botha, Pieter Willem (1916–), South African political leader. He was a full-time worker for the ruling National Party at age 20 and was elected to parliament in 1948. Named minister of colored affairs in 1961, minister of public works in 1964, and defense minister in 1966, Botha became National Party leader and prime minister in 1978, at a time of increasingly violent black revolt against white rule. A staunch supporter of apartheid, the South African system of racial segregation and white supremacy, Botha has nevertheless introduced limited reforms in an effort to appease critics of apartheid.

Bradley, William Warren (1943–), U.S. senator, former basketball star. From an early age he combined academic excellence with exceptional athletic talent. A member of the winning U.S. basketball team at the 1964 Olympic Games, he refused an offer from the New York Knickerbockers and took a Rhodes Scholarship to Oxford University. Bradley did sign with the Knicks in 1966 and played with the team for ten seasons. He entered the New Jersey senatorial race in 1978 and won the support of labor and minority groups with his liberal programs. As one of the youngest senators, he is considered an expert on energy issues.

Brennan, William Joseph, Jr. (1906–), U.S. associate justice of the Supreme Court. A graduate of Harvard Law School, he was a justice of the New Jersey Supreme Court from 1952 to 1956, when President Eisenhower appointed him to serve on the High Court. Brennan has been an advocate of individual liberties and equal justice for the poor.

C

Chandrasekhar, Subrahmanyan (1910–), Indian-born U.S. astrophysicist. He studied at Madras University in India and obtained a Ph.D. at Cambridge University in 1933. After moving to the United States to take up research at the University of Chicago, he formulated his theory of the evolution of stars in *An Introduction to the Study of Stellar Structure* (1939), thus preparing the way for the discovery of black holes. He has since changed his area of study every eight or ten years, determined to acquire "a perspective on an entire area" rather than a single problem. He shared the 1983 Nobel Prize for Physics with William A. Fowler.

Chavez, Cesar Estrada (1927–), U.S. labor leader and Chicano activist, founder of the United Farm Workers. Son of a migrant worker, he organized the National Farm Workers Association in California in 1962. In 1965 Chavez led 2000 NFWA members on a strike against the grape growers and called for a consumer boycott, attracting much sympathy and support for the workers and for his nonviolent methods. The NFWA merged with the AFL-CIO in 1966; growers began signing labor contracts with the unions in 1970. Since 1975 farm workers in California have had the legal right to collective bargaining.

Chirac, Jacques René (1932–), French politician, prime minister of France, 1974–1976 and 1986–1988. A graduate of the Institut d'Études Politiques de Paris in 1954, he quickly rose to the rank of minister. President Giscard d'Estaing named him prime minister in 1974. He resigned two years later after a falling-out with Giscard, and set about reorganizing the Union of Democrats for the Republic into a neo-Gaullist group. Chirac was elected mayor of Paris in 1977 and was appointed prime minister by the socialist president Francois Mitterand in 1986. He was replaced after the socialist victory in 1988.

Coppola, Francis Ford (1939–), U.S. film director and screenwriter who made his first film, *Dementia 13,* at the age of 23. One of the few directors with a graduate degree in filmmaking, he has written or collaborated on such films as *Reflections in a Golden Eye* (1967), *Patton* (1970), and *The Great Gatsby* (1974). Coppola wrote and directed *The Godfather* (1972) and *The Godfather, Part II* (1974), both winners of several Academy Awards, as well as *Black Stallion* (1979) and *Apocalypse Now* (1979).

Cosby, Bill (William Henry, Jr.) (1937–), U.S. comedian, actor, and author. Beloved by audiences of all ages and races, Cosby has built his gentle humor on the commonplace events of family life. He starred in several award-winning television series, such as *I Spy* (1965–1968) and the cartoon series *Fat Albert and the Cosby Kids* (1972–1984). Cosby's film experience includes roles in *Uptown Saturday Night* (1974) and *A Piece of the Action* (1977). His television series *The Cosby Show* in the 1980's became one of the most popular comedies in TV history.

Crumb, George Henry, Jr. (1929–), U.S. composer. He studied with Ross Lee Finney and Boris Blacher, and received a number of grants and awards, including the Pulitzer Prize (1968) for his *Echoes of Time and the River.* His works are innovative and varied in

BILL COSBY

UPI/BETTMANN NEWSPHOTOS

style, with frequent use of electric or amplified instruments, unusual vocal effects, and occasional citations from familiar works by other composers. Among his pieces are *Ancient Voices of Children* (to a text by Garcia Lorca, 1970), *Star-Child* (1977), and *Celestial Mechanics (Makrokosmos IV)* (1979).

D

Dukakis, Michael Stanley (1933–), governor of Massachusetts and Democratic Presidential nominee, 1988. Born in Brookline, Massachusetts, he was governor of Massachusetts from 1975–1979 and 1983– . Dukakis graduated from Swarthmore College and served in the Army in Korea from 1955–1957. He earned a law degree from Harvard University in 1960. He served three terms in the state House of Representatives but was defeated for lieutenant governor in 1970. Running for governor in 1974, he campaigned against poor management and excessive political patronage. In his first term he had to cut social programs and raise taxes to offset a $600 million deficit. He was defeated for nomination to a second term but was reelected governor in 1982 and 1986. Dukakis received national attention for the "Massachusetts miracle," an economic upsurge during his second term. In the Democratic Presidential primary, he emerged as front runner in a field of seven and clinched the nomination with victories in California and New Jersey.

F

Falwell, Jerry (1933–), U.S. fundamentalist clergyman, founder of the conservative political lobbying organization Moral Majority, Inc. He established the Thomas Road Baptist Church in Lynchburg, Va., 1956, and soon after presented his first religious television program, the *Old-Time Gospel Hour.* By mobilizing supporters into political action, Falwell is considered to have contributed to Ronald Reagan's victory in the 1980 Presidential election. He resigned from the Moral Majority in 1987 to devote full time to his ministry.

Ferraro, Geraldine Anne (1935–), U.S. politician and Democratic Vice Presidential nominee in 1984. Daughter of an Italian immigrant, she earned a law degree while teaching in Queens, N.Y., public schools. She practiced law as a civil attorney and assistant district attorney before winning election to the U.S. House of Representatives in 1978. She was chosen by Walter Mondale to be his running mate in the 1984 Presidential campaign, becoming the first woman to appear on a major political party's national ticket.

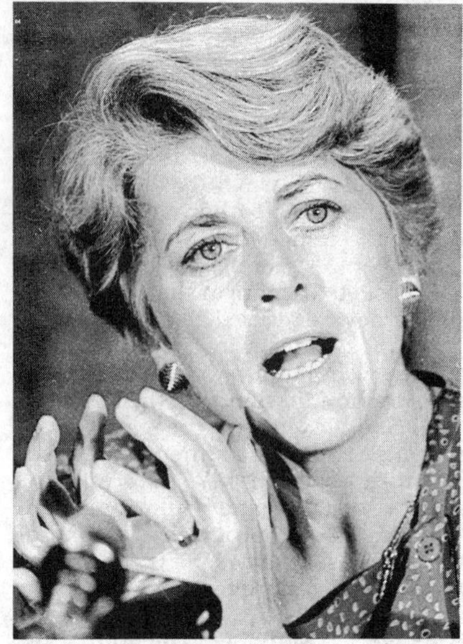
UPI/BETTMANN NEWSPHOTOS

GERALDINE FERRARO

Fossey, Dian (1932–1985), U.S. naturalist and author, one of the world's leading authorities on gorillas. She made her first trip to Africa in 1963, returning three years later at the invitation of anthropologist Louis B. Leakey to study the mountain gorillas of Zaire. Fossey spent the next 19 years in Rwanda examining gorilla habits and social structure and trying to ward off poachers. She was found murdered at her camp in the Virunga Mountains.

G

Gallo, Robert Charles (1937–), U.S. hematologist and virologist, head of the research team that identified human T-cell leukemia virus as the cause of AIDS (acquired immune deficiency syndrome). Publication of the discovery came one year after another team at France's Pasteur Institute indicated an imprecisely defined and differently named virus as the cause of the disease. After an intense scientific battle, the Albert Lasker Award was given to both Gallo and Dr. Luc Montagnier of the Pasteur Institute, with their respective teams, in recognition of their contributions to identifying the AIDS virus.

WAYNE GRETZKY

UPI/BETTMANN NEWSPHOTOS

García Márquez, Gabriel (1928–), Colombian novelist, winner of the 1982 Nobel Prize in Literature, and a major figure among Latin American authors. Many of his works are chronicles of the imaginary town of Macondo, blending a high degree of realism with elements of fantasy. His writings include *Leaf Storm and Other Stories* (1955), *One Hundred Years of Solitude* (1967), *The Autumn of the Patriarch* (1975), *Chronicles of a Death Foretold* (1981), and *Love in the Time of Cholera* (1988).

Gordimer, Nadine (1923–), South African novelist, short story writer, and civil libertarian, born in the Transvaal. A self-described natural writer, her fiction explores the confrontation between Europe and Africa, themes of alienation and exile. Among her best-known works are *A World of Strangers* (1958), *A Guest of Honor* (1970), *Burger's Daughter* (1979), which was banned briefly in South Africa, and *A Sport of Nature* (1987).

Gretzky, Wayne (1961–), hockey superstar known as the Great Gretzky. He began playing organized hockey at age six, turned professional at 17, and joined the Edmonton Oilers one year before its entry into the National Hockey League. He has since broken records for most points in one season, most assists in one season, and most points per game. He won the Ross Trophy and the Hart Most Valuable Player award six years running. In a controversial move, he was traded to the Los Angeles Kings in 1988.

H

Hesburgh, Theodore Martin (1917–), U.S. Roman Catholic clergyman, public servant and teacher, president of the University of Notre Dame for 35 years. After introducing social and educational reforms in the early years of his presidency, Hesburgh was able to increase Notre Dame's outside funding dramatically. New departments and graduate schools were created, along with a multitude of special projects. He was appointed to the U.S. Commission on Civil Rights in 1957 and became one of its most outspoken members. One of a few university leaders to survive the campus turbulence of the 1960's, he condemned the U.S. incursion into Cambodia and called for a restructuring of the military draft. He was chairman of the Overseas Development Council and headed the U.S. delegation to the UN Conference on Science and Technology for Development. He also has served on the board of numerous nonprofit organizations.

Hounsfield, Godfrey Newbold (1919–), British scientist and corecipient of the 1979 Nobel Prize in Medicine. After doing research on radar systems during World War II, he worked in solid-state computer design and in 1967 began to explore connections between computer technology and x-ray photography. In 1971 the first working model of his x-ray scanning system, called computerized axial tomography (the CAT or CT scanner), was installed in a hospital.

Hurt, William (1950–), U.S. film and stage actor. He earned a degree in theology at Tufts University and in 1972 began to study acting with John Houseman at the Juilliard School in New York. He worked with the Circle Repertory Company, winning an Obie Award for his role in the play *My Life,* by Corinne Jacker. Some of his best-known films are *Body Heat* (1981), *The Kiss of the Spider Woman* (1985), *Children of a Lesser God* (1986), and *Broadcast News* (1987).

I

Iacocca, Lee (Lido Anthony) (1924–), U.S. industrialist, president of the Ford Motor Company and chairman of the board of Chrysler Corporation. He began working for Ford upon graduating from college, and spent a decade in sales and marketing. In 1964 he introduced the Ford Mustang at the New York World's Fair; the resulting record sales of the car ensured his promotion in the company. He was named president in 1970. In 1978 Iacocca moved to Chrysler Corporation, where the part he played in saving the financially troubled company made him world famous. His books *Iacocca: An Autobiography* (1984) and *Talking Straight* (1988) became best sellers.

J

Jackson, Jesse Louis (1941–), U.S. clergyman and civic leader, chairman of the National Rainbow Coalition. He was chosen by Martin Luther King, Jr., to head the Chicago arm of Operation Breadbasket, 1966, a program to obtain more jobs and better conditions for blacks. In 1971 he founded Operation PUSH (People United to Save Humanity) and worked to stem the tide of drug abuse and other problems in urban schools and neighborhoods. Jackson entered the race for the 1984 Democratic Presidential nomination, gaining wide support after he negotiated with Syrian president Hafez al-Assad for release of a captive U.S. Navy pilot. Although Jackson lost the nomination, his campaign inspired millions of the underprivileged to register to vote and thus enter the political process. He ran for the nomination again in 1988, finishing second behind Michael Dukakis.

Jackson, Michael Joseph (1958–), U.S. singer, dancer, and song writer, a member of the popular family group the Jackson Five. With his high tenor voice, angelic face, and exuberant dancing, he became the idol of millions of teenagers. Among his most famous songs are "Blame It on the Boogie," "Don't Stop 'Til You've Had Enough," and the album *Thriller* (1982), produced by Quincy Jones. Jackson gave a memorable film performance as Scarecrow in *The Wiz* (1978), the black rock version of *The Wizard of Oz.* His autobiographical *Moonwalk* was a best-seller in 1988.

Jarvik, Robert Koffler (1946–), U.S. physician, inventor, and businessman, a major designer of the first artificial heart to be implanted in a human patient. As an assistant to Dr. Willem Kolff at the Institute for Biomedical Engineering of the University of Utah, he worked on increasing the efficiency of an existing artificial organ being tested in animals; he produced the Jarvik-3 in 1972. In the mid-70's he developed the smaller Jarvik-7 and assisted Dr. William DeVries in implanting the device in Barney Clark, a victim of degenerative heart disease; Clark lived for 112 days. The second recipient, William Schroeder, lived for a record 620 days. In 1988, however, the National Institutes for Health halted further funding for artificial heart research, citing continuing severe complications.

K

Karajan, Herbert von (1908–1989), Austrian conductor, lifetime director of the Berlin Philharmonic Orchestra, whose recordings are esteemed throughout the world. His career, spanning almost 60 years, has included the directorship of the Berlin State Opera (1938, where he succeeded Wilhelm Furtwängler), the Vienna State Opera, and the Vienna Philharmonic Orchestra, 1956. Denied official status as a conductor because of his alleged role in the Nazi Party during World War II, he was cleared by the Allied Denazification Commission in 1947. He has made countless appearances as guest conductor and led music festivals at Salzburg, Bayreuth, and Edinburgh.

ROBERT JARVIK

UPI/BETTMANN NEWSPHOTOS

Kennedy, Anthony M. (1936–), U.S. associate justice of the Supreme Court, appointed by President Reagan in 1987. Born in Sacramento, California, he earned a degree in politics from Stanford and a law degree from Harvard in 1961. In 1976 he was appointed to the Ninth Circuit Court of Appeals, where he participated in 1400 decisions and authored more than 400. He is generally regarded as a pragmatic conservative.

Khomeini, Ruhollah (1900–1989), Iranian Shiite Muslim religious leader, known as the Ayatollah Khomeini, born Ruhollah Hendi. He was arrested in 1963 and banished by Muhammad Reza Shah Pahlevi for his public denunciation of the Shah's efforts to westernize Iran. After the collapse of the Shah's government in 1979, Khomeini returned from Paris to declare an Islamic republic. He became the virtual dictator of Iran. His reign has been marked by the taking of U.S. hostages, 1979–1981, and by war with Iraq, 1980, in which a cease-fire was arranged in 1988. His policy of isolation and antiwesternism is said to have caused his authority to decline.

L

Le Carré, John (1931–), British novelist, born David John Moore Cornwell. After attending the universities of Berne and Oxford, he spent five years in the British foreign service. His third novel, *The Spy Who Came in From the Cold* (1963), challenged the popular romantic spy story with its use of bleak realism and subtle exploration of character. Other works include *A Small Town in Germany* (1968), *Tinker, Tailor, Soldier, Spy* (1974), *The Little Drummer Girl* (1983), and *A Perfect Spy* (1986).

M

Madonna (1958–), U.S. singer and actress, born Madonna Louise Veronica Ciccone, an idol of pop culture noted for her extravagant dress and exuberantly aggressive style. Her fame was established by her music videos, the album *Like a Virgin* (1984), and the song "Material Girl," as well as her starring role in the film *Desperately Seeking Susan* (1985). Her third album, *True Blue* (1986), was a huge commercial and critical success.

Mandela, Nelson Rohihlahla (1918–), South African lawyer and prominent black nationalist leader, sentenced to life imprisonment in 1964 for his activities against the ruling National Party's apartheid policies. He joined the African National Congress in 1944 and played an important role in the 1952 Defiance Against Unjust Laws campaign organized by the ANC and the Indian Congress. Jailed on several occasions, Mandela was given a life sentence for his involvement with the underground ANC military group known as Umkonto We Sizwe (Spear of the Nation). He received the Jawaharlal Nehru Award (1979) and the Bruno Kreisky Prize for Human Rights (1981). *No Easy Walk to Freedom* (1965) is a collection of some of his speeches and writings.

His wife, South African activist and community leader **Winnie Mandela** (?1936–), was exiled for an indefinite period to the rural town of Brandfort as punishment for her role in assisting victims of the 1976 Soweto uprising. After her house and clinic were bombed in 1985, she returned to her home near Johannesburg in defiance of government orders. Special restrictions on her activity were removed in 1986.

Marsalis, Wynton (1961–), U.S. trumpet virtuoso adept at both jazz and classical music. After studying at the Juilliard School on full scholarship, he joined Art Blakey and the Jazz Messengers, played with Herbie Hancock's V.S.O.P. quartet, and in 1981 formed his own band with his brother Branford Marsalis. He is noted for the beauty of his tone and his impressive technical facility.

Marshall, Thurgood (1908–), U.S. associate justice of the Supreme Court, 1967– . In 1935 Marshall joined the legal staff of the National Association for the Advancement of Colored People (NAACP) and in 1938 became its chief legal officer. He argued more than 30 civil rights cases before the Supreme Court, winning most of them, including the landmark school desegregation case (*Brown* v. *Board of Education,* 1954). In 1961 Marshall was appointed to the U.S. Court of Appeals, but in 1965 he resigned to become U.S. solicitor general. He was appointed to the High Court by President Lyndon Johnson.

McAuliffe, (Sharon) Christa (1948–1986), U.S. high school teacher, wife, and mother of two children. She was chosen in a nationwide competition in 1985 as the first nonprofessional to go into orbit aboard the space shuttle *Challenger.* She trained for the flight at the NASA center in Houston. She and six other astronauts were killed on January 29, 1986, when *Challenger* exploded a few moments after liftoff.

Morita, Akio (1921–), Japanese industrialist, co-founder and director of the Sony company. A 1944 graduate in physics of Osaka Imperial University, he organized the Tokyo Tsushin Kogyo (Tokyo Telecommunications Company) after World War II with a modest outlay of capital. Before the Sony enterprise was formed in 1958, Morita brought out the first transistor radio, 1955. All-transistor television was in-

AYATOLLAH KHOMEINI

UPI/BETTMANN NEWSPHOTOS

troduced in 1959, followed by transistorized video recorders in 1960. Rather than exporting cheap imitations of Western products, Sony has concentrated on offering consumers quality electronics at reasonable prices. The company was the first in Japan to offer stock on the U.S. exchanges, 1963.

Murdoch, (Keith) Rupert (1931–), Australian newspaper publisher and entrepreneur, known for his sensationalist journalism. The owner of newspapers on three continents, including the *Sunday Mail* and *The* (Adelaide) *News* in Australia, the London *Times* and the *Sunday Times* in Great Britain, and the Boston *Herald* in the United States, Murdoch has increased the circulation of many publications through his emphasis on stories of crime and scandal, extensive sports coverage, and conservative editorials. He acquired Twentieth Century-Fox Film Corporation in 1985 and then bought six independent U.S. television stations, consolidating all into a new enterprise, Fox, Inc.

REUTERS/BETTMANN NEWSPHOTOS

LUCIANO PAVAROTTI

N

Naipaul, V. S. (Vidiadhar Surajprasad) (1932–), West Indian novelist and essayist, born in Trinidad. Considered the West Indies' finest modern writer, and a winner of many literary awards, Naipaul first gained recognition with the publication of *A House for Mr. Biswas* (1961). His later works include travel essays such as *The Middle Passage* (1962) and *The Loss of El Dorado* (1969), a view of Trinidadian history, and the novels *Guerrillas* (1975) and *A Bend in the River* (1979). Naipaul is noted for his portrayal of today's "new synthetic world" and his sense of the tragicomic in ordinary people.

Nakasone, Yasuhiro (1918–), Japanese statesman. A lieutenant commander in the imperial navy during World War II, he entered politics in 1946 and the next year was elected to the House of Representatives for the first of 14 consecutive terms. As minister of state and director general of defense, 1970, he signed a U.S.-sponsored nuclear nonproliferation treaty for Japan. He became minister of international trade and industry under the Tanaka government, 1972–1974, later campaigning to introduce a system of public election of the prime minister. As prime minister from 1982 to 1987, he tried to strengthen ties with the United States through trade and to stimulate the Japanese economy.

Navratilova, Martina (1956–), a Czech-born tennis player, the powerhouse of women's tennis. Her left-handed serve has been timed at 93 miles an hour. Czech national champion from 1972 to 1975, she defected while on tour in the United States and became a U.S. citizen in 1981. Five-time winner of the Wimbledon singles and six-time doubles champion, her victories in the French, Wimbledon, U.S., and Australian championships have brought her six grand slam titles in a row. She was named to the Women's Sports Hall of Fame in 1984.

O

Oates, Joyce Carol (1938–), U.S. novelist, poet, and playwright. The characters in her stories are often desperate people trapped in a meaningless or precarious existence. *Them* (1969), a novel of the Detroit slums, won the National Book Award in 1970. Other works include *A Garden of Earthly Delights* (1967), *Unholy Loves* (1979), and the short story collection *The Goddess and Other Women* (1974).

O'Connor, Sandra Day (1930–), U.S. associate justice of the Supreme Court, considered a conservative. She was graduated from Stanford Law School in 1952 and took up law practice in Arizona. Active in Republican politics, she was assistant state attorney general, 1965–1969, state senator, 1969–1974, and judge in the state superior and appellate courts, 1974–1979. President Reagan named her to the seat vacated by Potter Stewart in 1981. She is the first woman to sit on the Supreme Court.

P

Palme, Sven Olof Joachim (1927–1986), Swedish politician and government official. Born to an aristocratic family, he completed part of his education in the United States. He joined the Social Democratic Party and was elected to parliament in 1956, later becoming minister of communications and minister of education. As prime minister from 1969–1976 and again from 1982–1986, he openly protested the U.S. presence in Vietnam and put great strain on U.S.-Swedish relations. He was assassinated in Stockholm by an unidentified man.

Pavarotti, Luciano (1935–), Italian tenor, the most idolized operatic singer since Enrico Caruso. After engagements throughout Europe in the 1960's, he made his debut with the Metropolitan Opera in New York in 1968 as Rodolfo in *La Bohème.* An unqualified success and able to command huge fees, he has starred in operas such as *Tosca, Rigoletto,* and *La Traviata* and has appeared in recitals in the United States, Europe, and Japan.

Penderecki, Krzysztof (1933–), Polish composer. The first major musical figure to benefit from the increased artistic freedom allowed in Poland after 1956, he has written works noted for unconventional sonorities and performance techniques. He designed a system of notation to indicate special effects such as hissing and shouting, percussive tapping of the fingers, white noise, and aleatory passages, in which some elements are left to the performer's discretion. Among his compositions are the *St. Luke Passion* (1963–1966) and *Dies Irae* ("Auschwitz Oratorio") (1967).

Perez de Cuellar, Javier (1920–), Peruvian diplomat and secretary-general of the United Nations, 1982– . A man of courtly manners with a deep love of art and music, he entered the Peruvian foreign service in 1944, rose to the rank of ambassador in 1962, and became Peru's first ambassador to the Soviet Union in 1969. After serving as permanent representative to the UN and later president of the UN Security Council, he was sent by Secretary General Kurt Waldheim to Cyprus

REUTERS/BETTMANN NEWSPHOTOS

ANDREI SAKHAROV

in 1975. There he helped ease tensions by persuading Greek and Turkish leaders to initiate talks. As a compromise candidate, he was elected to head the UN in 1981. He was widely praised in 1988 for mediating the Iran-Iraq war and the Afghanistan conflict.

Pickens, T(homas) Boone, Jr. (1928-), U.S. chairman of the board, president, and founder of Mesa Petroleum Company, one of the best known of the so-called corporate raiders. After receiving a degree in geology from Oklahoma State University in 1951, he organized the Petroleum Exploration Company, which became Mesa Petroleum in 1964. He made his first big takeover bid in 1982 with an attempt to buy out Cities Service Company; the resulting merger of Cities Service and Occidental Petroleum brought $31 million in profit to the Mesa group. Later maneuvers were aimed at acquiring a majority of shares in companies like General American Oil, Gulf Oil, Phillips Petroleum, and Unocal Corporation, with each effort earning substantial profits for Pickens and his shareholders.

Powell, Lewis Franklin, Jr. (1907-), U.S. associate justice of the Supreme Court, regarded as a strong force for moderation. He earned degrees from Washington and Lee University and Harvard Law School and practiced law in Virginia from 1931. He was president of the American Bar Association in 1964-1965 and was appointed to the Supreme Court in 1971 by President Nixon. Powell retired in 1987.

Q

Qaddafi, Muammar al- (1942-), Libyan army officer and chief of state, champion of Arab unity and a powerful ally of the Palestinian Arabs in their conflict with Israel. A man of puritanical standards and erratic behavior, he is said to have provided financial support to Palestinian terrorist groups. In April, 1986, President Reagan orderd a strike against Libya in retaliation for the Libyan bombing of a West German disco in which two died and 200 were injured.

Quayle, Dan (James Danforth III) (1947-), Vice President of the United States (1989-). Born in Indianapolis, Quayle is the son and grandson of prominent Indiana newspaper publishers. He graduated from DePauw University in 1969 and received a law degree from the University of Indiana in 1974. He served in the Indiana National Guard from 1969 to 1975. Elected to the U.S. House of Representatives in 1976, he served two terms, then was elected to the U.S. Senate in 1980, defeating the three-term Democratic incumbent, Birch Bayh. A champion of conservative causes, Quayle served on the Senate Armed Services Committee, the Budget Committee, and the Labor and Human Resources Committee.

R

Rehnquist, William Hubbs (1924-), U.S. chief justice of the Supreme Court, a strong supporter of law and order. After receiving his degree from Stanford Law School, 1952, he practiced law in Arizona and pursued his interest in Republican politics. An assistant attorney general in the Justice Department from 1968 until President Nixon appointed him to the Supreme Court, he was named chief justice in 1986 by President Reagan.

Rostropovich, Mstislav (1927-), Russian virtuoso cellist, conductor, and pianist. Winner of the International Competition of Cellists in Prague in 1950. A successful performer, he also showed himself to be an excellent pianist, accompanying his wife, the singer Galina Vishnevskaya, in recitals. His friendship with, and support of, dissident author Alexander Solzhenitsyn caused Soviet authorities to curtail his professional activities; in 1974 he and his family moved to the United States. After becoming conductor of the National Symphony Orchestra in Washington, D.C., he and his wife were deprived of their citizenship by the Soviet government.

S

Sakharov, Andrei Dimitrievich (1921-), Soviet theoretical physicist and political dissident, the first Soviet citizen to receive the Nobel Peace Prize, in 1975. Although he helped develop the Soviet hydrogen bomb, becoming a full member of the Academy of Sciences in 1953, he emerged in the 1960's as an outspoken critic of the nuclear arms race and of Soviet repression. His activities in defense of human rights caused him to be exiled to Gorky in 1980, where he remained under police surveillance. He was released from internal exile in 1986.

Scalia, Antonin (1936-), U.S. associate justice of the Supreme Court, the first Italian-American to sit on the High Court. He earned degrees from Georgetown University and Harvard Law School, and later taught law at several institutions, including the University of Chicago Law School. In 1982 he became a judge of the U.S. Court of Appeals for the District of Columbia. He was appointed to the Supreme Court by President Reagan in 1986. Regarded as a conservative, he is noted for his dedication to judicial restraint.

Shultz, George Pratt (1920-), U.S. secretary of state. He earned degrees in economics from Princeton University and Massachusetts Institute of Technology. From 1957 to 1968, he was professor of industrial relations at the University of Chicago Graduate School of Business; he was dean from 1962 to 1968. Under President Nixon, Shultz was named secretary of labor, 1969-1970, director of the Office of Management and Budget, 1970-1972, and secretary of the treasury, 1972-1974. He was professor of management and public policy at Stanford University from 1974 to 1982, when he was appointed secretary of state by President Reagan.

Spielberg, Steven (1947-), U.S. film director, writer, and producer, noted for his ability to tell a story on screen and for his visual inventiveness. Al-

KAGAN/PHOTO RESEARCHERS, INC.

MERYL STREEP

though he has been accused of relying too much on optical tricks and mechanical gadgetry, critics have praised his sense of composition and movement. Among his most successful and most highly acclaimed films are *Jaws* (1975), *Close Encounters of the Third Kind* (1977), and *The Color Purple* (1985), for which he won an Academy Award as best director. In 1987 he received the Irving G. Thalberg Memorial Award in recognition of his achievements.

Stevens, John Paul (1920–), U.S. associate justice of the Supreme Court, regarded as a moderate with conservative leanings. Educated at the University of Chicago and Northwestern University, he practiced law in Chicago and specialized in antitrust and corporate areas. He served on the U.S. Circuit Court of Appeals from 1970 to 1975. President Ford appointed him to the Supreme Court in 1975.

Streep, Meryl (1949–), U.S. actress noted for her perceptiveness and versatility, born Mary Louise Streep. After studies at Vassar and Dartmouth colleges and Yale Drama School, she acted in a number of New York theater productions, with particular success in Andrei Serban's staging of Chekhov's *The Cherry Orchard* (1977). She made her television debut in *The Deadliest Season* (1977). Some of her best-known films are *The Deer Hunter* (1978), *Kramer vs. Kramer* (1979), for which she won an Academy Award as best supporting actress, *Sophie's Choice* (1982), which earned her the Oscar for best actress, and *Ironweed* (1987).

Styron, William Clark, Jr. (1925–), U.S. novelist and essayist, known for his mastery of dialogue and his preoccupation with "the catastrophic propensity of human beings to dominate one another." His reputation was established with the novel *Lie Down in Darkness* (1951), a tale of life in a disintegrating Southern family. Among his other works are the novella *The Long March* (1955), *The Confessions of Nat Turner* (1967), for which he won the Pulitzer Prize, and *Sophie's Choice* (1979), a controversial novel of the World War II Holocaust.

T

Teresa of Calcutta, Mother (1910–), founder of the Order of the Missionaries of Charity (Roman Catholic), original name Agnes Gonxha Bojaxhiu. Born in Macedonia of Albanian parents, she went to India in 1928 as a teacher. She studied nursing and founded her order in 1948 in the slums of Calcutta. Mother Teresa organized and worked in schools and dispensaries for the poor, as well as at a leper colony (Shanti Nagar) and many centers for the blind, crippled, and aged. She received the Nobel Prize for Peace in 1979.

Trump, Donald John (1946–), U.S. real estate developer, one of New York's most grandiose and controversial builders, who has been called everything from megalomaniac to world-class salesman. He was instrumental in persuading the city of New York to build a multimillion-dollar convention center on a site for which he was given the option. His most noted project was the Trump Tower, New York's tallest reinforced concrete structure, completed in 1982.

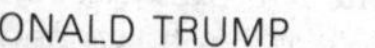
DONALD TRUMP

UPI/BETTMANN NEWSPHOTOS

BACHMAN/PHOTO RESEARCHERS, INC.

DESMOND TUTU

Tutu, Desmond Mpilo (1931–), South African Anglican prelate, a leading opponent of apartheid. After completing his education in South Africa and England, he became the first black Anglican dean of Johannesburg, in 1975. In 1978 he was chosen as the first black general secretary of the South African Council of Churches, an interdenominational group that under Tutu became an important agent of black protest. As Anglican bishop of Johannesburg and later archbishop of Cape Town, 1986, the witty and ebullient Tutu was a thorn in the side of government, publicly calling apartheid "vicious, evil, and immoral," exhorting foreign nations to withdraw their South African investments, and supporting many nonviolent demonstrations and boycotts. A Nobel Peace Prize winner in 1984, he has been an outspoken critic of U.S. policy in South Africa.

W

Walesa, Lech (?1943–), Polish labor leader, co-founder of the free trade union known as Solidarity, and winner of the 1983 Nobel Peace Prize. The son of a carpenter and one of eight children, he moved to Gdansk after completing vocational school and became an electrician in the shipyards. He was fired in 1976 for demanding better working conditions, and in 1979 helped organize Solidarity. After the Polish government doubled meat prices in 1980, causing widespread public outrage, Walesa led work stoppages and strikes. The Gdansk agreement, giving workers the right to form independent unions and to strike, was signed by Walesa and Prime Minister Jagielski in August, 1980, marking the first such agreement ever to be given in a Soviet bloc country. In 1981, however, Solidarity was outlawed by the Polish government and its leaders arrested. Walesa was detained for almost a year. He is known for his deep religious and nationalist convictions, and for his ability to steer a course between moderation and militancy.

Walker, Alice Malsenior (1944–), U.S. writer and social activist, known for her vivid evocations of life in the rural South. Her first book of poems was published in 1968, followed by works such as "To Hell With Dying" (1967), *The Third Life of Grange Copeland* (1970), *In Love and Trouble: Stories of Black Women* (1973), and *The Color Purple* (1982), a novel that won an American Book Award and the Pulitzer Prize for fiction.

Wang, An (1920–), Chinese-born U.S. business executive, philanthropist, and inventor of the magnetic core memory, a vital component in modern computer development. He studied electrical engineering at Shanghai's Chiao Tung University and applied physics at Harvard University, working as a research fellow at the Harvard Computation Laboratory from 1948 to 1951. After patenting his invention, he formed Wang Laboratories in 1951 and produced the first electronic justifying typesetter system and the first electronic scientific desk calculator. The 1200 Word Processing System, a so-called thinking typewriter, was brought out in 1972. In 1976 Wang launched the WPS, a cathode-ray tube-based word processor with television-style screen and high-speed printer.

Weinberg, Robert Allan (1942–), U.S. biochemist, professor at the Massachusetts Institute of Technology, a pioneer in the use of genetic engineering procedures to isolate genes from human tumor cells. In the early 1980's he and his colleagues were able to identify specific oncogenes (cancer-causing genes) as causes of specific types of human cancer. He theorized that genes affected by carcinogens undergo minute changes that cause the cell to produce a distorted protein, thereby disrupting the cell's regulatory mechanism and encouraging the growth of cancer.

UPI/BETTMANN NEWSPHOTOS

AN WANG

White, Byron Raymond (1917–), U.S. associate justice of the Supreme Court. A former professional football player and Rhodes Scholar, he was graduated from Yale Law School in 1946. In 1961 he was appointed deputy attorney general by President Kennedy; he was named to the High Court the following year.

Winger, (Mary) Debra (1955–), U.S. actress of Hungarian descent, acclaimed for the intelligence and intensity of her work and for her gravelly voice. Her best-known roles have been in the films *Urban Cowboy* (1980), *An Officer and a Gentleman* (1982), and *Terms of Endearment* (1983), which won her an Oscar nomination.

Wright, James C., Jr. (1922–), U.S. politician, Speaker of the House of Representatives (1987–). Born in Fort Worth, Texas, Wright joined the U.S. Army Air Force in World War II. He has held elected office since 1947, serving in the Texas state legislature (1947–1949), as mayor of Weatherford, Texas (1950–1954), and in the U.S. House of Representives from 1955 to the present. He was elected House majority leader in 1976, then succeeded Thomas P. ("Tip") O'Neill, Jr., as Speaker in 1987. He is credited by many for making the House more independent in its relations with the White House.

For Further Reference

American Council of Learned Societies staff, editors. *Concise Dictionary of American Biography* (3rd Ed.). Charles Scribner's Sons, 1980.

Avery, C. *The New Century Handbook of Leaders of the Classical World.* Prentice-Hall, 1972.

Biography Index. H. W. Wilson, 1946–1986.

Contemporary Authors. Gale Research, 1962–present.

Dictionary of American Biography. Charles Scribner's Sons, 1928–1988.

Dictionary of National Biography. Oxford University Press, 1917–1986.

Dictionary of Scientific Biography. Charles Scribner's Sons, 1976.

Encyclopedia of World Biography. Publisher's Guild, 1973–1987.

Hebert, Miranda C., and Barbara McNeil. *Biography and Genealogy Master Index* (2nd Ed.). Gale Research, 1980

International Who's Who. Europa Publications, 1935–present.

Kunitz, Stanley J., and Howard Haycraft. *A Biographical Dictionary of American Literature.* H. W. Wilson, 1977.

Kunitz, Stanley J., and Howard Haycraft. *British Authors Before Eighteen Hundred.* H. W. Wilson, 1952.

Kunitz, Stanley J., and Howard Haycraft. *British Authors of the Nineteenth Century.* H. W. Wilson, 1936.

Stetler, Susan L., editor. *Biography Almanac,* Gale Research, 1986.

Webster's Biographical Dictionary. G. & C. Merriam, 1976.

Who's Who. St. Martin's, 1849–present.

Who Was Who. St. Martin's, 1953–1981.

Who Was Who in America. Marquis Who's Who, 1943–1985.

VOLUME 20

Performing Arts

CULVER PICTURES

TIME-LINE OF PERFORMING ARTS

	1700–1900	1900–1940	1940–1990
MUSIC	Bach, *Well-Tempered Clavier* (1722) Handel, *Messiah* (1741) Mozart, *Magic Flute* (1791) Haydn, last symphonies (c 1800) Beethoven, *Fifth Symphony* (1808) Schumann, *Piano Concerto* (1845) Wagner, *Tristan und Isolde* (1859) Brahms, *Second Symphony* (1877) Debussy, *Afternoon of a Faun* (1894)	Rachmaninoff, *Piano Concerto I* (1908) Schönberg, *Erwartung* (1909) Stravinsky, *Firebird* (1910) Ives, *Concord Sonata* (1919) Berg, *Lulu* (1935)	Bartok, *Concerto for Orchestra* (1943) Cage, *Imaginary Landscape I* (1939) Copland, *Appalachian Spring* (1944) Stravinsky, *Rake's Progress* (1951) Britten, *Midsummer Night's Dream* (1960)
DANCE	*Les Indes Galantes* (1735) *Whims of Cupid* (1786) *Giselle* (1841) *Coppelia* (1870) *Sleeping Beauty* (1890)	Isadora Duncan (1900–1910) Ruth St. Denis, *Temple of Isis* (c 1910) Ballet Russe, *Rite of Spring* (1913) Balanchine, *Serenade* (1934)	Martha Graham, *Appalachian Spring* (1944) Merce Cunningham (1950–1960) Balanchine, *Jewels* (1967)
DRAMA/THEATER	Sheridan, *School for Scandal* (1777) Lessing, *Nathan the Wise* (1779) Schiller, *The Robbers* (1782) Goethe, *Faust* (Part I) (1808) Ibsen, *A Doll's House* (1879)	Chekhov, *Cherry Orchard* (1902) Shaw, *St. Joan* (1923) O'Neill, *Strange Interlude* (1928)	Williams, *Glass Menagerie* (1944) Beckett, *Waiting for Godot* (1952) Albee, *Who's Afraid of Virginia Woolf?* (1962)

AMERICAN POPULAR MUSIC		Joplin, "Maple-Leaf Rag" (1899)
		Growth of Jazz (1910–1950)
		  New Orleans/Chicago (1910–1925)
		  Gershwin, *Rhapsody in Blue* (1924)
		  New York/Kansas City (1925–1940)
		Be-bop (1940–1950)
			Oklahoma! (1943)
			My Fair Lady (1956)
			Hair (1967)
			A Chorus Line (1977)

FILM		*Birth of a Nation* (1915) Chaplin, *The Gold Rush* (1925) *The Jazz Singer* (sound) (1927) *Gone With the Wind* (color) (1939)	*High Noon* (1952) Bergman, *The Seventh Seal* (1956) *The Godfather* (1972) *Star Wars* (1978)
RECORDINGS		Caruso, others (1915–1920) Music for dancing (1920–1930) Basie, Ellington bands (1930–1945) Crosby, Sinatra (1930–1945)	Long-play record, high fidelity (1952) Elvis Presley (1957–) The Beatles (1964–) Protest songs (1968–) Rolling Stones (1972–) Disco (1978–)
BROADCASTING		First radio programming (1920) Radio comedy, soap opera (1930–1940)	War news (1940–1945) First FM stations (1948) "I Love Lucy" (1951–) "Gunsmoke" (1958–) First Presidential debates (1960) Instant replay (1964) Football's Super Bowl (1967) "All in the Family" (1972–) Cable TV, video recordings (1980–1990)

DANCERS IN WHITE: SIPA/BLACK STAR

VOLUME **20**

Performing Arts

CULVER PICTURES

CULVER PICTURES

MARTHA SWOPE

AMERICAN SHAKESPEARE THEATRE, STRATFORD CONN.

CULVER PICTURES

CULVER PICTURES

In prehistoric times, man had not yet divided his world into various "subjects." In seeking to understand himself and take some control over his natural surroundings, he used a wide variety of means. In seeking to befriend potential destroyers—gods, demons, storms, wild animals, even human enemies—he made sacrifices, developed rituals, made up stories, sang songs, danced, and acted out the parts of the destroyers.

From these beginnings have come such modern subjects as religion, which still seeks to put God and man into a right relationship; philosophy and science, which seek to understand and explain both the internal and external forces that play upon man; and literature, which records the ancient stories of man's aspirations, pleasures, and griefs.

From these same beginnings come the traditional performing arts: music, dance, and drama. Each was perhaps first used to communicate with gods or spirits, but each also became a center of communal celebration and eventually a means of self-expression intended for the pleasure of viewers and listeners as well as for the gods.

Unfortunately, our knowledge of the ancient performing arts is limited. We must rely for our information on drawings, ancient statuary, and written records. We will never know exactly what the music of ancient Egypt or Greece sounded like. In more recent times, even the mood and texture of the first performance of a play by Shakespeare can never be perfectly recreated. At the same time, however, each of the performing arts has been built on the traditions of the past—or on that part of the past that has been recorded or remembered.

Only in the century just past have men learned how to record sounds and images, preserving performances in a way never before possible. Through sound recording, film, and video, we now capture the voice of a great singer, the gestures and inflections of an outstanding actor, and even a whole performance of a ballet or an opera. Today a great performer's work is preserved for all future generations, whereas earlier performers lived on only in memory.

Together with broadcasting—the transmission of sound and images over wires or through the air—recording has become an art in itself, and new creators are using recording devices to produce works of a new kind—neither quite music, dance, nor drama, but works for a new medium.

The first section of this volume considers music, both as a "language" and as a tradition stretching from the dim past to the most recent times. Special attention has been given to the musical and other performing arts in America in the past century, a period of great innovation and creativity.

The second section provides a brief history of the dance, from its religious origins through modern dance. A third section follows the long history of drama in the Western world.

Finally, there is a section on the recording and broadcast arts. These arts are the ones most familiar to modern readers, yet they are so new that we are only now beginning to study their "language" and their history.

Other information pertinent to the performing arts may be found in other volumes of the *Volume Library*. The article on "Sound" in CHEMISTRY AND PHYSICS considers musical acoustics. The technical aspects of recording and broadcasting are described in INDUSTRY AND TECHNOLOGY. The volume on LITERATURE considers the importance of drama in literary history, and its glossary includes entries on many important dramatic works. Finally, the PEOPLE volume provides brief biographies of many outstanding creators and performers important to the performing arts.

MUSIC

We will probably never know how music began. Its roots are older than the roots of speech itself, and are deeply buried in the prehistoric past. But by studying the musical development of children and the music of primitive societies, we can get some idea of how it all began.

Perhaps the first musical instrument was a hollow tree trunk, accidentally struck by a hand-held stick. Perhaps it was a pair of dried animal or human bones, struck one on the other. That first thump, that first rattle, must have produced a sound so strange, so mysterious that our ancestors must have thought it magical.

From the simple yet magical sounds of these early percussion instruments, our forebears soon discovered the intoxicating power of rhythm, which propelled and organized ritual dance. From there it was simple to use rhythmic beats to match the movements of labor, magically lightening the burden of daily toil.

But the hollow-log drum and other percussion instruments were not the only sound-makers in primitive society. Our ancestors also possessed the most natural, most expressive, most flexible instrument of all: the human voice.

Those first musicians may have used their voices to imitate bird song, the cries and mating calls of animals, and the sounds of wind and rain. Or perhaps the first crude chants and songs grew out of the rising and falling inflections of everyday language. Hunters may have learned to use definite pitches—so different from the vague pitches of ordinary speech—to signal the sighting of their prey, or to announce the victorious kill.

GEORGE HOLTON/PHOTO RESEARCHERS

TRIBESMEN *from New Guinea chant and dance to the sound of primitive instruments.*

As early man grew more and more skilled in the use of tones of definite pitch, this element joined rhythm to create primitive melody. With the addition of words, or of mouth sounds that imitated natural sounds, came the magical incantations of priests in sacred rituals, or the songs to accompany dance.

As tribal societies evolved, music remained a part of social life, and a part of man's natural response to his environment and to daily events. Ceremonies were accompanied by singing, dancing, and playing. Laborers chanted their work songs. As they still do today, children spontaneously created their own little songs and dances. Mothers hummed the first lullabies to their sleeping children. Hunters and warriors bucked up their courage with chants and cries and calls, and the beat of sticks, bones, and drums.

From earliest times music was also tied to the deepest expressions of human emotions and desires: prayer, work, play, love. Our ancestors, like us, played and sang and danced to express their joy and sorrow and fears; to worship their gods; to accompany them in battle; to express their pain or longing; and to give form to their stories, passed on from one generation to the next.

Sounds and Sound-Makers

From the time of the first musicians, the forms and sounds of music have been influenced by the environment and by the state of human knowledge. The earliest instruments were adapted from natural elements. Drums were fashioned out of hollow logs, or made by stretching dried animal skins across the open mouths of simple log cylinders. Dried gourds were struck for their hollow sound, or—when still filled with loose, dried seeds—shaken to become rattles. Tubes of reed or cane or hollowed-out bone, cut to different lengths and later pierced with holes for variable pitch, became the first wind instruments.

As centuries passed, tools became more sophisticated and instrument makers refined their skills. Sound-makers became more intricate and offered more and more precise control of sound.

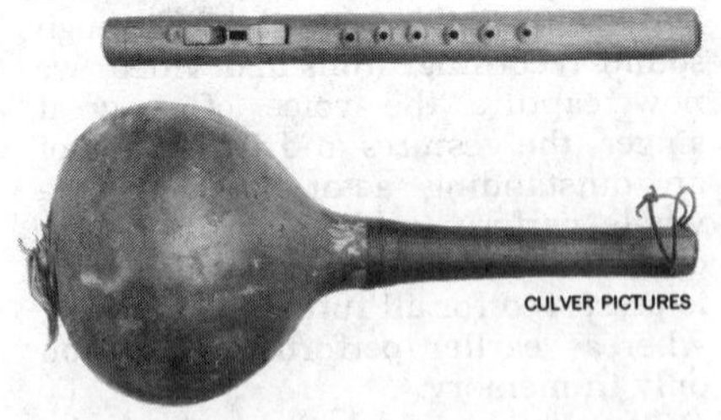
CULVER PICTURES

FLUTE AND RATTLE *used by Iroquois tribe in North America.*

Understanding Sound

In order to understand sound-makers, we must understand more about sound itself.

Vibrations. No matter how crude or sophisticated an instrument is, no matter what its shape or size or material may be, and no matter how it is played, each and every instrument depends on *vibrations* to produce its sound. Without vibrations we would hear no singing voice, no conch-shell horn or modern-day trumpet, no reed flute or saxophone, no rattle, kettledrum, violin, or xylophone.

When we drop a stone in the center of a still pond, waves of water ripple out from the point of disturbance. In the same way, the simple act of plucking a guitar string, blowing a bugle, or beating a tom-tom causes that instrument to vibrate and send out air disturbances in the form of *sound waves.* Those waves move outward from the instrument, through the air, to our ear's membrane, which picks up the vibrations and carries the sound message to our body's nerve center.

Waveforms and cycles. Before we touch a guitar string, for example, it is at complete rest:

But the moment we pluck it, the string is disturbed into movement: it vibrates (1) outward in one direction, (2) back past the point of rest, (3) outward in the opposite direction, and then (4) back again toward the point of rest:

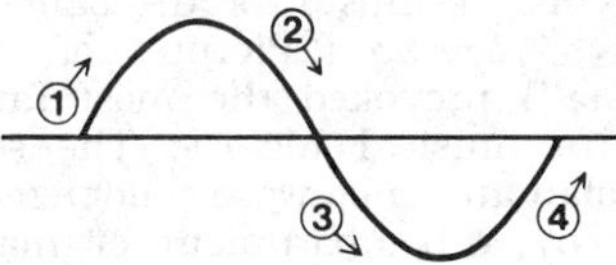

That one complete wave motion—which happens faster than the eye can see—is called a *cycle.*

Pitch and frequency. The *pitch* of that guitar sound—how high or low it is—depends on how many cycles occur in one second. The number of cycles per second is called *frequency.* The lower the frequency, the lower the pitch:

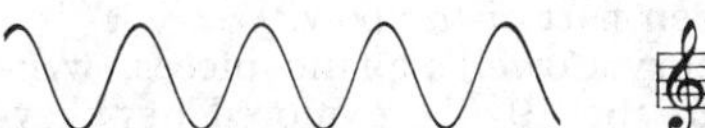

The higher the frequency, the higher the pitch:

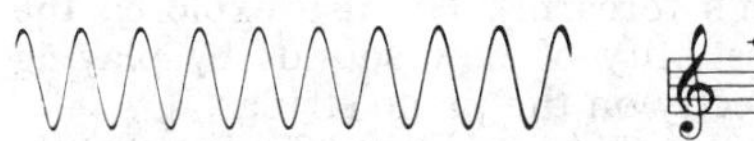

Although vibration speed has a tremendous range—from less than one cycle per second to thousands of cycles per second—the audible range for the human ear is very limited. We can only hear sounds produced by vibrations that move between about 20 cycles per second to about 16,000 cycles per second. Sounds produced by vibrations below this range (called *sub-audio*) or above this range (called *ultrasonic*) can only be heard by animals who are "tuned in" to those extreme frequencies. (Watch a dog, for instance, perk up his ears at a sound that is completely inaudible to us.)

Loudness and amplitude. The loudness or softness of a sound also depends on vibrations. But where pitch is determined by how many vibrations occur in one second, loudness depends on the height of the wave's peaks. This is called the wave's *amplitude.*

Plucking that guitar string with all your force will create a very large amplitude; barely strumming it will create a tiny amplitude. Here is a picture of a sound that begins loudly, then gradually dies away:

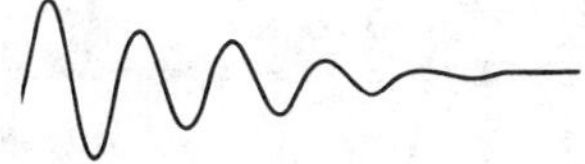

Timbre and overtones. The simple waveform we have been looking at is so pure that it can be produced only by a tuning fork or an electronic oscillator. But the sounds of our world are far from being so simple. Here are the more complicated waveforms produced by four common sound-makers:

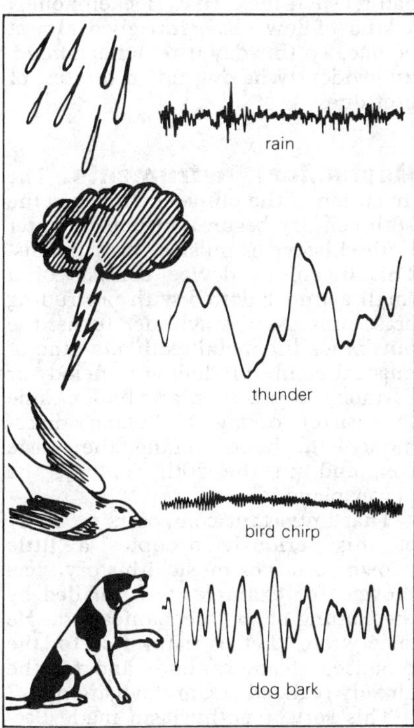

EDUCATIONAL AUDIO VISUAL INC.

These intricate shapes—with their peculiar peaks and dips and curves—determine the tone color, or *timbre,* of a sound.

In effect, each sound source creates its individual color just as a painter does by beginning with a pure base color, and then adding ingredients to produce subtle new shades and hues. In the world of sound, the pure base color is called the *fundamental;* the added ingredients (the color tones) are called *overtones* or *partials.* Just as our eyes perceive only the result of the painter's blended colors, our ears perceive only the result of an instrument's blended fundamental and special overtones. This end product of the blend—the timbre of a sound—is what permits our ears to identify a familiar voice, the distinctive color of a clarinet, and the difference between a clap of thunder and the roll of a bass drum.

The pictures below show the waveforms of three instruments playing the same pitch at approximately the same degree of loudness. Their frequencies are identical. Their amplitudes are similar. But their waveforms—and thus their timbres—are different:

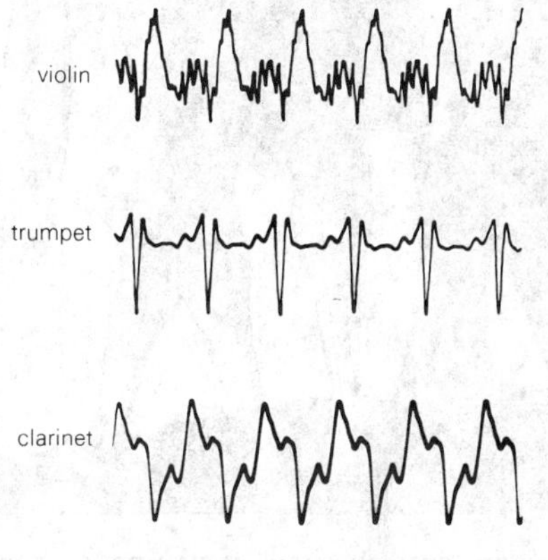

EDUCATIONAL AUDIO VISUAL INC.

Musical Instruments

Whereas early instruments were comparatively limited in the variety and quality of sounds they could produce, their modern counterparts are extremely versatile. An extremely old and very simple wind instrument, for example, is the so-called "Pipes of Pan"—a set of cane or wooden tubes cut to different lengths, with each tube producing but one mellow pitch. By comparison, our present-day silver or platinum flute—a single pipe with 15 holes and 23 levers—can produce a highly colored rainbow of more than three dozen pitches!

Despite the sensuous timbre of the Pipes of Pan (an instrument still played in remote villages around the world), this antique woodwind has been completely swept aside by its latest descendant. Not only can the modern flute play more pitches, but it can do so with great facility and with exceptional control of loudness, timbre, speed, duration, and overall quality.

Our modern winds, brass, percussion, and stringed instruments did not develop all at once. They evolved slowly over the centuries, adding improvements, refining their timbre, and gradually extending their range (the distance between lowest and highest pitches of an instrument).

This evolution came from the combined efforts of instrument makers, performers, and composers. The design of a new improvement or, in fact,

of an entirely new instrument, was only the first step toward its acceptance. That new design, above all, had to be useful. For the frustrated performer, it had to solve a previously unsolved technical problem (an easier fingering system, for example). For the demanding composer, the design had to be a means of expressing something that could not have been expressed before (an intriguing new timbre, for example, or a way to produce a special effect). Only then was the new design accepted as a new standard of excellence—as the "state of the art."

Orchestral instruments. With each improvement, musical instruments came closer to the designs we know today. The addition of rotary valves to the simple hunting horn led to the design of the modern French horn. The medieval sackbut (literally, "draw pipe") evolved into the slide trombone. The invention of a hammer mechanism for a keyboard instrument created the forerunner of the modern piano.

In the 1500's, Gasparo da Salò, the grandson of a lute maker, transformed the medieval viol into the first violin. A century later Antonio Stradivari perfected an improved design and a secret formula for varnish that gave the Stradivarius stringed instruments their special timbre and their reputation as the finest ever made.

By the 1800's, inventors (some were well known performers) brought important new changes to the family of woodwinds. Theobold Boehm—a goldsmith's son, and one of the finest flutists of his time—invented a new flute with a revolutionary key system. Hyacinthe Klosé, professor of music at the Paris Conservatoire, adapted Boehm's system to the clarinet. Johann Heckel brought improvements to the bassoon. (But his son, Wilhelm, had no such luck. His "Heckelphone," a kind of low oboe, intrigued almost no one. To this day it remains an oddity, evidently having failed the test of usefulness.)

Mechanical instruments. The invention of the pinned cylinder in the 18th century began a curious chapter in the history of musical instruments. This ingenious device consists of a small cylinder dotted with protruding brass pins. As the cylinder turns, the pins pluck the metal teeth of a kind of musical comb, producing a melody or harmony. From such a cylinder came the barrel organ, a "piano mécanique," the handle piano, the music box, and, in the 20th century, the player piano.

That important composers took any of this seriously occupies a little known corner of musical history. Beethoven, for example, was thrilled by the coming of the mechanical era. He once wrote "Let us thank God for the promised steam cannons and for the already realized steam navigation. . ."

This sort of enthusiasm made Beethoven a devoted friend of the new musical devices. He became fascinated by the inventions of Johann Maelzel, creator of the ear trumpet (for the hard of hearing), an automatic chess player, a mechanical trumpeter, and—by stealing another inventor's idea—the metronome. Beethoven agreed to compose a piece for Maelzel. The result was *Wellington's Victory,* created for Maelzel's Panharmonicon, a kind of glorified music box that combined military band instruments with a powerful bellows, all enclosed in a case. Beethoven's piece was, in fact, on the program of an 1813 charity concert, along with marches tooted by Maelzel's mechanical trumpeter.

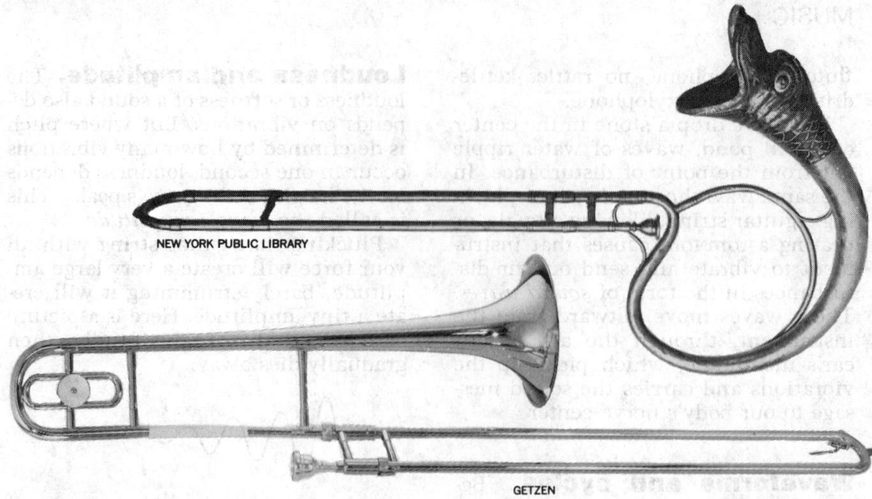

SACKBUT TO TROMBONE: *from the 1500's* (left) *to a decorative model in the 1800's* (above top), *the ancient sackbut was evolving into the modern trombone* (above bottom).

The search for new timbres. By the early years of the 20th century, composers had begun to explore a new possibility: that conventional instruments were capable of producing unconventional sounds.

On a spring evening in 1913, Igor Stravinsky's music for the ballet *The Rite of Spring* ("Pictures of Pagan Russia") provoked the most famous riot in musical history. The sedate Parisian audience was scandalized not only by a bombardment of massive orchestral discords, but by strange new instrumental timbres. A solo bassoon (traditionally a bass instrument) played at the very top of its range, producing eerie, unheard-of sounds. A vast array of deep drums pounded out jagged rhythms, a sound associated with tribal ritual, not the concert hall. Stringed instruments swept through glassy, odd-colored waves of high-pitched harmonics.

In his string quartets, Béla Bartók laced his music with slides, snapped strings, and rhythms played with the wooden part of the bow.

Henry Cowell's piano pieces, written in the 1920's, explored new keyboard sonorities (dense note groups called "tone clusters," and great, blurred "chords" played by the pianist's forearm). He also explored the possibility of new sounds by playing directly on the piano strings.

John Cage probed even deeper into the innards of the piano by inserting metal, wooden, and rubber objects between the strings, creating sonorities akin to the soft, muted gong-and-drum *gamelan* ensembles of Indonesia.

Edgard Varèse's *Ionisation* (1933) dealt with timbre alone (pitch and rhythm were secondary; harmony, in the conventional sense, was nonexistent). His use of bells and sirens, chains and anvils, together with piano and percussion instruments, demonstrated the musical resources of totally unconventional sound-makers. Tradition was overturned, and *any* sound was a legitimate source of music.

The electronic age. The miracle of electricity—which could supply power for the production, transmission, and recording of sound—opened up a new world for the 20th-century composer. Instruments were developed to produce sounds electrically: the vacuum tube to amplify sound, and the oscillator to generate sound electronically.

As new inventions appeared on the scene, composers like Varèse called for new instruments: "The composer and the electrician," he said, "will have to labor together."

To the general public, the newly invented tape recorder was a marvelous machine. But to composers—men like Varèse, and Otto Luening and Vladimir Ussachevsky at Columbia University—the tape recorder was a totally new musical instrument. It could be used to collect and transform sounds in ways never before possible. Tape could be used to alter the shape and speed of a sound, to play a sound backward, or to layer it with other sounds in complex combinations.

In Paris, composer Pierre Schaffer created a piece made from the recorded sounds of railroad trains. He called this type of composition *musique concrète,* to differentiate it from traditional composition, which begins as a written score and ends in sound. Schaffer's music began with concrete sounds that could be transformed through tape into a composition.

The synthesizer. Parallel to the development of the tape recorder was the invention and evolution of various electronic devices: oscillators, filters, modulators, and others. Each device produced or controlled sound in some way.

Finally these components were consolidated into a single instrument. This compact, all-in-one unit was called a *synthesizer.* The composer now had an instrument capable of unprecedented control over the creation and synthesis of sounds.

In 1955 the first and most elaborate synthesizer was unveiled: the room-size RCA Electronic Music Synthesizer, an instrument that today would cost several hundred thousand dollars to duplicate. But with the modern benefits of microminiaturization, some of the best and most sophisticated synthesizers are table-size instruments, available today at a tiny fraction of that cost.

The evolution of the synthesizer has been paralleled by an artistic evolution in its use: it is now regarded not as a gadget but as a functional part of a composer's complete storehouse of instruments. Milton Babbitt moved from his purely electronic *Composition for Synthesizer* (1961) to *Philomel* (1964), a work for soprano and taped synthesizer accompaniment. Mario Davidovsky (a director of the Columbia-Princeton Electronic Center) wrote his *Synchronisms No. 1* for flute and electronic sounds; Leon Kirchner, a chamber work for string quartet and electronic tape; and Luciano Berio, a work called *Visage* for an electronically modified human voice.

This tiny list barely suggests the variety and scope of the new music made possible by the synthesizer. Yet, seen as a part of the historical development of musical instruments, it is but one point on the long line of musical history. In time, as even more advanced instruments are invented and perfected, the synthesizer will be regarded as no more extraordinary than any of its predecessors.

THE SYNTHESIZER *can create a tremendous variety of sounds electronically.*

JOHN BOVA/PHOTO RESEARCHERS

AVAILABLE FORMS I, *by Earle Brown (1961) allows the five "areas" of the score to be played in any order.*

KING MUSICAL INSTRUMENTS/LATTIMER STUDIOS SELMER/CLOETINGH & DE MAN STUDIOS G.C. CONN ARTLEY FLUTE COMPANY KNEPP STUDIO/SELMER SELMER/RICK LA MAR & ASSOCIATES

The modern orchestra's instruments have developed over many centuries. Stringed instruments reached their modern state in the late 1700's. Brass and woodwind instruments received important technical improvements in the 1800's, making them easier to play and giving them a richer, fuller tone.

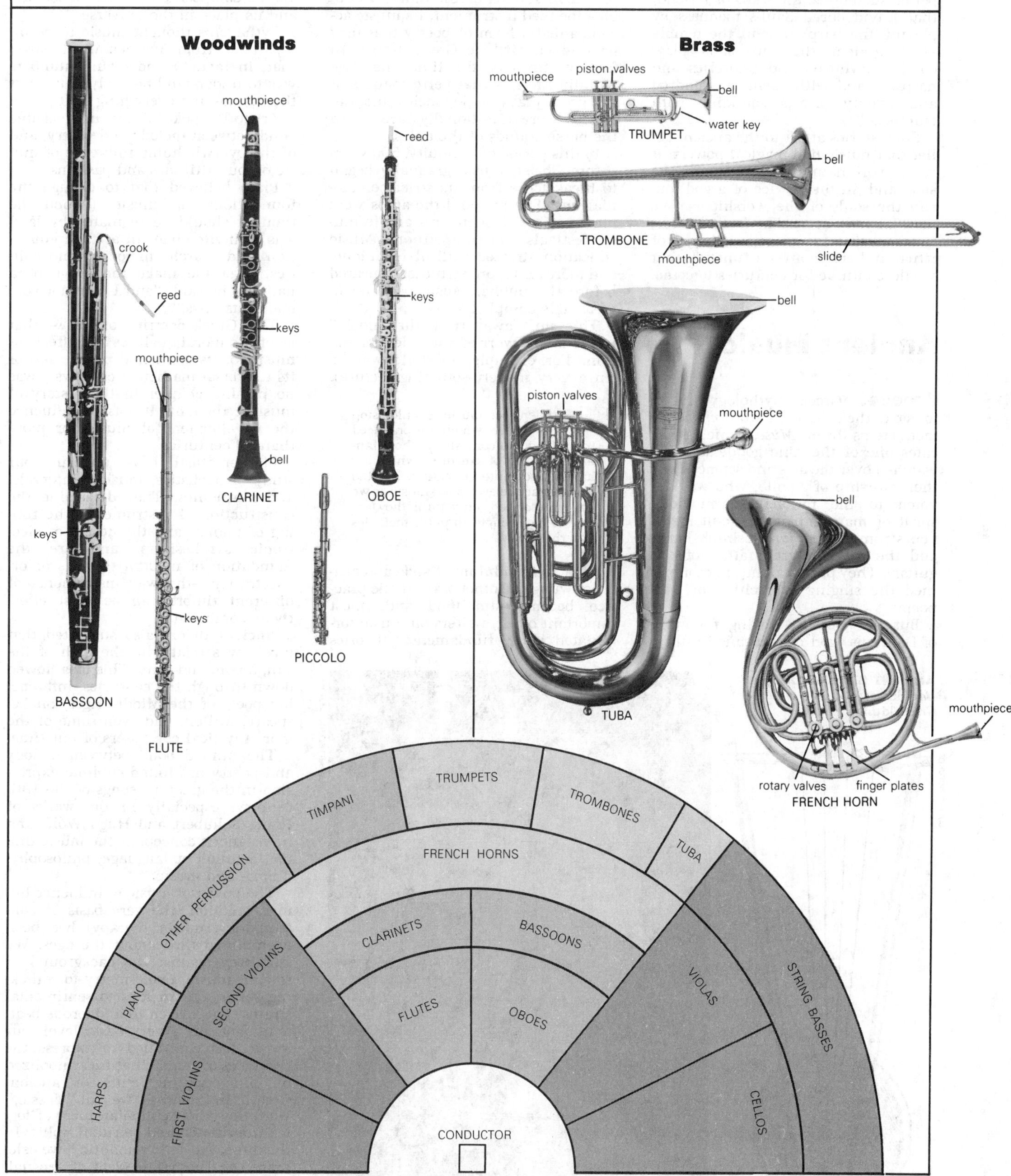

History of Western Music

The Bible tells us that Joshua's trumpet blasts toppled the walls of Jericho; that David cured Saul's madness by playing the harp; that in the temple at Jerusalem the musicians played ". . .cymbals and psalteries and harps. . .and with them an hundred and twenty priests sounding with trumpets."

Such stories attest to the ancient belief that music had magical powers: it could work natural miracles, cure the sick, and, in the service of a god, purify the souls of the worshipers. We have already seen that from earliest times music was an inseparable part of ritual and ceremony—a function that would continue for centuries to come.

Ancient Music

Greece. Greek mythology traced music to the gods. (The word *music,* in fact, stems from *Muse,* which indicates one of the nine goddesses who watched over the arts and sciences.) In their worship of Apollo, who was devoted to the rational, harmonious spirit of man and nature, cult members strummed the *lyre* (a simple harp) and the *kithara* (grandfather of the guitar). They played alone or accompanied the singing or reciting of epic poems.

But the pleasure-seeking followers of Dionysus (god of wine and fertility, sometimes called Bacchus) preferred the shrill sounds of the *aulos,* a double-pipe reed instrument. Its music accompanied a form of poetry that may have given birth to Greek drama. In fact, writings of the time and vase paintings tell us that performances of the great plays of Sophocles and Euripides were traditionally laced with the harsh sounds of the aulos.

In this period of antiquity, 500 years before Christ, music gradually began to break loose from its strict ceremonial ties. The lyre and the aulos were played as solo instruments and in music festivals and competitions. Music education stressed skillful technique, and more and more virtuosos appeared before the public. Music became increasingly complex.

This shift away from the "noble" use of music worried the older generation. For example, Aristotle warned (in a very modern-sounding lecture):

> . . . students of music [should] stop short of the arts which are practiced in professional contests . . . those fantastic marvels of execution which . . . have passed into education. Let the young practice even such music as we have prescribed, only until they are able to feel delight in noble melodies and rhythms . . .

Soon the pendulum of style and attitude swung the other way. Music practice became simplified and, most important of all, writers on music formulated clear, fundamental theories of music: about its nature, its materials, its composition, its use in society, and its place in the universe.

Pythagoras thought music to be inseparable from mathematical laws; that, in fact, to understand numbers was to understand not only music but the cosmos and everything in it.

Aristotle spoke of the unbreakable bond between melody and poetry, and of the overwhelming influence of music on our attitudes and passions.

Plato believed that to change the foundations of music (which he thought should be regulated by law) was to invite chaos in art and education, and anarchy in society and politics. "Let me make the songs of a nation," he said, "and I care not who makes its laws."

This Greek doctrine of *ethos*—that is, of the moral qualities and effects of music, of its emotional power, and of its universal mathematical laws—was no passing chapter in the history of musical thought. It was to influence the development of music for more than 20 centuries.

Mathematical laws underlie our study of acoustics, musical intervals, and harmonies. They determine the construction of instruments, the tuning of pianos, and the design of electronic synthesizers, and are the foundation of modern theories of orchestration—the way instruments of different timbre can be most effectively combined.

Ancient theory also suggested that music was related to the path of the sun, moon, and stars. This idea flowed down through the centuries, influencing poets of the Middle Ages, Shakespeare, Milton, and even some of the more mystical composers of our time.

The unified bond between melody and poetry has found sublime expression in the great art songs of the 19th century, especially in the works of Franz Schubert and Hugo Wolf, and in Wagner's concept of the music drama: a union of language, philosophy, drama, and music.

The power of music to influence human emotion (the very basis of contemporary music therapy) has been exemplified throughout the ages. We still pray against the background of solemn music, make merry to rollicking songs, fall in love to sentimental strains, and march to a vigorous beat.

In fact, on a very basic level, our music has continued to express the two faces of human nature symbolized by the opposing cults of ancient Greece. In the music we call "classic," we follow the Apollonian ideal of logic, orderliness, and spiritual uplift. In the music we call "romantic," we celebrate the Dionysian ideal of sensual-

ANCIENT STRINGS: *the Egyptian* kissar (below), *and the Greek* kithara (right).

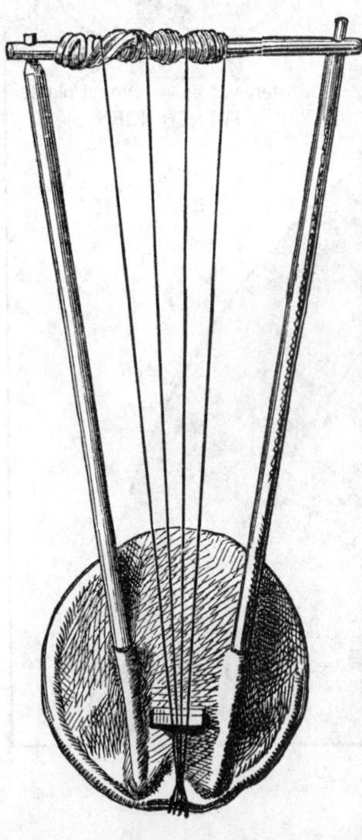

CULVER PICTURES

NEW YORK PUBLIC LIBRARY

ity, fantasy, and stimulation. As we will see, these opposite ideals have interacted throughout the entire history of music.

Early Christianity. With the exception of one shred of evidence—a mutilated scrap of papyrus "music paper," dating from the third century—we know of no direct historical link between the music of Greece and the music of the early Christian church. That scrap contains a single musical fragment: a hymn of praise to the Trinity, written in Greek words and using Greek vocal notation. But the musical style, as far as we can tell, suggests strong Eastern influences.

Early Christian church music was probably a collection of such influences. As the disciples of the new religion spread out through Asia Minor, Africa, and Europe, the young church probably adopted liturgical and musical practices from the Jewish synagogue, borrowed hymn-singing practices from the Eastern monasteries and churches of Syria and Byzantium (a powerful political and cultural center, now Istanbul), and absorbed further influences from the religious centers in Egypt, Greece, Milan, France, and Spain.

The early music of the church had certain characteristics: it was *monophonic* (that is, sung without harmony or an accompanying part); it was improvised within traditional musical formulas—a common practice in all ancient societies (no one performed from a written score); and it was intimately associated with a text. We can imagine a highly vocal musical tradition in the church, perhaps with simple hymn tunes and ornate, flowing chants sung in the florid style of the East.

From the fourth to the sixth century, the church—now richer and more strictly organized—graduallytransformed its practices. Large basilicas replaced informal places of worship. Liturgy and music were continuously revised and refined. The post of cantor (the chief solo singer) was established. And musical performance in church services was gradually taken away from the congregation and given over to a body of formally trained male singers.

Gregorian chant. But it was left to Gregory the Great, the pope from 590 to 604, to make the final and most important reform of liturgy and chant. Although there was a legendary belief that Gregory himself composed (through divine guidance) the entire body of chant that was finally and officially chosen for church use—the Gregorian chants—there is no evidence that this is true.

We now recognize that Gregory's contribution was not as a composer but as an organizer of great insight, artistic taste, and efficiency. In his 14 years as pope, he systematically redesigned the entire church liturgy, reorganized music training for church musicians, and stimulated the universal adoption of a uniform body of chant for church performance.

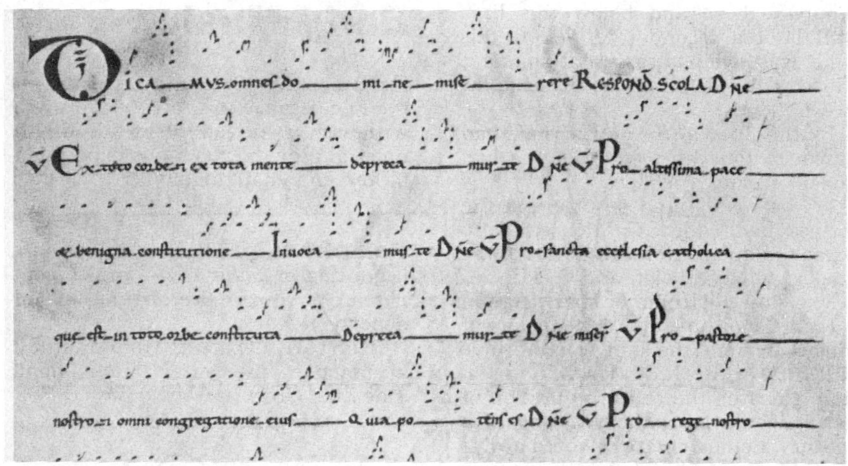

EARLY NOTATION: *words and music for a chanted prayer from a French cathedral in the eleventh century. The music appears as dots above the words.*

So great was his contribution that the liturgical music known worldwide as Gregorian chant has to this day remained one of the cornerstones of music in Western civilization. This noble music—a vast collection of pure melody—is not only a testament to religious faith but it has served as a source of inspiration for composers for over a thousand years.

So music was the servant of religion, sung in such a style and with such care in its choice as to open the mind of the worshiper to Christ and all holy thought. When one entered the church, one left behind the world of pagan spectacle and secular pleasure to hear (as one church father said) "mingled with the precepts of religion the sweetness of melody. . . ." Gregory, too, might have echoed this thought of Saint Ambrose: "Some claim that I have ensnared the people by the melodies of my hymns. I do not deny it."

The chant *Gaudeamus omnes in Domino* (Let us all rejoice in the Lord) is typical of the effortless, flowing Gregorian style. Here is the first line, written in modern notation: Note that the melody moves carefully, in small steps and within a limited range; that most of the text is set with only one or two notes to each syllable; but that the syllables of a key word like *Domino* (Lord) receive several notes to give the word prominence. These extensions, called *melisma,* are characteristic of Gregorian chant.

Musical notation. The same melody looks radically different in the square notation developed by the monks of Solësmes (*below*).

As odd as this notation may seem to the modern reader, it was a rather late development in the history of musical notation. We must remember that for centuries words and music had been transmitted orally. By the 700's, however, the number of chants had so greatly increased that some sort of written system seemed necessary.

The first attempts at notation were nothing more than reminders: it was enough to mark ⁄ or ⟍ or ∧ above a text to indicate a rising or falling pitch, or a combination of both.

By the 900's, in an effort to give a more precise idea about pitch, these signs, called *neumes* (from the Greek *pneuma,* for "breath"), were arranged more systematically. At first, scribes placed the neumes at varying heights above key points of the text. Later, a horizontal red line was drawn to represent the pitch *f,* and the neumes were

MODERN
A
Gau - de - a - mus om - nes in Do - mi - - no,
GREGORIAN
AUDE-AMUS omnes in Dó- mi- no

grouped above and below this line. Still later a second line, yellow this time, was added to represent *middle c,* thus further defining the distance between *c* and *f.*

By the 1000's, the music staff had grown to four lines, the neumes had taken on square shapes (/ = ┓, ~ = ▬ and so on), and the scribes had added Gothic letters to name the lines—the early forms of the modern G clef, F clef, and C clef.

The slow evolution of staff notation was an important step in the history of music. In time, the staff would evolve still further. By 1250, rhythmic notation (showing the relative duration of notes) would be refined; by the 17th century, neume notation would evolve into the shaping of notes as we now know them. The foundation had been laid for the physical preservation of a musical idea.

Secular music. Even while plainchant echoed through the great cathedrals, a vigorous, colorful, and decidedly unchurchly musical life swirled through the towns of medieval Europe.

In the 1000's, vagabond students and defrocked monks (the footloose *Goliards*) wandered from town to town, singing and playing their Latin songs of the bohemian life, of women and drink, of fighting and gambling:

On the great road I travel,
wrapped up in vice,
and careless of virtue.
Greedy more for lust,
I prize only my body.

Minstrels wandered the roads of Europe, performing for what coins they could gain, playing their stringed instruments, and singing their songs of love and great deeds. These struggling professional musicians would later organize fraternities and guilds, such as the famous *Meistersingers,* or "masters of song," of 15th-century Germany.

From about 1000 to 1300, noblemen sometimes became poet-musicians—the *troubadours* of France—creating pastorals, songs of religious devotion, and ballads of sensuous and courtly love:

She has stolen my heart
and my soul,
leaving me with nothing
but desire. . .

Spain heard songs of praise to the Virgin. Italy and Germany heard the powerful penitential songs of the flagellants, triggered by the black death that decimated Europe after 1350.

As they had always done, the people sang their popular songs, danced their regional dances, and played their bagpipes, wind and brass instruments, harps and zithers, drums and percussion. From all segments of everyday life, a musical vigor flowed through Europe.

Early Music

From about 900 to the beginning of the Renaissance in the 1400's, Europe witnessed a period of extraordinary musical growth, ingenious experimentation, and changing styles.

Polyphony. The first step was the beginning of *polyphony*—music composed of two or more distinct and independent lines.

In an early departure from traditional practice, the purely monophonic (one-line) Gregorian melody

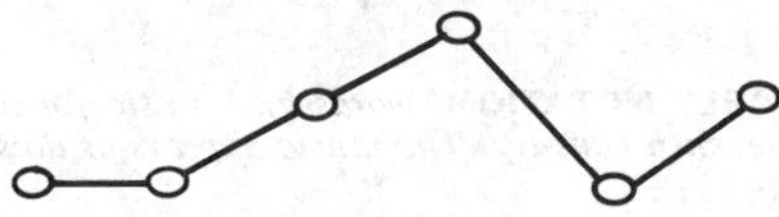

was joined by a second line that, for the most part, ran in parallel motion at a uniform distance:

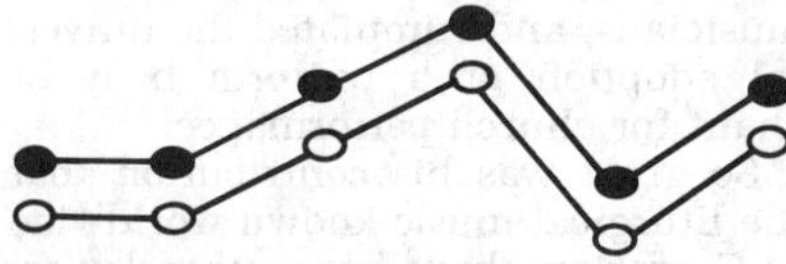

This writing style, called *organum,* expanded to four parallel lines when high and low voices sang the same parts, duplicating one another at the octave:

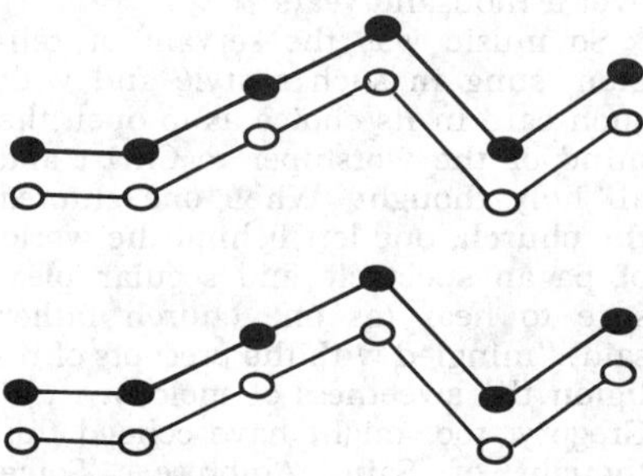

Before the year 1100, the lines were becoming melodically independent:

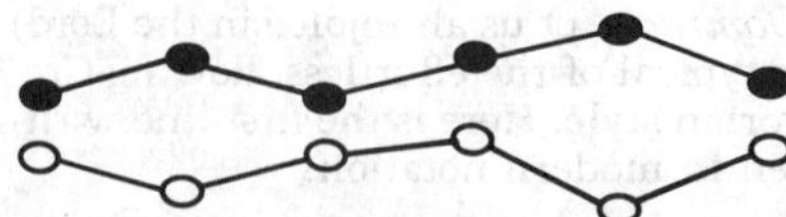

Before 1200 they were becoming rhythmically independent: the *plainsong* melody (another name for church chant) moved in long notes; the second voice moved quickly in a rhythmically free and ornamental fashion:

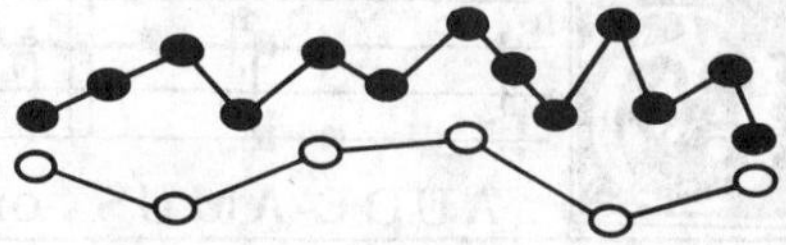

During the 1200's, the new polyphonic art, centered in France, had evolved still further. Composers expanded their textures to three melodically independent lines, and experimented with new ideas of consonance and dissonance. The long melismatic lines broke up into shorter phrases and repeated rhythmic patterns, and the flow of lines created colorful and dramatic clashes.

In secular polyphonic pieces, the use of Gregorian chant began to dissolve. Its texts gave way to Latin poems on sacred themes, moral issues, and historical events, and its music gave way to newly composed melodies, creating a more original, less "borrowed," work.

In all of these developments, composers worked within formal frameworks, balancing their musical elements and adhering to general principles of composition.

This spirit of the time, which we now label the "old art" (*ars antiqua*), to distinguish it from the "new art" (*ars nova*), was to reach its peak in the 1200's in a musical form called the *motet.*

This interesting polyphonic form occasionally combined completely diverse elements: love songs and hymns, popular dance tunes and plainsong—all in the same piece of music. An example follows.

(Top line: a joyous love song in quick notes, in French)

Sweet maiden, I adore you with all my heart.

(Middle line: a lovesick lament in even rhythm, in French)

I am weak with the sickness of love.

(Bottom line: a plainsong in long notes, with a single Latin word)

Domino (Lord).

To us, today, this potpourri seems odd, if not irreverent or sacrilegious. But to the medieval mind it was entirely appropriate for the motet to sum up all the diversity and unity of life itself—a polyphony of ideas, just as the music was a polyphony of sounds.

The "new art". The 1300's were a time of change. Social and cultural life, formerly based in a stability that centered around religion, now began to look at the individual and the dynamic diversity of everyday human life—an attitude that came to be called *humanism.*

The papacy was in turmoil. For part of the century, there were rival popes in Rome and in Avignon (in southern France). The aristocracy had weakened. Political power shifted: the French monarchy became powerful while anarchy beset Rome and all of Italy. The European economy was in a shambles, due partly to the Hundred

Years' War, and partly to the Black Death, a devastating plague that, at mid-century, killed perhaps half of all Europeans.

The music of this time made a radical move away from sacred composition. Composers felt freer to follow secular interests. They turned away from the systematic orderliness of the "old art"—now considered old-fashioned—and moved toward a musical expression that was freer, more personal, more sensuous. Their texts dealt with love, celebrated important secular occasions, spoke of political events, or even denounced the clergy.

Composers experimented with more complicated rhythms, delighting in the complexity and working out elaborate pitch and rhythmic formulas that only another composer could appreciate. Guillaume de Machaut, the leading poet-composer of the "new art" in France, demonstrated this approach in a piece called *My End Is My Beginning and My Beginning My End.* In a stroke of technical ingenuity, Machaut arranged for the melody of one voice to be the exact reverse of the melody of a second voice. A third voice reversed itself halfway through the music, running backward until the end. No listener would be likely to hear this "trick," but for Machaut it was enough that he had solved the problem and hidden it in his music.

Although sacred music was not forgotten (Machaut's *Mass of Our Lady* was the most famous composition of the century), secular music was everywhere, especially in Italy, where song and dance ruled the day.

Music in the 1400's. Music and musicians flourished throughout 15th-century Europe. Popes and princes competed for the services of important composers and performers. Music gradually took on an international flavor as musicians traveled widely, crossing national borders to take up new posts, or to join together in the courts of royal patrons.

Important musicians of the time, like John Dunstable, in the English court of the Duke of Bedford, and Guillaume Dufay, in the service of the Burgundian court of Philip the Good, began to move away from strong medieval influences. They worked toward a new clarity of writing and expression.

Their music, both sacred and secular, became more lyrical, expressive, transparent, and harmonious. Although strict and formal polyphonic works turned up for solemn occasions, it was the simpler, more appealing *homophonic* music that was clearly in favor: lighter-textured pieces with a tuneful melody and less important accompanying voices.

There was no less care in composers' linear writing, for Dufay and his contemporaries were masters of the polyphonic art. In their focus on clarity, harmonious sounds, and carefully integrated flowing lines, these composers were, in fact, harbingers of the Renaissance.

The Renaissance

Europe's focus on secular matters—embracing humanism and stressing man's interests and aspirations—was pressed forward by the rediscovery of the glories of ancient Greece and Rome. Artists everywhere magnified their achievements as revivals of ancient standards, as a rebirth, or renaissance, of rationality and the human spirit. For them, man was "the measure of all things" in this best of all times, this time of greatness.

Spurred on by the invention of printing in 1450 and by the first publications of printed music, in the late 1400's, the international spirit flourished. Beginning in 1501, new music, accurately reproduced, was available throughout Europe for study and performance, and musicians intermingled, learning from one another, and absorbing diverse national styles.

SECULAR MUSIC *of the 1400's concentrated on romantic themes: a harp and lute duet* (left) *and a love song written in the shape of a heart* (right).

NEW YORK PUBLIC LIBRARY

GIRAUDON

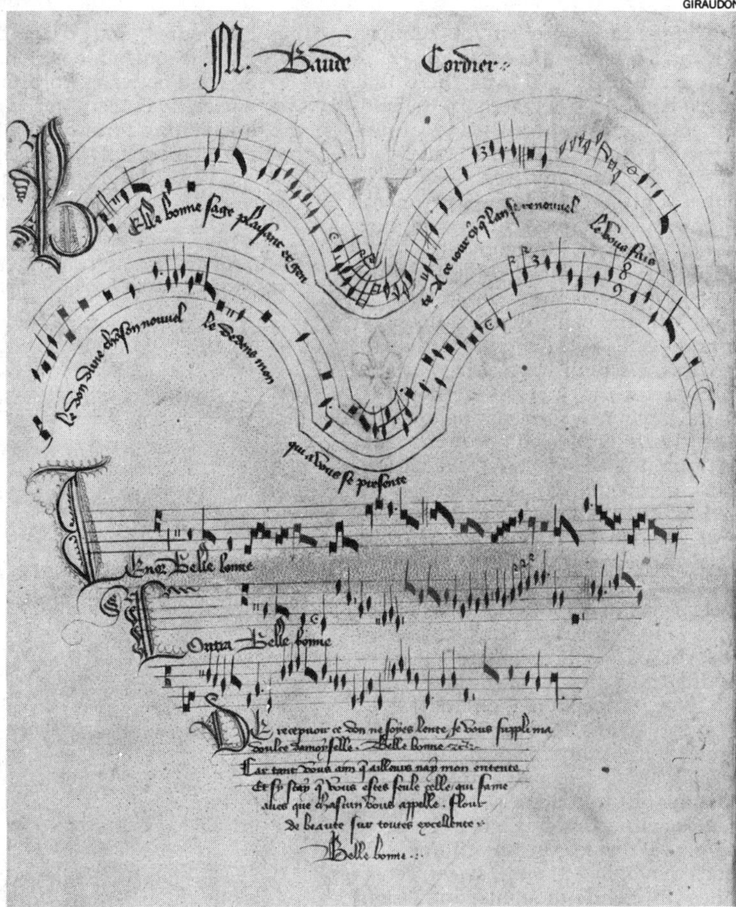

CULVER PICTURES

VARIETIES OF MUSIC: *A woodcut of 1512 shows organ, stringed instruments, recorder, and singers. Musical notation* (center) *is on a five-line staff.*

By the last quarter of the century, Italy had become the center of European cultural life. It was there that people came: to St. Peter's in Rome to immerse themselves in liturgical music, and to St. Mark's in Venice, considered the most progressive musical center of all Italy, to hear experiments with unheard-of sonorities and new uses of voices and instruments.

The master composers of the time were Josquin des Prez, the "Father of Music" in the early Renaissance; and Orlando di Lasso, the giant of the late Renaissance. Both were citizens of the European world, equally at home in several languages and national styles. Their skills embraced the appealing, rhythmic French *chanson;* the elegant Latin motet; the lyrical Italian *madrigal;* and the noble Latin Mass.

Music everywhere expressed the Renaissance spirit of clarity. In sacred music the Renaissance ideal took form in clear, balanced, harmonious, serene polyphony. In secular music, composers worked with regular, clear-cut rhythms and consonant harmonies, all in a lively homophonic (chordal) style.

In all styles, text was frequently connected to the musical line. The music was used to paint in sound the meaning of the poetry: a profound, descending line for "but go weeping to the grave"; a leaping motif for "the floods have lifted up"; sweet consonances for gentle thoughts; and, "sighing" melodies and dramatic, often daring, harmonies for laments.

This bond between words and music was especially evident in the madrigal, the outstanding form of secular music in Renaissance Italy and England. In Italy, Luca Marenzio ("the divine composer") and Carlo Gesualdo, prince of Venosa, set the great lyrical poems of their time, investing their madrigals of life and love with elegance and emotional power. In England, Thomas Morley and John Wilbye, and a whole school of skilled madrigalists, adopted the Italian form for their own.

Reformation and Counter Reformation. The treatment of music was also affected by the powerful religious movements and counter-movements of the 1500's. In their efforts to reshape Catholic church practices, and to bring the people back in touch with worship services, leaders of the Reformation—Martin Luther in Germany, John Calvin (Jean Chauvin) in France—developed a melodious unison music for congregational singing, with simple four-part settings for singing at home. To folksong melodies, popular tunes, and plainsong, the Lutheran chorale added new German words; the French psalter, translations of psalm texts.

By the 1500's, advocates of change took power in the Catholic church, arguing for new policies to counteract the church's slipping authority—in short, a Counter Reformation. Although music was only one of its problems, the Council of Trent (set up to purge the church of abuses) criticized distracting musical practices: too many secular elements in the Mass, complex polyphony that made sacred words unintelligible, noisy instruments, and careless performance.

Once the extremists were silenced (some wanted to return to pure Gregorian chant), the council settled for a more dignified service, a simpler vocal style, and more attention to sacred texts.

SECULAR AND SACRED: *a collection of English madrigals from Elizabethan times, and verses from the* Bay Psalm Book, *the first song book printed in America (1640).*

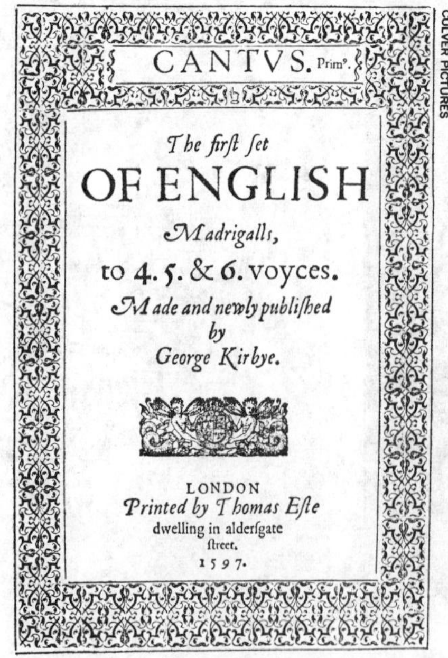

CANTVS. Prim°.

The firſt ſet

OF ENGLISH

Madrigalls,

to 4. 5. & 6. voyces.

Made and newly publiſhed by George Kirbye.

LONDON
Printed by Thomas Eſte
dwelling in alderſgate ſtreet.
1597.

CULVER PICTURES

PSALME xlix.

Pſalme 49
To the chief muſician a pſalme for the ſonnes of Korah.

Heare this all people, all give eare
that dwell the world all o're.
2 Sonnes both of low, & higher men,
joyntly both rich & poore.
3 My mouth it ſhall variety
of wiſdome be ſpeaking:
and my hearts meditation ſhall
be of underſtanding.
4 Vnto a ſpeech proverbiall
I will mine eare incline;
I will alſo upon the Harp
open my dark doctrine.
5 Why ſhould I be at all afrayd
in dayes that evill bee:
when that my heeles iniquity
about ſhall compaſſe mee.
(2)
6 Thoſe men that make their great eſtates.
their ſtay to truſt unto,
who in the plenty of their wealth
themſelves doe boaſt alſo:
7 Ther 's not a man *of them* that can
by any meanes redeeme
his brother, nor give unto God
enough to ranſome him.
8 So deare their ſoules redemption is
& ever ceaſeth it.

L 2 9 Than

It was left to Flemish composer Jacob de Kerle, and later to Giovanni Palestrina (composer, organist, and choirmaster at St. Peter's) to supervise these revisions. In their music, both exemplified the church ideal with compositions of a devotional spirit, free of personal drama, and based in a style that was transparent, harmonious, and unified.

Although Palestrina had turned away from key innovations in 16th-century polyphony, his influence later reached worldwide. His student Victoria, eventually chaplain to Empress Maria of Spain, was called "the Spanish Palestrina."

Toward Baroque. It is tempting to think of historical periods as clear-cut chunks of time, with specific dates and characteristics. But this is almost never true. Old styles linger on, new trends start early, and there is a great deal of overlapping from one style to the next. We can see all of this in the late Renaissance—the last half of the 1500's—a time that saw a continuation of old styles even as the foundations of the coming Baroque era were being built.

Composers began to seek an expanded musical language to express a greater, more intense range of emotions. They reached for new resources of harmony and dissonance, color, rhythm, and form. The powerful Venetian school at St. Mark's, led by Giovanni Gabrieli (a student of Lasso), experimented with massive colors, with new ways to use voices and instruments, and with multiphonic sound produced by up to five separate choirs, each with its own timbre and dynamics, echoing back and forth in brilliant *antiphonal* (answering) bodies of sound.

Succeeding Gabrieli, in 1613, as choirmaster at St. Mark's (the most desirable musical position in Italy), Claudio Monteverdi continued the transition toward the Baroque. Monteverdi, ranked as one of the greatest composers in all of Western music, moved toward modern tonalities, mixtures of polyphony and homophony (a trend that was well under way), and a focus on the solo voice and its supporting bass line—an approach to vocal writing that was to dominate music for four centuries.

Instrumental music, always a part of secular forms, became increasingly important during this transition period. Composers began to call for specific instruments and ensembles. They transcribed vocal music so it could be played by the lute, guitar, clavichord, virginal, and the harpsichord (an essential instrument in late Renaissance and early Baroque ensembles). They wrote dance music for ballets and for the very popular social dancing in the courts of Europe. And they experimented with improvisation, and with

METROPOLITAN MUSEUM OF ART, GIFT OF SUSAN DWIGHT BLISS, 1945

THE HARPSICHORD *became a favored instrument of the Baroque era. This one, ornately decorated, was made in Italy in the 1700's.*

pieces that would show off a performer's virtuosity.

Thus, with the arrival of the 1600's, many Baroque tendencies had already been anticipated, preparing the way for even greater and more elaborate personal expression through music.

Baroque, Classic, Romantic

Throughout the centuries, styles of music (and all art) have shifted between times of rationality and times of sensuality. Musical taste seems to move endlessly from the Apollonian ideal of logic, symmetry, clarity, and spiritual uplift to the Dionysian ideal of sensuality, irregularity, fantasy, and stimulation, and then back again.

This shift is especially clear in the years from the end of the Renaissance to the end of the 19th century.

In periods of logic and orderliness, like the Renaissance and the Classical era, the listener's attention is meant to focus not on the composer but on music *as an object,* as a design in sound. Hearing one of the earlier Haydn symphonies, for example, we are drawn to its balanced form, its clarity, the elegance of its construction. It stands apart from the hand that created it.

But in periods of dramatic expression (the Baroque), or of highly personalized sound-painting (the Romantic era), the listener's attention is meant to focus on the music as an expression of general states of the soul, or of the composer's capacity for feeling. Listening to Beethoven's *Eroica Symphony,* for example, we are drawn to the work as the composer's personal statement. We cannot separate the composition from the one who created it.

With the arrival of the 1600's, we embark on 300 years of familiar music. These are the times of Vivaldi and Bach, Haydn and Mozart, Beethoven, Schubert, Brahms, Wagner, and Verdi. We divide these centuries by affixing specific labels—the Baroque, the Classical, the Romantic—but, as we have seen again and again, art is a continuous phenomenon that responds to the continuous forces of human history. These labels, and the dates we associate with them, help us to understand changes in style and attitude, but they obscure the dynamic nature of art with all of its overlaps, inconsistencies, and dynamic movement.

The spirit of the times. The Baroque period was a time of powerful and contradictory currents. The visual arts valued ornate splendor, and yet looked toward greater simplicity and control. Wealth and power were concentrated among the nobility, and yet an increasingly powerful merchant class was competing for both. For composer and painter, sculptor and architect, there was no lack of patronage from the magnificent courts, the wealthy middle class of flourishing cities, and a divided church, struggling to capture the minds and hearts of the faithful.

By the 1700's, however, a clear shift in values had changed the complexion of European life. The merchant middle class had gained its power and wealth. Toward the end of the century, ideals of democracy helped set up revolutions in America and France. These revolutions demanded social reform and stressed the innate brotherhood of all men.

In this "age of enlightenment," the key word was naturalness. In the arts this meant simplicity and clarity instead of Baroque complexity. Art came to be judged on how it contributed to the well-being of the individual.

Replacing patronage from a slipping aristocracy, civic organizations and public concerts supported the arts. The people demanded and got music that was easy to understand and easy to play.

THE MINUET *is a stately form of an earlier fold or country dance.*

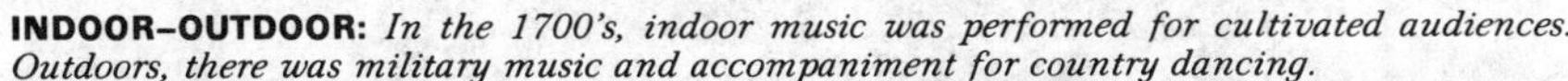

INDOOR–OUTDOOR: *In the 1700's, indoor music was performed for cultivated audiences. Outdoors, there was military music and accompaniment for country dancing.*

CULVER PICTURES

NEW YORK PUBLIC LIBRARY

As the artist moved into the 1800's, art and culture reached ever larger numbers of people. The Industrial Revolution changed the face of cities and the lives of people and artists.

For some, the growing impersonality of city life triggered a hunger for an imaginary world, for fantasy and mystery, and for expressions of intense personal emotion. For others, the age brought a renewed national spirit, and a longing for romantic heroes. At the same time, the diminishing aristocracy drew itself into tighter, more intimate circles.

These contradictory urges were all part of the Romantic movement. But there were hazards for the artist. He had to choose his course: to become the unknowable, fragile genius, patronized by and enclosed within a select salon society; or to be a highly visible superstar, supported by the vast and largely unsophisticated public in the concert halls that sprang up throughout Europe.

Either choice was a romantic choice, and the artist played a greatly increased personal role, as a hero, as the teller of fantastic tales, and as a bridge between the common man and those elements of life beyond the common man's reach.

Instrumental music: 1600–1900. By 1600, instrumental music easily rivaled vocal music in quality and quantity. Composers wrote for specific solo instruments and ensembles, seeking special colors and exploring the new capabilities of much improved wind, stringed, and keyboard instruments.

In their love for violent contrast, Baroque composers placed strikingly dissimilar pieces side by side: a brilliant, free-wheeling, rhythmically unrestrained and almost improvisational *toccata* or *fantasia* might be paired with a *fugue,* a grand architectural work of complex polyphony.

Just as composers loved to spin intricate webs of counterpoint around a given melody, in such favorite forms as the *passacaglia, chorale prelude,* and *theme and variations,* they delighted as well in shaping suites of lively dance pieces, borrowing from all national styles: the German *allemande,* French *courante,* Spanish *sarabande,* and Irish *gigue* (jig).

But by the early 1700's, a spirit of change was in the air. Music began to lose its massiveness and retain its decorative quality, but with a far lighter touch. Polyphony, with its wealth of simultaneous lines, gave way to homophony, with its emphasis on a clear melody supported by simple chords. The Baroque concept of a single spun-out theme, with a single mood and beat, gave way to contrasting themes, contrasting moods, and rhythmic flexibility. The "terraced dynamics" (a uniformly loud section followed by a uniformly soft one) of the Baroque era gave way to a constant fluctuation of volume.

The great Johann Sebastian Bach said in 1730, ". . . music is quite different from what it was. . . . Taste has changed unbelievably . . . the old style of music no longer pleases our ears."

These pre-classical years, from about 1720 to 1770, called the *Rococo,* saw the rise of music in the so-called *gallant style.* This was the time of elegantly polished keyboard music. It saw the courtly dance suites of France's François Couperin and Jean-Philippe Rameau; the delicate, miniature harpsichord sonatas of Domenico Scarlatti; and the late harpsichord music of Bach. The solo and ensemble music of Bach's second son, Carl Phillip Emmanuel, sometimes powerfully dramatic, sometimes charming and expressive, was to be a major influence on Haydn, Mozart, and Beethoven.

These influential pre-classical years also saw the rise of the great school of violin playing in Italy. For the wonderful stringed instruments of Amati and Stradivari, master composers like Arcangelo Corelli and Antonio Vivaldi wrote their melodious and vivacious *sonatas* and *concertos,* carrying music for chamber and orchestral ensembles to heights of lyricism and virtuosity.

CHAMBER MUSIC *for talented—and not-so-talented—amateurs reached its peak of popularity in the early 1800's.*

The foundation was laid for music in the great Classical era (the 30 or so years after 1770), the time of Haydn and Mozart. Its music was dignified but entertaining; restrained but expressive; harmonious, graceful, charming, symmetrical—and always pleasing to its audience.

By now instrumental groups, especially the string quartet and the symphony orchestra, had become favored ensembles, and their music followed fairly standard patterns. Later classical symphonies, for example, had four movements: a strong, expressive first movement, a lyrical slow movement, a minuet, and a vigorous finale.

Perhaps it was because of the comfortable formulas of the time—logical musical molds into which each composer could pour his straightforward melodies, simple harmonies, and regular rhythms—that such enormous quantities of instrumental music could be piled up. Haydn alone wrote 60 piano sonatas, 68 string quartets, and 106 symphonies (not to mention his other works, including 25 operas).

But the seeds of change, yet another swing from the rational to the sensual, were already planted in the late works of Haydn and Mozart. They flourished in the mature works of Beethoven. As the 1800's approached, artists became increasingly involved in the inner conflicts of the individual, in the world of nature, in fantasy, and in a search for mysterious cosmic truths.

It was in this new spirit, in the first quarter of the 1800's, that Ludwig van Beethoven wrote his gripping *Fifth Symphony* ("I will wrestle with Fate," he said, "it shall not overcome me"); painted the delicate scenes of his charming *Pastoral Symphony;* and glorified universal brotherhood in his mighty *Ninth Symphony.*

After Beethoven, nothing was the same, not even for composers like Franz Schubert and Felix Mendelssohn, who held on to Classical traditions; for Robert Schumann, endlessly torn between the old and the new; or for Johannes Brahms, who successfully merged Classical forms with Romantic expression.

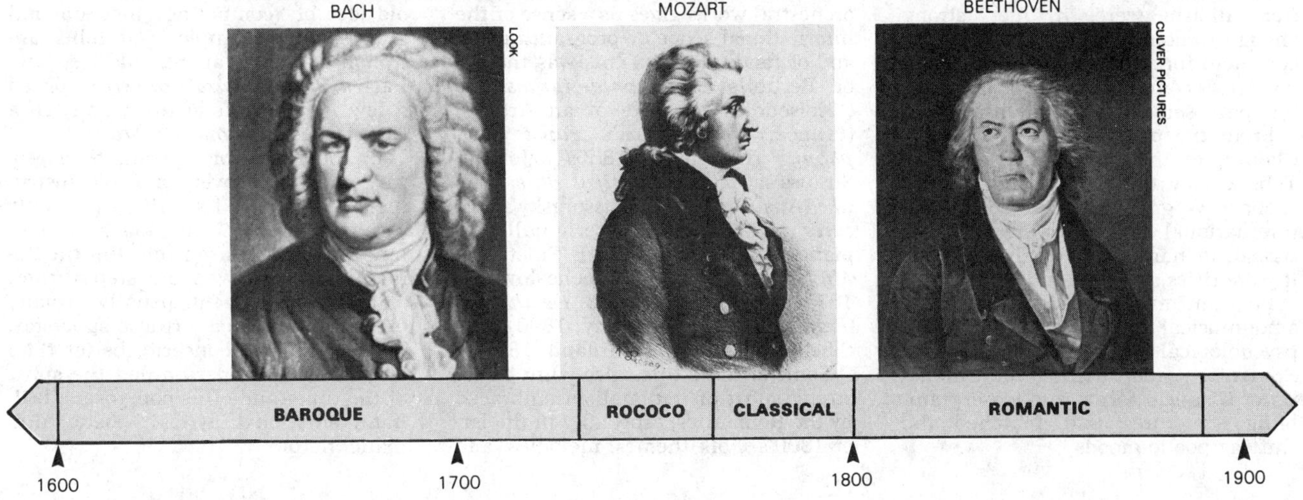

CULVER PICTURES

ARCHIV FÜR KUNST UND GESCHICHTE, BERLIN

KEYBOARD VIRTUOSITY: *classic and Romantic composers were also performers, from Mozart* (below) *to Brahms* (above), *to the legendary Liszt* (above right), *who wrote some music so difficult that only he could play it.*

CULVER PICTURES

The dual trends of Classicism and Romanticism were, in fact, strong enough to dominate music of a whole continent for a full century, creating a powerful common musical language for composers of all nationalities.

From the piano pieces of Frederic Chopin, to the symphonies of Peter Tchaikovsky, to the musical dramas of Richard Wagner, the melodies of this international language were intensely lyrical; its harmonies, richly complex; its sonorities, colorful and exotic.

Program music—pieces inspired by a nonmusical idea (a story, an image, a psychological mood)—dominated the Romantic scene, melting the symmetry of Classical forms into looser, rambling structures that matched the shifting poetic moods.

Even a short list of 19th-century orchestral works gives us a sense of the international scope of program music, and of its durability. This was the era of Berlioz's *Symphonie fantastique* ("Episode in the Life of an Artist") (France, 1829), Liszt's *Faust Symphony* (Hungary, 1855), Johann Strauss's *On the Beautiful Blue Danube* (Austria, 1867), Mussorgsky's *Pictures at an Exhibition* (originally for piano solo; Russia, 1874), Smetana's *My Fatherland* (Czechoslovakia, 1875), Richard Strauss's *Death and Transfiguration* (Germany, 1890), and Sibelius's *Finlandia* (Finland, 1899).

Some of these titles also point to the strong spirit of nationalism embraced by the Romantics, especially in the latter 1800's. Folk themes, melodies, and rhythms influenced not only the orchestral works of the time, from the *Peer Gynt* suites of Norway's Edvard Grieg to the *Slavonic Dances* of Czechoslovakia's Antonin Dvořák, but they flowed through much of the Romantic piano literature.

The piano, now much improved over the instrument Mozart knew, was, in fact, the supreme Romantic instrument. With its technical possibilities enormously expanded by composer-virtuosos Chopin, Liszt, and Brahms, the piano was the ideal medium for a massive outpouring of new music, including nationalistic dances (Chopin's mazurkas and polonaises), pieces based on folk tunes and rhythms (Liszt's *Hungarian Rhapsodies*), picturesque suites and intimate salon pieces (Schumann's *Scenes from Childhood,* Chopin's nocturnes and waltzes), and brilliant virtuoso displays (the *Etudes* of both Chopin and Liszt, the piano variations of Brahms).

The piano was also the star of the 19th-century *concerto.* This exciting form, virtually a symphony with a featured soloist, had its roots in the old idea of "competing" instrumental groups. For example, Gabrieli's antiphonal choirs at St. Mark's, and Bach's *Brandenburg Concertos,* pitted a few instruments against many in a form called the *concerto grosso.*

In the hands of Vivaldi, then Mozart, then Beethoven, the solo instrument expanded its role, eventually reaching a "star" position as important as the orchestra itself. But the Romantic concerto went one step further. The solo instrument, usually a piano or violin, became a virtuoso superstar. In this way the concerto, better than any other form, personified the spirit of the times and of its composers: brilliant, emotional, lyrical, poetic, dramatic, heroic.

Opera: 1600–1900. The intimate bond between words and music was already an ancient unbroken tradition when Baroque vocal music gave birth to a new form called *opera.* Using *monody*—a simple reciting-singing style for solo voice, lightly accompanied—the Camerata of Florence, Italy (a group of writers and musicians working around 1600), sought to use music to heighten the emotional power of their poetry. Applied to an entire story, the result was opera, a drama combining monologues and dialogues, scenery, action, and music.

Written for the princely courts of Europe, with stories originally drawn from ancient legends, 17th-century Italian opera soon developed features that would endure for 200 years. These included the overture, rapidly sung recitatives (a quick way to get through chunks of conversation), solo arias, duets, ensembles, dances, elaborate scenery, and assorted orchestral interludes.

By mid-century, opera spread throughout Europe, with the exception of France. Its *libretto,* or text, may have become ridiculous and dramatically unbelievable, but its vocal displays and stage effects were splendid. Its *arias*—elaborate songs that showed off the singer's virtuosity—were the highlights of the whole production. The Italian vocal style, full of intense expressions of pain, fury, and other emotions, dominated the show.

As popular as Italian opera may have been, France would have none of it. It was not until the late 1600's that France, under Louis XIV, developed its own brand of opera, called *lyric tragedy.* Under the leadership of composer Jean-Baptiste Lully (the king's favorite), French opera grew out of a blend of ballet (a court tradition) and French tragedy (especially the works of dramatists Corneille and Racine).

With its visual splendor, romantic stories, spectacular choruses, brilliant orchestral colors, and catchy ballet music, French opera became wildly popular, influencing composers into the early 1700's, and even touching early opera in England.

Although England's own Henry Purcell had produced the lovely *Dido and Aeneas,* it was left to a German composer to bring the full thrust of Italian opera to the courts and people of England. In 1710 the great George Frederick Handel stirred all of London with his opera *Rinaldo,* and Italian opera became the fashion of the day.

Italian opera soon became lighter, more vivacious, highly melodic, and ornately embellished. It gave rise to *bel canto*—an obsession with beautiful vocal sound and virtuosity.

The English boom, with Handel at its center, lasted until about 1730, when public taste turned away from tragic foreign opera and toward lighter theatrical amusements.

SPECTACLE *was an important part of opera from the late 1600's on. This stage set is for* Armide *by Lully, performed for Louis XIV of France.*

Thus was born the *comic opera,* the people's revolt against "serious" opera. The new, lightweight form took various names. In England it was called the "ballad opera" (the best was *The Beggar's Opera*); in Italy, the "intermezzo" (Pergolesi's *La Serva padrona* delights audiences to this day); in Germany, the "Singspiel" (a play with music); and in France, the "opéra comique."

Seeing that his kind of opera was now out of fashion, Handel, an astute showman, made a frank appeal to London's huge middle-class audience. In the 1730's he wisely turned his genius to the *oratorio,* a lengthy religious form that could be produced in a church or a concert hall without stage action or costly scenery and costumes.

With its potent Biblical themes, narrator, soloists, chorus, and orchestra, the oratorio was already a traditional form in Handel's native Germany. At Leipzig's St. Thomas's School, cantor Johann Sebastian Bach was writing his magnificent *Christmas Oratorio* at just about this time.

It was a smart move for Handel, for he surpassed even his earlier fame as an operatic composer. His new success with the English public was phenomenal. Handel's 26 oratorios (all in English)—including *Saul, Israel in Egypt* (both written in 1738), and, of course, *Messiah* (1741)—established his music once and for all as the single most powerful influence in British musical life for the next hundred years.

Handel's happy turn to the oratorio was only one of the far-reaching consequences of the collision between serious opera and comic opera. In the 1750's, just after Bach's death, and in Handel's last years, composers attempted to rescue serious opera, recognizing that its survival depended on badly needed reforms. It would have to reflect the new spirit of "naturalness," rid itself of deforming abuses, deepen its expressive qualities, tighten the bond between words and music, and adopt an international flavor.

Christoph Gluck transformed these ideals into a workable reality. Opera conductor, composer to the emperor at Vienna, and later a protegé of Marie Antoinette in Paris, Gluck said, ". . . my greatest effort should be directed to seeking a beautiful simplicity . . . music must serve the poetry. . . ."

In Vienna, just three years after Handel's death, Gluck's goals were reached in his exquisite *Orpheus and Euridice;* and in Paris, twelve years later, in 1774, in his tremendously popular *Iphigenia in Aulos.* The French public was overwhelmed by Gluck's synthesis of Italian grace, German solidity, and the noble magnificence of French lyric tragedy, qualities that were to influence operatic composers into the 19th century.

Operatic excitement in Paris and Vienna of the 1770's was rivaled by the activities at Prince Esterházy's lavish Hungarian estate. Here, under Haydn's directorship, had sprung up a new international center for opera. Although Haydn was devoted to opera and oratorio (he produced over 75 operas of other composers, 21 of his own, and wrote four oratorios, including *The Creation* and *The Seasons*), he felt himself overshadowed by the masters of his time.

Even at age 55, and famous throughout Europe, he could say of his 31-year-old friend that "scarely any man could stand comparison with the great Mozart"; and of Handel, upon hearing his *Messiah* in London, "He is the master of us all."

The greatness of Mozart lay not only in his miraculous gift of melody but also, throughout his operas, in his ability to probe human nature. At the same time, he summarized the theatrical music of a whole age and all national styles. *The Marriage of Figaro*

(1786) was the epitome of Italian comic opera; *Don Giovanni (Don Juan)* (1787) was a comic-dramatic Italian opera that would appeal to the 19th-century Romantic imagination; and *The Magic Flute* (1791) was perhaps the greatest of all German Romantic operas, a German "Singspiel," full of profound music and rich symbolism.

If Mozart was the master of theater, Beethoven was its slave, for few composers have ever struggled as he did wth his only opera, *Fidelio.* Its story of heroism reflected the same humanitarian ideals as his *Ninth Symphony,* but the operatic form, unlike the symphonic medium, seems to have eluded him. Beethoven was simply not a man of the theater.

The direction pointed out by Mozart was not lost on the Romantics who followed him. Side by side, to the end of the 19th century, there developed huge repertories of comic opera, grand opera (a spectacular feast of sound and action), lyric opera (something between comic and grand opera), and Romantic opera.

A partial list of 19th-century European operatic successes barely touches on the theatrical riches of this time and place: Rossini's *The Barber of Seville* (1816) and *William Tell* (1829); Bellini's *Norma* (1831); Donizetti's *Lucia di Lammermoor* (1835); Wagner's *Tannhaüser* (1845) and *Lohengrin* (1850); Verdi's *Rigoletto* (1851) and *La Traviata* (1853); Berlioz's *The Trojans* (1856); Offenbach's *Orpheus in the Underworld* (1858); Gounod's *Faust* (1859); Verdi's *Aïda* (1871); Johann Strauss's *Die Fledermaus* (1874); Bizet's *Carmen* (1875); Saint-Saëns's *Samson and Delilah* (1877); and Gilbert and Sullivan's *The Mikado* (1885)!

Sacred Music: 1600–1900.

Bach and Handel so dominate their chapter of history that we tend to ignore the fact that even these masters had their teachers. Works like the *St. Matthew Passion* and *Messiah* were in fact the direct products of trends well under way a century earlier.

Gabrieli's "colossal Baroque" style lent its vivid colors and multiphonic choirs and instrumental groups. Opera contributed the recitative, aria, chorus, and orchestral interludes. And the early Baroque composers showed how the new style could be artistically integrated with the traditional style of Palestrina.

To understand the roots of Bach's and Handel's devotional music we must look backward to Monteverdi's magnificent *Vespers* (1610), and especially to the long and productive career of Heinrich Schütz (1585–1672), the greatest German composer of the 17th century. Schütz studied with Gabrieli in Italy, then returned to Protestant Germany, where he developed a style all his own, using both the elaborate Italian polyphony and the solid homophonic materials of the German chorales.

Though they were exact contemporaries (both were born in 1685), Johann Sebastian Bach and George Frederick Handel led lives that were dramatically unalike. Bach was a systematic, hard-working provincial musician, content with steady work, secure patronage, and a limited reputation in his own time. Handel, on the other hand, was a flamboyant, imposing musician of international renown. Today we recognize these men as giants, not only of an age (the late Baroque) but of all time. In their work, both summed up the musical trends that preceded them, absorbed important styles and techniques of their own time, and anticipated future musical directions.

AN ORGAN PRELUDE *by Bach, one of hundreds of organ pieces, cantatas, and other works for church use by the great Baroque composer.*

CULVER PICTURES

Nowhere are these traits more evident than in Bach's extensive music for the church. For this devout Lutheran there was, in fact, no separation between his sacred and secular music. Everywhere he inscribed his scores "to the glory of God" or "in the name of Jesus."

Perhaps the outstanding symbol of Bach's devotion to both religion and tradition was his integration, into hundreds of his works, of the Lutheran chorale—that body of tunes that one historian has called "the battle hymns of the Reformation." Bach used these hymns as medieval and Renaissance composers had used Gregorian chant: as a broad fundamental melody (the *cantus firmus*) around which one wove polyphonic lines, as the basis for variations and fugue subjects, and as church anthems in majestic four-part harmonizations.

In his 20's, as the virtuoso court organist for the Duke of Weimar, Bach expanded the chorale in variations, fugues, fantasias, and intricately constructed chorale preludes.

In the last decades of his life, as cantor of St. Thomas's School in Leipzig, Bach turned frequently to the familiar chorale to help accomplish the enormous musical tasks demanded of him. In addition to his teaching duties, Bach was burdened with requests for special music for weddings, funerals, and city events, and was required to compose Passion music for Good Friday, Magnificats for church festivals, and, weekly, a new church cantata (a kind of oratorio-in-miniature) for that Sunday's service!

In these devotional works Bach, like Handel in his oratorios, produced the culminating work of a lifetime and of an historical age, merging craft, genius, and the intensity of a personal vision with the innovations of his predecessors.

Bach's 200 known church cantatas blended international forms and styles into a cohesive whole: the aria and duet, borrowed from opera; a flowing instrumental style, influenced by Vivaldi; France's majestic operatic overture; and, binding these diverse elements, the ever-present Lutheran chorale.

In his *St. Matthew Passion,* a majestic work as brilliant as any Baroque opera or Handel oratorio, Bach infused the traditional hymn tune with new power, united the operatic aria with his religious theme, and drew fully upon the dynamic theatrical colors and contrasts of Gabrieli's Venetian school of antiphonal writing.

It seems fitting that in his last great statement of Christian faith, the darkly majestic *Mass in B Minor,* Bach returned to Gregorian chant to set the words *Credo in unum Deum (I believe in one God).* This powerful *cantus firmus,* cementing a massive eight-part polyphonic texture, seems to symbolize both the continuity of Christian tradition and the end of four centuries of devotional music.

After 1750, the year of Bach's death, an era of great church music gradually came to an end. The new age of popular theater was already two decades old. Public attention was on comic opera, and on Handel's oratorios, which were intended more for the concert hall than for the church despite their religious subjects.

What had been an unbroken line of great devotional compositions, from Machaut's *Our Lady's Mass* of 1360 to Bach's *Mass in B Minor* of 1749, now became a scattering of isolated masterpieces: the Masses of Schubert, Haydn, Mozart, and Beethoven.

Both Haydn and Mozart knew Bach's work, but their music reflected a time of changing taste. Haydn's *Lord Nelson Mass* contains some traditional polyphonic writing, but his focus is clearly on the emerging symphonic style of the late 18th century. Mozart's unfinished *Requiem,* his last work, includes an intricate fugue on a theme used by both Bach and Handel, and it occasionally mirrors the massive choral style favored by Handel; but the work is infused with Mozart's love of grace and melodies in the lyrical Italian style.

Even Beethoven's *Mass in D* (the *Missa Solemnis* of 1823), considered to be second only to Bach's *Mass in B Minor* in its musical interpretation of the text, is more a tightly woven "symphony" in five movements than a liturgical setting in the Baroque style of independent movements. Beethoven, who idolized both Bach and Handel, may have borrowed his choral style from Handel, and even adapted one theme from the Hallelujah Chorus from *Messiah,* but his reverence for the past stops there. The work as a whole is pure Beethoven.

It is worth noting that after Bach's cantatas, the great composers wrote little for use in the normal services of the church. Bach's *Passions,* Handel's oratorios, and the Masses of Haydn and Mozart ignored the practical and liturgical needs of the church, and were better suited for concert performance. Music had declared its independence from its long-time sponsor and protector.

The new spirit of the classical era led, in fact, to a general neglect of Bach's great religious works for almost 80 years after his death. It was not until 1829 that the 20-year-old Felix Mendelssohn resurrected the forgotten *St. Matthew Passion,* leading Europe to a renaissance of the master's work.

The later Romantics were awed by Bach's and Handel's technique, but their ideal of sacred music was quite different. Liszt summed up this ideal as "devotional. . .and drastic, uniting on a colossal scale the theater and the church. . . ." Berlioz's *Grand Mass for the Dead,* an explosive work of vast dimensions, called for four brass choirs, four gongs, and 16 kettledrums! Brahms's *German Requiem* flowed with Romantic feeling, supported by intense Romantic harmonies. Verdi's *Requiem,* despite its gesture to the past in an elaborate fugue on the word *Sanctus,* glowed with theatrical fire and appeal, in the best traditions of Italian opera.

And so sacred music came to assume a less important role in the musical world. At the same time, in characteristically Romantic fashion, sacred music became the personal expression of the composer rather than an expression of corporate faith.

CULVER PICTURES

THE ORATORIO, *a new secular form, was perfected by Handel in England. This drawing by Hogarth makes fun of the amateur choruses of the day.*

The song. The song is the oldest of all musical forms. For centuries, people have sung folk songs, popular songs, sacred songs, and art songs ("serious" songs by trained composers). Songs have been written in all languages, for all occasions, and deal with almost every conceivable theme.

A Greek of the first century B.C. carved a song on the tombstone of his beloved wife. Love songs were written in the tenth century. The medieval Goliards sang of drink and gambling; the troubadours, of love and chivalry. Burgundian *chansons* of the 15th century, such as Josquin's *Farewell, my loves,* were so popular that their tunes soon appeared in solemn Masses. Elizabethan England embraced the charming lute songs of John Dowland and William Byrd. And, as we have already seen, Baroque monody led to Italian opera and its highlight, the aria, the epitome of theatrical song.

Monody in Germany, however, led not to the aria but, in the early 1800's, to the German art song, called the *Lied.* These *Lieder,* typically written as an intimate union of solo voice and piano, were short settings of poetry of the highest quality; they were probably the most successful of all attempts to bind words and music in a single art form.

In his tragically brief life, Franz Schubert wrote over 600 *Lieder.* Robert Schumann wrote 100 love songs in 1840 alone (the year of his marriage). Brahms published 260 *Lieder,* and Hugo Wolf (considered second only to Schubert in his genius for the art song) wrote 250.

Though many *Lieder* were conceived as individual pieces, a great number appeared as parts of a unified *song cycle;* that is, a group of songs related either by a single poetic theme or by having all been set to the lyrics of a single poet.

Thus Schubert composed *Winter Journey* (24 songs); Schumann, *Poet's Love* (on texts of Heinrich Heine); Brahms, his 15 *Magelone Romances;* and Wolf, the *Spanish* and *Italian Songbooks.*

By the time the 1900's dawned, the song-cycle tradition was being continued in Germany by Gustav Mahler *(The Song of the Earth)* and in France, by Gabriel Fauré *(The Good Song),* Claude Debussy *(Songs of Bilitis),* and Maurice Ravel *(Songs of Madagascar).*

As we will see shortly, a universal song tradition flowed uninterrupted into the 20th century. Although composers' interest in the art song gradually dwindled, it was replaced by an intensive search for folk songs as source material for new compositions.

Russian nationalism. Nowhere was this exploitation of folk materials more essential than in the work of the Russian nationalists of the 1800's. Other nationalist composers—Chopin or Liszt, for example—had touches of folk melody and rhythm, but they were written in a sophisticated cosmopolitan style. By contrast, the Russian nationalists were rooted in the soil of their homeland. They knew little of traditional European theory and practice, and so were forced to find their own voice in their native materials.

Launched by Mikhail Glinka's operas *A Life for the Czar* (1836) and *Russlan and Ludmilla* (1842), the Russian movement gained momentum in the work of "the mighty handful": Mily Balakirev (a professional musician and teacher), Alexander Borodin (a chemist), Modest Mussorgsky (a civil servant), and Nicolai Rimsky-Korsakov (a former naval officer).

It was Mussorgsky, the least educated of the group, who turned out to be the most thoroughly original composer of the movement and one of the most revolutionary innovators of *all* composers. Entirely unaware of European traditions, he had to invent his own "crude" harmonies, and carve out his melodies and rhythms from folk sources.

He was blessed with a flair for drama, a keen perception of human nature, and a sensitive ear for the rhythms of speech.

His music was extraordinarily powerful. The opera *Boris Godunov* (1872) is a masterpiece of psychological insight; *Pictures at an Exhibition* (1874), a piano suite later orchestrated by Maurice Ravel, is an exemplary display of realistic sound-painting.

By contrast, Rimsky-Korsakov moved away from extreme nationalism toward a broader, more refined cosmopolitan style. Although he never abandoned folk music as source material, his was a world not of dramatic realism but of vivacious fantasy and brilliant orchestral color.

Today we regard Rimsky-Korsakov as a bridge between the nationalists and the Russian composers of the 20th century—chiefly his pupils Alexander Glazunov and Igor Stravinsky.

No discussion of late 19th-century nationalism can omit the name of Peter Ilyich Tchaikovsky. Despite Stravinsky's claim that "He was the most Russian of us all," Tchaikovsky's music is a conglomeration of Western influences: Italian opera *(Eugene Onegin),* German symphony (the *Symphonie Pathétique*), and French ballet (*Swan Lake, Sleeping Beauty,* and *The Nutcracker*). A musical world apart from his countryman Mussorgsky, Tchaikovsky appealed immediately to Western tastes. He was even invited to New York to attend the opening of Carnegie Hall!

And so it was, in Mussorgsky's influence on the harmonies of Debussy, Rimsky-Korsakov's influence on the orchestral style of Stravinsky, and Tchaikovsky's universal appeal to the modern Romantics of the Western world, that the bridge was completed between 19th-century Russia and 20th-century Europe and America.

The 20th Century

Exploration and discovery in the 20th century have been carried out on a scale and with a momentum never before witnessed in human history. In three-quarters of a century we have moved from faltering airplane flight to the first manned moon landing; from the discovery of protons and electrons to nuclear energy; from the days of the wireless to an era of computerized telecommunication. Rapid world communication has linked distant communities and opened cultural channels. More and more, we have become a "global village."

In the world of music, our scores, recordings, broadcasts, and telecasts crisscross the globe. Composers and performers travel everywhere, exchanging ideas and exploring new resources, creating a musical cross-fertilization on a massive, international level.

As a result, 20th-century musical language reflects not one unified style but thousands of diverse influences. Every sort of musical element, old and new, traditional and radical, is fair game for the modern composer.

New uses of folk music. The incorporation of folk materials into classical compositions was, as we have seen, a traditional technique. Even in the American colonies, as early as 1794, composer James Hewitt used a death song of the Cherokee Indians in a ballad opera. But it was not until 1890 that researchers attempted to preserve American Indian tribal music. Their field recordings of Zuni melodies (on Edison's newly invented phonograph) was followed, in 1911, by an all-out government-sponsored program to seriously investigate and record the music of the native Americans.

In 1900, German researchers recorded the music of a visiting court orchestra from Thailand and of musicians from South Africa. At about the same time, scholar-composers in central Europe made the first extensive scientific studies of their regional folk music: Leoš Janáček, in Czechoslovakia; Béla Bartók and Zoltán Kodály, in Hungary and Rumania. Bartók went on to Bulgaria, Turkey, the Ukraine,

THE BOLERO *and other folk dances provided new material for early modern composers.*

CULVER PICTURES

and North Africa, publishing 2000 folk tunes in five books on native materials.

These ethnomusicologists saw that they had uncovered an enormously rich field of fresh, vital musical treasures. For composers, the materials suggested entirely new forms of musical expression. In England, his editorial work with English hymnody prompted composer Ralph Vaughan Williams to say that "Two years of close association with some of the best (as well as some of the worst) tunes in the world was a better musical education than any amount of sonatas and fugues."

Bartók's research revolutionized his music, infusing it with exotic melodic shapes and powerful irregular rhythms. Music of the Spanish gypsy richly colored the piano and orchestral works of Albéniz, Granados, and Manuel de Falla. Heitor Villa-Lobos's 1500 compositions consistently reflected the Indian and Spanish-Portuguese elements of his native Brazil.

In the United States, Charles Ives (an insurance executive by trade, a composer by calling) wove endless strands of folk and patriotic tunes into fantastic masses of dissonance. Scott Joplin (known best for his *Maple Leaf Rag*) attempted to blend native black idioms with European theatrical forms in his opera, *Treemonisha.* George Gershwin brought the blues—taken from black work songs and spirituals—into his "folk opera," *Porgy and Bess,* and jazz (the urbanized product of blues) into the concert hall in his *Rhapsody in Blue.*

Even into the 1930's and '40's, folk influences shaped American music. Aaron Copland wove Mexican songs into *El Salón México,* cowboy songs into his ballets *Billy the Kid* and *Rodeo,* and a Shaker hymn ("The Gift to Be Simple") into *Appalachian Spring,* his most famous piece.

Folk music fascinated the modern composer. It was direct and unsophisticated by Western standards, yet so technically complex that it often defied an accurate transcription into traditional notation.

The music of Africa was frequently antiphonal, polyphonic, and polyrhythmic. The music of Java and Bali, played by *gamelan* orchestras of gongs, drums, flutes, and lutes, often involved up to 25 different levels of simultaneous activity! Its pitched instruments had up to 18 different kinds of tuning.

The music of India, dating back to 4000 years before the Christian era, was based on ritual improvisation using enormously complex pitch and rhythmic formulas, systems of organization incomprehensible to Western ears.

The folk music of the Far East—of China, Japan, and Korea—was no less intricate. In China alone, with its 84 different scales, the first musical system was so old that it was already obsolete by the time of Confucius.

Modern research showed how interdependent musical traditions were. The music of Java and Bali was related to the traditions of Southeast Asia, China, India, and the Middle East. The music of North Africa seemed to draw from the music of Indonesia, Polynesia, India, and the Middle and Far East. In Central and South America, the Spanish conquest had merged Catholic church practices with native music; folk dances became a part of church ritual. In Peru, native flute melodies could be heard winding over the solemn tones of traditional church chord progressions.

The musical world also took folk tales and legends for its subject matter. The most influential models were the musical dramas of Richard Wagner: *Lohengrin* (1850), based on a tenth-century legend; *Tristan and Isolde* (1865), a love story set in legendary times; and especially *The Ring of the Nibelung* (1857–1874), a continuous tale, told over the course of four musical dramas, drawn from Germanic mythology.

With Wagner's models as a precedent, composers of the 20th century joined their integral use of folk melodies and rhythms with the dramatic possibilities of legend. In *Tapiola* and *The Swan of Tuonela,* Jan Sibelius turned to 13th-century Finnish epics; in *Alexander Nevsky* (a cantata, drawn from his 1938 film score), Sergei Prokofiev portrayed an episode from medieval Russian history. In three of the most revolutionary works of the early 20th century, Igor Stravinsky drew on the folk materials and tales of ancient Russia to write *The Firebird* (1910), *Petrushka* (1911), and *The Rite of Spring* (*Le Sacre du Printemps,* 1913), subtitled "Pictures of Pagan Russia."

20th-century conservatism. Their use of folk materials reflects only one aspect of modern composers'

FOLK MATERIAL *was used internationally by the 1900's—the Beatles learned from the Indian music of Ravi Shankar* (left), *French composers discovered ragtime, and Aaron Copland drew on the dances of the American West in his ballet* Rodeo (right).

F.B. GRUNZWEIG/PHOTO RESEARCHERS

MARTHA SWOPE

regard for tradition. Many other strong traditional elements have, to this day, continued directly out of the historical past.

Richard Strauss's *A Hero's Life* and Ottorino Respighi's *The Pines of Rome* are direct descendents of Liszt's tone poems, full of sweeping melodies, lush harmonies, and grandly theatrical Romantic gestures.

Mahler's ten symphonies—gigantic, programmatic, and ultra-Romantic—owe a lasting debt to Berlioz's concept of orchestral writing.

Sergei Rachmaninoff's piano concertos are pure Liszt, awash with sentimental tunes and supercharged virtuosity. The operas of Puccini and Menotti are pure Italian lyricism, traditional to the core.

In the world of popular theater, the American operetta—such as Sigmund Romberg's *The Student Prince*—grew out of a 200-year-old comic-opera tradition, evolving into musical comedy (Kern's *Showboat*), political satire (Gershwin's *Of Thee I Sing*), and finally into the Broadway musical (Rodgers' *Oklahoma!*, Porter's *Kiss Me, Kate,* Bernstein's *Candide,* and Loewe's *My Fair Lady*). Even Leonard Bernstein's revolutionary (for Broadway) *West Side Story* is rooted in the *verismo* (realist) tradition of late 19th-century opera. Its story of everyday people acting violently under the stress of powerful emotions only updated the sentiment-plus-violence formula of such standard operatic favorites as *Cavalleria rusticana* and *I Pagliacci.*

Innovation. Alongside the conservatives in any generation of composers there are always the restless innovators who are discontent with the "old art." These artists search for new means of expression and a new language with which to find fresh solutions for old problems. More than any other era in musical history, the 20th century has experienced radical innovations in all aspects of musical composition.

New concepts of tonality. The great bulk of music familiar to all of us is *tonal* music. This includes everything from a Bach cantata to a Beethoven symphony to a Verdi opera to our entire jazz-pop-rock repertory.

Such pieces are called tonal because their melodies and harmonies are systematically organized around the pitches of traditional major and minor scales. This gives us a comfortable feeling of being in a certain *key,* or *tonality.* Although our ears will readily accept slight departures from a given tonality—sometimes by momentary transitions to other tonalities (a process called *modulation*), sometimes by the slight intrusion of pitches foreign to that tonality (a use of "color" tones, called *chromaticism*)—we are comfortable in sensing that the piece will

IGOR STRAVINSKY, *drawn here by Picasso, was the major innovator in orchestral music in the first half of the 20th century.*

end with a satisfying return to a central point of rest, a "home" tone where all pitch movement and all dissonance come to a conclusive resolution.

Beginning in the 1800's, however, tonality began to slowly disintegrate. Composers gave more and more importance to the foreign "color" tones in order to enrich their melodies and add lively dissonances to their harmonies. At the same time they experimented with more frequent and closely spaced key changes, purposely blurring tonal centers of repose to create a "seamless" music. This tonal ambiguity (the loss of a strong "key feeling") produced music that seemed to endlessly unfold itself in a stream of heightened tension.

In his musical drama *Tristan and Isolde,* Wagner so extended these practices that the terms "Tristan melody" (unending melody) and "Tristan harmony" (seamless, chromatically rich, ambiguous modulations) became common terms in the modern composer's vocabulary.

Wagner's model opened the door to the complete dissolution of tonality. In *The Rite of Spring,* Stravinsky accomplished this by constructing massive, shatteringly dissonant chords that were sometimes *bitonal* (two different tonalities, played simultaneously), and sometimes *polytonal* (multiple simultaneous tonalities). In the second movement of his *Fourth Symphony* (1916), Ives accomplished this by interlocking a number of simultaneously played folk tunes, each in its own key, thus creating a thick mass of conflicting tonalities.

By far the greatest break with tonality came at the hands of Arnold Schoenberg. Beginning with a purposeful avoidance of any consonance whatsoever, Schoenberg evolved a revolutionary, highly systematized method of pitch organization called "composition with twelve tones." In place of a musical theme, he constructed a "tone row" of twelve different pitches of equal importance. Then, by rationally manipulating this fixed "note series" (backward, upside-down, inside-out, and so on), he was able to generate an entire piece of music that completely avoided the slightest hint of "key" or tonal center of repose.

The severity of Schoenberg's approach to writing was carried a step further by his pupil Anton Webern. Webern systematized not only the pitches of his music but *all* elements of composition: rhythm, harmony, dynamics, duration, and texture. He offered, in short, a thorough "serialization" of music.

By the end of World War II, Schoenberg's concepts and Webern's innovations were avidly embraced by younger composers throughout the world. "Twelve-tone writing" and "serial music" became an international vogue.

In the decades of exploration, from the turn of the century to the 1950's, other composers had struck out on paths that were equally innovative but far less drastic.

In France, Claude Debussy veiled his moody music with tantalizing glints of tonality, choosing his harmonies for their evocative color and sonority.

In Hungary, Béla Bartók, deriving his melodic lines from the chromatic folk tunes of Eastern Europe, wove dissonant polyphonic textures that were nevertheless anchored by clear key centers (and often interspersed with sections built on traditional Western harmonies).

In Germany, Paul Hindemith, disturbed by innovations that increasingly alienated the public, and concerned with the social obligations of the composer, wrote accessible pieces for the musical amateur and beautifully crafted, comparatively conservative works for the concert hall and opera house. *Mathis der Maler* (1934) is his best-known composition.

But it is the work of Schoenberg's pupil Alban Berg, especially the opera *Wozzeck* (1921), that most effectively merges the radical and the traditional. Berg uses both tonality and atonality to serve his dramatic purposes, with a structural foundation based on conventional forms.

Old and new techniques. The lessons learned from the natural evolution and modification of Schoenberg's break with tonality, and from Berg's resurrection of tonality in a new form, update one of the oldest lessons found in musical history: new methods and techniques may in time be absorbed into a common musical language (if they work), modified (if they are extreme), or rejected (if they fail to advance the cause of music).

Understanding this, modern innovators, no longer satisfied with conventional means, have systematically transformed traditional musical elements and explored new resources.

They have learned how to liberate

J. HEFFERNAN/METROPOLITAN OPERA

LULU *by Alban Berg brought atonality to dramatic use in opera. This dark setting is for a production by the Metropolitan Opera.*

rhythm from its conventional regularity, and how to work toward freer movement and a seamlessness far beyond Wagner's ideal of "endless melody." Ives's orchestral layers of tunes typically move at entirely different rates of speed. Elliott Carter's *Double Concerto* (1961) pits one instrumental group against another, each moving at its own tempo. Sometimes one group is slowing down and the other is speeding up at the same time.

These innovators have been intrigued by the delights of *aleatory* (chance) music, in which results are as random as the roll of dice: "I try to arrange my composing means," John Cage said, "so that I won't have any knowledge of what might happen." Surely this is the ultimate in total compositional freedom.

The innovators have learned to move beyond the conventional sounds of conventional instruments, coaxing new pitches and sound effects from the piano, from the flute, and from stringed instruments affixed with miniature contact microphones.

Some have elevated timbre to a dominant role in composition. Edgard Varèse's pioneer work *Ionisation* (1933) called for bells, chains, anvils, and sirens. Some have experimented with the use of physical space. Varèse used 425 loudspeakers to circulate the sounds of his *Electronic Poem* at the Brussels Exposition in 1958; Karlheinz Stockhausen's *Groups* (1957) surrounded his audience with three orchestras, all playing independently.

Composers have explored imaginative new sounds, and new ways to produce sound. George Crumb's *Ancient Voices of Children* (1970) uses, among other instruments, a toy piano, a musical saw, and Tibetan prayer stones. The composer asks his players to stretch the piano strings, to vocalize into an amplified piano, and to shout and whisper.

BEVERLY SILLS *has been a leading lady in opera, first as a singer, then as manager of the New York City Opera.*

NEW YORK CITY OPERA

Innovators have avidly explored the limitless resources of the synthesizer. Charles Wuorinen's *Time's Encomium,* a purely electronic work, won the 1968 Pulitzer Prize for Music; Leon Kirchner's poetic *Quartet No.3,* for string quartet and electronic tape, won the same prize for 1967.

The new music of the 20th century, like the new music of every previous era, has had its critics. Just as Brahms was once accused of having "no sense of melody," Chopin of visiting "tortured harmonies" on his listeners, and Bizet of having written a work *(Carmen)* that "had no chance of ever entering the repertoire of our opera companies," the composers of our time have often faced the charge of writing "nonmusic."

But without experimentation, change, and innovation, music would in time lose its function as an integral part of human society, and its vigor—traditional throughout recorded history—as a living art.

American Music

Beginning in the 1600's, they came to the New World with their father's tools and trades, their mother's heirlooms, their traditions, their old country customs, and their old, familiar songs. They sang tunes of praise, joy, and celebration.

"We gather together to ask the Lord's blessing," sang the early Dutch settlers, lending their traditional hymn of thanksgiving to the new territory. The English contributed "Old Hundredth" and "Greensleeves." Later the Spanish, French, German, and Irish immigrants would add their own favorites from church and field and home.

Popular songs as well as hymns flourished in the colonies. New song words, printed on large paper sheets called broadsides, boasted of local heroes, battle victories, and town news. They were sold on the streets for a penny a copy.

Tunes were everyone's property. During the Revolutionary War, for example, British troops fit their own words to "Yankee Doodle," a tune originally brought from England. This tune, however, became a special one for Americans. Within a few years, it appeared in the colonies' first stage play, Royall Tyler's *The Contrast* (1787), and in Benjamin Carr's patriotic *Federal Overture* (1795). It has been played and sung ever since.

1800–1880

During the early years, many colonists frowned on "popular" music, and on dance and theater. But by 1800, a new and lively spirit had grown up. Public entertainments were housed in empty stores, warehouses, courtrooms, and eventually in auditoriums and theaters. Concerts and musical plays, puppet shows, acrobats, and dancers held the stage.

Two popular forms are ancestors of modern entertainment: the *ballad opera* and the *pasticcio.* The first was a play sprinkled with favorite tunes, brightly fitted out with new topical verses. The second was a comedy with musical numbers contributed by various composers.

By 1800, music publishers were active in all major cities and some smaller towns, printing hundreds of songs, arrangements of operatic favorites, and vocal and keyboard collections. Before 1850, in fact, even while popular topical songs flooded the marketplace, publishers were quick to capitalize on the public hunger for adaptations of classical European favorites. Blake of Philadelphia brought out *A Selection from the Vocal Compositions of Mozart, United to English Verse,* joining countless sheet-music arrangements of arias and dances by Bellini, Rossini, Donizetti, and other popular masters.

The making of new words for old tunes was even applied to operatic arias. Such favorites as "The American Flag" and "Katy Darling" take their music from the opera *Norma* by Bellini.

Topical songs. The topical song, whatever its musical origin, helped record what Americans thought, felt, and witnessed. In those turbulent times of political and social change, appropriate songs sprang up overnight to commemorate important events. "The Liberty Song" (set, ironically to a British naval tune) denounced English tyranny: *"Come, join in hand, brave Americans all. . . ."* A hymn by William Billings, set to martial lyrics, became "Chester," called America's first great war song. The new republic was hailed in "Rise Columbia," to the tune of "Rule Britannia." Presidential candidates were hailed in "Jefferson and Liberty," "Monroe Is the Man," and "The Hunters of Kentucky" (for Andrew Jackson). And in 1840, songs for the Presidential campaign "sang Harrison into the Presidency."

For every event there were scores of songs, including a handful that became classics. For the War of 1812 there was "The Star-Spangled Banner"; for a new waterway, "The Erie Canal"; for the settling of the Appalachians and the Cumberlands, "Old Smokey"; for the western migration, "The Promised Land"; for the Mexican War, "Remember the Alamo"; and for the Gold Rush of 1849, "Oh! Susanna."

Some songs achieved the rank of national monuments, so great were their appeal. Of the Confederate Army's song of all songs, a commentator said, ". . . 'Dixie' has spread over the whole South. . . . It now bids fair to become the musical symbol of a new nationality, and we shall be fortunate if it does not impose its very name on our country." In the North, "The Battle Hymn of the Republic" far outlived the Civil War. It lent its tune to Presidential campaign songs (the 1932 version was "Battle Hymn of the Republican Party"). It was heard at President Lyndon B. Johnson's inauguration in 1965, and at his funeral in 1973. It was selected by the wife of Sir Winston Churchill to be played at her husband's funeral to honor his American mother. In moments both of joy and grief, it has been sung spontaneously by crowds of people, East and West, North and South.

Crusaders. A corner of early American musical history centers around the "singing families" that appeared on the scene around 1830. The Hutchinsons, changing personnel with each new generation, were the most durable, lasting into the 1880's; they were easily the most influential, too. The Hutchinsons were crusaders as well as musicians, using music to aid the causes of abolition, temperance, and women's rights. "The Hutchinsons," wrote a journalist of the time, "made the thousands at Faneuil Hall [in Boston] spring to their feet . . . and echo the anti-slavery appeal. . . . Oh, it was glorious! Slavery would have died of that music. . . ."

In the cause of temperance, the family performed such favorites as "Father Bring Home Your Money Tonight" and their own composition, "King Alcohol."

In support of women's rights, they sang their own version of "The Song of the Spirit":

Oh, men with sisters dear,
Oh, men with mothers and wives,
It is not linen you're wearing out,
But human creatures' lives.

The ballad. The Hutchinsons were also entertainers who know well the appeal of the sentimental ballad, a song form especially popular in the mid and late 19th century. Lyrics from "The Snow Storm," a real tearjerker, illustrate the type: "Oh, God, she cries in accents wild / If I must perish, save my child!"

Far less dramatic but no less sentimental were "Home, Sweet Home," probably the most popular song in 19th-century America, "The Old Arm Chair" (". . . a mother sat there / And a sacred thing is that old arm chair"), "Woodman, Spare That Tree," and such Stephen Foster favorites as the nostalgic "My Old Kentucky Home" and "Jeanie With the Light Brown Hair."

Where most of the protest songs have been forgotten, the sentimental songs—both words and music—had a lasting appeal. Among the favorites late in the 1800's were "Silver Threads Among the Gold," "Listen to the Mocking Bird," and "I'll Take You Home Again, Kathleen."

While the sentimental ballad touched the heart with nostalgia, the folk ballad painted a picture of America's growth westward in the years after the Civil War. Here were the songs of everyday life and work, and of folk heroes and folk myths. "I've Been Working on the Railroad," sang the laboring gangs, and "She'll Be Coming 'Round the Mountain," cheered the train crews, while "The Ballad of John Henry" preserved the tale of that steel driller of uncommon strength.

Of the Wild West's cowboys, vagabonds, and desperadoes, they sang "The Streets of Laredo," "Red River Valley," the ballad of "Frankie and Johnny," and the long story of "Jesse James."

The Irish musical heritage, always strong in young America, became even more pronounced in the late decades of the 1800's with the arrival of 1.5 million new immigrants. The caricature of the Irishman as rough and ready yet sentimental at heart fit ideally into the ballad tradition. "My Wild Irish Rose" and "Sweet Rosie O'Grady" nicely balanced the antics of "Down Went McGinty" and the muscle of the classic "Drill Ye Tarriers, Drill."

1880–1910

If we could put together a sound montage of all the music going on at the same time in the late 1800's, we would be astonished at its variety, scope, and sheer vitality. For this was a time of unbelievable activity.

From 1880 until the first decade of the 20th century, forms of popular musical entertainment evolved, overlapped, copied from each other, and jostled each other for acceptance by a music-hungry nation. No matter what the style, if it was appealing, chances are it would become a smash hit.

It was an era of hit shows, great names, superstar entertainers, wealthy song writers, and wealthier publishers. Minstrel shows, extravaganzas, burlesques, and variety shows (soon to be dubbed "vaudeville") ran side by side—and ran up record performances and profits.

European entertainments flooded the New York stage, from the operettas of Offenbach and Johann Strauss to the comic operas of Gilbert and Sullivan. *H.M.S. Pinafore* became such a hit that in its first American season, 1878–1879, 90 different companies performed it throughout the country, five of them in New York.

Spurred by the success of Gilbert and Sullivan, composers and librettists turned out scores of comic operas. Reginald De Koven's *Robin Hood* (1890) introduced "Oh Promise Me," which has been a favorite at weddings ever since. John Philip Sousa—not yet the "march king"—brought eleven comic operas to the stage. His *El Capitan* (1896) ran continuously for four years in America and Canada. Victor Herbert, a "classical" composer, wrote his first operetta, *La Vivandière,* in the 1890's. It was never produced, but Herbert was to produce a handful of enduring works, including *Babes in Toyland* (1903), *The Red Mill* (1906), and *Naughty Marietta* (1910).

Black music. More significant to American musical history was the appearance of a new strain of material late in the 1800's—the music of a black people only recently freed from slavery. To understand this new contribution, we must look at the history of black people in America.

Early history. Although Americans may have had some affection and family feeling for the house slave in the early 1800's, they saw the black man more as a caricature than a person. It was his walk, talk, tattered clothes, and color that represented the man. He was just the "Negro," the "black boy." On the stage, the black man (played by a white comedian) was little more than an object of amusement, even ridicule.

Comic black characters, talking and singing, appeared occasionally in English comic operas, light entertainments, and one-man shows. Tunes assigned to black characters were plainly European in style, however, modeled after an English air or a Scotch-Irish melody.

Beginning with English actor Charles Mathews, the black man became an object of greater interest. For his lively one-man shows of the 1820's, Mathews studied black dialect, phonetically transcribing what he heard in New York's streets, black churches, and black theaters.

Helped by Mathews' refinements, but with the old kind of pseudo-black music, blackface "minstrels" of the 1820's and '30's became popular. Wherever there was entertainment—a farce, a circus, even a Shakespeare play—one was sure to find an interpolated blackface dialogue, song, dance, comedy routine, or "lecture."

AMERICAN MUSIC *began with broadsides teaching new words to old songs* (left) *and with famous touring groups like the Hutchinson Family.*

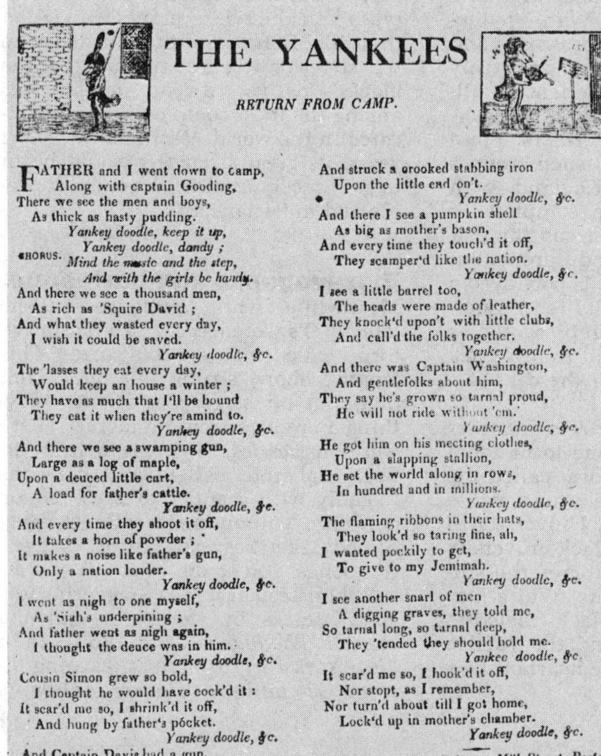

THE YANKEES

RETURN FROM CAMP.

FATHER and I went down to camp,
Along with captain Gooding,
There we see the men and boys,
As thick as hasty pudding.
CHORUS. *Yankey doodle, keep it up,*
Yankey doodle, dandy ;
Mind the music and the step,
And with the girls be handy.

And there we see a thousand men,
As rich as 'Squire David ;
And what they wasted every day,
I wish it could be saved.
Yankey doodle, &c.

The 'lasses they eat every day,
Would keep an house a winter ;
They have as much that I'll be bound
They eat it when they're amind to.
Yankey doodle, &c.

And there we see a swamping gun,
Large as a log of maple,
Upon a deuced little cart,
A load for father's cattle.
Yankey doodle, &c.

And every time they shoot it off,
It takes a horn of powder ;
It makes a noise like father's gun,
Only a nation louder.
Yankey doodle, &c.

I went as nigh to one myself,
As 'Siah's underpining ;
And father went as nigh again,
I thought the deuce was in him.
Yankey doodle, &c.

Cousin Simon grew so bold,
I thought he would have cock'd it :
It scar'd me so, I shrink'd it off,
And hung by father's pocket.
Yankey doodle, &c.

And Captain Davis had a gun,
He kind of clap'd his hand on't,
And struck a crooked stabbing iron
Upon the little end on't.
Yankey doodle, &c.

And there I see a pumpkin shell
As big as mother's bason,
And every time they touch'd it off,
They scamper'd like the nation.
Yankey doodle, &c.

I see a little barrel too,
The heads were made of leather,
They knock'd upon't with little clubs,
And call'd the folks together.
Yankey doodle, &c.

And there was Captain Washington,
And gentlefolks about him,
They say he's grown so tarnal proud,
He will not ride without 'em.
Yankey doodle, &c.

He got him on his meeting clothes,
Upon a slapping stallion,
He set the world along in rows,
In hundred and in millions.
Yankey doodle, &c.

The flaming ribbons in their hats,
They look'd so taring fine, ah,
I wanted pockily to get,
To give to my Jemimah.
Yankey doodle, &c.

I see another snarl of men
A digging graves, they told me,
So tarnal long, so tarnal deep,
They 'tended they should hold me.
Yankee doodle, &c.

It scar'd me so, I hook'd it off,
Nor stopt, as I remember,
Nor turn'd about till I got home,
Lock'd up in mother's chamber.
Yankey doodle, &c.

N. COVERLY, jr. Printer, *Milk-Street, Boston.*

NEW YORK PUBLIC LIBRARY, ASTOR, LENOX AND TILDEN FOUNDATIONS

NEW YORK PUBLIC LIBRARY, ASTOR, LENOX AND TILDEN FOUNDATIONS

CULVER PICTURES

MINSTREL SHOWS *like the one advertised in this poster had great popularity from the 1820's until near the end of the century. This company stresses family entertainment, as the words at bottom left suggest.*

George Washington Dixon was perhaps the first blackface to use burnt cork. Tom "Daddy" Rice clowned his way through his famous "Jim Crow" routine, sandwiched between the acts of a serious play:

An' he wheel about, he turn about,
He do jis so,
An' ebery time he wheel about
He jump Jim Crow.

"Jim Crow," a clearly racist ditty, helped bring the term into everyday language. Most of the other minstrel songs were similar, perpetuating the stereotype of the ignorant, awkward, carefree black man. The black stereotype lasted well into the 1900's. Early radio's "Amos 'n Andy" and the movies' clownish Stepin Fetchit preserved the image intact.

By the 1840's, blackface entertainment had evolved into a full evening's show by a minstrel troupe of singers, dancers, comics, and musicians. Audiences were treated to band overtures, marches, and dances, comic songs and sentimental ballads, banjo solos and duets for fiddle and "bones," comedy routines, and mock lectures (always in black dialect) on outlandish subjects. The larger troupes even managed to throw in a chorus or two from a favorite Italian opera. Among the most famous were the pioneering Virginia Minstrels and Christy's Minstrels.

In the 1840's and '50's, with the slavery issue increasingly in the air, the minstrel repertory reflected a slight shift toward a more sympathetic treatment of blacks. Typical "plantation songs" were written by Stephen Foster for Christy's Minstrels:

When Old Ned die,
Massa take it mighty bad . . .
("Old Uncle Ned")

All de world am sad and dreary,
Eb'ry-where I roam,
Oh! darkeys, how my heart grows weary,
Far from de old folks at home.
("Old Folks at Home")

Black minstrels. Although the black stereotype remained about the same, the minstrel show made dramatic changes after the Civil War. Productions became larger, more lavish, and more professional. What was truly drastic was the establishment of all-black minstrel troupes, some numbering more than 100 performers. From 1865 to the early '80's, such troupes toured America and England with great success. One even completed a profitable three-year tour of the Far East, the Middle East, and Europe. But even these black minstrels portrayed a distorted picture of black life in America. The "darkey" was represented as longing for "the good old times" back on the plantation, under the care of a beloved master.

Spirituals. In the 1870's another kind of black music came to national attention: a new song form called the spiritual. George White was a white faculty member of Fisk University in Nashville (the first all-black university in America), and director of the student Fisk Jubilee Singers. White harmonized traditional black melodies in a European style, and the Jubilee Singers used them as the heart of their repertory.

At the beginning of an international fund-raising tour, the group triumphed at the Gilmore Music Festival in Boston in 1872. An audience of 20,000 reportedly rose to its feet to shout "Jubilee forever!," so appealing and thrilling were the spirituals they heard:

Come down, Gabriel, blow your horn,
Call me home in de early morn;
Send de chariot down dis way,
Come and haul me home to stay, O!

Equally successful in Europe, the Jubilee Singers were considered to have introduced a genuine American folk music. But a main characteristic of the spiritual was not American but African: the singing style known as call-and-response. Here, heard for the first time in the white man's musical world, was an element that permeated native African music: the chorus responding to its leaders.

(Solo) *I looked over Jordan and what do I see,*
(Response) *Comin' for to carry me home,*
(Solo) *A band of angels comin' after me*
(Response) *Comin' for to carry me home.*
(Chorus)

Other kinds of black music, perhaps even closer to its African roots, also began to be heard. Field cries and work chants suggested an element of improvisation within firmly fixed traditional lines. Both the personal quality of the improvising and the form itself were to have far-reaching effects on American music—the one in what we know as jazz, the other in the form called the blues.

In 1890, however, there was little sign of what was to come. The white man had no perception of the true nature of black music. Old black stereotypes and the white man's conviction that his European musical heritage was superior obscured the fact that the blacks' native African music was among the most complex and sophisticated in the world. Within a few short years, its great strengths would begin to gain recognition from common people and musicians alike.

Extravaganza and burlesque. Meanwhile, white audiences in the late 1800's were treated to a new stage form called the extravaganza. This lengthy show, strung out on a slim plot, put on stage just about everything a producer could imagine. There were hurricanes, carnivals, demon rituals, elaborate ballets and can-cans (usually with scantily dressed female dancers), pantomimes, roller-skating, comedy sketches, caricatures, suggestive songs, and so on.

Public response was staggering despite attacks by the press and the church. *The Black Crook* (1866) ran in New York for 16 months, earning almost $2 million. *Humpty Dumpty*

(1868) ran for 483 performances. *The Brook,* one of the first extravaganzas to integrate music and story, was popular enough to bring to London, making it the first American musical ever given there.

A second stage form, called burlesque, soon followed, following the lines of the extravaganza but emphasizing parody and caricature. There was *Evangeline* (1874)—a takeoff on Longfellow's poem—the first American musical with an original score; *Adonis* (1884), parodying the Pygmalion theme that was to reappear 72 years later in *My Fair Lady;* and the enormously popular "Mulligan plays" of writers Harrigan and Hart, with music by David Braham (probably the most talented song writer of the '70's and '80's). These last were full of gentle, earthy humor and ethnic parody (the rowdy Irishman, the pompous German, the black dandy), the whole uplifted by Braham's delightful songs in the best tradition of the English music hall.

Vaudeville. Side by side with the minstrel show, the extravaganza, and the burlesque, there grew up yet another form of American musical stage entertainment: the variety show—later dubbed vaudeville.

At least one stage historian has said that American theater's most important moment came when Tony Pastor decided to entice women and their children into the theater, formerly the territory of men only.

Tony Pastor's idea was simple: prohibit smoking and drinking and, above all, provide wholesome entertainment—a clean show. Pastor's Opera House, set up in 1865, fulfilled his dream. Anticipating the wonderful wave of movie giveaways in the 1940's ("Soup bowls tonight! Complete your set of dishes! And see a great show inside!"), Pastor offered as door prizes sewing patterns, toys, pots and pans, and groceries.

And inside the theater, Pastor kept his promise by presenting a light evening of varied acts: a master-of-ceremonies (Pastor himself), singers, comedians, acrobats, animal acts, blackface entertainers, and short sketches. This was the true variety show, born out of the minstrel show tradition.

The idea worked so well that Pastor moved to larger quarters in 1875 and, in 1881, opened his famous Tony Pastor Music Hall—New York's showplace of clean variety entertainment. The name "vaudeville" was by this time in common use.

On his stage appeared not only the established stars of the day but unknowns who were to become legends. He auditioned the stunning Helen Leonard of Clinton, Ohio, and renamed her "Lillian Russell, the English ballad singer." He presented the new comedy team of Weber and Fields, teachers to two generations of vaudeville, radio, and early television comedians. And Pastor discovered the Four Cohans (including George M.), Pat Rooney, the Three Keatons (Buster was one), Eddie Foy, and Sophie Tucker.

Eventually, Pastor was the victim of his own success. As vaudeville swept the country, cut-rate competitors rose up around him, and Tony Pastor called it quits, closing his theater in 1908.

CULVER PICTURES

VAUDEVILLE *included everything—from visual spectacle (the "Myriophon,"* top*), to comedy (Weber and Fields,* left*), to the ubiquitous animal act.*

Tin Pan Alley. The songs sung in the big musical productions were soon published by a galaxy of music publishers in many large American cities. For the most part, they were gentlemen businesses, solid and reliable but unimaginative.

Tom and Alex Harms changed all that, altering permanently the character of popular music publishing. Their firm, T.B. Harms, learned to "plug" a new song. They stood along music publishers' row in New York, waiting to share aspiring singers, seeking to persuade the singers to take—and perform—a new song, or three or four. A popular performer might be plied with food, drinks, expensive cigars, even free rent—all to give a new song a chance; because if the song became a "hit," the publishers would show huge profits. The street the pluggers stood along was soon known as Tin Pan Alley.

The boom of popular song publishing, with its aggressive selling techniques, inspired a mass of imitators, all crowded near New York's Union Square. Later the major publishers moved to better quarters uptown, but they took Tin Pan Alley with them.

The get-rich-quick excitement of the

business is illustrated by the story of Charles K. Harris, a self-taught song writer. Shocked by a royalty check of only 85¢ from a major publisher for a song he had written, Harris set up his own company. Shortly afterward he wrote the music and lyrics for "After the Ball," a poignant little piece in the popular waltz style. Harris offered his song to one singer after the other unsuccessfully. Finally, he offered $500 to ballad singer J. Aldrich Libbey, to insert "After the Ball" in a show called *A Trip to Chinatown.*

At its first performance, the audience went wild, demanding six encores. May Irwin, a star of vaudeville, soon introduced the song at Tony Pastor's. "After the Ball" quickly rang up sales of $25,000 a week, and eventually reached a total sale of 5 million copies! Harris's fortune was made, turning him into one of the most powerful and effective publishers of popular songs in America.

Among other hits of the era were "A Bicycle Built for Two" (1892); "When You Were Sweet Sixteen" (1898); "Sweet Adeline" (1903); and "Wait 'Til the Sun Shines, Nellie" (1905).

As this sampling illustrates, American popular songs of the turn of the century seemed cut out of the same cloth, so similar were they in style and sentiment. They were "familiar" songs, designed to please and to sell—and the publishers, knowing their public, cashed in.

Ragtime. A new art form usually evolves out of a variety of influences and meets the need of an individual or a group to express its spirit in a different way.

Scott Joplin was born soon after the Civil War into a poor black family in Missouri. He was a musician from the start, a trained classical pianist and an aspiring "serious" composer. Gradually, he developed a new dream. He saw that within his own folk music were the seeds of an art form that could express the black spirit in a way that even whites would take seriously.

AFTER THE BALL, *a big Tin Pan Alley success, published by the author and picturing the musical comedy star who first performed it and helped make it a hit.*

CULVER PICTURES

ASCAP

SCOTT JOPLIN, *the master of ragtime, whose music was taken seriously only after his death.*

Others were using folk music for serious purposes. Franz Liszt used gypsy tunes and rhythms in his *Hungarian Rhapsodies.* Chopin's mazurkas and polonaises captured the native Polish dance spirit in refined classical form. In Joplin's lifetime, Béla Bartók would merge classical techniques and forms with the folk materials from Hungary, Bulgaria, Turkey, and North Africa.

But Joplin's job was harder. Very few black men were taken seriously in any field. Even as he was working toward his new music, there was a craze for "coon songs," old-fashioned tunes ridiculing stereotypical blacks, some even written by blacks themselves.

Joplin, like Liszt before him and Bartók after, became a collector and a collator. He found melodies in the black folk-tune snatches and fragments called "rags." These were already traditional in the backwoods plantations and towns of his native Missouri. With these rags, he heard the catchy, syncopated rhythms of plantation banjos, softer versions of the driving, polyrhythms of native African music.

Joplin also heard the back country dance music already widely exploited on the minstrel stage: the clog, breakdown, buck-and-wing, and especially the cakewalk, a kind of two-step grand promenade that was becoming a dance craze. He also knew the traditions of genteel ballroom dancing, centered around the quadrille, polka, two-step, schottische, and jig. Finally, Joplin heard the brass marches and parade music written by men like John Philip Sousa and by hundreds of small-town marching bands. For a composer with a dream, these were abundant materials.

Joplin fused these elements into a simple but formal piano composition. Its tunes echoed black rags; its rhythms, the feeling of banjo syncopations; its oom-pah bass, the marching beat of the two-step cakewalk and the brass band; its regular phrases and balanced form, the style of the ballroom dance; its potpourri of tunes, the qua-

CULVER PICTURES

THE MARCH KING, *John Philip Sousa, who won his first fame as a bandmaster. He is shown here with his U.S. Marine Band in 1880.*

drille; and its overall spirit, the spirit of dance.

In time, as in his first publication, "Original Rags," Joplin incorporated his own tunes, refined the form, and experimented with new compositional and piano techniques. Then, in September of 1899, John Stark of St. Louis published the work that brought Joplin his overnight fame: "Maple Leaf Rag."

Suddenly ragtime became an international passion. Publishers in Tin Pan Alley jumped on the ragtime bandwagon. Capitalizing on the voguish name, they flooded the market with ragtime songs, ragtime collections, and ragtime piano methods. Unfortunately, these were seldom more than dressed-up Tin Pan Alley songs. Classic ragtime by Joplin, James Scott, and Joseph Lamb (the "Bach, Beethoven, and Brahms of ragtime") was widely disseminated as a result of the craze, but only along with scores of shoddy imitations.

To a turn-of-the-century public accustomed to a diet of sentimental ballads and lightweight waltz tunes, the driving pulse and catchy syncopations of ragtime were a great attraction. It was a natural for that upright piano in the parlor, for the newly developed player piano, and for the improved commercial discs sold for early home phonograph play.

Sousa's and Arthur Pryor's bands snapped it up, emphasizing the links between the march, the cakewalk, and ragtime. It was perfect for vaudeville, substituting keyboard brilliance for razzle-dazzle banjo picking. Ragtime specialists like Tom Turpin, Eubie Blake, and Tony Jackson turned their performances into dazzling technical displays, and ragtime contests, played before foot-stomping crowds, pitted pianists against each other.

Ragtime's influence continued into the 20th century. It rode Irving Berlin to fame with "Alexander's Ragtime Band" (1911)—a song far more Tin Pan Alley than ragtime. It influenced Berlin's score for the revue *Watch Your Step* (1914), "a syncopated musical" starring Vernon and Irene Castle, the dance idols of Europe and America. During a vaudeville tour that reportedly earned the Castles $30,000 a week, ragtime enlivened their repertory with the Castle Walk and the Castle House Rag.

A sad postscript is the decline of Scott Joplin's dreams and fortunes, even as the commercialization of ragtime brought fame and wealth to others. Buried in a pauper's unmarked grave in 1917, Joplin would never know that his black opera *Treemonisha,* a failure in his lifetime, would one day run on Broadway; and that a "Joplin Renaissance" would bring his music to films *(The Sting),* to the recitals of classical artists, to ballet, and to records.

In granting him a posthumous award in 1976, the Pulitzer Prize committee recognized too late that Joplin had indeed created a black music of far greater significance than the musical world had been prepared to grasp.

Jazz

Although it had no single early hero of the stature of Scott Joplin, jazz was to have an even greater influence on the American scene. Like ragtime, it was made of a combination of earlier forms and styles, seeming to take first root in New Orleans (just down river from Scott Joplin's St. Louis) between 1900 and 1920.

The blues. Early jazz owed debts to ragtime, to brass band marches, and to popular dance forms of the day. But mostly early jazz was the blues: a bittersweet music that was part incantation, part drumlike dance beat. The blues was the private music of the field hand, the betrayed lover, the slave mother. It was the dragging, shuffling, stomping music of the Saturday night dance, when the work week was over and it was time to "swing the blues away." In its driving call-and-response form, it echoed the cadence of the black preacher and the chants and work songs originally brought from Africa.

Blues lyrics, in the typical three-line form that jelled out of the old "shouts," field hollers, and "stand ups," talked about that freedom that only a train could bring . . .

I'm leavin' here tonight if I have to ride the blinds,
Oh, I'm leavin' here tonight if I have to ride the blinds,
Take a freight train special, tell the engineer 'Lose no time.'

. . . or about homesickness . . .

I'm a po' boy 'long way from home,
Oh, I'm a po' boy 'long way from home,
I wish a 'schushion train would carry me back where I come from.

. . . or about a broken heart . . .

Ah well looka here mama, what in the worl' are you tryin'-a do?
Ah well looka here mama, what in the worl' are you tryin'-a do?
Don' know what makes me love you, you gonna break my heart in two.

So powerful is the blues tradition that it has lasted over the decades, fully intact in form and spirit. In the 1930's, Jimmy Rushing was singing this with Count Basie's Kansas City orchestra:

Sent for you yesterday and here you come today,
Sent for you yesterday and here you come today.
You can't love me baby and treat me that-a-way.

And in the rock 'n' roll era of the 1950's, Elvis Presley was pounding out:

You ain't nothin' but a hound dog, cryin' all the time,
You ain't nothin' but a hound dog, cryin' all the time.
Well, you ain't never caught a rabbit and you ain't no friend of mine.

Even today we can step into any jazz club in the world and hear the sound, spirit, and form of early vocal blues. The sultry trumpet and wailing saxophone imitate the bending, embellishing, improvising voice of the earliest blues singers.

CULVER PICTURES

CULVER PICTURES

BLUES TO JAZZ: *from the folkways of the black South Bessie Smith* (left) *and others brought the form and the mood called the blues. It was picked up by the King Oliver Band* (above right) *and became a part of jazz. Oliver's cornetist Louis Armstrong* (right) *helped spread the new music worldwide.*

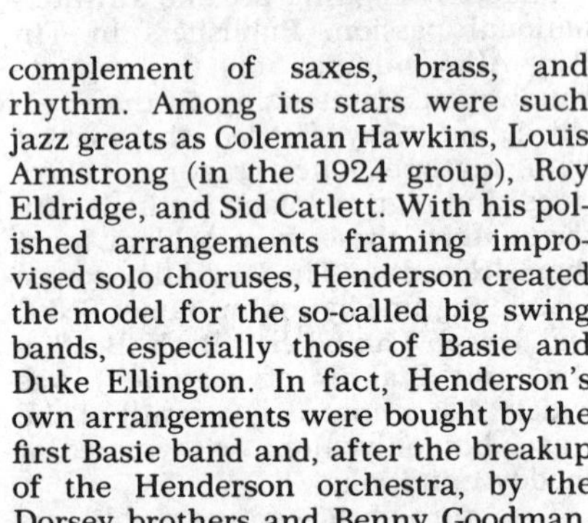
CULVER PICTURES

New Orleans. Blues music existed wherever there were field hands and dock workers and railroad gangs. But its urban center was in the city of New Orleans.

The black musicians there had to scramble to make a living. Some played for balls and picnics. Bessie Smith, the great blues singer, worked the theaters and vaudeville houses. Mamie Smith starred in vaudeville and musicals as a top ballad singer of the day. Blind Lemon Jackson, a blues-singing guitarist, played on street corners, in honky-tonks, and (like many black musicians) for house-rent parties. W.C. Handy toured as a bandmaster for the Mahara Minstrels, as a leader of street bands, and as a conductor of classical bandstand concerts.

The center of the new music was the raucous red-light district of New Orleans called Storyville. In its streets, bars, and brothels played the greats of the time: Tony Jackson, considered the most formidable of Storyville pianists; Jelly Roll Morton, flamboyant pianist, and thought to be the first great jazz composer ("Jelly Roll Blues," "King Porter Stomp," "Wolverines"—all written about 1905); and Buddy Bolden, a cornetist of remarkable blues-playing skill, and musical father to young Louis Armstrong.

The New Orleans sound also was heard in the streets when street bands, funeral-marching a friend to burial, would swing their way home, celebrating life, "ragging" (syncopating) the march beat and "jazzing" (embellishing) the tune. This special sound, shouted by clarinet, cornet, trombone, and drums eventually came to be called "Dixieland."

The spread of jazz. The government shut down Storyville just before World War I, and the last of the early jazz musicians left New Orleans. The exodus had begun long before. Tony Jackson left for Chicago by 1905. Jelly Roll Morton followed, working the honky-tonk joints as he went, later moving on to California and New York. In Chicago, King Oliver played at the Dreamland Cafe, giving way in 1924 to a group led by Louis Armstrong. The New Orleans Rhythm Kings took over at Friar's Inn, and Jelly Roll Morton arrived to organize his Red Hot Peppers.

By the "Roaring '20's," Chicago had become a new jazz capital as young stars joined the veterans: Bix Beiderbecke (one of the few great white jazzmen), Coleman Hawkins, Earl "Fatha" Hines, Fats Waller, and Gene Krupa.

In the same decade, in the Southwest, excellent black bands played dances, society engagements, and concerts. Alphonse Trent's polished band appeared at Dallas's Adolphus Hotel, the region's most glamorous white hotel, for a two-week stay. They stayed on for a year and a half—an unheard-of success for a black band. So rich and famous did the Trent orchestra become that its musicians wore silk shirts, drove Cadillacs, and were invited to play at the governor's inaugural ball.

The big bands. In Kansas City, ragtime pianist Benny Moten led a group that played all the popular styles from ragtime to Tin Pan Alley. In the 1930's Moten's band became the nucleus of the great Count Basie Orchestra (Basie had joined the group as pianist around 1929).

By the late '20's, the restless musicians moved on, leaving Chicago for New York or Kansas City. In New York, the remarkable Fletcher Henderson Orchestra was already a fixture at the Roseland Ballroom. Henderson's group was the first big band with a full complement of saxes, brass, and rhythm. Among its stars were such jazz greats as Coleman Hawkins, Louis Armstrong (in the 1924 group), Roy Eldridge, and Sid Catlett. With his polished arrangements framing improvised solo choruses, Henderson created the model for the so-called big swing bands, especially those of Basie and Duke Ellington. In fact, Henderson's own arrangements were bought by the first Basie band and, after the breakup of the Henderson orchestra, by the Dorsey brothers and Benny Goodman.

In New York, the Chicago and Dixieland traditions continued in new groups formed by Red Nichols (The Five Pennies), and by the influential Ben Pollack. Pollack, formerly a drummer with the New Orleans Rhythm Kings, combined commercialized jazz with Dixieland in a band that became a fixture at New York's Park Central Hotel and The Silver Slipper. That group, along with his earlier California band, was among the first large white jazz ensembles, including as "sidemen" such future greats as Glenn Miller, Charley Spivak, Muggsy Spanier, and Harry James.

Duke Ellington began his career in Washington, D.C., but soon moved to New York. In 1927 his enlarged group moved to Harlem's Cotton Club. There the Ellington sound blossomed into his

CULVER PICTURES

CULVER PICTURES

CULVER PICTURES

JAZZ TO SWING: *jazz took over American popular music through the big band of Duke Ellington, the swing bands of Benny Goodman, and the show music of composer George Gershwin.*

famous "jungle style"—a powerful, yet silky brand of jazz that quickly made the suave leader and his star-studded orchestra a major force in jazz. With Cootie Williams, Tricky Sam Nanton, Johnny Hodges, Harry Carney, and the great tenor saxophonist Ben Webster, Ellington produced such original classics as "Mood Indigo," "The Mooche," and "Black and Tan Fantasy." Later, with arranger-collaborator Billy Strayhorn, Ellington went further than any other big band leader in claiming "serious" status for his music, appearing in concert as well as in nightclubs and attracting the attention of classically trained as well as jazz audiences.

The 1930's also saw important activity in Kansas City. Jo Jones, up from Alabama, remembered that "You never knew what time in the morning someone would knock on your door and say they were jamming down the street." Jazz pianist Mary Lou Williams came from Pittsburgh to find music everywhere, all the time. Count Basie came from New Jersey; Andy Kirk, from Denver; Hot Lips Page, from Oklahoma City; Lester Young, called "Prez," from the deep South by way of the minstrel–circus–medicine show route.

It was here that Kansas City-born Charlie Parker—the immortal "Bird"—came of age. A serious and daringly innovative apprentice, he worked with the best saxophonists in the country, and ultimately became a master. By the 1940's, Parker was the acknowledged force behind an avant-garde jazz movement called bop, a movement that also produced such giants as Dizzy Gillespie, John Coltrane, and Miles Davis.

Society jazz. While the big jazz bands were forming, society bands continued to play their successful menu of cocktail music, lightweight ballroom dances, and slick arrangements of Tin Pan Alley hits. By the 1930's, dance crowds everywhere would be treated to the sweet sounds of orchestras led by Guy Lombardo, Lawrence Welk, and scores of others.

Perhaps the first—and most famous—of these groups was the internationally famous Paul Whiteman Orchestra. Many fine jazzmen played with the group. Whiteman came to be known as "the King of Jazz," but the orchestra was never a true jazz ensemble. Rather it was designed to give the public popular music dressed up in skillful "jazzy" arrangements.

Whiteman's successes were solid and steady: long hotel appearances, stardom in Broadway revues, visits to Europe. But one concert in 1924 immortalized the Paul Whiteman Orchestra: the world premiere of George Gershwin's *Rhapsody in Blue.*

George Gershwin. Like Scott Joplin two decades earlier, George Gershwin believed in creating a bridge between the folk/popular idiom and the "classical" idiom. For Gershwin, a child of New York's streets and an apprentice song plugger, the result was "symphonic" jazz tinged by Tin Pan Alley and colored by commercial blues songs.

Above all, Gershwin was a street-wise, innovative professional. Yet from the beginning he had something special: an original feel for jazzy rhythms and a special way with a tune.

Two years before *Rhapsody in Blue,* Gershwin tried to bridge the popular/classical gap in *Blue Monday Blues,* written for a Broadway revue. Although *Blues* was withdrawn as being too somber for the occasion, it caught the attention of the pit conductor, Paul Whiteman.

In late 1923, for a program of American popular music presented "in concert," Paul Whiteman came to Gershwin for a new jazz work to top off the evening. In February, 1924, Whiteman's historic concert took place at New York's Aeolian Hall. As the next-to-last item of a generally boring program, Gershwin himself appeared as soloist in *Rhapsody in Blue.*

The first reviews were mixed. Some said it was "stunning" or "ingenious"; others said "trite and feeble" . . . "empty, meaningless." But Gershwin's fame was assured. By 1930, the Roxy Theater in New York was paying the composer $10,000 a week to play the work on stage. A film company paid $50,000 to use the music in a motion picture. And Gershwin's total royalties amounted to a quarter of a million dollars over the next two decades.

Although *Rhapsody* was not the first piece of serious American music to incorporate jazz elements, it awakened the world to the appeal of "symphonic" jazz. The demand was on, and Gershwin followed up with his

Concerto in F (1925), three jazz *Preludes* for piano (1926), *An American in Paris* (1928), and other works in the same vein.

At the same time, Gershwin's major work was for the theater. Like Mozart, working a century and a half earlier, he wrote prolifically and at breakneck speed, tossing off such hit shows as *Lady Be Good, Funny Face, Strike Up the Band, Girl Crazy,* and *Of Thee I Sing.* Late in his career, he completed his most enduring dramatic work, the folk opera *Porgy and Bess,* a love story set in a black slum. Also like Mozart, Gershwin was not granted a long life. Mozart was dead at 35; Gershwin at only 39.

Records, Radio, Movies

With the evolution of phonograph records, radio broadcasting, and sound motion pictures—all within the first 25 years of this century—the American popular music industry enjoyed a stunning growth in revenues, profits, and royalties. No longer was the reputation and fortune of a musical group dependent solely on word of mouth, box-office sales, and press reviews. And no longer were the publisher and song writer dependent on sheet-music sales as a principal source of income.

A successful record amounted to a firsthand, in-home advertisement for the show it came from. A successful show encouraged the sale of records. And so it went, with live performances and recordings marching hand in hand, as America paid out its money to an increasingly powerful and wealthy entertainment industry.

Between 1906 and 1921, Enrico Caruso was said to have amassed over $2 million in record royalties. In 1920 alone, a recording by Paul Whiteman and his Ambassador Orchestra sold 2 million copies.

Broadcasters quickly tapped the entertainment possibilities of the new medium. Beginning with "The Happiness Boys," radio's first song and comedy show, a family tuned in for music. With the inauguration of network broadcasting, people were treated to a variety program starring storyteller Will Rogers, soprano Mary Garden, comedy team Weber and Fields, and the New York Symphony under conductor Walter Damrosch.

The poorer stations, looking for free entertainers in return for publicity, brought dance-band music into hundreds of thousands of homes through their "remotes": live broadcasts of bands directly from hotel ballrooms.

By 1932 the first full-fledged disc jockey arrived on the scene with Al Jarvis's talk-and-music show, "The World's Largest Make-Believe Ballroom," played over station KJWB in

CULVER PICTURES

ELLA FITZGERALD *became one of dozens of name vocalists, mixing jazz, popular standards, and novelties. Her distinguished career has run from the 1930's into the 1980's.*

Los Angeles. Martin Block's "Make-Believe Ballroom," heard over WNEW, New York, followed suit three years later, bringing new music and new names into homes around the country.

By the 1930's, records had transformed unknowns into stars and stars into legends. Decca recorded Bing Crosby ("Sweet Leilani"), Guy Lombardo ("It Seems Like Old Times"), Hoagy Carmichael ("Georgia on My Mind"), and Ella Fitzgerald ("A-Tisket, A-Tasket"). Brunswick made stars of the Mills Brothers ("Nobody's Sweetheart") and the Andrews Sisters ("Bei Mir Bist Du Schoen"). Columbia promoted not only cowboy Gene Autry ("That Silver-Haired Daddy of Mine") but the big bands as well: Artie Shaw's ("Begin the Beguine"), Harry James's ("Ciribiribin"), and Glenn Miller's ("Moonlight Serenade" and "Little Brown Jug").

With the advent of motion pictures, yet another medium fueled the already powerful entertainment industry. The pianist who played for silent films came in to add live music. Soon the song plugger livened up the show with song slides, songfests, and amateur nights.

With the appearance of film pioneer D.W. Griffith's *The Birth of a Nation* (1915) (music by Joseph Breil), and its sequel, *The Fall of a Nation* (1916) (music by Victor Herbert), motion pictures added their first original, custom-made scores—printed music to be played by the local pianist.

Al Jolson's *The Jazz Singer* (1927) is generally thought of as the first "talkie." In the midst of an otherwise silent film with synchronized background music, Jolson's own voice electrified audiences with the strains of "Blue Skies," "Toot, Toot, Tootsie," and "My Mammy" coming directly from the screen. Warner Brothers' Vitaphone film grossed $3 million, and Hollywood scrambled to acquire similar properties.

By 1929 MGM's *The Broadway Melody*—with commissioned music by Nacio Herb Brown and lyrics by Arthur Freed—gave the public its first "all talking, all singing, all dancing" screen musical. By 1930 Hollywood was raiding Broadway for musicals suitable for screen adaptation.

Warner Brothers' *Forty-Second Street* (1933) made the film musical a form in its own right. It combined a bright song-and-dance team (Ruby Keeler and Dick Powell), good performances, catchy songs, Busby Berkeley's spectacular dance routines, and inventive camera work to produce a huge success. Hollywood followed up with *Gold Diggers of 1933,* with Keeler, Powell, and Ginger Rogers, and a string of smash-hit musicals starring the sensational dance team of Fred Astaire and Ginger Rogers.

ASCAP and BMI. By the second decade of the 20th century, with Tin Pan Alley in its "golden age," it was clear to the publishers that a regulatory agency was needed to protect their valuable musical properties. Until 1914, copyright protection covered only the purchase and mechanical reproduction of published music. For live performances, however, there was no payment to the publishers, composers, and lyricists. This changed with the founding, in 1914, of a performing rights organization called the American Society of Composers, Authors, and Publishers (ASCAP).

Following a legal fight that reached the Supreme Court, ASCAP won the right to issue licenses—for a fee—to cover all music produced by its member writers and publishers played in any hotel, theater, dance hall, cabaret, or restaurant. Licensing rights were eventually extended to cover radio stations and motion picture studios.

All important writers and publishers soon joined ASCAP, sharing by the mid-1930's approximately $10 million in annual licensing fees, distributed according to ASCAP's own system of ratings.

A second performing rights organization was formed in 1940. Broadcast Music, Inc. (BMI) created its membership from composers and lyricists who had not been invited to join ASCAP or who dealt with kinds of music not then in favor with the older organiza-

Dance

The formal movements of ballet and modern dance *(right)* develop from the spontaneity of folk dances *(below)*, many of which have been done for centuries.

DON PERDUE

DAVID HURN/MAGNUM

Music

DOUG BRUCE/CAMERA 5

Individual performers become celebrities in many musical areas. Leonard Bernstein *(left)* is a world-renowned orchestra conductor as well as the composer of the classic musical, *West Side Story.* Mick Jagger of the Rolling Stones *(right)* brought rock to millions through live performances and recordings. Dizzy Gillespie *(below)* was a great innovator and performer in the improvisational world of jazz.

LYNN GOLDSMITH

BONNIE FREER/PHOTO RESEARCHERS

The Stage

Nashville's Grand Ole Opry carried on a long American tradition of variety on stage. Comedienne Minnie Pearl *(right)* alternates with country and western music. *Porgy and Bess* by George Gershwin used settings and music from black America to create a uniquely American opera.

JERRY COOKE/PHOTO RESEARCHERS

MARTHA SWOPE

Movies

From the burning of Atlanta in *Gone With the Wind,* the first full-color feature film, to the imaginary monsters of *Star Wars,* the movies have brought the excitement of spectacle to millions.

MEMORY SHOP

SILVER SCREEN

tion. From small beginnings it managed to sign up a massive number of new members over the next 30 years. Today, with shared revenues in classical, popular, rock, and especially country and western music, BMI rivals ASCAP in representation, income, and power in the entertainment industry.

1940 and After

From about 1940, the pace of development in American music slowed down. For the next half-century, musicians would be reworking and recombing the wealth of materials, idioms, styles, and forms laid down by their predecessors.

At the same time, there has been an increased emphasis on preserving and appreciating the past. One recent summer, straw-hat theaters in the Northeast were playing *The Burlesque Scandals of 1981,* and Sigmund Romberg's *The Student Prince; Show Boat,* and "The Musical Magic of George Gershwin."

Guy Lombardo's Royal Canadians, the Tommy Dorsey Orchestra, the Glenn Miller Orchestra, and the Duke Ellington Orchestra all survived their leaders' deaths, some for several decades. The jazz greats continued to appear into the 1980's: Ella Fitzgerald, Sarah Vaughan, the Count Basie Alumni, and Cab Calloway—still "stompin' at the Savoy."

Even on Broadway, the past does battle with the present. Recent years have seen Joplin's forgotten *Treemonisha,* and shows called *Duke Ellington's Sophisticated Ladies, Ain't Misbehavin'* ("The New Fats Waller Musical Show"), *Sugar Babies* (a slice of old-time vaudeville), and a stage version of the great movie musical *Forty-Second Street.*

Old song, new words. Setting new words to old melodies—a tradition since colonial days, continued on in "Full Moon and Empty Arms" (1946, Rachmaninoff), "You're Breaking My Heart" (1948, Leoncavallo), "Kisses Sweeter Than Wine" (1951, an Irish folk song), "Cindy, Oh Cindy" (1956, a sea chantey), and "Tom Dooley" (1958, a mountain tune).

The list, which is very long, also includes rock hits of the 1970's based on Bach, Chopin, and Beethoven.

Protest. The American tradition of socially and politically conscious song lyrics has remained as strong during the last 50 years as it was in the days of revolution and expansion.

Labor's exploitation in the coal mines was expressed in Aunt Molly Jackson's "Hard Times in Colman's Mines," and in Merle Travis's "Sixteen Tons" ("I owe my soul to the company store")—a song that sold over 1 million copies in Tennessee Ernie Ford's 1955 recorded version.

Woody Guthrie sang of migratory workers in "Blowing Down This Old Dusty Road," and of national pride in his classic "This Land Is Your Land." Equally nationalistic were Earl Robinson's cantata, *Ballad for Americans* and, in 1942, his famous tribute to Lincoln, *The Lonesome Train.*

The protest movements of the 1960's, in response to the war in Vietnam and civil rights issues, brought the young people to coffeehouses and rallies to hear Joan Baez and Bob Dylan sing songs about radical nonviolence: "We Shall Overcome," "Hard Rain's a-Gonna Fall," and Dylan's classic protest against prejudice and injustice, "Blowin' in the Wind"—a song that sold millions of records and that was performed by more than 60 different artists.

Buffy Sainte-Marie, a full-blooded Cree Indian, sang of racial oppression in "My Country 'Tis of Thy People You're Dying." Paul Simon expressed youth's pains and life's hypocricies in "The Sounds of Silence" and "Bridge Over Troubled Waters." Janis Ian spoke bitterly of adult prejudice in "Society's Child." And the women's rights movement, pressing intense social issues into the 1970's, produced Helen Reddy's "I Am Woman."

Country and western music. Nashville, the capital of the multi-million-dollar country and western music industry, is the single greatest center of music production in the United States, housing more musicians and music firms than any city in the world. Its current stars, including Loretta Lynn, Dolly Parton, Glen Campbell, and Roy Clark, are national headliners. Those of the older generation are nothing short of legendary: Johnny Cash, Hank Williams, Hank Snow, Roy Acuff, Eddy Arnold, the Carter Family, and many more.

But this formidable industry could not have had more humble beginnings. It came out of the mountain music of Appalachia, the work songs of the Kentucky coal mines, the blues of the backwoods rural South—all the grass-roots music called "hillbilly" in the 1920's. It was made of traditional folk tunes, lyrics about simple, elemental subjects—hardship, love, a day's work—and the sounds of simple folk instruments: the guitar, autoharp, dulcimer, and fiddle.

In 1924, radio's "National Barn Dance" began to spread the word. In 1927, Victor came to Tennessee to record Jimmy Rodgers ("The Singing Brakeman") and the Carter Family. In the same year the Grand Ole Opry began broadcasting its down-home blend of banjo pickers, singing fiddlers, and Kentucky mountain music called bluegrass.

The Grand Ole Opry, still running today—out of a $15-million auditorium called Opryland, U.S.A.—became more than a regional tradition; it was a national resource, a finishing

COUNTRY AND PROTEST: *the songs of country and western singer Ernie Tubbs, and those of protest hero Bob Dylan, both used folk material and forms to reach wide audiences.*

CULVER PICTURES

CULVER PICTURES

CULVER PICTURES

CULVER PICTURES

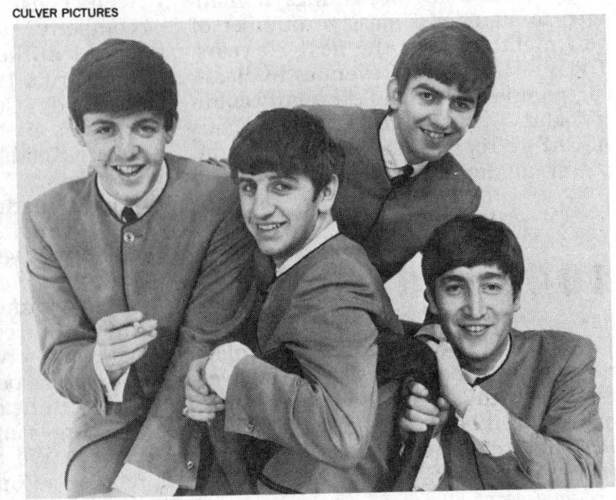

GIANTS OF ROCK: *Elvis Presley brought rock 'n' roll to the 1950's. In the 1960's the Beatles gave rock new sophistication and inventiveness.*

school, and a proving ground for country music, graduating star after star to national fame.

By the late 1940's, the growing industry centered in Nashville changed its image and name. Now called country and western, its stars shot to the top of the charts—the published tabulation of nationwide best sellers. Eddy Arnold's "Bouquet of Roses," Hank Williams' "Long Gone Lonesome Blues," and Johnny Cash's "I Walk the Line" and "Folsom Prison Blues" sold millions of records.

By the 1950's and '60's, country and western was a national craze; by the '70's, it was a major power in the United States, sharing equal radio and television time, record sales, and enormous revenues with rock, its only competitor.

Rock 'n' roll. The phenomenon of the mid-1950's known as rock 'n' roll was little more than a mixture of white country music and the old "stompin'" blues out of the rural South and Midwest. It was a percussive, pulsating, shouting, urgent brand of dance music, exaggerated by guitar amplification, heavy off-beat drumming, suggestive lyrics and—in Elvis Presley's stage act—wildly erotic body movement.

For the "war baby" generation of white, middle-class teenage Americans brought up on a diet of Tin Pan Alley's sentimental ballads, rock 'n' roll was a liberating, revolutionary escape into a kind of purely physical music.

Rock 'n' roll revolutionized the music industry. Because it was music in the oral tradition (one or two hearings were enough to learn it), sheet-music sales plummeted as record sales soared. Tin Pan Alley was in trouble.

To survive, Tin Pan Alley kept the new music's surface elements—the beat, instrumentation, and repertory—but signed up new teen idols (good-looking, white, young, middle-class singers) to record anything that even mildly resembled rock 'n' roll. Thus arrived Pat Boone, Frankie Avalon, Bobby Darin, Paul Anka, and the Everly Brothers.

The age of rock. By 1961, rock 'n' roll was just another item in a wildly diverse song market. Rock 'n' roll gradually gave way to a new "age of rock"—an era of a subtler, more profound, and more socially conscious "youth music." Among the influences on this new music were the Beatles, an English group strongly influenced by American rock 'n' roll, and a revival of folk music, headed by groups such as The Weavers and Peter, Paul and Mary, and singers Pete Seeger, Joan Baez, and Bob Dylan. But most important was the growing political-social awareness of these performers as they rallied American youth, by action and original songs, in the protest movements of the early 1960's.

At the same time, in California, the so-called hippie movement swept the campuses. The hippies swung away from traditional values and toward Eastern philosophies and religions, the moral leadership of spiritual gurus, and perception-altering drugs.

A new kind of music grew out of these complexities, spurred on by contact between the Beatles—who in 1964 accounted for 60 percent of *all* records sold in the United States—and the new counterculture. In *Rubber Soul,* a 1965 album, the surface glitter of rock 'n' roll was replaced by gentle introspection, the hypnotically shimmering sounds of the Indian sitar, enigmatic lyrics, and strange sound effects. The Beatles developed this approach still further in powerful but curiously veiled albums such as *Sgt. Pepper's Lonely Hearts Club Band.*

The new gentleness soon caused a reaction, however. The counterculture also produced "acid rock." The Rolling Stones and Mick Jagger, The Who, the Jimi Hendrix Experience, and Janis Joplin with Big Brother and the Holding Company presented a different face, one of sexual strutting, anger, frenzy, ear-splitting amplification, bizarre costumes, psychedelic light shows, and smashed guitars.

By the 1970's, rock settled down into a period of consolidation, reworking previous styles. New composer-singers appeared on the scene: Elton John, Carly Simon, and Billy Joel among them. "Fusion" groups, like Emerson, Lake and Palmer, brought a new blend of rock, jazz, pop, classical, and electronic elements.

Musical theater. In America, musical theater proved, on the other hand, that the old 19th-century models were as good as ever. Whether produced for the live stage or for television, shows rarely needed to depart from the form of the operetta, revue, variety show, or musical comedy to be popular.

Beginning in the 1930's, musical theater increased its capacity to draw audiences into its staged world. The musical's book (its story) became more real. Earlier, the book was little more than an artificial framework on which the composer and lyricist hung songs and dances. The laundress in Victor Herbert's *Sweethearts* (1913), for example, implausibly turns out to be a crown princess.

Jerome Kern's *Show Boat* (1927; book and lyrics by Oscar Hammerstein II) was the first musical to seriously approach an integration of plot and music. George Gershwin's *Strike Up the Band* (1930; based on a book by George S. Kaufman) introduced political satire, and Kurt Weill's *Knickerbocker Holiday* (1938; book and lyrics by Maxwell Anderson) took political and philosophical ideas seriously.

The 1940's produced Richard Rodgers' and Lorenz Hart's *Pal Joey* (1940), a work of cynical social commentary, and the utterly simple small-town story of *Oklahoma!* (1943), Rodgers' and Hammerstein's first collaboration. *Street Scene* (1947; music by Kurt Weill, book by Elmer Rice, lyrics by Langston Hughes) looked at life in New York tenements. Burton Lane's *Finian's Rainbow* (1947) spoke of Southern sharecroppers; Alan J. Lerner and Frederick Loewe's *Brigadoon* (1947) told a touching Scottish legend; Cole Porter's *Kiss Me, Kate* (1948) dressed Shakespeare in modern clothes; and Rodgers' and Hammerstein's *South Pacific* (1949) interwove three of James A. Michener's *Tales of the South Pacific* into one of musical theater's most entertaining and masterful evenings.

The 1950's and 1960's saw even greater emphasis on themes of substance and on the tight integration of book, lyrics, and music. Broadway was treated to Irving Berlin's *Call Me Madam* (1950), Cole Porter's *Can-Can* (1953), Harold Rome's *Fanny* (1954), Lerner and Loewe's *My Fair Lady* (1956) and *Camelot* (1960), Leonard Bernstein's *West Side Story* (1957), and Rodgers' and Hammerstein's *The Sound of Music* (1959).

New talents in the 1960's and '70's brought controversial and previously forbidden topics to the musical stage. Jerry Bock and Sheldon Harnick's *Fiddler on the Roof* (1964) brought Sholom Aleichem's world of impoverished Jews in czarist Russia to audiences ignorant of this corner of history. John Kander and Fred Ebb's *Cabaret* similarly brought audiences the terror of early Nazi Germany in brilliant song and dance.

The conception of dance as an integral part of musical theater owes much to the pioneering contribution of Agnes de Mille in *Oklahoma!*, to Jerome Robbins' innovations in *West Side Story*, and to Bob Fosse's highly stylized conceptions for *Cabaret* and his all-dance revue, *Dancin'*.

The musical comedy of the 1980's is a complex form, capable of handling a broad range of subjects and types of theater. From religion (*Godspell*) to spectacle to experimental works in search of new forms (*Sweeney Todd* and *A Chorus Line*), it continues to surprise with its inventiveness and flexibility.

CULVER PICTURES

MARTHA SWOPE

THE MUSICAL: *from* Oklahoma! *(1943) to* A Chorus Line *(1975), the Broadway musical combined drama, music, and dance in ever-changing ways.*

Other trends. Carried on out of old traditions, too, were the sentimental ballad—whether warbled by Bing Crosby in the 1940's or belted out by Frank Sinatra or Barbra Streisand in a Las Vegas nightclub in 1980; the spiritual—a 19th-century black classic, typified by Gospel singer Mahalia Jackson's moving performance of "He's Got the Whole World in His Hands"; and the soul music of the 1960's—right out of the backwoods roots of rhythm and blues.

Social dancing, too, is part of an unbroken line. The wild vigor of the twist or the frug matched the old Charleston and black bottom; and the Latin dance craze of the 1950's was no less potent than Vernon and Irene Castle's Argentine tango. But even while a discotheque of 1980 features no-touch dancing, Lawrence Welk waltzes his audience on national TV.

Motion picture music has occasionally reached both popular and artistic heights. The new works of Maurice Jarre, John Williams (*Star Wars*), John Barry, and Quincy Jones pick up where an earlier generation—Max Steiner, Dmitri Tiomkin, Miklos Rozsa, and Franz Waxman—left off. At the same time, Bernard Herrmann's classic scores for the Hitchcock films are models of dramatic effect and integration for new writers.

Although jazz ripped wildly through the bop (or be-bop) era of Dizzy Gillespie, Miles Davis, and John Coltrane, and stepped softly through the "cool" jazz era of the 1960's, led by the quiet earthiness of the Modern Jazz Quartet, its blues base was never much in doubt. Even the crossovers of recent year—jazz-rock and Latin jazz, to name two—have not altered its profile beyond recognition.

The big band is certainly not what it used to be, although its alumni are still playing concerts and dances here and there. And the 70- and 80-year-olds of New Orleans are still playing Dixieland in Preservation Hall. "That's the way jazz used to be played," they say, remembering how it all began.

Our long history of popular musical entertainment began back on the street corners of colonial America. Where it will go, we cannot be sure, but this corner of American life can certainly be described as "very much alive and in excellent health."

The Materials of Music

This piece of music is an excerpt from the aria "Qui sedes," from Johann Sebastian Bach's *Mass in B Minor.* The musical terms refer to specific elements of musical notation. The number next to each term refers to the numbered sections below, in which each term is explained. Terms that carry the same number are related musically, and are therefore covered in the same section.

1. Instrumentation refers to all instruments and voices required to perform a given piece of music. The excerpt above calls for an *alto* (a low female voice), an *oboe* (a woodwind instrument), *violins* (high-voiced stringed instruments), a *viola* (a middle-voiced stringed instrument), and a *cello* (a low-voiced stringed instrument).

In preparing a *score* (the complete notation of a composition), the composer draws a vertical line at the beginning of the music to connect all instruments and voices that are to play at the same time. This grouping is called a *system.* The score is read from left to right, then from one system to the next.

2. Pitch. A *note* is a musical symbol that represents a sound of a specific length. A *rest* is a musical symbol that represents a silence of a specific length. (Notes and rests are further explained in Section 4, below.)

Notes and rests are written on a five-line *staff:*

Low sounds are represented by notes placed on the lower lines or in the lower spaces of the staff. As the pitches ascend, the notes ascend on the staff. As pitches descend, the notes descend on the staff.

A pitch that is too high or too low to be included within the staff is written on or next to a *ledger line:*

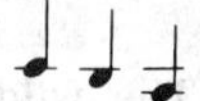

The ledger line is a temporary extension of the five-line staff; it is added only as needed.

The sign placed at the beginning of a staff is called a *clef.* The *treble clef* indicates that the notes on its staff are treble (high) pitches. The *bass clef* indicates that the notes on its staff are bass (low) pitches.

The treble clef is also called the *G-clef* because the lower curl of the clef encircles the line called "G". The bass clef is also called the *F-clef* because the two dots to the right of the clef enclose the line called "F".

Ascending from the bottom of the bass clef to the top of the treble clef, the pitch names follow this alphabetical order: A B C D E F G / A B C D E F G / (etc.).

3. Pitch names. Using the piano keyboard as a convenient reference, the pitch names of the white keys are as follows:

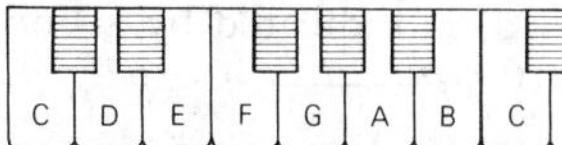

These white-key pitches may also be called *natural* (C-natural, D-natural, and so on).

The distance between any key and its closest neighbor (white or black), either above it or below it, is called a *half-step.* When a pitch is raised one half-step, that pitch becomes *sharp.* The sign ♯ means "sharp" (C♯, D♯, and so on).

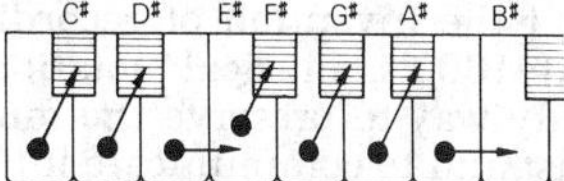

When a pitch is lowered one half-step, that pitch becomes *flat.* The sign ♭ means "flat" (G♭, A♭, etc.).

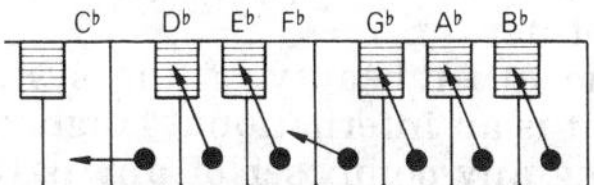

Since the number of keys on the piano are limited, they all do double duty: F♯ and G♭, for example, refer to the same black key; B and C♭ refer to the same white key. The choice of one name or the other is determined by the music's *key signature* (see below).

The signs ♯ and ♭ are part of a family of signs called *accidentals.* Other accidentals include the *natural* ♮ (meaning restore the sharped or flatted pitch to its natural position); the *double-sharp* 𝄪 (meaning raise the pitch two half-steps); and the double-flat ♭♭ (meaning lower the pitch two half-steps). There is no "double natural."

The *key signature* of a composition, placed to the right of the clef, indicates which pitches of the music are to be raised or lowered at all times.

The result of raising or lowering specific pitches at all times is a pitch pattern called a *key,* or *tonality.* Each pitch pattern forms a specific *scale* when the pitches are written in alphabetical order:

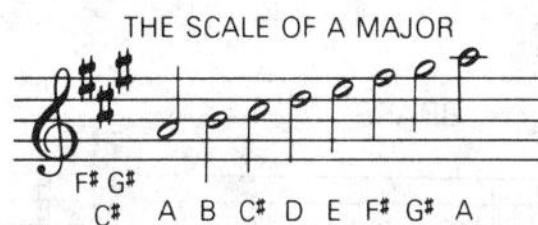

Traditional music may be written in any one of 15 *major* keys or 15 *minor* keys (the quality of being major or minor depends on the specific pitch pattern of the key). However, because our notational system provides for a total of only 15 key signatures, each one does double duty. Thus a given key signature refers to a specific major key in addition to what is called its *relative minor key* (see chart above).

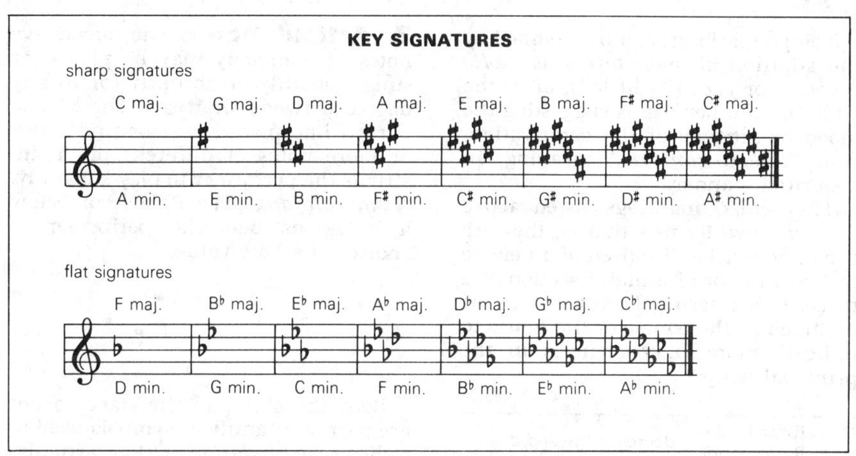

4. Rhythm. All music consists of combinations of sounds and silences. In traditional notation, all sounds are written as notes; all silences, as rests. *Rhythm* refers to the duration (length) of these notes and rests in relationship to one another.

The chart below shows the relative values of different notes, from the *whole note* 𝅝 at the top, down through its division and subdivision into shorter note values. Although the chart ends with the 16th note, further subdivisions into 32nd notes and 64th notes are possible. Rests of equivalent value are shown in the left margin.

The *beats,* or pulse, of a composition are grouped into *measures* (or *bars*), separated by *barlines.*

The *time signature* of the music, placed to the right of the key signature, is a simple number formula (not a fraction) that provides two pieces of information.

The top number indicates how many beats are grouped in one measure. The bottom number indicates the kind of note value that visually represents the beat.

In the excerpt, the time signature is $\frac{6}{8}$ ("six-eight"). This means that there are 6 beats in one measure, and that the 8th note represents one beat. Other time signatures may use other bottom numbers: "4" for a quarter note ($\frac{4}{4}$, $\frac{6}{4}$, etc.); "2" for a half note ($\frac{2}{2}$, $\frac{3}{2}$, etc.); "16" for a 16th note ($\frac{4}{16}$, $\frac{7}{16}$, etc.), and so on.

Tempo refers to the speed of the beat. Although a tempo marking may be in any language, the following Italian terms are commonly used:

TEMPO MARKINGS

Adagio Largo Lento	very slow
Andante Moderato	moderately slow
Allegro Vivace	fast
Allegro molto Presto	very fast

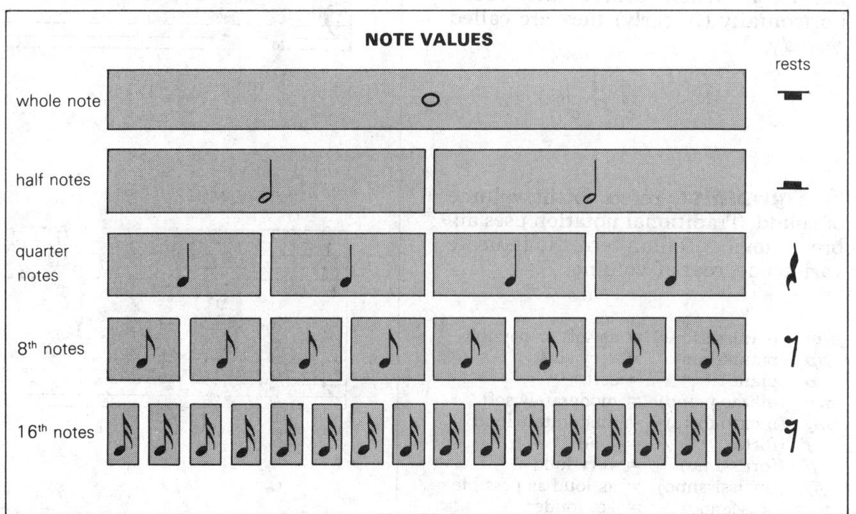

Tempo markings can be modified by the addition of such terms as *molto* ("very") or *poco* ("a little"); or by the addition of other words suggesting the mood or attitude of the composition, as in "allegro *con brio*," meaning "in a spirited manner."

The tempo markings listed above are *principal* terms—that is, they are used to describe the speed of an entire composition or of a major section of a piece. Other terms, however, may be included in the course of the music to indicate momentary changes in the principal tempo:

Ritardando Rallentando	decrease the speed
Allargando	broaden the tempo
Accelerando	increase the tempo
A tempo	return to the original tempo

These terms are usually abbreviated as: *rit., rall., allarg.*, and *accel.*

A tie is a curved line connecting two identical pitches. It is used to lengthen the duration of a sound:

tie

A *double barline* ‖ is placed after the last measure of a composition, indicating the end. The double barline in the excerpt has been added only to demonstrate this symbol.

5. Harmony.

A *chord* consists of three or more pitches played simultaneously. If the chord is perceived as pleasant-sounding, it is considered to be *consonant*. If it is perceived as discordant, it is considered to be *dissonant*. Consonance and dissonance are entirely subjective concepts. They depend on individual taste and listening experiences.

When sounds are heard as vertical (piled-up) structures they are called *harmony*. When sounds are heard horizontally (linearly) they are called *melody*.

6. Dynamics

refers to the volume of sound. Traditional notation uses abbreviations of Italian terms to indicate various degrees of volume:

ppp	(pianississimo)	= as soft as possible
pp	(pianissimo)	= very soft
p	(piano)	= soft
mp	(mezzo-piano)	= moderately soft
mf	(mezzo-forte)	= moderately loud
f	(forte)	= loud
ff	(fortissimo)	= very loud
fff	(fortississimo)	= as loud as possible
	(crescendo)	= get louder
	(diminuendo)	= get softer

7. Articulation.

The successive notes of a melody may be played or sung smoothly or abruptly (or in any degree between the two). The *slur*, a curved line placed over or under two or more notes of different pitch, instructs the performer to play smoothly. A *staccato dot*, placed above or below a note, instructs the performer to shorten the note value.

Both the slur and the staccato dot are part of a family of symbols used to indicate *articulation*. Other articulation symbols include the *tenuto* (—) (meaning stress the note slightly); the *accent* (>) (meaning emphasize the note); and the *"hammered" accent* (∧) (meaning accent the note as strongly as possible).

8. Text.

The traditional English translation of the *text* of the excerpt is:

Qui sedes ad dextram
Thou that sittest at the right hand
Patris
of God the Father

The text, or *lyrics*, of a vocal work is placed under the voice part. Word syllables are aligned with the notes at the composer's discretion.

When two syllables of a word are separated by a number of notes, several hyphens are placed between the syllables: *se - - - - des.*

The musical extension of a one-syllable word (or of the last syllable of any word) is indicated by a line after the word: *Qui*______

• • •

Musical notation is, as we have now seen, a compilation of numerous terms, signs, and symbols, each with its own specific meaning. All of these elements have been adopted, after centuries of evolution, because they are useful and clear. Brought together in a score, they constitute a functional language with which to communicate the composer's intentions to others.

Until the invention of recording in the late1800's, musical notation was the only way to preserve the music of the past and to communicate it to later generations. Had it not been invented, the music of the past 500 years would be lost to us, except (perhaps) as it has been passed down from performer to performer.

The other beauty of the system is that it is an international language, allowing any composer of any nationality to speak clearly to other musicians. In order to appreciate the great poets of Germany, for example, one must speak and read German (or settle for a rough understanding through translation). But the great composers of Germany speak to us directly, both through printed music in international notation and through the performance of their works. One need not speak German to appreciate Bach or Beethoven.

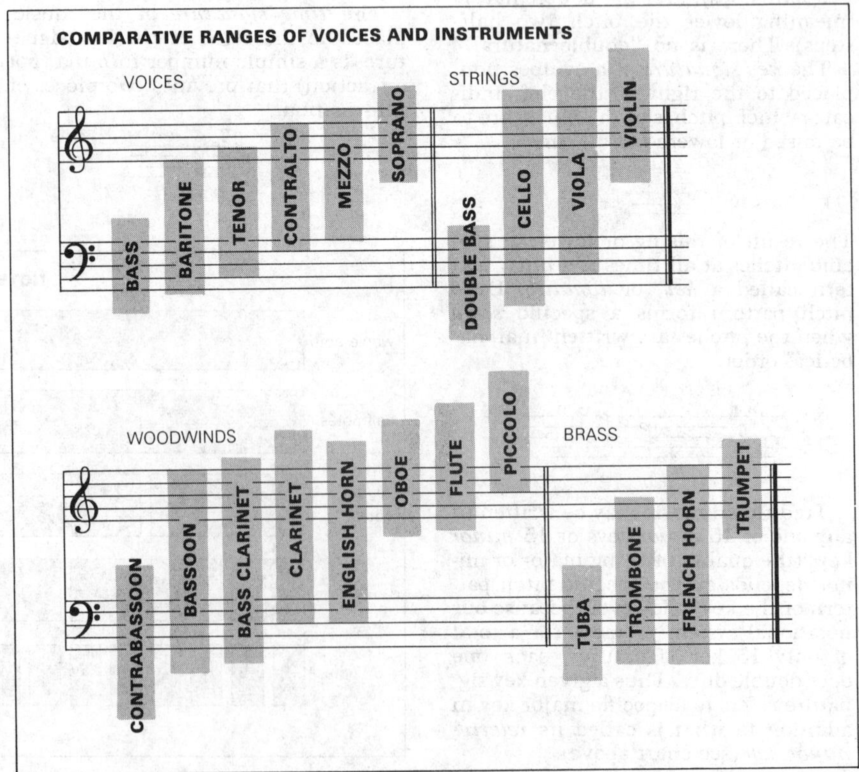

A SHORT DICTIONARY OF BASIC MUSICAL TERMS

Absolute music. Music conceived as abstract designs in sound, unrelated to story, image, or other nonmusical elements.

Accelerando. See Materials of Music, Rhythm.

Accent. See Materials, Articulation.

Accidental. See Materials, Pitch names.

Accompaniment. Music intended as a background for a melody, soloist, narrator, etc.

Acoustics. The science of sound; also, the qualities of a room, concert hall, etc., that make it good or bad for carrying sound.

Adagio. See Materials, Rhythm.

Ad libitum. Instructions to the player to choose any tempo or kind of expression.

Agitato. Agitated.

Aleatory. "Chance" music, whose elements are prescribed by the composer, but put together by the performer.

Allargando. See Materials, Rhythm.

Allegro; Allegretto. See Materials, Rhythm.

Alto. The lower female voice, also called contralto.

Andante; Andantino. See Materials, Rhythm.

Anthem. A piece of sacred music, usually with words taken from the Bible.

Antiphonal. A style of music using responsive (answering) voices and/or instruments.

Aria. An extended lyrical vocal solo.

Arpeggio. The notes of a chord played in rapid succession instead of simultaneously.

Atonal; Atonality. The absence of tonality.

Bar; Barline. See Materials, Rhythm.

Bass. The lowest male voice; also, the double bass, the lowest of the stringed instruments.

Beat. See Materials, Rhythm.

Bolero. A Spanish folk dance in three-quarter time.

Brass. Orchestral instruments, including the trumpet, French horn, trombone, and tuba.

Brio. Spirit, vivacity.

Cadence. The melodic and/or harmonic formula that marks the end of a musical phrase, section, etc.

Cadenza. A virtuosic passage for solo instrument, generally found near the end of a concerto movement.

Canon. The strictest form of melodic imitation between two or more successive voices of a composition.

Cantabile. In a flowing, singing manner.

Cantata. An extended work for voices and instruments.

Cantus firmus. A "fixed song"—that is, a given melody, often in long note values, that flows through a fabric of accompanying polyphonic voices.

Chorale. A hymn tune of the Lutheran Church; or a hymn tune of similar style.

Chord. See Materials, Harmony.

Chromatic. Relating to pitches foreign to a given tonality (key) or chord.

Chromatic scale. A succession of twelve half-steps, in ascending or descending order, beginning with any pitch.

Clavichord. An early keyboard instrument.

Clavier. A general name for any keyboard instrument except the organ.

Clef. See Materials, Pitch.

Coda. A concluding section of a composition.

Concerto. An extended work for a solo instrument and orchestra.

Consonance. See Materials, Harmony.

Continuo (also **basso continuo**). A continuous bass line that follows the beat of the music and suggests the harmonies to be added above it (a prominent stylistic element of Baroque music); also, the instruments that play such a bass line.

Contrapuntal. See *Counterpoint.*

Counterpoint. A musical texture consisting of two or more independent and simultaneous lines.

Crescendo. See Materials, Dynamics.

Degree. One of the tones of a scale.

Diatonic. Pertaining to a major or minor scale; also, music based on such scales, with an infrequent use of chromatic tones.

Diminuendo. See Materials, Dynamics.

Dissonance. See Materials, Harmony.

Divertimento. A composition of light, often festive, character.

Dolce. Sweet, soft.

Dominant. The fifth degree of a major or minor scale; also, a chord built on this degree.

Double barline. See Materials, Rhythm.

Double Bass. See *Bass.*

Downbeat. The first beat of a measure.

Dynamics. See Materials, Dynamics.

Ear training. That part of musical education devoted to sensitizing the ear to pitch patterns, harmonic progressions, and rhythmic figurations.

Eighth note; Eighth rest. See Materials, Rhythm.

Electronic music. Music that derives part or all of its sound materials from electronic components or instruments (such as the synthesizer); also, music that uses electronically modified natural or traditional instrument sounds.

Embellishment. A decorative element added to any pitch or note value. Common embellishments include the trill, the grace note, the turn, and the mordant.

Enharmonics. Any two pitches that sound exactly the same but are given different names (such as F♯-G♭).

Espressivo. Expressively.

Fantasia. A free-form composition, often of a virtuosic character.

F-clef. See Materials, Pitch.

Fermata. A momentary pause or hold in music.

Flag. The short curved line attached to the stem of an eighth note.

Flat. See Materials, Pitch names.

Form. The arrangement of materials within a composition.

Forte; Fortissimo. See Materials, Dynamics.

Fugue. A type or style of composition using counterpoint in which a single theme, called the *subject,* appears in different voices.

Gavotte. An old French dance form of dignified character, somewhat resembling the minuet.

G-clef. See Materials, Pitch.

Gigue. A country dance, a jig.

Glissando. A rapid slide through a succession of neighboring pitches.

Grace note. A single embellishing note, quickly played without time value, preceding a note.

Gregorian chant. Medieval church chant, named for Pope Gregory the Great; also called *chant, plainchant, plainsong.*

Half note; Half rest. See Materials, Rhythm.

Harmonic. A musical texture consisting mostly of chords or of melody accompanied by chords; also, any one of the *partials,* or high-frequency components, of a sound that contribute to the timbre of that sound.

Harmony. Any simultaneous combination of sounds; also, the style of a composition with respect to its use of chords.

Harpsichord. An early keyboard instrument.

Homophony (homophonic). A musical texture in which all parts move in more or less the same rhythm.

Imitation. In counterpoint, the restatement of a melodic idea by another voice part.

Improvisation. Music composed by the player simultaneously with its performance.

Interval. The distance between any two pitches.

Key; Key signature. See Materials, Pitch names.

Largo; Larghetto. See Materials, Rhythm.

Ledger line. See Materials, Pitch.

Legato. Smoothly.

Leggiero. Lightly.

Leitmotiv. A "leading motive": a term usually associated with Wagner's use of a short musical idea associated with a person, emotion, or situation.

Lento. See Materials, Rhythm.

Libretto. The words of a musical, opera, oratorio, etc.

Lied. A German song form.

Line. A melody or part of a melody, often considered as part of a contrapuntal texture.

Madrigal. The choral setting of a short lyrical poem of an amorous, pastoral, or descriptive character.

Maestoso. Majestically.

Measure. See Materials, Rhythm.

Melody. See Materials, Harmony.

Metronome. A mechanical device for measuring the speed of a beat.

Microtone. An interval smaller than a half-step.

Minuet. A stately dance of moderate speed in three-quarter time; popular in the 1700's.

Mode. A scale pattern outside of the major-minor system, especially such a pattern used in medieval music.

Modulation. Harmonic movement from one key, or tonality, to another.

Monody. A style of music in which the melody predominates over a subordinated background.

Monophony (monophonic). A musical texture consisting of a single line of melody without accompaniment.

Motive, motif. The smallest unit of a musical phrase.

Natural. See Materials, Pitch names.

Neume. In medieval musical notation, a character used to represent a tone or combination of tones.

Nocturne. A descriptive title for a short composition of dreamy, sentimental character.

Obbligato. An important independent instrumental line used in conjunction with a vocal solo.

Octave. The distance between any pitch and its doubled or halved frequency, as from middle C to the next C above or below it.

Opera. A dramatic work, usually staged, for solo voices and orchestra.

Oratorio. An extended composition for vocal soloists, chorus, and instruments, usually on a religious theme.

Ornamentation. Decorative notes added to a melodic line; embellishments.

Ostinato. A short melodic or rhythmic figure that is persistently repeated.

Partita. A suite of dance pieces.

Passacaglia. A musical form characterized by a continually repeated bass phrase of four or eight measures.

Percussion. Those orchestral instruments that are played by striking, including tympani, drums, bells, and sometimes the piano.

Phrase. A musical idea made of two or more motives.

Pitch. The relative highness or lowness of a sound.

Pizzicato. Plucked with the finger.

Plainchant, plainsong. See *Gregorian chant.*

Polyphony (polyphonic). A musical texture consisting of two or more melodically and rhythmically independent lines. See also *Counterpoint.*

Polyrhythmic. Music consisting of many independent simultaneous rhythms.

Polytonal. Music consisting of three or more simultaneous tonalities.

Program music. Descriptive music based on a story, image, scene, stated emotion, etc.

Quarter note; Quarter rest. See Materials, Rhythm.

Rallentando. See Materials, Rhythm.

Range. All pitches, from the lowest to the highest, capable of being played by a given instrument or voice.

Recitative. Vocal writing based on the rhythms and inflections of speech, with a minimum of musical structure.

Reed. A thin strip of wood, cane, metal, or plastic affixed to the mouthpiece of some woodwinds (oboe, bassoon, clarinet, saxophone, etc.) to transmit vibrations (produced by blowing) to the body of the instrument.

Register. A portion of an instrument's or voice's range.

Requiem. The Mass for the dead.

Resolution. The movement from a dissonant interval or chord to a consonant one.

Rest. See Materials, Rhythm.

Rhapsody. A free-form composition, characterized by distinct changes of mood, tempo, and materials.

Rhythm. Musical flow. See also Materials, Rhythm.

Ritardando. See Materials, Rhythm.

Rondo. A musical form in which the frequent repetitions of a musical theme are interrupted by the insertion of contrasting materials.

Root. The lowest note of a chord structure.

Rubato. A slight modification of the regularity of a tempo, introduced freely by the performer for expressive reasons.

Scale. A fixed arrangement of pitches, ascending or descending.

Score. See Materials, Instrumentation.

Semitone. A half-step. See also Materials, Pitch names.

Sequence. The continued repetition of a melodic motive, but on different pitches.

Sforzando. The sudden emphasis of a sound.

Sharp. See Materials, Pitch names.

Sixteenth note; Sixteenth rest. See Materials, Rhythm.

Slur. See Materials, Articulation.

Solfege. The system of musical training and performance in which the syllables *doh, ray, me, fah, sol, la,* and *te* are used to represent notes of a musical scale.

Sonata. Originally, a "sound piece." Now, an instrumental composition, usually in three or four movements, in which the first movement is generally structured along classical lines of exposition, development, and recaptitulation—the so-called *sonata-allegro* form.

Sonatina. A sonata in shortened, condensed form.

Soprano. The higher female voice.

Sostenuto. Sustained.

Staccato. See Materials, Articulation.

Stretto. A portion of a fugue in which the imitations of the theme occur at closer and closer intervals of time, possibly overlapping.

Strings. Those orchestral instruments including the violin, viola, cello, and double bass.

Subject. The theme of a fugue.

Suite. A set of related pieces, traditionally of dance forms.

Symphony. A long work for orchestra, usually in three or four contrasting movements.

Syncopation. The displacement of the normal accent of a meter by shifting strong emphasis to a weak beat or to a weak part of a beat.

Tempo. See Materials, Rhythm.

Tenor. The higher male voice.

Tenuto. See Materials, Articulation.

Texture. The "fabric" of music in terms of its density, color, and the relative activity of its different simultaneous parts.

Theme. The principal musical idea of a composition.

Timbre. The characteristic tone color of a voice or instrument.

Time signature. See Materials, Rhythm.

Toccata. Originally, a "touch piece." Now, a free-form work similar to the *fantasia,* characterized by rapid, brilliant passages and virtuoso displays.

Tonality. The sense of being in a key. See also Materials, Pitch names.

Tone. A musical sound of definite pitch.

Tone poem. A work for orchestra illustrating a poetic idea through sound.

Tonic. The first note, or degree, of a scale; also, a chord built on this degree.

Triad. A chord consisting of three notes: the root; a second tone, the interval of a third above the root; and a third tone, the interval of a fifth above the root.

Unison. A tone of the same pitch as a given tone; by extension, a higher or lower octave of a given tone.

Upbeat. The last beat of a measure.

Variation. The transformation of a theme by alterations in its melody, harmony, rhythm, form, texture, etc.

Vivace. See Materials, Rhythm.

Voice. A melodic line, especially in a contrapuntal texture.

Waltz. A dance in three-quarter time popular in the 1800's.

Whole note; Whole rest. See Materials, Rhythm.

Woodwinds. Those orchestral instruments including the piccolo, flute, oboe, English horn, clarinet, bass clarinet, bassoon, and contrabassoon.

—Ronald Herder

DANCE

To dance is to move the body in a rhythmic and expressive way. *Rhythmic* means that there is a beat of some kind to the movements. Usually the rhythm is supplied by music that accompanies the dance, although it is possible to move rhythmically, and so to dance, without music. *Expressive* means that the movements express ideas or emotions, or both. The expression may take the form of a narrative story, or it may be an abstract manifestation of feelings, without any story line.

Movement that is rhythmic but not expressive is not dancing. Marching is an example. Movement that is expressive but not rhythmic is called *mime.* Often there are elements of mime in dances, and the line that separates mime from dance is a vague one.

The Beginnings of Dance

Dance is one of the oldest and most widespread forms of artistic expression. There is probably no culture in which people do not dance, and in many cultures the dance traditions go back thousands of years.

The roots of dance go back at least as far as the neolithic (later Stone Age) cultures that preceded the development of civilized societies. Different cultures passed through the neolithic phase at different times in history; some neolithic cultures survived into the 20th century. A few of these cultures remain today in such places as New Guinea, the Amazon rain forest, and parts of Africa. Of these, many have preserved their dance traditions. Other dance traditions, such as those of certain American Indian tribes, have been kept alive by members eager to preserve the ancient rites of their people.

TOMAS D.W. FRIEDMAN/PHOTO RESEARCHERS

TRIBAL DANCE: *African pygmies dance in the characteristic circle. Their traditional dwellings may have been round rather than rectangular, as seen in the background.*

In neolithic cultures, dance is a kind of magic. There were many things that affected people's lives that were not understood. Magic helped to explain some of these things and, so people believed, to control them. Dance was one of the ways that magic was practiced.

From the beginning, there seem to have been two basic kinds of dance. In one kind, the thing that the dancer hoped to influence was depicted. The dancer might act out a battle that the tribe expected to fight, or imitate an animal that the tribe expected to hunt.

In the other kind of dance, the dancer did not try to create an image. Instead he tried through the dance to achieve a state of religious ecstasy, believing that this kind of escape from self would give him magical powers.

In some cultures, masks came to be used to intensify the meaning of dance. In a hunting dance, for example, the mask might make the image of the hunted animal more real; or in an imageless dance, it might suggest the fantastic and magical world that the dancer hoped to escape into.

The earliest dances probably had no musical accompaniment; most likely, the only sounds were the sounds made by the dancers. In fact, music probably developed out of these sounds. Dancers clapped their hands, slapped their knees, and made rhythmical noises with their mouths. They may have attached noise-making articles, such as shells, to their arms, legs, and hips. When their noise-making articles became larger and more complex, they were probably turned over to nondancers and played as accompanying musical instruments. The dancers' cries evolved, through a similar process, into singing.

In most tribal dancing, the basic form of the group was a circle. Often the subject of the dance, such as a sick person to be cured, or a dancer representing an animal to be hunted, was in the center of the circle. In some tribes, however, the dancers lined up in rows. People who lived in round structures, such as huts or tepees, tended to have circular dances, while those who lived in rectangular structures tended to dance in rows.

In some cultures there also developed dancing in couples. In some of these dances, the partners represented two complementary ideas, such as the light and dark sides of the moon. Other dances with couples had definite sexual meaning, often related to fertility.

Dances can be classified by the types of movements in them. Dances that are wild and frenzied are called *convulsive.* The purpose of these dances was to work the dancer into a state of ecstasy and collapse. The cultures whose dancing was convulsive were those in which witch doctors or medicine men figured prominently.

Dances that are not convulsive are called *harmonic* and are of two kinds, those that have expanded movements and those that have closed movements. Expanded movements are leaping, jumping, running, and the like. Closed movements are quieter and gentler, including such things as swinging and swaying.

Another way of classifying dances—all dances, not only neolithic ones—is by their arm and torso movements. Arm movements are of three kinds: straight, or one-dimensional; curved, or two-dimensional; and spiral, or three-dimensional.

There are two basic kinds of torso movements. In one kind, called single-unit, the torso is held relatively stiff and straight. In the other kind, called multi-unit, the different parts of the torso move independently in a sinuous, undulating way. Both kinds can now be found in American dancing, the single-unit deriving from European dance traditions and the multi-unit from African dance traditions.

CULVER PICTURES

SALOME *dances before Herod. This Victorian illustration of the biblical story suggests the connection between dance and sexual allure.*

Dance in Ancient Cultures

Dance figured prominently in the cultures of the ancient world around the Mediterranean Sea. Although elements of these dances have no doubt survived, the dances themselves have been lost. Only surviving written and pictorial records provide a certain amount of information about these dances.

Egypt. In ancient Egypt, priests danced both in regular religious observances and in various special celebrations that took place each year. The Egyptian nobility danced little themselves. They were, instead, the first people in the history of dance whose main function was to watch. The dancers themselves were either slaves or hired professionals who entertained the nobility at banquets and celebrations of various kinds.

Throughout most of Egypt's long history, its dancing was stiff, angular, highly stylized, and very formal. In the period called the New Kingdom, which began about 1570 B.C., foreign influences—mainly from India—brought about a more relaxed and sinuous style of dancing.

The Hebrews. Less is known of ancient Hebrew dance. Hebrew law prohibited depictions of the human form in art so there is no pictorial record. But various passages in the Bible make it clear that dancing was a part of Hebrew life from a very early time. The first mention of dance is in the Book of Exodus: "And Miriam, the prophetess, Aaron's sister, took up her tambourine, and all the women followed her, dancing to the sound of tambourines . . . " Another famous dance, also in the Book of Exodus, is that of the people around the golden calf that had been fashioned while Moses was on Mount Sinai. Perhaps the best known of the dances told of in the Bible is that of Salomé before her stepfather, King Herod, and his guests. As a prize she asked for the head of John the Baptist.

The Greeks. Many early Greek dances were dedicated to Apollo, god of the sun, prophecy, medicine, music, and poetry. On the whole, these dances were dignified, reflecting the Greek admiration for harmony and balance.

But along with these "Apollonian" dances, there also developed a kind of wild, unrestrained dance dedicated to Dionysus, the god of wine. In these Dionysian rites, men wore goatskins, horned masks, and sometimes beards and tails. Women called *maenads* ("madwomen"), danced with similar abandon.

It was from these primitive Dionysian rites that Greek tragedy eventually developed. As these tragedies were first performed, they fused poetry, music, and dance into a total theatrical experience. Today we still have the poetry, but the music and the dance have been lost.

The Romans. In Rome's early years, dance was an integral part of Roman religious observances. But as Rome's power increased and its conquests multiplied, dancing came to be regarded as an activity appropriate only for slaves and foreigners. Respectable Romans enjoyed watching dancers, but seldom danced themselves.

The Early Christians. Many early leaders of Christianity were opposed to dancing because of its association with other religions. As a result, dancing has rarely been a significant part of Christian religious worship. This is not to say that Christians abandoned dancing, for in most countries that became Christian, the old dances continued long after the introduction of the new religion. But the dances gradually lost the religious and magical meanings that they once had had, and became instead mainly a form of social activity.

Dance in the Orient

Oriental dances are generally much more restrained than those in other parts of the world. There is little jumping or leaping; the feet are usually planted firmly on the ground, and sometimes the dancers are even seated. But the movements of these dances can be extremely complex and subtle. This is particularly true of the traditional dances of India.

India. According to the Hindu religion, the universe was created by the Lord Shiva, who then set it in motion by himself doing a dance. Indeed, dance has been a fundamental part of Hinduism, still the principal religion of India, from its very beginning. The principles and methods of Indian dance were first put into writing about 500 A.D.; they are traceable to a sage named Bharata, who lived almost a thousand years earlier.

Bharata gave instructions on how to use every part of the body. For example, there are six ways to move the eyebrows, eight ways to move the eyes, nine ways to move the head, and more than 4000 ways to move the hands. Some gestures symbolize such things as animals; others are abstract, symbolizing ideas and emotions.

There are now four major schools of Indian dance: the *Manipuri,* the *Bharatya Natyam,* the *Kathakali,* west, and the *Kathak.* All derive directly from the early Hindu dance of Bharata. The Kathak also shows the influence of the Muslims who ruled the northwest of India for several centuries. It is characterized by a combination of graceful arm movements and vigorous foot movements and somewhat resembles the Spanish flamenco, which also shows strong Islamic influence.

The dances of Indonesia, including the well known temple dances of the island of Bali, derive from the Indian tradition and share many of its characteristics and conventions.

China and Japan. The dance of China is very much of this world. It tells of people rather than of gods, and is performed with mime, singing, and orchestral music.

ORIENTAL DANCE: *a Thai dancer uses traditions inherited from India and China.*

UNITED NATIONS

Chinese dance has eleven basic positions, and consists mainly of slow, stately changes from one of these positions to another. It is a static kind of dancing, delicate and dignified.

The Japanese dance tradition derived from the Chinese, and resembles it in many ways. But the spirit and style of the courtly *No* plays and the more dramatic *kabuki* plays are uniquely Japanese.

The Ballet

Ballet is the variety of theatrical dance that developed in Europe. It originated in France, but its roots are in Renaissance Italy. Italian dance, in its turn, derived from the courtly dances of the Middle Ages.

In the early Middle Ages, European dance was robust and earthy. But as the nobility came to see themselves as distinctly superior to the peasantry, they tended to reject the existing dance tradition. The peasantry continued dancing as before, but the nobility's dances became slower and more stately, emphasizing stylized, symbolic movements. Instead of dancing in circles, as did the peasants, the nobility more often danced in couples and moved in procession.

In the Renaissance, dancing became more elaborate and ostentatious. The Italian nobility used dance to demonstrate their wealth and refinement. They were quickly imitated by the rising class of wealthy bankers and merchants in the cities. Dancing masters—teachers of the dance—appeared on the scene, and about 1400 one of them wrote the first known European book on how to dance.

By 1500, dance spectacles, organized and directed by the dancing masters, had become very elaborate indeed. At banquets and other entertainments, costumed dancers, often representing figures from classical mythology, presented series of carefully rehearsed and polished dances. These spectacles were somewhat like amateur floor shows.

By 1600, both ballroom dancing and the more elaborate spectacles based on it had spread to every court of Europe. It was at the court of France that the first ballet was created.

Ballet at the French court.

In 1581, Catherine de Médicis, the Italian-born mother of the king, arranged a great dancing spectacle. She engaged the Italian musician and dancing master named Baldassarino de Belgiojoso to prepare it.

The resulting entertainment was called *Le Ballet Comique de la Reine* ("The Queen's Dramatic Ballet"). It took place in a large hall with raised platforms at each end, one occupied by the royal family, the other by sets depicting the castle and gardens of the evil enchantress Circe. The side walls were decorated. The action told of Circe's evildoings and of her eventual defeat by the Greek gods. Besides the dancing, there were songs, recitations, and the display of several large, elaborately decorated chariots, resembling modern floats. The action began about ten o'clock in the evening and lasted almost six hours.

The choreographer—that is, the person who devised and arranged the dances—was just about the only professional dancer involved in the proceedings. The rest were amateurs, members of the French aristocracy, including even the reigning queen, Catherine's daughter-in-law. For the next century, dance entertainments of this kind were a principal diversion of the nobility of Europe. A principal feature of the choreography—that is, of the planning—of these dances, was the forming and reforming of elaborate patterns, which the audience, seated in balconies, viewed from above. The spectacles were not unlike the halftime shows at modern football games.

During the reign of Louis XIII (1610–1643), the dancing courtiers were first joined by professional entertainers. By that time the principal form was the *ballet à entrée,* which consisted of a series of scenes that were related in theme but otherwise largely independent of one another. The scenes ranged from the grotesque to the solemn and called for dancing skills that required professionals.

Another important change was the gradual shifting of activity from ballrooms to theaters. The stage and proscenium arch of the theater brought a gradual change in choreography, away from elaborate formations and toward emphasis on individual dancers.

French court ballet reached its peak in the first half of the long reign of Louis XIV (1643–1715). The self-styled "Sun King" was probably the most theatrical monarch in history. He enlisted some of the leading talents of the day to produce his ballets, most notably Jean Baptiste Lully, a gifted comic dancer as well as the preeminent composer of the time. In the early decades of his reign, Louis himself often danced in the ballets. In one of his earlier appearances, at 15 years old, he became a living embodiment of the sun.

Louis became rather pudgy as he approached middle age, and in 1670 he stopped appearing in ballets. When the king quit ballet dancing, many of his courtiers followed suit. Louis also established the Royal Academy of Music, today the Paris Opéra, where ballet was from the beginning an important part of the productions. Thus ballet became a totally professional enterprise. The aristocracy continued dancing such elegant ballroom steps as the minuet, but ballet became the province of professionals.

WESTERN DANCE: *the elegant classical ballet, shown in the white act from* Giselle, *grew from the courtly dances of the nobility in Renaissance Europe. The first formal dance spectacles were produced for the entertainment of royalty.*

Ballet in the 1700's. By the early 1700's the old *ballet à entrée* had evolved into a form called *opéra-ballet.* The two forms were similar, but opéra-ballet brought both singing and dancing to new technical heights, and the elaborate staging made these productions some of the most spectacular ever presented. The leading composer and producer of these spectaculars was Jean Philippe Rameau, whose *Les Indes Galantes* (1735) has been successfully restaged in the 20th century.

After Rameau, the balance between singing and dancing tilted in favor of singing, and ballet gradually became a relatively minor part of operatic productions. Yet the tradition of balletic interludes in opera continued through the 1700's and, especially in France, well into the 1800's.

In a kind of countermovement, ballet came to be seen as an independent art, one consisting solely of the dance and its musical accompaniment. This development was forwarded by the appearance of the first superstars of dance. Among men, who originally predominated in ballet, the greatest were Louis Dupré, Dupré's pupil Gaetan Vestris, and Vestris's son Auguste, whose careers collectively spanned the 1700's. There were also, for the first time, memorable female dancers. In the early decades of the century the most famous were Marie Sallé, who tried to convey the emotions of the character she was portraying, and Marie Camargo, who emphasized the technical and acrobatic aspects of dance.

A new kind of ballet, the *ballet d'action,* gradually replaced the earlier forms. It consisted of a series of dances joined as a unified, coherent narrative. This kind of ballet brought increasing importance to the choreographer. By the middle of the century, two choreographers had attained particular prominence, Gasparo Angiolini and Jean Georges Noverre. Both were associated with the principal composers of the time. Angiolini choreographed works of Gluck and Noverre collaborated with Mozart. Noverre is particularly important for his *Letters on Dancing and Ballets* (1760), in which he argued that ballets should be a unified work in which every element contributes to the main theme, rather than a demonstration of the dancers' technical skill.

In 1786 Vincenzo Galeotti, a pupil of Angiolini working in Denmark, staged a comic ballet called *The Whims of Cupid and the Ballet Master.* This would probably not have been an important event in the history of ballet but for one thing: the ballet has ever since been preserved in the repertory of the Royal Danish Ballet. It is the oldest ballet extant and the only one from the 1700's whose choreography has survived.

Romantic ballet. In the early 1800's, Romanticism took hold in ballet as in every other art. Romanticism had many facets; those that most affected ballet were an interest in the humble life in the countryside; an interest in madness, hallucination, suicide; and an interest in the supernatural. All three found expression in the quintessential ballet of the period, *Giselle.*

Giselle, choreographed by Jules Perrot and Jean Coralli to music by Adolphe Adam, was first presented at the Paris Opéra in 1841. It is in two acts. The first act is set in a peasant village somewhere in Germany. Giselle, a lovely peasant girl, is loved by Hilarion, also a peasant. A stranger, accompanied by some friends, arrives on the scene; this young man is dressed as a peasant, but he is actually a prince in disguise. He and Giselle fall instantly in love; but Hilarion discovers his identity. It is revealed that the prince is already engaged to a princess, and the prince and his entourage depart. Giselle goes mad and dies shortly thereafter, either by suicide or of a broken heart, depending on the production.

The second act is set at Giselle's tomb deep in a forest. Giselle has become a Wili (pronounced VEE-lee), a ghost of a woman who died unhappy in love. The Wilis emerge from their tombs at night and lure men to their deaths by dancing them to exhaustion. Hilarion appears and falls victim to them. When the prince arrives, Giselle's ghost must dance with him; but because she still loves him, she manages to keep him dancing until dawn, when the Wilis must return to their graves. The prince is thus spared, presumably to grieve for Giselle to the end of his days.

Giselle offers everything the Romantics prized: country life, madness, ghosts. The second act, in particular, epitomizes an aspect of ballet that remained a fixture well into the 20th century, the so-called "white" act. In a white act, the principal ballerina and the corps de ballet are dressed all in white; usually the setting is at night; and often the dancers represent ghosts or similarly enchanted beings. The effect is ethereal and very delicate, and to this day it stands, in the minds of many, for ballet at its best. Much of the delicacy is achieved by dancing *en pointe,* on the toes of specially constructed slippers, a technique introduced in Romantic ballet.

Romantic ballet exalted the ballerina, consigning male dancers generally to supporting roles. Among the foremost ballerinas were Marie Taglioni, whose greatest role was in *La Sylphide,* an important predecessor to *Giselle* that is still performed occasionally; Fanny Elssler, a dancer of warmth and passion, who made a wildly successful tour of America; Carlotta Grisi, the first Giselle; Fanny Cerrito; and Lucile Grahn, who danced mainly in Denmark.

The Royal Danish Ballet was at this time under the direction of August Bournonville, one of the principal choreographers of the time. Bournonville established a tradition that the Danes have ever since maintained. Bournonville's choreography is the only major body of work that survives from this period.

Toward the end of the Romantic period there appeared another great ballet that is still in the repertory of most companies, *Coppélia.* Choreographed by Arthur Saint-Leon to music by Léo Delibes, *Coppélia* was first performed at the Paris Opéra in 1870. It is the charming story of a high-spirited girl who, by impersonating a life-sized doll, regains the attentions of her lover and at the same time plays a joke on a would-be sorcerer.

Coppélia was the last great ballet of the Romantic period. After 1870 the ballet of the Paris Opéra went into a decline, and the creative center of ballet shifted to Russia.

Russian classical ballet.

There were ballet companies in St. Petersburg and Moscow in the 1700's, and touring virtuosos, such as Taglioni, had always enjoyed good audiences there. But in the last decades of the 1800's Russian ballet reached its peak.

The name most associated with the great years of the Russian ballet is Marius Petipa. Petipa was a French dancer whose career flourished in Russia after 1847. In 1869 he was placed in full charge of the Imperial Ballet in St. Petersburg, and remained there until shortly before his death in 1910. In the later years of his tenure he was assisted by another brilliant choreographer, the Russian Lev Ivanov.

Petipa and Ivanov are today best remembered for the three ballets that they choreographed in the 1890's to scores by Tchaikovsky: *The Sleeping Beauty, The Nutcracker,* and *Swan Lake.* Of these, the first was choreographed by Petipa, the second by Ivanov, and the third by both, each taking responsibility for two of its four acts. The choreography of all three follows a formula that by the 1890's had become well established. Each has a rather slight story line designed mainly to provide a framework for various kinds of dancing. Dramatic and "character" dancing, incorporating elements of mime, advance the story line and establish the minor characters. At some point there is a *divertissement,* a series of dances unrelated to the plot, usually inserted under the guise of entertainment at a party. There is always a *pas de deux,* a duet for the principal ballerina and the principal male dancer. As in Romantic ballet, there is also a white act in which the principal ballerina and the corps de ballet, dressed in white, do a series of dances representing something more or less supernatural.

Some other ballets choreographed by Petipa have been preserved by the principal Russian companies, but many have been lost.

Ballets Russes and Diaghilev.

Ballet was brought into the 20th century by Sergei Diaghilev, a Russian impresario who, in 1909, presented a season of ballet in Paris. The name of Diaghilev's company was *Ballets Russes* ("Russian Ballets"). The dancers and the choreographer were Russian, as were the set and costume designer; most of the ballets were based on Russian themes. But what the Parisian audience saw was very different from what they might have seen in St. Petersburg.

NIJINSKY: *the great Russian dancer in Stravinsky's* Petrouchka *(1916).*

CULVER PICTURES

Diaghilev's principal choreographer was Michel Fokine. Fokine's ideals harked back to the principles of Noverre, for he believed that ballet should be a coherent, dramatic whole, rather than a framework holding together a series of unrelated dances. He favored relatively short, one-act ballets. Diaghilev added his own ideas. He believed that in ballet, the entire production—choreography, music, sets, costumes—should be of the first class. And to Diaghilev nothing was first class that was not innovative.

During the 20 years of the Ballet Russe's existence, the dancers and choreographers—and the company's name—remained Russian; but the composers, the artists, and the ballets' themes took on a decidedly international cast. Among the artists associated with *Ballets Russes* at one time or another were Léon Bakst, Pablo Picasso, Georges Braque, Maurice Utrillo, Joan Miro, Henri Matisse, and Georges Rouault. The composers included Igor Stravinsky, Claude Debussy, Serge Prokofiev, Maurice Ravel, Manuel de Falla, Erik Satie, Darius Milhaud, Francis Poulenc, and Richard Strauss.

Besides Fokine, Diaghilev's choreographers were the great dancer Vaslav Nijinsky; Nijinsky's sister Bronislava Nijinska; Léonide Massine; and George Balanchine. Among the great musical scores first presented by *Ballets Russes* were Stravinsky's *Firebird, Petrouchka, Rite of Spring,* and *Apollo;* Falla's *Three-Cornered Hat;* and Debussy's *Afternoon of a Faun.*

Most of the ballets choreographed by Fokine and his successors stressed the dramatic unity that was Fokine's ideal, but there was a significant exception. The exception was *Les Sylphides,* also by Fokine, choreographed to the music of Chopin (not to be confused with the much earlier *La Sylphide*). *Les Sylphides* is in the Romantic tradition, but, unlike the Romantic ballets, it is not tied to a supernatural story line. It is, rather, pure dance, for its own sake, dance in the abstract. As such it introduced what was later to become a major element in 20th-century dance.

After Diaghilev's death in 1929, a successor company, called *Ballet Russe de Monte Carlo,* was formed. It toured widely in the 1930's, but then split into two companies, both of which soon went out of business.

Ballet continued in the Soviet Union, and promising companies were established in England and the United States. In the United States, too, another kind of dance, theatrical like ballet, but otherwise unrelated to it, had by the 1930's become well established.

The Beginnings of Modern Dance

Modern dance is essentially American. It is true that in its early years it had a German counterpart; but the budding German movement was wiped out by Hitler in the 1930's, leaving the stage largely to Americans.

Modern dance is not easily defined. It resembles ballet in that it is expressive dance for the theater, often requiring a high degree of technical skill; but it rejects the highly conventionalized steps of ballet, its elaborate costuming, its sets, and sometimes even its music. Generally, it is a good deal more earnest than ballet. More than anything, it asks that dancers and choreographers find the exact movements to express whatever they feel, without regard for conventions. The emphasis, in short, is on invention and discovery.

The first dancer of this kind to attract widespread attention was Isadora Duncan, known as much for her unorthodox lifestyle as for her dancing. In the early 1900's, she began to perform expressive solos to the music of Beethoven, Wagner, and other major composers, on a bare stage, with bare feet, and wearing a simple tunic or robe. Although her basic movements were little more than walking, running, and skipping, her senses of rhythm and dynamics made them tremendously effective. In her personal life she was an outspoken feminist, believing in a woman's right to love and to bear children when and as she pleased, a belief that she put into much-commented-upon practice.

If Isadora Duncan can be regarded as modern dance's prophet, Ruth St. Denis and Ted Shawn may equally be considered its parents. St. Denis created *Radha* in 1906. Set in an Indian temple, it attempted to capture some of the spirit of India—not so much the real India as the India of St. Denis's imagination—by depicting both the mysticism and the sensuality of a temple idol come to life. Shawn, a young man who had taken up dancing as therapy for a temporary paralysis, met and married St. Denis in 1914. Together they organized Denishawn, both a touring dance company and a Los Angeles dance school.

Both the dance company and the school featured a wide variety of dancing styles, from ballet to austere modern dance. Denishawn included such diverse traditions as the Oriental, the Spanish, and American Indian. By the time it disbanded in 1932, it had both started the careers of the creators of modern dance and created an audience for them. Shawn was later the founder and guiding spirit of the Jacob's Pillow Dance Festival, held each summer in a large barn at his farm in western Massachusetts.

In 1926 a young dancer who had recently left Denishawn presented the first of her own dance programs. This event launched what has undoubtedly been the greatest career in modern dance, that of Martha Graham. She reigned for more than 50 years as the "high priestess" of American dance.

Graham continually invented new styles for herself. In the first and immensely creative stage of her career, in the 1920's and early 1930's, Graham's style was austere and angular; then, during a period lasting to about 1945, it was more lyrical; thereafter, it became more dramatic. Throughout these stages, what remained constant was her absolute integrity, her fierce devotion to drawing "a graph of the heart." The subjects for her dances ranged from religious visions (as in the early *Primitive Mysteries*) to the spirit of women on the American frontier (as in *Frontiers* and *Appalachian Spring*) to humanity's universal fears (as in the later *Errand into the Maze*).

After Graham, the most influential modern dancer was Doris Humphrey. Humphrey and her partner Charles Weidman left Denishawn in 1928 to establish their own group. Humphrey devised a dance technique that focused on balance, with falling and recovering its key concepts. From this principle she created a distinguished choreographic repertoire. Weidman was the only significant modern dancer noted for his comic abilities. Humphrey's later associate, José Limon, was himself the creator of a number of important dances, of which *The Moor's Pavane* (1949), based on *Othello*, is best known.

Two other important figures in the early years of modern dance were Helen Tamiris and Hanya Holm. Holm came from Germany to teach German modern dance, but was converted instead to the dance of her adopted country.

MODERN DANCE: *Isadora Duncan* (left) *was the prophet of this new form. One of its great creators and performers was Martha Graham* (right).

CULVER PICTURES

CULVER PICTURES

The Recent Past

Since the end of World War II in 1945, dance has flourished as never before. Both in America and Europe, ballet and modern dance companies have proliferated, and the dance audience has grown rapidly.

Ballet in Europe. The most important centers of ballet in Europe have been Britain and the Soviet Union.

In the Soviet Union the two great ballet companies are Moscow's Bolshoi and Leningrad's Kirov, the latter the continuation of Petipa's Imperial Ballet. In both the quality of the dancing is extraordinary. The traditions of Russian classical ballet have been lovingly maintained, especially in Leningrad; and some important new ballets have been created, most notably *Romeo and Juliet* (1940), to a magnificent score by Prokofiev. But the Soviet Union's restrictions on innovation have tended to stifle creativity in ballet, as in many other arts.

Another result of the restrictions on Soviet ballet has been the defection to the West of some of its finest dancers. The first was Rudolf Nureyev, a dancer of tremendous magnetism, who left the Kirov during a visit to Paris in 1961. Nureyev centered his activity in London, but he appeared with, and choreographed for, many other companies. More recent defectors include Natalia Makarova and the superb Mikhail Baryshnikov, who joined American companies.

The greatness of British ballet is traceable to two remarkable women. Marie Rambert acquired an interest in ballet by working with Diaghilev and Nijinsky on the original production of *Rite of Spring.* Her own company, the Ballet Rambert, tended to nurture young talents only to lose them to other companies. It continues today, now emphasizing modern dance.

The company that Ninette de Valois founded in 1931 has found a firmer footing. Originally the Vic-Wells Ballet, later the Sadler's Wells Ballet, it has been the Royal Ballet since 1956. It owes its distinction chiefly to de Valois's talents as an administrator and to Frederick Ashton, principal choreographer from 1935 until his retirement in 1970. Ashton created an unusually varied repertory, noteworthy especially for its sparkling comic ballets. Foremost among the Royal Ballet's many fine dancers has been the radiant Margot Fonteyn, whose partnership with Nureyev in the 1960's has become legendary.

Ballet has also flourished in Germany. The Stuttgart Ballet reached international stature under the direction of John Cranko, a former associate of Ashton's; and the Berlin Ballet has also achieved distinction. France's most prominent choreographer, Maurice Béjart, focused his career in Belgium, where he directed the somewhat radical Ballet of the Twentieth Century. In Copenhagen, the Royal Danish Ballet maintains a distinguished tradition. Many other cities throughout Europe support companies.

MARTHA SWOPE
DANCE NOTATION BUREAU

MODERN BALLET: *Mikhail Baryshnikov walks through a part, coached by choreographer George Balanchine. Dance notation* (inset) *is a recent effort to preserve choreography, which must otherwise be passed down from dancer to dancer.*

Ballet in America. Touring dancers and ballet companies had enjoyed enthusiastic audiences in America since the 1800's. But it was not until the 1940's that ballet took firm root in America.

The New York City Ballet was established in 1948, but its roots go back to 1933, the year in which a would-be impresario named Lincoln Kirstein invited George Balanchine to come to America. Balanchine, an early (1924) defector from the Leningrad ballet, was already a distinguished choreographer, having been the last to fill that role for Diaghilev. He and Kirstein made the company one of the world's finest in an astonishingly short time.

As a choreographer, Balanchine is particularly noted for his plotless, so-called "abstract" ballets. The music for these ballets ranges from Bach to Sousa to Stravinsky, and the moods conveyed by the ballets are equally various. Often the dances evoke emotional relationships, and here again the range is wide. Balanchine's abstract ballets may be thought of as modernism at its best, for they can possess profound significance without relying on specific images. He also choreographed traditional versions of many of the classic ballets, among them *The Nutcracker,* one of New York's best-loved Christmas traditions.

America's other major company is the American Ballet Theatre. Founded in 1939, it came under the direction of Lucia Chase and Oliver Smith in 1945. From the beginning, its repertory has been eclectic, including versions of the classics of many styles and periods. The company's strength in the classics has been reinforced by the engagement of several Soviet defectors. One of them, Mikhail Baryshnikov, became its director in 1980.

America boasts a number of other fine ballet companies. Both the San Francisco Ballet and Salt Lake City's Ballet West were founded in the 1930's. New York is home to the City Center Joffrey Ballet and the Dance Theatre of Harlem. Others include Philadelphia's Pennsylvania Ballet and the companies of Boston, Atlanta, Cincinnati, Houston, and Chicago.

Modern Dance. In the 1950's a new generation of modern dancers and choreographers came to prominence. Surely the most controversial among them was Merce Cunningham, whose productions typically are greeted with either enthusiasm or rage. Cunningham's dance relies on the principle of indeterminacy: in every performance some things are not planned but are left to chance to happen as they will. A second principle is that the dance takes place on all parts of the stage; there is no one place on the stage that is the focus of the viewer's attention at any given moment. A third principle states that the elements of the production—dance, music, decor—are to be treated as individual entities that happen to have come together in one time and place but that are otherwise unrelated. Thus, for example, dancers need not dance in time with the music.

Others who came to prominence in the 1950's include Erick Hawkins, whose works are characterized by unusual, almost Oriental softness and gentleness; Alwin Nikolais, who choreographed, composed electronic music, and designed sets, costumes, and lighting for his dazzling productions; and Paul Taylor, a dancer and choreographer of wit and grace.

More recently modern dance that derives from black dancing traditions has attracted large and enthusiastic audiences. Combining elements of tap dance and jazz, of African, Caribbean, and Southern traditions, and of modern dance, it can be dance of tremendous energy—and, sometimes, rage. Its pioneers include Katherine Dunham and Pearl Primus in the 1940's. Today its principal figure is Alvin Ailey, leader of a New York-based company whose exuberant *Revelations,* set to spirituals, invariably brings down the house.

There are many more dancers and companies on the contemporary modern dance scene, many of great talent and originality. One among them, Twyla Tharp, created two works for the adventurous Joffrey Ballet in 1973. The event symbolized what many hope will be the next great development in the dance: an increasing friendliness, cross-fertilization, perhaps even merging of the two great traditions of ballet and modern dance.

—Samuel C. Plummer

DRAMA

Spoken drama stands in the middle of the performing arts. It points backward to prehistoric religious rituals in which, combined with music and dance, it served magical purposes. At the same time, it points forward to our own age of popular entertainment, as the ancestor of the movies, soap operas, situation comedies, and dramatic programs that fill a hundred hours or more per week on modern television.

But drama itself remains an important art form. We can trace significant parts of our cultural heritage back through the lively theatrical tradition that runs from the modern American theater through the works of Shakespeare and, ultimately, to the ancient Greeks. The very word drama comes from the ancient Greek word meaning "to act."

TYPES OF WESTERN DRAMA

Name/Period	Era	Characteristics
GREEK	400's B.C.	Stately poetic dramas; tragic stories from early Greek legend. Bawdy and satirical comedy.
ROMAN	200 B.C.–100 A.D.	Comedies with elaborate plots, stock characters. Violent, bloody tragedies.
MEDIEVAL	1000–1400	Mystery plays based on biblical stories. Morality plays, allegories of good vs. evil.
RENAISSANCE	1500–1700	*Italy:* Commedia dell'arte, improvised comedies with stock characters; classical imitations. *England:* poetic tragedies based on English and ancient history; prose comedies. *Spain:* Tragedy, comedy, and mixed plays in polished rhymed verse. *France:* Tragedy on Greek models; comedy of manners satirizing society.
PERIOD DRAMA	1700–1850	Tragicomedies, melodrama based on lives of middle class; romantic dramas about outcasts, artists.
MODERN DRAMA	1850–present	Plays of social significance. Psychological dramas. Plays of the absurd.

Classical Drama

Drama and theater as we know them in the Western world began sometime before 500 B.C. in the Greek city of Athens. In just over a hundred years, the Athenian Greeks established the form of theatrical presentation as we know it, and produced four of the greatest dramatists in history—Aeschylus, Sophocles, Euripides, and Aristophanes.

Even the basic language of the theater comes from the Greek. *Theater* derives from *theatron,* "a place for viewing"; *comedy* is a combination of *comos* ("revellers") and *ode* ("song"); *tragedy* apparently derives from *tragoidia* or "goat song," possibly because the performers wore goatskins.

The Greek theater grew out of religious rituals associated with Dionysus, the god of wine and of the resurrection of living things. In the spring, at the time of the great Dionysian festival, the people of Athens gathered in the theater of Dionysus at the foot of the Acropolis in Athens.

This first theater was outdoors, and the performers were surrounded on three sides by the spectators. The chorus, which often communicated directly with the audience, performed in a circular area known as the *orchestra.* The actors performed behind them in front of a building called the *skene* (the origin of our "scenery").

CULVER PICTURES

THEATER OF DODONI, *where the works of the Greek dramatists were produced. Action took place on the stage and in the semicircle in front of it, surrounded on three sides by the audience. The actors wore masks* (inset), *which intensified the solemn mood.*

The tragic actors wore distinctive robes, elevated boots *(cothurni),* and masks frozen into distinctive, fixed expressions. When the actors (three of them and all male) changed roles, they simply changed masks.

Greek tragedy. Near the end of the great dramatic age of Greece, the philosopher Aristotle formulated a definition for the plays called tragedies. His definition described the form and effects of the early Greek dramas and established an ideal for drama that is still influential nearly 2500 years later.

According to Aristotle, a tragedy cannot be a random series of events. The pieces must fit together into a meaningful whole. Moreover, the events depicted must be important, not trivial, and they must be treated seriously and in an elevated tone. The language must be "artistic" or poetic. And, finally, the viewers should experience a catharsis, a sense of uplifting release after experiencing the tragedy.

The early tragedies were divided into parts. To begin, the scene was set by a dialogue known as the prologue. The chorus entered and performed a choral ode *(stasimon),* and then the actors began the first "act" or episode. After each episode, the chorus would comment on the action in another *stasimon.* The tragedy concluded with a final episode known as the *exodos.* This basic structure was modified into a looser form by later dramatists.

These early dramas evolved from the *dithyramb,* or purely choral hymn. In 534 B.C., a performer named Thespis introduced the first actor (or "answerer"). His function was to respond to the questions of the chorus. Only one more step was necessary for the creation of true drama—the introduction of a second actor to respond to the first and create an actual dialogue.

Aeschylus (c 525–456 B.C.). Aeschylus, the first dramatist whose work has survived, is credited with introducing this second actor. But Aeschylus was no "primitive" playwright. He is one of the greatest dramatists who ever lived. He produced dramas that are rich, powerful, and fully mature. He shows great destinies played out in the midst of world-shaking events. In *Prometheus Bound* (466/459? B.C.) he shows the magnificent endurance of the defiant hero who suffers perpetual torture at the hands of Zeus for bringing the gift of fire to mankind. In his masterpiece, the trilogy *Oresteia* (458 B.C.), which deals with a seemingly unbreakable chain of murder and revenge, Aeschylus combines great dramatic impact with a sophisticated portrayal of the evolution of justice.

Sophocles (c 496–406 B.C.). The second of the great Greek tragedians, Sophocles was about 30 years younger than Aeschylus. His plays are less grand and formal than the old master's, but their language is subtler and more polished and the characters are more finely drawn and well rounded. His three surviving plays deal with the story of Oedipus and his family. In *Oedipus the King* (c 430/426 B.C.), Oedipus struggles to avoid the prophecy that he will murder his father and marry his mother. Yet at the end he discovers he has unwittingly done both. *Antigone* (c 442/441 B.C.) relates the misfortunes of Oedipus's daughter. Finally, in *Oedipus at Colonus* (c 404/401 B.C.), the cycle of agony and misfortune is broken, the avenging Furies are appeased, and Oedipus becomes a minor deity at Athens.

Euripides (485?–?406 B.C.). Euripides was the third of the great tragedians. His plays are still looser and less formal than Sophocles', but they contain probing psychological portrayals of recognizable characters. Belief in traditional values was eroding in Athens, and Euripides often seemed skeptical or disillusioned. In *Electra* (413? B.C.) he depicts Orestes' royal sister as a peasant's wife. His *Medea* (431 B.C.) is a barbarian who slaughters her children in a rage against her faithless husband. In a somewhat more traditional play, the masterful *The Bacchae,* posthumously produced in 405 B.C., Euripides portrays a conflict between the gods against a background of demonic human fury.

Greek comedy. Comedy, as has been noted, was a "reveller's song" and, in its earliest form, a joyous and explicitly sexual celebration of the processes of reproduction.

Thus, from the beginning, comedy was associated with the continuity of life and the happy ending. But quite early in its tradition it also became a medium for satire. The comedies of Aristophanes (c 448–c 380 B.C.) examine and ridicule the shortcomings of Greek society.

There are three periods of Greek comedy—Old, Middle, and New. Aristophanes' eleven plays are the only surviving examples of the first two. In his early plays, the emphasis is on strong, broad satire aimed at political targets such as militarism (*Peace,* 421 B.C.), intellectualism (*The Clouds,* 423 B.C.), and the status of women (*Lysistrata,* 411 B.C.). His last two plays, representative of Middle Comedy, have tighter plots but are less lively.

The New Comedy is represented by fragments of Menander (342–292 B.C.), who wrote a full century after Aristophanes. In his work, the plot has become a major concern. Menander holds audiences in suspense over how the story will end. His work was studied and admired by the Roman dramatists of the next century.

Roman drama. Roman tragedy was a pale imitation of its Greek model. The plays of Seneca (4 B.C.–65 A.D.) are the sole surviving examples of Roman tragedy. Their fascination with violence and death, and their bombastic language make them seem vastly inferior to the Greek tragedies. Seneca was admired and imitated by Renaissance dramatists, however.

Far more important are the comedies of Plautus (c 251–c 184 B.C.) and his successor, Terence (195?–c 159 B.C.). While Plautus's plays were based on the model of the Greek New Comedy, he owes a debt to Aristophanes in the robust earthiness of his plays. By comparison, Terence's plays are more urbane and sophisticated, but they are not as funny.

More important than their differences are the characteristics shared by the two dramatists. Both used complex, suspenseful plots based on mistaken identity or deception and manipulation. And both used characters that were to become familiar stock figures throughout the history of comedy. These include the young man *(adulescens),* the old man *(senex),* the slave *(servus),* the married woman *(matrona),* the female servant *(ancilla),* and the courtesan *(meretrix).*

Some 1500 years later, these characters would be rediscovered and would become stock figures in the Italian *commedia dell'arte.*

Medieval Drama

With the fall of the Roman Empire, the drama, too, went into decline. Drama was considered pagan and sinful by the church, and the theater ceased as a living institution.

Ironically, the rebirth of drama began in the liturgy of the church itself. In the Middle Ages, a "trope," or response, was inserted into the Mass on special occasions to create a primitive dialogue not too different from that of the actors and chorus in the earliest Greek dramas.

One of the earliest tropes was the *Quem Quaeritis* in the Easter Mass. Actors portraying the women who came on Easter morning to anoint the body of Christ are met by an angel who asks: *"Quem quaeritis in sepulchro, o Christicolae?"* (Whom do you seek in the sepulcher, O followers of Christ?). In a short dialogue it is explained that Christ is risen and has departed. From this brief exchange, the drama begins its long journey back.

As the years passed, these dialogues became more complex and ambitious. They were clearly inappropriate to the Mass and were moved out of the churches, first to the church steps and then into the streets where they were performed on wagons known variously as "pageants" or "carros." Each of these wagons was equipped to present one scene or vignette from the Bible, or another appropriate religious subject. Thus, the action of the performance took the form of a procession in which the wagons moved in order from one group of spectators to another, performing their particular scene over and over.

Mystery plays. Throughout Europe, the forms were remarkably similar.

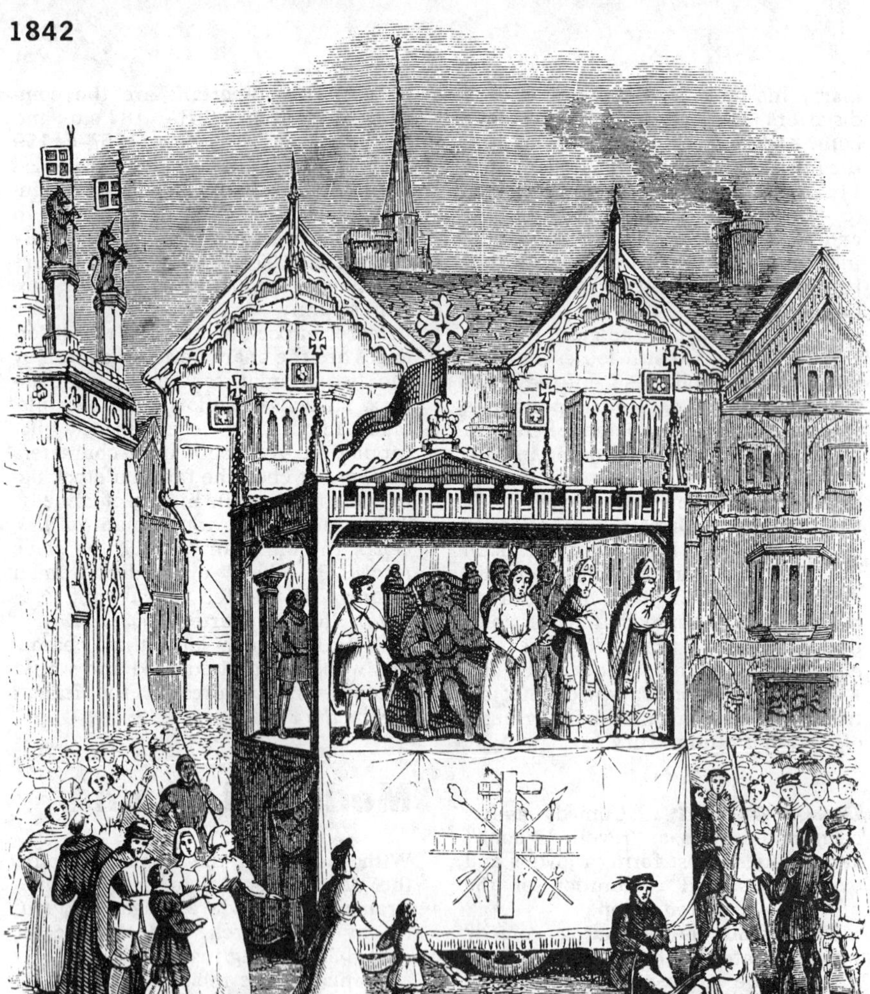

NEW YORK PUBLIC LIBRARY

A PAGEANT, *the movable wagonlike stage on which miracle plays and mystery plays were performed for holiday crowds during the Middle Ages.*

The original Latin text soon gave way to the language of the common people. In England, these pageants came to be known as "mysteries" or "mystery plays" because they dealt with the story of, or the events leading up to, the "mystery" of Christ.

The texts of the plays of a number of major cycles (the Chester, York, and Wakefield) have survived. These cycles were major local events, performed over a number of days, with the various guilds (for example, the bakers or the shipwrights) each assuming responsibility for a particular episode. Similar to these were the so-called "miracle" plays that dealt with the lives of the saints.

As the form continued to mature, "morality" plays began to appear. These were allegories or dramatic parables emphasizing the snares of vice and the eventual triumph of virtue. Among the most famous is *Everyman* (before 1500), in which the titular figure, a symbol of mankind, must give an account of his life as he faces death.

So drama returned, born again from a religious impulse. But the ancient plays of the Romans and Greeks were soon to be rediscovered, and that discovery would change the course of the theater still again.

Renaissance Drama

It was in Italy that the Renaissance first made itself felt. When learned men (many of them monks) brought the ancient classical plays back to light, the nobles of Italy took them as models for courtly entertainments. Their deep desire to reestablish the ancient standards of Greek and Roman times was reflected not only in drama but also in the painting, sculpture, and architecture of the period.

Italy. The early attempts to resurrect classical tragedy based on Seneca are hardly worth mentioning. Study of the Greek and Roman poets led the Italians to develop a new tradition of pastoral drama. These pastoral plays were set in elegant rural surroundings and peopled by dainty shepherdesses and handsome shepherds, unlike any country folk the world has ever seen. In such plays as Torquato Tasso's *Aminta* (1573) and Battista Guarini's *The Faithful Shepherd* (1585), these romanticized shepherds acted out their pathetic tragedies and delicate comedies. Though popular at the time, these plays seem precious to modern tastes.

More successful was the *commedia erudita* ("learned comedy"). Among the most successful were the plays of Pietro Aretino (1492–1556) and Ludovico Ariosto (1474–1533). The most famous was *The Mandrake* (1520) by Niccolo Machiavelli (1469–1527), who is better known for his "Machiavellian" political philosophy. The play is a cynical tale of a stupid husband who is gulled into becoming an accessory to his own cuckoldry.

Commedia dell'arte. The pride of Italian comic achievement was the *commedia dell'arte.* Unlike the *commedia erudita* (or other plays we have considered), the dramas of the *commedia dell'arte* were only plot outlines called *scenarii.* The actors filled in the outline with traditional bits of dialogue and action.

Each character had a set of *lazzi,* or standard routines that suited his or her personality. A great favorite was one traditionally associated with *Arlecchino* (the clown figure who became Harlequin in France and England). Having received a blow on the head that causes his brains to spill out, Arlecchino, ever the glutton, proceeds to gobble them up. The result is that he becomes even more stupid than before. So popular was this *lazzi* that audiences would demand that it be included in every performance.

ARLEQUIN, *a French version of the clown in the Italian commedia dell'arte.*

NEW YORK PUBLIC LIBRARY

The stock character types such as Arlecchino gave the *commedia dell' arte* a certain predictability. An actor frequently played the same role for life. Most of the plots involved the efforts of two young lovers (the *inamorato* and *inamorata*) to overcome obstacles, usually parental objections, that keep them apart. Their fathers were most frequently *Pantalone,* a miserly and misanthropic merchant, and *Il Dottore,* the very epitome of hollow pedantry. In their struggles, the lovers often had the help of lively but unscrupulous servants such as the glib, acrobatic Arlecchino; the cowardly rogue *Brighella;* or the clownish *Pagliaccio* and *Pedrolino* (Pierrot). They were assisted in their rascalities by such servant lasses as *Columbine.*

While other Italian forms influenced the later drama, the impact of the *commedia dell'arte* has been continuous: in later serious drama, in the puppet tradition of the Punch and Judy shows, in comic opera, and even in modern situation comedies.

CULVER PICTURES

KING LEAR, *one of the great tragic heroes of Shakespeare, speaks with his two evil daughters Goneril and Regan. Their efforts to usurp the kingdom drive him to madness.*

Elizabethan England. In the late 1500's, the excitement of the Renaissance produced a great age of drama in England. The period is generally called the Elizabethan age, after Queen Elizabeth I, who reigned from 1564 to 1603. But in drama, the years of great excitement extended into the reign of James I (1603–1625). The plays of this period are sometimes called Jacobean (from the Latinized form of "James").

At the beginning of Elizabeth's reign, there was little or no formal drama in England. There was a small class of strolling players who performed in the courtyards of inns. They were not far removed from jugglers, clowns, and swindlers, and were held suspect by respectable people.

By 1576, however, a permanent public theater, known simply as "The Theater," had been built in London exclusively for the production of plays. In the next 40 years, it was joined by eight others. Professional acting companies, made up of men and boys, offered public dramatic performances and were also available for private shows to be performed in the halls of noblemen.

Marlowe. The greatest of the dramatists for this young theatrical tradition was William Shakespeare. But before he made his mark, another poet and playwright did much to create the Elizabethan drama. He was Christopher Marlowe, who was born in 1564 and died before reaching his 30th birthday. In 1586 or 1587, his sweeping drama of the barbarian conqueror Tamburlaine was presented in London. A year or two later, his masterpiece, *Dr. Faustus,* revived the legend of the man who sold his soul to the Devil. Marlowe's plays offered plenty of opportunity for spectacle and violence. But his greatest achievement was his mastery of blank (unrhymed) verse, a poetic form that seemed to suit English perfectly. Marlowe's verse could be both exalted and natural and allowed him to achieve great dramatic effects. But his plays and his verse were soon eclipsed by those of Shakespeare himself.

Shakespeare. William Shakespeare was born in the same year as Marlowe. But when Marlowe died in 1593, Shakespeare had his greatest achievements still ahead of him. He was, in a phrase common in his day, a "man for all seasons," excelling any dramatist of his time in nearly any genre he attempted. He began writing historical dramas such as *Richard III* (c 1592) and comedies such as *The Taming of the Shrew* (c 1593). But he is best remembered for his great tragedies, written around the turn of the century. The three greatest, *Hamlet* (c 1600), *Macbeth* (c 1605), and *King Lear* (c 1605), are among the masterpieces of world drama.

It is difficult to single out any aspect of Shakespeare's art because his weaknesses were so few and his range of talent so enormous. He is perhaps most admired for the beauty and flexibility of his language and the extraordinary range of perception and imagination that he brought to the depiction of character.

The Jacobeans. Even without Shakespeare, the Elizabethan era in England would still have been a remarkable theatrical time. After Shakespeare, certainly the most famous dramatist was the formidable wit, Ben Jonson (1572–1637), a university man who drew heavily upon classical sources and used them as frameworks for sharp satires on London life of the time. He attacked cupidity and lust in *Volpone* (c 1605), chicanery and avarice in *The Alchemist* (1610), and a veritable grab bag of foibles and vices in *Bartholomew Fair* (1614). The latter is an example of the comedy of humors, based on the medieval physiological belief that a man's temperament was controlled by one of the four basic humors, or fluids, that make up his body.

Along with Jonson, the reign of James I produced the collaborators Francis Beaumont (c 1584–1616) and John Fletcher (1579–1625) and their tragicomic plays; John Marston (1575–1634), a brilliant, if often excessive, satirist; and John Webster (c1580–c1634) a particularly powerful and intense dramatist who wrote *The White Devil* (c 1612) and *The Duchess of Malfi* (c 1613), two of the finest tragedies of the period.

By the death of James I in 1625, the English theater was in decline. The Puritans, whose strength was great among the merchants of London, considered drama sinful and campaigned for the closing of the theaters. Although plays continued to be performed into the 1630's, the excitement had left the theater. In 1649, King Charles I was murdered by the Puritans, and for the next eleven years the production of plays was forbidden by law. Only in 1660, with the restoration of the monarchy, was the theater allowed to function once again. And by that time, the mood of the country had changed greatly.

The Spanish Golden Age. In August, 1588, the "invincible" Spanish Armada sailed into the English Channel to attack England. The Armada suffered a disastrous defeat at the hands of the English in one of the great naval battles of history. At the time, William Shakespeare was an actor and beginning playwright in London. Some 80 miles away, aboard a ship in the Armada, was Lope de Vega, soon to become the presiding genius of the Spanish *siglo de oro* ("Golden Age"). These two men, and the cultures they represented, were never so close again.

The great ages of both the English and the Spanish drama had many things in common. Both were products of the Renaissance and owed great debts to Italian popular theater and literature. Both rode in on a crest of nationalism and both were written in languages that had just evolved into magnificent vehicles of expression, rare combinations of youthful exuberance and maturity.

But there the similarities end. The plays of the English were longer, more substantial, and more intense. They contained major characters who had many (often conflicting) facets to their personalities. English dramas were largely written in blank verse, a form flexible enough to attain poetic heights while retaining prosaic rhythms of natural speech. The Spanish plays were in three *jornadas* (acts) and took no more time to perform than a modern Broadway play. Whatever the subject, serious or light, it was handled with smoothness and dispatch. The plays were skillfully, even facilely, constructed and plotted and briskly paced. The characters were sharply drawn with clear strokes.

This facile effect was heightened by the Spanish language itself, in which it is sometimes easier to find a rhyme than to avoid one. An abundance of verse forms was used, many of them formal, and they added to the delight of the experience without detracting from the flow of the dialogue or the action.

While the English drama was essentially secular, the Spanish drama was firmly grounded in the Catholic perception of the world. Good is rewarded and evil punished, if not in this world, then in the next. There are no tragedies in the Greek sense. The plays are called *comedias* (literally, comedies) in the sense that there is a "happy ending" since God's will is done to His greater glory and the good of all mankind.

As in England, plays in Spain were originally performed out of doors in the courtyards or *corrales* of inns. In Spanish, the word *corral* came to mean theater even after formal theaters were built.

Lope de Vega. Once plays became popular, Spanish audiences clamored for new plays every week. To keep up with this demand, the dramatists turned out a staggering number of plays. Lope de Vega, whom Cervantes called a "monster of nature," claimed to have written over 2000 plays (an average of just over 33 plays a year for 60 years). More than 300 of these have survived. Lope also wrote enough lyric and epic poetry to establish the reputation of half a dozen poets. His fellow Spaniards were almost as prolific.

Lope Felix de Vega Carpio was both the founder of the drama of the Spanish Golden Age, and its principal genius. In Elizabethan terms he was Marlowe and Shakespeare rolled into one. Characteristically, Lope wrote no great masterpiece such as *Hamlet* or *King Lear*—his genius lay rather in a general standard of excellence and a sizable collection of first-rate plays. Among the best known is *Fuenteovejuna* (1612), in which villagers kill an oppressive nobleman and seek the protection of the king. The rest range over every conceivable style and approach from the lighthearted *Dog in the Manger* (c 1614) to the stern *Knight from Olmedo* (c 1620).

During the early years of the Golden Age, Lope had two chief rivals, Tirso de Molina and Juan Ruiz de Alarcón. Tirso, a Mercedarian monk with a keen sense of irony and paradox, is best remembered for *The Rogue of Seville* (1625?), the play that introduced the legend of the charismatic Don Juan to the world. Alarcón, a polished writer specializing in comedies of manners, was author of *The Truth Suspected* (c 1619).

Calderón. In the second half of the Golden Age the characteristics of the *comedia* were heightened and exaggerated. The leading dramatist was Pedro Calderón de la Barca, author of the remarkable *Life Is a Dream* (c 1632). The hero's soliloquy reminds one of similar soliloquies in Shakespeare:

What is life? It's only madness.
What is life? A thing that seems,
A mirage that falsely gleams,
Phantom joy, delusive rest,
Since life is a dream at best,
And even dreams themselves are dreams.

Calderón was also noted for the Spanish dramatic form called the *auto sacramental*. This was a short play, usually a theological or moral allegory such as *The Great Theater of the World* (c 1645) in which the world is portrayed as a theatrical performance.

France. Few dramatic movements were as deeply influenced by the Greeks and Romans as that of 17th-century France. The very name "neoclassic," applied to French drama of that time, particularly tragedy, suggests a deep sense of respect for and indebtedness to the writers of the ancient world. Sometimes devotion to the classicists was carried to absurd lengths.

The development of the theater in France roughly paralleled that in England and Spain. But control of the drama was firmly in the hands of critics who established the "rules" by which it was to be written. Critical standards were enforced with tremendous social and artistic pressure.

According to the French critics, the ancients had established the form and structure of drama once and for all, and any dramatist was required to work within these limits. Aristotle's famous definition of tragedy was transformed into the law of the three unities: action, time, and place. Unity of action meant simply that a single plot must progress without interruption to its proper conclusion. Subplots were frowned upon. There were to be none of the multiple plots or comic interludes so common in Elizabethan drama.

Unity of time meant that the action on the stage should take the same amount of time to unfold as a similar action in real life. Ideally then, the events of two hours would take two hours to unfold upon the stage. Since this proved almost impossible to accomplish, the rules were generally relaxed to permit the portrayal of the events of a single day.

The second unity all but dictated the third. There could be no skipping from country to country or town to town as the action unfolded. Everything had to occur in a single place, preferably a locale identical in size to the playing area of the stage.

Under these almost crippling strictures, the wonder is that French neoclassicism produced two dramatists of the stature of Corneille and Racine.

Corneille. Of the two, Pierre Corneille (1606–1684) was the more prolific and wide-ranging. He was uncomfortable with the limits of neoclassicism. At times he seemed almost Elizabethan in the scope and grandeur of his work. He could write in the limited mode, as in such tragedies as *Horace* (1640) and *Cinna* (1641), but he was at his tragic best in *Polyeucte* (1642), which portrays the clash of Roman and Christian values.

Corneille is, however, best known for the tragicomedy, *Le Cid* (1637), based on the exploits of the famous Spanish national hero.

Racine. A late contemporary of Corneille is Jean Racine (1639–1699), whose work perhaps best represents French neoclassic tragedy. Racine not only managed to conform to the unities but to exploit them to considerable dramatic effect. His tragedies usually revolved around a single dominant passion, the intensity of which tended to control and unify all other aspects of his plays. Usually the theme is love, either unrequited or in conflict with affairs of state. This is true in his best works, *Andromache* (1667), *Britannicus* (1669), and the famous *Phaedra* (1677).

MOLIÈRE'S COMEDIES *are usually played in the elaborate costumes of the France of Louis XIV. The clothes contrast with the flawed characters Molière delighted in ridiculing.*

After Racine, French neoclassic tragedy went into decline. It was widely imitated, but its restrictions were so limiting that later dramatists found both new forms and new subject matter. Racine, however, continued to be a great influence on French drama, especially his clarity and delicacy of expression, which the French call *sensibilité.*

Molière. French comedy proved far more durable and influential than its tragedy. Jean-Baptiste Poquelin (1622–1673), who wrote under the name Molière, was one of the great comic writers in theater history. He borrowed plots and ideas from the Roman comedies of Terence and Plautus, from the comedies of the Spanish Golden Age, and from the Italian *commedia dell'arte.*

Like Shakespeare, Molière was a practical theater worker, serving as an actor and manager as well as a dramatist. Most of his plays were produced by his own company, with Molière himself in a major role. The company was, in fact, the principal partner in the merger (1680) that produced the famed Comédie Française.

While Molière excelled in such comedies of manners as *The Bourgeois Gentleman* (1670), which mocked social pretentiousness, he was perhaps at his best in those plays that explored a single, dominant character trait. *The Misanthrope* (1666), and *Tartuffe* (1664), a portrait of a hypocrite so scathing that it could not be publicly performed for five years, are examples.

After Molière the grand comic tradition of the Renaissance rapidly declined, giving way to a new middle-class kind of comedy. But there was to be a "last hurrah": Alain René Le Sage's *Turcaret* (1709), at first rejected by the Comédie Française, was a savage attack upon financiers, the very cornerstone of the coming bourgeois era.

The end of an age.

Vestiges of Renaissance styles and manners continued well into the 1700's, even though other dramatists were working in new directions.

The Restoration. In England, with the restoration of the monarchy under Charles II in 1660, the royalists returned from a 20-year exile in France. They proceeded to produce a drama that combined the old vigor of the English with the polish of the French. This is particularly evident in the witty and licentious comedies of manners of Sir George Etherege (1634–1691), such as *The Man of Mode,* or *Sir Fopling Flutter* (1676). William Wycherley (1640–1716) followed the same tradition, but was coarser and more savage in the comic attacks in *The Country Wife* (1675) and *The Plain Dealer* (1676). The Restoration period lasted a scant 40 years, culminating in the brilliance of William Congreve (1670–1729), whose *Love for Love* (1695) and *The Way of the World* (1700) are among the finest of English comedies.

In England and elsewhere, a new sensibility was taking over by 1700, and it seemed that the old aristocratic comedy was dead. But nearly three-quarters of a century after Congreve's last play, there was a brief resurgence of "laughing" comedy in England, producing a handful of plays that are produced to the present day. Oliver Goldsmith (1728–1774) offered a great hit in *She Stoops to Conquer* (1773), and his younger contemporary, Richard Brinsley Sheridan (1751–1816), wrote *The Rivals* (1775) and *The School for Scandal* (1777).

Italy and France. Nowhere were the older forms more alive than in Italy, where Vittorio Alfieri (1749–1803) tried his hand at neoclassical tragedy and embellished it with a touch of Italian bravura. Of more lasting interest is the work of two comic writers, Carlo Goldoni (1707–1793) and Carlo Gozzi (1720–1806). Goldoni was a sort of Mediterranean Molière, who modeled many of his plays after those of his master. Gozzi also exploited the *commedia dell'arte* for his own purposes. He took the old form, with all its lively crudity, and polished it until the characters and the actions were marked by elegant exaggeration and considerable finesse.

In France, the great satirist Voltaire (François Marie Arouet, 1694–1778) attempted to revive the classical tragic tradition, but his many tragedies, such as *Zarius* (1732), are good examples of the dictum: "too little, too late." Far more successful was Pierre de Beaumarchais (1732–1799), whose two brilliant comedies about a shrewd and irrepressible barber loose in an aristocratic world, *The Barber of Seville* (1775) and *The Marriage of Figaro* (1784), became the bases for great operas by Rossini and Mozart.

Period Drama

By 1700 the old aristocratic ideals of chivalry and heroism were being replaced by the values of the rising merchant and commercial class. While a few dramatists continued to write in the traditional manner, they were not in the mainstream of the theater.

Bourgeois drama.

The new style transformed drama by taking a different point of view. The new leading characters were bourgeois, or middle class. The life of the bourgeois was thrifty, ordered, and utilitarian. Thus we have well ordered plots (influenced in part by the tidy neoclassicists) that serve a purpose by instructing the audience on morals and proper behavior. The heroes and heroines are not sacrificed in some noble, tragic death at the end, but are tidily saved in a satisfactory ending. At the same time, they are taken too seriously to be ridiculed. The result is drama that is not quite tragedy or comedy, but something in between.

In 1722 in England, Sir Richard Steele (1672–1729) produced *The Conscious Lovers,* a comedy in which the audience's taste for sentimental thoughts took precedence over laughter. From here it was but a step to the *comédies larmoyantes* ("tearful comedies") of Pierre Claude Nivelle de La Chaussée (1692–1754), which produced teardrops in full flood. George Lillo's *The London Merchant* (1731) calls itself a "domestic tragedy," but any real tragic values are engulfed in a tide of moralizing.

The French dramatist Denis Diderot (1713–1784) flatly rejected tragedy and coined a new term for the modern stage, *drame bourgeois.* This new drama, he said, was to help improve mankind. At the same time, it was to be more realistic and more relevant to the lives of its audience.

Melodrama. The problem with the *drame bourgeois* was that it could be realistic to the point of being mundane and dowdy. Because of this, it soon caused a reaction—a new kind of play known as melodrama. The melodrama was flamboyant, theatrical, and passionate. In fact, "melodramatic" still means overemotional.

Such able practitioners as August Von Kotzebue (1761–1819) in Germany and Guilbert de Pixérécourt (1773–1844) in France made melodrama enormously and universally popular. A movement to give melodrama some semblance of literary respectability began in Germany in the late 18th century. Its essence is nicely summed up in the name by which it is known—*Sturm und Drang* ("Storm and Stress").

The Romantic movement. *Sturm und Drang* was a link to the next major dramatic movement—the Romantic. Romanticism is usually characterized as a reaction to the rules and manners of the neoclassicists. Like the neoclassicists before them, the Romantics sought their roots in the past but, instead of the Greeks, chose the Elizabethans (particularly Shakespeare), as their model. They admired the natural, unrestricted flow of Shakespeare's plays and the sense of expansiveness and freedom that they conveyed.

But things were very different in 1800 than they had been in 1600. The new dramatists were in revolt against the middle class. They were the sons of shopkeepers or merchants and professed to despise bourgeois values. They wrote flamboyantly, dressed flamboyantly, and outraged their bourgeois audience. When Victor Hugo's *Hernani* (1830) opened in Paris, the event caused rioting.

Germany. The Romantic movement began some 60 years before *Hernani,* and its first champion was the German Gotthold Ephraim Lessing (1729–1781). An articulate critic, Lessing loved Shakespeare and opposed French neoclassicism. His *Emilia Galotti* (1772) and *Nathan the Wise* (1778) were perhaps the first truly Romantic dramas.

Romanticism found its home in Germany in the latter years of the 1700's. Its two major figures were Schiller and Goethe. Friedrich von Schiller (1759–1805) depicted a somewhat idealized world, grander in feeling and action than the one we live in. His ideas are best exemplified by his *Wallenstein* trilogy (1798–1799), in which the hero approaches the protagonist of a Greek tragedy in grandeur.

Schiller's older contemporary, Johann Wolfgang von Goethe (1749–1832), is generally considered the greatest of all German writers. He was a major figure in the Romantic movement. His *Gotz von Berlichingen* (1773), *Iphigenia in Tauris* (1779), and *Torquato Tasso* (1789) were all important contributions to the drama, but they were overshadowed by his poems and novels.

The major work of his later years was *Faust,* a poem-play not intended for production, published in two parts (1806 and 1832). In *Faust,* Goethe took the story of the scholar who sold his soul to the Devil and transformed it into a great poem that exemplified the restless Romantic search for new experience.

The well made play. While the Romantics were busy rekindling the fires of the past, others, such as Eugene Scribe (1791–1861) in France, were working new variations on the *drame bourgeois* to keep the audience's attention. This Scribe called the *pièce bien fait* ("well made play"), and in it he pushed the social problems and heroic themes into the background—they were merely the raw materials—and concentrated on form and structure. His purpose was to construct plays so skillfully and carefully that each piece fell neatly into place and led logically to the next, keeping the audience's full attention until the satisfactory, and usually expected conclusion. Scribe wrote hundreds of plays, not one of them memorable, but he set a standard for dramatic structure. Many modern dramatists learned from Scribe and adopted his passion for structure.

One of the happy immediate results of the *pièce bien fait* was the 19th-century farce which, because of its origin, is sometimes called "French farce" or, because of a frequent subject, "bedroom farce." The two master practitioners of this form were Eugene Labiche (1815–1888), best known for *An Italian Straw Hat* (1851), and Georges Feydeau (1862–1921), author of a whole string of successful farces, including *How to Get Rid of Your Mistress* (1894). The farce, in its most sophisticated form, takes its basic structure from the *pièce bien fait* and increases the intensity of the action until the pace becomes hysterical and logic runs amok. Neglected for many years, the farce has recently enjoyed a worldwide revival.

Modern Drama

The term "modern," as applied to drama and theater, is a very imprecise and relative term. It is usually used to describe serious drama beginning with the mature works of Ibsen in about 1880.

The standard for modern drama is the serious, "realistic" play, usually dealing with a few human relationships within a broader social context. Its characters are from the middle or lower classes, and often the play considers a set problem.

In the early years of the modern era, "realism" was the norm. It was followed by a series of "movements" that altered its outlook. "Naturalism" sought realism in ripping away the facade of society and presenting a slice of life in all its stark (and usually ugly) reality. At the opposite pole, "expressionism" looked inward and sought realism in an individual's mind, presenting a wholly subjective view of life.

As early as 1810, dramatic elements began to appear in Germany that were characteristic of the modern drama. In that year, Heinrich von Kleist (1777–1811), generally considered a Romantic, wrote *The Prince von Homburg,* a disturbing and realistic study of heroism and disobedience.

Some years later, Georg Büchner (1813–1837) rejected the overblown emotions of Romanticism and the precise structure of the well made play. *Danton's Death* (1835) and *Woyzeck* (1836) are both episodic and almost expressionistic in style. Friedrich Hebbel (1813–1863) presented *Maria Magdalena* in 1844, and shocked his audiences with brutal realism resembling the later dramas of naturalism.

These were only isolated experiments, however. The real beginning of the modern era came from an unexpected part of Europe.

Scandinavia. The modern drama really began with two great Scandinavian dramatists.

Ibsen. Henrik Ibsen (1828–1906) was a Norwegian whose work as a dramatist spanned nearly 40 years. His reputation has survived almost every calamity: some have read their own ideas and social platforms into his plays; some dismissed his work because it discussed taboo subjects and questioned traditional values; still others concluded that his plays soon dated and lost their relevance. Despite all this, Ibsen's work continues to be performed and studied throughout the Western world, and his place as the father of modern drama is secure. Ibsen's two early Romantic masterpieces, *Brand* (1865) and *Peer Gynt* (1867), were more Romantic than modern, but already they reveal his deep concern over the differences between appearance and reality.

By the end of the 1870's, Ibsen had begun to write in prose rather than verse, and his ideas began to harden. In *A Doll's House* (1879), praised as an early feminist drama, a wife revolts against her husband to face a freedom for which she is ill-prepared. *Ghosts* (1882) considers the taboo of venereal disease. It was extravagantly praised and damned in its own time because of its subject matter. But beneath the surface it is a study of the lies ("ghosts") that come back to haunt us.

In *An Enemy of the People* (1883), the greedy residents of a resort town defeat an idealistic scientist who discovers that the water supply is tainted. Ibsen's skill at social and moral comment can be measured by the opposition his plays aroused. Where the Romantics thumbed their noses at the middle classes, Ibsen convicts them of sins against their own standards. Ibsen continued his successes and gained more enemies with *The Wild Duck* (1885), *Hedda Gabler* (1891), *John Gabriel Bjorkman* (1897), and other plays.

Strindberg. As Ibsen's fame spread worldwide, Sweden produced a formidable rival in August Strindberg (1849–1912). While Ibsen was the shrewd observer, Strindberg was generally the emotionally charged participant. His range was impressive: from the naturalistic studies of the male-female, love-hate relationships in *The Father* (1887) and *Miss Julie* (1889), to the expressionistic drama of *A Dream Play* (1902) and *The Ghost Sonata* (1907). This same man, often labeled "mad" during and after his lifetime, also composed a brilliant cycle of historical plays chronicling Swedish history from the 13th to the 18th centuries.

Russian drama.

The development of the theater in Russia was somewhat slower than in the rest of Europe. It begins to reach maturity only with the rise of Romanticism. Its early masterpieces include the tragedies *Boris Godunov* (1825) by the poet Alexander Pushkin (1799–1837) and *Masquerade* (1836) by Mikhail Lermontov (1814–1841).

At the head of modern Russian dramatic achievement stands the work of Nikolai Gogol (1809–1852), the great novelist and dramatist whose masterful comedy, *The Inspector General* (1836), was a brilliant satire of petty corruption under the czars.

Gogol's sharp comedies represent one reaction to Romanticism. The subtle, psychological studies of Ivan Turgenev (1818–1883) present another. In *A Month in the Country* (1850), Turgenev captured the nuances of delicate social situations without lapsing into cloying sentimentality.

Chekhov. Turgenev foreshadowed the achievements of Anton Chekhov (1860–1904), the most universally admired of all Russian dramatists. Chekhov's plays captured the decay and demise of the genteel culture of "Old Russia," stressing the need for fine illusions and the inevitable disasters that occur when real events cannot support them. He returned to this theme often, particularly in his four major plays, which he labeled comedies despite their unhappy endings.

In *The Sea Gull* (1896), idealism and frustration lead to tragedy in an atmosphere of suffocating boredom. Again in *Uncle Vanya* (1899), pettiness and sham are all-engulfing, resulting in an almost endless series of meaningless sacrifices. In *The Three Sisters* (1901), the sisters, crushed by the meanness and boredom of a provincial town, long for the life and vitality of Moscow. Finally, *The Cherry Orchard* (1904) marks the beginning of the end of the old order. The beautiful, but now useless, orchard is to be chopped down to make way for cheap summer cottages.

The drama of Chekhov, with its nuances, pauses, and conversational naturalism, cannot be separated from the emergence of the Moscow Art Theater. They rose together and each owed much of its success to the other. Konstantin Stanislavski (1863–1938), a founder of the theater, was the first and most influential exponent of the internationally influential acting style, often referred to simply as "The Method."

French drama.

In France, as elsewhere, realism was the dominant mode at the end of the 1800's. One important departure was the gritty naturalism of Emile Zola (1840–1902) and Henry Becque (1837–1899). The Théâtre Libre of André Antoine was devoted to the production of naturalistic plays and helped to promote "slice of life" realism.

But increasingly there was variety, from sardonic comedy in the case of *The Magnificent Cuckold* (1920) by Fernand Crommelynck (1885–1970) to the mystical mood plays of his fellow Belgian, Maurice Maeterlinck (1862–1949). Expressionism was represented in *The Dream Doctor* (1922) of Henri-Renè Lenormand (1882–1951) and in the great variety of Jean Cocteau (1889–1963), whose plays, variously described as surrealistic and symbolic, defy precise description. Greek themes were a favorite, as in *Orpheus* (1926) and *The Infernal Machine* (1934).

Traditional poetic drama found expression in *Cyrano de Bergerac* (1897), by Edmond Rostand (1868–1918), which became an international favor-

THE CHERRY ORCHARD *of Anton Chekhov is to be destroyed when its noble owners sell their estate to a former serf turned businessman and prepare to leave it forever.*

CULVER PICTURES

WAITING FOR GODOT: *the odd characters wait for the mysterious Godot but never meet him.*

ite. Paul Claudel (1868–1955) contributed deeply religious poetic dramas. Jean Giraudoux (1882–1944) brought back ironic humor and an element of fantasy in *The Madwoman of Chaillot* (1945) and other plays.

Since World War II, there have been two major dramatic movements in France. The first, existentialism, is roughly based on the philosophy that man imposes meaning on the universe through his actions. This concept found its fullest expression in the plays of Jean-Paul Sartre (1905–1980), particularly in *The Flies* (1943) and *Dirty Hands* (1948).

The second movement, theater of the absurd, focuses on the essential meaninglessness of life. Its principal exponent is Eugene Ionesco (b. 1912) in *The Bald Soprano* (1950), *The Chairs* (1952), and *Rhinoceros* (1959). Jean Genet (b. 1910), whose plays hover between existentialism and the absurd, is best known for *The Balcony* (1956) and *The Blacks* (1959).

Perhaps the finest example of the absurd, however, is *Waiting for Godot* (1953) by Samuel Beckett (b. 1906), an expatriate Irishman. *Godot* is a fascinating, if bewildering study of two tramps waiting interminably for Godot (God?), whom they have never seen.

German drama. Popular realism, in the form of the "well made play" ushered in the modern era in German-speaking lands. But Gerhart Hauptmann (1862–1946) brought naturalism to the German theater through such plays as the working class tragedy, *The Weavers* (1893), and a satirical comedy of village values, *The Beaver Coat* (1893).

In sharp contrast was the work of Frank Wedekind (1864–1918). His cynical contempt for society's values in *Earth Spirit* (1893) and *The Marquis of Keith* (1901) anticipated German attitudes after 1918.

Expressionism enjoyed its greatest vogue in Germany. Following Wedekind were Georg Kaiser (1878–1945) and Ernst Toller (1893–1939).

Brecht. The dominant dramatic figure of the mid-1900's in Germany was Bertolt Brecht (1898–1956), noted for his advocacy of the "epic theater," in which a procession of episodic scenes are punctuated with subtitles and film clips. The best of these include *Mother Courage and Her Children* (1941), *The Good Woman of Setzuan* (1943), and *The Caucasian Chalk Circle* (1948). They were given "definitive" productions under the author's supervision by the Berliner Ensemble in East Berlin, where Brecht settled after World War II. Brecht also wrote the libretti for a number of ballad and epic operas with music by Kurt Weill, among them *The Threepenny Opera* (1928).

With few exceptions, including the remarkable epic drama *Marat/Sade* (1964) by Peter Weiss (b. 1916), the major German contributions to the drama after World War II have been made by two Swiss, Dürrenmatt and Frisch.

Friedrich Dürrenmatt (b. 1921), a specialist in satirical comedy-drama bordering on the macabre, is the author of *The Visit* (1956), in which a town abandons its values under economic pressure. Disenchantment also runs through the drama of Max Frisch (b. 1911), author of *Biedermann and the Firebugs* (1958).

Italy and Spain. The modern era in Italian drama was initially characterized by the Neo-Romanticism of the flamboyant Gabriele D'Annunzio (1863–1938) and the equally flamboyant naturalism of Giovanni Verga (1840–1922).

Pirandello. The great modern dramatist of Italy, however, is Luigi Pirandello (1867–1936), author of the enigmatic *Six Characters in Search of an Author* (1921), in which "fictional" characters intrude upon the rehearsal of a play and insist upon acting out their own tragic drama. This deliberate confusion between appearance and reality, and the suggestion that they may be interdependent, runs through Pirandello's other plays, such as *Right You Are—If You Think You Are* (1917), and *Henry IV* (1922), in which a wealthy madman, who believes himself to be the Emperor, recovers his sanity, only to be forced forever back into his role to avoid a murder charge.

In a not too different vein, Ugo Betti (1892–1953) explores the nature of evil and the concept of justice in *Corruption in the Palace of Justice* (1944) and *The Queen and the Rebels* (1951). Eduardo De Filippo (b. 1900) brought new vitality to the Italian comic tradition in plays such as *Filumena Marturano* (1946).

Modernism reached Spain in the work of Jacinto Benavente (1866–1964) in a number of facile plays in every genre. Drama with a distinctive Spanish flavor was provided by Federico Garcia Lorca (1898–1936) whose *Blood Wedding* (1933) and *The House of Bernarda Alba* (1936) are among the very few successful attempts to write verse drama in the 20th century.

England. From the time of Sheridan in the late 1700's, England produced no great dramatists and few great plays. But in the wake of Ibsen, the British theater revived.

Shaw. George Bernard Shaw (1856–1950) was the first modern English dramatist of distinction. He was a continual source of irritation and embarrassment both to his friends and his critics since he chose to address the most serious of problems in comic form. He often caught his audiences in a net of paradox by triumphantly asserting in the end what he had presumably set out to destroy in the beginning. Shaw admired (and misread) Ibsen, and he resembled the great master in that his influence was broad and nearly impossible to define. He seemed unable to resist providing his villains with lines as eloquent and witty as those of his heroes.

In his romantic comedies, such as *Arms and the Man* (1894), *Candida* (1897), *The Devil's Disciple* (1897), and *Pygmalion* (1913), Shaw manages to give new and refreshing twists to conventional plots. Much the same is true of the historical plays *Caesar and Cleopatra* (1898), *Androcles and the Lion* (1913), and *Saint Joan* (1923). Even in the social satire, *Major Barbara* (1905), the philosophical *Man and Superman* (1905), and such serious dramas as *The Doctor's Dilemma* (1906) and *Heartbreak House* (1919), Shaw shows a keen awareness that he can lecture his audience as much as he pleases as long as he does not bore them.

Oscar Wilde (1854–1900) was a contemporary of Shaw who is best remembered for his brilliant comedy of manners, *The Importance of Being Earnest* (1895), which ridiculed the intense triviality of London society.

The tradition of serious drama in England was carried forward in the "well made plays" of Henry Arthur Jones (1851–1929) and Arthur Wing Pinero (1855–1934), and in the social problem plays of John Galsworthy (1867–1933).

Poetic drama of the traditional sort was represented in *The Tragedy of Nan* (1928) by John Masefield (1878–1967), while attempts at a newer and broader form were made by T.S. Eliot

(1888–1965) with *Murder in the Cathedral* (1935) and Christopher Fry (b. 1907) in *The Lady's Not for Burning* (1948).

The major figure in the comic field was Noel Coward (1899–1973), author of a long string of successes, including *Private Lives* (1930), *Design for Living* (1933), and *Blithe Spirit* (1941).

After 1945, younger writers were disillusioned with British society. John Osborne's play *Look Back in Anger* (1956) was an outcry of frustration and powerlessness, and it gave the name "angry young men" to a generation of British dramatists.

One of this generation, Harold Pinter (b. 1930), became England's leading exponent of the absurd. His surreal plays confuse the menaces from without and within the characters. Among his most successful productions are *The Caretaker* (1960) and *The Homecoming* (1965).

Ireland. The revival of Irish nationalism at the turn of the 20th century gave rise to a great Irish literary renaissance. The theatrical center of this movement was the Abbey Theatre in Dublin, directed by the poet William Butler Yeats (1865–1939) and Lady Augusta Gregory (1852–1932). The Abbey encouraged John Millington Synge (1871–1909), whose *Riders to the Sea* (1904) has been called the finest one-act tragedy ever written. Even better known is *The Playboy of the Western World* (1907), a grand, rollicking look at the Irish tendency to grandiloquent self-delusion. The play provoked riots at its opening.

As the Irish fight for freedom grew uglier and more intense, this was reflected in the plays of Sean O'Casey (1880–1964), whose *Juno and the Paycock* (1924) and *The Plough and the Stars* (1926) show the uneasy compound of idealism and terror that make up Irish patriotism.

The United States. From a slow start during the late 1700's, the theater in America grew gradually through the 1800's. But well into the present century, it had not produced a great dramatist.

O'Neill. American drama is generally considered to have come of age with the plays of Eugene O'Neill (1888–1953). The first American dramatist to achieve international stature, O'Neill gave early evidence of his talent in such plays as *The Emperor Jones* (1920) and *Anna Christie* (1921). His efforts to live up to this reputation led to such monumental works as *Mourning Becomes Electra* (1931), an Americanization of the classic story of Orestes.

As O'Neill's popularity declined, he wrote perhaps his best plays, which achieved success only after his death. These searing plays of false illusions and dashed hopes include *The Iceman Cometh* (1939) and *Long Day's Journey Into Night* (1941). They are among the finest plays in the American theater.

In the 1920's and 1930's, interest at home and influences from abroad led to increased vitality in the American theater. Social drama was much in evidence, as in *Street Scene* (1929) by Elmer Rice (1892–1967), *Awake and Sing* (1935) by Clifford Odets (1906–1963), and *The Little Foxes* (1939) by Lillian Hellman (b. 1905). A popular classic was the mildly experimental, *Our Town* (1938), a study of life in a small town, by Thornton Wilder (1897–1975).

The comedy of manners was represented by Philip Barry and S.N. Behrman. The more antic side of comedy, often not far from farce, was evident in *You Can't Take It With You* (1936), *The Man Who Came to Dinner* (1939), and other collaborations of George S. Kaufman (1887–1961) and Moss Hart (1904–1961).

The end of World War II brought a new generation of dramatists to the theater. They dealt with serious subjects in an earnest yet often affecting way.

The plays of Tennessee Williams (b.1911) focus on the destruction of a gentle, if decadent, civilization by brutal and vital forces, as in *The Glass Menagerie* (1944), *A Streetcar Named Desire* (1947), and *Cat on a Hot Tin Roof* (1955). Williams's dialogue brought an elegaic poetic quality to plays that were otherwise determinedly realistic.

Arthur Miller (b. 1915) is at once less poetic and more closely linked to socially conscious problem drama, as in *The Crucible* (1953), which used the 17th-century Salem witch trials as an analogy to the McCarthyism of the 1950's. But Miller's finest effort is *Death of a Salesman* (1949), in which a little man is destroyed by his illusions about "the American dream."

The plays of Edward Albee (b. 1928) reveal the drama of alienation, in which cruelty is not merely a weapon but the bond that holds an otherwise sterile society together. This was clear in his early *The Zoo Story* (1959) and was brilliantly explored in *Who's Afraid of Virginia Woolf?* (1962), where a couple's marriage depends upon mutual violence.

The future. The theater has died and been resurrected several times in its long history. In the mid-1900's, some believed it was about to die again. Film was stealing away its popular audience, and radio and television were bringing entertainment directly into people's homes. What was left for live drama?

There are two answers to that question. The first is that film, radio, and television depended directly on the performers, producers, and writers for the theater. Acting technique changed somewhat as the medium changed, and screenplays and broadcast dramas differed in detail from stage plays, but the tremendous appetite of the new inventions for new material seemed sure to employ more theatrical people than ever before. The medium might change, but drama would go on.

The second answer is that live drama seems to be getting healthier. Attendance on Broadway, New York's theater district and the drama capital of the United States, is higher than it has been for many years. Regional theaters seem to thrive as well. The educated audience of today seems to support not only current plays, but also classics. Film and television drama may gradually create new demand for live theater. —*Robert O'Brien*

A STREETCAR NAMED DESIRE: *the cast of this early production included Marlon Brando* (left) *and Jessica Tandy* (right) *as Tennessee Williams's bittersweet New Orleans characters.*

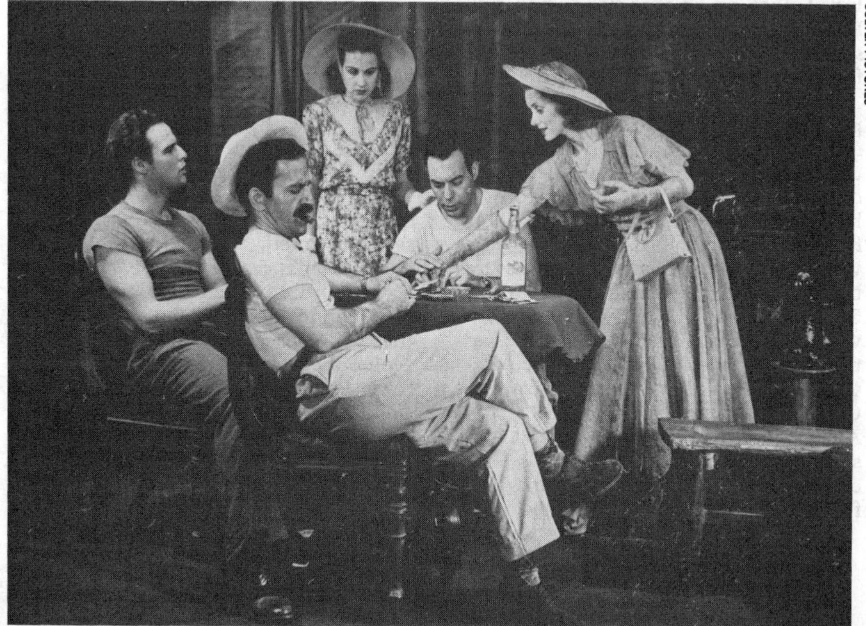

CULVER PICTURES

FILM AND BROADCASTING

Perhaps the most significant development in the performing arts in the 1900's was the birth of several new arts that were related to earlier forms, such as drama and music, but that required new approaches and were able to call on miraculous new technology to entertain, inform, and teach.

The new arts fall into two broad categories: the *recording arts* and *broadcast arts.* As we shall see, the two have influenced each other in many ways. But at least in the beginning, they grew from different interests and needs.

The Recording Arts

In a sense, the oldest and most important recording art is that of writing. Through writing, both the history of the human race and its greatest aspirations have been preserved for future generations. The beginning of civilization itself is often traced to the invention of writing. The visual arts, too, preserve a record of mankind, even of preliterate cultures.

Photography

In the 1800's, both scientists and artists were looking for a more precise way to preserve visual images. They looked back to the Renaissance invention of the camera obscura, which projected an image onto a blank piece of paper, allowing an artist to sketch the image more exactly than was possible with the naked eye. If the same image were projected onto a chemically treated surface, it might be captured permanently on paper. In 1839, both Fox Talbot, an Englishman, and Louis Daguerre, a Frenchman, discovered separate ways of fixing an image to a flat surface.

The daguerreotype was suited to portraiture and soon replaced painted miniature portraits. Each plate was unique and no copies could be made, but soon rich and poor could afford to have portraits of themselves and their families. Talbot's Calotype process was soon improved, and it became the basis of modern photography. Within 50 years of Talbot's and Daguerre's inventions, thousands of photographs of the world—the Holy Land, architectural treasures of Western civilization, the newly discovered wonders of the American West—were produced and sold in albums or as stereo cards. The camera was teaching people what the far reaches of the world looked like.

In the 1880's there were two important discoveries: the halftone method of printing, which allowed photographs to be printed easily and cheaply, and the Kodak, a camera designed by George Eastman in 1888, which allowed anyone to pick up a camera and take photographs ("you press the button and we'll do the rest"). In 1889, one year after the introduction of the Kodak, George Eastman made another important discovery: film rolls, a transparent, flexible film base that would later make moving pictures possible.

Moving Pictures

Interest in giving motion to photographs already existed. In 1887 Eadweard Muybridge published a series of sequential photographs that analyzed the gaits of different animals. He had lined up many cameras along a stretch of track, synchronized their shutters to open at regular intervals, and then assembled the individual prints to obtain a split-second-by-split-second record. Muybridge proved what the naked eye could not see: that at one point none of the horses' hooves were in contact with the track.

Thomas Edison was also fascinated with moving pictures. As cameras were developed, allowing a long sequence of film frames to be shot, Edison invented the kinetoscope, a machine that could show early "movies" to an individual who cranked the film loop by hand. By the early 1890's, these kinetoscopes were available to the public at penny arcades, offering a few seconds of racy or slapstick motion for a penny.

In 1896, the Lumiére brothers in Paris and Edison in New York held the first public showings of larger than life moving pictures on a screen for a large audience. By 1910, the movies had become a major form of popular entertainment, pulling in more money in admissions than vaudeville and Broadway together. People flocked to thousands of theaters across the country called nickelodeons. The success of the nickelodeons produced a great demand for films, and within only a few years the movie industry was born to produce them.

The early silent movies were little more than photographed vaudeville attractions. Then Edwin S. Porter introduced narrative into film in his movie, *The Life of an American Fireman,* by cross-cutting from one scene to another and creating a story. In effect, this method of editing film created a new theater.

Other film directors soon learned the new narrative language and helped improve it. One of the earliest story types was the chase. A camera could be mounted on a moving car or train; it could wheel around, looking over its shoulder at the pursuers. The scene might actually be shot with the cars moving slowly and safely, and then shown at breakneck speed.

It was a time of wild invention. By superimposing one shot over another, the filmmaker could also make it appear that a hero was hanging from a window hundreds of feet above the street, floating in the air, or even flying. By reversing the direction in which the film was run, he could show a man who had just fallen off a building leaping back to the roof.

The most important of the early film directors was D. W. Griffith, who made hundreds of short features for the nickelodeons. Griffith was the first to fully grasp the new language of film, learning to tell his stories economically, and often with intense emotion, by changing camera positions in the middle of scenes to direct the audience's attention to the dramatic content of a scene. He understood that the basic unit of film was not the scene or the actor but the shot. By the careful arrangement of the long shot, medium shot, and close-up, he learned how to manipulate audience response, helping make film capable of stirring the strongest human emotions.

Griffith's epics, *Birth of a Nation* and *Intolerance,* helped open up the nickelodeon to feature-length films. Griffith used vast resources: hundreds of extras, gigantic sets, and extravagant detail that all but overwhelmed the eye. He introduced the fadeout and cross-cutting between two or more plots; and filmed vast landscapes and juxtaposed them against close-ups showing the most personal human emotions.

The early movie stars established symbolic identities that appealed to their audiences. Douglas Fairbanks was the swashbuckling hero in a long series of feature films. Rudolph Valentino was an early matinee idol, the imagined paramour of millions of young women. Mary Pickford was the "all-American girl," Theda Bara, "the vamp."

CULVER PICTURES

CHARLIE CHAPLIN'S *silent comedy was admired internationally. Here, lacking any food, he experiments with eating his shoe, laces first.*

CULVER PICTURES

MARY PICKFORD, *leading lady of the silent movie era.*

The most durable figures, however, were the comics. Buster Keaton, Harold Lloyd, and Charlie Chaplin each established characters that deeply affected movie goers around the world. They revived the ancient style of pantomime comedy, aided by the great power of the close-up, and they used it to express not only pratfalls and gags but also a kind of loneliness and vulnerability that audiences found funny and moving at the same time. Chaplin's *Modern Times* released in 1936, which showed man faced with the machine age, was the last great silent picture and a classic.

Sound Recording

In the late 1920's, the movie business was faced with a revolution—the arrival of sound. Sound allowed the stars to talk or sing, the waves to roar, the explosions to deafen the audience. But to understand its importance, we must go back to the 1800's and early research into sound recording.

Among his many interests, Thomas Edison was fascinated with developing a "talking machine," a device that would preserve sound the way photography and moving pictures preserved visual images and movement. In 1877, Edison took out a patent on the first phonograph. A needle or stylus was used to transmit vibrations to the grooves of a cylinder wrapped with tin foil. A similar stylus could then be used to reproduce the original sounds by running over the grooves made by the recording needle.

The first recordings were very crude. Voices were barely understandable, and the sound of music was flat and distorted. But the appeal of a device that could capture the voice of a great singer or the exact words of a great orator encouraged continued research. By 1910, spring-operated phonographs were being sold for home use, and a recording industry to supply records was beginning. The great opera singer Enrico Caruso was one of the first musical artists to make a fortune on the sale of his recordings. The phonograph was especially important to the development of American popular music, including jazz and musical theater (see "American Music" above).

Most of the technical problems involved with synchronizing and amplifying recorded sound in movie theaters were solved by the mid-1920's, but the film companies resisted adding sound to their pictures. The new development would be too expensive, they said, and it was not really needed.

Then in 1927, a then little-known company, Warner Brothers, brought out *The Jazz Singer,* a sentimental story about a performer played by Al Jolson. It began silently, but in a scene with Jolson seated at a piano, he says a few words and then begins to sing. The effect on early audiences was terrific. Within weeks, it became clear to all movie studios that they must begin to produce sound films. Over the next five years, they did. Some silent stars—those with squeaky or unpleasant voices—disappeared from the screen. Others reached new heights of fame, and dozens of new stars were born. Three recording arts—photography, moving pictures, and sound—had been merged to create a new art and entertainment form.

AL JOLSON'S VOICE *in* The Jazz Singer *brought movies fully to life and began the Golden Age of Film.*

CULVER PICTURES

The Golden Age of Film

CULVER PICTURES

SPECTACLE: *extravagant visual effects—in this Busby Berkeley musical and in great outdoor epics—gave the movies both excitement and immediacy.*

The 1930's and '40's were troubled and difficult times both in America and around the world. The Great Depression caused widespread unemployment and suffering beginning in 1930, and by the end of the decade, a second world war had begun in Europe. It would involve every developed country and would last until 1945, causing death, destruction, and suffering on a vast scale. One of the few businesses to prosper through all these years was the movies.

The movies provided diversion for people during those seemingly hopeless years. In the movies people were powerful, rich, happy, and funny. Clouds rarely passed over the lens. Where private life was tedious or hopeless, the movies provided easy satisfaction. If people were afraid of the future, they could enjoy being scared to death by monster films starring Lon Chaney, Bela Lugosi, or Boris Karloff. If they were discouraged about justice in real life, they could sympathize with Edward G. Robinson playing a gangster. Fred Astaire and Ginger Rogers seemed to dance through life, and there was a steady diet of comedy and safe, predictable horse operas.

Hollywood, a district of Los Angeles, had become the center of the movie industry. The major studios made films on an assembly line basis, 400 to 500 a year to feed to their 10,000 theaters.

All America went to the movies. In 1929, 90 million people a week paid admission. The figure dropped during the deepest days of the Depression, but it rose again in the late 1930's and reached a peak in 1948. Movie palaces were built from coast to coast. They were the brightest and most striking pieces of architecture on the main streets of America, often decorated in the style of an Egyptian temple or an Italian opera house. The marquees held the brightest lights in almost any town.

Every week the show changed. The audience came to expect a double feature: a feature film, a "B" movie, a newsreel, cartoons, and the "trailers" or coming attractions. In 1933 these four hours of entertainment cost an average of 23 cents. As the lights dimmed and the curtain opened each member of the audience would prepare himself for a personal relationship with the characters on the screen.

The fans wanted to know about the "real" lives of their stars and a mini-industry of fan magazines grew. Heroes and heroines no longer came only from history, they came from the screen and became a part of the national legend.

Some movies were less concerned with stars. Busby Berkeley, a '30's musical director, developed the movie musical into a spectacle. Using hundreds of chorus girls, enormous sets, and enough fancy-dress gowns to make Cinderella weep, his camera would roll and tilt, rise off the ground, float up flights of stairs, and even out second story windows, following the ever-moving dancers. He made the camera the star and the spectacle the subject.

The '30's also produced a new kind of sophisticated comedy involving sharp-tongued, upper-class couples in outlandish situations. A monster movie, *King Kong,* introduced disaster, and the Marx Brothers introduced on-camera improvisation.

One technical advance in the movies helped to produce the most popular film of the golden age of motion pictures. Although the movies had added sound in 1927, through the 1930's it lacked color. Technicians wrestled with the problem of color film until late in the decade, when a color process developed by Technicolor finally worked. The first major film to use Technicolor was a blockbuster, a saga of the Civil War as it affected an elegant Southern plantation. It was called *Gone With the Wind* (1939). Starring Clark Gable, one of the great leading men of the 1930's, *Gone With the Wind* used color to great dramatic effect in such scenes as the burning of Atlanta.

Soon after *Gone With the Wind,* the United States was preparing for war. Movies turned toward making propaganda films as part of the war effort. A new interest in moral conviction and outside enemies characterized dozens of wartime films. Satanic villains, often with German accents or oriental features (resembling the enemy Japanese), were defeated again and again by American heroes played by the famous leading men of Hollywood.

The years after the war marked a high point in the movie business. Never before had so many people come out to the movies. Box office receipts were more than $1.5 billion. In less than 20 years since the coming of sound, the movies had brought an end to widespread live entertainment. The vaudeville circuit, which had once sent out thousands of musicians, comics, and other performers to tour the country, was dead. For many, the weekly visit to the movies was the only entertainment outside the home.

Decline and change. The huge popularity of the movies began to decline rapidly in the early 1950's. The major reason was not difficult to find. It was called television, and it could bring visual entertainment directly into the home. People stayed home in droves; movie theaters closed by the thousands, and the major studios began to lose money.

There were other reasons as well. The federal government brought suit against the major movie studios and required that they concentrate on the production *or* distribution of films, not both. Since they could not be assured of renting their films profitably without control of the movie theaters, the studios cut back on production. Independent producers, never happy with the monopoly of the big studios, began demanding new independence and power over their own films.

At the same time, the new booking system opened the doors to the films of foreign directors and producers for the first time. By the 1960's, there was a significant underground of film fans entranced with the productions of Sweden's Ingmar Bergman, Italy's Fe-

CULVER PICTURES

THE CHASE, *always a favorite movie device, was brought to a fine point by director Alfred Hitchcock in* North by Northwest.

derico Fellini, and many others. These same serious fans also studied the earlier productions of Hollywood and Europe searching for artistic merit rather than box-office appeal. Gradually film was being seen not only as entertainment, but as art, and the great movie makers, both past and present, were being honored for their contributions to a new art form.

Knowing who to honor for a successful film was often difficult. Making a major film had become one of the most intensely cooperative artistic ventures. The quality of a film depended on the imagination and skill of a producer, screenwriter, director, a large cast of actors, a cinematographer (cameraman), film editor, set designer, or special effects director. Just what part of a film's success any individual could claim was a matter of great dispute.

One solution to the problem was to give primary responsibility for a film to the director. Nearly all directors in Hollywood during the '30's and '40's were subsidiary to the "system." Only a few left personal signatures on their films. Among these was Alfred Hitchcock, who came to Hollywood from England in the late 1940's. His suspense films *(Rear Window, North by Northwest, Psycho)* won great popularity, yet they were admired by new young film directors for their innovative techniques and individuality.

Bergman and Fellini, working in Europe, were free to use their films more nearly as a mode of self-expression. Together they helped invent the *art film,* a feature-length movie not specifically designed for the commercial market. During the 1960's and '70's, they were followed by a flood of new directors, both in Europe and the United States, whose work owed much to their example.

In the meantime, Hollywood, though weakened, continued as a major force in the industry. Beginning in the 1950's it began to share stars and directors with television. In a larger sense, it was locked in a battle for the control of television itself. In its early years, the television industry had leaned heavily on the resources of radio. But the attraction of film as a way to fill the endless scheduled hours attracted television executives more and more to films. Huge rights agreements were concluded, giving television older movies for showing. Poor stations filled half or more of their schedules with old films—often the worst of the old low-budget variety. At the same time, however, this constant exposure of old movies brought younger generations all the material for a history of film. Students of Hollywood's golden age could do most of their research at home, as long as they were willing to stay up late or to watch in the daytime.

The movie studios also gained considerable control over the production of filmed shows for television—although it was often a question of who took control of whom. Beginning in the 1950's, many situation comedies and action shows were filmed in or near Hollywood, using the same pool of technicians, writers, and actors that supplied the studios. In the late 1960's, the studios went into the business of producing feature-length films expressly for television. These were generally blander and less likely to offend than films shown in movie theaters, but in many respects they resembled the "B" movies of the 1930's.

The wide availability of "family" entertainment on television also influenced the kinds of movies produced for group viewing in theaters. Movie producers began to specialize, doing "adult" films for adult audiences, "teenage" films featuring contemporary music and young romance for teenagers, and occasional special children's films. Restrictions on levels of violence and on explicit sex were relaxed, and moviegoers came to expect more explicit material than was available on television. When general release films were sold to television, they were often carefully edited or "laundered" to reduce the chance of offending home audiences. They might also be cut to fit the rigid time slots of the television schedule.

From the end of the golden age to the present, the Hollywood film never regained its sense of innovation and excitement. Instead, it continued to rework older material. Westerns, which began in the early days of film, were developed into a serious form in the 1940's and '50's by directors such as John Ford and Howard Hawks. Variations on the Western theme continue to appear up to the present, particularly the space "Westerns" such as *Star Wars* and *The Empire Strikes Back,* but with few significant additions. The gangster films of the 1930's reappeared in such sensational films as *Bonnie and Clyde,* which does not have a happy ending, and two installments of *The Godfather.* Similar variations appeared in comedies and in musicals. In the '50's, '60's, and '70's, the disaster movie came into its own as a predictable movie formula.

The growing edge of the medium was somewhere else. During the 1950's and early '60's, the producers of art films were the experimenters. But perhaps the most innovative of later cinematic work was in the neglected field of the documentary. A younger generation of directors, often producing films for television presentation, rejected scripts and sets and "artificiality" in favor of portraying something real. Frederick Wiseman's defiantly noncommercial films *Titicut Follies* (1967, about a mental institution), *Hospital* (1970), and others are perhaps the best representatives of the new documentary school. But Wiseman also owed much to the television documentary as it had been developed by the news bureaus of the major networks.

The development of film in the future is difficult to predict. Commercial film and television are hard to separate in any meaningful way. Avant-garde experiments in film and video have failed to gain public recognition. At the same time, film-making courses in high schools and colleges remain extremely popular, and improved equipment makes it possible for an amateur of small means to make a movie even of feature length. It seems likely that with training and experience so easy to obtain, new masters of the film are presently at work.

Broadcasting Arts

Running in parallel with the recording arts, a new field for entertainment grew and prospered. Just as the movie and sound recording industries sprouted from a desire to capture image and sound, broadcasting sprouted from a desire to send messages over long distances.

In 1837, Samuel F.B. Morse, an American painter and inventor, demonstrated the first practical telegraph, providing the first system of rapid communication. The next step was to transmit voices, rather than simple electrical impulses or codes, over the wires. In 1876, Alexander Graham Bell succeeded in doing that. He called his invention the telephone.

In 1895, a 21-year-old Italian experimenter named Guglielmo Marconi managed to send coded signals through the air to a receiver more than a mile away. The invention was called the "wireless." Within a few years, it was the basis of ship-to-shore communications for the British navy and was used by news organizations in Britain and the United States.

It remained for the Canadian Reginald A. Fessenden to make the final discovery. On Christmas eve, 1906, wireless operators on ships in the North Atlantic were listening for normal coded signals when they heard the voice of a woman singing, then of a violin playing. Finally, Fessenden himself read from the Christmas story. In the following years, Fessenden, Lee DeForest, and an eager band of amateur experimenters made many improvements on the first crude transmitters and receivers. During World War I the airwaves were reserved for military transmissions, but with huge subsidies from the government, radio equipment was improved and produced in large quantities for the first time. Thousands of men were trained in radio technology as well.

Radio

After the war, the possibilities of radio were revealed very quickly. In 1920, Frank Conrad, a radio enthusiast, began transmitting music from his home transmitter to other radio fans in the Pittsburgh area. Executives at the Westinghouse Corporation, which had been busy making wartime radio equipment, decided to try making receivers for home use. They asked Conrad to improve his transmitter so that purchasers of the new radios would have something to listen to. By the night of November 2, 1920, the new transmitter was in operation, and eager listeners heard the results of the Presidential election: Warren Harding defeated James M. Cox.

Only one question remained unanswered. Who would pay for the expense of transmitting radio programs? The American Telephone & Telegraph Company announced early in 1922 that its station, WEAF in New York, would offer time to any person who wanted to broadcast a message over the air. The first taker was a company seeking to rent apartments in a suburban area of the city. A company spokesman read the first radio commercial himself. The financing of broadcasting by advertisers was the pattern that survived.

Stations sprung up all across the country, and the power of transmitters was greatly increased. The RCA Corporation was the first to get simple, easy-to-operate receivers on the market, and its profits in the early 1920's were immense. By September, 1926, 5 million receivers had been sold.

At the same time, RCA was forming a "network," a nationwide group of stations connected by telephone lines, with the plan of offering national programs and attracting national sponsors. By January, 1927, it had two such networks, called the "red" and the "blue" networks of the National Broadcasting Company (NBC). That same year another network—the Columbia Broadcasting System (CBS)—began operations as David to NBC's Goliath. In 1941, NBC was forced by the government to sell off one of its networks, and the "blue" network became the American Broadcasting Company (ABC). These three organizations dominated national radio through the 1940's and carried their operations directly into television, where they continue to exercise control.

Early radio relied heavily on live music. It was broadcast from makeshift studios or from live performance halls—hotel ballrooms, auditoriums, nightclubs. As the quality of recorded music improved, stations found it more convenient and inexpensive than live broadcasts. The first true disc jockey show was broadcast in 1930, and a close link was formed between radio and the recording industry. Radio needed the records to fill its air time; recording companies came to rely on broadcast performances to promote their records.

Drama also was heard on radio from the earliest days. To suit the economic needs of stations and sponsors, it was usually confined to 15 or 30 minutes. Advertisers of household products found that women at home during the day liked melodramatic serials, and soon there were nearly a dozen to choose from. The soap opera, named for its original sponsor, eventually found its way to television. Other episodic programs were designed to appeal to young listeners. "The Lone Ranger" and similar adventure shows were often sponsored by breakfast food companies. For adults there were detective shows, horror and suspense shows ("The Shadow"), and some serious drama.

By the mid-1930's however, the most popular feature of radio was its

COMEDY AND NEWS *held the major appeal for radio audiences in the 1930's and '40's. Comedians Jack Benny, Bob Hope, and Groucho Marx also became movie and TV stars. Edward R. Murrow* (inset) *was a pioneering radio newscaster, and later an important force in TV news.*

CULVER PICTURES

CULVER PICTURES

CULVER PICTURES

CULVER PICTURES

MEMORY SHOP

TV FORMS *include the drama-action show, such as the 1950's hit* Gunsmoke; *the situation comedy, such as the 1970's hit* All in the Family; *and cartoons, such as* Tom & Jerry. *Action-drama and animation are film forms, while situation comedy grew from radio.*

comedy. Vaudeville, which made use of many live stand-up comedians, was dying in the early '30's, a victim of the new sound movies and of the Depression. Many of the best comics made the transition to radio. Some, like Jack Benny and Fred Allen, established shows with minimal plots and a regular cast of "guest" characters. Others—Bob Hope most famous among them—continued their stand-up routines on variety shows. At the same time, other creators were developing the serial comedy, which relied on plot as well as the personality of a star. The most successful was "Amos 'n Andy," a serial about two comic black men. To later tastes, the show treated black characters with disrespect, but for many listeners in the 1930's, the show was one bright spot in an otherwise discouraging time. The form of the situation comedy would dominate radio—and later, television—for the next half century.

Radio news developed more slowly. Listeners early came to rely on the radio for information, but news shows were not as popular with sponsors as music and comedy. The CBS network, struggling against the all-star entertainment lineup of NBC, was the first to give serious attention to the subject. Only with the coming of World War II in the 1940's did news gain wide respect and importance.

One of the great performers of early radio was President Franklin D. Roosevelt. Elected in 1932, Roosevelt soon recognized the potential power of the new medium, and he arranged to speak to the nation in a series of informal "Fireside Chats" during the darkest days of the Depression. For the first time, a majority of the electorate could hear a President all at one time; the effect was a sense of national unity in a troubled and dangerous era.

The golden age of radio ran almost exactly parallel to the golden age of Hollywood. Both ended in about 1950 for the same reason—television. Once home audiences came to rely on their TV sets instead of their radios for entertainment during the evening hours (what the sponsors called prime time), the most profitable part of the business was gone. For a time, it seemed that radio might disappear. The importance of the radio network was greatly reduced, and the day-to-day burden fell on local stations. At the same time, a new kind of radio—FM—which offered much better reception but required a new receiver, was also being introduced.

Radio did not disappear, of course. Instead, it changed direction. By the 1960's, millions relied on clock radios to wake them in the morning, car radios to entertain them on the way to work, and elaborate hi-fi sets with FM tuners to bring them music reproduced with the fidelity of live performance. When small, inexpensive transistor sets became available, some people carried a radio with them wherever they went.

Stations learned to specialize. Some offered rock, some country and Western music, some relaxing dinner music, some jazz or the classics. In large cities there were often stations directed at black audiences and Spanish-speaking audiences. Some stations began to offer news 24 hours a day, carrying the specialization ever further.

In the 1980's there were more radio stations than ever before. Although the medium had lost its dominant position in modern communication, it had found its niche, and it was in no danger of disappearing.

Television

The idea of television sprang up even before radio had been invented. The word itself was first used in the magazine *Scientific American* in 1907. Early visionaries assumed that a signal would be carried into people's homes by wire, much as with a telephone. After the invention of radio, experimenters concentrated on airborne systems.

In theory, the development of television was easy—it would differ from radio only in that the signal had to provide more information and that the signal would be translated into a visual pattern rather than a sound one. In practice, however, a system was difficult to design. Development was retarded first by the Depression and later by World War II, but much of the technical work was done in the 1930's and early '40's.

The war ended in the summer of 1945. Within a year, wartime assembly lines had been converted to make television sets. New stations, often using men who had received electronics training in the armed forces, were coming on the air, and the networks were busy adapting their radio organization to television. Consumers, who had been starved for entertainment during the war, were eager to have the new sets, and advertisers were eager to pick up the broadcasting bills in order to sell their wares.

In the next five years, television was still an infant. Most cities had only one station and advertisers were testing how well the new invention could sell products. By 1952, however, not only had TV succeeded in winning over the American public, it had succeeded in threatening the very existence of other forms of entertainment. Movie houses closed down; minor league sports teams went out of business; and radio entered a period of decline.

The first ten years of active broadcasting—from 1948 to 1958—set patterns that would persist into the present. Lucille Ball and her husband Desi Arnaz produced "I Love Lucy," the longest running and most successful of all situation comedies. A newspaper columnist named Ed Sullivan became producer and master of ceremonies of an hour-long variety show that ran for 20 years and that set the pattern for numerous shows of the kind. Half-hour drama and adventure shows included police stories ("Dragnet," a carry over from radio), Western series ("Gunsmoke"), and spy series ("I led Three Lives"). The game show was represented by Groucho Marx's "You Bet Your Life," which traded on humor, and "The $64,000 Question," which offered suspense and seemingly incredible prizes.

The development of television news was also far advanced. The pioneering news features of Edward R. Murrow (already famous as a radio correspondent during World War II) dared to explore sensitive issues and learned to make use of film images, interviews, and dramatic presentation. By the end of the 1950's, each network offered half-hour news programs presided over by familiar (and seemingly friendly) anchormen. Even sports had become a major attraction. Sunday football telecasts assured the prosperity of the National Football League by bringing its games to millions of prospective fans.

Hour-long drama shows flourished in the early 1950's and brought serious material and high performing standards to television. One of the original TV plays, *Marty,* was quickly made into a movie that won many awards. But these drama shows persisted in a kind of gritty realism, considering unhappy as well as happy people, poor as well as rich. The sponsors began to complain that such "negative" program material seemed to conflict with the content of their advertisements. One by one, the drama shows disappeared from the screen, illustrating the control commercial sponsors continued to have over what was shown on the magic tube.

The 1960's and '70's brought changes of mood to television programming, but few changes in basic approach. John F. Kennedy made masterful use of television in gaining election to the Presidency in 1960. Three years later, he was assassinated, and television's coverage of his death and funeral illustrated the immense power of TV to bring the nation together in a crisis. The coverage lasted three days and was watched at one time or another by a great majority of Americans.

The first manned moon landing in 1969 was actually planned as a television spectacular. A camera had been specially placed in the landing craft to capture the image of the astronaut's foot touching the moon's surface.

Just as television helped elect Presidents, in 1973–1974 it helped unseat one. The televised Senate Watergate hearings, and the later impeachment hearings, mobilized public opinion against Richard Nixon and helped pave the way for his resignation. Yet in the same time period, the network news teams provided full coverage of Nixon's triumphant visits to China and the Middle East.

Meanwhile, prime time entertainment rolled on. Network battles for the ratings—estimates of the percentage of viewers watching any given show, which helped determine advertising rates—caused most shows to come and go with startling suddenness. Successful shows such as the situation comedy "All in the Family," were mined for spinoff shows. Minor characters in one show became stars of other shows.

Through the 1960's, more and more recent feature films were made available to television for prime-time viewing. By the 1970's, the film studios were making feature-length films specially for television. Most were undistinguished, resembling the "B" movies of the 1930's. The more successful ones were often developed into new series shows.

The feature film was even lengthened into the "mini-series," a multipart movie shown on successive evenings. In 1978, one such series, "Roots," an eight-hour saga about the ancestors of a black American, received the highest ratings of any comparable show in history.

From the earliest days of radio, educators had been lobbying for reserving some broadcasting channels for educational uses. Not until the 1970's did educational television gain a strong enough foothold to be recognized. Then, through its award-winning children's shows ("Sesame Street"), its sometimes lively coverage of national affairs, and its sponsorship of serious drama and music, it gained a considerable following. Educational broadcasting faced a rather uncertain future, however, because it was supported largely by private foundations whose assistance was dwindling and by the government, whose interest was only lukewarm. Perhaps its greatest economic strength was the willingness of viewers to contribute to its support.

The influence of American television was not limited to America. Leading shows, from situation comedies to Olympic Games, were beamed to all parts of the world. The most popular entertainment shows were dubbed into dozens of languages, and some, such as "Sesame Street," were even adapted to various countries, acquiring new characters and local dress along the way. Many of the world's peoples took their ideas of America from its films and television presentations, coming to believe that people still ride horses in California, that the crime-ridden life of a favorite detective program showed the real picture of New York, and so on.

The future of the medium has been called into doubt by still another invention. Inexpensive video recording and playback devices may make it possible for families to collect their favorite movies and other entertainment much as they now collect long-playing records of their favorite music. The recording capability, allowing viewers to tape right from network transmissions, is a special problem—especially since commercial messages can be ignored by the amateur recorder.

The growth of cable television systems, promising recent movies, live sporting events, continuous news, and other features for a monthly fee, was potentially even more revolutionary since it could free the medium from the control of networks and commercial interests. For the first time since the 1940's, broadcasting—and related recording businesses—seemed at the edge of still another revolution that could change still again the entertainment patterns of America.

—Lawrence Lorimer, Donald Lorimer

For Further Reference

Music

Collier, James L. *The Making of Jazz: A Comprehensive History.* Houghton Mifflin, 1978.

Grout, Donald J. *A History of Western Music.* W. W. Norton, 1960.

Grout, Donald J., and Hermine W. Williams. *A Short History of Opera* (3rd Ed.). Columbia University Press, 1987.

Miller, Jim, editor. *The Rolling Stone Illustrated History of Rock & Roll.* Rolling Stone Press, 1976.

Robinette, Richard. *Historical Perspectives in Popular Music: A Historical Outline.* Kendall-Hunt, 1980.

Salzman, Eric. *Twentieth-Century Music: An Introduction.* Prentice-Hall, 1967.

Ulrich, Homer, and Paul A. Pisk. *A History of Music and Musical Style.* Harcourt, Brace, and World, 1963.

Dance

Chujoy, Anatole, and Phyllis W. Manchester, editors. *The Dance Encyclopedia.* Simon & Schuster, 1967.

Sorell, Walter. *Dance in Its Time.* Columbia University Press, 1986.

Drama

Bellinger, Martha F. *A Short History of the Drama.* Century Bookbindery, 1980.

Esslin, Martin. *The Field of Drama: How the Signs of Drama Create Meaning on Stage and Screen.* Routledge Chapman and Hall, 1987.

Broadcasting and Film

Barnouw, Erik. *Tube of Plenty: The Evolution of American Television.* Oxford University Press, 1975.

Brooks, Tim, and Earle Marsh. *The Complete Directory to Prime Time Network TV Shows, 1946-Present.* Ballantine Books, 1979.

Monaco, James. *How to Read a Film: The Art, Technology, Language, History & Theory of Film & Television.* Oxford University Press, 1977.

VOLUME 21
Plants
PLANTS

Plant Life 1859
Growing Plants 1870
Plants Glossary 1874
For Further Reference 1922

APPEARANCE OF PLANT LIFE ON EARTH (from earliest known fossils)
(in "days" relative to one year)

JAN	FEB	MAR	APR
1 (5 billion years ago) **algae, fungi, and bacteria**			
MAY	**JUNE**	**JULY**	**AUG**
SEPT	**OCT**		

NOV	DEC
18 (600 million years ago) **FIRST EVIDENCE OF LAND PLANTS** **spores** **25** (500 million years ago) **30** (425 million years ago) **PRIMITIVE VASCULAR PLANTS** **club mosses**	**2** (405 million years ago) **liverworts, horsetails, ferns** **6** (345 million years ago) **mosses, seed ferns, conifers** **11** (280 million years ago) **seed ferns extinct** **15** (230 million years ago) **cycads** **18** (180 million years ago) **flowering plants** **22** (135 million years ago) **31** (1 million years ago)

LEAVES: PAM PORDE

Plants

PLANT LIFE

All living organisms on earth are either animals or plants. The main characteristics that distinguish plants are ability to manufacture their own food from raw materials through the process of photosynthesis; general presence of chlorophyll; fixed location in their environment; and cellulose in their body structure.

These differentiating qualities are quite obvious in the higher forms of plant life. The acacia tree, for example, could hardly be confused with the giraffe that browses on its leaves. In the lower forms, however, the differences are not so clear: the molds and fungi, lacking in chlorophyll, cannot manufacture their own food and therefore must live parasitically on other plants; some plants ingest and devour insects; the algae, diatoms, bacteria, and many seaweeds move about freely and often vigorously in water, soil, and air; the slime molds are totally lacking in the characteristic plant building materials, cellulose. Yet all of these are plants.

In the very lowest orders the distinctions between plants and animals cannot be made at all, and in the realm of microbiology, plants and animals are considered as a single group of living organisms. This provides still more evidence of the common ancestry of plant and animal life.

Plants are literally vital to all animal life on earth. Without plants there would be no oxygen; without grass the grazing animals—and man—could not survive. Plants make up the staple food of mankind throughout the world, and only with great difficulty can man adapt himself to land where they do not thrive.

Even in the arctic wastes the chain of life depends on the simplest plants. The caribou and reindeers feed on lichens, a simple combination of algae and fungi; the seal, whose body furnishes the Eskimo with almost all the necessities of life, feeds on fish that feed on other fish, which in turn are all dependent on the simple protozoan plankton—floating sea plants.

METROPOLITAN MUSEUM OF ART: THE CLOISTERS

NATURAL SCIENCE in the Middle Ages was studied with a naive naturalism that often wandered into the fantastic. The unicorn in this fourteenth-century tapestry is a product of the imagination; the plants are not. Most have been identified by genus and species.

BOTANY

The branch of biology dealing with all aspects of plant life is called *botany*. It includes the study of structure, activities, distribution, origin, classification, and uses of plants.

Botany also touches on many other areas of study, some of which are *taxonomy*, or *plant systematics*, the grouping of related forms in a systematic order; *morphology*, the description of physical forms; *anatomy*, the phase of morphology dealing with structure; *histology*, the study of tissues; *physiology*, dealing with the processes, activities, and phenomena incidental to and characteristic of living matter; *cytology*, the study of the structure and physiology of individual cells; *pathology*, the description and investigation of the causes and control of diseases; *genetics*, the study of inheritance and breeding; *ecology*, the relationship of living organisms to their environment; and *paleobotany*, the study of fossilized plants and the evolution of plants.

In addition, there are several botanic specialities dealing with particular groups of plants. Some of these are *microbiology*, the study of microscopic forms of life; *bacteriology*, the study of bacteria; and such other branches of botany as *algology*, *mycology*, and *lichenology*, dealing with algae, fungi, and lichens, respectively.

Other related fields, once considered parts of botany but now regarded as practical sciences are *agronomy*, dealing with field-crop production; *horticulture*, dealing with greenhouse, garden, and orchard plants; and *forestry*, dealing with trees and forests.

HISTORY. The first studies of plants were primarily concerned with their magical and medicinal values; and the early stages of botany are more closely allied to myth, magic, and poetry than to the scientific method. Yet such contemporary drugs as digitalis, quinine, paregoric, and morphine had their origins in medicinal plants that for centuries have been man's pharmacological storehouse.

The first actual botanist was Theophrastus (c. 372–c. 287 BC), a pupil of Aristotle. He described and categorized plants, dividing them arbitrarily into *trees*, *bushes*, and *herbs*. In the first century AD Dioscorides and Pliny the Elder described many plants, stressing medical uses.

It was not until the 1500s that botany, and especially the classification of plants, became systematized. The invention of printing made possible the publication of the first *herbals*, books describing wild and cultivated plants and illustrated with woodcuts. One of the best of these herbals was written by Otto Brunfels (1488–1534), a German botanist.

Contemporary with Brunfels were Hieronymus Bock, author of *Materia Medica*, and Leonhard Fuchs (1501–1566), who wrote a glossary of technical terms, the first terminology of botany. Up to this point, attempts at systematic classification were crude at best; and the main concern of botanists was still with the medicinal virtues of plants.

Taxonomy. The need to distinguish useful plants led gradually to greater accuracy of description and eventually to an interest in *taxonomy*, the organization of the myriad plant forms in a scheme demonstrating their interrelationships.

The Italian botanist Andrea Cesalpino (1519–1603) made the first formal attempt at a methodical classification of plants. In his *De Plantis* (1583), he divided the 1,520 plants then known into 15 classes, basing his divisions on the character of the fruit. John Ray (1627–1705), an English naturalist, developed a system of natural affinities. He separated the flowering from the flowerless plants, calling them *dicotyledons* (having two seed leaves) and *monocotyledons*

NEW YORK PUBLIC LIBRARY

LINNAEUS, naturalist, physician, and philosopher, founded systematic botany.

(having one seed leaf), respectively. The same names are used today.

Linnaeus. Karl von Linné (1707–1778), the Swedish botanist who is also known by his Latin name Carolus Linnaeus, founded a system of nomenclature that was based on the characteristics of stamens and pistils; since these are the reproductive organs of the flower, the system is often called the *sexual system.* It was essentially an artificial arrangement, as Linnaeus himself knew; he considered it only a temporary method, to be used until a natural system of classification was developed.

Linnaeus also contributed much to *nomenclature*, or the naming of plants; and his *binomial method*, with one name for the *genus* and a second, qualifying word for the *species*, is universally accepted.

DARWIN was often caricatured and his ideas mocked by an angry and skeptical public.

A notable advance was made by Antoine de Jussieu (1748–1836), professor of botany at the Jardin des Plantes in Paris. The necessity for logical arrangement of the plants caused him to devote considerable time to the problem, and in his *Genera Plantarum* (1789) he outlined a plan that included the best features of Ray's and Linnaeus' systems. It was based on a close study of plant organs, made use of Linnaeus' simple definitions, and showed in general the natural relationships of plants, thus forming the basis for the natural classification predicted by Linnaeus.

Augustin de Candolle (1778–1841) showed that the natural affinities of plants must be found by a study of morphology, not of physiology.

Darwin. The most important influence on taxonomy was Darwin's theory of evolution and the origin of species by natural selection, published in 1859. "Natural" came to mean related by descent, and any classification scheme became a cross section of the course of evolution. This relationship of systematics and evolution, together with the identification and classification of new species, is the main concern of taxonomists now.

CLASSIFICATION OF PLANTS. The ordering of the more than 350,000 known forms of plants into groups of related organisms is the task of taxonomy. In the taxonomic system, every living plant form has its place in relationship to all other forms, both living and extinct.

Plants that seem to be related because of similarities in form and structure are assigned to a definite group; and smaller groups, based on some common characteristics, are formed within larger divisions. Some organisms do not fit well into any group, or perhaps they fit indifferently into several groups, for during the course of evolution all types and degrees of diversity have developed.

Nature is not concerned with the maintenance of groups, and organisms may be shifted from one group to another as taxonomic knowledge increases. The purpose of classification is to present a natural system of relationships; ideally, it aims not to create an artificial ordering but to discover the order inherent in the working of natural forces. Thus, a truly natural system of classification is also an evolutionary system, reflecting in its organization progressive differentiation of plant forms.

Logic of Classification. The logic of the taxonomic system is that of describing the order and connection of the various forms in terms of their relative similarity or, stated conversely, in terms of their progressive differentiation. Starting from the most general or inclusive group, all living organisms belong to the *Organisma;* this expresses the similarities between all animals and plants and their differences from all nonliving forms.

The next step in differentiation is that between plants and animals: all plants belong to the kingdom *Planta*, whose members share some of the properties of animals and are differentiated from them in other commonly shared properties. Differentiation continues in this fashion, with each group sharing certain characteristics with the preceding group, yet also differing from it in other characteristics.

In each case the succeeding group is a function of the preceding one and branches from it like a limb on a tree. Each limb in turn has smaller branches, and these branches give rise to even smaller ones. When a particular group has been so closely defined that there can be found no further characteristics to differentiate its members, the system is closed.

Every property of every plant in the series has a place in the system at some level. Thus, every member of the last group in each series can be placed in relation to every other plant, and organism, in the world.

As just described, the taxonomic system represents a progression from overall similarity to greater and greater differentiation, or *heterogeneity*. Viewed from the other direction, that is starting from the most differentiated unit, the same system presents a picture of greater and greater similarity, or *homogeneity*.

In order to find the position of a particular plant—for example, a white oak tree *(Quercus alba)*—in the whole taxonomic system, it is necessary to start with the particular and proceed through the more and more general groups. From this standpoint, the units of classification are ranged in order of increasing inclusiveness, from the most differentiated to the most undifferentiated.

The basic unit is the *species*, in this case *alba* (the white oak); the next step is the *genus* (plural *genera*), which for the oak is *Quercus*. (In some cases there are also types or *varieties* of species, but these are generally artificial and are not maintained in nature.) A group of closely related genera is a *family*; the oaks belong to the family *Fagaceae*, together with the chestnuts and beeches.

Families are in turn grouped in *orders*, and the *Fagaceae* belong to the order *Fagales*, which includes two other families, the birch and the beech. Groups of related orders are called *classes*, in this case the *Dicotyledoneae*, a large class of 47 orders that includes most flowering trees and many flowering plants.

The class *Dicotyledoneae*, together with the *Monocotyledoneae*, forms the important subdivision *Angiospermae*, to which belong all flowering trees and plants. The largest group within the plant kingdom is the *phylum*, and the oak is a member of the seed-bearing *Spermatophyta*.

The divisions into orders, classes, and phyla, and the groupings of the phyla into subkingdoms, has not been conclusively determined; and a number of systems are current. Many botanists hold that the *Thallophyta* as formerly constituted and the *Pteridophyta* do not represent true natural groupings; some have designated two main subkingdoms as *Thallophyta* and *Embryophyta*. Other systems propose a phylum *Tracheophyta*, which groups together all of the vascular plants.

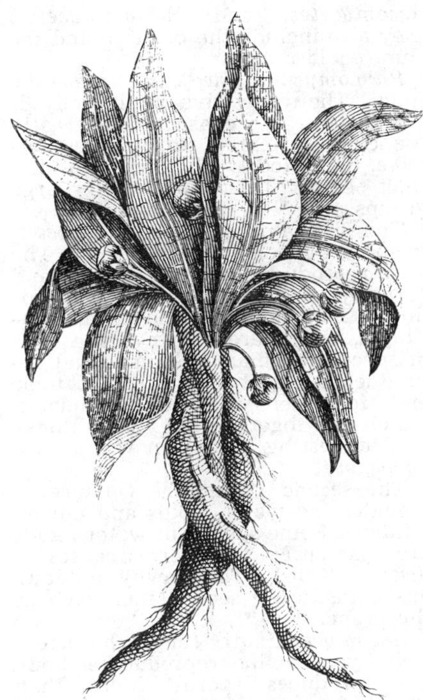

MANDRAKE, long believed to possess magical powers and credited with human attributes, was thought to shriek if uprooted.

Kingdom Planta

Phylum **Thallophyta** (simple plants without roots, stems, leaves; usually one-celled reproductive organs).
- Subdivision **Algae** (containing chlorophyll, e.g., pond scums, seaweeds).
- Subdivision **Fungi** (lacking Chlorophyll, e.g., molds, mushrooms).

Phylum **Bryophyta** (simple plants without roots, stems, leaves; many-celled reproductive organs).
- Class **Hepaticae** (live worts)
- Class **Musci** (mosses)

Phylum **Pteridophyta** (complex plants with true roots, stems, and leaves, and possessing vascular tissue, but lacking seeds).
- Class **Filicineae** (ferns)
- Class **Equisetineae** (horsetails)
- Class **Lycopodineae** (club mosses)

Phylum **Spermatophyta** (complex plants with true roots, stems, and leaves, vascular tissue, and bearing seeds).
- Subdivision **Gymnospermae** ("naked seed" plants, bearing cones, e.g., pines, spruce).
- Subdivision **Angiospermae** ("covered seed" plants or true flowering plants; e.g., grasses, maples, roses, orchids)
  - Class **Monocotyledoneae** (embryo bearing one cotyledon and flower parts typically in 3's; e.g., tulips, orchids).
  - Class **Dicotyledoneae** (embryo bearing two cotyledons and flower parts in 4's or 5's; e.g., roses, beans).

The classification given above, although not the most recent or the most accurate in terms of evolutionary relationships, is still common.

LIVING PLANTS

THALLOPHYTES. The phylum *Thallophyta* consists of plants possessing neither true roots, stems, nor leaves. They may be unicellular or multicellular; each type may be found in various forms.

Two divisions are recognized, algae and fungi. Algae are usually "independent," possess chlorophyll, and are able to manufacture their own food. Fungi do not possess chlorophyll and are dependent upon an outside source of carbon-furnishing food, such as the carbohydrates.

Algae. The oldest and simplest of all green plants, the *algae* range from simple unicellular organisms to complex, multicellular colonies. They vary in size from diatoms only a fraction of an inch in diameter to seaweeds 150 to 200 feet long. Although primarily water plants, algae grow all over the globe, from the ice and snow of the Arctic regions to the backs of certain turtles living in tropical regions.

While many species are attached, others constitute much of the floating life of aquatic habitats. The smaller forms especially are an important source of food for aquatic animal life. Reproduction may be effected bv simple *fission* (splitting off) or by nonsexual spores that may be motile or nonmotile.

Except for the flowering plants, the algae are the most numerous and widespread of all green plants; but they are a heterogeneous group whose exact interrelationships are not known. They include over 50,000 known species, grouped under different systems in various phyla. Some of the most important types are the following:

Green algae, the *Chlorophyceae*, are those algae in which chlorophyll is conspicuous. They are more numerous than all others combined and include about 10,000 species. The more primitive forms are unicellular, and some possess whiplike motile organs (cilia) in the active state.

Reproduction is primarily by simple fission—a parent cell becoming quiescent and dividing in two. Since death of the parent cell does not occur, any cell may be immortal. Sexual reproduction also occurs when two motile cells (or gametes) fuse to form a new cell.

The simple green algae are of special interest as steps in the chain of evolution. *Euglena*, a single-celled form with one whiplike cilia, may stand at the diverging point of plants and animals. Other green algae may be ancestors of the higher plants.

Filamentous forms of the green algae are numerous; these are the typical pond scums. Green algae of various types also occur in the sea, from the many one-celled forms that constitute large parts of plankton to such complex seaweeds as *Ulva*, the sea lettuce, which consists of colonies of cells forming broad ribbons or leaflike structures.

Diatoms are peculiar unicellular algae whose cell walls are impregnated with silica and fitted together in a boxlike shape. The hard, glass-like walls persist after the death of the cells and settle to the ocean floor, forming large deposits of *diatomaceous earth*, an exceptionally fine abrasive. Much petroleum is also of diatom origin.

Blue-green algae, the *Myxophyceae*, owe their common name to the occurrence of a blue pigment along with the chlorophyll. They may occur as single cells, but colony-forming species are more common. A gelatinous sheath or extensive jelly may enclose the colony, and in stagnant water the blue-green algae may give off a disagreeable odor. There are simple algae, apparently with less organization of the cell than any other algal group. Reproduction is by simple fission.

Brown algae, the *Phaeophyceae,* show great structural complexity and include the largest of all algal forms. They are almost exclusively marine, and include common rockweed and seaweeds. Species of *Laminaria,* or kelp, occur in deeper, colder waters. On the Pacific coast a giant kelp *Nereocystis,* often grows to exceed one hundred feet in a season. Many species break loose and float with the ocean current, often in great quantities; the Sargasso Sea is named after one algae genus, *Sargassum.* Chlorophyll is present in these algae, but is masked by the occurrence of another, golden-brown pigment in the plastid.

Reproduction in the brown algae is by spores or, often, by gamete production. The common rockweeds, *Fucus,* reproduce only by sexual gametes, and their life cycle resembles that of the flowering plants. The brown algae are used for food, especially in the Orient, and supply iodine and considerable fertilizer.

Red algae, the *Rhodophyceae,* are generally red and typically marine. They may be filamentous, massive, and highly differentiated; or they may be membranous. They often frequent deep waters, and in regions of plentiful sunshine have been found at depths exceeding three hundred feet.

FUNGI. The second great division of the thallophytes, the *fungi,* are commonly filamentous in the vegetative condition and are distinguishable from the algae primarily by the absence of chlorophyll.

Practically speaking, fungi occur wherever organic matter exists, since one or more species may inhabit any dead or non-living material and many species attack living tissues, especially those of seed plants. The chief classes of fungi are *Phycomycetes,* *Ascomycetes,* and *Basidiomycetes;* they also include the bacteria and the slime molds.

Phycomycetes are the alga-like fungi. The vegetative plant body is a *mycelium* and consists of a greatly branched system of threads, or *hyphae,* not clearly divided into distinct cells. There are two large groups.

The first group, the *zygomycetes,* includes the common bread mold. The mold reproduces both nonsexually and sexually. Nonsexual spores are produced in structures known as *sporangia,* which are borne at the ends of specialized filaments; in sexual reproduction, hyphae cut off at their ends form cells that act as gametes, which fuse together and form a thick-walled resting spore known as the *zygospore.*

The second group, the *Oomycetes,* includes the water molds and downy mildews. Some species of water molds are parasitic; one form causes a disease of fish. The downy mildews are parasitic on seed plants, such as the grape.

Ascomycetes are fungi characterized by a saclike reproductive body that produces spores. More than 10,000 species of ascomycetes are known, and they occur in many different situations.

The *saprophytic* species (those inhabiting dead material) are found abundantly upon decaying vegetation and in or on the soil. The blue and green molds of foods, such as *penicillium,* from which the drug penicillin is made, belong to this group. It also includes a few families of fungi with large and fleshy fruit bodies, such as the edible morels and truffles. Another useful group is that of the *yeasts.*

Parasitic species are likewise numerous, and cause such plant diseases as apple scab and rose mildew.

Basidiomycetes are a class of fungi that comprises orders and families varying in both structure and habitat, but the different subclasses are all related through the possession of *basidia* (club-shaped cells) that typically bear four spores. *Rusts* and *smuts* constitute the main parasitic groups; other divisions include the vast majority of the fleshy or woody fungi, such as mushrooms. Smut fungi are most recognizable during the spore stage.

Some rust fungi exhibit an exceedingly complicated life history. The black-stem rust of wheat has one stage on the wheat and related plants and another on the barberry. The apple rust passes from the apple to the red cedar and from the red cedar back to the apple. On the host plant the fungi are ordinarily characterized by the occurrence of rusty spots; these are the beds of the fungal spores.

Woods and fields yield hundreds of fungi variously known as mushrooms, toadstools, and puffballs. They grow in the soil or on decaying logs and vegetation, and a considerable number cause heartwood or sapwood decay of trees. Among fleshy forms there are both edible and poisonous species. They vary in texture from soft, spongy forms to hard, woodlike growths; in size, they range from the microscopic to two feet across.

Bacteria. Among the fungi there are usually included the smallest plants known, the *bacteria,* or *schizomycetes.* They seem, however, to constitute an independent group, perhaps related to some of the lower algae. They are so small that they are visible to the unaided eye only when growing in colonies of many hundreds or thousands. If they were arranged end to end, it would require about 500 of these bacteria of average size to reach across the head of a pin.

Under favorable conditions, bacteria reproduce by fission at an astonishingly rapid rate. Some also produce spores at the rate of a single spore per cell; these enable them to survive hostile conditions.

Bacteria are universally found in air, water, and soil, as well as on and within all living bodies. They have harmful effects as producers of disease in plants, animals, and man, but they are also beneficial as agents of the decay that return nutrients to the soil, and as the *nitrogen bacteria* that are vital in completing the cycle of this important element. Bacteria are also the agents of many useful fermentation processes. They are used commercially in the dairy industry, in wine-making, and in the curing of tobacco.

Slime Molds. *Myxomycetes,* or *slime molds,* are organisms sometime classed as plants and sometimes classed as animals. They form a slimy mass of naked protoplasm in decaying matter in moist, warm places.

The multinucleate protoplasm moves in amoeboid fashion and can ingest solid food, a characteristic that links the slime molds closely to the animal world.

Lichens. A *lichen* consists of a fungus and an algae growing together in a *symbiotic,* or mutually helpful, relationship to form a dual colony so closely associated that the colonial composite acts as one. To a degree the fungus is parasitic upon the alga and

BETTMANN ARCHIVE

BENEATH THE FOREST FLOOR, the mushroom plant extends a network of filaments. The familiar cap, with its spore-producing gills, makes up the "fruit," or reproductive body.

NATIONAL COAL ASSOCIATION

HELEN BUTTFIELD

FERNS have survived almost unchanged from the time 350 million years ago when they left their imprint (*left*) fossilized in the earth.

holds it captive, but the alga is thus enabled to grow in many places where it could not otherwise exist. Within the lichen, the alga multiplies vegetatively; the fungus has its characteristic spore reproduction.

Lichens commonly grow on trunks and branches of trees, on rocks, and on soil. Some are flat and leafy, and some are mosslike. Reindeer moss, really a lichen, is typical of the mosslike group. Lichens are often gray-green and are very resistant to extremes of cold and drought. In the Arctic, they sustain the vast reindeer herds.

MOSSES AND MOSSLIKE PLANTS. Members of the class *Bryophyta,* mosses and mosslike plants, constitute a considerable group of green plants higher in the scale of development than the algae, but less complex than seed plants. In some classifications they are considered the lowest members of the subkingdom *Embryophyta,* plants that form embryos. However, they lack the vascular tissues characteristic of the higher forms.

Mosses. Small, green, flowerless plants, the mosses grow erect but are usually no more than one to two inches high. They occur commonly in moist environments as miniature velvety or feathery growths carpeting the ground, growing on rocks, on the trunks of trees, and even in ponds or running water. The parts of the mosses usually visible look like those of higher plants; they have a stemlike axis with numerous leaves. But there is no true stem or root, such as characterize seed plants.

The mosses are among the most primitive of plants and have persisted almost unchanged since they arose about 300 million years ago. Because they have given rise to no other forms, the mosses are considered a terminal evolutionary group.

Liverworts. Primitive land and fresh-water plants, the liverworts are closely related to the mosses. Their growth pattern is flat and branching, and they resemble some seaweeds in appearance. They are the simplest land plants surviving, and may have evolved from certain algae.

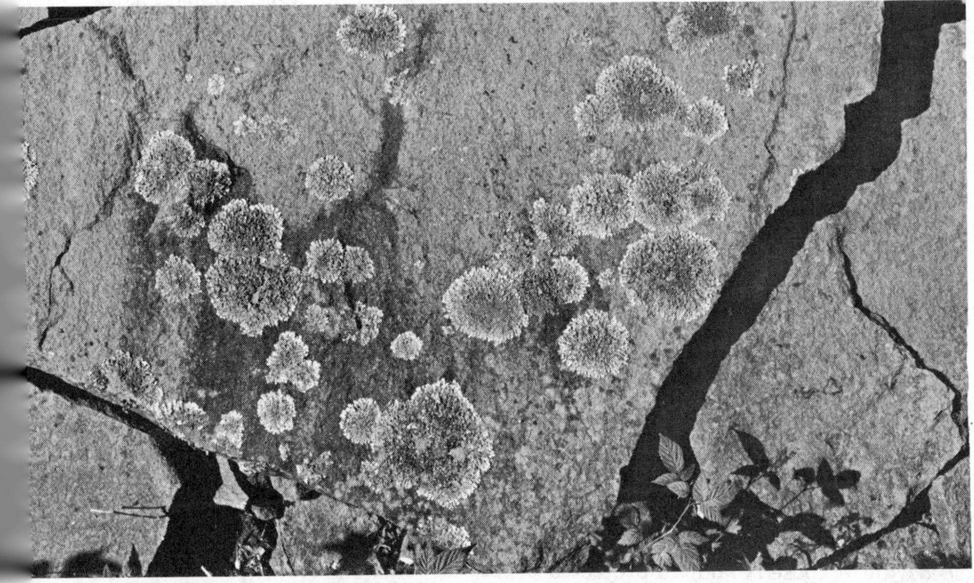

HELEN BUTTFIELD

LICHENS, as enduring as the stone they cover, are among the most primitive land plants.

FERNS AND FERN ALLIES. The *ferns,* together with a few related families of the class *Pteridophyta,* are the remnants of a once flourishing form of plant life that dominated the earth's vegetation for years. Geologically one of the oldest groups, the ferns originated in the Paleozoic era, 350 million years ago. Giant *tree ferns* once covered the earth, and the energy they gathered from the sun and stored in their tissues is preserved in the earth's great coal deposits.

Ferns are characterized by large, divided, feather-like leaves, or *fronds,* which usually uncurl from the tip. They have short stems that often grow underground. Unlike the mosses, they have true roots. Ferns, like the higher plants, have vascular tissues that transport nutrients and water from the roots to the leaves.

Ferns are abundant on the moist, shaded, forest floor and along streams; some species, however, thrive on rocky cliffs or slopes. Geographically, these plants range from the Arctic to the equatorial jungles and rain forests, where tree ferns often reach heights of forty feet.

Alternation of Generations. Reproduction in the ferns is marked by a distinct *alternation of generations,* which involves two different forms: the first is the familiar fern plant, which has a root, stem, and leaves; the second is a thin, flat, heart-shaped plant called the *prothallium.* Prothallia produce male and female sex organs in which gametes are developed. A male gamete fuses with an egg, and

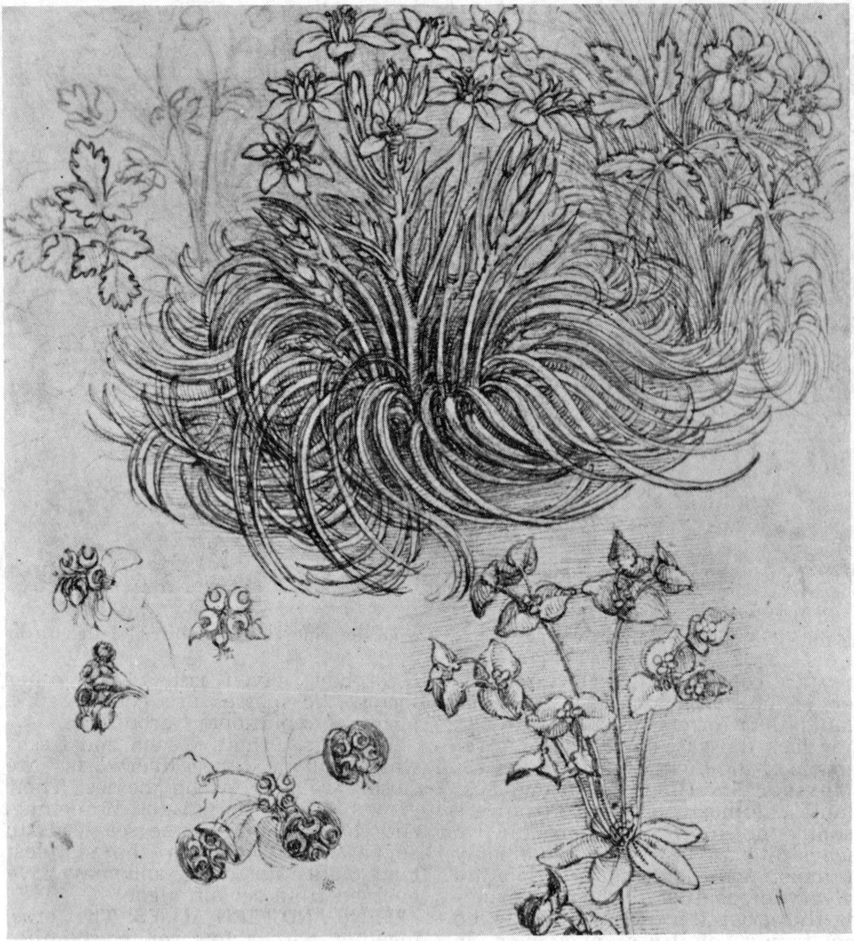

STAR OF BETHLEHEM, BY LEONARDO DA VINCI; ALINARI-ART REFERENCE BUREAU

THE FLOWERING PLANTS are the highest evolutionary form in the plant kingdom and the flower itself is the most effective means of reproduction evolved by any of the plants.

from the fertilized egg develops the fern plant with its roots, stem, and leaves.

On the underside of the fern's leaves there are small spore cases, or *sporangia,* which are often distributed as dots, rows, or larger masses. In these spore cases, large numbers of single-celled spores are produced; when they germinate, they give rise to the prothallia. Thus, the prothallia are *gametophytes* producing gametes, and the leafy fern is a *sporophyte* producing spores.

Club Mosses. Also called *ground pines, club mosses* are rarely more than three feet high. These relatives of the fern are neither mosses nor pines; they are small evergreen plants that have simple leaves resembling pine or hemlock needles. Sometimes they grow upright, but often they trail on the ground, where they propagate by means of *runners,* or elongations of the root stock that send up new sprounts. They also reproduce spores.

Horsetails. Only twenty-five living species of *horsetails* are known, and all of these belong to a single genus. Many extinct forms, however, have been found in fossils. Horsetails are the only surviving representatives of a group containing members that grew to over ninety feet.

Horsetails are composed of underground stems that send up tall, vertical, jointed stalks and of branches covered with scalelike leaves. These plants are also called *scouring rushes,* a name derived from the rough texture imparted by the silica they contain.

Cycads and the Ginkgo. The *cycads* are plants that resemble tree ferns in general appearance, but reproduce by means of seeds. Few in number today, they are the remains of a once dominant group which flourished in the great fern forests of the Permian age.

The *ginkgo,* also called the maidenhair tree, has fan-shaped leaflets, similar in form to those of the maidenhair fern. This leaf-form is found on no other flowering plant and the ginkgo represents a missing link between ferns and flowering plants.

SEED PLANTS. The *spermatophyta,* or seed plants, the highest division in the plant kingdom, contains all plants that reproduce by means of seeds. It includes all living trees and flowering plants. Seed plants form the dominant part of the vegetation of the earth today and thus can be considered the highest, or most successful, plant form.

Seed plants embrace two major divisions: the *gymnosperms,* or "naked seed" plants, in which the seeds lie exposed and unprotected on the cone scales, and the *angiosperms* or "enclosed seed" plants in which the seeds are borne inside a jar-shaped swelling, the ovary, located at the base of the flower pistil.

Gymnosperms. Familiar examples of gymnosperms are the pines, spruces, and other evergreen trees or shrubs with conelike fruits, known as the *Coniferae.* This group forms the great coniferous forests of the temperate zones and includes the largest plants on earth, the giant redwoods.

Vascular or woody tissues reach a high state of development in the stems and roots of conifers. The leaves of mature pines are called *needles;* they are retained for more than a year, giving rise to the name *evergreen.* These needles are highly specialized in structure and are adapted to resist extremes of cold and dryness. Morphologically they are grouped in *fascicles* (clusters) of two, three, or five needles, depending upon the species.

In the conifers the spore-bearing leaves or scales *(sporophylls)* do not constitute a flower. As the scales of the seed-bearing cones separate, the winged seeds may be seen, a pair under each scale.

In the pine, the embryo plant within the seed is surrounded by a considerable food-storage layer, called the *endosperm,* and the whole is enclosed by the seed coat, or *integument.*

Maturity of the seed is accompanied by a certain amount of drying out and by a period of inactivity, or *dormancy.* The seed remains dormant until it absorbs water, and *germination,* or sprouting, ensues. The young seedling, free of the seed coat, consists of root; bud, or *plumule;* and a whorl of long, green seed leaves, or cotyledons.

Angiosperms. The angiosperms, or true *flowering plants,* include the great majority of the familiar flowers and weeds, as well as all the trees and shrubs except the gymnosperms. The angiosperms have seeds and a complex tissue system in which vascular or woody elements attain a further advanced state of differentiation, and they exhibit the highest evolutionary development through the production of flowers.

The angiosperms, which include more than half the known plants—about 200,000 species—are subdivided into two groups. In the *monocotyledons* the young seedling bears a single seed leaf, or *cotyledon. Dicotyledons* bear two seed leaves, sometimes thickened, that provide reserves of organic food. Another characteristic of dicotyledons is apparent in the mature plant: the *venation,* or vein system, of the monocotyledons is parallel, as in corn; in dicotyledons it is netted, or *reticulate,* as in the rose.

There are other characteristics, of both floral parts and inner structure, that are generally distinctive of the two groups, such as the three-part flower structure of the monocotyledons, as opposed to the four or five parts that are found in dicotyledons.

Monocotyledons include such families as the grasses *(Gramineae)* which furnish the cereal grains, pasture grasses, and ornamental grasses;

tropical palms *(Palmaceae)*, including the date and coconut palms; lilies and related plants *(Liliaceae)*; bananas and plantains *(Musaceae)*; and the highly prized orchids *(Orchidaceae)*, famous both for the delicacy and variety of their waxlike flowers and for the remarkable modification in floral parts, the latter having come about in adjustment to insect pollination.

The orchids and the grasses show extreme differences in floral anatomy. The orchid flower's extreme complexity represents a high point in evolutionary development; the grass flower, also an advanced form, shows a high degree of reduction of parts, consisting of a pistil with ovary, style, and two feathery stigmas, and three stamens enclosed in scalelike leaves, or *bracts.*

Dicotyledons are nearly five times as numerous as monocotyledons; they are also regarded as geologically the older group. They have attained far greater diversity in form and have advanced to higher types of development.

Among families exhibiting less complex types of floral structure are the willows and the poplars *(Salicaceae)*, which have simple flowers in spikelike branches called *catkins.* Related to the willows are other families without showy floral parts, such as the walnut-hickory family *(Juglandoceae)* and elms *(Ulmaceae)*.

In a varied group of families that includes the pinks, sweet Williams, carnations *(Caryophyllaceae)*, water lilies *(Nymphaeceae)*, buttercups, columbines, peonies, and clematis *(Ranunculaceae)*, there are many wild and garden plants. All of these have distinct petals (are *polypetalous)*, and the carpels are either separate or united.

The rose family *(Rosaceae)* and the pulse family *(Leguminosae)* are closely related, and together they constitute a very considerable part of the separate-petal series of families. As a whole, the rose family is rather heterogeneous; its members include the blackberries, roses, and cherries.

In the pulse family there are several thousand species, among which are the lupines, clovers, beans, peas, and acacias. Generally the *corolla* (floral leaf) is *papilionaceous* (butterfly-like); the fruit is characteristically a pod or legume.

Among the families of dicotyledons in which the petals are united are the mints *(Labiatae)*, fragrant herbs, and shrubs with flowers that are commonly two-lipped. The nightshade family *(Solanaceae)* includes the potato, tomato, eggplant, tobacco, and petunia; the flowers are prevailingly rotate, and the fruit is a *berry* (as in tomato) or a capsule (as in Jimson weed). Melons are the fruit of certain members of the gourd family *(Cucurbitaceae)*.

Botanists generally agree in placing the composite family *(Compositae)* at the pinnacle of development in the plant kingdom. This is the family of sunflowers and goldenrods, asters and thistles, chrysanthemums and dahlias. It also includes lettuce, globe artichoke, and salsify. It is a huge family with perhaps 12,000 species, nearly all of which are annuals or perennial herbs; the woody members are not trees.

The outstanding characteristic of the composite family is the compact head of many flowers—some with ray flowers (as in sunflowers) and some without (as in thistles). The fruits are hard and one-seeded *(achenes)*, and are often provided with a feathery appendage, or *pappus* (as in dandelions), that helps wind distribution of the seeds.

AMERICAN MUSEUM OF NATURAL HISTORY

DECIMATED by the caddis fly, these leaf skeletons reveal the supporting venation.

PLANT STRUCTURE

From the smallest bacteria, 1/50,000 of an inch long, to the largest angiosperm, 372 feet tall, plants are made up of *cells,* the basic units of life. The study of cell structure and function is called *cytology.*

CELLS. A typical plant cell is enclosed by the *cell wall,* which is composed primarily of cellulose and nonliving substances and gives support and form to the cell and the whole plant. The enclosed *protoplasm* is a viscous, transparent, living matter composed of water, proteins, sugars, fats, acids, and salts.

Protoplasm is differentiated into two aspects. The dark, usually round *nucleus* controls the chemical activities of the cell and bears the *chromosomes,* carriers of hereditary traits. Surrounding the nucleus is the *cytoplasm,* in which are the structures that carry on the physiological cell functions: the *plastids,* including chlorophyll-bearing *chloroplasts* that are capable of photosynthesis; the *chromoplasts,* containing red and yellow coloring; the *leucoplasts,* which build sugar into starch grains; *mitochondria,* which produce chemical regulators; *vacuoles,* liquid-filled spaces that serve as storage areas; starch grains and crystals.

TISSUES. In all multicellular plants the individual cells are organized into *tissue. Histology* is the study of these groups of structurally similar cells that are organized to perform physiological functions.

Embryonic Tissue. *Meristem,* or young tissue, consists of thin-walled, active cells rich in protoplasm. They are able to divide by cell division and thus to continue the growth of the organ. All other tissues are derived from meristem by differentiation or modification. *Cambium,* the layer of active growth and cell formation in stems and roots of dicotyledons, is a form of meristem.

Permanent Tissue. The new cells produced by division and differentiation of the meristematic cells become the permanent tissue of the plant. As these cells mature, they no longer reproduce by cell division but expand in size. The cell walls stretch and, in many instances, thicken; the cytoplasm thins out and the major portion of the cell interior is taken up by the enlarged vacuole. Further modifications in shape and structure occur as the cell takes its place within one of the various types of permanent tissue.

There are two kinds of permanent tissues: *simple tissues,* in which each tissue is composed of similar cells; and *complex tissues,* in which different types of cells work together as a unit to perform certain physiological functions. Most plant parts are composed of simple tissues. However, the *xylem* and *phloem,* the vital carriers of water and food, are complex tissues consisting of parenchyma, fibrous, sieve, and vascular tissues.

Parenchyma, or soft tissue, consists of mature, thin-walled, usually short cells that have attained their growth, such as the tissue of ripened fruits and the green tissue of leaves.

Collenchyma tissue consists of long cells with thick angles. In many stems it occurs as a strengthening tissue just beneath the epidermis.

Sclerenchyma, or stone tissue, consists of thick-walled usually short cells, so tightly packed that they form a hard mass, as in nutshells and the "stones" of many fruits.

Fibrous and bast tissue consists of thick-walled, elongated cells so tightly packed together that they make up wood fibers (fibrous tissue) and bark (bast tissue) of the stems of most higher plants. Bast fibers are used in ropemaking and linen making.

Sieve tissue consists of elongated, usually large cells, more or less united into tubes and having only slightly thickened walls. The name derives from the perforation of the transverse partitions between the cells in a sievelike pattern; through these perforations the protoplasm connects from cell to cell. Sieve tissue occurs primarily in the young bark and is important in conveying organic food.

Vascular tissue is also tubular, but the continuity of the cavity is usually more complete than in sieve tissue. When they are young, these tubes contain protoplasm; but eventually they contain water or air. Vascular tissue occurs in the woody parts of stems and leaves.

Epidermal tissue, a single layer of cubical cells, constitutes the outer layers of leaves, young stems, and roots.

ANATOMY OF SEED PLANTS

Although the lower plants have developed quite complicated forms and structures and have adapted very successfully to a wide range of environments, the most highly differentiated and evolved structures are found in the angiosperms.

The bodies of typical seed plants are composed of four kinds of parts: *roots, stems, leaves,* and *flowers* (which in turn produce *fruit* and *seeds*). The first three structures are found also in the mosses, ferns, liverworts, and other lower forms; but flowers and their accessory products are exclusive to seed plants.

ROOTS. All living organisms, including the plants, are descended from forms which originated in the sea; and no cells, animal or vegetable, can exist without access to that most important element, water.

In the higher plants, the *root* is the vital link between the plant and its lost aquatic environment. Through its roots a plant absorbs the water that makes up most of its tissues and that it uses to carry on its life processes, as well as some oxygen and most of the mineral nutrients it requires.

Root Structure. All roots are covered at the growing tip with a *root cap* which protects the sensitive tip and serves as a boring point to push into the soil. Behind the root caps, the sides of the roots are covered with many fine *root hairs,* made up of single cells, which penetrate the soil and increase the roots' absorption.

Root Systems. The slender, branching roots of grasses, corn, and wheat are *diffuse systems* spreading over wide but relatively shallow areas. *Tap-root systems,* such as those of the carrot and beet, are made up of a single primary root that probes deeply into the soil and often is thickened to serve in food storage.

Specialized Roots. Adaptations to particular needs are the *aerial roots* of ivy and other *epiphytes* (plants that grow on other plants but are not parasitic); *prop roots* of corn and fig trees, which act as buttresses; *adventitious roots,* which drop down from the stem to lend additional support to many tropical trees; and the *aerating roots* of the cypress and mangrove, which grow above water to obtain oxygen.

STEMS. The *stem* is the part of the plant that supports the leaves and reproductive organs and supplies them with water and mineral nutrients absorbed by the roots. It also serves to carry food back down to roots and other parts for storage.

Most stems grow above the ground *(aerial stems)*, but some grow below the surface *(subterranean stems)*. Aerial stems are either *herbaceous* or *woody,* an important feature distinguishing groups of plants. All gymnosperms have woody stems, while those of angiosperms can be either woody or herbaceous.

It is generally believed that woody stems are the more primitive and that herbaceous stems have evolved from them. Herbaceous stems are soft and green, covered by an epidermis; they grow in length but little in diameter and are chiefly *annual* (confined to a single growing season). Woody stems are hard and are covered with a tough layer of bark. They grow considerably in diameter and are chiefly *perennial* (surviving through many growing seasons).

Woody Stems. Internally, *woody stems* are made up of two kinds of tissue, the outer *bark* and the inner *wood*; these are separated by a single layer of cells, the growing *cambium* layer. As the cambium cells divide the outer portions become differentiated into a layer of cells called *phloem,* and the inner cells form the *xylem.*

Phloem cells transport food, and the xylem cells conduct moisture throughout the plant. This formation of new cells causes a thickening in the diameter of the stem, and it is thus that the trunks of trees continue to increase in girth. The cells produced in the summer are larger and therefore lighter in color; the winter cells are smaller and appear darker.

This color differential creates the *annual rings* marking a year's growth. As a tree grows, the inner layers become clogged and loaded with tannins, resins, and gums. These make up the hard, dark *heartwood,* while the outer, more active layers constitute the *sapwood.*

Herbaceous Stems. Herbaceous stems resemble young woody stems in structure except that the xylem and phloem are arranged in clusters called *vascular bundles,* which are either scattered throughout the stem (monocotyledons) or arranged in a circle (dicotyledons). Herbaceous stems are chiefly annual, and growth is primarily in the length, not the diameter.

Buds. Buds are the growing ends of the stems of both woody and herbaceous plants and are the immature forms of leaves and flowers. *Terminal buds* provide growth at the tip of a stem or twig; *lateral buds* or *axillary buds* form side branches as well as leaves and flowers.

In annuals and tropical woody plants, the buds grow continuously; but in woody plants of temperate climates they become dormant when the plant slows its metabolism during the winter.

Subterranean Stems. *Rhizomes* are horizontal stems growing on or beneath the ground; they serve for storage of food and for reproduction. They are perennial and send up new shoots each year. *Tubers* are the enlarged tips of rhizomes; highly specialized for the storage of food, they are also, as with the potato, important means of propagation.

Bulbs, such as those of the onion and tulip, and *corms,* such as those of the gladiolus and crocus, are enlarged stem buds with overlapping leaves. They serve for storage and reproduction and as a means of carrying the dormant plant through seasons unfavorable to growth.

LEAVES. Leaves are the plant structures specialized primarily for the manufacture of food through photosynthesis. Thus, most leaves are constructed so as to provide the greatest possible surface area and are ar-

HELEN BUTTFIELD

POWERFUL ROOTS anchor the beech tree firmly in the ground while, deep in the soil, their growing tips spread out, searching for the moisture that nourishes the crown.

ranged so as to expose this surface to the maximum amount of sunlight.

Leaf Form. Most leaves consist of a slender stalk, or *petiole*, and a broad, expanded blade, or *lamina*. From the apex of the petiole, *veins* extend into the blade. Veins serve for mechanical support, for the transport of raw materials through the leaf, and for carrying away the products elaborated by the green cells.

Leaves vary in size from a fraction of an inch up to 60 feet, as in the palm tree. In shape they range from the long, thin blades of grass to the circular leaves of the nasturtium and water lily; there are many irregular forms also, as in the maples and oaks.

The *venation* (arrrangement of the vein) is characteristic for different kinds of plants: *net* venation in dicotyledons and *parallel* venation in monocotyledons. In *pinnate* net venation, the petiole extends as a main vein or midrib through the center of the leaf, lateral veins extending off it on each side to give a featherlike appearance; this is found in the apple and elm. In *palmate* net venation, several larger veins radiate from the apex of the petiole, as in the maple.

The leaf blade may be simple, as in the apple, or compound, consisting of *leaflets*. The leaflets may have the pinnate arrangement, as in the pea and tree of heaven; or the leaf may be palmately compound, the leaflets arranged at the end of the petiole like the fingers on a hand.

The leaves of grasses are specially modified in that, instead of a distinct petiole, the basal part of the petiole is a sheath that closely surrounds the stem. At the base of the blade there is a special growing zone, so that grass leaves continue to increase in length for long periods.

Leaves may undergo many modifications. *Bud scales* are greatly reduced leaves that overlap and protect the delicate bud tissues during cold and drought. The thick, fleshy leaves of sedum and other succulent plants store quantities of water.

Some barberry leaves are modified into *spines;* and in the pea, some of the leaflets are modified into *tendrils* that assist the plant in climbing. Very curious modifications occur in the insectivorous plants, such as the pitcher plants and Venus's flytraps; the latter's leaves are modified to attract and capture the insects that are digested by these plants.

Longevity. The leaves of most of the temperate zone plants do not continue to grow as do the grasses; they live for a single season and then fall. Such plants are *deciduous,* as opposed to the evergreens, which retain their leaves for a longer period—normally not for more than four years.

The falling of the leaves is the result of chemical changes in which the substance *auxin* plays a considerable part. In autumn, a special layer of cells, called the *abscission layer,* forms at the base of the petiole; these cells block the flow of water and nutrients. As a result, the chlorophyll decomposes, resulting in the yellow and orange pigments typical of autumn foliage. The red colors are new pigments that develop within the

HELEN BUTTFIELD

THE WINGED SEED of the Jeffrey Pine and the feathery seed of the dandelion are two examples of highly efficient seed dispersal: these need merely the air and the wind.

cells. Meanwhile, the middle cells of the abscission layers disintegrate and the leaf breaks off and falls, leaving a *leaf scar* on the stem.

Leaf Arrangement. Leaves usually are arranged on the stem in one of three ways: *spiral,* or *alternate,* one leaf at a node, the leaves forming a continuous ascending spiral on the stem, as in the apple or elm; *opposite,* two leaves that usually are directly opposite each other, as in the maple; *whorled,* three or more leaves at the same node, as in the lily.

Buds are regularly found in the *axils* of the leaves and, under favorable conditions, will grow into branches bearing leaves or flowers.

Internal Structure. In a cross section of a leaf blade, different types of tissues and cells are observed.

Epidermis.—The *upper epidermis* and *lower epidermis* each consists of a single layer of cells that covers the entire leaf surface, protecting the tissues within from mechanical injury and drying out. The epidermis, particularly the upper one, is usually covered with a waxy *cuticle,* which further prevents loss of water.

The epidermal cells are longer and wider than they are deep and, as viewed from the surface, have wavy cell outlines. Among the epidermal cells are special crescent-shaped *guard cells,* which contain chloroplasts. Between the guard cells are openings called *stomata* (singular, *stoma).* The size of these openings is regulated by the movements of the guard cells. It is through the stomata that the gaseous exchange takes place between the interior of the leaf and the air. Water vapor escapes and carbon dioxide enters for the process of photosynthesis; oxygen escapes as a product of photosynthesis or enters in connection with respiration.

Mesophyll.—Between the upper and lower epidermis there are specialized chlorophyll-bearing cells. Beneath the upper epidermis, long, narrow cells are arranged in a palisade fashion, and between these and the lower epidermis are more or less rounded or irregularly shaped cells arranged to form a loose, spongy tissue, with abundant air chambers between. These cells are largely concerned with carbohydrate manufacture.

Vascular bundles.—These are the veins of the leaves, as seen from the surface; the larger ones branch into smaller bundles, which may end in a single cell.

FLOWERS. From the standpoint of the continuation of the species, which is the only *natural* purpose, the flower and its resulting fruit and seed are the most important structures of the plant. It is for the flower's support that the entire plant is designed. The flower is the reproductive organ of the higher plants; its function is to produce the seed containing the male and female gametes that will unite in sexual reproduction and produce the new generation.

Flower Parts. The basic flower parts can be divided into four sets of structures. The outer set of parts (green in some plants) is the *calyx,* the individual leaves of which are the *sepals.* Next there is a set of showy leaves known as the *corolla,* the individual parts of which are *petals;* these are brightly colored and often secrete an aromatic and sweet substance *(nectar)* that attracts insects. Within the petals are a group of small sporophylls, the *stamens.* A stamen consists of a slender stalk *(filament)* with a pollen-bearing *anther* at its tip.

The central and last structure constitutes a united set, termed a *pistil,* that is made up of several parts, or *carpels.* Each group of carpels has an enlarged basal *ovule sac,* a terminal *stigma,* and a connecting shank known as the *style.* In the ovule sac there are differentiated ovules within which the egg gametes are produced.

The sepals and petals are known as *accessory parts* because they are not directly concerned with reproduction. The *essential parts* are the stamens (male parts) and the pistils (female parts).

Pollination. The development of the seed is preceded by the process of *pollination. Pollen* is produced on certain specialized structures and carried by the wind or by insects to the female structures. *Self-pollination* is the transfer of pollen within a single flower or from one flower to another on the same plant; *cross pollination* is the transfer of pollen from one plant to the female structures of another plant. There the pollen germinates, giving rise in a short time to male gametes that fuse with the female gamete. The latter develops into the embryo plant that, surrounded by protective structures, becomes the seed.

SEEDS AND FRUITS. The *seed* develops from the ovule and consists of the young embryo plant with its surrounding nutritive and protective tissues. The seeds are enclosed in the ovary during their development; the fully developed ovary with its adjacent parts constitutes the *fruit.*

Seeds. The seed consists of a *seed coat,* usually tough and partly impervious to the water that is necessary for germination; an *embryo,* the miniature plant that develops from the fertilized egg, or *zygote*; and the *endosperm,* or food-storage tissue that nourishes the germinating plant or seedling.

Effective seed dispersal is vital to the angiosperms because the parent plant is not mobile; seeds must be widely scattered to provide optimum conditions for germination and growth. Most of the striking characteristics of seeds and fruits are adaptations that aid dispersal: by wind, as in the wings of the maple seed and plumes of the dandelion; by spines and burrs that adhere to animals, as in the cockleburs; by floating, as in the coconut; or by the fleshy fruits of such plants as apples and cherries, which are eaten by animals and thus have their seeds distributed.

Fruits. There are several different kinds of fruits.

Fleshy fruits.—Soft and pulpy at maturity, *fleshy fruits* include the *berries* (grape, tomato, orange, squash); the *drupes* (cherry, peach, olive); and the *pomes* (pear, apple).

Dry fruits—Dry and hard at maturity, dry fruits fall into two types. Those that split open at maturity are the *dehiscent* fruits and include *follicle* (milkweed); *legume* (pea); and *capsule* (iris, lily). Fruits not splitting open are *indehiscent: achene* (buckwheat, sunflower); *caryopsis,* or grain (cereals); *samara,* or winged (maple, ash, elm); and *nut* (oak, chestnut).

Structural differences.—Fruits are called *simple* when they develop from a single or a compound ovary within the flower. If there are several separate carpels in the flower, an *aggregate* fruit is formed; in the raspberry there is an aggregation of many drupes. A *multiple* fruit arises when the fruits developed from separate flowers remain united, as in the mulberry and pineapple.

PLANT PHYSIOLOGY

ABSORPTION OF WATER AND NUTRIENTS. Active living plants contain a high percentage of water, and every growing plant must in some way be in contact with a water supply. While the seaweeds and floating algae are surrounded by water, the land plants have had to develop specialized structures, the roots, to penetrate the soil in search of moisture.

In such complex plants the cell walls are in close contact; and thus, although the leaf cells may be many feet from the absorbing roots, the distribution of water is so perfect that there is indirect water contact with the soil through long chains of tissue cells.

Each cell takes its water from some other cell or conducting vessel nearer the constant supply. Unless a plant contains a quantity of dead tissue, as in trees or shrubs, the water content is usually 75 percent to 80 percent of its weight.

Chemical Nutrients. Plants contain the chemical elements carbon, hydrogen, oxygen, nitrogen, phosphorus, sulfur, potassium, calcium, magnesium, and iron. Carbon, hydrogen, and oxygen enter into the composition of the carbohydrates as starch, cellulose, and dextrins. Proteins contain these same three elements, plus nitrogen, and minute traces of phosphorus and sulfur. In addition to these ten elements, minute traces of copper, manganese, boron, and zinc have been found to be necessary for plant growth.

Carbon, in the form of carbon dioxide, and oxygen are obtained mainly from the air; the other elements, usually in the form of nitrates, phosphates, and sulfates, are obtained in solution from the soil.

Absorption and Conduction. All the elements except carbon and oxygen, as well as the vital water molecules in which these elements are dissolved, must somehow be absorbed by the roots and carried, sometimes hundreds of feet, upward through the stem or trunk to the leaves. This task, which is actually an extraordinary and complex chemical and physical process, begins in the single-celled root hairs.

The walls of the root-hair cells are made up of *semipermeable membranes* that permit the passage of liquids from a less dense to a more dense solution, a process known as *osmosis.* Since the protoplasm inside the cells is of greater density than the water outside, the root cells absorb water; the cells become *turgid* from the increasing water content, and *root pressure* then forces the water up into the stem. However, this force is not strong enough to raise water more than a few inches off the ground.

The force that moves the nutrient-laden water up to the leaves is actually a form of suction and results from the plant's loss of water vapor through its leaves *(transpiration).* Thus, the actual force that draws the water upward is the great absorptive capacity of the dry, waterless air surrounding the plant.

Transpiration. The water and mineral nutrients absorbed by the roots are conducted through the xylem to the leaves, where they are utilized in food production. A large proportion of water absorbed is there transpired through millions of small pores, or *stomata,* on the leaf surfaces, which open or close according to the water pressure in surrounding cells.

PHOTOSYNTHESIS. *Photosynthesis* is the unique process of green plants in which they manufacture not only their own food, but also the food for all higher organisms. The raw materials are carbon dioxide from the air and water from the soil; the energy for the process is obtained from sunlight.

Photosynthesis takes place in the chlorophyll-bearing part of the living cells. Since most green cells are found in the leaf, the latter is the principal site of photosynthesis. The chief product synthesized is sugar; oxygen is given off.

Leaves are thin, broad, expanded structures and thus expose a large surface for the absorption of sunlight. The carbon dioxide necessary for photosynthesis enters the leaf through the same pores that function in transpiration, the stomata. The number of stomata varies greatly in different plants. Sometimes they are confined to one surface of the leaf; in other cases they are found on both.

FOOD STORAGE AND DIGESTION. The sugar manufactured in the leaves and other green portions of the plant may be stored temporarily in the form of starch. Most of it is soon transported to other parts of the plant, where it is utilized for building up the plant tissues. Some of it is used in the synthesis of proteins, which are manufactured in any living plant cell; the nitrogen for the proteins is derived from salts absorbed through the roots.

The legumes, such as peas and clover, are able to utilize the free nitrogen of the air through the presence of certain bacteria, called *nitrogen-fixing bacteria,* that develop characteristic nodules on the roots of these plants.

Much of the organic material manufactured during the growing season is stored as carbohydrates, fats, and proteins in the seeds and fruits, tuber, and roots. Upon the return of growing conditions, the plant utilizes this stored material; but, before it can do this, it must change it from an insoluble form to a soluble form for transportation. This is the process of *digestion* and is carried out by means of enzymes.

RESPIRATION. The plant must have a supply of energy in order to carry on the various life processes. This energy

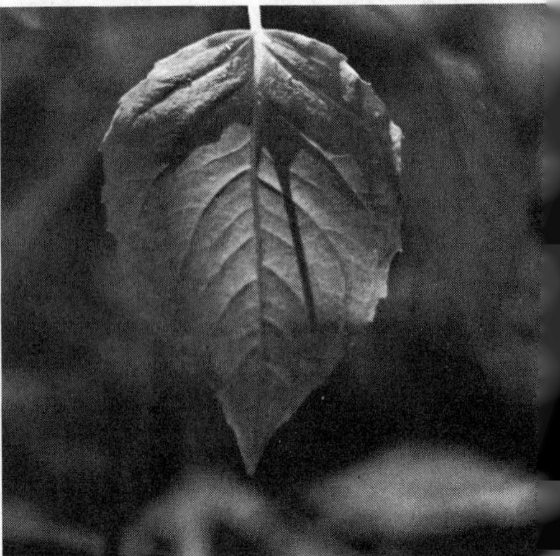

HELEN BUTTFIELD

SUNLIGHT AND AIR surround the growing, green leaf. Within the leaf, the mysterious processes of life are carried on; these include: respiration, transpiration, and the chemical transformations of photosynthesis.

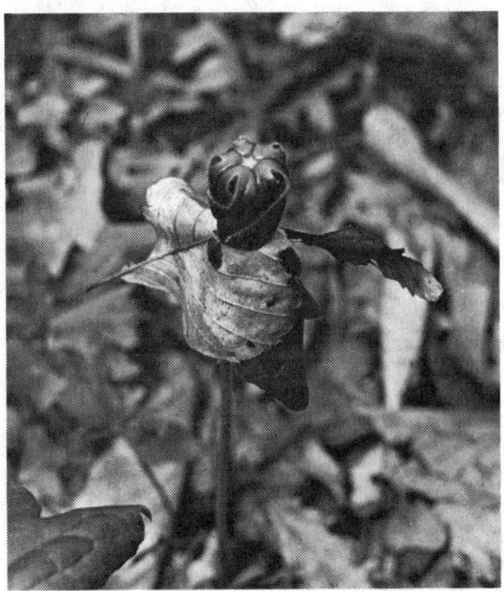

HELEN BUTTFIELD

PUSHING UP through the dead leaves in the forest, the young May apple will break free, expanding in a delicate umbrella. Tendrils uncoiling toward the light exemplify every plant's constant growth.

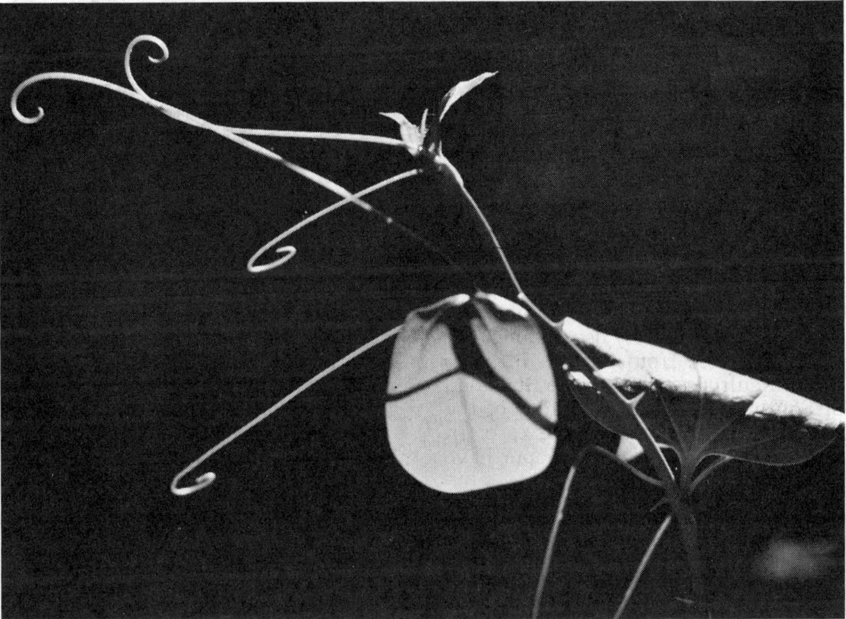

comes from the breaking down of the complex organic compounds within the cell; most of these breakdowns are associated with *respiration.*

It is a common mistake to confuse photosynthesis and respiration. Respiration is the same in green plants, nongreen plants, and animals. The chief end product of respiration is carbon dioxide, but one of the end products of photosynthesis is oxygen.

ASSIMILATION. The final conversion of carbohydrates, fats, and proteins into living material (protoplasm) is called *assimilation,* a process whose inner working still eludes the scientists' grasp. Very little is known except that assimilation can take place only where life already exists.

Since assimilation is the process by which living, organic protoplasm is created out of nonliving, inorganic materials, the problem of its mechanics is very close to the mystery of life itself.

STIMULUS AND RESPONSE. One of the basic characteristics of living matter is a property known as *irritability.* It is this that enables living protoplasm to be stimulated by outside forces and to respond to them, either positively or negatively. Without this capacity to respond to outside stimuli, no organism could live and grow. Although plants are less sensitive than animals in some respects, there are many stimuli to which they respond quickly and intensely.

Tropisms. In general, the most important stimulus to almost all plants is light, and their response to it is called *phototropism.* If a sunflower seedling, for example, is illuminated from one side, the stem will bend and the plant grow toward the source of light. This bending is the result of the concentration of auxin, a growth-stimulating hormone, on the side of the stem away from the light. Since the cells on that side grow more rapidly they force the stem to bend gradually toward the light. *Mimosa pudica* and certain other legumes close their leaves when they are placed in darkness and expand them when moved to the light.

Another important though invisible force is the pull of the earth itself. If a seedling is laid horizontally in the dark, the stem will grow upward and the root will bend and grow downward; both growths are in response to the influence of gravity and are, respectively, negative and positive forms of *geotropism.* Roots are also sensitive to the closeness of water and will grow toward it; this is known as *hydrotropism.*

Other Motions. Movements called *turgor movements* are responses of certain plants to light, temperature, and touch, and are usually more rapid than the tropisms. The leaves of clover fold up at night in *sleep movements;* the leaves of the mimosa will fold and droop on being touched; and the specialized leaves of the Venus's flytrap are extremely sensitive to contact, closing to entrap any insect that lights on them.

Photoperiodism. A recent development in physiology is the discovery of *photoperiodism,* the effect of the daily duration of light exposure on reproductive activity. Some plants are *short-day* plants that require brief periods of light in order to reach the flowering stage; others are *long-day* plants and flower only when they are exposed to long periods of light.

PLANT GROWTH. Growth is a familiar characteristic of all living organisms and a vital one for plants, for, unlike animals, when plants cease to grow, they will soon die. Growth is closely related to movement, which is obvious in the slow upward growth of the young seedling, less apparent in the steady spiraling motion made by growing shoots and even by roots.

Germination. Within each seed is a dormant embryo plant, conceived and nurtured on the parent plant, then dispersed and arrested in its growth until it finds the conditions necessary to renew its activity. Primary among these conditions are warmth and water, although other factors will also affect the chances of germination. Most seeds are able to withstand fairly long periods of inactivity before germinating—some up to 2,000 years, as in the case of certain lotus seeds.

When water permeates the hard seed coat, it permeates the cells, expanding their length up to one hundred times. The root of the sprouting plant emerges, the cells growing actively at the tip. Behind the tip, the cells elongate rapidly, continually increasing the length of the root.

As soon as the cells in any zone cease elongating, root hairs develop to establish the vital connection with the soil and water. The same elongation takes place in the stem until the young seedling is formed. Further growth requires new cells produced by cell division, which takes place in the *meristematic zone* at the tip of both stem and root.

Growth Regulation. The hormone *auxin,* present in the growing tips, has been shown to control growth in the young stem and root. This growth is precisely regulated, for each plant has a certain pattern that it must follow. Buds are formed and the leaves set out at exact and regular intervals, and modifications of the various parts are controlled to produce the proper structures when and where they are needed.

Growth rate, as well as form, is a function of the specific inheritance of the plant and of the favorableness of the environment. The bamboo grows with great rapidity, the oak and the bristlecone pine with extreme slowness; the maximum relative-growth rate of each is highest with adequate sunlight, warmth, moisture, and soil nutrients.

Every structure, organ, or individual plant has growth characteristics peculiar to itself and different requirements as to growth conditions. Therefore, some plants grow primarily in the spring or in midsummer; some grow in all seasons.

—Helen Buttfield

GROWING PLANTS

At first, people merely used plants that were available from nature. In some human cultures, such as the Bushmen of South Africa or the Tasaday of the Philippines, this is still the case. In most cultures, however, people have taken over in part from nature and have grown plants for thousands of years. The first experiments with growing plants probably took place about 10,000 years ago in the Near East—possibly in what is now Turkey or Syria. The "invention" of agriculture occurred independently in several other places as well, notably in Southeast Asia and in Mexico. From these centers, the idea spread through most of the world.

Reasons for Growing Plants

The main reason that the growing of plants spread so far is that plants are used for food. Plants are food not only for mankind, but also for that other "invention" of early human beings—domesticated animals. With domesticated plants and animals as the basis of their economy, farmers could develop enough food to feed large populations. The latest theories of archaeologists say that increases in population led to agriculture. Agriculture could sustain larger populations than could hunting animals and gathering plants.

Some plants that are not, strictly speaking, food plants are also grown. These plants include herbs and spices, grown for flavor, and various flora grown for their chemical effect on human bodies. In the latter category are tobacco, coffee, opium, and many beneficial drugs. The line between food plants and plants grown for flavor or medicinal purposes is often hard to detect. For example, the tomato supplies a lot of Vitamin C, but not very much in the way of food energy (which is measured in calories). Because it is an essential flavor in many dishes, people think of a tomato as food rather than as a drug or herb.

Plants are attractive and useful in other ways. A large tree in a yard provides shade for a house, and it makes the yard look better. Small plants near a house look nicer than the foundations of the house do. Using plants for these purposes is called landscaping. Although the idea of formal landscaping is quite recent—about as old as the United States in Western society—informal landscaping and gardening have been practiced by plant growers for thousands of years.

If plants look nice growing outdoors, then why not bring them in the house too? While houses with central courtyards could have plants, it was not until the development of glass windows that house plants could become a regular part of many people's lives.

THE YARD OR TERRACE OF A SMALL HOUSE *can be improved by careful landscaping.*

HALSTED WELLES

Principles of Plant Growing

The basic difference between plants and animals is that most plants obtain their energy from sunlight, but most animals must seek other sources. Therefore, depriving a plant of light is equivalent to depriving a pet bird of food. Almost all plants require an adequate amount of sunlight or other light. They use this light, water, and carbon dioxide to make food. This is called photosynthesis. (Fungi, such as mushrooms, are usually classed as plants, but they do not obtain energy from light.) In the absence of sunlight, fluorescent lamps provide plants with the kind of light they need. Incandescent lamps, however, are a poor substitute for sunlight, unless they are specially modified to be used for growing plants.

Like most other living things, plants require air and water. Supplying air is seldom difficult, but keeping a proper supply of water for each plant is often a troublesome problem for the plant grower. If the plants are growing outside, then drought must often be coped with. If the plants are inside, inattention or a vacation away from home can produce an indoor drought.

It is easy for a plant to get too much of a good thing. Many plants cannot grow in full sunlight. Almost all plants—except those accustomed to growing in swamps or similar conditions—cannot live with too much water around their roots for long.

While the basic growth process of plants involves just light, air, and water, many functions of plant growth are based on chemicals that plants get from the soil or some other source. For example, like animals, plants use proteins for many purposes. Proteins cannot be made without nitrogen. Plants that cannot get an adequate supply of nitrogen will not grow vigorously. Their leaves may also turn yellow. Although air is almost 80 percent nitrogen, plants have no direct way to take the nitrogen from the air. Some plants, such as peas, beans, and clover, have developed relationships with bacteria that can take the nitrogen from the air and put it into a usable form for plants.

Two other chemical elements are needed in substantial quantities by most plants—phosphorus and potassium. Potassium is often called potash, a name that refers to the potassium compound found in wood ashes. Nitrogen, phosphorus, and potassium percentages are identified—in that order—for most fertilizers. For example, a fertilizer that is labeled 10-5-10 is 10 percent nitrogen compounds, 5 percent phosphorus compounds, and 10 percent potash, or potassium compounds. A 10-5-10 fertilizer is usually a chemical fertilizer, meaning that people made the compounds in it. Most organic fertilizers, which are rock dust or animal or plant wastes, do not contain such a high percentage of nitrogen, phosphorus, and potassium compounds.

On the other hand, organic fertilizers are more likely than chemical fertilizers to contain elements that plants need in very small amounts. These elements, called trace elements, are usually not put into chemical fertilizers. Trace elements include calcium, magnesium, boron, manganese, sulfur, iron, and zinc. If any of these are missing from the soil and not added by the grower, the plants will not grow well.

In addition to having the right chemicals in the soil, the soil must not be too acid or too alkaline for the kind of plants being grown. Some plants, such as rhododendrons and blueberries, grow better in very acid soil, but most plants grow better when the soil is just slightly acid. A few plants, such as cabbages and carnations, grow best when the soil is not acid at all. The acidity of any substance is measured by a number called the *p*H. The lower the number, the more acid the soil. A *p*H of 7.0 is neither acid nor alkaline. Most plants grow best when the *p*H is between 6.0 and 7.0.

People who grow plants pay a lot of attention to the soil. Soil that is in good shape will hold water for the time that a plant needs it. It will also let air get through to the roots, and will contain abundant nitrogen, phosphorus, and potassium, as well as small amounts of many other necessary minerals. The correct *p*H for the plants to be grown will also be present.

For most plants, the soil fills another need. It provides the medium that the plant uses to keep upright. The plant must arrange itself so that it can receive the sunlight that it uses for energy. Most plants do this by anchoring themselves in the soil and growing up on stems. Others climb in various ways. Such plants, which are vines, need something to climb on if they are to grow properly.

Starting Plants from Seed

Most plants that people grow are flowering plants, which means that they produce flowers and seeds. Every plant that flowers can be grown from seed, although not all are grown that way. Even plants that are not thought of as flowering plants must have flowers if they have seeds. For example, people usually eat lettuce before it flowers, carrots live two years and flower only in the second year, and many ornamental house plants are kept under conditions that prevent them from blooming. Still, these are all flowering plants, grown from seeds (the cheapest and best way to obtain most plants, though many perennial flowers are bought as plants).

Very small seeds may be mixed with sand or coffee grounds to make them easier to handle. Very large seeds may have coverings that are so thick that seedlings will have difficulty getting through them. Large seeds, such as squash or sunflower seeds, may start better if a small nick is cut in them to give the seedlings a better chance.

The key process in starting a seed is called germination, which means "sprouting." Germination occurs when the seedling emerges from the seed. It is usually triggered by moisture. Seeds can often sprout in a jar with a small amount of water or in a damp cloth. People often sprout beans or other seeds to get the sprouts to eat, but the same method can be used to sprout seeds for planting. Sometimes seeds that do not germinate well are sprouted before they are planted.

It is generally more convenient to get seeds to germinate in soil. If you are starting seeds indoors, it is best to use special starting soils (available from plant stores) or artificial soil substitutes, such as vermiculite or perlite. Such sterilized soils will not contain weed seeds and will help minimize fungus diseases. Also, they are formulated to hold moisture well, which improves the rate of germination.

In general, seeds are most easily started indoors in "flats." A good homemade flat is a milk carton that has been cut in half lengthwise. Holes should be punched in the bottom for drainage. Fill the flat nearly to the top with starting soil. Plant the seeds an inch or two apart—or nearer for very small seeds. Do not plant seeds too deeply. They should be about as deep as each seed is long. Water the soil by letting the flat stand in a pan of water until the surface of the starting soil is moist. Then store the flat out of direct sunlight for a few days. When seedlings begin to emerge from the soil, move the flat to a place where the seedlings can get a good supply of sunlight or fluorescent light.

Outside, the matter is simpler. Watering after the seeds are planted is often enough to insure germination. A few seeds, such as parsley and carrot seeds, do not germinate very easily. Germination of these seeds can be improved by pouring boiling water over the ground after the seeds have been planted.

BARRY FEIG

HEALTHY SEEDLINGS *growing indoors under fluorescent lighting.*

Seedlings growing indoors need continuing care. Unless it is possible to give the seedlings access to strong sunlight, they should be placed a few inches from fluorescent lamps. Otherwise, they will grow too tall and weak. When the seedlings begin to look like adult plants (that is, when their first leaves are replaced by two or three leaves of the adult type), the indoor plants must be transplanted. Each plant should be moved from its flat to an individual pot filled with starting soil. (Small paper cups with holes punched in the bottom make good, inexpensive pots.) In both the flats and the pots, the plants must be kept watered, but the soil cannot be allowed to actually become wet. Wet soil promotes a fungus disease called damping off that can kill a whole flat overnight.

Plants that have been grown inside cannot be planted directly in a garden. First they must get used to conditions outdoors, including cold, more intense light, and wind. Before planting them, leave them outside in fine weather for a few days. At first, they should be out for only an hour or so. The time can be increased until they are set outside permanently. This process is called hardening off, and it is essential to a plant's proper growth after it has been transplanted into a garden.

Other Ways to Start Plants

While most plants for an outdoor garden are started from seed, house plants, and some outdoor plants, are often started in other ways.

Division. Unlike most higher animals, most plants can grow back parts that have been cut off. Thus, one good way to get new plants from old is to cut them in half vertically, through the roots. Sometimes a plant can be cut, or divided, into several smaller plants. Older plants often need such a division to restore lost vigor.

Cuttings. Taking a cutting is a less drastic operation than division. A small branch of an adult plant, or even just a leaf, can be made to grow into a new plant. All it needs to form roots is a good supply of water, though a commercial starting powder will help. When roots have formed, the cutting can be planted. The parts of plants that were growing vigorously usually form roots the most easily.

Layering. A part of a plant that is brought into contact with moist earth often develops roots. If the part is then cut from the parent plant, a new plant will grow independently. When you want to encourage such a development, bury a small portion of a branch in the ground, with the tip of the branch above ground. This process is called layering.

Air layering. When a plant is not flexible enough for layering, the same effect can be obtained by wrapping a part of the branch in moist earth. Even though the branch may be several feet from the ground, it will soon develop roots in the earth that is wrapped around it. The branch can then be cut off the parent plant. The roots will continue to develop when the branch has been planted with its new roots in the ground.

Bulbs and other ways to start plants. Many plants store energy underground in parts of the plant called bulbs, rhizomes, or tubers. To plant these underground storage compartments is the best way to start new plants of the same type. Such plants include tulips, onions, irises, and potatoes. Put the storage compartment in the soil at the proper depth. In the spring, or when conditions are right, the plant will emerge from its storage compartment.

Outdoor Gardening

While the basic principles of growing plants apply to any situation, there are special considerations involved in growing plants either outdoors or indoors.

Although some kinds of plants will grow in almost any soil, the flowers, vegetables, herbs, and grasses that you are most likely to want to grow need improved soil. It is a good idea to test the soil first, to find out what its *p*H is and whether any minerals are in short supply. If you live in a part of the world that has fairly abundant rainfall, the chances are that the soil will be on the acid side. This can be corrected by adding ground limestone (known to gardeners as lime, but not to be confused with the caustic lime used in some manufacturing processes). Other deficiencies can easily be made up by using chemical or organic fertilizers.

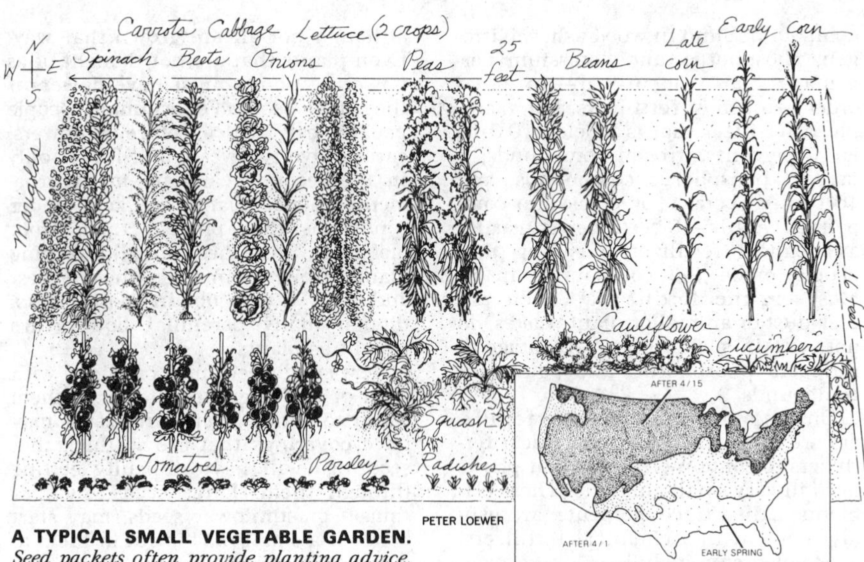

A TYPICAL SMALL VEGETABLE GARDEN.
Seed packets often provide planting advice.

Compost.

Most soils can be greatly improved by the addition of organic materials—that is, plant or animal wastes. For efficient use of these wastes, it is better for them to decay to a stable substance before they are added to the garden. This stable substance is called compost. Although it is possible to buy compost at a garden store, the process of making it in your own "compost pile" is useful in itself, for it recycles many lawn and garden wastes that would otherwise have to be removed.

Any dead plant matter can be used to make compost, for example, grass clippings, leaves, and weeds. Wood, however, will take a long time to decay unless it is chopped into very small pieces. Decay proceeds best when the materials are slightly moist (but not so wet as to keep air out), and when there is the right balance between the carbon that forms the tissues of the plant and the nitrogen compounds. Usually there is too much carbon, so animal manure or fertilizer is added to the plant wastes to provide more nitrogen. Some wastes, such as grass clippings, have too much nitrogen. Then dead leaves can be mixed in to produce better compost, faster.

Generally, compost is made in a bin in layers. It may take a year for the wastes to become stable compost—a brown substance that shows few traces of its origin. This time can be shortened by mixing the pile every so often so that the outside part becomes the center and the former center is put outside. This mixing operation is called turning the compost pile.

Preparing soil.

In the spring, in much of the country, the soil may be too wet to dig. In that case, wait until it has dried to the point where a ball of soil will shatter when dropped.

Digging is useful for removing any rocks larger than a hen's egg from the soil. Loosening the soil makes it easier to plant some seeds and to work fertilizer or lime into the soil.

Digging can be overdone, however. Only the topsoil should be dug up and turned over. When the soil below the top layer changes color, you are beneath the topsoil. In that case, you are digging too deep.

Compost can be added as the soil is being dug, but unless you have a very large supply of it, you would be better off using compost only where you are actually putting the plants.

Planting.

The proper time for plants or seeds to go outdoors depends on where you live. The United States is divided into ten climate zones that range from Zone 1, with an average winter temperature below −50° F, to Zone 10, where it rarely ever freezes, even in the depths of winter. It is a good idea to study the information on seed packets to make sure that your plants are suited to the weather in your area.

Seeds should be sown at the right depth for their size. A common mistake is to put seeds too deep into the ground. For very small seeds, you can put them on top of the ground and sprinkle them with a small amount of compost or dirt.

Plants that have been started inside can be transplanted into holes that have been partially filled with compost. Most plants need to keep the same depth in the ground as they are used to in their pots. A few, including tomatoes and their relatives, do better if they are planted deeper outdoors than they were planted in their pots.

Distances that should be left between plants are given on seed packets. When starting seeds, plant somewhat closer than you need, in case some seeds do not germinate. Plants that are too close are removed when they begin to get crowded. This process is known as thinning.

Mulches. When plants have been growing for a few weeks, they will benefit from having a protective cover on the ground around them. Such a cover is called a mulch. A mulch protects the plant in several ways: by preventing evaporation, the mulch keeps the soil moist, insuring a more even water supply; by shading the soil, it prevents weeds from growing that would compete with your plants. Such shading also gives the plants' roots a more stable environment. If the mulch is made of plant materials, it will work itself into the soil as compost.

Some common mulches include seed hulls, wood chips, hay and straw, newspapers covered with grass clippings, stones, and black plastic. Each has advantages and disadvantages. The kind to use would depend on the kind of garden to be made. Hay or straw might be suitable for a vegetable garden, but wood chips would look better in a rose garden.

Pests. Pests ranging from bacteria to raccoons attack garden plants. The best defense against most pests is to grow plants that are resistant to them, and to make sure that the plants have a good supply of water and minerals. In that way, the plants' natural defenses are most effective. For larger pests, such as rabbits or deer, you may need a fence.

Perennials. A plant that lives more than two years is called a perennial. Many flowers and herbs, and a few vegetables, are perennials. Because they will stay in the same place year after year, the soil needs to be prepared very carefully for them. They should get much more compost when they are planted than shorter-lived plants. Some perennials, such as rhubarbs and irises, may need to be divided every few years. Others, such as roses or thyme, may need to be protected in winter.

Trees and Shrubs

When a perennial is woody and fairly big, it is often called a shrub. If it is bigger still, especially if it has just one stem, it is a tree. There is no sharp dividing line. Trees and shrubs need special care when they are planted, since they will be in the same spot for many years. Some trees and shrubs also need the cutting of some branches each year. This is called pruning.

Young trees need protection from the sun because trees are not accustomed to places where there is no shade. In the summer, trees shade themselves for part of the day. In the winter, when the leaves are gone from most trees, the bright sun can be harmful to the bark. The tree can be protected by wrapping paper or cloth around its trunk for the winter.

Some animals, including rabbits and mice, will eat bark in the winter, especially from a young tree. A wire mesh protector that reaches a few inches above the expected snow line is a good idea.

The roots of a tree you have bought may not be the same kind of plant as the rest of it. Such trees have been deliberately made that way by a process called grafting. Grafting is used for many purposes. For example, apple trees grown from seed are usually not much like the parent tree. But a part of an apple tree can be grafted to the roots of a wild apple, and that part will grow to be a whole tree exactly like the one from which it came. Sometimes a particular kind of root is resistant to a pest or produces dwarfing in the tree that is grafted to it. These can be desirable properties. For example, many people do not have room for a full-sized fruit tree. But they have room for a dwarf tree.

After trees or shrubs are planted, it is just as important to keep them properly fertilized as it is for any other perennial. For example, lilacs grow best in soil that is not very acid and that is rich in potash. Therefore, it is a good idea to spread wood ashes (from a fireplace, for instance) around a lilac each spring. Mountain laurels, on the other hand, like very acid soil, and may need a chemical that will make the soil more acid, such as sulfur.

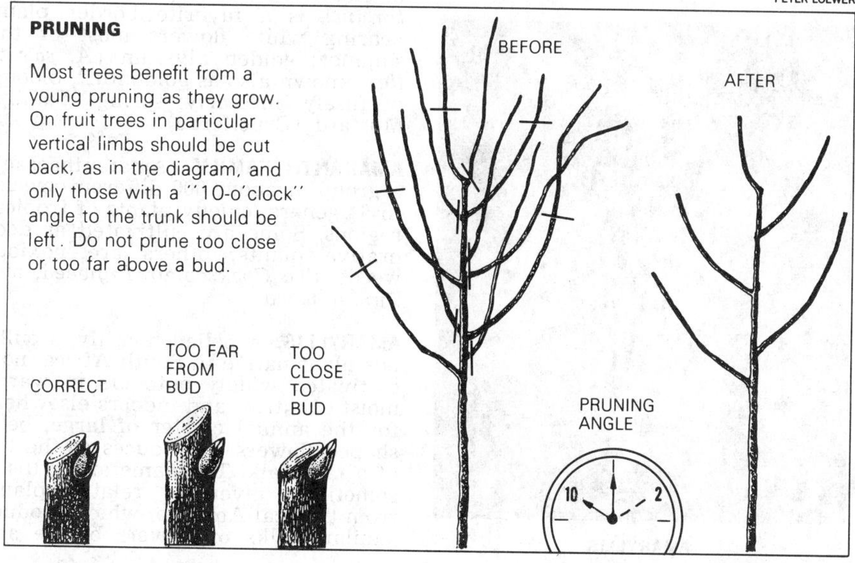

PRUNING

Most trees benefit from a young pruning as they grow. On fruit trees in particular vertical limbs should be cut back, as in the diagram, and only those with a "10-o'clock" angle to the trunk should be left. Do not prune too close or too far above a bud.

House Plants

Indoor conditions are not a natural environment for plants. Most houses are dark, dry, and too hot—conditions that are not exactly found anywhere in nature. There are steps to take to improve a plant's environment. South-facing windows get almost all of the sun; north-facing windows do not get much at all. Humidity can be raised by putting a plant on a tray that is filled with marbles and with water up to the top of the marbles. Even heat can be controlled by keeping the plant on a porch or next to a window in winter. The essential thing is to imitate the plant's natural environment as much as possible.

There may be other problems with indoor plants, such as difficulties with soil. It is best to use imitation soil of some sort with house plants, rather than soil fresh from the garden. Potting soil, as the soil used for indoor plants is called, can be made sterile to eliminate weeds and diseases. Potting soil can be bought or made. The easiest way to make your own is to sterilize garden soil over a charcoal grill for several hours. Then mix the sterilized soil with vermiculite, two parts soil to one vermiculite.

Some plants need a lot of space for their roots. These will need to be repotted as they grow. Others do better when they are "pot-bound"—that is, when their roots take up much of the space in the pot. If you are not sure about a particular plant, it is a good idea to check with a florist or a standard reference book on house plants.

Even though potting soil has been sterilized, there are still some kinds of pests that may attack your house plants. If you find that insects are eating a house plant, a good way to discourage them is to dip the entire plant (except the pot) into a sink or bathtub that has been filled with lukewarm water with a mild detergent, such as dishwashing liquid. If this fails, you may have to use poisons.

The ideal way to grow house plants is to have a greenhouse. It is particularly useful to have a greenhouse that is attached to your house, for the greenhouse can also be a free source of heat for the house. This is because the sun's heat builds up inside the greenhouse during the day. A fan can move the heat to the rest of the house and keep the greenhouse at a better temperature for plants at the same time.

PLANTS

ABACÁ, an important plant native to the Philippine Islands, cultivated for the long strong fibers in its leaves. Known as Manila hemp, the fibers are 6 to 12 feet in length and are used in better grades of rope and cable because they wear well and do not easily jam or kink in pulleys.

Abacá bears 12 to 20 clusters of leaf stalks, each 15 to 25 feet tall, from which large, undivided leaves rise. It requires a warm, damp climate and deep, rich soil. Attempts to introduce its culture into other tropical islands and into America have largely failed. Family: Banana (Musaceae); genus and species *Musa textilis.*

ACACIA, a large genus consisting of about 500 different kinds of woody shrubs and trees, found mostly in warm climates throughout the world. Acacias have pinnately compound or featherlike leaves, clusters of small, yellow or white flowers, and, usually, long, sharp thorns. Those of Australia are called wattles. An African species yields gum arabic. An Indian species, called cutch, provided the original dye for khaki cloth. Family: Pea (Leguminosae).

ACANTHUS, a genus consisting of about 25 different kinds of handsome, thorny shrubs native to the tropics and subtropics of the Old World. Their leaves are usually broad, shiny, and deeply notched.

Acanthus flowers are in spikes, generally white, purple, or red. They are familiar because they were the models used by the ancient Greeks and Romans for decorative designs on architectural columns. In Christian painting and sculpture the acanthus leaf often symbolizes heaven. Family: Acanthus (Acanthaceae).

ACONITE, any of about 75 different kinds of hardy, perennial herbs found in mountain regions of the North Temperate Zone. They have palmate leaves, ornamental, yellow or purplish-blue flowers, and a dangerous poison in all parts. The uppermost sepal is helmetlike, giving these plants the common name of monkshood.

The European yellow aconite is called wolfsbane; it is cultivated as a garden plant and for medicinal purposes. The drug derived from it can be used in small doses as a sedative for certain respiratory and cardiac ailments. Family: Buttercup (Ranunculaceae); genus *Aconitum.*

AGAVE. See *Century Plant.*

AGERATUM, or flossflower, a genus of about 30 different kinds of tropical American herbs with opposite leaves and flowers in small, tassel-like, clustered heads. *A. mexicana,* the most easily grown as a border plant, is usually blue, but it may be white or rose-colored. Family: Daisy (Compositae).

AGRIMONY, any of about 10 different kinds of coarse, perennial herbs native to temperate regions of Eurasia, North America, Brazil, and South Africa. The pointed and toothed leaflets on the pinnately compound leaves are generally of several sizes on a single leaf. Small, yellow flowers grow in stiff spikes at the top of the 2- to 4-foot stems and develop seeds enclosed in a spiny bur. Family: Rose (Rosaceae); genus *Agrimonia.*

AKEE, or vegetable brain, a tropical African tree that grows to 40 feet; its fruit, which is straw-colored to magenta, is also called akee. The fruit is about 3 inches long and encloses 3 shiny, spherical seeds to which are attached a corresponding number of spongy, ivory-white arils.

At exactly the correct stage of ripeness, the arils can be cooked to make a delicious vegetable with a nutty flavor. At any other stage, the whole fruit is deadly poisonous. Cultivation of the akee is forbidden in the United States, but it is a favorite food tree in Jamaica and some other Caribbean areas. Family: Soapberry (Sapindaceae); genus and species, *Blighia sapida.*

ALDER, any of about 20 different kinds of small, deciduous trees with toothed leaves and conelike fruits, most of which are native to the North Temperate Zone, although some are found south along the Andes. Alders usually grow in swamps and along the edges of streams.

The alder's wood is soft and unsuited for construction purposes, but has been used for turning and in making charcoal. Yellow, red, and brown dyes are obtained from the wood, and the bark is a source of tannin. Family: Birch (Betulaceae); genus *Alnus.*

ALFALFA, or lucerne, one of the world's leading forage plants for cattle, probably native to southwestern Asia or southeastern Europe, but now grown extensively in the United States. Its roots grow very deep, helping the plant to resist drought.

Alfalfa leaves have a high content of protein, and they can be dried to form an alfalfa meal. The flowers are small, purple, and followed by a twisted pod resembling a snail shell. Family: Pea (Leguminosae); genus and species, *Medicago sativa.*

BURPEE SEEDS

AMARYLLIS

ALLIGATOR PEAR. See *Avocado.*

ALLSPICE, or Jamaica pepper, or pimento, a small evergreen tree of the West Indies with fragrant, leathery leaves; the spice that is made from its fruits, which are picked unripe and cured by artificial heat, is also called allspice. The flavor seems to combine and suggest those of cinnamon, clove, and nutmeg. Jamaica and Grenada are the most important sources of allspice. Family: Myrtle (Myrtaceae); genus and species, *Pimenta officinalis.*

ALMOND, a small tree native to central Asia, but now cultivated extensively around the Mediterranean and in California for its seeds, which resemble those of a peach and develop similarly inside a stony covering coated with a soft flesh and outer skin. The blossoms of the almond are beautiful, suggesting those of the peach and cherry trees, to which the almond is related.

Bitter almonds are often used for flavoring extracts; at one time they were the chief source of the poison called prussic acid, which is chiefly hydrocyanic acid. Sweet almonds are used in candy and desserts; horticultural varieties are hard-shelled, soft-shelled, and paper-shelled. Family: Rose (Rosaceae); genus and species, *Prunus amygdalus.*

ALOE, a genus consisting of about 200 different kinds of shrubby or treelike perennial plants with succulent leaves in dense rosettes either at the ground or the ends of the branches. They are native chiefly to South Africa, particularly to the Karroo deserts, where local people have learned to use them to make tonics, purgatives, and dyes. Family: Lily (Liliaceae).

ALYSSUM, a genus containing about 100 different kinds of herbs native to Europe and west-central Asia, mostly with fragrant, white or yellow flowers in clusters. Sweet alyssum *(A. maritimum)* is a favorite border plant, bearing white flowers most of the summer; golden alyssum *(A. saxatile),* known also as goldentuft, blooms profusely in early spring. Family: Mustard (Cruciferae).

AMARANTH FAMILY (Amaranthaceae), a group of about 800 different species in 64 genera, chiefly plants of tropical regions. Some are cultivated as decorative plants; others are noxious weeds. See *Cockscomb, Pigweed,* and *Tumbleweed.*

AMARYLLIS, or belladonna lily, a bulbous plant native to South Africa, now cultivated widely outdoors in warm, moist countries and indoors elsewhere for the annual cluster of large, bell-shaped flowers it produces at the top of a tall stalk. The name amaryllis is sometimes given to related plants from tropical America, which produce similar stalks of flowers before any leaves appear. Family: Amaryllis (Amaryllidaceae); genus and species, *A. belladonna.*

AMARYLLIS FAMILY (Amaryllidaceae), a group of about 1300 different species in 90 genera, many of them highly adapted for survival in arid parts of tropical and subtropical regions. See *Amaryllis, Century Plant, Narcissus, Rose of Sharon, Sisal, Snowdrop,* and *Tuberose.*

ANEMONE, a genus of about 100 different kinds of perennial herbs, mostly from the North Temperate Zone, but some from the Andes. They produce divided leaves from the base of the plant and showy flowers with sepals but no petals.

The delicate, starlike flower of the wood anemone, or windflower *(A. quinquefolia),* is characteristic of early spring in North American forests. The European pasque-flower *(A. pulsatilla)* and American pasque-flower *(A. patens)* bloom before the leaves expand. The blood-red poppy anemone *(A. coronaria)* grows in the open on rocky ground all around the Mediterranean Sea. Family: Buttercup (Ranunculaceae).

ANISE, an aromatic herb of eastern Mediterranean countries, raised for its seeds and the oil that can be obtained from them. The seeds are used for flavoring in condiments, candy, and cheese, and for making a liqueur. The oil is helpful in hiding the unpleasant flavor of medicines and in adding fragrance to soap and some perfumes. The leaves can be used for seasoning and garnishing. Family: Carrot (Umbelliferae); genus and species, *Pimpinella anisum.*

APPLE, any of a large number of different horticultural varieties of fruit trees native to the North Temperate Zone. The greenish-gray, oval leaves grow thickly on the spreading branches, making a pleasant shade tree. In early spring it bears small clusters of beautiful, 5-petalled blossoms that are white, tinged with pink.

The fruits ripen in summer. Each is round, reddish or yellow outside, with a central core that is star-shaped in cross section. Named varieties have been developed according to the flavor of the fruits (from sweet to sour), the color, the keeping and cooking qualities, and the normal range of sizes. Family: Rose (Rosaceae); genus and species, *Pyrus malus.*

APRICOT, a small fruit tree native to central Asia but now grown in mild, temperate climates throughout the world. The oval, orange-colored fruit has a flavor similar to that of the related peach and plum. Apricots require careful handling because they bruise easily. They are used fresh, dried, and canned. Family: Rose (Rosaceae); genus and species, *Prunus armeniaca.*

ARAUCARIA FAMILY (Araucariaceae), a group of 37 different species in 2 genera, all evergreen, coniferous trees and shrubs, mostly of the South Temperate Zone, where they are often the dominant and most valuable native timber trees. The kauri pine *(Agathis australis)* of New Zealand is important for lumber and also for Manila-copal resin, used in paints and varnishes.

The monkey puzzle tree *(Araucaria araucana)* of Chile is widely cultivated in warm countries as a curiosity because of its short, stiff leaves, which completely cover the branches. See also *Norfolk Island Pine.*

ARBOR VITAE, literally "tree of life," a small or medium-sized, cone-bearing, evergreen tree of eastern North America from Tennessee to Canada, producing small, flat, soft leaves pressed close to the stems and hiding them. Family: Cypress (Cupressaceae); genus and species, *Thuja occidentalis.*

ARBUTUS, or ground laurel, or mayflower, or trailing arbutus, a creeping plant with oval, hairy, evergreen leaves and clusters of fragrant, white or pink blossoms in early spring. It grows in light, sandy loam, but is becoming extinct or rare in many areas of New England and the eastern United States where it was formerly common because people often tear out the plants when they pick the flowers.

Arbutus is also a genus consisting of about 20 kinds of evergreen shrubs and trees native to western North America (such as the madroño, *A. menziesii,* which yields timber), Central America, and Mediterranean countries. Family: Heath (Ericaceae); genus and species, *Epigaea repens.*

T.H. EVERETT

ARBUTUS

ARNICA, a genus containing about 18 different kinds of perennial herbs, found in temperate and mountainous regions in Eurasia and North America, including mountain tobacco *(A. montana),* which has large, yellow heads of flowers. The roots and leaves of several species yield an extract used in liniments for sprains and bruises. Family: Daisy (Compositae).

ARROWHEAD, any of about 40 different kinds of marsh plants that produce ribbon-shaped leaves under water and arrowhead-shaped leaves in air. A leafless stalk bears whorls of white flowers, each with 3 white petals. American Indians and the Chinese, as well as other people in both hemispheres where arrowhead is native, dig the fleshy, tuberous roots as a source of starchy food. Family: Water plantain (Alismataceae); genus *Sagittaria.*

ARROWROOT, any of a number of distantly related and unrelated plants with large, tuberous, underground stems from which a nutritious starch similar to sago can be extracted. According to tradition, arrowroot starch is particularly easy to digest, and, therefore, is a good food for infants and invalids.

West Indian arrowroot *(Maranta arundinacea)* is a member of the arrowroot family (Marantaceae); East Indian arrowroot *(Curcuma angustifolia)* is a member of the ginger family (Zingiberaceae); Queensland arrowroot *(Canna edulis)* is a tropical American member of the canna family (Cannaceae); Portland arrowroot, from the European cuckoo-pint *(Arum maculatum),* is a member of the arum family (Araceae); Hawaiian arrowroot, or pia, is from a Polynesian, liliaceous plant *(Tacca pinnatifida)* of family Taccaceae; and Florida arrowroot, or Seminole bread, or coontie, is from a member *(Zamia floridana)* of the cycad family (Cycadaceae).

ARTICHOKE, a herbaceous plant with long, prickly leaves and an upright stem 2 to 3 feet high, bearing heavy heads of white- or violet-colored flowers, each head surrounded by edible, fleshy, green bracts. Native to Mediterranean countries, the artichoke is widely cultivated (particularly in Tunisia and California) as a source of edible bracts, which are cooked as a vegetable. The Jerusalem artichoke *(Hellanthus tuberosus)* is a North American sunflower with edible, tuberous roots. Family: Daisy (Compositae); genus and species, *Cynara scolymus.*

ARUM FAMILY (Araceae), a group of about 1500 species in 105 genera, mostly of tropical regions, including plants of marshes, woodland herbs, climbing shrubs, and perching plants with aerial roots. Although the roots, stems, and leaves vary so greatly, the flowers are clustered on a cylindrical stalk (the spadix) partly surrounded by a prominent and brightly colored, leaflike bract (the spathe). See *Arrowroot, Calla lily, Jack-in-the-pulpit, Skunk cabbage,* and *Taro.*

ASH, any of about 65 different kinds of trees 50 to 125 feet high when mature, with opposite leaves that are pinnately compound and flowers that are followed by winged seeds called samaras or ash-keys. Native to north temperate regions, ash trees are valued for shade and as a source of strong, lightweight wood. Several are grown and harvested commercially, the wood used particularly for oars, baseball bats, and tool handles. The inner bark from some yields a dyestuff. The Mediterranean flowering ash *(Fraxinus ornus)* is unusual because of its showy, white petals; most European species and all those native to North America lack petals, making the flowers inconspicuous. Family: Olive (Oleaceae); genus *Fraxinus.*

ASPARAGUS, a large genus of about 300 different kinds of herbaceous plants in which the true leaves are mere scales on the green stems at the places where short, green side-shoots, called phylloclades, arise and serve in photosynthesis. All are native to the Old World particularly Africa.

One kind of asparagus *(A. officinalis)* is cultivated for its edible young stems; when these are permitted to grow they appear feathery and produce either yellow-green, bell-shaped flowers bearing pollen, or less conspicuous, smaller flowers that mature to red berries containing seeds. Florists raise asparagus-fern *(A. plumosus)* and a related, thorny species they call smilax *(A. asparagoides)* and use as a hardy decorative material that can be added to floral bouquets. Family: Lily (Liliaceae).

ASPEN. See *Poplar.*

ASPHODEL, any of about 12 different hardy, stemless, herbaceous plants with fleshy roots, long, gray-green leaves, and tall clusters of white or yellow flowers. They are native to warmer parts of Europe and Asia, and figure prominently in Greek mythology because they were regarded as flowers of the dead. The asphodel referred to by Shakespeare and other poets of England and France is believed to have been the related daffodil. Family: Lily (Liliaceae); genus *Asphodelus.*

ASTER, a genus composed of about 600 different kinds of tall, hardy perennials native to North America, where they are particularly abundant, and to Eurasia and Africa. They characteristically bloom in autumn, bearing flowers in starlike heads varying in color from white to pink, violet, and purple. The wild aster of Britain has been hybridized with several kinds form North America to produce the handsome horticultural Michaelmas daisy, which blooms as late as Michaelmas (September 29). Family: Daisy (Compositae).

AVOCADO, or alligator pear, a medium-sized tree of the West Indies and tropical America, with thick, oval, evergreen leaves and clusters of small, greenish flowers. The avocado can be used as a shade tree, or trimmed low in cultivation so that its fruits are easy to pick. The fruit is about the size of a large pear, green or purple outside, with a thick, soft, greenish-yellow, oily pulp around a single, large, central seed.

The pulp is eaten alone or used in salads. The seeds yield a black dye. Oil from the fruit can be used in soaps and in oil lamps. While avocados are taken for granted because they are so common in the American tropics, they are prized as a delicacy in temperate regions. Family: Laurel (Lauraceae); genus and species, *Persea americana.*

U.S. DEPARTMENT OF THE INTERIOR

AZALEAS

AZALEA, any of a large number of deciduous shrubs in the vast genus *Rhododendron,* native to arctic and north temperate regions, and to tropical mountains as far south as New Guinea and Australia. The leaves are small, smooth-edged, oval, and dull-green; the flowers fragrant, funnel-shaped, and white, yellow, pink, or flame-colored. Many horticultural varieties have been developed, but the wild flame azalea *(R. calendulaceum)* of the Appalachians, and the rhodora *(R. canadense)* are highly esteemed. Family: Heath (Ericaceae); genus *Rhododendron.*

BABY'S BREATH, a fine-stemmed, narrow-leaved plant with feathery stalks of tiny pink or white flowers, characteristic of limy soil and native to Eurasia. It is widely cultivated as a perennial in gardens, where it grows to 1 to 3 feet, and is used in decorative bouquets. Family: Pink (Caryophyllaceae); genus and species, *Gypsophila paniculata.*

BACHELOR'S BUTTON. See *Cornflower.*

BALD CYPRESS, a swamp tree of the southeastern United States, that grows in water or waterlogged soil; air reaches its roots through blunt, porous, upward projections called cypress knees. Attaining a height of 150 to 170 feet, the tree sheds all of its needles in autumn and grows new needles in spring. Like the larch, the dawn redwood, and a few other conifers it is deciduous. Its wood is hard and especially valuable for shingles. Family: Bald cypress (Taxodiaceae); genus and species, *Taxodium distichum.*

BALD–CYPRESS FAMILY (Taxodiaceae), a group of about 16 species in 9 genera, all but one native to the North Temperate Zone; the exception is found in Tasmania. All are trees or shrubs with needle-like or scalelike leaves and woody cones. See *Bald Cypress, Cedar,* and *Sequoia.*

BALM, an aromatic, perennial herb with lemon-scented, paired leaves, growing 1 to 2 feet high and producing clusters of almost white flowers all summer. Native to Eurasia, it has been adopted as a garden plant and has escaped from cultivation to grow on roadsides and open woodlands. Family: Mint (Labiatae); genus and species, *Melissa officinalis.*

BALM OF GILIAD. See *Poplar.*

BALSA, or corkwood, a small tree of the West Indies, Central America, and northern South America, with palmately compound leaves, white flowers as much as 6 inches across, and the lightest wood known. The wood is used for airplane floats, for such rafts as the *Kon-Tiki,* and for model-making. Family: Bombax (Bombacaceae); genus and species, *Ochroma lagopus.*

BALSAM, or garden balsam, an erect, branching, annual herb 1 to 2½ feet in height, with succulent, pale-green branches, narrow, finely-toothed leaves, and short-stalked flowers in pastel colors ranging from white to deep crimson. Native to humid mountain valleys in northern India, it has been planted widely in gardens of temperate zones. The most popular variety is double-flowered. Family: Jewelweed (Balsaminaceae); genus and species, *Impatiens balsamina.*

BALSAM FIR. See *Fir.*

BAMBOO, any of about 200 different kinds of tall grasses bearing leaves at well-marked joints, between which the strong stems are hollow. They form dense thickets in tropical and subtropical countries, or clamber, vinelike, over trees, forming impenetrable tangles. Tallest is the giant bamboo *(Dendrocalamus giganteus)* of India and Malaysia, which attains a height of 120 feet.

Most widely cultivated is a smaller bamboo *(Bambusa vulgaris)* of Madagascar and tropical Asia, used to build bridges, houses, pipelines, and supports for climbing crops (such as beans and yams), and to make utensils of many kinds. Young bamboo shoots are cut as food for people in various countries; they are also a major part of the diet of gorillas in the Congo. Family: Grass (Gramineae).

BANANA, a tall, treelike, herbaceous plant of the Old World tropics, sometimes growing to more than 30 feet, with leaves 5 to 20 feet long. As each upright stem matures, it forms a terminal cluster of flowers that becomes pendant. As each spathelike bract of the flower bud opens, it exposes about a dozen flowers; the fruits from these ripen as a "hand" of bananas. Thus a single stem of bananas at the harvesting stage supports many hands, with the greener fruit closer to the remains of the bud. Additional stems from the same root system perpetuate the life of the plant after each stem load of fruits matures and the stem dies. Cultivated bananas have no seeds and must be propagated from cuttings of the root system. Bananas are second only to coconuts as commercial products of tropical countries. Family: Banana (Musaceae); genus and species, *Musa sapientum.*

BANANA FAMILY (Musaceae), a group of about 150 species in 5 genera, widely distributed in the tropics. Most are large herbs, often treelike, with broad leaves and a flower cluster that opens between spathelike bracts. It includes the famous traveler's-tree *(Ravenala madagascariensis)* of Madagascar, the decorative bird-of-paradise flowers *(Strelitzia* species) of South Africa, the handsome baliser (one of about 50 species of *Heliconia),* which is the national flower of Trinidad, and the various kinds of bananas. See *Abacá* and *Banana.*

BANEBERRY, any of about 12 different kinds of perennial herbs of the North Temperate Zone, growing 1½ to 2 feet tall, with coarsely toothed, compound leaves. The sepals drop from the small, fuzzy, white flowers as soon as they open. The flower clusters are soon followed by bright-red or waxy-white, poisonous berries on conspicuous red stalks. A Eurasian species *(Actaea spicata)* and 2 in North America *(A. alba* and *A. rubra)* are called herb Christopher. Family: Buttercup (Ranunculaceae); genus *Actaea.*

BANYAN TREE. See *Fig.*

BAOBAB, or cream-of-tartar tree, any of about 10 different kinds of tropical, deciduous trees with enormously thick trunks to 30 feet in diameter. They are native to open savannas of continental Africa, Madagascar, and northern Australia. During prolonged dry seasons in Africa, elephants sometimes use their tusks to break through the bark of baobab trees to get at the moist, pulpy interior. The inconspicuous flowers are followed by a gourdlike fruit with a woody shell and a soft, edible, slightly acid pulp. These fruits offer a generous supply of food where monkeys can get at them and are known as monkey bread. Family Bombax (Bombacaceae); genus *Adansonia.*

UNITED NATIONS

BANANAS

BARBERRY, any of about 175 different kinds of thorny shrubs native to the North Temperate Zone, particularly Asia and the Andes. Japanese barberry *(Berberis thunbergii),* which has smooth-edged leaves, simple spines, and rather dry, plump, scarlet fruit scattered along its spreading stems, is used as a prickly hedge.

The fruit of the European barberry *(B. vulgaris),* in which many of the leaves are reduced to triple or branching spines, is borne in clusters at the tips of the branches; cultivation of this plant is prohibited in places where wheat is grown in the United States because it is the alternate host for the fungus disease known as wheat rust. A native American barberry *(B. canadensis),* which does not grow in Canada, produces fruit in flat clusters on stiff stems that grow as much as 3 feet tall. Family: Barberry (Berberidaceae).

BARBERRY FAMILY. (Berberidaceae), a group of about 300 species in 10 genera, all perennial herbs and shrubs of the North Temperate Zone. See *Barberry, May Apple,* and *Oregon grape.*

BARLEY, an annual grass native to Asia but now cultivated throughout the world for its grain. The individual seeds are small, and, like wheat, are produced in heads among stiff, projecting hairs; they contain no gluten and cannot be made into raised bread. Flat bread and porridge can be made of this cereal, however, and these have been customary foods in North Africa and the Near East since at least 5000 BC.

In North America, barley is raised chiefly as a food for stock animals, for use in the manufacture of malt beverages, as a breakfast cereal, and as baby food. Malt is sprouted barley seeds. Family: Grass (Gramineae); genus and species, *Hordeum vulgare.*

BASSWOOD. See *Linden.*

BAYBERRY, or candleberry, or wax myrtle, any of several different kinds of densely branching shrubs with aromatic, leathery foliage, fragrant bark, and small berries that yield wax when boiled in water. The bark is sometimes used in astringents and tonics; the wax is commonly made into candles. Family: Bayberry (Myricaceae); genus *Myrica.*

BAYBERRY FAMILY (Myricaceae), a group of about 40 species in 2 genera, all aromatic shrubs or trees of temperate and subtropical regions. They include sweet fern *(Comptonia asplenifolia)* of eastern North America, and sweet gale *(Myrica gale)* of bogs in northern and temperate Eurasia and North America, as well as bayberry. See *Bayberry.*

BAY-RUM TREE. See *Myrtle.*

BEAN, any of a large number of different erect or climbing plants with small, white, purplish, scarlet, or yellow flowers that are followed by elongated pods containing several somewhat flattened seeds. Usually the leaves are compound, consisting of 3 leaflets. The broad bean *(Vicia faba)* of the Old World is generally dried and ground up with peas and lentils, and made into soup or porridge.

Lima beans *(Phaseolus limensis)* and kidney beans *(P. vulgaris)* are from the New World and are regarded as vegetables; while still in their green, immature pods, they can be cooked as snap beans or string beans. Soybeans *(Glycine soja),* which have long been eaten by Asian peoples, from Manchuria to Japan, are now cultivated extensively as food for livestock and as a source of useful oils. Family: Pea (Leguminosae).

BEAR GRASS, any of a number of different North American, liliaceous plants with grasslike leaves and a conspicuous cluster of flowers borne on a tall, upright stalk. The name is given to several species of *Yucca* in the Gulf States and deserts of the Southwest, to some of the aloe-like sotols *(Dasylirion)* of Texas and Mexico, to camass or quamash *(Camassia),* which grows from edible bulbs in western North America, and to plants *(Xerophyllum tenax)* of western mountainsides that bear baton-like heads of creamy-white, fragrant flowers. Family: Lily (Liliaceae).

BEDSTRAW, any of about 300 different kinds of weak-stemmed, sprawling, flowering herbs found in most temperate regions, all with square stems, leaves in whorls, and clusters of small, white, yellow, or purple flowers.

Those varieties with minute hooks on the stems and leaves show resistance to crushing. This feature, and their pleasant fragrance, have made them favorite materials with which to stuff mattresses. Family: Madder (Rubiaceae); genus *Galium.*

BEECH, any of 10 different kinds of symmetrical, deciduous trees native to temperate parts of the Northern Hemisphere, generally with ash-gray bark that is so smooth that it tempts people to carve their initials into it. In medieval Germany, beechwood boards were inscribed with runes and symbolic charms. Today, the water-resistant, fine-grained wood of beech trees is valued for furniture, flooring, and tool handles because it does not split easily.

Some kinds of beech attain a height of 100 feet, with silky, oval leaves that bear coarse teeth along the sides; the flowers are small with both staminate and pistillate flowers on the same tree. Prickly husks open to drop the beechnuts, which are small, triangular, with a rich, delicate flavor. Beechnuts and acorns from oaks were formerly referred to as the mast, which was important for fattening hogs. In the Southern Hemisphere related trees called Antarctic beech (*Nothofagus* species) form large forests. Family: Beech (Fagaceae); genus *Fagus*.

BEECH FAMILY (Fagaceae), a group of about 600 species in 6 genera, many of them important timber trees. Half of the species are oaks. Equally famous, although far fewer, are the beeches and chestnuts of the North Temperate Zone. South America, New Zealand, Australia, Tasmania, and the East Indies have comparable forests of Antarctic beech trees *(Nothofagus)*, including the myrtle tree *(N. cunninghami)* of Australia, which yields valuable timber. See *Beech, Chestnut*, and *Oak*.

BEET, a biennial herb native to northern Europe, where for centuries it has been cultivated for both its luxuriant tops and its straw-yellow, enlarged roots, which develop in the first year of growth. The tops can be cooked as potherbs; a favorite variety is called Swiss chard. A different variety with red instead of yellow roots appeared in the 16th century, and has been propagated widely in Britain and Anglo-America.

Sugar beets, which have a higher than normal concentration of sucrose in the roots, were developed in the late 18th century as a source of refined table sugar. In its second year the beet plant produces a new whorl of leaves and a tall branching stem bearing flower clusters and a large number of small seeds. Family: Goosefoot (Chenopodiaceae); genus and species, *Beta vulgaris*.

BEGONIA, a genus of tropical flowering plants containing more than 800 different kinds, most numerous in northern South America. The individual flowers are often showy, but always either pistillate or staminate, although both types may be included in the same cluster. The ovary bears winglike extensions, which remain conspicuous on the capsule.

Many kinds and horticultural hybrids are also cultivated for their handsome leaves, which may be shiny with wax or fringed with long hairs, and for their flowers. Some have fibrous roots, and others have tuberous or bulbous roots. Family: Begonia (Begoniaceae, which includes four other small genera of similar plants).

BELLADONNA, or deadly nightshade, a coarse herb growing 2 to 5 feet tall from a thick, perennial root, with large, smooth-edged leaves and dull-purple, solitary flowers that are followed by plump berries that range in color from purple to black when ripe. Native to Europe, it has escaped from cultivation in other temperate lands. It is the source of the poisonous alkaloid atropin. Crude extracts of this substance from the roots and stems were formerly used in Europe by actresses who wished to make

T.H. EVERETT

BEGONIA

their eyes appear more attractive by chemically dilating their pupils. The purified extract can be used to relieve pain, particularly in spasms. Family: Potato (Solanaceae); genus and species, *Atropa belladonna*.

BELLADONNA LILY. See *Amaryllis*.

BERGAMOT, a small tree of southern Europe and Asia Minor, with leaves and flowers resembling those of orange trees and small, lemon-yellow fruits shaped and formed like oranges, but yielding a fragrant, essential oil used in the manufacture of perfumes, cosmetics, and liqueurs. Wild bergamot *(Monarda fistulosa*, of the mint family, Labiatae) is an entirely different fragrant herb of North America, bearing terminal clusters of lilac-colored, pink, or white flowers. Family: Rue (Rutaceae); genus and species, *Citrus bergamia*.

BIGONIA FAMILY (Bignoniaceae), a group of about 750 species in 110 genera, chiefly tropical shrubs, trees, or woody creepers (lianas). Included are some of the world's most beautiful flowering trees, such as the species of *Jacaranda* native to Brazil and the West Indies, which have showy, blue or purple flowers, and the African tulipan or flame-tree *(Spathodea campanulata)*.

The sausage trees *(Kigelia* species) of tropical Africa and Madagascar, which produce elongated, woody fruits on long stalks, and the calabash tree *(Crescentia cujete)* of tropical America, which bears huge, spherical, hard-shelled fruits on its trunk and branches, are among the most unusual. See *Calabash tree, Catalpa*, and *Trumpet creeper*.

BINDWEED, or wild morning-glory, any of several different trailing, herbaceous vines from perennial roots, native to Eurasia but now widespread as weeds on roadsides and vacant land in temperate North America. It clambers on other plants, winding around them and spreading its spear-shaped leaves and pink to white, bell-shaped flowers in the sun. Family: Morning-glory (Convolvulaceae); genus *Convolvulus*.

BIRCH, any of about 40 different kinds of woody plants of arctic, alpine, and temperate areas of the Northern Hemisphere, with saw-edged leaves that open after pollen has been distributed from long, staminate catkins and caught from the wind by shorter clusters of pistillate flowers. Arctic and alpine birches are often mere shrubs, but in the Temperate Zone the species include many graceful, trees as much as 70 feet tall.

The bark is conspicuously marked with crosswise, narrow slits (lenticels) and may be white, gray, brown, black, or red, according to the species. From canoe, or paper, birch *(Betula papyrifera)* of Canada and the northern United States, Indians cut the bark to make coverings for canoes and wigwams. Today white birch is grown as an ornamental tree.

The aromatic bark of the black birch *(B. lenta)* of eastern North America yields oil for wintergreen. The sap of others can be used instead of maple sap to produce a sweet syrup or the raw material for birch beer. Family: Birch (Betulaceae); genus *Betula*.

BIRCH FAMILY (Betulaceae), a group of about 105 species in 6 genera, all deciduous shrubs and trees with simple leaves and flowers in pendant catkins. See *Alder, Birch, Hazel*, and *Hornbeam*.

BIRTHWORT FAMILY (Aristolochiaceae), a group of about 400 species in 6 genera, 300 of them in *Aristolochia* (including *A. durior)*, most of which are tropical, twining shrubs and perennial herbs. Wild ginger *(Asarum canadense)* of eastern North America is a woodland wild flower with a few kidney-shaped leaves shading peculiar, globular, chocolate-brown flowers growing at ground level. See *Dutchman's pipe*.

BITTERROOT, a low-growing, perennial herb of western North America, with starchy, edible roots, small, succulent leaves, and large, pink- or rose-colored flowers close to the ground. The roots were eaten by the Indians and early white colonists. It is the state flower of Montana. Family: Purslane (Portulacaceae); genus and species, *Lewisia rediviva*.

BITTERSWEET, either of 2 different types of woody vines bearing simple, ovate leaves and small, conspicuous fruits. One, the nightshade *(Solanum dulcamara)* of temperate Eurasia, which has been introduced and become widespread in other parts of the world, bears small clusters of pink or violet flowers, followed by bright-red, poisonous berries. It is a member of the Potato Family *(Solanaceae)*.

The other, known also as waxwork, is a climbing plant *(Celastris scandens* of the eastern United States or *C. orbiculatus* from eastern Asia) with inconspicuous clusters of greenish flowers at the tips of side branches.

In autumn, the ivory-colored coverings of the fruits split open and drop off, exposing brilliant scarlet or crimson seeds in a tight, spherical cluster. It is a representative of the Staff-tree Family (Celastraceae).

BLACKBERRY, any of 20 or more different kinds of thorny brambles of North America, with stalked leaflets in the compound leaves, and raspberry-like, edible fruits borne in terminal clusters. The canelike, arching stems grow 5 to 6 feet high and usually bear fruit in their second or third year. Family: Rose (Rosaceae); genus *Rubus.*

BLACK-EYED SUSAN, or yellow daisy, a handsome, North American wildflower, 1 to 2 feet tall, bearing a flower head the center of which is composed of numerous tiny, brown flowerets closely packed, surrounded by gay, yellow petals of flowers that have lost their reproductive parts. It thrives in dry fields, blooms from June to September, and is the state flower of Maryland. Family: Daisy (Compositae); genus and species, *Rudbeckia hirta.*

BLACK HAW, or sweethaw, or stagbush, a coarse shrub or small tree growing 15 to 40 feet tall, with spreading branches, oval leaves that turn bright red in autumn, and clusters of white flowers in April or May. Native to eastern North America, it is used as a decorative tree. Family: Honeysuckle (Caprifoliaceae); genus and species, *Viburnum prunifolium.*

BLADDERWORT, any of about 250 different kinds of carnivorous water plants found throughout the world but most varied in South America and the East Indies; they are always found in sluggish streams and ponds.

The submerged leaves, which are finely divided, bear bladder-like traps ⅛ to ¼ inch long, with hinged doors that swing inward suddenly, sucking small animals into the interior where they are held and digested. Bladderwort produces upright stems bearing white or yellow flowers, which are pollinated by flying insects. Family: Bladderwort (Lentibulariaceae); genus *Utricularia.*

BLADDERWORT FAMILY (Lentibulariaceae), a group of about 260 species in 6 genera, mostly carnivorous plants growing in moist places in the North Temperate and South Temperate zones and on mountains of tropical America. See *Bladderwort* and *Butterwort.*

BLEEDING HEART. See *Dutchman's-breeches.*

BLOODROOT, a delicate, herbaceous, perennial flower of woodlands in eastern North America, which produces an upright stem with a single, circular leaf tightly rolled around the single flower bud. The leaf opens in early spring; the flower expands its 8 to 12 white petals and lasts only a day or two. All parts of the plant contain an orange-red juice. Indians formerly gathered the thick, underground stems of bloodroot to obtain the juice for use as warpaint and basket dye. Family: Poppy (Papaveraceae); genus and species, *Sanguinaria canadensis.*

BLUEBELL, any of a number of low-growing plants with blue, bell-shaped flowers, particularly the widespread harebell *(Campanula rotundifolia,* of the bellflower family, Campanulaceae) of temperate Eurasia and North America, which bears one flower at the nodding tip of each of its hairlike stems, and has been made famous in poetry and prose as the "bluebell of Scotland." The name bluebell is also given to the European wood hyacinth *(Scilla nonscripta)* and the grape hyacinth *(Muscari botryoides),* both of the lily family (Liliaceae).

In New Zealand the name bluebell is used for some kinds of tuftybells *(Wahlenbergia,* a large genus of the bellflower family). In North America, bluebells may be the Virginian cowslip *(Mertensia virginica,* of the borage family, Boraginaceae), the American brooklime *(Veronica americana,* of the figwort family, Scrophulariaceae), the Jacob's ladder *(Polemonium reptans,* of the phlox family, Polemoniaceae), or the leatherflower *(Clematis crispa,* of the buttercup family, Ranunculaceae).

BLUEBERRY, any of a number of different kinds of shrubby plants of wide distribution, bearing small, bell-shaped, pink or white flowers and blue-black berries, which are usually edible and often confused with those of the related huckleberry. Many horticultural varieties have been developed from the highbush blueberry *(Vaccinium corymbosum)* of dry uplands in eastern North America, which yield large crops of berries with a delicious flavor, highly esteemed when eaten fresh, dried, frozen, or canned. Family: Heath (Ericaceae); genus *Vaccinium.*

T.H. EVERETT

BOUGAINVILLEA

BLUEBONNET. See *Lupine.*

BLUEGRASS, any of several different pasture grasses with a bluish color on the upright stems (culms). In North America, bluegrass is generally either Kentucky bluegrass (or june-grass, or speargrass, *Poa pratensis),* which is native to subarctic meadows and moist slopes in Eurasia and North America but grows well in Kentucky and other regions, or Canada bluegrass (or wiregrass, *P. compressa),* which is native to Eurasia but is now widespread in North America. Unrelated grasses are given the same name in Australia and New Zealand. Family: Grass (Gramineae).

BOMBAX FAMILY (Bombacaceae), a group of about 140 species in 22 genera, all trees of the tropics, often of vast girth or with enormous buttresses. See *Balsa, Baobab,* and *Kapok.*

BONESET, any of several different related American herbs with a stout, hairy stem growing 2 to 5 feet tall and bearing wrinkled, saw-edged leaves and clusters of flowers in shaggy heads; the flowers are usually greenish-white or pale pink. The Indians used extracts from the flowers and leaves in treating ague and fevers. Family: Daisy (Compositae); genus *Eupatorium.*

BORAGE, a coarse, hairy, annual or biennial herb native to Europe, where it is cultivated as a source of nectar for bees. It has been introduced and become widespread in many other temperate areas of the world, and is noted for its clear, blue flowers. Family: Borage (Boraginaceae); genus and species, *Borago officinalis.*

BORAGE FAMILY (Boraginaceae), a group of about 2000 species in 100 genera, widely distributed, mostly herbs, commonly with simple, smooth-edged leaves covered with rough, bristly hairs. See *Bluebell, Borage, Forget-me-not,* and *Heliotrope.*

BOSTON IVY, a hardy, deciduous, woody vine native to China and Japan that climbs by means of branching tendrils with expanded, adhesive pads at the tips. Its long-petioled, simple leaves turn red or orange in autumn and usually fall before the petioles do, exposing clusters of dark purple fruits.

Introduced into New England and Canada, the plant provides wall covering in places where English ivy is killed by cold. A close relative in eastern North America is the Virginia creeper *(Parthenocissus quinquefolia)* with compound leaves consisting mostly of 5 leaflets. Family: Grape (Vitaceae); genus and species, *Parthenocissus tricuspidata.*

BOUGAINVILLEA, a genus of South American vines that bear flowers in groups of 3, surrounded by 3 purple or red conspicuous bracts. A Brazilian species *(B. spectabilis)* is cultivated in warm countries as a decorative covering for walls. Family: Four-o'clock (Nyctaginaceae).

BOUNCING BET, or soapwort, an attractive, perennial herb with a sturdy, smooth stem, smooth, oval leaves, and clusters of pink or white flowers. Native to Europe, it has become a roadside weed in North America. Colonial housewives crushed its leaves into water to produce a lather possessing some of the qualities of a soap solution. Family: Pink (Caryophyllaceae); genus and species, *Saponaria officinalis.*

BOX, a popular evergreen shrub native to western and southern Europe, cultivated in many temperate and cool climates as a hedge plant. It grows slowly to a height of 16 feet, producing small, oval leathery leaves so close together that they provide privacy and a screen from the wind. The flowers are inconspicuous. The pale yellow wood is very hard and sometimes used for wood engraving and for making wind instruments. Family: Box (Buxaceae); genus and species, *Buxus sempervirens.*

BOX ELDER. See *Maple.*

BRACKEN, or brake, any of several kinds of tall, coarse ferns growing 2 to 14 feet tall, their fronds divided into 3 branches and bearing spore cases underneath the edges. Found throughout the world, particularly in dry, rocky pastures, these ferns can be dug up to extract a solution used as a bitter beverage or for tanning from their thick, underground stems. Family: Polypody (Polypodiaceae); genus *Pteridium.*

BRAZIL NUT, a tree that grows in moist soil along river banks in northern South America, where it attains a height of 100 to 150 feet, and bears huge, oval, leathery leaves, creamy-white flowers, and large, globular pods containing 18 to 24 wedge-shaped, oily seeds, each in a hard seed coat. The seeds, called brazil nuts, are flavorful and edible, and yield an oil used by watchmakers and artists, as well as by native people for fuel in lamps. Family: Brazil nut (Lecythidaceae); genus and species, *Bertholletia excelsa.*

BRAZIL–NUT FAMILY (Lecythidaceae), a group of 315 species in 18 genera, all tropical trees with simple leaves clustered at the ends of the branches. Included is the strange cannonball tree *(Couroupita guianensis)* of northern South America and the West Indies, which bears large rust-colored, woody, seed-filled capsules on short, twisted side branches extending from the main trunk; it is a source of good timber. See also *Brazil nut.*

BREADFRUIT, a tropical tree with thick, oval leaves that are deeply indented around the edge. Native to the South Pacific islands, where it rarely grows to more than 40 feet tall, the breadfruit is valued for its large, spherical, green fruits, each pebbled on the outside and full of a starchy pulp that is edible when baked or fried. A sticky substance that oozes from wounds in the bark can be used as birdlime or to seal the seams of small boats. Strong bast fibers can be removed from the inner bark and woven into tapa cloth. The wood itself can be used to build houses or canoes. First described by Capt. James Cook, breadfruit was introduced into the West Indies as food for Negro slaves by Capt. William Bligh after an expedition to Tahiti aboard the famous ship *H.M.S. Bounty.* Family: Mulberry (Moraceae); genus and species, *Artocarpus incisa.*

BRIDAL WREATH. See *Spiraea.*

BROCCOLI. See *Mustard.*

BROOM, any of several related plants with long, slender, stiff, green branches, small leaves, and showy, yellow flowers resembling those of a sweet pea. Scotch broom *(Cytisus scoparius),* which is native to Britain and temperate parts of Europe, has been introduced into North America, South Africa, and New Zealand, where it grows well. A medicine made from the foul-tasting twigs and seeds has been used as a diuretic.

Other plants to which the name broom is applied include several kinds of gorse *(Genista* and *Ulex* species) of Europe, western Asia, and north Africa. Family: Pea (Leguminosae).

BROOMCORN, a tall coarse, annual sorghum native to warm parts of Eurasia, but cultivated in America since colonial days. It has escaped from cultivation. It raises jointed stems either 4 to 6 feet tall (dwarf variety) or 10 to 14 feet tall (standard variety), which bear long leaves and terminate in a brushlike cluster of inconspicuous flowers. After the seeds have ripened the long "broom straws" of the flower cluster are gathered and used to make brooms and brushes. Family: Grass (Gramineae); genus and species, *Sorghum vulgare technicus.*

T.H. EVERETT

BUCKTHORN

BRUSSELS SPROUTS. See *Mustard.*

BUCKEYE. See *Horse chestnut.*

BUCKTHORN, any of about 100 different kinds of woody shrubs, mostly from the North Temperate Zone. They include some that attain a height of 12 feet, with black bark, small, scalloped leaves, tiny 4-petalled, yellowish-green flowers, and blue-black berries which yield a purgative juice and a pigment used by painters. Most buckthorns have thorny branches.

Dried bark of the western North American *Rhamnus purshiana* is called *cascara sagrada* (sacred bark), and is the source of a mild laxative. Family: Buckthorn (Rhamnaceae); genus *Rhamnus.*

BUCKTHORN FAMILY (Rhamnaceae), a widely distributed group of about 550 species in 45 genera, all tree or shrubs with simple leaves and flowers that, strangely, have stamens that are opposite to the petals instead of alternate with them. Several kinds are valued for their fruits, as well as for drugs or ornamental planting. See *Buckthorn* and *Jujube.*

BUCKWHEAT, an annual herb with a slender, jointed stem, 2 to 3 feet tall, bearing heart-shaped leaves and clusters of small, white, pink, or purplish-red flowers. Although the plant is not a grass, the ripened seeds are regarded as a cereal crop.

Cultivated for many centuries in the Orient, buckwheat was introduced into Europe and then into North America where it is grown in the northeastern United States as a food for cattle and poultry, or made into a flour for griddle cakes. Buckwheat honey has a distinctively dark color, and a strong flavor. Family: Buckwheat (Polygonaceae); genus and species, *Fagopyrum sagittatum.*

BUCKWHEAT FAMILY (Polygonaceae), a group of about 800 species in 32 genera, mostly herbs of the North Temperate Zone, but including also some shrubs, climbing vines, and trees. They are encountered as small trees on tropical beaches, for example, the sea grape *(Coccoloba uvifera),* which has edible fruits; or as coral-vine *(Antigonum leptopus)* of Mexico and Central America, which climbs trellises or tall trees and bears a profusion of pink flowers. See *Buckwheat, Dock, Rhubarb,* and *Sheep sorrel.*

BULRUSH, any of about 200 different kinds of grasslike herbs with narrow leaves in 3 rows that provide a sheath for the triangular stem. Widely distributed, they are plants of shallow water or wet soil, particularly characteristic of bogs, marshes, and wet moorland in areas where the climate is cool. The end of the stem bears many flowers in a clublike cluster. The "bulrushes" of which the floating cradle of the infant Moses was made were probably *Iris* because bulrushes do not grow in Egypt, whereas *Iris* leaves are still used for such purposes along the Nile. Family: Sedge (Cyperaceae); genus *Scirpus.*

BUNCHBERRY, a low-growing herb of cool, damp woodlands in northeastern North America, producing 4 to 6 oval leaves above which a slender stalk bears 4 to 6 conspicuous, white bracts resembling petals around the central cluster of inconspicuous green flowers. When ripe, the clustered scarlet berries are edible. Family: Dogwood (Cornaceae); genus and species *Cornus canadensis.*

BURDOCK, a coarse biennal herb native to temperate Eurasia but now widespread as a weed in North America. In its first year it produces broad, wavy-edged leaves, and stores nourishment in a sturdy root. The following year it raises a branched, leafy stem with flowers opening in heads from July until the first frost arrives in the fall.

Hooked bristles cover the flower heads, which have pink or purplish florets packed tightly together, converting the cluster of ripened seeds into a bur that catches on to clothing or the fur of passing animals. New burdocks grow along paths, fences, and walls where the burs are scratched free or fall. Family: Daisy (Compositae); species chiefly *Arctium lappa,* the great burdock, *A. minus,* the common burdock, and *A. nemorosum,* or hybrids among these.

BURNING BUSH. See *Euonymus.*

BUTTERCUP, or crowfoot, any of about 300 different kinds of wildflowers with tough, green, branching stems 3 to 30 inches tall, bitter juice, small, deeply-cut leaves, and cup-shaped flowers, generally golden-yellow and intensely reflecting. They are found in wet areas of cool and temperate regions, in the Arctic, north temperate, and alpine areas of the Americas and New Zealand. The Mt. Cook lily *(Ranunculus lyalli)* has large, white flowers and is the national flower of New Zealand. Family: Buttercup (Ranunculaceae); genus *Ranunculus.*

BUTTERCUP FAMILY (Ranunculaceae) a group of about 1500 species of herbs, vines, or shrubs in 5 genera, common to both the North Temperate and South Temperate zones. See *Aconite, Anemone, Baneberry, Bluebell, Buttercup, Clematis, Columbine, Hellebore, Hepatica, Larkspur, Marsh marigold, Peony,* and *Woodbine.*

BUTTERFLY BUSH, a decorative, tall, branching herb of northwest China, with showy clusters of small, lilac-colored flowers that attract butterflies and other insects. Widely introduced as a garden plant, it thrives in sunny, warm climates. Family: Logania (Loganiaceae); genus and species, *Buddleia alternifolia.*

BUTTERFLY FLOWER, a tall, herbaceous plant native to Chile but widely introduced into gardens for its lacy, fernlike leaves and varicolored flowers, each of which has small, winglike petals suggesting those of a butterfly. Family: Potato (Solanaceae); genus and species, *Schizanthus pinnatus.*

BUTTERFLY WEED. See *Milkweed.*

BUTTERNUT. See *Walnut.*

BUTTERWORT, any of about 40 different kinds of small, herbaceous plants that grow in wet soil. They are prevalent in the North and South Temperate zones and the mountains of tropical America.

Thick oblong leaves arise in a rosette close to the ground; first they capture and then they digest insects that alight and are caught on the sticky surface. Small clusters of violet-like flowers, generally blue or purple, are borne on an upright stalk, which is about 4 inches tall. Family: Bladderwort (Lentibulariaceae); genus *Pinguicula.*

BUTTONWOOD. See *Plane-tree family.*

CABBAGE. See *Mustard.*

CACAO, a small tree native to Central America and northern South America, with a thick trunk that grows to 40 feet, spreading branches with a downy covering, leathery, oval leaves that hang downward, and inconspicuous, pink flowers on cushion-like projections from the trunk; the large fruits, 10 to 14 inches long and 5 inches in diameter, are dark purplish-red on the outside, and have 25 to 50 purple seeds embedded in a mucilaginous, pink pulp.

The seeds, or cocoa beans, can be removed by hand, cured by fermentation, and dried. Later they can be ground and processed to make cacao powder and chocolate. Cacao orchards that provide the world with chocolate have always been planted with a cover of taller trees to provide the necessary shade; this is particularly true of tropical Africa. Family: Sterculia (Sterculiaceae); genus and species, *Theobroma cacao.*

CACTUS FAMILY (Cactaceae), a group of about 1700 species in 120 genera, originally from the New World, most with fleshy stems armed with spines and bristles, leaves that drop off without expanding, and large flowers followed by a fleshy berry. Many are cultivated for their unusual form and handsome flowers. Prickly-pear *(Opuntia* species), barrel cactus *(Ferocactus* species), Christmas cactus *(Zygocactus truncatus)* from Brazil, and organ-pipe cactus *(Cereus marginatus)* are among the forms that have attracted widespread attention. See *Night-blooming Cereus* and *Saguaro.*

CALABASH TREE, a small tree native to tropical America, with opposite leaves on its small branches but with flowers extending from the bark of large branches and the trunk. The fruits develop as much as 12 inches in diameter, with a hard rind. Native people clean out the central pulp and seeds, thus creating a woody calabash

U.S. DEPARTMENT OF THE INTERIOR

CACTUS

that can be used to carry liquids or as a drinking utensil. Family: Bignonia (Bignoniaceae); genus and species, *Crescentia cujete.*

CALCEOLARIA, or slipperwort, a genus containing about 200 different kinds of herbaceous, perennial plants native to America from Mexico to Tierra del Fuego, growing 1 to 2 feet tall, bearing oval leaves and usually, yellow flowers with red markings, each flower with a large, saclike, lower lip and a small, erect, upper lip. Family: Figwort (Scrophulariaceae).

CALENDULA. See *Pot marigold.*

CALLA LILY, a cultivated South African herbaceous plant with thick, starchy, horizontal, underground stems and green, upright stems bearing large, white, flower-like spathes around a bright yellow spadix of minute flowers. A golden calla *(Zantedeschia elliottiana)* has white-spotted leaves and a yellow spathe.

The name calla is actually that of the genus of a related but small-flowered water arum *(Calla palustris),* which is native to the bogs and marsh edges of the North Temperate Zone. Family: Arum (Araceae); genus and species, *Zantedeschia aethiopica.*

CALTROP, any of more than 20 different kinds of Eurasian, African, and American perennial herbs and shrubs with opposite, leathery leaves, the inconspicuous flowers of which produce hard fruits with sharp, rigid spines. These fruits, called caltrops, may puncture the tires of bicycles and automobiles as well as wound the feet of man and animal; *Tribulus terrestris,* which is a native weed from the Mediterranean to Tibet that has been introduced and become widepsread elsewhere, is therefore called puncture weed.

In the Middle Ages arms makers used the caltrop fruit as a model for a metal device with 4 sharp spikes equally spaced in radial directions; one of these spikes always pointed upward no matter how the device rested, thus readily maiming a horse or man who stepped on it. Family: Caltrop (Zygophyllaceae); genera *Tribulus* and *Kallstroemia.*

CALTROP FAMILY (Zygophyllaceae), a group of about 250 species in 27 genera, chiefly plants of warm regions, all with opposite leaves. Several kinds are grown as ornamentals and some are useful trees. Bean capers *(Zygophyllum fabago)* of Asia Minor yield buds than can be pickled for use as a condiment. See *Caltrop, Creosote bush,* and *Lignum vitae.*

CAMELLIA, a genus of Asian shrubs with glossy, pointed, slightly toothed, evergreen leaves and waxy, roselike flowers, 3 to 7 inches in diameter, ranging in color from red to white. Of the 80 different species, many are cultivated widely in temperate areas as house plants.

C. sinensis, native to the area from Japan to India, is raised on plantations to yield young twigs and partly opened leaves that are cured, dried, and later steeped to yield a tea. Tea bushes or tea trees can naturally attain a height of 30 feet, but they are usually pruned to a height of 3 to 5 feet to enable workers to reach more easily the young growth that is to be picked. Family: Tea (Theaceae).

CAMOMILE, or chamomile, any of several related branching herbs with pinnately dissected leaves and solitary, terminal heads of small, daisy-like flowers. These plants have long been gathered or cultivated for their aromatic foliage and young stems, which are the source of a drug used to induce perspiration and to inhibit muscular spasms. Some species are grown as decorative garden plants. Family: Daisy (Compositae); genera *Anthemis* and *Matricaria.*

CAMPHOR. See *Cinnamon.*

CANDYTUFT, any of about 30 different kinds of herbaceous, branching, stiff plants with toothed or deeply cut, narrow leaves and showy white or crimson flowers in which the lowest 2 of the 4 petals are larger than the others. The first species introduced as low-growing garden plants were annuals from Candia on the island of Crete; hence the name candytuft. Others that are now widely cultivated are evergreen perennials, produced primarily in Mediterranean countries. Family: Mustard (Cruciferae); genus *Iberis.*

CANNA, a genus of about 60 different kinds of tropical American plants that comprise a separate family. Many are cultivated for their large, sheathing leaves, which are green, bronze, or red, and for their terminal clusters of red, white, or yellow flowers in which the conspicuous parts are 1 to 5, petal-like, modified stamens. The underground stem of *C. edulis,* from Central America, is starchy and edible and known as Queensland arrowroot. Family: Canna (Cannaceae).

CANTALOUPE. See *Melon.*

CAPE JASMINE. See *Gardenia.*

CAPER, any of about 350 different kinds of shrubs and small trees found in warm climates, some climbing by means of tendrils from the axils of the simple leaves. The showy flowers have 4 sepals, 4 petals, and numerous stamens.

The flower buds of a Mediterranean species called capers *(Capparis spinosa)* are dried for use as seasoning; the plants are cultivated for this purpose. Family: Caper (Capparidaceae); genus *Capparis.*

CAPER FAMILY (Capparidaceae), a group of about 700 species in 46 genera, all tropical or subtropical herbs, shrubs, or trees. One kind, the Spiderflower *(Cleome spinosa)* of tropical America, is a widespread, cultivated, garden ornament, named for its extraordinarily long, projecting stamens. See also *Caper.*

CARAWAY, an erect, biennial herb with aromatic, pinnately compound leaves, and white or pink flowers in clusters, producing small seeds with a distinctive flavor. The plants are cultivated in many temperate countries.

Plants were introduced from Europe to obtain seeds that are dried and added as flavoring to bread, cheese, candy, soups, and sauces. An oil extracted from the seeds is used in soaps and perfumes. Family: Carrot (Umbelliferae); genus and species, *Carum carvi.*

CARDAMOM, an East Indian herb with elongated, sheathing leaves and a stem growing to 10 feet, topped by a spike of white-striped, purple flowers that are followed by 3-cornered pods containing aromatic, brown, white-lined seeds.

It is cultivated for its seeds, particularly in Ceylon, India, and Latin America. Cardamom is the source of medicinal substances with stimulant and purgative qualities as well as the preferred source of a spice that is added to curries.

The name cardamom (or cardamon or cardamum) is also given to alternate spices from a related plant, *Anomum cardamon,* of Java. Family: Ginger (Zingiberaceae); genus and species, *Elletaria cardamomum.*

CARDINAL FLOWER. See *Lobelia.*

CARNATION. See *Pink.*

CAROB. See *Locust.*

CARROT, or Queen Anne's lace, a biennial, herbaceous plant with finely divided leaves and flat-topped clusters of small white flowers. It is native to Europe but has been introduced and become widespread as a weed all over the world.

A cultivated variety, with a large, edible, yellowish or reddish-orange root from its first year of growth, is valued as a food because of its high content of vitamin A and minerals. Family: Carrot (Umbelliferae); genus and species, *Daucus carota.*

T.H. EVERETT

CAMELLIA

CARROT FAMILY (Umbelliferae), a group of about 2900 species in 125 genera, represented on all continents but most numerous in the North Temperate Zone. Most are biennial or perennial herbs with aromatic leaves, the stalks of which enclose the stems, and with flat-topped clusters of flowers (umbels). See *Anise, Caraway, Carrot, Celery, Dill, Fennel, Parsley, Parsnip,* and *Poison hemlock.*

CASCARA SAGRADA. See *Buckthorn.*

CASHEW, a small tree native to the American tropics, with alternate, simple leaves, clusters of 5-part flowers, and distinctive fruits called cashew apples, each with a large, pearlike, fleshy portion below which a hard-shelled seed, called a cashew nut, projects. The cashew apple is edible; the seeds can be made edible by roasting to destroy a poisonous, irritating compound and break the shells. Family: Sumac (Anacardiaceae); genus and species, *Anacardium occidentale.*

CASSAVA, or manioc, or yuca, either of 2 kinds of erect, slender, woody plants of tropical America, with stems growing to 9 feet tall and bearing large leaves that are deeply notched into 3 to 7 long, narrow, spreading lobes. The fleshy underground stems, which may be 3 feet long and 9 inches in diameter, are dug up, purified of any bitter poisonous substances present, and converted into either a flour from which a flat bread can be made or into a pudding known as tapioca.

These foods are produced from cultivated cassava plants; they provide a poor diet but are the principal sources of nutritional calories in many parts of Latin America, tropical Africa, and from Malaya through the East Indies and the South Pacific islands. Family: Spurge, (Euphorbiaceae); genus and species, *Manihot esculenta* (bitter) and *M. palmata* (sweet).

CASTOR-OIL PLANT, or palma Christi, a tropical perennial shrub or small tree of Africa and Asia, which reaches a

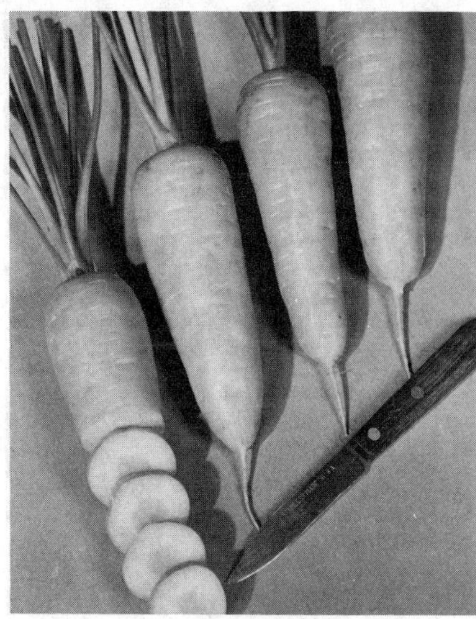
BURPEE SEEDS

CARROTS

height of 30 to 40 feet, with palmately compound, bronze-green leaves, small flowers in loose clusters, and spiny capsules that contain poisonous, mottled seeds.

The castor-oil plant grows quickly and produces fruits even in temperate climates, where it is killed by winter frosts and can therefore be cultivated only as an annual. Castor oil can be extracted from the seeds; it is used as a violent laxative and as a fine lubricating oil. Family: Spurge (Euphorbiaceae); genus and species, *Ricinus communis.*

CATALPA, a genus comprised of 10 different trees of East Asia and eastern North America, including the West Indies, several of which have been introduced and become widespread beyond their native areas for their attractive, large, heart-shaped, mostly opposite leaves; their tall, open clusters of 2-lipped, frilled flowers; and their useful wood. They produce drooping, cylindrical pods 6 to 20 inches long for which the trees are often called Indian beans or cigar-trees. Family: Bignonia (Bignoniaceae).

CATNIP, an aromatic, perennial herb native to Eurasia, with an erect, square stem, opposite, pointed, serrate, velvety leaves, and terminal whorls of white, purplish, or blue-tinged flowers. Introduced and widespread in most temperate parts of the world, it was long valued as the basis of a catnip tea used for colic and colds. Cats are attracted by the odor of the fresh or dried aerial parts of the plant. Family: Mint (Labiatae); genus and species, *Nepeta cataria.*

CATTAIL, any of 12 different perennial herbs found in marshes all over the world, with starchy, horizontal stems in water-soaked soil and erect, sword-shaped leaves partially sheathing upright stems that end in club-shaped spikes of minute flowers. The top of the spike consists of staminate flowers which soon drop off, leaving a naked length of stem beyond the clustered, pistillate flowers, which have a furry appearance. The single genus is in a family by itself. Family: Cattail (Typhaceae); genus *Typha.*

CAULIFLOWER. See *Mustard.*

CEDAR, in the strict sense, any of 4 different kinds of handsome, evergreen, coniferous trees native to Eurasia, where 3 are becoming rare because of the excessive harvesting of the fragrant wood. Only the deodar *(Cedrus deodara)* in its native Himalayan forests is not yet seriously threatened.

The famous cedar of Lebanon *(C. libanotica)* is represented today by a few dwindling forests in Turkey and scattered trees introduced elsewhere. The Cyprus cedar *(C. brevifolia)* is threatened in addition by goats and fires. The Atlantic cedar *(C. atlantica)*, which was once widespread in Algeria and Morocco, is now scarce.

All cedars have rather short, sharp needles arranged in spirals on spurlike side branches; they shed their winged seeds when the ovulate cones disintegrate, dropping their scales and leaving only the central supporting stem attached to the branch.

Many unrelated coniferous trees with fragrant wood belonging to genera *Chamaecyparis* (North American), *Juniperus* (North Temperate), *Libocedrus* (Pacific coasts), *Thuja* (North American and East Asian), and *Widdringtonia* (African, in the cypress family, Cupressaceae), and *Cryptomeria* (Japanese, in the bald-cypress family, Taxodiaceae), are commonly referred to as cedars. Family: Pine (Pinaceae); genus *Cedrus.*

CELANDINE, a European biennial herb 1 to 2 feet tall, with a sprawling, brittle stem, deeply notched, alternate leaves, and odorless, yellow flowers; its yellow juice, which stains skin and clothing, contains a dangerous poison. Family: Poppy *(Papaveraceae)*; genus and species, *Chelidonium majus.*

CELERY, a biennial herb native to Europe but widely cultivated for its fleshy petioles, which are eaten raw or cooked, and for its seeds, which are dried for use as a condiment. It has fibrous roots, a very short stem, and deeply divided leaf blades. When allowed to flower, it produces small blossoms in flat topped clusters. Family: Carrot (Umbelliferae); genus and species, *Apium graveolens.*

CENTURY PLANT, any of about 230 different kinds of succulent-leaved plants of arid and semiarid areas from northern South America to the southern United States. Most have stems that remain very short and produce an ever greater whorl of thick sword-shaped leaves until a critical amount of nourishment has been accumulated. Then, during a month or two of rapid growth, the stem extends upward to a height of as much as 20 feet, displaying a large cluster of fragrant, yellow, tubular flowers. After blooming, the plant develops seeds and sometimes suckers, but the leaves and main stem die. Originally believed to require a century to bloom, century plants normally need 20 years or less. Many are cultivated for the strong fibers in their leaves, which include henequen (from *Agave fourcroydes)*, sisal (from *A. sisalana* and *A. letonae)*, istle (from *A. lophantha* and *A. funkiana)*, Mauritius hemp (from *Fourcroya gigantea)*, cabuya (from *F. cabuya)*, and fique, the fibers of which are used in making Colombian coffee bags (from *F. macrophylla)*. Family: Amaryllis (Amaryllidaceae); genera *Agave* and *Fourcroya.*

CHARD. See *Beet.*

CHERIMOYA. See *Custard apple.*

CHERRY, any of several trees of the North Temperate Zone with small, smooth, oval leaves usually finely toothed around the edge, beautiful clusters of fragrant, white or pinkish flowers, and edible fruits with a soft pulp and a central, armored seed.

Some, such as the black cherry *(Prunus serotina)* of eastern North America, attain a height of 100 feet and are sought after for their hardwood. Others such as the sweet cherry *(P. avium)* of southern Europe and the sour cherry *(P. cerasus)* of Asia, are appreciated for their fruit. Still others, such as the flowering cherry *(P. serrulata)* of Japan, are planted for their spring flowers and attractive foliage; the small and rather tasteless fruits are left for the birds. Family: Rose (Rosaceae); genus *Prunus.*

CHESTNUT, any of 10 different kinds of shrubs and trees of the Northern Hemisphere, bearing alternate leaves that are coarsely serrate and have conspicuously straight side veins. The staminate flowers are borne in cream-colored, loose catkins; the pistillate flowers are small but produce 2 or 3 nuts grouped in a leathery bract, which opens to release them.

Best known is the Spanish or Italian chestnut *(Castanea sativa)* of the Mediterranean region, with large, edible nuts, sold freshly roasted on street corners in many large cities. The American chestnut *(C. dentata)*, of the eastern United States and Canada, was formerly important as a timber and nut tree, but it has almost been exterminated by a fungus blight that still prevents it from becoming reestablished. Family: Beech (Fagaceae); genus *Castanea.*

CHICKWEED, any of about 200 different kinds of frail, quick-growing, herbaceous perennials of temperate regions, rarely more than 8 inches tall, with small, oval leaves in pairs at swellings on the slender stems, and with solitary or clustered white flowers bearing 5-notched petals. Both flowers and seeds are produced throughout the spring and summer. Family: Pink (Caryophyllaceae); evenly divided between genera *Stellaria* and *Cerastium.*

CHICORY, or succory, a perennial herb of the Mediterranean region, now cosmopolitan as a weed. The lower leaves are oval, the upper leaves on the stiff, flowering stems are very small and bractlike, and the flower heads are 1½ inches across and composed entirely of strap-shaped florets in varying shades of blue.

In Europe the long, heavy taproots are dug up, dried, and pulverized to make a substitute for coffee or to adulterate the coffee. The blanched lower leaves can be used for salads. A close relative, the endive *(Cichorium endiva)*, has frilly, bitter, edible leaves. The endive is cultivated largely for use in salads. Family: Daisy (Compositae); genus and species, *Cichorium intybus.*

CHINABERRY, or bead tree, or pride of India, a fast-growing, spreading tree native to eastern Asia and northern Australia but introduced widely. It has alternate, pinnately compound leaves, large clusters of fragrant, purplish flowers, which are followed by nearly spherical, yellow fruits ½ inch in diameter. The thin pulp soon dries over the armored seed, producing a "bead." Family: Mahogany (Meliaceae); genus and species, *Melia azedarach.*

CHOCOLATE. See *Cacao.*

CHRISTMAS BERRY, a shrub or small tree native to California and used there in place of holly for Christmas decorations. Growing 5 to 25 feet high, the tree has pale, aromatic bark, glossy, serrate, evergreen leaves, loose clusters of white flowers, and bright red berries which are edible, pleasant tasting, and ripen during the coldest part of winter. Family: Rose (Rosaceae); genus and species, *Heteromeles arbutifolia.*

CHRISTMAS ROSE. See *Hellebore.*

CHRYSANTHEMUM, a genus of about 150 different kinds of annual and perennial herbaceous plants of the Northern Hemisphere and Africa, some of which are attractive weeds, and others of which are cultivated for their handsome flowers. All have notched or pinnately divided leaves and flattened flower heads.

The oxe-eye daisy or whiteweed *(C. leucanthemum)* of Eurasia is now almost cosmopolitan in temperate regions. The East Asian species (particularly *C. morifolium)* were cultivated in early times, leading Japan to adopt a stylized chrysanthemum with 16 florets as its national emblem; horticultural varieties include many in which all florets are strap shaped and twisted, the flower heads as much as 10 inches across and in many colors. Family: Daisy (Compositae).

CINCHONA, a genus of perhaps 40 different kinds of trees native to mountain slopes from Peru northward to Costa Rica, with red bark, spreading branches, opposite, ovate leaves, and open clusters of pink flowers. The fruit is a capsule that opens to release its many seeds. Known since about 1630 as a source of an anti-malarial drug, quinine, cinchona trees have been cultivated in India and Java; the latter country is the principal commercial producer of the drug itself, which is extracted from the bark, called Peruvian bark. Family: Madder (Rubiaceae).

CINERARIA, the florist's name for a herbaceous perennial plant from the Canary Islands, with large, ovate leaves, short, branching stem, and large, daisy-like flowers with purple disc florets and white, red, or purple ray florets. *Cineraria* is a genus of South African herbs and low shrubs with thistle-like flowers. Family: Daisy (Compositae); genus and species, *Senecio cruentus.*

CINNAMON, a small evergreen tree native to Ceylon, but cultivated in China, tropical America, Florida, and California for the inner bark of its young shoots and branches, which yields a popular flavoring, cinnamon. The tree itself has large, ovate, paired leaves, loose clusters of malodorous, greenish flowers, and small, fleshy fruits. Oil can be extracted from the fruit and leaves as well as from the bark, but only the light, yellowish-brown bark can be powdered as a spice; the spice has a sweet, warm taste from the aromatic oil it contains.

A closely related tree native to Formosa, Japan, and China *(Cinnamomum camphora)* is now cultivated in California, Texas, and Florida as a shade tree, a windbreak, and a source of gum; it is the principal source of camphor, which is distilled from young shoots or old trees cut into chips. Family: Laurel (Lauraceae); genus and species, *Cinnamomum zeylanicum.*

CITRON, a small evergreen tree with irregular branches, large, oval leaves, and bluish blossoms. It is native to India, China and Southeast Asia but is cultivated chiefly in southern Europe, primarily for its greenish-yellow lemon-shaped fruits, 5 to 6 inches long; the fruit rind is candied and the juice used as a beverage or concentrated to a syrup. An oil extracted from citron leaves is used in making perfume. Family: Rue (Rutaceae); genus and species, *Citrus medica.*

CLEMATIS, a genus containing about 230 different kinds of vines and climbing shrubs with opposite compound leaves the petioles of which are tendril-like and curl around supports. The flowers of all lack petals but have 4 showy sepals and many stamens. Represented on most continents in areas with cool summers, the genus is best known in eastern North America as virgin's bower, or old-man's-beard *(C. virginiana)*, which has feathery plumes attached to the many seeds in each cluster of a flower. Family: Buttercup (Ranunculaceae).

CLOVER, any of about 300 different kinds of herbaceous plants native to temperate and subtropical regions, bearing palmately compound leaves with 3 to 5 leaflets, and round heads of tiny, closely packed, white, pink, or purplish flowers. Bees make some of the most delicious honey known from their nectar. Clovers are valuable forage plants for livestock, and are often grown as part of a rotational sequence for soil improvement. Family: Pea (Leguminosae); genus *Trifolium.* See also *Sweet clover.*

DURPEE SEEDS

CINERARIA

CLOVE TREE, a tropical evergreen tree with large oval leaves, native to the East Indies, where it grows to a height of 50 feet. It is cultivated near the seacoasts and on tropical islands of South America, the West Indies, and Africa, particularly Zanzibar. It is pruned as a low shrub from which the buds of the clustered, crimson flowers can easily be picked in order to be dried and used as spice cloves. Each tree yields from 5 to 75 pounds of cloves annually.

The spice is used for making candy and clove liqueur, and for flavoring. Oil of cloves, extracted by distillation, is used in medicine, soaps, and perfumes. Family: Myrtle (Myrtaceae); genus and species, *Eugenia aromatica.*

CLUB MOSS, any of about 180 different kinds of creeping herbaceous plants found almost all over the world, with upright stems clad in evergreen and bractlike leaves, bearing spore cases either among the leaves or clustered to form the club-shaped ends of the vertical stems. The spores are carried by wind, and can germinate in moist soil into ½-inch, carrot-shaped plants with sex organs. Fertilized eggs in these develop into the club moss.

Because of a fancied resemblance, various club mosses are known as staghorn evergreen, ground pine, ground fir, and ground cedar. Few grow more than a foot tall, and most live in moist forests. Family: Club moss (Lycopodiaceae); genus *Lycopodium.*

COCA, a small shrub of mountain slopes in Bolivia and Peru, with straight branches growing to a height of 8 feet, bearing small, oval leaves distinctly marked with a transparent area on each side of the midrib; the small, white flowers are followed by small, black berries. The native people have learned to pluck the leaves as soon as each is stiff enough to break when bent, to dry them, and to keep them dry. The product, which resembles tea

UNITED NATIONS

CORN

leaves, is chewed by Indians at work or on long journeys, dulling hunger and fatigue and apparently giving them strength and endurance; or it is marketed as a source of the drug cocaine, which is used as a local anesthetic in surgery. Coca belongs to a genus of about 200 different species native to the American tropics, many of which contain smaller amounts of cocaine. They form a small family. Family: Coca (Erythroxylaceae); genus and species, *Erythroxylum coca.*

COCKSCOMB, a low-growing, herbaceous plant of tropical Asia, widely cultivated in temperate gardens as an annual because, about its long, pointed, green leaves, it produces a monstrous flower head suggesting a rooster's comb. The flower head is sometimes as wide as the plant is tall and consists of crimson, orange, or creamy-white flowers at the ends of multiple stalks that grow in a fan-shaped bundle. Family: Amaranth (Amaranthaceae); genus and species, *Celosia aristata.*

COCOA. See *Cacao.*

COFFEE, any of about 45 different kinds of small trees with paired, oval, shining, evergreen leaves and clusters of fragrant, white flowers from which, after about 7 months, crimson, cherry-like fruits develop, each containing 2 flat seeds known as coffee beans.

Native to Arabia and tropical Africa, particularly Ethiopia and Madagascar, a few species have been intensively cultivated for their beans in Ceylon, Java, and elsewhere in the East Indies, as well as in Brazil, Cuba, Central America, and Colombia. These beans are cured and dried and later ground and brewed to make a mildly stimulating beverage containing caffeine. Family: Madder (Rubiaceae); genus and species, *Coffea arabica.*

COFFEE TREE. See *Kentucky Coffeetree.*

COLUMBINE, any of about 50 different kinds of graceful, perennial herbs of the Northern Hemisphere, with long-stalked palmately compound leaves and large, showy flowers at the end of the branches; each flower has 5 sepals and 5 long-spurred petals that secrete nectar. Family: Buttercup (Ranunculaceae); genus *Aquilegia.*

COREOPSIS, a genus that comprises about 115 different kinds of weak-stemmed herbs ranging from 12 to 15 inches tall, mostly native to North America but found also in Africa and Hawaii. They produce a few narrow leaves and many long-stalked, yellow or pink, daisy-like flowers. Several species are cultivated as ornaments in temperate gardens. The most notable is an annual, *C. calliopis,* the ray florets of which are red, maroon, or yellow.

The name tickseed is given to many species, particularly *C. major* of eastern North America, because the small, flat fruits have tiny hooks that cause them to adhere to fur and clothing. Family: Daisy (Compositae).

CORN, or Indian corn, or maize, an erect, herbaceous, annual grass native to mountainous tropical America, domesticated by the Indians and developed horticulturally into many diverse genetic strains, chiefly for the fruits (called kernels) borne in a tight spiral (the cob) within a sheath of spathe-like leaves (the husk), from the end of which the long, threadlike filaments (the silk) extend. Pollen from a terminal cluster of stamens (the tassel) is carried by the wind, pollinating each of the separate, clustered, pistillate flowers from which the kernels develop.

Various strains of corn grow 2 to 30 feet tall; the chief food varieties are dent, flint, flour, pod, pop, and sweet corn. Corn stalks, with their partly sheathing, elongated, coarse leaves are cut for storage and fermentation in farm silos. They are used to provide winter food for livestock. Family: Grass (Gramineae); genus and species, *Zea mays.*

CORNEL. See *Dogwood.*

CORNFLOWER, or bluebottle, or bachelor's button, a slender annual herb of southern Europe, now common in gardens throughout the temperate zones. It grows 1 to 2 feet tall, with small, grayish leaves and fringed, trumpet-like flower heads containing many blue, pink, or white florets. Family: Daisy (Compositae); genus and species, *Centaurea cyanus.*

COTTON, any of several different cultivated, annual, branching, erect herbs of tropical and subtropical regions, with alternate, 3-lobed leaves, and large, showy, creamy flowers that turn red on the second day after opening. The fruit is a globular capsule, called a boll, filled with fluffy fibers attached to the flattened seeds.

Wild cotton grows more than 15 feet tall, but domesticated species are short to facilitate picking the ripe bolls, from which the fibers are removed for use in making textiles and the seeds for the extraction of a commercial cottonseed oil. Family: Mallow (Malvaceae); genus *Gossypium.*

COTTONWOOD. See *Poplar.*

COWPEA, or black-eyed pea, a sprawling, herbaceous plant native to tropical Asia, now cultivated in warm parts of Europe, North America, and Africa for its edible seeds, which may be eaten fresh or dried for storage and later soaked before cooking.

The plant itself is a twining annual with 3-part leaves and a few purplish flowers; it produces pods growing to 12 inches long, with kidney-shaped seeds, each usually with a black spot around the point of attachment. Family Pea (Leguminosae); genus and species, *Vigna sinensis.*

COWSLIP. See *Marsh marigold* and *Primrose.*

CRABGRASS, a coarse, annual European grass, now almost cosmopolitan on cultivated land and wasteland in temperate regions. It has a creeping stem, rough, hairy leaves 2 to 10 inches long, and radiating spikes of minute, grayish-yellow flowers that produce red or purple seeds. In some parts of Europe crabgrass is raised as forage for livestock. Family: Grass (Gramineae); genus and species, *Digitaria sanguinalis.*

CRANBERRY, either of 2 closely related, slender, creeping, shrubby plants with alternate, leathery, small, evergreen leaves which are dark above and paler below, the edges curving downward. The plants have up to 10 nodding, pink or white, bell-shaped flowers on each branch, followed by red, spherical fruits that float on water. Cranberries grow on boggy or peaty soil, along swamp edges, and on floating bogs.

The small-berried species is found across Eurasia and North America, and at higher elevations in the south; the larger-berried North American species is cultivated in artificial bogs that can be flooded at harvest time. The fruits are used for canning, preserving, and in baking. Family: Heath (Ericaceae); genus and species, *Vaccinium oxycoccus* (small-fruited) and *V. macrocarpon.*

CRAPE MYRTLE, an Oriental shrub or small tree with paired, oval, glossy, green leaves and showy, open clusters of lavender-colored flowers, often called "lilac-of-the-South" in the southeastern United States, where it is commonly planted as an ornament. Family: Loosestrife (Lythraceae); genus and species, *Lagerstroemia indica.*

CREOSOTE BUSH, a tough, perennial shrub of deserts in Mexico and the adjacent United States, growing 3 to 4 feet tall, with gray stems marked with black paired leaflets at the end of each petiole; after a rainfall, it produces yellow flowers.

Few animals will eat the foliage or stems because of the strong, tarry odor, even though the creosote bush is one of the few types of vegetation that has adapted well to conditions of extreme chronic drought. Family: Caltrop (Zygophyllaceae); genus and species, *Larrea tridentata.*

CRESS, any of several different kinds of small, perennial herbs that grow prostrate or buoyed up by running water, with hot-tasting leaves sought as ingredients for salads, or as a garnish or seasoning. They can be cultivated for home use in tubs or frames that hold water. If allowed to flower, all produce small clusters of white or yellow blossoms, each with 4 petals.

The most common kinds are the European watercress *(Nasturtium officinale)*, the garden cress or peppergrass *(Lepidium sativum)* from Mediterranean countries, the wild peppergrass *(L. virginicum)* from North America, which has been introduced into Europe, and the winter cress *(Barbarea verna)*, from the North Temperate Zone. Family: Mustard (Cruciferae).

CROCUS, a genus of about 70 different kinds of bulbous, herbaceous plants, most of which are native to the Mediterranean region. They blossom in early spring before extending their narrow, stiff, white-lined, green leaves, a characteristic that makes them attractive as ornaments. A fall-flowering species *(C. vernus)* is harvested in Spain for the stigmas of its blossoms, which yield saffron dye.

The name autumn crocus, or meadow saffron, is given to an unrelated bulbous plant *(Colchicum autumnale* of the lily family, Liliaceae) that produces flowers in autumn after its leaves of the year have shriveled and disappeared; its bulbs and seeds are the source of the poisonous alkaloid colchicine, which is used in medicine and horticulture. Family: Iris (Iridaceae).

CROTON, a genus that comprises about 600 different kinds of tropical shrubs native to the Old World and the New, many of them with handsomely mottled leaves in shades of green, yellow, and dark red, usually with long, terminal spikes of small flowers, the staminate flowers commonly nearer the tip of the same spike than the pistillate ones. An Asian species *(C. tiglium)* yields croton oil, which is a strong purgative. The cascarilla *(C. cascarilla)* of the Bahamas and Florida yields a bark known as Eleuthera bark or cascarilla bark and is used to make a tonic and an incense. Family: Spurge (Euphorbiaceae).

CUBEB. See *Pepper.*

CUCUMBER, a trailing annual, herbaceous plant that probably originated in Asia south of the Himalayas, but is now cultivated throughout the world for its edible fruits. The hairy stem bears 3-lobed leaves and bell-shaped, yellow flowers on short stalks; the green, fleshy, oblong fruit is eaten fresh, cooked, or pickled. A close relative from the West Indies *(Cucumis anguria)* bears prickly, small fruits called gherkins. Family: Gourd (Cucurbitaceae); genus and species, *Cucumis sativus.*

CURRANT, any of a small number of branching, shrubby perennials with smooth stems, round, scalloped leaves, clusters of small, yellowish or purple flowers, and, later, similar clusters of red, black, striped, or white berries. Cultivated in many temperate countries are the Eurasian red currants *(Ribes rubrum* and *R. vulgare)* and Eurasian black currants *(R. nigrum)*; they bear edible fruits that can be eaten raw, cooked, or preserved. The fruits of the golden currant *(R. aureum)* of the western United States are regarded as less important than their bright yellow, fragrant blossoms, which are unusual because they are tubular rather than bell-shaped. Family: Saxifrage (Saxifragaceae); genus *Ribes.*

CUSTARD APPLE, a small, West Indian tree with large, leathery leaves and solitary, nodding flowers bearing 3 sepals and usually 6 petals, as well as numerous stamens and separate pistils. The fleshy fruits of the separate pistils unite as they ripen, often becoming very large.

Introduced into many other parts of the tropics, custard apples are cultivated for their fruits, which are too soft to ship, and are generally eaten with a spoon. Related trees from the American tropics, yielding different but delicious fruits, include the sweetsop or sugar apple *(Annona squamosa)*, the soursop *(A. muricata)*, and the cherimoya *(A. cherimolia)*, all used in making drinks, ices, jellies, and preserves. Family: Custard apple (Annonaceae); genus and species, *Annona reticulata.*

CUSTARD–APPLE FAMILY (Annonaceae), a group of about 850 species in 80 genera, chiefly woody plants—shrubs, vines, or trees—with aromatic, simple leaves. See *Custard apple* and *Papaw.*

CYCAD, any of about 100 different kinds of woody shrubs and trees widely distributed in the tropics and subtropics, with thick, slow-growing stems that have a very large pith, alternate, pinnately compound, leathery, evergreen leaves, and separate staminate and ovulate cones, the seeds often brightly colored and with a fleshy covering.

Many cycads are palmlike, two kinds *(Macrozamia* species) in eastern Australia growing to a height of 60 feet. The "palms" of hotel lobbies in many parts of the world are actually either *Cycas revoluta* of southeastern China and southern Japan or *Dioon edule* of Mexico. The seeds of the latter are starchy and can be ground into an edible meal.

The pith of the sago palm *(Cycas circinalis)* of the East Indies yields sago starch, which is almost indistinguishable from that of many true palms (family Palmaceae). In Florida, the Seminole Indians dug the heavy, short, underground stems of the native cycads (chiefly *Zamia floridana)*, called coonties, as a source of starchy flour. Family: Cycad (Cycadaceae).

CYCLAMEN, a genus of 13 different kinds of herbaceous, perennial plants native to southern Europe and Asia Minor, with leathery, kidney-shaped leaves on long stalks, and nodding flowers with reflexed petal lobes, white, rose, pink, or purple in color. One species *(C. persicum)* is cultivated in greenhouses and homes of northern Europe and North America for its flowers. Family: Primrose (Primulaceae).

CYPRESS, any of 12 different kinds of evergreen, coniferous trees native to warm parts of the Northern Hemisphere. All grow tall, with tiny leaves less than 1/4 inch long, closely pressed to the branchlets, and small cones composed of less than 20 cone scales. None tolerates hard frosts or extended cold weather.

The funeral cypress *(Cupressus funebris)* of China, which grows like a tall, dark green column with branches that hang down and are said to "weep," is planted in cemeteries in many warm countries. Family: Cypress (Cupressaceae); genus *Cupressus.*

CYPRESS FAMILY (Cupressaceae), a group of about 140 species in 15 genera, all shrubs or trees with scalelike or needlelike leaves and mature cones that are dry and woody or fleshy and berry-like. See *Arbor vitae, Cedar, Cypress,* and *Juniper.*

DAFFODIL. See *Narcissus.*

DAHLIA, a genus of perennial plants native to Mexico and Central America, including about 9 different kinds, of which one, *D. pinnata,* is grown widely as an ornamental garden flower. The wild plant grows 2 to 6 feet tall and bears compact heads of red flowers, each with a yellow center.

More than 10,000 horticultural varieties have been developed in every color except blue. Although many of the varieties produce seeds that will germinate, the named kinds are usually grown from the tuberous roots, which have buds at the stem end. Family: Daisy (Compositae).

DAISY, any of a number of different plants that produce flat flower heads surrounded by a radiating row of white petals. The lawn daisy *(Bellis perennis)*, a stemless little plant that produces 1-inch flower heads on 2- or 3-inch slender stalks from spring until autumn is widespread in Britain and has been introduced by Europeans into many parts of North America, Asia, and New Zealand. A field full of tall, white daisies usually consists of the ox-eye, marguerite, or whiteweed *(Chrysanthemum leucanthemum)* of Eurasia, which has become a pasture weed in Canada and the United States.

The Shasta daisy, with flower heads up to 4 inches in diameter, is a hybrid developed by Luther Burbank chiefly from the smaller *Chrysanthemum maximum* of the Pyrenees. Daisy-like flowers also open on more than 125 different kinds of daisy-bushes *(Olearia)* in New Zealand, Australia, and New Guinea, where these shrubs often form thickets. Family: Daisy (Compositae).

DAISY FAMILY (Compositae), the largest family of flowering plants, with more than 20,000 species in 950 genera, widely distributed and including shrubs and a few trees as well as herbs. All are easy to recognize by their flower heads, in which many florets are attached side by side to the broad end to the stalk and surrounded by a row of bracts called an involucre. See *Ageratum, Arnica, Artichoke, Aster, Black-eyed Susan, Boneset, Burdock, Camomile, Chicory, Chrysanthemum, Cineraria, Coreopsis, Cornflower, Dahlia, Daisy, Dandelion, Edelweiss, Elecampane, Everlasting, Gaillardia, Golden glow, Goldenrod, Guayule, Hawkweed, Ironweed, Joe-Pye weed, Lettuce, Marigold, Mayweed, Pot-marigold, Ragweed, Rubber Tree, Safflower, Sagebrush, Salsify, Sunflower, Tarragon, Thistle, Wormwood, Yarrow,* and *Zinnia.*

DANDELION, or blowballs, a common weed of lawns introduced from Europe and now kept widespread in the United States by its light-weight fruits, each with a terminal tuft of silky hairs that catches the wind. The bright yellow flowers are borne on tall, hollow stalks that rise from a flat rosette of leaves; the leaves, which are toothed along the edges, have led to the name dandelion *(dents-de-leon,* "lion's teeth").

Europeans commonly gather the leaf rosettes and boil them as potherbs, or collect the flowers and extract their sugar as the basis of dandelion wine. Family: Daisy (Compositae); genus and species, *Taraxacum officinale.*

DASHEEN. See *Taro.*

DEVIL'S-PAINTBRUSH. See *Hawkweed.*

DEWBERRY. See *Blackberry.*

DILL, a biennial herb of southern Europe and North Africa, originally cultivated in Asia Minor, India, and North America for its seeds, but more recently for its immature flower clusters and leaves as well. From all these an extract called dill herb oil can be obtained for use in flavoring. Like caraway and anise extracts, it apparently reduces gas in the human digestive tract. Family: Carrot (Umbelliferae); genus and species, *Anethum graveolens.*

DOCK, any of several coarse weeds of Eurasia, now widespread, each a perennial with a long, stout taproot, broad, ruffled leaves, and a stem 1½ to 3 feet tall, topped by clusters of small, green flowers. They grow on poor, acid soil, where other plants do not find enough nourishment, and provide some food for livestock. In Eurasia the young shoots are used as a vegetable. Mexican tanner's dock *(Rumex hymenosepalus)* yields canaigre, an extract used in tanning hides. Family: Buckwheat (Polygonaceae); genus *Rumex.* See also *Burdock.*

DODDER, any of about 160 different kinds of rootless, leafless, non-green, parasitic vines that grow as annual plants, twining around the stalks of other vegetation. They are native to most temperate and tropical countries. At intervals along the yellow, red, or white, threadlike stems are short suckers that extend into the tissues of the host plant and absorb nourishment. The pink flowers generally appear in small clusters from July to September, and are followed by capsules of minute, ripe seeds that travel as impurities among seeds of crop plants. Family: Morning-glory (Convolvulaceae); genus *Cuscuta.*

DOGBANE, any of about 25 different kinds of herbaceous perennial plants native to the North Temperate Zone, with paired, simple leaves on branching stems 1 to 4 feet tall, and small clusters of pinkish-white, bell-shaped flowers. Family: Dogbane (Apocynaceae); genus *Apocynum.*

DOGBANE FAMILY (Apocynaceae), a group of about 1300 species in 300 genera, widely distributed but best represented in the tropics. They include trees, shrubs, tropical woody vines, and herbs, all with milky sap and simple, smooth-edged leaves. Some yield drugs, latex, tannins, and other valuable substances, whereas others are valuable chiefly as ornaments. Frangipani or temple tree *(Plumeria rubra),* native to tropical America, is grown for its perfumed, clustered flowers. See *Dogbane, Indian Hemp, Oleander, Periwinkle,* and *Rubber Tree.*

DOGTOOTH VIOLET, or dog's-tooth-violet, any of several similar and related fawn lilies with a pair of mottled, basal leaves, producing in early spring a nodding, single flower at the top of a slender stalk. The Eurasian dogtooth violet *(Erythronium denscanis)* has a red or purple flower. The eastern North American area has a yellow violet, adder's-tongue *(E. americanum),* and a white one *(E. albidum).* A rosy-pink dogtooth violet *(E. propullans)* is native to Minnesota. Family: Lily (Liliaceae); genus *Erythronium.*

DOGWOOD, any of about 40 different kinds of shrubs and trees with simple leaves, native to the North Temperate Zone and to tropical mountains. Their small but often conspicuous fruits remain after the leaves drop in autumn, providing winter food for birds. The widespread red osier dogwood *(Cornus stolonifera)* forms thickets that may be identified by the many smooth, red stems and, in autumn, white or lead-colored fruits; its flowers are inconspicuous.

The flowering dogwoods, small trees in which the flower clusters are conspicuous because of the 4 to 7 white or colored, petal-like bracts associated with them, include the Cornelian cherry *(C. mas)* of central and southern Europe and western Asia, the western dogwood *(C. nuttallii)* of British Columbia to California, and the eastern dogwood *(C. florida)* of eastern North America, including eastern Mexico. Family: Dogwood (Cornaceae); genus *Cornus.*

DOGWOOD FAMILY (Cornaceae), a group of about 125 species in 18 genera found in temperate areas in the Northern and Southern hemispheres, including the higher slopes of tropical mountains. They are undershrubs, shrubs, and trees with simple leaves. See *Bunchberry, Dogwood,* and *Tupelo.*

DOUGLAS FIR, a tall, straight tree of western North America, with flattened needles on short stalks and pendant cones 2 to 4 inches long, which are unique because every cone scale is accompanied by a 3-pronged bract that projects half an inch or so beyond the scale. When the leaves drop off the stem is smooth, as in a true fir; the cones, however, remain attached until after the seeds have been dispersed, whereas those of a true fir disintegrate to release the seeds.

Douglas fir grows to a height of 221 feet, and is the leading timber tree in America today, yielding about a quarter of the lumber produced in the United States and Canada. Family: Pine (Pinaceae); genus and species, *Pseudotsuga taxifolia.*

DUTCHMAN'S-BREECHES, a woodland wildflower of northeastern North America, with delicate, green leaves and slender stalks 5 to 10 inches high, bearing rows of small, heart-shaped, spurred, white or pink flowers shaped somewhat like the ballooning breeches once worn by Dutch peasants.

Closely related are the bleeding heart *(Dicentra spectabilis)* of China and Japan, which is cultivated in gardens because of its rosy-red and pink flowers, and the squirrel corn *(D. canadensis),* named for the yellow, tuberous knobs on its buried, horizontal stems. Family: Fumitory (Fumariaceae); genus and species, *Dicentra cucullaria.*

DUTCHMAN'S-PIPE, a woody, climbing vine native to eastern North America, from Pennsylvania to Georgia and Alabama, now widely cultivated for its smooth, heart-shaped leaves and its clusters of showy flowers, each resembling a Dutch pipe. The showy part is the calyx, for petals are lacking. Family: Birthwort (Aristolochiaceae); genus and species, *Aristolchia durior.*

EBONY, any of several related trees of equatorial Africa and tropical Asia, the intensely hard, black, heartwood of which can be given a high polish. India and Ceylon are the principal sources for *Diospyros ebenum,* which attains a height of 100 feet, and has oblong leaves, fragrant, yellow flowers, jet-black bark, and almost white sapwood surrounding the valuable heartwood. Family: Ebony (Ebenaceae); genus *Diospyros.*

EBONY FAMILY (Ebenaceae), a group of 325 species in 5 genera, all shrubs or trees with simple, smooth-edged, leathery leaves. They are most numerous in Southeast Asia but are widely represented in tropical and subtropical regions. See *Ebony* and *Persimmon.*

EDELWEISS, an alpine plant with narrow, wooly, white leaves and flowers with many separate heads, which are clustered so close together that insects can walk from one to the next, obtaining nectar and pollinating the blossoms. Native to high peaks in the European Alps, where it is endangered by excessive picking, it is now cultivated in gardens in many temperate parts of the world. In cultivation it sometimes grows to 6 feet. Family: Daisy (Compositae); genus and species, *Leontopodium alpinum.*

EGGPLANT, a bushy, annual plant native to northeastern India, domesticated and cultivated in warmer parts of Eurasia, North America, Australia, and New Zealand for the pendant, oblong, edible fruits, which may be purple, yellow, or white. The stems are spiny, the leaves large and lobed, and the flowers are violet-colored. Family: Potato (Solanaceae); genus and species, *Solanum melongena.*

ELDER, any of about 20 different kinds of shrubs and trees native to temperate and tropical lands, with pinnately compound leaves and flat clusters of tiny flowers that are followed by juicy fruits, each containing 3 tiny, armored seeds.

The fruits of the European elder *(Sambucus nigra),* native to western Asia and North Africa and to Europe, and of the common American elder *(S. canadensis)* in eastern Canada and the United States are eaten by birds unless they are harvested. The berries are made into elderberry pie or used as the basis of elderberry wine. Family: Honeysuckle (Caprifoliaceae); genus *Sambucus.*

ELECAMPANE, or horseheal, a tall, coarse herb of Eurasia, with large, egg-shaped tubers on the roots, and 4-inch heads of daisy-like flowers bearing golden-yellow petals around the rim and disc florets that change in color from yellow to tan as they mature.

The root tubers yield a medicinal agent rich in the carbohydrate inulin, with a warm, bitter taste and an odor suggestive of that of camphor. Family: Daisy (Compositae); genus and species, *Inula helenium.*

ELEPHANT'S EAR. See *Begonia.*

ELM, any of about 30 different kinds of trees native to the North Temporate Zone and the mountains of tropical Asia, bearing simple leaves that are oblique at the base and winged fruits with the seed at the center. The American elm *(Ulmus americana)* develops a wide-spreading crown, making it a valuable shade tree. It rises to a height of 160 feet with a top 75 feet across; the wood is so cross-grained that it can hardly be split.

The slippery elm *(U. rubra)* of the eastern United States has a mucilaginous inner bark that has been used medicinally. Like the European elm or the English elm *(U. campestris),* and the Chinese elm *(U. parvifolia),* it is a lesser tree but is immune to the fungus infection known as the Dutch elm disease, which is destroying the New England elms. Family: Elm (Ulmaceae); genus *Ulmus.*

ELM FAMILY (Ulmaceae), a group of nearly 160 species in 15 genera, all shrubs or trees with simple leaves that are native to the North Temperate Zone and mountains of tropical Asia. See *Elm* and *Hackberry.*

BURPEE SEEDS

EGGPLANT

ENDIVE. See *Chicory.*

EUCALYPTUS, or gum trees, a genus of tall trees including about 600 different kinds native to Australia, New Guinea, and the adjacent islands. The leaves are usually narrow and pendant, casting little shade. The sepals and petals drop from the flowers as they open, exposing a tuft of stamens that are commonly bright red, gold-tipped, and attractive to pollinating insects. The fruits are hard and dry.

A fast-growing eucalyptus, the Australian bluegum *(E. globulus),* has been introduced in many temperate areas as a windbreak and as a quick source of wood. It grows to a height of 50 feet in about 5 years. Tallest is the gum tree *(E. regnans)* of eastern Australia, which attains a height of 326 feet and a diameter of 25 feet at chest height. Oil of eucalyptus, used medicinally for colds and bronchial infections, is extracted from the young twigs and leaves of several different kinds. Family: Myrtle (Myrtaceae).

EUONYMUS, a genus of shrubs and trees native to the Northern Hemisphere and Australia, with about 100 different species, many of them evergreen. All have spreading branches, pointed, serrate leaves, open clusters of drooping, purple flowers, and seeds covered by bright orange or red arils, which are exposed in autumn when the fruit capsule breaks open.

The European spindle-tree *(E. europaeus)* and the burning-bush or wahoo *(E. atropurpureus)* of eastern North America are often raised as ornamental shrubs or trees partly because their leaves turn a rich purplish-red in autumn before dropping; they grow to 25 feet tall. The winged spindle-tree *(E. alatus)* also displays such rich fall coloring; it is native to eastern Asia and has corky, winglike projections from its branches. Family: Staff tree (Celastraceae).

EUPHORBIA, a large genus of latex-bearing plants native to subtropical and warm, temperate parts of Africa and America. Most have succulent, spiny stems, simple leaves, and tiny flowers with large, nectar-producing glands.

Of the 1600 different kinds, the most widely cultivated are the poinsettia *(E. pulcherrima)* of Mexico and Central America, the flower clusters of which are made conspicuous by an open whorl of adjacent, bright red or white leaves, and the prickly crown-of-thorns *(E. splendens)* of Madagascar, often planted as a hedge; the latter bears a succession of slender stems from its woody branches, holding 2 or 4 scarlet "flowers," each of which is a diminutive cluster.

Africa south of the Sahara has tree euphorbias, which resemble organ-pipe cacti, and have adapted in a similar way to store water in arid highlands. Family: Spurge (Euphorbiaceae).

EVENING PRIMROSE, any of about 100 different kinds of American herbs found from the Arctic to Patagonia. Most bear bright butter-yellow or white flowers that open late in the day and close again permanently the following dawn, often changing to a pink or magenta color as they fade.

Hawkmoths are attracted by scent to serve as pollinators. The seeds have a thin membrane that catches the wind; in this fashion any gust can distribute them widely. The root and upper foliage of some kinds are edible. Family: Evening primrose (Onagraceae); genus *Oenothera.*

EVENING-PRIMROSE FAMILY (Onagraceae), a group of about 650 species in 20 genera, widely distributed, growing as herbs, shrubs, or trees with simple leaves. See *Evening primrose, Fireweed, Fuchsia,* and *Godetia.*

EVERLASTING, any of several different kinds of annual plants the dried blossoms of which have a strawlike texture; they retain their color and form and can be displayed as decorations throughout the winter.

The flower heads, cut before they open fully, are often hung upside down to be dried and then dyed in assorted colors. This custom presumably began with the wild immortelle *(Helichrysum orientale)* of Asia and Africa, which is cultivated in southern Europe, but it has also been followed with the Australian *Waitzia* and the North American species of *Anaphalis, Antennaria,* and *Gnaphalium.* Family: Daisy (Compositae).

FENNEL, a stout, aromatic, perennial herb native to Europe, bearing leaves that are divided into threadlike projections from the midrib, flat heads of yellow flowers, and slender seeds about ¼ inch long. The young leaves are sometimes eaten as salad greens, and the seeds used as a relish or as the source of a fragrant oil used in perfumes and soaps. Introduced into North America, it has sometimes become a troublesome pasture weed. Family: Carrot (Umbelliferae); genus and species, *Foeniculum officinale.*

FIG, any of about 800 different kinds of tropical and subtropical shrubs and trees, which have a palatable, milky juice in their alternately arranged leaves and produce a unique, pear-shaped, inverted receptacle enclosing tiny flowers that produce small fruits. The edible part of the fig is the fleshy receptacle, which may be eaten raw, fresh, dried, cooked, or preserved, or may be used as the base from which wine and other alcoholic beverages are made.

The commercial fig is the product of a 20-foot tree *(Ficus carica)* of western Asia, now cultivated in all Mediterranean countries and the United States; its fruits vary in color from white to yellow, purple, and black. The India-rubber plant *(F. elastica)* of India and Java, which was formerly a commercial source of rubber, is now widely cultivated as a house plant with glossy, oblong leaves.

The pipal tree, or bo tree *(F. religiosa)*, which is sacred to Gautama Buddha, is planted outside Buddhist shrines, providing shade, a useful lac, and an extract useful in tanning leather. The banyan tree *(F. benghalensis)* of the East Indies supports its outspread, heavy limbs on strong, adventitious roots that grow down to the soil and become thick; a single tree can extend itself in this way over a broad area. Family: Mulberry (Moraceae); genus *Ficus.*

FIGWORT, any of about 150 different kinds of coarse herbs native to the North Temperate Zone, found especially in Asia, with a 4-sided stem, mostly opposite leaves, and a loose, terminal cluster of flowers shaped like those of the snapdragon. The flowers are usually greenish, purple, or blood-red. Fleshy knobs on the horizontal, underground stems of some species were once believed to be evidence that the plants could be used to cure fig-warts and scrofula. Family: Figwort (Scrophulariaceae); genus *Scrophularia.*

FIGWORT FAMILY (Scrophulariaceae), a group of about 2600 species in 200 genera, represented on all continents, mostly herbs and low shrubs with simple leaves and bilaterally symmetrical flowers, the 5-part corolla typically 2-lipped. Included are the imperial tree *(Paulownia tomentosa)* of China and Japan, which grows 40 feet tall with large, heart-shaped leaves and clusters of white flowers; the louseworts *(Pedicularis* species), which are partially parasitic on tree roots; and the paintbrush *(Castilleja* species), chiefly of western North America, in which the upper leaves and bracts near the inconspicuous flowers are brightly colored in orange and red. See *Bluebell, Calceolaria, Figwort, Foxglove, Mullein, Snapdragon,* and *Veronica.*

FILBERT. See *Hazel.*

FIR, any of about 40 different kinds of coniferous, evergreen trees native to Eurasia and North America, which release their winged seeds when their upright cones disintegrate. Balsam firs, particularly the North American

BURPEE SEEDS

FORGET–ME–NOT

Abies balsamea, yield a fragrant resin from numerous "blisters" on the trunk that is used in medicine. With the exception of the noble fir *(A. nobilis)* of the northwestern United States and adjacent Canada, the firs are less valuable than the spruces for lumber; young firs are favored as Christmas trees. Family: Pine (Pinaceae); genus *Abies.*

FIREWEED, or great willow herb, a perennial, herbaceous plant of cool, temperate, and arctic-alpine parts of the Northern Hemisphere, where its lightweight, hair-tufted seeds germinate on cleared and burned-over land, leading to a conspicuous stand of stout stems 5 to 7 feet tall; these stems are generously clad in narrow, green leaves shaped like those of the willow, and end in a conspicuous, elongated cluster of magenta or pink flowers. Family: Evening primrose (Onagraceae); genus and species, *Epilobium angustifolium.*

FLAX, a slender, upright, herbaceous plant native to Eurasia, with almost grasslike leaves and few branches. At the tip of each branch it produces a delicate, violet-blue flower with petals that spread about ¾ inch across. The seeds, from which linseed oil is extracted, ripen in globular capsules.

To obtain fibers to be made into linen thread, the plants are harvested when the seeds are not yet fully ripe; at this stage, the fibers in the stems are at their best for removal and working. Weaving linen from flax plants is one of man's oldest technical achievements. Today, most of the fibers are from the Soviet Union and Europe from Poland to France. Family: Flax (Linaceae); genus and species, *Linum usitatissimum.*

FORGET–ME–NOT, or scorpion grass, any of about 300 different kinds of low herbs of temperate regions, some of which are supposed to have curled clusters of flower buds suggestive of a scorpion's upturned tail, and others to have leaves resembling mouse-ears, thus inspiring the generic name *Myosotis.* The European forget-me-not *(M. scorpioides)* has been widely introduced as a decorative plant for flower borders, where its small, pink buds open into pale blue blossoms; when it escapes from cultivation, it thrives in its normal surroundings—partly shaded banks of shallow streams as well as other wet places. Family: Borage (Boraginaceae).

FORSYTHIA, or golden bells, a genus with just 4 species of shrubs native to temperate parts of Eurasia, but now widely cultivated for their arching stems on which bright yellow flowers open before the leaves expand in spring. The four pointed petals diverge symmetrically from the rim of a bell-like throat. The pointed leaves have saw-teeth along the edges, and are arranged alternately along the stems. Family: Olive (Oleaceae).

FOUR-O'CLOCK, or marvel of Peru, a handsome herb with opposite leaves and clustered, trumpet-shaped flowers that open petal-like sepals with amazing regularity about four o'clock every afternoon, stay open through the night, and close again around sunrise. In its native Peru and in warm parts of the United States, four-o'clock is a perennial, whereas in temperate regions it is cultivated as a garden annual. Family: Four-o'clock (Nyctaginaceae); genus and species, *Mirabilis jalapa.*

FOUR-O'CLOCK FAMILY (Nyctaginaceae), a group of about 250 species in 28 genera, mostly herbs or woody plants of the tropics and subtropics, in which the floral parts seem reversed: the 5, united sepals are petal-like, the petals are absent altogether, and the imitation corolla is backed by green, sepal-like bracts. See *Bougainvillea* and *Four-o'clock.*

FOXGLOVE, any of about 25 different kinds of tall herbs of the Old World from the Canary Islands to central Asia, growing to a height of about 5 feet, with scattered, ovoid leaves and a tall spike of yellow, white, pink, or purple, spotted, tubular flowers that hang like inverted bells. *Digitalis purpurea* from western Europe has been widely introduced as an ornament, and is the principal source of the powerful heart stimulant digitalis. Family: Figwort (Scrophulariaceae); genus *Digitalis.*

FREESIA, a genus composed of 3 different kinds of herbaceous plants native to South Africa that grow from bulbs and produce an upright stem with small leaves and linear clusters of trumpet-shaped, fragrant flowers varying in color from white to cream, yellow, rose, and lavender. They are raised as house plants in many countries. Family: Iris (Iridaceae).

FRITILLARY, or checkered lily, any of about 50 different bulbous herbs of the North Temperate Zone, which produce nodding clusters of bell-

BURPEE SEEDS

GAILLARDIA

shaped flowers the petals of which are checkered or spotted. Among the most handsome species cultivated as an ornament is the crown imperial *(Fritillaria imperialis)* of Iran. Family: Lily (Liliaceae); genus *Fritillaria.*

FUCHSIA, a genus of shrubs and trees, chiefly from Central and South America, with about 75 different species, including 2 in New Zealand. The plants have dark green, paired, oval leaves and funnel-shaped, pendant flowers on slender stalks. The sepals are usually a different color from the petals, providing such striking color contrasts as red and blue, red and cream, or scarlet and green. The plumlike fruits contain red seeds.

Many ornamental fuchsias are found in outdoor gardens of warm regions or grown as house plants in colder climates. They are often of hybrid origin. Family: Evening primrose (Onagraceae).

FUMITORY, a leafy-stemmed, branching, annual plant of Mediterranean countries, now cultivated in the United States and elsewhere in warm temperate parts of the world, that escapes from cultivation into waste ground. The dense spikes of small, spurred, irregular, purplish flowers are followed by cylindrical capsules, each with a single seed. The name refers to the odor of the roots when they are first pulled from the soil. Family: Fumitory (Fumariaceae); genus and species, *Fumaria officinalis.*

FUMITORY FAMILY (Fumariaceae), a group of about 425 species in 19 genera, widespread in the North Temperate Zone and in South Africa. All are weak, smooth herbs with a watery sap and bilaterally symmetrical flowers. See *Dutchman's-breeches* and *Fumitory.*

FURZE. See *Gorse.*

GAILLARDIA, or blanket flowers, a genus of stiff, herbaceous wildflowers comprising 12 different kinds native to the western United States, all growing 2 to 3 feet tall, with a few oval, notched leaves and conspicuous flower heads, the red or yellow ray flowers of which form a bright halo around a golden center. Several have been developed by horticulturalists as garden flowers, which are popular because they bloom until late autumn. Some are annuals and others perennials. Family: Daisy (Compositae).

GARDENIA, a genus of about 100 different woody shrubs native to the Old World tropics, with broad, simple, opposite, evergreen leaves, and attractive, regular flowers. The fruits are bright orange and as much as 1½ inches long in cultivated gardenias such as the cape jasmine *(G. jasminoides)* of China, so named because the first plants brought to England came from the Cape of Good Hope.

Bearing fragrant, white or yellow flowers that have a waxy texture and last a long time, gardenias have become popular greenhouse plants in cool places; in warm regions, such as southeastern United States, they bloom outdoors and are used for decorative hedges. Family: Madder (Rubiaceae).

GARLIC, a strong-smelling, small onion native to southern Eurasia, with spearlike leaves rising from a hard bulb that reproduces itself as it grows, providing additional small bulbs (called cloves) within the tough outer skin. Cultivated for use as a flavoring, garlic has been introduced into many regions and has escaped from cultivation to roadsides and fields.

Along with such related plants as wild garlic *(Allium oleraceum* from Europe and *A. canadense* from eastern North America) and European field-garlic *(A. vineale),* it has become a hazard in pastures because cows tend to eat it, thus spoiling the taste of their milk. Family: Lily (Liliaceae); genus and species, *Allium sativum.*

GENTIAN, any of about 500 different kinds of herbaceous plants of temperate, cool, and especially alpine regions all over the world. They bear single or clustered, showy flowers late in the growing season. Most have deep, purplish-blue flowers, but some (particularly in the Andes) have pink or red, and a few have yellow flowers.

Several kinds are known as closed or bottle gentians because the petals of their deep, tubular corollas never spread; bumblebees force their way into these flowers to get nectar and attend to pollination. Gentian seeds are small, winged, and wind-distributed.

Those of the fringed gentian *(Gentiana crinita)* of moist woodlands from Maine to Minnesota and southward have had so little chance to ripen in recent years because people pick the flowers, that the plant is facing extermination. The flowers are lovely azure, urn-shaped blossoms with fringed edges that turn down. Because it is an annual in the southern parts of its range and a biennial in the northern parts, the fringed gentian depends for survival upon producing seeds from each flower.

The roots of the yellow gentian *(G. lutea)* of southern Europe and Asia Minor yield a drug formerly used as a tonic. Many other gentians produce a dye called gentian violet, which can be extracted and used in treating various skin and respiratory infections. Family: Gentian (Gentianaceae); genus *Gentiana.*

GENTIAN FAMILY (Gentianaceae), a group of about 800 species in 70 genera, widely distributed, some in the Arctic and on high mountains. All have opposite, simple leaves and clusters of regular flowers. The petal tips of the flowers uncurl as the bud opens.

A very different related plant is the water snowflake, or floating heart. Twenty different varieties of this plant grow in shallow ponds and slow-flowing streams, their heart-shaped leaves floating like waterlily pads on the surface; water snowflakes are often cultivated in garden pools and large aquaria. See also *Gentian.*

GERANIUM, a name applied widely and without discrimination to herbaceous plants of two related genera. About 300 of them are known as cranesbills *(Geranium)* from the shape of the fruit, and 250 are known as storksbills *(Pelargonium).*

Cranesbills have 5 similar petals, with no sepal, extended in the form of a hollow spur. The upper 2 petals of storksbills are smaller, larger, or bear different markings, and the sepal behind these is extended into a long, hollow spur that is joined for its whole length to the flower stalk. Cranesbills include the wild geranium *(G. maculatum)* of eastern North American meadows, thickets, and woodlands, and the herb Robert *(G. robertianum),* found on gravelly shores and rocky woodlands of much of North America, Eurasia, and North Africa.

The hardy house plant known as geranium, which survives in poor soil with little attention as long as it gets warmth, sun, and an occasional watering, is a storkbill developed horticulturally, primarily from a South African ancestor; most are aromatic, with stiff stems, luxuriant, round, or nearly heart-shaped leaves, and large heads of red, rose, pink, yellow, or white, irregular blossoms.

The essential oil extracted from leaves and stems of *Pelargonium* is called geranium oil and is used in perfumes. Family: Geranium (Geraniaceae).

GESNERIA FAMILY (Gesneriaceae), a group of about 1200 species in 85 genera, most of them tropical and subtropical herbs with opposite leaves. A number are widely enjoyed as ornamental plants for house or greenhouse. Cape primrose *(Streptocarpus* species) is native to South Africa and Madagascar.

African violet (horticultural varieties from 3 species of *Saintpaulia),* native to East Africa, propagates

PLANT TYPES

IRVIN L. OAKES FROM NATIONAL AUDUBON SOCIETY

MOREL MUSHROOM

© WALT DISNEY PRODUCTIONS

AIRPLANT BLOSSOM

ANTHONY MERCICA FROM NATIONAL AUDUBON SOCIETY

BEAR GRASS

EL AL

BARLEY FIELD

EL AL

DWARF BANANA

© WALT DISNEY PRODUCTIONS

HEDGEHOG CACTUS

© WALT DISNEY PRODUCTIONS

BARCO

© WALT DISNEY PRODUCTIONS

PAPAYA

FLOWERS

CHRYSANTHEMUM

LOTUS

CLEOME (CASPER PLANT)

WATER LILY

SINGLE DAHLIA

COSMOS

PETUNIA

PHOTOS BAUMAN/LOOK

GLADIOLUS

HELIOTROPE

DAHLIA

PHLOX

JAPANESE CHRYSANTHEMUM

ROSES

TREES

WILLIAM HARLOW FROM NATIONAL AUDUBON SOCIETY

TWO CROWN SHAPES OF AMERICAN ELM

DENNIS BROWN FROM NATIONAL AUDUBON SOCIETY

REDWOOD

ARTHUR W. AMBLER FROM NATIONAL AUDUBON SOCIETY

NORWAY MAPLE

RICHARD PARKER FROM NATIONAL AUDUBON SOCIETY

ASPENS

easily from leaves in water. The Brazilian gloxinia *(Sinningia)* is similar in many ways, although with much larger flowers and a need for an annual period of inactivity. See also *Gloxinia.*

GILLYFLOWER. See *Stock* and *Wallflower.*

GINGER, a herbaceous perennial of tropical and subtropical Asia, generally a cultivated species with alternate, narrow, grasslike leaves along an upright, reedy stem rising from a fleshy, underground rhizome (horizontal stem), which also produces slender stalks topped with clusters of flowers.

The cultivated species is no longer found wild; it is believed to have been adapted by early man in tropical Asia. The spice ginger is made from the rhizomes, which may be scrubbed, dried, and then ground, or cooked while fresh and then candied.

In North America, an unrelated perennial herb *(Asarum canadense* and other species of the birthwort family Aristolochiaceae) is called wild ginger; it has an aromatic rhizome that produces 2 kidney-shaped, furry leaves and a bell-shaped flower without petals, which is purple inside and green outside. Family: Ginger (Zingiberaceae); genus *Zingiber,* particularly *Z. officinale.*

GINGER FAMILY (Zingiberaceae), a group of about 1400 species in 47 genera, chiefly tropical, perennial herbs with fleshy, underground stems and 2-ranked leaves or whorls of basal leaves. Several yield valuable spices. Others are outstandingly beautiful, such as the brilliant torch-flowers *(Hedychium* species) native to Madagascar and Southeast Asia, and the shellflower *(Alpinia speciosa)* of the East Indies. See *Arrowroot, Cardamom,* and *Ginger.*

GINKGO, or maidenhair tree, an erect, generously branching Oriental tree that attains a height of 60 to 80 feet and bears clusters of fan-shaped leaves on short, woody spurs rising from the main branches. The staminate trees produce stamens in clusters resembling catkins. The ovulate trees form ovules in pairs on short spurs and, later, seeds that appear plumlike, with a fleshy outer covering over an inner stony layer. When ripe, the fleshy covering decomposes, emitting a fetid odor.

Staminate trees are therefore preferred for ornamental planting. They are hardy and grow well in cities, despite soot, exhaust fumes, and pavement reaching to within a few inches of the trunk on all sides. The single species *(Ginkgo biloba)* is a "living fossil," with no wild representatives known. It has been perpetuated by Oriental monks in temple grounds. Fossil ginkgoes have been found in many parts of Eurasia and North America. Family: Ginkgo (Ginkgoaceae).

GINSENG, any of about 6 different kinds of herbaceous, woodland plants of tropical and eastern Asia and temperate North America, growing 1 to 4 feet high, with alternate compound leaves and flat or globular clusters of small, yellow flowers that produce scarlet, fleshy fruits.

The Chinese have long considered the fleshy roots a valuable medicine and pay a high price for those of the Manchurian species *(Panax schinseng)* and a lower price for the kind native to eastern North America *(P. quinquefolius).* Family: Ginseng (Araliaceae); genus *Panax.*

GINSENG FAMILY (Araliaceae), a group of about 800 species in 65 genera, most abundant in tropical America and Southeast Asia, all with 5-part, small flowers in clusters that are flat-topped or spherical. It includes the devil's club *(Echinopanax horridus),* a dangerously spiny shrub native to western North America from California to Alaska, and the rice-paper tree *(Tetrapanax papyrifera)* of Formosa, from which rice-paper is made. See *Ginseng, Ivy,* and *Spikenard.*

GLADIOLUS, a genus of bulbous plants with narrow, linear leaves and spikes of large, stemless, irregular, trumpet-shaped flowers. In addition to the 250 different species native to Africa and southern Europe, many horticultural varieties have been developed. They are propagated by natural division of the bulbous corms and produce large flowers that are white, yellow, pink, rose, purple, or combinations of more than one color. Family: Iris (Iridaceae).

GLOXINIA, a low-growing, tuberous, Brazilian herb with large, thick, hairy, deeply-veined, spreading leaves and large, bell-shaped flowers. Cultivated as a decorative house plant, it has developed horticultural varieties with red, rose, pink, or white flowers, rather than the violet-colored flowers characteristic of the wild plants. Family: Gesneria (Gesneriaceae); genus and species, *Sinningia speciosa.*

T.H. EVERETT

GINKGO

GODETIA, a genus of herbaceous plants native to western North America, with about 25 different species of which one, called summer's darling or farewell-to-spring *(G. amoena),* bearing large, satiny petals ranging in color from white to deep red, is widely cultivated as a garden ornament. Family: Evening primrose (Onagraceae).

GOLDEN BELL. See *Forsythia.*

GOLDEN CHAIN. See *Laburnum.*

GOLDEN GLOW, a coarse, perennial, garden plant developed by horticulturalists from a flower of eastern North America. Golden glow has spherical heads of golden-yellow disc florets 2 to 4 inches across and hardly any, or no ray florets. Family: Daisy (Compositae); genus, species, and named variety, *Rudbeckia lacinata hortensis.*

GOLDENROD, any of about 90 different kinds of perennial herbs, one native to Britain and parts of Europe, one to the Azores, a few found in temperate Asia and South America, and the vast majority in North America where they brighten forest, field, and roadside with feathery sprays of small flowers, usually golden-yellow but sometimes white or greenish in color.

They are flowers of late summer and autumn, some of them growing on rough, hairy stems 7 feet tall that bear many small leaves all the way up. Family: Daisy (Compositae); genus *Solidago.*

GOOSEBERRY, a low-growing, spiny shrub, sometimes 3 feet tall, native to North Africa and much of Europe, producing 3-lobed leaves, small, pale yellow blossoms in loose clusters, and spherical, shiny fruit with minute seeds. Cultivated varieties, with edible green or purple fruit, are raised in cool parts of Europe, North America, South Africa, New Zealand, and Australia. The fruit is eaten raw or used in cooking and in making preserves. Family: Saxifrage (Saxifragaceae); genus and species, *Ribes grossularia.*

GOOSEFOOT FAMILY (Chenopodiaceae), a group of about 1400 species in 102 genera, widely distributed but especially well represented in arid and salty or alkaline areas. They include annual and perennial herbs, shrubs, and some small trees, often with fleshy enlargements on the stems where leaves are attached or where leaves would have been attached had the stem not been leafless.

Glasswort, or samphire *(Salicornia* species), are fleshy, leafless herbs of seacoasts, often changing in color from bright green to brilliant red in autumn. See *Beet, Lamb's-quarters, Pigweed, Saltbush, Spinach,* and *Tumbleweed.*

GORSE, or furze, or whin, any of about 20 different kinds of spiny, woody shrubs; its green spines are modified leaves. It is native to Europe and North Africa, but has been widely introduced as a soil-binding plant, a hedge, and a source of young growth appealing to sheep and other livestock. It is also grown for the large, yellow, fragrant flowers that precede the conspicuous brown pods. Family: Pea (Leguminosae); genus *Ulex.*

GOURD, a fleshy fruit with a thick, firm, outer part (the rind) surrounding a more fibrous, soft part (the pulp) in which the seeds are embedded; also, the plant that produces such a fruit. Most are members of the gourd family (Cucurbitaceae) and are usually vines native to Africa or warm and temperate parts of the Northern Hemisphere.

Some gourds are raised for their fruits, others as ornaments, and still others to be dried, cleansed of their pulp, and made into drinking vessels, dishes, and musical instruments.

GOURD FAMILY (Cucurbitaceae), a group of about 850 species in 100 genera, mostly tropical and subtropical prostrate or climbing herbs with tendrils that appear along the length of the stems. Many are cultivated for food or for their decorative value. See *Cucumber, Gourd, Melon, Pumpkin, Squash,* and *Vegetable sponge.*

GRAPE, any of about 60 different kinds of woody vines mostly native to temperate parts of the Northern Hemisphere. The spherical fruits are also called grapes. The grape plant or grapevine bears simple, heart-shaped leaves, and climbs by means of tendrils that are highly adapted terminal buds growing out of side branches that lack leaves. The flowers are small, green, and generally hairy; the fruits are small or large, seeded or seedless, tart or sweet, green, red, blue, or greenish-white in color.

Grapes may be eaten raw, dried as raisins, or used in fermentative processes to make many kinds of wine. Until the 1600s, almost the only grape in cultivation was the one that was domesticated in prehistoric times in southern Europe and Asia Minor. Its culture was introduced into America before the value of the American species was recognized.

The principal species used are the European *Vitis vinifera* and the North American *Vitis labrusca*, as well as numerous hybrids and horticultural varieties. Family: Grape (Vitaceae); genus *Vitis.*

GRAPE FAMILY (Vitaceae), a group of about 600 species in 11 genera, native to the tropics, subtropics, and some temperate regions, chiefly climbing shrubs with terminal buds that become tendrils, requiring the stem to continue growth by an apparent bend as the axillary bud extends into a new branch. The flowers are clustered and produce berries.

Among cultivated plants in this family are the trailing begonia *(Cissus discolor)* of Java and the peppervine *(Ampelopsis arborea)* of the southern United States. See *Boston ivy, Grape,* and *Woodbine.*

GRAPEFRUIT, a small tree with large, ovate leaves and fragrant, white flowers, discovered first in the West Indies and probably derived from the

BURPEE SEEDS

GOURDS

pomelo or shaddock *(Citrus grandis)* of Southeast Asia. The fruits of the grapefruit grow in clusters of 5 to 15, and include among the varieties developed by horticulturalists a number of thin-skinned and seedless types differing considerably from the original stock. The fruit is eaten fresh, canned, or made into juice. Family: Rue (Rutaceae); genus and species, *Citrus paradisi.*

GRAPE HYACINTH, any of about 40 different kinds of small, bulbous plants with bladelike leaves and clusters of bell-shaped flowers at the top of upright stems. The clusters suggest bunches of blue, white, or yellow grapes. Native to Mediterranean Europe, they have been introduced widely as decorative plants used in flower borders and rock gardens. Family: Lily (Liliaceae); genus *Muscari.*

GRASS FAMILY (Gramineae), a very large family with about 4500 species in 500 genera, the most widely distributed of vascular plants. Many have the ability to lie dormant during protracted droughts.

They have colonized prairies, plains, savannas, campos, pampas, steppes, and veldts, and are a source of food for grazing animals, a great variety of seed-eating birds, and rodents. They have fibrous roots, typically hollow stems, and parallel-veined leaves. Their flowers are clustered and so specialized that only the stamen and pistil seem to correspond to parts of flowers in other plant families.

See *Bamboo, Barley, Bluegrass, Broomcorn, Corn, Crabgrass, Millet, Oat, Pampas grass, Reed, Rice, Rye, Sorghum, Sudan grass, Sugarcane, Timothy,* and *Wheat.*

GROUND IVY, or gill-over-the-ground, a delicate but prolific creeping and trailing plant with a square stem, round or kidney-shaped leaves on short petioles, and clusters of blue or yellow flowers. It is native to Europe but has been introduced into many parts of the world and has escaped from cultivation to become a weed. Family: Mint (Labiatae); genus and species, *Glechoma hederacea.*

GROUNDNUT. See *Peanut.*

GROUND PINE. See *Club moss.*

GUAIACUM. See *Lignum Vitae.*

GUAVA, a small tree with square stems, opposite leaves, fragrant, white flowers with four petals, and mildly acid, yellow fruits about the size of a hen's egg. Native to the West Indies, it is now cultivated extensively in the southern United States, North Africa, Malaya, and China. The pinkish flesh of the fruit is too soft to withstand transportation, but it is eaten raw where grown or made into jams and jellies. Family: Myrtle (Myrtaceae); genus and species, *Psidium guajaba.*

GUAYULE, a branching shrub with luxuriant, silvery leaves, native to the North American southwest, and now cultivated in Texas and Mexico for its latex, which contains solid particles suitable for extraction and manufacture into a valuable rubber.

When about 4 years old the whole plant is pulled up, dried, crushed, and immersed in water. The particles that have been suspended in the cell sap then float to the top and can be skimmed off. Between 150 and 200 million pounds of this material are used annually. Family: Daisy (Compositae); genus and species, *Parthenium argentatum.*

GUNNY. See *Jute.*

GUTTA-PERCHA. See *Rubber Tree.*

GYPSOPHILA. See *Baby's-Breath.*

HACKBERRY, any of about 60 different small trees of the Northern Hemisphere, with elmlike leaves and plumlike fruits. The bark of the most widespread species in eastern North America *(Celtis occidentalis)* is silvery and deeply grooved into a checkered pattern. The wood is soft, easily broken by strong windstorms and accumulations of sleet, but useful for making boxes, baskets, and some kinds of furniture.

Hackberries are often planted as windbreaks and as shade trees in the southern United States. Family: Elm (Ulmaceae); genus *Celtis.*

HAREBELL. See *Bluebell.*

HAWKWEED, any of perhaps 2000 different kinds of herbaceous perennial plants of temperate and cool climates in the Northern Hemisphere, the Andes, and South Africa. Most have hairy, simple leaves in a whorl close to the ground and hairy, upright stalks bearing one or more flower heads. All of the florets in each head bear strap-shaped corollas, which are commonly orange, yellow, or scarlet. Many are noxious weeds that reproduce by seeds and runners. Family: Daisy (Compositae); genus *Hieracium.*

HAWTHORN, any of perhaps 1000 different kinds of woody shrubs and small trees of the North Temperate Zone with alternate leaves that are deeply cut into lobes, prominent spines on the stems, and clusters of pink or white flowers that open in spring. The flowers are followed by small, red, yellow, blue, or black, apple-like fruits called haws. Family: Rose (Rosaceae); genus *Crataegus.*

HAZEL, any of 8 different shrubs and small trees of the North Temperate Zone, with oblong to round leaves that are folded lengthwise in the bud, drooping catkins of staminate flowers, budlike, pistillate flowers with conspicuous red stigmas in early spring, and hard-shelled seeds released from leaflike bracts that develop around the ripening fruit.

The seeds of the European hazel *(Corylus avellana)* are produced commercially by orchards in Italy, Turkey, Spain, and the state of Oregon for sale as filberts. A filbert differs from the hazelnuts of other species in that it is larger but shows no distinctive difference in shape, texture, or taste. Family: Birch (Betulaceae); genus *Corylus.*

HEATH, any of about 500 different tough, branching shrubs and trees of Europe, southwestern Asia, and South Africa, with small, white, pink, or purple, cuplike flowers, and 4-chambered capsules that open to release small seeds. A great many heaths are characteristic of moorlands. The tree heath *(Erica arborea)* of the Mediterranean region grows to a height of 65 feet and furnishes brierwood for briar pipes. Family: Heath (Ericaceae); genus *Erica.*

HEATH FAMILY (Ericaceae), a group of about 1900 species in 70 genera, almost all woody shrubs and trees. The heaths constitute the characteristic vegetation of moors, many mountain slopes and swamps in temperate and subarctic lands, and the higher slopes of tropical mountains. See *Arbutus, Azalea, Blueberry, Cranberry, Heath, Heather, Huckleberry, Madroña, Manzanita, Mountain laurel, Pipsissewa, Rhododendron,* and *Wintergreen.*

HEATHER, or ling, a low-growing evergreen shrub native to Greenland, Europe, and western Asia but now introduced into eastern North America and covering large areas of moorland. The leaves are minute, overlapping, and in opposite pairs. The small pink, purple, or white flowers generally arise on one side of the stem or its branches, near the tip. The bright color is in the calyx, which overlaps and hides the small corolla.

In true heaths *(Erica),* on the other hand, the calyx is small and the corolla shows the color. Family: Heath Ericaceae); genus and species, *Calluna vulgaris.*

HELIOTROPE, any of about 250 different kinds of herbs, vines, shrubs, and small trees, chiefly native to tropical South America, but found also in warm parts of Eurasia and North America. All have simple leaves and

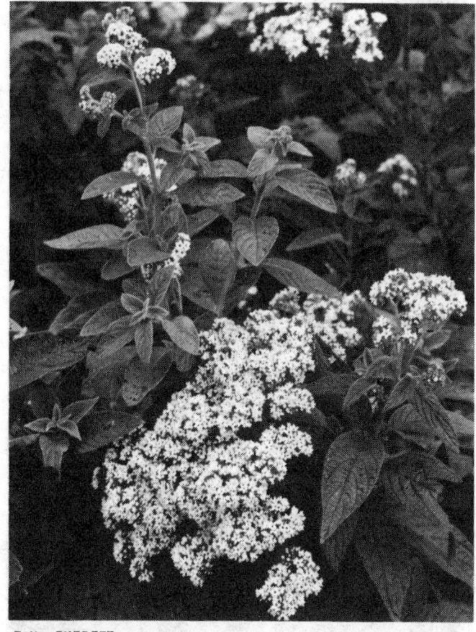

T.H. EVERETT

HELIOTROPE

funnel-shaped or tubular flowers with flaring petals borne in spikes. Many horticultural varieties of the cherry pie *(Heliotropium arborescens),* native to Ecuador and Peru, are cultivated for their perfumed flowers. Family: Borage (Boraginaceae); genus *Heliotropium.*

HELLEBORE, any of about 22 different kinds of evergreen plants native to southern Europe, with glossy, palmately compound leaves, and showy, cupshaped flowers that lack petals but have white, pink, or purple sepals. The powdered roots of some have been used in medicine as a sedative and in agriculture as an insecticide.

A cultivated ornamental plant is the Christmas rose or black hellebore *(Helleborus niger),* which blooms in winter and often pushes its rather stiff, 2-inch flowers through the snow. Each flower has 5, widely spreading, white, petal-like sepals and numerous golden stamens. Family: Buttercup (Ranunculaceae); genus *Helleborus.*

HEMLOCK, any of 12 different coniferous, evergreen trees characteristic of forests in China, Japan, and North America, but not native to Europe or other continents. The needles are flat, with 2 white lines beneath, and are arranged on the 2 sides of drooping branches. Tan colored cones grow on the under-sides of the branches and release winged seeds.

The eastern hemlock *(Tsuga canadensis)* of North America grows well in the shade of hardwood forests and is valuable for the tannins in its bark. Western hemlock *(T. heterophylla)* of the Pacific Northwest is a much larger, stronger tree, rising to about 260 feet, and yielding inportant timber, as well as bark that is rich in tannins. Family: Pine (Pinaceae); genus *Tsuga.* See also *Poison hemlock.*

HEMP, an erect or twining annual plant native to Asia, growing 3 to 18 feet high, with 3 to 7 narrow, toothed leaflets on each of its palmately compound leaves. The inner bark is valuable for its tough fibers, which are made into twine, rope, canvas, and sailcloth. Resin extracted from hairs on the stem and leaves contains a mixture of narcotic compounds responsible for the drug effects obtained from smoking the dried unextracted plant materials, known as marijuana, hashish, or charas. Hemp seeds are used to feed cage birds and to make a commercial oil resembling linseed oil. Family: Hemp (Cannabinaceae); genus and species, *Cannabis sativa.*

HEMP FAMILY (Cannabinaceae), a small group of 3 species in 2 genera, often included in the Mulberry family (Moraceae). The genus *Cannabis* has only one species, hemp *(C. indica).* See *Hemp* and *Hop.*

HENEQUEN. See *Century Plant.*

HEPATICA, or liverleaf, a small genus of woodland wildflowers blooming in early spring in the North Temperate Zone. Each plant consists of a basal whorl of 3-lobed leaves on slender, hairy petioles and, in season, a number of white, pink, or lavender flowers with many stamens but no petals, the petal-like sepals providing the color.

There are two species native to eastern North America; one, *H. triloba,* is native to Eurasia but not to the British Isles. Family: Buttercup (Ranunculaceae).

HERB CHRISTOPHER. See *Baneberry.*

HERB ROBERT. See *Geranium.*

HIBISCUS, or rose mallow, a genus of herbs, shrubs, and small trees native to tropical and subtropical countries, with large, showy flowers. One *(H. rosasinensis),* known as rose of China, or shoeblack plant, or shoeflower, has almost become a symbol of the tropics because of its wide cultivation as a decorative hedge plant. Its blossoms collapse permanently at the end of a day. They contain a black dye that makes them suitable for polishing and cleaning black shoes.

More than 1000 horticultural varieties of the hibiscus plant with distinctive names and petals of many colors and forms have been developed.

Among the 200 other species of the genus, the Asian rose of Sharon *(H. syriacus)* with 3-lobed leaves and cupshaped, red flowers is commonly planted as an ornamental shrub; okra, or gumbo, or bandakai *(H. esculentus),* which probably originated in northeastern Africa, is cultivated extensively in tropical West Africa, southeastern United States, Turkey, and India for its edible, partly ripened capsules, which are mucilaginous unless properly cooked. Family: Mallow (Malvaceae).

HICKORY, any of several kinds of trees native to eastern North America and Southeast Asia, with large, shiny, pinnately compound leaves, trunks 60 to 160 feet tall, tough, close-grained wood, and small flowers in separate clusters, the staminate flowers in yellow, tassel-like catkins and the pistillate flowers in stiff spikes. The leathery coverings of the fruits crack open, releasing the armored seeds, which fall to the ground.

Some species are shagbark or shellbark hickories; these shed their old bark in long, flat strips that loosen gradually and curl slightly away from the trunk. Others are more smooth-barked, marked only by deep surface furrows. Most have edible kernels in the seeds. The pecan *(Carya pecan)* grows to a height of 150 feet, and yields the best nuts of any member of the group; a native of the Mississippi Valley, the Southwest, and into Mexico, it is now cultivated in large orchards in Georgia and adjacent states. Family: Walnut (Juglandaceae); genus *Carya*.

HOLLY, any of about 280 different kinds of shrubs and trees with alternate, simple leaves and small clusters of regular flowers that are followed by berry-like fruits containing several nutlets. They are widely distributed, although Europe has only one, *Ilex aquifolium:* a small tree with very hard wood, leathery, glossy, evergreen leaves, and bright red fruits that remain in place until mid-winter. The European holly was used in pagan rituals, and later found a place in Christmas ceremonies.

An American holly *(I. opaca)* with prickly leaves that are only slightly less glossy than those of the European holly is used for Christmas purposes in the New World, although fruits develop only on the pistillate trees when they are near the fruitless staminate trees. Some hollies, such as black alder *(I. verticillata)* of swamps in the eastern United States, are deciduous. Others are appreciated because their prickly leaves contain caffeine and can be brewed into the popular beverage, *yerba maté,* or Paraguay tea (from the South American evergreen shrub *I. paraguariensis)*. Family: Holly (Aquifoliaceae); genus *Ilex*.

HOLLYHOCK, a tall, biennial herb with large wrinkled leaves on an erect stem that grows 5 to 6 feet high, producing an ascending progression of saucer-shaped flowers in white, pink, yellow, lavender, and even a violet so dark that it seems black. Native to the Balkans, the plant was brought to western Europe by returning Crusaders and adopted as a stately garden flower. In Egypt its leaves are sometimes cooked as a vegetable. Family: Mallow (Malvaceae); genus and species, *Althaea rosea*.

HONEYDEW MELON. See *Melon*.

HONEY LOCUST. See *Locust*.

HONEYSUCKLE, any of about 180 different kinds of erect or climbing shrubs with opposite, simple leaves and paired flowers that are bilaterally symmetrical and often both fragrant and supplied generously with nectar. Native to the Northern Hemisphere, they include several shrubs that have been introduced widely and cultivated for their flowers and, in some cases, the evergreen cover the climbing species provide over unwanted native vegetation Family: Honeysuckle (Caprifoliaceae); genus *Lonicera*.

T.H. EVERETT

HONEYSUCKLE

HONEYSUCKLE FAMILY (Caprifoliaceae), a group of about 275 species in 18 genera, chiefly native to the Northern Hemisphere, mostly trees or shrubs, but many climbing vines, all with opposite leaves and clustered flowers. It includes the twinflower *(Linnaea borealis),* found in the far north of both Eurasia and North America. See *Black haw, Elder, Honeysuckle, Viburnum,* and *Woodbine*.

HOP, a perennial climbing vine of Eurasia, with rough stems 15 to 20 feet long, coarse, lobed leaves, staminate flowers on some plants and pistillate flowers on others. The pistillate flowers are enclosed by green bracts (the "hops" of brewers) which bear yellow, dustlike grains of a bitter substance used to give flavor and sparkle to beer. Family: Hemp (Cannabinaceae); genus and species, *Humulus lupulus*.

HOREHOUND, a perennial herb with a square stem, opposite, hairy, silvery leaves, and clusters of small, white flowers in the leaf axils. Native to the Mediterranean countries from the Canary Islands to western Asia, it has been cultivated and naturalized elsewhere for an extract used in candies and in syrups designed to treat colds and coughs. Family: Mint (Labiatae); genus and species, *Marrubium vulgare*.

HORNBEAM, any of about 20 different small trees of the North Temperate Zone, with gray bark, hard wood, drooping branches, oval, serrate leaves that turn orange in autumn, and separate clusters of staminate and pistillate flowers in catkins. The small, one-seeded fruits are winged. Family: Birch (Betulaceae); genus *Carpinus*.

HORSE CHESTNUT, a handsome, deciduous tree attaining a height of 60 feet, with opposite, palmately compound leaves. The leaflets are wedge-shaped and toothed along the edges. Pyramidal clusters of creamy flowers are followed by prickly fruits that open to release large, inedible seeds resembling chestnuts.

Native to the Balkans and the Caucasus, the horse chestnut is cultivated widely as an ornamental tree. Relatives from South America and the North Temperate Zone include the buckeyes of California, the north central states, and the southeast. The light wood of these trees is used for paper pulp and the manufacture of artificial limbs. Family: Horse chestnut (Hippocastanaceae); genus and species, *Aesculus hippocastanum*.

HORSERADISH, a perennial herb native to Eurasia, growing to about 2 feet in height, with narrow leaves, clusters of white flowers, and white, fleshy roots that are edible and used as a condiment. The plant is now widely cultivated and used to give flavor to relishes. Family: Mustard (Cruciferae); genus and species, *Armoracia rusticana*.

HORSETAIL, any of about 25 different kinds of perennial rushlike herbs with hollow, jointed stems. They have neither leaves nor flowers and are found throughout the world except in the Australasian region. Most are less than 3 feet tall, but the *Equisetum giganteum* of the West Indies and tropical South America may attain a height of 36 feet.

Several species are native to both Eurasia and North America, such as the scouring rush *(E. hyemale),* the stems of which are so harsh because of the siliceous material they contain that poineers and peasants have used them to scour pots, floors, and other surfaces. All horsetails develop terminal clusters of spore cases. The spores germinate on suitable moist surfaces and grow into small, special plants bearing the sexual reproductive organs. Fertilized eggs from these grow into the familiar herbs. Family: Equisetaceae; genus *Equisetum*.

HUCKLEBERRY, any of about 40 different kinds of shrubs 1 to 6 feet tall, with smooth, oval, leathery leaves, white or pink, bell-shaped flowers, and clusters of glossy, black berries containing 10 minute, hard seeds. Native to the Americas, they are often confused with blueberries *(Vaccinium),* which have somewhat less acid berries and no armor around the seeds. Family: Heath (Ericaceae); genus *Gaylussacia*.

HYACINTH, any of about 30 different kinds of hardy, bulbous herbs native to Mediterranean countries and South Africa. They are cultivated widely for their early spring flowers, which are fragrant, bell-shaped, white, pink, blue, or violet, and grow in tall, compact clusters that precede the stiff, bladelike leaves.

The name is also given to some related plants of other genera, such as the wood hyacinth *(Scilla non-scripta)* of the Old World, and the wild hyacinth *(Camassia scilloides)* of eastern North America. Family: Lily (Liliaceae); genus *Hyacinthus*. See also *Grape Hyacinth*.

HYDRANGEA, a genus containing about 80 different species of woody shrubs native to the North Temperate Zone. They attain a height of 8 to 20 feet, and bear large, paired leaves and round heads composed of globular flowers. The Oriental species *(H. paniculata)* is the most common ornamental species, with flowers ranging from white to pink and blue. The wild hydrangea *(H. arborescens)* of eastern North America attains a height of 10 feet and grows mostly on wet soils rich in lime. Family: Saxifrage (Saxifragaceae).

ICE PLANT, a succulent, low-growing plant of South Africa, with leaves densely covered with small, bladder-shaped hairs that glisten like ice crystals. Grown as a ground cover, rather than for its small white or pink flowers, the plant is cultivated extensively in southern California and elsewhere. It does not tolerate hard frosts.

The juice of the plant can be used as a diuretic and demulcent. In Spain the ashes of its leaves and stems are often added to the mixture used in making glass. Family: Carpetweed (Aizoaceae); genus and species, *Mesembryanthemum Crystallinum.*

INDIAN HEMP, a widespread North American perennial herb with a milky juice in tough stems 2 to 4 feet tall. It has paired, oval leaves, and bell-shaped, white or greenish flowers in terminal clusters. Indians used the fibers of the inner bark for making rope. Family: Dogbane (Apocynaceae); genus and species, *Apocynum cannabinum.*

INDIAN PIPE, a colorless, saprophytic plant of moist woodlands in North America. It lives on dead vegetable matter in the soil with the help of a fungal partner. The upright stems are covered with waxy, white scales, and they terminate at a height of 4 to 10 inches in a nodding, white, cylindrical flower. The stem and flower turn black when picked. As the seeds ripen, the stem straightens, shrivels, and turns blackish-brown, holding an upright capsule. Family: Pyrola (Pyrolaceae); genus and species, *Monotropa uniflora.*

INDIAN TOBACCO. See *Lobelia.*

INDIAN TURNIP. See *Jack-in-the-pulpit.*

INDIGO, a shrubby plant native to the East Indies. The blue dye obtained by fermenting and oxidizing the juice from the odd-pinnate leaves of this plant is also called indigo. Cultivation of indigo for the dye industry was formerly a major occupation in India and other warm parts of Asia and South America, but operations virtually ceased when cheaper synthetic dyes became available. Family: Pea (Leguminosae); genus and species, *Indigofera tinctoria.*

IRIS, a genus of about 200 different species found in the North Temperate Zone, all with grasslike or sword-shaped leaves, usually growing from a fleshy underground stem. The flowers have 3 showy sepals which turn down (called by horticulturalists "the falls") while 3 similar petals turn up ("the standards"); the 3 branches of the style on the pistil are often petal-like, arching over the stamens.

Many species, hybrids between species, and horticultural varieties are cultivated for their flowers. The Florentine iris *(I. florentina)*, with white flowers, is probably the model for the French emblem, the fleur-de-lis ("flower of the lily"). The dried and powdered roots of this and a few other European irises, known as orris root, are used to give an imitation violet fragrance to perfumes, tooth pastes, and other cosmetics. Family: Iris (Iridaceae).

IRIS FAMILY (Iridaceae), a group of about 1500 species in 58 genera, native to all but the coldest regions, mostly herbaceous plants with storage organs in underground stems or roots, and sword-shaped or grasslike leaves rising from the base. Their flowers differ from those of lilies and related families in having only 3 stamens instead of 6. See *Crocus, Freesia, Gladiolus,* and *Iris.*

IRISH MOSS, or carrageen, a soft seaweed growing attached to rocks at moderate depths along North Atlantic coasts, where it is often torn loose and cast ashore in vast quantities by winter storms. Although technically a red alga, it may be green, yellow, purplish, or brown.

When gathered, washed, and dried in the sun, it can be pulverized to make a flourlike material of some food value. Soaked in water, it becomes mucilaginous and is used to give body to soups and desserts such as blancmange, or to medicines such as cough mixtures. Family: Gigartina (Gigartinaceae); genus and species, *Chondrus crispus.*

T.H. EVERETT

JACK–IN–THE–PULPIT

IRONWEED, any of about a dozen North American, rough-stemmed, coarse, herbaceous perennials growing as high as 10 feet, with many alternate, narrow, pointed leaves and clusters of purplish-red or white flowers that resemble thistle heads without prickles. They produce prodigious numbers of seeds, and spread quickly over neglected or overgrazed land, offering little that attracts livestock but providing abundant nectar for honeybees.

Some of their relatives in Africa are valuable timber trees. These are perhaps the largest representatives of the family. Family: Daisy (Compositae); genus *Vernonia.*

IVY, or English ivy, a vigorous climbing plant native to temperate Eurasia, with dark glossy, oval or 5-lobed, evergreen leaves, yellowish flowers, and clusters of black berries. It clings by means of short, aerial roots penetrating small cavities in wood or stone surfaces.

Garlands of ivy were used in ancient Greece to decorate statues of Dionysus or Bacchus, and became a symbol of those establishments where wine was sold by the glass. Later, ivy-clad walls became a mark of institutions of learning. Introduced into the New World, ivy forms an attractive ground cover in the southern United States, but is often killed by winter cold in northern states and Canada.

The name ivy is commonly given to other creeping and climbing plants. Family: Ginseng (Araliaceae); genus and species, *Hedera helix.* See *Boston Ivy, Poison Ivy,* and *Woodbine.*

JACK-IN-THE-PULPIT, or Indian turnip, any of several herbaceous, woodland plants of temperate North America, bearing one or more palmately compound leaves. It has a single flower cluster with a spathe extended into a flaplike hood (the "pulpit") around the central column (the spadix, or "Jack") bearing the tiny staminate and pistillate flowers.

The thick, short, underground stem is made acrid by a sap containing needle-like crystals of poisonous calcium oxalate, which the Indians removed with boiling water to obtain an edible food. Family: Arum (Araceae); genus *Arisaema.*

JAPONICA, or flowering quince, a popular Oriental ornamental shrub. It has spreading spiny branches 3 to 6 feet tall, glossy leaves, scarlet or orange flowers blooming early in the year, and 2-inch, globular, hard fruits rich in pectin and suitable for making into a jelly. Family: Rose (Rosaceae); genus and species, *Chaenomeles lagenaria.*

JASMINE, any of about 200 different erect or climbing shrubs native to all continents except Africa and Australasia. Several are cultivated in warm, temperate, and tropical countries for their attractive and fragrant white or yellow starlike flowers borne on climbing, slender stems among delicate, pinnately compound leaves. The fresh flowers are used to make perfume. Dried flowers are often added to tea in China and Japan.

The name jasmine is often given to the unrelated yellow jessamine *(Gelsemium sempervirens* of the strychnine family, Loganiaceae), an evergreen vine with clustered, golden flowers native to swamps in the southeastern United States. Family: Olive (Oleaceae); genus *Jasminum.*

JEWELWEED, or touch-me-not, or snapweed, any of several herbaceous plants of the North Temperate Zone, with hollow, juicy stems 2 to 5 feet tall, oval leaves, and clusters of pendant, orange flowers shaped like those of the snapdragon but with a spur formed by the extended calyx.

The fruits are explosive capsules that shatter when ripe, scattering the pellet-like seeds over a radius of several feet. Sparkling drops of water often adorn the leaves in the early morning, giving them the name of jewelweed. Family: Jewelweed (Balsaminaceae); genus *Impatiens.*

JIMSONWEED, or thorn apple, a malodorous and dangerously poisonous coarse annual native to the Asian area between India and the Caspian Sea. It is now almost cosmopolitan as a rank weed growing to 5 feet, with broad leaves toothed around the margin and white, trumpet-shaped flowers that are followed by a prickly, ovoid seed capsule. The sweet-tasting seeds are deadly poisonous; all other parts of the plant are almost equally dangerous. Family: Potato (Solanaceae); genus and species, *Datura stramonium.*

JOE-PYE WEED, a herbaceous perennial of eastern North America with oval, serrate leaves whorled around its thick stems; the stems are 3 to 10 feet tall and bear flat-topped clusters of pink or purple flowers. It was named after Joe Pye, a traveling Indian medicine man of New England, who advertised a tonic made from this plant. Family: Daisy (Compositae); genus and species, *Eupatorium purpureum.*

JONQUIL. See *Narcissus.*

JUDAS TREE. See *Redbud.*

JUJUBE, a shrub or small tree of southern China and the East Indies, attaining a height of 20 to 50 feet, with alternate leaves, hooked spines, and plumlike fruits about the size of olives. These fruits are known as jujubes or Chinese dates. It has been introduced into the southern United States as an ornamental tree, but preserved jujubes are still imported from Mediterranean countries and Japan. Family: Buckthorn (Rhamnaceae); genus and species, *Zizyphus jujuba.*

JUNIPER, any of about 60 different kinds of shrubs and trees native to the North Temperate Zone, with scale-like or needle-like, evergreen leaves and one-seeded, fleshy cones known as juniper berries. Oil of juniper, extracted from these cones, is used medicinally as a diuretic, and commercially in the manufacture of varnish and the flavoring of gin.

Eastern red cedar *(Juniperus virginiana)* provides long-lasting posts, railroad ties, and wood for making lead pencils, but because it is an alternate host for the fungus causing apple rust, some states prohibit the planting of this tree near apple orchards. Western juniper *(J. occidentalis)* grows at moderate altitudes in the mountains of western North America, sometimes reaching the age of 2000 years. Family: Cypress (Cupressaceae); genus *Juniperus.*

JUTE, or gunny, the fiber from the inner bark of either of two East Indian shrubs, which are raised as annuals and grow 6 to 12 feet tall. They are planted so close together that they produce almost no branches. The fiber is used for cheap twine, cording, burlap, bagging, oakum, and strong wrapping paper. Family: Linden (Tiliaceae); genus and species, *Corchorus capsularis* and *C. olitorius.*

KAFIR CORN. See *Sorghum.*

KALE. See *Mustard.*

KAPOK, or silk-cotton tree, a tropical American tree of moderate height, with large, 5-lobed leaves; a heavy, ridged trunk; bark studded with conical, blunt spines; bell-shaped flowers; and pods full of fluffy, silky fibers that can be separated from the seeds.

These fibers are water-resistant, buoyant, elastic, but not useful for spinning. Kapok trees are cultivated extensively in Java, Malaysia, Ceylon, and the Philippine Islands to obtain the fibers. The fibers are used to stuff mattresses, life-preservers, and pillows, and for the manufacture of wallboard, ceiling insulation, and even bathing suits. The oil from kapok seeds is used in foods and soap. Family: Bombax (Bombacaceae); genus and species, *Ceiba pentandra.*

KENTUCKY COFFEE TREE, a deciduous, hardwood tree of the southeastern United States. It grows 50 to 100 feet tall and has rough, scaly, reddish-gray bark; twice pinnately compound leaves; terminal clusters of white flowers; and pods containing black seeds, which were used by the colonists as a substitute for coffee beans. The hard wood is useful for fence posts. Family: Pea (Leguminosae); genus and species, *Gymnocladus dioica.*

KOHLRABI. See *Mustard.*

KUDZU, a hairy, twining vine native to southeastern Asia. It has luxuriant foliage and clusters of purple flowers. In the United States it has been planted as a decorative porch vine capable of climbing 60 feet or more, and in the southern states, as a soil binder to control erosion on slopes. Family: Pea (Leguminosae); genus and species, *Pueraria lobata.*

KUMQUAT, any of 6 different Asian shrubs 6 to 8 feet tall, with glossy, green, simple leaves, fragrant, white flowers, and fruits the size of an olive resembling miniature oranges. The fruits may be eaten raw or preserved, and are now the basis for the cultivation of kumquats in the southern United States. Family: Rue (Rutaceae); genus *Fortunella.*

LABURNUM, a genus consisting of 3 different kinds of small European and western Asian trees with dark 3-parted leaves and pendant sprays of bright yellow flowers. *L. anagyroides* is cultivated for Easter decorations and as the principal source of the alkaloid cytisine, used in medicine. Golden chain *(L. vulgare),* is popular in the southern United States for decorative outdoor planting. The wood of all of these trees is used in fine cabinet work. Family: Pea (Leguminosae).

LACQUER TREE, or varnish tree, any of several unrelated trees from which substances can be extracted for the production of lacquer or varnish. Most notable is a small tree of China and Japan, with handsome, pinnately compound leaves that turn orange-red in autumn. A mildly toxic latex can be obtained from these trees by slashing the bark on the trunk or stripping the bark from branches less than an inch in diameter. The viscous latex turns black upon exposure to air.

Chinese workmen who have become immune to its irritating effect upon the skin paint the blackened latex on boxes, trays, and other objects, and later smooth the coating with a stone tool to produce a handsome, high luster. The practice began in prehistoric times and reached the greatest perfection during the Ming dynasty (1364–1644 AD). Family: Sumac (Anacardiaceae); genus and species, *Rhus vernicifera.*

LADY'S SLIPPER, any of about 30 different kinds of perennial, woodland orchids of the North Temperate Zone, with coarse, fibrous roots, broad, pleated leaves that clasp the stem, and mostly solitary, showy flowers atop a tall stalk. The lower lip (labellum) of the corolla resembles the toe part of a shoe or moccasin, inspiring the other common names of shoeflower or moccasin flower.

The lady's slipper flower may be white, pink, purple, yellow, brown, orange, or red, plain or attractively mottled. The large yellow lady's slipper *(Cypripedium pubescens)* is often grown in shady gardens. Family: Orchid (Orchidaceae); genus *Cypripedium.*

LAMB'S-QUARTERS, an annual plant native to western Asia but now cosmopolitan as a weed of roadsides and neglected land, growing as a straight stem to 1 to 9 feet, with narrow, serrate leaves and sprays of greenish-white flowers. In Eurasia the green portions of young plants are sometimes cooked and eaten. Family: Goosefoot (Chenopodiaceae); genus and species, *Chenopodium album.*

LARCH, any of about 10 different kinds of needle-leaved trees of the North Temperate Zone, bearing deciduous needles in clusters of 10 or more, and small cones from which winged seeds are distributed by the wind. All larches produce useful wood.

The European larch *(Larix decidua)* is the source of a yellow resin called Venice turpentine, used in lithography. The American larch *(L. laricina),* known also as the tamarack or hackmatack, grows in cold bogs across the continent from Alaska to New England. Family: Pine (Pinaceae); genus *Larix.*

LARKSPUR, any of about 200 different kinds of herbaceous plants found in the North Temperate Zone, with palmately lobed or divided leaves and an upright, sturdy stem growing to 2 to 7 feet. The stem is topped by a graceful cluster of handsome flowers, each with the top sepal prolonged into a spur that is hollow and surrounds similar extensions from the top 2 petals. The 5 sepals and 2 or 4 petals are all petal-like, in blue, purple, pink, pale yellow, white, or blended colors.

Horticulturists reserve the name larkspur for annuals and use the generic name for perennials. Many wild larkspurs are poisonous to cattle. Family: Buttercup (Ranunculaceae); genus *Delphinium.*

LAUREL, or sweet bay, a handsome tree of Mediterranean countries, with aromatic, glossy, evergreen leaves, yellow flowers, and purple fruits resembling cherries. Wreaths and coronets were made with its leafy branches as a traditional sign or honor for the winners in Greek games.

A similar and related tree, California laurel *(Umbellularia californica),* found in forests of California and Oregon and growing to a height of 80 feet, yields hard wood used a great deal in cabinetry. Family Laurel (Lauraceae); genus and species, *Laurus nobilis.* See *Mountain laurel.*

LAUREL FAMILY (Lauraceae), a group of about 1100 species in 45 genera, chiefly shrubs and trees with aromatic bark, aromatic, smooth-edged leaves, and clustered flowers, native to tropical and subtropical regions.

Some varieties such as the greenhart *(Nectandra rodioei)* of northern South America and the stinkwoods *(Ocotea* species) of South Africa, grow very slowly and produce exceedingly hard, strong wood.

Other varieties, such as the camphor-tree *(Cinnamomum camphora)* native to Formosa, Japan, and south China, and the cassia-bark tree *(C. cassia)* of southern China, rank along with cinnamon as a source of valued extracts and flavorings. See *Avocado, Cinnamon, Laurel, Sassafras,* and *Spicebush.*

LAVENDER, a low-growing, perennial, evergreen shrub of temperate Eurasia, with narrow, grayish-green leaves, and tall spikes of pale lilac-colored flowers. Both leaves and flowers are clad in fine hairs among which are glands containing a fragrant oil.

Fresh flowers are quite often used commercially to make lavender perfumes and other cosmetics; dried leaves and flowers are used in the manufacture of toiletries.

Southern France and Scotland have become centers of the lavender industry, although the plant itself is cultivated extensively as a garden ornament in North America. Family: Mint (Labiatae); genus and species, *Lavandula officinalis.*

LEEK, a slender, bulbous plant native to the Near East but now widely introduced and cultivated for its tasty, slender, cylindrical bulb and soft succulent leaves, which are milder than those of an onion. When it is allowed to mature it produces a cluster of white or pink flowers. Leeks are used commonly in the Old World and the New as a relish, a condiment, and to add flavor to soups. Family: Lily (Liliaceae); genus and species, *Allium porrum.*

LEMON, a low-growing, evergreen tree of Southeast Asia, 10 to 12 feet tall, with glossy, oval leaves and fragrant, white flowers. Its yellow, acid fruit is rich in citric acid and vitamin C. Cultivated for thousands of years in Asia and in warm parts of Europe, it is now grown extensively in subtropical America. The glandular rind of the fruit is frequently candied, preserved, or used in grated form to add a distinctive flavoring to foods. Family: Rue (Rutaceae); genus and species, *Citrus limon.*

LENTIL, an annual branching herb of the Mediterranean region, 6 to 18 inches tall, the pinnately compound leaves ending in climbing tendrils, the blue or white pealike flowers followed by small pods each containing 2 lens-shaped, gray or red seeds. The plant is cultivated extensively in the Old World for its edible seeds, which are made into soups and porridges. Family: Pea (Leguminosae); genus and species, *Lens culinaris.*

LETTUCE, an annual plant probably native to Asia Minor, cultivated for at least 2500 years as the most popular of salad ingredients. Until the Middle Ages, only the loose-leaved variety was known. Left to grow, it produces a stem 2 to 3 feet tall, topped by small clusters of white- or cream-colored flowers in which every floret is strap-shaped. Head lettuce, which was a new horticultural variety in the 1500s, is now generally preferred to leaf lettuce. Another variety is Cos, or romaine lettuce, with spoon-shaped leaves that have a broad midrib; it was first discovered on the Greek island of Kos. Lettuce contains important vitamins and minerals but virtually no food energy. Family: Daisy (Compositae); genus and species, *Lactuca sativa.*

BURPEE SEEDS

LEEKS

LICORICE, a herbaceous perennial plant native to Europe, with pale green, pinnately compound leaves, a stem about 3 feet tall, and purple flowers resembling those of peas and beans. It is cultivated extensively in southern Europe for its fibrous roots, from which a sweet black extract can be obtained for use in candies, soft drinks, and in flavoring medicines and tobacco.

A related plant, wild licorice *(Glycyrrhiza lepidota),* found widely in the plains and pasturelands between Mexico and central Canada, has sweet-tasting roots that yield their flavor when chewed. Family: Pea (Leguminosae); genus and species, *Glycyrrhiza glabra.*

LIGNUM VITAE, any of 6 different tropical American trees with extremely hard, heavy wood, pinnately compound leaves, blue, 5-petalled flowers, and seeds in capsules. Most grow to 15 to 30 feet and yield a gum (guaiacum) used in the treatment of rheumatic and skin diseases. The wood of the *Guaiacum officinale,* native to Forida, the West Indies, and northern South America, is the hardest and heaviest of commercial woods. Family: Caltrop (Zygophyllaceae); genus *Guaiacum.*

LILAC, any of about 25 different kinds of woody shrubs with thick, oval, paired leaves and clusters of white or purplish, 4-petalled flowers, which usually emit a strong and characteristic pleasant fragrance. Native to temperate Eurasia, lilacs are cultivated extensively in North America; many horticultural varieties have been developed, chiefly from *Syringa vulgaris* of southeastern Europe. Syringa is also the common name of an unrelated, different plant. Family: Olive (Oleaceae); genus *Syringa.* See also *Mock orange.*

LILY, in the strict sense, any of about 60 different kinds of herbaceous, perennial, bulbous plants of the North Temperate Zone, with upright stems, scattered or whorled, narrow, sessile leaves, and large, trumpet-shaped flowers, the 6 petal-like parts of which curve back upon themselves to display the inner surface.

Easter lilies are usually either the white-trumpet lily (or Bermuda lily, *Lilium longiflorum)* of Japan, which blooms in late March and early April, or they are the very similar madonna lily *(L. candidum)* of southern Europe, which flowers from late April through May. Handsome markings on the inner surface of the flower are features of the golden-banded lily *(L. auratum)* of the Orient and of the various tiger lilies with nodding blossoms, such as the Turk's-cap lily *(L. superbum)* of the eastern United States. Family: Lily (Liliaceae).

LILY FAMILY (Liliaceae), a group of more than 4,000 species in about 250 genera, widely distributed, mostly perennial herbs with a storage organ in the shortened stem, horizontal underground stem, or enlargement of the roots. Generally the flowers are regular, with a 6-parted display of petals and petal-like sepals, and a united ovary of 3 parts that ripens to form a capsule or a berry. See *Aloe, Asparagus, Asphodel, Bear grass, Bluebell, Dogtooth violet, Fritillary, Garlic, Grape hyacinth, Hyacinth, Leek, Lily, Lily of the valley, Mariposa lily, Onion, Rose of Sharon, Smilax, Solomon's seal, Trillium, Tulip,* and *Yucca.*

LILY OF THE VALLEY, either of 2 similar, small, perennial herbs of the North Temperate Zone, with freely spreading horizontal stems, scattered, oblong, upright leaves, and slender, one-sided sprays of small, fragrant, nodding, bell-shaped flowers which are followed by red, poisonous berries that contain a few seeds.

The North American species *(Convallaria montana)* is native to woodlands in the southern Appalachians; the European species *(C. majalis)* has been widely introduced and has become naturalized. Family: Lily (Liliaceae); genus *Convallaria.*

LIME, a small evergreen tree native to the East Indies, with glossy, oval, evergreen leaves, fragrant, white flowers, and small, greenish-yellow, acid fruits, the juice of which is used in beverages and for flavoring. Limes are cultivated throughout Mexico, the West Indies, parts of southern Florida, and southern Europe. Family: Rue (Rutaceae); genus and species, *Citrus aurantifolia.*

LINDEN, or basswood, any of 12 different fast-growing trees of the North Temperate Zone, with soft wood, heart-shaped leaves, and fragrant, creamy-white flowers in small clusters at the tip of pendant stalks to which a green, oval bract is attached for much of the length.

Bees obtain a large amount of nectar from basswood flowers, and the wood is often used in the manufacture of beekeeper's supplies, furniture, woodenware, charcoal, and paper pulp. Family: Linden (Tiliaceae); genus *Tilia.*

LINDEN FAMILY (Tiliaceae), a group of about 400 species in 41 genera, mostly tropical shrubs and trees with simple, alternate leaves and clustered regular flowers. The linden tree and jute are chief among those that grow in temperate regions. See *Jute* and *Linden.*

LITCHI, a genus of a single species *(L. chinensis)*. It is a handsome evergreen tree with large, pinnately compound leaves, small flowers, and oval or spherical fruits slightly more than an inch in diameter, each with a leathery skin, a pink pulp, and a central seed. When dried, the skin becomes wrinkled, brown, and brittle; the pulp becomes somewhat like that of a raisin. Cultivated extensively in the Far East since prehistoric times, its origin is uncertain. The tree is rarely raised in the western world. The fruits, dried or preserved and known as litchi nuts (also spelled lychi or leechee), are imported as expensive luxuries. Family: Soapberry (Sapindaceae).

BURPEE SEEDS

LILY

LIVE-FOREVER. See *Orpine.*

LIVE OAK. See *Oak.*

LOBELIA, a genus of about 250 different kinds of herbs, shrubs, and treelike plants widely distributed in tropical and temperate regions. All have tubular flowers with 2 upturned upper petals and 3 lower petals forming a sort of lip.

Several kinds of lobelia with showy blossoms have been cultivated and developed horticulturally as garden plants. These include the shrubby little blue lobelia *(L. erinus)* of South Africa, used as an edging for flower beds in the Northern Hemisphere, and the cardinal flower *(L. cardinalis)* native to meadows and freshwater shores in eastern North America, its stem 2 to 4 feet tall topped by an open cluster of scarlet flowers.

Colonists in the eastern parts of North America found the Indians drying and smoking the leaves of another native kind *(L. inflata)*, now known as Indian tobacco. It has large, oval leaves, small, blue flowers, and inflated capsules, and contains at least one alkaloid that is poisonous if taken internally.

In the Old World, lobelias include extraordinary species, such as the tree lobelia *(L. keniensis)* of high, misty mountain slopes in equatorial Africa, which produces leafy stems 10 to 15 feet tall, from which sturdy flower spikes rise another 6 to 8 feet. Family: Lobelia (Lobeliaceae).

LOCOWEED, any of several different kinds of bushy, herbaceous plants of the western United States and adjacent parts of Canada and Mexico. The plants are sometimes eaten by starving livestock. Within a few months, however, the animals develop symptoms of poisoning, such as an inability to drink or eat; these symtoms are usually soon followed by death. This effect has been attributed to at least 8 species of genus *Astragalus* and 3 of *Oxytropis.* Family: Pea (Leguminosae).

LOCUST, any of several different trees with pinnately compound leaves and flowers resembling those of peas. The flowers are followed by seed pods that turn brown and release the seeds. The name was originally given to the carob tree *(Ceratonia siliqua)* of the Mediterranean region, the unripened pods of which are edible and called St. John's bread. Its seeds may have been the original weights of "carats" used by jewelers. Black locust *(Robinia pseudoacacia)*, a valuable timber tree of eastern North America which is now planted in many other parts of the world, grows to a height of 80 feet, producing very hard, durable wood and drooping clusters of showy, white flowers. Its branches bear pairs of sharp spines.

The honey locust *(Gleditsia triacanthos)* attains a height of 140 feet, its branches and bark armed with stiff spines that fork repeatedly. Its pods are filled with a sweet natural gum that children like to chew. Family: Pea (Leguminosae).

LOGANBERRY, a hybrid bramble produced from a cross between the western dewberry *(Rubus ursinus)* of California and the widespread red raspberry *(R. idaeus)*. It was discovered in 1881 by Judge J. H. Logan and named for him *(R. loganobaccus)*. It thrives in the northwestern United States, producing large fruits resembling purplish raspberries; it has not been grown with as much success elsewhere in the United States. Family: Rose (Rosaceae).

LOGANIA FAMILY (Loganiaceae), a group of about 800 species in 32 genera, including herbs, shrubs, climbing vines, and trees, all native to tropical and subtropical regions and most with opposite, simple leaves. It includes the Carolina, yellow jessamine *(Gelsemium sempervirens)*, sometimes erroneously called jasmine, which is grown as a porch vine and is the state flower of South Carolina. See *Butterfly bush* and *Nux vomica.*

LOGWOOD, a small Central American tree with peculiarly ribbed bark, thorny branches, pinnately compound leaves, and almost symmetrical, 5-petalled, yellow flowers. Its dark red heartwood yields a valuable dye called haematoxylon, which can be used to dye felt, woolens, and silk a permanent black, purple, blue, or red color. An astringent extract from the wood is also used in medicine. Family: Pea (Leguminosae); genus and species, *Haematoxylon campechianum.*

LOOSESTRIFE FAMILY (Lythraceae), a group of about 475 species in 23 genera, widely distributed but most numerous in tropical America, including herbs, shrubs, and trees with simple, smooth-edged leaves, usually paired or in whorls, and flowers in which sepals, petals, and stamens all arise from the rim of a tubular part.

The henna plant *(Lawsonia inermis)*, a small shrub native to countries from northern Australia to India and East Africa, has shoots and leaves that yield the orange-red dye used for religious purposes and personal adornment.

The 25 kinds of loosestrife *(Lythrum)* are slender herbs with pink or magenta flowers, often giving their color to great areas of low, wet ground where they grow to 3 feet and bloom in mid-summer. The name loosestrife is also used for yellow-flowered herbs *(Lysimachia* species of the primrose family, Primulaceae). See also *Crape myrtle.*

LOQUAT, a small, Oriental, evergreen tree with large, oblong leaves, rust-colored underneath; fragrant, white flowers; and acid, yellow fruits shaped like miniature pears. In cultivation the tree grows to 10 to 12 feet, blossoms in autumn, and produces its fruits in spring. The fruits can be eaten raw, cooked, or preserved. Orchards of loquats have been established in California and the Gulf states. Family: Rose (Rosaceae); genus and species, *Eriobotrya japonica.*

LOTUS, any of several aquatic plants of the Old World as well as their close relatives in America. The pink-flowered, sacred lotus of China, Tibet, and India *(Nelumbo nucifera)*, like the yellow-flowered lotus *(N. lutea)* of the West Indies and the eastern United States, usually raises its circular leaves and flowers out of the ponds and quiet streams in which it grows.

The Egyptian lotuses include one with blue flowers *(Nymphaea caerulea)* and one with white *(N. lotus);* the latter is the floral emblem of Egypt. In both, the leaves ordinarily float on the water surface and the flowers extend little, if at all, on exposed stalks. The mythical lotus tree, which yielded fruits reputed to cause forgetfulness of all responsibilities, may have been the jujube. Family: Water-lily (Nymphaeaceae). See also *Jujube.*

LUFFA. See *Vegetable sponge.*

LUPINE, any of about 100 different kinds of herbaceous plants native to North America and Europe, with palmately compound leaves and tall, upright spikes of pealike flowers. The flowers of the lupine are usually blue, but they may also be white, yellow, red, or purple.

Many lupines contain poisonous substances in their foliage, flowers, and seed pods, causing loss of life to deer and livestock that eat them in times of extreme hunger. The bluebonnet *(Lupinus subcarnosus)* is the state flower of Texas. Family: Pea (Leguminosae); genus *Lupinus.*

MADDER, a perennial herb native to Eurasia, with a thick root, a slender stem bearing repeated whorls of leaves, and small clusters of yellow flowers which are followed by fleshy berries. Until 1869, madder was cultivated extensively for the dye alizarin, which could be extracted from its roots. The discovery of a cheap way to synthesize the dye from coal tar put an end to the industry.

When animals eat madder, the coloring becomes concentrated in their bones, claws, and beaks, and these parts of their bodies become orange-red. Madder dye was used to give color to many mummy cloths found in old Egyptian tombs. Family: Madder (Rubiaceae); genus and species, *Rubia tinctorium.*

MADDER FAMILY (Rubiaceae), a group of more than 5,000 species in 400 genera, chiefly of tropical and subtropical regions, all with smooth-edged, opposite leaves with large stipules, clustered, regular flowers, stamens attached to the petals, and the corolla attached to the ovary.

They include the delicate Eurasian herb *(Rubia tinctorium)* from which madder dye ("turkey red") was formerly obtained, the low-growing bluets *(Houstonia caerulea)* of North America, the partridgeberry *(Mitchella repens)* of North American woodlands, the shrubby buttonbush *(Cephalanthus occidentalis)*, and the many kinds of shrubby gardenias from the Old World, of which the fragrant-flowered ancestor for most cultivated varieties is the Chinese *Gardenia jasminoides.* See *Bedstraw, Cinchona, Coffee, Gardenia, Madder.*

MADROÑA, or madroño, either of two closely related evergreen shrubs or trees of western North America, growing to 125 feet, with smooth, red bark that peels in strips, large, glossy leaves that are white below, edible, orange-red fruits called "madrona apples," and a fine-grained wood that can be made into a superior grade of charcoal which is ideal for use in gunpowder. Family: Heath (Ericaceae); genus and species, *Arbutus menziesii* (Pacific coast) and *A. xalapensis* (northwest Mexico).

MAGNOLIA, a genus of about 20 different species of decorative shrubs and trees native to eastern Asia and North America, with aromatic bark, large, fragrant, waxy, white, yellow, or rose-colored flowers as much as 12 inches in diameter, and cone-shaped clusters of fruits. A hybrid between two Chinese species is cultivated in the northern United States and Europe for its flowers, which open in spring before the leaves.

The large-flowered magnolia *(M. grandiflora)*, native to the southern states and the state flower of both Louisiana and Mississippi, is an evergreen tree growing to 70 feet, with handsome, dark green, glossy leaves and lemon-scented, creamy flowers 8 inches or more across. A smaller evergreen, the sweet bay *(M. virginiana)*, is native to swamplands in the southeastern states, which are then known as "bay-lands." Although it attains a height of only 15 feet, its thick, short trunk is used to make wooden bowls and utensils. Family: Magnolia (Magnoliaceae).

MAGNOLIA FAMILY (Magnoliaceae), a group of about 100 species in 10 genera, all woody shrubs or trees with simple, alternate leaves and, usually, large, showy flowers in which the receptacle is elongated beyond the petals, bearing first a spiral of many stamens and then a spiral of carpels which mature and convert the floral cluster into a large, aggregate fruit. See *Magnolia* and *Tulip tree.*

MAHOGANY, any of several related tropical trees that produce a valuable hard, red-brown wood suitable for cabinetmaking. Most highly esteemed is *Swietenia mahogani,* native to the West Indies and Central America, and cultivated in Florida and India.

Mahogany has compound leaves resembling those of the honey locust, clusters of small flowers, and large, dull brown, pearshaped fruits. African mahogany *(Khaya senegalensis)*, Indian mahogany *(Toona ciliata)* of India and northern Australia, and Philippine mahogany *(T. calantus)* are similar. Family: Mahogany (Meliaceae).

MAHOGANY FAMILY (Meliaceae), a group of about 1000 species in 50 genera, chiefly tropical shrubs and trees with compound leaves and clustered, regular flowers. It includes the West Indian cedar *(Cedrela odorata)*, which provides the fragrant wood used in cigar boxes and is supposedly insect-repellent. See *Chinaberry* and *Mahogany.*

MAIDENHAIR TREE. See *Ginkgo.*

MAIZE. See *Corn.*

MALLOW, any of about 30 different kinds of Eurasian and north African herbs, many of them annuals and biennials. Most have alternate lobed leaves, pink, white, or blue flowers, and flattened fruits commonly called cheeses, which are enclosed in 2 or 3 tough, leaflike bracts rather than the 6 to 9 bracts of the closely related marshmallow and hollyhock.

The high mallow *(Malva sylvestris)* and round-leaved mallow *(M. rotundifolia)* have been introduced into North America and other continents, escaping from cultivation to become roadside weeds. Family: Mallow (Malvaceae); genus *Malva.*

MALLOW FAMILY (Malvaceae), a group of about 1500 species in 82 genera, widely distributed but most numerous in tropical America. Whether they appear as herbs, shrubs, or trees, they have simple, alternate leaves and, in each regular flower, a central column of stamens beyond which the style and stigma protrude. See *Cotton, Hibiscus, Hollyhock, Mallow, and Marshmallow.*

MANDRAKE, a herbaceous plant of southern Europe and northern Africa, with a thick taproot that is often forked equally, suggesting a human torso with legs. The short stem bears a tight whorl of spreading, ovate leaves, and a single, purplish flower. Many ancient superstitions developed in relation to this plant, including the claim that it shrieked when pulled from the ground.

Dried, powdered mandrake root was used to increase fertility in women and as an emetic, purgative, and mild narcotic throughout Europe and the Orient. The name mandrake is sometimes applied to the American May apple *(Podophyllum peltatum)*. Family: Potato (Solanaceae); genus and species, *Mandragora officinarum.*

MANGEL-WURZEL. See *Beet.*

MANGO, a small tree of the East Indies, growing to 50 feet, with glossy, oval leaves, sprays of yellow flowers, and large, pear-shaped, green fruits with a delicious, yellow pulp around a central, flattened seed. The fruit of the wild mango is smaller and less palatable than that of horticultural varieties now in cultivation in most tropical and subtropical countries. The roasted seeds are occasionally eaten. Family: Sumac (Anacardiaceae); genus and species, *Mangifera indica.*

MANGROVE, any of several different low-growing trees of tropical and subtropical shores, which grow in shallow sea water and form dense thickets. Red mangrove *(Rhizophora mangle)* of tropical America and West Africa has opposite leaves, and multi-branched aerial roots that grow downward from spreading branches.

The seeds germinate while still attached to the parent plant and fall free only after developing a long, dagger-shaped root and a terminal bud from which leaves can quickly spread. Black mangrove *(Avicennia nitida)*, an unrelated tree of the vervain family (Verbenaceae), generally grows in water-soaked soil, and gets air to its roots through upright, pencil-sized, leafless stems that grow upward for 4 to 6 inches until exposed.

The white mangrove *(Laguncularia racemosa)* of tropical America and Africa, and button mangrove *(Conocarpus erecta)* of the same regions, are members of the combretum family (Combretaceae); their bark is often harvested as a source of tannin. Family: Mangrove (Rhizophoraceae).

MANILA HEMP. See *Abacá.*

MANIOC. See *Cassava.*

MANZANITA, a stiff, branching, evergreen shrub native to the Pacific coast of North America, where it forms dense thickets or contributes to the harsh chaparral vegetation of arid areas. It produces smooth leaves, white or pink flowers, and brown fruits resembling small apples. The bark is conspicuously reddish or chocolate-brown. Family: Heath (Ericaceae); genus and species, *Arctostaphylos pungens.*

MAPLE, any of about 150 different kinds of trees and shrubs of the Northern Hemisphere and of mountains in Java and Sumatra, all with paired leaves and paired, winged fruits (samaras) commonly known as maple keys. Many are tall trees with palmately lobed, simple leaves on long stalks and valuable hardwood. In early spring they yield a slightly sweet sap that can be boiled to make syrup or maple sugar.

BURPEE SEEDS

MARJORAM

Most valuable are the sugar maple *(Acer saccharum)* of the northeastern United States and adjacent Canada, which attains a height of 120 feet, and the slightly smaller sycamore maple *(A. pseudoplatanus)* of central Europe and Asia Minor. Faster growing and with softer wood are the Norway maple *(A. platanoides)* of Eurasia, and the silver maple *(A. saccharinum)* and red maple *(A. rubrum)* of eastern North America.

Box elder *(A. negundo)* of eastern Canada and the northeastern United States, which, peculiarly, has pinnately compound leaves, is a still weaker tree, growing best in wet woodlands and near streams. The largest assortment of maples is native to Japan. In autumn the foliage of most maples undergoes a spectacular change in color through all shades from yellow and orange to deep red. Family: Maple (Aceraceae); genus *Acer.*

MARGUERITE. See *Daisy.*

MARIGOLD, any of about 20 different kinds of daisy-like, herbaceous plants native to the New World from Argentina to the southern United States, with aromatic, dissected leaves and orange-red flower heads firmly supported by a cluster of green bracts. The two kinds cultivated most widely are the tall, straight-stemmed "African" species *(Tagetes erecta)* and the dwarf "French" marigold *(T. patula)*, both originally from Mexico. The related pot-marigold *(Calendula officinalis)* of Mediterranean Europe, Asia Minor, and North Africa was formerly used for flavoring and raised widely as a potherb. Now it is cultivated as an ornament which produces flowers much of the summer; each flower head is large and orange-gold. Family: Daisy (Compositae); genus *Tagetes.*

MARIPOSA LILY, any of about 40 different kinds of bulbous herbs of western North America, with narrow leaves and tulip-like flowers handsomely marked with colorful spots on white, red, yellow, or lilac petals. A mariposa lily, *Calochortus nuttalii*, is the state flower of Utah. Family: Lily (Liliaceae); genus *Calochortus.*

MARJORAM, any of several related aromatic, perennial herbs native to the Mediterranean coasts. They are widely cultivated and have also escaped from cultivation to grow naturally along roadsides. They have square stems, paired, oval leaves, and either short clusters of purple flowers *(Origanum,* especially *O. vulgare)* or grayish leaves and white flowers *(Majorana hortensis)*. Family: Mint (Labiatae).

MARSHMALLOW, an erect perennial herb of temperate Eurasia and North Africa, growing to 4 feet, with oval leaves and delicate, pink flowers. Formerly its roots were gathered and used in the manufacture of a sweet, white confection which is now produced artificially from cane syrup. Family: Mallow (Malvaceae); genus and species, *Althaea officinalis.*

MARSH MARIGOLD, a perennial herb of eastern North America and northern Europe and Asia. It grows in wet places, producing glossy, kidney-shaped leaves on hollow stalks, and, usually, bright yellow flowers in spring. Young leaves and stems are eaten as greens, but older ones are poisonous. The plant is often called cowslip. Family: Buttercup (Ranunculaceae); genus and species, *Caltha palustris.*

MATÉ. See *Holly.*

MAY APPLE, an erect perennial herb of eastern North America, with a long, branching root, umbrella-shaped leaves on tall, stout stalks, and solitary, nodding, waxy, white flowers followed by oval, yellow, fleshy fruits.

The fruits are the least poisonous part of the plant. The roots are the most dangerous part because they contain several toxic materials; these poisons have been used in primitive medicine. May apple is sometimes known as the American mandrake, or wild jalap. Family: Barberry (Berberidaceae); genus and species, *Podophyllum peltatum.*

MAYFLOWER. See *Arbutus.*

MAYWEED, or dog fennel, a branching perennial herb native to Eurasia and North Africa, now widespread as a weed, with pinnately dissected leaves emitting a strong, unpleasant odor, and yellow-centered, white-rayed flower heads an inch in diameter resembling daisies. The leaves were formerly employed in preparing a tea used in treating colic. The garden camomile *(Anthemis nobilis)* is a closely related plant with a pleasant odor; a tea from its foliage was once used as a blood purifier. Family: Daisy (Compositae); genus and species, *Anthemis cotula.*

MEDLAR, a small, branching tree native to Eurasia and much cultivated in Europe for its globular fruits, which resemble crab apples and have a tart flavor in the freshly-ripened, gritty pulp. When they are killed by the frost and partially decayed, the unpreserved fruits have a better flavor. Family: Rose (Rosaceae); genus and species, *Mespilus germanica.*

MELON, a prostrate vine, or the large, spherical, or egg-shaped fruit, with a thick, fleshy rind and a fibrous, seed-filled center. The term is generally used to describe all horticultural varieties of the muskmelon *(Cucumis melo)* of tropical Asia and Africa, such as cantaloupes, cassaba melons, honeydew and Persian melons, and rock melons, and the varieties of the watermelon *(Citrullus vulgaris)* of tropical Africa, including the citron, or preserving melon. Insects carry pollen from the starlike, yellow, staminate flowers to the similar pistillate flowers on the same hairy prickly stems, partially concealed below large, round leaves.

Cantaloupes have an orange pulp and a hard skin raised in ridges, often in a netlike pattern. Cassaba melons are large, round, and smooth-skinned, with a rich, creamy pulp; they mature late and are often called winter muskmelons. Honeydew melons are oval in shape, ivory to white externally, with thick, green, sweet flesh. Rock melons, or European cantaloupes, are hardly grown in the United States and Canada; they are small, with a tough skin raised in high ridges, and a comparatively shallow, orange-red flesh.

Watermelons, which were cultivated in Egypt in ancient times, have a thick, green or green and white rind surrounding a sweet red pulp, and may weigh 50 pounds or more when mature; the pulp is eaten raw, the rind pickled, and the seeds sometimes enjoyed as if they were thin-shelled nuts. Family: Gourd (Cucurbitaceae).

MESQUITE, any of about 30 different kinds of tropical and subtropical thorny trees and shrubs native to arid regions and most conspicuous in the American Southwest, South America, and Hawaii where, after locally heavy rains, the seeds germinate and send down extremely long roots. The taproots attain a depth of as much as 60 feet, reaching underground supplies of water that other plants have failed to reach. Wherever mesquite grows into unstunted trees 40 to 50 feet tall, there is water within 40 feet of the earth's surface.

The branches bear decidous, twice pinnately compound leaves, and spikes of odorous, greenish-yellow flowers followed by yellow or brown seed pods. The pods of the common mesquite *(Prosopis juliflora)* are long and straight; those of the screw bean *(P. pubescens)* are twisted into spirals. The seeds are eaten by Indians and Mexicans, and the foliage by livestock. As fodder, mesquite provides an inadequate diet and symptoms of a fatal deficiency develop in cattle that continue to eat virtually no other foods for a few months. Family: Pea (Leguminosae); genus *Prosopis.*

MIGNONETTE, any of about 50 different kinds of small, herbaceous plants native to arid areas around the Mediterranean Sea and Asia. They have small, alternate leaves and spikes of fragrant flowers with tufts of brownish stamens on the upper petals. Beekeepers sometimes plant mignonette as a nectar-producing plant that gives a pleasant flavor to the honey made by their bees.

Two Mediterranean species have become roadside weeds in the New World, one *(Reseda alba)* with white flowers and the other *(R. lutea)* with yellow flowers. Horticulturalists have developed larger, greenish flowers in the common mignonette *(R. odorata)*, which has broad leaves and grows very close to the earth, forming a dense blanket over the soil or providing attractive edgings for flower beds. Family: Mignonette (Resedaceae); genus *Reseda.*

MILKWEED, any of about 90 different kinds of perennial herbs native to America and Africa, with erect stems, opposite or whorled leaves, an abundant milky juice that may contain poisonous substances. The clustered, small flowers have 5 petals that turn backward, exposing pairs of pollen masses linked by peculiar fibers that catch onto the legs of insects. Weak insects are often caught, whereas strong bees and butterflies carry the paired masses of sticky pollen and often accomplish cross-pollination. A pollinated flower develops into an inflated pod that splits along one side to release flat seeds, each with a tuft of satiny, white hairs that catch the wind.

The common milkweed *(Asclepias syriaca)* of eastern North American fields and roadsides, which was accidentally introduced into Asia Minor and later spread through much of Eurasia, has purple-pink or brownish-pink blossoms. Butterfly weed *(A. tuberosa)* of North America is often cultivated in gardens for its bright orange flowers. Family: Milkweed (Asclepiadaceae); genus *Asclepias.*

T.H. EVERETT

MIGNONETTE

MILKWEED FAMILY (Asclepiadaceae), a group of about 1700 species in 100 genera, mostly tropical, perennial herbs or shrubs (including climbing vines), usually with a milky sap, simple, paired, smooth-edged leaves, and clustered flowers. It includes the strange carrion flowers *(Stapelia species)* of South Africa, which resemble cacti in their succulent green stems and reduced leaves. See *Milkweed* and *Waxflower.*

MILKWORT, any of about 500 different kinds of herbaceous and shrubby plants native to Eurasia and Africa, with bitter-tasting, simple leaves and attractive, irregular flowers in which the conspicuous parts are two petal-like sepals; of the five sepals, only these two are red, white, blue, or yellow instead of green.

According to superstition, a decoction made from the leaves of the common milkwort *(polygala vulgaris)* would induce more production of milk in nursing mothers. Seneca snakeroot *(P. senega)* of eastern North America is the source of an irritant drug. Family: Milkwort (Polygalaceae); genus *Polygala.*

MILLET, any of a number of different grasses cultivated in the Orient for more than 5,000 years, and generally regarded as the "poor man's cereal" although the nutritional quality of the grains is higher than that of rice as it is eaten. Common, or proso, millet *(Panicum miliaceum)* is cultivated in the Soviet Union, whereas little millet *(P. miliare)* is the favorite in India; both are members of the huge genus of panic grasses.

Italian millet *(Setaria italica)*, grown in the Near East and China, is a foxtail grass. Pearl millet, known also as cattail millet *(Pennisetum glaucum)*, is favored in parts of India and in the Sudan. More distantly related grasses include finger millet *(Eleusine coracana)* and broomcorn millet *(Sorghum vulgare technicus)*, which are popular in Africa and India.

All millets yield grains that can be used to thicken soups or mixed with wheat to make a bread flour that will rise when baked. In North America and much of Europe millets are cultivated chiefly for poultry feed. Family: Grass (Gramineae).

MIMOSA, a genus of tropical and subtropical trees, shrubs, vines, and herbs containing about 350 species native to America, Africa, and Asia.

All have feathery, pinnately compound leaves, white or pink flowers in fuzzy, globular clusters, and seeds in bivalved pods. The sensitive plant *(M. pudica)*, a roadside weed in tropical America, has become famous because its leaflets and leaves fold quickly when touched. Family: Pea (Leguminosae).

MINT, any of about 15 different kinds of aromatic herbs native to the Northern Hemisphere, with square stems, opposite leaves, and clusters of blue, pink, or white flowers. Several are cultivated for the volatile oil that can be extracted from the leaves. It is used to flavor candies and to give a pleasing odor to perfumes and soaps.

Whole, fresh leaves of peppermint *(Mentha piperita)* are often added to beverages or chopped and cooked gently to make a sauce for meat. Spearmint *(M. spicata)* has become most famous as a flavoring for chewing gum. European pennyroyal *(M. pulegium)* and an American substitute, mock pennyroyal *(Hedeoma pulegioides)*, are also used to flavor foods. Family: Mint (Labiatae); genus *Mentha*.

MINT FAMILY (Labiatae), a group of about 3200 species in more than 200 genera, widely distributed but most numerous in Mediterranean countries, chiefly herbs with square stems and opposite leaves but sometimes shrubs, climbing vines, or trees. The epidermal cells secrete aromatic oils and the flowers are clustered, usually with a 2-lipped corolla and the 4 stamens of different lengths—2 long and 2 short. See *Balm. Catnip, Ground ivy, Horehound, Lavender, Marjoram, Mint, Oswego tea, Rosemary, Sage, Self-heal,* and *Thyme*.

MISTLETOE, any of more than 1000 different kinds of herbaceous and shrubby parasitic plants, principally of tropical regions, growing at the expense of trees to which the mistletoes are attached by modified roots called haustoria. Most have opposite or whorled, simple leaves on branching stems, small, green or colored flowers, and a sticky covering over the seeds. Birds that pick the small fruits have difficulty swallowing the sticky seeds and scrape them off on tree branches to which the seeds adhere while germinating.

European mistletoe *(Viscum album)* grows on many trees, especially apple, and was used in pagan ceremonies. The magic attributed to the mistletoe is the source of the custom of kissing under the plant at Christmas time. In the New World the plant used for this purpose is the American mistletoe *(Phoradendron flavescens)* of the eastern United States. Family: Mistletoe (Loranthaceae).

MOCK ORANGE, a hardy European shrub that grows to 6 to 12 feet, with brown bark, oval leaves about 4 inches long, and large, sweet-scented, white or cream-colored flowers that open late in spring. Often called a "syringa" because its stems were made into pipe stems, it is not related to the lilac *(Syringa)*. The state flower of Idaho, known there only as the syringa, is *Philadelphus lewisii*. Family: Saxifrage (Saxifragaceae); genus and species, *Philadelphus coronarius*.

MONKSHOOD. See *Aconite*.

MORNING GLORY. See *Bindweed*.

MORNING-GLORY FAMILY (Convolvulaceae), a group of about 1200 species in 50 genera, chiefly climbing herbs and woody vines of the tropics, but including shrubs and trees, some of which are thorny and adapted for arid conditions. See *Bindweed, Dodder*, and *Sweet potato*.

MOUNTAIN ASH, a small North American tree with pinnately compound leaves, clusters of creamy flowers that produce bunches of orange-scarlet berries, and soft, weak wood. Its flowers and fruits are decorative, and attract bees and fruit-eating birds. Moose and deer often eat the leaves and young twigs. Closely related is the Eurasian rowan *(Sorbus aucuparia)*. Neither tree commonly grows taller than 30 feet and both live best in cool climates protected from the wind. Family: (Rosaceae); genus and species, *Sorbus americana*.

MOUNTAIN LAUREL, a small evergreen shrub of eastern North America, with leathery leaves and beautiful clusters of rose-pink flowers. It is the state flower of Pennsylvania. A close relative is sheep laurel or lambkill *(Kalmia angustifolia)*, which is poisonous to young sheep. Family: Heath (Ericaceae); genus and species, *Kalmia latifolia*.

MULBERRY, any of about 12 different kinds of small trees native to the North Temperate Zone, which have leaves of many different shapes (oval, notched, and lobed) on the same tree, and clusters of small flowers followed by very sweet fruits. Most favored for eating raw, cooked, or preserved are the black fruits of black mulberry *(Morus nigra)*, native to western Asia. Red mulberry *(M. rubra)* of the eastern United States also produces edible fruits as well as wood that is resistant to decay. White mulberry *(M. alba)* of China is raised to provide leaves on which silkworms can feed. Family: Mulberry (Moraceae); genus *Morus*.

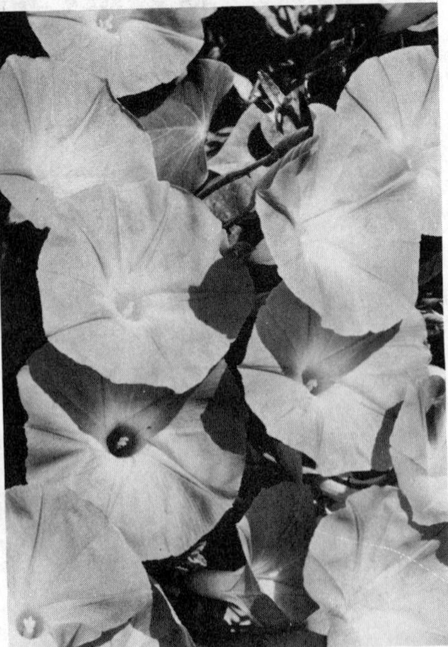

BURPEE SEEDS

MORNING GLORY

MULBERRY FAMILY (Moraceae), a group of about 1000 species in 73 genera, all with a milky juice and alternate, smooth-edged leaves. Most are plants of tropical and subtropical regions and many are important for their edible fruits. It includes the breadfruit *(Artocarpus altilis)*, a tall tree with large, deeply lobed leaves and hard, spherical fruits that can be eaten baked, boiled, or fried, and the jackfruit *(A. heterophyllus)*; both are from Southeast Asia but are widely cultivated in the tropics.

One of the fast-growing pioneer trees in tropical America is the trumpet tree *(Cecropia peltata)*, which harbors fierce, biting ants in hollow spaces reached through small holes in the axils of the leaves. See *Breadfruit, Fig, Mulberry, Osage orange,* and *Paper mulberry*.

MULLEIN, any of about 260 different kinds of tall, biennial herbs of the temperate parts of Eurasia, many now introduced and naturalized elsewhere. Best known is the common mullein *(Verbascum thapsus)* which, in its second year, raises an upright stem 2 to 7 feet tall above large, hairy, whorled lower leaves. On this stem a succession of flowers open, each for a single day. The plant is sometimes called flannel leaf or feltweed because of the felty texture of the leaves. Family: Figwort (Scrophulariaceae); genus *Verbascum*.

MUSKMELON. See *Melon*.

MUSTARD, any of several related annual, biennial, and sometimes perennial herbs native to Eurasia, where they have been cultivated for thousands of years as a source of small, round seeds producing a pungent oil. The plants themselves have stiff, branching stems 1 to 6 feet tall, and loose clusters of yellow flowers, each with 4 petals about ½-inch long. Young plants (mustard greens) are cooked as a slightly bitter potherb in some regions.

Black mustard *(Brassica nigra)*, a hairy plant with black seeds, is the principal source of the mustard seeds that are dried and pulverized for use as a condiment in Europe, excluding the British Isles, and as the major ingredient of mustard in North America. White mustard *(B. hirta)*, a rough plant with less hair and pale gray seeds, is preferred in Britain and many former British colonies for its "hotter" flavor. Small amounts are blended with black mustard powder and starch to make the mixture milder to suit the tastes of inhabitants of the New World.

Rape *(B. rapa)* is an annual with leaves that clasp the stems. Now known only in cultivation, rape is raised as a forage crop as well as for its seeds, which yield rape oil (useful as a food, lubricant, and lamp fuel). Its seeds are also used as bird food. The closely related turnip *(B. napus)*, like the rutabaga *(B. napobrassica)*, stores a great amount of food in a swollen root during its first year of growth, and is cultivated as a root crop for human use and as fodder for livestock.

Chinese cabbage *(B. pekinensis)*, sometimes called celery cabbage or pe-tsai, grows in a lettuce-like head of tightly wrapped, edible leaves. The inner leaves are white, crisp, and tasty. It has been raised as a salad green and vegetable in China since the first century AD and has been introduced into the United States.

Ordinary cabbage *(B. oleracea)* has been developed horticulturally from a wild Eurasian cliff plant to include the varieties known as cabbage *(B. oleaceae capitata)*, eaten raw, cooked, or slightly fermented and salted as sauerkraut; kale *(B. oleracea acephala)*, a headless variety with curly leaves; kohlrabi *(B. oleracea gongolodes)*, which has a turnip-like enlargement of the stem just above the ground; Brussels sprouts *(B. oleracea gemmifera)*, which has tight edible buds 1 to 2 inches in diameter clustered on the thick stalk; broccoli *(B. oleracea italica)*, with narrow, long, erect leaves around a large, round-topped cluster of flower buds; and cauliflower *(B. oleracea botrytis)*, which produces an edible head of misformed but delicately flavored, white flower stalks and buds. Family: Mustard (Cruciferae); genus *Brassica*.

MUSTARD FAMILY (Cruciferae), a group of about 2500 species in some 350 genera, mostly native to the North Temperate Zone, particularly to Mediterranean countries. All are herbs with alternate, simple leaves. Flowers with 4 sepals and 4 petals, 4 long stamens and 2 short ones around a pistal mature to become a pod that opens to release its seeds. See *Alyssum, Candytuft, Cress, Horseradish, Mustard, Peppergrass, Radish, Shamrock, Shepherd's purse, Stock,* and *Wallflower.*

MYRTLE, any of about 75 different kinds of tropical and subtropical shrubs and trees with glossy, green leaves and white or faintly pink flowers that are followed by small, black, fleshy berries. The classical myrtle *(Myrtus communis)*, from which wreaths were fashioned as crowns for victorious athletes, is a strong-scented ornamental shrub native to the Mediterranean region but now grown as a hedge in the southern United States.

Myrtle wood is fine grained and useful in turning fine gunstocks. An oil extracted from the leaves has medicinal value. Various parts of the plant, all pleasantly strong smelling, are used for perfumes and cosmetics. Family: Myrtle (Myrtaceae); genus *Myrtus*. See also *Crape Myrtle.*

MYRTLE FAMILY (Myrtaceae), a group of about 3000 species in 80 genera, all shrubs or trees of warm climates, most numerous in America and Australia, with leathery, simple leaves

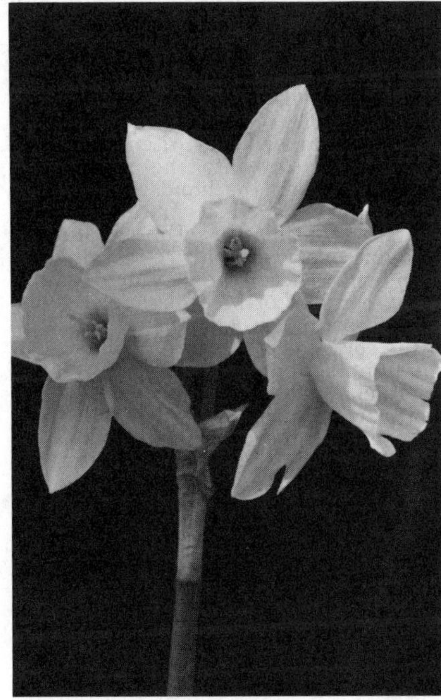

BURPEE SEEDS

NARCISSUS

dotted with glands containing volatile oils, and regular flowers usually in clusters. Among members of this family are many of the tall timber trees of Hawaii, New Zealand, Australia, and the East Indies, including not only members of the huge genus *Eucalyptus*, but also of *Metrosideros, Leptospermum, Melaleuca,* and *Callistemon* (bottlebrush); for most of these, only local common names have been developed. See *Allspice, Clove tree, Eucalyptus, Guava, Myrtle, Pomegranate.*

NARCISSUS, a genus of bulbous Eurasian herbs with slender leaves and white or yellow flowers on tall stalks, each flower with a 6-part perianth opening to display a ruffled disc- or trumpet-shaped crown. Cultivated all over the world as early spring garden flowers, several of the 40 different species have become well known.

The common name narcissus is usually restricted to *N. incomparabilis*, in which the crown is well developed and edged in reddish-orange, while the rest of the flower is white. The poet's narcissus *(N. poeticus)* has a much smaller crown, making the white perianth itself the most conspicuous part of the blossom.

The daffodil *(N. pseudo-narcissus)* bears solitary flowers on each stalk; its yellow fragrant blossom has a prominent crown of the same color. Jonquils *(N. jonquilla)* have clustered, pale yellow, fragrant flowers and crowns that are small and somewhat flattened. The polyanthus narcissus, or Chinese sacred lily *(N. tazetta)* produces a flat-topped cluster of yellow or white flowers with small crowns. Family: Amaryllis (Amaryllidaceae).

NASTURTIUM, a weak-stemmed, clambering herb of South America, now cultivated in gardens on many continents. It has circular leaves with stalks attached at the center, and with handsome, spurred, irregular flowers. The 5 petals of the flower may be yellow, scarlet, or maroon. All parts of the plant, including the seed capsules, have a pleasant, pungent aroma, which can be used to add flavor to salads. Pickled seed pods are sometimes used as a garnish for meat.

Dwarf horticultural varieties of nasturtium grow only a few feet tall, whereas others climb by sensitive leaf stalks to a height of 20 feet or more. The similar and closely related canary-bird flower *(Tropaeolum peregrinum)* is also cultivated for ornamental purposes. Watercress (genus *Nasturtium* of the mustard family, Cruciferae) is unrelated. Family: Nasturtium (Tropaeolaceae); genus and species, *Tropaeolum majus.*

NECTARINE. See *Peach.*

NETTLE, any of a number of related plants belonging to several genera native to most continents, and notable for the intensely irritating effect of a toxic material contained in stiff glandular hairs on the leaves. These hairs break after penetrating skin and release the irritant, which causes acute but usually temporary itching. Yet the young plants of some species are gathered and cooked as edible greens, and the roots of a few are harvested as a source of a lasting yellow dye.

Many nettles have strong stem fibers, but preparation for textile use is often difficult. Chinagrass, or ramie *(Boemeria nivea)*, of Southeast Asia, yields the toughest and silkiest fiber known. Nettletree *(Laportea gigas)* of Australia grows to a height of 90 feet. A close relative, the wood-nettle *(L. canadensis)*, is a perennial herb of eastern North America, growing no more than 3 feet tall.

Most famous of the nettles are the cosmopolitan members of genus *Urtica*, of which more than 30 species are known. Some are annuals easy to eradicate by cutting off the tops before their inconspicuous greenish flowers produce seeds, and others annuals that must be dug out or killed with herbicide chemicals. Family: Nettle (Urticaceae).

NIGHT-BLOOMING CEREUS, any of several climbing cactus plants with stems ribbed lengthwise, supporting themselves by means of aerial roots. They open solitary, huge, creamy, fragrant flowers as much as a foot in diameter for an hour or two in late evening, only to close them permanently before dawn. These cacti are native to the southwestern United States, Mexico and Central America, and the West Indies. Horticultural varieties and hybrids have been developed, partly from a spectacular wild species *(Cereus grandiflorus)*. Family: Cactus (Cactaceae).

NIGHTSHADE, loosely, any of 1700 different kinds of herbs, shrubs, and trees of tropical and temperate regions classified in genus *Solanum* of the potato family (Solanaceae). Specifically, either the common Eurasian nightshade *(Solanum nigrum)*, which is now almost cosmopolitan as a prostrate or erect herb with small clusters of white flowers followed by bunches of poisonous black berries, or the bittersweet *(Solanum dulcamara)*.

Enchanter's nightshade, 9 different north temperate and arctic plants growing from underground stems, is unrelated (genus *Circaea* of the evening-primrose family, Onagraceae). It produces paired leaves and short upright clusters of small white or pink flowers followed by similar clusters of dry fruits with hooked bristles that travel as burs. Family: Potato (Solanaceae). See also *Bittersweet*.

NORFOLK ISLAND PINE, an evergreen coniferous tree native to South Pacific islands, now widely introduced in warm climates or grown indoors in tubs for its symmetrical whorls of branches bearing luxuriant, short, needle-like leaves. Family: Araucaria (Araucariaceae); genus and species, *Araucaria excelsa*.

NUTMEG, an evergreen tree native to the Molucca Islands in the East Indies, now cultivated in the West Indies and tropical America. It grows 50 to 60 feet tall and has simple, oval leaves and tiny sprays of bell-like flowers that are either staminate or pistillate.

The flowers produce a peachlike, fleshy fruit of which the central seed is eggshaped and enclosed in a waxy, red membrane. The flesh of the fruit is preserved to be eaten as a candy, or made into a jelly. The membrane, which turns yellow, is dried for sale as the spice mace; the seed is grated or ground as the spice nutmeg. Family: Nutmeg (Myristicaceae); genus and species, *Myristica fragrans*.

NUX VOMICA, a medium-sized tree native to India and Ceylon and cultivated elsewhere in the tropics, with shining, oval leaves, clusters of greenish flowers, and globular, white fruits about the size of an orange. The bark, often called false Angostura bark, yields a bitter tonic. The green seeds embedded in the fruit are the principal source of the poisonous alkaloid strychnine. Family: Logania (Loganiaceae); genus and species, *Strychnos nux-vomica*.

OAK, any of about 300 different kinds of hardwood trees, native to the North Temperate Zone and islands of the South Pacific, with simple leaves and separate staminate and pistillate flowers. The staminate flowers are clustered in pendant, loose catkins; the pistillate flowers are solitary or in small groups close to the stem. The fruits are acorns, borne in a cup.

They mature in one year on members of the white-oak group, which bear round-lobed leaves and include the widespread Eurasian brown oak or English oak *(Quercus robur)*, the only oak in Britain, and such American trees as the eastern white oak *(Q. alba)*, Californian white oak *(Q. lobata)*, post oak *(Q. Stellata)*, bur oak *(Q. macrocarpa)*, and overcup oak *(Q. lyrata)*. The acorns take 2 years to ripen and usually germinate in the third year on members of the red-oak group, which have sharp-pointed lobes on the leaves and include the American trees known as red oak *(Q. rubra)*, black oak *(Q. velutina)*, water oak *(Q. nigra)*, pin oak *(Q. palustris)*, and willow oak *(Q. phellos)*. Many of these trees grow to a height of 100 to 170 feet, and produce valuable lumber. They often hold their dead leaves far into the winter, although by then the handsome autumn colors have faded to a dull brown.

In the southeastern United States a valuable evergreen oak *(Q. virginiana)* is known as live oak. A much smaller evergreen oak of Mediterranean countries, growing only about 40 feet tall, is the cork oak *(Q. suber)*, from which the light, spongy, bark can be stripped in thick sheets about once every 9 years to be made into the cork products of commerce. Some cork trees are grown in the United States, but the world's major cork supply comes from Portugal and Spain. Family: Beech (Fagaceae); genus *Quercus*.

OAT, an annual grass native to temperate regions of the Old World, cultivated in Eurasia for thousands of years as a forage plant, as a cereal for human use, and as food for horses. The plant grows 3 to 5 feet tall, with thin, narrow, long leaves beyond which the stem continues upward, arching over because of the weight of the many grains, each of which is surrounded by chaffy bracts. Family: Grass (Gramineae); genus and species, *Avena sativa*.

OKRA. See *Hibiscus*.

OLEANDER, a small evergreen shrub or tree 7 to 15 feet tall, with narrow, stiff leaves and sprays of attractive flowers in colors ranging from white to rose. Native to the Orient and southern Europe, the oleander has been cultivated for ornamental purposes for many years in warm parts of both hemispheres, often as a hedge, though all parts of the plant are poisonous if eaten. Family: Dogbane (Apocynaceae); genus and species, *Nerium oleander*.

BURPEE SEEDS

OXALIS

OLIVE, a small evergreen tree native to warm, semiarid areas of Eurasia and North Africa, cultivated for thousands of years and introduced into western North America, South America, and Australia as a source of fruits (olives) and oil. A branch from an olive tree, with its dull, willow-like, gray-green leaves, has long been regarded as a symbol of peace.

Olive flowers are shining-white, clustered, and followed by small, egg-shaped, plumlike fruits which turn black as they ripen. Olives are bitter and inedible until treated with lye and given time to ferment under careful control. Olive oil is obtained from pressed, ripe olives. Family: Olive (Oleaceae); genus and species, *Olea europaea*.

OLIVE FAMILY (Oleaceae), a group of about 500 species in 22 genera, all shrubs, climbing vines, or trees of tropical and warm temperate climates with opposite leaves and clusters of regular flowers, usually with just 2 stamens. See *Ash, Forsythia, Jasmine, Lilac, Olive*, and *Privet*.

ONION, a biennial herbaceous plant native to southwestern Asia, but now widely cultivated for the pungent flavor in its succulent leaf bases, which form a bulblike enlargement just below ground level. In its second year an onion plant produces a tall, upright stalk with a cluster of inconspicuous, white flowers from which the seeds may germinate before being shed from the fruits.

Horticultural varieties of large size, or flattened instead of spherical shape, or red instead of white color, or sweeter and less "hot" flavor are raised on every continent and are often known as Bermuda or Spanish onions, although the seed may be imported from the Canary Islands. Closely related are the chive *(Allium schoenoprasum)*, the leek *(A. porrum)*, and the shallot *(A. ascalonicum)* from Mediterranean countries, cultivated widely as flavoring for salads, stews, and cooked meats. Family: Lily (Liliaceae); genus and species, *Allium cepa*.

ORANGE, any of a number of closely related, small trees native to southern Asia, yielding some of the world's most important fruits. The unpruned trees may grow to 35 feet, with glossy, oval, evergreen leaves on short stalks that bear a narrow wing along each side. The fragrant, white flowers are followed by spherical fruits composed of 10 to 12 fleshy sections surrounding the seeds, enclosed in a tough rind beset with oil glands.

The rind may be dried or candied, or its oil may be removed for separate uses as bitter flavoring. Orange pulp is particularly rich in vitamin C, and is commonly crushed to make a nourishing beverage that can be frozen or concentrated for later use. Whole oranges are made into marmalade. For this use, the sour, or Seville, orange *(Citrus aurantium)* is often preferred; it is native to Malaysia, but much cultivated in Spain. The sweet orange *(C. sinensis)*, native to China and Southeast Asia, has been horticulturally developed to produce the seedless navel orange (introduced from Brazil and cultivated extensively in California), and the Washington and Valencia oranges. The Temple orange is believed to be a hybrid between the sweet orange and the mandarin orange or tangerine *(C. reticulata)*, a native of the Philippines and Southeast Asia; its rind is removed with special ease, making it a luxury fruit, raised extensively in the Gulf States. Family: Rue (Rutaceae); genus *Citrus.*

ORCHID FAMILY (Orchidaceae), an immense group of about 15,000 different species in 450 genera, often regarded as the most highly developed of all the monocotyledonous plants. Widely distributed, those of all arctic regions and most temperate regions are terrestrial, whereas the majority in tropical regions are perching plants (epiphytes) that perch on forest tree branches and bark. All family members are perennial herbs, the terrestrial ones with thickened roots, the perching ones with aerial roots specialized for absorbing water and with the stem swollen at the base to form a water-storage organ called a pseudobulb. The flowers are bilaterally symmetrical, often very showy, solitary or in clusters, with the lowest (innermost) of the 3 petals generally larger and often extended to form a spur or sac.

The fruit is a capsule containing a large number of exceedingly minute seeds that have almost no store of food and, hence, are dependent upon germinating soon after they ripen.

Lady's slippers (genus *Cypripedium)* of North Temperate woods have showy, solitary flowers, whereas the showy orchis *(Orchis spectabilis)* of eastern North America and many of its relatives produce spikes of smaller blossoms. Of the tropical perching orchids, the American species of genus *Cattleya* are especially favored for corsages because of their large size and handsome colors.

A climbing orchid, with glossy, oval leaves, is the vanilla plant *(Vanilla fragrans)* native to Mexico, and cultivated in the West Indies and Asia for its long, slender fruit capsules, which can be cured and from which the flavoring vanilla can be extracted. Artificial vanilla is now available at lower cost from other plant sources.

OREGON GRAPE, a small shrub native to the Pacific coast of North America, growing to about 5 feet, with spiny, compound leaves and clusters of yellow flowers followed by dark berries resembling grapes. Its flower is the state flower of Oregon. Family: Barberry (Berberidaceae); genus and species, *Mahonia aquifolia.*

ORPINE, or live-forever, an erect, perennial, succulent herb native to Eurasia. It is cultivated in rock gardens around the world for its 1- to 4-inch thick, tooth-edged leaves and its 15-inch fleshy, gray-green stems bearing clustered, white, purple, pink, or yellow flowers. Named live-forever because of the long survival of separated parts of the plant, which take root if given an opportunity, it was kept on hand during the Middle Ages for its supposed value in promoting the healing of wounds. It is a member of a genus containing about 500 species, known generally as stonecrops, of which *Sedum acre,* with its creeping, succulent, evergreen leaves and yellow, starlike flowers, is widely grown in gardens. Family: Orpine (Crassulaceae); genus and species, *Sedum telephium.*

ORPINE FAMILY (Crassulaceae), a group of about 1300 species in 33 genera, widely distributed but primarily found in arid regions of the Mediterranean, the American Southwest, and south-central Asia. Many are cultivated in rock gardens for their novel, often cactuslike shapes. Jade plant *(Crassula arborescens)* is a treelike member of a large genus.

Cigarette plant *(Kalanchoe verticillata),* and various kinds of life plants *(Bryophyllum* species) from the Old World tropics produce new small plants with leaves and roots in the notches of their leaves; they drop these smaller leaves to the ground as an asexual mode of reproduction. Other members of the family are known as hen and chickens because of their ability to produce new plants on short runners, thus covering the ground with close-set rosettes of fleshy leaves; live-forever or houseleek *(Sempervivum tectorum)* of southern Europe has this characteristic. See also *Orpine.*

ORRIS ROOT. See *Iris.*

OSAGE ORANGE, or bowwood, a sprawling, thorny tree 30 to 60 feet tall, native to the region between Texas and Missouri, the home of the Osage Indians. It has glossy, green leaves, staminate and pistillate flowers on separate trees, and hard, round, inedible, yellow fruits formed by the joining together of the receptacles, floral parts, and ripened ovaries of several adjacent flowers. The bark yields yellow, tan, orange, gold, and olive-colored dyes, and the wood has the strength and flexibility needed for the construction of bows for archery, tool handles, posts, and woodenware. Family: Mulberry (Moraceae); genus and species, *Maclura pomifera.*

OSIER. See *Willow.*

OSWEGO TEA, or bee balm, a perennial herb native to eastern North America, with a square stem that grows to about 3 feet, opposite, fragrant, pointed leaves, and shaggy clusters of showy, red flowers. A close relative of wider distribution in the United States and Canada is the taller, lavender-flowered, wild bergamot *(Monarda fistulosa).* Family: Mint (Labiatae); genus and species, *Monarda didyma.*

OXALIS, a genus of about 850 different species of small, perennial herbs with delicate stems filled with sour juice, small, clover-like leaves, and solitary or clustered regular flowers with 5 petals that may be pink, lavender, yellow, or white and that generally close at night and in dull weather, as do the leaflets of the compound leaves. Known generally as wood sorrels, they are widely distributed, but are most numerous in South Africa, on the slopes of the Andes, and in wet parts of Central America and Mexico. Those native to North America and Europe are often marketed in pots as shamrocks at St. Patrick's Day celebrations. Family: Oxalis (Oxalidaceae).

OYSTER PLANT. See *Salsify.*

PALM FAMILY (Palmaceae), a group of about 1500 different species in 200 genera, mostly thick-stemmed, unbranched, evergreen trees topped by a cluster of large, simple, palmate leaves (in fan palms) or pinnately compound leaves (in feather palms).

Palms have enormous economic importance in tropical and warm, temperate climates for almost every part of the tree is useful. Dead leaves are used to thatch the roofs of native houses; strips from fresh leaves are woven into mats, baskets, and wall panels; buds and many kinds of palm fruits are edible and nutritious, or yield raw materials for making sugar, wine, cosmetics, and waxes; whole trunks and strips cut lengthwise from the trunks provide valuable building materials; and fibers from the leaves are made into textiles, clothing, and hats. Door mats in countries far from the tropics are commonly composed of fibers known as coir, made from the husks of coconuts and called coco mats.

Fan palms include the cabbage palm *(Sabal palmetto),* which attains a height of 80 feet on the higher ground of some of the isolated areas in the Florida Everglades, and the prostrate scrub palmetto *(Serenoa repens),* found in neglected pastures from the Carolinas to Texas. The clambering fan palms of the Old World tropics include the *Raphia ruffia* of Madagascar, the extraordinarily long leaves of which are a source of strong raffia fiber, and the sago palms *(Metroxylon rumphii* and *M. laeve)* of the East Indies, the pith of which yields sago starch. The largest known seeds are those of a fan palm, the double coconut *(Lodoicea sechellarum)* of the Seychelles, which in the husks weigh 30 to 40 pounds and take 10 years to ripen.

The coconut palm itself *(Cocos nucifera)* is a feather palm, thriving close to salt water, rising 60 to 100 feet, producing large fruits in clusters with each seed covered by a thick, buoyant husk as well as a hard shell, and containing a layer of nutritious "meat" surrounding a cavity filled with a juice called coconut milk. The dried meat is copra, a principal product of tropical coasts, which is made into soap, coconut oil, and animal food.

Other feather palms of great economic value include the date palm *(Phoenix dactylifera)* of tropical Africa and Asia, which yields edible fruits, date sugar, and structural materials, as well as shade under the equatorial sun; the oil palm *(Elaeis guineensis)* of West Africa, cultivated extensively in the East Indies and tropical America, which yields fruits from which palm oil is extracted for use in soaps, medicines, and industry; and the betel palm *(Areca catechu)* of Southeast Asia, which produces egg-sized fruits that are generally harvested before they ripen. The husk is torn off and the mottled seed boiled, sliced, and dried in the sun for sale as "betel nut." More than 300 million people enjoy chewing betel nut, which is prepared for consumption by wrapping a small piece in a leaf of the betel pepper *(Piper betle)*, along with a pellet of lime, and perhaps a pinch of some aromatic spice.

Still another feather palm is the royal palm *(Roystonea regia)* of Florida and Cuba, the smooth, gray, columnar trunks of which are greatly admired along public avenues.

PALMETTO. See *Palm Family.*

PALOVERDE, any of 3 related, small, spiny, desert trees of the North American southwest, with stiff branches, green, smooth bark, delicate, pinnately compound leaves that drop as soon as drought returns after a period of rain, and clusters of small, bright, yellow, 5-petalled flowers. Family: Pea (Leguminosae); genera and species, *Cercidium floridum, C. torreyanum,* and *Parkinsonia aculeata.*

PAMPAS GRASS, the common name given to an ornamental, tall, reedlike grass *(Cortaderia argentea)*, native to mountainous country in southern Brazil and Argentina. It is cultivated in California for the decorative effect produced by its massed, coarse, basal leaves, its waving, fluffy plumes of flowers, and its 6-to-12-foot-high clusters of seeds. A similar grass with the same name *(Gynerium argenteum)* forms natural hedges along waterways in the pampas of southern South America. Family: Grass (Gramineae).

PANSY. See *Violet.*

PAPAW, or pawpaw, any of 8 different kinds of shrubs or small trees native to southeastern and eastern North America, all with large, feather-veined, pointed leaves and solitary flowers where the leaves of the previous year joined the stems.

The dull purple flowers are followed by large, pulpy fruits containing several seeds, each enclosed within a fleshy part called an aril. The pulp of the common papaw *(Asimina triloba)* is sweet and edible in autumn, but all other parts of the tree give off an unpleasant odor when bruised. Family: Custard-apple (Annonaceae); genus *Asimina.*

PAPAYA, a tall, herbaceous plant of tropical America that grows to a height of 25 feet, with a crown of large, palmately lobed leaves on long stalks and clusters of yellow flowers high on the main stem followed by huge, ovoid, melon-like fruits weighing 15 to 20 pounds.

Each papaya fruit contains a thick, orange pulp surrounding a fibrous center filled with spherical black seeds. The ripe pulp has the consistency of muskmelon. Its distinctive, pleasant flavor is greatly appreciated in salads or as a breakfast fruit. An enzyme in papaya leaves is pepsin-like, and is used to tenderize meats. Family: Papaya (Caricaceae); genus *Carica,* particularly *C. papaya.*

PAPER MULBERRY, a small, attractive tree native to Southeast Asia and the Pacific islands, but cultivated in subtropical parts of the United States as well. It has evergreen, ovate leaves that give dense shade, small clusters of flowers followed by mulberry-like fruits, and a fibrous bark that is used throughout the tree's native range to make tapa (bark cloth) for decorative material and clothing. Family: Mulberry (Moraceae); genus and species, *Broussonetia papyrifera.*

PAPRIKA. See *Pepper, Red.*

PAPYRUS, a long-stemmed, reedlike sedge native to northeastern Africa, growing to 15 feet, the 3-ranked, narrow leaves and triangular stems of which are topped by an umbrella-shaped cluster of minute flowers borne on a radiating array of fine stalks. The ancient Egyptians cut the pith of this marsh plant into long strips, arranged them into layers, and soaked and pressed them to form long sheets and rolls of writing material.

Papyrus is grown in warm parts of Europe and the United States as a decorative plant. Closely related is the umbrella plant *(Cyperus alternifolius)* of Madagascar and the Mascarene Islands, raised as a house plant for its clumps of 3 to 10 stems, 1 to 3 feet tall, which bear whorls of rough, blade-like leaves arranged like the ribs of an umbrella. Clusters of greenish flowers appear at the tops of the stems in winter. Family: Sedge (Cyperaceae); genus and species, *Cyperus papyrus.*

BURPEE SEEDS

PARSLEY

PARSLEY, a low-growing, biennial herb of southern Europe, widely cultivated for its bright green, finely-divided leaves, which are used as a garnish and seasoning, and for the small, hard, paired fruits, which at the end of its second year, ripen from umbrella-like clusters of small, yellowish green flowers.

Parsley seeds can be used as a seasoning, and an oil from the seeds can be used as a medicine. One variety, Harburg parsley, has a thick root eaten as a vegetable. Family: Carrot (Umbelliferae); genus and species, *Petroselinum crispum.*

PARSNIP, a biennial, herbaceous plant that stores food in a thick taproot during its first year and produces a stem 2 to 5 feet tall with many compound leaves and flat-topped clusters of yellow flowers in its second year.

Native to Europe, it is used as a winter fodder for cattle and as a food for man. It is harvested after a killing frost at the end of the first growing season destroys the exposed parts and induces the formation of sugar from the starch in the underground root. Family: Carrot (Umbelliferae); genus and species, *Pastinaca sativa.*

PASQUEFLOWER. See *Anemone.*

PASSIONFLOWER, any of about 400 different kinds of tropical climbing vines, most of them native to western South America. They generally have simple, alternate leaves and a succession of paired flowers along the stem, each flower with a peculiar ring of petal-like parts growing out of the tubular support of the stamens.

The common passionflower *(Passiflora caerulea)* from Brazil, which is widely cultivated in warm countries, has flowers colored blue, purple, and white, followed by peach-sized berries. A delicious beverage can be prepared from the pulp.

A passionflower with 1-inch yellow blossoms *(P. lutea)* and another *(P. incarnata)* with 3-inch, white and purple flowers are native to the southern United States. Brazilian and West Indian species with particularly large fruits are often cultivated and called granadillas. Fruits of *P. quadrangulàris,* or giant granadillas, may be 10 inches long. Family: Passionflower (Passifloraceae).

PEA, any of 6 different related kinds of perennial herbs, mostly native to the Mediterranean region, with pinnately compound leaves, some leaflets modified to form tendrils used in climbing, and with characteristic bilaterally symmetrical flowers in which the lowest 2 petals join to form a pouch (keel). The fruits are straight pods containing a single row of spherical seeds.

Garden peas *(Pisum sativum)* have been cultivated for at least 1,000 years in Eurasia as a vegetable and as stock food. Often the whole pea plant is plowed under as "green manure" to enrich the soil. The living roots accomplish a great deal in this respect because they bear nodules in which bacteria use atmospheric nitrogen to produce nitrogenous substances nourishing to the pea plant and others in the same earth. Family: Pea (Leguminosae); genus *Pisum*.

PEA FAMILY (Leguminosae), a huge group with about 13,000 species in some 550 genera, probably the second largest family of plants, including herbs, shrubs, climbing vines, and trees. Many are thorny and most have nodules on their roots containing nitrogen-fixing bacteria. All produce a pod of some kind as the fruit. See *Acacia, Alfalfa, Bean, Broom, Clover, Cowpea, Gorse, Indigo, Kentucky coffee tree, Kudzu, Laburnum, Lentil, Licorice, Locoweed, Locust, Logwood, Lupine, Mesquite, Mimosa, Paloverde, Pea, Peanut, Redbud, Sandalwood, Shamrock, Sweet clover, Sweet pea, Tamarind, Tonka bean tree, Tumbleweed, Vetch, Wattle tree, Wisteria,* and *Yellowwood.*

PEACH, a small, many-branched tree easily injured by frost, native to southern China and introduced first in Europe and then the southern United States. Many varieties have been developed and some with more attractive flowers than others, producing larger fruits with special features, for instance, "freestone" instead of "clingstone" flesh.

All have simple leaves, attractive, pink, 5-petalled flowers, and edible fruits with a juicy flesh outside an armored, central seed. Smooth-skinned nectarines differ from most other varieties of peach, which have a downy or velvety covering over the fruit. Family: Rose (Rosaceae); genus and species, *Prunus persica.*

PEANUT, a sprawling, annual, herbaceous plant native to Brazil, with pinnately compound leaves and bright yellow flowers, which give rise to pods on long stalks. The ripening pods bend downward, enter the earth, and mature hidden in the soil. The peanut commonly eaten is not a nut, but the dried seed of this plant.

It has been known in South America since prehistoric times and cultivated in Africa for more than 400 years. In Africa it is known as groundnut or goober. The green parts are made into hay for livestock and the seeds are eaten raw, boiled, roasted, in cakes and candies, or crushed into peanut butter and peanut oil. Family: Pea (Leguminosae); genus and species, *Arachis hypogaea.*

PEAR, a small Eurasian tree with glossy, pointed, wavy-edged leaves, white flowers, and sweet, sometimes gritty, ovoid fruits. Dwarf trees are preferred for cultivation, because the fruits can be harvested easily.

Among the varieties, the Bartlett has a sweet fruit, the Seckel or sugar pear, a small, hard, sweet fruit, and the Kieffer pear, a coarse fruit with less flavor but a firmness that lasts into winter. The closely related sand pear *(Pyrus sinensis)* of China and Japan is often used as a strong root upon which to graft fruit-bearing tops of more desirable kinds of pears. Family: Rose (Rosaceae); genus and species, *Pyrus communis.*

T.H. EVERETT

PEACH

PECAN. See *Hickory.*

PEEPUL, or pipal. See *Fig.*

PELARGONIUM. See *Geranium.*

PENNYROYAL. See *Mint.*

PEONY, any of several different kinds of herbaceous perennials with deeply divided leaves on long stalks. All except the wild peony *(Paeonia browni)* of mountains in the Pacific states are native to Eurasia.

About 700 named varieties have been developed from the European common peony *(P. officinalis)* hybridized with the Chinese and Siberian white peony *(P. albiflora).* These are remarkable for the size of their flowers, the "doubleness" through development of extra petals instead of stamens, and the variety of colors ranging from white to pink to red to magenta.

Tree peonies, which produce an upright, woody stem 3 to 6 feet tall and flowers of a particularly satin-like texture as much as 12 inches across, have been developed from the mountain peony *(P. suffruticosa)* of eastern Asia through hybridization with a closely related species *(P. lutea).* In colonial times extracts from the roots of common peonies were used as a nerve tonic. Family: Buttercup (Ranunculaceae); genus *Paeonia.*

PEPPER, the most valuable spice in commerce today, produced from the fruits of a climbing, woody vine native to India. It has stems reaching 20 to 30 feet above the ground, ovate leaves, and spikes of inconspicuous flowers followed by yellowish-red, globular berries, each about ¼-inch in diameter, with a single seed (the peppercorn) covered by a thin pulp. Unripe fruits are gathered, dried, and ground whole to produce black pepper, whereas ripe fruits are dried, peeled, and soaked in water to free the seeds which are ground to make white pepper.

Cultivated in the Orient since ancient times, pepper became so important to the traders of the 1400s that they explored the world, seeking a shorter route to tropical India to obtain the spice. Pepper is still produced in Indonesia, India, and Thailand, as well as in some parts of Africa and tropical America.

A related plant, the betel pepper *(Piper betle)* of the East Indies provides the fresh leaves chewed with dried fragments of betel nut. Another East Indian relative is cubeb *(P. cubeba),* a woody, climbing shrub the aromatic, bitter berries of which are dried and used in remedies for respiratory ailments. Family: Pepper (Piperaceae); genus *Piper.* See also *Palm Family.*

PEPPER FAMILY (Piperaceae), a group of about 1400 species in 12 genera, chiefly herbs and shrubs of the tropics with stems jointed or swollen where the leaves arise and with the inside conducting tissue more or less scattered.

The flowers are clustered in spikes and produce small, fleshy fruits with a single, central seed. Most of the species are members of the large genus *Piper* or of the genus *Peperomia,* of which several among the 500 species are cultivated as house plants for their handsome foliage. See also *Pepper.*

PEPPERGRASS, or pepperwort, any of about 130 different kinds of annual herbs widely distributed in temperate regions, with branching stems to 2 feet high, curly, notched leaves, and ascending clusters of small, white flowers. The foliage is edible and has a "hot" taste, which has led to the cultivation of one species *(Lepidium sativum)* from Mediterranean countries as garden cress. It has escaped from cultivation in many regions and become a weed. Family: Mustard (Cruciferae); genus *Lepidium.*

PEPPERIDGE. See *Tupelo.*

PEPPERMINT. See *Mint.*

PEPPER, RED, a woody shrub native to tropical America, perennial in warm climates, but grown as an annual where frost occurs in winter. The leaves are generally pinnately compound; the flowers are small, solitary, and followed by a hollow berry with a thick rind containing many small, flat seeds. Cultivated by the Indians, the plant was discovered by Spanish explorers and introduced into Europe, where the sweet, or bell, pepper was developed horticulturally to be eaten green or ripe (red). Paprika is made from dried, ripe, bell peppers.

Another mild variety is the Spanish sweet pepper, known as pimento. The smaller, "hotter" varieties are used in making chili and tabasco sauce as condiments. Cayenne pepper is made from the dried, ground fruits of the Guinea pepper *(Capsicum annuum)* and the spur pepper *(C. fastigiatum)*. Peppers are rich in vitamin C and have a variety of medicinal uses. Family: Potato (Solanaceae); genus and species, *Capsicum frutescens.*

PEPPER TREE, an evergreen tree native to America from Mexico to Chile, with graceful, drooping branches bearing pinnately compound leaves, clusters of small, whitish, staminate or pistillate flowers, but not both on the same tree, and bright red or rose-colored firm fruits, each with a central armored seed. It has been introduced into Florida and California, where winters are mild, as an ornamental and hedge tree capable of growing 20 to 50 feet tall. Family: Sumac (Anacariaceae); genus and species, *Schinus molle.*

PERIWINKLE, or running myrtle, a perennial, trailing plant with glossy, dark, paired, evergreen leaves and solitary, purplish-blue flowers. Native to the Old World from western Europe to Asia Minor, it has been widely introduced into temperate lands as a ground cover thriving in shady areas. A tropical relative *(Vinca rosca)* from Madagascar tolerates greater summer heat but is susceptible to winter cold. Family: Dogbane (Apocynaceae); genus and species, *Vinca minor.*

PERSIMMON, any of several different shrubs and small trees, native to the Northern Hemisphere, that grow to 50 feet and produce simple, leathery, smooth-edged leaves, bark splitting into a pattern of squares, and staminate flowers on separate trees from the pistillate flowers.

The flowers are followed by spherical, orange-brown fruits, resembling tomatoes and as much as 3 inches in diameter. The flesh is sour until touched by frost and completely ripe. The cultivated persimmon *(Diospyros kaki)* of Japan comes in seedless as well as seeded varieties; it is grown in the Pacific states as well as in the Orient. The wild persimmon of the southern United States *(D. virginiana)* and the date plum *(D. lotos)* of China also produce edible fruits. Family: Ebony (Ebenaceae); genus *Diospyros.*

PE-TSAI, or Chinese cabbage. See *Mustard.*

PETUNIA, a genus of tropical American, herbaceous annuals with weak, hairy, stems 6 to 24 inches tall, smooth, oval leaves, and fragrant, trumpet-shaped, ruffled flowers of white, purple, violet, or mixed colors. Most frequently cultivated as a garden flower in the United States are the Argentinian purple petunia *(P. violacea)*, the white petunia *(P. axillaris)*, and hybrids between these and other species. Family: Potato (Solanaceae).

PHLOX, a genus of about 50 different kinds of annual and perennial herbs, one species of which is native to northeastern Siberia. The others are native to North America. They produce stiff stems, narrow, stalkless leaves, and clusters of white, pink, red, purple, or mottled flowers in which the corolla is 5-lobed with a slender tube expanded into a flat display.

Many cultivated annual varieties are horticultural forms of the Texan species *(Phlox drummondii)*, with red or purple blossoms. Dwarf phlox, chosen as a rock-garden ornament, is generally the moss pink or ground pink *(P. subulata)* of eastern North America; it has tiny tufted leaves and clusters of magenta, pink, or lilac flowers that open early in the spring.

A taller related plant is wild sweet william *(P. maculata)*, about 2½ feet tall, with clusters of pink or purple flowers. It is native to stream edges and rich woodland soil in eastern North America. Family: Phlox (Polemoniaceae).

PIGNUT. See *Hickory.*

PIGWEED, any of several related herbaceous plants, chiefly annuals of almost cosmopolitan distribution as weeds, flowering inconspicuously late in the summer, and belonging to genera *Chenopodium* (especially the European *C. lanceolatum* and *C. paganum*), *Cycloloma* ("American winged pigweed") and *Axyris* ("Russian pigweed," of the goosefoot family, Chenopoliaceae), and *Amaranthus* (especially the cosmopolitan *A. hybridus* and *A. retroflexus* of the amaranth family, Amaranthaceae).

PIMENTO, or Pimiento. See *Pepper, Red.*

PIMPERNEL, a low spreading herb native to Europe, with small, oval leaves and solitary, scarlet, white, or blue petals united at the base and closing in dull weather and at night; hence the popular English name "poor man's weatherglass." The many-seeded capsules contain fruits resembling peppercorns, which has led to the introduction of this plant along most coasts of the world and in fields a long distance inland. Family: Primrose (Primulaceae); genus and species, *Anagallis arvensis.*

BURPEE SEEDS

PETUNIA

PINE, any of about 90 different kinds of evergreen coniferous trees with needles of two types: one borne singly in spirals around stems, the other in bundles of 2 to 5 enclosed in papery sheaths at the base. The needles, ranging from 1 to 24 inches long, may be retained on the tree from 2 to 8 years according to the species.

Among 5-needle pines, the most valuable for timber are the North American white pine *(Pinus strobus)*, found east of the Rockies and as far south as Guatemala; the western white pines *(P. monticola)* of the North American Pacific coast; and the sugar pine *(P. lambertiana)* of California and Oregon, which attains a height of about 250 feet and produces cones 20 inches or more in length.

Three-needle pines include the western yellow pine *(P. ponderosa)* and the longleaf pine *(P. palustris)* of the American southeast, a valuable source of turpentine and resins. Included among the 2-needle pines are the important Scotch pine *(P. sylvestris)* of northern Eurasia, the lodgepole pine *(P. contorta)* of western North America, and the stone pine *(P. pinea)* of Mediterranean countries, which yields edible seeds called pignolias.

Edible pine seeds, known as piñon nuts, were gathered as winter food by American Indians in the southwest, chiefly from the nut pine *(P. edulis)* and the singleleaf pine *(P. monophylla)*, which has solitary leaves. Family: Pine (Pinaceae).

PINE FAMILY (Pinaceae), a group of about 210 species in 9 genera, all coniferous trees with winged seeds, yielding more lumber than any other family of plants. See *Cedar, Douglas Fir, Fir, Hemlock, Larch, Pine, Spruce.*

PINEAPPLE, any of 5 different spiny plants native to tropical America, with a basal rosette of long, stiff, saw-edged, and sharply pointed leaves among which the stem eventually grows upward to terminate in a cluster of inconspicuous greenish or purple flowers. The ovaries join together as they ripen, forming one multiple fruit from each flower cluster.

Often the stem continues for a short distance between the ovaries and beyond the multiple fruit to bear a short cluster of harsh, stiff, green leaves. *Ananas sativa* has been developed to yield juicy, large, sweet fruits, weighing from 3 to 20 pounds, which are cut from the plant with the terminal tuft of shorter leaves still in place.

About three-quarters of all edible pineapples and pineapple products are raised and produced in the Hawaiian Islands; additional large plantations have been established in Puerto Rico and other parts of the West Indies, and in Malaysia. Wild pineapple, or pinguin *(Bromelia pinguin)*, from tropical America forms almost impenetrable tangles along the edges of rain forests and yields a valuable fiber from its leaves. It is sometimes grown in the tropics as a fruitbearing plant or as an ornament. Family: Pineapple (Bromeliaceae); genus *Ananas.*

PINEAPPLE FAMILY (Bromeliaceae), a group of about 1500 species in 65 genera, all but one species native to America. Most are short-stemmed, often with stiff, fleshy leaves in a rosette which holds rain water. Included are the most conspicuous perching plants of the tropical rain forests. They are epiphytes, frequently called "air plants" because they take no nourishment from the tree branches on which they grow. See *Pineapple* and *Spanish moss.*

PINK, any of almost 300 different kinds of low-growing or sprawling perennial herbs native to Eurasia and Africa, with narrow, paired, grasslike leaves and showy, fragrant flowers the 5 petals of which are conspicuously notched or "pinked" at the outer edge. Many are cultivated as garden flowers or have escaped to become widespread on other continents to which they were introduced.

The garden or grass pink *(Dianthus plumarius)* commonly has flowers almost 2 inches in diameter. The carnation *(D. caryophyllus)* produces solitary blooms of larger size; horticultural varieties are often double in size. Sweet william *(D. barbatus)*, with a flat-topped cluster of flowers the petals of which usually have a line of color across, has long been a favorite of English gardeners. Family: Pink (Caryophyllaceae); genus *Dianthus.*

PINK FAMILY (Caryophyllaceae), a group of about 1800 species in 80 genera, all herbs with simple, opposite leaves and flowers with notched ("pinked") petals. See *Baby's breath, Bouncing Bet, Chickweed,* and *Pink.*

PINK, GROUND. See *Phlox.*

PIPSISSEWA, or prince's pine, a small, perennial herb of dry woodlands in the northern parts of the North Temperate Zone. Its extensive horizontal, creeping, underground stems give rise to short, upright stems bearing thick, glossy, evergreen leaves and loose, terminal clusters of white flowers with waxy, concave petals and expanded filaments on the stamens. Family: Heath (Ericaceae); genus and species, *Chimaphila umbellata.*

PISTACHIO, a tree native to the Mediterranean countries, growing 25 feet tall with compound leaves and producing three leaflets and olive-like fruits containing an edible green seed, much prized for its delicate flavor. A close relative from the same region is the terebinth tree *(Pistacia terebinthus)*, which yields Chian turpentine, the only oily resin of this kind not obtained from a conifer. Family: Sumac (Anacardiaceae); genus and species, *Pistacia vera.*

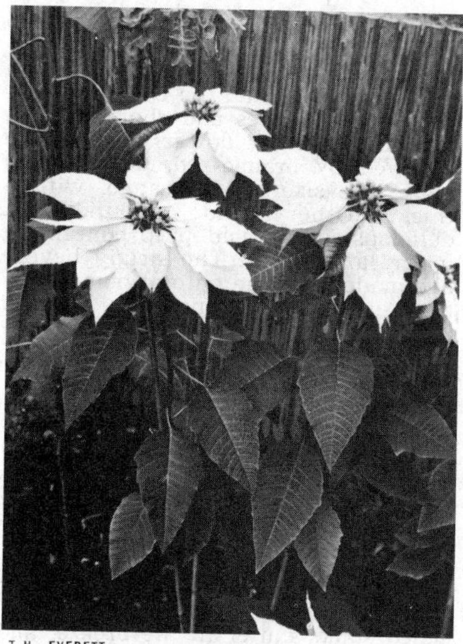

T.H. EVERETT

POINSETTIA

PITCHER PLANT, any of several insectivorous plants with pitcher-like leaves that hold rainwater in which insects drown, are digested, and soluble products absorbed as nitrogenous nourishment for the plant. Native to bogs and swamps in the New World are the members of the pitcher-plant family Sarraceniaceae, including 7 or more (genus *Sarracenia)* in eastern North America, 1 (genus *Darlingtonia)* in northern California and southern Oregon, and 4 (genus *Heliamphora)* in high mountains of Venezuela and the Guianas.

In the tropics of Asia and of Australia, particularly in the jungles of Borneo and adjacent parts of the East Indies, are 66 members of the monkeycup family, Nepenthaceae, all in genus *Nepenthes.* These are herbs or climbing shrubs with pitchers at the ends of the leaves or climbing tendrils. An Australian pitcher plant *(Cephalotus follicularis)*, found in marshes of Western Australia, is the sole member of family Cephalotaceae; only its lower leaves form insect-catching pitchers.

PLANE-TREE FAMILY (Platanaceae), a group of 8 different kinds of trees in a single genus *(Platanus)*, native to the Northern Hemisphere, with massive trunks growing to 170 feet tall; tough wood; broad, deciduous leaves with 3 pointed lobes; leaf stalks concealing the axillary buds; and pendant clusters of minute flowers that mature into spherical heads of small, pyramidal, brown fruits.

The plane tree *(P. orientalis)*, which is native to Eurasia, from the Mediterranean to the Himalayas, is widely planted along city avenues for its pleasant shade. Like the sycamore tree *(P. occidentalis)* of eastern North America and the California sycamore *(P. racemosa)*, the plane tree has a thin, brittle bark which scales off in large patches leaving chalky white or yellow areas, as though the tree had been painted for camouflage purposes.

PLANTAIN FAMILY (Plantaginaceae), a group of about 200 species in 3 genera, almost all members of the cosmopolitan genus *Plantago* and chiefly weeds of temperate areas. They have fibrous roots, rosettes of thick, long leaves, short stems, and spikes of tiny, greenish or white flowers atop slender stalks 8 to 10 inches tall.

The common broad-leaved plantain *(P. major)* is found in lawns, and its seeds are eaten by birds. The narrow-leaf plantain or buckhorn *(P. lanceolata)* tends to crowd out valuable grasses in meadows and pastures. The name plantain is also given to certain tropical bananas that are cooked before being eaten.

PLUM, one of several related small trees native to Asia, with smooth, oval, saw-edged leaves, close-grained wood frequently used for cabinet work, a bitter sap containing cyanides, clusters of white flowers that open early in the year (sometimes before the leaves), followed by smooth-skinned, fleshy fruits containing a single, smooth, armored seed.

Damsons, greengages, and prune plums are varieties of the common plum *(Prunus domestica)* which has been grown extensively for its fruit in Europe and North America. Prunes, or dried plums, include certain varieties developed for cultivation in California, or those from a West Indian tree *(P. occidentalis)*.

Also cultivated in the United States are the native American wild plum *(P. americana)*, the hardy Canadian black plum *(P. nigra)*, and the Japanese plum *(P. salicina)*. Family: Rose (Rosaceae); genus *Prunus.*

POINSETTIA, a small tree of tropical America with large, jagged-edged leaves and similar brilliant leaves in irregular whorls near the tips of the branches, radiating from under the strange small flowers; these are borne in cuplike clusters, each with one pistillate and several staminate flowers. Reaching the peak of display before Christmas and lasting well through the holiday season, poinsettias are cultivated for sale as indoor decorations; the cut ends of the stems should be dipped in boiling water or sealed with paraffin or flame to prevent the loss of the milky juice.

There are a number of related herbaceous plants that are native to the southeastern United States. Among these is painted leaf *(Euphorbia heterophylla)*, which has a splash of orange-red across the stalk end of its green leaves, near its terminal clusters of equally inconspicuous flowers. Family: Spurge (Euphorbiaceae); genus and species, *Euphorbia pulcherrima.*

POISON HEMLOCK, an erect, perennial herb native to southern Europe, introduced and well established in eastern North America, Mexico, South America, and elsewhere, and growing to 5 feet tall. Only the lower leaves are long-stalked but all leaves are twice pinnately compound. The small flowers are borne in umbrella-like clusters to 3 inches across followed by paired, small, dry fruits. The thick root might easily be mistaken for a parsnip. All parts of the plant, and especially its seeds, are deadly poisonous. A cupful of poison hemlock juice was a standard dose for suicide or execution of prisoners in ancient Greece. Family: Carrot (Umbelliferae); genus and species, *Conium maculatum.*

POISON IVY, an erect shrub or climbing, woody, perennial vine with deciduous, compound leaves of 3 oval leaflets, the middle one larger than the lateral ones, but all bearing a few small teeth along the sides. Small, greenish flowers in clusters are followed by hard, gray, globular berries.

All of the plant, including the underground horizontal stems and roots, is poisonous, causing the affected skin or stomach lining to swell and blister. Highly susceptible people react from contact with domestic animals that have walked through poison ivy plants in underbrush, or from smoke from fires in which poison ivy plants are burning. The active agent is urushiol, an oily substance.

Similar effects are caused by related poison sumac *(Rhus vernix)* of eastern North America, and poison oak *(R. diversiloba)* of California. Family: Sumac (Anacardiaceae); genus and species, *Rhus radicans.*

POKEWEED FAMILY (Phytolaccaceae), a group of about 125 species in 17 genera, chiefly herbs and woody perennials of the American tropics and subtropics. The most familiar of them in the United States and Canada is the pokeweed or pigeonberry *(Phytolacca americana).* It has a large, poisonous root from which a stout, smooth stem grows upward each spring bearing drooping, large leaves pointed at each end, and short spikes of petal-less flowers, each with 5 white or pinkish, petal-like sepals.

By midsummer, elongated loose clusters of plump, black berries ripen, their enclosed seeds probably distributed by birds that are immune to the poison. All parts of the plant are poisonous, except young shoots under 4 inches long in the spring; these may be cooked and eaten after the root is removed. They taste much like asparagus. Pokeweed is found along roadsides and in wasteland.

POLYPODY FAMILY (Polypodiaceae), a group of more than 7000 species in about 170 genera, most with compound leaves rising from large underground stems. They are the largest family of ferns.

The family includes the fern *(Onoclea sensibilis)* of eastern North America and eastern Asia, the fronds of which are very sensitive to frost; the Christmas fern *(Polystichum acrostichoides)* of North America, which is evergreen; the spleenworts *(Asplenium* species) and the maidenhair ferns *(Adiantum* species) of temperate and tropical regions; and the large staghorns *(Platycerium* species) of Australia, Southeast Asia, and Africa, which are handsome perching plants often displayed in greenhouses of temperate regions. See *Bracken* and *Walking fern.*

POMEGRANATE, a small tree native to northern India and Afghanistan, cultivated throughout the Orient and in parts of Europe and the United States, with glossy leaves and short-stalked, bell-like, scarlet flowers which are followed by orange-red, fleshy fruits about the size of an orange, with a thick, leathery rind surrounding a delicious, juicy, acid pulp containing many large seeds. The sirupy beverage made from the pulp of pomegranates is called grenadine. Family: Myrtle (Myrtaceae); genus and species, *Punica granatum.*

POMELO. See *Grapefruit.*

POND LILY. See *Water lily.*

POPLAR, any of about 40 different kinds of quick-growing trees native to the North Temperate Zone, with soft wood and thin bark, used commonly for fuel and paper pulp. Their broad, triangular leaves on long flattened stalks flutter in the breeze, and turn golden-yellow in autumn.

Drooping catkins of staminate or ovulate flowers are borne on separate trees and appear in spring before the leaves. The seeds are dropped when ripe and carried by the wind which catches on the cotton-like fibers extending from the seed covering.

These trees were frequently planted along streets and avenues until city planners discovered how quickly the roots invade and clog sewers. The European white poplar *(Populus alba),* the leaves of which have a feltlike coating of white hairs beneath, the gray poplar *(P. canescens),* and the columnar Lombardy poplar *(P. nigra italica)* were introduced into America.

Native American types include the widespread quaking aspen *(P. tremuloides),* the balsam poplar *(P. balsamifera)* of Canada, the cottonwood *(P. deltoides)* of eastern states, and the black cottonwood *(P. trichocarpa)* of the Pacific coast from California to Alaska, which attains a height of 225 feet. Family: Willow (Salicaceae); genus *Populus.*

POPPY, any of nearly 200 different kinds of related herbaceous annuals and perennials native to the Northern Hemisphere, South Africa, and Australia, about 100 of them in the large genus *Papaver.* Most have deeply-cleft, hairy leaves, a milky juice, and long stalks supporting hairy, nodding, egg-shaped flower buds from which the green sepals drop off when the 4 to 6 or more thin, white or colorful petals open.

On opening, the flower turns upright, exposing its many stamens and flat-topped crown formed by the union of the stigmas. The crown then becomes the top of the seed capsule. When ripe, the capsule opens 4 to 20 small pores, through which the seeds are shaken free.

The Oriental poppy *(P. orientale)* produces large, orange or scarlet flowers as much as 10 inches in diameter. The Iceland poppy *(P. nudicale),* which is native to all the arctic lands, is a dwarf plant with delicate petals up to 2 inches across in pastel shades ranging from white to pink, or yellow. The common European poppy *(P. dubium)* and the opium poppy *(P. somniferum)* of Mediterranean countries are cultivated far beyond their native regions.

The opium poppy is grown for the milky juice that can be collected from the unripe capsules. Although a dangerous narcotic when smoked, it is also a valuable medicine when prepared in various forms such as laudanum, morphine, paregoric, and codeine. All of these are sedatives capable of relieving acute pain, but also habit-forming. The California poppy *(Eschscholtzia californica)* is the state flower of California; it produces silvery foliage and cup-shaped, orange or yellow flowers. Family: Poppy (Papaveraceae).

POPPY FAMILY (Papaveraceae), a group of about 250 species in 28 genera, mostly of the Northern Hemisphere, chiefly herbaceous plants with showy, solitary flowers and a milky or colored sap. See *Bloodroot, Celandine,* and *Poppy.*

PORTULACA. See *Purslane.*

POTATO, a branching, herbaceous plant native to western South America, with pinnately compound leaves on a stem 1 to 2 feet high, and small, white or purple flowers that produce bitter, yellow, seed-filled berries. The fibrous roots produce underground stems with fleshy, swollen tips (tubers) that are starchy and edible.

Potato plants are generally propagated from pieces of tubers which have buds ("eyes") that grow into leafy stems. Over 600 varieties have developed. Family: Potato (Solanaceae); genus and species, *Solanum tuberosum.*

POTATO FAMILY (Solanaceae), a group of about 2200 species in 85 genera, principally in tropical and temperate regions of Central and South America. Included are herbs, shrubs, climbing vines, and trees, with clustered flowers distinguished by a 5-parted, wheel- or tubular-shaped corolla.

The very stiff and spiny Kaffir thorn *(Lycium afrum)* of South Africa, used for hedges and as a lion-proof temporary fence around cattle pens is a close relative of the widely cultivated matrimony vine *(L. halimifolium),* a climbing shrub with purple flowers and orange berries native to Asia. Chinese lantern *(Physalis alkekengi)* and gooseberry tomato *(P. peruviana)* have their fruits concealed within paper-thin bracts resembling Oriental paper lanterns.

See *Belladonna, Bittersweet, Butterfly flower, Eggplant, Jimson weed, Mandrake, Nightshade, Pepper (red), Petunia, Potato, Salpiglossus, Tobacco,* and *Tomato.*

POT MARIGOLD, a large annual herb native to Mediterranean countries, with simple, pointed leaves to 5 inches long, the leaf base more or less clasping the stout, straight, somewhat hairy stem. The leaves and terminal flower heads, which have orange-yellow ray petals around a darker center, are cultivated for use as potherbs. Horticulturalists have developed many varieties with larger and more decorative flowers. The dried flowers have been used as a laxative, a healing agent for wounds, and a kidney stimulant. Family: Daisy (Compositae); genus and species, *Calendula officinalis.*

PRIMROSE, any of about 500 different kinds of low-growing perennial herbs native to the Northern Hemisphere, particularly to mountainous or northern regions. The simple leaves are mostly in a basal whorl, above which hairy stalks raise flat-topped clusters of flowers with fringed petals that are white, yellow, rose, red, or lavender.

Many primroses are grown as garden ornaments or house plants, particularly those that bloom early in the spring, such as the Eurasian cowslip *(Primula veris)*, the European primrose *(P. vulgaris)* of Mediterranean countries, and the horticultural hybrid known as polyanthus *(P. polyantha* or *P. variabilis)*. Family: Primrose (Primulaceae); genus *Primula.*

PRIMROSE FAMILY (Primulaceae), a group of about 800 species in 28 genera, widely distributed but most numerous in the North Temperate Zone. They are almost all perennial herbs with opposite or whorled leaves, and flowers with the 5 petals united and the 5 stamens opposite the petals, the ovary ripening as a capsule. See *Cyclamen, Pimpernel, Primrose,* and *Shooting star.*

PRIVET, any of about 50 different kinds of shrubs with dark, oval, small leaves, clusters of fragrant, white flowers at the ends of the branches, followed by black berries. Several kinds tolerate trimming and pruning, even into artistic shapes, and remain evergreen except where the winter weather is severe.

The common privet *(Ligustrum vulgare)* of the Mediterranean region is a favorite in Europe as a hedge plant. "California" privet *(L. ovalifolium)* is native to Japan. Family: Olive (Oleaceae); genus *Ligustrum.*

PRUNE. See *Plum.*

PUMPKIN, a trailing vine native to America, with a prickly stem, dark green, 3- or 4-lobed leaves, large, yellow, bell-shaped flowers, and huge, globular, dull-orange fruits with vertical ribs, the white seeds of which are in a fibrous pulp surrounded by a medium-hard rind.

Cultivated by the Indians as a vegetable, the pumpkin can be eaten boiled, baked, canned, crushed, or used for livestock food. Pumpkins are popular for use on Halloween, at which time they are hollowed out and carved as jack-o'-lanterns. A burning candle is placed inside the pumpkin and glows through the translucent rind.

Horticultural varieties of economic value are the summer squash *(Cucurbita pepo condensa)*, of many different shapes, and the yellow-flowered gourd *(C. p. ovifera)*. Family: Gourd (Cucurbitaceae), genus and species, *Cucurbita pepo.*

PURSLANE, or pussley, a trailing, succulent herb of tropical America, now almost cosmopolitan as a weed except in Mexico, India, China, and France, where it is cultivated and sold as a salad green or potherb.

The smooth, fleshy stem is green, branched, easily broken, and supports successive whorls of fleshy leaves that are rounded at the tip and break readily from the stem. The inconspicuous yellow flowers, 1/4 inch across, open for a few hours in early morning, are pollinated by insects, and close permanently, soon to be followed by small seed capsules that shed ductlike, flattened seeds. The seeds survive hard winters, permitting the purslane to grow as an annual in cold climates; it reproduces readily from fragments of stem and leaves.

Closely related succulent plants widely cultivated in rock gradens and flower beds include the garden purslane or rose moss *(Portulaca grandiflora)*, native to South America, which opens to the sun large, cup-shaped flowers with rose, red, or orange petals. Family: Purslane (Portulacaceae); genus and species, *Portulaca oleracea.*

PUSSY WILLOW. See *Willow.*

PYROLA FAMILY (Pyrolaceae), a group of 70 species in 10 genera, chiefly of the North Temperate Zone and Arctic, either perennial evergreen herbs or non-green plants nourished by the decay of vegetable matter in the soil. See *Indian pipe, Snow plant,* and *Wintergreen.*

QUEEN ANNE'S LACE. See *Carrot.*

QUINCE, a small shrub or tree growing to 15 feet, native to central Asia, with crooked branches bearing downy, oval leaves and white or pink flowers, followed by hard, fragrant, acid, yellow fruits. Widely introduced and cultivated for the fruit, quince trees are hardy and deciduous, their fruits inedible raw but esteemed for making jelly and as a source of pectin for marmalade. The seeds are coated with a mucilaginous substance used in making cosmetics. The related flowering quince *(Chaenomeles lagenaria)*, or "japonica," is a cultivated, ornamental shrub from Japan, with spiny branches, handsome rose or orange flowers opening very early in spring, and edible fruits. Family: Rose (Rosaceae); genus and species, *Cydonia oblonga.*

BURPEE SEEDS

RADISHES

RADISH, a small, herbaceous annual, probably of Asiatic origin, cultivated as a vegetable by the Chinese for over 3000 years, widely adopted for the pungent flavor of its enlarged edible roots, red, white, gray, or black in color, from which coarse, lobed leaves arise in a basal whorl. Late in the summer the stem grows upward, bearing erect clusters of pink, 4-petalled flowers, which are followed by short pods full of black, spherical seeds. Family: Mustard (Cruciferae); genus and species, *Raphanus sativus.*

RAFFIA. See *Palm.*

RAGWEED, any of about 20 different kinds of coarse herbs native to America and Africa, usually with deeply lobed or dissected leaves and inconspicuous, greenish flowers the fine pollen of which is windblown, causing allergic symptoms of "hay fever" in many people. Several species are widespread weeds in grain fields, growing as annuals but with hardy seeds that often live several years before germinating. Family: Daisy (Compositae); genus *Ambrosia.*

RAMIE. See *Nettle.*

RAPE. See *Mustard.*

RASPBERRY, any of several related kinds of thorny shrubs with arching, woody branches bearing toothed, compound leaves, white flowers, and edible red, black, purple, yellow, or white fruits formed as aggregates from many separate pistils on the same finger-shaped receptacle. Unlike blackberries, raspberries are easily separated from the receptacle. They can be eaten raw or cooked, and are preserved. Wild raspberries are commonly called thimble berries.

The most common cultivated kinds are the red raspberry *(Rubus idaeus)* of Eurasian and North American north country, the blackcap raspberry *(R. occidentalis)* of eastern North America, and the decorative, pink-flowered, fragrant, flowering raspberry *(R. odoratus)* of eastern North America. Family: Rose (Rosaceae); genus *Rubus.*

REDBUD, a small tree native to eastern North America, with heart-shaped leaves and clusters of small, pealike, magenta flowers, followed by oblong, flat pods that are winged along the upper edge.

The redbud is cultivated in many parts of the country for its decorative value because its flowers open before the leaves in early spring. The redbud is the American counterpart to the similar Judas tree *(Cercis siliquastrum)* of Mediterranean countries. Family: Pea (Leguminosae); genus and species, *Cercis canadensis.*

REDWOOD. See *Sequoia.*

REED, an almost cosmopolitan grass growing from branching, horizontal, under-ground stems, from which stout, hollow, upright stems rise to 10 or 15 feet, clad in wide, flat leaves to 2 feet long and topped with sprays of rose, lavender, or silvery flowers partly hidden among long bristles.

The horizontal stems growing in swampy or marshy areas catch decaying vegetable matter and sediments and help make new land. Some roofs in Europe are thatched with reeds.

The related giant reed *(Arundo donax)* of southern Europe, which grows in clumps to 15 feet high, has strong stems that are often used for fishing poles and said to be of bamboo; hard, dry, thin pieces from the stem are used in making musical reed instruments. Family: Grass (Gramineae); genus and species, *Phragmites communis.*

RHODODENDRON, a genus of about 850 different kinds of shrubs native to arctic and north temperate regions and to tropical mountains southward through New Guinea to Australia. They have simple leaves, smooth edged or toothed, and showy flowers in clusters from terminal buds. Most of the deciduous species are called azaleas.

Several of the evergreen rhododendrons are cultivated. Some have been horticulturally developed into many varieties. The rosebay, or great laurel rhododendron *(R. maximum)* is the state flower of West Virginia; the western rhododendron *(R. californicum)* is the state flower of Washington. Family: Heath (Ericaceae). See also *Azalea.*

RHUBARB, or Pie plant, a herbaceous perennial native to Central Asia, with thick, horizontal, underground stems from the ends of which coarse, triangular, wrinkled leaves grow on long, green, pink, or red stalks. The leaves and underground stems are poisonous, but the leaf stalks are edible, acid but sweet, and are commonly used in cooking.

A related species *(Rheum officinale),* which is native to China and Tibet, is the source of a root extract used in Oriental medicine for indigestion and diarrhea for over 4000 years. Family: Buckwheat (Polygonaceae); genus and species, *Rheum rhaponticum.*

RICE, an annual grass, probably native to Southeast Asia, usually cultivated in shallow ponds ("paddies") in warm parts of the Orient and the United States, but raised on drier land in Latin America with smaller yields of fruit (grain). Rice grows 2 to 6 feet tall, with narrow leaves and terminal clusters of inconspicuous flowers that produce the fruits.

When ready for harvesting, the water is drained from the paddy, the plants cut, threshed to free the fruits, and the grains polished to remove the seed coats. The product becomes edible when boiled in a little water. About 90 percent of the world's rice is grown in the Orient.

UNITED NATIONS

RUBBER TREE

A related plant, wild rice *(Zizania aquatica)* of the North American marshes, is an important food for water birds. Indians formerly beat out the grains into their canoes as they paddled among the rice plants; now it is a delicacy highly prized in modern cooking. Family: Grass (Gramineae); genus and species, *Oryza sativa.*

ROSE, any of about 150 different species, as well as an immense number of horticultural varieties of erect or climbing shrubs with pinnately compound leaves, the stalks of which are expanded into large, leaflike stipules where they join the stem; to a European the large stipules distinguish a briar *(Rosa)* from a bramble *(Rubus,* raspberries and blackberries), which has small stipules.

Roses usually have thorny stems and bear single or double flowers that are generally fragrant, ranging in color from white to yellow, pink, and many shades of red. The fruits, called hips, are enclosed within a fleshy receptacle and are edible. Rose petals, too, may be candied and eaten.

Roses, particularly the damask rose *(R. damascena),* are cultivated on a large scale in Bulgaria as the source of a rich perfume known as attar of roses, and of a rose oil.

Roses are native to the northern temperate regions and to the tropical mountains; many species, particularly from Eurasia, have been developed to produce flowers of outstanding beauty, such as the named varieties of tea roses *(R. fragrans* and *R. odorata)* of China, the multiflora rose *(M. multiflora)* of China and Japan, the sweetbriar *(R. eglanteria)* of western Asia, the cinnamon rose *(R. cinnamomea),* and the Scotch rose *(R. spinosissima)* from all across Eurasia into the British Isles. Family: Rose (Rosaceae); genus *Rosa.*

ROSE FAMILY (Rosaceae), a large group of about 3200 species in some 115 genera, widely distributed but particularly numerous in the North Temperate Zone. They include herbs, shrubs, and trees with alternate leaves and flowers in which the corolla is attached to the rim of a short tube that bears the numerous stamens.

See *Agrimony, Almond, Apple, Apricot, Blackberry, Cherry, Christmas berry, Hawthorn, Japonica, Loganberry, Loquat, Medlar, Mountain ash, Peach, Pear, Plum, Quince, Raspberry, Rose, Serviceberry, Spiraea,* and *Strawberry.*

ROSEMARY, a fragrant shrub with square stems and small, simple, opposite leaves, native to arid coasts of Mediterranean countries, but cultivated in other regions for the pungent, warm taste which the leaves and young stems add to foods and medicines. The small flowers are unusual in having just 2 stamens. They are sometimes gathered to add a distinctive character to perfumes. Family: Mint (Labiatae); genus and species, *Rosmarinus officinalis.*

ROSE OF CHINA. See *Hibiscus.*

ROSE OF SHARON, any of several unrelated plants, including the meadow saffron *(Colchicum autumnale* of the lily family, Liliaceae), narcissus *(Narcissus* of the amaryllis family, Amaryllidaceae), a creeping, succulent plant *(Hypericum calycinum* of the mangosteen family, Guttiferae), and the shrubby Oriental mallow *(Hibiscus syriacus),* which grows 10 to 20 feet tall, with saw-edged, sharp-pointed, oval leaves and wide-open, bell-shaped flowers in a white, purple or rose color, resembling those of hollyhocks. See also *Hibiscus.*

ROWAN. See *Mountain Ash.*

RUBBER PLANT. See *Fig.*

RUBBER TREE, Brazilian or Pará, a tropical forest tree 60 to 100 feet tall, with long-stalked leaves, green flowers in highly specialized clusters partially surrounded by an enlarged receptacle, and with dry capsules full of small seeds.

Amazon Indians long ago learned to cut the bark to collect the milky juice (latex) from the vertical tubes, and to use the latex to make rubber balls for games. Rubber trees are set out in vast plantations, particularly in Southeast Asia and, to a lesser extent, in Africa.

Many other unrelated plants of different plant families also yield latex that can be converted into special kinds of rubber. These include the gutta-percha *(Palaquium gutta),* a Malaysian tree of the sapodilla family (Sapotaceae); the India-rubber plant *(Ficus elastica),* a small tree of India and Java now cutivated indoors for ornamental purposes; the guayule *(Parthenium argentatum),* a low-growing herb native to the southwestern United States, resembling a small sunflower, and a Russian dandelion *(Taraxacum kok-saghyz),* both of the daisy family (Compositae); and various members of the mulberry (Moraceae) and dogbane (Apocynaceae) families.

Family: Spurge (Euphorbiaceae); genus and species, *Hevea brasiliensis.*

RUE, a strongly scented shrub native to southern Europe and Asia Minor, now introduced widely and widespread, with a woody stem 1 to 2 feet high bearing notched, bitter leaves and clusters of yellow flowers. An oil extracted from its leaves was formerly regarded as a valuable medicine.

Meadow rue is unrelated. It includes any of about 10 different herbs (*Thalictrum* species, of the buttercup family, Ranunculaceae) that grow to 7 feet, with dissected leaves and plumelike clusters of flowers in which the white, yellow, or rose-colored sepals are the most conspicuous parts. Family: Rue (Rutaceae); genus and species, *Ruta graveolens*.

RUE FAMILY (Rutaceae), a group of about 1300 species in 140 genera, most abundant in Australia and South Africa, but well represented in other tropical and temperate regions. They include herbs, shrubs, and trees, usually with compound leaves dotted with glandular spots containing an aromatic oil, and with clustered flowers in which the stamens are attached at the base or on the rim of a peculiar, elevated extension of the stalk (receptacle). See *Bergamot, Citron, Grapefruit, Kumquat, Lemon, Lime, Orange,* and *Rue*.

RUSH, any of about 225 different kinds of herbaceous plants native to most countries, with narrow, grasslike leaves on stiff, upright, slender stems rising from a creeping, horizontal, buried stem; inconspicuous flowers are borne atop the tallest stems. Many rushes are marsh plants; the most widespread is the common rush (*Juncus effusus*), which also forms dense stands in wet meadows.

In Japan, mats are made from rush stems. In Europe, rush stems 3 to 4 feet high are collected to be made into chair seats, baskets, and rope. The pith from the thickest stems can be removed, soaked in tallow, and used for lampwicks or "rush lights." Family: Rush (Juncaceae); genus *Juncus*.

RUTABAGA. See *Mustard*.

RYE, a hardy, annual grass, probably native to southern Europe and Asia Minor, cultivated as a cereal in southeastern Europe for at least 2000 years. It grows 7 to 10 feet tall, with ribbon-like leaves and long, bearded spikes of flowers.

The straw is useful in making hats, paper, packing, and mattress stuffing. The grains can be ground to make flour for black bread, mixed with wheat flour to make a softer rye bread, or used as the base for rye whiskey.

Rye is often sown as a cover crop or grown to be plowed under as a green manure. Wild rye or lyme grass (*Elymus arenarius*) of northern Eurasia and North America is a related plant that grows well on bare sand and is often used to anchor sand dunes or bared soil. Family: Grass (Gramineae); genus and species, *Secale cereale*.

SAFFLOWER, an annual herb native to the East Indies but cultivated extensively in warm parts of North Africa, India, southern Europe, and the United States. It grows 1 to 3 feet tall, with prickly leaves and heads of bright orange, daisy-like flowers. In the Old World it is raised mostly for the pale red dye that can be obtained from the flowers, and which is used for rouge and for coloring silks. An oil used in cooking and in drying paints and varnishes can be extracted from its seeds.

The safflower plant is sometimes called bastard saffron or false saffron because a drug can be obtained from its dried flowers and used medicinally in place of the drug saffron. Family: Daisy (Compositae); genus and species, *Carthamus tinctorius*.

SAFFRON. See *Crocus*.

SAGE, any of about 550 different kinds of herbaceous and shrubby plants native to temperate and tropical countries and to all continents, usually with square stems 1 to 2 feet tall, paired leaves, and clusters of blue, purple, scarlet, pink, or white flowers.

Garden sage (*Salvia officinalis*) is a European perennial that is cultivated widely in the United States as well. Its aromatic leaves are dried and used to flavor sausages, cheeses, and dressings; in addition, a tea, which served as a tonic, was formerly brewed from its leaves. The showy scarlet sage (*S. splendens*), native to Brazil, is a tropical annual with spikes of vivid scarlet, 2-lipped flowers; it is commonly grown as a garden plant. Family: Mint (Labiatae); genus *Salvia*.

SAGEBRUSH, any of several different shrubs of arid areas in the southwestern United States and Mexico, with stiff branches 1 to 12 feet tall, notched, silvery leaves, and sprays of yellow flowers resembling small daisies. The common sagebrush (*Artemisia tridentata*) is the state flower of Nevada. Sagebrush is eaten to a limited extent by cattle and sheep and is used as an emergency fuel. Family: Daisy (Compositae); genus *Artemisia*.

SAGO PALM, any of several different true palms or palmlike cycads from the pith of which an edible starch can be obtained. See *Cycad* and *Palm*.

SAGUARO, a giant tree cactus native to the Arizona-Sonoran desert of the American southwest. Largest of all cacti, it grows to 60 feet, the spiny, fluted, columnar trunk sometimes supporting 1 or more armlike side branches, each of which may be crowned at the tip with waxy white, yellow-centered, night-blooming flowers that produce pear-shaped, edible fruits. Family: Cactus (Cactaceae); genus and species, *Cereus giganteus*.

SALPIGLOSSIS, a genus of branching herbs native to Chile, with branching stems growing to 2 feet, alternate pointed leaves, and large, trumpet-shaped flowers from which a tongue-like stamen protrudes. One of the 5 species (*S. sinuata*) is called painted tongue and is commonly cultivated in gardens of the Temperate Zone for its velvety night-opening flowers of white, yellow, or red, which are often marked with brilliantly colored veins; for these qualities it has sometimes been described as the "orchid of hardy annuals." Family: Potato (Solanaceae).

SALSIFY, or oyster plant, a herbaceous biennial native to southern Europe, with smooth-edged, grasslike leaves and a thickened, edible, tapering taproot that is creamy-white and has an oyster-like flavor when cooked. In its second year the plant produces an upright stem that grows to 3 feet and is topped by large, solitary heads of purple, daisy-like flowers. Family: Daisy (Compositae); genus and species, *Tragopogon porrifolius*.

SALTBUSH, any of several different kinds of herbaceous or woody shrubs adapted for living conditions on alkaline and arid soils, primarily in Australia and the American southwest.

Saltbushes have gray-green leaves with a salty taste, attain a height of as much as 10 feet, and bear clusters of separate staminate and pistillate flowers, in some instances on the same plant. The most widespread American species (*Atriplex argentea*) has been introduced into wasteland as far east as Ohio and westward to the Pacific coast. Family: Goosefoot (Chenopodiaceae); genus *Atriplex*.

SALVIA. See *Sage*.

SANDALWOOD, any of a number of unrelated tropical trees with close-grained, fragrant wood, used for incense, boxes, and fine furniture.

Most important of these is white sandalwood (*Santalum album*) of India and Malaysia; its wood is used for funeral pyres, powdered to form, with colored solutions, a paste that is used for caste marks, carved for decorative purposes, or processed to yield a fragrant oil. Red sandalwood (*Lingoum santalinus*, of the pea family, Leguminosae) from the East Indies is less valuable. Family: Sandalwood (Santalaceae); genus, chiefly *Santalum*.

SAPODILLA, or naseberry, a small tree of tropical America that grows to 60 feet and bears stiff, evergreen leaves, white flowers, and reddish-brown berries the size of oranges, with a dark yellow, juicy pulp. On large plantations, particularly in Yucatan. the milky latex from the bark, called chicle, is tapped, collected, and used in making chewing gum. Family: Sapodilla (Sapotaceae); genus and species, *Achras zapota*.

SAPODILLA FAMILY (Sapotaceae), a group of about 600 species in 40 genera, almost all trees with a milky sap, alternate simple, leathery, smooth-edged leaves, and stamens in 2 or 3 whorls. The outer stamens are modified and become petal-like and sterile. See *Rubber tree, Sapodilla,* and *Sapote*.

SAPOTE, or marmalade plum, or mammee apple, a small West Indian tree with simple leaves and white flowers, producing large, sweet, edible berries containing a single, large seed.

The russet-brown fruit resembling a ripe pear in taste, is a local favorite, but does not ship well. A rich oil can be extracted from the seed to be used in confections. Family: Sapodilla (Sapotaceae); genus and species, *Calocarpum sapota.*

SARSAPARILLA. See *Smilax.*

SASSAFRAS, a shrub or tree native to eastern North America, growing 40 to 100 feet high in southern states, and 3 to 5 feet high in northern states. It has oval or lobed leaves, soft, yellow wood, corky roots, greenish-yellow flowers (the staminate and pistillate flowers on the same plant), and purplish-red berries with red bracts.

The wood is sometimes used for fence posts and small boats. An extract from the aromatic red bark of the roots is used in sassafras tea, and as the flavoring for root beer and other confections. The oil of sassafras, which is also obtained from the roots, is used in medicine and cosmetics. The leaves are sometimes used, along with okra, to flavor soups. Family: Laurel (Lauraceae); genus and species, *Sassafras albidum.*

SAXIFRAGE, any of about 300 different kinds of herbaceous plants native to lands from the highest Arctic to Tierra del Fuego. Many of the plants are alpine, low-growing annuals and perennials, usually with a basal whorl of leaves, and a short, upright stalk bearing a cluster of small flowers.

Some are among the first plants to bloom in the year; others are among those that grow highest on mountain slopes, where they bloom on rocks or in crevices between boulders. Family: Saxifrage (Saxifragaceae); genus *Saxifraga.*

SAXIFRAGE FAMILY (Saxifragaceae), a group of about 1200 species in 80 genera, widely distributed, growing as herbs, shrubs, or small trees with clustered, regular flowers. It includes grass-of-Parnassus *(Parnassia palustris)*, a perennial herb of northern and alpine parts of the Northern Hemisphere that bears a single large, white flower from a basal whorl of leaves on each upright 12-inch stalk. See *Currant, Gooseberry, Hydrangea, Mock orange,* and *Saxifrage.*

SCHIZANTHUS. See *Butterfly flower.*

SCREWPINE, any of 180 different kinds of shrubs and small trees native to the Old World, from Africa, through Indonesia, to Australia, with stiff, shiny, sword-shaped leaves in a conspicuous spiral around the branching stems.

The trunk produces a good many stiltlike, prop-roots from above the ground, which sometimes remain after the lowest part of the trunk itself has died and decayed. Clusters of inconspicuous flowers, either staminate or pistillate, develop close to the branches; an aggregate fruit develops from them, on the outer surface of which the pattern of individual ovaries can be traced, much as on a pineapple. Family: Screwpine (Pandanaceae); genus *Pandanus.*

SEDGE, any of perhaps 1000 different kinds of grasslike herbs, chiefly of temperate regions and tropical mountains, with triangular, upright stems that are solid (never hollow like grass stems) and grow from a few inches to a few feet tall with narrow leaves that may be saw-edged and sharp enough to cut human skin.

Small green or brown flowers are borne in bristly spikes, the pistillate flowers in a saclike structure which persists and covers the hard nutlets that contain the seeds. Sedges are found mostly on marsh edges and in wet, poorly drained ground. Family: Sedge (Cyperaceae); genus *Carex.*

SEDGE FAMILY (Cyperaceae), a large group of more than 3000 species in about 85 genera, chiefly marsh plants of temperate and frigid regions, and widely distributed. Cotton grass *(Eriophorum* species), found in bogs and moorlands of the Northern Hemisphere, shows ball-like, white masses on tall, slender stalks, each ball composed of fine bristles that become hairs as they extend out in radial directions from each pistillate flower.

Sawgrass *(Cladium jamaicense)* is the most common plant in the Everglades of Florida, and with its sharp-edged leaves makes travel difficult through marshes and swamps in much of the southern United States and West Indies. See *Bulrush, Papyrus,* and *Sedge.*

SEDUM. See *Orpine.*

SELF-HEAL, or heal-all, a low-growing perennial herb native to the Northern Hemisphere, with a subterranean, creeping stem, many upright square stems, opposite leaves, and dense clusters of blue or purple, 2-lipped flowers. At one time it was believed to be useful as a salve for cuts and wounds. Family: Mint (Labiatae); genus and species, *Prunella vulgaris.*

SENECA SNAKEROOT, a perennial herb native to North America east of the Rockies but restricted to higher elevations in the Southeast. It grows to 18 inches, with smooth, pointed, alternate leaves clasping the erect stem at regular intervals, and a terminal cluster of greenish-white flowers; this green color appears in the petal-like sepals as well as the 3 petals. The medicine senegin was formerly extracted from the roots. Family: Milkwort (Polygalaceae); genus and species, *Polygala senega.*

SENSITIVE PLANT. See *Mimosa.*

SEQUOIA, a genus of mammoth, coniferous trees native to the western United States, with ridged, cinnamon-colored bark, short branches, sharp, scalelike needles barely longer than the diameter of the young stems in the big tree *(S. gigantea)* or flat, stiff needles growing to 1 inch in the coastal redwood *(S. sempervirens).*

It is thought that some sequoia trees may range in age from 3000 to 4000 years. The big trees grow at elevations of 5000 to 8500 feet on the west side of the Sierra Nevada in California. The trunks grow to 280 feet in height, 35 feet in diameter, and produce egg-shaped cones 2 to 3¾ inches long.

Coastal redwood trees often attain a height of 369 feet, a diameter of nearly 18 feet at chest height, and have cones ¾ to 1 inch in diameter; they grow in the fog belt of western California and Oregon in groves never more than 30 miles from the Pacific Ocean. Their lightweight, fungus-resistant wood is valuable for the construction of houses and furniture. Family: Bald cypress (Taxodiaceae).

SERVICEBERRY, or Juneberry, or shadbush, any of about 25 different kinds of shrubs or trees of the temperate Northern Hemisphere, growing to 30 feet, with simple leaves and white or pink flowers in loose clusters opening in early spring, followed by sweet, edible, purple fruits containing up to 10 seeds. Family: Rose (Rosaceae); genus *Amelanchier.*

SESAME, a woody plant native to India but now cultivated throughout the East, growing 2 to 4 feet tall, with lobed leaves and pink or yellow, trumpet-shaped flowers.

An oil is obtained from sesame leaves and seeds for use in cooking, confectionary, soap-making, lighting, medicine, and the manufacture of India ink. Sesame seeds themselves are flat, ivory-colored, and used to garnish baked goods or made into candy. Family: Pedalium (Pedaliaceae); genus and species, *Sesamum indicum.*

SHALLOT. See *Onion.*

SHAMROCK, the floral emblem of Ireland and the common name of several plants that bear 3-part, compound leaves with almost circular leaflets, including clovers *(Trifolium* species) and black medic *(Medicago* species) of the pea family, Leguminosae, the wood sorrel *(Oxalis* species) of the oxalis family, Oxalidaceae, and the European watercress *(Nasturtium officinale)* of the mustard family, Cruciferae.

SHEEP LAUREL. See *Laurel.*

SHEEP SORREL, or field sorrel, or garden sorrel, a small annual or perennial herbaceous plant native to Europe but introduced into America and elsewhere, and widespread as a weed indicative of poor, acid soil. From a subterranean, branching, creeping, tough, horizontal stem, it sends up many erect, vertical stems growing to 1 foot, usually from the middle of a whorl of leaves shaped like arrowheads on long stalks.

The flowers, in a loose, branching cluster atop the stem, are either yellow and staminate or red and pistillate, on separate plants, flowering most of the summer and producing small seeds that drop to the ground and quickly germinate. The leaves have a pleasant, sour taste from the oxalic acid they contain but are poisonous if eaten in quantity. It is unrelated to wood sorrel *(Oxalis).* Family: Buckwheat (Polygonaceae); genus and species, *Rumex acetosella.*

SHEPHERD'S PURSE, a low-growing annual or perennial herb native to Eurasia but now cosmopolitan, with a basal rosette of notched leaves and a slender upright stem growing to 10 inches and bearing small, white flowers and, later, 3-cornered, pouchlike pods that open to release minute seeds. It is one of the most familiar of small weeds. Family: Mustard (Cruciferae); genus and species, *Capsella bursa-pastoris.*

SHOOTING STAR, any of about 30 different kinds of herbaceous perennials native to Eurasia and western North America, with basal, stemless leaves and pink or white flowers on tall stalks, suggesting those of cyclamens. Each blossom possesses stamens that protrude from the folded corolla. Family: Primrose (Primulaceae); genus *Dodocatheon.*

SISAL, a large perennial plant of arid and semiarid regions of tropical America, now cultivated in Florida, the West Indies, Africa, and the Far East, with a basal whorl of succulent, swordlike leaves about 5 feet long and 4 inches wide, containing sturdy fibers useful for making cord, twine, and rope.

At maturity sisal produces a tall, upright stem growing to 12 feet, with clustered, malodorous flowers. Family: Amaryllis (Amaryllidaceae); genus and species, *Agave sisalana.*

SKUNK CABBAGE, a coarse herb, with broad leaves, growing in wet woodlands in eastern North America and eastern Asia. In very early spring before its leaves unfurl, it produces a number of greenish-yellow flowers on short stalks (spadixes), partly surrounded by purple-streaked, green hoods (spathes). The disagreeable odor of the flowers appears to attract flies, which act as pollen carriers. Family: Arum (Araceae); genus and species, *Symplocarpus foetidus.*

SMILAX, a genus containing about 300 different species of herbs, vines, and climbing shrubs, mostly of tropical and subtropical regions, with net-veined leaves and tendrils that are modified stipules. The prickly greenbrier *(S. rotundifolia),* native to dry woodlands in the eastern parts of North America, is regarded as an obnoxious pest.

Sarsaparilla is an oil extracted from the roots of several different kinds, particularly from *S. officinalis* of Honduras, *S. medica* of Mexico, and *S. ornata* of Jamaica. The "smilax" sold by florists is actually the mature, finely-divided foliage of either the prickly asparagus *(Asparagus asparagoides)* or of the asparagus-fern *(A. plumosus);* these are quite different plants of the same family. Family: Lily (Liliaceae).

SMOKE TREE, either of two shrubs or small trees, with leathery leaves and large clusters of minute flowers on fine stalks with multiple branches; these give the cluster the appearance of a cloud of brownish smoke. The cultivated European smoke-tree *(Cotinus coggygria)* is smaller than the

BURPEE SEEDS

SNAPDRAGON

American species *(C. americanus),* which is also known as chittamwood. In both the European and American species the staminate and pistillate flowers are on separate plants, and the few fruits consist of small, round berries. Family: Sumac (Anacardiaceae); genus *Cotinus.*

SNAPDRAGON, an annual or perennial herb native to the Mediterranean region, cultivated as an ornament and horticulturally developed into many varieties popular in gardens of both hemispheres. The plants grow from 8 to 36 inches tall and are topped with handsome spikes of 2-lipped flowers with white, yellow, orange, rose, red, or purple corollas that open when squeezed at the sides and snap shut when released. Family: Figwort (Scrophulariaceae); genus and species, *Antirrhinum majus.*

SNOWDROP, an early-blooming, bulbous herb native to the Mediterranean region but widely cultivated for the small, bell-shaped, white flowers that often push through the late snows of winter, before the long, narrow, grasslike leaves appear. Family: Amaryllis (Amaryllidaceae); genus and species, *Galanthus nivalis.*

SNOW PLANT, a brilliant, red, saprophytic plant of California mountain country, often seen under big trees. It attains a height of 3 to 12 inches and opens waxy-red, bell-like flowers. The plant lacks chlorophyll and derives all of its nourishment from the decay of organic matter; it is a relative of the Indian pipe. Family: Pyrola (Pyrolaceae); genus and species, *Sarcodes sanguinea.*

SOAPBERRY, an evergreen shrub or small tree native to warm countries from Mexico to northern Argentina, with pinnately compound leaves, open clusters of small, white flowers, and globular, ivory-colored berries that blacken in autumn. The berries contain saponins that act like soap in water but may cause severe irritation of human skin.

A related deciduous tree *(Sapindus drummondi)* of the central and southwestern United States attains a height of 50 feet and yields wood used in making baskets and packsaddle frames. Family: Soapberry (Sapindaceae); genus and species, *Sapindus saponaria.*

SOAPBERRY FAMILY (Sapindaceae), a group of about 1100 species in some 130 genera, mostly tropical shrubs and trees with alternate leaves and clustered flowers. Many provide timber, edible fruits, or serve decorative purposes. See *Akee, Litchi* and *Soapberry.*

SOAPWORT. See *Bouncing bet.*

SOLOMON'S SEAL, any of about 30 different kinds of herbaceous perennials native to the North Temperate Zone, with large, fleshy, subterranean, horizontal stems marked with seal-like scars where the upright, vertical stems of previous years have separated at death. The vertical stems, growing to a height of 8 feet, arch over gracefully, bearing paired, oval leaves at the tip and paired, short stalks with pink or ivory, pendant, bell-like flowers and, later, purplish berries.

An allied genus *(Smilacina),* with about 20 different species native to America, is called false Solomon's seal or plumelily; the flowers and fruits are clustered in a terminal plumelike group. Family: Lily (Liliaceae); genus *Polygonatum.*

SORGHUM, a genus of coarse, tall grasses native to the Old World, found chiefly in tropical and subtropical regions, with 13 different species, of which several have been cultivated and developed horticulturally as important crops. Egyptian millet, or Johnson grass *(S. halepense),* is a valuable forage grass where it has been introduced in the southern United States, but it is a weed of cultivated fields farther north. The Eurasian broom corn or guinea corn *(S. vulgare)* is cultivated as a cereal in the Mediterranean countries.

Specialized varieties include kaoliang (var. *nervosum,* a cereal of China), durra (var. *durra,* a cereal of North Africa), kafir corn (var. *caffrorum,* a cereal of South Africa), shallu (var. *roxburghii,* a cereal of India), molasses sorghum (var. *saccharatum,* which yields a sweet juice similar to cane juice), and broomcorn (var. *technicus,* in which the stiff stalks that support the flowers and seeds are particularly long and useful in making brooms). Family: Grass (Gramineae).

SORREL. See *Sheep sorrel.*

SOURSOP. See *Custard apple.*

SPANISH MOSS, a feathery, silver-gray, epiphytic plant native to the southern United States, the West Indies, and Central America, with slender, threadlike stems several feet long, bearing short, pointed, scalelike leaves and small, yellow flowers, but no roots. It absorbs moisture and mineral nourishment from water vapor and dust in the air, and can grow equally well on a telephone wire or the outstretched limb of a live oak tree. It is often gathered for use as upholstery packing. Family: Pineapple (Bromeliaceae); genus and species, *Tillandsia usneoides.*

SPEEDWELL. See *Veronica.*

SPICEBUSH, a shrub native to eastern North America, growing to 15 feet, with flexible, aromatic, young branches, alternate leaves tapering at both ends, and small, yellow, fragrant flowers appearing in spring before the leaves. Some plants are staminate and others are pistillate; they produce oval, red, fleshy, aromatic fruits.

The older wood will burn while still green. The bark and fruit can yield an astringent oil of supposed medical value; this oil is not related to the drug benzoin, which is extracted from Oriental trees of the genus *Styrax* (family Styracaceae). Family: Laurel (Lauraceae); genus and species, *Lindera benzoin.*

SPIKENARD, either of 2 unrelated herbaceous plants with enlarged, underground stems from which a fragrant, medicinal extract can be prepared.

The Old World spikenard *(Nardostachys jatamansi)* of the Far East is a member of the valerian family (Valerianaceae). The New World spikenard *(Aralia racemosa)* of eastern North America is a woodland plant with compound leaves and spherical clusters of minute, greenish flowers followed by purple-black berries; like its close relative, wild sarsaparilla *(A. nudicaulis),* it is a member of the ginseng family (Araliaceae).

SPINACH, a hardy, annual, herbaceous plant native to Asia, introduced into Europe in the 15th century and brought to America by early settlers. It has a thick cluster of oval or arrow-like, dark green leaves rich in iron, vitamins A, B complex, and C, and an upright branching stalk attaining a height of 2 to 3 feet in summer and bearing inconspicuous flowers in a cluster. It is regarded as a table vegetable and is prepared by boiling. Family: Goosefoot (Chenopodiaceae); genus and species, *Spinacia oleracea.*

SPINDLE TREE. See *Euonymus.*

SPIRAEA, a genus consisting of about 80 different species of shrubs native to the North Temperate Zone, found particularly in central and eastern Asia, many of them widely cultivated for their clustered flowers, each of which has 5 small petals of a red, pink, or white color.

Several of the wild species of spiraea found in North America are known as meadow sweet, while one, *S. tomentosa,* commonly found in pastures of eastern Canada and the northeastern states, is called steeple-bush or hardhack. Bridal wreath *(S. prunifolia),* with delicate white flowers in clusters on a dense shrub about 10 feet tall, is an Oriental species raised in gardens of the temperate zones. Family: Rose (Rosaceae).

SPRUCE, any of about 45 different kinds of evergreen, coniferous trees native to cool and cold, temperate parts of the Northern Hemisphere, with needles borne on short, woody projections. These projections remain as roughness on the stem after the needles fall. The needles are angular in cross-section, but can be rolled between thumb and forefinger. The cones, which vary in size from 1 to 10 inches in length according to species, are always pendant.

Spruces yield valuable timber and are the world's most important source of pulp for paper. Norway spruce *(Picea abies),* a timber tree that is a handsome ornament, has been introduced to America from Europe. Sitka spruce *(P. sitchensis),* native to western America from California to Alaska, grows to 300 feet. The principal pulp spruces are eastern American red spruce *(P. rubra)* and black spruce *(P. nigra).* Family: Pine (Pinaceae); genus *Picea.*

SPURGE, any of several hundred different herbaceous and shrubby plants with milky juice, classified in genus *Euphorbia* and related genera, mostly native to warm, temperate, and subtropical regions, varying remarkably from one species to another in manner of growth, form of leaf, and details of flower. A spurge native to the north-central United States, but now widely cultivated as a decorative plant for gardens, is snow-on-the-mountain *(E. marginata),* an erect annual with broad, oval leaves; the uppermost leaves have broad, white edges.

Flowering spurge *(E. corollata)* of the eastern United States has conspicuous, white, round or oval appendages around its inconspicuous flower clusters; the flowers thus acquire a distinctive appearance without giving the impression that they have essentially the same form as the "flowers" of poinsettia (another spurge). Family: Spurge (Euphorbiaceae).

SPURGE FAMILY (Euphorbiaceae), a large group of about 7300 species in 283 genera, commonly cactus-like or heathlike, although many are herbs, shrubs, climbing vines, and trees. See *Cassava, Castor-oil plant, Croton, Euphorbia, Poinsettia, Rubber tree, Spurge, Tallow tree,* and *Tung tree.*

SQUASH, any of a number of closely related, coarse, prostrate, annual herbs or climbing vines native to tropical America, with large, rough leaves on thick, hollow stems and large, yellow flowers followed by edible fruits of many shapes. Fruits of winter squash *(Cucurbita maxima)* sometimes weigh more than 100 pounds.

Before Europeans arrived, the Indians were cultivating squashes in every section of the United States and depicting squash flowers in their cultural and religious rites. Family: Gourd (Cucurbitaceae); genus *Cucurbita.* See also *Pumpkin.*

SQUIRREL CORN. See *Dutchman's breeches.*

STAFF TREE, a low-growing evergreen tree native to the East Indies, bearing large clusters of small, regular flowers and, later, spherical, fleshy fruits with bright orange appendages attached to the seeds. From the seeds a medicinal oil called oleum nigrum is obtained. Family: Staff-tree (Celastraceae); genus and species, *Celastrus paniculatus.*

STAFF-TREE FAMILY (Celastraceae), a group of about 500 species in 45 genera, widely distributed, growing as shrubs, climbing vines, and trees, with simple leaves and clustered, small, greenish flowers. They usually have brightly-colored fleshy appendages (arils) attached to the seeds. See *Bittersweet, Euonymus,* and *Staff tree.*

STOCK, or gillyflower, a somewhat woody, erect biennial or perennial plant native to Mediterranean countries, growing 2 feet high, with narrow, blunt leaves. Both stem and leaves are coated with short hairs giving them a grayish, feltlike, or wooly appearance. The attractive flowers in terminal clusters are in pastel shades of yellow, orange, rose, blue or magenta, or white, and are usually fragrant. Many horticultural varieties have been developed for cultivation in gardens. Family: Mustard (Cruciferae); genus and species, *Mathiola incana.*

STONECROP. See *Orpine.*

STRAWBERRY, any of several related plants native to Europe and North America, with very short stems, 3-part, coarse, saw-edged leaves on long stalks, attractive white flowers, and bright red fruits. The fruits are composed of the fleshy, edible receptacle in the surface of which small, hard nutlets with seeds are embedded.

Cultivated berries are larger, softer, and often sweeter than the wild forms. American strawberries and some of the horticultural hybrids cultivated for this favorite fruit reproduce by runners (horizontal, naked stems above ground that produce new plants with roots at the tip). Family: Rose (Rosaceae); genus *Fragaria.*

SUDAN GRASS, a coarse cereal grass native to central Africa, introduced into the central United States as a drought-resistant hay and pasture plant, growing 5 to 9 feet tall with long clusters of tiny blossoms from which small, edible seeds develop. Family: Grass (Gramineae); genus and species, *Sorghum vulgare sudanensis.* See also *Sorghum.*

SUGARCANE, a tall grass, probably native to Southeast Asia, now cultivated throughout the tropics and subtropics for the sweet juice that can be obtained from its upright stems; it is the world's principal source of sugar. The plant grows to 6 to 16 feet, bearing coarse, narrow, grasslike leaves at intervals along its many-jointed stems, and a handsome plume of minute flowers at its summit.

The crop is prepared for harvesting when ripe by burning off the dry leaves and cutting the stems (canes) close to the ground. At the sugar mill the canes are crushed, their juice extracted, and the refuse (bagasse) used for fuel or processed into paper or wallboard. The juice is concentrated to produce molasses and purified to yield crystalline cane sugar.

Major producers of sugarcane are Cuba, India, Java, Hawaii, and countries of tropical America. Family: Grass (Gramineae); genus and species, *Saccharum officinarum.*

SUMAC, any of several shrubs and low trees native to North America and warm parts of Europe, with pinnately compound leaves, a milky juice, 4- or 6-lobed flowers, and clusters of bright red, hairy berries. The staghorn sumac *(Rhus typhina)* of eastern North America is often grown as a decorative plant. It grows to 30 feet, with angular branches; all of its young growth is covered with velvety hairs.

Some sumac plants produce clusters of greenish-yellow, fragrant, staminate flowers, and others, less conspicuous, pistillate flowers that mature into upturned, pyramidal clusters of crimson fruits. Aromatic sumac *(R. aromatica)*, or polecat bush, of the central and eastern United States, which grows to 6 feet, is often planted along roadsides.

Related species include the poison sumac *(R. vernix)*, which is also known as poison elder and poison dogwood and grows in swamps, and the poison oak *(R. toxicodendron)* of dry, sandy uplands in eastern North America. Like poison ivy *(R. radicans)*, they cause a severe irritation of human skin. Family: Sumac (Anacardiaceae); genus *Rhus.* See also *Poison Ivy.*

SUMAC FAMILY (Anacardiaceae), a group of about 600 species in 73 genera, chiefly tropical, growing as shrubs or trees, with a milky sap and resin ducts, the leaves alternate and the flowers in clusters. Many cause inflammation of the skin. See *Cashew, Lacquer tree, Mango, Pepper tree, Pistachio, Poison Ivy, Smoke tree,* and *Sumac.*

SUNDEW, any of about 90 different low-growing, insectivorous plants native to all continents but most numerous and varied in Australia. They have basal rosettes of leaves bearing sticky, glandular hairs and slender, upright stems topped by clusters of small, white flowers. The glandular hairs produce shining droplets of secretion to which insects are attracted, and thus caught, enfolded by movements of the leaf, and digested.

The long-leaved sundew *(Drosera longifolia)* and the round-leaved sundew *(D. rotundifolia)*, which has round leaves on narrow stalks, live on poorly drained hillsides and bog margins in cool, temperate, and arctic regions of Eurasia and North America. Family: Sundew (Droseraceae); genus *Drosera.*

SUNDEW FAMILY (Droseraceae), a small group of about 100 species in 5 genera, all insectivorous herbs with highly specialized leaves and small clusters of regular flowers supported by slender, upright stalks. *Aldrovanda vesiculosa,* a floating plant with no roots, native to the Old World from Central Europe to Australia, has whorls of leaves that close on and catch aquatic insects and worms. See *Sundew* and *Venus's-flytrap.*

BURPEE SEEDS

SUNFLOWER

SUNFLOWER, any of about 60 different kinds of herbaceous annuals and perennials native to North America, with large, daisy like flowers distinguished by a flat, central area of seed-producing disc florets surrounded by a handsome display of sterile ray florets, the strap-shaped petals of which are commonly bright yellow.

The common sunflower *(Helianthus annuus)* is native to Texas and Mexico, sacred to the Incas of Peru, and now the state flower of Kansas. It is widely cultivated as an ensilage crop and for its edible seeds, from which a valuable oil can be extracted. Its hairy stem grows 3 to 20 feet high, with coarse, saw-edged leaves and a flower head up to 18 inches in diameter. Sunflower stalks are used as fuel in many parts of eastern Europe and Asia.

The Jerusalem artichoke *(H. tuberosus)* is a sunflower native to central North America and cultivated by Indians for its edible, thick, underground stems, which grow to 4 inches long. It is an attractive garden plant and its roots are nourishing for livestock. Family: Daisy (Compositae); genus *Helianthus.*

SWEET BAY. See *Laurel.*

SWEET CLOVER, an erect tough annual or perennial herb, native to Eurasia but widespread in America. It has a deep, strong taproot, small, 3-part, compound leaves, and many slender spikes of small white or yellow flowers from which bees obtain a nectar that gives a distinctive flavor to honey.

It is grown extensively as hay, known as Bokhara clover, helps anchor the soil, and also enriches it with nitrogenous compounds produced by bacteria in the root nodules. Family: Pea (Leguminosae); genus and species, *Melilotus alba* (white-flowering) and *M. officinalis* (yellow-flowering).

SWEET GUM, a deciduous tree native to wet forests in North and Central America, growing to 150 feet in annually flooded areas of Mississippi, and often cultivated as an ornamental shade tree because of the strange, corky ridges that distinguish its younger stems and the gorgeous red or orange color that appears when its large, simple, star-shaped leaves take on their fall coloration. Its flowers lack a corolla and appear on the same plant in tight clusters that are either staminate or pistillate, the latter developing into spherical, burlike masses that drop ½-inch, winged seeds in autumn.

The reddish-brown wood of sweet gum is used instead of mahogany or walnut in furniture, flooring, and veneers. A related Asian species *(Liquidambar orientalis)* and an unrelated tree *(Styrax offiicinalis* of the storax family, Styracaceae) yield an aromatic resin called storax from their bark. Family: Witch-hazel (Hamamelidaceae); genus and species, *Liquidambar styraciflua.*

SWEET PEA, a herbaceous annual plant native to Sicily, introduced into northern Europe and then America in the 18th century for its handsome, fragrant butterfly-shaped flowers in white, lavender, blue, peach, pink, or red. The flowers grow in clusters of 3 or 4 on slender, climbing stems. The stems have pinnately compound leaves and twining tendrils, which are formed from modified, terminal leaflets. Family: Pea (Leguminosae); genus and species, *Lathyrus odoratus.*

SWEET POTATO, a perennial, trailing vine native to South America, introduced to Europe by Columbus, now widely cultivated in warm countries for its swollen, starchy, edible roots. It produces heart-shaped leaves and purple flowers. Although it is the original plant to be called a potato, and the "Irish" or white potato was named after it, the horticultural variety of sweet potato with the sweetest flavor is often incorrectly called a yam. Family: Morning-glory (Convolvulaceae); genus and species, *Ipomoea batatas.*

SWEETSOP, or Sugar Apple. See *Custard Apple.*

SWEET WILLIAM. See *Pink.*

SWISS CHARD. See *Beet.*

SYCAMORE. See *Plane-tree Family.*

SYRINGA. See *Lilac* and *Mock Orange.*

TALLOW TREE, a small tree native to China and Formosa, introduced to Europe and America as an ornament with glossy, oval leaves and long clusters of very small flowers, followed by seeds with a waxy covering. The wax has long been valued in China and India as a dressing for cloth, a material that could be made into soap, and a tallow for making candles that give a very clear light. The hardwood is sometimes used for engraving. Family: Spurge (Euphorbiaceae); genus and species, *Sapium sebiferum.*

TAMARACK. See *Larch.*

TAMARIND, an evergreen shade tree native to tropical Africa, but cultivated in India and other tropical countries. It grows to about 80 feet, with pinnately compound leaves bearing many leaflets, and clusters of white, yellow, or pink flowers followed by long, narrow, knotty, brown pods containing a juicy, brown pulp and small seeds. The pulp can be used to make a cooling drink, jellies, and preserves. The leaves yield a mordant used in dyeing cloth. The wood is hard and durable, suitable for cabinetmaking. Family: Pea (Leguminosae); genus and species, *Tamarindus indica.*

TAMARISK, any of about 80 different kinds of shrubs and small trees native to warm and tropical regions of the Old World, introduced also into semi-arid parts of America, many of them tolerating extended drought and salty or alkaline soil. The densely branching stems bear smooth-edged, thick, or scalelike leaves, often suggesting those of heaths, and small, white flowers in slender spikes.

In desert areas, tamarisks provide shelter and break the wind. Along rivers and intermittent streams in arid lands, they absorb a great deal of water, which they lose in transpiration at the expense of other adjacent plants that are less well adapted to desert conditions. Family: Tamarisk (Tamaricaceae); genus *Tamarix.*

TANGERINE. See *Orange.*

TAPIOCA. See *Cassava.*

TARO, a horticultural variety of a perennial herb native to India and Malaysia, cultivated widely as the source of a staple food in much of the world's tropics, particularly in the Orient and the Pacific islands. The plant grows best in wet soil, producing long stalks, large, triangular leaves shaped like arrowheads, inconspicuous flowers resembling miniature calla lillies, and large, starchy, edible, underground stems (corms).

The wild ancestor of taro, dasheen *(Colocasia esculenta),* has sweeter but more slender corms containing less starch. Taro corms can be boiled or dried and ground into a meal; in the Hawaiian Islands the meal is fermented to a paste called poi that is often regarded as the native delicacy.

Florists sometimes offer dasheen or taro leaves, which they call elephant's ear, for decorative purposes. The term elephant's ear is also used to describe cultivated members of a related genus *(Caladium)* and certain unrelated begonias. Family: Arum (Araceae); genus, species, and horticultural variety, *Colocasia esculenta antiquorum.*

TARRAGON, a perennial herb native to Europe, with smooth branches, aromatic, simple leaves, and globular heads of tubular flowers. The foliage, which has a bitter taste, is used to flavor vinegar, pickles, and salads. The flavor is contained in an oil that can be extracted from the plant; the oil is known as tarragon oil or estragon oil. Family: Daisy (Compositae); genus and species, *Artemisia dracunculus.*

TEA, an evergreen shrub or small tree that grows to 30 feet, native to eastern Asia from India to Japan and cultivated extensively in Asia and equatorial Africa. The tree is pruned to 3 to 5 feet tall to facilitate the harvesting of its buds and young shoots. If these are allowed to mature, the shrub bears many leathery, oval, saw-edged leaves with thick veins and fine hairs below, as well as clusters of faintly fragrant, ivory-white or pink flowers, which produce woody fruits containing several seeds resembling hazelnuts.

The cultivated tea plants include many hybrid strains but the method of harvesting is much the same for all. Tea leaves are picked from the same bushes 20 to 30 times a year. The first picking (flush) yields buds and very young leaves, which contribute to the best grades of tea. New buds and leaf shoots induced to grow by the first plucking provide for the next pickings.

The final picking of the year includes the old leaves and completely strips the shrubs, providing the coarsest grade of tea. After the picked buds and leaves have wilted, they are rolled by hand. Those dried with a minimum of fermentation make green tea; those allowed to ferment more extensively before drying make black tea. Family: Tea (Theaceae); genus and species, *Camellia sinensis.*

TEA FAMILY (Theaceae), a group of about 500 species in 30 genera, chiefly of tropical and subtropical regions, growing as trees or shrubs with simple leaves and flowers bearing several whorls of stamens. The franklinia, or lost camellia tree *(Gordonia alatamaha),* is now extinct except in cultivation, although it was discovered in Georgia as recently as 1765; it has large, white flowers suggesting waxy poppies. See *Camellia* and *Tea.*

TEAK, a tall tree native to India and Malaysia, cultivated on huge plantations, with a straight trunk growing to 200 feet, a spreading crown, 4-sided branchlets with a central pith, and leaves attaining 24 inches in length and 12 in width, suggesting those of tobacco. The branches terminate in upturned clusters of small, white flowers.

The timber is fragrant, the heartwood a golden yellow that becomes darker and mottled with seasoning; it ranks with mahogany in value and is used for expensive furniture, homes, temples, and ships. Some teak carvings preserved in Indian temples are more than 2000 years old. In Burma an oil extracted from teak wood is used in medicine and commerce. Family: Vervain (Verbenaceae); genus and species, *Tectona grandis.*

TEASEL, any of 12 different kinds of prickly, stemmed, biennial plants native to Mediterranean countries, East Africa, and across the Caucasus to India. Wild teasel *(Dipsacus sylvestris)* is now a widespread weed, with long leaves that are toothed and prickly on the edges, the stem attaining a height of 5 or more feet and branching near the top to bear cone-shaped clusters of lavender, purple, or blue flowers among stiff bristles, each whole head guarded by about 6 narrow, modified leaves.

A cultivated variety of teasel, called fuller's teasel *(Dipsacus sylvestris fullorum),* has particularly stiff hooked bristles between the flowers in the head. When firm ripe heads are split lengthwise, they can be mounted on long wooden rollers under which new woolen cloth is shifted back and forth during the fulling process; the bristles raise the nap by picking gently at the cloth surface. Family: Teasel (Dipsacaceae); genus *Dipsacus.*

THISTLE, any of several different coarse, prickly, herbaceous plants, many widespread or cosmopolitan as weeds. Most are members of the daisy family (Compositae), with tubular flowers clustered in cylindrical heads, often surrounded by prickly, green bracts. The Scotch thistle *(Onopordum acanthium),* the national emblem of Scotland, falls into this category; it grows to 10 feet, bearing lobed, toothed, prickly, cotton-wooly leaves with a covering of gray hair. It is widespread as a weed.

Russian thistle *(Salsola kali tenuifolia)* is a very different plant. Native to Eurasia but now grown in America, it has short, stiff, prickly leaves on a repeatedly branched stem growing to 4 feet, which dries as a huge, loose, open globe and breaks loose from the root to become a tumbleweed, scattering its seeds as it rolls along in the wind; it is a member of the goosefoot family (Chenopodiaceae).

THORN APPLE. See *Jimsonweed*

THYME, any of about 40 different kinds of low-growing, perennial shrubs native to Eurasia and Africa, most with a square, woody stem 1 to 2 feet high, narrow, aromatic, paired leaves, and clusters of lilac-colored, 2-lipped flowers. The garden thyme *(Thymus vulgaris)* of Mediterranean Europe and North Africa grows straighter than the wild, creeping thyme *(T. serpyllum).*

Thyme is much favored as a source of leaves, as a condiment, or as a source of the essential oil of thyme, which is used medicinally. Wild thyme has been introduced to America and has escaped from cultivation to become a weed. Family: Mint (Labiatae); genus *Thymus.*

TIMOTHY, a perennial grass native to Europe but widely introduced and cultivated as a leading hay crop. It is tolerant of cold weather and withstands drought well; some varieties have bulbous enlargements for food storage in the region where the stems arise from the roots. The minute, purple flowers are borne in an elongated, club-shaped head resembling a miniature cattail head; the purple color is that of the long stamens. Family: Grass (Gramineae); genus and species, *Phleum pratense.*

TOBACCO, a broad-leaved, annual herb native to Central and South America. Long before the coming of the Europeans to the New World, it was cultivated in the Caribbean islands and North America for the leaves, which were smoked in special pipes. The plant grows upright, bearing handsome leaves, a straight stem growing to 6 feet, and attractive white or pink tubular flowers. The leaves are stripped from the stems either before or after the stalks have been cut; they are dried and processed for manufacture into cigars, cigarettes, smoking tobacco, chewing tobacco, or snuff. Today the United States leads in all-purpose tobacco production.

Several related plants with larger flowers are favorites in gardens. They are known generally as nicotine and their flowers open mostly at night. Family: Potato (Solanaceae); genus and species, *Nicotiana tabacum*.

TOMATO, a herbaceous annual plant native to tropical South America, with a straggling, hairy stem, notched, pinnately compound leaves, small clusters of yellow flowers, and spherical, red or yellow berries. Introduced as a curiosity into Europe by Spanish explorers, tomatoes were known as "love apples" and thought to be poisonous.

Only within the last century has the tomato been widely recognized as harmless, edible, delicious, and rich in vitamins, whether eaten raw, cooked, pickled, canned, or crushed into juice. Family: Potato (Solanaceae); genus and species, *Lycopersicon esculentum*.

TONKA BEAN TREE, a tree of tropical South America, growing to 80 feet, with pinnately compound leaves and irregular flowers, producing fleshy pods containing black, fragrant seeds called tonka beans. The beans contain coumarin, a sweet-smelling carbohydrate. They are used in flavoring tobacco and in making artificial vanilla and perfumes. Family: Pea (Leguminosae); genus and species, *Dipteryx odorata*.

TREE OF HEAVEN, a deciduous tree native to China but commonly introduced into urban areas of Europe and North America, escaping from cultivation to become widespread. It grows to 90 feet in height and 40 inches in diameter at chest height, with large, pinnately compound leaves and either ill-smelling, small, greenish, staminate flowers or inconspicuous, pistillate flowers, which produce strange, 2-inch fruits with a seed at the center resembling twisted strips of brown paper.

The tree survives in cities despite polluted air and the paved soil that surrounds it. Family: Quassia (Simaroubaceae); genus and species, *Ailanthus altissima*.

TRILLIUM, a genus of delicate woodland wildflowers, native to North America and eastern Asia, with about 30 different species, all with short, thick, underground, horizontal stems from which they produce upright stems every spring. Each stem has a single whorl of 3 net-veined leaves and a terminal flower with 3 large petals.

In eastern North American woodlands, the most familiar are the large, white trillium *(T. grandiflorum)*, the ill-smelling red trillium *(T. erectum)*, and the attractive, painted trillium *(T. undulatum)*, which has red stripes on its white petals. Family: Lily (Liliaceae).

TRUMPET CREEPER, or trumpet vine, either of two woody vines with bright-green, pinnately compound leaves and clusters of orange or scarlet, trumpet-shaped flowers. The stout stem clambers with the aid of tendrils over rocks, walls, trellises, trees, and sometimes roofs, occasionally reaching a height of 80 feet. Family: Bignonia (Bignoniaceae); genus and species, *Campsis radicans* (eastern North America) and *C. grandiflora* (native to China, but widely introduced as an ornament).

TUBEROSE, a herbaceous perennial plant native to Mexico, grown widely in gardens and greenhouses in temperate regions of both hemispheres for its long spikes of heavily perfumed, waxy, white, tubular flowers on stalks about 3 feet tall. The name tuberose has nothing to do with tubes or roses; instead, it refers to the tuberous, rather than bulbous, roots from which the narrow leaves and flower stalks grow. Family: Amaryllis (Amaryllidaceae); genus and species, *Polyanthes tuberosa*.

TULIP, any of about 50 different kinds of bulbous, perennial herbs native to north temperate parts of Eurasia, particularly to the steppes of Central Asia. Many kinds are now cultivated, especially in Holland, as the basis of an important horticultural industry. All tulips have sheathed bulbs, broad, tapering leaves, and large, showy, cup-like flowers. The original wild species *(Tulipa gesneriana)* is sometimes called the cottage tulip. The early-blooming, yellow-tipped, red, Van Thol tulips were derived from another wild tulip *(T. suaveolens)* from the vicinity of the Caspian Sea. Family: Lily (Liliaceae); genus *Tulipa*.

TULIP TREE, a handsome, tall, straight, deciduous tree native to the eastern United States, growing to 200 feet, with a cone-shaped top composed of branches bearing broad, simple, lobed leaves and strikingly tulip-like, greenish-yellow flowers. The soft wood, sometimes known as whitewood or canoewood, is still used for woodenware and interior finishes; for many years the Indians used the wood to make large canoes. The only close relative is a Chinese tree with similar blossoms. Unrelated tropical trees, such as the African tulipan *(Spathodea campanulata* of the bignonia family, Bignoniaceae), are sometimes called tuliptrees. Family: Magnolia (Magnoliaceae); genus and species, *Liriodendron tulipifera*.

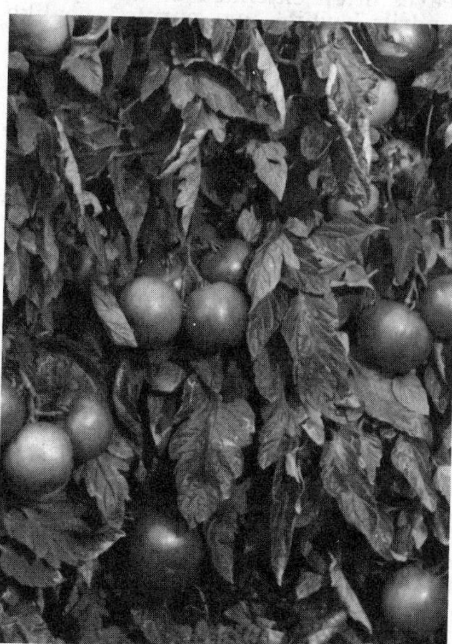
BURPEE SEEDS

TOMATO

TUMBLEWEED, any of a number of mostly unrelated plants of plains and prairies that break loose from their roots when mature and dry, curl into almost spherical masses, and tumble over and over, scattering their small seeds, as they are blown by the wind.

The native tumbleweed, covering much of North America, is usually *Amaranthus graecizans* of the amaranth family (Amaranthaceae). It might also be a winged pigweed *(Cycloloma)*, a bugseed *(Corispermum)*, a Russian thistle *(Salsola tragus)* of the goosefoot family, Chenopodiaceae, or a member of the pea family (Leguminosae), such as the scurf pea *(Psoralea)* or wild indigo *(Baptisia)*.

TUNG TREE, either of two kinds of small, deciduous trees native to China, now cultivated in vast orchards in the southeastern United States for the valuable oil that can be extracted from the seeds. The tree itself grows to 40 feet, flowering in early spring before leafing out. One to several pistillate flowers in the same cluster grow together with many staminate flowers; the apple-shaped fruit matures in early autumn.

Tung oil from the seeds is used in varnishes as a drying agent; it is also used in the manufacture of paints, oilcloth, linoleum, waterproof textiles, electrical insulation, and printing ink. Family: Spurge (Euphorbiaceae); genus and species, *Aleurities fordii* (semitropical) and *A. montana* (more cold-resistant).

TUPELO, or pepperidge, or sour gum, any of different kinds of small, water-loving trees native to India, eastern Asia, and North America, growing to 40 to 60 feet, with drooping lower branches, leathery simple leaves, and clusters of separate staminate and pistillate flowers on the same tree. The fruits are red, blue, or purple. Like the cherry, they have a central seed in a fleshy pulp. Both the cotton-gum or water tupelo *(Nyssa aquatica)*, and the black gum *(N. sylvatica)* produce useful timber, and are often grown in parks for their brilliant red autumn foliage. Family: Dogwood (Cornaceae); genus *Nyssa*.

TURNIP. See *Mustard*.

UMBRELLA PLANT. See *Papyrus*.

VALERIAN, any of about 200 different sun-loving, hardy, perennial herbs of cool and alpine regions in the Northern Hemisphere, with thick, strong-scented roots and underground stems, simple or delicate pinnately compound leaves, and luxuriant clusters of tiny, sweet-smelling, pink, lavender, or white flowers. Common valerian (*Valeriana officinalis*), often called garden heliotrope, is frequently grown in the New World and the Old as a border plant. Its dried roots and underground stems yield a valuable drug used in nervous disorders. Unrelated plants with blue, cuplike flowers and showy foliage (genus *Polemonium* of the family Polemoniaceae) are often called Greek valerian or Jacob's ladder. Family: Valerian (Valerianaceae); genus *Valeriana*.

VALERIAN FAMILY (Valerianaceae), a group of about 370 species in 10 genera, chiefly of the North Temperate Zone and high elevations in the Andes. Most are herbs, usually with a 5-parted corolla, the calyx often developing later as a bristly appendage to the small dry seed. See *Spikenard* and *Valerian*.

VANILLA. See *Orchid Family*.

VEGETABLE SPONGE, or dishcloth gourd, or Loofah, a tropical vine with large, coarse leaves, yellow, bell-shaped flowers, and a slender fruit, 10 to 40 inches long, with a fibrous skeleton through the pulp. Although the fruit rind is edible, the fibrous portion is commonly saved, washed, and used as a sponge or in the preparation of cloth and hats. Family: Gourd (Cucurbitaceae); genus and species, *Luffa cylindrica*.

VENUS'S-FLYTRAP, a low-growing, insectivorous plant of North and South Carolina, displaying a rosette of shiny, green leaves with winged stalks and bilobed blades. The blades are edged with long, coarse projections and the upper surface of each lobe is armed with 3 sensitive bristles. If these are agitated, as by an insect crawling over them, the 2 lobes of the leaf fold abruptly and the long projections fit together, forming a cage.

Slowly the plant brings the leaf surfaces against the insect, secretes digestive juices, and absorbs the products of digestion. After closing without catching an insect, or after absorption is complete, the leaf blades spread apart, ready to act as a trap again. Mature plants send up a slender, vertical stalk to 7 inches high, with a cluster of white flowers at the top. Family: Sundew (Droseraceae); genus and species, *Dionaea muscipula*.

VERBENA, a genus of herbaceous plants native to temperate and tropical regions of both hemispheres, with about 230 species, bearing opposite leaves and spikes of flowers all through the summer. A few kinds, such as Eurasian vervain (*V. officinalis*), have been introduced and grown in North America; it has branching, smooth stems and purple flower spikes.

Horticultural verbena hybrids include the sweet-scented verbena (referred to as *V. hybrida*). European moss verbena (*V. erinoides*) is often grown in hanging baskets. A related plant is the lemon verbena (*Lippia citriodora*) native to South America and cultivated in North America and Europe for the lemon fragrance of its leaves and its large pyramidal clusters

BURPEE SEEDS

WALLFLOWER

of flowers, which are smaller than those of true verbenas. Family: Vervain (Verbenaceae).

VERONICA, or speedwell, a genus of about 150 different species of small, herbaceous plants native to the North Temperate Zone, mostly with opposite, simple leaves on creeping or erect stems, and spikes of small, wheel-shaped, blue flowers. All contain large amounts of vitamin C, and some can be cooked as potherbs. One, called American brooklime (*V. americana*) because it grows along stream edges, has been recommended as a preventative for scurvy. Family: Figwort (Scrophulariaceae).

VETCH, any of about 150 different kinds of prostrate and climbing perennial herbs native to the Northern Hemisphere and temperate South America, with pinnately compound leaves often extended at the tip into tendrils, white or purple, pealike blossoms in short or solitary spikes, and a compressed pod from each flower.

The narrow-leaved, common vetch (*Vicia sativa*) of Europe and the British Isles, and the hairy or winter vetch (*V. villosa*) of eastern Europe are among those that have been widely introduced and become widespread in most temperate climates, sometimes planted and plowed under as a green manure, and often harvested as forage for livestock. Family: Pea (Leguminosae); genus *Vicia*.

VIBURNUM, a genus of shrubs and small trees native to temperate and subtropical regions, especially of Asia and North America, with simple leaves and clusters of white or pink flowers followed by fleshy fruits, usually red or black, for which the plants are sometimes called "wild raisins." The Eurasian guelderrose (*V. opulus*), which has spherical flower clusters instead of flat-topped ones, has been developed into a widely cultivated ornamental shrub, the snowball bush (*V. o. roseum*), which must be propagated by cuttings because its large flowers are sterile. Tree viburnums 15 to 30 feet tall include the nannyberry or sweet viburnum (*V. lentago*), of eastern North America, and the twistwood or wayfaring tree (*V. lantana*), native to Europe but introduced and widespread in the New World. Family: Honeysuckle (Caprifoliaceae).

VIOLET, any of about 400 small, herbaceous plants native to the North Temperate Zone, mountains in tropical Latin America, and tropical and southern Africa. They grow best in moist places, spreading oval or heart-shaped leaves on long stalks, and raising irregular, 5-petalled flowers on individual, long stalks; one long-spurred petal contains the nectar.

The widely cultivated perennial pansies, with flowers of many colors and patterns resembling human faces, have been developed by horticulturists from the wild European violet (*V. tricolor*) known as heart's-ease. Pansies escape from cultivation into lawns and wild areas, their flowers shrinking in size; the plant is then known as a Johnny-jump-up. A majority of violets have purple flowers; indeed, the flower gives its name to the color purple. Family: Violet (Violaceae); genus *Viola*.

VIRGINIA CREEPER. See *Boston Ivy*.

WAKE-ROBIN. See *Trillium*.

WALKING FERN, or walking leaf, a small fern native to eastern North America, with simple, lance-shaped, leathery, evergreen leaves tapering to slender, elongated tips, which droop down to the earth and take root, starting new plants. The base of each leaf is heart-shaped, and the spore cases are irregularly scattered on both sides of the midrib over the under surface of the blade. Family: Polypody (Polypodiaceae); genus and species, *Camptosorus rhizophyllus*.

WALLFLOWER, or gillyflower, a tall, herbaceous plant native to eastern Mediterranean countries, often cultivated in gardens as an ornament behind the flower bed or on the wall. The wild plant has yellow flowers with 4 petals, but horticultural varieties in many pastel shades have been developed. Family: Mustard (Cruciferae); genus and species, *Cheirinia cheiri*.

WALNUT, any of 15 different kinds of tall timber trees native to the Old World and the New, growing to 70 or 150 feet, with large, pinnately compound leaves; tiny, staminate and pistillate green flowers borne on the same tree; and usually, spherical, hard-shelled seeds enclosed in a leathery or fibrous husk. The commercial nuts, called walnuts, are from the Circassian or Persian walnut tree (*Juglans regia*), native to western Asia from Iran to India, but much cultivated in England and known there as the English walnut; its seeds are particularly sweet and large, and its hard, gray-brown, mottled wood warps so rarely that it is prized for furniture-making.

The Black walnut *(J. nigra)* of the eastern United States is equally valuable for fine timber, but its seeds have a stronger flavor. Butternut *(J. cinerea)* of the eastern United States is less valuable, with smaller fruits that are oblong, pointed, and contain an oil from which a stain for dyeing homespun woolens was made in colonial days.

The California walnut *(J. californica)* is frequently used in walnut orchards of the western United States as the best root upon which to graft fruit-bearing branches of the Persian walnut; the trees are then called California budded walnuts. Family: Walnut (Juglandaceae); genus *Juglans.*

WALNUT FAMILY (Juglandaceae), a small group of about 60 species in 6 genera, all deciduous shrubs or trees with alternate, pinnately-compound leaves. The staminate flowers grow in catkins and the solitary, pistillate flowers mature into a hard shell around the seed that is enclosed by a leathery or fibrous husk. See *Hickory* and *Walnut.*

WATER CHESTNUT, or horn-nut, or water caltrop, an aquatic herb native to tropical Eurasia, with mottled, oval, floating, feathery, underwater leaves and spongy stalks. The small, white flowers are raised above the water surface, and produce large, horned, or spiny fruits with a thin shell that encloses a sweet, edible seed. In the Orient these seeds are roasted or eaten raw, whereas in Mediterranean countries they are ground into a flour. Family: Water chestnut (Hydrocaryaceae); genus and species, *Trapa natans.*

WATERCRESS. See *Cress.*

WATER LILY, any of several related kinds of aquatic plants native to ponds and shallow, slow-moving streams of many parts of the world. The fleshy stems grow in the bottom sediments of the marshes and produce flat, padlike leaves on long, slender stalks. The leaves float on the water's surface; the shiny green upper surface of the leaf is normally dry while the bottom is wet. Some kinds extend their flowers into the air, while others allow the flowers to float with the leaves on the water's surface.

The yellow pond lily *(Nuphar advena)* of the eastern United States and Canada has almost spherical flowers. The yellow parts are sepals; the petals are tiny and usually overlooked. More fragrant is the white water lily *(Nymphaea odorata)* of the same region, with almost indistinguishable white sepals, and white petals that open widely, displaying the yellow stamens. The giant among water lilies is the *Victoria regia,* with leaves to 6 feet across that are turned up at the edges and prickly beneath; it is native to the Amazon valley and northeastern South America. Family: Waterlily (Nymphaeaceae).

WATER-LILY FAMILY (Nymphaeaceae), a small group of about 90 species in 8 genera, widely distributed in shallow, fresh waters. Aquarium fanciers often provide extra oxygen and food for their fish by cultivating fish grass *(Cabomba* species), native to tropical America, which has brushlike, green stems of finely divided leaves and grows completely submerged; or water shield *(Brasenia schreberi),* which has floating leaves on long stalks that come to the center of the under surface of the leaf. See *Lotus* and *Water lily.*

WATERMELON. See *Melon.*

WATER PLANTAIN, any of 6 different marsh plants of temperate regions, with fleshy stems growing in the bottom sediments of the marshes, and long-stalked leaves differing in shape according to the depth of the water in which they grow. Those that are submerged are generally grasslike; those that emerge from the water into the air are oval or lance-shaped and pointed at the tip; and those on the shore are more heart-shaped.

Submerged plants rarely open their flowers, which are self-pollinating; on the other hand those that grow in the air have small clusters of white or purple flowers that are visited by insects. Family: Water-plantain (Alismataceae); genus *Alisma.*

WATER-PLANTAIN FAMILY (Alismataceae), a small group of about 75 species in 14 genera, widely distributed, found mostly in wet ground or shallow, fresh water, and most common in the Northern Hemisphere. See *Arrowhead* and *Waterplantain.*

WATTLE TREE, any of several different kinds of low branching trees native to Australia, with pinnately compound leaves and clusters of bright yellow flowers. Young saplings are easily bent and are used for making fences and primitive dwellings. The common wattle *(Acacia longifolia)* is the national flower of Australia. Family: Pea (Leguminosae); genus *Acacia.*

WAXFLOWER, a climbing, evergreen, perennial plant native to southern China, with stiff, cylindrical stems, leathery, shiny, oval leaves, and clusters of pink, fragrant flowers, from which a copious and sweet nectar often drips. Cultivated indoors in temperate climates or outdoors where frost is rare, it is usually propagated by cuttings and requires much water. Family: Milkweed (Asclepiadaceae); genus and species, *Hoya carnosa.*

WAYFARING TREE. See *Viburnum.*

WHEAT, an annual grass native to central Asia and southern Europe, cultivated since prehistoric times for its cereal grains, and now one of the world's chief crops. It has tall, slender stems, ribbonlike leaves, and bearded, terminal clusters of flowers that mature into heads of grain. Wheat contains more gluten than many other cereal grains, and is especially suited for making into bread flour.

Spring wheat, planted in the spring and harvested in early summer, is grown in the northern United States, Canada, and other cold temperate regions. Winter wheat, planted in the fall and harvested late in the following spring, is preferred in warmer regions. Durum wheat has particularly hard, starchy grains, and yields semolina flour, which serves as the basis for most macaroni products. Family: Grass (Gramineae); genus *Triticum,* particularly the species *T. sativum.*

WILLOW, any of about 300 different kinds of fast-growing shrubs and trees with simple, narrow leaves and flowers in catkins; the pistillate flowers mature as loose capsules with numerous hairy seeds. Willows are found throughout the world—as creeping perennials between boulders in the Arctic and on high mountains, and as 100-foot trees along streams and in wet soil in warmer countries.

The young branches of many willows are used in making baskets and wicker furniture. These branches are called osiers. They take their name from a European basket willow *(Salix viminalis).*

One of the largest species is the black willow *(S. nigra)* of eastern North America. Weeping willow *(S. babylonica),* native to China, is popular as an ornamental tree because of its gracefully arching, drooping branches. Pussy willows (chiefly the eastern North American *S. discolor* and *S. humilis)* have gray, furry catkins that open in early spring before the leaves appear, generally after dropping their stiff, shiny brown bud scales on the snow. Family: Willow (Salicaceae); genus *Salix.*

WILLOW FAMILY (Salicaceae), a group of about 340 species in two genera, widely distributed, but most numerous in the North Temperate Zone and the Arctic. See *Poplar* and *Willow.*

WINTERGREEN, either of 2 unrelated types of evergreen plants with shiny, leathery leaves; one is native to heaths and northern woodlands in both the Old World and the New, and the other is characteristic of similar places in the eastern part of North America. The original wintergreens, members of genera *Chimaphila* and *Pyrola* of the pyrola family (Pyrolaceae), were so named before the discovery of America, and are known in the New World as "false wintergreens" to distinguish them from "true wintergreen" or checkerberry *(Gaultheria procumbens* of the heath family, Ericaceae).

Wintergreen oil, used medicinally or as a flavoring, can be obtained from the leaves of *Gaultheria* or made synthetically. The leaves, the white, waxy flowers in small clusters, and the brilliant red berries all have the same pleasant flavor.

WISTERIA, or *wistaria,* a genus consisting of 6 species of climbing, woody vines native to eastern Asia and eastern North America, with pinnately compound leaves and handsome clusters of pea-shaped, white or lavender flowers. In horticultural varieties of the Chinese *(W. chinensis)* and

Japanese *(W. floribunda)* wistaria, the flower clusters range from 1 to 5 feet in length, and the pods that follow the flowers are hairy. In the shrubby species native to southeastern United States *(W. frutescens* and *W. macrostachya)*, the clusters are smaller and more fragrant, the pods bare. Family: Pea (Leguminosae).

WITCH HAZEL, any of 6 different kinds of shrubs or trees native to eastern Asia and eastern North America, with alternate, simple leaves, and fragrant, yellow flowers with long, twisted, narrow petals that open in late autumn and sometimes again in early spring.

The fertilized ovules, enclosed by the hairy ovary wall, develop in the spring amid a mucilaginous material that becomes compressed as the fruit dries. Eventually the tip of the fruit opens and the brown seeds are shot out explosively for many feet. The astringent extract from the leaves and scaly bark is used in lotions and medicines. Family: Witch hazel (Hamamelidaceae); genus *Hamamelis.*

WITCH-HAZEL FAMILY (Hamamelidaceae), a group of about 100 species in 23 genera, all trees or shrubs with alternate simple leaves, chiefly Asiatic but found also in eastern North America, Africa, and Australia. See *Sweet gum* and *Witch hazel.*

WOLFSBANE. See *Aconite.*

WOODBINE, a common name given to several different, unrelated, climbing plants with tough stems that tend to tie together the bushes and trees upon which they grow.

They include the Virginia creeper *(Parthenocissus quinquefolia)* of the grape family, (Vitaceae); the common woodbine *(Lonicera periclymenum)* and Italian woodbine *(L. caprifolium)* of the honeysuckle family (Caprifoliaceae); and the virgin's-bower *(Clematis virginiana)*, native to eastern North America and a member of the buttercup family (Ranunculaceae). See *Boston ivy* and *Clematis.*

WOOD SORREL. See *Oxalis.*

WORMWOOD, a coarse, perennial herb native to southern Europe and central Asia, with hairy, branching stems growing to 3 feet from a thick, subterranean branching stem. The twice or thrice pinnately compound leaves growing low on the stem have long stalks, whereas those higher up have short stalks. Several small heads of yellow flowers develop on each wormwood plant.

Once cultivated in Eurasia and introduced into North America, wormwood is generally regarded as a historically interesting weed, for a dark green, bitter oil extracted from it gave much of the flavor to absinthe and various tonics. Family: Daisy (Compositae); genus and species, *Artemisia absinthium.*

YAM FAMILY (Dioscoreaceae), a group of about 650 different species in 10 genera, mostly plants of warm, temperate, and tropical regions with herbaceous or woody climbing stems, large, net-veined leaves, and clusters of small, inconspicuous flowers followed by a fleshy berry or a dry capsule.

T.H. EVERETT

WITCH HAZEL

Most useful to man are members of the large genus *Dioscorea,* which have thick, starchy, underground stems or tubers worth cultivating for food. The edible parts of the common white yam *(D. alata)* grow to a length of 8 feet, weigh 30 to 100 pounds, and are made edible by roasting or boiling. In the United States the name yam is sometimes applied incorrectly to some varieties of the unrelated cultivated sweet potato.

YARROW, a milfoil, a herbaceous perennial, native to Europe but now widespread as a weed found on roadsides and in fields, bearing finely-divided leaves that have a pleasant aromatic fragrance and upright stems terminating in a flat-topped cluster of small, white or (rarely) pink flowers.

The name milfoil refers to the thousands of fine divisions on each soft leaf of the yarrow. Family: Daisy (Compositae); genus and species, *Achillea millefolium.*

YELLOWWOOD, a branching tree native to the central and southern United States, from 40 to 60 feet tall, with pinnately compound leaves that turn yellow in autumn. The tree has brittle, yellow wood from which a dye can be extracted, and long sprays of sweet-smelling, white flowers. It is sometimes known as gopherwood. Family: Pea (Leguminosae); genus and species, *Cladastris lutea.*

YEW, any of about 9 different kinds of shrubs and small trees native to the Northern Hemisphere, with evergreen needles more or less borne in 2 ranks along the outstretched branches. The seeds are dry or nutlike, surrounded except at their tips by a soft, fleshy, colorful enlargement of the tip of the flower stalk. English yew *(Taxus baccata)* has tough, flexible wood, and was formerly important in the construction of bows for archery. Western yew *(T. brevifolia)* of the Pacific coast of North America is a relatively scarce, medium-sized tree with fine-grained wood valuable in cabinetmaking and for canoe paddles. Ground-hemlock *(T. canadensis)*, a shrub of thickets in east-central North America, is often used decoratively around buildings and for making wreaths.

The foliage, bark, and seeds of all yews contain poisonous substances; English yew, in fact, is regarded as the most poisonous plant in Britain. Cattle will eat yew branches if given an opportunity, and children may be harmed if they swallow yew seeds while sampling the attractive, red, fruitlike covering. Family: Yew (Taxaceae); genus *Taxus.*

YUCA. See *Cassava.*

YUCCA, a genus of perennial plants native to southern North America and Central America, with a woody stem bearing a dense whorl of long, pointed, swordlike leaves, and majestic clusters of waxy, ivory-white flowers with a sticky pollen that is distributed only by certain small moths *(Pronuba* species).

A spirelike yucca *(Y. filamentosa)* of the eastern United States is called Adam's needle. A branching species *(Y. brevifolia)* of the southwestern United States, which grows up to 20 to 30 feet in height, is known as the Joshua tree.

New Mexico has chosen the Spanish bayonet *(Y. gloriosa)* as its state flower. Other species of the genus are known as Spanish dagger, beargrass, and candle-of-God. Family: Lily (Liliaceae).

ZINNIA, a genus of 12 different species of herbaceous plants native to southern North America, with opposite leaves lacking stalks, and handsome, terminal heads of daisy-like flowers. The common cultivated zinnias of gardens are horticultural varieties of the species *Z. elegans,* introduced from Mexico. Family: Daisy (Compositae).

For Further Reference

Bold, Harold Charles. *The Plant Kingdom* (2nd Ed.). Prentice-Hall, 1964.

Hunken, Jore, and New England Wildflower Society staff. *Botany for All Ages.* Globe Pequot, 1989.

Muller, Walter Henry. *Botany: A Functional Approach.* Macmillan, 1963.

Northern, Henry T. *Introductory Plant Science* (3rd Ed.). Ronald Press, 1968.

Ray, Peter, and Taylor Steeves. *Botany.* Saunders College Publishing, 1983.

Selsam, Millicent. *Plants That Move.* William Morrow, 1962.

Wilson, Carl Lewis, and Walter E. Loomis. *Botany* (4th Ed.). Holt, Rinehart and Winston, 1967.

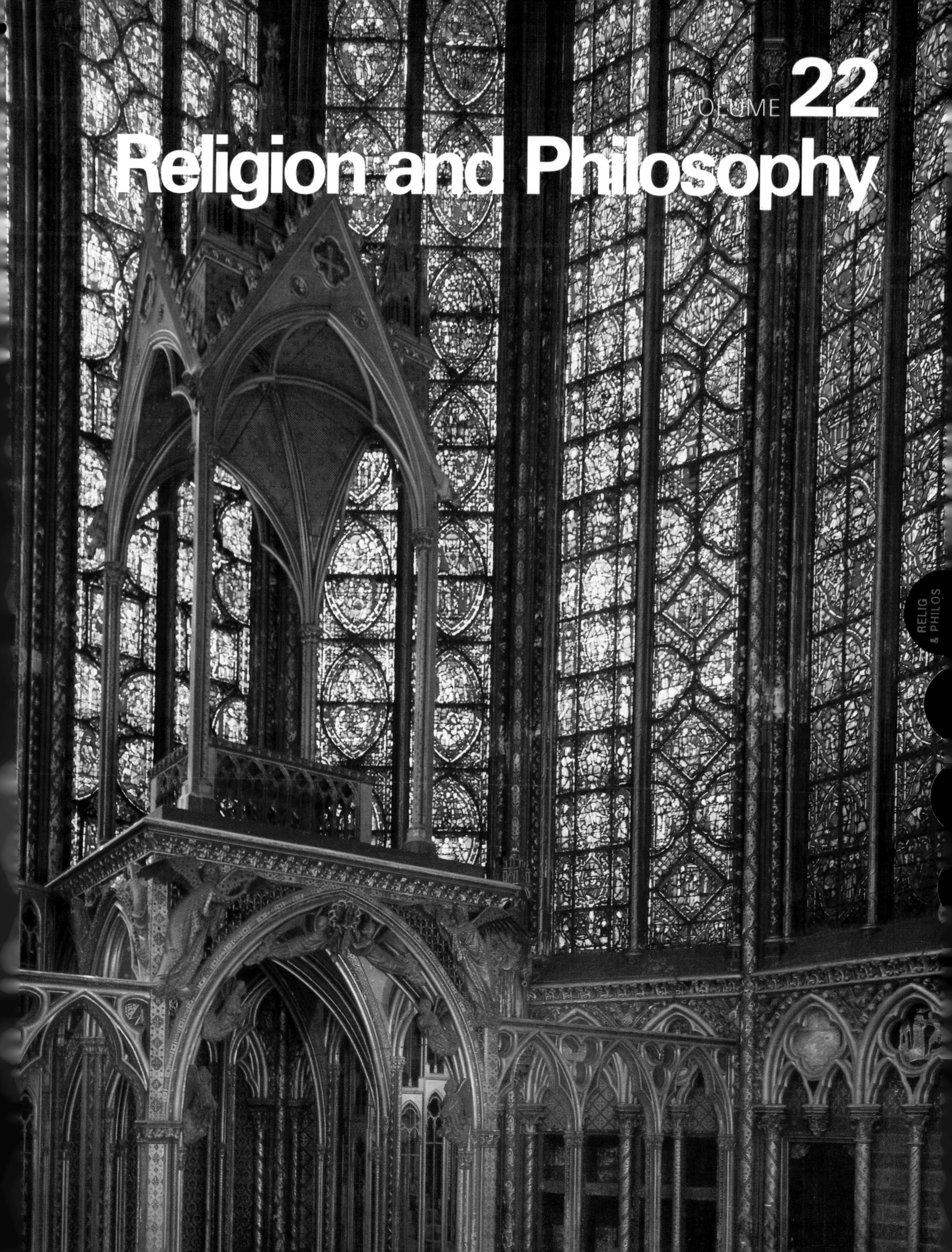
VOLUME 22
Religion and Philosophy
RELIG & PHILOS

BETTYE LANE/PHOTO RESEARCHERS

APPROXIMATE MEMBERSHIP IN RELIGIOUS BODIES, U.S.A.
(millions)

Religion	Adherents
CHRISTIAN	
Catholic Churches	
Roman Catholic	49.4
Eastern Orthodox Churches	5.1
Other	.4
Total Catholic	54.9
Protestant Churches	
Baptist	16.4
Methodist	13.0
Lutheran	8.6
Presbyterian	4.0
Episcopal	3.0
Pentecostal Churches	2.7
Churches of Christ	2.5
United Church of Christ	1.8
Disciples of Christ	1.3
Christian Churches	1.1
Adventists	.6
Jehovah's Witnesses	.5
Church of Christ, Nazarene	.5
Other	2.2
Total Protestant	58.2
Total Christian	113.1
JEWISH	5.8
LATTER DAY SAINTS (Mormons)	2.7
OTHER (includes Muslims, Buddhists, Unitarian-Universalists)	1.5
TOTAL RELIGIOUS MEMBERSHIP	123.1

APPROXIMATE MEMBERSHIP IN WORLD RELIGIONS
(millions)

Religion	Adherents
CHRISTIAN	
Roman Catholic	575
Eastern Orthodox	75
Protestant	350
Total Christian	1000
MUSLIM	600
HINDU	550
BUDDHIST	250
CONFUCIAN	170
SHINTO	55
TAOIST	30
JEWISH	15
Total adherents	2670

ST. CHAPELLE, PARIS: SCALA/EPA

VOLUME 22

Religion and Philosophy

PATTERSON/MONKMEYER
NEW YORK PUBLIC LIBRARY
PAN AMERICAN
METROPOLITAN MUSEUM OF ART, WOLFE FUND, 1931
DIRK BOUTS/ST. PETERS, LOUVIAN

Religion and philosophy are among the oldest of mankind's concerns. From the very dawn of human history, man has sought to control the unseen forces that bring prosperity or disaster, good or ill fortune.

Over the centuries, the religious impulse has resulted in not only religion as we know it, but also the fine and performing arts, literature, and philosophy itself. Music, dance, and drama all originated in prereligious magic and ritual. For untold centuries there was no clear division between the questioning spirit of the religious man and the questioning spirit of the philosopher.

Ironically, the arts and sciences have often been seen as the enemies of religion, the "parent" from which they sprung. Yet no perfection of art, no new scientific discovery, has ever managed to eradicate the religious impulse. The world's major religions still claim the allegiance of a majority of the human race, as suggested by the table to the left. Religious men have sought a relationship between themselves and the unseen even when faced with hostile critics or repressive political systems.

Philosophy, which once included all of man's efforts to understand himself and his world, has lost huge parts of its territory to the ever-growing disciplines of the sciences and social sciences. What was once known as "natural philosophy," for example, is now called physics.

Yet philosophy remains an important field in its own right, often asking questions whose answers other disciplines take for granted. How do we know what we know? What is the relationship between mind and body? What does it mean to be good? Philosophers consider the answers to such questions with great rigor. Their devotion to the power of reason in asking and answering such questions is the quality that sets them off most clearly from religious thinkers.

This volume is arranged in three main sections. The first considers the major religions of the world. It begins with the monotheistic faiths most familiar in the Western world—Judaism, Christianity, and Islam. All three find their roots in the faith of the ancient Hebrews, and they share to this day many traditions. The section on Christianity gives special attention to the larger Christian denominations in the United States, each of which is described briefly.

Descriptions of the major religions of the East—Hinduism and Buddhism—are then described, followed by discussions of other religions that have substantial followings in the modern world. In general, the religions of the East are less tightly organized than those in the West, and the distinction between religion and philosophy is less clear.

A second major section of the volume is a glossary of biblical characters, places, and books. This may be used to identify any of the major personalities who play a part in the Jewish and Christian scriptures.

The third and final section provides a brief history of philosophy in the Western world, from ancient times to the present. Early philosophy grew from the secular tradition of the Greeks and Romans. From the 400's A.D. until the 1500's, however, most Western philosophers were also Christian churchmen, accepting the concerns and assumptions of Christian theology. Since the 1500's, philosophy and religion have parted ways once again, and the mainstream of philosophy is secular in its interests.

Other information relating to religion and philosophy may be found in biographies of the leading religious figures and philosophers in the PEOPLE volume; in the histories of various regions of the world; and in the volumes on ART and LITERATURE.

RELIGION

All human societies today, and all societies that people know about from history or archaeology, have some form of religion. Even in nations where the official state policy is determinedly against religion, millions continue to practice their religions. Although some individuals may profess no religion or an opposition to all religions, the overwhelming majority of the people alive today, or who have lived in the past, believe at least some of the following to be true:

The universe was not created by accident. Some being capable of knowledge and thought created it.

Beings that do not live on Earth can change what happens on Earth. The behavior of human beings is of interest to these beings. Humans can behave in ways that please or displease the beings.

After a human being dies, some part of the human lives on in some form.

Most people who follow any religion today believe most or all of these ideas, although many Buddhists believe the last sentence only.

It has been known for many years that this tendency toward religious practice goes back to the beginning of the human species. The Neanderthal people, who are considered by most anthropologists to be a part of our species, were discovered in 1856. The Neanderthals lived from about 100,000 years ago until about 40,000 years ago. Although it was not apparent to the original discoverers, the very first Neanderthal found had been buried. Burial indicates that the Neanderthals had some belief in a form of life after death. By 1908, a Neanderthal grave had been found with tools and animal bones buried alongside the man in the grave. More dramatic evidence of Neanderthal burial practices came from modern techniques of analysis.

In 1960, Arlette Leroi-Gourhan was checking for flower pollen in soil from a Neanderthal grave found in Iraq. She found a great amount of pollen from flowers similar to hyacinths, bachelor's buttons, and hollyhocks. Evidently, the Neanderthal had been buried in a grave strewn with flowers.

The Neanderthal part of our species was replaced by a group known as the Cro-Magnons about 40,000 years ago. Like the Neanderthals, the Cro-Magnons buried their dead. Some Cro-Magnon graves have been found with many ivory ornaments. Furthermore, many works of art that are of Cro-Magnon origin are generally believed to have religious significance.

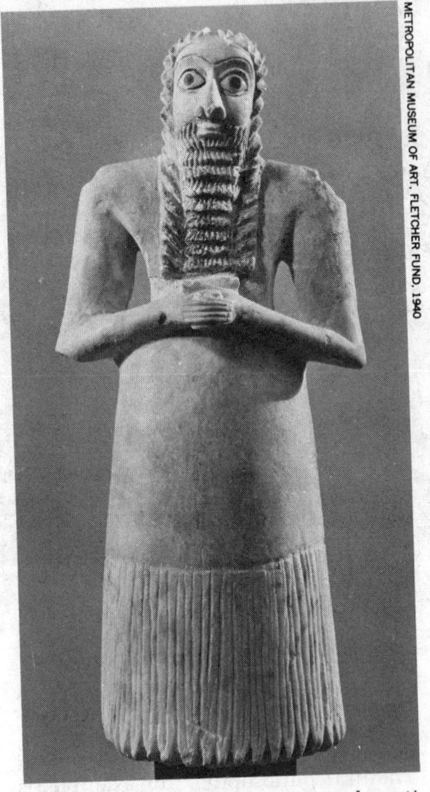

METROPOLITAN MUSEUM OF ART, FLETCHER FUND, 1940

SUMERIAN STATUE *from a temple, estimated to be 5000 years old.*

A Cro-Magnon female figure, called the "Venus" by anthropologists, has been found in many parts of Europe. It is believed to represent a Cro-Magnon concept of a goddess. In the depths of caves, Cro-Magnons painted pictures of many animals and of a few people. These figures are generally believed to have some religious or magical connection. Because these paintings are in nearly inaccessible parts of the caves, it is possible that the rooms they are in were used for ceremonies initiating young Cro-Magnons into the mysteries of their religion.

By the time recorded history began, about 6000 years ago, even advanced societies were deeply involved in religion of one form or another. Many peoples left records of their religious beliefs. For the most part, people in ancient times believed in the creation of the world by a god. They pictured the gods as living much like people do on Earth, although some early gods were pictured with animal or part animal forms. The gods could change events on Earth by magic or other great powers. Many of these gods were identified with the sun, the moon, particular stars, or certain high mountains. Others were thought to control the seas or the weather. The gods could be influenced through sacrifices, generally made by killing animals that could be used for food, or by offering other forms of food. After a person died, his or her spirit might go to live with the gods.

In many cases, religions were localized. If a person traveled to another country, he or she would worship the gods of the other country. The gods from home were not powerful in a strange land.

Today the religions of the world are largely universal in scope. Their believers assume that the values of the religion are the same everywhere. Most of the major religions have traveled great distances and only one of them (Hinduism) is largely limited to the land where it was born. In fact, Christianity and Buddhism are not very prominent in the lands of their origin.

Today, four religions—Christianity, Islam, Hinduism, and Buddhism—have a total of more than 2 billion followers. They reflect the religious thinking of most of the people on Earth. A fifth religion, Judaism, is also classed as a major religion, although it has many fewer followers.

These five religions are best considered in two groups. Judaism is particularly significant, not only for its own important beliefs but because it forms the historical and religious background for both Christianity and Islam. Jews, Christians, and Muslims worship the same god. This section considers these three religions in their historical order. In a somewhat similar manner, Hinduism, itself a major religion, also forms the historical and religious background for Buddhism.

In addition, there are several lesser religions whose followers number in the millions. Found primarily in Asia and the Middle East, they are also a part of the world religious scene.

Judaism

Although much smaller than any of the other major religions, Judaism is generally considered to be a major world religion. Its followers are spread over much of the world. There are only about 15 million followers of Judaism, but they have had an influence far beyond their numbers.

Judaism is the religion of a people called the Jews. The Jews are a people or national group as well as a religion. A few followers of Judaism do not consider themselves to be a part of the Jewish people, and many who consider themselves Jews do not follow or practice the religion of Judaism.

For the sake of simplicity, we will generally use the word Jew to mean a follower of Judaism. It should be understood, however, that the word can also be used to mean any member of the Jewish people, without regard to religion.

Judaism was probably the first truly *monotheistic* religion, devoted to the worship of a single all-powerful God. The Jewish faith holds that God acts through history to change events on Earth. Thus, history is important to Jews in a way that is different from its importance to the people of most other religions. It is possible to imagine Buddhism without Buddha ever having lived, but Judaism without Abraham and Moses would amount to a contradiction in terms.

Both Christianity and Islam inherited this sense of history from the Jews. In fact, both of these later religions consider the history of the early Jewish nation to be part of the record of God's actions, so in a sense the three share a common tradition. Much of the Jewish Bible, which is the same as the Christian Old Testament, is devoted to reporting the acts of God in the history of the Jews.

Early History

The history of the Hebrews opens with God's Creation of the universe. Before the universe was created, God existed, but His form then is unknowable. At the end of Creation, God brought man and woman into being and gave them the responsibility for the care of Earth. But they were tempted into sin against God, and lost their direct relationship with God. In the course of time, people began to believe in many local gods, forgetting the one God who had created the universe.

The Jews trace their history to a man named Abram, a seminomadic shepherd who lived about 4000 years ago. God told Abram to take his family and followers (called the Hebrews) to the land of Canaan, a land that today we identify with Israel. From the first, God promised Abram that he would have many descendants and that they would live in Canaan. Later, as Abram and his family traveled from place to place, God reinforced this promise by a making it a *covenant,* a solemn agreement, binding on both parties. The covenant bound Abram (whom God renamed Abraham) and his descendants to faithfulness to God in return for His everlasting care, as long as they abided by His precepts.

With this covenant, the Hebrews (who were known later as the Israelites and finally as the Jews) became God's chosen people, chosen to represent God to the rest of the world. The Bible shows over and over again that when God chooses someone, He does not make it easy for them. The history of the Jewish people is one of many difficulties.

Indeed, after the Hebrews had lived in Canaan for several hundred years, a famine arose in the land. They moved their families to Egypt, where there was plenty of food. Although Egypt welcomed the Hebrews initially, after a time the rulers that had welcomed them were overthrown. The new rulers, known as the Pharaohs, made slaves of the Hebrews (or Israelites, as they were coming to be called). The Pharaoh ordered that all male babies born to the Israelites be killed. However, God aided the Israelite mothers in helping many of their sons escape death.

One who escaped death was Moses, often considered the founder of the Jewish religion. Moses forced the Egyptians to let the Israelites go and led them out of Egypt and into the desert. His goal was Canaan, the land that God had promised to Abraham. As the Israelites escaped Egypt, God destroyed the army of the Pharaoh, which was pursuing the fleeing Israelites. While in the desert, Moses received a new covenant from God in the form of the Law. The centerpiece of the Law was the Ten Commandments, rules written by God himself on two stone tablets. These tablets were the center of Jewish religious life for nearly a thousand years. They were

ABRAHAM *takes Isaac to the mountain to sacrifice him.*

CULVER PICTURES

kept in a wooden chest called the Ark of the Covenant. At first the Ark was housed in a tent that was carried wherever the Israelites wandered. When they occupied Canaan, the tablets were kept in a tent at Shiloh for over 200 years. The Ark itself was sometimes carried by Israelite armies into battles and was hidden from enemies in moments of danger.

Eventually, the Israelites formed a kingdom called Israel. The second king, David, moved the capital to Jerusalem and laid plans for a temple for the Ark of the Covenant. His son Solomon built the Temple and moved the Ark to it.

After Solomon's death, Israel broke into two nations, Israel in the north and Judah, whose capital was Jerusalem, in the south. In 722 B.C., Assyria conquered the northern kingdom and carried off people, many as slaves. The northern kingdom of Israel was never reestablished.

Some 135 years later, in 586 B.C., the Babylonians conquered Judah, the southern kingdom, and destroyed the temple in Jerusalem. They transported most of the Jews in Judah to Babylon. This period, known as "the Babylonian Captivity," did not last long, however, for the Persian Cyrus defeated Babylon in 539 B.C. and began to allow Jews to return home. By 515 B.C. the returning Jews had built a second Temple in Jerusalem, which lasted over 500 years. The Ark of the Covenant, however, was perhaps destroyed with the first Temple.

The Babylonian Captivity marked a major turning point in the development of Jewish thought. Jews began to look for a person who would restore the glories of the kingdom of Israel as it had been at its height, under David. Such a person would be sent by God and would make Israel and Jerusalem central among all nations. The Jewish term for the restoring king is the Messiah. Jews today still believe that a Messiah will come to usher in a period of peace and brotherhood throughout the world.

JAN LUKAS/PHOTO RESEARCHERS

THE WAILING WALL *at Jerusalem, a remnant of the second temple, is now a place of prayer and penitence.*

The Jewish Scriptures

The first five books of the Old Testament summarize what Moses had to report on how God wanted the Jews to behave. They also record the early history of the Jewish people. To Jews they are known as the *Torah.* Although Moses is considered to be the author of the Torah, the Torah is also the basic word of God. Over the years, a long series of commentaries has been written on the Torah. These commentaries were first organized into one document in the third century A.D. Over the next 300 years, treatises were written on that first organized group of commentaries. All of these were assembled in the sixth century A.D., and the whole set of commentaries on the Torah and commentaries on the commentaries is known as the *Talmud.*

Besides the Torah, Jews also consider many other historical writings, books of prophecy, songs, and sayings as a part of their sacred literature. Taken with the Torah, these writings make up what the Jews know as the *Bible,* which corresponds to what Christians call the *Old Testament* of the Bible.

From the Bible and the Talmud, Jews can learn how to conduct themselves on almost every occasion in life in ways that please God. If a Jew holds to a strict monotheistic understanding of God and conducts himself according to the laws God has laid down, then he or she is fulfilling the requirements of the religion. This leaves great latitude with regard to beliefs. In other words, if you act like a Jew and believe in God, you can freely form your own opinions about other questions of religion. Thus, some Jews believe in eternal life after death in much the same terms as Christians or Muslims do. Others, however, believe that the soul becomes a part of God after death, but the body and the individual person cannot be recovered after death.

Later History

After their return from the Babylonian Captivity, the Jews were dominated most of the time by whichever state was most powerful in the Middle East. Over and over the Jews tried to revolt against these powerful rulers, but only the Hasmoneans (also known as the Maccabees) succeeded, and their success was short-lived. In Jesus's time, the Roman Empire dominated the Jews through a puppet kingdom. A revolt against the Romans in 70 A.D. led to the destruction of all but one wall of the second Temple. This wall is known today as the Wailing Wall. Once again the Jews were taken from their promised land and dispersed.

Most of the Jews no longer lived in Israel after the destruction of the second Temple. Jewish communities spread throughout the world; together they are known as the Diaspora. Since the Temple no longer existed as a focus for worship, an entirely new centerpiece had to be found. While synagogues had existed before the destruction of the second Temple in 70 A.D., the synagogue now became one of the focal points for Judaism. Any group of ten Jewish males could form a body of worship, and any member of the congregation could read to the rest from the Torah.

Many of the main observances of faith, however, were centered in the home. Observances at home include Passover, which celebrates the escape from Egypt and the destruction of the Pharaoh's army, and Hanukkah, which celebrates the rededication of the Temple after the defeat of the Syrians in 165 B.C. These private, familial forms of worship were particularly needed by people who were dispersed into small communities.

By the 1800's A.D., there were Jewish communities in many parts of Europe, in North Africa, the Middle East, and (in lesser numbers) in Australia and North and South America. Many of these communities had been persecuted (especially by Christians in Europe), and some had been driven from place to place in fear for their lives.

The greatest trial for the Jewish people came in the 1930's and 1940's. The Nazi government of Germany based part of its ideology on hatred of the Jews. First in Germany and later in countries the Germans occupied in World War II (1939–1945), the Nazis systematically killed every Jew they could locate. Millions fled Europe (many coming to the United States), but about one-third of all the Jews alive at that time were killed before the Nazis were defeated. This systematic destruction of the Jewish people is known as the Holocaust.

After World War II, the United Nations set up the modern state of Israel, in 1948. Many Jews from around the world moved to Israel, but many others decided to stay in the places where they were used to living. Although the state of Israel has had to engage in several wars against neighboring Arab states to maintain its independence, the Jews are once again in control of the land that was promised to them.

Judaism Today

Today the largest number of Jews live in the United States and Canada. The second largest group of Jews is in Israel. Other large groups of Jews live in the Soviet Union, France, the United Kingdom, Latin America, and South Africa. There has long been a population of Jews in India, although its numbers have never been great.

Jewish religious practice developed in somewhat different ways in different parts of the world over the centuries. But each community maintained the study of Hebrew (the language of the Jewish Scriptures), and there were no clear breaks into "denominations" until the 1800's. Jews in the United States today are divided into four groups: Orthodox, Conservative, Reform, and Hasidic. The first three of these denominations are separated largely by the freedom with which they interpret the Torah, but the Hasidic Jews, or Hasidim, form a tradition all their own.

Orthodoxy. Before the 1800's, it could be said that all Jews were Orthodox, although there have always been different schools of Jewish thought. (For example, in Jesus's time, there were the Pharisees, the Sadducees, and the Essenes.) Beginning in 1810 in Germany, however, some Jews decided that the strict interpretation of the Law found in the Talmud no longer applied. Jews who continued to follow a strict interpretation came to be called Orthodox.

Orthodox Jews today continue to apply all of the ancient rules of worship, including services in Hebrew, the separation of men and women during the service, and various rituals at home, including the strict observance of dietary laws. Men wear head coverings at all times, not just during worship services. However, even among Orthodox Jews there are some disagreements, and the Orthodox congregations in the United States are formed into several different national organizations. About a million or a million and a half of the Jews in the United States are members of Orthodox congregations.

Reform. Abraham Geiger and Samuel Holdheim were among the early leaders of the Reform movement. The first Reform service was held in 1810.

Reform Judaism does not accept the traditional interpretations of the Law. Thus, Reform Jews do not wear head coverings during services, and services may be conducted in a language other than Hebrew. Dietary laws may not be observed at all, or some laws may be observed and others ignored. Cremation, prohibited to Orthodox Jews, is allowed. Reform Jews call their places of worship temples, not synagogues. There are about a million Reform Jews in the United States.

Conservatism. The Conservative movement started in 1845 as a dispute among Reform Jews on the use of Hebrew in the worship service. Those who wanted to maintain Hebrew left the Reform movement to start the first Conservative group. Conservative Jews try to maintain a balance between the traditional ways of Judaism and the modernist spirit of Reform. For example, men and women are not separated at services, but men must wear a head covering during the service. There are about a million and a quarter Conservative Jews in the United States.

If you add up the number of Orthodox, Reform, and Conservative Jews in the United States, the sum will be over a million short of the more than five and a half million American Jews. While a small number of these other Jews are Hasidim, many Jews are not affiliated with any one denomination, although they may worship at home and sometimes visit synagogues or temples.

Hasidism. In observance of Jewish law, the Hasidim are Orthodox Jews, but their movement maintains separate congregations and often separate communities from other Jews. The Hasidic movement was founded in the 1700's in Poland by Israel Ball Shem Tov. He taught that religion should be joyous and that the senses obscured the spark of the Divine that was in every object. His followers spend much less time studying the Talmud and Torah than Orthodox Jews. Instead, they devote themselves to dancing, singing, and love of nature as ways of worshiping God. There are small communities of Hasidim in the United States, concentrated largely in New York City, but the Hasidim also have communities throughout Europe and in Israel.

Christianity

The religion with the most followers in the world today is the Christian religion. There are about 1 billion Christians. About one person in four throughout the world is a Christian. Christianity is the dominant religion of Europe, both Americas, and Australia, with significant numbers of followers in Asia and Africa as well.

Beliefs

Like Judaism, from which it grew, Christianity is monotheistic—its followers believe that there is one and only one God. Christians also believe that God acts in history and that He is the God of the early Jewish people—the God of Abraham. The Scriptures of Judaism are part of the Christian Bible.

The earliest Christians were Jews who came to believe that Jesus of Nazareth was the Messiah that the Jews had been awaiting. Jesus was born in a village called Bethlehem, near Jerusalem, about 2000 years ago.

During his time on Earth, Jesus taught in the synagogues and outdoors, healing the sick and welcoming particularly the poor and the outcast. He said he had come to establish a new kingdom in which men's wrongdoings would be forgiven, allowing them to achieve a new relationship with God.

When he was about 33 years old, Jesus was arrested by the official Jewish court and turned over to the Romans, who controlled the country as a part of the Roman Empire. The Romans put Jesus to death by nailing him to a cross made of wood. Three days after he died, according to the Gospels, he rose from the dead and visited many of his followers. Then he went to be with God the Father until the time for his return.

The night before he was arrested, Jesus ate and drank with his closest followers. In this Last Supper, he admonished his followers to observe a similar meal to remember him. He suggested that his suffering, death, and resurrection would make a new covenant with God, replacing the covenant (or testament) made between God and the Jewish patriarchs, Abraham and Moses. In this new covenant, God forgives the sins of those who follow Jesus and offers them eternal life with God. The two parts of the Christian Bible are the Old Testament (the Jewish Scriptures), which describes God's agreement with the Jewish people, and the New Testament, which describes His new agreement.

ALINARI/EPA

THE LIFE OF CHRIST *is pictured in much of early Western art.* Left, *a Byzantine mosaic of Mary and the child Jesus.* Right, *Mary and Jesus after his crucifixion in the famous* Pietà *by Michelangelo.*

Early Christians came to believe that Jesus, whom they called the *Christ* or the Messiah, was the Son of God, both man and God at the same time. They eventually formulated their belief in the doctrine of the Trinity. The one God expresses Himself through three different natures: God the Father, God the Son (Christ), and God the Holy Spirit. The Trinity, one God in three different Persons, is a central mystery of the Christian faith.

After Christ went to be with God, the Holy Spirit became the principal means of continuing God's messages to people on Earth. Inspired by the Holy Spirit, the followers of Jesus started the Christian Church, which is the formal, organized expression of their religion on Earth. The church and its members spread the *gospel,* or good news, about Christ. The church also performs the few rites that are basic to Christianity. These include *baptism,* or ritual purification with water, and *communion,* a rite that commemorates the Last Supper that Jesus had on Earth with his followers. Prayer to God is a part of the faith.

The main symbol of the Christian religion is the cross, which reminds Christians that Christ died for their sins. A schematic fish is also sometimes used.

The Early Church

Christianity began when Peter, one of the disciples of Jesus, accepted Jesus as the Christ or Messiah. Then, on the seventh Sunday after the resurrection, the Holy Spirit came to the disciples. This event, known as Pentecost ("the 50th day"), is considered by many Christians to be the birth of the Christian Church. Peter preached a sermon that day that converted 3000 people to the church, after which the converts lived communally and worshiped together. At this point, however, the early Christians thought of themselves as Jews who had recognized Jesus as the Messiah.

Some Jews who did not recognize Jesus as the Messiah persecuted the early Christians. However, one of the persecutors, Saul of Tarsus, had a vision of Jesus and was converted to Christianity. Under the name of Paul, he became the main missionary of the early church to non-Jews (gentiles). As Paul converted gentiles in Syria, Greece, and Rome, the church grew to be separate from its Jewish beginning. Paul's preaching and letters, known as "the epistles," described a church that welcomed both Jews and gentiles.

Starting in 64 A.D., while Nero was the Roman emperor, the Romans began to persecute the Christians. The persecution by Romans continued with varying degrees of severity for about 250 years. It ended in 313 A.D., when the emperor Constantine made Christianity the state religion of the empire.

In the meantime, despite the persecutions, the church was growing. The letters of Paul and other followers, which were copied and read aloud at various churches, became the first part of a scripture for the new church. A few years later, the gospels, which are summaries of Jesus's ministry, were written. Together with a history of the early church, which we know as *The Acts of the Apostles,* and the difficult book of *Revelations,* these letters and summaries became the New Testament, the second part of Christian Scripture. It is believed that all 27 of the books of the New Testament were written between 50 A.D. and 100 A.D.

By 95 A.D., there were bishops and deacons working for the church. The bishop of Rome claimed from early on to have received authority over the rest of the church, and he can be found exercising such authority by 190 A.D. In 325 A.D. the Council of Nicaea affirmed the basic beliefs and organization of the church, with the bishop of Rome, or pope, at its head. The summary of beliefs, or *creed,* formulated at Nicaea is still used in many Christian churches.

The Roman Catholic Church

The church that took shape at the Council of Nicaea is still the largest Christian denomination. In fact, there are almost as many Roman Catholics as there are Muslims, who form the second largest religion after Christianity. More than half the Christians in the world are Roman Catholic.

From the very beginning of the church, Christians disagreed on many points of doctrine and belief. These disagreements were the subjects of discussion at many councils, such as the one at Nicaea. Once a council decided on an issue, people who disagreed with its decision were termed *heretics* by the church. Some of the heretics had large followings and set up rival Christian churches, some of which lasted for hundreds of years. But the majority of Christians remained in a single church, calling it Catholic, which means "universal."

The Roman Catholic Church traces its existence back through this majority church. The bishops of Rome traced their office back to St. Peter, and gained authority over and respect from the rest of the church. Today the bishop of Rome is called the pope or "the Holy Father," and is considered the supreme authority in matters of faith and discipline. The senate of the Roman Catholic Church is the College of Cardinals, a group of bishops and priests who assist the pope in running the church. While many of the cardinals live in Rome, others are scattered around the world, in charge of large bodies of Catholics. Most of the cardinals who do not live in Rome are also archbishops. When a pope dies, all of the cardinals come to Rome to elect a new pope.

The bishops of the Roman Church are viewed as the bearers of the apostolic succession, an unbroken line of authority that traces back to Christ's earliest followers. Therefore, only a bishop can ordain another bishop or a priest, and only a bishop can confirm a person as a member of the church.

In every Roman Catholic Church there are one or more priests. The priesthood is open to men only and priests are required to take an oath of celibacy. Priests can perform the main rituals of the church, called *sacraments,* except for ordination and confirmation. Roman Catholics believe that the sacraments are the means by which the grace of God is transmitted to the individual. All seven sacraments of the Roman Catholic faith must ordinarily be performed by either a priest or a bishop.

Besides priests and bishops, the Roman Catholic Church has many different kinds of monks and nuns, men and women who have taken special vows of poverty, chastity, and obedience. They may be teachers, medical workers, or workers in other helping professions. During the centuries after the fall of the Roman Empire, monasteries preserved the learning of the classical as well as the Early Christian world. Most monks are not priests.

The Roman Catholic Church is distinguished from most other Christian churches by various special beliefs, most notably the belief that the pope is supreme on Earth in matters of faith and discipline. While most Protestant churches rely solely on the Bible as their authority, Roman Catholics accept the traditions of the church as the authority for many of their beliefs and practices. This has led the Roman Catholics to accept seven sacraments instead of the two that most Protestants accept. In addition to Communion (called the Mass or Holy Eucharist by Roman Catholics) and baptism—the two sacraments of the Protestants—Roman Catholics believe that ordination (holy orders), confirmation, penance (confession and absolution by a priest), anointing the sick (formerly known as extreme unction or the last rites), and marriage are also sacraments.

Roman Catholics believe that most people after death enter a place or condition called *purgatory,* where they stay until they have been punished for their sins. People on Earth can reduce the length of time that a person spends in purgatory by prayer and other means. Roman Catholics also believe that certain holy men and women, called *saints,* can intercede with Christ for people on Earth.

Mary, the mother of Jesus, occupies an important place in the Roman Catholic Church, and she is frequently asked through prayer to intercede with Christ. While almost all Christians believe that Mary was a virgin when Jesus was born, Roman Catholicism states Mary was herself free from sin and that after death Mary's body entered heaven.

All Christian churches celebrate some form of Communion, or the Lord's supper, but there is considerable disagreement about the interpretation of this sacrament. Since the 1200's, however, Roman Catholics have believed that the bread and wine used in the Mass change into the true substance of the flesh and blood of Christ (although their appearance stays the same). This belief is called *transubstantiation.* Roman Catholics also believe that the sacrament of Communion represents the sacrifice of Christ on the cross.

Roman Catholicism is the predominant faith in much of southern Europe (France, Spain, Portugal, Italy), in Ireland, and in South and Central America. In addition, it represents a sizable minority in the United States and Canada, Great Britain, Germany, and many parts of Africa.

THE MASS *or Holy Eucharist is the central observance of Roman Catholicism. It is shown here in an illuminated manuscript from the 1400's.*

GIRAUDON

Other Early Churches

A few of the churches that parted ways with the Roman Catholic Church in the first thousand years of Christianity have survived independently. Most prominent among these is the *Coptic Church,* which left the Roman Catholics in 451. There are about a million Coptic Christians in Egypt today. Like several other of the early churches that have survived, the Coptic Christians are *monophysites.* Monophysites believe that Jesus Christ was only divine and did not partake of a human nature. Other surviving monophysite churches include the *Armenian Church* and the *Christian Church of Ethiopia.*

The *Nestorians* were another early church group. They became the leading Christian church of Persia. Nestorians held that Jesus was two distinct persons, the Word and the man. They opposed the title Mother of God for Mary. They sent out many missionaries, some in the Middle Ages reaching China and India, where they founded thriving churches.

After the conquest of Persia by the forces of Islam, the Nestorians, although tolerated by the Muslims, gradually reduced in number. Today only a small Nestorian Church survives in the mountains along the Iran-Turkey border.

Eastern Orthodox Churches

To some degree, the church in the eastern part of the Roman Empire went on a different course from the Western church for centuries. In 1054 A.D., as a result of a dispute over whether the Holy Spirit emanated from God the Father alone or from both God the Father and Jesus Christ, the church split into two parts. The part that reaffirmed the older tradition (the Holy Spirit emanating from God the Father alone) became the Eastern Church. The Eastern Church rejected the authority of the pope, but was similar in most other respects to the Roman Catholic Church. However, the Eastern Church maintained traditions that had been part of the Eastern pattern of worship even before the "great schism" with Rome.

Originally the Eastern Church was the church of the Byzantine Empire, while the Roman Catholic Church was becoming the religion of the Frankish Holy Roman Empire. Although the Eastern Church was centered in Constantinople (modern-day Istanbul, Turkey), the domination of Constantinople by Muslim forces after 1453 led to a period when the Eastern Church was centered in Russia. Today the Eastern Church has separate branches in the Soviet Union, Rumania, Bulgaria, Yugoslavia, Greece, Cyprus, Czechoslovakia, Poland, and Finland. The Eastern Church also includes the Christians supervised by the patriarchs of Constantinople, Antioch, Alexandria, and Jerusalem, among the earliest bishoprics in the Christian religion.

The Eastern Church accepts as valid the first eight councils of the church. Because it holds to many early traditions of the church, the Eastern Church is called Orthodox. The state church of Greece, for example, is usually known as the Greek Orthodox Church, although officially it is the Church of Greece. In the United States, the largest group following the Eastern rite is probably the Russian Orthodox Greek Catholic Church of America, which is most commonly called the Russian Orthodox Church.

Although the various Eastern Orthodox churches have no central authority, their beliefs and practices are quite similar from church to church. The Eastern churches believe in the same seven sacraments as do the Roman Catholics, but the actual administration of each of them is somewhat different. More recent traditions in the Catholic Church, such as belief in purgatory or in the immaculate conception of Mary, are rejected by Orthodox churches. Orthodox priests are not required to be celibate, but bishops are all celibate.

The Orthodox churches have a long tradition of venerating religious paintings called *icons.* Icons are considered to be more than just paintings on wood; they are thought to have a power of their own. While three-dimensional statues are not acceptable to the Eastern churches, each church building includes a place for icons in front of the altar.

The Protestant Churches

In 1517, the German monk Martin Luther started a dispute with the Roman Catholic Church over several of its doctrines. He objected particularly to the sale of *indulgences,* certificates that were said to shorten one's time in purgatory. Luther found no authority in Scripture for such a practice. On October 31, Luther posted 95 objections to prevailing church practices. Although no one knew it, the Protestant Reformation had begun.

Luther's confrontations with the defenders of the Roman Catholic practices quickly led him to state the basic principles that varied from those of both the Roman and Orthodox churches of the time. Luther, using the Bible as his single guide, said that Christians do not require priests or the church to intervene between them and God, that God's grace is the only thing that saves sinful believers, and that only the sacraments of Communion and baptism carry with them the promise of God's grace.

Within three years of Luther's posting the 95 theses, the pope issued an order that Luther recant or be excommunicated. To be excommunicated is to be formally deprived of the sacraments and the prayers of the church, although the person who is excommunicated does not cease being a Christian. Luther burned the order and was excommunicated. Although he was given one more chance to recant, he refused.

Luther tried at first to avoid becoming the leader of a separate church, but his many reforms and innovations became the basis of the Protestant Reformation. These included his reform of the liturgy (the rites of worship), his stupendous translation of the Bible into German, still the Bible of German Lutherans, his introduction of hymns sung by the congregation, and his composition of the Small Catechism. Luther also changed the development of Protestantism by marrying.

Lutherans. Soon the church based on Luther's ideas was known as the Lutheran Church. As such, it spread across Germany and Scandinavia—although parts of Germany remained Roman Catholic. By 1638, Lutheran Swedes were worshiping in what is now Delaware in the United States. In the great migrations of 1840–1910 from Europe to the United States, the largest number of Protestant immigrants were Lutherans from northern Europe.

When these Lutherans reached the United States, each group brought the liturgy of its own nation. By 1900, there were German, Swedish, Norwegian, Danish, and Finnish Lutherans, each with separate organizations and worshiping in different languages. Since then, a series of mergers has reduced the number of Lutheran bodies to three large and a handful of very small ones. Two of the large bodies, the American Lutheran Church and the Lutheran Church in America, emphasize the importance of social action. They are fairly liberal in interpreting both the Bible and the teachings of Luther. The other group, the Lutheran Church–Missouri Synod, is quite conservative.

Lutheran worship is formal and follows the general pattern of the ancient Catholic forms. Lutherans believe that Christ is actually present in the bread and wine of Communion, but that the bread and wine are not changed by transubstantiation. A characteristic Lutheran practice requires that all children go through a year or more of study (sometimes as much as four years) of the Small Catechism before they are confirmed as full members of the church.

Reformed Churches. Besides the Lutheran churches of northern Europe, other churches were started in the 1500's in reaction to the Roman Catholicism of that time. Collectively, these are known as the Reformed Churches. The Reformed Churches were very strong in Switzerland, the Netherlands, Scotland, and Hungary. There were also widespread, but often officially suppressed, Reformed Church movements in England and France.

The Reformed Churches can be traced to a 1529 disagreement between Martin Luther and Ulrich Zwingli about Christ's actual presence during Communion. Zwingli's interpretation that only the spirit of Christ was present became the doctrine of the Reformed Churches.

But the principal architect of Reformed thought was the Frenchman John Calvin. In 1533 Calvin escaped persecution in France by fleeing to Switzerland, which was already Protestant. There he promoted his views with a systematic exposition of Protestant thought. While Calvin relied on many of the same ideas as Luther, Calvin's logical mind led him from Luther's ideas to conclusions that Luther did not share. Most members of today's successor churches to the early Reformed Churches no longer believe in the strict Calvinist doctrine, but historically Calvin's ideas dominated the Reformed Churches.

While Calvin differed with Luther on the nature of baptism and Communion, the most influential part of his doctrine concerned sin, heaven, and hell. Calvin's approach to these subjects is known as "the five points":

1. Total depravity (people cannot do anything that God sees as good until they are among God's elect);
2. Predestination (God has elected some people to go to heaven and others to go to hell);
3. Limited atonement (Christ's death on the cross benefits only the elect);
4. Irresistibility of grace (God's decision that a person is to be among the elect cannot be resisted by the person); and
5. Perseverance of the saints (the elect cannot fall from grace).

While the five points did not say so explicitly, they suggested to many people that Calvin's "elect" would be rewarded by God with material wealth.

Calvin eventually became the ruler of Geneva in Switzerland, which he tried to govern by strict Christian rules. From Switzerland, Calvin's ideas spread to start the Reformed Church in other lands. In Scotland, the church became known as the Presbyterian Church (to avoid confusion with the Church of England, which was also sometimes called "Reformed"). In France, the followers of Calvin were called the Huguenots. The Huguenots were suppressed by the state most of the time. In England, Calvin's ideas had a major influence on the Puritans, who tried to reform the Church of England along Calvinistic lines. After failing in this, the Puritans won control of the nation under Oliver Cromwell, but England rejected the Puritan faith after Cromwell's death in 1658.

JOHN CALVIN, *father of the Reformed Protestant denominations, was Swiss by birth and French by adoption. Calvinism flourished in Holland and Scotland.*

Suppression of the European followers of Calvin in the 1600's led many of them to come to North America. Both the Pilgrims of Plymouth, Massachusetts, and the Puritans of the Massachusetts Bay Colony were Calvinists. The church that they brought to the United States became the Congregationalist Church and, later, the United Church of Christ. Another migration of followers of the Reformed Churches brought Scottish Presbyterians to the United States in great numbers, along with Huguenots and members of the Dutch and German Reformed Churches.

Today most followers of the Presbyterian Church or of the United Church of Christ are no longer strict Calvinists. Only a few members of the United Church of Christ believe in predestination. Many Presbyterians no longer believe that people are unable to cooperate with God in obtaining salvation.

Anglicans. At the same time as the Roman Church was losing members to the Lutheran and Reformed Churches, it also lost all of England. King Henry VIII questioned the authority of the pope, and declared himself head of the English church in 1534.

Under Henry's successors, Edward VI and Elizabeth, the church became increasingly like the Lutheran and Reformed Churches of the Continent. Elizabeth deliberately tried to keep the church halfway between Protestantism and Roman Catholicism.

Most Englishmen who came to settle the American colonies did not want to conform to the Church of England, but Church of England followers came as well.

Individual colonies were often organized by religion, and in the 1600's only Virginia was particularly hospitable to Anglicans. In the 1700's, however, all colonies allowed diverse Christian churches, and Anglican churches were established in all of them. In the South and in New York City the Church of England was supported with tax money (as it is to this day in England).

The American Revolution nearly ended Anglicanism in the colonies, since Church of England members were also often Loyalists. Many Anglicans moved to Canada or back to England. The church survived, however, and changed its name to the Protestant Episcopal Church.

The Anglican churches remain both Catholic and Protestant. As in the Catholic and Orthodox churches, the Anglican Church preserves the apostolic succession of bishops and priests. Thus, only properly ordained bishops and priests can administer Communion or preach sermons.

Yet many of the beliefs of Anglican churches are Protestant. There is a wide latitude of practice in the church, ranging from churches with simple services that focus on the sermon to churches that emphasize elaborate liturgical rites. All seven of the traditional sacraments are maintained, as in the Roman Catholic and Orthodox churches, but only Communion and baptism are viewed as necessary. Like other Protestant churches, the Anglican churches use the Bible as their sole authority.

The churches that grew out of the Church of England form the Anglican communion. The Anglican communion is a group of separate churches around the world that have a line of ordination that goes back to the Church of England. They also share a liturgy based on the *Book of Common Prayer,* the liturgy originally prepared for the Church of England in the 1500's. There are major groups of Anglicans in England, North America, Australia, and Africa.

Baptists and Mennonites. Baptists form the largest Protestant group in the United States. Baptist-like believers can be found throughout the history of Christianity, but it is not clear just which of these earlier groups modern Baptists come from.

Around the time of the Reformation, there were scattered groups called Anabaptists in Europe. Anabaptists believed that baptism is valid only for persons who have reached faith on their own, a belief shared by Baptists today. Anabaptists in Switzerland also argued for the separation of church and state, another Baptist tenet. Soon after, a former priest named Menno Simons organized Anabaptists into a church known as the Mennonite Church. The earliest Baptist churches in England were formed on the basis of Mennonite ideas.

It is not clear what influence either Mennonites or English Baptists had on the American Baptist Church. In the United States, the Baptists began to organize in the 1600's. The first Baptist churches in the New World were begun independently in Rhode Island.

Several of the basic beliefs of the Baptists enabled their churches to spread rapidly in the late 1700's and early 1800's. Baptists strongly believe in the independence of each congregation, a belief that is helpful to a church spread out through a wilderness. The Baptist belief in religious liberty and the independence of church and state was in tune with the principles of the new nation. The Baptists made a serious effort to reach the settlers of the frontier. They ordained many part-time ministers who supported themselves by farming but who also organized congregations.

Baptists practice baptism by immersion (submerging a person completely in water), and restrict baptism to people who have come to faith in Christ; infants are not baptized. Only people so baptized can be members of the church. Baptists view communion as a memorial to Jesus Christ, and they believe that neither the body nor the spirit of Christ is present in the bread and wine.

Mennonites, although their ideas influenced the early Baptists, are not considered Baptists themselves. For one thing, Mennonites do not baptize by immersion. While the Baptists are the largest Protestant denomination in the United States, the Mennonites are one of the smallest.

CULVER PICTURES

THE CIRCUIT RIDER, *traveling from one small settlement to another, brought Methodism to the American frontier in the 1800's.*

Methodists. Although the Baptists, when taken all together, are the largest Protestant denomination in the United States, the largest single Protestant organization is the United Methodist Church. Methodism grew out of 18th-century reform efforts in the Church of England. Starting in 1738, the Anglican priest John Wesley and his brother Charles set up "societies," or clubs, for prayer and Bible reading. Members of these societies were expected to attend worship services in an Anglican church. By the 1760's, similar Methodist societies were started in the United States.

After the American Revolution, Methodists in the United States started to break with the Church of England. In 1784, John Wesley sent Thomas Coke and Francis Asbury from England to help organize a Methodist Church. (In England, the Methodist Church was not fully separated from the Church of England until 1791, after John Wesley's death.)

The Methodist Church grew rapidly in the United States throughout the 1800's. One important tool was the use of circuit preachers. A circuit preacher traveled a circuit of hundreds of miles, preaching to a different group every day, returning to the same group every week, every two weeks, or every four weeks, depending on the length of the circuit. Another factor in the Methodists' growth was their sponsorship of popular outdoor gatherings for preaching and singing called "camp meetings." Most who were converted at camp meetings became Methodists.

The beliefs of the Methodists are similar to those of the Anglican communion, although Methodist worship is focused more on the sermon and on hymn singing. John Wesley taught that people could become free of sin in this life, and, in general, opposed Calvin's ideas of total depravity and of an elect. Methodists today tend to avoid theological complexities, focusing more on Christ as a guide to living.

Christian churches. Early in the 1800's, several different reform churches started in the United States. These churches believed that worship should be modeled more closely on the practices of the early church of the apostles. While these reform groups had much in common with the Baptists, especially in their belief in the independence of each congregation, there were enough differences to insure that the reform groups never allied themselves with the Baptists.

One aim of this reform movement was the elimination of denominations. Therefore, the churches that are part of the movement call themselves simply Christian churches or churches of Christ. (The United Church of Christ, which has a Calvinist heritage, includes some churches that were part of this reform movement.) Some member churches of the Christian church prefer the name Disciples of Christ.

The first Christian churches were formed in 1803 under the leadership of Barton W. Stone. The Disciples of Christ grew out of efforts by Thomas Campbell, and his son Alexander, that first took organized form in 1809. In 1832, Stone and Alexander Campbell urged their followers to unify, and many of the reform churches began to work together. Although the cooperating churches could not agree on a single name for themselves, their group grew rapidly. In 1906, the conservative wing of the church left to form the Churches of Christ. The Churches of Christ opposes the use of instrumental music during services and the formation of missionary societies. The present name for the part of the church that did not form the Churches of Christ is the International Convention of Christian Churches (Disciples of Christ.)

Pentecostal churches. The fastest growing group of churches in the United States today is the group that is identified with the Holiness movement or the Pentecostal movement that began in 1906. Among the members of this group of young churches, the church called the Assemblies of God is the largest, but other large churches in the group are the Church of God in Christ, International; the Church of God in Christ; and the Church of God (Cleveland, Tennessee). The characteristic emphases of the Pentecostal bodies are on fundamentalist principles, revivalism, and a postconversion experience called baptism in the Holy Spirit, accompanied by the sign of speaking in tongues, as experienced by followers of Jesus at Pentecost.

The Church of the Nazarene, once classed with this group, dropped "Pentecostal" from its name in 1919 to disassociate itself from the others. Positioned to the right of the Pentecostals in terms of emotionalism, Nazarenes oppose the practice of speaking in tongues; otherwise, their doctrine has close similarities.

Other Denominations

The Protestant denominations, from Lutheranism to the Pentecostals, share as basic the authority of Scripture, the two sacraments of Communion and baptism, a belief in the Trinity (although some churches prefer not to use the term), and similar notions about heaven and hell. There are also large churches in the United States that are neither Protestant nor Roman Catholic.

Quakers. The Quakers first formed in England under the leadership of George Fox in 1647. Although Fox called his group the Society of Friends, the Friends have been known as Quakers since early in their history. Fox taught that a seed of God exists in every person, and that this seed produces an Inner Light that can lead to new revelations about God. While the Bible was revealed by God, the new revelations of the Inner Light should also be taken into account. The Friends were against all ceremonial forms of worship, including sacraments, churches, and ministers.

Many Quakers came to the New World to escape persecution in England, although they were also persecuted in some of the colonies. Today there are a number of different denominations of Friends, ranging from those that avoid all ceremonies to those that are somewhat like traditional denominations. All are known for their pacificism, and many Friends speak out on social issues.

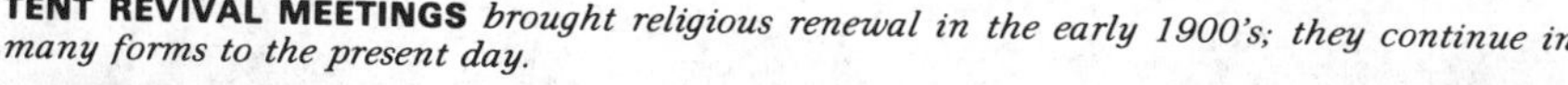

TENT REVIVAL MEETINGS *brought religious renewal in the early 1900's; they continue in many forms to the present day.*

BRUCE ROBERTS/PHOTO RESEARCHERS

Unitarians. Opponents of the idea of the Trinity go back at least as far as the start of the Reformation. The actual organization of a Unitarian church, however, did not begin until the time of the American Revolution. Historically, the Unitarians were strict monotheists, who believed that God the Father was proclaimed as supreme in the Bible. Today, the followers of the Unitarian Universalist Association each believe what his conscience dictates. Many do not believe in any sort of a God.

Mormons. The Church of Jesus Christ of Latter-Day Saints (the larger and better known group) and the Reorganized Church of Jesus Christ of Latter-Day Saints are generally known as the Mormon churches. Both result from a series of visions of angels that Joseph Smith had near Palmyra, New York, between 1820 and 1830. Mormons believe in the continuous revelation of God to people on Earth, as shown by God's revelation to Joseph Smith.

The separation between the two main branches of Mormonism occurred after Joseph Smith was killed by a mob in Carthage, Illinois, when he was less than 40 years old. While the main body of the church followed Brigham Young to Utah (to escape persecution), a smaller group founded the Reorganized Church around Joseph Smith's son. Because Mormons use authorities beyond the Bible or Christian tradition, they have many beliefs about the Trinity, the sacraments, the last judgment, and other matters that are different from the beliefs of most other Christians.

Jehovah's Witnesses. Members of the Watch Tower Bible and Tract Society are known as Jehovah's Witnesses. All Jehovah's Witnesses consider themselves missionaries, warning others in their literature and door-to-door visitations of the impending apocalyptic Battle of Armageddon. They believe in a God whose personal name is Jehovah and reject the Trinity. In the Bible they find justification for condemning a long list of activities, including drinking and the formation of the United Nations; they refuse to vote, serve in the armed forces, salute the flag, and recite the oath of allegiance. Their membership and publishing activities are worldwide in scope.

Christian Science. The official name of this religion is First Church of Christ, Scientist. Christian Science is the work of one woman, Mary Baker Eddy, whose book, *Science and Health with Key to the Scriptures* (1875), is read from (along with the Bible) in place of a sermon at Christian Science services. Mrs. Eddy regarded Christian Science as "divine metaphysics" and her system of healing as "the scientific system of divine healing." Scientists hold that God the Creator is wholly good, and that evil, sickness, suffering, and other things unlike God are the result of human alienation from God, with no foundation in reality. Christian Science sets out to teach its adherents how to find and experience the true reality.

Unification Church. The full name of this organization is the Holy Spirit Association for the Unification of World Christianity. The church was founded by Sun Myung Moon in Korea in 1954. The theological basis for the church is Moon's book, *Divine Principle,* which claims that Jesus achieved spiritual redemption for people on Earth, but not physical redemption. The physical redemption is being brought by a new savior, the "Lord of the Second Advent," or "True Parent." The principal task of the True Parent is to father "perfect children" who are free from Eve's original sin, which has tainted all human beings. Although it is not stated directly, there are many hints that Moon himself is the Lord of the Second Advent. The National Council of Churches of Christ in America declared in 1977 that the Unification Church is not a Christian Church.

Seventh Day Adventists. This church grew out of the prediction associated with William Miller that the second coming of Christ would occur on October 22, 1844. After that date, and the "Great Disappointment" that occurred when the second coming failed to happen, three followers of Miller gradually put their views together to form the Seventh Day Adventists. One of them, Joseph Bates, argued that God did not intend for His commandments to be changed; therefore, the Sabbath should be kept as described in the Old Testament. Also, the Old Testament dietary laws should be maintained. Most other Seventh Day Adventist beliefs resemble those of the Baptists.

Islam

The second largest religion today is Islam, whose followers are called Muslims. (Islam is sometimes incorrectly called Muhammedanism after its founder Muhammad. Followers of Islam object to this name because they think it causes people to believe that they worship Muhammad, which they do not.) There are nearly 600 million followers of Islam throughout the world. The largest numbers are in Asia and Africa, particularly in that part of Asia called the Middle East and in North Africa.

Islam is also a monotheistic faith. In fact, the main creed of Islam is a very simple one: "There is no God but God, and Muhammad is his prophet." A *prophet* is a human being who has been chosen by God to tell his message on Earth. Muslims believe that Muhammad was the last major prophet, but the earlier prophets included the people who founded Judaism and also Jesus Christ. As a result, Muslims believe many of the same things that Jews and Christians do, although not always in exactly the same way.

Muhammad

The great prophet of Islam lived in Arabia about 1400 years ago (570–632). When Muhammad was about 40 years old, God began to speak to him. Muhammad often spent nights alone in the hills, where he received his first messages from God. Soon, however, God's messages came to him wherever he was. God told Muhammad to transmit His message to the people of Arabia. God also dictated a book to Muhammad. This book was later written down and is known today as the *Koran.*

In 622 A.D. the people of Mecca, where Muhammad lived with his wife and daughters, were so upset by Muhammad's teachings that Muhammad and his followers had to flee. His escape to the city of Medina is known as the Hegira. The date of the Hegira is usually taken as the beginning of Islam.

Eight years after the Hegira, Muhammad returned to Mecca. By then he had so many followers that he took over the city without a struggle. From that point on, the followers of Islam built a mighty empire that stretched at its height from Spain to India.

Muhammad used many Arab elements in describing Islam. The name

THE KAABA *at Mecca (now in Saudi Arabia) is the holiest place in Islam. All Muslims hope to make a pilgrimage to Mecca at least once in their lives.*

PHOTO RESEARCHERS

he used for God was Allah, which was also a name used by some Arabs for their principal god. When Muhammad returned to Mecca, he declared it a holy city. He also declared that the Kaaba, where Arabs had worshiped for many, many years, was to be a shrine for Allah.

The Koran retells many stories that are familiar to Jews and Christians from the Bible. It tells that the Arabs are descended from the same Abraham as are the Jews. Abraham had two sons, Isaac and Ishmael. Isaac became the ancestor of the Jews, and Ishmael became the ancestor of the Arabs. The Koran, however, also tells the stories of Isaac's descendants: Jacob, Joseph, Moses, David, Solomon, and Jesus Christ.

Islam is not as complicated a faith as Christianity. It is based on five principles only:

1. Faith that there is no God but God (Allah), and Muhammad is His prophet;
2. Prayer to God five times daily;
3. Charity, as shown by helping the poor and by providing the upkeep for the places of prayer;
4. Fasting in two ways—by never drinking alcohol or eating pork and certain other foods; and by not eating, drinking, or smoking at all during daylight for one month each year (the Muslim month of Ramadan); and
5. Pilgrimage to Mecca at least once in each Muslim's life.

Muslims believe in a life after death in a paradise that is described in detail in the Koran. Paradise is for all those who keep the faith. People who are evil will spend eternity in a fiery hell.

Muhammad was effectively the ruler of Arabia when he died, as well as its religious leader. Because the state and the religion were one, there was no need for a separate church. The leaders of Islam are those that people recognize as learned and holy. There is no central organization as there is in the Christian church.

Islam After Muhammad

When Muhammad died, he left his followers in control of Arabia. While he had made it clear that the state and worship of God were to be unified, he had not left instructions on how this was to be achieved. He also did not leave detailed guidelines for worship or for living.

Muslims tried to develop specific policies from what Muhammad had done or said in various situations. The reports of Muhammad's actions and sayings, or Muhammad's *Sunna,* were gathered into written collections called *hadith.* From these collections and from the Koran, scholars in the seventh and eighth centuries developed a set of specific rules for worship and for life. These rules, which exist in several slightly different forms, are called the *Sharia,* or Islamic law. The Sharia bears a relation to the Koran and to Muhammad's Sunna that is similar to the relation that the Talmud has to the Torah.

After Muhammad's death, the problems of government also had to be resolved. A small group in Medina elected Abu Bakr as *caliph* ("successor") in charge of both state and religious matters. Abu Bakr selected the second caliph, Umar I, who expanded the Muslim state beyond Arabia and appointed a group of elders to elect the next caliph. This system resulted in the election of Muhammad's son-in-law, Ali, as the fourth caliph. However, Ali made a series of blunders that led to his assassination. The fifth caliph then started a dynasty by naming his own son as his successor.

The *Sunnite* Muslims accept the first three caliphs as genuine. But a minority, called the *Shiites,* believe that it was Muhammad's wish that Ali be the first caliph.

The separation of Islam into Sunnites and Shiite factions has no exact parallel in other religions. Within each faction, there are several denominations or sects with somewhat differing beliefs. (There are also denominations that are neither Sunnite nor Shiite, but these are very small.) Because of the identification of church and state in Islam, many of the differences between Sunnites and Shiites concern political power.

Most of the denominations or sects of Islam are centered in particular geographic regions. Saudi Arabia, for example, has Wahhabism as its state religion. Wahhabi is a Sunni denomination that is based on 18th-century reforms of Muslim practices. In Iran most of the people are Imamis. Imami is a Shiite denomination that awaits the second coming of the "hidden imam," a caliph who disappeared in 873 A.D. Many of the Muslim denominations expect the hidden imam to appear near the time of the end of the world. Such a person, called the Mahdi, will rule the Earth along with Jesus, who will also return at that time. Different denominations have different ideas as to the identity of the Mahdi. For example, in Syria, the Druses are Shiites who regard Caliph al-Hakim as a manifestation of God, who will return as the Mahdi.

Not all Muslim denominations are located in geographic regions. The Shiite Ismailis are scattered all over Asia and Africa. They are mainly held together by their hereditary religious leader, the Aga Khan.

THE SHAH MOSQUE *in Isfahan, Iran, suggests the beauty and subtlety of Islamic architecture. The four minarets have balconies from which the faithful are called to prayer.*

PAN AMERICAN

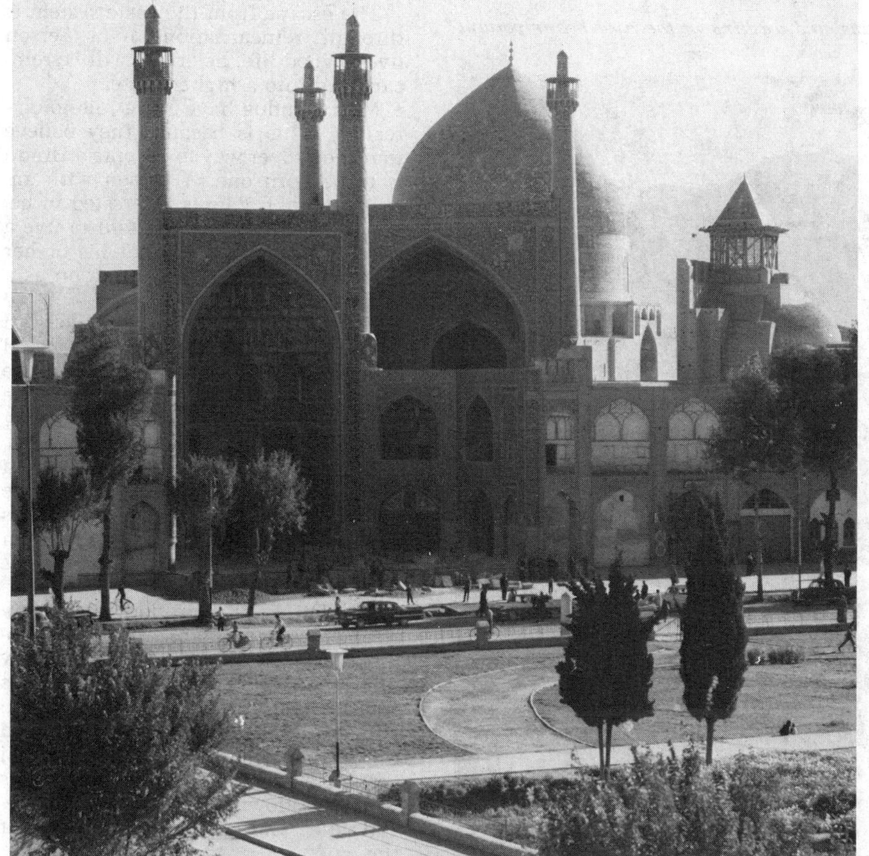

Hinduism

The third largest religion and the oldest major religion is Hinduism. No one is certain how old Hinduism is. Its followers believe that it has existed since people were first created. This belief is very different from that of the Christians, Muslims, Buddhists, and Jews, who all date the creation of their religions to a specific point in time.

There are about half a billion Hindus in the world. Nearly all of them live in India, although there are Hindus in Bangladesh, Sri Lanka, Burma, Indonesia, and Africa. Most of the Hindus outside of India, however, are ethnic Indians whose families have traveled to other lands.

Beliefs

Like Christianity, Hinduism in theory is a complicated form of monotheism. Hindus believe in a single universal spirit called Brahman. This spirit exists in three persons: Brahma, the creator; Vishnu, the preserver; and Shiva, the destroyer. However, the Hindu religion as actually practiced is not monotheistic at all. Very many gods and goddesses are worshiped, often in more than one form for a particular god or goddess. Local groups of Hindus often worship just one form of one god or goddess, although they may believe to one degree or another in all the other gods and goddesses of the Hindu faith. Taken as a whole, then, Hinduism is *polytheistic* (worship of many gods or goddesses), with an intellectual overlay of monotheism.

The Hindu religion has a strong set of beliefs that are shared by all followers of the religion. Hindus believe that when any living thing dies, it is almost always immediately reborn on Earth. This is called *reincarnation.* The soul of a person who dies today becomes the soul of a person who is being born today—or the soul of an animal in some instances.

The law of *karma* determines what happens to a soul in reincarnation. As each person or other living thing goes through one particular life, he, she, or it can perform good acts or evil ones. The sum of the holiness or the evil in a soul is its karma. Karma includes all past lives. If the karma is good, then the soul will be reborn as a higher being than in the life just past. If the karma is bad, then the soul will be reborn into a lower being.

For much of the long history of Hinduism, the determination of what was a higher or lower human being was based on a class system that was built into the religion. This system is less important today than it once was, but it still forms a part of many Hindus' beliefs. To begin with, there were four classes formed when Brahma created human beings: Brahmins, or priests; kings and warriors; merchants and farmers; and laborers and servants. A fifth class appeared as the Hindu warriors conquered other peoples around them. Since these people were not in one of the four classes created by Brahma, they were viewed as outcasts. The old name for this group in English is *untouchables,* but Mahatma Gandhi (1869–1948) renamed these people harijans, "children of God." The harijans were considered to be below the other classes to such a degree that any contact with a harijan would defile a member of one of the higher classes. This attitude has been outlawed in modern India, but traces of it are still strong in many areas.

Over thousands of years of Hindu culture, the classes were broken up into thousands of smaller groups called *castes.* Each caste had a traditional occupation. Marriage was only permitted between members of the same caste. A Hindu was born into a caste and stayed in it all of his life.

The escape from the caste system is through reincarnation. If a person lives a good life, he or she will be reincarnated into a higher caste.

Most Hindus have little missionary feeling. This is because they believe that the proper way to become a Hindu is to be born one. A person with another religion who is interested in becoming a Hindu may be told to live a good life and to hope that his or her karma will lead to reincarnation as a Hindu.

If a person builds up a lot of bad karma, he or she may be reincarnated as an animal, even an insect. Because of this possibility, Hindus on the whole are reluctant to kill any living thing. Many of them are vegetarians.

If a person builds up good karma over many succeeding lives, he or she can escape the otherwise endless round of lives, returning to Brahman and becoming a part of Him. This is the goal of all Hindus.

The Hindu religion does not have a strong central organization. Ceremonies are conducted at temples by priests, but the average Hindu attends such ceremonies only to watch them. His or her devotions are performed mainly at home. These include ritual greetings to the sun each morning as well as following a multitude of special rules and ceremonies throughout the day.

THE GANGES RIVER *in India is sacred to Hindus, and washing in the river has important religious significance.*

LOOK

Most Hindus are devoted to a particular manifestation of one god or goddess. Certain things are holy for all Hindus, however. These include cattle, monkeys, water in any form, the Ganges River, and the city of Benares on the Ganges.

History of Hinduism

The origins of Hinduism are complex. The religion of the ancient civilization of the Indus valley probably contributed some ideas to the Hindu religion, but the earliest known Hindu scriptures are the Vedas. The Vedas describe the religion of invaders from the north, the Aryans, who overran part of India about 1500 B.C. The Vedic religion was not Hinduism, although Hindus consider the Vedas as scripture. From the Aryan invasion until the time of the Buddha and the Mahavira (sixth century B.C.), the Vedic religion was characterized by complex animal sacrifices. During this period, the Vedic religion was slowly turning into Hinduism. For example, in the Upanishads, which were written over several hundred years preceding the Buddha's time, there are such characteristic Hindu ideas as the unity of a soul with Brahman, karma, reincarnation, and escape from reincarnation. The notion of class and caste, absent from the Vedas, began to appear in this period also.

MUSEUM OF FINE ARTS, BOSTON/KEITH MC LEOD FUND

VISHNU *the preserver, a major Hindu god, in a bronze from Nepal c850 B.C.*

After the sixth century B.C., animal sacrifice assumed much less importance and Hinduism began to have its own recognizable form. Still, many of the most important elements of Hindu religious writing, including the Bhagavad-Gita, would not be composed for nearly a thousand years.

While the main gods of Hinduism are generally identified as Brahma, Vishnu, and Shiva, the relative importance of the gods has varied greatly. Of the Hindu "Trinity," only Vishnu appears in the oldest Veda. In the Buddha's time, Brahma was Hinduism's main god. Today there is only one temple to Brahma left in India. In the thousand years after the Buddha, both Vishnu and Shiva became much more important. The concept of Brahma the creator, Vishnu the preserver, and Shiva the destroyer dates from around 500 A.D. Around that time also, a new importance began for a goddess who appears in many forms, Shakti, Shiva's wife or consort.

Today most Hindus belong to one of three groups, characterized by which god they consider to be most important. The *Shaivas* are devoted to Shiva, whom they see as the creator and maintainer of the universe, as well as its destroyer. The *Vaishnavas* assign these roles to Vishnu, while the *Shaktas* consider Shakti as the one whose energy produced, sustains, and will destroy the universe. While other gods and goddesses are worshiped, especially various children of Shiva and Shakti, none of the others has the kind of central role that Shiva, Vishnu, or Shakti do.

These divisions of Hinduism are not quite the same as denominations of Christianity, for Hindus do not form congregations. The essential part of worship is done at home, and it is not strange for a Vaishnava to visit or worship in a Shakta temple.

Local gods or goddesses are often considered another reincarnation of one of the main Hindu gods or goddesses. As a result, the major gods and goddesses of Hinduism are worshiped by many names and in many forms.

Buddhism

The fourth largest religion in the world is Buddhism. It has 250 million followers, largely in Asia. Although Buddhism originated in India, today there are more Christians in India than Buddhists. The strongholds of Buddhism are the places where Buddhist missionaries from India carried the religion: Sri Lanka, Southeast Asia, China, Tibet, and Mongolia. Japan and Korea also have many Buddhists, but their missionaries came from China. There is a small but growing number of Buddhists in the United States.

A STUPA, *an early Buddhist shrine, is to be circumambulated (or walked around) by the Buddhist faithful as an act of devotion or meditation.*

INFORMATION SERVICE OF INDIA

Beliefs

Buddhism is sometimes described as *atheistic*—believing in no god at all. The followers of Buddhism, however, would dispute this, for the founder of their religion said, "There is an unborn, an unoriginated, an unmade, an uncompounded." The Buddhist concept of God does not have the "personhood" that concepts of God have in other religions.

Buddhism was founded by Sidharta Gautama, known as Buddha, who lived from about 566 B.C. until 486 B.C. The Buddha grew up in the Hindu religion, in northern India in the foothills of the Himalayas. Buddhism contains many concepts that grew out of Hinduism. Some have compared this relationship to the relationship between Christianity and Judaism. Both Buddhism and Christianity used elements of the older religions, but are essentially different from them.

In particular, Buddhists retain the concepts of reincarnation and karma. They see an end to reincarnation as the major goal of the religious life. Buddha rejected caste, however, and was not interested in the many gods and goddesses of Hinduism. His followers do not hold sacred the holy things of the Hindus.

Instead, Buddhism concentrates on the way an individual should live to escape the otherwise endless round of reincarnation. Buddha declared that all life is suffering; therefore, one should devote one's life to escaping from this suffering. In fact, the central dogma of Buddhism, the Four Holy Truths, summarizes this point in a simple way:

1. Human existence involves much suffering;
2. Human suffering occurs because human beings are self-centered;
3. Self-centeredness can be overcome;
4. The way to overcome self-centeredness is the Eightfold Path.

The Eightfold Path is the Buddha's prescription for correcting false values and attaining true knowledge. Like the Four Holy Truths, the Eightfold Path consists of simple statements:

Right understanding: You must clearly see what is wrong with your life.

Right purpose: You must decide to correct what is wrong.

Right conduct: You must act to correct what is wrong.

Right speech: You must speak in ways that will help.

Right vocation: Your occupation must not conflict with your efforts to correct what is wrong.

Right effort: You really have to work at making a change.

Right awareness: Your effort at making a change must always be on your mind.

Right meditation: You must meditate on correcting what is wrong; you must get your effort for change into your subconscious mind as well as your conscious mind.

The goal of the Eightfold Path is achieved when the follower attains perfect peace and escape from the constant round of reincarnation. This state is called *nirvana,* which means enlightenment.

UPI

A STANDING BUDDHA *in a temple in Mandalay, Burma.*

When the Buddha attained nirvana, he could have immediately left the Wheel of Life, as the round of reincarnation is called. Instead, he decided to stay with his fellow people and to teach them how they, too, could go from ignorance to nirvana. He did not leave the Wheel of Life until his earthly body died.

Before he left the Wheel, he founded the Buddhist monastic order. (Although it is not very common, women can become Buddhist nuns.) The order, known as the Sangha, is much like a Christian monastic order. Monks take vows of poverty, cut their beards and hair, and wear special yellow robes. A monk owns nothing but a bowl for begging, his robe, his razor, a string of 108 beads, and a filter. The string of beads is to remind the monk of the 108 characteristics of the Buddha. The filter is to remove insects from his drinking water so that he will harm no living thing. A monk begs for all his food and devotes most of the rest of his time to meditation. The monks also perform at a few rites including funerals. Most Buddhist monks are celibate.

Buddhist Sects

While the Four Noble Truths, the Eightfold Path, and the Sangha are the core of Buddhism, since the Buddha's time—2500 years ago—many Buddhists have added other elements to the religion. Some have included the worship of various gods or goddesses as part of the faith. Others believe in a long string of Buddhas stretching back through time. In one version that invokes several Buddhas, *Amida Buddhism,* the Buddha Amida promises salvation through faith; the historical Buddha said that salvation could only be achieved by working for it and by meditating. Amida Buddhism has been popular in Japan. Other Buddhists await the arrival of a sort of second coming of Buddha.

Another form of Buddhism that is well known in the United States is *Zen Buddhism,* or Zen. Zen is heavily influenced by the Chinese religions of Taoism and Confucianism. All three religions are alike in de-emphasizing God and emphasizing humanity. Even more than other Buddhist sects, Zen concentrates on methods to obtain nirvana, or enlightenment. Zen is particularly differentiated from other forms of Buddhism by the methods it uses, which include the holy riddles, called *Koans,* and several specialized forms of meditation.

History of Buddhism

The life of the Buddha was not put into writing until 500 years after his death. Because of this, the beliefs that are attributed to him may have been distorted. Almost from the beginning of Buddhism, scholars have tried to determine both what the Buddha really said and what he may have meant by saying it. These questions have been resolved, for the record at least, in councils. The First Council was held shortly after the Buddha's death, in 483 B.C.

The development of two major schools of Buddhism was already apparent by the time of the Second Council (383 B.C.). At the Third Council (around 250 B.C.), the two schools split completely, with the majority leaving the council over a disagreement about which oral recitations were actually the words of the Buddha. The minority at the council, which had gained control of the council before the walkout, then set up a canonical group of scriptures in the Pali language. This is known as the Tripitaka. The majority wanted to add other works to the Pali canon.

Today, the scriptures of the majority school of Buddhism are written in

Sanskrit, Chinese, Japanese, and Tibetan, while the minority school of Buddhism maintains the Tripitaka. Because of this difference, the Buddhists who belong to the majority school call themselves *Mahayani Buddhists* ("Great Vehicle" Buddhists) and they call the members of the minority school *Hinayani Buddhists* ("Small Vehicle" Buddhists). The minority school, however, calls itself *Theravada Buddhists* ("Way of the Elders").

The Theravadians became the dominant Buddhists in the south, while the Mahayani Buddhists are located in the north. Thus, Sri Lanka, Burma, and most of Indochina are Theravada, while Buddhists in Japan, China, Korea, Tibet, Nepal, and Mongolia are Mahayani. A Sixth Council in 1956 A.D. was held in Burma and was sponsored by (and largely attended by) Theravada Buddhists.

The differences between the Mahayani and the Theravadians go far beyond the scriptures that they accept. Although both stem from Buddha's teaching, they are like two different religions. For example, the Mahayani believe in a universal spirit (similar to the Brahman of the Hindus), while the Theravadians believe that no such universal spirit exists. Thus, the Mahayani conception of nirvana is union with the universal spirit, but the Theravadians see nirvana as simple cessation of the endless round of reincarnation.

The Theravadians, perhaps because their religion is based on a short scripture, are essentially a single denomination or sect. The Mahayani, who have many scriptures to draw upon, have formed many diverse groups. For example, the Amida Buddhists and Zen Buddhists are both considered Mahayani. Buddhism in Tibet, which is often called Lamaism, is a Mahayani sect that incorporates many rituals. Another well known group within Buddhism is the Shingon school of Japan, which is based upon secret teaching brought from China in the eighth century A.D.

Lesser Religions

The place of other religions that claim millions or hundreds of thousands of followers is not as clear as that of the major religions. There are many Chinese who are considered followers of Confucianism or of Taoism, but numbers are almost meaningless because one may follow both at the same time. The same problem of counting followers exists with the Shinto faith in Japan. Many followers of Shintoism are also Buddhists, at least some of the time. The Sikhs and Jains in India are sometimes viewed as followers of two separate religions, but their religions are also seen as "denominations" within Hinduism. The Bahai faith can be seen as an offshoot of Islam. Theosophy is closely related to the Tibetan form of Buddhism. Only the followers of Zoroaster seem to stand apart from all the rest.

Nevertheless, we will treat all of these as if they were truly separate. In their own ways, each is practiced by its followers as a distinct religion, or as a mixture of several religions.

Far Eastern Religions

Confucianism. The minor religion that is generally judged to have the largest number of followers is Confucianism. As with Buddhism, the original leader, Confucius, was not religious in the usual sense of the word. Confucius is the Latinized name for K'ung Fu-tzu, a Chinese scholar and official who lived in China from 551 B.C. until 479 B.C., around the same time as the Buddha. From the reports of his life, Confucius had no intention of starting a religion, but his followers came to venerate him. For nearly 2000 years, Confucianism was the official state religion of China, complete with sacrifices of oxen to Confucius and Confucian temples in every major city.

The original teachings of Confucius were largely ethical. He was especially concerned with how government should be run for the benefit of all. For example, he said that the three necessities of good government were food for everyone, soldiers, and leadership, but of these leadership was most important, for you cannot govern at all without leadership.

The Chinese people had worshiped the spirits of their ancestors long before the time of Confucius. He encouraged this practice and also the practice of venerating the ruler. He did not speak of a God or of gods, and he once said that he himself did not pray very much. Most of the Chinese people who followed Confucius's teaching continued to pray to various spirits, such as the god of the earth, the god of the waters, and the god of wealth. Since Confucius believed strongly in the virtue of ritual, he probably would not have disapproved of the worship of these various spirits, although he did not speak directly of it.

CONFUCIUS, *the Chinese philosopher whose teachings became a religion.*

Shintoism. In Japan a similar form of religion was also practiced since ancient times. Today we know it as Shintoism. After Confucianism, Shintoism probably has the greatest number of followers of any of the minor religions. In Japan, as in China, a person may follow more than one religion at a time. Even Japanese Christians may keep a small Shinto shrine in their homes and go on a two-week retreat to a Zen Buddhist monastery.

Unlike Confucianism, Shintoism has no one founder or leader connected with the religion. Shintoism originally evolved out of the folk practices of the Japanese people. The word *Shinto* is usually translated as "The Path of the Gods." Shintoism is a polytheistic religion with more than 3000 recognized gods and goddesses, including spirits associated with particular places as well as gods or goddesses associated with major natural phenomena, such as the sun, the moon, storms, and earthquakes. But the principal deity of Shintoism has always been the sun goddess Amaterasu. She has been considered the ancestor of the original emperor of Japan, and the emperor has also been worshiped as a Shinto god. Shintoism, like Confucianism, includes ancestor worship.

Shintoism has no scriptures and no full-time priests. The shrines that celebrate one of the thousands of gods or goddesses are maintained by priests who also have secular professions.

Shintoism can be divided into four main historical periods. Before about 600 A.D., Shintoism was the single, unwritten folk religion of Japan. After 600, Buddhism dominated court life, but Shinto goddesses and gods continued to be worshiped at Shinto shrines.

In 1868 a group of Japanese warrior–noblemen (*samurai*) took over the government and made Shintoism the official state religion. The result is known as State Shinto, beginning the third period in the history of Shintoism. Efforts were made to separate Shintoism from Buddhism but they did not fully succeed. Since World War II, Shintoism without the trappings of the state is practiced comfortably alongside Buddhism.

Taoism. A third religion of the Far East is Taoism. Taoism is believed to come after Shintoism in the number of followers.

Taoism, even more than Confucianism, is heavily embedded in the Chinese folk religion of ancestor worship, spirits in natural objects, and magic. As in Confucianism, the founder of the religion was really concerned with something else. The religious practices that grew up many years after the founder's death may have little to do with his views. Both founders lived in the sixth century B.C. Taoism, however, is the mystical side of the Chinese culture, while Confucianism is its practical side.

Lao-tze, the founder of Taoism, was born about 50 years before Confucius. Lao-tze is a title that may be translated as "The Old Philosopher" or "The Old Man." Little is known of his life.

Lao-tze, after a few years in government service, retired to the mountains to live as a hermit. Near the end of his life, war reached the mountains, disturbing his retreat. He fled the area riding on a black ox (which is how he is often shown in Chinese art). When he reached a pass in the mountains, he was stopped by the keeper of the pass. The keeper demanded an unusual price for passage: that Lao-tze write out the sum of all his wisdom. Lao-tze did this, in just 5000 Chinese ideograms, and was allowed to pass. The short book that Lao-tze wrote has come to be known as the *Tao Ching,* the *Tao Te Ching,* or simply the *Lao-tze.* Many experts think that the *Tao Ching* is actually a compilation of works by several authors that was made in the second century A.D., more than 600 years after Lao-tze's death.

The Tao, which is often translated as "the Way" or "the Path," is the essence of the universe. It is not God, but rather it is the way the universe works. The Tao itself cannot be found by approaching it; in fact, the Tao cannot be approached. Yet it does have practical uses. Much of the *Tao Ching* suggests the strategy that is the foundation of the Chinese and Japanese martial arts, of which the best known is judo. As in judo, the *Tao Ching* tells us that one can win a battle by offering no force to oppose a force. Instead, one can let the opposing force overcome itself.

About 300 years after Lao-tze there arose in China a philosopher named Chuang-tse. While the *Tao Ching* consists solely of aphorisms such as "Law begets crime," the writings of Chuang-tse, known as the *Chuang-tse,* include discussions of other philosophers and many parables. Like the *Tao Ching,* the *Chuang-tse* emphasizes the unknowability of the Tao, the importance of doing nothing, and the futility of greatness. The philosophical basis of Taoism comes both from the *Tao Ching* and the *Chuang-tse.*

When Confucianism became the official Chinese religion, Taoism became something of an underground religion. In the process, it lost much of its philosophical content and merged with Chinese folk religion. Taoist monasteries were founded, and by 666 A.D. Lao-tze came to be venerated. The Tao was thought of as a kind of magic force that could be invoked. Many spirits were thought to rule the affairs of people on Earth.

Religions of India

Although India is predominantly Hindu, several important lesser religions are also found there. These religions are Sikhism, Jainism, and Zoroastrianism. It is easiest to follow the development of the three religions in historical order.

Zoroastrianism. Zoroastrianism is one of the many religions that were founded around the sixth century B.C. In fact, the founder, Zoroaster, lived from around 660 B.C. until 583 B.C., so his life overlaps that of both Lao-tze and the Mahavira, who founded Jainism. Zoroaster lived in the country we now call Iran, which was then known as Persia. At the time of his birth, Persian religion was similar in many ways to Hinduism. The Persians were polytheistic and made animal sacrifices to many gods and goddesses. Zoroaster was brought up as a priest and participated in these rituals. Little else is known of his life.

His teachings eventually became the state religion of the powerful Persian Empire. But all known copies of the Avesta, the sacred book of Zoroastrianism, were destroyed by Alexander the Great in the fourth century B.C. Some portions were reconstructed from the memories of followers, but at least two-thirds of it was completely lost. The Avesta was written in Zend, a language that is known only from the Avesta, and this has made translation of the book exceedingly difficult.

Zoroastrianism is monotheistic, but the god of Zoroastrians, Ahura Mazda, is engaged in a lengthy struggle with the powerful spirit of evil, Ahriman.

Zoroaster preached that Ahura Mazda would defeat Ahriman in 9000 years (revised by later Zoroastrians to a long, unknowable time). While the Zoroastrians believe that a soul enters a kind of heaven or a kind of hell four days after death, someday a savior, known as Saoshyant, will appear. At that time, Ahura Mazda will put all the souls back in their original bodies and bring the people who died back to life. He will judge all and condemn the wicked to hell.

Unlike the Christian Last Judgment, however, Ahura Mazda's judgment will not condemn anyone to eternal fire. The fires of hell will, instead, burn away all the evil within three days. At that time, the good remnant, if any, will be taken back to live with Ahura Mazda. This belief in a future savior resembles the Jewish belief that a Messiah will come to start an age of peace when God triumphs.

Faith in Zoroastrianism was widespread when the Persian empires were at their height, but when the last of these empires was conquered by the Muslims in 641 A.D., the religion of Zoroaster was suppressed. While a few followers of Zoroaster have continued to live in Muslim Iran, the principal group of Zoroastrians in the world today are the descendants of those who fled to India in the eighth century A.D. to escape Muslim persecution.

Today there are only about 300,000 Zoroastrians, most living in the area around Bombay, India. In India they are known as the Parsees, a corruption of *Persians.* The Parsees live an elaborate religious life, with prayers five times a day while facing the sun and many ceremonies and rituals. Their dead are taken to "Towers of Silence" and left to be devoured by vultures. Although they live to some degree in separation from the surrounding Hindus, the Parsees have become successful merchants who are influential beyond their small numbers.

Jainism. About the same time that Zoroaster was preaching monotheism in Persia, the Mahavira was preaching atheism—or the absence of any god—in northern India. In fact, the Mahavira lived and taught in the same general part of India as the Buddha, but about 30 years earlier. Their lives overlapped, but it is believed that they did not meet. The Mahavira is generally believed to be the founder of Jainism, a religion that has about 3 million followers in India today. The Jains themselves believe that their religion is the oldest in the world and that the Mahavira was merely the last of 24 "ford crossers" who advanced the faith that started with King Rsabbha, who is regarded by the Hindus as an incarnation of Vishnu.

Both Buddhism and Jainism emphasize that an individual can achieve his or her own salvation (escape from rebirth), but they differ as to what the world is really like. Jains use the word *karma* to mean a substance that binds the soul to the physical world. Actions, such as causing the death of any creature, cause the formation of karma. Other actions, such as fasting and meditation, burn away karma. Only when all the karma that has been accumulated in past lives has been burned away can the soul leave the material world.

The Mahavira put forth five ways to eliminate karma:

1. Be nonviolent and do not destroy life even through carelessness;
2. Speak only what is true, pleasant, and good;
3. Take nothing that is not freely given;
4. Be celibate;
5. Own nothing.

Following all five precepts requires one to become a monk. Other Jains follow as far as they can, concentrating mostly on the first precept. For example, Jains cannot become farmers because tilling the soil requires killing small insects. Water is strained several times before drinking it to remove any insects that might be accidentally swallowed. Some Jains wear face masks to avoid breathing in any flying insects.

The Mahavira also preached against many of the traditional beliefs of Hinduism. He rejected all the Hindu gods and goddesses, and for this reason is usually considered an atheist. The Mahavira also rejected caste, as the Buddha did.

There are only about 3 million Jains today, and their number seems to be decreasing. Although the number of Jains is small, their influence is large in two ways. Their doctrine of nonviolence has influenced Hindu thought (Gandhi, for example, was known to have gotten part of his concept of nonviolence from the Jains). Also, the Jains' rule against entering many professions has led them to become merchants and bankers.

Sikhism. While Jainism claims to be the oldest religion in the world, Sikhism is one of the newest. Sikhism was founded in the 1400's A.D. by yet another warrior-caste Hindu, Nanak. Although some religions are younger than Sikhism, there are more Sikhs than there are followers of any other religion founded since Islam. Today there are about 12 million Sikhs, mostly in the Punjab region of India.

Nanak lived from 1469 to 1538, making him a contemporary of Martin Luther. In his region of India, Islam and Hinduism were practiced side by side. He based his new religion on combining compatible elements of Islam and Hinduism. The result was distinctly different from either of the parent religions. A religion that is formed from others in this way is called *syncretic.*

DENIS BRIHAT/PHOTO RESEARCHERS

CHESTER HIGGINS, JR./PHOTO RESEARCHERS

RELIGIOUS DRESS: *the Sikhs of India and the Rastafarians of the West Indies use distinctive headdresses and hairstyles to set themselves apart.*

Sikhism is like Islam in being strictly monotheistic. It is like Hinduism in its acceptance of karma (as the sum of past actions), and rebirth. Although the Sikh god, known as the True Name, is a personal god, there is neither judgment nor paradise. Instead, true followers of god will someday cease to be reborn and become a part of god.

A life acceptable to god does not involve denial, as in Hinduism, Buddhism, or Jainism, however. Sikhs can eat meat (but not pork), marry, and live a life in the world, and still escape from the cycle of rebirth. Such a redemption comes by the grace of god, not by a person's striving. In this last respect, Sikhism strikingly resembles the teachings of Luther about the Christian faith.

Every Sikh must have a religious leader, or guru, that he or she follows. The submissiveness of the Sikh to the guru's teaching is the basis on which god grants his grace and the escape from rebirth.

Although Nanak is the first Guru of the religion, the nine Gurus that followed him did much to shape the religion. Nanak started public kitchens where all could eat together regardless of caste. The second Guru turned the public kitchens into an essential part of the Sikh temple. The fifth Guru put together the first version of the Sikh scriptures. The tenth Guru completed the scriptures, now known as the Granth Sahib. At his death, the tenth Guru also directed that from then on the only guru for the Sikhs was to be the Granth Sahib, which today is placed in the center of each Sikh temple as their most sacred object.

The tenth Guru also started a special order of Sikhs, whose distinctive dress is today often associated with India. Members of this order, known as the Khalsa, do not cut their hair or beards (although they cover their long hair with a turban), and wear a comb in their hair, a steel bangle on their right wrists, short drawers, and a sword. Although most Sikhs are farmers in the Punjab region of India, many are also found in most of the large cities of India.

Other Faiths

While the five major religions (Christianity, Islam, Hinduism, Buddhism, and Judaism) and the six minor religions (Confucianism, Shintoism, Taoism, Sikhism, Jainism, and Zoroastrianism) just discussed include among them almost all the followers of religion around the world, there are a number of religions today besides these. These include Bon, the ancient religion of Tibet; Bahai, an independent religion that grew out of Islam in 1844; Theosophy, developed by Helena Petrovna Blavatsky in the early 1870's out of a mixture of Tibetan Buddhism and spiritualism; Ethical Culture, founded in 1876 by Felix Adler as a society devoted to ethics; Cao Dai, a syncretic religion based on Judaism, Christianity, Confucianism, Taoism, and Buddhism, founded in 1919 in Indochina by Ngo-van-Chieu; and Rastafarianism, which is devoted to the worship of the Ethiopian Emperor Haile Selassie, but is centered in the West Indies. In addition, many local groups in isolated places in the world continue to practice traditional religions whose origins are unknown.

—*Bryan H. Bunch*

BIBLE GLOSSARY

Please consult also the glossary of literature and mythology for biblical references in, and influences on, literature. The symbols OT *and* NT *signify the Old and New Testaments respectively.*

A

Aaron, OT: brother of Moses; the first high priest and ancestor of the priests and high priests of Israel. He was spokesman for Moses in appealing to Pharaoh to let the Israelites leave Egypt (Ex. 7); in the wilderness, when Moses was on Mount Sinai, Aaron set up a golden calf for the people to worship (Ex. 32). He died on Mount Hor (Num. 20).

Abel, OT: second son of Adam and Eve; a shepherd. God accepted his sacrifice, but not that of his brother Cain. Out of jealousy, Cain then killed Abel (Gen. 4).

Abraham, or Abram (meaning "father of a multitude"), OT: founder of the Hebrew nation and the first patriarch. Born in Ur, a city in Chaldea, he was called by God to be the founder of a new nation. He migrated to Canaan, where he became very prosperous (Gen. 11–13). After renewing the covenant, with circumcision as its sign, God changed his name from Abram to Abraham (Gen. 17). God tested him by ordering him to sacrifice his only son Isaac; Abraham obeyed without question. Just before he killed his son, however, an angel stopped him, pointing out a ram that he was to sacrifice instead. God then promised to bless Abraham and his descendants forever (Gen. 22).

Absalom, OT: son of David. He rebelled against his father but was defeated in battle. While escaping, he rode under an oak tree, where his head caught hold of the tree. He was found by David's commander Joab, who slew him (II Sam. 18).

Acts of the Apostles, NT: fifth book, giving an account of what happened to the disciples after the death of Jesus. Scholars agree that it was written by Luke as a sequel to his Gospel. The first twelve chapters trace the history of the church in Palestine from Pentecost to the death of Herod, with Peter as the central character. The remainder of the book deals chiefly with the work of Paul, whose conversion (Acts 9) is the most graphic and significant of the events narrated.

FRICK COLLECTION, NEW YORK

AN ANGEL *as perceived by a sculptor of the Middle Ages.*

Adam (meaning "the man"), OT: first man. God made Adam out of the dust of the earth, placed him in the Garden of Eden, and gave him dominion over all the rest of the animals created. When he and Eve disobeyed God's command not to eat the fruit of the tree of knowledge of good and evil, they were driven out of the Garden of Eden; Adam was forced to get his food by his own labor. Adam's sin, called the Fall of Man, is supposed to have been the origin of all later sin (Gen. 3).

Ahab, OT: king of Israel, c 874–853 B.C. His wife, Jezebel, a Phoenician princess, wished to induce the Israelites to worship Baal. When Ahab coveted Naboth's vineyard, she had Naboth killed so that Ahab could seize it. Elijah prophesied a terrible death for Ahab and Jezebel. Ahab repented and eventually died in battle (I Kings 21–22); Jezebel died according to the prediction (II Kings 9).

Ahasuerus: See *Esther.*

Amos, OT: book of a minor Hebrew prophet who was a shepherd from Tekoa, in Judah. About the year 760 B.C., he went to the northern kingdom of Israel and proclaimed its coming destruction. During a long period of peace and prosperity, Israel had become corrupt; Amos told the people that God would bring the Assyrians down upon them as a punishment for their sins. He is considered the first prophet of doom.

Andrew, NT: brother of Peter. He was sent to Jesus by John the Baptist, and was one of the first called to be a disciple (Matt. 4:18). Tradition says he brought the gospel to Scythia, which lay north of the Black and Caspian seas; he became the patron saint of Russia. Scotland also adopted him.

Angels: in Jewish, Christian, and Muslim theology, creatures that rank above man and below God in the divine order of creation. The early church fathers listed nine orders of angels: seraphim, cherubim, thrones, dominions, virtues, powers, principalities, archangels, and angels. In Judeo-Christian tradition, the four archangels are Michael, the warrior; Gabriel, the herald; Raphael, the healer; and Uriel, the angel of light. In Muslim tradition, they are Michael; Gabriel; Azrael, the angel of death; and Israfel, the angel of music.

Antichrist, NT: chief opponent of Christ, or a false Christ. The term

"Antichrist" appears in the Epistles of St. John (I John 2: 18–22; 4: 3; II John 7), but the concept of a ruler who is an enemy of God, and who is to appear at the end of time, is also to be found in the Old Testament (Dan. 8: 23–25). Jesus predicted (Matt. 24) that the coming of the Son of Man would be preceded by "false messiahs."

Early Christians applied the term to any enemy of Christ, whether a person or a power. During the Reformation, Protestants regarded the pope as the Antichrist; the pope, in turn, held Martin Luther to be the Antichrist.

Apocalypse (Greek for "revelation"): See *Revelation.*

Apocalyptic literature: Book of Daniel, Book of Revelation, and certain other works not accepted in the biblical canon, such as the books of Enoch. Such literature claims to have special knowledge of the end of time. Certain apocalyptic works promise the coming of a messiah and a heavenly kingdom.

Apocrypha (Greek for "hidden"; "spurious"): books of uncertain authorship and authority. The Old Testament Apocrypha comprises certain works that were known by the Jews, but not included in the Hebrew Bible. They were included in the Septuagint and in the Vulgate (see *Bible*). They are included as canonical in Roman Catholic Bibles, but are either excluded from Protestant Bibles or included in a separate section called "Apocrypha." The New Testament Apocrypha is a body of writings by early Christian sects, which failed to gain acceptance. It includes writings attributed to apostles, e.g., Peter and Thomas.

Apollyon, NT: destroying angel, angel of the bottomless pit (Rev. 9: 11).

Ararat, OT: mountain on which Noah's ark rested after the flood (Gen. 8). Ararat is a mountain massif in western Turkey, near the junction of the Turkish, Soviet, and Iranian borders.

Ark, OT: ship Noah built to keep his family and the animals safe (Gen. 6); also, the Ark of the Covenant: a wooden chest in which the Israelites kept the stone tablets of the Law (Ex. 25).

Armageddon, NT: place of the final conflict between the forces of good and evil (Rev. 16: 16). The place is usually identified with the ancient city of Megiddo, which commanded the main route from Egypt to Damascus.

Ashtaroth, OT: plural form of Ashtoreth, a Canaanite fertility goddess known also as Astarte and to the Assyrians and Babylonians as Ishtar. The Israelites periodically fell to worship her (Judges 2:13; 10:6) in various manifestations, hence the plural form.

B

Baal, or Bel: (literally, "lord" or "god"), OT: ancient Semitic god of rain and fertility. There were many baals, belonging to different tribes and places, overseeing the crops of each region (such as the Tyrian Baal or the Babylonian Baal). In some areas, the cult of Baal developed into an orgiastic form of nature worship. God was angered by the Israelites' repeated backsliding into baalism (Num. 25).

Babel, Tower of, OT: tower intended by its builders to reach to the heavens. For their presumption God mixed up their language, causing confusion and a stoppage of construction. The account (Gen. 11) is an explanation of the origin of language.

Babylon: capital city of the ancient Babylonian Empire, which reached its height during the early sixth century B.C. Its king, Nebuchadnezzar, captured many Jews and led them into exile in Babylon after he had destroyed Jerusalem in 586 (called the Babylonian Captivity, or Exile; see Psalm 137). Cyrus the Great, founder of the Persian Empire, captured Babylon in 538 and freed the Jews.

At its height, Babylon was a rich city; its Hanging Gardens were one of the Seven Wonders of the World. Its name later became synonymous with luxury, wickedness, and a place of exile.

Balaam, OT: soothsayer in the early days of the conquest of Canaan by the Israelites. He was summoned by Balak, king of the Moabites, and told to curse the Israelites. The ass on which he rode saw an angel in the way and refused to go on. Balaam was therefore led to bless the Israelites instead of cursing them (Num. 22–24).

Barabbas, NT: prisoner in Jerusalem at the time of Jesus' crucifixion. Pilate told the crowd to choose a prisoner for him to release to them at Passover. Egged on by the chief priests, the people chose Barabbas, a rebel who was in jail for murder after a recent uprising, instead of Jesus.

Barnabas, NT: an early convert to Christianity, active in the church at Antioch, and associate of Paul in his first missionary journey. They split after the Jerusalem conference.

Bartholomew, NT: one of the twelve apostles (Matt. 10). John's Gospel makes no mention of an apostle by that name; it is assumed that the Nathanael named in John 1:45 is the same as Bartholomew, who is named in the other three Gospels.

Baruch, OT: friend and secretary of Jeremiah. Jeremiah dictated his doomful prophecies to Baruch, who read them to the people. The prophecies aroused the wrath of King Jehoiakim, who had the roll burned, but Baruch rewrote it. With Jeremiah, he was taken to Egypt. I and II Baruch are Apocryphal books addressed to the exiles in Babylon, to whom they were intended to give encouragement and comfort.

Bathsheba, OT: wife of Uriah the Hittite and, afterward, of King David; she was the mother of Solomon. After David fell in love with her, he plotted to have Uriah killed in battle so he could marry her. Bathsheba gained the throne for Solomon when David died, and was influential during her son's reign (II Sam. 11–12; I Kings 1–2).

Beatitudes, NT: nine verses from Jesus' Sermon on the Mount (Matt. 5: 3–11), each of which begins with "Blessed are. . . ." In the Beatitudes, Jesus praised the poor in spirit, those that mourn, the meek, those who hunger for justice, the pure in heart, the peacemakers, and the persecuted, promising them great rewards in heaven.

Beelzebub (literally, "lord of flies"): god of the ancient Philistine city of Ekron. In the New Testament he is called a prince of demons.

Beersheba, OT: residence of the patriarchs Abraham and Isaac, on the extreme southern boundary of the territory held by the twelve tribes of Israel (Gen. 21: 31; 26: 23–33). As Dan was at the extreme north, the saying "from Dan to Beersheba" indicated the entire extent of the territory (Judg. 20).

Bel and the Dragon: one of the stories in the Apocryphal part of the Book of Daniel. Bel was an idol who, with the dragon, was worshiped by the king of Babylon until Daniel exposed them.

Belial: personification of evil; the devil. The word seems to mean worthless. In the New Testament, Satan is called Belial.

Belshazzar, OT: son of King Nabonidas of Babylonia. He was not only crown prince but co-regent of Babylon in the years preceding its fall to Cyrus, king of Persia, in 539 B.C. Until the 19th century, he was known only from the story about his feast and death (Dan. 5), and from allusions to him by Greek historians. Since 1854 many references to him have been found in Babylonian writings discovered by archaeologists.

Benjamin, OT: youngest of the twelve sons of Jacob. Rachel was his mother and Joseph his full brother. Traditionally, he was the ancestor of the tribe of Benjamin, whose territory lay just north of Jerusalem. King Rehoboam forced some of its towns to join his southern kingdom after the revolt of the northern tribes (II Chron. 11:5–12).

Bethany: town near Jerusalem, on the eastern slope of the Mount of Olives, where in Jesus' time Mary, Martha, and Lazarus lived. It was the place where Jesus raised Lazarus from the dead (John 11).

Bethel: originally called Luz, an ancient city in Palestine. After Israel was divided into the kingdoms of Israel and Judah (tenth century B.C.), it was for a time the most important shrine of the northern kingdom of Israel. In modern times, the village of Beitin, eleven miles north of Jerusalem, occupies the site.

Bethlehem: town in western Jordan, located about five miles southwest of Jerusalem. Bethlehem was the birthplace of Jesus. The Church of the Nativity, built by Emperor Constantine in 330 A.D., occupies the reputed site of the stable where Jesus was born.

Bible (Greek for "book"): sacred scriptures of Judaism and Christianity. The Jewish Bible consists of the Old Testament; the Christian Bible consists of the Old and New Testaments. Several books that do not appear in the Hebrew Bible, but were included in the Septuagint—the Greek translation of the Hebrew Bible made in the third century B.C.—are called the Apocrypha. These books were included in the Latin Vulgate and subsequently in Roman Catholic Bibles. Protestant Bibles either exclude these books or place them in a separate section called "Apocrypha."

The Old Testament, originally written in Hebrew, consists of the religious literature and history of the Jews. The Hebrew Bible was divided into three parts: the Pentateuch, or Torah ("Law"); the Prophets; and the Hagiographa, or Holy Writings. According to scholars, the main historical events took place over a period of about 1000 years, from the Exodus of the Jews from Egypt in about 1300 B.C. to the return of Ezra to Palestine in about 400 B.C.

The Pentateuch—made up of the five books, Genesis, Exodus, Leviticus, Numbers, and Deuteronomy—begins with the creation of the world and ends with the death of Moses. It tells of God's covenant with Abraham, in which Abraham's descendants are chosen as a special people; of the captivity of the children of Israel in Egypt; of the Exodus from Egypt and wanderings in the wilderness; and of God's giving the law to Moses.

The books known as the Prophets tell of the messages given by men who felt they were inspired by God; they also tell much of the history of the Israelites. The Hagiographa, or Holy Writings, is made up of several books that contain history, prophecy, songs, poems, and maxims.

The New Testament, originally written in Greek and Aramaic, is an account of the life and teachings of Jesus Christ, and the growth of the early Christian Church. The four Gospels—Matthew, Mark, Luke, and John—tell of Jesus' life, death, and resurrection, and recount his sayings and parables. The first three are called the Synoptic Gospels.

The Acts of the Apostles, a continuation of Luke, tells about the early Christian Church in Jerusalem under the leadership of Peter, and the missionary trips of Paul.

The 21 Epistles, or letters, were written by various authors and deal with problems encountered by the early Church. The Revelation of John, or the Apocalypse, is the last book. It tells of visions seen by the author that deal with the end of the world and the establishment of God's kingdom.

Around 400 A.D. St. Jerome translated the Bible from Greek and Hebrew into Latin. This translation, the Vulgate, became the official Bible of the Catholic Church. The first complete English translation appeared about 1385 and was based on the Vulgate. It is believed to be the work of a group led by John Wycliffe. The Douay, or Reims-Douay, English translation used by Roman Catholics was also made from the Vulgate version and was published in France in 1582 (NT) and 1610 (OT).

The King James Version, or Authorized Version, was published in English in 1611. It was prepared by 54 biblical scholars who were assigned the project by James I of England. The King James Version remained the standard English translation for Protestants for more than 300 years.

A group of British scholars produced the Revised Version (1881–1885), on which was based the American Standard Version (1901). While these versions were accepted by scholars, they did not replace the King James Version in worship services. The Revised Standard Version (1946; 1952), produced by U.S. scholars, gained wide acceptance.

In 1961 the main Protestant churches of the British Isles published the New Testament of the New English Bible, a translation from the Hebrew and Greek. The complete Bible, called the New English Bible, was published in 1970. The New American Bible, published by Roman Catholics to replace the Douay Version, appeared in 1970. Numerous other English translations have been made.

An outstanding translation of the Bible was that of Martin Luther (1522; 1534), which influenced many subsequent translations of the Bible in many languages. It is still the official Bible for German Protestants. The Gutenberg Bible, the first book to be printed with movable type (1455), is an edition of the Vulgate.

BOOKS OF THE BIBLE

Old Testament		New Testament	
PENTATEUCH ("BOOKS OF MOSES")		GOSPELS	
Genesis	Numbers	Matthew	Luke
Exodus	Deuteronomy	Mark	John
Leviticus			
		Acts of the Apostles	
PROPHETS			
Joshua	Obadiah	EPISTLES (LETTERS) ATTRIBUTED TO PAUL	
Judges	Jonah	Romans	Colossians
Samuel I and II	Micah	Corinthians I and II	Thessalonians I and II
Kings I and II	Nahum	Galatians	Timothy I and II
Isaiah	Habakkuk	Ephesians	Titus
Jeremiah	Zephaniah	Philippians	Philemon
Ezekiel	Haggai		
Hosea	Zechariah	OTHER EPISTLES	
Joel	Malachi	Hebrews	John I, II, III
Amos		James	Jude
		Peter I and II	
HAGIOGRAPHA ("HOLY WRITINGS")			
Ruth	Psalms	The Revelation of John (Apocalypse)	
Chronicles I and II	Proverbs		
Ezra	Ecclesiastes	**The Apocrypha**	
Nehemiah	Song of Songs	Esdras I and II	Letter of Jeremiah
Esther	Lamentations	Tobit	Song of the Three
Job	Daniel	Judith	Daniel and Susanna
		Esther (continued)	Daniel, Bel, and the Snake
		Wisdom of Solomon	
		Ecclesiasticus	Prayer of Manasseh
		Baruch	Maccabees I and II

Boaz: See *Ruth*.

C

Cabala, or Kabbalah (Hebrew for "tradition"): originally, the Jewish oral tradition, said to have been handed down from Moses through the rabbis. During the Middle Ages, the term referred to the traditions of Jewish mysticism, which later Christians equated with magic.

Caiaphas, NT: high priest before whom Jesus was tried (John 18).

Cain, OT: oldest son of Adam and Eve, and the first murderer in the Bible. After murdering his brother Abel, Cain became a fugitive and vagabond. God put a mark on him so no one would kill him (Gen. 4).

Calvary: See *Golgotha.*

Cana, or Cana of Galilee: a village near Nazareth where Jesus, while attending a wedding, performed a miracle, turning water into wine (John 2).

Canaan: ancient name of Palestine. The Canaanites were conquered by the Israelites some time before 1000 B.C., and probably afterwards they intermarried.

Canticle (from the Latin *canticulum* meaning "little song"): song or hymn in honor of God, or of some special sacred event. Canticles is another name for The Song of Songs.

Capernaum: ancient city near the Sea of Galilee where Jesus resided after he left Nazareth (Matt. 4). Three of his disciples—Peter, Andrew, and Matthew—were from Capernaum. The city eventually disappeared and its location was unknown for many years. A ruined site at Tell Hum in Israel, where excavations were begun in 1905, has been identified as the site of Capernaum.

Carmel, Mount: promontory in the northwest part of Palestine, overlooking the Mediterranean Sea. Closely associated with the lives of Elijah and Elisha, it was venerated as a holy place and was famous for its beauty and fertility.

Chaldea: seacoast region south of ancient Babylonia (modern southern Iraq). The Chaldean kings became kings of Babylonia about 626 B.C., and the names Babylonian and Chaldean, as used in the Bible, usually mean the same thing.

Chronicles, Books of, OT: two books that give the history of the children of Israel from a priestly point of view; probably written about 300–200 B.C. The Chronicles begin with a genealogy from Adam to Saul, until about the reigns of David and Solomon, and finish with the destruction of Jerusalem and the Babylonian captivity. Much of its material is found in the four books constituting Samuel and Kings. The new material in Ezra and Nehemiah is a continuation of the same narrative.

City of God, The *(de civitate Dei)*: treatise in 22 books by St. Augustine, written between 413 and 426 A.D., in defense of Christianity, which some said had been responsible for the fall of the Roman Empire. St. Augustine saw human history in terms of a struggle between the City of God, devoted to eternal truths, and the Earthly City, emphasizing lesser values. He predicted ultimate victory for the inhabitants of the City of God, thanks to divine protection.

Colossians, Epistle to the, NT: letter written by Paul to the Christian Church in Colossae, a city in Phrygia, on the main route from Palestine to the East. The letter emphasizes the mission of Christ as redeemer and head of the church. An erroneous doctrine leading to the worship of angels is especially attacked.

Confessions of St. Augustine, The: spiritual autobiography by the saint, bishop of Hippo in North Africa, dating from 397–401, important as the first of many such literary examinations of an author's spiritual and emotional life. It describes the experiences of his profligate youth, his growing interest in matters philosophical, and his ultimate, though reluctant, conversion to Christianity. The message of the *Confessions* is that the "real," or the "good," consists in a return to "ourselves" away from inferior outward pleasures.

Corinthians, Epistles to the, NT: two letters to the Christian Church in Corinth from Paul, both probably written in 56 A.D. Paul had lived and worked in Corinth for 18 months, and had then gone to Palestine and to Ephesus. In I Corithians, Paul rebukes the church for having factions and disputes; then he writes of marriage as being wise and honorable; then of regard for others' opinions, even though one may not agree with them (as in the case of eating meat offered to idols); then of matters regarding public worship. The 13th chapter contains the well known lines about faith, hope, and charity. The later chapters of II Corinthians indicate that many people in the church were hostile to Paul, and the writer expresses his grief.

Cornelius, NT: "a devout man and one that feared God" (Acts 10). Though he was a Gentile, Peter received him into the church; when Peter's colleagues reproached him, he told them of a vision in which he saw that salvation was for all men.

D

Dagon, OT: a god of the Philistines (Judg. 16: 23). Dagon was probably a fertility god.

Damascus, or Dimashq: now the capital and largest city of Syria, situated in the southwestern part of the country on the Barada River. The city is an oasis that has been continuously inhabited since before the time of Abraham. It was a noted marketplace on the Mediterranean caravan routes. Saul of Tarsus, traveling from Jerusalem, was converted to Christianity on the road outside Damascus (Acts 9).

Dan, OT: son of Jacob and ancestor of one of the twelve tribes of Israel. The tribe's position was in the extreme north of the territory. They established a city named Dan, which was a national shrine for a time (I Kings 12: 29). See also *Beersheba.*

Daniel, OT: prophet whose triumphs on behalf of his faith are recorded in the Book of Daniel. Most scholars agree that it was written between 167 and 164 B.C., although it purports to be about a young Jew in Babylon under Nebuchadnezzar in the sixth century B.C. Daniel was brought up at court, where he displayed a flair for visions and interpreting dreams. This brought him to the king's attention. When he solved the king's dream about the image with iron and clay feet destroyed by a stone uncut by human hand (Dan. 2), he became, in effect, chief court seer. His friends Shadrach, Meshach, and Abednego were cast into the fiery furnace for refusing to worship a golden image, but their angelic rescue (Dan. 3) brought Judaism the king's protection. Daniel's exploits continued under the next king, Belshazzar, and the Persian conqueror Cyrus: he read the handwriting on the wall at Belshazzar's feast (Dan. 5), and was left unharmed in the lion's den (Dan. 6). The rest of the book relates a series of visions about the history of great empires to come.

David, OT: king of Israel whose reign of about 40 years began c 1000 B.C. The youngest son of Jesse, he grew up on a farm near Bethlehem. In his youth he learned to play the lyre. Called to the court of King Saul, he played to the troubled king to quiet him, and became the friend of Saul's son Jonathan. While he was still a youth, he had his famous fight with the Philistine giant Goliath, whom he killed with a stone from a sling. He married Saul's daughter Michal, but Saul became jealous of David's growing power and sought to kill him. David escaped and became leader of a band of refugees (I Sam. 17–31).

After Saul's death, David became king. He united the kingdoms of Israel and Judah, and made Jerusalem the seat of his government, making it the religious capital as well by bringing the Ark of the Covenant to the city (II Sam. 6).

His love for Bathsheba led him to command that her husband Uriah be placed in "the forefront of the hottest battle" and then be deserted. Uriah was accordingly killed, and David took Bathsheba as another wife. When his son Absalom rose in rebellion and was defeated and killed, David was overcome with grief (II Sam. 13).

Though much of David's life was occupied with wars, he was able to organize his government, to develop a sense of loyalty in his people, and to unite them in their religious attitude. He was famous as a poet, and many Psalms are attributed to him.

Old Testament prophecies of the Messiah say that he is to come from the house of David, and the gospels of Matthew and Luke both trace the descent of Jesus from King David.

Dead Sea Scrolls: collection of scrolls from the Judean desert, the first of which were discovered in the Qumran caves, above the northwest shore of the Dead Sea. The first scroll was found in 1947; since then, hundreds of scrolls have been found in the area. The original find was the library of a Jewish sect that lived at Qumran at the time of Christ. The scrolls include Old Testament and Apocryphal books or portions of books, commentaries, rules for the sect, psalms, and many other works. Scrolls discovered at other nearby sites include records of the Jewish revolt led by Simon Bar Cocheba in 132–135 A.D., and a collection of legal documents.

Deborah, OT: prophetess and judge of Israel. With Barak she caused the defeat of the Canaanites in a battle by the river Kishon. The victory is celebrated in a stirring poem (Judg. 5).

Delilah, OT: Philistine woman loved by Samson. She cut off his hair and betrayed him, causing his loss of strength and his capture by his enemies (Judg. 16). See also *Samson.*

Deuteronomy (literally, "the second law"), OT: fifth book, the main portion of which consists of the farewell of Moses to the people of Israel. In it, he proclaimed and explained the laws that were to govern them, and told what would befall them if they disobeyed. Deuteronomy ends with an account of the death of Moses.

Many scholars believe that Deuteronomy is the "Book of the Law" found in the Temple of Jerusalem in the seventh century B.C. (II Kings 22: 8). Great reforms, apparently based on Deuteronomy, were then carried out under King Josiah of Judah.

Devil: See *Satan.*

E

Ebenezer (literally, "stone of help"), OT: town in central Palestine where the Philistines defeated the Israelites (I Sam. 4). Some 20 years later, when the Israelites under Samuel had driven back the Philistines at Mizpah, Samuel erected a stone there and called it Ebenezer (I Sam. 7: 12).

Ecce homo (Latin for "behold the man"), NT: words spoken by Pontius Pilate when he brought Christ before the people (John 19: 5). The phrase has also been used by Western authors with the meaning "behold man," in the general sense.

Ecclesiastes (Greek for "the preacher"), OT: one of the Wisdom books, named for its anonymous author who calls himself "the preacher." The skeptical preacher stresses that "all is vanity," that virtue is not necessarily rewarded, and that God is remote and incomprehensible; but man can only go on living as if there were purpose and reward in life. See also *Wisdom Literature.*

Ecclesiasticus, or the *Wisdom of Jesus the Son of Sirach,* OT: Apocryphal book that contains good advice on many subjects. It is an excellent example of Wisdom Literature, and shows some resemblance to the Book of Proverbs. See also *Wisdom Literature.*

Eden, OT: luxuriant garden (sometimes translated as "paradise") created by God as a home for the first man, Adam. The Garden of Eden lay east of Palestine, at the headwaters of the Tigris and Euphrates rivers (Gen. 2: 8–14).

Elijah, or Elias, OT: great prophet of the kingdom of Israel in the time of King Ahab (ninth century B.C.). He was uncompromising in leading the Israelites away from idolatry (I and II Kings).

Elijah prophesied the drought that would result from Ahab's sins, and was fed by ravens as he hid from Ahab. In Phoenicia he performed the miracles of keeping full a widow's supply of oil and meal, and restoring her son to life (I Kings 17). According to the scriptural account, Elijah did not die but was taken to Heaven in a chariot of fire (II Kings 2: 11). Elijah appeared with Moses at the transfiguration of Christ (Matt 17: 1–4).

Elisha, OT: Hebrew prophet, the successor to Elijah (II Kings 2–13). He had many followers and succeeded in completing the work begun by Elijah—the elimination of Baal worship in Israel (see *Baal*). He performed many miracles, including the curing of Naaman the leper (II Kings 5: 1–27), and appointed Jehu to rid Israel of Ahab's descendants and become king (II Kings 9).

Enoch, OT: father of Methuselah. Enoch walked with God and was taken away by God (Gen. 5: 18–24). Enoch was also the name of Cain's son, for whom Cain named a city he was building (Gen. 4: 17). There are three ancient Jewish writings called books of Enoch.

Ephesians, Epistle to the, NT: letter traditionally attributed to Paul, though some scholars believe that the letter was written by an admirer of Paul's. Many biblical manuscripts indicate that the letter was sent to Ephesus, but other manuscripts omit the destination. It may have been a circular letter, to be read in various churches in turn and not merely in the church at Ephesus. The letter emphasizes the harmony brought about by God in Christ. It also consists of moral reflections and exhortations, especially urging unity between Jews and Gentiles, and includes the well known exhortations to wives and husbands, children and parents.

Ephraim, OT: son of Joseph and ancestor of one of Israel's twelve tribes (Gen. 41: 50–52; 48: 13–20). Ephraim was one of the strongest tribes in the northern kingdom. Its strength and central position led to the frequent use of the name for the whole kingdom.

Esau, OT: firstborn of the twin sons of Isaac and Rebekah (Gen. 25–28). He was his father's favorite, a hunter and outdoorsman. One day when he was famished, he sold his birthright to his twin brother Jacob for a "mess of pottage," that is, a bowl of soup. Later, Jacob, pretending to be Esau, deceived their dying father Isaac, and Isaac gave Jacob the blessing Isaac intended for Esau. Esau afterward forgave Jacob (Gen. 32–33).

Esther, OT: book that tells the story of Esther, a Jewess, who was chosen queen of Persia by King Ahasuerus (Xerxes I, who invaded Greece in 486 B.C.). Her foster father Mordecai angered the king's vizier Haman, who formed a plot to exterminate all the Jews in Persia; but Esther foiled the plot, Haman was hanged on the gallows he had prepared for Mordecai, and the Jews killed those who had plotted to kill them, as commemorated by the feast of Purim. The Rest of Esther is a book of the Apocrypha with those parts of Esther included in the Septuagint, but not in the Hebrew, Bible.

Eve, OT: first woman, the wife of Adam. She was created by God from Adam's rib. Tempted by the Serpent, she ate the fruit of the tree of knowledge, which God had forbidden them to eat, and she gave Adam some of the fruit as well. As a result of their disobedience, Adam and Eve were driven from the Garden of Eden by God. Eve was condemned to give birth to children in great pain. She was the mother of Cain, Abel, and Seth (Gen. 2–4).

Exodus, OT: second book, telling of the escape of the Israelites from Egypt under Moses, of their life in the wilderness, of the sealing of the covenant between God and his people, and of the giving of the Ten Commandments (Ex. 20). It also gives detailed instructions for building and furnishing the Tabernacle.

Ezekiel, OT: book recounting the career of the prophet Ezekiel. He was a priest and one of the Jews carried into captivity in Babylon in 597 B.C. There he became the religious leader of the exiles and prophesied the destruction of Jerusalem; after this took place in 586 B.C., he prophesied its rebuilding and future greatness (Ezek. 37).

Ezra and Nehemiah, OT: originally one book in the Hebrew canon. It became two separate books in English Bibles, usually called I and II Esdras in the Vulgate Bible. These books continue the history of Israel that was begun in the Book of Chronicles, and purport to be written by Ezra, a Babylonian Jew of the fourth or fifth century B.C., and Nehemiah, fifth-century governor of Judea.

The Apocrypha contains two additional books known in English Bibles as I and II Esdras, and in the Vulgate as III and IV Esdras. The first is a Greek Septuagint version of the history contained in II Chronicles 35 to Nehemiah 8, the second, an apocalyptic work that is partly from the Christian era.

F

Fall, The: common name for Adam's and Eve's fall from grace and expulsion from the Garden of Eden after having eaten the fruit of the tree of knowledge (Gen. 3).

Four Horsemen of the Apocalypse, NT: allegorical riders who appear as ominous portents (Rev. 6: 1–8). They are subject to different interpretation, but usually the rider on the red horse personifies war, that on the black horse, famine, that on the pale horse, death, and that on the white horse, pestilence; together they represent the horrors of war.

G

Gabriel: in Jewish and Christian legend, the archangel who is the announcer of God's messages to men. He annouced to Zacharias that he would be the father of John the Baptist, and to Mary that she was to be the mother of Jesus (Luke 1). According to Christian legend, Gabriel will blow his horn to announce Judgment Day.

Gad, OT: son of Jacob and ancestor of one of the twelve tribes of Israel (Gen. 46).

Galatians, Epistle to the, NT: letter from the Apostle Paul addressed to the people of Galatia, a Roman province in Asia Minor. Paul warns them against pride and jealousy, and the guidance of false teachers; he also writes of his own life and mission, and follows with a careful analysis of the principles of Christian faith.

Galilee: northern portion of Palestine, extending as far east as the Jordan River. It was at one time a Roman province governed by a tetrarch. The Sea of Galilee, closely associated with the ministry of Jesus and his disciples, is the largest freshwater lake in the country, fed from the north and drained to the south by the Jordan River.

Gath, OT: home of the giant Goliath, and one of the principal cities of the Philistines, of which David sang in his lament when Saul and Jonathan died, "Tell it not in Gath" (II Sam. 1: 20).

Gaza: city by the Mediterranean Sea, about 40 miles southwest of Tel Aviv, Israel. Its known history dates back to the 1400's B.C., and it is mentioned several times in the Bible. During the 1100's B.C., it was the chief city of the Philistines. Samson carried off the gates of Gaza and was afterwards imprisoned there after Delilah betrayed him to the Philistines (Judg. 16).

Genesis (Greek for "beginning"), OT: first book, describing the Creation, and telling the stories of the three patriarchs, Abraham, Isaac, and Jacob (Israel). It concludes with the death of Joseph.

Gethsemane, NT: garden, probably on the slope of the Mount of Olives, where Jesus went with three of his disciples on the night before he was crucified. He was betrayed by Judas and captured in Gethsemane (Mark 14).

Gideon, OT: one of the judges of Israel, called Jerubbaal (Judges 6:25–32) because he cast down his father's altar to Baal. He and 300 Israelites put the Midianites, Amalekites, and their allies to flight by attacking their camp at night. Against the Midianites he led an army of 32,000 men and, by two tests, reduced their number to 300. The 300 threw the Midianites into panic by blowing the trumpets and breaking the pitchers.

Gilead: name given to a large, but not clearly defined, section of Palestine east of the Jordan. It is a hilly region of beautiful scenery and was noted for its rich balsam—balm of Gilead—that was used for the treatment of wounds. The phrase is now a figurative expression meaning anything that will soothe pain.

Gog and Magog: Magog, the second son of Japheth (Gen. X), later referred to as the land over which Gog, an enemy of God and Israel, is ruler (Ezek. 38). Later still, Gog and Magog are leaders of Satan's host at Armageddon (Rev. 20).

Golgotha (Aramaic for "skull"), NT: also called Calvary: scene of the Crucifixion of Jesus (Matt. 27: 33; Luke 23:

EVE, *grasping the fruit of the tree of knowledge, from a sculpture at the Cathedral of Autun, France. The temptation of Adam and Eve and their expulsion from the Garden of Eden were favorite themes of sculptors and painters in the Middle Ages and the early Renaissance (see* ART *volume).*

VANGUARD PRESS

33). Guides to modern Jerusalem hold it is where the Church of the Holy Sepulchre now stands.

Goliath, OT: Philistine giant whom David fought and slew (I Sam. 17).

Gomorrah: See *Sodom and Gomorrah.*

Goshen: northeastern part of Egypt, where the Israelites lived before the Exodus.

H

Habakkuk, OT: minor prophet who prophesied the devastations caused by the Chaldeans, which he saw as the punishment of the wicked, sent by God. His book concludes with a prayer of praise and adoration.

Hagar, OT: handmaiden of Sarah and mother of Ishmael by Abraham (Gen. 16). She and her son were sent away into the wilderness because the childless Sarah, Abraham's wife, was jealous. See also *Ishmael.*

Haggai, OT: prophet who urged the rebuilding of the Temple of Jerusalem after the Israelites returned from the Babylonian exile. The Book of Haggai tells how God spoke through Haggai and told the Israelites that their tribulations would cease as soon as they rebuilt the temple.

Ham, OT: one of the sons of Noah; traditionally the ancestor of the Egyptians and of other peoples of North Africa (Gen. 10).

Haman: See *Esther.*

Hannah, OT: childless wife of Elkanah, who vowed that if she were granted a child, he would be dedicated to the Lord. She became the mother of Samuel (I Sam. 1).

Harrowing of Hell: transformation of Hell from the abode of all dead souls to the exclusive province of the wicked. According to Christian legend (not supported by Scriptures but seemingly referred to in the Creeds), Christ descended into Hell after the Crucifixion. There he held judgment over the dead; those found worthy joined Christ in Paradise after the resurrection and ascension. Hell then became the place for sinners after death. See also *Hell.*

Heaven: in Judaism and Christianity, the firmament, believed to be the abode of God and innocent, righteous souls. Originally, in Judaism, Sheol was the province of all dead souls—a place neither of torment nor reward, but of lifeless existence cut off from God, similar to the Greek Hades. In the third and second centuries B.C., influenced by the Greek belief in Elysium as a blissful place for those favored by the gods, the Jews developed the concept of Heaven as the destination of the good after death. In the New Testament, Christ is believed to have come from, and returned to, Heaven (Mark 16), which is also the destination of his followers (John 14). He spoke of Heaven as "my father's house," a place where those who love God will dwell with him forever.

Hebrews, Epistle to the, NT: primarily an argument in favor of Christianity as the final and true religion; rather a sermon on faith than a letter. It is unlikely that Paul wrote it, and the precise group to whom it was addressed is not known.

Hebron, or Al-Khalil: city in ancient Palestine near Jerusalem. One of the oldest cities in the world, it is mentioned frequently in connection with David and Absalom (II Sam.). According to tradition, Abraham, Sarah, Isaac, Rebekah, Leah, and Jacob were buried in a cave at Hebron.

Hell: place of torment for the wicked after death. The idea developed from the ancient concept of the underworld, a gloomy place under the earth where the shades of the dead resided. In Western tradition, this idea was common to both the ancient Greek and Jewish religions; the Greeks called it Hades, after their god of death; the Jews called it Sheol, meaning "the grave." The Greeks also spoke of Tartarus, a region below Hades where those guilty of heinous crimes suffered unique punishments. Influenced by the Greeks and the Persians, the Jews developed the idea of judgment after death, with reward for the good in Heaven and punishment for the wicked in Gehenna (where punishment could not exceed twelve months except in cases of heresy).

The punishments of Hell are believed by most Christians to be eternal, but certain Protestant sects have developed the idea of Hell as a temporary state. This is akin to the Roman Catholic and Eastern churches' concept of purgatory, where basically good believers who died in sin are temporarily tormented until they are deemed purified enough to enter Heaven. Christ spoke of Hell as a place of "everlasting fire prepared for the devil and his angels" (Matt. 25: 41). He also spoke of the punishment of the wicked—primarily the rich, the selfish, and the hypocritical—in Hell, as in the parable of the rich man and Lazarus (Luke 16), and the parable of the talents (Matt. 25).

Hermon, Mount: beautiful, snow-capped mountain, 9200 feet high, on the border of Syria and Lebanon. It is often referred to in the Psalms, and was believed by some to be the Mount of Transfiguration (Mark 9: 2).

Herod: name of several puppet kings of Roman Palestine. Herod the Great, king at the time of the birth of Jesus, rebuilt the Temple and created a new port and capital city, Roman style, at Caesarea. His son, Herod Antipas, executed John the Baptist.

Hezekiah, OT: king of Judah, c 715–c 686 B.C. He joined with the neighboring countries to resist the Assyrians, which led to the invasion of the country, the plundering of many cities, and almost to the capture of Jerusalem. The miraculous affliction of the Assyrian army saved the city (II Kings 19). See also *Sennacherib.*

Hiram, OT: king of Tyre who helped Solomon to build the Temple at Jerusalem (I Kings 5).

Holy Land: name given to the former country of Palestine (now divided mostly between Israel and Jordan) because of its associations with Judaism and Christianity.

Holy of Holies: internal chamber of the Temple in Jerusalem. There, the Ark of the Covenant was kept sacred, and only the high priest was allowed to enter. See also *Ark.*

Horeb: See *Sinai, Mount.*

Hosea (meaning "deliver"), OT: one of the minor prophets who lived in the eighth century B.C. After Amos prophesied the destruction of the northern kingdom, Hosea saw the same catastrophe approaching and called the people to repent. He believed that if they repented, God would forgive and spare them. He spoke of the love of God for his people as like that of a husband and a father.

I

Imitation of Christ: devotional book written between 1390 and 1440, giving clear and simple instruction for modeling a Christian spiritual life on that of Christ. The authorship is generally credited to an Augustinian monk, Thomas à Kempis, although several other authors have been proposed; some authorities assert that it is the work of several unknown authors.

Isaac, OT: only son of Abraham and Sarah. He was born after God made a covenant with Abraham, and promised that the aged Sarah would bear a son. To test Abraham's faith, God told him to offer Isaac as a sacrifice. Abraham obeyed, but God intervened and saved the boy. Isaac married Rebekah, his kinswoman, and became the father of Esau and Jacob (Gen. 17; 21–22; 24–27). See also *Abraham.*

CULVER PICTURES

JERUSALEM, *from a photograph of the late 1800's, shows Christian, Jewish, and Islamic places of worship. The city is holy to all three faiths.*

Isaiah, or Isaias, OT: one of the major prophets (eighth century B.C.). He opposed joining the league against Assyria (Is. 7), and may have kept Jerusalem from sharing the fate of Damascus and Samaria. He also opposed seeking aid from the Egyptians, whom he did not trust. His faith that God would save Jerusalem led him to advise Hezekiah not to surrender to Sennacherib when the city was besieged in 701 B.C.; this may have postponed the downfall of Judah for over a century. Beginning with the 40th chapter, the Book of Isaiah is a Messianic prophecy in poetry; many scholars consider it a separate, later work. It has been taken by Christians to refer to the coming of Jesus.

Ishmael, OT: son of Abraham and Hagar, half-brother of Isaac, and ancestor of the Ishmaelites. He and his mother, a servant of Sarah, were cast out into the desert because of the jealousy of Sarah, Abraham's wife. "Ishmaelite" is proverbial for an outcast (Gen. 16; 17; 21; 25).

It is not known who the ancient Ishmaelites were, but the Arabs have considered themselves as descendants of Ishmael.

Israel (Hebrew for "contender with God"): name given to Jacob after he wrestled with the angel (Gen. 32: 28). The children of Israel were the twelve sons of Jacob and their descendants. The name "Israel" was applied to the twelve tribes until the division of the kingdom after the death of Solomon (c 934 B.C.). From then on it was applied to the ten tribes that made up the northern kingdom; the two tribes (Judah and Benjamin) of the southern kingdom were called Judah.

The northern kingdom was destroyed by the Assyrians (721 B.C.), however, and its people lost their political and cultural identity. The people of Judah came to be known as Jews. After returning from Babylonian captivity, this remaining fragment of the once-united nation of Israel resumed the name to indicate that they were the survivors and heirs of the faith of Israel.

J

Jacob, OT: son of Isaac, who with the help of Rebekah, his mother, tricked his father into giving him the blessing intended for his brother Esau (Gen. 27). His wives were Leah and Rachel, and he had twelve sons, founders of the twelve tribes of Israel. God told him his name would be Israel rather than Jacob (Gen. 35: 10). In his old age, Jacob took his family to Egypt, where the children of Israel eventually became slaves of the Egyptians.

Jael, OT: wife of Heber, remembered as a Jewish heroine. Sisera, leader of the Canaanites, who were fighting Israel, was fleeing for his life. Jael offered him hospitality, and while he slept she killed him by driving a tent nail into his temple (Judg. 4–5).

James, Saint, NT: son of Zebedee, brother of John, and one of the twelve apostles. He was killed by Herod Agrippa I. According to tradition, his body was carried to Spain, where his shrine at Santiago de Compostela attracts many pilgrims.

James, Saint "the Less," NT: one of the apostles. He is identified as the son of Alphaeus, but little is known about him. He has been identified with James, "the Lord's brother" (Gal. 1: 19), but this identification has been challenged by scholars.

Japheth, OT: third son of Noah (Gen. 5:32; 10:1). His descendants were supposedly the Indo-European peoples.

Jehovah (meaning "I am"): name by which God revealed himself to Moses (Ex. 3). Only the consonants JHVH (or YHWH) were used in the Hebrew, which is written without vowels; the four-letter name (called the Tetragrammaton) was too sacred to be spoken, and was read aloud as "Adonai" or "Elohim." The original pronunciation is probably "Yahweh."

Jehu, OT: soldier who became king of Israel after he had led a revolt against the house of Ahab and killed Jezebel and the kings of both Israel and Judah. A watchman recognized him by his chariot driving, "for he driveth furiously" (II Kings 9: 20), giving rise to the saying "to drive like Jehu."

Jephthah, OT: judge of Israel, who turned back the Ammonite invasion. Before the battle, he vowed to sacrifice the first living thing to meet him if he returned victorious. The first one to meet him was his daughter, his only child. Before she died, she was allowed to roam the hills for two months and mourn that she must die a virgin (Judg. 11–12); mourning her became a yearly ritual among young Israelite women.

Jeremiah, OT: one of the greatest Hebrew prophets. He began to prophesy about 626 B.C., when the Scythians were devastating Judah; he considered this God's punishment and called the people to reform. After the destruction of Jerusalem in 586 B.C., Jeremiah was taken to Egypt, where, tradition says, he was put to death.

Two books of the Old Testament are attributed to him. In addition to the Book of Jeremiah, he is believed to be the author of the Book of Lamentations, five poems about the sufferings of his people.

Jericho, OT: first city of importance captured by the Israelites under Joshua in their conquest of Canaan. Its walls fell down as a result of the Israelites' marching around the city, blowing their trumpets (Josh. 6).

Jeroboam, OT: first king of the northern kingdom of Israel (922–911 B.C.). He led the revolt of the ten tribes against Rehoboam, son of Solomon (I Kings 11–14). As king, he "led Israel into sin," namely idolatry. The same charge is made against another Jeroboam, son of Joash, king of Israel about 200 years later (II Kings 14: 24).

Jerusalem: city in the Judean Hills, a holy city for Jews, Christians, and Muslims. Jerusalem was captured from the Jebusites by David, who made it his capital (II Sam. 5). It has since been a center of religious and political activity, central in the later ministry of Jesus, in the Crusades, and in the history of Israel, both ancient and modern.

Jesse, OT: father of David (I Sam. 16), and so considered the source of Jesus' genealogy. The "tree of Jesse"—portraying Jesse as the root, with Christ and Mary as branches—was a favorite religious motif during the Middle Ages.

Jesus, also called Jesus of Nazareth and Jesus Christ, NT: considered by Christians the son of God as well as the central figure of the Christian religion. The principal sources for the events in Jesus' life are the first four books of the New Testament, the Gospels as told by the evangelists Matthew, Mark, Luke, and John. Indirect references to his teachings and to his early followers can be found in the writings of late first-century Jewish and Roman historians.

According to the Gospels, Jesus was born in Bethlehem, in Judea, near the Jewish religious center of Jerusalem. He grew up in Nazareth, in the Judean province of Galilee, then under the rule of the Romans.

In about 27 A.D., having been baptized by John the Baptist, Jesus began his ministry. He recruited twelve disciples and went about the countryside teaching in the synagogues, preaching to large crowds, and healing the sick. His teaching showed considerable knowledge of contemporary Jewish thought but was critical of the established leadership. He proclaimed the coming of a "kingdom of God" and was believed by his followers to be the Messiah, the savior foretold by the Hebrew prophets and awaited by the Jewish people.

Jesus became increasingly unpopular with Jewish religious leaders. In the third year of his ministry, when he was in Jerusalem for the Jewish feast of Passover, Jesus was betrayed to hostile authorities by his disciple Judas Iscariot in the garden of Gethsemane. He was arrested, accused of blasphemy, tried, and convicted by the ecclesiastical court for calling himself the son of God. Pontius Pilate, the Roman procurator of Judea, yielded to popular pressure and passed the death sentence. Jesus was crucified on a hill called Calvary (or Golgotha), near Jerusalem, and, according to Christian doctrine, rose from the dead on the third day.

JESUS CHRIST *as pictured by an artist more than 1000 years after the death of Christ.*

NORTH CAROLINA MUSEUM OF ART, RALEIGH

Jethro, OT: Midianite priest, the father-in-law of Moses (Ex. 2–3).

Jezebel: See *Ahab.*

Joab, OT: nephew of David and commander of his armies; a faithful but cruel soldier who was usually involved in David's court intrigues. He sent Uriah the Hittite to his death (II Sam. 11), and killed Absalom (II Sam. 18).

Job, OT: pious man who was tested by God and suffered many misfortunes. He was restored to health and prosperity in greater measure than before because he stood the test.

In the Book of Job, one of the most dramatic and poetic books of the Bible, Job debates this problem of evil—why God sends suffering—with his three friends, Eliphaz, Bildad, and Zophar ("Job's comforters"). They maintain that he must have sinned greatly to be afflicted as he is. When these three are silenced, a younger man, Elihu, takes up the argument. Then God answers Job out of the whirlwind, stressing his power and jurisdiction over men and all things.

Joel, OT: book of one of the minor prophets, who foretold a great locust plague in terms that suggest an invading army, and called the people to repentance. The date of the prophecy is uncertain.

John, NT: called the "beloved apostle." He is considered the author of the fourth Gospel, three Epistles, and Revelation. The Gospel According to St. John differs from the other Gospels in that it is not so much a history of the life of Jesus as it is an interpretation of his life and significance to the world, with special stress on the idea that Christ is the Word of God made flesh. See also *Revelation.*

John the Baptist, NT: son of Elizabeth and Zacharias, a kinsman and forerunner of Jesus who called the people to repent and prepare for the Messiah. He baptized his followers in the Jordan, and Jesus came to him and was baptized (Mark 3). John was decapitated at the order of King Herod when Salome asked for his head in return for dancing before the king (Matt. 14).

Jonah, OT: prophet who did not want to obey God's command to go to Nineveh and prophesy its destruction. He got on a boat going in the opposite direction, but the sailors, learning of his flight, threw him overboard to appease God during a storm.

The Lord prepared a great fish that swallowed Jonah (Jon. 1: 17). He remained in the fish for several days, but God heard his prayers and the fish vomited him out on dry land. Jonah then went to Nineveh and made his prophecy; the people repented and were spared. Jonah felt that God had made a fool of him, but was shown that Nineveh was more important than his pride. The fish that swallowed Jonah is called a whale only in the New Testament (Matt. 12: 40).

Jonathan, OT: eldest son of Saul and the close friend of David (I Sam. 18); Jonathan protected his friend from his father's wrath.

Jordan: river in the Middle East that flows south for some 200 miles in Israel and Jordan through the Sea of Galilee and into the Dead Sea.

The Jordan River is important in the history of Judaism and Christianity. After the exodus from Egypt, the children of Israel finally reached the Promised Land when they crossed the Jordan. Jesus was baptized in the Jordan by John the Baptist.

Joseph, OT: favorite son of Jacob. His brothers were jealous of him (particularly of the "coat of many colors" given him by his father), and they sold him to a band of Midianites who took him to Egypt. There he interpreted the Pharaoh's dream of fat and lean cattle, and of ripe and withered ears of corn, as meaning that seven years of plenty would be followed by seven years of famine. The Egyptians were prepared when the famine came, and so Joseph rose to great power and influence. During the famine, his brothers arrived to buy food and had to appeal to Joseph, whom they did not recognize. After a series of tests, Joseph revealed himself; the family was reconciled, and Joseph had them all come to settle in Egypt (Gen. 37–50).

Joseph, Saint, NT: Mary's husband, about whom little is known. He was a descendant of King David and was betrothed to Mary at the time of Jesus' birth in Bethlehem. He had had a vision assuring him that Mary's pregnancy was no impediment to their marriage; in Bethlehem, he was instructed to take Mary and Jesus to Egypt to escape Herod. When the family lived in Nazareth, he followed the trade of a carpenter (Matt. 1–2; Luke 1–3). Later, nonbiblical, works have stated that he was a widower with children when be was betrothed to Mary.

Joseph, Saint, of Arimathea, NT: wealthy Jew who buried the body of Jesus Christ in the tomb he had bought for himself. He held a high office, probably as a member of the Sanhedrin in Jerusalem. Evidently a secret follower of Jesus, he wished to give Jesus an honorable burial.

According to British legend, Joseph went to Britain to teach Christianity and founded the monastery at Glastonbury; he was believed also to have brought the Holy Grail to Britain.

Joshua, OT: successor of Moses as leader of the Israelites; their commander in the conquest of Canaan. The Book of Joshua gives an account of this conquest, including the famous Battle of Jericho. See also *Jericho.*

Josiah, OT: a king of Judah (640–609 B.C.). When the "Book of Law" was discovered in the temple and read to him, he instituted a great reform. He was killed in the Battle of Megiddo, attempting to resist an invasion of the Egyptians (II Kings 22–23).

Jotham, OT: youngest of the 70 sons of Gideon. He was the only one who escaped when his brother Abimelech killed the others, setting himself up as king. Jotham spoke against him and told the fable of the trees who chose a bramble as their king (Judg. 9).

Judah, OT: one of the sons of Jacob and ancestor of one of the twelve tribes, Judah, which united with that of Simeon to form the southern kingdom of Judah.

Judas, NT: one of the apostles of Jesus, possibly called Thaddaeus and Lebbaeus in other places (Mark 3:18; Matt. 10:3). He should not be confused with Judas Iscariot.

Judas Iscariot: apostle who betrayed Jesus for 30 pieces of silver and then hanged himself (Matt. 27). "Iscariot" seems to mean a man who comes from Kerioth, in Palestine. Many modern scholars believe that Judas was a political revolutionary, a Zealot, who betrayed Jesus because he thought Jesus had undermined the Zealot cause.

Judas Maccabeus: See *Maccabees.*

Judea: name of the southern division of ancient Palestine, the other two divisions of which included Samaria in the center and Galilee to the north. It covered the approximate area of the Old Testament kingdom of Judah, which was destroyed by Babylonia in 587 B.C. The area became known as Judea after Alexander the Great captured it in the fourth century B.C.

Jude, Epistle of, NT: one of the so-called catholic (universal) epistles, because it was addressed to Christians in general and not to a particular group. It warns against false teachings and false practices. The author refers to himself as "Jude . . . the brother of James," but little is known about him.

Judges, The Book of, OT: book that deals chiefly with the men and women who judged Israel. They were the rulers of the people for four centuries before the establishment of the kingdom. The book begins with the story of the death of Joshua and closes with records of the time of Samuel; it contains the stories of Gideon and of Samson.

Judith: heroine of the Apocryphal Book of Judith; she was a beautiful Jewish widow of the city of Bethulia when it was besieged by Holofernes, a general of Nebuchadnezzar. She went to his tent, and, when he was in a drunken sleep, cut off his head. The Jews were inspired by Judith's heroic deed to defeat their enemies and free their city.

K

Kings, Books of, OT: two historical books that continue the narrative in I and II Samuel. They begin with recounting the death of David and the choosing of Solomon as his successor, and end with the taking of Jerusalem and the carrying of the Jews in captivity to Babylon.

L

Laban, OT: brother of Rebekah, uncle of Jacob, and father of Jacob's wives, Leah and Rachel (Gen. 28–31).

Lamentations, OT: book of poetic laments over the fall of Jerusalem and the consequent sufferings of the Jews. The book is probably the product of several authors, although it has traditionally been assigned to Jeremiah.

Lazarus, NT: brother of Mary and Martha; he was raised from the dead by Jesus (John 11). In his parable of the rich man and the beggar, Jesus gave this name to the beggar (Luke 16).

Leah, OT: first wife of Jacob (Gen. 29–30).

Lebanon, Mount: a mountain region in Lebanon along the Mediterranean Sea where the famous cedars of Lebanon, prized from ancient times for their fragrance and hardiness, were found. In classical and biblical references to the cedars, they symbolize power and longevity. They were used by Solomon to build the Temple of Jerusalem (I Kings 5). A few groves still exist.

Levi, OT: one of the twelve sons of Jacob. He was the ancestor of the tribe that supplied the Levites, the priests and priests' helpers, for the other tribes of Israel (Josh. 18:7).

Leviathan, OT: formidable sea monster, used figuratively in passages that stress the great power of God the Creator (Job 41:1; Ps. 104:26; Isa. 27:1).

Leviticus, OT: third book, containing the laws and ordinances that governed the priests and people in their religious observances. The word means pertaining to the Levites, who were the priests.

Lot, OT: kinsman of Abraham who settled in the plain of Jordan. When the cities of Sodom and Gomorrah were to be destroyed, he was warned by an angel to fly from the region with his household and not to look back. Lot's wife did look back and was turned to a pillar of salt (Gen. 13; 19).

Lucifer (Latin for "light-bearer" or "morning star"): used originally in reference to the fall of the formerly splendid king of Babylon (Is. 14:12). The name became associated with Satan, the fallen archangel.

Luke, NT: Gentile, probably a Greek, who was a physician, a friend, and coworker with Paul. He was probably the author of the third Gospel and of the Acts of the Apostles. Both books are addressed to Theophilus, apparently a man of rank who was not familiar with the events recounted. The Gospel According to St. Luke is similar to Matthew's Gospel in that both have material that is not in Mark.

M

Maccabees: Jewish patriots of the second century B.C., notably Judas, called Maccabeus, whose restoration of the Temple of Jerusalem is commemorated in the Jewish festival of Hanukkah. The Apocryphal books I and II Maccabees give an account of their wars against Syria, as do III and IV Maccabees, which are not included in the Vulgate Bible or Protestant Apocrypha. (See also PEOPLE volume.)

Magdalene, or Mary of Magdala, NT: the woman from whom Jesus cast out seven demons (Luke 8). She is sometimes identified with the sinner who anointed his feet (Luke 7). The term is commonly used for a repentant fallen woman.

Magi, NT: three wise men from the East who brought gifts of gold, frankincense, and myrrh to the Christ child (Matt. 2). The word "magi," plural of *magus,* denotes a member of a Persian priestly caste. The biblical Magi were probably astrologers, guided to Bethlehem by the star. Later Christian legend calls them kings and gives them the names of Melchior, Gaspar, and Balthazar.

Magnificat, NT: first word (in Latin) of a canticle in which Mary tells her cousin Elizabeth the joyful news of her conception (Luke 1: 46–55). This song of praise, "My soul doth magnify the Lord," is used in the liturgies of the Roman Catholic and Anglican churches. Its many musical settings include a well known harmonized setting by Bach.

Malachi (Hebrew for "messenger"), OT: book written by a prophet about whom little is known. It deals chiefly with the need of keeping the law and with the coming judgment that will separate the wicked from the good.

Mammon, NT: personification of wealth, greed, and worldliness. Jesus taught that one cannot serve God and Mammon (Matt. 6:24; Luke 16:13).

Manasseh, OT: firstborn son of Joseph and ancestor of one of the twelve tribes called by his name. Another Manasseh was king of Judah (II Kings 21) who sacrificed infants to Moloch but later repented (II Chron. 33).

Mark, or John Mark, NT: author of the second Gospel. Very little is known about him. His Gospel is the shortest and is generally believed to be the earliest written of the four. Tradition links him to the founding of the Egyptian church, and he is the patron saint of Venice.

Martha, NT: practical sister of Mary and Lazarus of Bethany (Luke 10: 38–42). Her interest in serving food to Jesus is contrasted with Mary's spiritual hunger.

Mary, NT: name of several women: Mary Magdalene; Mary, the sister of Martha; Mary, mother of James and Joseph, and a witness of the Crucifixion (Mark 15: 40). Preeminent is the Virgin Mary, mother of Jesus, a descendant of the House of David espoused to Joseph at the time of the Annunciation (Luke 1: 26–38), and honored in Catholic churches; with the infant Jesus, she has been the subject of many of the world's greatest paintings.

Matthew, NT: one of the twelve apostles. According to tradition, he was the author of the first Gospel, although many scholars do not accept this. He was a publican (tax gatherer or customs officer) when Jesus called him (Matt. 9: 9). The Gospel According to Matthew begins with the genealogy of Jesus and his nativity, and ends with the announcement of the resurrection by the angel and the appearance of Jesus to his disciples with his last words to them (Matt. 28).

Matthias, NT: apostle chosen to take the place of Judas Iscariot among the twelve apostles (Acts 1: 26).

Melchizedek, OT: priest and king who bestowed a blessing on Abraham (Gen. 14; 18–20). In the New Testament, Christ is likened to Melchizedek (Heb. 5–7) since he also is both a priest and a king. The words "Thou art a priest forever, according to the order of Melchizedek" (Ps. 110) are used in the ordination of Roman Catholic priests, and his name is mentioned in the canon of the mass.

Messiah (Hebrew for "the anointed"): title both of the kings of Israel, especially Saul and David, and of the expected savior of Israel (Is. 9: 1–6; 11: 1; 40: 1–11). He is usually connected with the line of David. The messianic prophecies contain the most exalted imagery and the highest hopes of the great prophets—a common heritage of the pious Jew and the Christian believer. In the New Testament the Gospel of Matthew in particular points out the different ways that Jesus fulfilled these prophecies.

Methuselah, OT: grandfather of Noah, said to have lived to be 969 years old (Gen. 5: 27), thus inspiring the expression "old as Methuselah."

Micah, OT: minor prophet who was a contemporary of Isaiah. He prophesied that the coming destruction of Samaria and Jerusalem, a punishment for the sins of the people, would be followed by an age of deliverance and restoration. The Book of Micah is also notable for the prophecy that the Messiah would come from Bethlehem.

Michael: one of the archangels in Jewish, Christian, and Muslim tradition. He usually appears in the Bible as the militant leader of the angels, as guardian of the nation of Israel (Dan. 10: 13; 21), and leader of the heavenly forces in casting out the dragon (Rev. 12:7). In the Christian calendar, Michaelmas Day is September 29.

Midianites, OT: Arabian people sometimes identified with the Ishmaelites. A band of them carried Joseph to Egypt (Gen. 37: 28). Moses found refuge with them and married the daughter of their priest Jethro (Ex. 2: 15). They appear later as a hostile people against whom Gideon fought (Judg. 7).

Miriam, OT: sister of Moses and Aaron. She may have been the "sister" who watched the Pharaoh's daughter take the baby Moses from the Nile (Ex. 2: 1–5). When the Israelites had crossed the Red Sea, she led them in a celebration (Ex. 15: 20–21), but was made a leper because she joined Aaron in criticizing Moses' wife. Her affliction was later removed through the intercession of Aaron and Moses (Num. 12: 1–14).

Mizpah (Hebrew for "watch tower"), OT: name applied to several places.

NASH/MONKMEYER

MOSES, *the patriarch who led the Jewish nation out of bondage in Egypt, as portrayed by Michelangelo.*

When Jacob made his covenant with Laban, he gave the name to a heap of stones set up as a witness and said, "The Lord watch between me and thee, when we are absent one from another" (Gen. 31: 49).

Moab, OT: son of Lot, born of his incestuous union with his eldest daughter; also the kingdom of his descendants. The Moabites were among the most bitterly hated of the peoples that surrounded Judah. The ancient historian Josephus writes that the Babylonians subdued Moab in 582 B.C.; after that, nothing is known of them.

Moloch, OT: ancient Semitic god to whom living children were sacrificed. He is the same god as Milcom of the Ammonites.

Mordecai: See *Esther.*

Mosaic Law: law of the ancient Hebrews set forth by Moses. it contains the Ten Commandments, other laws of the Hebrew religion, and instructions for ritual. It is upon this code that Judaism was founded. See also *Ten Commandments.*

Moses, OT: great leader and lawgiver of the Jews in their exodus from Egypt and their 40-year journey to the Promised Land of Canaan. As an infant in Egypt, he escaped death when his mother hid him in an ark of bulrushes on the banks of the Nile; there he was found by Pharaoh's daughter and was brought up at court. When grown, he killed an Egyptian for striking a Jew and fled to Midian, where he married Zipporah (Ex. 2).

God appeared to Moses in a burning bush and told him to deliver his people from Egypt (Ex. 3). Moses and Aaron, his brother, appealed to Pharaoh, but only a series of dreadful plagues, culminating in the death of every Egyptian family's firstborn child, won the ruler's consent. As the Israelites left Egypt, the waters of the Red Sea divided for them to pass ahead of the pursuing Egyptians (Ex. 14).

Throughout the entire journey in the wilderness, Moses acted as leader of the Jews, transmitting to them the laws and instructions he received from God, though he met opposition. He received the Ten Commandments on Mount Sinai (Ex. 20) and engraved them upon stone tablets. He died at last on Mount Nebo, overlooking the Promised Land, where he could not go (Deut. 34).

Moses is one of the great heroic figures of Judaism; the first five books of the Old Testament (the Pentateuch) are called the "Books of Moses."

Mount of Olives, or Olivet: mountain ridge near Jerusalem. In the Old Testament, it was a place of refuge and prayer for David (II Sam. 15), and subject of a prophecy by Zechariah (Zech. 14: 4; Ezek. 11; 23). In the New Testament, it was a place Jesus often went, and the site of his last agony and his ascension.

N

Naaman: See *Elisha.*

Naboth: See *Ahab.*

Nahum, OT: one of the minor prophets, called "the Elkoshite." The Book of Nahum is an exultant chant of magnificent poetry written in anticipation of the fall of Nineveh.

Naomi: See *Ruth.*

Nathan, OT: prophet who rebuked David for his sin with Bathsheba (II Sam. 12).

Nathanael, NT: man who originally doubted that "any good thing can come out of Nazareth," but who was later convinced that Jesus was the Christ (John 1: 45–49).

Nazareth: city in modern Israel, the home of Jesus in his childhood and youth. Never mentioned in the Old Testament, it is mentioned frequently in the Gospels.

Nebuchadnezzar, or Nebuchadrezzar, OT: Chaldean king of Babylonia (605–562 B.C.). After he established his supremacy in western Asia in 605 B.C., he also received the submission of the Palestinian king, but Judah, despite the protests of Jeremiah, revolted. Nebuchadnezzar then took Jerusalem and carried the leading Jewish families to Babylon in 597 B.C., the First Captivity. The Second Captivity occurred in 586 B.C., when Zedekiah, the ruler appointed by Nebuchadnezzar, rebelled; Jerusalem was destroyed and the remaining Jews were taken to Babylon (II Kings 24–25).

Nehemiah: See *Ezra and Nehemiah.*

New Testament: See *Bible.*

Nicodemus, NT: Pharisee and ruler of the Jews who came to Jesus by night and received answers to his questions (John 3). He assisted Joseph of Arimathea in preparing the body of Jesus for burial (John 19:39).

Nimrod, OT: "mighty hunter" who built Nineveh (Gen. 10).

Nineveh: ancient city, the capital of Assyria, frequently mentioned in the Old Testament books of Jonah and Nahum. It was located on the Tigris River, across from modern Mosul, Iraq. Jonah was sent to warn the people to repent, and Nahum celebrated the city's destruction which occurred in 612 B.C. when the Assyrian Empire fell.

Noah, OT: hero of the flood story (Gen. 6–10). When God decided to destroy mankind because of the evil on Earth, Noah was chosen to take his family and two animals of each kind on an ark. After the flood had covered Earth and destroyed everything, Noah, his family, and the animals he had saved replenished the Earth.

Numbers, OT: fourth book, so named because it contains a census of the people. It also records various incidents concerning the Israelites during their wanderings in the wilderness.

O

Obadiah, OT: minor prophet whose book foretells the doom of Edom as a result of the Edomites' pride and their mistreatment of the Israelites.

Old Testament: See *Bible.*

P

Palestine, previously called Canaan: country occupied by the Israelites in biblical times. Now the republic of Israel, it lies between the Mediterranean Sea and the Arabian Desert.

Paul, NT: known before his conversion as Saul of Tarsus; a Jewish convert to Christianity who became the foremost missionary of the early church and the author of many epistles in the New Testament. See PEOPLE volume.

Pentateuch, OT: first five books, also called the Torah or the Five Books of Moses. They are: Genesis, Exodus, Leviticus, Numbers, and Deuteronomy.

Peter, NT: foremost apostle of Jesus and an early church leader. Originally called Simon, he was a fisherman of Capernaum, called by Jesus with his brother Andrew, according to two Gospels, to become a fisher of men. Jesus gave him the name of Peter (meaning rock), and said that he would found his church on him (Matt. 16: 17–19).

Peter was the first apostle to whom Jesus revealed himself after his resurrection; he took a leading part in the early history of the church, and is the central character of the first part of the Book of Acts. Later in life he went to Rome where, according to tradition, he was the first bishop of the Roman church, founder of the papacy, and the probable author of at least the first of the two New Testament Epistles named for him. He suffered martyrdom c 64 A.D.

Pharaoh: title of the king of Egypt. The pharaoh from whom the Israelites fled was probably Ramses II (1292–1225 B.C.). Pharaoh Necho II (609–593 B.C.) defeated Josiah at Megiddo in 609 B.C. but was defeated at Carchemish by Nebuchadnezzar in 605 B.C.

Pharisees: Jewish sect that stressed the importance of the oral law, believed to have been transmitted to Moses with the Torah. They believed in judgment after death and resurrection. They disappeared as a separate sect after the first century A.D. because their beliefs were assimilated into mainstream Judaism. In the New Testament, Jesus often criticized the Pharisees for their pride, exclusiveness, and rigidity.

Philemon, Epistle to, NT: short, personal letter from Paul asking Philemon to take back a runaway slave and promising to make good whatever loss the slave had caused him.

Philip, NT: one of the twelve apostles (Mark 3: 18).

Philippians, Epistle to the, NT: written by Paul during one of his imprisonments; he had gone to Philippi in answer to the call to "come over to Macedonia and help us" (Acts 16: 9); the letter is based on this personal acquaintance. It expresses his love, joy, and peace; unlike most of the Epistles, it attacks no error either of doctrine or of practice.

Philistines, OT: ancient people who lived along the Mediterranean coast (Philistia) when the Israelites were occupying Canaan. A civilized, town-dwelling people whose army had iron weapons, they dominated the area for many years and were a constant threat to the survival of the Israelites. Among the events characterizing the long enmity are the carrying off of the Ark of the Covenant (I Sam. 5–6), the defeat of the Israelite hero Samson (Judg. 16), and the battle of David with the Philistine champion Goliath (I Sam. 17). The Philistines eventually were conquered by Saul and David.

Pilate, Pontius, NT: Roman governor of Judea at the time of Jesus' trial. When he sentenced Jesus to death at the insistence of the high priests and the people, Pilate washed his hands before the crowd, saying, "I am innocent of the blood of this just person" (Matt. 27: 24).

Potiphar, OT: officer of Pharaoh. Joseph was sold into his service in Egypt and became his trusted steward. But when Joseph scorned the advances made to him by Potiphar's wife, she falsely accused him of attempting to seduce her, and Potiphar cast him into prison (Gen. 39).

Potter's Field: place for the burial of strangers and the poor, usually located next to but separate from a cemetery. The name comes from the New Testament: when the repentant Judas returned the 30 pieces of silver he was paid for betraying Christ, the chief priests "took counsel and bought with them the potter's field to bury strangers in"(Matt. 27: 7).

Proverbs, OT: book of maxims and longer poems of wisdom, many of which have been attributed to Solomon, famous for his wisdom.

Psalms, OT: book of lyrical religious poems, attributed to David. The Psalter or Book of Psalms was used as a hymn book in the Second Temple in Jerusalem. The Psalms express both personal and national feeling, and often rise to great heights of exaltation and beauty.

Q

Queen of Sheba, OT: wealthy Arabian queen who visited Solomon and was amazed at his wisdom (I Kings 1–10).

R

Rachel: See *Jacob.*

Rahab, OT: harlot of Jericho who aided the spies of Joshua and therefore was spared when the Israelites conquered the city (Josh. 2; 6).

Rebekah: See *Isaac; Jacob.*

Red Sea: inland sea between northeastern Africa and the Arabian peninsula. Its waters parted at the command of Moses, enabling the Israelites to pass through and escape from slavery in Egypt (Ex. 14: 21).

Rehoboam, OT: son of Solomon and king of Judah 931–914 B.C. Rather than reducing the heavy taxes levied earlier by Solomon, he declared that he would greatly increase them, thus bringing on the revolt of the ten northern tribes under Jeroboam, leaving only two tribes to form Rehoboam's kingdom of Judah (I Kings 12).

Reuben, OT: firstborn son of Jacob and Leah, and ancestor of one of the twelve tribes of Israel (Gen. 37:21–22; 46:8–9).

Revelation, also called the Apocalypse, NT: last book, traditionally ascribed to St. John the Divine, who is thought to have received the revelation on the island of Patmos. The book is addressed to the churches of Asia to encourage them in their faith. The highly figurative language makes the book difficult to interpret. It is concerned with Satan's attempt to destroy the church, the great judgment, and the final overthrow of Satan, who is to be cast into the bottomless pit while the church lives on as the bride of the lamb.

Romans, Epistle to the, NT: first of Paul's epistles in canonical order, though definitely not the first written. It was addressed to the congregation at Rome before Paul's visit to them (about 60 A.D.), and presents a full account of his ideas and purpose. It deals mainly with the idea that only righteousness is acceptable to God, and that one can be made righteous by faith through Christ's sacrifice.

Ruth, OT: book telling of the devotion of a Moabite woman, Ruth, to her Israelite mother-in-law, Naomi, and of Ruth's second marriage to Boaz, a wealthy Jew. The story ends with the statement that David was descended from Ruth and Boaz. Ruth's declaration of loyalty to Naomi, "Whither thou goest, I will go . . . thy people shall be my people . . . ," is sometimes used today in marriage ceremonies.

SATAN, *from Doré's illustrations for Milton's epic* Paradise Lost.

S

Salome, NT: daughter of Herodias; at the instigation of her mother, she asked for John the Baptist's head as a reward for dancing at Herod's feast (Mark 6: 22–25).

Samaritan: inhabitant of Samaria, which was one of the three main divisions of Palestine—between Judea on the south and Galilee on the north. Because of the enmity between Jews and Samaritans, both groups were surprised at Jesus' preaching to them (John 4), and at his featuring a Good Samaritan as a hero of one of his parables (Luke 10: 30–35).

Samson, OT: Hebrew champion and one of the judges of Israel (Judg. 13–16). In his inspired feats of strength, he bears a striking resemblance to Greek heroes such as Ajax or Hercules. His deeds include slaying a thousand Philistines with the jawbone of an ass and carrying off the city gates of Gaza. When he told the Philistine woman Delilah that his strength lay in his long hair, she cut it off while he slept; he was then captured by the Philistines, blinded, and forced to drive the grindstone in the prison house. When he recovered his strength, he pulled down the pillars of the temple in which the Philistines were gathered, thus killing numerous Philistines at the sacrifice of his own life.

Samuel, OT: early prophet and the official judge or leader of Israel before the establishment of the monarchy (I and II Samuel). As a child under the care of the priest Eli, he heard the voice of God and foretold the destruction of Eli's house. By divine command, he anointed Saul to be king; Saul proved unworthy and at God's command, he anointed David to succeed Saul at his death.

Sarah, or Sarai, OT: wife of Abraham and, in her old age, the mother of Isaac (Gen. 11–12; 16–18; 20–21).

Satan (Hebrew for "adversary"): opponent of God and of goodness, personified as the Prince of Darkness or the Devil. In the Book of Job (1–2), he is a cynical and skeptical being who has a special, if limited, jurisdiction on Earth. In the New Testament, he is called "that old serpent" (Rev. 12: 9; 20: 2), and hence identified with the tempter of Eve (Gen. 3). Matthew represents him as tempting Jesus (Matt.

4), and Peter describes him as walking about like a roaring lion "seeking whom he may devour" (I Pet. 5: 8).

Saul, OT: first king of Israel. He was a brave and patriotic man, but was given to brooding and to fits of violent jealousy. Saul freed his people from the Philistines, but was later defeated by them at Mount Gilboa. He took his own life to avoid being captured (I Sam. 9–31).

Saul of Tarsus, NT: name of Paul before his conversion (Acts 9). See also *Paul.*

Semites: traditionally, descendants of Shem, one of Noah's three sons (Gen. 10–11). In the modern world, Semites (a word derived from Shem) are represented by Jews and Arabs. But in antiquity, his descendants included the Assyrians, Babylonians, Phoenicians, Canaanites, and Hebrews.

Sennacherib, OT: king of Assyria in about the eighth century B.C. During his siege of Jerusalem in 701, a plague broke out in his camp, forcing his army to withdraw; the biblical explanation (II Kings 19: 35) is that the angel of the Lord smote the invaders. See also *Hezekiah; Isaiah.*

Septuagint (Latin for 70): See *Bible.*

Seth, OT: third son of Adam and Eve, born after the death of Abel (Gen. 4:25).

Shadrach, Meshach, and Abednego, OT: three young Jewish men of sixth-century Babylon. With their friend Daniel, they were raised in the royal court with other outstanding young men of Judah. They held to their Jewish faith, however, even after they had risen in the royal administration, and were condemned to be thrown into a fiery furnace because they would not worship a golden image that the king had set up. An angel appeared in the furnace, and the three emerged unharmed, which so impressed Nebuchadnezzar that he gave orders to respect their God, and gave them even higher posts in Babylon (Dan. 1–3).

Shem, OT: oldest son of Noah (Gen. 5: 32). See also *Semites.*

Shibboleth, OT: word the Gileadites used as a test to distinguish the Ephraimites (Judg. 12: 6). The Ephraimites pronounced the word *sibboleth,* for they did not know the "sh" sound. The term is now used for a word, manner of speaking, or custom that betrays its user as belonging to a particular group or class.

Shiloh, OT: place where the Tabernacle was set up (Josh. 18: 1) and the Ark of the Covenant remained when not carried into battle (I Sam. 4: 3–6).

Silas, NT: companion of Paul; he was also a prophet (Acts 15: 32).

Simeon, OT: son of Jacob and Leah, and ancestor of one of the twelve tribes of Israel (Gen. 29; 34; 37; 42–49). In the New Testament, another Simeon was a holy old man in the Temple at Jerusalem who declared that the infant Jesus was the savior and prophesied his future (Luke 2: 25–35).

Simon, NT: name of nine men, among the better known of whom are: Simon Peter (see also *Peter*); Simon the Canaanite, one of the twelve apostles; the man who carried Jesus' cross on the way to Calvary (Mark 15: 21); and Simon Magus, a famous sorcerer converted by Philip, who sought to buy the power he saw in the apostles (Acts 8: 9–24).

Sinai, Mount, also called Mount Horeb, OT: the peak on which Moses talked with God and received the Ten Commandments (Ex. 3; 19). It is in the southern Sinai peninsula.

Sodom and Gomorrah, OT: cities of the plain, destroyed by God with fire and brimstone because of their wickedness (Gen. 19). Only Lot and his family were allowed to leave, with the aid of angels.

Solomon, OT: son of David and second king of the united nation of Israel (I Kings; II Chronicles). He became king in the tenth century B.C., and during his reign he extended his dominion by peaceful alliances, which were often sealed by marriage. He built a gorgeous palace for himself; many people, including the Queen of Sheba, were dazzled by his magnificence. In building the Temple of Jerusalem, he gave the Jews an inspiration that long outlasted the temple itself, but he himself was led astray by his wives to worship other gods. Solomon was credited not only with great riches but with great wisdom; much of the Book of Proverbs, as well as the Song of Songs, has traditionally been attributed to him.

Song of Songs, OT: called in the King James Version The Song of Solomon; also often called Canticles, it is a poetic book traditionally considered the work of King Solomon, but now regarded as a group of marriage songs. Many religious interpretations have been given to it.

Stephen, Saint, NT: first Christian martyr. For accusing the Sanhedrin of persecuting prophets and of causing Christ's death, he was stoned to death. Saul of Tarsus (later Paul) participated in his murder (Acts 6–7).

Summa Theologica (Latin for "summary of all theology"): major treatise by the medieval philosopher and theologian St. Thomas Aquinas, dating from c 1265–1274, and, for several centuries following, an important codification of the Roman Catholic Church's doctrinal thought. It has three sections. The first is about God's existence and nature, and about the universe; the second deals with moral theology; and the third, unfinished at Aquinas's death, is about revealed religion and the sacraments.

Susanna: Apocryphal book that is an addition to the Book of Daniel. The beautiful young wife of a rich Jew of Babylon, Susanna was surprised by two elders while bathing in her private garden. When she turned down their propositions, they charged her, before the assembly, with entertaining a young lover. By examining her accusers separately, Daniel discovered their falsity and had them punished, and Susanna's name was cleared.

T

Tabernacle: portable place of worship in which the Ark of the Covenant was housed. Carried by the Jews during their wanderings in the wilderness, it was built by Moses according to detailed instructions from God (Ex. 25–27; 30–31; 35–40). This tentlike structure was always placed in the center of every camp where the Israelites halted.

In the Roman Catholic Church, the term indicates the small cupboardlike container on an altar where the Host is reserved.

Talmud: compilation of Jewish oral law arising from discussions and applications of the Torah, the written law. It is divided into two parts: the *Mishna,* in Hebrew, completed in 200 A.D., which contains the commentaries of many earlier generations of scribes; and the supplementary *Gemara,* in Aramaic. The Talmud is not only a collection of legal decisions but a repository of knowledge about religion, philosophy, history, astronomy, ethics, medicine, and folklore. In the Middle Ages, when most Europeans were illiterate, many Jews derived intellectual stimulation from Talmudic studies.

Ten Commandments, or Decalogue, OT: series of laws given by God to Moses on Mt. Sinai. These laws form a basis for the Jewish, Christian, and Muslim ethical systems. The text of the Decalogue is given in Exodus 20 and Deuteronomy 5, but various groups disagree on the numbering of the commandments.

In general, the commandments prohibit stealing, killing, adultery, bearing false witness, or coveting another's possessions; they command worship of one God, keeping the Sabbath, and honoring one's parents.

Thaddaeus, NT: one of the twelve apostles, apparently sometimes called Judas (not Iscariot) and sometimes Lebbaeus.

Thessalonians, Epistles to the, NT: two letters written by Paul to the church at Thessalonica, a city in Macedonia. They show his affection for his converts and his indignation at those who were hindering the spread of Christianity.

Thomas, NT: "doubting apostle" who refused to believe in the Resurrection until he had seen Jesus' wounds with his own eyes and touched him with his own hands (John 20: 24–29).

Timothy, NT: disciple and fellow worker of Paul; he remained close to the apostle to the end of his life. Paul's Epistles, I and II Timothy, are filled with friendly advice about carrying on their work.

Titus, Epistle to, NT: letter of advice from Paul to one of his missionary assistants.

Tobit: Apocryphal book telling the story of a good man named Tobit who lost his eyesight, but had it restored. The central part of the story is concerned with the journey of Tobit's son, Tobias, and his marriage to a woman whose seven previous husbands had all been killed by an evil spirit. The angel Raphael, who guided Tobias on his journey, taught him how to banish the evil spirit and to cure the blindness of Tobit.

Torah: first five books of Jewish Scriptures, also called the Pentateuch. Torah also refers to the parchment scrolls on which the books are written, and which are used for liturgical purposes. See also *Pentateuch.*

Twelve Tribes of Israel, OT: divisions of the ancient Hebrew nation that descended from the twelve sons of Jacob, to whom God gave the name Israel.

The descendants of Joseph split into two tribes named after his sons, still making twelve tribes because the sons of Levi became a priestly caste. See also *Israel.*

U

Ur: known in the Bible as Ur of the Chaldees; ancient city of the Sumerian civilization and the home of Abraham, father of the Hebrews. The site of ancient Ur lies about 140 miles south of Babylon. It was the capital of a small wealthy empire during the third millenium B.C. Most of the great ziggurat of Ur is still standing. The royal tombs, excavated during the 20th century, revealed the ancient practice of burying a king's servants and officials with him.

V

Vulgate (Latin for "popular speech"): See *Bible.*

W

Wisdom Literature: name applied to some ancient Oriental texts and to several books of the Bible that contain philosophical speculation and ethical maxims. Sometimes the philosophy is in brief proverbs, as in the Book of Proverbs; sometimes it is in essays; and sometimes it is in parables and dialogues, as in the Book of Job. Ecclesiasticus and the Wisdom of Solomon in the Apocrypha are also works in this same spirit.

Wisdom of Solomon, or Book of Wisdom: book of the Apocrypha; not proverbs but rather discourses on wisdom as the governing power of the world and its salvation. It was written in Greek, probably in the first century B.C., and is not the work of King Solomon.

THE TORAH *is used in Jewish religious services. The Hebrew text is written on parchment and kept in the ancient form of a scroll.*

ARNOLD EAGLE

Z

Zaccheus, NT: wealthy tax collector who, being short, climbed a tree to see Jesus as he passed (Luke 19: 2–10). Noticing him, Jesus spoke to him and asked to be a guest in his house; Zaccheus later gave half his wealth to the poor.

Zacharias, NT: priest to whom the angel Gabriel appeared, announcing that he and his wife Elizabeth, despite their old age, would become parents of John the Baptist. Because Zacharias questioned the angel's words, he was struck dumb until the child was born (Luke 1).

Zealots: radical Jewish political group that flourished about the time of Jesus. Inheritors of the Maccabean tradition, the Zealots violently opposed Roman rule. They were instrumental in raising the revolt that began in 66 A.D., and ended with the razing of the Temple in Jerusalem in 70 A.D. One of the apostles, Simon, was a Zealot (Acts 1: 13). Some believe that Judas Iscariot was one. He may have expected Jesus to overthrow Roman rule.

Zechariah, OT: one of the minor prophets who, with Hagai, urged the rebuilding of the Temple of Jerusalem in about 520 B.C., after the Jews returned from the Babylonian captivity. His prophecy is given in the form of visions. Only the first eight chapters of the Book of Zechariah are usually assigned to him.

Zephaniah, OT: minor prophet whose dominant theme was that the "day of the Lord" was coming upon his people as a result of their sins. He prophesied c 640–625 B.C., during the reign of Josiah.

Zion: originally the name of the eastern one of the two hills of Jerusalem. The name came to stand for Jerusalem, or sometimes the kingdom of Judah. Jerusalem is also called the daughter of Zion. In Christian hymns and literature, Zion stands for the heavenly city or the perfect community on Earth.

PHILOSOPHY

Philosophy is a subject that considers questions stemming from reflections on everyday events in life. The term philosophy comes from the ancient Greek, meaning *love of wisdom.* The ancient Greeks were not the first people to pursue the subject, but they were the first to leave a rich body of writings in philosophy. The philosophical questions they discussed are very much like the questions thoughtful people wonder about today, and will continue to wonder about for all time.

For example, a few moments before you awake in the morning, you think you see your blue sweater lying on a chair by your bed. Later, when you awake, you notice that your blue sweater is not lying on the chair. You wonder if someone has moved it, since you saw it there just moments ago. But, you realize, no one is home but yourself, and you do not remember moving the sweater.

You then begin to doubt whether you saw the sweater there at all. Perhaps it was only a dream. Yet your recollection is so real! How do you *know* what really happened? Once you ask this question, you have opened one of the doors to philosophy. Philosophy is the search for answers to this question and to related ones. Reaching entirely adequate answers to such baffling questions is far more difficult than it seems, yet the search itself is exciting and illuminating.

One of the numerous questions we will examine in this article is, "What is knowledge in general?" If we could answer this broad question, perhaps we could answer the specific question about the blue sweater and a related one: "How do we distinguish between events that happen in our minds and those that happen in the world of physical objects?" We may wonder what led us to dream in the first place: we didn't *choose* to dream about the blue sweater. What caused us to dream about it, and why weren't we free to dream about something else? All of these questions have been asked over and over during the history of philosophy.

In thinking of this vast world of minds and physical objects in which we live, people have long been moved to wonder how this world came to be and how it is organized or governed. Many have concluded that God created the world and that He has some part in its organization and governance. How we know whether God exists is another important philosophical question that will occupy our attention.

ANDERSON/ART REFERENCE BUREAU

REALITY AND ILLUSION *are the concerns of philosophers and artists alike, as suggested by this drawing by Goya.*

Philosophy and Theology

In early times, there was no clear distinction between philosophy and theology on the one hand, and philosophy and science on the other. Only in modern times have these subjects gained fairly clear boundaries, although there are still areas where they overlap. Theology is the study of God and His relationship to the world. Philosophy, like theology, is concerned with the characteristics that we ascribe to God and with arguments about God's existence. The nature of the arguments that philosophy and theology employ, however, are rather different.

To appreciate this difference, we must first understand what is meant by an argument. An argument is a unified collection of reasons in support of a specific conclusion, such as "God exists." If we claim that it will rain today because there are dark clouds overhead, and it usually rains when there are dark clouds overhead, we have offered an argument in support of our conclusion that it will rain today. We encounter arguments in virtually every phase of life.

In theology, authoritative arguments may be drawn from holy writings or from commentaries written by recognized church fathers. By contrast, the reasons offered in philosophy rely on experiences common to everyone, ideas thought to be inherently reasonable, or conclusions of other arguments. Whereas theology may appeal to authority, philosophy does not. The theologian may hold a belief not because he has a strong argument to support it, but because he has *faith* in it or in the reasons leading up to it. The philosopher, on the contrary, believes only when he has strong reasons to support his belief. To recognize a strong argument is, he says, to use his *reason.* The possible relationship between faith and reason is a problem that has occupied both philosophers and theologians.

Philosophy and Science

Philosophy and science share many of the same concerns. Both seek to understand the ultimate nature of the world, and both do so in part by constructing imaginative hypotheses or theories, and by deducing various consequences from these hypotheses. Their methods, however, diverge in many ways. The scientist often tests a theory by designing an elaborate experiment. The philosopher relies on observations that nearly every person of normal physical abilities can make. Whereas the scientist often uses mathematics to deduce his conclusions, the philosopher rarely does so, although he is often intrigued by mathematics. The scientist rarely questions why mathematics is useful in his work, but the philosopher may study how mathematics is essential to the scientist's work and judges the extent to which scientific methods are valid.

Ancient Philosophy

The Pre-Socratics

The close affinity between science and philosophy has been evident since the time of the earliest philosophers of ancient Greece.

These early philosophers, whose writings have come down to us in fragments, are called the pre-Socratics because they predate Socrates and the "golden age" of Greek philosophy.

Thales (640?–546 B.C.), of the city of Miletus, is recognized as the first philosopher. He was also an astronomer who predicted a solar eclipse, probably in 585 B.C. Thales wanted to know the ultimate nature of physical objects, and he maintained that everything is composed of water. Although his idea may strike us as silly today, it reveals two features of a good philosopher—concern with explaining the complexity of things in terms of an apparently simple idea, and reliance upon pervasive features of the world in doing so.

One difficulty in ascertaining the ultimate nature of things has always been the constant change and movement that we find all around us—the sun moves across the sky, night falls, birds fly, trees grow and sway in the breeze, and people act. Heraclitus (c 540–c 470 B.C.) was a philosopher who argued that *everything* is in a state of perpetual change. He is renowned for his remark, "You cannot step into the same river twice, for fresh waters are always flowing by."

Many people seek things that do not change in a world that is never static. Parmenides (c 450 B.C.) responded to Heraclitus by arguing not merely are there things that do not change, but that, despite all appearances, *nothing* ever changes at all! There is, he said, just one unchanging thing. He defended his position with clever and provocative arguments that Plato later reconstructed in his dialogue, the *Parmenides.* Parmenides influenced his student Zeno (c 490–c 430 B.C.), who devised several related arguments (called Zeno's Paradoxes) to show that motion is impossible. The arguments of Parmenides and Zeno are important because their conclusions seem so mistaken, yet the flaws in the arguments are very difficult to discover. Without discovering them, we cannot be sure that another convincing argument whose conclusion is apparently correct is not in fact riddled with flaws as well.

Another Pre-Socratic, Democritus (c 460–c 370 B.C.), argued that there was not one unchanging thing in the world, but many. These things he called *atoms.* He argued that they constituted all things, but that they themselves were indivisible, indestructible, and always in motion. More than 2000 years later, these ideas were adopted and developed by chemists whose atomic theory of matter was the forerunner of today's physical and chemical theories.

Perhaps the most famous of the Pre-Socratic philosophers is Pythagoras (c 582–c 500 B.C.). He was also an important student of mathematics and music. One of his school (not necessarily Pythagoras himself) discovered the Pythagorean theorem, which states the relationship of the lengths of the sides of a right triangle, familiar to every student of geometry. Pythagoras declared that everything is composed of numbers. He was one of the first to recognize the importance of mathematics for understanding and controlling the physical world.

Socrates

One of the most revered figures in the history of philosophy is Socrates (470?–399 B.C.). He was an Athenian who wandered about the city, engaging people in philosophic conversation. Contemporary accounts suggest that he was physically unattractive and badly clothed. Our knowledge of Socrates, though, derives mainly from the dramatic dialogues of Plato (427–347 B.C.), who was one of Socrates' students, and who himself was to become a great philosopher. In Plato's dialogues, Socrates appears as an amusing individual, able to converse wittily and wisely all day and all night.

Socrates often raises a question with a person, elicits a brief and confident answer from him, and then proceeds to raise further questions that cast doubt on the original answer. He ultimately concludes that the true answer to the question is very difficult to find after all.

An example of this Socratic method occurs in the dialogue the *Euthyphro,* in which the major question is, "What is piety?" Euthyphro, a pompous man, replies that piety is what he is doing now (filing questionable murder charges against his father). Socrates relies that he is not seeking an *example* of piety. Rather, he wants to know "what is the essential form of piety which makes all pious actions pious?" Euthyphro then declares that "piety is what is pleasing to the gods." But Socrates answers that what is pleasing to the gods—or to God, as we would say—is so because He loves it, whereas what is pious is *not* so because He loves it. To the contrary, God loves something *because* it is pious. Consequently, what is pious is not the same thing as what is pleasing to God, although the two may often be found together. This argument provokes discussion up to the present day. Socrates concludes that he does not know what piety is, while Euthyphro scurries away, too weak to admit that he is ignorant.

From this and other dialogues, one can see how Socrates could inspire the love and devotion of his students, while reaping the ill will of individuals who resented being made to appear foolish. He was also not quite the humblest of men—he often remarked that he knew nothing, but was wiser than others because he knew that he knew nothing.

Eventually, the enemies of Socrates brought a false charge against him, that of impiety, the very notion he had investigated with Euthyphro in the dialogue just discussed. The formal indictment accused him of corrupting the young and of preaching that the Greek gods do not exist.

Plato describes the trial of Socrates in the *Apology* (meaning "the explanation"). Socrates plainly refutes the charges, but is judged guilty. During the month before his execution, Socrates' friend Crito visits him, as described in the dialogue by that name, and tries to persuade him to let his friends carry out their plan for his escape. But Socrates refuses, arguing that even though the laws of Athens have been unjustly applied in his case, he would be wrong to violate them by trying to escape.

The *Phaedo* describes his last day in this life. He is calm, and offers several arguments in support of his belief that the human soul is immortal. He looks forward to his future life, in which he can pursue his questions without being put to another death. Finally, with his friends sitting by, softly weeping, he drinks the poison hemlock, lies down, and dies.

Plato

After Socrates' death, Plato wrote a number of his Socratic dialogues in the manner of his teacher and friend. Socrates continues to be a character in Plato's dialogues, but the subject matter broadens and the views change in the later dialogues, reflecting more of Plato and less of Socrates.

The state and the soul. Plato was deeply concerned with creating a government that would be free of the evils he saw around him. His major work, the *Republic,* reveals much of his philosophy of the ideal government. The central question of this dialogue is "What is justice?" but the work also considers the nature of the soul or mind and the nature of knowledge. After rejecting various common definitions of justice, the character Socrates suggests that since justice is thought to be a property of both individuals and states, and since states (or countries, as we sometimes say) are so very much larger than individuals, we should begin by investigating justice within the state, where it will be more easily discerned. He then argues that an ideal, just state is one in which everyone performs his or her proper function. Some should be craftsmen, others farmers, still others hunters, etc. When people do not perform their proper function, they create an unjust society.

All people, the *Republic* argues, can be divided into three classes—the rulers, the guardians, and the common people. These classes correspond to the sections or parts of the human soul—the rational, the spirited, and the appetitive. The rational represents our understanding, the spirited pursues honor, and the appetitive desires the pleasures of sex, food, sleep, and drink. Any two of the three can be in conflict. For example, when one desires to drink, but refrains from doing so because he believes the water is polluted, the appetitive part of his soul is in conflict with the rational part, or reason. In this and other situations, the just state of the soul consists of the rational part controlling the other two.

In another dialogue, the *Phaedrus,* Plato offers an allegorical description of the relationship among the three parts of the soul in love. The soul is a chariot, controlled by a horseman (the rational) and drawn by two powerful horses, one white (the spirited element), the other black (the appetitive element). The white horse is generally obedient to the charioteer. The black horse, overcome with sexual desire for the beloved, is more difficult. Only when the charioteer controls and the horses pull together is the soul in balance or harmony.

Forms and knowledge. Influenced by both Heraclitus and Parmenides, Plato distinguishes two worlds—one constantly in change, the other wholly without change. The World of Change or Becoming is the world of appearance, which we perceive by means of our five senses. Since our senses often deceive us, the world of appearance does not offer us genuine knowledge. It provides us, at best, with the source of everyday beliefs or opinions, which, unlike knowledge, are often false.

In sharp contrast, the world without change is the World of Reality or Being, not mere appearance. It is invisible to our senses, but is apparent to our reason. Plato calls the real objects of knowledge Forms. They include the Forms of justice, beauty, truth, and love, as well as roundness, heaviness, hardness, and softness. These Forms are what ultimately gives objects in the world of appearance their properties or characteristics. The Forms themselves are not part of the world of appearance. Yet the Form of justice, for example, makes all just actions just; the Form of beauty makes all beautiful things beautiful; and the Form of softness makes all soft things soft.

In general, there is a Form corresponding to every adjective or verb, although Plato hesitates to admit the existence of a Form of dirt and a few others. He divides the world of Forms into two groups, mathematical objects and the rest, claiming that our knowledge of mathematical objects is different from our knowledge of other Forms. Mathematics begins with premises from which we deduce theorems. But since we cannot verify these premises, our knowledge of theorems is not of the highest kind.

The Good. At the top of the World of Being is the greatest Form of all, the Good, the source of all good things in the universe, and what later thinkers often likened to God. To understand the Good is the highest aim of Plato's philosophy. Through the search for the Good, Socrates' pursuit of the definition of important concepts has been transformed by Plato into an almost religious quest. Plato argues that only a philosopher with the proper training can hope to experience this vision of the Good. Once the philosopher does so, and only then, can he be fit to become a philosopher-king and rule the ideal state.

Aristotle

Plato's best student was Aristotle (384–322 B.C.), the other Greek philosopher whose ideas have so greatly influenced the thought of Western civilization. Aristotle studied at Plato's Academy for 20 years, until Plato's death. He tutored the young Alexander the Great, and founded his own school, the Lyceum, in Athens. When Alexander died, the Athenians revolted and threatened to kill Aristotle because of his earlier association with the cruel conqueror. Aristotle fled Athens, vowing that "Athens would not sin twice against philosophy." He died a year later.

In numerous respects, Aristotle's ideas contrast with those of Plato. This can be seen in his view of Plato's

IDEAL FORM *was sought by the Greeks in thought and art, as in these temple statues* (left). *Early oriental carvings* (right) *were intended to gain liveliness and appeal through exaggeration instead.*

METROPOLITAN MUSEUM OF ART, PURCHASE, 1890, LEVI HALE WILLARD BEQUEST

CEYLON (SRI LANKA) TOURIST BOARD

Forms. Plato argued that Forms must exist independent of the world of sense experience. Aristotle argued to the contrary, that the forms, or *universals,* to use his terminology, must exist *within* our world of sense experience in order for them to truly explain why physical objects have the properties they do. He criticized Plato for maintaining that the universal is something even capable of existing independent of things in the sensory world; he believed that a universal is what "is said of" things, and thus is dependent upon them. It is not clear whether Aristotle meant that universals are *in* objects themselves or whether they are simply ideas. This issue has been discussed (and argued) ever since.

Four causes. Aristotle distinguished four causes to explain the occurrences of our world. The *material* cause is the stuff of which something is composed; the stone or wood constituting a statue is its material cause. The *efficient* cause is the sequence of events that bring something about; the sculptor's working with his hammer and chisel to turn the stone into a statue is an example. The *formal* cause is the pattern or idea that sets limits to the object and makes it what it is; in the statue, this is the shape that the sculptor keeps in mind as he works (in a living organism, the formal cause is its soul). The *final* cause is the purpose or end for which something occurs, such as the payment the sculptor looks forward to receiving once he completes the statue.

The formal cause or form (not capitalized, as with Plato) was one of Aristotle's central concepts. It relates to his notions of potentiality and actuality. Without form, matter is simply potentiality; it is able to *become* actual matter of our sensible world, but is in fact not yet real or actual matter. Once it acquires form, it is actual matter. Indeed, the more form something has, the more actual it is.

Aristotle distinguished three types of soul, each having more form and more actuality than the preceding one. The first is the *vegetative* soul, which enables the body to grow and to provide itself with its necessary nutrients or food; plants have this soul. The second is the *animal* soul, which is the source of the power of sensation and of motion that animals possess. Finally, there is the *rational* soul, which thinks; it characterizes man and the gods. Aristotle generally argued that every type of "soul is inseparable from its body." Just as "the wax and the shape given to it by the stamp are one," so are the soul and the body one. At other times, however, he suggested that the rational soul may be separable from the body, and thus that the rational soul may be immortal, as Plato argued.

The first mover. Aristotle's thoughts on motion led him to formulate an interesting argument for the existence of God (or of several gods). He argued that every moving thing must be moved by something. Where a moving thing is moved by another moving thing (as when a baseball is moved by a player's throwing arm), "that again is moved by something else in motion, and so on." But, "the series cannot go on to infinity; there must be some first mover." This first mover is God. Aristotle wrote that this first mover is itself unmoved, forever contemplating itself, and is pure thought and nothing else. Aristotle's conception of God differed from the Judeo–Christian conception, since in contemplating itself alone, it does not concern itself with the affairs of man at all.

Logic. One of Aristotle's great achievements was his work in logic, which he considered to be the study of demonstration or deductive argument, the means by which we acquire new knowledge from old. The focus of Aristotle's logic was his investigation of a class of arguments called *syllogisms.* Each of these consists of two premises and one conclusion; three *terms* are involved (a different pair in each of the premises and the conclusion). The standard example is:

All men are mortal.
All Greeks are men.
Hence, all Greeks are mortal.

Here, the terms are *men, mortal,* and *Greeks.* This syllogism is *valid*: if the premises are both true, the conclusion must be true as well. Aristotle attempted to distinguish all the valid forms of the syllogism from the *invalid* ones. An example of an invalid syllogism is: "All apples are fruits. Some apples are red. Hence, all fruits are red." Here, the premises are true, but the conclusion is false; the argument is therefore invalid.

There are some flaws in Aristotle's logic. He exaggerated the importance of the syllogism to the exclusion of other forms of valid reasoning. Yet his successors were so impressed with his work that they did not develop this subject significantly until the 1800's. Nonetheless, logic, like much of the rest of philosophy, owes its beginnings to Aristotle.

Later Philosophers

After Plato and Aristotle, the ancient period produced several notable philosophers. Epicurus (342?–270 B.C.) and Marcus Aurelius (121–180 A.D.) were the principal representatives of two schools of *ethics,* the study of how men ought to behave. The Epicureans emphasized finding happiness in everyday pleasures of this world. The Stoics, of whom Marcus Aurelius (Emperor of Rome) is a late representative, stressed a more sober approach, disciplining themselves for whatever life might bring. They sought to remain placid and unchanged through both good and ill fortune. Plotinus (205?–270? A.D.) was the most prominent philosopher of the Neo-Platonist school, which extended and developed Plato's thought. None of these philosophers were of the stature of the two great thinkers of Greece, however.

Medieval Philosophy

In the Middle Ages (extending from approximately the fourth through the 15th centuries A.D.), philosophy was dominated by the thinkers of the Christian church, but the influence of Plato and Aristotle on their thought was immense. Plato's influence predominated for the first several centuries, partly because many of Aristotle's writings were unknown in Europe. Only in the early 1200's were these writings rediscovered, causing Aristotle's influence to overshadow Plato.

The overriding task of medieval philosophers was to develop a philosophy that harmonized with the tenets of Christianity. One of their first concerns was to reconcile faith with reason. The early church fathers were more theologians than philosophers, concerned with the scriptures and creeds of the growing body of Christians. The first to combine Christian theology and philosophy in a convincing way was St. Augustine.

St. Augustine

St. Augustine (354–430 A.D.) was born in the North African town of Tagaste to a devoutly Christian mother and a

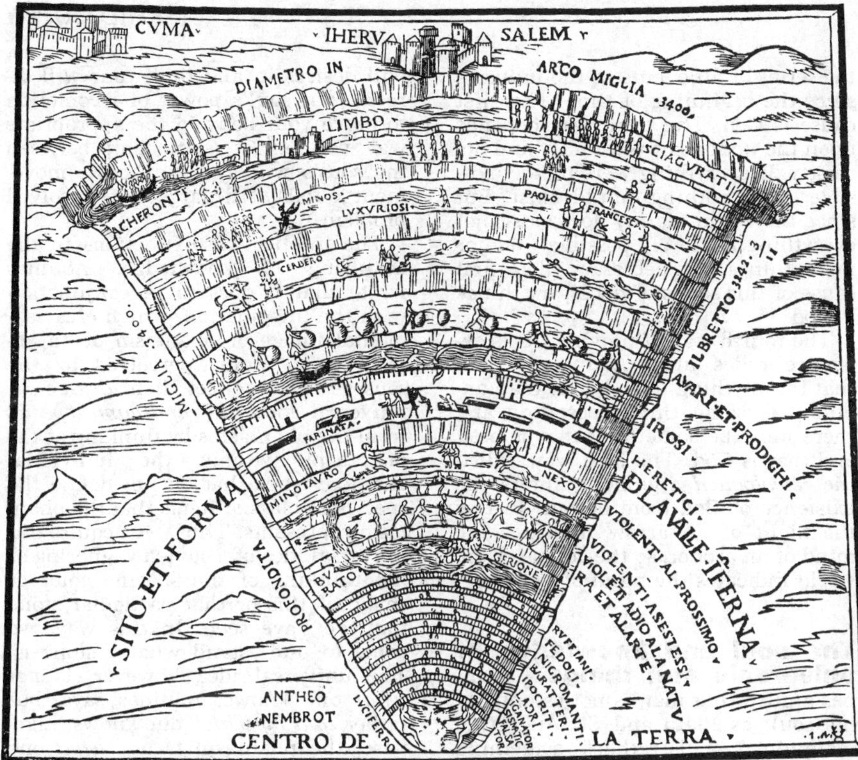

MEDIEVAL THINKERS *sought the grand scheme of God's universe as suggested by Dante's ordered vision of Hell itself.*

pagan father. According to his own testimony, in his autobiographical *Confessions*, he led a most sinful youth, marked by lustful behavior and even petty thievery. After much soul-searching and philosophic exploration, however, he converted to Christianity at the age of 32. Thereafter he led a life of study, writing, and celibacy. He supervised a monastery in Hippo, a town near his birthplace, and ultimately became a bishop of the church.

Faith and reason. Central to St. Augustine's thought is his conception of the relation between faith and reason. Like much of his philosophy, his conception of reason is quite Platonic. Reason, he said, is that faculty of the soul that in the wise man controls the other faculties, such as "the love of praise and glory and the desire for power." It is also the clear vision of the truth, providing one with knowledge and understanding.

Faith, on the other hand, is a belief in what is not clearly understood. It is voluntary, he argued, and it requires that we first think through, however hazily, what we believe. Moreover, we must believe, or have faith, in order to best understand certain truths, such as the existence of God.

Reason alone can demonstrate numerous truths. For example, by means of our reason, each of us can demonstrate that he or she exists. In the case of physical objects, which we perceive with the aid of our senses, it is *conceivable* that all those objects do not exist, and are just deceptions. But, St. Augustine argued, we *cannot* be deceived that *we* exist, because "if I am deceived, I exist. For he who does not exist cannot be deceived." To be deceived, then, is a sure sign that one exists.

St. Augustine does not make this fascinating argument the starting point of his philosophy, although he views it with great importance. Later, Descartes independently developed a similar argument, as we shall see, and by making it his starting point he conferred a lasting prominence upon it.

God, evil and free will. St. Augustine argued that there are three natures or levels of reality. The lowest is the bodily or *corporeal*, that which is capable of change both from place to place and from time to time; the next is the *spiritual*, that which is incapable of change with regard to place, but is capable of change from one time to another; the highest level is *God*, whose nature cannot be changed at all—neither with respect to place nor with respect to time.

Plato's Forms, St. Augustine maintained, are God's Ideas, the true reasons why things are the way they are. Consequently, everything has been created in accord with God's reason and is good. Any evil is merely apparent—it is the absence of good. For example, disease is simply the absence of health. This argument has not persuaded many later philosophers, who see evil as a real force in the world. But St. Augustine's reasoning does offer an interesting solution to the problem of evil, the question of how evil can exist in a world created by a God who is good.

Another challenging problem St. Augustine discussed is the conflict between our free will and God's foreknowledge of what we will do. If God knows what we will do on a specific occasion, how can we be *free* to act? If He knows, was not the act fore-ordained? St. Augustine replied that God does have foreknowledge *that we will act of our own free will.* Indeed, because God *knows* this, it is *true.* Since God knows that we will act freely, we do act freely. St. Augustine's argument was not the last word, however. The question of free will continued to haunt philosophers and became a major theological issue at the time of the Reformation.

St. Anselm

After St. Augustine, philosophy entered a dark age. Boethius (480–525) wrote a philosophical book that greatly influenced later thinkers, and the church (chiefly the monasteries) preserved many early writings. But it was nearly 700 years before the tradition of philosophy was revived.

St. Anselm (1033–1109) was an Italian philosopher who became Archbishop of Canterbury in England. He invented an argument for the existence of God that has captivated the minds of many philosophers and theologians. St. Anselm began his argument by defining God as the greatest being that can be conceived. He then claimed that for something to exist in reality is greater than for it to be merely conceived. But "if God existed in the understanding alone" then He would not be the greatest being that can be conceived, since one could conceive of Him existing in reality as being still greater. But God *is* the greatest being that can be conceived, and therefore He exists not in the understanding alone, but in reality as well. Philosophers have raised a number of objections to this argument. St. Thomas Aquinas found it unsatisfactory. Later, in the modern era, Descartes and Leibniz defended the argument, and then Kant renewed the attacks upon it.

St. Thomas Aquinas

After St. Anselm, there were several other notable Christian philosophers, including Peter Abelard (1079–1142) and Duns Scotus (1270?–1308). The next major thinker, however, was St. Thomas Aquinas (1225?–1274), whose influence is great even today in Catholic philosophy.

Most of Aristotle's previously lost writings had only begun to be read in the West during the years from 1150 to 1250, thanks to the influence of Arab philosophers such as Averroes (1126–1198), who developed Aristotle's thought and wrote commentaries upon it. Aquinas began with Aristotle's philosophy, modifying it in his own striking way. He helped raise the reputation of Aristotle so high that he was eventually able to refer to Aristotle simply as "The Philosopher."

The five ways. Aquinas drew a sharp distinction between knowledge by faith and knowledge by reason. Faith does not at all contradict reason; yet it is able to reach "certain things about God so sublime that reason cannot reach them by means of demonstration." Among these are the Christian doctrines of the Trinity and the Incarnation. Reason can, however, demonstrate the less sublime proposition that God exists.

St. Thomas argued that reason can do this in any of five ways. Three of these ways are somewhat different versions of what has become known as the *cosmological* argument; they all rely on the impossibility of an infinite series extending back through time. The first of these three ways is essentially Aristotle's argument, that there is a first unmoved mover. The second way argues that every series of causes must have a first cause, in particular the series of all events in the universe since the beginning of time. This first cause is God. The third way depends upon the notions of possibility and necessity. If everything were merely possible, then nothing would exist. But since the world plainly does exist, not everything is merely possible—one or more things are necessary. The first cause of this series of necessary things is God.

The fourth way of proving God's existence relies upon Aquinas's claim that for anything to be better than another, as some things certainly are, there must be something that is best, and that is God. The fifth way, called the *teleological* argument, infers the existence of God from design. Just as the flight of an arrow indicates the mind of an archer, so the course of the world indicates the mind of God.

The soul and knowledge of universals and things. Aquinas argued that man is not essentially his soul, as Plato and St. Augustine maintained, but rather "something composed of soul and body." The soul itself, however, has several faculties, among which are the will and the intellect. The intellect first apprehends some end, then the will desires it and directs the other faculties of the soul to carry out the means to attain that end. Thus, on a hot summer afternoon, your intellect apprehends that to go swimming is a good idea, next your will desires it, and then your will directs your soul's power of locomotion to move your body in the appropriate way. (The exact relationship between the soul's will and the body's movement is today still largely an unsolved problem.)

The intellect also functions in the acquiring of knowledge. Aquinas wrote that it does so in conjunction with the imagination, which creates a mental image or phantasm of an object, say a stone, perceived by the senses. The intellect then *abstracts* a universal idea or *intelligible species* from the phantasms by thinking of the phantasm without the individual characteristics that do not define the species or class of items that the phantasm represents. Thus, we acquire our universal idea of a stone by ignoring or not thinking of the specific color or shape of this or that particular stone that we have seen. In this way, we come to understand what a stone is. The universal idea however, is not *what* one knows, Aquinas says, but rather *that by which* one knows. Likewise, the phantasm is not *what* one knows, but rather *that by which* one knows objects, such as a particular stone or chair. This clever way of stating the matter avoids saying that we really cannot know physical objects, such as stones and chairs, *themselves.* Later philosophers have sometimes concluded that we can know *only* our ideas or phantasms, not the physical objects themselves.

Modern Philosophy

The modern period begins in the late 1400's. Within some 100 years, the discoveries of Copernicus, Kepler, and Galileo signaled the rise of modern science; Luther and Calvin began the Protestant Reformation; and the Americas were discovered and explored. At the same time the political hold of the Catholic Church was loosening, modern nation-states were forming, and an international system of commerce was being built.

All of these events helped produce a strong wave of optimism and a vibrant sense that man was on the verge of a new era. In philosophy, this feeling was especially apparent in the work of René Descartes.

René Descartes

René Descartes (1596–1650) was born in Touraine, France, and was educated at the Jesuit College of La Flèche. He was fortunate to receive an inheritance from his well-to-do father. He settled in Holland, where he devoted himself to his research, not only in philosophy, but in mathematics and science as well. In mathematics, he developed analytic geometry. In philosophy, he argued that reason alone can provide us with knowledge; he is thus called the first of the *rationalist* philosophers. He was also a splendid literary stylist; his philosophic writings are a model of French style.

Doubt. Descartes' first published work was the *Discourse on Method* (1637), in which he explained his rules for discovering truths, and illustrated their fruitfulness with treatises on optics, meteorology, and analytic geometry. A few years later, in the *Meditations,* he returned to the basis of his philosophy. He began his first meditation by noting that he has made so many errors in the past that he feels he cannot with justification be certain about anything at all. He has often believed, for example, that he was sitting by the fire, when in fact he was fast asleep in his bed and merely dreaming of himself by the fire.

Descartes argued that all such examples show that, at least once in a person's life, he should doubt everything. So doubt everything Descartes did; or at least he "pretended" that his firm convictions "are entirely false and imaginary." To aid him in this all-inclusive or *hyperbolic doubt,* Descartes supposed that some "evil genius" has thoroughly deceived him into believing that there are stars in the heavens, that he is awake at his desk, even that he has hands.

Cogito. Descartes then asked if there is anything that is *incapable* of being doubted, or of being supposed false. If so, he would have a *certain* truth on which to build an edifice of knowledge. His answer to the question was *yes,* for he could imagine himself without a body; could suppose that there is no heaven or earth; and could doubt that there are other minds; but he could not truly suppose that he

Cogito ergo sum
I think, therefore I am.
Because I think, I know I exist.

MODERN PHILOSOPHY *even wonders whether we exist. Descartes' only proof that he existed was that he could think or reason about the problem.*

himself does not exist, since *he* has been thinking of all the doubts he has recently embraced. Thus, even if an evil genius "deceives me, . . . he can never cause me to be nothing so long as I think I am something."

In the *Discourse,* Descartes summarizes this reasoning process in the famous Latin phrase, *Cogito, ergo sum,* meaning "I think, therefore I am," or, "I am thinking, therefore I exist."

Descartes' *Cogito* is a very special reasoning process; its very *occurrence* makes it true.

Clear and distinct ideas. After discovering this single firm truth, Descartes inquired what it is *about* this truth that assures him that it is so. He replied that it is so because he "so clearly and distinctly" perceives it to be true. Therefore, he adopted the premise, ". . . all things which I perceive very clearly and very distinctly are true."

Philosophers have often objected that what makes a perception "clear and distinct" is itself not clear. Have not many, if not most, of our perceptions of things been clear and distinct? In fact, just those things that Descartes resolved to doubt seem often to be clearly and distinctly perceived.

God's existence. Descartes argued that in order to trust his clear and distinct perceptions, he must first demonstrate that God exists. Descartes offered two arguments for the existence of God. One was a version of the cosmological argument in which God is the cause of his idea of God. The other was a reformulation of St. Anselm's ontological argument. Descartes used Aristotle's notion of *essence*: the set of characteristics that make something exactly the thing, or kind of thing, it is. The essence of a mountain, for example, is that it rises up from a valley. Similarly, he argued, it is of the very essence of God that He has existence. Just as a mountain cannot be conceived of without a valley, so God cannot be conceived of without existence. With his demonstration that God exists, Descartes concluded that he could now trust his rule that whatever he clearly and distinctly perceived to be true is true, for "God is not a deceiver."

Mind and body. With his newfound assurance, Descartes concluded that he could know many things, such as the truths of mathematics, which he perceived clearly and distinctly. He himself is a *thinking* thing, because even if he is mistaken that he talks, walks, or eats (actions that seem to involve a body), he knows that he thinks—he doubts, conceives, imagines, feels, etc.

But what of his body? Could Descartes conclude now that he has a body, consisting of hands, feet, arms, eyes, etc.? He answered *yes,* because he has a clear and distinct idea of his body and of other bodies. Since he has a clear and distinct idea of himself as a mind only, and a similar idea of his body as something different from his mind, he concluded that he "is entirely and absolutely distinct from my body and can exist without it." A body, he said, is an unthinking and extended substance, in contrast to a mind, which is a thinking and unextended substance. Extension is the essential attribute of bodily substance, whereas thought is the essential attribute of mental substance, although both types of substance have additonal characteristics or attributes.

A major question that Descartes raised but did not solve to his satisfaction is the nature of the interaction between mind and body. Descartes argued that, as common sense indicates, each brings about changes in the other. For example, when your body is hit, your mind or soul experiences pain and anger; and conversely, when your mind has a specific thought, your body's tongue is able to move and thus speak. Yet, if the two substances are as distinct as Descartes argued, their interaction remains very mysterious. Other philosophers' attempts to solve this problem will soon be addressed.

Leibniz

The next major philosopher after Descartes was Baruch Spinoza (1632–1677), who, because of his heretical view that God and nature were identical, was excommunicated from his Jewish community in Amsterdam. He made a bare living grinding lenses and influenced others by teaching Descartes' philosophy as well as his own.

One philosopher who visited Spinoza was Gottfried Wilhelm Leibniz (1646–1716), who was himself becoming one of the most remarkable intellectual figures of the age. Leibniz, the son of a professor of moral philosophy at the University of Leipzig, studied philosophy and law, and so impressed his professors at Altdorf that upon his graduation, they asked him to remain as a professor. He declined the offer, saying he "had other things in view," and soon became a diplomat for the Elector of Mainz, a German prince. Utilizing his diplomatic position to meet the leading intellectual figures of the day in mathematics, science, history, technology, religion, and politics, Leibniz made significant contributions to all of these fields. He invented machines to aid calculation and mining; he discovered the differential and integral calculus; and he labored to reunify the Christian churches. In philosophy, he created one of the most fascinating and original pictures of the world.

Monads. The central concept in Leibniz's philosophic view of the world is that of the *monad.* The monad is the basic substance or building block of which all things are composed, but it is quite different from the contemporary physicist's notion of an atom. A monad has no parts, is unextended, has no shape, and is indivisible. Groups of monads work together to form what we normally understand to be a body or a physical object. But the extension that bodies seem to have (and that for Descartes was the essence of body) for Leibniz was an illusion, since even in the infinitely large groups constituting bodies, monads do not acquire extension.

Monads differ from each other considerably with respect to the states or *perceptions* through which they pass. The perceptions of each monad, Leibniz said, reflect the entire universe from the monad's distinctive point of view. Some monads are not conscious of their perceptions. Others, like the monads constituting people, are conscious of their perceptions. The latter class of monads, at least, can thus be understood to be minds.

Monads do not affect each other at all. They merely *appear* to do so. This line of thought, which seems odd at first, helped Leibniz solve the problem of mind/body interaction. He claimed that they do not interact at all. Then how is it, one asks, that, as Descartes and common sense point out, they *seem* to interact? Leibniz replies that God, the supreme monad, has created a *pre-established harmony* between the conscious perceptions of any one monad and another. For example, your perceptions agree or harmonize with those of your friend. When you slap your friend's hand in a gesture of pleasure or excitement, the two of you have (visual) perceptions of your hand moving in a downward arc to contact his, followed by (tactile) perceptions of the sting of contact. It is God's prior arrangement of the order of these perceptions, according to Leibniz, that constitutes what we mistakenly take to be the interaction between mind and body. Leibniz draws an analogy between two independent clocks that keep the same time thanks to the work of the clockmaker (God).

Although this view seems strange at first, it neatly avoids Descartes' problem of describing mind and body as two very distinct substances. In Leibniz's view, there is only one type of substance, namely that of minds or monads, and there is no true interaction even between them.

Truths of reason and of fact. Leibniz is perhaps the first philosopher to divide all true propositions into two kinds, "those of reason and those of fact." Leibniz argued that truths of reason are necessary in that they are true in all possible worlds, or every universe that might have been. Their opposite, he says, is thus impossible, and we can come to know this through our reason alone by analyzing the concepts involved and seeing that the one concept, the predicate, is contained in the other, the subject. Mathematical truths, such as Euclid's "All right angles are equal," are prime examples of truths of reason, but there are many others. Truths of fact, on the other hand, cannot be completely analyzed by us to see why they are true, although they can be so analyzed by God. Every truth of fact, such as "Caesar crossed the Rubicon," is true because of what Leibniz calls the *principle of sufficient reason*, which states that "no fact can be real . . . unless there is a sufficient reason why it is so and not otherwise." We cannot know completely, however, what this sufficient reason is. Thus, Caesar crossed the Rubicon because he wished to conquer more people, but this is not sufficient to explain completely why Caesar crossed the Rubicon. (Why, for example, did Caesar wish to conquer more people?) There are other reasons, some of which you may understand and some of which you may not. What we do know of truths of fact, and of the sufficient reasons for them, we know by means of our experience working together with our reason, not through reason alone.

The best of all possible worlds. Leibniz argued that God follows the principle of plenitude, which states that the world with the greatest amount of perfection should exist. Every possible object in a possible world, Leibniz said, has a need for and a right to existence, but the existence of object A might not be possible *together* with, or *compossible* with, other objects, such as B or C. The sole possible world God has brought into existence is the one whose perfection of the set of all its compossible objects is the greatest; it is therefore *the best of all possible worlds*. Some later thinkers ridiculed this idea, as did the Frenchman Voltaire (1694–1778) in his comic novel *Candide*. But it is difficult to find a more imaginative attempt to reconcile the religious doctrine that God is all-good with the obvious presence of evil in the world.

Locke

During Leibniz's lifetime, there arose in England another highly influential philosophic movement. Its leading doctrine was directly opposed to the rationalist doctrine of Descartes, Spinoza, and Leibniz.

The new movement was called *empiricism*, and its chief doctrine was that *all* of our ideas and knowledge derive purely from sense experience; by contrast, the rationalists believed that some ideas and knowledge derived from reason. The empiricist philosophers said reason often reflects on sense experience, but it does not have any ideas or knowledge of its own.

John Locke (1632–1704), the first major figure of British empiricism, was born near Bristol, England, and studied chemistry, physics, Greek, medicine, and philosophy at Oxford. He was a lecturer in philosophy at Oxford for a few years, and later obtained his degree in medicine, but for most of his life he worked in various governmental posts. He was interested not only in "pure" philosophy, but also in problems of political philosophy. He wrote two *Treatises on Government*, which attacked the longstanding doctrine of the divine right of kings, and promoted the doctrine that the executive and legislative powers of government should be separated; this concept became one of the foundations of the U.S. Constitution. His political views were so repugnant to King James II that Locke was forced to flee England for a few years.

The empiricist principle. Locke began his chief philosophic work, *An Essay Concerning Human Understanding*, with an extended criticism of the doctrine that some ideas and knowledge are derived from reason, or are *innate*. Locke argued that he could justify all the knowledge we have without assuming that this rationalist doctrine is true. He divided all knowledge into two types, speculative and practical (or moral). "Whatever is, is" and "It is impossible for the same thing to be and not to be" are examples of speculative knowledge. The rationalists believed that such statements derived from reason, and claimed in their own defense that mankind universally consents or agrees to them. Locke argued that this is false, since "all children and idiots have not the least apprehension or thought of them." Moreover, he claimed, even when we do assent to these truths, we must first know what the words by which they are expressed mean, and this knowledge comes from sense experience.

As for practical or moral knowledge, it is highly doubtful, he said, that there is any such knowledge about which everyone will agree. Many may *say* that they believe, for instance, that all contracts should be honored, but their actions all too often belie their words.

Since there are no innate ideas or principles, they must all originate in experience. Locke distinguished simple ideas from complex ones. He said the mind is "wholly passive in the reception of its simple ideas," examples of which are sweetness, loudness, and hardness. But the mind is active in creating complex ideas out of simple ones. For instance, our idea of gratitude is composed of the simple ideas that we have had on past occasions when we have been thankful or have seen others expressing gratitude.

Another important distinction, according to Locke, is that between primary and secondary qualities. Primary qualities are the genuine properties of bodies that really "cause perception" in our minds; these qualities include the "bulk, figure, texture, and motion" of bodies. Secondary qualities, however, are "nothing in the objects themselves," but rather are effects of the primary qualities (generally, motion) in bodies or physical objects; examples are "colors, sounds, tastes, etc."

Universal ideas. Locke argued that the only things that exist are particular objects. He is thus led to face the question of how we come to know general ideas, or terms. Recall that Plato's answer to this question was that reason has an insight into the world of Forms. Locke argued that there is no need to assume the existence of Platonic forms. Our minds, he said, form general or universal ideas from their particular ideas by a process he called *abstraction*. This involves the mind actively separating the characteristics common to several of our ideas from the characteristics specific to each of them. For instance, we create the universal idea of *man* by abstracting the common features of individual men (and disregarding their individual features). By comparing this universal idea and a particular idea we have of a particular person, we can frame the proposition, "My friend is a man."

Substance. Locke believed that physical objects do exist outside of our perceiving them. He argued that every set of qualities constituting a complex idea—for example, the hardness, shape, weight, etc., of an apple—must reside in something, or in a "substratum wherein they do subsist." This is *substance*, but it is something about which we cannot say or know anything further. If we try to describe substance, we end up simply mentioning another one of the qualities that rests or inheres within it, and we are thereby not talking about substance itself. It is thus a strange thing, we "know not what." Yet, like Descartes, Locke concluded that there are two kinds of substance, the corporeal and the spiritual.

Hume

After Locke, the next great British empiricist was Bishop George Berkeley (1685–1753), who argued that there is only one kind of substance, namely spirits or minds with their ideas. "To be is to be perceived" is the slogan he used to summarize his philosophy. His view is a natural development from the empiricist principle that all of our knowledge derives from our ideas of sense perception.

David Hume (1711–1776), the third of the major British empiricists, developed the principle still further. He argued that we cannot even know that there are spirits or minds; we can know only our ideas and their characteristics. Born in Edinburgh, Scotland, Hume ventured to France at the age of 23, and wrote *A Treatise of Human Nature* at La Flèche, the town where Descartes had studied. When published in 1738, the *Treatise*, he wrote, "fell deadborn from the press." Hardly anyone seems to have read it at first. He resumed his writing, however, and soon acquired recognition with his *Essays, Moral and Political.* His earlier *Treatise* eventually became his most famous work. Hume later worked as a librarian, wrote a three-volume history of England, and assisted the British ambassador to France.

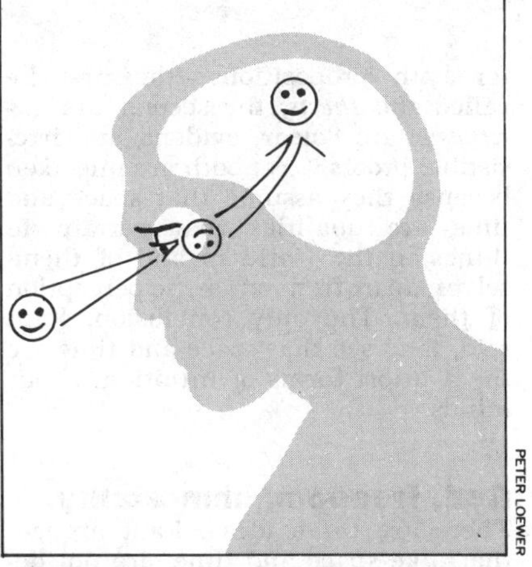

PETER LOEWER

THE SENSES *fascinated 18th-century thinkers. They wanted to understand how we receive and process information about the world.*

Impressions and ideas. Hume separated all of our sense perceptions into two classes, impressions and ideas. Impressions are our perceptions of our senses and emotions, "as they make their first appearance in the soul"; ideas are our copies or "faint images of these in thinking" on our past impressions.

Hume argued that our impressions and ideas are the only objects about which we can truly claim to know anything. Locke had argued that we can know physical objects and minds because we know our ideas, but he did not explain how we make the jump from ideas to things. Hume said there is no possible argument to support this jump, though we may find ourselves nonetheless compelled to believe in the existence of minds and bodies.

We may argue with Locke that there must be bodies to explain our ideas of sight, sound, etc., but Hume responded that we cannot really know this. We have no genuine idea of body at all, since all of our ideas are of the *qualities* of bodies, not of body itself. Here Hume is developing Locke's argument on substance to its natural conclusion. If bodily substance is something we cannot talk meaningfully about, then we cannot even claim to know that there *is* any bodily substance. The word "body" signifies nothing apart from our ideas of its properties.

The same argument applies to our supposed notion of minds or spirits, including our own: we do not truly know that there are such things, because we have no idea of them apart from their qualities—for example, intelligence, quickness, or imaginativeness. Descartes, according to Hume, should only have concluded that there are thoughts, not that there was an *I* that had them. Hume thus rejected minds and bodies as unproven, as Berkeley had rejected bodies.

Analysis of causality. Hume wrote that in order to understand completely any ideas we have, we must study the impressions from which they come, since impressions supply us with the originals of the ideas in their most vivid forms. He applied this maxim, in particular, to the principle of cause and effect, which says that there is a necessary connection between a cause and its effect or that "every effect *must* have a cause." Aquinas, for example, and Leibniz had maintained the truth of this principle of causality.

But when we examine our ideas about any specific cause, say a waitress giving prompt and cheerful service, and its effect, a bigger tip, we cannot find that there is any necessity in our ideas either of the cause, the effect, or the relation between the two. Nothing binds the effect to the cause; it is merely that "one does actually in fact follow the other." In fact, the effect does not *always* follow the cause, as it should if there were a necessary connection between the two. The waitress's customer may be preoccupied with another matter, or short on change one day; despite the waitress's prompt and cheerful service, her tip may not be forthcoming. Hume claimed we can say the same of any other instance of cause and effect.

Hume believed that the inference we make from a cause to its effect, although usually correct, results simply from the custom or habit we have developed from our past experience, in which the cause was usually followed by the effect. This custom usually stems from the vividness of the impression of the cause and the impression of the effect generally following it. But though these vivid impressions may explain our *belief* in the necessary connection between a cause and its effect, they do not give us certainty that there *is* such a connection.

Kant

One of the first philosophers to endeavor to meet Hume's challenge was Immanuel Kant (1724–1804). He was born in Königsberg, Germany, and spent his life there, first as a student and later as a professor at the University of Königsberg. He was quite regular in his habits; housewives were said to have set their clocks when they saw him taking his daily walks. He wrote on many topics, including the nature of a world government. His philosophic work, especially *The Critique of Pure Reason*, constitutes a fascinating effort to bring together the rationalist and empiricist traditions.

Judgments. One of Kant's aims was to justify the principle of causality that Hume had thrown into great doubt. To understand how he did this, we must first understand two important distinctions that Kant drew. Propositions, or, as he called them, "judgments" can be divided into analytic and synthetic. Analytic judgments (like Leibniz's truths of reason) have predicates that express what is already in the concept of the subject, though perhaps not clearly; they do not increase our knowledge. Analytic judgments are arrived at by our understanding. "All bodies are extended" is an example. Synthetic judgments have predicates not in their subjects; they *do* increase our knowledge, as in "All bodies have weight."

Kant's second distinction was between *a priori* and *a posteriori* judgments. A priori judgments are known without any sense experience at all, whereas a posteriori judgments are known "through sense experience." All analytic judgments are a priori. Synthetic judgments may be either a posteriori or a priori. The class of synthetic a priori judgments is of particular interest. Among the most important judgments in this class is the principle of causality.

Hume demonstrated that the principle of causality is not analytic, Kant said, and that it is not derived from sense experience. He claimed, however, that it is an idea that we have a priori, that is, without experience, and is *applicable* to our sense experience. In fact, our minds are so constituted that they *must* apply the concept of cause and effect to experience. Thus, Kant claimed, we know that the synthetic a priori principle is true, because it states a fact at least as much about our minds as about the world, and our minds presumably know themselves. Whether or not Kant satisfactorily answered Hume is a matter of continuing controversy.

Space and time. Kant also placed space and time among the synthetic a priori judgments. He argued that they are not particular things characterizing the objects of the universe in themselves. Rather, they are the means of our perceiving or our *forms of intuition* of the physical objects of the world. They are not derived from sense experience; they are a priori particular things that our minds must necessarily *apply* to our sense experience so that we can experience the world.

Kant supported this position by considering pairs of conflicting arguments that he called the antinomies of pure reason. One of these antinomies is that the universe appears to have a beginning in time and in space and appears to have *no* beginning in time and in space, but is infinite in both respects. Kant argued that the demonstrations for both propositions (the first he called the *thesis,* the second the *antithesis*) are "clear, evident, and irresistible proofs." Yet both are mistaken because they assume that space and time are qualities that pertain to things in the world in and of themselves, apart from our sense perception of them. The only conclusion, Kant said, is to see that space and time are the a priori forms of intuition of our minds.

God, freedom, immortality. There are three ideas, Kant argued, that, like space and time, are not derived from sense experience. But, unlike space and time, they are not applicable to sense experience. These ideas of pure reason are our ideas of God, freedom, and immortality. Kant criticized the traditional arguments for the existence of God because they mistakenly attempt to apply the idea of God to the world of our sense experience. Nonetheless, Kant argued that the ideas of God, freedom, and immortality are quite significant. All three show us how we can best lead our lives. They suggest that we can act *as if* there were a God, *as if* we were free, and *as if* we were immortal. By acting so, we demonstrate that in a certain sense these ideas of pure reason are real.

Hegel

Kant had suggested that we could know an object as we constructed it in a space and time of our own making, but we could never know the thing in itself (*ding an sich*) as it exists outside of time and space. It was a natural development of this suggestion to simply deny that there are any such things in themselves. All that certainly exist are minds alone. This doctrine is known as *idealism.*

We have already met idealism, in Leibniz and Berkeley, for example, but the 1800's produced a flood of idealist philosophers. This group includes Johann Fichte (1762–1814), Friedrich Schelling (1775–1854), Arthur Schopenhauer (1788–1860), and, the most provocative and influential of all, Georg Wilhelm F. Hegel (1770–1831). Hegel was born in Stuttgart, Germany, studied at Tübingen, and became a professor at the universities of Jena, Heidelberg, and Berlin.

The Absolute Spirit. The central concept of Hegel's philosophy is the Absolute. It is the developing organism constituting the universe as a unified whole. It is purely spiritual—all bodily properties, such as extension, are merely illusion. Every part of the Absolute Spirit derives its reality from its relation to the whole Spirit. Thus, you, your acquaintances, the Empire State Building, the Mississippi River, and the planet Mars all are real only insofar as they are part of the Absolute Spirit.

It follows, Hegel argued, that in order for us to know truly any specific thing, we must know its relation to other things. In order for Brown, an expert welder, to know the piece of metal he shapes, he must know how it facilitates the smooth functioning of the automobile or airplane of which it is a part. In order for us to know truly our acquaintances at work, we must know what they do once they leave work each day. All knowledge, like the Absolute Spirit that it is about, forms a system. "It is only as science or system that knowledge is actual."

But since no knowledge perceives *all* of the relations that something has to other parts of the Absolute, all knowledge is, to different degrees, false or deficient. It is the purpose of what Hegel calls the *Phenomenology of the Spirit* to take the "long journey" to discover more and more of these relations that constitute the Absolute Spirit, or Truth. Philosophy thus becomes, as Hegel conceives it, a grand enterprise encompassing all avenues of thought, knowledge, and creativity.

The dialectic. The Absolute, Hegel says, "is never at rest, but is always engaged in an ever progressing motion" that involves a cycle of three stages. Hegel called this cycle the *dialectic.* It consists of the *thesis,* the *antithesis,* and the *synthesis.* (Here we

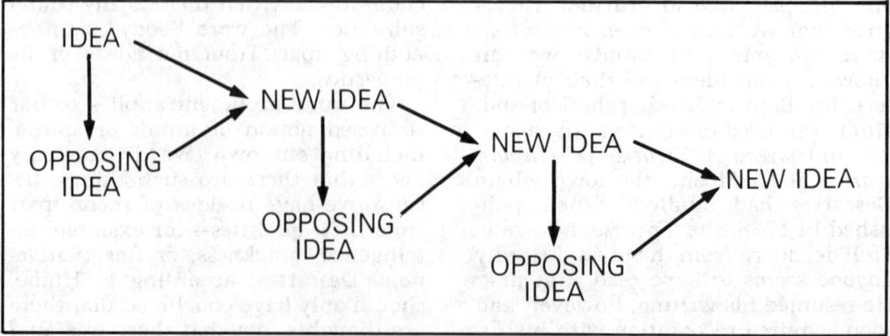

THE DIALECTIC *of Hegel suggests that the universe is continually changing and developing rather than fixed and constant.*

can see the influence of Kant.) The thesis is one particular state in which the Absolute finds itself at a given moment. The thesis gives rise to its opposite, the antithesis. The two together create a temporary resolution that Hegel called the synthesis. The synthesis becomes a new thesis promoting the further development of the Absolute Spirit.

The movement of the dialectic pertains both to the Absolute Spirit itself and to our knowledge of it, limited as it is. Accordingly, our knowledge is neither quite true nor quite false, partly because the relations of things to one another are so complex, and partly because they are constantly developing.

History, nations, freedom.

Hegel compared the development of the Absolute Spirit to the growth of a child into an adult. The Absolute is becoming ever richer and more perfect. Hegel found his conception of progress especially realized in the history of nations. Nation states, especially Germany, have become, Hegel claimed, the complete embodiment of human reason and freedom, toward which the Absolute is developing.

Freedom, as Hegel understood it, is quite different from our political conception of it. He condemned freedom of speech and democracy, and argued that to follow the laws established by the leader of a state constitutes true freedom. Freedom so conceived acquires its full reality only insofar as it is part of a whole nation's development. Many have found this doctrine offensive, in that it seems to justify a tyrannical dictatorship. Whether this is what Hegel intended has been one of the intriguing questions about his philosophy.

SOVFOTO

NATIONAL DESTINY *was a concern of 19th-century philosophers. Their speculations became fighting words in the disastrous conflicts of the 20th century.*

Marx

There were numerous thinkers who were captivated by the dynamic and all-embracing nature of Hegel's thought. In the course of creating their own philosophies, they often retained and modified certain ideas of Hegel's. One of these thinkers was Karl Marx (1818–1883), whose thought has inspired the economic and political development of many nations during the last 100 years.

Marx was born in Trèves, Germany, studied at the University of Jena, edited a journal, and participated in the French and German revolutions of 1848. He settled in London, and befriended Friedrich Engels (1820–1895). Together and independently, they wrote numerous books and essays, such as the *Communist Manifesto* and *Das Kapital,* and organized workers to bring about an economic revolution.

Dialectical materialism.

Marx transformed Hegel's concept of the dialectic. He agreed with Hegel that the world must be understood from a developing historical point of view, but whereas Hegel argued that the primary causal force in the world was spiritual in nature, Marx argued that it was bodily or material. Marx did not claim that the mind does not exist. Rather, he argued that man's material needs for food, clothing, and shelter have largely determined his bodily activities and behavior, and indeed, his thoughts. There is a Hegelian-like dialectical relationship here, since man's activities, themselves revealing his mind, in turn shape the kind, quality, and quantity of material goods that he produces. Marx's dialectical materialism thus led him naturally into an economic analysis of society.

Class struggle and freedom.

Marx argued that society develops in accordance with truly scientific laws, as rigorous as those in physics. One of these laws deals with the so-called class struggle. Historically there are three economic classes in society—the landowners, the capitalists (or factory owners), and the workers (or wage earners). The landowners were the dominant force in the feudal Middle Ages (thesis); the capitalists have been dominant since the Industrial Revolution of the 18th century (antithesis); and the workers will become dominant in the future (synthesis).

Marx argued that the production of material goods is presently controlled by the capitalists because of the existence of private property. In the synthesis stage, he said, the right of private property will be eliminated, goods will be justly distributed, and wage earners will receive fair payment for the goods they produce.

Since the capitalists will lose their right to own machinery, there will be a struggle with the wage earners in bringing about the synthesis stage. Whether the synthesis stage can come about peacefully is a matter on which Marx was not clear, and which later became a source of contention among his followers. Marx argued that since the future stage will satisfy people's material needs more efficiently, it will create a world of freedom for all. Because some governments, such as the Soviet Union's, claim to have created Marx's ideal third stage, despite political repression, many have viewed

Marx's claims with skepticism. Others, however, argue that those governments have not in fact realized Marx's ideal.

Peirce

While Hegel's influence grew steadily in 19th century England, thanks to the work of philosophers such as F. H. Bradley (1846–1924), in the United States a more independent brand of philosophy arose. One of its proponents, Charles Sanders Peirce (1839–1914), was perhaps the greatest philosopher America has produced. Peirce was born in Cambridge, Massachusetts, and studied at Harvard, where his father was a distinguished mathematician. He was a physicist with the U.S. Geological Survey, made major contributions to logic and mathematics, and taught at Harvard and Johns Hopkins universities. He was dismissed from Johns Hopkins, apparently because of bitter disputes with his colleagues, and retired to his home in Milford, Pennsylvania, and continued his study and writing. He struggled to make a living from irregular freelance writing assignments.

The pragmatic maxim. Peirce founded the pragmatic movement in philosophy with the 1878 publication of "How to Make Our Ideas Clear." As the title suggests, the purpose of the article is to provide a way to insure that our concepts are clear so that we can put ourselves on the right path to acquiring knowledge.

Peirce claimed that "what a thing means is simply what habits it involves." The meaning of the chemical term sodium, for example, involves the habits or actions that the chemical exhibits when the chemist subjects it to various tests in his laboratory.

Accordingly, the pragmatic maxim states that in order to ascertain completely what a concept means, we should consider what effects "we conceive the object of our conception to have." Peirce claimed that following the maxim had helped him greatly in developing many of his thoughts and that the maxim later aided other philosophers and physicists in coming to understand their disciplines. The maxim was, however, capable of many different interpretations, chiefly because of the vagueness of the notions of *conceiving* and *practical effects.* Philosophers and others often disagree as to what, for example, is a practical effect.

Tychism and mind. Peirce is one of the few philosophers who argued vigorously against Leibniz's principle of sufficient reason and Kant's principle of causality.

FORD MOTOR COMPANY

PRAGMATISM WAS A PHILOSOPHY *for practical men: Henry Ford's automobile was not the first or most elegant, but it "worked."*

He offered at least two arguments to show that the principles are false. First, no law of nature, he said, is ever exactly verified—there are always small variations from the numbers expected on the basis of scientific laws. For example, physics may predict that a shell fired from a gun will land precisely 2.4 miles from where it was fired, but it in fact always lands either a little less or a little more than that distance from the gun.

Second, there is a wonderful diversity of things—plants, animals, colors, shapes, tastes—in the world. This diversity, he argued, could not be explained if nature always did everything the same way in accordance with certain laws.

Despite the existence of laws, there is considerable *chance* in the world. Chance occurrences are spontaneous; they explain feeling and consciousness; and they constitute life itself. Once they occur, they can create new laws or habits. For example, you may spontaneously think of a new line of encouragement to shout to your teammates in the midst of a game, and liking it so much, you may thereafter acquire the habit of shouting it during every game.

Peirce called his view that chance is pervasive in the world *tychism.* In light of 20th century developments in physics regarding quantum mechanics, where chance occurrences are essential to the theory, Peirce's ideas seem to have been ahead of their time.

James

One of Peirce's closest friends was the famous philosopher and psychologist, William James (1842–1910). James studied at Harvard and taught psychology and philosophy there for his entire adult life. He was a charming and attractive person, who was loved by nearly all who knew him.

The pragmatic conception of truth. James transformed Peirce's pragmatic maxim into a tool not only for determining the meaning of specific scientific concepts, but for determining when particular beliefs are true. He stressed the importance of the practical consequences or effects of our beliefs and argued that since "truth is one species of good," a true belief is one that it is good for us to believe, good in the sense that it supports our other beliefs and is "helpful in life's practical struggles."

James argued that this conception of true belief explains a common everyday belief such as "Tom is in the room with me now." This belief supports other beliefs—that Tom is speaking with you now—and is helpful in your dealings with Tom. James also argued that this pragmatic conception of true belief can justify one's belief that God exists, since such a belief may be "good for us to believe," in the way described.

James's pragmatic conception of truth is important because it is an interesting and influential alternative to the traditional and common sense view that a true belief is one that *corresponds* to the facts. The notion of correspondence here is very difficult to explain, and a view such as James's, which avoids the problem even if it raises other problems in its place, is thereby attractive.

Russell

Bertrand Russell (1872–1970) is a towering giant in the philosophy of the 20th century. He has made remarkable contributions to mathematical logic and the philosophy of mathematics, and significant contributions to every branch of philosophy. He often spoke out publicly on political and ethical issues, and thus became a model of the activist philosopher, one whose life guides others in the pursuit of their own goals. One of Russell's great concerns was the modern threat of the nuclear annihilation of mankind.

Born in Trelleck, Wales, Russell, the grandson of a British prime minister, was orphaned at an early age and was raised by his grandmother. He attended the University of Cambridge, and taught there intermittently throughout much of his life.

Logic and philosophic analysis. Russell did his first major work in the foundations of mathematics. He argued that although mathematics and logic historically had developed independently, mathematics was actually identical with logic. Recent work in logic and mathematics had seemed to support this view, but did not demonstrate it.

With Alfred North Whitehead (1861–1947), Russell wrote the monumental classic *Principia Mathematica,* which endeavored to deduce all of mathematics from purely logical axioms to demonstrate that mathematics was logic. In this work, Russell defined old concepts in terms of just a few others. For example, he defined a number as a class of all classes similar to each other, where similarity is itself further defined in mathematical terms.

When he turned his attention to the problems of mind and body and existence in general, he employed the same technique he had used in logic. For example, he argued that physical objects could be defined in terms of classes of sense perceptions. Standing here, I see the tabletop as shaped like a rectangle; standing there, I see it as shaped like a diamond. The tabletop itself is the class of all such perceptions of it. Russell argued that we can show that the universe does not consist in quite as many kinds or classes of objects as common sense or even physics indicates.

The Logical Positivists

One of Russell's close friends, G. E. Moore (1873–1958), developed philosophy by defending our common-sense claims to know various things, and by painstakingly analyzing how we perceive objects.

Another friend and student of Russell's, Ludwig Wittgenstein (1889–1951), wrote a book during World War I called the *Tractatus,* which admirably defended a detailed version of the correspondence theory of truth (the so-called picture theory); but it also argued that certain features of the world could not be described with language at all.

In Vienna, in the late 1920's and early 1930's, there arose a group of philosophers who were especially influenced by Wittgenstein's *Tractatus,* Bertrand Russell, and David Hume. They became known as the Vienna Circle of Logical Positivists because they stressed the importance of formal logic and reliance on sense experience for philosophy. Their number included their founder, Moritz Schlick, A. J. Ayer, Rudolph Carnap, and the logician Kurt Gödel.

One of the Vienna Circle's notable achievements was the formulation of the empiricist criterion of meaningfulness. They argued that most traditional metaphysical arguments, such as Hegel's claims regarding the Absolute, and debates over the existence of God, are not false but completely meaningless. Their criterion stated that in order for a sentence to be meaningful, it must be either *empirically verifiable* or *analytic.*

By analytic, the logical positivists meant sentences of mathematics or logic ("If the sky is blue, then the sky is blue"), which they argued were true not because, as Leibniz and Kant had said, their predicates were contained in their subjects, but rather because the meanings of the terms involved made them true.

By empirically verifiable, the logical positivists meant that our sense experiences could show that the sentence was either true or false. For example, you look above and see that the sky is gray; that is *direct* verification. An elaborate scientific experiment, on the other hand, would yield *indirect* verification.

Controversy flourished as to the precise nature of empirical verification, but the logical positivists contributed greatly to the development of the philosophy of science, the study of the nature of scientific knowledge.

Linguistic Analysis

After Ludwig Wittgenstein wrote his *Tractatus,* he left philosophy for a few years to pursue other interests; but later he returned to philosophy.

Wittgenstein's later philosophy (expressed in his posthumous classic *Philosophical Investigations*) developed in a direction quite different from his earlier views. He no longer maintained that there is any fundamental correspondence between a class of things called propositions and another class called facts of the world. His conception of meaning had changed. Meaning is not, he argued, anything that words have or express. Meanings are simply the *uses* to which words, and language in all its marvelous variety, are put. Accordingly, in order to understand what meaning is, we must study the ways in which people use language, what Wittgenstein called our "language games."

For example, it is a mistake, Wittgenstein argued, to pursue the search for a universal (or Form) common to many things—such as the universal, mentioned earlier, of *gratitude* common to all acts of gratitude, and the universal of *game* common to all games—since there is nothing common to these various instances of the universal at all. Rather, there is a large, undefined and changing set of characteristics between one situation in which we use the given word, say *game,* and another. Some games use dice, others cards, others a ball; some require two players, others nine, etc. There is no universal; there are only "family resemblances."

Another problem we can free ourselves from, Wittgenstein argued, is Descartes' problem of how we know that there is a world of people in addition to ourselves. The mere fact that Descartes can use a language shows that others exist who use the language as well. For it is impossible, Wittgenstein argued, for anyone to develop a language in pure isolation. Language, by its very nature, is a social phenomenon. The development of this line of thought is called the Private Language Argument and it, like the rest of Wittgenstein's philosophizing, has encouraged others to pursue philosophy in a similarly interesting way.

European Philosophy After 1900

Philosophy in Europe for the most part has taken a sharply different direction from philosophy in England and America. Despite differences among themselves, Russell, Wittgenstein, and the logical positivists agreed that philosophy must seek to solve problems one at a time rather than try to solve all problems by constructing a sweeping, panoramic view of the entire universe in the manner of Hegel.

European philosophers of the interacting existentialist and phenomenological movements have maintained to the contrary that it is the purpose of philosophy to offer a unified picture of the entire universe. Only in this way, they claim, can we determine man's place within it.

Phenomenology. Edmund Husserl (1859–1938), the founder of phenomenology, was a professor at the universities of Göttingen and Freiburg, Germany. His influence today is widespread throughout Europe, Latin America, and parts of the United States. Husserl argued that in order to understand the world, we should begin, as Descartes suggested, with our own sense perceptions, or what Husserl called "the forms of my manifold and shifting spontaneities of consciousness." In examining these, we eventually discover certain invariable features of our consciousness. One of these is the fact that our perceptions have the property of being *about* or *of* certain things. Our different visual perceptions of the tabletop, for instance, seem to be about or of a tabletop, whether or not there really is a tabletop there.

This consciousness of objects (real

or not) Husserl calls the *intentionality* or object-directedness of our consciousness. By detaching ourselves from other studies, and by attending to this and other properties of our consciousness with the utmost care—what Husserl calls "bracketing our experience"—we can come to know numerous things about our world. In this way, we can establish a science of knowledge.

Existentialism. Jean-Paul Sartre (1905–1979) was one of the leading proponents of existentialism. Born in France, Sartre taught philosophy for several years, but resigned to devote himself to writing. He became very popular as a playwright and novelist as well as a philosopher. During World War II, he fought in the French Resistance, was captured, and escaped. He was deeply concerned with the problem of human freedom. His major philosophic work is *Being and Nothingness.*

Sartre expressed his central existentialist doctrine by saying that "existence comes before essence." What this means is that every person exists first and his nature or essence comes about later through the manner by which he chooses to live his life. This view contrasts sharply with the traditional views of Plato, Aristotle, and the major religions of the world, which assert that man's nature or essence is determined before any given individual is born. What man can and should do are defined or limited by this essence. Sartre argued that there is no prior conception of man in God, because God does not exist.

This fact, Sartre claimed, liberates man to create himself in any way he chooses, but it also confers great responsibility upon him for what he does. He cannot blame his actions upon his nature, as if that were something distinct from himself, for he has created that very nature or essence. Moreover, in choosing to act in a certain way, say by joining the Resistance, one chooses in a way for all mankind. One affirms by one's actions that this is the way all men should act. Such responsibility for one's actions creates a great sense of anguish or pain in each one of us, to the extent that we recognize our predicament. But our freedom to create ourselves, our essence, knows no bounds. What we are and will be will thus be seen in our actions of today and tomorrow.

Recent Analytic Philosophy

Philosophy continues to be a vibrant subject, eliciting novel and stimulating ideas on the problems that have always intrigued people. Willard V.O. Quine (1908–) has considered the analytic/synthetic distinction, and argued provocatively that the distinction is not valid. We have seen that the distinction was employed by various philosophers to show, first, that there were two broad ways in which a proposition could be true (by meanings or by the facts of sense experience, according to the logical positivists), and that there were two associated ways in which the truth or falsity of the proposition could be known (by reason alone or by sense experience, according to Leibniz). Quine argued that this "dogma of empiricism" is false, and attempted to show that *all* propositions (or *sentences*) are true for basically the same kinds of reasons, and that their truth or falsity is known through basically the same means. He asserted that all of our knowledge forms an intricate network, with some pieces of it readily confirmed or refuted by experience and other pieces (for instance, mathematics) not so readily confirmed or refuted by experience. The distinction is not sharp, as the logical positivists would have it. All pieces of knowledge differ only in the degree to which they relate to experience, but all *do* relate to experience.

Another major thinker, Hilary Putnam (1931–), has argued that all knowledge falls into several different networks or conceptual schemes. The analytic/synthetic distinction, he claimed, should be drawn only with respect to a specific conceptual scheme. Each of these schemes has its own statements that are quite central and others that are close to the outer surface of the network. Those near the center are analytic with respect to the conceptual scheme of which they are a part. Those at the edge are synthetic with respect to that conceptual scheme. A statement that is analytic in one conceptual scheme may be synthetic in another, or vice versa.

Whether it be Plato's majestic Forms, Descartes' captivating *Cogito,* Peirce's spontaneous universe of chance, or Sartre's anguish in the face of man's freedom, philosophers' ideas will forever excite the imaginations of thoughtful people everywhere. By reflection upon them, new models to enrich people's lives are created, and new philosophers are born.

—Stephen H. Levy

For Further Reference

Religion

Abbott, Lyman. *The Evolution of Christianity.* American Biography Service, 1985.

Anderson, Bernhard W. *Understanding the Old Testament* (3rd Ed.). Prentice-Hall, 1975.

Baron, Salo W. *A Social and Religious History of the Jews* (2nd Ed.). 2 volumes. Columbia University Press, 1952–1958.

Brandon, Samuel George, editor. *Dictionary of Comparative Religion.* Charles Scribner's Sons, 1970.

Conze, Edward. *Buddhism: Its Essence and Development.* Harper & Brothers, 1959.

Coomaraswamy, Ananda. *Hinduism and Buddhism.* South Asia Books, 1986.

Handy, Robert T. *A History of the Churches in the United States and Canada.* Oxford University Press, 1976.

Holt, P. M., et al. *The Cambridge History of Islam.* 2 volumes. Cambridge University Press, 1971.

Johnson, Paul. *A History of Christianity.* Atheneum, 1979.

Kee, Howard Clark, et al. *Understanding the New Testament.* Prentice-Hall, 1973.

Ling, Trevor. *A History of Religion East and West.* Macmillan, 1968.

Radin, Paul. *Primitive Religion: Its Nature and Origin.* Viking Press, 1937.

Yang, Ch'ing-K'un. *Religion in Chinese Society.* University of California Press, 1967.

Philosophy

Copleson, Frederick J. *History of Philosophy. Volumes I–III.* Doubleday, 1985.

Creel, Herrlee G. *Chinese Thought From Confucius to Mao Tse-tung.* University of Chicago Press, 1953.

Fakhry, Majid. *A History of Islamic Philosophy.* Columbia University Press, 1970.

Flew, Anthony. *Introduction to Western Philosophy.* Bobbs-Merrill, 1971.

Guttman, Julius. *Philosophies of Judaism.* Routledge, 1964.

Jones, William T. *A History of Western Philosophy* (2nd Ed.). Harcourt, Brace, and World, 1969.

Maurer, Armand A. *Medieval Philosophy.* Random House, 1962.

Takakusu, Junjiro. *The Essentials of Buddhist Philosophy* (3rd Ed.). Asia Publishing House, 1956.

Westphal, Fred A. *Art of Philosophy: An Introductory Reader.* Prentice-Hall, 1972.

VOLUME 23
Social Sciences

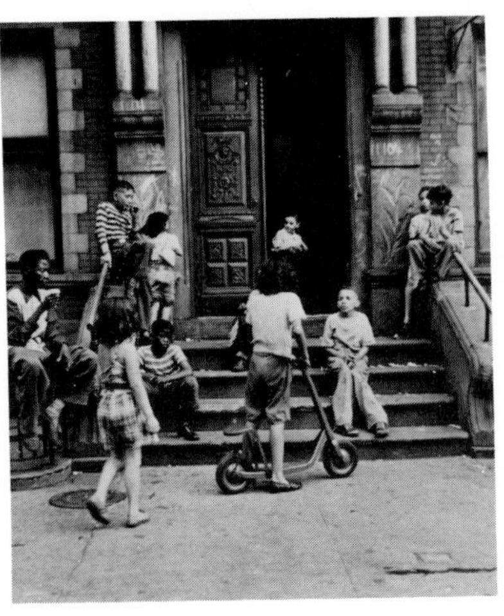

LEADERS OF SOCIAL SCIENCE

Psychology	Wilhelm Wundt 1832–1920
	William James 1842–1910
	Ivan Pavlov 1849–1936
	Sigmund Freud 1856–1939
	Alfred Binet 1857–1911
	Alfred Adler 1870–1937
	Carl Jung 1875–1961
	John Watson 1878–1958
	Jean Piaget 1896–1980
	Erik Erikson 1900–
	Carl Rogers 1902–
	Bruno Bettelheim 1903–
	B.F. Skinner 1904–
Sociology	August Comte 1798–1857
	Herbert Spencer 1820–1903
	Emile Durkheim 1858–1917
	George Herbert Mead 1863–1931
	Max Weber 1864–1920
	Talcott Parsons 1902–
	C. Wright Mills 1916–1962
	Erving Goffman 1922–
Anthropology	Franz Boas 1858–1942
	Ruth Benedict 1887–1948
	Margaret Mead 1901–1978
	Louis Leakey 1903–1972
	Oscar Lewis 1914–1970
	Marvin Harris 1927–

(Timeline scale: 1800, 1850, 1900, 1950, 2000)

TOTEM POLE: SJÖSTEDT/ALPHA PHOTO ASSOCIATES

VOLUME 23

Social Sciences

DO YOU NEED TO
TALK TO SOMEONE?
Call 914-8501

MIMI FORSYTH/MONKMEYER

PETER ARNOLD

PAUL CONKLIN/MONKMEYER

ERIC KROLL/TAURUS PHOTOS

The social sciences are both the oldest and the newest of the fields of human study. They are the oldest because humans have been interested from prehistoric times in their own thoughts, feelings, and actions (psychology), in their associations with others in their family, tribe, or region (sociology), and in their own origins and connections to other tribes or nations (anthropology). Early writings are filled with speculations and observations on matters that are now a part of social science.

In another sense, the social sciences are among the newest disciplines because they did not take their present form until the 1800's. Until then, psychology was the concern of philosophers, who speculated on the nature and organization of the mind. Sociology developed as a part of a field called political economy, which contained elements of political science and economics. Explorers brought back information on exotic peoples and discovered artifacts from earlier civilizations, but systematic study of this information, now known as anthropology, did not begin until the late 1800's.

Gradually, each of the major social sciences claimed its place as a separate discipline. In the early years, however, the social sciences combined the findings of widely separated fields. For example, psychology made use of studies by philosophers such as William James; reports of physiological experiments, such as those of Ivan Pavlov; and the findings of medical doctors like Sigmund Freud, who were seeking ways to treat patients with mental and emotional disturbances.

Early sociologists included both researchers who used statistics to help understand communities and political activists eager to improve the lot of the poor and oppressed. Even today, social scientists are often interdisciplinary in their approach, and the lines between disciplines are not always distinct. This bridging of traditional lines has led to development of new specialties within disciplines and increased interest in the entire field.

This volume concentrates on the three major social sciences mentioned above. The largest section, "Psychology," describes a vast field ranging from studies in brain chemistry to educational programs to encourage creativity.

The section on "Sociology" outlines the variety of ways in which the discipline studies the behavior of men and women in groups. A group may include two collaborators producing a musical comedy or a nation with millions of citizens.

The section on "Anthropology" describes that discipline's interest in man's origins and in the amazing variety of cultures in today's world. It includes a feature on archaeology, a multidisciplinary science that has provided important material for anthropological studies of the past.

The final section, "Applications of the Social Sciences," talks about some of the many practical uses of these disciplines, ranging from marketing and advertising to government social services.

Many other parts of the *Volume Library* provide additional information on the social sciences. The volume GOVERNMENT AND LAW provides an introduction to political science, often considered one of the social sciences. Economics, also sometimes included among the social sciences, is discussed in the volume BUSINESS AND FINANCE. A special branch of psychology concerned with the stages of mental and emotional growth is the subject of the volume CHILD AND FAMILY, which follows human development from birth through to old age. That volume also includes a guide to service agencies that may be able to help individuals or families in crisis.

PSYCHOLOGY

Psychology is the scientific study of behavior and of the mental processes that cause behavior. It is the study of *all* behavior and mental functioning, whether human or animal. The study of animals often has the dual purpose of learning about animal behavior and, by extension, about human behavior.

The terms psychiatry, psychoanalysis, and psychology are often confused.

• *Psychiatry* is a branch of medicine dealing with emotional disturbances. A psychiatrist, besides being trained in psychology, is a medical doctor qualified to prescribe medicines and perform surgery.

• *Psychoanalysis* is a particular method based on the personality theories and treatments developed by Sigmund Freud. In theory, anyone can undergo the training necessary to become a psychoanalyst; in practice, nearly all psychoanalysts are psychiatrists. Not all psychiatrists are psychoanalysts, however; only about 10 percent so identify themselves.

• *Psychology* is a much broader field than psychiatry or psychoanalysis. Its practitioners, almost all of whom hold advanced academic degrees, work in a variety of ways and settings. About half work in clinical psychology and counseling; that is, they deal with the specific problems of individual clients. About a fourth are primarily teachers in colleges and medical schools. Some 15 percent apply their knowledge to the specific needs of industry, government, hospitals, and school districts. And 10 percent are engaged in the basic research that continually broadens and refines psychology's understanding of behavior.

BARBARA PFEFFER/PETER ARNOLD

LOOKING AT ONESELF *is a principal aim of the study of psychology.*

Basics of Psychology

The subject matter of psychology, behavior and its causes, has been of interest to people for a long time—probably for as long as mankind has existed. Yet psychology itself is barely a century old. The difference between psychology and earlier approaches to understanding behavior lies in the methods used.

Modern psychology uses the methods of science. The essence of science is the ability to make accurate predictions: when Condition A exists, then Behavior B will occur. Such a statement, when not supported by direct evidence, is called a *hypothesis*; it is a kind of educated guess. The basis of the scientific method is the formulating of hypotheses and the search for evidence of their validity. The stronger the evidence for a hypothesis (and the weaker the evidence for contradictory hypotheses), the greater its validity. But a hypothesis is never proved or disproved, only supported or not supported. The possibility always exists that evidence yet to be discovered will cast it in a new light.

When evidence supports several related hypotheses, a *theory* can be developed. A theory is a broad set of concepts and principles, a sort of framework for existing hypotheses. It demonstrates how supported hypotheses relate to one another, and it suggests new hypotheses for further investigation. A theory serves a useful purpose even if subsequently disproved, for it often leads to new knowledge and better theories.

Because psychology's theories are much less precise than those of such sciences as chemistry and physics, some people question whether psychology is in fact a science. Psychologists respond, first, that their subject matter is more complex; second, that generalizations are more difficult because of the many individual differences among people and even among animals of the same species; and third, that notwithstanding these differences, psychology's commitment to the methods and principles of scientific inquiry makes it a true science.

In practice, some phases of psychology are more scientific than others. Psychologists who do basic research—especially with animals under controlled conditions—observe the scientific method very carefully. Psychological counselors, on the other hand, use art and common sense as well as science.

Research Methods

Psychology employs several research methods according to the nature and limitations of a particular line of investigation.

Controlled experiments. The preferred method of investigation is the controlled experiment. In a controlled experiment, the experimenter is in control of all the elements of the experimental situation; no outside elements can enter and affect the experiment's outcome. After establishing the experimental situation, the experimenter then changes it in some way—by adding something to it, taking something from it, or changing some element of it. This changed element is called the *independent variable.* To determine whether this change has the effect predicted by the hypothesis being tested, some other element—the one that the hypothesis predicted would be affected—is measured. This element is called the *dependent variable.*

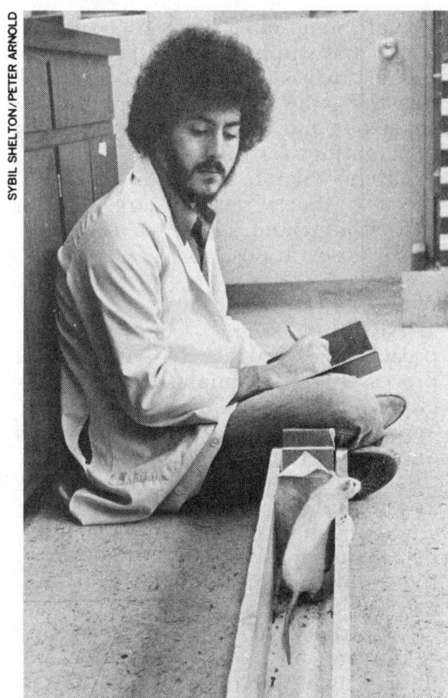
SYBIL SHELTON/PETER ARNOLD

GEORGE ROOS/PETER ARNOLD

RESEARCH: *Psychologists may study problems by devising controlled experiments* (above left), *usually with animal subjects; by directly observing the performance of individuals, or even participating with them* (above); *or by correlating two sets of variables, as with an inkblot test* (left). *Research on the test has shown that disturbed individuals "see" particular themes in the patterns. Once validated, a test such as the inkblot test can be used to validate other tests, to screen subjects for testing or treatment, to treat the emotionally disturbed, etc.*

Normally, the dependent variable is measured in two groups, an experimental group and a control group. In the experimental group, the independent variable has been introduced; in the control group, it has not. In all other respects the two groups are the same. If there is a significant difference in the measurements of the dependent variable between the two groups, there is a significant likelihood that the independent variable is the cause. Thus, a cause-and-effect relationship is established.

Controlled experiments require *operational definitions* of the independent and dependent variables. In an experiment testing the hypothesis that anger affects people's work in some way, the independent variable cannot be simply "making people angry"; the specific action that is intended to make them angry must be defined. Similarly, the dependent variable cannot simply be "work"; it must be something measurable, such as a typist's speed, measured in words per minute, or perhaps the number of errors a typist makes in a given number of words.

The controlled experiment is simple in principle; in practice, however, it can be extremely difficult to create appropriate operational definitions and to control the situation so that nothing changes except the independent variable. Also, there are many situations in which controlled experiments cannot ethically be applied; one cannot, for example, study the effects of malnutrition on children's learning abilities by deliberately starving a group of children. There are many ethical limits that restrict the design of psychological experiments, especially those with human subjects.

Direct observation. The goal of observation is to make objective and precise observations of realistic behavior. Observation is a more open-ended kind of investigation than the controlled experiment in that the expected behavior in a given situation may be more variable and less predictable.

There are two basic kinds of observation: laboratory and naturalistic. In a laboratory observation, the researcher creates a setting and situation for the observation. The researcher might, for example, bring together a group of people of a certain age (or combination of ages) and ask them to discuss a particular topic. The researcher's interest probably is not so much what is said about the topic as his data on who talks the most, who interrupts, and so forth.

Naturalistic observations take place in a natural setting; for example, the reactions of passengers on a bus to a passenger who acts in a particular way. In some situations, hidden videotape or movie cameras aid researchers in recording what takes place.

In one kind of naturalistic observation, called participant observation, the observer takes an active part in what he or she is observing. An observer might, for example, join some sort of organization in order to learn about the behavior of its members. This kind of observation makes possible close contact with the persons being observed, but it has the disadvantage that the observer's own participation in the group can affect what the other group members do.

Correlation. Correlation is a statistical method that can be usefully applied in psychology. Correlation determines the relationship between two sets of measures. Both measures are variables; but no variable is manipulated by the researcher, who simply gathers the data and correlates it.

Suppose, for example, a researcher hypothesizes that Situation A is associated with Behavior B. Gathering and correlating the data will show either a *positive* correlation (A and B often occur together), a *negative* correlation (A and B rarely occur together), or a *zero* correlation (there is no relationship between them).

It is important to note that a positive correlation between two variables does not necessarily mean that there is a cause-and-effect relationship. The correlation could mean that A caused B; that B caused A; that some other factor (C) caused both A and B; or some combination of these. A positive correlation merely indicates that two factors occur together, not that one caused another.

Case studies. A case study is an intensive investigation of an individual or, less often, of a group or an event. Because each study has only one subject, scientific generalizations cannot be made. But the mass of data gathered about one case, or a few cases, can help to confirm or refute the validity of existing theories and may suggest fruitful areas for further research.

Surveys and tests. Surveys—data obtained from questionnaires or interviews—are valuable in some kinds of psychological research. They are particularly useful when information cannot be gained by direct observation. Much knowledge of sexual behavior, for example, can only be gained by surveys.

Psychological tests are essentially exercises in correlation. Researchers have established that certain answers to certain questions correlate with certain behaviors, attitudes, personality traits, and the like. Tests based on such correlations make possible the gathering of large amounts of data in a relatively fast and inexpensive manner.

Approaches to Psychology

Given the complexity of the field, it is not surprising that several different approaches to the study of behavior have evolved. Psychologists differ among themselves about the best subject matter, the best methods, and even the fundamental goals of their investigations.

Today there are five basic points of view in psychology. Most psychologists associate themselves to some degree with one of these; some adopt an eclectic approach, combining two or more viewpoints.

Biological. The biological approach has its basis in the evolutionary theory of Charles Darwin. According to this theory, the genetic makeup of all species, including human beings, has evolved through a process called "natural selection." This means that certain genetic (inheritable) traits that help individuals survive become established in the species because individuals with those traits are likelier to survive and reproduce. Genetic traits include both physical characteristics and behavioral characteristics that are essentially inherited traits of the human nervous system.

Because it assumes an evolutionary relationship of human beings to other forms of life, the biological approach to psychology assumes that human and animal behaviors are related. Therefore, investigations of animal behavior can help to shed light on human behavior.

Studies of animal behavior have become an important part of research in psychology. Such studies have definite advantages over experiments with human subjects. Many animals have much shorter reproductive cycles than do people, so many generations can be studied in a relatively short time. In addition, some experiments that cannot be undertaken with human subjects for ethical reasons can be undertaken with animal subjects.

Because inherited traits are so fundamental to human behavior, the biological approach is sometimes not considered a separate approach at all, but rather a fundamental part of each of the other four points of view.

Psychodynamic. This point of view, also called "psychoanalytic," derives from the research and theories of Sigmund Freud. Freud theorized that individuals have strong basic drives that come into conflict with the behavior expected by society. Individuals deliberately banish these basic drives from their conscious mind or, in Freudian terms, repress them. But the drives persist in the unconscious part of the mind and sometimes break through the defenses that the conscious mind has constructed. These drives may also find expression in disguised behavior that is considered socially acceptable.

In Freud's theory, the strong but repressed inner drives are basically sexual. Some later theorists have disputed that emphasis, but all psychodynamic theorists follow Freud in emphasizing the dynamic interaction of conscious and unconscious motives as explanations for behavior.

Psychodynamic theory is an example of a theory derived largely from case studies and supported by subsequent observations.

Cognitive. The cognitive approach is also concerned with mental processes, but it emphasizes a different kind. Where the psychodynamic approach emphasizes the unconscious and the irrational aspects of the mind, the cognitive emphasizes the mind as a system that processes information. It studies such specifically human activities as thought, perception, remembering, problem-solving, and language use.

Cognitive psychology's roots go back to the work in the late 1800's of such figures as Wilhelm Wundt and William James, both considered to be among psychology's founders. More recently the dominant figure has been Jean Piaget, who devoted his life to studying the ways in which children think and solve problems. His theories, derived mainly from naturalistic observation, suggest that the mind of a growing child goes through different stages of development, changing the ways it responds to and processes information. Such stages are difficult to explain simply by the older child's greater number and variety of experiences. Piaget and other cognitive psychologists explain these stages in terms of development of the rational, creative, and interpretive qualities of the mind.

More than other points of view, cognitive psychology assumes that people are rational beings whose behavior is determined largely by their own perceptions and choices. Thus, each individual's world is to a large extent what that person's mind has made of it.

Behavioral. Much more than other psychological perspectives, the behavioral point of view sees behavior as determined by environmental influences. According to behaviorists, people learn to associate certain behaviors with rewards and others with punishment. These associations largely determine, or "condition," their subsequent behavior. Even mental processes—which behaviorists tend to minimize—are thought of as externally conditioned behaviors.

Research by behavioral psychologists has emphasized learning processes. Much of the research has been conducted with animal subjects, as behaviorists believe that the same principles apply to both human and animal learning. Underlying all re-

PIAGET AND SKINNER: *The great modern psychologists are each associated with a particular approach. Piaget is a cognitive psychologist, Skinner a behaviorist.*

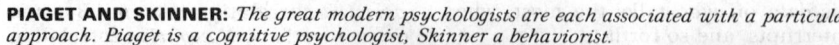

JEAN-PIERRE LANDENBERG

T. POLUMBAUM/COURTESY OF ALFRED A. KNOPF

search is the behaviorist's basic belief that observable behavior, not unobservable mental processes, is the proper subject of psychology. John Watson and, later, B. F. Skinner, have been the preeminent figures in behavioral psychology.

Humanistic. As its name suggests, humanistic psychology focuses on the uniquely human: the inner lives, goals, and hopes of people. It rejects the notion, shared by the psychodynamic and the behavioral psychologists, that behavior is largely determined by forces beyond people's control. Humanists argue that this idea takes away people's essential dignity as human beings. Instead humanists encourage studies of such topics as creativity, personal responsibility, and values. Humanistic psychologists hope to help people to understand themselves and to develop their fullest potential.

Humanistic psychologists tend to be less insistent on a "pure" scientific approach; they use some research procedures, such as analysis of their own feelings and impressions, that other psychological perspectives reject.

Humanistic psychology has emerged only in the years since World War II, but it is deeply rooted in the great religious and philosophical traditions of Western society. Its leading figures include Abraham Maslow, Carl Rogers, Rollo May, and R. D. Laing.

Biological Bases of Behavior

The Nervous System

Of the various systems within the human body—the digestive system, the circulatory system, and so on—psychologists are mainly concerned with the nervous system. The nervous system receives and processes information and determines what to do with that information. In other words, it determines behavior.

The basic building blocks of the nervous system are cells called *neurons.* The system itself has two major divisions, the central nervous system, consisting of the brain and spinal cord, and the peripheral nervous system, whose neurons conduct impulses between the central nervous system and the rest of the body.

Neurons. A neuron is a body cell and, like all other cells, it consists basically of a cell wall, a nucleus, and protoplasm. Its shape, however, is quite different from that of other cells. The largest part of the cell, where the nucleus is located, is called the *soma.* Radiating from the soma are numerous small fibers called *dendrites.* Also extending from the soma is a single fiber called the *axon,* at the end of which are branches leading to terminals. Axons vary in length from a fraction of an inch to several feet.

Neurons work by an electrochemical process. Chemical changes in the neuron create an electrical current, which flows along the neuron as a nerve impulse. An impulse enters the neuron at a dendrite, passes through the soma, and goes out the axon to its end, where it may be transferred to a muscle, a gland, or another neuron.

Between the axon of one neuron and the dendrite of another is a microscopic space called a *synapse.* In the synapse are several chemicals called *neurotransmitters.* Some neurotransmitters facilitate the passage of an impulse across the synapse; others inhibit it. Neurotransmitters are in a constant state of flux, and whether an impulse passes from one neuron to another depends upon the combination of neurotransmitters in the synapse at that particular instant.

In most persons, the delicate balance of neurotransmitters keeps the nervous system functioning well. The balance can, however, be affected by drugs, by disease, and by electrical stimulation of certain parts of the brain. For example, if the neurotransmitter dopamine is absent or insufficient, the result is the muscular rigidity and tremors known as Parkinson's disease; too much dopamine is associated with the psychotic disorder called schizophrenia. The drug amphetamine, which acts in some ways like dopamine, is useful in treating Parkinson's disease, but when used to excess, it produces symptoms resembling those of schizophrenia.

Another group of neurotransmitters called endorphins can reduce pain by lowering the number of impulses between pain-transmitting neurons. The body's production of endorphins can be increased by electrical stimulation of certain parts of the brain, or by inserting needles at specific places in the body, as in acupuncture. Opium-derived drugs, such as morphine and heroin, work much like endorphins, but also have less desirable effects.

The human nervous system contains billions of neurons—estimates range from 12 to 200 billion—distributed throughout the body, but the largest number are in the brain. The number of neurons is greatest at birth, declining thereafter at an estimated rate of 10,000 per day (and at a greater rate when alcohol is consumed). A neuron, once dead, is not replaced. Even when large numbers of neurons are destroyed, however, as in an accident or stroke, other neurons often take over the functions of the destroyed neurons. Apparently, the surviving neurons begin using synapses that were previously unused, thus creating new paths for nerve impulses. Some neurons also extend their axons to make new connections. The nervous system's ability to recover in this way is greatest in childhood.

THE SYNAPSE *is where two nerve cells meet and where information is exchanged. This electrochemical exchange is the subject of intense research.*

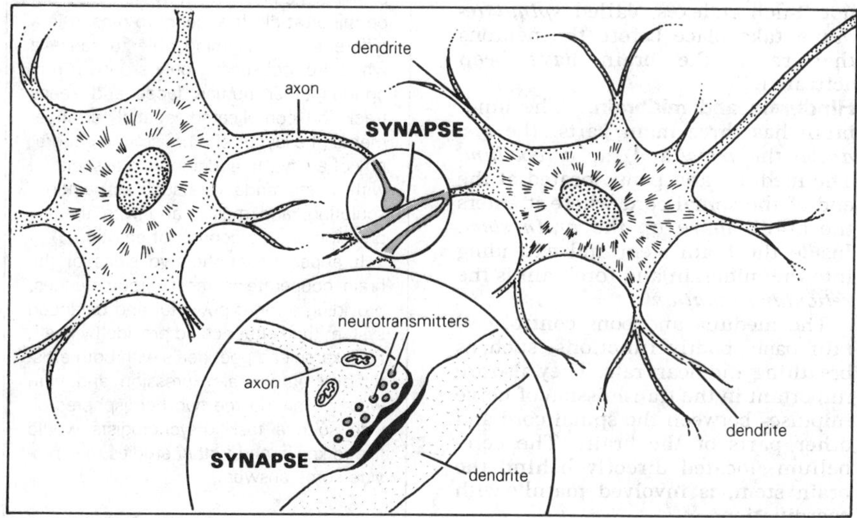

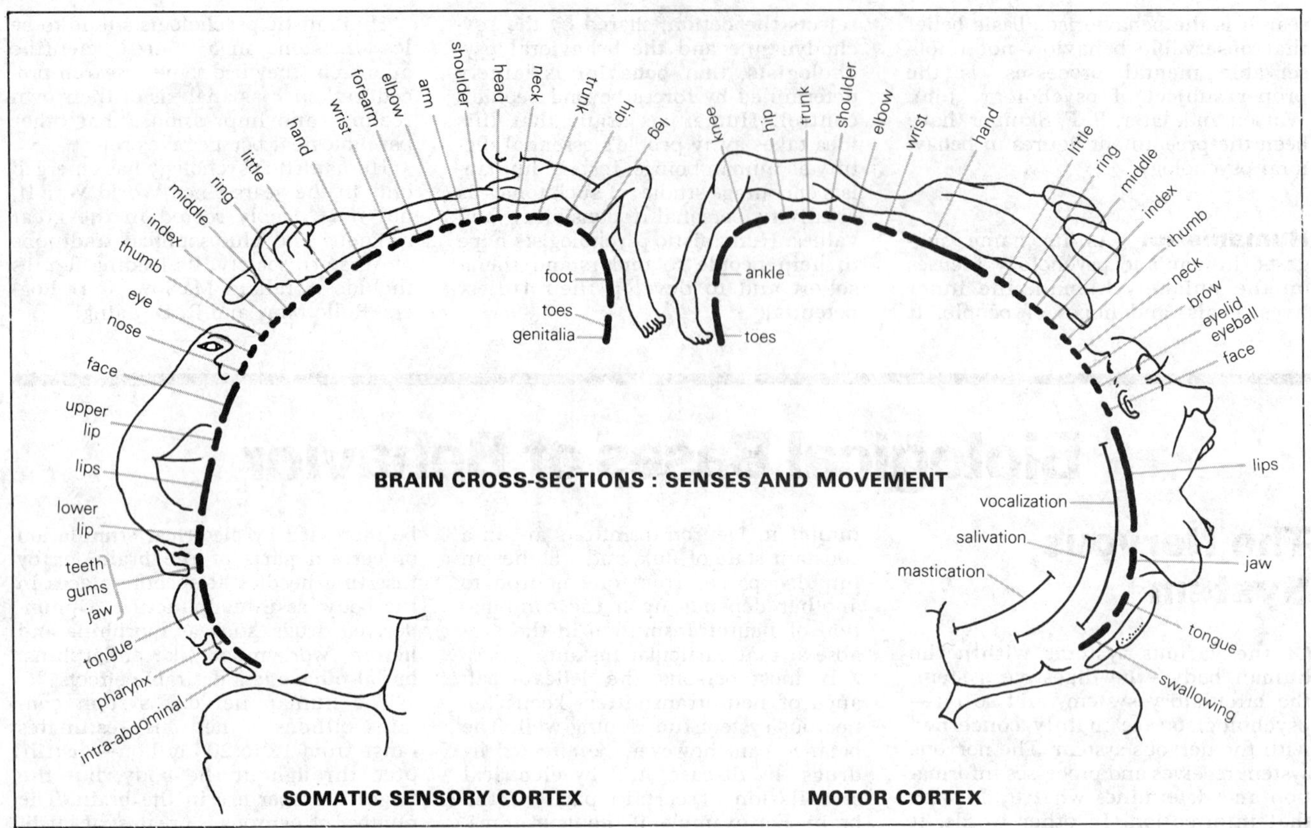

SENSES AND MOVEMENT *are monitored and controlled by different parts of the cerebral cortex. These drawings of the sensory region* (left) *and the motor region* (right) *show the major prominence of the face and hands, which are well supplied with nerve endings.*

Central nervous system.

The central nervous system consists of the spinal cord and the brain. The three main parts of the brain are the hindbrain, the midbrain, and the forebrain; each has further subdivisions.

Spinal cord. The spinal cord extends the length of the neck and torso. It is protected by the 33 bones called vertebrae or, collectively, the backbone.

The spinal cord serves mainly to conduct nerve impulses between the brain and other parts of the body. It also controls certain basic reflexes, such as the knee-jerk reflex and the reflex response to touching something hot. Such reflexes, called *spinal reflexes*, take place before the neurons that reach the brain have been activated.

Hindbrain and midbrain. The hindbrain has three main parts: the *medulla*, the *pons*, and the *cerebellum*. The medulla and pons, located at the end of the spinal cord where it enters the brain, make up the *brain stem*. Inside the brain stem and extending into the midbrain and forebrain is the *reticular formation*.

The medulla and pons control certain basic bodily functions, such as breathing and heart rate. They also are important in the transmission of nerve impulses between the spinal cord and other parts of the brain. The cerebellum, located directly behind the brain stem, is involved mainly with coordination.

LEFT BRAIN—RIGHT BRAIN

In recent years, psychologists have discovered amazing differences between the left and right sides (or hemispheres) of the brain—differences that may cast important light on the nature of the brain itself.

The left side of the brain, which is the dominant side in most humans, is associated with speech and with analytical reasoning. In some ways, it resembles a super-computer in its ability to receive and process information. The right side, or minor hemisphere, however, may not be minor at all. It appears to reason in a different way, seeming able to sense a whole from observing only a part. It recognizes other human faces and keeps track of complicated spatial arrangements (the layout of a house, the geography of a city). In addition, it is associated with artistic endeavors such as painting, sculpting, and music, and with the expression and perception of emotion.

It appears that the two sides of the brain cooperate in most circumstances, providing a more powerful and balanced system than either could provide by itself. For example, a poet deals with both artistic and emotional expression and with words. How do the two hemispheres divide such a task? Psychologists would like to know, and further studies may provide some answers.

The reticular formation is important in consciousness, attention, and sleep. It has an important role in determining which nerve impulses reach the rest of the brain and which do not. The ability of the brain to "tune out" parts of the environment while concentrating on other parts is a function of the reticular formation.

The midbrain, just above the hindbrain, is mainly a relay system between the forebrain and the other parts of the central nervous system. It also controls eye movements.

Forebrain. The forebrain consists mainly of a large mass of neurons called the *cerebral cortex*. Its surface is wrinkled and folded, so that the majority of its neurons are near a surface. Certain deep folds, called *fissures*, divide it into right and left halves and divide each half into four major divisions called *lobes*. Buried deep within the cortex, near the midbrain, are other structures called the *thalamus*, the *hypothalamus*, and the *limbic system*.

The cerebral cortex has *sensory*, *motor*, and *association* areas. The sensory areas deal with information coming into the brain from the senses, by way of neurons connecting with the eyes, the ears, the skin, etc. The motor areas determine body movements. Interestingly, the two largest areas have to do with movement of the hands and of the speech-producing organs of the mouth—the tongue, lips, jaw, etc. The association areas, the largest part of the cerebral cortex, have to do with such specifically human functions as language, thought, and problem-solving.

There are important differences between the right and left halves, or *hemispheres*, of the cerebral cortex. In all right-handed and most left-handed people, the left hemisphere controls language and all the mental processes based on it: the memorization of facts; thinking in terms of past, present, and future; and reasoning logically, including mathematically. The right hemisphere has to do with space perception, such as sense of direction; with emotions, both one's own and the perception of them in others; and with artistic expression and appreciation, as in music and the fine arts. The left hemisphere thinks logically: it puts things into sequences. The right hemisphere is intuitive: it looks at the "big picture." A band of nerve fibers called the *corpus callosum* connects the two hemispheres, allowing them to combine their information and share their abilities.

Of the small structures within the cortex, the thalamus is a kind of relay station for sensory nerve impulses and the limbic system has to do with motives and emotions. The hypothalamus has to do with emotion; with regulation of such body processes as eating, drinking, and temperature regulation; and with control of the pituitary gland, which in turn controls all the other glands of the endocrine system.

Peripheral nervous system. The peripheral nervous system connects the central nervous system to the rest of the body. It has two major parts, the *somatic* and the *autonomic* systems.

The somatic system has two kinds of neurons: sensory, which carry perceptions from such sense organs as eyes, ears, and skin to the central nervous system; and motor, which carry instructions for movement to all of the body's various voluntary muscles. These include not only the muscles used in such activities as walking and lifting, but also those used in such complex activities as speaking, singing, drawing, or playing a musical instrument.

The autonomic system has to do with the body's various glands and with its involuntary muscles, such as those of the heart and the intestines. Its two subdivisions, the *sympathetic* and *parasympathetic* systems, both coordinate such activities as breathing, heart rate, and digestion, but in different ways. In emergency or stress situations, for example, the sympathetic system can increase heart and respiration rates and stimulate the adrenal glands to produce adrenalin (or epiniphrene), preparing the body for "fight or flight." The parasympathetic system works in the opposite way, by bringing the same functions back to the levels appropriate to a more relaxed state.

Sensation and Perception

Sensation is the process by which the nervous system reports stimuli to the brain. *Perception* is the process by which the brain organizes and interprets sensations to give them meaning. Perception is a creative process. Since no two people's perceptions are identical, each of us, in a sense, creates his or her own world.

Senses. The body's various sense organs have in common the ability to detect certain forms of energy in the environment and to change that energy, by a process called *transduction*, into nerve impulses. The specialized cells that accomplish this process are called *receptors*.

Different receptors respond to different kinds of energy. Those in the eye respond to electromagnetic energy, giving us the sense of sight. Receptors in the ear respond to sound waves, a form of mechanical energy. The senses of smell and taste are responses to chemicals in the air or dissolved in saliva.

The so-called sense of touch is in reality several different senses whose receptors are in the skin and many internal organs: touch and pressure (sometimes regarded as one sense, sometimes as two distinct senses), pain, warmth, and cold.

There are, in addition, two senses called "body" senses. The *kinesthetic* sense, whose receptors are in muscles, tendons, and joints, is the sense of movement of the various parts of the body. Close your eyes and, without its touching anything, wiggle your thumb or one of your fingers; it is the kinesthetic sense that tells you of the thumb's or finger's changing position.

The other body sense is the *vestibular* sense, sometimes called the sense of balance or of orientation. The vestibular sensors, located in the inner ear, respond to gravity and to acceleration and deceleration. It is this sense that enables us to stand and walk upright and that, when disturbed, produces dizziness.

Attention. Sensory receptors are constantly sending information—as much of it as they possibly can—through the neurons of the peripheral nervous system. Yet at any given moment, a person is aware of only a very small fraction of these messages. The process by which the central nervous system sorts out information, concentrating on some and largely ignoring the rest, is called *attention*.

Psychologists differ as to whether attention is mainly a matter of focusing on what one wishes to perceive or of filtering out what one wishes not to perceive. They agree, however, that it is limited in capacity: a person can pay attention to more than one thing at a time only when one of the activities, such as driving a car, is largely automatic. Experiments have shown that a person wearing headphones, each headphone carrying a different message, can follow one message and "tune out" the other. When the messages are on familiar subjects, so that a person can fill in information from his own experience, the person can shift attention back and forth from one message to the other and so get the general sense of each message without a complete understanding of either.

Factors in the environment can also attract attention. For example, increases or decreases in the intensity of a stimulus—the dimming of a light, the flaring of a candle—attract attention. So, too, does movement. A stimulus that is repeated, such as the sound of a continually dripping faucet, is likelier to attract attention than is the same stimulus occurring only once or at infrequent intervals.

ATTENTION *is divided when one is skating, blowing bubbles, and listening to a radio all at once.*

ERIC KROLL/TAURUS PHOTOS

Attention is also affected by factors within a person. One who is thirsty, for example, is likelier to notice the sound of running water than is the same person when not thirsty. Interests play a part. A painter, an art historian, and a person who is neither will each notice different details of a painting. Previous experiences also affect attention. A person who has studied the oboe is likely to hear more of the oboe's parts in a symphony concert than is someone who has never studied music; a person who has been through some kind of disaster is likely to be especially sensitive to the sounds, smells, or other sensory stimuli that he associates with that disaster.

Information that agrees with their beliefs tends to attract people's attention more than does contradictory information. Similarly, people's attention tends to filter out information that they find threatening or anxiety-producing.

Visual perception. Perception is the process, or series of processes, by which the brain organizes the information it receives. In a sense, it is the interpretation of that information, based on what the person has learned in his or her previous experiences.

Of the various kinds of sensory stimulation that the brain processes, most is known about visual perception. The brain employs many different strategies in interpreting visual information.

Constancy. When you look at something nearby and something similar that is several hundred feet away—two cars of the same make and model, for example—the images of the cars, as they register in the retina of your eye, are of different sizes, the nearer being much much larger. But you do not perceive the cars as being of different sizes. As part of its perceptual processes, your mind interprets the cars as being the same size, even though the information coming to it from the eye is different for each car.

The mind interprets shapes similarly. For example, a circular object will, when viewed from an angle, register in the eye as an oval. But the mind adjusts for the angle of vision, and so perceives the circle as such.

Besides making allowances for distance and for angle of vision, the mind also makes allowances for degrees of light and darkness. The ability to make these allowances is called *constancy.*

Figure and ground. The mind perceives objects, or "figures," as standing out against a background, or "ground"; indeed, an object cannot be clearly seen as such unless it has been distinguished from its ground. A given object may be perceived either as a figure or as part of the ground, depending on how the attention is directed, but not as both at once. For example, the words you are now reading are figures against the ground of the page. If you put your hand on the book and look at your hand, both letters and page will become part of the ground.

The figure-ground principle applies to sounds as well as sights. For example, most music is perceived as a melody (the figure) against a ground of accompanying notes.

Grouping. Grouping is the process by which the mind perceives individual figures as parts of larger wholes. Among the principles of grouping are (1) similarity: elements that are alike are perceived as being together; (2) proximity: elements close to one another are similarly perceived as belonging together; (3) symmetry: elements that relate to one another as regular, well-balanced shapes are perceived as being together; (4) continuity: elements that form a continuous line or pattern are perceived as being together; and (5) closure: elements that group to form an incomplete figure are usually formed into a complete figure by the mind.

Depth and distance. The eyes receive information in only two dimensions (left-right and up-down), yet the third dimension of depth or distance is easily perceived. Depth perception is made possible by a number of "cues." The cues are both binocular and monocular.

Binocular cues are those that depend on the simultaneous use of two eyes. Because the eyes are slightly differently located, each receives an image that is fractionally different from that received by the other eye. This difference is called binocular disparity. The two two-dimensional images from each eye are processed by the brain into a single perception in three dimensions. A second binocular cue, convergence, derives from the need of the eyes to turn in toward each other in order to see something close by. The input from the kinesthetic sense in the eye muscles is used by the brain in perceiving the relative depth of nearby objects (within 30 feet).

Monocular cues make possible a certain amount of depth perception even when using only one eye. They also make possible the perception of depth in pictures (including moving pictures).

A few monocular cues are related to motion. You know, for example, that

VISUAL PERCEPTION *depends on the way the brain processes information. It searches for* constancy (left) *by assuming that these balloons are the same size (the smaller is farther away).* Grouping (right) *suggests that the pattern (A) is made up of the elements shown in (B).* Figure and ground (below) *in the Escher drawing deliberately confuse the viewer.*

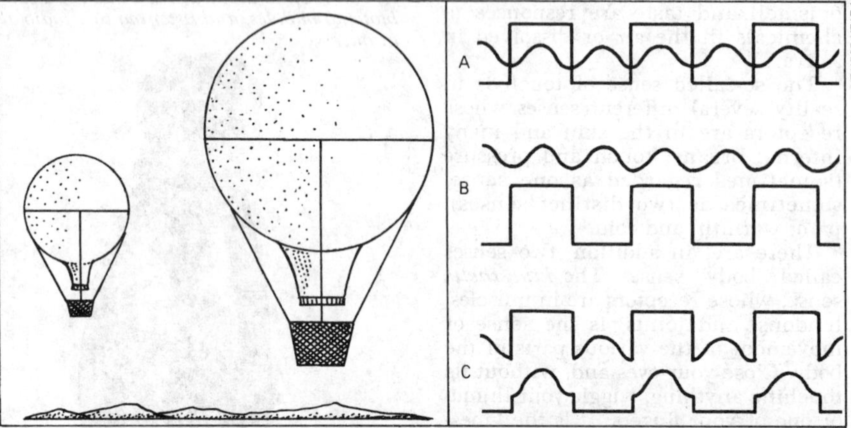

PETER LOEWER

EPA/SOTHEBY PARKE-BERNET

when you are riding in a car or a train, an object in the distance appears to go by much more slowly than does one nearer by. The difference in the speeds is perceived by the brain as a difference in distances.

Most monocular cues apply to still images as well as to moving images. There are several such cues. A small object is interpreted as farther away than a larger but otherwise similar object. Straight lines that converge, or tend toward convergence, are perceived as parallel lines receding into the distance, as seen when looking along railroad tracks or along a road. Patterns caused by light hitting an object are perceived as indications that the object is three-dimensional. (Photographers know that early morning and late afternoon, when sunlight strikes objects from the side and casts deep shadows, are the best times for taking pictures.) Objects that are clear and detailed are perceived as nearby, those less distinct as farther away; for example, a tree whose individual leaves can be seen seems closer than one that is just a mass of green. Finally, an object that partially blocks the view of another object is perceived as nearer than the blocked object.

Perceptual hypotheses. While other kinds of perception have been less thoroughly studied than vision, it may be assumed that the perceptual processes involved are similarly complex. In hearing, for example, our two ears make possible the perception of the direction from which a sound comes; other cues make it possible to judge the distance of a sound. The perceptual processes involved in the understanding of language and other symbolic systems are doubtless even more complex.

One psychologist has suggested that each perception, of whatever kind, is a kind of hypothesis. When the brain receives a piece of information from the senses, it seeks other information within the brain with which to compare it. Of this information, some may be innate, but most is the result of earlier perceptions. The brain compares the incoming sensory data with the information already stored, and, on the basis of those comparisons, forms a hypothesis about its meaning. The more a perceptual hypothesis resembles the earlier perceptions stored in the brain, the more confident a person will be about it.

Sometimes these perceptual hypotheses are erroneous; the brain misinterprets the sensory data it is receiving. This kind of perceptual error, resulting from a misinterpretation of perceptual cues, is called an illusion. The illustrations at left show some examples of visual illusions.

Perceptual abilities. Some perceptual abilities may be present at birth, at least in part, but most must be learned. It appears that there are certain critical periods in learning to perceive, after which a perceptual ability can be learned only incompletely or not at all. Persons blind from birth whose vision has been fully restored in adulthood show the importance of these periods; their visual perceptions remain severely limited.

Extrasensory perception. A small group of psychologists has made studies of modes of perception that do not rely on the generally accepted senses. Although there is great popular interest in people who claim to be able to find lost objects, predict future events, or receive messages from people far away, there is no generally accepted proof that such feats really occur.

Consciousness

Consciousness is a person's awareness of his sensations and thoughts. There are two basic states of consciousness, the normal waking state and various altered states. Altered states may be further subdivided into those that occur naturally, as a result of sleep or of disease, and those that are induced, as by hypnosis, meditation, or drugs.

Consciousness, being an internal mental state, has proved difficult to study scientifically. Physiological measures, as of brain waves, heart rate, and blood pressure, can be made of people in various states; but these tell little of the person's thoughts. Most studies of the normal waking state are based on people's reports of their thoughts at a series of given moments, as, for example, when an electronic device sounds. Studies of altered states, as during dreaming, must rely on memories whose reliability is often questionable.

Normal waking state. It has been suggested that the brain consists of several different but parallel subsystems, all active all or much of the time, but with only one in control of the consciousness at any given moment. Control shifts from one to another of these subsystems, such as those that underlie memories, emotions, and fantasies, with remarkable frequency. One study reported shifts in thinking at intervals of approximately five seconds. Attention plays an important role in determining which sensory experiences will enter the consciousness.

There appear to be two basic functions of waking consciousness. In the active function, the consciousness

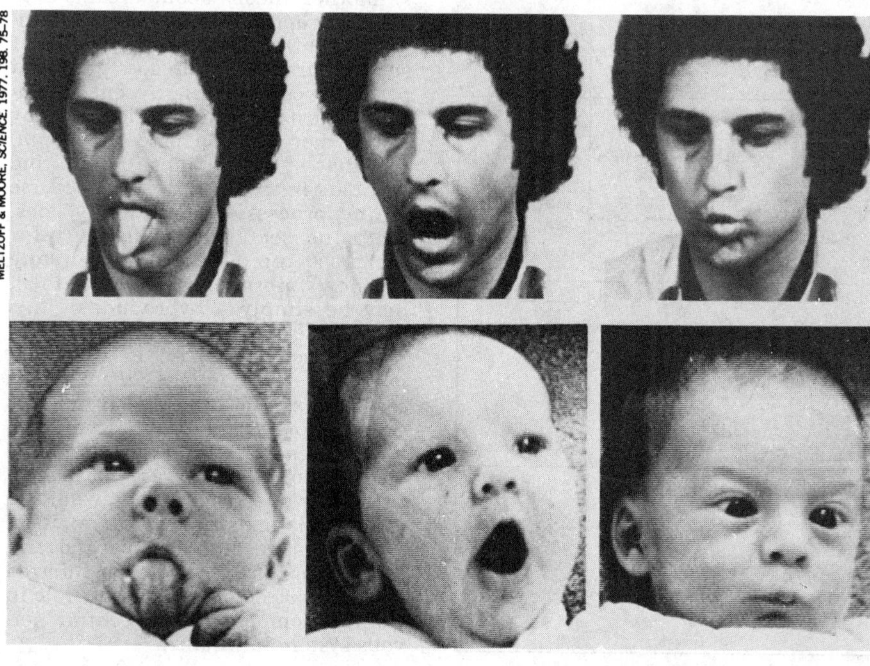

MELTZOFF & MOORE, SCIENCE, 1977, 198, 75–78

PERCEPTUAL LEARNING: *Tests have shown that babies two or three weeks old can see and mimic simple behavior.*

DREAMLIKE PAINTING *by Chagall shows that normal rules of logic do not apply.*

MUSEUM OF MODERN ART

plans, directs, and monitors behavior. Receptive functions include perception and the awareness of thoughts, emotions, and memories.

Consciousness can be affected by a number of factors. Fatigue (or its absence) is one such factor; another is mood, such as joy or depression. Biological rhythms, the regular cycles followed not only by such biological functions as body temperature, heart rate, and hormone levels, but also by various moods, also affect consciousness. Posture plays a role as well. Persons lying down tend to think more about the past and future than do standing and sitting persons, whose consciousness is more in the present.

Most conscious thought appears to be realistic and related to the present situation, but with interludes controlled by memories, fantasies, emotions, and the like. Individual patterns, however, vary widely.

Sleeping and dreaming. No one knows why sleep is necessary, though necessary it clearly is. Studies of people who have been deprived of sleep for several days show them developing various physiological and mental symptoms such as irritability, confusion, lack of eye focus, and tremors of the hand. These, however, are relatively mild symptoms, and only a good night's sleep is required for virtually complete recovery. In some cases, several days' lack of sleep will lead to hallucinations in a small group of individuals.

Whatever the purpose of sleep may be, it is not to rest the brain, for the brain is as active during sleep as during waking hours—perhaps even more active.

Stages of sleep. The primary tool for research into the nature of sleep is the electroencephalograph (EEG), which measures the electrical activity of the brain. In the course of a normal night's sleep, several different kinds of brain waves register on the EEG, indicating the different stages of sleep through which the sleeper passes.

The first sleep stage, immediately after falling asleep, is called Stage One. At this level, the body is somewhat relaxed and the sleeper can easily be awakened. The sleeper then passes through Stage Two and Stage Three, becoming more relaxed and more difficult to awaken, to the deepest stage of sleep, Stage Four, characterized by total relaxation and extreme difficulty in awakening. At each of these stages the EEG registers a noticeably different kind of brain wave.

Throughout the period of sleep, the sleeper moves from one sleep stage to another. After the first period of Stage Four sleep, the sleeper moves briefly to Stage One or Two, then, typically, back to Stage Four. After two or three such cycles, which take place in the first hours of sleep, the remainder of the sleeping period is spent mainly at Stage One and Stage Two.

At Stage One there are two distinct kinds of sleep. During REM (Rapid Eye Movement) sleep, the eyes move about rapidly beneath the closed lids. The brain-wave measurements suggest a high level of activity in the brain, but the sleeper is as difficult to awaken as in Stage Four. As the sleep period progresses, the periods of REM sleep become progressively longer. Sleepers awakened from the various stages of sleep during experiments indicate that REM sleep is typically a time of emotional and pictorially vivid dreams. (It has been suggested that the moving eyes may be following the action of the dream.)

During NREM (Non-Rapid Eye Movement) sleep, many people also report dreamlike activity when awakened, sometimes as vivid as that of REM sleep but much more often of a less emotional character. It appears that many people are mentally active through most or all of the night, and that almost all are active during REM sleep. It seems almost certain, then, that all normal people dream; their ability to recall dreams upon awakening, however, varies considerably.

Dreams Information on the content of dreams is gathered in two ways: by asking people to write about their dreams after they wake up or, in a laboratory setting, by waking them up and taking an immediate report. The second method produces better data but is much more expensive and time-consuming.

The content of a person's dreams seems to be considerably influenced by that person's waking concerns. It can also, at least in some cases, be influenced by stimuli in the sleeper's environment, such as the music or talk of a radio left on overnight. Interestingly, the content of about two-thirds of reported dreams is emotionally negative, characterized by anger, fear, and hostility.

The purpose of dreaming is not clear. Sigmund Freud theorized that what he called the manifest content of a dream—essentially its action and story line—is the surface manifestation, disguised and dramatized, of the latent content. The latent content is the hidden desires and motives that, according to Freud's theory, the conscious mind has repressed. If the latent content is not sufficiently disguised, the result is frightening to the dreamer—a nightmare. Freud's hypothesis has been partially supported by subsequent research, but much of it has also been questioned.

Another theory about dreams suggests that approximately every 90 minutes—the frequency with which REM sleep recurs—the brain goes through a period of consolidating recent experiences with the information already stored there. It is a process, not unlike that of a computer, of inserting new data in the memory. In the course of the process, so the theory goes, the mind searches the memory for the most appropriate place to store the new information. Dreams, then, may be simply a byproduct of this memory search.

Whatever its purpose, REM sleep is not limited to humans; all mammals seem to experience it, and in roughly the same proportions as humans. Newborn babies (and the newborn young of other mammals that are born with their nervous systems not yet fully developed) experience more REM sleep than do older people and animals. From this it has been inferred that REM sleep may play some role in the development of the central nervous system in infants.

MEASUREMENT OF BRAIN ACTIVITY *shows differences between the waking state* (top), *NREM sleep* (middle), *and REM sleep* (bottom). *The pattern during REM sleep is very active, resembling that of being awake.*

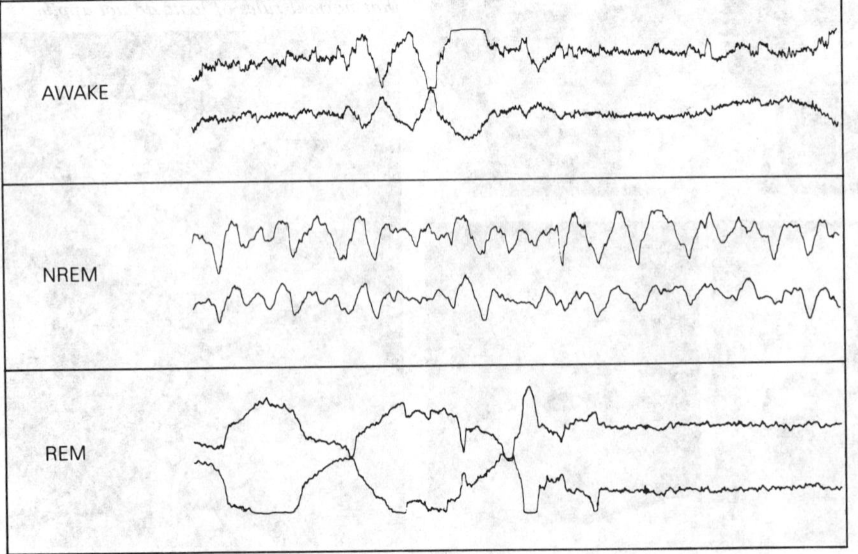

MIMI FORSYTH/MONKMEYER

MEDITATION

The following are typical instructions for meditation:

1. Choose a quiet place where you can spend 20 minutes without being disturbed. Sit in a comfortable position.
2. Close your eyes. Concentrate gently on relaxing your body, one part at a time: toes, feet, ankles, legs, etc.
3. When you are thoroughly relaxed, concentrate on your breathing. Choose a pleasant syllable (those ending in "n" or "m" are popular), and say it to yourself each time you exhale.
4. Use the syllable to gently exclude everything else. If outside sounds or other thoughts distract you, return to your syllable and relaxed breathing.
5. Continue for 15 to 20 minutes, then gradually come out of the meditative state.

This discipline requires practice. Ideally, you should use it twice a day, morning and evening. Most people are more successful meditating before eating rather than after.

HYPNOSIS AND MEDITATION *may both be valuable tools for dealing with stress. The hypnotist at left has put his patient into a trancelike state. The procedure at right describes one simple type of meditation.*

Hypnosis. A person enters the hypnotic state through *hypnotic induction*, a process in which the hypnotist first asks the subject to concentrate on some object, such as a spot on the wall or a watch dangling from a chain, and then suggests various changes in the subject's feelings and perceptions. Often a trancelike state is induced. Once hypnotized, the subject is very susceptible to suggestions from the hypnotist. The hypnotist may suggest that a part of the body cannot be moved, that the subject is hearing music, or that there is no feeling in some part of the body. Subjects may also be induced to unusual kinds of behavior, such as imitating an animal or acting like a child.

Persons in the hypnotic state will wait for suggestions rather than initiate activity on their own. Often they perceive only what the hypnotist directs them to perceive, blocking out other perceptions and even accepting gross distortions of reality. Some suggestions made under hypnosis, such as that cigarettes taste awful, can carry through after the hypnotic trance has ended. This phenomenon, known as *posthypnotic suggestion*, is useful in helping people overcome bad habits.

Not everyone is susceptible to hypnosis, and of those who are, some are more susceptible than others. The most responsive people seem to be those who often fantasize.

Hypnosis is not well understood. One theory suggests that in hypnosis the various systems that alternate in controlling attention become dissociated from one another. Another holds that hypnosis works because some people are willing, often eager, to engage in a kind of experimental role-playing, entertaining new ideas and playing by new rules.

Meditation. To meditate is to concentrate the attention on some single thought, word, or sensation. Meditation can be active, requiring strenuous exercises, as in the whirling of Turkish dervishes and in some yoga techniques. More often, however, it is passive, involving relaxation in a quiet atmosphere while concentrating on a single word or on one's own breathing.

Meditation does not dramatically alter consciousness so much as it relaxes it. There is evidence that meditating for one or two 20-minute periods daily helps one better adapt to stress. Apparently, meditation decreases the activity of the sympathetic nervous system, that part of the autonomic system that arouses the body to respond to emergencies, or increases the activity of the calming parasympathetic system, or both. It achieves this through the *relaxation response*, which has both somatic (body) and cognitive (mental) aspects.

Some have suggested that meditation brings the right half of the brain temporary dominance over the left half, which is usually in control of waking consciousness. There is evidence that people who meditate regularly do better on certain right-brain tasks and not as well on certain left-brain tasks as do nonmeditators. This, however, may simply reflect the personalities of persons who choose to meditate rather than any direct result of meditation.

Drugs. A drug is any nonfood chemical substance that affects the functioning of the body in some way. Certain drugs can, by altering the chemistry of the nervous system, affect the state of a person's consciousness. Such drugs, called *psychoactive* drugs, work by either increasing or decreasing the rate of synaptic transmission. Some drugs do this by replacing the natural neurotransmitters, others by affecting the quantities of the natural neurotransmitters.

People can become tolerant of certain drugs, dependent on them, or addicted to them. *Tolerance* means that, because of the body's natural reactions to a drug, increasingly large doses are required to produce the same effect. *Dependence* is of two kinds, physical and psychological. *Physical dependence* means that the body's natural defenses continue to fight a drug for some time after the person has stopped taking it, producing withdrawal symptoms. *Psychological dependence* means that the person is unwilling to do without the pleasurable effects of the drug. *Addiction* is unusually strong dependence beyond the person's control.

Psychoactive drugs are generally classified into five groups: depressants, stimulants, narcotics, hallucinogens, and cannabis.

Depressants. Depressants are drugs that interfere with synaptic transmissions and so decrease the level of the nervous system's activity. In mild doses, they produce feelings of relaxation and well-being. Larger doses, however, can lead to such conditions as psychological depression and, in extreme cases, to death. Use of depressants may often lead to dependence, both physical and psychological, and addiction.

Alcohol, barbiturates, and tranquilizers are the major depressants. They are by far the most widely used of psychoactive drugs, and they are the most frequently abused, a fact often overlooked because of their general social acceptability. While alcoholism remains the most serious and widespread of all forms of drug abuse, addiction to such tranquilizers as Valium is far more common than is generally realized.

Stimulants. Stimulants are the opposite of depressants. They activate the nervous system by increasing the rate of synaptic transmissions.

Caffeine, found in coffee, tea, many soft drinks, and some headache remedies, is the most widely used stimulant. Its effects are relatively mild in most people, although physical dependence is common ("I can't function in the morning until I've had my coffee").

Less widely used but far more dangerous are the amphetamines and cocaine. Amphetamines, marketed under such trade names as Dexedrine and Benzedrine, are also known as "speed," "uppers," and "bennies." Used in moderation—to prevent fatigue, reduce appetite, and in the treatment of certain diseases—they seem not to be particularly harmful. Tolerance develops rapidly, however, so that larger and larger doses are required for the same effect. Large doses may cause heart failure, stroke, or serious brain damage if continued. If use is suddenly discontinued, the user may experience acute depression and exhaustion.

Cocaine stimulates the nervous system in similar though not identical ways, producing euphoria in some cases but anxiety in others. In large doses it can lead to convulsions, delusions, and hallucinations, including the feeling of bugs crawling under the skin. It is considered to be a dangerous drug.

CHRIS SHERIDAN/MONKMEYER

ERIC KROLL/TAURUS PHOTOS

DRUG REHABILITATION *takes many forms.* Left, *a patient relaxes in a treatment center that provides a peaceful retreat for former addicts.* Right, *a former heroin addict takes methadone, a heroine substitute that is addictive but allows the addict to function normally.* Below, *drug addicts and alcoholics participate in a rap session in which they are required—perhaps for the first time—to express their doubts, fears, and anger to a sympathetic audience that shares many of their feelings.*

SYBIL SHELTON/PETER ARNOLD

Narcotics. Narcotics are opium and its derivatives, such as morphine and heroin. They reduce the activity in the synapses of pain-transmitting neurons and so are widely used in medicine to relieve pain. They also produce intense but temporary feelings of happiness and well-being.

Tolerance and dependence, both physical and psychological, develop rapidly; the physical dependence is such that withdrawal symptoms are severe.

Hallucinogens. Hallucinations are mental images that are misperceived as sensory perceptions. Hallucinogens are drugs that affect the nervous system so as to cause hallucinations; they may also distort or intensify actual sensory perceptions. Their effects are highly unpredictable, with differences occurring not only from one person to another but also within one individual on different occasions.

Certain naturally occurring hallucinogens, such as mescaline and psilocybin, have long been used in the religious ceremonies of certain cultures. Much more dangerous, because they are many times more potent, are the laboratory-manufactured hallucinogens LSD and PCP, the latter also known as "angel dust." Both can lead to severe mood disorders and even to long-term psychoses. PCP, because of the severity of its psychotic effects, may be an even more dangerous substance than LSD; unfortunately, it can be manufactured very inexpensively and so is often substituted for LSD or other psychoactive drugs by dealers in illicit drugs.

Cannabis. Cannabis, or marijuana, is a mild hallucinogen. It is now regularly used by an estimated 25 million Americans, particularly those of college age, and is estimated to have been tried at least once by about 25 million more.

Although various long-term ill effects from marijuana use have been suggested, none other than lung irritation has been conclusively established. Like alcohol, marijuana makes driving hazardous. In other respects, it is probably less dangerous than alcohol if used in moderation. Overdoses, particularly in inexperienced users, can cause anxiety, disorientation, and psychoses. The recent introduction of more potent forms of the drug may well introduce new hazards to its use.

Basic Psychological Processes

Every person differs from every other person both because of different genetic characteristics and because of a lifetime of experiences that differ. At the same time, there are a number of basic human psychological processes. Studying these basic processes, the foundations of human behavior, is the central concern of most psychologists.

CULVER PICTURES

RESPONDENT CONDITIONING: *The classic demonstration was developed by Ivan Pavlov, whose dogs were conditioned to salivate at the sound of a bell at feeding time.*

Learning

Learning is basic to behavior; most behaviors, including those that make us specifically human, are learned. Lower animals also learn—indeed, research into their learning processes provides the basis for much of our understanding of human learning—but no animal has anything resembling the human ability to profit from learning experiences.

Learning may be defined as a lasting change in potential behavior based on experience. This definition excludes behaviors that are temporary, such as those caused by fatigue or drugs, as well as those that seem to be innate or instinctive, such as smiling and crying. While people do learn, from family and culture, to control and modify these behaviors, basic behavior is not learned. The important word "potential" in the definition suggests that people can learn to perform behaviors without actually putting them into practice; most of us, for example, have the knowledge (learning) necessary for committing a wide variety of crimes, but have refrained from putting that learning to use.

There are three ways in which learning takes place: (1) respondent conditioning (also called classical or Pavlovian conditioning); (2) operant conditioning (also called instrumental conditioning); and (3) observational learning. However complex a learning experience may be, it is based on some combination of these three principles.

Respondent conditioning.

Respondent conditioning was discovered by the Russian physiologist Ivan Pavlov in a famous series of experiments with salivating dogs. Pavlov was originally studying digestion, and as part of his study was taking precise measurements of the quantities of saliva secreted in response to various kinds of food. He noticed as the tests proceeded that dogs began to salivate before they had actually received the food. For example, salivation started as soon as they heard the footsteps of the person bringing the food. Pavlov decided to experiment by ringing a bell shortly before the dogs were fed. Soon the ringing of the bell would, by itself, cause the dogs to salivate.

The dogs' response to the bell is called a *conditioned response*, and the bell itself a *conditioned stimulus*. (When the dogs respond the same way to actual food, the food is called an *unconditioned stimulus* and the reaction an *unconditioned response*.) The basic premise of respondent conditioning is that a neutral stimulus—one that previously had had no special meaning—becomes a conditioned stimulus when it comes to be associated in the mind with an unconditioned stimulus.

Pavlov found that if he repeatedly rang the bell but did not then give the dogs food, the dogs would eventually stop salivating in response to the bell. This breaking of the association between conditioned stimulus and unconditioned stimulus is called *extinction*. Subsequent research has shown that the rate with which a conditioned stimulus is acquired or extinguished may vary considerably.

Other characteristics of respondent conditioning are *generalization* and *discrimination*. Generalization means that stimuli that resemble a conditioned stimulus can elicit the same or similar responses. If a child has come to associate the cat next door with the painful experience of being scratched, he may generalize the association and so be afraid of all cats. Discrimination, the opposite of generalization, refers to the ability to tell stimuli apart. When the child becomes aware that not all cats are like the cat next door, he has learned to discriminate among cats.

Recent research indicates that what is most important in respondent conditioning is how predictably the conditioned and unconditioned stimuli occur together. It is less important that the pairing occurs often than that it remain predictable, always producing the same result. If several stimuli are presented together—different kinds of noises, for example—but only one of them is paired with the unconditioned stimulus, the paired noise will not become a conditioned stimulus until the person has determined which of the noises is the relevant one.

Once a conditioned stimulus has been established, it can be the stimulus for additional conditioned stimuli without the original unconditioned stimulus. This phenomenon is called *higher-order conditioning* and has much to do with language and its use. Most words are conditioned stimuli: one can associate a word like "good" or "nice" with some new stimulus without going back to the original unconditioned stimulus that gave meaning to the words.

Operant conditioning. Respondent conditioning has to do with involuntary responses: a bell makes a dog salivate; the sight of a cat makes a child afraid. Operant conditioning, by contrast, has to do with voluntary behavior and its results. Its basic principle, the law of effect, says that if a behavior is followed by something pleasant or satisfying, the behavior will be strengthened; that is, one will become more likely to do it again. If the behavior is followed by something unpleasant, the behavior will be weakened; one will be less likely to do it again.

Much of the basic research in operant conditioning was conducted by B. F. Skinner in experiments with animals. In a typical experiment, a hungry rat was placed in a small cage, on one wall of which was a lever. As the rat wandered around the cage, he accidentally pressed the lever, and a bit of rat food instantly dropped into a nearby cup. Later the rat pressed the lever, again accidentally, and again received some food. Gradually the rat came to associate pressing the lever with receiving food. In due course the rat began to press the lever with regularity. The food is positive reinforcement: it increases the likelihood that the rat will repeat the behavior—continuing to press the lever.

Suppose, on the other hand, that each time the rat had pressed the lever, he had received an electric shock. In that case he would gradually come to associate the lever with the shock, and so be careful to stay away from the lever. The shock is punishment; it decreases the likelihood that the rat will repeat the behavior of pressing the lever.

Many animals can be conditioned, by positive reinforcement, to perform not just one but a whole series of behaviors, called a *behavior chain*. The training process, called *shaping*, is the method used by trainers in circuses and similar shows.

Partial reinforcement. As with respondent conditioning, a learned response to operant conditioning can be extinguished if it is no longer reinforced. It is not necessary, however, for a behavior to be reinforced each time it occurs. Partial reinforcement—reinforcement after only some percentage of like behaviors—is also effective.

Partial reinforcement can be at either a fixed or a variable rate, and it can be on the basis of either ratio or time interval. In a fixed ratio reinforcement, a behavior might be reinforced every third time it occurs, or every tenth time, or every hundredth. In a variable ratio reinforcement, it is reinforced irregularly, as, for example, after the third, eleventh, thirteenth, twenty-fourth, and thirty-third times. In time-interval reinforcement, the behavior is reinforced after a certain amount of time has elapsed, regardless of how many times it has taken place during the interval. The intervals may be regular—every ten minutes, for example, or every hour—or they may be irregular.

Reinforcement on a ratio schedule, either fixed or variable, usually maintains a behavior at a high rate. An example of fixed-ratio reinforcement is piecework wages, in which a worker might be paid for every ten of an item that he produces. The classic example of variable-ratio reinforcement is compulsive gambling, in which a person doggedly continues a behavior despite irregular and usually infrequent reinforcement.

Learning occurs most rapidly on a continuous schedule when the behavior to be learned is reinforced every time; but it is longer lasting if learned on a partial schedule, especially a variable schedule. If continuous reinforcement stops, one notices immediately and discontinues the behavior more readily than one does on a partial schedule, where another reinforcement is likely to be just around the corner.

Negative reinforcement. Negative reinforcement, like positive reinforcement, encourages a specific behavior, but it does so because the behavior prevents a negative reinforcement. The discomfort that most people feel in hot weather is negative reinforcement for such behavior as going swimming or staying in an air-conditioned room. A hangover is negative reinforcement for staying sober.

One kind of learning that negative reinforcement produces is called *escape conditioning*. One escapes from unpleasant circumstances, such as the hot weather in the example above, by some behavior such as going swimming. Another kind, *avoidance conditioning*, is remarkable for the durability of the behaviors that it fosters. Avoidance conditioning has elements of both respondent and operant conditioning. Suppose, for example, that one of Pavlov's dogs learned to associate the sound of a bell with an electric shock a few seconds later (respondent conditioning), and that the dog further learned that he could escape the shock by moving to another part of his cage (operant conditioning). The dog would soon become conditioned to move to another part of the cage every time he heard the bell, so as to avoid the electric shock. If the electric shocks were discontinued, the dog's escape behavior would no longer

OPERANT CONDITIONING *relies on the voluntary acts of its subjects. The pigeons try to win at "Ping-Pong" for a reward of food. Similarly, slot machine gamblers use hundreds of coins for a rare payoff.*

WALTER FLEISCHER/HARVARD UNIVERSITY

MICHAEL KAGAN

be necessary; but the dog is not likely to find that out, as he will continue to escape at each sounding of the warning bell. Avoidance conditioning helps explain why behaviors based on fear are among the most difficult to change. The fear itself tends to prevent one's knowing when the fear is no longer appropriate.

Punishment. When a behavior's result is such that it makes occurrence of the behavior less likely, the behavior's result is called *punishment.* Note that punishment, which decreases a behavior, is not at all the same as negative reinforcement, which increases a behavior.

Punishment takes two forms. One attempts to discourage a certain behavior by countering it with something unpleasant, called an *aversive stimulus.* Spanking is a classic example of an aversive stimulus. The other form takes away something pleasant; that is, removes positive reinforcers. Forbidding some activity, such as watching television, to counter some generally unrelated behavior, such as lateness, is an example.

Punishment can be effective, but it has its drawbacks, particularly the aversive stimulus type. One drawback is that undesirable behavior can reappear when the threat of punishment is not present. Another is that the person being punished may interpret the behavior for which he is being punished too broadly. For example, a child punished for sexual behavior may become an adult with sexual inhibitions. Another disadvantage is that people who are punished may come to perceive punishment as a means of getting one's way, and so attempt to punish others.

Punishment is most effective when it occurs immediately after the behavior that is to be discouraged. Delayed punishment, or the threat of it, can also be effective, but not with animals. Sometimes, immediate reinforcement can be a stronger determiner of behavior than the threat of punishment. Smoking, drinking, and drug use are examples of behaviors whose immediate reinforcements are, for many people, stronger than the threat of later ill consequences.

Observational learning.

Observational learning, also called modeling, means that people can and do observe the behavior of others and the consequences of that behavior. Depending on what they perceive as the consequences of the observed behavior, people may adopt or reject such behavior for themselves.

It is not necessary for behavior to be observed directly; it can also be "observed" through language, either heard or read. As a rule, however, direct observation is a stronger stimulus than verbal description or instruction.

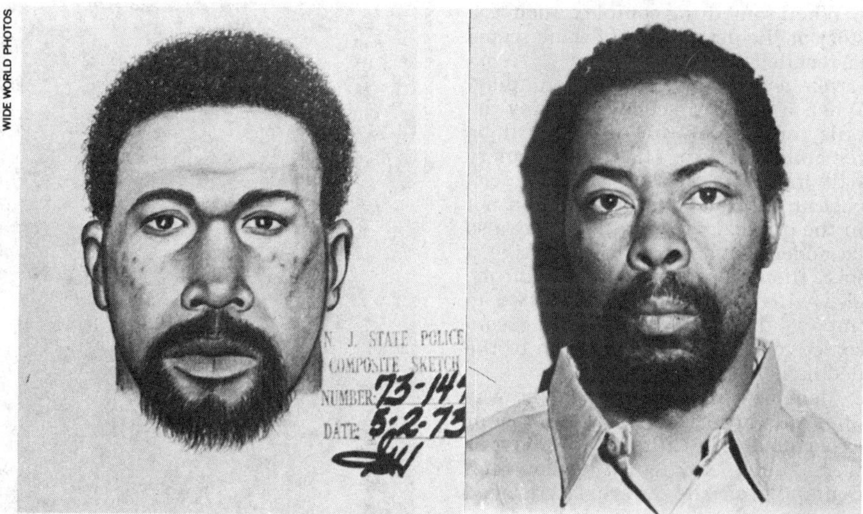

MEMORY *plays a part in law enforcement. The sketch at left, based on victims' descriptions, helped capture the suspect at right. Memory is notoriously unreliable, however, and in general other physical evidence is required in order to convict a suspect.*

Memory.

The brain has a tremendous capability to store perceptions. How this capability, called memory, works is not fully understood; indeed, there is no one theory that at present fully explains the workings of memory, although several offer partial explanations.

One widely held theory suggests a division of memory into short-term and long-term. It is known that sensory perceptions, such as sights and sounds, stay in the brain for a very short time in their original forms—about one second for something seen, four seconds for something heard. If, before it fades, a perception passes into the short-term memory, it will be on its way to being remembered; otherwise it will, once it has faded, be gone.

The short-term memory has a limited capacity, and normally it remembers something for only about 15 seconds. It is the short-term memory that, for example, is storing the memory of these words as you read them, so that these words make sense as a sentence, and so that the sentence relates to the one that preceded it. You can, if you like, keep this sentence (or almost any other that is not too long) in your short-term memory by repeating it over and over. This repeating process is called *rehearsal,* and as long as it is maintained, it can keep a small piece of information—a short sentence, a telephone number—in the mind indefinitely. But if the information is not rehearsed, it will either pass into the long-term memory or be forgotten. The more it has been rehearsed, the likelier it is that the information will pass into the long-term memory.

A modification of this theory suggests that there are two kinds of rehearsal. One kind does nothing more than keep information available for immediate use. A telephone number that is to be used only once is an example; as soon as the number has been dialed, it will be forgotten, so quickly that a busy signal may require its being looked up again.

The other kind of rehearsal, called *elaboration,* is used when a person wishes to remember something. Elaboration means finding some way of associating the new information with what is already in the memory. The larger the number of such associations, the likelier it is that the information will be remembered.

A newer theory does not separate short- from long-term memory, suggesting instead the concept of one memory, a small part of which is active at any one time. Incoming perceptions activate those parts of the memory that are needed to make sense of the perceptions. For example, the sight of a familiar face activates various memories connected with that person; a conversation with that person will activate additional memories and at the same time introduce new information, which will be processed and stored in the memory in association with the information that was already there. A stranger with whom you have a conversation—someone that you ask directions of, for example—is much less likely to be remembered because the associations with that person will be few; there will be less already in the memory to attach the new information to.

Remembering. To remember something is to retrieve it from the memory. There are two basic kinds of remembering, *recognition* and *recall.* Recognition is just that: one recognizes a perception—a face, a tune, the smell of frying onions—because earlier perceptions of that same stimulus are stored in the memory. Recall is somewhat more difficult, as it requires searching the memory for the answer to a question: What is the name of this person? Of that tune?

When something complex, such as a story or the description of some scene, is recalled from the memory, *reconstructive memory* comes into play. When a story or scene has many details, not all of the details will be remembered; often, then, the memory will find details from other experiences to fill the gaps. Information not in the original story or scene may also be added. It is rather like hearing a joke, then telling the joke to someone else with an added detail or two to improve the story. In the case of reconstructive memory, the addition of the details is not done consciously.

Memory can be affected by the way questions are asked. In one series of experiments, a number of persons were shown movies of traffic accidents. When they were later asked questions about what they had seen, some persons were asked how fast the cars were going when they "hit," others when they "smashed." Persons questioned with "smashed" remembered higher speeds than did those questioned with "hit."

ERIC KROLL/TAURUS PHOTOS

CHARLES GATEWOOD/EPA

MIMI FORSYTH/MONKMEYER

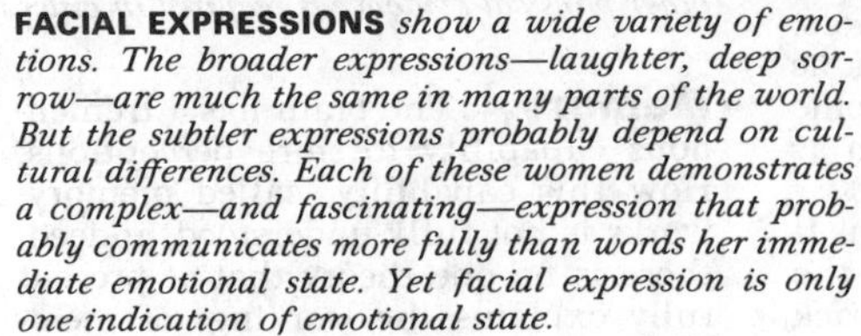

FACIAL EXPRESSIONS *show a wide variety of emotions. The broader expressions—laughter, deep sorrow—are much the same in many parts of the world. But the subtler expressions probably depend on cultural differences. Each of these women demonstrates a complex—and fascinating—expression that probably communicates more fully than words her immediate emotional state. Yet facial expression is only one indication of emotional state.*

Forgetting. Sometimes when a person is unable to remember something, it seems as if the information has simply disappeared from his mind. Whether information can actually be lost from the memory in this way, or whether every instance of forgetting is in fact a failure in the ability to retrieve information, is not known.

Certainly most forgetting is a failure to retrieve information. Cognitive psychologists suggest that remembering requires *retrieval cues*, cues as to where in the memory the information being sought is stored. Until the appropriate retrieval cues are brought to bear, the information cannot be retrieved from the memory. Reminders and hints are essentially retrieval cues provided to one person by another.

According to Freudian theory, certain unpleasant or frightening memories are deliberately forgotten, or *repressed.* Other theories hold that some memories get in the way of other memories. Recent research has suggested that, at least in some circumstances, a new memory may completely displace an older memory.

Emotion and Motivation

Emotions and motivation are closely related. Emotions are reactions to certain events. They are basically internal, having both cognitive and physiological elements, although they also prompt behaviors—both expressive behaviors, such as laughter and weeping, and instrumental behaviors, such as striking out at someone or taking flight. Motives are in some respects mirror images of emotions, being the internal processes that determine the goals of a person's behavior and the degrees of energy and persistence with which any specific goal is pursued.

Emotions.

A person's emotions are responses to events or stimuli. The stimuli may be in the environment (something seen, heard, or otherwise perceived that prompts an emotional response) or they may be internal (a memory, or a train of thought).

Whatever the stimulus, there are both cognitive and physiological aspects to the response. The cognitive element is an appraisal of the situation, interpreting the stimulus and thereby giving meaning to it. There are cultural differences in appraisals of stimuli. What seems an innocent gesture in one culture may be highly insulting in another. There are also great differences among individuals within a culture. What excites one person may amuse another and disgust a third. Even an individual will respond to a person or event in different ways at different times.

The physiological aspect of emotion is a state of physical arousal prompted by the stimulus. The arousal may be strong or mild depending on various factors. Here, too, there are cultural and individual differences. The state of arousal involves mainly the autonomic nervous system, the endocrine system—secretions of adrenaline, for example—and certain parts of the brain. The patterns of physiological response seem to be quite similar for all emotions. The polygraph, or "lie detector," is one instrument that measures physiological responses to emotion. It is useful in detecting and measuring emotional responses, but unfortunately cannot distinguish the emotional response to lying from any other emotional response.

The precise relation between the cognitive and physiological aspects of emotion has long been a matter of study for psychologists. The fundamental question is how and to what extent each influences the other. A widely held recent theory holds that each element influences the other simultaneously and in equal degree, with the cognitive element determining what the emotion is, and the physiological elements determining its intensity.

Expression of emotion. Of the various ways in which emotion is expressed, by far the most important is facial expression. The cues for recognizing the various emotions are found in different parts of the face: the forehead (surprise), the eyes (fear, sadness), the mouth (happiness, disgust). Some facial expressions are innate, others learned. There are also wide differences in interpreting expressions from one culture to another.

Emotion and performance. Athletes and performing artists have long known that the degree of their emotional arousal affects the quality of their performance. Evidence suggests that emotional arousal improves performance—up to a point. If emotional arousal increases beyond that optimum point, performance begins to decline. The optimum point of emotional arousal varies depending on the

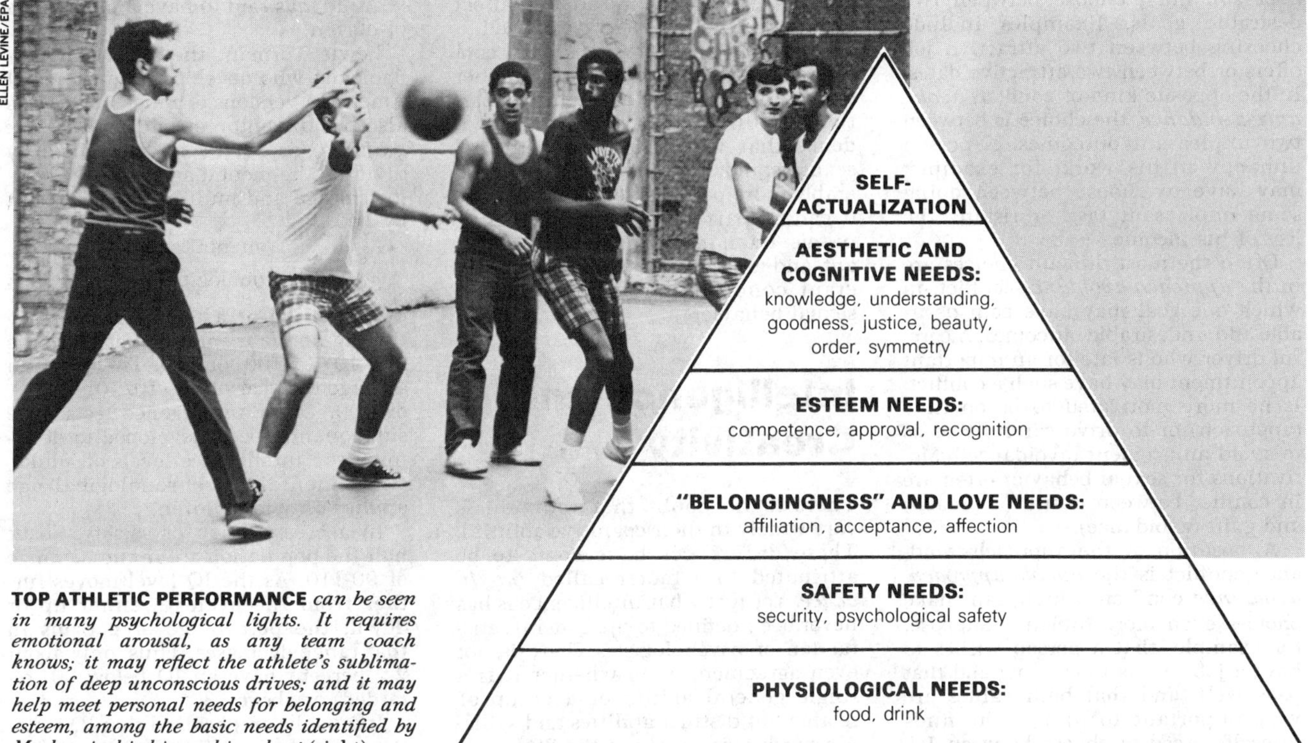

TOP ATHLETIC PERFORMANCE *can be seen in many psychological lights. It requires emotional arousal, as any team coach knows; it may reflect the athlete's sublimation of deep unconscious drives; and it may help meet personal needs for belonging and esteem, among the basic needs identified by Maslow in his hierarchies chart* (right).

complexity of the task. Thus, the optimum point for playing a piano or violin solo is relatively low compared with that for running in a dash.

Motives. Motives are the internal processes that determine the goals of behavior and the persistence and vigor with which those goals will be pursued. Motives that satisfy basic physiological needs are called *drives.*

Theories of motivation. Freudian, cognitive, and humanistic psychologists have developed important theories of motivation. A basic principle of Feudian psychology is that much motivation results from the conflict between basic drives, which continuously seek to express themselves, and the defenses with which the conscious mind attempts to control or suppress those drives. Through a process called *sublimation,* drives are channeled into socially acceptable behavior, and so motivate such behavior.

Cognitive psychologists emphasize the role in motivation of such mental processes as anticipation and imagination. One important theory holds that motives are the product of the *value* of a particular goal to a person and the *expectation* that particular behavior will achieve that goal. The strongest motives are those in which both value and expectation are high, the weakest those whose goals are neither desired nor perceived as attainable.

Cognitive psychologists have also addressed the relation of intrinsic and extrinsic motivation. An *intrinsic* motive is one that comes from within: one does something because one enjoys doing it. An *extrinsic* motive is one that comes from without: one does something because one expects to be rewarded for it. There is evidence that extrinsic rewards can displace intrinsic ones. Suppose, for example, that a child enjoys doing some household task. If a parent begins giving the child money (an extrinsic reward) for doing the task, then later withdraws the money, the former intrinsic motivation will not return, at least in its original strength. On the other hand, extrinsic rewards can be used to develop intrinsic motivations that did not previously exist; but the timing of the discontinuation of the extrinsic reward is important. There is evidence, too, that a person is motivated to continue a behavior after extrinsic rewards have been discontinued if that behavior makes the person feel more competent.

One of the most widely known of the current theories of motivation is that developed by the humanistic psychologist Abraham Maslow. Often referred to as the *hierarchy of needs,* Maslow's theory arranges a person's needs in a pyramid. At the bottom of the pyramid are the basic physiological needs, such as the need for food. On the next highest level are the need to be free from danger and threats. The next two levels encompass the need to feel accepted and loved and the need for approval and recognition. Near the top of the pyramid are aesthetic and cognitive needs, such as the needs for beauty and knowledge. At the pyramid's peak are what Maslow calls self-actualization needs, the need to achieve the fullest development of an individual's potential. The first four levels are called *basic* or *deficiency* needs, the top levels, *higher* or *growth* needs.

In Maslow's theory, a person is not motivated to satisfy his needs at any one level until his needs have been satisfied at all prior levels. Thus, at the lowest level, a person who is starving is not motivated to seek safety; at a higher level, a person is not motivated to seek approval and recognition from the world at large if his basic need for love has not been satisfied. Conversely, once the needs at any one level have been satisfied, the needs at the next highest level come into play, providing new motives for new and different behaviors.

Among individuals, needs at any one level vary considerably. At the lowest level, for example, motivation to eat is related to a number of physiological and psychological factors, with the result that many people eat more (or sometimes less) than is needed to keep them at their optimum weights. At higher levels, too, motivations and needs vary considerably.

Conflicting motives. It often happens that goals come into conflict with each other. Three basic kinds of conflict have been identified, based on a differentiation between *approach* motivation, the desire to achieve some outcome, and *avoidance* motivation, the desire to avoid or prevent some outcome.

One kind of conflict, called *approach-approach* conflict, occurs when a person must choose between two desirable goals. Examples include choosing between two attractive job offers or between two attractive dates. In the opposite kind of conflict, *avoidance-avoidance*, the choice is between two unpleasant outcomes. A person unhappy in his work, for example, may have to choose between doing some unpleasant task or risking the loss of his income.

Often the most difficult choices are in the *approach-avoidance* conflict, in which one goal may have both desirable and undesirable outcomes. A careful driver who is late for an important appointment may have such a conflict. Is he more motivated to be on time (approach) or to drive carefully so as to avoid an accident (avoidance)? Motivations for sexual behavior often are in conflict between desire (approach) and guilt (avoidance).

A variation of the approach-avoidance conflict is the *double approach-avoidance* conflict, which can make choices even more difficult. Suppose, for example, that a person wishes to have a job that is interesting and that pays well, and that both values are very important to him. If he finds himself forced to choose between Job A, which pays poorly but promises to be very interesting, or Job B, which pays well but seems likely to be exceedingly boring, he is faced with a double approach-avoidance conflict.

Sexuality. One of the most complex aspects of emotion and motivation is sexuality. A person's sex is determined at the moment of conception, when a so-called X chromosome from the mother pairs with either an X or a Y chromosome from the father. The different pairings cause different kinds of gonads (sex glands) to develop in the embryo: an XX pairing results in the development of ovaries; an XY pairing, the development of testes. Sexual behavior and development are affected by hormones secreted by these glands. The differences between the hormones secreted by the male and female sex glands control sexual differentiation.

Sex hormones are produced in large amounts around the time of birth. They particularly affect the development of the central nervous system, thereby determining sex-related behavior to some extent. But how much sex-related behavior is so determined, and how much it is later learned, is an area of considerable disagreement.

Sex hormones are again produced in large quantities beginning at about age eleven, the time known as *puberty*. The hormones stimulate development of the sex organs, so that a person becomes capable of reproducing. They also stimulate the development of secondary sexual characteristics, such as the growth of breasts in women and the growth of beards and change of voice in men. The hormones affect behavior in noticeable ways as well.

Specific sexual practices vary considerably from one culture to another and among subgroups within a particular culture. There is much evidence that within our own culture, sexual standards have become considerably more permissive in the past two decades, particularly among young people. In an individual, various pleasant and unpleasant experiences—operant conditioning—strongly affect sexual behavior.

Intelligence and Creativity

There is no doubt that individuals vary widely in their cognitive abilities. These differences have come to be attributed to a factor called *intelligence*. Yet just what intelligence is has never been defined to the general satisfaction of psychologists. There is not even agreement as to whether it is a single general ability or a group of related but distinct abilities and skills. A remark made early in the 20th century, that intelligence is "the capacity to do well on an intelligence test," remains the only widely accepted definition.

Intelligence tests. The first intelligence tests were developed at the beginning of the 20th century by the French psychologist Alfred Binet. They tested such cognitive functions as memory, logical thinking, and comprehension. Their purpose, as with many subsequent intelligence tests, was to aid in assigning children to the appropriate levels in school.

It was Binet who developed the concept of *mental age*. A ten year old who performed at the average level for all ten year olds was said to have a mental age of ten. A ten year old who functioned at the level of an average eleven year old was said to have a mental age of eleven.

IQ CLASSIFICATIONS

IQ	CLASSIFICATION	% OF THE POPULATION
130+	Very superior	2.2
120–129	Superior	6.7
110–119	Bright normal	16.1
90–109	Average	50.0
80–89	Dull normal	16.1
70–79	Borderline	6.7
Below 69	Mental defective	2.2

Lewis Terman, the American psychologist who developed the principal American versions of Binet's tests, was also the inventor of the *intelligence quotient*, or *IQ*. IQ is determined by dividing the mental age by the chronological age and multiplying the result by 100:

$$IQ = \frac{\text{mental age}}{\text{chronological age}} \times 100$$

Thus the IQ of a ten year old functioning at the mental age of eleven is (11/10) × 100, or 110. The IQ of an average ten year old is (10/10) × 100, or 100. Other intelligence tests have subsequently been developed to determine the intelligence levels of adults, since mental vs. chronological age applies only to children.

In a cross-section of society, about half the population are in the IQ range of 90-110. As the IQ level moves further from the average, either up or down, the percentage of persons in that range decreases. Thus, only about 2.2 percent have an IQ below 70 (retarded) or above 130.

It must be emphasized that IQ is not the same thing as intelligence. IQ is a test score; whether the tests used to determine IQ are actually measuring intelligence (whatever intelligence may be) is a matter of considerable uncertainty. IQ scores do, it is true, correlate well with performance in school—in the kind of schooling, that is, that is traditional in Europe and America. But there may well be more to intelligence than the mental abilities needed to do well in a certain kind of school.

Tests may have a *culture bias*. They may contain questions based too narrowly on the experiences of only some members of society, so that people with dissimilar experiences do not do well on the tests, regardless of their inherent intelligence. Conscientious and largely successful efforts have been made to remedy culture biases, but tests may contain other biases as yet undiscovered.

Heredity vs. environment. There is no question that both heredity and environment influence IQ test scores, but no precise relationship has been established.

The effects of heredity are difficult to document. Most studies have compared the IQ scores of persons who are related but who have been reared apart from each other: siblings and, in a few cases, identical twins. While the correlation of scores of siblings reared apart is not so high as that of siblings reared together, it is nonetheless remarkably high, suggesting that inherited abilities do strongly affect IQ scores. On the other hand, it should be kept in mind that siblings, even when reared apart, are likely to be in families with similar social and educa-

KAREN COLLIDGE/TAURUS PHOTOS

CHARLES GATEWOOD/EPA

SOCIO-ECONOMIC DIFFERENCES *correlate with differences in measured intelligence, even though there are many individual exceptions. As these pictures suggest, however, socio-economic differences may not necessarily correlate with happiness.*

tional backgrounds, so that environment may very well have some positive effect on the correlations.

There is a correlation between IQ scores and socioeconomic status, not only among employed adults but also among their children. Generally, the lower the socioeconomic status, the lower the IQ. It seems likely that in many instances a kind of vicious cycle is at work: an environment of poverty is not conducive to developing the kinds of mental abilities that enable people to escape that environment.

The early years seem to be crucial. In one experiment, educators worked intensively with poor mothers, all of whom had an IQ below 70, to enrich the environment of their children from birth to age five and a half. At five and a half, the IQ difference between the experimental group and a control group was fully 30 points (124 vs. 94). In Israel there is a 20-point difference between the average IQ of Jewish children from European backgrounds (105) and those from Middle-Eastern backgrounds (85); but for children of either background, when reared in the highly stimulating environment of a kibbutz, the average IQ is 115.

The preponderance of evidence suggests that differences in the IQ scores of different racial groups are due to environmental rather than inherited factors. But there is not enough evidence for firm conclusions, and the relation of race to IQ remains a controversial question.

Creativity. Although the inventor of the term IQ defined "genius" as having a very high IQ, there seems to be little relationship between IQ and creativity. Apparently, anyone who is capable of becoming competent in a field, be it dishwashing or nuclear physics, is sufficiently intelligent to be creative in that field.

At one time it was thought that creativity derived from *divergent thinking*, the ability to break loose from conventional ways of solving problems. However, persons of acknowledged creativity in their fields seldom do remarkably well on tests of divergent thinking.

What seems more likely is that creative accomplishment is due to certain personality traits. Creative people seem to have a strong need to make sense of the world in their own terms and to impose their own sense of order on their experiences. They spend more time than others in exploring and defining problems, and they are more open to new ideas. Above all, they are persistent, often intensely so. Thomas Edison no doubt had that trait in mind when he commented that genius is "10 percent inspiration and 90 percent perspiration."

Personality

Just as no two persons are exactly alike physically, so no two persons are exactly alike mentally. Each person displays certain patterns of behavior in interacting with his environment. The term *personality* refers to the entire complex of behavior patterns that, together, go to make up a person's identity.

The term personality is a *construct*, or concept. There really is no separate, identifiable entity called personality. The term is used, rather, as a basis for constructing theories that attempt to explain how each person's unique complex of behavior patterns came about.

There are many theories of personality. Among the most important are the following.

Freudian theory. The psychoanalytic personality theory of Sigmund Freud is deservedly famous. It is a cornerstone both of psychology and psychiatry, and it has influenced modern philosophy, literature, and social policy. Many of the terms that Freud coined have become common currency, though not always with the precise meanings that he intended.

The unconscious. Probably Freud's greatest contribution was his theory of the *unconscious* mind, which he distinguished from the *conscious* and *preconscious* minds. Conscious mental events are those that a person is aware of at any given moment; preconscious events are those that are in the memory, to be drawn on as needed. The unconscious is, by contrast, beyond one's awareness, although it constitutes the largest part of the mind. Basic drives are part of the unconscious mind, as are many "forgotten" past events, particularly early childhood experiences that involve painful psychological conflicts. The unconscious surfaces only in disguised form, such as in dreams, in slips of the tongue ("Freudian slips"), or in other kinds of mistakes or accidents.

Ido, ego, superego. Superimposed on these three parts of the mind are the three components of personality, the *id*, the *ego*, and the *superego*. The id is entirely within the unconscious.

It is a chaos of basic drives, having no contact with reality and functioning in a wholly irrational and often contradictory way. It operates according to the *pleasure principle*: it seeks immediate gratification of its demands. The id is present from birth.

Gradually, as a person moves through infancy and into childhood, the *ego* develops out of the id. The ego operates on the *reality principle*: it seeks socially acceptable ways of gratifying the demands of the id and postpones gratification until those ways are found. The ego operates mainly at the conscious level.

Finally, the *superego* develops out of the ego. It is much the same as the conscience, the locus of the sense of right and wrong. It seeks moral perfection, rewarding the ego for behavior it considers acceptable and punishing it, by means of guilt feelings, for those it considers unacceptable. Like the id, it is completely unrealistic, seeking only the satisfaction of its moralistic goals.

Thus, the ego, the part of the personality that deals with reality, is a battleground between the conflicting basic drives of the id, the moralistic goals of the superego, and the perceived demands of the real world. The conflict produces *anxiety*.

INFORMATION SERVICES, CLARK UNIVERSITY

PIONEER PSYCHOANALYSTS: *Seated from left to right are Sigmund Freud, G. Stanley Hall, and Carl Jung; standing are A.A. Brill, Ernest Jones, and Sandor Ferenczi.*

Defense mechanisms. Sometimes the ego can find a course of action that resolves the anxiety. At other times, however, it must resort to *defense mechanisms*; it does this at the unconscious level, not realizing what it is doing. A defense mechanism is a kind of self-deception that wards off anxiety. The basic defense mechanism is *repression*, in which the ego simply prevents something that will arouse anxiety from reaching the consciousness. If the repressed impulse persists, it may be released indirectly through any of several other defense mechanisms that disguise the nature of the impulse from the ego and the superego. These defense mechanisms include

- *sublimation*, finding a different, acceptable way of expressing the impulse;
- *rationalization*, finding an acceptable reason for otherwise unacceptable behavior;
- *displacement*, finding a substitute object for one's feelings, often a scapegoat;
- *denial of reality*, refusing to acknowledge something unpleasant;
- *intellectualization*, dealing with a stressful situation in a detached, analytic way, as if one were not emotionally involved;
- *reaction formation*, transforming a strong drive into its opposite, as a strong sex drive into excessive prudery, or dislike for someone into excessive displays of affection;
- *projection*, attributing one's own feelings to someone else; and
- *regression*, returning to a way of behavior characteristic of an earlier stage of one's life.

Stages. Freud held that personality is largely shaped by a series of *psychosexual stages* during one's first five years of life. These stages are the *oral*, the *anal*, and the *phallic*; in each the *libido* (sexual energy) is centered in a different part of the body. If a child is either overindulged or unduly frustrated at a particular stage, he will become *fixated* at that stage. The degree of fixation will depend on the severity of the indulgence or frustration. In other words, he will become an adult who retains some of the traits or attitudes that characterize the stage when the fixation occurred. A person fixated at the oral stage, for example, is likely to be dependent, passive, and greedy, as in infancy, and to be preoccupied with such oral functions as eating, smoking, and talking.

Freud believed that two further stages followed these crucial first three. After age five the person enters a period of *latency* from the ages of 5 to about 13 during which concerns about sexual matters are repressed. At puberty, the last or *genital* stage begins and lasts until old age.

DEFENSES *can sometimes be recognized in speech. Those illustrated below include rationalization, denial, intellectualization, projection, and regression.*

I'm only doing this for your own good.
It hurts me as much as it hurts you.

I AM *NOT* ANGRY !!*@#!

Divorce is not so bad, you know. I read a study the other day that showed divorced people are much more happy than those who . . .

YOU'RE THE ONE WHO'S *SHOUTING* !!!

You wouldn't blame poor little me, would you?

STEPHANIE FITZGERALD/PETER ARNOLD

PHENOMENOLOGICAL THEORIES *stress the importance of social relationships in childhood. These Irish girls show spontaneous pleasure in each other's company.*

Neo-Freudian theories. Following Freud, a number of theories were developed that accepted some part of Freud's premises but disagreed with other parts.

One of the first to modify Freud's theories was Alfred Adler, who believed that people are drawn toward positive social goals, rather than simply driven to escape anxiety. Adler believed that everyone feels inferior to what he might be, and that well-adjusted individuals strive to perfect themselves by achieving socially beneficial goals. The maladjusted seek selfish goals, such as power or fame, or develop an *inferiority complex,* a set of behaviors that overcompensate for perceived inadequacies.

Carl Jung labeled what Freud had called the unconscious the *personal unconscious,* unique to each individual, and added to it his own idea of a *collective unconscious,* shared by everyone. The collective unconscious contains *archetypes,* memories accumulated by humanity throughout its history. These memories characteristically express themselves in mythological images common to all cultures. The unconscious was, to Jung, more a source of knowledge and wisdom than of anxiety.

A third important neo-Freudian is Erik Erikson, who outlines a set of *psychosocial* stages that each person passes through. The first four stages parallel those of Freud, though with different emphases. Thereafter, in place of Freud's single genital stage, Erikson posits four additional stages: adolescence, early adulthood, middle age, and later adulthood. Each of these stages presents the individual with characteristic conflicts that must be faced and resolved. For example, the characteristic conflict of adolescence is between the individual's desire to be unique and his desire to be seen as part of a larger group. This produces an "identity crisis," according to Erikson, and the term has become a familiar one to laymen as well as psychiatrists. How well early conflicts are resolved will affect how subsequent conflicts are handled, although success at one stage does not necessarily guarantee success at later stages. A table of Erikson's stages of development is in the *Child and Family* section, page 495.

Adler, Jung, Erikson, and other neo-Freudians have in common an acceptance of much of Freud's theoretical framework. They differ most significantly in their view that Freud overemphasized the role of infantile sexuality in the development of personality.

Phenomenological theories. Phenomenological personality theories are a part of psychology's humanistic tradition. Their focus is on the *self,* or the sum of a person's perceptions about himself.

Everyone's self-concept develops slowly. People become aware of their own consistent behaviors and assign names and values to them. The more in accord an experience is with one's self-concept, the likelier it is that the concept will be perceived accurately. Experiences that deny or contradict the self-concept tend to be perceived inaccurately and excluded from the consciousness.

Social relationships are important, especially in childhood; and the need for approval (from parents or others) can cause distortions in a child's self-image, causing it to be incomplete or unrealistic. This leads to the construction of rigid defenses against what are perceived as attacks on the self-image.

Like Maslow (see Motives, above), Carl Rogers holds that self-actualization is each person's highest motive. To the extent that a person's self-image is realistic, movement toward self-actualization is possible. If a person is open to experience and able to use it in reaching decisions, he is well adjusted. To be poorly adjusted means that one's self-image is poorly adjusted to reality, leading to inevitable frustrations.

Other theories. Other theories include the trait theory, developed by Raymond Cattell. This theory identifies 16 *source traits* as the bases of personality. Each trait is expressed as a continuum between two opposites, such as reserved-outgoing or trusting-suspicious. By identifying a person's position on each continuum, a profile of his personality can be developed. Such a profile can then be compared with various composite profiles to determine, for example, a person's suitability for a particular kind of work.

The body type theory suggests that particular body types correlate with personality types. William Sheldon identified three basic components of the human body: *endomorphy, mesomorphy,* and *ectomorphy.* The endomorph is essentially fat and flabby; the mesomorph, muscular; and the ectomorph, thin and delicate. Endomorphs typically enjoy eating, sleeping, and relaxing, and depend on others for approval. Mesomorphs are assertive, energetic, and resolute. Ectomorphs are inhibited and restrained. Each individual contains all three categories in some combination. In some persons, one type will predominate; in others, the types are more balanced.

Research has not strongly substantiated Sheldon's theory, although it seems likely that a person's body type will strongly influence his or her self-image, and hence personality.

Some behaviorists, such as B.F. Skinner, reject the concept of personality. Skinner holds that all behaviors are *situation specific*; that is, they arise in response to specific situations and not according to any pattern. A person may have been conditioned to respond aggressively in one kind of situation and submissively in another, relaxed in some situations and tense in others.

Other behaviorists have adapted Freudian theory to behavioral terms, pointing out, for example, the near relationship between "repression" (Freudian) and "avoidance reaction" (behavioral).

Stress and Abnormal Behavior

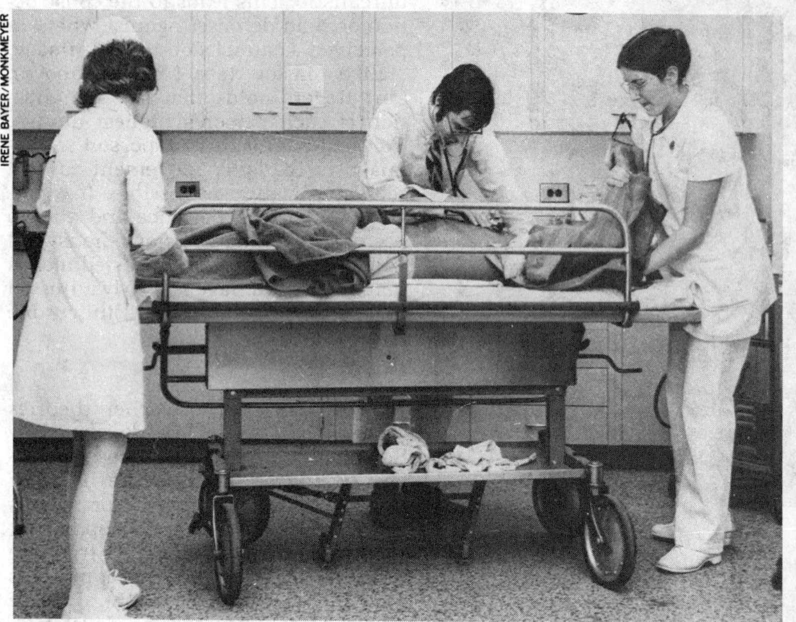

IRENE BAYER/MONKMEYER

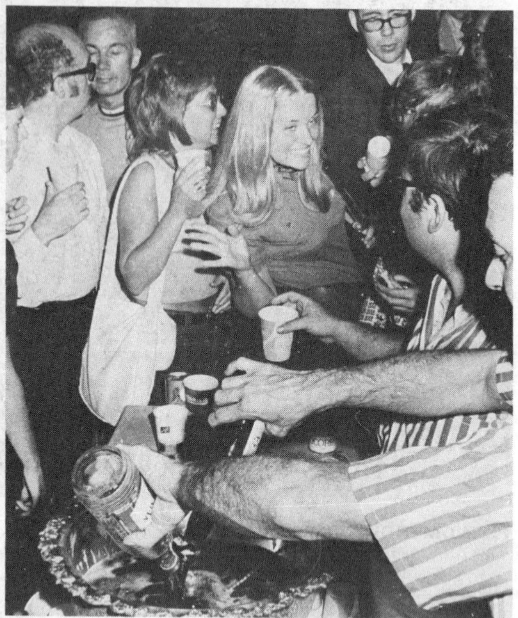

BRUCE ANSPACH/EPA

STRESS *may come from heavy responsibility on the job* (left) *or from social occasions—even when people are enjoying themselves. Too much stress can result in occupational "burnout" or in a variety of other emotional troubles.*

Just as every person has problems, so every person has ways of responding to problems. Ways that are generally successful are called *coping*. Ways that are unsuccessful lead to behavior disorders, or abnormal behavior.

Stress

Life constantly presents challenges to every person. When there is an imbalance between the challenge and the person's evaluation of his ability to cope with that challenge, the result is *stress*. Absence of stress, or finding a resolution to it, is called *adjustment*.

Adjustment. There are two kinds of criteria in evaluating a person's success in addressing a problem. *Objective* criteria are those that anyone can observe. Winning a race or achieving a certain score on a test are objective criteria; there is no disagreement that the race was won or the score achieved.

Subjective criteria are the bases of an individual's self-evaluation. They relate to and derive from a person's self-image, so that the identical test score may represent success to one person and failure to another. Subjective criteria do not always agree with reality; for example, a person's self-image may be that he is witty and charming, when in fact he is a self-centered bore. A different kind of self-image may cause a person to be silent when, in fact, people would be very interested to hear what he has to say.

There are three basic stages in addressing a problem. The first is becoming aware of it; the second is making a plan for dealing with it; and the third is carrying out the plan. Adjustment is having the resources to satisfactorily address a problem through all three stages.

Stressful situations. There are a wide variety of situations that can cause stress, but they fall into two general categories.

Some stresses are *situational*; that is, they arise from some change in the circumstances of one's life. Major situational causes of stress, affecting many people at once, include such calamities as war, natural disasters, and accidents. Others, called *life changes*, are more personal. Among those that cause great stress are the death of a spouse, child, or parent; divorce; and being dimissed from a job. Also stressful, but somewhat less so, are such experiences as getting married, changing jobs or schools, or changing place of residence.

Other situations are stressful to some but not others. A particular social gathering, for example, may be pleasant and relaxing to some but stressful in varying degrees to others. Reactions to various testing situations can vary from great anxiety to none at all. Some people are in a state of almost perpetual anxiety, perceiving danger—and so experiencing stress—in almost any situation.

Stresses that are not situational are *transitional*. Transitional stresses, such as those associated with the various stages of childhood, adolescence, and adulthood, are experienced during the normal course of life.

Coping with stress. In some situations stress is so severe and yet unavoidable that the most effective way of coping with it is to fantasize. For example, a prisoner who has no way of knowing when, or whether, he will ever be released can often best cope with the situation by imagining that he is somewhere else.

In most situations, however, coping requires a realistic effort to gain control of the situation. The fewer surprises a situation presents, the less stressful it is likely to be. It is important that stress not be allowed to distort one's perception of reality. Realism requires accurate assessments of both the situation and of one's own resources for dealing with it. It may well be that a realistic appraisal includes acknowledging one's anxiety, but the feeling should not be exaggerated or allowed to take control.

Besides realism, the second major requirement for coping with stress is self-control. Self-control is not what is often called "willpower." It is, rather, an accurate assessment of how one can affect or alter a situation, free from excuses, rationalizations, and unrealistic expectations.

Coping with challenging situations may be aided by social support, particularly strong family support. Those who try to make it alone usually cope less effectively. In fact, the most "self-reliant" people are those who are able to rely on others.

Stress reactions. Stresses that are too strong or that continue too long can lead to stress reactions, or "breakdowns." In some cases, the stress is beyond the person's control, as in the case of the prisoner; in others the stress has not been coped with effectively. The reaction may be either psychological of physical or both.

One of the more frequent kinds of stress reaction is the *post-traumatic* reaction, often experienced by the survivors of disasters. The survivors continue to relive the event and often feel guilty, depressed, irritable, and restless. Such reactions typically subside over a period of several months following the traumatic event.

Burnout is a kind of emotional exhaustion, usually concerning one's job. It is most often experienced by those who have come to feel frustrated and unappreciated. Nurses and teachers are among those who often experience burnout; feeling underpaid and overworked, they find themselves incapable of caring any longer about their patients or students. Those likeliest to burn out are persons who cannot leave their problems at work and who react personally to professional failures.

Stress reactions are also likely when stress-producing situations occur simultaneously or in quick succession, or when stress is prolonged or intensified by inappropriate ways of attempting to cope with it.

Depression, anger, and anxiety are common psychological reactions to stress. When these reactions are prolonged and persistent, their effects on the chemistry of the nervous and endocrine system can lead to physical disorders. Diseases in which psychological factors often play a role include asthma, arthritis, high blood pressure, ulcers, certain skin conditions, colitis, and heart disease.

Abnormal Behavior

When a person's responses to changing situations are inappropriate, and when that person is unable to change from the inappropriate responses to more appropriate ones, the person may be said to be behaving abnormally. Abnormal behavior is often called mental illness.

The various kinds of abnormal behavior are called *behavior disorders*. Most disorders can vary in degree from mild to severe. Behavior disorders fall into several broad categories.

Personality disorders. Everyone develops patterns of responding to stressful situations; such patterns are a basic component of the personality. In some people, however, a particular pattern will come to predominate to the extent that it is applied inflexibly, regardless of its appropriateness to the situation. Such inappropriate patterns are known as personality disorders. Personality disorders develop early in life, usually being evident by adolescence; very little is known about how to prevent or modify them.

The *paranoid* personality is characterized by extreme mistrust, prejudice, hostility, and deviousness. The *introverted* personality is the classic loner who prefers solitude to social relationships and who finds most contacts with others stressful. The *histrionic* personality acts out feelings in a very dramatic way, and often overreacts. And the *antisocial* personality is largely incapable of loyalty, guilt, cooperation, or self-sacrifice.

COMMON EMOTIONAL DISORDERS *include compulsive eating* (above), *which may lead to physical ailments associated with overweight; and depression* (below), *which is especially common among women.*

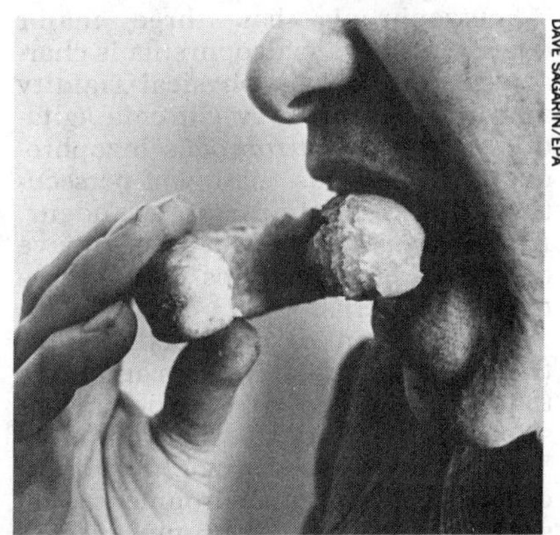
DAVE SAGARIN/EPA

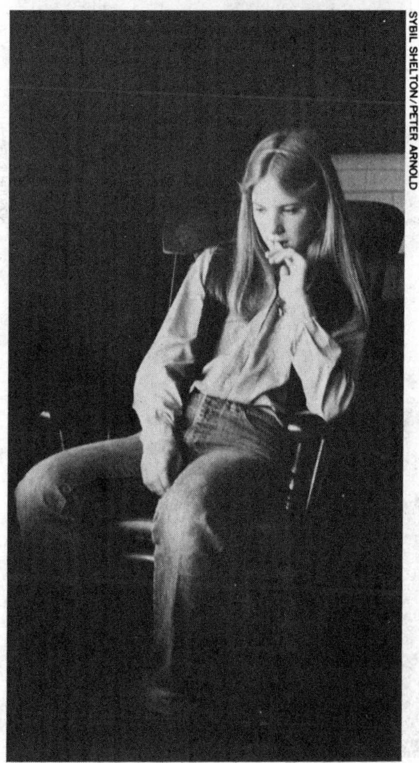
SYBIL SHELTON/PETER ARNOLD

Anxiety disorders. An anxiety disorder was, until recently, called a *neurosis*. Anxiety so intense that it interferes with daily life characterizes anxiety disorders. What prompts anxiety and what results from it varies greatly, but in each case anxiety represents a great overreaction to a particular situation.

Generalized anxiety exists when a person is continually afraid, without being able to specify why or of what. *Panic* exists when fear is not continuous, but rather appears with great intensity at sudden and unpredictable intervals. *Phobias* are fears of one specific thing or situation that are magnified out of all proportion to reality.

Obsessive-compulsive anxiety disorders are characterized by thoughts that the person cannot get out of his mind, and compulsive behavior that the person cannot stop repeating. Some obsessions and compulsions are relatively harmless, like not walking under ladders; others can become rituals that interfere with daily life.

Most psychologists view anxiety disorders in essentially Freudian (psychodynamic) terms. The causes are seen in terms of repressed unconscious impulses, characterized by conflict and guilt, against which the troubled person's defenses are inappropriate or inadequate.

Affective disorders. Affective disorders are so called because their most obvious manifestation is the mood (or "affect") of the person. They include *depression* and *bipolar disorder*, formerly called manic-depressive disorder.

Depression. The behavior disorder called depression, or clinical depression, must be distinguished from the occasional periods of sadness or discouragement that everyone feels from time to time. In clinical depression, these periods are both more severe and more long-lasting than any objective situation warrants.

Depression always is characterized by a sad, hopeless feeling and by loss of interest in things that normally are enjoyed. Other characteristics may be feelings of self-reproach; loss of energy and an inability to concentrate; a gain or loss in weight; and insomnia. Thoughts of death and suicide are frequent; in fact, depression is by far the most frequent cause of suicide.

Depression is the most common of behavior disorders—and probably the most common of all ailments after the common cold. In the course of a year, about 15 percent of the U.S. population display one or more symptoms of clinical depression. A disproportionate part of the sufferers are women.

Cognitive theories seem to offer the best perspective on depression. One characteristic of depression is *overgeneralization*, the tendency to draw broader conclusions from a situation than it warrants. Thus, a failure in one situation will cause a depressed person to reflect self-critically on all of his or her failings, real and imagined.

Another characteristic of depression is *learned helplessness*, a belief that there is nothing one can do to change an unpleasant situation. A person who feels that there is little relation between the quality of his work and the salary increases or promotions that he receives, for example, is likely to develop an attitude of learned helplessness. This, in turn, will affect his job performance: if nobody cares, why bother? The idea of learned helplessness thus is in accord with the view of behavioral psychologists that depression is caused by inadequate reinforcement of behavior, causing a partial extinction of what has been inadequately reinforced.

Depression is also associated with an insufficiency of certain neurotransmitters.

Bipolar disorder. Bipolar disorder is characterized by alternating phases of depression and mania. In the manic state, a person has seemingly unlimited energy and enthusiasm, frequently undertaking wildly unrealistic projects and resisting any attempts to curb them.

Biopolar disorder is relatively rare compared with depression. A disposition to it seems to be inherited, and there is evidence that it may have a physiological cause. It usually appears in early adulthood and, if untreated, episodes occur with increasing frequency. There is, however, a medication that is usually effective in treating it.

Schizophrenia. Schizophrenia is a very severe and, unfortunately, rather common behavior disorder. It has many distressing symptoms, including (1) confused thought patterns: thoughts and speech often make little or no sense, and speech becomes a form of self-expression rather than of communication; (2) inappropriate emotional responses, varying from apathy to happiness or rage; (3) hallucinations: the perceiving of mental images as sensory perceptions (hearing voices, having visions, imagining smells, and the like); and (4) delusions: misinterpretations of reality, such as perceiving nonexistent threats or feeling all-powerful.

Schizophrenia has three major types. *Catatonic* schizophrenia is characterized either by physical rigidity and inflexibility or by extreme agitation. Sufferers of *paranoid* schizophrenia have delusions, mainly of persecution but sometimes of grandeur. *Hebephrenic* schizophrenics also have delusions, hallucinations, and bizarre thought patterns.

Psychodynamic theorists believe that fear, prompted by urges and ideas that break through from the unconscious, is the basis of schizophrenia. This fear causes schizophrenics to disengage from the environment, substituting for it an environment constructed in their own minds. Unrealistic thought, then, is a way to defend oneself against anxiety; it both causes and is reinforced by isolation from others.

Certain neurotransmitters are associated with schizophrenia, but whether they are a cause or a result of the disease has not been established. The same is true of the relationship between abnormalities of brain structure and schizophrenia. An increasing body of evidence suggests that schizophrenia is hereditary.

Organic brain disorders. Organic disorders are those whose cause is known to be actual brain damage or impairment of some kind.

Sometimes the brain is affected by a condition in another part of the body. High fevers, for example, can cause *delirium*, characterized by confusion and disorientation. So, too, can excessive alcohol consumption (*delirium tremens*, or *the DT's*) and certain vitamin deficiencies. Delirium is usually a temporary condition.

Certain poisons, such as lead and mercury, can affect the brain permanently, and syphilis in its advanced stages causes irreversible brain damage leading to psychosis and paralysis.

In some people, the brain deteriorates rather rapidly at some point after the age of 60. This condition, known as *senile dementia*, may be caused either by changes in the brain tissue or by circulatory problems in the brain. It leads to a gradual loss of short-term memory, with resulting confusion, impaired cognitive abilities, and personality changes.

Dementia that begins before the age of 60 is called *presenile dementia*. Huntington's disease, a rare hereditary disorder, is a cause of severe presenile dementia. Alzheimer's disease, whose relationship to heredity is less clear, is a major cause of both presenile and senile dementia.

The brain can be damaged by accidents, tumors, and strokes, with widely varying effects on behavior depending on the location of the damage.

Psychologists have learned a great deal about brain function by studying the behavior and responses of brain-damaged patients. By correlating behavior to the precise location of the injury or damage, they have been able to construct a more accurate "geography" of the brain.

Sudden electrical charges in the brain are the cause of the condition called *epilepsy*. Epileptic seizures may be severe and accompanied by convulsions (*grand mal*), or be brief and without convulsions (*petit mal*). A third variety, called *psychomotor* epilepsy, causes temporary lapses in judgment. Epilepsy can be caused by brain damage and is also related to stress. Most cases can be successfully treated by drugs. —*Samuel C. Plummer*

MENTAL DISORGANIZATION *can be expressed in drawings, as in this elaborate sketch by a patient suffering from schizophrenia.*

THAMES & HUDSON

SOCIOLOGY

Sociology is the scientific study of human interaction. In a way it is the most social of the social sciences because it deals with the behavior of people in groups. Sociologists look for answers to questions like these: Does racial integration improve scholastic achievement? Is American society dominated by a small establishment? What values do we derive from watching television? Why do people become criminals? Topics like these interest students of government, psychology, and other disciplines, but sociologists approach them from the perspective of group membership. In studying the origins of criminal behavior, for example, sociologists are interested primarily in an individual's affiliations with others, whether through family, social class, or community.

In its concern with human behavior, sociology is linked to other social sciences, especially psychology and anthropology. But its emphasis is different. Psychologists are concerned chiefly with individual attitudes and behavior, not with groups. Anthropologists focus primarily on behavior in prehistoric or primitive societies, while sociologists usually study various aspects of modern industrial societies. Sociology is a *synthetic* discipline: it uses information provided by all the social sciences, interpreting the information from the perspective of group membership.

HUMAN INTERACTION *is the concern of sociology. Here buyers and sellers, family members, and bystanders discuss the purchase of some vegetables.*

Like other social sciences, sociology strives for objectivity, and sociologists use the scientific method. They collect data and analyze and present it logically and systematically. But sociologists disagree about the purpose of sociological inquiry. Some feel that sociologists should simply present what they have learned. Others believe that sociology can help make society more just and humane.

History

The workings of society have interested scholars since ancient times. Plato, for example, described an ideal state based on his conception of various social classes and their functions. Several philosophers of the Enlightenment—among them Thomas Hobbes and Jean Jacques Rousseau—were concerned with human nature as evidenced by group behavior.

The founders of sociology. Beginning in the 1800's, a few thinkers began to analyze society in a scientific way. Industrialization was causing rapid change in social structure and in living conditions, and different ways of approaching these changes seemed called for. The new discipline originated with the French philosopher Auguste Comte (1798–1857), who coined the word sociology from the Latin *socius* (associate) and the Greek *logos* (science). Comte was a reformer, and he saw sociology as a means of achieving harmony by uncovering laws of social order.

Another influential early sociologist was the Englishman Herbert Spencer (1820–1903). His *Principles of Sociology* applied the theory of Darwinian evolution to human societies. Spencer argued that a society is like a living organism, with each part (the economy, religion, and so on) serving a function in maintaining stability. Spencer opposed any attempts at social reform. He believed that society ought to be allowed to evolve without interference.

Just the opposite view was held by the great German thinker Karl Marx (1818–1883). He was not a sociologist, strictly speaking. But his insights into human society greatly influenced the discipline. Marx believed that social structure is determined by economic factors, and he regarded class conflict as the key to history. Only through violent revolution, he wrote, could mankind achieve a truly humane (classless) society.

Two later sociologists, Emile Durkheim (1858–1917) of France and Max Weber (1864–1920) of Germany, helped make the new study a formal discipline. Durkheim, like Spencer, was interested in how various elements of society contribute to the operation of the whole. A pioneering work was his careful statistical study of suicide, undertaken with the aim of showing that many outside forces, including the size of an individual's community, affect even this most personal of acts.

The interests of Max Weber were varied, ranging from law and bureaucracy to religion and music. He disagreed with Marx on the overriding importance of economic forces, holding that people's perception of social forces help to determine their behavior. Almost all later sociologists have been influenced by Weber's insistence on value-free research—sociological investigation unbiased by personal convictions.

Sociology in the United States. The new study caught the interest of Americans quite early. One of the first prominent American sociologists was Lester F. Ward (1841–1913), who, like Comte, believed that humans could and should improve society by directing its course. A contrary view was that of Spencer's chief disciple in the United States, William Graham Sumner (1840–1910). Sumner agreed with Spencer that the aim of sociology was understanding rather than political or social action.

The first department of sociology was opened at the University of Chicago in 1893, and it dominated the field for decades. One of its well known teachers was George Herbert Mead (1863–1931), who helped develop the concept of the social self. Three others, Robert E. Park (1864–1944), Ernest W. Burgess (1886–1966), and Louis Wirth (1897–1952), analyzed urban growth and problems.

Today most sociologists are associated with one of three broad perspectives:

Functionalists, in the tradition of Spencer and Durkheim, see society as a stable structure in which each part has a definite function. Even conditions condemned by society may have some practical use. For example, prostitution may serve as a sexual outlet for unattractive males. Talcott Parsons (1902–) and Robert Merton (1910–) are among those associated with functionalism.

Conflict theorists are descended from Marx in that they emphasize some form of conflict (not necessarily class conflict). To them, continual struggles among competing forces—for example, the old versus the young—mean that society is not stable, but in a constant state of flux. C. Wright Mills (1916–1962), who studied American political and economic institutions, was a prominent conflict theorist.

Symbolic interactionists, influenced by Weber, are interested not so much in big issues, like the distribution of wealth, as in individual perceptions of social factors. They stress everyday interchanges in which language, gestures, and so on have meanings that go beyond surface expression. Erving Goffman (1922–), a leading symbolic interactionist, sees social life as theater, with all of us playing various parts at various times.

The Nature of Society

During the 150 years that sociology has existed as a discipline, those who have practiced it have developed a sizable body of knowledge about how society is put together. Their findings form the basic vocabulary of sociology today.

Culture

One of the most basic concepts in sociology (and in anthropology as well) is that of *culture*, which may be defined as the sum total of all distinctively human activities that can be transmitted from one generation to another. Social scientists speak of both material and nonmaterial culture. *Material culture* includes all the physical objects created by humans, from pizza and sneakers to calculators and hydrogen bombs. *Nonmaterial culture* consists of abstract creations, such as religious beliefs, language, and marriage customs.

Culture is learned behavior, and it sets humans apart from animals. Ants and other creatures act from instinct and behave like others of their species the world over. Humans act out of shared experience and have developed strikingly different patterns of living, ranging from that of the Arabian Bedouin to that of the Alaskan Inuit (or Eskimo). The distinctive pattern of a particular group of people is called an individual culture. The word culture is thus used both in a broad general sense and in a more specific one. The idea of pattern is important, for the elements of a given culture fit together and depend on each other: the camels, tents, and roast lamb of desert herders; the dogs, igloos, and raw fish of Arctic hunters.

The terms culture and society are sometimes used interchangeably, but they have somewhat different meanings. Strictly speaking, culture refers to all the *products* (material and nonmaterial) of a group, while society refers to the *people* (usually in a common territory) who share this way of life. Thus we speak of Western culture as a way of life shared by American society, French society, and so on.

Norms. Sociologists are particularly interested in those aspects of culture that affect people's relations with each other. Paramount among these are *norms*—guidelines that state what a person should do or not do in given situations.

Norms vary a great deal from one culture to another. Americans commonly greet each other with a handshake or a kiss; the Japanese bow. Our society allows a person to have multiple marriages, but only one at a time; a Muslim man may have as many as four wives at once.

Norms also vary within a culture from group to group, time to time, and situation to situation. Ordinary citizens are forbidden to take a human life, but members of the armed forces are trained to do just that. Until re-

MATERIAL AND NONMATERIAL CULTURE: *sociologists learn much about a culture from such things as the objects people gather around them, left. The statues by George Segal suggest the behavior of commuters—their patient waiting. Objects are part of our material culture, while behavior is a part of our nonmaterial culture.*

FORSYTH/MONKMEYER

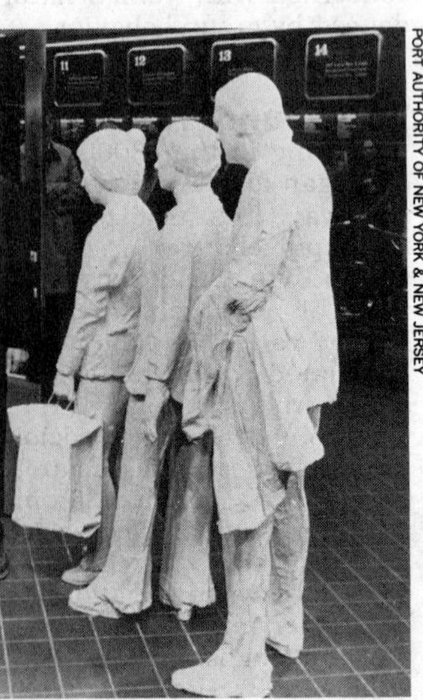

PORT AUTHORITY OF NEW YORK & NEW JERSEY

GREETINGS *or expressions of agreement are different in different cultures—from the handshake in Western culture to the courtly bow in traditional Japan.*

NORMS AND THE LAW

Social norms and folkways sometimes find their way into law. Because norms change, laws based on them may soon become outdated. Among laws that have been on the books in the United States are the following:

Health and Sanitation

No citizen may take more than one bath per week (Boston).
Citizens may not blow their noses in public (Waterville, Me.).
No one may bring a mule into a saloon (Lourdsburg, N.M.).

Modesty and Personal Appearance

Women's skirts may be no more than 2 inches above the ankle (Terre Haute, Ind.).
Men are required to grow beards (Brainerd, Minn.).
Men must wear bathing suit tops (Prichard, Ala.).

Men and Women

A man may not buy liquor without written permission from his wife (Cold Spring, Penn.).
A woman may not rearrange furniture in a house without her husband's permission (Ky.).
A woman may not telephone a man for a date (Dyersburg, Tenn.).

—*From You Can't Eat Peanuts in Church and Other Little-Known Laws* by Barbara Seuling, Doubleday, 1975

cently, men and women were criticized severely if they lived together without being married. Although this behavior may still be criticized, it has become far more common and is even recognized in official census reports. A full-throated rendition of the national anthem is expected at a football game but frowned on in a public bus.

As can be seen from these examples, norms are not all of equal significance. Those that are treated least seriously are known as *folkways*—ordinary habits of social behavior. American folkways include being on time for appointments, hiding a yawn behind one's hand, and applauding to show approval. People who consistently disregard folkways may be thought of as odd or eccentric, but not immoral.

Mores (pronounced MO-rays) are more serious. They reflect deeply held convictions about proper behavior toward others: caring for children and parents, respecting the property of others, and the like. Those who violate mores by committing child abuse or theft are regarded as immoral and even dangerous.

Laws are guidelines formalized by statute and enforced by the authority of the state. They may codify existing folkways (by prohibiting driving on the left side of the street) or mores (by outlawing rape). Sometimes laws do not reflect cultural norms. These are often difficult to enforce. From 1918 to 1933, the manufacture or sale of alcoholic beverages was illegal in the United States. Drinking alcoholic beverages was so deeply rooted in American culture, however, that millions of people continued to do so even though it was illegal.

Values. The norms of a society are derived from its *values*—ideas about what is right and desirable. While norms are guidelines for behavior in specific situations, values are abstract, generalized principles.

Sociologists have identified a number of values underlying norms in the United States. Although none is unique to our society, the combination is distinctively American. Sociologist Robin Williams has listed 15 values. Among them are worldly success, work, a moral orientation, practicality, progress, equality, freedom, and democracy.

The relationship between values and norms becomes clearer if we look at some of the norms associated with the American value of success. Schoolchildren openly strive for grades and other forms of recognition. Their parents display such tangible signs of success as stylish clothes and expensive cars. People in many walks of life engage in competitive sports (with winning as the object) and spend hours watching televised games.

Cultures that attach less importance to success have different norms. For example, Pueblo Indian schoolchildren, reared to regard cooperation as more important than competition, hesitate to volunteer answers or take part in spelling or math contests. The Tangu people of New Guinea, who value equivalence, play games not to win but until each side scores the same number of points.

Language. Language is humans' way of transmitting what they know, whether it be tribal traditions or chemical formulas. Societies whose language is written down are *literate*; those without writing are known as *preliterate*.

A culture's language expresses the concepts its people regard as important. Vietnamese, for example, have several different pronouns corresponding to the English "you." Traditional Vietnamese society had a highly developed sense of etiquette, and it needed more ways of expressing respect than does a less formal society. Nouns, too, proliferate as needed. The Aztecs, who lived in the tropics, had only a single word for snow, frost, ice, and cold; English speakers differentiate among the four; the Inuit, who live above the Arctic Circle, have 20 words describing types of snow alone.

Language reflects culture, and it may be that culture comes to reflect language. The Sapir-Whorf hypothesis, named for the two linguists who advanced it, argues that the structure and vocabulary of a language force its speakers to perceive reality in certain ways. For example, English speakers may be incapable of distinguishing among 20 different kinds of snow, or of comprehending the complexity of traditional Vietnamese society—all because of the language they grew up with.

Social Structure

Because sociologists are concerned primarily with humans as social beings, they have taken special care in analyzing *social structure*—the orderly, patterned ways individuals and groups relate to each other in society. The most important components of social structure are status, role, and group.

Status. Although the word status is often used to mean prestige, sociologists define it differently. To them, *status* is any position, high or low, that determines where a person fits in society. Every individual occupies several statuses at any given time. Thus one person may be described as a collection of the various relationships he or she has with others. For example, female, black, teenager, student, cheerleader, friend, Methodist, daughter, and sister are each a status. Each status serves to place the individual in a social relationship with others.

Statuses fall into two groups, ascribed and achieved. An *ascribed status* is one over which we have no control; it is assigned when we are born or as we grow older. The ascribed statuses of the high-school junior mentioned above are her sex, race, age, and family relationships.

An *achieved status* is one that results at least partly from our own actions. The achieved statuses of the young high-school woman are student, cheerleader, friend, and Methodist. Later in life she may occupy such achieved statuses as lawyer, wife, and mother. The "achievement" of status is not necessarily positive; other achieved statuses are school dropout, convict, and bankrupt.

Role. To a sociologist, *role* is the conduct associated with a status—that is, the behavior, rights, and duties expected in a given social position. The role of a child usually involves the following: carefree play, economic and psychological dependence on parents, and obedience toward parents and other older people. A person with the status of physician is expected to diagnose illness, prescribe treatment, collect fees for services, and so on.

Because we occupy many different statuses at the same time, there is a constant possibility of *role conflict*; this arises when expectations are in opposition. If a man's boss asks him to work late on the evening of his son's piano recital, there is a conflict between his role as employee and his role as father.

Group. Although most people use the word group rather loosely in everyday speech, sociologists give it a specific meaning. To them, a *group* is a collection of people who interact in terms of related statuses and roles and who feel a sense of belonging. A family is a group; its members interact in their statuses as husband/father, wife/mother, son/brother, daughter/sister, and so on. The workers at a restaurant form a group too. Host, chef, waiters, busboys, and dishwashers each have their own statuses and roles. On the other hand, a crowd of strangers watching a football game is not a group, for its members do not interact on the basis of related status and role.

Groups may be based on similar roles (a union local) or complementary ones (an opera company). They may be small (an engaged couple) or large (employees of a big corporation). They may be formal (a Little League team) or informal (neighbors playing a game of touch football).

All groups fall into two main categories, primary and secondary. The *primary group* is close, personal, and relatively permanent. Its members are bound together by generalized ties of affection. The family is a primary group, as are cliques of friends.

The *secondary group* is more formal, impersonal, and temporary. Members interact in terms of specific tasks in order to achieve a common purpose. Most work groups are secondary groups; so are clubs and other voluntary associations (although primary groups may develop within them).

A form of secondary group prevalent in modern society is a *bureaucracy*, a hierarchically organized, task-oriented group. Although we tend to associate bureaucracy primarily with government, it is also characteristic of big business, labor, and nonprofit organizations.

All groups have boundaries; "we" belong, while "they" remain outside. Sociologist William Graham Sumner named these "we" and "they" categories the *ingroup* and the *outgroup*. Being a part of the ingroup gives members a sense of identity, often strengthened by the group's feelings of hostility to those outside. Some of the most enduring and appealing fictional situations involve outgroup characters who break into the ingroup.

Whether we are on the inside looking out or on the outside looking in, all of us use *reference groups* to evaluate our own behavior. A reference group may serve as a positive or negative model. The norms and values of the

FORSYTH/MONKMEYER

GROUPS *may be of any size—from the baseball team in the dugout to the two bricklayers working together on the wall. The baseball fans, however, are not a group in the sociological sense because an individual does not have a recognized status or role with respect to the others. But there may be many smaller groups—families, clubs, friends—within the crowd.*

WOOD/TAURUS

family next door, for instance, may be the object of either imitation or avoidance.

Interactions within groups, especially small groups, have been carefully studied by sociologists. Specific areas of interest include leadership (how leaders emerge and exercise authority); decision making (the effectiveness of group decisions); and conformity (the extent to which members are influenced by group pressure).

Social Institutions

All societies have certain basic needs. To provide for them they develop social institutions. A *social institution* is a cluster of norms, values, statuses, and roles associated with a particular need. The social institution of education in the United States may serve as an example. Children are compelled to attend school for a certain number of years (a norm). Attendance is required because of the shared belief (value) that a democracy needs educated citizens. Schools employ teachers (statuses) who are expected to instruct students (roles).

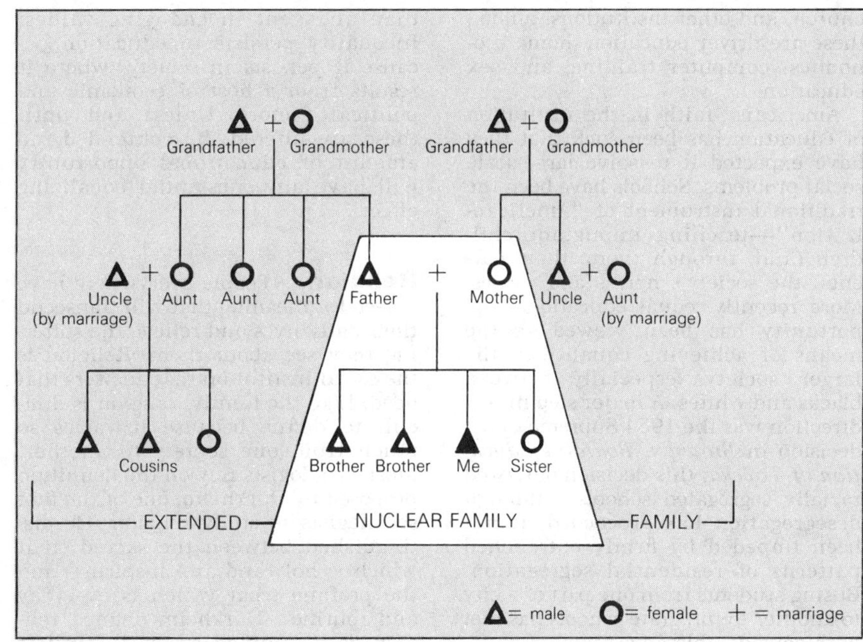

NUCLEAR AND EXTENDED FAMILY: *The nuclear family consists of a couple and their children; the extended family includes other fairly close relatives on both sides of the family. In this diagram, the maker of the chart is a child in the nuclear family, and all others are named by their relation to him. Most people are children in one nuclear family, then form another by marrying and having children.*

The family. Every culture makes provision for the family as a social institution. Defining a family, however, is difficult because its form varies so much. In one culture, a mother's parents, not the father, assume responsibility for her children. In another, the marriage partners are actually women, who raise children fathered by nonfamily members. Whatever form the family takes, its primary responsibility is the care of family members, especially children.

In the United States, as in other industrialized nations, the family has undergone considerable change in this century. It has altered economically, from being a unit of production (the family running its own farm) to being a unit of consumption (the family as purchaser of goods and services). When children were producers, working from an early age, there was economic incentive for having a large family. Today, children are consumers, and since there is no economic incentive to have many children, family size has declined. The average family now has about three members, as compared with about five in 1890.

It used to be thought that the extended family (three or more generations living under one roof) was the norm in American society before the present century. Recent research indicates that, on the contrary, the nuclear family (parents and their dependent children living together) was the commonest form. Family composition in earlier times was limited both by the small size of houses and by the fact that fewer people lived to old age.

What *has* been happening in this century is a shift away from the nuclear family to other forms, especially single-parent families. The main cause of this change is the soaring incidence of divorce. The rate per thousand Americans more than doubled between 1940 and 1980. There has also been an increase in the number of people remaining single and in unmarried singles living together.

Roles within the family have changed, too. For a long time the American norm was breadwinner/father and homemaker/mother. These norms are less common than they used to be, mainly because more women have joined the paid work force. In 1950 less than a third of women over 16 held jobs; by 1980 the total had increased to almost 60 percent. By the late 1970's only 16 percent of all American families consisted of a working father, housewife, and dependent children. As a result, there has been an increasing tendency for men to share such responsibilities as household maintenance and child care.

Education. Education, the social institution charged with teaching a society's values and skills to new members, exists in all cultures. In simple ones it is informal, with parents or other older persons imparting knowledge to children in the course of everyday life. In modern industrial societies, professional teachers provide formal instruction to students in fixed settings (schools).

Education in the United States differs from education in most comparable societies. For one thing, the nation is committed to mass education. Everyone has the right to at least twelve years of schooling at public expense, and the number taking advantage of this right has grown steadily. In 1900 less than 10 percent of 17-year-olds were high school graduates; today almost 80 percent of them are. In 1900 about 4 percent of high school graduates attended college; today over 40 percent do. (In European countries only 10 percent of high school graduates pursue further study.)

A second characteristic of American education is that it has traditionally been controlled by local communities rather than by the national government. Public schools may receive some state and federal funds, but the bulk of their financial support comes from local property taxes. This system fosters independence and flexibility in curriculum. But it also means that schools vary enormously in the amount of money they have at their disposal. Figures compiled in 1975 showed that the average annual per-pupil expenditure by state ranged from $2000 in New York to less than $900 in Mississippi. Discrepancies between individual districts were even more pronounced.

A third feature of education in the United States is its utilitarian emphasis. Schools are expected to teach practical skills and provide information that will help students in their working years. Schools also have been entrusted with a number of tasks that other countries leave to the family, the church, and other institutions; among these are driver education, home economics, computer training, and sex education.

Americans' faith in the institution of education has been such that they have expected it to solve large-scale social problems. Schools have been the traditional instrument of "Americanization"—teaching immigrant children (and, through them, their parents) the society's norms and values. More recently, equal educational opportunity has been viewed as the means of achieving equality in the larger society, especially between blacks and whites. A major step in this direction was the 1954 Supreme Court decision in *Brown* v. *Board of Education of Topeka*; this decision outlawed racially segregated schools. Although desegregation has proceeded, it has been impeded by firmly entrenched patterns of residential segregation. Busing students from one part of a city to another to integrate schools has met with considerable opposition.

Sociologists have been interested in how effective schools can be in fostering equality. James Coleman conducted a large survey of black and white students in the 1960's. He expected that students in predominantly black schools would score lower academically because such schools are generally older and poorer. He did, indeed, find differences, but the schools did not account for them, since whites did consistently better than blacks *in the same schools*. The important factor, Coleman concluded, was class. White students tended to come from middle-class homes that prepared and motivated them for school. Most black students came from lower-class environments and were less motivated.

A study in the 1970's by Christopher Jencks reinforced Coleman's conclusions. Jencks wrote that schools are more a reflection of American values than an agent in changing values. Inequality persists in education because it persists in society, where it results from a host of economic and political factors. Unless and until these are altered, he contended, no amount of educational opportunity will have any substantial equalizing effect.

Religion. People everywhere have a need for meaning that will transcend their daily lives and relieve the suffering they see about them. Religion is the social institution that answers that need. Like the family, religion is difficult to define because it varies so much from one society to another. Most sociologists rely on the definition proposed by Durkheim, one of the first sociologists to study religion. He distinguished between the sacred (that which is holy and awe inspiring) and the profane (that which is everyday and routine). Durkheim defined religion as "a unified system of beliefs and practices relating to sacred things, uniting into a single moral community all those who adhere to those beliefs and practices."

The idea of a "moral community" is important. Although religious beliefs are deeply personal, they are shared with others and are usually expressed through group rituals: a Roman Catholic mass, a Jewish seder, a Muslim communal prayer, the Sun Dance of the Cheyenne Indians.

Americans regard themselves as religious people. Most polls show that at least 90 percent of the respondents believe in "God or a universal spirit." Almost two-thirds of Americans are affiliated with a church or synagogue. Yet attendance at religious services has declined steadily for decades, and many observers feel that American society, like those of other industrialized countries, is becoming increasingly secular.

ENDS AND MEANS: *surveys suggest that most Americans favor desegregation of schools; but they have reacted strongly against busing to achieve desegregation.*

UPI

The decline in religious observance and orientation has affected established denominations such as the Presbyterians, Methodists, and Episcopalians. At the same time, growing numbers of Americans have turned to more informal, evangelical sects: Pentecostal Churches, Seventh-Day Adventists, and small cults whose followers are sometimes known as "Jesus freaks." Some young people have embraced non-Christian and extra-Christian mystical cults such as the Hare Krishna sect and the Unification Church of Sun Myung Moon (the "Moonies").

Separation of church and state is written into the American Constitution. Strong feelings are aroused when potential breaches, such as proposals for federal aid to parochial schools, threaten. Yet our national life is full of religious elements. Our currency proclaims our trust in God; our politicians pepper their speeches with references to the Almighty. We pledge allegiance to one nation "under God" and swear courtroom oaths on Bibles. The prevalence of such elements has led some sociologists to describe the real religion of the United States as a "civil religion" that worships the American way of life.

Government. All societies have to allocate power among their members; government is the social institution that channels that power. The term government is usually reserved for the formal kinds of organizations—with written laws and professional bureaucracies—characteristic of developed nations. Simpler cultures maintain political order through unwritten norms, tribal councils, and similar informal controls.

Sociologists who study political life are indebted to Max Weber, who formulated some of the basic concepts involving government. One was the idea of power itself, which Weber defined as the ability to control other people, even against their will. Those who have power may rule without the right to do so; history offers many examples of tyrants controlling through military force. Those who rule rightfully are said to have *legitimacy*. Weber called this rightful power authority, and distinguished three types.

Traditional authority usually derives from inheritance, through either birth (monarchs) or bequest (Roman emperors). Tribal elders and parents also exercise traditional authority. *Charismatic authority* depends on charisma, a personal quality inherent in individuals. People with charisma (Julius Caesar, Joan of Arc, Napoleon) inspire strong personal devotion. *Rational-legal authority* grows out of an office, not inherited position or personal appeal. This type of authority characterizes most statuses in constitutional governments (presidents, ministers of state, legislators, judges, and the like).

Since its beginnings as a nation in the 1700's, the United States has had a republican form of government—one in which power is held by the voters. With the passage of time, the country became a democracy—a republic in which the majority of citizens can vote. Through a complex system of federalism and of checks and balances embodied in the Constitution, elected and appointed officials carry out the actual executive, legislative, and judicial functions.

Sociologists are concerned not only with the formal apparatus of government but with how the system actually works. For example, the proportion of eligible U.S. voters taking part in Presidential elections has averaged less than 60 percent in this century. This figure compares with an average of 85 percent in Britain and 90 percent in West Germany.

At the same time, voters identify less strongly with political parties and seem increasingly disillusioned with the process of government itself. Interest in large political questions has been replaced by interest in special issues. Voters mobilize around such causes as abortion, gun control, the draft, or nuclear power plants.

American sociologists have advanced conflicting theories about who really wields power in our society. C. Wright Mills argued that it is held by a "power elite" made up of white males prominent in government, business, and the military. Although they do not conspire to rule, they "occupy the strategic command posts of the social structure." This view has been challenged by David Riesman and others, who emphasize the pluralist nature of American politics. Power is held not by any single group, they say, but rather by alliances and coalitions that are constantly shifting.

The economy. While the political order allocates power, the economic order allocates resources. In every society, goods and services are scarce—which is another way of saying that there is not enough to go around. Therefore, a social institution must be devoted to determining who gets what.

Industrialization, the key event in shaping the modern world, has made economic systems extremely complex. Huge amounts of capital are invested in the mass production of goods, and the division of labor results in a high degree of specialization. Industrialized nations have various ways of organizing their economies, but these fall into two main categories.

Capitalism, or free enterprise, rests on a belief in private ownership of the means of production, with the goal of making profits. Production and distribution are regulated through the forces of supply and demand in a competitive market. *Socialism* rests on a belief in public ownership of the means of production, with the goal of social equality. Production and distribution are regulated by the government. Capitalism, or a market economy, characterizes the United States, some Western European nations, and Japan. Socialism, or a planned economy, is the system in the Soviet Union, Eastern Europe, and China. It is usual to characterize the systems maintained by Russia and its satellites as communist. Actually, Marxist communism envisions a classless society where the state has withered away; in this sense, communism does not exist anywhere.

It is hard to draw firm distinctions between economic systems because elements of socialism exist in capitalist countries, and vice versa. This is certainly true in the United States, where some segments of the economy are publicly owned (Conrail, TVA) and government regulation does much to control the market (by restraining monopolies and setting safety standards). For this reason the American system is often termed modified capitalism, or a mixed economy. Britain and the Scandinavian countries also have mixed systems, but the government actually owns major manufacturing industries.

Sociologists emphasize the immense power of large corporations in the American economic system. The top hundred of these corporations own more than half the manufacturing assets of the country. Multinational corporations (those with operations in at least six countries) often have annual incomes greater than those of the nations in which they operate. The dangers of corporate capitalism include the concentration of wealth in a few hands and the domination of political processes by business interests. When a few large firms dominate a market (to form an *oligopoly*), true competition cannot flourish, and consumers may end up paying high prices for poor quality or even dangerous products.

Socialization

Human beings, unique as culture-producing animals, also undergo a distinctively human process of learning how to be members of society. This process, called *socialization*, is never-ending because people are constantly adapting to new statuses, roles, and groups.

Infancy and childhood. Young humans are the most helpless of all creatures: unable to feed themselves, walk, or talk for many months, and not fully independent for many years. Babies have the biological potential to learn human skills, but they cannot do so alone. The few known cases of children reared in isolation—children who survived with an absolute minimum of care—indicate that humans cannot even learn to walk without social contact.

The nature of early human interaction was of particular interest to the American sociologists Charles Horton Cooley and George Herbert Mead. Cooley developed the concept of the "looking-glass self"—the idea that we develop individual identity by imagining how others see us. Mead elaborated on this idea with his notion of "significant others"—people whose judgments are important to us. Children first shape their behavior according to norms enforced by significant others. In time, they obey guidelines on their own. They have developed a conscience through a process that sociologists call *internalization*.

PUBLIC ISSUES *often become the nucleus around which a group can organize. These demonstrators are protesting American involvement in the Vietnam War in the early 1970's.*

WIDE WORLD

DRAWING BY ROBT. DAY; © 1970

"Don't you understand? This is life, this is what is happening. We can't switch to another channel."

Humans learn the ways of society from *agents of socialization.* The most important of these in a child's early years is the family. Through it the child acquires the first statuses and roles (son or daughter, brother or sister) and learns basic values and norms (for instance sex-role socialization—the different behaviors expected of males and females).

At an early age, at least in American society, a child is also exposed to another agent—television. While TV entertains and communicates knowledge, it also imparts such values as competitiveness (through game shows) and violence as a solution to problems (through spy and police melodramas). Commercials tend to reinforce traditional masculine-feminine roles by depicting men in situations outside the home and women as domestic workers. Other agents of socialization in a child's early years are the school (and its teachers) and the peer group—that is, playmates and other children of the same general age.

Adolescence and adulthood. In preindustrial societies, a child becomes an adult upon physical maturation. In our own and other industrial societies, however, there is a middle period called adolescence. For most young people, the peer group becomes the primary agent of socialization and many of the norms and values inculcated earlier (obedience, neatness, politeness) are questioned and even abandoned, at least temporarily.

In adulthood, people enter the world of work and embark on a new kind of socialization as unskilled or skilled laborers, white-collar workers, or professionals. Adulthood is also the time when people establish families of their own, and are socialized to be spouses and parents. Studies by such social scientists as Daniel Levinson have shown that socialization continues in definite stages throughout the entire adult life cycle.

Social Problems

Deviance

Every society includes people who do not conform to its norms. Nonconformity may be simply a harmless departure from standard behavior. Misers, hermits, mediums, devotees of religious cults—any or all might be regarded as nonconformists.

When nonconformity involves essential norms and causes widespread and severe disapproval, it is called *deviance.* Like a society's values, deviance is relative. For example, homosexuality, once widely condemned as a shameful sin, has become more acceptable in recent years.

Types of deviance. One type of deviance that particularly concerns sociologists is crime. Many focus on specialized areas such as white-collar crime or organized crime. Studies of violent crimes against persons and property are of special interest, too. Even though such crimes constitute only a small fraction of the total crime and most Americans are never the victims of violent crime, it inspires a great deal of fear. The United States is a violent society: its homicide rate is much higher than that in most other industrialized nations, including Britain, Canada, and Japan.

Another type of deviance, addiction, involves a compulsive craving for certain mood-altering substances. Some of these substances, especially alcohol and tobacco, are legal. Others, such as tranquilizers and amphetamines, are legal when prescribed, but they are also widely obtained illegally. Still others, notably narcotics and hallucinogens, are illegal. The term drug abuse usually refers to the habitual use of such drugs as marijuana, cocaine, and heroin, but it may also apply to alcoholism and dependency on stimulants ("uppers") and depressants ("downers").

Although alcohol and tobacco harm far more people than other drugs do, their users are rarely labeled as addicts; in fact, many Americans do not regard these substances as drugs at all. Some sociologists suggest that we may judge drug abuse more by the users than by the drugs themselves and the damage they cause. Drinking and smoking are vices of all classes, but drugs like heroin and cocaine have been associated with marginal social groups such as musicians, hippies, and the ghetto poor.

A third type of deviance, suicide, is ironically not a crime unless it fails. Durkheim's classic study of the 1890's reported, among other findings, that suicide occurred more often in large cities than in small towns and more frequently among single than among married people. Durkheim concluded that the common element in these situations was a loosening of social bonds and a consequent weakening of society's norms against taking one's life. Durkheim coined the word *anomie* to describe this state of normlessness.

More recent research into suicide in the United States has revealed a number of trends: that it is commoner among males than females; that it is the third most prevalent cause of death among teenagers; and that, as a group, American Indians have the highest rate of suicide.

What causes deviance? Some theories of deviance stress biological factors. Early in this century the Italian criminologist Cesare Lombroso, after studying dozens of criminals, wrote that the majority were characterized by certain physical traits, including shifty eyes and strong jaws. His theory was effectively demolished when other researchers measured ordinary citizens and found the incidence of shifty eyes and strong jaws to be the same in the general population.

More recently, investigators have linked criminal behavior in males to an extra chromosome. Normal males have an XY chromosome structure; less usual is an XYY makeup. Although the XYY type does seem commoner in criminals than the XY type, most XYY males lead normal lives. Thus the chromosomal irregularity does not seem to have much causal significance, at least in terms of crime.

Social theories offer several different explanations of deviance. One is built on Durkheim's idea of anomie. Robert Merton has elaborated on this concept, using it to define the gap in our modern society between socially approved goals (wealth, social position) and the means of attaining them. An individual deprived of legitimate channels of succeeding (because of racial discrimination, for example) then adopts one of several patterns. One type, the "innovator," tries to attain success by illegal means, such as prostitution or embezzlement. Another, the "retreatist," drops out of the race by becoming an alcoholic or a heroin addict. A third, the "rebel," not only rejects society's goals, but sets up new ones, such as overthrowing society altogether.

Another social theory of deviance, called cultural transmission, holds that people learn deviant behavior from those around them. If someone is exposed to, say, pimps, drug pushers, and thieves at an early age, he or she is likely to adopt similar behavior. In fact, it is not regarded as deviant in the context in which the person lives.

Some sociologists use labeling theory to explain deviance. They believe that almost everyone engages in deviant behavior at one time or another, whether it be shoplifting, illegal drug use, or income tax evasion. Some people, however, are labeled "thief," "addict," and so on. Their self-concept is altered and they then adopt the deviant behavior as a way of life.

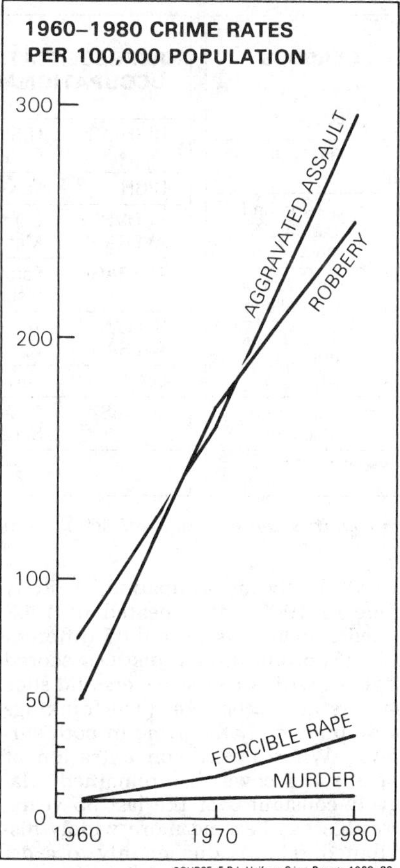

VIOLENT CRIME *has increased rapidly in the United States in recent years. Crime rates are much higher here than in other developed countries.*

Social control. Social control—the means society uses to enforce its norms—encourages conformity and discourages deviance. For the majority of people, informal sanctions are sufficient. For some, however, formal means must be used to prevent or punish deviance.

The criminal justice system is one agency of social control. Many Americans are dissatisfied with it as it exists in the United States today. For one thing, it fails to apprehend thousands of wrongdoers. Some criminologists estimate that the actual crime rate is two to three times higher than that reported in official statistics. Another problem is that the burden of punishment is not borne equally. Studies show that, other things being equal, lower-class and/or black offenders are far more likely than upper-class and/or white ones to be arrested, prosecuted, convicted, sentenced, and imprisoned.

What is the function of prison itself? Lip service is given to the idea of rehabilitation, yet the rate of recidivism (repeated offenses) is so high that this aim cannot be viewed as realistic. What of the ultimate punishment, the death penalty? Cyclically in and out of favor with the public, its use is much debated. Evidence that it deters crime—or fails to do so—is spotty and unreliable.

Sociologist Erving Goffman has called prison a *total institution.* Other total institutions include mental hospitals, military training installations, and religious orders. In all of these, the aim is *resocialization*—supplying people with new values and norms. First initiates are stripped of their old identities, then they are taught new roles. Goffman holds that, by their nature, total institutions are not able to help inmates (or patients, or trainees, or the religious) take up normal responsibilities in the society at large.

TOTAL INSTITUTIONS *can resocialize a group of people very rapidly. These West Point cadets look, walk, and are probably thinking alike—an important part of military training.*

KROLL/TAURUS

CHARACTERISTICS OF AMERICAN SOCIAL CLASSES

Class	Population Range	Income	Property	Education
UPPER	1–3%	Very high	Great and inherited wealth	Elite colleges
UPPER-MIDDLE	10–15%	High	Property and savings	College and graduate school
LOWER-MIDDLE	30–35%	Modest	Savings	High school and college
WORKING	40–45%	Low	Some savings	Grade school and high school
LOWER	20–25%	Poverty level	No savings	Little or no education

—Source: adapted from Rossides, *The American Class System* (Boston: Houghton Mifflin, 1976)

REPRESENTATIVE PROFESSIONS RANKED BY OCCUPATIONAL PRESTIGE

HIGHEST	U.S. Supreme Court justice, Physician, Scientist, College professor, Congressman
HIGH	Lawyer, Dentist, Minister, Pilot, Priest, Schoolteacher
ABOVE AVERAGE	Contractor, Novelist, Economist, Union leader, Machinist
AVERAGE	Farm owner, Policeman, Newspaper reporter, Insurance agent
BELOW AVERAGE	Tenant farmer, Mailman, Plumber, Mechanic
LOW	Taxi driver, Bartender, Farmhand, Janitor
LOWEST	Sharecropper, Garbage collector, Street sweeper, Shoe shiner

—Source: Robert W. Hodge, et al., "Occupational Prestige in the United States, 1925–1963," *American Journal of Sociology*, 70 (Nov. 1964), pp. 286–302.

U.S. CLASS STRUCTURE *is less rigid than in other countries, but it is very real* (left). *Prestige* (right) *is one aspect of class.*

Social Stratification

In every society, some people rank higher than others. When a society is structured so that inequality affects whole categories of people, sociologists speak of it as having *social stratification*. Stratification may be based on caste, as in India. Caste is an ascribed status, because a person is born into a certain level. Stratification is more commonly based on class, as in most Western societies. Class is an achieved status in that it depends on factors other than birth. Most sociologists rely on Weber's definition of class as having three components: wealth, power, and prestige.

Classes in the United States.

The American Declaration of Independence proclaims that "all men are created equal," and, indeed, equality is a value much admired in the United States. But many kinds of inequality are obvious. To begin with, wealth is very unevenly distributed. If the total population is divided into fifths according to earnings, the top fifth has over 40 percent of the total income, and the bottom fifth only about 5 percent. To put it another way, there are about 180,000 millionaires in the United States and over 25 million poor people.

Power is also concentrated in a few hands. Whether or not there is an actual "power elite," a small proportion of citizens do wield a great amount of power. According to G. William Domhoff, approximately 11,000 white, middle-aged Protestant males—about one twenty-thousandth of the population—constitute a powerful establishment that controls most American institutions, including corporations, governments, and education.

Prestige in the United States is based chiefly on occupation. A study done in 1947 and repeated in 1963 asked respondents to rate 85 different jobs. Supreme Court justices scored highest, with street sweepers and shoe shiners at the bottom. (The rankings were practically the same in both surveys.) Whereas the concentration of wealth and power has remained relatively constant over the last 35 years, prestige has become more widely distributed. This is due mainly to a decline in low-prestige jobs, such as sharecropper and coal miner, and an increase in higher-prestige positions, such as those held by white-collar workers.

Using the three criteria of wealth, power, and prestige, many social scientists divide Americans into five classes: upper, upper-middle, middle, lower-middle, and lower. Classes shade fuzzily into one another so that the exact number in these classes can only be estimated. The upper classes in the United States not only have a disproportionate share of wealth, power, and prestige, they also participate more in political processes, are better educated, enjoy superior health care, and can expect to live longer.

Sociologists are interested not just in class divisions, but also in movement from one class to another—*social mobility*. They measure social mobility mainly by comparing the occupations of people with those of their parents. (Most studies have involved fathers and sons, so they cannot be applied with confidence to today's population as a whole.) Sons whose jobs have higher prestige than those of their fathers are considered upwardly mobile. Findings indicate that, in our open society, upward mobility is a fact, but that the movements are not very big. The log cabin-to-White-House story is an exception. More often the step is relatively small: from insurance salesman to college professor; from dressmaker to department store buyer.

Poverty. One of the most intractable problems in the modern United States is poverty. Definitions of poverty vary. A useful concept is the federal government's poverty line—the minimum income required to provide a family of four with the basic necessities of life. The official poverty line in 1980 was $8380, and about 13 percent of Americans fell below it. This percentage represents an improvement over the high rate of 22.4 in 1957, but there was little change throughout the 1960's and 1970's in spite of such all-out efforts as President Lyndon Johnson's "War on Poverty."

Poverty is much commoner among certain groups than others. Racial minorities, women, and the elderly are the most poverty-stricken groups. This fact has been linked to a number of causes, such as unemployment, discrimination, and the like, but no single factor fully explains the phenomenon.

The abolition of poverty remains a goal in the United States, but Americans themselves have ambivalent attitudes toward the poor. Polls reveal, for example, that many people blame poverty on the idleness of the poor, though the majority of poor people actually work. Most social scientists agree that until there is a genuine commitment to reduce the society's extremes of inequality, poverty will continue to afflict tens of millions of Americans.

Racial and Ethnic Inequality

While stratification results from class differences based on wealth, power, and prestige, other social inequalities result from physical and cultural differences, particularly race and ethnicity. One sociologist who specializes in

CULVER PICTURES

MEDIAN INCOME OF FULL-TIME WORKERS BY SEX

YEAR	WOMEN	MEN	WOMEN AS % OF MEN
1970	5,440	9,184	59%
1975	7,719	13,144	59%
1979	10,550	17,514	60%

DISCRIMINATION —*because of race or sex—has been violent* (left) *or economic* (right). *Women still receive unequal pay for their work.*

this field defines *race* as "a category of persons who share a certain combination of inherited physical traits." As a biological term, race is practically meaningless, and many social scientists prefer not to use the word at all. But race has a social meaning; people attach certain values to being black, white, Oriental, and so on. In other words, race is important because people *think* it is.

An *ethnic group* is comprised of people who share certain cultural features passed on from one generation to another. A feeling of kinship, or ethnicity, sometimes characterizes whole nations (Poland, for instance) and smaller groups within nations, such as Basques in Spain.

People everywhere make "we/they" distinctions, almost always regarding their own group as superior. This attitude has become especially crucial in modern times because societies in many industrialized countries are so varied. The United States is but one of many countries that include numerous minorities. The classic definition of a *minority*, formulated by Louis Wirth, is "a group of people who, because of their physical or cultural characteristics, are singled out from the others in the society . . . for differential and unequal treatment."

Prejudice—discrimination. Minorities are frequently the object of hostile attitudes (*prejudice*) and actions (*discrimination*). The latter runs the gamut from simple avoidance, as in "white flight" from city to suburb, to the extreme violence of lynching and genocide. One of the worst features of discrimination is the self-fulfilling prophecy. When a dominant group limits a minority to an inferior status, its members cannot obtain decent education, good jobs, and the like. The fact that the members of the minority group are ill-schooled and poor is then used to "prove" that they are incapable of sharing fully in the society.

Social scientists who have studied prejudice and discrimination disagree on their causes. Some stress psychological roots: people faced with failure vent their frustrations on weaker people (scapegoats). Others say that prejudices are not abnormal individual reactions, but rather learned behaviors transmitted to members of a given society, like other norms and values.

Whatever the origins of prejudice, it always involves *stereotypes*—generalized, unverified images associated with groups. Stereotyped individuals have no identity; they are usually seen as sharing negative group traits: laziness (blacks), greed (Jews), criminality (Italians), stupidity (Poles), and so on.

The American experience. From the beginning, the United States has had a diverse population, racially and ethnically. Its record in regard to minorities has not been noteworthy for tolerance, in spite of American ideals of brotherhood and opportunity.

American Indians were dispossessed, both territorially and culturally, and even hunted down and exterminated. Blacks, kept in slavery until the mid-1800's, were for decades systematically deprived of basic civil rights. Asian-Americans suffered arbitrary exclusion; during World War II Japanese-Americans were relocated to internment camps. Hispanics—Puerto Ricans, Mexican-Americans, and other Spanish-speaking people—found opportunities limited because of their brown skins. Jews faced anti-Semitism that kept them out of certain neighborhoods, schools, and professions. The U.S. government acted to limit the immigration of certain "white ethnics," especially those from Eastern and Southern Europe.

Progress has been made in both attitudes and actions, as any study of the recent civil rights movement will show. There has also been a change in American values. The earlier ideal of a "melting pot" that would obliterate racial and ethnic differences has given way to an ideal of pluralism, with individual groups retaining some degree of separate identity.

Sex Discrimination

Every society differentiates among its members on the basis of sex, and almost every one assigns women an inferior status. Sex differences between males and females—anatomical, genetic, and hormonal—are biologically transmitted. But gender differences—expected masculine and feminine behaviors—are socially learned. A few personality traits may be inborn: boy babies seem to be more active and girl babies seem to smile more. Even these traits, however, may be learned, since parents treat boy and girl babies differently from birth.

Men's superior status may result from their greater physical strength. Strength could mean the difference between life and death in the days when cave dwellers were menaced by wild animals. Dominance then became ingrained in and perpetuated by societal norms. The Judeo-Christian tradition, for example, is strongly patriarchal and anti-female. Western cultures have taught for generations that certain learned behavior traits are "natural" to males: bravery, aggressiveness, independence, and rationality. Female stereotypes include timidness, passivity, dependence, and emotionalism. Men were expected to go into the world, while women were expected to remain in the home.

Some of the costs of sexism can be seen in the United States, which is less discriminatory than many other societies. Throughout most of the country's history, women had second-class citizenship. They were barred from most professions, and were not allowed to vote until 1920. Although their numbers in the work force were constantly increasing, they were generally restricted to low-paying, low-status jobs.

A revitalized feminist movement began to affect American norms after the publication of Betty Friedan's *The Feminine Mystique* in 1963 and the founding of the National Organization for Women (NOW) three years later. American women made many gains during the 1970's and early 1980's, but they still face discrimination. For instance, women's earnings consistently lag behind those of men. The Equal Rights Amendment (ERA), passed by Congress in 1972, subsequently failed to win ratification by the states. Its opponents included women as well as men. Clearly, centuries of sex-role socialization had had its effect both on those who dominated society and on those who had been relegated to an inferior status.

Social Change

Most of us accept without thinking the cliché that ours is a world of rapid change. Sociologists are interested in getting at the truth behind the truism. They study specific trends, such as population growth, but also try to understand root causes so they can make predictions about the future.

Population Growth

Demographers—social scientists who study population—estimate that for thousands of years the number of people in the world was fairly small and stable. Population began to grow with the neolithic revolution (the shift from hunting and gathering to farming), which started around 8000 B.C. The increase was gradual until about 1650 A.D. Then, during the next 325 years, the rate of growth went from about .001 percent to about 1.8 percent a year. Today's world population is approximately 4.4 billion. To put it another way, almost 10 percent of the humans who ever lived are living now. By the year 2000, world population will reach at least 6 billion. The phenomenon has aptly been named a population explosion.

Measuring change. In measuring overall population change, demographers consider two factors. One, the crude birthrate, is the ratio of births per thousand members of the population. It is affected not only by sheer numbers—the total women of childbearing age—but also by such cultural factors as marriage (since in most societies marriage is a prerequisite for childbearing) and the use of birth control. The second factor is the crude death rate, the ratio of deaths per thousand population. It is related to both infant mortality and life expectancy. Net growth rate is determined by subtracting the crude death rate from the crude birthrate. (In individual societies, a third factor, the migration rate, also comes into play; it is the ratio between migrants and immigrants per thousand.)

In developed nations, the overall rate of population increase is about .7 percent a year; in developing countries it is over 2 percent. In other words, the already poor nations of the Third World are growing almost three times as fast as the richer industrial countries. In poor countries, improved health care and sanitation have allowed people to live longer, so the death rate has declined. But the birthrate remains very high. It is widely believed that numerous children prove a man's virility. And children can care for their parents in old age—an important consideration where there is no institutionalized form of old-age security.

High birthrates and declining death rates produce the great population explosion. At a growth rate of 2 percent per year, a country's population will double in only 35 years. Developed countries grow at a much slower rate. The United States population increased by only 1.1 percent per year during the 1970's, and in some European countries population was approaching equilibrium, with births just offsetting deaths.

WORLD POPULATION *increased 130 percent between 1920 and 1980 (right). A major cause was high birthrates in less developed countries* (left).

HIGH AND LOW NATIONAL BIRTHRATES (ANNUAL, PER 1000 POP.) BY REGION

REGION	HIGH RATES		LOW RATES	
AFRICA AND MIDDLE EAST	Senegal	55.4	Israel	24.3
	Niger	51.4	Egypt	37.6
	Rwanda	51.0	South Africa	37.9
NORTH AMERICA	Honduras	47.1	Cuba	13.9
	Guatemala	41.8	Canada	15.5
	Haiti	41.8	U.S.	15.9
SOUTH AMERICA	Bolivia	46.6	Uruguay	18.3
	Ecuador	41.6	Chile	22.2
	Peru	39.6	Argentina	25.2
EUROPE	Albania	33.3	West Germany	10.1
	Ireland	21.9	Denmark	10.4
	Poland	18.9	Italy	11.2
	U.S.S.R.	18.3	Sweden	11.3
ASIA AND AUSTRALASIA	Bangladesh	47.0	Japan	13.0
	Papua New Guinea	42.5	Australia	15.3
	Vietnam	40.1	New Zealand	16.3

—Source: UN Population and Vital Statistics Report 1982

TOTAL, WORLD AND URBAN, POPULATIONS 1920-2000

YEAR	TOTAL	URBAN	PERCENT URBAN
1920	1,860,000,000	267,000,000	14.3
1940	2,295,000,000	432,000,000	18.8
1960	2,991,000,000	760,000,000	25.4
1980	4,318,000,000	1,354,000,000	31.3
2000	6,111,000,000	2,337,000,000	38.2

—Source: *UN Population Studies, No. 44*, "Growth of the World's Urban and Rural Population, 1920–2000"

Analyzing trends. One of the first people to study population was an English clergyman, Thomas Malthus. In a book published in 1798, he argued that population increases geometrically while food supplies increase only arithmetically. He predicted that, since population could not be controlled, the world was doomed to "war, pestilence, and famine."

While some demographers believe that Malthus's gloomy prediction is essentially correct, others see hope in the theory called *demographic transition.* This theory, developed from studies of population patterns over the last two centuries, describes three periods of growth. In the first, characteristic of preindustrial societies, both the birthrate and the death rate are high, so population does not change much. In the second, found in developing societies beginning to industrialize, the birthrate is high but the death rate falls, so population rises. In the third, common to advanced industrial societies, the birthrate drops, so population is again relatively stable.

At present, many African nations are considered to be in the first stage, but the most populous Third World nations are in the second stage. Developed countries in North America and Europe, plus Japan, have progressed to the third stage. It could be expected that population will level off for second-stage nations as they industrialize, so that overall growth will slacken. But critics of the demographic transition theory argue that it describes what has happened, not necessarily what will happen. There is evidence, for example, that birthrates in preindustrial Europe were lower than those in preindustrial Third World countries today, thus casting doubt on comparisons. Also, some say, the world simply does not have the resources for all developing nations to industrialize; therefore, population rates cannot decline in Third World countries as they have in Europe and North America.

The future. Social scientists take three main approaches to the problem of world population and hunger. One group stresses the need to increase the food supply through more efficient agriculture. Another argues that the world produces enough food, but that it has to be distributed more equally. The third group emphasizes that population limitation is the only solution. Its proponents advocate *zero population growth* (ZPG)—population that replaces itself but does not increase.

It is worth noting that, even when ZPG appears possible—as it does in the United States—other population problems occur. For instance, as growth slows, the population as a whole ages. Aging in turn leads to a smaller work force and increases society's burden of providing old-age assistance to those who need it.

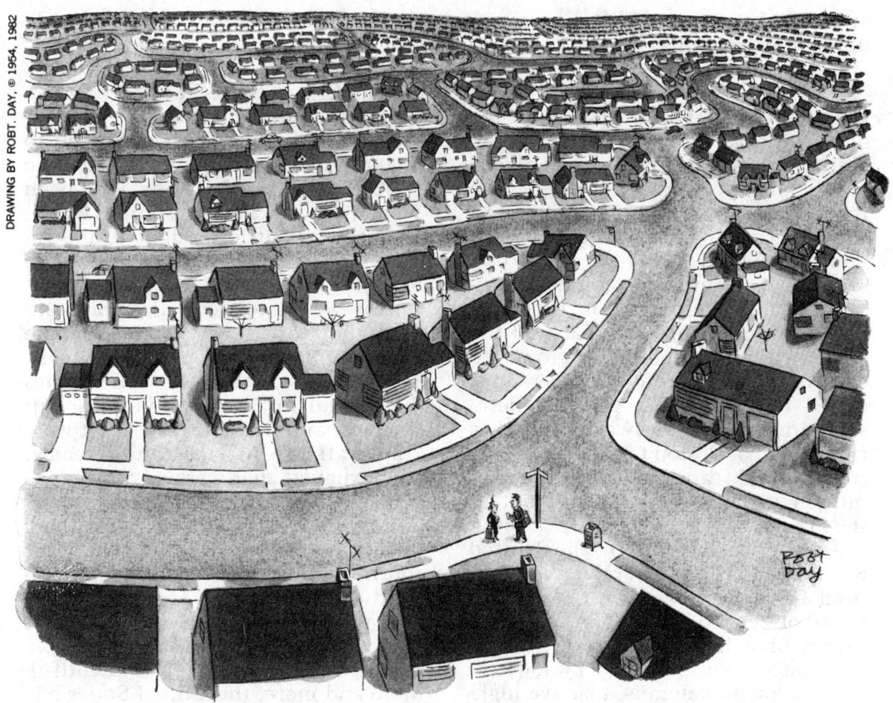

"I'm Mrs. Edward M. Barnes. Where do I live?"

Urbanization

World population growth has been accompanied by a trend toward increasing urbanization. Cities have been particularly important in the development of civilization; they have served as centers of trade, government, and learning. But they contained only a small proportion of the world's population until the massive industrialization that began in the 1800's. It is estimated that, even as late as 1850, only 5 percent of Earth's people lived in cities. Then the urbanizing trend gathered force, even in undeveloped countries. According to one projection, over 80 percent of the total population will live in cities by the year 2000.

The quality of city life. The discipline of sociology grew as cities grew, and its practitioners have always been interested in the social effects of urban living. A German sociologist, Ferdinand Tönnies, developed the concepts of *Gemeinschaft* and *Gesellschaft.* The former, meaning "community," describes a small population characterized by close personal relationships in primary groups. The latter, meaning "association," designates a large concentration of people whose interaction is impersonal, mainly through secondary groups. Tönnies associated *Gemeinschaft* with rural society and *Gesellschaft* with cities.

Durkheim made a similar distinction, using different terminology. He argued that members of rural societies are linked by "mechanical solidarity," leading similar lives and sharing norms and values. Urban society, he held, exhibits "organic solidarity," with members engaging in many different kinds of activities and socialized to a variety of norms and values. It was this kind of living that could produce anomie.

The so-called "Chicago school" of sociology tended to agree with the Tönnies–Durkheim view that urban living is dehumanizing. Louis Wirth defined cities as population centers characterized by large size, high population density, and great social diversity; he believed that these features tended to loosen vital social bonds and encourage lawless behavior.

There is certainly ample evidence that urban living can lead to alienation. (The term alienation was used by Marx to describe industrial workers' sense that they had lost control over their lives; it has since been extended to mean estrangement in general.) City people may feel cut off from and indifferent to each other. Some findings link high rates of mental illness, suicide, and crime to urban living. This may also suggest, however, that troubled people tend to congregate in cities.

On the other hand, a number of studies reveal that a sense of community can develop in cities through networks of families, friends, and the kinds of neighborhoods Herbert Gans calls "urban villages." Moreover, the greater size, concentration, and diversity of cities can give individuals the scope and freedom that they could never find in smaller societies.

City growth in the U.S. Like other industrialized nations, the United States is highly urbanized; almost three-fourths of its people live in urban settings. Metropolitan areas—central cities together with nearby suburbs and fringe exurban areas shading into open countryside—are the characteristic form urbanization now takes. In some parts of the country, metropolitan areas grow into each other to create huge super-cities called megalopolises. One of these, sometimes called Boswash, stretches from north of Boston to south of Washington, D.C., and includes over 40 million people, nearly 20 percent of the U.S. population.

The general trend in the United States over the last several decades has been for suburbs to grow at the expense of central cities. The American dream of a home of one's own was aided after World War II by low-cost home loans to veterans, massive highway building programs, and cheap gasoline.

Unfortunately, the shift to suburbs involved mainly middle-class families. Increasingly, the population of central cities became comprised of low-income minority families in particular need of social services. This pattern of wealth in outlying regions and poverty near the center of the city is a reversal of the earlier pattern. In the 1800's, the wealthy lived near the center of town, and the poor in outlying regions.

As the urban tax base declined, commercial taxes rose, and businesses as well as families moved to suburbs. This situation in turn resulted in fewer city jobs and a lessening of economic opportunities in the central core. In some cases city property owners abandoned their buildings, and downtown areas became deserted.

Social scientists have suggested a number of solutions to arrest the spread of urban decay: urban renewal (tearing down slums and building low-cost housing); improved public transportation; and tax credits to encourage city businesses. However, given Americans' traditional hostility to cities, plus the hard times of the late 1970's and early '80's, sustained improvement seems far in the future.

The Environment

A great concern of social scientists in recent decades has been the environment. The developments that endanger the environment, of course, involve Earth as a whole, but ecologists (those who study the relationship between living organisms and their surroundings) focus especially on the changes brought on by large-scale industrialization.

Environmental change in a country like the United States results from two main processes: pollution and resource depletion. Americans began to become aware of pollution in the 1960's. For decades they had been despoiling the nation's land, water, and air with little thought to the future. A book published in 1962—*Silent Spring*, by Rachel Carson—alerted people to the danger of pesticides that threatened to contaminate and possibly destroy plants, animals, and humans. A host of other issues then began to arouse public concern: chemical and human wastes that were killing all life in lakes and streams; auto exhausts that were creating smog blankets over major cities; high levels of noise that were causing stress; and unsightly garbage dumps that were sprawling over many parts of "America the beautiful."

At the same time, the once bountiful resources of the North American continent began to seem less plentiful. More and more, the United States had to import raw materials in which it had once been self-sufficient; and it used a disproportionate amount of them. With only 6 percent of the world's population, the United States consumes a fourth of its steel, a third of its energy, and half its rubber. A worldwide oil crisis in the 1970's underscored the fact that many resources on which industry depends are nonrenewable. When the world's supply of petroleum runs out, there will be no more.

The United States initiated efforts to cut down on pollution and conserve resources, but progress was slow. The pessimistic view is that, at present rates of growth, the planet will become unlivable in a century. Optimists argue that present predictions, made on the basis of resources now known, cannot account for the new technology and resources that industrial societies are constantly discovering.

The Mechanics of Social Change

Social change has always been a factor in human history. Empires rise and fall; societies are modernized; communities are destroyed. What forces lead to such phenomena? How can they be explained?

Social movements. One of the most important factors behind social change is people acting together to bring it about. This is what social movements are all about.

Sociologists categorize social movements according to their goals. *Regressive* movements (sometimes called countermovements) try to stop or reverse change. An example is the Ku Klux Klan, which wants to restore white supremacy and racial segregation. *Reform* movements want to change certain aspects of society: to eliminate alcohol abuse (Prohibition); to end slavery (abolition); or to abolish legal penalties against homosexual acts (gay liberation).

THARPE/MONKMEYER

Secessionist movements aim to free some segment of society, often a nationality, from a larger entity. American Southerners at the time of the Civil War were secessionists; so are sizable numbers of today's Scots, French Canadians, and Kurds. *Revolutionary* movements work to overturn one social system and replace it with another. The Bolsheviks did this in Russia in 1917, and Castro's followers did it in Cuba in 1959.

The changes wrought by social movements are often different from intended goals. For example, one aim of the French Revolution was to lessen government centralization. After the overthrow of the monarchy, France became more centralized than ever before.

Other factors. Social change has many other causes, less planned and less overt. One is the forces of nature. The last ice age froze enough water in the Arctic region to expose a land connection between Siberia and Alaska; this served as a bridge over which the ancestors of the American Indians could cross from Asia and people the American continents. Sudden disasters, such as volcanic eruptions and floods, can have devastating effects on entire regions.

The growth, decline, and migration of large segments of the population have significant consequences for society. North America was transformed from a sparsely populated, culturally isolated continent into a leader of Western society after the immigration of millions of people from Europe, Africa, and Asia.

Technology, according to some sociologists, is the single most important generator of social change. In the United States, the automobile helped bring about the development of the

CAUSES OF SOCIAL CHANGE *need not be economic or political. The beliefs or prejudices of a small group like the Ku Klux Klan,* far left, *an act of God such as a flood or tornado, or an invention like the automobile may cause huge and unpredictable social changes.*

petroleum industry, the growth of suburbs, and a vast network of highways, motels, and shopping centers. It also led to air pollution, the destruction of neighborhoods, and the decline of railroads and other public transportation systems. Recent technological developments with far-reaching implications include television, computers, and artificial organs.

Cultural diffusion—the adoption by one culture of elements from another—has had profound repercussions, especially since the expansion of Western culture in modern times. While today we think of examples like Coca-Cola in Kuwait and jeans in Japan, we tend to overlook earlier borrowings, such as "Arabic" numerals from India, steel from Damascus, and paper from China.

Social change usually results from a combination of factors rather than any single one. In the United States, the growth of the Southern Sun Belt states and the declining influence of the Northern Frost Belt states had many causes. One was a social movement: the rise of organized labor in the Northeast led to higher manufacturing costs, making the less unionized South more attractive for businesses such as textiles. Another cause was the scarcity and expense of heating fuels—far less of these are needed in the South. Technological improvements also contributed: Southern towns and cities became far more comfortable with the widespread use of air conditioning. Finally, there were human factors less easy to define. The promise of more time outdoors for recreation and relaxation seemed to be a factor in the decision of many to move; and a large number of the new residents of the Sun Belt settled in towns much smaller than the ones they left in the heavily urbanized North.

Theories of change. No one has yet developed an explanation of social change that can satisfactorily predict future directions. The theories that have been advanced fall into three main categories.

Evolutionary theories stress gradual change for the better. Comte and Spencer were among those who saw societies evolving from the simple to the complex; less developed cultures would pass through definite stages until they were as advanced as Western society. Evolutionary theories are generally discredited today because of their pro-Western bias and because they assume that change and progress are identical.

Functionalist theories argue that, while societies change, their basic tendency is to maintain stability. If equilibrium is disturbed in one institution, others react so that order is restored. In the United States, for instance, women have joined the work force in increasing numbers. Lest this economic change disrupt society, the institution of the family has adapted, with husbands sharing more responsibility for home and children. Critics of the functionalist approach maintain that it does not take into account the strains modern societies exhibit; if societies strive for stability, how and why do revolutions occur?

Conflict theories, in the tradition of Marx, emphasize struggle and disequilibrium. Although Marx focused on class struggle, more recent conflict theorists attribute disturbances to quests for power and authority. These may involve race (blacks versus whites in South Africa) or religion (Protestants versus Catholics in Northern Ireland). Conflict theories are more useful in explaining the past than in predicting the future, say their critics. For instance, they can analyze revolutions in Russia or China, but seem to have little success in predicting where other violent upheavals might take place.

How Sociologists Work

Clearly, sociologists are interested in a wide range of topics ranging from intimate relations between people to long-range trends in world affairs. A distinction is sometimes made between "micro" sociology (denoting interest in small-scale topics) and "macro" sociology (denoting interest in large-scale topics). Whatever the range of interest, however, sociologists are committed to seeking a scientific approach in their investigations. They begin with the logic of the scientific method, which is used by all scientists.

The Scientific Method

For scientists in any discipline, the basic research method is the same; it consists of four main steps. The first is to identify the issue or topic. A sociologist working within one of the broad areas discussed in this article (the family as an institution, or socialization, or urbanization) narrows the field down to a specific concern, such as the divorce rate or the effects of communal living.

The second step is to form a hypothesis about a specific issue. This is a sort of hunch about the relationship between two items (variables). A sociologist may guess that the divorce rate (variable) has risen since the advent of no-fault divorce procedures (variable), or that living in a commune (variable) encourages cooperation (variable). The hypothesis may be formulated as a question: *Has the divorce rate in State A risen since it adopted a no-fault law?*

Or it may be a statement: *The inhabitants of Commune B exhibit more cooperative behavior than similar people living in society at large.* In any case, terms must be clearly defined before research can proceed. For instance, what does the sociologist mean by "cooperative behavior"? How will it be measured?

The third step in the scientific method is to gather data. Sociologists use one of four procedures: examination of existing sources, such as census records; survey, which may be either a written questionnaire or an oral interview; observation; and experimentation. The student of divorce rates would probably research existing records, while the investigator of communal living might rely on a survey or on observation.

Finally, an investigator must analyze the data collected and present findings. The relations between variables must be summarized in words and/or figures. Here a researcher must be careful not to confuse correlation with causation. Correlation means that variables are associated in some regular way: both may rise or decline comparably, for example. Causation means that one variable has a direct causal effect on the other. The divorce rate may have risen in State A after it instituted no-fault procedures. (This is known as a positive correlation.) However, the rate in three neighboring states that lack no-fault laws has risen similarly. Thus the researcher cannot infer a causal relation between the no-fault law and the increasing divorce rate; some other factor must be at work.

Gathering Data

The range of sociological interest and practice can be most readily appreciated if one takes a closer look at the four methods by which sociologists collect data. The method a researcher chooses is directly related to the issue he or she is examining.

Existing sources are useful in determining broad trends, especially if a historical perspective is desired. Durkheim used official statistics in developing his classic study of suicide. Almost any kind of record, including diaries and novels, can serve as raw material for the sociologist. One group of women studying sex-role socialization examined children's story books. (They found that boys, pictured eleven times as often as girls, were shown having adventures, while girls daydreamed or helped their mothers.) Researchers studying social stratification in an Arizona town sifted through tons of garbage to compare use and waste patterns in middle- and lower-income neighborhoods.

MATERIAL CULTURE *includes junk and garbage. Sociologists have learned from studying wastes just as archaeologists have learned from prehistoric waste heaps.*

BECKWITH/TAURUS

Surveys are conducted when new data must be gathered. In his mammoth investigation of integration in education, James Coleman submitted thousands of questionnaires to students, teachers, and parents. Another kind of survey, the interview, is more flexible, and also more time-consuming. Interviews have been used to learn more about racial prejudice, sexual practices, social class, and many other topics.

Surveying demands painstaking research techniques. The sample (the people surveyed) must be representative of the universe (the total group being studied). Questions must be carefully phrased. An inquiry such as "Are you religious?" is practically useless because it is so vague.

Participant observation is especially helpful in gaining an inside view of a way of life. Some participant observers disguise themselves as group members. This is what David Owen, a writer in his mid-20's, did when he went back to high school to "find out what teenagers are up to these days" (*High School,* 1981). Some of the most famous of all sociological studies have resulted from participant observation: Robert and Helen Lynd's *Middletown* (1929), a portrait of Muncie, Indiana; William Foote Whyte's *Street Corner Society* (1943), a look at an Italian neighborhood in Boston; and Erving Goffman's *Asylums* (1961), a sensitive account of life in a mental hospital.

Experimentation is used when a researcher wants to collect data in a highly controlled setting in order to isolate cause and effect. Experiments have the disadvantage of artificiality, but many have yielded provocative results. One conducted by Albert Bandura aimed to test the effects of television violence on children. He separated children into two groups; one watched violent action scenes on TV, and the other did not. Hidden observers, watching the two groups later, found that the television viewers were more apt to attack dolls and other children.

Another well-known experiment, conducted by Philip Zimbardo, was designed to test the importance of assigned roles in an institutional setting. Arbitrarily dividing some two dozen college students into "guard" and "prisoner" groups, Zimbardo put them into a mock prison for a stay of two weeks. The experiment had to be cancelled after six days because the youths played their parts all too realistically. Some formerly humane young men begame tyrannical overseers, while others, normally self-respecting, groveled in servility. Much of the dehumanization of prison life, Zimbardo concluded, results from the structure of total institutions themselves rather than the personalities of individual guards and inmates.

—*Paula Franklin*

ANTHROPOLOGY

Anthropology is a fairly new social science that covers a large spectrum of concerns and issues. Many anthropologists look to the day when anthropology is recognized as a "hard" science; one of its two major branches, *physical anthropology*, relies heavily on scientific methods and values. Other anthropologists seek to develop the human element in their research; the field's other main branch, *cultural anthropology*, remains as much an art as a science.

Anthropology is the study of man, or more properly, the study of human beings. It was first developed in a formal, organized way only late in the 1800's. Among the aims of this new study from the beginning were

- to learn where human beings came from and how they got to be the way they are today; and
- to analyze and classify the systems human beings have developed to control their lives.

Two important developments led to the founding of anthropology. The first of these was a series of events that started in the 1400's. Before that time, people in Europe knew little or nothing about many of the peoples of the world. By their understanding of the Arabs and their slight acquaintance with China, Europeans concluded that "foreign" peoples were odd in some ways, but were essentially like themselves. These societies all had kings or emperors, armies, marriage, funeral rites, religion, and so forth.

Then explorers began to bring back word of other peoples—in Africa south of the Sahara, the Americas, Indonesia, Polynesia, and Australia. These peoples were very different from Europeans. At first they were

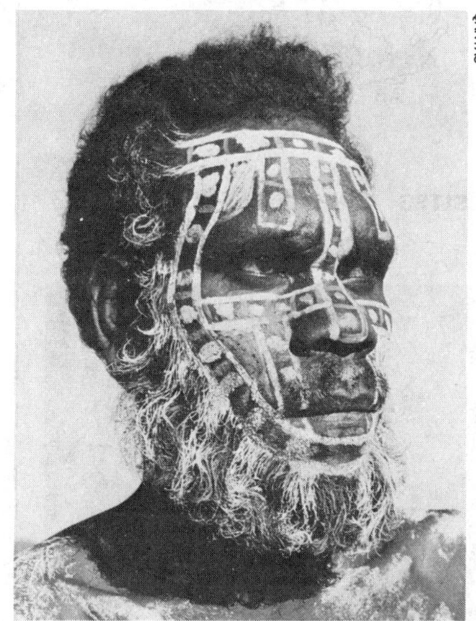

FACE PAINT *would seem eccentric in the United States, but it is a normal and valued part of life to an Australian aborigine.*

dismissed as "savages" or "barbarians," but at the same time, students of human nature showed a lively curiosity about these new societies. The study of such human differences would come in time to be known as anthropology.

The second major development can be more exactly pinpointed in time. In 1856 a skull was found in a cave in the valley named Neanderthal near Düsseldorf, Germany. After much scientific controversy, the world gradually accepted the opinion that the skull was very old and that it had belonged to a person who was physically different in some significant ways from people living today. As the controversy raged, other very old human bones were found. By 1891 even older bones with more marked differences—but still recognizably "human"—had been located. As men became alert to the existence of such fossil remains, the "history" of humanlike creatures extended several millions of years into the past.

The extension of human knowledge through space to include all the many peoples of the world led to the development of cultural anthropology. The extension of human knowledge through time to include the physical evidence of early humans led to the development of physical anthropology. There is, however, continuing crossover between the two disciplines. Physical anthropologists rely on the findings of cultural anthropologists to gain insight into how the creatures they study may have lived. Also, physical anthropologists have widened their interests to include the physical differences found in the peoples on Earth today. In fact, there is a gradual shading from physical to cultural anthropology.

At one end of the spectrum, a specialist in classifying teeth is a physical anthropologist; at the other extreme, a specialist in interpreting religious practices is a cultural anthropologist. But in the middle are many who use elements of both kinds of study. For example, an anthropologist may study the diets of early peoples by examining scratches on fossil teeth. The following discussion divides the two branches for convenience, but it is important to keep in mind the contributions that each branch makes to the other.

Physical Anthropology

The Discovery of Early Man

When quarry workers discovered a pile of old bones in the Feldhofer Grotto in the Neanderthal, they threw them out. But a local teacher quickly recognized that old human bones could be scientifically valuable, and he recovered as many of the bones as he could. The Neanderthal discovery came in 1856, just three years before publication of Darwin's *Origin of Species.* Interest in fossil remains as a part of the record of prehistoric times was already high.

Many who examined the Neanderthal bones thought they belonged to a human being of the same type as modern man, but one whose skeleton was deformed by disease. The thigh bones were heavier than those of modern man and were slightly bowed. The skull was thick, and had heavy ridges over the eyes. A few scientists argued that the Neanderthal bones were those of a species that had preceded the human species.

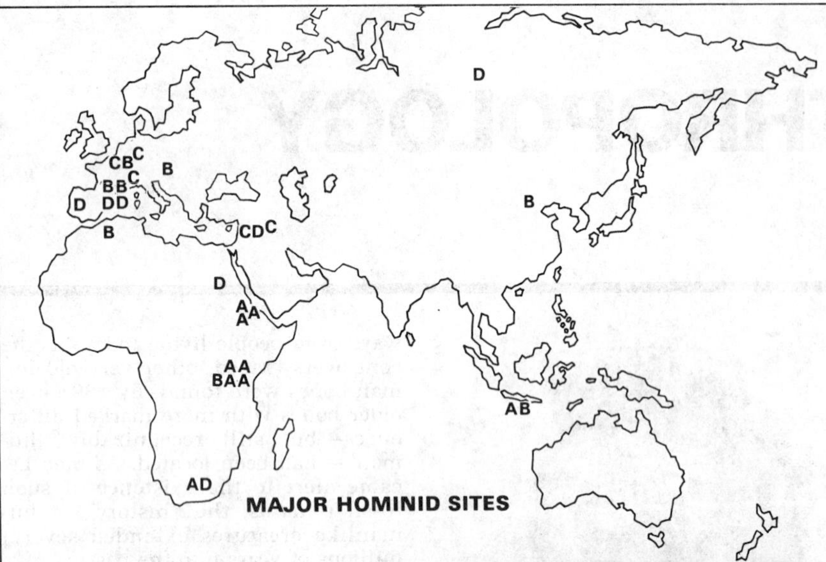

A AUSTRALOPITHECINE
HOMO HABILIS
South Africa
Ethiopia (3)
Kenya (2)
Tanzania (2)
Indonesia (Java)

B HOMO ERECTUS
Indonesia (Java)
China
France (2)
Germany
Algeria
Tanzania
Hungary

C NEANDERTHAL
Germany
Iraq
Belgium
France
Israel

D PREAGRICULTURAL
HOMO SAPIENS
France (2)
Spain
Israel
Egypt (Sudan)
Siberia
South Africa

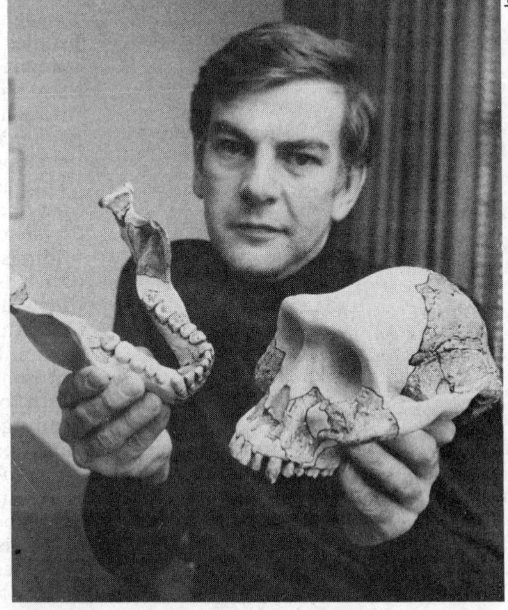

LUCY, *the oldest and most complete hominid ever found, is displayed by anthropologist Donald Johanson, who discovered her. The fossil fragments have been assembled with plastic to fill in missing parts. Lucy was less than 4 feet tall and according to dating tests, she lived more than 3 million years ago in what is now Ethiopia.*

In 1868 workmen building a road in France discovered five very old skeletons in a cave named Cro-Magnon in France. Judging from the geological stratum where they were found, the bones were about 35,000 years old. Yet they showed fewer oddities than the Neanderthal bones and they clearly belonged to the human species.

It was not until 1886 that skeletons of the Neanderthal type were found again. These new discoveries cast doubt on the old "disease" theory, and scientists were gradually concluding that Neanderthal-type skeletons were older than Cro-Magnon ones. But were the Neanderthal remains of the human species *Homo sapiens*? Advocates of Darwin's ideas of evolution could accept the concept of a species that was clearly human but not *Homo sapiens.* But the scientific community was still in great doubt, and most people believed that early creatures must either be human or not human.

A Dutchman named Eugene Dubois was an evolutionist who organized an expedition to the island of Java, hoping to find evidence of the "missing link" between humans and apes. Dubois believed (erroneously) that the apes of Indonesia, the orangutan and gibbon, were the animals most closely related to *Homo sapiens.* Even though his theory was wrong, he found what he believed to be the skull of a member of the "missing link" species. In 1895 Dubois brought his collection of fossils to Europe. They caused great excitement and controversy. Scientists could not agree on the place of the new Java man, and the general public was outraged at the suggestion that man had descended from monkeys. Dubois was so upset by the controversy that he buried his collection of bones under the floor of his dining room, and did not show them again for 25 years.

Many more human fossils were found in the early 1900's, mainly of the Neanderthal type. But the big news was the bones of the Piltdown Man, discovered in England in 1911 and 1912. These bones were clearly more "primitive" than any found earlier, resembling primate apes more than humans. They caused great controversy for 40 years until they were proven to be part of a hoax. The bones had been buried and then "discovered" by an anthropology student hoping to be recognized as a discoverer of artifacts in England.

The next true discovery of significance took place in 1924. A small skull was given to Raymond Dart, an anatomy professor in Johannesburg, South Africa. The skull, which was that of a child, had been found in a quarry at a nearby place called Taung. In 1925, Dart correctly identified the Taung "baby" as the remains of a previously unknown species. He stated that the species was more closely related to humans than it was to any nonhuman species. Most scientists at the time disagreed with Dart's conclusions. Instead, anthropologists believed the Taung skull to be that of a close relative of the African apes.

After 70 years of fossil discoveries, the only generally accepted true fossils of early humans were those of the Cro-Magnon and Neanderthal types. This situation was to change very fast, however. By 1929, teeth and part of a skull had been found near Peking in China. Soon many specimens were found at the same site. This time the fossils were quickly recognized as human, but of a different species from *Homo sapiens.* Also, in the 1930's parts of three fossil skeletons were found in Java, confirming the discoveries of Dubois; and an adult relative of the Taung "baby" was found in South Africa. Finally, Robert Broom, an anthropologist who had confirmed Dart's discovery in South Africa, found remains of a species that was related to the Taung specimen, but different from it as well.

Then World War II intervened and most fossil collecting stopped for the duration. The Peking collection of fossils disappeared during the war, never to be seen again; but the fossils had done their job. Most scientists were convinced of the existence of more than one species that could be called human. All such humanlike creatures were called *hominids*, and *Homo sapiens*, or modern man, was only one of several species to share that name.

After the war, many more fossils of all the previously discovered types were found. Eventually, two new species were found. In the early 1960's, the family of Louis and Mary Leakey found still earlier evidence of hominids in East Africa. In 1974, a team headed by Don Johanson and Maurice Taieb found a third relative of Dart's Taung "baby" in Ethiopia. One of Johanson's finds was "Lucy," 40 percent of a single skeleton of a small, young female of the species. "Lucy" is more than 3 million years old; she is both the oldest and the most nearly complete fossil of a hominid species ever found.

Hominid Types

With the finding of "Lucy" and her relatives, the story of discovery stops for now. The fossils are pieces of a puzzle that still has an unknown number of pieces missing. When the puzzle is put together with our presently available pieces, however, a definite picture emerges.

The fossil record has revealed what most anthropologists believe to be six species of hominids. Hominids are human beings together with their close relatives that walk upright, have relatively large brains, and share certain other characteristics. Apes are not hominids. In fact, the only species of hominid alive today is *Homo sapiens.* The six known species of hominids are (in order of their appearance):

- *Australopithecus afarensis*: "Lucy" and her relatives
- *Australopithecus africanus*: Dart's Taung "baby" and its relatives
- *Australopithecus robustus*: Broom's discovery
- *Homo habilis*: the discovery of the Leakeys in East Africa
- *Homo erectus*: Peking Man, Java Man, and others
- *Homo sapiens.*

Both the Neanderthal and Cro-Magnon specimens are usually considered to be *Homo sapiens.* Neanderthal is sometimes considered a subspecies, and some argue that it should be a separate species altogether. The evidence strongly suggests, however, that Neanderthal specimens are very late developments in the history of hominids.

Australopithecus. How can one separate the *Australopithecus* hominids from the *Homo* hominids? While there are a number of technical ways to do this, an easy way is the "subway test," inspired by a 1950's anthropologist's remark that a Neanderthal who was suitably shaved, trimmed, and dressed would not seem strange if seen on the subway in a big city. Later reconstructions of *Homo habilis* and *Homo erectus* also show creatures close enough to *Homo sapiens* to be able to pass the subway test (although Don Johanson has said that seeing *Homo habilis* might make you walk to the other end of the car). On the other hand, none of the *Australopithecus* species would pass the test.

Little is known about the way of life of the *Australopithecus* species, which appeared on Earth more than 3 million years ago. Study of the skeletal remains shows that all the *Australopithecus* species walked upright and did it with ease. *Australopithecus afarensis,* the earliest, was quite small. "Lucy," although in her 20's when she died, was only about $3\frac{1}{2}$ feet tall. The tallest *afarensis* specimens are almost 5 feet tall.

As time went by, other *Australopithecus* species appeared to replace *afarensis.* The slim, 4-foot *africanus* appeared more than 2 million years ago. It in turn was replaced by the stocky *robustus*, perhaps 2 million years ago.

Apparently *Australopithecus robustus* and *Homo habilis* were both living in nearby locations in Africa at the same time, before a million and a half years ago. This presents a problem. Microscopic examination of *africanus, robustus,* and *habilis* teeth suggests that all three species lived on a diet similar to that of the modern chimpanzee—wild fruits supplemented by occasional meals of termites, bird's eggs, and monkeys or other small animals. If two species compete directly for the same food in the same place, one species is usually displaced and vanishes. It is not known what kept *habilis* and *robustus* from direct competition, but they lived too long in the same place at the same time for such competition to have existed.

Homo habilis. Finally, about 1.5 million years ago, the last *Australopithecus* species disappears from the fossil record. Perhaps *Homo* began to compete more directly with *Australopithecus,* or perhaps baboons provided the competition that caused the demise of *robustus.* In any case, *Homo* survived.

One reason for the persistence of *Homo* is probably that *Homo habilis* made tools (the name *Homo habilis* means handyman). *Australopithecus* may have *used* tools, since the size of its brain indicates more intelligence than a chimpanzee is thought to have, and chimpanzees are known to use tools—but it appears that *Australopithecus* did not *make* tools. When primitive stone tools are found, eventually evidence of *Homo* is found nearby. The stone tools that were probably made by *Homo habilis* are barely recognizable as artificial. Nevertheless, anthropologists have made modern versions of these tools and used them successfully to butcher animals. Marks on fossilized animal bones near where the tools were found suggest that the tools were used for this.

DRS. LOUIS AND MARY LEAKEY *made many discoveries in the Olduvai Gorge in Africa. Their son has continued explorations in that region.*

UPI

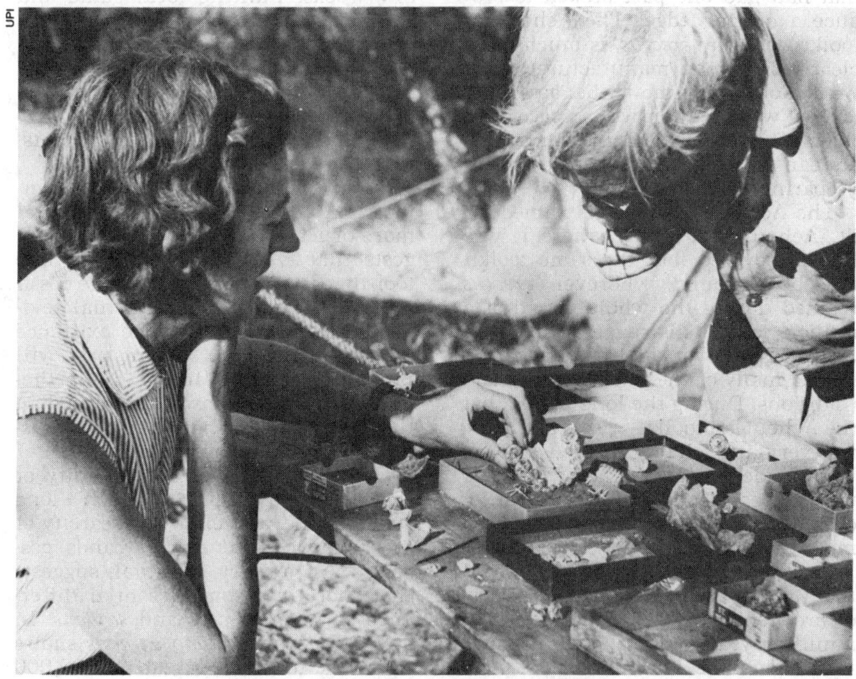

Homo erectus. About a million and a half million years ago *Homo erectus* appeared, probably first in Africa. Some anthropologists believe that all hominids were confined to Africa before *erectus*; others think that the fossil record shows examples of *Australopithecus* and *habilis* in Asia as well. In any case, *erectus*, with a slightly larger brain than *habilis*, became the only hominid on Earth for the next million years or more. During that time, its range extended over virtually all of the tropic and temperate zones of Africa, Europe, and Asia.

One reason for the success of *erectus* is a change in basic diet. Studies of tooth wear show that *erectus* had added roots, bulbs, and tubers to the basic *habilis* diet of wild fruits, insects, and occasional meat. Having foods such as wild versions of carrots, onions, and potatoes (although not necessarily those species) available opened up many desertlike areas that would not have supported *habilis's* way of life.

Another change in the diet of *erectus* was a significant increase in the amount of meat eaten. While *habilis* probably consumed more meat than, say, modern chimpanzees or baboons, it seems likely that *habilis* only hunted sporadically and supplemented its meat supply by scavenging. *Erectus* evidently hunted animals as large as elephants. He also gathered plant materials and small animals, much as a few groups of *sapiens* do to this day.

One of the reasons we believe that *erectus* was engaged in these activities is the kind of tools associated with sites where *erectus* lived. Anthropologists call the range of tools used by a certain group its "toolkit." The Oldowan toolkit, which was used by *habilis*, consisted of simple pebble tools that had had one part broken to produce a cutting edge. The Acheulean toolkit, used by *erectus*, is much more clearly of human manufacture; while we do not always know what a particular tool was used for, we can recognize that such tools as hand axes and cleavers can be used in butchering and in preparing plant materials.

The Acheulean toolkit is named for St. Acheul in France, where it was first discovered, but the same toolkit has been found wherever *erectus* roamed during the whole period of a million years. This suggests that *erectus* bands all over the inhabited world shared many of the same customs and traditions. During the long period that the Acheulean toolkit was in use, there was very little change in the way tools were made. In fact, some of the later tools appear cruder to us than earlier ones do (although they may have been more efficient to make and to use).

Another important discovery of *erectus* was the use of fire. Good evidence of fires tended by *erectus* is about half a million years old, although fire may have been in use for hundreds of thousands of years earlier without modern anthropologists having been lucky enough to find the evidence.

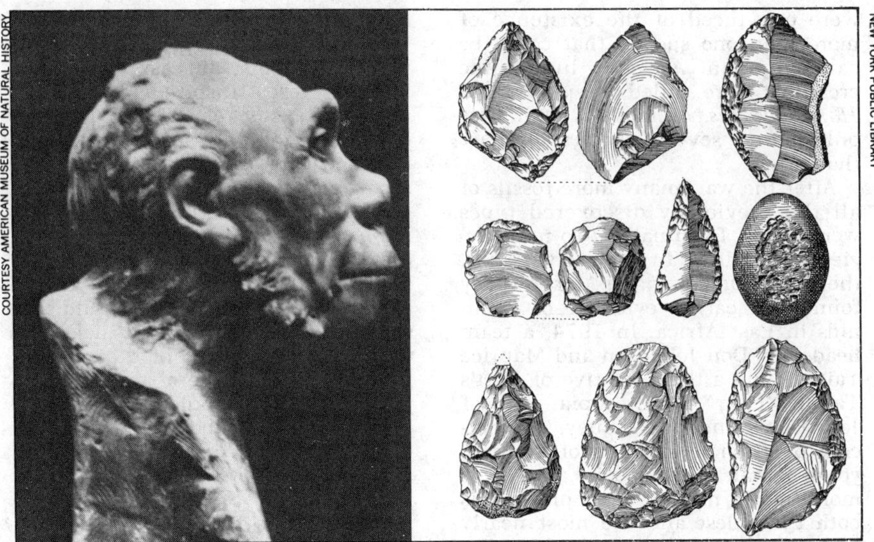

NEANDERTHAL MAN *(named for the Neander Valley in Germany) used tools called Mousterian (after a cave in France). Remains of similar men and tools have also been found in Asia.*

It is believed that the *Australopithecus* species did not make long-term camps, but roamed each day and camped in a new place each night as modern chimpanzees do. There is some evidence of camps from the *habilis* period, and good evidence of long-term habitation of caves and the building of regular shelters by *erectus*. Near Nice in France there is a seaside site about 400,000 years old to which bands of *erectus* returned each spring. We know they came in the spring from analyzing fossil pollen—it comes only from flowers that bloom in the spring. There beside the sea the bands built rough huts of branches and lived for a few weeks, hunting local game and gathering shellfish. As summer approached, they abandoned their huts, which soon collapsed and were buried in the sand, where the remains were preserved. The following spring, *erectus* would return to build new huts, nearly always on the same site.

Such evidence—well-made, symmetrical tools, the use of fire, and more-or-less long-term camps—suggests that *erectus* probably had one tool that is not preserved in the fossil record—language. The actual evidence that could prove the existence of language in the distant past will probably never be found. Nevertheless, language seems so ingrained in the human brain that one has to suspect that it has a long ancestry.

On the other hand, the rigidity of the *erectus* way of life over such a long span of time, as well as the scarcity of any evidence that *erectus* bands possessed art, jewelry, or ritual, suggests that there was some essential difference between *erectus* and *sapiens*. In any case, when *Homo sapiens* shows up in the fossil record, about 100,000 years ago, so does diversity, change, and ritual, which have remained typical *sapiens* characteristics to this day.

Our Ancestors: Homo Sapiens

Sometime after *Homo erectus* appeared, Earth began to go through a radical change of climate. Thick ice that did not melt in summer formed in Northern Europe (and elsewhere). Eventually the ice covered most of Scandinavia and Britain, and reached far into France, Germany, and Russia. Over a million years, the ice formed and then retreated several times. Somewhere along the way, *Homo sapiens* arrived on the scene. The youngest fossil (currently known) of *erectus* is about 300,000 years old. The oldest known fossil of *sapiens* is about 100,000 years old, appearing during one of the warm periods between the advances of the ice. Somewhere in the period between 300,000 and 100,000 years ago, there began to be people much like us on our planet. Many anthropologists believe that we are creatures of the ice ages, since the latest retreat of the ice was only 10,000 years ago or so; in fact, we may be merely in a period between ice advances now.

Neanderthals. The earliest fossils of *Homo sapiens* are of the Neanderthal type, with characteristically shaped skulls, including heavy brow ridges and other facial features that are different from those of modern-day people. In fact, from 100,000 until 40,000 years ago, all the known people on Earth were of this type.

The Neanderthals occupied much the same territory as had *Homo erectus*, at least when the ice permitted it (in Africa, Europe, and Asia). Although most of the known Neanderthal fossils are from Europe and the Middle East, it is believed that the distribution reflects where anthropologists have looked and where suitable sites for preservation exist. In fact, some anthropologists think that the highest population density during Neanderthal times was in Africa.

With the advent of the Neanderthals, the million-year-old Acheulean toolkit was finally put aside. The Neanderthals developed their own toolkit, which is known as the Mousterian, named for the cave in France where tools of this type were first found.

The Mousterian toolkit is based on a much more efficient way of working stone. In the Acheulean method, a single stone was gradually shaped to form a typical Acheulean tool, such as a hand ax. In the Mousterian method, a large stone is flaked into smaller stones of the desired general shape. The small flakes are then used to make the tools. Measurements have shown the Mousterian method to be five times as efficient in using a given amount of suitable stone, a distinct advantage when the right kind of stone is scarce.

Although the basic toolkit of the Neanderthals was Mousterian, there is considerable variation from site to site, even from sites that are close together and occupied around the same time period. This diversity suggests that Neanderthal people, unlike *erectus*, were separated into a number of different groups, each of which had its own customs.

Anthropologists know about some of the Neanderthal customs because of traces in the fossil record. One such custom was burial of the dead. In fact, the first recognized Neanderthal skeleton, the 1856 find in the Neanderthal itself, had probably been buried at the site. Burials can be recognized in many ways. Sometimes a characteristic posture is used, with the knees curled up against the chest. Often there is evidence that the body has been painted with a red substance called ocher. (Red ocher had special significance to Neanderthal peoples.) In some cases, tools or food are buried along with the body.

One of the most intriguing Neanderthal burials took place early in June some 60,000 years ago in a cave in Iraq. Pollen analysis has shown that a man we know today as Shanidar IV was buried on a bed of flowers. We know the time of year because the pollen is of grape hyacinth and hollyhock, which bloom in June.

Burial of the dead indicates a level of social organization that was probably not present in *erectus*. Such organization is further indicated by evidence that the Neanderthals wore clothing, took care of their injured and aged, and engaged in more complex hunting techniques than did *erectus*. It seems clear that Neanderthals had developed language.

About 40,000 years ago, Neanderthals suddenly disappear from the fossil record. There are a number of theories as to why. One is that the Neanderthal tooth structure and brow ridge were a result of the need to bite off pieces of meat from larger pieces. When better tools became available, this need disappeared, and with it the brow ridge and powerful teeth. Another theory is that the "modern" strain of human beings overwhelmed the Neanderthals in terms of population, simply by breeding faster. Still another theory holds that modern humans either bested the Neanderthals in competition for food or killed them off in war. Objections have been raised to all of these theories, and we will probably never know the truth. In any case, about 40,000 years ago people who were anatomically almost identical to people today became the only human population on Earth. This new population is sometimes called Cro-Magnon for the site where the early modern *Homo sapiens* were first found in France.

These near ancestors of ours extended the range of *Homo* to include both Australia and North and South America, lands that had never before been visited by hominids. The modern form of *Homo sapiens* very quickly became a worldwide species.

The recent past. Modern *Homo sapiens* has been present on Earth for only a small fraction of the total time hominids have existed: 40,000 years of perhaps 3.5 million, a little more than 1 percent. But to us, even 40,000 years is an unimaginably long time—2000 generations. Written records began only about 4000 years ago, and we often call humans who lived before that time "prehistoric." There is another development in those 40,000 years, however, that can be a more useful marker.

Agriculture began to be commonly practiced about 10,000 years ago, and that practice marks a major step toward life as we know it. The word "preagricultural" can thus be used to refer to those modern *Homo sapiens* who lived between 40,000 and 10,000 years ago.

Many anthropologists today view the preagricultural time as a "golden age," when there was little disease, plenty of food, not much required work, and a rich artistic and social interchange. This view is in sharp contrast to the older belief that life without agriculture was "nasty, brutish, and short."

While it is all too easy to romanticize the preagricultural way of life, careful studies of the few preagricultural peoples left on Earth have led to the modern conclusion that this way of life was easy, healthy, and interesting—at least when the cold of the ice ages did not destroy game and freeze people.

One of the great discoveries about preagricultural peoples was made by a young girl in 1879. Her father had been exploring a cave at a Spanish farm called Altamira. He was looking for evidence of life in the cave from the most recent of the ice ages. When Maria Sautuola joined her father one day, she spotted something he had missed. Maria was short enough to

ANTHROPOLOGICAL STAGES

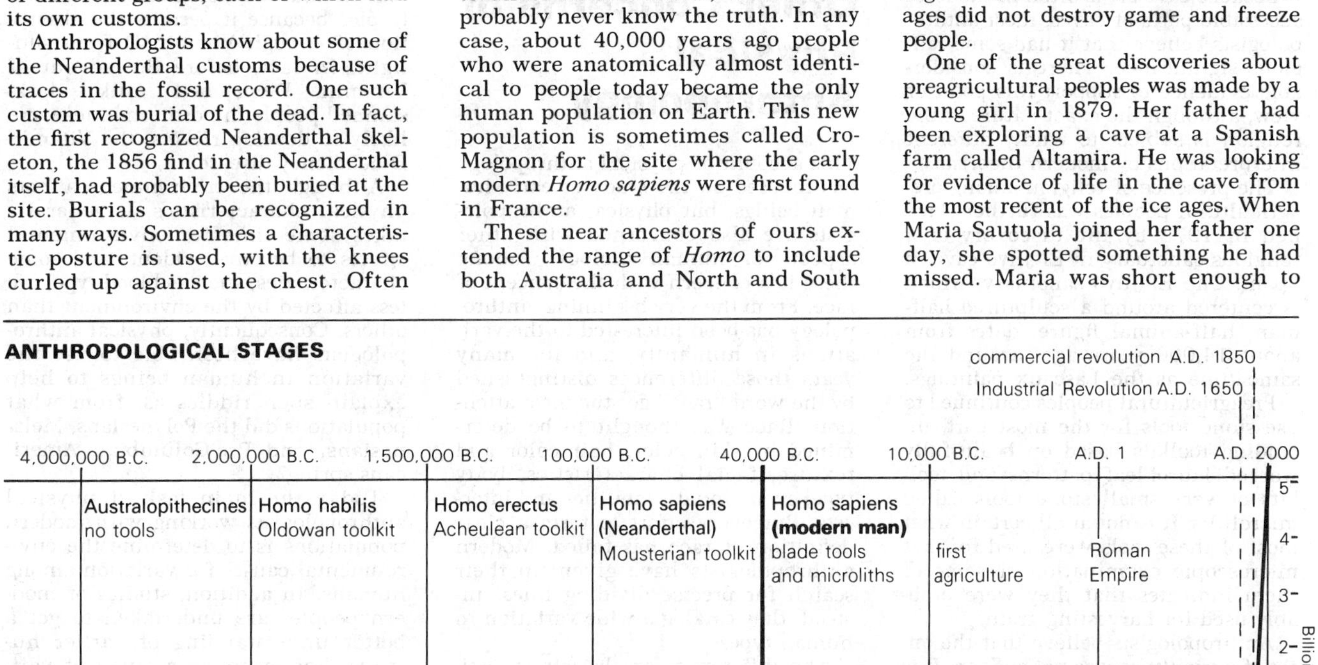

commercial revolution A.D. 1850
Industrial Revolution A.D. 1650

4,000,000 B.C.	2,000,000 B.C.	1,500,000 B.C.	100,000 B.C.	40,000 B.C.	10,000 B.C.	A.D. 1	A.D. 2000
Australopithecines no tools	Homo habilis Oldowan toolkit	Homo erectus Acheulean toolkit	Homo sapiens (Neanderthal) Mousterian toolkit	Homo sapiens **(modern man)** blade tools and microliths	first agriculture	Roman Empire	

Billions of people: 0 1 2 3 4 5

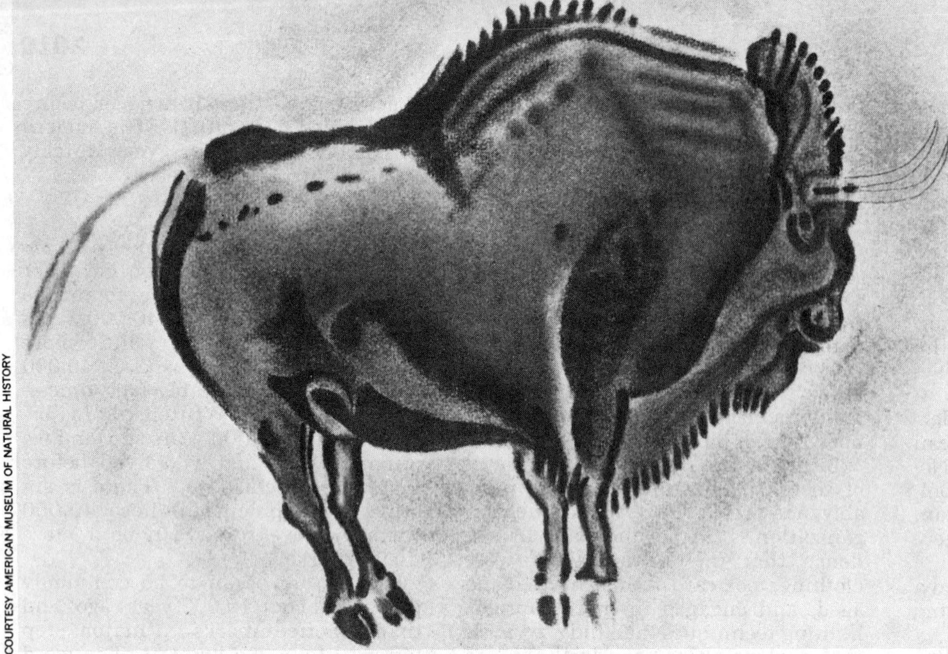

THE ART OF EARLY MAN *includes this elegantly stylized bison and other animals painted on the walls of caves (and discovered only in the past 100 years). The ominous human face,* right, *is from a relief sculpture discovered in a cave at El Juyo, Spain, in 1978.*

stand upright in places where Sautuola had to go on his hands and knees, so she was the first person in over 10,000 years to see a herd of bison painted on the ceiling of the cave.

Since then, other examples of ice-age cave art have been found. Some of this art, such as that found in the Lascaux cave in France in 1940, is as artistically vital as any painting done since. Some of its conventions are different from ours, but cave art is clearly the product of talented people who had the time and energy to do more than search for food.

Because cave art is often in the least accessible parts of caves, most anthropologists believe that it had some religious significance. There is considerable evidence to support this point of view, although the exact nature of the religion is subject to wildly different interpretations by modern theorists.

The presence of religion among preagricultural peoples was further clarified in 1978 by the discovery of a religious sanctuary in El Juyo cave in Spain. The El Juyo sanctuary, which is centered around a sculptured half-man, half-animal figure, dates from about 14,000 years ago, around the same time as the Lascaux paintings.

Preagricultural peoples continued to use stone tools for the most part, including toolkits based on beautifully worked laurel-leaf patterns and toolkits of very small stone tools called microliths. It is not at all certain what most of these tools were used for, but microscopic examination of some of them indicates that they were probably used for harvesting grain.

Anthropologists believe that the onset of agriculture was not sudden. It is likely that preagricultural humans already understood how to grow plants from seeds and had domesticated horses and reindeer to some extent. But sufficient available wild food made the labor of farming seemed unnecessary. Various anthropologists have suggested that either population pressure, climatic change at the end of the most recent ice age, or simple exhaustion of resources led people to take up farming about 10,000 years ago. Whatever the cause, the result was a major change in the way of life for *Homo sapiens.* The development of society after the triumph of agriculture is a major concern of cultural anthropology (see below).

Other Concerns of Physical Anthropology

This account of physical anthropology has focused on the study of early human beings, but physical anthropologists are also concerned with other aspects of human biology. Among these is a concern with the concept of race. From the very beginning, anthropology has been interested in the variations in humanity, and for many years those differences distinguished by the word "race" got the most attention. Race was thought to be determined by skin color, hair color and texture, facial characteristics, body type, even "innate" abilities and interests. But every effort to form a clear definition of race has failed. Modern anthropologists have given up their search for precise dividing lines; instead, they catalog a wide variation in human types.

The differences are largely statistical. For example, there are more blond Scandinavians than blond Italians. But there are thousands of dark-haired Swedes, some blond Italians, and similar traits in other populations.

Other characteristics, such as the shape of various parts of the body, the pattern of body fat, and the texture of hair, also vary from place to place, but only in a statistical fashion. Most human characteristics are determined in the long run by environment. For example, it is apparent that dark skin is adaptive in the tropics because it protects the body against absorbing too much ultraviolet light. Consequently, populations in Africa and in the South Pacific that do not share other characteristics do share a dark skin color. Similarly, light skin is adaptive in the regions that are north or south of the tropics because it permits the absorption of enough Vitamin D from sunlight. In fact, before the advent of Vitamin D-enriched milk, dark-skinned people in northern cities were likely to develop rickets, the Vitamin D deficiency disease.

Although the environment affects physical characteristics, it generally takes some time for environmental effects to become evident, and some characteristics, such as blood type, are less affected by the environment than others. Consequently, physical anthropologists have been able to use the variation in human beings to help explain such riddles as, from what populations did the Polynesians, Melanesians, and Pre-Columbian Americans spring?

Today the main task of physical anthropologists working with modern populations is to determine the environmental causes for variation among humans. In addition, studies of modern peoples are undertaken to get a better understanding of earlier humans. For example, a study of variation in teeth or skulls in a modern population can be used to help understand the amount of difference between populations of *Homo erectus.*

ARCHAEOLOGY

Beginnings. The first "archaeologists" were grave robbers. To this day, it is the custom in many cultures to bury prominent people with their riches. Grave robbers have located the graves of many of these wealthy people successfully, and have removed the treasures they have found. Grave robbers are not interested in the meaning of the societies that built the graves, and they usually melt down the treasures for their content of precious metal or otherwise destroy the treasures in order to profit from them.

Egypt. By the end of the 1700's, general interest developed in learning about earlier cultures. Napoleon took scientists with him on an invasion of Egypt in 1798; there one of his soldiers found the Rosetta stone near the mouth of the Nile in 1799. The Rosetta stone contains identical inscriptions in three versions: Egyptian hieroglyphic, Egyptian demotic, and classical Greek. Jean François Champollion, who knew classical Greek, soon developed a system for deciphering the Egyptian inscriptions. By the end of the 1800's, many Egyptian inscriptions and ancient documents had been read. Life in Egypt 3000 years ago was perhaps better understood than, say, life in England 1000 years ago.

Bible lands. Before archaeologists began to work in Egypt, the principal source of information about ancient civilizations was the Bible. This ancient book told of many fabulous civilizations of the Near East. Soon after the Egyptian excavations began in earnest, early archaeologists were spurred by biblical accounts to excavate mounds in what is now Iraq. There they uncovered the ancient civilizations of Assyria, Babylonia, Sumeria, and Ur (each one more ancient than the last). These excavations, along with others in what are now Syria, Israel, Lebanon, Jordan, and Turkey, confirmed and expanded on the historical accounts offered in the Bible.

Greece and Crete. Meanwhile, Heinrich Schliemann began confirming the historical basis of another ancient document—the *Iliad* of Homer. In 1866, he correctly identified the site of Troy in what is now Turkey and conducted extensive investigations.

Then, at the turn of the century, Arthur Evans discovered the lost civilization of the Minoans, centered on the island of Crete. Evans's excavations continued through the 1930's and uncovered many beautiful and important artifacts. But none of the three written languages used by the Minoans could be translated. Only in 1952 did Michel Ventris, an architect whose hobby was ancient languages, decipher one of the scripts, Linear B. It turned out to be a form of Greek, however, and not the key to the earlier Minoan language. That language has still not been deciphered, limiting modern knowledge of the culture.

The Americas. Although it was apparent from the early encounters of Hernán Cortés and Francisco Pizarro with the Aztecs and Incas that complex civilizations had developed in the Americas before Columbus, there was little European interest in these civilizations after they had been exploited for their gold and silver. With the archaeological awakening at the beginning of the 1800's, however, the 300-year-old remains of Aztec and Inca cities, temples, fortresses, and roads captured the interest of Alexander Humboldt. His 1814 book on the subject started William Prescott and John Lloyd Stephens on the routes that led to public awareness of the civilizations and new discoveries. By 1839, Stephens had begun his explorations, which led to the first clear account of the Maya civilization. Over the course of the next century, various explorers came to understand that the Inca and Aztec civilizations were actually latecomers to the Americas, having been preceded by a series of brilliant societies in what are now Peru and Mexico.

EPA

AN ARCHAEOLOGICAL DIG *near the Snake River in Washington state. The workers are uncovering an early Indian village.*

Modern trends. Although the excavation and interpretation of major past civilizations was the priority of archaeologists, and certainly the most dramatic part of archaeology for most people, there was a gradual realization that facts about daily life were as important as treasures or works of art. Today, archaeologists have come to concentrate on learning about the daily lives of the peoples they study. A broken piece of pottery, called a potsherd, is as sought after as any other find, for pottery styles have varied from culture to culture in such a way that potsherds have become the "fingerprints" of societies.

In the nearly 200 years of archaeological research, there has been a gradual change from the "grab and exploit" techniques of the grave robbers to the cautious methods used by modern archaeologists. Today, archaeologists no longer try to restore all of a site to some approximation of its original condition. Instead, the site is mapped into a grid, and only portions of the grid are excavated. This leaves major parts of the site untouched for later archaeologists, who may have improved techniques and tools. Every bit of soil that is excavated is sifted for tiny artifacts that can reveal the details of daily life. Instead of carting most of the material to faraway museums or private collections, as much as possible is returned to local repositories. Today's scientific archaeology is a far cry from the work of the grave robbers.

Cultural Anthropology

What Is Culture?

Some early anthropologists specialized in analyzing and classifying the systems human beings use to control their lives. They called themselves "social anthropologists." Gradually these social anthropologists developed a new concept—that of *culture.* A group of people develops characteristic kinds of social arrangements and interactions, as well as its own way of manufacturing tools, of eating, of picturing the universe, of speaking and gesturing, and even of sitting or sleeping. Culture is all of the traits that humans learn from the other humans around them. The study of culture, especially of unfamiliar cultures, came to be known as "cultural anthropology."

Beyond its broad general meaning, the word "culture" came to be used for more specific purposes. Anthropologists study the culture of particular groups or societies, such as the culture of the Arapesh of New Guinea, or of the Polish-Americans of Buffalo, New York, or of teenage gangs in England. Often one culture is part of another—for example, English teenage gangs are part of the larger culture of England. In such cases, the smaller culture is called a subculture.

When a culture is broken down into its components, each component is called a *cultural trait.* Cultural traits range from the way marriages are arranged to the use of certain gestures for emphasis.

Cultural anthropology, then, is the study of the cultural traits of different groups of people. In the beginning, most anthropologists devoted themselves to the study of small groups of people whose ways of life were different from the ways of westerners—the residents of Europe and North America. Western culture and technology were spreading rapidly to other parts of the world, and older cultures were being overwhelmed by the new. By 1900, for example, the cultures of most North American Indian groups were known only to a few older people who remembered how things had been done in the past. Later anthropologists extended their study to the subcultures of developed Western nations.

Because cultures disappear, anthropologists use a method of comparison called the *ethnographic present.* All cultures are discussed as if they still existed. Using the ethnographic present, an anthropologist treats the customs of, say, the Mohawk Indians as if the Indians still lived in the 1600's, even though the Mohawk have largely adopted Western ways today.

EARLY MIGRATION *to America from Asia over a prehistoric land bridge was a theory substantiated by early anthropological studies of Siberian natives like the one shown. Some Siberian peoples seem culturally related to American Indian tribes.*

Pioneers of Cultural Anthropology

Although anthropology as a scientific study did not begin until late in the 1800's, writing typical of anthropologists began much earlier. Indeed, many stories of the early Greek historian Herodotus dealt with the strange customs of people in faroff lands. (His facts were often wrong or wildly exaggerated, but Herodotus showed a lively anthropological curiosity.) At a later stage, the early explorers of the New World and the South Seas provided much information that is still of use to anthropologists.

In the United States, various explorers and later visitors began to describe the customs of the different groups of North American Indians. In 1851 Lewis Henry Morgan undertook to base a theory of cultural development on his study of the Iroquois. He assumed that culture could be developed in three stages: savagery, barbarism, and civilization. Later anthropologists found this approach far too simplified, but Morgan was a pioneer in advancing an anthropological theory of development.

Starting in 1896, modern anthropology was established at two institutions in New York City. Frank Boas, a German-born physicist, had developed a great interest in the Indians of North America. In 1896 he came to Columbia University in New York and established the first university department of anthropology. There he became the first great leader of the new discipline and trained a whole generation of anthropologists. Boas believed that anthropologists should study other cultures in the field, living with and observing people in their natural settings. Among Boas's many famous students were Ruth Benedict and Margaret Mead.

The second New York institution was the American Museum of Natural History. It became involved in anthropology almost by accident. One of the large questions of human history in the 1800's was how American Indians had arrived in the Americas. One popular theory was that they had migrated from Asia across a land bridge in the far north, but there was little direct evidence of such a migration.

KIRK/PETER ARNOLD

FUJIHIRA/MONKMEYER

GSCHEIDLE/PETER ARNOLD

CULTURES *vary widely both in time and place. They include that of a Stone Age tribe in South America (shown looking at an instant photograph of themselves); the Hopi Indians of Arizona, who mix their ancient culture with that of modern America; and modern subcultures such as Hell's Angels.*

Around 1900, the museum initiated a large program to seek evidence for this theory. It involved collecting cultural data from northern groups of Indians and Inuit (then known as Eskimos) and from groups of people living in eastern Siberia. This project tended to confirm the migration theory, and it gathered a vast number of artifacts and observations on Indian and Siberian cultures. Indeed, the study is still the main source on some cultural groups that have since vanished. The museum followed up its great northern study with others of interest to anthropology. In the 1920's it hired Margaret Mead, who became one of the best known anthropologists in the world.

Another early anthropologist who contributed to new ways of studying culture was Bronislaw Malinowski. During World War I, Malinowski found himself confined to the Trobriand Islands in the South Pacific. He made the most of this experience by living among the peoples of the islands and studying their culture. Later anthropologists have also tried to live in the native style while in the field.

By the 1930's the Great Depression severely reduced funds for field studies in faraway places. Many anthropologists began to consider societies that were closer to home. Ruth Benedict studied the Zuni and Hopi cultures in the American Southwest. After 1930, she wrote an influential book on comparative anthropology, *Patterns of Culture* (1934), and then turned to the study of race relations. Margaret Mead studied the passage from childhood to adulthood in non-Western societies—*Growing Up in Samoa* (1928) and *Growing Up in New Guinea* (1930). During the Depression, she turned her attention to growing up in the United States.

World War II found most American anthropologists in Washington, D.C. They had been called there by the federal government to study the cultures of various groups involved in the war, including the Chinese, Rumanians, Czechs, and Japanese. Just after the war, Ruth Benedict published her study of Japanese culture in *The Chrysanthemum and the Sword* (1946). In general, anthropologists broadened their interests to the study of all cultures, including those close to home. In fact, the war had Westernized many remote peoples, leaving only a few cultures in South America, the Philippine Islands, and New Guinea relatively unaffected by Western ideas and devices.

While anthropological fieldwork continues among the few non-Western societies, many leaders in cultural anthropology are seeking theories that may help explain the development of culture in general and the wide variations among peoples. Theories range from the deeply psychological, such as the structural anthropology theory of

Claude Lévi-Strauss, to the purely economic, such as the hypothesis put forward by Marvin Harris that cannibalism is a natural outgrowth of depletion of food resources.

Meanwhile, a general body of knowledge and theory that is widely accepted among cultural anthropologists has been developed. This basic information includes a broad explanation of how society has developed, and some understanding of kinship patterns, religion, and language.

The Organization of Societies

The work of both physical and cultural anthropologists has shown that until quite recently there were two main types of economic organization for human societies: *hunter-gatherer* and *agricultural.*

For the million and a half years since the emergence of *Homo erectus*, almost all societies have been of the hunter-gatherer type. Anthropologists believe that human beings developed many of their most characteristic cultural traits as a result of this. Since we have no direct access to the hunter-gatherers of the past, modern hunter-gatherer societies, such as the San (formerly known as Bushmen) of southern Africa, have been studied to provide an understanding of the hunter-gatherer organization.

One of the fundamental organizational principles of hunter-gatherer societies is division of labor between the sexes. Men do almost all of the hunting and women do almost all of the gathering. Most of the gathering involves finding and bringing fruits, nuts, and roots or tubers into camp, but women also gather small, slow animals such as snails or edible insects. The food gathered by the women forms the basis of the hunter-gatherer diet. The meat obtained by the men's hunting is viewed as the more important food source, but it does not provide many of the calories.

Hunter-gatherers live in fairly small bands of about 30 individuals. These bands must travel frequently to new camps because they exhaust local resources or must take advantage of seasonal food or water supplies. In this respect, their way of life is somewhat like that of chimpanzee or gorilla troops. There are significant differences, however. Apes do not divide food-gathering tasks by sex.

Human hunter-gatherer bands get together periodically with several other related bands in large camps that include hundreds of individuals, a practice also not shared by the apes. These large get-togethers serve many purposes, including the opportunity to find spouses and the exchange of information and goods.

Hunter-gatherer bands are loosely organized. Usually there is no one person directly in charge of everything, but leadership develops in specific situations. Also, the bands are not permanent. One person or family may leave a band at any time and join another.

When farming and herding replaced the hunter-gatherer way of life, the society needed more internal organization. Anthropologists have classified the organization of agricultural groups in various ways. Here is one system:

1. *Tribes.* Tribes have an organization not far removed from that of the loose hunter-gatherer band. Each family may govern itself, although some individuals may be recognized as "big men" who have more prestige than others in the tribe. Such "big men" gain respect by holding large feasts.
2. *Chiefdoms.* When a "big man" gains the power to make decisions for others (that is, as a judge) and to compel people to provide supplies and soldiers for war, the society has become a chiefdom. Usually the chief rules over a federation of villages. Anthropologists believe that this form of organization begins when there is a food surplus.
3. *Feudal states.* The feudal state expands upon the chiefdom, in which society is separated into two classes: a large class of serfs or peasants, who are controlled by a small class, and the nobility. Anthropologists find that the feudal organization does not require additional food surpluses, but rather develops from the concentration of wealth over time. The nobility acquire control over more and more of the food, while the serfs or peasants have less control.
4. *City-states.* Urbanization, or the development of cities, is a poorly understood phenomenon. The main difference between a city and other settlements is that in a city a significant number of people are no longer engaged directly in producing food. The traders or artisans in cities form a third class of people, between

HUNTERS AND FEUDALISM: *hunter-gatherer cultures survived into the 1900's in remote parts of the world. Feudalism flourished in the European Middle Ages. It was an elaborate form of chiefdom in which people's status and social roles were firmly differentiated.*

NEW YORK PUBLIC LIBRARY

NEW YORK PUBLIC LIBRARY

the nobility and the serfs. The government officials who manage the increasingly complex organization often constitute a fourth class. These government officials may also be priests.

5. *Empires.* When one city-state gains sufficient control over the others around it, the group of city-states becomes an empire (a small-scale empire is called a kingdom). An empire is a larger version of the city-state.

Evidence indicates that human population density did not rise significantly from the emergence of *Homo erectus* until the development of agriculture. Some anthropologists believe that increased density led people to adopt agriculture. Others believe that the rise of agriculture led to increases in population.

City-states and empires have tended to grow in regions where irrigation or similar massive enterprises were required to maintain the food supply for an increasing population. In some cases, the need for more useful land produced the organization and leadership for large earth-moving projects. While many classic empires, including the Sumerian, Egyptian, Chinese, Aztec, Maya, and Inca, may be explained in this way, some anthropologists feel that the case is still not proven.

In the past 200 years there has been another change, one which may well be as significant as the development of agriculture—industrialization. Industrialization has led to unprecedented population growth and to the development of cities on a scale never seen before. Sociologists have been active students of these new phenomena, but in the scale of anthropological time, 200 years is very short. It is too soon to tell what the ultimate effects of the new industrialized way of life will be.

Kinship

More important to the day-to-day life of individuals than the overall organization of society is the internal organization of families. All human societies are based upon families, people related by marriage or blood. Often the family consists of parents and their children: the *nuclear family*. There are many variations on the nuclear family, however, and many different forms and customs for the development of the family. Anthropologists believe that family arrangements are cultural inventions whose purposes include reducing conflict between groups and between individuals, protecting against economic crises, and improving or protecting the physical and cultural inheritance of the culture.

Endogamy vs. exogamy. Endogamy is the practice of marrying within one's general hereditary group. The Hindu caste system in India provides a good example. In the Hindu culture, people in a given subculture must have the same occupation, eat certain foods, and marry only within their own subculture, which is called a caste. In the United States, social pressure encourages a kind of endogamy: people tend to marry within their economic class, religion, and "race."

Exogamy requires that a person marry outside of the group that has the same general heredity. Some societies accomplish this by establishing kinship groups called *clans.* A person must marry out of his or her own clan. Other societies require that marriage be between people from different villages.

There are obvious virtues to both systems. Endogamy promotes solidarity within the group that is closely related, and it encourages the hereditary traits of that group to be passed on to future generations. Exogamy reduces conflict between clans or villages and promotes genetic diversity.

Patrilocal vs. matrilocal. In many cultures, newlyweds have a particular responsibility to one side of the family. Where exogamy between villages is practiced, tradition usually specifies that the new couple shall live in the husband's village or the wife's. Society decides, and the couple has no choice in the matter. If the newlyweds move to the husband's village or household, the culture is patrilocal. If, as among the Zuni, they move to the wife's village or household, the culture is matrilocal. In matrilocal societies, women usually play a more important role than in patrilocal societies.

In the United States and other Western societies, customs are neither matrilocal nor patrilocal. Most often, the newlyweds set up new households, sometimes thousands of miles from either set of parents.

Some matrilocal societies are also *matrilinear.* In a matrilinear society, the mother is recognized as the parent and lines of descent go through her. Other societies recognize the father only; they are *patrilinear.* The United States is a *bilinear* society in terms of recognition, but the custom of having a bride take her husband's name tends to obscure the female line of descent over several generations.

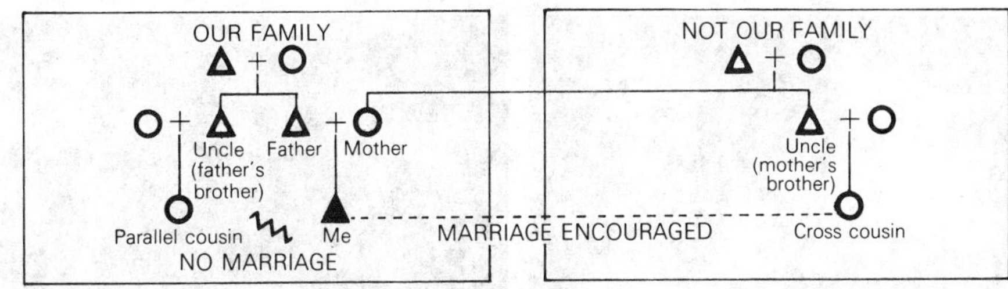

MARRIAGE RULES *in some cultures forbid marriages to parallel cousins, considering them incestuous* (left), *while encouraging marriage to cross cousins, who are considered to be outside the family* (right).

Monogamy vs. polygamy. In most Western societies, both men and women may be married to only one person at a time. This custom is called monogamy. In many other cultures, however, polygamy—having more than one spouse at a time—is acceptable in one form or another. If men may have more than one wife, the system is called *polygyny.* In most cases of polygyny, each of the wives has a separate household; either the husband visits each wife in turn, or the wives visit the husband one at a time. *Polyandry,* in which women may have more than one husband, is rare. Among the Toda of India, a woman marries a group of brothers. The economic benefit in this case stems from the fact that Toda brothers receive their inheritance equally, making each brother's portion too small to enable him to set up a household by himself.

Rules about marriage and kinship are often extremely complicated. Even in endogamous societies there is a prohibition against incest (sexual relations with anyone too closely related). All cultures prohibit marriage between members of the nuclear family. But beyond that, customs show wide variations. One pattern is based on treating one's father's brothers as equivalent to one's father. In that case, one cannot marry a father's brother's child (a *parallel cousin*) because that person would be the same as a sister or brother. On the other hand, marriage between *cross cousins* may be encouraged. A cross cousin would be a mother's brother's child. In matrilinear societies, this pattern may be reversed, forbidding marriage to cousins on the mother's side.

The economic and practical advantages of marrying a cross cousin are easy to see. In a patrilinear society, if you marry your parallel cousin, you do not gain any new relatives, for you are already related to your father's brothers and their children. On the other hand, if you marry your cross cousin, you gain his or her mother's brother and his children as relatives. These new kin can be counted upon as allies in times of trouble.

PRO PIX/MONKMEYER

LIBRARY OF CONGRESS

JANGOUX/PETER ARNOLD

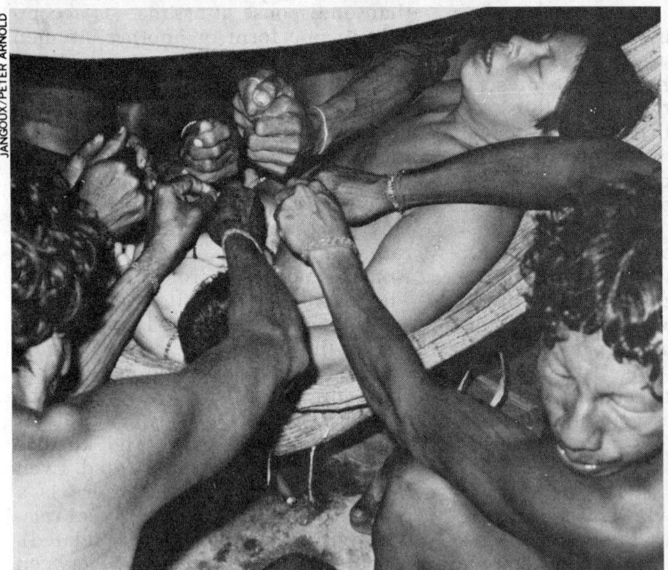

MCKINNEY/EPA

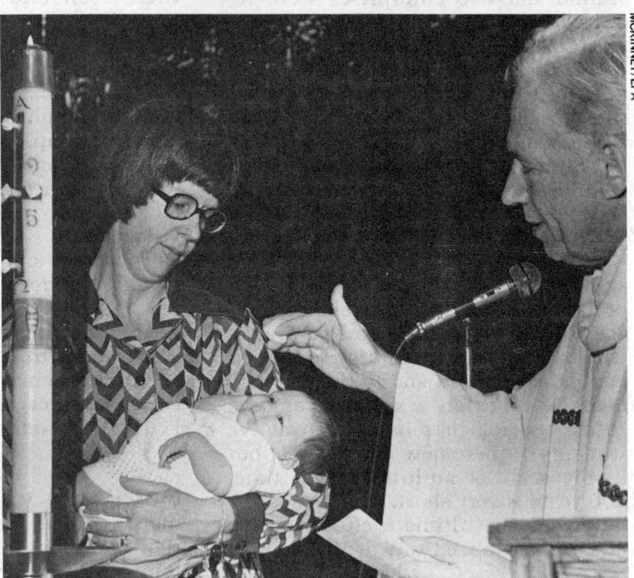

THE POWER OF RELIGION *is illustrated by the Inuit (Eskimo) shaman or medicine man, and by a trancelike healing ceremony* (left). *In Western culture, we distinguish between evil and good uses of supernatural power; one we call witchcraft, and the other religion* (right).

Religion and Magic

From the time of the Neanderthals at least, and perhaps as early as the appearance of *Homo erectus*, there are indications of rituals that suggest beliefs that can be classified as religion or as magic. Such beliefs have persisted in all known cultures, although their importance in daily life varies from culture to culture.

Unlike the dissimilar organization of societies and of kinship relationships, magic and religion are remarkably alike in many ways from culture to culture. Magical healing powers, belief in the soul, prayer, and sacrifice are inherent in all. But efforts by anthropologists to find one set of magical or religious beliefs that is basic to all have failed. These beliefs can range from simple to complex, but it is not always clear whether "simple" beliefs (such as a belief in "high gods" that rule the world) developed from more complex systems of ritual and magic, or whether the complex developed from the simple.

Because many similar beliefs and practices occur in many different cultures with many different names, anthropologists have adopted a general terminology. Thus, they use the Polynesian words *mana* and *taboo*, the English word *witch*, the Siberian word *shaman*, and the English word *priest* to refer to similar cultural traits in many different societies.

Mana is a mysterious quality that all people and objects possess. It is necessary to make anything happen. Certain people or things may have so much mana that they become taboo (too much mana will harm you). Other people have a harmful form of mana that they can direct against you without your knowing who they are. Such people are witches and the harmful form of mana is called witchcraft.

While a person is born with the power to be a witch and keeps that power a secret, a person has to train to become a shaman. The community knows who the shamans are, since the shamans are involved in healing the sick as well as other forms of public magic. Magic is the control of animate or inanimate objects by supernatural means. If the magic ritual is performed correctly, the desired result is considered to be inevitable.

Shamans may fall into trances, often assisted by strong tobacco or mind-altering drugs, as part of their ritual. In the trances the shamans appear to be dead, but they often call upon spirits, who may answer back.

The priests, like the shamans, perform rituals, but there are essential differences. The priest is not thought to be in control of events or objects. The control belongs to spirits or gods, and the priests' rituals merely influence the spirits or gods. In general, the priests help interpret a belief system that is the culture's basis for understanding how the universe works.

Priests in many religions administer the rituals that are called *rites of passage* and *rites of intensification*. Rites of passage include those associated with birth, puberty, marriage, and death. Rites of intensification are those used to guarantee good crops or other good fortune, such as welcoming the change of seasons or performing rituals that bring rain. They are called rites of intensification because it is believed that their adaptive purpose in the culture is to help intensify the feelings of the participants and observers.

A common practice that may involve either a shaman or a priest is divination. Generally, divination is foretelling the future, although it can also refer to the ability to find hidden objects or hidden resources.

There are counterparts to many of these terms in the United States today. Mana is called luck, good fortune, or destiny. People who have little control of events around them, such as gamblers, sailors, or baseball players, seem to place great importance on luck, but nearly everyone believes in it at least some of the time. Often something will be thought to possess intrinsic bad luck, such as a black cat. While most people in the United States do not believe in witches, there is widespread interest in accounts of possession of evil spirits, exorcism, and various "supernatural" occurrences.

Although there is no single equivalent to a shaman, there are faith healers, psychics who predict the future, and diviners who claim they can find water or lost objects. Organized religions have priests who perform such rites of passage as bar mitzvahs, baptisms, marriages, and funerals. Such festivals as Christmas, Passover, and Easter have elements of rites of intensification.

Language and Culture

Anthropologists in the field were often the only Western people who understood a language that was spoken by a very few people. (For example, in the early 1970's there were only eight people in the world who regularly spoke Selknam to each other; the eight lived in Tierra del Fuego, a remote part of South America.) Because anthropologists "collected" the languages, they also studied them. Often the grammar and vocabulary of a language can tell many things about the past of a cultural group and about its relationship to other cultures. A people's language may also tell something about how the group views the world.

In the late 1700's students of language recognized similarities between Sanskrit, the ancient language of Hinduism, and Greek. The family resemblance of these languages helped scholars to theorize that at some time in the prehistoric past, a people (whom we call Indo-European) spoke a language from which Sanskrit, Greek, and most European languages (including English) developed.

Such evidence is difficult to interpret, however. For example, the fact that most American Indian groups in the United States speak English tells nothing about their ancestors. Similarly, many cultural groups in Peru, Bolivia, and Ecuador speak Quechua, the language of the Inca Empire. Quechua was most likely imposed on their ancestors after the Inca conquest. Anthropologists know this because they are familiar with the Inca Empire. What influence a prehistoric empire had by imposing its language on outsiders is more difficult to judge. For this reason, it is dangerous to assume that all who speak a single language are closely related.

We do know that culture affects language. Skiers and Inuit need to have a good vocabulary for describing snow—and they do. To a skier, *corn* is a name for granular snow and *mashed potatoes* is the heavy, wet snow of a warm day in early spring. The Inuit are so dependent on snow that they have many words to describe specific kinds of snow.

Language may affect culture as well. For example, in a patrilinear culture, such as the Arapaho, the word *father* may mean not only one's biological father but also the biological father's brothers. At some point in the distant past, the Arapaho understanding of how people are related was expressed by this use of language. But to succeeding generations, having a single word to express "father-uncles" may help shape the way they look at human relationships.

Language may also affect culture in other, more subtle ways. In most Germanic and Romance languages, nouns tell the gender or sex of the person, place, or thing to which they refer. In German *der Lehrer* is a male teacher and *die Lehrerin* is a female teacher. In English "teacher" may refer to a man or woman. English has pronouns that indicate sex or gender (he, she), but many languages in West Africa have no way to indicate sex except by using the specific words that mean male and female. What effect such differences have on a culture is not at all clear. Modern feminists assume that the differences *are* significant, and have demanded changes in English in cases where males seem to be favored over females.

There are cultures in which more than one language is spoken as a matter of course. At one time in South America there were Carib groups in which the husbands and the wives spoke different languages, although they shared the same culture in other ways. Apparently this curious situation arose because the warlike Caribs regularly obtained their wives from the peaceful Arawak by conquest. The husbands continued to speak Carib while the wives continued to speak Arawak, although both groups understood both languages. Carib and Arawak are more different from each

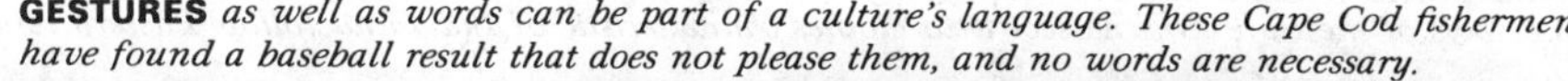
GESTURES *as well as words can be part of a culture's language. These Cape Cod fishermen have found a baseball result that does not please them, and no words are necessary.*

PFEFFER/PETER ARNOLD

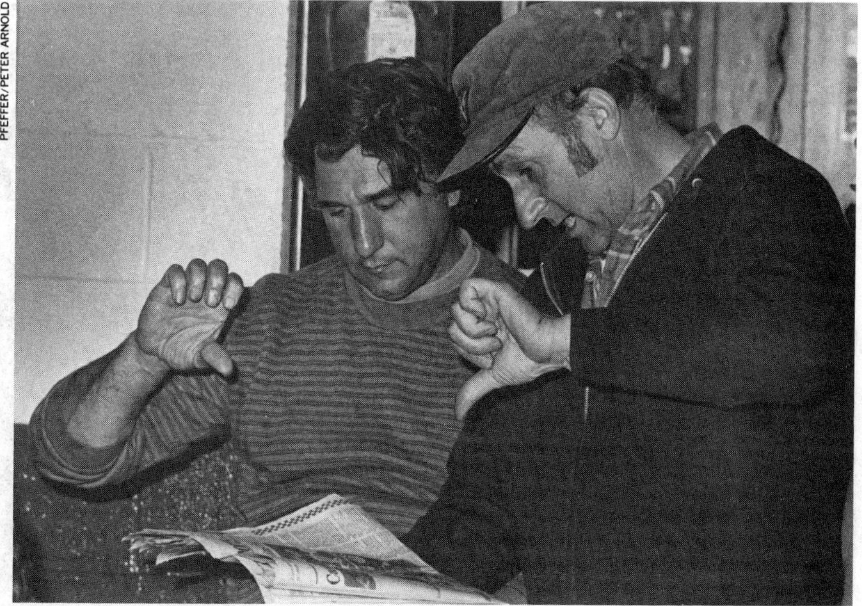

other than English and Russian. It is interesting to note that the Carib groups living today all speak a form of Arawak.

Another example of double language comes from the upper Amazon region where there are more than 25 different culture and language groups that practice strict exogamy. As a result, in any marriage, the husband and wife have grown up speaking different languages. The children of these marriages are raised largely in the father's language, although they are also exposed to the mother's language. All of these cultures also practice preferential cross cousin marriage. Thus, if a son marries a cross cousin—one on his mother's side—the son will already have some knowledge of his wife's language, since his wife's language will be the same as his mother's.

Westernization

In the development of human societies, one cultural pattern has often been superimposed on another, usually by conquest.

The legacy of a conquering people may be shown physically. The Mongol occupiers of Russia in the 1200's and 1300's intermarried with earlier peoples, and Mongol features in central Russia today reflect those marriages. Often, a conqueror may change a whole culture. Modern France owes much to its long occupation by the Romans before 400 A.D. A conquering army may even be "conquered" itself in a cultural sense. Many of the "barbarians" who invaded Rome stayed and took on Roman ways and values.

On the other hand, a culture can be amazingly resistant to change, even when conquered and occupied. In Peru before the Inca conquest, the Ica Valley was famous for the excellence of its pottery. The nearby cultures imported Ica pottery and valued it more than their own. Nearby cultures also imitated Ica designs.

When the Incas occupied the land, they suppressed local pottery styles. Ica ware continued to be made and used locally, but the Ica Valley people made high-quality Inca-style ware for sale outside the valley. After the Inca rule was ended, the original Ica style was revived.

In the past several hundred years, Western culture has come to influence virtually every other culture in the world. The culture has been carried by invading armies and imposed by political regimes. But it has also been adopted by choice in many areas since it promises material improvement and prestige. People in remote corners of the world have learned about the West from radio, films, television, and visits from Western businessmen.

Examples of Western cultural domination are easy to find. In nearly all of the nations of North and South America the only official language is a Western language. (In the past few years, some nations have begun to permit a second official language, such as Quechua; Paraguay has always used Guaraní as a second official language.) In Japan, Western-style clothing, food, and even sports compete with the traditional Japanese styles for popularity. African mothers feed their babies formula from bottles rather than nursing them. Traditional slash-and-burn farming in the tropics has been replaced by the planting of single cash crops such as peanuts or soybeans. Even in the farthest reaches of the jungle or highest mountains, Western manufactured objects have replaced some locally made objects from the traditional culture.

Non-Western cultures have dealt with this challenge in several ways. One of the most unusual was the response of the cargo cults of the South Pacific. During World War II, Western armed forces suddenly arrived on non-westernized islands, built airstrips, flew in men and supplies, and changed the local economy for a while. When the war was over, the forces left and abandoned their airstrips. The cargo cults came to believe that the Western armed forces would return, bringing their "cargo" of tools and food with them. The cults even built airstrips in the jungle, hoping to attract airplanes bearing gifts.

Many cultures have sought to reject westernization. In the United States, the Ghost Dance Revival of the 1880's was an effort to counter the European whites, who had destroyed the great buffalo herds of the Plains and occupied Indian territory. In its original form, the Ghost Dance was supposed to return the good life (that is, the traditional culture) to the Indians who performed the five-day ritual. As the revival spread, however, it came to include such promises as the destruction of the white invaders and invulnerability of the dancers to bullets. The revival ended in 1890 in Wounded Knee, South Dakota, when about 300 Indians were shot to death by white soldiers.

Rejection of Western culture continued into modern times. The 1979 revolution in Iran sought to destroy Western cultural influence without giving up the advantages of Western technol-

WESTERNIZATION *is clear in small things such as the factory-produced pacifier in this Afghan child's mouth. At the same time, American members of the Hare Krishna sect wear clothes characteristic of India and follow Eastern religious practices.*

KELER/EPA

EPA

ogy. Even as Western culture has spread, however, it has been changed in the process. In the second half of the 1900's, for example, the influence of Eastern music, religion, and philosophy has grown steadily in the United States. Where two cultures are of similar complexity and economic power, acculturation brings change to both. The relations between the West and China seem likely to change both cultures in ways difficult to predict.

When the power of two cultures is unequal, however, the results are often tragic. For people who are hunter-gathers, such as the Inuit, or who are at the tribe or chiefdom stage, as many Amazonian Indians are, Western culture tends to be destructive. As the Inuit accept Western technology and values, they lose their ancient culture and find themselves lost in the new way of life. They are often prey to disease or to alcohol, and become people without a cultural home.

Anthropology and Western Society

Since the 1930's, cultural anthropologists have studied their own societies as well as the cultures of non-Western groups. Therefore, it is sometimes difficult to sort out what is anthropology and what is simply reporting by other social scientists or comentators.

In 1928, Frank Boas wrote *Anthropology and Modern Life.* He noted that cultural change has occurred more and more rapidly over the span of human existence. In his time, the most noticeable example of cultural change in Western society was a changing definition of what was viewed as modest behavior. Boas sought to apply his anthropological learning to modern times. He defended the need for strong leaders in society and the equality of the sexes; he questioned the importance of monogamy and refused to accept the Marxian notion that economics determines culture.

Writing after World War II, two of Boas's students had different concerns entirely. In the course of her book on Japanese culture, *The Chrysanthemum and the Sword*, Ruth Benedict contrasted Western culture with pre-Western Japanese culture. One of her main concerns was how child-rearing in each society influenced the cultural beliefs and practices of adults. She identified an "arc" in Western human growth and development; in infancy, there is a strict schedule and little freedom, but freedom of expression and behavior increase into adulthood, then return to restriction in old age. The corresponding "arc" for the Japanese has freedom in infancy and old age, with the strictest controls in adulthood.

Benedict also contrasts Japanese education, in which the instructor physically guides the child's hand or body through the desired behavior, to the Western way, in which the child observes the teacher and does the writing, walking, or other activity alone. She believed that the Western method promoted more independence and less passivity.

Margaret Mead's *Male and Female: A Study of the Sexes in a Changing World* (1948), ascribed many of the manifestations of Western culture to the way children are raised. In the United States, despite the immense differences among subcultures, there was one common cultural trait. People in the United States are brought up to look to the future, not to the past. In other cultures, including much of Western Europe, people shaped their lives around what their families had been. In the United States, the important thing in life was what an individual could *become.* Advertising, movies, and popular books all reinforced the hopeful future and encouraged everyone to consider his or her possibilities.

Mead also considered the differences between the way boys and girls were raised, showing how the spouses' differing expectations from marriage, family, and career, could bring frustration and disillusionment.

More recently, Marvin Harris, in *Cannibals and Kings* (1977) and other books, looked at Western society from a broader perspective. He wrote that Western culture has reached the point at which it can escape from the economic cycle of past cultures. He believes that the exhaustion of resources, mainly because of increasing population, produced in each culture of the past a series of events that resulted in more and more people being forced to live marginally, while very few live well. Harris pins his hopes for Western culture on its ability to limit population. If the West succeeds in achieving such a limitation, Harris thinks its culture can endure and change for the better.

The preoccupations in this brief selection suggest some of the concerns that face anthropologists trying to study a culture of which they are a part. Boas's observation that culture seems to change at a faster and faster pace still seems true. As a result, there continues to be much to be studied by anthropologists. *—Bryan H. Bunch*

MARGARET MEAD, *a pioneer in anthropological field studies, is shown with Manus children in 1928. She was a major influence on the field until her death in 1976.*

UPI

APPLICATIONS OF THE SOCIAL SCIENCES

The disciplines discussed in this volume—psychology, sociology, and anthropology—affect aspects of our daily lives ranging from the products that stock our kitchen shelves to the principles that govern our most vital institutions.

The disciplines are applied in various ways. One way is through social scientists themselves, practicing in fields as varied as industrial management, advertising, and prison administration. Employment in the business world and in various institutions is commonest among psychologists; most sociologists and anthropologists still work primarily as teachers.

Social science is also applied in techniques that social scientists have developed, such as testing, polling, and participant observation, and in the use of principles learned through research. Research has provided psychological findings on how learning occurs (basic to education); sociological findings on public opinion (important to the political process); and anthropological data on cultural differences (crucial in relations with developing countries).

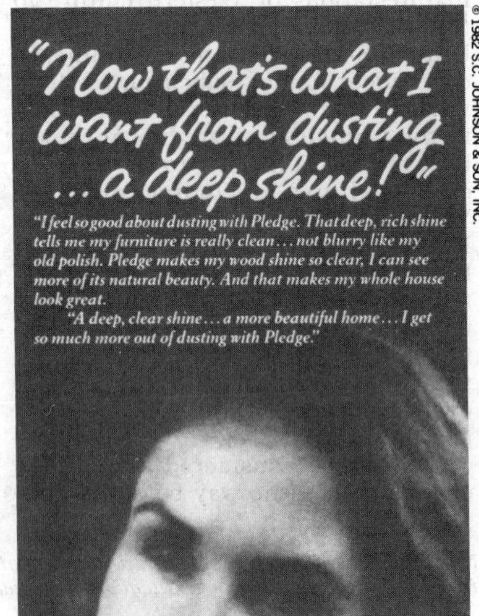

"Now that's what I want from dusting ... a deep shine!"
"I feel so good about dusting with Pledge. That deep, rich shine tells me my furniture is really clean... not blurry like my old polish. Pledge makes my wood shine so clear, I can see more of its natural beauty. And that makes my whole house look great.
"A deep, clear shine... a more beautiful home... I get so much more out of dusting with Pledge."
© 1982 S.C. JOHNSON & SON, INC.

ADVERTISING SLOGANS *often use applied psychology to help sell a product.*

Demographics, the scientific study of human populations, is a sociological technique worthy of special mention; it is, as one scholar puts it, "a general servant of other social sciences." The United States was a pioneer in the collection of demographic data. It provided for a census in its Constitution. Since 1790, census counts have been taken every ten years. In modern times, more frequent censuses in many fields have registered and projected trends in population size and composition, economic conditions, and other areas of concern.

The examples that follow have been chosen to give an idea of the breadth of applied social science. They suggest rather than exhaust the possibilities in this vast field.

The World of Work

The human being as worker, particularly as factory worker, became an object of serious study as industrialization accelerated in Europe and the United States in the late 1800's. One of Karl Marx's key concepts was the development of an industrial working class, the proletariat, that would be the prime mover in reshaping society. In the free market economy of the United States, however, social scientists tend to place less emphasis on workers as a political force and more on the productivity and motivation of workers.

Scientific management.

"Systematizing Shop Management and Manufacturing Costs a Specialty" read the business card of Frederick W. Taylor, America's first "efficiency expert." Active in the late 1800's and the early years of this century, Taylor observed various processes, such as steel manufacturing, in order to see how men and machines could best be combined for maximum output. Another pioneer in the field, Frank Gilbreth, produced a classic investigation of bricklaying. These efforts came to be known as time and motion studies. (Gilbreth also found uses for time and motion studies in the home—he was the father of the twelve children made famous in the comic reminiscence of family life called *Cheaper by the Dozen.*)

Men like Taylor and Gilbreth regarded workers chiefly as sources of power. Believing that a laborer's sole incentive was money, they established quotas that awarded higher rates of pay for extra units produced. The recommendations of Taylor and Gilbreth did result in increased productivity—more steel was poured, more bricks were laid per hour—but their approach, known as scientific management, had its limitations.

Hawthorne and human relations. A new dimension was added by a landmark series of experiments at the Hawthorne plant of the Western Electric Company, near Chicago. These experiments were carried out in the late 1920's and early 1930's under the supervision of Elton Mayo, a professor of industrial research at Harvard. Mayo's background was mainly in philosophy and psychology, but his team of researchers also included anthropologists and sociologists.

In one phase of the Hawthorne studies, five young women who assembled parts for telephones were moved into a separate room. There they were subjected to several experimental changes in work conditions, including morning and afternoon breaks and shorter work days. Their rate of production increased, as expected. However, the rate continued to rise even when the original conditions (no breaks, a longer day) were restored.

This unexpected outcome has been explained in various ways according to different perspectives in the social sciences. One explanation suggests that the women realized that they were getting special attention, enjoyed it, and did their best to please. This kind of experimental "contamination" resulting from subjects' awareness that they are being studied has been known ever since as the *Hawthorne effect.* Other explanations hold that productivity remained high because the young women felt a sense of solidarity and cohesiveness, or that they responded to a new kind of interaction with their employers.

This experiment and others at Hawthorne made clear the importance of social relations in working life and gave rise to a new applied science known as human relations. Companies were encouraged to foster informal groups among workers and to improve communications between labor and management. Direct results were difficult to measure. But investigations did indicate that no one strategy alone improved working conditions. Workers found satisfaction not simply in high pay but in a combination of factors that included security, opportunity for advancement, and friendly relations with coworkers and supervisors. Job satisfaction in turn led to lower rates of absenteeism, accidents, and turnover.

Present-day approaches.

Today social science approaches the working world from two main outlooks. One focuses on the work process itself, while the other stresses the people who do the work.

Improving the work process is the goal of the field known variously as human engineering, human factors engineering, or ergonomics. Some of the objectives of human engineering have to do with the workplace: finding and maintaining the best levels of light, ventilation, noise, and so on. Other objectives have more to do with so-called man-machine systems, particularly equipment design. Air and space travel present extreme conditions under which humans and machines must interact. The United States Air Force has employed physical anthropologists to help design cockpits, seats, and other equipment.

Personnel psychology is descended from Mayo's Hawthorne studies and the field of human relations. Its practitioners work in three main areas: (1) selecting and classifying personnel, chiefly through tests; (2) training personnel to improve both labor and management skills; and (3) improving motivation and morale. A number of innovations in recent years have aimed at increasing workers' personal satisfaction. They include job rotation, flexible working hours (flex-time), and self-managing work teams.

Marketing

In the 1920's psychologist John B. Watson became involved in divorce proceedings that shocked the staid academic community. He was forced to leave Johns Hopkins University and found himself effectively barred from the field of teaching. Watson became an account executive at the J. Walter Thompson advertising agency, and remained in the advertising business for the rest of his working life. His career, linking academic psychology and advertising, personifies the close ties between social science and the world of marketing.

Marketing in its broadest sense involves all the activities that have to do with directing and encouraging the flow of goods and services from producers to consumers. These include product development, packaging, distribution, and advertising. Marketing is a vital aspect of all capitalist economies, where competition and choice rule the marketplace. All the social sciences, but especially psychology and sociology, are brought into play to learn the whats, whys, and hows of consumer behavior.

MUSEUM OF MODERN ART

ZALE CORPORATION

CORPORATE EMPLOYERS, *satirized by Charlie Chaplin as huge, impersonal (and dangerous) machines, have been encouraged by social science research to be more attentive to workers' needs. The Zale Corporation, for example, has a child-care center where working mothers can leave their children during business hours.*

NABISCO CO.

SAVING MONEY *is one of the most potent appeals in marketing campaigns.*

Psychological perspective.

As might be expected, marketing psychology stresses the individual response—for instance, what emotional needs affect a buyer who is making a decision? The application of psychology to marketing ranges from determining the best shape for a mustard jar to changing the image of a multinational corporation.

Perception. Perception plays an important part in marketing. For example, researchers have learned that the greater the number of colors in a print advertisement, the greater its readership; other tests have shown that women respond to color more readily than do men. Visual cues do much to create a mood in packaging. There is a world of difference between the stark, no-nonsense black and white of generic products and the lavish, lively color illustrations on boxes of cereal designed to appeal to children.

Perception may have subtle ramifications. Because people perceive the smell of lemon to be fresh and clean, its scent is added to such products as dishwashing detergent, furniture wax, and oven cleaner. The fragrance has no functional benefit, but it does sell goods.

Marketing is also concerned with the phenomenon known as perceptual screening. In the modern world of mass communications, we are subjected to a barrage of commercial messages—some 150 a day according to one estimate. Through the process called perceptual screening, we tune out the vast majority of these messages. Advertisers have concluded that their messages must either be intriguing enough to break the "boredom barrier" or be repeated very often. Repetition may be maddening, but there is little doubt that it works. Most of us can easily remember much-repeated advertising slogans that have long since been discontinued.

Learning. How people learn obviously makes a difference in how they acquire or change their attitudes toward products and services. Advertising often uses classical conditioning, the simple pairing of stimulus and response. Classical conditioning seems to be at work in the recognition of many well-known trade symbols such as Morton Salt's girl and umbrella and RCA Victor's listening dog. Certain trade names, such as Kodak, Xerox, and Kleenex, have become commonly used for any brand of their principal products (cameras, photocopiers, facial tissues). Kodak has even adopted a color—a particular shade of yellow—that millions of people immediately associate with the company's photographic products.

Reliance on the opposite behavior, discrimination, is more frequent, however. Sellers go to great lengths to create an image of uniqueness for their product: it works better, costs less, or gives some special benefit to the purchaser.

Operant conditioning, which combines stimulus and response with reinforcement, is widely used as well. In essence, the marketer conveys the message that, by acting, the consumer will be rewarded. Makers of shampoo imply that users will look as glamorous as the models, while "fast relief" is promised for buyers of headache pills and other home remedies.

Motivation. The motives behind buying decisions are crucial to marketers, many of whom have spent millions of dollars to learn how to motivate consumers to buy particular goods and services. A glance through any popular magazine will reveal the many needs and emotions to which sellers appeal.

Banks, insurance companies, investment firms, and the like offer security. Advertisers play on our need for love when they show mothers serving foods that their families enjoy. Fear underlies a number of appeals, especially those having to do with personal hygiene (toothpaste prevents cavities) and grooming (mouthwashes guard against bad breath). Makers of Cadillacs and fine perfumes often base their selling strategies on the needs for self-esteem and approval. Almost every psychological tool has been used to gauge motivation, from the galvanometer, which measures skin changes, to the Thematic Apperception Test, which measures attitudes.

WORKING WOMAN

CAMPBELL SOUP COMPANY

DEMOGRAPHICS *help marketers to target their products. If many women join the work force, magazines for them will appear. If many people are living alone, convenience products will be created for them.*

Motivation research has called attention to emotional needs that do not seem obvious at first glance. For instance, Miles Laboratories found that mothers who applied an antiseptic to children's cuts and scrapes were motivated not only by a desire to protect against germs but also by the need to show their affection (by comforting the child when the antiseptic stung). For this reason, Miles restored the sting to its previously too-soothing antiseptic, Bactine.

Personality. Attempts have been made to relate various personality traits to buying habits, but correlations between specific traits and actual purchasing behavior seem difficult to establish. Personality profiles of users of particular products can, however, be useful in future sales efforts. The technique of developing and using such profiles is known as psychographics. Research has shown, for example, that heavy beer drinkers are mostly male, tend to look for approval from their peers (other men), and value physical pleasures and accomplishments. Since such drinkers account for some 80 percent of beer sales, it is little wonder that so many beer commercials feature men drinking together and appear during telecasts of major sports events.

Sociological perspective.

With its emphasis on group behavior, sociology is identified chiefly with marketing strategies aimed at the consumer as a group member.

Demographics. The discipline of demographics charts not only the number of potential buyers and where they live, but also their age, education, income, and marital status.

A good example of demography in marketing is afforded by the "baby boom" in the United States after World War II. Between 1950 and 1960, an extraordinarily high birthrate helped increase the U.S. population by 20 percent. The baby boom generation (known to social scientists as a *cohort*) has been inelegantly compared to the bulge of a pig passing through the digestive tract of a boa constrictor. The effects of the generation were first seen in the increased sales of baby food and strollers, and later seen in school construction, textbook purchases, and the youth market for jeans, records, and so on. By the 1980's, the members of this generation, as independent adults, were in the market for furniture, automobiles, and insurance.

Nearly all large broadcasting stations, newspapers, and magazines have demographic profiles of their audience to help potential advertisers make marketing decisions. Clearly, the readers of *Cosmopolitan* form a very different group from those who regularly scan the pages of *Road and Track* or *Architectural Digest.* For each medium the nature of its audience helps determine the goods and services to be promoted there, while circulation figures determine the cost of such promotion.

In a special class is the rating system of the A. C. Neilsen Company, which monitors television viewing. Some 1200 households throughout the United States are equipped with electronic devices that record what is happening on all TV sets in the house. Data are regularly transmitted by a special telephone line to the Nielsen offices. The resulting Nielsen ratings reflect, in theory at least, the television viewing habits of the entire country. Ratings are used not only to price commercial time but also to make programming decisions. New shows are added and old ones are dropped or moved in order to gain points in "rating wars."

Cultural traditions. Marketing executives find many uses for a sociological understanding of American values and traditions. The widely held values of worldly success and material comfort are reflected in the very existence of such luxury items as designer clothes and vacation tours. Other goods and services, from sliced bread to disposable diapers, attest to the value Americans place on practicality. Advertising appeals take American values into account. For instance, our admiration for progress inclines us favorably (if warily) toward almost any product touted as "new" or "improved."

The norms of American society—its guidelines for behavior—also play a vital part in the marketplace. The celebration of Christmas as a gift-giving holiday has become an economic as well as a cultural value. A poor Christmas season can spell failure for entire retail businesses. While many Americans resent the commercialism of this holiday, vast numbers continue to observe it; hence, the continuing success of Hallmark cards and telephone company appeals to "reach out and touch someone."

Roles. Roles are of interest to market researchers, although people play so many roles in life that is difficult to target any single one. Advertisers must be careful not to violate role expectations. An ad campaign featuring identical hairdos for mother and daughter was headlined "A Double Header Hit with Dad." It was withdrawn after testing because women objected strenuously to the idea of competing with their daughters for their spouses' affection. The ad, in other words, called attention to the role conflict that can arise when a man is both a husband and a father.

In recent years, changes in women's roles have been of prime concern to market researchers, especially since women between 18 and 34 control a great deal of the nation's discretionary income. There has been a trend toward portraying women in more varied ways: not solely as homemaker-mothers or decorative models, but also as independent professionals. Symbolic of the change toward a more "liberated" view of women are two slogans for Clairol hair coloring. In 1960 the message was, "What would your husband do if suddenly you looked ten years younger?" Twenty years later a happy user proclaimed, "This I do for *me*!"

Social class. Class is related to consumer behavior chiefly as it pertains to income. Membership in a social class may affect a person's choice of housing, automobile, clothing, and leisure activities. Class is also a factor in media selection. One study showed that lower-middle-class readers identified with *Reader's Digest*, while those of the upper middle class read *Time* and *The New Yorker*. Research into television habits has indicated that, compared with upper-class families, those in lower strata watch more television, prefer CBS to NBC, and like quiz and variety shows more than dramatic programs and movies.

Politics

Social science applications in the field of politics are numerous. From psychology's point of view, behavioral factors in an individual's response, particularly as a voter, are of prime concern. The sociological perspective is concerned more with public opinion, political socialization (the process by which people learn the norms of their political system), and demographics. Demographics has become especially important with the development of ever more sophisticated systems of computerized data collection. It allows seekers of political office to be more efficient in mobilizing support and raising funds.

Of the many political areas where social science is applied, two—promoting candidates and polling—are of greatest interest. For the sake of simplicity, the following concentrates on Presidential elections.

Candidate promotion. After the 1968 election, in which Richard Nixon defeated Hubert Humphrey for the Presidency, newspaper reporter Joe McGinniss published a book called *The Selling of the President 1968.* McGinniss's main point was that candidate Nixon had been marketed to the public as if he were a commercial product. Efforts to convince voters that there was a "new Nixon" (the old one had a reputation for deviousness) were carried out not only through advertisements but also through campaign coverage that purported to be news. The stress, said McGinniss, was on image rather than substance.

Nixon's advisers characterized their candidate as "a funny-looking guy" whose speeches were "incredible pap." One way of coping with this problem was to create ads that used a Nixon voice-over narration but no shots of the candidate. Other ads featured filmed "Dick Nixon community receptions," where the candidate could look statesmanlike in friendly surroundings. One Nixon adviser wrote: *"We have to be very clear on this point: that the response is to the image, not to the man. . . .* It's not what's *there* that counts, it's what's projected—and, carrying it one step further, it's not what *he* projects but rather what the voter receives."

Nixon's advisers were not alone. Winning candidates from Kennedy in

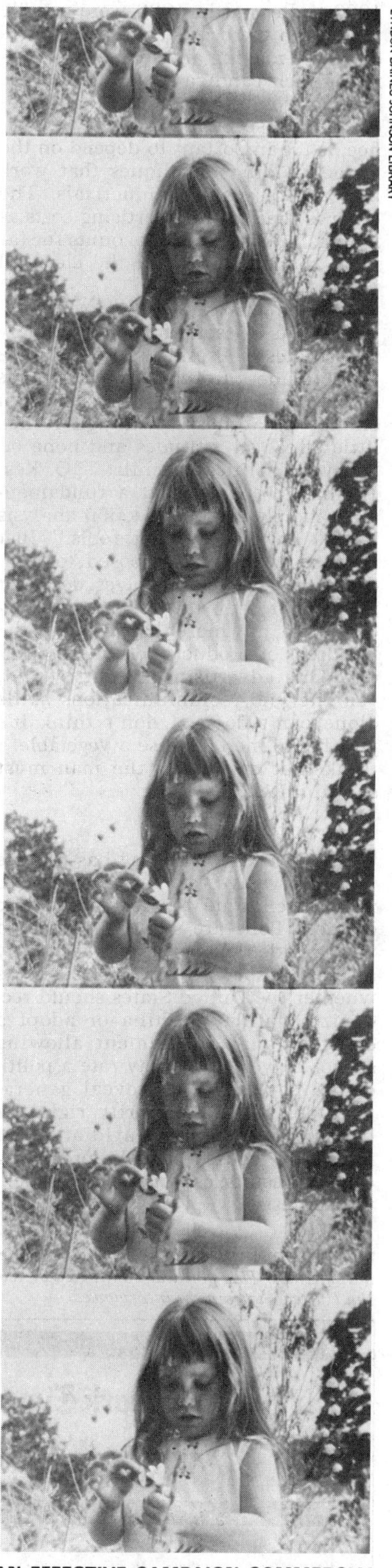
LYNDON BAINES JOHNSON LIBRARY

AN EFFECTIVE CAMPAIGN COMMERCIAL *(and one considered unfair by many) showed this little girl pulling petals off a daisy until, suddenly, a nuclear explosion lit up the television screen. The voice-over implied that Barry Goldwater was dangerously unreliable on war and peace issues and that a concerned voter would vote for Lyndon Johnson. Johnson won the election.*

1960 to Reagan in 1980 were usually those with the best "technical" advice on image-making and marketing. Critics of such candidate marketing raise two main objections. One is that political office, especially high political office, is too important to depend on the image-building techniques that work best in 30-second commercials. The other is that, with advertising costs as high as they are, money counts for far more than it should in the electoral process.

How effective *is* candidate promotion in its present form? Relatively few studies of Presidential races have been made. Recent investigations seem to indicate that mass media can change awareness, although it has little effect on attitudes and none on behavior. Political scientist V. O. Key, Jr., has suggested that a fundamental principle of good election analysis is that "voters are not fools." Just because people are exposed to hundreds of political messages does not mean that they unquestioningly accept them, any more than they buy the hundreds of products advertised every day. One advertising executive said: "In the end, communications skills alone can't do it. I don't think it's possible to merchandise a vegetable. I think that eventually the man must show himself."

Polling. As marketing has become more pervasive, so has polling, the major technique for gauging public opinion. Polls are surveys concerned with a wide range of issues. They may assess a specific policy, such as whether the United States should recognize mainland China or adopt a constitutional amendment allowing school prayer. They may rate a politician's popularity or reveal general attitudes toward minority rights or bureaucracy. The most avid attention is usually focused on polls predicting election results, especially in Presidential contests.

Polling in the United States can be traced back at least as far as 1824, when a newspaper in Harrisburg, Pennsylvania, predicted the election of Andrew Jackson in his campaign against John Quincy Adams (he lost). The newspaper printed sample ballots, which readers submitted. Informal surveys of this sort are known as straw polls, or straw votes.

The first systematic polling began in the 1930's. Three Americans working independently for various magazines—Archibald Crossley, George Gallup, and Elmo Roper—developed scientific sampling, using small groups chosen at random to represent the population at large. All three men correctly predicted the victory of Franklin D. Roosevelt over Alf Landon in the Presidential election of 1936. Their success was all the more notable in view of a widely publicized poll of $2\frac{1}{2}$ million Americans conducted by the *Literary Digest,* which predicted a win for Landon. The *Digest* results, a warning to pollsters ever since, were obtained through an unrepresentative straw vote.

Sample surveys solicit opinions from relatively few people—usually no more than 2000. These surveys are generally accurate to within about 4 percent because of the operation of probability. According to the theory of probability, a coin tossed in the air 1000 times will come up heads about 500 times; the same percentage would result no matter how many times the coin were tossed. What this means in terms of polling is that the number of respondents is less important than their being representative.

Critics of polls do not question their accuracy so much as their constant use, or overuse. Reliance on polling, they say, turns campaigns into horse races; the media, and thus the voters, become obsessed with questions of "Who's ahead?" and "Who's gaining?" rather than concentrating on who is best qualified or who would follow the most enlightened policies.

PUBLIC OPINION POLLS *provide statistically reliable information about attitudes toward many issues. This poll was conducted by telephone over five days; 1,489 adults in all regions of the United States were interviewed.*

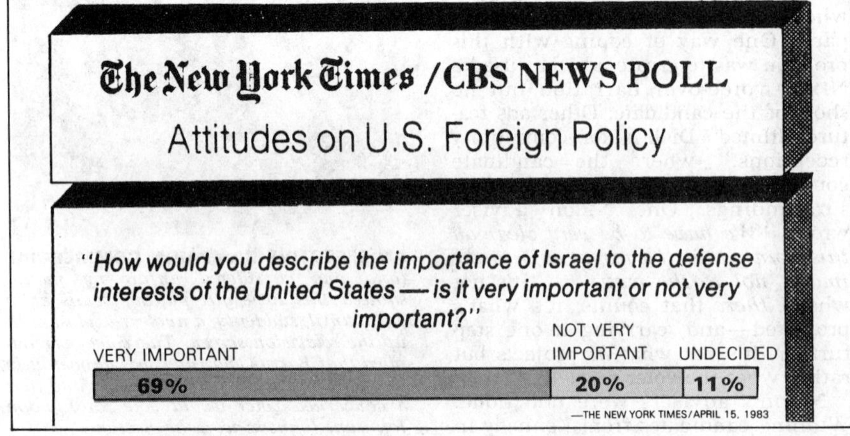

The New York Times /CBS NEWS POLL
Attitudes on U.S. Foreign Policy
"How would you describe the importance of Israel to the defense interests of the United States — is it very important or not very important?"
VERY IMPORTANT
NOT VERY IMPORTANT
UNDECIDED
69%
20%
11%
—THE NEW YORK TIMES/APRIL 15, 1983

A serious drawback of polling is how quickly circumstances (and opinions) seem to change. In 1980 pollsters predicted a close election in the Ronald Reagan–Jimmy Carter campaign, but Reagan won by a landslide. In the words of one critic: "If a Presidential election can swing from a nip-and-tuck battle to a landslide within forty-eight hours, then what is the point of the constant reporting of state and national polls weeks before the election?"

Another polling technique that has aroused criticism is the precinct poll (first used in Boston in the 1880's), whereby election outcomes are predicted on the basis of the vote in selected precincts. The television networks, feeding precinct data into computers, have been able to make correct forecasts early in the evening of election day. In 1972, for example, NBC predicted a victory for Nixon at 8:30 P.M. Eastern Standard Time, when most of the actual vote had not yet been counted. Many feel that such projections influence people farther west, where voting is still taking place. So far evidence concerning the possibility or extent of such influence is inconclusive.

Education

The application of the social sciences in the field of education has led to considerable controversy in the United States. The man considered to be the very first educational psychologist, Edward L. Thorndike, aroused strong feelings with his learning theories. As a professor at Teachers College of Columbia University from 1899 until 1940, Thorndike was an advocate of what has since come to be called operant conditioning. He taught that children learn by being rewarded for the proper response to a stimulus. He emphasized not only the activity necessary for learning but also its specificity—that is, the notion that learning results from a specific stimulus joined to a specific response. This idea contradicted the long-held belief that certain studies were useful because they "disciplined the mind."

Thorndike's teachings were influential in making American education more utilitarian and diversified. So were the contributions of his somewhat older contemporary, philosopher John Dewey. Dewey advanced a concept called "intelligent action." Learning occurs, he said, as the student constantly evaluates experience in light of its consequences and the goals being pursued. Dewey emphasized problem-solving and individual instruction. He thus became the father of progressive education, with its stress on "learning by doing," a broader curriculum, and greater freedom in the classroom.

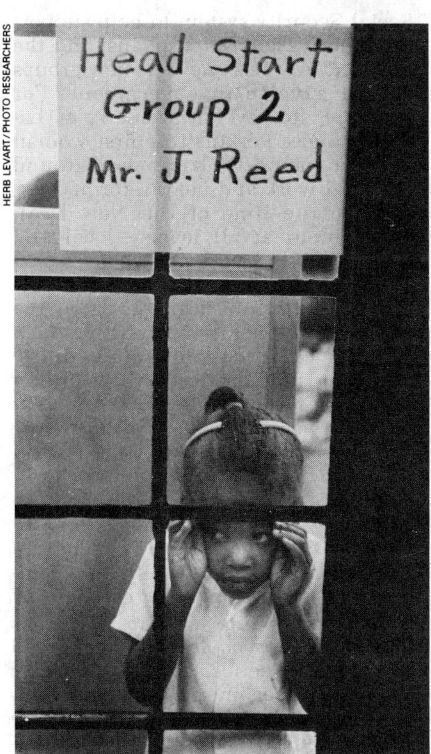

HERB LEVART/PHOTO RESEARCHERS

HEAD START *was an effort to give children from disadvantaged homes an even start with more privileged children by the time they reached school age.*

TEACHERS' EXPECTATIONS

What teachers expect can have a major influence on students' performance. A researcher once sent letters to all teachers in a school predicting that certain children in each class would "blossom" in the upcoming school year. In fact, the children's names had been chosen at random. But many of those children did "bloom" that year because the teachers respected the researcher and his predictions. Clearly, the students themselves sensed that the teachers were expecting more of them, and so they gave more, making better than average progress, all because of their teacher's confidence.

Many social scientists believe that the most damaging kind of discrimination against racial and ethnic minorities is teachers' unconscious signals that nothing much can be expected from certain children. The children come to believe this themselves and are thus "programmed" to fail.

Race and intelligence. By the middle of this century, attention was also directd to the social environment of educational institutions and the role of testing.

Could education do more to narrow the gap between whites and blacks? Years of intelligence testing indicated that middle-class children do better than poor children, and that whites (most of whom are middle class) do better than blacks (many of whom are poor). The difference in scoring came to be regarded as a class difference. It was argued that if poor (and therefore many black) children could be provided with some of the cultural advantages of middle-class children, their IQ levels could be raised.

Various compensatory programs were launched, the most notable being Project Head Start, initiated in 1965. This enrichment program for preschoolers, which originally enrolled some half million children in an eight-week summer course, was later expanded to include full-year programs. By 1980, the project had reached $7\frac{1}{2}$ million children, and was serving about 20 percent of all the poor children in the United States.

The mid-1960's also produced the Coleman Report (see Sociology, Social Institutions, Education). It concluded that class is a major determinant of IQ, or at least of school achievement. But psychologist Arthur Jensen disagreed. In 1969 he published an article stating that "the average difference in IQ scores between black and white people may be attributable as much to heredity as environment." Enrichment programs, he said, did not raise IQ scores. Nor could they be expected to, since inheritance accounted for some 80 percent of an individual's score. There was a good possibility, he suggested, that blacks might be genetically rather than culturally disadvantaged.

Jensen's theories aroused a storm of protest. Some argued that hereditary factors, although they might account for individual differences in IQ, could not be extended to racial groups. Others held that most tests are culturally biased in favor of the white middle class. Still others questioned the value of *any* IQ testing as a measure of intelligence. It has been shown, for example, that scores are affected by teacher expectations. In one experiment, when teachers were told that certain children (selected at random) would show great improvement during the school year, they did so—possibly because they received more classroom attention.

Studies of this complex question continue, and the evidence is far from complete. It is important to remember that IQ variation is far greater within groups than between groups, and that it is the individual's score that matters, not that of the group.

School effectiveness. By the 1970's a growing number of Americans were questioning the value of education itself. A report by sociologist Christopher Jencks (*Inequality,* 1972), which focused on education as a means of reducing income inequality, concluded that education made practically no difference. Income is unequal because of deeply rooted societal inequalities, Jencks said; a more just distribution of wealth, not schooling, is the only way to right the imbalance.

Americans were worried by another trend that seemed to signal growing weakness in their educational institutions. This was a steady decline in the scores of students taking the Scholastic Aptitude Test (SAT).

What did this decline mean in terms of American education? Several things, according to a report by the College Board and the Educational Testing Service, which develops and administers the SAT. A larger proportion of high school juniors and seniors began taking the tests; this accounted for the drop in scores in the 1960's. A college education was being sought by more women (who score lower in math) and more poor and minority students (many of whom lack adequate preparation). But educational standards were also slipping, which accounted for the drop in the 1970's, when the scores of top achievers started to fall. The report blamed several trends in the schools, among them grade inflation, social promotion, relaxed homework requirements, and inferior textbooks.

By the 1980's, two contradictory trends had developed. One was the adoption by many states of minimum competency tests, which students had to pass before receiving a high school diploma. The other was an attack on standardized testing itself. Some states, under pressure from consumer groups, passed "truth-in-testing" laws, whereby students could demand to see their tests to ensure that they had been scored correctly. More fundamental was the accusation that the SAT and similar tests continued to discriminate against poor and minority students.

Law

As the institution through which norms are codified, law has long interested sociologists. They have investigated not only how the process occurs, but also various aspects of law enforcement. A number of studies have been concerned with police officers as a social group, noting how they are socialized to the demands of their special type of work and how they interact with the public at large.

The lie detector. One well-known application of psychology in law enforcement is the use of the polygraph, or lie detector. The polygraph is based on the psychologist's practice of measuring emotional states by physiological responses (and, in

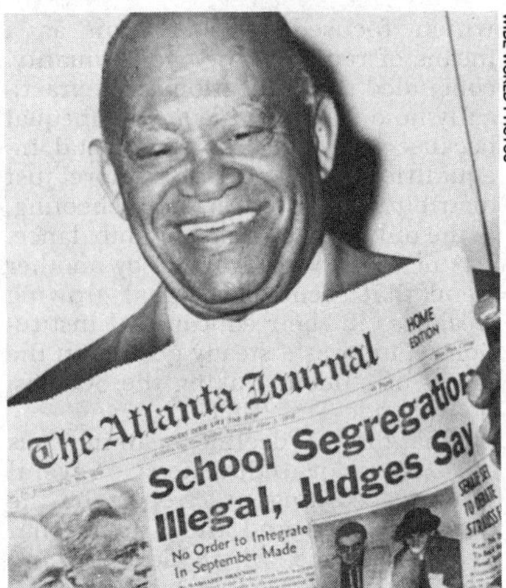

THE BROWN DECISION *is announced in headlines. The case made use of social science research into racial discrimination.*

turn, on the assumption that telling a lie is an emotional experience for most people). The polygraph registers changes in a subject's blood pressure, pulse rate, breathing, and galvanic skin response. No single sign indicates that a person is lying, but a combination of higher blood pressure, irregular pulsebeat, and so on is frequently persuasive. Much depends on the skill of the interrogator. Summing up the evidence of field studies, a major advocate of the polygraph estimates that it is accurate about 90 percent of the time. Because the lie detector is not totally reliable, however, polygraph evidence is rarely allowed in court.

Two landmark cases. In the early years of this century, some states passed laws setting limits on working hours and conditions for women. Employers appealed the laws all the way to the Supreme Court. Then, in 1908, in *Muller* v. *Oregon,* the state of Oregon, represented by lawyer Louis Brandeis, argued that it had a legal right to limit women's working hours to ten a day.

Brandeis delivered a brief consisting of two pages of legal citations and over a hundred pages of data from medical and social science experts. Social scientists contended that long working hours were harmful for women, for their children, and even for succeeding generations. This form of argumentation, stressing social facts rather than law, has ever since been known as the "Brandeis brief." It was successful in *Muller* v. *Oregon,* and the Court took the unusual step of mentioning Brandeis and his "very copious collection" of "expressions of opinion from other than judicial sources" in its opinion.

In the landmark case on school segregation, *Brown* v. *Board of Education of Topeka* (1954), argued before the Supreme Court by Thurgood Marshall, much of the argument depended on testimony by noted psychologists, who attacked segregation for its harmful effects on the self-image of black children and on their motivation to learn, and for creating hostility between racial groups. Marshall won the case, which brought sweeping changes in the years following.

The insanity defense. The opinion of social scientists was controversial enough in matters of racial segregation. But nowhere did expert testimony arouse stronger feelings than in criminal cases involving insanity. Nationwide attention was focused on this issue during the trial of John W. Hinckley, Jr., in 1982. He had shot at President Ronald Reagan a year earlier, wounding him and several others. It was a violent attack that was recorded by television cameras. Yet the jury found Hinckley "not guilty by reason of insanity" and he was sent, but not sentenced, to a mental institution.

Insanity, a legal rather than a medical term, is defined differently in various jurisdictions. In the federal court that tried Hinckley, a man is judged insane if he lacks "substantial capacity to conform his conduct to the requirements of the law" and "to appreciate the wrongfulness of his conduct." Many Americans were distressed by the spectacle of psychiatrists and psychologists testifying both for the prosecution, which tried to prove that Hinckley was sane and therefore guilty, and the defense, which tried to prove that Hinckley was insane and therefore not guilty.

In actual practice, the insanity defense is used very rarely, and is successful even less often. But the Hinckley case put pressure on the legal system to make changes. Some states, for example, have an additional verdict, "guilty but insane," which allows for sentencing.

Government and Social Welfare

It has been said that social science came to Washington with the New Deal. The Great Depression had wreaked such havoc on American society that traditional remedies, such as private charity, and traditional government, were no longer adequate. President Roosevelt and his "brain trust" of lawyers and scholars had no clear plan of action in 1933, but they did believe in an expanded social role for government. "We have a human problem as well as an economic problem," said Roosevelt.

The New Deal initiated a variety of programs that heralded a fundamental shift in political philosophy. Most important was the establishment of a Social Security system to help support the elderly, widows, orphans, and the disabled. At the same time new groups gained a voice in government. For example, Roosevelt's Secretary of Labor, Frances Perkins (the first woman Cabinet member), had a background in social work and labor reform.

Since the time of the New Deal, government at all levels—local and state as well as national—has become involved in a vast range of social programs. Some Americans question the wisdom of federal intervention in a number of these, including family planning and day care for working mothers. Most agree, however, that only government can deal effectively with such problems as poverty and unemployment.

Uses of psychology. The entire field of mental health is dependent on professionals in the field of psychology. While many psychiatrists and clinical psychologists are engaged in private practice, a sizable number work in government-supported community mental health centers. The centers were created after the Community Mental Health Centers Act of 1963 mandated a center for every 50,000 members of the population; there were 2000 by 1980. The centers provide ongoing therapy and emergency counseling for such psychological traumas as drug overdoses and suicide attempts.

The development of powerful new drugs to control symptoms of mental illness resulted in major public policy changes in caring for the mentally ill in the 1960's and '70's. States "deinstitutionalized" as many of the patients in mental hospitals as possible and returned them to semblance of normal life. In the first 15 years of deinstitutionalization, the number of in-patients in public hospitals fell from almost 560,000 to fewer than 250,000. Some large hospitals closed their doors entirely.

The overall results were mixed, at best. Cutbacks in government spending meant that less money was available for the community centers and other facilities that most former patients needed. In some big-city neighborhoods, released patients made up sizable groups of residents, who, while not dangerous, could not cope with the pressures of modern life.

An unusual application of psychology followed a nuclear accident at Three Mile Island, Pennsylvania, in 1979. A malfunction at a power plant there, which threatened explosion or meltdown, caused nationwide alarm. Three years later a federal court ruled that even the undamaged reactor at the site could not be reactivated until the government had made every effort to assess the effect of psychological stress on nearby residents. "Health encompasses psychological health," said the opinion, and must take account of "post-traumatic anxieties accompanied by physical effects and caused by fears of recurring catastrophe."

Uses of sociology. Given sociology's interest in social problems, its application to them is pervasive. Unlike psychologists, sociologists usually do not themselves work in the many public programs concerned with social welfare. The largest group of professionals who do are social workers. Social work itself was once a subfield of sociology, but it is now established as a discipline in its own right.

Sociology is applied to government programs in three ways. Its first contribution is in policymaking. Sociology asks such questions as: Should our attack on crime give priority to eradicating poverty or to building more prisons? Studies of the roots of crime and of the effectiveness of prisons can influence policymakers, and the written or oral testimony of sociologists may be taken by legislatures and other governing bodies.

Second, sociology can inform people who are developing actual programs. Urban planners, for instance, have learned about slum inhabitants from such imaginative participant observers as William Foote Whyte (*Street Corner Society,* 1943) and Elliott Liebow (*Tally's Corner,* 1967). While the horrors of big-city public housing are graphically presented in *The Vertical Ghetto* (1969) by William Moore, Jr., a more positive view of urban existence emerges from Herbert Gans's *The Urban Villagers* (1962).

A sociological concept that has proved helpful to city planners is the notion of the "dispersed" social network—a peculiarly urban chain of communication that creates a sense of community amid impersonal surroundings. "Telephone communities," as one sociologist has called them, may link scattered family members or elderly people who live alone.

Finally, sociology performs the function of evaluating policies and programs after they have been put into effect. When President Lyndon Johnson lauched his "War on Poverty" in the 1960's, the result was a multitude of programs to help the poor. How well did they work? Both students and social activists provided a wide range of answers, many unfavorable. Sociologist Daniel Patrick Moynihan's report, *The Negro Family* (1965),

SYBIL SHELTON/PETER ARNOLD

SYBIL SHELTON/PETER ARNOLD

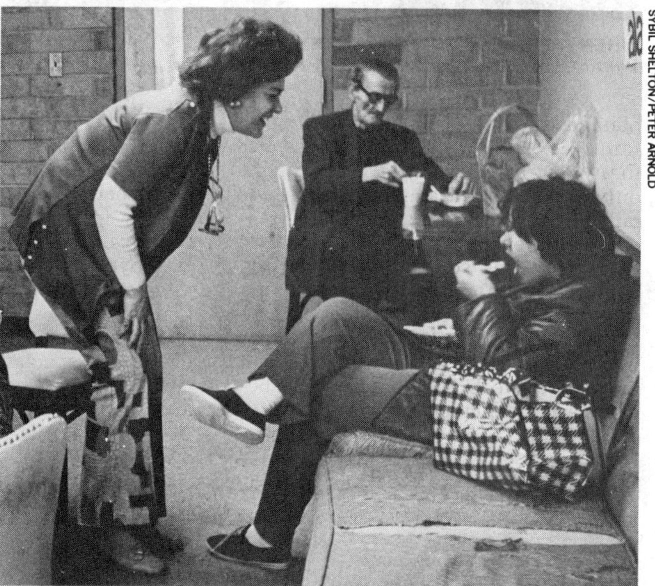

PUBLIC INSTITUTIONS *use social science research in providing care for the mentally and emotionally handicapped* (above), *and in planning for better use of public space, as shown by the plea for a people's park and a finished vest-pocket park* (below).

ERIC KROLL/TAURUS PHOTOS

KAREN COLLIDGE/TAURUS PHOTOS

WHEN DIFFERENT CULTURES MEET, *the insights of anthropology can smooth the way. Here World War II American soldiers pose with children in the South Pacific.*

U.S. NAVY/MONKMEYER

blamed the system for contributing to family breakdown among blacks. In many states, payments were made only to women and children, and then only if there was no adult male present—thus encouraging men to desert their families so that the families could qualify for benefits. Moynihan's report was widely criticized, especially by policymakers. It is significant, however, that Moynihan himself was elected to the U.S. Senate and so became a policymaker himself.

Uses of anthropology. Many anthropologists, in line with the discipline's long-standing interest in preliterate societies, have continued to work mainly in the setting of non-Western cultures. For instance, they have been employed as consultants in technical-assistance projects sponsored by the United States and the United Nations in developing countries. Others, however, have specialized in the two relatively new areas of medical and urban anthropology.

Medical anthropologists emphasize the role of cultural factors in treating the sick. For example, they have worked to encourage cooperative relationships between "native curers" (shamans, voodoo practitioners, and the like) and physicians. Research indicates that the approaches of the nonprofessionals can be especially helpful in treating mental illness.

Urban anthropologists have focused particularly on rural migrants to the city and on how they preserve and change former cultural patterns. Redfield's concept of a "folk-urban continuum" stresses a blending of elements rather than a sharp break between country and city ways of life. Oscar Lewis, in chronicling a Puerto Rican family in San Juan and in New York City (*La Vida,* 1966), introduced another concept: the culture of poverty. In Lewis's words, such a culture "is not just a matter of deprivation or disorganization." Instead it is "a culture in the traditional anthropological sense in that it provides human beings with a design for living."

Urban anthropology has tended to counteract the ideas of Moynihan and other observers who emphasize the pathological in their studies of poor blacks and other ethnic minorities in America. Its approach encourages social workers, among others, to avoid patronizing their clients, and instead to view their responses as resourceful ways of coping with their particular (and often serious) problems and discontents.

—Paula Franklin

For Further Reference

Abrams, Philip. *Historical Sociology.* Cornell University Press, 1983.

Barbu, Zevedei. *Society, Culture, and Personality: An Introduction to Social Science.* Schocken Books, 1971.

Bell, Daniel. *The Social Sciences Since the Second World War.* Transaction, 1981.

Benedict, Ruth. *Patterns of Culture.* Humanities Press, 1961.

Bonjean, Charles M., et al., editors. *Social Science in America: The First Two Hundred Years.* University of Texas Press, 1976.

Braybrooke, David. *Philosophy of Social Science.* Prentice-Hall, 1987.

Brown, Geoffrey, et al. *Experiments in Social Science.* Harper & Row, 1975.

Calhoun, Donald W. *Social Science in an Age of Change.* Harper & Row, 1978.

Erikson, Erik. *Childhood and Society.* W. W. Norton, 1964.

Freud, Sigmund. *New Introductory Lectures on Psychoanalysis.* W. W. Norton, 1965.

Kagan, Jerome, and Julius Segal. *Psychology: An Introduction* (5th Ed.). Harcourt Brace Jovanovich, 1984.

Kline, Paul. *Psychology and Freudian Theory.* Routledge Chapman and Hall, 1985.

Kruskal, William H. *The Social Sciences: Their Nature and Uses.* University of Chicago Press, 1982.

Leakey, Richard. *The Making of Mankind.* E.P. Dutton, 1981.

Levin, William C. *Sociological Ideas: Concepts and Applications* (2nd Ed.). Wadsworth Publishing, 1988.

Lienhardt, Godfrey. *Social Anthropology.* Oxford University Press, 1966.

MacRae, Duncan, Jr. *The Social Function of Social Science.* Yale University Press, 1976.

Maslow, Abraham. *Motivation and Personality.* Harper & Row, 1954.

Mausner, Bernard. *A Citizen's Guide to the Social Sciences.* Nelson-Hall, 1979.

Mayer, Robert R. *Social Science and Institutional Change.* Transaction, 1982.

Mead, Margaret. *Anthropology: A Human Science.* Van Nostrand Reinhold, 1964.

Morris, Charles G. *Psychology: An Introduction* (6th Ed.). Prentice-Hall, 1988.

Nisbet, Robert A., and Robert G. Perrin. *The Social Bond: An Introduction to the Study of Society.* Alfred A. Knopf, 1977.

Piaget, Jean, and Bärbel Inhelder. *The Psychology of the Child.* Basic Books, 1968.

Scientific American editors. *Scientific American Resource Libraries: Readings in the Social Sciences.* W. H. Freeman, 1973.

Smith, Robert B., and Peter K. Manning. *The Handbook of Social Science Methods.* Irvington Press, 1982.

Sorokin, Pitirim. *Social and Cultural Dynamics.* Transaction, 1982.

Toffler, Alan. *Future Shock.* Bantam Books, 1971.

Welty, Paul T., and Carol R. Simone. *The Human Expression: A History of People and Their Cultures.* Harper & Row, 1977.

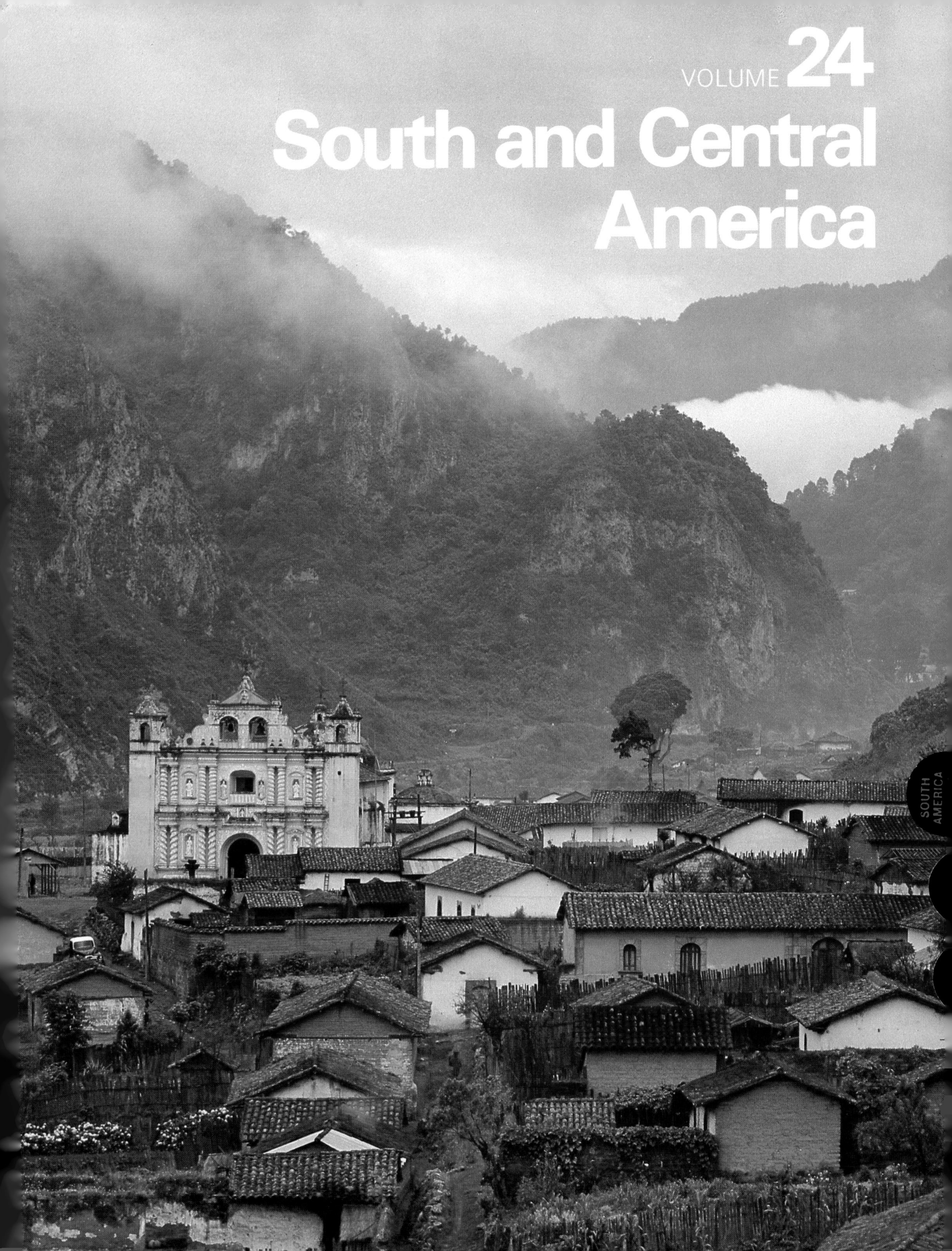
VOLUME 24
South and Central America
SOUTH AMERICA

A. JONGEN/UNITED NATIONS

For national flags see VOLUME 12: GOVERNMENT AND LAW.

SOUTH AND CENTRAL AMERICA

PACIFIC OCEAN
Galapagos Is.
The Netherlands Antilles
The Lesser Antilles
ST. VINCENT AND THE GRENADINES
TRINIDAD AND TOBAGO
L. Nicaragua
VENEZUELA
GUYANA
SURINAM
French Guinea
The Llano Plains
COLOMBIA
Negro
Branco
ECUADOR
Japurá
Amazon
Madeira
Juruena
Juruá
Marañón
BRAZIL
São Francisco
Araguaia
PERU
L. Titicaca
BOLIVIA
Andes Mts.
Atacama Desert
PARAGUAY
Grande
Laguna mar Chiquita
Paraná
Uruguay
Pampas Lowlands
URUGUAY
Rio de la Plata
CHILE
ARGENTINA
ATLANTIC OCEAN
Patagonia
Falkland Is.
Tierra del Fuego
Drake Passage

Colorado
Baja California
Yaqui
Sierra Madre Mts.
Rio Grande
MEXICO
Gulf of Mexico
Atlantic Ocean
BAHAMAS
CUBA
The Turks and Caicos Is.
Yucatan Pen.
Cayman Is.
HAITI
Puerto Rico
Virgin Is.
ANTIGUA
Montserrat
Guadeloupe
BELIZE
JAMAICA
DOMINICAN REPUBLIC
DOMINICA
Martinique
HONDURAS
ST. LUCIA
Caribbean Sea
Pacific Ocean
GUATEMALA
EL SALVADOR
NICARAGUA
BARBADOS
GRENADA
PANAMA
L. Maracaibo
COSTA RICA
Panama Canal
VENEZUELA
COLOMBIA

ALMALONGA, GUATEMALA: GIANNI TORTOLI/PHOTO RESEARCHERS

VOLUME 24

South and Central America

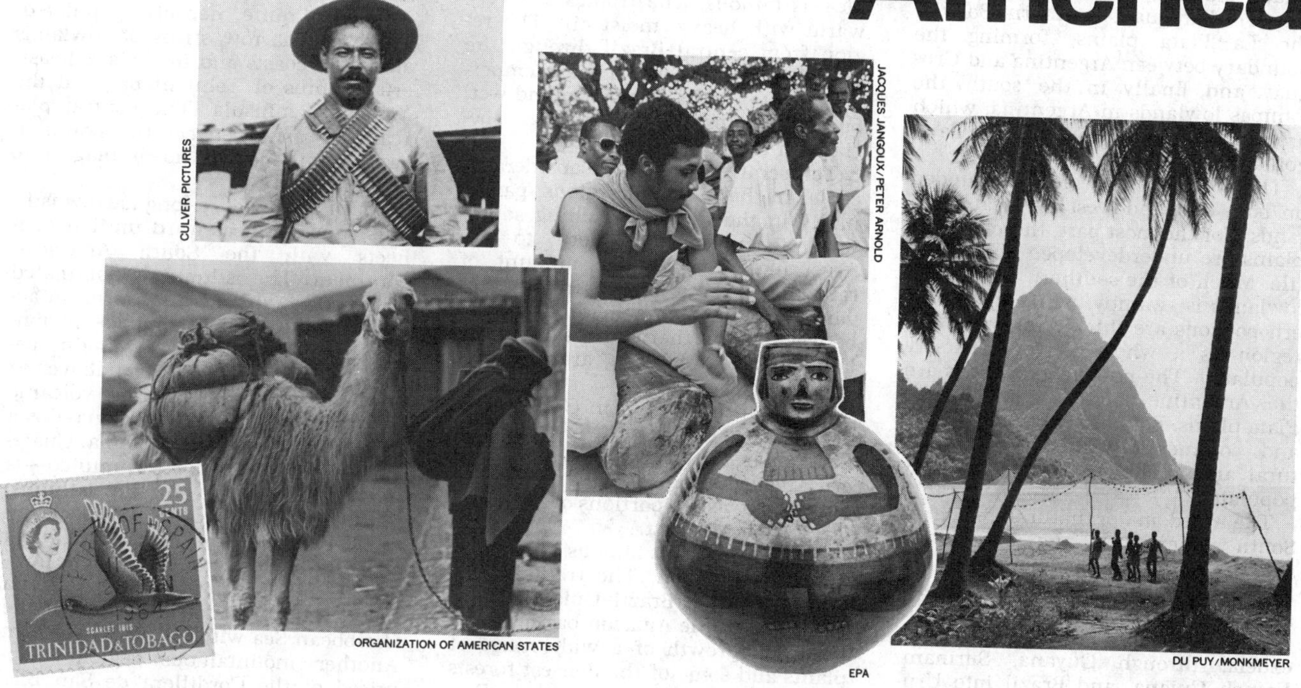

CULVER PICTURES
ORGANIZATION OF AMERICAN STATES
JACQUES JANGOUX/PETER ARNOLD
EPA
DU PUY/MONKMEYER

This region comprises the vast area of the Americas that lies south of the United States. It includes the entire continent of South America, the country of Mexico, the long isthmus that links the two American continents—consisting of the nations of Guatemala, El Salvador, Honduras, Nicaragua, Costa Rica, Panama, and the former British dependency of Belize, which became independent on September 21, 1981—and the islands of the Caribbean Sea, usually referred to collectively as the West Indies. In this volume we will consider, first, South America (the continent) and then Central America (the remaining areas described above).

South and Central America as a whole has often been called Latin America, since most of the countries in the area derive their modern civilizations from Spain and Portugal, which colonized them following the discovery of the Americas in 1492 A.D.

Although most of the nations south of the United States are actually Latin American, there are exceptions, particularly the small republics of Guyana and Surinam on the northern coast of South America, and several of the Caribbean islands that were colonized by the British, French, and Dutch. In this volume we will not distinguish between the Latin and non-Latin countries, since they share common geographic and economic features as well as common social and political problems; and also because they are neighbors.

The population of South and Central America—so defined—is approximately 375 million people. South America's total population roughly doubles that of Central America. The average annual rate of growth in most of these countries is high—approximately three percent. The problems of poverty and social conflict that face this area are in no small degree created by the failure of most of the nations to control the rapid rate of population growth.

The Land.

South America. South America, the world's fourth largest continent, is located in the southern half of the western hemisphere. It has an area of nearly 7 million square miles. It is bordered on the north by the Caribbean Sea, on the east by the Atlantic Ocean, on the south by the Drake Passage, which separates it from Antarctica, and on the west by the Pacific Ocean. It is connected to Central America by the Isthmus of Panama.

South America may be generally divided into three geographic regions. In the west is the great cordillera that is dominated by the Andes and that runs parallel to the Pacific. The high mountains of the Andes system tower over a narrow coastal plain in the west, isolating it from the interior lowlands. Mt. Aconcagua in Argentina is the highest peak in the western hemisphere, standing 22,834 feet above sea level.

The Andes run along the entire western coast of the continent and are frequently interspersed with deep river valleys and plateau regions. Many of the mountains are volcanic, and over the ages they have deposited over the adjacent valleys a thick crust of lava, resulting in extremely fertile soil deposits. Earthquakes are frequent in the great mountain system.

Large, dry deserts are another main feature of the cordillera, notably the Atacama Desert in northern Chile. Lake Titicaca, on the border between Peru and Bolivia, is the largest lake on the continent other than Venezuela's Lake Maracaibo, which is actually an inlet of the Caribbean Sea.

The second of South America's major natural regions is the interior lowlands, which are densely forested in the north and swampy or arid in the south. The lowlands are formed by the basins of the continent's mighty river systems—the Orinoco, Amazon, and Paraná-Paraguay. These great frontier plains include, running southward, the Llanos formed by the Orinoco basin in Venezuela, the Amazon basin, one of the world's most extensive lowland regions, the Paraná-Paraguay plains that slope down from the eastern base of the Andes to form the Gran Chaco plains of northern Argentina, western Paraguay, southern Bolivia, the La Plata plains, forming the boundary between Argentina and Uruguay, and, finally, in the south, the Pampas lowlands in Argentina, which are bounded on the south by the Patagonia Plateau.

This vast plains region is bounded on both east and west by great highlands. For the most part, these interior plains are underdeveloped and unfertile. Much of the southern part of the lowlands is swampy, while the northern portions are thickly forested. The region as a whole is very sparsely populated. The notable exceptions are the Argentine Pampas and the La Plata plains. Both are extremely fertile and commercially thriving agricultural areas. The La Plata is heavily populated.

The third major natural region of South America is the continental shield, which is comprised of the Brazil-Guiana Highlands. Averaging about 3000 feet above sea level, the highlands extend eastward from Venezuela, through Guyana, Surinam, French Guiana, and Brazil into Uruguay. They run along most of the continent's northeastern and eastern Atlantic coastline. They are highest on the Venezuela-Guyana border and in eastern Brazil, where peaks reach over 9000 feet above sea level.

The eastern highlands are much older and lower than the Andes in the west. Some scientists believe that the Brazilian Highlands formed the point where South America once joined with Africa, prior to a hypothetical "continental drift," which may have occurred over 100 million years ago.

The Guiana Highlands, which lie mainly between the Orinoco and Amazon rivers, are quite rugged, wild, and very sparsely populated. The Brazilian Highlands are much more rolling and rounded, and they hinder access to the Atlantic. There are practically no coastal plains between the Atlantic Ocean and the Brazilian Highlands, which are much more densely populated than the Guiana Highlands.

Most of South America's great river systems flow through the Brazil-Guiana Highlands and empty into the Atlantic Ocean. The main exception to this is the Magdalena River, which rises in the cordillera and flows northward into the Caribbean Sea.

Most of the continent's coastline is rocky and high, and has very few good harbors, with the notable exception of that of Rio de Janeiro. Nonetheless, because of the wild and barren conditions of the continent's interior region, 90 percent of the South American population is clustered near the coasts.

Climate and vegetation. South America is extremely varied both in climate and in vegetation. Most of the continent is in a tropical zone, characterized by the heavy rainfall for which the Amazon basin region—for example—is famous. The tropics are very warm with heavy, moist air. The region from central Brazil through the Gran Chaco in Argentina has a temperate climate that is also warm and wet, but broken by long droughts, especially in the cool winters.

Temperatures become considerably cooler in the highland regions, particularly in the Andes stretching southward from southern Peru to the Argentine Pampas. The amount of rainfall in these mountain climates varies, but the area generally tends to be wet. The northern Andes, from Colombia to central Peru, are both hot and wet.

The Atacama Desert in Chile is one of the world's more arid regions. The Patagonian-Fuegian Steppe in southern Argentina is also an extremely dry desert area, as are portions of Venezuela's Caribbean coast.

South America is famous for its rich natural vegetation. The tropical rain forests of the Brazil-Guiana Highlands and of the Amazon basin have a luxuriant growth of a wide range of plants and some of the densest forests in the world, while the Atacama Desert is one of the most barren areas in the world. The central plains are characterized by mixed forests and grasslands in the north, shading into broad grasslands that extend southward from central Brazil to east-central Argentina. Most of Venezuela and Colombia is grassland or desert.

Central America. Central America is a very mountainous region. Mexico, for instance, has two major mountain ranges—the Sierra Madre Oriental in the east and the Sierra Madre Occidental in the west—that run parallel to each other. They border the main interior region of the Mexican Plateau, which is quite densely populated. There are narrow strips of lowlands along the coasts and in the southeastern Isthmus of Tehuantepec and the Yucatán Peninsula. The central plateau has basins between the mountain ranges, but there is no drainage into the sea.

South of Mexico, a long narrow isthmus runs southeastward until it connects with the South American continent. The isthmus is dominated by central highlands that form an active volcanic and earthquake region. Elevations vary greatly, averaging between 4000 and 12,000 feet above sea level. A series of interior volcanic ranges runs from the Nicaragua-Costa Rica border to central Panama. Guatemala's volcanic peak—Tajumulco—is the highest peak on the isthmus, standing 13,846 feet above sea level.

In Panama, the great highland chain is broken suddenly by the lowland Canal Zone, where the Panama Canal was constructed to connect the Caribbean Sea with the Pacific Ocean. Another mountainous region—comprised of the Cordillera de San Blas and the Serranía del Darién—runs east from the Canal Zone to the Colombian highlands of South America.

TORTUOUS MOUNTAIN ROADS *lead up to La Paz, Bolivia, the highest capital in the world. South America's varied and hostile landscape has much to do with its fragmented history.*

UNITED NATIONS

Other than the narrow plains of southern Mexico, the isthmus has few lowlands. There are some very narrow strips of lowland along the Pacific coast, but the plains that run along the Caribbean coast are more extensive, notably in Belize and Guatemala. Most of the plains, however, are swamplands, and some are thickly forested.

Many small rivers and streams run into the Caribbean, making it generally more accessible than the Pacific. The Caribbean coast has many small towns with ports and harbors, and it is much more densely populated than the Pacific coast.

The Caribbean islands—the West Indies—are also dominated by mountainous terrains that feature considerable volcanic activity. For the most part, the West Indies' highlands are an extension of the mountain systems that cover the isthmus from southern Mexico to Nicaragua. These mountain structures run from west to east and rise beneath the Caribbean to form the Greater Antilles archipelago.

Most of the islands have only narrow strips of lowlands that, typically, run along the coastlines. Cuba has larger plains regions along the shores, as well as among the central interior hills—a large region that is flanked on the east by the extremely rugged Sierra Maestra mountains, and on the west by the lower Sierra de los Órganos range.

Rivers are not a very significant feature of Central America. The most important ones in Mexico are the Río Bravo (called the Rio Grande in the United States), the Yaqui, the Río Grande de Santiago, and the Río Balsas. On the isthmus, the chief rivers are the Polochic and Motagua in Guatemala; the Ulúa, Agúan, Paulaya, and Patuca in Honduras; the Coco along the Honduras-Nicaraguan border; the Prinzapolca, Tuma, and Escondido in Nicaragua; and the San Juan, which runs along the Nicaragua-Costa Rica border. In the West Indies, the only notable river is the Cauto in Cuba.

The only important lakes in Central America are Lake Nicaragua and Lake Managua, both part of Nicaragua's Pacific lowland region.

Mexico is bordered on the north by the United States, part of the North American continent, and Panama is bordered on the southeast by Colombia, which lies in the northwest corner of the South American continent. Otherwise, all of Central America is bordered by water. Mexico is bordered on the west by the Pacific Ocean and on the east by the Gulf of Mexico and the Caribbean Sea. The isthmus is bordered on the west and south by the Pacific Ocean, and on the north and east by the Caribbean Sea. The West Indies lie mainly in the Caribbean Sea, and are also washed by the Atlantic Ocean and the Gulf of Mexico.

The presence of extensive and rugged coastal mountains results in fewer good harbors than might otherwise exist. The chief ports include those in the Canal Zone of Panama, Veracruz, Coatzacoalcos, and Mazatlán in Mexico, and Havana and Nuevitas in Cuba.

GERHARD E. GSCHEIDLE/PETER ARNOLD

BRAZILIAN LABORER, *a mestizo, or European-Indian mix, typical of the continent.*

Climate and vegetation. The climate of Central America varies with the elevation of the land. Even in the highest regions, though, temperatures are cool, not cold, and as elevations drop, temperatures become extremely high.

Rainfall is very heavy in the eastern portions of Mexico and the isthmus, where moist Caribbean wind currents prevail. The lowlands in these areas are extremely hot as well as wet. While the Pacific coast plains are nearly as hot, they are much drier since they are shielded from the Caribbean currents by mountain ranges.

Dense forests cover most of the isthmus, particularly on the Caribbean coasts. The interior plateau of Mexico is extremely dry in contrast to the coasts, and vegetation there is scant, consisting mostly of sparse grasslands.

The West Indies, in general, have hot year-round temperatures and are frequently hit by hurricanes that sweep across the Caribbean. Most of the islands receive fairly large annual rainfalls, while Jamaica and Puerto Rico receive very heavy rains. Vegetation consists mostly of relatively thick rain forests.

The people.

South and Central America share a similar variety of ethnic and cultural backgrounds. The predominate races are American Indian, European, and Negro (black). For the most part, these races have been mixed by intermarriage, notably between white Europeans and Indians, resulting in the mestizo population.

The American Indians inhabited the area for many centuries prior to the Iberian (Spanish and Portuguese) conquests, which began after 1492 A.D. The types of Indian cultures, however, varied widely, as they were largely isolated from each other. The most advanced cultures existing at that time were those of the Aztecs of Mexico's central plateau and the Incas of the Andes in Peru. The great Mayan civilization that flourished in Central America before 1000 A.D. had deteriorated by the time of the conquests.

In addition, there were many other Indian groups, like the Caribs, who lived in the West Indies islands, notably in the Lesser Antilles; the Chibchas were in the Colombian Andes. There were hundreds of different tribes and at least as many different languages spread throughout South and Central America. Many of the tribes were highly civilized and sustained themselves as agriculturalists. They lived in permanent villages and developed elaborate social and political organizations. Many other tribes consisted essentially of nomadic rovers who were constantly at war with neighboring tribes, and who seldom developed any stable socio-political or economic system.

During the Iberian (mainly Spanish) conquests, large numbers of the native population were killed defending themselves against the white intruders. Even more died from prolonged disease epidemics that resulted from contact with the European peoples. Most of the Indians that did survive were enslaved and their civilizations disappeared.

By 1700 A.D. only a handful of the native Indians had survived. Most of those who survived lived in the South American interior, where the Europeans did not care to venture. Many of these tribes still exist today, in essentially the same isolated condition in which they have survived for centuries.

While the Spanish were conquering most of South and Central America, the Portuguese were colonizing Brazil. Between 1550 and 1850 the Spanish and Portuguese brought millions of Africans to the New World to use as slave labor. Since then, blacks and mulattoes have constituted a third major racial group in the area.

Today, the populations of most of the countries in South and Central America are overwhelmingly mestizo—mixed European and Indian. There are countless numbers of different mestizo strains. Black populations are particularly heavy where the colonial plantation economic system had thrived—especially in Haiti, Cuba, and Brazil.

In Central America—between Mexico and Panama—about three-quarters of the people are mestizo, although Costa Rica is predominantly European. In the West Indies, blacks constitute a majority of the population.

In South America there is more diversity. The countries along the Pacific coast, except for Chile, have considerable numbers of Indians. Mestizos make up most of the remaining population in those countries, while the people of Chile, Argentina, and Uruguay are mostly of white European stock. Brazil has a wide range of racial mixtures, and mulattoes make up a large proportion of the population. The interior regions of the continent (except in Argentina) are populated mostly by Indians.

Nearly all the people of South and Central America live in highlands and plateau regions. In South America these regions are rarely over 200 miles from the coastlines, and nearly two-thirds of the continent's population is clustered along the Atlantic coast that extends southward from Brazil. In Central America the populated highlands also tend to be near the coast, except in Mexico and Cuba, where many people also live on interior plateaus. The interior of South America is very sparsely populated and is virtually isolated from the modern world. Roughly 250 million people live in South America, with about half that amount in Brazil alone. Mexico and the Central American isthmus have the greatest concentration of people. Mexico alone has 70 million of Central America's total population, which is close to 125 million. Cuba, with 10 million people, is the most populous country of the West Indies.

High birthrates and rates of immigration (now being limited in most countries), along with increased life expectancies, have given South and Central America one of the fastest growing populations in the world. This phenomenal increase has contributed heavily to the serious economic, social, and political problems that these nations face.

Populations are generally growing in urban areas, but rural areas also have growing populations, though to a much smaller degree. There is keen competition for good farmland, since most of it is owned and managed by the landed aristocracy, which constitutes only a tiny percentage of the total number of farmers.

Most of the cities in Central and South America were founded early in the colonial era. They were carefully planned and usually laid out symmetrically around a central plaza. Areas are often set aside in these cities for the Indian population, which retains, to some degree, its own cultural unity.

With the rapid increase of urbanization in the 20th century, there has also been a widespread and massive development of peripheral squatter settlements. These shantytowns are usually crudely constructed and are dangerously overcrowded with people who migrated to the cities and found jobs, but no homes. Housing shortages plague most of the cities in this part of the world.

Economy.

South America. Fourth in size of the continents, South America is handicapped by its location, for more than two-thirds of its area lies within the tropics and the tropical rain belt. The present underdeveloped nature of much of South America may be attributed directly to the inefficiency of humans working in hot and humid climates; and indirectly to the impossibility of crossing the huge and tangled forests resulting from these natural conditions.

The great forest of the Amazon basin is the largest equatorial forest in the world and one of the world's greatest sources of natural rubber. The Amazon River, in the northern part of South America, is the great, and was for many years the only, waterway system making it possible to penetrate the vast forests. No river rivals the Amazon in volume and in number and size of tributaries.

Increasingly the Amazon region is being penetrated by highways, and air transport now links once inaccessible areas with the developed parts of South America.

Southern South America is separated by the Andes mountain system into two major countries and two major economic units—Argentina and Chile. Southern Brazil and northern Argentina, the northern part of this southern peninsula area of South America, constitute one of the world's leading food-exporting regions. Production is far beyond consumption, and the area around the Plata River (Río de la Plata) is one of the greatest surplus food-producing regions in the world.

Argentina is a principal maize (corn) exporting country, supplying as much as half that commodity and also nearly half the linseed that enters international trade. Wheat is the principal export of Argentina.

This great food-producing region is also important as a grazing land for cattle and is one of the world's important sources of meat. Argentina exports considerable quantities of beef, wool, and mutton.

The wealth of Chile, a narrow country bounded by the Andes on the east and the Pacific on the west, is chiefly in minerals. It ranks high as a world producer of copper, and a large share of its exports consists of nitrates.

COFFEE BERRIES *being stripped from a branch. Brazil leads the world in coffee, and also exports other crops.*

MONKMEYER

The western coast of South America, including Peru, Ecuador, and Colombia, produces minerals chiefly, but Ecuador until very recently led the world in the production of the cacao bean, which is still a leading export. Colombia has important platinum mines and supplies a large part of the world's demand for that metal. The emerald mines at Muzo in the eastern Andes are famous.

Coffee makes up more than one-half the value of Brazil's exports. Other leading exports include cotton and cacao. Bolivia is the world's most important producer of tin and antimony. These and other metals account for practically all of the country's exports.

Venezuela ranks high in world oil production. The chief source is found in the Lake Maracaibo area, but newer fields in other areas are also significant. Venezuela's vast interior Orinoco region is important for its iron ore and hydroelectric power potential. This industry enables Venezuela to enjoy a healthy balance of trade.

Brazil occupies an area greater than that of the conterminous United States and lies almost completely in the tropics. To the climate and the volcanic soils, rich in iron, may be attributed the fact that nearly 70 percent of the world's coffee is grown in Brazil, nearly half the world's total coming from the state of São Paulo alone, where more than 3 million acres are planted in coffee. The Brazilian highlands in the east have vast mineral resources, with reserves of high-grade iron ore among the richest in the world.

To a large extent, South America is still a producer of raw materials. The continent as a whole lacks the capital and skills on a broad enough scale to launch needed development. It is hoped that funds available from the Alliance for Progress and other sources will aid South America to realize its great potential wealth.

Long-distance surface transport is difficult, as the vast interiors are almost impenetrable and the mountains of the west form great barriers to communication between the two coasts. There are no good seaports in the west and few in the east and south.

As yet, South America maintains its motto, "Down to the sea and away to the North," meaning that there is little internal trade, but raw materials from mines and farms are sent down the rivers, railroads, and highways to the sea and are then shipped to other countries, especially to Britain and the United States. From these countries South America imports manufactured goods: machinery, cotton textiles, iron and steel.

Central America. Central America is also handicapped by many of its natural features. Located mostly in the tropical zone, its low-lying plains are frequently too hot and barren for successful cultivation. Mountains cover

URBAN RENEWAL *in Castro's Cuba. A new, modern day-care nursery for poor working mothers has been built in the midst of a famous slum in Havana; the slum is slowly disappearing.*

most of the area and act as isolating factors between countries. They often shield coastal areas (particularly the Pacific coast of the Central American isthmus) from receiving greatly needed rains. Many parts of Central America are subject to periodic volcanic destruction, and the West Indies are often hit by devastating hurricanes. There are only a few usable rivers and access to the sea is often hampered by rocky highlands and mountains that rise sharply off the coast. Thus, because of poor overland communication, the oceans provide the primary means of transporting goods into and out of Central America. Highways and rail systems are generally discontinuous and inadequate for heavy traffic.

Most economic activity occurs in the more temperate highland regions and along the seacoast. Although there is a scarcity of fertile land, agriculture is a major source of income in Central America, and a great number of people live as subsistence farmers. Bananas and coffee are the chief cash crops, and cacao is also important. Sugar cane is the leading crop in Cuba and on several other islands. Maize (corn) is widely grown for domestic use and is the staple food crop for most of the rural families.

Large plantations—often owned and operated by U. S. businesses, except in Cuba, and to a lesser degree, Mexico—account for most of the agricultural production. Cuba's chief crop, sugar, is grown on state-owned farms and collectives. The Mexican government has slowly (since the early 1900's) converted large private holdings into farm collectives run by groups of individual small farmers.

Outside of Cuba and Mexico, most plantations and large farms are owned—as they have been for generations—by a landed aristocracy that dominates the rural economy and often has more political power than the merchants, businessmen, and industrialists in the cities. Small farmers are left with scarce bits of leftover land that they are barely able to cultivate. Most farmers do not own land, but work under peasantlike conditions for the wealthy landlords. For this reason, rural poverty is widespread and is a major source of political discontent. Many communist and left-wing activists base their popularity on their appeal to the rural poor, to whom they promise land reform and redistribution of wealth.

Mining is a traditional source of profits in Central America, particularly in Mexico and along the isthmus. For many years the production of iron ore, copper, gold, silver, zinc, and lead, have contributed to Mexico's national income, and in recent years petroleum has been added to this list. With important discoveries in the 1970's Mexico's production of oil has considerably increased.

The great mountain systems of Central America are rich in mineral deposits. Honduras mines large quantities of silver, while El Salvador, Guatemala, Nicaragua, and Costa Rica all produce considerable amounts of gold. Copper is mined in Guatemala, and manganese in Panama. Bauxite—used in aluminum production—is now being mined in the West Indies, particularly in Jamaica, Haiti, and the Dominican Republic.

Forestry and fishing are minor economic activities in the region. Mexico has the largest fish intake, while Honduras is an important exporter of wood products.

Food processing is the major industrial activity of Central America. Outside of Mexico, there is very little heavy industry. Mexico is easily the industrial giant of the region. Iron and steel, petrochemicals, and consumer goods are all produced in large quantity. Petroleum refining is active.

Guatemala and El Salvador have led the way toward developing diverse and thriving light industries as a basis for strengthening regional cooperation and trade activity through the Central American Common Market (CACM; organized in 1960). The CACM members are Guatemala, Honduras, El Salvador, Nicaragua, and Costa Rica. They are protected by a common tariff that has resulted in a significant increase in trade activity among them. Mexico is a member of the Latin American Free Trade Association (LAFTA). Its co-members are all South American nations. Several of the West Indies nations have been united economically and culturally to each other and to several of the small South American Caribbean coast republics by the Caribbean Community and Common Market (CARICOM).

The rise of industrialization in Central America has spurred urbanization and has given rise to a new social class. The urban middle class—merchants, small businessmen, and workers (especially when united through labor unions)—now rivals the landed aristocracy in economic and political power. This development has caused considerable political tension, because the aristocracy has controlled political life in most Central American countries for generations, and because the industrial middle classes are growing steadily in numbers and in importance. Left-wing activists generally support the workers' cause, thereby gaining popular approval.

Central America's economy is essentially based on supplying the United States, Canada, and Western Europe with raw materials (minerals and wood products) and food products (sugar, coffee, and bananas). In return, machinery, consumer goods, fuels, and foodstuffs are imported.

One of the weakest features of most of the national economies is an overdependence on one or few basic products. A bad crop one year, a drop in the market value, or natural crop devastation may cause a serious economic depression with resulting food shortages, inflation, and unemployment in the affected country. Diversification attempts have been slow and still have a long way to go.

Another typical problem is the need to attract foreign investments (usually from the United States, Canada, or Britain) to finance economic development. This has led to charges of foreign interference and exploitation, yet national capital is rarely available to replace lost foreign dollars. Incidents of foreign business firms persuading government officials to grant special favors have added fuel to this controversy. Even when there are no cases of corruption or interference, there are still charges that profits made in Central America by foreigners do not benefit the exploited regions.

Meanwhile, when attempts have been made to nationalize major aspects of the economy, lack of the necessary capital has often led to failure. Foreign investors are naturally wary about investing in politically unpredictable situations, where there is no capital available to sustain the economy. Thus, without foreign investment economic chaos results and, very often, political turmoil follows.

JANE LATTA/KAY REESE & ASSOCIATES

AMERICAN MUSEUM OF NATURAL HISTORY

THE INDIAN CULTURES *of Central America were rich and varied. The earliest was the Olmec, whose huge stone heads* (left, above) *survive. Most advanced were the Maya, who fashioned the clay censer* (right); *in New Empire days they built the Castillo* (below) *in Yucatán.*

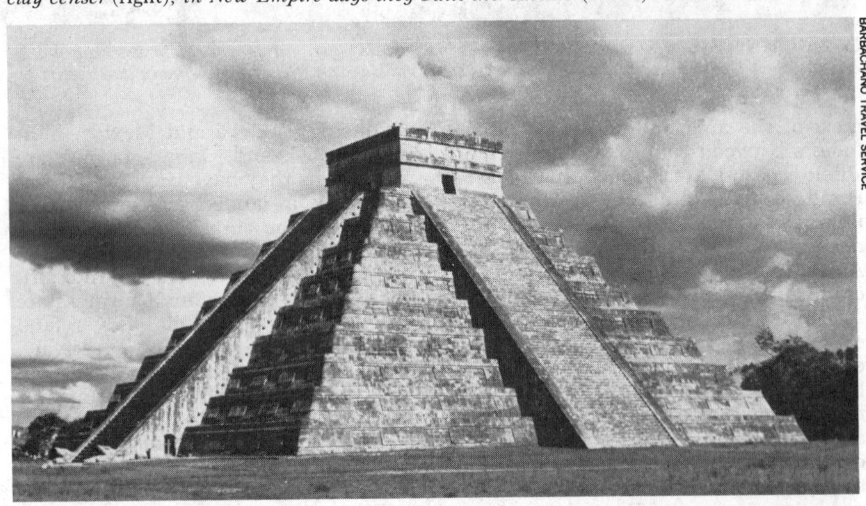

BARBACHANO TRAVEL SERVICE

History

After Christopher Columbus discovered the Americas in 1492, Spanish and Portuguese forces sailed toward South and Central America in search of gold and silver that could be shipped home. The Spaniards were particularly successful in their endeavor. In the process of stripping bare the accumulated wealth of many great Indian centers, they brought South and Central American history into a new era—the colonial period.

While most modern histories of this region begin with the Spanish-Portuguese (and later, to a much smaller extent, the French and British) conquests and colonization, there is a long Indian history that predates Columbus and the Age of Discovery. This period is called the pre-Columbian era.

The pre-Columbian era. Indians inhabited many areas in South and Central America in prehistoric times. Most of them were hunters and nomads before the extinction of the large mammals that sustained them.

One of the earliest civilizations was created by the Central American Olmec between about 500 B.C. and 1150 A.D. The Olmec were sedentary farmers whose culture first appeared in the lowlands along the coast of the Gulf of Mexico. It eventually extended as far south as Costa Rica. The Olmec developed a crude commercial economy based on local intertribal trade, and they fashioned huge sculptures, built pyramids, and apparently worshiped a nature deity.

About 200 B.C. a great religious and commercial center had its early beginnings in the metropolis of Teotihuacán, located near modern-day Mexico City, in Mexico's east-central valley region. The civilization that radiated from this great city covered vast areas (between Mexico and Guatemala) during its greatest era, between 300 A.D. and 900 A.D. It is called the Old Empire. Sophisticated systems of religion and commerce were developed at Teotihuacán, and high forms of culture that featured grandiose architecture with rich sculptural detail. The city was, perhaps, the most splendid one in all of pre-Columbian America. The famous and imposing Pyramids of the Sun and the Moon graced the city, as well as several temples, lesser pyramids, and a palace.

The Maya. Farther south the mighty Mayan civilization also flourished between about 300 A.D. and 900 A.D. The Maya Indians inhabited Mexico's Yucatan Peninsula and neighboring regions, vast portions of Guatemala, and a small part of western Honduras. Very early in Mayan history, sedentary agricultural communities arose. Also prior to the Old Empire of 300 A.D. to 900 A.D., the Maya developed an elaborate hieroglyphic writing system along with a calendar.

Probably influenced by the Olmec culture, the Maya made great advances in art, language, and mathematics. They constructed magnificent temples, huge pyramids, and carved stone stelae. They produced brilliantly colored frescoes and wall murals, as well as sculptural reliefs and ceramics to adorn the interior walls and rooms of their public buildings, pyramids, and temples. Their art and architecture are considered to be the finest, and their mathematics and writing systems the most original and advanced, of the pre-Columbian period.

After 1000 A.D., Mayan culture was centered in northern Yucatán, and the period from 1000 A.D. to about 1400 A.D. is known as the New Empire. During this period the Toltec Indians invaded Yucatán from the Mexican plateau, exerted great influence on Mayan civilization, and in turn were absorbed into a fusion of Mayan and Toltec cultures.

The Mayan-Toltec culture never reached the heights achieved during the Old Empire. Other neighboring tribes warred against them and civil strife dominated the post-Old Empire period and the decadent years that followed 1400. By the time of the Spanish conquest of the area, the Mayan-Toltec culture had long since suffered a major decline.

Mixtec and Zapotec. The Mixtec and Zapotec Indians both inhabited southern and southwestern Mexico. The Mixtec were most numerous in the modern states of Oaxaca and Puebla, while the Zapotec lived primarily in southern Oaxaca and on the Isthmus of Tehuantepec. It is not certain when either culture first appeared, but both seem to have been influenced considerably by the Olmec, and later, by the Toltec. The Zapotec had established a thriving civilization with an advanced culture as early as 200 B.C. Monte Albán was their capital and Mitla was their religious center. Both cities—exquisite examples of Zapotec architecture—were captured, after 1300 A.D., along with most other Zapotec cities, by the Mixtec, who staged an invasion from the north.

The Zapotec and Mixtec, who had been at war with each other for many years, united in the mid-1400's against a common foe—the mighty Aztec. The Zapotec eventually betrayed the Mixtec, allying themselves with the Aztec. Early in the next century, they betrayed the Aztec as well, by joining the ranks of the Spanish armies that had recently arrived to conquer the Indian nations. The Mixtec carried on a relentless battle against the Spaniards, but were finally subdued.

The Andes. In South America, the most significant pre-Columbian cultures were located in the Andes, from Colombia to Chile, and particularly in Peru. In northeastern Peru, the Chavín established what may have been the earliest Andean civilization of any importance. It developed about the same time as the Olmec culture in Mexico, and there are many similarities between the two, notably in art, architecture, and religion. The Chavín culture flourished between about 700 B.C. and 200 B.C. It was highly advanced for its time, and featured elaborate temples and exquisite pottery. Chavín culture had a great impact on later developments in the surrounding region, particularly influencing the Paracas, also of Peru.

The Mochica, on Peru's northern coast, developed a sophisticated social and political system, and were adept in architecture and engineering. Their civilization rose about 100 B.C. and ended late in the first millennium A.D. After Mochica's fall, the Chimu—strongly influenced by the Mochica—built a string of highly organized cities in the same area. The most important of these was the desert metropolis of Chan Chan, set in an extensively irrigated area. The Chimu were finally conquered by the Inca in the mid-1400's A.D.

Contemporaneous with the Mochica–Chimu empires, was that of the Nazca on the southern coast of Peru. Apparently influenced by the Chavín and Paracas, the Nazca excelled in their crafting of ceramics and textiles. They were apparently absorbed into the great Inca empire at about the same time as the Chimu.

Another outstanding culture was established at Tiahuanaco in western Bolivia. It flourished roughly from 1000 A.D. to 1300 A.D., and had a great impact on other contemporary Andean civilizations. It is especially famous for its magnificent stone construction.

In Colombia, the Chibcha had a stable agricultural society that was complex and industrious, if not splendid. Other agricultural states were established by the Aymara around Lake Titicaca in Peru and Bolivia, and by the Araucanians in central Chile. The Guaraní in southern Brazil and Paraguay, and the Tupi in Brazil's Amazon basin region, were also successful agriculturalists. They had elaborate mythologies and religious systems. All were conquered by the Spaniards, who were disappointed by the lack of wealth and grandeur found in most of these Indian civilizations—except those of the Inca and the Aztec.

The Inca. Cuzco, in Peru, was the capital of the great Inca empire that extended over vast regions along the west coast of South America, from Ecuador to Chile. The Inca first rose to power about 1200 A.D., but the empire reached the height of its expansion under the reigns of Pachacuti (c 1440–1471) and his son Topa Inca (1471–1493).

The Inca empire was tightly unified under a strong central administration. It was controlled by an emperor, the Inca, who ruled by divine right. The priests and nobles constituted the upper echelons of Inca society.

Great advances were made in field irrigation and drainage by the Inca, since agriculture was central to the economic life of the nation—even though the natural terrain was not promising. Manufacturing activities included sophisticated textile and ceramic crafting, and metal works industries. Although the Inca are well known for their vast stores of gold and silver, mostly robbed by the Spanish, they also mined great quantities of copper and produced bronze.

The Inca established a thriving centralized state. The emperor had absolute authority and the state owned all mines, roads, cultivated fields, and buildings other than houses. The state also controlled most aspects of Inca lives, but it in turn gave them military protection and provided economic and social stability.

The Inca were adept in architecture and engineering, as evidenced by their elaborate road systems and imposing public and religious buildings, built of stone with incredible precision. Their religion was organized around elaborate rituals and the worship of a pantheon of deities, foremost being the sun god.

In 1532 the Spanish adventurer Francisco Pizarro, welcomed by the Inca, seized and executed the emperor, Atahualpa, and proceeded to lead his tiny Spanish army to a swift and total conquest of the proud Inca civilization. The cities were plundered and stripped of their wealth as South America entered a dramatically new period in its history.

The Aztec. Tenochtitlán, in Mexico's central valley, was the capital of the mighty Aztec empire. It is the site of modern-day Mexico City. At its height—just before the Spanish conquest—the empire included territories north of the great valley, and extended as far south as modern-day Guatemala. The Aztec gradually filtered into the valley in the 1100's and 1200's. From the northern highlands they

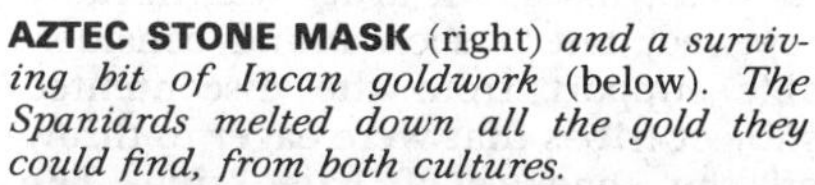

AZTEC STONE MASK (right) *and a surviving bit of Incan goldwork* (below). *The Spaniards melted down all the gold they could find, from both cultures.*

LAIMA/DRUSKIS/EPA

EPA/SCALA

AZTEC DRAWING *of a battle between fierce Aztec warriors and the Spanish and Indian allies. The Spanish were helped by the horses, unknown to the Indians, and their own iron swords.*

brought with them an essentially nomadic culture that had been greatly influenced by several of the more prosperous tribes that also roamed the hills. Already a mixture of various tribal traditions, the Aztec culture was reshaped further by its contacts with the powerful Toltec, who had been established in the valley several centuries before the arrival of the Aztec.

The Aztec were fierce and skilled warriors who established their capital in the early 1300's, and who then embarked on an era of conquest and expansion. Their greatest conquests were made in the 1400's. One of their most notable was that of the Mixtec and Zapotec, who had been fighting with each other for years before joining arms against the Aztec.

The Aztec culture made great strides in architecture and engineering, and mathematics, art, and sculpture also were extensively developed. Tenochtitlán, in the midst of a lake, was a beautiful city, with dikes, canals, and a great sacred pyramid. It represented the zenith of Aztec cultural achievement.

The Aztec also had a thriving economy based on highly advanced forms of agriculture, commerce, and marketing. Precious metals were extensively mined and the dazzling Aztec wealth in gold and silver was a major reason for the Spaniards' campaigns against them.

The Aztec religion had an elaborate pantheon headed by the war god, Huitzilopochti, to whom, unfortunately, thousands of human beings were sacrificed each year. Aztec society was dedicated to war, heroes, and deities. The most important priesthood was that of Huitzilopochti. Most of the nobles were high-ranking officials in the Aztec army, which was powerful, strict, and efficient. The ranks of the army were filled largely by captured Aztec subjects, the remainder of whom were used for field and public works labor, or were sacrificed on the bloody altars of the war god.

In general, the many lesser tribes that had been conquered, subjugated, and incorporated into the Aztec empire were exploited and kept in line by sheer force. When the Spaniard Hernán Cortés invaded this mighty nation in 1520, his small army was initially repelled, but it soon found considerable support from the discontented subject tribes that were eager to throw off the shackles of Aztec rule. The tribes soon discovered, however, that they had not gained freedom, only a new master.

Indian influence. A large number of Indians were wiped out during and after the Iberian conquests that swept through the great civilizations of South and Central America. They were killed in battle and above all were decimated by European diseases. Those who survived were held in bondage and forced into hard labor and slavery. For centuries, Indian culture was repressed and the Indian population only gradually increased again to the numbers it had attained before the conquests.

The value of Indian cultures, however, has received more recognition in the present century, and many of these cultures have been to a certain extent renewed. Indian influence today, is particularly strong in areas where great Indian civilizations existed, as in Mexico and Peru, and in areas where there was a large Indian population, as in Paraguay. There the language of the Guaraní Indians is still spoken by a majority of the people.

In other areas, where there were fewer Indians, or where the Indians had not developed high cultures, the Indian population was rapidly absorbed or driven into remote areas that were found unattractive by European settlers.

Iberian background.

The two nations of Europe's Iberian Peninsula, Portugal and Spain, were the earliest colonizers of South and Central America. Situated on one of the frontiers of medieval Christianity, they had a varied heritage from both Latin Christian and Muslim sources. They also had a tradition of religious warfare between Christianity and Islam.

Spain. In 1469 Ferdinand of Aragon and Isabella of Castile had married, and together they forged a united kingdom. In 1492 their Christian forces conquered the Muslim kingdom of Granada in southern Spain. This victory brought to a close the period of conflict that was waged for the control of Spain, known as the *Reconquista,* or Reconquest.

Unification resulted in a great surge of energy and a drive for further expansion. The Spanish monarchs sponsored a voyage of discovery to find a new route to the Indies, the source of spices and luxury goods important in the markets of Europe. Christopher Columbus, a Genoan by birth, was equipped with a fleet of three ships, and he set out to find the Indies by sailing west.

Portugal. The Portuguese directed their energies to commerce and maritime exploration, but had a smaller population and fewer material resources than the Spanish. Portuguese seamen discovered and explored the west coast of Africa, however, and in 1487–1488 Bartholomeu Dias succeeded in rounding the southern tip of Africa. This led in 1498 to the even greater discovery by Vasco da Gama of the sea route to India and the establishment of a Portuguese commercial empire in Asia.

New World. In October, 1492, Columbus reached the western hemisphere, or the New World, as it came to be known. When land was sighted on October 12, 1492, the existence of this vast new world to the west of Europe was unknown, and the islands that were sighted were thought to be those of the East Indies.

Columbus's return to Europe created great excitement and stimulated the Spanish rulers to seek concessions from Pope Alexander VI to exploit and rule the newly discovered lands. When Portugal protested, the pope granted Spain control of lands lying 100 leagues west of the Azores. By a later treaty (1494) the line was relocated 370 leagues west of the Cape Verde Islands. This dividing line was known as the Line of Demarcation.

Conquest and settlement.

In 1493 Columbus set forth on a second voyage to the New World. This time he was accompanied by hundreds of colonists and adventurers. Soon Spaniards poured into the continent by the thousands, spreading from the West Indies across the mainlands of South, Central, and North America. They founded scores of cities, subdued and exploited millions of Indians, and acquired fabulous riches of gold and silver. This American treasure provided Spain with the means to establish predominance in Europe.

Central America. The expansion of Spanish dominion in the West Indies proceeded rapidly. Santo Domingo, on the island of Hispaniola, became the first colonial capital in the Spanish empire in the New World. Between 1508 and 1511 Puerto Rico and Jamaica were conquered and settled, and between 1511 and 1515 Cuba was conquered and the cities of Santiago and Havana were founded.

After establishing themselves in the islands, the Spaniards began to move to the mainland. Between 1509 and 1513 two colonies had been established on the Isthmus of Panama. In 1513 they were united by Vasco Núñez de Balboa, who was appointed the first governor of Panama. In the same year Balboa crossed the isthmus and sighted the Pacific Ocean. From Panama, the Spaniards conquered present-day Nicaragua and Costa Rica.

The northern coast of South America was explored and raided, but only a few coastal ports were established until long after other regions had been explored.

New World settlements. One of the most important Spanish New World settlements was New Spain. Hernán Cortés conquered the Aztec confederacy, 1519–1521, and established one of the two main centers of Spanish power in America. In 1535 Mexico City became the seat of the viceroyalty of New Spain.

The firm establishment of Spanish colonial rule in New Spain made possible further exploration and conquest. Between 1523 and 1526, Guatemala, El Salvador, and Honduras were added to the viceroyalty of New Spain. The conquest of the Maya in Yucatán was completed in 1546, and expeditions were sent northward into what is now California, New Mexico, Texas, Colorado, Kansas, and Oklahoma.

The second of the most important Spanish conquests in the New World came with the discovery, 1524, and the destruction, 1532, of the Inca empire by Francisco Pizarro. Lima, established as Peru's capital in 1535 by Pizarro, became one of the early centers of education and cultural activity.

After a period of dissension marked by a power struggle among the various Spanish conquistadores and royal officials, Peru was finally pacified. Viceroyal authority was successfully established in 1551. In 1545 one of the world's largest silver mines had been discovered at Potosí, high in the Andean mountains.

DESPITE FIVE VOYAGES *to the New World, Columbus always thought he had reached Asia.*

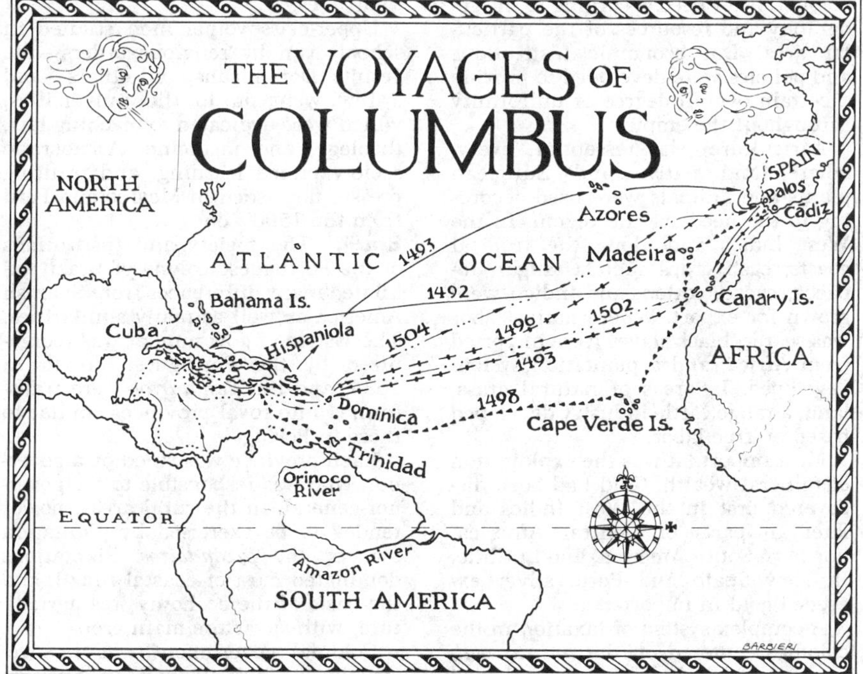

In 1569 Francisco de Toledo was made viceroy of Peru. He brought relative stability and increased prosperity to the viceroyalty. He was also responsible for issuing a colonial code of laws.

The viceroy of Peru became the most powerful and important of all Spanish colonial officials in the New World. His jurisdiction extended over almost all of South America with the exception of Brazil and Venezuela.

After the conquest of Peru, Spanish expansion was directed southward to the valleys of Chile. There the conquistadores under the leadership of Pedro de Valdivia founded the city of Santiago in 1541.

But the Spaniards were stopped by the Araucanians, the most warlike of all the Indians encountered by the Spaniards. The Spaniards finally routed the Araucanians by 1561, but they faced continual frontier resistance in the south throughout the colonial era.

During the same period as the settlement of Peru, the conquest of the tropical plateaus and highlands began. Settlements were established in modern Colombia at Santa Marta in 1525, at Cartagena in 1533, and at Bogotá in 1538. The *audiencia,* or judicial region, of New Granada was created in 1549 with Bogotá as its capital.

On the Colombian plateau, the Spaniards encountered another rich Indian culture, that of the Chibchas. Gonzalo Jiménez de Quesada conquered the Chibchan empire after a formidable struggle. Meantime, Spaniards seeking gold explored the valley of the Orinoco River in Venezuela.

The first exploration of the Río de la Plata, the estuary of the Paraná and Uruguay rivers, was led by Sebastian Cabot between 1526 and 1532. The son of the explorer John Cabot, Sebastian sought a southwest passage to the Orient.

In 1535 the Spanish crown assigned the conquest and permanent colonization to Pedro de Mendoza, who founded the city of Buenos Aires in 1536. The settlement failed, but survivors moved up the Paraná and founded Paraguay. Buenos Aires was reestablished in 1580.

Rio de la Plata, as the area was called, was a subdivision of the viceroyalty of Peru until 1776, when it became a separate viceroyalty. The area of La Plata included modern Argentina, Uruguay, Paraguay, and after 1776, Bolivia, then called Upper Peru.

Portuguese America. During the early years of European expansion into the Americas, Portugal played a smaller role than Spain. According to the terms of a 1494 treaty with Spain, the Treaty of Tordesillas, which established the Line of Demarcation, the Portuguese held title to territory in eastern South America. This land had been discovered in 1500 by Pedro Álvares Cabral, and it was named Brazil.

For the first decades of the 1500's, Portugal did little more than trade with the Indians of the coastal area. But when the area was threatened by the French, the Portuguese king, John III, began to send colonists to establish permanent settlements.

Early colonial rule was based on a proprietary system under which hereditary feudal powers and titles to lands were given to royal favorites. A series of unconnected settlements, called *capitanias donatarios,* were established, and they remained the basis of colonial organization for several years. In 1549 the first attempt to enforce the royal prerogatives occurred when Tomé de Sousa was appointed the first governor-general of the Portuguese colonies.

Colonial patterns. Colonial institutions in Spanish America evolved as the conquest and colonization of the New World proceeded. Colonial government was based primarily on the laws and institutions of Castile, modified and supplemented as needed to control the colonies in the royal interest.

Administration. At first the royal system was one of private governments. The crown awarded capitulations or contracts to individuals, called *adelantados.* The adelantado bore the expense of conquest, and his contract assured him almost complete authority and hereditary privilege over the area he had conquered for the crown. A small measure of local autonomy was permitted in the municipalities, however, where there were elected councils known as *cabildos.*

The private governments soon became inadequate to the needs of orderly administration and protection of royal revenues. At first the crown restricted the privileges of the adelantados, and then finally it cancelled all capitulations and contracts. Royal control was established through the appointment of royal officials at every level of government.

The most important colonial institution was the *audiencia,* which was a body of judges appointed by the king. Where the audiencia was not near the administrative capital, it exercised all functions of government within a fixed territory. In the capital cities, it functioned as an advisory body to the ranking official of the region, who in turn presided over the audiencia.

The most powerful official in the colonial administration was the viceroy. He performed all duties of government as the king's representative and he had authority over all lesser officials in his viceroyalty.

In Spain itself, the evolution of colonial administration followed similar lines. At first there was a single royal adviser for each area. By 1500, however, Juan Rodríguez de Fonseca had become virtual minister of the Indies, and he was largely responsible for the development of the colonial administrative system.

In 1503 the House of Trade (*Casa de Contratacion*) was established to supervise commerce, travel, and royal revenue between Spain and the colonies. By 1524 the Council for the Indies (*Consejo de Indias*) had become the judicial, legislative, and ecclesiastical body for colonial government.

Indian policy. Spanish treatment of the Indians was based largely on a system known as the *encomienda.* Under this system, Spanish settlers were granted the labor of a particular group of Indians.

The receiver of a grant, or *encomendero,* was responsible for the Christianization, civilizing, and protection of the Indians in his charge. But in fact, the encomienda was a form of forced labor for the Indians, and the system was responsible in part for the decimation of the Indian population in many areas.

Attempts to protect the Indians had been made as early as 1512, in the Laws of Burgos. But abuses continued, especially under the encomienda, which came under bitter attack, particularly from churchmen. The most famous was Bartolomé de Las Casas, a Dominican missionary.

Reform efforts met with the opposition of the conquistadores, who regarded control over the Indians as a reward for services to the crown. In 1542 the New Laws of the Indies were passed, and they included a provision for ending the encomienda. Settlers in Mexico threatened rebellion, and in Peru actually rebelled, and the offensive provisions were eventually watered down.

Economic life. The economic base of colonial life varied according to the geography and resources of the particular area. But economic institutions and policies were developed to provide a certain overall degree of uniformity throughout the empire.

Agriculture was essential everywhere, and native and European plants and animals were used according to the needs of the region. In the West Indies and along the tropical coasts, cash crops such as sugar, tobacco, cacao, cotton, and indigo were grown for export. Where native labor was scarce, black slaves were imported from Africa, and a plantation system developed. In areas of natural grassland, a range cattle industry developed based on free labor.

Most important was the exploitation of mineral wealth. Gold had been discovered first in the West Indies and later in parts of Central America, northern South America, and in Chile. In New Spain and Peru, silver exceeded gold in importance.

A complex system of taxation in the colonies centered on the *quinto real,* or royal fifth, which the crown levied on the production of precious metals. One set of taxes supported local government; another supported the costs of trade protection and regulation.

As a protection against raiding British, Dutch, and French privateers, the Spanish employed a system of two transatlantic convoys a year. The convoy system increased the cost of transportation and thus limited the volume of commerce.

Church and society. The key institution that integrated the government, economic life, and cultural life in Spanish America was the Roman Catholic Church. Between 1493 and 1508 the popes had granted extraordinary privileges to the Spanish crown. These empowered the crown to control the church officials through the power of appointment and made the church in America almost a branch of government.

Through its missionary orders, the church served as the chief organ of acculturation of the Indian populations. Through its religious and educational activities, the church became the conscience and the critic of colonial society. The church also served as the patron of artistic and intellectual activity in the New World.

Colonial society was organized in a hierarchical, stratified fashion. An upper-class minority of American-born Spaniards, or Creoles, and European-born civil and military officials, *peninsulares,* dominated a vast laboring population made up of Indians and black slaves. People of mixed race, called *castas* or mestizos, occupied an intermediate position.

The upper class was dominated by a few great families who lived in large mansions and controlled vast estates. The festivals and observances of the church played an important part in their lives.

Upper-class young men studied in schools run by religious orders—the Jesuits, Dominicans, and others—and a few went on to the universities, which were dedicated to teaching law, theology, and medicine. Aristocratic society prized learning, and printing presses flourished in Mexico and Peru from the 1500's on.

Brazil. The society and institutions of the Portuguese colony of Brazil exhibited many differences from Spanish America as well as many similarities. The system of government was reorganized by the Portuguese crown in 1534, and the *donatarios* were transformed into royal provinces similar to those in Portugal.

Each province was ruled by a governor, who was responsible to the governor-general. In the rural areas, power tended to be exercised by plantation owners, the *fazendeiros.* Plantations dominated most of coastal Brazil, and the basis of the economy was agriculture, with sugar the main crop.

Colonial government was less restrictive in Brazil than in Spanish

UNITED NATIONS

TOWN IN EL SALVADOR *with its Spanish-style church, open-air market, mestizo or Indian natives, and looming volcano could be almost anywhere in South or Central America.*

America, and municipal government was a vital element in political life. In general, each city had a representative body made up of local leaders on the basis of heredity or limited suffrage. Their responsibilities included supervision of shipping, taxes, public works, defense, police, and public health.

From 1580 to 1640 Portugal was ruled by the Spanish crown, and some Spanish colonial institutions were applied to Brazil. These tended to remain after Portugal regained its independence, but there was less centralized control than in Spain's colonies.

A feature of the 1600's was large-scale exploration of the interior. Adventurers in search of gold and slaves made important discoveries of gold mines in the late 1600's and were largely responsible for the expansion of Brazil into territory beyond the Line of Demarcation.

From 1630 to 1654, serious conflicts developed between the Brazilians and the Dutch, who conquered much of northeastern Brazil. The Brazilians eventually dislodged the Dutch without aid from Portugal, and the success contributed to a sense of pride among the Portuguese-speaking inhabitants. In the 1700's a gold-mining boom led to the founding of new towns in the interior and increased the wealth and population of the south.

Brazilian colonial society was dominated by the twin institutions of slavery and the plantation. Indian slavery declined to insignificance as increasing numbers of African slaves were imported after 1570.

The economic importance of the plantation was paralleled by the key social role of the plantation owners, the masters of the "big houses." Society became paternalistic, oligarchical, and decentralized.

International conflicts. During the 1500's British and French ships had raided the coasts of Spanish and Portuguese America, but neither Britain nor France succeeded in establishing permanent settlements. The British adventurers, led by John Hawkins and Francis Drake, raided Spanish ships and ports and took great treasures.

During the 1600's, the chief commercial threat to both Spain and Portugal was the newly independent Dutch republic. In the 1700's, however, Spain's chief rival was once again Britain, then allied with Portugal. Spain and France, both ruled by Bourbon monarchs, had become allies.

The Caribbean became the focus of conflict between the two sets of allies. Britain and France fought each other for control, while Spain, unable to enforce its monopoly of trade with its colonies, was weakened economically by an extensive illegal trade carried on by British, Dutch, and French ships.

Independence struggle.

The movement for independence in South and Central America came in the early 1800's. It reflected both internal conditions and external influences and events. Internally, the rigidity of Spanish colonial administration and continued dominance by the *peninsulares* gave rise to increasing resentment. Attempts at reform by the Spanish crown served only to weaken the colonial administration.

At the same time that internal strains were increasing, inflammatory doctrines from the newly independent United States and revolutionary France reached the colonies. The climax of external shocks came in 1808, when Napoleon Bonaparte of France invaded the Iberian Peninsula. The Spanish royal family was toppled, and the Portuguese royal family fled to Brazil.

Within Spain, a national, anti-French struggle developed and this provoked revolts in the Americas that were also largely anti-French. The colonial uprisings were scattered and uncoordinated at first, but gradually they coalesced into three main movements centered in New Spain (Mexico), Venezuela and New Granada, and La Plata and Chile.

Brazil, where the Portuguese royal family had reestablished its court, achieved its independence in 1822.

New Spain. The first revolutionary activity in Mexico came in the capital where Creole aristocrats attempted to depose the Spanish authorities. They failed, but another rebellion broke out in the north in 1810. This rising was led by a Creole priest, Miguel Hidalgo, who was supported by mestizos, those of mixed Spanish and Indian blood, and Indians.

Hidalgo, in his call to revolution, the Cry of Dolores (*Grito de Dolores*), demanded social as well as political changes. The leaders, including Hidalgo, were soon captured and were executed. However, the rebellion was continued in the south, led chiefly by José María Morelos. In 1815 Morelos was captured and shot.

Venezuela, New Granada, and the south. Early revolts in Venezuela under the leadership of Francisco de Miranda failed, but the Creoles were able to overthrow the royal government in 1810 and they declared independence in 1811. The rebels under Miranda had been defeated in 1806, and they had mixed fortunes under his successor, Simón Bolívar, but by 1815 the rebels were in exile, except for a few guerrilla bands inland.

In New Granada, royalists offered little serious opposition, but the provinces quarreled among themselves and reached the point of civil war.

Ferdinand VII was restored to the Spanish throne in 1814, after the defeat of Napoleon, and in 1815 a large force was sent to America under the leadership of Pablo Morillo. Morillo had very little difficulty in consolidating Spanish power in Venezuela and in then overcoming resistance in New Granada.

Peru remained firmly under the control of Spain, but farther south in La Plata and Chile, patriots had risen against the colonial authorities in 1810. The patriots sought to incorporate all of the former viceroyalty of La Plata into the new state, including Upper Peru (Bolivia), Paraguay, and the Banda Oriental (Uruguay). The patriots at Buenos Aires had to fight on two fronts—against royalists at Montevideo, in Uruguay, across the Río de la Plata; and against Spanish forces in Upper Peru in the northwest.

In the northwest, the patriots were not able to defeat the Spanish but they were able to prevent the colonial forces from moving south. In 1814 they succeeded in dislodging the Spanish from Montevideo, but the Buenos Aires government was not able to bring the Banda Oriental and Paraguay under its control. The independence of the United Provinces of Río de la Plata was finally declared by a congress that met at Tucumán in 1816.

The people of Paraguay had determined to become independent and in 1811 they defeated patriot armies sent from Buenos Aires. A constitution that had been drawn up under a junta was adopted in 1813.

By 1814 Dr. José Gaspar Francia, secretary of the junta, had executed a coup d'etat and had himself proclaimed "perpetual dictator." He shut Paraguay off from the outside world and ruthlessly dominated the small European and large Indian population until his death in 1840.

Uruguay's separation from the government at Buenos Aires was more complicated. Problems between the two provinces began in 1813, when the congress of the United Provinces of Río de la Plata refused to seat a Uruguayan delegation in a dispute over which form of constitution should be adopted.

When the patriot armies were besieging Montevideo, José Gervasio Artigas, leader of the ousted Uruguayan delegation, withdrew his troops from the siege. Artigas was then outlawed by Buenos Aires, and when the Spanish were defeated in 1814, Artigas lacked the resources necessary to protect his small country. Portugal occupied the area from 1816 to 1825. An independence movement supported by Buenos Aires drove out the Brazilians and in 1828 Uruguay was made a buffer state.

In 1817 José de San Martín, together with Chilean exiles led by Bernardo O'Higgins, began the liberation of Chile. A victory in February, 1817, gave the rebels the capital, Santiago, and in April, 1818, the Spaniards were totally routed at Maipú, and Chile was liberated.

The final stages. The war for liberation in the interior plains of Venezuela was revived by Simón Bolívar. With his brilliant lieutenant Antonio José de Sucre, he moved from success to success. By 1822 the whole of New Granada and Venezuela had been freed from Spanish rule and united in the republic of Greater Colombia, made up of present-day Colombia, Ecuador, Panama, and Venezuela.

The last stages of the struggle for independence in South America took place in the greatest Spanish fortress—Peru and Upper Peru (Bolivia). There the northern and southern revolutionary forces joined together and waged successive campaigns against the Spanish.

San Martín began the liberation of coastal Peru in 1821 with a joint Argentinian-Chilean army backed by a Chilean fleet commanded by a British admiral, Lord Thomas Cochrane. San Martín entered Lima, the capital, in July, 1821, and proclaimed Peruvian independence.

SIMÓN BOLÍVAR, *the brilliant liberator of much of South America.*

San Martín and Bolívar met at Guayaquil, in Ecuador, in July, 1822, and San Martín turned over the conduct of the final stages of the war to Bolívar. Bolívar fought a two-year campaign in which he commanded troops from all over the continent.

The climax of the struggle came on December 8, 1824, at the battle of Ayacucho, in the central Peruvian highlands. There Bolívar's lieutenant, Sucre, defeated the Spanish, and the republic of Bolívar (Bolivia) was proclaimed in 1825 in what had been Upper Peru.

Central America. Independence in the northern parts of the Spanish American empire was achieved between 1819 and 1821 more rapidly and suddenly than in South America. There was neither the extensive fighting nor the great climatic battles that marked the struggle on the southern continent.

In 1815 Central America was quiet under Spanish rule, and in Mexico only the embers of revolt smoldered in the backlands. The sudden rise of revolutionary activity was due to two related occurrences—the accession to political and military leadership of Augustín de Iturbide and a liberal revolution in Spain in 1820.

Iturbide had been a commander in the royalist army in New Spain, but in 1819 he assumed the leadership of the revolutionary movement. He managed to unite almost all Mexicans under his Plan of Iguala, which called for Mexican independence, the equality of all Mexicans, and continued allegiance to Roman Catholicism.

Ironically, Iturbide's plan was supported by upper-class, conservative Mexicans, who were dismayed by the Spanish revolution of 1820. They favored independence rather than trusting the country to Spanish liberals. Negotiations to establish a monarchy under a Spanish prince failed, and on July 25, 1822, Iturbide had himself proclaimed emperor.

In the captaincy of Guatemala, a junta was convened by the captain-general, and independence was proclaimed. Iturbide invited the Central Americans to join Mexico, but only Guatemala accepted. Iturbide fell from power in 1823, and a constituent assembly was convened in Guatemala City. On November 22, 1824, a proposal to form a confederation of Central American states was adopted.

West Indies. In the West Indies, most of the islands were initially conquered by Spaniards who practically annihilated the Carib and Arawak Indian populations there. By the 1700's, most of the larger islands had developed thriving plantation economies that were dependent on large numbers of African slaves brought in in shiploads.

Haiti was actually the first country in South or Central America to attain independence. Led by the famous nationalist hero, Toussaint L'Ouverture, a former slave, Haiti's rebellion began during the Napoleonic Wars, and before the new republic was established in 1804, the Haitians, with United States aid, had driven out the French and had withstood sea attacks by the British.

The Dominican Republic, formerly the colony of Santo Domingo, was controlled by the Spanish until 1795. After that time, it was ruled alternately by the French, Spanish, and neighboring Haitians who inhabited the western third of the island of Hispaniola. Haitian rule was overthrown in 1844, when the republic was established.

Jamaica was conquered by the Spaniards in 1509, but in 1670 it was ceded to the British, who allowed its people a considerable degree of autonomy. In the 1700's, though, as Jamaica became an important plantation colony, the colonial reins were pulled tighter. Independence was not achieved until 1962.

Cuba, inspired by its famous nationalist hero, José Martí, gained independence from Spanish rule in 1898. It

BLACK SLAVERY. *To work the profitable sugar plantations in the West Indies in the 1700's, large numbers of blacks from Africa were brought in and held under inhuman conditions.*

did so, however, only after United States military aid and intervention in the Spanish-American War. Cuba's freedom ended nearly four centuries of Spanish rule.

Brazil. Unlike Spanish America, Brazil achieved independence with little violence. The Portuguese royal family had made Rio de Janeiro its capital, and both Rio and Brazil benefited. Many changes occurred that stimulated economic and cultural activity.

Brazil's trade was opened to all nations. A national bank and a mint were introduced; schools, libraries, and a military academy were established. Artists and scientists had accompanied the court to America, and a cultural renaissance began in Rio. Finally, in 1815, Brazil was declared a kingdom coordinate with Portugal.

The revolutionary spirit spread to Brazil from Spanish America as well as from France and the United States. As a result, in 1817 a republican revolt broke out in Recife, but it was quickly suppressed.

The event that sparked the movement for independence came in 1820, when a liberal revolt similar to the one in Spain occurred in Portugal. A Parliament was convened in Lisbon, Portugal's capital, and it demanded the return of the king from Brazil. The key issue was Portuguese resentment and jealousy over the political status given Brazil.

The king reluctantly returned to Lisbon in 1821, but he left his son, Dom Pedro, as regent in Brazil with instructions to declare Brazil independent should the liberal Parliament impose restrictions on Brazil. The Lisbon authorities soon demanded the return of Dom Pedro, however, and indicated that Brazil would revert to its old colonial status.

The Portuguese attitude created a community of interest between the young prince and Brazilian nationalists. Dom Pedro declared that he would remain in Brazil. In 1822 he was proclaimed emperor as Dom Pedro I. José Bonifácio de Andrada e Silva, a leading Brazilian intellectual known as the "Father of Brazil," became prime minister and chief adviser to the emperor. In 1823 a constitutional convention was convened, but Pedro dissolved it and issued a new constitution by decree in 1824.

The Lisbon government opposed independence, but had few means to enforce its will. Moreover, Britain, interested in maintaining profitable trade relations it had established with Brazil, pressured the Portuguese government to accept a settlement. In August, 1825, Portugal finally recognized the independence of Brazil.

Foreign relations surveyed. Neither Spanish America nor Brazil received official aid from foreign governments, as the United States did during its war for independence. But the attitudes of foreign powers were important at times, as in the case of Brazil.

When the revolts first began, Europe was involved in the wars of the French Revolution and the Napoleonic era. Britain was fighting the French and was allied with Spain. British policy therefore was to work for a settlement of disputes between Spain and its American colonies. Soon, however, the revolutionary governments' removal of trade restrictions became important to British commercial interests and led to English opposition to Spain's efforts to suppress the revolts.

The revolutionaries had hoped for aid and encouragement from the United States, but the United States was involved in its own difficulties with Britain and France. It did little more than show general good will and a desire for commercial relations. There was no official military aid, and political support was limited to the activities of private individuals.

During the War of 1812, a British blockade cut off U.S. contact with the rebels, but after the war relations were renewed. By then, however, the United States was involved in negotiations with Spain for the cession of Florida and settlement of the western boundary of the Louisiana Territory, and the United States preferred to maintain a cautious neutrality.

In 1821 a U.S.-Spanish treaty was ratified, and during 1821 and 1822 the revolutionaries achieved their great victories over the Spanish. In 1822 U.S. President James Monroe granted diplomatic recognition to the new governments to the south.

Following the defeat of Napoleon in 1814–1815, the victorious European powers were in a reactionary mood and dedicated to the restoration of monarchic rights. Between 1817 and 1823 the continental powers occasionally considered intervention in Latin America, though no decision to act ever was reached. Only Britain, which had established profitable trade relations with the new governments, remained apart from the policy of restoration.

The British prime minister, George Canning, proposed to the United States that the two governments issue a joint statement opposing foreign intervention in the Americas. But opposition to joint action by the U.S. Secretary of State John Quincy Adams led to the issuance of a unilateral statement by President Monroe in 1823.

The major points of the Monroe Doctrine, as the declaration came to be known, were that the American continents were no longer open to colonization and that any intervention by European powers to control or subjugate those parts of the Americas that had won their independence would be regarded as dangerous to the peace and safety of the United States. Although the immediate effect of the declaration was small, it was received enthusiastically in South and Central America as a sign of good faith.

In 1824 Britain granted recognition to the new countries, and in 1830 France did the same. Spain and other European governments delayed still longer, however.

New republics.

The newly independent states had many problems to solve—economic and social as well as political. Widespread destruction during the independence struggle made reconstruction the most urgent need, but instability and conflicting forces prevented political cooperation and economic and social development.

The political scene remained confused and unstable. The efforts of Simón Bolivar and other far-sighted leaders to inhibit the growth of sectional rivalries by creating large political units were unsuccessful.

La Plata separated into the modern states of Argentina, Bolivia, Paraguay, and Uruguay. Bolívar's Greater Colombia broke into Ecuador, Venezuela, and New Granada. New Granada became modern Colombia, which included Panama until 1903.

The confederation of Central American provinces established in 1824 broke up in 1839, when the five small components separated and formed the independent nations of Costa Rica, El Salvador, Guatemala, Honduras, and Nicaragua.

Chile remained roughly the same territorially until 1884, when important coastal lands were ceded by Bolivia and Peru. Brazil gradually expanded control over the unoccupied South American heartland.

Government and politics. The new governments lacked the traditional authority of the old monarchy. Moreover, the personal ambitions of military leaders made a mockery of constitutional principles providing for legal transfers of power.

Essential to an understanding of the early period is the phenomenon of *caudillismo,* the tendency to follow a charismatic leader regardless of principles or issues. Two outstanding examples of the *caudillo* during the new national period were Juan Manuel de Rosas, who ruled Argentina from 1835 to 1852, and Antonio López de Santa Anna, who dominated Mexican politics from 1833 to 1853.

The caudillo usually won popular support by appealing to a developing sense of nationalism, and he ruled through the use of propaganda, terror, and military force.

During this same early period, a division of Latin American politics into conservative and liberal factions was developing. The conservatives, although strongly in favor of independence, had no intention of broadening the base of government.

The higher clergy of the church also tended to support the conservatives. All had a stake in the status quo and therefore favored preserving the stable, hierarchical society of the colonial past as well as close cooperation between church and state.

The liberals were the heirs of the French Enlightenment. They proclaimed the "natural rights" of man, popular sovereignty, and the separation of church and state. They generally supported the ideas of federalism and decentralized government and accepted the economic doctrine of free enterprise. Both conservatives and liberals were of the upper classes. The masses played no part in politics.

Liberalism also tended to ally itself with nationalism, which gradually became a characteristic attitude of the middle and upper classes and a source of emotional appeal to the masses.

Economic and social problems. The years immediately following independence saw the establishment of basic patterns that continue to mark the economies of South and Central America. With independence, the Spanish trade monopoly was broken, and international commerce flourished.

NEW YORK PUBLIC LIBRARY

LÓPEZ DE SANTA ANNA, caudillo *of Mexico in the first half of the 19th century.*

Agriculture and mining remained the most important economic activities, and even greater reliance was placed on cash crops. The emphasis on agriculture also served to strengthen the plantation system, which was especially strong in northeastern Brazil, the Caribbean islands, coastal Peru, and parts of Mexico.

Industrial activity received little encouragement. Transportation linking the mines and plantations to ports did improve, however, and South and Central America became a field for European and North American investment.

Independence brought the abolition of slavery by mid-century, but peonage and oppression of freed men and Indians continued. On the whole, blacks remained a vast, untrained, and uneducated segment of the population. In fact, they were perhaps more exploited than before independence because the colonial legislation that protected them had been removed. Although the status of the mestizos was considerably higher than that of the Indians or blacks, even the mestizos formed a culturally unassimilated, economically dependent, and discontented group.

Wealth was overwhelmingly concentrated in the hands of a small upper class, and there was only a small middle class. Factions within the elite fought for power with little or no involvement of the masses.

International relations. Despite the professed sentiments among South and Central American countries that they were sister republics, nationalism and rival territorial claims prevented the establishment of peaceful relations. Ill-defined boundaries and ambitious dictators all too often led to the intervention by one country in the affairs of others.

Such interference in the former provinces of La Plata culminated in the War of the Triple Alliance (1864–1870), in which Argentina, Brazil, and Uruguay defeated the military dictator of Paraguay, Francisco Solano López, in one of the bloodiest wars in South or Central American history. Paraguay lost more than 50,000 square miles of land and its male population was decimated.

Prolonged civil and national wars not only caused a drain on resources and manpower, but often led to involvement with the countries of Europe and North America. Foreign intervention now and then occurred when foreigners suffered losses in civil strife. This was the case in the French and English blockades of Río de la Plata in 1835–1850.

In the 1840's and 1850's, Mexico suffered losses of territory to the United States. From 1846 to 1848 the United States fought Mexico for land that now makes up parts of the southwestern United States. In 1853 more territory was gained in the Gadsden Purchase. Both losses created bitter resentment in Mexico.

France, allied with England and Spain, intervened in 1862 after the Mexican civil war known as the War of Reform, which ended with the establishment of a liberal government under Benito Juárez. Using accumulated Mexican debts as an excuse, France established Archduke Maximilian, a Hapsburg, as emperor of Mexico. Another bitter conflict followed, ending in 1867, when Juárez was victorious and ordered Maximillian executed.

National development.

Beginning with the crucial period of 1870–1880, the effects of increasing European and North American industrialization began to be felt in South and Central America. The new industrial plants needed greater amounts of raw materials, such as leather, copper, tin, nitrates, wool, and cotton. Moreover, Europe's growing population needed ever greater supplies of food from the Americas—wheat, coffee, sugar, cacao, and meat.

In addition to an increased demand for the region's goods, industrial growth in Europe and North America provided growing supplies of capital funds for investment. The first areas of investment were communications and transportation. Railroads, steamship lines, port facilities, and cable and telegraph lines were all developed with foreign capital, and all helped to stimulate the production of foodstuffs and raw materials for export.

Waterworks, street railways, telephone networks, and electric-power systems multiplied as foreign concessionaires provided the capital at profitable rates of return. Capital from the United States and Europe also was invested in the mining industry to develop new and more efficient methods of producing metals, nitrates, and later, petroleum.

The major impact of these new economic forces came in the temperate zone of South America—Argentina, Chile, Uruguay, and southern Brazil. The livestock industry was revolutionized in Argentina, Brazil, and Uruguay. Large-scale cereal production began on the pampas, and nitrate production boomed in Chile.

The wealth of the countries in the temperate zone grew rapidly, and there was a huge tide of immigration that brought millions of Italians, Spaniards, Portuguese, Germans, and French to the southern parts of the continent. There was little impact on the economies of most of the smaller tropical republics, however.

In the north, Mexico also received important amounts of foreign capital although it did not share in the large-scale immigration to the New World.

Political evolution. The political ramifications of this economic development were the growth of nationalism and the greater stability of government. It became clear to the new leaders that frequent coups and revolutions discouraged the inflow of capital and of immigrants.

Some countries achieved stability by a union of all major economic interests in a single powerful political machine. Older violent party conflicts were resolved by the establishment of constitutional oligarchies, a course followed in Argentina, Chile, and Brazil.

In other nations, order was achieved by the establishment of a dictatorial regime allied with, supported by, and operated in the interests of the new economic forces. The classic example of this pattern was the regime of Porfirio Díaz in Mexico.

In Brazil, the traditional conservative empire was overthrown in 1889 by a combination of military, business, and professional men imbued with the idea of progress. These groups dominated the first Brazilian republic throughout its early days.

Whichever political path was taken, there was a common ideology for the leaders in politics, education, and business. The idealistic or conservative concepts of the earlier period were replaced with evolutionary social doctrine as expressed by "positivism," derived from the philosophy of August Comte.

The positivists stressed the importance of social structures and institutions of the kind that favored "order and progress," and they abandoned talk of natural rights. They felt that social progress would come through hard work and the accumulation of wealth. Government, they thought, should aid the accumulation of wealth by offering subsidies and special favors to business and by suppressing labor organizations.

War and interventionism. The changing nature of Spanish America was illustrated by the War of the Pacific (1879–1884). This was a conflict between Chile and an alliance of Bolivia and Peru over rich nitrate fields in southern Bolivia and Peru.

At the beginning of the war, Bolivia was in a state of confusion following years of dictatorship under Mariano Melgarejo. Peru was in an equally chaotic state after a series of brief, unstable revolutionary governments. Chile, in contrast, had enjoyed almost 60 years of relative stability and constitutional government, and had a more efficient army and navy.

The war was fought bitterly, and looting and destruction of property occurred in Lima, Peru's capital, which was occupied by Chilean forces. Hostilities were ended on October 20, 1883, when the parties signed the Treaty of Ancón. Chile was completely victorious. It gained the disputed nitrate-rich territory, leaving Bolivia without access to the sea.

The war both stimulated and reflected the nationalistic spirit of the age, and the hostilities encouraged the new economic and nationalistic forces. One result was increased political representation and power for the new economic interests, which became equal to that of the traditional landowning oligarchy.

Government generally came to work in the interest of expanding economic activity and declined to restrict or regulate the activities of business. These developments were expressed in one form or another in almost every South and Central American country. They were similar to developments taking place in Europe and the United States.

Another major development of the late 1800's was increasing awareness of the growing power of the United States. Having enjoyed a century of spectacular economic, territorial, and population growth, the United States had emerged from a bitter civil war with renewed strength.

In the two decades that followed the Civil War, the United States avoided expansionist adventures in the Caribbean area, but the situation changed in the 1890's. One development stemmed from a boundary dispute between Venezuela and the British colony of British Guiana, now the nation of Guyana. When Britain refused U.S. offers to arbitrate the dispute, the U.S. secretary of state, Richard Olney, was instructed to notify the British government that the United States was "practically sovereign on this continent, and its fiat is law upon the subject to which it confines its interposition." This theory of interposition was both feared and resented by the peoples of South and Central America.

In 1898 the United States intervened in Cuba, then a colony of Spain, and a war with Spain followed. By the terms of the Treaty of Paris ending the Spanish-American War, Spain withdrew from Cuba and ceded Puerto Rico, along with the Philippines and Guam, to the United States.

Cuba became a U.S. ward, and in 1902 the U.S. Congress forced the inclusion of the Platt Amendment in the Cuban constitution. It gave the United States broad powers of intervention in Cuba. During the next two decades, the United States managed to establish five protectorates in the Caribbean: Cuba, Panama, the Dominican Republic, Nicaragua, and Haiti.

Following the Cuban episode, the United States tried to obtain concessions from Colombia to construct a canal across the Isthmus of Panama. Officially, the concession belonged to a French company, but it had failed to complete the task by 1899 and was bankrupt.

When the Colombian Senate delayed in approving the transfer of the concession to the United States, the province of Panama rebelled against Colombia. The United States prevented Colombian forces from suppressing the revolt and recognized the new government of Panama.

THE PANAMA CANAL *on June 12, 1914. It opened on August 15. The advantages to U.S. and world commerce perhaps offset the questionable circumstances surrounding its planning.*

PAN AMERICAN UNION

The affair was settled on November 18, 1903, by the Hay-Bunau-Varilla Treaty between the United States and Panama. The United States received a zone five miles wide on each side of the proposed canal and broad powers of intervention to preserve order. Panama received a cash settlement and an annuity.

On August 15, 1914, the canal was opened to world commerce. In 1921 the United States finally ratified the Thompson-Urrutia Treaty, which provided for a cash settlement with Colombia for the loss of the canal route and Panama.

At the same time that it used force, the United States also attempted to win the support of the Latin American nations for Pan-Americanism. Aiming essentially to exclude European influence from the Americas, the United States tried to develop an ideology of "continentalism." Thus, it was hoped, Pan-Americanism would accomplish what the United States alone was attempting to achieve by a more vigorous enforcement of the Monroe Doctrine.

South and Central Americans had made efforts to form a cooperative union of the Americas in 1826, but the United States did not participate. Later conferences were held in Lima, Peru, in 1847 and again in 1864 and 1865; and in Santiago, Chile, in 1856. Most meetings were concerned with threats to the territorial and political integrity of nations threatened by European encroachment.

Under the vigorous leadership of U.S. Secretary of State James G. Blaine, a new Pan-American conference convened in Washington in 1889. It was attended by all the American nations except the Dominican Republic. Less was achieved at the conference than the United States had hoped. No continental peace treaty or arbitration convention resulted, and there was opposition to U.S. leadership from Argentina as well as other South American nations.

A continuing official organization did come out of the 1889 conference. A secretariat, later named the Pan-American Union, was set up as an information bureau.

Modern era. South and Central America in the first half of the 20th century tended to be nationalistic, and there was a strong movement to incorporate the masses of the people, urban and rural, into national life. Opposition to this came from the entrenched oligarchy, frequently supported from abroad. Rapid urbanization became a prominent feature, and organized labor became a potent force in political affairs.

The dominant ideology in the first decades of the century was a democratic one. It included elements of socialism and a rejection of laissez-faire economic doctrines, and was hostile to foreign capital.

Political trends. In many countries of South and Central America the new tendencies burst on the scene only after the world economic depression of the 1930's. This was true especially of countries in the Caribbean, Central America, and the Andean region. In Argentina and Uruguay, the change was evolutionary. In Chile there was a combination of evolutionary development and the coup d'etat.

In Argentina, a relatively new middle-class party, the *Union Civica Radical,* dedicated to achieving economic and political reform through a broader franchise, gained power in 1916. In Uruguay, political reformer José Batlle y Ordóñez created a new constitutional system in 1919 that aimed at the gradual establishment of a welfare state. In Chile, an era of political and social reform was ushered in by the rise to power of a popular socialist, Arturo Alessandri, in the early 1920's.

The strongest expression of these political and social developments was the Mexican revolution of 1910. Moreover, the international impact of the revolution made it one of the outstanding movements in South and Central America during the 1900's.

The revolution began as a more or less conventional protest against the excesses of the Porfirio Díaz regime. Although led by political liberals and reformers, it was not intended to be a social revolution.

A MOVIE ACTOR? *No—Emiliano Zapata himself, a hero of the Mexican revolution.*

NEW YORK PUBLIC LIBRARY

Between 1911 and 1917, the rebellion developed into an almost anarchical struggle among rival leaders such as Francisco Indalecio, Madero, Victoriano Huerta, Francisco (Pancho) Villa, Venustiano Carranza, and Emiliano Zapata. Each fell by the wayside, but the movement that each had led contributed to a far-reaching national and social revolution.

In 1917 a new constitution included a revolutionary program. It embodied demands for land reform, including the limitation of private property rights in the interest of the nation, and the right of laborers to organize and strike. It also called for an end to peonage and granted land to rural communities. Other provisions established a secular state, extended public education, and eliminated foreign influence.

Although the revolution frequently faltered, many of the objectives were finally secured, and eventually, in 1938, foreign-owned petroleum corporations were expropriated and their facilities nationalized. Despite reforms, poverty and illiteracy continued to slow development, however.

The nationalistic trend in South and Central America was more pronounced after 1930. A concern for the welfare of the masses was often combined with militarism and a distrust of political democracy.

The best example of the new politics of the 1930's was the regime of Getulio Vargas in Brazil. Vargas was proclaimed president in 1930 by a military junta. As the head of a liberal coalition, he framed a new liberal and progressive constitution in 1934, but he moved steadily to the right and in the period 1937–1945 his regime acquired many fascist features. Argentina also moved in the same direction during the 1930's.

In most of Central America and the Caribbean, however, dictatorial regimes supported by the military maintained a firm hold on power. There were also countries such as Colombia and Venezuela in which a moderate, middle-of-the-road reformism dominated the 1930's.

Economic change. The United States emerged from World War I with a prosperous economy, and it surpassed Europe as the primary investor and supplier of South and Central America. U.S. products flooded their markets, and for the first time their governments borrowed in the United States rather than in the European money markets.

Modernization of transportation facilities was accelerated, and improved and extended radio and cable connections made rapid communications increasingly effective.

The world depression, beginning about 1930, had great political as well as economic impact on South and Central America. Few political systems were able to withstand the domestic economic crises following the decline in industrial demand for their countries' export products. Governments in Argentina and Brazil, among others, fell in that year. Chile, which began suffering severe economic setbacks following the World War I invention of artificial nitrates, also experienced political instability, but somewhat earlier, beginning in the mid-1920's.

While politically destabilizing, the depression caused fundamental questions to be raised about undue dependence on one or two export products and the consequent vulnerability to the fluctuations of international market prices; this was to lead, especially in the decades of the 1940's and 1950's in the major countries, to programs of industrialization. The depression also placed a focus on the serious social problems of the South and Central American countries, especially the poverty of the urban and rural poor. Programs for the advancement of urban labor were launched in several countries as well as less often, programs for land reform.

Mexico, which had identified its major social problems in the course of its revolution, beginning in 1910, significantly advanced in the 1930's a land reform program that had been begun earlier. President Lázaro Cárdenas (1934–1940) gave land reform a new momentum by moving rigorously against most of the existing large landholdings, so that in the 1970's, almost one-half of the cultivated land of the country was held in the form of *ejidos.* These are villages that have received lands from the government and are worked, usually by members on an individual family basis, for subsistence. Many urban workers were also encouraged to organize in Mexico in the 1930's. They began receiving important social guarantees in the form of social security and limited work days, as well as higher wages through collective bargaining. The rural and urban workers who were to benefit were organized respectively in the National Confederation of Peasants and the Confederation of Mexican Workers, both of which continue as the most populous components of the present governing Institutional Revolutionary Party (PRI). Beginning in the 1940's, Mexico launched an industrial revolution that transformed the economy's emphasis on agricultural and mineral primary products to manufacturing industries of all kinds. The PRI candidate, José López Portillo, won, as expected, the presidential election in 1976 and was inaugurated for a six-year term.

Brazil began in the 1930's a more limited program of social reform that especially benefited a portion of the urban workers during the increasingly authoritarian regime of Getulio Vargas (1930–1945). Vargas also created an important base for the country's industrialization. His programs advancing manufacturing industries continued under later democratic governments (1946–1964), but they have been given special impetus since the assumption of power by the Brazilian military establishment, beginning in 1964. Since 1964, Brazilian economic growth has been among the highest in the world. Criticism has often been leveled, however, at the lack of economic distribution among the lower classes, and at the repressive policies of the military governments.

After a period of economic stagnation in the 1930's, Argentina experienced unprecedented social and industrial change during the unusual regime of General Juan Domingo Perón (1946–1955). He organized most of the urban labor force of the country and used it as a political base for pushing ahead a program of very rapid industrialization. The costs of the program, increased enormously by the political need for satisfying workers' wage and social benefit demands, drove the country to the brink of bankruptcy before he was overthrown. Then in 1973 Perón was permitted to return and, after a brief unsuccessful government by one of his supporters, was elected to the presidency, serving until his death in 1975. His widow, Vice President Isabel Perón, succeeded to the presidency but was removed shortly afterward on charges of corruption. General Jorge Videla assumed presidential power on behalf of the military establishment and governed by decree to deal with problems of widespread terrorism and severe inflation. As of late 1977, much of the terrorism had been brought under control, and the inflation, which at its height reached about 400% per year, became significantly reduced.

While several other South and Central American countries experienced dictatorships as a result of the worldwide depression, Chile reestablished constitutional democracy as of 1932 and maintained stable democratic government until 1973. Alongside this impressive political record was a move toward limited industrialization. The increased demand during World War II for copper—which replaced natural nitrates as Chile's principal export product—provided an extraordinary prosperity. When Chile later began experiencing balance of payments deficits, primarily because of its need for the importation of food for its increasing population, as well as because of fluctuating international demand for copper, it received significant economic assistance from the United States and from international financial institutions. Chile also faced severe social problems involving the rural and urban poor. There was extensive landholding with a serflike labor base and few benefits for the urban working classes. In addition, the ownership of most of the copper resources of the country by foreign companies created nationalistic tensions.

ORGANIZATION OF AMERICAN STATES

THE FAMOUS EVITA PERÓN, *influential wife of dictator Juan Perón of Argentina.*

The administration of Eduardo Frei (1964–1970), the first Christian Democratic Party leader to come to power in South America, sought to redress these inequities by launching a land reform program and by inaugurating a program of "Chileanization," that is, gradual government purchase of the foreign copper firms. In the election of 1970, the leftist candidate of the socialist-Communist coalition, Salvador Allende, won the most votes and was inaugurated. He advanced significantly the land reform program and immediately nationalized the foreign-owned copper resources, indicating that compensation was inappropriate because of the companies' alleged excess profits. On this issue and on Allende's Marxist orientation, tensions developed with the United States. Allende was overthrown in 1973 by military force. The chief of staff of the Chilean army, General Agosto Pinochet, has since governed by decree.

Social revolutions in two smaller South and Central American countries took place in the 1950's. In Bolivia, a civilian political party, the National Revolutionary Movement, was elected in 1952, and after temporary obstruction by the military, was inaugurated and initiated a major social and economic transformation. Almost all of the large landholdings were broken up and divided among the peasants—a reform that has continued to the present. The tin mines—source of the country's major export product—were nationalized and the mineworkers organized into a national confederation. These reforms were accompanied by the regular and peaceful transfer of executive power until President Victor Paz Estenssoro sought reelection. Because of the political tensions that had been generated, he was overthrown shortly after his inauguration. Both elected and imposed governments followed. More recently, Bolivia has been largely governed by the military.

The social revolution in Cuba was led by Fidel Castro, who overthrew a long-lived dictatorship and changed Cuba's close economic relationship with the United States. He opened diplomatic relations with the Soviet Union and entered into a trade agreement there for the sale of Cuban sugar that had been previously traded chiefly to the United States under a special, protected quota. He nationalized all of the sugar plantations, almost half of which were owned by U.S. companies. He then moved to create a society that was to be guided by the precepts of Marxism-Leninism, and an authoritarian party was created to guide political decision-making. The economy was almost entirely brought under government control. In addition, a vast program was launched to reduce illiteracy. After an unsuccessful attempt in the early 1960's to pursue rapid industrialization, the Castro government returned to the old policy emphasizing increased sugar production for exportation. The authoritarianism of the regime has been somewhat modified in recent years by permission for the election of some local officials. Material incentives in the form of increased wages for increased output are now allowed. Diplomatic relations with the United States, broken since 1961, were partially resumed with an agreement between the two countries in 1977 to exchange lower-ranking diplomatic officers.

While there has been an increase in military-controlled governments in South and Central America, Venezuela has maintained a civilian, constitutional regime. After a ten-year experience with the despotism of Marcos Pérez Jiménez, the country overthrew the dictatorship in 1958; a democratic reform government was then established under the Acción Democrática, a moderate leftist party.

Despite growing pressure from the extreme left and intraparty divisions, peaceful elections have been held every five years since 1958. A representative of the Acción Democrática, Carlos Andrés Pérez, was elected president in 1973; in 1979 Luis Herrera Campins succeeded him.

Civilian government has also prevailed in Colombia, where Alfonso López Michelsen was elected president in 1974; and J. C. T. Ayala in 1978.

The population growth rate of South and Central America has been extremely high. The problems of unemployment, public health, education, and housing seemed insoluble. Teeming masses of people in shantytowns came to surround almost every major city and constituted a threat to orderly government.

The accumulated wartime earnings of South and Central American nations were soon exhausted, and demands arose for large-scale U.S. aid, but the United States, beset by major challenges in Europe and Asia, provided only minimal financial and technical assistance.

Since 1955 there have been only limited economic advances in most of South and Central America. Only Brazil, Colombia, Mexico, and Venezuela showed appreciable progress. Industrial production expanded, but the expansion was accompanied by inflation everywhere, except in Mexico and Venezuela, where petroleum revenues have been used to support development programs.

U.S. military intervention in several Caribbean countries clouded inter-American relations during the first three decades of the 20th century. When in 1933, as a part of the "good neighbor" policy of President Franklin Roosevelt, the United States committed itself to the principle of nonintervention, a new era in hemisphere relations began. As World War II loomed, the United States agreed to consult with the South and Central American countries on hemisphere defense, thereby modifying a policy of unilateralism that dated from the Monroe Doctrine (1823). The goodwill thus engendered provided a base for wartime solidarity, with only one western hemisphere country—Argentina—remaining neutral. The wartime cooperation led after the war to a Treaty of Reciprocal Assistance (1947) that continues in force. In the following year, a charter was approved for a formally constituted inter-American association, the present Organization of American States (OAS).

Three Central American countries became focuses of the Cold War. The government of Guatemala, perceived by the United States to be Communist-controlled, was overthrown in 1954 by forces to which the United States gave clandestine support. Since then, however, extreme rightist and leftist guerrillas have fought for control of the government, and since the early 1970's terrorist activities have been excessive. Following the 1978 election of President Romeo Lucas Garcia, Guatemala has been the scene of a virtual civil war.

After the Cuban government of Fidel Castro opened diplomatic and commercial relations with the Soviet Union and expropriated properties of U.S. companies, the United States supported an unsuccessful invasion by anti-Castro exiles in 1961. In the same year, and largely with a view toward preventing the expansion of the Cuban revolution to other Latin American countries, President John Kennedy launched a program of support for South and Central American social and economic development; he named the program the Alliance for Progress.

Cuba was subsequently expelled from the OAS on the grounds that the commitment of its government to Marxism-Leninism was incompatible with the democratic principles of the inter-American system. After evidence was uncovered of Cuban clandestine intervention in Venezuela, the OAS countries voted to sever diplomatic and commercial relations. Cuba was thus diplomatically isolated within the hemisphere during much of the 1960's, although most of the South and Central American countries reopened relations in the 1970's.

Cuba is still a leading advocate of communism in the western hemisphere as well as in Africa. It is quick to support communist revolutions with military and economic aid and advice. In 1979 the United States learned that Soviet combat troops were stationed in Cuba, but the Cubans and Soviets insist that they are there in a strictly advisory capacity.

El Salvador has become the latest hot spot of international concern in this part of the world. Both rightist and leftist terrorists went on a rampage after the hated General Carlos Humberto Romero was elected to the presidency in the disputed election of 1977. In 1979 a revolutionary junta replaced the deposed president, but it has been unable to restrain the terrorist activities.

As the United States, Cuba, and the Soviet Union contend for allies in South and Central America, the issue of human rights becomes more and more significant. Many of the region's dictators and military regimes have been accused of gross violations of human rights. They are charged with unfair and wanton incarceration of political foes, as well as torture and mass executions for political ends.

The last U.S. President, Jimmy Carter (1977–1981), insisted that the United States could not maintain proper relations with governments that were guilty of such atrocities. He believed basic human freedoms to be more important than the facilitation of political programs, ideals, or international friendships.

Reagan's administration (beginning in 1981) has reversed this trend. Condemning Carter's foreign policy as too idealistic, Reagan hopes to gain and maintain many more political allies in South and Central America through his foreign policy.

Most of the countries of this region, meanwhile, are working toward improved cooperation among themselves. Several organizations hoping for increased economic cooperation have been formed. Among these are the Latin American Free Trade Association; the Central American Common Market; the Caribbean Free Trade Association; and the Andean Economic Integration Group. The Latin American Economic System was founded by Mexico and Venezuela with a goal of increasing the economic integration of all of South and Central America.

COUNTRIES OF SOUTH AND CENTRAL AMERICA

Antigua and Barbuda

Official name: *Antigua and Barbuda*
Area: *171 sq. mi., 442 sq. km.*
Population: *(1987 est.) 83,598*
Capital: *St. John's (Pop., 1982, 30,000)*
Language: *English*
Religion: *Anglican, other Christian denominations*
Currency unit: *East Caribbean dollar*

Antigua and Barbuda is comprised of the islands of Antigua, Barbuda, and Redonda. They are located in the eastern Caribbean, part of the Lesser Antilles, about 250 miles southeast of Puerto Rico.

The land and the people. Antigua is a low-lying island though hills rise in the south and west. Its irregular coastline provides several natural harbors. Barbuda is a flat, wooded coral island. Antigua and Barbuda have a dry climate.

The people of Antigua and Barbuda are mostly of African descent. There is a small number of Europeans and mixed minorities. Almost 40 percent of the population live in urban areas. The largest city is St. John's.

Economy. The economy of Antigua and Barbuda is dominated by the tourist industry, which accounts for 40 percent of the gross domestic product and employs 60 percent of the population. Also important are cotton, fruit, and sugar cane cultivation. Most manufacturing has to do with the processing of agricultural products.

In 1987 exports, mostly clothing, fruit, and rum, were an estimated $30.8 million, while imports, chiefly fuel, food, and machinery, were an estimated $278.9 million.

Government. The head of state of Antigua and Barbuda is the Queen of England, who is represented by a governor-general. The head of government is a prime minister. Legislative power rests with a bicameral Parliament, made up of a House of Representatives and a Senate, each with 17 members.

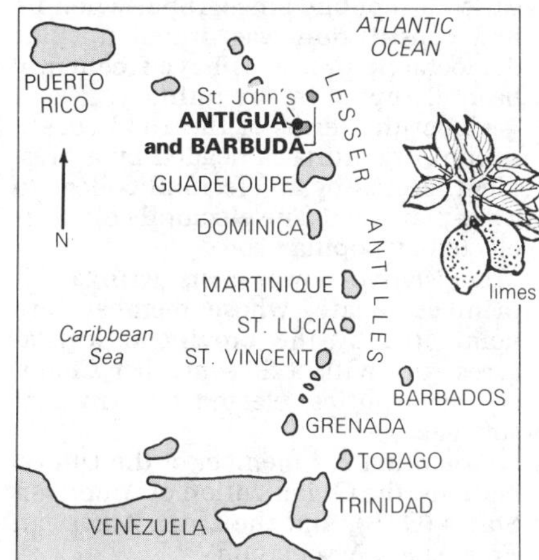

History. The earliest known inhabitants were Arawak and Carib Indians. Antigua was discovered by Columbus in 1493, but early Spanish attempts at colonization were unsuccessful. Englishmen from St. Kitts settled there in 1632, introducing sugar cane cultivation. Barbuda was settled by colonists from Antigua in 1661.

From 1871 to 1956 Antigua was administered as part of the Federation of the Leeward Islands. In 1967 the islands became an Associated State of Great Britain, and enjoyed total internal autonomy.

Independence came on November 1, 1981, though some problems were encountered with the rise of a strong separatist movement on Barbuda. The political life of the islands has been dominated by the Antigua Labour Party. Its leader, Vere Bird, became prime minister upon independence.

Argentina

Official name: *Argentine Republic*
Area: *1,072,163 sq. mi., 2,776,889 sq. km.*
Population: *(1990 est.) 32,291,000*
Capital: *Buenos Aires (Pop., metro. area, 1990 est., 11,600,000)*
Language: *Spanish*
Religion: *Roman Catholic*
Currency unit: *Austral*
National holiday: *Independence Day, May 25*

Argentina is a republic in the southern part of South America. It is the second largest Latin American country in area and the fourth largest in population. Argentina is bounded on the north by Brazil, Paraguay, and Bolivia; on the east by Brazil, Uruguay, and the Atlantic Ocean; on the west by Chile; and on the south by Chile and the Atlantic Ocean.

The land. Argentina has four major land regions: the pampas, the north, the Andes, and Patagonia.

The pampas, great level plains, are divided into the Humid Pampa, in the east of Argentina's central region, and the Dry Pampa, in the west. The rich, black soil of the Humid Pampa makes it one of the most fertile agricultural areas in the world.

The pampas form the economic, political, and social heartland of the nation. The half circle around Buenos Aires, with a radius of 250 miles, includes only 24 percent of the country's total area but contains some 75 percent of the total population.

The north contains the semiarid, forested plains of the Chaco, the rolling hills and the floodplains of Mesopotamia, which lie between the Paraná and Uruguay rivers, and the Paraná Plateau.

The Andes region includes the "Monte," or foothill zone, with elevations below 2500 feet, and the Andes cordillera (range) itself. In the northwest the cordillera reaches a height of 22,834 feet at Mt. Aconcagua, the highest point in the western hemisphere.

Patagonia is a dry, windswept plateau south of the Río Colorado. Rainfall ranges between 20 inches a year near the Andes and less than eight inches along the Atlantic Coast. Patagonia's dryness is an obstacle to both farming and grazing, and it is sparsely populated.

The people. About nine out of every ten of Argentina's people are of European descent, and approximately one out of five Argentinians was born in Europe. In the 1800's a large number of Europeans, primarily Italians and Spaniards, emigrated to Argentina and their influence has made the country in many ways more European than Latin American. The dwindling indigenous population consists of small groups of Guaraní Indians in the north and Patagonian Indians in the south.

One-third of the people of Argentina lives in the metropolitan area of Buenos Aires, the capital.

The larger provincial cities include Mar del Plata, about 250 miles from the capital, a beach resort; Rosario, the country's wheat exporting center, about 200 miles from Buenos Aires on the Río Paraná; Cordoba, an educational and commercial center in the heart of the country that has recently become important in manufacturing; and Tucumán, the major metropolis of northwestern Argentina and capital of the sugar-growing area.

Economy. Industry contributes over one-third of the gross national product and employs one-quarter of the labor force. Agriculture employs about 20 percent of the labor force, but only contributes about ten percent of the gross national product. Before World War II the *estancieros,* ranch and farm owners whose wealth derived from the old colonial economy, formed the dominant economic and social class in Argentina. Since then, however, middle-class urban-based industrialists have made broad economic gains and have replaced the *estancieros* as the dominant economic class, although the latter have retained much of their traditional social and political power.

Most farming activity occurs in the Humid Pampa, where corn, wheat, oats, barley, and potatoes are grown. Argentina is a world leader in wheat, corn, and cotton production. Beef cattle are raised in the pampas, and sheep in Patagonia.

Mining had been limited mainly to copper, lead, and zinc, in the northwestern Andes, and coal in the Río Turbio area. Petroleum and natural gas, however, have now become Argentina's main mineral resources; 21.3 million metric tons of crude oil were produced in 1987.

After World War II Argentina made an effort to broaden the base of its economy. Industrial development has increased gradually since then. However, Argentine industry is largely confined to the processing of food and agricultural products. Meat packing, flour milling, sugar refining, and wine making play an important role. Argentina has developed more heavy industry in recent years. It now manufactures automobiles, machinery, chemicals, and iron and steel. Aluminum production, which began in 1970, is becoming quite important as well.

In 1987 Argentina's imports cost \$5.8 billion while its exports earned \$6.3 billion. The main exports are agricultural goods, such as grain, meat, wool, and vegetable and linseed oil. Imports consist mostly of manufactured goods, including machinery and wood products.

Argentina imports mainly from the United States, Brazil, West Germany, Italy, France, and Japan. Exports go primarily to Italy, the Netherlands, Britain, Brazil, West Germany, the United States, and Communist China.

Government. Argentina has been called a republic since 1853, when its first constitution was drawn up. But democractic processes have frequently been disrupted by the military.

Under the terms of the 1853 constitution, Argentina is headed by a president elected by an electoral college to a six-year term. The electoral college is elected by popular vote.

Legislative power rests with a 46-member senate, whose members are nominated by the provincial legislatures, and with a 254-member Chamber of Deputies, elected by universal suffrage.

Argentina is a member of the United Nations, the Organization of American States (OAS), and the Latin American Free Trade Association.

History. In the 1400's the Inca empire extended into the northern corner of what is now Argentina. Its drive south, however, was permanently halted by Argentina's more primitive Indians, who were largely nomadic.

beef cattle

The first European to explore Argentina was the Spaniard Juan Díaz de Solis, who discovered the Río de la Plata in 1516. In 1536 an expedition headed by Pedro de Mendoza built a village on the site of present-day Buenos Aires. A majority of the early settlers, however, were Spanish colonists who crossed the Andes from Chile and Peru in the late 1500's.

The hostility of the Indians and the relative lack of precious metals at first made Argentina a neglected and sparsely settled part of the Spanish empire. It was not until the late 1700's that the colony acquired major economic importance as an exporter of cattle products, principally hides. In 1776 its capital, Buenos Aires, became the seat of the Spanish colonial viceroyalty of Rio de la Plata, which also included modern-day Bolivia, Paraguay, and Uruguay.

Independence. The Argentinians acquired a new sense of their own power and importance in 1806, during the Napoleonic wars, when they expelled a British force that had seized Buenos Aires. Four years later, on May 25, 1810, they established an autonomous junta to rule during the captivity in France of Spain's King Ferdinand VII. Although independence was not formally declared until 1816, in practice the Argentinians had been self-governing since 1810.

Within Argentina a strong rivalry had developed between Buenos Aires and the inland provinces. The capital favored a centralized government and was receptive to liberal reforms; the interior desired a federal system that would provide almost complete local autonomy and was politically conservative.

In the early 1820's, the liberal and centralist faction, the Unitarios, consolidated its control of the city and surrounding province of Buenos Aires under the leadership of Bernardino Rivadavia. The Unitarios encouraged immigration and investment, reformed the tax system, and restricted the influence of the Roman Catholic Church.

But they were unsuccessful when they tried to establish a centralized government over the entire country. The move provoked bitter Federalist resistance, which coincided with a war fought against Brazil over control of Uruguay (1825–1828).

Rosas era. In 1829 the Unitarios lost even Buenos Aires, which came under the control of the wealthy rancher and Federalist leader, Juan Manuel de Rosas. Rosas ruled the Buenos Aires province as dictator from 1829 to 1832 and from 1835 to 1852. He brutally suppressed political opponents, repealed many of the reforms of the Unitarios, and governed in the interest of his own class of great ranchers.

Rosas fought a brief war with Bolivia in 1837–1838 and continually intervened in Uruguay's affairs. He also engaged in disputes with France and Britain, which resulted in a hostile blockade of the Argentine coast from 1845–1848.

The European powers failed to humble Rosas, but eventually some of his own collaborators in the interior provinces turned against him. One of these, General Justo José de Urquiza, formed a coalition with the Unitarios and in 1852, with aid from Brazil, drove Rosas from power.

Federalism. Urquiza sought to reorganize the government of Argentina, and in 1853 a new constitution providing for a federal system was adopted. The province of Buenos Aires at first remained outside the union, but it agreed to join in 1859. In 1862 its governor, Bartolomé Mitre, became the first president of a fully united Argentina, serving from 1862 to 1868. During his administration, Argentina joined Brazil and Uruguay in the War of the Triple Alliance against Paraguay (1865–1870), when Paraguayan troops ignored Mitre's refusal to allow them to cross Argentine territory.

Domingo F. Sarmiento, president from 1868 to 1874, was an ardent admirer of the United States and especially of U.S. educational methods. Sarmiento established a public school system that became the best in Latin America. Moreover, the nation experienced a period of rapid economic expansion during the latter 1800's and early 1900's. Argentina built up an elaborate railway network, attracted a flood of European immigrants, and became a major world supplier of meat and wheat.

This ruling class was in many respects able and progressive, but it frequently stayed in power by irregular election practices and the use of arbitrary federal intervention in provincial affairs. The result was a gradual increase in political unrest, which found its most important expression in the Radical Party, organized in the 1890's. The Radicals had special appeal for the middle class.

Enactment of an electoral reform law in 1912 finally opened the way for the Radicals to elect a president, Hipólito Irigoyen, in 1916. The Radicals did not introduce any fundamental changes in social and economic policy, and Irigoyen, the first Argentine president ever chosen in a truly democractic election, was best known outside Argentina for his course of strict neutrality in World War I.

Irigoyen resigned in 1922, but was reelected in 1928. He was overthrown by a military coup in 1930, however, amid the crisis of the world economic depression.

This first revolutionary change of government in almost 70 years was followed in 1932 by the resumption of an outwardly constitutional government under a wealthy oligarchy similar to the one that had ruled prior to 1916. Another revolt occurred in June, 1943, however, and led to the establishment of a military regime under General Pedro Ramírez and later under General Edelmoir Farrell. Juan Perón ultimately emerged as the leading figure of this regime.

DIEGO GOLDBERG/SYGMA

ARGENTINE COWBOYS, *or gauchos, round up beef cattle on the pampas. Argentina's exports run heavily to meat and agricultural products, coming largely from the fertile pampas.*

Perón dictatorship. The new regime was politically repressive, but through Perón's inspiration and that of his famous wife, Eva, it gained working class support by expanding social security and other benefits. During World War II it continued the neutral policy that it had inherited from the preceding administration, but with pro-Axis overtones. In March, 1945, however, when the conflict was almost over, Argentina declared war on Germany and Japan.

Perón was briefly stripped of power in October, 1945, but he scored an impressive victory early in 1946 in a free election and became president.

As president, Perón expanded his labor policy into a doctrine called *justicialismo,* which claimed to be a middle course of true social justice between the extremes of communism and capitalism. Workers received a stream of wage increases and benefits.

Perón also gave special encouragement to industry. His extravagant spending and economic favoritism, however, severely damaged grazing and agriculture and produced grave inflation. In addition, he quarreled with the Roman Catholic Church and alienated the army. Dissatisfaction with his policies steadily increased, and he was finally overthrown by a military coup on September 19, 1955.

Contemporary Argentina. A series of provisional military governments ruled from 1955 until 1958. Then, in the first free elections held in twelve years, Dr. Arturo Frondizi was elected president. However, he soon lost popular and military support in his efforts to stabilize the economy, and he was overthrown in a coup in 1962.

None of the governments since Frondizi has gained lasting popular support owing to economic difficulties.

Civilian government was restored when President Alejandro Lanusse called for national elections in 1973. Hector Campora, a Perón supporter, was elected president. He subsequently resigned and, after 18 years in exile, Juan Perón was elected. He was in office only nine months when he died in July of 1974. His third wife, Isabel, succeeded him. Economic failures continued to plague the country, and when her administration's policies faltered she was replaced by a military regime in March of 1976. The new military regime, under president Jorge Videla, immediately took up the chore of suppressing the Marxist and Peronist guerrilla activities that sought to undermine it. In its iron-fisted attack on political opposition, the junta was accused of countless executions, torture, and wanton incarceration. The situation became so bloody and arbitrary that the 1980 Inter-American Human Rights Commission issued a scathing declaration of condemnation against the government of Argentina.

In April, 1982, Argentina invaded the British colony of the Falkland Islands, which it has claimed since 1833. After more than a month of fighting, Britain recaptured the islands.

In 1983 the junta allowed elections to be held. The Peronist Party, for the first time in almost 40 years, was defeated by the Radical Civic Union Party and its presidential candidate, Raul Alfonsin. One of Alfonsin's first actions was to order an investigation into human rights abuses by the junta.

The economy declined rapidly during the 1980's. Inflation reached phenomenal levels in 1989, causing looting and riots in supermarkets and other establishments.

The Peronist Carlos Saul Menem

was elected president in May, 1989. He was inaugurated in July rather than December because of Alfonsin's inability to control the economic situation.

Bahamas

Official name: *Commonwealth of the Bahamas*
Area: *5,380 sq. mi., 13,935 sq. km.*
Population: *(1990 est.) 251,000*
Capital: *Nassau (Pop., 1980, 135,437)*
Language: *English*
Religion: *Protestant*
Currency unit: *Dollar*
National holiday: *Independence Day, July 10*

The Bahamas form an archipelago in the Atlantic Ocean off the southeastern tip of Florida. The islands became an independent nation within the British Commonwealth on July 10, 1973, ending nearly 200 years of British rule.

The land and people. The 22 islands and 650 islets of the archipelago have low, rocky, flat, or rolling terrain and are ringed with coral reefs. The climate is warm throughout the year. About 50 inches of rain falls each year. Three-quarters of the people are black; the rest are of European or mixed descent. The people are English speaking.

About 60 percent of the people live in urban areas, mostly in the capital city of Nassau on New Providence Island. Only seven percent of the labor force is occupied by agriculture, and most of the workers are employed in the trade and service industries, especially tourism.

Economy. Tourism is the prime factor in the economy, but agriculture is also significant on most of the islands. Bananas, citrus fruits, and vegetables are grown. Forestry and salt production are important and, with food processing, constitute the only industrial activities.

Since 1960 government programs have sought to persuade businesses to make their headquarters on the islands. The poor balance of trade caused by the need to import necessities is partially offset by the expenditures of tourists.

Nassau is the commercial and corporate headquarters of the Bahamas. It has also become the center of a relatively new and very thriving business—international banking and investment management.

Oil transshipment to the United States has become increasingly important to the economy. There are several large refineries in the Bahamas.

Most of the Bahamas' small-volume trade is carried on with the United States, Saudi Arabia, and Iran.

Government. According to the democratic constitution of 1973, the Bahamas are ruled by an elected prime minister and a bicameral legislature. The General Assembly consists of a Senate and a House of Assembly, with 16 and 49 members, respectively. Queen Elizabeth II is chief of state, represented by a governor-general.

The Bahamas is a member of the United Nations and the Commonwealth of Nations, and it is an associated state of the European Common Market (EEC).

History. The Bahamas were discovered in 1492 by Christopher Columbus, but the first settlements were made by the English in the 1600's. Plantations were established, and black slaves were imported. The islands became a British colony in 1783 and retained that status until 1964, when self-government was granted. In 1967 the islands' first black prime minister took office and began to move the colony toward independence from Britain.

The Bahamian prime minster, Lynden O. Pindling, led the nation to independence in 1973; he has remained in office since then. His opposition comes mostly from black dissidents who oppose white minority rule on the islands.

Barbados

Official name: *Barbados*
Area: *166 sq. mi., 431 sq. km.*
Population: *(1990 est.) 260,000*
Capital: *Bridgetown (Pop., metro. area, 1988 est., 102,000)*
Language: *English*
Religion: *Anglican, Protestant*
Currency unit: *East Caribbean dollar*
National holiday: *Independence Day, Nov. 30*

Barbados, a small island nation at the extreme eastern end of the Windward Islands in the Lesser Antilles, West Indies, lies about 300 miles north of Guyana, on the South American mainland. Barbados achieved its independence in 1966 after some 300 years of British control.

The land. Barbados is a triangular-shaped island about 20 miles long and 14 miles across at its widest point. Most of the island is a low-lying plateau, but there is a small highland area in the northeast. There are good beaches along the western and southwestern coasts.

Barbados has an adequate supply of fresh water, but there is little natural vegetation. The climate is comfortable. Temperatures range between 70°F and 87°F, and the trade winds blow across the island all year.

The people. Most of the island's people are of African origin. Persons of mixed African and European background make up about 17 percent of the total, and those of European origin represent about three percent.

The island is densely populated, and population growth creates serious economic and social problems. There are over 1500 people per square mile, one of the highest population densities in the world. Over half of these people live in rural areas. Another 40 percent live in St. Michael parish, which includes Bridgetown, the nation's chief port and capital.

About 15 percent of the nation's labor force is occupied by agriculture, and twice that amount is employed in industry.

Economy. The economy of Barbados has only recently been successfully diversified. Traditionally based on sugar production, the economy has developed a thriving tourist industry that is now considered to be the main support of the island. Light industry

has been growing, and other activities, such as fishing, have been promoted.

Sugar cane is grown on about 80 percent of the cultivatable land, and sugar and sugar products—rum and molasses—account for approximately 80 percent of export earnings. Yams, peas, beans, and corn are grown for local food needs.

In 1985 imports cost $610.8 million while exports earned only $353.9 million. Most trade is carried on with the United States and Great Britain.

Government. The head of state is the British monarch, represented on the island by a governor-general. Actual executive powers are exercised by a prime minister and a cabinet. The prime minister is normally the leader of the majority party in the legislature.

The legislature has two houses, the Senate and the House of Representatives. The 21 members of the Senate are appointed by the governor-general. Twelve are named on the advice of the prime minister, two on the advice of the leader of the opposition party, and seven to represent religious, economic, and other interest groups. The 27 members of the House are popularly elected.

Barbados is a member of the United Nations, the Commonwealth of Nations, the Organization of American States (OAS), and the Caribbean Community and Common Market (CARICOM). It is also an associated state of the European Common Market (EEC).

History. Arawak Indians lived on Barbados until about 100 years before the arrival of the first British voyagers in 1625. An English merchant group had won control of the island by 1629, but during the English civil wars of the 1600's the English government took direct control. In doing so, the British granted the islanders the Charter of Barbados, providing for government by a governor, council, and elected assembly, and taxes levied only with the express consent of the inhabitants.

British rule. Barbados was a prosperous island. Coffee, tobacco, cotton, and other crops were grown for export, and cassava and corn were raised for local needs. In the late 1600's sugar became the major crop, and large numbers of African slaves were brought to work on sugar plantations.

The abolition of slavery in 1834 had little effect on the island's economic, social, or political life. Prosperity continued until late in the 1800's, when home-grown sugar beets began to meet Europe's sugar needs, and the world price of sugar dropped.

The economy revived in the early 1900's as a result of British financial aid, improvements in sugar production, and the beginnings of the export of labor. Many Barbadians went to Central America to work on the construction of the Panama Canal.

Federation. Political progress was rapid after World War II, and universal suffrage was introduced in 1951. Political parties were formed during the postwar years, and elections held in 1951 were won by the Barbados Labor Party (BLP), led by Grantley Adams.

In 1958 Barbados became a member of the short-lived Federation of the West Indies, which united ten of Britain's West Indian and Caribbean territories; Adams was the federation's prime minister. Adams's BLP lost the 1961 elections. The victor was the Democratic Labor Party, led by Errol Barrow, which had been formed in 1955 by dissident BLP members.

Independence. The Federation of the West Indies began to break up in 1962, when Jamaica and Trinidad withdrew to become independent nations. In 1965 Barbados decided to seek independence from Great Britian and achieved it on November 30, 1966.

Prime Minister Barrow quickly brought the new country into the United Nations and the Commonwealth of Nations. In 1967 Barbados became a member of the Organization of American States (OAS). Later, it became a leader in developing Caribbean economic and cultural organizations.

In 1985, on the death of John Adams, Bernard St. John became prime minister.

In 1986 Barrow became prime minister again; however, he was succeeded by Lloyd Erskine Sandiford in 1987.

Belize

Official name: *Belize*
Area: *8867 sq. mi., 22,963 sq. km.*
Population: *(1990 est.) 180,000*
Capital: *Belmopan (Pop., 1986, 3500)*
Language: *English, Creole*
Religion: *Roman Catholic, Protestant*
Currency unit: *Belize dollar*

Belize, formerly British Honduras, is located on the Caribbean coast of Central America. It is bounded on the north by Mexico, on the west and south by Guatemala, and on the east by the Caribbean Sea.

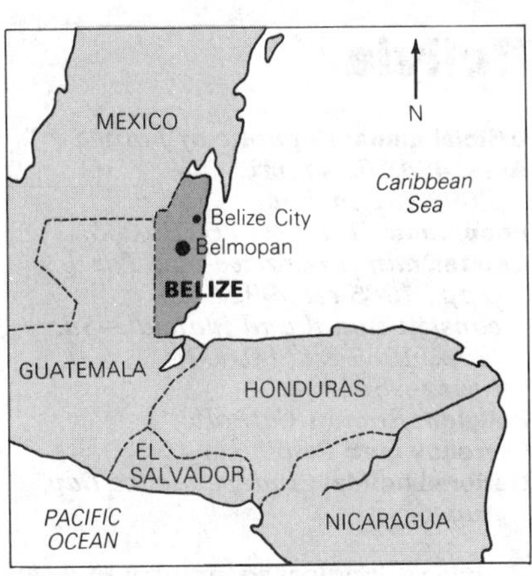

The land and the people.

The southern half of Belize is dominated by the Maya Mountains; the highest point, Victoria Peak, reaches 3681 feet. The northern part of the country is mostly lowlands, much of which is swamp. The vegetation throughout most of the country is tropical jungle. About 15 miles off Belize's long Caribbean coastline lies the second largest barrier reef in the world.

About 50 percent of the population is of African descent. Mestizos and Indians make up the next largest groups. There are also small minorities of East Indians and Europeans. The largest cities are Belize City, with about 50,000 inhabitants, and Orange Walk, with about 8500.

Economy. Agriculture is the most important sector of the Belizean economy. Major crops include sugar, fruit, rice, and tobacco. Manufacturing is dominated by the clothing, beverage, construction materials, and tobacco industries. In 1985 exports earned about $64 million, while imports cost about $105.4 million. Belize's major trading partners are the United States, Great Britain, and Canada.

Government. The Queen of England is the head of state; she is represented by a governor-general. The head of government is a prime minister. Legislative power is held by a bicameral National Assembly, made up of a House of Representatives with 28 members, and a Senate with eight members.

History. The first recorded European settlement was begun in 1638 by shipwrecked English sailors. Over the next several hundred years, more English settlements were established.

Until 1798 Belize was dominated by the struggle between the English settlers and the nearby Spanish colonists. Then the English defeated the Spanish in the battle of St. George's Cey.

In 1862 Belize became the Crown Colony of British Honduras. In the period just before World War I, Belize enjoyed a time of prosperity, but the colony remained undeveloped. In 1964 Belize received a new constitution that gave the colony internal autonomy.

Belize became independent in 1981, and another new constitution was promulgated. Relations with neighboring Guatemala are strained because of Guatemalan claims to a large part of Belize.

Bolivia

Official name: *Republic of Bolivia*
Area: *424,162 sq. mi., 1,098,581 sq. km.*
Population: *(1990 est.) 6,730,000*
Capital: *administrative—La Paz (Pop., 1985 est., 992,592) constitutional and judicial—Sucre (Pop., 1985 est., 86,609)*
Language: *Spanish*
Religion: *Roman Catholic*
Currency unit: *Peso*
National holiday: *Independence Day, Aug. 6*

ORGANIZATION OF AMERICAN STATES

INDIAN WOMAN *weaving in mountainous Bolivia. Indians predominate in the mountain area, along with mestizos, and some still speak the old Incan language, Quechua. Many work in the tin mines.*

Bolivia, a landlocked country in west-central South America, is bounded on the north and east by Brazil, on the west by Peru and Chile, and on the south by Argentina and Paraguay. Titicaca, on the Peru-Bolivia border, is the largest lake in South America.

The land. The basic natural division of the country is between lowland Bolivia and mountain Bolivia. The lowlands, or Oriente, in the east, occupy about 70 percent of the country. Mountain Bolivia includes four regions—the Altiplano, the Western Cordillera, the Northeastern Cordillera and Yunga Zone, and the Eastern Bolivia Highland.

Lowland Bolivia. The lowlands are sparsely inhabited, although pioneer activity begun in the 1950's attracted a number of people from the overpopulated upland areas. The humid, tropical condition of the north, situated within the southern part of the Amazon basin, contrasts with the southeastern Chaco, which has frosts as well as temperatures of over 100°F. Rainfall can vary 25 inches a year from an average of 38 inches.

Mountain Bolivia. The heartland of mountain Bolivia is the vast central plateau of the Bolivian Andes, the Altiplano (literally, "high flat area"). The Altiplano, averaging 12,000 to 13,000 feet above sea level, is composed of a series of high and gently rolling basins surmounted here and there by snow-capped mountains. The region is cool and dry in the south but more humid in the north.

The Western Cordillera, separating Bolivia from Chile, is a long series of dry slopes among which are several extinct volcanoes. The Northeastern Cordillera forms the edge of the Altiplano. Its streams have carved steep valleys in the course of their rapid descent to the broad Beni River system, which empties into the enormous Amazon River. The area has a large population and supplies food to the highland communities.

The remaining area of mountain Bolivia is the Eastern Bolivia Highland, or the Puna, a sloping region connecting the Northeastern Cordillera with the plains. The important regional centers of Cochabamba, Sucre, and Tarija provide markets for the corn, wine, and fruit grown in the area.

The people. Over half of the people of Bolivia are Indians. A small percentage of the population is of European descent. The remainder of the people are mestizo, of mixed Indian and European origin.

The Indians in the Lake Titicaca area speak Quechua, the Inca language, but the majority of the Andean Indians speak Aymara. Most of the mestizo and white population is found in the eastern valley towns of the Yungas and in the south.

La Paz, lying more than 12,000 feet above sea level, is the social, political, and economic center of the country. It occupies the position of political capital formerly held by Sucre, still the constitutional and judicial capital.

Bolivia's third largest city is Cochabamba, the focus of the road and rail routes that link mountain Bolivia with the lowlands. It is also the center of a populous farming area.

Economy. Bolivia's economy is based on mining. The country depends on the export of its mineral resources to earn the foreign exchange necessary to import essential goods. Bolivia is the second largest tin-producing country in the world, and in 1986 production was 16,800 metric tons. There are also large deposits of lead, copper, silver, oil, and natural gas.

Approximately three out every four workers are engaged in agriculture, but farm production meets only about 75 percent of Bolivia's food needs. The Altiplano, where most of the people live, is ill-suited for agriculture. Nevertheless, some barley, wheat, corn, beans, and potatoes are grown there. Coffee is a major crop and sugar cane is also grown.

Industry is limited and mainly produces simple consumer goods for domestic needs. La Paz is the country's manufacturing center. The lack of an adequate transportation system has been a major obstacle to economic growth.

Bolivia usually imports more than it exports, and the deficit has been met by foreign economic aid, principally from the United States. However, in 1985 Bolivian exports were valued at $663 million, and imports cost $552 million.

Minerals are Bolivia's major export, and foodstuffs and manufactured goods make up the bulk of imports. Bolivia exports primarily to the United States and Britain. Most imports come from the United States, although Japan is increasingly important as a supplier of imports.

Government. Bolivia is a republic with a strong executive branch headed by a president. Legislative power is vested in a bicameral congress consisting of a 27-member Senate and a 130-member Chamber of Deputies.

History. The Andean portion of what is now Bolivia was long a center of advanced Indian civilization. It formed part of the Inca empire from the 1300's to the 1500's. The Inca empire was overthrown by the Spanish in 1533, and in 1538 an expedition led by Gonzalo and Hernando Pizarro conquered Bolivia.

In 1559 Bolivia became part of the Spanish colonial viceroyalty of Peru and was known as Upper Peru. It later became important to Spain as a supplier of precious metals, especially silver. Spanish rule was harsh, and from 1661 to 1780 there were many Indian uprisings.

Independence. In 1809, after Napoleon had conquered Spain, the people of the city of La Paz deposed the Spanish authorities. A junta led by Pedro Domingo Murillo was soon overthrown by the Spanish, and Argentine patriots were unsuccessful at liberating Bolivia from the south.

In December, 1824, Simón Bolívar's forces under the command of Antonio José de Sucre, won a decisive victory at Ayacucho, Peru, that set the stage for the final defeat of the Spanish in Bolivia the following year. Bolivians were then faced with the alternatives of joining Argentina, joining Peru, or becoming a separate nation. An assembly in 1825 chose independence and adopted the name Bolivia.

The early republic. Antonio José de Sucre was elected Bolivia's first president in 1826. His administration was enlightened but brief. Unrest among his own troops combined with an invasion by Peru forced him from power in 1828. Sucre was succeeded by Andrés Santa Cruz, who remained in office until 1839. For roughly the next 50 years, government consisted largely of a rapid succession of dictatorships.

One recurring feature of the mid-1800's was the interference in each other's affairs by Bolivian and Peruvian military dictators. From 1835 to 1839 Santa Cruz united both countries in a confederation, but a war with Chile brought about its collapse.

Bolivia again fought Chile in the War of the Pacific (1879–1884), which resulted from Chilean designs on the nitrate deposits controlled by Bolivia and Peru in the Atacama desert along the Pacific coast. Bolivia was defeated and lost its portion of the Atacama desert, which included Bolivia's only outlet to the sea.

Modernization. Bolivia began to modernize rapidly in the early 1900's under presidents Ismael Montes (1904–1909; 1913–1917) and Eleodoro Villazón (1909–1913). Railroads were constructed, industries developed, and tin mining greatly expanded. During World War I Bolivia remained neutral until 1917, when it broke off diplomatic relations with Germany.

In the late 1920's an old boundary dispute with Paraguay over the Chaco region was renewed. War broke out in 1932, and in 1935 Bolivia was defeated. The final settlement, negotiated in 1938, gave three-fourths of the disputed territory to Paraguay.

New political parties arose with programs aimed at modernizing the country and improving the condition of the masses. One of these new parties, the National Revolutionary Movement (MNR), came to power in 1943 with a program calling for sweeping economic and social reforms.

Contemporary Bolivia. The MNR was overthrown in 1946 before it could accomplish a great deal, but it staged a successful uprising in 1952 after its leader, Victor Paz Estenssoro, had been cheated of his victory in a presidential election. The MNR managed to consolidate its position and carry out a series of reforms that included nationalization of the tin mines and distribution of large private estates among the Indian peasantry.

The MNR incurred huge deficits in operating the tin industry, and the drastic land reforms resulted in a sharp drop in production. Severe food shortages in the cities followed. Only massive U.S. aid kept the government functioning and saved many Bolivians from starvation. Nevertheless, progress was made in expanding education and in developing the fertile but sparsely populated eastern lowlands.

Paz Estenssoro remained in power from 1952 until 1956, when he resigned in favor of a party colleague, but he returned as president in 1960. After a period of strikes and rioting, especially in the tin mining region, he was overthrown in 1964 by the military, and a junta took power.

This was the first in a series of coups. The government changed its leadership seven times before Hugo Banzer Suarez took over in August of 1971, when an alliance of political parties, the armed forces, and several middle-class social organizations, overthrew the regime of Juan Jose Torres.

Under Banzer, nearly a decade of political stability was enjoyed. In 1978 he permitted presidential elections, but when they were declared to be corrupt, he fled to exile. Two years of chaos ensued. In 1980, as leftist Hernán Siles Zuazo was on the verge of winning a presidential election, a three-man junta staged a military coup on July 17. Civilian rule was restored in 1982 and elections have been held since, although military coups have temporarily overthrown the government.

In 1985 Victor Paz Estenssoro was chosen president by Congress after a popular election was inconclusive. In 1989 Jaime Paz Zamora was declared president by Congress.

In 1988 the United States Drug Enforcement Agency and the Bolivian government joined together to crack down on illegal drug trafficking and massive coca production.

Brazil

Official name: *Republic of Brazil*
Area: *3,286,488 sq. mi., 8,511,965 sq. km.*
Population: *(1990 est.) 157,940,000*
Capital: *Brasília (Pop., metro. area, 1986 est., 1,649,000)*
Language: *Portuguese*
Religion: *Roman Catholic*
Currency unit: *Cruzeiro*
National holiday: *Independence Day, Sept. 7*

Brazil, South America's only Portuguese-speaking nation, covers almost half of the South American continent and contains nearly half its people. Brazil borders every country in South America, with the exception of Chile and Ecuador. It is bounded on the north by Colombia, Venezuela, Guyana, Surinam, and French Guiana; on the northeast and east by the Atlantic Ocean; on the south by Uruguay; and

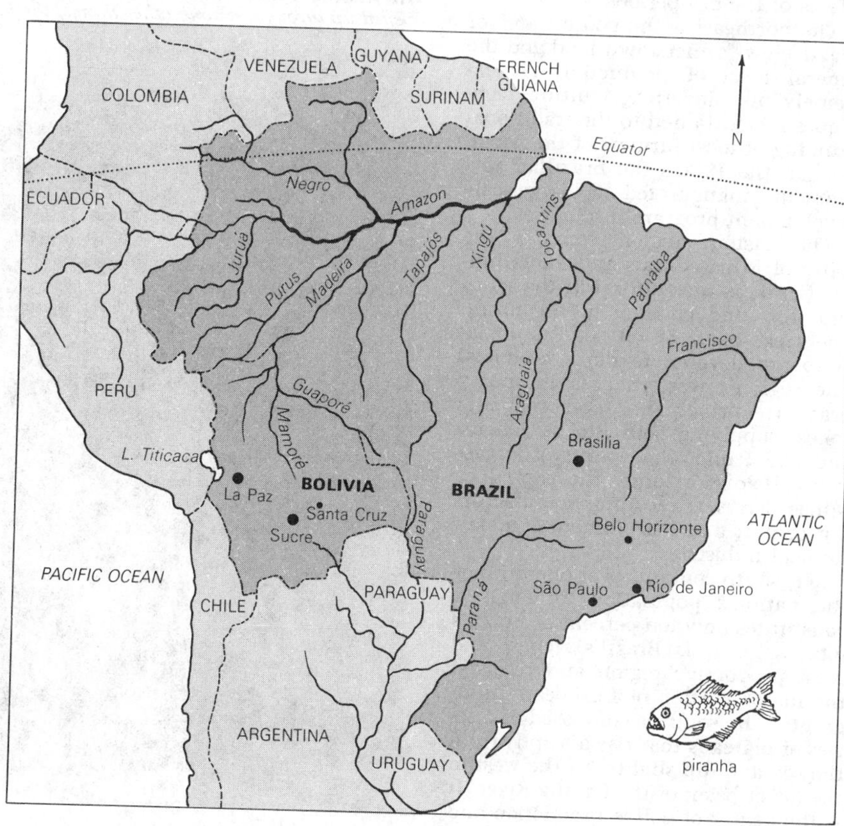

on the west by Argentina, Paraguay, Bolivia, and Peru.

The land. Brazil has a widely varied landscape, but there are two major types of terrain: the broad lowlands of the northern third of the country, which include the Amazon basin, and the Brazilian Highlands, which consist of low plateaus and mountains.

Brazil's land surface is unusual in that the highest areas lie just behind the Atlantic coast, and most of the rivers flow toward the interior, where they empty into the Amazon River or the Paraná-Paraguay river systems.

The north, which includes more than half the nation's land area, has less than ten percent of its total population. The area's few inhabitants live mainly within the floodplains of the Amazon River and its numerous tributaries. Since the 1950's, the exploitation of jute, cacao, tropical hardwoods, medicinal plants, oil-bearing nuts, and black pepper has improved the economic situation of the north. A number of Japanese immigrants have settled in the north.

The northeast is a region of great physical diversity. A wet, tropical, coastal plain is separated from desert, or *sertão,* by a dry forest area, the *agreste,* which forms a narrow zone between the two. Droughts have always afflicted the desert, and it is only within the last two or three decades that the building of reservoirs and the development of drought-resistant forage plants for cattle have lessened the effects of the dry periods.

The northeast is the poorest area of Brazil. Few farmers own land and the general level of productivity is extremely low. Modern agricultural techniques are still alien to the traditional thinking of most farmers of the northeast. In the 1960's the Brazilian government inaugurated a large-scale development program in the area.

The eastern region contains the states of Minas Gerais and Bahia. Minas Gerais is agricultural in the south and west and pastoral in the north. The areas near the city of Rio de Janeiro are devoted to dairy products. The region's western area is one of Brazil's principal food-producing zones, supplying both Rio de Janeiro and São Paulo, the country's largest cities. Belo Horizonte, the capital of Minas Gerais, is a leading manufacturing center, and has numerous metallurgical industries.

The south contains over one-third of the nation's population although it constitutes only ten percent of Brazil's total area. It is Brazil's richest and most productive region and received the major portion of European immigrants. The south is composed of a series of plateaus that rise abruptly from the sea and dip slightly in the west to the lower basin of the Paraná River. It is the center of coffee production and is also important for its forests, which provide softwoods.

The central west, the fifth region, includes almost 22 percent of the total area, but is occupied by only three percent of the country's population. It is an area of extensive grasslands with scattered trees, known as *campo cerrado,* or savanna. These *cerrados* occupy high plateaus at elevations of between 2000 and 3000 feet and are dry for most of the year.

In the south, it snows during the winter months in the highest areas, but usually the snow does not stay on the ground for more than a day. The vast western central interior of Brazil experiences sporadic showers three to four months a year from November through March or April, followed by a dry season during which the scrub vegetation turns brown.

The people. Brazil's population is composed of three main stocks: Indians, descendants of the original inhabitants; whites, descended from Portuguese and other European colonists; and blacks, brought as slaves from Africa by the Portuguese in the 1500's.

The bulk of the population is concentrated along the coast in a strip extending approximately 250 miles inland. The few remaining pure-blooded Indians live within the remote interior, particularly in the Amazon basin. Blacks live primarily in the northeast, especially near the coast, where once there were many sugar plantations.

The major cities of Brazil are on or near the coast. The largest city is São Paulo, which has more than 10 million people. Rio de Janeiro, the capital of Brazil until 1960, is the country's second largest city, with almost 6 million people. Rio remains the artistic and cultural center of the country, although it has been superseded in economic importance by São Paulo.

The capital, Brasília, in the central west, is a model of modern architecture and city planning. It is designed to link the heavily populated coast with the still underdeveloped interior.

Economy. Historically, Brazil's economy has depended heavily on the export of one commodity at a time. Sugar was the mainstay in the 1500's and 1600's, minerals, gold, and diamonds in the 1700's. In the mid-1800's coffee became Brazil's most important product. Although the coffee boom declined, the country has continued to rely heavily on the export of coffee for foreign exchange.

In recent years Brazil has developed a more diversified economy. It is now the leading industrial state of South America and easily has the largest gross national product. Although agriculture occupies two-fifths of the labor force, it accounts for less than ten percent of the gross national product. Industry occupies only one-fifth of the

THE AMAZON BASIN, *remote and enormous, the haunt of primitive Indians, is now being opened up through, among other things, the building of new highways.*

ORGANIZATION OF AMERICAN STATES

labor force, but contributes nearly 40 percent of the gross national product.

Nonetheless, agricultural output has increased markedly in the last decade, although not as much as industrial output. Agricultural products account for three-quarters of all exports and food processing is a major industry.

In addition to coffee, Brazil produces much of the world's cacao and considerable amounts of sugar, vegetable oils, and tobacco. Brazil is also a world leader in cotton production.

Brazil is rich in natural resources, including a vast, largely untouched supply of minerals, and one of the largest hydroelectric capacities in the world. Oil is produced on a small scale and most of the rest of it must be imported. To offset this expense, Brazil has been rapidly developing hydroelectric facilities and is beginning to develop nuclear energy.

Mining has changed from the production of gold and diamonds to the exploitation of iron ore and bauxite. Coal is mined in southern Brazil, principally in Santa Catarina, but it is of poor quality. The iron ore and coal are consumed in the various iron and steel mills located at Volta Redonda, on the route between Rio de Janeiro and São Paulo, and in Minas Gerais.

Since World War II there has been an accelerated growth of both light and heavy industry, centered primarily in the state of São Paulo. The major Brazilian industries produce textiles, iron, steel, motor vehicles, and foodstuffs.

Transportation. The transportation situation in Brazil has changed markedly since World War II. The physical integration of the country is being accomplished by building roads to the cities of the interior. Airlines have also come to serve the entire country. As a result, physical isolation, one of the primary barriers to development, is rapidly being overcome.

Trade. In 1986 Brazil's exports earned $22.4 billion and its imports cost $14.04 billion. Coffee normally makes up about half the value of Brazil's exports. Other major exports include cacao, sugar, pinewood, iron and bauxite ores, and cotton. Brazil imports large quantities of manufactured goods, machinery, fuels, vehicles, industrial raw materials, and foodstuffs.

Brazil exports chiefly to the United States, Japan, West Germany, and the Netherlands. Imports come largely from the United States, Saudi Arabia, and Iran.

Government.

Brazil was proclaimed a republic in 1889, but democratic processes have often been disrupted. The military overthrew the constitutional government in 1964 and instituted a new constitution in 1967.

The 1967 constitution strengthened the central government considerably, changing Brazil from a federal union of states into a centralized republic. It vested executive powers in the president, no longer elected by popular vote but chosen indirectly, by the congress. Strong powers were given to the president; they were increased even more in 1969 when the constitution was further revised.

In 1988 a new constitution was drafted; it is gradually introducing many changes to the existing government. Presidential elections were reinstituted and the president can no longer issue laws by decree. Many social and economic changes were also enacted, including new benefits for workers and incentives for Brazilian companies to develop.

The congress, consisting of the Senate and the Chamber of Deputies, continues to be elected by popular vote, but the franchise is restricted to those able to read and write. The 487 deputies are directly elected, as are two-thirds of the 72 senators. The remaining senators are indirectly elected.

History.

In 1494 Spain and Portugal, rivals in the establishment of colonies, signed the Treaty of Tordesillas, which granted Portugal all the territory east of a north-south line that extended from the mouth of the Amazon River to the São Paulo coast, neither of which had then been discovered. Thus, in 1500, when the Portuguese explorer Pedro Alvares Cabral claimed Brazil for the Portuguese crown, the claim was incontestable.

Brazil was at first overshadowed by Portugal's Asian and African possessions. It had no great Indian civilization or readily apparent mineral wealth, and early Portuguese contacts consisted mainly of sporadic expeditions to obtain dyewood and to trade with the Indians. Other Europeans, however, especially the French, began frequenting the Brazilian coast for the same reasons, and the rivalry spurred Portugal into taking more effective possession of the vast land.

Colonial administration. In 1534 Portugal carved Brazil into a series of "captaincies," under proprietary governors called "captains donatary," who were authorized to colonize and rule in the name of the king. In 1549 Portugal also sent out a royal governor–general to the city of Salvador, on Brazil's northeast coast, to exercise general jurisdiction over the entire colony.

Gradually, from the mid-1500's through the 1600's, sugar plantations worked by African slaves took root in the northeastern coastal belt. The export of sugar yielded huge profits and became the backbone of Brazil's economy. It was basically sugar that enticed the Dutch to carve out a short-lived colony in northeastern Brazil in the second quarter of the 1600's. Farther south, there arose a more varied agricultural and grazing economy that relied on Indians and mestizos rather than on black slaves for labor.

At the same time, some settlers, especially those of São Paulo, ranged far and wide through the interior, seizing Indians to work as slaves and searching for gold. In the process they pushed the boundaries of the colony far to the west of the zone allotted to Portugal by the Treaty of Tordesillas. In the late 1600's they found gold and diamonds in the region of Minas Gerais.

In the 1700's population growth and the increased importance of the south with its gold and diamond deposits brought a number of administrative changes. The last vestiges of the powers of the captains donatary, already largely superseded by royal officials, were eliminated, and in 1763 the capital was transferred from Salvador to Rio de Janeiro. It was also at that time that the first agitation for independence, which drew inspiration from the revolutions in France and the United States, began to occur.

In 1789 in Minas Gerais, a militia subaltern called Tiradentes, meaning "toothpuller," headed a conspiracy against the government. The Tiradentes conspiracy was easily suppressed, but it set a precedent for later attempts.

Brazil's status was altered without a struggle early in 1808, when Prince Regent Dom João and the Portuguese court arrived on Brazilian soil in flight from the armies of Napoleon. Rio de Janeiro became the temporary capital of the Portuguese empire, and Brazil obtained many of the advantages of independence. Moreover, Dom João lingered in Brazil even after Portugal was evacuated by Napoleon's forces. When he did return to Portugal in 1821, he left his eldest son, Pedro, in Brazil as regent, and advised him to become an independent monarch if a final separation of the two countries should prove unavoidable.

The empire. The eventuality feared by Dom João became a reality in 1822, when the Portuguese government attempted to return Brazil to a subordinate position within the empire. A resistance movement developed, and on September 7, 1822, Pedro declared Brazil independent. On December 1, 1822, he was crowned Emperor Pedro I of Brazil.

Although Brazil was organized as a limited, constitutional monarchy, Pedro I was unable to work smoothly with the Parliament. His government's popularity also suffered because of an unsuccessful war with Argentina over control of Uruguay and dislike of Pedro's numerous Portuguese advisers. In 1831 the emperor was forced to abdicate in favor of his infant son, Pedro II. From then until 1840 Brazil was governed by a series of regencies chosen by Parliament.

The regency period was marked by

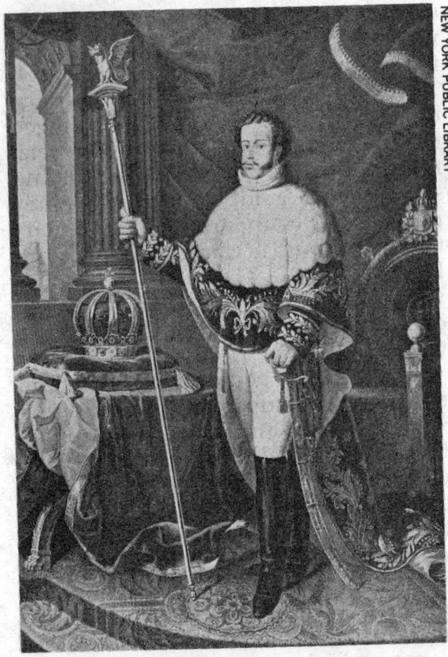
NEW YORK PUBLIC LIBRARY

EMPEROR PEDRO I, *who ruled Brazil from 1822 to 1831, when he was forced to abdicate in favor of his son, Pedro II.*

outbreaks of republicanism, regional separatism, and general political turmoil, but the monarchy survived. Demands for regional autonomy were partially met by the Additional Act of 1834, which amended the constitution to grant limited self-government to the provinces.

Pedro II. In 1840 Pedro II was declared of age, and he began performing his duties personally. During his reign of almost 50 years, Brazil attained a high degree of political freedom and stability. Brazil's two political parties, the Conservatives and the Liberals, peacefully alternated in power under prime ministers chosen from first one and then the other party.

Pedro II wielded substantial personal power, but civil liberties were guaranteed even to the small republican minority. However, the monarchy was slow to deal with the problem of black slavery. The slave trade had been outlawed by a treaty signed with Great Britain in 1827, but it continued in practice until the mid-1800's.

Slavery itself was completely ended only in 1888. The fact that slavery was abolished without compensation alienated the slave-owning aristocracy. By that time, moreover, the monarchy had also begun to weaken in other ways.

In the 1870's a serious clash with the Roman Catholic Church had occurred as a result of government interference with a strong anti-Masonic campaign launched by a group of bishops. Brazil's participation in the war of the Triple Alliance against Paraguay (1865–1870), although it ended in victory, added little to the empire's prestige.

After the war the army aspired to a greater role in Brazilian life, and thus came into conflict with the civilian-minded emperor and his ministers. Finally, republicanism increased steadily after 1870. The aging Pedro II still retained great personal popularity, but there was no serious resistance on his behalf when a military coup led by Marshal Manoel Deodoro da Fonseca overthrew the monarchy in 1889.

The republic. In 1891 the new Brazilian republic adopted a federal constitution modeled after that of the United States. The first two presidents, however, were military officers, and both showed arbitrary tendencies that provoked wide unrest. The first president to serve a full term was a civilian from São Paulo, Prudente José de Moraes Barros (1894–1898). His administration was harassed by military upheavals and by a revolt in the back country of northeastern Brazil led by a religious fanatic, Antônio Conselheiro. But when Barros left office, the republic appeared to be firmly established.

Subsequent administrations until 1930 were mostly controlled by a narrow oligarchy representing the large and wealthy states of São Paulo and Minas Gerais. Nonetheless, constitutional and democratic forms were generally maintained.

During the mid-1800's coffee had replaced sugar as Brazil's chief crop and major export. Coffee production steadily increased until in the early 1900's serious overproduction appeared. The government then began to restrict coffee planting and later to buy up surplus stocks, hoping to support coffee prices. Meanwhile a great rubber boom had swept the Amazon basin, only to collapse on the eve of World War I in the face of Asian competition.

The economy recovered with the wartime and early postwar demand for Brazilian products, but slumped with the later return to normal conditions. The 1920's were characterized by serious social and economic unrest.

The world economic depression of the 1930's caught Brazil in a highly vulnerable position because of its heavy dependence on coffee as an export. The government was unable to halt a disastrous drop in coffee prices. Moreover, the economic crisis coincided with an attempt in 1930 by the outgoing president, Washington Luís Pereira de Souza, to assure the election of Julio Prestes as his successor. Prestes won, but a revolution by the military installed the more popular opposition candidate, Getulio Vargas, in the presidency.

The Vargas era. Although he had condemned undemocratic practices of the previous regime, Vargas himself ruled by decree, which provoked demands for a return to constitutional procedures and an uprising in São Paulo in 1932. The revolt failed, however, and Vargas remained in power as dictator.

From the beginning, Vargas recognized the need for social and economic reforms. On assuming office, he initiated labor legislation, supported labor unions, and expanded educational facilities and social services in the larger towns and cities. He also encouraged industrialization in an attempt to diversify the economy, and with foreign financial assistance began the creation of a Brazilian steel industry.

In World War II Vargas sided with the Allies and sent Brazilian troops to fight in Italy. Toward the end of the war Vargas found himself subject to increasing public pressure to observe in Brazil the democratic principles for which he was ostensibly fighting abroad. He therefore began to modify his dictatorship and promised free presidential elections in 1945.

Fearing that Vargas would go back on his word, the military ousted him from office in October, 1945. The 1945 elections were won by Enrico Gaspar Dutra, who took office on January 1, 1946. In September a new constitution was adopted, completing the restoration of political freedom and representative government.

In 1951 Vargas returned to the presidency by popular election. His new administration, however, was characterized by blatant corruption and demagoguery. Vargas did create a government petroleum monopoly, Petrobras, which was designed to save Brazil from exploitation by foreign oil interests. Nonetheless, he was generally unable to solve Brazil's postwar economic problems.

An attempt by men close to the president to assassinate an opposition publisher brought forth a new move by the military to oust Vargas. Rather than resign as demanded, he committed suicide in August, 1954.

BRASÍLIA, THE CONGRESS BUILDING. *An ultra-modern planned city, the new capital of Brazil is centrally sited.*

PAN AMERICAN AIRWAYS

Contemporary Brazil. After a period of political confusion, Juscelino Kubitschek took office as president for the next full term (1956–1961). Kubitschek's main accomplishments were the creation of a new capital city, Brasília, located near the geographic center of the country, and the building of highways and hydroelectric works.

To finance these and other expenditures, Kubitschek issued vast amounts of paper money. By doing so he added to an inflationary spiral that had begun before his presidency. Economic growth nonetheless continued.

Jânio da Silva Quadros was elected president in 1960. His government resumed diplomatic relations with the Soviet Union and decorated the Argentine-born Cuban guerrilla expert Ernesto "Ché" Guevara. In general, Quadros proved to be a highly erratic leader, and he resigned in less than a year. The military unsuccessfully tried to prevent Vice President João Goulart from succeeding him because of Goulart's strong leftist leanings.

During the Goulart administration (1961–1964), inflation rapidly increased. Much was said about fundamental social reforms, including agrarian reform, but little was done. In March, 1964, a new military coup ousted Goulart.

A provisional military government had some success in slowing the pace of inflation. It conducted a widespread purge of prominent politicians, and gained control of the congress by barring opponents. General Humberto Castello Branco was elected president by the purged congress on April 11, 1964.

In December, 1966, Castello Branco had pushed through congress a new constitution providing for the consolidation of federal power and the election by congress of the president, who was granted semidictatorial powers. Under this constitution, extensively amended in 1969, the president is elected to a six-year term by an electoral college composed of members of the congress and representatives of the state legislatures.

Since Branco's regime, Brazil has been ruled by a succession of military governments that have somewhat improved economic conditions, but that have also used severe tactics in quieting political opposition. Church liberals and labor groups have been repressed, as have human rights in general. The abrogation of human rights has led to deteriorating relations with the United States, which publicly condemned the government in 1977.

Democratic reforms were begun in 1979. In that year, General João Baptista Figueiredo was elected president in the country's first open election since Goulart's deposition in 1964. Baptista promised more democratic reforms and granted relative freedom of political expression.

In January 1985 Brazil received its first civilian president in 21 years when an electoral college chose Tancredo Neves as the new president. Neves died in April, before being sworn in, and his vice president, José Sarney, succeeded to the presidency.

Brazil has a mixed economy that blends state, private, and international corporate ownership. The problem is that a very small proportion of the population owns the land and reaps the profits from farms, businesses, and industries.Widespread poverty results from this unequal distribution of land and income.

A 1989 election declared Fernando Collor de Mello president.

Chile

Official name: *Republic of Chile*
Area: *292,256 sq. mi., 756,945 sq. km.*
Population: *(1990 est.) 13,016,000*
Capital: *Santiago (Pop., 1985 est., 4,318,305)*
Language: *Spanish*
Religion: *Roman Catholic*
Currency unit: *Peso*
National holiday: *Independence Day, Sept. 18*

Chile is a long, narrow country on the western coast of South America. It stretches 2650 miles from north to south, but averages only 100 miles in width. The country has imposing natural boundaries. On the north the Atacama Desert separates Chile from Peru; on the northeast and east the Andes separate the country from Bolivia and Argentina; on the south the Drake Passage separates Chile from Antarctica; and on the west is the Pacific Ocean.

The land. The highest mountain in the western hemisphere, Mt. Aconcagua (22,834 feet), lies on the Chile–Argentina border. The Chilean Andes form a single mountain range in the east, and there is a low coastal mountain range in the west. A central valley nearly 500 miles long nestles between the two parallel ranges.

Northern Chile, the desert region, is very dry, and there are weather stations there that have no record of rain ever having fallen. The region has rich

CHILE'S ATACAMA DESERT, *rich in nitrates, copper, and iron ore. Chile fought and won the War of the Pacific in 1879–1883, against Bolivia and Peru, over the nitrate-rich region.*

COLVIN/MONKMEYER

mineral resources. The central valley has a mild climate, with a winter rainy season and summer drought. It is the heartland of the country. Almost 90 percent of the people live there, and it produces most of the country's domestic food supply.

Southern Chile is wet and heavily forested. The land is said to resemble Switzerland because of its high, snow-capped mountains and glacial lakes. Temperatures average in the low 50°s F. In the extreme south, at the end of the continent, are Patagonia and Tierra del Fuego, inhabited by extremely primitive natives who were of great interest to Charles Darwin when he visited the southern tip of the continent on the *Beagle*. The area has steep slopes, heavy rainfall, low temperatures, and high winds. It is very sparsely populated.

CULVER PICTURES

THE WAR OF THE PACIFIC, 1879–1883. *The capture of the Peruvian ironclad,* Huascar, *by the Chileans. Chile emerged victorious with most of the nitrate-producing areas in its hands.*

The people. Approximately 25 percent of Chile's population is of European descent. Most of the rest is mestizo, of mixed Spanish and Indian heritage.

About 100,000 Araucanian Indians live in the forests of south-central Chile. Changos live along the northeastern frontier and are employed in the mines. Groups of nomadic Fuegians inhabit Tierra del Fuego.

A dominant trend in Chile is the movement of people from the rural areas to the urban centers, which now contain four-fifths of the population. The capital, Santiago, has nearly one-third of the country's people. Vina del Mar is the second largest city, followed by Valparaiso, the principal port. Concepción is located in the center of Chile on the Bío Bío River, and other smaller cities, such as Talcahuano, Puerto Montt, and Punta Arenas, the most southerly city, are important ports.

Economy. Chile is largely dependent on the exploitation of its mineral resources, which are found primarily within the Atacama Desert. Copper, iron ore, and nitrates make up three-quarters of the total value of Chilean exports.

Chile has long been a world leader in copper and nitrate production, but in the early 1960's iron ore replaced nitrates as the country's second most important export. Chile produces the world's total supply of natural sodium nitrate, and most of the world's supply of iodine, a byproduct of nitrate.

Agreements with foreign mining companies provide for a portion of the profits to remain in Chile, and the income has aided the development of the entire economy. All of Chile's mines were nationalized in 1971, but many of them were returned to private ownership in 1975.

Mining employs a small percentage of the nation's labor force, but accounts for most of its international trade and over ten percent of its gross national product. Agriculture employs nearly one-third of the labor force, but provides less than ten percent of the gross national product.

Only a fraction of Chile's total land area is suitable for cultivation, and only a small part of that is used. Chile's Central Valley is the main agricultural region. The principal crops are wheat, barley, and oats. Livestock raising is also important, but neither cattle nor crop production is adequate for Chile's needs, and foodstuffs must be imported.

Chile is one of the most industrialized nations of South America. Industry employs a quarter of the labor force and provides for over one-fifth of the gross national product. The Huachipato steel plant, inaugurated in 1951, meets almost all Chile's requirements. Chile also manufactures a variety of consumer goods for domestic consumption including textiles, medicines, shoes, paper, and cement. The major industries are located in the provinces of Santiago, Valparaiso, and Concepción.

In 1987 Chile's exports were valued at $5.2 billion while imports cost $4.4 billion. Major exports are copper, iron ore, nitrates and iodine, fish meal, beans, lentils, wool, and paper. Principal imports include industrial raw materials, industrial and agricultural machinery and equipment, vehicles, petroleum, and consumer goods.

Most exports go to the United States, Britain, West Germany, the Netherlands, and Japan. Imports come largely from the United States, Argentina, West Germany, and Britain.

Government. Chile is a republic with a strong tradition of constitutional government. Since the coup of 1973, however, it has been ruled by a four-man military junta that is headed by a president. The legislature—which had consisted of an elected Senate and Chamber of Deputies—was dissolved in 1973. A new constitution was approved in 1980, but the country remains under military rule.

Chile is a member of the United Nations, the Organization of American States (OAS), and the Latin American Free Trade Association.

History. During the 1400's, the northern part of Chile had come under the influence of the Inca empire. The extent of Inca control is not known, but it did not extend to the warlike Araucanian Indians who lived in the southern forest region. The Spaniards, under Pedro de Valdivia, conquered Chile in 1541 but they were unable to defeat the Araucanians, who were not subdued until the late 1800's.

In the more open central portion of Chile, Spain created a stable agricultural colony, and Chile was part of the viceroyalty of Peru until the 1800's.

The first move toward independence was made in September, 1810, when Chileans established an autonomous junta to rule during the absence of the Spanish king, Ferdinand VII, who was held prisoner by Napoleon. The patriot regime was suppressed in 1814 by loyalist forces from Peru.

The Spanish were finally defeated in 1817–1818 by the army of José de San Martin, which crossed the Andes from Argentina. San Martin's Chilean comrade in arms, Bernardo O'Higgins, was made provisional ruler of Chile with the title of supreme director.

Independence. O'Higgins gave Chile a generally sound and progressive administration. Nonetheless, he antagonized Chile's powerful class of wealthy landowners by his efforts at mild social reform and his concentration of authority in his own hands. In 1823 he was forced to resign. Chile was then plunged into a brief period of turmoil during which rival political factions battled for control.

In 1830 the conservatives came to

ARAUCANIAN INDIANS *dance to the music of a long horn in southern Chile. These once-fierce warriors, never subdued by the Incas, only submitted to the Chileans in the late 1800's.*

power under the leadership of Diego Portales. Although he never assumed the presidency, Portales nonetheless created a strong centralized government while holding various cabinet posts. Portales was assassinated in 1837 while organizing a military campaign against a confederation of Peru and Bolivia, which he believed posed a threat to Chile. Chile won the war and broke the confederation in 1839.

Era of growth. From the 1840's through the 1880's, Chile made notable social and material progress, although those who benefited most were the upper and middle classes. Educational facilities were expanded, and religious toleration and the abolition of entailed estates were peacefully achieved. Economic development was aided by the extension of railway and coastal steam navigation, and by the final subjugation of the Araucanians.

From 1879 to 1883 Chile fought Bolivia and Peru in the War of the Pacific, which began as a dispute over Bolivia's treatment of Chilean nitrate interests in the Atacama region. Chile won the war and annexed the nitrate-producing provinces of Peru and Bolivia. A Chilean nitrate boom followed and lasted until the development of synthetic nitrates during World War I.

Commerce, manufacturing, and coal and copper mining grew during the same period. This progress was accompanied by the rapid growth of an urban and mining proletariat, whose poor working conditions led to serious unrest in the early 1900's.

Reforms. Chile had moved toward a system of constitutional rule in which the legislative branch established its supremacy over the executive. Confirmation of this trend was assured by a civil war in 1891, in which an attempt by President José Manuel Balmaceda to reassert presidential authority was defeated. Congress was controlled by parties representing the landed aristocracy and the allied urban upper class, and little was done to improve the conditions of Chilean labor.

Chile remained neutral during World War I. The economy was stimulated by the wartime need for nitrates, but was badly hurt when prices dropped after peace was declared. Social and political dissatisfaction on the part of the middle and working classes increased and resulted in the election in 1920 of Arturo Alessandri, who had run on an ambitious reform platform. Once in office, however, Alessandri had little success in carrying out his program and was forced to resign.

From 1924 to 1932 constitutional government was severely shaken. There were numerous changes of administration and even a mild dictatorship from 1927–1931 under reform-minded General Cárlos Ibanez. Nevertheless, Chile emerged from this period of turmoil with a start in labor legislation and a new constitution designed to end congressional domination of the executive.

Alessandri, allied with both conservatives and liberals, returned to the presidency in 1932 and successfully restored the pattern of constitutional government. He was succeeded in 1938 by Pedro Aguirre Cedra, whose Popular Front administration drew support from both socialists and Communists, although Aguirre Cedra himself was from the generally moderate Radical Party.

The Popular Front sponsored additional benefits for labor, including government medical programs and low-cost housing. It collapsed during World War II, and for the following 20 years Chile was ruled by a succession of middle-of-the-road and right-of-center administrations.

Contemporary Chile. Despite a high degree of political freedom and stability, and a seemingly impressive body of social legislation, Chile still had social problems. Almost nothing had been done for the landless rural masses, and the standard of living of urban workers did not keep pace with overall national economic gains.

Persistent inflation became a major problem, and in the late 1950's a vigorous socialist-Communist alliance showed signs of growing political strength. This was counterbalanced by the rapid rise of the Christian Democratic Party, which gained power in 1964 when its leader, Eduardo Frei Montalva, was elected president.

In 1970, a coalition of socialists, Communists, radicals, and dissident former Christian Democrats backed Dr. Salvadore Allende Gossens of the Socialist Party to a narrow presidential victory. Abrupt economic changes, recurring strikes, and general social unrest thwarted his programs for nationalizing the copper mines and taking over foreign-owned industries and banks. Allende was overthrown by a military coup in September of 1973.

Although Marxism was replaced by a self-styled "democracy," the ruling military junta—headed by President Augusto Pinochet Ugarte—has been repressive and dictatorial. The United States, which aided the 1973 coup, has led world criticism of the regime's disregard for human rights.

Since 1973 Chile has benefited from an influx of foreign (chiefly U.S.) investments. Allende's socialist policies had resulted in a loss of foreign capital and subsequent economic chaos.

In 1988 Chileans rejected Pinochet in a plebiscite as the military junta's choice for presidential candidate. In the 1989 elections, Patricio Aylwin was declared president of the civilian government.

Colombia

Official name: *Republic of Colombia*
Area: *439,737 sq. mi., 1,138,914 sq. km.*
Population: *(1990 est.) 32,598,000*
Capital: *Bogotá (Pop., 1985, 4,185,174)*
Language: *Spanish*
Religion: *Roman Catholic*
Currency unit: *Peso*
National holiday: *Independence Day, July 20*

Colombia is unique among the South American nations in facing both the Caribbean Sea and the Pacific Ocean. Colombia is bordered on the north by the Caribbean, on the east by Venezuela and Brazil, on the south by Peru and Ecuador, and on the west by the Pacific Ocean and Panama.

The land. The country is crossed by three distinct ranges of the Andes, which create serious barriers. Most of the country's people and economically important areas lie in scattered valleys, separated by the Andes and by climate and different ways of life.

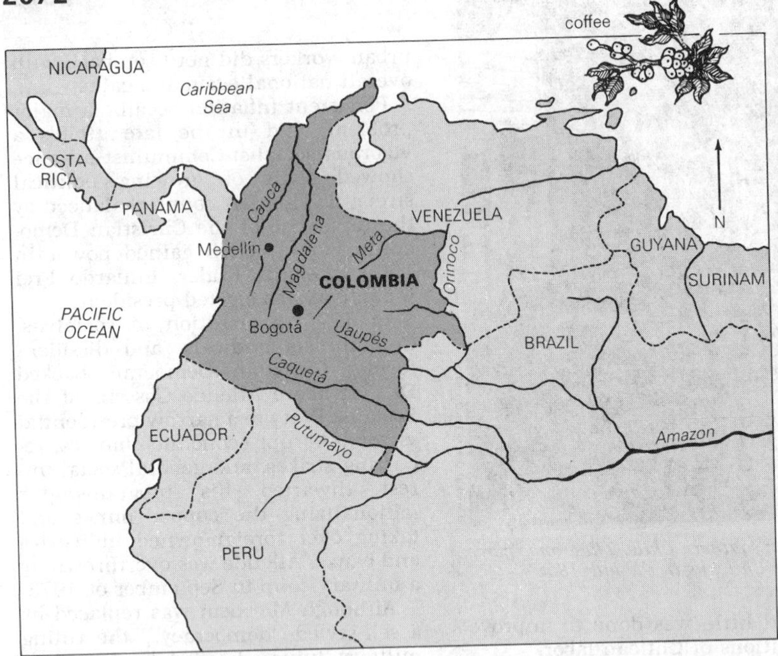

COLOMBIAN INDIANS *cast their votes. Although it is a rare functioning democracy, Colombia has been plagued by violence and unrest, a series of bloody civil wars in the late 19th century and early 20th, and in the 1950's ten years of mindless violence.*

Physical regions. Colombia has two main land regions—the Andes, in the west, and the lowlands, in the east. The Andean region is a continuation of the broad Andes mountain system, which runs almost the entire length of the western side of the South American continent. The Colombian Andes fan out in an east-west direction in the southwest to form three ranges: the Cordillera Occidental, the Cordillera Central, and the Cordillera Oriental.

The Cordillera Central has peaks that rise more than 18,000 feet above sea level. The cordilleras Occidental and Oriental are somewhat lower. The Cordillera Oriental widens in the north and forms a narrow plateau in the vicinity of Bogotá. The Magdalena River separates the Cordillera Oriental from the Cordillera Central, and the Cauca River separates the Cordillera Central from the Cordillera Occidental. Both rivers flow northward and empty into the Caribbean Sea.

The eastern lowlands drain into the Amazon and Orinoco river systems. The southern section of the region is tropical rain forest and is sparsely populated. The northern section consists of savannas, or *llanos.* Although flooded for a large portion of the year, it is suitable for livestock raising.

Climatic zones. Climate in Colombia varies with altitude. The lower areas, from sea level to about 3000 feet, comprise the *tierra caliente,* or hot country. It has average temperatures of from 75°F to 85°F, and tropical crops such as rice and bananas are grown there.

The *tierra templada,* or temperate country, lies between 3000 and 6500 feet above sea level. It has year-round temperatures of 65°F to 70°F, and coffee flourishes on the Andean slopes.

The third level is the *tierra fría,* or cold country, between 6500 and 10,000 feet above sea level. Wheat, maize, and fruit are grown there. Above 10,000 feet but below the 15,000-foot snow line, the land is unsuitable for cultivation and is devoted to pasturing livestock.

The people. About 70 percent of the Colombian population is mestizo, of mixed Spanish and Indian descent, and mulatto, mixed black and white. Whites constitute about 20 percent of the total and are concentrated in the major cities. Blacks make up less than seven percent of the population and live mainly along the Caribbean and Pacific coasts. Indians represent about three percent of the population.

Nearly three-quarters of the people live in urban areas, particularly in the Andean valleys. Bogotá, the capital, lies more than 8500 feet above sea level. Cali, in the fertile Cauca Valley, is a market point for agricultural products and an industrial center. Medellín, in the Cordillera Central, is the commercial center of the coffee and textile industries.

Barranquilla, on the Caribbean coast, is the country's largest port. Cartagena, one of the oldest South American cities, is Colombia's foremost tourist center. It is also the shipping point for petroleum and petroleum products from a large local refinery.

Economy. Agriculture is the most important part of Colombia's economy. Although only four percent of the nation's total land area is cultivated, about two-fifths of the population is employed in agriculture. Coffee is the chief crop and Colombia relies heavily on its export to earn foreign exchange. Other major commercial crops are bananas, sugar cane, tobacco, cotton, and cacao. Cattle are also important and are raised on the *llanos* of the country's eastern lowlands.

Colombia is rich in mineral resources, and mining plays an important role. Petroleum is the country's second most valuable export, and in 1979, 6.5 million metric tons of oil were produced. Colombia leads South America in gold production and is the world's most important source of emeralds.

Although industry is not highly developed, it has been growing. It now contributes about 20 percent of the gross national product, just slightly less than agriculture does. Manufacturing is largely devoted to textiles and food processing, but beverages, shoes, steel, and a variety of chemicals are also produced. The growth of both industry and mining, however, is hampered by a lack of capital for investment, poor transportation facilities, a small domestic market, and political instability.

In 1979 Colombian exports were valued at $3.4 billion and imports cost $4.4 billion. Coffee accounts for about 65 percent of the value of all exports. Other exports include petroleum, bananas, tobacco, cotton, and sugar. Chemicals, machinery, steel products, paper, and vehicles are the country's main imports. Colombia's major trading partner is the United States. Other important trading partners are West Germany, Japan, and Venezuela.

Government. Colombia is a constitutional republic. The chief executive and head of state is the president, who is popularly elected to a term of four years. He may not serve consecutive terms.

The congress is composed of the 114-member Senate and the 199-member House of Representatives. Senators serve for four years, and representatives for two.

Colombia belongs to the United Nations, the Organization of American States (OAS), the Andean Group, and is a member of the Latin American Free Trade Association.

History. Before the Spanish conquest in the 1500's, the high Andean region of Colombia stretching northeastward from Bogotá was the home of the Muiscas, a Chibcha-speaking American Indian people who had a stable agricultural society and who were highly skilled at goldwork. They were easily subdued by the Spaniards, who began exploring the Caribbean coast as early as 1500.

Spanish era. The first permanent Spanish communities were established at Santa Marta in 1525 and Cartagena in 1533. Santa Marta later served as the base for an expedition under Gonzalo Jiménez de Quesada that moved inland to conquer the Muiscas and resulted in the founding of Bogotá in 1538.

To the west, the Spaniards discovered what was to become the chief gold-producing area of their empire. Cartagena, on the Caribbean coast, became the principal naval base of the Spanish Main. Nonetheless, most of Colombia remained virtually uninhabited throughout the Spanish colonial period. Its few people were engaged chiefly in raising cattle and growing crops for local consumption.

Colombia's struggle for independence began in 1810, when local leaders deposed the Spanish authorities and established a number of juntas, ostensibly to rule in the absence of Spain's King Ferdinand VII, who was held captive by Napoleon. Spanish armies reoccupied the principal regions of the country in 1815–1816, but in 1819 Simón Bolívar returned from Venezuela and decisively routed the Spanish forces at Boyacá.

Independence. In the same year, 1819, the former viceroyalty of New Granada—which included modern Colombia, Panama, Venezuela, and Ecuador—was organized by the leaders of the independence movement into the republic of Gran Colombia. Bolívar was elected president, but he had to leave to continue the war against Spain and turned over the government to his vice president, Francisco de Paula Santander.

Santander proved an able administrator, but was harassed by separatist movements in Venezuela and Ecuador. Not even the return of Bolívar could prevent the final dissolution of the republic of Gran Colombia in 1830.

In 1831 the territory of modern Colombia and Panama was established as the Republic of New Granada. Santander became its first elected chief executive in 1832. Soon, however, a long and often violent struggle began between liberals and conservatives over church policy and constitutional organization of the state.

Era of conflict. During the 1850's and 1860's, the liberals established freedom of worship and separation of church and state, but they also seized church lands, abolished monastic orders, and placed restrictions upon the Roman Catholic clergy. Politically, they carried the concept of states' rights to such extremes that the national government itself was often rendered ineffective.

The liberals' extreme approach to local autonomy and their church policy brought a strong reaction against them in the 1880's. Although originally a liberal, President Rafael Núñez joined forces with the conservatives to adopt a rigorously centralist constitution in 1886 and to remove the major restrictions placed upon the church.

The policies of Núñez did not end internal strife. Liberals fought to undo his work by launching civil wars, the longest and bloodiest of which raged from 1899 to 1902. This war, plus the secession of Panama in 1903, shocked the leaders of both factions into laying aside some of their bitterness.

Civil wars abruptly ceased, and for nearly 50 years Colombia enjoyed relative stability and constitutional government. In the meantime, economic growth continued. The production of coffee increased. New commodities, such as bananas and petroleum, and the beginnings of light manufacturing, especially of textiles, did a great deal to broaden the base of the economy. But it was not enough.

Reforms. Until the liberal administration of Alfonso López (1934–1938), however, neither party had given much attention to the great majority of Colombians, who remained illiterate, impoverished, and beyond the reach of modern health facilities and social services. To deal with this problem López launched a program that included labor reform and social welfare legislation.

Although his program was generally moderate, it aroused strong opposition from wealthy Colombians. At the same time, it aroused among the working class hopes that could be only partially satisfied. Colombia thus faced a new period of strife in which inherited political rivalries were aggravated by new social and economic conflicts.

Tensions reached a climax on April 9, 1948, when the leftist liberal leader Jorge E. Gaitán was assassinated in Bogotá and his followers staged a riot in protest. A year later, interparty relations broke down entirely, and violence began to spread to large areas of Colombia. Beginning as a struggle between liberals and conservatives, it often degenerated into banditry.

Contemporary Colombia. A dictatorship by General Gustavo Rojas Pinilla, from 1953 to 1957, brought a slight decline in civil strife but failed to stop the violence, which in the decade following Gaitán's death claimed roughly a quarter million lives. The violence of the 1950's and the growing unpopularity of the Rojas regime led liberals and conservatives to cooperate once again.

After joining to overthrow the dictator in May, 1957, the two factions created a National Front coalition government. The terms of the coalition agreement provided for the alternation of liberals and conservatives in the presidency and the division of other offices on a 50-50 basis for a 16-year period. Under the National Front, violence decreased but did not disappear.

A new approach was made to the nation's fundamental social and economic problems, including efforts at agrarian reform. But Colombia's difficulties were compounded by an extremely high rate of population increase, large scale migration to the cities, and a sharp drop in the world price of coffee, which limited the financial resources available for carrying out reform programs.

The last president to serve under the National Front alternating system was Misael Pastrana, a conservative elected in 1970. Elections returned to the traditional parties in 1972.

Since 1970 the left-wing Movement of April 19 (M-19) has steadily increased its guerrilla and terrorist activities as the government has lagged in effecting adequate social and land reform. There is a legal Communist Party, but it has only slight support.

Colombia has been troubled by inflation, high unemployment, and illegal drug traffic that reached monumental levels in the 1980's. Although illegal, drugs are Colombia's largest export. In 1989 the Colombian government began a serious drug crackdown by seizing drug cartels' property and confiscating their drugs. The government continued the battle despite the traffickers' violent retaliations.

In 1985 a devastating volcanic eruption buried the town of Armero in a river of mud, killing about 23,000.

Costa Rica

Official name: *Republic of Costa Rica*
Area: *19,575 sq. mi., 50,700 sq. km.*
Population: *(1990 est.) 3,039,000*
Capital: *San José (Pop., 1984, 241,464)*
Language: *Spanish*
Religion: *Roman Catholic*
Currency unit: *Colón*
National holiday: *Independence Day, Sept. 15*

The Republic of Costa Rica, a small country in Central America, is bounded on the north by Nicaragua, on the east by the Caribbean Sea and Panama, and on the south and west by the Pacific Ocean.

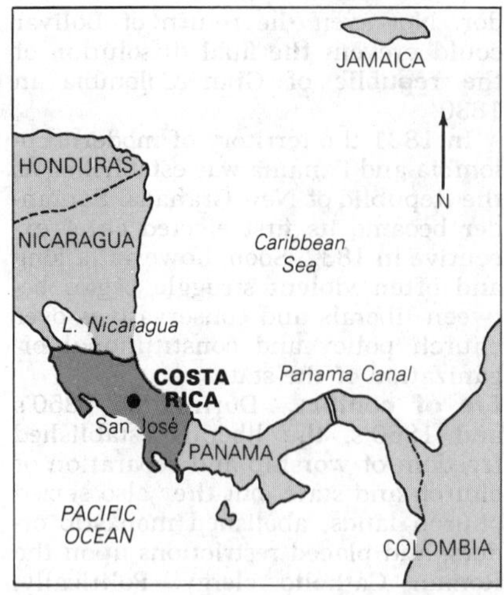

The land. Costa Rica has three major regions: a Caribbean coastal plain, a mountainous central area, and a Pacific coastal plain.

The Caribbean coast is rainy and covered with tropical evergreen forests and swamps. The central region, which has a temperate climate, consists of high flat basins formed by three mountain ranges—the Cordillera de Guanacaste, the Cordillera Central, and the Cordillera de Talamanca. The *Meseta Central,* or central plateau, the largest basin of the region, lies between the Cordillera de Guanacaste and the Cordillera de Talamanca.

The Pacific coastal plain, a region of tropical forests and savanna, has alternating wet and dry seasons.

The people. With the exception of a relatively small black population concentrated in the Caribbean coastal area, Costa Ricans are almost all of European, largely Spanish, descent. Most live in the Meseta Central, the site of San José, the industrial and cultural center as well as the capital of the country.

Costa Rica has a very high population growth rate, about $2\frac{1}{2}$ percent a year. This is considerably lower than it was in the 1960's, however.

Nearly two-thirds of the people live in rural areas. One-third of the labor force is occupied by agriculture, and another 15 percent by industry.

Economy. Costa Rica is one of the most prosperous and industrialized countries of Central America, and its prosperity is more evenly distributed than most. Since 1960, manufacturing has been rapidly developed; it now contributes about one-fifth of the gross national product, while agriculture contributes slightly more.

Most manufacturing involves the processing of agricultural products—food, cotton, and wood. Gold and manganese are the most important minerals produced, and bauxite is just beginning to be exploited. Membership in the Central American Common Market (beginning in 1963) has opened up new markets for the nation, which began to produce pharmaceuticals, textiles, tires, and other consumer items after its entry.

Hydroelectric power, the main domestic source of energy, has developed gradually. A huge facility at Arenal opened in 1979. It has added greatly to the nation's power reserves.

The main source of national income is still agriculture. Coffee and bananas are the main cash crops, followed by cacao and sugar. Fruits, vegetables, cereals, and cotton are also grown.

In 1987 Costa Rica imported $1.3 billion worth of goods, while exports earned $1.4 billion. Most trade is conducted with other Latin American states and with the United States. Imports consist of manufactured goods, machinery, chemicals, and petroleum. Coffee, bananas, cacao, abaca, cotton, and cattle are the major agricultural exports. Other significant exports are fish, lumber, gold, and manganese.

Costa Rica's economic progress is heavily dependent on foreign aid and investment. Through the Alliance for Progress the United States has helped finance Costa Rica's efforts to industrialize further.

Government. Costa Rica has a presidential form of government. The head of state and chief executive is the president, who is popularly elected to a four-year term. Legislative powers rest with the unicameral Legislative Assembly, whose 57 deputies are popularly elected to a four-year term.

Costa Rica is a member of the United Nations, the Organization of American States (OAS), the Organization of Central American States, and also of the Central American Common Market.

History. Columbus first discovered Costa Rica in 1502 on his last voyage to America. Expecting to find gold, he named it *Costa Rica,* or rich coast. Disappointed treasure hunters who followed him stayed only long enough to pillage the land. The first permanent European settlement was established in 1564 at Cartago, on the Meseta Central, by Juan Vásquez de Coronado.

Costa Rica was part of the Spanish colonial province ruled by the captain general of Guatemala. When Agustín de Iturbide proclaimed Mexico's independence from Spain in 1821, the Spanish Captain General Gabino Gaínza declared Central America independent. In 1822 Gaínza was overthrown and the region was annexed to Mexico.

Iturbide fell in 1823, and Costa Rica joined Guatemala, El Salvador, Honduras, and Nicaragua to form the United Provinces of Central America. Dissatisfaction with Guatemala's domination of the union soon developed and in 1839 Costa Rica withdrew

CUTTING BANANAS *in Costa Rica. A conveyor carries the bananas to a washing and packing station nearby. Costa Rica is one of the most prosperous nations in Central America.*

JANE LATTA

from the federation and became a separate nation.

Independence. Braulio Carrillo, a dynamic president, who served from 1834 to 1837 and again from 1838 to 1842, promoted the cultivation of coffee, which became a major export, and subdivided many large estates, thus increasing the number of small landholders.

In 1842 Carrillo's dictatorial methods led to a successful revolt under the leadership of Francisco Morazán. Morazán was himself shortly overthrown, and a period of anarchy followed. Order was finally restored in 1849.

In 1870 Tomás Guardia overthrew the government and dominated national affairs until his death in 1882. He modernized the economy and increased unity, partly through a large program of railroad construction.

Under President Bernardo Soto (1885–1890), free compulsory education was established, and in 1889 the first free elections were held. Costa Rican support of democratic principles was expressed in public hostility to a coup in 1917 led by Federico Tinoco Granados. His regime lasted for less than two years.

Conflict with Panama over Coto, a border region on the Pacific coast, dominated foreign affairs during the 1920's and 1930's. Costa Rica invaded the Panamanian-occupied territory in 1921, and the United States pressured Panama to accept Costa Rican control of Coto. The issue was finally settled in 1941, when both countries agreed to redefine their common boundary.

Contemporary Costa Rica. A fraudulent presidential election in 1948 prompted a revolution led by José Figuéres. The Figuéres victory was followed by 18 months of rule by a junta that introduced a new constitution that enacted many progressive social reforms into law. Otilio Ulate, the victorious moderate president, originally elected in 1948, was inaugurated in 1950 after Figuéres restored civilian rule in Costa Rica.

In 1953 Figuéres was elected president. Figuéres, a liberal, was a severe critic of Latin American dictators, in particular of President Anastasio Somoza of Nicaragua. Early in 1955 a Nicaraguan-instigated rebellion broke out, but the rebels were crushed.

Francisco Orlich, a supporter and friend of Figuéres, was defeated in the 1958 election by Mario Echandi Jiménez, a conservative. In 1962, however, Orlich won the presidency and, a year later, brought Costa Rica into the Central American Common Market. The resulting economic progress led to greater political stability and unity.

Since 1966 the National Liberation Party has become the dominant political force in Costa Rica. Under the Liberation presidents, José Figuéres (elected in 1970) and Daniel Oduber Quirós (elected in 1974), Costa Rica began to reverse some of the trends toward socialism that had preceded them.

Rodrigo Carazo Odio was elected president in 1978, as head of the new Unity Party. He ordered a break in relations with neighboring Nicaragua when rebels from that country used Costa Rica as a base for military operations. The National Liberation Party returned to power in 1982 with the election of Luis Alberto Monge; it remained in power with the election of Oscar Arias Sanchez in 1986.

In 1987 Sanchez won the Nobel Peace Prize for his regional peace plan that became an agreement accepted by five Central American countries.

Cuba

Official name: *Republic of Cuba*
Area: *44,218 sq. mi., 114,524 sq. km.*
Population: *(1990 est.) 10,548,000*
Capital: *Havana (Pop., 1986 est., 2,014,800)*
Language: *Spanish*
Religion: *Roman Catholic*
Currency unit: *Peso*
National holiday: *Anniversary of the Revolution, Jan. 1*

Cuba, the largest island in the Greater Antilles, occupies a strategic position dominating the sea lanes that link the Atlantic Ocean, the Caribbean Sea, and the Gulf of Mexico. The island lies about 100 miles southeast of the United States, from which it is separated by the Straits of Florida. There is a major U.S. naval base in southeastern Cuba, at Guantanamo Bay.

A revolutionary government was established in Cuba in 1959 under the leadership of Fidel Castro. Under Castro's leadership, Cuba became closely tied to the communist bloc of nations, especially the U.S.S.R. itself.

The land. Cuba is made up largely of level or rolling land. There are only three mountain areas—all small. The Sierra Maestra and associated highlands lie in the extreme southeast and reach a maximum elevation of about 6500 feet. The heavily eroded, limestone Sierra de los Organos, with a maximum elevation of some 2500 feet, is in the dry and barren northwest. The Trinidad Mountains, rising less than 4000 feet, are on the south coast, east of Cienfuegos.

The island has two rainy seasons, one in summer and one in winter. Hurricanes frequently occur in the fall and winter.

The people. The people of Cuba are largely of Spanish, African, and mixed origins. More than half the population lives in urban areas. The major cities include Havana, the capital; Camaguey, a center of the sugar industry; and Santiago, a major port.

The rate of population increase is high, but there has been a heavy emigration since the early 1960's, when the Castro government launched a socialist program. Many of the émigrés settled in the United States, and especially in Miami, opposite Cuba. They included large numbers of professional people, managerial personnel, and technicians.

Economy. Cuba is a rich country and it is among the most economically developed nations of Latin America. The island has rich soil and considerable mineral wealth. There are abundant deposits of iron ore, chromite, manganese, nickel, cobalt, and copper ore. There is also some petroleum, although not enough to meet the country's needs. There is a good transportation system, with an excellent road and rail network and a number of well equipped ports.

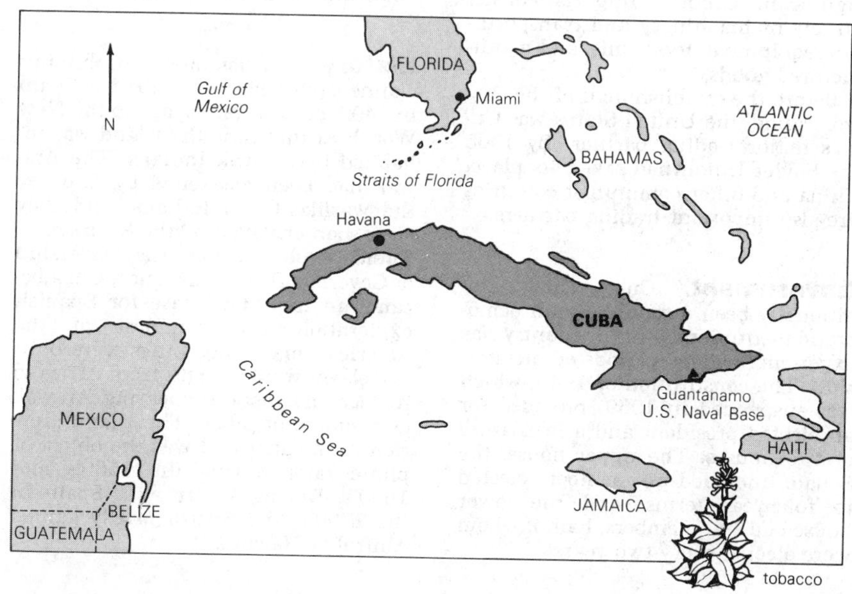

UPI

THE U.S. MAINE EXPLODES *in Havana harbor in 1898—cause unknown. The incident sparked a war in which Spain's decaying empire collapsed. The United States inherited Cuba.*

Cuba has long been one of the world's leading producers of sugar, and is also known for its tobacco, which is grown in the region east of the Sierra de los Organos. Coffee is produced in southeastern Cuba. Other important crops include henequen, sweet potatoes, citrus fruits, vegetables, and pineapple.

Manufacturing has grown rapidly, and it now accounts for over 40 percent of the gross national product. It occupies one-quarter of the labor force. Sugar processing is the most important activity, but Cuba is also on a par with several European countries in the production of several types of goods—synthetic fibers, for example. Steel and power consumption are also high. But industry has been hampered by a shortage of technicians and parts since the Castro revolution.

In 1983 Cuba's exports earned $6.5 billion and its imports cost $7.2 billion. Sugar represents about 75 percent of export earnings. Tobacco, ores, especially nickel, and chemicals are also significant exports. Imports consist largely of machinery and transportation equipment, foodstuffs, and manufactured goods.

Before the establishment of the Castro regime, the United States was Cuba's major trading partner. By 1965 the Soviet Union had taken its place. China and other communist countries are also important trading partners.

Government. Cuba has traditionally been a republic with democratic institutions. But the country has experienced long periods of dictatorship. The constitution of 1940, which was suspended in 1959, provided for an elected president and a legislature of two houses. The upper house, the Senate, included 54 members elected to four-year terms, and the lower house had 140 members, half of whom were elected every two years.

Castro instituted a dictatorship under his personal control. The head of state was still nominally the president, but power rested in Castro's hands as prime minister and first secretary of the Communist Party of Cuba, or PCC, from its initials in Spanish.

The United Party of the Cuban Socialist Revolution (PURSC), formed in 1962 by the merger of Cuba's old Communist Party with Castro's Integrated Revolutionary Organizations (ORI), was renamed the Communist Party of Cuba in 1965. Castro's followers remained the dominant group. In 1967 Castro promised that Cuba would have a new, "socialist," constitution by 1970. It was finally granted by 1976.

According to the new constitution, there is now a unicameral National Assembly of People's Power. Its 481 deputies are elected to five-year terms. The real power remains, however, with the Communist Party and its politburo.

Cuba is a member of the United Nations, and of the Council for Mutual Economic Assistance (Comecon).

History. Christopher Columbus claimed the island of Cuba for Spain in 1492, on his first voyage to the New World. At that time the island was inhabited by Arawak Indians. The Arawak had been weakened by raids by the warlike Carib Indians, and they were soon enslaved by the Spanish.

Spanish rule. Under the leadership of Governor Diego Velázquez, Cuba became an important base for Spanish exploration and conquest of the American mainland. Cities were built and slaves were brought from Africa to replace the fast-disappearing Arawak as a source of labor. The island grew rich from sugar and was the object of pirate raids during the 1500's and 1600's. During a war with Spain in the 1700's, the British briefly gained control of Havana.

Cuba remained aloof from the general struggle for independence from Spanish rule that occupied the mainland during the early 1800's. Although in 1812 a slave revolt was led by José Aponte, Spanish rule remained secure, based on capable administrators, loyal troops, and an aristocracy that feared the loss of its wealth should relations with Spain be changed. Resentment against Spain developed by the mid-1800's, however, as Spanish rule became increasingly corrupt.

The first serious attempt to organize an independence movement was made by Narciso López, a veteran of the mainland independence struggles. López was captured and executed, but his death served to strengthen Cuban nationalism. In 1868 a group of Cuban patriots, including Carlos Manuel de Céspedes, drew up the *Grito de Yara,* or "Cry of Yara," a call for independence. The new movement fought a bitter ten-year struggle, the Ten Years' War (1868–1878), which ended in a truce.

Resentment against Spanish rule intensified in the early 1890's, when the island was struck by an economic depression and North American tariff restrictions were raised against Cuban tobacco and sugar exports. In 1895 a new rebellion broke out, sparked by the poet and journalist José Martí, Cuba's national hero.

The rebel forces were led by men such as Máximo Gómez, Antonio Maceo, and Calixto García. The Spanish colonial troops were commanded by General Valeriano Weyler. Within a short time, Weyler had the rebellion under control. He launched a bitter campaign of repression, during which many thousands of Cubans died of mistreatment.

U.S. rule. The Spanish repression kindled cries in the United States for support of the Cubans, and in 1898 war broke out between the United States and Spain after the U.S. battleship *Maine* blew up in Havana harbor. The Spanish-American War lasted but 100 days. Spain gave up Cuba, but instead of granting Cuba independence, the United States sent forces to occupy the island, remaining until 1902.

During the U.S. occupation, Cuba benefited from improved sanitary conditions, and public education was extended. Yellow fever was wiped out after a Cuban doctor, Carlos Finlay, discovered that it was carried by a mosquito. But Cuban resentment grew as the United States continued from year to year to refuse to withdraw its troops.

The United States set as a condition for withdrawal the inclusion in the Cuban constitution of the Platt Amendment. The amendment provided the United States with naval bases in Cuba, including a base at Guantanamo Bay, and allowed the United States to intervene if it felt Cuban sovereignty to be threatened.

CASTRO OF CUBA *visits a sugar plantation in Jamaica. Castro has greatly improved Cuba's lot since 1959, but at the expense of reliance on the U.S.S.R. and driving thousands into exile.*

Independence. The Cuban constitution was promulgated in 1901, and in 1902 a conservative, Tomás Estrada Palma, became Cuba's first president. Liberal opposition and popular unrest led to the resignation of Estrada in 1906, and U.S. forces were again landed in Cuba.

In 1909 José Gómez, a liberal, was elected president. Instability continued, and in 1917 U.S. troops again returned. In 1925 General Gerardo Machado won the presidency and changed the constitution to keep himself in power. Machado instituted an era of tyranny that lasted until 1933, when he was toppled by an army revolt led by Fulgencio Batista.

Batista remained in control of Cuba until 1944, when he unexpectedly allowed fair elections. Dr. Ramón Grau San Martín, once an associate of Batista, but by then a bitter political foe, was elected president. Grau was succeeded in 1948 by Carlos Prío Socarrás. In 1952 Batista again seized power and gradually instituted a repressive regime that became increasingly unpopular.

Castro revolution. In 1953 a young law-school student, Fidel Castro, and his brother, Raúl, led a revolt against Batista. On July 26 the rebels unsuccessfully tried to seize the Moncada army base in Santiago. Captured, but later pardoned in a general amnesty, the Castros went into exile.

In 1956 Castro returned with a small band of followers that included an Argentinian, Ernesto (Ché) Guevara. They succeeded in reaching the rugged Sierra Maestra, and gradually their strength grew as students and peasants from Oriente Province joined them. Large-scale fighting broke out in 1958, and on January 1, 1959, Batista fled the country.

Castro took power on a wave of popular support, but his popularity quickly waned at home and abroad. Former associates broke with him over Communist influence in the new government, and in 1960 a socialist program was launched resulting in the nationalization of much of the economy. Hundreds of thousands of Cubans fled, most of them finding refuge in the United States.

U.S. property was among that seized, and the United States retaliated by reducing sugar imports from the island. In 1961 Cuba signed a trade agreement with the Soviet Union, and Castro announced his acceptance of Marxist-Leninist doctrine.

U.S. diplomatic relations with Cuba were severed in 1961, and in that year the United States sponsored an invasion of Cuba by a force of Cuban exiles. The force landed at the Bay of Pigs, and was soon destroyed. In 1962 Castro exchanged the survivors of the invasion for needed foodstuffs and medical supplies from the United States.

A new crisis in Cuban-U.S. relations occurred in 1962, when U.S. President John F. Kennedy charged that Soviet missiles were being installed in Cuba. A blockade of Cuba was announced by the United States, and the Soviet Union agreed to dismantle the missile bases.

Castro attempted to spread his form of revolution throughout Latin America, and Cuban-supported insurrections broke out in many countries. In 1962 the Organization of American States (OAS) suspended Cuba's participation in the work of the organization. Prominent among the Cuban revolutionaries active in promoting Castro-type revolutions in other countries was Ché Guevara, who lost his life fighting with a rebel band in Bolivia in 1967. Cuba has also played a very active role in support of communist revolutionary groups in Africa.

In 1979 the United States learned that Soviet combat troops were based in Cuba, but the Soviets insisted that their mission was strictly advisory.

In 1977 the United States and Cuba agreed to exchange diplomats. In 1980 Castro allowed massive emigration from Cuba. Thousands of people left the country, most of them going to the United States.

The emigrations were instigated, partly, by recent drastic reversals in Cuba's economic well-being. A U.S. boycott of Cuban sugar led to a large drop in sugar production. As sugar prices dropped and a poor balance of trade developed, emergency Soviet aid was needed to help offset severe depression and food shortages, and a general decrease in the standard of living.

Dominica

Official name: *Commonwealth of Dominica*
Area: *290 sq. mi., 750 sq. km.*
Population: *(1990 est.) 86,000*
Capital: *Roseau (Pop., 1981, 20,000)*
Language: *English, French patois*
Religion: *Roman Catholic*
Currency unit: *Dominican dollar*

Dominica is one of the Windward Islands of the Lesser Antilles, lying between the Caribbean Sea and the Atlantic Ocean. It lies south of Guadeloupe and north of Martinique. Dominica became an independent nation on November 3, 1978, and is now a full member of the Commonwealth of Nations.

The land and people. Dominica has a rugged, densely forested, and mountainous terrain. The climate is hot throughout the year, and rainfall is heavy.

Dominica's population is of mixed African, European, and Carib Indian descent. Most of the population is black, two percent is white, and a

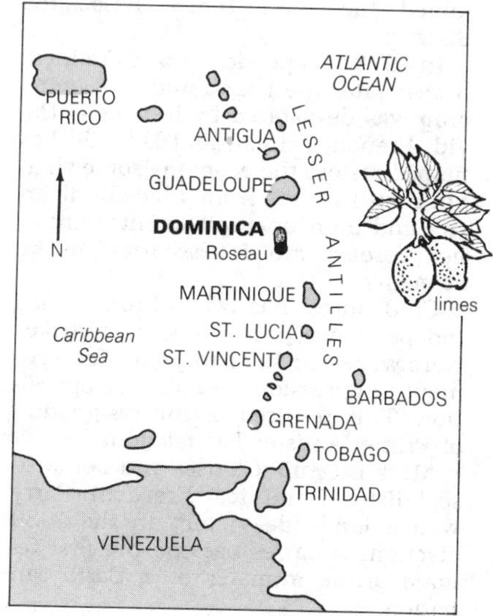

small minority is Carib. English is the official language, but French patois is also commonly spoken. Most people are agricultural laborers.

Economy. Agriculture employs more than 40 percent of the labor force and fuels the economy. Banana production, accounting for approximately 50 percent of the gross domestic product, dominates the economy.

In addition to bananas, limes and other citrus fruits, cacao, vanilla, and coconuts are the chief crops. The only industries process farm products and manufacture straw goods. Exports of bananas, copra, and lime juice are outweighed by imports of foodstuffs, machinery, and other necessities. Most trade is with Britain, the United States, and other islands of the West Indies. In 1986 imports cost $63.2 million and exports totaled $35.4 million.

Government. According to its democratic constitution of 1978, Dominica is ruled by a powerful prime minister, although there is also a president. The legislature is the unicameral House of Assembly, which has 21 elected representatives and nine appointed senators.

Dominica is a member of the United Nations and of the Commonwealth of Nations.

History. The island was inhabited by Indians when discovered by Christopher Columbus in the 1490's. Between the 1600's and the 1800's it was settled by colonists from several European countries. They developed plantations worked by imported African slave labor.

In 1814 the island became British, and it was governed as part of the Leeward Islands until 1940, when it became a separate colony. In 1967 Dominica gained self-government as a state in association with Britain, and it joined the West Indies Associated States.

In 1978 independence was attained. A year later the island and its banana crop was devastated by hurricane David. French, British, and U.S. aid has helped restore the economy somewhat, but it still suffers from a lack of diversity and high unemployment. Continued foreign aid is essential to the economy.

Civil unrest has been chronic since independence. Nationwide strikes were waged in 1979 to protest government suppression of political opposition. This resulted in the resignation of Prime Minister Patrick John.

Mary Eugenia Charles and her antisocialistic Dominica Freedom Party won a landslide victory in the 1980 elections. Charles became the first female prime minister of a Caribbean nation.

DOMINICA DESTROYED. *In 1979 hurricane David all but wrecked the island. These roofless houses are in the capital, Roseau. The United States has provided a great deal of relief.*

Dominican Republic

Official Name: *Dominican Republic*
Area: *18,816 sq. mi., 48,734 sq. km.*
Population: *(1990 est.) 7,501,000*
Capital: *Santo Domingo (Pop., metro. area, 1981, 1,550,739)*
Language: *Spanish*
Religion: *Roman Catholic*
Currency unit: *Peso*
National holiday: *Independence Day, Feb. 27.*

The Dominican Republic occupies the eastern two-thirds of the Caribbean island of Hispaniola. The western third of the island is occupied by Haiti. Hispaniola is situated between Cuba on the west, Jamaica on the southwest, and Puerto Rico on the east.

Santo Domingo, the country's capital, was founded in 1496 by Bartholomew Columbus and is the oldest permanent European settlement in the western hemisphere.

The land. The Dominican Republic has four mountain ranges, which lie roughly parallel to each other. The narrow Cordillera Septentrional is the northernmost range. The Cordillera Central, with peaks over 10,000 feet, is the backbone of the country. To the south are the Sierra de Neiba and the Sierra de Bahoruco.

The Cibao plain, the largest lowland in the republic, separates the Cordillera Septentrional from the Cordillera Central. In the eastern part of the

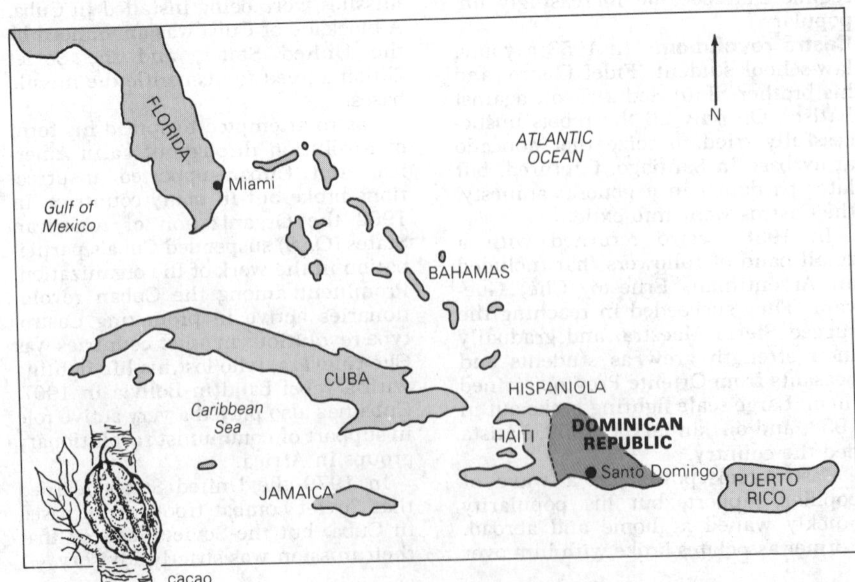

plain is the humid and rich Vega Real, which is drained by the Río Yuna in the east and by the Río Yaque del Norte in the northwest.

Southwest of the Cordillera Central is the San Juan Valley, and south of the Sierra de Neiba lies the Cul de Sac, a semi-arid lowland area watered by Lake Enriquillo. A broad Caribbean coastal plain contains Santo Domingo.

The climate of the Dominican Republic is generally subtropical. Extremes in temperature do not often occur, and rain is abundant in most areas. The higher inland regions, however, are cooler, and rainfall is greatest on the slopes facing northeast, toward the trade winds.

The people. Most Dominicans are mulatto, of mixed white and black origin, but there are white and black minorities. The Vega Real and the Caribbean coastal plain are the most heavily populated regions.

Economy. Fertile soil and a favorable climate have made agriculture and stock raising the principal economic activities. Sugar, cacao, coffee, tobacco, and bananas are grown for export. Meat and dairy products are also exported.

Farming methods in the Dominican Republic are backward, and agricultural production is inefficient. Approximately 20 percent of the labor force is occupied by mining and manufacturing compared with 45 percent occupied by agriculture. Yet both occupations contribute equally (about 20 percent) to the gross national product.

There is a great variety of mineral resources, and gold, silver, copper, iron, and bauxite are mined for export. Textiles and lumber are manufactured mainly for domestic use.

The Dominican Republic has an unfavorable balance of trade. In 1986 its exports earned $720 million while its imports cost $1.2 billion. The United States, followed by Venezuela, is its leading trade partner. Sugar and sugar products, such as molasses and rum, make up about 50 percent of all exports. The major imports are machinery, textiles, iron and steel products, and petroleum products.

Government. The head of the government is the president, who is popularly elected to a four-year term. He is assisted by a cabinet, whose members are appointed by him. Legislative power rests with the bicameral National Congress, which is comprised of a 30-member Senate and a 120-member Chamber of Deputies. All legislators are popularly elected to four-year terms.

The Dominican Republic is a member of the United Nations and the Organization of American States (OAS).

History. Christopher Columbus discovered the island of Hispaniola in 1492 and claimed it for Spain. In 1697 Spain ceded the western third of Hispaniola to France, and in 1795 it also surrendered the eastern two-thirds of the island, Santo Domingo. Spain regained Santo Domingo in 1809 with British and Dominican help.

Independence. In 1821 the middle class rebelled against Spain and proclaimed the country's independence. But in 1822 Haitian forces occupied Santo Domingo, and for 22 years Dominicans suffered under oppressive Haitian rule. In 1844 the Dominicans expelled the Haitians and established the Dominican Republic, with Pedro Santana as president.

During the following years, a fierce power struggle between Santana and Buenaventura Báez, and the continued fear of Haitian aggression, threatened the existence of the republic. To protect the state and maintain himself in office, President Santana, in 1861, proclaimed the reannexation of the Dominican Republic to Spain, with himself as governor-general. Spanish forces occupied the country, but sporadic uprisings, called the War of Restoration, forced the withdrawal of Spanish troops in 1865.

CHRISTOPHER COLUMBUS MONUMENT *in Santo Domingo, the Dominican Republic's capital. Discovered by Columbus in 1492, Hispaniola was one of the first European colonies in America.*

TIERS/MONKMEYER

Under Báez's intermittent rule, from 1865 until 1878, the country continued to be poor and backward and accumulated large foreign debts. In 1869 Báez negotiated a treaty of annexation with the United States. Although the measure was supported by President Ulysses S. Grant, it was rejected by the Senate.

In 1882 Ulises Heureaux gained the presidency and ruled the country until he was assassinated in 1899. Although he greatly increased the foreign debt, he managed to maintain internal peace, launched public works programs, and developed industry.

U.S. role. With the death of Heureaux, violence and disorder again erupted. In 1905 President Theodore Roosevelt, fearing aggression by foreign nations demanding repayment of loans, agreed to place Dominican customs duties under the control of U.S. collectors, who would use the customs revenues to pay the foreign debts. In addition, U.S. loans reassured both foreign creditors and Dominicans.

Political instability continued, however, and in 1911 President Ramón Cáceres was assassinated and a military government installed. Peace was temporarily restored in 1912 by a U.S. mission, and in 1914 by U.S. supervision of elections.

Further difficulties in 1916 led President Woodrow Wilson to send troops and to establish a U.S. military government in the Dominican Republic. Although material improvements were made during the occupation, Dominicans resented foreign rule. The occupation forces were withdrawn in 1924, but U.S. control of Dominican customs continued until the 1940's.

Trujillo regime. Horacio Vásquez was elected president of the republic in 1924. When he attempted to remain in power indefinitely, his government was overthrown in 1930 by Rafael Leonidas Trujillo Molina. Trujillo ruled the country, directly or indirectly, with an iron hand, until he was assassinated in 1961.

Trujillo achieved political stability and economic progress at the expense of civil liberties. Dominicans had the highest per capita income of any of the small Caribbean republics, the budget was balanced, and debts were paid. The expansion of industry and public works projects broadened the economy and raised the standard of living.

Nonetheless, no opposition was tolerated and Trujillo, supported by the army, ruled by a system of terror. In 1960 the Trujillo regime was censured by the Organization of American States (OAS) for trying unsuccessfully to assassinate President Romulo Bétancourt of Venezuela.

Trujillo was assassinated in 1961, and the army and the bureaucracy, both controlled by the Trujillo family and their supporters, seized power. But they were forced out when the United States threatened to intervene.

Search for stability. A provisional council of state governed until 1962, when elections were held. Juan Bosch, a popular intellectual and a member of the Dominican Revolutionary Party, became president.

Seven months later the military deposed Bosch and established an army-backed civilian triumvirate, headed by Donald Reid Cabral, which initiated considerable economic reforms. On April 24, 1965, however, civil war broke out between government forces led by General Elias Wessin y Wessin and Bosch supporters under Colonel Francisco Caamaño Deñó.

President Lyndon B. Johnson, fearing Communist infiltration of the pro-Bosch faction, sent troops to the republic. After bitter fighting, a military occupation of U.S. and OAS forces was established. Despite the condemnation by some Latin American countries for this violation of the nonintervention provisions of the OAS charter, an OAS-sponsored provisional government headed by Héctor García-Godoy was formed.

Elections were held in June, 1966, and Joaquín Balaguer, a former puppet president under Trujillo, defeated former President Bosch. The U.S. and OAS forces were withdrawn by September, 1966, and the country set about restoring its war-shattered economy and attempting to develop democratic processes.

Balaguer, reelected in 1970 and again in 1974, used dictatorial powers and military support to suppress opposition. He succeeded, however, in establishing a period of relative peace and stability for the republic.

Antonio Guzmán Fernández, a moderate, defeated Balaguer in the 1978 elections. Guzmán concentrated on agricultural development and the improvement of human rights.

Despite these efforts, the economy received a severe blow in 1979 when hurricane David devastated the nation. Massive U.S. aid was given during the crisis, and this aid is still important to the economy.

In 1982 Guzmán declined to run for a second term, and was succeeded by a member of his own party, Jorge Blanco. Blanco instituted several economic recovery programs.

In 1986 Balaguer was again elected and he emphasized the need for economic diversification.

Ecuador

Official name: *Republic of Ecuador*
Area: *109,483 sq. mi., 283,561 sq. km.*
Population: *(1990 est.) 10,790,000*
Capital: *Quito (Pop., 1982, 1,110,248)*
Language: *Spanish, Quechua*
Religion: *Roman Catholic*
Currency unit: *Sucre*
National holiday: *Independence Day, Aug. 10*

Ecuador, a republic in northwestern South America, is bordered on the north by Colombia, on the east and south by Peru, and on the west by the Pacific Ocean. Ecuador's territory also includes the Galapagos Islands, situated about 600 miles from the mainland.

The land. Ecuador has three major geographical zones: the coastal lowlands in the west, the Andes, and the eastern lowlands.

The Andes in Ecuador form two parallel chains: the Cordillera Occidental and the Cordillera Oriental. The mountains of these ranges, which have elevations of between 10,000 and 20,000 feet above sea level, are frequently volcanic. The ranges are highest in the north, where there are three towering, dormant volcanoes—Chimborazo, Cotapaxi, and Sangay.

Between the ranges is nestled a long trough, with an elevation of between 6000 and 9000 feet. This trough is composed of a series of interconnected mountain basins cut by rivers flowing west to the Pacific or east to the Amazon. Over three-fourths of the population lives within this central valley region. Livestock, poultry, grains, and vegetables are produced there, mainly for local consumption. Cotton and sugar cane are also cultivated in the lower basins.

The Cordillera Occidental descends abruptly to a warm coastal plain that is 40 to 50 miles wide. The northern part of the plain is well watered and forested, but the southern region is semi-arid and grades into the desert of the Peruvian coast.

The coastal plain is crossed by rivers, the most important of which is the Guayas, which flows south and empties into the Gulf of Guayaquil. It is in this region that Ecuador's banana, coffee, and cacao plantations are found.

The eastern lowlands form a humid, tropical area that is almost uninhabited, except for the primitive Jivaro Indians.

The people. Most of the people of Ecuador are Indian or mestizo, of mixed Indian and European origins. About ten percent of the population is of European origin, and some ten percent is black. The Indians live mainly in the Andes, and the mestizos are concentrated in the Andes and in the coastal areas. The Europeans, largely of Spanish descent, live primarily in the large cities, particularly Quito and Guayaquil. The blacks live mainly along the coast.

The capital, Quito, lies at an elevation of about 9500 feet above sea level. The chief commercial center and largest city is Guayaquil, located on the warm coastal plain. It has a population of over 1.3 million. Guayaquil sends out about 75 percent of Ecuador's exports and receives about 90 percent of all imports. It is linked with Quito by a narrow-gauge railroad, the country's major rail line.

Economy. The economy has been revolutionized since the discovery of oil in eastern Ecuador in the 1960's. Isolated from the coast by the Andes Mountains, oil was not effectively incorporated into the economy until after 1972, when the construction of a trans-Andean pipeline was completed. In 1987 nearly 8.5 million metric tons were produced, but at that rate of extraction, deposits will be largely depleted by the turn of the century.

Oil is Ecuador's leading export, replacing the traditional agricultural products. Bananas rank second. In the 1970's Ecuador's economic growth more than doubled the 1960's rate. Oil refining has resulted in increased in-

ECUADOR *means equator, marked by this monument. The equator runs just north of Quito. Nevertheless Ecuador, being mountainous, has a generally mild climate.*

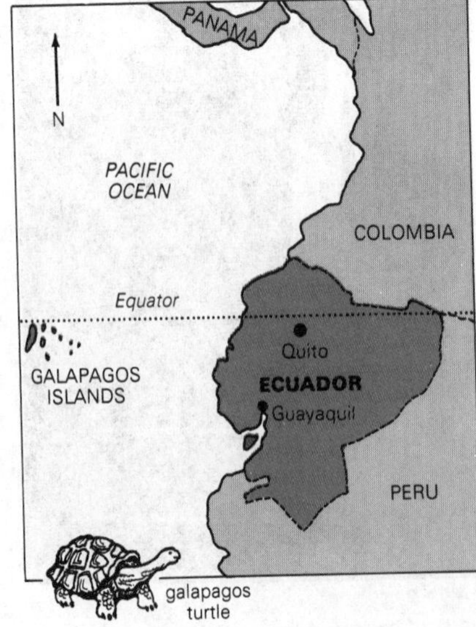

dustrial output, although food processing is still the leading manufacture. The government has nationalized over 60 percent of the oil industry.

Agriculture, previously the most important sector of the economy, still employs most of the country's labor force. Bananas, coffee, and cacao are the chief crops.

Despite its recent increase in revenues, Ecuador remains largely underdeveloped. Most farming is on a subsistence level, and lacks, as does industry, technological sophistication. Land distribution is grossly unequal, causing considerable social and political tensions.

Ecuador's exports earned $2.9 billion in 1985 while its imports cost $1.8 billion. The United States is its leading trading partner, and Japan and West Germany are also important. After oil and bananas, other important exports are coffee, cacao, fish products, rice, sugar, and balsa wood. Ecuador also exports "Panama hats," so named because they were shipped through the Panama Canal. Ecuador's imports consist primarily of manufactured goods —machinery, motor vehicles, chemicals, textiles, and paper.

Government. Ecuador is officially a republic, but it has a long tradition of political upheaval and coups d'etat have been frequent. Traditionally, the head of state and chief executive is a popularly elected president. Legislative powers have rested with a congress consisting of a Senate and Chamber of Deputies.

According to its 1979 constitution, Ecuador has a unicameral congress with 12 national and 59 provincial deputies. The president is elected to a four-year nonrenewable term.

Ecuador is a member of the United Nations, the Organization of American States (OAS), and the Organization of Petroleum Exporting Countries (OPEC).

History. Present-day Ecuador was originally the Indian kingdom of Quito. The Incas, however, conquered Quito and incorporated it into their empire. After the Spanish conquest of Peru by Francisco Pizzaro in 1533, an army led by one of his captains, Sebastián de Belalcázar, conquered Ecuador and in 1534 established the city of San Francisco de Quito on the site of the ancient Indian capital. At first Ecuador was part of the Spanish colonial viceroyalty of Peru, but after 1740 it belonged to the viceroyalty of New Granada.

During the Spanish American struggle for independence in the early 1800's, Quito was one of the first cities to establish an autonomous government, or junta (August, 1809). This junta was quickly suppressed by forces loyal to Spain.

PANAGRA

QUITO'S ANCIENT CATHEDRAL, *founded in 1534, at the end of the Spanish conquest.*

A second patriot government created in 1810 was also suppressed. In 1820, however, the port of Guayaquil threw off Spanish rule. Two years later, the rest of Ecuador was liberated with the help of one of Simón Bolívar's lieutenants, Antonio José de Sucre, who decisively defeated the Spaniards at the battle of Pichincha.

Independence. After gaining its freedom, Ecuador joined with Venezuela and Colombia to form the republic of Gran Colombia. But separatist feeling was strong, and in 1830, with the dissolution of Gran Colombia, Ecuador became independent.

Ecuador's first president was General Juan José Flores, another of Bolívar's lieutenants and a Venezuelan by birth. Flores remained a dominant figure until 1845, serving twice as president (1830–1835, 1839–1845) and keeping control of the army even during the four years he was out of office. His last administration was followed by 15 years of political instability. Some attention, however, was given to liberal reforms—slavery, for example, was completely abolished in 1854.

A new era began in 1860 with the election of Gabriel García Moreno as president. From then until 1875 he exercised firm control over Ecuador. García Moreno launched an ambitious public works program and expanded the school system, but his rule is remembered chiefly for its close alliance with the Roman Catholic Church, to which García Moreno gave wide control over both education and culture.

García Moreno was assassinated in 1875, and during the following two decades political anarchy reigned. In 1895 Ecuadoran Liberals, led by General Eloy Alfaro, gained control of the government. Over the next few years they attempted to weaken the influence of the church and enacted a series of laws that included the legalization of divorce and the granting of religious freedom. In addition, the completion in 1908 of a railroad from Guayaquil to Quito was a major step toward modernization of the country.

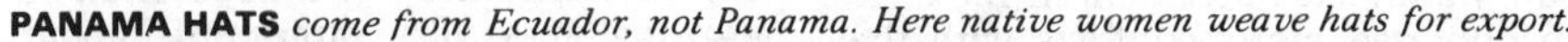

PANAMA HATS *come from Ecuador, not Panama. Here native women weave hats for export.*

ORGANIZATION OF AMERICAN STATES

Various factions of the Liberal Party generally remained in control until the mid-1940's, despite numerous coups and periods of political chaos. During the period 1925–1948, for example, Ecuador had more than 20 presidents or chiefs of state, and none completed a normal term of office.

Contemporary Ecuador. An undeclared border war with Peru broke out in 1941. The conflict was settled by the Rio de Janeiro Protocol of 1942. Under its terms Ecuador was forced to give up most of its claims to territory in the Amazon basin, Ecuador's Eastern Region. In 1961 Ecuador unilaterally denounced the 1942 Rio agreement, however, and renewed its claims.

In 1956 Camilo Ponce Enríquez, a conservative, was elected president. He was succeeded in 1960 by José María Velasco Ibarra, an independent. In 1961, owing to violent demonstrations, Velasco resigned in favor of Vice President Carlos Julio Arosemena Monroy.

Arosemena was overthrown in 1963. A military junta ruled until widespread civil protest, beginning in 1966, led to the temporary restoration of civil rule in 1968, when Velasco Ibarra was elected president again.

In 1970 Velasco used his full dictatorial powers to control opposition from those who resented his tax increases.

Velasco was ousted in 1972. A new military junta ruled until 1979, when it provided for a transfer of power to democratic civilian rule. In 1979 Jaime Roldós Aguilera won a disputed presidential election. He was killed in an airplane crash in 1981. Osvaldo Hurtado, Roldós's vice president, became president. His plans for economic development were often obstructed by financial problems.

Leon Febres Cordero, a Social Christian, was elected president in 1984. He encountered many conflicts with the opposition-dominated congress. In 1988 Social Democrat Rodrigo Borja Cevallos was elected president.

El Salvador

Official name: *Republic of El Salvador*
Area: *8,260 sq. mi., 21,393 sq. km.*
Population: *(1990 est.) 5,659,000*
Capital: *San Salvador*
(Pop., 1984, 452,614)
Language: *Spanish*
Religion: *Roman Catholic*
Currency unit: *Colón*
National holiday: *Independence Day, Sept. 15*

The Republic of El Salvador is the smallest and most densely populated of the Central American states. It is bounded on the north and east by Honduras, on the southeast by the Gulf of Fonseca, on the south by the Pacific Ocean, and on the northwest and west by Guatemala.

GUERRILLAS IN EL SALVADOR. *The tiny country has been torn apart by endless civil war since 1977. In 1982 the country returned to civilian rule after three years under a military junta. The government has tried to lessen violence from extremists of both left and right.*

The land. The backbone of El Salvador is formed by two volcanic mountian ranges that run parallel to the Pacific coast. Between the two ranges is a large, high plateau with rich volcanic soil. The plateau is the most densely populated region of the country. There is a narrow plain along the Pacific coast. The Río Lempa cuts El Salvador in two and also provides hydroelectric power and much needed water for irrigation.

The climate of El Salvador is tropical, but the heat is modified by elevation. Rainfall is heavy from May to October and slight from November to April. There are frequent earthquakes and volcanic eruptions.

The people. Most of the people are mestizo, of mixed European and Indian origin, but there are white and Indian minorities. The population is growing at a very rapid rate, about three percent a year. El Salvador has about 580 people per square mile, a high population density. Agriculture employs about half of the nation's labor force.

Economy. El Salvador suffers from a grossly unequal distribution of land and wealth. Most farmers live like peasants, while nearly all of the best farmland is owned by only a handful of rich people. Social reform is traditionally scorned as being communistic, with the result that the country has been on the verge of a massive peasant revolt for years.

Agriculture is El Salvador's main source of income and the source of most of the country's exports. Coffee, cotton, sesame, and balsam are grown for export, and corn, sorghum, beans, rice, sugar cane, and fruits are raised largely for domestic consumption. Cattle raising is also important.

Mineral resources include gold, lead, zinc, mercury, sulfur, gypsum, alum, limestone, iron, and coal. The major manufactured products are cement, refined sugar, cotton textiles, coffee concentrates, and henequen bags for the coffee industry.

In 1986 El Salvador's imports cost $1.1 billion while exports earned $769 million. The United States is its main trading partner, but trade is also active with its co-members of the Central American Common Market.

Coffee and cotton are the major exports. Other exports include gold, silver, and balsam. The chief imports are machinery, chemicals, textiles, wheat, and petroleum products.

Government. The constitution of El Salvador provides for a system of checks and balances similar to that of the government of the United States. Executive power is vested in a president, who is popularly elected to a five-year term. Legislative power rests with the Legislative Assembly, which has a single house, or chamber. Assembly members are popularly elected to two-year terms.

Since the coup of 1979, however, all real authority has been transferred to the five-man revolutionary junta.

El Salvador is a member of the Central American Common Market, the United Nations, the Organization of American States (OAS), and the Organization of Central American States.

History. In 1524 Pedro Alvarado led an expedition southeast from Guatemala into El Salvador to continue the Spanish conquest of the area. In 1525 Alvarado founded San Salvador de Cuscatlán.

As a Spanish colony, El Salvador was part of a province under the control of the captain-general of Guatemala. The whole province, including El Salvador, declared its independence from Spain on September 15, 1821.

Soon after, Augustín de Iturbide,

who had been crowned emperor of Mexico, sent troops to El Salvador and incorporated the country into his empire. In 1822, however, the government in El Salvador petitioned to be included in the United States as a sovereign state, but the U.S. Congress rejected the appeal.

In 1823 Iturbide's empire fell and El Salvador joined the other Central American states to form the United Provinces of Central America. In 1828 El Salvador, prompted by the threat of Guatemalan dominance within the federation, withdrew and in January, 1841, independence was proclaimed.

Independence. The history of the republic has been turbulent. During the 1800's there were frequent presidential successions and revolutions reflecting much factional strife between liberals and conservatives. Internal unrest was complicated by foreign aggression and the country's participation in numerous wars. The period from 1900 to 1930 was relatively peaceful, however. The coffee industry grew and the country prospered.

In 1931 General Maximiliano Hernández Martínez seized power, ruling until 1944. Although he instituted one of the most brutal regimes in the country's history, the period was one of the most prosperous for El Salvador.

Contemporary El Salvador. The final overthrow of Martínez in 1944 was followed by a new period of political instability. In 1945 General Salvador Castañeda Castro became president. Castro was removed from office at the expiration of his term in 1948, however, when he tried to alter the constitution to retain power indefinitely as a dictator.

Castro was replaced by a junta, and in 1950 Major Oscar Osorio, a member of the junta, was elected president. His administration grew increasingly autocratic, and in 1956 a follower of his, Lieutenant Colonel José Mariá Lemus, was chosen president.

Lemus ruled until 1960, when he was deposed by a junta. In 1961, a military directorate seized control and Colonel Julio Adalberto Rivera became president. He was succeeded in 1967 by Colonel Fidel Sanchez Hernández. In 1972 Colonel Arturo Armando Molina was elected to a five-year term.

In 1969 the first of several bloody clashes erupted between El Salvador and Honduras when Salvadorans pushed across the Honduran border. In 1976 the two countries agreed to permit third-party mediation of any future border conflicts.

When General Carlos Humberto Romero won the disputed presidential election of 1977, the country was upset by a stream of violent protests from both right and left extremists. Romero was deposed on October 15, 1979, and the revolutionary junta took control.

In 1980 the junta appointed José Napoleón Duarte, a moderate, as president. Despite attempts at agricultural reform, violence by both right- and left-wing extremists continued.

A high turnout in elections in 1982 brought a right-wing coalition to power, with Alvaro Alfredo Magana as president. The new government's first act was to suspend the land redistribution laws enacted in 1980.

A new election in May, 1984 brought Duarte back to the presidency. He has the difficult task of trying to keep the country on a moderate course, to ensure that the United States continues to provide military and economic aid.

In 1989 Alfredo Cristiani, a conservative, was elected president.

Grenada

Official name: *State of Grenada*
Area: *133 sq. mi., 344 sq. km.*
Population: *(1990 est.) 84,000*
Capital: *St. George's (Pop., 1981, 29,369)*
Language: *English*
Religion: *Roman Catholic, Protestant*
Currency unit: *East Caribbean dollar*

Grenada is one of the Windward Islands of the Lesser Antilles, which lie between the Caribbean Sea and the Atlantic Ocean. Grenada Island makes up most of the land mass (120 square miles) of the country, which also includes the southern Grenadines islets of Carriacou and Petit Martinique.

Grenada became an independent nation on February 7, 1974, ending over 150 years of British rule.

The land and people. Volcanic in origin, the islands of the State of Grenada have few rivers and a mountainous terrain. The climate is hot throughout the year and rainfall is heavy. The population is of mixed African, European, and Carib Indian origin.

Economy. Grenada's economy is based on agriculture. Cacao, nutmeg, mace, and bananas are the chief crops. Processing these products constitutes the only industry. There is ongoing exploration for offshore oil and gas.

In recent years tourism has become significant. It now rivals agriculture as the country's economic mainstay.

Grenada's farming is done mostly at a subsistence level and production is insufficient to meet domestic demand. Grenada must therefore import considerable amounts of food, as well as consumer goods. Its exports consist of agricultural products, which in 1986 earned only $27.8 million; imports, mostly from Great Britain and the United States, cost $83.1 million.

Government. Grenada has a parliamentary system of government based on the British model. The British monarch, represented by a governor-general, is the head of state. The prime minister is the most powerful executive figure, and there is a 15-seat elected House of Representatives and a 13-seat appointed Senate.

ST. GEORGE'S HARBOR, *Grenada. The island state, independent in 1974, has now fallen into the hands of a revolutionary government under socialist Prime Minister Maurice Bishop, a British-educated lawyer who rules through a revolutionary council.*

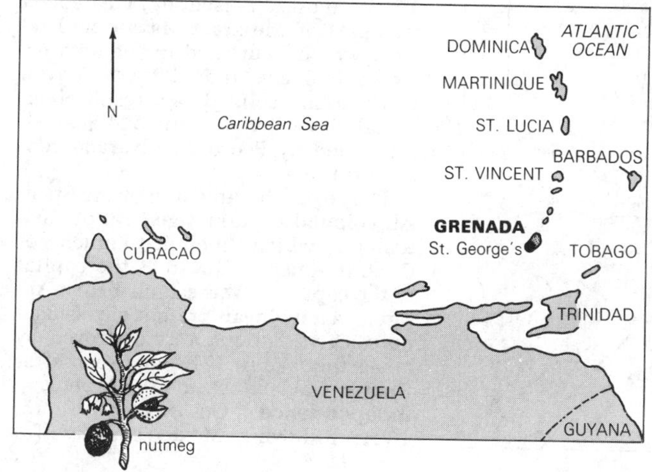

Grenada is still a member of the Commonwealth of Nations, and also of the United Nations, the Organization of American States (OAS), the Caribbean Community, and the Caribbean Community and Common Market (CARICOM). It is also an associated state of the European Common Market (EEC).

History. The island was inhabited by Indians when discovered by Christopher Columbus in the 1490's. Colonists from several European countries settled in Grenada in the 1600's and 1700's. They established plantations worked by slaves brought from Africa. In 1814 the island became British.

Grenada was governed as a unit with the other Windward Island colonies until 1967, when it gained self-government as a state in association with Britain.

Following independence in 1974, Grenada became the scene of political turmoil. Prime Minister Eric Gairy, accused of abusing his power in dictatorial fashion, responded by establishing a reactionary regime, backed by a secret police unit. Nonetheless, he was reelected in 1976.

On March 13, 1979, Maurice Bishop led a military overthrow of the government, which he replaced with the radical socialistic People's Revolutionary Government. He has sought close ties with Cuba and the Soviet bloc.

In October, 1983, Bishop was overthrown in a second military coup. The new regime had been in place for about a week when a force made up of troops from other Caribbean nations and the United States invaded Grenada with the announced intention of halting a growing Cuban presence on the island.

Guatemala

Official name: *Republic of Guatemala*
Area: *42,042 sq. mi., 108,889 sq. km.*
Population: *(1990 est.) 9,249,000*
Capital: *Guatemala City (Pop., 1983 est., 1,300,000)*
Language: *Spanish*
Religion: *Roman Catholic*
Currency unit: *Quetzal*
National holiday: *Independence Day, Sept. 15*

Guatemala, the third largest country in Central America, is bordered on the west and north by Mexico; on the east by Belize, the Gulf of Honduras (an arm of the Caribbean Sea), and Honduras; and on the south by El Salvador and the Pacific Ocean.

The land. Guatemala is a mountainous land. The Central American Cordillera, which lies roughly parallel to the Pacific coast, includes the highest peak in Central America, the volcanic Mt. Tajumulco, 13,812 feet above sea level.

A narrow plain borders the Pacific coast. Inland from the plain are the central highlands, which include about one-fifth of the country's land area. In the southeast are the Caribbean lowlands. In the north is the Petén district, a sparsely settled forest region containing about one-third of the country's area.

The Caribbean lowlands are hot and rainy. The Pacific coast has dry winters and wet summers. The central highlands have a cool, dry climate.

The people. More than half of Guatemala's people are of American Indian stock, descendants of the Mayas, and about 30 percent are *ladino,* or mestizo, of mixed Indian and European background. A small minority, perhaps ten percent of the population, claims unmixed European descent. Most live in the highlands, where Guatemala City is located.

Nearly two-thirds of the people live in rural areas, and over half the labor force is employed in agriculture. Guatemala has a high rate of population increase, about three percent a year.

Economy. The economy is based on agriculture, which provides a fairly high standard of living for farm owners, and which is supported by relatively advanced technology and cheap Indian labor. Most Indians work for poverty wages on prosperous plantations, and land distribution is grossly unequal.

Coffee is the most important crop, accounting for one-third of all exports. Sugar and cotton are also important, but banana production—previously very significant—has decreased because the United Fruit Company, an American firm, has cut back on its Guatemalan investments.

Agriculture is concentrated in the central highland valleys and the narrow coastal plains. The main commercial crops are coffee, cotton, sugar cane, and bananas. The major food crops include corn, rice, wheat, and beans. Livestock include cattle, sheep, and pigs.

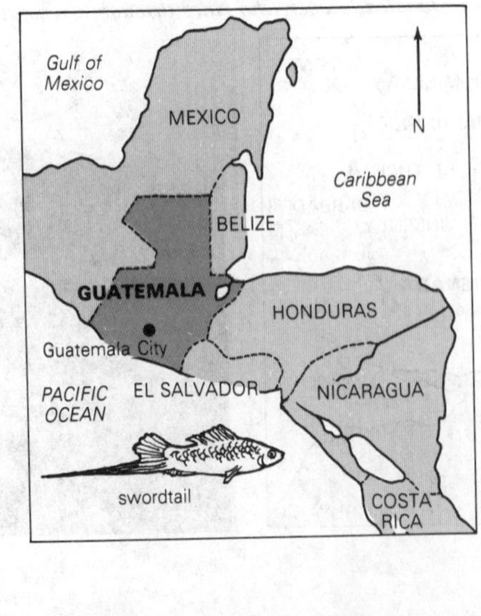

Forests cover about 40 percent of the country's land, and forest resources are increasingly exploited. The country's mineral resources include antimony, chromium, lead, and zinc, but only salt is produced in appreciable quantities.

Industry has grown steadily in recent years, particularly since Guatemala joined the Central American Common Market (CACM) in the 1960's. Textiles, chemicals, and tires are the newer industries, and food processing is traditionally significant.

In 1985 Guatemala's exports earned $1 billion while imports cost $1.1 billion. CACM co-members are significant trading partners, but most of Guatemala's trade is with the United States. After coffee, cotton, meat, sugar, bananas, chicle, and essential oils, such as citronella, are valuable exports. Manufactured goods are of growing importance. Imports include foodstuffs, petroleum products, machinery and vehicles, and manufactured goods.

Government. Guatemala has a long tradition of political upheaval and dictatorial rule. A new constitution was drawn up in 1985 and put into effect in 1986.

The 1986 constitution vests executive powers in a president who serves a five-year term. The president cannot be reelected. Legislative powers rest with a one-house, 100-member congress that also serves a five-year term. If no presidential candidate wins a majority in a popular election, a runoff election is held between the two candidates who receive the most votes.

Guatemala is a member of the United Nations, the Organization of American States (OAS), and the Central American Common Market.

History. Long before the Spanish conquest of Central America in the 1500's, most of present-day Guatemala was part of the great Mayan civilization, which flourished in the area between 300 B.C. and 800 A.D. Mayan civilization declined as a result of internal dissension, and in 1524 Spanish forces led by Pedro de Alvarado conquered the area.

The region became part of the Spanish colonial captaincy-general of Guatemala, which included much of Central America. In 1543 the capital of the captaincy was established at Antigua, a city near present-day Guatemala City. Antigua was destroyed by an earthquake in 1773, and soon after Guatemala City became the capital.

Independence. On September 15, 1821, following Mexico's successful

MAYAN TIKAL, *the plaza and a temple of the ancient city in Guatemala. Mayan ruins, relics of the area's greatest Indian civilization, are also found in Yucatán, Belize, and Honduras.*

independence struggle, Guatemala was peacefully separated from Spain and joined to the Mexican empire of Augustín de Iturbide. Quickly dissatisfied with Mexican control, Guatemala joined El Salvador, Honduras, Costa Rica, Nicaragua, and Chiapas (now part of Mexico) in the United Provinces of Central America. The United Provinces were torn by internal conflicts, and in 1838 the federal system collapsed.

Guatemala became a sovereign state in 1839 under the leadership of Rafael Carrera, who remained the country's strongman until his death in 1865. Carrera had the complete support of the Indians, and his conservative policies won the support of the upper classes and the army. He made Guatemala a republic in 1847, and in 1851 he was elected president. He assumed the presidency for life in 1854. Conservatives remained in power until a liberal revolt in 1871.

Guatemala was ruled by a liberal dictator, Justo Rufino Barrios, from 1873 to 1885. His administration was characterized by great progress in railroad construction, educational reforms, and encouragement of foreign investment. In an attempt to reestablish the Central American Federation under his leadership, he launched a war against Guatemala's neighbors and was killed in battle.

Manuel Estrada Cabrera gained control of the country in 1898. During his administration, the United Fruit Company, a U.S. firm, entered Guatemala and began to play an influential role in Guatemalan politics. Estrada Cabrera was toppled from power in 1920.

Jorge Ubico Castañeda ruled Guatemala from 1931 to 1944. He led the country through the world economic depression of the 1930's, but his despotic rule provoked widespread dissatisfaction. He was removed from power by the military, which attempted to replace him with Federico Ponce. But student riots and a general strike forced the military to allow free elections and grant a new constitution.

Guatemala in recent times. The "revolutions" of October 20, 1944, raised the hopes of many Guatemalans for a new era of social reform. Serious inequalities in the distribution of wealth and income plagued the country. A small number of wealthy people had controlled economic and political life, and the masses had little land and lived in poverty.

Dr. Juan José Arévelo was overwhelmingly elected president, and he launched a program that included support for trade unions and the introduction of social security programs. Although opposition from the privileged minority threatened his administration, he became one of the few presidents to complete his term of office. In 1951 he was peacefully succeeded by Colonel Jacobo Arbenz Guzmán.

Arbenz attempted to continue the reforms. He initiated an extensive land reform program and restricted the activities of the United Fruit Company. His administration was charged with being Communist dominated, and in 1954 an armed force led by Colonel Carlos Castillo Armas, and supported by the United States, invaded Guatemala from Honduras and toppled Arbenz.

Castillo Armas took control and promulgated a new constitution in 1956. Castillo Armas was assassinated in 1957, and in 1958 General Miguel Ydígoras Fuentes became president. Attempts at moderate reform won Ydígoras the enmity of the conservatives, who thought he was going too far, and of those on the left, who felt he was not going far enough.

In 1963 the military overthrew Ydígoras and Colonel Enrique Peralta Azurdía was placed in power. Peralta's administration abrogated the 1956 constitution. Considerable economic growth was achieved under Peralta's rule, and in 1964, bowing to popular pressure, a constituent assembly was convened to draw up a new constitution. The new basic law, promulgated in 1965, outlawed Communist and other totalitarian groups.

Elections were held in 1966, but the military split into two major factions and a civilian candidate, Julio César Méndez Montenegro, led the *Partido Revolucionario* (PR—Revolutionary Party) to victory.

Carlos Arana Osorio was elected president in 1970, succeeded by Kjell Laugerud Garcia in 1974.

In 1975 the Guerrilla Army of the Poor was founded. Its terrorist activities on behalf of the oppressed Indians has underscored the existence of two societies in Guatemala—an Indian one and a Spanish one. There has also been increased terrorism from the extreme right since 1975.

General Romeo Lucas Garcia was elected president in 1978, and a bloody civil war has raged since then.

In 1982, following presidential elections that were widely believed to be fraudulent, a group of junior military officers led a coup and established a junta. The junta immediately annulled the election, suspended the constitution, and banned the activities of all political parties.

In 1985 the military permitted new elections. The candidate of the Christian Democrat Party, Marco Cerezo Arévalo, was chosen president.

For many years Guatemala and Britain have disputed the possession of British Honduras (now called Belize). Controlled by Spain until 1821, it had been settled by the English as far back as the 1630's. In 1981 they agreed that Belize would become independent by the end of that same year.

Guyana

Official name: *Cooperative Republic of Guyana*
Area: *83,000 sq. mi., 215,000 sq. km.*
Population: *(1990 est.) 765,000*
Capital: *Georgetown (Pop., metro. area, 1983, 188,000)*
Language: *English*
Religion: *Hindu, Christian, Islam, Roman Catholic*
Currency unit: *Dollar*
National holiday: *Republic Day, Feb. 23*

Guyana, a small country on the northeast coast of South America, is bounded on the north by the Atlantic Ocean, on the east by Surinam (formerly Dutch Guiana), on the south and southwest by Brazil, and on the west by Venezuela. Guyana received its independence from Britain in 1966. It was formerly British Guiana.

The land. Guyana's land surface consists of a low coastal plain that rises gradually into the heavily faulted Guiana Highlands. The coastal plain, from 10 to 40 miles in width, represents only three and a half percent of Guyana's total land area, yet it is the home of 90 percent of the population. The coastal plain is the only area suitable for agriculture, and the country's two main crops, sugar cane and rice, are raised there.

South of the coastal plain is an inland forest region that covers 86 percent of Guyana. The inland forest contains great quantities of commercially valuable wood, but transportation is poor and the region has remained largely unexploited. Guyana also has about 8000 square miles of grassland savannas, located primarily in the southwestern interior and off the northeast coast.

Guyana has four major rivers—the Essequibo, Demerara, Berbice, and Courantyne—as well as a number of small rivers, but they are generally navigable only from about 40 to 100 miles upstream. Farther inland the irregularity of the highland terrain creates numerous falls and rapids, which have hindered access to the interior.

Guyana has a humid tropical climate. The coastal plain is cooled by the northeast trade winds and has an average temperature of 80°F, but the savannas and inland forest have somewhat higher temperatures. Annual rainfall ranges from about 80 inches on the coast to about 100 inches in the interior. The coast has two rainy seasons, from April to August and from November to January.

The people. About 50 percent of the population is descended from East Indian laborers who came to work on the sugar plantations in the mid-1800's. About 31 percent is descended from black slaves. Twelve percent is mixed. The remainder consists of indigenous Indians (Amerindians), as well as Chinese, Portuguese, and other Europeans.

The diversity of Guyana's people is reflected in their religious beliefs. Some 30 percent of the population is Hindu, 15 percent Muslim, 35 percent Protestant, and 15 percent Roman Catholic.

One-third of the labor force is occupied by agriculture, and another third by industry and mining. Two-thirds of the population lives in rural areas.

Economy. Guyana's economy is based on agriculture and mining. The government has sought to decrease dependence on sugar, the country's chief agricultural product. Rice has also become an important crop. Coconuts, coffee, cocoa, citrus, and other fruits are grown largely for domestic consumption. Increased land cultivation is a major goal of the country's economic planning.

Guyana's most important mineral is bauxite, from which aluminum is made. In 1986 almost 1.5 million metric tons of bauxite were produced. Manganese has been discovered in the northwest, at Matthews Ridge, and large-scale mining operations began in 1960. Small amounts of gold and diamonds are also mined.

Most of Guyana's industry is based on bauxite production and food processing. The country seeks to increase the output of consumer goods to reduce imports of those items.

In 1986 Guyana's exports earned $241.7 million while its imports cost $231.2 million. Bauxite is the leading export. Other exports include sugar, rice, fish, uncut diamonds, manganese ore, rum, and wood. Principal imports are foodstuffs, petroleum products, textiles, iron and steel products, machinery, transportation equipment, and chemicals. Guyana trades primarily with Britain, Canada, the United States, and Trinidad and Tobago.

Government. Guyana has a modified parliamentary system of government. The country became a republic on February 23, 1970. In 1980 a new constitution was introduced. The president is elected by the National Assembly. Executive power is exercised by the president and his nine-member appointed cabinet, consisting of a prime minister who is the first vice president, several deputy prime ministers who are also vice presidents, and four senior ministers. The president is normally the leader of the majority party in the legislature.

Legislative power is vested in the unicameral National Assembly, whose 53 members are elected directly under a complicated system of proportional representation. Local councils appoint an additional 12 members.

The president is elected to a six-year term and legislators are elected to five-year terms.

History. The Guyana coast was one of the first parts of South America to be discovered by Europeans. There was no immediate attempt at colonization, but the legend of the golden land of El Dorado and tales of fabulous riches to be found farther inland led to the exploration of the interior by Sir Walter Raleigh, who led expeditions in 1595 and 1617.

CULVER PICTURES

NEVVES
Of Sr. Walter Rauleigh.
WITH
The true Deſcription of GVIANA:
As alſo a Relation of the excellent Gouernment, and much hope of the proſperity of the Voyage.
Sent from a Gentleman of his Fleet, to a moſt eſpeciall Friend of his in London.
From the River of Caliana, *on the Coaſt of* Guiana, *Nouemb.* 17. 1617.
LONDON,
Printed for *H. C.* and are to be ſold by *J. Wright*, at the ſigne of the Bible without New-gate. 1618.

SIR WALTER RALEIGH'S *second expedition to Guyana (1617) was a desperate attempt to win the favor of James I of England. But Raleigh was beheaded the next year. In 1595 he had also visited the South American coast, sailing 300 miles up the Orinoco.*

During the 1600's the Dutch, French, and English established small settlements along the coast. For 200 years different parts of the Guianas passed back and forth among the three powers, and it was not until the Congress of Vienna in 1814–1815 that the Guianas were formally divided into British, French, and Dutch areas.

British rule. The economy of British Guiana was based on sugar, which was raised on large plantations worked by black slaves. During the early 1800's there was a great deal of unrest among the slaves, partly fostered by abolitionists in England. Slavery was abolished in 1833, and the economy suffered when the former slaves drifted off into the unsettled backlands and established themselves as small farmers.

Efforts were made to find an alternative labor force, and East Indians were eventually brought to work on the sugar plantations under a system of indentured labor. By 1883 they constituted one-fourth of the population. Sugar production rose in step with East Indian immigration, but friction began to develop among groups of different backgrounds.

The British kept the colony under tight political control and allowed only a few wealthy Guyanese to have some voice in its government. Serious discontent, however, did not become evident until the 1900's. There was some minor labor unrest as a result of the world economic depression of the 1930's, but it did not reach major proportions until after World War II.

In 1949 Cheddi Jagan, of East Indian origin, established the People's Progressive Party (PPP) to work for social and economic reforms, and to aim toward self-government. Britain granted the colony a constitution providing for a good deal of autonomy in 1953. The PPP won elections held in April, 1953, under the new constitution, but in October Britain suspended the constitution, charging that the PPP was under strong Communist influence.

In 1955 the PPP split along ethnic lines. Forbes Burnham led most of the black members into a new party, the People's National Congress (PNC). New elections were held in 1961 under a new constitution, and the PPP returned to power. But communal violence and fear of Jagan's left-wing connections led the British to intervene once more.

Independence. Elections were held under a system of proportional representation in 1964, and the PNC gained control of the government. Britain granted Guyana independence on May 26, 1966, and Forbes Burnham became the country's first prime minister. Burnham was returned to power in 1968, 1973, and 1978.

As the executive authority of South America's only Marxist socialist state, Burnham initiated a program of broad nationalization in the mid-1970's. The government now owns all of the bauxite industry and most of the commercial enterprises. Burnham died in 1985. His prime minister, Desmond Hoyte, succeeded to the presidency.

On November 18, 1978, members of a fanatic religious community at Jonestown, Guyana, were victims of a mass murder-suicide engineered by their leader, Jim Jones. Jones, leader of the People's Temple of Disciples of Christ (based in San Francisco, California), ordered the "suicides" after his aides had assassinated five members of an investigative committee from the United States, led by U.S. Congressman Leo Ryan. Ryan had come to investigate the Jonestown community after he had been informed that some of its members were being held against their will. The "suicides" were front page news.

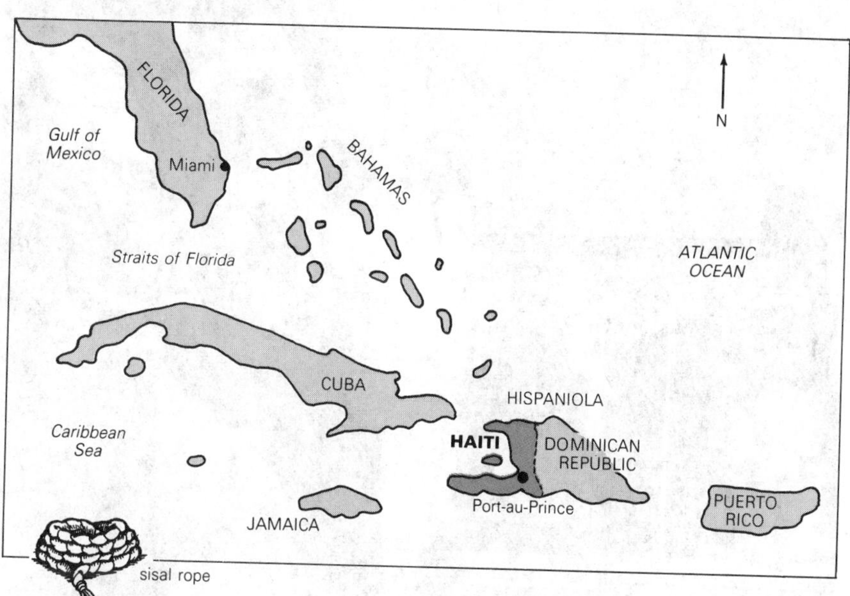

Haiti

Official name: *Republic of Haiti*
Area: *10,714 sq. mi., 27,750 sq. km.*
Population: *(1990 est.) 6,509,000*
Capital: *Port-au-Prince (Pop., metro. area, 1982, 763,188)*
Language: *French, Creole*
Religion: *Roman Catholic*
Currency unit: *Gourde*
National holiday: *Independence Day, Jan. 1*

The Republic of Haiti occupies the western third of the island of Hispaniola in the Greater Antilles. The Dominican Republic occupies the eastern two-thirds of the island. Hispaniola is bounded by the Atlantic Ocean on the north and by the Caribbean Sea on the south. Cuba lies to the west, and Puerto Rico to the east.

The land. Haiti is a mountainous country. The principal ranges are the Massif du Nord, in the north; the Montagnes Noires, in the center; the Montagnes du Trou d'Eau, the Chaine des Matheux, and the Massif de la Selle, all in the southeast; and the Massif de la Hotte, in the south.

Between the mountains is a system of plains and valleys. Among the most important are the Cul-de-Sac in the south, where Port-au-Prince is situated, the Plaine du Nord in the northeast, the Plaine de l'Artibonite in the center, and the Plaine Centrale in the east. Haiti's most important river is the Artibonite.

Haiti has a tropical climate, but temperatures are modified by altitude, rainfall, and sea winds.

The people. Haiti's people are mainly of black African origin, but about ten percent of the population is mulatto, of mixed African and European background. The mulattoes dominated the political, economic, and social life of Haiti for many years.

Most of the people live in the mountain valleys, but transportation facilities through the mountains are poor and the cities lie along the coasts.

Three-quarters of the nation's people live in rural areas. With over 540 people per square mile, Haiti is one of the most densely populated countries of Latin America. There is heavy emigration into both the Bahamas and the neighboring Dominican Republic.

Most of Haiti's black population is illiterate, while the mulattoes, who dominate the political scene, are relatively well educated. Roman Catholicism is the chief religion, but it is commonly blended with primitive voodoo practices. Nearly four-fifths of the labor force is employed by agriculture.

Economy. Agriculture, the mainstay of the economy, accounts for nearly half of the gross national product. The importance of tourism has risen significantly in the last two decades, and it now accounts for nearly one-quarter of the gross national product. Mining is underdeveloped, but it still contributes about 15 percent of the gross national product.

Most farmers work at subsistence levels on very small plots of land in the mountain valleys. The leading cash crops are coffee, cacao, and sugar cane. Sisal, essential oils, and castor beans are also important export crops. Cotton, bananas, tobacco, fruits, and rice are grown as well.

Manufacturing industries produce cotton textiles, soap and pharmaceuticals, sisal rope and plastics, furniture and building materials, foodstuffs, and molasses and rum.

Bauxite is mined for export, and there are deposits of other minerals,

"PAPA DOC" DUVALIER, *absolute ruler of Haiti, addresses the nation. He used his secret police to maintain control. The rule of his son, Jean-Claude, is a shade less autocratic.*

UPI

including copper, manganese, gold, silver, iron, tin, and coal.

In 1986 Haiti's exports earned about $200 million and its imports cost $340 million. The major exports include coffee, sugar, bauxite, and sisal. Imports include machinery, vehicles, petroleum products, and manufactured goods. The United States is Haiti's chief trading partner.

A major barrier to economic development is the increasing pressure of people on the land. Only about one-third of the country's land can be cultivated, and it is estimated that there are some 1500 persons per square mile in the agricultural areas. Although the government has instituted programs to encourage industrial development and increase agricultural production, Haiti remains one of the world's most underdeveloped nations.

Government. Haiti is a republic. In 1987 a new constitution instituted a democratic form of government. A system of checks and balances was introduced and local and national elections were organized.

Executive power is vested in a popularly elected president and his cabinet of ministers. The directly elected bicameral legislature consists of a 195-member House of Representatives and a 27-member Senate.

In 1988, shortly after the new system was introduced, the government was overthrown and the new constitution was suspended.

History. Christopher Columbus discovered the island of Hispaniola in 1492 during his first voyage to the New World. The peaceful Arawak Indian inhabitants called the island Haiti, "land of mountains," but Columbus named it Española, which later became Hispaniola.

Columbus described the Arawak in a letter to the Spanish monarchs as "timid, full of fear, and lovable." Nonetheless, the Indians were soon subjected to severe exploitation by Spanish colonists, and by the end of the 1500's the Arawak had been almost completely exterminated.

Although Spain claimed the entire island, Spanish settlements were concentrated in the east, and French and English pirates were able to establish themselves on the western coast. The French eventually drove out the English, and in 1697 Spain ceded the western end of the island to France, which called it St. Dominique.

French rule. The French established sugar and tobacco plantations, importing slaves to work the land. They gradually succeeded in building a flourishing colony in which many mulattoes prospered and became slaveholders themselves. But social class rivalry was intense, and the slaves were kept in atrocious conditions.

In 1791, sparked by the French Revolution in Europe, civil war broke out in Haiti. Toussaint L'Ouverture, a former slave, led the blacks in a victorious revolt. He forced the French to abolish slavery in 1793, and in 1801 became head of an autonomous government. He successfully expelled Spanish and British forces that attempted to intervene, but in a struggle to achieve complete independence from the French he was captured and sent to prison in France, where he died.

Independence. Jean Jacques Dessalines, another former slave, assumed leadership of the struggle and ultimately led a black army to victory. Independence was declared on January 1, 1804, and Dessalines proclaimed himself governor-general for life. He was later crowned Emperor Jacques I. His despotic rule over a war-ravaged country ended with his murder in 1806.

Two states emerged in Haiti following Dessalines' death, and there began a struggle for power between Henri Christophe, in the north, and Alexandre Pétion, in the south. Christophe ruled as a benevolent despot from 1811 to 1820, and the north made considerable economic progress. Pétion's rule in the south during the same period had disastrous results.

North and south were reunited in 1820 under the rule of Jean Pierre Boyer, who had succeeded Pétion in the south in 1818 and then extended his rule to the north when Christophe committed suicide. Boyer ruled ineffectively until 1843, when he was exiled. At that time the inhabitants of Santo Domingo, in the eastern part of the island, broke away and established the Dominican Republic.

U.S. intervention. The next 70 years were marked by almost constant misrule, misery, and revolution. Dictators rapidly succeeded each other, and Haiti fell into a state of chaos. In 1915 U.S. marines landed in Haiti. The U.S. occupation was ordered by President Woodrow Wilson, who feared that Haiti's political and economic breakdown and recurring violence would spread throughout the Caribbean.

Although considerable progress was made during the occupation, Haitians expressed continued resentment of foreign interference. Under President Herbert Hoover, a U.S. commission met with leading Haitian citizens to discuss withdrawal of U.S. troops; by 1934, under the administration of President Franklin Roosevelt, evacuation of the marines was completed.

Contemporary Haiti. Following the end of the U.S. occupation, several enlightened mulatto leaders ruled Haiti. In 1946 the blacks revolted and restored leadership to the "authentiqué," the blacks. The government changed hands often during the next several years, and disorder and misery increased. Then, in 1957, François Duvalier, a physician, was elected president.

"Papa Doc," as Duvalier became known, established an oppressive dictatorship. Duvalier's rule rested in large part on his secret police, popularly called the *tonton macoute* (Haitian Creole for "bogeyman").

Duvalier died in 1971. He had designated his son, Jean-Claude "Baby Doc," to succeed him as president.

After assuming the presidency, Jean Claude Duvalier increasingly showed himself to be a harsh ruler. Like his father, Duvalier maintained control with the terror of the Tonton Macoute.

Though the national economy improved marginally, Haiti remained the poorest country in the western hemisphere. Large numbers of impoverished Haitians fled the country, many going to the United States.

In early 1986, in the face of rising antigovernment demonstrations and riots, Duvalier fled the country, leaving power in the hands of a five-man military junta led by Lieutenant General Henri Namphy.

In 1987 a new constitution was approved. It ensured a changeover to a democratic form of government. In June, 1988, six months after Leslie F. Manigat was elected president, Namphy ousted Manigat, declaring himself president of a military government.

In September, 1988, Lieutenant General Prosper Avril was declared president after a coup led by noncommissioned officers overthrew Namphy. Avril promised to improve the economy and ensure democracy.

Honduras

Official name: *Republic of Honduras*
Area: *43,277 sq. mi., 112,088 sq. km.*
Population: *(1990 est.) 5,286,000*
Capital: *Tegucigalpa (Pop., 1985, 571,400)*
Language: *Spanish*
Religion: *Roman Catholic*
Currency unit: *Lempira*
National holiday: *Independence Day, Sept. 15*

Honduras, the second largest in extent of the Central American republics, is bounded on the north by the Caribbean Sea; on the east by Nicaragua; on the south by the Gulf of Fonseca, an arm of the Pacific Ocean, and El Salvador; and on the west by Guatemala. Honduras includes the Bay Islands, or Islas de la Bahía, which lie off the north coast.

The land. Honduras is a mountainous country. The Central American Andes dominate the landscape, running from northwest to southeast. The highlands are cut through by fertile river valleys, the largest of which is the valley of the Río Ulúa.

A fertile, well watered plain stretches inland from the Caribbean coast. The plain is narrow in the west, near the border with Guatemala, and broad in the east along the border with Nicaragua. The eastern part of the plain is known as the Mosquito Coast. There is another, smaller lowland region along the Pacific coast.

The Caribbean lowlands have a hot, humid tropical climate. The Pacific coastal region has wet summers and dry winters. The uplands have a pleasant temperate climate.

The people. Most Hondurans are mestizo, of mixed Indian and European origin. There are some Indians, whites, and blacks.

The population of Honduras is increasing at a rapid rate, estimated at 3 percent a year. This rapid rate of growth places heavy strains on the economy for more food, housing, and jobs.

Economy. Honduras is an agricultural land. In the mid-1960's, two out of every three working people were employed in agriculture, which contributed one-half the gross national product. The chief crops raised for export are bananas, coffee, cotton, and beef. Before 1960 bananas accounted for three-quarters of the country's total exports, but banana production has dropped off with crop failures, and because the economy has become more diversified. Nonetheless, bananas still account for over half the exports.

Sugar cane, corn, sorghum, beans, and rice are grown for local food needs.

Honduras has rich forest resources, and lumbering is an important economic activity. The country also has considerable mineral resources, including gold, silver, lead, and zinc. But there is little manufacturing, and the major products of Honduran industry are consumer goods, such as clothing.

Despite attempts to diversify the economy, transportation remains poor, there is a lack of skilled labor, and actual growth has been very slow. The country's vast potential hydroelectric power is still largely untapped.

In 1985 Honduras's exports earned $958 million while imports cost $1.3 billion. Exports consist almost entirely of agricultural products and raw materials. The major exports include bananas, coffee, cotton, wood, and minerals. Imports consist largely of manufactured goods, machinery, transportation equipment, chemicals, and foodstuffs.

Honduras is a member of the Central American Common Market, and its foreign trade is increasingly with fellow market members, especially El Salvador. Nonetheless, the United States remains the country's major trading partner.

Government. Honduras is officially a republic with democratic institutions. But there is a strong tradition of political instability and of military interference in government.

In 1981, a revision of a 1965 constitution was adopted by a constitutional assembly. It provides for a president as the head of state. Legislative power is held by a 78-member unicameral Congress.

Honduras is a member of the United Nations and the Organization of American States (OAS), as well as the Central American Common Market.

History. Christopher Columbus discovered the area of Honduras in 1502, on his final voyage to the New World. But it was not until 1524 that the first Spanish colony was established. The American Indian inhabitants fiercely resisted the Spanish conquest, and the Indian chief Lempira is regarded as a national hero for his bravery in the struggle against the Spanish.

In 1539 Honduras was included in Spain's captaincy-general of Guatemala. Silver was discovered in the 1570's, and an influx of prospectors led to the founding of Tegucigalpa.

Independence. Following Mexico's achievement of independence in 1821, the Central American region proclaimed its independence of Spanish rule. The area was annexed to Augustín de Iturbide's Mexican empire, but after Iturbide's fall in 1823 it regained its freedom. Honduras then formed part of the United Provinces of Central America, which also included Costa Rica, El Salvador, Guatemala, and Nicaragua.

By the late 1830's the federation was divided by bitter rivalries among its members, as well as by divisions within the member states. In 1838 Honduras withdrew to become a separate nation, and in 1841 Francisco Ferrara became the country's first constitutional president.

During the later 1800's and early 1900's, Honduras struggled to remain independent in the face of threats posed by its neighbors, particularly Guatemala and Nicaragua.

In 1841 Britain gained control of the Bay Islands, withdrawing only in 1859. From 1871 to 1874 Honduras was at war with Guatemala and El Salvador, and in 1906 Honduras and El Salvador fought Guatemala.

By 1912 the troubled political situation led President William Howard Taft to send troops to protect U.S. business interests, mainly the United Fruit Company. U.S. forces intervened again in 1919 and in 1924.

Contemporary Honduras. Tiburcio Carías Andino ruled from 1933 to 1948. He improved the country's economy, built roads, and opened schools and hospitals.

In 1948 Carías Andino gave the presidency to Juan Marval Gálvez, who permitted the organization of trade unions, a free press, and open political debate. He retired in 1954, a year marked by a ten-week strike against the United Fruit Company.

No candidate won a majority of the votes in 1954 elections, and Julio Lozano Díaz assumed the presidency. He was overthrown in 1956 and an army-supported junta took power.

The junta held elections for a constituent assembly in 1957. The assembly drafted a new constitution and chose Dr. Ramón Villeda Morales president. Villeda brought Honduras into the Central American Common Market but was overthrown by a military coup in 1963 led by Oswaldo López Arellano. He was elected president by a new constituent assembly in 1965 and a new constitution was promulgated.

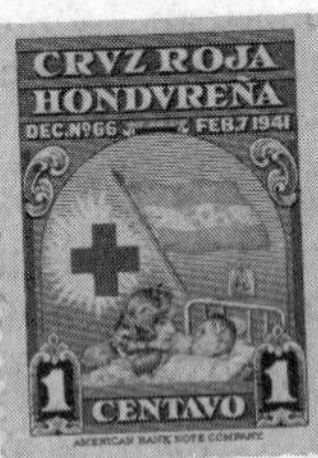

Elections were held in 1971 and Ramón Ernest Cruz was chosen president. But one year later, following another coup, López regained the presidency. In 1975 he was deposed after his involvement in a bribery scandal with U.S. businessmen.

In 1978 there was another change of leadership as a new military government deposed President Juan Melgar (1975–1978), who was too slow in effecting promised social and economic reforms.

In elections held in 1981, the right-of-center Liberal Party candidate Roberto Suazo Cordova was elected president. His party gained an absolute majority in Congress.

In 1985 Liberal Party candidate José Azcona Hoyo was elected president. Since his inauguration in 1986 he has concentrated on economic improvements and on the establishment of a democratic system.

Honduras has a standing border dispute with neighboring El Salvador. A short war broke out in 1969, and several clashes since prompted an agreement in 1976 that future border disputes would be mediated by a third party.

Tensions between Honduras and Nicaragua have heightened because of border conflicts and Honduras's acceptance of Nicaraguans escaping the Sandinista regime.

Jamaica

Official name: *Jamaica*
Area: *4,232 sq. mi., 10,962 sq. km.*
Population: *(1990 est.) 2,513,000*
Capital: *Kingston (Pop., 1987, 104,041)*
Language: *English*
Religion: *Anglican, Protestant, Roman Catholic*
Currency unit: *Dollar*
National holiday: *Independence Day, first Monday in Aug.*

Jamaica, an island nation in the West Indies, lies 90 miles south of Cuba in the Caribbean Sea. Jamaica received its independence in 1962 after more than 300 years of British control.

The land. Jamaica is a mountainous island. A central mountain axis runs from west to east, reaching elevations above 7000 feet in the Blue Mountains in the east. There is a narrow coastal plain in the north and a wider coastal plain in the south, where Kingston, the capital and chief port, is located.

The climate varies with elevation. Temperatures throughout the year average in the low 80's F in the plains, but it is much cooler in the mountain areas. The mountains also affect the distribution of rain. The slopes facing northeast receive the heaviest rainfall, about 200 inches a year. The southern coast is blocked off from rain-bearing winds and receives little rain.

The people. Most Jamaicans are of African and mixed African and European descent. There are also people of Chinese, East Indian, European, and Near Eastern origins.

Jamaica is a densely populated island, with about 520 people per square mile. In the cultivable areas, there is an average of more than 2000 people per square mile. Many Jamaicans migrated to other countries, particularly to the United States and Britain, in search of work.

Immigration restrictions, however, have reduced the possibilities for employment abroad. Thus, the country constantly must find more jobs for its growing population, which increased at an annual rate of 1.2 percent during the 1980's. This rate of increase is much lower than the annual two and a half percent rate of the 1960's, and it is currently one of the lowest rates in Latin America.

Three-quarters of the people are Protestants and the remainder are Roman Catholics. About 30 percent of the labor force is occupied by agriculture, about 20 percent by mining and construction.

MICHAEL MANLEY *with his mother, wife, and daughters at a People's Party rally.*

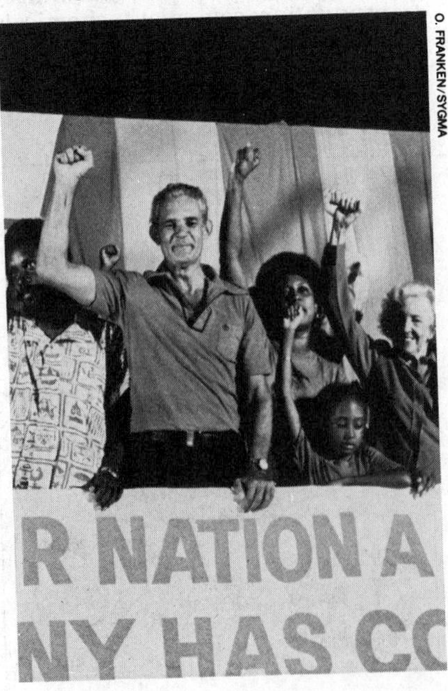

O. FRANKEN/SYGMA

Economy. Agriculture and mining are the mainstays of the Jamaican economy, and they form the basis for the island's developing industry. The country has rich soils and produces valuable tropical crops. Jamaica is one of the world's major sources of bauxite, from which aluminum is made. The island also earns a great deal of money from tourism. Resorts such as Montego Bay, on the northwest coast, are popular.

The most valuable export crops are sugar cane and bananas. Sweet potatoes, rice, and corn are important food crops. Other crops include coffee, citrus fruits, cacao, ginger, pimento, cassava, and tobacco.

Jamaica's mineral resources include gypsum as well as bauxite, but bauxite is the most valuable product of the island. In 1986 bauxite production was almost 7 million metric tons, while alumina production was about 1.5 million metric tons.

Industry and construction have grown rapidly since the mid-1970's. They now contribute about one-quarter of the gross national product, compared with about ten percent each contributed by the important mining and agriculture industries.

Industry is based on processing agricultural and mineral products. Sugar and sugar products, alumina (enriched bauxite ore), and cement are all produced. Oil refining is an important activity.

In 1985 Jamaica's exports earned $568.5 million and imports cost $1.1 billion. The major exports are bauxite and alumina, which account for about half of all export earnings, and foodstuffs, especially sugar and sugar products—rum and molasses. Jamaica trades mainly with Britain, the United States, and Canada.

Government. Jamaica has a parliamentary system of government patterned on that of Great Britain. The head of state is the British monarch, who is represented by a governor-general. Executive powers are wielded by a prime minister and cabinet responsible to the Parliament. The prime minister is normally the leader of the majority party in the Parliament.

The Parliament has two houses, a 21-member Senate and a 60-member House of Representatives. Senators are appointed by the governor-general—13 on the advice of the prime minister and eight on the advice of the leader of the opposition party. House members are popularly elected to a term of five years.

Jamaica is a member of the United Nations, the Commonwealth of Nations, and the Organization of American States (OAS). It is also an associated state of the European Common Market (EEC).

History. Christopher Columbus claimed Jamaica for Spain in 1494, during his second voyage to the New World. The island, called Xaymaca by its Arawak Indian inhabitants, became a Spanish colony in 1509. Under Spanish rule, the Arawak were exterminated and slaves were brought from Africa to provide labor for the colony in their place.

Britain captured Jamaica in 1655. During the British conquest, many of the slaves fled to the mountains, where they developed a distinct culture. Known as Maroons, they successfully fought off the British for more than 100 years. Jamaica had become a haven for pirates, but piracy was suppressed after 1670, when British control was officially recognized in the Treaty of Madrid.

British rule. Jamaica became a prosperous colony, thriving as the major slave market of the western hemisphere and as a producer of tropical produce, especially sugar and coffee. The slave trade was abolished in 1807, and slavery itself was ended in 1838, after a serious slave revolt. Before the island could recover from the loss of slave labor, Britain, in 1846, removed its protective colonial tariff and the plantation economy was ruined.

Economic hardship and misgovernment combined in 1865 to provoke a black uprising at Morant Bay. The rebellion quickly spread throughout the island and was suppressed only after a bitter struggle marked by violent excesses on both sides.

In 1866 Jamaica was made a Crown colony and Sir John Peter Grant was sent from Britain as governor. He initiated political, economic, and social reforms and introduced the cultivation of bananas, which soon became an important export. The colonial administration introduced by Grant lasted into the 1900's.

Self-government. World War II led to an economic depression. The conflict cut Jamaica's trade and virtually eliminated tourism. But political progress was rapid. In 1944 the island received a large measure of self-rule, and in 1945 universal suffrage was introduced.

Jamaican politics had come to be dominated by two figures—Alexander Bustamante, leader of the Jamaica Labor Party, and Norman Manley, leader of the People's National Party. Both parties rested on trade union support. Bustamante won elections held in 1945 and in 1949, but Manley was victorious in 1955.

In 1958 Manley brought Jamaica into the Federation of the West Indies, which united several British Caribbean and West Indian territories. Jamaicans voted in 1961 to withdraw from the federation, and in 1962 general elections were held.

Independence. Bustamante returned to power in April, and on August 6, 1962, led the island to independence. The Labor Party remained in power under Bustamante (1962–1967) and Hugh Shearer (1967–1972). It was defeated in the 1972 elections by Michael Manley and the People's National Party, marking the beginning of new strides toward socialism.

Manley, reelected in 1977, permitted private enterprise, but only for businesses owned by Jamaicans. In 1976 he bought a 50 percent interest in the foreign-owned mining companies, and nationalized many plantations and industries. He initiated welfare programs and made a determined effort to increase industry and tourism.

The results of Manley's program, though, were dismal. The new socialist policies scared off foreign investors as well as tourists. Production dropped as emigration reached new heights. Manley sought to quiet dissension by harshly restricting human and political rights, while seeking economic aid from other socialist countries.

In 1980 Manley was defeated by Edward P. G. Seaga, a conservative who has reversed Manley's policies. The economy has begun to recover.

In September, 1988, Hurricane Gilbert struck Jamaica, killing 45 people, causing damage totaling over $300 million, and leaving 500,000 people homeless. The banana crop was destroyed and the coffee crop was greatly diminished.

Mexico

Official name: *United Mexican States*
Area: *761,604 sq. mi., 1,972,547 sq. km.*
Population: *(1990 est.) 86,888,000*
Capital: *Mexico City (Pop., 1985 est., 18,000,000)*
Language: *Spanish, Indian languages*
Religion: *Roman Catholic*
Currency unit: *Peso*
National holiday: *Independence Day, Sept. 16*

Mexico, a republic at the southern end of the North American land mass, is bounded on the north by the United States, on the east by the Gulf of Mexico, on the southeast by Belize and Guatemala, and on the south and west by the Pacific Ocean.

The land. The physical geography of Mexico is very complex, partly because Mexico is formed by both North American and Central American land structures. North American land forms end in the volcanic region south of Mexico City. The mountains of Oaxaca, which lie west of the Isthmus of Tehuantepec, together with all the highlands to the south, are Central American.

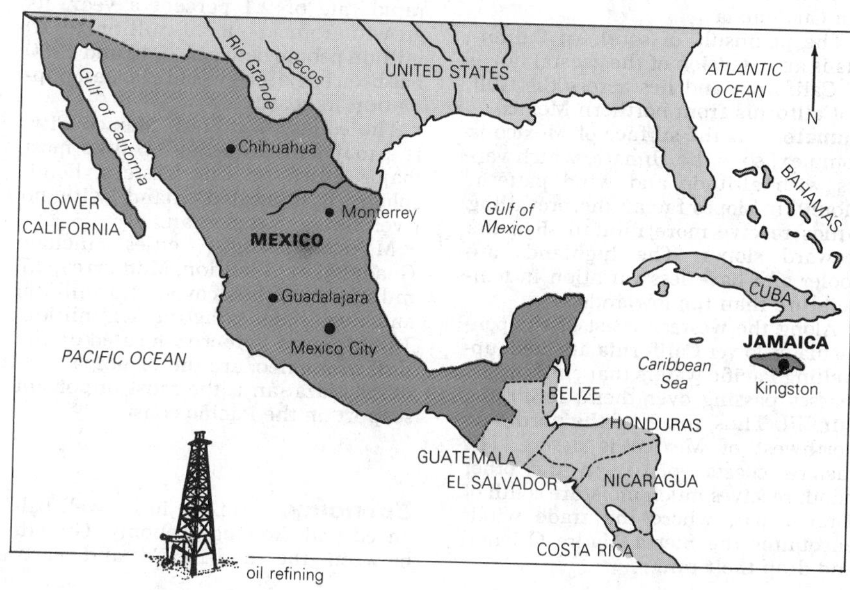

Eastern Mexico, north of Oaxaca, consists of a coastal plain. This plain is broad near the U.S. border, where it forms a continuation of the Texas Gulf coastal plain, but it narrows sharply south of Veracruz, ending with Mt. San Martin, the beginning of the Tabasco coastal lowlands and marshes.

West of the coastal plain are the eroded valleys and peaks of the Sierra Madre Oriental, whose elevations exceed 13,000 feet above sea level. The Sierra Madre Oriental forms the eastern border of the Central Plateau, which is subdivided into a northern and southern region by the Sierra de Zacatecas. The southern region of the Central Plateau contains Mexico City and most of the country's people.

The Sierra Madre Occidental forms a barrier of chasms, canyons, and arid pocket valleys between the Central Plateau and the narrow Pacific coastal plain. These mountains are so rugged that in Jalisco the land plunges 5000 feet into the Pacific within a distance of only 275 miles. Only one pass through this range is used extensively for transportation, and Guadalajara, Mexico's second largest city, is located at that strategic point.

A cordillera of volcanic mountains extends from east to west across Mexico south of Mexico City. Peaks like Popocatépetl, over 17,880 feet, and Iztaccíhuatl, over 17,340 feet, are scenically striking, but form a barrier that isolates the southern plateau region from the Balsas Valley to the south.

The Sierra Madre del Sur, to the southwest, forms a barrier between the Balsas Valley and the very narrow Pacific coastal plain. This range runs eastward into Oaxaca and forms a tangled mountain knot west of the Isthmus of Tehuantepec.

The Central American portion of Mexico includes the Tabasco lowlands, the limestone plateau of the Yucatán Peninsula, and the mountain and plateau system of Chiapas, which extends into Mexico from northwestern Guatemala.

The peninsula of southern California is an extension of the coastal range of California and lies across the Gulf of California from northern Mexico.

Climate. As the surface of Mexico is complex, so is the climate, which varies with altitude and wind pattern. Mountain slopes facing the prevailing winds receive more rainfall than the leeward slopes. The highlands are cooler and have less variation in temperature than the lowlands.

Along the western coast of the peninsula of lower California are cold, upwelling Pacific waters that chill the air masses passing over them, inhibiting rainfall. Thus, much of the north and northwest of Mexico is desert. The eastern coastal plain, on the other hand, receives much moisture south of Tamaulipas, where the trade winds encounter the Sierra Madre Oriental and drop their rain.

MARILU PEASE/MONKMEYER

THE LANDSCAPE OF OAXACA, *a rural scene in mountainous southern Mexico. The piled-up maguey hearts will be boiled and distilled into mescal, the fiery "brandy of Mexico."*

The people. Approximately 75 percent of the people of Mexico are mestizo, of mixed European and Indian ancestry. About ten percent of the population is of European descent—primarily Spanish. The remaining 15 percent of the Mexican population is Indian.

Spanish is the official language, but more than 2 million Mexicans speak Indian languages. These fall into more than 30 major linguistic groups and range from Nahautl, or Aztec, and Otomi, which are spoken by large groups of people, to tribal languages spoken by only a few family groups.

The overall Mexican population density of 114 people per square mile is not overwhelming, but more than 50 percent of the people live within the Central Plateau, which represents only 14 percent of the national territory. Mexico's population is increasing at a rapid rate of 2.1 percent a year. Its growth from about 20 million to 70 million people between 1940 and 1980 has been one of the world's largest population increases.

The country's capital, Mexico City, is a major urban center. Unlike most major cities in the western hemisphere, it is located inland, with no river access to the ocean.

Mexico's largest cities include Guadalajara, 3 million; Monterrey, 2.7 million; Netzahualcóyotl, 1.3 million; and Puebla de Zaragoza, 1.1 million. Tampico and Veracruz, located on the Gulf of Mexico, are the principal seaports. Mazatlán is the most important seaport on the Pacific coast.

Economy. Mexico has a well balanced and growing economy. Growth between the mid-1950's and early 1970's averaged six and a half percent a year, but this high rate has dropped considerably since then. Industrial development and oil exploitation are chiefly responsible for the growth of the economy since World War II.

Natural resources. Mexico is rich in natural resources. It is one of the world's leading producers of silver and it ranks high in the production of antimony, graphite, sulfur, mercury, lead, zinc, copper, and gold. The country also mines quantities of iron ore, cadmium, molybdenum, tungsten, manganese, arsenic, and bismuth.

Mexico has an abundance of oil, producing 165 million metric tons in 1985. The oil industry is totally nationalized, as are many of the country's industries and businesses. Coal and natural gas are plentiful.

Mining employs about 15 percent of the labor force and it is traditionally the country's greatest source of wealth. Oil and silver mining are particularly prosperous.

Agriculture. Over two-fifths of Mexico's labor force is engaged in agriculture, which contributes just over ten percent of the gross national product. Only ten percent of the land is arable, and a considerable quantity of food is imported. Nonetheless, production has increased significantly since 1960. This increased production is largely the result of government irrigation projects.

A major share of Mexican farming is devoted to the production of basic food crops such as corn, wheat, beans, and rice. Commercial crops, which are also important, include sugar cane, cotton, coffee, and henequen, a fiber plant.

Industry. Industry employs about one-fifth of the country's labor force and has grown rapidly since World

MEXICAN GOVERNMENT TOURISM DEPT.

UNIVERSITY OF MEXICO, *the library, an urban scene typical of Mexico City, which is famous for its modern arts. The bold style and bright colors owe much to the Indian heritage.*

War II. Hydroelectric power is well developed and the geothermal plant at Baja California is the largest in the western hemisphere. Nuclear power is also being developed.

Oil refining is rising steadily in importance, and in recent years the government has made a concerted effort to develop the manufacture of chemicals, synthetic fibers, plastics, industrial machinery, and automobiles.

In spite of major advances in these areas, Mexico's most important industries are textiles, food processing, and beverages. The country also produces cement, iron and steel, and a variety of consumer goods.

About 40 percent of Mexico's industry is concentrated around Mexico City. Monterrey and Guadalajara are also important industrial centers.

Trade. In 1987 Mexico's exports earned \$20.6 billion and its imports cost \$12.1 billion. Mexico usually imports more than it exports, but tourism helps to make up the gap. The country's chief exports include cotton, oil, sugar, coffee, fish, wheat, and metals. Principal imports are chemicals, machinery, food, appliances, and transportation equipment. Over half of Mexico's trade is with the United States.

Government.

Mexico is a federal republic composed of 31 states and a federal district in which the capital, Mexico City, is located. Each state has its own governor and popularly elected legislature.

The head of state and chief executive is the president, who is directly elected by popular vote to a six-year term. He may not serve more than one term. The president is assisted by a cabinet appointed by him.

Legislative power is vested in the Congress, which consists of the Senate and the Chamber of Deputies. The Senate has 64 members, who are elected to six-year terms. The members of the Chamber of Deputies are directly elected to three-year terms. Senators and deputies may not serve two consecutive terms.

Mexico is a member of the United Nations and the Organization of American States (OAS).

History.

Before Columbus discovered the New World in 1492, Mexico was the site of one of the greatest Indian civilizations on the North American continent.

THE FEATHERED SERPENT, *a Mayan motif, at Xochicalco, a pre-Aztec Mexican site from the 800's. Aztec glyphs* (bottom) *spell out the conquest of Tehuantepec.*

MARDEN FITCH/TAURUS

NEW YORK PUBLIC LIBRARY

The civilization of the Mayas, which was at its height from about 300 B.C. to 800 A.D., was centered in Guatemala and southern Mexico. The Mayas built great cities and were skilled at astronomy and mathematics. They also developed a calendar that was probably more accurate than the one used in Europe at the time, and they had a well developed system of writing.

In the 800's the Mayas, for unknown reasons, abandoned their cities and reestablished themselves in the Yucatán Peninsula. Gradually, the Mayas became weakened by attacks made on them from the north by the Toltec Indians of the Central Plateau. By the 1400's Mayan civilization was in decline.

The Toltecs, whose capital was in the Valley of Mexico in the Central Plateau, were subjugated in the early 1400's by the Aztecs, whose original homeland is unknown.

The Aztecs built an empire ruled from their capital, Tenochtitlán founded in 1325 on the site of present-day Mexico City. Nearly invincible, Tenochtitlán was constructed upon a group of islands in the middle of Lake Texcoco and connected to the mainland by a series of causeways.

In 1517–1518 the Spanish governor of Cuba sent two expeditions to investigate rumors of the existence of mainland civilizations rich in gold. Both expeditions retreated to Cuba after brief and bloody encounters with the Indians. In 1518–1519 Hernán Cortés, undaunted by the failures of his predecessors, undertook the conquest of Mexico with fewer than 600 men.

The conquest of the Aztec empire was accomplished primarily by the skillful use of horses and guns, which terrified the Indians, who had never seen them before. In addition, the Indians believed that the light-skinned, bearded Spaniards riding on horses were gods, and Cortés was allowed to enter Tenochtitlán. He captured Montezuma, the Aztec emperor, and by the mid-1500's all Mexico had been won.

Spanish rule. Following the Spanish conquest, the Indians were reduced to the level of slaves. They were forced to work in the mines or on the estates of the Spaniards. Gold and silver were taken from the land with unceasing zeal.

In 1535 Mexico City became the capital of the viceroyalty of New Spain, which included a large part of Central America as well as Mexico. The immediate subordinates of its governor, or viceroy, were the *peninsulares,* Spaniards born in Spain. Native-born Spaniards, known as Creoles, were not permitted to hold high government office.

During the colonial period the Creoles grew to resent the privileged position of the *peninsulares.* Discontent also surged among the rapidly growing population of mestizos, those of mixed

Spanish and Indian parentage. The successful American and French revolutions of the late 1700's further increased native resentment of Spanish injustice and exploitation.

In 1808 Napoleon Bonaparte of France conquered Spain and imprisoned Spain's king, Ferdinand VII, thus leaving Mexico without a legitimate ruler.

Struggle for independence. On September 16, 1810, a Creole priest in the town of Dolores, Miguel Hidalgo y Costilla, issued the famous "Cry of Dolores," in which he denounced the injustices of the Spanish government and cried out for social reform. With Indian support, Hidalgo and his followers were able to dominate southern Mexico.

The Creoles would not support Hidalgo's social revolution, which threatened their own position. Without Creole support, the revolt could not succeed. Hidalgo was defeated and executed. The struggle was renewed by another priest, José María Morelos, a mestizo, but he too was eventually defeated and executed, in 1815.

Hope for independence lay dormant until 1820, when Ferdinand VII, who had been restored to the Spanish throne after Napoleon's armies were expelled from Spain, was forced by internal pressures to approve a new liberal constitution. Mexican Creoles feared that the liberal reforms would weaken their position in Mexico and they aligned themselves with the struggle for independence.

Independence. Then in 1821 General Augustín de Iturbide led another revolution. He declared Mexico independent and established himself as Emperor Augustín I. In 1823 he was overthrown by Antonio López de Santa Anna, another ambitious general, who proclaimed a republic. Santa Anna remained the dominant political figure in the new republic until 1855. For most of those years, he was either president or dictator, although he was intermittently overthrown.

In 1836 the territory of Texas, which had been settled largely by people from the United States, declared its independence. Santa Anna attempted to prevent the secession, but after an initial victory at the Alamo he was decisively defeated at the battle of San Jacinto, in April, 1836. The United States annexed Texas in 1845, which angered the Mexicans, who had never recognized the independence of Texas.

War broke out between Mexico and the United States in 1846. Mexico was defeated, and under the terms of the Treaty of Guadalupe Hidalgo (1848) Mexico was forced to cede a large section of land north of the Río Grande to the United States. The land lost included New Mexico and California, as well as Texas. In 1853 Santa Anna, short of government funds, sold the Mesilla Valley to the United States in the Gadsden Purchase. This final loss of territory gravely insulted Mexico.

CULVER PICTURES

PANCHO VILLA, *a colorful bandit who for many years, with his cavalrymen,* Los Dorados, *played a leading part in the Mexican revolution. He was assassinated in 1923.*

Revolution and reform. Shortly afterward, bands of guerrillas gathered in the mountains and stormed the capital, demanding liberal reforms. Led by Juan Álvarez and Benito Juárez, the rebels declared their intention to institute many reforms for the good of the people of Mexico. They planned to assert civilian control over the church and the military; to eliminate sharp class distinctions by breaking up large estates and distributing land among the peasants; and to unite the country to prevent further losses to the United States.

In 1855 Santa Anna was overthrown by the rebels and Álvarez became acting president. Various edicts outlining the reforms were issued from Mexico City, and in 1857 a new constitution, which provided for a more liberal and democratic government, was adopted. The liberals were staunchly opposed by the army, the church, and the upper classes. The ultimate result was civil war lasting from 1858 to 1860, when Benito Juárez led his liberal forces to a costly victory.

During the war Mexico had become deeply indebted to Spain, Britain, and France. In 1861 Juárez, faced with national bankruptcy, suspended payment on these debts. A combined army of French, Spanish, and British troops invaded Mexico in December, 1861, to force payment. Napoleon III of France seized this opportunity to conquer the country. A Mexican victory at the battle of Puebla in May, 1862, only temporarily halted the French advance, and with reinforcements the French won control in 1863.

In 1864 Napoleon declared Maximilian, an Austrian prince, emperor of Mexico. In 1867, under strong diplomatic pressure from the United States, which objected to French intervention, France withdrew its troops. Maximilian, under the erroneous impression that he had popular support, refused to leave the country and was captured and shot. Juárez returned as president and held office until 1872.

Díaz era. Juárez and his successor, Sebastián Lerdo de Tejada, attempted to enact liberal reforms, but in 1876 the government was overthrown by Porfirio Díaz, who ruled as dictator from 1876 to 1911. Under his rule the upper class again enjoyed prosperity, foreign investments multiplied, and the government budget was balanced. The Indians and the growing working class were neglected, however. The slogan, "Mexico, mother of foreigners, stepmother of Mexicans," expressed the growing popular resentment.

Discontent with Díaz's rule culminated in revolution in 1910. In an imprudent interview with a U.S. news correspondent, Díaz expressed the view that Mexico was prepared for a democratic election. Although his comments were intended to be read only in the United States, translations of his statement reached Mexico. Francisco Madero, a Creole from northern Mexico, challenged Díaz to hold free elections, and Díaz was forced to uphold the declaration he had made.

The elections were rigged, however, and Madero was imprisoned after his defeat by Díaz. Resentment surged throughout the country, and the people revolted. In the north, Francisco ("Pancho") Villa and Pascual Orozco led armies of peasants in rebellion. In the south, Emiliano Zapata and an army of Indians raided large estates. In May, 1911, Díaz was forced to flee from the country.

Civil strife. Francisco Madero became the popularly acclaimed president in November, 1911. His term of office brought some extension of democratic institutions, but no sorely needed economic and social reforms. The Indians and workers remained dissatisfied and once again revolted. In 1913 Madero unwisely enlisted the support of General Victoriano Huerta, who betrayed Madero and had him assassinated.

Huerta ruled as dictator until 1914, when violent revolutionary movements erupted throughout Mexico. Venustiano Carranza, Álvaro Obregón, and Pancho Villa led the revolutionary movements in the north. In the south, an army of peasants was again led by Emiliano Zapata. Huerta's army was defeated and he fled to the United States.

Peace was not restored to Mexico, however, for the victorious troops then fought among themselves for control of the government. Villa and Zapata seized Mexico City, while Carranza and Obregón held Vera Cruz. With promises of extensive liberal reforms, the Obregón forces triumphed. In 1917 Carranza became president and a liberal constitution was drawn up.

Reform era. The constitution protected labor, limited church authority, and provided for the division of large estates into the ancient Indian communal land system known as the *ejido.* The constitution was not implemented, however, and when Carranza tried to choose his own successor, he was overthrown by Obregón. In September, 1920, Obregón was elected president, and during his four-year term a modest, but solid, program of reforms was initiated.

In 1924 General Plutarco Elías Calles was elected president. Disputes with the church and with foreign investors plagued his administration. In 1928 Obregón was again elected, but he was assassinated before taking office. From 1928 to 1934 a series of puppet presidents, under the control of Calles, ruled Mexico. During this period the strongly reformist party, *Partido Nacional Revolucionario* (PNR), or National Revolutionary Party, was formed and came to dominate Mexican politics.

In elections held in 1934, the PNR candidate, Lázaro Cárdenas, was elected to the presidency. Under the Cárdenas administration, reforms demanded during the revolution were enacted. Millions of acres of land were distributed to the *ejidos,* and schools, hospitals, and roads were constructed. In 1938 both the U.S. and British oil industries were nationalized.

Contemporary Mexico. In 1940 Manuel Avila Camacho was elected president. Although Camacho made no innovations during his own term of office, he consolidated the gains that had already been made. In 1942, after German submarines had sunk Mexican tankers, Mexico declared war on the Axis. Mexico contributed strategic raw materials to the war effort. Mexicans enlisted in the United States armed forces, and a squadron of the Mexican air force was sent to the Pacific. In 1945 Mexico became a charter member of the United Nations.

Postwar administrations basically followed the domestic reforming policies of President Camacho and focused on increasing food production and developing transportation. President Adolfo Ruiz Cortines (1952–1958) greatly extended Mexico's farmland through irrigation projects. Under Adolfo López Mateos (1958–1964) Mexico's educational system was expanded.

In 1964 Gustavo Diaz Ordaz was elected president. During his administration, on October 28, 1967, Mexico signed a treaty with the United States that settled a century-old border dispute caused by the shifting course of the Rio Grande.

Also during the administration of Díaz Ordaz, Mexico enjoyed great prosperity. There were huge increases in industrial production and in the national income. But the wealth was unevenly distributed, and by 1970 the demands for social reform began to be met by the newly elected socialist regime of President Luis Echeverria (1970–1976).

The new president initiated land redistribution and firmly restricted foreign investments. Relations with the communist world were improved.

José López Portillo was elected president in 1976 and he immediately began to reverse the leftist policies of his predecessor. In 1982 Miguel de la Madrid Hurtado was elected president. He immediately had to face a deeply troubled economy marked by high inflation and the weakening of the peso.

In 1985 Mexico was hit by two earthquakes that caused severe damage in Mexico City. More than 4500 people were killed and as many as 50,000 left homeless.

Carlos Salinas de Gortari of the ruling Institutional Revolutionary Party (PRI) was elected to the presidency in 1988. The voters, however, showed unexpectedly strong support for opposition candidates.

Mexico has a high unemployment rate and a large poverty-stricken peasant class. Many destitute Mexicans emigrate illegally into the United States each year in search of a higher standard of living.

Nicaragua

Official name: *Republic of Nicaragua*
Area: *50,200 sq. mi., 130,000 sq. km.*
Population: *(1990 est.) 3,606,000*
Capital: *Managua (Pop., 1985, 682,111)*
Language: *Spanish*
Religion: *Roman Catholic*
Currency unit: *Córdoba*
National holiday: *Independence Day, Sept. 15*

Nicaragua, the largest of the Central American republics, is bounded on the north by Honduras, on the east by the Caribbean Sea, on the south by Costa Rica, and on the west by the Pacific Ocean.

The land. Most of Nicaragua is occupied by the Central American Cordillera of the Andes, which extends in a north-south direction through the center of the country. The cordillera separates the wide Caribbean coastal plain from a narrow Pacific coastal plain.

A long, narrow depression runs diagonally across Nicaragua from the Gulf of Fonseca in the northwest into Costa Rica. This depression contains two large lakes, Lake Nicaragua and Lake Managua. Lake Nicaragua, about 100 miles long and 45 miles wide, is one of the largest bodies of fresh water in Central America.

The mountains to the west of the depression are actively volcanic, and eruptions and earthquakes are a constant hazard.

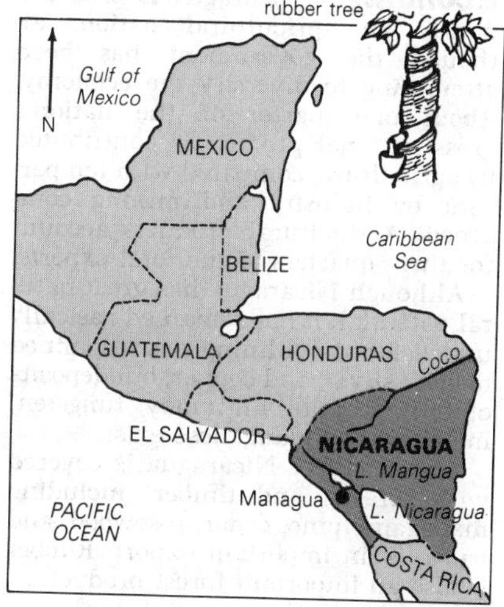

EARTHQUAKE DAMAGE *in Nicaragua. The country is subject to frequent severe earthquakes, and a string of active volcanoes lines the west coast, just where most of the people live.*

Nicaragua has a hot climate. Temperatures seldom drop below 75°F, although it is generally cooler in the central mountain region. Rainfall is moderate on the Pacific coast and in the mountains. It is extremely heavy, however, along the Caribbean coast, where some places receive as much as 200 inches a year.

The people. Over 70 percent of the people of Nicaragua are mestizo, of mixed Indian and European ancestry. About 15 percent are of European descent. The remainder of the population is composed of the indigenous Mosquito Indians and blacks.

Much of Nicaragua is thinly settled. The Mosquito Indians and most of the blacks live on the Caribbean coastal plain. The bulk of the population is concentrated along the Pacific coast and in the area around Lake Nicaragua and Lake Managua. It is in this area that Nicaragua's three largest cities—Managua, León, and Granada—are located.

Economy. Nicaragua is predominantly an agricultural nation, although the government has been attempting to diversify the economy. About one-quarter of the nation's gross national product is contributed by agriculture, compared with ten percent by industry and mining combined. Agricultural products account for three-quarters of the total exports.

Although Nicaragua has great natural potential, it has remained basically undeveloped. Mining is confined to gold, silver, and copper, but deposits of iron, bauxite, antimony, tungsten, mercury, and manganese exist.

About half of Nicaragua is covered with forests; and timber, including mahogany, pine, cedar, rosewood, and balsa, is an important export. Rubber is also an important forest product.

Agriculture. Agriculture still employs about 60 percent of the labor force. A major share of the country's crops are raised in the west, where extensive tracts of fertile soil are ideal for mechanized farming, but a large percentage of Nicaragua's arable land is not cultivated.

Corn, beans, rice, and sugar cane are raised for domestic consumption. Cotton, coffee, and sesame are the leading commercial crops. Tobacco, cacao, and fruits are grown, and cattle are important in the west.

Industry. Nicaraguan industry is almost entirely limited to food processing and the manufacturing of a few consumer items for local consumption. The largest industry is sugar refining. Factories produce cement, insecticides, cigarettes, soap, liquor, and clothing.

Industry has been spurred somewhat in the last decade by Nicaragua's membership in the Central American Common Market (CACM).

Trade. Nicaragua's exports in 1985 earned $260 million while imports cost $843 million. Most trade is with the United States and with other CACM members. Major exports are cotton, coffee, copper, oilseeds (cotton and sesame), meat, and timber. Principal imports include machinery, equipment for transportation, chemicals, textiles, and foodstuffs.

Government. Nicaragua was formerly a republic headed by an elected president. The Congress consisted of a Senate and a Chamber of Deputies, and all legislators were elected.

On July 20, 1979, a five-man junta seized control of the government. It abrogated the 1974 constitution and replaced Congress with a single Council of State, which has 47 members of diverse political persuasions.

Nicaragua is a member of the United Nations, of the Organization of American States (OAS), and of the Central American Common Market.

History. Nicaragua was discovered in 1502 by Christopher Columbus on his last voyage to the New World, but it was not explored until 1522, when Gil González Dávila led an expedition from Panama. In 1524 the Spanish founded the cities of León and Granada in the western lowlands, and except for sporadic raids by English pirates during the latter half of the 1600's, the colonial period in Nicaragua was peaceful.

Independence from Spain was won in 1821, but Nicaragua was annexed to the Mexican empire. When the Mexican empire collapsed in 1823, Nicaragua joined the United Provinces of Central America, which included El Salvador, Honduras, Guatemala, and Costa Rica. In 1838 Nicaragua left the United Provinces and declared itself independent.

Sovereignty. As a sovereign nation, Nicaragua suffered from intense rivalry between liberals, centered in León, and conservatives, in Granada, who battled for political control of the country. In 1856, when the conservatives gained power and attempted to establish a strong and stable government, the liberals invited an adventurer from the United States, William Walker, to help oust the conservative administration.

With a following of approximately 60 men, Walker managed to capture control of Nicaragua and install himself as president. The U.S. financier, Cornelius Vanderbilt, who feared that a steamship monopoly he held would be restricted by Walker and the liberals, took an active role in Nicaragua's politics.

Vanderbilt helped organize an invading army recruited in neighboring countries, and after only one year in office, Walker was forced to flee. In 1860 he was captured in Honduras and executed. Following Walker's death, tension between liberals and conservatives was temporarily abated and Nicaragua enjoyed peace and prosperity under several consecutive conservative administrations.

Zelaya era. A revolution by liberal forces in 1893 brought José Santos Zelaya to power. Zelaya moved the capital from León to Managua, promoted railroad construction, brought the Indians of the east coast under the government's jurisdiction, and promoted agricultural development. Zelaya also involved Nicaragua in revolutions in nearby Central American countries.

In 1909 Zelaya executed two U.S. engineers, whom he maintained were implicated in a plot to overthrow his government. The United States severed diplomatic relations with Nicaragua, weakening the prestige of the Zelaya administration. The conservatives rebelled, forcing Zelaya to resign.

U.S. intervention. For several years political and economic conditions in Nicaragua were in a chaotic state. In 1912 the United States sent marines to restore order at the request of provisional President Adolfo Díaz.

In the same year Díaz was elected president, and in 1914 Nicaragua signed the Bryan-Chamorro Treaty with the United States. The treaty gave the United States the right to construct a trans-isthmian canal through Nicaragua and to establish military bases on both coasts. Except for a brief period in 1925, the U.S. Marines remained in the country until 1933.

Contemporary Nicaragua. In 1936 General Anastasio Somoza, commander of the U.S.-trained National Guard, established himself in the presidency and assumed dictatorial powers. His administration was characterized by economic development and political repression. During World War II Somoza actively cooperated with the United States.

In 1947 Leonardo Arquello was elected president, but Somoza had him removed from office. Victor Manuel Roman y Reyes was then selected by a constituent assembly to occupy the presidency. Roman y Reyes died in May, 1950, at which time Somoza again became president. Somoza was assassinated in September, 1956, and his son, Luis Somoza Debayle, was appointed acting president for the duration of his father's term. The next year he was elected president.

Luis Somoza's administration, contrary to expectations, proved to be less oppressive than that of his father. Civil liberties, freedom of the press, and political opposition were now permitted to a limited extent.

In 1963 René Schick Gutiérrez was elected president. Schick died in 1966, and Congress elected Lorenzo Guerrero Gutiérrez to finish his term. In 1967 General Anastasio Somoza Debayle, the brother of Luis Somoza, was elected president amid charges of election fraud. He was reelected in 1974.

During General Somoza's rule the Sandinist National Liberation Front (FSLN) became a highly active guerrilla force. A moderate socialist coalition, it was dedicated to ending the Somoza family's domination of Nicaragua, which began in 1933. It sought to redistribute the country's land more evenly, to relieve the miserable living conditions of the peasantry, and to end the severe political repression imposed by the Somozas.

General Somoza countered FSLN terrorism by imposing strict martial law in 1975. His regime lost prestige after reports of torture and gross violations of human, as well as civil, rights.

When one of Somoza's foes—publisher Pedro Joaquín Chamorro—was murdered in 1978, the nation erupted into civil war. In 1979 Somoza fled the country and the FSLN, with U.S. support, tried to improve the economy.

Relations between the U.S. and the Sandinista government worsened steadily through the first half of the 1980's. Accusing the Sandinistas of supporting leftist guerrillas in El Salvador, the U.S. gave support to anti-Sandinista rebels, the contras. In 1985 President Reagan ordered an embargo on U.S. trade with Nicaragua.

Panama

Official name: *Republic of Panama*
Area: *29,762 sq. mi., 77,082 sq. km.*
Population: *(1990 est.) 2,423,000*
Capital: *Panamá City (Pop., 1985 est., 976,800)*
Language: *Spanish*
Religion: *Roman Catholic*
Currency unit: *Balboa*
National holiday: *Independence Day, Nov. 3*

Panama, a Central American republic situated on the Isthmus of Panama, is bounded on the north by the Caribbean Sea, on the east by Colombia, on the south by the Pacific Ocean, and on the west by Costa Rica. The Panama Canal cuts through the country at its narrowest point. The canal runs through the Canal Zone, a strip of land five miles wide on each side of the canal, leased to the United States by the Panamanian government in 1903.

The land. Panama's land surface is mostly hilly and mountainous. The highest mountains rise in the west, near the Costa Rican border, and are volcanic. The highest peak is Chiriquí Volcano, 11,410 feet above sea level. These mountains gradually slope down toward a hilly central lowland, which separates them from jungle-covered highlands in the east. It is through this lowland that the Panama Canal runs.

The only other significant lowlands are plains along the Caribbean and Pacific coasts. The Caribbean plain, along the north coast, is extremely rainy. Tropical evergreen rain forests predominate. The Pacific plain, along the south coast, has a wet and a dry season, producing semideciduous forest mingled with savanna.

Panama's climate varies with elevation. The lowlands have a tropical climate, with an average annual temperature of about 80°F. Temperatures in the mountains range from 50°F to 66°F.

The people. The inhabitants of Panama are largely mestizo, of mixed European and Indian parentage, but there are small groups of whites, blacks, and Indians. The overwhelming majority of the population is Roman Catholic. Spanish is the national

INDIAN CHILDREN *in their finery. They live on Panama's San Blas islands off the Caribbean coast. The effigy is not explained. The most important aspect of Panama is the Panama Canal, dominated by the United States. Panama is now due to take over the canal by the end of the century.*

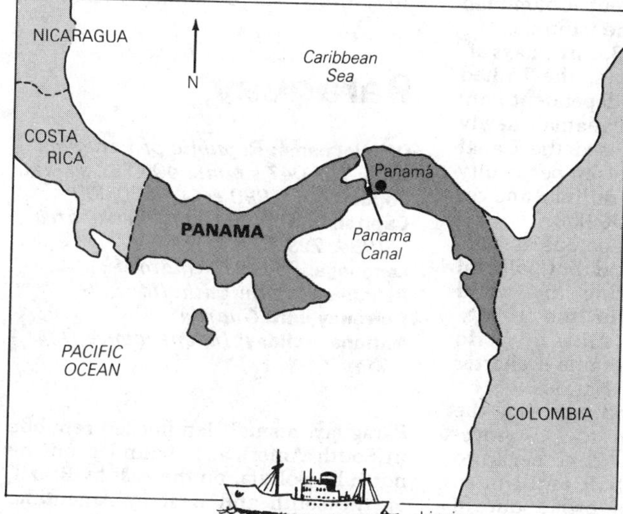

language, although English is widely understood.

Colón, near the northern end of the canal, and Panamá, at its southern end, are the country's major seaports and urban centers. Outlying areas are sparsely settled, especially the region east of the Canal Zone.

Economy. The economy of Panama is largely based on providing goods and services for the Canal Zone. In recent years the government has sought to lessen Panama's dependence on the canal and diversify the economy by increasing agricultural production and expanding industry.

Panama has rich natural resources, but they are mostly unexploited. Only small quantities of gold, silver, and manganese are mined. Limestone is quarried and it supplies the cement industry. Panama also has valuable timber and an abundance of fish in its coastal waters, but neither has been adequately exploited.

Only a fraction of Panama's arable land is cultivated, and farms traditionally are small and primitive. Rice and corn are the basic food crops, but a variety of fruits and vegetables are also grown. Bananas are by far the most important commercial crop. Coconuts, cacao, sugar cane, and coffee are also significant.

The rising importance of international banking and industry has spurred a period of economic expansion since 1960. While light industries are still the most important ones, chemical and plastic manufacturing and oil refining are growing steadily. Small factories produce cement, shoes, soap, soft drinks, alcoholic beverages, furniture, and clothing. There is also some food processing and a variety of home handicraft industries.

Trade. In 1986 Panama's exports were estimated at $327 million while imports cost an estimated $1.2 billion. Oil transshipment has figured in the economy since a port for this traffic was built in 1979 on Panama's Pacific coast. The country's poor balance of trade is compensated for by income from the Canal Zone and by fees from the registry of foreign vessels under the Panamanian flag.

Panama's chief exports are bananas, petroleum products, fish—especially shrimp—sugar, and coffee. Principal imports include petroleum, machinery, motor vehicles, textiles, chemicals, and foodstuffs. The bulk of Panama's trade is with the United States.

Government. Panama is a democratic republic. The president, who is directly elected to a term of five years, is the head of state and chief executive. Legislative power is vested in the unicameral Legislative Assembly, whose 67 members are elected from regions throughout the country.

Panama is a member of the United Nations and the Organization of American States (OAS).

History. Panama was discovered in 1501 by Rodrigo de Bastidas. In 1502 Christopher Columbus explored the Caribbean coast and claimed the territory for Spain. In 1513 Vasco Núñez de Balboa crossed the isthmus and discovered the Pacific Ocean, thereby putting the western coast within Spanish reach.

In 1519 the small village of Panamá, on the Pacific coast, was made the capital of the isthmus. The Spanish explorer Francisco Pizarro used Panama as the base for expeditions to Peru in 1531. The cities of Nombre de Dios and, later, Portobelo became the ports through which gold and silver were shipped to Spain.

During the late 1600's and the 1700's Spain entered a period of political and economic decline and the importance of Panama began to wane. In 1751 Panama lost its autonomy and became part of the viceroyalty of New Granada, which included present-day Colombia.

In 1821 Panama gained independence from Spain and joined with Colombia, Ecuador, and Venezuela to form the Republic of Gran Colombia. Gran Colombia was dissolved in 1830, but Panama remained part of Colombia. A spirit of Panamanian nationalism began to grow, however, and political relations with Colombia deteriorated as Panamanians grew to fear that their interests might be sacrificed.

Independence. In 1903 the Colombian government refused to ratify the Hay-Herrán Treaty, which would have permitted the United States to build a canal through the Isthmus of Panama. Fearing that the United States would build the canal through Nicaragua instead, the Panamanians revolted and declared their independence from Colombia. U.S. President Theodore Roosevelt insured the success of the revolt when he ordered a U.S. warship to prevent Colombian troops from entering the isthmus.

On November 6, 1903, three days after the revolution began, the United States recognized an independent Panamanian government. Panama's newly formed government leased the Canal Zone to the United States in perpetuity for a payment of $10 million and an annual payment of $250,000.

Panama became prosperous as a result of the Panama Canal, but political unrest developed during the world economic depression of the 1930's. Panama sided with the Allies in World War II and in 1945 became a charter member of the United Nations.

Contemporary Panama. During the mid-1950's opposition to U.S. sovereignty over the Canal Zone began to grow. In November, 1959, anti-United States demonstrations broke out in Panamá and Colón.

In January, 1964, Panamanian students led violent anti-United States riots. The two countries agreed to negotiate their differences, and in 1967 a new treaty was drafted providing for Panamanian sovereignty over the Canal Zone and a joint board to govern the canal itself. In 1974 the United States and Panama agreed that the United States would operate and protect the canal for a certain period with Panama sharing the revenues. They also agreed to set a date for final transfer of the canal to Panama.

In 1977 the two countries proposed a plan for Panama's gradual takeover of the canal, to be completed in 1999. In 1978 the U.S. Senate approved the plan, which included a guarantee of the canal's neutrality. In 1979 the Canal Zone was transferred to Panama. In 1980 Japan and Panama together began to study the construction of a second canal in Panama—one that could accomodate full-size tankers.

A breakdown of order in 1968 resulted in a military coup on October 1. The National Assembly was dissolved and the constitution was suspended. In 1969 Brigadier General Omar Torrijos Herrera took command of the junta now in power. By 1972 he had assumed virtual dictatorial powers, had given the country a new constitution, and had promised to restore civilian rule by 1978. He brought an era of stability to Panama and championed causes for the underprivileged classes.

In 1982 General Manuel Antonio Noriega became commander of the National Defense Forces. Noriega virtually controlled the civilian government. He was also implicated in Panama's drug trafficking. In 1984 the first direct presidential elections in 16 years were held.

In December, 1989, U.S. troops invaded Panama because increasing violence in the country was threatening American citizens. The constitutionally elected leaders from the 1989 elections were installed in the government and Noriega went into hiding. Eventually Noriega surrendered to U.S. forces.

Paraguay

Official name: *Republic of Paraguay*
Area: *157,047 sq. mi., 406,752 sq. km.*
Population: *(1990 est.) 4,660,000*
Capital: *Asunción (Pop., metro. area, 1984, 729,307)*
Language: *Spanish, Guaraní*
Religion: *Roman Catholic*
Currency unit: *Guaraní*
National holiday: *Independence Day, May 14*

Paraguay, a small landlocked republic in South America, is bounded on the north by Bolivia, on the east by Brazil, on the south and west by Argentina.

The land. The Paraguay River, which flows down from Brazil and joins the Paraná River in the southwestern corner, at the Argentine border, divides Paraguay into two contrasting regions. The western region, or Chaco Boreal, is a hot, parched wasteland, partially covered with scrub forest. The eastern region consists of fertile plains, grasslands, and dense forests.

In the extreme east is the heavily forested Paraná Plateau, which ranges in altitude from 1000 to 2000 feet above sea level. In the northern part of the plateau the forests give way to grasslands or savannas. West of the plateau are rolling, grassy plains.

Climate. Because of its location within the interior of the continent, Paraguay experiences wider temperature fluctuations than almost any other part of South America. Summer temperatures average about 80°F, but temperatures over 100°F are fairly common. Winter temperatures average 55°F.

Annual rainfall varies, although it is generally quite dry in the west and becomes progressively wetter toward the east. The average annual rainfall at Asunción, on the Paraguay River, is 62 inches, but near the Brazilian border it increases to about 80 inches.

The people. The overwhelming majority of the people are of mixed Guaraní Indian and Spanish ancestry. Although the admixture of Spanish blood in the population is small, there are few pureblooded Indians left in Paraguay; they mostly inhabit the remoter regions of the Chaco. There are also small numbers of foreigners who have settled in agricultural communities. They include Germans, Japanese, Italians, Brazilians, Argentines, and Canadian Mennonites.

The official language is Spanish but Guaraní is spoken almost universally. Most Paraguayans belong to the Roman Catholic Church.

giant anteater

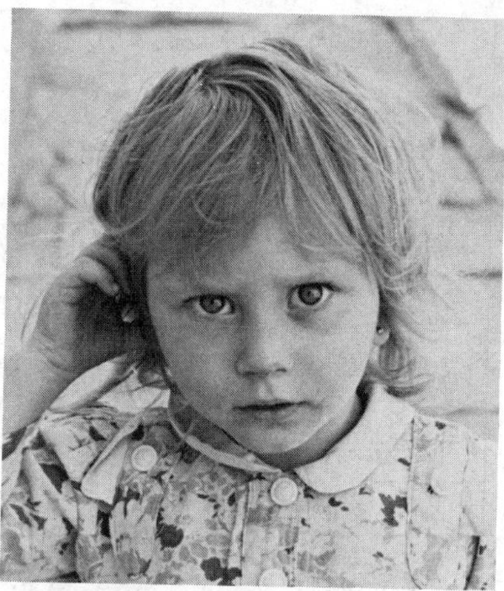
IRELL/MONKMEYER

A BLOND IN PARAGUAY. *The little girl's parents are German settlers.*

Over half the labor force is employed in agriculture, with about 15 percent in manufacturing. Paraguay is very sparsely populated, with only about 20 people per square mile. Nearly two-thirds of the people live in rural areas.

Economy. Paraguay is one of the least developed nations in South America. The government owns many of the nation's public utilities, but encourages private enterprise and depends heavily on foreign investment.

The economy is based on agriculture and forestry, and these activities account for almost all the country's exports.

Paraguay has deposits of manganese, iron, copper, kaolin, mica, talc, and bauxite, but the only two minerals mined are limestone and salt. The country's most important natural resource is its forests, which yield valuable hardwoods and a variety of other products. Two of the most important forest products are tannin, used in tanning, dyeing, ink, and medicine, and yerba maté, from which a tealike beverage is made.

Agriculture. Although most of the people are engaged in agriculture, only a fraction of Paraguay's arable land is cultivated. Farming methods are primitive and most farmers raise only enough to feed their own families.

Food crops include manioc, corn, sugar cane, sweet potatoes, rice, and citrus and other fruits. The country's most important commercial crops are cotton, tobacco, coffee, and oilseeds.

Cattle have long been an important source of income, and meat products are Paraguay's most valuable export. Cattle are raised chiefly in the area between the Paraguay and Paraná rivers, in Concepción near the northwestern border, and in the Chaco.

Industry. Paraguay is one of the least industrialized countries in South America. The nation's few industries are limited to the processing of its agricultural products and the manufacture of a small number of consumer goods and also construction materials, such as soap, matches, glass, cement, and bricks.

Trade. Paraguay's exports in 1985 earned $304 million and imports cost $478 million. The major exports are meat, wood, tobacco, cotton, tannin, and coffee. Imports include machinery, wheat, iron and steel products, transportation equipment, fuel oil, and chemicals.

Brazil, Argentina, Japan, and the European Common Market countries are Paraguay's chief trading partners.

Government. Paraguay is a republic. The head of state and chief executive is the president, who is directly elected to a term of five years. He is assisted by a cabinet, which he appoints.

The legislative branch of government consists of the Chamber of Deputies, with 60 members, and the Senate, with 30 members. All legislators are elected to five-year terms.

Paraguay is a member of the United Nations, the Organization of American States (OAS), and the Latin American Free Trade Association.

History. Paraguay was discovered in 1524 by Alejo García, a Portuguese explorer. Two years later Sebastian Cabot explored the Paraná and Paraguay rivers for Spain, and in 1537 a permanent Spanish settlement was made in Asunción, on the Paraguay River.

Spanish rule. In 1609 the Jesuits arrived in Paraguay to convert the Guaraní Indians. The Jesuits were highly successful in their missionary work and they founded more than 30 *reducciones,* self-sufficient, autonomous mission communities. Between 150,000 and 200,000 Indians lived and worked within this system.

The Jesuits were not popular with the Spanish colonists. They wanted the Indians to work for them and resented the competition from mission agricultural produce. In 1767 Spain expelled the Jesuits from South America, and the *reducciones* collapsed.

In 1776 Paraguay was incorporated into the newly formed viceroyalty of Río de la Plata, which included present-day Argentina and was governed from Buenos Aires. In 1810 the Argentinians rebelled against Spain and set up a junta, or government council, at Buenos Aires. Paraguayans refused to recognize this government, but the following year they threw off Spanish rule and established a junta of their own at Asunción.

Independence. In 1814 one of the members of the junta, José Gaspar Rodríguez de Francia, took over the government and became president. Francia exercised strong autocratic control, aided both by an internal spy network and by the reverence that he managed to inspire in the common people. He followed a policy of political isolation, which protected Paraguay from outside influences and encouraged economic self-sufficiency.

Francia died in 1840, and in 1844, after a brief period of transition, his nephew, Carlos Antonio López, became president. López made education free and compulsory, built roads, and loosened Francia's policy of isolation. But whereas Francia had been personally honest, López and his family profiteered at the nation's expense. When López died in 1862, his son Francisco Solano López became president.

The central feature of the regime of Francisco Solano López was the War of the Triple Alliance, which pitted Paraguay against Argentina, Brazil, and Uruguay. In 1864 López attacked Brazil, ostensibly because of Brazil's interference in the affairs of Uruguay. Also at stake was López's ambition to expand Paraguayan influence and territory at the expense of Argentina and Brazil, with which Paraguay had long-standing territorial disputes.

In 1865 the conflict expanded into a general war. Paraguay was victorious at first, but the overwhelmingly superior resources of the allies assured Paraguay's eventual defeat. In 1870 López was killed and the war ended. The devastation from the war was tremendous. Paraguay's population had fallen from approximately 1 million to about 220,000, of whom fewer than 30,000 were adult males. Paraguay also lost some territory, but rivalry between Argentina and Brazil prevented Paraguay's complete dismemberment.

Contemporary Paraguay. Recovery was slow and political conditions were unstable. Between 1870 and 1932 Paraguay had 29 presidents. Nonetheless, Paraguay made some economic progress in these years. Foreign capital and enterprise, much of it from Argentina, assisted the nation's development, and a number of small colonies of immigrants were established.

In 1932 Paraguay fought a war with Bolivia over the Gran Chaco, a semi-wasteland between the two countries. Paraguay defeated Bolivia owing superior leadership and shorter lines of communication. A truce was declared in 1935, and a 1938 treaty allotted Paraguay three-fourths of the disputed territory.

General José Félix Estigarribia, the commander of Paraguay's forces during the Chaco War, became president in 1939. He was killed in an airplane accident and was succeeded by Higinio Morínigo. Morínigo was forced out of office by a revolt in 1948.

In 1954, following a series of short-lived governments, the army under General Alfredo Stroessner took over the government. Running without opposition, Stroessner was elected to the presidency later that year.

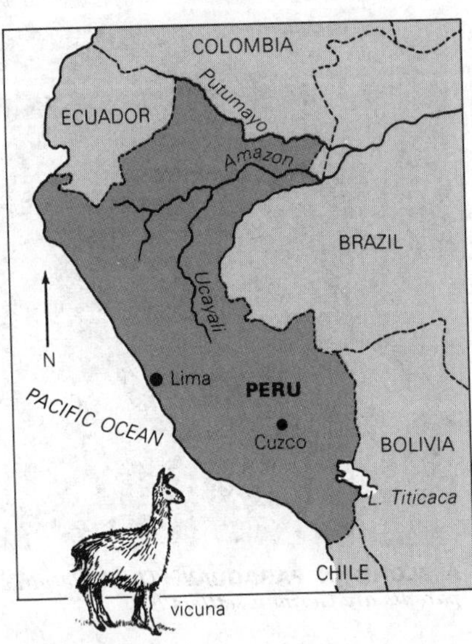

vicuna

Stroessner established a rigid dictatorship. He gave the country stability and relative prosperity but was still accused of severe oppression. With little opposition, Stroessner was consistently reelected until a coup led by General Andrés Rodríguez ousted him in February, 1989.

Rodríguez was immediately sworn in as president; he promised to introduce democracy to Paraguay. In April a free election confirmed Rodríguez as president, ending a long history of dictatorial rule. He planned to reinstate relations with the Roman Catholic Church and ensure human rights.

Hydroelectric production on the Paraná River has stimulated economic growth since the 1970's. The facility built through a joint effort with Brazil is the largest in the world, and a second is scheduled to be built.

Peru

Official name: *Republic of Peru*
Area: *496,224 sq. mi., 1,285,216 sq. km.*
Population: *(1990 est.) 22,353,000*
Capital: *Lima (Pop., 1983, 5,258,600)*
Language: *Spanish, Indian languages*
Religion: *Roman Catholic*
Currency: *Sol*
National holiday: *Independence Day, July 28*

Peru, a republic on the west coast of South America, is bounded on the north by Ecuador and Colombia, on the east by Brazil and Bolivia, on the south by Chile, and on the west by the Pacific Ocean.

The land. Peru is a country of striking diversity. Within its borders are humid tropical lowlands in the east; ice covered peaks in the Andes; and rainless coastal desert in the west. The country has three main geographic regions: the coastal desert, or *costa*; the Andean highlands, or *sierra*; and the eastern Andean slopes and Amazon lowlands, or *montaña*.

The coastal zone extends from Ecuador to Chile and is generally less than 30 miles wide. It is extremely dry. Winds blowing in from the ocean are chilled by the cold Peru, or Humboldt, Current and yield no moisture. The only oases are the valleys of 50 or 60 seasonal rivers that drain the western slopes of the Andes.

The Andean highlands consist of a broad altiplano, or plateau, that lies between 10,000 and 15,000 feet above sea level and is surmounted by mountain peaks. The grassland vegetation of the altiplano, known as *puna*, provides good pasturage for livestock, and the mountain valleys contain Peru's most fertile land.

The *montaña* is part of the Amazon basin and is covered with tropical forest and jungle. Although it constitutes 60 percent of the nation's territory, it is very thinly populated. Development of the area has been impeded by its physical isolation.

Climate varies from region to region. The climate on the coast is dry and temperate. Temperatures in the *sierra* vary with altitude from temperate to frigid, and most of the area is fairly dry. The *montaña* is hot and humid, with temperatures in the 70°s and 80°s F. Rainfall often exceeds 100 inches a year.

The people. About half of the population is Indian and most of the remainder is mestizo, of mixed Indian and Spanish ancestry. About ten percent is of European origin. Spanish is the official language, but it is spoken by only about half of the population. The Andean Indians speak either Quechua or Aymara, and the Amazon tribes of the *montaña* have their own Indian languages.

Peru's principal city is Lima, the capital, which is the largest and most important city on the Pacific coast of South America. Other major urban centers of Peru are Arequipa, population 706,580; Callao, now the chief port, 443,413; Chimbote, 216,406; and Chiclayo, 280,244.

Since 1960 the population has shifted drastically toward urban centers, where nearly two out of every three people now live. Two-fifths of the people live on the Pacific coast, which consists of just over ten percent of Peru's total area.

Economy. Peru's economy is based largely on agriculture and mining, and the Peruvian Andes are rich in minerals. Although the country has deposits of a wide variety of minerals from which it could prosper, copper, iron, zinc, lead, silver, and oil are the mainstays of the mining industry. Eight million metric tons of oil were produced in 1987. Mining earns half of Peru's total export revenues.

Fish abound in Peru's offshore waters, and as recently as the late 1960's the country had the world's largest catch. Since then, however, overexploitation and shifting marine conditions have resulted in a large drop in fish production.

The forests of the *montaña* cover more than half the country's territory. Although still largely unexploited, they produce valuable quantities of cedar, mahogany, and other tropical hardwoods, as well as rubber, leche caspi (used in making chewing gum), jute, and a variety of medicinal plants.

Agriculture. Agriculture employs approximately half the labor force and is the backbone of the Peruvian economy, although it only contributes just over ten percent of the gross national product, with nearly 25 percent contributed by industry (based on the processing of agricultural products).

Agricultural production is slowed down by a lack of well watered arable land. Farming methods are often inefficient. As a result, Peru cannot raise enough food for its own use and foodstuffs must be imported.

Potatoes and corn are the major food crops. They are raised in the *sierra*, which has 60 percent of the country's cultivated land. Large quantities of rice and beans are also grown. The leading commercial crops are sugar cane and cotton, which are grown in the coastal valleys and in the *montaña*. The *montaña* also produces coffee, tobacco, cacao, fruit, and nuts.

Peru has very few cattle, and meat and dairy products must be imported. Sheep, vicuñas, and alpacas are raised in the southern Andes and their wool is exported.

Industry. Peruvian industry is limited largely to the processing of agricultural products, smelting and refining, and the manufacture of a variety of domestic consumer goods. The most important of these include textiles, beverages, footwear, leather goods, construction materials, paper and cardboard, chemicals, pharmaceuticals, and synthetic fertilizer.

Trade. In 1986 Peruvian exports earned $2.5 billion and imports cost $2.4 billion. The country's major exports are fish meal, cotton, sugar, iron ore, copper, lead, zinc, oil, and silver. Peru's principal imports include machinery, transport equipment, foodstuffs, chemicals, and pharmaceuticals. Major trade partners are the United States, West Germany, Japan, and Great Britain.

Government.

Peru is a constitutional republic. It has a popularly elected president who serves a five-year term. He is assisted by a Council of Ministers, which he appoints. Legislative power is vested in the 60-member Senate and the 180-member Chamber of Deputies. All legislators are also elected to five-year terms.

Peru is a member of the United Nations, of the Organization of American States (OAS), the Andean Group, and of the Latin American Free Trade Association.

History.

Before Christopher Columbus reached the New World in 1492, Peru was the center of a great American Indian civilization, that of the Incas. In about 1200 the Incas began to move from their original homeland in the southern Peruvian Andes and to subjugate neighboring Indian peoples living in the highlands and on the coast.

By the late 1400's the Incas had established an empire that stretched along the western coast of South America from Ecuador to Chile. This vast empire was joined together by an intricate network of roads. It was ruled from the city of Cuzco, high in the Andes of southern Peru.

In 1531 a small army of Spaniards led by Francisco Pizarro invaded Peru. Despite their small numbers, the Spanish easily conquered the Incas, who were weakened and divided by civil war and terrified by the guns and horses of the Spaniards.

Spanish rule. In 1542 the Spaniards transformed what had been the Inca empire into the viceroyalty of Peru, ruled from Lima, which Pizarro had founded in 1535. Rich deposits of precious metals, particularly silver, made Peru for many years the most prized of Spain's American colonies.

In the 1700's Peru's importance was diminished by the creation of the viceroyalties of New Granada, in 1717, and Río de la Plata, in 1776. Internal tranquility was shaken by a number of Indian uprisings, the most serious being that of Tupac Amaru, between 1780 and 1783. Nevertheless, during the first years of the 1800's, when Spain's other South American colonies were seeking independence, Peru remained a loyalist stronghold.

It was not until 1820, when the Argentine leader José de San Martín, who had already defeated the Spaniards in Chile, landed with an Argentine-Chilean army of liberation, that the Peruvian struggle for independence began in earnest. San Martín captured Lima and a year later, on July 28, 1821, declared Peru independent. But Spain's power was not finally broken until December, 1824, when the forces of Simón Bolívar, who had replaced San Martín, routed the Spanish at the battle of Ayacucho. The independence of Peru marked the end of Spain's empire in South America.

Independence. For nearly 20 years after gaining independence, Peru was controlled by a succession of military dictators, or *caudillos*, including Luis José Orbegosa, who drew Peru into a

MACHU PICCHU, *evocative ruin some 9000 feet high in the Andes, the best preserved of all Incan cities. Lost to the world after the Spanish conquest, it was rediscovered in 1911.*

ORGANIZATION OF AMERICAN STATES

ALFREDO LINARES/MONKMEYER

BALSA BOATS *tended by an Indian on the edge of Lake Titicaca, which runs 22 miles across the Bolivia-Peru border. It is 45 miles wide. The lake lies 12,500 feet above sea level.*

short-lived confederation with Bolivia from 1836 to 1839.

In 1845 the presidency was assumed by General Ramón Castilla, who, except for a brief interval from 1851 to 1854, ruled the country until 1862. Castilla brought about the abolition of black slavery and a reduction in the special privileges of the church. He developed Peru's guano and nitrate sources, and provided the country with a large measure of stability.

The ten years following Castilla's regime were marked by a growing public debt, political corruption, and internal disorder, all of which were intensified in 1865–1866 by a brief war with Spain, which sought redress for the mistreatment of Spanish citizens in Peru. Chile, Ecuador, and Bolivia came to the aid of Peru, and the Spanish ultimately withdrew.

Dissatisfaction with the military in Peruvian politics increased. As a result, in 1872 Manuel Pardo, a civilian who represented a coalition of landed aristocrats and financial and commercial interests, was elected president. Pardo aided higher education, sought to reduce the size and influence of the army, and tried to improve the economy. He was hindered in his efforts by a decline in the important guano industry, which was only partially offset by increased nitrate production in the southern coastal province of Tarapacá.

Through an alliance that Pardo had made with Bolivia in 1873, Peru became involved in the War of the Pacific, from 1879 to 1883, which resulted from a dispute between Bolivia and Chile over the Atacama nitrate fields. Chile was victorious, and under the terms of the peace treaty Peru was forced to yield its nitrate province of Tarapacá as well as to permit Chilean occupation of the adjoining provinces of Arica and Tacna. Peru was left bankrupt and exhausted.

Contemporary Peru. Peru did not fully recover until the early 1900's. Progress was especially notable during the second administration of Augusto B. Leguía y Salcedo, which stretched from 1919 to 1930. Leguía managed to bolster the economy by securing foreign loans and investments. He also supported large-scale public works.

Leguía was relatively popular until 1930, when the world economic depression cut off the flow of foreign capital and reduced the earnings of Peruvian exports. He was then overthrown by Colonel Luis Sánchez Cerro, who remained in power until 1933, when he was assassinated. Under his successor, Oscar Benavides, in office until 1939, Peru gradually recovered from the depression.

Nevertheless, the Indian population of the Andean region received little direct benefit from the progress that had taken place. Control of Peruvian society remained in the hands of a small, wealthy minority and protest movements arose. One of these was the growing *Alianza Popular Revolucionaria Americana* (APRA—American Popular Revolutionary Alliance), founded by Victor Rául Haya de la Torre.

APRA's original program was pro-Indian, socialistic, and extremely hostile to foreign capital. During the 1930's, APRA became the strongest political movement in Peru, but it was distrusted by the military and repeatedly frustrated in its efforts to gain power, even though it gradually became more conservative.

The moderately leftist and pro-democratic *Partido de Acción Popular* (PAP—Popular Action Party), founded and led by Fernando Belaúnde Terry, had more success. Belaúnde was elected president in 1963. He sponsored agrarian reforms and supported measures beneficial to the Indians, while seeking to involve more people in the government. He also put special emphasis on the development of the *montaña.* In 1968 Belaúnde was overthrown by an army coup and General Juan Velasco became head of a new government.

Elections were last held in 1963, and the military government insisted that it would not relinquish power until its reforms were irreversible. Its program was to implement a social democracy with full popular participation, and to formulate a nationalist approach to industrialization.

Velasco's regime, however, became authoritarian and intolerant, and he was deposed by his military commanders on August 29, 1975. They placed General Francisco Morales Bermudez in the presidency. He vowed not to change the revolutionary process of Velasco, and asserted that all Peruvians would be permitted to take part in forming a "new society."

The sweeping social and agrarian reforms that Velasco was responsible for remained in effect, but inflation, unemployment, and severe food shortages became worse. Stringent austerity programs were begun by Morales in 1977 to counter foreign debt. The programs were met with nationwide labor strikes. In 1978 a state of emergency and martial law was declared. Political opponents of the regime were severely repressed.

Elections were held in 1978 for the first time in 15 years. A Constitutional Assembly was elected to draw up a new democratic constitution and pave the way for a return to civilian rule. These plans became a reality in 1980, and Fernando Belaúnde Terry, deposed in 1968, was reelected to the presidency. Severe economic and social problems decreased Belaúnde's popularity.

In 1985 Alan García Pérez was elected president. García planned to tackle the economic problems by limiting payments on Peru's foreign debt, but inflation continued to rise.

Peru is still sadly beset with most of its traditional economic problems. Wealth and land are unequally distributed among regions and among social and ethnic groups. Racial tensions also dangerously persist among whites, mestizos, and Indians.

St. Kitts-Nevis

Official name: *Saint Kitts-Nevis*
Area: *104 sq. mi., 269 sq. km.*
Population: *(1990 est.) 35,000*
Capital: *Basseterre (Pop. 1980, 15,000*
Language: *English*
Religion: *Anglican, Roman Catholic*
Currency unit: *East Caribbean dollar*

St. Kitts and Nevis are two islands in the Lesser Antilles chain in the eastern Caribbean.

The land and people. St. Kitts is about 68 square miles. Its topography is dominated by a volcanic ridge that occupies the center of the island. Nevis, which lies about two miles from St. Kitts, is about 50 square miles, and is also mountainous. The islands have a tropical climate with an average yearly rainfall of 55 inches and a mean temperature of 79 degrees.

The majority of the islands' inhabitants are of African or African-European decent. Nearly a third of the people live in the two main cities, Basseterre and Charlestown.

Economy. The sugar industry is the mainstay of the islands' economy. It is the largest employer and sugar products are the largest export. Cotton and pineapples are also cultivated. As with many other Caribbean islands, tourism is becoming an increasingly important part of the economy.

Government. St. Kitts-Nevis has a parliamentary form of government, with a prime minister as the head. He presides over a cabinet. The legislative body is the House of Assembly.

History. St. Kitts and Nevis were both discovered by Christopher Columbus in 1493, and were settled by the English in 1623 and 1628, respectively. The French also established a colony, and possession of the islands was disputed until the 1783 Treaty of Versailles, when the question was settled in favor of the British.

St. Kitts and Nevis, along with the nearby island of Anguilla, were granted internal self-government as an associated state of the United Kingdom in February of 1967. Anguilla withdrew from the association later that year. St. Kitts-Nevis became an independent country on September 19, 1983.

St. Lucia

Official name: *Saint Lucia*
Area: *238 sq. mi., 616 sq. km.*
Population: *(1990 est.) 143,000*
Capital: *Castries*
(Pop., 1986 est., 52,000)
Language: *English, French patois*
Religion: *Roman Catholic*
Currency unit: *East Caribbean dollar*

St. Lucia is one of the Windward Islands of the Lesser Antilles chain, which lies between the Caribbean Sea and the Atlantic Ocean. It is located just south of French Martinique, and northeast of St. Vincent.

St. Lucia attained independence on February 22, 1979, ending over a century and a half of British rule.

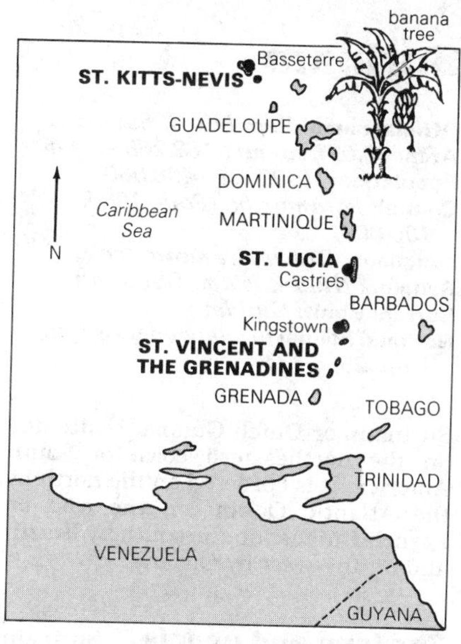

The land and people. Volcanic in origin, St. Lucia has a rugged, mountainous terrain. The capital, Castries, has an excellent harbor. The climate is hot and dry throughout the year, and rainfall is abundant.

The population is of mixed African, European, and Indian origin. Most of the people are blacks or mulattoes. English is the official language, but a French patois is in common use.

Castries is the only sizable city, and over one-third of the population resides there. With over 470 people per square mile, the island is very densely populated.

Economy. Agriculture is still the mainstay of the economy, and bananas, copra, cocoa, and spices are the chief commercial crops.

The economic importance of industry and tourism are rising very rapidly. About one-third of the labor force is now employed in industry, just slightly less than in agriculture. Tourism has become the nation's largest single source of income. There is also considerable manufacturing growth, although food processing remains of prime importance.

A major oil transshipment port and free trade zone are under construction; these should improve St. Lucia's economy.

In 1985 St. Lucia's exports earned $53 million, while its imports cost $127 million. The bulk of exports go to Britain, the United States, and nearby islands. Imports are fertilizer, fuels, machinery, and other manufactured goods.

Government. St. Lucia has a parliamentary form of government. Queen Elizabeth II is the nominal head of state and she appoints a governor-general to the island.

The prime minister is the head of the government. The legislature consists of the House of Assembly, with 17 elected members, and the Senate, with eleven members—six appointed by the prime minister, three by the opposition, and two by the British governor-general.

St. Lucia is a member of the United Nations, the Commonwealth of Nations, and also a member of the Caribbean Community and Common Market (CARICOM).

History. St. Lucia was inhabited by Indians when it was discovered by Europeans in the late 1400's and settled by colonists in the 1600's. During the 1700's slaves were brought from Africa to work on plantations. St. Lucia became a British colony in 1814 and gained self-government in 1967.

After 1967, the United Workers Party, led by Prime Minister John Compton, became the chief political force on the island. Compton pushed for full independence and closer economic ties with other CARICOM nations and with oil-rich Venezuela.

In 1979 the island won its independence and the socialist-oriented Labor Party won two-thirds of the assembly seats. Its leader—Allan Louisy—became the new prime minister.

In 1982 Compton became prime minister and the United Workers Party regained control of parliament.

St. Vincent and the Grenadines

Official name: *Saint Vincent and the Grenadines*
Area: *150 sq. mi., 389 sq. km.*
Population: *(1990 est.) 110,000*
Capital: *Kingstown*
(Pop., 1982, 33,694)
Language: *English, French patois*
Religion: *Methodist, Anglican, Roman Catholic*
Currency unit: *East Caribbean dollar*

St. Vincent and the northern islets of the Grenadines are part of the Windward Islands of the Lesser Antilles. They lie between the eastern Caribbean and the Atlantic Ocean, south of St. Lucia and north of Grenada.

The islands became an independent nation on October 27, 1979, following over a century and a half of British rule.

The land and people. St. Vincent is the main island of the group. It accounts for 133 of the 150 square miles of the nation's total area. St. Vincent consists of a heavily forested spine of mountains flanked by coastal plains. In the north is the imposing

Soufrière volcano, which had a violent and destructive eruption in 1902, and a smaller eruption in 1979. The climate is hot throughout the year and rainfall is abundant.

The population is mostly black, although of mixed African, European, and Indian origin. With a population density of nearly 750 people per square mile, the islands are extremely crowded, and the annual growth rate of two percent is fairly high.

Economy. Agriculture and tourism are the basis of the economy. Bananas, arrowroot, copra, cotton, fruits, spices, and yams are the chief crops.

Manufacturing has grown modestly since 1970, and still consists mainly of food processing.

In 1986 the country's imports cost $87 million while its exports earned only $68 million. Farm products are the main exports, and foodstuffs, raw materials, and machinery are the main imports. Most trade is conducted with Great Britain and neighboring islands.

Government. Queen Elizabeth II, the nominal head of state, is represented by her appointed governor-general. The prime minister is the head of government. There is a unicameral legislature—the House of Assembly—that has 13 elected members, plus six appointed senators.

St. Vincent and the Grenadines is a member of the United Nations, the Commonwealth of Nations, and the Caribbean Community and Common Market (CARICOM).

History. Inhabited by a few Indians when discovered by Christopher Columbus in the 1490's, St. Vincent and the Grenadines were settled in the 1600's by Europeans from several countries. They established plantations worked by slaves brought from Africa. The islands became British colonies in 1814 and were governed with the other Windward Islands until gaining self-government in 1967.

Milton Cato and his moderately socialist Labor Party came to power in 1974. The party has remained the islands' chief political force. Independence was achieved October 27, 1979, and Cato was reelected prime minister on December 5. Two days later, Union and Palm islands rebelled. The secessionist violence was put down, although a state of emergency remained in effect for half a year. In 1984 James Mitchell was elected prime minister.

The eruption of Mt. Soufrière on April 13, 1979, devastated the nation's banana crop and emergency foreign aid (mostly from Britain) was needed to sustain the economy. This along with a chronic high unemployment rate has not allowed the economy to recover from the disaster.

Surinam

Official name: *Republic of Surinam*
Area: *63,037 sq. mi., 163,265 sq. km.*
Population: *(1990 est.) 408,000*
Capital: *Paramaribo (Pop., 1984, 180,000)*
Language: *Dutch, Sranantongo*
Religion: *Hindu, Islam, Christian*
Currency unit: *Guilder*
National holiday: *Independence Day, Nov. 25*

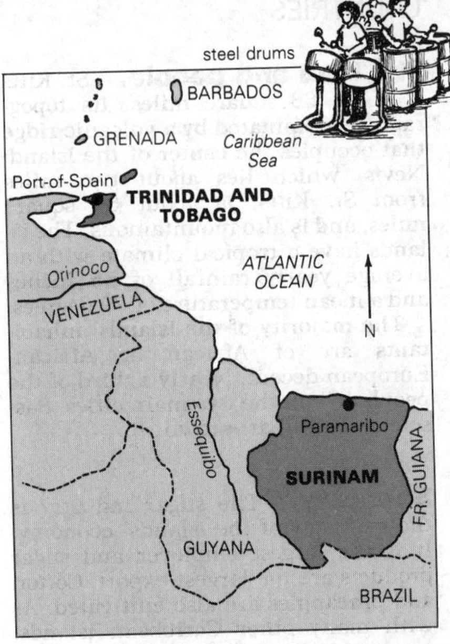

Surinam, or Dutch Guiana, is situated on the northeastern coast of South America. It is bordered on the north by the Atlantic Ocean, on the east by French Guiana, on the south by Brazil, and on the west by Guyana.

The land and people. Surinam has a flat, narrow, fertile coastal plain and a hilly, forested interior, from which flow many rivers. The climate is warm and damp.

The population is of varied origins, but most of the people are of East Indian, Indonesian, African, and mixed descent. There are some American Indians (Amerindians), Chinese, and Europeans. A mixed Creole group is the most politically significant.

The population rose at an extremely rapid rate in the 1960's, but since independence was attained in 1975, mass emigration has reduced the population by nearly one-third. The East Indians emigrated more than other groups because they resented a Creole-dominated government and economy; most of them went to the Netherlands.

Dutch and Sranantongo, a local language, are the chief languages. Religious life is as diverse as the people, and there are Hindus, Muslims, Protestants, and Roman Catholics. Indeed Surinam is an example of a multinational new nation, recently created.

Economy. Surinam has rich deposits of bauxite, from which aluminum is made, and excellent timber resources. Farming is important, and rice, sugar, cacao, fruits, and coffee are raised. Mining and forestry are the only important industries.

Nearly one-third of the labor force is engaged in agriculture along the coastal plains, but the backbone of the economy is bauxite and aluminum production. Bauxite provides about two-fifths of the gross national product and 90 percent of the national export income. Surinam produces ten percent of the world's supply of bauxite, most of it mined at Moenga and Paranam. Gold is also mined.

There are great potential water-power resources in the country. Most of it is undeveloped, however, and industrial production is backward.

Surinam's imports cost $320 million in 1986 while exports earned $332 million. Bauxite, timber, and fruits are exported and foodstuffs, raw materials, textiles, and consumer goods are imported. The United States, the Netherlands, and Canada are Surinam's chief trading partners.

Government. In 1980 the National Military Council overthrew the government but it was replaced by a 51-member National Assembly and a State Council in 1985. Democracy was restored in 1988. Surinam's government is a parliamentary democracy. The president and vice president are assisted by the National Assembly and the State Council. The military is still involved in the government.

Surinam is a member of the United Nations and the Organization of American States (OAS).

History. Surinam was first visited in the 1500's by Spaniards in search of gold. They abandoned the territory. In the 1600's and 1700's Surinam changed hands among Britain, the Netherlands, and France.

In 1815 the area was ceded to the Netherlands by the Treaty of Paris. The Dutch established plantations and began extensive mining and timber operations in the late 1800's and early 1900's, when they brought Indian and Indonesian laborers to Surinam.

During the 1900's Surinam gained an increasing measure of popular government, and in 1954 it became a self-governing part of the Kingdom of the Netherlands. Surinam faced severe economic and social problems because of its rapid rate of population growth and the variety of ethnic groups constituting its population. In the 1950's and 1960's the government concentrated on expanding industry and improving agriculture. But the colony became increasingly a burden to the Netherlands, a very small country.

Led by Prime Minister Henck Arron (1973–1980) and the National Party Coalition, Surinam became independent on November 25, 1975. The East Indians who, along with the blacks, had strongly opposed independence, left the country in droves. The economy was severely damaged by the loss of many people from this highly educated and skilled group.

Additional economic problems have arisen recently because of heavy migrations of people from the farms to the cities. This trend toward urbanization has caused food shortages, high rates of urban unemployment, and labor unrest. The Netherlands has pledged economic aid to Surinam to help alleviate its plight.

Trinidad and Tobago

Official name: *Republic of Trinidad and Tobago*
Area: *1980 sq. mi., 5128 sq. km.*
Population: *(1990 est.) 1,270,000*
Capital: *Port-of-Spain (Pop., metro. area, 1988, 300,000)*
Language: *English*
Religion: *Roman Catholic, Christian, Hindu, Islam*
Currency unit: *Dollar*
National holiday: *Independence Day, Aug. 31*

Trinidad and Tobago, an independent island country in the West Indies, lies off the eastern coast of South America between the Caribbean Sea and the Atlantic Ocean. Venezuela, on the South American mainland, is only seven miles from Trinidad.

The country consists of two islands, Trinidad, the second largest island in the West Indies, 1864 square miles in area, and Tobago, some 20 miles northeast of Trinidad, 116 square miles in area and some tiny islets.

The land. Trinidad is crossed by three mountain ranges—the Central, Southern, and Northern ranges. The mountains rise to a peak of more than 3000 feet and are separated by lowlands. Tropical forests cover about one-half of Trinidad. There are many small streams, and the east-central coast is swampy.

Tobago's terrain is rugged. A central core of volcanic hills rises over 1800 feet and drops sharply to the sea in the northeast. Except for some isolated coastal plains, flat land is limited to the southwestern tip of Tobago.

The climate of the islands is tropical, with temperatures averaging 77°F throughout the year. Rainfall ranges from about 120 inches a year on Tobago and northern Trinidad to about 50 inches a year in southwestern Trinidad.

The people. Most of Trinidad and Tobago's people are of African descent. About one-third of the population is of East Indian origin and 14 percent is mulatto, of mixed European and African origin. There are also people of Chinese, European, and Near Eastern background.

English is the official language, but a dialect combining English with French, Spanish, and other tongues is widely spoken.

About 90 percent of the country's population lives on Trinidad. The population has rapidly increased, resulting in high rates of unemployment and emigration to Britain and the United States. With 575 people per square mile, the country is very densely populated.

Economy. Trinidad and Tobago has a moderately prosperous economy based on international trade, tourism, and on the exploitation of its rich natural resources, especially petroleum and asphalt.

Half the labor force is occupied by manufacturing, which is dominated by the oil and asphalt industries. In 1979, 11.5 million metric tons of oil were produced. Natural gas reserves are an important source of energy for domestic use, as is electricity, the production of which has increased sharply in recent years.

Agriculture. Arable land is limited in Trinidad and Tobago, but agriculture employs about 13 percent of the labor force and provides important exports.

Sugar cane is the most important commercial crop and is grown in western Trinidad. Cocoa, second in importance, is raised mainly on Tobago and in the wetter regions of Trinidad. Coffee, citrus fruits, and vegetables are grown for local consumption.

Industry. Industry is of prime importance in the economy, and the processing of petroleum is the leading industrial activity. The major oil-producing areas are in Trinidad's Southern Range and off its western coast.

The processing of asphalt extracted from Pitch Lake at La Brea, one of the world's largest sources of natural asphalt, is also important, as is the quarrying of building stone. Other significant manufactures are rum, cement, chemicals, paper products, and metal goods.

Trade. In 1986 exports earned $1.4 billion and imports cost $1.3 billion. The principal imports are crude petroleum, foodstuffs, machinery, transportation equipment, and iron and steel. Petroleum products, sugar, fruit, and cocoa are the main exports.

CARNIVAL TIME IN TRINIDAD. *The whole island joins in the annual festival, the big event of the year. The elaborate costumes, many designed in England, are produced in local shops.*

ORGANIZATION OF AMERICAN STATES

The country's main trading partners are the United States and the nations of the Caribbean Community. Tourism is important, and in 1978 nearly 180,000 foreigners visited the islands.

Government. Trinidad and Tobago is a republic with a parliamentary system of government. An elected president is head of state. Actual executive powers are wielded by a prime minister and cabinet responsible to the legislature, which consists of an appointed Senate and a popularly elected House of Representatives.

The prime minister is appointed by the president. The 31 senators are appointed, the 36 representatives are elected, and all serve five-year terms.

Trinidad and Tobago is a member of the United Nations, the Organization of American States (OAS), the Commonwealth of Nations, and the Caribbean Community and Common Market (CARICOM). It is also an associated state of the European Common Market (EEC).

History. Both Trinidad and Tobago were visited by Christopher Columbus on his third voyage to the New World in 1498. Trinidad was at that time inhabited by Arawak Indians. Tobago was uninhabited when Dutch settlers arrived in 1632.

Trinidad was settled by Spain, which made it a colony about 1550. The island was subject to constant raids by French, Dutch, and British privateers, and the Spanish maintained their control only with difficulty. Cocoa crop failures in the early 1700's led to the abandonment of most settlements on the island.

The colony revived after 1783, when the Spanish government invited Roman Catholics from other countries to settle in Trinidad. Many Frenchmen moved to the island, bringing with them sugar cane, cotton, coffee, and new types of cocoa. Plantation agriculture prospered, based on the labor of slaves imported from Africa.

British rule. In 1798 Britain captured Trinidad and its control was recognized in 1802 by the Treaty of Amiens. The treaty gave Tobago to France, but the French ceded the island to Britain in 1814. The sugar and cocoa industries prospered and were expanded under British colonial rule.

In the 1830's the slaves were freed, and a critical labor shortage in the second half of the 1800's led to contract workers being brought from India. Oil was discovered in the early 1900's and soon played a key role in the economy.

The islands had been made a single colony in 1889, and they began to move toward independence in 1925, when popular representatives were first elected to the governing council. Popular participation in government gradually increased. In 1958 the colony entered the Federation of the West Indies, which united a number of Britain's West Indian and Caribbean colonies, but it withdrew in 1961 when Jamaica left the federation.

Independence. In 1962, a year after complete internal self-government had been granted, Trinidad and Tobago became independent. Dr. Eric Williams, leader of the People's National Movement (PNM), was chosen as the first prime minister.

Trinidad and Tobago was admitted to the Organization of American States in 1967. It thus became the second English-speaking member state in the organization.

Eric Williams was consistently reelected and the PNM has remained the country's dominant political force since it was founded in 1956. The PNM, which draws its strongest support from black citizens, has been opposed by the Democratic Labor Party, which chiefly represents the East Indians, and by the United Labor Front, which mostly represents the leftist trade unions. In the 1976 elections the United Labor Front made a strong showing, winning about one-third of the legislative seats.

Unemployment was a chronic problem for Williams and the PNM. Following labor strikes and civil riots in 1970, a state of emergency was declared. The economy did not improve.

Williams's family planning programs to reduce overpopulation and unemployment were mildly successful. He also sought to attract foreign investment to help develop his country, but there is still a deficiency of working capital. Williams died in 1981 but the PNM remained in power, holding a large majority in parliament.

In 1986 A.N.R. Robinson of the National Alliance for Reconstruction Party was elected prime minister with a large parliamentary majority.

Uruguay

Official name: *Oriental Republic of Uruguay*
Area: *68,536 sq. mi., 117,508 sq. km.*
Population: *(1990 est.) 3,002,000*
Capital: *Montevideo (Pop., 1980, 1,362,000)*
Language: *Spanish*
Religion: *Roman Catholic*
Currency unit: *Peso*
National holiday: *Independence Day, Aug. 25*

Uruguay, a small republic on the east coast of South America, is bounded on the north and east by Brazil, on the south by the Atlantic Ocean, and on the west by Argentina.

The land. Most of Uruguay consists of low, gently rolling plains. There are two long ranges of hills known as *cuchillas*, or "knives"—the Cuchilla de Haedo in the west and the Cuchilla Grande in the east. The eastern coast is edged by tidal lakes, lagoons, and sand dunes. The southern coast is characterized by wide, sandy beaches.

The climate of Uruguay is subtropical. The summers are warm and winter temperatures are generally above freezing. Rainfall is fairly evenly distributed throughout the year and averages about 35 inches.

The people. The people of Uruguay are mostly of Italian and Spanish descent. The native Churrúa Indians were almost completely driven out during the Spanish colonial period, and today less than ten percent of the population can be classified as Indian or mestizo. Spanish is the official language and Roman Catholicism the principal religion.

Uruguay's population increases at one of the lowest rates in South America. Uruguay averages only 43 people per square mile and over 80 percent of the people live in urban areas. Nearly half the people live in the capital city of Montevideo.

Economy. Uruguay is fairly well developed, with a relatively high standard of living and little subsistence farming. Slightly over one-tenth of the labor force is employed in agriculture, which contributes about 15 percent of the gross national product. About one-third is employed in industry, which contributes one-third of the gross national product. There are rich but unexploited fish reserves.

The economy is based on agriculture. About 70 percent of the country's land is devoted to the raising of cattle and sheep, and almost 90 percent of exports consist of wool, hides, meat, and various meat products.

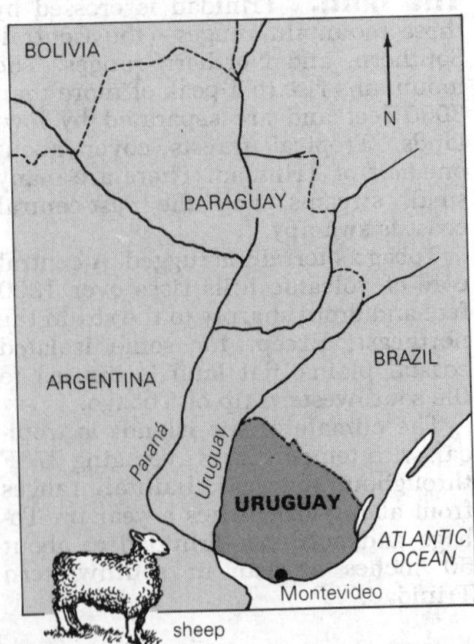

About eleven percent of the total land area is under cultivation. Wheat is the principal crop but rice, oats, corn, and barley are grown in large quantities. Sunflower seeds and linseed are also major crops.

Uruguay's industry—largely government owned and operated—is almost totally dependent on imported oil, although domestic electric capacity is being rapidly increased. Still insufficiently developed, the country's industry consists mostly of meat packing, food processing, and the manufacture of a few domestic consumer goods. Manufactured products include textiles, glass, rubber, paper, cement, ceramics, beverages, and tobacco.

Trade. In 1986 Uruguay's exports earned $1.088 billion and imports cost $870 million. Principal exports are wool, meat, and hides. Major imports include motor vehicles and parts, machinery, chemicals and pharmaceuticals, raw cotton, and paper.

Uruguay's exports go primarily to the United States, Britain, the Netherlands, West Germany, and Brazil. Most imports come from Brazil, Argentina, and the United States.

Government.

Uruguay is a republic. Its executive branch is headed by a president who is elected to a five-year term. The legislative branch consists of a bicameral General Assembly with a 30-member Senate and a 99-member Chamber of Deputies.

Uruguay is a member of the United Nations, the Organization of American States (OAS), and the Latin American Free Trade Association.

History.

Uruguay was discovered by the Spanish navigator Juan Díaz de Solís in 1516 and further explored in 1520 by the Portuguese captain, Ferdinand Magellan. It was not colonized until 1680, however, when Portugal built a fort at Colonia. Uruguay's location between Brazil and what is now Argentina made it a bone of contention between the Portuguese and Spanish empires during the 1700's.

Spain had a better legal title to Uruguay than Portugal, however. Furthermore, Uruguay was too close to the Spanish military and administrative center of Buenos Aires for Spain to allow it to remain in hostile hands. In 1776 Spain included Uruguay in the newly formed viceroyalty of Río de la Plata, and in 1777 seized control of the Portuguese settlement at Colonia.

In 1810 Argentina began its struggle for independence from Spain, and in 1811 Uruguay followed suit under the leadership of José Gervasio Artigas. Artigas favored the formation of a loose confederation with Argentina, but Argentina was unwilling to accept this solution.

A complex struggle soon developed among the forces of Artigas, Argentina, and Spain, as well as Portugal, which took advantage of the general confusion to revive its earlier claim to the country. The Portuguese were successful, and when Brazil gained its independence in 1822, Uruguay became a Brazilian province.

Independence. In 1825 a new group of Uruguayan revolutionaries rose up against Brazil and declared Uruguay annexed to Argentina. The result was a war between Argentina and Brazil that ended in a military stalemate. In 1828 British mediation brought about a peace treaty, which provided for Uruguay's independence. But its independence was precarious.

Independence did not mark the end of foreign intervention in Uruguayan affairs. Uruguay soon developed two political parties, the Blancos and the Colorados, and Argentina, Brazil, and Paraguay frequently intervened in the struggles for power between the two. In 1865 a five-year war broke out, in which Uruguay was allied with Argentina and Brazil against Paraguay.

During the last two decades of the 1800's, Uruguay began to achieve a degree of stability. Educational facilities were expanded, agricultural production increased, and large-scale immigration took place, increasing the European component in the population.

Batlle era. It was not until the early 1900's, however, under José Batlle y Ordóñez, that Uruguay made major social and economic progress. Batlle twice served as president (1903–1907, 1911–1915) and exerted a strong influence over the country until his death in 1929.

Batlle helped make Uruguay a model of democratic government and encouraged such social and economic reforms as workers' accident compensation and a minimum wage. He also initiated government enterprises in banking, meat packing, and other areas.

Contemporary Uruguay. Some of the democratic procedures were suspended during the world economic depression of the 1930's under the administration of Gabriel Terra (1931–1938), but constitutional procedures were reinstated later in the 1930's. In 1942 Uruguay broke diplomatic relations with the Axis powers and in February, 1945, declared war on them. Later that year Uruguay became a charter member of the United Nations.

In 1951 Uruguay adopted a new constitution, which replaced the president with a nine-member executive council. In the late 1950's the country began to suffer from serious economic difficulties caused in part by a decline in foreign trade and the heavy financial burden of extensive social welfare programs.

The executive council proved unable to provide the leadership necessary to deal effectively with these and other problems, and in November, 1966, a new constitution reinstating the presidential system was approved in a referendum.

Oscar Gestido was elected president in 1966. Gestido initiated an austerity program and took strong fiscal measures that slowly began to improve the country's economic situation.

Gestido died in 1968 and was replaced by Jorge Pacheco Areco. Areco turned to repressive tactics when faced with massive labor strikes, but he could do nothing about the skyrocketing price of imported oil, which led to inflation and very much poorer living standards.

In the early 1970's an upper class left-wing terrorist group known as the Tupamaros stepped up guerrilla activity. Juan Maria Bordaberry became president in 1971, but by 1973 he was forced to accept military rule over his government.

Relations with the United States were damaged by reports of oppressive government tactics and disregard for human rights. The economy continued to decline as Maria Bordaberry promised a gradual return to democracy. But he was ousted in the military coup of 1976 and Aparicio Méndez became president. In 1984 there was finally a return to democratic civilian rule when Julio Maria Sanguinetti of the Colorado Party was elected to the presidency.

Venezuela

Official name: *Republic of Venezuela*
Area: *352,144 sq. mi., 912,250 sq. km.*
Population: *(1990 est.) 19,753,000*
Capital: *Caracas (Pop., 1981, 1,816,901)*
Language: *Spanish*
Religion: *Roman Catholic*
Currency unit: *Bolivar*
National holiday: *Independence Day, July 5*

OIL FROM VENEZUELA. *Oil rigs in Lake Maracaibo in northern Venezuela. The country today depends on its vast export of petroleum, which will be exhausted in about 18 years.*

Venezuela, a republic on the northern coast of South America, is bounded on the north by the Caribbean Sea, on the east by Guyana, on the south by Brazil and Colombia, and on the west by Colombia. Seventy-two small offshore islands are also part of Venezuela. The largest of these is Margarita Island, which is famous for its pearl fisheries.

The land. Venezuela has four major geographic regions—the northern highlands, the Maracaibo lowlands, the Orinoco *llanos,* or plains, and the Guiana highlands. The northern highlands, part of the Andes mountain system, extend from the Colombian border in the southwest to the Paria peninsula in the northeastern part of the country.

The mountainous highland area has five subdivisions: the Sierra de Perijá in the extreme west; the Sierra Nevada de Mérida in the southwest; the Segovia highlands, which run eastward from the Sierra Nevada de Mérida along the coast; the central highlands, which run parallel to the coast; and the northeastern highlands in the Araya and Paria peninsulas.

Although the northern highlands cover only about twelve percent of Venezuela's land area, they contain three-fifths of the population and constitute the economic, political, and cultural core of the country.

The Maracaibo lowlands lie to the northwest of the northern highlands. In the center of this region is Lake Maracaibo, which has an area of 6300 square miles and is the largest lake in South America.

The Orinoco *llanos* extend from the northern highlands south to the Orinoco River. This region is a rolling savanna, or grassland, dotted with a few scattered trees and bushes, and crossed by the numerous streams that feed the Orinoco. These streams swell enormously during the rainy season, and large areas in the *llanos* are flooded for almost half the year.

The Guiana highlands lie to the south of the Orinoco and cover roughly half of the country's territory. This area is a high, jungle-covered tableland with elevations ranging between 3000 and 6000 feet above sea level. It is not easily accessible and parts of the area have not been thoroughly explored.

The country's major river is the Orinoco, which rises in the south and flows northeast for about 1500 miles before emptying into the Atlantic Ocean. The Orinoco and its many tributaries provide Venezuela with excellent water transportation routes.

Climate. Venezuela lies entirely within the tropics, but its climate varies widely according to altitude. The lowlands are hot and humid, and Maracaibo has an annual average temperature of 86°F, the highest registered in South America. The capital, Caracas, in the central highlands at an altitude of about 3000 feet, has an annual average temperature of 71°F. Temperatures become cooler as the elevation increases.

Venezuela has a wet summer season from May to November and a dry winter season from December to April. Rainfall is generally heavier at higher altitudes. It ranges from about 17 inches a year at Maracaibo on the coast to over 70 inches at Mérida in the northern highlands.

The people. About 70 percent of Venezuela's population is mestizo, of mixed Indian and European descent. Pureblooded Indians are few in number and live in the more remote parts of the Guiana highlands, the Orinoco delta, and the western Maracaibo lowlands. Europeans constitute about 20 percent of the population and are mainly concentrated in the larger cities. Blacks and mulattoes, who make up about seven percent of the population, live largely along the coast.

Spanish is the official language and Roman Catholicism the predominant religion.

Venezuela is sparsely populated, with three-quarters of the people living in urban areas. Major cities include Caracas, Maracaibo, Barquisimeto, and Valencia.

Economy. The Venezuelan economy depends heavily on petroleum, which should be depleted around the year 2000 at the present rate of extraction. In 1987 90.2 million metric tons of crude oil were produced, accounting for more than 95 percent of the country's exports.

In recent years the government has made an attempt to diversify the economy by expanding industry and strengthening agriculture through agrarian reform measures.

Natural resources. Venezuela's most important natural resource is its petroleum deposits, most of which are located in the Maracaibo lowlands. The country is currently the world's largest exporter of oil, and the fifth largest producer.

Hydroelectric power is an abundant resource in Venezuela. A large portion of this power comes from the huge Guri Dam on the Caroní River.

The country also has extremely valuable iron ore deposits at El Pao and Cerro Bolívar in the Guiana highlands. Iron ore ranks as the second largest export. In 1988 production amounted to 17 million metric tons. Gold, diamonds, natural gas, asbestos, bauxite, sulfur, copper, gypsum, limestone, and salt are also mined.

Agriculture. Agriculture and industry each employ about 20 percent of the labor force. While industry contributes over 15 percent of the gross national product, agriculture contributes just over five percent. Actual food production, though, has increased over 70 percent since 1960, despite generally poor development in technology.

The major crops are sugar cane, corn, bananas, and rice. Coffee and cacao are important commercial crops. Beans, sesame, cotton, cassava, sisal, potatoes, and tobacco are also raised in large quantities.

Cattle are raised in the Orinoco *llanos*, but they are generally of poor quality. The government has been working to improve the breed and to better grazing conditions. In 1986 Venezuela had more than 12 million head of cattle.

Industry. Venezuelan industry has expanded rapidly since World War II. In recent years oil refining has become one of the most important industries.

Aluminum production—totally supplied by Venezuelan bauxite—is rapidly increasing in importance. Steel production is also rising steadily.

Other than these, the country's major industries include cotton and wool textiles, leather goods, cement, petrochemicals, and automobile assembly. Other industries are food processing, meat packing, construction materials, fats and oils, tires, automobile parts, soap, matches, and liquor.

The greatest industrial area in the country is Ciudad Guayana, along the Caroní River, 300 miles southeast of Caracas. Located near hydroelectric reserves and iron ore deposits, this region includes Santo Tomé de Guayana, Puerto Ordaz, and Palúa.

Trade. In 1985 Venezuela's exports earned $14.2 billion and imports cost $7.3 billion. Major exports include petroleum, iron ore, coffee, and cocoa. Principal imports are industrial raw materials, machinery, transportation equipment, construction materials, foodstuffs, and many consumer goods.

Venezuela exports primarily to the United States, the Netherlands Antilles, Canada, and Britain. Imports come from the United States, West Germany, Canada, Britain, Japan, and Italy.

Government.

Venezuela is a republic. The head of state and chief executive is the president, who is popularly elected to a five-year term. Legislative power is vested in the Congress, which consists of the Senate and the Chamber of Deputies.

Two senators are elected from each of Venezuela's 20 states and from its Federal District, Caracas. Additional senators are appointed to represent minorities. There is one seat in the Chamber of Deputies for every 50,000 inhabitants. Both senators and deputies are elected to five-year terms.

Venezuela is a member of the United Nations, the Organization of American States (OAS), the Latin American Free Trade Association, and the Organization of Petroleum Exporting Countries (OPEC).

History.

Venezuela was discovered in 1498 by Christopher Columbus on his third voyage to the New World. The first permanent settlement was made by Spain about 1520 at Cumaná, on the Caribbean coast. In 1528 Charles I of Spain (Charles V of the Holy Roman Empire) granted a contract to settle Venezuela to the Welser mercantile firm of Augsburg, Germany. The Welsers were ruthless administrators, and in 1546 the contract was cancelled.

In 1526 the original colony of Venezuela was placed under the jurisdiction of the Audiencia of Santo Domingo. Later it was included in the viceroyalty of New Granada (Colombia). In 1777 Venezuela became the Captaincy-General of the United Provinces of Venezuela, and in 1786 the Audiencia of Caracas was created. In the last half of the 1700's, Venezuela became prosperous from plantation agriculture and a flourishing cattle industry.

Struggle for independence. In 1806 a Venezuelan patriot, Francisco de Miranda, and a group of volunteers attempted to free the country from Spain. But most Venezuelans remained loyal to Spain, and the attempt failed. In 1808 Napoleon Bonaparte of France deposed Spain's King Ferdinand VII and placed his brother Joseph Bonaparte on the throne. In 1810 a successful revolt took place at Caracas; it deposed the Spanish captain-general of Venezuela and installed a junta, or ruling council.

In 1811 Venezuela declared its independence from Spain, but for several years control passed back and forth between Venezuelan patriots and forces loyal to Spain. Leadership of the struggle passed to Simón Bolívar.

In 1819 Bolívar defeated the Spanish at the battle of Boyacá, in what is at present Colombia. He subsequently formed the Republic of Gran Colombia, which included the territories of Venezuela, Colombia, Panama, and Ecuador. In 1821 Bolívar virtually completed the struggle for independence with a decisive victory at the battle of Carabobo.

Independence. In 1830, under the leadership of General José Antonio Páez, Venezuela seceded from the Republic of Gran Colombia. Páez, an outstanding military leader during the struggle for independence, governed Venezuela from 1830 to 1846. He gave the country stability without resorting to oppression, but those who benefited most were the members of a small elite of the educated and well-to-do.

During the 1850's and 1860's the government was often dictatorial, and the political scene was marked by confusion and instability. Nonetheless, a few constructive measures were undertaken, including the abolition of slavery in 1854.

In 1870 Antonio Guzmán Blanco seized power and ruled the country for 18 years. During his dictatorship there was relative peace, and although corrupt and autocratic, Guzmán Blanco did much to extend public education and to stimulate economic development. In 1889 he lost control, which led to a new period of turmoil.

During 1895–1896 Venezuela engaged in a dispute with Britain over its border with British Guiana, the present-day republic of Guyana. In 1902–1903 the country was blockaded by Britain, Germany, and Italy as the result of financial claims of their citizens against the Venezuelan government. The United States intervened to promote a settlement.

In 1909 domestic peace returned following the seizure of the presidency by Juan Vicente Gómez, who ruled the country with a heavy hand for 26 years. Gómez encouraged the rapid growth of the petroleum industry through liberal concessions to British and U.S. companies, but he used the oil revenues for personal gain, military expenses, and showy public works rather than for education, public welfare, or development.

Reform and reaction. Gómez died in 1935 and his immediate successors gradually dismantled the apparatus of dictatorship and devoted attention to social and labor legislation. Nevertheless, many Venezuelans were dissatisfied with the pace of change. In 1945 a popular rising brought the leftist Acción Democrática Party, led by Rómulo Betancourt, to power.

The new regime's most notable achievement was an agreement with the oil companies that stipulated that half their profits were to go to the Venezuelan government, which hoped to use this income for a far-reaching program of social betterment. Presidential elections were held in 1947, and Rómulo Gallegos, the Acción Democrática candidate, was elected.

In 1948 the government was overthrown by the army, which set up a military junta. In 1952, after an interlude of confusion, Marcos Pérez Jiménez was made provisional president. He soon established a new military dictatorship that was in many ways a repetition of the Gómez regime.

Public opposition to the dictatorship was strong, and in 1958 Pérez Jiménez was forced to resign. A brief provisional government restored political liberty, increased the government's share of oil industry profits, and in December, 1958, held free elections. The elections returned the Acción Democrática to power with Betancourt.

Betancourt launched a program of agrarian reform, agricultural and industrial development, and educational expansion. He was bitterly opposed by supporters of Pérez Jiménez and harassed by Communist terrorists. Carlos Andrés Pérez was elected president in 1974. The Pérez administration emphasized industrial development, and agricultural production was allowed to drop. In 1977 there were severe food shortages and in 1978 Luis Herrera Campins was elected president.

During Herrera's term the Contadora Group was formed. It consisted of several Central American countries concerned with peace and democracy.

The elections in 1983 declared Jaime Lusinchi president. In 1985 he refinanced Venezuela's $25 billion debt.

In 1988 Carlos Andrés Pérez was elected president. In 1989 Pérez's price increases and other economic measures in response to the large debt caused rioting and looting. Pérez temporarily revoked constitutional rights and imposed a nationwide curfew in response to the chaos.

DEPENDENCIES IN SOUTH AND CENTRAL AMERICA

British Dependencies

Anguilla (35 square miles), one of the Leeward Islands of the Lesser Antilles chain, between the Caribbean Sea and the Atlantic Ocean, northwest of St. Kitts (Christopher) and near St. Martin. Its population (1990 est., 7000) is mostly of African origin, although there is a small white minority. The capital is The Valley. Sheep and goat herding and salt production are the island's main economic activities.

St. Christopher-Nevis-Anguilla became a federated state in 1967, but Anguilla seceded later that year. The British took possession of the island again in 1969, and granted it self-rule in 1976.

Bermuda (21 square miles), an archipelago of 20 inhabited islands and numerous uninhabited islets in the Atlantic Ocean, some 600 miles east of the United States. Around two-thirds of the population (1990 est., 58,000) is of African descent, with the remainder of British descent. Hamilton is the capital. Tourism is the mainstay of the economy.

Discovered in 1503 by a Spaniard, it was first settled by the British in the early 1600's. It soon became a thriving plantation colony as thousands of Africans were brought to the islands for slave labor. In the 1900's Bermuda became a popular resort for the wealthy. Racial hostility flared in the early 1970's following the assassination of the colony's governor and several other high officials. British troops were called in to restore peace.

British Antarctic Territory (600,000 square miles) consists of the South Orkney and the South Shetland islands, in the South Atlantic Ocean off the southern tip of South America; Graham Land, on the Antarctic peninsula; and Coats Land and Caird coast, along the Antarctic's Weddell coast.

A separate colony since 1962, it is uninhabited. Research stations are located on the islands, which are also claimed by Argentina.

The British Virgin Islands (59 square miles) lie in the northern Lesser Antilles in the eastern Caribbean. The colony consists of three large islands and over 30 islets. The population (1990 est., 12,000) lives on 16 of the islands, and is almost entirely of African descent. Road Town on Tortola is the capital. Agriculture and tourism are the economic mainstays.

Discovered by Christopher Columbus in 1493, the islands were a base for pirates until the early 1700's, when plantations, worked by African slaves, first appeared. The islands became a British colony in 1774.

The Cayman Islands (100 square miles)—Grand Cayman, Little Cayman, and Cayman Brac—lie in the Caribbean Sea some 100 miles northwest of Jamaica and about 100 miles south of Cuba. The population (1990 est., 25,000) includes people of European, African, and mixed origins. Since becoming (early 1970's) a tax-free haven for foreign funds, the islands have developed a thriving commercial, banking, and tourist economy. Georgetown is the capital.

First inhabited by British Jamaicans in the 1700's, the Caymans did not gain independence from Jamaica until 1962.

The Falkland Islands (6198 square miles) and its two small dependent islands lie in the South Atlantic Ocean off the southeastern coast of Argentina. The population (1916 in 1986) is mostly of British origin. Sheep-raising and wool manufacturing are the main economic activities. Stanley on East Falkland is the capital.

First settled by the French in the 1760's, the islands were abandoned and then resettled in the 1820's by Argentina and in the 1830's by Britain. Argentina continues to claim the Falkland Islands. In 1982, angered at the failure to negotiate a transfer of the islands, Argentina seized the Falklands. The British retaliated by sending a force to the islands. After a bloody war that lasted for more than two months, Britain was able to regain the islands.

Montserrat (40 square miles), north of Guadeloupe, is one of the Leeward Islands of the Lesser Antilles, which lie between the Atlantic Ocean and the Caribbean Sea. The population (1990 est., 12,000) is mostly of mixed African and European origin. Agriculture is the main feature of the economy, with cotton and sugar the major crops.

WAR IN THE FALKLAND ISLANDS. *British army vehicles line the streets in Stanley, the capital of the islands, following the surrender of the Argentine forces in June, 1982.*

UPI

Plymouth is the capital.

Discovered by Columbus in 1493, Montserrat was settled by Irish colonists in 1632. A British possession since 1783, it was granted self-rule in 1962, and chose, by a 1967 referendum, to remain a British colony.

St. Helena (162 square miles) and its two dependencies, Ascension and Tristan de Cunha, are located between South America and Africa, in the South Atlantic Ocean. Its population (1990 est., 9000) is mostly of European origin. A United States satellite tracking center is on Ascension. St. Helena Island is mostly agricultural. Jamestown is the capital.

Claimed by the British in 1673, St. Helena was the place of Napoleon's exile between 1815 and 1821. Ascension was the site of a vital Allied air base during World War II. Tristan de Cunha was devastated by a volcanic eruption in 1961.

The Turks and Caicos Islands (166 square miles), numerous small islands of the Bahama Archipelago, lie in the Atlantic Ocean about 100 miles north of the island of Hispaniola.

The population (1990 est., 10,000) is mainly of African origin. Fishing and salt-raking are the main economic activities. Cockburn Town, on Grand Turk Island, is the capital.

The islands were incorporated into the British colony of Jamaica in 1873. When Jamaica became independent in 1962, the Turks and Caicos were made a separate colony.

Chilean Dependencies

Chilean Antarctica (482,502 square miles) is located in Antarctica between 59° and 67° west. It is uninhabited.

Juan Fernández (70 square miles) is an island group in the Pacific Ocean, 360 miles off the coast of Chile. Its two main islands are Robinson Crusoe and Alejandro Selkirk. The islands have a population of 540. Lobstering is the main economic activity. The islands, discovered in 1572, are best known for Daniel Defoe's 18th century classic, *Robinson Crusoe,* which used an island of the same name for its setting.

San Ambrosio Island and San Felix Island (1.3 square miles) are uninhabited islands located in the Pacific Ocean, 600 miles off the coast of Chile. They were discovered in 1574.

French Departments

French Guiana (35,135 square miles), on the northeastern coast of South America, is bordered on the north by the Atlantic Ocean, on the east and south by Brazil, and on the west by Surinam. The population of 98,000 (1990 est.) consists mostly of people of mixed African and European descent. Guiana is rich in bauxite and gold, and mining is its main industry. Logging is also a significant industry. French aid and investment is important.

The capital, Cayenne, has nearly half of the total population of French Guiana, which includes the Îles du Salut group.

Guiana was sighted by Christopher Columbus in 1498, and in the early 1600's Frenchmen established a settlement at present-day Cayenne. Captain Dreyfus was once incarcerated (1894–1899) at the famous prison colony on Devil's Island in Guiana.

Guadeloupe (687 square miles) is one of the Windward Islands of the Lesser Antilles, which lie between the Caribbean Sea and the Atlantic Ocean. It consists of two adjacent islands, Basse-Terre and Grande-Terre, and four smaller islands to the east. Guadeloupe's population (1990 est., 344,000), comprised mostly of the black descendants of slaves and of mulattoes, is growing rapidly.

Basse-Terre (on Basse-Terre Island) is the capital, but Pointe à Pitre is the largest city. Guadeloupe has fertile land. Agriculture (mainly sugar and banana crops) is the main economic activity. Tourism is also an important industry.

Discovered by Columbus in 1493, Guadeloupe was first settled by the French in 1635. In 1674 France annexed the islands and developed plantation agriculture, employing slaves imported from Africa. Slavery was abolished in the 1800's. In 1946 Guadeloupe was made an overseas department of France.

Martinique (425 square miles) is one of the Windward Islands of the Lesser Antilles. It lies 130 miles south of Guadeloupe, between Dominica and St. Lucia. The population (1990 est., 333,000) is of mixed African, European, and Carib descent. The island is of volcanic origin, with a generally chilly or mountainous terrain. In 1902 Mount Pelée erupted, burying the city of St. Pierre in volcanic ash and lava.

The capital, Fort-de-France, has nearly one-third of the island's total population. Agriculture, especially the cultivation of bananas, sugar cane, and pineapples, is the mainstay of the economy. Tourism is also very important. Close economic ties with France are maintained and French aid is significant in the economy.

Discovered by Columbus in 1502, Martinique was first settled in 1635 by Frenchmen; it was annexed by France in 1674 and became a thriving plantation colony before slavery was abolished in the 1800's. In 1946 the island

GUADELOUPE, *with Martinique and lesser islands, has belonged to France since the 1600's. Both Guadeloupe and Martinique are volcanic, and Guadeloupe's La Soufrière* (below) *still smokes. Peopled largely by blacks and mulattoes* (right), *Guadeloupe attracts many tourists.*

FRENCH GOVERNMENT TOURIST OFFICE

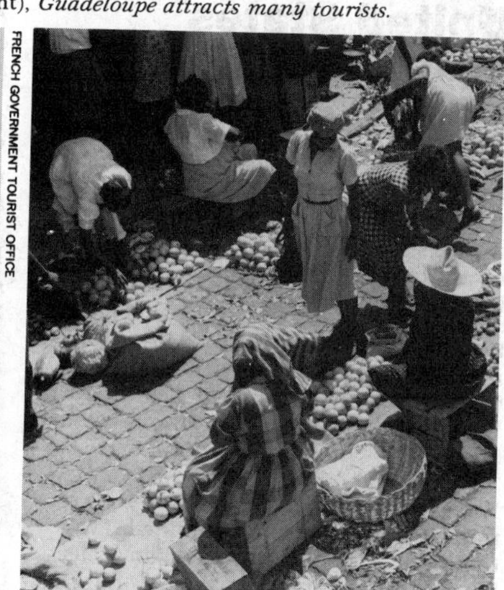

FRITZ HENLE/MONKMEYER

was made an overseas department of France. Napoleon's empress, Josephine, was born here in the 1700's.

Martinique's high population density has contributed to its chronic high unemployment rate. National labor strikes in 1980, resulting in violence and chaos, were blamed on Cuba. Castro denied the charges as French troops restored order.

Netherlands Dependency

The Netherlands Antilles (385 square miles) consists of six islands in the Caribbean Sea. The islands of Aruba, Bonaire, and Curaçao lie off the northwest coast of Venezuela, on the South American mainland. They are part of the Leeward Islands. Saba, St. Eustacious, and St. Maarten, which is shared with France, are in the Windwards, some 200 miles east of Puerto Rico.

The population (1990 est., 183,000) is mostly of mixed African and Indian origin, although there are also European descendants. Over one-third of the people live in the capital city of Willemstad on Curaçao.

Curaçao is the most important island of the six, followed closely by Aruba. The two islands together have most of the islands' population and prosperity. They enjoy a high standard of living, the result of their lucrative oil (imported from Venezuela) refining industry. Tourism is also important, while agriculture is the basis of the economy on the other four islands.

The islands were taken by the Dutch in 1815, after being claimed and occupied by Spain (in the early 1500's) and then by Portugal and Britain. Curaçao was an important center for the Caribbean slave trade between 1700 and 1860. The Netherlands Antilles attained self-rule in 1954.

United States Dependencies

Navassa (2 square miles) is a Caribbean island that lies between Jamaica and Haiti. A U.S. possession since 1865, it is uninhabited except for workers at a U.S. Coast Guard lighthouse that was established on the island in 1916.

Puerto Rico (3421 square miles) is an island lying between the Atlantic Ocean and the Caribbean Sea, about 1000 miles southeast of the United States. Its population (1990 est., 3,415,000) is almost totally Hispanic. With nearly 1000 people per square mile, it is very densely populated. Two-thirds of the people live in urban areas. San Juan, the capital, has nearly half a million people. Roman Catholicism is the chief religion and English and Spanish are both commonly spoken languages.

SYBIL SHELTON/PETER ARNOLD

PLAZA IN RINCON, *Puerto Rico, where young people meet. With a healthy economy, Puerto Rico enjoys a high standard of living, but overpopulation forces many to emigrate each year.*

Puerto Rico has one of the highest standards of living in all of South and Central America. For centuries, its economy was based on one crop—sugar cane. Since World War II, however—aided by the U.S.-initiated "Operation Bootstrap" program—Puerto Rico has been rapidly industrialized. Both heavy and light industries now form the leading economic activities, employing one-fifth of the labor force. Tourism is also very important.

Discovered by Christopher Columbus in 1493, Puerto Rico was conquered by the Spaniard, Ponce de León, in 1508. It flourished as a plantation colony following the introduction of sugar cane in 1515, and African slaves in 1518. Plantation society deteriorated after slavery was abolished in 1873.

U.S. troops occupied the island in 1898 during the Spanish-American War, making it a U.S. possession. Self-rule began in 1900 (U.S. Foraker Act), and U.S. citizenship was granted in 1917 (U.S. Organic Act). Luis Muñoz Marin was the first governor popularly elected by Puerto Ricans. He served from 1948 to 1964.

Puerto Rico attained commonwealth status in 1952, and by popular referendum in 1967 it chose to maintain that status rather than become a state. A Puerto Rican independence movement has been active on the island for many years, but it enjoys only scant support. Its counterpart in the United States engages in frequent acts of terrorism to gain sympathy for its cause.

Quita Sueño Bank, Roncador, and Serrana are tiny uninhabited Caribbean islands lying between Jamaica and Nicaragua. They are partly owned by Colombia.

The U.S. Virgin Islands (133 square miles) are located 35 miles east of Puerto Rico between the Caribbean Sea and the Atlantic Ocean, in the western part of the Lesser Antilles. Their population (1990 est., 116,000) is mostly of African origin, with about 15 percent being white. English is the chief language. Although there are some 100 islands in the group, most of the people live on St. John, St. Croix, and St. Thomas. With over 750 people per square mile, the islands are crowded. Charlotte Amalie on St. Thomas has one of the best Caribbean harbors, and it is the capital of the islands.

The Virgin Islands have a pleasant, low-humidity, subtropical climate; this has helped make tourism the chief source of income. Agriculture—mainly sugar production—was the main economic activity before World War II. Since then, oil refining and bauxite processing have largely replaced it in importance.

Discovered by Columbus in 1493, the Virgin Islands were settled by the Spaniards in 1555; they became Danish in the 1700's. Plantations worked by African slaves formed the economic-social base of the islands during the colonial period. The United States bought the islands from Denmark in 1917 for defense purposes. U.S. citizenship was granted to the inhabitants in 1926, and the islands began electing their own governor in 1970.

CITIES OF SOUTH AND CENTRAL AMERICA

Acapulco, seaport in southwestern Mexico, on the Pacific Ocean. It is an international resort with lavish facilities for recreation. It is the shipping point for bananas, coconuts, beans, and farm produce grown in the area. Pop., 456,655.

Arequipa, in southern Peru, on the Chili River. It is a commercial center and its manufactures include textiles, leather goods, processed foods, and plastics. Pop., 302,316.

Asunción, capital of Paraguay and a port on the Paraguay River about 630 miles (1014 km.) north of Buenos Aires. It is the country's chief city.

Paraguay has no seacoast and Asunción's river port handles most of the country's trade. Its industries consist for the most part of food processing and the manufacture of textiles and footwear. Pop., 729,307.

Barranquilla, seaport in northern Colombia, on the Magdalena River, 10 miles (16 km.) from its mouth. It is Colombia's chief port, and its industries include shipbuilding, sugar refining, brewing, textile mills, and publishing. Pop., 691,728.

Basse-Terre, capital of St. Kitts Island and the St. Kitts-Nevis territory in the Leeward Island colony, British West Indies. The city lies on the southwest coast. Pop., 15,000.

Basse-Terre, capital of Guadeloupe in the French West Indies, on the southwest coast of Basse-Terre Island. It is commercially underdeveloped. Pop., metro. area, 135,341.

Belem, or Pará, seaport and the capital of Pará State, Brazil, located on the Pará River, about 90 miles (145 km.) inland from the Atlantic Ocean. The city lies at the mouth of the Amazon River system and is a transshipment point for Amazon River traffic. It is linked by highway and railroad with Brasília. Belem's exports include nuts, pepper, cocoa, timber, and jute. Pop., 771,665.

Belmopan, capital of Belize (formerly British Honduras) since 1970. It is situated inland, southwest of the former capital, Belize city, which was devastated by a hurricane in 1961. Pop., 5000.

Belo Horizonte, in southeastern Brazil, the capital of Minas Gerais State. The first planned city in South America, it was inaugurated in 1897. Belo Horizonte processes iron ore, manganese, gold, and precious stones mined in the state. Other industries include food processing, meat packing, and the manufacture of textiles. The city has several universities and is the educational center of Minas Gerais. Pop., 1,557,464.

Bogotá, capital of Colombia, located in the central part of the country on a fertile plateau 8660 feet (2640 m) above sea level. The city is the political, economic, and cultural center of Colombia. Industries produce a variety of goods for domestic consumption. Bogotá is the seat of the National University and has a number of other educational institutions. Pop., 4,185,174.

Brasília, capital of Brazil, located in the interior of the country, about 600 miles (965 km.) northwest of Rio de Janeiro. Brasília is a planned city that was built in the late 1950's and inaugurated as the capital in April, 1960. It was designed by Lucio Costa and Oscar Niemeyer. The city is linked by highways and air routes to the rest of Brazil. Pop., metro. area, 1,649,000.

Bridgetown, capital, largest city, and chief port of Barbados, in the West Indies. The city is located on the southwest coast of the island, on Carlisle Bay. Bridgetown is a railroad terminus and the financial, commercial, and tourist center of Barbados. Exports include sugar, molasses, and rum. Pop., metro. area, 102,000.

Buenos Aires, capital of Argentina and the largest city in Latin America, located on the Río de la Plata. The city is the financial, commercial, and industrial center of Argentina. The chief industries are meat packing, tanning, flour milling, and the manufacture of textiles and chemicals. Buenos Aires has one of the world's largest and busiest ports and is an important rail and air center. The city has many libraries, museums, and theaters. It is the seat of the University of Buenos Aires. Pop., metro. area, 11,600,000.

Cali, in western Colombia, on the Cali River. The city is an industrial and commercial center that ships farm products, timber, and minerals. Its chief manufactures are textiles, chemicals, building materials, and paper. It is also a tourist center and the seat of two universities. Pop., 990,304.

Callao, chief seaport of Peru, on the Pacific Ocean, 8 miles (13 km.) west of Lima. The city exports minerals, refined metals, wool, fish meal, and fish oil. Its industries include breweries, sugar refineries, and shipbuilding. Pop., 296,220.

BUENOS AIRES, *a city of over 8 million and capital of Argentina. The Plaza del Mayo.*

PAN AMERICAN AIRWAYS

Caracas, capital and largest city of Venezuela, in a mountain basin more than 3000 feet (915 m) above sea level. It is linked by superhighway with nearby La Guaira, its port on the Caribbean. Earnings from the nation's oil industry have financed extensive development. Central University and Simón Bolívar University are in the city. Manufactures include chemicals, textiles, glass, and cement. Pop., 1,816,901.

Cartagena, seaport on the northwest coast of Colombia, 60 miles (96 km.) southwest of Barranquilla. Its principal industries are the manufacture of textiles, leather products, sugar, and tobacco. It is also a tourist center with many old landmarks. Pop., 345,735.

Castries, capital, largest city, and chief port of St. Lucia, in the West Indies. Castries has a fine, landlocked harbor. Chief exports are bananas, cocoa, copra, and coconut oil. Castries is also the tourist center of St. Lucia. Pop., 52,000.

Cayenne, the capital and principal port of French Guiana, on an island near the mouth of the Cayenne River. Nearby Devil's Island was the site of a French penal colony from 1851 to 1945. Exports include tropical woods, rosewood essence, rum, and gold. Its most famous product is Cayenne pepper. Pop., 38,091.

Charlotte Amalie, capital, largest city, and chief port of the Virgin Islands of the United States. The city is located on the south-central coast of St. Thomas Island, about 40 miles east of Puerto Rico. It was formerly called St. Thomas. The city is the chief commercial and tourist center of the Virgin Islands. Pop., 52,660.

Concepción, in south-central Chile, on the banks of the Bío Bío River. Concepción is one of Chile's larger cities and an industrial and commercial center. Its port, Talcahuano, lies nearby, to the northwest. Its industries produce textiles, timber, steel, sugar, and hides. Pop., 189,929.

Córdoba, city in central Argentina, on the Primero River. It is a cultural and commercial center for an agricultural region. It exports cattle, wheat, and minerals, and its manufactures include leather goods, textiles, and glass. It has several museums, two universities, and an astronomical observatory. Pop., 791,000.

Curitiba, in southern Brazil, on a plateau near the Iguaçú River, about 65 miles (105 km.) west of Paranagua, its port on the Atlantic Ocean. Curitiba is the capital of the state of Paraná and an important transportation, trade, and industrial center. The city's products include timber, coffee, maté, and cattle. Pop., 765,716.

Cuzco, in southern Peru, about 350 miles (565 km.) southeast of Lima. It lies at an altitude of about 11,000 feet (3360 m) above sea level in the Andes. Cuzco, the capital of the Inca empire, was captured by the Spanish in 1533. The city's Inca ruins and Spanish colonial buildings attract many tourists. Cuzco is also a commercial center. Pop., 120,881.

Fortaleza, on the northeast coast of Brazil, about 270 miles (435 km.) northwest of Natal. Fortaleza is a port and the capital of the state of Ceara. The city manufactures textiles and processes agricultural products. Coffee, sugar, and cotton are exported. Pop., 1,109,837.

Fort-de-France, capital and largest city of Martinique, French West Indies. Located on the Bay of Fort-de-France, on the southwest coast of the island, the city has a large, landlocked harbor. Exports include sugar, rum, and bananas. Pop., 99,844.

Georgetown, capital, largest city, and chief port of Guyana, on the northeastern coast of South America. Georgetown is located at the mouth of the Demerara River, on the Atlantic Ocean. It is a railroad terminus and Guyana's communications and transportation center. Chief exports are sugar, bauxite, and rice. Pop., urban area, 188,000.

Guadalajara, second largest city in Mexico and capital of the state of Jalisco, located about 280 miles (450 km.) northwest of Mexico City. Guadalajara is the commercial center for a rich agricultural and mining region and is an important rail and highway hub. Its industries produce flour, textiles, leather goods, pottery, and glassware. Pop., 3,000,000.

Guatemala, or Guatemala City, capital and largest city of Guatemala. It is located in the central highlands, at an altitude of about 5000 feet (1525 m) about 75 miles (120 km.) from the Pacific Ocean. It is the commercial, cultural, educational, financial, and political center of the country. Manufactures include textiles, soap, cement, and furniture. Pop., 1,300,000.

Guayaquil, in western Ecuador, on the Guayas River, about 40 miles (65 km.) from the Pacific Ocean. It is the major seaport and largest city in Ecuador and its economic and commercial center. It exports bananas, cacao, cattle, sugar, and coffee, and its industries manufacture textiles, iron, leather goods, machinery, wood products, and cement. It is the seat of two universities. Pop., 1,020,000.

Hamilton, free port and the capital of Bermuda, on Bermuda Island. It is a bustling tourist center with important fisheries. Pop., 3000.

Havana, capital and chief commercial city of Cuba, located on the island's northwestern coast. Havana is Cuba's major port and exports the island's chief commercial crops, sugar and tobacco. Cigars, cigarettes, consumer goods, and heavy machinery are manufactured in the city.

Havana is also Cuba's cultural center. It has universities, libraries, museums, and other cultural amenities. Pop., urban area, 2,014,800.

Holguin, in north-central Oriente Province, eastern Cuba. The city is a transportation and commercial center in a rich agricultural area that produces cattle, coffee, tobacco, and sugar cane. It is served by the port of Gibara, about 19 miles (30 km.) to the north. Pop., 422,329.

Juárez, or Ciudad Juárez, in northern Mexico, opposite El Paso, Texas, on the Rio Grande. It is the marketing and processing center for a large cotton-growing area and a highway and railroad terminus. It handles an extensive trade with the United States. Pop., 570,401.

Kingston, capital and chief port of Jamaica, located on the southeastern coast of the island in the western Caribbean Sea. It exports Jamaica's rum, sugar, molasses, bananas, bauxite, and alumina. Pop., 104,041.

Kingstown, capital and seaport of St. Vincent in the Windward Islands, located on the southern coast, in the eastern Caribbean Sea. Pop., 33,694.

La Paz, administrative capital and largest city of Bolivia, in west-central South America. Situated at an altitude of more than 11,000 feet (3355 m) on the high plateau of western Bolivia, La Paz is the industrial, commercial, political, and cultural center of Bolivia. Sucre is the legal capital and seat of the judiciary. Manufactures include textiles, cement, glass, and furniture. Pop., 992,592.

La Plata, seaport and capital of Buenos Aires Province, about 35 miles (56 km.) southeast of Buenos Aires, Argentina. It has a large, artificial harbor and exports grain, meat, and oil. Its industries include oil refining, chemicals, and electrical goods. It is also a major cultural center, with museums and colleges. Pop., 391,000.

León, in central Mexico, on the Turbio River. The city is located in a fertile river plain and was once subject to frequent floods; it is now protected by a dam. It is an agricultural, commercial, and industrial center whose manufactures include shoes, textiles, flour, and leather goods. Local artisans produce knives, metal goods, and distinctive gold and silver embroideries. Pop., 557,030.

Lima, capital and largest city of Peru, on the Rimac River, about 8 miles (13 km.) inland from the Pacific Ocean and its port, Callao. The city is the political, economic, and cultural center of Peru. Its diverse industries include textiles, cement, leather goods, foundries, and oil refineries. Founded in 1535 by Francisco Pizarro, Lima retains many buildings from its colonial past and the oldest university in South America. It is connected by rail and road to Callao and other cities in Peru. Pop., 5,258,600.

Managua, capital and largest city of Nicaragua, situated on the southern shore of Lake Managua. It lies on the main rail and road transportation routes and is the economic and cultural center of the country. It has food-processing plants, textile mills, pharmaceutical factories, and other industries. Pop., 682,111.

Maracaibo, seaport in northwestern Venezuela, on the western shore of a channel connecting Lake Maracaibo and the Gulf of Venezuela. It is a commercial and industrial center and the oil capital of South America. In addition to oil, its exports sugar, cacao, coffee, and timber, and its manufactures include textiles, rope, building materials, and soap. Pop., 792,000.

Medellín, in Colombia, in a mountain valley at an altitude of about 5000 feet (1524 m) above sea level. Medellín is the capital of the department of Antioquia and the second largest city of Colombia. Medellín is an educational center and the nation's chief industrial city. Its principal products are steel, textiles, chemicals, sugar, and coffee. Pop., 1,159,194.

Mendoza, in west-central Argentina, 60 miles (96 km.) southeast of Aconcagua. The city is the center of an extensive wine-producing area irrigated by the Mendoza River. Pop., 471,000.

Mexico City, capital of Mexico, located in the southern part of the Central Plateau. Mexico City is one of the oldest cities in North America. The Aztecs built their capital, Tenochtitlan, on the site. Today one of the largest cities in the western hemisphere, Mexico City is a major cultural, commercial, and industrial center. Its manufactures include steel, petroleum, textiles, machinery, chemicals, and food products. Mexico City's fine buildings, sites of historical interest, beautiful location, and pleasant climate attract many tourists from all over the world. Pop., 18,000,000.

UPI

MONTEVIDEO: *a voting line in Uruguay's sophisticated capital. Once a showpiece of democracy and social legislation, Uruguay has come on hard times and has lost its freedom.*

Monterrey, one of Mexico's largest cities, the capital of Nuevo León State, located about 440 miles (710 km.) north of Mexico City. Second only to Mexico City as an industrial center, Monterrey produces iron and steel, refined nonferrous metals, cement, flour, textiles, and beverages. The city is an important financial center and the rail and highway hub of northern Mexico. Monterrey is the site of the University of Neuvo León. Pop., 1,054,029.

Montevideo, capital, largest city, and chief port of Uruguay. It is located on the north shore of the Rio de la Plata, about 135 miles (215 km.) east of Buenos Aires, Argentina. Montevideo is the industrial, commercial, and cultural center of Uruguay. The city's leading industry is meat packing. Chief exports are wool, meat, and hides. Pop., 1,362,000.

Nassau, port and capital of the Bahamas, on the northeast coast of New Providence Island. It exports salt, wood pulp, crawfish, rum, and cement. Tourism is the most important industry. Pop., 135,437.

Nova Iguaçu, municipality northwest of Rio de Janeiro, in the Sarapui River valley, Brazil. Its manufactures include chemicals, pharmaceuticals, soft drinks, and canned foods. Pop., 931,954.

Panama City, capital city of Panama, situated at the Pacific end of the Panama Canal. The city is a transportation and commercial center with an important tourist industry. Its manufactures include food products and clothing. The city is the seat of two universities. Pop., 976,800.

Paramaribo, capital of Surinam, situated in northeastern South America. The city is a port that has good rail and road connections with the interior. Its exports include bauxite, coffee, timber, and citrus fruits. Pop., 180,000.

Pointe-à-Pitre, capital and chief city of Guadeloupe, in the West Indies. The city is a seaport that exports food products, especially sugar, rum, cacao, coffee, and bananas. Pop., metro. area, 163,668.

Port-au-Prince, capital and chief port of Haiti, situated on the west coast of Hispaniola, on the Caribbean Sea. The chief exports of Port-au-Prince are coffee, bananas, rum, sugar, and sisal. Pop., metro. area, 763,188.

Pôrto Alegre, seaport in southeastern Brazil, on an inlet at the northern end of the Lagoa dos Patos. It is a major industrial and commercial center of Brazil and exports the products of a rich agricultural region. Its manufactures include leather goods, textiles, metal products, and candles. It has shipyards, meat-packing plants, and foundries. It is also a cultural and educational center. Pop., 1,043,964.

Port of Spain, or Port-of-Spain, seaport and capital of Trinidad and Tobago, on the northwest coast of the island of Trinidad. It is the commercial and industrial center of the country and one of the principal shipping centers for the Caribbean. It exports oil, citrus fruits, coffee, and asphalt. Pop., 250,000.

Puebla, in east-central Mexico, about 75 miles (120 km.) southeast of Mexico City. The city is an agricultural, commercial, and industrial center noted for its onyx work, glazed colored tiles, textiles, pottery, and glass. It is also a popular tourist center. Pop., 516,197.

Quito, capital and second largest city of Ecuador, located on a plateau in the Andes near the equator. An important city in the empire of the Inca Indians, it still has a large Indian population. Quito is primarily an administrative center. Pop., 742,858.

Recife, capital of Pernambuco State, in northeastern Brazil, located at the mouths of the Capibaribe and Beberibe rivers on the Atlantic Ocean. The city's economy is based on processing and exporting the agricultural products of the interior, including coffee, cotton, sugar, and hides. A rail and road network links Recife with other parts of Brazil. The city has two universities and many fine churches, some of which date from the colonial period. Pop., 1,249,821.

Rio de Janeiro, second largest city in Brazil, located on Guanabara Bay, on the Atlantic Ocean. It served as the capital of the country from 1763 to 1960. Rio de Janeiro is Brazil's cultural center and a major port, ranking second only to São Paulo. It has three universities and several museums. Local industries produce shoes, clothing, furniture, drugs, and processed foods. Pop., 5,600,000.

Rosario, river port in east-central Argentina, on the Paraná River. It is the second largest city of Argentina and a commercial center. Its principal industries include sugar refining, meat processing, and flour milling. Pop., 807,000.

Roseau, capital and largest city of Dominica in the Windward Islands. The city is located on the Caribbean Sea. Primarily a port, Roseau exports the island's limes, lime juice, bananas, and spices. Pop., 20,000.

St. George's, capital and principal town of Grenada, in the Caribbean Sea. The town, on the island's southwestern coast, has a deep natural harbor and exports locally grown cocoa, bananas, and spices. Pop., 29,369.

Salvador, formerly Bahia, a port and industrial city on the east coast of Brazil. It processes and exports sugar, cotton, cacao, and tobacco grown in the surrounding region, and it manufactures textiles and cigars. One of Brazil's oldest cities, it was for 200 years the capital of the Portuguese colony. Pop., 1,237,373.

San José, capital and largest city of Costa Rica, situated on the Rio Grande near the center of the country. It is on international air and rail routes and is the commercial center for a coffee-growing region. It produces furniture and textiles. Pop., 241,464.

San Juan, seaport and the capital of Puerto Rico, on the island's northeast coast. It has an excellent harbor and is an exporting center for agricultural goods such as sugar, tobacco, and fruit. It was first settled in 1509 by Spaniards commanded by Ponce de León. Pop., 434,849.

San Salvador, capital and largest city of El Salvador, situated in the mountains in the west-central portion of the country. It is a commercial center whose manufactures include textiles, leather goods, liquor, and tobacco products. The city is subject to severe earthquakes and has frequently been badly damaged. Pop., 452,614.

Santa Cruz, in central Bolivia, on the Piray River. The city is a trade, commercial, and processing center for coffee, rice, cattle, and timber. It is connected by rail to both the Pacific and Atlantic oceans. Pop., 255,568.

Santiago, capital of Chile, situated in a high valley near the center of the country. In addition to being the political, cultural, and commercial heart of Chile, it manufactures iron and steel, chemicals, textiles, paper, and other products. Pop., 4,318,305.

Santo Domingo, capital and largest city of the Dominican Republic. Its refineries and distilleries process locally grown sugar cane. The city has textile mills and is the chief port of the country. Founded in 1492, it has been continuously inhabited longer than any other city in the western hemisphere. Pop., metro. area, 1,550,739.

São Paulo, capital of São Paulo State in southeastern Brazil. It is the largest city and principal commercial and industrial center of Brazil, with oil refineries, chemical plants, and factories manufacturing heavy machinery, vehicles, pharmaceuticals, electrical devices, and textiles. The city is a cultural and educational center with extensive libraries, museums, and four universities. It is the location of the famous Butantan Institute, where snake serums are produced. Pop., 7,198,608.

Sucre, legal capital of Bolivia and seat of the judiciary, situated in a high Andean valley in the south-central part of the country. Although Sucre is the site of the national university and many government buildings, La Paz is the administrative capital. Sucre is important mainly as a commercial center for an agricultural and mining region. Pop., 86,609.

Tegucigalpa, capital and largest city of Honduras, situated in the south-central part of the country. It produces textiles, soap, cigarettes, plywood, and plastics. Pop., 316,500.

Tijuana, in Baja California, northwestern Mexico, just south of the United States border. The city is a popular tourist resort, with casinos, racetracks, and bullfights, and a principal point of entry on the U.S.-Mexico border. It is the center of an irrigated agricultural region that produces wheat, barley, and grapes. Pop., 571,400.

Tucuman, or San Miguel de Tucuman, in northwestern Argentina on a branch of the Dulce River. The city is the commercial center of a region that produces sugar, grains, fruit, and timber. Pop., 366,000.

Valencia, in northwestern Venezuela, 80 miles (130 km.) west of Caracas, near the western shore of Lake Valencia. It is a major transportation and industrial center whose products include animal feeds, motor vehicles, textiles, fertilizers, chemicals, processed foods, and paper. The city lies in a fertile agricultural region and is the market for the crops, dairy products, sugar cane, cotton, and cattle from the surrounding area. Pop., 439,000.

Valparaíso, principal seaport of Chile, on the west-central coast. The city handles most of the imports and is also an industrial center that manufactures textiles, paint, shoes, leather goods, metal products, and chemicals. Pop., 248,972.

Viña del Mar, seaside resort on the central coast of Chile, about 6 miles (10 km.) northeast of Valparaíso. It has a pleasant summer climate and many hotels, clubs, public gardens, and fine beaches, along with museums and theaters. The city's industries include oil refining, textiles, food processing, and sugar refining. Pop., 229,000.

GLOSSARY OF SOUTH AND CENTRAL AMERICA

Aconcagua, a South American mountain in the Andes chain, situated on the Chile-Argentina border. Aconcagua is the highest mountain in the western hemisphere, rising to 22,834 feet (6965 m) above sea level.

Alcalde, the title used in the Iberian Peninsula since the 1000's, and later in the Spanish colonies, to designate a local official. The term, derived from the Arabic *al qadi,* the judge, was also part of many government titles indicating some judicial authority.

Alliance for Progress, a pan-American program initiated in 1961 by U.S. President John F. Kennedy. It called upon the Americas to unite in their attempts to install and protect democratic governments while working toward economic prosperity. This enthusiastic and idealistic program called for labor and agrarian reforms to insure that all people would share equitably in the resulting progress.

Altiplano, in Spanish, a high, flat area or plain, especially a high South American plateau in Peru and Bolivia. The plateau has an average altitude of about 12,000 feet (3660 m) above sea level and has a gently rolling surface. The eastern edge, or *montaña* zone, is deeply cut by rivers. Its climate is cool and dry. The altiplano was the heartland of the Inca empire.

Amazon, a South American river, the largest in the world in volume and catchment area. It extends 4000 miles (6440 km.) across Brazil and Peru, and its tributaries form a basin of some 2.7 million square miles (7 million sq. km.) in central South America. Its basin includes the floodplain, or *varzea,* which is fertile after rains between November and May, and the unflooded areas, or *terra firme,* which have sterile soils.

Andes, a massive mountain system of western South America. The Andes stretch for more than 5000 miles (8050 km.) in a great crescent from northeastern Venezuela westward and then southward to the southernmost tip of the continent. Elevations range generally from 10,000 to 20,000 feet (3050 to 6100 m), but there are several peaks over 20,000 feet, including Aconcagua.

Angel Falls, the highest waterfall in the world, located in southeastern Venezuela on a tributary of the Caroni River. Actually a series of falls, it drops a total of 3212 feet (980 m), and its highest fall is 2650 feet (808 m).

Antilles, a large archipelago between North and South America lying partly in the Caribbean Sea and partly in the Atlantic Ocean. The Greater Antilles, at the northwestern end of the curving chain, includes the large islands of Cuba, Jamaica, Hispaniola, and Puerto Rico.

The Lesser Antilles, the southern and eastern portions of the archipelago, includes the many small islands off the coast of Venezuela in the south and the islands of the Windward and Leeward groups in the east. Many of the Antilles are volcanic in origin, and most are mountainous.

Article 123, a revolutionary provision of Mexico's constitution of 1917 that granted political recognition of the country's labor groups. It guaranteed wage controls, an eight-hour workday, an end to child labor, occupational safety provisions, and the right of labor to organize. It is often called the Magna Carta of Mexican labor.

Atacama, a desert region that extends for about 600 miles (1000 km.) in northern Chile. It lies between the Pacific coastal range on the west and the Andean piedmont on the east. The desert proper, with an elevation of about 2000 feet (610 m) is a series of dry salt basins rich in nitrates.

AMAZON INDIAN *and palm basket, used to collect wild fruit. The huge Amazon basin is home to very primitive tribes.*

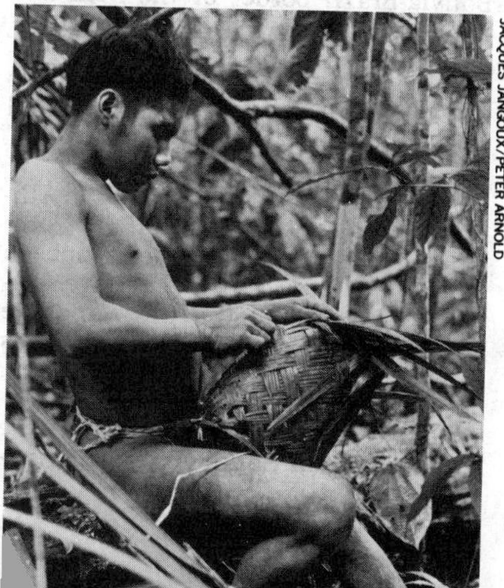

JACQUES JANGOUX/PETER ARNOLD

Audiencia, a Spanish royal court of appeal that came into existence in Spain in the 1200's. The institution was carried to Spain's colonial possessions beginning in the 1500's. The first audiencia in the Americas was established in 1526 on the island of Santo Domingo (Hispaniola).

The audiencia had judicial and administrative functions. In the Americas these bodies came to function as councils of state, often acting as checks on the exercise of arbitrary power by the Spanish governor.

Baja California, or Lower California, a long, narrow peninsula about 750 miles (1208 km.) long in western Mexico south of California. The Pacific Ocean lies to its west, and the Gulf of California to the east separates it from the rest of Mexico. Mountain ridges occupy the eastern and central portions of the peninsula. Most of the land is desert or arid plains.

Bandeirantes, profit-seeking slave catchers in the colonial Portuguese empire in Brazil. They pushed into the Brazilian frontier regions in search of new groups of slaves that could be sold on the coastal plantations.

California, Gulf of, an arm of the Pacific Ocean extending northwest for about 750 miles (1208 km.) between Baja California and the Mexican mainland.

Caribbean Sea, a body of water between North and South America at the western edge of the Atlantic Ocean. On the north and east it is ringed by the islands of the Greater and Lesser Antilles. The Caribbean Sea is approximately 1 million square miles (2.6 million sq. km.) in area.

Caudillos, leaders that rose to power in the early 1800's in most of the South and Central American republics, most notably Brazil, Venezuela, Colombia, Bolivia, and Mexico. They were usually powerful military figures who gained political control through violence, and who maintained it with repression and terrorism.

Colorado, a river 530 miles (853 km.) long in southeastern South America. It rises in the Andes near the Chilean border and flows southeast across south-central Argentina to the Atlantic Ocean.

Creoles, the second highest class of citizens (behind the *peninsulares,* born in Spain) in colonial Spanish America. They were Spaniards or Europeans but were American-born. They held high positions in government, and were important landholders and artisans.

Cuquenán Falls, or Kukenaam, a waterfall in eastern Venezuela, northwest of Mt. Roraima. Dropping some 2000 feet (610 m), it is one of the world's highest waterfalls.

Devil's Island, an island in the Atlantic about 6 miles (10 km.) off the northern coast of French Guiana. It was the site of a famous penal colony, closed in 1945.

Donatários, recipients of large land grants that carried economic and political privileges in the colonial Portuguese empire in Brazil. The donatário enjoyed more privileges than a feudal lord, including tax exemptions and the right to use Indian slaves. He was, in return, obliged to improve his grant by settling it and developing it.

Drake Passage, a channel separating the southern tip of South America from the Antarctic Peninsula, joining the Pacific and the Atlantic oceans.

Good Neighbor Policy, the U.S. policy of nonintervention in the internal affairs of South and Central American republics. It was first announced by U.S. President Franklin D. Roosevelt in his 1933 inaugural address. It was a departure from prior U.S. policies, which often allowed unilateral intervention in the affairs of the American republics "for their own good."

Gran Chaco, a lowland plain, about 300,000 square miles (777,000 sq. km.) in area, of south-central South America, divided among Argentina, Bolivia, and Paraguay. Much of the region is arid, but there are swampy areas. The climate is quite hot, and the area is barren and sparsely populated.

Hay-Pauncefort treaties, agreements negotiated in 1899 and 1901 between the United States and Britain, giving exclusive rights to the United States for construction, ownership, operation, and fortification of the Panama Canal. They included an abrogation of the Clayton-Bulwer Treaty (1850), which had provided for U.S.-British joint control of the projected canal.

Hispaniola, a large island of the West Indies between the Caribbean Sea and the Atlantic Ocean. Its two mountain ranges are separated by a deep valley and ringed by narrow coastal plains. The climate is tropical and the vegetation is lush. Hispaniola is shared by Haiti and the Dominican Republic.

EPA

THE MOUNTAINS OF TIERRA DEL FUEGO *at the bottom of South America. Before the Panama Canal opened, Pacific-bound shipping had to round Cape Horn in this cruel environment. Many ships were lost in "rounding the Cape."*

Horn, Cape, the southernmost point of South America, on Horn Island in the Tierra del Fuego Archipelago.

Jamaica Letter, a famous philosophic exposition on independence. It was written in 1815 by "The Liberator," Simón Bolívar, who was dedicated to assisting South America's attempts to rid itself of European control. The Jamaica Letter was very influential among independence movements.

Japurá, a river that rises in southwestern Colombia and flows southeast for about 1750 miles (2818 km.) across the Brazilian border into the Amazon.

Juruá, a river flowing from the Andes in east central Peru across northwestern Brazil for more than 2000 miles (3200 km.) into the upper course of the Amazon.

Llanos, a low-lying plains region of South America, in eastern Colombia and the Orinoco basin of Venezuela.

Madeira, a river in central South America formed from the union on the Bolivia-Brazil border of the Beni and the Mamoré rivers, which rise in Bolivia. The Madeira, from the headwaters of the Mamoré, is 2082 miles (3352 km.) long and flows north and east to join the Amazon.

Magdalena, a river that flows northward for 956 miles (1540 km.) through Colombia into the Caribbean Sea. It lies between the massive Cordillera Central, to the west, and the Cordillera Oriental, to the east. It is joined near its mouth by the Cauca.

Magellan, Strait of, a passage at the southern tip of South America, winding between the mainland and Tierra del Fuego. It is 350 miles (564 km.) long and connects the South Pacific and South Atlantic oceans.

Managua, a lake in western Nicaragua, with an area of about 400 square miles (1036 sq. km.).

Maracaibo, a lake, 130 miles (209 km.) long and 75 miles (120 km.) wide, in northwestern Venezuela. It is a major petroleum-producing area.

Marañón, a river rising in the Andes in west central Peru and flowing northwest and then east for about 1000 miles (1600 km.) to combine with the Ucayali to form the Amazon.

Mestizos, the mixed Indian-Spanish populace in Spanish America. As a group, they have generally been rejected as bastard by both pure Indians and Spaniards. They are middle class citizens, usually working as merchants and artisans.

Monroe Doctrine, a foreign policy first promulgated in 1823 by U.S. President James Monroe. Its main statement concerned U. S. insistence that European nations should not interfere in the affairs of the western hemisphere, particularly by attempting to recapture recently freed states in South and Central America.

Nicaragua, the largest lake in Central America, with an area of 3100 square miles (8930 sq. km.). It is located in southwestern Nicaragua.

Organization of American States (OAS), an organization of 23 countries in the western hemisphere. The OAS was established in 1948 to promote mutual assistance between the nations of Latin America and the United States.

In 1889 the International Union of the American Republics was established, with both the United States and Latin American nations participating. The International Union was reorganized in 1910 as the Pan American Union.

Despite the existence of the Pan American Union, relations between the United States and Latin America deteriorated during the first two decades of the 1900's, and under the administration of President Theodore Roosevelt, the United States asserted its right to intervene in the internal affairs of Latin American countries. This policy made the Pan American Union virtually useless.

In the 1930's, the "Good Neighbor" Policy was put forth under U.S. President Franklin Roosevelt, and attempts were made to revive the pan-American movement. A conference in Lima, Peru, in 1938 established the principle of nonintervention.

The outbreak of World War II tightened the bonds between the nations of the western hemisphere. In an attempt to provide for mutual defense, most of the Latin American countries joined the United States in declaring war on the Axis powers. Only Argentina and Chile remained on friendly terms with the Axis through most of the war.

In 1945, after the war had ended, the members of the Pan American Union signed a mutual security treaty, known as the Act of Chapultepec. In 1947 the Inter-American Treaty of Reciprocal Assistance was signed in Rio de Janeiro, Brazil, and in 1948, at a meeting in Bogotá, Colombia, the OAS was established.

The OAS is recognized as a regional organization under the UN Charter. It was formed to consolidate the policies and treaties of the pan-American organizations that preceded it. Its charter members were the United States and the then 20 sovereign nations of Latin America. Subsequently, independent Jamaica, Trinidad and Tobago, Barbados, and Grenada joined the organization. In 1962 Cuba was excluded from all organizational activities; however, its membership was not rescinded, although a diplomatic and commercial embargo was invoked.

Orinoco, a river of South America that flows for about 1300 miles (2090 km.) from the Parima Mountains of Venezuela west, then north along the Venezuela-Colombia border, and then northwest through central Venezuela to the Atlantic Ocean. The Orinoco forms a wide delta at its mouth.

Pampas, the grassy treeless plains of South America. They extend some 1000 miles (1600 km.) through central Argentina from the lower Paraná River south to the Colorado River.

Panama, Isthmus of, a narrow S-shaped neck of land between Costa Rica and Colombia, separating the Caribbean Sea from the Gulf of Panama. An arm of the Pacific Ocean, it is occupied by Panama and by the Panama Canal Zone.

Pará, a 200-mile (320 km.) river in northeastern Brazil, forming the estuary of the Tocantins and a navigable mouth of the Amazon south and east of Marajó.

Paraguay, a river of South America, rising in southwestern Brazil and flowing generally south for some 1585 miles (2550 km.). The Paraguay forms parts of the boundaries between Brazil and Bolivia, Brazil and Paraguay, and Paraguay and Argentina before it empties into the Paraná River in the southwestern corner of Paraguay.

Paraná, the second longest river in South America. Formed by the junction of the Grande and Paranaíba rivers in south-central Brazil, it flows generally southwest for some 2500 miles (4025 km.).

The river forms part of the boundary between Brazil and Paraguay and between Paraguay and Argentina. It continues south through northeastern Argentina to the Río de la Plata.

Parícutin, a volcano 200 miles (320 km.) west of Mexico City that grew out of a corn field in 1943 and now reaches 7451 feet (2271 m) in height.

Patagonia, a barren tableland of southern Argentina lying between the Andes and the Atlantic Ocean. It extends south of the Negro River to the Strait of Magellan.

Patos, Lagoa dos, a shallow lagoon in southern Brazil, covering an area of about 4000 square miles (10,360 sq. km.) and separated from the Atlantic by a sandy peninsula about 15 miles (24 km.) wide. Porto Alegre lies at its northern end. The port of Río Grande at its southern end is linked to the Atlantic by a narrow opening.

Peasant leagues, local organizations formed to help alleviate the desperate suffering, starvation, and squalid living conditions of the landless, homeless, poverty-stricken peasants that populate large areas of Brazil's northeast region. The first peasant league was formed in 1955, and others followed, particularly under the leadership of the social reformer and humanitarian Francisco Julião. The leagues received support from the Roman Catholic pope, encouraging the social activism of Brazil's clergy.

Peninsulares, New World Spaniards in the colonial period who were born on the Iberian Peninsula.They were considered first-class citizens in Spanish America, and they generally held the highest government and church positions.

Plata, Río de la, an estuary on the southeast coast of South America. It forms part of the border between Uruguay and Argentina, stretching some 250 miles (400 km.) from the Atlantic Ocean to the mouths of the Paraná and Uruguay rivers.

Platt Amendment, U.S. legislation that rejected the idea of U.S. intervention in Cuban affairs, while declaring its duty to "protect" the island. Devised in 1902, its execution proved cumbersome and unpopular as the distinction between protection and interference became increasingly difficult to decipher. It was abrogated in 1934 as part of President Franklin Roosevelt's "Good Neighbor" Policy.

Popocatépetl, a volcano in south-central Mexico. It is perpetually snow-capped and rises to a height of 17,887 feet (5452 m).

Putumayo, a river rising in southwestern Colombia and flowing southeastward for about 1151 miles (1853 km.) into the Amazon. It forms a great part of the border between Colombia and Ecuador and Peru before entering Brazil, where it is called the Içá.

Repartimiento, the practice whereby the Spanish conquerors of the New World enslaved native Indians and forced them to labor on public projects and private plantations. Indian families were often divided by this system, and entire villages were frequently converted into virtual labor camps.

Rio Pact, (Inter-American Treaty of Reciprocal Asistance), a treaty signed in 1947 stating that an attack on any member would be considered by the others as an attack on them, and that collective steps would be taken to repel the aggression. Originally there were 22 members, including the United States, but in 1964 Cuba was suspended.

Sierra Madre, three high mountain ranges that dominate the landscape of Mexico. The Sierra Madre Oriental runs from north to south in eastern Mexico. The Sierra Madre Occidental lies in the west. The Sierra Madre del Sur is in the southwest. All three have peaks above 10,000 feet (3050 m).

Tehuantepec, Gulf of, an inlet of the Pacific Ocean on the coast of the Isthmus of Tehuantepec, in southwestern Mexico. Its irregular coastline is backed by steep mountains.

Tierra del Fuego, an archipelago at the southern tip of South America, comprising all the islands south of the Strait of Magellan. The islands are divided between Chile and Argentina.

Titicaca, a lake in South America on the border of Peru and Bolivia. It lies 12,500 feet (3810 m) above sea level in the altiplano of the central Andes. Lake Titicaca is about 120 miles (193 km.) long, 45 miles (73 km.) wide, and 920 feet (280 m) at its greatest depth.

Tocantins, a river rising in south-central Brazil and flowing north for about 1700 miles (2740 km.) into the Pará River.

Uruguay, a 1000-mile-long (1610 km.) river of southeastern South America. It rises in the Serra do Mar of southern Brazil and flows west, southwest, and then south into the Río de la Plata.

Vinson Massif, the highest Antarctic peak, 16,864 feet (5140 m) above sea level. It is in the Ellsworth Mountains near the Ronne Ice Shelf, at the head of the Weddell Sea.

Weddell Sea, an arm of the South Atlantic Ocean, extending into Antarctica between the Antarctic Peninsula and Princess Martha Coast, in Coats Land.

West Indies, a group of islands in the western hemisphere, lying between southeastern North America and northern South America, and enclosing the Caribbean Sea. The group is divided into the Greater Antilles (Cuba, Hispaniola, Jamaica, and Puerto Rico), the Lesser Antilles (the Virgin, Leeward, and Windward islands, including Trinidad and Tobago and Barbados), and the Bahama Islands off Florida.

Yucatán, a large peninsula off Mexico's southeastern coast. It lies between Campeche Bay and the Caribbean Sea and is separated from Cuba, to the northeast, by the Yucatán Channel. The terrain is barren and consists largely of swamps and semidesert. Nevertheless, Yucatán was the site of such Mayan cities as Chichen Itzá.

For Further Reference

South and Central America

Atkins, G. Pope. *Latin America in the International Political System* (2nd Ed.). Westview Press, 1988.

Burns, E. Bradford. *Latin America: A Concise Interpretive History* (4th Ed.). Prentice-Hall, 1986.

Burns, E. Bradford. *The Poverty of Progress: Latin America in the Nineteenth Century.* University of California Press, 1981.

Farer, Tom J. *The Future of the Inter-American System.* Frederick A.Praeger, 1979.

Gibson, Charles, editor. *The Spanish Tradition in America.* Harper Torchbook, 1968.

Haring, Clarence H. *The Spanish Empire in America.* Harcourt, Brace, and World, 1963.

MacDonald, Scott B. *Dancing on a Volcano: The Latin American Drug Trade.* Frederick A. Praeger, 1988.

Mecham, J. Lloyd. *Church and State in Latin America* (Revised Ed.). University of North Carolina Press, 1966.

Odell, Peter R., and David Preston. *Economies and Societies in Latin America: A Geographical Interpretation* (2nd Ed.). Wiley, 1978.

Perkins, Dexter. *History of the Monroe Doctrine* (Revised Ed.). Little, Brown, 1955.

Skidmore, Thomas E., and Peter H. Smith. *Modern Latin America.* Oxford University Press, 1989.

Stuart, G. H., and J. L. Tigner. *Latin America and the United States* (6th Ed.). Prentice-Hall, 1975.

Thorp, Rosemary, and Lawrence Whitehead, editors. *Inflation and Stabilization in Latin America.* Holmes & Meier, 1980.

Wiarda, Howard J. *National Development in Latin America.* Westview Press, 1980.

South America

Barager, Joseph R. *Why Perón Came to Power.* Alfred A. Knopf, 1967.

Bello, José M. *History of Modern Brazil, 1889–1964.* Stanford University Press, 1966.

Browman, David L., editor. *Advances in Andean Archaeology.* Beresford Book Service, 1978.

Isenberg, Irwin, editor. *South America: Problems and Prospects.* H. W. Wilson, 1975.

Johnson, John J. *Simón Bolívar and Spanish American Independence, 1783–1830.* Van Nostrand, 1968.

Mulhall, Michael G. *The English in South America.* Arno Press, 1977.

Munck, Ronaldo, et al. *Argentina from Anarchism to Peronism: Workers, Unions, and Politics, 1855–1985.* Humanities Press, 1987.

Normano, J.F. *The Struggle for South America: Economy and Ideology.* Gordon Press, 1977.

O'Leary, Daniel F. *Bolívar and the War of Independence.* University of Texas Press, 1970.

Prago, Albert. *The Revolutions of Spanish America: The Independence Movements of 1808–1825.* Macmillan, 1970.

Weaver, Frederick S. *Class, State, and Industrial Structure: The Historical Process of South American Industrial Growth.* Greenwood Press, 1980.

Wilgus, Alva C., editor. *South American Dictators During the First Century of Independence.* Russell Publications, 1963.

Wynia, Gary W. *Argentina: Illusions and Realities.* Holmes & Meier, 1986.

Central America

Barchfield, J.W. *Peasants, Politics and Development in Mexico.* Intercult Press, 1980.

Brown, Gene, editor. *Central America and the Caribbean.* Arno Press, 1980.

Bulmer-Thomas, Victor. *The Political Economy of Central America Since 1920.* Cambridge University Press, 1987.

Dunn, Richard S. *Sugar and Slaves: The Rise of the Planter Class in the English West Indies, 1624–1713.* W. W. Norton, 1973.

Elkins, W.F. *Black Power in the Caribbean.* Revisionist Press, 1976.

Gooding, Earl. *The West Indies at the Crossroads.* Schenkman Publishing, 1980.

Hay, Clarence L., et al., editors. *The Maya and Their Neighbors: Essays on Middle American Anthropology and Archaeology.* Dover Publications, 1977.

Lowenthal, David. *West Indian Societies.* Oxford University Press, 1972.

McCuen, Gary E., editor. *Political Murder in Central America: Death Squads and U.S. Policies.* G. E. McCuen Publishing, 1985.

McNeil, Frank. *Reality or Illusion: War and Peace in Central America.* Scribner's, 1988.

Meyer, Michael C. *The Course of Mexican History.* Oxford University Press, 1979.

Perkins, Dexter. *The United States and the Caribbean* (Revised Ed.). Harvard University Press, 1966.

Sherman, William L. *Forced Native Labor in Sixteenth-Century Central America.* University of Nebraska Press, 1979.

Thompson, V.B. *Africa, the Atlantic Slave Trade and the West Indies: African Background to West Indian History.* NOK Publishers, 1979.

Vaillant, George C. *Aztecs of Mexico.* Doubleday, 1962.

Williams, Eric. *From Columbus to Castro: The History of the Caribbean, 1492–1969.* Harper & Row, 1971.

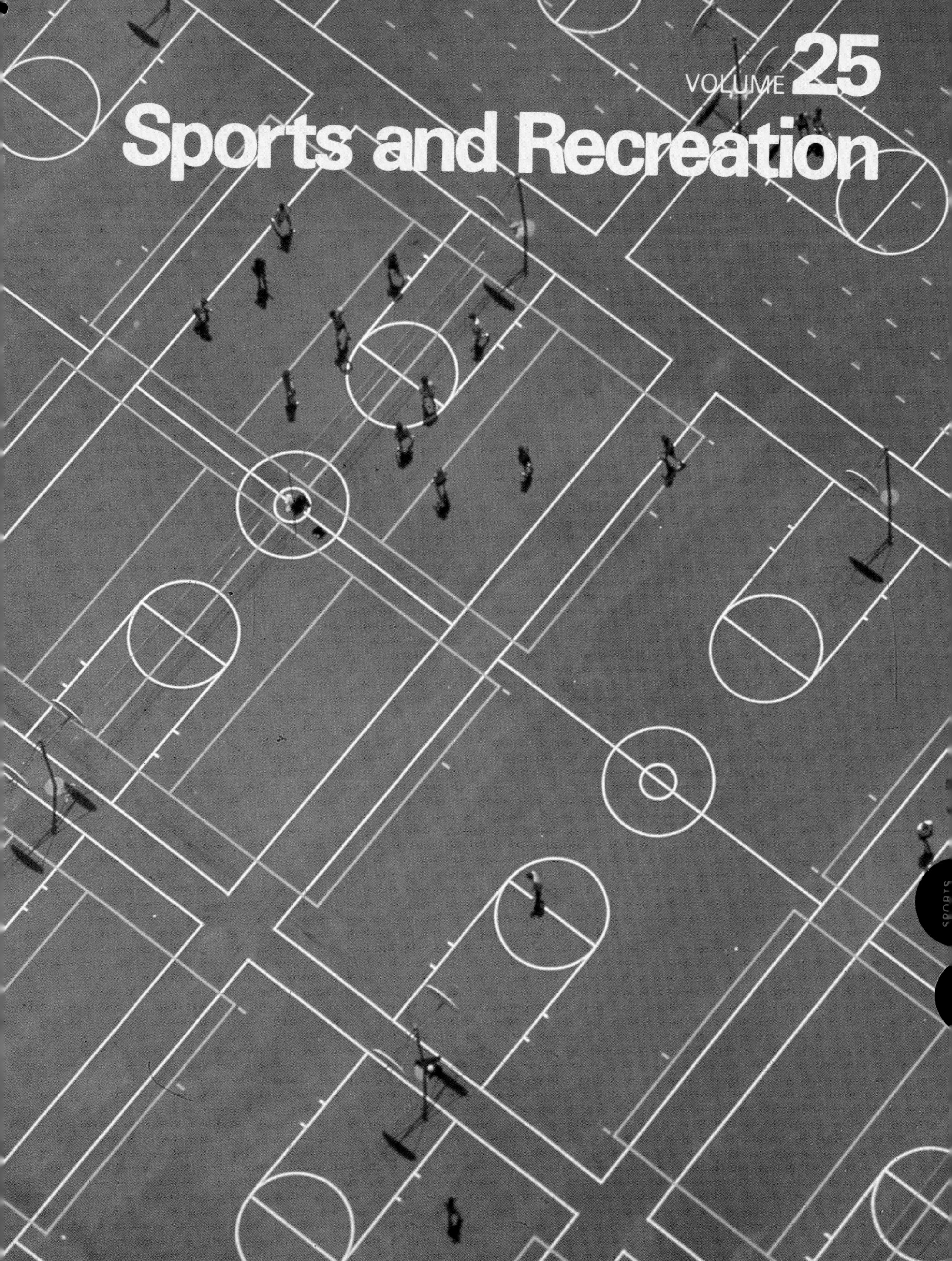
VOLUME 25
Sports and Recreation
SPORTS

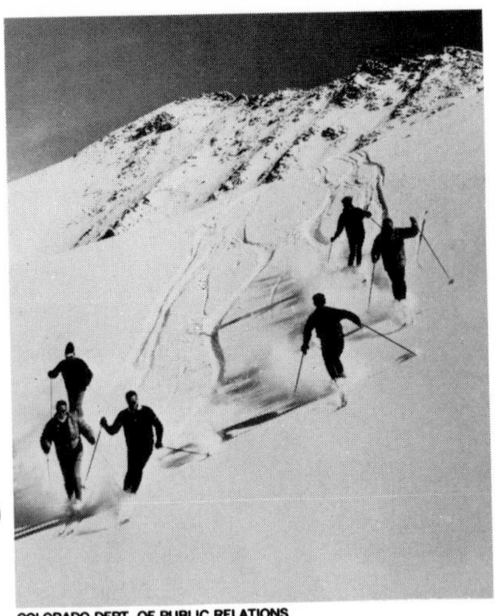

COLORADO DEPT. OF PUBLIC RELATIONS

INDEX TO SPORTS AND RECREATION

BASKETBALL: GEORG GERSTER/PHOTO RESEARCHERS

VOLUME 25

Sports and Recreation

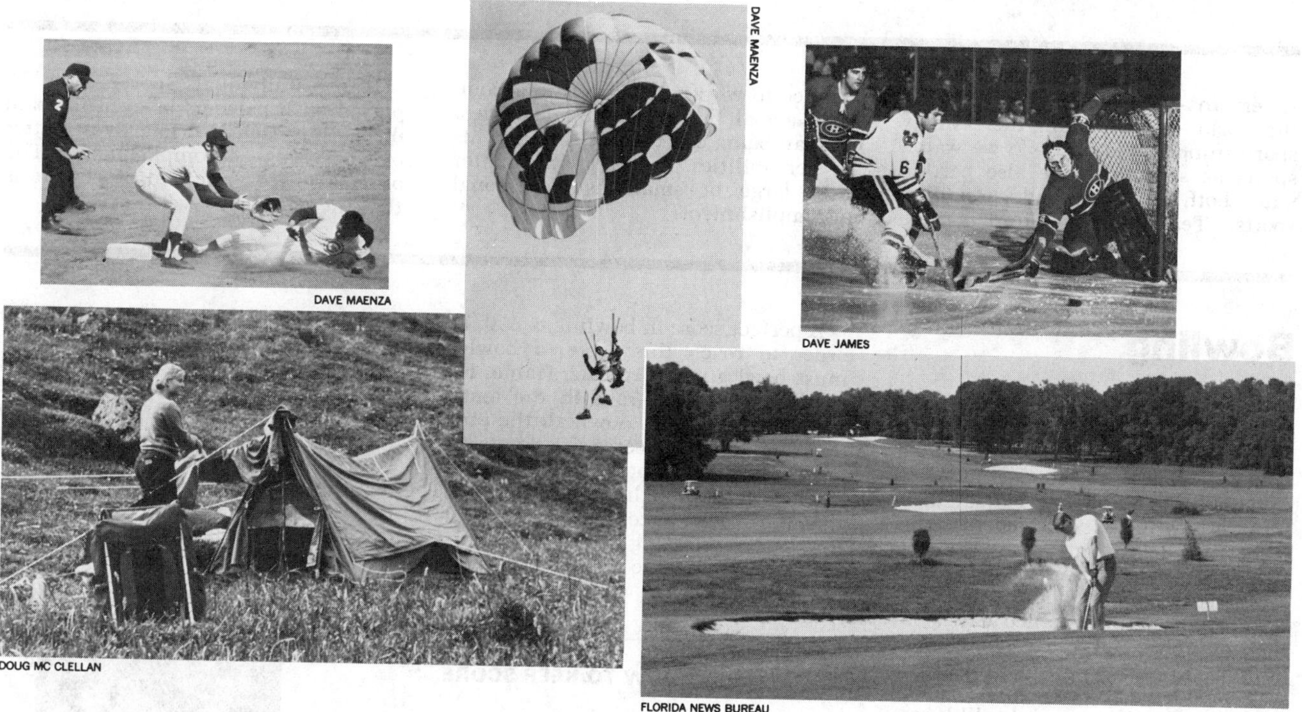
DAVE MAENZA

DAVE MAENZA

DAVE JAMES

DOUG MC CLELLAN

FLORIDA NEWS BUREAU

The human instinct to play seems almost universal. Even among the poorest and least civilized cultures, people play games of some kind for amusement and recreation.

The leap from such games to the modern idea of sport is not as long as it might appear. Many of the athletic events of modern sports have obvious connections with the way our distant ancestors lived. Hunting and fishing—now recreations—were originally jobs required for survival. Many early tribes were organized specifically to hunt wild animals for food. Combat sports are clearly related to military campaigns in the days before powerful modern weapons. The first footrace was almost certainly a race for survival—in flight from a stronger enemy or in pursuit of food.

As civilization grew, men had more time to play, and they had the luxury of separating the sporting instinct from the battle for survival. Races and combat sports were organized, and the rules protected participants from harm while preserving the excitement of competition. Men came to compete not for survival but for a token—a simple laurel wreath or a small trophy whose value is only symbolic.

No doubt early sports competitions were also related to the need for physical conditioning and military preparedness. The personal battles described in Homer's *Iliad* suggest that the well conditioned athlete was also the heroic warrior. Only a century or two after the *Iliad*, the Greeks established the Olympic Games. Yet the association of sport with some physical danger persisted. In ancient England, an early version of football involved whole towns in combat, and one or more participants were often maimed or killed before the match came to an end. Deaths in combat sports and in modern motor sports still occur today.

The dozens of sports we recognize today grew in many ways. Some, like the wall and racket sports, developed among monks and the nobility in their partially enclosed courtyards (sites of the first handball and tennis courts). Others grew among the common people—footraces and such team sports as football.

Many of our sports took their current form less than a hundred years ago. A great wave of interest in physical fitness and competitive games in the last half of the 1800's brought popularity to organized football and soccer, cricket, and baseball. During the same years, many new sports, including lawn tennis, basketball, and badminton, were invented.

The sports world has always been divided into two kingdoms—that of the participant and that of the spectator. Participant sports are largely for amateurs, those who play for the simple pleasure of the game. Amateurs usually find both physical fitness and emotional release in their sports. They take pleasure at excelling in the heat of competition and enjoy (especially in team sports) associating with other enthusiasts.

Spectators most often watch games—either in person or, more recently on television—that are expertly played by professional athletes. Watching a championship game in which the home team is involved—whether a high school team or a major league baseball team—brings the spectators together not only for the moment but also for years to come, whenever the great game is mentioned and replayed in the mind's eye.

This volume is arranged to give brief descriptions of the most prominent sports and recreations in America today. The first section considers individual sports; the second describes major team sports; later sections deal with equestrian, motor, water, and winter sports and noncompetitive recreations. An index to specific sports is provided on the page at the left.

INDIVIDUAL SPORTS

Americans—indeed, people all over the world—are becoming increasingly sports-minded. Not only do we watch sports as spectators, we also participate, both in team and individual sports. Team sports afford a fine chance to work with others to accomplish a goal, but in individual sports, a human being can test the limits of his or her abilities. A victory, no matter how large or small, is a personal accomplishment.

Many individual sports may be played with partners or even in team meets, but each is primarily a matter of individual accomplishment. The only teamwork required of players is that they do their level best.

Bowling

A form of bowling was enjoyed by the Egyptians as far back as 5200 B.C., and the ancient Polynesians also rolled polished stones at objects along a smooth path. Romans called their form of bowling *boccie.* Modern forms of bowling began in Germany during the fourth century A.D. as a form of religious ceremony. Pious peasants set up clusters of pins, called *kegels,* in their churches and rolled round stones at them. Knocking down all the kegels was considered a good sign. The game came to America around the 17th century, when the Dutch settled in New York City. A section of lower Manhattan is called Bowling Green.

In the modern game, a bowling *lane* is an area of polished maple or pine boards 42 inches wide. On both sides of the lane are shallow trenches called *gutters.* The distance from the *foul line* to the head pin is 60 feet; there is an *approach* area behind the foul line of about 15 feet. Ten bowling *pins* are set up in a 36-inch triangle at the far end of the lane. The bowler uses a ball made of composition rubber measuring not more than 27 inches in circumference and weighing not more than 16 pounds. He rolls it at the pins and tries to knock them all down. The ball has two or three finger holes that the bowler uses to lift the ball and control its course.

A bowling game consists of ten frames. The bowler rolls a maximum of two balls at the pins in each frame. If all ten pins are knocked down with the first roll, the second roll is eliminated, for the bowler has scored a *strike;* this is marked on a score sheet with a cross. The bowler is credited with ten points plus the number of pins knocked down on the next two rolls. If the bowler knocks down ten pins with two rolls, that is called a *spare.* He gets ten points plus the pins knocked down with the next roll. A spare is marked with a diagonal line.

A perfect score in bowling is 300. In order to reach this score, a bowler must bowl a strike in each frame. He receives two extra rolls in the tenth frame. If he knocks down all the pins on each roll, he scores 30 points in each frame, for a total of 300.

The *approach* is the number of steps that the bowler takes toward the foul line before releasing the ball. Bowlers usually take three to five steps in their approach. If they step over the line, no pins will be credited to the score.

Duckpins is another popular form of bowling, but the ball and the pins are much smaller. Scores are usually lower in duckpins because the pins are harder to knock down. Bowling is under the supervision of the American Bowling Congress, and duckpins under the National Duckpin Bowling Congress.

HOW TO KEEP SCORE

A *strike* is noted by an X in the left small box; no score for that frame is entered until the bowler bowls his next two balls. The bowler receives a score of 10 for the strike *plus* the total pins knocked down on his next two rolls.

A *spare* is noted by a slash (/) in the right small box. A spare earns 10 points *plus* the pins knocked down on the next roll.

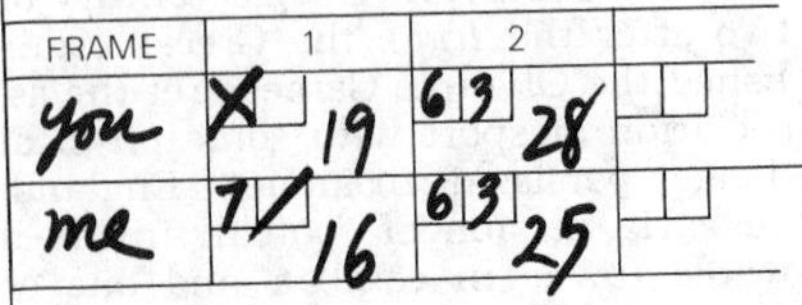

FRAME
1
2
you
X
19
6 3
28
me
7 /
16
6 3
25

You scored a strike in the first frame; *me* scored a spare. Both scored nine pins in the second frame.

A *perfect game* consists of 12 strikes in a row; the bowler receives a score of 30 for each frame, for a total of 300.

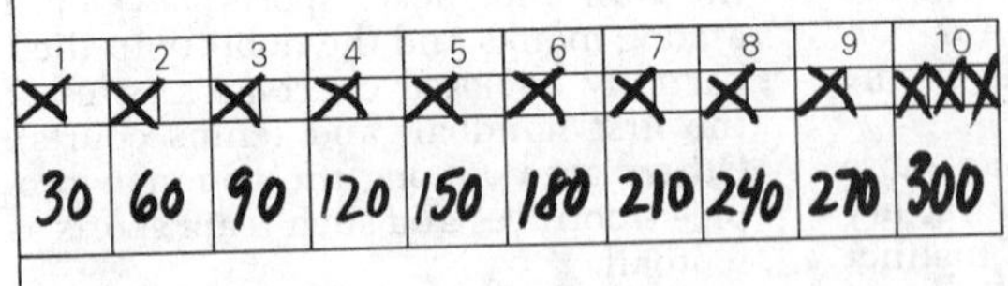

1 2 3 4 5 6 7 8 9 10
X X X X X X X X X XXX
30 60 90 120 150 180 210 240 270 300

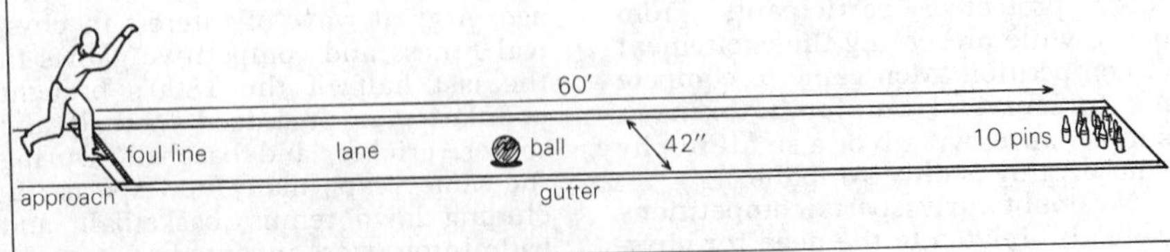

Combat Sports

For the purposes of this section, combat sports will be defined as one-on-one physical encounters without the aid of weapons. Fencing, which is a form of combat sport, will be dealt with under "Other Individual Sports".

Boxing. The most popular of combat sports is boxing, in which two contestants of almost equal weight, strike each other about the head and torso for a preset number of three-minute rounds (two–minute rounds in amateur bouts between young boxers).

Boxing can trace its origins back to the days of ancient Greece and Rome. Bouts were usually fought to the death or until one man was seriously injured. Opponents could punch, kick, gouge, wrestle or do whatever was necessary in order to win. Theagenes of Greece, a famous Olympic champion of about 450 B.C., killed most of his 1400 opponents. Roman gladiators wore wrappings with protruding spikes on their fists. The fights were so brutal that for many centuries this "sport" was banned.

It was in England that boxing started on the road to a more scientific approach. James Figg, England's bare–knuckle champion from 1719 to 1730, was an expert fencer who used fast footwork, parrying and thrusting instead of kicking and wrestling. Other boxers, noting his success, tried to follow suit. However, during Figg's reign, a fight continued without letup until one man was knocked out or otherwise disabled. Jack Broughton, the champion from 1734 to 1750, introduced a rule requiring a rest period after a knockdown. Still, there was no limit to the length of a match. The longest bare-knuckle fight took place near Melbourne, Australia, in November, 1855, when James Kelly and Jonathan Smith fought for six hours and 15 minutes.

Finally, in 1867, under the auspices of the eighth Marquis of Queensberry, a code of rules was formulated by John F. Chambers, a British lightweight boxer and authority on the sport. The rules were designed to eliminate the brutal aspects of boxing, such as fighting with bare knuckles. Essentially, these are the same rules that are in force today.

In America, the Queensberry rules were not widely adopted until 1892, when the reigning heavyweight champion, John L. Sullivan, was defeated by James J. Corbett in a bout under the new rules.

The rules of modern boxing are fairly simple. The contestants, in both amateur and professional boxing, must fight opponents in their own weight classification. These classes are shown in the table above.

CULVER PICTURES

WEIGHT CLASSES

Flyweight, not over 112 lbs.
Bantamweight, not over 118 lbs.
Junior featherweight, not over 122 lbs.
Featherweight, not over 126 lbs.
Junior lightweight, not over 130 lbs.
Lightweight, not over 135 lbs.
Junior welterweight, not over 140 lbs.
Welterweight, not over 147 lbs.
Junior middleweight, not over 154 lbs.
Middleweight, not over 160 lbs.
Light heavyweight, not over 175 lbs.
Heavyweight, all weights over 175 lbs.

Each match consists of a specified number of three-minute rounds (two minutes in some amateur bouts). A match may last from three rounds (Olympics) up through 15 rounds (for professional championship bouts).

Boxing matches are conducted in a ring, which is raised, padded, and roped off. Fighters wear padded gloves that weigh eight ounces (amateur gloves can weigh ten ounces). Certain blows are illegal, such as a punch below the belt line, a rabbit punch to the back of the neck, or a backhand blow. Legal punches are the straight jab, the hook or cross, and the uppercut.

BOXING: *Jim Corbett* (above) *won the heavyweight crown in 1892. Muhammad Ali* (below, *vs. Sonny Liston) was only the second to lose the title and win it back.*

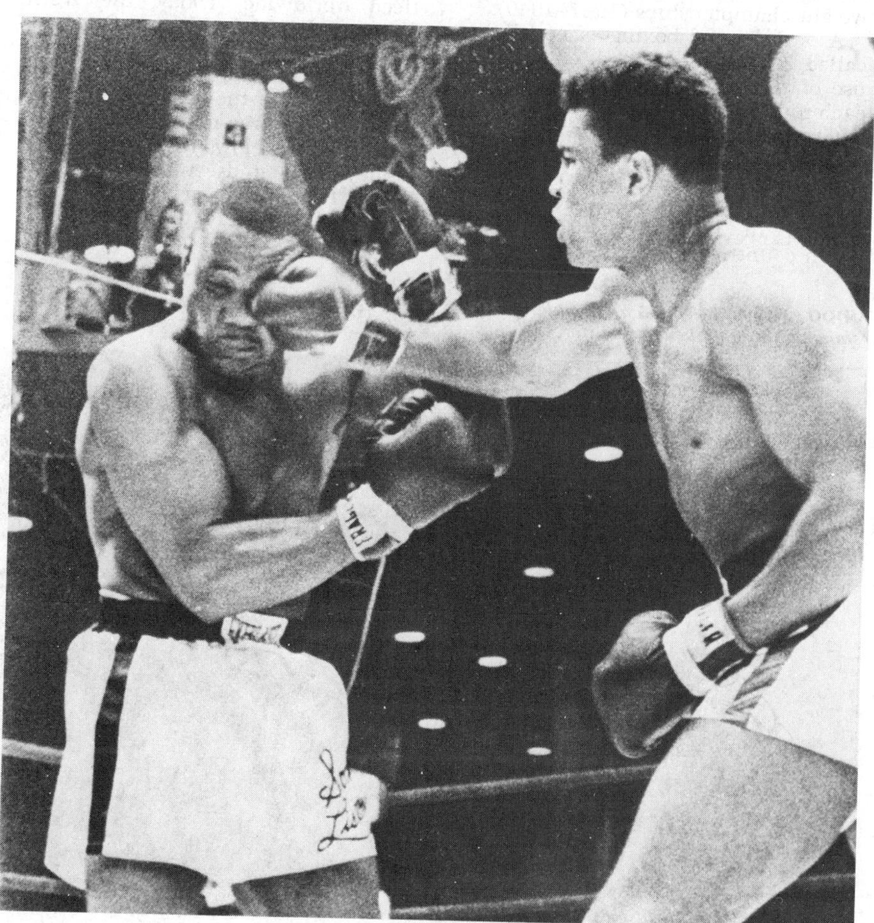

WIDE WORLD

"Roundhouse" blows are permitted, but they usually leave the puncher open to a counter punch.

A match ends in a knockout (KO) when one boxer is knocked down and fails to stand up before the referee counts off ten seconds. When one boxer has taken severe punishment and is in danger of suffering grave injury, the referee can stop the fight and award the winner a technical knockout (TKO). When a match reaches the end of a predetermined number of rounds, the referee and two judges determine the winner by decision, awarding the match to the boxer who has scored the most and the hardest punches. When the bout is considered even, it is called a draw. A boxer may lose a fight if he persistently commits fouls, such as repeatedly hitting his opponent below the belt.

Over the last half century, a number of boxers have stood out over the rest. Among the heavyweights, Joe Louis, Rocky Marciano (who was never beaten in a professional bout), and Muhammad Ali (born Cassius Clay) are notable. "Sugar" Ray Robinson, who held the welterweight championship from 1946 to 1951, and who later became middleweight champion, was judged "the best pound-for-pound fighter" of his era. Henry Armstrong was the only boxer to hold three titles simultaneously, having won the featherweight, lightweight, and welterweight championships (1937–1940).

A variation of boxing is popularly called *kick-boxing,* since it entails the use of feet as well as hands. During each round a boxer must deliver a predetermined number of kicks at his opponent, as well as punches with his fists. Kicks, like punches, must not be delivered below the belt. The sport is popular in Thailand and in other Asian countries.

Martial arts. The martial arts consist of a series of hand-to-hand unarmed combat tactics, the most popular being karate, judo, jujitsu, and kung fu. Some experts believe kung fu does not belong in the category of unarmed self-defense because it can become a killer art in its most violent form.

Chinese *jujitsu* and its offshoot, *judo,* are thousands of years old; they arose in China and Japan. In Japan during the Middle Ages, common people were forbidden to carry weapons, so they devised a self-defense technique that involved a series of trips, holds, strangles, and falls. By the 1700's, judo and jujitsu were no longer required for self-defense. But they survived as sports stressing grace, physical discipline, and intense spiritual concentration.

In 1882 a Japanese named Jigaro Kano founded the first of the modern judo schools. It was Kano who introduced the system of "belts," with a white belt for a novice and a black belt for an expert; the system has been extended to other forms of the martial arts, such as karate. Judo came to America in 1902, and it is now sanctioned by the Amateur Athletic Union (AAU). It was an Olympic event in 1964 and 1972.

Karate was introduced in an Okinawa school in 1905, and by 1922 it had spread to Japan; later it was practiced worldwide. Today, the World Union of Karatedo (Karate) Organization sets the rules governing the use of punching, striking, and kicking on various parts of the body. Matches last from two to three minutes and points are scored for blows to the face, neck, kidneys, and midsection of an opponent. The blows are not actually landed: if they were, they could kill or disable.

Wrestling. Wrestling is one of mankind's oldest sports, dating back to the days of ancient Greece and Rome. Homer's *Iliad* gives an account of a wrestling match between Ulysses and Ajax, and in the seventh century B.C., the sport was an important part of the Olympic Games. Today, it is still a popular amateur sport. The modern form of professional wrestling is more show business than athletics.

Amateur wrestling, as practiced in schools and colleges, can be divided in two types: freestyle and Greco–Roman. Both are performed on a mat 24-feet square; matches consist of three three-minute periods, with the wrestlers using various grips and holds while trying to pin their opponents to the mat. A "fall" is awarded to the wrestler who can pin his opponent's shoulders to the mat for two full seconds. Points are awarded for "take downs" or "near falls," as well as for escapes. A wrestler can be penalized for stalling, illegal holds, or other infractions cited by the referee. If a wrestler is cautioned three times, he is eliminated. If a fall occurs, the match is ended. If no fall occurs, the decision is rendered on the point system. The basic difference between freestyle and Greco–Roman wrestling is that Greco–Roman forbids any hold below the waist or use of the legs in any manner to take down an opponent.

Sumo wrestling is practiced primarily in Japan, where it is extremely popular. Many sumo wrestlers weigh 400 pounds. In some ways it resembles Greco–Roman wrestling in that a fall is scored when any part of the body touches the ground except the feet.

Although modern *professional wrestling* has many fans, few experts view it as a true sport. Matches are staged for the enjoyment of the audience rather than for genuine competition.

JUDO AND WRESTLING *are popular combat sports. The bottom drawing shows the beginning of an over-the-shoulder throw. The top drawings show winning maneuvers—a forceful throw and a lift. At right, a wrestler seeks to pin an opponent in Olympic competition.*

PETER LOEWER

UPI

Golf

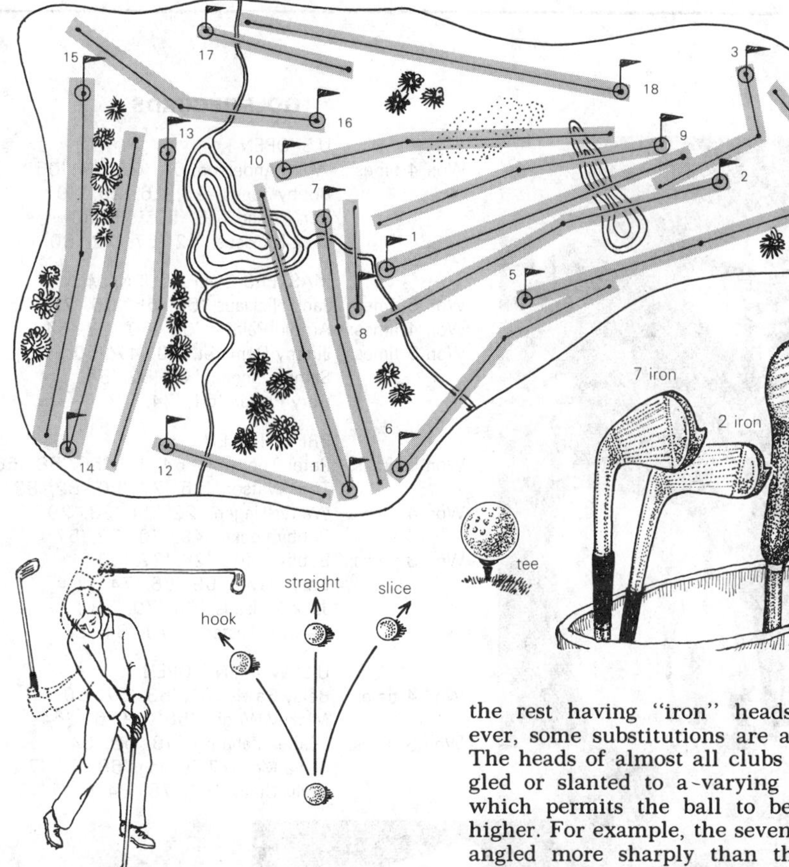

GOLF: *a typical course layout* (above) *shows the length and direction of fairways. Clubs* (right) *are of three kinds. An errant drive may hook or slice* (above).

In a way it can be said that the invention of gunpowder was responsible for furthering the popularity of golf. Young soldiers of the 15th century were so busy playing "fute ball" (now called soccer in America) and "golfe" that they had little time to practice archery. In those days of castles, moats, and battlements, sharpshooting bowmen were vital, and King James II of Scotland finally banned both games. However, after gunpowder was invented, cannons could be fired from relatively long range. Suddenly archers were no longer the first line of defense, giving them time once more for golf and football. Soon even royalty realized that "golfe" could be fun.

Golf probably began as a field game played by the Romans, which they called "paganica." The legions used sticks to hit a "ball" stuffed with feathers toward a stick in the ground. The original version may have been a team game something like field hockey. But when individual players began to study how to move the ball toward the goal in the fewest possible strokes, they were playing a primitive kind of golf. Exactly when the hole became a part of golf is not known, but in the year 1500 an illustrated book shows three golfers standing on a green with a hole in it.

The first great golfers were the Scots. In 1754 they formed the St. Andrews Society of Golfers and established a set of rules. The ball used was still kind of "featherie." Then in 1845, the Reverend Dr. Robert Patterson fashioned the *gutta percha* ball, made of a resin from a species of Malayan tree. Still later, Dr. Coburn Haskell made one of rubber.

Golf arrived in America with the Dutch and English settlers, but the game was almost unnoticed until 1888, when John Reid of Yonkers, New York, and four friends, founded the American St. Andrews. Golf's popularity began to spread, and in 1894 the Newport Club held what was perhaps the first "all star" match, with 20 of the best golfers meeting for a 36–hole contest. That same year the U.S. Golf Association was formed, giving the game some organization.

At the turn of the 20th century, golf was considered a rich man's game. But beginning about 1910, communities began to build public courses. In the 1940's and '50's new courses sprang up all over America. Millions were playing the game, and a regular "circuit" was established for professional golfers.

The course. No two golf courses are exactly alike, although all have many similarities. Generally, they have 18 holes (some have nine, but they are *never* used in tournament play). The golfer encounters many obstacles as he plays the course, including sand traps, bunkers, creeks, lakes, trees, and high grass. The distance from tee to hole varies. Some short holes cover a distance of less than 180 yards; the medium holes range from 280 to 480 yards; the long holes can be more than 500 yards.

The short holes are usually adjudged par three, meaning that a good golfer will put the ball into the hole in three strokes: a drive off the tee, an approach shot that takes the ball up on the green, and a putt into the "cup." The medium holes are par four, the long ones par five. Most courses are divided so that there are eight medium holes, with the rest split between long and short holes.

Rules. Golf is governed by the U.S. Golf Association (USGA) and the Royal Academy of Golf Clubs (St. Andrews, Scotland). The rules are the same except for the size of the ball. In the United States, the minimum diameter is 1.68 inches; the British ball is smaller. Golfers are limited to a maximum of 14 clubs. Generally, a bag contains four clubs with wooden "heads," the rest having "iron" heads; however, some substitutions are allowed. The heads of almost all clubs are angled or slanted to a varying degree, which permits the ball to be lofted higher. For example, the seven-iron is angled more sharply than the two-iron; therefore, a seven-iron shot will carry higher but will not travel as far as a two-iron shot. The *wedge* affords the most loft and is used to explode out of sand traps. The *putter* is not angled at all; it is used on the greens to tap the ball into the cup.

Grips and stances. When preparing to hit the ball off the tee (the first shot for a particular hole), the great golfers employ similar grips and stances. Each one, of course, adjusts to his own particular need or style.

The most popular grip is the *overlapping* grip. A right-handed golfer grasps the shaft of the club with the little finger of the right hand placed over the index finger of the left hand. The club is held securely but not too tightly. The *interlocking* grip has the little finger of the right hand placed under the index finger of the left hand.

There are three different stances (with slight variations). In the *square* stance, the ball is played from an equal distance between the feet with the toes lined up evenly. Theoretically, the ball should sail straight down the fairway. Moving the front foot back slightly with the toe pointing outward creates the *open* stance, which causes a *slice,* or left-to-right arc of the ball (when a right-handed golfer hits the ball). Moving the rear foot back with the toe pointing out induces the *hook;* the ball arcs from right to left in this *closed* stance.

GOLF RECORDS

U.S. OPEN

Won 4 times:	Willie Anderson, 01, '03, '04, '05
	Bobby Jones, '23, '26, '29, '30
	Ben Hogan, '48, '50, '51, '53
	Jack Nicklaus, '62, '67, '72, '80

MASTERS GOLF TOURNAMENT

Won 6 times:	Jack Nicklaus, '63, '65, '66, '72, '75, '86
Won 4 times:	Arnold Palmer, '58, '60, '62, '64
Won 3 times:	Jimmy Demaret, '40, '47, '50
	Sammy Snead, '49, '52, '54
	Gary Player, '61, '74, '78

BRITISH OPEN

Won 5 times:	Peter Thomson, '54, '55, '56, '58, '65
	Tom Watson, '75, '77, '80, '82, '83
Won 4 times:	Walter Hagen, '22, '24, '28, '29
	Bobby Locke, '49, '50, '52, '57
Won 3 times:	Bobby Jones, '26, '27, '30
	Gary Player, '59, '68, '74
	Jack Nicklaus, '66, '70, '78
	Steve Ballesteros, '79, '84, '88

U.S. WOMEN'S OPEN

Won 4 times:	Betsy Rawls, '51, '53, '57, '60
	Mickey Wright, '58, '59, '61, '64
Won 3 times:	"Babe" Zaharias, '48, '50, '54
	Susie Maxwell Berning, '68, '72, '73
	Hollis Stacy, '77, '78, '84

CULVER PICTURES

BOBBY JONES

UPI

JACK NICKLAUS

UPI

JOHNNY MILLER

CULVER PICTURES

ARNOLD PALMER

The swing. All golfing manuals stress two basic points: first, keep the head down, eyes on the ball, until the swing and follow-through have been completed; second, keep the left arm stiff at all times (assuming a right-handed golfer), the elbow locked in place.

Scoring. In tournaments, there are two different methods of scoring: match play and medal play. Match play is a hole-by-hole manner of scoring; the player requiring the fewest strokes to sink the ball into the cup wins the hole, and the player winning the most holes wins the match. In medal or stroke play, the strokes for the entire course are counted. The player who uses the fewest strokes traversing the course wins. In professional tournaments, the player with the lowest total for four circuits of the course (played on four consecutive days) is the winner.

Golfers and tournaments. In 1913 very few people followed golf or knew much about world-class golfers. That year, two of England's greatest golfers, Harry Vardon and Ted Ray, came to the United States to play in the U.S. Open. They were heavily favored, but a 20-year-old former caddy named Francis Ouimet (pronounced "we met") tied both at the end of regulation play, and then defeated them in a playoff round. The match caught the imagination of U.S. sports fans and made golf a spectator sport for the first time.

Perhaps the greatest American golfer was Bobby Jones. He is the only golfer ever to complete the "Grand Slam" of golf, winning the four most important tournaments in the same year (1930). Lists of the greatest players also include Walter Hagen, Ben Hogan, Sam Snead, Arnold Palmer, Jack Nicklaus, and Johnny Miller.

The most notable tournaments are played in the United States or Great Britain, although there are a number of other nations that boast important tournaments. In America, the top contests are those of the Professional Golf Association (PGA), the Masters, and the U.S. Open. Along with the British Open, they make up the modern "Grand Slam"; no golfer has ever won this modern Grand Slam in one year.

Women golfers. In no recognized tournament do men and women compete against each other. Women pros belong to the Ladies Professional Golf Association (LPGA) and have their own set of tournaments. Prizes for women are not as large as those for men, but they have been increasing rapidly.

Among the greatest women golfers, Mildred "Babe" Didrickson (Zaharias) has a special place. She was also a great all-around woman athlete. Other greats include Mickey Wright, Patty Berg, Betsy Rawls, and Nancy Lopez.

Gymnastics

Until the 1960's, gymnastics was confined to gymnasiums; few people, even sports fans, were familiar with the grace and beauty to be found in gymnastic events. Since then, the attention given the sport by television and other media, and the appeal of such stars as Olga Korbut of the Soviet Union and Nadia Comaneci of Rumania, have brought gymnastics great popularity, both as a spectator event and as an active sport for participants.

Gymnastics began in ancient Greece as exercises intended to develop both mind and body. All exercises were considered gymnastics, including running, jumping, discus throwing, and wrestling. The Greek enthusiasm for physical culture was rekindled in the 1800's by the Germans and Scandinavians. By 1900, many schools and colleges in the United States had built gymnasiums where the gymnastic arts could be taught and practiced. At first, however, gymnastics was considered a personal discipline rather than a competitive sport. Only in recent years has gymnastics become a popular competition in the United States.

Today, U.S. gymnastics competition is regulated by the Amateur Athletic Union (AAU) and the National Collegiate Athletic Association (NCAA). In both national and international competition, there are six major events for men and four for women:

MEN'S EVENTS

Horizontal bar—continuous swinging and vaulting on a steel rod

Parallel bars—vaulting, swinging, balancing, and handstands on bars made of wood

Stationary rings—maneuvers such as handstands and body swings on suspended rings that ideally remain stationary

Long horse—vaulting of a stuffed apparatus after a running start; athletes land on the horse with their hands and vault over it in various ways

Side horse—continuous series of maneuvers such as scissors, swinging circles, and double leg circles on apparatus resembling a long horse but with two curved "pommels"

Free exercises—graceful and poetic movement over a 12- by 12-meter floor mat, including cartwheels, balances, handsprings, and held poses

There are other men's gymnastics that are not a part of international competition but that are popular, nevertheless, in America. They include tumbling, which consists of a long series of handsprings, mid-air twists and cartwheels; flying rings, in which the rings are not stationary; trampoline, which is "rebound tumbling"; and rope climbing.

WOMEN'S EVENTS

Long horse—see Men's Events

Free exercise—same as men's event except that women do exercises to music and emphasize grace more than strength

Balance beam—a series of tumbles, splits, cartwheels, and a tumbling dismount on a slab of wood about 16 feet long and 4 inches wide suspended 4 feet above the floor

Uneven parallel bars—breathtaking series of maneuvers, including swinging from the high bar to the low, with hand changes, swings, flips, and a dazzling dismount, on two bars set parallel to each other but at different heights

All exercises are awarded points on the basis of style, grace, and difficulty. Judging of gymnastics events is subjective. In international matches, judges are often criticized for seeming to favor contestants from their own country or region.

GYMNASTICS: *Mary Lou Retton performs on the balance beam and Kurt Thomas on the side horse, two events in international competition. Retton won the all-around gold medal at the 1984 Olympics. Thomas won the U.S. men's title in 1979.*

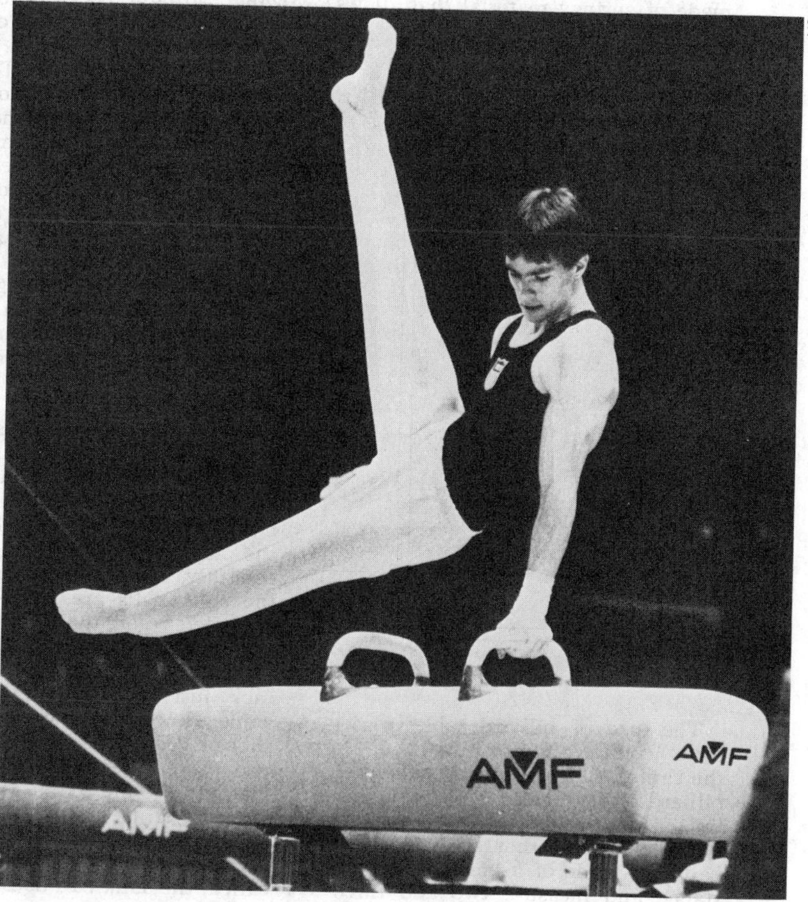

UPI

Pool and Billiards

Billiards was developed at a time during the 14th century when lawn bowling was very popular. When rain forced the bowlers indoors, innovators devised a table and a stick to push the balls. The word billiards derives from the French *billart,* which means "playing cue."

Many of the game's refinements can be credited to a French army captain named Mingaud who was sentenced to a prison term in the Bastille by the emperor Napoleon. He was granted permission to have a pool table in his cell. To pass the time he began to experiment with different methods of executing various shots. Mingaud found that after filing down his cue tip so that it was rounded, he could make a number of apparently "impossible" shots. About 1825 an Englishman named Jack Carr, who became the first billiards champion, discovered that if he struck the cue ball from an odd angle, it would react erratically but effectively, thus giving birth to the phrase, "putting English on the ball."

The first pool tables were made of wood, but humidity caused them to warp. For a time marble was used, but it tended to "sweat" in hot weather. Finally, slate, with a smooth cloth stretched tautly over it, proved to be the best material for the table top. Modern tables have "cushioned" sides made of springy material that allows the ball to carom.

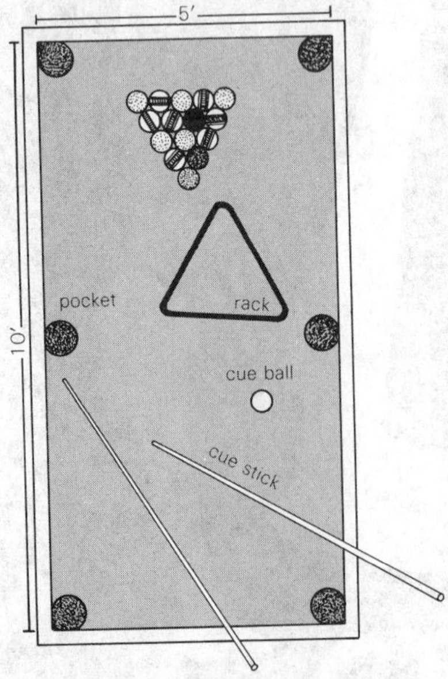

The size of billiard tables varies from country to country, but in the United States a full-size regulation billiards table measures five feet wide by ten feet long (tables are always twice as long as they are wide). The balls are made of a hard elastic substance and measure two and three-eighths inches in diameter. Cue sticks weigh between 14 and 22 ounces, tapering from about one and one-half inches at the base to one-half inch in diameter at the tip. They are usually made of wood.

Billiards. Modern billiards is a game played with three balls, one white (the cue ball) and the others solid colored. The object of *three-cushion billiards* (the most popular form of the game) is to strike the cue ball with the stick so that it will carom off three sides of the table *and* strike both object balls. Contestants take turns at the table, with one contestant retiring if he fails to make his shot.

Pocket billiards (pool). A pocket billiards table is different from a billiards table in two respects: generally, it is somewhat smaller, measuring four and a half feet wide by nine feet long. Also, it has six "pockets" into which a ball may be driven. There are pockets at each of the corners and pockets midway along each long side of the table.

In pocket billiards, 15 numbered object balls are used in addition to the white cue ball. Seven of the balls are solid colored, seven are striped, and one, the 8-ball, is black.

There are several variations of pocket billiards, the most popular being "straight pool." The object of the game is to drive the cue ball so that it knocks one (or more) of the object balls into a pocket. The shooter must "call his shots," announcing before shooting which ball he will sink into which pocket. Combination shots may be attempted; in these the cue ball first strikes an unannounced ball which then strikes the announced ball, driving it into the appropriate pocket.

At the beginning of the game all 15 balls are placed inside a triangular *rack* so that the first ball is on a *spot.* The cue ball may be placed anywhere behind another spot at the other end of the table.

Then one player "breaks" the rack, driving the white cue ball into the triangle of racked balls. He need not call the ball that might drop into a pocket, but he must call all shots thereafter. If the player should "run" 14 balls successfully, leaving one numbered ball, the sunk balls are reracked, with a space left where the 1-ball would ordinarily be placed. The shooter then drives the remaining ball into the rack, just as at the beginning of the game. He continues until he misses a shot or commits some error. The second player then takes up where the first left off, and so on.

A player is guilty of a "scratch" when the cue ball is driven into a pocket. Even if a shot is successfully called, the sunk ball does not count if the cue ball also falls into a pocket; in addition, a point is deducted from the score. The sunk ball is returned to the table and placed on the spot. A scratch can also be called if the cue ball is shot and fails to touch any of the object balls on the table.

Should a player send the wrong ball (not the one called) into a pocket, it does not count and is respotted on the table. Similarly, if the called ball falls into the wrong pocket, it does not count and is respotted. Should the player successfully sink the called ball and in so doing sink another ball as well, both balls count. Usually, 50 points wins the game.

A popular variation of pocket billiards is *rotation* (also called "Chicago"), in which the object balls must be pocketed in numerical sequence. Another is *8-ball.* If, after the opening break, a striped ball is sunk, the player must sink all striped balls, leaving the black 8-ball for last. Should he accidentally sink the 8-ball before he has run all the striped balls, he loses the game.

Shooting Sports

In a philosophical sense, man first learned how to shoot when he discovered methods of hurling a missile through the air by mechanical means. The bow and arrow probably came first, followed in turn by the crossbow, and finally by gunpowder and firearms. All these devices had many practical applications. Man made war with them, hunted food, protected himself and his family from human and animal marauders, and later, when he was safe, well-fed and at peace, learned to use his shooting weapons for sport.

Archery. In the Middle Ages, English rulers considered archery such an important skill that they outlawed other sports so that their sharpshooters would have more time to practice with their longbows. Even when firearms made the archer obsolete as a fighting man, British rulers insisted their bowmen continue to hone their skills. Roger Ascham, considered the father of modern archery, wrote a treatise in 1545 called "Toxophilus" (love of archery). King Charles II, a sports buff, offered prizes to his best shooters. The Grand National Archery Association was formed in England in 1844.

In America, the Club of the United Bowmen of Philadelphia was formed in 1828, but archery was not very popular at the time. Not until after the Civil War did the bow become popular, mostly because of the work of two brothers, Maurice and Will Thompson. They returned from service with the Confederate army, found their

SHOOTING: *Archery* (left) *is the oldest target sport. Trapshooting, in which a marksman must hit a moving target, grew from hunting* (inset).

land in ruins, and decided to live in the forest. They hunted their food with bows and arrows, and wrote several articles and books about archery when they returned to civilization.

The first important archery contest in the United States, under the jurisdiction of the new National Archery Association, was held in 1879 at the Chicago baseball stadium. The contest was won by the old master, Will Thompson.

The modern bow varies in size and cost. Adult bows are from five to six feet long and may be relatively inexpensive or worth several hundred dollars. They come in two principal styles: the curved bow, modeled after the English longbow, or the recurved bow, of ancient Turkish design. Bows are made of red cedarwood, lemonwood, yew, fiberglass, or aluminum. A crossbow is a kind of short bow attached to a block of wood; the arrow is fired by a device similar to the trigger of a rifle.

Arrows are usually made of cedar or aluminum and are tipped with brass. They are from 24 to 32 inches long. Targets are four feet in diameter, with the bull's–eye 9.6 inches in diameter. Other archery equipment includes a leather cuff for the wrist of the hand holding the bow, a three-fingered glove for the shooting hand, and a quiver for arrows.

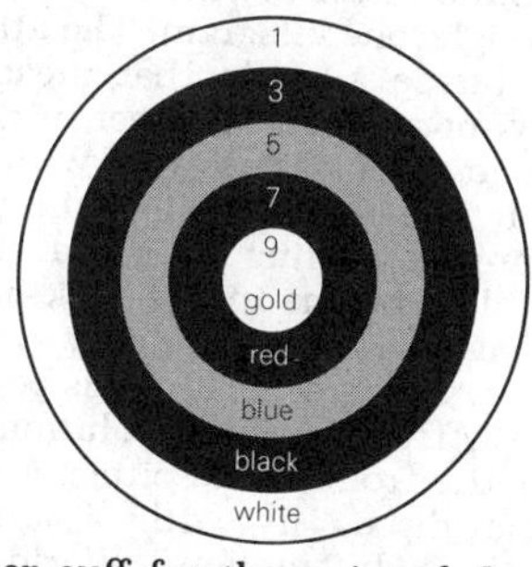

In the United States Men's National Championships, the rules decree that each archer shoot off two rounds, the American and the York. In the American Round, each archer lets fly a total of 90 shots: 30 arrows from a distance of 60 yards, 30 more from 50 yards, and 30 from 40 yards. In the York Round the archer fires off 144 shots: 72 arrows from 100 yards, 48 from 80 yards, and 24 from 60 yards.

The target has five rings counting the bull's-eye. An arrow in the outside ring counts as one point; in the next inner ring, three points; the next inner one, five points; the ring next to the bull's-eye, seven points; and the bull's-eye nine points. If an arrow hits on the line dividing two rings, the higher number is allowed. The winner is the archer whose total points for the two rounds is highest.

Women also fire off two rounds in their national championships, the Columbia and the National. In the Columbia Round, 24 arrows each are fired from 50, 40, and 30 yards. In the National, 48 arrows are fired from 60 yards and 24 from 50 yards.

Boys and girls can compete in the Junior American Round. They shoot a single round, consisting of 30 arrows each from 50, 40, and 30 yards, a total of 90 arrows.

Trap- and skeet shooting. More than a century ago, British landowners amused themselves by shooting at birds. These sportsmen, called "high hats," released captured birds from their high-hat prisons and fired as the birds flew away. When the bird supply diminished, a new method of shooting was devised: substitute "pigeons" made of clay were released from boxlike spring contraptions for the shooter to shatter. In the late 1870's the Amateur Trapshooting Association was formed, and since 1900 that governing body has sponsored the annual Grand American Handicap in the United States to determine the American champion. Shooters aim at 100 targets from distances between 16 and 25 yards.

Skeet shooting is a variation of trapshooting. It got its name through the efforts of the *National Sportsman,* which sponsored a contest to find a name for what had been called "round the clock shooting." Mrs. Gertrude Hurlbutt of Dayton, Montana, submitted the word "skeet," from the Scandinavian word meaning shoot.

In skeet there are two target houses located 42 yards apart. Targets are hurled at different angles from each house over a center post between the two houses. Seven shooting stations are located along a curved line resembling the half face of a clock, with another station in the center of the circle halfway between the target houses. Shooters fire shotguns from each station at targets thrown alternately from each house. Some targets come out in pairs, one from each house and at different angles. The shooter tries to hit both.

Pistol shooting. Pistols are seldom used for hunting. They are used for target shooting, however. Events include the Rapid-Fire Pistol from 25 meters and the Free Pistol from 50 meters. Pistol shooting is also part of the modern Pentathlon.

Track and Field

The first known running champion in Olympic competition was a Greek named Coroebus. In the year 776 B.C. he won a *one-stade* race, the distance measuring slightly more than 200 yards. That was the only "track and field" event at that time, but over the years other contests were added—even for runners wearing armor.

Modern track and field meets include long and short footraces, both over a flat track and over hurdles, and a variety of throwing and jumping events. One overall event, the *decathlon,* asks an athlete to compete in a series of ten events that include all the major categories. The winner of the decathlon is the athlete whose overall performance is best. The decathlon is one of the most demanding tests in the world of sports.

Track events. Track events consist of running various distances; they can be short straightaway dashes down a track, or very long races, such as marathons, over an outdoor course. A variation on the shorter races puts a series of obstacles called *hurdles* into each lane; the runner must leap over them. Another variation is the *relay race,* in which four sprinters each run one-quarter of the race, passing a baton to the next runner in turn.

The marathon is the longest race in competitive sports. Runners cover a distance of 26 miles 385 yards, moving through city streets, over country roads, and on to the finish line, which, in the Olympics, is in the stadium itself. The name of the race comes from the ancient Greek city of Marathon, and the distance is said to be that between Marathon and Athens. In 400 B.C., Athenian troops were in battle at Marathon. A messenger named Pheidippides was sent to Athens with news of their victory. After announcing the news, the exhausted runner fell dead.

Other principal long-distance races include the 5000- and 10,000-meter runs. These distances (equal to about 3.1 and 6.2 miles) require great stamina and resistance to pain. Among the great athletes to win at long distances are Paavo Nurmi of Finland (1920's), Emil Zatopek of Czechoslovakia (1950's), and Akebe Bikila of Ethiopia (1960's). Distance runners seem often to be solitary people, quiet and stoic.

Middle distance races include the 1500-meter run, sometimes called the "metric mile," and the mile run, which has been an event of great interest in U.S. and British meets for decades. The mile run is about 120 yards longer than the 1500-meter run.

During the early 1950's, track fans speculated on whether any athlete would ever run the mile in less than four minutes. World record time had been decreasing in that direction, but the four-minute mark seemed a barrier. But in May, 1954, Roger Bannister of England ran the mile in a meet at Oxford in 3:59.4. Within ten years, sub-four-minute miles became common in world-class competition.

Middle distance races also include the 800-meter and 880-yard (half mile) runs.

Among the most exciting events in all sports are the dashes, races over short distances that require sudden and intense bursts of speed from the runners. The most avidly followed are the 100-meter and 100-yard dashes. World-class sprinters cover 100 meters in ten seconds and 100 yards in just over nine seconds.

Dashes also include the 200-meter and 220-yard. The 400-meter and 440-yard (quarter mile) races are sometimes considered dashes and sometimes middle-distance runs.

Track events also include the hurdles. A hurdle is a vertical obstacle that the athlete must leap over without losing speed. High hurdles are three feet six inches high, low hurdles are two feet six inches high (heights differ slightly in women's competition). The hurdles are placed at regular intervals along the track. Distances of the major hurdles races are 110 meters (100 meters for women) and 400 meters. The equivalent races in conventional measure are the 120-yard and 440-yard hurdles.

Field events. At most track meets, field events take place on the infield (often a football field) around which the track runs.

The discus. Discus throwing dates back to the Olympics of 708 B.C. A discus is circular in shape, made of wood with metal plates set into the sides. It is thick at its center and tapers to the rim. A standard discus for men weighs two kilograms (just under four and a half pounds); for women, the discus used weighs one kilogram. The athlete stands inside a circle that measures slightly more than eight feet in diameter. The discus is thrown with one hand; it is held flat against the palm with fingers curling over the edges. The athlete begins in the back of the circle. After a few preliminary swings, he moves forward, turning his body as he goes. After two full revolutions, he is near the front of the circle, and he lets the discus fly with a straight across-the-body motion. World-class discus throwers can achieve distances of more than 200 feet.

Hammer throw. Throwing a heavy weight, such as a sledge hammer, was considered a fine sport by Englishmen in the 16th century. The hammer throw has since become one of the Olympic events.

UPI

UPI

The modern hammer is a round ball made of brass or iron, to which is attached a steel handle, nearly four feet in length. The hammer weighs 16 pounds. Standing inside a seven-foot circle, grasping the handle with both hands, the thrower begins to swing the hammer around his body; then, with a sweeping movement, he lets it fly.

Shot put. Shot putting began many centuries ago when soldiers staged cannon ball throwing contests among themselves. Like the hammer and discus throws, it is executed from a throwing circle.

The modern shot is a brass or iron ball weighing 16 pounds. The sphere is held at the base of the fingers with the hand resting at the hollow of the neck. The athlete executes a 180-degree turn and thrusts rather than throws the sphere from in front of the shoulder. World-class athletes can put the shot more than 60 feet. Women also compete in shot put events, but their sphere weighs only eight pounds.

Javelin. Javelin throwing began many centuries ago, when soldiers wagered on how far they could throw their spears. The modern javelin weighs slightly more than one pound twelve ounces for men, and about one pound five ounces for women. It has a metal tip and a cord grip that the thrower must grasp when throwing.

Holding the javelin with one hand, the thrower takes a running start and with an overhand motion lets it fly. The metal tip must touch the ground first. Measurement is made from the throwing line to the spot where the tip makes contact with the ground.

High jump. High jumping dates back to the days of early Greece, although there is no record of the event having been included in the ancient Olympics. In modern track and field meets, the jumper takes a running start and tries to clear a horizontal bar that is raised higher each time it is successfully cleared. In the 1960's, two innovations made all other techniques of high jumping obsolete. One was an air bag substituting for the sawdust in the landing pit. The other was the introduction of the "Fosbury Flop." Under former standard procedure, the jumper would take his or her running start, approach the bar with the side of the body, and leap up on the inside foot. Then the body would "roll" over the bar. Dick Fosbury, an American jumper, introduced a new technique that would have been outlawed in earlier Olympic meets. Fosbury ran up to the bar and took off on his outside foot. As he rose, he turned his back and went over the bar head first, with his back to the bar; he landed on his shoulder blades. His seven-foot-four-and-a-half-inch leap was a new Olympic record. Other jumpers, noting his success, quickly adopted the new method.

Long jump. Long jumping dates back to the ancient Olympic Games. There is a record of a Spartan athlete named Chionis who leaped more than 23 feet in the year 656 B.C. During the 1800's, jumpers were permitted to carry weights in their hands in order to build up momentum, but that is no longer permitted. In this event, the jumper has a running start up to the takeoff, a slab of wood set into the ground. If the jumper's foot crosses the farthest edge of the takeoff, it is a foul. The jumper lands in a sand pit, and the measurement taken extends from takeoff wood to the nearest imprint of his rear foot. The world record jump is more than 29 feet.

Pole vault. Pole vaulting probably evolved from pole jumping, a pastime popular in certain sections of England for the purpose of leaping over sections of marshy ground. It did not become a competitive sport until the late 1800's.

In modern pole vaulting, the jumper, gripping his pole, races down the approach run, which is not less than 120 feet long. The pole is shoved into a wedge-shaped box near the crossbar and the jumper's momentum helps him to rise. He pulls himself as high as he can as the pole rises, then pushes it away and soars over the crossbar.

Until World War II, poles were usually made of bamboo and heights of 15 feet were considered outstanding. The introduction of fiberglass poles in the early 1960's sent jumpers soaring over 18 feet as the flexible material seemed to whip the jumpers over the bar. Air bags set on platforms under the crossbar reduce the distance the jumper must fall and reduce the chance of serious injury.

Triple jump. Another jumping event in international meets is the triple jump, or the hop, step, and jump. The athlete gains momentum in an approach run as in the broad jump. In the triple jump, however, he lands on hard ground on his takeoff foot, leaps ahead a second time, lands on his opposite foot, and leaps a third time. The combined length of the three jumps is measured. The triple jump is not an event in most U.S. meets.

TRACK AND FIELD: *track events include dashes* (far left), *runs for longer distance, and hurdles* (near left). *Field events include the discus throw* (below left) *and other throwing events, and jumping competitions such as the high jump* (below right).

THE OLYMPICS

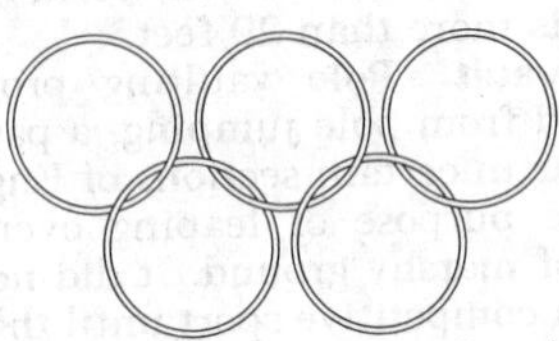

According to legend, Hercules was commanded by the gods to clean out the huge stables of Augeas, king of the Greek city of Elis. Hercules accomplished the task in one day by diverting the direction of two rivers so that they flowed through the stables. To celebrate, Hercules began the Olympic Games, in honor of Zeus, the chief Greek god.

The cities of Pisa and Elis each claimed to have created the idea of the Olympics in the Olympia valley. In 884 B.C. a truce was declared so that the games could be held in peace. Emissaries were sent to inform others of the truce; they bore a message engraved on a metal disc with the words in five circles. The five linked circles are still the Olympic symbol.

No records were kept of the earliest Olympic Games. Indeed, the whole affair lasted just one day and consisted of a race of about 200 yards (one *stade*). The first champion was a young cook, Coroebus of Elis, who was the victor in 776 B.C.

In time, additional events were added, including boxing, wrestling, chariot racing, jumping, discus and javelin throwing, and races for runners wearing armor. The games took on a carnival atmosphere.

Olympic winners were considered heroes. The crowning achievement was to win the pentathlon, which consisted of five events: jumping, foot racing, discus throwing, javelin throwing, and wrestling. Whoever won three of the first four events was the champion; if no one won three, wrestling was the deciding event.

A particularly vicious "sport" of the later games was called *pancratium;* it was a fierce combination of boxing and wrestling. There were no holds barred. During one match a boxer named Arrachion had a toehold on his opponent, who gripped Arrachion's throat and began to choke him. With one last effort Arrachion twisted his opponent's leg severely, causing him to raise one arm in defeat. At that instant Arrachion choked to death. He had won the match but lost his life. Perhaps the greatest of all pancratium champions was Theagenes of Thasos, who was reputed to have won a total of 1400 matches.

As the Olympic Games grew in popularity, contestants came from Rome, Asia, and Africa. The games became a travesty. More and more professional athletes were entered. By the time Rome conquered the Greek cities, the Olympics were more spectacle than athletic event.

At last, in 394 A.D., the games were outlawed by the Christian emperor of Rome, Theodosius I. For almost 16 centuries the Olympics were forgotten. Only legends and poems remained to tell of the ancient glory of the games, the high ideals, the great champions.

Between 1875 and 1881 German archaeologists uncovered in Greece the area that had once been the site of the temples and the stadium. One visitor to the excavation was a French scholar named Baron Pierre de Coubertin. Coubertin's suggestion that the Olympics be started again finally was implemented, and the first "new" Olympiad was held in 1896 in Athens.

An "unofficial" team represented the United States. A crowd of 50,000 saw the lighting of the torch, which had been carried by relays of runners from the Olympia valley to the Greek capital. Athletes from 13 nations marched into the stadium and were greeted by the cheering throng, as a choir sang the Olympic hymn. The U.S. athletes won most of the events; however, the honor of Greece was upheld when a 25-year-old country shepherd named Spiridon Loues won the great marathon race.

After the success of the 1896 Olympics, there was considerable sentiment to hold all future games in Athens, but Baron de Coubertin believed the site should be changed for each Olympiad. Paris was chosen for 1900, then St. Louis in the United States in 1904. A special Olympics was held in 1906 in Athens and the regular Olympics in 1908 were in London.

The 1912 Olympics took place in Stockholm, Sweden. Many additional events had been added, including swimming, various racing distances, yachting, and the shot put.

CULVER PICTURES

SONJA HENIE

UPI

JESSE OWENS

REUTERS/BETTMANN NEWSPHOTOS

FLORENCE GRIFFITH JOYNER

Also, women competed for the first time.

The 1916 games were never held because of World War I and its effects. In 1924 the winter Olympics were begun at Chamonix, France, with events in hockey, skiing, and figure skating. The summer games were held in Paris. The Olympics had become a truly international event, with two sections of the games (winter and summer sports) held in different cities every four years. They were held every fourth year thereafter except for 1944, during World War II. In 1980 the United States did not participate in the summer Olympics, held in Moscow, as a protest against Russia's invasion of Afghanistan. Many nations of the world did send teams.

The modern Olympics have produced numerous athletes who have won everlasting fame. Among them are:

- Jim Thorpe of the United States, a Sac and Fox Indian who attended Carlisle College, a school for Indians. In 1912 Thorpe won both the pentathlon and decathlon events; however, he was deprived of his medals when it was discovered that he had played professional baseball, thus losing his amateur standing.
- Jesse Owens of the United States. Of the 66-man American track and field squad for the 1936 Olympics in Berlin, Germany, ten were blacks. These ten outscored every other national team, winning a total of eight gold, three silver, and two bronze medals. Owens himself won three golds. Adolf Hitler, the leader of Germany, believed black people were an inferior race, and refused to award the medals to black Americans personally.
- Sonja Henie of Norway. The first of a series of outstanding figure skaters, "the Norwegian doll" won the gold medal in her event in 1928, 1932, and 1936 before turning professional and becoming a movie star.
- Emil Zatopek of Czechoslovakia. In 1952 Zatopek broke three running records: the 10,000 meter, the 5000 meter, and the marathon.
- Mark Spitz of the United States. In 1972 Spitz broke all previous records by winning seven gold medals in swimming events.
- Olga Korbut of the Soviet Union and Nadia Comaneci of Romania, two of the world's greatest gymnasts. Korbut won two gold medals in the 1972 games, Comaneci won three gold, one silver, and one bronze medal in 1976.
- The 1980 United States hockey team. This squad, made up of amateurs from college teams, scored one of the great upsets in Olympic history, defeating the heavily favored national team of the Soviet Union, and going on to win a gold medal.
- Florence Griffith Joyner of the United States. In 1988 Griffith Joyner became the first woman to win four Olympic running medals—three gold and one silver.
- Katarina Witt of East Germany. Witt was the first woman since Sonja Henie to defend the women's Olympic title in figure skating. She won gold medals in 1984 and 1988.
- Greg Louganis of the United States. Louganis was the first diver to win the same gold medals in successive Olympics. He won golds in 1984 and 1988 in the 3-meter springboard and 10-meter platform dive.

SITES OF MODERN OLYMPIC GAMES

Year	Summer Games	Winter Games
1896	Athens, Greece	
1900	Paris, France	
1904	St. Louis, U.S.A.	
1906	Athens, Greece	
1908	London, England	
1912	Stockholm, Sweden	
1920	Antwerp, Belgium	
1924	Paris, France	Chamonix, France
1928	Amsterdam, The Netherlands	St. Moritz, Switzerland
1932	Los Angeles, U.S.A.	Lake Placid, U.S.A.
1936	Berlin, Germany	Garmisch-Partenkirchen, Germany
1948	London, England	St. Moritz, Switzerland
1952	Helsinki, Finland	Oslo, Norway
1956	Melbourne, Australia	Cortina d'Ampezzo, Italy
1960	Rome, Italy	Squaw Valley, U.S.A.
1964	Tokyo, Japan	Innsbruck, Austria
1968	Mexico City, Mexico	Grenoble, France
1972	Munich, Germany	Sapporo, Japan
1976	Montreal, Canada	Innsbruck, Austria
1980	Moscow, U.S.S.R.	Lake Placid, U.S.A.
1984	Los Angeles, U.S.A.	Sarajevo, Yugoslavia
1988	Seoul, S. Korea	Calgary, Canada
1992	Barcelona, Spain	Albertville, France

UPI

MARK SPITZ

UPI

U.S. HOCKEY TEAM

Wall and Racket Sports

In the Middle Ages, monasteries and castles had courtyards, outdoor areas surrounded by buildings. These courtyards became the playing areas for a whole family of sports that involved hitting balls against walls or back and forth from one player to another.

The back-and-forth court games include tennis and its later cousins, badminton and Ping-Pong (table tennis). The wall games include handball, squash, and jai alai.

Tennis. Evidence exists that the ancient Egyptians, Arabians, Greeks, and other peoples played some sort of game using a ball and an object to hit it with, but whatever rules they might have adopted are lost. In the Middle Ages, monks in European monasteries developed a game in monastery courtyards that used both a net and the surrounding walls. The game, now known as court tennis, is still played in English-speaking countries, but it requires an elaborate special court.

During the 1860's and 1870's there was a burgeoning of interest in sports, but most of them were for men only. People wanted a game that both sexes could enjoy. Croquet was tried but proved to be too slow. Then some young men decided to try court tennis on the croquet lawns, using court tennis rackets and a hollow rubber ball. The new sport seemed to catch on, and in 1873 British army major Walter C. Wingfield published a book of rules. Most of the rules have been changed, but Major Wingfield helped popularize the new game, known as lawn tennis. Mary Ewing Outerbridge learned the game from her British friends and brought it to America in 1874. Soon afterward the United States Lawn Tennis Association (USLTA) was founded. Rules and equipment were standardized. The game assumed international importance in 1900 when Dwight F. Davis, a Harvard student, organized the Davis Cup matches, pitting the best players of America and England against each other. In 1923 the Wightman Cup was offered in American-English women's competition. Professional tennis began in 1926 when promotor C. C. Pyle organized a tour of the United States; he featured the French champion, Suzanne Lenglen. However, the game was mostly for amateurs until 1960, when Texas oil millionaire Lamar Hunt organized the World Championship Tennis Group (WTC) and many outstanding players left the amateur ranks. Today, nearly all world-class players are professionals.

Rules of the game. Tennis balls must be two and a half to two and five-eighths inches in diameter and weigh two to two and one-sixteenth ounces. The ball is made of rubber and covered with a wooly layer of synthetic fiber. It is hollow and inflated to give it a "live" high bounce. There are few restrictions concerning rackets. They may be made of wood or aluminum; most weigh between 11 and 15 ounces. They are tightly strung with nylon or animal gut, which gives the strings their "bounce."

The court is marked out so that it can be used for singles or doubles play. For singles, the section of the court used measures 78 by 27 feet; for doubles, the width is 36 feet. A net, dividing the court in half, stands three feet six inches high. A *service line* crosses the court on each side, 21 feet from the net; the *center service line* runs down the center of the court touching both service lines. The court surface may be of concrete, clay, grass, or one of several synthetic substances. Different surfaces have different playing qualities and they may affect the speed and strategy of the game.

The scoring of tennis seems unaccountable to most beginners. A player wins a *point* when his or her opponent hits the ball into the net or out of bounds. Four points usually win a *game.* The points are named as if they were being scored on a clock: the first point is "15," the second "30." The third point, which one would expect to be "45," is "40" instead, probably because it is shorter and easier to say. The fourth point has no number score; it is simply called "game."

There are two further complications to game scoring. The first is that in tennis, the word for zero is "love." If player A scores the first two points in a game, she leads "30-love." The second complication is that a player must win a game by a margin of two points. If player A is leading 40-30, and her opponent wins the next point, the game is "at deuce," which means it is tied.

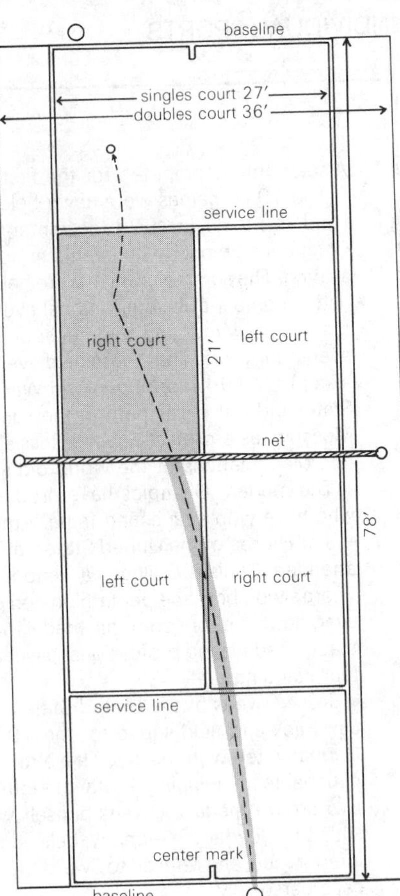

THE SERVE: *the first serve of a game is from the right side of the server's court into the left service area* (shaded). *The second serve is from the server's left into the right service area. The side then continues to alternate.*

EARLY TENNIS: *the game began as a gentle pastime on the same lawn that often accommodated croquet. Women's dress did not encourage acrobatics.*

CULVER PICTURES

LEADING WINNERS OF THE BRITISH NATIONALS

MEN'S SINGLES

Won 7 times:	Willie Renshaw, 1881, '82, '83, '84, '85, '86, '89
Won 5 times:	Laurie Doherty, 1902, '03, '04, '05, '06
	Björn Borg, 1976, '77, '78, '79, '80
Won 4 times:	Reggie Doherty, 1897, '98, '99, 1900
	Tony Wilding, 1910, '11, '12, '13
	Rod Laver, 1961, '62, '68, '69
Won 3 times:	Wilfred Baddeley, 1891, '92, '95
	Arthur Gore, 1901, '08, '09
	Bill Tilden, 1920, '21, '30
	Fred Perry, 1934, '35, '36
	John Newcombe, 1967, '70, '71
	John McEnroe, 1981, '83, '84

WOMEN'S SINGLES

Won 8 times:	Helen Wills Moody, 1927, '28, '29, '30, '32, '33, '35, '38
	Martina Navratilova, 1978, '79, '82, '83, '84, '85, '86, '87
Won 7 times:	Dorothea Douglas Lambert Chambers, 1903, '04, '06, '10, '11, '13, '14
Won 6 times:	Blanche Bingley Hillyard, 1886, '89, '94, '97, '99, 1900
	Suzanne Lenglen, 1919, '20, '21, '22, '23, '25
	Billie Jean King, 1966, '67, '68, '72, '73, '75
Won 5 times:	Lottie Dod, 1887, '88, '91, '92, '93
	Charlotte Cooper Sterry, 1895, '96, '98, 1901, '08
Won 4 times:	Louise Brough, 1948, '49, '50, '55
Won 3 times:	Maureen Connolly, 1952, '53, '54
	Maria Bueno, 1959, '60, '64
	Margaret Smith Court, 1963, '65, '70
	Chris Evert Lloyd, 1974, '76, '81

LEADING WINNERS OF THE U.S. NATIONALS

MEN'S SINGLES

Won 7 times:	Richard Sears, 1881, '82, '83, '84, '85, '86, '87
	Bill Larned, 1901, '02, '07, '08, '09, '10, '11
	Bill Tilden, 1920, '21, '22, '23, '24, '25, '29
Won 5 times:	Jimmy Connors, 1974, '76, '78, '82, '83
Won 4 times:	Robert Wrenn, 1893, '94, '96, '97
	John McEnroe 1979, '80, '81, '84
Won 3 times:	Oliver Campbell, 1890, '91, '92
	Malcolm Whitman, 1898, '99, 1900
	Fred Perry, 1933, '34, '36
	Ivan Lendl, 1985, '86, '87

WOMEN'S SINGLES

Won 7 times:	Molla Bjurstedt Mallory, 1915, '16, '18, '20, '21, '22, '26
	Helen Wills Moody, 1923, '24, '25, '27, '28, '29, '31
Won 6 times:	Chris Evert Lloyd, 1975, '76, '77, '78, '80, '82
Won 5 times:	Margaret Smith Court, 1962, '65, '69, '70, '73
Won 4 times:	Elisabeth Moore, 1896, 1901, '03, '05
	Hazel Hotchkiss Wightman, 1909, '10, '11, '19
	Helen Jacobs, 1932, '33, '34, '35
	Alice Marble, 1936, '38, '39, '40
	Pauline Betz, 1942, '43, '44, '46
	Maria Bueno, 1959, '63, '64, '66
	Billie Jean King, 1967, '71, '72, '74
	Martina Navratilova, 1983, '84, '86, '87
Won 3 times:	Juliette Atkinson, 1895, '97, '98
	Mary K. Browne, 1912, '13, '14
	Margaret Osborne duPont, 1948, '49, '50
	Maureen Connolly, 1951, '52, '53

UPI

CHRIS EVERT LLOYD

UPI

JOHN McENROE

UPI

BJÖRN BORG

After that, no further number scores are used. If player A wins the next point, the score is "advantage A." If A wins a second point in a row, she wins the game, but if her opponent wins the next point, the score is "deuce" once again. A game may go to deuce any number of times.

A player must win at least six games to win a *set*. Traditionally, the "deuce" rule also applied to games. If a set was tied at five games all, one player had to win two games in a row to take the set. In the 1940's, one doubles set was won by a score of 49-47.

To keep a set from lasting too long, a tie breaker was introduced in the 1970's. If a set is tied at six games all, a special game consisting of nine or twelve points is played. The winner of this tie breaker game wins the set.

In men's competition, the player who wins three sets wins the *match*. In women's competition, two sets wins.

The game begins after the toss or spin of a racket to determine who serves first. The server serves for one full game. He stands with both feet behind the baseline, to the right of the center line, tosses the ball into the air and hits the ball over the net into the opposite service area. If his service hits the net or goes out of bounds, a *fault* is called. Two faults in succession loses a point for the server. A ball hitting the net but bouncing into the correct service area is a *let*, and no fault is assessed. After the point is completed, the server serves from the left of the center line.

A service or any other return must be hit on the fly or after only one bounce. A return into the net or out of bounds loses the point.

Tennis greats. The earliest tennis stars were British. But by the 1920's the United States was a tennis power. America's Bill Tilden was the greatest star of that period. He was challenged only by Helen Wills Moody, also an American; her dominance of women's tennis has never been equaled. Among later stars were Don Budge, Jack Kramer, "Pancho" Gonzales, and Maureen Connolly. During the 1960's, Australians Ken Rosewall and Rod Laver dominated the game. In recent years, tennis has become a multi-million dollar business, and its stars, Bjorn Borg, Chris Evert, John McEnroe, Tracy Austin, and many others, have become international celebrities.

Badminton. Badminton, originating in India, was called "poona" and was brought home by British army officers during the 1870's. The game got its name because it was first played on exhibition at Badminton, the country estate of the Duke of Beaufort. It was introduced into the United States in the early 1900's and became quite popular. The game is relatively simple and requires very little room outdoors. However, since the *shuttlecock* is so light and can be blown around by any breeze, tournaments are usually played indoors.

A badminton playing area is about 30 by 60 feet. There are no rules about rackets, but they are light, usually around five ounces. The traditional shuttlecock ("bird") has feathers stuck into its cork head. Modern birds have rubber heads and plastic "feathers." The net is strung so that it is five feet at its highest point. Badminton may be played either singles or doubles, and 15 points wins a game (11 in some women's matches).

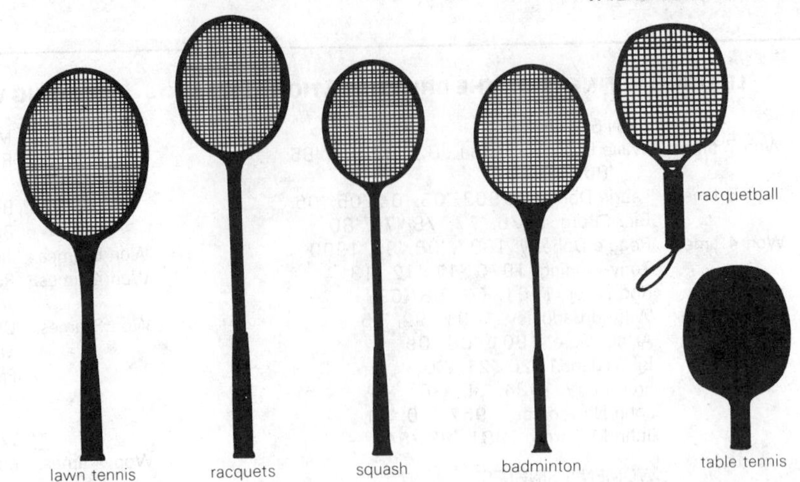

RACKETS *for wall and net sports differ in size, shape, weight, and construction.*

Table tennis (ping-pong). In 1899 an engineer named James Gibb, who was also a founder of the Amateur Athletic Union (AAU), fixed a piece of string across a table and hit a small rubber ball over it to other members of his family. Later he found some small celluloid balls and discovered they were more fun to use.

Table tennis is played on a table measuring 9 feet 5 inches long by 6 feet wide and 30 inches high. A net 6 inches high bisects the table. The ball is made of celluloid and rackets (really paddles) are made of wood covered with a layer of stippled rubber, or foam rubber. Ping-Pong can be played singles or doubles.

The server hits the ball so that it bounces first on his or her side of the table, clears the net, and bounces on the other side. Failure to return a shot—hitting the ball into the net or off the table—gives a point to the opposition. Service is alternated after five serves, and a game is 21 points. If the score is tied at 20-all, the service is alternated after each serve, and a player must win two points in a row to win the game.

Paddle tennis. In 1924 Dr. Frank P. Beal of New York City invented paddle tennis in order to teach children to play lawn tennis easily. He cut down the size of the court, used paddles instead of rackets, and introduced a lively sponge ball. In 1938 Murray Geller, an attorney from Brooklyn, New York, changed Beal's game by making the court larger (it is now 50 by 20 feet), substituting a deadened tennis ball, and outlawing the use of the overhand smash. An underhand serve was adopted. The scoring system is about the same as for lawn tennis, although no tie breaker is used and a player must win two out of three sets.

PING-PONG *became a part of international diplomacy in 1972 when an American team made a visit to the People's Republic of China.*

WIDE WORLD

Handball. The Irish are credited with inventing handball in the tenth century, although man probably batted a ball with his hand long before that. Because the hand was used, the Irish called it *fives.* The game was relatively obscure until the 19th century, when a skilled player from Tipperary named Meham Baggs showed the spins, curves, and rebounds that were possible. When another Irish handball star named Phil Casey came to New York in the 1880's, he spread the game by giving lessons and building courts. Today, one-wall handball is played by children wherever they can find a suitable wall and a ball to bounce against it. Three-wall and four-wall handball is much more difficult. Championship matches are sponsored by the Amateur Athletic Union (AAU).

Handball is played with a hard rubber ball that weighs 2.3 ounces and measures $1\frac{7}{8}$ inches in diameter. Five-finger gloves are worn to protect the hands from the ball's impact. The game may be played by two, three ("cutthroat"), or four (doubles). Only the server can score points. In four-wall handball, the server drops the ball between the short and service lines and strikes the ball on the bounce, hitting it against the front wall. The ball must rebound behind the short line either before or after striking one of the side walls. The ball must be returned by the server's opponent to the front wall directly, or after having bounced off a side wall or the ceiling. If the return fails, a point is scored by the server.

FLORIDA NEWS BUREAU

JAI ALAI, *the fastest of all racket sports, is played with a special curved basketlike racket called* a cesta. *The hard ball can travel at more than 100 miles per hour.*

UPI

VASSILY ALEKSEYEV *of the Soviet Union broke records in the super-heavyweight class.*

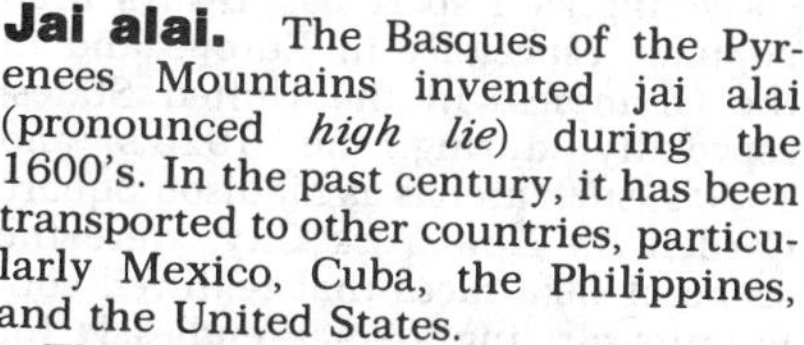

Jai alai. The Basques of the Pyrenees Mountains invented jai alai (pronounced *high lie*) during the 1600's. In the past century, it has been transported to other countries, particularly Mexico, Cuba, the Philippines, and the United States.

The game resembles handball to a great extent, in that it is a multi-walled game. Players use a curved straw basket called a *cesta* over one hand. The ball, called the *pelota,* is made of rubber with a layer of nylon thread and coats of specially hardened goatskin. Rebounding from a wall, the pelota zooms back at speeds of 150 miles an hour or more. It is caught and thrown back against the wall using the cesta. The return is made in one fluid motion.

Squash. Squash was invented by students of Harrow School in England during the 19th century. They called their game squash racquets. In the United States, it is called squash tennis, or just squash. Although the rules are about the same, Americans use a bouncier ball and a lighter racket, making for a livelier, faster game. The National Squash Tennis Association governs the game in America.

A squash tennis ball resembles a lawn tennis ball. The racket is also similar to that used in tennis, except that it is somewhat shorter.

A regulation squash singles court measures 32 feet long, $18\frac{1}{2}$ feet wide, and 16 feet high at the front wall. A *floor service line* is marked 22 feet from the front wall, and a line bisects the back court in half, much as it would a tennis court. A *front-wall service line* is marked $6\frac{1}{2}$ feet above the floor, and all serves must hit above it. Returns must strike above a strip of metal called the *telltale,* 17 inches above the floor. A score of 15 points usually wins.

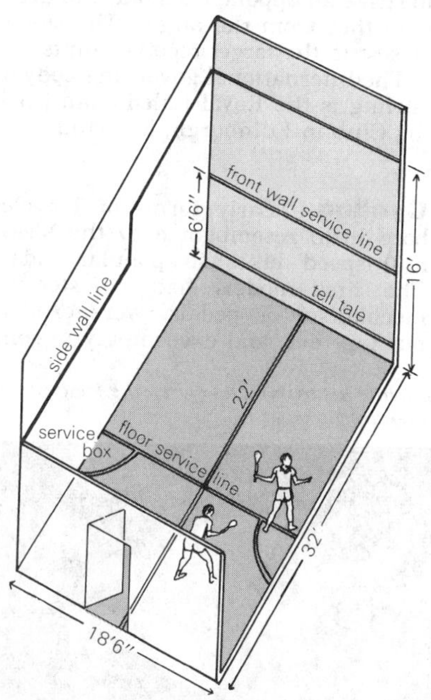

Racquetball. Racquetball is a combination of handball and tennis. The court is a standard four-wall handball court; the racket is like the one used in tennis, but the handle is much shorter. The ball is extremely lively. A game is won when 21 points are scored, and two out of three games wins the match.

Weight lifting

Weight lifting as a sport began in central Europe early in the 1800's. It quickly spread all over the world, becoming an Olympic sport when the Games were revived in 1896. In 1920 the International Weight Lifting Federation was established.

There are three basic lifts in the sport: the *snatch,* the *clean and jerk,* and the *press.* In the snatch, the weighted bar is brought overhead in one continuous movement and held there for the count of two by the referee. In the clean and jerk, the barbell is first brought to chest level and then raised overhead. The press is similar to the clean and jerk, except that the barbell must be raised overhead by arm strength alone, without the accompanying heave by the legs and body. Scores are determined by the weights lifted in each event and the poundage totaled. As in boxing, contestants compete in their own body weight class.

A new wrinkle in weight lifting was introduced in 1972 in the form of power lifting. As governed by the International Power Lifting Federation, three new tests were devised: *two hands bench press, deep knee bend* or *squat,* and *two hands dead lift.* Also, body development is judged. A large number of American universities hold power lifting competitions sanctioned by the Amateur Athletic Union (AAU).

Among the great weight lifting champions of the past are Louis Cyr of Canada, Eugene Sandow and Arthur Saxon of Germany, Paul Anderson of America, and Vassily Alekseyev of the Soviet Union.

Other Individual Sports

DEN HANNA/PHOTO RESEARCHERS

CYCLING: *races along the steeply banked wooden tracks are popular in Europe and have been an Olympic event.*

Croquet. Although croquet is thought of as an English game, it was actually first played in France. The word croquet is derived from the French word *croc,* which means crooked stick. It is a game that can pit one player against another or be played by teams. British rules are different from American rules.

The American game is played with a *mallet,* a wooden stick with a hammerlike head that weighs between two and three-quarter and three and three-quarter pounds. The ball is made of compressed cork or plastic; balls of several colors are used.

The object of the game is to drive a ball through wire hoops set into the ground in the correct sequence, moving first in one direction, then doubling back in reverse sequence. The game is over when the winner's ball hits a wooden peg behind the last wire hoop.

Curling. Although curling has few devotees in the United States, it is a popular sport in Scotland, Holland, Canada, and other countries. It is quite old; a pond in Scotland that was drained revealed a curling stone dated 1551.

Curling can be called a variation on the Italian game boccie, or the game of shuffleboard, except that curling is played on ice. Curlers slide a large stone, fitted with a handle, toward a fixed target, using a slight twist in the delivery that causes it to rotate or "curl" as it moves. As the stone leaves the curler's hand, a teammate, using a broom, sweeps the ice ahead of the stone to remove stray particles of ice. This adds to the distance the stone will travel. The curler tries to avoid the stones of his teammates, but hopes to strike an opponent's stone and drive it farther from the target. The stones closest to the target receive points.

The international governing body of curling is the Royal Caledonian Curling Club in Edinburgh, Scotland.

Cycling. Early forms of bicycles bore little resemblance to the sleek, multispeed bikes so popular today. The first models had no steering mechanism or pedals, were crudely put together, and exceedingly uncomfortable to ride. Several of the models were nicknamed "boneshakers."

By 1886 the "safety cycle" was introduced. It featured a diamond frame and chain drive, a design that is, in many respects, the same one used today. In many countries, the bicycle is a primary means of transportation.

Cycling as a sport has always been popular, especially in Europe and in the Olympics. In the United States, especially during the 1920's and 1930's, such arenas as Madison Square Garden, in New York City, were the scene of bike races that featured contestants circling a track endlessly for six full days. Bicycling has also been an Olympic sport since 1894. Several cycling events are featured, including road races, sprints, and competition for bicycles built for two.

Fencing. The use of a sword to kill or maim an opponent dates back thousands of years.

Fencing as a sport seems to have begun in the 1200's in Frankfurt, Germany, with the establishment of the Marxbruder (Fencing) Guild, but the swords used were heavy and clumsy double-bladed affairs with no hand guards. The lighter, more useful rapier, was invented in Italy.

In modern sport fencing, three different types of weapons are used: the foil, épée, and saber. The most popular, the foil, is a limber steel weapon, approximately 43 inches long and weighing about 17 ounces. The épée, also a pointed dueling sword, is a little heavier and more rigid. The saber has cutting edges on the front and back.

Fencers wear protective equipment, including face masks, gloves, and padded jackets or vests. Hits are scored when the weapon (which has a "button" on its tip to prevent injury) touches any part of the body, from the collar to the groin to the hip bone in back. There are eight different attack points and a parry (defense) to counter each of them.

CURLING: *the curler slides the stone along the ice, while his teammates sweep the ice clear in front of it so that it will travel on a true path to the target.*

UPI

Horseshoe pitching. About 2000 years ago, Greek and Roman armies began to shoe their horses. When the crude pieces of iron were worn out, they were discarded, but they were promptly salvaged by camp followers who tried to toss them as they would a discus. Eventually, the "game" was modified so that the shoes were pitched at a stake in the ground. A kind of army game was born; as peasants also began to shoe their horses, they picked up the game and made it a pastime.

Horseshoe pitching is a very simple game and almost anyone of any age can become proficient with practice. It can be played by two people or four, the latter method utilizing teams. Each player tosses two horseshoes at a metal stake 40 feet away. A "ringer" (a shoe that encircles the stake) counts for three points; a "leaner" (a shoe that leans against the stake) counts for two points. A shoe within six inches of the stake counts for one point. Tournament games consist of 50 points.

The National Horseshoe Pitchers of the United States governs professional horseshoe pitching, while the Amateur Athletic Union (AAU) supervises amateur events.

Roller skating. The first practical four-wheel roller skates were designed by an American named James Plimpton in 1863. A few years later Plimpton opened the first public roller rink in Newport, Rhode Island, but skating did not really strike the public fancy until 1884, when ball-bearing skates werre introduced. Before long, every major city on both sides of the Atlantic Ocean boasted at least one roller rink. Today, roller skating has become both a popular pastime and a recognized sport.

International rules for figure skating and speed skating apply almost equally to roller and ice skaters. Speed skaters on ice are only slightly faster than those on wheels.

A number of team sports, such as roller hockey, have been played on wheels, but the most popular, at least from a spectator's point of view, is the Roller Derby, a contest of speed, skill, and endurance.

Roller Derby teams are composed of five men and five women; when competing, men skate against their male opponents and women against women. A contest is divided into eight twelve-minute periods, with the male and female sections of the team getting equal playing time. Points are scored during "jams," when players from one team try to pass their opponents, who try to prevent them from passing by hard blocking, elbowing, and other rough tactics. Once a jammer (or more than one jammer) has broken free of the pack, a point is scored for every opponent passed within a time span of 60 seconds.

Shuffleboard. Shuffleboard, like billiards, is an offshoot of lawn bowling, although it is more closely related to curling or the Italian game of boccie. Probably the game originated in England in the 1200's. Several English rulers considered it too frivolous, and for a time the game was banned. At that time it was called *shove beard, shove groat,* or *slide groat,* and was played on a dirt court. Shuffleboard was introduced to America in New England in the 1840's; it was banned there, too, as it was termed "a gambler's pastime." The game's sudden rise in popularity occurred at the end of the 19th century among tourists crossing the oceans by steamer. In 1913 a hotel owner in Daytona Beach, Florida, Robert Ball, marked off the first shuffleboard court on the sidewalk near his property. Thus shuffleboard is always thought of as a resort-oriented game.

Shuffleboard can be played singles or doubles. The hard surface court measures 52 feet long by 6 feet wide. At each end is a triangle divided into numbered scoring areas with different scoring values. Each player uses a long stick that has a kind of "pushing" attachment at one end. The object of the game is to push four disks into the scoring areas of the target triangle to gain points. Opponents try to block the shots with strategic sliding of their own disks, or to knock their opponents' disks out of scoring areas.

The National Shuffleboard Association, founded in 1913, makes the rules and regulations. Tournaments are held twice a year: during the winter, at St. Petersburg, Florida, and during the summer at Traverse City, Michigan.

Skateboarding. A skateboard is a piece of plastic material mounted on roller skating wheels. It is a variation of several devices (some of which are homemade, such as the "pushmobile") that use roller wheels. Skateboarding in America enjoyed great popularity during the late 1950's and 1960's; its popularity waned for a time, as with many fads, but it was revived with even greater success in the late 1970's.

Expert skateboarding requires great balance and coordination and is therefore restricted mostly to young people. In tournament competition, skateboarders perform a variety of stunts, including handstands while moving, slaloms, and climbs up banked walls with sudden reversals of direction. Falls are frequent and can be painful; therefore skaters wear helmets, knee, and elbow pads.

OLD AND NEW: *fencing* (left) *is one of the most ancient sports, dating from the Middle Ages or earlier; skateboarding is one of the newest.*

UPI

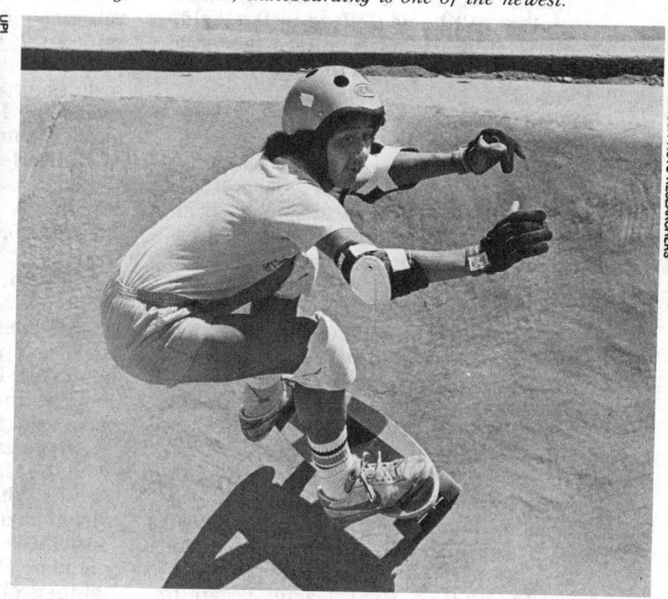

ROBERT A. ISAACS/PHOTO RESEARCHERS

TEAM SPORTS

Participating in team sports offers an athlete a sense of camaraderie, sportsmanship, and discipline that is all but impossible to define. The team is dedicated to one end, and when that goal has been attained there is a spirit of excitement that outsiders cannot share. Almost always, an athlete who has set a record in a team sport, but whose team has come out second best, will say, "I'd trade my record in a minute if only my team could have won the championship." Years after a championship has been won, athletes of a winning team can get together and relive the glorious moment when they, as a group, were the best of their time and their sport.

Baseball

According to historians, baseball evolved from an English children's game called *rounders,* which was in vogue beginning in the early 1800's. In rounders a ball was hit with a stick, but a fielder could throw the ball at a runner who was trying to reach some kind of base. If the runner was hit, he was out.

If anyone merits credit for America's national pastime, it should be Alexander Cartwright, who wrote the first rules and sketched out the first baseball diamond. Cartwright also organized the first baseball club, the New York Knickerbockers. In 1846 the Knickerbockers engaged the New York Nine in what is now deemed to be the first real baseball game. It was played on a picnic field in Hoboken, New Jersey. The game lasted four innings and the New York Nine beat the Knickerbockers, 23-1.

CULVER PICTURES

EARLY BASEBALL: *the Cincinnati Red Stockings of 1869 won 65 games in a row.*

The first intercollegiate baseball game was played in 1859. Amherst took on Williams College in Pittsfield, Massachusetts. Each college fielded a team of 13 players, and Amherst won, 66-32.

In 1869 the Cincinnati Red Stockings became baseball's first professional team. By then the National Association of Baseball Players had been formed, with teams in a dozen states, but they were considered amateurs, or semiprofessionals. The Red Stockings traveled the country, taking on all comers. They won 64 games and tied one. In 1870 the Red Stockings ran their unbeaten streak to 93 games.

More and more teams turned professional. In 1876, at a meeting in the Grand Central Hotel in New York City, the National League was formed. On April 22, 1876, Boston defeated Philadelphia, 6-5, in baseball's first big-league game. The teams changed from time to time, but the National League continued.

In 1900, a rival league began to form. By 1903 it was known as the American League. The upstart group raided the older league of some 100 players and soon was its equal. Both leagues prospered, and a playoff between the league champions was discussed from the start. Thus was the World Series born in 1903, pitting Boston of the American League against Pittsburgh of the National League. Boston defeated Pittsburgh, five games to three.

The two major leagues played from 1903 to the early 1950's with the same teams. Then teams began to shift locations and the leagues decided to expand. The leagues now have 26 teams. Each league is divided as shown in the table at right.

At the end of each baseball season, which lasts from the first week in April to the end of September, the division champions meet in a best-three-out-of-five playoff to determine the pennant winner. Then the pennant winners of both leagues meet in a best-four-out-of-seven World Series to determine the baseball champion of the year.

NATIONAL LEAGUE

East	West
Chicago Cubs	Atlanta Braves
Montreal Expos	Cincinnati Reds
New York Mets	Houston Astros
Philadelphia Phillies	Los Angeles Dodgers
Pittsburgh Pirates	San Diego Padres
St. Louis Cardinals	San Francisco Giants

AMERICAN LEAGUE

East	West
Baltimore Orioles	California Angels
Boston Red Sox	Chicago White Sox
Cleveland Indians	Kansas City Royals
Detroit Tigers	Minnesota Twins
Milwaukee Brewers	Oakland A's
New York Yankees	Seattle Mariners
Toronto Blue Jays	Texas Rangers

Rules of the game. Baseball is played with teams consisting of nine players on each side. In the American League, however, the pitcher does not bat for himself. Another batter is "designated" to bat for him when he is due to come to the plate. This *designated hitter* is the tenth man on a team, although the team fields only nine players and sends only nine players to bat.

Baseball fields may vary in size, but all are uniform in many ways. At one corner is *home plate.* Three bases form a perfect square with home plate—first base to the right, second base straight ahead, and third base to the left. The bases are 90 feet apart. From home plate they form a diamond shape, and the playing field is often called the diamond. In the middle of the diamond, 66 feet 6 inches from home plate, is the *pitching rubber,* the spot from which the pitcher throws the ball. The area enclosed by the bases is called the *infield.* Beyond the infield is a vast expanse of territory called the *outfield.*

At the beginning of the game, one team (usually the one playing at home) takes the field. The catcher's position is just behind home plate. The pitcher is in the middle of the diamond. There are four infielders, one to cover each base, and a shortstop, who plays between second and third bases. The remaining three players are outfielders. The left fielder plays beyond the infield on the third base side, the center fielder straight out behind second base, and the right fielder on the first base side.

The batting team sends one man at a time to home plate. This batter stands just in front of the catcher and tries to hit the ball when the pitcher throws it. The batter may either get safely on base or be put out. If he hits the ball into fair territory (between the first- and third-base lines), he runs to first base, trying to reach it before the fielders can catch the ball and throw it to the first baseman. The batter may also reach first base if the pitcher throws four *balls,* pitches that are not within the strike zone, or if a pitch strikes him. The batter is out if any of the following happen: a ball he hits is caught by a fielder before it touches the ground (a *fly ball*); a ball he hits is thrown to the first baseman before he touches first base; he swings at three pitches and misses them (three *strikes*); or the umpire calls three strikes.

When the first batter has reached base or gone out, the second batter comes to the plate. A player on base may run to the next base when the next batter gets a hit. The object of the game is for a player from the batting team to reach each base safely. When he touches home plate without being put out, he scores a run.

The batting team may bat until three of its batters have gone out. Then that team takes the field and the fielding team comes to bat. When both sides have batted, one *inning* is finished. A regulation game is nine innings, and the winning team is the one that scores the most runs. If the score is tied at the end of nine innings, the teams play extra innings until one team ends an inning with more runs.

If a batter hits the ball far enough, he may try for more than one base. A one-base hit is a single, a two-base hit is a double, a three-base hit is a triple. If the ball is hit over a fence, or far enough for the batter to circle the bases, it is a home run.

A base runner can be put out if a teammate hits a ball on the ground where it is fielded and thrown to the base immediately ahead of the runner, before he reaches that base. However, if a runner is on second or third base and there is no runner on the base immediately behind him, he is not forced to run to the next base. A base runner may not advance to the next base when a fly ball is hit, unless he returns to his base and tags it after the ball is caught.

Baseball game officials are called umpires. They determine balls and strikes, fair hits or foul, and whether a runner is safe or out.

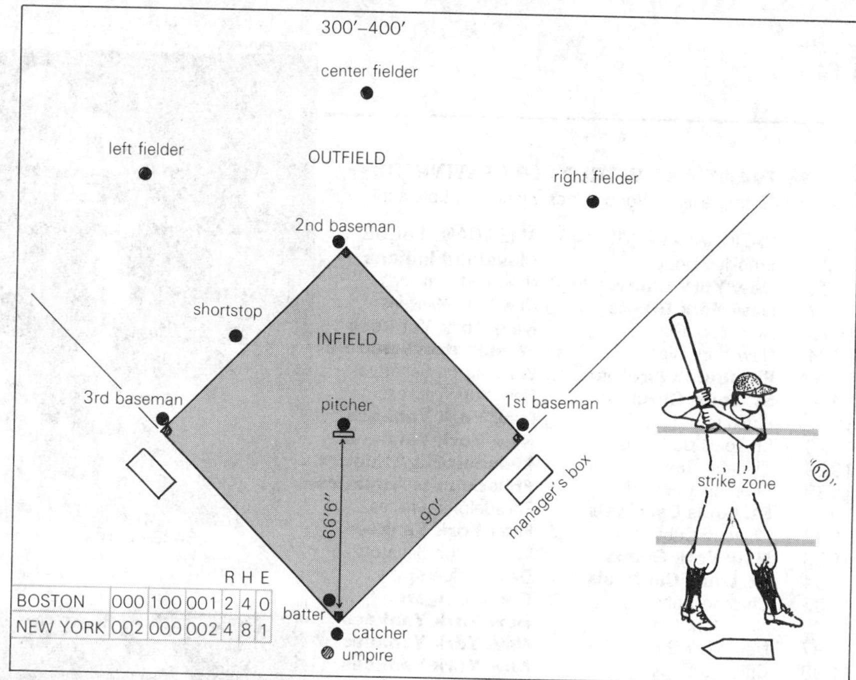

				R	H	E
BOSTON	000	100	001	2	4	0
NEW YORK	002	000	002	4	8	1

SCORING, FIELD, STRIKE ZONE: *a line score* (left) *is given inning by inning, with total runs, hits, and errors at right. The field is the shape of a fan, though called a diamond for the shape of the infield. The strike zone is from the batter's armpits to his knees and over the plate.*

Equipment. A regulation baseball is between nine and nine and a quarter inches in circumference and must weigh between five and five and a quarter ounces. The core of the ball is made of rubber or cork, wrapped tightly with yarn and covered with horsehide or cowhide, which is sewed together. Major league bats must be made of wood (amateur players sometimes use aluminum bats). Baseball gloves vary in shape and size. The catcher also uses a face mask, a chest protector, and shin guards.

Great players. The greatest players of major league baseball are remembered at the Baseball Hall of Fame in Cooperstown, New York. Some baseball feats are known by nearly every baseball fan, young or old. A few of the great players and their accomplishments are shown in the following box.

Other forms of baseball. There are literally thousands of teams besides those playing big league baseball, including Little League, a number of leagues for teenagers (Babe Ruth League, American Legion Baseball), college teams, and minor professional leagues. Baseball is also a major sport in Japan, Taiwan, Mexico, Central America, and the Caribbean islands.

Softball is a variation of baseball, with many of the same rules.

LITTLE LEAGUE BASEBALL *is played by millions in the United States. Many of the Little World Series champions, however, have come from Taiwan, where baseball is a major sport.*

UPI

PENNANT AND WORLD SERIES WINNERS

1920 to present (World Series winners in boldface)

	NATIONAL LEAGUE	AMERICAN LEAGUE
1920	Brooklyn Dodgers	**Cleveland Indians**
1921	**New York Giants**	New York Yankees
1922	**New York Giants**	New York Yankees
1923	New York Giants	**New York Yankees**
1924	New York Giants	**Washington Senators**
1925	**Pittsburgh Pirates**	Washington Senators
1926	**St. Louis Cardinals**	New York Yankees
1927	Pittsburgh Pirates	**New York Yankees**
1928	St. Louis Cardinals	**New York Yankees**
1929	Chicago Cubs	**Philadelphia Athletics**
1930	St. Louis Cardinals	**Philadelphia Athletics**
1931	**St. Louis Cardinals**	Philadelphia Phillies
1932	Chicago Cubs	**New York Yankees**
1933	**New York Giants**	Washington Senators
1934	**St. Louis Cardinals**	Detroit Tigers
1935	Chicago Cubs	**Detroit Tigers**
1936	New York Giants	**New York Yankees**
1937	New York Giants	**New York Yankees**
1938	Chicago Cubs	**New York Yankees**
1939	Cincinnati Reds	**New York Yankees**
1940	**Cincinnati Reds**	Detroit Tigers
1941	Brooklyn Dodgers	**New York Yankees**
1942	**St. Louis Cardinals**	New York Yankees
1943	St. Louis Cardinals	**New York Yankees**
1944	**St. Louis Cardinals**	St. Louis Browns
1945	Chicago Cubs	**Detroit Tigers**
1946	**St. Louis Cardinals**	Boston Red Sox
1947	Brooklyn Dodgers	**New York Yankees**
1948	Boston Braves	**Cleveland Indians**
1949	Brooklyn Dodgers	**New York Yankees**
1950	Philadelphia Phillies	**New York Yankees**
1951	New York Giants	**New York Yankees**
1952	Brooklyn Dodgers	**New York Yankees**
1953	Brooklyn Dodgers	**New York Yankees**
1954	**New York Giants**	Cleveland Indians
1955	**Brooklyn Dodgers**	New York Yankees
1956	Brooklyn Dodgers	**New York Yankees**
1957	**Milwaukee Braves**	New York Yankees
1958	Milwaukee Braves	**New York Yankees**
1959	**Los Angeles Dodgers**	Chicago White Sox
1960	**Pittsburgh Pirates**	New York Yankees
1961	Cincinnati Reds	**New York Yankees**
1962	San Francisco Giants	**New York Yankees**
1963	**Los Angeles Dodgers**	New York Yankees
1964	**St. Louis Cardinals**	New York Yankees
1965	**Los Angeles Dodgers**	Minnesota Twins
1966	Los Angeles Dodgers	**Baltimore Orioles**
1967	**St. Louis Cardinals**	Boston Red Sox
1968	St. Louis Cardinals	**Detroit Tigers**
1969	**New York Mets**	Baltimore Orioles
1970	Cincinnati Reds	**Baltimore Orioles**
1971	**Pittsburgh Pirates**	Baltimore Orioles
1972	Cincinnati Reds	**Oakland A's**
1973	New York Mets	**Oakland A's**
1974	Los Angeles Dodgers	**Oakland A's**
1975	**Cincinnati Reds**	Boston Red Sox
1976	**Cincinnati Reds**	New York Yankees
1977	Los Angeles Dodgers	**New York Yankees**
1978	Los Angeles Dodgers	**New York Yankees**
1979	**Pittsburgh Pirates**	Baltimore Orioles
1980	**Philadelphia Phillies**	Kansas City Royals
1981	**Los Angeles Dodgers**	New York Yankees
1982	**St. Louis Cardinals**	Milwaukee Brewers
1983	Philadelphia Phillies	**Baltimore Orioles**
1984	San Diego Padres	**Detroit Tigers**
1985	St. Louis Cardinals	**Kansas City Royals**
1986	**New York Mets**	Boston Red Sox
1987	St. Louis Cardinals	**Minnesota Twins**
1988	**Los Angeles Dodgers**	Oakland A's
1989	San Francisco Giants	**Oakland A's**

CULVER PICTURES

BABE RUTH

UPI

CASEY STENGEL

MILWAUKEE BREWERS BASEBALL CLUB

HANK AARON

WIDE WORLD PHOTOS

NOLAN RYAN

INDIVIDUAL RECORDS

(Since 1900)

LIFETIME

Highest batting average

Ty Cobb (1905–1928)	.367
Rogers Hornsby (1915–1937)	.358

Most home runs

Hank Aaron (1954–1976)	755
Babe Ruth (1914–1935)	714

Lowest earned run average

Ed Walsh (1904–1917)	1.82
Addie Joss (1902–1910)	1.88

Most victories (pitcher)

Cy Young (1890–1911)	511
Walter Johnson (1907–1927)	416

No-hit games

Nolan Ryan (1966–1981)	5
Sandy Koufax (1955–1966)	4

SEASON

Highest batting average

Nap Lajoie (1901)	.426
Rogers Hornsby (1924)	.424

Most home runs

Roger Maris (1961)	61
Babe Ruth (1927)	60

Lowest earned run average

Dutch Leonard (1914)	1.01
Three Finger Brown (1906)	1.04

Most victories

Jack Chesbro (1904)	41
Ed Walsh (1908)	39

TEAM RECORDS

(since 1900)

Most pennants won

New York Yankees	34
Brooklyn/Los Angeles Dodgers	20

Most World Series won
(began 1903)

New York Yankees	23
St. Louis Cardinals	8

MANAGER RECORDS

Most seasons managed

Connie Mack (1895–1950)	53
John McGraw (1899–1932)	33

Most pennants won

Casey Stengel (1934–1965)	10
John McGraw (1899–1932)	10
Connie Mack (1895–1950)	9
Joe McCarthy (1926–1950)	9

Basketball

Basketball is probably the most widely played team sport in the world. It has been estimated that in the United States, perhaps 98% of all high schools, and virtually all colleges, have varsity teams. The game is popular in every nation on every continent, and is played indoors in gymnasiums and huge arenas, and outdoors in playgrounds. Basketball is one of the major events of the Olympic Games.

In 1891 Dr. James Naismith, an instructor at the International Young Men's Christian Association Training School (now called Springfield College) in Massachusetts, realized that there was no team sport to keep the students occupied between the end of the football season and the beginning of the baseball season. He recalled an old childhood game called "Duck on a Rock," and he set about adapting it to his needs. He fixed peach baskets ten feet off the ground to the walls of a gym and asked players to throw a soccer ball through them. The first players were his 18 secretarial students. Naismith served as referee. He also devised a set of 13 rules. Most of them have been modified over the years, but the basic aim of the game has remained unchanged.

The game caught on swiftly as college and amateur teams were formed everywhere. In fact, basketball became so popular that for a time it was banned from YMCA gyms because it was interfering with other gymnasium work. It was that ban that led to the first professional basketball players. Teams would rent gyms and charge admission to pay the rent. If money was left over, they shared it among themselves. This playing for money lost the players their amateur standing. Since they could no longer play for school teams, they began to set up frankly professional teams. A well known player of the time, Lambert Will, was deemed a pro because he accepted 50 cents.

A National Basketball League (not the same as the present professional organization) was formed before the turn of the 20th century, and in the years that followed numerous pro leagues formed and faded away.

By 1981 the National Basketball Association (NBA), the dominant pro league, consisted of 23 teams divided into an Eastern and Western Conference, with each conference having two divisions:

NBA

EASTERN CONFERENCE

Atlantic Division	Central Division
Boston	Atlanta
New Jersey	Chicago
New York	Cleveland
Philadelphia	Detroit
Washington	Indiana
	Milwaukee

WESTERN CONFERENCE

Midwest Division	Pacific Division
Dallas	Golden State
Denver	Los Angeles
Houston	Phoenix
Kansas City	Portland
San Antonio	San Diego
Utah	Seattle

The National Collegiate Athletic Association (NCAA) governs most of college play. Also involved in amateur basketball is the Amateur Athletic Union (AAU). College basketball is broken into divisions, according to the size and enrollment of each school.

EARLY BASKET *for basketball was a bushel basket. Since it had a bottom, a bystander stood on a ladder to retrieve the ball after a score had been made.*

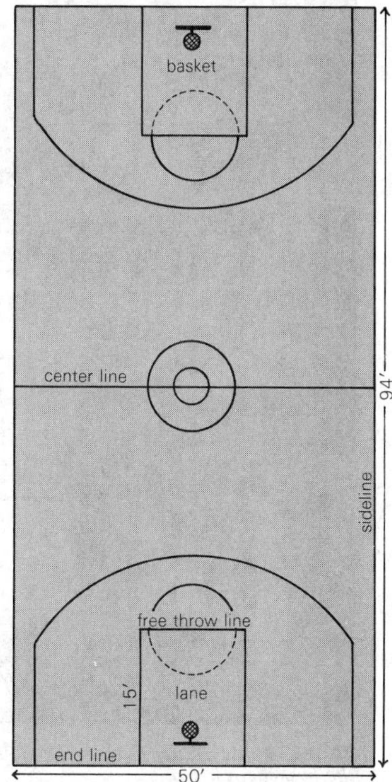

Rules of the game. A basketball team fields five players: two forwards, two guards, and one center. The object of the game is to score points by tossing the ball through the hoop of the opponent's basket. A *field goal*—a shot from anywhere on the court that enters the basket—counts two points. (In professional play, a shot from beyond 25 feet has sometimes counted three points.) A *foul shot* is taken only from the free throw line and counts for one point.

The game begins with the center jump. The referee tosses the ball up between the two centers, who leap up and try to tap the ball to a teammate. The ball is advanced by throwing, bouncing, or rolling it to a teammate, or by bouncing it while running (called dribbling). The ball remains in play after a missed shot, unless it goes out of bounds or is ruled "dead" by an official. A referee and one or two umpires, plus timers and scorers, officiate at a basketball game. Following a field goal or a successful foul shot, the team scored upon puts the ball in play by passing it from behind the end line.

Free throws are awarded for personal or technical fouls. A personal foul may be called by an official when a player is guilty of charging, tripping, pushing, holding, or "hacking"—interfering with the arm movement of an opponent in the act of shooting for the basket. Depending on the situation, the fouled player is awarded one or two free throws (in pro basketball, under certain conditions, a fouled player is given three chances to score two free throws). A technical foul is awarded for unsportsmanlike conduct, deliberate delay of the game, or abuse

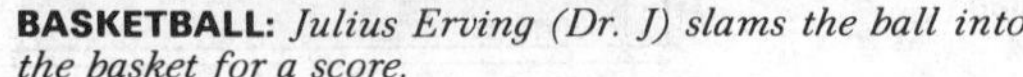
BASKETBALL: *Julius Erving (Dr. J) slams the ball into the basket for a score.*

CRICKET: *the batsman* (right) *seeks to hit the ball and keep it from hitting the wicket* (center).

of an official. The team that does not commit the violation gets a free throw and is given possession of the ball.

Violations of some rules do not call for a free throw; instead, possession of the ball is awarded to the other team. Common violations (all on the offensive team) include double dribbling (dribbling with the ball, holding it, then dribbling again), traveling (running with the ball without dribbling), or staying in the opponent's foul lane longer than three seconds without having possession of the ball.

The playing time of the game varies according to the participants. High-school games consist of four eight-minute periods, college games have two 20-minute halves, and pro games require four twelve-minute quarters. In case of a tie after regulation time, teams play overtime periods, five-minute sessions in college and pro contests, three-minute periods for high-school games.

In the professional game, teams are allowed 24 seconds to make a shot at the basket. If they hold the ball longer than this without making a shot, possession is awarded to the other team. In college and high-school games, a team may hold the ball indefinitely. A team in the lead can "stall," keeping possession, but attempting no shots.

Equipment. The size of a regulation court can vary, but it may not be larger than 94 by 50 feet or smaller than 74 by 42 feet. The basket consists of a metal ring or hoop 18 inches in diameter from which dangles white cord or netting. Baskets are at opposite ends of the court, affixed to a backboard; they are ten feet above the floor. A regulation basketball is made of rubber or leather and inflated so that it measures between $29\frac{1}{2}$ and 30 inches in circumference; it weighs between 20 and 22 ounces.

Great players. Ed Wachter was probably the first great basketball player in the United States. In 1909, he helped form the Troy club of New York, which won 38 games in a row against all comers. The 1920's saw the rise of the Original Celtics, which amassed a record of 1320 victories against only 66 defeats. Among the Celtics' stars were Nat Holman and Joe Lapchick, who both became famous coaches. Only two teams have been entered in basketball's Hall of Fame, Naismith's first group of 1891 and the Original Celtics.

Other greats include Hank Luisetti, who revolutionized the game in the 1930's with his one-handed shots. Early professional stars in the National Basketball Association were George Mikan, Oscar Robertson, and Bob Cousy. The great Wilt Chamberlain once scored 100 points in an NBA game. He was overshadowed, however, by his great opponent, Bill Russell of the Boston Celtics, a brilliant defensive player. More recent stars include Kareem Abdul Jabbar and Julius "Dr. J." Erving.

Cricket

Cricket is considered the national game among British Commonwealth nations; it has been played in England for at least 700 years. The name of the game stems from an Anglo-Saxon word, *Cryce,* which means "a wooden stick used to hit a ball." The game has some similarities to baseball in that it is a contest between a batter and a bowler (pitcher), and the object is to score runs without going out. In other respects, however, the games are quite different.

A cricket pitch (field) can be any size, but generally it measures from 450 by 500 feet to about 525 by 550 feet. In the center of the field, two *wickets* are set in the ground, 66 feet apart, parallel to the short ends of the field. A wicket consists of three wooden stumps between 27 and 28 inches high, lined up so that there is a distance of between eight and nine inches between the first and third stumps. Atop the stumps are placed two strips. The strips, called *bails,* measure between four and four and a half inches in length. The wicket is centered in a white line, eight feet eight inches long, called the *bowling crease.* Four feet in front of the bowling crease is another white line called the *popping crease.* Much of the game is between the batter, who stands between the popping crease and the bowling crease, and the bowler who delivers the ball from behind the opposite bowling crease.

A cricket ball is made of cork and twine covered by leather, somewhat the same as a baseball. It weighs about six ounces and is nine inches in circumference. The cricket bat looks something like a paddle and its average weight is about two pounds six ounces, although there are no restrictions as to weight. The blade (the wide part) is made of willow, and the handle is cane reinforced with rubber and tied with twine. A bat cannot exceed 38 inches in length by $4\frac{1}{2}$ inches in width.

A cricket team consists of eleven players. In a match, one team bats while the other team bowls and fields. The game lasts one or more, usually two, innings; an inning is not over until all eleven players on the batting have been put out. A cricket match can last several days.

At the start of a game, two batters go to the wickets, one stationed at each. A bowler stands behind one bowling crease and "bowls" the ball. His aim is to get the ball past the batter on one bounce and hit the wicket, knocking the bails off. If he succeeds, the batter is out. Behind that wicket stands the wicketkeeper. The other nine players of the fielding team take up positions in various parts of the field. There is no distinction between fair and foul territory as in baseball, so the fielders play behind and to the sides of the batter as well as in front of him.

The bowler pitches the ball with a stiff-armed motion so that the ball will bounce between the popping crease and the wicket. The spin the bowler puts on the ball makes it bounce unpredictably. The batter can hit the ball in any direction: to the front, to either side, or even behind him. If he does hit the ball, he can run or not run. If he does run, he moves toward the opposite wicket while the second batter runs from wicket to wicket in the opposite direction. If both runners reach their wickets before an out is made, a run scores.

A batter may be put out in a number of ways. If he hits the ball and it is caught on the fly, he is *caught out.* If the ball delivered by the bowler gets by him and knocks the two bails off the wicket, he is *bowled out.* He is also out if the bails are knocked off the wicket by a fielder or a bowler while he is running without having reached the crease. If the delivered ball hits his leg, and in the opinion of the umpire it interfered with the ball striking the wicket, he is out as well.

If a batter hits the ball to the extremity of the field, he scores four runs without bothering to run from his wicket. If he hits the ball completely out of the field (akin to a home run in baseball), he scores six runs. After hitting safely, the batter remains at bat, continuing to hit until he is put out. An outstanding batter can hit almost indefinitely, scoring 100 or more runs in one turn at bat.

When the bowler has delivered six throws, a second bowler takes his place behind the first batter's wicket and pitches to the second batter. Actually, the game has now switched directions. When the second bowler has delivered six throws, the first bowler and the first batter resume their duel. In each case, the fielders must shift their positions for maximum effectiveness in retrieving a hit ball.

Football

Several different games are called football, the most popular worldwide being soccer. Variations include rugby, Gaelic football, and American football, which is the most widely known in the United States.

American football. Football as played in the mid-1800's was a violent melee centered on the ball, with a lot of pushing, punching, and piling on. If there were any rules, no one bothered to enforce them. Often huge teams played each other, and the event was more like an initiation rite than a sport. Angered school authorities finally banned the "game" from their campuses. Only when some of the roughness was eliminated and rules enforced were students again permitted to resume their sport.

A group of boys below college age first brought some order to the game. The lads in the Boston area, attending such schools as Roxbury High and Boston Latin, formed teams and played on Boston Common around the time of the Civil War. They played a combination of rules from English football (soccer) and rugby, another English game that was popular in schools.

The colleges at first seemed to favor a rough version of soccer, in which the ball could not be handled with the hands. In fact, the first intercollegiate football game, played on November 6, 1869, between Princeton and Rutgers, was more like soccer than today's American football.

Harvard, meanwhile, chose to play "The Boston Game." Their first intercollegiate game under Boston rules was against McGill University of Canada in 1874. In 1879, Yale, Harvard, Columbia, and Princeton finally agreed to a set of rules. The game would still undergo many changes before it would become the sport we recognize, but the basic principles and rules were in place.

College football. Intercollegiate football is governed by the National Collegiate Athletic Association (NCAA). Most universities are members of a conference and have agreed to play other conference members regularly. The most famous are the Ivy League, in the Northeast; the Big Ten, made up of Midwestern state universities; the Pacific-Ten; Southwest Conference; and the Southeast Conference. Some major schools, such as Notre Dame, prefer to remain independent. Many great rivalries attract huge crowds. Among the traditional grudge matches are Harvard vs. Yale, Ohio State vs. Michigan, and Southern California vs. UCLA.

The college season runs from September to early December. Late in the season, a handful of the most powerful teams are invited to play in post-season bowl games. The most important of these are the Rose Bowl, played in Pasadena, California; the Sugar Bowl, in New Orleans, Louisiana; the Cotton Bowl, in Dallas, Texas; and the Orange Bowl, in Miami, Florida.

Professional football. Professional football was born on August 31, 1895, in Pennsylvania, when the home team, Latrobe, played a team from the neighboring town of Jeanette. The game was won by Latrobe, 12-0.

The modern National Football League (NFL) was begun in 1920

FOOTBALL: *San Francisco 49er quarterback Joe Montana* (center and inset) *breaks clear of the Cincinnati Bengals in an attempt to pass during Super Bowl XXIII in 1989.*

REUTERS/BETTMANN NEWSPHOTOS

when the managers of several barnstorming pro teams agreed to band together. Their meeting was held in an automobile showroom in Canton, Ohio. Today, the pro football Hall of Fame is in Canton. Other pro leagues have succeeded in popularizing the sport in new cities, but each has finally been absorbed by the NFL.

Today there are 28 teams in the NFL, divided in two conferences and six divisions:

NFL

AMERICAN CONFERENCE

Eastern Division
Baltimore Colts
Buffalo Bills
Miami Dolphins
New England Patriots
New York Jets

Central Division
Cincinnati Bengals
Cleveland Browns
Houston Oilers
Pittsburgh Steelers

Western Division
Denver Broncos
Kansas City Chiefs
Oakland Raiders
San Diego Chargers
Seattle Seahawks

NATIONAL CONFERENCE

Eastern Division
Dallas Cowboys
New York Giants
Philadelphia Eagles
St. Louis Cardinals
Washington Redskins

Central Division
Chicago Bears
Detroit Lions
Green Bay Packers
Minnesota Vikings
Tampa Bay Buccaneers

Western Division
Atlanta Falcons
Los Angeles Rams
New Orleans Saints
San Francisco 49ers

Professional football begins with an exhibition season in August; the regular season lasts from early September through mid-December. The top teams qualify for the playoffs, which culminate in the Superbowl game, played in mid-January between the American and National conference champions.

Football rules. Football teams play eleven players at one time, but they make frequent substitutions. The offensive unit is used when the team has the ball; the defensive unit when the opponent has the ball; a special unit is used for kickoffs, punts, etc.

The football itself is pointed at both ends and round through the middle. It was formerly made of pigskin, but today it is often made of a grainy rubber or plastic material. It is about 11 inches long from point to point, and just over 21 inches in circumference at the middle.

The football field measures 120 yards long by $53\frac{1}{3}$ yards wide. Ten-yard end zones at either end of the field are behind the goal lines. The actual playing length is 100 yards. White stripes run across the width of the field at five-yard intervals. The midfield line is the 50-yard-line, and the other lines are numbered downward toward each goal. At the back line of each end zone is an H-shaped crossbar, which is a target for kickers on certain scoring plays.

teammate in the backfield. The moment the center moves the ball, players from both teams go into motion. The offensive players try to protect the ball carrier, and the defensive players try to tackle him. A ball carrier behind the line of scrimmage may throw (pass) the ball to a teammate downfield.

If a team fails to gain ten yards in four tries, possession is awarded to the other team. Often, when the offensive team has used three plays (downs) and has not gained ten yards, it will kick (punt) the ball far down the field in order to keep its opponents as far from its own goal as possible.

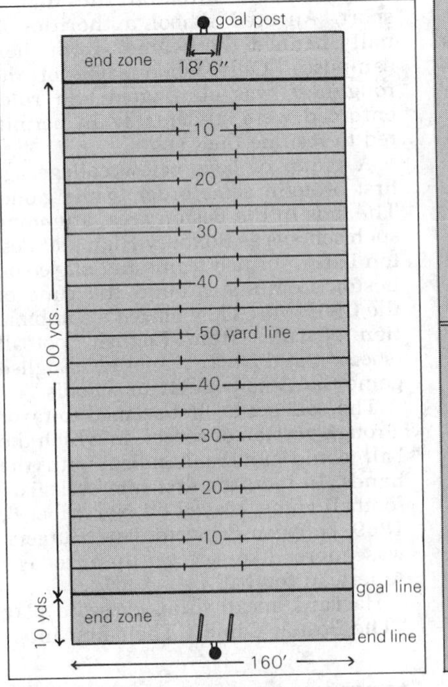

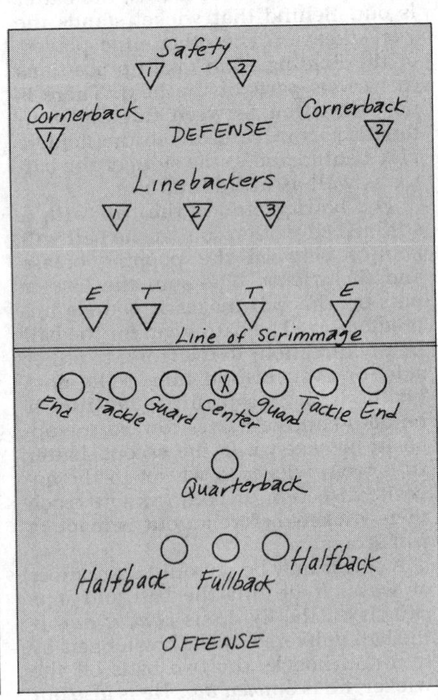

FIELD, FORMATION: *the field is numbered upward from both goals to the 50-yard line. On a play from scrimmage, the offensive team* (bottom) *lines up opposite the defense* (top).

The game begins when one team kicks the ball to the other. The player who receives the kickoff attempts to run it back upfield as far as possible while his teammates try to protect him by blocking out opposing players who are trying to tackle him. The place where the runner is tackled (or steps out of bounds) marks the first *line of scrimmage,* an imaginary line where the two teams face each other.

The team with the ball then has four tries (downs) to move the ball forward at least ten yards. If the team succeeds, it gets another four downs to move ten yards farther. Its aim is to put the ball over the opponent's goal line, scoring a touchdown, which is worth six points.

On each play, the opposing teams line up on opposite sides of the line of scrimmage. The offensive team's center has his hands on the ball. At an agreed-upon signal, he centers the ball, passing it through his legs to a

Offensive teams often use the *T-formation,* or some variation of it, on offense. The offensive line consists of two ends (one usually split away from the rest of the linemen), two tackles, two guards, and a center. The quarterback, who usually decides which type of play to use, stands directly behind the center, ready to receive the ball from him. Behind him are a halfback and a fullback. To one side, nearer the line, the flanker back is positioned. The defense (more often in the pros than in college) will have four linemen, consisting of two ends and two tackles, facing the offensive line. They charge through the offensive line as soon as the ball is in play and try to tackle the ball carrier. Three linebackers stand behind the line. They tackle any ball carrier who comes into their area and watch for short passes. Two cornerbacks and two safety men are stationed farther from the line of scrimmage. On pass plays, they try to bat the ball down or catch it themselves (intercept it) before an offensive player can get it. They must also try to tackle ball carriers who have gotten away from the other defenders.

The team with the ball can score in three different ways. If it moves the ball across the opponent's goal, it scores a *touchdown* (six points). If it is near the goal on last down, it may try for a *field goal* (three points). The ball is centered to a player who holds the ball in position for a kicker. If the ball is kicked far enough and accurately enough to go between the uprights of the crossbar, the field goal is good. Finally, a team is allowed a field-goal-like kick from the two yard-line immediately after a touchdown. This *point-after-touchdown* is worth one point. (In college football, a team may elect to run the ball over the goal after a touchdown to score two points instead of one.) After any offensive score, the scoring team kicks off to the team scored against. The defensive team may score in only one way. If it tackles an opposing ball carrier behind his own goal, the defensive team scores a *safety* (two points) and gains possession of the ball.

If one team breaks a football rule or is guilty of unnecessary roughness, it is penalized by having the ball moved toward the goal it is defending. Minor penalties move the ball 5 yards, major penalties 15 yards.

College and professional games last 60 minutes, divided into quarters of 15 minutes each. The clock is stopped when a ball carrier goes out of bounds, when an attempted pass is incomplete, after a score has been made, or for a time out. Substitutions are permitted after every play.

Football greats. The first great man in football was Walter Camp, who played for Yale in its very first game against Harvard. After his student days, Camp was largely responsible for refining the rules of the game—limiting teams to eleven men, restricting the size of the playing field, and other important changes. He also named the first All-American team. Among other great originators were Amos Alonzo Stagg, who coached for over 60 years; Glenn "Pop" Warner, who originated the three-point stance and taught his players the knack of the spiral punt and the spiral pass; John Heisman, who insisted on the use of the forward pass; and Knute Rockne, the fabled coach of Notre Dame, who adapted and improved many innovations conceived by others.

One of football's first great stars was William Walter "Pudge" Heffelfinger, who played for Yale in the 1880's. Jim Thorpe and Harold "Red" Grange were magnificent early ball carriers. Later great runners include Jim Brown and O. J. Simpson. Quarterbacks famous for their passing include Sammy Baugh, Johnny Unitas, Joe Namath, and Terry Bradshaw.

PROFESSIONAL FOOTBALL CHAMPIONS

(playoff winners in bold face)

SEASON		SEASON	
1921	Chicago Bears	1927	New York Giants
1922	Canton Bulldogs	1928	Providence Steamrollers
1923	Canton Bulldogs	1929	Green Bay Packers
1924	Cleveland Indians	1930	Green Bay Packers
1925	Chicago Cardinals	1931	Green Bay Packers
1926	Frankford Yellow Jackets	1932	Chicago Bears

	NFL EAST	NFL WEST
1933	New York Giants	**Chicago Bears**
1934	**New York Giants**	Chicago Bears
1935	New York Giants	**Detroit Lions**
1936	Boston Redskins	**Green Bay Packers**
1937	**Washington Redskins**	Chicago Bears
1938	**New York Giants**	Green Bay Packers
1939	New York Giants	**Green Bay Packers**
1940	Washington Redskins	**Chicago Bears**
1941	New York Giants	**Chicago Bears**
1942	**Washington Redskins**	Chicago Bears
1943	Washington Redskins	**Chicago Bears**
1944	New York Giants	**Green Bay Packers**
1945	Washington Redskins	**Cleveland Rams**
1946	New York Giants	**Chicago Bears**
1947	Philadelphia Eagles	**Chicago Cardinals**
1948	**Philadelphia Eagles**	Chicago Cardinals
1949	**Philadelphia Eagles**	Los Angeles Rams
1950	**Cleveland Browns**	Los Angeles Rams
1951	Cleveland Browns	**Los Angeles Rams**
1952	Cleveland Browns	**Detroit Lions**
1953	Cleveland Browns	**Detroit Lions**
1954	**Cleveland Browns**	Detroit Lions
1955	**Cleveland Browns**	Los Angeles Rams
1956	**New York Giants**	Chicago Bears
1957	Cleveland Browns	**Detroit Lions**
1958	New York Giants	**Baltimore Colts**
1959	New York Giants	**Baltimore Colts**
1960	**Philadelphia Eagles**	Green Bay Packers
1961	New York Giants	**Green Bay Packers**
1962	New York Giants	**Green Bay Packers**
1963	New York Giants	**Chicago Bears**
1964	**Cleveland Browns**	Baltimore Colts
1965	Cleveland Browns	**Green Bay Packers**
1966	Dallas Cowboys	**Green Bay Packers**
1967	Dallas Cowboys	**Green Bay Packers**
1968	Cleveland Browns	**Baltimore Colts**
1969	Cleveland Browns	**Minnesota Vikings**

SUPER BOWL CHAMPIONS

		NATIONAL FOOTBALL LEAGUE	AMERICAN FOOTBALL LEAGUE
I	1966	**Green Bay Packers**	Kansas City Chiefs
II	1967	**Green Bay Packers**	Oakland Raiders
III	1968	Baltimore Colts	**New York Jets**
IV	1969	Minnesota Vikings	**Kansas City Chiefs**
		NFL—NATIONAL CONFERENCE	NFL—AMERICAN CONFERENCE
V	1970	Dallas Cowboys	**Baltimore Colts**
VI	1971	**Dallas Cowboys**	Miami Dolphins
VII	1972	Washington Redskins	**Miami Dolphins**
VIII	1973	Minnesota Vikings	**Miami Dolphins**
IX	1974	Minnesota Vikings	**Pittsburgh Steelers**
X	1975	Dallas Cowboys	**Pittsburgh Steelers**
XI	1976	Minnesota Vikings	**Oakland Raiders**
XII	1977	**Dallas Cowboys**	Denver Broncos
XIII	1978	Dallas Cowboys	**Pittsburgh Steelers**
XIV	1979	Los Angeles Rams	**Pittsburgh Steelers**
XV	1980	Philadelphia Eagles	**Oakland Raiders**
XVI	1981	**San Francisco 49ers**	Cincinnati Bengals
XVII	1982	**Washington Redskins**	Miami Dolphins
XVIII	1983	Washington Redskins	**Los Angeles Raiders**
XIX	1984	**San Francisco 49ers**	Miami Dolphins
XX	1985	**Chicago Bears**	New England Patriots
XXI	1986	**New York Giants**	Denver Broncos
XXII	1987	**Washington Redskins**	Denver Broncos
XXIII	1988	**San Francisco 49ers**	Cincinnati Bengals
XXIV	1989	**San Francisco 49ers**	Denver Broncos

Soccer. Soccer is by far the most popular spectator sport in the world. The world champion game, known as the World Cup, is played between national teams every four years, and may be watched on television by $1\frac{1}{2}$ *billion* viewers.

A form of soccer was played by the Chinese 2500 years ago. They called it *tsu chu,* which means "kicking a ball with the foot." The Roman version of the game was called *harpastum;* it was played with the inflated bladder of a pig. Legend has it that in medieval times, some Danish raiders invaded an English town. The people fought on until help arrived from London and the Danes were defeated. The Danish leader's head was then cut off and kicked around the village. The incident happened on Shrove Tuesday, and the event has since been celebrated with a kicking game.

Like its offspring, American football, soccer was a disorganized, rough game until the late 1800's. It came to be known in England as association football to distinguish it from rugby and other football games. An abbreviation of "association" gives Americans the name "soccer."

Soccer rules. Soccer is the easiest of all team sports to understand. Like basketball, hockey, and American football, it is a goal game, with each team seeking to move the ball into its opponent's goal.

A soccer field is 115 yards long by 75 yards wide. A halfway line at midfield is the spot from which the ball is kicked to begin play. At each end of the field there is a goal 24 feet wide, 8 feet high, and 3 feet deep into which one team is seeking to kick the ball. Marked out on the field directly in front of each goal is the *goal area,* 20 by 12 yards. Beyond the goal area is marked the *penalty area,* 44 by 18 yards. A *penalty arc* is marked at the outside edge of each penalty area, and a *penalty spot* is marked inside the penalty area. At all four corners of the field are flags, and a small arc is marked just inside the field.

A soccer ball is 27 to 28 inches in circumference and weighs 14 to 16 ounces. A game is governed by three officials, and lasts 90 minutes, divided into two 45-minute halves.

A soccer team consists of eleven players: five forwards, three halfbacks, two fullbacks, and one goalkeeper. The goalkeeper plays directly in front of the goal and is the only player permitted to touch the ball with his hands when it is in play. All other players must control the ball using their feet, knees, torsos, and heads. In general, substitutions in a soccer match may be made only in case of injury to a player.

Attacking players (those whose team has control of the ball) cannot get between the ball and the goal they are aiming for unless there are at least two defenders between them and the goal line (one being the goalkeeper). If they do, their team is called for an offside violation and the other team is awarded a free kick. The rule does not apply if the ball was last touched by an opponent.

The free kick is something like a free throw in basketball. It is the means of assessing penalties and gives the innocent team a chance to score. An *indirect* free kick is awarded on offside violations, and for certain other violations such as intentionally blocking or charging an opponent not in possession of the ball. An indirect kick is taken from the point where the infraction occurred, but it may not be made directly at the goal. Another player must play the ball after the first player has kicked it.

Direct free kicks are awarded for intentional and dangerous tripping, pushing, hitting, holding, charging, charging from behind, or deliberately playing the ball with the hands. In this case, the ball may be kicked directly at the goal. On all free kicks, defending players must be at least ten yards from the ball until it is kicked.

If a foul is committed inside the penalty area, the innocent side receives a *penalty kick.* The ball is placed on the penalty spot (twelve yards from the goal) and all defensive players must remain outside the penalty area. The kicker shoots at the net with only the goalkeeper before him.

When the attacking team sends the ball over the back goal line, the ball is given to the opposing goalkeeper, who kicks it away up field; this is called a *goal kick.* When the defending team sends the ball over the back goal line, a member of the attacking team puts the ball in play from the arc at the corner of the field (a *corner kick*). If the ball goes out of bounds across a side line; the team that did not touch it last puts the ball in play at the point it left the field. One player stands out of bounds and makes a two-handed overhead throw to a teammate. This is the only situation in which a player other than a goalkeeper touches the ball with his hands.

A game that ends in a tie may be resolved by playing an overtime period in which the first team to score wins. If a second overtime is played and neither team has scored, the tie remains

SOCCER: *the game is played on a field both longer and wider than that for American football.* Below, *the player at right tries for a score.*

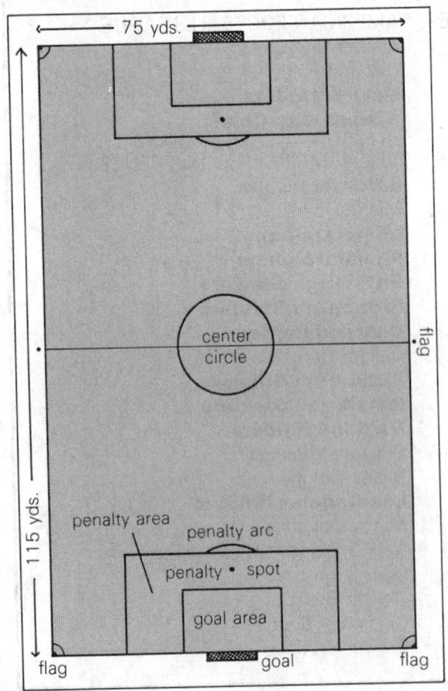

UPI

PELE, *the Babe Ruth of world soccer.*

for the record. In the North American Soccer League (NASL), however, rules call for a "shootout" after two overtime periods. Each side takes five penalty kicks. The team scoring the most goals is the winner.

Soccer greats. Soccer is a comparatively recent game in the United States, but in much of Europe the list of soccer heroes goes back to the early 1900's. The greatest player of all time, by general agreement, was Edson Arantes do Nascimento of Brazil, known simply as "Pele." His popularity throughout the world was all but indescribable. He could perform feats with a soccer ball that no one else could even approach. Pele concluded his career with the New York Cosmos of the NASL while a cheering crowd of some 77,000 fans watched him play his last game. Other stars who played in American arenas and helped popularize the game include Gordon Banks, George Best, Franz Beckenbauer, and Georgio Chinaglia.

Indoor soccer. Indoor soccer is a comparatively new variation of regulation soccer; it can be called a mixture of soccer and ice hockey. Some soccer rules prevail, such as the one restricting the use of hands to the goalkeeper, but the ball can carom off the boards or the glass partitions just as a hockey puck might bounce around a rink. Like hockey, the game features six-man teams. The governing body in professional indoor soccer is the Major Indoor Soccer League (MISL).

Rugby.

Rugby was born at Rugby School in England. In 1823, during a primitive soccerlike football game, a student named Webb Ellis suddenly picked up the ball and ran over the goal line with it. Running with the ball was not part of the game, but it was an exciting way to move the ball. Officials decided to legalize running with the ball, thus creating a new type of football—one that contributed greatly to the later development of American football.

Rugby is played on a field measuring about 110 yards long by 75 yards wide. The ball resembles an American football, but is less pointed at its ends. Teams consist of 15 players on a side. The ball may be kicked, carried, or passed laterally. Points are scored when the ball is carried over an opponent's goal line. Players do not wear protective gear and substitutions are not permitted.

Gaelic football.

Still another variation of soccer is Gaelic football, which originated many centuries ago in Ireland and became popular during the 1500's. In its earliest form, it was a kind of pitched battle between two towns, in which citizens of one town tried to drive the ball across the other town's boundary line. The modern rules were formulated in 1884 by the Gaelic Athletic Association, which also governs Irish hurling (see below).

Gaelic football is played by 15-man teams. The ball is advanced by kicking, punching, punting, or dribbling. Throwing the ball or carrying it is not permitted. Kicking or punching the ball over the crossbar counts for one point, punching or kicking it into the net counts for three.

Irish hurling.

This game resembles football except that each player carries a three-foot stick shaped like a hockey stick with a short blade. The ball is advanced by carrying it on the blade of the stick, or more frequently by "hurling" it—tossing it into the air and striking it with the stick, like a fungo batter in baseball. A hurling team has 15 players.

Both Gaelic football and hurling are popular in Ireland; they are also played in the Northeastern U.S.

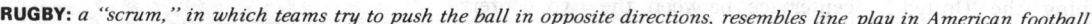

RUGBY: *a "scrum," in which teams try to push the ball in opposite directions, resembles line play in American football.*

UPI

Hockey

HOCKEY: *Gordie Howe* (right) *scores during his 32nd season in major league hockey—a record for endurance in a rough game.*

Hockey games resemble other goal games, such as football and basketball. As in hurling, players use a stick to propel an object toward its goal. The term hockey usually refers to ice hockey in North America, but in Britain and India, the word usually refers to field hockey.

Ice hockey. Without doubt ice hockey is the fastest and roughest of all team sports. A top Olympic sprinter can fly over the lane in the 100-yard dash at 9.1 seconds or so, which translates into roughly 23 miles per hour. A top hockey player has been timed at 33 miles an hour. Most hockey players have lost some of their teeth, and nearly all have been stitched together after suffering cuts.

Ice hockey is the national game of Canada. The first form of the game was played by soldiers of the Royal Canadian Rifles stationed near Kingston, Ontario. A patch of ice was cleared of snow on Kingston Harbor, and the players began to knock objects around using tree limbs, brooms, or whatever kind of stick was handy. It was a disorganized affair, and not until 1879 were any rules devised. Two students at Montreal's McGill University, W. F. Robertson and R. F. Smith, formulated a game that combined ideas from field hockey and several other goal games.

The first hockey team to play by prearranged rules was the McGill University Club. Within three years other hockey teams were formed, and they began to play in indoor rinks once reserved exclusively for ice skaters. Over the years many of the old rules were changed and the popularity of the game spread, reaching the United States during the 1890's.

In 1893 Canada's governor general, Frederick Arthur, Lord Stanley of Preston, offered a trophy to the hockey champions of the land. The trophy came to be known as the Stanley Cup, and today it is awarded each year to the champion team of the National Hockey League (NHL).

The NHL was formed in 1917. Today there are 21 teams in two conferences, which in turn are divided into four divisions as shown at right.

Rules of ice hockey. Hockey rinks vary in size, but the average is 200 feet long by 85 feet wide. The rink is surrounded by a four-foot wall topped with plexiglass, which allows spectators to see the action, but keeps the hockey puck from flying into the crowd. Ten feet from the ends of the rink are goals with nets affixed to them. The goal opening is four feet high and six feet wide. The rink is divided into three zones: the zone nearest a team's goal is the defense zone; the middle is the neutral zone; and the farthest one the attack zone.

Teams consist of six players: a center, two wingmen, two defensemen and a goalkeeper. Each player carries a stick that is not longer than 53 inches, with a blade not more than $14\frac{3}{4}$ inches (the goalkeeper's blade may be wider). The hockey puck is made of hard rubber and measures an inch thick by three inches in diameter. A goal is scored when the puck is driven into the opponents' goal.

The game is divided into three 20-minute periods, with a change of goals at the end of each period. Games can (and often do) end in a tie, but in playoff and championship games, a winner is decided in overtime play. The first team to score wins the game.

Play is begun with a *face-off,* in which the referee drops the puck at center ice between the two centers, who are poised, facing each other. The puck is batted along the ice by means of the sticks. No player except the goalkeeper may touch it with his hands. If a pass crosses into a team's attacking zone ahead of the players, it is considered offside, and a face-off ensues where the offside occurred.

Penalties are assessed for various infractions, such as tripping, "high-sticking," spearing, slashing, or other unnecessarily rough play. The offending player is sent off the ice for a stated period of time, and his team must play shorthanded until the penalty time is ended. Otherwise, substitutions are frequent.

Most of hockey's great players have been Canadian by birth, although many played for American teams. Perhaps the greatest hockey player was Gordie Howe, who played professional

NATIONAL HOCKEY LEAGUE

CAMPBELL CONFERENCE

Norris Division	Smythe Division
Chicago Black Hawks	Edmonton Oilers
Minnesota North Stars	Calgary Flames
St. Louis Blues	Winnipeg Jets
Toronto Maple Leafs	Vancouver Canucks
Detroit Red Wings	Los Angeles Kings

PRINCE OF WALES CONFERENCE

Patrick Division	Adams Division
Philadelphia Flyers	Quebec Nordiques
Washington Capitals	Montreal Canadiens
New York Islanders	Boston Bruins
New York Rangers	Hartford Whalers
Pittsburgh Penguins	Buffalo Sabres
New Jersey Devils	

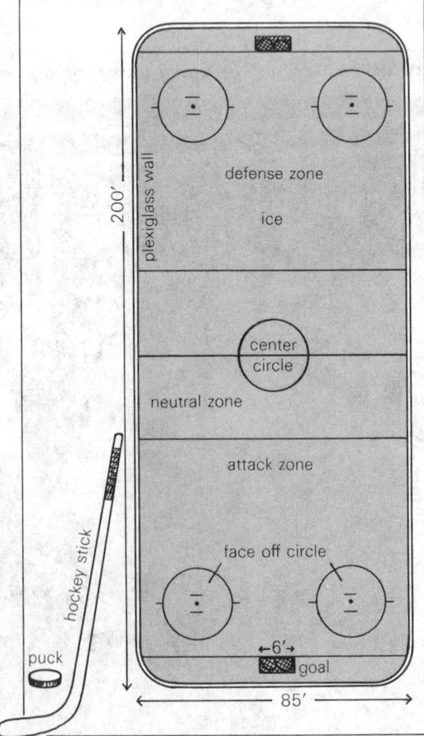

hockey for 30 years and scored over 1000 goals. Among other all-time stars are forwards Bobby Hull and Maurice "Rocket" Richard; defense players Eddie Shore and Bobby Orr; and goalkeepers Jacques Plante, Terry Sawchuck, and Frank McCool.

Field hockey. Field hockey in some form was played by the ancient Greeks and Persians centuries before the birth of Christ. It got its name from the French word *hoquet,* but it was popularized by the British, who took the game with them to their colonies. During the early years of the Olympic Games, perennial champions were teams from India and Pakistan, both of which had been ruled by England. It is one of the few sports played by women as much as it is by men.

Field hockey is played on a field 100 yards long by 55 to 60 yards wide. At each end of the field are netted goals, with a 16-yard *striking circle* before the goals. A curved stick and a ball similar to a baseball are used. Teams consist of eleven players: five forwards, three halfbacks, two fullbacks, and a goalkeeper. The object of the game is to knock the ball into the goal from the striking circle.

WIDE WORLD

VOLLEYBALL *is an exciting Olympic sport both for men and women. Here Japan plays South Korea in 1976.*

Lacrosse

European explorers and missionaries who came to the Great Lakes region in the 1600's found the Indians playing a game they called *baggataway;* this was the ancestor of modern lacrosse. They used sticks backed with nets made of *wattup,* the small roots of spruce trees, and balls made of deerskin. Teams, which sometimes consisted of entire villages, used open fields of any size; sometimes they were 500 yards long or more. The referees were the medicine men and their decisions were final. The French called the game lacrosse because the stick looked like a bishop's crozier, *la crosse* in French.

During the French and Indian War, the Indians used a game of lacrosse to fool the British troops at Fort Mackinac. "Teams" of Sac and Chippewa Indians invited the British to watch them play on a field outside the fort. When the soldiers opened the gates to get a better view, the Indians seized tomahawks hidden under their squaws' blankets, rushed in and massacred the soldiers.

About 1840 the Montreal Lacrosse Club and several others were formed, but competition was limited because there were no definitive rules to the game. It remained for Dr. G. W. Beers of Montreal to compile a manual of play, in which he not only drew up rules but also named positions. Lacrosse spread slowly and reached the United States late in the 1800's, when the United States Lacrosse Association was organized. Today lacrosse is an intercollegiate sport among colleges in the eastern United States.

Lacrosse is played on a field 110 yards long and 60 to 70 yards wide. The goals are 80 yards apart, with 15 yards of playing space behind each goal. A *center line* divides the field in half, with a cross in the middle serving as the *face-off spot.*

Lacrosse uses ten-man teams. Each player carries a *crosse,* which is a kind of stick-and-net, that may not measure more than 72 inches or less than 40 inches (the goalkeeper may use any length he likes). The ball is made of rubber, weighs about five ounces, and is slightly less than eight inches in circumference. The game is divided into four 15-minute periods, and in case of a tie, two five-minute overtimes may be played. If the game is still tied, the score stands.

The game starts with a *face-off,* as it does in ice hockey. Players try to pass the ball to each other using the net end of the stick to pass and receive. Three players plus the goalkeeper must be in the defensive area at all times, and three players in the attack area. A point is scored when a player succeeds in flinging the ball into his opponents' goal. Most defensive moves are made with the crosse in a "poke-check" attempt, but only against the player in possession.

Volleyball

In 1895 Dr. William G. Morgan, a YMCA instructor, invented volleyball. For a long time the game was played only in New England, and the first rule book was not published until 1916, but after that the growth of volleyball was rapid. Today, although the game is not considered a major sport, it is part of the Olympic Games, and it is popular throughout the world.

In the United States, a volleyball court measures 30 by 60 feet; it is divided by a tightly strung net eight feet from the floor (seven feet four and a quarter inches for women). Six players constitute a team.

The game resembles tennis and other net sports. The aim is to force the opposing team to hit the ball into the net or out of bounds. The ball may be hit three times on one side of the net (never twice in succession by the same player). Practiced teams try to set up a "spike"—a heavy downward hit into the opposing team's court by a player positioned near the net.

Only the serving team may score points. If the receiving team forces an error, it wins the right to serve next. One team continues to serve until it commits an error. Game is usually 15 points, and matches between two teams consist of a best-of-three or best-of-five series.

WATER SPORTS

Water sports have been part of man's recreation ever since he first learned that he could float or propel himself through water.

Canoeing

Although canoeing was practiced by American Indians for sport, it was made a formal sport by a British lawyer named John MacGregor. He canoed through the rivers of Europe and the Middle East in the 1860's.

In 1865 MacGregor helped found the Royal Canoe Club in London, and soon more than 300 racing canoes were registered. The New York Canoe Club, founded in 1871, was perhaps the first canoe racing club in the United States. The club's first secretary-treasurer, Nathaniel Bishop, astounded everyone by going from Quebec to the Gulf of Mexico in a paper canoe named *Maria Theresa*.

Modern racing events use the canoe or the kayak and include flat water racing and white water and slalom.

Diving

What is known as "fancy diving" was begun in England in 1905; it has since become an international competitive event, regulated by the International Amateur Swimming Federation. In the United States the regulatory body is the Amateur Athletic Union (AAU).

Divers used a stationary platform until the invention of the springboard. Three-meter springboard and ten-meter platform diving are major events in modern competition.

Dives are classified into three types: *layout,* in which the body is not bent, the feet are together and the arms straight; *pike,* in which the body is bent at the hips, knees rigid; and *tuck,* in which the body is compacted, the diver clasping his ankles with his hands. A swan dive is an example of the layout, a jackknife is a pike. All dives are variations of these basics; a somersault contains a tuck, but can become another type of dive in midair.

In competition, divers are evaluated by a group of judges on the difficulty and form of their dives. The winner is the diver whose total score over a set number of dives is greatest.

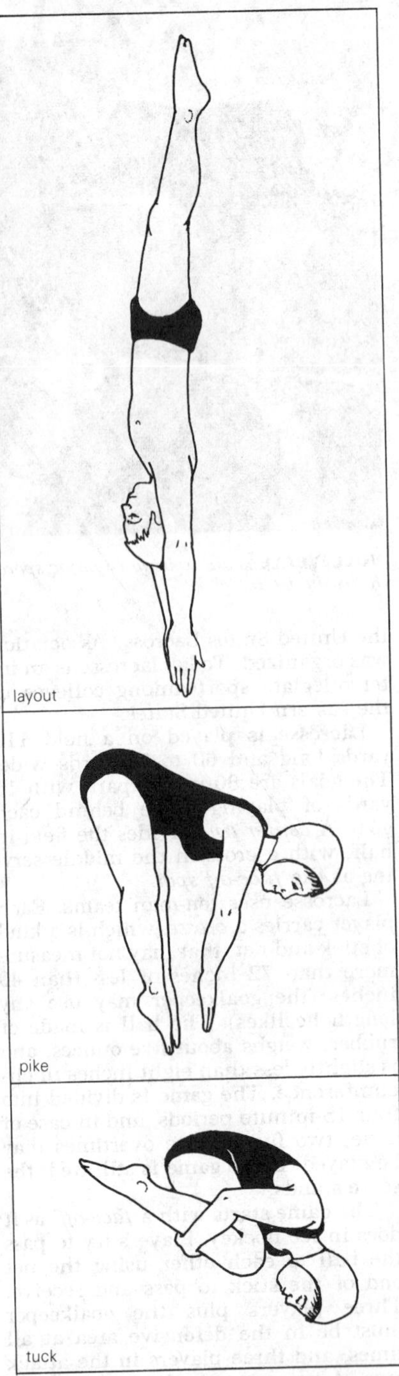

DIVING FORM *is judged during competition by a panel of judges. Basic forms such as the layout* (top), *the pike* (middle), *and the tuck* (bottom) *are combined with twists and somersaults to produce competitive dives.*

Rowing

Galley slaves were the first oarsmen. They powered both warships and cargo ships in ancient times. The first modern rowing contest took place in 1716 on the Thames River in London. Six rowers competed for Doggett's Coat and Badge, named for Thomas Doggett, a popular comedian of that era. The distance covered was from London Bridge to Chelsea.

In 1829 English intercollegiate rowing began with a two-mile race between oarsmen from Oxford and Cambridge, now an annual event. Five years later, rowing came to the United States when the Castle Garden Boat Club Association was organized; the first intercollegiate race was held in 1852 on Lake Winnepesaukee between Harvard and Yale.

The sport falls into two basic categories, *rowing* and *sculling.* A sculler uses two oars, a rower uses only one. The *coxswain,* important in rowing, does not dip an oar into the water; his function is to call out the pace for his teammates.

The International Rowing Association governs the sport in such events as coxed fours, coxless twos, single sculls, double sculls, and eights.

Sailing and Yachting

When man discovered that the wind filling sheets of cloth could propel his craft through water with almost no effort on his part, the sport of sailing and yachting was born. Although races are probably as old as competitive instinct, the first yacht race of note took place in 1662 when King Charles II of England raced his yacht *Mary* against a craft owned by the Duke of York.

There are numerous types of sailing craft on the water today. At the Olympic Games, one sees many small sailboats grouped into "classes" such as Star, Firefly, and Finn Mono-type. A Dane named Paul Elvstrom, nicknamed "The Master," won gold medals in 1948, 1952, 1956, and 1960 racing various small sailboats.

In the large yacht category, the great prize is the America's Cup. Yachts competing for the America's Cup cost

PHILIP WALLICK/FPG

STEVE LISSAU/RAINBOW

ALEX BARTEL/FPG

Aerial Sports

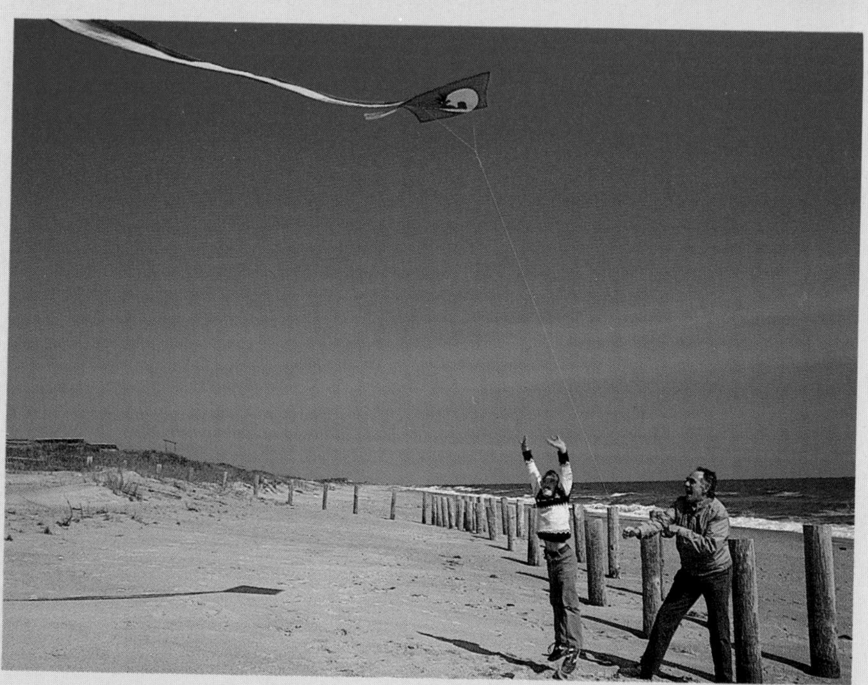

M. NELSON/FPG

Here are illustrated several aerial sports; on the next two pages, water sports; on the last page, land sports. A balloonist *(upper left)* hovers over Reno, Nevada, while a boy enjoys kiting *(below).* A woman hang gliding *(top)* exploits air currents to stay aloft over a seacoast, and a skydiver *(lower top)* employs her skill in parachuting over Kent, England.

Water Sports

A fisherman casts for trout, while a scuba diver confronts his fish. An iceboat maneuvers to attain high speed, and a couple speed along in a kayak. Windsurfing tests skill against wind and water.

ROY MORSCH/THE STOCK MARKET

H. SCHWARTE/FPG

KIM MASSIE/RAINBOW

LEONARD HARRIS/LEO DE WYS

JEFF DIVINE/FPG

Land Sports

The young girls *(right)* are mastering skiing cross country; the land sailors *(middle left)* speed across flatlands; and the spelunker *(bottom left)* explores caverns. The rock climber *(bottom right)* faces a steep cliff.

NORMAN R. THOMPSON/TAURUS PHOTOS

CRAIG AURNESS/WOODFIN CAMP

WILLIAM J. SYDOR/TAURUS PHOTOS

NORMAN R. THOMPSON/TAURUS PHOTOS

many hundreds of thousands of dollars. American yachts have won the cup against challengers from several nations in every race since 1851.

Surfing

In 1778 Captain James Cook, the English explorer, noted in his ship's log the sight of Polynesians happily skimming the Pacific waters on long flat boards. Surfing today is extraordinarily popular, especially among young people along the West Coast of the United States, and anywhere else in the world where waves rise up and come pounding toward the shore.

A surfboard may range in size anywhere from six to twelve feet in length. The best ones have a keel and some drain mechanism. Surfing competition includes standing races, paddling races, and contests for best style. In international championships, surfers may compete in pairs (tandem).

UPI

THE BREASTSTROKE *record was broken by American John Henken in the 1976 Olympics.*

Swimming

Anthropologists theorize that swimming began when a prehistoric man got into water over his head and frantically dog paddled for his life.

The first nation to take swimming seriously was Japan, whose emperor decreed that schools must compete against each other. Swimming developed as a sport in Europe in the 1800's. The National Swimming Association of England, the first national body, was organized in 1837.

It was in Australia that the sport took a giant leap forward, however. In 1846 a 440-yard event was won by W. Redmond in Sydney; that race is considered to be the first championship contest. A dozen years later a "world championship" of sorts was held in Australia again. While the English may have pioneered swimming, they learned the "crawl stroke" from South Americans, and the improved "Australian crawl" from the natives of the South Seas Islands.

Modern swimming competition features four basic strokes: freestyle (usually the Australian crawl, the fastest of all swimming strokes), backstroke, breast stroke, and butterfly. The *medley race* requires each swimmer to use all four strokes. In Olympic competition, the distances covered range from 100 to 1500 meters.

ON THE WATER: *from luxurious yachts to simple surfboards, watercraft provide both sport and recreation.*

UPI

RON CHURCH/PHOTO RESEARCHERS

Long-distance swimming is more of a stunt than an actual competition. The first person to swim across the English Channel was Captain Matthew Webb of England, who accomplished the feat in 1875 using the breast stroke. In 1926, Gertrude Ederle, an American, became the first woman to match that distance. Since then, several swimmers have swam both directions in the same effort.

Great Olympic champions include Mark Spitz of the United States, who captured seven gold medals in 1972, and Roland Matthes of East Germany. Early swimming stars include Johnny Weissmuller and Clarence (Buster) Crabbe, both of whom became movie stars.

Water Polo

Water polo can be thought of as a combination of hockey and basketball played in a pool. The ball must be put past a goalkeeper into a net. There are seven players on a side.

The pool's measurements can vary greatly. According to the rules, it must be from 8 to 20 yards wide, between 20 and 30 yards long and at least 3 feet deep. Players can swim underwater, but the ball must remain on the surface. Technically, no body contact is permitted unless one player has the ball. Fouls include deliberately ducking an opponent not in possession of the ball, and kicking or punching an opponent.

Water polo originated in England about 1870. In 1897 Harold Roeder of New York City introduced the first set of rules. It has since become an Olympic sport, with the strongest nations traditionally being Hungary, Russia, Yugoslavia, and Italy.

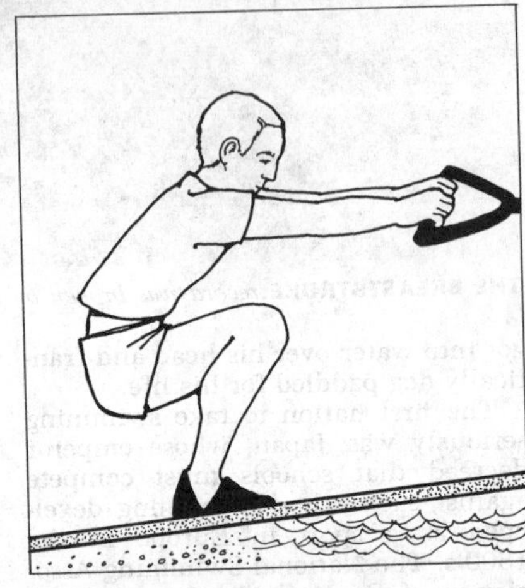

STARTING POSITION *for a beginning water skier is in shallow water near shore.*

Water Skiing

The popularity of water skiing has increased rapidly from its beginnings in the 1920's. In 1939 there were about 500 devotees, today there are perhaps a million. The American Water Ski Association sanctions a number of tournaments that feature three categories: slalom, trick riding, and jumping. Skiers move through the slalom course twice, once going down and again in the opposite direction. A fall eliminates a contestant. Speeds sometimes reach almost 40 miles an hour.

In trick skiing the skiers perform various maneuvers, such as turning in midair, going backward, or holding the tow line with the toes of one foot. Contestants are judged on the degree of difficulty of the trick.

Jumping competition uses jump ramps about 20 feet long and up to 6 feet high. Three jumps are taken and the best two count.

White Water Boating

White water boating is a relatively new Olympic sport. The slalom event uses both Canadian canoes and kayaks. The course is no longer than 800 meters (about half a mile) through swiftly flowing water that creates a strong current. Along the course are 12 to 30 gates, each consisting of two poles hung from overhead wires. The gates may be in mid-river, behind rocks, or some other place. The race is run downstream and then upstream. Time is important in these races, and so is execution. A boat touching one of the poles causes loss of seconds added on to actual time.

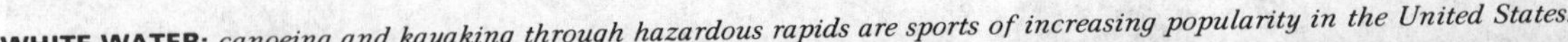

WHITE WATER: *canoeing and kayaking through hazardous rapids are sports of increasing popularity in the United States.*

UPI

WINTER SPORTS

The concept of winter sports is relatively new, although the implements of movement over snow and ice have been known for many centuries. Peoples of the northern climates used crude sleds and beasts of burden (dogs, reindeer, etc.) to travel from place to place and transport their household goods.

The Olympics hesitated before introducing winter games. In 1908 figure skating was introduced, but few seemed interested. Not until 1920 did winter sports become popular as an Olympic series of events. By 1924 a separate Winter Olympics was staged at Chamonix, France. Today, winter sports vie in popularity with sports of all seasons, both in organized competition and as recreation. Numerous ski resorts flourish all along the northern section of the United States and in neighboring Canada, plus in countries in Europe and the Far East. The advent of the snowmobile has added yet another dimension to the enjoyment of the outdoors in winter.

UPI

FOUR-MAN BOBSLED *of the German national team negotiates a banked curve in the 1976 Olympics.*

Bobsledding, Luge

Sleds were first used for transportation, but in modern sporting events they are used in downhill racing. Bobsled and luge races test the courage and split-second timing of athletes.

A modern bobsled is constructed of steel and aluminum and has a steering wheel up front. A four-man model weighs about 500 pounds, while a two-man model weighs about 400 pounds.

The first bobsled competition was held at St. Moritz in 1898. However, this course, called Crest Run, was considered too dangerous and a new one was constructed in the same area. In 1928 bobsledding was included in the Winter Olympics.

In four-man bobsledding, the team captain rides up front and does the steering while the rear rider handles the brakes. The two center riders are there for the added weight and to aid in "bobbing" the sled by the way in which they lean: flattened out to reduce wind resistance, then forward in unison to increase speed. Bad timing can have disastrous effects.

A bobsled run ranges from one to one and a quarter miles, and has numerous curves, causing the sled to shoot around high on the icy bank. Each team makes four descents, the winner being the team with the fastest aggregate time.

In luge racing, one or two persons compete. The riders are practically flat on their backs and steering is done with the feet. Luge racing was introduced in the Winter Olympics in 1964. The luge course is about two-thirds of a mile.

Dogsledding

Dogsled racing, also known as "mushing," is popular in the northern United States, Canada, and especially in Alaska. Fairbanks is the dogsled racing capital of the world. The races vary from 6 to 15 miles in length; from 3 to 16 dogs are used. The dogs fall into the general category of "Eskimo dogs." By breed they would include Huskies, Malemutes, Samoyeds, and crossbreeds. Dogsledding is both an amateur and professional sport. The North American Championships are held each March at Fairbanks.

Iceboating

Scandinavians were the first to develop iceboating. They were seafarers and knew how to handle sailboats. During the winter they learned to use their knowledge to transport large loads across ice. Iceboats were used by early settlers in the United States and Canada to haul goods in winter. As has happened in many sports, the skippers of these vessels took to racing to amuse themselves.

In 1850 the three-point iceboat was developed, with two forward runners and one aft for steering. When a jib forward of the mast was added, speeds increased appreciably. Large modern iceboats can attain speeds of 100 miles an hour. Races are held in the United States and other countries where large bodies of water freeze in winter.

Sporting iceboats are small craft that generally carry less than 100 square feet of sail. One of the most popular is the *skeeter,* which accommodates one person. The skipper sits upright in the cockpit and controls both steering and the sail.

Ice-Skating

Ice-skating probably began in Scandinavia or Holland many centuries ago. The word "skates" is derived from the Dutch. However, the Scots promoted sport skating initially with the formation of the Skating Club of Edinburgh in 1642. The steady improvement of skates has been a major factor in the popularity of the sport. Bone and wood skates gave way to iron skates in the 17th century, and the introduction of steel blades in the mid-1800's set the stage for figure skating.

ANCIENT SKATE *was bound to the boot. The blade was made of wood.*

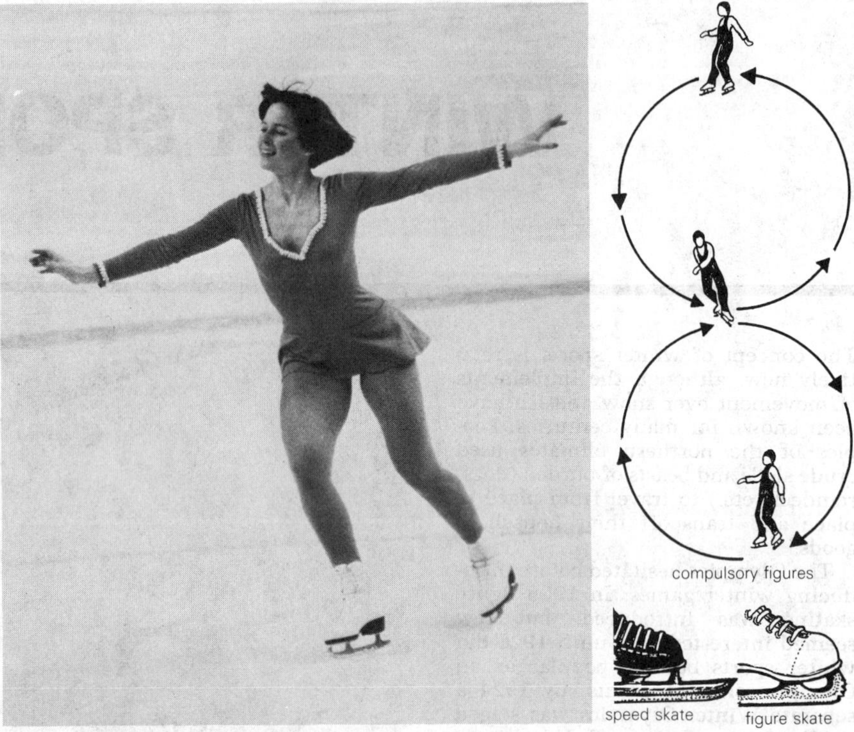

FIGURE SKATING *includes both free skating events as shown by U.S. champion Dorothy Hamill and compulsory figures* (right). *Figure skates have toothed points.*

In 1863 Jackson Haines, an American ballet teacher, went to Vienna to escape the Civil War and to further his profession. He watched as Viennese skaters moved about the ice aimlessly, and he thought that perhaps skating set to waltz music would offer a new dimension to the sport. Haines began to teach "dancing on ice" to his pupils, rhythmic movements that included spirals, arabesques, gliding, and turning gracefully. Haines became so famous in Europe that when he died in 1875, the Finns erected a statue in his honor.

The first renowned figure skater in North America was a Haines pupil, Louis Rubinstein of Canada. He taught his friends the new techniques; this led to the formation of the Amateur Skating Association of Canada in 1878. In 1887 the Skating Club of the United States was organized.

Irving Brokaw of New York helped organize the first American figure skating tournament in 1914, but skating as a competitive sport did not gain a large following. It remained for a beautiful Norwegian girl named Sonja Henie to popularize figure skating on an international level. In three Olympics—1928, 1932, and 1936—she won gold medals and attracted admiration around the world for her grace and athletic ability. After 1936, she turned professional and became a major attraction with a series of commercial ice shows.

Olympic ice-skating is divided into two categories: speed skating and figure skating. Men and women compete in separate categories.

Figure skaters must compete in a series of compulsory or "school" figures; in a short program, using prescribed moves; and in free skating, in which they devise their own routines to recorded music. The free skating is a popular event, giving skaters a chance to perform with a combination of daring and grace. Women are allowed four minutes for a free-skating routine, and men are allowed five. Contestants choose their own music and often help devise their own choreography. The winner of a figure skating tournament is the skater whose combined marks for compulsory and free skating are highest.

In addition to individual events for men and women, international competitions feature pair skating and ice dancing. Among the great U.S. figure skaters have been Richard Button, Tenley Albright, Peggy Fleming, and Dorothy Hamill.

Speed skaters race in distances varying from 500 to 10,000 meters. In Olympic competition, two lanes are used. Because the inside lane is shorter, the skaters must change lanes at stated intervals so that each skater skates the same distance. American Eric Heiden won five speed skating gold medals in the 1980 Olympics.

ERIC HEIDEN *of the United States won five gold medals in the 1980 Winter Olympics and held several world records simultaneously.*

Skiing

Of all recreational winter sports, skiing is by far the most popular.

The oldest known ski was found in Norway; it is thought to date from the year 5000 B.C. The Hoting ski, found in a Swedish peat bog, dates back to the Bronze Age, 2500 B.C. In ancient times, three types of skis were used. The northern type, still used in some parts of Siberia, was short and wide with a hide-covered bottom. The southern type, used from the Ural Mountains to southern Norway, looked somewhat similar to today's skis. The central Nordic ski, used in what is today Lapland, was grooved and uneven in size, the left ski being longer than the right. The shorter ski had fur on the bottom for traction.

Recreational skiing began in Austria during the latter part of the 1600's. The first true ski competition was a military meet at Christiana, Norway, in 1767. The first modern jumping meet was held on Huseby Hill in Norway in 1879. Scandinavians of the Minnesota area helped popularize skiing in the United States, and interest soon spread to other regions.

Mathias Zdarsky of Austria is considered the father of Alpine skiing, contributing the snowplow and stem turn to the sport. Sir Arnold Lunn of England organized the first slalom race in 1928, subsequently adopted into the Olympic program. Rudolph Lettner, an Austrian, invented the steel edge, which permitted skiers to move downhill with their feet closer together and their bodies more erect.

Skiing competition is divided into two basic categories: Alpine and Nordic. The three major Alpine events are the downhill, the slalom, and the giant slalom. The Nordic events include ski jumping and cross-country racing.

Downhill. The downhill is exactly what its name implies, a speedy run down a course in the fastest possible time. The trail is not less than 800 meters for men (400 for women), but often it is between $1\frac{1}{2}$ and 2 miles long, not less than 100 feet wide, with a vertical drop of at least 1400 feet.

Slalom. The slalom course is shorter than the downhill, and is controlled by gates. A gate is simply a set of two flags of the same color, no closer than eleven feet apart, through which the skier must pass. The gates set a zigzag course down the slope, testing the skier's control and skill at high speed.

Giant slalom. The giant slalom is a compromise between a downhill and a slalom, shorter than a downhill and with fewer gates than the slalom.

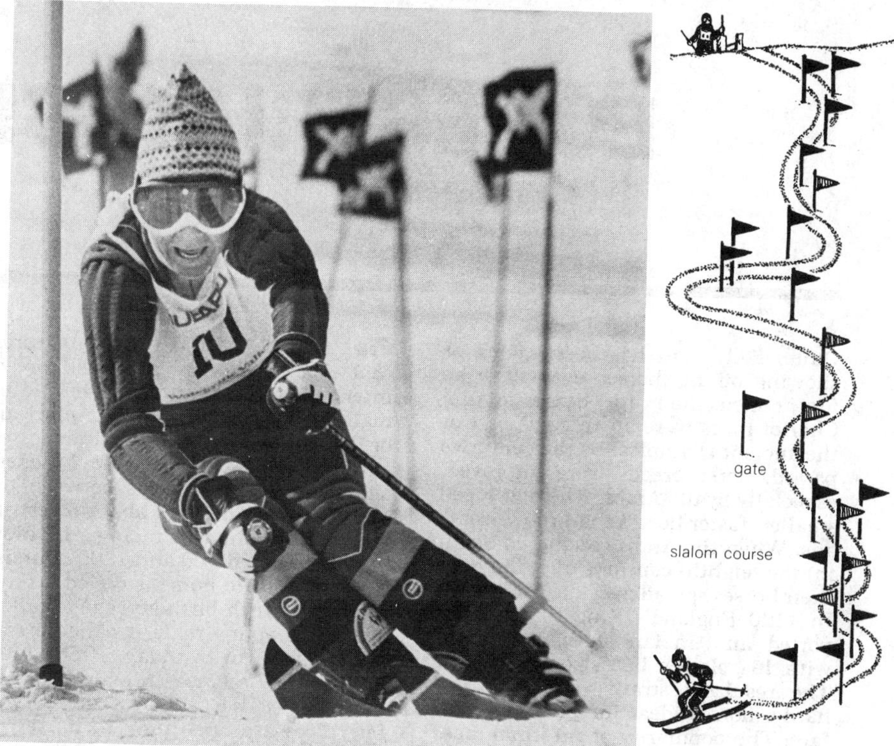

UPI

SLALOM SKIING *requires great agility, strength, and balance to follow the irregular course marked by flags on the slope.*

Jumping. Jumping is the most spectacular of all ski events. Jumping skis are longer, wider, and heavier than downhill skis and have no steel edges. Instead, the bottoms have three grooves for increased traction. The bindings are looser, allowing the jumper to lean far forward while keeping his skis horizontal. A ski jump is a manmade platform built into the side of a slope. The *inrun* is the steep artificial slope from which the jumper starts. At the very edge of the platform is the *lip,* from which the skier flies into midair. The *landing hill* is the section of slope on which the jumper lands and continues on to the *outrun,* where the hill flattens out and leads to the end of the jump.

The jumper speeds down the inrun in a crouch, skis almost together. As the ski tips reach the lip, the jumper uncoils like a spring and goes up and forward. In flight the jumper leans forward, arms ahead or at the sides. The landing should have the skis together, both knees slightly bent.

Jumpers are judged both for the distance they achieve from lip to landing and for their form.

Cross-country skiing. Cross-country skis are also different from downhill skis, being narrower and lighter and without steel edges. Ski poles are also longer and lighter. Boots are cut low, and are light and soft. The binding holds only at the toe so that the heel can lift. Cross-country technique consists of a "sliding–running" step, with the skis being lifted as little as possible. Cross-country races, which include stretches of level, uphill, and downhill skiing, test a competitor's form, determination, and stamina.

Snowmobiling

Snowmobiling is the newest and fastest growing of winter sports. It is sometimes called "motorcycling on skis," imparting the same flavor of youthful zest as associated with driving a motorcycle.

Historians credit Carl J. Eliason of Wisconsin with being the first builder of a snowmobile; he received a patent for a "motor toboggan" in 1927. However, in 1923, a 15-year-old French Canadian named Joseph Armand-Bombardier designed and built a snowmobile. He was the first to produce the machines commercially.

Ordinary snowmobiles, used for recreation, can travel at speeds in excess of 35 miles per hour, while the racing models can skim the snow at better than 90 miles per hour. During the winter, numerous snowmobile races are staged, some around race tracks and some cross-country. One annual marathon is run from Winnipeg, Manitoba, to St. Paul, Minnesota, a distance of more than 500 miles. The United States Snowmobile Association (USSA), founded in Wisconsin in 1965, sets competitive standards for racing events.

EQUESTRIAN SPORTS

Quite likely man has been racing or showing off his horses ever since he first tamed them for domestic use. Chariot races were an integral part of the ancient Olympics. As the centuries passed, horse breeds were improved, especially by the Arabs, who developed smaller, faster horses than the Europeans. When the Arabs conquered Spain in the eighth century, the fame of their horses spread over the Continent. In 1120 England's King Henry I imported an Arabian stallion to mate with his slower but stronger mares. The resulting strain was swift and hardy, horses ideal for mounted warfare. The popularity of informal races led to the construction of Smithfield Track in England, the first public racetrack built since Roman times. The first racetrack in North America was built near New York City, in 1665.

Horse Racing

Horse racing can be divided into three different types of events: *flat racing* around an oval track (or part of the track); *harness racing,* in which a horse pulls a light two-wheeled cart called a sulky; and *steeplechase racing,* in which the horse must hurdle over high hedges and wide water trenches.

Flat racing. Flat racing features *thoroughbred* horses, a special breed intended only for racing. These animals are listed in the official American or British registries, and their ancestry is traced back very carefully. An average thoroughbred stands between 62 and 65 inches high, is about 8 feet in length, and when in racing condition weighs between 900 and 1200 pounds. A young female horse is called a filly; after her fourth birthday, she is called a mare. A young male is called a colt until his fourth birthday, after which he is merely a horse. A male who has been unsexed is called a gelding. A few races are open only to horses of one sex, but in most races both sexes can compete.

Quarter horses are a uniquely American breed. They are heavily muscled and bred as sprinters. A typical quarter horse race is a straight dash of two furlongs (a quarter of a mile), hence the name quarter horse.

The more typical races run by thoroughbreds range in distance from five-eighths of a mile to about a mile and a half. In some events, called *handicaps,* the weight of the jockey (rider) is taken into consideration. The favored horses must carry more weight than the others. This is accomplished by inserting weights into the saddlecloth pockets.

The three most notable races in America constitute the "Triple Crown" of horse racing. These events are open only to three-year-olds. They consist of the Kentucky Derby, run at a track in Louisville, Kentucky; the Preakness, at Baltimore, Maryland; and the Belmont Stakes, Long Island, New York. Only eleven horses have won all three of the Triple Crown races. They include some of the most famous of all American race horses: War Admiral (1937), Whirlaway (1941), Citation (1948), Secretariat (1973), and Seattle Slew (1977).

For many years only male jockeys rode the thoroughbreds, but on February 7, 1969, Diane Crump became the first woman to ride in a regular race at a major track. Two weeks later, Barbara Jo Rubin became the first woman to win a race. Other female riders include Robyn Smith and Mary Bacon. Among the greatest jockeys in history are Eddie Arcaro, Willie Shoemaker, and Johnny Longden.

Harness racing. Harness racing horses are called *standardbreds,* a special breed trained not to gallop but to trot or pace. A trotter moves its left front leg and right back leg simultaneously, while a pacer moves with a lateral gait—both legs on the same side of the body moving in the same direction at the same time.

HORSE RACING: *in harness racing* (below) *horses trot or pace and pull a light sulky. In flat racing, horses gallop and carry jockeys on their backs.*

DAVE MAENZA

FLORIDA NEWS BUREAU

Harness racing began in the United States and became very popular at state and county fairs. The most notable trotting race in the United States is the Hambletonian, held in Du Quoin, Illinois, open to three-year-olds. Other important races include the Roosevelt International Trot, the Dexter Cup, and the Little Brown Jug.

Harness races are held on oval tracks covered with prepared dirt or clay. A race usually consists of two one-mile heats, with the winner being the horse that performs best overall.

The great harness horses of the past have included Dan Patch, Albatross, Cardigan Bay, and Bret Hanover among the pacers; and Un de Mai, Fresh Yankee, Roquepine, and Nevele Pride among the trotters. Leading drivers include William Haughton, Stanley Dancer, and Herve Filion.

Steeplechase racing. Steeplechase racing is most popular in England and Ireland; the outstanding event is the Great National Steeplechase, held annually at Liverpool, England. In the United States, this type of racing has dwindled in popularity; the important races include the American National Steeplechase at Aqueduct, New York, and the Laurel and Havre de Grace in Maryland.

Horse Show Events

The American saddle horse, a mixture of breeds including thoroughbreds, standardbreds, Arabians, and Morgans, is most commonly seen in horse show events. The famous Lippizaner breed of the Spanish Riding School in Vienna, Austria, has been specially bred for *dressage:* the exhibition of a horse's obedience and deportment.

The first horse show in the United States was held in 1883 at Gilmore Gardens, an exhibition hall in New York City. It was an informal affair with 299 horses of all classes, and even a few donkeys for added revelry. It was a great success for the rich people who attended during the shows' early years. The people were more concerned with being seen in all their finery than in watching the horses. However, with the passing of time, and the establishment of the American Horse Shows Association, the event became more serious and less of a social event. Today, horse shows are an international attraction, with presentations in several American cities as well as numerous countries throughout Europe and South America.

Horses compete in one of several main classes, including Hunter and Jumper, Light Harness, Polo, Stock Horse, and Draft Horse. In the Hunter and Jumper classification, horses leap over obstacles, such as a high wooden rail flanked on two sides by lower rails.

During dressage horses execute complex maneuvers in response to barely perceptible movements of the riders' hands, legs, and weight. Some of the movements judged are the *pirouette,* a turn on the haunches in four or five strides at a controlled canter; the *levade,* in which the horses raise and draw in their forelegs while balanced on hind legs; and the *capriole,* in which horses jump straight up, forelegs drawn in and hind legs kicking back simultaneously in mid-air. There are contests for three-gaited horses (walk, trot, and canter) and five-gaited horses (walk, trot, canter, step, and pace).

Horses are also judged on conformation, which includes height, weight, and form, quality or degree of refinement in build, soundness of bone and limb, and health, training, and fitness.

Rodeos

Rodeos were created shortly after the Civil War in America, when Texas cowboys, after having driven huge herds of longhorns to railroad towns, wanted some amusement. Initially, the fun consisted of some wild bronco rides, with bets placed in a ten–gallon hat while cheering crowds looked on. During the 1870's promoters began to charge admission and part of the money was awarded in the form of prizes to the contestants. Finally, the Rodeo Cowboys Association was formed to control rodeos for men, and the Girls' Rodeo Association was formed for women.

Certain standard events are featured in rodeos, including bull riding, calf roping, and bareback riding. The most popular event is saddle-bronco riding. In order to qualify for prize money, a rider must stay aboard his bucking bronco for at least eight seconds.

Polo

Polo is a game played on horseback between two four-man teams. The playing field is 300 yards long by 150 yards wide, with goals at each end measuring 8 feet wide.

Polo resembles hockey in that an object is struck by a stick in order to send it into a goal. A polo match is divided into periods called *chukkers,* each lasting seven and a half minutes. There are eight chukkers in a match, with a three-minute timeout between chukkers in order to change ponies. There is also a five-minute halftime break.

Players carry a *mallet* (stick), usually made of cane, which is 48 to 52 inches long. They strike at a ball made of willow or bamboo, which weighs about four and a half ounces.

ELISABETH WEILAND/PHOTO RESEARCHERS

ELEGANCE AND ACTION: *the dressage event in horse show competition contrasts with the rough and ready action of steer roping in the Western rodeo.*

COLORADO VISITORS BUREAU

MOTOR SPORTS

Since the invention of the steamboat in the early 1800's, men have been putting mechanical contraptions to sporting use. Races between steamboats and railroad locomotives never became regular events. But with the rise of the automobile and the airplane, motor sports attracted thousands of participants and millions of spectators.

Auto Racing

For almost a century auto racing has been one of the most popular of all international sports. Over the years many different types of cars have competed, including steam cars, electric cars, and cars of various shapes and sizes that use internal combustion engines. One special type of car even uses jet or rocket engines.

The first scheduled auto race with rules and regulations took place in France in 1894. The following year a town-to-town race was held in the United States. Several gasoline and electric cars started the 55-mile round trip between Chicago and Evanston, Illinois, but only three cars finished. The winning car covered the distance in 10 hours and 23 minutes, averaging just over ten miles per hour. All the cars required repair at one time or another during the race.

The first really important auto race was staged on a three-mile track at Grosse Pointe, Michigan. It was won by a four-cylinder, 80-horsepower car called "999." The winning driver was Barney Oldfield, the first great race driver, who had begun by racing bicycles. The man who built the car was a machine shop mechanic named Henry Ford.

CULVER PICTURES

EARLY RACING: *legendary driver Barney Oldfield crosses the finish line in the Vanderbilt Cup Race in 1914.*

Classifications. In modern auto racing, cars are classified into groups and categories. In many races, such as a Grand Prix event or the Indianapolis 500, only certain types of cars can be entered. Some mixed races include several types of car.

Category A includes five groups of cars, all various types of sports cars. The cars are basically production models. The best known cars in this category include the Corvette, Alfa Romeo, MG, Ferrari, and Porsche. In most of the groups, only a few modifications can be made on the cars for races, and then primarily for greater safety and efficiency.

Category B (group six), consists of experimental cars or prototypes built only for racing. Among them are the Ferrari, Matra, and Alfa Romeo.

Category C includes groups seven, eight, and nine. Group seven includes the powerful "sports/racing cars," which are manufactured by Ferrari, Porsche, and other companies.

Group eight consists of the *formula* racing cars. These are the "pure" racers, with open wheels (meaning no fenders) and open cockpits for the drivers. A formula is a set of specifications that limit the size and power of the cars. The most important part of the formula is the measurement of the capacity or volume of the car's cylinders. This space inside the cylinders, between the top and bottom of a piston's stroke, is measured in cubic centimeters (cc's) or in liters. One liter is equal to 1000 cc's. The larger the volume, the more powerful the car will be. Formula I cars, the most powerful in this group, are entered in Grand Prix races. Formula II and smaller cars compete in other types of races.

Group nine takes in all the other cars not covered in the previous groups. These include the Indianapolis 500 cars, stock cars, drag racers, and the cars trying to break the land-speed record.

The Indianapolis 500. America's most important auto race is run each Memorial Day. In 1910 several automobile executives built an oval track outside Indianapolis, Indiana, for the purpose of testing auto products. Since it was paved with bricks it was nicknamed "The Brickyard." It is now paved with asphalt. The first 500-mile race was held in 1911 and was won by Ray Harroun with an average speed of 74.59 miles per hour.

Recent winners have averaged more than 160 miles per hour.

Indianapolis cars also compete in a circuit of races sanctioned by the United States Auto Club (USAC), which also has divisions for sprint, midget, and stock cars. USAC races are run on paved oval tracks, including those at Ontario, California; Pocono, Pennsylvania; and Milwaukee, Wisconsin. Drivers accumulate points based on how high they finish in the various races. The driver with the highest total becomes the year's champion driver. Top performers in this type of racing include A.J. Foyt, Johnny Rutherford, Al Unser, and Bobby Unser.

Grand Prix. Grand Prix racing, which is open only to Formula I cars, consists of an international series of races.They are held on road courses in Monte Carlo; Watkins Glen, New York; Zandvoort, Holland; Spa Francorchamps, France; and elsewhere. Each course is different and each offers its own special challenge to drivers. In Monte Carlo, for example, the race is run through the streets of the town and the drivers must contend with hairpin turns, zigzags, hills, and tunnels. The course at Spa Francorchamps runs through the Ardennes Forest. This race, like several others, is run over public roads that are closed only for the day of the race. All courses have different lengths. A lap around the Monte Carlo course measures 1.9 miles while the Spa course runs 8.76 miles per lap.

The governing body for Grand Prix racing is the *Federation Internationale de l'Automobile* (FIA). The *Commission Sportive Internationale* (CSI) is a kind of special committee of the FIA. The Automobile Competition Committee of the United States (ACCUS) is the American arm of the international governing body.

Grand Prix racing also has its championship ratings according to the order of finishes over the racing season. Juan Manuel Fangio of Argentina won the title five times, including four in succession from 1954 through 1957. Other champions were Scotland's Jim Clark and Jackie Stewart, Niki Lauda of Austria, and Mario Andretti of the United States.

UPI

MODERN RACING: *an Indianapolis car* (top) *is designed only for racing; stock cars are modified versions of commercially available cars.*

Stock car races. Stock car races are held on dirt or paved tracks and are sponsored by the National Association for Stock Car Auto Races (NASCAR). These vehicles might look like ordinary production cars, but they certainly are not. Their bodies, frames, and suspensions have been greatly strengthened and their engines are extremely powerful. Legend has it that stock car racing began in America's southern states with men who operated illegal alcohol distilleries. These bootleggers, who paid no taxes on their products, needed expert drivers who could deliver the whiskey from the stills, which were located in the backwoods, to their customers in town. Since local police and federal agents were always on their trail, the drivers learned how to soup up their cars in order to outrun the "revenuers." When they were not on duty, the whiskey drivers raced each other for amusement. Owners of small race tracks organized the contests and began to charge admission.

Stock cars today run over all sorts of tracks, from half-mile dirt ovals to two-and-a-half-mile paved superspeedways, such as the one at Daytona Beach, Florida. In order to qualify as a super-speedway, a track must be paved, cover a distance of at least one mile, and have banked turns so that drivers can reach speeds up to 200 miles an hour. Actually, stock cars achieve running speeds higher than those at the Indianapolis 500.

Divisions of stock car racing include the Grand National for late model cars (the last three production years); Grand American for late model cars of the sports sedan type; a "modified" division for cars three years old and older, in which technical restrictions are waived; and a hobby division for amateurs and novices driving cars ten years old or older. Stock car racing has included such star drivers as Lee Petty, Joe Weatherly, Richard Petty, and Cale Yarborough.

Endurance racing. Endurance racing is just what its name implies, racing that lasts a long time. The most notable of the endurance races are those held at Le Mans, France (24 hours); Sebring, Florida (12 hours); and Watkins Glen, New York (6 hours). Two-man teams, often including the best racers in the world, try to cover more distance in the allotted time than their competitors. The races are held under the sanction of the FIA.

Often different types of cars compete in the same endurance race. The less powerful cars may not finish first overall and yet still win "first in class" honors, meaning that they finished ahead of their rivals with similar engine power.

Drag races. Drag races are short sprints on a straightaway course. Most drag racing cars are simple metal frames with skinny wheels and extremely powerful engines. The most exotic of them burn special fuels. Beginning from a standing start, the dragsters cover a quarter of a mile. The fastest drag racers can reach a speed of some 200 miles an hour and cover the quarter-mile course in less than seven seconds. Parachutes are required to bring these cars to a halt.

Rallies. Rallies are not really speed races; they are run for accuracy. A long course is laid out, often running through several countries (the East African Safari uses roads running through Kenya, Tanzania, and Uganda and covers 3100 miles), with designated stops for rest along the way. Officials determine exact times for various legs of the race; the car coming closest to those times is the winner. Each car has a driver and a navigator; the latter, with the aid of stop watches and calculators, keeps track of elapsed time. Often, if a car has been going too fast during the race, it will slow down to stay within the time limits.

Group seven events. Group seven cars are unlimited in body weight, engine size, wheels, or tires. By rule, the cars must be two-seaters, run on pump gasoline, and have a self-starter. Each car must have a dual brake system activated by the same foot pedal, so that if one brake system fails the other operates automatically. Otherwise, designers have complete freedom. These amazing vehicles can run at 100 miles an hour in low gear and brake to a stop almost instantly. The best such car has been clocked at almost 250 miles an hour.

There are not many events for this group of cars. Sometimes they run in European hill climbs or in Japan; in North America they are featured in the Can-Am (Canadian-American Challenge Cup). The same drivers who compete in the Indianapolis 500 and the Grand Prix often drive in the Can-Am series.

The land-speed record. The land-speed record is not a race between cars; it is a contest to see who can become the fastest driver alive. The runs are made at the Bonneville Salt Flats in Utah, a barren stretch of land that was once the bottom of Lake Bonneville. The cars are powered by jet or rocket engines.

In attempting to set a record, a car must make two runs (after a running start) over a measured mile, first moving from west to east, then, after a suitable pause to check the vehicle, making the return run from east to west. The time of both runs is averaged out to reach the final result. The event is sanctioned by the FIA.

The drivers of these cars are a special breed and do not usually compete in other races. The record for the land-speed trials is nearly 640 miles per hour, well over the speed of sound. At that speed, the one-mile course flashes by in less than six seconds.

Motorcycling

There is more motorcycle racing in Europe than in the United States, but motorcycle events are increasing here. The first practical motorcycle was developed by George Hendee of Springfield, Massachusetts, in 1901, with a model he called The Indian. A year later the Harley-Davidson model was introduced by the Davidson Brothers of Milwaukee, Wisconsin. Among the earliest riders was "Cannonball" Baker, who set many records making transcontinental runs from California to New York.

Motorcycle races are staged at many tracks in America. In addition to flat races, there are road events, motocross events, and hill climbs. The governing body is the American Motorcycle Association.

Flying

Man's longing to imitate the birds is as old as man himself. At first he succeeded only in legend. In mythology, a Greek named Daedalus fitted himself and his son Icarus with wings to escape from King Minos of Crete. Father and son soared away, but Icarus flew too close to the sun, causing the wax fastening the feathered wings to melt. Icarus plunged into the sea, but Daedalus flew home safely.

Centuries later, Leonardo da Vinci (1452–1519) designed a form of flying device. But though his understanding of the principles of flight was amazing, his device was impractical and soon forgotten. Not until 1783 did a man finally soar up and way from Earth.

Ballooning. The first successful balloons were constructed and flown in France in 1783. Two years later a Frenchman named Blanchard and an American named Jeffries made the first balloon crossing of the English Channel. The first balloon in America rose in 1793 in Philadelphia, Pennsylvania. The balloon was used in military operations for observation purposes, particularly in the Franco–German War of 1870 and in World War I. Ballooning as a sport caught the public fancy starting in 1906 with the advent of the Gordon Bennett Balloon Trophy Races, which were held each year in the 1920's and '30's.

Attempts to set long-distance records by balloon have often ended in disaster, since balloons are at the mercy of wind direction. However, in August of 1978 a balloon named Double Eagle II, with balloonists Ben Arbruzzo, Max Anderson, and Larry Newman, succeeded in sailing all the way across the Atlantic Ocean from the United States to Europe.

Hang gliding. Hang gliding is one of the fastest growing sports, especially among young people. It is extremely popular in the western United States, where enthusiasts like to soar off from high elevations and glide along beaches and the ocean.

Although many hang gliding fans think theirs is a new sport, actually it is almost a century old. One of the pioneers, Otto Lilienthal, helped pave the way for the Wright Brothers' engine-driven airplane through experiments in the 1890's.

Hang glider pilots can choose from one of two types of craft, *sailwing* and *rigid wing*. The craft weigh about 100 pounds and can be constructed for between $200 and $300.

MOTORCYCLE RACING: *contestants compete on a dirt track in an international motocross competition in Massachusetts.*

ABRAM G. SCHOENFELD/PHOTO RESEARCHERS

BOB WILSON

UPI

UPI

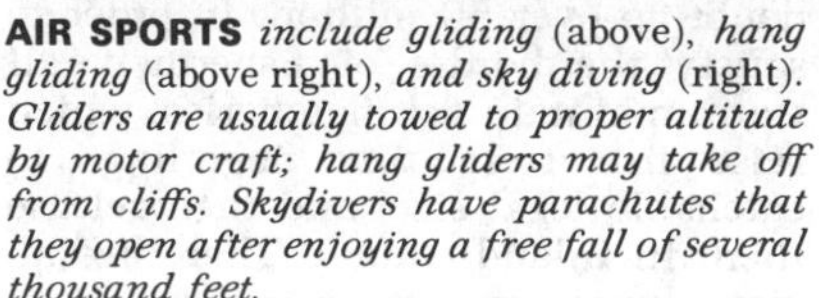

AIR SPORTS *include gliding* (above), *hang gliding* (above right), *and sky diving* (right). *Gliders are usually towed to proper altitude by motor craft; hang gliders may take off from cliffs. Skydivers have parachutes that they open after enjoying a free fall of several thousand feet.*

Gliding. Essentially, a glider is an airplane without an engine. Like an airplane, a glider is controlled with a series of elevators, ailerons, and a rudder. A glider pilot must be licensed, much as an airplane pilot must be.

Gliders stay aloft using wind and thermal (heat) currents; these allow the craft to glide downward or soar upward. Under proper conditions, a glider can stay aloft for long periods of time. Gliders are fairly light, being constructed of lightweight metal or of wooden frames covered with treated cloth. They become airborne by being launched from some elevation or by being towed by an automobile or airplane.

Air racing. Before World War I flying was considered too dangerous to become a popular sport, and even during the war pilots were considered daredevils of the sky. Later, during the 1920's, pilots barnstormed around the country, giving exhibitions of skill and daring at fairs, using old surplus biplanes left over from the war. Slowly, as planes were improved, many people began to take up flying as a sport, and after World War II the number of licenses issued increased impressively.

In recent years, as the prices of planes, and of fuel and insurance, have climbed, owning a small private plane for sport has become prohibitively expensive. However some competitive events—both racing and air acrobatics—are still held. The world sanctioning body is the *Fédération Aéronautique International* (FAI).

Skydiving. Oddly, man learned to drop from a height before he learned to fly in a plane. During the 1500's, the Chinese used parachutes to leap from the Great Wall. However, 20th-century man's experience with the parachute was, for a long time, limited to survival when jumping from a plane that had been disabled.

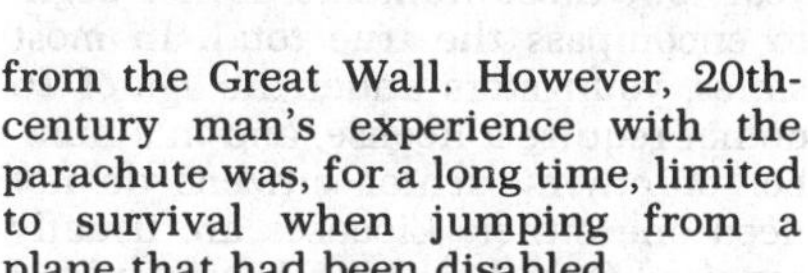

Air shows featured parachuting in the early barnstorming years, but that was done by professionals for exhibition. Skydiving as practiced today did not exist then because the equipment did not permit maneuverability. Even during World War II, when the armies of both sides introduced parachute troops, the chutes were intended only to permit the soldier and/or his equipment to reach the ground safely.

International competition in skydiving began in 1951 in Yugoslavia, when five countries sent jumpers. It was not until 1954 that America had a representative; a soldier named Fred Mason finished in 23rd place. In 1958 a Marine reserve named Jacques Istel, who had studied French parachute techniques, opened a sports jumping center in Massachusetts. Soon other centers sprang up throughout the country. Istel and Lew Sanborn, a former paratrooper with the 82nd Airborne Division, helped develop the first truly maneuverable parachute.

Skydivers today can make their bodies perform loops, rolls, and turns as they drop through the sky at 120 miles per hour. By forming delta wings with their arms they can soar cross-country, covering one foot of ground horizontally for every foot they fall vertically. Groups of jumpers can perform acrobatic feats, form geometric patterns, and exhange objects in midair.

In skydiving competition, the two basic goals are accuracy and style. In the accuracy events, the skydiver starts with 200 points when he enters the plane in the 1000-meter competition. After jumping, he delays up to ten seconds before opening the chute. If he delays more than ten seconds, 50 points are lost, and then 2 additional points for each meter he lands away from the target. Scoring is based on the best three out of four jumps. The 1500-meter competition is similar, except that the time delay is different. The chutist has between 15 and 21 seconds to open the chute. Opening it before the 15th second or after the 21st loses 50 points.

In style competition, accuracy of landing is not a factor. The jump is made from 2000 meters, and the contestant is graded on the difficulty and style of his aerial maneuvers.

RECREATION

BERTRAND DE GEORFOY/PHOTO RESEARCHERS

There is a very fine distinction between sport and recreation. Sports, whether team or individual, usually have a fixed set of rules and are pursued partly for the pleasure of competition. Records are sometimes kept in recreational pursuits such as fishing, but few fishermen judge their success by record catches. Their primary interest is the fun of the pastime. So it is with other recreational activities.

Fishing

Fishing in one form or another is as old as man's quest for food. Several thousands of years ago man used some kind of sharp bone as a hook, or he waded into a stream with a spear hoping to find an unwary fish in the shallows. There were few refinements over the centuries; ancient Greeks also used the "gorge," a bone shaped so that a fish could swallow it easily but not easily spit it out. By the Middle Ages, with the production of the first iron hooks, fishing became more of a sport. Fish ponds could be found near many monasteries throughout Europe. Still, the first interest was food, and most people had little leisure time for fishing as a hobby.

It remained for a retired English linen draper named Izaak Walton (1593–1683) to write the first thorough treatise on the delights of fishing. In 1653 his book, *The Compleat Angler or the Contemplative Man's Recreation,* was published; it has since gone through 350 editions and is still the most widely read book on fishing in the world. Walton's close friend, Charles Cotton, later added a supplement on fly fishing.

Since Walton's day there have been improvements in fishing gear far too numerous to cite in any single volume. In hooks alone, the variations are almost too many to count. Hooks are graded by size, by the presence or absence of barbs, by whether they are single or come in "gangs," and whether they have spinners. No store, no matter how large its fishing department, can stock even a fraction of all the lures, flies, and plugs.

Fishing is by far the single most popular recreation in the world. It has been estimated that in the United States alone, between 30 and 40 million fishing licenses are issued each year, but those numbers do not begin to encompass the true total. In most states, youngsters under the age of 16 do not require a license, and in a number of others, senior citizens do not need one either. Licenses are usually required for others who fish in inland waters (lakes, rivers, streams, and ponds), but saltwater fishing, in the Atlantic and Pacific oceans and in the Gulf of Mexico, has no license requirements for the average fisherman. Therefore, a more accurate count of the number of fishermen would no doubt go over 50 million. In order to satisfy the hordes of fishermen, all states maintain fish hatcheries, which raise fish from tiny fingerlings to catchable legal size, and then release them in inland waters. There are always limits on catches according to date, size, and number. In Pennsylvania, for example, trout season begins at 8 a.m. on the first Saturday after April 11th. Anglers may catch only eight trout and they cannot be less than six inches in length in some sections of the state or less than twelve inches in other sections. In New York State, trout season opens on April 1st. Anglers are advised to consult local fishing laws.

Types of fish. It is a misconception, even among seasoned anglers, that a given fish may be found either in fresh- or in saltwater. Certain species, known as *amphidromous,* move freely from fresh- to saltwater. Examples include the milkfish of the Pacific and Indian oceans and the snook of the South Atlantic. *Anadromous* fish are those that move from the saltwater of the ocean into freshwater in order to spawn. The Atlantic salmon, shad, and alewife are examples. *Catadro-*

FLY FISHING: *the fisherman, wearing waders, stands in a mountain creek and casts his line. When it has floated downstream, he reels it in and casts again.*

UPI

mous fish, such as the American eel, reverse the procedure, moving from freshwater into the oceans in order to breed. However, for the most part, freshwater fish remain in their own habitats and saltwater fish in theirs.

Several types of fish taste somewhat different from each other, but have some similarities in appearance and are related to each other. Trout, salmon, char, and steelhead are part of the same "family"; the various catfish are related to bullheads, and there are a number of fish belonging to the bass family, both saltwater and freshwater.

The most prized freshwater fish include trout, salmon, bass, pickerel, walleye (considered by some to be the best tasting of all freshwater fish), northern pike, perch, catfish, and muskellunge. The "muskie," as it is often called, is referred to as "the tiger of freshwater" because it is a ferocious adversary when hooked. Found in the colder waters of the northern United States and southern Canada, muskies can grow to more than 60 pounds. When finally landed, they must be handled with great care because of their strong, sharp teeth. Other popular pan fish are sunfish, crappies, and rock bass.

Saltwater fish may be divided into two categories: those that swim in coastal waters, and the great fighting game fish that are sought as trophies rather than for food. In the former category can be listed striped bass, bluefish, channel catfish, flounder, haddock, pollack, whiting, fluke, blackfish, mackerel, cod, and snapper. The trophy fish include tarpon, sailfish, large tuna, marlin, and swordfish. Saltwater also has its pan fish, the most popular being butterfish.

Fishing gear. The simplest form of fishing employs the time-honored cane pole, line, bobber, and hook. This is referred to as "still fishing," simply lowering a baited hook into the water and waiting for a pan fish to investigate the worm. Although still fishing brings to mind visions of Huckleberry Finn, even the most sophisticated fisherman can enjoy a lazy morning with a cane pole.

Of all fishing rigs, the *fly rod* requires the most skill in handling. The fly rod is long; about eight and a half feet is a good size. Originally such rods were made of bamboo, but most are now made of fiberglass. Because of its length, the fly rod is made in sections, with one half fitting snugly into the other. The fly reel sits at the base of the rod, affixed underneath it. Fly lines are usually made of plastic monofilament, thick where it is on the reel, and tapering down at the other end. The lures most commonly used are dry flies, which rest on the surface of the water, and wet flies, which sink beneath the surface. Both types simulate some type of insect or other natural food eaten by fish.

Fly casting correctly is difficult, for it involves "stripping line" from the reel with successive casts until the desired length is reached. Accuracy and distance are achieved only by long practice. An experienced fly fisherman can drop his lure almost 200 feet from where he stands.

A *bait-casting rig* uses a shorter, stronger rod, perhaps six feet long, and a level-wind reel. The level-wind is a metal slot through which the line is threaded onto the reel. It moves back and forth on the reel so that the line, normally braided nylon, is wound onto the reel in even layers. The reel rests on top of the handle, fitting into a screw slot.

Spinning tackle consists of a rod somewhat similar to a bait casting rod, except that the guide rings are larger and the reel is mounted on the bottom of the rod handle. The handle of a spinning reel is on the left. Because of the way it is constructed, a spinning reel affords the longest cast with the lightest possible bait or lure. Spinning reels are referred to as "open face."

A *spin-casting rig* is a compromise between a bait casting rig and spinning (open face) tackle. The rod resembles a bait casting rod, except that the guide rings are larger, but the reel sits on top of the rod. Pressing down on a small "button" at the rear of the reel releases the line for casting. The spin-casting reel is referred to as "closed-face."

Depending on the size of the fish being sought, all four types of freshwater tackle listed above can also be used in saltwater. However, for the larger game fish and for surf casting, larger, stronger, and heavier rods and reels must be used. Surf casting requires a two-handed cast to throw the hook and bait any appreciable distance from shore. When angling for the big game fish, the rods are usually slipped into a socket for added support.

Baits and lures. As a rule, a hungry fish will snap at anything living that it comes across, including smaller fish. The most popular live baits are those the fish is familiar with, such as worms and night crawlers, minnows, suckers, chubs, frogs, grasshoppers and other insects, crayfish, shrimp, fish eggs, hellgrammites, and tadpoles. Artificial lures are fashioned to attract the fish's attention.

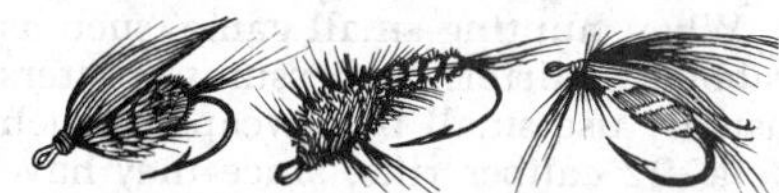

They flutter, dive, wobble, float, and some even make noises. Lures are made of plastic, wood, or metal. Some have shiny red bits of glass or plastic, or rotating spinners, or feathers, or a combination of all three. Some attract more fishermen than fish, others work very well.

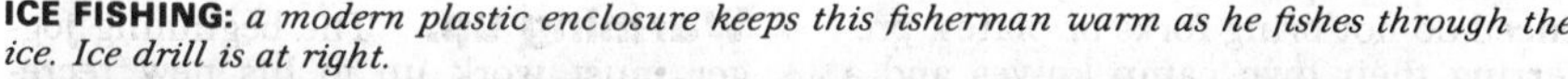

ICE FISHING: *a modern plastic enclosure keeps this fisherman warm as he fishes through the ice. Ice drill is at right.*

UPI

Ice fishing. A frozen lake or pond is no deterrent for many fishermen. They chop holes through the ice and catch many of the same fish as in warmer weather.

Ice fishing requires the use of a *jig,* which is a very short pole with one guide ring at the very tip. Often no reel is necessary; the line is wound around the handle or some other device. Live bait, such as minnows, worms, or grubs, is used almost exclusively, since artificial lures do not seem to work well. For added comfort, some fishermen use small huts out on the ice, complete with stoves for heat. If an angler has chopped two or three holes through the ice, he may also require the use of a *tip-up,* a device that is triggered when a fish takes the bait, allowing the angler to keep track of several lines at once.

Hunting

While not as widely popular as fishing, hunting also provides millions with a chance to get away singly or in groups.

Clearly, hunting is much older than recorded history. But hunting for sport, rather than for food, is a fairly recent development. Country squires in England in the 1700's developed elaborate fox-hunting techniques, using men on horseback and trained dogs.

Sport hunting in the United States today, for such game as duck, pheasants, and deer, is a part of individual states' wildlife management programs. Hunting seasons and licensing procedures are set to help control wildlife populations and to protect endangered species. Although some wildlife organizations object to hunting on principle, it is not true that hunted species are endangered. More often, the animals killed by hunters would face sickness and starvation and might endanger other natural forms if allowed to multiply without limit.

Most states have a limited season set aside only for bow and arrow hunters; no firearms are permitted during this season. For deer and other large game, the firearms season is divided: in "buck" season, only the male may be shot, and in "doe" season, only the female. Generally, the doe season is shorter than the buck season, and a separate license is required for each.

When hunting small game, such as rabbits, squirrels, or possums, hunters usually use small bore weapons, such as a .22 caliber rifle, since they have sufficient power to bring down the quarry. More powerful rifles are used for larger game, such as deer, since small bore would only wound the animal or cause it to die a painful death. Shotguns are used in hunting birds such as quail.

To hunt ducks and geese, hunters usually construct a "blind" to camouflage their presence. Also, trained dogs, such as retrievers, will swim out into the water to fetch the birds knocked down by the hunter. In the field, pointers and setters sniff out the presence of pheasant or quail and become rigid in their tracks, "pointing" to the location of game birds.

HUNTING SAFETY

1. Make certain both gun and ammunition are in good condition.
2. Sight-in the gun before hunting. Know your gun and how it works.
3. Practice marksmanship. A poorly aimed shot can be dangerous.
4. *Never* point a gun at anybody.
5. Keep you finger out of the trigger guard until ready to fire.
6. When crossing a fence, put the gun down first. Go over the fence, then retrieve the gun.
7. Wear an outer garment that can be readily seen by another hunter.
8. Know and observe all local game laws.
9. When the hunt is over, store guns locked and unloaded in a safe place, separate from the ammunition.

Hiking, Camping, Backpacking

Concern for our environment has caused many people to renew the quest for the beauties nature has to offer. The number of hikers, backpackers, and campers has increased steadily for more than two decades. A number of interested community groups, supervised by Forest Service agencies, help maintain important trails over which hikers travel. An interesting example is the Appalachian Trail, which attracts thousands of outdoor enthusiasts annually.

The Appalachian Trail is the longest marked continuing footpath in the world, extending 2020 miles from Maine to Georgia, mostly along the crest of the Appalachian Mountains. In some areas it rises to elevations of more than 6000 feet. Backpackers can write to the U.S. Forest Service for detailed maps of trails and parks throughout the country.

After World War II, the introduction of convenience products helped make backpacking more enjoyable than ever. Dehydrated and freeze-dried foods eliminate the need for bulkier canned goods; lighter, warmer clothing and improved camping equipment keep the tenter more comfortable, and reduce the weight the backpacker must carry.

The average adult backpacker carries between 50 and 55 pounds, and soon learns to include only the most essential equipment. The most experienced do not bring forks or plates, preferring their own camp knives and a utility spoon, plus nested bowls. They do not overload with water, since they have detailed maps showing where drinkable water is to be found. Their soap is in liquid form, carried in a plastic dispenser. Bread travels poorly, so biscuit mix is used, which can also serve to flour freshly caught fish. Margarine keeps better than most other fats or oils and can be used for cooking or spreading on biscuits.

If there is one single most important factor in camping, it is the need for safe practices. Campfires must never be left unattended, and must be kept small enough to be extinguished easily. The fire should be doused with a little water and then covered with dirt. A first-aid kit is as necessary as food and water. A thoughtful camper always leaves the campsite in good condition for the next camper.

Jogging

Jogging has become one of the most popular of all forms of exercise. Joggers can be seen on the streets of every city, in the suburbs, and in rural areas, morning, noon, and evening. Numerous books for beginners and more advanced runners have been snapped up by eager exercisers. The benefits of a steady jogging regimen are self-evident in loss of weight, toning of muscle, and a general feeling of fitness and pride in one's body.

Before jogging. It is important that any beginning jogger over the age of 35 who has not exercised regularly in the past have a thorough physical examination. Even strong young athletes, such as football or basketball players, should have a physical after a post-season layoff. It takes time to build the body, and deterioration can set in very quickly. Most doctors suggest a stress test, which determines how much stress the body can withstand in its present condition.

Equipment. Beginning joggers sometimes try to use standard tennis shoes or basketball sneakers to start jogging. Such footgear can harm the joggers' feet. Proper running shoes are flexible, with uppers of leather, suede, or nylon. The better shoes have two-layer soles: a strong outer layer that is ridged in a pattern and a cushioned insole. Joggers who have flat feet may require an arch support. The fit should be snug but not too tight. Socks should be cotton or light wool; heavy wool socks are too bulky and absorb perspiration. Winter jogging requires layers of clothing, depending on the temperature. Head, face, and ears can be covered with a ski mask.

Warming up. The beginning jogger must work up to his new recreation in much the same way a baseball player does when he goes to spring training camp. There must be a warmup period for the body, to prepare it for the strain to come. Begin with a five-minute period of normal calisthenics, including stretching from side to side, deep breathing, knee bends, pushups, and neck rotation. These calisthenics need not be strenuous, but they will increase blood circulation and limber up the body.

Beginning joggers should walk before they run. The walking period can last from one to four weeks, depending on the person's age and weight. People in their mid-20's who are in fairly good condition and about five or ten pounds overweight can finish the walking in one week. Those over age 40 and 20 or more pounds overweight need more time. It is important to put no needless stress on the heart, lungs, and circulatory system. During the first couple of days, about one mile is sufficient. The distance can be increased gradually until two or three miles have been covered.

An intermediate period is taken up with the walk-jog, consisting partly of brisk walking and slow jogging. At this point, jogging form is perfected. The heel of the foot contacts the ground first and then rolls forward to the ball in a very slight rocking motion. The toes are pointed straight ahead. The jogging stride is longer than the walking stride. The jogger will notice that in walking, both feet are always in contact with the ground. In jogging, for at least an instant, both feet are off the ground. The arms are somewhere between the bottom ribs and the waist, hands loosely cupped, swinging inward across the body, with the swing natural, not exaggerated. The body should be as erect as possible, since leaning forward can unnecessarily strain the leg and back muscles. All breathing should be done through the mouth. Whether walking briskly or jogging slowly, the technique should be the same.

The walk-jog will lead to jogging only. It is best to begin by walking 100 yards swiftly and then jogging 25 yards for at least two days. The walking period can be shortened and the jogging extended gradually, until at last the walking is eliminated entirely. By then a week should have passed and the beginner can jog a quarter of a mile with no difficulty. Afterward, it is merely a matter of increasing the distance covered and the time consumed. Actually, neither time nor distance matter. It is up to the jogger, who should now be in fairly good physical condition. Most joggers pursue their activity for one-half to one hour every day.

There are, of course, certain times when it is wiser not to jog. Moving through a blizzard is foolish, particularly in the city, when the stinging particles of snow and ice obscure vision for both the jogger and the motorist. Extreme cold, when the wind–chill factor drops dangerously low, can result in frostbite, especially in the toes. Extremely high temperatures with accompanying humidity also present risk, especially for those who are past the age of 40 or those who have a great deal of weight to lose. Loss of blood pressure, dehydration, and heat exhaustion are among the perils. Should any of those symptoms occur, the jogger should stop immediately. Cool, not cold, fluids should be drunk, and the jogger should lie down immediately. If the symptoms persist, a physician should be summoned.

Running

Jogging is not running. It is more than a question of speed. The stride is different and so is the end result. A jogger's aim is physical fitness, the runner is testing his or her body, strength, stamina, and desire. Of course, a running regimen will strengthen the heart, lungs, and circulatory system even further. But even more than with jogging, constant training is necessary with running.

Many joggers who have been covering two or three miles a day get interested in running. They require a buildup period just as they did when they began jogging.

In walking and jogging, the heel of the foot makes contact with the ground first, the body is nearly erect, and arm action is easy and relaxed. Running means sprinting. The ball of the foot makes contact with the ground, the heel is raised, the foot is flexed at the arch, placing added stress on the arch, instep, and calf muscles. The body is leaning forward more, and the arm action is much faster.

Just as walking led to jogging after a period of time, so does jogging lead to running. The beginning runner should jog for some yards, sprint, then return to jogging. Gradually, the periods of jogging are decreased and the periods of running increased. The distances covered are likewise increased. This type of training will gradually increase stamina and overall running speed. The actual pace in running any long-distance race, from five miles to a marathon, is a compromise between the jog and the sprint. In the final phase of jogging, three miles is about maximum. In distance running, three miles is the beginning. The new runner may cover 21 miles per week (three each day). Working toward a marathon, he must work toward being able to run *26 miles* in one day. Thus preparing for a marathon means running an average of 40–45 miles a week, double the previous distance.

MARATHON: *some 16,000 runners start the New York Marathon, crossing the Verrazano Bridge on the first leg of the 26-mile race.*

UPI

MOUNTAIN CLIMBING: *a climber pulls himself up a sheer ice wall.*

The additional distance should be added gradually, perhaps at the rate of one mile a week for three or four weeks, so that six to seven miles are covered in each day's run. Running for a marathon race is an exhausting, grueling grind.

After every exercise period, whether jogging or running, it is advisable to "cool out." Just as a racehorse is walked around after crossing the finish line, so should a runner-jogger ease to a halt. Swinging the arms, rotating the shoulders, walking slowly, and breathing properly are extremely valuable. Regardless of how uncomfortable one may feel, cold showers or cold drinks are unwise immediately following a workout.

Running injuries. Both the beginning walker and the veteran runner experience some sort of disability or injury from time to time. Problems arise with toenails, calluses, blisters, sprains, shin splints, cramps, athlete's foot, stitches in the side, and sometimes dizziness. Some of these inconveniences can be self-treated by rest, massage, simple medication (such as anti-fungus foot powder for athlete's foot), or warm baths. Others, such as recurring dizziness, might require the aid of a physician.

Mountain Climbing

The classic answer to the question, "Why do you want to climb the mountain?" is, "Because it is there." In one way or another, whether it be racing, rocketing into outer space, or climbing a mountain, man has always tested himself against nature and his own environment, often disregarding the consequences. Mountain climbing presents one more opportunity for man to show personal courage, physical stamina, and daring.

Mountain climbing as a sport began in the mid-1800's, when English sportsmen took on the challenge of climbing the Alps. At first climbing was restricted to men, who were assisted by professional guides, but gradually women took up the sport and climbers began to ascend without using guides. The great successes began in 1854 when the Englishman Sir Alfred Wills reached the top of the Wetterhorn in the Swiss Alps, an elevation of 12,149 feet. Edward Whymper scaled the Matterhorn (14,780 feet) in 1865. By the end of the 1800's, American climbers joined in the assault on the heights, climbing mountains in the Andes and the Alaskan Rockies. In 1932 an American party reached the top of Minya Konka (24,891 feet), the highest peak in China. In 1950 a French party scaled Annapurna (26,493 feet) in the Himalayas, and in 1953 a party of British and Nepalese climbers reached the summit of Mt. Everest (29,141 feet), the highest mountain in the world.

The basic equipment for mountain climbing includes strong leather boots with cleated heels, a 120-foot length of strong nylon rope, pitons (iron spikes with an eye through which a rope can be threaded), a hammer to drive the pitons into rock, and carabiners (rings that snap to the eyes of the pitons to hold a running rope). Climbing in snow and ice requires dark glasses to guard against snow blindness and an ice axe, which doubles as a walking stick to probe for hidden crevasses and test the snow bridges crossing them. Using the axe, "steps" are cut into hard snow. Climbing involves the use of legs more than arms. The hands and arms supply balance and grasp outcroppings or pitons or rope, but the actual lifting of the body is done mostly with the legs. Usually the most experienced climber will lead the ascent, and the entire climb is slow and laborious. A vertical ascent of 1000 feet an hour is considered good. In difficult climbs sometimes even 100 feet an hour cannot be covered.

Climbing societies in North America include the Appalachian Mountain Club located in Boston, the Sierra Club in San Francisco, the Mazamas Club in Portland, Oregon, and the Alpine Club of Canada.

For Further Reference

Arlott, John, editor. *The Oxford Companion to Sports and Games.* Oxford University Press, 1975.

Benagh, Jim. *Football: Startling Stories Behind the Records.* Sterling, 1987.

Bridge, Raymond. *America's Backpacking Book.* Charles Scribner's Sons, 1973.

Browning, Robert. *A History of Golf.* Classics Golf, 1985.

Carruth, Gorton, and Eugene Ehrlich. *Facts and Dates of American Sports.* Harper & Row, 1988.

Danzig, Allison, and Peter Schwed, editors. *The Fireside Book of Tennis.* Simon & Schuster, 1972.

Diagram Group. *Rules of the Game.* Bantam Books, 1976.

Fixx, James F. *The Complete Book of Running.* Random House, 1977.

Fox, Robert A. *Basketball: The Complete Handbook of Individual Skills.* Prentice-Hall, 1988.

Frommer, Harvey. *Primitive Baseball: The First Quarter-Century of the National Pastime.* Atheneum, 1988.

Hollander, Zander, editor. *The American Encyclopedia of Soccer.* Everest House, 1980.

Liss, Howard. *They Changed the Game: Football's Great Coaches, Players, and Games.* J.B. Lippincott, 1975.

Lorimer, Lawrence, and John Devaney. *The Football Book.* Random House, 1977.

Nemel, David. *Great Baseball Feats, Facts, and Firsts.* New American Library, 1987.

Reichler, Joseph L., editor. *The Baseball Encyclopedia: The Complete and Official Record of Major League Baseball* (6th Ed.). Macmillian, 1985.

Ritter, Lawrence S., editor. *The Glory of Their Times: The Story of the Early Days of Baseball as Told by the Men Who Played It.* Macmillan, 1976.

Schaap, Richard. *The Illustrated History of the Olympics* (3rd Ed.). Alfred A. Knopf, 1975.

Sports Illustrated editors. *Sports Illustrated Ice Hockey.* J.B. Lippincott, 1971.

Sports Illustrated editors. *Sports Illustrated Squash.* J.B. Lippincott, 1971.

Sports Illustrated editors. *Sports Illustrated Swimming and Diving.* J.B. Lippincott, 1973.

Treat, Roger, editor. *The Encyclopedia of Football* (16th Ed.). A.S. Barnes, 1979.

VOLUME **26**

United States and Canada

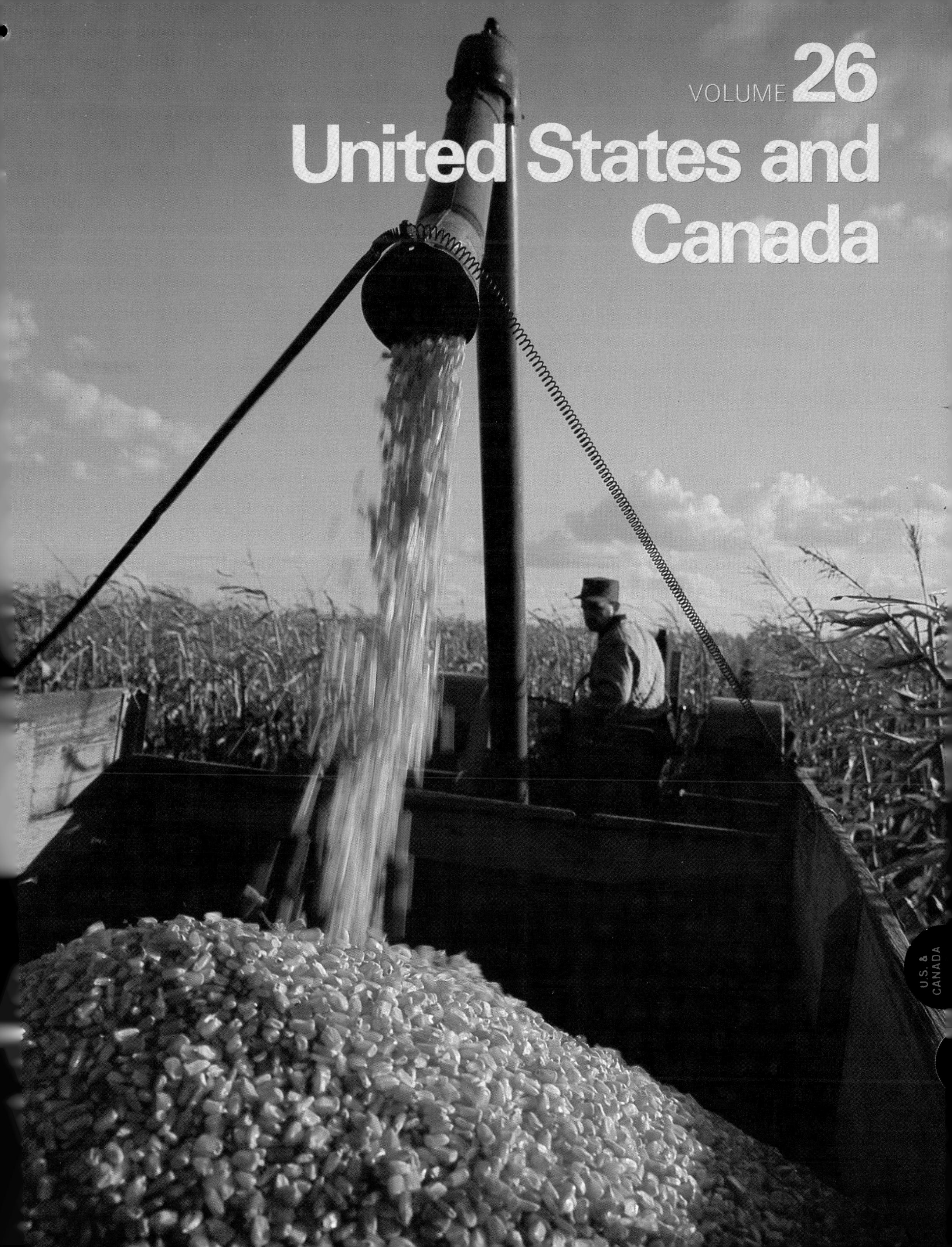

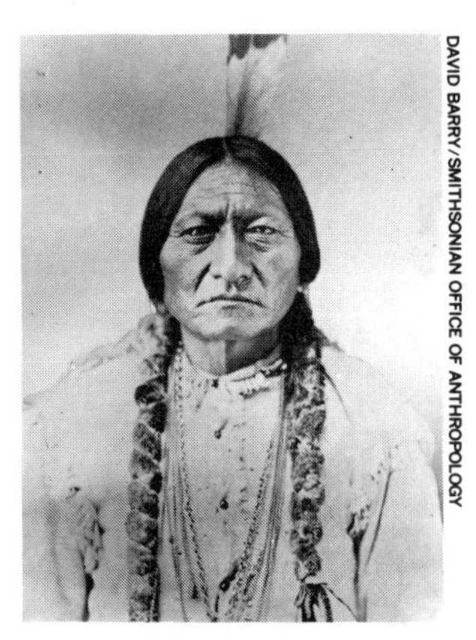

DAVID BARRY/SMITHSONIAN OFFICE OF ANTHROPOLOGY

UNITED STATES AND CANADA

CORN HARVEST: JOE MUNROE/PHOTO RESEARCHERS

VOLUME 26

United States and Canada

PROVINCIAL ARCHIVES OF BRITISH COLUMBIA

CULVER PICTURES

LAIMUTE DRUSKIS/EPA

MONTEREY COAL COMPANY

The United States and Canada occupy the vast majority of the continent of North America. Each country ranks among the largest in the world in area; the United States is also among the most populous. The two countries rank high in economic development and in per capita wealth.

Although independent of each other, the countries share a complex web of cultural, social, and economic ties. English is the predominant language in each, and both were dependent on British political and cultural ideas during their formative years. Today these two North American giants have a combined population more than four times that of Great Britain. They have also developed a social and cultural life enriched by immigrants from many other nations.

(Mexico, which shares the North American mainland with the United States and Canada, is covered in the volume SOUTH AND CENTRAL AMERICA, along with the smaller countries of the Caribbean.)

This volume is divided into four main sections; three consider the United States; the fourth is devoted to Canada.

The first section, "The United States Today," provides an overview of the physical and social aspects of the United States in the 1980's. The section outlines the major U.S. land areas and its climate, then pays special attention to the characteristics of its people. The country is divided into eleven regions and their differences are described.

The second section, "United States History," is a narrative account of the political and social history of lands that now make up the United States, from early exploration to the present. Special boxes on principal wars and other major events are included for quick reference.

The third section, "U.S. States and Territories," includes detailed information on each of the eleven regions and on each of the 50 states. Among the important elements are maps of each region and essential information on each state, including area, population, capital city, state bird, and state flower.

The final section, "Canada," follows the general organization of the three sections on the United States, providing a profile of the country today, an extended history, and information on provinces and territories. Material on the provinces is similar to that given for the U.S. states.

There are many other places in the *Volume Library* where additional material on the United States and Canada may be found. Among the most important are GOVERNMENT AND LAW, which includes a large section on "United States Government," with the full text of the Constitution, a table of U.S. Presidents, and other useful information; and PEOPLE, which provides brief biographies of many prominent U.S. and Canadian men and women.

In addition, the material in BUSINESS AND FINANCE concentrates on American business. CHILD AND FAMILY contains information on vital statistics and social trends. There are special sections on "American Art" in ART and on "American Music" in PERFORMING ARTS. Color maps of the United States and Canada may be found in the ATLAS.

Readers seeking similar information on other countries should consult the other regional volumes (ASIA AND AUSTRALASIA, EUROPE, MIDDLE EAST AND AFRICA, and SOUTH AND CENTRAL AMERICA). These volumes contain general regional histories and, in the case of larger countries, national histories as well. Country entries also contain essential information, including area, population, capital city, etc.

Those seeking information on other topics concerning the United States and Canada should consult the INDEX.

THE UNITED STATES TODAY

The United States of America is one of the largest countries in the world, both in area and in population. In area, it ranks fourth behind the U.S.S.R., Canada, and China. In population, it also ranks fourth, behind China, India, and the U.S.S.R. Economically, it is the most powerful nation in the world. Its standard of living is by far the highest of all large countries, but it ranks behind several smaller countries in the oil-rich Middle East and in Northern Europe.

Two great forces have formed the United States—immigration and development. In 1600, the present-day United States was a vast wilderness, inhabited by fewer than $1\frac{1}{2}$ million American Indians. In 1790, the first census taken by the United States government counted 3.9 million residents, mostly immigrants from Europe. These people were sparsely spread along the Atlantic coast from Massachusetts to Georgia.

In 1980, the U.S. census counted some 226 million residents, spread

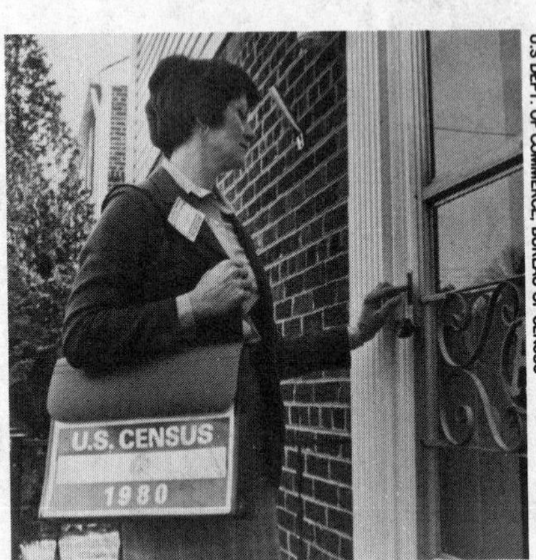

U.S DEPT. OF COMMERCE, BUREAU OF CENSUS

from coast to coast, and from the Arctic shores of Alaska to the year-round beaches of Hawaii. For every American counted in that first census, there are now about 60. Much of this increase has come from the tens of millions of immigrants. They have given the country a diversity and a sense of energy unmatched in any other nation. Nearly every American can trace his ancestry to someone who has arrived in America in the past 200 years.

The new immigrants brought with them a determination to conquer the vast and nearly empty continent. They invented new means of transportation to cross it, new communications to keep in touch across its great distances, and new implements to farm its lands, recover its natural resources, and encourage trade. They developed a new kind of federal government as well, one that was suited to a country of huge dimensions, and combined the virtues of central and local administration. Even social relations were modified; compared with the ancient countries of Europe and Asia, the United States was less rigidly formed into social and economic classes.

The story of immigration and development is to a large degree the story of American history. But to understand it fully, one must know about the land itself and about the people of the United States today.

U.S. LAND FORMS *include western plateaus, midwestern plains, and eastern coastal regions, separated by mountain ranges.*

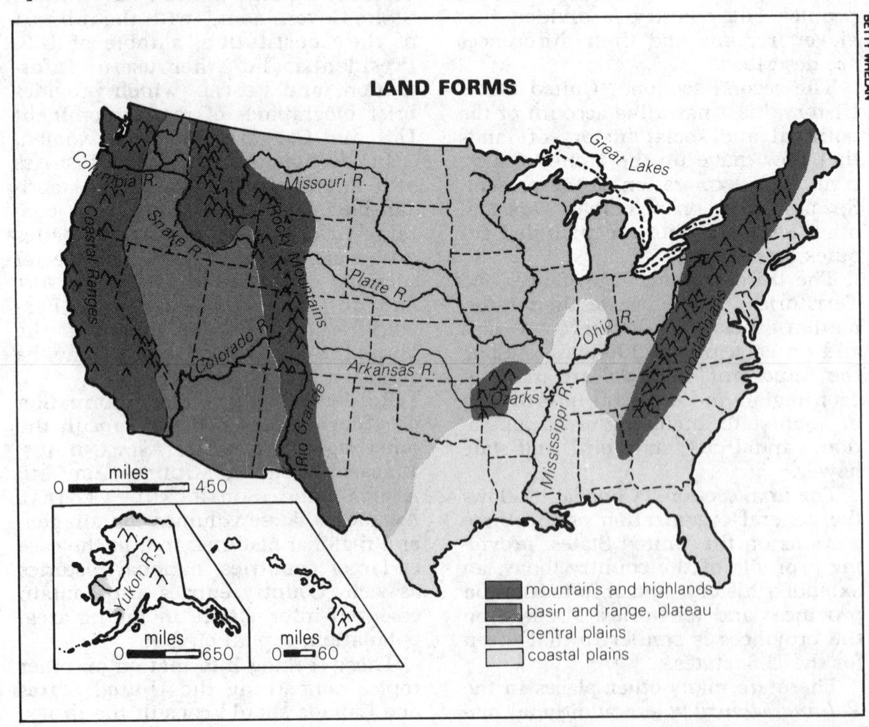

BETTY WHELAN

The Land

The main land mass of the United States, accommodating 48 of its 50 states, occupies the central part of the North American continent, bordering Canada to the north and Mexico to the south. U.S. lands stretch from a long Atlantic coastline in the east to the Pacific in the west.

The state of Alaska is a vast frigid region in the northwest corner of North America, separated from the 48 contiguous states by the Canadian Province of British Columbia. Hawaii is an island chain in the Pacific, some 2000 miles southwest of California.

The land mass of the 48 contiguous states is defined by four regions of mountains and highlands. The first of these is the Coastal range, running parallel to the Pacific shoreline. The range includes the Cascade Mountains in Washington and Oregon, and the Sierra Nevada in California. The second range is the Rocky Mountains, which run from northern Idaho and Montana south and east as far as north-central New Mexico. At their southern extreme, the mountains are 1000 miles from the Pacific.

A third mountain chain, the Appalachians, runs roughly parallel to the Atlantic coast from Maine in the north to Alabama in the south. These older and less precipitous mountains were the first great obstacle to the development of the continent.

The fourth mountain region is the Ozark-Ouachita Highlands, an isolated area of hills centered in Arkansas and southern Missouri.

The other main land forms of the United States can be defined in relation to these mountain ranges. In the West, between the Coastal and Rocky Mountain ranges, is the Basin and Range region, a huge arid plateau covering a part of nearly every Western state. In the East and South, along the Atlantic and Gulf of Mexico coasts, are the coastal plains, which cover a part of nearly every Southern state. Finally, in the great midland region between the Rockies and the Appalachians is the Inland Plain. These prairies and flatlands have become the principal agricultural region of the United States and one of the most productive such regions in the world. Most of this section is drained by the Mississippi River and its tributaries, the largest and most important river system in the country.

Alaska has immense ranges of coastal mountains, including the highest point in North America (Mt. McKinley, 20,320 feet above sea level), which separate a narrow coastal area from the state's vast Arctic interior. The Hawaiian Islands are of volcanic origin, and each of the principal islands has one or more volcanic peaks.

Climate

In general, the climate of the United States is temperate—neither as cold as the vast reaches of Canada to the north, nor as hot and dry as large parts of Mexico to the south. Temperatures are generally higher in the south and lower in the north. Precipitation is, for the most part, higher in the east and lower in the west. These two weather patterns produce four principal weather regions.

The Northeastern states are generally cool and damp. Winter low temperatures range from 0° F to 30, and summer highs range from 70 to 90. Precipitation is moderate, ranging from 30 to 45 inches. The Southeast is warm and humid. Summer highs average near 90, and winter lows range from 30 to 60. In southern Florida and along the Gulf coast of Alabama and Mississippi, precipitation is over 60 inches a year; in the rest of the region it ranges from 45 to 60 inches.

The Southwestern region is warm and very dry. Except in high mountain regions, summer high temperatures average above 90, and precipitation averages between 10 and 25 inches. The deserts of Arizona and California receive less than 10 inches of rain a year and routinely record high temperatures over 100.

In general, the Northwestern region is cold and dry. Winter lows average from 0 to 20, and summer highs approach 90. The inland regions show the greatest temperature extremes in the country: readings over 100 in summer and well below zero in winter are common. Precipitation ranges from 15 to 30 inches. A narrow strip between the Pacific and the Coastal mountains in Washington, Oregon, and northern California have a much damper and more temperate climate because of the warm, moist Pacific current.

As in the Northwestern states, the Pacific shore of Alaska has a damp, temperate climate. Inland regions east and north of the Coastal mountains are bitter cold, and in the far north, average temperatures do not rise above freezing even in summer. Temperatures in Hawaii vary from 60 to 80 year-round. Precipitation varies from moderate at low altitudes and along southwest shores to over 100 inches per year at high altitudes and along northeast shores.

U.S. POPULATION 1790–1980

YEAR	POPULATION	INCREASE	% INCREASE
1790	3,929,214	—	
1800	5,308,483	1,379,269	35.1
1810	7,239,881	1,931,398	36.3
1820	9,638,453	2,398,572	33.1
1830	12,866,020	3,227,567	33.5
1840	17,069,453	4,203,433	32.7
1850	23,191,876	6,122,423	35.9
1860	31,443,321	8,251,445	35.6
1870	38,558,371	7,115,050	22.6
1880	50,155,783	11,597,410	30.1
1890	62,947,714	12,791,931	25.5
1900	75,994,575	13,046,861	20.7
1910	91,972,266	15,977,691	21.0
1920	105,710,620	13,738,354	14.9
1930	122,775,046	17,064,426	16.1
1940	131,669,275	8,894,229	6.8
1950	150,697,361	19,028,086	14.5
1960	179,323,175	28,625,814	19.0
1970	203,302,031	23,978,856	13.3
1980	226,504,825	23,202,794	11.4

U.S. POPULATION *doubled between the early 1920's and 1980.*

The People

The population of the world has increased rapidly in the last 200 years, but the rate of increase in the United States is even greater than the world average. From a base of fewer than 4 million in 1790, it increased to 10 million by about 1822; multiplied by five times in less than 60 years to 50 million in 1880; reached 100 million by 1920; 150 million in 1950; and 200 million in 1970.

In recent years, the rate of population growth has decreased, yet in absolute numbers, the country gained more than 23 million between 1970 and 1980 to record a total of 226,504,-825. Population experts predict that the total in 1990 will exceed 250 million.

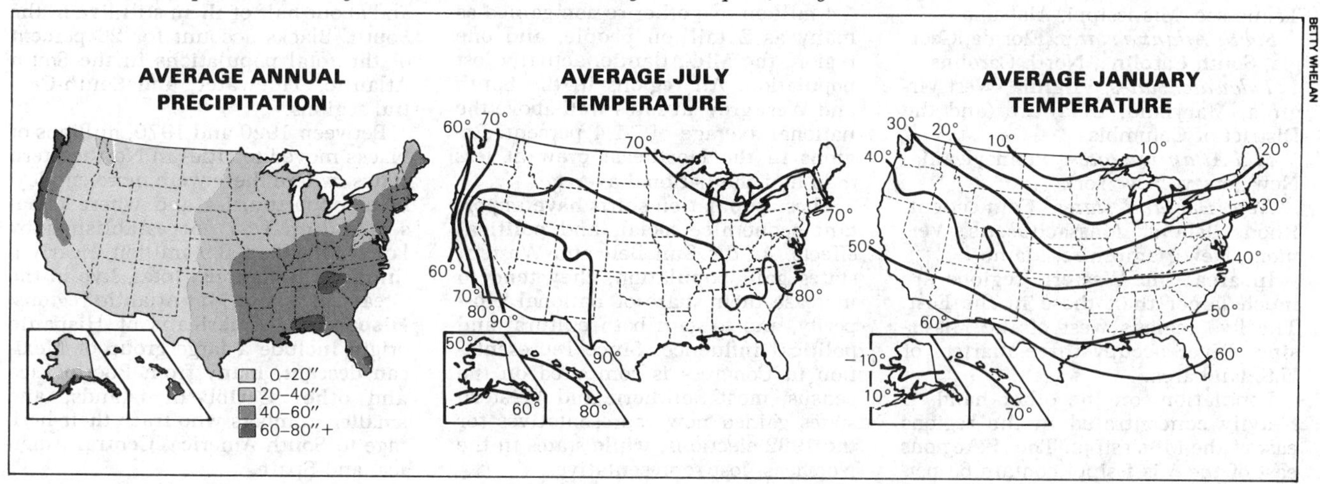

U.S. WEATHER: *Precipitation increases generally from west to east, while temperatures—both summer and winter—increase from north to south. These trends produce four large climatic areas, with small regions excepted from general rules.*

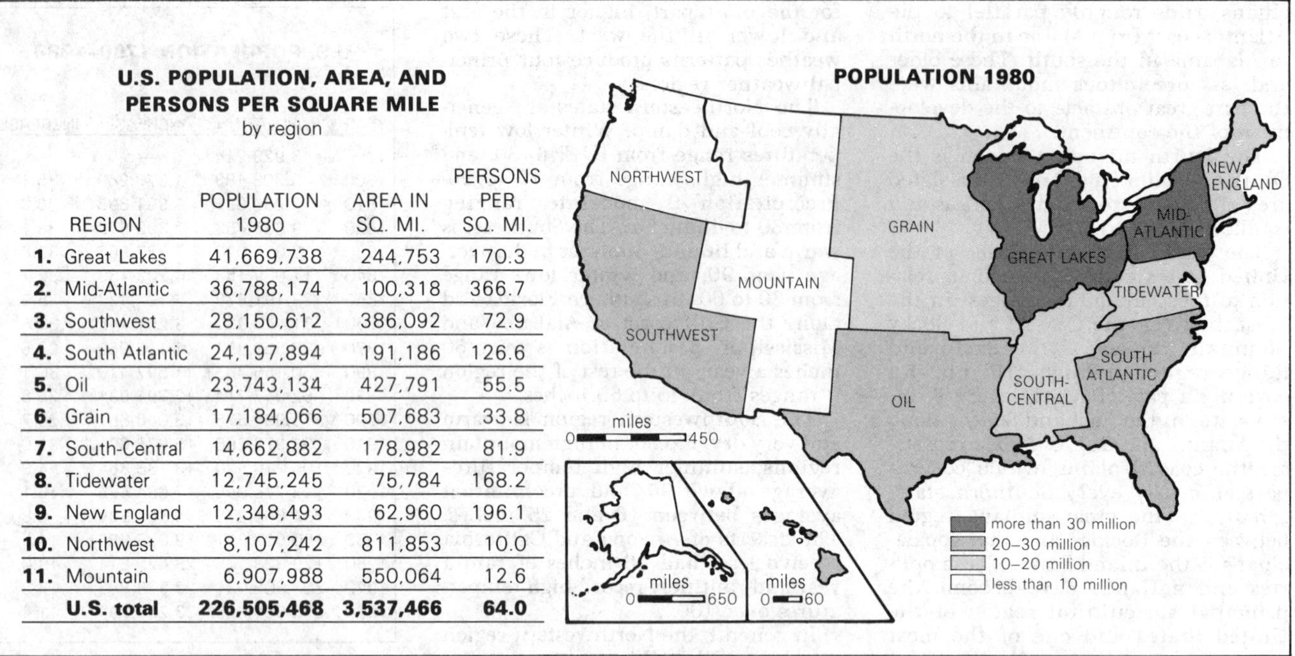

U.S. POPULATION, AREA, AND PERSONS PER SQUARE MILE
by region

REGION	POPULATION 1980	AREA IN SQ. MI.	PERSONS PER SQ. MI.
1. Great Lakes	41,669,738	244,753	170.3
2. Mid-Atlantic	36,788,174	100,318	366.7
3. Southwest	28,150,612	386,092	72.9
4. South Atlantic	24,197,894	191,186	126.6
5. Oil	23,743,134	427,791	55.5
6. Grain	17,184,066	507,683	33.8
7. South-Central	14,662,882	178,982	81.9
8. Tidewater	12,745,245	75,784	168.2
9. New England	12,348,493	62,960	196.1
10. Northwest	8,107,242	811,853	10.0
11. Mountain	6,907,988	550,064	12.6
U.S. total	**226,505,468**	**3,537,466**	**64.0**

U.S. POPULATION DISTRIBUTION IN 1980: *Two northeastern regions claim more than 35 million people each. Three others, along the southern rim, claim between 20 and 30 million. Together these five regions have more than two-thirds of the total population.*

The regions. Population is not distributed evenly throughout the country, and population growth and other characteristics differ from one section to another. In order to make these differences clear, the United States has been divided into eleven regions.

The regions, as shown in the map above, are defined as follows:

Southwest states: California, Arizona, Nevada, Hawaii

Northwest states: Oregon, Idaho, Washington, Alaska

Mountain states: Montana, Wyoming, Utah, Colorado, New Mexico

Oil states: Texas, Louisiana, Olkahoma, Arkansas

Grain states: Missouri, Kansas, Nebraska, Iowa, South Dakota, North Dakota, Minnesota

Great Lakes states: Wisconsin, Illinois, Indiana, Michigan, Ohio

South-Central states: Kentucky, Tennessee, Mississippi, Alabama

South Atlantic states: Florida, Georgia, South Carolina, North Carolina

Tidewater states: Virginia, West Virginia, Maryland, Delaware (and the District of Columbia)

Mid-Atlantic states: Pennsylvania, New Jersey, New York

New England states: Connecticut, Rhode Island, Massachusetts, Vermont, New Hampshire, Maine

In area, the Western regions are much larger than those in the East. The five regions west of the Mississippi River occupy three-quarters of U.S. land area.

Population, on the other hand, is heavily concentrated in the regions east of the Mississippi. The six regions east of the Mississippi contain 63 percent of the population on only 25 percent of the land.

Population distribution can be most easily seen by examining *density*—the number of persons per square mile in each region. Five of the six regions in the East have more than 100 persons per square mile. The Western regions range between 10 and 73.

Population growth. As a whole, the United States grew by more than 23 million, or 11.4 percent, between 1970 and 1980. This was the third largest population increase in any decade of the country's history, but the second lowest growth rate in history.

Growth was very unevenly distributed among the regions. Over 60 percent of the increase occurred in only three regions. The Southwest and the South Atlantic each gained more than 5.1 million, and the Oil states gained 4.4 million. No other region gained as many as 2 million people, and one region, the Mid-Atlantic, actually lost population. All regions in the South and West grew at rates well above the national average of 11.4 percent. Regions in the Northeast grew at less than half the national average.

These population shifts have important economic, social, and political effects. As the Sun Belt and Western states gain population, they tend to increase their share of national prosperity, and to gain both cultural and political influence. Since representation in Congress is computed on the census, most Southern and Western states gained new representatives for the 1982 elections, while states in the Northeast lost representatives.

Minorities and ethnic groups. During the 1800's Americans of foreign birth or parentage constituted a large part of the total population. Today the foreign born make up less than 5 percent of the total population. There are, however, several important minority and ethnic groups in the United States.

Of a total population of 226.5 million,

• 26.5 million, or 11.7 percent, of all Americans are black, most of them descendants of slaves brought from Africa before 1808;

• 14.6 million, or about 6.5 percent, are of Hispanic descent;

• 11.7 million, or about 5.1 percent, are designated "other" by the census; these include those of Asian, American Indian, Inuit (Eskimo), and Polynesian descent.

Blacks. Most black Americans have ancestral roots in the Southern states, and about half of them still live in the South. Blacks account for 20 percent of the total populations in the South Atlantic, Tidewater, and South-Central regions.

Between 1920 and 1970, millions of blacks moved to cities in Northeastern states, where there were more employment opportunities and where racial segregation was not established by law. More than 8.9 million, nearly a third of the national total, live in the Great Lakes and Mid-Atlantic regions.

Hispanics. Americans of Hispanic origin include a large group of Mexican descent; many from Puerto Rico and other Caribbean islands; and smaller numbers who trace their heritage to South America, Central America, and Spain.

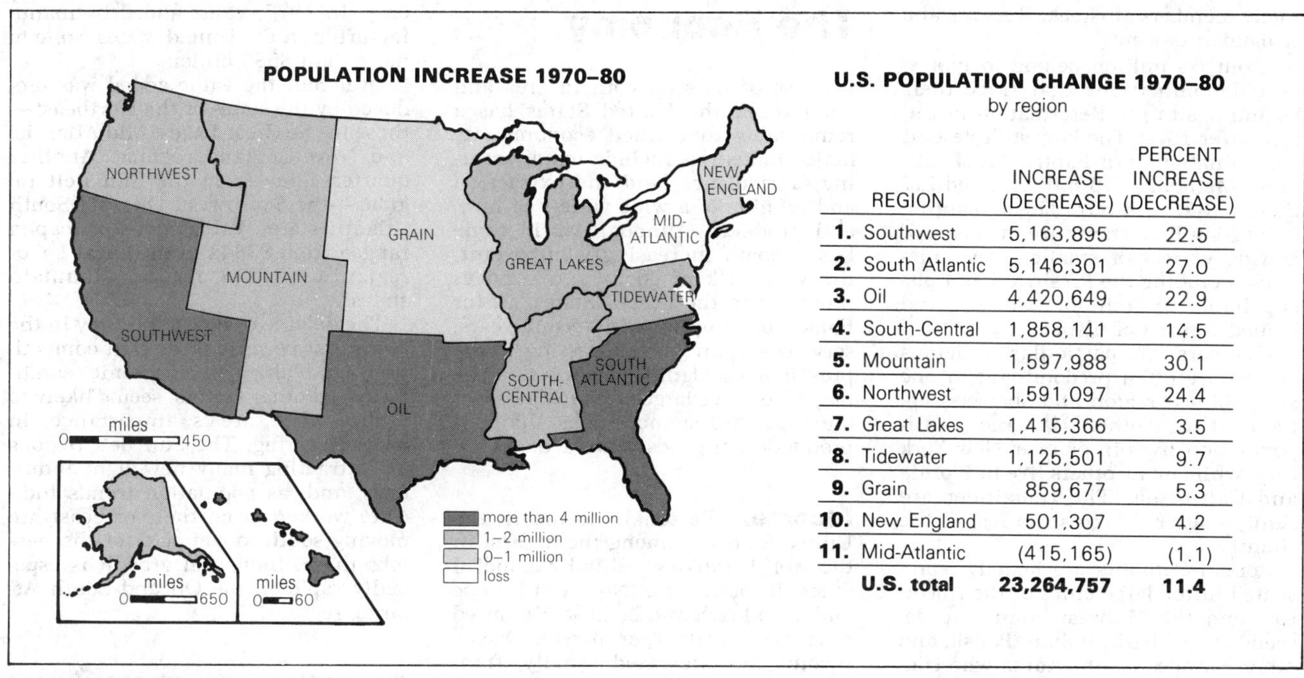

U.S. POPULATION CHANGE 1970–80
by region

REGION	INCREASE (DECREASE)	PERCENT INCREASE (DECREASE)
1. Southwest	5,163,895	22.5
2. South Atlantic	5,146,301	27.0
3. Oil	4,420,649	22.9
4. South-Central	1,858,141	14.5
5. Mountain	1,597,988	30.1
6. Northwest	1,591,097	24.4
7. Great Lakes	1,415,366	3.5
8. Tidewater	1,125,501	9.7
9. Grain	859,677	5.3
10. New England	501,307	4.2
11. Mid-Atlantic	(415,165)	(1.1)
U.S. total	**23,264,757**	**11.4**

U.S. POPULATION INCREASE *between 1970 and 1980 was greatest in the Southwest, South Atlantic, and Oil regions. These regions accounted for more than 60 percent of the country's total increase. The Mid-Atlantic region actually lost population.*

Americans of Hispanic descent are heavily concentrated in the Southwest. They account for 18 percent of the population in the Southwest region and for more than 13 percent in the Mountain and Oil regions. All together, nearly two-thirds of all Hispanics live in these three regions.

There are also considerable concentrations of Hispanic-Americans in the Mid-Atlantic states (principally around New York City), and in the Great Lakes and South Atlantic regions. Miami, Florida, has the largest population of Cuban-Americans in the country.

Asians and others. The majority of those reported by the Bureau of the Census in the "others" category are of Japanese, Chinese, Korean, Filipino, Vietnamese, or other Asian ancestry. Also included, however, are smaller numbers of American Indians, Inuit (Eskimo), and Polynesian peoples, including descendants of the native Hawaiian Islanders.

By far the largest concentration of Asians and others is in the Southwest states. California alone numbers nearly 4 million in the category, and a majority of Hawaii's population claims descent from the native islanders. As a result, more than 17 percent of the region's population falls into this category. The percentage of Asians and others is greater than the national average in the Mountain, Oil, and Northwest states as well.

MINORITIES: *The Southwest and Oil states have the highest representation of minority populations; the regions along the northern border from the Pacific Northwest to New England have the lowest.*

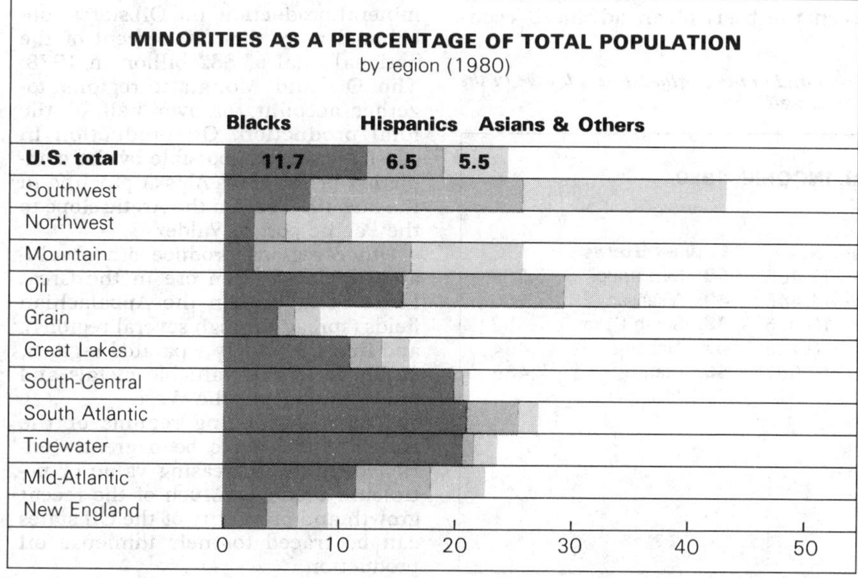

Total minorities by region. In the Southwest and Oil regions, various minorities make up more than 35 percent of the total population, compared with a national average of 23 percent. Five regions have minority populations near the national average, and four regions have substantially smaller minority populations, forming an arc across the northern United States from the Northwest to New England.

Religion.

About 55 percent of Americans report affiliation with a religious group. Of these 123 million, about 113 million are members of a Christian church. Nearly 6 million are Jewish; about 3 million, those commonly known as Mormons, are members of the Church of Jesus Christ of the Latter-Day Saints, a denomination that grew up in the United States and that combines elements of Christianity with special non-Christian doctrines. Finally, 1.5 million adhere to a variety of other religions, including Islam and various branches of Buddhism.

Of the 113 million people affiliated with Christian churches, the largest single group is Roman Catholic, with about 50 million people. Five million belong to several Eastern Orthodox Catholic churches, which include many members of Greek, Russian, and Armenian descent.

About 58 million belong to Protestant denominations that trace their beginnings to the Reformation in Europe after 1500. The largest Protestant denominations are Baptist (16.4 million), Methodist (13 million), and Lutheran (8.6 million). The remaining 20 million Protestants are members of a wide variety of smaller denominations including the Presbyterian, Episcopalian, Church of Christ, and United Church of Christ.

Members of particular religious groups are often predominant in one geographical region and sparsely represented in another. Half the Jewish population lives in or near New York City, while many others live in Florida and California. The remainder are thinly scattered across the rest of the country.

Roman Catholics are heavily represented in the large cities of the Northeast and the Midwest. Many are descendants of Irish, Italian, Polish, and other European immigrants who continue to follow the religions of their ancestral homes. In addition, many Hispanic-Americans, who are heavily concentrated in the Southwest, are Roman Catholics.

Protestant denominations are not too heavily represented in Northeastern cities, but they make up the overwhelming majority in most of the South and Midwest. Baptist churches are predominant in the South, while Methodist churches predominate in the Midwest outside of large cities. A majority of blacks who claim a religious affiliation are Baptists, but there are also sizable black memberships in some other Protestant denominations and in the Roman Catholic Church.

The Mormon church is a special case. Its headquarters are in Salt Lake City, Utah, and members of the church account for a majority of that state's population. There are also sizable numbers of Mormons in other Western states.

The Economy

Because of its size, both in area and population, the United States has a remarkably diversified economy. Its major industries include manufacturing, agriculture, and the extraction and refining of a wide variety of mineral products. Although world trade has become increasingly important, the vast bulk of goods and services produced in the United States are for home consumption. In recent years, services—from data processing to the provision of lodging for tourists—have played an ever larger role in the economy, providing more jobs than all production of goods combined.

Income. Personal income in the United States is among the highest in the world, ranking behind a handful of small countries in Northern Europe and the oil-rich Middle East. Measured on a per capita (per person) basis, income has increased rapidly, from less than $600 in 1940 to $9458 in 1980. Although the cost of living has also increased rapidly during that period, the average American has far greater purchasing power in the 1980's than his predecessors in the 1940's and '50's. Between 1940 and 1980, per capita income increased sixteenfold, while the cost of living, as measured by the consumer price index, increased only sixfold.

Per capita income varies from region to region. In general, the more industrialized areas along the Atlantic and Pacific coasts and the Great Lakes had per capita incomes above the national average, while the Southern and interior regions had incomes below the average. Cost of living differences may partially offset income differences, however.

Manufacturing. Production of manufactured goods has traditionally been the basis of an advanced economy. In 1977, value added by manufacturing in the United States came to more than $585 billion.

Over half the value added was produced by the states of the Northeast—those in the Great Lakes, Mid-Atlantic, and New England regions. Another quarter came from the Sun Belt regions—the Southwest, Oil, and South Atlantic states. Value added per capita ranged from $3842 in the Great Lakes region to $1218 in the Mountain states.

The decline of heavy industry in the Northeast because of foreign competition, and sluggish economic conditions and other factors, seems likely to reduce that area's importance in manufacturing. The Sun Belt regions are attracting many new light industries, and, as population trends indicate, workers from the Northeast are moving south to compete for the new jobs there. Industrial growth is especially rapid in the Oil and South Atlantic regions.

Agriculture. In 1979, farm marketings in the United States exceeded $131 billion. Fully a quarter of this total was produced by the Grain states. Combined with the output of the Oil and Great Lakes states, the total for the central regions is more than half the national output. On a per capita basis, the Mountain and Northwest regions are also over the national average in agricultural production. The Southwest, which includes California, the largest agricultural state in the union, contributed more than 11 percent of the national total, with a range of crops from citrus to cotton to wine grapes. As would be expected, agricultural production is lowest along the heavily populated northern Atlantic coast.

Minerals. The most important mineral product economically is oil. In mineral production, the Oil states contributed more than 40 percent of the national total of $82 billion in 1978. The Oil and Mountain regions together account for over half of the total production. Oil production in Alaska was made possible by the completion of the trans-Alaska pipeline in the late 1970's from the Arctic slope to the Pacific port of Valdez.

Other regions produce other valuable products—iron ore in the Great Lakes area; coal in the Appalachian fields (spread through several regions), and in other widely separated regions; and a variety of valuable metals and other minerals in the West.

The oil-producing regions of the United States have been greatly enriched by the increasing value of petroleum products. Much of the recent growth and prosperity of the Oil states can be traced to their immense oil production.

PERSONAL INCOME *is highest along the Pacific Coast and in the Northeast. It is lowest in the Southern states, but the cost of living may be lower as well.*

PER CAPITA PERSONAL INCOME, 1980
by region

U.S. average $9,458		Highest States		Lowest States	
1. Southwest	$10,600	**1.** Alaska	$12,406	**50.** Mississippi	6,508
2. Mid-Atlantic	10,000	**2.** Connecticut	11,445	**49.** Arkansas	7,180
3. Northwest	9,900	**3.** California	10,856	**48.** South Dakota	7,452
4. New England	9,900	**4.** New Jersey	10,755	**47.** Alabama	7,484
5. Great Lakes	9,800	**5.** Wyoming	10,692	**46.** Utah	7,485
6. Tidewater	9,600				
7. Grain	9,200				
8. Oil	9,000				
9. Mountain	8,900				
10. South Atlantic	8,300				
11. South-Central	7,500				

Trade and services. The contribution of trade and services to the total economy is more difficult to assess. Altogether, wholesale, retail trade, and service establishments paid more than $200 billion in wages and salaries in 1977. The heaviest activity is in the densely populated urban areas in the Mid-Atlantic, Great Lakes, and Southwest regions. These three areas account for 52 percent of the total payrolls in these fields.

Retail trade is especially strong along the Pacific coast and in the Great Lakes region. Wholesale trade is centered along a line from New York to Nebraska. The service economy is most active in California and along the East Coast, from Washington, D.C., to Boston, Massachusetts.

Major Cities

For political purposes, cities are still defined by city limits. But for most other purposes, they are better defined as metropolitan areas—clumps of cities and towns that most often center around the largest city in the area. People in metropolitan areas often live in one town, work in another, and shop in still another; but they tune in the same radio and television stations, follow the same sports teams, and participate in the same regional economy. All populations in this section are given for standard metropolitan areas as defined by the U.S. Census Bureau.

In all, the United States had 38 cities with metropolitan populations of more than 1 million in 1980. The seven largest have between 3 and 10 million; nine have between 2 and 3 million; and the remaining 22 have between 1 and 2 million. Together these 38 metropolitan areas have over 90 million people or about 40 percent of the national total.

All of the U.S. regions, except the South-Central, have at least one city of a million or more. But the large cities are not evenly distributed. They tend to develop in long corridors or in clusters.

Six of the eleven largest cities are part of a corridor that runs from Boston, Massachusetts, to Washington, D.C., along the Atlantic seaboard. The corridor centers on New York City and includes Philadelphia, Baltimore, and several metropolitan areas surrounding New York. In all, the corridor is the home of more than 30 million people.

A second corridor stretches along the southern shores of the Great Lakes, from Pittsburgh, Pennsylvania, and Buffalo, New York, in the east, to Chicago, Illinois, and Milwaukee, Wisconsin, in the west. There are six metropolitan areas with over a million people, including Detroit and Cleveland. This corridor has traditionally been the industrial heartland of the United States, but in recent years, its heavy industries have declined, and its cities have begun to lose population.

A third urban corridor is growing along the Pacific coast from San Francisco to San Diego, California. The largest center along this corridor is the Los Angeles area, a vast region that includes not only the Los Angeles metropolitan area, but also Anaheim–Santa Ana–Garden Grove, Riverside–San Bernardino–Ontario, and

U.S. ECONOMY: *The major manufacturing centers are in the Northeastern states. Agriculture is centered in the Midwest. Oil and mineral production is highest in the Oil and Mountain regions. The Great Lakes and Southwest regions rank high on all three lists.*

BETTY WHELAN

MANUFACTURING

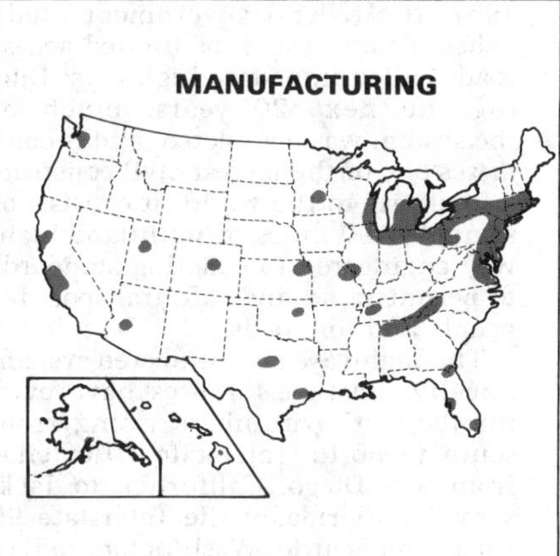

AGRICULTURE

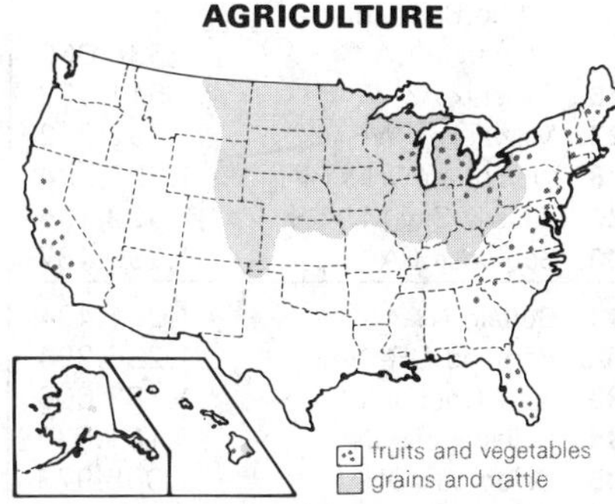

MINING

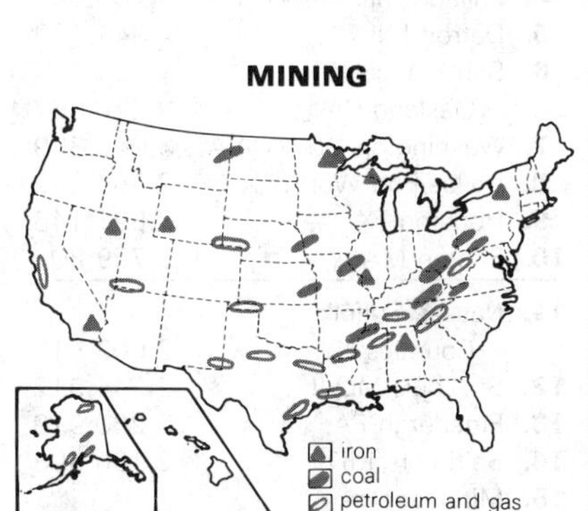

VALUE ADDED BY MANUFACTURING, 1977
by region

REGION	TOTAL (MILLION $)	PERCENT OF U.S. TOTAL
1. Great Lakes	160,223	27.4
2. Mid-Atlantic	103,160	17.6
3. Southwest	59,476	10.2
4. Oil	52,043	8.9
5. South Atlantic	48,221	8.2
6. Grain	40,666	6.9
7. South-Central	36,234	6.2
8. New England	35,587	6.1
9. Tidewater	24,084	4.1
10. Northwest	17,027	2.9
11. Mountain	8,408	1.4
U.S. totals	**585,096**	**100.0**

FARM MARKETINGS, 1979
by region

REGION	TOTAL (MILLION $)	PERCENT OF U.S. TOTAL
1. Grain	35,884	27.3
2. Great Lakes	21,157	16.1
3. Oil	18,001	13.7
4. Southwest	14,982	11.4
5. South Altantic	11,311	8.6
6. South-Central	7,972	6.1
7. Mountain	6,909	5.3
8. Northwest	5,836	4.4
9. Mid-Atlantic	5,171	3.9
10. Tidewater	2,817	2.1
11. New England	1,419	1.1
U.S. totals	**131,459**	**100.0**

VALUE OF MINERAL PRODUCTION, 1978
by region

REGION	TOTAL (MILLION $)	PERCENT OF U.S. TOTAL
1. Oil	33,655	41.2
2. Mountain	8,988	11.0
3. Southwest	6,518	8.0
4. Great Lakes	6,469	7.9
5. South-Central	6,012	7.3
6. Grain	5,046	6.2
7. Tidewater	4,538	5.6
8. Mid-Atlantic	3,773	4.6
9. Northwest	3,663	4.5
10. South Atlantic	2,813	3.4
11. New England	265	.3
U.S. totals	**81,740**	**100.0**

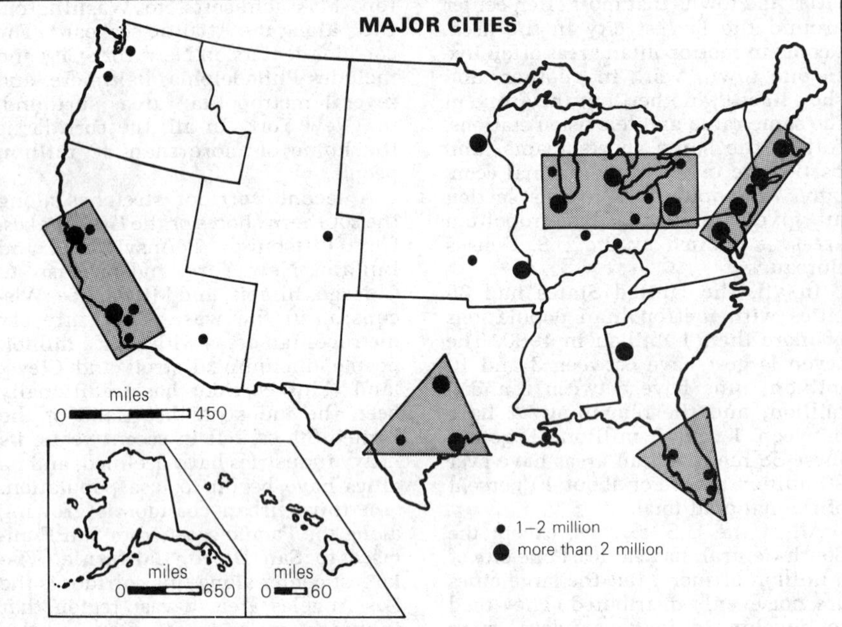

CITIES WITH METROPOLITAN POPULATIONS OVER 1 MILLION (1980)

1.	New York NY-NJ	9,080,777
2.	Los Angeles-Long Beach CA	7,445,721
3.	Chicago IL	7,057,853
4.	Philadelphia PA-NJ	4,700,966
5.	Detroit MI	4,344,139
6.	San Francisco-Oakland CA	3,226,867
7.	Washington DC-MD-VA	3,045,399
8.	Dallas-Fort Worth TX	2,964,342
9.	Houston TX	2,891,146
10.	Boston MA	2,759,800
11.	Nassau-Suffolk Counties NY	2,603,817
12.	St. Louis MO-IL	2,344,912
13.	Pittsburgh PA	2,260,919
14.	Baltimore MD	2,166,308
15.	Minneapolis-St. Paul MN-WI	2,109,207
16.	Atlanta GA	2,010,368
17.	Newark NJ	1,963,600
18.	Anaheim-Santa-Ana Garden Grove CA	1,925,840
19.	Cleveland OH	1,895,997
20.	San Diego CA	1,859,253
21.	Denver-Boulder CO	1,615,442
22.	Seattle-Everett WA	1,600,944
23.	Miami FL	1,573,817
24.	Tampa-St. Petersburg FL	1,550,035
25.	Riverside-San Bernardino-Ontario CA	1,538,066
26.	Phoenix AZ	1,511,522
27.	Milwaukee WI	1,392,872
28.	Cincinnati OH-KY-IN	1,392,394
29.	Kansas City MO-KS	1,322,156
30.	San Jose CA	1,290,487
31.	Buffalo NY	1,241,434
32.	Portland OR-WA	1,236,294
33.	New Orleans LA	1,183,606
34.	Indianapolis IN	1,161,539
35.	Columbus OH	1,088,973
36.	San Antonio TX	1,070,245
37.	Sacramento CA	1,010,989
38.	Fort Lauderdale-Hollywood FL	1,005,507

MAJOR CITIES *form large corridors of high population density and business activity. The metropolitan areas may each contain many smaller cities.*

other smaller metropolitan areas. This region contains nearly 12 million people, and it continued to grow rapidly in the 1970's.

Two other clusters of large cities have grown more recently in Texas and Florida. More than 7.5 million people live in the triangle whose corners are Houston, Dallas, and San Antonio, Texas. In Florida, rapid development along both the Atlantic and Gulf coasts has fostered six large metropolitan areas, including Miami, Tampa, and Fort Lauderdale, with a combined population of more than 6 million.

These corridors and clusters contain 27 of the 38 cities with populations over 1 million. The remaining cities are regional centers that serve as economic capitals of less developed or less populated regions. They include Seattle, Washington, Portland, Oregon, Phoenix, Arizona, and Denver, Colorado, in the West; Minneapolis, Minnesota, St. Louis, Missouri, Kansas City, Kansas, and Cincinnati, Ohio, in the Midwest; and Atlanta, Georgia, and New Orleans, Louisiana, in the South.

There are 40 additional metropolitan areas in the United States with between 500,000 and 1 million people. They include some cities that will have more than 1 million by 1990—Salt Lake City, Utah; Memphis, Tennessee; Oklahoma City; and perhaps Nashville, Tennessee.

Transportation

The development and prosperity of the United States has always depended on efficient transportation because of the country's vast distances. The economic development of the Northeastern states depended on good ocean ports, and later on rivers, canals, and roads leading to the interior. The railroad made the rapid development of the Midwest and Far West possible. More recently, the use of air transportation has been essential to the statehood and economic well-being of Alaska and Hawaii.

The principal means of transportation in the late 1900's, however, has been the automobile. A vast system of paved roads was developed by the states in the 1930's and 1940's. In 1957, the federal government established a new system of limited access roads called interstate highways. During the next 20 years, much of the system was completed, and it comprises one of the largest civil construction efforts in the world. It consists of some 42,500 miles of multilane highway engineered to exacting standards to permit rapid and safe transport for people and for goods.

The highways are numbered systematically. East-west routes have even numbers, the numbers rising from south to north. Interstate 10 extends from San Diego, California, to Jacksonville, Florida, while Interstate 90 runs from Seattle, Washington, to Boston, Massachusetts. Perhaps the most heavily traveled is Interstate 80 between San Francisco and New York.

North-south routes have odd numbers ascending from west to east. Interstate 5 parallels the Pacific coast from Seattle to San Diego; Interstate 95 runs from northern Maine to Miami, Florida.

Many spurs and city bypasses marked with prefix numbers help drivers avoid local traffic and find the fastest way to their destinations. In large metropolitan areas, the interstate highways have become an important part of local traffic patterns, enabling workers and shoppers to travel long distances in relatively short times. The system also provides a major means of transporting goods from farms and factories to market.

Long-distance travel, both for business and pleasure, has shifted more and more to the air. The United States has the largest domestic airline industry in the world. Airports in important regional centers such as Atlanta and Chicago are among the busiest in the world. International travel is especially important to airports in New York, Los Angeles, and Seattle.

Communications

Rapid communication has played an important role in the country's development. A telegraph network was already being developed before the Civil War and was proving its usefulness both for business and military communication.

The telephone was developed in the United States by Canadian Alexander Graham Bell, and it was welcomed particularly by residents of rural areas who were miles from neighbors and from towns. Today, about half of all the telephones in the world are in use in the United States. Electronic switching equipment and advanced satellite technology have allowed direct dialing and automatic billing of almost all calls within the country and of many international calls. The telephone system is also used as a connection between computers, typesetting equipment, and many other electronic devices.

The United States was a pioneer in the development of radio and television. Today hundreds of television stations and several thousand radio stations provide local programming and bring both entertainment and news from distant parts of the country and the world. At its best, broadcasting has helped promote understanding between various regions of the country and has provided a sense of unity in moments of national crisis.

Education

The American system of education has historically differed from European systems in seeking to provide more years of public education for a larger proportion of the population. A large majority of Americans receive both elementary and secondary education in local public schools. Half the adult population has completed more than twelve years of schooling, and more than half of recent high-school graduates enroll for college.

More than 11 million Americans are enrolled in over 3000 institutions of higher education. Nearly 80 percent are enrolled at publicly supported institutions, and the remaining 20 percent are in private colleges or universities.

There are heavy concentrations of colleges and universities in many major cities—especially around Boston, New York, Chicago, and San Francisco. But many important universities are located in smaller cities and towns; for example, there are major state universities in Austin, Texas, in Iowa City, Iowa, and in Bloomington, Indiana.

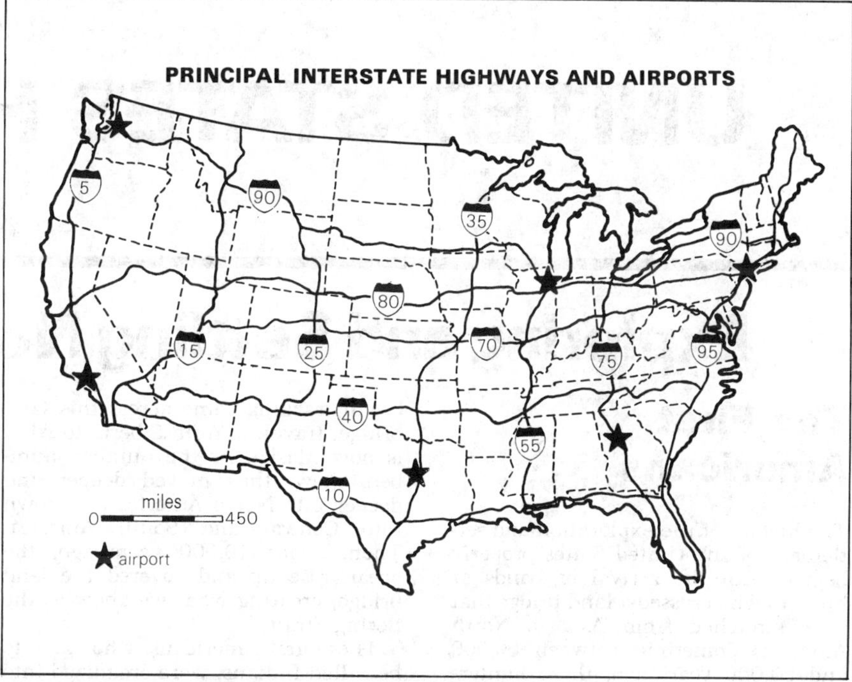

MAJOR INTERSTATE HIGHWAYS *connect all major cities and serve to transport goods as well as people over both long and short distances.*

The Arts

Aspiring writers, painters, and musicians have traditionally flocked to the large cities of the Eastern seaboard. In the 1800's, Boston and Philadelphia were the major cultural and art centers. In the early 1900's, New York was the major center of the arts, rivaled only by Chicago. As recently as the 1960's, the "Big Five" symphony orchestras were those in Boston, New York, Philadelphia, Cleveland, and Chicago.

Although the Eastern cities remain important in the arts, many Southern and Western cities are becoming important as well. Any listing of important musical centers, for example, would include Los Angeles, Minneapolis, Houston, and Santa Fe. An increasing number of important visual artists and writers live on the Pacific coast, and important new publishing centers are developing both in the West and in the South.

World Prospects

The 1900's have been called "The American Century," and through the first half of the century, the United States gradually took on a role of world leadership. Since 1960, however, the country has faced serious challenges, both from within and without. Perhaps the most serious of these have been the economic challenges of decreasing fossil fuel supplies and increasing international competition in the manufacture of such basic industrial goods as steel, automobiles, and home appliances.

Politically, the rise of China as a world power and the rising sense of nationhood among the densely populated regions of Asia, Africa, and South America make world leadership a difficult task. The continued threat of nuclear war with the Soviet Union poses a threat not just to leadership but to the survival of the United States and the rest of the world.

At home, the country continues to wrestle with racial issues that have haunted it since the Constitution was drawn up nearly 200 years ago. Problems of poverty and unemployment bring suffering to many and inspire a wide range of suggested solutions from public officials and private groups. The depletion of our natural resources and the pollution of our air and water make us wonder how profligate we can afford to be without turning nature against us.

Despite all these problems, and the responsibilities they suggest both for the U.S. government and for its citizens, the country remains more prosperous and more peaceful than any country of its size in the history of the world. After a long period of growth and development, the United States has come of age. It is learning to accept both the privileges and responsibilities of adulthood.

UNITED STATES HISTORY

Exploring and Settling North America

The First Americans

The history of the exploration and settlement of the United States properly begins with the arrival of bands of hunters who crossed a land bridge that once stretched from Asia to North America. Sometime between 50,000 and 20,000 years ago, these hunters began tracking game across this land bridge, traveling from Siberia to what is now Alaska. As the hunters' numbers grew, they moved deeper and deeper into North America and down into Central and South America. Then, about 10,000 years ago, the ocean rose up and covered the land bridge, creating what we know as the Bering Strait.

These first Americans, who came to be called Indians, were organized into a variety of tribes. It is estimated that at their most numerous, there were 2000 tribes in North America alone. They spoke at least 200 different languages and followed different ways of life. Perhaps a million Indians lived in the area that has since become the United States and Canada. Modern researchers suggest that 3 million lived in what is now Mexico and Central America, and another 20 million lived in South America.

INDIAN WAMPUM

INDIAN LAND REGIONS

Indian land regions. Geography was the main factor in determining the way of life of the first Americans. Different tribes developed different cultures, largely influenced by the characteristics of the land region in which they made their homes. In the area that would become the contiguous United States, there were five land regions that were home to five major cultural groups of Indians.

The Eastern Woodlands. This area, stretching all the way from Canada to the Gulf of Mexico and from the Atlantic coast to west of the Mississippi River, was the largest land region. The Eastern Woodlands were characterized by abundant inland waterways and coastal waters, forests filled with game, and good soil. In this environment, the tribes of the area became hunters and farmers.

The many tribes that occupied the Eastern Woodlands fell into three language groups. The largest group, the Algonkian, was scattered from Canada to Virginia; the Iroquoian group was centered in present-day New York State; and the Muskgogan group occupied the southeast.

The Plains. Stretching from the Mississippi River westward to the Rocky Mountains and from Canada southward to Mexico, the Plains were flatlands covered by tough grass. The Plains Indians lived for the most part in villages along streams and rivers. The men were hunters, and the women were farmers, raising mainly corn, squash, and beans.

The buffalo was central to the life of the Plains Indians. It is estimated that at one time from 45 to 50 million buffalo roamed North America, grazing mainly in this region. The Plains Indians hunted the huge beasts and used buffalo meat for food; buffalo skins for tepees, blankets, and shields; and even dried buffalo manure for heating fuel.

Winters on the Plains were often harsh, as cold arctic weather swept down from the north. During winter, the Plains Indians stayed close to home, in their villages. But with the coming of summer, they packed up to go on long buffalo hunts, during which they lived as nomads.

The Pacific Northwest. This area extended along the Pacific coast from southern Alaska through present-day Oregon and Washington. It was an area of great abundance. In the mild, wet climate, wild berries and other foods grew easily and plentifully. The many rivers were rich in salmon, and the coastal waters teemed with sea mammals that could be captured for their meat and warm furs. Thick forests of cedar and fir trees reached all the way down to the beaches, so wood was plentiful for building houses and hollowed-out seagoing canoes. Within the forests, game abounded. Farming was largely unnecessary because there was enough food that could be gathered or hunted. All in all, the Indians of the Pacific Northwest were well provided with food and the materials needed for shelter.

The California – Intermountain. Resources were not quite so abundant in much of this region, which included what is now California and the Great Basin that lies between the Rocky Mountains and the Cascade and Sierra Nevada ranges. The mild climate of California made it suitable for farming and for gathering foods that grew wild, like berries, acorns, and roots. Clothing and housing could be quite simple, requiring a minimum of raw materials.

Life was much harder for the Indians of the Intermountain area. Here the climate was dry and ill-suited to farming. Winters amid the mountains were harsh, and finding food was nearly impossible. People traveled in small hunting bands, finding what food they could and storing it in caves to carry them through the winter storms.

The Southwest. This huge, dry land region covers present-day Arizona, New Mexico, and southern Colorado and Utah. It is marked by steep-walled canyons, few rivers, and stretches of flat desert land. Yet the Indians who settled here were able not only to survive, but also to develop highly organized and comfortable societies. Some of the groups built their villages, or pueblos, against the canyon walls, making them resemble today's apartment buildings. They reached their "apartments" by climbing ladders. These ladders could be pulled up in case of attack.

The dry land and climate of the Southwest did not provide much food naturally, but some of the Indians devised methods of irrigation that allowed them to grow much of the food they needed, mainly corn, beans, and squash. They supplemented this with foods they could hunt or gather.

The Age of Discovery

Far to the east of the American continents, events were taking shape that would one day bring profound changes to the lives of American Indians. In Western Europe, new and powerful nations were emerging from the feudal Middle Ages. By the 1400's, nations like England, France, Spain, Portugal, and the Netherlands had been organized and strengthened by strong monarchs. A new merchant class had become increasingly important, and it was eager to extend its buying and selling powers to new markets and products. Europeans began to take an interest in the world outside their own boundaries. They sought new learning and discoveries.

Travels of the Vikings.

The first Europeans to "discover" the Americas probably did so centuries before the 1400's. The Vikings were daring seafarers who sailed from Norway, Sweden, and Denmark westward into the Atlantic Ocean from the 800's on. Having explored and settled Iceland and then Greenland, they went on to the North American coastline around 1000 A.D. Their travels took them to present-day Labrador and Newfoundland, where they attempted to establish settlements. But repeated attacks by the Indians, or *skrellings*, as the Vikings called them, drove the would-be settlers away and back to Greenland.

Voyages of the Portuguese.

As the Vikings were looking to the West, the people of several other European nations were looking to the East. The Crusades of the 1100's and 1200's had acquainted Europeans with the useful and beautiful goods of the Middle East and Asia—spices, silks, polished steel, perfumes, and fine pottery. The overland routes to these regions were slow, expensive, and often dangerous. Merchants and sailors were looking for faster and more economical sea routes.

The Portuguese were the first to succeed in this search. In 1487–1488, Bartholomeu Dias sailed down the western coast of Africa into the then mysterious and forbidding waters near the southern tip of the continent. A few years later, in 1497–1498, Vasco da Gama followed Dias's route and continued on up along Africa's east coast, through the Indian Ocean, and on to India. Soon the sailors and traders of other Atlantic nations were following the same route to successful trade.

Columbus and the Spaniards.

In the meantime, an Italian seaman from Genoa, Christopher Columbus, believed he could find a sea route to the East that was even shorter. Like most knowledgeable people of his time, Columbus believed that Earth was round rather than flat. Thus, he determined, it was possible to reach the East by sailing west. He judged the distance to Asia to be only about 3500 miles. In 1492, he convinced Queen Isabella of Spain to finance his voyage.

In August, 1492, Columbus set sail from Palos, Spain. Two months and about 3500 miles later, he landed on a tiny island that he named San Salvador, today one of the islands of the Bahamas. Thinking he had reached the Indies—the islands of present-day Indonesia—he called the people of the island Indians. He sailed on and reached what he thought was China. Actually, it was the large island of Cuba. In later years, he made three more voyages. He never found the riches of the East that he sought, but he died thinking that he had indeed reached Asia. His calculation of reaching Asia in 3500 miles was at least 7000 miles short of the true distance to the Orient.

Future Spanish explorers found the golden treasures of the great Indian civilizations of the Aztecs of Mexico, the Mayans of Central America, and the Incas of Peru. These finds encouraged more Spanish exploration, some of it farther to the north. In 1513, Juan Ponce de León, who had already found gold on the island of Puerto Rico, traveled farther west in search of a legendary "Fountain of Youth." His explorations took him up and down the coasts of Florida. In 1539, Hernando De Soto began a search for gold. His travels took him from Florida through what are now the Carolinas and as far west as present-day Oklahoma. During the same period, Francisco Coronado led an expedition in search of another legend, "the Seven Cities of Gold." His search was as fruitless as Ponce de León's had been, but he did explore the U.S. Southwest, including the Grand Canyon.

The French, English, and Dutch. The wealth that Spain was finding in the newly found lands aroused the interest of other European nations. They wanted riches from the new lands, and they also wanted a way through North America to Asia, a "Northwest Passage."

In 1524, the king of France sent Giovanni da Verrazano to explore the North American coast and find a likely waterway west. Verrazano did not succeed, but on the basis of his explorations, France laid claim to North America. Later explorers for France, like Jacques Cartier, began penetrating the continent by way of the St. Lawrence River in Canada. Following this route, Louis Jolliet and Jacques Marquette, and then Robert de La Salle, penetrated as far as the Mississippi River and down to the Gulf of Mexico.

England had begun sending its explorers to North America as early as 1497. In that year, John Cabot reached the continent's shores and claimed the "new-found-land" for England. About 80 years later, another English explorer, Martin Frobisher, tried to find a Northwest Passage. His voyage took him as far as Frobisher Bay in Canada. About 35 years later, Henry Hudson, an English seaman sailing for the Dutch, penetrated still farther into Canada in search of passage to China. He reached Hudson Bay. The previous year, he had made another attempt, following the Hudson River in what is now New York. On the basis of this expedition, the Dutch laid claim to an area extending up the Hudson River and down the Delaware River south of the Delaware Bay.

CULVER PICTURES

MARQUETTE AND JOLLIET *explored the rivers of the Midwest and claimed most of the great fertile region for France.*

Colonizing America

The nations of Western Europe began by seeking treasure in the New World. But gradually they decided to colonize the lands to which they laid claim. A colony could supply raw materials to the mother country and provide markets for goods that the mother country produced. In that way the mother country could become self-sufficient and eliminate the need to buy from other nations.

Spanish, French, and Dutch settlement. The Spanish were the first to actually establish colonies in the New World. They had claimed part of South America as well as the islands of the Caribbean, Central America, Mexico, Florida, and the region west of the Mississippi River through to California. They called the North American portion of their claim New Spain.

In 1565, the Spanish founded the first permanent European settlement in what would one day be the United States. They established the fort and village of St. Augustine along the Atlantic coast of Florida. In years to come, the Spanish would found many more settlements along the Pacific coast in California.

Cartier and the French explorers who followed him informed France of the vast riches in fish to be found along the coast of North America, especially on the Grand Banks of Newfoundland. Their explorations along inland waterways called France's attention to a potential fortune in furs in the New World from a seemingly endless supply of fur-bearing animals.

These attractions brought French settlers to New France, as the French called the territory they claimed. The territory included the St. Lawrence River valley, the Great Lakes, and the Mississippi River valley. The French established most of their larger settlements, such as Quebec and Montreal, in Canada, but they also founded smaller communities around their trading posts, especially along the Mississippi River.

The Dutch acted on their claims to North American territory too. Dutch settlers left their own land-poor nation to start farms along the rich river valleys of New Netherland. Their major settlement was New Amsterdam, established in 1626 on the island of Manhattan, which the Dutch governor Peter Minuit had bought from the Manhattan Indians for $24 worth of goods. New Amsterdam soon became an important trading center for shipping farm products and furs back to the Netherlands and elsewhere.

Early English settlements. Nearly a century passed after John Cabot's explorations before England finally began its first attempts at settlement on North America. In 1587, Sir Walter Raleigh, an English adventurer, sent 121 settlers to Roanoke Island, off the coast of what is now North Carolina. The ship that brought the settlers had to return to England for supplies and was unable to come back to Roanoke Island until 1591. When it did, it found no sign of the settlers, only the word CROATOAN carved on a tree. This was the name of an Indian tribe that lived in the area. The fate of the settlers of the "Lost Colony" remains a mystery.

Jamestown. The next attempt at settlement was made in 1607. A group

CULVER PICTURES

THE DUTCH *brought their architecture, customs, and trading instincts to the New World and soon established a prosperous colony around New Amsterdam.*

of about 120 settlers arrived in present-day Virginia and founded a community they called Jamestown. These settlers had come better prepared with supplies than the Roanoke settlers, but life was still very hard for them. The land they had chosen for their settlement was low and swampy and not good for farming. When winter came, it was very harsh and many settlers died.

For the next three years, the settlers were often on the verge of starvation. Indian attacks were common. More settlers died. Yet somehow, thanks in part to the strong leadership of Captain John Smith, Jamestown survived. It became England's first permanent settlement in the New World and the Virginia colony was established.

Plymouth. The Pilgrims, a group of people who were persecuted for their religious beliefs in England, founded the next permanent settlement. They came to America in search of a place where they might worship as they pleased. In September of 1620, 102 Pilgrims—men, women, and children—crowded aboard a tiny ship called the *Mayflower* and set sail from England to America. They headed for Virginia, but storms drove them off course and sent them northward toward Cape Cod Bay in what is now Massachusetts.

In December, they anchored in the bay and drew up a plan of government for themselves in which they promised to make "just and equal laws . . . for the general good." In their "Mayflower Compact," they agreed to abide by the will of the majority in governing themselves. After signing the compact, they went ashore. They named their settlement Plymouth after the port in England from which they had sailed.

Like the settlers at Jamestown, the Pilgrims faced great hardships that first winter. Half of them died, yet the remainder did not want to return to England. Instead, they stayed on and, with the help of Indians who were friendly to them, they learned how to farm, fish, and hunt in their strange new home. In autumn, they harvested their first crops and with the Indians celebrated the first Thanksgiving.

Massachusetts Bay Colony. Eight years after the Pilgrims arrived in Massachusetts, another, larger group of people in search of religious freedom came to settle there. They were called the Puritans because they thought that the established Church of England, of which they disapproved, was in need of purification. The Church of England did not agree, and forced the Puritans to pay taxes to support the established church. The Puritans came to the New World to escape persecution.

The new settlers established their first community at Salem and soon founded many other settlements in Massachusetts, among them Boston. The Massachusetts Bay Colony grew and thrived. In 1632, Boston became its capital, and in 1691, Plymouth joined in as part of Massachusetts Bay.

The Thirteen Colonies

The English government colonized the New World by granting charters to lands it claimed to corporations and individuals. The recipients of land grants then recruited settlers and financed the establishment of their colonies. In return, they hoped the colonies would become profitable.

Between 1607 and 1730, 13 English colonies were established along the Atlantic coast, stretching from Maine (then a part of Massachusetts) in the north to Georgia in the south. The colonies can be divided into three groups—New England, the Middle Colonies, and the Southern Colonies.

New England. In addition to Massachusetts, the colonies of New England included Rhode Island, Connecticut, and New Hampshire. The founding of these latter colonies stemmed in large part from trouble in Massachusetts. The Puritan leaders of Massachusetts were very serious about their religion and demanded that people living in Massachusetts follow Puritan beliefs and practices. But not all Puritans agreed. Roger Williams, a brilliant young Puritan minister, came to Massachusetts from England in 1631. He disagreed strongly with many practices of both the Puritan church and the government it ran. As a result, he was forced to flee the colony. In 1636, he and a few followers founded a new settlement, which they called Providence. This was the beginning of the colony of Rhode Island. Williams established a government independent of religious belief, and he encouraged toleration for the members of most religious faiths. Williams was able to get a charter from the English king for his new colony, which soon grew and prospered.

Other Puritans also left Massachusetts in disagreement with the government there. Thomas Hooker, also a Puritan minister, sought greater religious and governmental freedom. He and his followers founded a town they called Hartford. It became the basis for the colony of Connecticut. New Hampshire was also settled in part by those who dissented from the religious tenets of Massachusetts.

The Middle Colonies. New York, Delaware, New Jersey, and Pennsylvania constituted the Middle Colonies. The first settlers in this area had been Dutch, and much of the region was claimed by the Netherlands. But in 1664, the English sent four warships into the harbor of New Amsterdam and demanded that New Netherland come under English rule. The governor of New Netherland, Peter Stuyvesant, was highly unpopular with the Dutch settlers. The settlers put up no resistance to the English and thus New Amsterdam became New York, named for the Duke of York, whom the English king had named proprietor of the settlement.

The Duke of York then gave the territory south of New York to two of his friends, Lord John Berkeley and Sir George Carteret. They divided the land into East Jersey and West Jersey and became proprietors of the two areas, which would eventually become New Jersey. The colony of Delaware also went from Dutch to English control at this time.

In 1680, another colonial proprietor arrived, hoping to create a colony where the people of his religious sect could find religious freedom. William Penn, the son of a wealthy English admiral, had joined the Society of Friends, or Quakers, in England. Like the Pilgrims and the Puritans, the Quakers suffered from religious persecution in England.

When Penn's father died, it was discovered that the king of England owed him a large sum of money. William Penn asked that the debt be paid in the form of a charter that would give him the right to establish a colony. The king granted Penn an area of some 48,000 square miles.

When Penn came to visit this heavily wooded territory, he named it Pennsylvania ("Penn's woods"). There he set out a plan of government for his colony, the Great Charter and Frame of Government. In it he stated that all colonists in Pennsylvania would have the freedom to follow the religion of their choice and that all men who owned land or paid taxes would have the right to elect representatives to make the colony's laws. Pamphlets advertising Penn's new colony were distributed throughout Western Europe. Soon settlers from the British Isles, Germany, Scandinavia, and France were pouring into Pennsylvania.

The Southern Colonies. Of the Southern Colonies—Virginia, Maryland, North Carolina, South Carolina, and Georgia—Virginia was the oldest, going back to the founding of Jamestown in 1607. Maryland was next. About 25 years after Jamestown, the English nobleman George Calvert (Lord Baltimore) sought to establish a colony that offered religious freedom to Roman Catholics. Like the Quakers, Catholics were denied freedom of religion in England.

The king granted Lord Baltimore 12,000 acres just north of the Virginia colony. In 1634, about 200 settlers came to the colony, which they called Maryland.

North and South Carolina were the next Southern Colonies to be settled, although at first they were one big colony called Carolina. Carolina is the Latin form of Charles, named in honor of Charles II, England's king from 1660 to 1685. Charles had given the land grant for Carolina to eight noblemen who became proprietors of the colony. As time wore on, though, the proprietors did not feel they were making the profit they should from the colony, so they sold it back to the king. It was then divided into the two colonies of North Carolina and South Carolina.

Georgia was the last of the colonies to be established. In 1732, an English nobleman, James Oglethorpe, wanted to establish a place where people who had fallen into debt could start again. The usual procedure for dealing with such unfortunates in England was to send them into overcrowded debtors' prison, where they would be confined until someone paid their debts for them or they died.

The king, George II, granted Oglethorpe and 19 other men a generous tract of land south and west of the Savannah River. Oglethorpe and 30 fam-

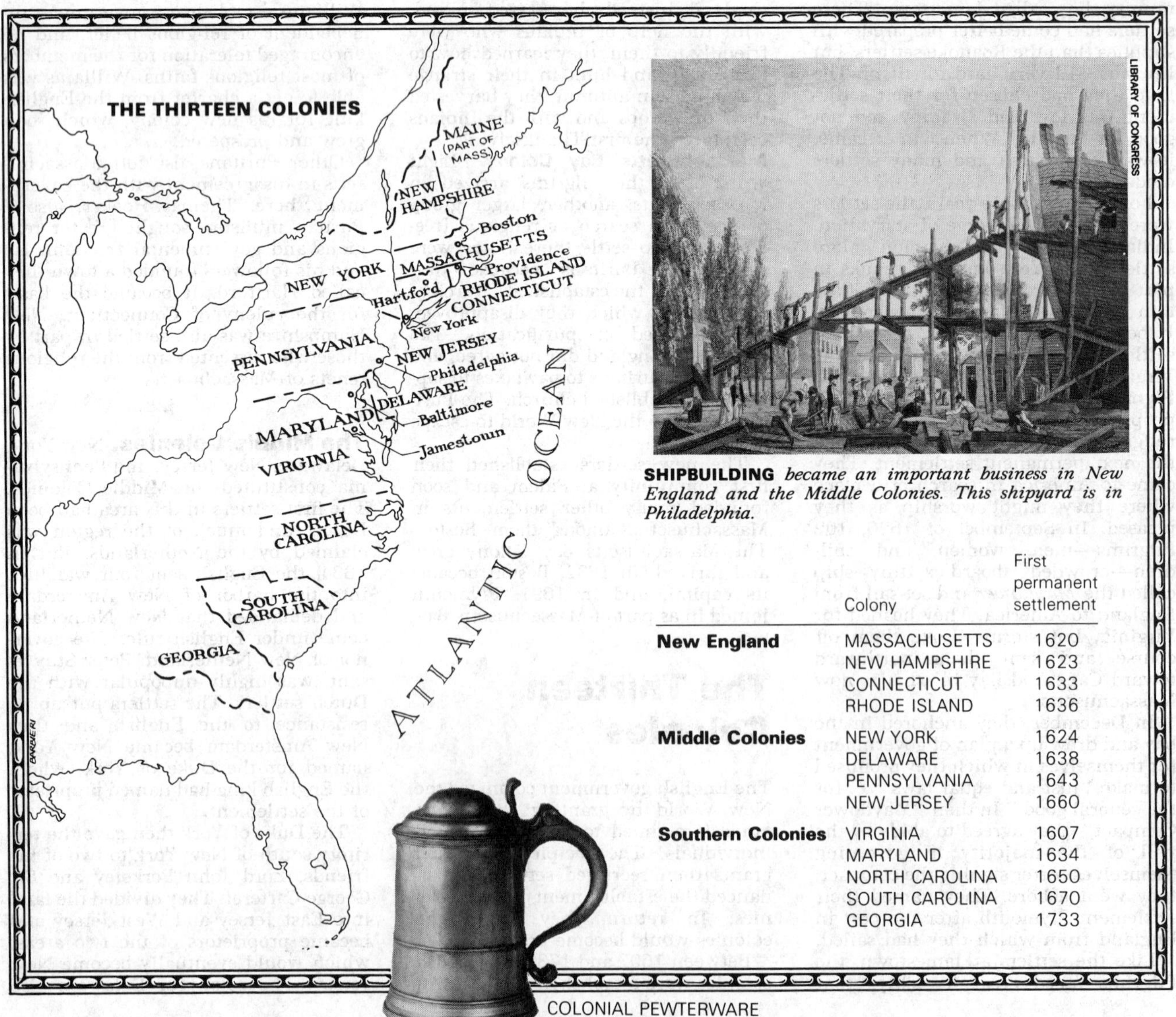

SHIPBUILDING *became an important business in New England and the Middle Colonies. This shipyard is in Philadelphia.*

	Colony	First permanent settlement
New England	MASSACHUSETTS	1620
	NEW HAMPSHIRE	1623
	CONNECTICUT	1633
	RHODE ISLAND	1636
Middle Colonies	NEW YORK	1624
	DELAWARE	1638
	PENNSYLVANIA	1643
	NEW JERSEY	1660
Southern Colonies	VIRGINIA	1607
	MARYLAND	1634
	NORTH CAROLINA	1650
	SOUTH CAROLINA	1670
	GEORGIA	1733

COLONIAL PEWTERWARE

ilies set out for Georgia, named for their benefactor, and there they began the difficult work of carving a settlement out of the wilderness. The colony did not grow quickly: debtors did not seem willing to migrate to the rough new land. Oglethorpe and the other proprietors grew disheartened, and in 1751 they turned over ownership of the colony to the king. Soon after that, Georgia began to grow and prosper.

Colonial Life

By the 1750's, the population of the 13 colonies stood at about a million and a half people, spread fairly thinly along the Atlantic coast. Most people lived on farms. A few important cities had developed: Philadelphia, Boston, New York, and Charleston, South Carolina. But even the largest of them, Philadelphia, still had fewer than 20,000 people. The colonists were overwhelmingly from the British Isles.

Representative government. The desire for representative government, for having a voice in making the laws under which all live, ran deep and strong in the colonies. The Mayflower Compact 130 years earlier had established a pattern of developing a set of written laws, of "government by law and not by men." Even before the Mayflower Compact, in 1619, the House of Burgesses had been formed in Virginia. The burgesses were the elected representatives of the Virginia colonists, and they met to determine what laws they would live under and what taxes they would pay.

By 1640, the Fundamental Orders of Connecticut had been drawn up. This plan of government was based on an earlier one in the Massachusetts Bay Colony. It provided for the election of a governor and representatives to an upper and lower house of legislature by the eligible voters of the colony. The earlier Massachusetts plan had made membership in the Puritan church a prerequisite for voting, but the Connecticut plan did not.

The government of each colony was also determined by the kind of colony it was. Royal colonies were under the direct authority of the king (New Hampshire, Massachusetts, New York, New Jersey, Virginia, North Carolina, South Carolina, and Georgia); proprietary colonies were under the authority of one or more proprietors (Maryland, Delaware, and Pennsylvania); the self-governing colonies had no direct supervision (Rhode Island and Connecticut).

All of the colonies had a governor, a council to advise the governor, and an assembly (like the House of Burgesses). In royal colonies, the king selected the governor and the governor chose his council. The voters elected the members of the assembly. In proprietary colonies, the proprietor selected the governor who then selected his council. In self-governing colonies, the voters elected the governor, his council, and the assembly.

For laws to be enacted by colonial governments, they had to be approved by the governors and the assemblies. Then they had to be approved by the English government. This need for mutual approval sometimes led to disagreements between assemblies and governors and between colonial governments and England.

The colonial economy. The economy created by the colonists was based largely on agriculture. For nearly 90 percent of the people, farming was the major source of income. The kind of farming and other economic pursuits differed from section to section.

In New England, farms were generally quite small, not more than five or ten acres of frequently rocky soil. Corn was the basic crop, and the colonists made it a staple of their diet, as cornmeal bread or mush. They fed the stalks to their livestock and used the husks to make mattresses.

The sea was also important to the New England economy. Many fishing villages sprang up along the coast, and hundreds of fishing boats went out to gather cod and haddock from the rich waters. Shipbuilding flourished as the colonists used their forests for this new industry. Ships were in demand as New England merchants developed a busy trade with Europe, Africa, and even China.

The Middle Colonies were blessed with richer soil than New England, and soon they had developed into the breadbasket of American colonies. Wheat was the main crop, and the Middle Colonies grew so much of it that it soon became a major export. Port cities like New York and Philadelphia attracted artisans who produced a wide variety of useful and fine goods, like hats, furniture, wigs, and carriages.

In the Southern Colonies, rich soil, flat land, and a warm climate combined to promote the development of large plantations that produced tobacco, rice, cotton, and indigo. Plantation owners found ready markets for these goods, and they traded agricultural products for manufactured goods.

The need for workers on the plantations led to the introduction of slavery. From the earliest days of colonization, there had been people in servitude. Indentured servants were people who agreed to work as servants for a predetermined period of time, perhaps five or seven years, in return for their passage to America and for some land and tools with which to start off on their own. In 1619, Africans were brought to Jamestown in Virginia as indentured servants. But before long, Africans were being brought to American shores as slaves, to work for masters for their entire lives.

Creating the American Republic

War and Disagreement

France and Great Britain had pressed conflicting claims in North America. Both nations claimed the Ohio River valley, west of the Appalachian Mountains. They were attracted by the fur-trapping and the rich farmland there. Since 1689, the two nations had often fought over their claims, but the matter was never settled.

The French and Indian War. In 1754, Britain sent a trained army of about 1400 soldiers, along with 450 soldiers of the Virginia militia under the command of 22-year-old George Washington, to attack the French in the Ohio River valley. This attack set off the French and Indian War. The British lost this first battle, but they won later ones. In 1763, they could claim victory over the French. The peace treaty gave the British the land west of the Appalachians to the Mississippi River and all of Canada.

The colonists looked happily toward settling the new lands to the west. But now the British government forbade settlement west of the Appalachians because it did not want to have to provide troops to protect settlers from Indian attacks. In addition, the British demanded more taxes from the colonists to help pay off the debts incurred in fighting the French. The colonists objected, saying that their assemblies had already collected taxes to support the war. Resentment of the British government began to grow.

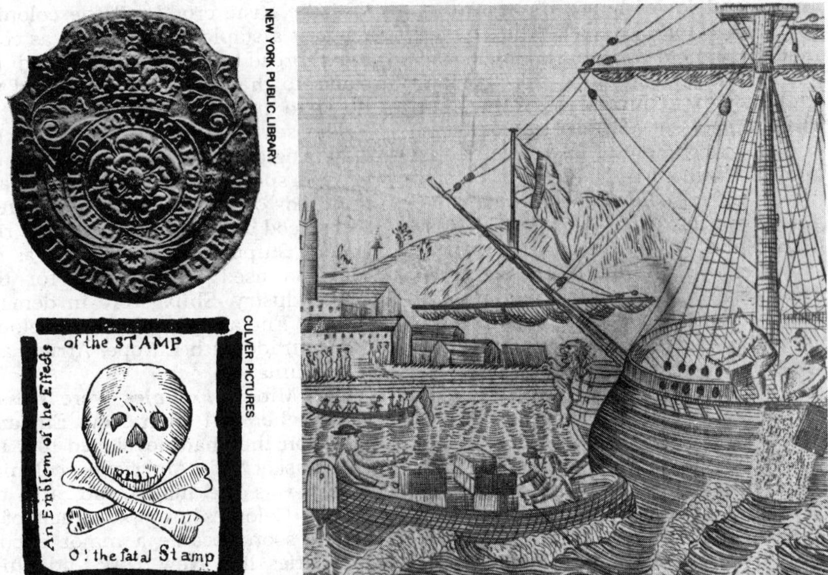

NEW YORK PUBLIC LIBRARY

CULVER PICTURES

CULVER PICTURES

TAXES AND RESISTANCE: *the Stamp Act (1764) required paying for a stamp,* upper left, *to be placed on newspapers and documents. The* Pennsylvania Journal *published one last issue under the skull and crossbones,* lower left, *then ceased publication rather than pay. Nine years later, the British monopoly of tea resulted in the famous Boston Tea Party,* above.

Actions and Reactions

For 150 years, the people of the American colonies had lived in relative freedom. British rule over them had been lax, partly because the British government did not have any centralized authority to oversee colonial affairs.

Following the French and Indian War, however, British rule began to tighten. The mother country had always placed some trade restrictions on the colonies. For example, the Navigation Acts passed during the 1600's stated that all goods shipped into and out of the colonies had to be transported on British-owned or colonial-owned ships; that goods going from the colonies to other nations of Europe had to first pass through British ports, where the British could collect taxes on them; and that some colonial goods—like tobacco, sugar, rice, cotton, molasses, and indigo—could be shipped only to Britain, and never sold to any other markets.

There were also some restrictions on the goods the colonists were allowed to manufacture (so they would not be competitive with British manufactures). Enforcement of these restrictions was never very firm, and colonists engaged in massive smuggling to get around them. As the British government sought new revenues, it wanted to enforce these trade laws and impose new ones.

The Grenville Acts. In 1764, Lord George Grenville, Britain's prime minister, began a campaign to strengthen British authority over the colonies. The Sugar Act imposed new duties on many goods shipped to the colonists from Britain. The Quartering Act required colonial governments to provide quarters and supplies for British troops stationed in the colonies. The Stamp Act ordered colonists to pay for a tax stamp every time they bought a newspaper or playing cards or received a legal document.

American protest against these measures was immediate and loud. Colonial merchants complained that the Sugar Act duties were more than they could afford. Colonial governments refused to obey the Quartering Act. But the Stamp Act drew the greatest fire. In Virginia's House of Burgesses, Patrick Henry rose up to condemn it and the English king, saying "If this be treason, make the most of it!"

Groups of angry colonists organized the Sons of Liberty, who openly defied the act by attacking stamp tax collectors. Representatives from nine colonies formed a Stamp Act Congress, which sent a formal protest to King George III asserting that only colonial assemblies had the right to tax the colonists. "Taxation without representation is tyranny," they cried. In response to this protest, the hated Stamp Act was repealed. But new laws were on the way.

The Townshend Acts. Grenville was forced to resign, but his ideas still had support in Charles Townshend, the head of the British treasury. In 1767, Townshend persuaded the British Parliament to place a new set of revenue-producing duties on glass, lead, paper, pepper, and tea brought into the colonies. The colonists saw these duties as thinly disguised taxes.

Some Americans determined to avoid paying the new duties by smuggling goods into the colonies. Others decided to do without the goods rather than pay. Imports of the listed goods went down by 50 percent. Boston became a hotbed of resistance. Britain stationed troops there to keep the peace and enforce the duties.

The citizens of Boston, forced to quarter the British troops, grew more and more angry. On March 5, 1770, their anger exploded into violence. As a crowd of Bostonians taunted redcoated soldiers standing guard near the Customs House, a shot rang out, and the soldiers opened fire on the crowd. When the smoke cleared, five of the colonists lay dead in the snow. Word of this "Boston Massacre" spread quickly through the colonies.

The next month, the British government once again backed down. It repealed all the Townshend duties except the one on tea. It left that as a symbol of its right to tax the colonists.

Organized resistance.
Following the Boston Massacre, Samuel Adams, a Boston lawyer, began organizing a large number of Committees of Correspondence. Their purpose was to keep tabs on British actions in the colonies and to pass information along to other colonists. The committees encouraged opposition to British actions. Soon there were Committees of Correspondence in nearly every colony. In addition to Sam Adams, members included John Hancock and James Otis of Massachusetts and Patrick Henry and Thomas Jefferson of Virginia.

In 1773, the British passed the Tea Act, which favored a British tea-selling company and threatened to put colonial tea merchants out of business. In the dark of night on December 16, 1773, 50 Sons of Liberty disguised as Indians stole aboard three ships in Boston Harbor that were loaded with tea from the hated British tea company. Within an hour's time, all of the tea had been thrown overboard into the harbor. This "Boston Tea Party" enraged the British government.

The Intolerable Acts. The British were quick to retaliate. Early in 1774, Parliament began passing a series of Coercive Acts, called "Intolerable Acts" in America. The first act, the Boston Port Bill, closed Boston harbor to all shipping. This threatened the people of Boston with shortages of food and with business failures. Another act took the Massachusetts government out of colonial hands and placed it under British military rule. It also forced the colonists to quarter the 10,000 British soldiers sent to administer the new laws.

Toward Independence

The British government intended the Coercive Acts to punish and isolate Massachusetts. Instead, the acts served only to rally the other colonies to Massachusetts's support and defense. At first news of Boston's fate, the Virginia House of Burgesses called for a meeting of representatives to come from all the colonies and draw up a united protest.

The First Continental Congress. In September of 1774, 56 delegates from twelve colonies (only Georgia was absent) met in Philadelphia, where they took the following steps:

1. Declared the Coercive Acts null and void and therefore not to be obeyed.
2. Pledged that their colonies would not buy goods from Britain.
3. Urged the colonists of Massachusetts not to pay any taxes to their military government.
4. Encouraged Massachusetts to organize a militia.
5. Sent a formal protest to King George III.
6. Planned to meet again the following May.

Parliament and the king replied to the protest by sending more troops to the colonies to put down any unrest.

Lexington and Concord. The British troops would soon be needed. The military governor of Massachusetts, General Thomas Gage, learned that the colonists were training a militia of "Minutemen" who could mobilize at a minute's notice. The Minutemen had a supply of guns and ammunition in a warehouse at Concord, a few miles outside Boston. Gage ordered 800 British soldiers to march from Boston to Concord and capture the supplies in a surprise raid. But the colonists set up a system to warn the people when the British troops made their move.

On the night of April 18, 1775, a light flashed from the tower of Boston's Old North Church. It alerted Paul Revere and William Dawson to race along the roads to Concord on horseback, warning that "the British are coming."

When the British got to Lexington, they were met by Captain Thomas Parker's company of 70 Minutemen. "If they mean to have war," said Parker, "let it begin here." Gunfire exploded and seven Minutemen fell dead. The British continued on to Concord, where Minutemen drove them away and back on the road to Boston. By that time, some 30 towns in eastern Massachusetts had been roused, and their 3700 Minutemen sniped at the retreating British troops from behind walls and trees, killing 240 of them.

The Second Continental Congress. Less than a month later, on May 10, 1775, the Second Continental Congress assembled in Philadelphia. This time all the colonies sent delegates, among whom were George Washington, John Adams, Benjamin Franklin, Thomas Jefferson, and John Hancock.

Once again, the Congress petitioned the English king, this time to repeal the Intolerable Acts and to refrain from any more "unprovoked attacks" such as those at Lexington and Concord. The Congress also asked the colonies to send soldiers to help the Minutemen who were still fighting around Boston. It named George Washington as the commander of the American forces.

Before he could reach Boston, however, a major conflict flared between Americans and British there. The Americans had dug in at Breed's Hill and Bunker Hill north of Boston. In June of 1775, General Gage sent 2400 British troops to dislodge them. The Americans stuck to their guns, but after three charges, the British troops drove them out. This victory in the Battle of Bunker Hill cost the British nearly 1000 casualties.

Still, the Continental Congress did not call for total revolution against Britain. Many Americans were still willing to stay loyal to the British Crown; they simply wanted to end what they saw as Britain's unfair and wrongful actions toward them. Then, in September of 1775, the colonists learned that the British Parliament not only refused to grant the petition of the Continental Congress, but also declared that the colonies were in revolt and that Britain would take military action against them.

In May of 1776, the Second Continental Congress met once more and declared, "It appears absolutely irreconcilable to reason and good conscience for the people . . . to support any government under the Crown of Great Britain."

The Declaration of Independence. In June, 1776, Richard Henry Lee of Virginia brought a motion before the Continental Congress: "*Resolved,* that these United Colonies are, and of right ought to be, free and independent States." Five delegates—Thomas Jefferson, Benjamin Franklin, John Adams, Robert R. Livingston, and Roger Sherman—began preparing a declaration to embody this motion. Thomas Jefferson did most of the writing, and in July, the Declaration of Independence was presented to the Continental Congress.

THE DECLARATION OF INDEPENDENCE

Adopted by the Continental Congress, July 4, 1776

WHEN in the Course of human Events, it becomes necessary for one People to dissolve the Political Bands which have connected them with another, and to assume among the Powers of the Earth, the separate and equal Station to which the Laws of Nature and of Nature's God entitle them, a decent Respect to the Opinions of Mankind requires that they should declare the causes which impel them to the Separation.

We hold these Truths to be self-evident, that all Men are created equal, that they are endowed by their Creator with certain unalienable Rights, that among these are Life, Liberty, and the Pursuit of Happiness—That to secure these Rights, Governments are instituted among Men, deriving their just Powers from the Consent of the Governed, that whenever any Form of Government becomes destructive of these Ends, it is the Right of the People to alter or to abolish it, and to institute new Government, laying its Foundation on such Principles, and organizing its Powers in such Form, as to them shall seem most likely to effect their Safety and Happiness. Prudence, indeed, will dictate that Governments long established should not be changed for light and transient Causes; and accordingly all Experience hath shewn, that Mankind are more disposed to suffer, while Evils are sufferable, than to right themselves by abolishing the Forms to which they are accustomed. But when a long Train of Abuses and Usurpations, pursuing invariably the same Object, evinces a Design to reduce them under absolute Despotism, it is their Right, it is their Duty, to throw off such Government, and to provide new Guards for their future Security. Such has been the patient Sufferance of these Colonies; and such is now the Necessity which constrains them to alter their former Systems of Government.

. . .

(Here follows a list of specific complaints against the King and the British government.)

. . .

We, therefore, the Representatives of the UNITED STATES OF AMERICA, in GENERAL CONGRESS, Assembled, appealing to the Supreme Judge of the World for the Rectitude of our Intentions, do, in the Name, and by Authority of the good People of these Colonies, solemnly Publish and Declare, That these United Colonies are, and of Right ought to be, FREE AND INDEPENDENT STATES; that they are absolved from all Allegiance to the British Crown, and that all political Connection between them and the State of Great-Britain, is and ought to be totally dissolved; and that as FREE AND INDEPENDENT STATES, they have full Power to levy War, conclude Peace, contract Alliances, establish Commerce, and to do all other Acts and Things which INDEPENDENT STATES may of right do. And for the support of this Declaration, with a firm Reliance on the Protection of divine Providence, we mutually pledge to each other our Lives, our Fortunes, and our sacred Honor.

This historic document was composed of two parts: a preamble that justified the colonists' rights as God-given, and a list of grievances that showed how the tyrannical King George III had mistreated them. On July 4, 1776, the Congress adopted the Declaration. The new United States were on their way to full revolution.

The American Revolution

By July 4, 1776, the Revolution was actually more than a year old. Following Lexington and Concord, Boston lay under siege for nearly a year as the Americans continued to fight to drive the British out. Finally, on March 26, 1776, the British forces under the command of General William Howe pulled out and sailed to a friendlier base in Canada.

War in the Middle Colonies.

In the summer of 1776, General Howe landed 30,000 British troops in New York City. Washington had moved his troops there from Boston, but they were no match for the British force. Howe easily defeated the Americans and occupied New York City.

Trenton and Princeton. Washington retreated through New Jersey and into Pennsylvania in the autumn. As winter set in, the British believed that the war would wind down, but Washington surprised them. On Christmas night, Washington and 6000 troops crossed the icy Delaware River to attack the British garrison at Trenton, New Jersey. The force there, made up of Hessian (German) mercenaries hired by the British, quickly surrendered. Washington moved on to Princeton, where his men captured two British regiments and their guns and supplies.

Saratoga. In 1777, British General John Burgoyne presented a plan he thought would crush all effective American resistance. He believed that the Hudson River valley was the key. If the British could win control there, they could gain full control of New York and cut off New England from the other colonies.

Burgoyne's plan called for him to lead an army south from Montreal in Canada to the Hudson River. A second army, under the command of Colonel Barry St. Leger was to enter western New York from Canada over Lake Ontario and sweep in from the west. A third army, under General Howe, was to move up the Hudson River from New York City toward Albany.

Unfortunately for the British, the plan did not work. St. Leger's force was stopped by an American force under the command of General Nicholas Herkimer and retreated to Canada. General Howe had a plan of his own, to capture Philadelphia, the American capital. Instead of moving north up the Hudson, he moved south, capturing Philadelphia after defeating Washington at Brandywine and Germantown. Burgoyne's troops marched south as far as Saratoga on the Hudson north of Albany, where the Continental Army surrounded them and forced their surrender on October 17, 1777.

NEW YORK PUBLIC LIBRARY

GEORGE WASHINGTON *reviews his troops at Valley Forge, 1777–1778.*

The Battle of Saratoga proved the turning point of the American Revolution. It weakened the British and strengthened American morale, and it also helped to convince France that the Americans just might be able to win the war. The French concluded that they should offer to support the Americans with troops and supplies against the common enemy, and they signed a treaty of alliance on February 6, 1778.

Valley Forge. Following the loss of Philadelphia, Washington moved his troops to Valley Forge in Pennsylvania for winter encampment. The winter of 1777–1778 was a terrible period of starvation, disease, and suffering for the American troops. Yet they endured, and thanks to military drill and training, they came out a stronger army than before.

War at sea.

The powerful British navy had little to fear from the rebellious Americans. The Continental Congress had tried to create an American navy, but there was little money to build ships and the British easily destroyed most of the ships that were built. Some owners of fishing boats or merchant ships equipped their vessels with guns and went to sea as privateers, harassing British shipping and sometimes capturing trading ships.

The most famous naval battle of the American Revolution was fought off the coast of England in 1779 between the American ship *Bonhomme Richard*, an old French warship under the command of Captain John Paul Jones, and the larger British ship *Serapis.* After several hours of battle, the *Bonhomme Richard* was close to sinking when Jones brought it near to the *Serapis.* Thinking that the American ship wanted to surrender, the British captain asked, "Have you struck your colors?" Jones shouted his famous reply, "I have not yet begun to fight!"

With that, Jones's men leaped aboard the British ship and engaged its crew in hand-to-hand combat. More than half the Americans were killed or wounded, but Jones captured the *Serapis* as the *Bonhomme Richard* sank behind him. Jones then set sail for the friendly shores of France.

War in the South.

In 1778, the British developed a new plan to defeat the rebellious colonists. They attacked the Southern Colonies with plans to march northward. In December, British forces attacked Savannah, the major port of Georgia. The attack succeeded and the British soon took control of most of the colony. In 1780, British forces under the command of General Charles Cornwallis sailed into the South Carolina port of Charleston and captured it. British troops began the march north to capture the Carolinas. Britain's southern strategy seemed to be working.

However, when Cornwallis's men reached King's Mountain in North Carolina, they were in for a surprise. A few hundred Kentucky and Tennessee riflemen wiped out half of Cornwallis's army. In the next few months, the British lost more battles in the Carolinas to Americans under the command of Generals Nathanael Greene and Daniel Morgan. In the end, the British were able to hold onto Savannah and Charleston but nothing else.

Yorktown. In June, 1781, the British government ordered Cornwallis to invade Virginia. It was defended by a small American force under the command of the Marquis de Lafayette, a young French nobleman who had offered his military services to the Continental Congress. Cornwallis and Lafayette fought to a stalemate. Cornwallis made camp at Yorktown, Virginia, on the Chesapeake Bay, where he waited for the British navy to resupply him with fresh troops, ammunition, and provisions.

Before Cornwallis could receive help, however, Washington and his army, along with French troops commanded by Marshall Rochambeau, moved south to Virginia to attack by land. The French fleet arrived to blockade Chesapeake Bay, cutting off any possibility of resupply or escape by sea for the British. Surrounded and cut off, Cornwallis was forced to surrender. He and his 8000 men laid down their arms on October 18, 1781. Sporadic fighting continued in the colonies for the next year, but essentially the American Revolution was over and a new independent nation was born.

THE AMERICAN REVOLUTION 1766–1783

In the following listing of battles and events in the American Revolution, (A) indicates an American force and (B) a British force. The winning generals appear in italics. The symbol (k) denotes killed in action.

1766–1774

Mar. 8, 1766 Repeal of the Stamp Act.
Mar. 5, 1770 Boston Massacre.
June 9, 1772 Burning of the Gaspé.
Dec. 16, 1773 Boston Tea Party.
Sept. 5 to Oct. 6, 1774 First Continental Congress.

1775

Apr. 18 Paul Revere's ride.
Apr. 19 Fight at Lexington and Concord—*Capt. John Parker (A)*; Maj. John Pitcairn (B).
May 10, 1775 to Mar. 3, 1789 Second Continental Congress.
May 10 Capture of Ticonderoga—*Ethan Allen (A)*; Capt. Delaplace (B).
May 12 Capture of Crown Point—*Seth Warner (A)*.
June 17 Battle of Bunker Hill—*William Prescott (A)*; Gov. Thomas Gage (B).
July 3 Washington assumes command of the Continental Army at Boston.
July 1775 to Mar. 1776 Siege of Boston—*Washington (A)*; Sir William Howe (B).
Sept. to Dec., 1775 American invasion of Canada—Richard Montgomery (A); Sir Guy Carleton (B).
Nov. 12 Capture of Montreal—*Gen. Richard Montgomery (A)*: Sir Guy Carleton (B).

1776

Mar. 17 British evacuate Boston.
July 4 Declaration of Independence adopted by Continental Congress in Philadelphia.
Aug. 27 Battle of Long Island, N.Y.—Washington (A); *Sir William Howe (B)*.
Sept. 15 Occupation of New York City by British.
Sept. 16 Battle of Harlem Heights—Washington (A); *Sir William Howe (B)*.
Sept. 22 Execution of Nathan Hale (A) as a spy.
Oct. 11-13 Naval battle on Lake Champlain—Benedict Arnold (A); *Sir Guy Carleton (B)*.
Nov. 16 Loss of Fort Washington, N.Y.—Col. Robert Magaw (A); *Sir William Howe (B)*.
Nov.-Dec. Washington's retreat through New Jersey.
Dec. 25 Washington crosses the Delaware River.
Dec. 26 Battle of Trenton, N.J.—*Washington (A)*; Johann G. Rall (B).

1777

Jan. 3 Battle of Princeton, N.J.—*Washington (A)*; Lt. Col. Mawhood (B).
Apr. 25-26 British raid and burn Danbury—*Benedict Arnold and David Wooster (A)*; Col. William Tryon (B).
July 6 Americans evacuate Ticonderoga—Arthur St. Clair (A).
Aug. 4-22 Siege of Ft. Stanwix (Schuyler—now Rome), N.Y.—*Peter Gansevoort (A)*; Barry St. Leger (B).
Sept. 11 Battle of Brandywine, Pa.—Washington (A); *Sir William Howe (B)*.
Sept. 18 Continental Congress flees Philadelphia to York, Pa.
Sept. 21 The Paoli "Massacre," Pa.—Anthony Wayne (A); *Gen. Grey (B)*.
Sept. 25 British occupy Philadelphia, Pa.
Oct. 4 Battle of Germantown, Pa.—Washington (A); *Sir William Howe (B)*.
Oct. 6 British capture Forts Montgomery and Clinton, N.Y., on the Hudson—James Clinton (A); *Henry Clinton (B)*.
Oct. 17 Surrender of the British Army at Saratoga, N.Y., by Sir John Burgoyne.
Nov. 15 Articles of Confederation submitted to the States for ratification.
Dec. 19, 1777 to June 17, 1778 Washington's army encamped at Valley Forge, Pa.

1778

Jan. Exposure of the Conway Cabal seeking removal of Washington from command of American army.
Feb. 6 Franco-American treaty of alliance signed in Paris.
June 18 British evacuate Philadelphia.
June 28 Battle of Monmouth, N.J.—*Washington (A)*; Sir Henry Clinton (B).
July 4 Wyoming (Pa.) Massacre—Col. Zebulon Butler (A); *Col. John Butler (B)*.
July 4-Aug. 12 Court-martial of Gen. Charles Lee for conduct at Battle of Monmouth.
July 11 Arrival of French fleet under Comte d'Estaing off Sandy Hook, N.Y.
Aug. 8-11 Siege of Newport, R.I.—Washington (A); *Sir Henry Clinton (B)*.
Nov. 11 Cherry Valley (Pa.) Massacre—by Indians led by Chief Joseph Brant (B).
Dec. 29 Capture of Savannah, Ga., by British—Gen. Robert Howe (A); *Lt. Col. Archibald Campbell (B)*.

1779

Jan. 29 British conquest of Georgia completed—Gen. Robert Howe (A); *Lt. Col. Archibald Campbell (B)*.
Feb. 24 Capture of Vincennes, Ind.—*George Rogers Clark (A)*; Henry Hamilton (B).
Mar. 3 Battle of Briar Creek, Ga.—Col. John Ashe (A); *Lt. Col. Prevost (B)*.
July 5 Plundering and burning of New Haven, Conn., by British led by Gov. William Tryon.
July 16 Storming of Stony Point, N.Y.—*Anthony Wayne (A)*; Lt. Col. Henry Johnson (B).
July 25 Penobscot (Me.) Expedition—Solomon Lowell (A).
Sept. 23 Naval action, *Bon Homme Richard* and *Serapis*—*John Paul Jones (A)*; Richard Pearson (B).
Sept. 29 to Oct. 9 American siege of Savannah, Ga.—Benjamin Lincoln (A); *Sir James Wright (B)*.
Oct. 9 American assault at Savannah and death of Pulaski—Lincoln (A); *James Wright (B)*.

1780

Apr. 10-May 12 British siege of Charleston, S.C.—Benjamin Lincoln (A); *Sir Henry Clinton (B)*.
May 12 American surrender of Charleston, S.C.—Lincoln (A); *Henry Clinton (B)*.
July 10 Arrival of French troops under Rochambeau at Newport, R.I.
July 25 Gen. Horatio Gates assumes command of American army in the South.
Aug. 6 Battle of Hanging Rock, S.C.—*Thomas Sumter (A)*; Banastre Tarleton (B).
Aug. 16 Battle of Camden, S.C.—Horatio Gates (A); *Lord Cornwallis (B)*.
Sept. 21 Benedict Arnold's (A) treason.
Oct. 2 Execution of John André (B) at Tappan, N.Y., as a spy.
Dec. 4 Gen. Nathanael Greene assumes command of the American army in the South.

1781

Jan. 1 Mutiny of Pennsylvania line in Washington's army at Morristown, N.J.
Jan. 17 Battle of Cowpens, S.C.—*Col. Daniel Morgan (A)*; Tarleton (B).
Jan. 20 Mutiny of the New Jersey line in Washington's army at Morristown, N.J.
Mar. 1 Articles of Confederation become effective.
Mar. 15 Battle of Guilford Courthouse, N.C.—Greene (A); *Lord Cornwallis (B)*.
May 22 to June 5 Siege of Augusta, Ga.—*Andrew Pickens (A)*; Lt. Col. Thomas Browne (B).
Sept. 8 Battle of Eutaw Springs, S.C.—*Greene (A)*; Lt. Col. Alexander Stewart (B).
Sept. 28 to Oct. 19 Siege of Yorktown, Va.—*Washington (A)*; Lord Cornwallis (B).
Oct. 19 Surrender of Yorktown, Va.—*Washington (A)*; Cornwalis (B).

1782

July 11 British evacuate Savannah, Ga.
Nov. 30 Preliminary Treaty of Peace between United States and Great Britain signed in Paris.
Dec. 14 British evacuate Charleston, S.C.

1783

Mar. Newburgh Addresses to Congress.
Sept. 3 Definitive Treaty of Peace between the United States and Great Britain signed in Paris.
Nov. 25 British evacuate New York City.
Dec. 2 Washington delivers his Farewell Address to his officers in Fraunce's Tavern, New York City.
Dec. 23 Washington resigns as commander-in-chief of the American army.

Establishing a New Government

Now that the war had ended, it was time to draw up the terms of peace. The Continental Congress sent Benjamin Franklin, John Jay, and John Adams to Paris to meet with the commissioners of the British government. The British wanted to grant little more than independence to their former colonies, but through sheer tenacity, the American commissioners gained further concessions: fishing rights in Canadian waters and ownership of the entire Ohio River valley. By the Treaty of Paris, signed in 1783, the United States stretched from Canada to Spanish Florida and from the Atlantic coast to the Mississippi River. Now the nation had to set about the task of governing itself in peacetime.

The Articles of Confederation. Shortly after the Declaration of Independence had been adopted in 1776, the Second Continental Congress had drawn up a plan of government under which the rebellious states would live. The plan was called the Articles of Confederation. The Articles provided for the continuation of Congress, with state delegates appointed and paid by each state, and they gave Congress the right to declare and carry on war, build a navy, manage all foreign and Indian affairs, settle interstate disputes, coin money, and create post offices.

Weaknesses within the Articles became obvious all too quickly. Under them, Congress could neither levy nor collect taxes; it could only name the amount needed and wait for the states to supply it. It could pass laws, but it had no way of enforcing them. Also, no change or improvement could be made in the Articles without the unanimous vote of all the states, which meant that one state could thwart the will of the other twelve.

Under the Articles of Confederation, Congress was able to shape one far-reaching measure—the Ordinance of 1787, also called the Northwest Ordinance—which determined the future of the Northwest Territory, the area west of the colonies and north of the Ohio River. The ordinance divided the area into smaller territories and declared that each territory would become a self-governing state when its population reached 60,000. Slavery was forbidden in the area, but this provision did not affect slaves already there. Five states grew out of the old Northwest Territory—Ohio (1803), Indiana (1816), Illinois (1818), Michigan (1837), and Wisconsin (1848). The nation now had a working method by which future states would enter the Union.

But this one success was not enough to save the Articles. They were unable to alleviate the growing rivalries and disputes among the states and the nation's inability to deal adequately with foreign affairs. In 1787, Congress called a convention to draw up a plan that would correct the weaknesses of the Articles of Confederation.

Writing the Constitution. In May, 1787, 55 delegates from twelve states (Rhode Island was absent) met in Philadelphia. Among them were the nation's most prominent leaders. George Washington was chosen president of the convention. James Madison, Alexander Hamilton, Benjamin Franklin, and Gouvernor Morris were among the delegates. The delegates soon determined that it would not be enough merely to revise the existing Articles. Instead, they decided to prepare an entirely new Constitution.

Problems became obvious immediately. States with large populations clashed with smaller states over the matter of representation in Congress. Small states feared that lesser representation would put them at the mercy of larger states. Connecticut proposed a solution: Congress would be divided into two Houses. One, the House of Representatives, would represent the people of the states on the basis of population. Large states would have more representatives than small states. The other House, the Senate, would include two senators from each state, large or small.

Another problem arose between states that had large slave populations and states that did not. The slave states wanted the slaves counted as part of their populations in determining how many representatives they would have in the House. But they did not want slaves counted as part of their populations when it came to determining what taxes each state should pay. The nonslave states could not agree. Once again, a compromise was found. Only three-fifths of the slaves would be counted, for both representation and tax purposes.

The convention agreed that the national government should be divided into three branches—legislative (Congress), to make laws; executive (President), to carry out laws; and judicial (Supreme Court and other national courts), to interpret laws. The convention also agreed that the United States should have a federal system of government in which the national, or federal, government would share power with the governments of the separate states.

On September 17, 1787, the convention delegates adopted the Constitution. Now they had to go back to their states to convince the state governments to vote for its adoption too. Only when two-thirds of the states ratified the Constitution would it become the law of the land.

Ratification. The Constitution met with a great deal of opposition in the various states. Numerous groups opposed it, as did some prominent patriots who had been active in seeking independence. Men like Patrick Henry and Samuel Adams fought ratification because they believed that the Constitution created too strong a central government; they feared tyranny. Other Americans argued that the Constitution created a government that would favor the rich over the poor and middle classes. Men like Thomas Jefferson thought that the Constitution must include a "bill of rights" that would protect citizens' personal liberties—for example, freedom of speech, press, and religion—against the powers of the new government.

The Federalist Papers, a series of essays written by Alexander Hamilton, James Madison, and John Jay, defended the Constitution and helped win support for it. Gradually, the states began ratifying the Constitution, on condition that a bill of rights be added to it. (They were, as the first ten amendments, or Bill of Rights.) On June 21, 1788—about nine months after the Constitutional Convention adopted it—the vote of the ninth ratifying state (New Hampshire) made the Constitution "the supreme law of the land."

(See also *Government and Law:* the Constitution.)

Founding a New Nation

The first step in implementing the Constitution was to elect a President and the members of Congress. The Constitution provided for an electoral college, composed of elected representatives from each state, to cast votes for the President and Vice President. On the first Wednesday in February, 1789, the electoral college chose George Washington as President and John Adams as Vice President. On April 30, Washington took the oath of office in New York City, the nation's temporary capital. (In 1790, it would be moved to Philadelphia and in 1800 to Washington, D.C.)

Congress met and quickly established a Cabinet system to aid the President. Executive departments of state, treasury, and war as well as an office of attorney general and postmaster general were included. By passing the Judiciary Act of 1789, Congress set up the Supreme Court and 16 lower federal courts.

Domestic problems. The Revolutionary War had left the nation deeply in debt, both to American citizens and to foreign governments. The nation was also in need of many costly internal improvements—roads, for example. Secretary of the Treasury Alexander Hamilton felt that the central government should take strong actions to solve these monetary problems. He proposed that tariffs be raised and that new taxes be levied on certain American goods, like liquor. He further proposed that a national bank, a Bank of the United States, be established by private investors to handle tax revenues and print money. (Previously, each state printed its own money.)

Secretary of State Thomas Jefferson opposed Hamilton's plan, feeling that it favored the wealthy, landed class at the expense of the farmers. He also objected to the national bank because the Constitution had not called for it.

Hamilton's plan was put in place, but it pointed up a deep division in beliefs about how the nation should be governed. Rival political factions developed. One faction, the Federalists, led by Hamilton, favored a strong and active federal government. They thought national power should take precedence over state or individual rights. The other faction, the Democratic-Republicans, led by Jefferson, did not want to see a strong central government. They felt that strong state powers were the surest way to protect the individual rights of the common people. In the following years, these two factions hardened into rival political parties, forming the basis of the two-party system.

Hamilton's new taxes soon led to rebellion. Farmers in Pennsylvania, who made whiskey from the grain they grew, objected to the tax on whiskey. In 1794, they banded together and refused to pay the tax and drove the tax collectors away. President Washington saw this "Whiskey Rebellion" as a defiance of the federal government. He sent troops to put down the rebellion and to show that federal law must be obeyed.

Foreign affairs. In 1789, the United States' old ally France had a revolution of its own, overthrowing the monarchy. In 1793, the new republican government went to war with Britain and Spain. France expected American support, but President Washington proclaimed that the nation would remain strictly neutral.

Remaining neutral proved very difficult. Both French and British ships harassed American shipping, and the British even began taking American sailors off their ships and impressing them into the British navy.

These and other problems prompted President Washington to open negotiations with the warring nations. In 1794, he sent John Jay to Britain as his representative. The result was the Jay Treaty; it did not succeed in ending British impressment, but it did extract a promise that British troops would be removed from the Northwest Territory, reducing the threat of war in North America.

The next year, Washington sent Charles C. Pinckney to Spain. The result was the Pinckney Treaty, which gave Americans free use of the Mississippi River and let them establish warehouses in New Orleans.

The XYZ Affair. In 1797, John Adams, a Federalist, became President, and he continued negotiations with foreign governments. The French had broken off diplomatic relations with the

FOUNDING FATHERS

LIBRARY OF CONGRESS

BENJAMIN FRANKLIN

LIBRARY OF CONGRESS

GEORGE WASHINGTON

LIBRARY OF CONGRESS

JOHN ADAMS

LIBRARY OF CONGRESS

THOMAS JEFFERSON

LIBRARY OF CONGRESS

CULVER PICTURES

FOUNDERS OF A NEW NATION *included some remarkable men.* Left *to* right: *Benjamin Franklin was already 70 years old at independence, but still young enough to serve as a diplomat and to help frame the Constitution when past 80; George Washington, war hero and the most universally admired man of the age; John Adams, first framer of American foreign policy; and Thomas Jefferson, scholar, architect, author of the Declaration of Independence, and defender of the rights of the common man.* At left *is the Senate wing of the Capitol as it looked when Jefferson was elected President.* Above *is the first official flag of the new nation.*

United States because of continuing American trade with Britain. President Adams sent diplomats to France to try to reestablish peaceful relations, but the French minister of foreign affairs, Talleyrand, not only refused to see the Americans but also sent three French agents to them to demand huge bribes as the payment for a peaceful settlement. When the American people learned of this XYZ Affair (the French agents were never named and were referred to simply as X, Y, and Z), they were outraged. Federalists demanded that the United States declare war on France. The Democratic-Republicans resisted, and tensions grew.

Alien and Sedition Acts. Popular feeling at the height of the French crisis led the Federalists to push Congress to pass the Alien and Sedition Acts in 1798. The first act gave the President the power to deport any foreigner who seemed a menace to the nation; the second imposed fines and imprisonment upon anyone who opposed government measures or published "false and malicious" attacks on Congress or the President.

The Democratic-Republicans accused the Federalists of a "reign of terror" that was sweeping away the freedoms of press and speech pledged by the Constitution. The states of Kentucky and Virginia passed resolutions in 1798 that denied the federal government any powers not explicitly given by the Constitution, and declared that the states had the right to nullify what they believed to be unconstitutional acts of Congress.

Jeffersonian democracy.

In 1800, John Adams was defeated for another term as President by Thomas Jefferson, and the Democratic-Republicans took over. Jefferson, a firm believer in limited government, promised to preside over "a wise and frugal government which shall restrain men from injuring one another, and shall leave them otherwise free to regulate their own pursuits in industry and improvement."

LEWIS AND CLARK, *with help from the Indian Sacajawea, explored the wild Missouri River.*

The Louisiana Purchase. In 1803, President Jefferson was offered an opportunity to double the size of the United States in just one stroke. France under Napoleon had been embroiled in European wars for several years and was in terrible need of money to keep fighting. Napoleon agreed to sell the Louisiana Territory, a vast area between the Mississippi River and the Rocky Mountains, for only $15 million, or a few cents an acre. Afraid that Napoleon would change his mind, Jefferson snapped up the offer, then asked Congress for approval. Congress voted to ratify the Louisiana Purchase, and the United States redrew its boundaries.

Embargo Act of 1807. Britain and France continued to fight each other and to interfere with American freedom on the seas. Both sought to keep the other from benefiting from American trade. Finally, Jefferson persuaded Congress to pass an Embargo Act, a law forbidding American ships to call on any foreign port. He hoped this loss of American goods would make Britain and France stop their interference. But the only effect it had was to hurt American traders. In 1809, trade was resumed with all nations but Britain and France.

The War of 1812.

In 1809, James Madison, another Democratic-Republican, from Virginia, succeeded Jefferson as President. British offenses against American shipping continued. In addition, the British were encouraging Indians along the western frontier to attack American settlers. Members of Congress called "war hawks" were calling for a declaration of war on Britain. In June of 1812, President Madison called on Congress to support this declaration, and the War of 1812 began.

The young nation was really too weak to fight a war against a major power, but the British were fighting the French at the time, so they could spare few troops or ships to fight the Americans. At first, the Americans lost battle after battle. The British were even able to capture Washington, D.C., and set it afire. But they did not press their advantage, and soon the Americans began winning battles. Their most stunning victory took place at New Orleans, at the mouth of the Mississippi River. American troops led by General Andrew Jackson drove the British out of New Orleans in December, 1814.

Actually, this final battle never even had to be fought. Representatives of Britain and the United States had been meeting in Belgium to discuss peace. A few days before the Battle of New Orleans took place, they had signed a peace treaty, but news of it had not reached the United States.

The 1814 peace treaty, the Treaty of Ghent, marked the beginning of better relations between the United States and Britain. The European wars had finally ended, so interference with American shipping ended too. The agreement marked a settlement between Britain and the United States that assured peace and tranquility for a generation. The settlement allowed the United States to enter a long period of uninterrupted westward expansion and development.

National Growth and Expansion

The Era of Good Feelings

Following the War of 1812, America took its place as a full-fledged nation in the world. At home, there was a growing sense of unity and nationalism. Even party differences seemed to fade as the Federalist Party lost support and only the Democratic-Republican Party remained. In 1816, the Democratic-Republican candidate, James Monroe of Virginia, easily won the Presidency, to which he was reelected in 1820. The years of his Presidency are often referred to as "the Era of Good Feelings."

Economic growth.

The Federalist Party may have faded away, but many of its principles had not. The Democratic-Republicans had gradually adopted many of Hamilton's ideas for strong federal government and federal participation in the nation's economic life. Therefore, they passed the Tariff of 1816, which placed high tariffs on British-made goods coming into the country so that the goods would not compete with budding American manufactures.

That same year, Congress chartered the Second Bank of the United States (the first one had been chartered for only 20 years). Like its predecessor, it was owned by private investors and it handled government revenues and issued bank notes, the national currency. It also regulated the policies of state banks and extended loans to encourage the growth of industry.

Recognizing that if industry were to grow it would require a good transportation system to tie the nation together, the federal government contributed public subsidies to aid in the construction of "a perfect system of roads and canals." Among these important arteries were the National Road, running westward from Baltimore, Maryland, to Vandalia, Illinois, and the Erie Canal, which opened a shipping passage from the Atlantic Ocean to the Great Lakes. This transportation system aided not only the growth of industry, but also the movement of hundreds of thousands of settlers westward.

Expanding boundaries. President Monroe's secretary of state, John Quincy Adams, the son of the former President, felt very strongly that the United States must expand its "natural boundaries" (take over all of North America). He believed that any foreign power on American borders was a threat to the nation.

In 1819, he was able to gain Florida from Spain, for the sum of $5 million, under the terms of the Adams Onis Treaty. The previous year, under the provisions of the Convention of 1818, the United States gained some land from Canada, in what is now North Dakota, South Dakota, and Minnesota.

The Monroe Doctrine. Secretary of State Adams believed there was a threat to the United States from Europe far to the south of the nation's borders as well. Many of the Spanish colonies in Latin America were rebelling against their European masters and declaring themselves independent nations. Several of Spain's European allies expressed interest in helping Spain to regain the lost colonies. The idea of European nations coming to conquer areas in the western hemisphere greatly alarmed Adams; he feared they might also come to conquer the United States.

On Adams's advice, President Monroe enunciated a new doctrine in his State of the Union message to Congress in 1823. He warned Europe that any attempt at conquest or colonization with the western hemisphere would be looked on as an "unfriendly disposition to the United States." The new nation had little power to back up this "Monroe Doctrine," but fortunately the British agreed with it and the powerful British navy was able to

LIBRARY OF CONGRESS

MONROE'S *famous diplomatic doctrine warned Europe to stay out of disputes in the Americas.*

prevent European intervention in the western hemisphere. The Monroe Doctrine was never embodied into actual law, but it became part of the nation's political practice.

The Development of Economic Sections

By the end of Monroe's second term, the Era of Good Feelings was drawing to a close. In the election of 1824, the candidates—John Quincy Adams of Massachusetts, William Crawford of Georgia, Henry Clay of Kentucky, and Andrew Jackson of Tennessee—were called Republicans, but they were divided along sectional lines.

The nation was developing distinct economic sections—the North, the South, and the West. Each section favored a particular candidate. Jackson won the most popular votes, but he did not have a majority in the electoral college. The election was thrown into the House of Representatives, where Adams was chosen President.

The industrial North. As early as the late 1700's, the Industrial Revolution, already well established in Britain, was moving to the United States, most particularly to the North, which included the New England and Mid-Atlantic states. The many rushing waterways of the North supplied a ready source of energy to power factory machines. In 1790, Samuel Slater built a cotton thread spinning mill in Pawtucket, Rhode Island. Within the next 25 years, textile mills sprung up all over New England, and the American factory system was born.

At about the same time, the young and inventive Eli Whitney developed a new method of gun manufacture by creating interchangeable parts. He used machinery to cut uniform parts for guns. Then guns could be easily assembled. This was a vast departure from the old way, in which a gunsmith turned out one gun at a time by hand.

The emerging factory production system gave impetus to many other industries. Iron and steel were needed for factory and farm machines. Coal was necessary to help make the iron and steel and to power factory machines.

Growing industry demanded improved transportation, and during the period from the 1820's to the 1850's, new canals and roads were being built throughout the North. At the same

THE ERIE CANAL *helped open the land west of the Appalachians to settlement and trade. It also brought prosperity to New York, which it connected with the Great Lakes.*

BETTMANN ARCHIVE

time, new forms of transportation were also appearing. A practical steamboat had been developed by Robert Fulton in 1807, and by 1820 steam navigation was common on the rivers and lakes of the North. With the development of the steam locomotive in 1830, a great railroading boom began. By the 1850's, the Northeastern United States was connected by rail to Chicago, St. Louis, Memphis, and New Orleans.

The need for labor to run the North's growing industries brought on rapid population growth. Immigrant workers came by the thousands and the at-home birthrate rose as well. Between the 1820's and the 1850's, the population of the North more than doubled. Philadelphia tripled and New York City and Boston quadrupled in size. A large wage-earning class was emerging in the North.

The agricultural South. As the North became more industrialized and urbanized, the South maintained a very different character, remaining agricultural and rural. It also developed an economic system and a social structure that differed greatly from that of the North.

The economic system of the South was dominated by the production of cotton. Prior to 1793, cotton had not been particularly important because it was expensive to produce. Before it could be sold, sticky seeds had to be cleaned out of it by hand, a process that produced only one pound of cotton per day per worker. But in 1793, Eli Whitney, traveling in the South, recognized the problem and invented a cotton gin (short for *engine*) that made it possible for one worker to clean 50 pounds of cotton a day.

Now cotton became highly profitable. Planters in search of cheap land left the seaboard states and established large plantations in western Georgia, Alabama, Mississippi, and even farther west. Labor was needed to work the plantations, and the planters relied on slaves. Slavery, an institution that had been diminishing somewhat in the South, experienced a burst of growth. Gradually, the South became the producer of two-thirds of the world's supply of cotton.

The South benefited from its plantation economy, but it had to share the benefits with the North. Northern shippers handled most of the cotton, and Northern manufacturers sold many goods to the South, which had not built up manufactures of its own.

The frontier West. For most of the colonial years, the Mid-Atlantic region had been the breadbasket of the nation. But as droves of settlers crossed the Appalachian Mountains following the War of 1812, the rich lands of the West became the new breadbasket. Many of the settlers headed for the Old Northwest, which grew in population more than tenfold between the 1820's and the 1850's. Others headed for the area south of the Ohio River and settled in Kentucky and Tennessee. Still others moved farther on, across the Mississippi River into Iowa, Missouri, and beyond.

The fertile prairie lands took quickly to the plow, especially to the

IMMIGRATION AND THE UNITED STATES

The United States has taken in more immigrants than any other nation in the history of the world. During colonial times, about 1 million immigrants arrived, mostly from the British Isles. In the decades following American independence, immigrants kept arriving at the rate of about 10,000 a year. Then, in the 1830's alone, more than 600,000 arrived, an average of 60,000 per year.

In the 1840's, the surge of immigrants nearly tripled. Famine in Ireland and political unrest in Germany drove citizens to scrape together the steerage fare, crowd into sailing ships, and suffer the uncomfortable and treacherous trans-Atlantic journey. In that decade, 1,700,000 immigrants arrived in the United States, to be followed in the 1850's by 2,600,000 more. Over the next three decades, another 10 million arrived, mainly from Great Britain, Ireland, and Germany, joined by farmers from soil-poor Scandinavia.

The migration preceding 1885 is often referred to as the "old migration"; it consisted mostly of people from Northern and Western Europe. The migration after 1885 is known as the "new migration"; it consisted of many more immigrants from Southern and Eastern Europe. Poverty, political unrest, and religious persecution in Austria-Hungary, Italy, Russia, Greece, Rumania, and Turkey impelled more than 8 million people to leave for the United States between 1890 and 1910. In the two decades following, another 16 million followed them.

It was not until the United States was more than a hundred years old that it placed any restrictions on immigration. In 1882, Congress passed the Chinese Exclusion Act, which barred any further immigration from China. In 1907, the United States concluded a "gentlemen's agreement" with Japan to exclude any further immigration from that country.

Legislation during the 1920's cut back severely on the number of immigrants admitted and set up quotas that discriminated against immigrants not from Northern and Western Europe.

More recent waves of immigration have included refugees from Europe made homeless before and after World War II. In 1965, a new Immigration and Nationality Act abolished the old quotas and opened up immigration to Hispanics from Latin America and to Asians. Each year, more than 300,000 of these people are taken in legally, but this number cannot keep pace with the number who want to enter. As a result, illegal immigration is today at an all-time high.

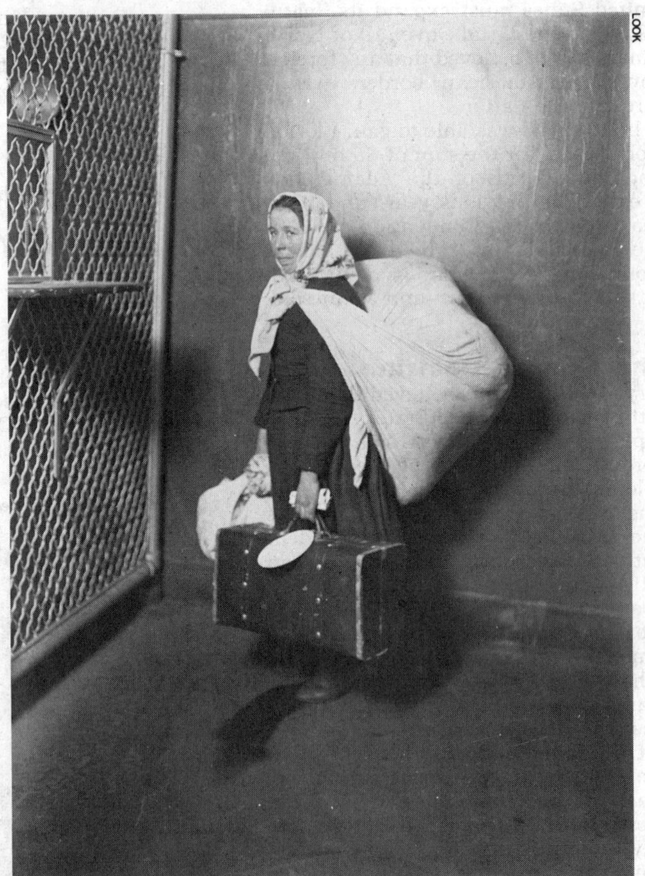
LOOK

A YOUNG IMMIGRANT, *arrives at Ellis Island, the immigrant processing center in New York Harbor, in 1910. Millions landed like this, carrying everything they owned.*

cast-iron one invented in 1820 and then to the steel one developed by John Deere in 1837. Bumper crops of corn and wheat soon provided not only enough grain to feed the United States, but also enough for export. Beef, pork, and poultry joined grain as important Western farm products.

The federal government favored this Western settlement. Its first service to the settlers was removing the Indians from the land by driving them farther west. In 1820, Congress passed the Land Act, which provided land to be sold in 80-acre tracts at only $1.25 an acre. Such prices were irresistible to farmers from small, largely worn-out farms in New England, as well as to immigrant farmers from Ireland, Germany, and Scandinavia.

Improvements in transportation helped fuel the great growth of the West. Steamboat shipping on the Mississippi brought farm products down to New Orleans, a port from which they could be shipped by sea. Products could also be shipped along the Great Lakes, then placed on canal barges and sent to the East Coast through the canal systems. These same shipping arteries made it easy to get manufactured goods to markets in the West. The extension of railroads made shipment even faster and cheaper. By 1850, Chicago had become the nation's largest railroad center.

The development of the agricultural West made greater industrialization of the nation possible. The West provided the food the North needed to feed its ever-growing numbers of industrial workers.

The Growth of Democracy

The election of 1824 had pointed up the differing interests of the developing economic sections. For example, the industrial North wanted high tariffs on manufactured goods entering the United States to reduce competition. The agricultural South believed that high tariffs raised the prices of manufactured goods it had to buy, and so favored low tariffs. The West, the newest and least developed section, favored federal spending on roads and other improvements, but other sections resisted the higher taxes that would pay for Western development.

Then, too, there was the issue of slavery. The South believed its economy was thoroughly dependent on slavery and therefore defended it strongly. Elements in the North, however, objected to it just as strongly.

The Missouri Compromise. The issue of slavery became a national problem for the first time when Missouri applied to become a state in 1818. Missouri had been settled by people from the South who expected it to become a slave state. Up until that time, slave states and nonslave, free states had been evenly represented in the Senate. But if Missouri were brought in as a slave state, the balance would be destroyed. In 1820, Henry Clay, the speaker of the House of Representatives, worked out the Missouri Compromise—Missouri would be admitted as a slave state while another applicant for statehood, Maine, would be admitted as a free state, thus maintaining the balance. The compromise also outlawed slavery in the remaining lands of the Louisiana Purchase north of the parallel 36°30′. The compromise settled the immediate problem, but the issue of slavery would continue to plague the nation.

The party system. Andrew Jackson, a Westerner, had been the popular vote winner but the ultimate loser in the Presidential election of 1824. He and his followers were enraged at the outcome. They accused the winner, John Quincy Adams, of making a "corrupt bargain" with Henry Clay. They claimed Clay threw his influence behind Adams in return for the office of secretary of state and Adams's support for Clay's eventual election as President.

Jackson began campaigning for the election of 1828 as soon as the 1824 decision was reached. By this time, the Republican Party was splitting along ideological lines. Adams and his supporters were calling themselves the National Republicans, reflecting their belief in strong and active national government. Jackson and his supporters characterized the National Republicans as the "aristocratic" party of the wealthy and the powerful. The Jacksonians called themselves Democrats, to stress their concern for the common man.

Jackson's triumph. Several factors favored Jackson's election over Adams in 1828. Since the Revolution, the right to vote had been gradually extended to "the common man" to whom Jackson appealed. Property qualifications and payment of land taxes generally ceased to limit suffrage. The right to vote continued to be limited to white adult males (excluding women and blacks), but between 1824 and 1828 alone, the number of voters doubled.

Another factor favoring Jackson was his attack on the "Tariff of Abominations," passed under Adams. Manufacturing interests in the North favored the tariff because it placed high taxes on foreign goods. But the agricultural South was enraged by it, causing many Southerners to support Jackson (as did many Westerners, who were voting for one of their own).

NEW YORK PUBLIC LIBRARY

ANDREW JACKSON *exemplified the rough virtues of the frontier West.*

Jackson won by a landslide. Adams took only New England, Delaware, and New Jersey. Jackson easily took the South and the West, as well as states with many wage earners, such as New York and Pennsylvania. His election ushered in "the Era of the Common Man," during which Jackson would attack government policies that he thought protected privileged groups and suffrage would be extended still further. (The number of eligible voters casting ballots would double again during Jackson's Presidency.)

The spoils system. Jackson believed that people should not remain in government service for a very long time. If they did, he believed, they lost their concern for the public welfare and instead concentrated on holding their own jobs. He therefore advocated a policy of rotation in public office. He also believed in the adage, "To the victor belong the spoils." So he began replacing people who opposed him with people who had supported his candidacy and were faithful to him.

Although Jackson set a precedent for this so-called "spoils system" in filling government jobs, he actually replaced only about one-fifth of federal officeholders. Later Presidents would extend the system, causing a massive turnover of officeholders with each new administration.

Removal of the Indians. Jackson often spoke out for retaining the rights of the states in the face of attempts by the federal government to exercise its power. He argued for these rights when he supported Georgia's attempt to take over the land of the Cherokee Indians and relocate the Cherokees west of the Mississippi River. The Cherokees brought their case against removal to the Supreme

Court in 1832. The Court, under Chief Justice John Marshall, declared that "the laws of Georgia can have no force" in removing the Indians.

Jackson agreed with Georgia; indeed, he favored the removal of all Indians to west of the Mississippi. He refused to enforce the High Court's decision. "John Marshall has made his decision," Jackson remarked, "now let him enforce it." As a result, the entire Cherokee nation was marched westward, under U.S. Army guard. Fully one-fourth of them died along the way.

Nullification. Another issue concerning states' rights arose in response to the Tariff of Abominations. The South began proposing resistance to the tariff. John C. Calhoun of South Carolina, Jackson's Vice President, was a vociferous opponent of the tariff. In 1828 he had written a tract (which was published anonymously) stating that if Congress passed legislation that did undue injury to any state, that legislation was unconstitutional and the state had a right to declare it null and void. (In this, Calhoun echoed the contentions of the Virginia and Kentucky resolutions of 1798.)

In 1830, on the floor of Congress, Daniel Webster, senator from Massachusetts, and Robert Hayne, senator from South Carolina, debated the matter of federal versus states' rights. Webster argued that the federal government had final authority because it was the agent of all the people, not merely the people of one state. He went on to argue that only the Supreme Court, not the states, had the right to decide whether laws were constitutional. He warned that if this proposition were not accepted by all states, the states would one day go to war against each other. "Liberty *and* Union, now and forever, one and inseparable!" was his final plea.

In 1832, however, the Tariff of Abominations was renewed, and Southern opposition sprang up again. South Carolina passed a law in November, 1832, that declared the tariff null within the state, and prepared to defend this stand by force of arms if necessary. Jackson was personally opposed to the tariff, but he would not tolerate a possible disruption to the Union. He sent South Carolina a sharp warning emphasizing that the law would be enforced; he also sent two warships into Charleston harbor to support his threat. Once again, "the Great Compromiser," Henry Clay, pushed a compromise through Congress; it provided for a ten-year decrease in tariffs so that all tariffs would be lowered by at least half. This satisfied South Carolina for the time, and talk of nullification ceased.

The bank fight. A prime Jackson target as a bastion of special privilege was the privately controlled Second Bank of the United States. Jackson saw it as a tool of the rich to oppress the poor and to prevent state banks and small businesses from expanding their commercial activities. He also saw that stockholders could grow rich on government funds.

In 1832, Congress voted to renew the bank's charter, and Jackson vetoed the bill. Renewal of the charter became a campaign issue later that year as Jackson's opponent, National Republican Henry Clay, campaigned against Jackson's veto and for the bank. Jackson won the election easily and set out to destroy the bank, even though its charter still had four years to run. He did so by withdrawing government funds and by making no more deposits. Instead, the government deposits were given to state banks owned by Democrats—"pet banks" they soon came to be called. The effect was to cripple the U.S. bank and eventually cause it to fail.

Panic and depression. Jackson's crippling of the U.S. bank had severe financial repercussions for the nation. In 1836, shortly after the election of Jackson's hand-picked successor, Martin Van Buren, the nation neared financial collapse. Without the restraining influence of the Second Bank of the United States on issuing money, a great deal of currency was printed that had little backing in gold or silver. Credit was easy and borrowing reached record heights. Inflation was rampant. Jackson attempted to cool the heated economy by returning, in part at least, to the use of gold or silver—hard currency—in place of paper money. This action dealt a severe blow to the boom, and soon mortgages were going unpaid, banks were failing, and factories were closing. This Panic of 1837 led to the worst depression in the nation's history to date.

The financial gloom helped to defeat President Van Buren's bid for reelection in 1840. By that time, the National Republicans had joined together with many of Jackson's enemies to form the Whig Party. The party's candidate in 1840 was a popular Indian-fighting hero, William Henry Harrison, who won the election. But just one month after taking office, he died of pneumonia. His Vice President, John Tyler, succeeded him.

Manifest Destiny

As Americans filled up the Ohio and Mississippi valleys, the nation looked farther west, to the lands beyond. Said writer John Louis Sullivan in 1845, "Our manifest destiny is to overspread the continent allotted by Providence for the free development of our yearly multiplying millions." But the area was not simply the Americans' for the taking. Not only were there hundreds of thousands of Indians there, many of them driven westward by earlier American settlement, but other nations were laying claim to the West. The Oregon Territory had been claimed by Britain. Mexico, now free of Spanish rule, included the area from Texas to California. The American drive toward the Pacific, toward living out its "manifest destiny," would be fraught with many difficulties.

The Oregon Territory. In 1818, the United States and Britain had agreed to share the rights to the Oregon Territory, which included what is now Oregon, Washington, Idaho, and part of Canada.

The first non-Indians to come to the Oregon Territory were the rugged "mountain men," hunters and trappers of the valuable fur-bearing animals there, especially beaver. Although these were wandering men, permanent settlements were founded on the sites of fur-trading posts. One was Astoria, on the Pacific coast, named for John Jacob Astor, founder and owner of the American Fur Company.

By the 1830's, the mountain men had destroyed most of the beavers, but there was now a new job they could take on, leading wagon trains of American settlers to the fertile land west of the Rockies. The route they followed was the Oregon Trail, beginning in Independence, Missouri, and stretching as far as Portland, Oregon.

Soon American settlers vastly outnumbered the British in the Oregon Territory, and expansionist-minded Americans were calling for the United States to take sole ownership of the entire Pacific Northwest, up to the parallel 54°40′. "Fifty-four forty or fight" became their rallying cry. For a while, war with Britain threatened, but neither nation wanted war; both sent representatives to work out a solution. The Oregon Treaty of 1846 divided the Oregon Territory at the 49th parallel, a continuation of the boundary between Canada and the United States from Minnesota east.

Texas. From the 1720's, the Spanish had claimed all of what is now Texas, but only about 4000 Spanish settlers lived there by the 1820's. In 1821, Mexico gained its independence from Spain and wanted to make Texas its northern province. Eager to attract settlers there, the Mexican government granted permission to Moses Austin and 300 other American settlers to start a colony in Texas. Under Moses's son Stephen, the colony was founded in 1821, and thus began a mass movement of American settlers into Texas. By the end of the 1820's,

CULVER PICTURES

WAGON TRAINS *moved pioneers across half the continent to California, Utah, and Oregon. The trip took as long as six months, and some who began the trip did not survive it.*

there were about 20,000 Americans living there, versus 4000 Mexicans.

It was not long before there was severe friction between the Texans and the Mexican government. The Mexicans were Roman Catholics, and the Americans predominantly Protestants. Misunderstandings were caused by the language difference between the Spanish and the English. In addition, the Americans were mainly Southerners who had brought slaves with them, while Mexico outlawed slavery. Political tensions arose when the American community refused to pay taxes to

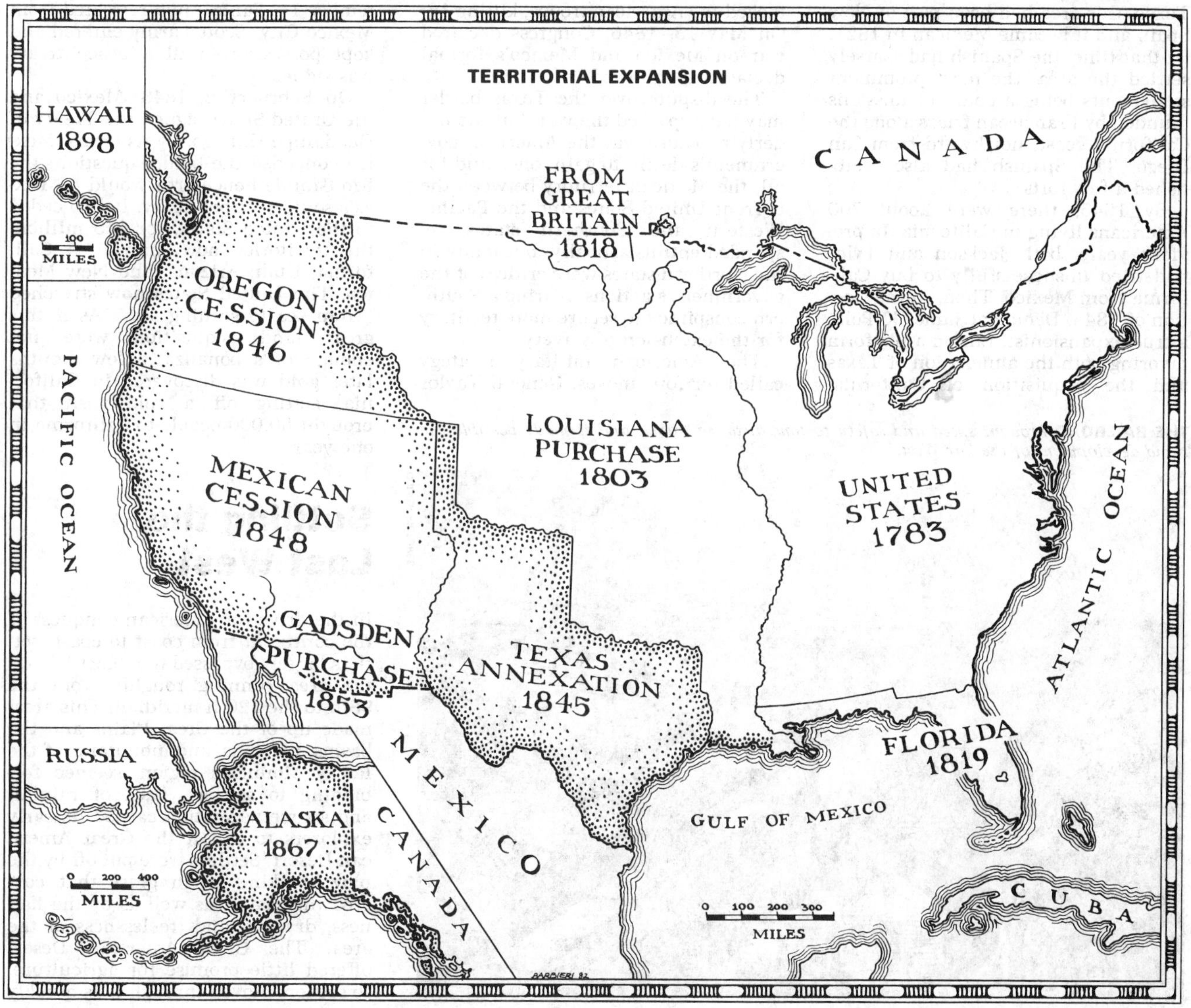

TERRITORIAL EXPANSION

Mexico. Mexico retaliated by prohibiting any further American immigration into Texas.

In 1836, the Texans rebelled and declared themselves the independent Lone Star Republic, with Sam Houston as president. After defeating a Mexican attempt to kill the rebellion, Houston applied for permission for Texas to enter the United States. President Jackson favored annexing Texas, but he saw two problems: probable war with Mexico and the admission of a slave state that would tip the delicate balance between North and South. Jackson refused to support annexation.

In 1843, Houston again approached the United States government on annexation. President Tyler, eager for American expansion, was able to get a joint resolution through Congress, and in 1845 Texas became the Union's 28th state. Mexico broke off diplomatic relations with the United States.

California. During the same period, the area west of Texas, through California, was also in ferment. Like Texas, this area had been part of New Spain and it became Mexican in 1821. By that time, the Spanish had sparsely settled the area, the most prominent settlements being a chain of missions founded by Franciscan friars along the California coast, northward from San Diego. The Spanish had also established a few forts.

By 1845, there were about 700 Americans living in California. In previous years, both Jackson and Tyler had tried unsuccessfully to buy California from Mexico. Then, in the election of 1844, Democrat James K. Polk, a true expansionist, ran on a platform favoring both the annexation of Texas and the acquisition of California. When he won, he too made an attempt to buy California, but to no avail.

Polk encouraged Americans in California to rebel against the Mexican government. They did, and on June 15, 1846, American rebels proclaimed the California Republic and raised their flag, showing a grizzly bear and a lone star. U.S. Army Captain John C. Frémont took command of the rebel forces and succeeded in driving all Mexican troops out of northern California. As the "Bear Flag Revolt" raged, news arrived that war between the United States and Mexico had finally come.

War with Mexico. The immediate cause of the war with Mexico was Texas's claim that the Rio Grande was its southwestern boundary. Mexico claimed the region as far north and east as the Nueces River. In May, 1845, President Polk sent General Zachary Taylor and his troops to the disputed border, and in July the American forces advanced to the Rio Grande. On April 25, 1846, Mexican forces crossed the Rio Grande and attacked the American troops, killing 16. On May 13, 1846, Congress declared war on Mexico and Mexico's formal declaration followed.

The dispute over the Texas border may have sparked the war, but the underlying cause was the American government's desire to gain, once and for all, the Mexican territory between the current United States and the Pacific. Western and Southern states responded enthusiastically, but many in the Northern states were critical of the government's actions, fearing a Southern conspiracy to secure more territory for the extension of slavery.

The American military strategy called for four moves. General Taylor was to hold the Rio Grande; General Winfield Scott was to land at the Mexican port of Veracruz and advance on Mexico City, the capital; Colonel Stephen Kearny was to take and hold New Mexico, then push on to California to join the forces there under Captain Frémont; and Commodore R. F. Stockton was to position a fleet in the Pacific off the California shore.

All four campaigns were marked with success. Taylor followed up his early victories by taking Matamoras and Monterey. He then took some 10,000 men south to reinforce Scott's march from the coast to Mexico City. Mexican General Santa Anna, with an army of 20,000, attacked a force of about 4000 Americans at Buena Vista. The American force held, and after a desperate two-day battle in February, 1847, routed the Mexicans. This battle made Taylor the hero of the war and put him in the White House in 1849.

In March, 1847, Scott landed at Veracruz, took the city, and began his march on the Mexican capital. He drove Santa Anna from the pass at Cerro Gordo and continued his advance, taking city after city. On September 14, Santa Anna retreated from Mexico City. Scott's army entered and kept possession until a peace treaty was signed.

On February 2, 1848, Mexico and the United States signed the Treaty of Guadalupe Hidalgo. By its terms, Mexico conceded the border question: the Rio Grande henceforth would be Texas's southwest boundary. It also ceded to the United States, for $15 million, the territories now known as California, Utah, Arizona, and New Mexico. The United States now stretched "from sea to shining sea." As if this great land acquisition were not enough of a bonanza, a few months later gold was discovered in California, setting off a gold rush that brought 80,000 people to California in one year.

THE RAILROAD *brought speed and safety to long-distance travel, and it made possible the rapid development of the Far West.*

CULVER PICTURES

Settling the Last West

In the drive for American conquest of the continent from coast to coast, settlers largely bypassed the "Last West," the area running roughly from the 98th to the 120th meridian. This area, made up of the Great Plains and the basins, plateaus, and mountains of the Rocky Mountain region, seemed forbidding to settlers. Lack of rainfall and sparse vegetation caused its early explorers to call it the Great American Desert. Settlers were put off by the plow-breaking tough grass that covered the plains, as well as by the flatness, dryness, and treelessness of the area. The Great American Desert offered little promise for agriculture, so settlers moved through it as quickly as they could and on to the more inviting lands of California and the Pacific Northwest.

Mining and cattle. During the 1850's, though, settlers began coming in large numbers. Some were drawn by mining strikes, as prospectors discovered that the Rocky Mountain region was rich in precious ores. A gold strike near Denver, Colorado, caused the Pike's Peak rush of 1859, which brought 50,000 prospectors in just a few months. In the same year, the greatest deposits of gold and silver ever found were discovered in the Comstock Lode, near Virginia City, Nevada, drawing 20,000 prospectors. Two years later, a gold strike at Last Chance Gulch in Montana brought thousands more. In 1875, gold was discovered in the Black Hills of the Dakotas, producing the Homestake Mine near Deadwood.

A growing cattle industry was also bringing in settlers. Millions of longhorns, descendants of cattle brought by the Spanish settlers, roamed lower Texas. As the demand for meat grew in the increasingly populous East, cowboys rounded up the cattle and moved them northward on "the long drive" to such railroad towns as Abilene and Dodge City in Kansas. From these towns the cattle could be shipped to meat-packing houses in Chicago.

Western railroads. By approximately 1860, the American government was eager to link the nation with transcontinental railroads. It granted huge tracts of government-owned land to private railroad companies with the provision that they use the money made by selling the land to build new railroads. A great race to build railroads began, with the Central Pacific building eastward from California and the Union Pacific building westward from Omaha, Nebraska. On May 10, 1869, the two sets of tracks met at Promontory, Utah. It was now possible to cross the nation in only a few days. By 1890, the entire Last West could be crossed by such railroads as the Great Northern, the Northern Pacific, and the Southern Pacific.

Farming. The railroads did a great deal to attract farmers to the Great Plains. Railroad companies advertised their land sales all over the East and Europe. The Homestead Act of 1862 was another attraction. Through it, the government offered settlers 160-acre plots of land at no cost if they lived on the land and developed it for five years. Farmers could also buy plots for $1.25 an acre after living on them for only six months.

Improvements in farm machinery made the Great Plains more suited to agriculture than it had been. Modern steel plows could cut through the tough sod. Improved reapers and threshers made it possible for one farmer to till ever-larger plots of land. In addition, it was found that a hard-kerneled variety of wheat from Russia grew well in the Great Plains climate. By the 1880's, Kansas and Nebraska were covered with wheat fields. Farm production from the newly settled area soared.

The Indians. American settlers had at last conquered the Last West, but the losers were the Indians. To them the Last West was their last home. Many of the Indians had been forced there by white settlements in other parts of the country; of course, the Plains Indians had always been there.

In 1851, the American government began a reservation policy under which it tried to restrict the Indians to designated areas (very often the poorest ones, which the settlers did not want), allowing settlers to take over the rest of the land. However, if a designated area became attractive, as when gold was discovered in the Black Hills of South Dakota, the Indians were driven off, so that American fortune-hunters could exploit the new riches the land offered.

For the next 40 years, clashes between protesting Indians and the U.S. Army were all too frequent—as in the Sand Creek Massacre in Colorado in 1864, Custer's Last Stand in Montana in 1876, and the Battle of Wounded Knee in South Dakota in 1890. But the outcome was inevitable. The Indians were finally subdued and restricted to their reservations. The Dawes Severalty Act of 1887 dissolved Indian tribes by law and divided the reservation land among individual Indians, weakening the tribes' collective power.

A House Divided

Toward Disunion

The acquisition and settlement of the new lands of the West during the 1840's and 1850's worsened the tensions that had developed between North and South. The South wanted to be able to extend slavery into the new areas, but the North firmly objected. Whether new states would be admitted to the Union as slave or free states was a frequent point of contention on the floor of the Senate. Neither North nor South wanted the other to gain the upper hand in representation in that body.

Compromise of 1850. By 1849, the number of free and slave states stood at 15 each. But now California was applying to enter the Union as a free state, a prospect the South did not favor since it would tip the balance in favor of the North.

Northerners objected to the trading of slaves in Washington, D.C., virtually in the shadow of the Capitol Building. Southerners complained that there were no effective laws to help them reclaim fugitive slaves who were escaping to the North. Southerners were also concerned about the admission of other states from the Southwest—New Mexico, for example. Would slavery be prohibited there? Tempers flared and debate in the Senate was heated.

Henry Clay, now a senator from Kentucky, proposed a compromise, as he had 30 years earlier with the Missouri Compromise. In the North's favor, he proposed that California be admitted as a free state and that slave trade be abolished within Washington, D.C. In the South's favor, he proposed that New Mexico be divided into two territories—New Mexico and Utah—and that each have the right to *popular* sovereignty (the right to choose for themselves whether they wanted to be slave or free). He also proposed that a strict new Fugitive Slave Law be adopted.

Congress enacted this Compromise of 1850, but once again, compromise did not settle the slavery question. Newspapers in the North were soon protesting the new Fugitive Slave Law, calling it "a hateful statute of kidnappers." Protest and outrage grew with the publication in 1852 of abolitionist Harriet Beecher Stowe's *Uncle Tom's Cabin*, which movingly described the cruelties of slave life and the desperation of the slaves who fled from it. While the book was not a literary masterpiece, it stirred antislavery feelings to a fever pitch in the North.

Kansas-Nebraska Act. In 1854 came another direct confrontation over slavery. Senator Stephen A. Douglas of Illinois proposed a bill that would start the vast, unorganized territory west of Minnesota, Iowa, and

Missouri on the way to statehood. But Southerners objected that his bill, following the terms of the Missouri Compromise of 1820, in which slavery was prohibited in this territory, would create several new free states and overpower the South in the Senate.

Once again, a compromise was reached. The Kansas-Nebraska Act, passed in May, 1854, divided the territory into Kansas and Nebraska. The provisions of the Missouri Compromise were repealed and the doctrine of popular sovereignty was applied—the settlers, not Congress, would decide whether to permit slavery when the territories became states.

Immediately, proslavery and antislavery interests began sending armed settlers to the new territories, especially to Kansas, neighbor of the slave state of Missouri. When it came time to vote for representatives to the Kansas legislature, proslavery settlers outnumbered antislavery forces. But to make sure of victory, proslavery Missourians crossed the border, voted illegally, and gave the proslavery party an overwhelming victory. Antislavery settlers, calling it a stolen election, set up their own legislature. For the next four years, a state of civil war existed in "Bleeding Kansas," marked by murders, pillagings, and burnings.

Sectionalism and politics. Both the Whig Party and the Democratic Party had supporters in the North and South, and since Tyler's time, they had more or less alternated in winning the White House. Democrat Polk was succeeded by Whig Zachary Taylor, who died in office and was replaced by Whig Millard Fillmore. In 1852, Democrat Franklin Pierce was elected President. But as sectional strains worsened, so did party stability.

In 1854, antislavery forces from both the Whig and the Democratic parties met in Jackson, Michigan, and formed a new party, which they called the Republicans. By 1856, the Republicans had become strong enough to run their antislavery candidate, John C. Frémont, for President. His Democratic opponent, James Buchanan, won by only a narrow margin. The Whig Party faded away.

Two days after Buchanan's inauguration, the Supreme Court handed down a momentous decision brought on by the suit of Dred Scott, a black man who insisted he was a free man rather than a slave by virtue of having lived in a free state. The High Court declared that no slave and no individual of slave ancestry could be a citizen of the United States or appeal to a federal court. It further decided that slaves were "property" to be transported from state to state, and that Congress could not prohibit slavery in the territories and was bound by the Constitution to protect it.

This decision delighted the South because it implied that slavery was protected throughout the nation by constitutional guarantees. Northerners were outraged at the ruling, and the Republican Party continued to insist upon congressional legislation against the extension of slavery into the territories. Republicans knew, however, that they could reverse the ruling only by winning control of the government

THE MOVEMENT FOR ABOLITION OF SLAVERY

Black slavery was established in the American colonies shortly after the first Africans were brought to America in 1619. In the next two centuries, slavery became an economic necessity in the minds of many Southern planters, especially after the invention of the cotton gin. By 1820, more than 2 million black slaves labored in the United States, and by 1860, the number had grown to nearly 4 million.

There had always been some moral qualms about slavery in the nation—Thomas Jefferson, a Southern slaveholder himself, had voiced some of them before 1800. But in the 1800's, antislavery feeling grew, especially in the Northern and Western states. In 1816, the American Colonization Society was founded; its aim was to buy slaves, free them, and return them to Africa, to a newly founded country called Liberia. The society met with very limited success—by 1831, only about 1400 former slaves had been relocated in Liberia.

In the meantime, other attempts were being made to abolish slavery in the United States. In 1829, David Walker, a free black, published the *Appeal,* in which he urged black Americans to strike for their freedom. In 1831, William Lloyd Garrison began publishing a newspaper called the *Liberator,* in which he demanded freedom for slaves, claiming that slavery was forbidden by the Declaration of Independence.

In 1833, Garrison helped organize the American Anti-Slavery Society, and served as its president for two decades. Other prominent abolitionists were the poets John Greenleaf Whittier and James Russell Lowell; reformers Wendell Phillips and Theodore Weld; Lucretia Mott; and the Grimke sisters, Angelina and Sarah, Southerners who had left South Carolina in protest against slavery.

One of the most effective speakers of the 1000-chapter Anti-Slavery Society was Frederick Douglass, a former slave who had educated himself and who had proved to be a formidable fighter against unwilling servitude. Sojourner Truth, another freed slave, sought, like Douglass, to influence public opinion.

In 1840, abolitionists formed the Liberty Party and ran a Presidential candidate who favored abolition. With the formation of the Republican Party in 1854, abolitionists found their political home.

While advocating that the nation end slavery through law, many abolitionists acted to free slaves by helping them to escape along the "underground railroad." Slaves seeking freedom would follow the North Star, to make their way up to Canada. Abolitionists along the way hid the fleeing slaves in their homes and farms by day.

The Civil War, the Emancipation Proclamation, and the 13th Amendment brought the abolitionist movement to a successful conclusion.

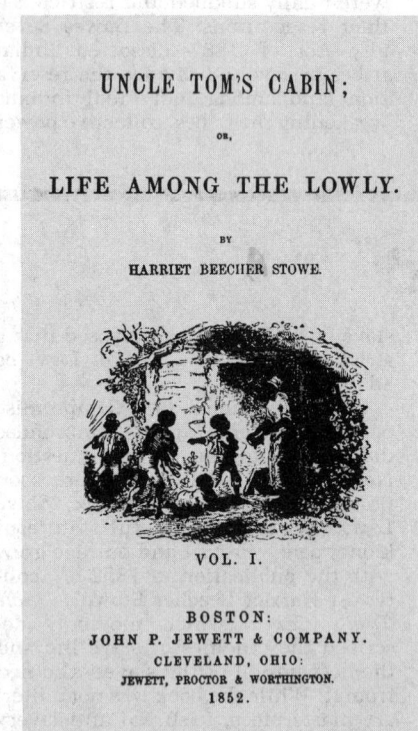

UNCLE TOM'S CABIN; OR, LIFE AMONG THE LOWLY. BY HARRIET BEECHER STOWE. VOL. I. BOSTON: JOHN P. JEWETT & COMPANY. CLEVELAND, OHIO: JEWETT, PROCTOR & WORTHINGTON. 1852.

NEW YORK PUBLIC LIBRARY

UNCLE TOM'S CABIN, *the melodramatic story of a slave family, created tremendous sympathy for abolition in the 1850's.*

and then staffing the Supreme Court with their own appointees.

John Brown. In the midst of the sectional ferment, an antislavery veteran of the "Bleeding Kansas" fights named John Brown took the first step in a fanatic design to arm the slaves of the South to attack their masters. On the night of October 15, 1859, he and a small band of followers attacked and took the federal armory at Harpers Ferry, Virginia. President Buchanan ordered a force of U.S. Marines under the command of Colonel Robert E. Lee to retake the armory and capture Brown. After a two-day siege, the Marines succeeded. Brown was tried for treason and then hanged on December 2, 1859.

The episode horrified and terrified the South, bringing as it did the specter of slave uprisings. The South now felt its existence as a slave-holding territory might well depend on separation from an antislavery Union.

The election of 1860. The entire nation anxiously awaited the next election. When the Democratic convention met, Democrats from the North had a majority who favored Senator Stephen A. Douglas of Illinois, an advocate of popular sovereignty. This so upset the Democrats from the South, who thought that the slavery issue had been solved by the Dred Scott case, that the convention adjourned without having nominated a candidate. When it reconvened two months later, delegates from the deep South were absent. Douglas was chosen the candidate of the Northern Democrats. The Southern Democrats split off and nominated John C. Breckinridge of Kentucky.

The jubilant Republicans, sensing victory over a divided opposition, nominated a relatively unknown and moderate candidate, Abraham Lincoln of Illinois. He ran on a platform that did not push abolition of slavery but did restrict its extension into territories. The platform also favored a tariff and a homestead act for Western lands, thus strengthening its appeal to the North and the West.

Lincoln won only 40 percent of the popular vote, but he easily captured a majority of votes in the electoral college.

Secession. The election of Lincoln, the representative of a party that had support only in the North, galvanized the South into action. Fearful of being unable to maintain its power in the federal government and to protect itself against the power of the industrial North, the South began to seriously entertain ideas of secession. "Fire eaters" preached the need for secession and maintained that it could

CULVER PICTURES

SEIDMAN PHOTO SERVICE

LINCOLN *in 1864 seemed to have aged ten years in three.* Below, *a Union recruiting poster using Daniel Webster's battle cry, and an 1864 Confederate bill.*

be accomplished without civil war because the North, threatened with the loss of cotton and the Southern market, would not dare to oppose secession forcibly.

South Carolina, long a place where a belief in the doctrine of nullification had thrived, led the movement for secession. On December 20, 1860, it declared itself a free and independent state. By February, 1861, all the other states of the lower South—Mississippi, Florida, Alabama, Georgia, Louisiana, and Texas—had taken similar action. These seven states then met in Montgomery, Alabama, to form the Confederate States of America with Jefferson Davis as president and Alexander H. Stevens as vice president. The Confederate constitution stressed state sovereignty, prohibited high protective tariffs, and recognized "the institution of Negro slavery as it now exists in the Confederate States."

During the early days of secession, the Confederacy took over many federal forts and arsenals in the South. In April, 1861, Fort Sumter in the harbor of Charleston, South Carolina, still lay in federal hands, but it was under siege. Lincoln, hoping to keep the states of the upper South—Virginia, Arkansas, Tennessee, and North Carolina—from seceding and hoping to avoid war, had thus far not acted to oppose the Confederate takeovers. But he did order Fort Sumter to be resupplied with food. On April 12, Confederate batteries began bombarding the fort. The next day, the beleaguered federal force under Major Robert Anderson evacuated Fort Sumter. The first shots of the Civil War had been fired.

The Civil War

The day after the surrender of Fort Sumter, President Lincoln made a formal declaration of war and called for 75,000 volunteers. Regiments sprang up overnight. By December, 1861, 600,000 men were in the Union army. In the South the call for volunteers met with an equally ardent response, and many brilliant officers resigned from the U.S. Army to go home and serve their states. Among them was the unparalleled Robert E. Lee, who refused Lincoln's offer of the command of the Union forces. Instead, Lee chose to serve the South.

Within a month, four more states went over to the Confederacy. First went Virginia, but its western section remained loyal to the Union and was admitted to the Union as the state of West Virginia. Arkansas, Tennessee, and North Carolina followed. The capital of the Confederacy was moved from Montgomery, Alabama, to Richmond, Virginia. President Davis licensed Southern privateers to seize U.S. vessels. Lincoln proclaimed a blockade of Southern ports.

Unequal sides. At the outset of war, the North and South each proclaimed confidence in gaining victory in a short war—90 days perhaps. But only one side could be victorious and the war would be a prolonged one—four years in all.

The South had the advantage in military talent. In addition to Lee, it boasted West Point-trained Generals Pierre G. T. Beauregard, Thomas J. (later "Stonewall") Jackson, J. E. B. Stuart, and Joseph E. Johnston. Among the South's disadvantages was the weakening effect of a states' rights ideology on the execution of the war.

Among the North's advantages were its much larger population (23 million in the North versus fewer than 9 million in the South), allowing it to raise a much larger army; its factories (110,000 versus 18,000), capable of being converted to the production of war supplies; and its railroad mileage (27,000 miles versus 8,400 miles), for moving troops and supplies.

Strategy. As war began, the South had no intention of invading the North. It planned to wage a defensive

THE AMERICAN CIVIL WAR 1861–1865

In the following listing of battles and events in the Civil War, (U) represents the Union (Northern) army, while (C) represents the Confederate (Southern) army. Italics denote winning generals; (k) signifies killed.

1860

Nov. 6 Election of Lincoln.
Dec. 20 Secession of South Carolina.

1861

Feb. 9 Jefferson Davis elected president of The Confederate States of America (C.S. of A.).
Feb. 18 Davis inaugurated at Montgomery, Ala.
Mar. 4 Lincoln inaugurated at Washington, D.C.
Apr. 12-13 Bombardment and surrender of Ft. Sumter, Charleston Harbor, S.C.
Apr. 19 Blockade of Southern ports declared by President Lincoln.
May 6 Confederate Congress passes act recognizing state of war between the U.S. and the C.S. of A.
May 26 Richmond, Va., becomes capital of the C.S. of A.
July 21 First Battle of Bull Run (Manassas, Va.): McDowell (U); *J. E. Johnston and Beauregard (C)*.
Aug. 10 Battle of Wilson's Creek, Mo.: Lyon (U); *Ben McCulloch (C)*.
Oct. 21 Battle of Ball's Bluff, Va.: C. P. Stone (U); *N. G. Evans (C)*.
Nov. 7 Battle of Belmont, Mo.: U.S. Grant (U); *L. Polk (C)*.
Nov. 8 Removal of Mason and Slidell from the British steamer *Trent*.
Nov. 20 Creation of Committee on the Conduct of the War by Union Congress.

1862

Jan. 19 Battle of Mill Springs (or Logan's Cross Roads), Ky.: *G. H. Thomas (U)*.; G. B. Crittenden (C).
Feb. 6 Fall of Fort Henry, Tenn.: *U. S. Grant (U)*; L. Tilghman (C).
Feb. 14-16 Siege and surrender of Ft. Donelson, Tenn.: *Grant (U)*; Buckner (C).
Feb. 21 Battle of Valverde, N.M.: *E. R. S. Canby (U)*; H. H. Sibley (C).
Mar. 9 Battle of Monitor and Merrimack in Hampton Roads, Va.: *J. L. Worden (U)*; Catesby ap Roger Jones (C).
Apr. 5-May 4 Siege of Yorktown, Va.: *G. B. McClellan (U)*; J. B. Magruder (C).
Apr. 6-7 Battle of Shiloh (or Pittsburgh Landing), Tenn.: *Grant (U)*; A. S. Johnston (k) and Beauregard (C).
Apr. 16 First Confederate Conscription Act.
Apr. 29 Surrender of New Orleans, La.: *B. F. Butler (U)*; Mansfield Lovell (C).
May 8-25 Jackson's Valley (Va.) campaign: N. P. Banks (U); *T. J. Jackson (C)*.
May 31-June 1 Battle of Seven Pines (or Fair Oaks), Va.: *McClellan (U)*; J. E. Johnston and G. W. Smith (C).
June 1 R. E. Lee (C) appointed to command Army of Northern Virginia.
June 25-July 1 Seven Days battles, Va.: McClellan (U); *Lee (C)*.
July 17 Second Confiscation Act (U) passed.
Aug. 29-30 Battle of Bull Run (or Groveton), Va.: John Pope (U); *Lee (C)*.
Sept. 16-17 Battle of Antietam (or Sharpsburg), Md.: McClellan (U); Lee (C). *Draw*.
Sept. 19 Battle of Iuka, Miss.: *W. S. Rosecrans (U)*; Sterling Price (C).
Sept. 24 Presidential (U) suspension of writ of *habeas corpus*.
Oct. 3-4 Battle of Iuka, Miss.: *Rosecrans (U)*; Van Dorn (C).
Oct. 8 Battle of Perryville, Ky.: D. C. Buell (U); *Braxton Bragg (C)*.
Nov. 16-July 4, '63 Vicksburg (Miss.) campaign: *Grant (U)*; J. C. Pemberton (C).
Dec. 13 Battle of Fredericksburg, Va.; A. E. Burnside (U); *Lee (C)*.
Dec. 20 Holly Springs, Miss., depot captured and burned; R. C. Murphy (U); *Van Dorn (C)*.
Dec. 31-Jan. 1, '63 Battle of Stone River (or Murfreesboro), Tenn.: Rosecrans (U); Bragg (C). *Draw*.

1863

Jan. 1 Emancipation Proclamation (U).
Jan. 1 Galveston, Tex. recaptured: I. S. Burrell (U); *Magruder (C)*.
Feb. 25 National Bank Act effective (U).
Mar. 3 Federal Draft Act (U).
Apr. 11-May 4 Siege of Suffolk, Va.: *John J. Peck (U)*; James Longstreet (C).
Apr. 27-May 5 Campaign and battle of Chancellorsville, Va.: Joseph Hooker (U); *Lee (C)*.
May 20-July 4 Siege and surrender of Vicksburg, Miss.: *Grant (U)*; Pemberton (C).
May 27-July 8 Siege and surrender of Port Hudson, La.: *Banks (U)*; Franklin Gardner (C).
June 9 Cavalry battle of Brandy Station, Va.: Alfred Pleasanton (U); *Jeb Stuart (C)*.
June 20 West Virginia admitted to the Union.
June 23-30 Tullahoma (Tenn.) campaign: *Rosecrans (U)*; Bragg (C).
July 1-3 Battle of Gettysburg, Pa.: *G. G. Meade (U)*; Lee (C).
July 4 Surrender of Vicksburg, Miss.: *Grant (U)*; Pemberton (C).
July 8 Surrender of Port Hudson, La.: *Banks (U)*; Gardner (C).
July 13-16 New York City draft riots.
Sept. 19-20 Battle of Chickamauga, Ga.: Rosecrans (U); *Bragg (C)*.
Sept. 21-Nov. 24 Siege of Chattanooga, Tenn.: *Rosecrans and Thomas (U)*; Bragg (C).
Oct. 25-Nov. 27 Chattanooga, Tenn. campaign: *Grant (U)*; Bragg (C).
Nov. 17-Dec. 5 Siege of Knoxville, Tenn.: *Burnside (U)*; Longstreet (C).

1864

Feb. 3-Mar. 5 Meridian (Miss.) campaign: Sherman (U); Polk (C). No decision.
Feb. 20 Battle of Olustee (or Ocean Pond), Fla.: Truman Seymour (U); *Jos. Finegan (C)*.
Mar. 10-May 22 Red River (La.) campaign: Banks (U); *Richard Taylor (C)*.
Mar. 12 Grant appointed general-in-chief of Union armies.
Apr. 12 Capture of Fort Pillow, Tenn.: L. F. Booth (k); *N. B. Forrest (C)*.
May 5-7 Battles in the Wilderness, Va.: *Grant (U)*; Lee (C).
May 5-Sept. 1 Atlanta (Ga.) campaign: *W. T. Sherman (U)*; J. E. Johnston and J. B. Hood (C).
May 8-21 Operations about Spotsylvania Court House, Va.: *Grant (U)*; Lee (C).
May 11 Cavalry battle at Yellow Tavern, Va.: *P. H. Sheridan (U)*; Jeb Stuart (k) (C).
May 15 Battle of New Market, Va.: Franz Sigel (U); *C. Breckinridge (C)*.
May 27 Battle of New Hope Church, Ga.: Joseph Hooker (U); *P. R. Cleburne (C)*.
June 3 Battle of Cold Harbor, Va.: Grant (U); *Lee (C)*.
June 10 Battle of Brice's Cross Roads, Miss.: S. D. Sturgis (U); *N. B. Forrest (C)*.
June 17-Apr. 1, 1865 Siege of Petersburg, Va.: *Grant (U)*; Lee (C).
June 19 Naval battle, *Alabama* and *Kearsarge*, off French coast; *John A. Winslow (U)*; Raphael Semmes (C).
June 27-Aug. 7 Early's (C) raid on Washington, D.C.
July 9 Battle of Monocacy, Md.: Lew Wallace (U); *J. E. Early (C)*.
Aug. 5 Naval battle in Mobile Bay, Ala.: *D. G. Farragut (U)*; Percival Drayton (C).
Aug. 7-Oct. 25 Shenandoah Valley (Va.) campaign: *P. H. Sheridan (U)*; Early (C).
Sept. 1 Evacuation of Atlanta, Ga.: *Sherman (U)*; Hood (C).
Sept. 27 Battle of Pilot Knob, Mo.: *Thomas Ewing, Jr. (U)*; Price (C).
Oct. 19 Battle of Cedar Creek, Va.: *Sheridan (U)*; Early (C).
Oct. 23 Battle of Westport, Mo.: *S. R. Curtis (U)*; Price (C).
Nov. 16-Dec. 20 Raid through Georgia from Atlanta to coast: *Sherman (U)*; G. W. Smith and W. J. Hardee (C).
Nov. 8 Lincoln reelected president.
Nov. 20-Dec. 17 Hood's Tennessee campaign: *Thomas (U)*; Hood (C).
Dec. 15-16 Battle of Nashville, Tenn.: *Thomas (U)*; Hood (C).
Dec. 20 Capture of Savannah, Ga.: *Sherman (U)*; Hardee (C).

1865

Jan. 13-15 Battle of Ft. Fisher, N.C.: *A. H. Terry (U)*; W. H. C. Whiting (k) (C).
Feb. 5 Hampton Roads (Va.) peace conference.
Feb. 6 Lee appointed general-in-chief of all Confederate forces.
Feb. 17 Charleston, S.C., evacuated by Confederate troops.
Feb. 17 Columbia, S.C., burned by Sherman's troops (U).
Mar. 4 Lincoln inaugurated for second term.
Apr. 1 Battle of Five Forks, Va.: *Sheridan (U)*; G. E. Pickett (C).
Apr. 2 Capture of Selma, Ala.: *J. H. Wilson (U)*; N. B. Forrest (C).
Apr. 2 Confederate evacuation of Richmond, Va.
Apr. 9 Confederate surrender at Appomattox Court House, Va.: *Grant (U)*; Lee (C).
Apr. 12 Capture of Mobile, Ala.: *Canby (U)*; D. H. Maury (C).
Apr. 15 Death of President Lincoln—Andrew Johnson inaugurated as president.
Apr. 26 Confederate surrender at Durham, N.C.: *Sherman (U)*; J. E. Johnston (C).
May 4 Surrender of Confederate forces in Louisiana: *Canby (U)*; Taylor (C).
May 10 Jefferson Davis captured at Irwinsville, Ga.
May 26 Surrender of Trans-Mississippi Dept.: *Canby (U)*; E. Kirby Smith (C).
June 2 Surrender of Galveston, Tex.: *Henry K. Thatcher (U)*; Kirby Smith (C).
Nov. 6 Final Confederate surrender—*Shenandoah*, Capt. James Waddell, to British authorities at Liverpool, England.

war against Northern attacks, with the hope that repeated defeats would cause the North to wear down and finally leave the South alone. The North had to invade so that it could defeat the Southern armies and thus force the Confederate states back into the Union.

The North's broad strategy was proposed by General Winfield Scott, a veteran of the war with Mexico. Named the Anaconda Plan (for the python that crushes its victims to death), it aimed to split the South into three parts, first by capturing the Mississippi River valley and thus isolating the states west of the Mississippi River; second by splitting the sections east and west of the Appalachians. Once the areas were isolated from one another, a naval blockade, extending from Virginia to Texas, would further weaken the sections by cutting them off from supplies and reinforcements from overseas.

Early battles. Implementing this broad strategy would take time, but some Northern strategists had a more immediate plan—to capture the Confederate capital of Richmond and so demoralize the South that its surrender would follow.

First Bull Run. To that end, in July, 1861, Lincoln sent the Army of the Potomac, though poorly trained and inexperienced, to attack a Confederate force camped at Manassas Junction in northern Virginia, not far south of Washington, D.C. The two sides joined in battle at Bull Run. At first, the Union forces under General Irvin MacDowell seemed to be winning against the Confederate forces under Beauregard. But their advance was stopped by Jackson (with a "stonewall" of his troops), and the Confederate reinforcements put them to rout. The North could now see that a long war was probably ahead.

Peninsular campaign. Lincoln then named General George B. McClellan as general in chief of the Union forces. After a period of retrenchment and training, McClellan and his troops marched on Richmond in Spring of 1862. The Union forces reached as close as 5 miles to Richmond when Confederate forces under Lee drove them back, and they returned to Washington.

Second Bull Run. Lincoln created a new army, the Army of Northern Virginia, under the command of General John Pope. This army marched on Richmond in Summer of 1862. But like the Army of the Potomac, it was stopped at Bull Run in a battle waged there on August 29th and 30th; it sustained 16,000 casualties. The Army of Northern Virginia, as unsuccessful as that of the Potomac, was disbanded.

Antietam. The defeat of the Union in its attempts on Richmond freed Lee and his troops. To the amazement of the North, Lee set out to invade the border state of Maryland, in an effort to demoralize the North. In late summer, McClellan moved his troops to stop Lee. On September 17, 1862, Union and Confederate forces met in the bloodiest battle of the war, at Antietam Creek in Maryland. McClellan succeeded in forcing Lee's army to retreat, but he failed to press his advantage and destroy the scattering troops. Upset by McClellan's lack of aggressiveness, Lincoln relieved him of command.

Fredericksburg and Chancellorsville. Union troops, now under the new general in chief Ambrose Burnside, made another attempt on Richmond in mid-December, 1862. Once again, Lee's army stopped the Army of the Potomac, this time at Fredericksburg, and sent them reeling back to Washington. Lincoln next tried General Joseph "Fighting Joe" Hooker, who again marched on Richmond, in late April of 1863. This time Union troops reached only as far as Chancellorsville, where once again they met defeat at Lee's hand, suffering a loss of 17,000 Union troops. When hearing the news of yet another defeat, Lincoln cried, "My God! My God! What will the country say? What *will* the country say?"

Emancipation Proclamation. That the Union "cease to be divided" had been Lincoln's aim from the beginning. "The Union must be preserved with or without slavery," he said. Toward the end of 1862, he sensed, however, that the long, discouraging war could be won only with the impetus provided by a new emotional lift. He decided that now was the time to take a moral stand and raise the banner for the slave.

On January 1, 1863, the Emancipation Proclamation was issued. It proclaimed that all slaves in areas still in a state of rebellion were henceforward free. It did not state that slaves in Union-held territories or in border states loyal to the Union were free. Since the Union was not in control of the areas the proclamation covered, the Emancipation Proclamation did not actually free any slaves. But it did change the nature of the war, from one of political patriotism to one of a crusade for the oppressed.

Turning points. While war raged in the East, it was also being fought in the West, as Union troops tried to capture control of the entire Mississippi River valley. Combined Army and Navy operations, under the command of General Ulysses S. Grant and Commodore Andrew H. Foote, were bringing the Union a number of stunning victories. From February to June, 1862, through victories at Fort Donelson and Fort Henry and at Shiloh and Memphis, Union forces recaptured western Tennessee. On April 26, Union Admiral David S. Farragut's naval squadron captured New Orleans, at the mouth of the Mississippi River. Now only Confederate control of Vicksburg, Mississippi, kept the Union from succeeding in taking the entire Mississippi valley and cutting off the Confederate states west of the Mississippi.

Vicksburg. Surrounded by many swamps and rivers, the Confederate fortress at Vicksburg was very difficult to attack. After several failures, Grant decided to attack from the south. In April, 1863, he moved 20,000 men down the Mississippi to a point south of Vicksburg. Using every sort of draft animal to be found on the surrounding plantations and farms to carry their supplies, Grant's troops marched north toward Vicksburg. Then they suddenly turned right—away from Vicksburg. First they captured and destroyed Jackson, Mississippi, an important Southern railroad and munitions center. The next day they turned west, and on May 16, they defeated a considerable part of the Vicksburg garrison. Two days later, Grant had completely surrounded Vicksburg. After a 47-day siege, the city finally surrendered on July 4. The Mississippi valley part of the Anaconda Plan had been achieved.

Gettysburg. At exactly the same time, another momentous battle was raging in the East. President Davis and General Lee had decided that Lee should bring the war up into Pennsylvania, to strike a death blow after the North's failures at Fredericksburg and Chancellorsville. The Southern plan was to march up to Harrisburg, capture it, and continue to capture Philadelphia and New York if the North did not surrender. Lincoln sent Union troops under General George C. Meade to stop Lee. The two forces met unexpectedly near Gettysburg. The bloody struggle continued from July 1 through July 3, 1863. The Confederates, victorious the first two days, confidently charged the Union center on the third day. Here they met defeat, and General George C. Pickett's division, which led the charge, was almost annihilated. It is estimated that the total number of losses were between 40,000 and 50,000. This devastating Confederate loss marked the beginning of the end for the South.

Union victory. After Vicksburg and Gettysburg, the South could never again gain momentum. The Union naval blockade had strangled the South's export of cotton and its import of goods, including war materiel. The South grew steadily weaker.

General Grant, now general in chief of all Union armies, devised a three-point plan to end the war. Union forces under General Philip Sheridan were to invade the rich Shenandoah valley and destroy it so that crops could not grow. Grant and his troops were to march from Washington and capture Richmond. General William T. Sherman and his forces were to march from Chattanooga, Tennessee, to Atlanta, Georgia, destroying everything in their path.

All three campaigns succeeded. A totally debilitated South sued for peace. On April 9, 1865, General Lee surrendered to General Grant at Appomattox Courthouse in southwestern Virginia. The Civil War had ended.

Death of Lincoln. Five days later, President Lincoln was attending a performance of a play entitled *Our American Cousin* at Ford's Theater in Washington, D.C. At about 10 o'clock on the night of April 14, a shot rang out. Someone shouted, "Sic semper tyrannis!" ("Thus ever to tyrants"—the state motto of Virginia.) "The South is avenged!" the man shouted as he leaped to the stage, ran off behind the scenes, and disappeared. John Wilkes Booth, once an actor, was the crazed assassin of the one man who might have put through the difficult postwar policy of "malice toward none; charity for all." The war was over, but Lincoln was dead.

Reconstruction

The Civil War produced two major consequences. First, the Union victory, emphasizing the supremacy of the federal government over the states, ended the doctrines of nullification and secession and laid down the principle of an "indestructible Union of indestructible states." Second, the war destroyed the influence of the Southern planters in national government, giving dominance to the Northern industrialists. This so enhanced the prestige of the Republican Party that it controlled the federal government until well into the 20th century. As a result, businessmen carried the nation into a new period of industrialization and Western expansion.

Lincoln's plan. Lincoln's desire had been to restore civil government throughout the broken South as quickly as possible. "Let us bind up the nation's wounds. Let us do all we can to achieve and cherish a just and lasting peace," he had urged. In 1863, he proclaimed that each formerly rebellious state could reestablish its own government when it met two conditions. First, 10 percent of its citizens who had voted in 1860 had to swear an oath to "faithfully support and defend the Constitution of the United States" in order to be pardoned. Lincoln withheld pardons from high-ranking Confederate leaders, former U.S. congressmen and judges who supported the rebellion, and military officers, effectively cutting them off from political power. Second, the state had to abolish slavery. When these conditions were met, the state could be received back into the Union.

Many Republicans in Congress believed that Lincoln's plan was far too lenient. These "Radical Republicans" insisted that Congress, not the President, determine how to deal with the South. In 1864, the Radical Republicans pushed through the Wade-Davis Bill, which set forth a harsher plan. It required that a majority of white males (not just 10 percent) had to swear allegiance before the state could reestablish its government. Further, it ordered that anyone who wanted to vote or take part in government swear never to have supported the Confederacy. Finally, the state government not only had to abolish slavery, but to repudiate Confederate debts and its act of secession. Lincoln pocket vetoed the Wade-Davis Bill, but support for its ideas persisted in Congress.

Lincoln's assassination brought Andrew Johnson to the Presidency. Johnson, a former congressman and senator from Tennessee, had bitterly opposed his state's secession, and in 1864 had been chosen as Lincoln's running mate.

At first, Johnson seemed to share the Radical Republicans' views on how the South should be treated, and they rejoiced. But their joy was premature. Johnson continued to demand of reorganized states that they repudiate Confederate debts and acts of secession and that they legally end slavery, by ratifying the 13th Amendment abolishing it. But he offered a full pardon to anyone who would swear allegiance to the Constitution, including many Confederate officials. He asserted that Reconstruction policy was for the President, and not Congress, to make.

By December, 1865, all the former Confederate states except Texas had met Johnson's terms and had reorganized their state governments. Now they wanted to send their representatives to Washington to take part in the federal government, but Congress was not willing to take them back on Johnson's terms.

The Black Codes. The reorganized states may have ratified the 13th Amendment, but that did not mean that they wanted to give equal rights to the newly freed blacks, called *freedmen.* In March, 1865, Congress established the Freedmen's Bureau, to help impoverished freedmen to make new lives. The bureau offered funds for food and education and protection in labor contracts and local troubles. But life remained desperate for the former slaves, as it did for all the South's poor. As the reorganized state governments drew up their laws in 1865 and 1866, they incorporated a number of acts called Black Codes, designed to limit the freedom of freedmen severely and to keep them on in the South as an available labor supply.

The Black Codes denied the freedmen many rights of citizenship. They forbade blacks from carrying arms, required that they serve an apprenticeship while under age, governed their employment, and instituted curfews. Thus blacks were once again relegated to social, economic, and political inferiority in America.

Johnson and Congress. Many members of Congress were outraged by the Black Codes. In February, 1866, they voted to renew the Freedmen's Bureau and extend its powers to protect blacks. Johnson vetoed the bill. (In July, a new version of the bill was passed, overriding Johnson's veto.) In April, Congress passed the Civil Rights Act, which declared that freedmen were U.S. citizens entitled "to full and equal benefit of the laws." Johnson vetoed this act, too, stating that it was unconstitutional and granted the federal government power at the expense of the states. This time, an angry Congress overrode Johnson's veto, but fearing that the Supreme Court might agree with the President, it proposed the 14th Amendment, which guaranteed citizenship to blacks.

Johnson objected to the 14th Amendment, too, as an invasion of states' rights, and advised Southern states not to ratify it. In the congressional elections of 1866, Johnson sought to gather strength for his policies in Congress by campaigning for candidates that would support them. The effect was disastrous. Republicans who opposed him won overwhelmingly. Control of Reconstruction was now firmly in the hands of Congress.

Congressional extremists. Congress was quick to pass the Reconstruction Act of 1867, over Johnson's veto. The act made new demands on the reorganizing Southern states before they could be taken back into the Union. It divided the South into five military districts, each under the control of a military commander. The commander was to register the voters, exclude prominent Confederate leaders, and include all other male citizens "of whatever race, color, or previous condition of servitude." These voters were to elect a state convention to frame a state constitution. If this constitution satisfied Congress, and if the state legislature ratified the 14th Amendment, the state would be readmitted to the Union.

Impeachment of Johnson. Congress backed up its Reconstruction Act with other laws that limited John-

BETTMANN ARCHIVE

A CARPETBAGGER *was a Northerner who came South to profit from defeat.*

son's role in Reconstruction. One was the Tenure of Office Act, which denied the President the right to dismiss civilian government officials without Senate approval. Through this act, Congress would be able to keep in office those officials who were friendly to Congress, in spite of Johnson's wishes.

In 1867, Johnson came into conflict with Secretary of War Edwin M. Stanton over the appointment of commanders of the military districts in the South; Johnson removed Stanton from office. Radical Republicans saw this as an opportunity to get rid of Johnson, so the House brought articles of impeachment against him on February 2, 1868, outlining what it saw as the President's "misdemeanors and crimes."

From March 25 to May 26, Johnson stood trial on the charges, with the Senate as jury and Chief Justice Salmon P. Chase as judge. Thirty-five senators voted Johnson guilty, one short of the necessary two-thirds majority. Johnson could remain in office, but his power was greatly diminished. That fall, he did not attempt to run again. General Grant, now a popular war hero, was elected President.

The South reacts. By 1871, all the former Confederate states had reorganized their governments, under generally Republican domination, and had been readmitted to the Union. Thanks to the newly passed 15th Amendment, blacks now had the right to vote, which they did, generally for Republicans. Several black representatives were elected to state and federal office. Much to many white Southerners' chagrin, carpetbaggers—Northerners who had moved to the South following the war—were exerting some power in Southern state governments. So were scalawags, Southerners who had stayed loyal to the Union during the war and supported Reconstruction under the Republicans.

Economic conditions were desperate following the devastating war. Planters and farmers faced ruin, with much of their land destroyed and their labor supply now freed. Landless former slaves turned to sharecropping to survive, often working a plot of their former masters' land and living no better than they had, and in some cases worse. Little by little, though, the South began rebuilding itself, and conditions improved for many. A "New South" was emerging.

It soon became obvious that many white Southerners wanted to maintain strict control over blacks and to end black participation in voting and government. Secret groups like the Ku Klux Klan and the Knights of the White Camellia were formed to keep both blacks and white Republicans intimidated and away from elections. To try to combat such actions, Congress passed the Force Act in 1870 and the Ku Klux Klan Act in 1871.

Reconstruction ends. As time wore on, the North began losing interest in Reconstruction. Radical Republicans, notably the fiery Thaddeus Stevens, were dying out. Government corruption, which seemed to flourish during Grant's administration, became the new focus of attention. Union troops that had long occupied the South were being pulled out. The last of them left in April, 1877, one month after the inauguration of Rutherford B. Hayes as President. Southern governments moved out of Republican hands and into Democratic ones. Reconstruction had come to an end.

Coming of Age

An Industrial Giant

Though the beginnings of industrial growth in the United States are usually traced to the 1830's and 1840's, the greatest surge of growth began after the Civil War. In the next 50 years, industrial expansion completely changed the United States—from agricultural to industrial, from rural to urban, from inward-looking to outward-looking. The United States evolved from a torn young nation into a major world power.

Growth of industry. The nation's phenomenal industrial growth was spurred by four fortuitous circumstances. First, the United States was blessed with a seemingly endless supply of natural resources—vast reserves of coal, iron ore, oil, copper, zinc, gold, and silver. It also had generous supplies of lumber and excellent conditions for agriculture. Second, markets for American industrial output were growing. During this period, 25 million immigrants came to the United States, and the birthrate of the native-born population increased, causing the population to grow from 40 million to 100 million. Home markets alone were able to absorb nearly 95 percent of American output.

Third, favorable government attitudes toward industry also favored growth. With the defeat of the South and the triumph of the Republicans in federal government, business enjoyed high tariffs and many other encouragements. Finally, innovative industrial leaders appeared: clever, talented inventors, resourceful business organizers, and ingenious investment bankers who could assemble necessary capital.

All of these forces combined to cause American industrial production to grow fivefold by 1900, and to continue this phenomenal growth into the 20th century. The United States was becoming the greatest industrial producer in the world.

Rise of big business. Before 1865, most businesses had been owned by a single proprietor or by partners. As businesses grew, it became apparent that many small, competing businesses were not necessarily the most efficient way to turn a profit. Instead, financiers formed large corporations by buying and merging small firms.

One example was Andrew Carnegie's steel corporation. Carnegie assembled all of the elements that go into steel production—coal and ore mining, water and rail shipping to steel plants, steel-making, shipping to customers—into one corporation. Another example was John D. Rockefeller's corporation. Rockefeller brought together many small, independent oil refineries and combined them into the giant Standard Oil.

Such businesses as these contributed to economic growth, but they also created monopolies that often destroyed free competition in various industries. Soon the cry went up that the government must intervene and control the power of monopolies. Said one advocate of control, Henry Demarest Lloyd, "If the tendency to combination is inevitable, control of it is imperative."

The federal government responded with some legislation. The Interstate Commerce Act of 1887 established the Interstate Commerce Commission to keep railroads from giving lower prices through rebates to some large businesses. The Sherman Antitrust Act of 1890 was passed "to protect trade and commerce against unlawful restraints and monopolies." Both laws were ineffective, however, since those in high government office had little interest in placing limits on large industrial combinations.

Communication and transportation. It is impossible to imagine America's dramatic industrial growth without advances in communication and transportation. Telegraphy introduced rapid communication before the Civil War. In 1866, Cyrus Field laid the first transatlantic cable, linking Europe and the United States. In 1876, Alexander Graham Bell marked the nation's centennial by showing his "speaking machine," which would one day be the basis of American Telephone & Telegraph. At about the same time, Thomas Edison began demonstrating new methods of recording (the phonograph) and a revolutionary means of transporting power through wires for lighting and for running machinery.

THE HOMESTEAD STRIKE *in 1892 became a pitched battle between strikers and hired Pinkerton guards. The state sent the militia and crushed the union. Homestead was owned by Andrew Carnegie* (inset).

CULVER PICTURES

LIBRARY OF CONGRESS

Transportation was totally transformed with the massive expansion of the railroads. Electric trolley cars, elevated trains, and subways allowed cities to expand beyond all previous dreams. Finally, there came the automobile. In 1900, there were about 3500 cars in the United States. By 1920, there were 9 million, thanks in large part to the enterprise of Henry Ford. He made the automobile an ordinary possession of the average family, through the economy of assembly line mass production. Between 1910 and 1917, his company sold more than a million and a half Model T's, and each year the price went *down*—beginning at $950 and ending at $360.

During the same period, another form of transportation was literally spreading its wings. Two bicycle mechanics, Orville and Wilbur Wright, developed an airplane, which they first flew successfully on the beach at Kitty Hawk, North Carolina, on December 17, 1903. Air transportation did not affect the economy until after 1920, but its development gave hopes that one day no mountain, jungle, or ocean would stand between one man or country and another.

Struggles of labor. The Carnegies, the Rockefellers, and the Fords were growing rich, and a comfortable middle class, made up largely of business managers and clerical workers, was growing as well. But a large mass of people were not benefiting from the rapid industrialization. Industrial laborers worked 70- and 80-hour weeks for less than 20 cents an hour, often in dirty and unsafe conditions. Immigrants made up a large percentage of these workers, and the children of the poor were well represented—as many as 2 million in 1900.

Life for the working class was very uncertain. An injury could throw a person out of work, and when it did, there was no pay. Depressions, too, were common, causing unemployment and want every ten years or so. There was no unemployment compensation or other public assistance to replace wages.

Following the idea that "In union there is strength," workers made several attempts to unionize themselves, to try to get management to agree to higher wages, shorter hours, better working conditions, and an end to child labor. An early attempt was made by the Knights of Labor, formed in 1869. By 1886, their membership, made up of skilled and unskilled laborers in many industries, had risen to 700,000. But on May 4 of that year, a riot in Haymarket Square in Chicago, brought on by a strike of workers demanding an eight-hour workday, led to bloodshed and death. The riot turned many Americans against the idea of labor unions. Union supporters were accused of being socialists or communists and were widely thought to be "un-American."

The American Federation of Labor, founded in 1881 under the leadership of cigar-maker Samuel Gompers, weathered this storm, though. By 1904, its membership had grown to over a million mostly skilled workers.

Business owners and managers were generally hostile to labor unions, fearing the loss of profits and loss of control if they granted union demands. The government, too, had little use for unions, declaring that they defied antitrust laws when they went on strike because they were "in restraint of trade." Nevertheless, strikes were frequent and often bloody. In 1892, a strike at the Carnegie Steel Works at Homestead, near Pittsburgh, resulted in nine strikers and three company guards dead. In 1894, a strike at Pullman's Palace Car Company near Chicago caused federal troops to be brought in, on the side of management. Labor agitation for both freedom to unionize and better wages and conditions would be a continuing struggle for industrial workers for many decades.

Growth of cities. Cities were where the large work forces were, and so industrialists built their plants in or near cities. Once the plants were there, more workers moved to the cities, causing them to grow at astounding rates, doubling or tripling in size in as short a time as 20 years. In 1880, less than a quarter of the American population lived in cities; by 1900, well over half did.

The cities were exciting places, with such attractions as giant department stores like Marshall Field's in Chicago, Wanamaker's in Philadelphia, and Macy's in New York. They were also centers of theater, music, the arts, and sports. New trolley cars and elevated trains could carry the wealthy and the middle class to nice homes at the outskirts of the cities.

But cities had their seamier sides, too. Housing for the poor was dark and overcrowded. The mortality rate among the occupants of tenements, especially of children, was shockingly high. City governments paid little attention. Powerful political "machines" were too busy stealing money from city treasuries or accepting generous bribes from builders and other "interests" who could pay for favored treatment.

The Drive for Reform

Corruption in city government simply reflected corruption at state and federal levels. During the Grant administration (1869 to 1877), members of Grant's official family were convicted of taking bribes and of stealing from tax revenues. During the same period, the weaknesses of the "spoils system" became all too obvious, as the Presidential right to name people to public offices, high and low, led to still more corruption, allowing unworthy appointees to use government jobs to make money illegally.

Civil service. Agitation to end the spoils system became particularly strong after the assassination of James A. Garfield, in 1881. Garfield was shot by Charles J. Guiteau, a man who had wanted an appointment to a government job but had not gotten it. Garfield's successor was Chester A. Arthur, who fought tenaciously against the spoils system. In 1883, the Pendleton Act was passed; it set up a Civil Service Commission and decreed that many government jobs were to be given, awarded by competitive examination rather than political favor.

Populism. Industry may have been booming, helping industrialists and bankers in the East to grow rich, but agriculture was suffering during the late 1800's. Farm production was up, but farm prices were steadily declining, and farmers in the South and Midwest were sinking deeper into debt. The farmers saw the railroads as their enemies. They believed the railroads charged them too much to ship their farm products. They also did not trust the bankers, whom they believed hoarded gold and did not allow enough money to circulate to help the farmers pay their debts. The farmers favored the "free coinage of silver," which would allow the government to print paper money backed by the nation's plentiful silver supply to give the farmers the dollars they needed to become solvent again.

CHILDREN *at a cotton mill in 1911. Some were under ten years old but worked a twelve-hour day.*

NATIONAL CHILD LABOR COMMISSION

In 1891, agrarian interests formed the Populist Party, which favored, in addition to the free coinage of silver, government ownership of the railroads, a graduated income tax, an eight-hour workday, and direct election of senators by the people (at the time, senators were elected by the state legislatures). The Populist Party ran candidates in the Presidential elections of both 1892 and 1896, but the party never really gained much power. Farm prices began to rise, diminishing farmer discontent, and populism faded away.

Progressivism. Populism may have faded away, but many of its reform ideas had not. They were picked up and expanded by a new movement—Progressivism. The Progressives, who came from both the Republican and Democratic parties, believed that continuous progress was possible, that life in the United States could improve for everyone. They believed that the nation's rapid industrialization and urbanization had harmed the working poor, and that big business had become too powerful and was crushing small business. They further believed that individual citizens did not have enough power in determining how their government was run and that government corruption at all levels had therefore flourished.

Housing and labor. Many Progressives concentrated mainly on the awful living conditions in many of the nation's cities. They made more comfortable citizens aware of the poverty and lack of sanitation in the city tenements. Through their efforts, cities began passing laws that set building standards to alleviate some unhealthful conditions. Cities also began setting up public boards of health.

In the early 1900's, state legislatures, with the urging of Progressives, began passing laws to reduce the length of workdays, to force employers to make machinery safer, and to outlaw or limit child labor. Public systems of industrial accident insurance were also set up to help compensate workers injured on the job.

State and city government. The Progressives used two methods to reclaim state and city government from corruption and inefficiency. One struck at the power of party bosses. "Give the government back to the people!" was the cry. The second method was to hire experts to run government, rather than trust party professionals.

The state of Wisconsin, under Robert Marion ("Fighting Bob") La Follette, its Progressive Republican governor, took the lead in reforming state government. As part of the "Wisconsin Idea," the state legislature decreed the *direct primary,* giving citizens, not party bosses, the right to choose candidates for office. Soon other states were adopting other measures for "direct democracy." In 1913, the states ratified the 17th Amendment, which provided for the election of senators by popular vote.

Other Progressive measures included the *secret ballot,* assuring that voters need not express their preferences in front of bosses, officials, or others who might disapprove; *initiative,* which gave voters the right to suggest laws to their legislators; *referendum,* which gave voters the right to vote directly on certain bills; and *recall,* which gave voters the right to remove officials they believed were not doing a good job.

Many city governments adopted a city manager type of government. The city manager was a professional administrator who was expected to run city government along the most efficient, rather than the most politically rewarding, lines.

Roosevelt's Square Deal

The Progressives achieved real national power when one of their own, Republican Theodore Roosevelt, became President in 1901. He unexpectedly came to office at age 42 when President William McKinley died on September 14, eight days after being shot at the Pan-American Exposition in Buffalo, New York.

Roosevelt firmly believed that all Americans should get what he called "a square deal," that government should protect all segments of the population, not just a few chosen ones. This belief was put to the test in May, 1902, when 150,000 coal miners went on strike in Pennsylvania's anthracite mines, owned by a combination of coal-carrying railroads. In previous strikes, the federal government had sided with management rather than labor, but under Roosevelt, the government came to the aid of the striking workers, forcing the reluctant owners to grant a shorter workday and a 10 percent pay increase to the miners.

Trust busting. Roosevelt quickly made known his distaste for what he

LIBRARY OF CONGRESS

TEDDY ROOSEVELT, *a famous hunter, shot down "bad trusts" and restrained good ones.*

called "bad trusts," business combinations that used their great financial power to kill competition and thus increase their profits. The government brought many prosecutions against trusts, 44 of which were decided in the government's favor. Many railroads and shippers were convicted of rebating. Among the most famous trust exposures of this period was the suit against the Standard Oil Company, which was convicted of receiving and giving rebates and was ordered to dissolve in 1907.

Conservation. In May, 1908, Roosevelt called the Conservation Congress to take up the question of saving the nation's rapidly dwindling natural resources. The Reclamation Act of 1902 had already provided for the irrigation of Western arid areas. The renewal of forests, the protection of wildlife, and the development of waterpower were provided for as a result of the Conservation Congress.

Consumer protection. Through reading a book by Upton Sinclair entitled *The Jungle,* which described the unsanitary conditions of a meat-packing plant in Chicago, Theodore Roosevelt became an avid supporter of legislation to protect consumers from unsanitary or otherwise harmful products. In 1906, both the Meat Inspection Act, giving government inspectors the right to check sanitary conditions in meat-packing plants, and the Pure Food and Drug Act, which prohibited the use of harmful ingredients in products, were passed.

After Roosevelt. In 1908, Roosevelt decided not to run again and helped his friend William Howard Taft to win the Republican nomination and ultimately the election. Taft followed many of Roosevelt's Progressive reform policies, including prosecuting trusts and improving the lot of labor. A separate Department of Labor was established, and government workers were given an eight-hour workday.

Even so, Taft fell into disfavor with Roosevelt, and in 1912, Roosevelt decided to try for the Republican nomination. But the Republicans stuck with Taft, and Roosevelt bolted to become the candidate of the newly established Progressive Party. This split among the Republicans ensured the election of the Progressive Democratic candidate, Woodrow Wilson.

Wilson, too, had reformist aims. He lowered tariffs, which had remained high during so many Republican administrations; reformed the banking system, giving the government more control over finance; and continued the work of controlling the trusts.

The Clayton Antitrust Act of 1913 listed in detail all the practices condemned by the courts, particularly rebates, secret agreements, price privileges, and interlocking directorates between banks, railroads, and coal companies. It asserted that the labor of a human being is not a commodity, and it exempted from antitrust laws all nonprofit-making labor and farm groups. This provision gave labor unions new freedom to organize and operate.

Becoming a World Power

Prior to the Civil War, the United States took little part in world affairs. But its burgeoning industrialization following the Civil War led to a demand for foreign markets and raw materials. From then on, the United States played an ever-increasing role in world affairs. By the turn of the century, it had become a leading world power and an imperialistic nation with possessions scattered all over the globe, especially in Latin America and Asia.

Imperialism. The first American stirrings toward empire occurred in 1867 when Secretary of State William H. Seward prevailed on Congress to buy Alaska from Russia for $7.2 million. The purchase was derisively called "Seward's Folly" until great reserves of gold were found there 30 years later, setting off a mad gold rush. In 1867, Seward also got the United States to buy the Midway Islands in the Pacific. In 1889, the United States joined Germany and Britain in taking control of the Samoan Islands in the South Pacific for use as a refueling base for American ships trading in China.

Nearer at hand, some 2000 miles off the California coast, lay the Hawaiian Islands, where American missionaries had gone to convert the islanders and had stayed to become prosperous sugar growers and traders. By the 1890's these business interests were eager to take total control of the islands by removing the Hawaiian monarch, Queen Liliuokalani, from the throne. In 1893, with the help of U.S. Marines, they achieved their goal, and in 1898, Congress annexed the Hawaiian Islands to the United States.

War clouds. The United States's neighbor Cuba, lying just a few miles off the Florida shore, had long been under Spanish rule, and since 1868 had been trying to get out from under it, through guerrilla warfare and uprisings. Following an insurrection in Cuba in 1895, Spain sent General Valeriano Weyler to crush the rebellion. Reports of his pitiless treatment of the Cuban people earned American sympathy for the Cuban cause. This sympathy was not lessened by the $50 million in American capital tied up in Cuba. Many important and influential Americans wished to oust Spain from the western hemisphere for economic and strategic reasons, and to acquire Spain's possessions in both the Caribbean and the Pacific.

In 1898, riots in Havana prompted President McKinley to send the U.S. battleship *Maine* to the harbor there to protect American citizens and property. On the night of February 15, the *Maine* blew up in the harbor, killing 266 American sailors. It was never proven that Spain was responsible for the disaster, but newspapers played up the incident until the American public was eager for war. On April 19, Congress demanded that Spain relinquish Cuba. On April 24, Spain declared war, and on April 25, the United States resolved that a state of war had existed since April 21.

The Spanish-American War. The war's activities began at once. The U.S. North Atlantic Squadron was ordered to blockade Cuba and head off the Spanish fleet assumed headed there. Commodore George Dewey, in command of the Pacific squadron, was ordered to the Philippine Islands to destroy the Spanish fleet stationed there. Dewey was in Manila Bay by midnight, April 30. He began his bombardment about 5 a.m. and had destroyed the Spanish fleet by 12:30 with no losses. The elusive Spanish Atlantic fleet sailed into Santiago harbor in Cuba in May, and Commodore Winfield S. Schley blockaded the harbor by May 28.

General William R. Shafter and 17,000 troops (including the famous Rough Riders led by Colonel Theodore Roosevelt) landed at Daiquiri near Santiago in June. El Caney was taken by General Henry Lawton on July 1. The same day, the Rough Riders stormed and captured San Juan Hill. Fearing the destruction of Admiral Pascual Cervera's fleet, which was caught between land and sea, General Ramón Blanco in Santiago ordered the fleet to make a run for the open sea. On July 3, Cervera sailed out of the harbor to dare the blockade, and the battle that followed left not one Spanish vessel afloat. The U.S. Navy then bombarded Santiago unhindered, and

THREE AMERICAN CRUSADES

KEYSTONE VIEW COMPANY

SUFFRAGE AND PROHIBITION: *women camp in front of the White House in 1919, demanding Wilson's support for the 19th Amendment. That same year, Prohibition took effect and thousands of gallons of liquor were publicly poured into sewers.*

The Progressive movement, like its predecessor, the Populist movement, was made up of crusaders and activists. Three of the movement's causes helped change American institutions in the years before 1920—the graduated income tax, Prohibition, and women's voting rights.

Why would anyone crusade for an income tax? Farmers especially favored it as a way to get nonlandowning city dwellers to share the tax burden. The farmers opposed high tariffs, a common way to raise revenues at the time. Income taxes had been levied previously, but in 1894 the Supreme Court declared them unconstitutional. Agitation for them continued, though, and in 1913, the 16th Amendment was ratified, giving Congress "the power to lay and collect taxes on income." Today, income taxes are the government's single largest source of revenue.

The drive for Prohibition began in the early 1800's, led by concerned women and churchmen who deplored the effect of hard drinking on the family. They began a crusade for *temperance*, by which they meant the avoidance of all use of alcohol. In 1874, the Women's Christian Temperance Union (WCTU) was formed, and its members went into saloons where they prayed and sang hymns to discourage drinking. Carry Nation, one of the most vociferous crusaders, took a hatchet into saloons and smashed the liquor kegs.

By 1917, the crusade against alcohol had succeeded in getting Congress to approve the 18th Amendment, and in 1919 the amendment was ratified by three-quarters of the states. However, Americans found that they did not like living "dry," and in 1933, the 21st Amendment was passed; it repealed Prohibition.

The WCTU was helpful in working for another constitutional amendment, one that would not be repealed: extension of voting rights to women. The suffrage movement began in 1848 in Seneca Falls, New York. There, under the leadership of Lucretia Mott and Elizabeth Cady Stanton, a women's rights convention met; it demanded equal rights for women, including the right to vote. In 1869, Stanton and Susan B. Anthony formed the National Woman Suffrage Association; its aim was to get Congress to pass an amendment giving women the vote. The struggle was a long one. It was not until 50 years later, in 1920, that women got what they wanted—the 19th Amendment guaranteeing women's suffrage.

the city surrendered on July 17.

An armistice was signed on August 12; on December 10, 1898, a peace treaty was signed in Paris. Spain gave up all claims to Cuba, Puerto Rico, and Guam, and sold the Philippine Islands to the United States for $20 million.

Aftermath. Now that the United States had expanded its territory and influence in the Caribbean and Pacific, it had to work out ways to deal with it.

Cuba. Cuba received a provisional government under General Leonard Wood, whose military rule greatly improved education and sanitation on the island. Yellow fever was wiped out because of the sacrifices of Major Walter Reed, a U.S. Army surgeon. The provisional government developed, with self-government as its goal. In February, 1901, Cuba framed a constitution patterned after the U.S. Constitution. As a condition of American withdrawal from the island, the Cubans added an amendment that guaranteed that Cuba would permit no foreign interference or control by treaty of any kind, and reserved to the United States the right to intervene, at its own will, in behalf of Cuba's peace or independence.

Puerto Rico. Puerto Rico remained under U.S. military control until the Foraker Act of 1900 established a civil government with an American governor and executive council appointed by the President, and a house of representatives elected by the inhabitants. This was far from satisfactory to the Puerto Ricans because control of their government actually rested with the American executive council, and because U.S. citizenship was denied them. Finally, an act passed in 1917 gave them their own legislature and U.S. citizenship.

The Philippines. American desire for overseas expansion came to a head over the question of the Philippines. Living on approximately 80 islands more than 6000 miles from America's west coast were some 7 million Filipinos from over 80 tribes. A common desire to be free from United States rule united them. Under the leadership of Emilio Aguinaldo, the Filipinos tried, in February, 1899, to oust the temporary American regime established in Manila.

The United States countered mercilessly with a force of 50,000 troops that engaged in a three-year guerrilla war, killing hundreds of thousands of Filipinos before putting down the revolt and restoring order.

Antiimperialists denounced U.S. occupation of the Philippines, but the imperialists carried the day. They argued that the United States would now increase its national prestige, promote new business enterprises, tap the expanding trade with the Orient, frustrate the designs of other expanding powers in the Pacific, particularly Germany, and "uplift and civilize" the people of the islands.

In July, 1901, William Howard Taft, who had previously headed a commission to organize a civil government for the Philippines, became the islands' first civil governor. The Filipinos were promised independence in 1916, but did not achieve it until 1946.

The Troubled Hemisphere

Now that the United States had possessions and imperial ambitions, it took an even more militant stand in the western hemisphere.

The Panama Canal. With navies and political interests in the Atlantic and Pacific, U.S. politicians and businessmen wanted to move ships more quickly between the oceans. President Roosevelt eagerly supported a project to dig a canal across the Isthmus of Panama, in what was part of Colombia. In 1903, Secretary Hay concluded the Hay-Herrán Treaty between the United States and Colombia. The treaty provided that the United States would buy a strip of land six miles wide across the isthmus. The U.S. Senate readily ratified this treaty, but then Colombia rejected it. With the tacit assistance of President Roosevelt, the inhabitants of Panama rebelled against Colombia and established an independent republic of their own.

U.S. naval forces prevented Colombian troops from opening fire in Panama to quell the rebellion. The new government was recognized within three days by the United States, and its independence was immediately guaranteed. In February, 1904, the Hay-Bunau-Varilla Treaty between the United States and the new Panamanian government was ratified. Panama by the treaty permanently leased a zone 10 miles wide across the isthmus for $10 million and a perpetual annuity of $250,000.

Digging began at once, but no great progress was made until 1907, when Roosevelt transferred the job to the Army engineers under Colonel George W. Goethals. At a cost of $400 million and thousands of lives, the "big ditch" was completed in 1914.

The Roosevelt Corollary. Several European nations had made large loans to Latin American countries and were now demanding repayment. In fact, they were threatening to use force. This threat prompted Roosevelt to promulgate a new policy. According to the Monroe Doctrine, the United States became the guardian of the western hemisphere; now it must also have the right to police all of the international difficulties in the area. If any nation of the hemisphere were unable to meet its financial obligations, or protect the lives and property of foreigners, the United States would intervene. Roosevelt and his successors Taft and Wilson made frequent use of this declared right to intervene in Latin America's affairs—in Nicaragua, the Dominican Republic, and Haiti, for example—to the lasting consternation of the Latin Americans.

Trouble with Mexico. During the early 1900's, Mexico underwent a series of revolutions. In 1913, the self-proclaimed military dictator General Victoriano Huerta seized control of the government. President Wilson adopted a strong moral tone. He refused to recognize Huerta's new regime, charging that it did not represent the will of the Mexican people and that it rested only on force. Wilson's stand was a departure from the traditional American policy, which was to recognize any government firmly in power, no matter how it was installed. Wilson went so far as to engage in efforts to bring down the Huerta regime.

Huerta retaliated against American citizens and their property, arresting American naval personnel in 1914. The United States promptly seized the Mexican port of Veracruz. War between the two neighbors seemed imminent. It was averted only when a reform leader, Venustiano Carranza, seized power, and Wilson immediately recognized his government.

But the trouble between the two neighbors was not over. Pancho Villa, an anti-Carranza revolutionary, showed his displeasure with the American recognition of Carranza by raiding Columbus, New Mexico, in March of 1916 and killing 17 Americans. With Carranza's permission, Wilson sent a punitive military expedition under General John J. Pershing into Mexico to capture Villa. Pershing failed, and the Americans withdrew in January, 1917. Other foreign problems were demanding American attention.

America in World War I

The drive for empire among European nations had created bitter rivalries. Fearful and jealous of one another, the European countries formed alliances for their mutual protection. In 1907, two major alliances faced each other—the Allies, including Britain, France, and Russia; and the Central Powers, including Germany and Austria-Hungary. The situation grew increasingly volatile.

UPI

VIDE WORLD PHOTOS

MILITARY SERVICE: *a stern Uncle Sam glared from recruitment posters in 1917 as America entered World War I. The popular leader of the American Expeditionary Forces was General "Black Jack" Pershing, shown here with troops in Mexico in 1916.*

On June 28, 1914, the heir to the Austro-Hungarian throne, Archduke Franz Ferdinand, was riding in an open limousine through the streets of Sarajevo, Bosnia, a part of the Austro-Hungarian empire. In the crowd stood a young student from Serbia, Gavril Princip, who believed that Bosnia should be freed from Austria-Hungary and become a part of Serbia. As the limousine paused before Princip, he raised a gun and fired twice, killing both the archduke and his wife.

This single act propelled all of Europe into war, as Austria-Hungary declared war on Serbia, Russia (considering itself Serbia's protector) prepared to fight Austria-Hungary, and Germany declared war on Russia. World war had begun between the two alliances.

Neutrality. In August, 1914, President Wilson urged Americans to stay neutral: "Be impartial in thought as well as in action, neutral in fact as well as in name." At first, Americans seemed willing to follow this course. After all, 3000 miles of ocean separated them from Europe. In addition, the war provided an economic opportunity. The warring nations were anxious for the food and munitions that the United States could provide. Orders for such goods flooded the United States from both sides.

Britain, however, was using its navy to set up a blockade of Germany in an effort to starve that nation out. Americans were angered when British ships harassed American shipping headed for Germany, but in an effort to stay neutral, the United States took no action. To break the blockade, Germany resorted to its underwater U-boats, which could strike British ships and ships heading for Britain. The United States protested U-boat warfare, since it sometimes cost American lives and property.

On May 7, 1915, a German U-boat sank the British passenger liner *Lusitania* off the coast of Ireland, with the loss of nearly 1200 lives, including 128 Americans. Americans feared that they were losing their "freedom of the seas." The sinking of the *Lusitania* aroused great anger in the United States, and as a result Germany promised to stop sinking passenger ships.

Closer to war. In 1916, Wilson was reelected, using the slogan "He Kept Us Out of War." But three events would combine to end American neutrality. The first was Germany's return to "unlimited submarine warfare" on February 1, 1917, causing Wilson to break off diplomatic relations. The second was the discovery in early March of the so-called Zimmerman telegram. Written by German Foreign Minister Arthur Zimmerman to the German minister in Mexico, it instructed him to urge Mexico to join the Central Powers and to go to war against the United States should the United States declare war on the Central Powers. In return, Germany offered Mexico the return of Texas, New Mexico, and Arizona after the defeat of the United States. The third decisive event was the revolution in Russia, ending Russian contributions to the cause of the Allies.

On April 2, 1917, President Wilson asked Congress for a declaration of war against the Central Powers. "The world must be made safe for democracy," he stated. On April 6, Congress declared war and the United States joined the Allies.

Into battle. By this time, the Allies were in a desperate situation. They had been fighting for nearly three years, and the war was at a stalemate. Troops on both sides faced each other from trenches stretching down a long front through France. The British had lost one-third of their troops, the French over half. They were fast running out of food and military supplies.

The first task for the United States was to raise an army. Within three months, over a million men had volunteered, but many more would be needed. So on May 18, 1917, the Selective Service Act was passed, providing for the draft of what eventually turned out to be nearly 3 million men.

The next task was to mobilize American agriculture and industry to provide for both the American forces and those of the hard-pressed Allies. The government tripled the amount of food sent to the Allies, through both greater farm production and conservation of food on the home front. (Citizens were encouraged to save food by honoring "wheatless Mondays" and "meatless Tuesdays.") Federal agencies also took control of the American economy, telling manufacturers what to produce for the war effort.

On the home front, women rushed in to fill the jobs left by departing volunteers and draftees. For the first time, women became auto mechanics, mail carriers, and trolley conductors. Also for the first time, women lawyers and doctors were allowed to work for government agencies. Morale was kept up by the Committee on Public Information, which sent out 75,000 speakers to rally enthusiasm for the war. Movie stars and other entertainers appeared before large groups to encourage them to buy "Liberty Bonds" to help the government finance the war. To aid in that financing, income tax rates were raised.

War in France. Since it took a long time for the Army to mobilize, relatively few American troops reached France until March of 1918. President Wilson had chosen General John J. Pershing, veteran of the Pancho Villa search, to head the American Expeditionary Force (AEF). Pershing insisted that the AEF fight as a separate force, not as a part of British or French forces. By spring and summer of 1918, the AEF was in the thick of the fighting, at Cantigny, Chateau-Thierry, Belleau Wood, the Marne River, and San Mihiel. In September, 1918, the Americans mounted a huge offensive between the Argonne Forest and the Meuse River. More than a million Americans fought there, and in November, they triumphed. On November 11, 1918, Germany signed the terms of surrender. Wilson's "war to end war" was over.

A search for a just peace. Before the war had ended, Wilson had proposed "Fourteen Points" on which he thought the peace should be built. Among these was the proposition that all peoples should have the right to *self-determination.* Former colonies, for example, and nations within the Austro-Hungarian empire should be able to choose for themselves how they wanted to be ruled. Another point proposed that the nations of the world join together in a League of Nations, where they might settle their differences peaceably.

For a while, Wilson thought he might make his Fourteen Points a reality; he was enthusiastically welcomed by European crowds as he made his way to Versailles to work out the peace treaty. But the other Allied leaders were more interested in punishing Germany than in implementing Wilson's ideals. The Treaty of Versailles did provide for a League of Nations, but it demanded huge reparations from a war-impoverished Germany; this helped to assure that European war would come soon again.

Wilson fared little better at home, where he found bitter opposition to the United States joining a League of Nations. Fearing that such a league would have too much power over American foreign affairs, Congress voted against approving the Treaty of Versailles. Wilson found his hopes for a "just peace" irreparably broken.

The American Age

Feast and Famine

As American troops began arriving home, the nation was in a mood to forget war and foreign entanglement and the rapid social changes brought on by war. Americans welcomed the message of Warren G. Harding, Republican senator from Ohio: "America's present need is not heroics but healing, not nostrums but normalcy . . . not surgery but serenity. . . ." In 1920, the American people elected Harding President and looked forward to "a return to normalcy."

Unrest. The 1920's are often looked back on as a crazy, fun-loving era—the Roaring Twenties, the Era of Wonderful Nonsense, the Jazz Age. But the '20's had its deeply serious side. The decade began with a recession, marked by rising prices and unemployment. Labor unrest followed, and with it frequent strikes.

The Red scare. Many Americans were quick to blame the strikes on Communist influences within labor unions. A wave of bombings, blamed on "foreign anarchists," many of them immigrants from Southern and Eastern Europe, only exacerbated American fears that the "Reds" were plotting to overthrow the American government.

In January of 1920, Attorney General A. Mitchell Palmer ordered a series of raids to be made on groups suspected of "un-American" ties. During these raids, 6000 suspects were arrested in 33 cities, and over 500 of them were deported. Yet no overthrow plots were ever uncovered, and many Americans began to feel that the raids were trampling on the Bill of Rights. By the end of the year, the Red scare had died down.

Immigration restricted. American distrust and dislike for the large numbers of immigrants arriving from Southern and Eastern Europe did not die down, however. In 1921, Congress passed the Emergency Quota Act, which severely limited the number of immigrants who could enter the United States. In 1924, Congress passed the Immigration Act. It decreed that only a small number of immigrants from Southern and Eastern European countries could enter the United States; immigrants from Northern and Western Europe were favored. In 1929, the total number of all immigrants allowed in annually was lowered to 150,000.

The Ku Klux Klan. Fear of the new and the strange was especially strong in the small towns of the South and Midwest. Here prejudice against blacks had long been strong, but now it was joined by hatred of Catholics and Jews, groups that included many of the new immigrants. These prejudices and hatreds led to a revival of the Ku Klux Klan, reestablished in Georgia in 1915. By 1923, the Klan's membership had grown to 4 million people bent on preserving America for white, "native-born" Protestants. The Klan's methods were to terrorize those who did not fit their definition of an American.

Political scandal. It has been said that the only qualification Harding had to be President was that he looked like one. Harding was an affable man, given to playing poker with his pals. His cronyism was the basis for his selection of many Cabinet and executive officers, and their greed resulted in massive political corruption. His attorney general, Harry Daugherty, made a fortune selling government favors. Harding's friend Charles Forbes, whom he named head of the new Veterans' Bureau, helped himself and his friends to $200 million of the bureau's funds. Harding's secretary of the interior, Albert B. Fall, took over $400,000 in bribes to rent out government oil land reserved strictly for U.S. Navy use, at Teapot Dome in Wyoming and Elk Hills in California, to private oil developers. The scandals were the most serious since those of the Grant era 50 years earlier.

Word of all this corruption was just starting to come out when, on August 2, 1923, Harding died suddenly on a trip to the West Coast. He was succeeded by his Vice President, a dour and laconic former governor of Massachusetts, Calvin Coolidge.

WIDE WORLD PHOTOS

CULVER PICTURES

THE ROARING '20'S *brought new American heroes like Charles Lindbergh, who flew alone across the Atlantic in 1927, and new American crazes like the Charleston, a dance adored by the short-haired, short-skirted young women called "flappers."*

Prosperity. The advent of "Silent Cal" began a period that came to be called "Coolidge prosperity." During this time tariffs went up and income tax rates went down. Antitrust legislation was not enforced. These circumstances combined to provide a good climate for business growth, and Coolidge's attitude toward business could not have been more encouraging: "The business of America is business," he declared. During the 1920's, industrial production nearly doubled.

Not everyone was sharing in Coolidge prosperity, though. Agricultural production had grown impressively during World War I as American food entered world markets. Farmers had taken mortgages on new land and put it under cultivation. Now, as Europe got back on its feet and could meet much of its own agricultural need, prices for American farm products fell. It was becoming increasingly difficult for American farmers to meet their mortgage payments, and banks began repossessing their farms.

Organized labor was also not faring well during the 1920's. In a highly business-oriented country, hostility toward labor unions ran high, and the unions lost several of the safeguards that they had won during the Progressive Era. Once again, the Supreme Court was finding unions in violation of antitrust legislation.

Boom to bust. In 1928, Coolidge announced, "I do not choose to run," and the Republicans nominated Herbert Hoover as their candidate. To run against him, the Democrats named Alfred E. Smith, governor of New York, the first Roman Catholic to run for the Presidency for a major party. Satisfied with the prosperity under the two previous Republicans, the voters overwhelmingly elected Hoover.

Problems. Farm problems continued to plague the country. The remedy might have been to lower the tariff barriers and thus facilitate world buying and selling. Instead, in 1930, Congress passed the highest protective tariff in its history, the Smoot-Hawley Tariff. Within two years, the United States lost over $5 billion in world trade.

With its world trade down, the nation had an excessive supply of manufactured goods. High productivity had, by the end of the 1920's, produced a great overstock. Factories began cutting back on production, thus cutting back on jobs.

The crash. One of the causes of the seeming prosperity of the 1920's was the busy stock market. Speculation in stocks became nothing short of a national mania. Stock prices kept going up and up until they were dangerously overpriced. Speculators kept borrowing more money to buy more stocks. By 1929, $9 billion was owed to banks in stock speculation. Then, on October 29, 1929, the bubble finally burst. Prices had been going down steadily, and nervous speculators were trying to sell their stocks as quickly as they could. On that "Black Tuesday," they dumped 16 million shares on the market and there was no one who wanted to buy. The stock market had crashed. Soon the nation's other economic ills would become apparent to all, and the worst depression in the nation's history was under way.

The Great Depression. In the three years following the crash, the national situation became desperate and human suffering grew. Between 1929 and 1932, farm income shrank by 50 percent. Industry was operating at one-half its former rate. In 1932 alone, 32,000 businesses failed, and so did nearly 1500 banks, wiping out the life savings of millions of Americans. Unemployment reached over 12 million—fully one-quarter of the work force. One million Americans took to the road, trying to find work. Local and state charities could not deal with the widespread destitution.

Hoover opposed measures for federal relief on various political and moral grounds, but he launched a huge program of public works in 1930 to try to stem unemployment. In 1932, he secured passage of the bill for the Reconstruction Finance Corporation, which lent $2 billion to banks, railroads, and other industries. But nothing short of world recovery could stem the economic disaster, because the Great Depression was worldwide.

Election of 1932. Amid growing domestic economic crises, the Republicans renominated Hoover. The Democrats chose New York Governor Franklin D. Roosevelt, a distant cousin of Theodore. As governor, Roosevelt had set up a relief program for New York, and he promised to set up relief programs on a national scale if elected.

Despite having suffered a crippling attack of polio in 1921, Roosevelt was one of the most active and appealing young Democrats; he had made a dramatic appearance on crutches at the 1924 convention to nominate Al Smith and, at Smith's urging, had run for governor in 1928. Roosevelt toured the country promising people a "New Deal." He won a landslide victory as voters rejected Hoover's administration, which many of them blamed for their economic problems.

The New Deal. As soon as he was elected, Roosevelt and his advisers, called his "brain trust," began shaping a series of domestic social and economic programs—the New Deal. The New Deal had three main objectives: *relief* for those hit hardest by the Depression; *recovery* for the nation's economy; and *reform* to prevent another depression.

Roosevelt took office on March 4, 1933, saying: "The nation asks for action and action now. We must act and act quickly." In the "first hundred days," Congress responded to the President's programs by passing a raft of emergency recovery measures in banking, industry, and agriculture. (See chart below.)

The first thing Roosevelt did was declare a "bank holiday," closing all the banks to allow bank inspectors to determine which were sound enough to continue doing business. Then Congress passed the Emergency Banking Law, giving the President the power to reorganize insolvent national banks. To help revive industry, Congress passed the National Industrial Recovery Act (NIRA), to establish codes for industries to eliminate unfair competition, abolish child labor and sweat shops, establish minimum wages and maximum hours, create additional jobs for the unemployed, and assure labor the right to organize freely and bargain collectively. To aid agriculture, Congress passed the Agricultural Adjustment Act (AAA), to control production of farm goods through subsidies aimed at lowering production, and to lend money to farmers.

Congress also passed a number of relief acts, some offering direct aid to the needy and some offering jobs in public works. The Civilian Conservation Corps and Public Works Administration employed millions. Other measures created the Tennessee Valley Authority (TVA) to develop a depressed area covering parts of seven states; the Securities and Exchange Commission (SEC) to regulate the stock market; Social Security legislation to provide old-age insurance; and the National Labor Relations Board (NLRB) to monitor labor disputes.

UPI

PRESIDENT ROOSEVELT *heartened victims of the Depression with his confidence.*

THE FIRST HUNDRED DAYS

LIBRARY OF CONGRESS

USDA/SOIL CONSERVATION SERVICE

THE POOR *stood in line for soup,* above, *and western farmers were ruined by drought* right.

Franklin D. Roosevelt took office on March 4, 1933. In the first months of his term, aided by a sense of crisis in the country and a Democratic majority in the Congress, he passed bills designed to help the needy and shore up the economic structure of the nation. The major acts were:

Emergency Banking Relief Act, March 9	Imposed federal regulation on the banking business
Civilian Conservation Reforestation Relief Act, March 31	Provided jobs for young men on federal conservation projects
Federal Emergency Relief Act, May 12	Granted funds to states for relief of the poor; provided 4 million civil works jobs
Tennessee Valley Authority Act, May 12	Created Tennessee Valley Authority to provide jobs, electrical power, and flood control
Agricultural Adjustment Act, May 21	Paid farmers subsidies for reducing production and made federal loans available
Federal Securities Act, May 27	Tightened regulation of securities markets; required fuller disclosure about securities in order to protect investors
Home Owners' Refinancing Act, June 13	Provided federal mortgages to those in danger of losing their homes because of unemployment
Glass-Steagall Banking Act, June 16	Created the Federal Deposit Insurance Corporation to insure bank deposits up to $5000
National Industrial Recovery Act, June 16	Suspended antitrust laws; granted new rights to labor; created the National Labor Board

Some of these acts were temporary and some provisions were later ruled unconstitutional; but many provisions endured and some agencies are still active and important.

Roosevelt and the Supreme Court. Many of the New Deal measures represented incredible departures from previous governmental practices, and their constitutionality was called into question. The Supreme Court found both the AAA and the NIRA unconstitutional. An angry President Roosevelt blamed this defeat of his policies on the fact that the Supreme Court was made up of "nine old men," six of them over 70 years old and seven of them appointees of Republican Presidents. In February, 1937, Roosevelt proposed that Congress reorganize the High Court, giving the President the right to name a new justice for each one who did not retire by age 70. This would allow Roosevelt to install his own appointees, who would be more likely to be sympathetic to the laws he proposed. Congress angrily accused him of trying to "pack the court," and denied his proposal, leaving the Court as it was.

Effects of the New Deal. The New Deal did not return the nation to prosperity at once. Indeed, when Roosevelt began his second term in 1937, he had to state that he still saw "one-third of the nation ill-housed, ill-clad, ill-nourished." But the New Deal, which by 1938 was running out of steam, had made the most profound, dramatic, and lasting changes in government in American history. Government had grown larger than ever before and it had moved into many new phases of American life. Direct government intervention and regulation—in business, social welfare, and human security—reached heights undreamed of a few years earlier. Even after the Depression ended, government's right to intervene and regulate was widely accepted.

War and Responsibility

The worldwide Depression had paved the way for the rise of rightist military dictators in Europe. Adolf Hitler and the Nazi Party took control of Germany and Benito Mussolini and the Fascists ruled Italy. Half a world away, in Japan, another government dominated by the military came to power. The German, Italian, and Japanese dictatorships were bent on expansion, and soon each was on the move—Japan into China in 1931, Italy into Africa in 1935, and Germany into Czechoslovakia in 1938. In the mid-1930's, the three signed a series of mutual agreement pacts and became known as the Axis powers.

War in Europe. At first, the Allies, Britain and France, had regarded fascism as the best defense against encroachments into Western Europe by Soviet communism, under the iron rule of Stalin. To appease Hitler, the Allies agreed to sacrifice Czechoslovakia to German expansionism by the terms of the 1938 Munich Pact. But on September 1, 1939, Hitler's tanks rolled into Poland, which was an ally of Britain and France, and the Allied nations were forced to declare war on Germany.

The Germans were prepared for war and the Allies were not. In the spring of 1940, in a *blitzkrieg* (lightning war), Hitler rapidly conquered Denmark, Norway, the Netherlands, Belgium, and France, leaving Britain to fight alone. In 1941 Hitler tore up a mutual nonaggression pact he had signed with Stalin and attacked the Soviet Union, which immediately joined Britain as an ally.

From neutrality to aid. Once again, popular sentiment in the United States favored staying out of foreign troubles. In 1935 and 1937, Congress passed a series of laws known as the Neutrality Acts to ensure that the United States would isolate itself from war. But as in 1917, the United States would find neutrality impossible to maintain.

In the fall of 1940, Roosevelt had won an unprecedented third term as President, all the while maintaining that the United States would not involve itself in any foreign war. But by that time, it had become clear that the nation could no longer remain uninvolved. In a radio "fireside chat," Roosevelt told Americans that their nation must become the "arsenal of democracy," providing money and military equipment to those nations resisting German forces. In his January, 1941, message to Congress, Roosevelt asked for a lend-lease plan to assist the Allies. He also set forth the "four freedoms" that he believed were the birthright of all human beings: freedom of speech and of worship, freedom from want and from fear.

In March, Congress approved the Lend-Lease Act, which supplied beleaguered Britain with guns, tanks, ships, and planes. Later in 1941, Congress repealed the Neutrality Acts, as American shipping was already fighting an undeclared naval war with Germany in the Atlantic.

Pearl Harbor. As the European colonial powers were weakened by the war in Europe, the Japanese militarists saw their opportunity to step up their plan to drive all colonial powers, including the United States, from East Asia, and to establish their own "New Order" there. President Roosevelt and Secretary of State Cordell Hull resisted these efforts. When the Japanese occupied French Indochina (Vietnam and Cambodia) in July of 1941, the President froze Japanese assets in the United States and embargoed shipments of the oil and scrap iron desperately needed in Japan. Britain followed suit. In November, 1941, negotiations over trade, the status of China, and territorial expansion in Asia began between the United States and Japan. Japan demanded an end to all U.S. and British influence in Asia. While the talks were going on, a Japanese fleet set out across the Pacific toward Hawaii.

On the morning of Sunday, December 7, 1941, Japanese fighters, bombers, and submarines attacked the American naval base at Pearl Harbor in Hawaii. Nineteen U.S. ships were sunk or badly damaged; more than 2300 Americans were killed. The following day, President Roosevelt spoke to Congress, referring to the "day which will live in infamy" and asking for a declaration of war against Japan. Within a few hours, war was declared. Three days later, the other Axis powers, Germany and Italy, also declared war on the United States.

The United States now found itself facing war on two fronts—in Europe and in the Pacific. Roosevelt determined that the situation in Europe was the more desperate—if Britain and the Soviet Union fell, the United States would be totally on its own.

Americans in wartime. Industry and agriculture mobilized to create a giant wartime production apparatus, shifting as quickly as possible from consumer goods to military supplies and equipment. The wartime economy provided millions of new jobs, higher wages and overtime pay, factory jobs for women, and profitable war contracts for manufacturers.

Many government agencies were set up to regulate prices, wages, and rents; allocate materials; and coordinate production. Rationing systems were set up for scarce goods such as gasoline, sugar, coffee, and rubber.

Fearful of further Japanese attacks and of enemy spies and sabotage, many Americans, particularly on the West Coast, became suspicious of all people of Japanese ancestry, even those born in the United States, the Nisei. President Roosevelt authorized inland "relocation camps" and the forced removal of 100,000 Japanese-Americans from their homes and property.

As early as September, 1940, Congress passed the Selective Service Act, the first U.S. peacetime draft. In December, 1941, the age limits were broadened to include men 20 to 44 years of age. In May, 1942, Congress authorized the formation of women's noncombat branches in the Navy (WAVES), Army (WACS), Air Force (WAFS), Coast Guard (SPARS), and Marines. In all, about 16 million Americans served in military units during the war.

Allied cooperation. Throughout the war, the leaders of the "Big Three"—Roosevelt for the United States, Churchill for Britain, and Stalin for the Soviet Union—as well as other Allied civilian and military leaders, met regularly to work out wartime strategy and to plan for postwar peace. The major disagreement among the three was the timing of the Allied invasion of Western Europe. The Soviet Union was fighting heroically on the eastern front and insisted that Britain and the United States invade France without delay. British and American troops landed instead in North Africa, and then invaded Italy.

The fall of the Axis. In 1943 American and other Allied forces invaded Sicily and Mussolini and the Fascist government in Italy were soon overthrown. The new Italian government then joined its armies with the Allied forces against Germany.

The long-awaited invasion of Western Europe came on June 6, 1944, with the invasion of Normandy. With massive air support, American and British troops moved across France into Germany. The Soviet army moved on Germany from the east. At the end of April, 1945, Hitler and many top Nazis committed suicide; others fled. Germany surrendered unconditionally on May 8, 1945.

War in Asia raged on with no sign of abating as American forces moved on Japan from the east. In July the United States, Britain, and the Soviet Union met in Potsdam, near Berlin, to decide how Germany would be occupied. On August 6, 1945, the newly developed atomic bomb was dropped on the Japanese industrial city of Hiroshima, killing 100,000 people. On August 9 a second bomb was dropped on Nagasaki. The next day Japan surrendered. Allied victory was declared on August 15. Japanese officials signed the document of surrender on September 2. World War II was over, after the loss of over 405,000 American lives among millions of casualties worldwide. In addition, the atomic age had begun and the stage was set for a new kind of conflict.

Roosevelt to Truman. President Roosevelt did not live to see either the German surrender or the use of the atom bomb and the Japanese surrender. In 1944, although aging and ill, the President had run for a fourth term and had easily beaten the Republican candidate, New York State governor Thomas E. Dewey. Less than three months after his fourth inauguration, Roosevelt died, on April 12, 1945, after suffering a stroke at his winter home in Warm Springs, Georgia. He was succeeded by his Vice President, Harry S. Truman, a blunt, plainspoken former senator from Missouri.

During the war Roosevelt had urged the formation of a new international organization to replace the League of Nations as a stronger, more effective, force for peace. On April 25, 1945, 50 nations met in San Francisco in order to draft a charter for the new United Nations.

A serious disagreement between the United States and the Soviet Union on use of the veto in the Security Council delayed the signing of the UN Charter until June 26, 1945.

MAJOR EVENTS OF WORLD WAR II

CULVER PICTURES

UPI

PEARL HARBOR, left, *shocked the nation on December 7, 1941, and the United States entered the war. By June, 1944, the Allies had landed in France,* right, *and Germany and Japan were in retreat.*

1939–1941 The German armies of Adolf Hitler attack Poland September 1, 1939. The Allied powers, led by Britain and France, declare war on the Axis (Germany and Italy). By July, 1940, the Axis powers overrun Denmark, Norway, Belgium, Holland, and France, and threaten Britain. In June, 1941, they invade the Soviet Union.

Meanwhile, the Japanese, allied with the Axis, take control of south Asia and the Pacific. On December 7, 1941, they attack Pearl Harbor, a U.S. Navy base in Hawaii. Within days, the United States declares war on all Axis nations.

Events in Europe/ • Events in the Pacific

1942
- • *Jan.-May.* Japanese capture the Philippines and Burma.
- • *May.* U.S. forces drive off Japanese fleet in Coral Sea.
- • *June.* U.S. defends Midway Island, defeats Japanese fleet.
- • *Aug.* U.S. forces land on Guadalcanal, face bitter fight.
- *Nov.* U.S. and Allied forces land in North Africa.

1943
- *Feb.* Soviets begin long offensive to retake Stalingrad and drive Germans from U.S.S.R. in bloodiest campaign of war.
- • *Feb.* U.S. completes conquest of Guadalcanal.
- *May.* Allied forces drive all Axis troops from North Africa.
- *July-Aug.* Allies invade and occupy Sicily.
- • *July.* U.S. begins drive on Solomon Islands.
- *Sept.* Allies invade the mainland of Italy.

1944
- *Jan.-May.* Allied air forces begin heavy bombardment of Germany.
- • U.S. defeats Japanese in New Guinea.
- *June-Aug.* Rome liberated June 4; Allies invade France at Normandy beaches June 6; Paris liberated August 25.
- • *June.* U.S. forces capture Saipan, Guam.
- • *Oct.* U.S. fleet crushes Japanese fleet at Leyte Gulf, gains foothold in Philippines.
- *Dec.* Battle of the Bulge: German counteroffensive drives Allies back in Belgium. Allies hold at Bastogne.

1945
- • *Feb.* Manila, capital of the Philippines, is liberated.
- • *Apr.-June.* U.S. approaches Japan, captures Okinawa.
- *Apr.-May.* Fall of Germany: British, U.S., and Soviet forces meet; Berlin falls May 2. Germany surrenders May 8.
- *May-June.* U.S. bombards Japan, prepares for invasion.
- • *Aug. 6 and 9.* U.S. drops atom bombs on Hiroshima and Nagasaki.
- Japan surrenders August 14.

Prosperity and Suspicion

When the war ended, the United States found itself to be the world's leading industrial and military power. Its wartime Allies and the Axis nations were severely war-damaged and they faced the monumental task of rebuilding. The United States, on the other hand, was relatively untouched. Its most pressing problems were to convert from a wartime to a peacetime economy and to absorb the returning military veterans into daily life.

Readjustment. America converted to peace with surprising ease. The armed forces were demobilized rapidly, and returning service personnel were aided by the G.I. Bill of Rights. The bill offered money for tuition and living expenses to those who wanted to go to college or to training schools; low-cost loans to those who wanted to buy homes or start up businesses; and unemployment benefits to those who were seeking jobs. Millions of veterans took advantage of these opportunities, at once raising the educational level of the nation and sending the building industry into a period of unprecedented boom.

Inflation. Americans had built up savings of over $135 billion during the war, and now they were anxious to spend it. Consumer demand for goods that were scarce during the war kept the factories busy. But the supply of consumer goods could not keep pace with the demand, and prices soared as soon as wartime price controls were lifted. Within a single year, the cost of living rose by 50 percent.

The Taft-Hartley Act. The inflation brought on a rash of strikes as workers demanded pay increases that would allow them to keep up with rising prices. A wave of antiunion feeling resulted, and in 1947, a Republican Congress passed the Taft-Hartley Act, which took away some of the power that labor had gained in the New Deal. Among other provisions, it banned the closed shop, required an 80-day cooling-off period before a strike could begin in a vital industry, and forbade unions from contributing to political campaigns. Denounced by labor and rejected by Truman, the bill was passed over his veto.

Cold War. The Soviet Union insisted on keeping a tight hold on the nations of Eastern Europe, and by 1947 it was evident that they wanted to expand Communist influence into Greece and Turkey, a move that the Western Allies vehemently opposed.

The Truman Doctrine. Civil war in Greece, in which Communists were trying to gain control of the government, caused Truman to take steps to stop further Communist expansion. In March, 1947, he announced what came to be called the Truman Doctrine, that it "must be the policy of the United States to support free people who are resisting attempted subjugation." He asked Congress to authorize millions of dollars in economic and military aid for Greece, Turkey, and any other nation that wanted to fight Communist takeovers.

The Marshall Plan. Truman's policy was carried even further by his secretary of state, George C. Marshall. Seeing that the economically dislocated countries of Europe were all subject to Communist influence, Marshall announced on June 5, 1947, that the American government was willing to provide economic aid to any country that agreed to work for its own recovery. This was the basis of the European Recovery Plan (ERP), also called the Marshall Plan, for the reconstruction and rehabilitation of Europe.

Through this plan, Congress supplied $12.5 billion worth of aid to countries in Western Europe (the countries of Eastern Europe were offered the same aid, but the Soviet Union did not allow them to accept). This aid helped Western Europe to become independent and self-supporting once again.

The Berlin blockade. The next year, a direct confrontation between the Western nations and the Soviet Union arose in Berlin. All of eastern Germany had been occupied solely by the Russians, with the exception of the German capital of Berlin. Here Americans, French, British, and Russians controlled different zones within the city. Wanting to drive the Western nations out of this eastern area, Soviet troops blocked the routes of access—highways and railroads—that the Western powers had to the city in an effort to cut off the city's supplies.

But the Western powers would not be driven out. They mounted a massive airlift into Berlin, flying in enough cargo each day to keep Berlin's 2 million residents, as well as their own troops, supplied. After 321 days, the Russians lifted the blockade.

NATO. Recognizing that an "iron curtain" now separated Europe into two parts, the Western powers established the North Atlantic Treaty Organization (NATO), a regional mutual security alliance, in April, 1949. The original members were the United States, Canada, eight Western European nations, Turkey, and Greece.

The election of 1948. Inflation, the spread of communism, and accusations of corruption in his administration had made Truman look like an easy candidate to beat in 1948. The platform he offered, which he called the Fair Deal, promised to extend many New Deal programs—higher minimum wage and Social Security benefits; more support for housing, agriculture, and education; and a system of government insurance for medical expenses. But left-leaning Democrats wanted more; they broke away to form the Progressive Party, with former Vice President Henry A. Wallace as their candidate. Truman's insistence on equal rights for blacks and other minorities alienated many Southern Democrats, so they too broke away to form the States' Rights Party with South Carolina Governor J. Strom Thurmond as their candidate.

Jubilant Republicans chose Thomas E. Dewey again and awaited a landslide victory. But Truman began an extensive "whistle-stop campaign," traveling by train through communities across the nation and stopping to address the voters at the stations along the way. He polled about 2 million more votes than Dewey.

The Korean War. Cold war turned hot on June 25, 1950, when Communist North Korean troops crossed the 38th parallel and attacked non-Communist South Korea. During the previous year, a long civil war in China had ended with the triumph of the Communists. The People's Republic of China was now the ally of the Soviet Union and of North Korea. Fearful that if one Asian nation were conquered others would soon fall to the Communists, the United States sent its troops as part of a United Nations force to aid South Korea.

By November the UN troops had driven the North Koreans back behind their border and were continuing north. At that point, the Chinese intervened, sending the UN troops retreating south. For the next two and a half years, the fighting continued, until finally a cease-fire was signed on July 27, 1953, essentially restoring the old border between North and South Korea. The war cost 157,530 U.S. casualties, including 54,246 dead.

TRUMAN *made hard decisions and stuck by them. "The buck stops here," he said.*

LIBRARY OF CONGRESS

MAJOR EVENTS OF THE KOREAN WAR

1950	
June 25	North Korean forces invade South Korea.
June 27	UN authorizes the use of UN forces to repel the North Koreans. President Truman orders U.S. forces to South Korea.
June 28	Seoul falls to North Koreans.
July 8	General Douglas MacArthur is named UN commander in Korea.
Aug. 6	North Koreans open a major drive to destroy UN forces.
Sept. 15	UN forces land at Inchon, near Seoul and the 38th parallel, and within weeks drive the North Korean army north toward Manchuria.
Nov. 24	General MacArthur launches an end-the-war offensive in northern Korea.
Nov. 26	Chinese launch a massive counterattack. UN forces begin retreat, then stabilize front near 38th parallel.
1951	
Apr. 11	General MacArthur is relieved of command. General Matthew B. Ridgway is named UN commander in Korea.
July 10	Armistice talks begin.
1953	
July 27	Armistice is signed and goes into effect.

The Korean War demonstrated the strong determination of the United States to resist Communist aggression around the world, but it also revealed the dangers and the tremendous cost of American involvement in a land war in Asia.

Disagreement on the conduct of the war between General Douglas MacArthur, commander of UN forces in Korea, and President Truman led to MacArthur's removal from command. MacArthur had publicly advocated air and naval strikes against targets in China in order to secure the defeat of Chinese and North Korean forces. Truman, seeking to prevent the conflict from expanding into a full-fledged world war, opposed such measures.

This tactical disagreement highlighted the flaw inherent in so-called limited warfare: military objectives and political objectives do not necessarily coincide.

In Korea, UN forces halted North Korean aggression, but the 1953 armistice produced little more than a fragile armed truce.

McCarthyism. A fear of Communist activity both abroad and at home dominated much American thinking during the late 1940's and early 1950's. Senator Joseph McCarthy of Wisconsin charged that there were Communists in American government in 1950, claiming he had a list of 205 Communists or pro-Communists working in the State Department. In that same year, former State Department official Alger Hiss, accused of spying for the Soviet Union 20 years earlier, was convicted of perjury. In 1953 Ethel and Julius Rosenberg, convicted of treason for stealing sketches of the atomic bomb, were executed.

Other private and public investigations went on throughout the country; they involved former members of the Communist Party, their associates, and others simply suspected of radical tendencies. Many people were unfairly dismissed from their jobs and many organizations and institutions required "loyalty oaths" of their employees. Though few charges were ever proved, many people were labeled "security risks."

Then, in early 1954, McCarthy accused the United States Army of harboring known Communists. The televised Army-McCarthy hearings showed the American public McCarthy's unfair tactics and public opinion began turning against him. In December McCarthy's colleagues in the Senate censured him for "conduct unbecoming a member," and with that, "McCarthyism" faded away.

Eisenhower years. In 1952 the Republicans chose war hero and organizer of NATO General Dwight D. Eisenhower as their candidate for President. Adlai E. Stevenson, governor of Illinois, was the Democratic candidate. A respected liberal, Stevenson failed to overcome the popular sentiment for "Ike," and Eisenhower won by a large margin.

Domestic affairs. The Eisenhower years saw the development of unprecedented prosperity in the United States. Population growth, brought on largely by a "baby boom" after the war, encouraged a tremendous building boom —houses (mostly in new suburbs), highways on which to reach them, schools, and shopping centers. In addition, science and technology, pushed ahead by wartime research, helped create new industries, such as plastics, electronics, and television.

Foreign affairs. Eisenhower appointed John Foster Dulles as his secretary of state. Dulles committed the United States to the theory of "massive retaliation"—which relied on the use of the U.S. nuclear arsenal against Communist aggression.

The United States and the Soviet Union began competing furiously in an arms race, constructing new and more potent nuclear weapons. Rockets carrying nuclear warheads and atomic submarines equipped with missiles were stockpiled in huge numbers.

In the mid-1950's, following the death of Stalin, there was something of a thaw in Soviet-American relations as the two powers attempted to move closer to peaceful coexistence. The two nations planned a summit conference in 1960. But shortly before the meeting, an American U-2 reconnaissance plane was brought down inside the Soviet Union. The pilot, Francis Gary Powers, confessed to his spy mission but President Eisenhower refused to apologize for the spying, so the Soviet Union angrily withdrew from the planned summit.

FREEWAYS AND EXPRESSWAYS *revolutionized travel and the transport of goods in the 1950's. The federal interstate highway program helped finance a nationwide grid of limited access highways.*

LOS ANGELES CHAMBER OF COMMERCE

New Challenges

Crises and Crusades

JOHN KENNEDY *announces the Cuban missile crisis in 1962. The great victories of his space program were achieved after his death. The first men landed on the moon in 1969.*

The decade of the 1960's began on a note of hope. In November, 1960, Democrat John F. Kennedy, at the age of 43, became the youngest man ever elected to the American Presidency, as well as the first Roman Catholic. He narrowly defeated Republican Richard M. Nixon. During his campaign, Kennedy had promised the voters that he would name a "ministry of talent" as Cabinet advisers. Fulfilling that promise, he gathered around him people distinguished by their youthfulness, academic background, informality, and vigor. Kennedy's inaugural address was an inspiring appeal to his fellow citizens to join him in pushing toward a "New Frontier," both at home and abroad.

Kennedy offered several innovative programs. He pressed for new and better relations with Latin America through a $10 billion Alliance for Progress. To strengthen the image of the United States abroad, and at the same time to help underdeveloped nations, he suggested and implemented the unique and successful Peace Corps. The corps was comprised mainly of youthful volunteers who served overseas at subsistence wages as teachers, agricultural advisers, public health workers, engineers, and community advisers.

At home Kennedy offered new programs in housing, education, urban renewal, and medical care for the aged, but nearly all his proposals were blocked by Congress. His single important legislative victory was the passage in 1962 of the Trade Expansion Act, designed to stimulate American foreign trade by giving the President new powers to negotiate tariff reductions.

The Cuban crisis. In 1959 Fidel Castro, a young lawyer, had successfully led a revolution in Cuba against the government of dictator Fulgencio Batista. As premier, Castro turned increasingly to Communist nations for aid. Cuban-American relations were strained in May, 1959, when Castro promulgated a law permitting Cuban seizure of American property in Cuba without compensation. Because of Castro's obvious ties with the Soviet Union, President Eisenhower ordered the severing of diplomatic relations with Cuba.

The Eisenhower administration also began secretly making plans for an invasion of Cuba. Shortly after taking office, Kennedy decided to carry out the plan, and on April 17, 1961, an American-equipped army of about 1500 anti-Castro Cuban exiles landed at the Bay of Pigs. American officials had believed that the Cuban people and Castro's own troops would support the invaders, but the attack was decisively repulsed and most of the invaders captured or killed. The Bay of Pigs fiasco aroused anti-American sentiment throughout Latin America and the world, and the United States was regarded as an aggressor.

In October of 1962, the U.S. Central Intelligence Agency (CIA) informed Kennedy that the Soviet Union was establishing nuclear missile launch sites in Cuba. In a bold, dramatic television speech, Kennedy announced that in response to this threat to the western hemisphere, he had ordered a naval "quarantine" of Cuba. Any ships carrying offensive weapons to Cuba would be turned back by the U.S. Navy. He also demanded that the Soviet Union dismantle the existing missile bases in Cuba, and stated bluntly that the United States would use military action against the Soviet Union if it did not comply.

Five tense days followed, but at last Soviet Premier Nikita Khrushchev backed down, and the 16 Soviet ships heading toward Cuba turned back.

Following the Cuban missile crisis, Kennedy took steps to ease the threat of nuclear destruction. In the spring of 1963, a "hot line" teletype connection was set up between Washington and Moscow; it afforded direct communication between the two heads of state in times of crisis. After further efforts, the United States, the Soviet Union, and the United Kingdom signed a nuclear test ban treaty in 1963 banning testing of nuclear weapons in the atmosphere and under water.

Race for space. In 1957, as the United States was beginning to develop a satellite to send into orbit around Earth, Americans were stunned when they learned that the Soviet Union had succeeded in placing its satellite *Sputnik* into orbit. Fearing that the United States was falling behind in rocket technology, the United States stepped up its space program, and on January 31, 1958, it launched *Explorer 1*. The United States and the Soviet Union vied with each other to see who could build more powerful (and potentially weapons-carrying) rockets.

In 1961 Kennedy announced a new goal for the space program: to land a man on the moon and return him safely to Earth. The Mercury program launched the first American in space, Alan Shepard, on May 5, 1961. On February 20, 1962, astronaut John Glenn made the first U.S. orbital flight around Earth. In the mid-1960's, the Gemini program followed, sending a two-man spacecraft into orbit.

With the Apollo program that followed, Kennedy's goal was achieved. In July of 1969, astronauts Neil Armstrong, Edwin Aldrin, and Michael Collins accomplished the first manned landing on the moon. As Armstrong set foot on the moon on July 20, he said, "That's one small step for a man, one giant leap for mankind."

On November 22, 1963, while riding in a motorcade in Dallas, Texas, Kennedy was shot by a gunman hiding in a nearby building. He died shortly after of a rifle bullet wound in his brain. Police soon arrested 24-year-old Lee Harvey Oswald, a former Marine who had once defected to the Soviet Union. Two days later, the accused assassin was himself killed by Jack Ruby, a Dallas nightclub owner, as police were moving Oswald from one jail to another. Millions of television watchers saw the shooting.

There was much speculation as to whether Oswald had acted alone or as part of a conspiracy. A commission directed by Chief Justice Earl Warren was set up to study the murder. The commission concluded that the action had been Oswald's alone, but many remained unconvinced.

Lyndon Baines Johnson was sworn in as President. Johnson had had a long career as a congressional leader. He had been elected to the House of Representatives from his Texas district in 1937 and to the Senate in 1948. In 1953 he had become Senate majority leader.

The Great Society. Johnson pledged himself to carry out Kennedy's domestic program and to build a "Great Society" in the United States. Thanks to his long, close association with Congress, Johnson was able to get much of his legislation passed. Almost immediately, Congress passed a major tax cut that decreased individual income tax rates. In August of 1964, Congress passed the Economic Opportunity Act, which began a federal "war on poverty." The Office of Economic Opportunity (OEO) was created to operate a federal Job Corps, VISTA (Volunteers in Service to America), community action programs, a program for migrant workers, and the Head Start program for disadvantaged preschool children.

After overwhelmingly defeating Republican Presidential candidate Barry Goldwater in 1964, Johnson got Congress to pass many more programs to assist public schools, the aged, and the poor. Other measures increased Social Security benefits and the minimum wage.

MARTIN LUTHER KING *and his followers marched on Selma, Alabama, to demand voting rights.*

WIDE WORLD

Struggle for civil rights. The Great Society also sought to extend full civil rights to the nation's blacks. The crusade for civil rights had begun during the 1950's. An early target was desegregation of American public schools. In May, 1954, the Supreme Court, under Chief Justice Earl Warren, handed down a momentous decision forbidding school segregation. The unanimous ruling in *Brown* v. *Board of Education of Topeka* held that "separate but equal" schools were "inherently unequal." The High Court ruled that school desegregation should begin at once. Widespread resistance in the South slowed implementation. Federal troops and federal marshals were sometimes called in to enforce school desegregation.

In an effort to desegregate public transportation, the 26-year-old Reverend Martin Luther King led a year-long boycott of the buses of Montgomery, Alabama, beginning in December, 1955. "Freedom Riders" helped force desegregation of long-distance buses. The boycott was successful, as were many "sit-ins" for the purpose of desegregating eating and entertainment establishments.

By 1963 King was recognized as the major leader of the black civil rights movement. On August 28, 1963, more than 200,000 civil rights supporters joined in a march on Washington to show Congress their desire for civil rights legislation. King addressed the vast crowd, describing his dream of full equality and respect between blacks and whites.

Congress responded with the Civil Rights Act of 1964, which outlawed racial discrimination in employment and public accommodations, and the Voting Rights Act of 1965, which provided for federal supervision to allow blacks to register where they had been previously denied the right to vote. The Civil Rights Act of 1968 attempted to guarantee blacks the right to open housing.

With all this legislative action, though, blacks were still struggling for the opportunities that full civil rights were intended to afford them. In 1967 the Kerner Commission, a government group that had studied riots in black neighborhoods of Los Angeles and other cities, concluded that "Our nation is moving toward two societies, one black, one white, separate and unequal."

Vietnam. When the French were driven out of their former colony of Vietnam in 1954, the nation was divided in two. Beginning in the late 1950's, Communist North Vietnam, under leader Ho Chi Minh, was backing Vietnamese guerrillas who were fighting to overthrow the non-Communist regime of South Vietnam. The Northerners wanted to reunite Vietnam under a Communist government. Presidents Eisenhower and Kennedy had sent military advisers and supplies to help South Vietnam.

As the situation grew more and more desperate for South Vietnam, President Johnson began increasing American involvement in the fighting. In 1964 he persuaded Congress to pass the Gulf of Tonkin Resolution, which authorized him "to take all necessary measures to repel any armed attack against the forces of the United States and to prevent further aggression."

Soon American planes were bombing targets in North Vietnam, and great numbers of American troops were being shipped to South Vietnam, half a million by the end of 1967. Johnson's hope was to hold off the North Vietnamese and guerrilla forces long enough to give the South Vietnamese a chance to build up their army and their government. But as time passed, it became obvious that this strategy was not working.

Antiwar movement. Protest against the seemingly endless war began when college students staged "teach-ins" to explain the costs of the war and to portray it as a civil war in which the United States should not be involved. Their disillusion spread to other citizens until the antiwar movement claimed millions of supporters.

Fight for women's rights. The activism of the 1960's spawned a new crusade for women's rights. One spark for the movement was the publication in 1963 of Betty Friedan's book *The Feminine Mystique*. The book identified many of the inequalities women suffered in American life—social, political, and economic. Three years later, Friedan founded NOW, the National Organization for Women, which demanded, among other things, equal educational opportunities for women; equal pay for equal work; wider job opportunities; publicly funded day-care centers; and the repeal of laws banning abortion.

The Equal Pay Act of 1963 had guaranteed equal pay for equal work, and the Civil Rights Act of 1964 prohibited job discrimination on the basis of sex as well as race, but the passage of legislation did not guarantee compliance. The crusade for allowing abortion was advanced by a Supreme Court ruling in 1973 striking down antiabortion laws. But strong opposition on religious and moral grounds continued.

In 1972 Congress passed the Equal Rights Amendment (ERA), which stated "Equality of rights under the law shall not be denied or abridged by the United States or any state on account of sex." But the amendment failed to be ratified by the necessary 38 states, so it did not take effect.

The End of Optimism

In February, 1968, the North Vietnamese staged an ambitious offensive that showed how little control non-Communist forces had in South Vietnam. On April 4 Martin Luther King was shot dead in Memphis, Tennessee, by sniper James Earl Ray. Rage swept the nation and riots broke out in over 170 cities. That same month antiwar riots broke out at Columbia University.

In March President Johnson, undermined by lack of success in Vietnam and by antiwar protests at home, announced that he would not seek reelection. Robert Kennedy, brother of the slain President, sought the Democratic nomination. In June, following his victory in the California Presidential primary, Kennedy was killed by gunman Sirhan Sirhan.

In August a deeply divided Democratic Party met in Chicago for a turbulent convention marked by violent clashes between police and antiwar protestors. Vice President Hubert Humphrey won the nomination over Senator Eugene McCarthy of Minnesota, who had campaigned as the peace candidate. Humphrey's running mate was Senator Edmund Muskie of Maine. The Republicans chose former Vice President Richard M. Nixon and Governor Spiro Agnew of Maryland. A major third-party contender, Governor George Wallace of Alabama, ran for the American Independent Party, stressing law and order and states' rights. Nixon won the election by one of the narrowest popular vote margins in U.S. history, receiving 43.4 percent of the popular vote to Humphrey's 42.7 percent.

Nixon came to office with the promise of ending the Vietnam War. "The greatest honor history can bestow is the title peacemaker," he said in his inaugural address. On the domestic scene, the economy was slowing down, resulting in increased unemployment and inflation.

Ending the Vietnam War.

Nixon's original plan was to "Vietnamize" the war—to withdraw U.S. troops gradually and turn the war over to the South Vietnamese. Antiwar protestors, however, continued to demonstrate for an immediate end to American involvement; a nationwide "moratorium" was held in October, 1969. The administration, with Vice President Agnew as its spokesman, roundly criticized dissenters.

Despite Nixon's policy of troop withdrawal, in April, 1970, he sent American and South Vietnamese troops into Cambodia to clear out border sanctuaries used as supply bases by North Vietnamese and guerrilla forces. The public's reaction to the move was intense. Antiwar demonstrations were held across the nation. Four students at Kent State University were killed by National Guard troops during a demonstration on May 4, 1970, and 448 colleges closed down in protest.

In February of the next year, South Vietnamese forces, with U.S. air and artillery support, invaded neighboring Laos to cut off the "Ho Chi Minh Trail," a well-worn Communist supply line. Again there was intense reaction against American involvement. Congress repealed the Gulf of Tonkin Resolution, the original mandate for massive U.S. involvement; bills were introduced to curb the President's power to commit the United States to war without the consent of Congress; and proposals were made for a fixed deadline for the withdrawal of all American forces.

Peace negotiations had begun in Paris, but they stalled over the deadline for withdrawal. Finally, on January 27, 1973, an agreement was signed. Terms included a cease-fire, withdrawal of American troops, and return of all American prisoners of war.

In April, 1975, the last Americans were evacuated, and within days, South Vietnam was entirely in Communist hands. The unsuccessful U.S. involvement had cost 57,000 American lives, many billions of dollars, and a crisis of confidence in government.

MAJOR EVENTS OF THE VIETNAM WAR

UPI/BETTMANN NEWSPHOTOS

THE FINAL AMERICAN EVACUATION *from Saigon, South Vietnam, came only hours before North Vietnamese troops captured the city.*

1945 Ho Chi Minh declares independence of Vietnam September 2, but French soon move to reassert authority in Indochina.

1954 French are defeated at Dien Bien Phu May 7. Truce agreement at Geneva in July divides Vietnam pending nationwide elections. Ho establishes Democratic Republic of Vietnam in north; former emperor Bao Dai sets up rival government in south with Ngo Dinh Diem as prime minister.

1955 Diem refuses to participate in nationwide elections.

1960 National Liberation Front, or Vietcong, founded; organizes guerrilla operations in south.

1964 North Vietnamese gunboats attack U.S. destroyer *Maddox* August 2. Gulf of Tonkin Resolution passed August 7. U.S. warplanes bomb North Vietnam.

1965 First sustained bombing of North Vietnam begins February 24. First U.S. combat troops land at Da Nang March 8.

1968 Tet offensive launched January 31. My Lai massacre committed in March. Paris peace talks begin in May. U.S. troop strength rises to 540,000.

1969 President Nixon announces withdrawal of 25,000 troops June 8. Troop level down to 480,000 by year's end.

1970 U.S. and South Vietnamese troops invade Cambodia April 30.

1971 U.S. and South Vietnamese forces invade Laos February 8.

1972 President Nixon orders mining of Haiphong harbor in May, bombing of Hanoi and Haiphong in December.

1973 Cease-fire agreement signed in Paris January 27. Last U.S. forces withdrawn from Vietnam March 9.

1975 North Vietnamese launch new offensive in January, capture Saigon April 30.

TRIUMPH AND TRAGEDY: *the Nixon years brought diplomatic relations with China,* left, *and the disillusioning Watergate scandal, which was pursued by the Senate committee of Sam Ervin,* right, *and which ultimately led to Nixon's resignation.*

The Soviet Union and China. Nixon's other steps to promote world peace had more positive results. In November, 1969, the United States and the Soviet Union ratified the nuclear nonproliferation treaty. Two years later, Nixon visited the People's Republic of China, ending nearly 25 years of diplomatic separation. Nixon and the Chinese leaders agreed to increase trade between the two nations and to allow journalistic, scientific, and cultural exchanges. A few months later, Nixon visited the Soviet Union and signed a treaty limiting antiballistic missiles, a result of the Strategic Arms Limitation Talks (SALT).

The faltering economy. As American participation in the Vietnam War wound down, the economy became the major political issue. The unemployment rate climbed steadily until 5 million were out of work. At the same time, inflation reduced the value of the dollar, industry produced below capacity, and many American goods were uncompetitive on the world market. The nation was entering a period of "stagflation," economic stagnancy combined with inflation.

Nixon announced in August, 1971, a program that included a wage-price freeze, tax cuts, a surcharge on certain imports, and devaluation of the dollar. For a while, it seemed that stagflation might be beaten, but when the wage-price controls were lifted in early 1973, prices leapt once again.

Oil crisis. A major contributor to continuing high inflation in the United States was the high price of oil. As a long-time ally of Israel, the United States incurred the wrath of the Arab nations, which provided 25 percent of all American oil. The Arabs punished the United States by refusing to export oil in 1973, and prices for petroleum and gasoline soared, raising inflation rates. Even when the oil embargo was ended in March, 1974, American oil problems did not end. The Organization of Petroleum Exporting Countries (OPEC) continued to raise oil prices for the rest of the decade, further fueling inflation.

Watergate. In November, 1972, Richard Nixon and Spiro Agnew were easily reelected. But prior to the election, during the night of June 16–17, there had been a puzzling break-in at Democratic National Headquarters in the Watergate apartment complex in Washington, D.C. Five men employed by the Committee to Reelect the President were arrested after breaking in to plant electronic surveillance equipment in the offices.

The Watergate break-in was treated as a minor incident and had no real impact on the 1972 election. But when the five defendants went on trial in early 1973, it became apparent that the break-in was instigated, and then covered up, by high White House officials. Nixon denied any role in planning the break-in or the cover-up, but in April of 1973 he announced that two of his top aides, H. R. Haldeman and John Ehrlichman, were resigning. Later disclosures connected these aides to the scandal.

In May a Senate select committee was formed to investigate the Watergate affair. White House counsel John Dean testified that Nixon was involved in the cover-up. Testimony from Attorney General John Mitchell and others uncovered various other illegal activities directed by the White House. Another revelation disclosed that Nixon's office contained recorders on which all conversations had been taped. Several investigative bodies tried to get these tapes in order to prove or disprove the diverse accounts of the Watergate events. Nixon refused to surrender them on grounds of executive privilege. He finally gave up some tapes, one with a crucial erasure, to the federal court demanding them. Then, under Supreme Court direction, he surrendered other complete tapes that were later used to convict his former aides and Mitchell of conspiracy to obstruct justice.

Agnew resigns. In the midst of the Watergate investigations, Vice President Agnew was undergoing an investigation on a totally unrelated matter—the alleged acceptance of bribes from construction companies while he was governor of Maryland. On October 10, 1973, he resigned as Vice President, shortly after entering a no-contest plea on a single charge of income tax evasion.

Under the provisions of the 25th Amendment, Nixon selected a successor to Agnew. His choice was Representative Gerald R. Ford of Michigan, a 25-year veteran of Congress.

Nixon falls. In early 1974, the House Judiciary Committee began studying the possibility that Nixon had committed impeachable offenses. On July 30 the committee approved three articles of impeachment charging Nixon with obstruction of justice in connection with Watergate; abuse of Presidential powers; and evading the impeachment process by ignoring committee subpoenas for evidence.

A few days later, Nixon released a statement and a transcript showing that he had ordered the FBI to cover up the Watergate break-in six days after it occurred. This revelation eroded most of Nixon's remaining support. On August 8, 1974, Nixon announced his resignation.

Gerald Ford was sworn in as President. One month later he issued a pardon to Nixon for all federal crimes he "committed or may have committed or taken part in" while President.

Ford's Presidency. In accordance with the 25th Amendment, Ford nominated a Vice President to replace himself. He chose former governor Nelson A. Rockefeller of New York. For the first time since the Constitution was adopted, both the President and Vice President were appointed rather than elected.

Ford acted to carry out both the domestic and foreign policies set forth by Nixon and Secretary of State Henry Kissinger. Domestically, the dual problem of the 1974–1975 recession and high inflation placed the country's economy in serious condition. By early 1975, nationwide unemployment had passed 8 percent while prices continued to rise.

WIDE WORLD PHOTOS

HOPES FOR PEACE: *President Carter smiles as Anwar el-Sadat of Egypt and Menachem Begin of Israel ratify the Camp David accords, a plan for peace in the Middle East.*

Carter is elected. In 1976 Ford chose to seek a full elected term as President. The Democratic nominee was former governor Jimmy Carter of Georgia, who chose Senator Walter Mondale of Minnesota as his running mate.

Ford's pardon of Nixon, in effect putting the former President above the law, hurt him in the election. Carter defeated Ford by a 51 percent edge in the popular vote.

Relinquishing the Panama Canal. After 13 years of negotiation, in September, 1977, the United States and Panama reached agreement on the terms of a new Panama Canal treaty. The treaty would place the canal and the Canal Zone under complete Panamanian control by the end of the century. Debate over the treaty was heated. Opponents contended that "giving away the Panama Canal" threatened national security. Finally, Congress ratified the treaty by a close vote in the spring of 1978.

Camp David. Carter's greatest triumph came in April, 1979, when he called together Israeli leader Menachem Begin and Egyptian leader Anwar el-Sadat at the Presidential retreat at Camp David, Maryland. There, for 13 days, the leaders worked out a treaty to end 30 years of war between Egypt and Israel. The treaty provided a framework for the Israeli return of captured land to Egypt, a process that was eventually completed in 1982.

Hostage to Iran. One of the staunchest allies of the United States in the Middle East was the Shah of Iran, Mohammed Riza Pahlevi, who had sought to modernize his oil-rich country. In 1979 he was overthrown by political and religious opponents who believed modernization undermined the religious beliefs and practices of Islam.

The Shah fled his country and eventually came to the United States for medical treatment. When the United States refused to return him to Iran, Iranian militants seized the American embassy in the capital at Teheran on November 4, 1979, and took 52 Americans hostage. Despite all American efforts, both diplomatic and military, the hostages were not freed until January, 1981, after spending 444 days in captivity. By then the Shah had died and Jimmy Carter had been replaced as President.

The Carter Doctrine. In December, 1979, the Soviet Union invaded Afghanistan, on Iran's border. Carter tried to punish the Russians by cutting off the sale to them of such American products as grain. He also withdrew the United States team from the 1980 Olympics held in Moscow. Then, in an effort to keep the Soviet Union from moving any farther into the Middle East, he declared the "Carter Doctrine" —that any Soviet moves on the Persian Gulf would be met by American military response.

Changing Direction

By the time the election of 1980 approached, President Carter's popularity was at a very low ebb—a poll showed that he had the approval of only 21 percent of the American people. Energy shortages and high fuel costs, unemployment and inflation, and seemingly worsening international relations had sadly disillusioned the American electorate.

Reagan elected. The election of Ronald Reagan, a former movie actor and governor of California, to the Presidency in 1980 brought the first basic change in federal government policy in nearly half a century. Reagan said he would cut government spending, balance the budget, reduce taxes, and rebuild defense forces. He also promised to return to the states powers and functions that had been assumed by the federal government.

Inaugurated on January 20, 1981, Reagan had no chance to put his policies into effect before he was seriously wounded on March 30 by John W. Hinckley in an assassination attempt. He made a rapid recovery.

The economy was sluggish and inflation and unemployment were high. Reagan's economic policy came to be known as "Reaganomics" or as "supply-side economics." It called for tax cuts that would spur savings and presumably increase capital investment and create jobs. This policy was designed to reduce inflation, lower interest rates, and increase government revenues.

On August 4 Congress approved a Reagan tax reduction bill that cut income tax rates by 25 percent in three stages, ending July 1, 1983. The economy began to improve but the budget deficit began to rise, partly because of large increases in military expenses. The Reagan administration attempted to cut domestic programs in such fields as social welfare and education but largely failed because the Democrats controlled the House of Representatives throughout Reagan's Presidency.

The Gramm-Rudman Act of December 12, 1985, specified deficit totals for the coming years with a view to eliminating the deficit by 1990. Automatic spending reductions were required if necessary to meet this goal. Two years later the problem remained, and Reagan and Congress worked out an agreement to reduce 1987–1989 spending by $30 billion.

Foreign affairs. The Reagan Presidency faced numerous problems, including war in the Middle East, terrorism, civil war in Nicaragua, and negotiations with the Soviet Union.

On August 20, 1982, some 800 U.S. Marines landed in Beirut, Lebanon, as part of a multinational peacekeeping force. On October 23, 1983, an explosive-laden truck leveled the Marines' headquarters, killing 241 Marine and Navy troops. Earlier, on April 18, another bomb had nearly destroyed the U.S. embassy in Beirut, killing 63 persons, including 17 Americans.

With Iran and Iraq at war, there was danger to the heavy traffic of oil tankers in the Persian Gulf. Accordingly, U.S. Navy ships were sent there in Feburary, 1984; they later began to convoy neutral shipping. On May 17, 1987, an Iraqi warplane mistakenly fired a missile at the U.S. frigate *Stark,* killing 37 crewmen. An even greater tragedy came on July 3, 1988, when the U.S. cruiser *Vincennes* mistakenly shot down an Iranian passenger jet, killing all 290 persons aboard.

The Reagan administration had earlier identified Libya as an abettor of worldwide terrorism. On April 14, 1986, Reagan ordered an air strike against Libya. Air Force and Navy planes blasted five military bases and terrorist training centers near Tripoli and Benghazi.

The administration exhibited a particular dislike for the Marxist-oriented Sandinista regime in Nicaragua. Opposed to it were the Contras, representing both democratic forces and the remnants of the brutal regime the Sandinistas had overthrown. Reagan sought throughout his Presidency to secure financial aid for the Contras, whom he called "freedom fighters." At first Congress obliged, but later it resisted appropriations for any but humanitarian aid.

More successful was the invasion of the Caribbean nation of Grenada on October 25, 1983, undertaken to oust a pro-Cuban Marxist group that had seized power in a bloody coup. The invasion succeeded, although a discouraging lack of preparation and coordination was revealed. American casualties were 18 killed and 115 wounded.

Also a success was U.S. participation in negotiations for the withdrawal of Soviet troops from Afghanistan. On April 14, 1988, the U.S.S.R. agreed to begin a phased withdrawal to be completed in February, 1989.

LEADERS *Reagan and Gorbachev signed an historic nuclear arms agreement in 1987.*

REUTERS/BETTMANN NEWSPHOTOS

During his Presidency, Reagan held four summit meetings (in Geneva, Reykjavik, Moscow, and Washington) with General Secretary Mikhail Gorbachev of the U.S.S.R. The meetings did not yield any specific results but led to the first treaty in history to provide for nuclear arms reductions. Signed on December 9, 1987, and ratified by the U.S. Senate on May 27, 1988, the treaty provided for the destruction of 2611 U.S. and Soviet medium- and short-range missiles in Europe.

Reagan's second term was marred by scandal. It was revealed on November 3, 1986, that the United States had been secretly selling arms to Iran in the hopes of securing the release of Americans held hostage in Lebanon by Islamic terrorists. Some funds from the sales had been secretly diverted to the Nicaraguan Contras. John M. Poindexter, the national security adviser, resigned and his assistant, Oliver L. North, was dismissed. The President appointed a commission to investigate the Iran-Contra affair. Its report, issued on February 26, 1987, was critical of Reagan for his failure to understand or control the dealings. On November 18 a congressional report also criticized Reagan. An independent prosecutor was named to pursue the investigation and on March 16, 1988, Poindexter and North were indicted on federal charges of conspiring to defraud the United States.

Domestic matters. In the area of domestic legislation, several significant laws were enacted. On October 22, 1986, Reagan signed a bill providing the most sweeping tax reform in 40 years. It lowered tax rates but also eliminated various deductions. A major reform of the immigration laws was signed on November 6, 1986. It prohibited employers from hiring illegal aliens, but it also provided the means for many aliens to secure legal status in the United States.

The first major expansion of the Medicare program was the subject of an act signed July 1, 1988. It increased hospital, nursing home, and medical benefits. A bill requiring employers to give 60 days notice of plant closings became law on August 2.

In a series of domestic scandals, three of the President's top aides were targets of investigation. Two were convicted, one for illegal lobbying and the other for perjury. In addition, Edwin Meese III, the attorney general, who was the focus of much criticism for alleged wrongdoing, announced on July 5, 1988, he would resign. On July 18 an independent counsel found no grounds for bringing criminal charges against Meese.

On July 10, 1986, Warren E. Burger retired as chief justice of the United States. The President named Supreme Court Justice William H. Rehnquist to succeed him.

In 1984 Reagan had been reelected in such a landslide that he carried 49 of the 50 states against the Democratic candidate Walter Mondale.

In November, 1988, Vice President George Bush was elected President, defeating his Democratic opponent, Governor Michael S. Dukakis of Massachusetts. Senator J. Danforth Quayle of Indiana was elected Vice President. The unsuccessful Democratic Vice Presidential candidate, Senator Lloyd Bentsen of Texas, was reelected to the Senate.

The nation in 1988. By the end of 1988, unemployment was at its lowest level since June, 1974, inflation seemed under control, and the massive foreign trade deficit declined slightly. But the public debt was now well over $1 trillion and the annual federal budget deficit was more than $100 billion. In foreign affairs, the U.S. military buildup and a new, more flexible regime in the Soviet Union pointed to the possibility of more arms reduction treaties.

Energy. The energy crisis of the 1970's had subsided and oil prices fell in 1988 as a result of overproduction around the world. But hopes that nuclear power would replace oil were given up in the face of a serious accident at the Three-Mile Island nuclear power plant in Pennsylvania in March, 1979, and the skyrocketing cost of plant construction.

The environment. There was much concern about pollution of the environment. Pesticides were among the first contaminants to be regulated, but toxic waste from manufacturing processes, as well as from nuclear facilities, was growing in volume with no clear program for disposing of it safely. Acid rain, a product of the contaminants from the chimneys of the nation's factories, damaged forests and lakes, especially in the eastern United States. Emission standards were finally set for automobiles, a major cause of air pollution. The Environmental Protection Agency (EPA) had been established in 1970 to coordinate antipollution efforts. Environmentalists charged that the Reagan administration had done little to protect the environment.

Future. As the nation approached the 1990's, a number of major problems remained to be addressed: balancing the federal budget; protecting the environment at an affordable cost; meeting the competition of foreign manufacturers; fighting the growing incidence of crime, much of it drug related; improving race relations; and providing health care for the elderly, the poor, and victimes of the disease AIDS. Reagan's successor would find some aspects of American life had indeed improved since 1981, but many national problems were far from being solved.

THE STATES AND TERRITORIES

Regions and States

The states that make up the United States each have considerable independence in pursuing their own affairs; they are given important powers in the Constitution itself. In recent years, the federal government has grown more powerful than individual states. But in spite of this, the states have maintained a strong sense of diversity, owing to a combination of geographical, historical, social, political, and economic differences.

Regional differences have played an important part in the development of the United States, both for good and for ill. They have allowed flexibility, encouraged rapid development of new land and new resources, and promoted a sense of cultural diversity and tolerance. On the other hand, these same regional differences led to the nation's greatest tragedy—the Civil War, in which social, political, and economic differences were resolved by force.

In this section, the United States is divided into eleven regions, each consisting of between four and seven states. A general overview of the region and the characteristics that set it off from other regions is presented first. A regional map shows how member states fit together. Then information on each state in the region is presented separately. The regions are arranged geographically, running generally from west to east. In order of appearance they are:

- Southwest States
- Northwest States
- Mountain States
- Oil States
- Grain States
- Great Lakes States
- South-Central States
- South Atlantic States
- Tidewater States
- Mid-Atlantic States
- New England States

The map at the right shows which states are in each region, and the index of states will enable a reader to find any particular state. The reader should examine the material on a region for additional information on its states. More information on regional characteristics and trends will be found in "The U.S. Today".

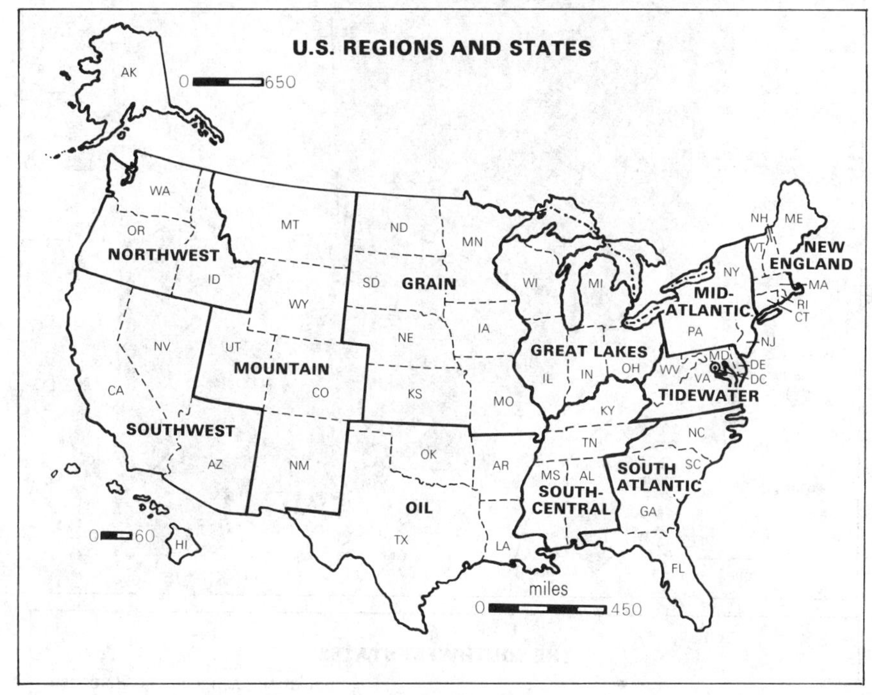

WHERE TO FIND EACH STATE

The Southwest States

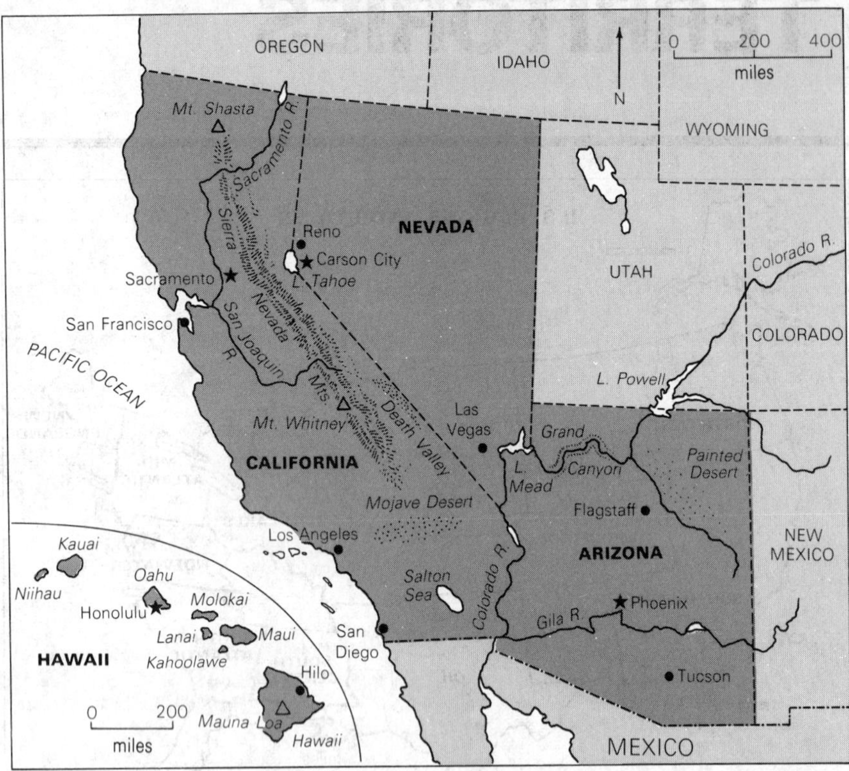

THE SOUTHWEST STATES

State	Area (sq. mi.)	Population 1985	Population change 1980–85 number	Population change 1980–85 percent	Persons per sq. mi.
California	156,361	26,365,000	+2,697,000	+11.4	169
Arizona	113,417	3,187,000	+ 469,000	+17.2	28
Nevada	109,889	936,000	+ 135,000	+16.9	9
Hawaii	6,425	1,054,000	+ 89,000	+ 9.2	164
Region totals	386,612	31,542,000	+3,390,000	+12.0	82

The Southwest states are California on the Pacific coast, Nevada and Arizona on California's eastern border, and the chain of Hawaiian Islands in the Pacific, 2000 miles southwest of California. The continental Southwest borders the Northwest region to the north and the mountain states to the east.

Once ignored as a barren desert region relieved only by forbidding mountains, the continental Southwest has experienced a population explosion in the 20th century. In 1880 the population was less than 1 million, or about 2 percent of the U.S. total. A century later, in 1980, the population was more than 28 million, or about 13 percent of the U.S. total. The growth of California has been the most dramatic: in 1960 it became the most populous state in the country, and in 1980 nearly 24 million people, 10 percent of the U.S. population, lived there. California accounts for 84 percent of the population of the entire Southwest region. It continues to add huge numbers of residents each year. Nevada and Arizona, though much less populous, have the highest growth rates in the country.

The land. Two principal topographical features unite the continental Southwest: the plateau called the Great Basin and the Colorado River. The Great Basin dominates Nevada and touches both California and Arizona. It includes some of the major desert areas in the United States, including the Mojave Desert in California and the Sonoran Desert in Arizona. All three states have borders formed by the Colorado River, the principal freshwater resource in the region. Where it crosses the Great Basin in northern Arizona, the Colorado has created the Grand Canyon, 217 miles long and some 1500 feet deep. Dams along the Colorado are also an important source of hydroelectric power, supplying electricity to southern California as well as to parts of Arizona and Nevada.

The Southwest also includes significant mountain ranges, notably the Sierra Nevadas along the California–Nevada border and the Coastal Ranges along the California coastline. Hawaii, the only state not part of the North American continental landmass, is a remote cluster of volcanic islands, six of which support large populations.

Climate. The climate of the continental Southwest varies with distance from the sea and elevation. The coastal regions of northern and central California are cool and damp; the south of the state has a moderate year-round "Mediterranean" climate attractive to winter visitors. The Coastal Ranges separate the shore areas from the generally dry and warm interior valleys and plains. Much of the moisture blown inland from the Pacific is trapped by the high Sierra Nevadas along the California–Nevada border. Sierra peaks are snow-covered much of the year, but regions east and south of these mountains are left with the semi-arid or desert conditions common in southeastern California, most of Arizona, and all of Nevada.

At low elevations, daytime temperatures in the desert may exceed 110° F, but nights in these areas are cool. At higher elevations, daytime temperatures in the 80° F range may be followed by night temperatures dropping to 40°. In the Hawaiian Islands, a region of climatic extremes because of high mountains and small land areas, regions near sea level are dry and warm year-round, but at higher elevations rainfall is greater and temperatures cooler.

History. The continental Southwest, alone among U.S. regions, was explored and settled from the south and west. California was first visited by Spanish sailors in 1542, although permanent missions were not established until 1769. Arizona was first explored in 1539 by Spaniards in quest of the mythical "Seven Cities of Gold." Nevada, farther inland, waited until 1776 for its first Spanish settlement. In 1778, Captain James Cook from England discovered Hawaii and named it the Sandwich Islands.

Most of the continental Southwest was ceded by Mexico to the United States at the end of the Mexican War, in 1848. Immediately after becoming part of the United States, the region attracted a large influx of settlers because of a series of mining bonanzas:

gold at Sutter's Mill in California in 1848; silver at the Comstock Lode in Nevada in 1859; then gold again in Tombstone, Arizona, in 1877. California and Nevada became states soon after their mining booms, but Arizona remained a territory until 1912. Hawaii was an independent nation through most of the 1800's. It became a U.S. territory in 1900 and a state in 1959.

The people. Today the population of the Southwest is heavily concentrated in urban areas. All of the Southwest states have urban populations far above the national average, and the metropolitan regions of Los Angeles, San Francisco, and San Diego in California account for more than half the Southwest's total population.

The population contains high proportions of three ethnic groups: Mexicans, who immigrate across the Mexico–U.S. border; Asians, who began settling in California in gold-rush times; and American Indians, who are more numerous in Arizona than in any other state. Many residents of the Southwest are recent arrivals. Only a third of those in the region were born in the states in which they now live.

Economy. Because of their varied and dramatic natural features, tourism is the largest industry in two Southwestern states, Hawaii and Nevada. It is also among the largest industries in the other two states. California is the leading agricultural producer among the 50 states; it is the national leader in manufacturing as well.

California

Abbreviations: *Calif., CA*
Area: *156,361 sq. mi., 404,975 sq. km.*
Rank (of 50) *3rd*
Population:
1985 *26,365,000*
Rank (of 50) *1st*
Change 1980–85 *+2,697,000*
Percent change *+11.4*
Persons per sq. mi. *169*
Percent urban *91.3*
Capital: *Sacramento*
Largest city: *Los Angeles*
Metro. pop. 1985 *8,109,000*
Entered Union: *Sept. 9, 1850 (31st)*
State bird: *California valley quail*
State flower: *Golden poppy*
State tree: *California redwood*

California has an 850-mile coastline on the Pacific Ocean at the extreme southwest of the contiguous 48 states. It ranks first in population and third in area, after Alaska and Texas. Its phenomenal growth in population and prosperity has changed the social and economic complexion of the United States. If California were a separate country, it would rank seventh in the world in gross national product. If metropolitan Los Angeles were a separate state, its population would rank seventh in the United States. California's remarkable growth continued through the 1970's, contrary to expectations. Its population grew by 3.7 million, and the metropolitan regions of southern California (Anaheim, San Diego, Los Angeles, Riverside–San Bernardino) alone gained 1.8 million.

Much of this growth defies common logic. The southern part of the state lacks both water and power resources; the economy after World War II was based too heavily on wartime industries; and the state as a whole is far from other large population centers. Yet California leads the United States in agricultural production, and its manufacturing businesses have managed remarkably successful diversification. For example, "Silicon Valley," near San Francisco, so named for the tiny chips used in microcircuitry, is a major electronics center.

Despite frequent alarms about the state's economy, more than 16 million people have immigrated from other states. They have succeeded in creating a giant market of their own, as well as in exporting goods to other regions of the United States. California's growth and prosperity are based largely on the attractiveness of its climate and the affluence of its own local markets.

The land. California's topographical pattern is one of contrasts. Along the northern two-thirds of the ocean shore the mountains of the Coastal Range come almost to the water's edge. Inland from the Coastal Range lies the semi-arid Central Valley, stretching some 400 miles from north to south. Since the advent of modern irrigation this low-lying valley has become one of the most productive farm regions in the world. Inland from the Central Valley rise the Sierra Nevada, among the steepest mountains in North America. The range includes Mt. Whitney (14,494 feet), the highest point in the 48 contiguous states; four national parks, Yosemite, Sequoia, Kings Canyon, and Lassen; and Squaw Valley and other well-known skiing resorts.

Along the southern third of the state the ocean shore alternates between rocky stretches and wide beaches. A ring of mountains surrounds the large coastal plain on which Los Angeles is built and separates it from the great Mojave Desert, which covers 15,000 square miles of inland southern California. Here the lowest point in the United States, Death Valley, 282 feet below sea level, lies only 80 miles southeast of Mt. Whitney.

Climate. The climates of northern and southern California contrast as much as their topography. The southern coast enjoys year-round sun and pleasantly warm temperatures, while the northern coast is far cooler and damper. Temperatures above 100° F are frequent in the southern inland deserts, and heavy snows and intense cold are common in the northern high Sierra.

Principal cities. California's two great metropolitan regions are representative of the contrasts in the state between north and south. In the north, San Francisco became the state's principal city in the late 1800's, after a new population of prospectors flocked there in the wake of the 1849 gold rush. The city was almost totally destroyed by an earthquake in 1906, but it was soon rebuilt. Today San Francisco is the center of a large metropolitan region stretching from San Jose, 30 miles to the south, to a string of cities, including Oakland and Berkeley, on the inland shores of the bay.

By contrast, Los Angeles, 400 miles to the south, experienced no dramatic growth until after 1920. Then, in the 1950's, out-of-state immigrants (many from the Midwest and the South) began arriving at the rate of 1000 per week. Because of its rapid expansion, Los Angeles today lies sprawled out in all directions, linked by a complex system of freeways. This sprawl has overtaken many formerly separate cities, and today it stretches almost without break 60 miles eastward to Riverside and San Bernardino, 50 miles north and east to Ventura, and 75 miles south toward San Diego.

The people. California boasts a wide variety of people. One person in three is a member of an ethnic group. Five million (19 percent) are of Hispanic, chiefly Mexican, descent; more than 2 million (8 percent) are black; and 1.6 million (6 percent) are of Asian descent. Only one-third of the population were born in the state, and the newcomers, even after many years in California, often continue to identify themselves by their states of origin. Because of its large metropolitan areas, California also has the highest proportion of urban population in the United States.

Economy. Agriculture is the largest industry, chiefly because of production in the Central Valley of a variety of crops ranging from cotton to wine grapes. Citrus fruits declined in importance as residential developments replaced orange groves. The most important farm products are grapes, tomatoes, grain for livestock feed, and dairy products.

The state's early reliance on aerospace industries has been corrected in recent years by manufacturing diversification, and various manufactures, including food products and fabricated metals, now bring the state $62.5 billion per year. Tourism is another major source of income, with visitors from both the United States and abroad spending nearly $13 billion per year. The most famous industry in the state is entertainment: the film and television businesses are largely centered in and around Hollywood, a section of Los Angeles.

MONKMEYER

SUMMER/MONKMEYER

SPRAWLING CITIES AND GHOST TOWNS *both characterize the Southwest. At* left, *Los Angeles, connected by snakelike freeways, stretches as far as the eye can see.* Right, *the mining town of Rhyolite, Nevada, once had 12,000 residents, but it is now deserted.*

Places of interest. California offers a wide range of appealing attractions. Among its spectacular natural landscapes are the Yosemite Valley, the giant redwood and sequoia forests, and the wide beaches and desert expanses of southern California. Among the most popular manmade attractions are Disneyland and Hollywood in the south, and San Francisco, known for its picturesque harbor and its literary and artistic community, in the north.

Arizona

Abbreviations: *Ariz., AZ*
Area: *113,417 sq. mi., 292,750 sq. km.*
Rank (of 50) *6th*
Population:
1985 *3,187,000*
Rank (of 50) *27th*
Change 1980–85 *+469,000*
Percent change *+17.2*
Persons per sq. mi. *28*
Percent urban *83.8*
Capital: *Phoenix*
Largest city: *Phoenix*
Metro. pop. 1985 *1,847,000*
Entered Union: *Feb. 14, 1912 (48th)*
State bird: *Cactus wren*
State flower: *Sequaro cactus blossom*
State tree: *Paloverde*

Arizona is an arid state in the southwest United States bordered to the south by Mexico and to the west by California. Once a territory of Mexico, most of present-day Arizona was ceded to the United States at the end of the Mexican War in 1848 as part of a huge area then called "New Mexico." Named Arizona from the Indian word meaning "few springs," it was organized as a U.S. territory in 1863, but considered a desert wasteland populated by hostile Indians. In modern times, however, the warm, dry climate and improvements in transportation, irrigation, and air conditioning have brought Arizona a rate of population growth second only to Nevada.

The land. Arizona is crossed diagonally from northwest to southeast by mountain ranges collectively known as the Mexican Highlands. North and east of this mountain system lies the Colorado Plateau. The Colorado River enters the state from the north, then turns east, flowing through the highlands in the gigantic cut known as the Grand Canyon. After emerging from this canyon, the river turns south and forms Arizona's border with Nevada and California.

The river is dammed at several points in Arizona for irrigation, hydroelectric power, and water supply. Two of these dams, Hoover on the Nevada border and Glen Canyon on the Utah border, are among the largest in the United States.

The region to the south and west of the highlands is an extension of the great western basin and range and is drained by the Gila River and its tributaries.

Climate. The climate of Arizona varies with elevation. Phoenix, in the south-central region, has average high temperatures of more than 100 degrees in summer. Midwinter temperatures range from highs in the 70's to lows below freezing. Yuma, in the southwest corner of the state, is generally warmer than Phoenix, while Flagstaff, in the highlands to the north, is considerably cooler. There is an average rainfall of under 8 inches in Arizona, most of it falling in the northern mountains. The state receives the highest percentage of available sunshine, 86 percent, in the United States. The sun and the low relative humidity make for a generally pleasant climate.

Principal cities. Phoenix, the business and transportation center of Arizona, contains more than half the state population in its metropolitan area. A former U.S. Cavalry hay camp incorporated as a city in 1881, Phoenix is now the eleventh largest metropolitan area in the United States with 1.5 million people. Arizona's second largest city is Tucson, 120 miles southeast of Phoenix, with a population of 500,000. No other city in Arizona has as many as 50,000 residents.

The people. The population of Arizona doubled in the 20 years before 1960 and then doubled again between 1960 and 1980. Only 20 percent of Arizona's residents were born in the state. The largest single ethnic group is Hispanic, representing 19 percent of the population. Arizona has the largest American Indian population in the United States, 145,258, or 6 percent of the total population.

Economy. Arizona was once dependent on copper, cotton, and cattle, but by 1960 manufacturing surpassed farming and mining. The chief manufactured goods are electronic equipment and primary and fabricated metals. The total value added by manufacture exceeds $4 billion per year. Tourism is the second largest industry, also approaching $4 billion in value. Visitors come for warm winter weather and to visit the state's national parks.

Arizona's mines produce half the country's supply of copper ore, a business valued at $2 billion. Large quantities of nonmetallic minerals such as sand, gravel, and lime are also mined. The chief agricultural products are livestock, cotton, grains, and citrus fruits.

U.S. military installations brought the state its first significant growth in the 1950's, and today the federal government continues to be the state's largest single employer, commanding 20 percent of the work force.

Places of interest. The main natural attraction in Arizona is the Grand Canyon. There are many other areas of dramatic desert scenery in the state, including the Painted Desert and the Petrified Forest. The town of Tombstone commemorates the state's cowboy history, and the numerous Indian reservations also attract many visitors. Hoover Dam and Lake Mead on the Colorado River are among the premier engineering marvels in the United States.

Nevada

Abbreviations: *Nev., NV*
Area: *109,889 sq. mi., 284,613 sq. km.*
Rank (of 50) 7th
Population:
1985 936,000
Rank (of 50) 43rd
Change 1980–85 +135,000
Percent change +16.9
Persons per sq. mi. 9
Percent urban 82.7
Capital: *Carson City*
Largest city: *Las Vegas*
Metro. pop. 1985 557,000
Entered Union: *Oct. 31, 1864 (36th)*
State bird: *Mountain bluebird*
State flower: *Sagebrush*
State tree: *Single-leaf piñon*

Nevada is a southwestern state situated between the Sierra Nevada and Rocky Mountain ranges, with a long border to the west and southwest with California. The state is unusual because it is mostly desert, yet its limited population is generally prosperous. In 1859 the discovery of the famous Comstock silver lode transformed a barren territory into a mining property of such value that Nevada was admitted to the Union in 1864 without the required number of inhabitants. Then, in 1931, gambling was legalized in Nevada and divorce requirements eased. Since then Nevada's principal cities, Las Vegas and Reno, have grown rapidly by attracting large numbers of visitors, helping to make tourism the largest growth industry in the American West.

The land. The largest topographical area in Nevada is the Great Basin, a desert plain more than 3000 feet above sea level running north-south between the Sierra Nevadas on the west and a spur of the Rocky Mountains on the east. Only near the Colorado River, at Nevada's southern border with Arizona, is its altitude below 1000 feet. Many of Nevada's rivers carry water only after rainfall, and many of its alkaline lakes exist as dry beds, or sinks, for much of the year. The largest body of water in the state is Lake Mead, a manmade lake formed by the construction of the Hoover Dam on the Colorado River.

Climate. Nevada has the lowest annual rainfall of any state, averaging under 7 inches. Winds from the Pacific drop most of their moisture on California's Sierra Nevada, leaving very little for Nevada. In most of the state days are hot and nights cold, regardless of the season.

Principal cities. More than 80 percent of the state's population live in its two metropolitan areas. Nevada's largest city is Las Vegas, in the southern corner of the state near the Colorado River. Originally settled because of its mineral springs, the city began to expand with the legalization of gambling and the construction of nearby Hoover Dam in the 1930's. Since then, a steady stream of tourists, many from southern California, has caused huge increases in the resident population. Between 1970 and 1980 metropolitan Las Vegas grew at a rate of 69 percent to approach the half-million mark. The city is especially famous for the gambling casinos, nightclubs, and luxury hotels that line its central avenue, "The Strip."

The second largest city is Reno (metropolitan population 193,623), more than 300 miles northwest at the base of the Sierra Nevadas near the California border. Reno is an older and more traditional city than Las Vegas, and its casinos and hotels attract tourists from the San Francisco area, about 200 miles to the west.

The other cities in the state, all much smaller, include the cattle town of Elko, the mining town of Ely, and Carson City, the capital.

The people. Nevada is sparsely populated, ranking 43rd in population in the United States. Its growth has been rapid, but the limited base from which it began accounts for the exceptionally high 63.5 percent growth rate of the 1970's. Less than a quarter of the people residing in Nevada were born in the state, and most newcomers are attracted by the solid economic base that gives the state the eighth highest per capita income in the country and a lower than average unemployment rate. The population is heavily urban.

Economy. The major industry in Nevada is tourism, which brings the state $1.5 billion in revenues yearly. Taxes on gambling alone account for nearly half of Nevada's total tax revenues. The second leading industry is mining, which now far exceeds the production levels of the state's early boom years. In addition to large quantities of copper and a variety of other minerals, Nevada accounts for 26 percent of the total U.S. output of gold. Manufacturing of electronic equipment and chemical products now constitutes an increasingly important sector of the economy. Livestock and feed provide most of the state's agricultural income.

Places of interest. In addition to the large resorts in Las Vegas and Reno, Nevada has major resort areas near Lake Tahoe, along the California border, and Lake Mead, along the Arizona border. Among the principal attractions associated with the state's desert geography are Carson Hot Springs, Cathedral Gorge State Park, and many preserved fossil beds. Other places of interest include such former boom towns as Virginia City, and the many ghost towns and abandoned mines scattered across the state.

Hawaii

Abbreviations: *Haw., HI*
Area: *6425 sq. mi., 16,641 sq. km.*
Rank (of 50) 47th
Population:
1985 1,054,000
Rank (of 50) 39th
Change 1980–85 +89,000
Percent change +9.2
Persons per sq. mi. 164
Percent urban 86.5
Capital: *Honolulu*
Largest city: *Honolulu*
Metro. pop. 1985 815,000
Entered Union: *Aug. 21, 1959 (50th)*
State bird: *Hawaiian goose*
State flower: *Hibiscus*
State tree: *Kukui (candlenut)*

Hawaii is the 50th state and the only one situated outside continental North America. Located in the Pacific Ocean 2000 miles southwest of California, Hawaii is a 1500-mile-long archipelago of over 100 islands with a total area less than that of New Jersey. The principal islands are clustered in the southeastern end of the chain. They are, in descending order of size: Hawaii, Maui, Oahu, Kauai, Molokai, Lanai, and Niihau. One other significant island, Kahoolawe, is a cattle station with no permanent population.

Despite its small land area and limited population, Hawaii is a remarkably diversified state. In addition to the tropical beaches that most visitors from the mainland expect to see, the state includes cattle ranches, pineapple and coffee plantations, winter skiing on the volcanic cone of Mauna Kea, large suburban neighborhoods, and a citizenry of unusual ethnic mixtures.

History. The first European to report on the Hawaiian Islands was Captain James Cook of England. In 1778 he discovered a thriving civilization of

Polynesian peoples on the main islands. Hawaii attracted more visitors, including Christian missionaries from the United States, in the next 50 years, but kept its independence. It was recognized as an independent country by the United States in 1842.

U.S. business investments in the islands increased in the late 1800's, and businessmen sought the advantages of closer ties to the United States. In 1894, the traditional Hawaiian monarchy gave way to a republic. Four years later, the United States annexed Hawaii, and in 1900 Hawaii became a territory. The Navy base at Pearl Harbor increased both in size and in strategic importance after World War I. On December 7, 1941, the base was attacked by Japanese war planes and mostly destroyed, with great loss of life. The next day, the United States entered World War II.

After the war, sentiment for statehood grew rapidly, and finally, in 1959, Hawaii became the 50th state.

The land. The Hawaiian Islands are volcanic in origin, which makes many of them natural reservoirs because rainwater collects in the inactive volcanic cones. The largest island, called Hawaii, is the creation of the twin volcanic peaks Mauna Loa (13,680 feet) and Mauna Kea (13,796 feet); it has a total land area of 4021 square miles. The second largest island is Maui (728 square miles), an agricultural plantation dominated by the volcanic peak that gives Haleakala National Park its name. The island of Oahu (595 square miles) is the location of the capital city, Honolulu. The remaining populated islands of Kauai, Molokai, Lanai, and Niihau are all dominated by single volcanic mountains and have coastlines of steep cliff faces broken by small natural harbors.

Climate. The climate of Hawaii is relatively mild because the ocean winds moderate temperatures usual in such subtropical latitudes. Temperatures in the most populous areas remain in the 70° F range year-round. Rainfall varies greatly, from 15 inches per year along the southwestern shores to more than 100 inches along northeastern shores and at high altitudes. The higher peaks may be snow-covered part of the year.

Principal cities. The major city is Honolulu on Oahu. Nearly 80 percent of the state's people live in the metropolitan area. The city is situated southwest of Pearl Harbor, the largest natural harbor on the islands. In addition to being the seat of state government, Honolulu is also the tourist capital of Hawaii, with large vacation hotels stretching along the beaches to the east of the older city center.

The second largest city in the state is Hilo (population 37,017), the chief commercial port and tourist center on the larger island of Hawaii.

The people. Native Hawaiians are descended from Polynesian peoples who first settled the island in the seventh century. The state's other major ethnic groups are Japanese, Chinese, and Filipino. Intermarriage and influences from the mainland have led to the integration of these ethnic groups, but 65 percent of the population consider themselves of Asian-American or Pacific Islander heritage. The total population of the state is now more than four-fifths urban and enjoys both a higher per capita income and a lower unemployment rate than the national average.

Economy. Tourism brings Hawaii more than $4 billion per year, far more than any other industry, and provides the principal employment of the work force. Since the 19th century, however, Hawaii has been known for its agriculture. Pineapple, sugar cane, and coffee are the largest crops. They are grown and processed on huge corporate plantations that occupy the entire area of some smaller islands. Large herds of cattle are also grazed on isolated islands. Recent years have seen an increase in other businesses in the state, including electronics research sponsored by the U.S. military and businesses associated with trade and shipping.

Places of interest. The major geological places of interest in Hawaii, identified by island, include Hawaii Volcanoes National Park (Hawaii) and Haleakala National Park (Maui). Places associated with the islands' Polynesian heritage include Puuhonua o Honaunau National Historical Park (Hawaii), the Polynesian Cultural Center (Oahu), and Iolani Palace (Oahu), the only royal palace in the United States. Sights near Honolulu include the *U.S.S. Arizona* memorial at Pearl Harbor, Waikiki Beach, and Diamond Head.

The Northwest States

The Northwest states include Oregon and Washington on the Pacific coast, Idaho immediately inland, and Alaska separated by a coastal strip of Canada. Together, these states represent one-fifth of the total land area of the United States. The population is sparse, representing less than 4 percent of the U.S. total. The region is growing rapidly, however, and in the 1970's, the rate of population growth was more than double the national average.

The land. The principal topographical features of the Northwest are mountain ranges and powerful rivers. Oregon, Washington, and Alaska have in common Coastal Ranges that rise from 4000 to over 10,000 feet in altitude. Another mountain range, the Cascades, is shared by Washington and Oregon. These two states are touched by the spurs of the Rocky Mountains that also cover the western half of Idaho. Alaska contains the spectacular Alaska and Brooks ranges within its enormous area. All Northwestern states lie to the west of the Continental Divide, and their principal rivers flow toward the Pacific Ocean. The contiguous northwestern states are dominated by the Columbia River and its inland tributary, the Snake River. Alaska is traversed from east to west by the Yukon River.

In addition to sharing mountain ranges, Washington, Oregon, and Idaho also have in common upper branches of the Great Basin that covers major portions of Nevada and Utah to the south. The variety of relief characteristics gives the states a full range of contrasting landmarks. The extremes include the highest mountain in North America, Mt. McKinley (20,320 feet); the deepest gorge, Hell's Canyon (7900 feet deep) on the Snake River at the Idaho–Oregon border; the largest rain forest in the United States, on Olympic Peninsula in Washington; and the extensive, barren lava beds called Craters of the Moon in Idaho.

Climate. The greatest influence on the climate of the Northwest is the Cascade Range. Areas west of the range along the Pacific have mild climates with heavy rainfall. Areas to the east of the Cascades are dry and have greater seasonal variations in temperature. A similar pattern holds in Alaska.

History. The lower Northwestern states were first explored by the Spanish Captain Bruno Heceta in 1775. Earlier, in 1741, Alaska was discovered by Vitus Bering, a Dane in command of Russian ships. In 1792 Robert Gray, captain of the British vessel *Columbia*, sailed up the principal river of "The Oregon Country" and named it after his ship. The most important exploration came from inland, however, when Lewis and Clark spent the winter of 1805–1806 in the Northwest. Their reports encouraged fur trappers to settle in the region. Present boundaries were fixed by the Oregon Treaty of 1846.

The Northwest was first made acces-

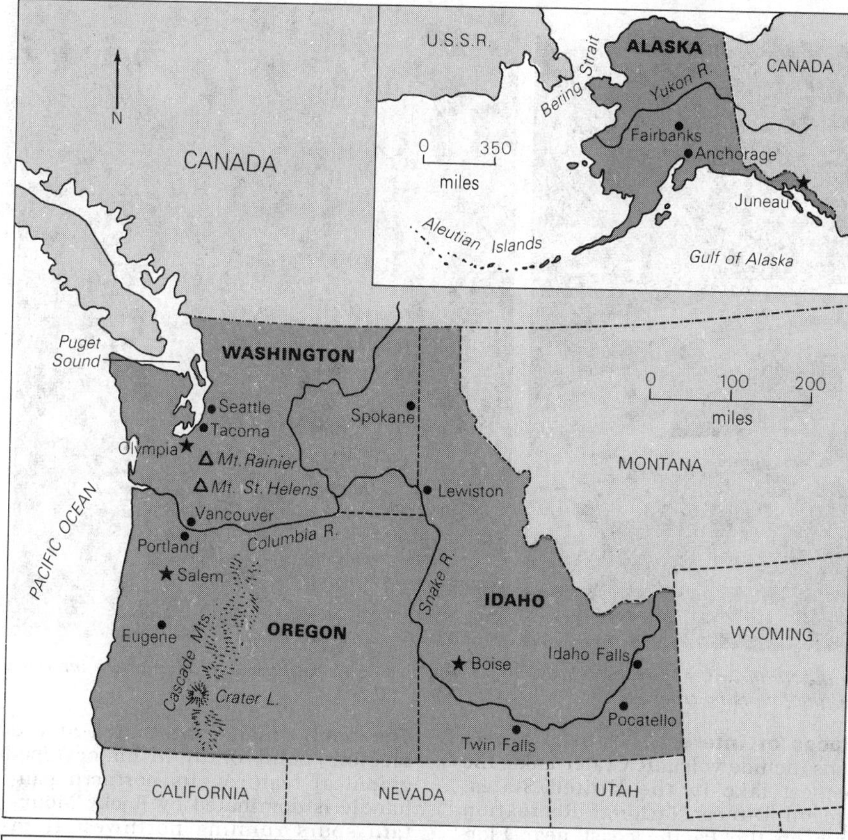

THE NORTHWEST STATES

State	Area (sq. mi.)	Population 1985	Population change 1980–85 number	Population change 1980–85 percent	Persons per sq. mi.
Oregon	96,184	2,687,000	+ 54,000	+ 2.1	28
Idaho	82,667	1,005,000	+ 61,000	+ 6.4	12
Washington	66,570	4,132,000	+277,000	+ 6.7	66
Alaska	566,432	402,000	+119,000	+29.7	1
Region totals	811,853	8,622,000	+511,000	+ 6.3	11

sible to settlers by the opening of the Oregon Trail from Independence, Missouri, in 1843. During the late 1800's, gold rushes attracted many people. The completion of transcontinental railroad lines helped change the Northwest into a settled region.

The people. Present-day migration to the Northwest has been encouraged by manufacturing businesses made possible by the region's huge hydroelectric dams. The discovery of enormous oil deposits is the main cause of the rapid growth of Alaska. Because new residents are attracted by these industrial operations, the Northwest's population has become increasingly concentrated. Two-thirds of the total population now live in urban areas, and the Seattle and Portland metropolitan areas alone account for one-third of the region's population.

Economy. About one-quarter of all U.S. forestland lies within the Northwest states, and the region's lumber production more than doubles that of any other region in the United States. In recent years its rank in agriculture has declined, but the value added by manufacture tripled between 1967 and 1977. The chief manufacturing businesses are food processing, wood products, and technological, aerospace, and chemical enterprises.

Oregon

Abbreviations: *Ore., OR*
Area: *96,184 sq. mi., 249,117 sq. km.*
Rank (of 50) *10th*
Population:
1985 *2,687,000*
Rank (of 50) *30th*
Change 1980–85 *+54,000*
Percent change *+2.1*
Persons per sq. mi. *28*
Percent urban *67.9*
Capital: *Salem*
Largest city: *Portland*
Metro. pop. 1985 *1,147,000*
Entered Union: *Feb. 14, 1859 (33rd)*
State bird: *Western meadowlark*
State flower: *Oregon grape*
State tree: *Douglas fir*

Oregon is a Northwestern state on the Pacific Ocean. It borders Washington on the north and California on the south. It is generally rectangular, with some irregularities because of shoreline and river boundaries. Second among Northwestern states to Alaska in area and to Washington in population, Oregon is distinguished for the 30 million acres of forestland that cover about half its total land area. The concentration of population in a relatively small area has left these forest tracts, parts of the state's 300-mile Pacific coastline, and arid volcanic regions of the interior largely undisturbed.

The land. The Cascade Mountains run north-south through Oregon about 100 miles inland from the ocean. This range defines the state's principal topographical and climatic areas. The Pacific coast is composed of rocky cliffs that rise into Coastal Ranges such as those found in Washington to the north and California to the south. Heavily forested in Oregon, these ranges reach a maximum height of about 4000 feet within the state borders.

Inland from the Coastal Ranges lies the Willamette Valley, a lowland farming region that now includes most of the state's population. This valley widens to the north and adjoins the Puget Trough in Washington. The eastern limit of the Willamette Valley is defined by the wall of the Cascades, rugged mountains with several peaks higher than 10,000 feet.

Inland from the Cascades lies two-thirds of Oregon's area, an immense plateau extending to the Idaho border. In its eastern reaches this plateau is broken by minor mountain ranges into distinct areas related to the Columbia Plateau in Washington, the Snake River Plateau in Idaho, and the Great Basin that covers most of Nevada.

Climate. From the Pacific coast inland to the Cascades, Oregon has a mild climate influenced by the warming effects of the ocean's Japan Current. Temperatures in this area range from 30° to 50° F in January and from 50° to 85° in July, with heavy rains falling in winter. The Cascades effectively block rains from the eastern plateau, however, where precipitation averages only about 12 inches per year. On the plateau winters are far colder and summers are warmer than in coastal areas.

Principal cities. The state's four largest cities are all clustered in the Willamette Valley. The largest city is Portland, which straddles the Willamette River near its meeting with the Columbia River at the Washington border. The Portland metropolitan area, which includes Vancouver, Washington, is the retail center of a large area of Washington as well as Oregon. The state's other principal population centers, Salem and Eugene–Springfield, both lie south of

PRO PIX/MONKMEYER

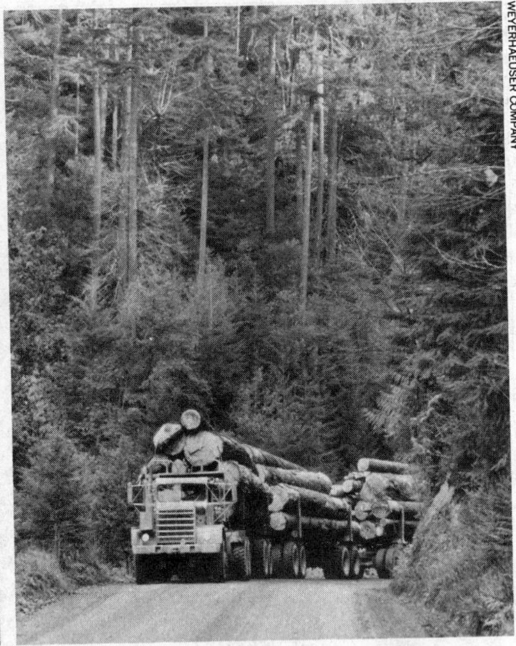

WEYERHAEUSER COMPANY

OIL AND TIMBER *are two of the major industries in the Northwest. At left, the Alaska oil pipeline weaves its way through the Alaskan interior. Once transported by water, timber now comes out of the forests by truck.*

Portland on the banks of the Willamette River. The remainder of the state, including its whole western half, is very sparsely populated.

The people. The state waited until the opening of the Oregon Trail in 1843 for its first significant wave of German, Scandinavian, and English settlers. Generous land-grant policies attracted hardy farmers in the 1850's. After 1870, the railroads brought another influx of settlers. Many more new residents arrived between 1950 and 1970.

Today the population is two-thirds urban, and the towns of the Willamette Valley attract most of the state's new residents. Only about 5 percent of the population are Hispanic, black, or Asian.

Economy. The economy of Oregon has been based on agriculture and lumber since the 1800's. The seats of agriculture are the Willamette Valley, where small dairy farms predominate, and the open eastern region, where large consolidated farms produce large quantities of wheat, potatoes, cattle, and sheep. The state's huge stands of virgin timber provide 431 billion board feet annually, one-sixth of the total U.S. output. These two industries have combined to spawn diversified manufacturing businesses based on the processing of food and wood products.

Tourism is also one of the largest industries, with out-of-state visitors to Oregon's forest and ocean areas spending over $1 billion each year. The largest known lode of nickel ore in the United States has been mined beneath Nickel Mountain in the southwest since 1954. Oregon also mines large quantities of gravel and cement from its eastern plateau.

Places of interest. Natural attractions include volcanic Crater Lake, the deepest lake in the United States; Oregon Dunes National Recreation Area on the Pacific coast near Florence; and Oregon Caves National Monument. Also of interest are Fort Clatsop, where Lewis and Clark spent the winter of 1805–1806; and numerous summer and winter resorts.

Idaho

Abbreviations: *Ida., ID*
Area: *82,667 sq. mi., 214,133 sq. km.*
Rank (of 50) *11th*
Population:
1985 *1,005,000*
Rank (of 50) *40th*
Change 1980–85 *+61,000*
Percent change *+6.4*
Persons per sq. mi. *12*
Percent urban *54.0*
Capital: *Boise*
Largest city: *Boise*
City pop. 1984 *107,000*
Entered Union: *July 3, 1890 (43rd)*
State bird: *Mountain bluebird*
State flower: *Syringa*
State tree: *White pine*

Idaho is the single landlocked state in the Northwest. Its rectangular southern region is defined by ruler-straight borders with other U.S. states, and its northern region is an irregular panhandle that narrows to a width of only 45 miles at the extreme northern border with Canada. A sparsely populated state, Idaho contains natural features as different as lava plateaus, subalpine lakes, desert tablelands, and deep river gorges.

The land. Idaho is situated at the meeting point of three major topographical features. Its northern panhandle is dominated by Rocky Mountain spurs running northwest from Wyoming and Montana. Southeastern Idaho touches the beginning of the Great Basin that extends south into Nevada and Utah. This plateau is volcanic in origin and includes extensive lava beds in Idaho.

The third distinct feature of the land is the Snake River Plateau, which follows the Snake River across the wide southern part of the state, and then northward along the Oregon border. This plateau is an arm of the Columbia Plateau that dominates eastern portions of Washington and Oregon, and it includes the finest farmland and open grazing land in Idaho.

Climate. Mountains to the north shelter Idaho from cold Arctic air, giving the state a moderate continental climate. July high temperatures at Boise average 91 degrees, and January lows average 20. Like western Oregon and Washington, Idaho has sparse rainfall, averaging 12 inches per year.

Principal cities. The only city in Idaho with a population over 100,000 is Boise, in the southwestern plateau. It is located near the Snake River's route across the state's lower rectangle, as are the other large cities of Twin Falls, Pocatello, and Idaho Falls. The only large city in the northern reaches of the state is Lewiston, a river port at the confluence of the Snake and Clearwater rivers beside the Washington border.

The people. Idaho's sparse population is an unusual ethnic blend. Among the earliest settlers were French trappers who gave many of the state's northern areas French names.

Since that time the state has been settled by large numbers of German, Scandinavian, and Dutch immigrants. Basque sheep herders from Spain also settled in Idaho to make use of land too hilly for cattle grazing. Today, Idaho is among the fastest growing states. The proportion of city dwellers is just over 50 percent, but it is increasing rapidly.

Economy. Profits from livestock now exceed those from crops in Idaho, but the state continues to grow one-quarter of the U.S. potato crop. The principal manufacturing business is food processing. Tourism has become the third most profitable industry. The other chief industries are lumber and mining. The state provides one-third of the U.S. silver output.

Places of interest. Natural places of interest in Idaho include Hell's Canyon on the Snake River, the deepest canyon in the United States; the volcanic Craters of the Moon National Monument and Lava Hot Springs; and the northern Lake Coeur d'Alene. The state is also known for its ski resort at Sun Valley and for numerous camping, fishing, and hunting areas.

Washington

Abbreviations: *Wash., WA*
Area: *66,570 sq. mi., 172,410 sq. km.*
Rank (of 50) *20th*
Population:
1985 *4,409,000*
Rank (of 50) *19th*
Change 1980–85 *+277,000*
Percent change *+6.7*
Persons per sq. mi. *66*
Percent urban *73.5*
Capital: *Olympia*
Largest city: *Seattle*
Metro. pop. 1985 *1,724,000*
Entered Union: *Nov. 11, 1889 (42nd)*
State bird: *Willow goldfinch*
State flower: *Rhododendron*
State tree: *Western hemlock*

Washington is located in the northwest corner of the contiguous 48 states, with borders on the Pacific Ocean and British Columbia, Canada. Its shape is retangular, except for a "notch" in the northwest formed by Vancouver Island, a part of Canada that extends south of the 49th parallel. The Strait of Juan de Fuca leads past Vancouver Island and into Puget Sound, which extends 100 miles into the state and provides its primary deep-water ports. Washington's southern border is formed primarily by the Columbia River, which flows south through the center of the state before turning at the "Big Bend" to form the boundary between Washington and Oregon. Its rapid flow and great volume give it huge potential for generating hydroelectric power, and a series of dams along its length make Washington the largest producer of hydroelectric power in the United States. These water resources, a mild climate, and extensive forestland have combined to make Washington the home of one-half the population of the Northwest states.

The land. Washington is characterized by four distinct topographical areas. The farthest west is the peninsula of Olympic Mountains. Isolated by the southern reaches of Puget Sound, surrounded by water, and subject to Pacific westerly winds, it contains the largest rain forest in the United States.

Immediately inland is the lowland Puget Trough that extends south from Puget Sound toward Oregon. About 100 miles farther east, the Cascade Mountains run parallel to the Pacific coastline. Geologically an extension of the Sierra Nevadas in California, this spectacular range is the principal topographical division of the state. Its peaks include Mt. Rainier (14,410 feet) and Mt. St. Helens, a long-dormant volcano that erupted on May 31, 1980.

Inland from the Cascades and covering the southeast quarter of the state is the Columbia Plateau, a semi-arid tableland between 500 and 2000 feet above sea level. At its northeast corner the state is touched by western spurs of the Rocky Mountains.

Climate. Washington has two distinct climates, defined by the Cascades. Western Washington has a moderate seasonal variation, with winter mean temperatures about 30° F and summer ones about 60. Rainfall near the coast is heavy, averaging about 35 inches at Seattle and over 100 inches on the Olympic Peninsula. East of the Cascades, however, rainfall diminishes to about 16 inches per year and temperature variations, depending on elevation, increase to the usual continental averages of 70 degrees in summer and below freezing in winter. The Cascade Range itself includes many peaks with year-round ice caps.

Principal cities. Washington's principal urban centers are at either end of the state. The Seattle–Tacoma–Everett metropolitan area on the east shore of Puget Sound contains nearly 40 percent of the state population. It is the business center of the Northwest. Across the state, Spokane, hub of a metropolitan area including parts of Idaho, is the center of the aluminum industry and a processor of agricultural and lumber products from Idaho as well as Washington.

The people. Having lain nearly barren until the opening of railroad links with the east in 1883, Washington developed as the gateway to Alaska and to the Orient. The major ethnic groups in those early years were German, English, and Norwegian. In recent years, the state has attracted a much wider range of people. Today about 3 percent of the population are of Hispanic descent, 3 percent are black, and 2 percent are of Asian descent.

Economy. Washington has come a long way since its early days as a collection of boom towns and erratic shipping businesses. Today Washington's manufacturing businesses have outgrown the traditional industries of timber and agriculture. By the 1960's manufacturing had come to dominate the work force, with most of it heavily concentrated on the Boeing Company, a producer of civilian and military aircraft.

Seattle is now the fourth largest containerized seaport in the United States, primarily because of manufactured exports. Manufacturing industries farther inland have prospered by processing the state's timber and agricultural produce. Another substantial factor in the state economy is the aluminum industry, which provides one-quarter of the nation's output of raw aluminum.

Washington's agricultural products are stratified into regions: dairy products in the west, apples in the central region, and wheat on the eastern plateau. Lumbering is an industry as old as the state, and production remains second only to Oregon among U.S. states. As in Oregon, the principal harvest is of Douglas fir, but in Washington the state tree, the western hemlock, is a close second.

Places of interest. The major attractions in Washington are Mount Rainier National Park, North Cascades National Park, and Olympic National Park. Also of interest are the state's Pacific beaches, the Columbia River Gorge, and Grand Coulee Dam.

Alaska

Abbreviations: *Alas., AK*
Area: *566,432 sq. mi., 1,467,059 sq. km.*
Rank (of 50) *1st*
Population:
1985 *521,000*
Rank (of 50) *49th*
Change 1980–85 *+119,000*
Percent change *+29.7*
Persons per sq. mi. *1*
Percent urban *64.3*
Capital: *Juneau*
Largest city: *Anchorage*
City pop. 1984 *227,000*
Entered Union: *Jan. 3, 1959 (49th)*
State bird: *Willow ptarmigan*
State flower: *Forget-me-not*
State tree: *Sitka spruce*

Alaska, the largest and least populated of U.S. states, is a peninsula extending north and west from Canada's Pacific shore to a point only 56 miles from Russia across the Bering Strait. Other than its single land border with Canada, the state is surrounded by the

Arctic Ocean to the north, the Bering Strait to the west, and the Gulf of Alaska to the south. The southern reaches of the state are distinguished by two extremely narrow panhandles: one running southeast along the Pacific coast toward Prince Rupert, Canada, and one reaching southwest toward the Aleutian Island chain, which extends far into the Bering Sea. The most westerly island in the Aleutian chain lies farther west than Honolulu on the same longitude as New Zealand.

Alaska was purchased from Russia in 1867 at a price of two cents per acre. Its strategic importance has only recently been realized, however, as its natural resources become more valuable in the world economy.

Alaska differs from all its sister states in its extensive reliance on air and water transportation. The Alaska Highway, completed in the 1940's, connects Anchorage and Fairbanks to the "south 48," running through British Columbia and the Yukon Territory before entering Alaska. But weather conditions, rugged terrain, water barriers, and the difficulties of building on permafrost have encouraged sea and air travel. Juneau, the state capital, and such settlements as Ketchikan, Sitka, and Kodiak are not connected to other large towns by road. Even where roads exist, they may not be passable for long periods during the winter.

The land. The area of Alaska, one-fifth the size of all the 49 other states combined, is comprised of the Coastal Ranges, an interior plateau, and the northern Arctic Slope. The mountains running the length of the state's southern shores are a continuation of the Coastal Ranges found along the entire Pacific coast of the United States. In Alaska, however, the mountains are far higher than any in the contiguous 48 states. Separated by fjords from the sea, many of these mountains are covered by the glaciers that envelop 15,000 square miles of the state.

Slightly inland these ranges rise to become part of the spectacular Alaska Range, which includes the highest point in North America, Mt. McKinley (20,320 feet). The chain of Coastal Ranges isolates the central plateau of Alaska from the warmth and rainfall of the Pacific winds; as a result, parts of the interior experience only temporary, superficial thaws in summer. This central plateau, traversed by the Yukon River, extends to the Brooks Range of mountains north of the Arctic Circle. Beyond the Brooks Range lies the Arctic Slope, a barren region of treeless tundra leading to the northernmost point in the United States, Point Barrow.

Climate. Large portions of Alaska enjoy warmer weather than might be expected. The southern and coastal regions benefit from the warm ocean currents. Juneau, the state capital, has average lows of 17° F in January and average highs of 63 in July. Inland, however, the climate is at once drier and colder, and the limited daylight in such northern latitudes increases the effects of the cold. Summer temperatures in the interior may reach 80 degrees, but these brief thaws never completely undo the effects of winter temperatures that may plunge to minus 60. At Point Barrow, the mean July temperature is 40 degrees and mean winter temperature is minus 19.

Principal cities. The largest city in Alaska is Anchorage, located at the center of the southern coast on the inland reaches of the huge Cook Inlet. With a population more than two-fifths that of the entire state, Anchorage is both the business and transportation center of Alaska. All other cities in the state have fewer than 25,000 in population.

The people. Throughout its term as a territory of Russia, Alaska's population remained almost entirely Indian, Eskimo, and Aleut. The gold rush of 1898 brought the first wave of American immigrants to the state, and in modern times the discovery of huge oil reserves has brought another wave of workers to "America's last frontier." As a consequence of the oil discoveries, the population today is less than one-quarter native. The new population remains clustered in towns; this accounts for the state's high percentage of urban residents. The largest employer in the state continues to be the government. Alaska has the highest per capita income in the United States, but this figure must be balanced against its unusually high cost of living.

Economy. Mining of crude oil and natural gas brings Alaska more than ten times the revenue of any other industry. The principal industrial achievement in the state's recent history was the 1977 opening of the $7.7 billion Alaska pipeline, stretching from Prudhoe Bay on the Arctic Ocean to the Pacific coast. Its presence promises diversification of the state's traditional reliance on government employment and defense spending. Other industries include limited agriculture, commercial fishing, and the processing of food products—principally fish—for export.

Places of interest. The primary attractions in Alaska are unusual natural features such as Mt. McKinley, the Mendenhall Glacier, and the volcanic "Valley of Ten Thousand Smokes." There are also many wildlife preserves and places devoted to Eskimo, Indian, and Aleut heritage.

The Mountain States

The Mountain states, the only U.S. region with borders on two other countries, cross the breadth of the American West from Canada 1200 miles to Mexico. The region is bounded by the Northwest and Southwest regions to the west and by the Grain states and Oil states to the east. The central ridge of the Rocky Mountains runs south through the region from western Montana through Wyoming and Colorado and about 100 miles into New Mexico. A branch ridge isolated by the Wyoming Basin runs south through Utah.

The region is one of the largest and most sparsely populated in the United States, with less than 7 million people living on half a million square miles. There are large areas of undisturbed natural beauty in all the states, including not only mountain scenery but sand dunes, deserts, salt flats, geysers, and glaciers. The region is now experiencing a population growth because of its beautiful natural surroundings and the recent expansion of its manufacturing businesses. During the 1960's all mountain states except Colorado lost residents to migration; during the 1970's all Mountain states grew from immigration.

The land. The Rocky Mountains that unite these states are the highest in the United States—twice as high as the Appalachian chain east of the Mississippi. The three main divisions of the Rockies are all represented in the Mountain states. The Northern Rockies cover western Montana and extend north across Canada to Alaska. The Middle Rockies cover Wyoming, where they are interrupted by the Wyoming Basin, and then divide into two ranges: the main chain, which runs southeast through the center of Colorado, and the Wasatch Range, which runs south through much of Utah. These Southern Rockies are the highest in the chain. Colorado contains the highest peaks. To the south the Rockies decline into the Sangre de Cristo Range, which extends 100 miles into New Mexico.

The central ridge of the Rocky Mountains forms the great watershed in North America, the Continental Divide. Rain falling to the west of this

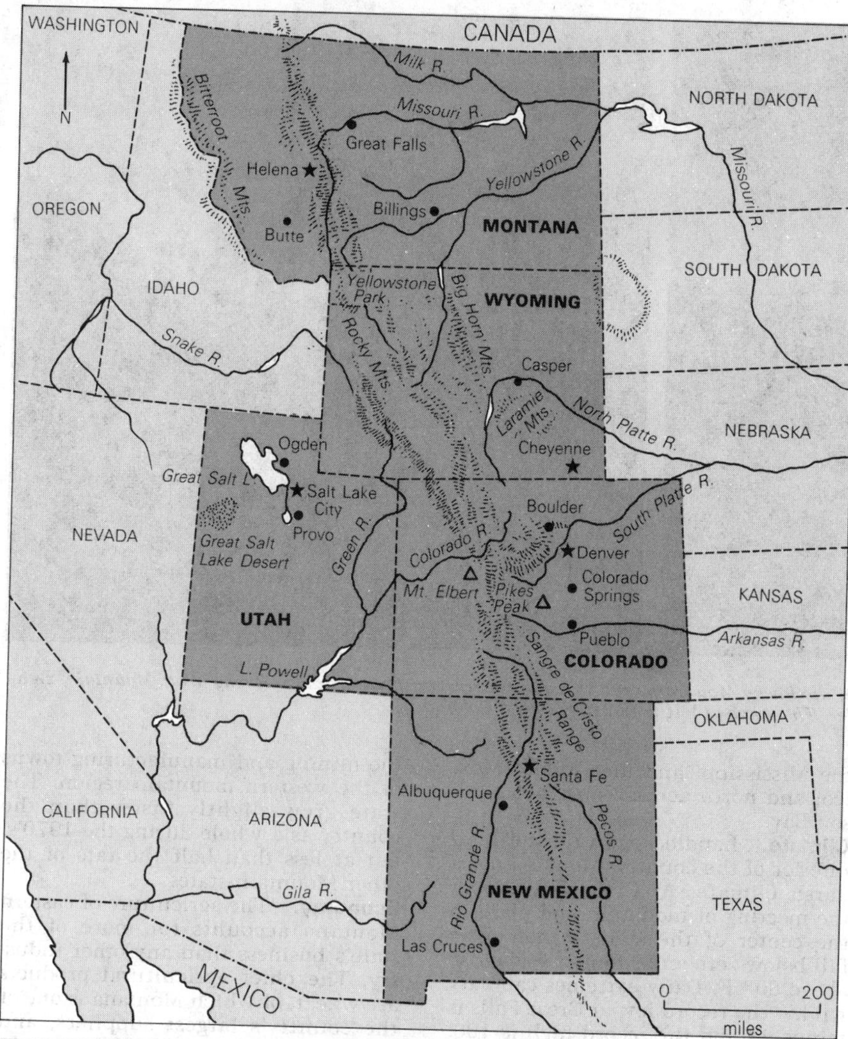

THE MOUNTAIN STATES

State	Area (sq. mi.)	Population 1985	Population change 1980–85 number	Population change 1980–85 percent	Persons per sq. mi.
Montana	145,587	826,000	+ 40,000	+ 5.0	6
Wyoming	97,203	509,000	+ 40,000	+ 8.5	5
Colorado	103,766	3,231,000	+341,000	+11.8	31
Utah	82,096	1,645,000	+184,000	+12.6	20
New Mexico	121,412	1,450,000	+147,000	+11.3	12
Region totals	550,064	7,661,000	+752,000	+10.9	14

imaginary line will flow west into the Pacific Ocean. Rain falling to the east of it will flow east and south into the Gulf of Mexico. Four of the major rivers in the United States have headwaters in the Rockies. The Missouri flows east to the Mississippi, and then to the Gulf of Mexico. The Rio Grande flows southeast directly to the Gulf. The Columbia flows west to the Pacific, and the Colorado flows west and then south to the Gulf of California, an arm of the Pacific.

Climate. The climate of the region varies north to south from the harsh winters and hot summers of Montana to the desert climate of warm days and cool nights throughout the year in New Mexico. Precipitation, however, is uniformly low throughout the region. The Mountain states average about 15 inches of precipitation per year, with New Mexico significantly lower. Much of it falls as snow in the highest elevations, running off to the east or west after spring thaws.

History. The Mountain states were the last U.S. region to be fully opened to settlement. French-Canadians were the first explorers in Montana and Wyoming, and the Spanish were the first European visitors to Colorado, Utah, and New Mexico. However, the region was not fully explored until well into the 1800's. The Great Salt Lake was not discovered until 1825, only 22 years before Brigham Young led his Mormon followers there. The northern half of the region's land area came into U.S. possession with the Louisiana Purchase of 1803. The southern half was ceded by Mexico after the Mexican War in 1848. Early settlers established huge ranches for grazing cattle because most of the land was too dry to support crops.

Principal cities. The only large metropolitan area in the region is Denver, a city near the center of the region that is also the commercial heart of the Mountain states. Its population of 1.6 million makes it half again as large as any other city in the area. Salt Lake City, 350 miles west of Denver, and Albuquerque, 300 south of Denver, are the only other populous cities. Although small by national standards, these three metropolitan areas account for more than 43 percent of the region's population.

The people. The major ethnic groups are Hispanic and American Indian. Both groups live in all Mountain states but they are especially numerous in New Mexico.

Economy. All Mountain states have three industries in common: tourism, mining, and ranching. Yellowstone in Wyoming was the first national park. Along with such natural preserves as Glacier in Montana, Grand Teton in Wyoming, and Rocky Mountain in Colorado, it is the basis of the tourism industry. In recent years winter sports have become an important business, especially in Colorado.

Wyoming and New Mexico lead the region in mining because of their oil and natural gas wealth. But Utah's Bingham Canyon copper mine is the world's largest open pit mine; Colorado leads all states in production of the industrially important element molybdenum; and Montana is rich in both coal and copper. Ranching is the traditional business of the region, and profits from cattle and sheep exceed those from crops in the agricultural economy of all Mountain states.

Montana

Abbreviations: *Mont., MT*
Area: *145,587 sq. mi., 337,070 sq. km*
Rank (of 50) *4th*
Population:
1985 *826,000*
Rank (of 50) *44th*
Change 1980–85 *+40,000*
Percent change *+5.0*
Persons per sq. mi. *6*
Percent urban *52.9*
Capital: *Helena*
Largest city: *Billings*
City pop. 1980 *66,798*
Entered Union: *Nov. 8, 1889 (41st)*
State bird: *Western meadowlark*
State flower: *Bitterroot*
State tree: *Ponderosa pine*

Montana is the most northern of the Mountain states, stretching more than

TAURUS

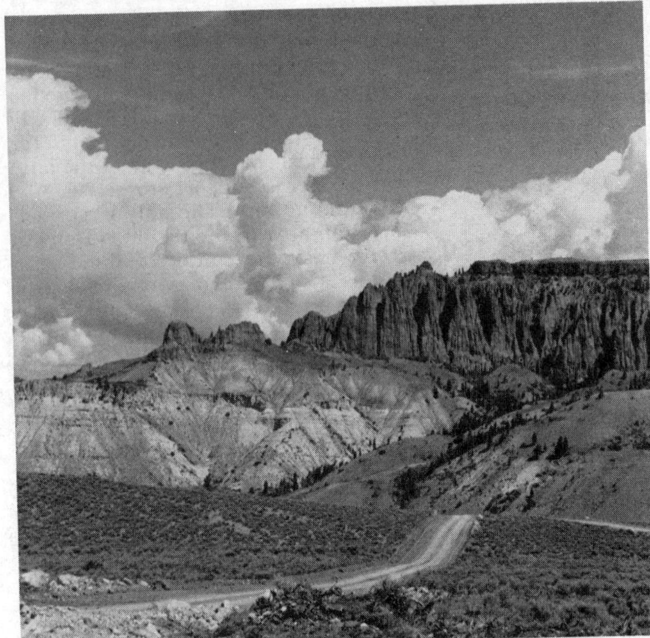

LEDING/MONKMEYER

FROM FRIGID PEAKS TO DESERT WASTELANDS, *the Rocky Mountains run through the western United States. Rising Wolf Mountain,* right, *is in Glacier National Park on the Canadian border. The scene at* left *is in arid western Colorado.*

650 miles along the Canadian border between the plains of North Dakota and the mountains of Idaho. Its eastern two-thirds is a precise rectangle, but the western third is a wider and more irregular area defined by the ridges of the Bitterroot Mountain. In surface area, too, the eastern two-thirds is more regular, for the most part consisting of the grazing lands of the "big sky country." The western third is a rugged mountain area that includes the Continental Divide ridge of the Northern Rockies.

Montana is a state more influenced by its western terrain than by the plains that occupy most of its area. Appropriately, it contains more U.S. government-defined wilderness areas than any other state. The population is sparse and the cities few, so the residents are inured to long trips for the limited social entertainments of small towns. Full of mineral resources that can only be estimated, Montana has been the stage for bitter clashes between protectors of the environment and supporters of industrial and economic development.

The land. The eastern two-thirds of Montana is a vast plain and prairie region crossed by the Missouri River in the north and the Yellowstone River in the south, with the two converging at the North Dakota border. In the western third, the central ridge of the Rockies extends from Yellowstone Park at the Wyoming border in a northwest direction to Glacier National Park on the Canadian border. In the Rockies are found the headwaters of rivers that drain in three directions: west via the Snake and Columbia rivers into the Pacific; east and south via the Missouri and Yellowstone rivers to the Mississippi and the Gulf of Mexico; and north across Canada to Hudson Bay.

Climate. Landlocked in the northern interior of the country, Montana has a harsh climate. At Great Falls, near the meeting of mountain and plain in the center of the state, winter lows fall below zero and summer highs rise above 80° F. Daily extremes can vary wildly: the record low at Great Falls is minus 43 and the record high is 106. Winter storms in the Rockies and along the Canadian border can be especially brutal.

Principal cities. Montana has no metropolitan areas, the largest city being Billings, an agricultural marketplace for northern Wyoming as well as Montana. All other major cities are located in the western, mountainous third of the state. Great Falls (population 56,725) grew dramatically when the hydroelectric power of the Missouri River was first tapped. The capital city of Helena (population 23,938) was originally a stockyard town for cattle grazed in the Big Belt Mountains. The Butte–Silver Bow–Anaconda area in the southwest was built on the profits of copper mines and was once the site of violent battles between union workers and the Anaconda Mining Company.

The people. The population of Montana, while sparse, is among the stablest in the American West. Social status is often measured by one's descent from pioneer stock, and half the residents were born in the state. Most migrations tend to be within state borders. Since the 1960's there has been a significant movement from the agricultural areas of eastern Montana, where farms are being consolidated, to the mining and manufacturing towns of the western mountain region. The state grew slightly faster than the country as a whole during the 1970's, but at less than half the rate of the other Mountain states.

Economy. The agriculture of eastern Montana accounts for more of the state's business than any other industry. The chief agricultural products are wheat, of which Montana is one of the country's largest suppliers, and cattle. Montana leads all Mountain states in both amount of forestland, with 22.5 million acres, and in lumber production, with more than 97 billion board feet.

The mining industry continues to be the principal support of the Mountain region, where in recent years coal has surpassed copper in importance. The state's 2 billion tons of coal reserves are strip mined, a process that has resulted in the imposition of environmental protection laws and severance taxes bitterly resisted by the industry. Tourism is also a substantial industry, with most visitors attracted by the hunting of big game, such as moose, elk, and bear, and the state's natural beauty.

Places of interest. From Yellowstone north to Glacier National Park the western region of Montana is full of impressive mountain, lake, cavern, and river landscapes preserved in virtually virgin condition. The plains areas in the eastern two-thirds of the state include places associated with the early history of the state, such as George Armstrong Custer National Battlefield (where Custer's troops were massacred by Indians in 1876), the Fort Union Trading Post, and the Museum of the Plains Indian.

Wyoming

Abbreviations: *Wyo., WY*
Area: *97,203 sq. mi., 251,756 sq. km.*
Rank (of 50) *9th*
Population:
1985 *509,000*
Rank (of 50) *50th*
Change 1980–85 *+40,000*
Percent change *+8.5*
Persons per sq. mi. *5*
Percent urban *62.7*
Capital: *Cheyenne*
Largest city: *Casper*
City pop. 1980 *51,016*
Entered Union: *July 10, 1890 (44th)*
State bird: *Meadowlark*
State flower: *Paintbrush*
State tree: *Cottonwood*

Wyoming lies in the heart of the Mountain region, and its rectangular borders enclose some of the most spectacular Rocky Mountain peaks. The mountains cross the state in isolated ranges from the rugged northwest to the southeast, where the capital city of Cheyenne is located.

The state was explored by John Colter, who first saw the Yellowstone area in 1807. From the 1840's on, the territory was an important way station on the Oregon and Mormon trails. Forts Laramie in the southeast and Bridger in the southwest were the major outposts.

Wyoming has a smaller population than any state with the exception of Alaska. To some extent it remains a frontier: men outnumber women and mining sometimes brings sudden wealth. The land wars of the 1890's have been replaced by the environmental battles of the 1980's.

The land. Wyoming is dominated by the Rocky Mountains, and the state's average elevation of 6700 feet is second only to Colorado's. There are several individual mountain ranges running from northwest to southeast through the state.

The ranges in the northwest corner of the state include some of the highest peaks in the United States and two national parks, Yellowstone and Grand Teton. In north-central Wyoming, the Big Horn Mountains rise above 13,000 feet, and in the southeast, the Laramie Mountains reach 10,000 feet. These ranges are separated by great arid basins, a wandering extension of the basin and range country to the south and west. Along the state's eastern edge, approaching the foothills of the Laramie and Big Horn ranges, are the western edges of the Great Plains.

Climate. Wyoming's climate is generally cool and dry, but it varies with elevation. The northwestern mountains include glaciers that remain frozen year-round, and the basin country is predominantly desert. In moderately elevated Cheyenne, in the extreme southeast, temperature averages are 20° F for winter lows, and 80 for summer highs. Precipitation averages about 15 inches per year, most of it falling in the mountains and drained by an extensive network of rivers.

Principal cities. Wyoming's cities lie clustered for the most part in the southeastern region. There is only one city with a population of 50,000, Casper. It stands on the North Platte River, which pioneer travelers to Oregon and California followed to the Rockies. Casper's modern growth has been encouraged by oil and mining businesses to its west. Cheyenne (population 47,283) and Laramie (population 24,410) both lie in the extreme southeast of the state, along the principal transcontinental railway and highway route as it crosses the Laramie Mountains.

The people. Wyoming experienced the highest growth rate among Mountain states in the 1970's. The major incentives drawing the new population were increasing oil and mining businesses and a surviving frontier spirit. More than a quarter of the population has resided in the state less than five years. The turnover of population in Wyoming has always been high, with newcomers arriving from the plains states and the Midwest and residents drawn farther west to California and the Northwest.

Economy. Wyoming raises significant quantities of wheat and grazes cattle and sheep on its northeast plains, but the major industry of the state is mining. Wyoming is the chief producer of crude oil among Mountain states and the leading producer of coal west of the Mississippi. In plains and in basin and range areas, large strip mines yield enormous quantities of a low-sulfur coal especially in demand because it burns more cleanly than most other varieties. The state also ranks second to New Mexico among Mountain states in its production of natural gas and uranium. What manufacturing exists in the state is concentrated around Casper, where food products and cattle are processed and some oil refined. Wyoming has also had a large tourist industry ever since Yellowstone became the first national park in 1872. Nearby Grand Teton Park and other mountain resorts currently bring the state more than $535 million annually.

Places of interest. Wyoming's principal attractions are its mountains and the nearly 10 million acres of forestland that cover them. Yellowstone and Grand Teton national parks are found beside each other in the state's northwest mountains, but across the state there are many natural landscapes of different character, such as Devil's Tower National Monument near the South Dakota border. Historic attractions include Fort Laramie, the restored fur-trapping and military outpost, the state historical museum in Cheyenne, and the Buffalo Bill Museum in Cody.

Colorado

Abbreviations: *Colo., CO*
Area: *103,766 sq. mi., 268,766 sq. km.*
Rank (of 50) *8th*
Population:
1985 *3,231,000*
Rank (of 50) *26th*
Change 1980–85 *+341,000*
Percent change *+11.8*
Persons per sq. mi. *31*
Percent urban *80.6*
Capital: *Denver*
Largest city: *Denver*
Metro. pop. 1985 *1,614,000*
Entered Union: *Aug. 1, 1876 (38th)*
State bird: *Lark bunting*
State flower: *Rocky mountain columbine*
State tree: *Colorado blue spruce*

Colorado is located in the heart of the Mountain region. It is divided roughly in half from north to south by the Southern Rockies, sharing the mountains with its neighboring states to the north, south, and west: Wyoming, New Mexico, and Utah. The most elevated of all U.S. states, Colorado contains some of the most spectacular mountain scenery in the United States and includes within its borders both the highest peak in the Rockies, Mt. Elbert (14,433 feet), and the highest city in the United States, Leadville (10,200 feet). The state is growing at a rapid rate, having gained nearly 700,000 residents in the 1970's. The new population is generally attracted by the state's sound economy, notable for its diversified manufacturing businesses, and by its lifestyle, notable for its outdoor pursuits in striking mountain scenery.

The land. Colorado contains three clearly defined topographical areas: the mountains running north-south through the center of the state; the Great Plains to the east; and the Colorado Plateau to the west. The Southern Rockies include 54 peaks over 10,000 feet in elevation within Colorado. They also contain the headwaters of rivers that supply water to six states and Mexico.

The entire eastern third of the state is part of the Great Plains that stretch east over most of neighboring Nebraska and Kansas. Eastern Colorado has poor, arid land, suitable only for grazing. The region is crossed by the South Platte River in the north flowing into Nebraska, and by the Arkansas River in the south flowing into Kansas.

Colorado's western plateau is comprised of horizontal rock broken by canyons, mesas, and subsidiary plateaus ranging in elevation from 5000 to 10,000 feet. The western plateau is drained by a network of waterways that converge to form the Colorado River.

Climate. The climate in Colorado is dry and sunny, with temperatures in

Denver, in the eastern foothills of the Rockies, ranging from winter lows below 20° F to summer highs of nearly 90. Alpine conditions prevail in the highest elevations, and both the western plateau and the eastern plains remain warmer than the center of the state. Statewide rainfall is low, averaging about 16 inches per year in Denver, but mountain regions receive heavy snows.

Principal cities. Metropolitan Denver, originally a gold mining camp situated where the South Platte River emerges from the mountains, contains well over half the state population. It is a manufacturing city and the center of rail, road, and air transport for a retail area that includes much of the Mountain states region. Colorado's other major cities lie clustered north and south of Denver along the eastern face of the Rockies. Colorado Springs (population 215,150), 60 miles south of Denver, is a resort and the home of the U.S. Air Force Academy. Pueblo (population 101,686), another 35 miles south, is an industrial city once known as the Pittsburgh of the West for its steel mills. For 50 miles north of Denver, along the same corridor, a chain of towns stretches from nearby Boulder (population 76,685) to the smaller northern towns of Greeley and Fort Collins.

The people. The population of Colorado is relatively urban and is concentrated in cities within 100 miles north or south of Denver. People of Spanish origin, chiefly Mexicans, are the only large ethnic group, numbering over 300,000, or 11 percent of the population. Nearly a third of the population settled in the state during the 1970's, attracted by available employment, a generally high standard of living, and proximity to natural beauty and outdoor activities.

Economy. Manufacturing is by far the most important sector of the state economy, and the state's manufactured goods are worth more than twice as much as those of any other Mountain state. The principal manufactures are electronic equipment and aerospace products. Mining is the second largest industry, valued at over $2 billion per year. The agricultural activities of the state are concentrated on livestock. Colorado is second among Mountain states in forestland and in the production of lumber, trailing only Montana in both respects. Tourism is also an important industry, particularly the ski resorts.

Places of interest. Mountains are the main attraction in Colorado, and the prime mountain reserve is Rocky Mountain National Park in the north-central region, within 40 miles of Denver. Also of interest are Pike's Peak, near Colorado Springs, and Great Sand Dunes National Monument, south of Pueblo. Colorado Springs, with its combination of mountain scenery, mineral springs, and the U.S. Air Force Academy, is also one of the great attractions in the Rockies. Colorado is rich in winter skiing resorts, the most famous being at Aspen and Vail.

Utah

Abbreviations: *U., UT*
Area: *82,096 sq. mi., 212,629 sq. km.*
Rank (of 50) *12th*
Population:

1985	*1,645,000*
Rank (of 50)	*35th*
Change 1980–85	*+184,000*
Percent change	*+12.6*
Persons per sq. mi.	*20*
Percent urban	*84.4*

Capital: *Salt Lake City*
Largest city: *Salt Lake City*
Metro. pop. 1985 *1,025,000*
Entered Union: *Jan. 4, 1896 (45th)*
State bird: *Seagull*
State flower: *Sego lily*
State tree: *Blue spruce*

Utah is located at the western edge of the Rocky Mountain region, bordered by the Mountain states of Wyoming and Colorado to the east, Idaho to the north, and the Southwestern states of Nevada and Arizona to the west and south. The state is almost perfectly rectangular, except for a chunk taken out of its northeast corner by Wyoming.

Nearly three-quarters of Utah's population are members of the Church of Jesus Christ of Latter-Day Saints, commonly called the Mormons. The church was founded in New York State in the early 1800's, but persecution in the East and Midwest prompted Brigham Young to lead the membership to the wilderness of Utah in 1847. Early Mormons practiced polygamy, and the United States refused on that ground to admit Utah as a state. Finally, in 1895, the church abandoned its policy of polygamy, and Utah was accepted as a state in 1896. The Mormon church continues to be an important factor in the economic, political, and social affairs of the state.

The land. The most important physical feature in the state is the Rocky Mountain range, which enters the state from the north and covers most of the northeastern region. Utah's principal cities cluster along the western slope of these mountains, which are called the Wasatch Range.

The eastern and southern region is a part of the great Colorado Plateau, which extends into Arizona to the south. The Colorado River enters the state from the east and is soon joined by the Green River, the principal watershed of eastern Utah. Glen Canyon Dam in northern Arizona has backed up the waters of the Colorado, creating Lake Powell in southern Utah, a large national recreation area. The Colorado Plateau itself is a huge area of sedimentary rock uplands cut by strikingly colored canyons and occasional lava flows.

The western third of the state is part of the Great Basin that covers Nevada and parts of neighboring states. It is characterized by smooth desert floors broken by parallel mountain ranges averaging 4000 feet in elevation. The Great Salt Lake Desert and the Great Salt Lake lie in the northwest. The lake, with a salt content of 25 percent, is approximately 75 miles long and, subject to dramatic variations from evaporation, averages about 1800 square miles in area, about the size of the state of Delaware.

Climate. The northeastern mountains and the eastern plateau are the coolest regions of the state. In Salt Lake City temperatures range from winter lows of 20° F to summer highs of 90. The basin and range region to the west is predominantly desert, warmer in both winter and summer than the rest of the state. As a whole, the state averages less than 15 inches of rain per year, but mountain regions receive much more, and extensive desert areas less.

Principal cities. Two-thirds of the population of Utah live on the western slope of the Wasatch Range in the north-central part of the state. Salt Lake City, Provo, and Ogden lie within 75 miles of each other. Salt Lake City, situated in a valley surrounded by mountains, is the headquarters of the Mormon church and a warehousing center for the entire U.S. West. Provo, 40 miles to the south beside freshwater Utah Lake, is the hub of the state's grain and mining businesses. Ogden, about the same distance north of Salt Lake City, lies at the center of the state's railroad network and is the home of its principal military defense and stockyard industries.

The people. The Mormon church is a stabilizing influence on Utah's population. Fully 52 percent of Utah's citizens are lifelong residents of the state, the highest percentage in the Far West. Utah also has the lowest per capita income of the Mountain states, yet the population increased nearly 40 percent in the 1970's.

Economy. Devastating droughts in the 1930's destroyed the Mormons' hopes for building a farm paradise in the desert. Since then the state economy has shifted to manufacturing. Manufactures such as food products, transportation equipment, primary metals, and aerospace weapons bring the state $2.3 billion per year.

Second in importance is mining. Utah ranks second only to Arizona in copper mining and ranks fourth among all states in gold and silver mining. Each county in the state has at some time contributed to its mining of over 200 different minerals. Nearly 80 percent of the state's farm income comes from livestock, and the range areas on the eastern plateau make the state eighth in sheep grazing in the United States. Tourism is becoming an increasingly important business as resorts are built in the central mountains for winter sports.

Places of interest. Utah's greatest natural attraction is the Great Salt Lake. Other sites of rugged scenery include Zion, Canyonlands, and Bryce Canyon national parks and unusual natural rock formations at Natural Bridges and Rainbow Bridge national monuments. Despite its reputation for deserts and salt flats, the state also includes 11,000 miles of fishing streams and 147,000 acres of freshwater lakes and reservoirs. The principal places associated with the Mormon church surround the Mormon Tabernacle in Salt Lake City.

New Mexico

Abbreviations: *N.M., NM*
Area: *121,412 sq. mi., 314,457 sq. km.*
Rank (of 50) *5th*
Population:
1985 *1,450,000*
Rank (of 50) *37th*
Change 1980–85 *+147,000*
Percent change *+11.3*
Persons per sq. mi. *12*
Percent urban *72.1*
Capital: *Santa Fe*
Largest city: *Albuquerque*
Metro. pop. 1985 *464,000*
Entered Union: *Jan. 6, 1912 (47th)*
State bird: *Roadrunner*
State flower: *Yucca*
State tree: *Piñon*

New Mexico is the most southern of Mountain states, directly south of Colorado. It borders Arizona on the west, Texas and Oklahoma on the east, and Texas and Mexico on the south. It is rectangular in shape, except for its irregular southern border with Mexico and Texas. The southern extreme of the Rocky Mountain chain extends into New Mexico from the north, and it is along the edges of the mountains that most residents of the state have settled.

New Mexico is unusual because it is the most Spanish-influenced of U.S. states, with traditions passed down by Spanish settlers of the 1700's. At the same time it is a center of America's most modern military technology, symbolized by the northern city of Los Alamos, where the first atomic bomb was constructed. The state also has a large American Indian population. In recent years the area around Santa Fe and Taos has attracted many artists and writers.

The state was nearly ruined by a long drought followed by the Depression of the 1930's, but since World War II it has experienced increasing prosperity because of government spending and improvements in living conditions provided by modern irrigation and air-conditioning techniques.

The land. New Mexico's complex topography begins with the foot of the southern Rocky Mountains in the north-central region. The mountains protrude 100 miles into the state to a point near Santa Fe and contain the headwaters of the Rio Grande River, which flows south through the center of the state. To the east of the river lie the southern reaches of the Great Plains. This flat tableland, averaging over 4000 feet in elevation, joins the high plains of Texas across the state's eastern and southern borders. West of the Rio Grande, New Mexico includes portions of the Colorado Plateau in the north and portions of the intermontane basin and range in the south. The Colorado Plateau is a scenic mesa, butte, and canyon region broken by mountain ranges approaching 10,000 feet in elevation. The southwest basin and range region is a semi-arid desert characterized by low mountain ranges separated by elongated dry desert floors.

Climate. The climate is one of warm days and cool nights, with winter temperature averages ranging from 55° F in the south to 35 in the north and summer ones ranging over 80 throughout the state. New Mexico is an exceptionally dry state. In Albuquerque precipitation averages about 8 inches annually, although high mountains receive much more rain.

Principal cities. A third of the state's population reside in metropolitan Albuquerque, established by the Spanish in 1706. The city is the financial, educational, and industrial center of the state. Santa Fe (population 48,899), 60 miles north at the foot of the Rockies, is the state capital and a popular resort center for artists, musicians, and writers. It was the capital of a Spanish overseas province as early as 1610, before the Pilgrims had landed in New England. The third largest city is Las Cruces (population 45,086), on the Rio Grande only 50 miles from El Paso, Texas, and Juárez, in Mexico.

The people. The population of New Mexico is 37 percent Hispanic, and Spanish is in common use among a third of the state's residents. New Mexico also contains a population of over 100,000 American Indians, making it second only to Arizona and Oklahoma. The major tribes in the state are Zuni, Apache, and Navajo. The growth rate of the population is not as high as that for Colorado or Arizona, but at 28 percent, it is still more than twice the national average.

Economy. The chief industry in New Mexico, accounting for three-fifths of its commerce, is mining. The state is the country's leading producer of potash, perlite, and uranium. New Mexico also produces large amounts of energy fuels. It ranks second to Wyoming among Mountain states in petroleum drilling, a business conducted in the southeastern region known as "Little Texas." New Mexico ranks fourth in the United States in natural gas production, an industry also based in the southeast. New Mexico's resources have combined to help the state rank ninth among U.S. states in mining.

The state's agricultural production is chiefly of livestock, with some hay and cotton crops. Manufacturers in New Mexico produce large quantities of stone, clay, and glass products, but the most important manufactures are electric and transportation equipment associated with the U.S. military.

Places of interest. Among the principal natural features of interest in New Mexico are the Carlsbad Caverns, located in the extreme southeast near the corner of the Texas border; they include the largest cave in the United States. The basin and range region in the southwest is the site of extensive ancient pueblo ruins at the Gila Cliff Dwellings National Monument. The Colorado Plateau in the northwest is the location of Indian reservations as well as places associated with the state's mining and cowboy history.

MORMON PIONEERS *sought religious freedom in a beautiful but demanding wilderness. This statue commemorating them stands in Salt Lake City.*

SEF/EPA

The Oil States

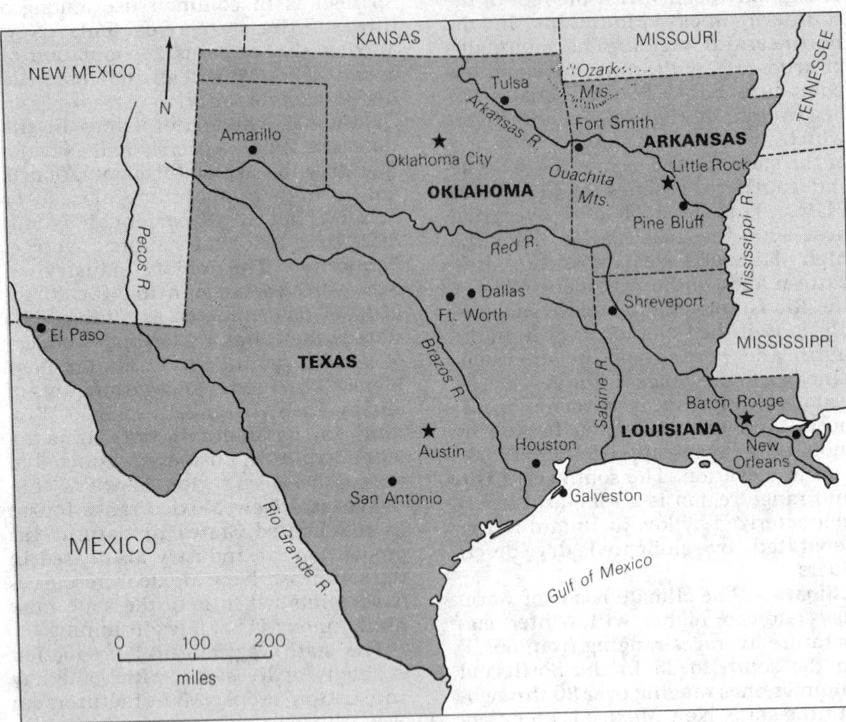

THE OIL STATES

State	Area (sq. mi.)	Population 1985	Population change 1980–85 number	Population change 1980–85 percent	Persons per sq. mi.
Texas	262,134	16,370,000	+2,140,000	+15.0	62
Oklahoma	68,782	3,301,000	+ 276,000	+ 9.1	48
Louisiana	44,930	4,481,000	+ 275,000	+ 6.5	101
Arkansas	51,945	2,359,000	+ 72,000	+ 3.2	45
Region totals	427,791	26,511,000	+2,763,000	+11.6	62

The Oil states, Texas, Oklahoma, Arkansas, and Louisiana, are in the south-central United States. In the southwest the region borders Mexico across the Rio Grande River, and in the southeast it has a long shoreline on the Gulf of Mexico. The U.S. borders are with the southernmost Mountain state of New Mexico on the west, the Grain states on the north, and the South-Central states across the Mississippi River on the east.

The Oil states are growing rapidly, both because of their reserves of fossil fuel and because of poor economic conditions in Northern states. In the 1960's the region's growth was sluggish and it lost 40,000 residents to employment opportunities elsewhere. In the 1970's, however, a general enthusiasm for "Sun Belt" life brought an influx of 1.5 million migrants, most of them to Texas.

The region had long been the principal oil producer in the United States, but skyrocketing fuel costs during the 1970's greatly increased the income of the oil industry. All states in the region produce large quantities of oil; they also account for most of the country's natural gas, an increasingly valuable fuel. In addition, the region exports drilling machinery and sends experts to oil-rich areas around the world.

The land. The major topographical feature within the region is the Gulf Coastal Plain. The plain extends north from the Gulf itself along the Mississippi embayment, or river valley, narrowing to a point and ending in southern Illinois. Consequently, the Gulf Coastal Plain covers a wide area of southeast Texas, all of Louisiana, and the south and east of Arkansas.

Along the region's eastern boundary is a strip of alluvial land built up by Mississippi River silt, and in southern Louisiana the Mississippi delta was created by the same process. Eastern Oklahoma and western Arkansas share a portion of interior highland consisting of the Ozark Plateau and the Ouachita Mountains. The western panhandle of Oklahoma and western Texas lie within the Great Plains, a treeless tableland reaching 4000 feet above sea level. The highest elevations in the region are found in extreme western Texas, which is a part of the Mexican Highlands.

Climate. The entire region has a moderate climate, with rainfall and temperatures highest along the Gulf Coast. Louisiana experiences temperatures over 70° F for much of the year and an annual rainfall of over 50 inches. Its climate is humid and semitropical. Farther inland, in Oklahoma and west Texas, however, rainfall declines to less than 30 inches per year. The weather is dry, and seasonal temperature extremes vary from below freezing in winter to more than 90 in summer.

History. The Oil states were first explored by the Spanish from Florida and the French from Canada in the first half of the 1500's. The region was subject to a series of conflicting claims after settlement had begun. Louisiana, Arkansas, and Oklahoma came to the United States as part of the 1803 Louisiana Purchase. The two eastern states gained statehood before 1840. Texas was still part of Mexico when that country became independent from Spain in 1821. The American settlers in Texas rebelled in 1836, and Texas entered the Union as a state in 1845 after existing nine years as a republic. Oklahoma was designated an Indian territory before being opened to homesteaders in the 1890's. It gained statehood in 1907.

The people. This history has left the region with an unusual mix of people. Texas has one of the highest proportions of Hispanic residents in the country, and Oklahoma contains a large American Indian population. Louisiana is unique in its population of Creoles, descendants of early Spanish and French peoples, and Cajuns, descendants of French Acadians from Canada. The black population is largest in Arkansas, where it represents 16 percent of the total, and Louisiana, where it represents 29 percent.

Principal cities. Two out of every three residents of the Oil states live in urban areas. The two largest metropolitan areas are Houston–Galveston, near the Texas Gulf Coast, and Dallas–Fort Worth, 200 miles north and inland from Houston. Other cities with more than a million metropolitan residents are New Orleans, Louisiana, and San Antonio, Texas. The major cities in the north are Oklahoma City and Little Rock, Arkansas.

Economy. Houston is the largest city in the region because it is the seat of the oil industry. The region produces 54 percent of the total U.S. output of crude petroleum and 80 percent of the nation's natural gas. In addition to the mining income fuels generate, manufacturing industries have been created in the Oil states, especially in Texas and Louisiana, to refine and ship the oil and gas and produce equipment for drilling. Although principally known for its fuels, the region is also third in the United States in agriculture. Cattle and irrigated grain crops for feed predominate in relatively dry Texas and Oklahoma, and large crops of soybeans and rice are harvested in Louisiana and Arkansas.

Texas

Abbreviations: *Tex., TX*
Area: *262,134 sq. mi., 678,927 sq. km.*
Rank (of 50) *2nd*
Population:
1985 *16,370,000*
Rank (of 50) *3rd*
Change 1980–85 *+2,140,000*
Percent change *+15.0*
Persons per sq. mi. *62*
Percent urban *79.6*
Capital: *Austin*
Largest city: *Houston*
Metro. pop. 1985 *3,222,000*
Entered Union: *Dec. 29, 1845 (28th)*
State bird: *Mockingbird*
State flower: *Bluebonnet*
State tree: *Pecan*

Texas, the largest in area of the 48 contiguous states, is located in the south-central United States between the Red River, which separates it from Oklahoma to the north, and the Rio Grande River, which separates it from Mexico to the south. Three extensions of the state give it its characteristic shape: the Panhandle in the north, the Pecos region extending west between Mexico and New Mexico, and the lower Rio Grande valley to the south, between the river and the Gulf of Mexico.

Once a territory of Mexico, Texas revolted and became an independent republic for nearly a decade beginning in 1836. Its independence and its enormous land area, greater than that of France, have combined to give Texans a special sense of pride in their state. Until 1900, this pride was associated with rugged ranchers and cowboys, but the discovery of oil at the turn of the century transformed the state's economy and glamorized oilmen of enormous wealth and buying power. The full importance of the Texas oil fields became apparent in the 1970's, when increased petroleum prices supported an expansion of the state's manufacturing sector and attracted more than a million Americans from other states.

The land. The surface of Texas is generally a series of plains rising in elevation as they extend north and west from the Gulf of Mexico. There are four principal divisions: Coastal Plain, Central Lowland, Great Plains, and Basin and Range. The Coastal Plain is the largest area, covering most of the eastern half of the state from the Red River in the north to the Rio Grande valley in the south. It rises in elevation from sea level at the water's edge to over 500 feet inland. The largest cities are within this region.

The Central Lowland covers north-central Texas from the Oklahoma border almost 200 miles south. Ranging in elevation from 1000 to 2000 feet, this hilly region is an extension of the Osage Plains in Oklahoma and Kansas. The Great Plains cover a belt from the Panhandle in the north to the Pecos and Rio Grande rivers in the south. This region includes flat and arid high plains in the north, the steep Central Texas Hills, and limestone escarpments in the south. The western extension of the state is a part of the Mexican Highlands of the Basin and Range region. It includes the highest elevations in the state.

Climate. Summer temperatures are fairly consistent throughout Texas, with highs averaging in the low 90's F, but the weather is humid near the Gulf Coast and very dry in the west and north. Winters are far colder in the interior, where snow falls, than on the coast, where frost is uncommon. Precipitation ranges from 60 inches per year in the far eastern section to only 7 inches in the extreme west. Winter may bring blizzards to the Panhandle in the north, and in summer, the Gulf Coast may encounter hurricanes.

Principal cities. Texas includes two of the largest and fastest-growing metropolitan regions in the United States. Houston–Galveston, near the Gulf Coast, includes 3 million people and increased by 1 million in the 1970's. Once an uninhabited swampland, the city has become the headquarters of many U.S. oil companies and the center of the aerospace industry. Dallas–Fort Worth, about 200 miles north, at the inland edge of the Coastal Plain, includes 2.9 million people in its metropolitan area and grew rapidly in the 1960's and '70's. It is also a banking and insurance capital. San Antonio, in the south-central region, has a population of over 1 million. It is the site of the famous fort called the Alamo, where defenders of Texas's independence were wiped out in a siege by the Mexican army. Other important cities include Amarillo, in the northern Panhandle, and El Paso, at the state's extreme western border with Mexico and New Mexico.

The people. The population of Texas nearly doubled between 1950 and 1980, making Texas both the fastest growing and most urban of the Oil states. Texas has the highest proportion of Hispanic population in the United States, 21 percent. Most are of Mexican descent. More than 1.8 million, or 13 percent of the population, are black Americans.

Economy. Mineral wealth is the historical and present basis of Texas's growth and prosperity. Oil has been found in 200 of the state's 254 counties, but the west Texas fields near Lubbock are the richest. Even after the Alaska oil pipeline was opened, Texas continued to produce as much crude oil as that state. The second most important mineral resource is natural gas; Texas ranks second to Louisiana. Texas is also among the U.S. leaders in sulfur production.

Next to California, Texas is the largest manufacturing state west of the Mississippi. Petroleum refining and production of drilling equipment are the largest industries. Other products include aerospace equipment, chemicals, and processed food.

Texas is also second to California among all U.S. states in total farm products. Five times as much land is devoted to livestock as to crops, and Texas produces twice as many beef cattle and sheep as any other state. Although most of its crop lands must be irrigated by wells or rivers, Texas produces half the crops of the Oil states region. It grows more cotton than any state in the United States, and it also produces large crops of sorghum, rice, and peanuts.

Places of interest. Padre Island National Seashore, along the southern Gulf Coast, and Big Bend National Park, along the Rio Grande, are among Texas's major tourist attractions. There are striking examples of desert, mountain, and plains scenery throughout the state, and many cultural and recreational attractions in the major cities. The principal historic attractions are the Alamo in San Antonio, the Lyndon Johnson birthplace and Presidential library 60 miles north of San Antonio, and the border cities of Laredo and El Paso on the Rio Grande.

Oklahoma

Abbreviations: *Okla., OK*
Area: *68,782 sq. mi., 178,145 sq. km.*
Rank (of 50) *19th*
Population:
1985 *3,301,000*
Rank (of 50) *25th*
Change 1980–85 *+276,000*
Percent change *+9.1*
Persons per sq. mi. *48*
Percent urban *67.3*
Capital: *Oklahoma City*
Largest city: *Oklahoma City*
Metro. pop. 1985 *976,000*
Entered Union: *Nov. 16, 1907 (46th)*
State bird: *Scissor-tailed flycatcher*
State flower: *Mistletoe*
State tree: *Redbud*

FORSYTH/MONKMEYER

PAKIS/OKLAHOMA TOURISM & RECREATION DEPT.

MODERN AND TRADITIONAL *compete for attention in the Oil states. The Hyatt Regency Hotel in Dallas,* left, *is a symbol of the dynamic and prosperous new cities. The main street of Cordell, Oklahoma, dominated by the county courthouse, recalls the Southwest of earlier times.*

Oklahoma is situated in the south-central United States, north of Texas. It also borders Kansas to the north and Arkansas and Missouri to the east. The shape of the otherwise rectangular state is distinguished by the 35-mile-wide panhandle that extends 165 miles due west to a New Mexico boundary.

Oklahoma was originally set aside by the U.S. federal government as an Indian territory. In 1889, however, the government decided to open the territory to homesteaders. Ten land rushes ensued in the following decade. Homesteaders lined up in wagons at the border, ready to rush across and claim their land. Those who sneaked across the border early were called "Sooners," a nickname now applied to state residents.

During the droughts of the 1930's, Oklahoma turned into a dust bowl. Thousands of people called "Okies" left for California in search of watered farmland. Since that time the state has returned to economic prosperity because of the extensive Arkansas River Navigation Project, soil and water conservation acts, and the construction of huge multipurpose dams. Once a predominantly agricultural state, Oklahoma's economic base has been broadened by tapping its mineral resources, especially oil and natural gas.

The land. The surface of Oklahoma is an irregular one, sloping gradually upward from 400 feet in the southeast to nearly 5000 feet in the extreme west. Rough distinctions can be drawn among three principal topographical areas: the Great Plains of the panhandle, the hills and mountains of the east, and the central lowland between them covering most of the state area.

The Great Plains cover the three counties in the panhandle, a 4000-foot high plateau bisected west to east by the Beaver River. The state high point of Black Mesa (4973 feet) is located in the extreme west of the panhandle beside the New Mexico border. The hills and mountains of the east comprise a 60-mile-wide strip of the Ozark Plateau in the north and the Ouachita Mountains in the south. The Arkansas River valley passes east through these hill regions, and the valley streams throughout it have been dammed to create reservoirs such as the Eufaula Reservoir between the Ozarks and the Ouachitas. Three-fourths of the state area is included in the central lowland between these extremities. The southern lowland region is characterized by low ranges such as the Arbuckle and Wichita mountains, which rarely rise above 1000 feet over ground level. The northern lowland region is characterized by the Redbud Plains, a tableland crossed by small streams lined by sand dunes.

Climate. Despite occasional temperature extremes in summer and winter, Oklahoma's climate is generally a temperate one. Summer highs average above 90° F and winter lows average just below 32. Rainfall is greatest in the southeast, where it averages over 50 inches per year; it declines sharply toward the west to less than 20 inches in the panhandle.

Principal cities. Oklahoma contains two large metropolitan areas. The largest is the capital, Oklahoma City, situated near the center of the state on the Canadian River. The area includes parts of five counties. The hub of a network of interstate highways, Oklahoma City is the state's financial and agricultural business center and the site of several major electronics components manufacturers. Tulsa (population 678,627) in the northeast is the center of the state's oil industry and a base for aerospace and airline businesses. The Arkansas River Navigation Project has helped make Tulsa an important inland port, receiving and sending goods by barge down the Arkansas to the Mississippi and the Gulf of Mexico.

The people. Oklahoma was populated by at least 67 Indian tribes, many of them transported there by the U.S. government before the land rushes brought a wave of settlers from eastern states. Between 1890 and 1910, the era of land openings for homesteaders, the population of Oklahoma rose from about 250,000 to more than 1.6 million, a number which the state has yet to double. Today the population is nearly 6 percent American Indian. This Indian population of about 175,000 is unique in the United States because the state has no formal Indian reservations. This has caused hardships for Indians, but it has also encouraged assimilation. The total population of the state shrank by 60,000 during the dust bowl drought of the 1930's, and it did not return to its 1930 level until nearly 1970. During the 1970's, however, nearly 300,000 Americans immigrated to Oklahoma from other states. Other than American Indians, the only significant ethnic group in the state today is black Americans, who represent nearly 6 percent of the population.

Economy. Oklahoma ranks fifth in the production of crude oil and third in natural gas among U.S. states. Mineral fuels account for 95 percent of the state's mining industry income, which is ranked fourth overall in the United States. The remaining mining products are principally sand, gravel, stone, and other quarry spoil. The largest oil fields are in the state's south-central regions, and the major natural gas fields are in the panhandle. Production of coal, once the state's primary mineral product, has diminished to insignificant levels.

Manufacturing actually exceeds mining in value, but most of the income from manufacturing is derived from refining mineral products or producing drilling equipment. Agriculture was the traditional basis of the local economy, and nearly 80 percent of the land area of Oklahoma remains farmland. Two-thirds of the state farm income is derived from livestock. The principal crops are winter wheat, sorghum, and cotton lint, all of which are grown on irrigated portions of the central lowland.

Places of interest. Oklahoma is rich in places of Indian interest, especially the Fort Gibson Stockade and Cherokee Cultural Center near Muskogee in the Arkansas River valley. Other attractions include the Ouachita National Forest, the National Cowboy Hall of Fame in Oklahoma City, and the Will Rogers Memorial in Claremore near Tulsa.

Louisiana

Abbreviations: *La., LA*
Area: *44,930 sq. mi., 116,369 sq. km.*
Rank (of 50) *33rd*
Population:
1985 *4,481,000*
Rank (of 50) *18th*
Change 1980–85 *+275,000*
Percent change *+6.5*
Persons per sq. mi. *101*
Percent urban *68.6*
Capital: *Baton Rouge*
Largest city: *New Orleans*
Metro. pop. 1985 *1,324,000*
Entered Union: *April 30, 1812 (18th)*
State bird: *Eastern brown pelican*
State flower: *Magnolia blossom*
State tree: *Bald cypress*

Louisiana lies in the south-central United States, bordering Texas to the west and Arkansas to the north. The state is shaped like an hourglass, wide at top and bottom and narrowest in the middle. Its eastern border with Mississippi is formed by the Mississippi River, except in the south, where the state has a large extension of land to the east of the river, which includes New Orleans and Baton Rouge, the two major cities. The state's southern boundary is the irregular shore of the Gulf of Mexico, formed principally by the Mississippi River delta.

Louisiana is the most culturally foreign of all U.S. states. Its local governmental units are 64 parishes, rather than counties. Its civil laws are greatly influenced by the legal systems of France and Spain, from which many of its original settlers came. Its population includes large numbers of Creoles, descendants of French and Spanish settlers, and Cajuns, descendants of French settlers who were driven from Nova Scotia in Canada by the British after 1760. The presence of French and Spanish influence is most obvious in New Orleans, with its French Quarter, Mardi Gras celebrations, and Creole cookery.

The land. All of the state area lies within the low Gulf Coastal Plain. Local elevations below sea level are common, and the highest point in the state, Driskill Mountain near Arkansas, has an elevation of only 535 feet.

The largest individual feature of the plain is the alluvial floodland west of the Mississippi crossed by the Red, Ouachita, and Alchafalaya rivers. Generally swampy, the floodland is protected from river waters by an extensive system of levees. Only near the state's northern borders with Arkansas and Mississippi does the plain rise into forested hills.

The southern portion of the state has been swollen by centuries of silt deposits brought downstream along the Mississippi. This delta region is a fertile lowland full of bayous, or freshwater inlets from the river. The entire Gulf Coast is a swampy region where marshes cover extensive mineral deposits.

Climate. Louisiana has a generally subtropical climate influenced more by the Gulf of Mexico than by inland weather patterns. At New Orleans, low temperatures rarely fall below 50° F, and high temperatures average 65 in winter and 90 in summer. Louisiana is one of the wettest states in the country, with rainfall averaging well over 50 inches per year.

Principal cities. Louisiana's major city is New Orleans, situated in the southeast 100 miles above the mouth of the Mississippi. Its metropolitan area of well over 1 million represents nearly 30 percent of the state's population. The city is the exportation point for most of the Mississippi valley and the second largest port in the country after New York. The capital city of Baton Rouge, 100 miles upstream from New Orleans, has a metropolitan area population of nearly one-half million and it is another large deepwater port. The only major city in northern Louisiana is Shreveport, a manufacturing center in the extreme northwest with a metropolitan population approaching 400,000.

The people. Rural northern Louisiana has a population and lifestyle similar to that of other Oil states. Southern Louisiana includes most of the state's Cajun and Creole population and cosmopolitan city centers. One in six state residents speaks French. The French-speaking community is almost entirely located in the southern swamplands and bayous near the Gulf Coast.

The state also has had a large black population since the Spanish slave-trade era. Today the black population is 29 percent of the state's total, a proportion that has declined slightly since 1960. The major population pattern within the state since World War II has been one of urbanization; between 1940 and 1980 the proportion of the population living in urban areas increased from 40 to nearly 70 percent.

Economy. After 1945 Louisiana was gradually transformed from an agricultural to an industrial state. Virtually all of its industry is located in the southern regions of the state. The oil industry, including both the drilling and refining of crude oil, is the largest and the fastest growing sector of the state economy. Louisiana is also the nation's largest producer of natural gas, and it ranks third to Texas and Alaska in production of crude oil.

Most oil drilling is located along the Gulf Coast, and in recent years offshore drilling rigs have accounted for 20 percent of the state's petroleum production. The principal oil refineries are located south of Baton Rouge, and the 100-mile river corridor between Baton Rouge and New Orleans is lined with manufacturers of food products and transportation equipment as well as oil-related industries.

Tourism, principally in New Orleans and the coastal region, is also a major industry. The agricultural businesses that once dominated the state economy continue to produce large soybean, rice, and cotton crops.

Places of interest. The principal attraction in Louisiana is New Orleans, where modern structures such as the Superdome have been added to older sites of historical and cultural interest. Plantations are preserved near New Iberia in the south-central region. The Mississippi delta region includes places of Cajun interest and Chalmette National Historical Park.

Arkansas

Abbreviations: *Ark., AR*
Area: *51,945 sq. mi., 134,538 sq. km.*
Rank (of 50) *27th*
Population:
1985 *2,359,000*
Rank (of 50) *33rd*
Change 1980–85 *+72,000*
Percent change *+3.2*
Persons per sq. mi. *45*
Percent urban *51.6*
Capital: *Little Rock*
Largest city: *Little Rock*
Metro. pop. 1985 *499,000*
Entered Union: *June 15, 1836 (25th)*
State bird: *Mockingbird*
State flower: *Apple blossom*
State tree: *Pine*

Arkansas is situated in the south-central United States on the west shore of the Mississippi River between Louisiana to the south and Missouri to the north. The state's principal western border is with Oklahoma.

For most of its history Arkansas was an agricultural state heavily reliant on the cotton crop grown near the Mississippi River, but more recently the state has focused on mining and manufacturing. Unlike the states in the Great Plains, Arkansas did not experience severe out-of-state migrations in the 1930's. But between 1940 and 1960, the population shrank by almost 200,000, prompting the state government to encourage a major shift from farming to industry. The result has been a strong resurgence of population, economic growth, and state pride.

The land. The land of Arkansas falls into two areas of approximately equal size: the coastal plain in the east and south, and the interior highlands in the west and north. The coastal plain consists in part of a 50-mile-wide strip of Mississippi alluvial land running parallel to the river. Only about 150 feet above sea level, this tract represents the state's finest farmland. The remainder of the coastal plain consists of plains slightly higher in elevation and much more heavily forested.

The interior highlands consist of the Ozark Plateau in the north and the Ouachita Mountains to the west, with the Arkansas River valley dividing them. The Ozark region is a plateau averaging over 1000 feet in elevation and heavily eroded by streams and rivers flowing east. Its northern extent includes the fertile Springfield Plateau; its southern extent rises into the rugged Boston Mountains. The Ouachitas south of the Arkansas River valley are steep, mineral-rich mountains. The Arkansas River valley itself is 30 to 40 miles wide, and the river falls 300 feet as it flows east to the Mississippi.

Climate. The climate of Arkansas is a mild one influenced by winds from the Gulf of Mexico. The capital city of Little Rock in the center of the state has winter lows of about 30° F and summer highs of 90. Portions of the state to the south have warmer winters, but those to the north have only slightly colder ones. The average rainfall in the state is about 50 inches, most of it falling in winter. Spring and autumn are especially long seasons in the Arkansas climate and they add to the state's growing season.

Principal cities. Arkansas is a state of small towns and a relatively rural population. The only major city is the capital, Little Rock. It is situated on the Arkansas River in the center of the state and is the site of most of the state's manufacturing businesses as well as the seat of the state government. Other manufacturing centers on the Arkansas River are Fort Smith (population 71,384), on the Oklahoma border, and Pine Bluff (population 56,576) 35 miles southeast of Little Rock.

The people. After its major population decline of almost 200,000 between 1940 and 1960, Arkansas managed to build an economy in the 1970's that attracted 136,000 immigrants from other states. Urbanization has increased as a result, but the state remains well below the national average in that respect. Blacks, the major ethnic group, represent 16 percent of the total citizenry.

Economy. During its decades of population decline Arkansas established an Industrial Development Commission to provide legislation beneficial to business. Today the state has extensive mining and manufacturing businesses. It produces most of the U.S. supply of bauxite, the ore from which aluminum is refined, and major portions of the national bromine and vanadium output. Oil and natural gas are drilled in the southern regions of the state.

Recently, manufacturing businesses have developed to process the state's mineral output, which generates more than $5 billion in income per year. Poultry processing has also become a major business since 1940. The state's agricultural decline was related to its small farms and reliance on the cotton crop, but in recent years heavily mechanized farming has converted the cotton fields along the Mississippi River to high-yield crops such as soybeans and rice. The forestry industry on the west Gulf coastal plains presently produces nearly 50 billion board feet of timber per year.

Places of interest. The major tourist attraction in Arkansas is Hot Springs National Park, 45 miles southwest of Little Rock, where mineral waters naturally flow at temperatures up to 147° F throughout the year. Blanchard Springs Caverns in the Ozarks, 60 miles north of Little Rock, are among the largest in the country, and Ouachita and Ozark national forests, covering thousands of acres in the western part of the state, are also of interest.

The Grain States

The Grain states include the heart of the central plains and prairies, occupying a large part of the north-central United States. The region looks west to the Rocky Mountains and east to the Great Lakes region. The Great Plains themselves run north deep into Canada and south into the Oil states of Oklahoma and Texas.

The Great Plains predominate in the western states of the Grain region, including most of North Dakota, South Dakota, Nebraska, and Kansas. Prairie, plateau, and hilly lands predominate in the eastern states of Minnesota, Iowa, and Missouri. The region is dominated by two great rivers: the Mississippi, which rises in Minnesota and forms most of the region's eastern boundary, and the Missouri, which flows through or touches each of the other six states, flowing into the Mississippi near St. Louis, Missouri.

The Grain states are literally at the center: the region contains the geographical center of North America, the geographical center of the United States, and the center point of the U.S. population.

In character, too, the Grain states represent the heartland of the United States. The region is the agricultural center of the nation, with an economy based on grain crops: wheat in Kansas, corn in Iowa, and oats in Minnesota. Much of the grain is intended for livestock feed. The region also exports enormous quantities of meat and dairy products.

From the air, the region is a patchwork of fields, laid out at right angles and differing in color and texture by season and crop. The importance of the Grain states' farm country has been realized since the 1800's, but the region's modern prosperity owes much to farming innovation: hybrid seeds for high yields, chemical fertilizers, and mechanized cultivation.

The land. The eastern Grain states lie in the central lowland drained by the Mississippi River. The plains covering the western Grain states are actually a plateau of this central lowland, rising gradually in elevation from east to west. The dividing line between the areas, known as the Break of the Plains, is a series of steep escarpments running north-south from North Dakota to Kansas. The plains are broken in western areas by mountains such as the Black Hills in South Dakota, where peaks rise more than 3000 feet above the level of the land.

Climate. The climate of the Grain states is known for dramatic seasonal variations. Arctic storms arrive from the northwest without obstruction, causing bitter cold and drifting snow

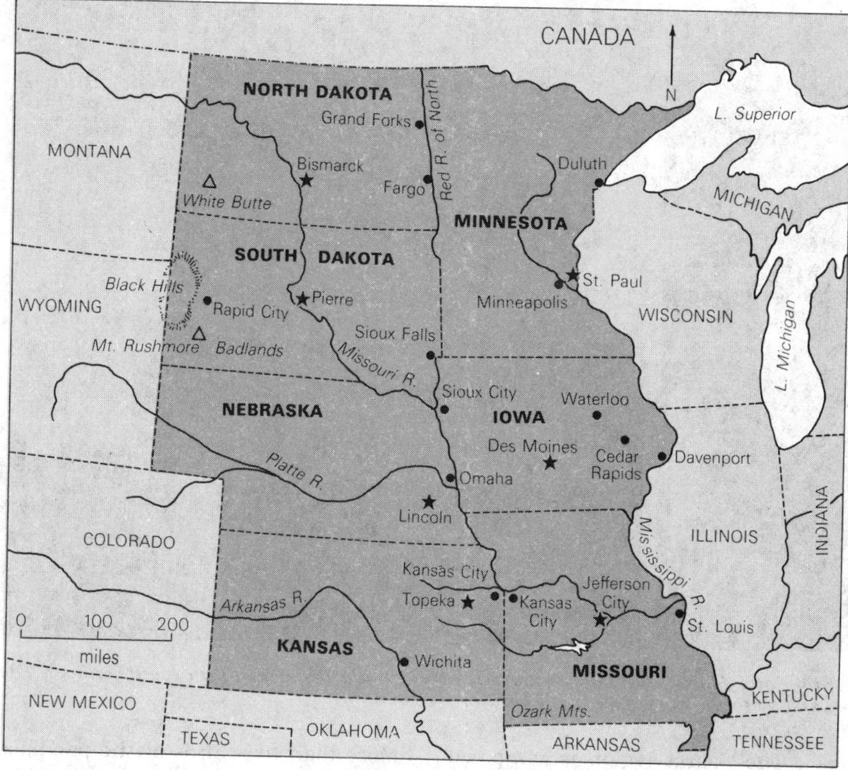

THE GRAIN STATES

State	Area (sq. mi.)	Population 1985	Population change 1980–85 number	percent	Persons per sq. mi.
Missouri	68,955	5,029,000	+112,000	+ 2.3	73
Kansas	81,787	2,450,000	+ 87,000	+ 3.7	30
Nebraska	76,483	1,006,000	+ 36,000	+ 2.3	21
Iowa	55,941	2,884,000	− 30,000	− 1.0	52
South Dakota	75,955	708,000	+ 17,000	+ 2.5	9
North Dakota	69,273	685,000	+ 32,000	+ 4.9	10
Minnesota	79,289	4,193,000	+117,000	+66.9	53
Region totals	507,683	17,555,000	+431,000	+ 2.5	35

in winter. In summer, warm moist air from the Gulf of Mexico brings high humidity to eastern parts of the region. The Grain states have the highest average wind speed of any U.S. region and startling temperature extremes. In North Dakota, for example, record lows are minus 40° F and record highs exceed 110. The region's normal temperatures range from about 80 in summer to about 10 in winter, with southern states more moderate in climate than northern ones. Rainfall averages over 30 inches per year near the Mississippi, where crops predominate, but it is significantly lighter on the plains, where cattle grazing is more common and agriculture only possible with irrigation in some areas. Rapid changes in weather are common in all seasons, with fast-moving weather fronts creating thunder showers, tornadoes, sudden changes of temperature, and winter blizzards.

History. The initial exploration of the Grain states was carried out by Francisco de Coronado in 1541, but it was the expeditions south from Canada by Marquette, Jolliet, and La Salle in the 1600's that first brought notice to the region. French influence continued until most of this land area came into U.S. hands with the Louisiana Purchase of 1803. In 1804, Lewis and Clark began their exploration of the new territory by following the Missouri River to its source.

The earliest settlers in most of the region were adventurous farmers from eastern territories looking for good farmland. As they established homesteads, violent clashes erupted between these pioneers and Indian tribes, notably the Sioux who hunted buffalo on the plains. The Indian wars flared from about 1810 until 1870, and skirmishes in remoter regions continued for another 20 years.

The Grain states grew rapidly from the 1880's to the 1930's, when drought in the western plains and economic depression ruined the agriculture-based economy. It was only after World War II that improvements in farming techniques and increasing manufactures restored the economy.

The people. Most Grain states, particularly those on the western plains, continue to lose residents to migration. Only the natural population increase, the result of a high birthrate and a decreasing death rate, accounts for the region's small population growth. Because of the pattern of migration from these states, the region has an overall population that is relatively old, rural, and low in ethnic mix.

Principal cities. Despite relatively low growth, the Grain states have several thriving cities, primarily in their eastern half. Kansas City, on the Missouri–Kansas line, is a major business and commercial center. Omaha, on the Nebraska–Iowa border, serves a large central area. Minneapolis–St. Paul, in the north, is the cultural and business capital of the northern plains. St. Louis, near the southeastern corner of the region, serves as a connecting city to the Great Lakes region to the east and to the nearby Southern states.

Economy. The Grain region includes all U.S. states with more than 90 percent of their land area devoted to agriculture: North Dakota, South Dakota, Nebraska, Kansas, and Iowa. The region also includes the nation's leading producers of wheat, corn, oats, soybeans, and several other crops. These crops support large livestock and dairy industries and serve as raw materials for the food processing industry. In addition, the region includes the principal U.S. producer of iron ore, in Minnesota, and of gold, in South Dakota.

Missouri

Abbreviations: *Mo., MO*
Area: *68,955 sq. mi., 178,697 sq. km.*
Rank (of 50) *18th*
Population:
1985 *5,029,000*
Rank (of 50) *15th*
Change 1980–85 *+112,000*
Percent change *+2.3*
Persons per sq. mi. *73*
Percent urban *68.1*
Capital: *Jefferson City*
Largest city: *St. Louis*
Metro. pop. 1985 *2,412,000*
Entered Union: *Aug. 10, 1821 (24th)*
State bird: *Bluebird*
State flower: *Hawthorne*
State tree: *Dogwood*

Missouri, the most southeastern of the Grain states, is situated on the west bank of the Mississippi River. It borders Iowa to the north and Kansas and Nebraska to the west. To the south and east, it touches states of several other

AMERICAN ANGUS ASSOCIATION

TUZLER/PETER ARNOLD

GRAIN AND LIVESTOCK *are the lifeblood of the Grain states. Most of the grain is stored in elevators like these, then fed to cattle or hogs. The final product—meat—is prepared in packinghouses and sent to food markets in all parts of the country.*

regions: the Oil states of Oklahoma and Arkansas, the South-Central states of Tennessee and Kentucky, and the Great Lakes state of Illinois. The Missouri River forms the upper third of the state's western border and then turns east to cross the state and join the Mississippi just north of St. Louis.

In the early 1800's, Missouri became the gateway between the upper and lower reaches of the Mississippi River. St. Louis became the principal city north of New Orleans and prospered from the river trade. Later in the century, Missouri became the "Gateway to the West." Independence, near the western border, became the starting point for generations of settlers taking the Santa Fe or the Oregon trails to the western lands. Independence and neighboring Kansas City later were important depots on the new transcontinental railroads. This prominence in commerce and transportation has made Missouri the most populous, urban, and industrial of the Grain states. In many ways it continues to function as a link between east and west. Its principal cities, St. Louis in the east and Kansas City in the west, lie almost 250 miles apart and face neighboring states as different as Illinois and Kansas. In 1980 the U.S. center of population, a symbol of the relations between east and west, moved west of the Mississippi River for the first time to the small town of De Soto, Missouri, near St. Louis.

The land. The area north of the Missouri River consists of fertile plains like those of Iowa to the north. South of the Missouri River are the Osage Plains along the western border. The remainder of the land consists of the hillier and more forested Ozark Plateau. The Ozarks region is composed of steep hills and manmade lakes, such as the Lake of the Ozarks near the center of the state. One unusual feature of the Ozarks is the number of springs, caves, and sinkholes created by groundwater dissolving the limestone bed of the plateau. In the extreme southeast of the state, the "boot heel" that extends into Arkansas includes a stretch of Mississippi alluvial plain, a fertile farming area.

Climate. Missouri has a mild, humid climate. High summer temperatures average near 90° F and winter lows average about 20. Rainfall averages over 35 inches per year, and it is heavier in the east than in the west of the state.

Principal cities. St. Louis in the east and Kansas City in the west are representative of Missouri's ties to neighboring states. With a metropolitan area including parts of Illinois, St. Louis is a city of heavy industry, resembling those in the Great Lakes states. It is second only to Detroit as a producer of automobiles and trucks and the home of a major aerospace manufacturer, the McDonnell-Douglas Corporation. The city ranks tenth in the United States in number of major corporations, and it is noted for its breweries, aluminum plants, and electrical component manufacturers. Kansas City (metropolitan population 1.3 million) lies in a metropolitan area that includes parts of Kansas. It is a center of the nation's food industry. The major businesses are stockyards and cereal grain mills.

The people. Missouri had a population of over 3 million before 1900. Its growth since then has been gradual, reaching 4.7 million in 1980. More than two-thirds of the populace are lifelong residents of the state. There has been considerable movement within the state, however: rural population declined and urban population increased rapidly. Black Americans represent 10 percent of the total population, and they are heavily concentrated in urban areas.

Economy. Missouri is the third largest manufacturing state west of the Mississippi, after California and Texas. Its combination of heavy industry and food processing, concentrated in St. Louis and Kansas City respectively, earns the state well over $15 billion each year.

Agriculture continues to be a major industry. Missouri grows a variety of crops because of its position between the Corn Belt to the north and the Cotton Belt to the south. Income derived from livestock is twice that from crops, with cattle grazing concentrated north of the Missouri River and dairy farming south of it. There is also a large mining industry operating in the Ozarks. It produces large quantities of lead, iron, and zinc. Tourism, principally to the Ozarks, brings the state $3 billion per year.

Places of interest. The principal natural attraction of Missouri is the Ozarks, which can be toured along the Ozark National Scenic Riverway. Mark Twain's boyhood hometown of Hannibal is located along the northern part of Missouri's Mississippi shoreline; it includes the Mark Twain Cave and many other places related to his life and works. Other notable sights include the 630-foot Gateway Arch in St. Louis, the Pony Express Museum in St. Joseph, and the Harry S. Truman Library in Independence.

Kansas

Abbreviations: *Kan., KS*
Area: *81,787 sq. mi., 211,828 sq. km.*
Rank (of 50) *13th*
Population:
1985 *2,450,000*
Rank (of 50) *32nd*
Change 1980–85 *+87,000*
Percent change *+3.7*
Persons per sq. mi. *30*
Percent urban *66.7*
Capital: *Topeka*
Largest city: *Wichita*
Metro. pop. 1985 *435,000*
Entered Union: *Jan. 29, 1861 (34th)*
State bird: *Western meadowlark*
State flower: *Sunflower*
State tree: *Cottonwood*

Kansas is located at the center of North America. The geodetic center, or reference point, for maps of the continent lies in Osborne County in north-central Kansas. Among the U.S. regions it lies in the southwest of the Grain states, bordering Colorado to the west and Oklahoma to the south, with a northeastern corner just brushed by the Missouri River.

Among Grain states, Kansas ranks first in land area and third to Missouri and Minnesota in population. Its history has been a turbulent one, with Civil War confrontations violent enough to give it the name "bleeding Kansas." With the coming of the first railroads, a period of wild cattle drives from Texas to railheads in Kansas made towns like Dodge City a symbol of the lawless West. Since those times Kansas has endured droughts and economic depressions to become the wheat state of America, producer of one-quarter of the national crop. More recently, diversified manufacturing has begun to challenge agriculture as the basis of the state economy.

The land. The topography of Kansas is entirely one of plains, but the surface of the state has significant detail. The elevation of the land rises from less than 1000 feet in the extreme east to over 4000 in the extreme west. Across this rising slope are three distinct areas. The eastern third includes the hilly Osage Plains and the glacial Till Plains that extend into Kansas from Nebraska. The central third is known as the Plains Border, a level region characterized by isolated low ranges such as the Blue Hills and the Red Hills. The western third is composed of High Plains, a flat, treeless expanse so arid that many of its rivers completely dry up for portions of the year. Kansas's agricultural prominence is related to its soil's natural growth of grasses, and each of its three regions is associated with a particular growth of grass: tall grass in the east, mixed grasses in the central third, and short grass in the west.

Climate. Like most Grain states, Kansas has a variable climate characterized by seasonal extremes because of the absence of mountains or bodies of water in the surrounding areas. Normal daily highs are above 90° F in summer and below 20 in winter. Rainfall is heaviest in summer, and it averages about 40 inches per year in the southeast and about half that in the west. Sudden changes of weather in Kansas often take the form of hailstorms, thunderstorms, or tornadoes. Winter blizzards are also common.

Principal cities. All of Kansas's large cities are in the state's eastern third. The largest city entirely in Kansas is Wichita, located in the southeast at the confluence of the Arkansas and Little Arkansas rivers. The principal manufacturer of private aircraft in the United States, Wichita is also the wholesale and retail center for a large area that includes northern Oklahoma as well as Kansas. Kansas City lies in the northeast of the state at the junction of the Kansas and Missouri rivers. Kansas City, Kansas, has a relatively small population of 161,087, but its metropolitan area, which centers around Kansas City, Missouri, has a total population of more than 1.3 million. It is also a distribution center for areas beyond the Kansas state borders. The capital city of Topeka, with a metropolitan population of 185,442, lies to the west of Kansas City. All three of these principal cities dropped in rank among metropolitan areas in the 1970's.

The people. Kansas was famous after the Civil War for opening its borders to freed slaves, and it continues to have a high proportion of blacks (5 percent) for a Grain state. The state was settled by Germans, Russians, and other European nationalities, and presently 8 percent of the population considers itself of foreign stock. Like all western Grain states, Kansas experienced a severe population decline during the 1930's. A severe drought destroyed the farm economy in the west, and thousands left the state in search of greener pastures. Migration from Kansas continued through the 1970's but its population increased slightly because of a higher birthrate than death rate.

Economy. Kansas leads all Grain states in farm acreage and produces more than twice the amount of wheat grown by any other state. Most of the wheat crop is grown in the central third of the state, and huge crops of sorghum grain are grown on irrigated lands in the western third. However, most of the state's farm income is derived from livestock, grazed on these same mixed grass and short grass plains. Since World War II Kansas has emerged as a leading manufacturing state. The manufacturing sector, mainly in Wichita, Kansas City, and Topeka, is based on food processing and transportation equipment. It employs nearly 20 percent of the state work force and is valued at $6.1 billion per year. Kansas also ranks 16th among all U.S. states in mining, chiefly because of the natural gas reserves in the western plains, where more helium is extracted from the natural gas than in any other state.

Places of interest. The primary attractions in Kansas are Dodge City, with its recreated Front Street, in the southwest; the Eisenhower Museum at Abilene near the center of the state; preserved landmarks of the Santa Fe Trail; and early military outposts.

Nebraska

Abbreviations: *Neb., NE*
Area: *76,483 sq. mi., 198,091 sq. km.*
Rank (of 50) *15th*
Population:
1985 *1,606,000*
Rank (of 50) *36th*
Change 1980–85 *+36,000*
Percent change *+2.3*
Persons per sq. mi. *21*
Percent urban *62.9*
Capital: *Lincoln*
Largest city: *Omaha*
Metro. pop. 1985 *612,000*
Entered Union: *Mar. 1, 1867 (37th)*
State bird: *Western meadowlark*
State flower: *Goldenrod*
State tree: *Cottonwood*

Nebraska lies at the very heart of the U.S. Grain states region. Its borders are with South Dakota to the north, Iowa to the east, and Kansas to the south. On the west, it touches the Mountain states of Colorado and Wyoming. Part of its northern border and all of its eastern border are formed by the Missouri River.

Nebraska is one of the principal agricultural states of the United States, second only to North Dakota in percentage of farmland (94.5 percent) and second only to Kansas and Texas in total acreage of farmland (46.3 million acres). From the beginning, corn and hogs have been the principal produce of the eastern third of the state, and wheat and cattle of the west. Change is apparent, however, in the increasing automation of the farms and in the urban growth of areas around Omaha and Lincoln.

The land. Nebraska contains two main topographical areas, a strip of central lowlands in the extreme east of the state and a huge expanse of the Great Plains covering the rest of its land area. The central lowlands are limited to lands extending about 80 miles west from the Missouri River. Although it represents less than one-quarter of the state area, this strip contains most of its population centers and the fertile lands on which most of the state's enormous corn crop is grown. The western three-quarters of the state, more than 60,000 square miles in area, is crossed from west to east by the Platte River.

Climate. The climate of Nebraska is known for its sudden changes, with fast-moving meteorological fronts often resulting in hailstorms or thunderstorms. Warm, moist air from the Gulf of Mexico gives Nebraska warm, humid summers, with temperatures above 80° F. Normal daily lows of about 10 in winter, but colder local extremes are common in the western regions. The state's average annual precipitation is about 30 inches.
Principal cities. The Omaha metropolitan area, on the Missouri River near the center of the state's eastern border, contains nearly one-third of Nebraska's total population. A regional center for portions of Iowa as well as Nebraska, it is one of the major meat-packing cities in the country, a large grain storage depot, the headquarters of the U.S. Air Force Strategic Air Command, and a transportation hub at the intersection of river, rail, and highway routes. The capital city of Lincoln (population 171,932), 50 miles to the southwest, is a center for grain and insurance businesses. Between them, Omaha and Lincoln have 42 percent of the state's population.
The people. The people of Nebraska are for the most part descendants of the European immigrants who settled the state before 1900. The state grew from 28,000 to 1.1 million between 1860 and 1890, but it has lost population to migration throughout the 20th century. Between 1930 and 1940 the total state population declined by 62,000. Loss to migration in the 1970's was 12,600. Birthrates now give the state a small population growth, but the trend of young people moving elsewhere for employment leaves the state with one of the highest proportions of senior citizens in the country: more than 13 percent of Nebraska's population is over 65 years of age.
Economy. Nebraska is one of the great food producers in the country. It ranks fourth in production of corn and hay, seventh in production of wheat, and high in production of sorghum grain, oats, and soybeans. Crops, however, account for less than half the state's farm income. On the plains of its central and western regions Nebraska raises more beef cattle than any state except Texas, and hog production in the east ranks fourth in the United States. Although not an extensively industrialized state, Nebraska's manufacturing businesses, chiefly food processing, account for $3 billion in commerce, or about half that of agricultural businesses.
Places of interest. The major places of striking natural scenery in Nebraska are the Scotts Bluff National Monument and the Chimney Rock National Historic Site, both near the Wyoming border. Also of interest are the Buffalo Bill Ranch; and the Oregon Trail, which follows the North Platte through the state.

Iowa

Abbreviations: *Ia., IA*
Area: *55,941 sq. mi., 144,887 sq. km.*
Rank (of 50) *25th*
Population:
1985 *2,884,000*
Rank (of 50) *29th*
Change 1980–85 *−30,000*
Percent change *−1.0*
Persons per sq. mi. *52*
Percent urban *58.6*
Capital: *Des Moines*
Largest city: *Des Moines*
Metro. pop. 1985 *372,000*
Entered Union: *Dec. 28, 1846 (29th)*
State bird: *Eastern goldfinch*
State flower: *Wild rose*
State tree: *Oak*

Iowa is an eastern Grain state situated between the Missouri River to the west and the Mississippi River to the east. Its northern and southern borders are formed, respectively, by the Grain states of Minnesota and Missouri.

Iowa is a state that falls near the middle of the U.S. range in both population and land area. It is known as a "balanced" state in other ways as well. As one of the principal U.S. exporters of food products, it is also the seat of extensive scientific research into plant hybrids and chemical fertilizers, and it is the home of considerable manufacturing. Widely known as the corn state for providing 50 percent of the U.S. crop, Iowa in fact earns more from livestock than from all crops combined.
The land. Virtually all of Iowa is considered part of the Central Lowland Plain. Two-thirds of the state is nearly level, varying in elevation from 800 to 1400 feet across its width of more than 300 miles. The two significant variations in this topography are the Till Plains in the south, the smoothest and most regular area in the state, and the hillier Young Drift Plains in the north, a region of recent, or young, glacial soil deposits. The extreme northeast also contains a hilly unglaciated area called the Wisconsin Driftless region. It is now the center of the state's dairy farming.
Climate. Iowa has an extremely changeable climate, with occasional variations in temperature of as much as 50° F in a single day. Ordinarily, high temperatures average over 80 in summer, and lows approach 10 in winter. The rainfall is heaviest in the southeast, where precipitation averages about 40 inches per year.
Principal cities. Iowa is relatively rural, even by Grain state standards. Des Moines, with scarcely 10 percent of the state population, is the largest city in the state. It is situated near the center of Iowa on the Des Moines River, and it is known for its insurance companies, farm equipment manufacturers, and publishing enterprises. Davenport, on the Mississippi River, is the largest of the "Quad-Cities," a metropolitan area of nearly 400,000 whose other cities are in Illinois. Similarly, Council Bluffs, on the Missouri River at the state's western border, is part of the Omaha, Nebraska, metropolitan area. Most of Iowa's other principal cities—Cedar Rapids, Waterloo, and Dubuque—are industrial centers located in the eastern third of the state.
The people. The population of Iowa passed 2 million before 1900, and it has yet to pass 3 million. Such limited population growth gives it the highest percentage of lifelong residents (67.4 percent) among the Grain states. Because of the consolidation and mechanization of farms, young people in Iowa tend to migrate to other states. Iowa lost 60,000 residents to migration in the 1970's, and the remaining population is one of the oldest in the region, with 13 percent of the residents older than 65 years.
Economy. Iowa ranks second only to California in agricultural produce, and its production of corn, soybeans, and hogs surpasses that of all other states. Corn production is based in the central and northern regions of the state, and it has soared since the introduction of hybrid seeds, new fertilizers, and automatic reapers. Most of the corn crop is intended for livestock feed. Given this ample supply of feed, the state's production of cattle and hogs has eclipsed that of all other crops in total value. These extensive agricultural businesses have spawned their own food processing industry, one which now virtually equals farm income in value and far surpasses it in number of persons employed.
Places of interest. The attractions in Iowa include the Herbert Hoover birthplace and Presidential library at West Branch, near Cedar Rapids; the Effigy Mounds National Monument in the extreme northeast corner of the state, a prehistoric burial site; and the Fort Dodge Stockade and Historical Museum, 70 miles up the Des Moines River from the state capital.

South Dakota

Abbreviations: *S.D., SD*
Area: *75,955 sq. mi., 196,723 sq. km.*
Rank (of 50) *16th*
Population:
1985 *708,000*
Rank (of 50) *45th*
Change 1980–85 *+17,000*
Percent change *+2.5*
Persons per sq. mi. *9*
Percent urban *46.4*
Capital: *Pierre*
Largest city: *Sioux Falls*
City pop. 1980 *81,343*
Entered Union: *Nov. 2, 1889 (40th)*
State bird: *Ring-necked pheasant*
State flower: *Pasqueflower*
State tree: *Black Hills spruce*

South Dakota is located in the upper Great Plains, bordered by Wyoming and Montana in the west, North Dakota to the north, and Minnesota and Iowa to the east. The state is bisected north-south by the Missouri River, which then turns east to form part of its southern border with Nebraska.

Most of South Dakota's population live east of the Missouri River, but most of the symbols of its identity lie to the west. Along the state's far western border with Wyoming lie the Black Hills, the highest mountains east of the Rockies and the site of the famous national monument at Mt. Rushmore. Just south and east of the Black Hills is the Badlands National Monument, in a region of strange and desolate rock formations and buttes carved by wind erosion.

The western region is also the home of most of the state's 42,000 Indians, and a symbol of the Indian presence is found in the west at Wounded Knee, the site of the final Indian conflict in 1890.

The land. The eastern third of the state is a region known as the Prairie-plains, rolling hills formed by glacial action and dotted by small lakes. The western two-thirds is the unglaciated area of the Missouri Plateau, uplands varying in elevation from 2000 to 3000 feet and crossed by the Missouri River. The river and its tributaries drain nearly all of South Dakota. Along the southwestern border with Wyoming are the Black Hills, an isolated mountain group including the state's high point, Harney Peak (7242 feet). These rocky mountains have been eroded down to their granite cores by centuries of wind action.

Climate. The climate of South Dakota is one of seasonal extremes. Winter lows average near 5° F, and summer highs average near 90. The state is also subject to high winds and blizzard conditions in winter. The average precipitation across the state is only 18 inches per year, with higher averages in the east and lower in the west.

Principal cities. Less than half the population of South Dakota live in urban areas, making it the most rural of Grain states. The largest city, Sioux Falls, is in the southeastern corner of the state. Its stockyards are the third largest in the United States, and it is near retail and wholesale markets in southern Minnesota, Iowa, and Nebraska. The second largest city in the state, and the principal urban seat of the western region, is Rapid City (population 46,492).

The people. South Dakota attained almost 60 percent of its present population by 1900, and it has experienced periodic population declines since that time. In the decade following 1930, a period of national economic depression and local drought, the total population declined by about 50,000, or more than 7 percent. In the 1970's overall population increased slightly, but the state lost about 27,000 residents to migration. Two-thirds of the present population were born in the state, descendants of the northern Europeans who settled South Dakota in its years of land bonanzas before 1900. South Dakota is also notable for its high proportion of American Indians, about 7 percent of the population. There are nine reservations, all in the western region, and the state area includes 5 million acres of lands owned by or allotted to the members of the Sioux tribe.

Economy. Agriculture is carried out on more than 90 percent of South Dakota's land area, and livestock production accounts for two-thirds of the state's farm income. Most of the cattle and hog production is based in the eastern area of the state. The central and northern regions of the state produce most of its crops, principally wheat, rye, and oats. Mining is the principal industry in the state's western region. The town of Lead, near the Wyoming border, is the site of the Homestake Mine, the largest single source of gold in the United States. South Dakota leads all states in gold mining, and it also mines large quantities of crude oil, stone, sand, and gravel.

Places of interest. The greatest attraction in the state is Mt. Rushmore, a 6200-foot granite peak with likenesses of Presidents Washington, Jefferson, Lincoln, and Theodore Roosevelt carved into its face by Gutzon Borglum. Mt. Rushmore is located in the Black Hills, which are themselves a principal tourist attraction that can be toured by car along the famous Needles Highway. Also in the western region are the Crazy Horse Memorial and the George Armstrong Custer State Park.

North Dakota

Abbreviations: *N.D., ND*
Area: *69,273 sq. mi., 179,417 sq. km.*
Rank (of 50) *17th*
Population:
1985 *685,000*
Rank (of 50) *46th*
Change 1980–85 *+32,000*
Percent change *+4.9*
Persons per sq. mi. *10*
Percent urban *36.4*
Capital: *Bismarck*
Largest city: *Fargo*
City pop. 1980 *61,308*
Entered Union: *Nov. 2, 1889 (39th)*
State bird: *Western meadowlark*
State flower: *Wild prairie rose*
State tree: *American elm*

North Dakota is a northern Grain state, bordering the Canadian provinces of Saskatchewan and Manitoba on the north and South Dakota on the south. It lies between the U.S. states of Montana, to the west, and Minnesota, to the east, near the center of the expanse of Great Plains stretching from northern Canada south to Mexico. The geographic center of North America lies in the north-central part of the state.

North Dakota is the most agricultural state in the country, with 94.8 percent of its total acreage given over to farms (principally in the east) and to ranches (in the drier western areas). A quarter of the population continue to live on farms and ranches.

The state landscape is one of broad horizons and grasslands, all virtually unchanged since the original 19th century plantings. Consolidation of many small farms into giant holdings more economical to cultivate have led to a gradual population decline. Yet

SIOUX ELDERS *meet in council on the Rosebud Reservation in South Dakota, not far from the scenes of the last Indian wars in the late 1800's.*

HERON/MONKMEYER

North Dakota today harvests more than 10 percent of the nation's crops, second only to Kansas in the Grain region.

The land. The principal topographical features of North Dakota are the central lowlands in the eastern half of the state and the Missouri Plateau in the west. The central lowlands consist of the fertile Red River Valley, which forms the state border with Minnesota; and farther west the Young Drift Plains, where the glaciers of the last ice age deposited rich soils, or "drift." This eastern dry-farming region extends from the Minnesota border to a north-south divide, near the center of the state, called the Missouri escarpment, a chain of hills rising 300 to 400 feet above ground level.

West of the escarpment lies the Missouri Plateau region of the Great Plains. Crossed by the Missouri River, this plateau, ranging in elevation from 2000 to 3000 feet, is covered by only a thin, easily eroded, layer of soil. In the southwest, along the Little Missouri River, are the Badlands, an area of chiseled buttes called *mauvaises terres à traverser* (bad lands to cross) by the first French-Canadian explorers.

Climate. North Dakota's climate is subject to great seasonal extremes. At Fargo, on the state's eastern border, January lows average minus 3° F and July highs average 84. The average precipitation is only about 16 inches, but 75 percent of it falls as rain during the growing season. The rest accounts for snow that often blankets the state under blizzard conditions.

Principal cities. The largest city in North Dakota, the second most rural of Grain states, is Fargo in the southern portion of the Red River Valley. The third largest city, Grand Forks (population 43,765), also lies in this river valley, farther north. Ranked between these two cities in population is Bismarck (population 44,485), located in the south-central area of the state on the Missouri River.

The people. Three-quarters of the people in North Dakota are descended from north European and Canadian settlers, and two-thirds of the present population were born in North Dakota. The devastating effects of drought and the Depression caused a population decline of 40,000 in the 1930's. Despite a small population increase due to birthrate, the state lost 17,000 residents to migration in the 1970's.

Economy. North Dakota's economy is based on agriculture, and two-thirds of the farm income is derived from the crops principally grown in the eastern half of the state. The third largest wheat crop in the United States is grown there, and the state ranks second only to Idaho in the production of barley. The livestock ranches in the western half of the state generate a third of the farm income.

Second to agriculture in the state economy is mining, with 70 percent of the mining income derived from oil drilling, principally in the Williston Basin in the southwest. The western areas of the state also mine significant quantities of coal, uranium, and clay.

Places of interest. One unusual attraction in North Dakota is the International Peace Garden near the center of the state's Canadian border, commemorating friendly relations between the United States and Canada. The Theodore Roosevelt National Park, in two parts of the southwest Badlands, preserves the President's ranch and its natural surroundings.

Minnesota

Abbreviations: *Minn., MN*
Area: *79,289 sq. mi., 205,359 sq. km.*
Rank (of 50) *12th*
Population:
1985 *4,193,000*
Rank (of 50) *21st*
Change 1980–85 *+117,000*
Percent change *+2.9*
Persons per sq. mi. *53*
Percent urban *66.9*
Capital: *St. Paul*
Largest city: *Minneapolis-St. Paul*
Metro. pop. 1985 *2,262,000*
Entered Union: *May 11, 1858 (32nd)*
State bird: *Common loon*
State flower: *Showy lady's slipper*
State tree: *Red pine*

Minnesota is situated near the northern center of the country, with a 350-mile border with the Canadian provinces of Manitoba and Ontario. It is the only Grain state with access to the Great Lakes, and its eastern border is with Wisconsin. The Dakotas are to the west and Iowa to the south.

Minnesota ranks second among the Grain states in area (to Kansas) and in population (to Missouri). Its landscape is one of great beauty and variety, including extensive bluff, prairie, and hill formations. It is especially noted for its lakes, which number more than 20,000. Its northern reaches are heavily wooded and are popular with vacationers from all parts of the Midwest. The state also claims enormous iron ore reserves in its northeastern corner and fertile farmland along its southern and western borders. This combination of natural assets gives the state an economy far more diversified than that of any state in the region.

The land. Minnesota contains two principal topographical areas of approximately equal size, the superior upland in the north and the central lowlands in the south. The central lowlands are the beginning of the fertile region of rolling hills and river valleys that stretches south along the route of the Mississippi River. In Minnesota the area consists of the Young Drift Plains, a fertile grassland of more recent, or younger, glacial deposits, or drift, than those found to the east or west.

The superior upland is characterized by 2000-foot hills in the east, beside Lake Superior, and a flat clay prairie in the west. Its eastern region, called the Arrowhead for its shape, contains the iron-rich Mesabi Range and other well forested ranges. Its western region was once covered by the glacial Lake Agassiz, which left behind fertile flats on which the state's large oats crop is grown.

The topography of Minnesota is also notable for its river drainage in three directions: south via the Mississippi to the Gulf of Mexico; north via the Red River into Canada and the Hudson Bay; and east via the Great Lakes to the Atlantic Ocean.

Climate. Minnesota is a generally cool state, with temperatures declining toward the west as well as toward the north. In the east-central city of Duluth, normal summer highs are in the 70° F range and winter lows are below zero. The Minneapolis–St. Paul area farther south is milder in both seasons. The state has a relatively light annual rainfall of about 30 inches, but most of it falls in the growing season.

Principal cities. Half the population of Minnesota live in the Minneapolis–St. Paul area. These Twin Cities at the junction of the Minnesota and Mississippi rivers process and distribute food products; both have developed modern manufacturing sectors. The second largest city is Duluth, at the western reach of Lake Superior. It is from Duluth's giant inland harbor that northern Minnesota's exports of iron ore are shipped.

The people. Many state residents are of Scandinavian descent, but among recent immigrants, Germans outnumber Scandinavians. The state's growth rate of 7 percent is the highest of the Grain states, but it is still well below the national average.

Economy. Minnesota ranks second among all U.S. states in cash receipts for agricultural products. The northeast hills grow the second largest hay crop in the United States; the northwest prairie grows the largest oat crop; and the southern region grows the third largest corn crop. About half of farm income is from livestock.

Minnesota also mines 60 percent of the U.S. iron ore yield, principally from open pits in the Mesabi Range. The state's manufacturing businesses, chiefly food processing in the Minneapolis–St. Paul area, generate $10 billion in commerce each year. Tourism and timber are also significant industries.

Places of interest. The principal attractions in Minnesota are year-round outdoor activities, including camping, fishing, and winter sports in all areas of the state. Of special interest is Voyageurs National Park at the Canadian border. The Twin Cities have many cultural attractions.

The Great Lakes States

THE GREAT LAKES STATES

State	Area (sq. mi.)	Population 1985	Population change 1980–85 number	Population change 1980–85 percent	Persons per sq. mi.
Wisconsin	54,464	4,775,000	+ 70,000	+1.5	88
Illinois	56,400	11,535,000	+108,000	+ .9	207
Indiana	36,097	5,499,000	+ 9,000	+ .2	153
Michigan	56,817	9,088,000	−174,000	−1.9	160
Ohio	40,975	10,744,000	− 53,000	− .5	262
Region totals	244,753	41,641,000	− 40,000	− .2	170

The Great Lakes states are located in the north-central United States. They are separated from the Grain states to the west by the Mississippi River, and from the South-Central states to the south by the Ohio River. Three of the five Great Lakes form the region's northern border, separating it from the Canadian Province of Ontario. Lake Michigan, the only Great Lake entirely in the United States, touches four of the five states in the region. The state of Michigan has 1700 miles of Great Lakes shoreline. The region's eastern boundary is with Pennsylvania.

The Great Lakes states are notable for the network of industrial cities along the southern reaches of the lakes, from Milwaukee and Chicago on Lake Michigan to Detroit and Cleveland on Lake Erie. The lakes themselves, connected to the Atlantic by the St. Lawrence River, afford a major transportation system and an important source of water for industrial use. Steel plants cluster along the lake fronts near Gary, Indiana, and Youngstown, Ohio. And the automobile industry made Detroit, halfway between Gary and Youngstown, the largest industrial complex in the world. Foreign competition, both in steel production and manufacturing, have led to a decline of these industrial cities and to a general population loss in the region. At the same time, a modest resurgence is taking place in the less industrial North Woods areas of northern Wisconsin and Michigan, attracting people leaving the industrial cities.

The land. Almost all of the land area of the Great Lakes states lies within the vast Central Lowland, which stretches from the Appalachian Plateau in eastern Ohio to the Mississippi River on the western border. This relatively flat plain, broken by low ranges of moraines, or glacial hills, is fertile and ideally suited to large, mechanized farming. Along the coastlines of the lakes themselves the region also includes strips of Great Lakes Plain, lower lying and marshy areas on which most of the region's major cities now stand. Northern Wisconsin and the western half of Michigan's Upper Peninsula also share a portion of Superior Upland, a glacial hill area containing the highest elevations in the region, about 1900 feet.

Climate. The Great Lakes states have a very consistent climate of cold winters and hot summers. The normal temperature range throughout the region runs from normal winter lows of about 10° F to normal summer highs of about 80. The average precipitation is about 35 inches per year, and the snowfall averages between 25 and 35 inches. In the North Woods area, however, winters are colder and snowfalls average over 100 inches per year.

History. The Great Lakes states were first explored by the French explorers Jolliet, Marquette, and La Salle in the 1600's. They remained a French territory until 1763, when France ceded the region to Britain. American claims to the region after the Revolution were disputed by Britain, which occupied Michigan. The disputes were ended by the War of 1812.

In the meantime, settlers had crossed the Appalachians and begun to live in Ohio, which entered the Union in 1803. Indiana and Illinois joined before 1820; Michigan and Wisconsin, less suited for agriculture and off the main thoroughfares, gained statehood in 1837 and 1848. When the railroads opened in the 1850's, the industrial cities began to grow and the population was increased by huge numbers of European immigrants.

Principal cities. The largest city in the region is Chicago, which includes 7.1 million residents of Illinois and Indiana; it is a metropolis of worldwide importance. Its diversified economy helped it avoid the decline experienced by other large Great Lakes cities—Detroit, Cleveland, and Milwaukee—in the 1970's. Only Indianapolis and Cincinnati, south of the Great Lakes and reliant on newer industries, continued to grow in population.

The people. The stream of people leaving the region because of the decline of the automobile and steel industries reached enormous proportions in the 1970's. Although all five states increased slightly in population, they lost 1.5 million people to other

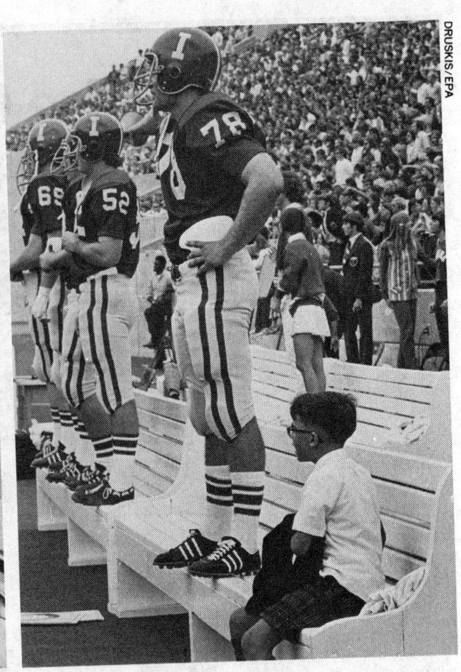

HARD WORK AND HARD PLAY *are characteristic of the Great Lakes region. Assembly line workers at a General Motors plant in Detroit carry on a long tradition of heavy industry. Another tradition is football: the region is a hotbed of enthusiasm for the game.*

regions. The inner cities today have increasing concentrations of poor black residents and decreasing tax bases and employment opportunities. The region also includes significant numbers of Hispanic people.

Economy. The principal industries of the region are the automobile plants in Detroit, Flint, and other Michigan cities, and the steel mills around Gary, Indiana, and Cleveland and Youngstown, Ohio. This economic core has spawned related machinery, shipping, and transportation industries that together make the Great Lakes states the manufacturing center of America. Across the Central Lowland the region also generates significant agricultural income, most of it in dairy farming and crops for cattle feed. Northern Wisconsin and Michigan rely on mining, timber, and tourism.

Wisconsin

Abbreviations: *Wis., WI*
Area: *54,464 sq. mi., 141,062 sq. km.*
Rank (of 50) *26th*
Population:
1985 *4,775,000*
Rank (of 50) *16th*
Change 1980–85 *+70,000*
Percent change *+1.5*
Persons per sq. mi. *88*
Percent urban *64.2*
Capital: *Madison*
Largest city: *Milwaukee*
Metro. pop. 1985 *1,379,000*
Entered Union: *May 29, 1848 (30th)*
State bird: *Robin*
State flower: *Wood violet*
State tree: *Sugar maple*

Wisconsin is north of Illinois between the Mississippi River, which forms part of its western border with Minnesota, and Lake Michigan to the east. Its northern border is formed by Lake Superior and the Upper Peninsula of Michigan.

Wisconsin is the least industrialized of Great Lakes states because of its northern location and relative lack of natural resources. It is also the least populated state in the region, and the population is more evenly dispersed throughout the state area than in the other, more urban, Great Lakes states. These apparent deficiencies became assets in the 1970's: Wisconsin was the only one of the region's states to gain more new residents from other states than it lost. In addition, the same forest and lake scenery that attracted residents has made tourism one of the state's major industries.

The land. Wisconsin has a complex topography consisting of two major land masses. The northern half of the state is a portion of the Superior Upland that extends northwest into Minnesota and northeast into the Upper Peninsula of Michigan. The rolling lands and glacial hills here are a part of the enormous Canadian Shield that extends into the far north. In north-central Wisconsin the state's high point at Timm's Hill (1952 feet) is found.

Southern Wisconsin lies within the Central Lowland and contains two distinct features. In the southeast uplands decline into the Great Lakes Plain lying only about 500 feet above sea level. In the southwest the lowlands include a portion of the Wisconsin Driftless Plain, a hilly region never covered by glacial ice sheets and so lacking the soil, or "drift," they left behind. This plain contains the state's most dramatic relief features, limestone hills as high as 1700 feet eroded by streams into steep valleys. Close to the Mississippi River this region drops off from the same 500-foot elevations found on the Great Lakes Plain beside Lake Michigan.

Climate. Wisconsin's climate is notable for its long frigid winters and short warm summers. At Milwaukee in the southeast normal winter lows are 10° F and summer highs approach 80. However, record temperatures in other state areas range from 54 below to 114 above. Precipitation is a consistent 29 inches per year throughout the state, and snows average 46 inches per year in Milwaukee and more in the northern regions.

Principal cities. The largest urban center in the state is a consolidated metropolitan area running 20 miles along the Lake Michigan shore from Milwaukee to Racine and including 1.6 million people, or one-third of the state's population. The Milwaukee metropolitan area, the state's industrial seat, declined in population during the 1970's. Its city population returned to its 1950 level. The second largest city in the state is the capital of Madison (population 323,109), 80 miles east of Milwaukee. Madison is an insurance and banking center and is the home of the largest campus of the University of Wisconsin. The western and northwestern parts of the state look toward metropolitan centers in Minnesota: Minneapolis-St. Paul and Duluth.

The people. The population of the state, once 66 percent urban, returned in 1980 to the less urbanized levels of the 1950's and 1960's. Nearly 17 percent of the people are immigrants or the children of immigrants; most are Germans who live in or around Milwaukee. The proportion of minority groups in Wisconsin is lower than that in any other Great Lakes state: blacks represent 4 percent of the total population and Hispanics 1 percent.

Economy. Although it is the least industrialized state in the region, Wisconsin's manufacturing businesses generate $19 billion in income per year and rank eleventh in the United States. The principal manufactures, mostly coming out of the Milwaukee and Madison areas, are machinery, electrical components, paper goods, and food products (including cheese). More than half the state is covered by farmland, making Wisconsin's agricultural businesses second only to Illinois' in the region. Dairy products generate the most income, and the chief crops are feed grains such as corn and oats. Tourism is the state's third largest business, with summer visitors from out of state spending $2.5 billion per year.

Places of interest. The major attractions in Wisconsin are natural preserves such as the Apostle Islands in Lake Superior, Lake Winnebago near Lake Michigan, and the Dells region in the south-central part of the state, where the Wisconsin River has carved picturesque sandstone canyons.

Illinois

Abbreviations: *Ill., IL*
Area: *56,,400 sq. mi., 146,076 sq. km.*

Rank (of 50)	*23rd*
Population:	
1985	*11,535,000*
Rank (of 50)	*5th*
Change 1980–85	*+108,000*
Percent change	*+.9*
Persons per sq. mi.	*207*
Percent urban	*83.3*

Capital: *Springfield*
Largest city: *Chicago*
Metro. pop. 1985 *6,177,000*
Entered Union: *Dec. 3, 1818 (21st)*
State bird: *Cardinal*
State flower: *Violet*
State tree: *White oak*

Illinois is at the southwest corner of the Great Lakes states, separated from Missouri and Iowa by the Mississippi River on the west, and from Kentucky by the Ohio River on the south. Its northern border is with Wisconsin and its eastern border is with Indiana. In the northeast, the state has a 50-mile shoreline on Lake Michigan, which is covered by the sprawling Chicago metropolitan area.

Illinois has been one of the most prosperous of U.S. states. Between 1850 and the 1960's, millions of people from other states and European countries gravitated to Illinois because of the immense economic advantages it enjoyed. The land is agriculturally fertile, rich in minerals, and watered by abundant rivers. The state is the geographical connection between north-south traffic on the Mississippi River and east-west traffic through the Great Lakes to the Atlantic Ocean.

In the late 1800's Chicago became the hub of a great railroad system, and in the 1900's it became a similar center for highway and air routes. Northern Illinois is one of the major U.S. manufacturing centers, and southern Illinois is one of the nation's major producers of agricultural goods. The clash between "downstate" agricultural interests and Chicago's manufacturing and business interests has helped determine much of the state's political and social history.

In recent years, Illinois' steady growth and traditional prosperity appear to have been stalled. More than 500,000 residents migrated to other states in the 1970's, and the state's 2.8 percent growth rate in the 1970's was one of the smallest in the country. The state also slipped from seventh to eighth in per capita income among U.S. states in the same decade.

The land. Nine-tenths of the land area of Illinois consists of predominantly flat central lowlands and till plains. This expanse is comprised of rich black loam covered by a thin layer of prairie sod. The periphery of the state includes small portions of other topographical areas. In the northwest there is a small section of unglaciated Wisconsin Driftless Plain. In the northeast, along the shore of Lake Michigan, there is a small hill and marsh region known as the Great Lakes Plain. In the far south, Illinois includes strips of Ozark Plateau extending northeast from Missouri; interior low plateau extending northwest from Kentucky; and the northernmost point of the Gulf Coastal Plain.

Climate. Illinois' climate is a temperate continental one with snowy winters and warm summers. Winter lows average below 20° F in the north but only 30 in the south. Summer temperatures throughout the state are above 80. Precipitation varies from 44 inches per year at the southern point to 33 inches per year in Chicago, in the northeast. Snowfall in the north averages 40 inches per year.

Principal cities. The Chicago metropolitan area is the third largest in the United States, after New York and Los Angeles. It is also part of a consolidated metropolitan area that extends along the southern shore of Lake Michigan to Gary, Indiana; it includes 7.7 million persons. The second largest population center is Peoria (population 365,864), in the north-central region of the state on the Illinois River. Rockford, to the northwest of Chicago, is the third largest city (population 279,514). Illinois shares metropolitan areas with Missouri at St. Louis and with Iowa at the Quad Cities (Davenport, Iowa, and Rock Island, Moline, and East Moline, Illinois).

The people. Illinois attracted major waves of European immigrants throughout the 1800's. First came the Irish, Germans, Scandinavians, and English, and later the Poles, Czechs, and Italians. After World War I, Illinois also attracted a steady stream of black Americans from the southern states. Today the black population is about 15 percent of the total, or about 1.7 million, and it is heavily concentrated in major cities. Other significant ethnic groups are Hispanics, who represent 6 percent of the population, and Asians, who represent 1 percent.

Economy. Among all U.S. states, Illinois ranks fourth in both manufacturing and farming. The principal manufactures include farm and earth-moving machinery, electrical goods, and processed food products. Although no longer "hog butcher to the world," Chicago is still an important food-processing center. It is also a banking and financial center for the whole north-central United States.

Illinois is second only to California in the exportation of manufactured goods, and second only to Iowa in the production of soybeans and corn. It also mines significant quantities of coal and oil in its southern regions, and it leads all states in the mining of fluorspar, a mineral important to the steel industry.

Places of interest. Various places associated with the life of Abraham Lincoln, around the capital city of Springfield near the center of the state, are preserved. Other places of interest include the Mormon settlement at Nauvoo, on the Mississippi River; and the many cultural attractions of Chicago.

Indiana

Abbreviations: *Ind., IN*
Area: *36,097 sq. mi., 93,491 sq. km.*

Rank (of 50)	*38th*
Population:	
1985	*5,499,000*
Rank (of 50)	*14th*
Change 1980–85	*+9,000*
Percent change	*+.2*
Persons per sq. mi.	*153*
Percent urban	*64.2*

Capital: *Indianapolis*
Largest city: *Indianapolis*
Metro. pop. 1985 *1,203,000*
Entered Union: *Dec. 11, 1816 (19th)*
State bird: *Cardinal*
State flower: *Peony*
State tree: *Tulip tree*

Indiana is situated between the Great Lakes states of Illinois to the west and Ohio to the east and just south of Michigan. Its southern border with Kentucky is formed by the Ohio River.

Like the surrounding Great Lakes states, Indiana has been industrialized for more than a century. The capital city of Indianapolis near the center of the state was once a crossroads for trails from the American east. This historical role is maintained by the networks of modern interstate highways that now converge near the city.

The entire commercial history of the state remains apparent in the distinct business interests of its three principal areas: industry in the north, farming in the central region, and mining and quarrying in the south.

The land. The land of Indiana shows three topographical divisions. A narrow band across the extreme north of the state is part of the Great Lakes Plain. This is a low-lying region with hundreds of lakes and ponds. The shoreline of Lake Michigan in the northwest corner consists of drained swamplands and sand dunes at the water's edge. The larger central region of the state is part of the Central Lowlands, a plain of rich soil characterized by ranges of low hills. In its southern region Indiana includes a portion of the Interior Low Plateau, a hilly region of limestone beds eroded by groundwater into caverns and sinkholes.

Climate. The climate of Indiana is one of hot summers and cold winters. At Indianapolis normal winter lows are below 20° F and summer highs are over 80. In the center of the state precipitation averages 39 inches and snowfall 20 inches per year. The extreme south remains about 10 degrees warmer in both summer and winter than the north, and snowfall in the north is twice that in the south.

Principal cities. The capital city of Indianapolis is twice as large in population as any other city in the state. It functions as the commercial center of Indiana's agricultural region and as an industrial center based on the manufacture of automobile and airplane engines. The other major cities are in industrial districts in the north of the state. Fort Wayne in the northeast (population 382,961) is a principal manufacturer of farm machinery and electronic equipment. The Gary–Hammond–East Chicago area beside Lake Michigan is an industrial center that includes 642,781 residents of the greater Chicago metropolitan area. South Bend (population 278,109), between Gary and Fort Wayne, is the home of Notre Dame University. The principal population centers in southern Indiana are Evansville in the southwest (population 307,103), and the New Albany region across the Ohio River from Louisville, Kentucky. All Indiana cities grew far less in the 1970's than in the 1960's.

The people. The population growth rate in Indiana declined from 18.5 percent in the 1950's to 11.4 percent in the 1960's and then to less than 6 percent in the 1970's. Between 1970 and 1980 150,000 state residents migrated to other states. Despite this, Indiana's population growth rate remains second only to Wisconsin among Great Lakes states. The present population is 8 percent black and 2 percent Hispanic. Indiana has the lowest proportion of foreign-born residents, about 7 percent, within the Great Lakes region.

Economy. The principal industry of Indiana is manufacturing, and most of the manufacturing centers are located in the north of the state. The most important center is in the Calumet region in the northwest, an area of steel mills and oil refineries where raw materials are imported and finished goods are exported via Great Lakes freighters. The state is also known for its specialty manufacturers concentrated in single towns. For example, musical instruments are made in Elkhart; Mason jars in Muncie; television sets in Bloomington.

The principal farmland is located in central Indiana. Crops, chiefly corn and soybeans, account for more than one-half the total farm income, and the greatest livestock production is of hogs and sheep. In southern Indiana mining businesses predominate. Coal is strip mined from the Interior Low Plateau in the southwest of the state. Elsewhere on the same plateau Indiana quarries more building limestone than any other state; it also quarries substantial quantities of stone and gravel.

Places of interest. Southern Indiana contains several extensive limestone cavern systems. The Wyandotte Cave near the Ohio River is the most noteworthy. Other natural attractions include the Indiana Dunes National Lakeshore, beside Lake Michigan, and the Hoosier National Forest. The principal annual attraction in the state is the Indianapolis 500 automobile race in the state capital.

Michigan

Abbreviations: *Mich., MI*
Area: *56,817 sq. mi., 147,156 sq. km.*

Rank (of 50)	*22nd*

Population:

1985	*9,088,000*
Rank (of 50)	*8th*
Change 1980–85	*–174,000*
Percent change	*–1.9*
Persons per. sq. mi.	*160*
Percent urban	*70.7*

Capital: *Lansing*
Largest city: *Detroit*

Metro. pop. 1985	*4,319,000*

Entered Union: *Jan. 26, 1837 (26th)*
State bird: *Robin*
State flower: *Apple blossom*
State tree: *White pine*

Michigan is a north-central state composed of two peninsulas with shorelines on four of the five Great Lakes. The Upper, or northern, Peninsula stretches from its southwestern border with Wisconsin 320 miles east between lakes Superior and Michigan toward Ontario, Canada. The Lower Peninsula, which is much larger and contains most of the population, extends north from borders with Indiana and Ohio between Lake Michigan on the west and lakes Huron and Erie on the east. The two peninsulas are separated from each other by the 5-mile-wide Straits of Mackinac that connect lakes Michigan and Huron. The Mackinac Bridge, one of the largest suspension bridges in the world, provides highway connections between the two parts of the state.

Michigan is the only Great Lakes state that has land borders with Canada. Detroit lies just across the Detroit River from Windsor, in the heavily populated southern region of Ontario. And the Upper Peninsula city of Sault Ste. Marie faces the Ontario town of the same name across the St. Mary's River.

There is a dramatic difference in character between the Upper Peninsula and the much larger Lower Peninsula of Michigan. The Upper Peninsula is a sparsely populated region including much North Woods wilderness. The Lower Peninsula is a densely populated area that includes some of the principal industrial cities in the United States.

The automobile industry, based in Detroit, is the focus of the state's economic interest. The increasing cost of motor fuel and competition from foreign automobile manufacturers brought a severe decline to the industry in recent years; as a result, Michigan lost 300,000 residents to migration during the 1970's.

The land. All of the Lower Peninsula of Michigan lies within the Central Lowland region, principally within the subdivision called the Great Lakes Plain. This central plain is characterized by ridges that rise in elevation from about 1000 feet in the south to about 1700 feet in the north, where some tablelands are found.

The Upper Peninsula consists of two topographical regions of equal area. In the east the Great Lakes Plains predominate, and maximum elevations of only 400 feet decline into marshy lands along the lake shores. In the west is the Superior Upland extending into Wisconsin. The state high point lies near Lake Superior.

Climate. The climate differs in the two peninsulas. In southeastern Detroit normal winter lows are 30° F and summer highs above 80. At Sault Ste. Marie, on the northern shore of the Upper Peninsula, normal winter lows are about 10 and summer highs 70. Precipitation averages 31 inches per year throughout the state, but Sault Ste. Marie receives almost four times as much snow as Detroit—about 112 inches per year.

Principal cities. All the large cities of Michigan are located in the Lower Peninsula. The largest is the "motor city" of Detroit, situated in the southeast on the Detroit River, part of the link between lakes Erie and Huron. The second largest is Grand Rapids (population 601,106), an industrial center in the western part of the state 40 miles from Lake Michigan. The third largest is Flint (population 521,541), about 40 miles northwest of Detroit. It is the state's second largest automobile manufacturer. Together these three urban seats account for 60 percent of the state's population. Marquette (population 22,000) is the largest town in the Upper Peninsula.

The people. Because of the growth of the automobile industry into one of the largest businesses in the United States, Michigan grew in population at a rate above the national average from 1910 to 1970. By contrast, growth in the 1970's was well below the national average, and the proportion of people living in urban places actually declined. Nearly 13 percent of the state population are black Americans, most of whose parents or grandparents migrated from the South seeking industrial jobs between 1920 and 1970. Hispanics are the only other large ethnic group within the population. They represent 2 percent of the total.

Economy. Michigan is the fifth largest manufacturing state in the United States, and one-third of its manufactures are related to the automobile industry. In addition to the principal car and truck builders in Detroit and Flint, major manufacturers of automobile parts and acccessories exist in cities such as Lansing, the state capital, Battle Creek, and Kalamazoo.

The second largest business in the Lower Peninsula is agriculture, with equal concentrations on livestock and crops. Most of the cattle are raised on dairy farms, and most of the crops are grown for feed. The principal businesses of the Upper Peninsula are timber, chiefly hardwoods, and mining, chiefly of iron, cement, and natural gas. The northern half of the Lower Peninsula and much of the Upper Peninsula are rich in lakes, streams, and shoreline areas, generating $3.8 billion in annual income from tourism.

Places of interest. There are many summer resorts along the Great Lakes shorelines throughout Michigan, including the Pictured Rocks National Lakeshore in the Upper Peninsula and Sleeping Bear Dunes in the northwest Lower Peninsula. The major attractions near Detroit are the automobile plants themselves, the Henry Ford Museum, and the preserved 19th-century Greenfield Village in Dearborn.

Ohio

Abbreviations: *O., OH*
Area: *40,975 sq. mi., 106,125 sq. km.*

Rank (of 50)	*35th*
Population:	
1985	*10,744,000*
Rank (of 50)	*7th*
Change 1980–85	*–53,000*
Percent change	*–.5*
Persons per sq. mi.	*262*
Percent urban	*73.3*

Capital: *Columbus*
Largest city: *Cleveland*
Metro. pop. 1985 *1,860,000*
Entered Union: *Mar. 1, 1803 (17th)*
State bird: *Cardinal*
State flower: *Scarlet carnation*
State tree: *Buckeye*

Ohio is the most eastern of the Great Lakes states. Its northern border is formed by Michigan and by Lake Erie, which separates the state from the Canadian Province of Ontario. Its entire southern border is formed by the Ohio River, which separates it from Kentucky in the southwest and West Virginia in the southeast. Ohio stretches about 200 miles from Indiana in the west to Pennsylvania in the east.

Ohio was the first part of the Northwest Territory to be settled after the American Revolution. The first settlement was established at Marietta in 1788 along the Ohio River on the state's southern border. It was only the advent of heavy industry along Lake Erie in the 20th century that made the northeast the most populous region of the state. Today Ohio is the most densely populated of Great Lakes states because of the extent of its manufacturing industries. The state ranks third nationally in manufacturing commerce yet only thirty-fifth in land area.

The land. Most of the land of Ohio lies within the central lowland that covers the central and western regions of the state. This is a generally flat plain of fertile soils deposited by glacial actions that left it covered with moraines, or rolling hills, of sand and gravel.

In the east and the southeast the state includes portions of the Appalachian Plateau, a hillier region rich in mineral deposits. In the extreme east this Appalachian Plateau includes the beginnings of the rugged Allegheny Mountains that extend into Pennsylvania. Along its northern border, Ohio includes a strip of Great Lakes Plain. Much of the region once lay beneath Lake Erie; for that reason it remained swampland until drained by modern engineering techniques. West of Lake Erie the Great Lakes Plain broadens into a fertile farming valley.

Climate. Ohio has a continental climate with seasonal extremes ranging from below 20° F in winter to over 80 in summer. Precipitation averages about 36 inches across the state. Winters are longer in Cleveland, on the shore of Lake Erie, than in the rest of the state, and the annual snowfall of more than 50 inches in Cleveland is nearly twice that in Columbus, near the geographical center of the state.

Principal cities. Ohio is a state of large cities, and it includes three metropolitan areas with more than 1 million residents. The largest is Cleveland, the center of a consolidated metropolitan area extending nearly 30 miles south to Akron and includng 2.8 million people. Cincinnati, on the Ohio River in the southwest, is part of another consolidated metropolitan area extending north to Dayton and into Indiana and Kentucky; it has 1.6 million people. Columbus, with a metropolitan population just over 1 million, is both the state capital and its central city. Other large cities are Toledo, on the Michigan border in the northwest, and Youngstown, near the Pennsylvania border in the east. The state's eastern border is only 30 miles

ACCESSORIES *for the automobile—from tires to tape decks—are a major Midwestern product. Rubber, glass, and a wide variety of plastics go into their manufacture.*

FIRESTONE

from Pittsburgh, and its northwestern border is 40 miles from Detroit.

The people. Population growth in Ohio virtually ceased during the 1970's, when the rate was only 1.3 percent. The natural population increase was 770,000, but 624,000 state residents moved to other states, principally to the South. The proportion of urban population actually declined. The state population is 10 percent black and 1 percent Hispanic. The population is also notable for the number of European groups, such as Germans in Cincinnati and Poles in Cleveland, who have retained their ethnic identity.

Economy. Ohio is one of the major manufacturing states in the United States. It is unusual for its diversification of manufacturing businesses and their dispersal across the state. Cleveland's steel industry is supplied with ore by Great Lakes barges. Across the state, Cincinnati is a leader in machine tools and electronic equipment. Other cities throughout the state are associated with particular products: Akron with rubber; Canton with steel bearings; Toledo with glass; and Youngstown with steel.

Ohio ranks twelfth among all states in mining, with the principal products being coal, natural gas, and limestone. The state also ranks twelfth in agricultural production. The major crops are soybeans, corn, and greenhouse vegetables. The livestock income, less than that of crops, is derived from hogs, sheep, and dairy products.

Places of interest. All of Ohio's major cities include special cultural attractions, and the smaller towns offer attractions such as the Air and Space Museum at Wapakoneta, the Air Force Museum at Dayton, and the Pro Football Hall of Fame at Canton. The state also preserves the homes of and memorials to five native U.S. presidents—Hayes, Garfield, McKinley, Taft, and Harding.

The South-Central States

The South-Central states extend 550 miles from the Ohio River south to the Gulf of Mexico and a maximum of 430 miles from the Mississippi River west to the Appalachian Mountains. These continental southern states are Mississippi and Alabama along the Gulf Coast, Tennessee along the northern border of Alabama and Mississippi, and Kentucky between Tennessee and the Ohio River.

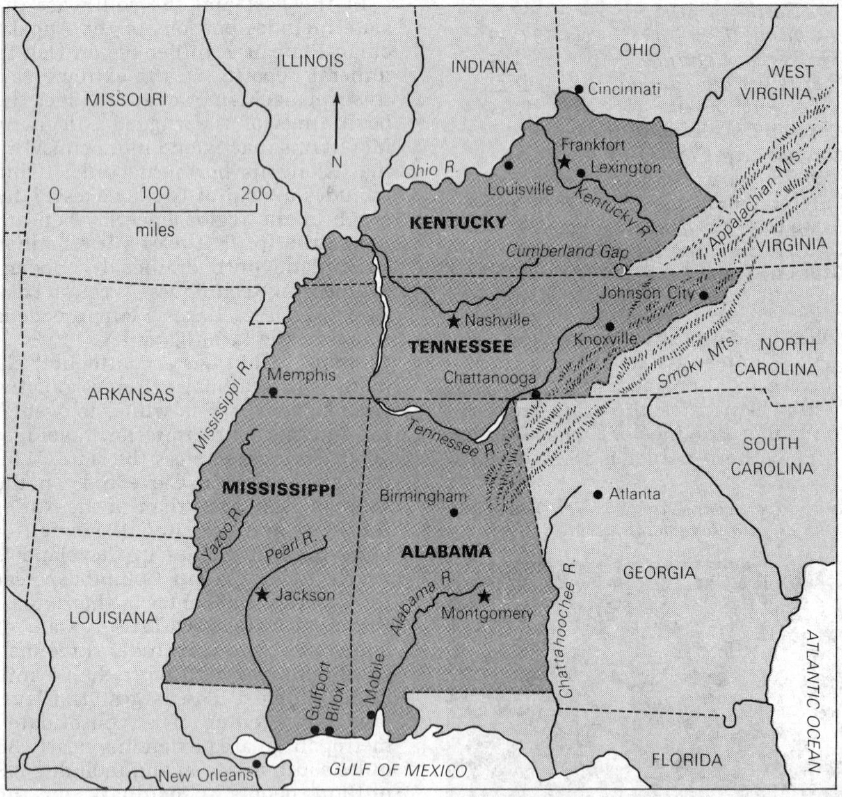

Until 1970 the South-Central states regularly lost population to employment opportunities in other regions, particularly the Great Lakes states north of the Ohio River. During the 1970's, however, fully 20 percent of the region's total population growth, or about 350,000 people, were immigrants to the region.

The change has been especially apparent among blacks, who traditionally migrated from the South-Central states for both economic and social reasons. By 1980 black migration from the region had virtually ceased, and the black proportion of the total population (approximately 20 percent in 1980) is expected to rise.

The primary economic factor in the rise of the "New South" has been the growth of its manufacturing businesses. Social factors have also been important. The increase in employment opportunities was accompanied by the end of the civil rights clashes of the 1950's and '60's.

The land. Topographically, all the South-Central states have in common portions of the Gulf Coastal Plain. The plain runs from southern Mississippi and Alabama to a narrow northern extreme in western Kentucky. To the west, along the Mississippi River, lies a narrow strip of swampy silt built up by the river. To the east lie the highland plateaus that eventually rise into the Appalachian Mountains. In the north the region includes a portion of the Interior Low Plateau running from the Great Lakes states south across central Kentucky and into the Nashville Basin in central Tennessee.

The lower Mississippi River that forms the western border of the region is the great trunk of the central U.S. drainage system. Running from its confluence with the Ohio River at the edge of western Kentucky to its mouth

THE SOUTH-CENTRAL STATES

State	Area (sq. mi.)	Population 1985	Population change 1980–85 number	Population change 1980–85 percent	Persons per sq. mi.
Kentucky	39,650	3,726,000	+ 65,000	+1.8	94
Tennessee	41,328	4,762,000	+171,000	+3.7	116
Mississippi	47,296	2,613,000	+ 92,000	+3.7	55
Alabama	50,708	4,021,000	+127,000	+3.3	79
Region totals	178,982	15,122,000	+455,000	+3.1	84

at the Gulf, the river travels 560 air miles. Its actual route, however, is approximately twice that distance because of wide bends that are especially serpentine along the Mississippi–Arkansas border.

Climate. The climate of the region ranges from moderate in Kentucky to subtropical along the Gulf Coast. Winter temperatures fall below freezing in the Appalachian Highlands but only to 40° F in the south of the region. Summers are warm throughout. Light snows are common in the north, but the Gulf Coast experiences year-round heavy rains surpassing 60 inches per year at Mobile in southern Alabama.

History. Most of the region was simultaneously explored in the 1500's by the French from Canada and the Spanish from Florida. Great Britain took possession at the end of the French and Indian War in 1763. Effective settlement was first accomplished from the American colony of Virginia. The major trauma in the region's history was the Civil War, initiated at the Convention of Confederate States in Montgomery, Alabama, on February 4, 1861. Following the defeat of the Confederate Army in 1865, the region entered a period of reconstruction by outsiders that devastated its economic and political future.

Principal cities. The South-Central states lack the major urban centers created in other regions by massive industrialization. No metropolitan area has as many as a million residents. The largest population centers are Memphis, Tennessee, on the Mississippi River, and Louisville, Kentucky, on the Ohio River. Both are on the periphery of the region and both include population from states outside the region. Many South-Central residents look toward major cities just outside the region: New Orleans to the southwest, Atlanta to the southeast, and Cincinnati to the north. The largest population center entirely within the region is Birmingham, Alabama, ranked only 44th among U.S. urban centers. The South-Central states have the lowest proportion of metropolitan residents of all U.S. regions, about 52 percent.

Economy. The principal industry in the region is now manufacturing, a sector of the economy that tripled in value between 1967 and 1977. Metal products and mineral refining are among the main manufactures. The region's fivefold increase in mineral production in the 1970's has helped these manufactures to thrive.

The principal river ports, such as Memphis and Louisville, and Gulf ports such as Mobile, have also benefited from the importation of raw materials for manufacturers. During this era of industrialization the agricultural income has remained stable and equally divided between livestock, including dairy products, and new crops, such as soybeans.

Kentucky

Abbreviations: *Ky., KY*
Area: *39,650 sq. mi., 102,694 sq. km.*

Rank (of 50)	*37th*

Population:

1985	*3,726,000*
Rank (of 50)	*23rd*
Change 1980–85	*+65,000*
Percent change	*+1.8*
Persons per sq. mi.	*94*
Percent urban	*50.9*

Capital: *Frankfort*
Largest city: *Louisville*

Metro. pop. 1985	*964,000*

Entered Union: *June 1, 1792 (15th)*
State bird: *Cardinal*
State flower: *Goldenrod*
State tree: *Coffeetree*

Kentucky is a South-Central state with a straight southern border with Tennessee and a long, irregular northern border formed by the Ohio River. The Ohio River separates it from the three Great Lakes states of Illinois, Indiana, and Ohio. The state extends 425 miles from the Mississippi River on the west to Virginia and West Virginia on the east.

Daniel Boone crossed the Cumberland Gap into eastern Kentucky in 1775. After the American Revolution he began to lead the first westward wave of American settlers from Virginia to the lush bluegrass region of north-central Kentucky. These early settlers found the bluegrass region congenial to the horse farms and cotton and tobacco fields favored in Virginia, and the central area of the state retains some of that character today.

The Ohio River was the traditional border between northern and southern states in the 1800's, but Kentucky has always looked north. Today it shares parts of three metropolitan areas that straddle the river, and its own fortunes are tied to those of the Great Lakes states. Manufacturing has become a major factor in the state economy and extensive coal mining in two parts of the state has brought heavy industry to Kentucky.

The land. The surface of Kentucky slopes down from Pine Mountains along its southeast border with Virginia across the Interior Low Plateau in the central region to a small area of Gulf Coastal Plain lying near sea level beside the Mississippi River in the extreme west. The eastern mountain region includes one-quarter of the state area. It consists of the chain of Pine Mountains, and a portion of the mineral-rich Cumberland Plateau, including the eastern coalfield. The Interior Low Plateau, covering more than half the state area, includes the bluegrass area around the city of Lexington, the Pennyroyal Plateau in the south-central area, and the western coalfield along the Indiana border. In the extreme west of the state there is a small area of Gulf Coastal Plain along the Mississippi River. It is isolated by the Tennessee and Cumberland rivers, which flow north across the state into the Ohio.

Climate. Kentucky has a moderate continental climate with warm summers and cool winters. Normal summer high temperatures approach 90° F and normal winter low temperatures fall into the 20's. Precipitation across the state averages about 45 inches per year and all regions of the state receive snow in winter.

Principal cities. Louisville, on the Ohio River in the north-central region of the state, is the largest urban center in Kentucky. It is an industrial river port, and it includes two counties of Indiana across the river within its metropolitan area. Lexington, in the midst of the meadowlands and grazing areas of the bluegrass region, is the second largest city, with a metropolitan population over 300,000. In the far northern corner, part of Kentucky is within the Cincinnati metropolitan region, with a total population of 1.5 million. It shares smaller metropolitan regions with Evansville, Indiana, in the northwest, and with Huntington, West Virginia, in the northeast.

The people. Kentucky added more people in the 1970's than it had in the previous 30 years, but its rate of growth was only slightly above the national average. Traditionally, the state had lost residents to industrial employment opportunities in the Great Lakes states. In the 1970's, however, this trend reversed itself and immigration to Kentucky accounted for nearly one-quarter of its total population growth. About 7 percent of the total population is black. There is no other large racial or ethnic group. Most of the population live in the central bluegrass region. The mountainous mining regions to the east remain sparsely populated and economically depressed.

Economy. Manufacturing is the major industry in Kentucky, which was once almost exclusively an agricultural state. The major manufactures are refined coal and tobacco products. One special manufacture is whiskey, in which Kentucky leads all states. Kentucky also leads all states in the mining of bituminous (soft) coal, principally from the eastern coalfield on the Cumberland Plateau and from the western coalfield on the Interior Low Plateau.

The bluegrass region contains most of the state's farmland, and agricultural income is equally divided between crops, principally tobacco and cotton, and livestock, including poultry and dairy products. The bluegrass region is also especially famous as a breeding ground for thoroughbred horses.

Places of interest. The single greatest attraction in the state is the annual Kentucky Derby horse race run at Churchill Downs in Louisville. The

GORO/MONKMEYER

U.S. ARMY CORPS OF ENGINEERS

RIVER TO MOUNTAINS: *the South-Central states run from the majestic Mississippi in the west to the coal country of the Appalachian slopes in the east. Much of the region's development has been influenced by its geography.*

Mammoth Caves beneath the Pennyroyal Plateau are spectacular examples of limestone caverns eroded by groundwater, and the Land Between the Lakes National Recreation Area near the Mississippi is the state's principal water resort. The U.S. gold depository is located at Fort Knox, 12 miles southwest of Louisville.

Tennessee

Abbreviations: *Tenn., TN*
Area: *41,328 sq. mi., 107,040 sq. km.*
Rank (of 50) 34th
Population:
1985 4,762,000
Rank (of 50) 17th
Change 1980–85 +171,000
Percent change +3.7
Persons per sq. mi. 116
Percent urban 60.4
Capital: *Nashville*
Largest city: *Memphis*
Metro. pop. 1985 945,000
Entered Union: *June 1, 1796 (16th)*
State bird: *Mockingbird*
State flower: *Iris*
State tree: *Tulip poplar*

Tennessee is a South-Central state with borders on the states of four other regions. It stretches more than 400 miles from its western Mississippi River border with Arkansas and Missouri to its irregular eastern border with North Carolina. Its north-south extent is over 100 miles from a northern border with Kentucky and Virginia to a southern border with Mississippi, Alabama, and Georgia.

The Tennessee River passes through the state twice. The upper Tennessee flows south through the eastern region and then, after a loop through northern Alabama, returns to flow north across the more populated western region to Kentucky and the Ohio River. The river divides Tennessee into eastern, central, and western regions that are distinct in topography, economy, and population. The river has also been the most important factor in making Tennessee an industrial state. The Tennessee Valley Authority, established in 1933, has created a network of dams and reservoirs that gives the state an abundance of cheap hydroelectric power.

The land. The traditional division of Tennessee into east, central, and west provides the primary distinctions within its rugged and complex topography. East Tennessee is a mountainous area of the Appalachian Highland. The highest mountains are the Unakas on the North Carolina border, where the state high point at Clingman's Dome (6642 feet) is located. East of the Unakas lies the Great Appalachian Valley, a 30- to 60-mile-wide region of parallel ridges that averages over 1000 feet in elevation. The western extent of the Appalachian Highland consists of the Cumberland Plateau, made up of rugged flat-topped hills.

Central Tennessee is part of the Interior Low Plateau and includes the Nashville Basin, farmland ringed in all directions but north by highland rims rising 600 feet from ground level. Western Tennessee is part of the Gulf Coastal Plain, a moderately hilly region extending north from Mississippi and Alabama. In the extreme west of the state, beyond a line of 150-foot bluffs, the Gulf Coastal Plain drops to a narrow strip of Mississippi bottomland varying in width with the bends of the river.

Climate. Tennessee has a moderate continental climate. Normal winter lows throughout the state are about 30° F, and normal summer highs are near 90. Rainfall throughout the state is about 50 inches per year, and substantial snows occur only in the eastern mountains.

Principal cities. The largest city in the state is Memphis, a Mississippi River port in the southwest whose metropolitan area includes nearby parts of Arkansas and Mississippi. The principal city in central Tennessee is the capital, Nashville. Its metropolitan population approaches 500,000, and it functions as the state's major industrial center. At the edge of the eastern mountains are three growing metropolitan areas: Knoxville, a mineral refining center; Johnson City–Kingsport–Bristol, on the northeastern border with Virginia; and Chattanooga, on the southeastern border with Georgia.

The people. Tennessee has a growing and increasingly urban population because of the spread of its manufacturing industries. In addition to natural growth, the population was swelled by more than 200,000 immigrants from other states during the 1970's. These new residents account for almost one-third of the total population increase. Most of the population growth has occurred in the metropolitan areas of the western and central regions. Eastern Tennessee remains in comparison an economically depressed Appalachian mining region. The black population represents 16 percent of the total.

Economy. Because of the Tennessee Valley Authority's hydroelectric power projects, manufacturing has come to exceed agriculture in value in the 20th century. A large portion of the manufacturing industry, which employs nearly 30 percent of the work force, is devoted to refining the state's mineral and agricultural produce, but there are also large manufacturers of transportation and electronic equipment. The mining industry produces large quantities of bituminous coal on the Cumberland Plateau in the east. Tennessee also leads all states in the production of zinc.

In agriculture, farm income from livestock slightly exceeds that from crops. Cattle ranches and dairy farms predominate in central Tennessee. In addition to the usual sources of agricultural income, there is extensive trade in show animals such as Tennessee walking horses. New soybean plantings exceed the traditional crops of cotton and tobacco in value.

Places of interest. The principal attraction in eastern Tennessee is Great Smoky Mountains National Park, a preserve within the Unakas on the North Carolina border. Reelfoot Lake, formed by an earthquake in 1811, is a major attraction on the far west Mississippi bottomland. There are several places of historical interest in Nashville, including the homes of Presidents Andrew Jackson, James Polk, and Andrew Johnson. Tennessee is also the home of two major American music centers: Memphis, an important jazz center and former home of Elvis Presley, and Nashville, a recording and performance center for country and western music. Knoxville was the host to a world's fair in 1982, attracting millions of visitors.

Mississippi

Abbreviations: *Miss., MS*
Area: *47,296 sq. mi., 122,497 sq. km.*
Rank (of 50) *31st*
Population:
1985 *2,613,000*
Rank (of 50) *31st*
Change 1980–85 *+92,000*
Percent change *+3.7*
Persons per sq. mi. *55*
Percent urban *47.3*
Capital: *Jackson*
Largest city: *Jackson*
Metro. pop. 1985 *385,000*
Entered Union: *Dec. 10, 1817 (20th)*
State bird: *Mockingbird*
State flower: *Magnolia*
State tree: *Magnolia*

Mississippi is a South-Central state on the east bank of the Mississippi River, bordering Louisiana and Arkansas to the west. Its southern border includes 44 miles of coastline on the Gulf of Mexico. It is otherwise separated from the Gulf by the 50-mile-wide eastern extension of Louisiana. The state's eastern and northern borders are with Alabama and Tennessee, two other South-Central states.

Historically Mississippi was the heart of a Southern plantation society in which aristocratic growers owned large numbers of slaves and cultivated cotton. This heritage continued to dominate the state's social, political, and economic character well into modern times. Until the 1940's blacks outnumbered whites, and although slavery had long been abolished, they were both poor and powerless. In the next 30 years, thousands of blacks moved out of the state, seeking better conditions in the North. During these same years, however, blacks in Mississippi gained greater economic opportunities and political power, and by 1970 the great Northern migration had slowed to a trickle. The state's new businesses brought it a larger population increase in the 1970's than it had seen in the previous 40 years. Yet Mississippi remains last among U.S. states in per capita income, a position it has occupied for most of the 20th century.

The land. There are two principal topographical areas in Mississippi: a 200-mile-long stretch of Mississippi delta along the river in the northwest, and a far larger expanse of Gulf Coastal Plain covering the rest of the state area. The delta, ranging from 10 to 85 miles in width, lies between the Mississippi River on the west and the Tallahatchie and Yazoo rivers on the east. It is separated from the rest of the state area by a line of rugged loess bluffs that runs north into Tennessee. The Gulf Coastal Plain to the east and south is a hillier region, with many individual relief features. From a sea-level elevation along the Gulf Coast the plain rises to the north. The state's high point is Woodall Mountain (806 feet) in the extreme northeast corner. The plain is broken along the state's eastern border by the Black Belt, a prairie of rich black soil that extends eastward into Alabama.

Climate. Mississippi has a warm, humid subtropical climate. Normal high temperatures in summer exceed 90° F, and normal lows in winter remain above 40. Rainfall throughout the state is a heavy 50 inches per year, and snows are rare even in the highest northeastern regions.

Principal cities. Although the urban proportion of the population has nearly doubled since 1950, Mississippi remains a predominantly rural state. The principal city is the capital, Jackson, near the center of the state on the Pearl River. Its metropolitan area population increased 24 percent in the 1970's to exceed 300,000. The second largest population center is Biloxi–Gulfport (population 191,918) on the Gulf Coast. Together these two large metropolitan areas account for only one-fifth of the state's population. Several important cities lie near Mississippi's border in adjacent states: Memphis to the north and New Orleans and Mobile to the south.

The people. Mississippi has one of the most stable populations in the United States. It has the fewest foreign-born residents in the country, only about 8000, and nearly 70 percent of the people were born in the state. For the first time in half a century, more people moved into Mississippi than out of it during the 1970's. Blacks represent about 35 percent of the population, the highest proportion of any state.

Economy. Manufacturing is now the principal industry in Mississippi. Diversified manufacturers employ 30 percent of the work force in the production of textiles, food, wood, and electrical goods. In agriculture soybeans have replaced cotton on the fields of the delta, and Mississippi has surrendered its traditional leadership in cotton to the irrigated farmlands of California and Texas. Dairy farms account for most of the state's livestock. Other principal industries include timber and petroleum and natural gas drilling along the Gulf Coast.

Places of interest. Mississippi is rich in Civil War monuments such as the Vicksburg National Military Park, Brice's Crossroads National Battlefield Site, and the Tupelo National Battlefield. Plantation mansions are preserved at Oxford in the north of the state and at Hattiesburg and Natchez, both in the south. Prehistoric Indian mounds are also preserved along the Natchez Trace National Parkway.

Alabama

Abbreviations: *Ala., AL*
Area: *50,708 sq. mi., 131,334 sq. km.*
Rank (of 50) *28th*
Population:
1985 *4,021,000*
Rank (of 50) *22nd*
Change 1980–85 *+127,000*
Percent change *+3.3*
Persons per sq. mi. *79*
Percent urban *60.0*
Capital: *Montgomery*
Largest city: *Birmingham*
Metro. pop. 1985 *904,000*
Entered Union: *Dec. 14, 1819 (22nd)*
State bird: *Yellowhammer*
State flower: *Camellia*
State tree: *Southern pine*

Alabama lies in the southern United States midway between the Mississippi River and the Atlantic Ocean. It has about 60 miles of shoreline on the Gulf of Mexico in the southwest, but it is otherwise separated from the Gulf by the 50-mile-wide panhandle of Florida. The state stretches 335 miles north-south from Tennessee to the Gulf, and its eastern border is with Georgia.

Nicknamed "the Heart of Dixie," Alabama, like Mississippi, was historically an agrarian state with large plantations of cotton worked by slave labor. It remained a symbol of the Confederacy long after the Civil War, and in recent times it was the scene of the most bitter racial confrontations in the United States: the bus boycott in Montgomery in 1955 and the Freedom March from Selma to Birmingham in 1965.

Today industry has supplanted agriculture as the state's leading business, and the manufacturing district centered around Birmingham in the north-central region of the state has made Alabama the principal heavy-industry state in the south.

The land. Alabama contains three major topographical areas: the Appalachian Highlands in the northeast, the interior plateau in the far north, and Gulf Coastal Plain in the south and west. The Appalachian region is the southernmost extension of the Appalachian mountain range, which runs northeast through the eastern United States and into Canada. The mineral-rich highlands represent more than one-third of Alabama's area. The mountain and valley region is flanked by the Cumberland Plateau on the northwest and the Piedmont Plateau on the southeast. The state's high point, Cheaha Mountain (2407 feet) is in the midst of the Appalachian region. The interior plateau in the far north is crossed by the Tennessee River, which enters the state at its northeast corner and flows out again at the northwest corner. The fertile Gulf Coastal Plain rarely rises above 500 feet in elevation, and it declines to sea-level swampland around Mobile Bay on the Gulf Coast. The principal feature of the plain in Alabama is the Black Belt of fertile prairie in the southwest quarter of the state.

UPI

BLACKS *have overcome many racial barriers in the South, including those to public office. Richard Arrington became the first black mayor of Birmingham, Alabama, in 1979.*

Climate. Alabama's climate varies from subtropical in the south to temperate in the northern highlands. Normal summer highs are over 90° F and winter lows range from 44 in the south to 32 in the northeast. Seasonal variations are far greater in the north than in the south. Rainfall is over 50 inches everywhere in the state, but Mobile has the greatest rainfall of all major U.S. cities, about 67 inches per year.

Principal cities. The largest metropolitan area in the state is Birmingham, located just northwest of the Appalachian ranges in the north-central part of the state. Known as "the Pittsburgh of the South" for its steel industry, this industrial center includes one-fifth of the state's population. Mobile has a metropolitan area population of nearly 500,000 and it is the second largest industrial center in the state. The capital city of Montgomery has a metropolitan population approaching 300,000. Together these three urban seats account for over 40 percent of the state's population.

The people. Alabama's rate of growth in the 1970's was higher than for any decade since 1900–1910, and for the first time in 50 years more people moved into the state than moved out. Hundreds of thousands of black citizens moved from the state between 1930 and 1970, but the exodus ended in the 1970's. Blacks constitute 26 percent of the total population.

Economy. The principal industry in Alabama is manufacturing. One-quarter of the total manufacturing income of over $10 billion per year is generated in Birmingham. Iron and coal are both mined in the highlands north of Birmingham, and the local industry is based on refining these products and smelting the pig iron into a variety of major manufactures such as cast iron pipe. The economy of Mobile is also based on refining mineral products, in this case petroleum and natural gas drilled near the Gulf Coast.

Agriculture is second to manufacturing, and principal products include livestock, dairy products, and poultry. A major field crop, replacing cotton in many areas, is soybeans. Alabama also leads all Southern states in timber production, principally softwoods harvested in the southwest of the state.

Places of interest. Alabama's capital city of Montgomery preserves the "White House of the South" occupied by Jefferson Davis during the Civil War. Bridgeport in the highlands at the extreme northeast corner of the state is the location of the Russell Cave National Monument, which was occupied by Indians in prehistoric times. Tuskegee Institute west of Montgomery is the home of the George Washington Carver Museum.

The South Atlantic States

The South Atlantic states are situated in the southeast corner of the United States. At the south, a peninsula, consisting of most of Florida, extends 450 miles south between the Atlantic Ocean and the Gulf of Mexico. The other three states, Georgia, South Carolina, and North Carolina, all extend from the Atlantic coast inland to the Appalachian Mountains. The region is bordered on the west by the South-Central states of Alabama and Tennessee, and on the north by the Tidewater state of Virginia.

The earliest settlement by Europeans in the New World occurred in this region. The Spanish established a colony at St. Augustine, Florida, in 1565. This city still bears traces of its Spanish heritage. Other states in the region have long colonial histories under British rule. All but Florida were among the original 13 colonies forming the United States. Later, all these states were members of the Confederate States of America, which seceded from the Union in 1861, at the beginning of the Civil War.

Today the greatest bond of the South Atlantic states is population growth. The South Atlantic states have the highest growth rate of any region except the Mountain states, and during the 1970's, they increased numerically more than any region except the Southwest. New jobs provided by manufacturing are a key factor in this growth, but an important additional factor is the region's combination of mild climate and recreational attractions, including both beaches and mountains.

The land. Topographically, these states all share portions of the Atlantic Coastal Plain, a lowland covering most of Florida and the eastern lands of Georgia, South Carolina, and North Carolina. The plain includes swamplands and shifting islands of sand just offshore that are part of the Great Barrier Reef. Along their western boundaries, Georgia and North Carolina include parts of the Blue Ridge Mountains. The highest peak in the eastern United States is Mt. Mitchell (6684 feet) in northwestern North Carolina. Between the mountains and the coastal plain lies the Piedmont Plateau, stretching northward from central Georgia across western South Carolina and central North Carolina. At the point where the rock beds of the plateau drop off to the lower lands of the plain, rivers turn to rapids. This fall line extends northeast from Columbus, Georgia, through South Carolina to Raleigh, North Carolina, and on into the Tidewater states.

Climate. The climate of the region ranges from subtropical on the islet keys south of Florida to moderate continental in inland North Carolina. In summer normal high temperatures are about 90° F throughout the region, and normal winter lows range from 45 in Florida to freezing in the northern states. Precipitation ranges from 60 inches in Florida to 42 inches in North Carolina. Only the western regions of North and South Carolina receive appreciable snow.

History. The Spanish kept possession of Florida until 1819, some 30 years after the establishment of the United States. The original colony of Carolina was divided into North and South in 1729. Georgia was established—originally as a colony where imprisoned debtors from England could get a new start—in 1732. The latter three states approved the U.S. Constitution in 1788 and 1789, and Florida entered the Union in 1845 as a slave state. The first shots of the Civil War in 1861 were fired by Confederate soldiers on Union-held Fort Sumter in Charleston Bay, South Carolina.

The people. Today the South Atlantic states, which were relatively slow-growing in population until World War II, attract immigrants from other U.S. regions. The greatest growth is in Florida, a haven for retired people, particularly from the eastern United States. But the other states also have significant population increases from migration and high birthrates. All of these states include a large proportion of black Americans, and Florida is unique among U.S. states for its large population of Cuban Americans.

Principal cities. The two largest metropolitan areas in the region are Miami, Florida, the center of the tourist and retirement business in Florida; and Atlanta, Georgia, a business and transportation center for the South Atlantic region as well as for nearby sections of northern Alabama and eastern Tennessee. The Carolinas have smaller cities, some clustered into sizable urban regions.

Economy. In the midst of their population growth, the importance of agriculture has receded in the economies of the South Atlantic states. The principal industry in all of these states except Florida is now manufacturing, especially of textile products. In Florida manufacturing ranks second only to tourism, an important industry in all South Atlantic states.

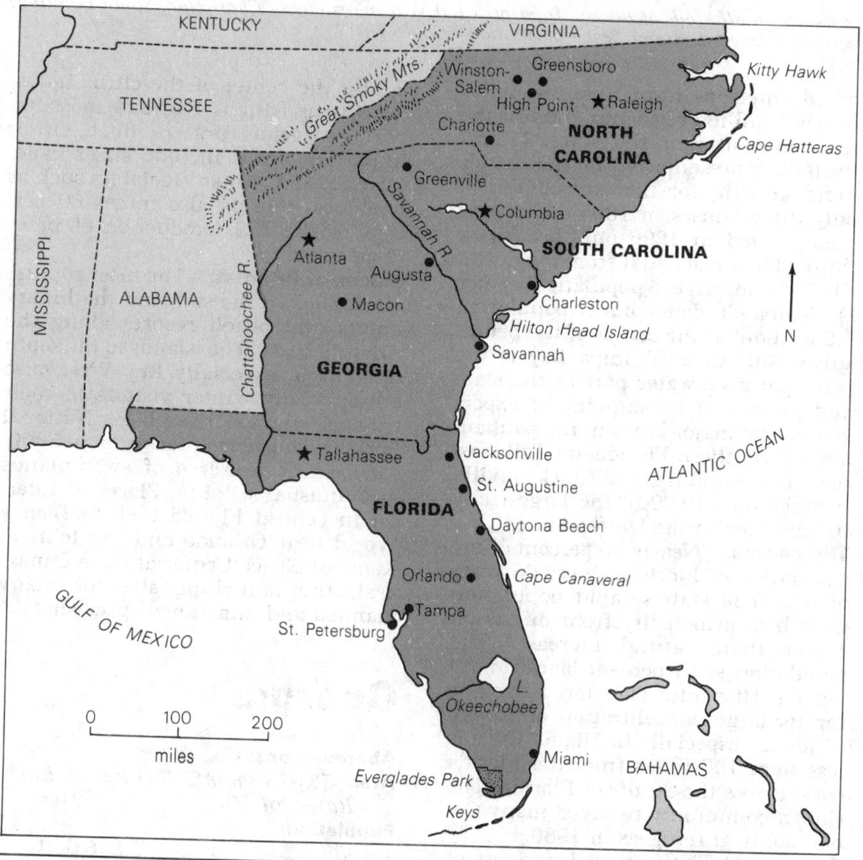

THE SOUTH ATLANTIC STATES

State	Area (sq. mi.)	Population 1985	Population change 1980–85 number	Population change 1980–85 percent	Persons per sq. mi.
Florida	54,090	11,366,000	+1,619,000	+16.6	210
Georgia	58,073	5,976,000	+ 513,000	+ 9.4	103
South Carolina	30,225	3,347,000	+ 226,000	+ 7.2	111
North Carolina	48,798	6,255,000	+ 374,000	+ 6.4	128
Region totals	191,186	26,944,000	+2,732,000	+11.3	141

Florida

Abbreviations: *Fla., FL*
Area: *54,090 sq. mi., 140,093 sq. km.*
Rank (of 50) *24th*
Population:
1985 *11,366,000*
Rank (of 50) *6th*
Change 1980–85 *+1,619,000*
Percent change *+16.6*
Persons per sq. mi. *210*
Percent urban *84.3*
Capital: *Tallahassee*
Largest city: *Miami*
Metro. pop. 1985 *1,753,000*
Entered Union: *Mar. 3, 1845 (27th)*
State bird: *Mockingbird*
State flower: *Orange blossom*
State tree: *Sabal palm (cabbage palmetto)*

Florida is situated in the extreme southeast of the continental United States. Most of the state area consists of a 450-mile-long peninsula extending southeast between the Atlantic Ocean and the Gulf of Mexico. The peninsula ends in a string of islets called the Florida Keys, the southernmost part of the contiguous 48 states. The state also includes a narrow northern panhandle extending 350 miles west from the Atlantic and separating Georgia and most of Alabama from the Gulf of Mexico.

The oldest European settlement in North America was a Spanish outpost at St. Augustine on Florida's Atlantic coast, and the state has a long history under Spanish, English, and American control. Its character, however, is entirely a product of the 20th century. There were fewer than 200,000 people in the state in 1880, and the population only reached 1 million a half-century later, in 1930. Between 1950 and 1980 the state had a greater numerical population growth than any

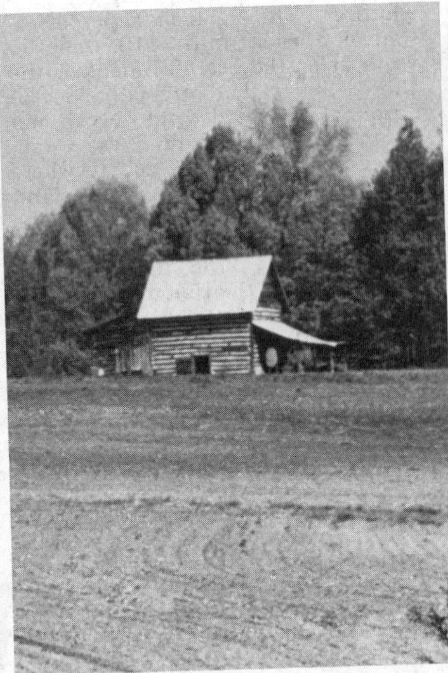

MANSIONS AND LEAN-TOS: *South Atlantic residents live in all kinds of houses, from pre-Civil War mansions in Charleston, South Carolina, to spartan sharecroppers' cabins to the modern luxury buildings of Miami Beach on Florida's Gold Coast.*

state except California: 7 million people, or 70 percent of the present population, in only 30 years. Many were retired people, and the populace is by far the oldest in the United States. The people were drawn by the state's 1300 miles of coastline beaches and the warm, sunny climate. Millions visit both winter and summer, making tourism the principal industry.

The land. Florida lies entirely within the Atlantic and the Gulf coastal plains. The peninsula is wholly a part of the Atlantic Coastal Plain. Along the Atlantic coast are the barrier beaches separated from the mainland by tidal lagoons. The interior of the peninsula consists of hills and lakes from the northern border south to Lake Okeechobee. The southern third of the peninsula is the great swamp known as the Everglades.

The northern panhandle is wholly a part of the Gulf Coastal Plain. South of Alabama the panhandle consists of highlands that reach a maximum elevation of 345 feet. South of Georgia it consists of the marshy Mariana lowlands and of the Tallahassee Hills in the extreme east.

Climate. Florida has year-round warm temperatures. Normal summer temperatures throughout the state are 90° F, and winter normal lows range from 45 in Jacksonville in the north to 60 in Miami, 350 miles to the south. Precipitation averages 60 inches per year in Miami and 55 inches in Jacksonville. Snowfall is rare anywhere in the state, but hurricanes are a threat in summer and early fall.

Principal cities. The major urban center in the state is the 100-mile-long "Gold Coast" of cities surrounding Miami in the southeast. This consolidated metropolitan area includes nearly 3 million residents, and it is the tourism center of the state. Miami itself is representative of the state's rapid growth, for the city contained only three houses in 1895 and it was incorporated in 1896 only because a railroad had reached it from the north. The second largest population center is Tampa–St. Petersburg (population 1.5 million) at the center of the peninsula's Gulf Coast. Tampa Bay is the principal deep-water port in the state and the site of its shipping of export goods. The major cities in the panhandle and northern Florida are Tallahassee, the capital, and Jacksonville (population 740,000), the largest city in land area in the United States.

The people. Nearly 20 percent of the population of Florida is over 65 years of age. The state's rapid population growth is principally from migration rather than natural increase. The population is 14 percent black, and 9 percent Hispanic. The state is unique for its large concentration of Cuban residents, especially in Miami. Cuba is less than 100 miles from the Florida coast across the Straits of Florida. The Cuban community received many Cuban political refugees in 1980.

Economy. The principal business of Florida is tourism, now a year-round industry that draws over 35 million visitors per year and produces an annual income of more than $16 billion. Manufacturing is the second most important sector of the state's economy. Florida's manufacturers concentrate on wood pulp and paper products, food processing, and electronics equipment associated with the space agencies surrounding Cape Canaveral on the Atlantic coast near Orlando. Orlando is also the center of the citrus industry. Citrus fruit is Florida's most important agricultural product. Other important crops include sugar cane, tobacco, and winter vegetables such as tomatoes. Florida also mines 80 percent of the U.S. production of phosphate rock.

Places of interest. The most popular attractions in the state are the luxury hotels and beach resorts along the Atlantic coast. The islands to the south of Florida, especially Key West, also attract many winter visitors to their tropical climate. Everglades National Park in southern Florida is a 5000-square-mile preserve of swamplands and unusual wildlife. Places of interest in central Florida include Disney World near Orlando and the John F. Kennedy Space Center at Cape Canaveral, the launching site for many manned and unmanned space shots.

Georgia

Abbreviations: *Ga., GA*
Area: *58,073 sq. mi., 150,409 sq. km.*
Rank (of 50) — *21st*
Population:
1985 — *5,976,000*
Rank (of 50) — *11th*
Change 1980–85 — *+513,000*
Percent change — *+9.4*
Persons per sq. mi. — *103*
Percent urban — *62.3*
Capital: *Atlanta*
Largest city: *Atlanta*
Metro. pop. 1985 — *2,472,000*
Entered Union: *Jan. 2, 1788 (4th)*
State bird: *Brown thrasher*
State flower: *Cherokee rose*
State tree: *Live oak*

Georgia is located in the southeast United States to the north of Florida. The state has 100 miles of coastline on the Atlantic Ocean, and a long northeastern border with South Carolina formed by the Savannah River. To the west it borders Alabama, and to the north Tennessee and North Carolina. Georgia is the largest state in land area east of the Mississippi River.

Georgia has endured a series of social and economic problems since the Civil War, most of them related to racial and economic inequalities. During the first half of the 1900's, thousands of blacks and poor whites left the state in search of opportunity elsewhere. Since 1950, however, the state has grown rapidly, and many state residents have moved to the cities. Animosity between blacks and whites and between city and country residents has cooled, and the state has experienced increased prosperity. More people now move into Georgia than move out of it each year. Atlanta has emerged as the commercial and financial center of the southeastern states.

The land. The land area of Georgia runs from the Appalachian Mountains in the north and west to the Atlantic coast. The northeastern part of the state includes a portion of forested Blue Ridge Mountains with a number of peaks over 4000 feet in elevation. Most of the northern half of the state, however, consists of the Piedmont Plateau, the agricultural and population center of the state. The rolling hills of the plateau decline in elevation from about 2000 feet in the north to about 1000 feet at the Fall Line Hills running east-west across the center of the state.

South of these hills lie the coastal plains. The western part slopes toward the Gulf of Mexico (only 30 miles from Georgia's southwest border with Florida), and the eastern half slopes toward the Atlantic. Waterpower generated by streams falling from the plateau to the plain made the hills the state's early industrial belt. The Atlantic Plain in the south covers more than half the Georgia land area. Individual features of it include the Okefenokee Swamp on the Florida border and the Sea Islands, part of the Great Barrier Reef, separated from the mainland by narrow tidal lagoons.

Climate. Georgia has a warm, humid climate with a long growing season. Normal summer highs approach 90° F, and winter temperatures usually remain above freezing. Precipitation throughout the state averages 48 inches per year, but the Blue Ridge Mountains in the northeast receive nearly 70 inches, some of it in the form of snow.

Principal cities. The major urban center in the state is Atlanta, on the northwestern portion of the Piedmont Plateau. Atlanta is the model for new cities throughout the South. Its city center has been rebuilt, major businesses have been attracted, and its metropolitan population increased nearly 30 percent in the 1970's. The other major cities lie on a line running northeast across the center of the state, along the Fall Line Hills. Columbus (population 239,196) is a textile city straddling the Chattahoochee River between Georgia and Alabama. Macon (population 254,623) is a manufacturing city in central Georgia. Augusta (population 327,372) is a food processing city on the Savannah River beside South Carolina. The only other major city is Savannah (population 230,728), a river port on the South Carolina border 20 miles from the Atlantic.

The people. Like the rest of the South Atlantic states, Georgia is growing at a rate well above the national average. Its central position in the region and the importance of Atlanta as a transportation and communications center suggest that its growth will continue, and that this often depressed state will see a period of increased prosperity and importance.

The other population movement over the past few decades has been from farms to cities. In the case of Atlanta, the movement has gone a step further, from cities to outer suburbs. The state gained 128,000 residents from migration in the 1970's. In addition, the exodus of black residents has ended. In the 1960's, 154,000 blacks migrated out of the state, but in the 1970's there was a small net in-migration. Blacks represent 27 percent of the state population, and Hispanics, the only other sizable minority group, represent 1 percent.

Economy. The chief industry of Georgia is manufacturing, and its principal product is textiles. All major cities in the state produce textiles ranging from cottons to synthetics; these are used in everything from clothing to carpets. Other major manufactures are paper, other wood products, and processed foods.

Georgia's agriculture was overdependent on cotton until the 1920's, when the crop was lost to boll weevil infestation. Now the farmland, principally on the Atlantic Coastal Plain, grows peanuts, tobacco, corn, and peaches. Livestock generates as much income as crops, primarily because of the state's enormous production of chickens and eggs. Tourism is the third largest industry, generating well over $2 billion per year.

Places of interest. The Okefenokee National Wildlife Refuge is a 660-square-mile preserve of swamplands on the Florida border. The Atlantic coast is lined with seashore beaches. Historical attractions include the "Little White House" near Columbus where Franklin Delano Roosevelt died in 1945, and various memorials to the Confederacy scattered throughout the state.

South Carolina

Abbreviations: *S.C., SC*
Area: *30,225 sq. mi., 78,283 sq. km.*
Rank (of 50) *40th*
Population:
1985 *3,347,000*
Rank (of 50) *24th*
Change 1980–85 *+226,000*
Percent change *+7.2*
Persons per sq. mi. *111*
Percent urban *54.1*
Capital: *Columbia*
Largest city: *Columbia*
Metro. pop. 1985 *439,000*
Entered Union: *May 23, 1788 (8th)*
State bird: *Carolina wren*
State flower: *Yellow jessamine*
State tree: *Palmetto*

South Carolina is a South Atlantic state bordered by North Carolina to the north and Georgia across the Savannah River to the south. The state's 190-mile Atlantic coastline is broken by large inlets and sounds and, at its center, a major harbor at Charleston.

South Carolina was the first state to secede at the beginning of the Civil War, and the first battle in the war took place at Fort Sumter in Charleston Bay. The Confederate sympathizers in South Carolina were so deeply disillusioned by the reconstruction that followed the war that a lingering resentment against government has remained, and voter participation is the lowest in the United States.

Throughout the "low" country of the southeastern plain, features of the antebellum South such as plantations remain to this day. In the northwest "up" country, however, urbanization and industrialization show evidence of the "New South."

The land. South Carolina includes a fringe of Blue Ridge Mountains in the extreme northwest. From that mountain fringe, the state lands decline in elevation across two major topographical areas. The northwest "up" country consists principally of the Piedmont Plateau. This area's rainfall and the sandy loams of its soil have left it heavily forested. The southeastern two-thirds of the state are part of the Atlantic Coastal Plain. This area consists of cleared lands of great agricultural value. The Atlantic coastline is an irregular one that includes the Sea Islands barrier reef in the south and an extensive intercoastal waterway in the north.

Climate. The climate of South Carolina is warm and humid. At the capital city of Columbia near the center of the state, normal summer high temperatures are over 90° F and normal winter lows remain above freezing. Precipitation throughout most of the state averages about 46 inches per year. Precipitation is significantly higher in the state's Blue Ridge Mountains area, and that area is the only one that receives occasional light snowfalls.

Principal cities. The major city in South Carolina is Columbia. In addition to being the seat of state government, the city is the state's principal commercial and educational center. The other major urban areas are clusters of towns with collective populations exceeding that of Columbia. The Charleston area (population 430,301) is the state's major shipping port and the commercial center of the "low" country plain. The Greenville-Spartansburg area (population 568,758) is a 35-mile-long cluster of industrial towns in the northwest "up" country.

The people. The population of South Carolina is becoming urbanized at a rapid rate: during the 1970's the proportion of urban population rose from 47 percent to 54 percent. The proportion of residents born in the state remains over 70 percent. The proportion of black population is 30 percent, the highest in the United States after Mississippi. There are no other major ethnic groups.

Economy. Manufacturing now accounts for an income nine times greater than that from farms. The state's manufacturing businesses employ a full third of the work force, and they produce nearly $10 billion in textile, chemical, and paper products each year. The state agricultural businesses are concentrated in the "low" country of the coastal plain. Crops generate twice the income of livestock because of the large harvest of tobacco and peaches and new plantings of soybeans to replace the old cotton crop. Tourism is the second largest industry in the state, generating $2.2 billion per year, or about twice the amount derived from agriculture.

Places of interest. Most of the attractions for out-of-state visitors to South Carolina are found along the Atlantic coast. The shore is lined with beach resorts from Myrtle Beach in the north to Hilton Head Island near the Georgia border. In addition, the coast includes some of the state's major historic attractions, such as the Fort Sumter National Monument.

North Carolina

Abbreviations: *N.C., NC*
Area: *48,798 sq. mi., 126,387 sq. km.*
Rank (of 50) *29th*
Population:
1985 *6,255,000*
Rank (of 50) *10th*
Change 1980–85 *+374,000*
Percent change *+6.4*
Persons per sq. mi. *128*
Percent urban *48.0*
Capital: *Raleigh*
Largest city: *Charlotte*
Metro. pop. 1985 *1,049,000*
Entered Union: *Nov. 21, 1789 (12th)*
State bird: *Cardinal*
State flower: *Dogwood blossom*
State tree: *Pine*

North Carolina is the most northern of the South Atlantic states. It has a 300-mile Atlantic coastline and is situated between Virginia to the north and South Carolina to the south. From the broad coastline the state narrows to a point more than 500 miles inland, where it borders Tennessee on the north and Georgia on the south.

The character of North Carolina belies its status as a heavily populated and economically powerful state. There is no city of national importance in the state, but North Carolina ranks tenth in the United States in population. There is no heavy industry in the state, but North Carolina also ranks tenth in the United States in manufacturing products. The industries in the state are among the oldest in the South, and the state's economic power derives from its national leadership in textiles, furniture, and tobacco, all industries related to agricultural produce. These businesses are evenly dispersed across the state, and so is the population: North Carolina is the only South Atlantic state with an urban population of less than 50 percent. The result of these factors is a state that prospers quietly, receiving less attention than one might expect.

The land. The land of North Carolina falls away from mountains in the western interior to sea-level elevations along the coast. The mountain region is the smallest in the state. The Great Smoky Mountains lie along the Tennessee border. Thirty miles farther east are the Blue Ridge Mountains, which include the highest peak in the eastern United States at Mt. Mitchell (6684 feet).

Two-fifths of the state land area consists of the Piedmont Plateau to the east of the mountains. This forested plateau ranges between 60 and 75 miles in west-east breadth and declines in elevation from 1500 feet in the west to 500 feet in the east. At its eastern extent there is a fall line at which the land drops away to the Atlantic Coastal Plain and the rivers pass through rapids and waterfalls. The Atlantic Coastal Plain of fertile sands and silts occupies the eastern two-fifths of the state land area. Along the Atlantic it includes tidewater areas where rivers are flooded into estuaries by the action of the sea. Tidewater areas are especially prevalent in the northeast; they are characterized by shifting banks of sand dunes, such as Cape Hatteras, and low-lying marshes such as the Great Dismal Swamp.

Climate. The climate of North Carolina is warm and humid except in the mountain region. Average temperatures on the Piedmont Plateau range from normal highs over 85° F in summer to normal lows around freezing in winter. Precipitation throughout the state averages 42 inches per year, including 5 inches of snow. The winters are longer and the snowfalls greater in the mountains.

Principal cities. All the major cities of North Carolina are located on the inland Piedmont Plateau, and the largest is the manufacturing center of Charlotte near the South Carolina border. Farther north on the plateau, three cities, Winston-Salem, Greensboro, and High Point form a triangular urban center 30 miles wide on a side that has a metropolitan area population of 827,385. These cities are the center of the state's tobacco industry as well as other manufactures. The capital city of Raleigh and nearby Durham form the third large urban area (population 530,673). They are located on the fall line between plateau and coastal plain. Together with Chapel Hill, the seat of the state university, Raleigh and Durham attracted new electronics and research business to the state in the 1970's.

The people. More than half of North Carolina's population growth during the 1970's was produced by immigrants from other states drawn to local employment opportunities. More than 70 percent of the residents were born in the state, but past migrations of young people from North Carolina have left the state with the oldest population in the region except for Florida; the result is an unusually low birthrate.

Many blacks have migrated from North Carolina; during the 1970's, however, this traditional loss by migration slowed to a trickle. Black residents now account for 22 percent of the total population. Hispanics represent 1 percent of the total, and there are a small number of Cherokees on the state's single Indian reservation.

Economy. North Carolina's manufactures generate $20.6 billion in income each year. Textile, tobacco, and wood products predominate. The state lacks such natural resources as coal and iron, which are required for heavy industry.

In farm produce the state ranks second in the region only to Georgia. The major crops are cotton for textiles and bright leaf tobacco for cigarettes. Poultry farms account for most of the income from livestock. North Carolina also ranks second in the region to Georgia in lumber, principally hard woods and pine harvested from the Piedmont Plateau. Much of the wood is used in the manufacture of furniture in the region around High Point. Tourism is also an important industry, and visitors to the state spend more than $2 billion per year.

Places of interest. The Cape Hatteras and Cape Lookout national seashores are the principal natural attractions in North Carolina, although the state shares some Smoky Mountain resorts with Tennessee. Historical sites include Revolutionary War memorials at Guilford Courthouse and Moore's Creek in southeastern North Carolina, and the Wright Brothers Museum at Kitty Hawk on Cape Hatteras.

The Tidewater States

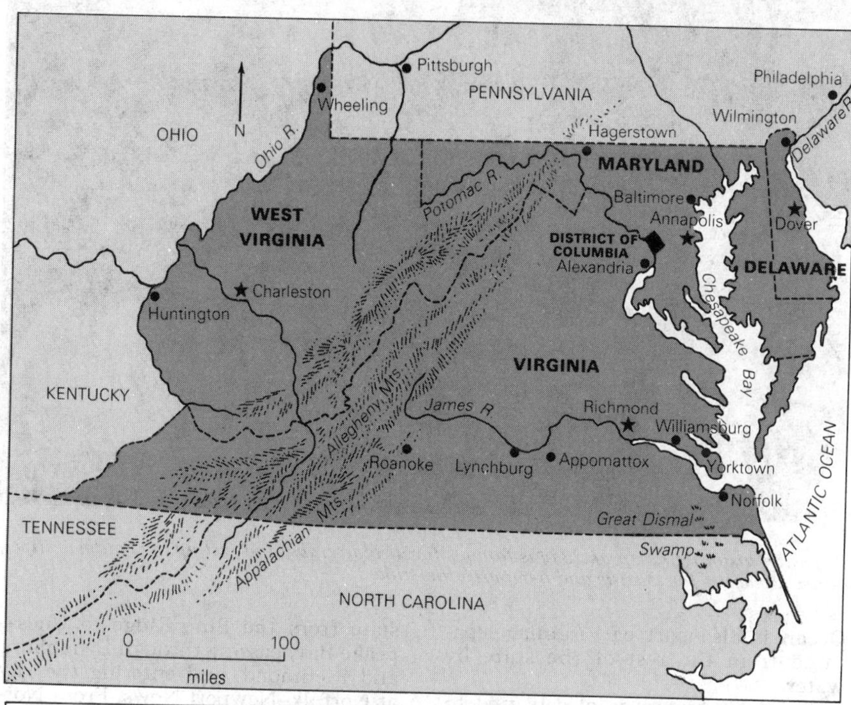

THE TIDEWATER STATES

State	Area (sq. mi.)	Population 1985	Population change 1980–85 number	Population change 1980–85 percent	Persons per sq. mi.
Virginia	39,780	5,706,000	+359,000	+6.7	144
West Virginia	24,070	1,936,000	− 14,000	− .7	80
Maryland	9,891	4,392,000	+175,000	+4.2	447
Delaware	1,982	622,000	+ 28,000	+4.6	322
District of Columbia	61	626,000	− 13,000	−2.0	9,931
Region totals	75,784	13,282,000	+535,000	+4.2	175

The Tidewater states are situated near the center of the Atlantic Ocean coastline. The region, including Virginia, West Virginia, Maryland, Delaware, and the District of Columbia, is roughly rectangular in shape. It is surrounded on its inland borders by Pennsylvania and New Jersey on the north, North Carolina on the south, and Kentucky and Ohio on the west.

The principal natural feature of the region and the source of its name is the Chesapeake Bay and its many tidal river estuaries. From its mouth just north of Norfolk, Virginia, the bay extends 180 miles north between the Delmarva Peninsula and the mainland. The western, or mainland, shore boasts many tidal rivers, including the Potomac and the Susquehanna. The peninsula contains all of the state of Delaware and parts of Maryland and Virginia.

The shelter provided by the bay and its inlets first attracted European settlers to the region. The shipping access it provides continues to support most of the region's industry. The Potomac River estuary between Virginia and Maryland divided the original 13 colonies into north and south. This led to the location on it of the country's "federal city," Washington, D.C.

The land. The region has a complex topography. The Allegheny Mountains, part of the great Appalachian chain, run through the western regions of Maryland and West Virginia. To the east of the mountains is a broader strip of the Appalachian ridge and valley region. Beyond the great Appalachian valley are the Blue Ridge Mountains, which run through northwestern Virginia and into Maryland. The land declines gradually toward the sea.

A strip of Piedmont Plateau runs through central Virginia and Maryland. The eastern border of the plateau is the fall line, where streams from the plateau fall in rapids to the coastal plain. This line often marks the highest point to which rivers are navigable; the rapids also provided industrial power from an early date.

The eastern reaches of the region are part of the Atlantic Coastal Plain. In the geological past, part of the plain fell below sea level. Several river mouths are submerged under Chesapeake Bay, leaving estuaries that are flooded for miles upstream by tidewaters.

Climate. The climate of the Tidewater states is generally moderate, influenced by its nearness to the sea and bay. Temperatures range between normal summer highs of 85° F (90 in Virginia) to normal winter lows of 25. Annual precipitation is between 40 and 46 inches. In the western reaches, winters are more severe, and snowfall is common, averaging 31 inches in West Virginia.

History. The Tidewater region was principally settled by the British, who built their first permanent settlement in America at Jamestown, Virginia, in 1607, and sent a party to settle Maryland the next year. It was, however, the Dutch who first occupied Delaware and the Swedes who established the first permanent settlement in the state at Wilmington in 1664. Virginia, Maryland, and Delaware were among the original 13 colonies. Washington, D.C., built on land along the Potomac River ceded by Maryland, became the capital of the country in 1800. Until 1861, West Virginia was part of Virginia. Then its residents, opposed to secession from the Union, requested statehood, which was granted in 1863.

Principal cities. Today the Tidewater region is predominantly urban, except for West Virginia. Two metropolitan areas alone, Baltimore, Maryland, and Washington, D.C., include 40 percent of the entire region's population. Although these cities are declining in population, other smaller cities are prospering.

The people. The movement of the people is primarily from cities to suburbs within the region. No Tidewater state except Virginia attracted significant numbers of new residents from migration in the 1970's. All Tidewater states except West Virginia include large numbers of black residents. In the District of Columbia, 70 percent of the population is black.

Economy. Manufacturing is the major industry of the Tidewater states, and it ranges from food processing throughout the region to heavy machinery manufacturing in Baltimore to chemical production in Delaware. Government employees make up a large proportion of the work force in Washington and nearby parts of Virginia and Maryland.

JANE LATTA

CONKLIN/MONKMEYER

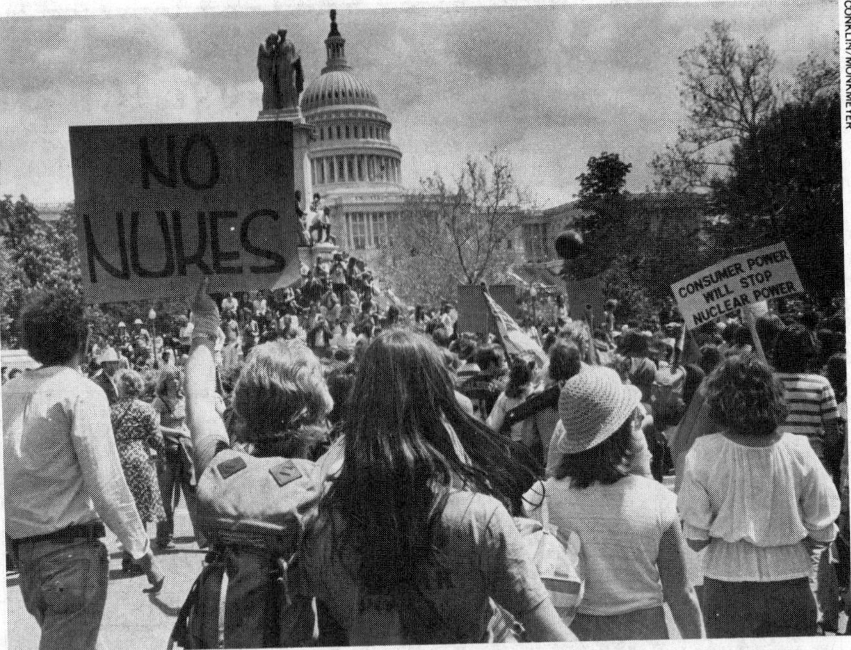

SEA LIFE AND POLITICAL LIFE *are both parts of Tidewater history. Chesapeake Bay is famous for its blue crabs, and just up the Potamac River, Washington, D.C., is the political center of the nation, a magnet for tourists and demonstrators alike.*

Tourism is the second most important source of income. Seaside resorts on the Delmarva Peninsula and the attractions in the nation's capital draw visitors. Agriculture is of far less importance, but all states in the region have in common poultry farming, and West Virginia and Virginia mine a substantial portion of the country's coal supply.

Virginia

Abbreviations: *Va., VA*
Area: *39,780 sq. mi., 103,030 sq. km.*
Rank (of 50) 36th
Population:

1985	*5,706,000*
Rank (of 50)	*13th*
Change 1980–85	*+359,000*
Percent change	*+6.7*
Persons per sq. mi.	*144*
Percent urban	*66.0*

Capital: *Richmond*
Largest city: *Norfolk*
Metro. pop. 1985 *1,289,000*
Entered Union: *June 25, 1788 (10th)*
State bird: *Cardinal*
State flower: *Dogwood blossom*
State tree: *Flowering dogwood*

Virginia lies near the center of the Atlantic seaboard. The state is triangular in shape, with a wide southern base that borders North Carolina and Tennessee. To the northwest the borders are with Kentucky and West Virginia, and to the northeast they are with Maryland, the District of Columbia, and Chesapeake Bay, an arm of the Atlantic Ocean. The southern portion of the peninsula separating Chesapeake Bay from the Atlantic Ocean is also part of Virginia, separated from the rest of the state by water.

America's history is closely tied to events in Virginia. The first permanent English colony in the New World was founded at Jamestown in 1607, and slave trade was introduced there in 1619 to support plantation society. The surrender that ended the American Revolution occurred at Yorktown in 1781, and the Civil War ended with Lee's surrender at Appomattox in 1865. Eight present-day states contain part of Virginia's original territory. Virginia has produced eight U.S. Presidents.

Today Virginia remains important to national affairs because it borders Washington, D.C. A large number of its residents are employed by the federal government. The state economy, however, is based on manufacturing, and most of its population centers are located southeast of Washington.

The land. The Appalachian Mountains lie along Virginia's northwestern border with West Virginia. This mountain and valley region includes part of the main ranges of the Allegheny Mountains and the Blue Ridge Mountains. The two ranges are separated by a great valley whose northern reaches are traversed by the Shenandoah River.

The central region of the state falls within the Piedmont Plateau, a rolling upland 40 miles wide in the extreme north broadening to 160 miles in the south. To the east of the plateau lies the Atlantic Coastal Plain, which reaches a maximum east-west breadth of 100 miles near the North Carolina border. The principal waterway is the James River, which runs across the state from the Blue Ridge to Chesapeake Bay, passing through Lynchburg and Richmond, and entering the bay at Norfolk–Newport News. From Norfolk north along the bay, river estuaries are flooded to points far inland by the action of the sea. South of Norfolk the land is marshy for lack of river estuaries, and the Great Dismal Swamp is located at the North Carolina border.

Climate. Virginia has a mild climate in which temperatures rarely rise above 90° F in summer or fall below 25 in winter except in high elevations. Precipitation at Richmond in the east-central region is 43 inches per year, including 13 inches of snow. Snowfall is lighter along the coast and heavier in the inland mountains.

Principal cities. The largest urban area in Virginia is on the banks of the James River at the mouth of Chesapeake Bay. Norfolk–Virginia Beach on the south bank of the river and Newport News–Hampton–Williamsburg on the north bank have combined metropolitan populations of nearly 1.2 million. They are the state's principal shipbuilding and shipping centers. Norfolk is connected to the end of the Delmarva Peninsula by the Chesapeake Bay Bridge–Tunnel, an 18-mile complex of trestles, bridges, and underwater tunnels, which was completed in 1964.

Nearly as large are the suburban centers surrounding Washington, D.C., in the northeastern corner of the state. Of 3 million in the Washington metropolitan area, 1.1 million live in Virginia, in Arlington, Alexandria, and a host of smaller cities. The capital city of Richmond is located 70 miles northwest of Norfolk and 110

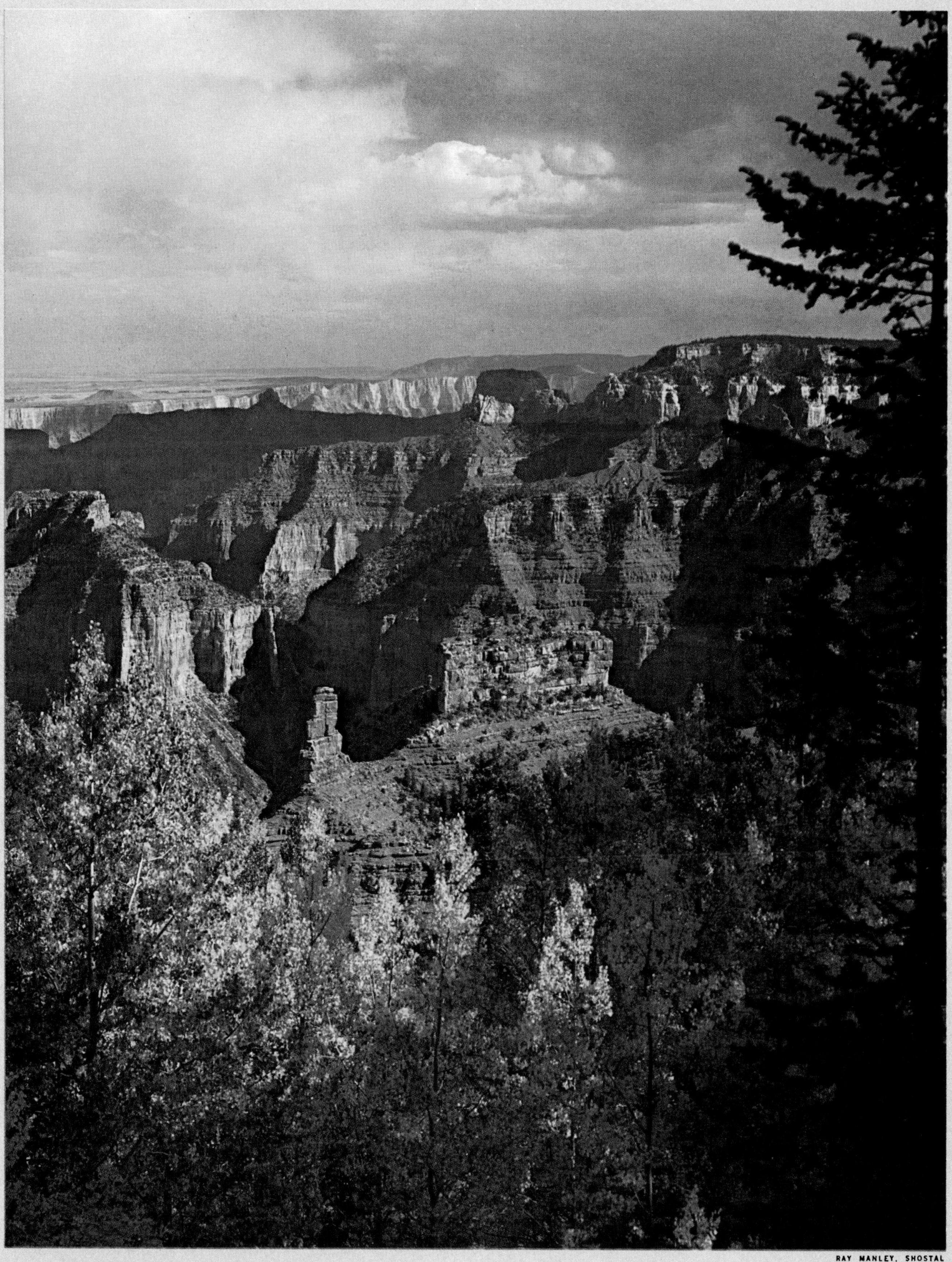

RAY MANLEY, SHOSTAL

AMERICA'S NATIONAL PARKS. A vast array of unusual geographic features characterize these sites, the first of which was established by Congress in 1872. Excellent views of the Grand Canyon, in Arizona, can be had from almost any spot, including the North Rim. The dull red walls of the Canyon, an immense and deep gorge cut by the Colorado River, give off a glow when lit by the sun.

FLAGS OF STATES AND POSSESSIONS: UNITED STATES

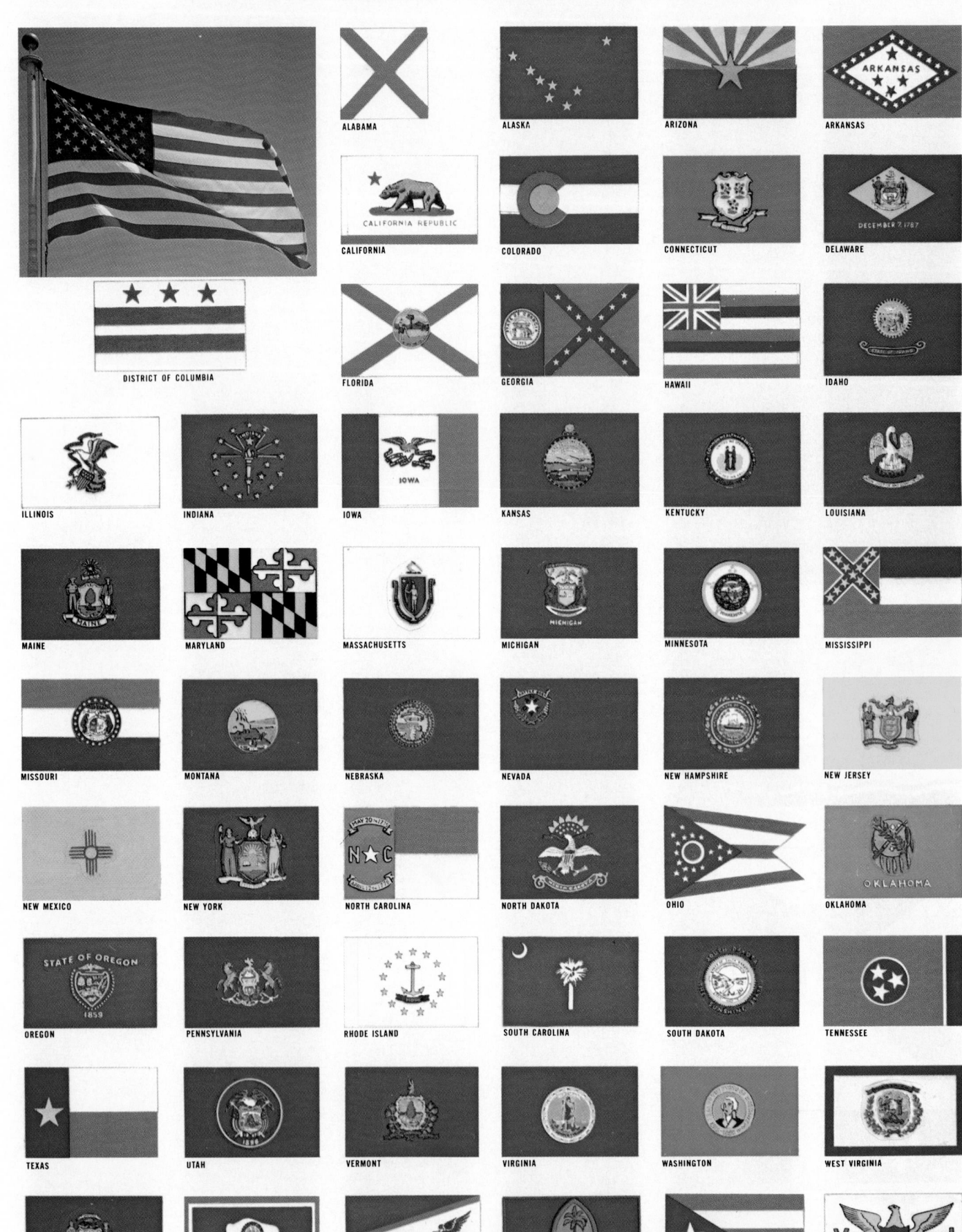

ALABAMA

ALASKA

ARIZONA

ARKANSAS

CALIFORNIA

COLORADO

CONNECTICUT

DELAWARE

DISTRICT OF COLUMBIA

FLORIDA

GEORGIA

HAWAII

IDAHO

ILLINOIS

INDIANA

IOWA

KANSAS

KENTUCKY

LOUISIANA

MAINE

MARYLAND

MASSACHUSETTS

MICHIGAN

MINNESOTA

MISSISSIPPI

MISSOURI

MONTANA

NEBRASKA

NEVADA

NEW HAMPSHIRE

NEW JERSEY

NEW MEXICO

NEW YORK

NORTH CAROLINA

NORTH DAKOTA

OHIO

OKLAHOMA

OREGON

PENNSYLVANIA

RHODE ISLAND

SOUTH CAROLINA

SOUTH DAKOTA

TENNESSEE

TEXAS

UTAH

VERMONT

VIRGINIA

WASHINGTON

WEST VIRGINIA

WISCONSIN

WYOMING

AMERICAN SAMOA

GUAM

PUERTO RICO

VIRGIN ISLANDS

FLAGS OF THE CANADIAN PROVINCES

ALBERTA

BRITISH COLUMBIA

MANITOBA

NEW BRUNSWICK

NEWFOUNDLAND

NORTHWEST TERRITORIES

NOVA SCOTIA

ONTARIO

PRINCE EDWARD ISLAND

QUEBEC

SASKATCHEWAN

YUKON TERRITORY

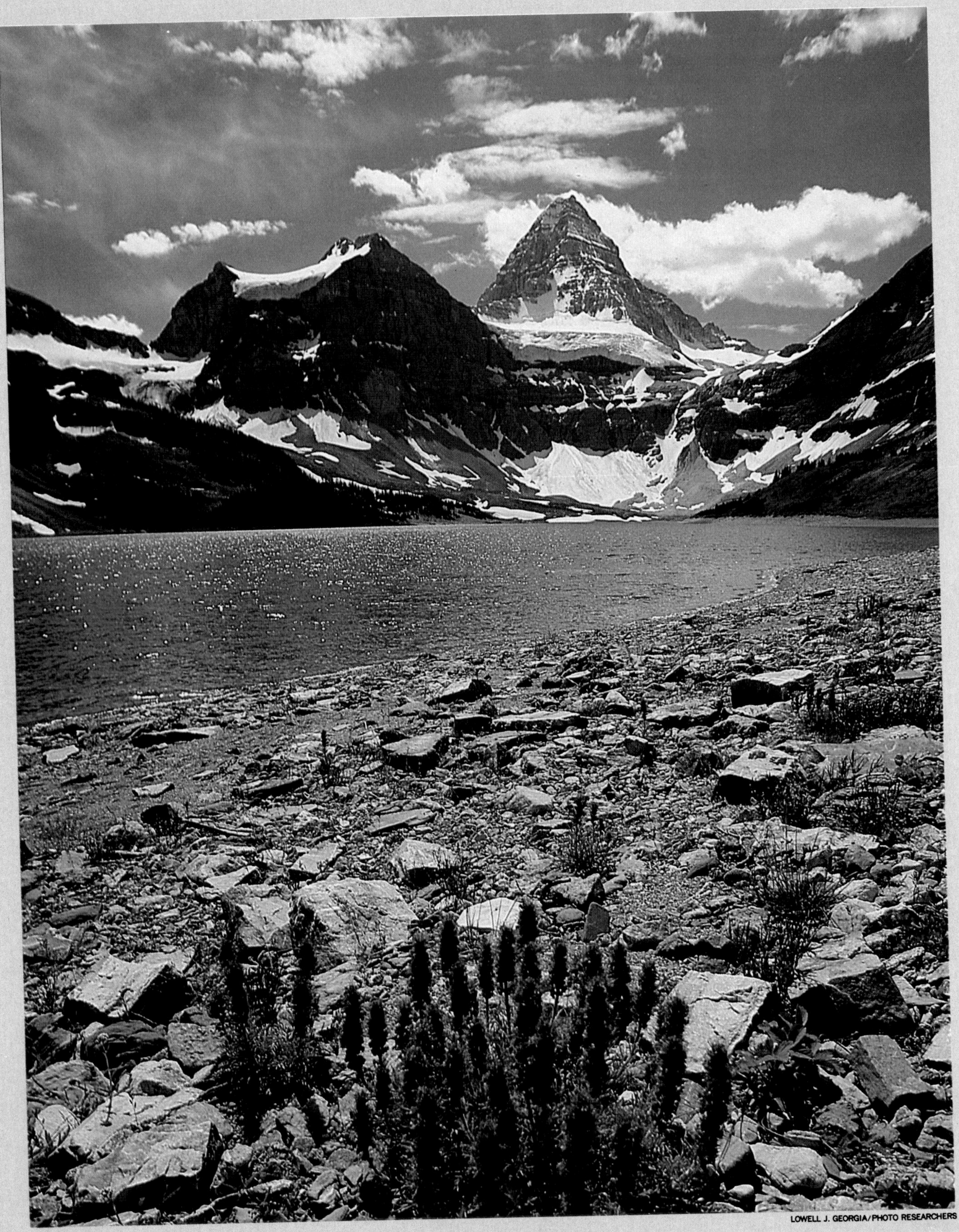

LOWELL J. GEORGIA/PHOTO RESEARCHERS

NATIONAL PARKS OF CANADA. Spectacular scenery is the specialty of Canada's parks. Typical is Mt. Assiniboine (*above*) in Assiniboine Provincial Park, established in 1922. It lies high up on the Continental Divide in the Rockies, on the Alberta-British Columbia border, and is close to three of Canada's most famous National Parks: Banff, established as early as 1885; Glacier (1886); and Jasper (1907). Waterton Lakes (1895) lies on the United States border to the south.

miles south of Washington. It has a metropolitan population of 632,015 and is the center of the tobacco processing industry. During the Civil War, Richmond was the capital of the Confederate States. Among the smaller cities farther inland are the Shenandoah Valley manufacturing town of Roanoke (population 222,548) and Lynchburg (population 153,260) in the Blue Ridge foothills.

The people. The population of Virginia grew slowly through the early 1900's. But beginning in the 1940's, its rate of growth suddenly increased, thanks in large part to increased federal payrolls in and around Washington. During the 1970's more than 300,000 people moved to Virginia from other states. Virginia grew more rapidly than any other Tidewater state and accounted for more than half of the region's population increase. In the past, black residents tended to move from Virginia, but during the 1970's this trend ended. The black population represents 18 percent of the total, and Hispanic residents make up 1.5 percent.

Economy. Virginia's manufacturing income of $12 billion per year exceeds that of all other businesses combined. With the exception of shipbuilding at Newport News, all of this industry is diversified, light manufacturing. The principal manufactures are chemical products exported from Norfolk, tobacco products processed in Richmond, and food and textile goods produced throughout the state.

Agriculture and mining each earn the state $1.3 billion per year. Crops exceed livestock in farm value. Virginia ranks third in the United States in tobacco production, most of it raised in the south and southeast of the state. The mountain and valley region grows large quantities of grain for feed. Poultry and cattle farms predominate in the region. Other important crops include peanuts, apples, and sweet potatoes. Dairy farming is common on the Piedmont Plateau.

Mining income is principally derived from coal, which is shipped from inland Virginia to Norfolk and Newport News for export. Tourism exceeds agriculture or mining in value. Visitors spend $2.4 billion per year.

Places of interest. Virginia's Atlantic Ocean shoreline, reached from the south by the Chesapeake Bay Bridge–Tunnel from Norfolk, includes beach resorts at Chincoteague and Assateague islands. Near the West Virginia border at the opposite extreme of the state is Shenandoah National Park. Virginia is unusually rich in historic monuments and preservations, including colonial Williamsburg near Newport News; the homes of Presidents Washington and Jefferson at Mount Vernon and Monticello, respectively; the Arlington National Cemetery near Washington, D.C.; and many Revolutionary and Civil War monuments.

West Virginia

Abbreviations: *W. Va., WV*
Area: *24,070 sq. mi., 62,341 sq. km.*
Rank (of 50) *41st*
Population:
1985 *1,936,000*
Rank (of 50) *34th*
Change 1980–85 *–14,000*
Percent change *–.7*
Persons per sq. mi. *80*
Percent urban *36.2*
Capital: *Charleston*
Largest city: *Charleston*
Metro. pop. 1985 *269,000*
Entered Union: *June 20, 1863 (35th)*
State bird: *Cardinal*
State flower: *Big rhododendron*
State tree: *Sugar maple*

West Virginia lies to the west of the Tidewater region and is extremely irregular in shape. To the south and east it borders Virginia, and to the west it borders Kentucky and Ohio. The northern borders are with Pennsylvania and Maryland. The outline of the state is unusual because of two panhandles. One stretches 60 miles north between Ohio and Pennsylvania and narrows to a breadth of only 7 miles. The other stretches 90 miles east between the Potomac River border with Maryland on the north and Virginia to the south.

West Virginia was the Trans-Allegheny region of Virginia until 1861. But it chose to part company with the rest of the state in the Civil War, joining the North rather than the Confederacy of the South. It remains distinct from all surrounding states in character because it is entirely mountainous and extremely rural. In modern times, the basis of the economy has been coal, and the fortunes of the state have varied with its value. The population grew during the peak mining years between 1930 and 1950. When coal suffered from competition from oil and natural gas fuels in the years that followed, West Virginia experienced the most dramatic population declines in recent U.S. history. Of late, the state has begun to show population growth again as rising oil and gas prices make coal competitive as an alternative fuel.

The land. All of West Virginia's topography is rugged and mountainous, and the state's average elevation of 1500 feet is the highest east of the Mississippi. The Allegheny Mountains, part of the vast Appalachian chain, run through the eastern panhandle and all along the state's southeastern border. To the west of the Alleghenies lies the Appalachian plateau, representing 80 percent of the state's land area. This land is cut into narrow valleys notable for river gorges and waterfalls, and it lacks large natural lakes. The state's high point is located at Spruce Knob (4862 feet), near the Virginia border.

Climate. West Virginia has a harsh climate relative to the region because it is inland and elevated. Normal temperatures at Charleston in the southwest range between 85° F in summer and 25 in winter, but record temperatures of 102 in summer and minus 12 in winter have been recorded. Prècipitation averages 41 inches per year at Charleston, which receives an average of 31 inches per year of snow. Winters are colder and snowfalls heavier along the eastern ridge of the Alleghenies.

Principal cities. Charleston, the capital, is the largest metropolitan area entirely within West Virginia. The state shares its other metropolitan areas with neighboring states. The Ohio River port of Huntington in the west of the state has more than 300,000 residents, of whom 150,000 live in the state; the remainder live in Kentucky and Ohio. Similarly, the area surrounding Wheeling, on the Ohio border in the northern panhandle, claims 100,000 West Virginia residents of 186,000 total.

The people. Between 1950 and 1970, the state lost more than 260,000 in population. In the 1970's, the resurgence of coal mining and some diversification of industry brought a healthy increase of 205,000, but the state still has fewer people than it claimed in 1950. Most of the growth can be attributed to natural increase—and to a reversal of the longstanding pattern of out-migration. During the '70's, the state received 28,000 more in immigration than it lost. Some 70 percent of the present population were born in the state. Blacks account for 3 percent, and there are no other large ethnic or racial groups. West Virginia has traditionally had a low per capita income. In 1980 it ranked 45th in the United States.

Economy. The principal industry in West Virginia is manufacturing based on the state's mining production. The largest center of manufacturers is in the Kanawha River valley, running northwest from Charleston to the Ohio River, where production is concentrated on chemical products and fabricated metals. The northern panhandle around Wheeling is an industrial region of blast furnaces and steel mills. In the eastern panhandle manufacturers produce textile goods.

Income from mining nearly equals that from manufacturing, and West Virginia ranks seventh among all states in total mining production. The principal ore is bituminous coal, which West Virginia produces in greater quantities than any state except Kentucky, but oil and natural gas are also drilled and clay and cement mined in large amounts. The only other large industry is tourism, which accounts for less than one-quarter of the income generated by either manufacturing or mining.

Places of interest. West Virginia contains 34 state parks and 9 state forests, as well as resorts at Berkeley Springs in the eastern panhandle and White Sulphur Springs in the south-central region. At the extreme of the eastern panhandle is the Harper's Ferry National Historic Park on the site where John Brown seized the U.S. Armory to protest slavery in 1859.

Maryland

Abbreviations: *Md., MD*
Area: *9,891 sq. mi., 25,618 sq. km.*
Rank (of 50) *42nd*
Population:
1985 *4,392,000*
Rank (of 50) *20th*
Change 1980–85 *+175,000*
Percent change *+4.2*
Persons per sq. mi. *447*
Percent urban *80.3*
Capital: *Annapolis*
Largest city: *Baltimore*
Metro. pop. 1985 *2,253,000*
Entered Union: *Apr. 28, 1788 (7th)*
State bird: *Baltimore oriole*
State flower: *Black-eyed Susan*
State tree: *White oak*

Maryland lies in the northern tier of Tidewater states. The bulk of its land is along upper Chesapeake Bay, including the mainland north of the Potomac River (the border with Virginia) and the eastern bay shores on the Delmarva Peninsula. Maryland's northern border with Pennsylvania is a straight line along the 40th parallel, and it is part of the famous Mason-Dixon line that separated the North from the South. To the west, the state has a long, irregularly shaped panhandle formed by the approach of the Potomac River to the 40th parallel. At one point, the state narrows to a north-south breadth of only 1.9 miles.

The state has a long irregular shoreline along Chesapeake Bay and a 30-mile stretch of Atlantic shore along the eastern edge of the Delmarva Peninsula. A square 10 miles on a side along the Potomac River was cut out of Maryland in 1790 to serve as the nation's capital; it is now the separately governed District of Columbia.

Maryland is a diverse state combining social characteristics of different U.S. regions. The far western counties between West Virginia and Pennsylvania are mountainous parts of the Appalachian region. Central Maryland includes the major manufacturing city of Baltimore and it is part of the heavily populated northeastern corridor that stretches from Washington, D.C., on Maryland's southern boundary, to Philadelphia, just to the north, and on to New York City and Boston. The eastern shore, a largely agricultural region, resembles the states to the south.

The land. Across its nearly 250-mile west-east extent, Maryland includes parts of three different topographical regions. The narrow western arm lies within the Appalachian Mountains. The individual features of this mountain region are the Allegheny Mountains in the far west, where the state high point is located at Backbone Mountain (3360 feet); a portion of Appalachian valley at the narrowest point on the western arm; and the Blue Ridge Mountains running north from Virginia.

The central region of the state includes an area on the Piedmont Plateau extending east of the Blue Ridge Mountains nearly to Washington and Baltimore. The fall line at which the plateau drops off to the Atlantic Coastal Plain runs through those cities from southwest to northeast.

Maryland's share of the coastal plain consists of rolling lands west of the Chesapeake Bay and flat, featureless lowlands on the eastern shore. Major tidewater estuaries are found on both sides of the bay in Maryland.

Climate. Most of Maryland has a warm and mild climate influenced by the moderating effects of the Atlantic Ocean and Chesapeake Bay. At Baltimore, on the bay in the north central region of the state, normal summer high temperatures are 85° F and winter lows are 25. Precipitation in Baltimore averages 46 inches per year, including 22 inches of snow. The eastern shore and Atlantic coast is generally warmer in both winter and summer. Winters in the western Allegheny Mountains are colder, and more snow falls.

Principal cities. The major population center in the state is the Baltimore metropolitan area, which contains 52 percent of the state's residents. The suburban areas around Baltimore are continuing to grow in population, but the central city population declined by 13 percent during the 1970's. Two Maryland counties along the Potomac River lie within the Washington, D.C., metropolitan area, and they account for nearly 30 percent of the total state population. In the northeast, farther along the transportation corridor running from Washington through Baltimore, parts of Maryland lie within the Wilmington, Delaware, metropolitan area.

The people. The state population is heavily concentrated in urban areas in central Maryland, leaving both the western arm of the state and the entire eastern shore rural and sparsely populated. Most growth continues to be in the suburban areas around Baltimore and Washington, and much of the population increase there is of black Americans. The black proportion of the state population is 23 percent. Hispanics and Asians each represent 2 percent.

Economy. Tourism generates more income in Maryland than any other industry, about $13 billion per year. In terms of employment, however, manufacturing is far more important. Baltimore is a center for heavy industries, including steel mills and manufactures of machinery, ships, and aircraft. Along the eastern shore, food processing of fish and vegetables predominates. The third major business is agriculture. Most farm income is generated by poultry farms on the eastern shore. In the west of the state there is limited dairy farming and some corn and soybean crops intended for feed.

Places of interest. The principal natural attractions in Maryland are the beach resorts around Ocean City on the Atlantic and the Catoctin and Piscataway Mountain parks in the west of the state. Other attractions in central Maryland include Fort McHenry and the *USS Constellation* in Baltimore, and the U.S. Naval Academy in Annapolis.

Delaware

Abbreviations: *Del., DE*
Area: *1,982 sq. mi., 5,133 sq. km.*
Rank (of 50) *49th*
Population:
1985 *622,000*
Rank (of 50) *47th*
Change 1980–85 *+28,000*
Percent change *+4.6*
Persons per sq. mi. *322*
Percent urban *70.7*
Capital: *Dover*
Largest city: *Wilmington*
Metro. pop. 1980 *524,108*
Entered Union: *Dec. 7, 1787 (1st)*
State bird: *Blue hen chicken*
State flower: *Peach blossom*
State tree: *American holly*

Delaware is the most northeastern of Tidewater states, bordered on both the west and the south by Maryland. The state borders Pennsylvania to the north, and its northern half faces New Jersey to the east across the Delaware River. The southern half of the state's eastern border is coastline on Delaware Bay and the Atlantic Ocean.

Delaware is ranked as the "First State" because it was the first to ratify the new U.S. Constitution in 1787. It is the smallest state in the United States, with the exception of Rhode Island, in land area, and it is the fourth smallest in population. The northern part of the state, however, is a heavily populated metropolitan area, part of the northeastern corridor of population stretching from Washington, D.C., to New York City and Boston.

Delaware also exerts considerable financial influence on other states because its liberal corporate regulations and low corporate taxes have caused many businesses to incorporate there. These include some of the country's largest companies.

The land. Virtually all of the state land area lies on the Atlantic Coastal Plain. This portion of the plain is 80 miles from north to south and broadens from 10 miles wide in the north to 35 miles wide in the south. Its maximum elevation is 60 feet, and its small rivers drain both east into Delaware Bay and west into Chesapeake Bay. These two bodies of water are linked in the north of the plain by the Chesapeake–Delaware Canal.

The northern tip of Delaware is a tiny portion of the Piedmont Plateau. There rolling pasturelands and wooded slopes include the state high point of 442 feet above sea level near Centerville. The Piedmont Plateau is separated from the Atlantic Coastal Plain by the northeastern route of the Christina River to the Delaware River.

Climate. Delaware's climate is relatively mild because of the moderating influence of the surrounding bodies of water. At Wilmington in the northern part of the state normal summer high temperatures are 85° F and normal winter lows are 25. Precipitation at Wilmington averages 40 inches per year, including an average of 20 inches of snow. Along the Atlantic coast in the south of the state summer temperatures are cooler and winter ones warmer than in the north.

Principal cities. The only major urban center in the state is Wilmington, on the Piedmont Plateau at the confluence of the Brandywine, Christina, and Delaware rivers. Wilmington is the heart of a large metropolitan area that includes the second largest city in the state, Newark, and portions of Pennsylvania and New Jersey. Its Delaware residents represent 75 percent of the total state population. The next largest city in the state is the capital, Dover, which has fewer than 25,000 residents.

The people. The population of Delaware was swelled slightly by immigration from other states in the 1970's, but the general population movement is from cities to suburbs. The city population of Wilmington, for example, dropped by more than 10,000 during the 1970's. The minority populations in the state are 16 percent black and 2 percent Hispanic.

Economy. The principal industry in Delaware is manufacturing, which generates four times as much income as agriculture. Most of the manufacturing is based in Wilmington, called the chemical capital of the United States because it is the home of Du Pont, a giant chemical company. Other major manufactures include food products, an outgrowth of Delaware's pioneering role in introducing fruit and vegetable canning in the late 1800's.

Half the state's land is farmland, and more than half the farm income in Delaware is from poultry farms. The principal crops are corn and soybeans for animal feed and fruits and vegetables for shipment to markets in the northeast. Banking and finance is also an important industry in Wilmington, and tourism brings in more than $300 million per year.

Places of interest. Points of interest around Wilmington include the Swedish–American Fort Christina Monument, the Francis du Pont Winterthur Museum, and the Holy Trinity Church, the oldest operating Protestant parish in the United States. Southern Delaware also includes stretches of Atlantic Ocean beaches.

District of Columbia

Abbreviations: *D.C., DC*
Area: *61 sq. mi., 158 sq. km.*
Population:

1985	*626,000*
Change 1980–85	*–13,000*
Percent change	*–2.0*
Persons per sq. mi.	*9,931*
Percent urban	*100.0*

Established as capital: *June 10, 1800*
District bird: *Wood thrush*
District flower: *American beauty rose*
District tree: *Scarlet oak*

The District of Columbia is the seat of the United States government. It is located on 61 square miles of land on the bank of the Potomac River surrounded on three sides by Maryland, and bordering northern Virginia across the Potomac.

THE WASHINGTON MONUMENT, *732 feet high, is the center of a wide variety of historic and cultural attractions in the District of Columbia.*

LUKAS/EPA

The District was originally a plot of land 10 miles on a side, through which the Potomac passed. But the land on the Virginia side was returned to that state in 1846. The city of Washington and the District have the same boundaries, although "District of Columbia" is also used to denote a smaller area in downtown Washington that is the center of the federal government.

A "federal town" had been contemplated by American leaders since 1783, and in 1790 the present site on the Potomac was chosen. The choice was a compromise worked out by Northern and Southern states. Including the original Virginia area, the new federal town would lie between the North and South. Philadelphia remained the U.S. capital until the new city, named for the first President, was ready to be occupied.

The Federal District of Columbia in Washington was designed as a spacious network of promenades and open vistas by Pierre Charles L'Enfant, who had come to America with Lafayette. The city he designed, completed by Andrew Ellicott and Benjamin Danneker, was burned by the British in 1814 but rebuilt in keeping with the original design.

Politically, Washington was incorporated as a town in 1802 and reorganized as the District of Columbia in 1871. In 1974 a new charter was approved that gave Washington residents an elected mayor and city council for the first time. The U.S. Congress retains veto power over the new local government. In 1978 a constitutional amendment to give the District of Columbia full voting representation in the House and the Senate was passed by Congress. It requires ratification by 38 states to become law.

Washington has experienced serious urban problems. More prosperous government employees have moved to suburbs in Virginia and Maryland, leaving the city with a poor population and a small tax base. It is unable to tax federal property. The Washington metropolitan area has a population of more than 3 million, but only a fifth of them live in the District itself.

The people. The population of Washington has been predominantly black since 1960, and in 1980 the population was 70 percent black. Hispanics from a variety of Third World countries represent 3 percent of the total city population. Half of all residents are employed by the government, and the major industry is tourism.

Places of interest. Some of the principal sights in Washington, D.C., are the Washington Monument, the Lincoln Memorial, the White House, the Capitol Building, and the Supreme Court Building.

The Mid-Atlantic States

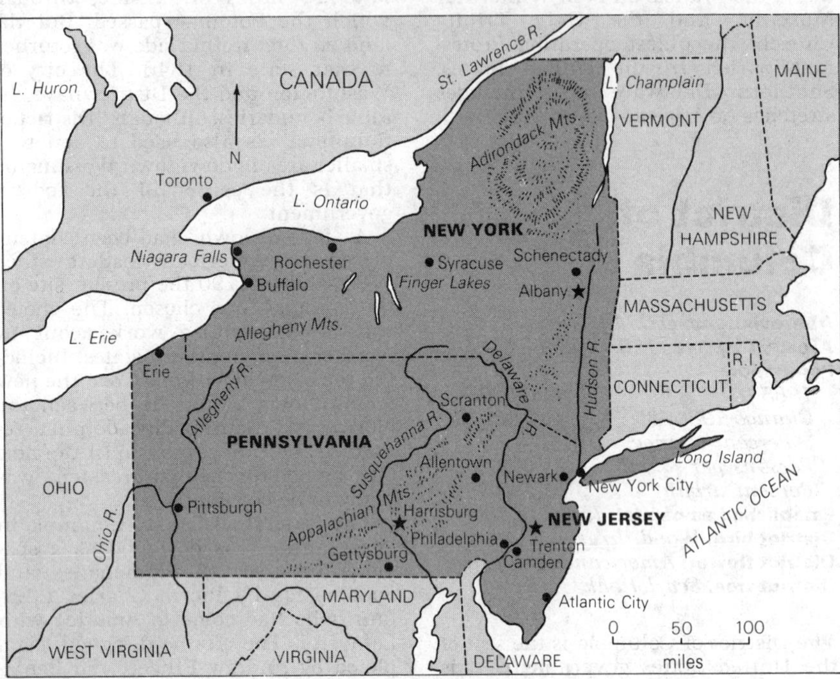

THE MID-ATLANTIC STATES

State	Area (sq. mi.)	Population 1985	Population change 1980–85 number	Population change 1980–85 percent	Persons per sq. mi.
Pennsylvania	44,966	11,853,000	− 11,000	− .1	264
New Jersey	7,521	7,562,000	+198,000	+2.7	1,013
New York	47,831	17,783,000	+225,000	+1.3	375
Region totals	100,318	37,198,000	+412,000	+1.1	371

The Mid-Atlantic states are Pennsylvania, New Jersey, and New York in the northeastern United States, bordering the New England states and the Atlantic Ocean on the east; the Tidewater states of Delaware, Maryland, and West Virginia on the south; and the Great Lakes state of Ohio on the west. The region's northern border is with Lake Ontario and the Canadian provinces of Ontario and Quebec.

The Mid-Atlantic states are the second most populous region after the Great Lakes states. The region is the most densely populated in the country, including 16 percent of the U.S. population on only 3 percent of its land area. In modern times, people were attracted by employment in the region's huge industrial complex. Earlier, trade flourished because of the states' Atlantic harbors and their river and canal transportation. The Erie Canal, completed in 1825, connected Lake Erie and the Atlantic by way of the Hudson River, bringing prosperity to New York State. The rivers of Pennsylvania offered access to the west via the Ohio and to the Eastern seaboard via the Susquehanna and Delaware rivers. New Jersey, facing harbors both at New York City and Philadelphia, shared in the commercial prosperity. All three states remain among the top seven in manufacturing production.

Like the Great Lakes states to the west, however, the Mid-Atlantic states experienced an economic decline beginning in the 1960's. Increased competition in manufacturing from the Southern states and from overseas, combined with difficult economic times in the 1970's, caused many residents to seek better opportunities elsewhere. The region was the only one to record an outright population decline during the 1970's.

The land. The Mid-Atlantic states share several topographical features. The Appalachian Mountains run northeast from south-central Pennsylvania through a corner of New Jersey and into New York. To the northwest of the mountains, the lands run down to the Great Lakes Plain beside Lake Erie and to the St. Lawrence and Champlain lowlands in northern New York. To the southeast of the mountains lie valley and upland regions in southeastern Pennsylvania and New York and northern New Jersey. The southern two-thirds of New Jersey and New York's Long Island consist of Atlantic Coastal Plain.

Climate. The climate of the region is cooler and drier in the west than in the east. Along Lake Erie normal summer highs are 80° F and winter lows are below 20. Precipitation in western New York and Pennsylvania averages 36 inches per year, including snowfall ranging from 46 inches in western Pennsylvania to 92 inches at Buffalo in western New York. In the coastal eastern areas, however, normal summer highs average a warmer 85 and winter lows are a milder 25. These eastern areas average about 40 inches of precipitation per year, including less than 30 inches of snow.

History. The Mid-Atlantic states were explored and settled by the Dutch and the British. The Dutch controlled southern New York and parts of New Jersey until 1664, when the British took control, and the Dutch city of New Amsterdam became New York. New Jersey was organized as a separate colony one year later, and in 1681 the English Crown granted the Quaker William Penn a charter to Pennsylvania. During the Revolutionary War, the colonial army under George Washington retreated from New York, leaving it to British control; the army later wintered at Valley Forge, Pennsylvania, near Philadelphia. It won a decisive victory, however, at Saratoga, New York. The region was largely untouched during the Civil War except for the monumental battle at Gettysburg in southern Pennsylvania.

Principal cities. Today the region is dominated by the metropolitan centers of Philadelphia and New York City. New York is the most populous metropolitan area in the country, and Philadelphia the fourth largest. Both include portions of New Jersey, and together they account for two-thirds of the region's total population. The largest metropolitan areas in the west of the region are Pittsburgh, in west-central Pennsylvania, with 2.2 million people, and Buffalo, on New York's Lake Erie shoreline, with 1.2 million people.

The people. All of these metropolitan areas experienced substantial population declines in the 1970's. New York City lost nearly 1 million people. New York was the only state in the nation to record a substantial population decline in the decade. The other states shared slight increases, but both lost substantial numbers to migration.

Economy. The leading industry in all Mid-Atlantic states is manufacturing, and the second leading industry is tourism. Coal and steel businesses based near the Great Lakes around Buffalo and Pittsburgh are the major heavy industries in the region. In the eastern areas, manufactures are more diversified, producing a variety of machinery, electrical, and chemical products.

Tourism earns the three states nearly $18 billion per year, most of it derived from summer activities throughout New York and Pennsylvania and from the coastal beaches of New Jersey. The region's agricultural income is lower than any other except New England, with most of it coming from dairy farms and greenhouse vegetables.

Pennsylvania

Abbreviations: *Pa., PA*
Area: *44,966 sq. mi., 116,462 sq. km.*
Rank (of 50) *32nd*
Population:
1985 *11,853,000*
Rank (of 50) *4th*
Change 1980–85 *−11,000*
Percent change *−.1*
Persons per sq. mi. *264*
Percent urban *69.3*
Capital: *Harrisburg*
Largest city: *Philadelphia*
Metro. pop. 1985 *4,784,000*
Entered Union: *Dec. 12, 1787 (2nd)*
State bird: *Ruffed grouse*
State flower: *Mountain laurel*
State tree: *Hemlock*

Pennsylvania is a Mid-Atlantic state lying south of New York and west of New Jersey. The New Jersey border is formed by the Delaware River. Its border with New York follows the 42nd parallel except in the far west, where a 35-mile northward extension gives the state a port on Lake Erie. Pennsylvania's western border is with Ohio and West Virginia, and its southern border is with West Virginia, Maryland, and the small northern tip of Delaware.

Pennsylvania is one of the most economically diverse states in the country, ranking in the top ten states in manufacturing and mining and in the top 20 in agriculture. Its 310-mile west-east extent also includes many sparsely populated mountainous areas.

Pennsylvania resembles the Great Lakes states to the west, in that its heavy industries have suffered from foreign competition. Like the automobile industry, Pennsylvania's steel and coal industries have declined in world-market importance. The state has not attracted enough modern industries to shore up its economy. As a result, total population growth is virtually nil, and the state actually lost almost half a million residents to migration during the 1970's.

The land. The great Appalachian Mountain range runs through the state from southwest to northeast. The Alleghenies are the principal mountain ridge. They enter the state from West Virginia in the south and trace a broad northeastern curve toward the Delaware River, the state's eastern boundary. To the west and the north of the mountains lies the Appalachian plateau, which covers half the state area. The plateau is a layered rock hill and valley region that declines along the shore of Lake Erie into a small fringe of Great Lakes plain. To the southeast of the mountains lie the Appalachian valley and the Piedmont Plateau. The Appalachian valley is a 40- to 50-mile-wide strip of parallel ridges that includes the Cumberland and Lebanon valleys. The small and low-lying farmland in the southeast corner of the state is part of the Piedmont Plateau.

Climate. Pennsylvania's climate varies from east to west. In Philadelphia, near the mouth of the Delaware River, normal summer highs are near 90° F and winter lows are 25; there is 40 inches of precipitation per year, including 21 inches of snow. Pittsburgh, in western Pennsylvania, is cooler in both summer and winter. It receives 4 inches less precipitation than Philadelphia but twice as much snow.

Principal cities. The major urban centers in Pennsylvania are Philadelphia and Pittsburgh, which lie 250 miles apart at the eastern and western ends of the state. Philadelphia, the fourth largest city in the country, has a consolidated metropolitan area, including parts of New Jersey, Delaware, and Maryland, of 6 million residents. Pittsburgh, where the Allegheny and Monongahela rivers meet to form the Ohio, is the 13th largest city, with 2.1 million people. Both Philadelphia and Pittsburgh are old manufacturing towns that lost population during the 1970's. Other large population centers are in the east of the state: Scranton–Wilkes-Barre (population 646,396) in the northeast, and Allentown–Bethlehem (636,714) at the center of the state's eastern border. The largest city in western Pennsylvania other than Pittsburgh is Erie (279,780) in the northwest on the shore of Lake Erie.

The people. Like other states in its region, Pennsylvania lost a sizable population to migration in the 1970's, most to states in the South and West. Natural increase barely stayed ahead of migration, giving the state a growth rate of less than 1 percent. Black population, concentrated in major cities, is 9 percent of the total, and Hispanics make up 1 percent. The rural regions of eastern Pennsylvania were settled in the 1800's by German immigrants popularly known as the Pennsylvania Dutch. This group is remarkable for having kept its language and cultural identity for over a century. A small proportion of these immigrants were Amish people who resisted such modern conveniences as electricity and automobiles on religious grounds. They still travel in horse-drawn vehicles and cultivate their farms largely by hand. The cities of Philadelphia and Pittsburgh have significant ethnic minorities as well, including Irish, Italians, Poles, and others from Eastern Europe.

Economy. Pennsylvania ranks sixth in the United States in manufacturing. Manufacturing generates more than six times the income of any other state business. The major manufacturing centers are Philadelphia, a diversified industrial town, and Pittsburgh, famous for coal and steel. All metropolitan areas in the state have economies based on manufacturing. Pennsylvania also ranks sixth in the United States in mining, chiefly because of its coal reserves. In western Pennsylvania soft bituminous coal for industrial use is mined, and northeastern Pennsylvania produces virtually all of the U.S. supply of hard clean-burning anthracite coal. Many mines were closed during the 1950's and '60's, but some were reopened as coal prices increased during fuel shortages in the 1970's.

Three-quarters of the state farm income is derived from livestock, principally from dairy farms. Tourism throughout Pennsylvania brings the state more than $6 billion per year, making it second only to manufacturing in the state economy.

Places of interest. Philadelphia, once the U.S. capital, contains historic attractions such as Independence Hall and the Liberty Bell. The National Historic Park at Valley Forge is near the Philadelphia city limits, and the Gettysburg National Military Park is in southeastern Pennsylvania. There are winter ski resorts in the mountains in central Pennsylvania and many summer fishing and camping areas throughout the state.

New Jersey

Abbreviations: *N.J., NJ*
Area: *7,521 sq. mi., 19,479 sq. km.*
Rank (of 50) *46th*
Population:
1985 *7,562,000*
Rank (of 50) *9th*
Change 1980–85 *+198,000*
Percent change *+2.7*
Persons per sq. mi. *1,013*
Percent urban *89.0*
Capital: *Trenton*
Largest city: *Newark*
Metro. pop. 1985 *1,882,000*
Entered Union: *Dec. 18, 1787 (3rd)*
State bird: *Eastern goldfinch*
State flower: *Purple violet*
State tree: *Red oak*

LANKS/MONKMEYER

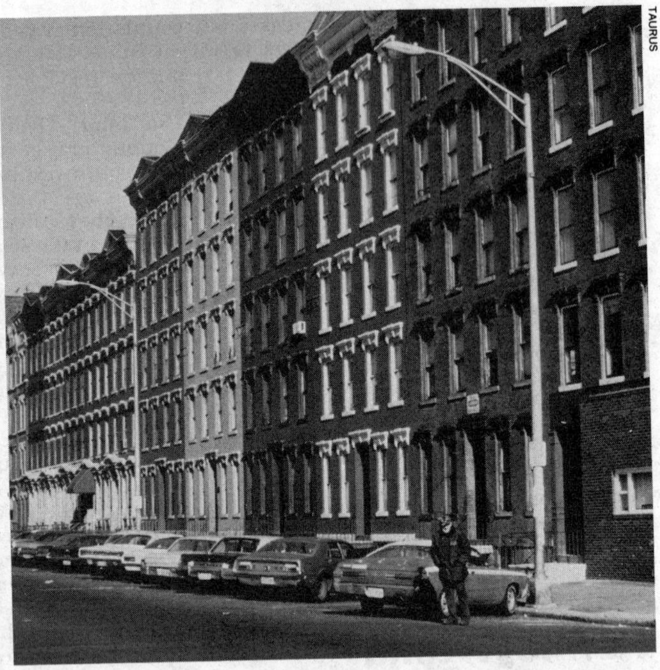
TAURUS

SOLITUDE AND CROWDS *are both characteristic of the densely populated Mid-Atlantic region. Historic Fort Ticonderoga in upper New York State commands the shore of Lake Champlain; many of the region's millions live in row houses like these in Hoboken, New Jersey.*

New Jersey is a Mid-Atlantic state located between Pennsylvania to the west and New York to the north and northeast. To the southeast, the state has a long Atlantic Ocean shore, and it shares a short water border with Delaware in the extreme south.

Among the top ten states in population and the bottom ten in land area, New Jersey is the most densely populated state in the country. Its population centers are clustered around New York City in the northeast and Philadelphia in the southwest and along the heavily developed corridor that connects the two cities. Many New Jersey communities are "bedroom" suburbs for those who work out of state in New York and Philadelphia. The remainder of the state, less heavily populated, includes pastoral hill and farm country in the northwest and sandy pine barrens in the southeast.

The land. New Jersey is divided in two by a diagonal line running from Trenton on the Delaware River northeast across the narrow center of the state to New York harbor. To the south of this line lies three-fifths of the state area consisting entirely of Atlantic Coastal Plain. The plain in New Jersey is flat, sandy land that stretches from the Delaware River to the Atlantic Ocean. The interior varies from farmland to sandier "barrens" of scrub pine, and the coastline is a uniformly sandy one characterized by the built-up sand bars of the Great Barrier Reef separated from the mainland by tidal lagoons.

North of the dividing line the state lands consist of a series of hilly formations running from southwest to northeast. Nearest the dividing line is the northernmost extension of the Piedmont Plateau, a lowland broken by isolated ridges. Northwest of the plateau is a range of higher hills related to the New England Highlands. The northeastern corner of the state is part of the Appalachian valley shared with Pennsylvania and cut by the Delaware River at the Delaware Water Gap, a picturesque canyon near the state's northwest corner.

Climate. The climate of New Jersey is moderate, influenced by its long Atlantic coastline. Normal winter lows throughout the state are above 20° F and normal summer highs are in the low 80's. Precipitation averages 45 inches per year, including an average of 16 inches of snow per year.

Principal cities. The largest urban area entirely within New Jersey is Newark, a port facility on the New Jersey side of New York harbor. However, Newark itself is part of the consolidated metropolitan area of New York City, which includes most of the area of New Jersey within a 40-mile radius of the harbor. The consolidated metropolitan area of Philadelphia includes major cities in southern New Jersey such as Trenton, the capital, and Camden. The only large city in the state not within one of these metropolitan regions is Atlantic City (population 194,119), a seaside resort on the Atlantic coast. Casino gambling was made legal in Atlantic City in 1977; creating a major increase in the tourist business.

The people. Between 1950 and 1970, New Jersey grew rapidly, increasing its population from 4.8 million to 7.2 million. The rate of increase in the 1970's was far lower, however, and the state lost 130,000 residents to other regions. Only half of New Jersey's residents were born in the state, the lowest proportion in the region. Large cities, like others in the region, showed significant population losses in the '70's, while some smaller towns continued to grow. The black population, concentrated in cities such as Newark, makes up 13 percent of the state population. Hispanics make up 7 percent and are concentrated in older manufacturing towns alongside New York harbor.

Economy. The principal business of New Jersey is manufacturing, which generates ten times the income of any other industry. Most of the manufacturers are based in northeastern New Jersey, where they produce $40 billion per year in chemicals, packaged foods, electrical equipment, and other goods. The container port of Newark is also a base for large oil-refining companies.

The second leading industry is tourism, principally in summer along the Atlantic coast. Crops represent 70 percent of New Jersey's limited agricultural income, most of it from the vegetable produce of southern truck farms within easy reach of major markets. Despite the small contribution of agriculture to its economy, New Jersey is still known as the Garden State for its vegetable production. Its vegetables, as well as poultry and dairy products, supply nearby urban centers.

Places of interest. The major tourist center in New Jersey is Atlantic City, a historic beach resort with a famous boardwalk. Atlantic City recently legalized gambling. It is the heart of the state's 127 miles of ocean beaches. Attractions in northern New Jersey include the Thomas Alva Edison Museum, the Grover Cleveland Birthplace, and Princeton University.

New York

Abbreviations: *N.Y., NY*
Area: *47,831 sq. mi., 123,882 sq. km.*
Rank (of 50) *30th*
Population:
1985 *17,783,000*
Rank (of 50) *2nd*
Change 1980–85 *+225,000*
Percent change *+1.3*
Persons per sq. mi. *375*
Percent urban *84.6*
Capital: *Albany*
Largest city: *New York*
Metro. pop. 1985 *8,466,000*
Entered Union: *July 26, 1788 (11th)*
State bird: *Bluebird*
State flower: *Rose*
State tree: *Sugar maple*

New York is the northernmost of the three Mid-Atlantic states, stretching 325 miles from Lake Erie in the west to the New England states and the Atlantic Ocean in the east. Along its eastern edge, the state stretches nearly 300 miles north to south, from a boundary with Canada near Montreal, Quebec, to New York Bay. From that bay, the state extends 90 miles farther east on Long Island, along the coast of Connecticut. Its southern borders are with Pennsylvania and New Jersey; to the east are Vermont, Massachusetts, and Connecticut. To the west and north, the state borders Lake Erie, the Canadian Province of Ontario across the Niagara River, Lake Ontario, and Canada again, across the St. Lawrence River.

For most of the 20th century, New York was the largest and most influential state in the Union. In the early 1960's, however, California's population exceeded that of New York, and in the succeeding years, the state entered a period of economic decline. Employment opportunities dwindled, and state residents began moving to more promising regions. In the 1960's the state's growth was below the national average, and in the 1970's, New York was the only state to record a substantial loss of population. More than 1.4 million residents moved to other states, and this loss was only partially offset by a natural increase of some 700,000.

Nevertheless, New York remains the second largest state. It is also one of the most diverse states, containing the nation's largest city and many other important commercial centers.

The land. The topography of New York is complex. More than half its area, along the southern border with Pennsylvania, is part of the Appalachian plateau, a hill and valley region covering all of south and central New York. To the east of the plateau is a lowland along the Hudson and Mohawk rivers, which join at Albany in the east-central part of the state. The Hudson runs south from Albany, reaching the Atlantic at New York Bay. The Hudson and Mohawk valleys represent a major break in the Appalachian Mountain chain, which stretches both southwest and northeast from the river lowlands. Early settlers recognized the importance of this break, and the Hudson–Mohawk system was connected to Lake Erie by a canal system completed in 1825. This system, linking Buffalo, Albany, and New York City, was the forerunner of modern rail and highway connections.

North of Albany lie the Adirondack Mountains, which include some of the oldest geologic formations in North America. The state high point is at Mt. Marcy (5344 feet). The northern reaches of the state are lowlands bordering the Great Lakes and the St. Lawrence River. Long Island, in the extreme southeast, is part of the Atlantic Coastal Plain.

Climate. New York has differing climates in the east and west. At New York City in the southeast normal summer highs are 85° F, winter lows 25; precipitation averages 40 inches per year, including snowfall of 29 inches. At Buffalo in the west on Lake Erie, normal temperatures are a cooler 80 in summer and 17 in winter, and precipitation averages 36 inches, including snowfall of 92 inches. (One inch of precipitation equals 10 inches of snow.) In the northern Adirondacks winters are colder and bring even more snow than in Buffalo.

Principal cities. New York City is the urban center of the state and the surrounding region. Its consolidated metropolitan area of New York, New Jersey, and Connecticut has a population of 17 million. In addition to its visible entertainment industry and cultural importance, New York City is a world banking and finance capital, and it serves as U.S. headquarters for numerous international corporations. It is also the headquarters of the United Nations.

The second largest urban center in the state surrounds Buffalo (population 1.2 million), a Great Lakes steel town that is also the commercial center of western New York. From west to east across the center of the state is a series of large industrial centers: Rochester (population 971,879) on Lake Ontario; Syracuse (population 642,375) in the center of the state; and Albany–Schenectady (population 795,619) near the Hudson River less than 30 miles from the Massachusetts border.

The people. Because of New York City's historical role as the port of entry for successive waves of European immigrants, the population of New York State continues to include the largest proportion of foreign-born residents in the United States, 11 percent or about 2 million people. The population also includes large numbers of black Americans (14 percent) and Hispanic Americans (9 percent). The population is divided almost equally between the New York City region and the rest of the state.

Economy. The leading industry in New York is manufacturing, and the state ranks second only to California in the total value of its manufacturing output. Virtually all products are represented, from steel in Buffalo to photographic and optical supplies in Rochester to machinery products in Syracuse to 10 percent of the U.S. apparel output in New York City.

Tourism is the second largest industry, with out-of-state visitors attracted both to the cultural landmarks of New York City and to the scenery of upstate New York. Agriculture ranks third in economic importance, with two-thirds of the farm income coming from dairy livestock and cattle. Crops include vegetables, apples, and the fourth-largest harvest of potatoes in the United States. There are also a variety of less important industries in the New York economy, including wine fermenting, timber, mining, and commercial fishing.

Places of interest. The greatest number of visitors to the state come to see the skyscrapers, museums, theaters, stock exchange, and many other attractions of New York City. Natural attractions in upstate New York include Niagara Falls near Buffalo, the Adirondack Mountain resorts, and the Thousand Islands of the St. Lawrence River in the northeast. Special points of interest include West Point, home of the U.S. Military Academy, 60 miles up the Hudson River from New York City; Fort Ticonderoga at the southern end of Lake Champlain; and the Baseball Hall of Fame at Cooperstown, 60 miles west of Albany.

NEW YORK CITY, *shown here at night, is the great international city of America, attracting businessmen, artists, performers, and laborers from around the world.*

NEW YORK STATE DEPT. OF COMMERCE

The New England States

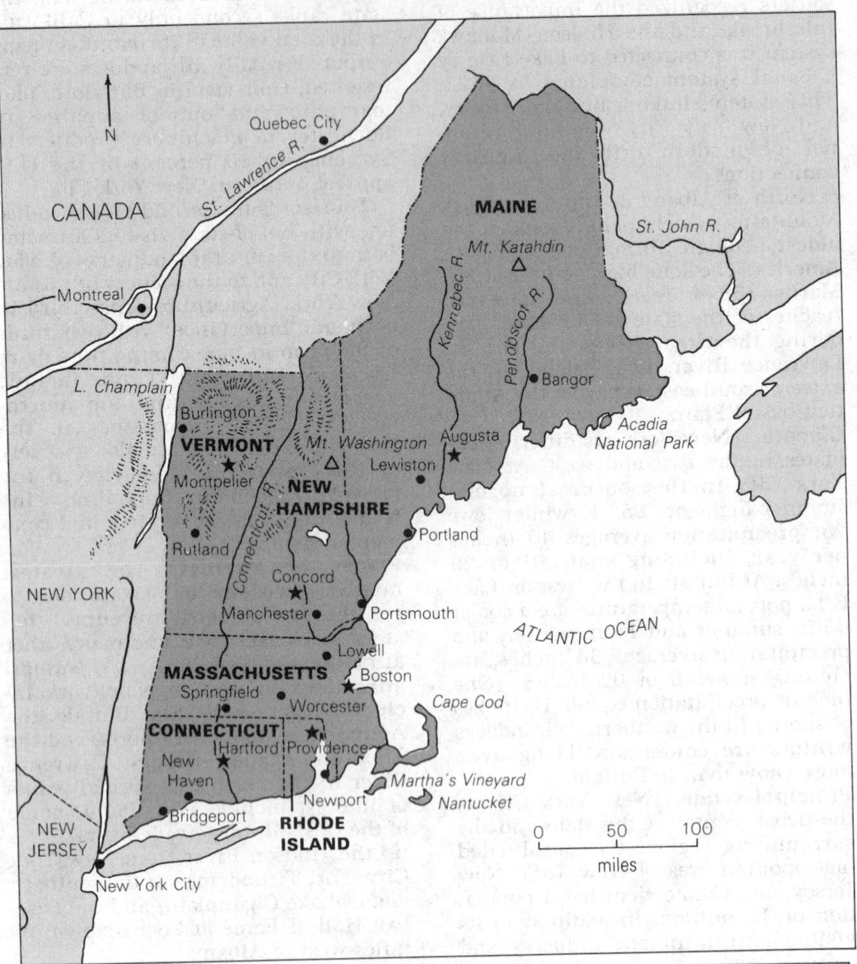

THE NEW ENGLAND STATES

State	Area (sq. mi.)	Population 1985	Population change 1980–85 number	Population change 1980–85 percent	Persons per sq. mi.
Connecticut	4,862	3,174,000	+ 66,000	+2.1	651
Rhode Island	1,049	968,000	+ 21,000	+2.2	918
Massachusetts	7,826	5,822,000	+ 85,000	+1.5	744
Vermont	9,276	535,000	+ 24,000	+4.6	58
New Hampshire	9,027	998,000	+ 77,000	+8.4	111
Maine	30,920	1,164,000	+ 39,000	+3.5	38
Region totals	62,960	12,661,000	+312,000	+2.5	201

The New England states occupy a narrow arm of land that extends to the northeast between the Atlantic Ocean and Canada. The region borders New York on the west and southwest. To the north are the Canadian provinces of Quebec and New Brunswick. Five of the region's states have southeastern Atlantic coastlines. Only Vermont is landlocked.

Of all the U.S. regions, the New England states are the smallest in area and the most homogeneous in character. The region's early farmers abandoned their fields and settled the Midwest, seeking better soil. The textile industry abandoned its plants, seeking cheaper labor and raw materials in other regions. Yet the region has survived its hard times, preserving its picturesque village greens and covered bridges, and developing new businesses to replace the old. New industries include the development and manufacture of electronics equipment. The region also attracts millions of visitors to its autumn foliage, winter skiing, and summer recreation along its Atlantic seashore and many lakes and streams.

The land. The topographical feature that joins the states of the region is the New England Upland. This hill and valley area covers all of Connecticut and half of Rhode Island in the south, and it extends northward across central Massachusetts, southeastern Vermont, southern New Hampshire, and central and northern Maine. To the northwest of the upland, the Taconics and the Green Mountains extend north and east across western Massachusetts and Vermont, and the White Mountains run from northeastern Vermont across New Hampshire and into central Maine. Southeast of the upland, the distinctive New England Seaboard Lowlands, partially submerged in the Atlantic, create a varied coastline with many peninsulas, islands, and deep harbors. Cape Cod, a narrow peninsula off eastern Massachusetts, is a tiny part of the Atlantic Coastal Plain and has a sandy shoreline characteristic of states farther south.

Climate. New England has a generally cool climate with winters that become harsher in elevated areas distant from the coast. Normal summer highs are in the low 80° F range throughout the region, but normal winter lows vary from 22 in coastal Massachusetts to 8 in Vermont. Precipitation varies from 43 inches per year in coastal areas to only 33 inches in Vermont. Snowfall, an indicator of the length of the winter, varies from 39 inches per year in Rhode Island to 80 inches per year in Vermont. In the highest mountain areas of the region, subzero temperatures and annual snowfalls over 100 inches are common.

History. Early explorers to the New England region included Dutch and British visitors to Connecticut and Vermont, but the effective settlement of the region began with the landing of the Pilgrims at Plymouth Rock in 1620. By 1623 the Pilgrims had sent parties to homestead New Hampshire and Maine. Another group of religious dissenters, the Puritans, established the Massachusetts Bay Colony in 1630. Within ten years, some had left the colony to settle Rhode Island and Connecticut.

The American Revolution brought the region its first sense of political unity. At the end of the war, Connecticut, Massachusetts, Rhode Island, and New Hampshire were among the original 13 states. Vermont became the 14th in 1791, and Maine, originally a part of Massachusetts, chose separation and statehood in 1819.

The people. Today the New England states are the third least populated region of the United States after the

Mountain and Northwest states. During the 1970's they recorded the second smallest population increase next to the Mid-Atlantic states. The population just remained stable in the heavily populated southern states of Connecticut, Rhode Island, and Massachusetts. But the northern three states—Vermont, New Hampshire, and Maine—grew at a rate greater than the national average. The central metropolitan area of the region is Boston, where the population declined by more than 135,000 in the 1970's. The greatest population growth in the region was recorded about 50 miles to the northwest in southern New Hampshire.

Massachusetts and Connecticut continue to account for nearly three-quarters of the region's population. These states also have the highest proportion of black and Hispanic residents.

Economy. The economy of the New England states is based on manufacturing and tourism. Manufacturing is the largest industry in all the states, with Connecticut and Massachusetts the leaders. Tourism ranks second in importance to the economy of each state. Tourism has increased in value with the rise in popularity of winter sports, for which the New England states are especially well suited. Agricultural output, chiefly of dairy products and greenhouse vegetables, is limited, but the region is known for special farm products such as cranberries in Massachusetts, shade-grown tobacco in Connecticut, and maple syrup in Vermont.

Connecticut

Abbreviations: *Conn., CT*
Area: *4,862 sq. mi., 12,593 sq. km.*
Rank (of 50) *48th*
Population:
1985 *3,174,000*
Rank (of 50) *28th*
Change 1980–85 *+66,000*
Percent change *+2.1*
Persons per sq. mi. *651*
Percent urban *78.8*
Capital: *Hartford*
Metro. pop. 1985 *732,000*
Entered Union: *Jan. 9, 1788 (5th)*
State bird: *American robin*
State flower: *Mountain laurel*
State tree: *White oak*

Connecticut is situated in the southwestern corner of the New England region bordering New York to the west and southwest. Rhode Island is to the east, and Massachusetts to the north. The southern boundary is the shoreline of Long Island Sound, an arm of the Atlantic between Connecticut and Long Island, a part of New York State. Connecticut is rectangular in shape, with a narrow southwestern extension reaching 15 miles toward New York City.

Connecticut was a relatively rural state until after 1945. Then the development of suburban communities in the southwest part of the state in the New York City metropolitan region sent the population soaring. It reached 1 million in 1950, and in the next 20 years it tripled to 3 million. Most of this growth occurred in the southwest, but there was also significant growth around the state capital, Hartford, near the center of the state. Suburban growth never reached the northwest and northeast, however, and in those areas the state retains its rural New England character, with small farms on rolling hills and solid wood frame houses in small towns facing handsome village greens.

The land. Connecticut consists almost entirely of New England Upland, divided through the center of the state by the lower Connecticut River valley. The uplands are highest to the west of the valley, and in the northwestern corner they reach a portion of the Taconic Mountains. The state high point is located at Mt. Frissell (2380 feet), near the New York and Massachusetts borders. The uplands to the east of the valley are lower, seldom rising more than 1000 feet above sea level; they are characterized by rolling hills and gentle river valleys. The Connecticut valley between these highlands is narrow in the north, but it broadens into fertile floodplains around Hartford, where most of the land is scarcely above sea level. Along its southern coast Connecticut also includes a narrow strip of New England Seaboard Lowland, a shoreline that mixes rocky peninsulas and deep bays with sandy beaches.

Climate. The climate of Connecticut is coldest in the elevated northwest and milder in the central valley. Normal winter lows at Hartford average 16° F and summer highs average 84. Statewide precipitation averages 43 inches per year, including snowfall of 54 inches per year. The northwest receives less total precipitation, but its long winters bring it greater snowfalls than the state average.

Principal cities. The largest metropolitan area within Connecticut is Hartford, a center for insurance companies and manufacturers as well as state government. The greatest portion of the state population, however, resides in a series of southwest coastal cities linked to New York City by highway and railroad routes. The largest of these cities is Bridgeport (population 395,455). The eastern limit of this metropolitan area is New Haven (population 417,592), 100 miles from New York City.

The people. Connecticut's growth leveled off during the 1970's, and more people moved out of the state than moved in. Since its suburban growth is so recent, Connecticut has a low proportion of lifelong residents (51 percent). The resident population is 7 percent black and 4 percent Hispanic, with the heaviest concentration of these groups in urban areas. Many ethnic communities are represented in Connecticut: 32 percent of the people are of foreign birth or parentage, most of them of Italian, Irish, or Polish descent.

Economy. Since the 1800's, Connecticut's principal industry has been manufacturing. In earlier times hardware was the chief product. This tradition led to large aircraft engine industries around Hartford and a shipbuilding industry around the U.S. submarine base in Groton on the southeast coast. Manufacturing in Connecticut now employs a third of the work force and generates $12.2 billion per year.

Another large industry in the state is finance, growing out of major corporate headquarters in the southwest of the state and large insurance companies in Hartford. Tourism to both coastal and inland areas is the third major industry, accounting for more than $1 billion per year. Connecticut's agriculture is a limited industry, based chiefly on dairy products but also noted for the shade-grown tobacco harvested on the floodplains around Hartford.

Places of interest. The state's Long Island Sound shoreline is its principal natural attraction. Mystic Seaport, along the southeastern coast, is a restored 19th-century whaling and shipbuilding village. Other places of interest include the P. T. Barnum Museum in Bridgeport; the Winchester Gun Museum and Yale University in New Haven; and the American Shakespeare Theater in Stratford.

Rhode Island

Abbreviations: *R.I., RI*
Area: *1,049 sq. mi., 2,717 sq. km.*
Rank (of 50) *50th*
Population:
1985 *968,000*
Rank (of 50) *42nd*
Change 1980–85 *+21,000*
Percent change *+2.2*
Persons per sq. mi. *918*
Percent urban *87.0*
Capital: *Providence*
Largest city: *Providence*
Metro. pop. 1985 *630,000*
Entered Union: *May 29, 1790 (13th)*
State bird: *Rhode Island red chicken*
State flower: *Violet*
State tree: *Red maple*

Rhode Island, the smallest of U.S. states in area, is situated in the southeast of the New England region. To the north and east the state borders Massachusetts, and to the west it borders Connecticut. Its southern border is the Atlantic coastline. The eastern part of the state is broken by Narragansett Bay, which extends 25 miles

STRICKLER/MONKMEYER

GREATER BOSTON CONVENTION & TOURIST BUREAU

COUNTRY LIFE AND HISTORY: *New England has lost several industries and thousands of residents to other sections of the country, but it cherishes such country arts as maple sugaring and such monuments to its history as the Old South Meeting House in Boston, built in 1713.*

inland from the sea. Rhode Island borders the bay on all sides and includes several large islands in its territory, including Rhode Island, for which the state is named. The rest of the southern coast is formed by Block Island Sound, named for an island 10 miles offshore included in the Rhode Island state lands.

Rhode Island is an unusual state in both history and demography. The colony was founded in 1636 when Roger Williams, a minister, led a group of followers south to Providence from the Massachusetts Bay Colony, where they had been persecuted. At the time of the American Revolution the tiny colony was reluctant to join the Constitutional Convention in Philadelphia, and it only became the 13th of the original American states after the war with England had begun. The state remains unusual today because virtually all of its population lives in and around Providence, at the northern head of Narragansett Bay.

The land. Rhode Island's lands include only two topographical features. The lands surrounding Narragansett Bay in the east of the state consist of New England Seaboard Lowlands. These lands have settled to the extent that the highest elevation in the area is only 200 feet above sea level, and the bay has submerged lands as far as 30 miles inland. The seaboard lowland also includes the coast of western Rhode Island, which is sandy and includes shifting Barrier Reef islands just offshore. Western and northern Rhode Island consists of New England Upland, a hilly region of lakes that rises to a maximum elevation of 812 feet at Jerimoth in the northwest of the state.

Climate. Rhode island's climate is slightly milder than that of the rest of New England because of its southern coastal location. Normal summer highs are 80° F and winter lows are 20. Precipitation averages 43 inches per year, including an average of 39 inches of snow.

Principal cities. All points in Rhode Island lie within 30 miles of the Providence metropolitan area, which includes 87 percent of the total state population and an additional 100,000 residents of Massachusetts. The only other large cities in the state are Woonsocket (population 45,914) in the north and Newport (population 29,259) on the southern coast. Both of these cities declined slightly in population in the 1970's, and during the same decade the population of the Providence metropolitan area declined by 10,000.

The people. Rhode Island lost 27,000 residents to migration in the 1970's. The state was the only one other than New York to record a total population decrease in the 1970's. Rhode Island's resident population is 3 percent black and 2 percent Hispanic. A third of its residents are of foreign birth or parentage, most of them of Italian and French Canadian descent.

Economy. It was in Pawtucket, Rhode Island, near Providence, that the first water-powered mill in the United States was built, in 1793. The state economy today is still based on light manufacturing. Its manufacturers continue to lead the United States in two traditional products, jewelry and silverware; they also produce large quantities of textile and electronics equipment. The second leading industry is tourism, chiefly to southern beach areas and the historic resort town of Newport. Rhode Island's agricultural produce is chiefly vegetables and potatoes, but some dairy farming is carried out on the hills of the western uplands.

Places of interest. The major attraction for visitors to Rhode Island is Newport, famous since the 19th century as a summer resort for the rich, and notable today for its large seaside mansions. Places of interest in Providence include the first Baptist Church in America and the Roger Williams National Memorial. In Pawtucket, just north of Providence, Samuel Slater's original 1793 water mill has been restored and preserved.

Massachusetts

Abbreviations: *Mass., MA*
Area: *7,826 sq. mi., 20,269 sq. km.*
Rank (of 50) *45th*
Population:
1985 *5,822,000*
Rank (of 50) *12th*
Change 1980–85 *+85,000*
Percent change *+1.5*
Persons per sq. mi. *744*
Percent urban *83.8*
Capital: *Boston*
Largest city: *Boston*
Metro. pop. 1985 *2,832,000*
Entered Union: *Feb. 6, 1788 (6th)*
State bird: *Chickadee*
State flower: *Mayflower*
State tree: *American elm*

Massachusetts is the central New England state, with borders on four of the other five states of the region. Two-thirds of the state area is a 50-mile-wide rectangle between Vermont and New Hampshire on the north and Connecticut and Rhode Island on the south. The state's western border is with New York. The eastern third of Massachusetts extends 90 miles from north to south; it has an irregular Atlantic Ocean coastline. The shape of the state is distinctive for the 75-mile-long peninsula of Cape Cod hooking to the north from the eastern coastline.

The commercial and population center of New England, Massachusetts has a historical importance that extends beyond the region. Its early settlements founded by Pilgrims and Puritans after 1620 were among the strongest in North America. In the years before the American Revolution, Massachusetts patriots were outspoken in their opposition to British excesses. The Boston Tea Party of 1773, defying a British tax on tea, became a symbol of American resolve. The war itself began at Lexington and Concord in 1775.

In the 1800's the state was the home of the preeminent American philosophers and writers, the testing ground for the earliest American manufacturers, and the port of entry for waves of Irish immigrants driven from their own country by potato famines. Today, Massachusetts is the home of 46 percent of the people of New England and it generates as much income from manufacturing as all other states of the region combined. It enjoyed consistent growth throughout the early 20th century, but that increase slowed in the 1970's, and the state recorded the fourth lowest rate of increase in the country: less than 1 percent.

The land. The western two-thirds of Massachusetts consists wholly of New England Upland. The far western region is Appalachian in character, consisting of narrow ranges of the Taconic Mountains, entering the state from New York, the Berkshire Hills, and the Green Mountains that extend northward into Vermont. Central Massachusetts is an upland plateau of rolling hills divided by the north-south Connecticut River valley. The eastern third of the state consists of New England Seaboard Lowlands with an irregular coastline that is generally rocky in the north and sandy in the south. The sandy peninsula of Cape Cod is a small part of the Atlantic Coastal Plain. Two large islands to the south of the cape, Martha's Vineyard and Nantucket, are also part of the plain.

Climate. The climate of Massachusetts is moderate for New England. At Boston on the Atlantic coast, normal summer highs are 81° F and winter lows are 22. Boston receives an average of 43 inches of precipitation per year, including 43 inches of snow. The winters are harsher and the snowfalls greater in the interior regions.

Principal cities. The great metropolitan area in Massachusetts is Boston, which contains 48 percent of the state's population. The city is the manufacturing and financial center of all eastern New England and a cultural and educational center of national importance. Its educational institutions include Harvard University, the Massachusetts Institute of Technology, Boston University, and a variety of other schools in professional and technical fields.

The second largest urban area is Springfield (population 530,668), a manufacturing center 60 miles southwest of Boston near the Connecticut border. Worcester, almost equidistant between these two, is the third largest city with a metropolitan population of 372,940. There is also a large urban population north of Boston around the towns of Lawrence and Lowell; their combined metropolitan areas include some 525,000 residents, some of them in New Hampshire.

The people. Massachusetts contains the greatest proportion of lifelong residents in New England, 66 percent. One-third of the population are of foreign birth or parentage, many of them members of the Italian and Irish communities of Boston and Springfield. Massachusetts showed only negligible growth in the 1970's. In that decade it lost nearly 150,000 residents to migration to other states. The state population is 4 percent black and 2 percent Hispanic, with most of these residents concentrated in and around Boston and Springfield.

Economy. Manufacturing far exceeds any other industry in value to Massachusetts's economy. The traditional manufactures are textiles and shoes, but the state manufacturers produce new products in addition, such as electronic equipment and machinery.

The second largest contributor to the state economy is tourism, particularly from resorts that extend the full range of the state from the Berkshire Hills in the west to Cape Cod in the east. The agricultural businesses of Massachusetts are evenly divided between livestock, chiefly from dairy and poultry farms, and crops, especially greenhouse vegetables and the largest U.S. harvest of cranberries. In addition, Boston is a major center for banking and insurance companies.

Places of interest. Boston is the principal attraction to year-round visitors to Massachusetts; it is the home of the Old North Church, many historical landmarks, Harvard University, and the John F. Kennedy Library. The summer resorts in both the Berkshire Hills and Cape Cod are noted for their cultural events. In addition to mountain scenery, the Berkshires offer concerts at Tanglewood and the Jacob's Pillow Dance Festival. The summer colonies on Cape Cod's beaches feature many artistic exhibits and theatrical performances, especially at Provincetown at the tip of the cape.

Vermont

Abbreviations: *Vt., VT*
Area: *9,276 sq. mi., 24,025 sq. km.*

Rank (of 50)	*43rd*

Population:

1985	*535,000*
Rank (of 50)	*48th*
Change 1980–85	*+24,000*
Percent change	*+4.6*
Persons per sq. mi.	*58*
Percent urban	*33.8*

Capital: *Montpelier*
Largest city: *Burlington*

City pop. 1980	*37,712*

Entered Union: *Mar. 4, 1791 (14th)*
State bird: *Hermit thrush*
State flower: *Red clover*
State tree: *Sugar maple*

Vermont is the most northwestern of the New England states. To the north it borders the Canadian Province of Quebec and to the west New York. Most of this western border is formed by the narrow north-south extent of Lake Champlain. To the south Vermont has a straight border with Massachusetts, and to the east it has an irregular one with New Hampshire formed by the Connecticut River. The state extends approximately 150 miles from north to south, and its east-west breadth broadens from about 40 miles in the south to about 80 in the north.

Vermont is the most rural of all U.S. states, and it is well known for its old New England ambience. The increased popularity of winter sports and increased interest in country living has brought recent growth to the state. Vermont had a population of 300,000 as early as 1850 and did not pass 400,000 until 1970. Between 1970 and 1980, however, the population increased by 66,000 to surpass 500,000. Even with this growth, Vermont remains the most sparsely populated New England state with the exception of Maine.

The land. All of Vermont is hilly or mountainous, but the state lands fall into three narrow regions that extend its entire length from Massachusetts to Canada. The western region consists of the Taconic Mountains running north from Massachusetts and the Champlain valley surrounding the lake, which drains into the St. Lawrence River 80 miles north in Canada. Central Vermont is the most mountainous, consisting of the 20- to 40-mile-wide range of Green Mountains. Eastern Vermont lies within the New England Upland, a hilly region declining slightly in elevation toward the Connecticut River along the New Hampshire border. In the northeast is one end of the White Mountains, which extend across New Hampshire and into Maine.

Climate. The climate of Vermont is very cold because of the state's elevation and inland location. Normal summer highs for the state are 81° F, but winter lows average 8 and extreme lows in the mountains fall below minus 30. Precipitation averages 33 inches per year. Winters are long in Vermont, and the state averages 80 inches of snow per year, with even heavier snowfalls in the mountains.

Principal cities. Vermont is unique in the eastern United States for its lack of a metropolitan area. The largest city in the state is Burlington, in the northwest on the shore of Lake Champlain. Chittendon County, in which Burlington is located, has 115,000 residents, more than twice that of the second largest county. The second largest city is Rutland (population 18,436) in the south-central region of the state within the Green Mountains. Other than suburbs of Burlington, there is no other city in the state with a population of 10,000.

The people. Vermont was one of only three states in the Northeast whose growth exceeded the national average. About one-third of the total population growth consisted of immigrants from other states. In addition to being the most rural in the United States, the population is the lowest in minority groups among New England states, with blacks and Hispanics each representing less than 1 percent of the total. Vermont also has the lowest number of residents of foreign birth or parentage among New England states. The foreign stock, about 18 percent of the population, is chiefly Canadian; these people live in northern communities near the U.S. border.

Economy. The chief industry of Vermont is manufacturing, mainly of machine tools, electrical equipment, and computers. Tourism is a much more visible industry, although it generates less than half the income of manufacturing. Vermont attracts numerous visitors in both winter and summer, but the winter ski resorts earn most of the income from tourism and support additional retail businesses throughout the central mountain region. Mining contributes a small portion of the state economy, but Vermont is the U.S. leader in the quarrying of monument granite and talc and ranks second in the country in asbestos mining. The state's agricultural businesses are virtually all devoted to dairy farming. Maple syrup is a Vermont specialty; Vermont produces greater quantities than any other state.

Places of interest. There are more than 50 ski areas in Vermont, the most famous being Stowe, Killington, Mt. Snow, and Sugarbush. Mountain landscapes and lakes also attract many summer visitors to the state, especially to Green Mountain National Forest and the shores of Lake Champlain. Also of interest are the Bennington Battle Monument in the southwest; the Vermont Marble exhibit in Proctor, just southeast of Rutland; and the Maple Grove Maple Museum at St. Johnsbury in the northwest.

New Hampshire

Abbreviations: *N.H., NH*
Area: *9,027 sq. mi., 23,380 sq. km.*
Rank (of 50) — *44th*
Population:

1985	*998,000*
Rank (of 50)	*41st*
Change 1980–85	*+77,000*
Percent change	*+8.4*
Persons per sq. mi.	*111*
Percent urban	*47.5*

Capital: *Concord*
Largest city: *Manchester*
Metro. pop. 1980 — *160,767*
Entered Union: *June 21, 1788 (9th)*
State bird: *Purple finch*
State flower: *Purple lilac*
State tree: *White birch*

New Hampshire is a triangular state situated in the northern tier of the New England region. The state is broadest in the south, where it has a 125-mile border with Massachusetts, and narrowest in the north, where its east-west breadth narrows to less than 20 miles at the northern border with the Canadian Province of Quebec. On the west New Hampshire has an irregular border with Vermont formed by the Connecticut River, and on the east it has a straight border with Maine. A short eastward extension between Maine and Massachusetts gives the state a 15-mile Atlantic Ocean coastline.

In the 1970's New Hampshire had the greatest numerical and proportionate population growth in New England. The state population grew by 100,000 in the 1950's and again in the 1960's, but in the 1970's it grew by nearly 200,000. The growth is especially striking in southern New Hampshire, where most of the people live, because it stands in contrast to the end of population growth in adjacent Massachusetts. In fact, many commuters to Boston have relocated across the New Hampshire border, and many companies have made similar moves because of tax advantages. At the same time, northern New Hampshire remains sparsely populated, but it attracts many tourists to the state.

The land. All of New Hampshire is hilly and forested, but the state lands fall into northern and southern topographical areas. The north is dominated by the White Mountains that cross the state from Vermont to Maine. The Presidential range within the White Mountains includes Mt. Washington (6288 feet), the highest peak in the northeast and the windiest spot in the country, with record gusts well over 200 miles per hour. The southern half of the state consists of New England Upland, a region that in New Hampshire averages 1200 feet in elevation and includes peaks over 3000 feet high. Along the small southeastern extension between Maine and Massachusetts to the Atlantic Ocean, New Hampshire includes a fringe of New England Seaboard Lowland, with sandy beaches and a major harbor at Portsmouth.

Climate. New Hampshire's climate typically consists of short summers and long, cold winters. At the capital city of Concord in south-central New Hampshire normal summer highs are 82° F and winter lows are 10. However, Concord has recorded temperatues as low as minus 37, and subzero temperatures are common in the northern mountains. Precipitation at Concord averages 36 inches per year with 66 inches of snow, but snowfall is heavier in the north.

Principal cities. The major cities in New Hampshire are all clustered in the southeast near the Massachusetts border. The largest is Manchester, an industrial city on the Merrimack River less than 20 miles from the Massachusetts border. The second largest city is Nashua (population 114,148), farther down the Merrimack and closer to Massachusetts. Each of these cities grew by more than 25,000 in population in the 1970's. The other large cities in the state are the capital of Concord (population 30,400) and harbor city of Portsmouth (population 26,254), both of which grew slightly in the 1970's.

The people. Well over half of New Hampshire's total population growth in the 1970's was from immigrants from other states. Most of these new residents settled in southern New Hampshire, which includes two-thirds of the total population. One-quarter of the residents are of foreign birth or parentage, chiefly Canadian. The black and the Hispanic populations in the state are each under 1 percent of the total.

Economy. Manufacturing is the principal industry of New Hampshire, producing three times the income of any other business. Because New Hampshire's lands are rocky and hilly, water-powered manufacturing was the traditional business of the state. The first products were leather and wood goods; these remain among the principal manufactures. New manufactures include electrical equipment and machinery, which are produced in the cities in the south of the state. The second leading industry is tourism, and most of this business is based in the northern, less populated areas of the state. The state's agricultural businesses are principally dairy farms, vegetable greenhouses, and fruit orchards.

Places of interest. The major attractions in New Hampshire are its mountains and more than 1000 lakes and ponds. Mountain attractions include the hiking trails around Mt. Washington, White Mountains National Forest, and the unusual "Old Man of the Mountain" granite formation in the Franconia range in the northwest of the state. The largest body of water in the state is 70-square-mile Lake Winnipesaukee in the east-central region; the lake and the Franklin Falls Reservoir both drain into the scenic upper reaches of the Merrimack River.

Maine

Abbreviations: *Me., ME*
Area: *30,920 sq. mi., 80,083 sq. km.*
Rank (of 50) *39th*
Population:
1985 *1,164,000*
Rank (of 50) *38th*
Change 1980–85 *+39,000*
Percent change *+3.5*
Persons per sq. mi. *38*
Percent urban *47.5*
Capital: *Augusta*
Largest city: *Portland*
Metro. pop. 1980 *183,625*
Entered Union: *Mar. 15, 1820 (23rd)*
State bird: *Chickadee*
State flower: *White pine cone and tassel*
State tree: *White pine*

Maine is the most northeastern of U.S. states. It is surrounded on three sides by Canada: the Province of Quebec to the northwest and the Province of New Brunswick to the north and east. Its only boundary with another state is the lower western one with New Hampshire. The southeastern edge of Maine is an irregular 230-mile Atlantic Ocean coastline that includes many islands and deep harbors.

Maine is the largest of all New England states. It contains a land area nearly equal to that of all the other states combined; it is also the most sparsely populated of New England states. After a history of slow growth since voting to separate itself from Massachusetts in 1819, Maine added more residents in the 1970's than in any decade of its history, passing 1.1 million. More than half of the new population growth is attributed to immigrants from other states, many of them retired persons attracted to resort areas along the southern coast. The total population is heavily concentrated in the southern half of the state, and large portions of northern Maine are forestland traversed only by private logging trails.

The land. The topography of Maine is a uniformly hilly and rocky one sharing three distinct features with the rest of New England. The White Mountains enter the state from the northern part of the New Hampshire border and extend northeast into the center of Maine, where the state high point is located at Mt. Katahdin (5268 feet). To the east and north of the mountains is the New England Upland, a region of rounded glacial "horsebacks," or low ridges. The upland declines in elevation toward the St. John River along the northern Canadian border and toward the southeastern coast. Perhaps the state's most remarkable feature is its varied and beautiful Atlantic coast. The New England Seaboard Lowlands provide a predominantly rocky and highly irregular shoreline. Mount Desert Island, two-thirds of the way from the New Hampshire to the Canadian borders, was the site of an early French settlement in the 1600's. In the early 1900's it was a wealthy seaside resort, and today it is preserved for all to enjoy as Acadia National Park.

Climate. The climate of Maine is one of long, cold winters and cool summers. Normal summer highs are below 80° F at Portland along the southeast coast and normal winter lows are 12. Summer highs may be higher inland, and winter lows are sure to be lower, reaching subzero in the far north. Precipitation averages 41 inches per year, with 75 inches of snow per year in Portland and more to the north.

Principal cities. The metropolitan area around Portland has twice the population of any other urban area in the state. The city is located on the large Casco Bay, and its harbor commerce is chiefly the transport of oil brought from Canada by pipeline and commercial fishing. The second largest population center is Lewiston–Auburn (population 72,445), located inland 25 miles due north of Portland. Bangor, farther north and 25 miles inland from the coast on the Penobscot River, has a city population of 31,643. The only other city with more than 20,000 people is the capital of Augusta on the Kennebec River 25 miles northeast of Lewiston.

The people. In population and rate of growth, Maine is third in the region. It has a high percentage of lifelong residents, 62 percent. After Vermont, it has the lowest population density and the lowest proportion of urban residents in the region. Black and Hispanic populations are both below 1 percent of the total. Most of Maine's small proportion of foreign stock is Canadian, with many of the people living in communities near the state's long Canadian border.

Economy. The economy of Maine is heavily based on manufacturing, which accounts for more income than all other industries combined. The principal manufactures are paper and wood products, textiles, leather goods, and processed foods. Tourism brings the state $479 million per year, particularly along the Atlantic coast and the many inland lakes in southern Maine. The state also contains 18 million acres of forestland, more than half the New England total, and from it Maine harvests 36 billion board feet of timber each year.

Agriculture accounts for slightly less income than tourism. Maine's agriculture is principally based on dairy and poultry farms, but its crop production is notable for producing 9 percent of the U.S. potato harvest. Commercial fishing generates far less total income than these other industries, but Maine is especially noted for its lobster catch, which represents 80 percent of the U.S. total.

Places of interest. The principal attraction for visitors to Maine is the state's rocky coastline, where Acadia National Park is found in the northern third and Boothbay Harbor in the southern third. There are also many inland lakes and streams that attract campers and fishermen in summer.

FACING EAST: *the coast of Maine is the easternmost part of the United States. Its lighthouses have guided generations of travelers past the rocky shores and safely into harbor.*

DU PUY/MONKMEYER

U.S. Territories

STYLE AND LEISURE: *Puerto Rico, the largest U.S. territory, traces its Spanish heritage to the voyages of Columbus. The governor's mansion in San Juan shows the elegance of Spanish design. At right, American Samoa offers a sense of leisure only dreamed about by mainlanders.*

The United States retains control of a number of outlying territories in both the Caribbean area and the west and central Pacific. The greatest number are in the Pacific, but many are uninhabited coral atolls. The most important territory and the only one with potential for statehood is Puerto Rico, between the Caribbean Sea and the Atlantic Ocean to the southeast of Florida. Puerto Rico is presently a commonwealth possession with powers of self-government similar to a state's, but without voting representation in Congress.

Of the rest, the greatest number are unincorporated territories, a status that grants autonomous elections for local governments under the administration of the U.S. Department of Interior. Micronesia, in the west Pacific, has a unique status, being a trusteeship under the mandate of the United Nations. The Canal Zone, in the Central American Republic of Panama, is governed by treaties that end U.S. control in 1999.

The political status of the populated U.S. possessions is frequently revised to permit greater self-government while protecting U.S. access to military installations. The many uninhabited U.S. territories are retained for their strategic importance. In addition to the official U.S. territories, there are some 25 Pacific islands of disputed sovereignty that have been claimed both by the United States and by either Great Britain or New Zealand.

Puerto Rico

Abbreviations: *P.R., PR*
Area: *3,421 sq. mi., 8,860 sq. km.*
Population:

1985	*3,282,000*
Change 1980–85	*+85,600*
Percent change	*+2.7*
Persons per sq. mi.	*924*
Percent urban	*66.8*

Capital: *San Juan*
Largest city: *San Juan*
Metro. pop. 1980 *1,200,000*
Declared Commonwealth: *July 25, 1952*
Bird: *Reinita*
Flower: *Maga*
Tree: *Ceiba*

Puerto Rico is an island located 1000 miles southeast of Miami, Florida. It is the easternmost of the chain of islands called the Greater Antilles, which stretch east-west between the Atlantic Ocean on the north and the Caribbean Sea on the south. Puerto Rico is the smallest of the major islands in the chain. The chain includes Cuba and the island of Hispaniola, which is shared by Haiti and the Dominican Republic. The island of Puerto Rico is roughly rectangular in shape, averaging 100 miles from east to west and 35 miles from north to south. The Commonwealth of Puerto Rico includes several smaller islands, notably Vieques and Culebra.

Officially known as *Estado Libre Asociado de Puerto Rico*, Puerto Rico was discovered by Christopher Columbus on his second voyage, in 1493, and ceded by the Spanish to the United States at the end of the Spanish-American War in 1898. Puerto Ricans became citizens of the United States in 1917, and began to elect their own governor in 1947. Since becoming a Commonwealth in 1952, the people have had nonvoting representation in Congress.

In the 1940's, Puerto Rico had a depressed economy; it was, in fact, known as "the poorhouse of the Caribbean." This inspired an industrialization program known as Operation Bootstrap. The program, a combination of tax incentives for investment and diversification of manufactures, has succeeded in bolstering the local economy. A constant flow of immigrants from Puerto Rico came to the U.S. mainland between 1945 and the late 1960's. New York City was the most popular destination and it has the largest community of Puerto Ricans outside of Puerto Rico. In the 1970's, however, migration slowed, and the Commonwealth gained more new residents than it lost in migration to other places.

The land. Three-quarters of the island of Puerto Rico is mountainous. The mountains rise to a maximum elevation of 4389 feet at Cerro de Punta, near the center of the island. From the central Sierra de Luquillo and Cordillera ranges, the land declines to coastal valleys on the east and west and sandy lowland beaches on the north and south.

Climate. The climate of Puerto Rico is warm and humid year-round. Normal winter temperatures along the coast seldom fall below 70° F, and normal summer temperatures remain above 80. The less populated areas in the central mountains are cooler in both summer and winter. Precipitation ranges from 20 inches per year on the southern coast to 200 inches per year in some mountain areas, with an average of 60 inches per year falling on the capital city of San Juan on the northeastern coast.

Principal cities. The major population center in Puerto Rico is San Juan, which accounts for almost 40 percent of the total population. One of the oldest cities in the Americas, San Juan is situated on a peninsula extending northwest from the island; it functions as the island's principal tourist and shipping center. The second largest city is Ponce, situated near the center of the southern coast, with a population of nearly 200,000. The third largest city is Mayaguez, a port and apparel center on the west coast with a population just over 100,000.

The people. The population of Puerto Rico is 99 percent Hispanic, two-thirds urban, and one of the densest in the world. The per capita income of the people doubled between 1965 and 1975, although it remains low in comparison with that of U.S. states. In the 1960's, Puerto Rico had a net migration loss of about 200,000 residents, but in the 1970's there was a gain of about the same number; this accounted for more than 40 percent of the total population increase for that decade.

The common language of the people is Spanish, but most Puerto Ricans are bilingual and official documents are published in both English and Spanish.

Economy. Once almost totally reliant on sugar and tobacco crops for its income, Puerto Rico now generates more than half its domestic income from manufacturing. The principal manufactures are metal products, foods, and apparel, but the most famous export is 75 percent of all the rum sold in the United States. Tourism is the second largest industry. More than 1.8 million visitors to Puerto Rico spent $615 million in 1980. Agriculture accounts for about half the income generated by tourism. The farm industry is based on sugar, from which molasses for rum is refined; coffee grown on the western mountains; and tobacco grown on the eastern mountains.

Places of interest. The principal attraction in Puerto Rico is Old San Juan, a walled city surrounded by historic forts at the tip of the San Juan peninsula. The city is also home to a number of museums, the Puerto Rican Botanical Gardens, and a music conservatory famous for the mid-June Pablo Casals Festival. Points of interest inland include the Cordillera Park and El Yunque Rain Forest.

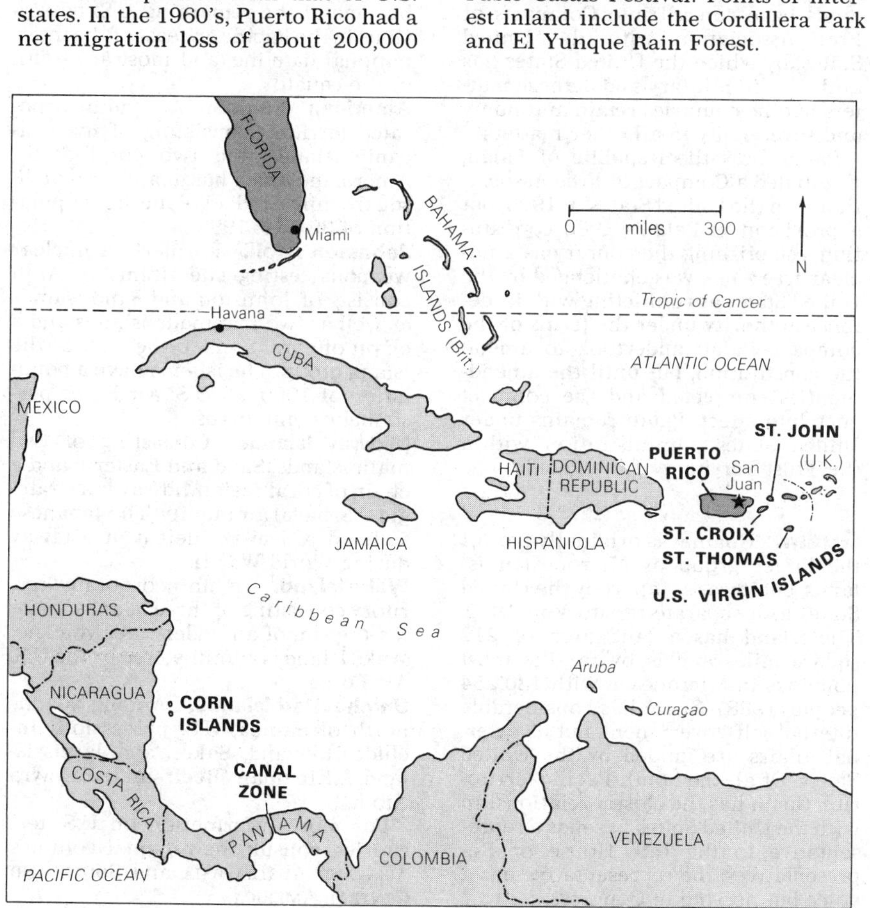

Other Territories in the Americas

The United States has a number of other possessions in the Caribbean area. The major ones are the Virgin Islands and the Panama Canal Zone.

The Virgin Islands. The U.S. Virgin Islands is an unincorporated territory 40 miles east of Puerto Rico. Great Britain retains possession of three major islands in the chain, but the United States governs St. Croix, St. Thomas, St. John, and about 50 minor islets. The three major islands under U.S. control are all volcanic in origin, with steep elevations and little arable land. They have subtropical climates cooled by trade winds, with average year-round temperatures of 78° F and annual precipitation of 45 inches. The total population is 95,214, of whom more than half live on St. Croix. Fewer than 3000 people live on St. John. The capital city of Charlotte Amalie, with a population of 13,000, is on St. Thomas.

The people of the Virgin Islands are English-speaking and 80 percent black; they were granted U.S. citizenship in 1927, and in 1970 elected their first governor. The islands lack agricultural lands, and the economy is based on tourism and exportation of manufactured goods such as rum, apparel, and costume jewelry.

The U.S. Canal Zone. The Canal Zone is a 10-mile-wide strip of land running through the Republic of Panama in Central America. The Canal Zone follows the Panama Canal, which was completed in 1914, between the Atlantic and Pacific oceans. In 1978 treaties were signed that will cede the Canal Zone and the Canal to complete Panamanian control on December 31, 1999.

Other territories. The Corn Islands off the east coast of Nicaragua in Central America are the only other inhabited U.S. possessions in the Caribbean. Great and Little Corn Islands have a combined land area of 4 square miles, and the population of about 1800 live entirely on Great Corn Island. Both islands are leased by the United States from the government of Nicaragua.

Quita Sueño Bank, Roncador, and Serrana are uninhabited cays in the Caribbean between Nicaragua and Jamaica. A 1972 treaty to cede them to Colombia has never been ratified by Congress. Navassa is an island of 2 square miles in the Caribbean between Jamaica and Haiti. It is a navigation point on which a U.S. Coast Guard lighthouse has been built.

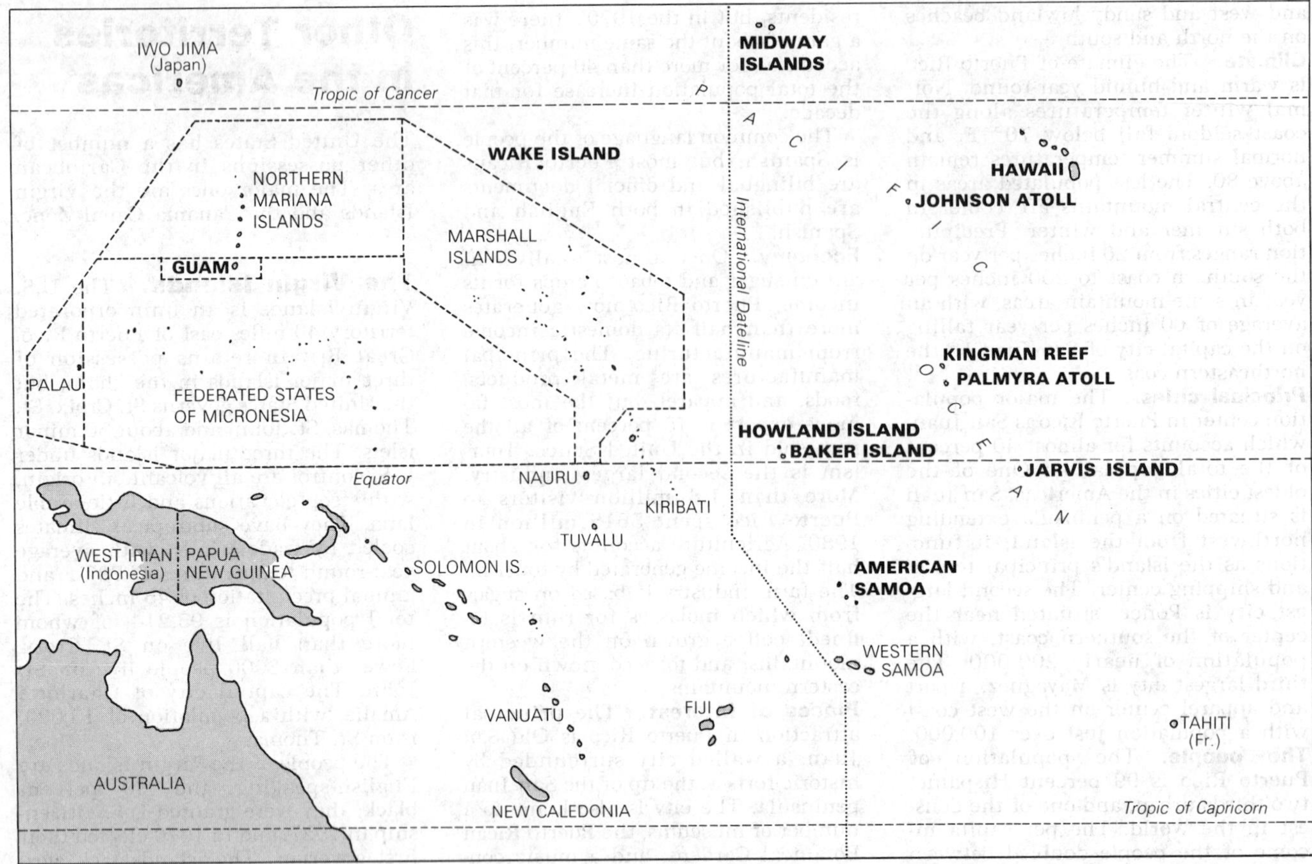

Pacific Territories

Trust Territory of the Pacific Islands. After World War II the United States was given a mandate by the United Nations to administer the islands in the western Pacific commonly known as Micronesia. There are 2100 identified islands spread over 3 million square miles just north of the large island of New Guinea and east of the Philippines. The southern extreme of the island region lies on the equator, and its western boundary is near the international dateline.

The islands were controlled by Spain from 1565 until 1898, when they were sold to Germany. In 1947 they became the UN-mandated Trust Territory of the Pacific Islands. The territory included the Northern Mariana Islands, a chain of islands running due north of Guam; the Federated States of Micronesia, located about 3200 miles southwest of Hawaii; the Marshall Islands, 2375 miles southwest of Hawaii; and Palau, about 530 miles southeast of the Philippines.

In 1986 the Northern Marianas achieved commonwealth status and were removed from the Trust Territory. Also that year, Micronesia became the independent Federated States of Micronesia and the Marshalls became independent as the Republic of the Marshall Islands. These too were removed from the Trust Territory, leaving only Palau.

Both Micronesia and the Marshall Islands have entered into Compacts of Free Association with the United States, by which the United States has authority in military and defense matters but the countries retain autonomy and sovereignty in all other matters.

Palau, now the Republic of Palau, negotiated a Compact of Free Association with the United States in 1986, but a provision in Palau's 1980 constitution, establishing the country as a nuclear-free zone, was challenged by the United States as conflicting with its defense authority under the terms of the compact. Palau undertook to amend the constitution, but until the amendment is completed and the compact goes into effect, Palau remains under United States administration within the Trust Territory of the Pacific.

Guam. Guam was originally part of the larger group of Micronesian islands, but it was set apart by the United States as a separate territory in 1950. The island has a land area of 212 square miles and is by far the most populous in Micronesia, with 130,254 people (1988). Guam has considerable internal self-government, but its external affairs are guided by the United States. Of all the South Pacific territories, Guam has the closest relationship with the United States. It sends a representative to the U.S. House of Representatives; the representative has a voice but no vote in Congress.

East Pacific Territories. All but one of the remaining U.S. possessions in the Pacific are east of the international dateline, and most are south of the equator.

American Samoa. An unincorporated territory consisting of five volcanic islands and two coral atolls, American Samoa has a land area of 76 square miles and a Polynesian population of 39,254 (1988).

Johnston Atoll. Formerly a nuclear weapons testing site, Johnston Atoll consists of Johnston and Sand islands as well as two manmade islands and a chain of coral reefs to the west of the island group. The islands have a population of 1000, all U.S. Air Force personnel or employees.

Midway Islands. Consisting of two main islands, Sand and Eastern, and a chain of coral reefs, Midway is a strategic U.S. naval air facility. The Japanese suffered a decisive defeat at Midway during World War II.

Wake Island. An unincorporated territory consisting of three islands forming the rim of an underwater volcano, Wake Island is administered by the U.S. Air Force.

Uninhabited Islands. Among islands north of Samoa, U.S. possessions include Howland, Baker, and Jarvis islands; Kingman Reef; and Palmyra Atoll.

For more information on U.S. territories, consult the regional volumes Asia and Australasia and South and Central America.

CANADA TODAY

Canada, a nation of more than 25 million people, derives its name from an Indian word, "kanata," meaning village or settlement. The population is made up of descendants of Canada's aboriginal groups, including Indians, Inuit (Eskimos), and Metis (people of mixed Indian and European, particularly French, descent); descendants of French, British, and other European settlers; and more recent immigrants.

Geographically, Canada comprises the northern half, excepting Alaska, of North America and adjacent islands. Canada's relatively small population is concentrated largely in urban centers within 100 miles of its long, undefended border with the United States. Canada's largest physical region, the Canadian Shield, is a vast and inhospitable U-shaped area of about 1.6 million square miles around Hudson Bay.

Canada has developed economically and politically in three distinct stages. The first period, characterized largely by French domination, lasted from the early 1600's until 1759, when the British gained control of Canada during the French and Indian War, the North American phase of the Seven Years' War. The second period, initially one of direct British control, witnessed the emergence of Canada as a self-governing nation on July 1, 1867, and its voluntary continuance as a monarchical parliamentary democracy in the British tradition. Canada's third stage of development has been marked by increasingly close relationships with the United States.

The existence in Canada of two official languages—French and English—and the country's emphasis on multicultural traditions contribute to the fragility of the Canadian federation, as evidenced by the Quebec separatist movement.

The Land

The land mass of Canada occupies all of the North American continent north of the United States, except Alaska. Its area is 3,851,809 square miles, making it about 5 percent larger than the United States.

The southern border of Canada in the east runs mainly along the line of the St. Lawrence River and the Great Lakes. It then extends westward to the Pacific Ocean on the 49th parallel of latitude. This boundary is just under 4000 miles long. Canada is bordered on the east by the Atlantic Ocean, on the west by the Pacific Ocean, and on the north by the Arctic Ocean. There are many islands belonging to Canada off all three coasts.

On the east coast, the cold Labrador Current, which carries icebergs, flows down from Baffin Bay and meets the warmer, north-flowing Gulf Stream off southeast Newfoundland. The meeting of the two currents, with warm air passing over them, causes a steady, dense fog. Here, too, are the Grand Banks, an underwater plateau that rises from the continental shelf. The shallowness of the water over the Banks and the water currents provide a favorable environment for small sea life such as plankton that fish feed on. As a result, the Banks teem with cod, halibut, and other fish, making it the world's most important commercial fishing ground. Off Canada's Pacific coast, too, special conditions of current and temperature cause a concentration of fish. Halibut, cod, herring, and especially salmon, make this another major commercial fishing area.

During the Pleistocene epoch, which began nearly 2 million years ago, great sheets of ice formed and advanced as glaciers to cover Canada and parts of the United States. From time to time the climate became milder and the ice melted and retreated. The ice sheets eroded the land and hollowed out areas that later became lakes. When the ice completely retreated, the Atlantic Ocean flooded the northeastern United States and southeastern Canada because the weight of the ice had pushed this huge region below sea level. This most recent Ice Age ended about 11,000 years ago.

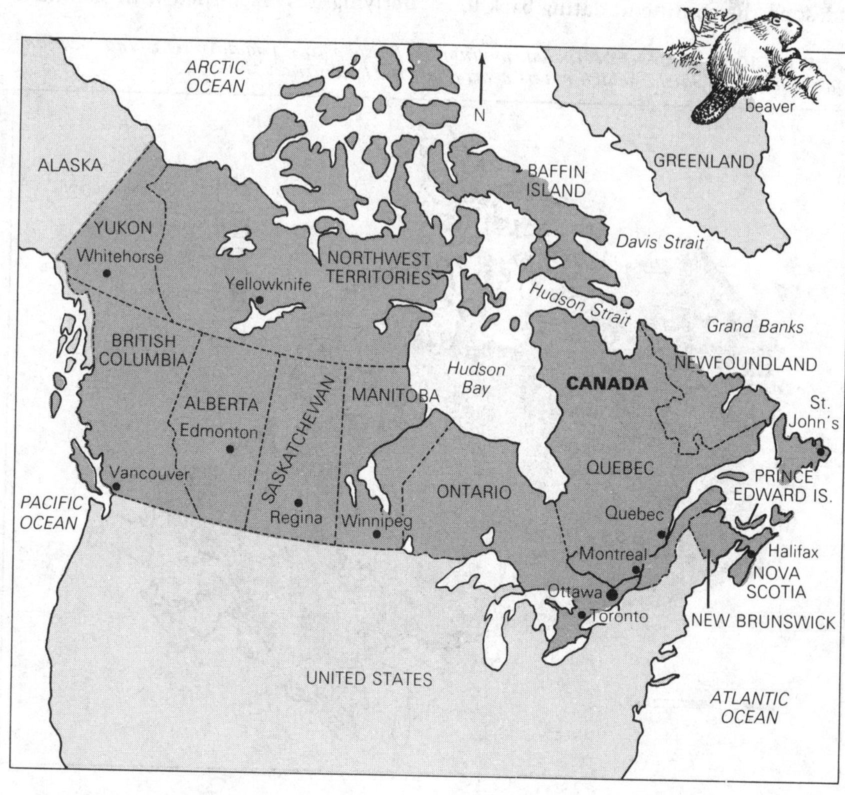

Geographic areas. Canada can be divided into five main geographic areas. The first of these is the southeastern region. On Canada's extreme east, the land is an extension of the Appalachian Mountain system running north from the United States. It continues to the Gaspé Peninsula and the island of Newfoundland. The Atlantic coast is quite indented, and provides excellent harbors.

Beginning at Quebec, the valley of the St. Lawrence River becomes broader, and there are fertile plains. This section merges into southeastern Ontario, the region north of Lake Ontario and between lakes Erie and Huron. This large triangle of fertile soil was left by the gradual disappearance of prehistoric lakes whose remains are now the Great Lakes.

The second principal geographic area is the Canadian Shield, which covers more than half of all of Canada and is the dominant physiographic feature of the dominion. The Shield, shaped like an enormous U, with Hudson Bay in the center, extends from Labrador on the Atlantic coast westward to the Great Plains, more than halfway across the country. Its western edge slants northwest until it reaches the Arctic Ocean. The northern boundary of the Shield is the coast of the continental mainland. In the south it pushes all the way down to the St. Lawrence valley and the Ontario peninsula.

The Shield was the first part of North America to be permanently elevated above sea level by natural forces. It consists mainly of metamorphic rock. This geologic formation is the oldest on the continent, dating back to the pre-Cambrian era of several billion years ago. Ice sheets and water have eroded the Shield for millions of years, so that today it is generally only 1000 to 2000 feet above sea level, with a few low mountain ranges. Much of the soil has been carried away and the erosion has created thousands of lakes, bogs, and rock formations.

The southern part of the Shield is heavily forested, but there is little or no land suitable for farming. As one goes north, the trees give way to scrub and then to the treeless tundra, a plain with bogs and some ground vegetation. Here the earth below is perpetually frozen in a condition called permafrost. Nevertheless, the Shield is rich in useful natural resources. It has minerals, especially gold and nickel, timber, fur-bearing animals, and great potential for waterpower development. Along the south and west shores of Hudson Bay, in the center of the Shield, are the Hudson Bay Lowlands, a generally marshy area.

West of the Shield and east of the Rocky Mountains lies a third important region, the interior plains of Canada. These plains are a part of the Great Plains that run from Texas in the south to the Arctic region. In general, it is a high grassland area, sloping upward from east to west, and covering parts of Manitoba, Saskatchewan, Alberta, and the Yukon and Northwest Territories. Its heart is a triangle, going west from eastern Manitoba to the foothills of the Rockies and north in Alberta for about 400 miles. Much of the area was at one time an inland sea and the sediment deposited there became the rock underlying it. It has filled with sediment from the higher lands to the east and west. There are a great many rivers and lakes.

Where the climate is favorable, the deep soil is excellent for farming. In general, rainfall decreases from east to west. There are some extremely productive grain-growing areas, and in many places conditions for livestock grazing are favorable.

From the western edge of the plains to the Pacific Ocean, a distance of about 400 miles, is the fourth and most mountainous area of the country. It is Canada's portion of the Cordillera, the mountain system that runs from northern Alaska all the way south to Nicaragua in Central America. These mountains are the result of the uplifting of the earth's crust over a period of millions of years. Even so, they are young as geological time goes. They run parallel to the coast and are very rugged. On the eastern side of the area are the Rocky Mountains, which extend south into the United States. Some of the Rockies' peaks are over 12,000 feet high, and present a barrier to travel. Along the Rockies runs the Continental Divide, which separates the westward flowing streams from those flowing eastward.

West of the Rockies lies a region of mountainous plateaus and basins with several small ranges of lower height. Then come the Coast Mountains, which extend for about 1000 miles in Canada and Alaska, and which meet the Cascade Range in southern British Columbia. There are a number of peaks from 10,000 to 13,000 feet high, with Mount Waddington being the highest at 13,260 feet. The mountains act as a barrier to keep much of the rainfall from reaching the inland plains.

Finally come the Coast Ranges, which run from Alaska south to lower California. In Canada they consist of the St. Elias Range in southwestern Yukon and islands off the coast, such as the Queen Charlotte Islands, where all but the peaks of the mountains have been submerged.

Far to the north, mostly beyond the Arctic Circle, is a fifth distinct geographic region, consisting of the Arctic Ocean, the mainland just south of it, and the Arctic Archipelago, comprising more than 50 large islands. The Arctic Circle, at 62.5 degrees north latitude, is the northernmost point at which the sun can be seen at the time of the winter solstice in December.

The smallest of the world's oceans, the Arctic is about 5,400,000 square miles and it is ice-covered all year except for its fringe areas. Directly across the ocean from Canada, a long expanse of the Russian coast borders on the Arctic Ocean. The Beaufort Sea is an arm of the Arctic Ocean that borders northwestern Canada and Alaska. It is covered with pack ice most of the year.

Off Canada's eastern and northeast-

LAND REGIONS OF CANADA *include mountains, fertile plains, frigid Arctic islands, and the giant Canadian Shield, which covers nearly half the land area.*

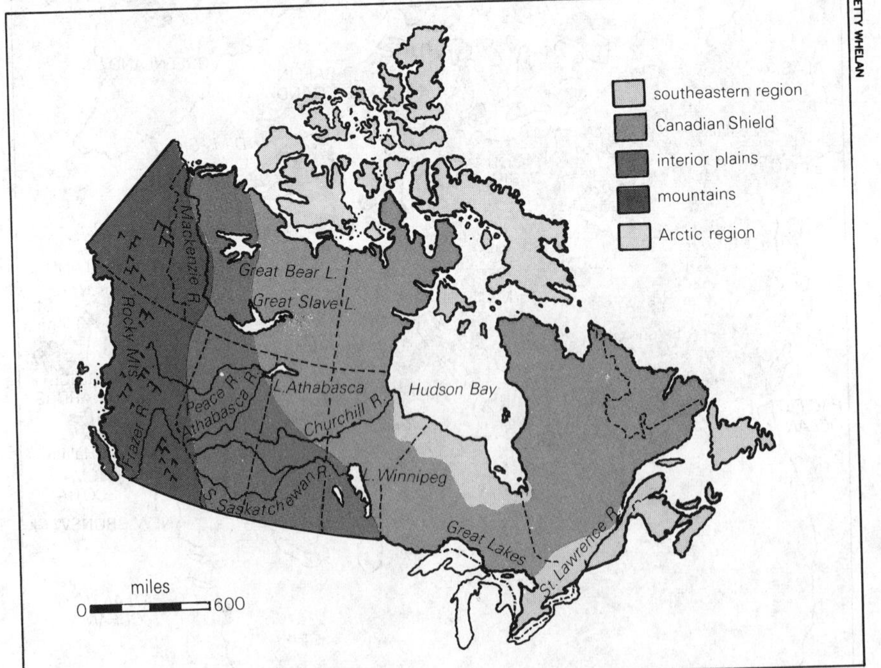

BETTY WHELAN

ern mainland is the Arctic Archipelago, whose islands are covered with areas of tundra and permanent ice. In the southern part of the archipelago, the main islands are Baffin, Victoria, Banks, Prince of Wales, and Somerset. Farther north are the Queen Elizabeth Islands, with Ellesmere the largest.

Climate. Because of its great expanse and its northern location, the climate of Canada shows wide variations, with some of the world's coldest weather in its northern regions. Except for southern Ontario and the Pacific coast, winters are cold. Both coasts are more moderate than the interior. The Atlantic is cool because it is open to the north, while the Pacific, more closed to the north, is warmed by ocean currents from the tropics.

The southern sections of Canada have a temperate climate, much like the areas of the United States just to the south. There is snow in winter and warm weather in summer. Along the St. Lawrence and around the Great Lakes, the mean temperature in winter is 10 to 20 degrees F and in the summer, 60 to 70. In the central plains, it gets colder to the north (zero to 10 below in winter is the mean), while the lower plains are about 10 degrees warmer in winter and are much like the eastern temperate region in summer.

The long north-south plains make it possible for polar air masses to move south and for subtropical air to move north into Canada. The Pacific mountains keep the polar air mass from reaching the coast, while the waters of Hudson Bay and the Great Lakes act to modify somewhat the climate in their areas. In the Arctic region, in the tundra areas, the average temperature of the warmest month is below 50 degrees F, while in areas permanently covered with ice and snow, the year-round average is below 32 degrees. In a good deal of the far north, the mean daily temperature in January is 10 to 20 degrees below zero F and, in certain areas, minus 20 to minus 30. Temperatures often plunge even further, while the cold Arctic winds add a chill factor. Canada's cold Arctic air masses tend to move south and to carry to the United States their bitter winter weather.

Precipitation varies greatly in different parts of Canada. The Arctic areas receive less than 20 inches a year, mostly as snow, but the winds make it seem as though it is constantly snowing. While precipitation along the Pacific coast may reach nearly 100 inches a year, the mean annual rainfall in the lower part of the interior plains is only 12 to 16 inches. The coastal areas of Newfoundland and Nova Scotia are on the damp side, with annual precipitation of around 56 inches. The St. Lawrence-Ontario heartland receives 32 to 48 inches of rain.

The People

Canada's population in the 1986 census was 25,354,000. This is about 11 percent of the population of the neighboring United States. It is estimated that by 2001 the population will be between 28 million and 31 million.

Until the 1800's, Canada's population grew quite slowly. It did not pass the 1 million mark until about 1840, and it did not cross the 5 million mark until the last decade of the century. For the past hundred years, population has risen at a faster rate, passing 10 million by 1930.

Approximately three-fourths, or about 18 million Canadians, live in the southern part of the country, within 200 miles of the United States border. In turn, more than half of these people dwell in the southern parts of Ontario and Quebec. In fact, these two provinces account for about 62 percent of Canada's total population, while another 11 percent is on the west coast in British Columbia.

As the population grew and as Canada became more industrialized, it also became more urban. Today, nearly 80 percent of the people live in urban areas.

Immigration. Like the United States, Canada has depended to a large extent on immigration for its growth in population. The earliest immigrants were from France, and they established a thriving French colony in eastern Canada before 1750. After the British victory in the French and Indian War (1757–1763), a new wave of immigration came from Britain. This wave was soon swelled by Loyalists who left the British colonies to the south during and after the American Revolution.

A new surge came after the War of 1812, and the newcomers were mostly from Scotland and Ireland. The potato famine in Ireland resulted in a large number of immigrants in the late 1840's. The great period of immigration, though, began in the latter part of the 19th century, and continued until 1914, when World War I began. More than 3 million persons came, and immigrants from continental Europe made up a much larger proportion of the whole than before. The 1920's brought large numbers, too, but the flow stopped when the Depression of the 1930's took effect. After World War II, in a period of a dozen years, a million and a half people arrived, about one-third of them from Britain.

There is still a steady flow of immigrants, but the countries of origin have changed. Of the 1985 arrivals, 46 percent were from Asia, only 5 percent from the United Kingdom and Ireland, and 8 percent from the United States.

There has also been a busy crossing and recrossing of the border by Americans and Canadians. By 1890 about 1 million persons of Canadian birth lived in the United States. This was also the start of a period when, in the course of 25 years, about 1 million Americans would move to Canada, mostly farmers settling in Alberta and Saskatchewan. In the 1920's there was another movement of Canadians southward, largely into the industrial Midwest. Many French-Canadians also left, mostly for New England.

CANADA'S POPULATION *is clustered on a corridor that runs from Windsor, Ontario, along the Great Lakes and the St. Lawrence to Quebec City.*

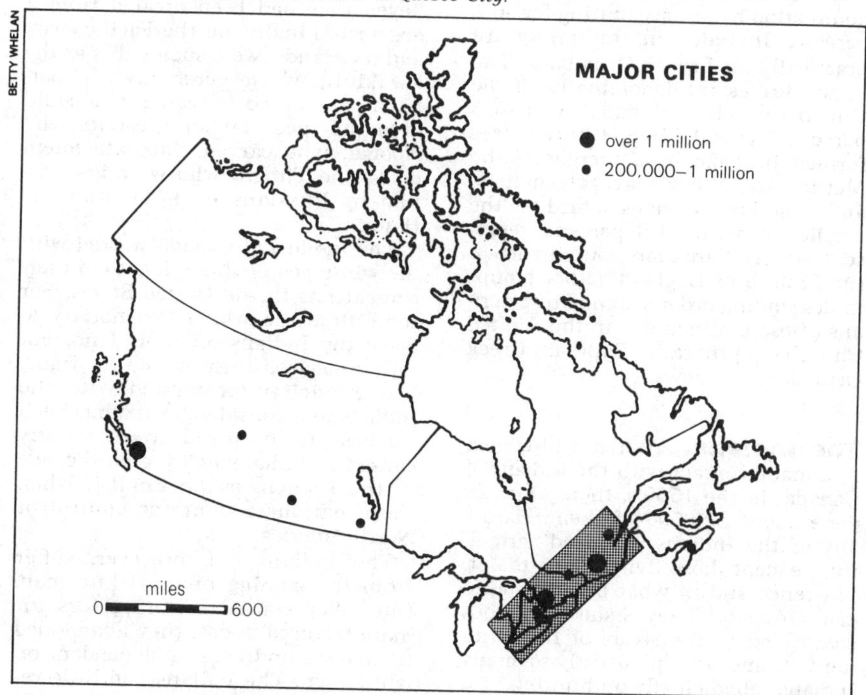

D. WILKINSON/NFB PHOTOTHEQUE

GLENBOW ARCHIVES

IMMIGRANTS OLD AND NEW: *when Europeans reached Canada, they met Inuit (Eskimo) and Indian peoples who had come from Asia in prehistoric times,* left. *Among the new immigrants were these Russian peasants who were fleeing religious persecution and arrived in 1899.*

The dominion today includes people of many ethnic backgrounds and religious beliefs. The largest ethnic group comprises those originally from the British Isles—45 percent. Those of French descent represent 29 percent of the population. (Of the slightly more than 6 million people in this group, all but about 1 million live in Quebec province.) The other large groups, in descending order, are the Germans, Italians, Ukrainians, Dutch, Scandinavians, Poles, Jews, Indians, and Eskimos.

Religion. Roman Catholics constitute the largest single religious denomination by far, accounting for 46.2 percent. Included in this group are practically all French-Canadians. The largest Protestant denomination is the United Church of Canada, with 17.5 percent. The United Church was formed in 1926 by a merger of the Methodists, the Congregationalists, and some Presbyterians. Third are the Anglicans, with 11.8 percent, representing the Canadian counterpart of the Church of England. Other groups in descending order are the Presbyterians (those not included in the United Church), Lutherans, Baptists, Greek Orthodox, and Jews.

The Indians. When white men first made contact with the Indians of Canada, in the 1500's, there probably were about 220,000 of them. Hardly any of the Indians practiced agriculture, except those living along the St. Lawrence and in what became southern Ontario. They fished on both coasts and in the rivers of the continent. Game was plentiful, so many Indians relied chiefly on hunting.

It was many years before the newcomers made contact with all the different tribes of Indians scattered over all parts of Canada. Among the tribes were, in the east, the Micmac and, especially, the Huron, who allied themselves with the French. Somewhat farther west were the Ottawa and the Cree, the former around Georgian Bay, the latter farther north. In the interior prairie region were the Ojibwa (or Chipewyans), the Nipissing, the Assiniboine, the Blackfoot, the Sioux, the Athabascan, and the Gros Ventre.

Far to the north were such small tribes as the Dogrib and the Nahani, the former so-called because they believed they had been created from a dog's rib. Finally, on the Pacific coast and its islands, were such tribes as the Kwakiutl, whose ceremony of "potlatch" amounted to seeing who could give the most lavish presents; the Nootka, who carved elaborate totem poles; the Tlingit, who were first visited by Russians in 1741, and the Haida.

The Indians of Canada warred with the white people much less than their compatriots in the United States. For some time the whites did not try to drive the Indians off their land, but rather engaged them in the fur trade. The French intermarried with the Indians to a considerable extent. Such clashes as occurred were mostly caused by Indians fighting on the side of the French or the English when those nations fought for control of North America.

The Indians did, however, suffer from the coming of the white man. Once they started bartering furs for manufactured goods, they abandoned their ways and became dependent on white men. The Indians had little resistance to European diseases, so epidemics, such as smallpox, wiped out half of whole tribes. Finally, many of the Indians came to love liquor, but were unable to cope with its effects.

In the late 1800's, the Canadian government began to secure Indian land by treaties, and to "civilize" the Indians. It was not until the 1960's that self-determination was recognized as a legitimate right of the natives.

Today there are more than 300,000 Indians in Canada, and the population is growing. Most of them are in registered bands (many groups are small and the term tribe is not used) or settled on government reserves, of which there are 2242, totaling about 10,000 square miles. Geographically, the Indians live chiefly in Ontario and the four western provinces. There are government programs in such areas as health, education, and vocational training, but unemployment is high.

The Eskimos. Except possibly for the Vikings, the first contact between Eskimos and whites came in the 1500's, all along the coast of Labrador. (The Eskimos call themselves Inuit, meaning "the people," and this is the term now officially used in Canada. To the Inuit, the white man is "kabloona.") It was the mid-1700's before there was much further contact, mostly with trading posts along the tree line. Because they were so isolated in the north, the Eskimos kept more to their own ways than did the Indians. It was the early 20th century before there were settlements where Eskimos could conveniently trade and live something like a modern lifestyle.

The Eskimos along the coastlines were hunters of seal, whale, and walrus, while those in the interior hunted

THE FUR TRADE *between Indians and Europeans flourished for nearly 300 years. Here, Cree Indians from northern Alberta display their wares at Fort Pitt in 1884.*

caribou. Contact with the whites brought tuberculosis to the Eskimos, and they had little resistance to it. Today, they are partly integrated with the rest of the economy, as fishermen, fur traders, tour guides, and producers of arts and crafts. Of the 100,000 or so Eskimos in the world, about 23,000 live in Canada—in Labrador, the Mackenzie delta, the mainland coast of the Northwest Territories, and the shores of the Hudson and Ungava bays. Since the 1950's, there has been an effort by the government to bring the Eskimos into the mainstream of Canadian life with schools and other benefits, and with provisions for self-government. In 1988 the Indians and Eskimos were awarded ownership of about 260,000 square miles of land in the Northwest Territories in response to their land claims against the government.

Culture.

As Canada grew, it began to seek its own identity in the realms of culture and entertainment. But there were three problems to face. First, and oldest, was the split between the British and the French-Canadians. The French-Canadians were interested in cultural matters, but were handicapped by being a minority group. French culture remained rather static and conservative.

Second, the Canadians of English background were torn between retaining their English heritage and developing a new, independent Canadian identity.

Finally, Canadians felt, and still feel, that they are in danger of being overwhelmed by American cultural values. Most Canadians do not want this to happen, much as they enjoy American magazines and television programs. The federal government has taken a positive role in promoting Canadian culture.

Literature. The first English-language writings to be popular were those that concerned Canada's frontier and explorations. Beginning in the last third of the 19th century, Canadian writers took up native themes.

By the first quarter of the 20th century, some Canadian novelists began to reach a wide audience outside their own land. *Anne of Green Gables* by Lucy Maud Montgomery, and the "Jalna" series by Mazo de la Roche, were best sellers in the United States. Compared with either the United Kingdom or the United States, however, the potential market in Canada alone is too small to be commercially attractive. Writers must appeal to an audience outside the dominion. Among successful and talented Canadian authors of the recent past are Margaret Atwood, Morley Callaghan, Matt Cohen, Robertson Davies, Jack Hodgins, Margaret Laurence, Hugh MacLennan, Farley Mowat, Alice Munro, Mordecai Richler, and Gabrielle Roy.

The arts. Canadian art, until quite recently, has been mostly nationalistic in spirit, concentrating on depicting life in the dominion. Eskimo artists turned to sculpture in bone, stone, and ivory to carve the Arctic animal life around them and ceremonial masks. Indians, especially those on the northwest coast, were also carvers, working in wood. The early French-Canadian artists expressed themselves chiefly in woodcarving, much of it of a religious nature. In the 1800's Canadian painters turned to landscapes and ordinary life for their themes. Paul Kane, after 1845, traveled in fur-trapping areas to paint Indians. Cornelius Krieghoff brought out the picturesque in French-Canadian life. Somewhat later, Horatio Walker, Emily Carr (in the far west), and David Milne carried these themes forward. In the 1920's the Group of Seven, led by Tom Thomson, broke from the more international tradition to emphasize Canada's unique natural features. In contrast, Alfred Pellan and James W. Morrice have concentrated on the international art movements of recent times.

The Ontario College of Art was founded in 1875; five years later, both the Royal Academy of Arts and the National Gallery in Ottawa came into existence. Today there are 1545 museums of all kinds.

AN ESKIMO SCULPTURE *of a seal hunter.*

Theater and music. Theater activities in Canada have had a long history. Today there are performing companies in many cities and modern facilities, such as the O'Keefe Centre for the Performing Arts in Toronto. In Montreal the Théâtre du Nouveau Monde, established in 1951, carries on the French tradition. In 1955 it was the first Canadian stage company to perform abroad, in Paris. The best known theatrical establishment is the Shakespeare Festival Theatre at Stratford, Ontario, established in 1952.

Performances of classical music, opera, and ballet are generally available through visiting companies or resident organizations. There are major symphony orchestras in Toronto and Vancouver, and others in Calgary, Edmonton, Quebec, Victoria, and Winnipeg. Toronto and Winnipeg have permanent ballet companies.

Education. The development of a nationwide system of education at all levels involved the problems of religious and linguistic minorities, as well as the usual ones of cost. When confederation came, education was reserved to the provinces, which meant that in Quebec education was in effect administered by the Roman Catholic Church. Elsewhere, school systems were secular institutions for the most part. There are now nearly 6 million Canadian children in primary and secondary schools.

Higher education developed slowly, with church-sponsored schools first, and, by the 20th century, six universities established by the provinces. Beginning in the late 1950's, there was a great increase in government support for higher education, and an even greater surge in the number of students. In Ontario alone nine universities were founded in ten years. Student enrollment in institutions of higher education increased from 65,000 in 1955 to nearly 350,000 today.

Canada's library system has also expanded over the years. There are almost 2800 libraries of all kinds, of which 778 are public. Academic libraries, special libraries, and government libraries account for the rest.

Communications. To Canada, as to all nations that extend over large geographic areas, the coming of the telegraph, the telephone, radio, and television has been a great boon. The telegraph first reached across the country in 1883, and the first telephone exchange opened in 1878. (Alexander Graham Bell, the inventor of the telephone, in 1876, was a Canadian.) There are now about 15 million telephones in use, and a microwave network is the backbone of a nationwide telecommunications system.

The federal government organized the Canadian Broadcasting Corporation (CBC) in 1936 for radio broadcasting. The CBC is government owned but controlled by an independent board. The CBC added television to its radio service in 1952. There are also private English and French networks. About 400 privately owned stations are associated with the CBC, and there are another 600 independent radio and TV outlets. Broadcast service began to reach out to the isolated north in the 1950's with radio, including one station north of the Arctic Circle. Television finally reached the north at Yellowknife in 1967.

Many Canadians hear and see more American programming than Canadian, often receiving U.S. stations directly. At least 60 percent of the programming in prime time on CBC must be Canadian, and CBC is seeking to reach a level of 80 percent.

STRATFORD, ONTARIO, *namesake of Shakespeare's birthplace in England, is the home of a renowned Shakespeare festival. This is a production of* A Comedy of Errors.

STRATFORD FESTIVAL

Publishing. Newspapers and magazines are widely published and distributed. The 117 daily papers have a combined circulation of over 5 million. The two largest papers in circulation are the *Toronto Star* (Saturday edition) and the *Toronto Sun* (Sunday edition), followed by the daily editions of the *Vancouver Province and Sun* and *Le Journal de Montréal.* Of the 16 papers with circulations of more than 100,000, four are French language. There are also more than 500 community papers across the dominion.

Among leading Canadian magazines are *Chatelaine*, *Homemaker's*, and *Maclean's.* The American leaders are *Reader's Digest* and *TV Guide.* Almost all magazines appear in English and French editions.

There has been a steady growth in books originating in Canada, and in the number of Canadian-owned publishing houses, yet in 1979 three-fourths of book sales, in dollars, were of imported books. Most of them came from the United Kingdom and the United States. A number of American and British publishers have branches in Canada. In all, about 4500 new books a year are issued in Canada.

Films. Although a feature film was made in Canada as early as 1914, the Canadian movie industry was held back by the smallness of its own market and the heavy flow of films from Hollywood. In 1939 Parliament established the National Film Board to produce films that would tell Canada's story to the world. The board has been very successful, having produced about 4000 films. It is now making about 100 films a year. In 1967 the government established the Canadian Film Development Corporation to give financial backing to private producers of feature films.

Sports. With plenty of ice to play on, it is not surprising that ice hockey has its historical roots in Canada. The game stems from the day in 1860 when some players at Kingston Harbor used a puck instead of a ball in their game. The sport grew and spread rapidly. The National Hockey League (NHL) of North America was formed in 1917 in Montreal, and the game became professional in 1924. Today there are 21 teams in the NHL, and seven of them are Canadian. The winning team each season receives the Stanley Cup. Many players of Canadian birth can be found on the American teams.

Canadian football, like American, developed from rugby. It closely resembles American football with these differences: a larger field, twelve players on a side, and only three downs to make 10 yards. Canadian football became professional in the 1930's. The nine teams in the Canadian Football League play for the Grey Cup.

In baseball, Toronto and Montreal have major league teams.

Canada also has 5 teams of 21 in the North American Soccer League.

The Economy

Canada's economic history is much like that of the United States, only on a smaller scale and somewhat later in time. Settlement of the west, growth in population spurred by immigration, the discovery and exploitation of natural resources, and the stimulus to manufacturing and trade from two world wars, have made Canada a developed nation. Her present-day advantages and problems are essentially the same as those of the rest of the Western world.

Canada's gross national product increased steadily during the 1980's, but the increase was in part caused by inflation. Consumer prices nearly doubled in the decade. Canada's per capita income was among the ten highest in the world.

Ever since the first furs were shipped out, Canada has been a trading nation. In the 1800's agricultural products were the most important export. By the 1950's, forest and mineral products had taken over first place. Today, the largest category is communications and transportation equipment, mostly motor vehicles. This category is followed by food and beverage products (about one-third of which is wheat), lumber, newsprint, wood pulp, natural gas, machinery, crude oil, chemicals, and precious metals. The United States is by far Canada's most important trading partner, followed by Japan and Great Britain.

Canada's major imports fall into much the same categories as her exports: transportation and communications equipment, a wide variety of fabricated materials, raw materials (including crude oil), machinery, miscellaneous equipment, such as office machines, and food products.

Canada's extensive forests were among the first of her resources to be exploited. The forests are treated as a renewable resource and the emphasis is on the use of spruce for pulp and paper. By 1913 Canada was the largest exporter of newsprint in the world. Nearly 10 million tons of newsprint are produced annually, and almost 90 percent of it is exported.

In addition to autos and paper, Canada manufactures a wide variety of products, from iron and steel and primary goods made from them, to refrigerators and washing machines. Important segments of industry turn out food and beverage products, rubber goods, textiles and clothing, shoes, railroad cars, ships, and tobacco products.

Labor. In late 1986 Canada's labor force totaled 12,870,000 persons, of whom 11,634,000 were employed; 1,236,000 were out of work, for an unemployment rate of 9.6 percent. Of those employed, 57 percent were men and 43 percent were women. Unemployment insurance benefits were being paid to 1,100,000 persons. Average hourly earnings in manufacturing were $11.59.

Although only about 4 percent of the work force is engaged in agriculture, this is one of the vital parts of the Canadian economy. For many years Canadian farm products were spread more or less evenly over a wide variety of produce. Then grain growing on the western prairies increased dramatically. This development made Canada a leading exporter of grains. In 1986 Canada exported 42 percent of the cereal grains it grew. Livestock, its products, and dairy products combined are the largest dollar element in agriculture. In the broad area of crops, wheat is by far the most valuable, followed by barley, rapeseed, and vegetables. Wheat is produced at an annual rate of about 900 million bushels.

Commercial fishing, which was one of Canada's first two great economic assets, no longer holds so high a position, but by no means has it disappeared. The total annual value of Canadian fisheries is nearly $2 billion, with cod and lobster the principal sea crops in the Atlantic and salmon off the Pacific coast.

Transportation. No nation can develop economically, especially in the area of world trade, without an adequate transportation system. Canada has had one great advantage and two conditions that work to her disadvantage in the area of transportation. Water transportation was an asset from the start, particularly the St. Lawrence–Great Lakes system and the lakes and rivers all over Canada's vast expanse. On the other hand, the great distances, combined with the sparse population, held back the development of transportation systems. Also,

ECONOMIC STRENGTHS OF CANADA *include huge oil reserves in Alberta,* left, *and an efficient network of water transport in the Eastern Provinces, including the Welland Canal around Niagara Falls. The canal is now part of the massive St. Lawrence Seaway.*

GEORGE HUNTER/NFB PHOTOTEQUE

DIETER F. GRABITZKY/MONKMEYER

THE CANADIAN PACIFIC RAILROAD, *a project of heroic proportions, united east and west in 1885. Here an early steam engine pauses in the Rocky Mountains.*

geographic and climatic factors have been a hindrance.

The arrival of the railroad age in the early 1800's was a blessing. The railroad could transport people and heavy and bulky goods quickly over long distances. The only drawback in Canada was the small amount of traffic available over large areas to pay the heavy cost of railroad construction. Nevertheless, by the 1850's Canada had about 2000 miles of track in the eastern and more heavily settled areas. By 1866, the Grand Trunk ran from the southern end of Lake Huron northeast to Quebec, with a branch south into New England. Somewhat later, the Intercolonial connected the St. Lawrence with the Atlantic seaboard.

Canada's first transcontinental line, the Canadian Pacific Railway, was built between 1880 and 1885. It ran for 2881 miles from Montreal to the Pacific coast, and soon acquired 500 more miles of track to carry it from Montreal to St. John, New Brunswick.

By 1915 two more cross-country railroads had been built, the National Transcontinental and the Canadian National Railway. The latter, with many branches, had 9362 miles of track. By this time Canada's total railroad mileage was 37,400. The new lines, however, were not successful financially. The government took over and combined the private lines into the Canadian National Railway. Canada's rail trackage reached its peak of 42,600 miles in 1930.

With the coming of the automobile, Canada followed, in its southern, well populated areas, much the same pattern as other countries. Roads were built, improved, and enlarged as passenger and commercial traffic increased. Canada's most notable achievement in highway construction has been the building of the Trans-Canada Highway, which was completed in 1962. At approximately 4800 miles, it is the longest national highway in the world. It runs from St. John's, Newfoundland, to Victoria, British Columbia.

The northern territories have posed special problems for road construction, and little was done until after 1940. Now there are roads providing access to Yellowknife and other towns. Leaving the Alaska Highway at Whitehorse, one can drive to Dawson. Following recent completion of construction, the road goes on to the Arctic Ocean at Tuktoyaktuk.

Aviation. The development of commercial aviation has been a great boon and has made some places, hitherto inaccessible for practical purposes, reachable for business or pleasure. The federal government established control over the airways in 1927, and ten years later set up Trans-Canada Airlines as a chartered government corporation and a subsidiary of Canadian National Railways, but it left other aviation to private enterprise.

Today there are two transcontinental lines, Air Canada and Canadian Airlines International. The former flies to Europe and to the United States. These two lines, together with the major regional airlines, carry about 30 million passengers a year. In addition, there are smaller airlines, especially in the Northwest Territories, that fly to Arctic settlements.

Waterways. For the Indians' canoes in the 1500's and for the ocean-going vessels of modern times, the St. Lawrence River and the Great Lakes have provided a pathway for commerce of the utmost importance to Canada's development. Even before the end of the 1700's, steps were taken to improve navigation on the St. Lawrence. Four short canals around rapids were built between 1779 and 1783. The Lachine Canal was constructed in 1821, and by 1850 there were several others. The project that finally made the river usable by ocean steamships going to and from all parts of the world was the St. Lawrence Seaway, a joint undertaking of Canada and the United States. Work began in 1954, and the seaway was officially opened in June, 1959. Another canal and seven locks were constructed between Montreal and Lake Ontario. Now a 2342-mile route from the mouth of the St. Lawrence to the heart of the continent exists.

A formidable obstacle to shipping through the lakes was Niagara Falls. This was overcome as early as 1829, when the Canadians completed the Welland Canal to take shipping around the falls. A fourth and larger Welland Canal, 27.5 miles long, was built between 1914 and 1932. It has eight locks and lifts or lowers ships the necessary 326 feet to get them between lakes Ontario and Erie.

Tourism. Canada is popular with tourists, especially Americans, 11.6 million of whom spent $3.7 billion in Canada in 1985. Tourism is a $20 billion business, accounting for 4.5 percent of GNP and employing 600,000 persons in over 100,000 establishments, including 4500 travel agencies.

Current problems. Canada has made great strides in economic growth. However, this expansion has been financed largely by foreign investors, and this is a continuing concern to Canadians. Furthermore, this foreign capital has been concentrated in manufacturing and natural resources, especially oil and gas.

In 1980 the government acted to limit foreign ownership to increase combined public and private Canadian ownership of the oil and gas industry to more than 50 percent over ten years. Petro-Canada, the government-owned oil company, is now exceeded in size only by Imperial Oil, which is 69.6 percent owned by Exxon.

Foreign investment between Canada and the United States is no longer a one-way street. Canadian investments in America exceed $10 billion. These interests, largely in real estate, are spread over 35 states.

Canada's level of economic activity remains strong, despite the Bank of Canada's continuing high interest rate policy. The Free Trade Agreement and debate over the proposed Goods and Services Tax, however, are clouds on the horizon.

CANADIAN HISTORY

The first human beings to inhabit what is now Canada were the ancestors of the present-day Indians and Eskimos. These ancient peoples began arriving by way of northeastern Asia and Alaska nearly 50,000 years ago.

Over the centuries, some of these aborigines, moving south and east, spread themselves sparsely over the huge expanse of northern North America. These people came to constitute the tribes that the Europeans called Indians. The tribes developed different languages, cultures, and ways of making a living.

The way of life of these people depended largely on the natural resources available to them. Most of the Indians lived by hunting and fishing along the seacoasts and the river valleys. Animals, birds, and fish were plentiful, but the Indians had only crude tools and weapons for catching them. The great forests provided wood for fuel and housing, while animals provided skins for clothing and shelter. The caribou, a large animal that existed in enormous herds, was the chief prize of the hunt for both the Indians and the Eskimos.

There was little agriculture, although it was practiced to some extent in the warmer region of southern Ontario and in the valley of the St. Lawrence River. For transportation, the Indian had only his own two feet or the light and useful birchbark canoe. There was a continual struggle to find enough food to survive, and when different tribes met while on hunting expeditions, armed conflict over choice areas sometimes resulted.

The far northern areas, mostly treeless tundra, were occupied by the Eskimos, who call themselves *Inuit,* which means people, or human beings. Although the term originated with the Cree Indians, to whom the word means "eaters of raw flesh," the Inuit cook their food whenever possible. They depend on fish, waterfowl, sea mammals, and the few land animals of the far north, such as bears and caribou, for food and for skins to be used for clothing and shelter. Some, but not all, Inuit live in igloos, domed houses made of snow. The total aboriginal population —Indians and Eskimos—was probably only about 200,000 when the Europeans arrived.

The term Canada was not applied to any part of the land until it appeared in an account by Jacques Cartier (1491–1557) of his voyage of exploration in 1535. It is a form of an Indian word meaning village or settlement.

Vikings. It has been claimed that Irish monks, sailing by way of Iceland, settled on Cape Breton Island, northeast of Nova Scotia, about 875 A.D. Legend has it that they were absorbed by the native population and the settlement died out.

The first white persons of whom it can be said with certainty that they landed on the North American continent were the Vikings, the Scandinavian warriors and traders who were active from the ninth to the twelfth centuries. They were the best shipbuilders and sailors of the time. Eric the Red (fl. 980–1000), a Norwegian explorer who named and settled Greenland, claimed he landed on what is now Baffin Island in 982.

According to the Icelandic sagas, Bjarni Herjulfsson sailed about 986 along the coast from Newfoundland to Labrador. It was Leif Ericson (fl. c 1000), however, the son of Eric the Red, who sailed to this same region and landed there about 1001. He probably first touched the mainland on the coast of Labrador and Belle Isle. The best evidence yet found indicates that the Vikings spent the winter in a settlement they built at L'Anse aux Meadows on the northern coast of Newfoundland. The remains of two large houses and of primitive ironworks have been uncovered there.

Thorwald Ericson, brother of Leif, spent two winters in Newfoundland, between 1005 and 1008, and was killed there. Beginning about 1010 or 1012, Thorfinn Karlsefni, who married Thorwald's widow, is said to have spent three winters in Newfoundland, but his settlement was abandoned. Thus, the Vikings never established a permanent settlement and knowledge of the European discovery of the continent was lost for nearly 500 years.

The Northwest Passage. It was almost the end of the 15th century before Europeans returned to Canada. When they did, they were not looking for it but, rather, for a way around it, through the fabled Northwest Passage, to the riches of Cathay, a mysterious far eastern region supposedly rich in gold and other treasures. Later, these explorers also nursed the hope that in the interior of North America they would find kingdoms as rich as those the Spaniards were conquering in Mexico and Peru.

The first of the explorers who tried to bypass the northern part of the western hemisphere was John Cabot (1450–1498). Cabot, an Italian born in Genoa who anglicized his name, sailed for America under the auspices of Henry VII, king of England. On June 24, 1497, he landed on either the southwest corner of Newfoundland or the northern tip of Cape Breton Island. He took possession of the land in the name of the king; England's first claim to Canada stemmed from this action.

On his return, Cabot, who was sure he had reached Asia, reported that he had sighted fish in great numbers. By the next year English fishermen began to work the area around Newfoundland. They were soon joined by Portuguese, French, and Spanish fishing boats.

Cabot made another voyage, in 1498, this time with five ships. The expedition disappeared; presumably all were lost. Cabot's son Sebastian (1476?–1557) led a voyage in 1509, also seeking the Northwest Passage. Whether he discovered Hudson Strait and saw part of Hudson Bay, as some have claimed, is disputable.

France's claim to Canada began with the voyages of Jacques Cartier, who was sent out by King Francis I in 1534. He saw the Labrador coast, found

VENETIAN NAVIGATOR JOHN CABOT *opened Canada to English exploration.*

PUBLIC ARCHIVES OF CANADA

Prince Edward Island and the Magdalen Islands, explored the Gulf of St. Lawrence, and landed on the Gaspé Peninsula to take possession for France on July 24 in the presence of a band of Indians.

When Cartier returned to France, he reported that in the New Brunswick region and on the Gaspé Peninsula there was fertile soil and a suitable climate for agriculture. Until then the region had been thought useful only for the fisheries off Newfoundland and Labrador. The French king sent Cartier back to America.

On this second voyage, in 1535, Cartier discovered the St. Lawrence River and sailed up it to the Indian village of Stadacona, the site of present-day Quebec City. Continuing on, he reached another village, Hochelaga, now the site of Montreal. Indians he met told him of three "kingdoms" farther west. Cartier and his men wintered near Hochelaga and returned to France the next spring. On the return voyage he determined that Newfoundland was an island. Cartier described this voyage in *Brief Récit et succincte narration* (1545). On Cartier's third and final voyage, in 1541, he went up the St. Lawrence to the Lachine Rapids, built a fort and wintered at Cape Rouge.

Jean François de la Rocque, sieur de Roberval (1500–1561), in April, 1542, sailed for America with three ships and colonists who planned to make France's first settlement in Canada. Meanwhile, tired of waiting for Roberval, Cartier started his return voyage to France and met Roberval in Newfoundland. Cartier refused to remain in Canada and went home, having failed to find the Northwest Passage or the riches of the Far East. He had, however, made important geographical discoveries, and they were the basis of French claims to the St. Lawrence River region. Roberval established his colony near Stadacona, but it lasted only about a year before the colonists returned to France.

It was not until the early 17th century that France was able to establish permanent colonies in Canada. This was accomplished under the leadership of Samuel de Champlain (c 1567–1635), a veteran soldier as well as a naval commander. He visited Canada in 1603 and returned the next year as joint leader of an expedition with Pierre du Gua, sieur de Monts (1568–c 1630), a wealthy Huguenot. They founded a colony on Saint Croix Island (now a U.S. national monument) off the coast of Maine. In 1605 they moved the colony across the Bay of Fundy to found Port Royal (now Annapolis Royal, Nova Scotia). Port Royal was abandoned for a while in 1607, but in 1608 Champlain set up a fur-trading post at Quebec and this became the first permanent establishment of France in Canada.

Champlain and the men he sent out began to learn much more about the interior of Canada. For example, Champlain explored the New England coast as far south as Martha's Vineyard. He discovered Lake Champlain in the spring of 1609. Here, with French troops and Indian allies, he fought a battle with some Iroquois. The guns of the French easily routed the Iroquois. Ever since, it has been believed that this incident caused the long-standing animosity between the Iroquois and the French.

In 1615 Champlain with a party of Hurons made an expedition to Georgian Bay on Lake Huron. He returned southeastward by way of Lake Ontario. Another time, Champlain accompanied a Huron war party on a raid on an Onondaga village in present-day New York State. He was wounded and had to spend the winter in an Indian village. This ended his own activities as an explorer, but in 1634 he sent west Jean Nicolet (1598?–1642), who explored Lake Michigan and went as far as Wisconsin. This was another aspect of the search for an easy route to Asia, but it also helped develop the fur trade, the profits from which were needed to enable exploration to continue.

In 1615 Champlain had brought Christian missionaries to Canada, four members of the Recollect branch of the Franciscan order. After an aborted attempt by Jesuits to establish a mission in Acadia and on Mount Desert Island (now in Maine) between 1611 and 1623, the Jesuits returned in 1625. They became leaders in the work of converting the Indians to Christianity until the downfall of New France in 1763.

In 1629, when the British seized Quebec, Champlain was captured along with the city. He was taken to England, where he was held for four years. While there he used the occasion to prepare a third edition of his *Voyages de la Nouvelle France* (1632).

FRENCH EXPLORERS *Jacques Cartier and Samuel de Champlain helped establish their country's claim to parts of Canada.*

NEW YORK PUBLIC LIBRARY

THE GRANGER COLLECTION

New France

Formal government came to Canada on October 8, 1611, when Louis XIII, king of France, appointed his nephew Louis de Bourbon, comte de Soissons, governor and lieutenant general of New France. New France consisted at that time of fur traders, trappers, and Catholic missionaries operating along the St. Lawrence River. The comte died on November 12, 1611, before he could take advantage of the trading monopoly and seigniorial rights that also had been granted to him.

Champlain had already been appointed deputy commander and so in effect became the first governor of New France. From 1633 until his death in Quebec on December 25, 1635, Champlain held the title of commandant and acted as the French king's viceroy in New France.

Many aspects of French law and government were transferred to New France. For example, on February 4, 1623, when Louis Hébert was granted a fief at Sault-au-Matelot, a system akin to feudalism was introduced in the New World. Later, especially after 1627, many more such fiefs were granted with the aim of stimulating the settlement of New France. Each *seigneur* undertook to bring in colonists at his own expense. By 1760 there were about 250 such landholdings, amounting to nearly 8 million acres. Most of them were on the St. Lawrence River, extending inland as long narrow strips. Since seigneurs were not actually liege lords of the king, this system was not strictly feudal; nevertheless, these landholders had considerable authority over the lives of their tenants.

In November, 1635, the French set up a separate government for Acadia

THE NEW YORK PUBLIC LIBRARY

ISLE STE. CROIX *was the earliest settlement in Acadia, which comprised part of Nova Scotia, New Brunswick, and Cape Breton Island.*

(which later became British Nova Scotia, New Brunswick, and Cape Breton Island). Charles de Menou, sieur d'Aulnay-Charisnay, and Charles de Saint-Étienne de la Tour (1593–1666) were named joint lieutenant generals. They quarreled to such an extent that civil war broke out, resulting in the recall of la Tour, who was reinstated after de Menou died, on May 24, 1650.

Much of the power of government was in the hands of those who had been granted monopolistic trading privileges, especially the Company of New France, or One Hundred Associates, established in 1627 by the French king. This group, which consisted mostly of wealthy nobles, proved incapable of maintaining power against the English, who were also attempting to claim and settle Canada. As a result, Louis XIV decreed in May, 1663, that New France was henceforth to be a royal province. Authority then was vested in a Sovereign Council (after 1703 called the Superior Council). It consisted of a governor, who was the military and political chief and who held the most power; an *intendant,* responsible for administration and finance; and the bishop of Quebec, the spiritual leader.

The fur trade. In the early 1600's, the French controlled the best routes for trading with the Indians in the interior. It was an especially favorable time for fur trading because of the then current style in Europe for felt hats. Beaver skins, which were plentiful in Canada, provided the best fur.

The trappers, whether white or Indian, spent the winter at their work. In the spring, in Indian canoes, they came east to trade the furs for knives, beads, cloth, firearms, liquor, and other valuable merchandise.

There were three key points for the fur trade along the St. Lawrence River. One was at the mouth of the Saguenay River. Tadoussac was founded there in 1600 by Pierre Chauvin, who built the first stone house in Canada. The other two posts were Trois-Rivière, founded in 1634, and on the site of Montreal, in 1642.

The French fur trade was officially a monopoly of the king, or his viceroy in Canada, or other individuals and groups chartered by the king. A large number of young Frenchmen defied the monopoly laws and took to the fur trade on their own account. They journeyed to the interior, lived like the Indians, and married Indian women. After 1660, when the Huron were badly defeated by the Iroquois, these *coureurs de bois*—runners of the woods—took the place of the Indians as middlemen to deal with the tribes farther west. The halfbreed descendants of these men and women, called Métis, later provided a large part of the fur trade's personnel.

As the French fur trade prospered, the competition grew. Iroquois Indians to the south of the French trade routes raided Huron canoes carrying furs. The Dutch and then the English began to give the French strong competition.

The fur trade rivalry also brought Indian tribes into conflict with each other. The Hurons, as allies of the French, were a steady source of supply. The Iroquois, on the other hand, were cultivated by the English, who supplied them with guns. They shut off the Richelieu River and made the Ottawa River unsafe for Huron trappers.

One center of Indian conflict, which also involved French missionaries, was Huronia, a region dominated by the Hurons, which lay in southern Ontario. It was a fertile area about 40 miles long and 20 miles wide. In 1616 Champlain estimated that 30,000 Hurons lived in the various towns and villages there. The Recollet fathers began their missionary work in Huronia in 1615. Later they were assisted by Jesuits. The Iroquois determined to exterminate the Hurons in the region and their attacks reached a climax from 1648 to 1649. In the attacks three Jesuit fathers were killed and the Hurons almost wiped out. Between the Iroquois attacks and epidemics of smallpox and influenza, only a few hundred survived in Huronia.

In 1660 the Iroquois were soundly defeated by the Marquis de Tracy. He led an expedition by way of the Richelieu River into present-day New York State and destroyed five Mohawk Indian villages. The Mohawks and other Iroquois tribes made peace with the French the next year.

The French answered this competition from the English by making more of an effort to explore the continent, by building trading and military posts, and by claiming large areas for the French king. Fort Frontenac (now Kingston) was founded in 1673 to control the point where Lake Ontario flows into the St. Lawrence. Sieur de la Salle (1643–1687), commandant of Frontenac, established a fort at the mouth of the Niagara River six years later. Among his explorations was the trip that took him to the mouth of the Mississippi River in 1682. Louis Hennepin (1640–1701?), Louis Joliet (1645–1700), and Jacques Marquette (1637–1675) also explored the western Great Lakes and the routes to the south.

French against English. Until the early 1600's, the French and English in America, while they competed for the fur trade and made conflicting territorial claims, had not clashed directly. The French did little to bring in settlers to populate Canada and little to encourage agriculture. The English, on the other hand, were starting to settle the Atlantic seaboard south of Canada in growing numbers.

France and Britain were also involved in Europe, in the perpetual rivalries of the European nations. In 1621 King James I granted to a Scotsman the right to colonize Nova Scotia, which the French claimed under the name of Acadia. In 1629 the British captured Quebec. Three years later, another king of England, Charles I, gave back by treaty Acadia and the rest of Canada to France in return for a badly needed sum of money.

During this period the French did make an attempt to strengthen New France, as they called their Canadian lands. The fur monopoly was taken away from the viceroy and in 1627 it was given to a new group known as the Hundred Associates. They not only

THE REPRESENTATIONS *of Henry Hudson (*left*) and of trading (*right*) at a Hudson's Bay Company outpost illustrate the rich early history of Canada.*

took over the monopoly but also were to arrange for 4000 immigrants to come to Canada. The Hundred Associates granted large estates to men who agreed to bring over these settlers, but most of them did far less than they were supposed to do. By 1663 the population of New France was only about 2500. French troops were sent over in 1665 and many of them remained as settlers.

Such success as the new settlers had was due largely to two energetic men. One was Count Louis de Frontenac (1620–1698), who was governor from 1672 to 1682 and again from 1689 to his death. Frontenac was both an able and a controversial character. He quarreled with the Jesuits and with the *intendant,* but he established posts and forts in new French territory. He enabled France to withstand English pressure on the colony at a difficult time.

Frontenac attempted to make New France more independent of King Louis XIV and his advisers, but he was always overruled. As a result of the controversies around him, he was recalled in 1682. When his successors were unable to solve the colony's problems, and the Iroquois became more troublesome, he was sent back to New France in 1689 as governor once more.

The other leader, Jean Baptiste Talon (1625?–1694), served as *intendant* from 1665 to 1668 and 1670 to 1672. Talon sent out prospectors and explorers, but he also encouraged more prosaic enterprises, such as brewing, lumbering, and shipbuilding. His efforts to bring in immigrants are reflected in the growth of the population to about 6700 in 1673.

The most important English explorer of northern North America was Henry Hudson (fl. 1607–1611). His voyages were attempts to find either the Northeast or the Northwest Passage. His first voyage was undertaken in 1607 for the English Muscovy Company; his second in 1608. Both of these attempts to sail east around northern Europe failed in their objective. In 1609 Hudson, making a voyage for the Dutch East India Company, discovered the Hudson River in New York State. His fourth and final voyage, in 1610, was financed by British adventurers. Entering Hudson Strait, between Greenland and Labrador, he discovered Hudson Bay. His ship then went down the east coast of the bay to James Bay at the mouth of the Rupert River. After wintering there, Hudson wanted to continue the voyage in the spring, certain that he had found the passage to Asia. The crew, however, mutinied, seized Hudson and his young son, John, and set them adrift in a small boat with six members of the crew, five of whom were suffering from scurvy. They were never seen again.

Hudson's explorations led to the chartering on May 2, 1670, by Charles II, king of England, of the Hudson's Bay Company. The charter granted to a group of courtiers and merchants all areas drained by the many rivers flowing into Hudson Bay. The company was given the right to trade, to settle, and to search for the Northwest Passage. The grant was known as Rupert's Land, for the leader of the company, Prince Rupert, who had been a capable general for his uncle Charles I in the English Civil War.

In the vast undefined region of western and northern Canada that was included in the grant, there were few people to govern for many years except for the company's fur traders. Though other high-ranking Englishmen were also governors of the Hudson's Bay Company, they, like Rupert, never went to Canada. James, duke of York, brother of Charles II, was elected to the post on January 3, 1683, but resigned on February 6, 1685, when he became

THIS MAP *indicates English and French claims to portions of the World.*

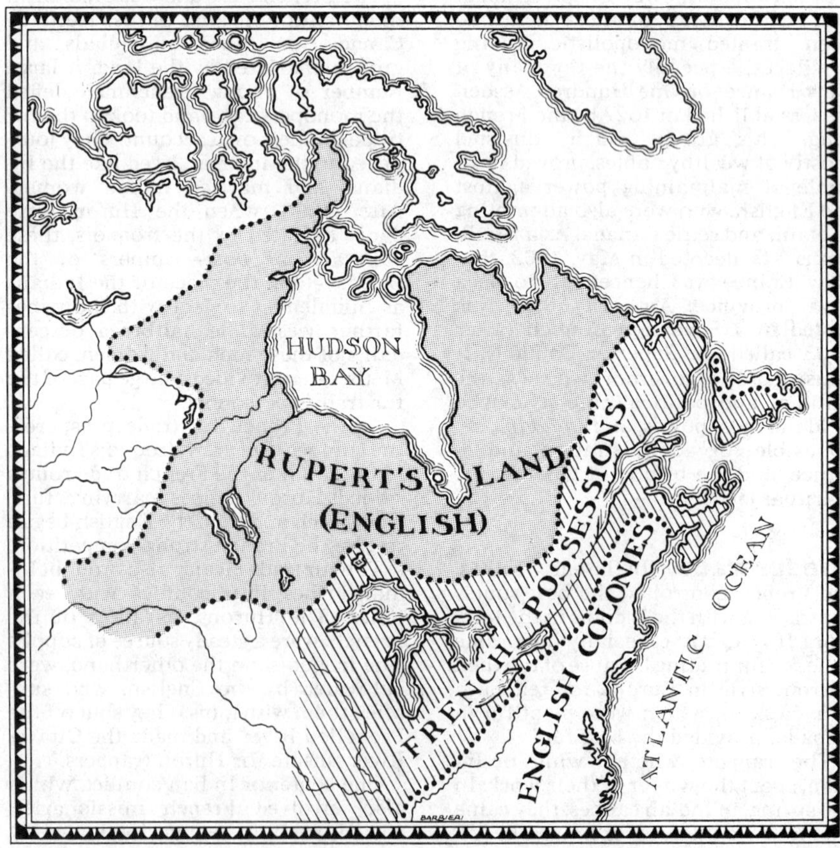

James II. York was succeeded on April 2 by John Churchill, later the first duke of Malborough. Rupert's Land was governed as a commercial company under the control of the governors of the Hudson's Bay Company until 1869.

These Englishmen had been encouraged in their enterprise by information they had obtained from two defecting French traders and explorers, Médard Chouat, sieur de Groseilliers (1618–?1696), and Pierre-Esprit Radisson (c 1640–1710). These Frenchmen believed it would be cheaper and faster to bring in supplies by ship to Hudson Bay and to take furs out by sending these goods down the rivers to the bay rather than via the Great Lakes-St. Lawrence route. They proved their point in 1668 by establishing a post on Hudson Bay and taking a valuable cargo to England. By 1685 the company had built four other posts at the mouths of rivers on Hudson and James bays. The French tried to cut into this operation by intercepting the Indian traders as they went down the rivers to the bay. One peaceful occasion was the signing on November 19, 1686, of a Treaty of Neutrality, which provided for a commission to settle the boundaries of New France and Rupert's Land, as all of western Canada was then known.

A century of wars. The competition between the two nations for land, fur, fish, and other commerce now moved to the battlefield. In 1689 there began the first of four wars that ended nearly a century later with the complete defeat of France. In Canada they are known separately as King William's War, Queen Anne's War, King George's War, and the Seven Years' War. In the United States they are known collectively as the French and Indian Wars (1689–1763). They were, in reality, the western hemisphere version of a worldwide struggle for empire that involved opposing coalitions of European nations. The four wars are known in European history as the War of the Grand Alliance, the War of the Spanish Succession, the War of the Austrian Succession, and the Seven Years' War. What the nations agreed on at the end of each war depended more on what had happened in Europe than in North America.

Even before King William's War began in 1689, the French had raided English shipping in Hudson Bay. In 1690 they attacked some of the Hudson's Bay Company posts. For several years posts were captured and recaptured. In 1690 the Count de Frontenac directed raids by the French and their Indian allies on English settlements in Maine, New Hampshire, and New York.

Reacting to these attacks, a force of New England sailors and militiamen, on seven ships, and under the command of Sir William Phips (1651–1695), a native of Maine, sailed for Port Royal in May, 1690. The fort was in no shape to defend itself and quickly surrendered. In August Phips headed a second expedition from Boston, consisting of 31 ships and about 14,000 men. Its object was to capture Quebec City. Bad weather, fever, and a strong defense led by Frontenac forced Phips to abandon the siege. On October 9 he gave up and sailed for home. The war ended in 1697 with each side giving back whatever territory or fort it had taken.

Queen Anne's War (1702–1713) was almost as indecisive in North America. Northern English settlements were raided again and New Englanders did the same to settlements in Acadia. In 1708 the French captured St. John's, Newfoundland. After failing twice, New Englanders captured Port Royal in 1710. This time the colonial expedition was led by Francis Nicholson (1655–1728), formerly a British army colonel and colonial administrator. His force was a combination of American and English troops. In 1711 Nicholson also led New England troops and Iroquois warriors in an expedition against Montreal; but, attacked by smallpox, they were forced to return without having made contact with the enemy.

In Europe, the French lost badly. The Treaty of Utrecht in 1713 put an end to French expansion and indicated the growing power of England. In America, France gave up claims to Hudson Bay, Newfoundland, and most of Acadia.

After two decades of peace, King George's War broke out in 1744 and lasted until 1748. French troops in 1745 failed to retake Port Royal (now named Annapolis Royal), but British troops successfully assaulted the fortress of Louisbourg on Cape Breton Island. On this expedition the land forces were commanded by Sir William Pepperell (1696–1759), who was an American colonial military leader. The accompanying British fleet was commanded by Sir Peter Warren (1703–1752). The next year a French attempt to retake Louisbourg failed. At the end of the war, Louisbourg was restored to France.

The Seven Years' War, the decisive conflict for control of North America, began in 1754. Fought on a larger scale than the others, it began badly for the British. The French routed them at Fort Duquesne (Pittsburgh, Pennsylvania) in 1755. This influenced the Indians of the Northwest to join the French side and left the English frontier settlements of Pennsylvania, Maryland, and Virginia open to attack.

In Acadia, which had a large French population, the British demanded in July, 1755, that representatives of the group swear allegiance to Great Britain. They refused, although the Acadians on the whole wished to remain neutral in the conflict. In August the British began rounding up Acadians preparatory to deporting them. There was considerable delay and confusion and some families were separated. The British distributed these exiles among the English colonies along the Atlantic coast, and even in the Caribbean and England. Some ended up in Louisiana, where their descendants, known as Cajuns, still retain a separate culture. Henry Wadsworth Longfellow's poem *Evangeline* (1847) tells of the expulsion in terms of two separated lovers. In all, between 6000 and 10,000 Acadians were transported into undeserved exile.

In the early part of the war, the French, under the leadership of Louis Joseph de Montcalm (1712–1759), a

GEN. EDWARD BRADDOCK, *after leading his British troops on a march to attack Fort Duquesne, died of wounds in the ensuing battle.*

THE NEW YORK PUBLIC LIBRARY

GOVERNORS AND ADMINISTRATORS OF NEW FRANCE 1612–1760

The intendant was the administrative officer in charge of commerce, finance, and police in New France. His duties were not clearly defined, so he and the governor often clashed over their jurisdictions.

GOVERNOR OR ADMINISTRATOR	TITLE	SERVED	INTENDANT	SERVED
Samuel de Champlain[1]	Lieutenant General of the Viceroy Commandant	1612–1629 1633–1635		
Marc-Antoine Bras-de-Fer de Chateaufort	Administrator	1635–1636		
Charles Jacques Huault de Montmagny	Governor	1636–1648		
Louis d'Ailleboust de Coulonge et d'Argentenay	Governor	1648–1651		
Jean de Lauzon	Governor	1651–1656		
Charles de Lauzon	Administrator	1656–1657		
Louis d'Ailleboust de Coulonge et d'Argentenay	Administrator	1657–1658		
Pierre de Voyer d'Argenson	Governor	1658–1661		
Augustin de Saffray de Mezy	Governor	1663–1665	**Louis Robert**[3]	1663–1665
Jacques Le Neuf de La Potherie	Administrator	1665	**Jean Baptiste Talon**	1665–1668
Daniel de Remy de Courcelle	Governor	1665–1672	**Claude de Bouteroue** **Jean Baptiste Talon**	1668–1670 1670–1672
Louis de Buade, Comte de Frontenac	Governor	1672–1682	**Jacques Duchesneau**	1675–1682
Joseph-Antoine Le Febvre de La Barre	Governor	1682–1685	**Jacques de Meulles**	1682–1686
Jacques-Rene de Brisay, Marquis de Denonville	Governor	1685–1689	**Jean Bochart de Champigny**	1686–1702
Louis de Buade, Comte de Frontenac	Governor	1689–1698		
Louis-Hector de Callieres	Administrator and Governor	1698–1703	**Francois de Beauharnois**	1702–1705
Philippe de Rigaud, Marquis de Vaudreuil	Governor	1703–1725	**Jacques Raudot**	1705–1710
Claude de Ramezay	Administrator[2]	1714–1716	**Michel Begon**	1710–1726
Charles Le Moyne, 1st Baron de Longueuil	Administrator	1725–1726		
Charles, Marquis de Beauharnois	Governor	1726–1747	**Claude-Thomas Dupuy** **Giles Hocquart**	1726–1728 1729–1748
Roland-Michel Barrin, Marquis de La Galissonière	Provisional Governor	1747–1749	**Francois Bigot**	1748–1760
Jacques-Pierre de Taffanel, Marquis de La Jonquière	Governor	1749–1752		
Charles Le Moyne, 2nd Baron de Longueuil	Administrator	1752		
Ange, Marquis Duquesne de Menneville	Governor	1752–1755		
Pierre de Rigaud, Marquis de Vaudreuil-Cavagnial	Governor	1755–1760		

[1]Quebec was in English hands from July 19, 1629, to July 13, 1632.
[2]While Vaudreuil was in France.
[3]Robert never went to New France.

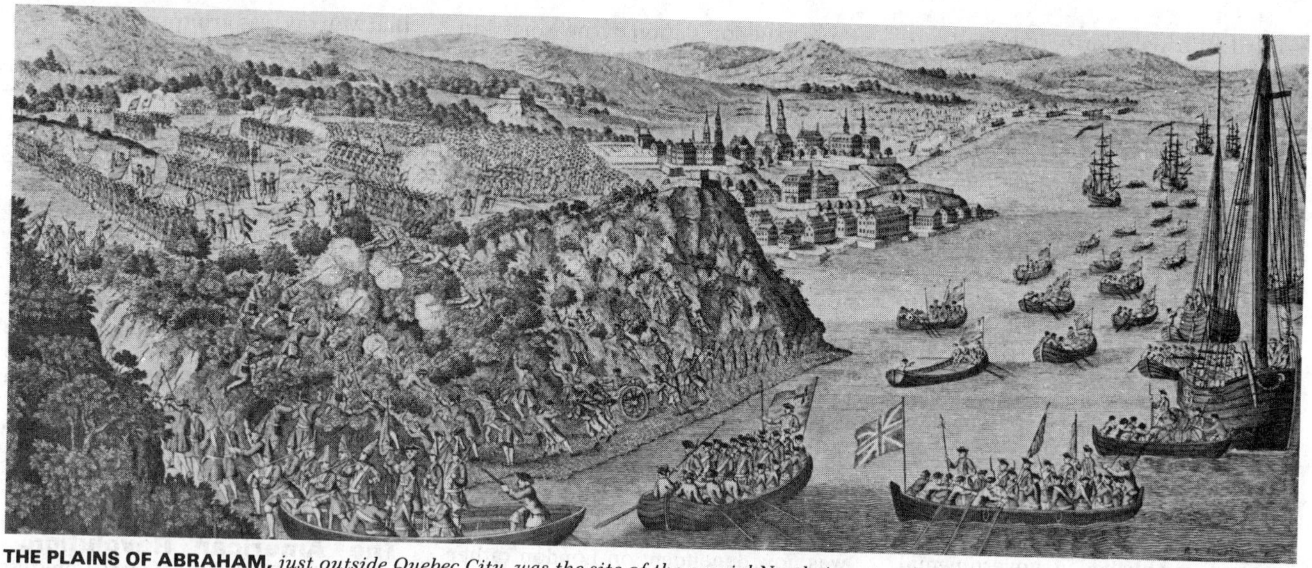

NEW YORK PUBLIC LIBRARY

THE PLAINS OF ABRAHAM, *just outside Quebec City, was the site of the crucial North American battle between the British and the French in 1759. The British forces defeated the French and strengthened Britain's claim to all of Canada.*

veteran of the War of the Polish Succession and the War of the Austrian Succession, took the initiative and gained some victories. In 1756 French forces captured Fort Oswego, on Lake Ontario, which the British had built in 1727, and destroyed it.

The following year British troops set out to capture Louisbourg. However, they were unable to rendezvous with the supporting fleet because of bad weather. This, combined with the French massing of strong reinforcements at the fort, defeated the plan. Montcalm won another victory for the French when in 1757 he attacked Fort William Henry at the foot of Lake George in New York; the fort surrendered after six days of bombardment. Unfortunately, the Indian allies of the French massacred the British prisoners in spite of Montcalm's attempt to control them.

France's fortunes began to decline in 1758 as the British government increased its military strength in America. Although British forces failed in an attempt to capture Fort Carillon (Ticonderoga) in New York, they reduced Louisbourg after a siege of seven weeks. Louisbourg was finally taken by an amphibious assault while a fleet prevented the French from reinforcing the stronghold. The British were under the command of Lord Jeffrey Amherst (1717–1797), who became after his victory the supreme commander of British forces in America.

Also in 1758 the English took Fort Frontenac on the northeast shore of Lake Ontario. The first French fort had been built there in 1673. In 1783 the city of Kingston, Ontario, was settled on this site by American Loyalists from New York State.

The year 1759 was even more disastrous for France. In July Fort Niagara, on the south shore of Lake Ontario at the mouth of the Niagara River, was captured by a force led by Sir William Johnson (1715–1774). At the same time the French withdrew from Lake George and Lake Champlain, destroying Fort Carillon and Fort Saint-Frédéric (Crown Point). The French had previously retreated from Fort Duquesne in the late fall of 1758.

The military climax to a century of struggle between France and England for control of northern North America arrived in September, 1759, with the fall of Quebec City. The British campaign to take this vital stronghold began with a naval blockade that closed the St. Lawrence River both above and below the city. In June, 9000 British troops landed opposite Quebec. They were under the command of James Wolfe (1727–1759), a brilliant young officer who had been second in command at the capture of Louisbourg. Montcalm meanwhile had gathered a force of 10,000 men to defend Quebec.

Wolfe's forces poured a heavy bombardment into the city, but the general could at first find no way to assault the French forces. At last a way was found to reach the Plains of Abraham, outside the walls of the city; this was done under cover of darkness on September 12. The next day Montcalm decided to risk all in a battle. A French attack was quickly repulsed and the British were victorious within 15 minutes. In the battle, however, both commanders were mortally wounded. Quebec was forced to surrender on September 18.

In 1760 the French made a futile attempt to retake Quebec, but they had to retreat to Montreal. In July the French fleet in the St. Lawrence was destroyed and on September 8, 1760, Montreal surrendered. The power of France in the New World was ended.

This defeat was formally acknowledged in the Treaty of Paris of 1763. France gave up Canada and ceded western Louisiana to Spain, its ally, to compensate for Florida, which Spain was forced to hand over to England. Besides keeping the islands of St. Pierre and Miquelon, south of Newfoundland, France recovered Guadeloupe and Martinique in the West Indies. In exchange, France ceded Grenada and the Grenadines to Great Britain.

Other terms agreed on among France, Spain, and England, involving other parts of the continent and other parts of the world, showed England to be the leading empire and sea power. France had been too concerned with European wars and too intent on keeping Canada Catholic and French to build up a strong colony. Canada's population in 1763 was still only a little more than 60,000.

The government of England now had to decide on important matters of policy affecting Canada. Most of the inhabitants were defeated enemies who spoke a different language and who were French Catholics rather than English Protestants.

British North America

A measure of self-government first came to Canada in 1758 when, on October 2, a legislative assembly met in Halifax as part of the government of Nova Scotia. Its members were popularly elected by property owners. The government also consisted of a governor, who wielded the most power, and a council nominated by the governor and formally appointed by the Crown. In 1773 Prince Edward Island was granted a similar kind of limited representative government.

On September 8, 1760, after the French surrendered Montreal to British forces, Jeffrey Amherst, the British commander, was appointed governor-general of British North America. Canada was put under a military government reporting to Amherst in New York City. This government consisted of three commands. Quebec, which had been formed into a British colony on September 3, 1759, was ruled by Brigadier General James Murray, who was appointed October 23, 1759. Brigadier General Thomas Gage commanded in Montreal, and Colonel Ralph Burton in Trois Rivières, both having been appointed September 22, 1760. After Amherst returned to England in 1763, civil government was again established in Canada under General Murray, who was appointed governor on August 10, 1764.

Further changes in government came after the Treaty of Paris of 1763. A British royal proclamation of October 7, 1763, set the boundaries of Quebec and established a governmental system. Quebec now consisted, approximately, of the valley of the St. Lawrence River from Nova Scotia on the east to Lake Nippissing in the west. A governor appointed by the king ruled Quebec. A council and a general assembly advised him, but only he had the power to summon the assembly. At this time Prince Edward Island and Cape Breton Island were made part of Nova Scotia, and Labrador was annexed to Newfoundland. On June 28, 1769, however, Prince Edward Island again became a separate colony.

Novia Scotia continued to have its own government and royal governor until the unification of Canada in 1867. New Brunswick was separated from Nova Scotia on August 16, 1784, and had its own governor until unification in 1867. Cape Breton Island was separated from Nova Scotia in 1764 and had its own government until October 9, 1820, when it was once more attached to Nova Scotia. Prince Edward Island came under the general government of Canada in 1873, six years after confederation. By 1867 most of what now constitutes eastern and central Canada had enjoyed some form of representative government for at least 20 years.

The Quebec Act. The Quebec Act of June 22, 1774, was a milestone in the history of government in Canada. Made law by the British Parliament, it introduced two important changes. First, it extended the boundaries of Quebec south of Lake Erie to the Ohio River; west to the Mississippi River; east to the Atlantic, including Labrador; and north and west to Rupert's Land, the domain of the Hudson's Bay Company. Second, it restored religious freedom to the Catholic population of Quebec and restored French civil law in place of English law. Both changes irritated the American colonies. Many of them claimed, by charter, lands extending west to the Mississippi River. The predominantly Protestant population of the American colonies resented what they saw as favoritism to a religious denomination they hated and feared. The Quebec Act became one of the Intolerable Acts cited by the American colonists against Great Britain and helped bring on the American Revolution. At the same time, though, the act helped keep Quebec loyal to England during that war.

British rule. The change from French to British rule brought economic changes as well as changes in the areas of law and government. British merchants followed the invading army and profited by supplying the soldiers and sailors with goods they needed or desired. Some of these tradesmen came from the English colonies to the south. In effect, Canada was now dependent on London rather than Paris for its economic lifeline to Europe.

In one way the change of government meant the replacement of a feudal Catholic system by a capitalistic and individualistic system. In turn, this resulted in a serious division in other areas, such as cultural life and religion, between the French and the English. However, most Frenchmen in Canada were not too disheartened by the change in their status because they, too, benefited by the improvement in economic conditions.

The British victory did not end the dominance of the fur trade in the Canadian economy; for a while, the French continued to be the most important element in this trade. The French traders and trappers had the experience to move confidently through western lands and to deal profitably with the Indian tribes. The tribes still disliked and distrusted the English, whom they had fought, and preferred to deal with the French. Nevertheless, English merchants became involved in the Canadian fur trade because they supplied the needed credit and had the business connections that opened European markets. In fact, the rivalry among the Canadian fur trade in the east, the Hudson Bay area to the west, and the trade centered on Albany, New York, to the south continued.

With the establishment in August, 1764, of a new civil government in the province of Quebec, problems arose because of the differences between the French and English legal systems. On the whole, the French establishment was not disturbed. For example, the seigniorial land tenure system was not abolished. The English rule that Catholics could not hold public office caused a problem because of few Englishmen to fill these positions. Governor Murray therefore allowed French citizens to serve on juries and to practice in the courts.

Murray and the growing merchant class did not get on well. The latter felt that Murray was arbitrary and his idea of civil government differed little in practice from harsh military rule. Murray in turn thought of the merchants as contentious and unruly, and disliked them, especially because so many of them came from the English colonies to the south. The businessmen asked the London government to recall Murray and this was done in 1765.

Murray's successor was Sir Guy Carleton (1724–1808), later Lord Dorchester, a man of high principles. He was a distinguished veteran of the French and Indian Wars, destined to play a leading role in the American Revolution. Carleton, who was hostile to Murray's rule, replaced Murray's officials and the province enjoyed a relatively peaceful period.

The American Revolution. When the First Continental Congress of the 13 American colonies met in 1774, a message was sent to Quebec. It invited delegates from Quebec to attend the next congress in 1775. No delegates came. Most of the French-Canadians resented the anti-Catholic bigotry of the colonies and preferred to remain neutral. Most of the English inhabitants of Canada, especially in Nova Scotia, reacted the same way, even though, of the 17,000 or so Nova Scotians, most of them were originally New Englanders.

The rebellious Americans invaded Canada, partly in the hopes of changing the people's minds, partly to forestall the use of Canadian ports and strongpoints by the British. The invasion was authorized by the Continental Congress in June, 1775, but little progress was made until fall. An expedition under Richard Montgomery (1736–1775), who had served in the British army in the French and Indian Wars and had then taken up residence in New York, moved northward. On November 2, 1775, his forces captured St. Johns on the Richelieu River in Quebec, the only remaining strong point before Montreal, the object of the invasion.

Governor Carleton had little with which to defend Montreal and the French inhabitants did not want to be involved in a siege. As a result, the city surrendered on November 13 and Carleton narrowly escaped to Quebec City. Meanwhile, Benedict Arnold (1741–1801) had been leading another American expedition up the Kennebec River and through the forests of Maine toward Quebec. Montgomery's force joined Arnold's and laid siege to Quebec, but they lacked artillery and Carleton had organized a strong defense. In the dark of the early morning of December 31, 1775, in a heavy snowstorm, the American forces attacked from two directions, but they were badly beaten and Montgomery was killed. The Americans continued the siege all winter to no avail. In May,

DURING AN ILL-FATED CAMPAIGN *by troops under command of Gen. Richard Montgomery, the American forces were badly beaten and their commander killed* (left). *When Loyalists fled north after the United States gained independence, they drew lots for land granted by the government of Nova Scotia* (right).

1776, a British force of 10,000 men reached Quebec and the Americans retreated to their own territory.

Carleton had a plan for ending the American rebellion by an invasion from Canada along the Lake Champlain-Hudson River route that would split the colonies in two. When it was later attempted, in 1777, it was not under his command. The result was a dismal failure.

Canada after the Revolution.

The Treaty of Paris, signed in that city on September 3, 1783, which gave the United States its independence, affected Canada in several ways. It established the boundary line between the two countries in such a way that the area of Quebec was greatly reduced. All the land north of the Ohio River, south of the midpoint of the Great Lakes (except for Lake Michigan), and east of the Mississippi River was now U.S. territory. Merchants in the fur trade protested to London against this surrender of western lands, but they got no satisfaction. The treaty also granted Americans the right to fish off Newfoundland and to cure fish in the uninhabited parts of Labrador and Nova Scotia, but not in Newfoundland.

Canada, with a sparse population, benefited from the American Revolution in one unusual way. In the years during and following the war, about 50,000 Loyalists moved to Canada from the colonies. These were persons who had sided with the British and did not favor independence. They were, on the whole, a substantial group economically and socially.

Among the first Loyalists to emigrate were a large number who were taken to Halifax from Boston in 1776 when the British army evacuated that city. Nova Scotia continued to be the haven for most Loyalists. In 1783, when the British evacuated New York City at the end of the war, another large group left for that region. Nova Scotia was conveniently reached by sea and there were large areas of vacant land. It is estimated that by the end of 1783, 30,000 Loyalists had arrived, almost doubling the size of the provincial population.

The government of Nova Scotia was supposed to supply these newcomers with land, tools, and help in the building of houses. However, it lacked the facilities and ability to provide so much help. The situation was worsened because some of the refugees arrived in destitute condition and many of them had been town or city dwellers who were not equipped to deal with the requirements of farming under pioneer conditions.

Some Loyalists moved on to England or the West Indies, but others settled in southern Ontario. Three districts were laid out where land would be granted them: along the upper St. Lawrence River; from Kingston to the Bay of Quinte; and on the Niagara Peninsula. Here, too, there were hardships of the kind suffered in Nova Scotia. In 1789, in fact, there was a near famine situation. Nevertheless, Loyalists, other settlers from the United States, and a number of German mercenary soldiers who had been disbanded in Canada, made up a population of about 10,000.

In 1789 it was officially decreed that Loyalists who had come to Canada before 1783 were to be designated "United Empire Loyalists"; those who came after 1783 were known as "late Loyalists." In fact, some of the latter were simply persons who had come from the United States to acquire land in Canada in the hopes of bettering themselves economically.

Fur trade. In spite of wars and changes of government, the fur trade continued to thrive and to expand westward. The Hudson's Bay Company no longer had French government competition, but it faced yet another rival in 1779 when a group of nine partnerships joined forces and in 1783 became the North West Company. The new organization built Fort Chipewyan on Great Slave Lake in 1789 as its headquarters.

The North West Company contributed a great deal to the exploration and geographical knowledge of the Canadian Far West. Alexander Mackenzie (1764–1820), Scottish born, was put in charge of the Athabasca district in 1788. In June, 1789, he set out from Fort Chipewyan on his first exploratory trek. He discovered the river named for him and followed it from its source to its mouth on the Arctic Ocean, which he reached on July 12. In 1793 Mackenzie made his way to the Pacific coast overland, but the route proved too difficult to be of practical value.

Another North West Company explorer, Simon Fraser (1776–1862), was Vermont born and the son of a Loyalist officer. His most important journey, which took him in 1808 along the river named for him, provided a great deal of new geographical information (though Fraser thought mistakenly that he was on the Columbia River). Fraser laid the groundwork for the future settlement of British Columbia by finding sites across the mountains suitable for agriculture. He also set up a series of posts for traders.

Another trader and explorer who helped open up the Canadian Far West was David Thompson (1770–1857), born in England, who first worked for the Hudson's Bay Company, then joined the North West Company in 1797. Among his accomplishments was the building in 1807 of Kootenae House, the first trading post on the

Columbia River. In 1811 he descended this river to its mouth, arriving on July 15 only to find some Americans already there. They had arrived by sea and had built Fort Astoria, named for New York's John Jacob Astor, whose American Fur Company carried on the leading U.S. fur trading operation.

In 1812, when war with the United States was approaching, Astor prudently sold this post to the North West Company. Meanwhile, that company and the Hudson's Bay group had been competing fiercely for the fur trade with the Indians. On March 21, 1821, however, the two companies merged under the Hudson's Bay Company name.

Pacific coast. In the late 18th century, controversy over territorial rights along the northwestern Pacific coast flared between England and Spain. First to land in the area, on May 13, 1778, was an English merchant ship captain, John Meares (1756–1809), who built a trading post. On May 29 Captain James Cook (1728–1779) of the British navy arrived and claimed possession of the area for Great Britain. These landings were on the west coast of Vancouver Island.

Because of the Spanish explorers Juan Pérez, who discovered British Columbia in 1774, and Bruno Heceta, who was said to have laid formal claim to much of the region in 1775, Spain claimed prior rights. On May 5, 1789, a Spanish sea captain, Estevan José Martinez, arrived, seized some British ships, but did not interfere with American ships trading there. Though Pérez and Heceta apparently did not make landings, Martinez took possession in the name of the Spanish king. Great Britain threatened to go to war with Spain over this incident, but the matter was resolved by the Nootka Sound Convention of October 28, 1790. By its terms, the Pacific coast was declared open to British subjects for trading purposes except within ten miles of any existing Spanish settlements.

The British sent Captain George Vancouver (1757–1798) to Nootka Sound in 1791 to arrange for the transfer back to English traders of the property the Spaniards had seized. The latter delayed matters as long as possible and did not withdraw until 1795. Meanwhile, Vancouver was conducting a survey of the coast. In 1793 he was off the mouth of the Bella Coola River, only a short time before Alexander Mackenzie arrived there on his overland trip.

The Canada Act. An important event in the history of Canadian government occurred on June 19, 1791, when the British Parliament passed the Constitutional Act of 1791, also known as the Canada Act. This legislation was intended to cope with changing political sentiment in Canada. There was a growing demand for more democratic government, stimulated partly by Loyalists who had fled the American colonies during the American Revolution and who were accustomed to more democracy than they found in Canada. Thus, it was felt in England that a more representative government, but one that retained a strong executive authority, would at once keep Canada peaceful and help it continue in the British tradition.

On August 24, 1791, after the Canada Act became law, Canada was divided into Lower Canada (roughly present-day Quebec) and Upper Canada (roughly present-day Ontario). In effect, this divided Canada in two: an English-speaking section and a French-speaking section. Though each was provided with a lieutenant governor with veto power, there was a council, with members appointed for life, and an elected assembly. The assembly was called to meet once a year, but it could not continue for more than four years without another election. The governor could dissolve it at will.

The Canada Act also provided for a land tenure system intended to result in development of a landed aristocracy. This never came about, probably because of lack of interest on the part of Canadians and Britons who had the means to participate in such a system.

Quebec City became the capital of Lower Canada. Newark (now Niagara-on-the-lake) was the temporary capital of Upper Canada, while York (now Toronto) was being prepared to be the capital city. York, founded in 1793 by British Loyalists, became the capital in 1797. The first legislature of Upper Canada convened on September 17, 1791, and that of Lower Canada on December 17, 1791.

In the end, the Canada Act resulted in political and economic oligarchies in both parts of Canada and caused resentment among the people. Nevertheless, the act helped establish a sense of unity and reduced the resentment against England that might have arisen if no form of free government had been permitted.

After the Americans burned the parliament building at York during the War of 1812, the seat of government of Upper Canada had to be moved to Kingston. Western Canada remained separate, still governed by the Hudson's Bay Company rather than by the British government. After this company and the North West Company merged in 1821, a new governing body was established. A governor and council were to run the overall commercial operation. Administration was divided into two departments. The northern section was made up of districts called Athabasca, Peace, Mackenzie, New Caledonia, and Columbia. According to its charter, the northern section was outside the limits of Rupert's Land; it was claimed by the North West Company. The southern department included the area between James Bay, at the south end of Hudson Bay, and eastern Canada, including the eastern shore of Hudson Bay.

War of 1812. A number of important engagements of the War of 1812 between Great Britain and the United

THE *NORTH WEST AMERICA* *was the first ship built in British Columbia, Canada.*

THE BETTMANN ARCHIVE

States were fought on Canadian soil. In addition, several of the war's battles on American soil involved British forces operating out of Canada. A faction of American members of Congress, the "war hawks," who had agitated for the war, saw it as an excuse for conquering Canada and driving the British out of North America.

War was declared by the United States on June 18, 1812. In July, General Isaac Brock (1769–1812), military commander and acting administrator of Upper Canada, declared martial law. Brock moved quickly to attack Detroit, which was defended by American forces under General William Hull (1753–1825). Brock outsmarted and outmaneuvered Hull, who surrendered Detroit on August 16. Hull, who had had an outstanding record in the Revolutionary War, was in this instance incompetent at best, a coward at worst. Earlier Hull had rashly invaded Canada, only to have his supply line cut and forcing him to retreat. Brock now considered that all of the Michigan territory had been restored to the British empire.

The Americans tried again to take the initiative on October 13, when troops under the command of General Stephen Van Rensselaer (1764–1839) crossed the Niagara River from New York and soon occupied Queenstown Heights, Ontario. Brock's forces defeated the Americans, who retreated to the United States, but Brock was killed in the battle. On November 28 the Americans again tried to cross the Niagara River, but they were repulsed.

The English benefited considerably from the help of their Indian allies, especially those led by Tecumseh, the Shawnee chief. British and Canadian forces, along with the Indians, defeated the Americans on January 22, 1813, at Frenchtown, Ohio, but they were unable to dislodge the army of General William Henry Harrison (1773–1841), the future president of the United States, at Fort Meigs, Ohio, May 1 to 9.

Both sides won victories on the Niagara Peninsula in 1813. On May 27 the Americans captured Fort George, Ontario, but on June 6 the British and Canadians, with their Indian allies, won the Battle of Stony Creek, while the Indians were victorious at Beaver Dam on June 24. The Americans retired from Fort George on December 10, but not before they had burned Newark (Niagara-on-the-Lake). The British pursued the Americans and on December 18 took Fort Niagara, New York. They then carried the war farther into New York, burning Lewiston, Manchester, Fort Schlosser, Black Rock, and Buffalo, ending their invasion on December 30.

Farther east, an American force on April 27, 1813, entered the harbor of Toronto and occupied the town. Public buildings, including parliament and the governor's residence, were burned. It was in retaliation for this deed that the British the next year burned the White House in Washington, D.C.

On Lake Erie on September 10, 1813, Captain Oliver H. Perry (1785–1819) and his small American fleet defeated a British fleet. This made it possible for General Harrison to move on Detroit and the British evacuated that post. Harrison moved into Ontario and on October 5 forced the British to join battle. The Americans totaled about 3000 while the British had only 300 regulars and 1000 Indians under Tecumseh. The British ranks broke under an American attack and Tecumseh was among those killed. This defeat, at the Thames River, put an end to the Indian confederacy that had been formed by Tecumseh.

About the same time, on October 26, an important and decisive victory was won by a Canadian force in Quebec on the Châteauguay River. Charles de Salaberry (1778–1829) and his small army of 750 Canadian Voltigeurs and some Indians defeated a much larger American force, numbering 7000, under General Wade Hampton (1752?–1835). This victory put a sudden and permanent halt to an attempt by the Americans to attack Montreal.

The fiercest battle of the war was fought at Lundy's Lane, just west of Niagara Falls, on July 25, 1814. The Americans were attempting to advance into Ontario but they were fought to a standstill, with casualties heavy on both sides. The American force withdrew to Fort Erie, on the Canadian side of the Niagara River, its previous position.

One further military engagement took place before the war ended. On Lake Champlain on September 11, 1814, an American force under Thomas Macdonough (1783–1825) soundly defeated a British fleet near Plattsburgh, New York, thus putting a stop to any plan to invade New York from Canada.

The war was formally ended by the Treaty of Ghent, Belgium, signed in that city on December 24, 1814. The two nations agreed to restore territory to each other on a prewar basis and to set up four commissions to settle the boundary line between Canada and the United States.

Rush-Bagot Convention. The boundary problem, as well as other matters, was settled, at least for the time being, by the Rush-Bagot Convention of 1817. It took its name from an agreement signed by Richard Rush (1780–1859), acting secretary of state of the United States, and Sir Charles Bagot (1781–1843), the British minister in Washington. Bagot later became governor of the province of Canada, from January, 1842, to March, 1843, when he was also governor-general of all the other colonies of British North America, e.g., Nova Scotia and New Brunswick. The American Senate approved the agreement in 1818, which gave it the force of a treaty.

By its terms, the boundary between the two countries in the west ran from the Lake of the Woods, partly in the present-day provinces of Ontario and Manitoba, and the American state of Minnesota, to the crest of the Rocky Mountains along the 49th parallel. The area west from there, known as the Oregon Territory, would be open to both countries for settlement and trade.

An unusual provision of the agreement brought disarmament to the U.S.-Canadian frontier. Each country was to have no more than four warships, not to exceed 100 tons each, on the Great Lakes.

The agreement set a precedent for the settling of Anglo-American differences by negotiation, although in 1864, during the American Civil War, when Canada was accused of harboring Confederate raiders and outfitting Confederate ships, the United States did, in fact, threaten to cancel the agreement. In 1865, however, with the end of the war, the notice of cancellation was withdrawn. Much later, during World War II, both countries agreed to ignore the provision concerning warships in order that both might build and sail such craft as allies.

Growth of Canada. In spite of this agreement, there was considerable anti-American feeling in Canada after the War of 1812. Many Canadians considered that they had been the victims of aggressors who sought to conquer and rule them. Some recent American settlers in Canada were believed to be outright disloyal, while those settlers who had come from the states as Loyalists after the Revolution boasted that it was they who had saved Canada from invasion.

One result of the anti-American feeling was the banning in 1815 of any more land grants to Americans. This inhibited the growth of Canada to some extent; nevertheless, Canada was growing. By 1825 the outlines of the eventual Dominion of Canada were becoming clearer. Canada now consisted of six settled areas: Lower Canada, Upper Canada, Newfoundland, Prince Edward Island, Nova Scotia, and New Brunswick. In the west, the Hudson's Bay Company continued to rule.

As time went on, the flow of emigrants from Europe, chiefly from the British Isles, increased. Most of the immigrants followed the St. Lawrence River route into Lower and Upper Canada, with the number increasing from about 12,000 in 1828 to 66,000 in 1832. By 1838 the population of Upper Canada was almost 400,000 despite its distance from Europe. Settlement in Lower Canada was impeded somewhat by the seigniorial system, left over from French rule. Immigrants also flowed into the maritime provinces. In the decade after 1815, nearly 40,000 arrived in Nova Scotia, the population of which was 200,000 by 1838. New Brunswick, with most of its influx coming from Ireland, had an average of 5000 or more newcomers per year.

This influx was not without its problems. Many of those who came were destitute, or very poor, farmers or artisans, all of whom were ill-equipped to become pioneers. In some areas land was not easy to acquire. Many immigrants found that the more prosperous United States had its attractions. As a result, a good many immigrants who arrived in Canada continued on to the United States, where land was more easily available.

THE BETTMANN ARCHIVE

TROOPS LED BY COL. WETHERELL *bivouac at St. Hilaire de Rouville, Quebec, in November, 1837.*

The Red River settlement. An experiment in settlement in the West in this period brought about clashes between fur trapping and farming interests. Seeking to do something to benefit impoverished inhabitants of Scotland and Northern Ireland, Thomas Douglas (1771–1820), 5th Earl of Selkirk, who had an interest in the Hudson's Bay Company, secured a grant of 116,000 acres from the company in 1811. The land lay chiefly in present-day Manitoba, on the Red River, but extended south into North Dakota and Minnesota. The North West Company bitterly opposed the Red River settlement, as it was known, because it lay across the company's trade route and deprived it of a source of food supply.

The company incited the Métis to resist settlers on the grounds that they were encroaching on land that rightfully belonged to the Métis as descendants of Indian forebears. The settlers were driven away to the Jack River, north of Lake Winnipeg, but were brought back in 1815 and reinforced. In March of 1816, the governor of the settlement seized a North West Company fort; in June he destroyed another. Meanwhile, the Métis were incited by the North West Company to harass the settlers and destroy two forts of the Hudson's Bay Company. Violence reached a climax on June 19, 1816, when the governor of the colony and 26 of his men came upon some Métis at Seven Oaks. A fight followed in which the governor and 20 of his men were killed and some of the bodies mutilated. Once more the settlers retired to the Jack River.

Lord Selkirk, who had come to Canada late in 1815, now brought a force of former soldiers west. They seized the North West Company's headquarters at Fort William in August of 1816. The provincial governor sent out a commissioner who arranged a peaceful settlement. Again the colonists were brought back from the Jack River, but their troubles were not over. There were floods and a plague of locusts. In the end, though, agriculture flourished on the western plains.

Rebellion of 1837. During the 1820's and 1830's, increasing unrest in both Lower Canada and Upper Canada led to the Rebellion of 1837. The unrest was both economic and political, stemming from the fact that in both provinces economic control and political power were held by a small group of individuals and families. Cooperating with the British-controlled government, those in control were ultraconservative socially, economically, and politically. In Upper Canada, this faction was known as the Family Compact. In Lower Canada, a similar group was known as the Château Clique, the name being derived from the residence of the governor, the Château Saint-Louis.

In the political arena, militant reformers demanded self-government, which was not about to be granted either by the Canadian Tories (Conservatives) or the government in London. A Royal Commission had demonstrated this. In Upper Canada the leader of the reformers was William Lyon Mackenzie (1795–1861), a Scot who emigrated to Canada in 1820 and in 1824 founded a journal, the *Colonial Advocate.* Elected to the House of Assembly in 1828, he was expelled in 1831 for libeling that body. Mackenzie's reform proposals were extreme, although some of them, such as the sale of public lands on easy terms, he adapted from the system in operation in the United States.

In Lower Canada Mackenzie's equivalent was Louis-Joseph Papineau (1786–1871), born in Montreal and a militia officer in the War of 1812. In 1834 he helped draw up the Ninety-two Resolutions. Though the resolutions stated grievances with which many agreed, and though they advocated democratic government, they were also extreme in their bitter attacks on the British and colonial administrations.

Armed rebellion broke out in a minor way on December 7, 1837, near Toronto, where some militants had gathered. They were attacked by the militia and some were captured; two were later convicted of treason and hanged on April 12, 1838. Mackenzie, however, escaped to the United States and on an island in the Niagara River he proclaimed optimistically a Canadian republic. He was arrested for violating the American neutrality laws and in June, 1839, was sentenced to 18 months in prison. Mackenzie returned to Canada under the Amnesty Act of 1849 and was elected to the House of Assembly in 1851, but he found little support. He retired from politics in 1858.

In Lower Canada there was rioting in Montreal on December 6, 1837, between members of a Tory club and a militant group calling itself *Fils de la liberté.* North of Montreal, on December 14, a group of rebels was dislodged from a church where they had gathered. Some of these rebels, Papineau among them, took refuge in the United States. He later went to Paris to live but returned to Canada in 1844.

Other militants participated in incursions into Canada from the United

WILLIAM LYON MACKENZIE *led demands for Canadian self-government.*

THE GRANGER COLLECTION

States between February and December, 1838. None of these ventures met with any success. Martial law was proclaimed and 733 rebels in all were taken prisoner. Of these, twelve were executed and 58 were transported to the penal colony in Australia.

The Aroostook War. While rebellion was taking place in Canada and spilling over into the United States, a border dispute between the two countries brought about a minor clash that became known as the Aroostook War. The trouble began in 1838 when both Maine and New Brunswick claimed territory along the border where no exact determination of the international boundary had been agreed upon. The area included the valley of the Aroostook River, whose fertile farmlands were of interest to Maine farmers and New Brunswick lumbermen. When the lumbermen appeared, Maine raised a force to eject them. The lumbermen, however, surprised the Maine posse and seized 50 of them.

Both sides armed for further conflict but cooler heads prevailed in March of 1839. Sir John Harvey (1778–1852), a veteran of the War of 1812 and lieutenant governor of New Brunswick, together with General Winfield Scott (1786–1866), who had been sent to command a small U.S. force, agreed on a truce. A final settlement was made by the Webster-Ashburton Treaty, signed on August 8, 1842. It took its name from Daniel Webster (1782–1852), the American secretary of state, and Alexander Baring (1774–1848), 1st Baron Ashburton, representing Great Britain. By its terms, more than 7000 square miles of the territory, including the Aroostook valley, were given to the United States. The treaty fixed the boundary between New Brunswick and Maine in part along the St. Croix River. Several rivers, including the St. John, which also formed part of the boundary, were opened to free navigation by both countries.

The same treaty also provided for cooperation between the two countries in suppressing the slave trade and in the mutual extradition of criminals. While some other problems, such as the boundaries of the Oregon Territory, were ignored, this treaty again demonstrated the desire of Great Britain, representing Canada, to settle differences peacefully.

Union

The Rebellion of 1837 convinced the British government that reform in the Canadian system of government was needed. Those who had rebelled had been extremists, but there was general dissatisfaction in the land. The need to replace the governing cliques with more democratic rule became evident.

The first step toward reform was the appointment of John George Lambton (1792–1840), 1st Earl of Durham, as governor-general and high commissioner of British North America. Durham had been an outspoken liberal in the British Parliament from 1813 to 1832 and had played a leading role in the passage of the milestone electoral Reform Bill of 1832. His activities and personality had earned him the nickname of Radical Jack. He arrived in Quebec on May 29, 1838, bringing with him colonial experts to help him determine a course of action that would keep Canada a contented part of the British empire. Between May and November 1, when he resigned and returned to England, he studied the problems in both Upper and Lower Canada.

Durham wrote his "Report on the Affairs of British North America" and submitted it to the Colonial Office on February 4, 1839. The report's basic proposal was that Upper and Lower Canada be united as the province of Canada, consisting of Canada East (Lower Canada, Quebec) and Canada West (Upper Canada, Ontario). This proposal was adopted by the British Parliament on July 23, 1840, and the whole measure, known as the Act of Union, was effective in Canada on February 10, 1841.

An elected House of Assembly was provided for, with an equal number of members from each of the two former provinces, as well as an appointed council. All legislative procedures were to be conducted in the English language. The power to impose duties for the regulation of commerce was retained by the British government but those duties, together with such other revenues as fines, land sales, and seigniorial dues, were to be used by the province for its budget. Kingston was chosen as the capital on February 10, 1841, but on May 10, 1844, the seat of government was removed to Montreal.

The section prohibiting the use of the French language in legislative proceedings was repealed in 1848. In 1854 the province was granted the power to alter the constitution of the legislative council, and in 1856 that council was granted permission to elect or appoint its own speaker.

One part of Durham's report, however, took a different tone from the progressive attitude shown in the recommendation for some measure of self-government. He was sharply critical of the French-Canadians and hoped that the governmental reorganization would officially and in practice make them subordinate to the English-speaking people of the province. Durham was willing to allow the French to retain their religious rights, but he wanted to wipe out the differences in language and law.

Durham's report and the Act of Union did not win unanimous praise. The Tories in both England and Canada, and the members of the Family Compact and the Château Clique, opposed the changes. The French were outraged, seeing the report as an attack on them. Nevertheless, the report and the Act of Union marked the beginning of a transition from the British empire as it existed in the first half of the 19th century to what in the 20th century became the Commonwealth of Nations.

Province of Canada. In 1839 Charles Poulett Thomson (1799–1841) was sent to Canada as governor-general to secure the consent of Upper and Lower Canada to the proposal to unite them as one colony. He did so and as a reward was created Baron Sydenham and named the first governor-general of the province of Canada. He had entered parliament in 1826 as a Liberal and was known as a reformer and as an exponent of free trade. At the same time, he wanted Great Britain to maintain strong imperial ties with its colonies.

Sydenham attempted to control the government by keeping the French-speaking region and the reformers in the minority in the new legislature. He was unsuccessful, however, when these two factions agreed to cooperate. Sydenham's administration brought useful changes, especially in municipal institutions and schools.

He balked, however, at accepting the idea of responsible government. In parliamentary terms, the phrase "responsible government" means that a governor-general accepts a prime minister and cabinet from the majority group or party of the elected legislature, which controls and manages legislation and so exercises effective governance, subject, in the case of a colony, to the formal approval of the British Crown and its representatives. Sydenham believed that the newly constituted council was simply an advisory body that the governor could consult or not as he wished and that the governor was the person who should make all executive decisions.

Lord Sydenham was killed in September of 1841 when he fell from his horse in Kingston. His successor as governor was Sir Charles Bagot. He found that the majority of the members of the House of Assembly, who were reformers, and the Tory members of the council, or ministry, appointed by Sydenham, had no confidence in each other. Bagot attempted to get the leaders of the reformers, Louis-Hippolyte Lafontaine (1807–1864) of Canada East, and Robert Baldwin (1804–1858) of Canada West, to join the ministry.

Lafontaine had been elected to the House of Assembly in 1830, but he did not approve of the Rebellion of 1837. Baldwin was elected to the House of Assembly in 1829, but he was defeated the following year. He and Lafontaine formed an alliance and in 1842

HEADS OF GOVERNMENT 1791–1841

Lower Canada

OFFICIAL	TITLE	SERVED
Sir Alured Clarke	Lieutenant Governor Administrator	Dec. 25, 1791– Oct. 1, 1793
Lord Dorchester (formerly Sir Guy Carleton)	Governor	Oct. 2, 1793– July 9, 1796
Robert Prescott	Lieutenant Governor Administrator Governor	July 12, 1796– Apr. 26, 1797 Apr. 27, 1797– July 29, 1799
Sir Robert Shore Milnes	Lieutenant Governor Administrator	July 30, 1799– Aug. 5, 1805
Thomas Dunn	Administrator	Aug. 12, 1805– Oct. 24, 1807
Sir James Henry Craig	Governor	Oct. 24, 1807– June 19, 1811
Thomas Dunn	Administrator	June 19, 1811– Sept. 14, 1811
Sir George Prevost	Administrator Governor	Sept. 14, 1811– July 15, 1812 July 15, 1812– Apr. 3, 1815
Sir Gordon Drummond	Administrator	Apr. 4, 1815– May 21, 1816
John Wilson	Administrator	May 21, 1816– July 12, 1816
Sir John Coape Sherbrooke	Governor	July 12, 1816– July 30, 1818
Duke of Richmond	Governor	July 30, 1818– Aug. 28, 1819
James Monk	Administrator	Sept. 20, 1819– Mar. 17, 1820
Sir Peregrine Maitland	Administrator	Mar. 17, 1820– June 19, 1820
Lord Dalhousie	Governor	June 19, 1820– June 6, 1824
Sir Francis Burton	Lieutenant Governor Administrator	June 7, 1824– Sept. 16, 1825
Lord Dalhousie	Governor	Sept. 17, 1825– Sept. 8, 1828
Sir James Kempt	Administrator	Sept. 8, 1828– Oct. 20, 1830
Lord Aylmer	Administrator Governor	Oct. 20, 1830– Feb. 4, 1831 Feb. 4, 1831– Aug. 24, 1835
Lord Gosford	Governor Commissioner	Aug. 24, 1835– Feb. 27, 1838
Sir John Colborne	Administrator	Feb. 27, 1838– May 29, 1838
Lord Durham	Governor	May 29, 1838– Nov. 1, 1838
Sir John Colborne	Administrator Governor	Nov. 1, 1838– Jan. 17, 1839 Jan. 17, 1839– Oct. 19, 1839
Charles Poulette Thomson (later Lord Sydenham)	Governor	Oct. 19, 1839– Feb. 10, 1841

Upper Canada

OFFICIAL	TITLE	SERVED
John Graves Simcoe	Lieutenant Governor	July 8, 1792– July 20, 1796
Peter Russell	Administrator	July 20, 1796– Aug. 17, 1799
Peter Hunter	Lieutenant Governor	Aug. 17, 1799– Aug. 21, 1805
Alexander Grant	Administrator	Sept. 11, 1805– Aug. 25, 1806
Francis Gore	Lieutenant Governor	Aug. 25, 1806– Oct. 8, 1811
Isaac Brock	Administrator	Oct. 9, 1811– Oct. 13, 1812
Roger Hale Sheaffe	Administrator	Oct. 20, 1812– June 19, 1813
Baron Francis de Rottenburg	Administrator	June 19, 1813– Dec. 13, 1813
Sir Gordon Drummond	Administrator	Dec. 13, 1813– Apr. 25, 1815
Sir Frederick P. Robinson	Provisional Lieutenant Governor	July 1, 1815– Sept. 21, 1815
Francis Gore	Lieutenant Governor	Sept. 21, 1815– June 11, 1817
Samuel Smith	Administrator	June 11, 1817– Aug. 13, 1818
Sir Peregrine Maitland	Lieutenant Governor	Aug. 13, 1818– Nov. 4, 1828
Sir John Colborne	Lieutenant Governor	Nov. 4, 1828– Jan. 25, 1836
Sir Francis Bond Head	Lieutenant Governor	Jan. 25, 1836– Mar. 23, 1838
Sir George Arthur	Lieutenant Governor	Mar. 23, 1838– Feb. 10, 1841

accepted Bagot's request that they take over the ministry. But in 1843 Sir Charles Theophilus Metcalfe (1785–1846), who had been governor of Jamaica, succeeded Bagot as governor of Canada and governor-general of all the British colonies in North America. He had received instructions in England from the colonial secretary not to allow responsible government. Metcalfe demonstrated his firm belief in his orders by making appointments without the advice of the members of the ministry and by taking other actions that bypassed them. Accordingly, Lafontaine and Baldwin resigned. Metcalfe received a baronetcy as a reward for his efforts, but he was dying and returned to England in 1845.

The situation was reversed after James Bruce (1811–1863), 8th Earl of Elgin, became governor-general of the British North American colonies on January 30, 1847. He carried new instructions from the British government to concede the right to govern. Accordingly on December 6, 1847, Elgin dissolved the assembly and, in the following election, reformers won a majority. Baldwin and Lafontaine formed a ministry on March 11, 1848. Their government became known as the Great Ministry because of the reforms it undertook and because it was the first real parliamentary cabinet in Canada.

The ministry passed a number of laws, some of them controversial. The Rebellion Losses Act of 1849 was intended to repay people in Canada East whose property had been damaged during the Rebellion of 1837. (A previous act in 1841 had compensated people in Canada West.) Lord Elgin approved the bill. The Tory faction revolted so strenuously that the parliament building in Montreal was burned and Elgin's carriage was stoned. Since passage and approval of the bill did make the point that the governor-general would accept the positions of a ministry, the act was a landmark in the constitutional development of Canadian government.

The Baldwin-Lafontaine ministry secularized King's College in 1849 and made it the University of Toronto, strengthened the school system, and provided a guarantee of funds to stimulate the building of railroads.

Reciprocal trade agreement. In Washington, in June, 1854, Lord Elgin and William L. Marcy (1786–1857), U.S. secretary of state, negotiated an agreement between the two countries. Complete free trade in many natural products was established, and the mutual use of fisheries in coastal and inland waters was agreed on. For example, the American market was opened to Canada for export of fur, fish, and timber, and Americans could freely sell in Canada such products as rice, turpentine, and tobacco.

The United States, however, abrogated the agreement in 1866, partly as the result of pressure from manufacturing interests, partly because the British government had favored the South in the Civil War that ended in 1865. Though the free trade agreement contributed a great deal to Canadian prosperity, British North America had also benefited from the demand for goods resulting from the Crimean War (1853–1856) in Europe and the American Civil War. A British and Canadian attempt was made in 1869 to renegotiate the agreement, but it failed.

Oregon Territory. After some strong words, especially on the American side, another agreement between the United States and Great Britain, acting for Canada, was reached in 1846. This concerned the Oregon Territory, a large and valuable region that eventually encompassed three whole American states, parts of two others, and part of British Columbia. Hawkish elements in the United States tried to insist on a boundary line at 54 degrees, 40 minutes of north latitude, which would give America the whole area. Great Britain wanted the boundary set farther south at the Columbia River.

On May 21, 1846, the United States gave England one year's notice that it would end the joint occupation agreement of 1818. Both countries were willing to compromise on the 49th parallel, which would extend to the Pacific Ocean the line, already accepted by both countries in the Rush-Bagot Convention (1817), from Lake of the Woods westward to the Rocky Mountains. However, neither country for a time wanted to be the first to propose the compromise. The British finally took the initiative and the U.S.-Canadian boundary from the Atlantic to the Pacific was settled. By the settlement, the United States received the larger part of the area, including the fertile Columbia River valley. But Great Britain received all of Vancouver Island, a portion of which lies south of the agreed upon line.

THIS POLITICAL CARTOON *deals with the Oregon Territory controversy.*

HISTORICAL PICTURES SERVICE, CHICAGO

NEW YORK PUBLIC LIBRARY

FORT LANGLEY, *built in 1827, was an early Canadian outpost on the Pacific.*

The Far West. At the same time that more democratic government was coming to the province of Canada, governmental institutions were appearing for the first time in the Far West. The first step was taken in 1843 when Vancouver Island was granted to the Hudson's Bay Company. The company was concerned by the threat to its interests of the influx of American settlers and trappers in the Oregon Territory. That year the company established Fort Camosun, which in 1851 was renamed Victoria. The first governor of the island was Richard Blanshard (1817?–1894), who arrived in 1850. The small population of the island chose its first assembly on August 12, 1856.

The population of the island and the adjacent mainland did not increase much for some time, largely because the Hudson's Bay Company was more interested in its fur trade than in bringing in farmers to settle the West. The situation changed in 1858 as the result of the discovery of deposits of gold along the Thompson River, the main tributary of the Fraser River. A throng of miners, mostly from the United States, poured in. This influx of miners and adventurers, some of whom did not stay long, prompted the British Parliament to establish on August 2, 1858, the colony of British Columbia. Fort Langley at the mouth of the

Fraser River was the capital for a short time, until in 1859 New Westminster, 20 miles up the river, was founded. On November 19, 1866, Vancouver Island, by act of the Parliament in London, was made part of the colony, although the Hudson's Bay Company continued to manage affairs there until April 3, 1867. Victoria became the capital of the province in 1868, displacing New Westminister.

New attempts at the Northwest Passage. The first half of the 19th century witnessed a number of expeditions to find the Northwest Passage through the Arctic lands and waters of northern North America. The leader of several expeditions, and an eventual tragic victim of the search, was Sir John Franklin (1786–1847) of the British navy, who led expeditions in 1819–1822 and 1825–1827 to explore the Arctic coast.

In 1845 Franklin sailed from England with two ships to seek the Northwest Passage. On July 26 a whaling ship met his ships in Baffin Bay; that was the last that was ever seen of Franklin or any of the members of his expedition. In 1848 three search parties were sent out to seek clues to the fate of the expedition and more than 40 others, looking for remains, followed in later years. It was not until 1854 that John Rae (1813–1893), another explorer, learned of Franklin's fate from Eskimos. The two ships had been frozen in the ice between Victoria Island and King William Island for more than a year, and Franklin had died on June 11, 1847. The other members of the expedition, scurvy-ridden, abandoned the ships in April, 1848, and tried to make their way back to civilization overland, but all perished. Relics and documents of the ill-fated expedition have turned up as recently as 1960.

Provincial government, 1851–1862. The arrival of the second half of the 19th century was marked by the end of the Baldwin-Lafontaine ministry. In 1851, the new minister was Francis Hincks (1807–1885), a reform leader in Canada West, and August-Norbert Morin (1803–1865), who had been the chief lieutenant of Lafontaine and speaker of the assembly from 1848 to 1851. Hincks was interested in economic affairs and especially in railroad promotion. In 1852 he secured the incorporation of the Grand Trunk Railway, which by 1856 was the longest rail system in the world, running for 1100 miles from Quebec westward to the southern end of Lake Huron. Because of its vast distances and scattered population centers, Canada badly needed railroads; their construction and financing played a major role in Canadian politics for many years.

Hincks also began negotiations that led to a reciprocal trade treaty with the United States in 1854. For his part, Morin, representing French-speaking Canada, was interested in assuring Catholic rights and in supporting the appropriation of funds for separate schools. The ministry lasted until 1854, when it was brought down by Hincks's involvement in questionable financial transactions.

Morin remained a leader in the next ministry with Allan Napier McNab (1798–1862), who had served in the War of 1812 and had been elected to the provincial assembly in 1841. He was a leader of the Tory and Conservative groups and when a Liberal-Conservative coalition was formed in 1854, he became its leader. The combination with Morin, a reformer, indicated that economic issues were more important to McNab than political principles.

Two important legislative actions were completed by the McNab-Morin ministry in 1854; one concerned the "clergy reserves." By the Constitutional Act of 1791, an area equal to one-seventh of all land granted to settlers in both Lower and Upper Canada was to be used for the support of a Protestant clergy. This act greatly angered the Catholics of Upper Canada and even some Protestants because the government at first chose to equate Protestantism solely with the Church of England. In 1819 it was agreed that the Church of Scotland, a brand of Presbyterianism, should share in the reserved land. Methodists and Baptists,

HEADS OF GOVERNMENT 1841–1867

Province of Canada

OFFICIAL	TITLE	SERVED
Lord Sydenham	Governor	Feb. 10, 1841–Sept. 19, 1841
Sir Richard Downes Jackson	Administrator	Sept. 24, 1841–Jan. 12, 1842
Sir Charles Bagot	Governor	Jan. 12, 1842–Mar. 30, 1843
Sir Charles Metcalfe	Governor	Mar. 30, 1843–Nov. 26, 1845
Lord Cathcart	Administrator	Nov. 26, 1845–Apr. 24, 1846
	Governor	Apr. 24, 1846–Jan. 30, 1847
Lord Elgin	Governor	Jan. 30, 1847–Dec. 19, 1854
Sir Edmund Walker Head	Governor	Dec. 19, 1854–Oct. 24, 1861
Lord Monck	Administrator	Oct. 25, 1861–Nov. 28, 1861
	Governor	Nov. 28, 1861–June 30, 1867

SIR JOHN FRANKLIN, *who led two expeditions to explore the Arctic coast, stopped here, at Point Lake, in 1821.*

THE GRANGER COLLECTION

on the other hand, did not believe the state should support any denomination. They wanted the money derived from the lands used for educational purposes. Finally, in 1854, the lands were given to the municipalities, except for enough to meet obligations already incurred to pay pensions for retired clergymen.

The same year seigniorial tenure rights were terminated. Unlike anything in the English legal system, those who held these rights had certain judicial powers and were conceded certain privileges in church affairs. The first of these grants had been made as far back as January 15, 1634. The Canada Tenures Act of 1826 had allowed holders of such rights to apply for a change to the English system of freehold.

Morin was appointed a judge in 1855 and the ministry then became that of McNab and Étienne-Paschal Taché (1795–1865), who was born in Lower Canada. He had served in the House of Assembly of the province of Canada, 1841–1846, and was a member of the Hincks-Morin ministry. In 1856 John A. Macdonald (1815–1891), who was born in Scotland and came to Canada in 1820, replaced McNab. Macdonald had first been elected to the provincial House of Assembly as a Tory in 1844. He now became the leader of the governing Liberal-Conservative coalition. George-Étienne Cartier (1814–1873) of Lower Canada, who had fought in the Rebellion of 1837, replaced Taché as the leader of the French-Canadian part of the coalition in 1857. Cartier had been banished for his part in the rebellion and took refuge in Burlington, Vermont, but he was able to return to Canada the next year. This alliance of Cartier and Macdonald became the foundation of the Conservative Party; it remained intact until Cartier's death in 1873.

Liberal groups in Canada East and Canada West were unable to form an effective alliance, so the Macdonald Cartier ministry, with one very short interruption, was in power until 1862. During its time in office, considerable attention was paid to the growth of railways, industry, and settlement in the West. The Huron district of Canada West was opened by the construction of roads, while settlement of the hinterlands of Canada East was also encouraged. In 1858 a decimal currency became legal tender. A tariff act of 1856 was expanded in 1859, at which time protective duties were placed on goods of British manufacture.

The early 1860's were marked by considerable controversy over the need for reforms in the system of government. Some political leaders wanted representation in the legislature to be by population; at the time, Canada East and Canada West were being equally represented. Some wanted a federation type of government that would give each province more autonomy. An even larger scheme was proposed for the confederation of all the British North American colonies and the acquisition of the vast lands of the Hudson's Bay Company.

The American Civil War. Canada became involved, involuntarily, in the American Civil War of 1861–1865. The British government made no secret of its support for the Confederacy in the South, even though most individuals in Great Britain and Canada favored the Union in the North and opposed slavery. Some of England's actions, such as allowing armed ships for the Confederacy to be built in its ports, outraged northern Americans and they took out some of their feelings on their northern neighbor.

Canada, entirely subordinate to Great Britain in the area of foreign relations, could not prevent agents of the South from using its ports as refuges and bases. Although most Canadians deplored the situation and had much more in common with the North than the South, there was a Tory minority of some influence that disliked the democratic North and feared another attempt at invasion. When events reached the point where it seemed that Britain and the United States might go to war over English support of the South, 15,000 British troops were sent to Canada to ward off possible invasion.

Worst of all to American northerners was the extremist element among the Confederates who slipped into Canada to use it as a base for raids into the United States. One plan was intended to free Confederate prisoners of war held in camps near the border. Another was to somehow incite an uprising in Chicago. The one raid of any consequence took place in September, 1864, when a band of southerners raided St. Albans, Vermont, from Canadian soil. About 25 men invaded the village, set fires, took $200,000 from three banks, killed one man, and wounded another. American anger was further inflamed when a Canadian judge, on technical grounds, ordered the raiders released after they had been captured. Canadian officials rearrested the raiders and hurriedly passed legislation intended to prevent any more such incidents.

In fact, Canada's contribution to the Union and antislavery cause far outweighed the importance of such incidents. Canada had long been the final haven on the underground railroad through which abolitionists in the North helped slaves escape from Southern states. About 40,000 blacks ended up in Canada. In addition, according to one historian, 53,532 men of British North America served in the Union Army. About two-thirds of them were French Canadians, prompted in part to enlist by the lack of economic opportunity in Canada East.

In early June, 1866, after the war was over, the tables were turned when a group of Irishmen, about 1600 members of the Fenian Brotherhood, crossed the border from the United States in the Niagara Falls, New York, area to seize Fort Erie in Ontario. The Brotherhood had been organized in New York City in 1857 with the purpose of securing the independence of Ireland from Great Britain by any means available. At the time of their raid, they were encouraged by the anti-Canadian feeling that had been building up in the North during the Civil War. The Fenians repulsed an attempt by some Canadian volunteers to dislodge them; but when regular army troops showed up, they retreated to American soil, where they were arrested and their arms seized. The Fenians remained a threat for five years, with rumors abounding of raids to take place from Maine to Minnesota. The last raid, into Manitoba in 1871, accomplished nothing.

Confederation

By the mid-19th century there was sensed, both in Canada and England, the need for a consolidation of British North America into a confederation that would eventually include the vast region from coast to coast and from the U.S. boundary to the Arctic north. It was perceived that representation in the House of Assembly was inequitable for both Canada East and Canada West and that the number of seats in the legislature should be based on population. There was a movement to bring the land of the Hudson's Bay Company under Canadian government control.

The idea of confederation was not new. A British officer suggested a form of union for defense as early as 1783. A plan for civil government with a central legislature for all of Canada was proposed in 1785 by William Smith (1728–1793), a Loyalist who had been chief justice of the colony of New York and who was named chief justice of Quebec in 1786. He later assisted in writing the Constitutional Act of 1791. Another proposal was made in 1807 by Jonathan Sewell (1766–1839), chief justice of Lower Canada; in 1824 he reformulated the plan with John Beverley Robinson (1791–1863), attorney general of Upper Canada.

Other proposals were made also. In 1826 the attorney general of Nova Scotia, Richard John Uniacke (1753–1830), presented a plan for confederation to the British Colonial Office. During the American Revolution, Uniacke had been jailed in Halifax under suspicion of aiding the colonies.

Lord Durham, the governor-general whose report resulted in the 1841 Act of Union, suggested in the report that confederation of British North America might come about later. As Britain's colonial secretary from 1846 to 1852, Henry George (1802–1894), Earl

BRITISH NORTH AMERICA ACT, 1867

(Now also known as the Constitution Act, 1867)

Some excerpts

WHEREAS the Provinces of Canada, Nova Scotia, and New Brunswick have expressed their Desire to be federally united into One Dominion under the Crown of the United Kingdom of Great Britain and Ireland, with a Constitution similar in Principle to that of the United Kingdom:

AND WHEREAS such a Union would conduce to the Welfare of the Provinces and promote the Interests of the British Empire:

AND WHEREAS on the Establishment of Union by Authority of Parliament it is expedient, not only that the Constitution of the Legislative authority in the Dominion be provided for, but also that the Nature of the Executive Government herein be declared:

AND WHEREAS it is expedient that Provision be made for the eventual admission into the Union of other Parts of British North America:

BE IT THEREFORE enacted and declared by the Queen's most Excellent Majesty, by and with the Advice and Consent of the Lords Spiritual and Temporal, and Commons, in this present Parliament assembled, and by the Authority of the same, as follows: . . .

II. UNION

3. It shall be lawful for the Queen, by and with the advice of Her Majesty's Most Honourable Privy Council, to declare by Proclamation that, on and after a Day therein appointed, not being more than Six Months after the passing of this Act, the Provinces of Canada, Nova Scotia, and New Brunswick shall form and be One Dominion under the Name of Canada; and on and after that day these Three Provinces shall form and be One Dominion under that name accordingly. . . .

Canada shall be divided into Four Provinces, named Ontario, Quebec, Nova Scotia, and New Brunswick.

6. The Parts of the Province of Canada (as it exists at the passing of this Act) which formerly constituted respectively the Provinces of Upper Canada and Lower Canada shall be deemed to be severed, and shall form two separate Provinces. The Part which formerly constituted the Province of Upper Canada shall constitute the Province of Ontario; and the Part which formerly constituted the Province of Lower Canada shall constitute the Province of Quebec. . . .

9. The Executive Government and Authority of and over Canada is hereby declared to continue and be vested in the Queen. . . .

12. All Powers, Authorities, and Functions which under any Act of the Parliament of Great Britain, or of the Parliament of the United Kingdom of Great Britain and Ireland, or of the Legislature of Upper Canada, Lower Canada, Nova Scotia, or New Brunswick, are at the Union vested in or exercisable by the respective Governors or Lieutenant-Governors of those Provinces, with the advice, or with the Advice and Consent, of the respective Executive Councils thereof, or in conjunction with those Councils, or with any Number of Members thereof, or by those Governors or Lieutenant-Governors individually, shall, as far as the same continue in existence and capable of being exercised after the Union in relation to the Government of Canada, be vested in and exercisable by the Governor General, with the Advice or with the Advice and Consent of or in conjunction with the Queen's Privy Council for Canada, or any Members thereof, or by the Governor General individually, as the Case requires, subject nevertheless (except with respect to such as exist under Acts of the Parliament of Great Britain or of the Parliament of the United Kingdom of Great Britain and Ireland) to be abolished or altered by the Parliament of Canada. . . .

17. There shall be One Parliament for Canada, consisting of the Queen, an Upper House styled the Senate, and the House of Commons.

18. The Privileges, Immunities, and Powers to be held, enjoyed and exercised by the Senate and by the House of Commons and by the members thereof respectively shall be such as are from Time to Time defined by Act of the Parliament of Canada, but so that the same shall never exceed those at the passing of this Act held, enjoyed, and exercised by the Commons House of Parliament of the United Kingdom of Great Britain and Ireland and by the Members thereof.

19. The Parliament of Canada shall be called together not later than six Months after the Union.

20. There shall be a Session of the Parliament of Canada once at least in every Year, so that Twelve Months shall not intervene between the last sitting of the Parliament of one Session and its first Sitting in the next Session.

21. The Senate shall, subject to the Provisions of this Act, consist of Seventy-two Members, who shall be styled Senators. . . .

37. The House of Commons shall, subject to the Provisions of this Act, consist of One hundred and eighty-one Members, of whom Eighty-two shall be elected for Ontario, Sixty-five for Quebec, Nineteen for Nova Scotia, and Fifteen for New Brunswick. . . .

58. For each Province there shall be an Officer, styled the Lieutenant-Governor, appointed by the Governor General in Council by Instrument under the Great Seal of Canada. . . .

91. It shall be lawful for the Queen by and with the Advice and Consent of the Senate and House of Commons, to make Laws for the Peace, Order and good Government of Canada, in relation to all Matters not coming within the Classes of Subjects by this Act assigned exclusively to the Legislatures of the Provinces: . . .

93. In and for each Province the Legislature may exclusively make Laws in relation to Education, . . .

95. In each Province the Legislature may make Laws in relation to Agriculture in the Province, and to Immigration into the Province; and it is hereby declared that the Parliament of Canada may from Time to Time make Laws in relation to Agriculture in all or any of the Provinces, and to Immigration into all or any of the Provinces; and any Law of the Legislature of a Province relative to Agriculture or to Immigration shall have effect in and for the Province as long and as far only as it is not repugnant to any Act of the Parliament of Canada. . . .

102. All Duties and Revenues over which the respective Legislatures of Canada, Nova Scotia, and New Brunswick before and at the Union had and have Power of Appropriation, except such portions thereof as are by this Act reserved to the respective Legislatures of the Provinces, or are raised by them in accordance with the special Powers conferred on them by this Act, shall form One Consolidated Revenue Fund, to be appropriated for the public Service of Canada in the Manner and subject to the Charges in this Act provided. . . .

145. Inasmuch as the Provinces of Canada, Nova Scotia, and New Brunswick have joined in a Declaration that the Construction of the Intercolonial Railway is essential to the Consolidation of the Union of British North America, and to the assent thereto of Nova Scotia and New Brunswick, and have consequently agreed that Provision should be made for its immediate Construction by the Government of Canada: Therefore, in order to give effect to that Agreement, it shall be the duty of the Government and Parliament of Canada to provide for the Commencement within Six Months after the Union, of a Railway connecting the River St. Lawrence with the City of Halifax in Nova Scotia, and for the Construction thereof without Intermission, and the Completion thereof with all practicable Speed.

146. It shall be lawful for the Queen, by and with the Advice of Her Majesty's Most Honourable Privy Council, on Addresses from the Houses of the Parliament of Canada, and from the Houses of the respective Legislatures of the Colonies or Provinces of Newfoundland, Prince Edward Island, and British Columbia, to admit those Colonies or Provinces, or any of them, into the Union, and on Address from the Houses of Parliament of Canada to admit Rupert's Land and the North-western Territory, or either of them, into the Union, on such Terms and Conditions in each case as are in the Addresses expressed and as the Queen thinks fit to approve, subject to the Provisions of this Act; and the Provisions of any Orders in Council in that Behalf shall have effect as if they had been enacted by the Parliament of the United Kingdom of Great Britain and Ireland. . . .

Grey, took the initiative by discussing the idea with the lieutenant governors of the provinces. In the early 1850's there was a move for confederation of the maritime provinces, comprising New Brunswick, Nova Scotia, and Prince Edward Island.

It was not until 1864, however, that a significant meeting was held among provinces to discuss confederation. The three maritime provinces agreed to meet at Charlottetown, Prince Edward Island, and they hastened into action when the province of Canada asked to send representatives. The conference met on September 1, 1864; when the talks took a favorable turn and the delegates of the provinces said they had a detailed plan to propose, it was agreed to hold another session in Quebec on October 10. Newfoundland joined this conference.

Presiding over the conference was Sir Etienne-Paschal Taché of Canada East, who had won respect for his work in public life and who had agreed in 1864 to head a coalition ministry pledged to achieve confederation. By October 29, when the conference adjourned, it had adopted 72 resolutions involving confederation.

Yet there remained considerable disagreement over the kind of confederation, or union, that would be best. One difference developed between those who wanted a national government that would leave the provinces with little power and those who wanted to safeguard provincial rights. In the end the provincial rights advocates prevailed. As a result, the resolutions of the October conference were rejected by both Newfoundland and Prince Edward Island.

British North America Act.

After a final conference in London, with both the Canadians and the British represented, Parliament on March 28, 1867, passed the British North America Act (later also called the Constitution Act). It provided that on July 1, 1867, the Dominion of Canada would be established. At first the intention had been to call the new confederation the Kingdom of Canada, but fears were expressed that there would be a hostile reaction to this designation in the United States.

To begin with, the new Dominion consisted of only four provinces: Ontario (formerly Canada West or Upper Canada), Quebec (formerly Canada East or Lower Canada), New Brunswick, and Nova Scotia. Although the other provinces, i.e., Prince Edward Island and Newfoundland, had participated in all the discussions of confederation, they did not join until later.

The Dominion of Canada had an upper house, called the Senate, and a House of Commons. The 72 senators were appointed by the governor-general, with 24 each from Ontario and Quebec and twelve each from New Brunswick and Nova Scotia. Among the qualifications for senators were that they be at least 30 years old and have real and personal property worth at least $4000 "over and above Debts and Liabilities." The House of Commons consisted of 181 members, apportioned on the basis of population so that Ontario would hold 82 seats, Quebec 65, Nova Scotia 19, and New Brunswick 15.

The largest part of the confederation would consist of the province of Canada, but Nova Scotia and New Brunswick were important parts of the new Dominion. Nova Scotia had been claimed and settled as Acadia by the French, but had been a British possession since 1713. It had first had a legislature in 1759; in 1838 separate legislative and executive councils were formed. Responsible government was granted in 1847 and the first liberal ministry took office in 1848. There was considerable opposition to the idea of confederation, but the forces in favor of joining the Dominion prevailed.

What became the province of New Brunswick (1784) had earlier been considered by the French part of Acadia. After the French were driven from North America, British and American colonial officers, as well as others, began to settle the region, causing friction with wealthy landholders of Nova Scotia who had grants there. As a result, in 1784 the British government created the province of New Brunswick, with its own governor, legislature, and judiciary. The first legislature met in 1786. As in Nova Scotia, there was some opposition to joining the confederation, but in the end New Brunswick became one of the four founding provinces of the Dominion of Canada.

The British North America Act gave Canada self-government internally. The British Parliament held reserve powers and could change the governmental system if it so desired. Executive authority continued to be vested in the British monarch. In effect, Canada had to ask Great Britain for permission to amend its constitution. Foreign affairs remained in British hands. The division of powers between the federal government and the provinces was spelled out: each province was to have a lieutenant governor appointed by the governor-general. Although the provincial lieutenant governor had extensive powers, each province had its own legislature. The provinces also had almost unlimited power over educational policy. Independence of judges was safeguarded. Provision was made for admitting other colonies as provinces of the federal Dominion.

Near the end of the act, special provision was made for the "immediate construction" by the federal government of an Intercolonial Railway. It was to be completed "with all practicable speed."

The city of Ottawa, in southeastern Ontario, just across the Ottawa River from the Province of Quebec, became the capital of the Dominion. It had been selected by Queen Victoria in 1857 as the permanent capital of the province of Canada and government departments had moved there in mid-November of 1865.

New Dominion.

The first prime minister of the Dominion was John A. Macdonald, who in 1864 had become one of the leaders of the "Great Coalition," which was the ministry pledged to bring about confederation. The other two leaders were George-Ètienne Cartier and George Brown (1818–1880). Brown was a Liberal who resigned in December, 1865, because he could no longer work amicably with his Conservative colleagues.

This ministry had played a leading role both in Canada and in England in bringing about confederation. Macdonald was one of the most influential members of the Charlottetown Conference in 1864. That same year, at the Quebec Conference, he wrote many of the resolutions approved by that body. He was disappointed, however, that the final confederation did not provide for a stronger union, with more power to the central government.

Macdonald became prime minister on July 1, 1867, and the first Canadian parliament met in November. Macdonald was eager to increase the influence of the Dominion, so he started a legislative process for acquiring the land of the Hudson's Bay Company. In 1859 the British government had refused to renew the license of the company and in 1863 its shares were taken over by the International Financial Society, a group that intended to establish telegraphic communications, among other systems, and to sell land to settlers.

JOHN A. MACDONALD *led the fight to bring about confederation.*

NATIONAL FILM BOARD OF CANADA

On June 22, 1869, this society agreed officially to sell Rupert's Land to the Dominion for £300,000, but it retained the rights to one-twentieth of the land in arable regions. Though most of the land taken over became the Northwest Territories, much of the area of Canada's western provinces was carved also out of this vast region.

Manitoba was the first province to be added to the Dominion from land formerly belonging to the Hudson's Bay Company. Established in 1870, it was at first known as the "postage stamp province" because of its shape and extent of only 14,240 square miles. Enlarged in 1881, in 1912 it reached its present size with its extension to Hudson Bay. Two more portions of the former Rupert's Land eventually became Alberta and Saskatchewan. They were first established as administrative districts in the southwestern part of the Northwest Territories in 1882 and became provinces in 1905.

On the Pacific coast, British Columbia, which had had its own government for some time, became a member of the confederation in 1871 by its own choice, but it did so with the proviso that a transcontinental railroad to link it to the eastern provinces be built within ten years. This the Macdonald government was happy to agree to.

Prince Edward Island, which had been claimed by France as early as 1534 and named by the French Île-Saint-Jean, became British territory in 1763 by the treaty that ended French rule in this region. It was renamed in 1799 in honor of Edward, duke of Kent, commander of British forces in Canada at the time, who later became the father of the future Queen Victoria. Representatives of the island's government took part in the conferences that preceded confederation, but they objected to many of the specific proposals for the union. Both a public meeting and the legislature rejected the proposed plan. In 1873, however, the island, which had a weak economy and which was nearly bankrupt, was willing to join the Dominion. It did so but asked and received from England an increase in its annual subsidy.

In 1880 and again in 1895, Great Britain transferred territory it claimed in North America to Canada so that the Dominion would include all of North America north of the United States, except for Alaska and Newfoundland, which remained a separate British colony. The Dominion thus stretched well above the Arctic Circle and included the islands of the Arctic Archipelago, which in 1897 were made part of the Northwest Territories.

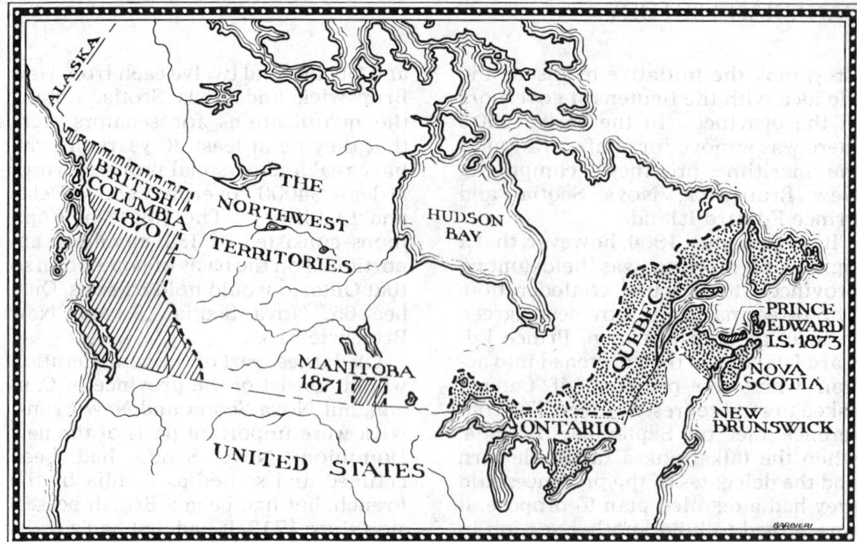

CANADA IN 1873 *consisted of the four original provinces (Ontario, Quebec, New Brunswick, and Nova Scotia) plus three new provinces—Prince Edward Island, Manitoba, and British Columbia.*

FORT GARRY (below)*, center of the Red River settlement, was seized briefly in 1870 by Louis Riel. Father André* (above, center)*, Chief Poundmaker* (left)*, and Little Bear* (right) *appear in the front row of this 1885 photo.*

The Red River Rebellion.

The early days of the new Dominion were not entirely peaceful. The move to take over the Hudson's Bay Company land and to establish the new province of Manitoba, which was centered on the Red River settlement, aroused mixed feelings among those who inhabited the area. Retired clerks and traders of the company did not want a change in government; this also applied to the so-called English halfbreeds, descendants of Scottish and English traders and their Indian wives, many of whom were now farmers. Even more resistant to change were the Métis, the French halfbreeds, who were also known as *bois-brûlés.* They thought, correctly, that any influx of settlers would bring in English and Protestant people opposed to their Catholicism and their somewhat nomadic way of life, which was built around the fur trade and the hunting of buffalo, much in the manner of the Indians of the western plains of Canada and the United States.

On the other side were newcomers from eastern Canada and a considerable number of Americans who had moved north of the border into the region. Both of these groups were in favor of Dominion rule as opposed to that of the Hudson's Bay Company. Some of the Americans advocated annexing the land to the United States. Actions of the Canadian government increased the fears of the Métis. A company of road builders came to the Red River area in 1868. In 1869 they were followed by surveyors who arrived to lay out townships. Both trespassed on farmland of the Métis.

At this juncture a leader stepped forward for the Métis. He was Louis Riel (1844–1885), who was born in the Red River settlement and educated in Montreal. Returning to the settlement in 1868, he organized resistance to the proposed takeover of Rupert's Land: he believed there was no guarantee of Métis rights. On October 11, 1869, Riel led a group that prevented a surveying party from carrying on its work on Métis land. The group stood on the chains of the surveyors, who withdrew in the face of the confrontation.

The Métis began to organize more formally; by October 24 they had formed a 200-man armed unit that soon grew to about 600 men. On December 1, 1869, William McDougall (1822–1905), representing the Dominion, crossed the border into what had been Rupert's Land and declared Canadian sovereignty. In reply, Riel on December 7 proclaimed an independent provisional government, retroactive to November 24. He and his followers were in possession of Fort Garry (present-day Winnipeg).

In March, 1870, Riel's illegal provisional government sent to Dominion officials in Ottawa a list of rights that they demanded be allowed them in any takeover of the land. A pro-Canadian government group raided Fort Garry and considerable turmoil followed. In the end, the main features of the list of rights were included in the act that established the province of Manitoba. Riel remained at Fort Garry and was prepared to turn over the government to Adams G. Archibald (1814–1892), a lawyer and an advocate of confederation who had been named the first lieutenant governor of Manitoba and the Northwest Territories. However, when a force of British and Canadian troops arrived ahead of Archibald on August 24, Riel fled.

Riel went to the United States only to return on September 17 to involve himself in a proposal that the Métis assist an invasion of Manitoba from the United States by the Fenian Brotherhood. He decided against such a plan and in October, 1871, led a Métis group that assembled to repel any such attempt. In 1873 Riel was elected to the House of Commons, then fled once more to the United States. He suffered a mental breakdown and was in institutions for two years from January, 1876, to 1878. Riel became an American citizen in 1883, but his career in Canadian affairs was far from over.

This unrest in the West was one reason for the establishment of the North West Mounted Police in 1873. Their original task was to control the Indians, to protect them from traders who supplied them with whiskey, and to police the new Dominion territory. King Edward VII granted the use of the prefix Royal in 1904, and in 1920 the official name became the Royal Canadian Mounted Police. The force now provides police service for all the provinces except Ontario and Quebec and numbers about 14,000.

Foreign affairs. The fact that Canada had no status in international affairs apart from its subordinate position in relation to Great Britain was demonstrated at the time the Treaty of Washington was negotiated in 1871. Prime Minister Macdonald attended, but only as a member of the British delegation. The negotiations concerned a number of matters that were at issue between the United States and Great Britain, but only two of them directly affected Canada.

One concerned fishing rights for Americans in Canadian waters. The Reciprocal Treaty of 1854 had given the United States certain rights, but these had expired when the United States abrogated the treaty in 1866. Canada then imposed a license fee on American fishermen which they resented and tried to evade. In Washington Macdonald made an effort to secure renewal of trade reciprocity in return for granting fishing rights again, but the British did not care to make an issue of this. Accordingly, the Americans were given the fishing rights for a ten-year period with no strings attached. To soothe the Canadians, the British agreed to reimburse them for losses resulting from the Fenian raids into Canada from the United States.

The other matter of Canadian interest concerned the San Juan boundary dispute, also called the Northwest boundary dispute, between England and the United States over the line to be drawn between British Columbia and

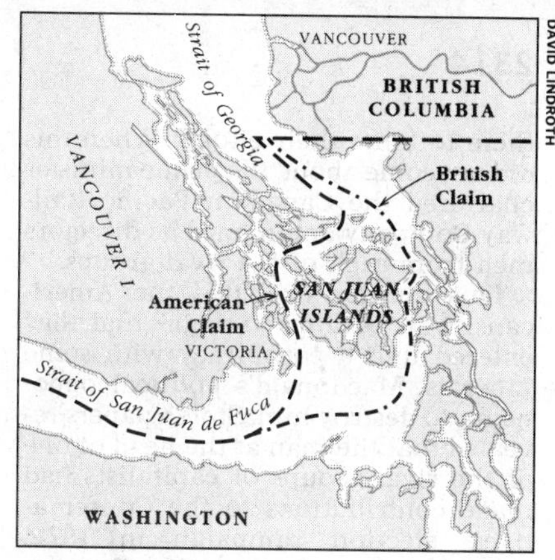

THIS MAP *shows 1872 British and U.S. Pacific boundaries.*

the state of Washington. In 1846 the agreement concerning the Oregon Territory had fixed a line through the middle of the channel between Vancouver Island and the mainland and through the middle of Juan de Fuca Strait. The strait, however, has several channels and so there was disagreement as to the ownership of several islands. One of them was San Juan Island, which had been occupied by U.S. troops in 1859. Joint occupation was then agreed on and the new treaty provided that Emperor William I of Germany would arbitrate the issue. In 1872 he decided on a line that gave the island to the United States.

In a gesture that to some extent acknowledged Canada had an official part to play in such negotiations, the British asked the Canadian parliament to ratify the treaty. Although there was considerable bitterness over the grant of fishing rights, the legislators did so.

In 1879 Canada began in a small way to have its own diplomatic representatives abroad. With the consent of the British government, Alexander Galt (1817–1893), who had been in the House of Assembly, had held other government positions, and had been active in the movement for confederation, was appointed to negotiate trade agreements with France and Spain. He became Canada's first high commissioner in London, a post he held from 1880 to 1883. In 1882 Hector Fabre (1834–1910), a journalist and lawyer who was appointed to the Dominion Senate in 1875, was named agent general for Canada in Paris. He held the post until his death.

Pacific scandal. Prime Minister Macdonald's moves to carry out the promise to British Columbia to build a transcontinental railway ended in political disaster for him. Two rival groups of capitalists wanted to secure the contract and one of them included some Americans. They were suspected of joining the enterprise merely to delay matters to protect the Union Pacific Railroad, in which they had an interest. One group of capitalists was centered in Montreal, the other in Toronto, and Macdonald tried to get them to unite their efforts. When this did not come about, the prime minister chartered the Canadian Pacific Railway Company and named as directors men from each of the rival groups.

This charter excluded the Americans, who became so angry that they entered into a conspiracy with some Liberals, Macdonald's political opponents, to destroy him. Stolen papers revealed that the man at the head of one of the rival groups of capitalists had made contributions to the Conservatives' election campaign in 1872. While some of the contributions seemed to have been given freely, others appeared to have resulted from demands for money. When a committee appointed to investigate the matter brought in a damaging report to parliament, the Conservative government of Macdonald was forced out of office on November 3, 1873.

Macdonald was succeeded by Alexander Mackenzie (1822–1892), who was born in Scotland and emigrated to Canada in 1842. He became active in reform politics in 1851 and was elected to parliament in 1867 when confederation took effect. In the election of January 22, 1874, Mackenzie and the Liberals won 133 of the 206 seats in the House of Commons. Overly cautious, he did not accomplish much. He preferred to have the government, instead of private interests, build the transcontinental railroad, but sufficient public funds for such a large project were not available. Mackenzie proposed therefore to build a series of portage roads to connect with the Great Lakes and to construct a short rail line on Vancouver Island. Public opinion in British Columbia was outraged at what appeared to be a failure to keep a promise and the province threatened to secede.

Macdonald returned to office in 1878 after an election on September 17 in which the Conservatives reversed the results of the previous election and won 137 of the 206 seats in the House. He then held the office of prime minister until his death in 1891. Among the problems he dealt with during that time was the issue of a transcontinental railroad. In 1880 the Canadian Pacific Railway Company was incorporated; the line was completed in 1885.

The Northwest Rebellion. In 1885 revolt flared up again with the start of the Northwest Rebellion. As in the earlier Red River Rebellion, Louis Riel was the leader of the Métis, this time along with two Indian leaders, Big Bear (d. 1888) and Poundmaker (1826–1886). Big Bear and Poundmaker were chiefs of the Crees. At this time in the valley between the North and South Saskatchewan rivers there was a good deal of discontent on the part of whites, halfbreeds, and Indians. They felt that the government in Ottawa had no understanding of their problems. The Indians and halfbreeds saw the buffalo, on which they had largely depended for food for a long time, disappearing. Farms and railroads were destroying their way of life. The English population, for its part, wanted representative government and a lowering of tariffs on American agricultural machinery and tools.

A petition setting forth all the grievances was agreed upon and sent to Ottawa on December 16, 1884, but there was no reaction. As a result, by February, 1885, Riel talked of forming a provisional, independent government. He was at this time suffering from delusions, believing he was a prophet, that changes should be made in the Catholic liturgy, and that the local bishop should become the pope of North America. As a result, he soon lost the support of the English-speaking settlers and of many of the Métis, who were staunch Catholics.

In March, 1885, hostilities began between the rebels and a military force that had been sent to keep order. On March 30 Poundmaker and his Indians overran a settlement, although the residents escaped to safety, but on April 2 Big Bear massacred all the whites at Frog Lake except for three who were taken prisoner and one who escaped. Further fighting was for a while inconclusive, but gradually the better organized government forces got the upper hand.

Eventually all three ringleaders were captured and tried; Riel was condemned to death. Though he was granted three reprives, and a commission considered the matter of his sanity, he was hanged on November 16, 1885. The two Indian chiefs were sentenced to prison. Eleven other Indians were sentenced to death, but three had their sentences commuted. Echoes of the rebellion and its aftermath were felt for some time in the East, where many in Quebec regarded Riel as a hero who had defended French-Canadian rights. To most of Ontario, however, he was a man who had rebelled against the legitimate government twice, taken to arms, and so deserved his fate.

Jesuits' Estates Act. An act of the Quebec provincial legislature in 1888 again raised controversial issues in the French- and the English-speaking sections of Canada, pointing up their separation in matters of religion and culture. This act was passed on July 12, 1888, at the insistence of Honoré Mercier (1840–1894), who had become premier of Quebec in 1886. Its purpose was to compensate the Jesuits for land that belonged to them before the pope suppressed the Society of Jesus in 1773.

After the last Jesuit missionary died in 1800, the land was taken over by the British Crown. The estates had been given to the Jesuits to provide funds for education, so in 1832 the revenues were assigned for educational purposes. The Jesuit order was revived in 1814 and in 1842 was invited to take up again its educational work in Quebec. By 1880 there was a growing opinion that the Jesuits should be compensated for their lost lands. Mercier's act appropriated $400,000 for this purpose, of which the Protestant School Board would receive $60,000. The rest was to be divided among Roman Catholic bodies in a manner to be left to the pope to decide.

The act was popular in Quebec but it did not please public opinion in Ontario, especially in the Orange Order, a militant Protestant group. They did not want the pope to be named in an act of a Canadian legislature. Efforts were made to get Prime Minister Macdonald and the Dominion government to cancel the act, but Macdonald refused, believing it to be a matter for the province to decide since it concerned education.

Manitoba Schools Act. Another act of a provincial legislature touched off a similar controversy between the French- and English-speaking people of Canada. This was the Manitoba Schools Act of March 31, 1890. When the province of Manitoba was created 20 years before, the school system was modeled on that of Quebec, with books, instruction, and funds shared between the two language interests. As time went on, however, further immigration into Manitoba was predominantly that of English-speaking people. This migration changed the balance in the schools as well as elsewhere. The situation was deliberately aggravated in 1889 by D'Alton McCarthy (1836–1898), a lawyer who served in parliament from 1876 until his death. He was a conservative Protestant who came into Manitoba to inflame opinion against the Jesuits' Estates Act.

Anti-Catholic and anti-French feeling built up. The result was the enactment of a law that abolished denominational schools and the use of the French language in schools. Not only French-Canadians in Manitoba, but those of Quebec, were outraged and appealed to the courts. The government in Ottawa was also asked to intervene, although by the terms of confederation, educational matters were to be supervised only by the provinces.

In 1897 a new Liberal ministry in Ottawa worked out an agreement whereby any school in Manitoba attended by ten or more children who spoke a language other than English would teach those children in their own language. In the long run, however, this arrangement did not work. After 1900 immigration to Manitoba consisted largely of persons who, when they came, spoke neither English nor

French. Multilingual schools then posed a formidable practical problem. The result was an act in 1916 making English the only language to be used in the schools for instructional purposes.

Laurier and the Liberals.

Macdonald's death in 1891 resulted in a breakup of the Conservative Party. The election of June, 23, 1896, confirmed Liberal strength when the Conservatives won only 89 seats in the House of Commons to the Liberals' 117. Wilfrid Laurier (1841–1919) became the new prime minister, the first French-Canadian to hold the post. He had already been active in politics, having held a seat in the Commons from 1874.

Laurier had a national outlook: he saw the Dominion as more important than its parts, and Canada as a nation independent of British empire interests though solidly loyal to the Crown. He organized a cabinet of likeminded leaders. His decision to expand the railway system, always a controversial subject in Canada, caused a rift in the party, but two new lines were begun, the Grand Trunk Pacific and the National Transcontinental.

UPI/BETTMANN NEWSPHOTOS

GOLD PROSPECTORS *in Dawson in the Yukon usually paid for their supplies with gold dust, as shown in this 1898 photo.*

Laurier took an active part in Canada's relations with Great Britain. He attended a colonial conference in London in 1897 at the time of Queen Victoria's Diamond Jubilee, and two others in 1902 and 1907. At all of these Laurier refused to commit Canada to proposals that, he believed, would pledge Canada to action in areas where it would not have a proper share in deciding on the policies involved, such as imperial defense. In 1907, for example, Laurier refused to allow Canada to contribute to the cost of the British navy, but three years later he proposed, without the full support of the Liberal Party, that Canada build a small naval force of its own. This issue helped lead to Laurier's defeat in 1911.

The problem of relations with Great Britain was especially acute at the outbreak of the Boer War (1899–1902) in South Africa. Laurier's government decided to send a contingent of soldiers to fight with the British forces. In all about 7300 Canadian troops went to South Africa. This action, however, caused another rift in the Liberal Party because the Quebec branch opposed helping England.

A longstanding dispute over the boundary between the Alaskan panhandle and British Columbia was settled in 1903 by a commission made up of Canadians, British, and Americans. The question of where the boundary should be located had become important in recent years because of the gold rush in the Yukon in 1896. The British representatives sided with the Americans, and awarded the United States almost all it claimed. The implication to the Canadians was that Great Britain was so eager to have America on its side in world affairs that it would sacrifice Canadian interests to do so.

In 1911 Canada and the United States negotiated a new reciprocal trade agreement. By its terms, Canadian food products could enter the United States free of duty. In return, Canada would reduce its tariffs on American manufactured goods. At first there was little opposition, although the Canadian Conservative Party was against it. Then Canadian industrialists, who were beginning to build up a substantial market in their own country, voiced opposition, as did the railway interests. The agreement was approved by the American Congress, although more trouble was caused in Canada when one influential congressman said that he saw the pact as a step toward joining Canada to the United States. In Canada 18 Liberals who had close ties to banking and insurance interests abandoned their party on the issue. Consequently, the agreement was not approved.

Laurier felt compelled to resign the prime ministership, and an election was held on September 21, 1911. The Conservative Party was voted into office with 132 seats in the Commons. The new prime minister was Robert L. Borden (1854–1937) of Nova Scotia, who had been elected to parliament in 1896 and who became the leader of the Conservative Party in 1901.

World War I.

As a dominion within the British empire, Canada had no official voice in matters of war and peace. Thus, when Great Britain declared war on Germany on August 4, 1914, Canada was at war as well. In fact, the Dominion had no hesitation about doing its part, although many French-Canadians were less than enthusiastic when it came to serving in the army. They felt that their language was a barrier to promotion. French-Canadians were badly underrepresented during the war, especially in the higher ranks.

By the time the war ended in 1918, Canada had put 628,000 men and women in uniform, about two-thirds of whom eventually saw service overseas. Casualties were high, with 48,121 dead or missing and about 175,000 wounded, these falling on a population of only 7.5 million people.

One reason for the high toll was the way in which the Canadian troops were used. Their spirit made them crack shock troops. Only two months after they arrived in France, in April, 1915, Canadian soldiers withstood the first gas attack in the history of warfare; it was launched against them by the Germans in the Ypres salient in northwest Belgium. By August, 1916, four divisions were in France, constituting a separate Canadian corps. During 1916 the Canadians fought in several desperate battles on the Somme, where casualties were overwhelming. It was there that these troops established their reputation.

The Canadians exhibited their valor again on April 9 and 10, 1917, at Vimy Ridge in northern France. The battle was predominantly a Canadian operation and it earned a well-deserved victory. Canada's memorial to its war dead was erected here after the war. Finally, the Canadian corps played a key role in the last great struggles of 1918 when the Hindenburg line was broken. On August 8, at the Battle of Amiens, Canadians were the spearhead of a vital breakthrough.

On the home front during the war, a bitter political battle arose over the

STATUTE OF WESTMINSTER, 1931

An Act to give effect to certain resolutions passed by Imperial Conference held in the years 1926 and 1930
11th December, 1931.

WHEREAS the delegates to His Majesty's Governments in the United Kingdom, the Dominion of Canada, the Commonwealth of Australia, the Dominion of New Zealand, the Union of South Africa, the Irish Free State and Newfoundland, at Imperial Conferences holden at Westminster in the years of our Lord nineteen hundred and twenty-six and nineteen hundred and thirty did concur in making the declarations and resolutions set forth in the Reports of the said Conferences:

AND WHEREAS it is meet and proper to set out by way of preamble to this Act that, inasmuch as the Crown is the symbol of the free association of the members of the British Commonwealth of Nations, and as they are united by a common allegiance to the Crown, it would be in accord with the established constitutional position of all the members of the Commonwealth in relation to one another that any alteration in the law touching the Succession to the Throne or the Royal Style and Titles shall hereafter require the assent as well of the Parliaments of all the Dominions as of the Parliament of the United Kingdom:

AND WHEREAS it is in accord with the established constitutional position that no law hereafter made by the Parliament of the United Kingdom shall extend to any of the said Dominions as part of the law of that Dominion otherwise than at the request and with the consent of that Dominion.

AND WHEREAS it is necessary for the ratifying, confirming and establishing of certain of the said declarations and resolutions of the said Conferences that a law be made and enacted in due form by authority of the Parliament of the United Kingdom:

AND WHEREAS the Dominion of Canada, the Commonwealth of Australia, the Dominion of New Zealand, the Union of South Africa, the Irish Free State and Newfoundland have severally requested and consented to the submission of a measure to the Parliament of the United Kingdom for making such provision with regard to the matters aforesaid as is hereafter in this Act contained:

Now, THEREFORE, be it enacted by the King's Most Excellent Majesty by and with the advice and consent of the Lords Spiritual and Temporal, and Commons, in this present Parliament assembled, and by the authority of the same, as follows:

1. In this Act the expression "Dominion" means any of the following Dominions, that is to say, the Dominion of Canada, the Commonwealth of Australia, the Dominion of New Zealand, the Union of South Africa, the Irish Free State and Newfoundland.

2. (1) The Colonial Laws Validity Act, 1865, shall not apply to any law made after the commencement of this Act by the Parliament of a Dominion.

(2) No law and no provision of any law made after the commencement of this Act by the Parliament of a Dominion shall be void or inoperative on the ground that it is repugnant to the law of England, or to the provisions of any existing or future Act of Parliament of the United Kingdom, or to any order, rule, or regulation made under any such Act, and the powers of the Parliament of a Dominion shall include the power to repeal or amend any such Act, order, rule or regulation in so far as the same is part of the law of the Dominion.

3. It is hereby declared and enacted that the Parliament of a Dominion has full power to make laws having extra-territorial operation.

4. No Act of Parliament of the United Kingdom passed after the commencement of this Act shall extend or be deemed to extend, to a Dominion as part of the law of that Dominion, unless it is expressly declared in that Act that that Dominion has requested, and consented to, the enactment thereof.

5. Without prejudice to the generality of the foregoing provisions of this Act, sections seven hundred and thirty-five and seven hundred and thirty-six of the Merchant Shipping Act, 1894, shall be construed as though reference therein to the Legislature of a British possession did not include reference to the Parliament of a Dominion.

6. Without prejudice to a generality of the foregoing provisions of this Act, section four of the Colonial Courts of Admiralty Act, 1890 (which requires certain laws to be reserved for the signification of His Majesty's pleasure or to contain a suspending clause), and so much of section seven of that Act as requires the approval of His Majesty in Council to any rules of Court for regulating the practice and procedure of a Colonial Court of Admiralty, shall cease to have effect in any Dominion as from the commencement of this Act.

7. (1) Nothing in this Act shall be deemed to apply to the repeal, amendment or alteration of the British North America Acts, 1867 to 1930, or any order, rule or regulation made thereunder.

(2) The provisions of section two of this Act shall extend to laws made by any of the Provinces of Canada and to the powers of the legislatures of such Provinces.

(3) The powers conferred by this Act upon the Parliament of Canada or upon the legislatures of the Provinces shall be restricted to the enactment of laws in relation to matters within the competence of the Parliament of Canada or of any of the legislatures of the Provinces respectively.

8. Nothing in this Act shall be deemed to confer any power to repeal or alter the Constitution or the Constitution Act of the Commonwealth of Australia or the Constitution Act of the Dominion of New Zealand otherwise than in accordance with the law existing before the commencement of this Act.

9. (1) Nothing in this Act shall be deemed to authorize the Parliament of the Commonwealth of Australia to make laws on any matter within the authority of the States of Australia, not being a matter within the authority of the Parliament or Government of the Commonwealth of Australia.

(2) Nothing in this Act shall be deemed to require the concurrence of the Parliament or Government of the Commonwealth of Australia, in any law made by the Parliament of the United Kingdom with respect to any matter within the authority of the States of Australia, not being a matter within the authority of the Parliament or Government of the Commonwealth of Australia, in any case where it would have been in accordance with the constitutional practice existing before the commencement of this Act that the Parliament of the United Kingdom should make that law without such concurrence.

(3) In the application of this Act to the Commonwealth of Australia the request and consent referred to in section four shall mean the request and consent of the Parliament and Government of the Commonwealth.

10. (1) None of the following sections of this Act, that is to say, sections two, three, four, five and six, shall extend to a Dominion to which this section applies as part of the law of that Dominion unless that section is adopted by the Parliament of the Dominion, and any Act of that Parliament adopting any section of this Act may provide that the adoption shall have effect either from the commencement of this Act or from such later date as is specified in the adopting Act.

(2) The Parliament of any such Dominion as aforesaid may at any time revoke the adoption of any section referred to in subsection (1) of this section.

(3) The Dominions to which this section applies are the Commonwealth of Australia, the Dominion of New Zealand and Newfoundland.

11. Notwithstanding anything in the Interpretation Act, 1889, the expression "Colony" shall not, in any Act of the Parliament of the United Kingdom passed after the commencement of this Act, include a Dominion or any Province or State forming part of a Dominion.

12. This Act may be cited as the Statute of Westminster, 1931.

issue of conscription. By 1917 not enough volunteers were coming forward to keep the ranks of the army filled in light of the unexpected length of the war and the heavy casualties. Prime Minister Borden's government felt it necessary to introduce a Military Service Bill in June, 1917. The Liberals were split on the issue, while the Conservatives, although on the whole favoring conscription, were not supported by their Quebec associates.

Conscription became law and the struggle over it was a main factor in bringing about a union government. An election on December 17 was fought between the Laurier Liberals, named for their leader, Wilfrid Laurier, who opposed conscription, and the Unionists led by Borden. The latter triumphed, winning 153 seats in the House of Commons. There were riots over conscription in Quebec City in March and April of 1918.

At the Paris Peace Conference in France after the war, Canada had its own representatives. It signed the Versailles Treaty on June 28, 1919, as a full national state. The important part Canada had played in support of Britain during the war thus paid off in enhanced status internationally. Canada began to expand its own diplomatic service and first exchanged ministers with the United States in 1927.

The war brought broad economic changes to the country. Agriculture expanded with the demand for foodstuffs. Prairie acreage under cultivation, for example, increased by four-fifths between 1913 and 1919. Industry also grew with the building of steel mills and shipyards. Overall the economy grew by 20 percent in this period, and Canada became a net lender instead of a borrower. On the other hand, a growing demand for goods and debt brought on by the large sums the government had to borrow to finance the war brought about an alarming inflation. The cost of living increased by 60 percent between the start of the war and 1918.

The wartime atmosphere speeded the granting of women's suffrage. The plains provinces allowed it in 1916 and others followed. The right to vote in Dominion-wide elections was granted in all provinces except Quebec by 1925. Quebec did not give the vote to women until 1940.

The 1920's. The dominant figure in Canadian politics between the two world wars was William Lyon Mackenzie King (1874–1950), grandson of the 19th-century leader William Lyon Mackenzie. He entered parliament as a Liberal in 1909 and the next year became a member of the cabinet as minister for labor. King was chosen leader of the Liberal Party in 1919 and rose to be prime minister after the election of December 6, 1921. The Liberals were a seat short of a majority in the House of Commons, but King secured the support of the Progressive Party. This new political group was organized in 1920, chiefly as a voice of western agricultural interests who thought they were neglected by the government in Ottawa. The Progressives won 65 seats in the 1921 election, 15 more than the Conservatives, making them the second largest party in parliament. A similar new political unit, the United Farmers of Alberta, governed that province from 1921 to 1935.

In the 1925 election, the Liberals lost seats, but King was able to stay in power until 1926. At that time he faced a vote of censure against his government because of a scandal in which the minister of customs was involved. Seeking to avoid the vote, King asked Julian Hedworth George (1862–1935), Lord Byng, the governor-general, to dissolve parliament and call an election. Normally such a request would not be made until the government had been defeated in parliament. Byng refused the request, whereupon King resigned without giving time, as was customary, for the governor-general to arrange for a successor. This was an unprecedented situation in terms of parliamentary procedure. It was not resolved until Arthur Meighen (1874–1960), the Conservative leader, King's successor, was defeated in a vote in the House of Commons, making it necessary to hold a general election. The Liberals won, increasing the number of seats they held, and King became prime minister again.

The Statute of Westminister. More formal recognition of the new status of Canada and the other self-governing British dominions resulting from their role in World War I came in 1926 at the Colonial Conference in London. Here Prime Minister King played a leading role in drafting the Balfour Declaration, named for Arthur Balfour (1848–1930), a former British prime minister. The declaration defined the dominions as "autonomous communities within the British Empire, equal in status and in no way subordinate one to another in any aspect of domestic or external affairs, though united by a common allegiance to the Crown and freely associated as members of the British Commonwealth of Nations."

The 1926 conference also established a committee to carry out a further study of the relationship of the dominions to the British government and the Crown. In 1929 this committee made its report, which was adopted at the next Colonial Conference in 1930. The end result was the Statute of Westminster, an act of the British Parliament on December 11, 1931. This statute made more legally binding the Balfour Declaration of 1926 and assured the dominions of their autonomous standing as full members of the Commonwealth.

The dominions could now make their own laws without the British Parliament having to legislate for them or approve their actions. The new statute also repealed some laws that had become obsolete in view of the new relationship between the mother country and the dominions. The Statute of Westminster applied in part to Australia, New Zealand, South Africa, the Irish Free State, and Newfoundland. It did not contravene the British North America Act of 1867, which remained in effect.

The Great Depression. The worldwide Depression that began with the crash of the American stock market in late October, 1929, demonstrated, as conditions worsened, that Canada was vulnerable to bad times in other lands. Agriculture was hit especially hard when other countries raised their tariffs on agricultural products, with the export of wheat suffering the most. Wheat production shrank from 567 million bushels in 1928 to 182 million by 1937, while the price of 38 cents a bushel by the end of 1932 did not cover the cost of growing it. In addition, drought in 1934 and 1937 ruined many crops.

The depression in agriculture was felt throughout the country. Railroads lost millions of dollars in freight revenue. Demand for manufactured goods slumped drastically, as did construction activity. By 1935 fully one-tenth of the population, both urban and rural, was receiving some kind of relief. With an estimated 23 percent of the labor force out of work by 1933, many Canadians left to emigrate to the United States, where the situation turned out to be no better.

An election on July 28, 1930, swept into power with a sizable majority the Conservative Party with Richard B. Bennett (1870–1947) as prime minister, showing that the Depression and the failure of the Liberal government under King to cope with it had turned Canadian politics around. In 1927 Bennett had succeeded Arthur Meighen as leader of the Conservative Party. Bennett was born in New Brunswick but moved west and in 1911 was elected to the House of Commons from Alberta.

The new administration promised to end unemployment by raising tariff barriers to eliminate competition from foreign goods of any kind. The general tariff level was raised by almost 50 percent in the hope that Canada would become self-sufficient by creating jobs to produce the goods that were to come in from foreign countries. Unfortunately for Canada, other nations had the same idea, especially the United States with its Smoot-Hawley tariff of 1930. For practical purposes, this tariff barred many of Canada's basic products from entering the United States. The government's action, however, did reduce imports and change a trade deficit into a surplus. It thereby kept unemployment from being as high as it might have been, but it raised costs for both producers and consumers and so did not do much to increase purchasing power.

Bennett also promised to stimulate the economy by building railroads, starting work on the St. Lawrence Seaway, and constructing a national highway. Parliament in September, 1930, not only raised tariffs but also voted $20 million for unemployment relief. At the Imperial Conference in London in 1930 and again at the Imperial Economic Conference in Ottawa in 1932, Bennett sought to improve matters by advocating a strong system of empire preference among the nations of the British Commonwealth. Thus Bennett for the most part adhered to conservative policies.

In January, 1935, however, Bennett suddenly announced a change of policy and advocated legislation much like that of the New Deal of President Franklin D. Roosevelt in the United States, calling for strong action by the federal government to deal directly with economic problems. Canada's parliament enacted legislation establishing minimum wages, limited hours of work per week, unemployment insurance, loans and credits for farmers, and control of unfair trade practices. These measures, however, did not remain in effect for long. Faced with court tests in 1937, they were held to be unconstitutional by the Privy Council in England.

As a political leader, Bennett was high-handed and unwilling to consult with his colleagues. For example, he demanded what amounted to a blank check for appropriations dealing with relief. He lost public confidence, resigned from the cabinet, and formed a faction of disgruntled Conservatives. A general election on October 4, 1935, put the Liberal Party in office with a large majority of the seats in the House of Commons. William Lyon Mackenzie King became prime minister once more, holding the office until November 15, 1948, when he was succeeded by a fellow Liberal, Louis St. Laurent (1882–1973).

The Depression brought into being new and radical political groups that began to influence Canadian life. Chief among them was the Social Credit Party, with its center in Alberta. Imported from England, the somewhat vague doctrine of "social credit" called for the redistribution of purchasing power. The ideas of social credit were picked up by William Aberhart (1878–1943), a Calgary teacher who was also a radio evangelist. One of his proposals was a "social dividend" of $25 a month to every person. Such ideas swept the province and in 1935 the Social Credit Party won control, with Aberhart as premier. That same year in the general election, the Social Credit Party won 17 seats in the federal parliament. In Alberta it stayed in power until 1971, although most of the social credit laws passed were declared unconstitutional.

UPI

THE ROYAL CANADIAN AIR FORCE *was famous for its courage during World War II. Canada went to war two years before the United States.*

In 1933, in Regina, the Cooperative Commonwealth Federation (C.C.F.) was founded, representing farm, labor, and socialist interests. In the 1935 election, the C.C.F. captured seven seats in the House of Commons; in 1961 it changed its name to the New Democratic Party.

Although a political opponent of Bennett, King now wished to carry out some of the same policies that, when submitted to the Privy Council in England, had been found to conflict with the British North America Act in that they would have allowed the central government to do what was reserved to the provinces. On the other hand, the provinces clearly could not cope with the Great Depression. King appointed a royal commission in 1937 to report on Canada's economic situation and on the measures to be taken to improve matters.

The commission's report in 1940 advocated what amounted to a rewriting of the British North America Act. However, when a provincial-federal conference was held, Ontario, Quebec, and British Columbia were so opposed to the recommendations that the meeting proved fruitless. An amendment that year to the act did allow the government in Ottawa to establish a system of unemployment insurance.

World War II. Such constitutional problems and conflicts of interest between the provinces and the central government were now overshadowed by World War II. Great Britain declared war on Germany on September 3, 1939, and Canada followed on September 10. Prime Minister King pledged that there would be no conscription for overseas service, which was to be voluntary; but under a national services act, men were drafted for defense within the western hemisphere.

As the war went on, with Germany inflicting crushing defeats on the Allies in 1940 and Japan entering the war in December, 1941, public support for conscription was voiced. Accordingly, a referendum was held on April 27, 1942, and the nation voted by a large margin to release the government from its no-conscription pledge. In the face of bitter opposition in Quebec, however, King did nothing to implement the vote until December, 1944, when his cabinet revolted because he had not acted.

One Canadian infantry division went to England in December, 1939. Later, two other infantry divisions, two armored divisions, and two armored brigades, along with other auxiliary services, went overseas. In all, Canada put about 1 million men and women into uniform: nearly 700,000 in the ground forces, 220,000 in the air force, and 90,000 in the navy. By the end of the war, 41,700 Canadians had been killed or were missing. Canada's representation in the air force was proportionately large because most of the training of pilots and air crews for the British Commonwealth was carried out in Canada, where space was available and facilities could be constructed with comparative ease and speed. In all, more than 131,000 airmen were trained.

On August 19, 1942, Canadian troops went into combat for the first time, in an action that proved disastrous. Two brigades and other units raided Dieppe, France, partly to test the German defenses and partly to keep Nazi forces pinned down. Of the approximately 5000 men who took part, 3367 were casualties, most of them taken prisoner.

As a unit of the British 8th Army, Canadian troops took part in the invasion of Sicily on July 10, 1943, and then engaged in the invasion of Italy. Eventually, Canadians participated in the capture of Rome on May 23, 1944.

The 3rd Canadian Division was one of the five Allied divisions to make the initial assault on the beaches of Normandy on D-Day, June 6, 1944. More Canadians were soon sent across the English Channel, and on July 23 the 1st Canadian Army was activated. These troops captured Caen on July 8–9, were worsted at Verrières Ridge on July 28, but captured Falaise on August 15. From then on, Canadians continued to fight on the left flank of the Allies, capturing the Scheldt area of Belgium against strong German resistance in November. In February, 1945, the 1st Army took part in the drive on the Siegfried Line and on into Germany. Some troops remained in Germany until April, 1946, as part of the Allied occupation forces.

In 1941, when Hong Kong fell to the Japanese, two Canadian battalions were present; they lost nearly as many men to harsh treatment in prison camps as in the defense of the colony. A squadron of the Royal Canadian Air Force fought in the Battle of Britain in 1940. The navy grew to 373 combat ships, its most valuable service in convoy operations. In 1943 the Canadian navy took over all such duties in the northwest Atlantic Ocean west of the 47th meridian.

Prime Minister King and President Franklin D. Roosevelt, in August, 1940, announced a Permanent Joint Board on Defense for their two countries. Canada took part in the crash research program that led to the atomic bomb, and cooperated with the United States in the construction of the 1523-mile Alaska Highway, which began in British Columbia and crossed the Yukon Territory to Fairbanks, Alaska.

As in World War I, Canada's economy expanded greatly during World War II. The passage of the National Resources Mobilization Act in June, 1940, was an indication of the determination of both the people and the government to make an all-out effort. By the end of the war, the government had invested $1.5 billion in the war industry. During the war, military products valuing more than $10 billion were produced. About two-thirds of these products went to Allied nations. The result of this stimulus to manufacturing was to accelerate the growth of Canada as a fully developed industrial state.

Agriculture suffered during the war because of the closing of many overseas markets, but the grain surpluses built up were badly needed after the end of hostilities. The cost of living was kept under control considering war time conditions, but the government had to borrow over $12 billion between 1939 and 1945. Nearly half of this came from individuals.

Postwar Canada. After the war, both Canada's standing and activity in international affairs increased. Canada joined the United Nations and all its specialized agencies. In 1949 Canada was the first nation to ratify the North Atlantic Treaty. In the Korean War, which began in 1950, Canada furnished an infantry brigade to the United Nations forces. In 1954 Canada became one of three nations that supervised the armistice in Southeast Asia. In 1956 the nation helped form the United Nations peacekeeping force in the Suez area, and in 1964 a similar force on Cyprus. Canada and the United States established a joint air defense command in 1958.

Several amendments to the British North America Act, passed by the British Parliament between 1949 and 1960, allowed the federal government to legislate in new areas. The most important amendment was that of December 16, 1949, which enabled the Canadian parliament to amend the constitution of its own accord in matters that affect the federal government but not the provinces. After this, the only area in which action by the British Parliament was necessary was in matters that affected both the Dominion and the provinces. However, formal assent of the British Crown was still required. An example was the royal assent given on August 10, 1960, to the passage of the Canadian Bill of Rights. Another amendment on May 31, 1951, approved the Old Age Security Act.

When King decided to retire in late 1948, he handpicked as his successor, Louis Stephen St. Laurent (1882–1973), a bilingual lawyer who had entered politics in 1941 as minister of justice in the King cabinet. St. Laurent was minister of external affairs from 1946 to 1948, and now became both leader of the Liberal Party and prime minister.

Canada enjoyed an economic boom while St. Laurent headed the government. He and the Liberals sponsored more social insurance legislation and supported the growth of educational facilities. The most permanent achievement of the St. Laurent administration was the construction of the St. Lawrence Seaway, although it was not completed until two years after St. Laurent left office.

THE 1600-MILE-LONG ALASKAN HIGHWAY, *built in seven months, officially opened to bus traffic in October, 1946*

HISTORICAL PICTURES SERVICE, CHICAGO

Built jointly with the United States, the seaway is a system of canals, dams, and locks that creates a shipping route from the Atlantic Ocean to the western end of the Great Lakes capable of handling oceangoing vessels. In all, it is 2342 miles long. The Canadian government first approved the start of construction in 1951. The seaway was formally opened by a ceremony at St. Lambert, Quebec, attended by Queen Elizabeth II and President Dwight D. Eisenhower of the United States.

By the second half of the 1950's, the Liberals, who had been in power for two decades, gave evidence of arrogance. This trend was apparent in 1956 when they used harsh parliamentary tactics to close down debate and force through parliament a questionable project for the building of the Trans-Canada Pipeline.

An election on June 10, 1957, proved the voters to be disenchanted with the Liberal Party. The Progressive Conservative Party, as the representatives of the right now called themselves, won the most seats in parliament, but not a clear majority. Even so, with the aid of third-party groups, John George Diefenbaker (1895–1979) took office as prime minister. He had first been elected to parliament in 1940 and was chosen the leader of the Progressive Conservative Party the year before he became prime minister.

Diefenbaker's ministry was not active, and little of a constructive nature was undertaken. In foreign affairs, Canadian policy became more nationalistic and more independent of both Great Britain and the United States. The United States, for example, imposed an embargo on the sale and shipment of grain to the People's Republic of China in 1960, but Canada made large wheat sales there.

Canadian voters approved of Diefenbaker, as shown in the election of March 31, 1958, in which they voted into the House of Commons 208 Progressive Conservatives as against only 57 candidates of all other parties. The tilt to the right, however, did not last long. A controversy over the use of nuclear warheads on Canadian strategic weapons was one factor in the defeat of Diefenbaker in the election of April 18, 1963.

In this election the Liberal Party won more seats than any other party; although it did not have an absolute majority, it was able to form a government with Lester Bowles Pearson (1897–1972) as prime minister. A veteran of World War I and a former university professor of history, Pearson had had a long and arduous career as a diplomat. In 1945 he had been Canada's most important diplomat at the conference in San Francisco that organized the United Nations. He then headed Canada's delegation to the new international body. For his work there in resolving the Arab-Israeli war of 1956, he received the Nobel Prize for Peace in 1957.

Pearson had been elected to parliament in 1948. He was minister of external affairs and a leader in the activities of the Commonwealth of Nations. He also played a major role in the formation of the North Atlantic Treaty Organization in 1949. He was elected leader of the Liberal Party in 1958. During his administration, a pensions act was passed in 1965 and a medical insurance law in 1966. Federal assistance to schools and universities was increased. While he was prime minister a new Canadian flag with a maple leaf design was adopted, in 1964, and the 100th anniversary of confederation, in 1967, was highlighted by a world's fair, Expo '67, in Montreal.

CANADIAN CONSULATE GENERAL

EXPO '67, *a major world's fair, was held in Montreal in 1967, attracting millions. In 1976, the city was host to the summer Olympic Games.*

The troubled provinces. The 1960's were a period of agitation because French-speaking Canadians, most of whom reside in Quebec, wanted to protect themselves from what they saw as a danger of being overwhelmed by English-speaking Canada. They believed they were politically and economically disadvantaged because the rest of Canada refused to adopt bilingualism to any extent. As a result of the unrest, the Ottawa government, in 1963, named the Royal Commission on Bilingualism and Biculturalism. The commission recommended in 1967 that both English and French be made official in the federal government and that in any province where the minority, either French or English, reached 10 percent, both languages should be official. This latter proposal was enacted into law in 1969. A second report the next year said that children should have the right to be educated in whichever of the official languages they chose.

A large number of French-Canadians wanted to go even further and declare Quebec independent of and separated from the Dominion. The situation was brought to a boil by President Charles de Gaulle of France when he visited Quebec in July of 1967. In a speech in Montreal, he seemed to promise support for independence, exclaiming, *"Vive Québec libre"* ("Long live a free Quebec").

When Pearson retired in 1968, he was able to pass on the leadership of the Liberal Party and with it the office of prime minister to Pierre Elliott Trudeau (1919–   ). Trudeau was a lawyer and a law professor who had been elected to the House of Commons in 1965. He came from Quebec and in part was of French descent. In the election of June 25, 1968, the Liberals won a decisive victory with 155 seats in Commons.

Trudeau was somewhat isolationist, or at least resolved to show that Canada was not subservient to the United States in international affairs. In 1970 he recognized the People's Republic of China despite U.S. opposition. He withdrew some Canadian troops from the NATO forces in Europe. When a Quebec separatist group, the *Front de Libération du Québec,* carried on terrorist activities in 1970, Trudeau declared martial law and had hundreds of suspects rounded up. In domestic affairs he pursued a policy intended to make sure that his nation controlled its own economy in answer to fears that America was trying to dominate Canada.

Trudeau had to deal not only with the demands of Quebec but also with dissatisfaction from other provinces on other issues. He called a conference of all the provinces in June, 1968, at which provincial leaders argued for more tax sharing between the central government and themselves. Little came of the conference except an agreement to keep on studying the various problems.

The Quebec secessionist movement scored a striking victory on its home territory on November 16, 1976, when the *Parti Québécois* won 89 of the 110 seats in the provincial legislature. The Liberal Party was the big loser. The leader of the Quebec nationalists was the man who became premier of Quebec as the result of the vote, René Lévesque (1922–1987), born on the Gaspé Peninsula. Lévesque had been a war correspondent in World War II and had also served as an interpreter between the American forces and the Free French. In 1967 he was one of the founders of the *Parti Québécois.* Now, as premier, he put through the provincial legislature popular measures intended to improve the status of the French language and culture and other acts to increase the province's power in the fields of education and social welfare.

The animosity between French- and English-speaking Canada, and between the provinces and Ottawa over other issues, came to a head in 1980. Trudeau proposed a tax on natural gas

THE BILINGUAL TRADITION *is firmly fixed in the life of Canada. Even highway signs reflect this diversity.*

ANTMAN/ IMAGE WORKS

that would transfer revenue from the provinces to Ottawa. The western provinces, where most of the natural resources are centered, were solidly against this. In Quebec, on May 20, a referendum was held on a proposal to take the province out of the Dominion politically, although Lévesque declared he wanted to keep economic relations intact. Even French-speaking citizens, however, rejected this move, about 54 percent of them joining the English-speaking minority in voting no. In 1985 the *Parti Québécois* was voted out of office.

On November 10, 1987, Pierre Marc Johnson (1946–) resigned as leader of the *Parti Québécois* and gave up his seat in the provincial legislature. He had been provincial premier for a short time in 1985 after Lévesque resigned. Johnson's resignation was forced by the militants in the party who wanted to renew the campaign for the independence of Quebec. Johnson had proposed deferring any such action until after the next election in the province, to be held before December, 1990. The renewal of the fight for independence seemed to have been fueled by the emotion arising from the death on November 1, 1987, of Lévesque. At present, the Liberal Party government of Quebec, headed by Premier Robert Bourassa (1933–) and in power since the December, 1985, election, continues to receive a high rating in public opinion polls.

UPI

QUEEN ELIZABETH *signs the Constitution Act in April, 1982, giving Canada the right to amend its own constitution.*

A New Constitution

In spite of continuing evolution toward complete sovereignty, the fact remained that the Canadian government would not be truly and fully sovereign until it could freely amend its own constitution, consisting of the British North America Act and other acts, without referring the amendments to England for parliamentary approval and royal assent.

A movement to change this situation had begun as far back as 1927; but, as was to be true throughout the process, the federal government and the provinces found it hard to agree on proposed constitutional revisions. Plans drawn up in 1961 and 1964 were withdrawn when the provinces were not unanimous in supporting them. After Prime Minister Trudeau and the provincial premiers failed to agree at a meeting in September of 1980, the federal government began to prepare its own plan in October. A Special Joint Committee of the House of Commons and the Senate worked from November 6, 1980, to February 13, 1981, to draw up proposals. On February 17, 1981, debate began in parliament.

In general, the proposed new constitution was perceived as increasing the power of the federal government in relation to the powers of the provinces. As a result, the western provinces opposed the plan on the grounds that it would give too much control of their natural resources to the central government in Ottawa. Another source of opposition came from Quebec, which feared that more federal power would bring with it domination by English-speaking Canada, resulting in the destruction of French culture and the Roman Catholic religion.

In the end, these two major points of contention centered on a proposed bill of rights and on the process that Canada would employ to amend its constitution. The proposed rights bill was revised to make explicit the rights of Indians, Inuit (Eskimos), and women. Educational rights of the French-speaking minority outside Quebec and the English-speaking minority inside Quebec were extended.

A complicated system for amending the new constitution was finally agreed on by nine of the provinces, with Quebec dissenting. If the House of Commons and the Senate propose an amendment, it must be approved by the legislatures of at least two-thirds of the provinces having at least 50 percent of the population of all ten provinces. Thus, at least seven provinces must approve. Another provision, however, allows a province, by a majority vote of its legislature, to dissent. If that occurs, the amendment has no effect in that province. It also provided that a province may repeal its dissent.

After 18 months of debate, the House of Commons, on December 2, 1981, approved the new constitution by a vote of 246 to 24. The Senate soon followed. In England, by a 177 to 33 vote, the House of Commons gave its approval on March 8, 1982; the House of Lords approved on March 25. On the following day, Queen Elizabeth II gave her royal assent. In April the queen journeyed to Canada and, in Ottawa on April 17, signed the constitution in a formal ceremony. This was 115 years after her great-great-grandmother Queen Victoria had assented to the British North America Act.

In this manner was "patriated" (brought home) the Canadian constitution. It consisted of 24 domestic documents: 13 acts of the British Parliament, 7 acts of the Canadian parliament, and 4 British Orders-in-Council. Elizabeth II remained queen of Canada and head of state, and Canada was willing to remain in the Commonwealth of Nations.

The 1982 constitution consists largely of a charter of rights and freedoms and a section outlining the amendment procedure. It is specific as to the right of all Canadians to "enter, remain in, or leave Canada." Everyone is equal under the law without discrimination based on "race, national or ethnic origin, color, religion, sex, age, or mental or physical disability."

English and French are the official languages and have equal rights in government. Language rights in some of the provinces are spelled out, and in all of them with regard to educational facilities. The existing aboriginal and treaty rights are affirmed. The term aboriginal here applies not only to Indians and Inuit but also to the Métis.

Recent trends and events.

Trudeau led the Liberal Party to victory in October, 1972, and again in July, 1974, but his role as head of government was briefly interrupted in 1979 when an election in May gave the Progressive Conservative Party more seats than the Liberals but not an absolute majority. Charles Joseph Clark (1939–) became prime minister, but only until March, 1980. An election the month before returned the Liberals to power with an absolute majority in

UPI/BETTMANN NEWSPHOTOS

THE SKYLINE OF CALGARY, *with the Saddledome in the forefront, will remind visitors for years that the city played host to the 1988 Winter Olympics.*

the House of Commons. The New Democratic Party reached its peak to date, winning 32 seats.

In June, 1984, Trudeau stepped down as prime minister. He was succeeded by John N. Turner (1929–), who served as prime minister for a short time. An election on September 4, 1984, gave the Progressive Conservatives an overwhelming mandate. The Progressive Conservatives won 211 seats in the House against 40 for the Liberals and 30 for the New Democratic Party.

The new prime minister was Brian Mulroney (1939–), who had not hitherto held any public office. On July 4, 1986, Prime Minister Mulroney began a drive to persuade Quebec to sign the new constitution. Quebec's government had demanded a unilateral veto over amendments, a right no other province would have. Mulroney, on April 30, 1987, met with the ten provincial premiers and the Meech Lake Agreement was worked out. It provided that Quebec be labeled a "distinct society," that it have three of the nine judges of the Canadian Supreme Court, and that no changes in federal institutions or provincial boundaries be made without the unanimous consent of the federal government and the provinces. All the provinces would now have the right to nominate members of the Senate and justices of the Supreme Court.

The final agreement, signed on June 3, 1987, further provided that Quebec has the right to pass laws to "preserve and protect" its special identity. On June 23 Quebec became the first province to ratify the agreement. The House of Commons on October 26 voted 242 to 16 to approve the agreement. The remaining nine provinces must vote on the proposal before June, 1990. Women's groups fear the "distinct society" clause will be used in Quebec to supersede equal rights provisions otherwise in effect. Indians and Inuit want further amendments to strengthen "aboriginal rights." A clause that would require approval of all provinces before any new ones are created is worrisome to residents of the Yukon and Northwest territories.

Apart from the agreement on the constitution, the most important action of the Mulroney government has been to negotiate a comprehensive trade agreement with the United States. Prime Minister Mulroney and President Reagan agreed in 1985 to seek a free trade arrangement; negotiations began in Washington, D.C., on June 17, 1986. The talks went on until the fall of 1987, at which time they seemed on the verge of collapse. On the one hand, the U.S. Congress had set a deadline for the completion of negotiations by October 3; on the other hand, on September 23 Canada's delegation walked out of the talks, saying the United States refused to yield on the matter of a binding arrangement for settling disputes that might arise under the agreement.

On October 3, an agreement was announced. The pact is intended to stimulate economic activity in both countries by eliminating all tariffs and other trade barriers within ten years, beginning January 1, 1989. Many topics are covered: the ending of all agricultural tariffs and import quotas; the ending of restrictions on investments in one country by businesses located in the other; the removal of restrictions on the import and export of automobiles and parts; the retention of existing laws dealing with subsidies and dumping; and the setting up of a mechanism for settling disputes by arbitration. Behind the agreement was the fact that trade between the two countries amounts to $150 billion a year.

The trade agreement required approval by the legislatures of both nations and in both countries opposition was at once voiced by economic interests that felt they would be damaged by the pact.

Mulroney had hoped that the agreements on the constitution and on trade would bolster his rating with the voters of Canada, but this did not happen initially. He and the Progressive Conservatives were not able to improve the economy as they had promised and the country continued to be plagued by a high rate of unemployment, among other problems. Both the Liberal Party and the New Democratic Party denounced the trade agreement as surrendering Canada's sovereignty. Although the denunciation was a political ploy, it echoed the long lasting fear of Canadians that their country might become an economic colony of the United States.

The championing of the Canadian-U.S. trade agreement by Prime Minister Mulroney during the fall, 1988, election campaign involved a key reversal on a major policy matter. Historically, the Conservatives had not been optimistic that Canada could survive politically over the long term if closer economic ties with the United States were forged. The Liberals, on the other hand, had held a more positive view.

In the November, 1988, national election, the Liberal and Progressive Conservative parties reversed their long-held positions on free trade with the United States. Some 56 percent of those who voted opposed Mulroney and the Progressive Conservative Party. Nonetheless, it remained the majority party in the Canadian House of Commons, winning 169 seats. The Liberals won 83 seats, and the New Democratic Party won 43 seats. Thus, even though a majority voted against supporters of the Free Trade Agreement, the Progressive Conservative majority in the House of Commons achieved ratification of the agreement.

Prospects for ratification of the Meech Lake Agreement are uncertain. Two provinces—Manitoba and New Brunswick—had not approved the accord by late 1989, and the Liberal government elected in Newfoundland in the spring of 1989 threatened to rescind that province's earlier ratification. Unless significant amendments to the Meech Lake Agreement are made, or a parallel accord is reached, it is likely that the proposal will fail.

A major factor in Prime Minister Mulroney's continued success is his thorough command of the French language spoken by the 6 million residents of Quebec, whose votes had helped the Progressive Conservatives to win in 1988. The leaders of the other two major parties, Edward Broadbent of the New Democratic Party and John Turner of the Liberal Party, retired in 1989.

PROVINCES AND TERRITORIES

The Western Provinces

The Western Provinces lie side by side and extend from the Pacific Ocean in the west to Hudson Bay in central Canada. Together they make up nearly 30 percent of Canada's land area. They are, from the Pacific, British Columbia, Alberta, Saskatchewan, and Manitoba. The southern border of the region is formed by the 49th parallel, which separates the Canadian provinces from a row of U.S. states extending from Washington in the west to Minnesota in the east. The northern border is formed by the 60th parallel, which separates the provinces from the Yukon and Northwest Territories. In the northwest, British Columbia is separated from the Pacific by the narrow southern panhandle of Alaska.

For much of their history the Western Provinces were the frontier of Canada, known only to fur trappers who worked their way slowly west from Lake Superior. The land itself was claimed at various times by France and Russia, but in 1792 Britain gained undisputed control. The following year Sir Alexander Mackenzie pioneered the first land route across the Canadian mainland to the Pacific. Part of the southern border with the United States was disputed until 1846, when Britain and the United States agreed to the 49th parallel by treaty. The Western Provinces were organized as territories after Canada gained independent status in 1867. British Columbia and Manitoba, the westernmost and easternmost, became provinces three years later. The territory between them entered the confederation as Alberta and Saskatchewan only 35 years later, in 1905.

Today the Western Provinces are no longer the most dynamic region of Canada. Consolidation after the hectic growth of 1971-1981 continues, as Alberta's major industry, petroleum, adjusts to difficult times. At the same time, disaffection with some national policies has reduced support for the Conservatives in Ottawa.

The land. Topographically, all four provinces share the vast plains that stretch southward into the central United States. These plains rise from the Manitoba Plains in the east to the Prairie-plains of Saskatchewan to the High Plains, which cover central and northern Alberta and extend into northeast British Columbia. To the west of the plains lies the Western Cordillera, a mountain region that covers the western edge of Alberta and nearly all of British Columbia. Northern Saskatchewan and the northern two-thirds of Manitoba are a part of the Canadian Shield, a vast plateau that runs from the Arctic Ocean in the northwest, around Hudson Bay, all the way to the Atlantic in the northeast. The extreme northeastern fringe of Manitoba lies in the Hudson Bay Lowlands.

Climate. The climate of the region varies from mild and humid in coastal British Columbia to extreme and semi-arid in the interior. Victoria, in the southwest corner of the region, has average winter temperatures above freezing and annual precipitation of 25 inches. In Regina, Saskatchewan, winter temperatures average minus 1°F, (minus 18°C), and annual precipitation is only 15 inches.

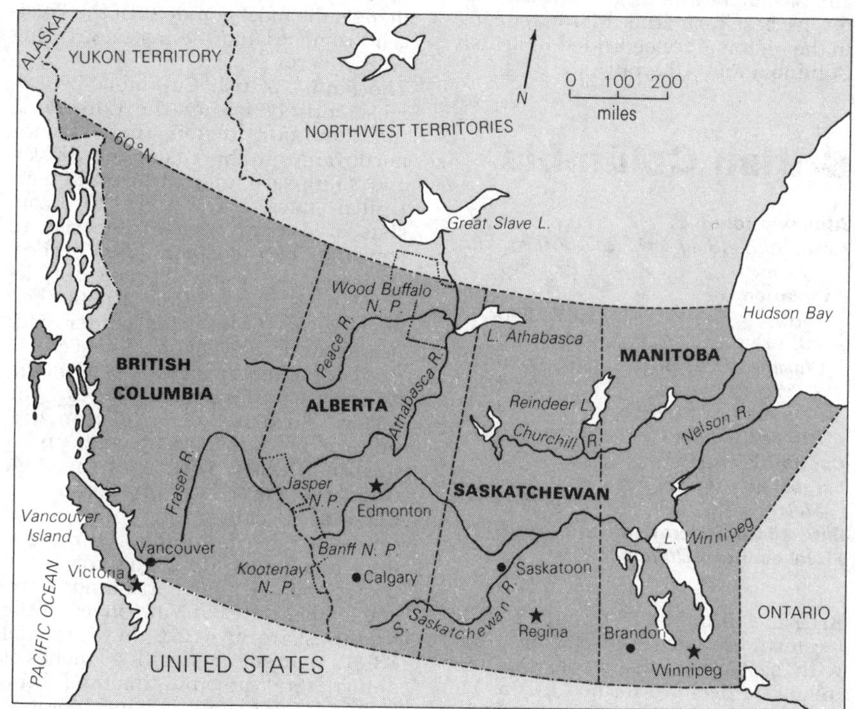

THE WESTERN PROVINCES

Province	Area (sq. mi.)	Population 1986	Population change 1971-86 Number	Percent	Persons per sq. mi.
British Columbia	365,948	2,889,200	+ 704,600	+32.3	8.4
Alberta	255,287	2,375,300	+ 747,400	+45.9	9.6
Saskatchewan	251,866	1,010,200	+ 84,000	+ 9.1	4.6
Manitoba	250,947	1,071,200	+ 83,000	+ 8.4	5.1
Totals	1,124,048	7,345,900	+1,619,000	+28.3	7.2

Principal cities. The largest urban centers of the region are found in its southern areas. The port city of Vancouver, with 1.4 million people, is the third largest in Canada. The fastest growing manufacturing cities are Edmonton and Calgary, in Alberta. The agricultural center of the region is Winnipeg, in southern Manitoba.

The people. The Western Provinces account for 29 percent of the Canadian population. Alberta and British Columbia, because of their mineral wealth, are the fastest-growing provinces in the country, but agriculture-reliant Saskatchewan and Manitoba and among the slowest growing. The region is largely English-speaking. The highest percentage of French is spoken in Manitoba, where 4 percent claim French as their mother tongue. The largest ethnic populations are German and Ukrainian. Canada's main concentration of Oriental peoples is in British Columbia.

Economy. The principal industries of the Western Provinces are forestry and manufacturing in the west and agriculture in the eastern plains. Alberta provides most of Canada's fuel output, and Saskatchewan and Manitoba supply its best farmland. Manufacturing in the region is concentrated in British Columbia and Alberta.

GEORGE HUNTER/NFB PHOTOTHEQUE

GRAIN AND OIL *are the principal riches of the Western Provinces. This scene in Alberta shows both in one landscape. Alberta is the dominion's fastest growing and most prosperous province.*

British Columbia

Abbreviation: *B.C.*
Area: *365,948 sq. mi., 947,800 sq. km.*

Rank	*3rd*

Population:

1986	*2,889,200*
Rank	*3rd*
Change 1971-86	*+704,600*
Percent change	*+32.3*
Persons per sq. mi.	*8.4*
Percent urban	*76.9*

Capital: *Victoria*
Largest city: *Vancouver*

Metro. pop. 1986	*1,380,729*

Entered Confederation: *July 20, 1871*
Floral emblem: *Dogwood*

British Columbia is Canada's most western province and the only one with a Pacific Ocean coastline. Its inland borders are formed by the Yukon and Northwest Territories to the north, Alberta to the east, and the U.S. states of Washington, Idaho, and Montana to the south. The upper third of the province's western border is separated from the Pacific by the narrow southern panhandle of Alaska. The lower two-thirds includes many offshore islands, the largest being 285-mile-long Vancouver Island across Queen Charlotte Strait in the extreme southwestern corner of the province.

British Columbia, the third largest of Canadian provinces in area, was not extensively settled until after the completion of the Canadian Pacific Railroad in 1885. Since then, however, its valuable forestland, ample natural resources, and hydroelectric power have made it the most populous of the Western Provinces and the fastest growing after Alberta.

The land. British Columbia lies almost entirely within the Cordillera, the mountain region that extends northward into the Yukon and Alaska, and southward into the contingous United States. The western third consists of coastal ranges that rise in elevation to the north. The highest peak in the Western Provinces is located at Mt. Fairweather (15,300 feet) near British Columbia's border with Alaska and the Yukon. The central third of the province consists of mountain plateaus and large lakes. The eastern third includes the principal ridge of the Canadian Rockies and a small northeastern fringe of the High Plains that cover most of Alberta.

Climate. Because of the coastal ranges, British Columbia's climate is mild and moist along the coast and cooler and drier farther inland. Average temperatures at Vancouver in the southwest are 36° F (2° C) in winter and 63° (17°C) in summer, with 43 inches of annual total precipitation and little snow. At east-central Prince George, however, average winter temperatures are 10° (minus 11.8°C). Although annual precipitation is lower at 25 inches, the longer winters bring 95 inches of snow per year.

Principal cities. Vancouver, only 15 miles from the U.S. border, is the third largest city in Canada and the busiest port in the country. Victoria (population 255,547), southwest of Vancouver on Vancouver Island, is the center of the province's tourism industry. Together these two cities account for more than half the population of the province.

The people. British Columbia is the third largest province in Canada, after Ontario and Quebec. In the 1970's it grew far faster than either of those provinces, taking second place only to the burgeoning growth of neighboring Alberta. This growth should continue as Canada's population shifts west. Among the Western Provinces, British Columbia has the highest proportion of native English speakers (80.9 percent) and the lowest of native French speakers (1.3 percent). The province also includes the highest proportion of Oriental people (3.8 percent) in Canada, most of them living in Vancouver's large Chinatown. The present population is one of the most mobile in Canada. More than half of the province's population increase in the 1970's consisted of migrants from other provinces.

Economy. Manufacturing, based on wood, paper, food, and fuel products, is the largest industry in British Columbia, generating $18 billion per year. Mineral production earns about $2 billion and is equally divided between ores such as zinc and copper and fuels such as petroleum and natural gas. Forestry is the major industry in the northern areas. The province's limited agriculture is carried out in the south, where fruits, vegetables, and grains are grown on irrigated lands. The commercial fishing industry in British Columbia is the second largest in Canada, earning the province nearly $500 million per year.

Places of interest. Vancouver Island includes Pacific Rim National Park; it is also the main departure point for cruises through the coastal islands to the north. The southeastern Rocky Mountain region is especially rich in natural attractions, such as those found within Mount Revelstroke, Glacier, and Kootenay national parks.

Alberta

Abbreviation: *Alta.*
Area: *255,287 sq. mi., 661,190 sq. km.*
Rank *4th*
Population:
1986 *2,375,300*
Rank *4th*
Change 1971–86 *+747,400*
Percent change *+45.9*
Persons per sq. mi. *9.6*
Percent urban *75.0*
Capital: *Edmonton*
Largest city: *Edmonton*
Metro. pop. 1986 *785,465*
Entered Confederation: *Sept. 1, 1905*
Floral emblem: *Wild rose*

Alberta lies to the east of British Columbia, sharing a border that runs from northwest to southeast along the ridge of the Canadian Rockies. The province borders the Northwest Territories to the north and Saskatchewan to the east. Its short southern border is with the U.S. state of Montana.

Once relatively neglected because of its limited agricultural resources, Alberta became the most dynamic and fastest growing of Canadian provinces owing to the wealth of its mineral reserves. Oil has been extracted near Calgary in the south since 1914, and near the central city of Edmonton since 1947. Increasing production and the boom in oil prices in the 1970's suddenly made the province the economic center of western Canada. During the 1970's Alberta had the highest growth rate in the country and the second greatest numerical increase after the province of Ontario.

The land. Most of Alberta consists of treeless High Plains that rise in elevation from east to west. Near the British Columbia border the plains rise into Rocky Mountains. The highest point in the province is Mt. Columbia (12,294 feet) in the southwest near Jasper.

Climate. Alberta's climate is one of short, pleasant summers and long, cold winters. In Edmonton winter temperatures average 5°F (minus 15°C) and summer temperatures average 63° (17° C), but extreme temperatures of minus 55° (minus 48°C) in winter and 94° (34° C) in summer have been recorded. Inland and isolated from the Pacific by mountains to the west, Alberta is a semi-arid province, with precipitation averaging 17 inches per year. Owing to the length of the winter, however, snowfall is 53 inches per year.

Principal cities. Alberta's two major cities, Edmonton and Calgary, account for 61 percent of the total population of the province. The capital city of Edmonton on the North Saskatchewan River is the center of the provincial oil industry; it grew in population by more than 41 percent between 1971 and 1986. Calgary (population 671,326), 200 miles south of Edmonton, is an agricultural and manufacturing depot as well as an oil town; its population increased by 66 percent in the same period.

The people. English is the native language of 80.7 percent of the people of Alberta, with 2 percent being native French speakers. The principal ethnic groups in the province are German and Ukrainian; each group represents about 4 percent of the total population. Until the 1980's, Alberta's population growth was rapid. Since 1981, movement from other Canadian provinces has declined and immigration has been reduced by 50 percent, to less than 10,000 persons per year.

Economy. Petroleum generates more than one-third of the total gross product of Alberta. The province provides 83 percent of Canada's total petroleum output and 87 percent of its natural gas. Agriculture is second in importance, but it accounts for less than one-quarter of the income generated by oil and gas. Large herds of cattle are grazed on the province's plains. In areas that can be irrigated, grain crops, including the country's largest harvests of oats and barley, are grown. Manufacturing is the third largest industry in the province, nearly all of it devoted to refining mineral and food products.

Places of interest. Alberta's tourism industry is based on attractions in its western mountain areas such as Banff and Jasper national parks near the British Columbia border. Other attractions include Wood Buffalo National Park on its northern border and the International Peace Park on the U.S. border.

Saskatchewan

Abbreviation: *Sask.*
Area: *251,866 sq. mi., 652,330 sq. km.*
Rank *5th*
Population:
1986 *1,010,200*
Rank *6th*
Change 1971–86 *+84,000*
Percent change *+9.1*
Persons per sq. mi. *4.6*
Percent urban *55.5*
Capital: *Regina*
Largest city: *Regina*
Metro. pop. 1986 *186,521*
Entered Confederation: *Sept. 1, 1905*
Floral emblem: *Prairie lily*

Saskatchewan is almost perfectly rectangular in shape, stretching 750 miles from north to south, and up to 350 miles from east to west. It borders Alberta in the west and Manitoba in the east. Its northern border is with the Northwest Territories, and its southern border is with the U.S. states of Montana and North Dakota.

Most of Saskatchewan lies within the region of Great Plains that extends south and east into the U.S. Grain states. The province is the major breadbasket of Canada. Saskatchewan includes more than half the improved farmland in Canada, typified by the rolling wheat fields of the south. It is the least populous of the Western Provinces; during the 1980's, however, growth has resumed, with a population gain of 4.3 percent from 1981 to 1986.

The land. The southern two-thirds of Saskatchewan consists of grassland plains that rise in elevation from an average of 2000 feet in the Prairie-plains of the southeast to an average of 4000 feet in the High Plains of the southwest. The northern third of the province is part of the Canadian Shield, a glacial plateau characterized by large lakes, such as Lake Athabasca on the northwestern Alberta border and Reindeer Lake on the northeastern Manitoba border. The division between the two regions is formed by the Churchill River and a series of small lakes that are its headwaters.

Climate. Saskatchewan has a continental Canadian climate, with cold winters, mild summers, and low precipitation. At the capital city of Regina in the south-central region, winter temperatures average minus 1°F (minus 18°C) and summer ones average 66° (19°C). Precipitation at Regina averages 16 inches per year, with 46 inches of snow. Northern Saskatchewan is both colder and drier than Regina.

Principal cities. Nearly 40 percent of the provincial population live in Saskatchewan's only two large cities, Regina and Saskatoon. Regina, 100 miles from the U.S. border, is the principal processing point for the province's agricultural products. Saskatoon (population 200,665), 160 miles to the northwest, is the province's manufacturing center and the processing point for its mineral products.

The people. The population of Saskatchewan is 81 percent native English speakers and 2 percent native French speakers. The major ethnic groups are German, Ukrainian, and native peoples, including Indians and Metis, people of mixed Indian and European descent. The province lost population to migration in the 1970's, but natural increase gave it a small net increase over the decade. Because its leading businesses are agricultural, Saskatchewan's population is the least urban among the Western Provinces.

Economy. Income from agriculture in Saskatchewan is the highest among the Western Provinces; it is more than twice that of any other provincial industry. The province supplies almost 60 percent of the Canadian wheat harvest; it also raises more beef cattle than any Western Province except Alberta. Manufacturing is Saskatchewan's second largest industry, concentrated largely on the processing of food and mineral products. Mining ranks third, with production of fuels and minerals, particularly potash and uranium, of equal importance.

Places of interest. The tourist attractions in central Saskatchewan include Prince Albert National Park and a series of provincial parks around the numerous lakes. Attractions in southern Saskatchewan include the Royal Canadian Mounted Police Museum in Regina and the Western Development Museums, with branches in Saskatoon, Yorkton, and Moose Jaw.

Manitoba

Abbreviation: *Man.*
Area: *250,947 sq. mi., 649,950 sq. km.*
Rank *6th*
Population:
1986 *1,071,200*
Rank *5th*
Change 1971–86 *+83,000*
Percent change *+8.4*
Persons per sq. mi. *5.1*
Percent urban *69.9*
Capital: *Winnipeg*
Largest city: *Winnipeg*
Metro. pop. 1986 *625,304*
Entered Confederation: *July 15, 1870*
Floral emblem: *Prairie crocus*

Manitoba is the easternmost of the Western Provinces. It stretches 750 miles from a southern border with the U.S. states of North Dakota and Minnesota to a northern border on the Keewatin District of the Northwest Territories. The breadth of the province from its western border with Saskatchewan to its eastern one with Ontario varies from about 240 miles in the south to a maximum of more than 400 miles in the northern third. The northeast border of the province is an irregular shoreline on Hudson Bay.

Most of Manitoba's population live in the lower third of the province, a rolling grassland notable for large lakes such as Winnipeg, Winnipegosi, and Manitoba. Northern Manitoba is a very sparsely populated wilderness of deep forests and scenic rivers draining northeast into Hudson Bay. The province is a popular summer camping, hunting, fishing, and boating site.

The land. The southwestern part of Manitoba, from its southern and western borders to the western shore of Lake Winnipeg, is a region of plains rising in elevation from southeast to northwest. The two-thirds of the provincial area that lie north and east of this division consist of the forested Canadian Shield and the Hudson Bay Lowland in the northeast corner south of the bay.

Climate. Manitoba has a continental Canadian climate consisting of cold winters caused by arctic winds from the north, and dry warm summers. At the capital city of Winnipeg in south-central Manitoba, normal winter temperatures average minus 1°F (minus 18°C) and normal summer temperatures average 67° (20° C). Extreme temperatures in Winnipeg, however, have ranged from minus 49° (minus 45° C) in winter to 104° (40°C) in summer. The total precipitation at Winnipeg averages 21 inches and includes 52 inches of snow per year.

Principal cities. The largest city in Manitoba is Winnipeg, which is the seventh largest metropolitan area in the country. Winnipeg is the capital and the principal agricultural marketplace and manufacturing center of the province. The second largest city is Brandon, which has a population of about 35,000 and is just over 100 miles due west of Winnipeg. The only large city in northern Manitoba is Thompson, which has a population of about 17,000 and is located 150 miles north of Lake Winnipeg.

The people. Manitoba is the least English of the Western Provinces. Some 74 percent of the population are native English speakers, and more than 5 percent are native French speakers. The population also has a high proportion of Germans (7 percent) and Ukrainians (6 percent). During the 1980's, agriculture-reliant Manitoba has experienced above-average growth under the influence of an expanding manufacturing sector. Population grew 4.4 percent from 1981 to 1986.

Economy. The principal business of Manitoba has shifted from agriculture to manufacturing. While farmland on the southern plains continues to be a significant producer of cereal grains and specialty crops, shipments of manufactured goods were $5 billion in 1986, more than double the cash receipts from farming. Products are primarily in the food, transportation, and farm machinery industries. Mining ranks third in importance, with the value of production reaching $664 million in 1986. Key minerals are nickel, copper, and zinc. Pulpwood and fish are also of economic significance.

Places of interest. Manitoba's large tourist industry is centered on the many lakes of the southern region and on such parks as Riding Mountain National Park in the southwest, and Whiteshell Provincial Park on the Ontario border in the southeast. There are also many places of historical interest, such as the restored Hudson's Bay Company post at Lower Fort Garry near Winnipeg.

Ontario

Abbreviation: *Ont.*
Area: *412,581 sq. mi., 1,068,580 sq. km.*
Rank *2nd*
Population:
1986 *9,113,500*
Rank *1st*
Change 1971–86 *+1,410,400*
Percent change *+18.3*
Persons per sq. mi. *26.5*
Percent urban *81.2*
Capital: *Toronto*
Largest city: *Toronto*
Metro. pop. 1986 *3,427,168*
Entered Confederation: *July 1, 1867*
Floral emblem: *White trillium*

Ontario is the most southern of the Canadian provinces. It lies just southeast of the geographical center of the country, bordering four of the five Great Lakes. It stretches nearly 1000 miles at its widest point from the Ottawa River, which forms most of its eastern border with Quebec, to its western border with Manitoba. To the north the province borders Hudson Bay and its southern extension, James Bay. To the south Ontario has a longer U.S. border than any other province, and it faces six U.S. states across the Great Lakes: Minnesota, Wisconsin, Michigan, Ohio, Pennsylvania, and New York. The crossings between Windsor and Detroit and into New York State at Niagara Falls are the two busiest between Canada and the United States.

Ontario is known as the "Heartland Province" because it is the population, government, metropolitan, and economic core of the country. The province is the home of more than 35 percent of the Canadian people, and it has 2.5 million more people than the second most populous province, Quebec. The triangle formed by lakes Huron, Erie, and Ontario contains Canada's largest city, Toronto, and ten other of the country's 25 largest cities. Economically, Ontario is the most industrial of the provinces, accounting for more than half the country's manufactured goods; it is also the leader in cash receipts from farms. Because of its many crossings into the United States, it is the most familiar province to Americans and the base for most U.S.–Canadian commerce.

The land. The central and western two-thirds of Ontario's land area consists of the Canadian Shield, a vast expanse of Precambrian sedimentary and volcanic rock leveled by glacial ice sheets to an average elevation of about 1000 feet above sea level. Along its northern limit Ontario also includes a strip of Hudson Bay Lowland, where forested land drops off to marshland at the shore of the saltwater bay. Eleva-

tions also decline in the extreme southeast, where there is a narrow strip of Great Lakes Lowland and St. Lawrence Lowland. These lowlands are the most fertile farmland in the province.

Climate. The climate of Ontario ranges from sub-arctic in the north near Hudson Bay to humid continental in the south. Most of the people live in the south, where the typical climate is one of clear, cold winters and mild to warm summers. At Toronto, on the north shore of Lake Ontario, normal winter temperatures average 24°F (minus 4°C), and summer ones average 71° (22°C). Annual precipitation of 32 inches includes 55 inches of snow. At Thunder Bay, on Lake Superior in the southwest, temperatures average 5° (minus 14° C) in winter and 64° (18° C) in summer, with lower annual precipitation (28 inches) but more snow (84 inches).

Principal cities. Ontario is the most urban of Canadian provinces, and it includes a large number of major cities. Toronto is the largest city in the country, and its rapid growth rate of 9 percent from 1981 to 1985 brought it close to the 3.5 million population mark. The Ottawa-Hull metropolitan area on the southeastern border with Quebec is second in population, with well over 800,000 people (part in Quebec); its 1980's growth rate of 10 percent exceeded that of Toronto. Ottawa is the center of the Canadian government. The next largest cities are Hamilton (population 557,000) on Lake Ontario west of Toronto and St. Catherine's-Niagara (population 343,000) on the south shore of Lake Ontario near Buffalo, New York. These two metropolitan areas are old industrial cities whose populations did not increase significantly in the 1970's. Kitchener, London, and Windsor, all farther east on the peninsula between the lakes, have more than 250,000 people each. The only large metropolitan areas outside the southern triangle are Thunder Bay, on the north shore of Lake Superior, and Sudbury.

The people. Ontario was first settled by French fur traders in the early 1600's, but the first large population growth occurred when Loyalists to the British Crown moved into the Great Lakes region from the American colonies during the American Revolution. In 1791 these English-speaking people established a separate province of Upper Canada, now Ontario, and ceded the nearby Lower Canada, now Quebec, to the French-speaking population.

The population of Ontario today consists of 76 percent English speakers and 5 percent French speakers. The largest ethnic groups in the province are Italian, representing 5 percent of the total population, and German, representing 2 percent. Ontario recorded the greatest numerical population increase in the country during the period of 1981 to 1986, although its proportionate rate of increase was second behind Alberta. Ontario's population is heavily concentrated in the Ottawa - Toronto - Windsor corridor, where nine-tenths of the provincial population live on one-sixth of the land.

Economy. Manufacturing accounts for nearly one-third of the province's gross domestic product. Ontario's manufacturers, like its population, are heavily concentrated in the southeast, where the largest numbers of automobiles, iron and steel products, and food and paper goods are produced. Although Ontario leads the provinces in farm goods, agriculture generates only

TORONTO, *on the shore of Lake Ontario, is the business and financial center of Canada. The Canadian National Tower,* left, center, *is the world's tallest free-standing structure.*

ONTARIO MINISTRY OF INDUSTRY & TOURISM

one-sixth the income of manufacturing. Two-thirds of the farm income is derived from livestock, especially cattle, which can be grazed in the rural central region, and poultry. The chief crops are grains for livestock feed, such as corn and soybeans, and cereals such as wheat and oats. Third in importance to the local economy is mining, with the Canadian Shield regions yielding 51 percent of world nickel production and large amounts of lead, zinc, and copper. Lumber is also an important industry in the north, and tourism is important in many parts of the province.

Places of interest. The Great Lakes region of Ontario includes a variety of attractions such as the Parliament buildings and the National Art Gallery in Ottawa, Niagara Falls on the New York State border south of Lake Ontario, and the CN Tower and Ontario Place in Toronto. Much of the shoreline of lakes Huron and Superior includes campgrounds and resorts popular in summer. Most of northern Ontario is unspoiled forestland with many lakes and streams. Polar Bear Provincial Park is a major attraction in the far north on the shore of Hudson Bay. In the northwest is an international park at Lake-of-the-Woods.

Quebec

Abbreviation: *Que.*
Area: *594,860 sq. mi., 1,540,680 sq. km.*

Rank	*1st*

Population:

1986	*6,540,300*
Rank	*2nd*
Change 1971–86	*+512,500*
Percent change	*+8.5*
Persons per sq. mi.	*12.5*
Percent urban	*79.1*

Capital: *Quebec City*
Largest city: *Montreal*

Metro. pop. 1986	*2,921,357*

Entered Confederation: *July 1, 1867*
Floral emblem: *Fleur de lys*

Quebec is largest in area of the provinces of Canada, occupying well over half a million square miles of the country's eastern mainland. The province's greatest north-south extent, well over 1100 miles, is along its western border, which is formed by Ontario in the south and west, James Bay in the west-central area, and the larger Hudson Bay in the northwest. The northern limit is defined by Hudson Strait and Ungava Bay, across which Quebec faces Baffin Island of the Northwest Territories. In the northeast Quebec extends to the border of Labrador, the mainland region of the province of Newfoundland, and in the east to the Gulf of St. Lawrence, both north and south of the Gulf. In the southeast Quebec borders the province of New Brunswick and the U.S. state of Maine; in the south it borders the U.S. states of New Hampshire, Vermont, and New York.

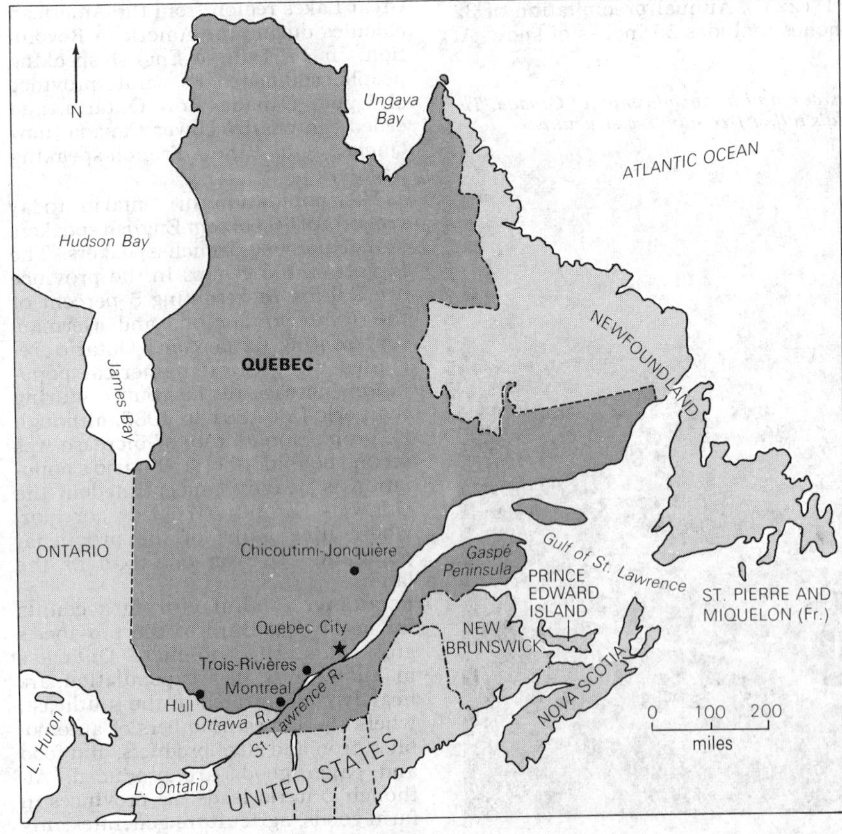

Although larger in area, Quebec ranks second to Ontario in population and economic importance. It is unique, however, because it is the most French of all the provinces.

Quebec is sometimes called "the cradle of Canada" because it was in the southeastern St. Lawrence area that Jacques Cartier landed in 1534 and named the region New France. Samuel de Champlain founded the original settlement at Quebec City in 1608. The province has remained thoroughly French in language and culture ever since. In recent years, French-Canadian supporters of Quebec's Parti Quebecois have begun to agitate for separation from the Canadian confederation as a means of resolving their differences with the federal government in Ottawa.

The land. Fully 90 percent of the Quebec land area lies within the topographical region called the Canadian Shield, the vast plateau that arcs around Hudson Bay. The shield reaches as far south as the Laurentian Mountains, 75 miles northwest of Montreal. It is poor farmland, with exposed Precambrian bedrock stripped of soil by glacial ice sheets, but it is rich in minerals and, in the south, well forested. Canada's tree line, however, crosses Quebec from James Bay in the west to the northeastern border with Labrador; above this line the frozen tundra supports only scrub vegetation.

The remaining 10 percent of the land area consists of the St. Lawrence Lowlands, which surround the river in the southeast, and the Appalachian Uplands, between the river and the U.S. border. The St. Lawrence Lowlands contain the most valuable farmland in the province, and the Appalachian Uplands include the mountains of the Gaspé Peninsula south of the river and north of New Brunswick.

Climate. Quebec's climate ranges from sub-arctic above the tree line to humid and continental in the south. At Fort Chimo on Ungava Bay in the north temperatures average minus 10° F (minus 23°C) in winter and 53° (11°C) in summer, with an annual precipitation of 20 inches, including 96 inches of snow. Most of the people live in the south, where the climate is one of cold winters and brief but warm summers. At Montreal, in the extreme south of the province, normal winter temperatures average 16°F (minus 9°C), normal summer temperatures average 70° (22°C), and there is an annual average precipitation of 40 inches with 97 inches of snow.

Principal cities. Montreal is the second largest city in Canada, after Toronto, Ontario, and the second largest French-speaking city in the world, after Paris. The metropolitan area includes 45 percent of the population of Quebec. For much of Canada's history, Montreal has been the largest and most important city, being surpassed by Toronto only in the early 1970's. Quebec City (population 603,267) is the second largest urban area, located 125 miles northeast of Montreal on the St. Lawrence River. Quebec City is especially French in character, and it is the only walled city north of Mexico. The only other metropolitan areas in the province are Chicoutimi-Jonquière (population 158,468), northeast of Quebec City on the Saguenay River; Trois-Rivières (population 128,888), on the St. Lawrence River between Montreal and Quebec City; and Ottawa-Hull, on the Ontario border (of 819,263 people, about a third live in Quebec). There are no large cities in the entire northern nine-tenths of the province.

The people. In population Quebec is both the second largest and the second most urban of the Canadian provinces after Ontario. As in Ontario, the overwhelming majority of Quebec's population is concentrated in the limited area of the southern lowlands. The population growth rate in Quebec, however, is only about half that of Ontario. In Quebec 80 percent of the population claim French as their mother tongue, and only 18 percent claim English. The largest ethnic group is Italian, representing 2 percent of the total population. There are a small number of Inuit, or Eskimo, people living in the far northern regions of the province.

PAUL LAMBERT / NFB PHOTOTHEQUE ONF

QUEBEC CITY, *overshadowed by Montreal in size, is still the capital of Quebec. It preserves the European charm of Quebec's French background.*

Economy. Quebec's largest industry, which generates almost a third of its gross domestic product of $144 billion, is manufacturing. Manufacturing in Quebec is based along the river systems of the southern region. Since 1960 it has been given a boost by the availability of hydroelectric power generated by the St. Lawrence Seaway, a joint Canadian–U.S. project that created an ocean-going ship route from the Atlantic to the Great Lakes. The principal manufactures are processed foods, textiles, and paper goods. Mining and agriculture are the most important industries after manufacturing. Quebec's northern mines produce large quantities of asbestos and structural metals, and its farms are equally divided between livestock, chiefly dairy cattle, and crops such as oats, corn, and potatoes.

Places of interest. Tourism is an especially successful industry in Quebec because of its uniquely French character. Quebec City's historic Old Quebec district, and Montreal's historic district preserve the flavor and charm of the mother country. Natural attractions in the province include the Gaspé Peninsula south of the St. Lawrence River, La Verendrye Provincial Park in the southwest, and the Laurentide Provincial Park north of Quebec City.

The Atlantic Provinces

The Atlantic Provinces surround the Gulf of St. Lawrence and separate it from the Atlantic Ocean. To the south are the three Maritime Provinces: New Brunswick to the southwest; the peninsula of Nova Scotia and its Cape Breton Island to the south; and Prince Edward Island, some 10 miles off the New Brunswick shore in the gulf itself. To the northeast of the gulf and separated from the other provinces by Cabot Strait lies Newfoundland Island. The Province of Newfoundland also includes Labrador to the north, a large, barren part of the Canadian mainland that faces the north Atlantic Ocean.

The Atlantic Provinces are the four smallest provinces in Canada both in terms of land area and population. They were perhaps the first Canadian lands seen by Jacques Cartier when he entered the Gulf of St. Lawrence in 1534, and have long histories of settlement. But the region has remained the most rural in Canada because of its scarcity of arable lands and natural resources. Today the region is Canada's great vacationland. All of the Atlantic Provinces are known for their dramatic coastal scenery of rugged cliffs interrupted by sandy beaches, their rustic fishing villages in secluded coves, and their unspoiled interior lands of forests and small farms.

The land. Newfoundland Island and all of the Maritime Provinces lie within the Canadian topographical area known as the Appalachian Uplands. This is the northern extreme of the mountain belt that runs southwest into the United States. The meeting of such mountain topography with the sea accounts for the coastal cliffs characteristic of much of the region's shoreline. Labrador, farther north, is

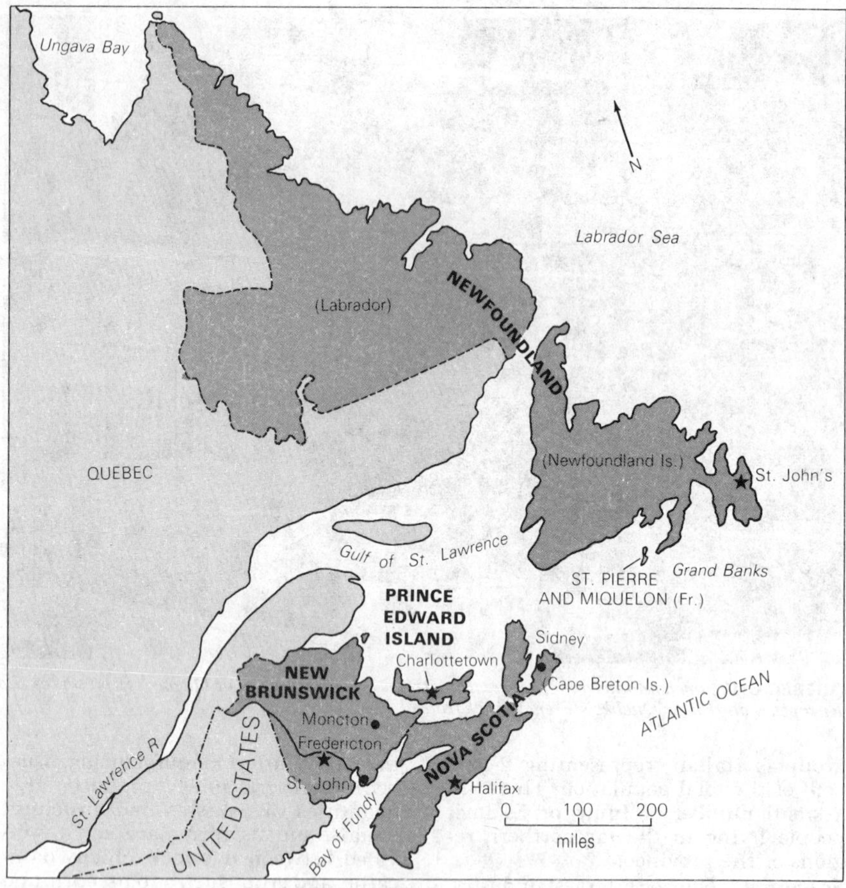

THE ATLANTIC PROVINCES

Province	Area (sq. mi.)	Population 1986	Population change 1971–86 Number	Percent	Persons per sq. mi.
New Brunswick	28,355	710,400	+ 75,800	+11.9	25.7
Nova Scotia	21,425	873,200	+ 84,200	+10.7	42.8
Prince Edward Island	2,185	126,600	+ 15,000	+13.4	57.9
Newfoundland	156,649	568,300	+ 46,200	+ 8.8	4.0
Totals	208,614	2,278,500	+221,200	+10.8	11.8

the most easterly part of the Canadian Shield, the glacially leveled area that covers much of northern and central Canada. Offshore of the Atlantic Provinces lies an unusually broad Continental Shelf of submerged banks that extend 300 miles east of the island of Newfoundland. These banks, teeming with fish, attracted early inhabitants to the region, and they continue to be one of the world's great fisheries.

Climate. The climate of the region varies with proximity to the sea. Mainland New Brunswick has relatively low winter temperatures and the highest summer readings. The island of Newfoundland is slightly warmer in winter and cooler in summer. Because of its more northerly position, however, Newfoundland receives more snow (146 inches) than New Brunswick. The climate of Labrador is subarctic—both colder and drier than the rest of the region.

Principal cities. The largest urban center in the Atlantic Provinces is Halifax, Nova Scotia, a deep-water port with 296,000 people. It ranks 13th in population among Canadian cities. The only other metropolitan areas in the region are the ports of St. John's on the island of Newfoundland, with a population of 96,000, and St. John in southern New Brunswick, with a population of 76,000. Most towns have fewer than 20,000 people.

The people. The population of the Atlantic Provinces is the most rural in Canada. The population growth rate is far below the national average, and as a unit the Atlantic Provinces experienced a net loss to migration during the 1970's. A sizable minority of the population is French-speaking.

Economy. Because of their spectacular coastal scenery, the southern Maritime Provinces rely on tourism for a large proportion of their local economy. Manufacturing is the next most important industry; it is chiefly based on the refining and processing of mineral, food, and forest products. The region's mining industries are chiefly devoted to ores rather than fuels, and its farm produce is chiefly of potatoes and fruits. Although it ranks behind these other businesses in contribution to the gross domestic product, commercial fishing is one of the most visible businesses throughout the region.

New Brunswick

Abbreviation: *N.B.*
Area: *28,355 sq. mi., 73,440 sq. km.*
Rank *8th*
Population:
1986 *710,400*
Rank *8th*
Change 1971–86 *+75,800*
Percent change *+11.9*
Persons per sq. mi. *25.7*
Percent urban *52.3*
Capital: *Fredericton*
Largest city: *St. John*
Metro. pop. 1986 *121,265*
Entered Confederation: *July 1, 1867*
Floral emblem: *Purple violet*

New Brunswick, the largest in size of the three Maritime Provinces, is situated to the east of the U.S. state of Maine. Its northern border is with Quebec. To the east of the province is the Gulf of St. Lawrence. Prince Edward Island lies 10 miles offshore in the southeast, near the Isthmus of Chignecto, a neck of land that connects New Brunswick to the large peninsula of Nova Scotia. To the south New Brunswick faces the Bay of Fundy, which separates it from the southern reaches of Nova Scotia by 30 to 50 miles of salt water. The bay, which has the highest tides in the world, opens into the Atlantic just opposite the New Brunswick–Maine border.

Lacking arable land, New Brunswick has developed more slowly than the provinces to the west. The population today is smaller than that of any province except Newfoundland and Prince Edward Island. Most of the population lives along the southern coast. The northern reaches are sparsely populated forestlands.

The land. Nearly all of New Brunswick lies within the Appalachian Uplands that extend southwest into New England in the United States. In New Brunswick the Appalachian Uplands are highest in the north, with Mt. Carleton (2690 feet) near the Quebec border being the highest peak. To the east and northeast New Brunswick also includes a small strip of lowlands along the Gulf of St. Lawrence.

Climate. Because its weather is determined by wind movement from west to east, New Brunswick has a

RON WEBBER/NFB PHOTOTHEQUE

FISH *were the original riches of the Eastern Provinces. The Grand Banks off Newfoundland attracted early settlers and explorers. Today, fishing is less important, but fish are still caught and processed by the millions. This scene is in Durrell, Newfoundland.*

humid continental climate despite its maritime location. At southwestern St. John, the long winters average 19° F (minus 7° C) and the short summers average 63 (17 C). Precipitation in New Brunswick is heavier than in the interior provinces, averaging 56 inches per year and including 82 inches of snow per year at St. John.

Principal cities. The only metropolitan area in New Brunswick is St. John. Located at the mouth of the St. John River on the Bay of Fundy, it is an ice-free port in winter and a ferry point for transportation to Nova Scotia. The only other large cities are Moncton, 80 miles northeast of St. John, with a population of about 55,000, and the capital city of Fredericton, which has a population of about 44,000 and is located 50 miles northwest of St. John.

The people. The population of New Brunswick is the most rural in Canada after Prince Edward Island. Between 1971 and 1986 the population grew by 75,000, an 11.3 percent rate of increase exceeded only by that of Prince Edward Island. The composition of the population by language is 64 percent English and 33 percent French. New Brunswick is the only officially bilingual province in Canada.

Economy. New Brunswick's leading industry is the manufacture of wood and paper products. This industry's output is valued at over $1.3 billion. Food processing is second in importance to the province, followed by mining. New Brunswick leads Canada in the production of specialized ores such as antimony and bismuth. Agriculture, located in the south of the province, is based on potato crops and dairy products and is valued at $225 million. Commercial fishing, most of it out of the Bay of Fundy, brings the province $75 million per year.

Places of interest. The principal historic attractions in New Brunswick are King's Landing, which recreates English village life of the late 1700's, and Village Historique Acadien, which does the same for French life of the same period. Bay of Fundy National Park is also a popular attraction, and the villages of inland New Brunswick contain many covered bridges.

Nova Scotia

Abbreviation: *N.S.*
Area: *21,425 sq. mi., 55,490 sq. km.*

Rank	*9th*

Population:

1986	*873,200*
Rank	*7th*
Change 1971–86	*+84,200*
Percent change	*+10.7*
Persons per sq. mi.	*42.8*
Percent urban	*55.8*

Capital: *Halifax*
Largest city: *Halifax*

Metro. pop. 1986	*295,990*

Entered Confederation: *July 1, 1867*
Floral emblem: *Trailing arbutus*

Nova Scotia consists of a long peninsula and the smaller Cape Breton Island just offshore its most northeastern point. The peninsula extends 250 miles from southwest to northeast and is joined to southeastern New Brunswick by the low-lying Isthmus of Chignecto. Its western arm is separated from New Brunswick by the Bay of Fundy, while its eastern arm extends eastward toward Cape Breton Island. Cape Breton, separated from mainland Nova Scotia by the narrow Strait of Canso, extends 100 miles north and east between the Gulf of St. Lawrence and the Atlantic Ocean.

Nova Scotia means New Scotland in Latin, the name given it in the original British charter of 1621. Rights to the land were contested by the French until 1713, when the British gained full control of Nova Scotia. While still under British rule in 1848, Nova Scotia became the first Canadian province with self-governing powers. Although the second smallest in area of all Canadian provinces, after Prince Edward Island, Nova Scotia is today the most developed of the Atlantic Provinces. It is especially noted for dramatic coastal scenery along its long southeastern shoreline with the Atlantic Ocean.

The land. Nova Scotia lies entirely within the region of Appalachian Uplands that cover most of the Atlantic Provinces. From a central spine of low mountains, the land declines in elevation to the north, with the Isthmus of Chignecto characterized by marshlands and bogs. Both the Atlantic coastline and the Bay of Fundy, which records the greatest tidal changes in the world, are irregular and dotted with rocky coves and harbors.

Climate. Owing to the influence of the surrounding bodies of water, Nova Scotia has the mildest climate of the Atlantic Provinces. At Halifax, near the center of the Atlantic Ocean coast, winter temperatures average 26°F (minus 3° C) and summer ones average 65° (18° C). Yearly precipitation averages 55 inches and includes 85 inches of snow.

Principal cities. Halifax is the only large city in Nova Scotia and the only metropolitan area in the province. It is the leading industrial center of the Atlantic Provinces. In recent years it has attracted a large number of diversified scientific research companies. The second largest city in the province and the largest on Cape Breton Island is Sydney, which has a population just over 30,000.

The people. Nova Scotia is the second most densely populated province of Canada, after Prince Edward Island. The composition of the population by mother tongue is 93 percent English and 4 percent French. An 11 percent rise in population from 1971 to 1986 was largely from natural increase, which countered the effects of a small population loss from net migration to other provinces in the 1970's.

Economy. The principal industry of Nova Scotia is manufacturing, which accounts for more than four times the income of any other business. The leading manufactures are paper and wood pulp products, processed foods, including fish, and refined petroleum and coal fuels. Mining is second in importance to the province, and mineral production is equally divided between fuels and structural metals. The majority of the agricultural businesses are dairy farms. Although it generates less income than agriculture, Nova Scotia's commercial fishing industry is second only to that of British Columbia among Canadian provinces. Forestry is also an important business.

Places of interest. Tourism is an important industry in Nova Scotia, with large numbers of visitors attracted to the beaches of the Bay of Fundy, the historic Citadel at Halifax, and Kejimkujik National Park in the southwest interior. Attractions on Cape Breton Island include the scenic Cabot Trail around the island, the restored fortress at Louisbourg, and the northern Cape Breton Highlands National Park.

Prince Edward Island

Abbreviation: *P.E.I.*
Area: *2185 sq. mi., 5660 sq. km.*
Rank *10th*
Population:
1986 *126,600*
Rank *10th*
Change 1971–86 *+15,000*
Percent change *+13.4*
Persons per sq. mi. *57.9*
Percent urban *37.1*
Capital: *Charlottetown*
Largest city: *Charlottetown*
Pop. 1986 *15,776*
Entered Confederation: *July 1, 1873*
Floral emblem: *Lady's slipper*

Prince Edward Island, Canada's smallest province, is located in the southern part of the Gulf of St. Lawrence. It is 120 miles across at its greatest east-west extent, and up to 35 miles wide. The island lies 20 miles north of the New Brunswick–Nova Scotia coast.

Prince Edward Island was discovered by the French explorer Jacques Cartier in 1534, and it was originally called Ile de St. Jean. It was formally ceded to England in 1763 and was named after a son of England's George III. It has been given the nickname "the cradle of confederation" because it was on Prince Edward Island that the initial Canadian self-rule talks were held in 1864.

Today, in addition to being the smallest in area, Prince Edward Island is the least populous and the most rural of Canadian provinces. It retains an old world, pastoral character, one typified by gently rolling fields bordered by low walls and hedges. Its coastal scenery is especially attractive to visitors, who are drawn to the island's extensive sandy beaches and quiet inlets.

The land. Prince Edward Island is a low-lying section of the Appalachian Uplands region notable for its underlying bed of red sandstone. Nowhere on the island do elevations rise to 500 feet, and the rolling hills are drained only by small streams. The coastline is sharply indented on all sides and uniformly sandy except for a stretch of low coastal cliffs along the southern shore.

Climate. Prince Edward Island has a slightly sunnier and drier climate than the other Atlantic Provinces. At Charlottetown, on the southern coast, normal winter temperatures average 20° F (minus 7° C) and normal summer temperatures average 65° (18° C). Average precipitation is 45 inches per year, the lowest in the Atlantic Provinces, but snowfall averages 129 inches per year, higher than in any Atlantic Province except Newfoundland.

Principal cities. The capital city of Charlottetown is the largest on Prince Edward Island. It is the hub of island life, the principal tourist center, and the major port, from which ferry service connects Prince Edward Island with New Brunswick and Nova Scotia.

The people. Because of its limited land area, Prince Edward Island's population is the densest in Canada; there are no uninhabited places on the predominantly rural island. The proportions of the population by mother tongue are 93 percent English and 4 percent French. The population is very stable and increased insignificantly from 1981 to 1986.

Economy. Tourism is the leading industry on the island, employing nearly one-third of the work force. Agriculture is second in importance, with the field crops being potatoes and grain and the livestock chiefly dairy cattle. Manufacturing accounts for $289 million in commerce per year. Commercial fishing is worth another $38 million per year.

Places of interest. Prince Edward Island is small enough to be conveniently toured in its entirety. Its 1000 miles of total shoreline include many harbor villages and campgrounds. Places of historic interest include the Province House, Fort Amherst National Historic Site, and the restored Micmac Indian village, all in Charlottetown.

Newfoundland

Abbreviation: *Nfld.*
Area: *156,649 sq. mi., 405,720 sq. km.*
Rank *7th*
Population
1986 *568,300*
Rank *9th*
Change 1971–86 *+46,200*
Percent change *+8.8*
Persons per sq. mi. *4.0*
Percent urban *58.9*
Capital: *St. John's*
Largest city: *St. John's Metro. pop. 1986: 161,901*
Entered Confederation: *Mar. 31, 1949*
Floral emblem: *Pitcher plant*

Newfoundland is an Atlantic Province consisting of two parts, the island of Newfoundland and mainland Labrador. The island accounts for less than one-third of the provincial land area but has 95 percent of the provincial population. Triangular in shape, it forms the eastern limit of the Gulf of St. Lawrence and is separated from Labrador in the north by the narrow Strait of Belle Isle. Labrador is the easternmost point of the Canadian mainland. Also triangular in shape, it is bordered on the west and south by Quebec and on the northeast by the Atlantic Ocean, where the more than 600-mile-long coastline includes many small offshore islands.

Newfoundland was probably one of the first points in North America seen by John Cabot on his 1497 voyage, but rights to the lands were disputed by France until 1783. Because most of the province's land area is barren and subject to harsh weather, it was settled very slowly. Labrador was only organized as a unit of Newfoundland in 1927, and Newfoundland remained a separate dominion of the British Commonwealth until it accepted provincial status in 1949. Today the province remains the most sparsely populated in Canada. Remote areas are still referred to by the names given them by frontiersmen, such as Heart's Content and Come By Chance. A unique dialect of English influenced by Irish and rural British Devonshire inflections prevails.

The land. All of the island of Newfoundland lies within Canada's Appalachian Uplands. Most of its area is a barren central plateau that drops off to the surrounding sea in rocky cliffs, but there is a small region of lowlands on the northernmost peninsula. All of Labrador is part of the Canadian Shield, a forested plateau of large lakes. Labrador's northernmost point lies above the tree line and consists of arctic tundra. Like Newfoundland, Labrador has a very irregular and rocky coast.

Climate. Most of Labrador has a sub-arctic climate, but the island of Newfoundland, home of virtually all of the provincial population, has a cool and stormy one. At St. John's at the southeastern tip of the island, normal winter temperatures average 25° F (minus 4° C) and normal summer temperatures average 60 (15 C). Precipitation averages 60 inches per year, more than anywhere in Canada except parts of British Columbia, and the annual snowfall averages 145 inches, more than in any other large city in the country.

Principal cities. The only metropolitan area in the province is St. John's, a deep-water port that served as an important military installation during World War II. Corner Brook, 250 miles west of St. John's on the western coast, has a population of 35,000.

The people. Almost 95 percent of the provincial population live on the island of Newfoundland. Fewer than 30,000 live in Labrador, most of them along its southeastern coast. Large areas of Labrador are totally uninhabited. The population by mother tongue is 98 percent English, with a small number of French-speaking people living in Newfoundland and a small number of Inuit, or Eskimo, people living in northern Labrador.

Economy. The major industry in Newfoundland is, without question, mining, which accounts for three times the income of any other business. The principal product is iron ore. Mines in Labrador account for more than half of Canada's production. In recent years there has been little offshore oil drilling. Newfoundland's other industries, ranked in order of importance, are manufacturing, commercial fishing, and lumber.

Places of interest. Newfoundland's tourist industry is limited because of the province's isolation, but the principal attractions for visitors are the numerous coastal fishing villages, Signal Hill National Historic Park in St. John's, and the Terra Nova National Park on Bonavista Bay 100 miles north of the capital city.

The Territories

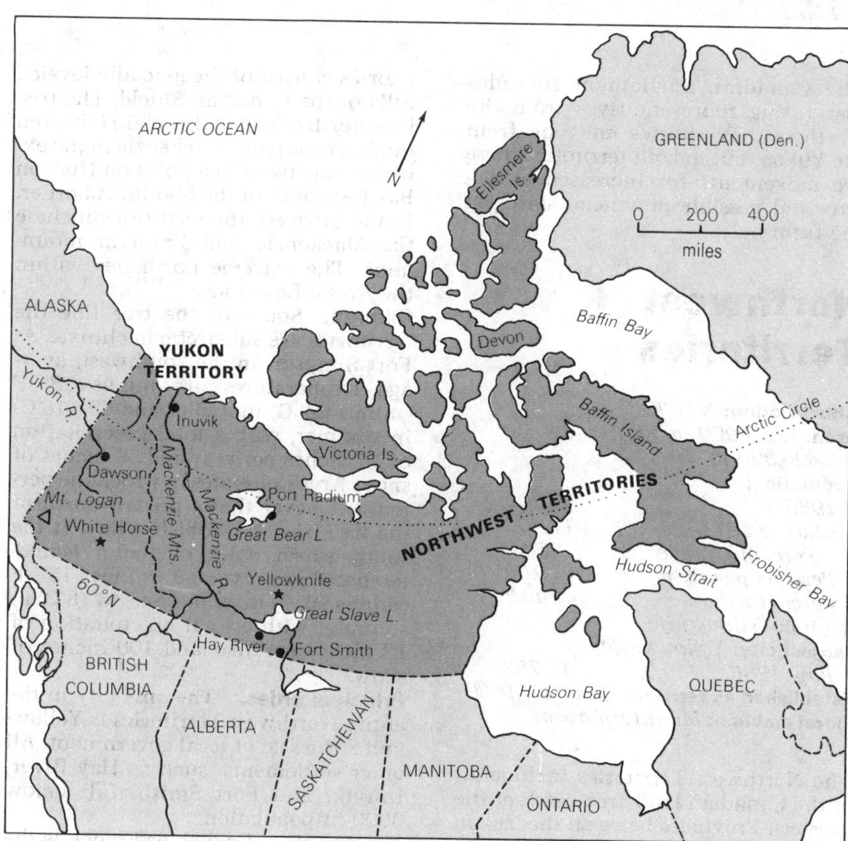

THE TERRITORIES

Territory	Area (sq. mi.)	Population 1986	Population change 1971–86 Number	Population change 1971–86 Percent	Persons per sq. mi.
Northwest	1,322,909	52,200	+17,400	+50.0	0.04
Yukon	186,661	23,500	+ 5,100	+27.7	0.13
Totals	1,509,570	75,700	+22,500	+42.3	0.05

The Yukon and the Northwest Territories occupy nearly the entire Canadian mainland north of 60° north latitude and include the numerous Arctic islands. Quebec's Ungava peninsula and the northern tip of Labrador are the only other Canadian lands above 60°. The Northwest Territories account for 87 percent of the area and two-thirds of the population. The Yukon, in the far west, accounts for the rest. The total expanse of over 1.5 million square miles represents 39 percent of the Canadian land area and is the home of only a fraction of 1 percent of the total population. Along with the U.S. state of Alaska, which forms its western boundary, this territorial area is the last great unexplored wilderness of North America.

The land. The land of the territories consists of the Canadian Shield, which covers the eastern two-thirds, and the western Cordillera, a mountain region that covers the western third. The Canadian Shield is a vast plain that averages between 600 and 1200 feet above sea level. Once mountainous in character, it was leveled by glacial ice sheets into rounded hills and depressed lake valleys. It is crossed from northwest to southeast by the tree line, north of which the frozen tundra cannot support forests. The Cordillera consists of the St. Elias Mountains, a coastal range in the southwest Yukon that is the highest in Canada; and the Mackenzie Mountains, in the western Northwest Territories, which are the northern end of the Rocky Mountain chain. Between these ranges lies a large mountain plateau that covers most of the Yukon Territory.

Climate. The climate of the territories varies from sub-arctic below the tree line to arctic above it. Winter temperatures are subzero in either

PRO PIX/MONKMEYER

BRYCE FLYNN/NFB PHOTOTEQUE

OLD AND NEW *live side by side in the northern territories. This ancient Indian woman lived through the boom and bust times in the Yukon. At* right, *a modern settlement on Frobisher Bay, Baffin Island.*

case, but the sub-arctic area experiences mild summers while the arctic region never experiences a complete thaw. Precipitation is uniformly low throughout the area, dropping to extremes of less than 10 inches per year far inland.

History. It is possible that the first European visitors to North America were Norse sailors who landed on Baffin Island in the Northwest Territories. The first permanent settlement was made by a party from the British vessel *Nonesuch* in 1668; two years later the British established the Hudson's Bay Company for fur trapping. The company owned the northern Canadian land area, called Rupert's Land, and gradually explored westward until it reached the Yukon Territory in the 1840's. In 1869 Canada took possession of the land, and in 1898, the year of the great Klondike gold rush, the suddenly valuable Yukon was set off from the Northwest Territories.

The people. The population of the territories is predominantly English speaking, but it is notable for its large proportion of Inuit (Eskimos) and Indians. The Northwest Territories include 75 percent of Canada's Inuit population. The Inuit are relatively unaffected by modernization because of the remoteness of the Arctic homelands. The Indian population is concentrated in the forested land south of the tree line; it includes a distinct group of mixed Indian and non-Indian ancestry called the Métis.

Government. Canada's two territories are administered by resident commissioners appointed by the government in Ottawa, which retains control of the as yet untapped fuel reserves. The Canadian Parliament includes two voting representatives from the Northwest Territories and one from the Yukon, but in both territories there are movements for increased autonomy and possible provincial status in the future.

Northwest Territories

Abbreviation: *N.W.T.*
Area: *1,322,909 sq. mi., 3,426,320 sq. km.*
Population:

1986	*52,200*
Change 1971–86	*+17,400*
Percent change	*+50.0*
Persons per sq. mi.	*0.04*
Percent urban	*49.7*

Capital: *Yellowknife*
Largest city: *Yellowknife*
Pop. 1986 *11,753*
Established as territory: *June 22, 1869*
Floral emblem: *Mountain avens*

The Northwest Territories include all of the Canadian land area north of the Western Provinces between the Yukon Territory on the west and Hudson Bay on the east. Its enormous area, exceeding that of the three largest provinces combined, includes an extensive archipelago of islands in the north; Baffin Island is the largest, and Ellesmere Island is the most northerly point in Canada. The Northwest Territories are divided into the districts of Mackenzie in the southwest, Keewatin in the southeast, and Franklin in the northern islands.

The land. Most of the Northwest Territories consist of the glacially leveled hills of the Canadian Shield. The tree line, north of which this plain is barren tundra, runs from Mackenzie in the extreme northwest to a point on Hudson Bay just south of the Manitoba border. In the far west, the territories include the Mackenzie and Franklin mountains. The extreme north lies within the Arctic Lowlands.

Climate. South of the tree line the territories are sub-arctic in climate. At Fort Simpson in the southwest, average temperatures are minus 18° F (minus 28° C) in winter and 60° (16°C) in summer, with a total precipitation of 14 inches per year and 59 inches of snow. Arctic climates in which the permafrost never thaws prevail north of the tree line. At Frobisher Bay, at the southeastern point of Baffin Island, temperatures average minus 15° F (minus 26° C) in winter and 46° (8°C) in summer, with a total precipitation of 17 inches per year and 100 inches of snow.

Principal cities. The only city in the entire Northwest Territories is Yellowknife, the seat of local government. All other settlements, such as Hay River, Inuvik, and Fort Smith, fall below 3000 in population.

The people. English or French is the mother tongue of only 56 percent of the territorial population. Of the remaining population, two-thirds are Inuit, the Eskimo people of the Arctic regions, and one-third are Indian, chiefly of the Athabascan tribe.

Economy. Mining is the only large industry of the Northwest Territories. Oil and gold were the earliest mineral products, but in recent years production has shifted to lead and zinc. Mining income was $659 million in 1986.

Places of interest. The many natural attractions of the Northwest Territories include Wood Buffalo National Park near the Alberta border, Nahanni National Park in the southwest, and Auyuittuq National Park above the Arctic Circle on Baffin Island.

Yukon Territory

Abbreviation: *Y.T.*
Area: *186,661 sq. mi., 483,450 sq. km.*
Population:

1986	*23,500*
Change 1971–86	*+5100*
Percent change	*+27.7*
Persons per sq. mi.	*0.13*
Percent urban	*61.0*

Capital: *Whitehorse*
Largest city: *Whitehorse*
Pop. 1986 *15,199*
Established as territory: *June 13, 1898*
Floral emblem: *Fireweed*

The Yukon Territory is located in the extreme northwest of Canada. It is triangular in shape, with a straight western border with the U.S. state of Alaska and a straight southern border with Alaska and the Western Province of British Columbia. The Yukon's irregular northeastern border with the Northwest Territories roughly approximates the ridge of the Mackenzie Mountains. The Yukon Territory remains an unspoiled wilderness notable for spectacular glaciers, even in its southern regions. A large portion of its dramatic mountain scenery has been accessible to visitors since the opening of the Alaskan Highway in 1942.

The land. The Yukon Territory lies entirely within the Cordillera, or mountain region, of western Canada. The highest mountain peaks are located in the southwest, where the St. Elias Mountains, part of the Pacific coastal ranges, include the highest point in Canada at Mt. Logan (19,525 feet). The interior of the Yukon is a mountain plateau that occupies more than half of the territorial area. Along the northeastern border the Yukon includes several individual ranges of the Mackenzie Mountains, a northern extension of the Rockies.

Climate. Because of its mountainous surface, the Yukon has a varied climate. At Dawson, near the center of the territory's western border, temperatures average minus 20° F (minus 29° C) in winter and 60° (15° C) in summer, with a total precipitation of 12 inches per year, including 55 inches of snow. The Yukon's inland plateau is far drier, with places averaging under 10 inches of precipitation per year, and colder, with temperatures that have dropped to the Canadian record low of minus 81° (minus 63° C).

Principal cities. The only city in the Yukon Territory is Whitehorse, which replaced Dawson as the territorial capital in 1951. Including surrounding towns, the city accounts for two-thirds of the total population. There is

THE FAR NORTH

Not until the 1500's did the North interest the people of Europe. Then, in a race to find a Northwest Passage to the Orient, a succession of explorers risked their lives in the cold, ice, and fog.

The fabled Northwest Passage was not discovered until the late 1800's, and it never proved practical for transportation or trade; but by then, a new breed of explorers were in a race to be the first to the North Pole. The first party to reach the Pole was led by Admiral Robert E. Peary of the United States. In the 1930's, U.S. Admiral Richard E. Byrd and others flew over the Pole, and in 1958, an American nuclear submarine, the *Nautilus*, sailed under the dense Arctic ice to the Pole.

By the 1950's, the Arctic regions had gained economic and strategic importance. Large deposits of iron, nickel, uranium, and other metals were found in northern Canada and the Soviet Union; and deposits of oil on the Arctic slope of Alaska and in the sea north of Norway have added to the world's fuel supply. Both the Americans and the Soviets, fearful of attack from the other, have set up monitoring stations around the edges of the Arctic region. These stations have provided valuable scientific data.

The region itself is bounded by the Arctic Circle, an imaginary line that marks the southernmost point where the sun never rises above the horizon on the shortest day of the year (about December 21st). The circle is about 1600 miles from the North Pole at 66.5 degrees north latitude.

Most of the Arctic is occupied by the Arctic Ocean, which has an area of more than 5 million square miles. Much of the ocean is covered year-round with ice, but near the Arctic Circle, it is navigable in the late summer. On land, although trees do not grow, a surprising variety of vegetable life, including many kinds of flowers, springs up during the short warm season. Both land and sea animals, including caribou, reindeer, bears, seals, and walruses, live in the area.

Small groups of people have also lived in or near the Arctic for centuries. Along its western shores from Greenland to Alaska, the Inuit (Eskimos) have mastered the art of hunting Arctic animals and fishing the icy waters. On the European shores, Lapps, Finns, and many isolated Siberian tribes still live. Many have abandoned their earlier patterns of life, however, and now rely on modern conveniences.

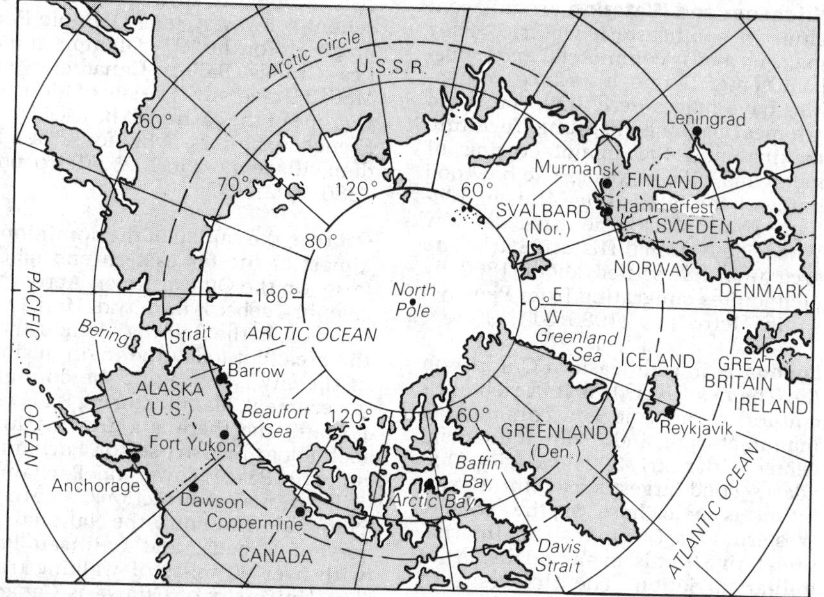

BETTY WHELAN

BROWN BROTHERS/LOOK MAGAZINE

ADMIRAL ROBERT E. PEARY

DAWSON, YUKON TERRITORY, *as it appeared at the height of the gold rush in 1899. In later years, the town became almost deserted.*

no other settlement with a permanent population of more than 2000.

The people. Most of the territorial population is English speaking. Nearly one-fifth of the population is comprised of Indian people. These include both the Indians of the Athabasca tribe and the Métis, who are of mixed Indian and non-Indian ancestry.

Economy. One-third of the Yukon's gross domestic product is derived from mining, principally of ores including copper, lead, zinc, gold, and silver. The only other significant industries are forestry and tourism.

Places of interest. The principal attractions in the Yukon, both of which are near the Alaskan Highway, are Kluane National Park in the southwestern Elias Mountains, and Dawson's restored gold rush town.

Cities of Canada

Calgary, Canada's fifth largest city, is located in the eastern foothills of the Rockies in southern Alberta. It is at the heart of a booming gas and oil-producing region, and is a major supplier of machinery and other goods to that industry. There are 900 industrial plants, and construction is also a major industry. In addition, Calgary acts as the processing, distributing, and service center for the bulk of Alberta's agricultural regions. Among cultural facilities are a symphony orchestra, museums, and the University of Calgary. Calgary was founded as a Northwest Mounted Police post in 1875. Metro. pop., 1986, 671,326.

Edmonton, the capital of the province of Alberta, is nearly in the center of the province, on the North Saskatchewan River. It is also in the heart of a growing oil, gas, and coal-producing region. It has many manufacturing plants, a large part of whose products supply the energy companies. Food and beverage production represent the second largest economic activity. Edmonton is an important transportation center for western and northern Canada. There is an opera company and a symphony orchestra, and Edmonton is the site of the University of Alberta. The city has extensive park lands. Metro. pop., 1986, 785,465.

Halifax, on the south coast of Nova Scotia, is one of the most important ports on the Atlantic seaboard. It is also a busy center of the commercial fisheries, with more than 800 fishing boats operating out of the area. In manufacturing, food and beverages account for the largest single sector. The city is also the center of retail trade for the province. Halifax has a professional repertory theater and is the home of Dalhousie University. The city was the first town in Canada settled primarily by the English. Metro. pop., 1986, 295,990.

Hamilton, at the western end of Lake Ontario, produces a little more than half the steel made in Canada. It has 800 industries in all, and machinery, food, and beverages play major parts in the city's industry. Hamilton has a large harbor that handles 900 ships a year. The Royal Botanical Gardens cover 2000 acres. The city is also the home of McMaster University, the Art Gallery of Hamilton, and the Canadian Football Hall of Fame. Hamilton was settled in 1778 by United Empire Loyalists. Metro. pop., 1986, 557,029.

Kitchener and Waterloo are adjacent cities in southeastern Ontario. They make up a busy commercial and industrial center. Large insurance companies have offices here. Important also are meat packing, distilling, furniture making, and the manufacturing of metal and rubber goods. The boyhood home of the late Prime Minister William Lyon Mackenzie King is now Woodside National Historic Park. The area was first settled about 1800 by Mennonites emigrating from Pennsylvania. Metro. pop., 1986, 311,195.

London is in southeastern Ontario on the Thames River. It is in a rich agricultural region and is a commercial, manufacturing, and regional financial center, with nearly 500 industries. Canada's second largest agricultural exhibition is held here at the 85-acre Western Fair Grounds. The International Air Show is an annual display of military aviation. The University of Western Ontario is here. The first white settlers in the region, in 1783, were United Empire Loyalists. The site of the city was first occupied in 1830. Metro. pop., 1986, 342,302.

Montreal, Canada's second largest metropolitan area and also the second largest French-speaking city in the world, is on an island in the St. Lawrence River. A cosmopolitan city with much evidence of French culture, it is also by virtue of its location on the St. Lawrence Seaway the chief gateway to the North American heartland and a focal point of all kinds of transportation. Montreal is also a banking and financial center, as well as a city of large and varied manufacturing operations, led by food and beverages. Of the total population, about 64 percent is French. Montreal is a favorite of tourists. Among its attractions are its excellent subway system; Olympic Park, first built for the 1976 Olympic games; Les Grands Ballets Canadiens; and McGill University. The site of Montreal was one of the earliest to be used by the French explorers, who found an Indian village there in 1535. Metro. pop., 1986, 2,921,357.

Ottawa, the capital of the dominion, is almost at the far eastern end of Ontario, on the Ottawa River. Across the river in Quebec is the city of Hull. Lumbering was the first major industry of the area, but today the main business of the city is managing the dominion government. Manufacturing is also important, and there is a growing high-technology industry sector. Parliament and the Peace Tower on Parliament Hill are major attractions, as are the National Arts Centre, the National Gallery of Canada, and Gatineau Park, with over 60 miles of walking trails. The University of Ottawa is Canada's largest bilingual university. Ottawa was first known as Bytown, named for Colonel John By who, with British army engineers, arrived in 1826 to build the Rideau Canal. Metro. pop., 1986, 819,263.

Quebec, on the St. Lawrence River, where the St. Charles River flows into it, is the capital of the province of Quebec. It is a center of government administration as well as a commercial and industrial city and a popular place for tourists. Food products, textiles, clothing, machinery, autos, and lumber are included in its output. The many historical attractions include La Citadelle, a fort restored in 1820–1832, and statues of Champlain and Cartier. A winter carnival is held every February. At the University of Quebec, teaching is in French. Only about 4 percent of the population come from English backgrounds. There was an Indian village on the site in 1535 when Cartier came to the area. Metro. pop., 1986, 603,267.

St. Catharines and Niagara Falls are the two largest of the twelve municipalities that make up the Niagara region, a wedge of land between Lake Ontario and Lake Erie. It is bounded on the east by the United States and on the west by the Hamilton, Ontario, area. St. Catharines, on the Welland Canal, is in the heart of Canada's wine country, and half of the fruit grown in Ontario comes from the immediate area. It also has nearly 250 manufacturing establishments, the largest product being transportation equipment. The Royal Canadian Henley Regatta is rowed here each year. Niagara Falls is a popular tourist attraction. The Rainbow Tower Carillon of 55 tuned bells is here, as is the Niagara Daredevil Exhibit. St. Catharines was founded after the American Revolution by Loyalists who came north. The first families on the site of Niagara Falls arrived in 1782. Metro. pop., 1986, 343,258.

Saskatoon, in south central Saskatchewan, is on the South Saskatchewan River. Its 210 manufacturing establishments produce a variety of goods, and the city has benefited from increased production of potash, uranium, and oil. It is also a processing and distributing center for agricultural products. There are two museums devoted to Ukrainian culture, and the University of Saskatchewan is here. Saskatoon was first settled in 1882 by members of the Temperance Colonization Society. Metro. pop., 1986, 161,901.

Toronto, located on the northwestern shore of Lake Ontario, is the capital of the province of Ontario and Canada's largest metropolitan area. It is a cosmopolitan city of commerce, industry, and retail trade, and is the financial center of the dominion. Its 5700 manufacturing establishments produce metal, electrical, rubber, plastic, chemical, paper, printing, food, and beverage goods, among others. Toronto is the home of many cultural and entertainment facilities. Among them are the Royal Ontario Museum, the Art Gallery of Canada, Ft. York (a reconstruction of the old fort), the Canadian National Exhibition (the oldest and largest annual exhibition in the world), the Hockey Hall of Fame, and the CN Tower (at 1815 feet the tallest free-standing structure in the world). The University of Toronto and York University are located here. The French built a fort on the city's site in 1749, and the British formally named the locality York in 1793. The name was later changed to Toronto, in 1834. Metro. pop., 1986, 3,427,168.

Vancouver, in the southwestern corner of the mainland of British Columbia, and only 15 miles north of the American border, is Canada's third largest metropolitan area. It is also Canada's gateway to the Orient as one of North America's busiest ports. Nearly 50 million tons of cargo go in and out of the port every year, and it can handle 375 million bushels of grain annually. Vancouver is a cosmopolitan city with a varied ethnic population, including among others the largest Chinatown on the continent outside of San Francisco. Among many attractions are the Vancouver Art Gallery, the Maritime Museum, and the H. R. MacMillan Planetarium. Simon Fraser University is here. The area was first sighted in 1791 by a Spanish explorer. It was claimed the next year for Great Britain by George Vancouver; however, there were no permanent settlers on the site until 1862. Metro. pop., 1986, 1,380,729.

Victoria, the capital of British Columbia, lies at the southeastern end of Vancouver Island. Tourism is the city's major business, followed by government, labor, and commercial fisheries. Although reputed to be "more English than England," Victoria holds a folkfest each July with a variety of ethnic performances. In the summer months, 650 flower baskets decorate the light standards of the business section. The Art Gallery of Greater Victoria is a major attraction. Victoria began in 1843 as a Hudson's Bay Company post known as Fort Camosun, but the name was soon changed to Fort Victoria. It became the capital of the Crown colony of Vancouver Island in 1862, and part of British Columbia in 1866. Metro. pop., 1986, 255,547.

Windsor, Ontario, is Canada's largest city on the United States border. It is on the Detroit River, opposite Detroit, Michigan, with which it is connected by a bridge and a vehicular and railway tunnel. Windsor is one of Canada's busiest ports of entry. Auto manufac-

VANCOUVER, *British Columbia, hosted Expo '86, where one of the big attractions was the waterfront Canadian pavilion.*

GOVERNMENT OF CANADA

turing is the largest single enterprise. Located in a region favorable to agriculture, Windsor is also a large producer of foods and beverage products. The Art Gallery of Windsor and the Hiram Walker Historical Museum are popular. Once a year Windsor joins with Detroit in an International Freedom Festival. The city was founded by French trappers in 1749. After the American Revolution many Loyalists arrived. Metro. pop., 1986, 253,988.

Winnipeg, in southern Manitoba, where the Assiniboine River joins the Red River, is the capital of the province. It is located, roughly, at the geographical center of the North American continent, and it is the chief market center of one of the world's largest grain-producing areas. Winnipeg's varied industries make it the most diversified secondary manufacturing city in Canada, and it is also important as the financial, distribution, and transportation center of western Canada. Winnipeg is also a lively home of culture and entertainment. It has a symphony orchestra, the Royal Winnipeg Ballet, and an art museum. The Folklorama is a popular annual festival featuring 30 ethnic groups. The first settlement here was a fort that was built by the French in 1783. Later, the English also built forts. In 1873 the city was incorporated as Winnipeg. Metro. pop., 1986, 625,304.

Natural Features of Canada

Athabasca, Lake, the fourth largest lake in Canada, covers about 3120 square miles. It is about 200 miles long and five to 35 miles wide. Lying in northeast Alberta and northwest Saskatchewan, the lake is part of the Mackenzie River system and drains north into Great Slave Lake by way of the Slave River.

Athabasca River and Pass. The river rises in the Rockies, flows north through Jasper National Park, and then northeast and north to Lake Athabasca. It is the most southerly tributary of the Mackenzie River. Near the headwaters of the Athabasca is Athabasca Pass, elevation 5736 feet, which leads across the Continental Divide to the Columbia River.

Baffin Island, the largest in the Arctic Archipelago, lies northeast of Hudson Bay. Its area is 183,810 square miles. It is about 1000 miles long and 130 to 450 miles wide. On the west it is mostly covered with tundra, while to the east mountains rise to about 8000 feet. The coastline is deeply indented and has many fjords.

Banff National Park is Canada's oldest park. It covers 2564 square miles in western Alberta. In the midst of the Rockies, the park has several peaks 12,000 feet high. There are hot mineral springs, ice fields, glaciers, and mountain lakes. Lake Louise, discovered in 1882 and named for a daughter of Queen Victoria, is a popular resort.

Fraser River, about 850 miles long, rises near Yellowhead Pass in the Rockies. It flows northwest, then south and west to the Strait of Georgia at Vancouver. The Fraser River canyon, with walls more than 3000 feet high, is noted for its scenery. The river was discovered in 1793 by Alexander Mackenzie. Simon Fraser first followed it to its mouth in 1808.

Fundy, Bay of, is an inlet of the Atlantic Ocean between New Brunswick and Nova Scotia. It is about 170 miles long and 30 to 50 miles wide. The bay is famous for its tides, the highest in the world, which reach a maximum of about 52 feet. The tide creates the unusual Reversing Falls Rapids in the city of St. John.

Gaspé Peninsula is a tongue of land in eastern Quebec that lies between the St. Lawrence River and Chaleur Bay on the south. It extends eastward into the Gulf of St. Lawrence. It is about 150 miles long and 60 to 90 miles wide. The backbone of the Gaspé is part of the Appalachian Mountain system; the highest part is called the Shickshock Mountains.

Great Bear Lake is the fourth largest in North America, bigger than Erie or Ontario. Its area is more than 12,000 square miles. It is 190 miles long, 20 to 110 wide. The lake lies on the Arctic Circle in the Mackenzie District of the Northwest Territories and is on the edge of the Canadian Shield. It is drained by the Great Bear River into the Mackenzie River.

Great Slave Lake, the second largest lake in Canada, covers about 11,000 square miles. It drains into the Mackenzie River. The lake is 300 miles long and is the deepest in North America at 2015 feet. The western shore is wooded, but the country around the long north and east arms is tundralike.

Hudson Bay is an inland sea of about 475,000 square miles in east central Canada. It is part of the Northwest Territories, but Manitoba, Ontario, and Quebec have shorelines on the bay. The bay is about 850 miles long and 650 miles wide. There is too much ice for navigation from October until July. The rivers flowing into the bay drain an area of almost 1,400,000 square miles. It is connected to the Atlantic Ocean by the Hudson Strait, which goes northwest from the northern end of Labrador for about 450 miles, and to the Arctic Ocean by Foxe Channel.

Jasper National Park, established in 1907, is the second largest of Canada's scenic parks and covers about 4200 square miles. It is in the Rockies, in western Alberta on the British Columbia border. There are many high peaks, part of the Columbia Icefield, hot springs, game reserves, and rivers and lakes. Among the lakes are Jasper and Maligne.

Klondike is an area of the Yukon Territory just east of the border with Alaska. The area is centered on the Klondike River and is about 100 miles in length. The river flows into the Yukon River at Dawson. In August, 1896, gold was found in a tributary of the Klondike, and when news of it reached the outside world the next year, a stampede began. By 1898 there were about 25,000 people where hardly any had been before. The rush soon died down and by 1920 fewer than 1000 persons lived in Dawson.

Laurentian Mountains are in southern Quebec, north of the St. Lawrence and Ottawa rivers. They form the watershed between Hudson Bay and the St. Lawrence. Mt. Tremblant is 3150 feet high. The Laurentians are a year-round recreation area, especially noted for skiing in the winter.

Logan, Mount, is the highest peak in Canada and the second highest in North America. It is 19,850 feet high and rises in the St. Elias Mountains in the southwestern corner of the Yukon Territory. Mt. Logan towers over a vast tableland and stands at the center of the largest glacial expanse on the continent.

Mackenzie River is about 1120 miles long, but with the rivers and lakes that flow into it, it constitutes a system of about 2600 miles, exceeded in North America only by the Mississippi–Missouri system. The Mackenzie begins in the western part of the Northwest Territories, flowing out of the west end of Great Slave Lake, and goes northwest into the Beaufort Sea. There

CANADIAN GOVERNMENT OFFICE OF TOURISM

THE MACKENZIE RIVER, *second longest river in North America, forms a large delta as it reaches the Arctic Ocean.*

is a large delta at its mouth. The system includes the Finlay, Peace, Liard, Athabasca, and Slave rivers, and Great Bear Lake. The system is navigable from June to October over almost 2000 miles of its length, with only one portage. The region was and is important for fur trapping, and in recent years valuable mineral and oil deposits have been found. The area was probably first entered in 1777 by Peter Pond, a Connecticut native and a representative of the North West Company. It is named for Alexander Mackenzie, who first followed it to its mouth in 1789. The river is flanked on the east by the Canadian Shield and on the west by the Mackenzie Mountains, part of the Rockies. They extend for about 500 miles, with one peak as high as 9049 feet. In the southern part is a game reserve, the Mackenzie Mountains Preserve.

Manitoba, Lake, in southwestern Manitoba, is about 130 miles long and 28 wide, and covers 1817 square miles. It drains into Lake Winnipeg. Manitoba, with Winnipeg, is part of the remains of Lake Agassiz, the vast body of water formed 10,000 years ago when the continental ice sheet melted.

Nelson River flows for about 400 miles from the northeastern end of Lake Winnipeg to Hudson Bay at Port Nelson. With the rivers that flow into the lake, the Nelson is the main part of a 1600-mile system from western Alberta to Hudson Bay. The river was a fur-trade route, and a trading post at its mouth, York Fort or Factory, was operated from 1684 by the Hudson's Bay Company for 273 years, until 1957.

Niagara Falls, in the Niagara River, between lakes Erie and Ontario, is shared by Canada and the United States. On the Canadian side is the Horseshoe, or Canadian, Falls, 176 feet high and 2600 feet wide. The falls were formed about 10,000 years ago when the ice age ended and the Niagara escarpment was exposed. This allowed water to flow north from Lake Erie over the escarpment.

Ottawa River, about 700 miles long, rises in the Laurentian Highlands of southwestern Quebec. For much of its length it forms the boundary between Quebec and Ontario, passing the city of Ottawa, and emptying into the St. Lawrence near Montreal. There are large hydroelectric developments on the river. From Ottawa there is a connection by the Rideau Canal to Kingston on Lake Ontario. Built but never used for military purposes, the canal system is a popular recreation route.

St. Lawrence River has been a prime commercial route since the earliest days of fur trapping. It starts at the northeast end of Lake Ontario and runs northeasterly 744 miles to the Gulf of St. Lawrence. Combined with the Great Lakes, all of which it drains, the St. Lawrence is part of a system of about 2300 miles. The first 114 miles form the border between Canada and the United States. In a stretch of about 50 miles near Lake Ontario is the Thousand Islands region.

Saskatchewan River is formed near Prince Albert, Saskatchewan, where the north and south branches meet. It flows 340 miles east into Lake Winnipeg. The North and South Saskatchewan Rivers both start in the Rockies of western Alberta. The former is about 760 miles long and the latter 550. The Saskatchewan system drains most of the prairie provinces. On the South Saskatchewan, near Outlook, is Gardiner Dam, of rolled-earth fill, one of the largest dams of its kind in the world.

Takakkawa Falls, the highest in Canada, falls about 1650 feet in three drops. It is in Yoho National Park. The park, 507 square miles, is in the Rockies in British Columbia, on the Alberta border. The park has several peaks over 10,000 feet.

Vancouver Island, a part of British Columbia, lies in the Pacific off the southwest coast of the mainland. It covers about 12,500 square miles and is 285 miles long and 30 to 80 miles wide. The island is a partially submerged section of the Coast Ranges, and is separated from the mainland by Georgia Strait and Queen Charlotte Strait. The greatest amount of precipitation anywhere in North America falls on the western side. Pacific Rim National Park is on the island.

Victoria Island, Canada's third largest, is in the Arctic Archipelago, north of Maude and Coronation gulfs. It covers nearly 82,000 square miles and has an irregular, deeply indented coastline. Prince Albert Sound is a deep inlet on the west coast.

Winnipeg, Lake, is 9465 square miles in extent and is Canada's third largest. It is about 264 miles long and 25 to 68 miles wide. Lake Winnipeg is in south central Manitoba and the Red, Winnipeg, and Saskatchewan rivers drain into it. It is drained by the Nelson River. Lake Winnipeg is a summer resort area, and fishing is important.

Yukon River, which rises in Atlin Lake in northwest British Columbia, is one of the longest in North America. It flows northwest, past Dawson, Yukon Territory, into Alaska, and eventually into the Bering Sea, a total distance of about 2000 miles. It is navigable for three months of the year as far as Whitehorse, in the southern Yukon.

—Fon W. Boardman, Jr.

For Further Reference

United States

Allen, Frederick Lewis. *The Big Change: America Transforms Itself, 1900–1950.* Harper & Row, 1952.

Billington, Ray Allen. *The Westward Movement in the United States.* Van Nostrand Reinhold, 1959.

Bonds, Ray. *The Modern U.S. War Machine.* Crown, 1987.

Boorstin, Daniel J. *The Americans.* 3 volumes. Random House, 1958–1973.

Boorstin, Daniel, editor. *An American Primer.* University of Chicago Press, 1966.

Burns, James McGregor. *The American Experiment.* 2 volumes. Alfred A. Knopf, 1982, 1985.

Carruth, Gorton, editor. *The Encyclopedia of American Facts and Dates* (8th Ed.). Harper & Row, 1987.

Catton, Bruce. *The American Heritage Short History of the Civil War.* American Heritage, 1982.

Countryman, Edward. *The American Revolution.* Hill & Wang, 1985.

Current, Richard N., et al. *Essentials of American History* (4th Ed.). 2 volumes. Alfred A. Knopf, 1986.

Degler, Carl. N. *Affluence and Anxiety: America Since 1945* (2nd Ed.). Scott, Foresman, 1975.

Degler, Carl N. *At Odds: Women and the Family in America from the Revolution to the Present.* Oxford University Press, 1980.

Dellinger, David. *Vietnam Revisited: Covert Action to Invasion to Reconstruction.* South End Press, 1984.

Dulles, Foster R. *A History of Recreation: America Learns to Play* (2nd Ed.). Appleton-Century-Crofts, 1965.

Dulles, Foster R. *Labor in America* (4th Ed.). Harlan Davidson, 1984.

Foote, Shelby. *The Civil War: A Narrative.* 3 volumes. Random House, 1958–1974.

Franklin, John Hope. *From Slavery to Freedom: A History of Negro Americans* (5th Ed.). Alfred A. Knopf, 1980.

Galbraith, John Kenneth. *The Great Crash, 1929.* Houghton Mifflin, 1955.

Garraty, John A. *A Short History of the American Nation* (4th Ed.). 2 volumes. Harper & Row, 1985.

Glaab, Charles N., and A. Theodore Brown. *A History of Urban America* (3rd Ed.). Macmillan, 1983.

Goldman, Eric F. *The Crucial Decade—And After: America, 1945–60.* Random House, 1960.

Hagan, William T. *American Indians* (Revised Ed.). University of Chicago Press, 1979.

Hopkins, J.G., editor. *Concise Dictionary of American Biography* (3rd Ed.). Charles Scribner's Sons, 1980.

Hudson, Winthrop S. *Religion in America* (3rd Ed.). Charles Scribner's Sons, 1981.

Kaufman, Burton. *The Korean War.* Alfred A. Knopf, 1986.

Kennedy, David M. *Over Here: The First World War and American Society.* Oxford University Press, 1980.

Leuchtenburg, William E. *Franklin D. Roosevelt and the New Deal, 1932–1940.* Harper & Row, 1963.

Lewy, Guenter. *America in Vietnam.* Oxford University Press, 1978.

Liddell Hart, B. H. *History of the Second World War.* G.P. Putnam's Sons, 1971.

Litwack, Leon. *The American Labor Movement.* Simon & Schuster, 1986.

McElvaine, Robert S. *The Great Depression: America, 1929–1941.* Times Books, 1984.

Morison, Samuel Eliot, Henry Steele Commager, and William E. Leuchtenburg. *A Concise History of the American Republic* (2nd Ed.). Oxford University Press, 1983.

Morris, Richard B. *The American Revolution: A Short History.* Krieger, 1979.

Morris, Richard B., and Jeffrey B. Morris. *Encyclopedia of American History* (6th Ed.). Harper & Row, 1982.

Nichols, Roger. *The American Indian: Past and Present* (3rd Ed.). Alfred A. Knopf, 1985.

Niemi, Albert W., Jr. *U.S. Economic History* (2nd Ed.). University Press of America, 1987.

O'Toole, G. J.A. *The Spanish War: An American Epic, 1898.* W. W. Norton, 1984.

Randall, J.G., and David Donald. *The Civil War and Reconstruction* (2nd Ed.). D. C. Heath, 1969.

Schlesinger, Arthur M., Jr., editor. *The Almanac of American History.* G.P. Putnam's Sons, 1983.

Shannon, David. *Between the Wars: America, 1919 to 1941* (2nd Ed.). Prentice-Hall, 1979.

Starr, Jerold M. *America at War in Vietnam: Decisions and Consequences.* Center for Social Studies, 1988.

Ver Steeg, Clarence L., and Richard Hofstadter. *Great Issues in American History.* 3 volumes. Random House, 1969.

Voorhees, David William, editor. *Concise Dictionary of American History* (3rd Ed.). Charles Scribner's Sons, 1983.

Washburn, Wilcomb E. *The Indian in America.* Harper & Row, 1975.

Weinstein, Allen, et al. *American Negro Slavery* (3rd Ed.). Oxford University Press, 1979.

Williams, T. Harry. *The History of American Wars: From 1745–1918.* Louisiana State University Press, 1985.

Canada

Barlett, G., and J. Galivan. *Canada: History in the Making.* Wiley, 1986.

Bothwell, Robert, et al. *Canada Since 1945: Power, Politics, and Provincialism.* University of Toronto Press, 1982.

Bothwell, Robert, et al. *Canada Nineteen Hundred to Nineteen Forty Five.* University of Toronto Press, 1987.

Bracken, Susan, editor. *Canadian Almanac and Directory.* Copp Clarke Pitman, 1986.

Clarke, C. E., editor. *Corpus Almanac and Canadian Sourcebook* (20th Ed.). Southam Communications, 1985.

Creighton, Donald G. *The Road to Confederation: The Emergence of Canada, 1863–67.* Greenwood Press, 1965, 1976.

Dawson, Robert M. *Democratic Government in Canada* (4th Ed.). University of Toronto Press, 1971.

Finlay, J.L., and D.N. Sprague. *The Structure of Canadian History* (2nd Ed.). Prentice-Hall, 1984.

Gough, Barry. *Canada.* Prentice-Hall, 1987.

Hill, Brian H.W., editor. *Canada: A Chronology and Fact Book. 875–1973.* Oceana, 1973.

Lowery, Arthur R. *Canadians in the Making: A Social History of Canada.* Greenwood Press, 1958, 1981.

Malcolm, Andrew H. *The Canadians.* Times Books, 1985.

Marr, William T., and Donald G. Paterson. *Canada: An Economic History.* Macmillan, 1980.

Marsh, James H., editor. *The Canadian Encyclopedia.* 3 volumes. Hurtig, 1985.

McInnis, Edgar W. *Canada: A Political and Social History* (4th Ed.). Holt, 1982.

Morton, Desmond. *A Short History of Canada.* Hurtig, 1983.

Story, Norah. *The Oxford Companion to Canadian History and Literature.* Oxford University Press, 1967.

United States and Canada

Borodayevsky, D. *Canada-U.S.A. Problems and Contradictions in Economic Integration.* Imported Publications, 1987.

Brebner, J. Bartlet. *North Atlantic Triangle: The Interplay of Canada, the United States, and Great Britain.* Russell, 1966, 1980.

Doran, Charles. *Forgotten Partnership: U.S.-Canada Relations Today.* Johns Hopkins University Press, 1983.

Doran, Charles, and John H. Sigler, editors. *Canada and the United States: Enduring Friendship, Persistent Stress.* Prentice-Hall, 1985.

Robins-Mowry, Dorothy, editor. *Canada-U.S. Relations: Perceptions and Misperceptions.* University Press of America, 1988.

VOLUME 27

Atlas

GAZETTEER—INDEX OF THE WORLD

This alphabetical list of grand divisions, countries, states, colonial possessions, etc., gives the area, population, capital or chief town, and index references and page numbers on which they are shown on the largest scale. The index reference shows the square on the respective map in which the name of the entry may be located.

COUNTRY	AREA SQUARE MILES	AREA SQUARE KILOMETERS	POPULATION	CAPITAL OR CHIEF TOWN	INDEX REF.	PAGE NO.
·Afghanistan	250,775	649,507	17,672,000	Kabul	A 2	2396
Africa	11,707,000	30,321,130	537,000,000	....	...	2364
Alabama, U.S.A.	51,705	133,916	3,893,978	Montgomery	M 6	2355
Alaska, U.S.A.	591,004	1,530,700	401,851	Juneau	F 8	2353
·Albania	11,100	28,749	2,590,600	Tiranë	B 3	2386
Alberta, Can.	255,285	661,185	2,237,724	Edmonton	E 5	2350
·Algeria	919,591	2,381,740	18,666,000	Algiers	D 3	2366
American Samoa	77	199	32,297	Pago Pago	J 7	2403
Andorra	188	487	39,940	Andorra la Vella	G 1	2381
·Angola	481,351	1,246,700	7,262,000	Luanda	C 5	2370
Anguilla	35	91	6,519	The Valley	F 3	2349
Antarctica	5,500,000	14,245,000	....	....	...	2406
·Antigua and Barbuda	171	443	77,000	St. John's	G 3	2349
·Argentina	1,072,070	2,776,661	30,097,000	Buenos Aires	H 10	2362
Arizona, U.S.A.	114,000	295,260	2,718,425	Phoenix	E 6	2353
Arkansas, U.S.A.	53,187	137,754	2,286,419	Little Rock	K 6	2355
Aruba	75	193	66,790	Oranjestad	D 4	2349
Ascension Island, St. Helena	34	88	719	Georgetown	A 5	2365
Asia	17,128,500	44,362,815	2,819,196,000	....	...	2390
·Australia	2,966,136	7,682,300	14,576,330	Canberra	...	2404
·Austria	32,375	83,851	7,555,338	Vienna	C 3	2385
·Bahamas	5,382	13,939	209,505	Nassau	C 1	2349
·Bahrain	240	622	350,798	Manama	F 4	2393
·Bangladesh	55,126	142,776	87,119,965	Dhaka	G 4	2396
·Barbados	166	430	248,983	Bridgetown	G 4	2349
·Belgium	11,781	30,513	9,848,647	Brussels	B 4	2379
·Belize	8,867	22,966	145,353	Belmopan	B 1	2357
·Benin	43,483	112,620	3,338,240	Porto-Novo	E 6	2367
Bermuda	21	54	67,761	Hamilton	H 3	2349
·Bhutan	18,147	47,000	1,301,000	Thimphu	G 3	2396
·Bolivia	424,163	1,098,582	6,082,000	La Paz; Sucre	G 7	2360
·Botswana	224,764	582,139	936,600	Gaborone	C 4	2372
·Brazil	3,284,426	8,506,663	119,098,992	Brasília	K 6	2361
British Columbia, Can.	366,253	948,596	2,744,467	Victoria	D 4	2350
British Indian Ocean Territory	29	75	2,000	(London, U.K.)	J 10	2391
·Brunei	2,226	5,765	192,832	Bandar Seri Begawan	E 5	2401
·Bulgaria	42,823	110,912	8,942,976	Sofia	D 3	2386
·Burkina Faso	105,869	274,200	7,919,895	Ouagadougou	D 6	2367
·Burma	261,789	678,034	36,747,000	Rangoon	B 1	2401
·Burundi	10,747	27,835	4,028,020	Bujumbura	E 3	2371
·Byelorussian S.S.R. (White Russian S.S.R.), U.S.S.R.	80,514	207,600	9,560,543	Minsk	C 4	2386
California, U.S.A.	158,706	411,049	23,667,826	Sacramento	C 5	2352
·Cambodia (Kampuchea)	69,898	181,036	5,756,141	Phnom Penh	C 3	2401
·Cameroon	183,568	475,441	9,432,000	Yaoundé	B 1	2370
·Canada	3,851,787	9,976,139	24,343,181	Ottawa	...	2350
·Cape Verde	1,557	4,033	296,093	Praia	B 8	2367
Cayman Islands	100	259	19,000	Georgetown	B 3	2349
·Central African Republic	242,000	626,780	2,442,000	Bangui	C 1	2370
Central America	197,480	511,475	25,000,000	....	...	2357
·Chad	495,752	1,283,998	4,309,000	N'Djamena	C 4	2368
Channel Islands	75	194	129,363	St. Helier; St. Peter Port	E 6	2376
·Chile	292,257	756,946	11,275,440	Santiago	F 10	2362
·China, People's Republic of	3,691,000	9,559,690	1,036,000,000	Peking (Beijing)	G 5	2398
China, Republic of (Taiwan)	13,971	36,185	18,029,798	Taipei	K 7	2399
Christmas Island	52	135	3,308	Flying Fish Cove	M 11	2391
·Colombia	439,513	1,138,339	28,217,000	Bogotá	F 3	2360
Colorado, U.S.A.	104,091	269,596	2,889,735	Denver	G 5	2353
·Comoros	719	1,862	345,000	Moroni	G 2	2373
·Congo	132,046	342,000	1,912,429	Brazzaville	C 3	2370
Connecticut, U.S.A.	5,018	12,997	3,107,576	Hartford	O 2	2354
Cook Islands	91	236	17,754	Avarua	K 7	2403
·Costa Rica	19,575	50,700	2,379,000	San José	C 3	2357
·Cuba	44,206	114,494	9,706,369	Havana	B 2	2349
·Cyprus	3,473	8,995	655,000	Nicosia	E 5	2394
·Czechoslovakia	49,373	127,876	15,470,000	Prague	C 1	2385
Delaware, U.S.A.	2,044	5,294	594,317	Dover	P 5	2354
·Denmark	16,629	43,069	5,114,000	Copenhagen	B 3	2377
District of Columbia, U.S.A.	69	179	638,432	Washington	O 5	2355
·Djibouti	8,880	23,000	330,000	Djibouti	H 5	2369
·Dominica	290	751	74,089	Roseau	G 4	2349
·Dominican Republic	18,704	48,443	5,647,977	Santo Domingo	D 3	2349
·Ecuador	109,483	283,561	9,251,000	Quito	E 4	2360
·Egypt	386,659	1,001,447	45,915,000	Cairo	E 2	2368
·El Salvador	8,260	21,393	4,999,000	San Salvador	B 2	2357
England, U.K.	50,516	130,836	46,220,995	London	F 5	2376
·Equatorial Guinea	10,831	28,052	300,000	Malabo	A 2	2370
·Ethiopia	471,776	1,221,900	33,680,000	Addis Ababa	G 5	2369
Europe	4,057,000	10,507,600	723,804,000	....	...	2374
Faeroe Islands, Denmark	540	1,399	45,000	Tórshavn	D 2	2374
Falkland Islands and Dependencies	6,198	16,053	1,813	Stanley	H 14	2362
·Fiji	7,055	18,272	671,712	Suva	H 8	2402
·Finland	130,128	337,032	4,869,858	Helsinki	E 2	2377
Florida, U.S.A.	58,664	151,940	9,746,421	Tallahassee	M 7	2355
·France	210,038	543,998	54,334,871	Paris	...	2380
French Guiana	35,135	91,000	73,022	Cayenne	K 3	2361
French Polynesia	1,544	4,000	166,753	Papeete	L 8	2403
·Gabon	103,346	267,666	555,000	Libreville	B 3	2370
·Gambia	4,127	10,689	695,886	Banjul	A 6	2367
Georgia, U.S.A.	58,910	152,577	5,463,087	Atlanta	N 6	2355
·Germany, East (German Democratic Republic)	41,768	108,179	16,732,486	Berlin (East)	...	2378
·Germany, West (Federal Republic)	95,985	248,601	61,306,667	Bonn	...	2378
·Ghana	92,099	238,536	12,205,574	Accra	D 7	2367
Gibraltar	2.28	5.91	29,648	Gibraltar	D 4	2381
·Great Britain and Northern Ireland (United Kingdom)	94,399	244,493	55,638,495	London	...	2376
·Greece	50,944	131,945	9,740,417	Athens	C 4	2386
Greenland	840,000	2,715,600	52,000	Nuuk (Godthåb)	P 2	2348
·Grenada	133	344	103,103	St. George's	F 4	2349
Guadeloupe and Dependencies	687	1,779	328,499	Basse-Terre	F 3	2349
Guam	209	541	105,979	Agaña	E 4	2402
·Guatemala	42,042	108,889	6,043,559	Guatemala	B 2	2357
·Guinea	94,925	245,856	5,143,284	Conakry	B 6	2367
·Guinea-Bissau	13,948	36,125	810,000	Bissau	A 6	2367
·Guyana	83,000	214,970	793,000	Georgetown	J 2	2361
·Haiti	10,694	27,697	5,053,792	Port-au-Prince	D 3	2349
Hawaii, U.S.A.	6,471	16,760	964,691	Honolulu	G 8	2353
·Honduras	43,277	112,087	4,092,000	Tegucigalpa	C 2	2357
Hong Kong	403	1,044	4,986,560	Victoria	H 7	2399
·Hungary	35,919	93,020	10,664,000	Budapest	E 3	2385
·Iceland	39,768	103,000	237,000	Reykjavík	C 2	2374
Idaho, U.S.A.	83,564	216,431	944,038	Boise	E 3	2352
Illinois, U.S.A.	56,345	145,934	11,427,414	Springfield	L 4	2354
·India	1,269,339	3,287,588	685,184,692	New Delhi	D 4	2396
Indiana, U.S.A.	36,185	93,719	5,490,260	Indianapolis	M 5	2355
·Indonesia	788,430	2,042,034	147,490,298	Jakarta	D 7	2401
Iowa, U.S.A.	56,275	145,752	2,913,808	Des Moines	K 4	2354
·Iran	636,293	1,648,000	43,414,000	Tehran	F 3	2393
·Iraq	172,476	446,713	14,110,000	Baghdad	D 3	2392
·Ireland	27,136	70,282	3,537,000	Dublin	B 9	2376
Ireland, Northern, U.K.	5,452	14,121	1,507,065	Belfast	C 3	2376
Isle of Man	227	588	64,679	Douglas	D 3	2376
·Israel	7,847	20,324	4,187,000	Jerusalem	B 3	2395
·Italy	116,303	301,225	56,243,935	Rome	...	2382
·Ivory Coast	124,504	322,465	9,300,000	Yammoussoukro	C 7	2367
·Jamaica	4,411	11,424	2,095,878	Kingston	C 3	2349
·Japan	145,730	277,441	121,047,196	Tokyo	E 3	2400
·Jordan	35,000	90,650	2,152,273	Amman	D 3	2395
Kalaallit Nunaat (Greenland)	840,000	2,175,600	49,773	Nuuk (Godthåb)	P 2	2348
·Kampuchea (Cambodia)	69,898	181,036	5,756,141	Phnom Penh	C 3	2401
Kansas, U.S.A.	82,277	213,097	2,364,236	Topeka	J 5	2353
Kentucky, U.S.A.	40,409	104,659	3,660,257	Frankfort	M 5	2355
·Kenya	224,960	582,646	19,536,000	Nairobi	G 2	2371
Kiribati	291	754	56,213	Bairiki	J 6	2402
Korea, North	46,540	120,539	18,317,000	P'yŏngyang	C 2	2400
Korea, South	38,175	98,873	37,448,836	Seoul	C 3	2400
·Kuwait	6,532	16,918	1,695,128	Al Kuwait	E 4	2392
·Laos	91,428	236,800	3,584,803	Vientiane	C 2	2401
·Lebanon	4,015	10,399	2,688,000	Beirut	F 6	2394
·Lesotho	11,720	30,355	1,339,000	Maseru	D 5	2372
·Liberia	43,000	111,370	1,873,000	Monrovia	C 7	2367
·Libya	679,358	1,759,537	3,356,000	Tripoli	B 2	2368
Liechtenstein	61	158	26,130	Vaduz	E 1	2383
Louisiana, U.S.A.	47,752	123,678	4,206,098	Baton Rouge	L 7	2355
·Luxembourg	999	2,587	364,606	Luxembourg	E 5	2359
Macau	6	16	261,680	Macau	H 7	2399
·Madagascar	226,657	587,041	9,400,000	Antananarivo	H 3	2373
Maine, U.S.A.	33,265	86,156	1,125,030	Augusta	R 3	2354
·Malawi	45,747	118,485	6,839,000	Lilongwe	F 5	2371
Malaya, Malaysia	50,806	131,588	11,138,227	Kuala Lumpur	C 4	2401
·Malaysia	128,308	332,318	13,435,588	Kuala Lumpur	D 5	2401
·Maldives	115	298	173,000	Male	J 9	2391
·Mali	464,873	1,204,021	7,719,000	Bamako	C 6	2367
·Malta	122	316	360,000	Valletta	E 7	2382

SATELLITE VIEW OF EARTH: NASA

Atlas

COUNTRY	AREA SQUARE MILES	AREA SQUARE KILOMETERS	POPULATION	CAPITAL OR CHIEF TOWN	INDEX REF.	PAGE NO.
Manitoba, Can.	250,999	650,087	1,026,241	Winnipeg	G 5	2350
Marshall Islands	70	181	30,873	Majuro	G 4	2402
Martinique	425	1,101	328,566	Fort-de-France	G 4	2349
Maryland, U.S.A.	10,460	27,091	4,216,941	Annapolis	O 5	2354
Massachusetts, U.S.A.	8,284	21,456	5,737,081	Boston	P 1	2354
*Mauritania	419,229	1,085,803	1,681,000	Nouakchott	B 5	2367
*Mauritius	790	2,046	993,000	Port Louis	G 5	2373
Mayotte	144	373	47,300	Dzaoudzi	G 2	2373
*Mexico	761,601	1,972,546	67,395,826	Mexico City	. . .	2356
Michigan, U.S.A.	58,527	151,585	9,262,070	Lansing	M 3	2357
Micronesia, Federated States of	275	712	73,160	Kolonia	E 5	2402
Midway Islands	1.9	4.9	468	. . . .	J 3	2402
Minnesota, U.S.A.	84,402	218,601	4,075,970	St. Paul	K 3	2354
Mississippi, U.S.A.	47,689	123,515	2,520,631	Jackson	L 6	2355
Missouri, U.S.A.	69,697	180,515	4,916,759	Jefferson City	K 5	2355
Monaco	368 acres	149 ha.	27,063	Monaco	G 6	2380
*Mongolia	606,163	1,569,962	1,732,000	Ulaanbaatar	F 2	2398
Montana, U.S.A.	147,046	380,849	786,690	Helena	F 3	2352
Montserrat	40	104	12,073	Plymouth	G 3	2349
*Morocco	172,414	446,550	20,419,555	Rabat	C 2	2366
*Mozambique	303,769	786,762	12,615,000	Maputo	E 4	2373
Namibia (South-West Africa)	317,827	823,172	1,009,000	Windhoek	B 3	2372
Nauru	7.7	20	7,254	Yaren (district)	G 6	2402
Nebraska, U.S.A.	77,355	200,349	1,569,825	Lincoln	H 4	2352
*Nepal	54,663	141,577	15,022,839	Kathmandu	E 3	2396
*Netherlands	15,892	41,160	14,599,430	The Hague; Amsterdam	C 3	2379
Netherlands Antilles	390	1,010	246,000	Willemstad	E 4	2349
Nevada, U.S.A.	110,561	286,353	800,493	Carson City	D 5	2352
New Brunswick, Can.	28,354	73,437	696,403	Fredericton	K 6	2351
New Caledonia and Dependencies	7,335	18,998	145,368	Nouméa	G 8	2402
Newfoundland, Can.	156,184	404,517	567,681	St. John's	L 5	2402
New Hampshire, U.S.A.	9,279	24,033	920,610	Concord	R 3	2354
New Jersey, U.S.A.	7,787	20,168	7,365,011	Trenton	P 4	2354
New Mexico, U.S.A.	121,593	314,926	1,303,445	Santa Fe	G 6	2353
New York, U.S.A.	49,108	127,190	17,558,072	Albany	P 4	2354
*New Zealand	103,736	268,676	3,175,737	Wellington	L 6	2405
*Nicaragua	45,698	118,358	3,058,000	Managua	C 2	2357
*Niger	489,189	1,267,000	5,686,000	Niamey	F 5	2367
*Nigeria	357,000	924,630	82,643,000	Lagos	F 6	2367
Niue	100	259	2,887	Alofi	K 7	2403
North America	9,363,000	24,250,170	395,000,000	. . . .	. . .	2348
North Carolina, U.S.A.	52,669	136,413	5,881,385	Raleigh	N 6	2355
North Dakota, U.S.A.	70,702	183,118	652,717	Bismarck	H 3	2352
Northern Ireland, U.K.	5,452	14,121	1,507,065	Belfast	C 3	2376
Northern Marianas	184	477	16,780	Capitol Hill	E 4	2402
Northwest Territories, Can.	1,304,896	3,379,683	45,741	Yellowknife	E 3	2350
*Norway	125,053	323,887	4,141,000	Oslo	B 2	2377
Nova Scotia, Can.	21,425	55,491	847,442	Halifax	K 7	2351
Ohio, U.S.A.	41,330	107,045	10,797,624	Columbus	N 4	2354
Oklahoma, U.S.A.	69,956	181,186	3,025,495	Oklahoma City	J 6	2353
*Oman	120,000	310,800	919,000	Muscat	G 6	2393
Ontario, Can.	412,580	1,068,582	8,625,107	Toronto	H 5	2351
Oregon, U.S.A.	97,073	251,419	2,633,149	Salem	C 4	2352
*Pakistan	310,403	803,944	83,782,000	Islamabad	B 3	2396
Palau	188	487	12,116	Koror	D 5	2402
*Panama	29,761	77,082	1,830,175	Panamá	D 3	2357
*Papua New Guinea	183,540	475,369	3,010,727	Port Moresby	B 7	2401
*Paraguay	157,047	406,752	3,026,165	Asunción	H 8	2360
Pennsylvania, U.S.A.	45,308	117,348	11,864,751	Harrisburg	O 4	2354
*Peru	496,222	1,285,215	17,031,221	Lima	E 5	2360
*Philippines	115,707	299,681	48,098,460	Manila	H 3	2401
Pitcairn Islands	18	47	54	Adamstown	O 8	2403
*Poland	120,725	312,678	37,003,000	Warsaw	. . .	2384
*Portugal	35,549	92,072	9,833,014	Lisbon	B 3	2381
Prince Edward Island, Can.	2,184	5,657	122,506	Charlottetown	K 6	2351
Puerto Rico	3,515	9,104	3,196,520	San Juan	E 3	2349
*Qatar	4,247	11,000	257,000	Doha	F 4	2393
Québec, Can.	594,857	1,540,680	6,438,403	Québec	J 5	2351
Réunion	969	2,510	515,814	St-Denis	F 5	2373
Rhode Island, U.S.A.	1,212	3,139	947,154	Providence	P 2	2354
*Romania	91,699	237,500	22,553,074	Bucharest	C 2	2386
*Rwanda	10,169	26,337	5,046,000	Kigali	F 3	2371
Sabah, Malaysia	29,300	75,887	1,002,608	Kota Kinabalu	F 4	2401
*Saint Kitts and Nevis	104	269	44,404	Basseterre	F 3	2349
Saint Helena and Dependencies	162	420	5,147	Jamestown	B 6	2365
*Saint Lucia	238	616	115,783	Castries	G 4	2349
Saint Pierre and Miquelon	93.5	242	6,041	Saint-Pierre	L 6	2351
*Saint Vincent and the Grenadines	150	388	124,000	Kingstown	G 4	2349
San Marino	23.4	60.6	22,000	San Marino	D 3	2382
*São Tomé & Príncipe	372	963	86,000	São Tomé	F 8	2367
Sarawak, Malaysia	48,202	124,843	1,294,753	Kuching	E 5	2401
Saskatchewan, Can.	251,699	651,900	968,313	Regina	F 5	2350
*Saudi Arabia	829,995	2,149,687	9,319,000	Riyadh	D 4	2392
Scotland, U.K.	30,414	78,772	5,117,146	Edinburgh	D 2	2376
*Senegal	75,954	196,720	6,316,000	Dakar	A 5	2367
*Seychelles	145	375	64,332	Victoria	H 5	2373
*Sierra Leone	27,925	72,325	3,571,000	Freetown	B 7	2367
*Singapore	226	585	2,413,945	Singapore	C 5	2401
*Solomon Islands	11,500	29,785	221,000	Honiara	G 6	2402
*Somalia	246,200	637,658	4,895,000	Mogadishu	H 2	2371
*South Africa	455,318	1,179,274	23,771,970	Cape Town; Pretoria	C 5	2372
South America	6,875,000	17,806,250	263,000,000	. . . .		2358
South Carolina, U.S.A.	31,113	80,583	3,122,814	Columbia	N 6	2355
South Dakota, U.S.A.	77,116	99,730	690,768	Pierre	H 3	2352
South-West Africa (Namibia)	317,827	823,172	1,009,000	Windhoek	B 3	2372
*Spain	194,881	504,742	37,746,260	Madrid	. . .	2381
*Sri Lanka	25,332	65,610	14,848,364	Colombo	E 7	2397
*Sudan	967,494	2,505,809	20,564,364	Khartoum	E 4	2368
*Suriname	55,144	142,823	354,860	Paramaribo	J 3	2361
*Swaziland	6,705	17,366	605,000	Mbabane	E 5	2373
*Sweden	173,665	449,792	8,431,000	Stockholm	C 3	2377
Switzerland	15,943	41,292	6,365,960	Bern	. . .	2383
*Syria	71,498	185,180	9,172,000	Damascus	G 5	2394
Taiwan	13,971	36,185	18,029,798	Taipei	K 7	2399
*Tanzania	363,708	942,003	21,015,000	Dar es Salaam	F 4	2371
Tennessee, U.S.A.	42,144	109,153	4,591,120	Nashville	M 6	2355
Texas, U.S.A.	266,807	691,030	14,227,574	Austin	H 7	2353
*Thailand	198,455	513,998	44,278,000	Bangkok	C 2	2390
*Togo	21,622	56,000	2,702,945	Lomé	E 7	2367
Tokelau	3.9	10	1,552	Fakaofo	J 6	2403
Tonga	270	699	96,592	Huku'alofa	J 8	2403
*Trinidad and Tobago	1,980	5,128	1,058,320	Port of Spain	G 5	2349
Tristan da Cunha, St. Helena	38	98	323	Edinburgh	J 7	2346
*Tunisia	63,378	164,149	6,886,000	Tunis	F 1	2366
*Turkey	300,946	779,450	51,420,757	Ankara	D 3	2394
Turks and Caicos Islands	166	430	7,436	Cockburn Town, Grand Turk	D 2	2349
Tuvalu	9.78	25.33	7,349	Fongafale, Funafuti	H 6	2402
*Uganda	91,076	235,887	12,630,076	Kampala	F 2	2371
*Ukrainian S.S.R., U.S.S.R.	233,089	603,700	49,754,642	Kiev	D 5	2387
*Union of Soviet Socialist Republics	8,649,490	22,402,179	280,000,000	Moscow	. . .	2388
*United Arab Emirates	32,278	83,600	1,043,225	Abu Dhabi	F 5	2393
*United Kingdom	94,399	244,493	55,638,495	London	. . .	2376
*United States of America	3,623,420	9,384,658	226,549,448	Washington	. . .	2352
*Uruguay	72,172	186,925	2,968,000	Montevideo	J 10	2363
Utah, U.S.A.	84,899	219,888	1,461,037	Salt Lake City	E 5	2352
*Vanuatu	5,700	14,763	111,251	Vila	G 7	2754
Vatican City	108.7 acres	44 ha.	733	. . . .	D 4	2382
*Venezuela	352,143	912,050	14,570,085	Caracas	G 2	2360
Vermont, U.S.A.	9,614	24,900	511,456	Montpelier	P 4	2354
*Vietnam	128,405	332,569	52,741,766	Hanoi	D 3	2401
Virginia, U.S.A.	40,767	105,587	5,346,797	Richmond	N 5	2355
Virgin Islands, British	59	153	12,000	Road Town	F 3	2349
Virgin Islands, U.S.A.	132	342	96,569	Charlotte Amalie	F 3	2349
Wake Island	2.5	6.5	302	Wake Islet	G 4	2754
Wales, U.K.	8,017	20,764	2,790,462	Cardiff	E 4	2376
Wallis and Futuna	106	275	11,000	Mata Utu	J 7	2755
Washington, U.S.A.	68,139	176,480	4,132,204	Olympia	C 3	2352
Western Sahara	102,703	266,000	165,000	. . . .	B 3	2372
*Western Samoa	1,133	2,934	158,130	Apia	J 7	2755
West Virginia, U.S.A.	24,231	62,758	1,950,258	Charleston	N 5	2355
*White Russian S.S.R. (Byelorussian S.S.R.), U.S.S.R.	80,154	207,600	9,560,543	Minsk	C 4	2387
Wisconsin, U.S.A.	56,153	145,436	4,705,642	Madison	L 3	2354
World . . . . (land)	57,970,000	150,142,300	4,763,000,000	. . . .	. . .	2346
Wyoming, U.S.A.	97,809	253,325	469,557	Cheyenne	F 4	2352
*Yemen, People's Democratic Rep. of	111,101	287,752	2,225,000	Aden	E 7	2392
*Yemen Arab Republic	77,220	200,000	6,456,189	San'a	D 6	2392
*Yugoslavia	98,766	255,804	23,018,000	Belgrade	B 2	2386
Yukon Territory, Can.	207,075	536,324	23,153	Whitehorse	C 3	2350
*Zaire	905,063	2,344,113	30,261,000	Kinshasa	D 3	2370
*Zambia	290,586	752,618	5,679,808	Lusaka	E 6	2370
*Zimbabwe	150,803	390,580	7,539,000	Harare	D 3	2372

*Member of the United Nations

MAP PROJECTIONS

by Erwin Raisz

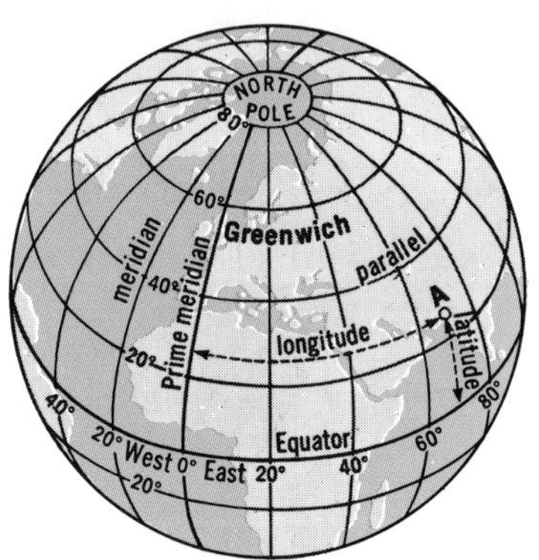

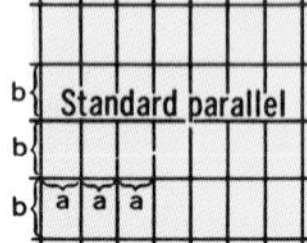

Rectangular Projection

Mercator Projection

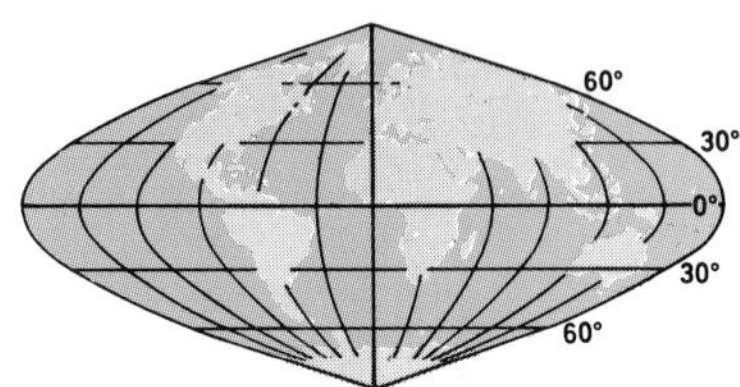

Sinusoidal Projection

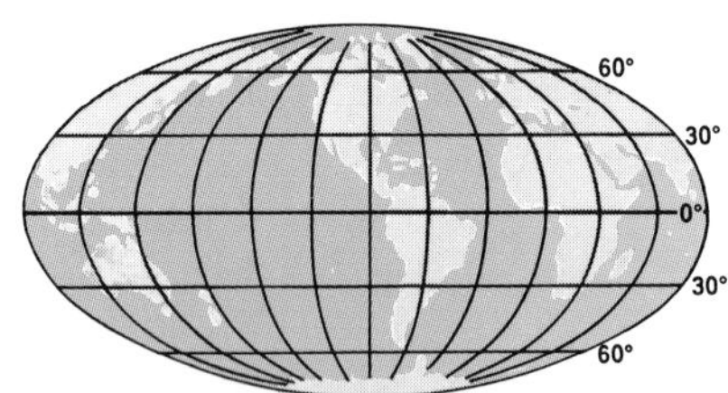

Mollweide Projection

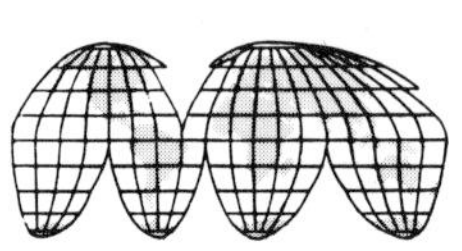

Goode's Interrupted Projection

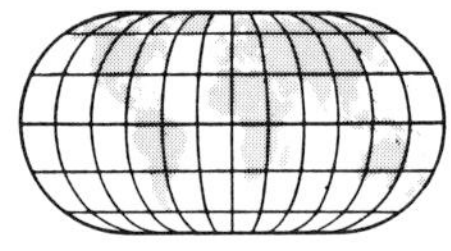

Eckert Projection

Our earth is rotating around its *axis* once a day. The two end points of its axis are the *poles;* the line circling the earth midway between the poles is the *equator*. The arc from either of the poles to the equator is divided into 90 *degrees*. The distance, expressed in degrees, from the equator to any point is its *latitude* and circles of equal latitude are the *parallels*. On maps it is customary to show parallels of evenly-spaced degrees such as every fifth or every tenth.

The equator is divided into 360 degrees. Lines circling from pole to pole through the degree points on the equator are called *meridians*. They are all equal in length but by international agreement the meridian passing through the Greenwich Observatory in London has been chosen as *prime meridian*. The distance, expressed in degrees, from the prime meridian to any point is its *longitude*. While meridians are all equal in length, parallels become shorter and shorter as they approach the poles. Whereas one degree of latitude represents everywhere approximately 69 miles, one degree of longitude varies from 69 miles at the equator to nothing at the poles.

Each degree is divided into 60 minutes and each minute into 60 seconds. One minute of latitude equals a nautical mile.

The map is flat but the earth is nearly spherical. Neither a rubber ball nor any part of a rubber ball may be flattened without stretching or tearing unless the part is very small. To present the curved surface of the earth on a flat map is not difficult as long as the areas under consideration are small, but the mapping of countries, continents, or the whole earth requires some kind of *projection*. Any regular set of parallels and meridians upon which a map can be drawn makes a map projection. Many systems are used.

In any projection only the parallels or the meridians or some other set of lines can be *true* (the same length as on the globe of corresponding scale); all other lines are too long or too short. Only on a globe is it possible to have both the parallels and the meridians true. The scale given on a flat map cannot be true everywhere. The construction of the various projections begins usually with laying out the parallels or meridians which have true lengths.

RECTANGULAR PROJECTION — This is a set of evenly-placed meridians and horizontal parallels. The central or *standard parallel* and all meridians are true. All other parallels are either too long or too short. The projection is used for simple maps of small areas, as city plans, etc.

MERCATOR PROJECTION — In this projection the meridians are evenly-spaced vertical lines. The parallels are horizontal, spaced so that their length has the same relation to the meridians as on a globe. As the meridians converge at higher latitudes on the globe, while on the map they do not, the parallels have to be drawn also farther and farther apart to maintai the correct relationship. When every very small area has th same shape as on a globe we call the projection *conforma*. The most interesting quality of this projection is that all *compass directions* appear as straight lines. For this reason it i generally used for marine charts. It is also frequently used fo world maps in spite of the fact that the high latitudes are ver much exaggerated in size. Only the equator is true to scale all other parallels and meridians are too long. The Mercato projection did *not* derive from projecting a globe upon a cylinder.

SINUSOIDAL PROJECTION — The parallels are truly spaced horizontal lines. They are divided truly and the co necting curves make the meridians. It does not make a goo world map because the outer regions are distorted, but th central portion is good and this part is often used for maps o Africa and South America. Every part of the map has the sam area as the corresponding area on the globe. It is an *equa area* projection.

MOLLWEIDE PROJECTION — The meridians are equally spaced ellipses; the parallels are horizontal lines spaced s that every belt of latitude should have the same area as on globe. This projection is popular for world maps, especially i European atlases.

GOODE'S INTERRUPTED PROJECTIONS—Only the goo central part of the Mollweide or sinusoidal (or both) projectio is used and the oceans are cut. This makes an equal-area ma with little distortion of shape. It is commonly used for worl maps.

ECKERT PROJECTIONS — These are similar to the sinusoid or the Mollweide projections, but the poles are shown as line half the length of the equator. There are several variants; th meridians are either sine curves or ellipses; the parallels a horizontal and spaced either evenly or so as to make the pr jection equal area. Their use for world maps is increasing. Th figure shows the elliptical equal-area variant.

CONIC PROJECTION — The original idea of the conic pr jection is that of capping the globe by a cone upon which bo the parallels and meridians are projected from the center the globe. The cone is then cut open and laid flat. A cone ca be made tangent to any chosen *standard parallel*.

The actually-used conic projection is a modification of th idea. The radius of the standard parallel is obtained as abov The meridians are straight radiating lines spaced truly on th

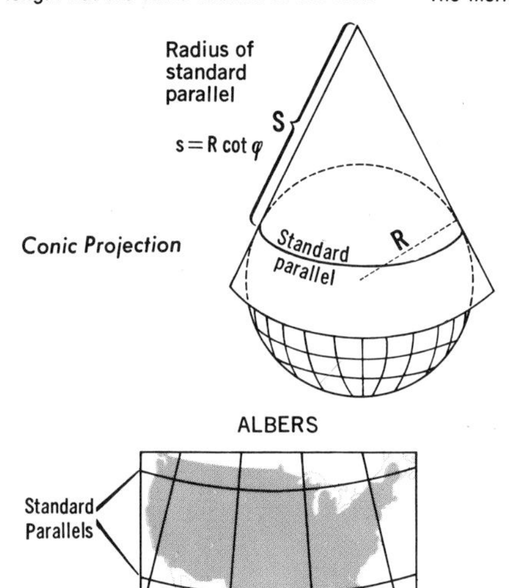

Conic Projection

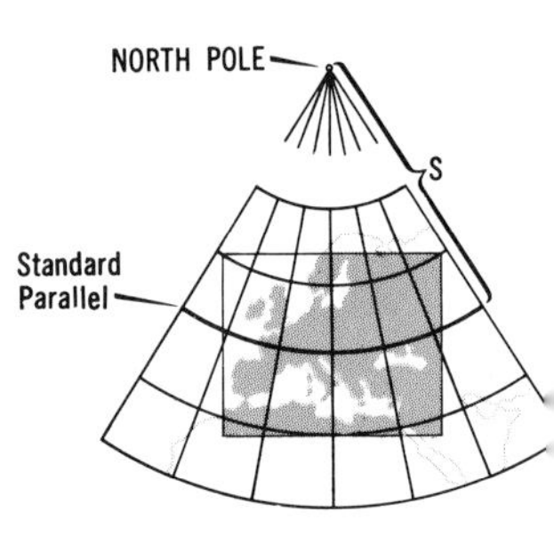

Albers Projection

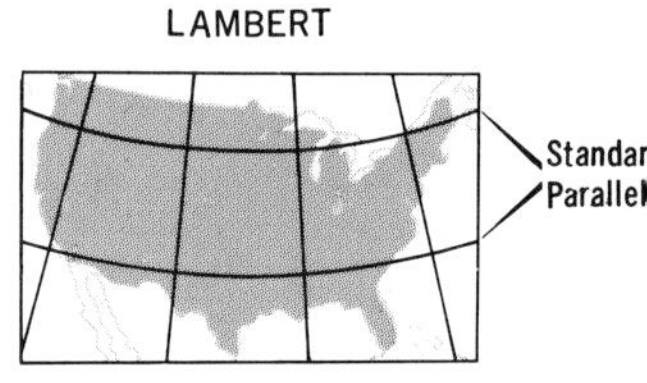

Lambert Conformal Conic Projection

standard parallel. The parallels are concentric circles spaced at true distances. All parallels except the standard are too long. The projection is used for maps of countries in middle latitudes, as it presents good shapes with small scale error.

There are several variants: The use of *two standard parallels*, one near the top, the other near the bottom of the map, reduces the scale error. In the *Albers projection* the parallels are spaced unevenly, to make the projection equal-area. This is a good projection for the United States. In the *Lambert conformal conic projection* the parallels are spaced so that any small quadrangle of the grid should have the same shape as on the globe. This is the best projection for air-navigation charts as it has relatively straight azimuths.

An *azimuth* is a great-circle direction reckoned clockwise from north. A *great-circle direction* points to a place along the shortest line on the earth's surface. This is not the same as compass direction. The center of a great circle is the center of the globe.

BONNE PROJECTION — The parallels are laid out exactly as in the conic projection. All parallels are divided truly and the connecting curves make the meridians. It is an equal-area projection. It is used for maps of the northern continents, as Asia, Europe, and North America.

POLYCONIC PROJECTION — The central meridian is divided truly. The parallels are non-concentric circles, the radii of which are obtained by drawing tangents to the globe as though the globe were covered by several cones rather than by only one. Each parallel is divided truly and the connecting curves make the meridians. All meridians except the central one are too long. This projection is used for large-scale topographic sheets — less often for countries or continents.

THE AZIMUTHAL PROJECTIONS — In this group a part of the globe is projected from an eyepoint onto a plane. The eyepoint can be at different distances, making different projections. The plane of projection can be tangent at the equator, at a pole, or at any other point on which we want to focus attention. The most important quality of all azimuthal projections is that they show every point at its true direction (azimuth) from the center point, and all points equally distant from the center point will be equally distant on the map also.

GNOMONIC PROJECTION — This projection has the eyepoint at the center of the globe Only the central part is good; the outer regions are badly distorted. Yet the projection has one important quality, all great circles being shown as straight lines. For this reason it is used for laying out the routes for long range flying or trans-oceanic navigation.

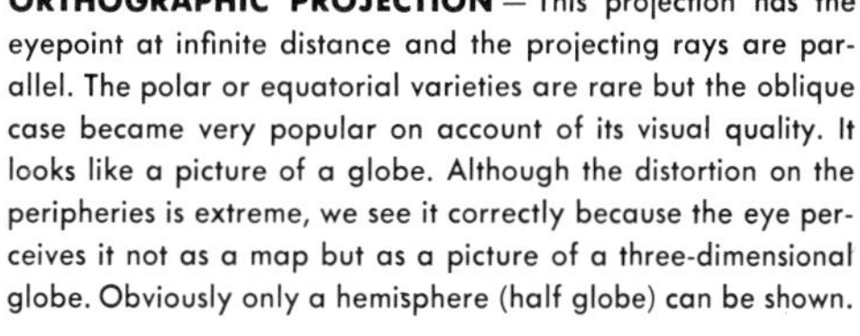

ORTHOGRAPHIC PROJECTION — This projection has the eyepoint at infinite distance and the projecting rays are parallel. The polar or equatorial varieties are rare but the oblique case became very popular on account of its visual quality. It looks like a picture of a globe. Although the distortion on the peripheries is extreme, we see it correctly because the eye perceives it not as a map but as a picture of a three-dimensional globe. Obviously only a hemisphere (half globe) can be shown.

Some azimuthal projections do not derive from the actual process of projecting from an eyepoint, but are arrived at by other means:

AZIMUTHAL EQUIDISTANT PROJECTION — This is the only projection in which every point is shown both at true great-circle direction and at true distance from the center point, but all other directions and distances are distorted. The principle of the projection can best be understood from the polar case. Most polar maps are in this projection. The oblique case is used for radio direction finding, for earthquake research, and in long-distance flying. A separate map has to be constructed for each central point selected.

LAMBERT AZIMUTHAL EQUAL-AREA PROJECTION—The construction of this projection can best be understood from the polar case. All three cases are widely used. It makes a good polar map and it is often extended to include the southern continents. It is the most common projection used for maps of the Eastern and Western Hemispheres, and it is a good projection for continents as it shows correct areas with relatively little distortion of shape. Most of the continent maps in this atlas are in this projection.

IN THIS ATLAS, on almost all maps, parallels and meridians have been marked because they are useful for the following:

(a) They show the north-south and east-west directions which appear on many maps at oblique angles especially near the margins.

(b) With the help of parallels and meridians every place can be exactly located; for instance, New York City is at 41° N and 74° W on any map.

(c) They help to measure distances even in the distorted parts of the map. The scale given on each map is true only along certain lines which are specified in the foregoing discussion for each projection. One degree of latitude equals nearly 69 statute miles or 60 nautical miles. The length of one degree of longitude varies (1° long. = 1° lat. × cos lat.).

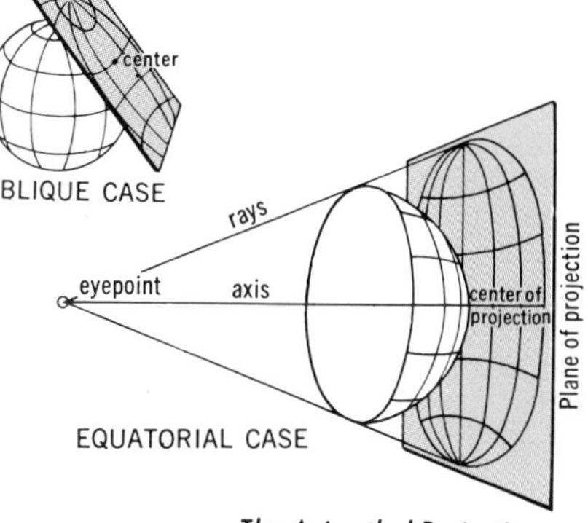

The Azimuthal Projections

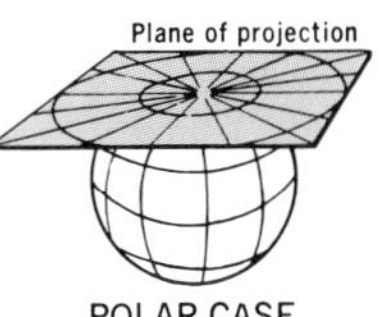

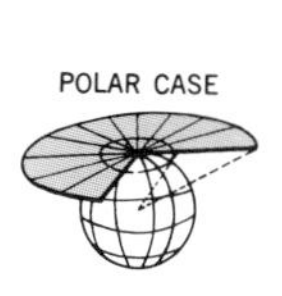

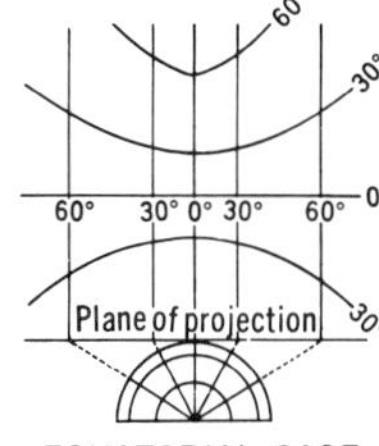

Gnomonic Projection

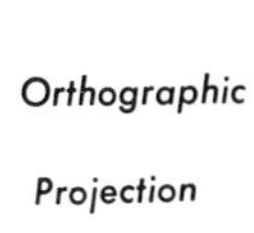

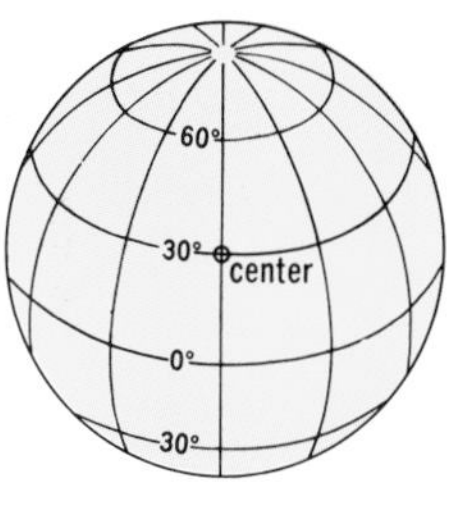

Orthographic Projection

OBLIQUE

center

Azimuthal Equidistant Projection

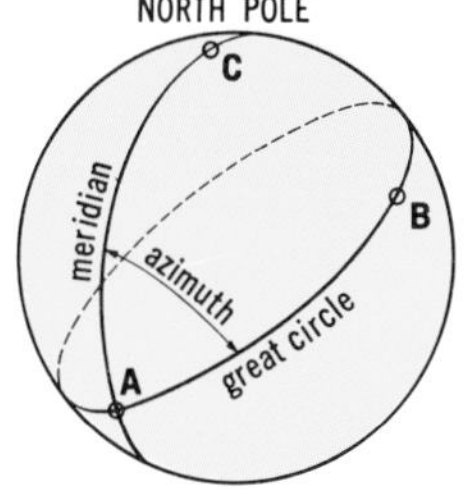

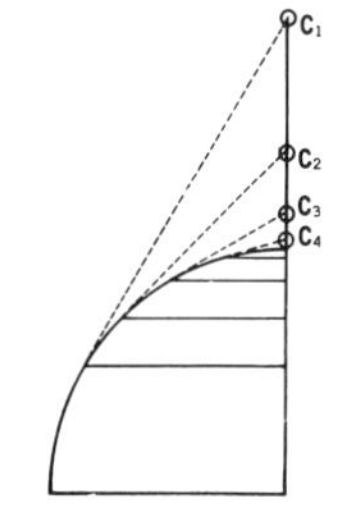

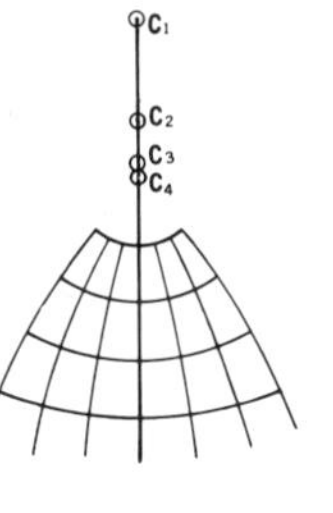

Polyconic Projection

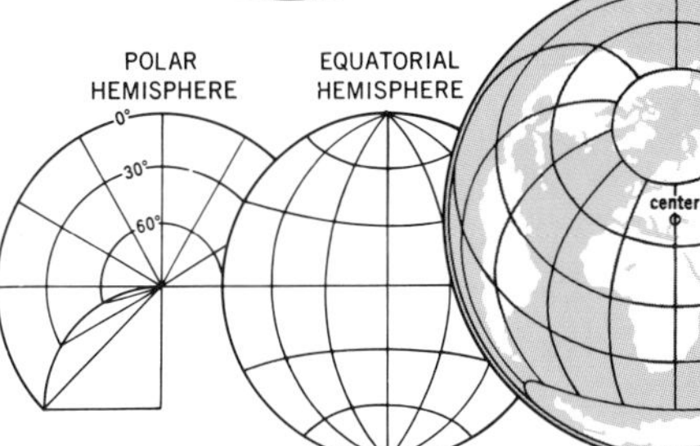

center

OBLIQUE WORLD MAP

Lambert Azimuthal Equal-Area Projection

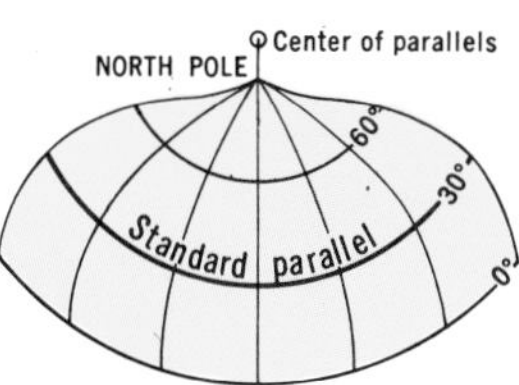
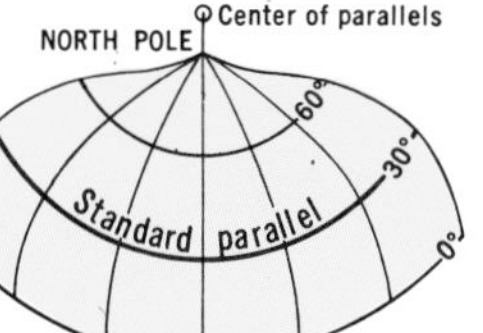

Bonne Projection

WORLD

Countries, Territories & Dependencies

Name	Ref.
Afghanistan	N 4
Albania. Not on map,	see p. 2386
Algeria	K 4
American Samoa. Not on map,	see p. 2403
Angola	K 6
Antigua and Barbuda. Not on map,	see p. 2349
Argentina	F 8
Ascension (isl.), St. Helena	J 6
Australia	S 7
Austria	K 3
Bahamas	F 4
Bahrain. Not on map,	see p. 2393
Bangladesh	P 4
Barbados	G 5
Belgium	K 3
Belize	E 5
Benin	K 5
Bhutan	P 4
Bolivia	F 6
Botswana	L 7
Brazil	G 6
British Indian Ocean Territory	N 6
Brunei	R 5
Bulgaria	L 3
Burkina Faso	J 5
Burma	P 4
Burundi	L 6
Cambodia	R 5
Cameroon	K 5
Canada	D 3
Cape Verde	H 5
Central African Republic	K 5
Chad	K 5
Chile	F 7
China, People's Rep. of	R 4
China, Rep. of (Taiwan)	S 4
Colombia	F 5
Comoros	M6
Congo	K 6
Cook Islands	B 7
Costa Rica	E 5
Cuba	E 4
Cyprus	L 4
Czechoslovakia	K 3
Denmark	K 3
Djibouti	L 5
Dominica. Not on map,	see p. 2349
Dominican Republic	F 5
Ecuador	E 6
Egypt	L 4
El Salvador	E 5
Equatorial Guinea	K 5
Ethiopia	M5
Faeroe Islands, Den.	J 2
Falkland Islands & Dep.	G 8
Fiji	U 6
Finland	L 2
France	K 3
French Guiana	G 5
French Polynesia. Not on map,	see p. 2403
Gabon	K 6
Gambia	J 5
Germany, East (German Dem. Rep.)	K 3
Germany, West (Fed. Rep. of Germany)	K 3
Ghana	J 5
Gibraltar	J 4
Greece	L 4
Greenland	G 2
Grenada. Not on map,	see p. 2349
Guadeloupe & Dep. Not on map,	see p. 2349
Guam	T 5
Guatemala	E 5
Guinea	J 5
Guinea-Bissau	H 5
Guyana	G 5
Haiti	F 4
Honduras	E 5
Hong Kong	R 4
Hungary	K 3
Iceland	J 2
India	N 4
Indonesia	R 6
Iran	M4
Iraq	M4
Ireland	J 3
Israel	L 4
Italy	K 3
Ivory Coast	J 5
Jamaica	E 5
Japan	T 4
Jordan	L 4
Kenya	L 5
Kiribati	A 6

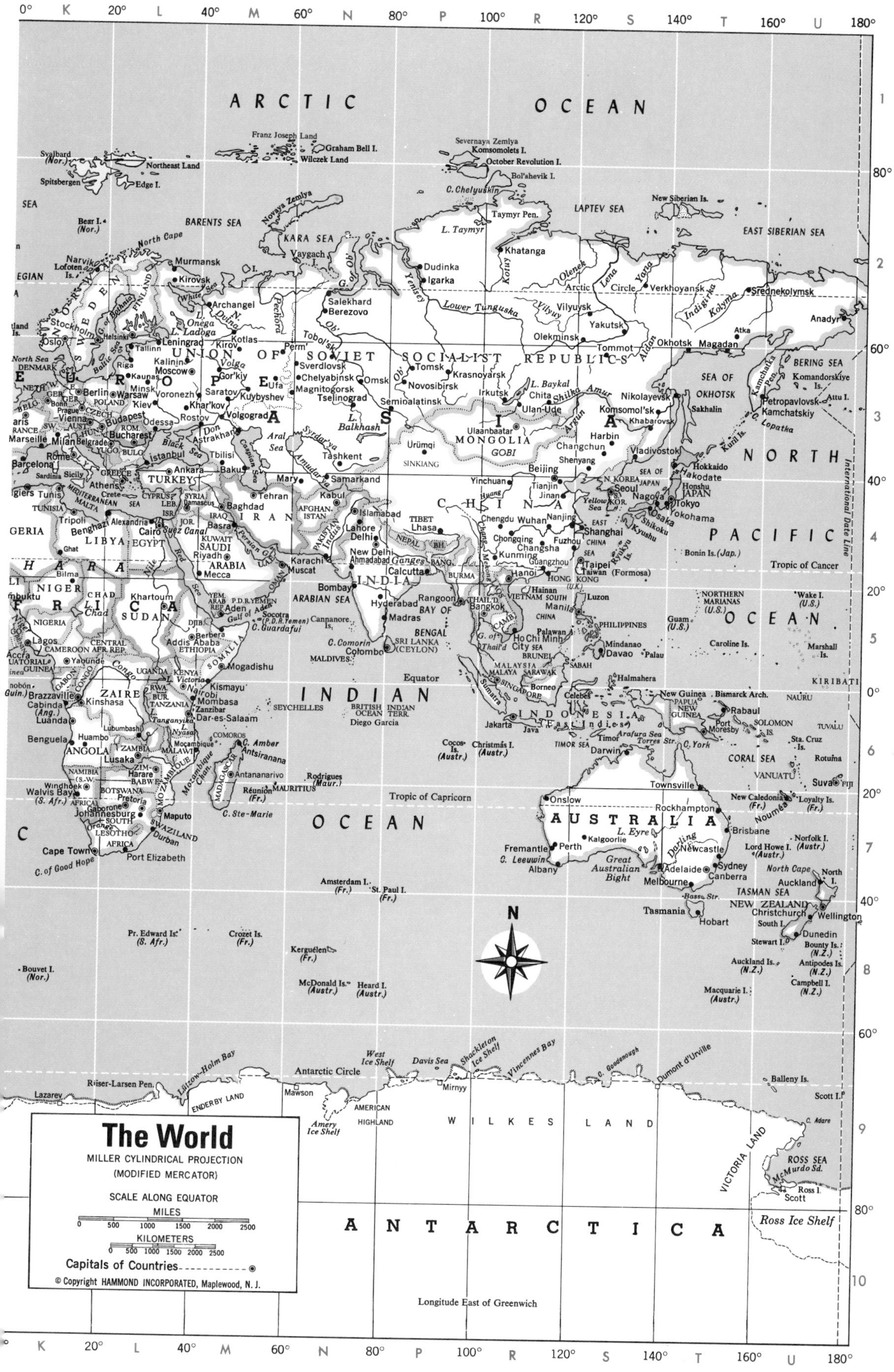

Korea, North .... S 4
Korea, South .... S 4
Kuwait M4
Laos .... R 5
Lebanon .... L 4
Lesotho .... L 7
Liberia .... J 5
Libya .... K 4
Luxembourg. Not on map, see p. 2379
Macau. Not on map, ... see p. 2399
Madagascar M6
Malawi .... L 6
Malaysia .... R 5
Maldives .... N 5
Mali .... J 5
Malta .... K 4
Martinique. Not on map, . see p. 2349
Mauritania .... J 4
Mauritius .... N 7
Mexico .... D 4
Mongolia .... R 3
Morocco .... J 4
Mozambique .... L 6
Namibia .... K 6
Nauru .... U 6
Nepal .... P 4
Netherlands .... K 3
Netherlands Antilles.
Not on map, ... see p. 2349
New Caledonia .... T 7
New Zealand .... U 8
Nicaragua .... E 5
Niger .... K 5
Nigeria .... K 5
Northern Ireland .... J 3
Northern Marianas .... T 5
Norway .... K 2
Oman M5
Pakistan .... N 4
Palau .... S 5
Panama .... E 5
Papua New Guinea .... T 6
Paraguay .... G 7
Peru .... F 6
Philippines .... S 5
Pitcairn .... C 7
Poland .... K 3
Portugal .... J 3
Puerto Rico .... F 5
Qatar. Not on map, ... see p. 2393
Réunion M7
Romania .... L 3
Rwanda .... L 6
Saint Kitts and Nevis.
Not on map, ... see p. 2349
Saint Helena .... J 6
Saint Lucia. Not on map, . see p. 2349
Saint Vincent and the Grenadines.
Not on map, ... see p. 2349
São Tomé & Príncipe.
Not on map, ... see p. 2367
Saudi Arabia M4
Senegal .... J 5
Seychelles .... N 6
Sierra Leone .... J 5
Singapore .... R 6
Solomon Islands .... U 6
Somalia M5
South Africa .... L 7
Spain .... J 4
Sri Lanka .... P 5
Sudan .... L 5
Suriname .... G 5
Swaziland .... L 7
Sweden .... K 2
Switzerland .... K 3
Syria .... L 4
Taiwan (Rep. of China) .... S 4
Tanzania .... L 6
Thailand .... R 5
Togo .... K 5
Tonga .... A 6
Trinidad and Tobago .... G 5
Tunisia .... K 4
Turkey .... L 4
Tuvalu .... U 6
Uganda .... L 5
Union of Soviet Socialist
Republics M3
United Arab Emirates M4
United Kingdom .... J 3
United States of America .... D 4
Uruguay .... G 7
Vanuatu .... U 6
Venezuela .... F 5
Vietnam .... R 5
Virgin Is. Not on map, ... see p. 2349
Western Samoa .... A 6
Yemen, People's Dem. Rep. of .. M5
Yemen Arab Rep. M5
Yugoslavia .... K 3
Zaire .... L 6
Zambia .... L 6
Zimbabwe .... L 6

The World

MILLER CYLINDRICAL PROJECTION
(MODIFIED MERCATOR)

SCALE ALONG EQUATOR
MILES
0 500 1000 1500 2000 2500
KILOMETERS
0 500 1000 1500 2000 2500

Capitals of Countries

Longitude East of Greenwich

NORTH AMERICA

CAPITALS

Name	Ref.
Belmopan, Belize	K 8
Guatemala, Guatemala	J 8
Havana, Cuba	K 7
Kingston, Jamaica	L 8
Managua, Nicaragua	K 8
Mexico City, Mexico	J 7
Nassau, Bahamas	L 7
Ottawa, Canada	L 5
Panamá, Panama	L 9
Port-au-Prince, Haiti	L 8
San José, Costa Rica	K 9
San Juan, Puerto Rico	M8
San Salvador, El Salvador	J 8
Santo Domingo, Dominican Republic	L 8
Tegucigalpa, Honduras	K 8
Washington, D.C., U.S.A.	L 6

PHYSICAL FEATURES

Name	Ref.
Alaska (pen.)	C 4
Anguilla (isl.)	M8
Appalachian (mts.)	K 6
Arctic (ocean)	B 2
Atlantic (ocean)	M6
Baffin (isl.)	L 2
Baffin (bay)	M2
Beaufort (sea)	D 2
Bering (sea)	A 3
Bermuda (isls.)	M6
Brooks (range)	C 3
California (gulf)	G 7
Canaveral (cape)	L 7
Caribbean (sea)	K 8
Cascade (range)	F 5
Cayman (isls.)	K 8
Chesapeake (bay)	L 6
Coast (mts.)	E 4
Coast (ranges)	F 5
Cod (cape)	M5
Colorado (riv.)	G 6
Columbia (riv.)	F 5
Davis (strait)	N 3
Ellesmere (isl.)	K 1
Erie (lake)	K 5
Florida (straits)	K 7
Great Bear (lake)	F 3
Greater Antilles (isls.)	K 7
Great Salt (lake)	G 6
Greenland (sea)	T 2
Guadeloupe (isl.)	M8
Hatteras (cape)	L 6
Hispaniola (isl.)	L 7
Honduras (gulf)	K 8
Hudson (bay)	K 3
Huron (lake)	K 5
Juan de Fuca (strait)	F 5
Labrador (sea)	N 4
Lesser Antilles (isls.)	M8
Lower California (pen.)	G 7
Mackenzie (riv.)	F 3
Manitoba (lake)	H 4
Martinique (isl.)	M8
McKinley (mt.)	C 3
Mead (lake)	G 6
Mexcio (gulf)	K 7
Michigan (lake)	K 5
Mississippi (riv.)	J 6
Missouri (riv.)	J 5
Newfoundland (isl.)	N 5
Nicaragua (lake)	K 8
Ohio (riv.)	K 6
Ontario (lake)	L 5
Pacific (ocean)	E 6
Panama (canal)	L 8
Panama (gulf)	L 9
Parry (chan.)	G 2
Queen Charlotte (isls.)	E 4
Queen Elizabeth (isls.)	G 2
Red (riv.)	J 6
Rio Grande (riv.)	H 7
Rocky (mts.)	F 4
Saint Lawrence (gulf)	M5
Saint Lawrence (riv.)	L 5
Santa Barbara (isls.)	F 6
Sierra Madre Occidental (mts.)	H 7
Sierra Madre Oriental (mts.)	H 7
Sierra Nevada (range)	F 6
Superior (lake)	K 5
Sverdrup (isls.)	J 2
Tanana (riv.)	D 3
Turks and Caicos (isls.)	L 7
Ungava (pen.)	L 3
Vancouver (isl.)	F 5
Virgin Islands (isls.)	M8
West Indies (isls.)	M7
Winnipegosis (lake)	H 4
Yucatán (pen.)	K 7
Yukon (riv.)	C 3

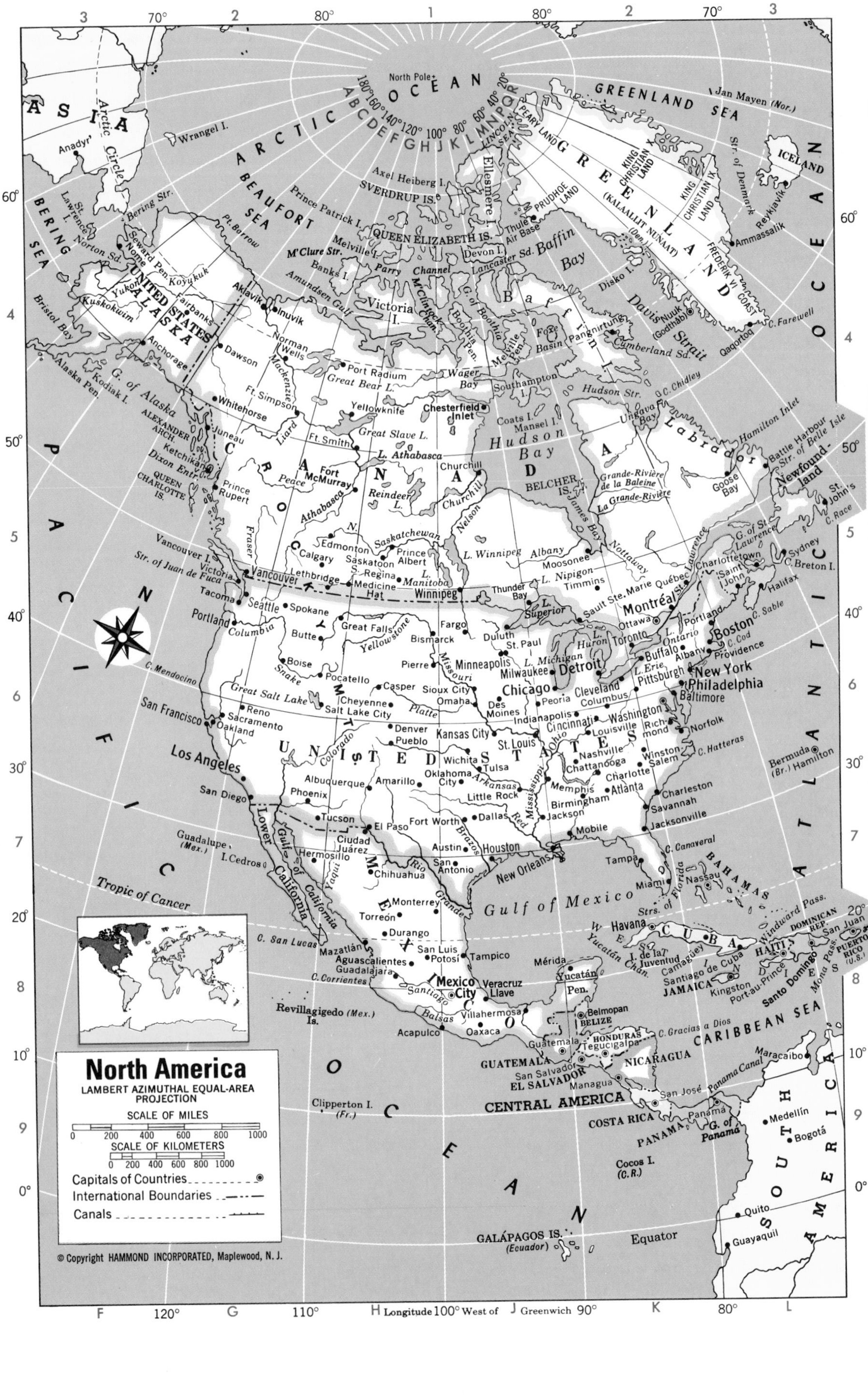

North America

LAMBERT AZIMUTHAL EQUAL-AREA PROJECTION

SCALE OF MILES: 0 200 400 600 800 1000

SCALE OF KILOMETERS: 0 200 400 600 800 1000

Capitals of Countries

International Boundaries

Canals

Longitude 100° West of Greenwich 90°

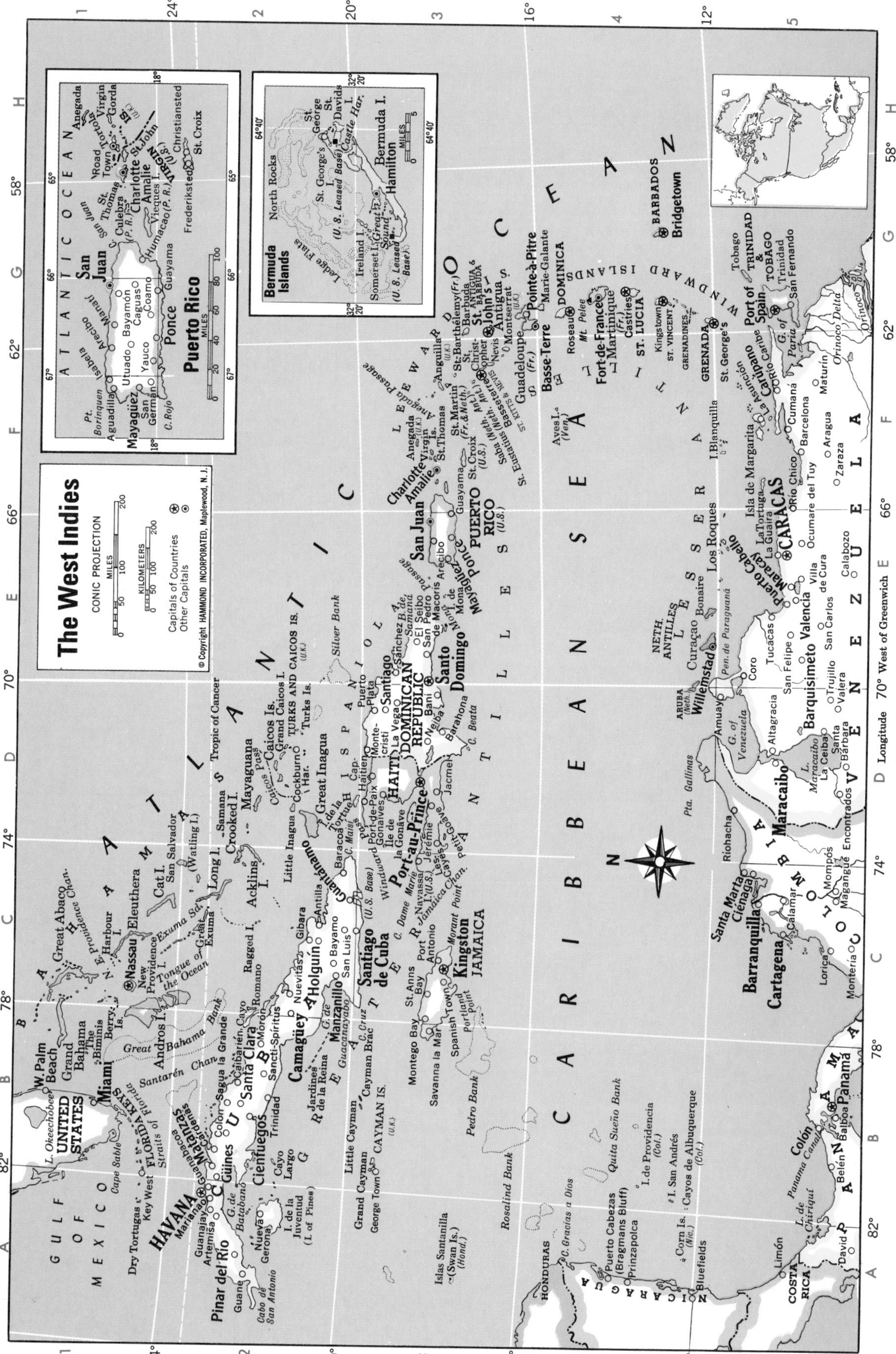
The West Indies
CONIC PROJECTION
MILES
KILOMETERS
Capitals of Countries
Other Capitals
© Copyright HAMMOND INCORPORATED, Maplewood, N.J.
Puerto Rico
Bermuda Islands
ATLANTIC OCEAN
CARIBBEAN SEA
Longitude 70° West of Greenwich

WEST INDIES

CANADA

Name Population	Ref.
Amherst, 9,684	K 6
Amos, 9,421	J 6
Athabaska, 1,731	E 5
Atikokan, 4,452	G 6
Banff, 4,208	E 5
Bathurst, 15,705	K 6
Battleford, 3,565	E 5
Biggar, 2,561	F 5
Bonavista, 4,460	L 6
Brandon, 36,242	F 6
Bridgewater, 6,669	K 7
Calgary, 592,743	E 5
Cambridge Bay, 815	F 2
Campbellton, 9,818	K 6
Camrose, 12,570	E 5
Cape Dorset, 748	J 3
Cardston, 3,267	E 6
Carman, 2,408	G 6
Chandler, 3,946	K 6
Channel-Port aux Basques, 5,988	L 6
Charlottetown (cap.), P.E.I., 15,282	K 6
Chatham, 6,779	K 6
Chibougamau, 10,732	J 6
Chicoutimi, 60,064	J 6
Chilliwack, 40,642	D 6
Cochrane, 4,848	H 6
Coppermine, 809	E 2
Coral Harbour, 429	H 2
Corner Brook, 24,339	K 6
Cornwall, 46,144	J 7
Courtenay, 8,992	D 6
Cranbrook, 15,915	E 6
Dartmouth, 62,277	K 7
Dauphin, 8,971	F 5
Dawson, 697	C 3
Dawson Creek, 11,373	D 4
Didsbury, 3,095	E 5
Drumheller, 6,508	E 5
Edmonton (cap.), Alta., 532,246	E 5
Edmundston, 12,044	K 6
Edson, 5,835	E 5
Estevan, 9,174	F 6
Eureka	N 3
Fernie, 5,444	E 6
Flin Flon, 8,261	F 4
Fort Frances, 8,906	G 6
Fort-George, 2,222	J 5
Fort Good Hope, 463	D 2
Fort Liard, 405	D 3
Fort Macleod, 3,139	E 6
Fort McMurray, 31,000	E 4
Fort McPherson, 632	C 2
Fort Nelson, 3,724	D 4
Fort Resolution, 480	E 3
Fort Saint John, 13,891	D 4
Fort Saskatchewan, 12,169	E 5
Fort Simpson, 980	D 3
Fort Smith, 2,298	E 3
Fredericton (cap.), N. Bruns., 43,723	K 6
Gander, 10,404	L 6
Gaspé, 17,261	K 6
Gjoa Haven, 523	G 2
Glace Bay, 21,466	L 6
Goose Bay, 7,103	K 5
Grand Falls, 8,765	L 6
Grande Prairie, 24,263	E 4
Grise Fiord, 106	H 1
Guelph, 71,207	H 7
Halifax (cap.), N.S., 114,594	K 7
Hamilton, 306,434	H 7
Harbour Grace, 2,988	L 6
Havre-St-Pierre, 3,200	K 5
Hay River, 2,863	E 3
Hearst, 5,533	H 6
High River, 4,792	E 5
Hope, 3,205	D 6
Hull, 56,225	J 6
Humboldt, 4,705	F 5
Inuvik, 3,147	C 2
Iqaluit, 2,333	K 3
Iroquois Falls, 6,339	H 6
Jasper, 3,269	E 5
Jonquière, 60,354	J 6
Kamloops, 64,048	D 5
Kapuskasing, 12,014	H 6
Kelowna, 59,196	E 6
Kenora, 9,817	G 5
Kindersley, 3,969	F 5
Kingston, 52,616	J 7
Kirkland Lake, 12,219	H 6
Kitimat, 12,462	D 5
Lacombe, 5,591	E 5
La Sarre, 8,851	J 6
La Tuque, 11,556	J 6
Leduc, 12,471	E 5
Lethbridge, 54,072	E 6
Lloydminster, 15,031	E 5
London, 254,280	H 7
Marathon, 2,271	H 6
Maricourt, 665	J 3

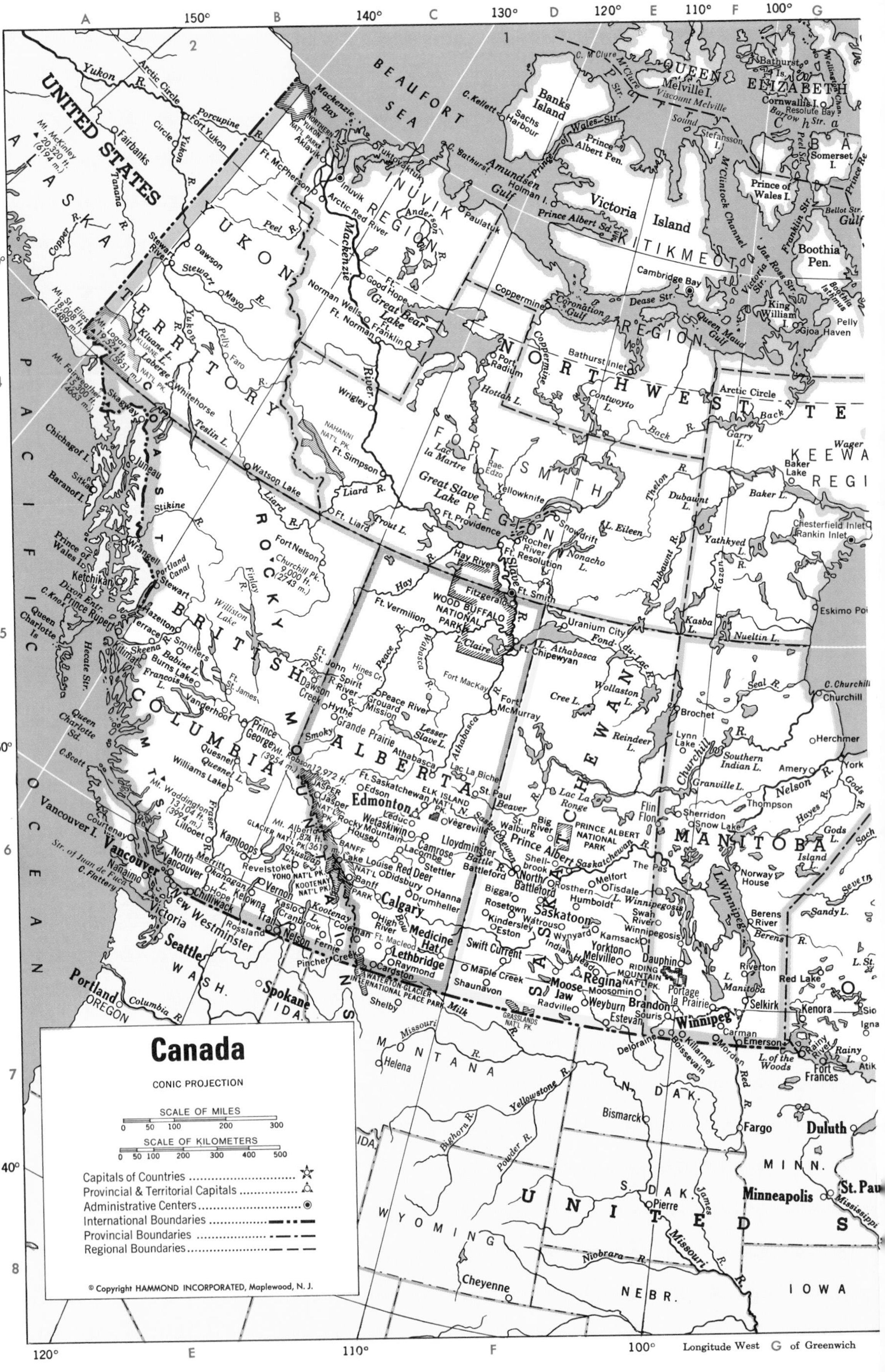

Canada

CONIC PROJECTION

SCALE OF MILES
0 50 100 200 300

SCALE OF KILOMETERS
0 50 100 200 300 400 500

Capitals of Countries
Provincial & Territorial Capitals
Administrative Centers
International Boundaries
Provincial Boundaries
Regional Boundaries

Longitude West G of Greenwich

Medicine Hat, 40,380 .... E 5
Melfort, 6,010 .... F 5
Melville, 5,092 .... F 5
Merritt, 6,110 .... D 5
Moncton, 54,743 .... K 6
Mont-Joli, 6,359 .... K 6
Mont-Laurier, 8,405 .... J 6
Montréal, 980,354 .... J 7
Moose Jaw, 33,941 .... F 6
Moosomin, 2,579 .... F 5
Morden, 4,579 .... G 6
Nanaimo, 47,069 .... D 6
Nelson, 9,143 .... E 6
Newcastle, 6,284 .... K 6
New Liskeard, 5,551 .... H 6
New Westminster, 38,550 .... D 6
Niagara Falls, 70,960 .... J 7
Nipigon .... H 6
Noranda, 8,767 .... J 6
North Battleford, 14,030 .... F 5
North Bay, 51,268 .... J 6
North Vancouver, 33,952 .... D 6
Ottawa (cap.), Canada, 295,163 . J 6
Owen Sound, 19,883 .... H 7
Parry Sound, 6,124 .... J 6
Peace River, 5,907 .... E 4
Pembroke, 14,026 .... J 6
Peterborough, 60,620 .... J 7
Portage la Prairie, 13,086 .... G 5
Port-Cartier, 8,191 .... K 5
Prince Albert, 31,380 .... F 5
Prince George, 67,559 .... D 5
Prince Rupert, 16,197 .... C 5
Québec (cap.), Que., 166,474 .... J 6
Quesnel, 8,240 .... D 5
Rankin Inlet, 1,109 .... G 3
Red Deer, 46,393 .... E 5
Regina (cap.), Sask., 162,613 .... F 5
Renfrew, 8,283 .... J 6
Resolute Bay, 168 .... G 1
Revelstoke, 5,544 .... E 5
Rimouski, 29,120 .... K 6
Rivière-du-Loup, 13,459 .... K 6
Roberval, 11,429 .... J 6
Rocky Mountain House, 4,698 .. E 5
Rouyn, 17,224 .... J 6
Saint John, 80,521 .... K 6
St. John's (cap.), Newf., 83,770 .. L 6
Saint Paul, 4,884 .... E 5
Saint Stephen, 5,120 .... K 6
Sarnia, 50,892 .... H 7
Saskatoon, 154,210 .... F 5
Sault Sainte Marie, 82,697 .... H 6
Selkirk, 10,037 .... G 5
Shawinigan, 23,011 .... J 6
Sherbrooke, 74,075 .... J 7
Smithers, 4,570 .... D 5
Souris, 1,413 .... K 6
Stephenville, 8,876 .... L 6
Stettler, 5,136 .... E 5
Stewart, 1,456 .... D 4
Stewart River .... B 3
Sturgeon Falls, 6,045 .... H 6
Sudbury, 91,829 .... H 6
Swan River, 3,782 .... F 5
Swift Current, 14,747 .... F 5
Sydney, 29,444 .... K 6
Terrace, 10,914 .... D 5
The Pas, 6,390 .... F 5
Thessalon, 1,620 .... H 6
Thompson, 14,288 .... G 4
Thunder Bay, 112,486 .... H 6
Timmins, 46,114 .... H 6
Tisdale, 3,107 .... F 5
Toronto (cap.), Ontario, 599,217 . H 7
Trail, 9,599 .... E 6
Trois-Rivières, 50,466 .... J 6
Truro, 12,552 .... K 6
Val-d'Or, 21,371 .... J 6
Vancouver, 414,281 .... D 6
Vègreville, 5,251 .... E 5
Vernon, 19,987 .... E 5
Victoria (cap.), B.C., 64,379 .... D 6
Wabush, 3,155 .... K 5
Wetaskiwin, 9,597 .... E 5
Weyburn, 9,523 .... F 6
Whitehorse (cap.), Yukon, 14,814 .... C 3
Williams Lake, 8,362 .... D 5
Windsor, 3,646 .... K 7
Windsor, 192,083 .... H 7
Winnipeg (cap.), Man., 564,473 .. G 6
Woodstock, 4,869 .... K 6
Yarmouth, 7,475 .... K 7
Yellowknife (cap.), N.W. Terr., 9,483 .... E 3
York Factory .... G 4
Yorkton, 15,339 .... F 5

UNITED STATES

Name Population	Ref.
Abilene, Texas, 98,315	J 6
Akron, Ohio, 237,177	N 4
Alameda, Calif., 63,852	D 8
Albany (cap.), N.Y., 101,729	O 1
Albuquerque, N. Mex., 331,767	G 6
Alexandria, La., 51,565	K 7
Alexandria, Va., 103,217	O 5
Alhambra, Calif., 64,615	D 8
Allentown, Pa., 103,758	O 4
Altoona, Pa., 57,078	O 4
Amarillo, Texas, 149,230	H 6
Ames, Iowa, 45,775	K 4
Anaheim, Calif., 219,311	D 8
Anchorage, Alaska, 174,431	F 8
Anderson, Ind., 64,695	M 4
Annapolis (cap.), Md., 31,740	O 5
Ann Arbor, Mich., 107,966	M 1
Appleton, Wis., 58,913	L 3
Arlington, Texas, 160,113	J 6
Asheville, N.C., 53,583	N 6
Athens, Ga., 42,549	N 6
Atlanta (cap.), Ga., 425,022	M 6
Atlantic City, N.J., 40,199	P 5
Augusta, Ga., 47,532	N 6
Augusta (cap.), Maine, 21,819	R 3
Aurora, Colo., 158,588	G 5
Aurora, Ill., 81,293	K 1
Austin (cap.), Texas, 354,496	J 7
Bakersfield, Calif., 105,735	D 6
Baltimore, Md., 786,775	O 5
Baton Rouge (cap.), La., 219,419	L 7
Bay City, Mich., 41,593	N 4
Beaumont, Texas, 118,102	K 7
Berkeley, Calif., 103,328	D 8
Bethlehem, Pa., 70,419	P 4
Billings, Mont., 66,842	F 3
Binghamton, N.Y., 55,860	P 4
Birmingham, Ala., 284,413	M 6
Bismarck (cap.), N. Dak., 44,485	H 3
Bloomington, Ill., 44,189	L 4
Bloomington, Ind., 52,044	M 5
Bloomington, Minn., 81,831	K 3
Boise (cap), Idaho, 102,160	E 4
Boston (cap.), Mass., 562,994	R 2
Bowling Green, Ky., 40,450	M 5
Bridgeport, Conn., 142,546	O 2
Bristol, Conn., 57,370	O 2
Brockton, Mass., 95,172	R 2
Brownsville, Texas, 84,997	J 8
Buffalo, N.Y., 357,870	O 4
Burbank, Calif., 84,625	D 8
Cambridge, Mass., 95,322	R 2
Canton, Ohio, 93,077	N 4
Carson City (cap.), Nev., 32,022	D 5
Casper, Wyo., 51,016	G 4
Cedar Rapids, Iowa, 110,243	K 4
Champaign, Ill., 58,133	L 5
Charleston, S.C., 69,510	O 6
Charleston (cap.), W. Va. 63,968	N 5
Charlotte, N.C., 314,447	N 6
Chattanooga, Tenn., 169,558	M 6
Cheyenne (cap.), Wyo., 47,283	G 4
Chicago, Ill., 3,005,072	L 1
Chicopee, Mass., 55,112	P 1
Chino, Calif., 26,603	D 8
Chula Vista, Calif., 83,927	D 6
Cicero, Ill., 61,232	L 1
Cincinnati, Ohio, 385,457	H 1
Clarksville, Tenn., 54,777	M 5
Clearwater, Fla., 85,528	N 8
Cleveland, Ohio, 573,822	N 4
Colorado Springs, Colo., 214,821	G 5
Columbia, Mo., 62,061	L 5
Columbia (cap.), S.C., 101,208	N 6
Columbus, Ga., 169,441	M 6
Columbus (cap.), Ohio 565,032	N 5
Compton, Calif., 81,286	D 8
Concord (cap.), N.H., 30,400	P 4
Coral Gables, Fla., 43,241	N 8
Corpus Christi, Texas, 231,999	J 8
Council Bluffs, Iowa, 56,449	K 4
Covington, Ky., 49,563	J 1
Dallas, Texas, 904,078	J 6
Daly City, Calif., 78,519	D 8
Danbury, Conn., 60,470	O 2
Davenport, Iowa, 103,264	L 4
Dayton, Ohio, 193,444	M 5
Daytona Beach, Fla., 54,176	N 7
Dearborn, Mich., 90,660	M 1
Decatur, Ala., 42,002	M 6
Decatur, Ill., 94,081	L 5
Denton, Texas, 48,063	J 6
Denver (cap.), Colo., 492,365	G 5
Des Moines (cap.), Iowa, 191,003	K 4
Detroit, Mich., 1,203,339	M 1
Dothan, Ala., 48,750	M 7
Dover (cap.), Del., 23,512	P 5
Downey, Calif., 82,602	D 8
Dubuque, Iowa, 62,321	L 4
Duluth, Minn., 92,811	K 3
Durham, N.C., 100,538	O 5

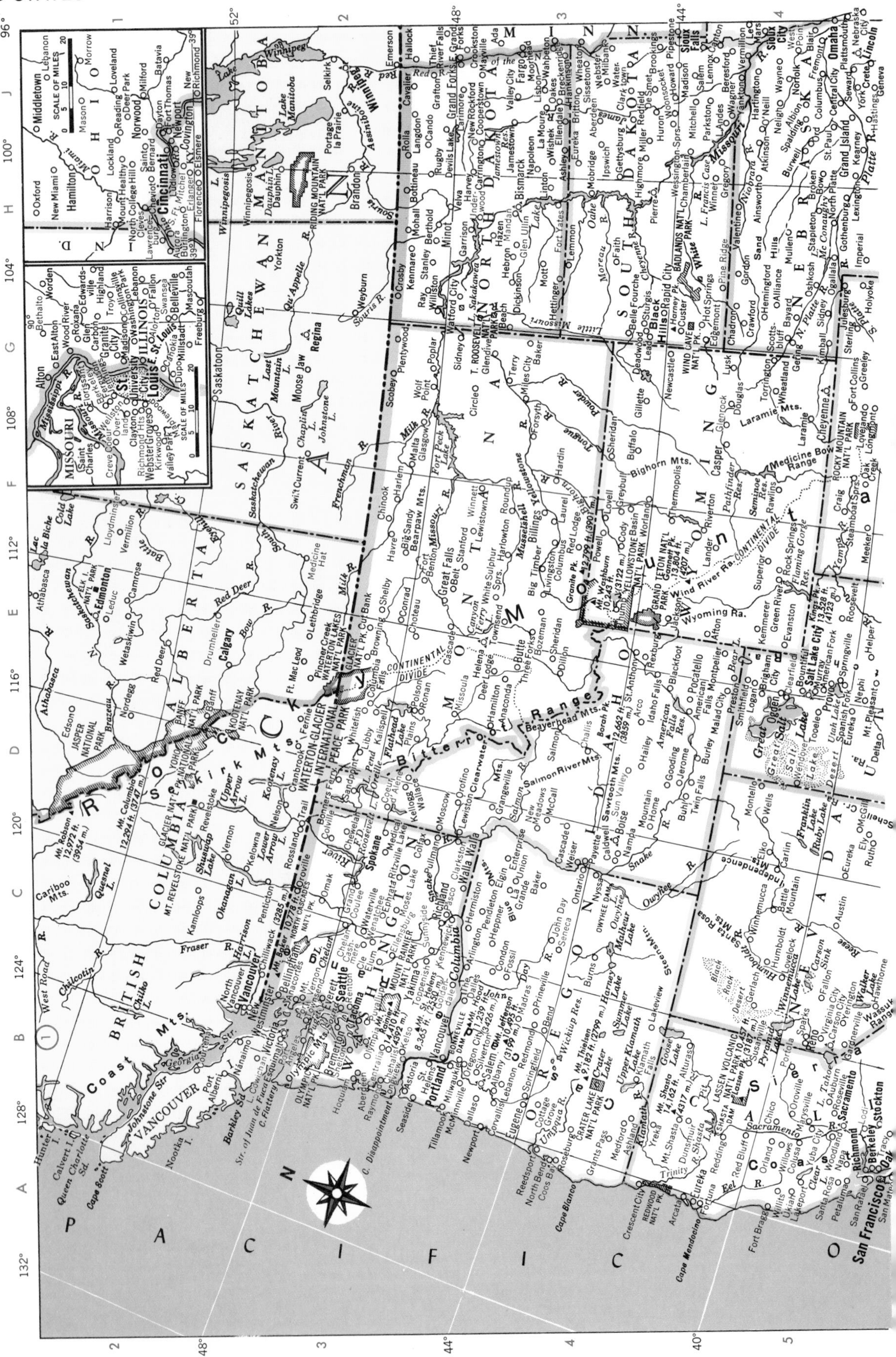

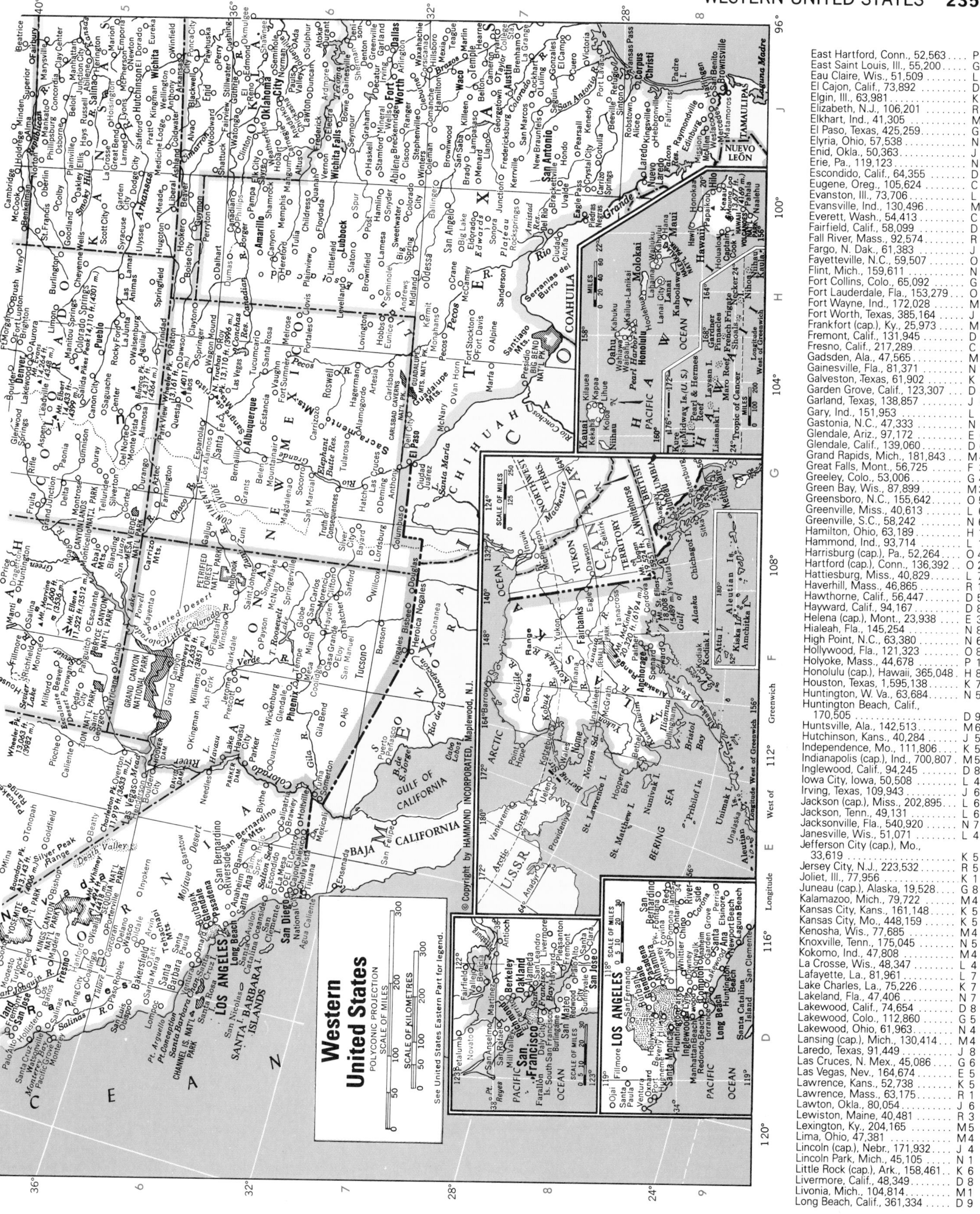

East Hartford, Conn., 52,563 .... P 2
East Saint Louis, Ill., 55,200 .... G 1
Eau Claire, Wis., 51,509 .... L 3
El Cajon, Calif., 73,892 .... D 6
Elgin, Ill., 63,981 .... K 1
Elizabeth, N.J., 106,201 .... R 5
Elkhart, Ind., 41,305 .... M 4
El Paso, Texas, 425,259 .... G 7
Elyria, Ohio, 57,538 .... N 4
Enid, Okla., 50,363 .... J 5
Erie, Pa., 119,123 .... N 4
Escondido, Calif., 64,355 .... D 6
Eugene, Oreg., 105,624 .... C 3
Evanston, Ill., 73,706 .... L 1
Evansville, Ind., 130,496 .... M 5
Everett, Wash., 54,413 .... C 3
Fairfield, Calif., 58,099 .... D 7
Fall River, Mass., 92,574 .... R 2
Fargo, N. Dak., 61,383 .... J 3
Fayetteville, N.C., 59,507 .... O 6
Flint, Mich., 159,611 .... N 4
Fort Collins, Colo., 65,092 .... G 4
Fort Lauderdale, Fla., 153,279 ... O 8
Fort Wayne, Ind., 172,028 .... M 4
Fort Worth, Texas, 385,164 ...... J 6
Frankfort (cap.), Ky., 25,973 ..... M 5
Fremont, Calif., 131,945 .... D 8
Fresno, Calif., 217,289 .... C 5
Gadsden, Ala., 47,565 .... M 6
Gainesville, Fla., 81,371 .... N 7
Galveston, Texas, 61,902 .... K 7
Garden Grove, Calif., 123,307 ... D 8
Garland, Texas, 138,857 .... J 6
Gary, Ind., 151,953 .... L 1
Gastonia, N.C., 47,333 .... N 6
Glendale, Ariz., 97,172 .... E 6
Glendale, Calif., 139,060 .... D 6
Grand Rapids, Mich., 181,843 ... M 4
Great Falls, Mont., 56,725 .... F 3
Greeley, Colo., 53,006 .... G 4
Green Bay, Wis., 87,899 .... M 3
Greensboro, N.C., 155,642 .... O 5
Greenville, Miss., 40,613 .... L 6
Greenville, S.C., 58,242 .... N 6
Hamilton, Ohio, 63,189 .... H 1
Hammond, Ind., 93,714 .... L 1
Harrisburg (cap.), Pa., 52,264 .... O 4
Hartford (cap.), Conn., 136,392 .. O 2
Hattiesburg, Miss., 40,829 .... L 7
Haverhill, Mass., 46,865 .... R 1
Hawthorne, Calif., 56,447 .... D 5
Hayward, Calif., 94,167 .... D 8
Helena (cap.), Mont., 23,938 .... E 3
Hialeah, Fla., 145,254 .... N 8
High Point, N.C., 63,380 .... N 6
Hollywood, Fla., 121,323 .... O 8
Holyoke, Mass., 44,678 .... P 1
Honolulu (cap.), Hawaii, 365,048 . H 8
Houston, Texas, 1,595,138 .... K 7
Huntington, W. Va., 63,684 ...... N 5
Huntington Beach, Calif., 170,505 .... D 9
Huntsville, Ala., 142,513 .... M 6
Hutchinson, Kans., 40,284 .... J 5
Independence, Mo., 111,806 ..... K 5
Indianapolis (cap.), Ind., 700,807 . M 5
Inglewood, Calif., 94,245 .... D 8
Iowa City, Iowa, 50,508 .... L 4
Irving, Texas, 109,943 .... J 6
Jackson (cap.), Miss., 202,895 ... L 6
Jackson, Tenn., 49,131 .... L 6
Jacksonville, Fla., 540,920 .... N 7
Janesville, Wis., 51,071 .... L 4
Jefferson City (cap.), Mo., 33,619 .... K 5
Jersey City, N.J., 223,532 .... R 5
Joliet, Ill., 77,956 .... K 1
Juneau (cap.), Alaska, 19,528 .... G 8
Kalamazoo, Mich., 79,722 .... M 4
Kansas City, Kans., 161,148 ...... K 5
Kansas City, Mo., 448,159 .... K 5
Kenosha, Wis., 77,685 .... M 4
Knoxville, Tenn., 175,045 .... N 5
Kokomo, Ind., 47,808 .... M 4
La Crosse, Wis., 48,347 .... L 4
Lafayette, La., 81,961 .... L 7
Lake Charles, La., 75,226 .... K 7
Lakeland, Fla., 47,406 .... N 7
Lakewood, Calif., 74,654 .... D 8
Lakewood, Colo., 112,860 .... G 5
Lakewood, Ohio, 61,963 .... N 4
Lansing (cap.), Mich., 130,414 ... M 4
Laredo, Texas, 91,449 .... J 8
Las Cruces, N. Mex., 45,086 ..... G 6
Las Vegas, Nev., 164,674 .... E 5
Lawrence, Kans., 52,738 .... K 5
Lawrence, Mass., 63,175 .... R 1
Lawton, Okla., 80,054 .... J 6
Lewiston, Maine, 40,481 .... R 3
Lexington, Ky., 204,165 .... M 5
Lima, Ohio, 47,381 .... M 4
Lincoln (cap.), Nebr., 171,932 .... J 4
Lincoln Park, Mich., 45,105 ...... N 1
Little Rock (cap.), Ark., 158,461 .. K 6
Livermore, Calif., 48,349 .... D 8
Livonia, Mich., 104,814 .... M 1
Long Beach, Calif., 361,334 ..... D 9

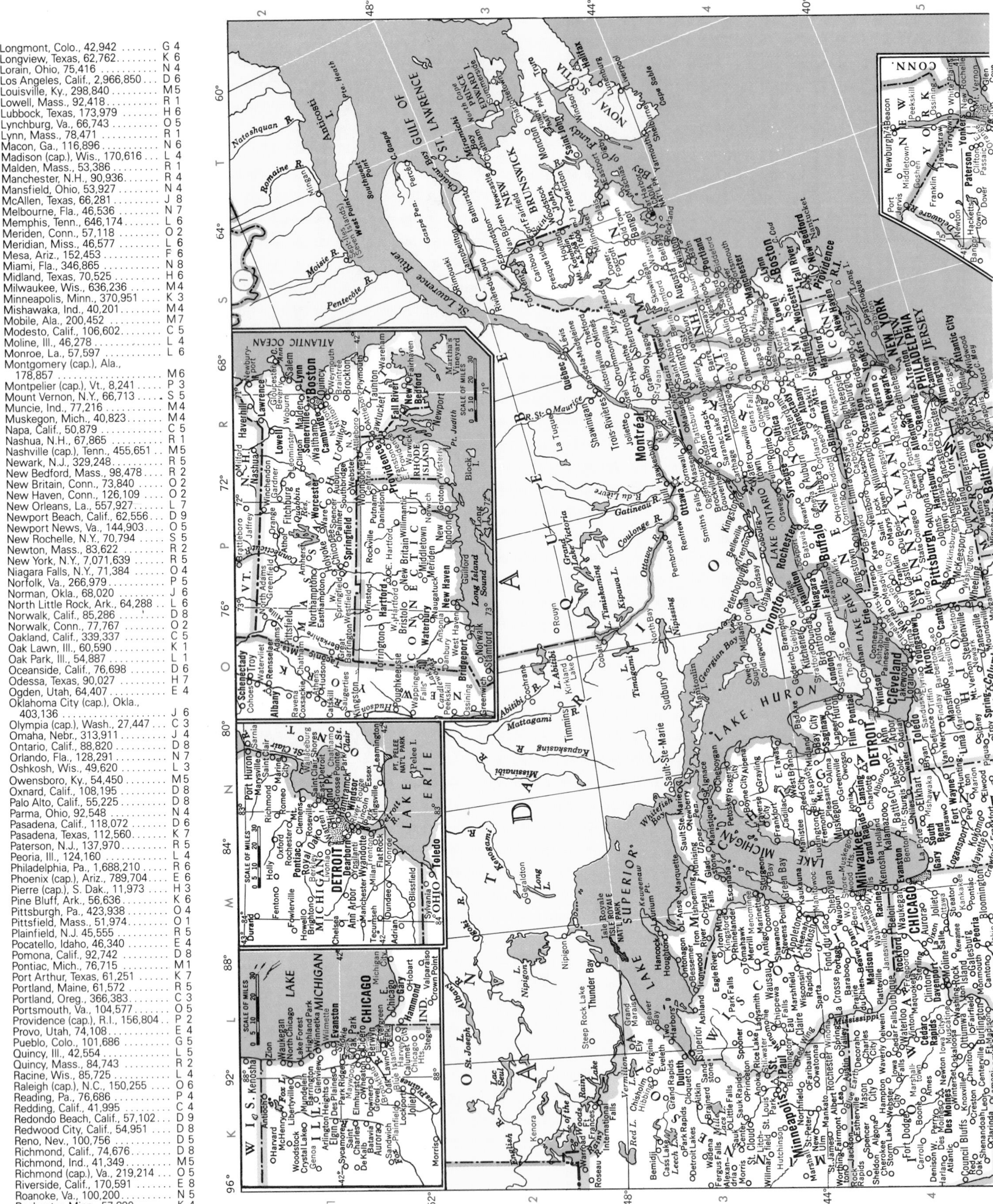

GULF OF ST. LAWRENCE
Anticosti I.
NOVA SCOTIA
NEW BRUNSWICK
ATLANTIC OCEAN
LAKE SUPERIOR
LAKE MICHIGAN
LAKE HURON
LAKE ERIE
LAKE ONTARIO
Québec
Montréal
Toronto
DETROIT
CHICAGO
Boston
NEW YORK
PHILADELPHIA

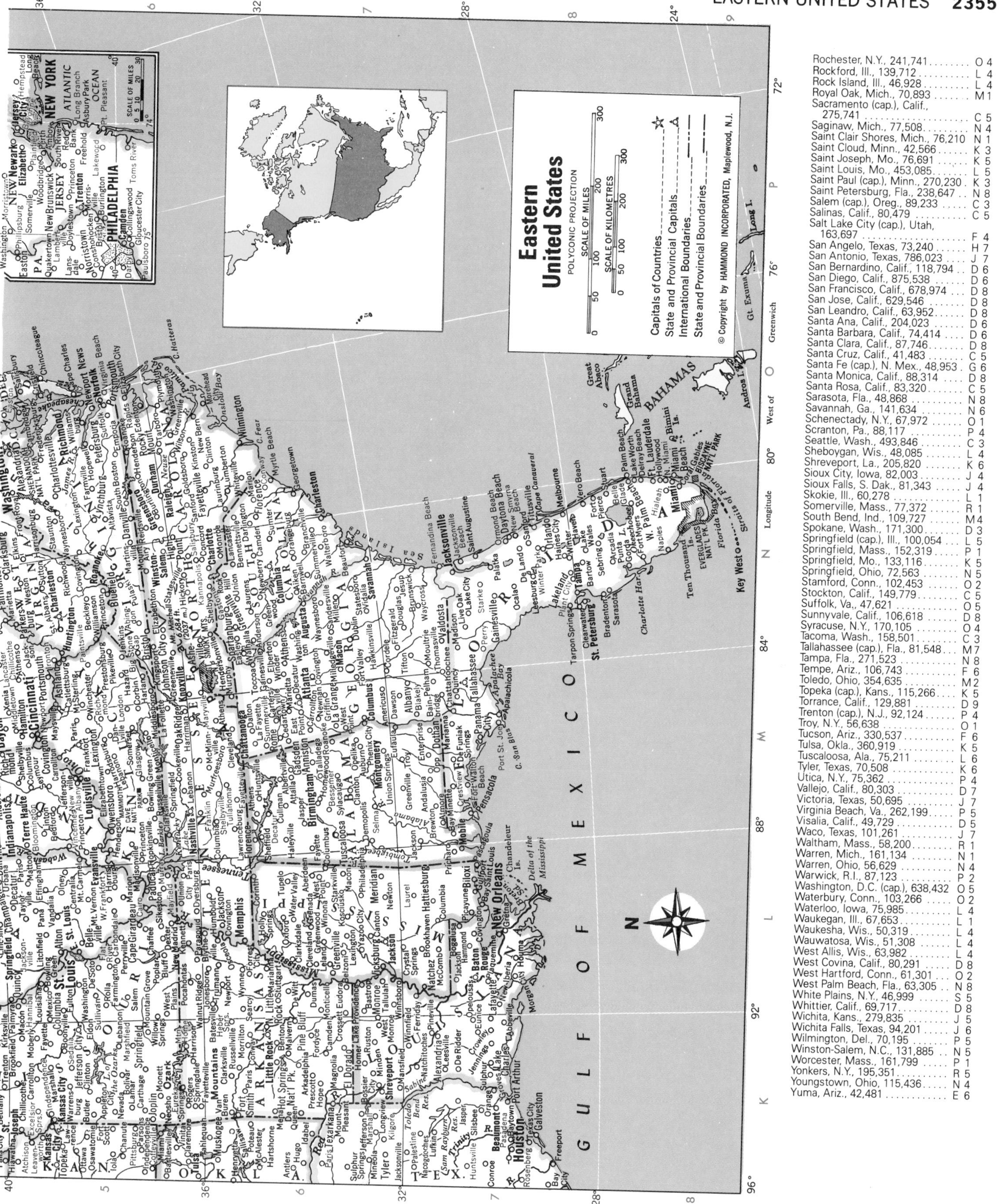

City	Key
Rochester, N.Y., 241,741	O 4
Rockford, Ill., 139,712	L 4
Rock Island, Ill., 46,928	L 4
Royal Oak, Mich., 70,893	M 1
Sacramento (cap.), Calif., 275,741	C 5
Saginaw, Mich., 77,508	N 4
Saint Clair Shores, Mich., 76,210	N 1
Saint Cloud, Minn., 42,566	K 3
Saint Joseph, Mo., 76,691	K 5
Saint Louis, Mo., 453,085	L 5
Saint Paul (cap.), Minn., 270,230	K 3
Saint Petersburg, Fla., 238,647	N 8
Salem (cap.), Oreg., 89,233	C 3
Salinas, Calif., 80,479	C 5
Salt Lake City (cap.), Utah, 163,697	F 4
San Angelo, Texas, 73,240	H 7
San Antonio, Texas, 786,023	J 7
San Bernardino, Calif., 118,794	D 6
San Diego, Calif., 875,538	D 6
San Francisco, Calif., 678,974	D 8
San Jose, Calif., 629,546	D 8
San Leandro, Calif., 63,952	D 8
Santa Ana, Calif., 204,023	D 6
Santa Barbara, Calif., 74,414	D 6
Santa Clara, Calif., 87,746	D 8
Santa Cruz, Calif., 41,483	C 5
Santa Fe (cap.), N. Mex., 48,953	G 6
Santa Monica, Calif., 88,314	D 8
Santa Rosa, Calif., 83,320	C 5
Sarasota, Fla., 48,868	N 8
Savannah, Ga., 141,634	N 6
Schenectady, N.Y., 67,972	O 1
Scranton, Pa., 88,117	P 4
Seattle, Wash., 493,846	C 3
Sheboygan, Wis., 48,085	L 4
Shreveport, La., 205,820	K 6
Sioux City, Iowa, 82,003	J 4
Sioux Falls, S. Dak., 81,343	J 4
Skokie, Ill., 60,278	L 1
Somerville, Mass., 77,372	R 1
South Bend, Ind., 109,727	M 4
Spokane, Wash., 171,300	D 3
Springfield (cap.), Ill., 100,054	L 5
Springfield, Mass., 152,319	P 1
Springfield, Mo., 133,116	K 5
Springfield, Ohio, 72,563	N 5
Stamford, Conn., 102,453	O 2
Stockton, Calif., 149,779	C 5
Suffolk, Va., 47,621	O 5
Sunnyvale, Calif., 106,618	D 8
Syracuse, N.Y., 170,105	O 4
Tacoma, Wash., 158,501	C 3
Tallahassee (cap.), Fla., 81,548	M 7
Tampa, Fla., 271,523	N 8
Tempe, Ariz., 106,743	F 6
Toledo, Ohio, 354,635	M 2
Topeka (cap.), Kans., 115,266	K 5
Torrance, Calif., 129,881	D 9
Trenton (cap.), N.J., 92,124	P 4
Troy, N.Y., 56,638	O 1
Tucson, Ariz., 330,537	F 6
Tulsa, Okla., 360,919	K 5
Tuscaloosa, Ala., 75,211	L 6
Tyler, Texas, 70,508	K 6
Utica, N.Y., 75,362	P 4
Vallejo, Calif., 80,303	D 7
Victoria, Texas, 50,695	J 7
Virginia Beach, Va., 262,199	P 5
Visalia, Calif., 49,729	D 5
Waco, Texas, 101,261	J 7
Waltham, Mass., 58,200	R 1
Warren, Mich., 161,134	N 1
Warren, Ohio, 56,629	N 4
Warwick, R.I., 87,123	P 2
Washington, D.C. (cap.), 638,432	O 5
Waterbury, Conn., 103,266	O 2
Waterloo, Iowa, 75,985	L 4
Waukegan, Ill., 67,653	L 1
Waukesha, Wis., 50,319	L 4
Wauwatosa, Wis., 51,308	L 4
West Allis, Wis., 63,982	L 4
West Covina, Calif., 80,291	D 8
West Hartford, Conn., 61,301	O 2
West Palm Beach, Fla., 63,305	N 8
White Plains, N.Y., 46,999	S 5
Whittier, Calif., 69,717	D 8
Wichita, Kans., 279,835	J 5
Wichita Falls, Texas, 94,201	J 6
Wilmington, Del., 70,195	P 5
Winston-Salem, N.C., 131,885	N 5
Worcester, Mass., 161,799	P 1
Yonkers, N.Y., 195,351	R 5
Youngstown, Ohio, 115,436	N 4
Yuma, Ariz., 42,481	E 6

MEXICO

Name	Population	Ref.
Acámbaro, 32,257		E 4
Acapulco de Juárez, 544,496		E 5
Aguascalientes, 293,152		D 4
Ameca, 21,018		D 4
Apizaco, 21,189		G 1
Atlixco, 41,967		F 2
Campeche, 128,434		G 4
Chetumal, 23,685		H 4
Chihuahua, 385,603		D 2
Chilpancingo de los Bravos, 36,193		E 5
Ciudad Camargo, 24,030		D 2
Ciudad del Carmen, 34,656		G 4
Ciudad Guzmán, 48,166		D 4
Ciudad Juárez, 597,096		D 1
Ciudad Madero, 132,444		F 3
Cioudad Mante, 51,247		E 3
Ciudad Obregón, 165,572		C 2
Ciudad Victoria, 153,206		F 3
Coatepec, 21,542		F 1
Coatzacoalcos, 186,129		G 4
Colima, 86,044		D 4
Comitán de Domínguez, 21,249		G 5
Córdoba, 126,179		H 2
Cuauhtémoc, 26,598		C 2
Cuernavaca, 192,770		F 2
Culiacán, 304,826		C 3
Durango de Victoria, 257,915		D 3
Empalme, 24,927		B 2
Ensenada, 120,483		A 1
Gómez Palacio, 116,967		D 3
Guadalajara, 1,540,016		D 4
Guanajuato, 48,981		E 4
Guasave, 26,080		C 3
Guaymas, 54,826		B 2
Hermosillo, 297,175		B 2
Heroica Nogales, 52,108		B 1
Irapuato, 170,138		E 4
Izúcar de Matamoros, 21,164		F 2
Jalapa Enríquez, 212,769		H 1
Juchitán de Zaragoza, 30,218		F 5
La Paz, 91,453		B 3
León, 593,002		D 4
Linares, 24,456		E 3
Los Mochis, 122,531		C 3
Manzanillo, 20,777		D 4
Matamoros, 238,840		F 3
Matehuala, 28,799		E 3
Mazatlán, 199,830		C 3
Mérida, 364,312		G 4
Mexicali, 341,559		A 1
Mexico City (cap.), *14,750,182		F 1
Minatitlán, 145,268		F 5
Monclova, 115,786		E 2
Monterrey, 1,044,608		E 3
Morelia, 297,544		E 4
Navojoa, 43,817		C 2
Nuevo Laredo, 203,840		E 2
Oaxaca de Juárez, 157,284		F 5
Orizaba, 114,848		H 2
Pachuca de Soto, 110,351		E 4
Papantla de Olarte, 26,773		F 4
Parral, 75,590		D 2
Piedras Negras, 41,033		E 2
Puebla de Zaragoza, 772,908		G 2
Puerto Vallarta, 24,155		D 4
Querétaro, 215,976		E 4
Reynosa, 211,412		E 3
Salamanca, 96,703		E 4
Salina Cruz, 22,004		F 5
Saltillo, 284,937		E 3
San Andrés Tuxtla, 24,267		F 4
San Cristóbal de las Casas, 25,700		G 5
San Luis Potosí, 362,371		E 4
San Martín Texmelucan de la Basti, 23,355		F 1
San Pedro de las Colonias, 26,882		D 3
Silao, 31,825		E 4
Tampico, 267,957		F 3
Tapachula, 85,766		G 5
Tecomán, 31,625		D 4
Tepic, 145,741		D 4
Teziutlán, 23,948		H 2
Tierra Blanca, 22,727		F 4
Tijuana, 429,500		A 1
Tlaxcala de Xicohténcatl, 9,972		G 1
Toluca de Lerdo, 357,071		E 4
Torreón, 328,086		D 3
Tulancingo, 35,799		F 4
Tuxpan de Rodríguez Cano, 33,901		F 4
Tuxtla Gutiérrez, 131,096		G 5
Uruapan del Progreso, 722,822		E 4
Veracruz, 305,456		F 4
Villa Acuña, 30,276		E 2
Villa Frontera, 25,761		E 2
Villahermosa, 158,216		G 5
Zacatecas, 80,088		E 3
Zitácuaro, 36,911		E 4

*City and suburbs.

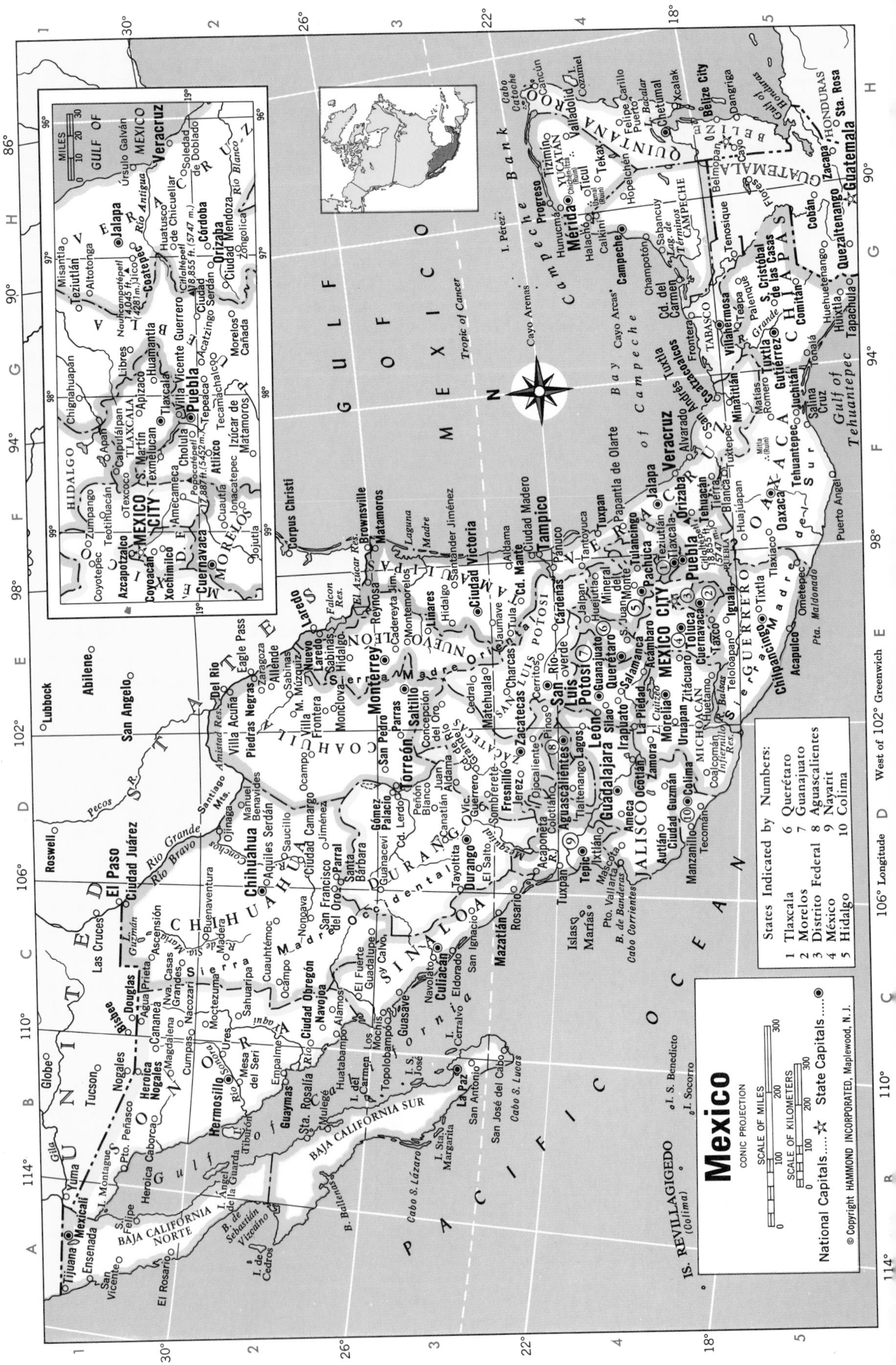

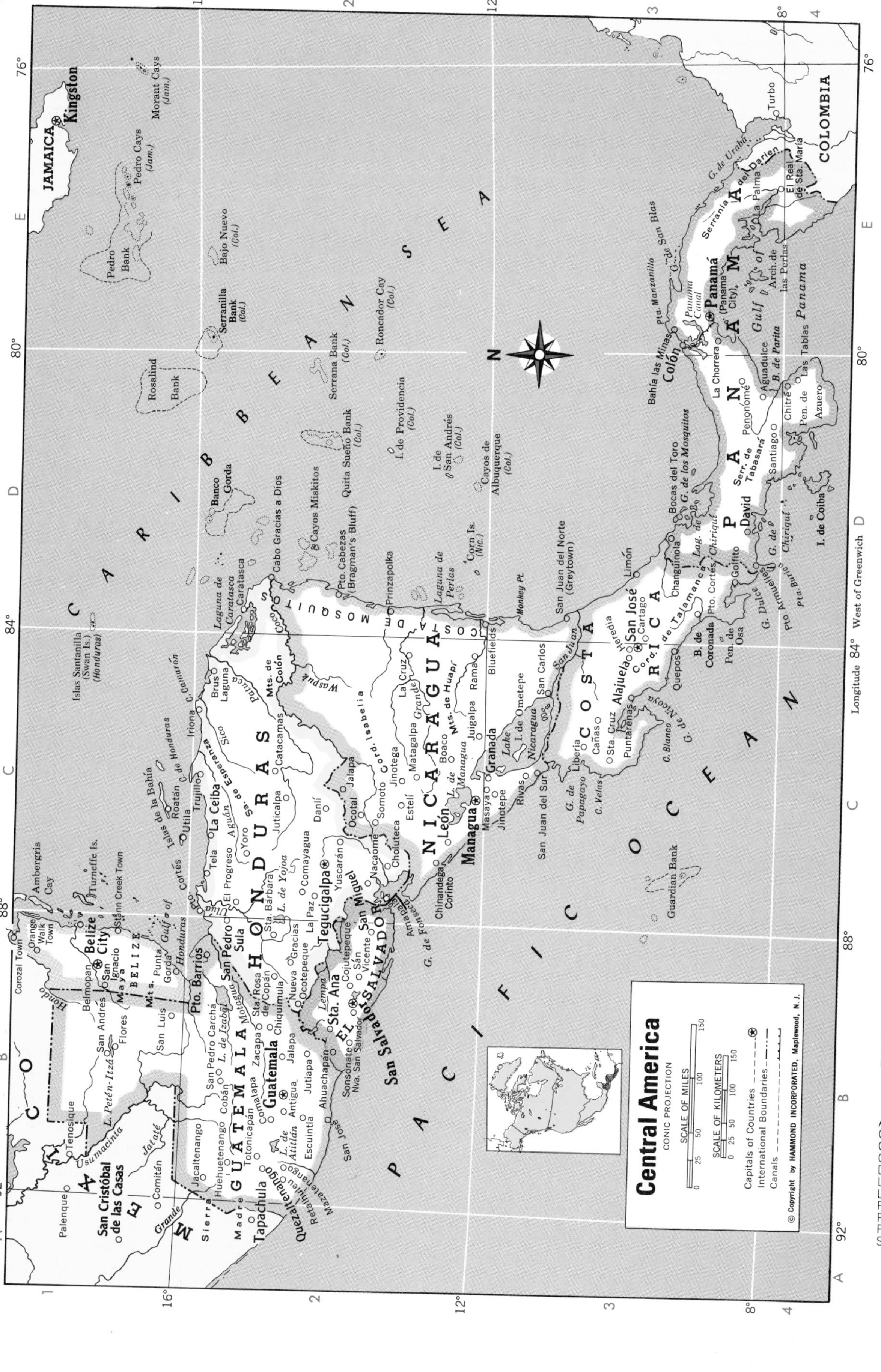

CENTRAL AMERICA

BELIZE

Name	Population	Ref.
Belize City, 39,771		B 1
Belmopan (cap.), 2,935		B 1
Orange Walk Town, 8,439		B 1

COSTA RICA

Name	Ref.
Alajuela, 33,122	C 3
Cañas, 6,053	C 3
Cartago, 21,753	D 3
Golfito, 6,962	D 3
Heredia, 22,700	D 3
Liberia, 10,802	C 3
Limón, 29,621	D 3
Puntarenas, 26,331	C 3
Quepos, 2,155	C 3
San José (cap.), 274,832	D 3
Santa Cruz, 5,777	C 3

EL SALVADOR

Name	Ref.
Nueva San Salvador, 35,106	B 2
San Miguel, 59,304	C 2
San Salvador (cap.), 335,930	B 2
Santa Ana, 96,306	B 2
Sonsonate, 33,562	B 2

GUATEMALA

Name	Ref.
Antigua, 17,994	B 2
Chiquimula, 16,126	B 2
Escuintla, 33,205	B 2
Guatemala (cap.), 793,336	B 2
Huehuetenango, 12,570	B 2
Jalapa, 13,788	B 2
Mazatenango, 23,285	B 2
Puerto Barrios, 22,598	B 2
Quezaltenango, 53,021	B 2
Retalhuleu, 19,060	B 2
Zacapa, 12,688	B 2

HONDURAS

Name	Ref.
Catacamas, 9,134	C 2
Choluteca, 26,152	C 2
Comayagua, 15,941	C 2
Danli, 10,825	C 2
El Progreso, 28,105	C 2
Juticalpa, 10,075	C 2
La Ceiba, 38,788	C 2
La Paz, 6,811	C 2
Neuva Ocotepeque, 4,724	B 2
Puerto Cortes, 25,817	C 2
San Pedro Sula, 276,826	B 2
Santa Barbara, 5,883	C 2
Santa Rosa de Copán, 12,413	B 2
Tegucigalapa (cap.), 444,230	C 2
Tela, 19,055	C 2

NICARAGUA

Name	Ref.
Bluefields, 14,252	C 3
Chinandega, 30,441	C 2
Corinto, 13,404	C 2
Estelí, 20,222	C 2
Granada, 34,976	C 3
Jinotega, 9,506	C 2
Jinotepe, 12,473	C 3
Juigalpa, 8,497	C 2
León, 55,625	C 2
Managua (cap.), 608,020	C 2
Masaya, 30,753	C 3
Matagalpa, 21,385	C 2
Ocotal, 8,215	C 2
Prinzapolka, 8,979	D 2
Rivas, 10,125	C 3

PANAMA

Name	Ref.
Aguadulce, 10,659	D 3
Changuinola, 9,528	D 3
Chitré, 17,156	D 4
Colón, 59,832	D 3
David, 50,621	D 3
La Chorrera, 36,971	D 3
Las Tablas, 5,230	D 4
Panamá (cap.), 389,172	E 3
Penonome, 7,389	D 3
Puerto Armuelles, 12,488	D 3
Santiago, 21,809	D 3

Central America

CONIC PROJECTION

SOUTH AMERICA

CAPITALS

Name	Ref.
Asunción, Paraguay	D 5
Bogotá, Colombia	B 2
Brasília, Brazil	E 4
Buenos Aires, Argentina	D 6
Caracas, Venezuela	C 2
Cayenne, French Guiana	D 2
Georgetown, Guyana	D 2
La Paz, Sucre, Bolivia	C 4
Lima, Peru	B 4
Montevideo, Uruguay	D 6
Quito, Ecuador	B 2
Santiago, Chile	B 6
Paramaribo, Suriname	D 2

PHYSICAL FEATURES

Name	Ref.
Altiplano (plat.)	C 4
Amazon (riv.)	D 3
Ancohuma (mt.)	C 4
Andes (range)	B 4
Angel (falls)	C 2
Angostura (falls)	B 2
Apurímac (riv.)	B 4
Araguaia (riv.)	E 3
Arauca (riv.)	C 2
Aripuaña (riv.)	D 3
Atacama (des.)	C 5
Bandeira (mt.)	E 5
Beni (riv.)	C 4
Bermejo (riv.)	C 5
Blanca (bay)	C 6
Branco (riv.)	C 2
Brazilian Highlands (plat.)	E 4
Buenos Aires (lake)	B 7
Caatingas (forest)	E 3
Campos (region)	E 4
Caquetá (riv.)	B 2
Caroni (riv.)	C 2
Cauca (riv.)	B 2
Caura (riv.)	D 2
Cerro Aconcagua (mt.)	C 6
Chimborazo (mt.)	B 3
Chiquita, Mar (lake)	C 6
Chonos (arch.)	B 7
Chubut (riv.)	C 7
Colorado (riv.)	C 6
Coluene (riv.)	D 4
Courantyne (riv.)	D 2
Cristóbal (mt.)	B 1
Cuyuni (riv.)	C 2
Deseado (riv.)	C 7
Desolación (isl.)	B 8
Espinhaço (mts.)	E 4
Essequibo (riv.)	D 2
Falkland (isls.)	D 8
Frio (cape)	E 5
Furnas (res.)	E 5
Gallinas (pt.)	B 1
Gran Chaco (region)	C 5
Grande (bay)	C 8
Grande (riv.)	E 5
Guainía (riv.)	C 2
Guajira (pen.)	B 1
Guaporé (riv.)	C 4
Guaviare (riv.)	B 2
Guayaquil (gulf)	A 3
Guiana Highlands (plat.)	C 2
Guri (res.)	C 2
Horn (cape)	C 8
Huallaga (riv.)	B 3
Huascaran (mt.)	B 3
Huila (mt.)	B 2
Iguaçu (riv.)	D 5
Iguazu (falls)	D 5
Itaipu (res.)	D 5
Itnay (riv.)	D 2
Japurá (riv.)	C 3
Jari (riv.)	D 2
Jequitinhonha (riv.)	E 4
Juan Fernández (isls.)	B 6
Jurua (riv.)	C 3
Juruena (riv.)	D 4
La Plata (est.)	D 6
Lima (riv.)	C 6
Llanos (plain)	B 2
Llullaillaco (mt.)	C 5
Loa (riv.)	C 5
Madeira (riv.)	C 3
Madre de Dios (riv.)	C 4
Magdalena (riv.)	B 2
Magellan (strait)	C 8
Mamoré (riv.)	C 4
Mar (mts.)	E 5
Maracá (isl.)	E 2
Maracaibo (lake)	B 2
Marajó (est.)	E 2
Marajó (isl.)	E 3
Marañon (riv.)	B 3
Margarita (isl.)	C 1

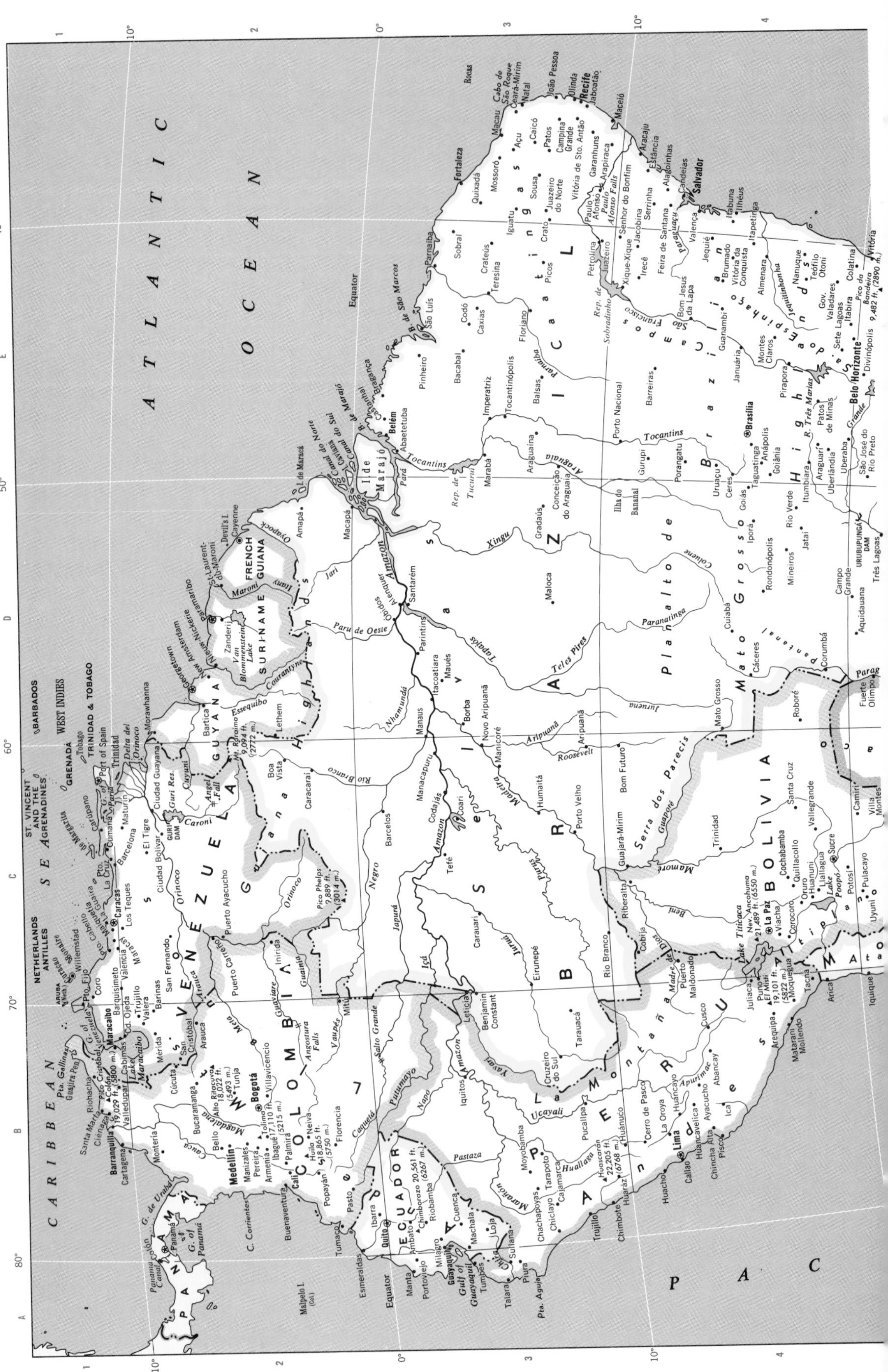

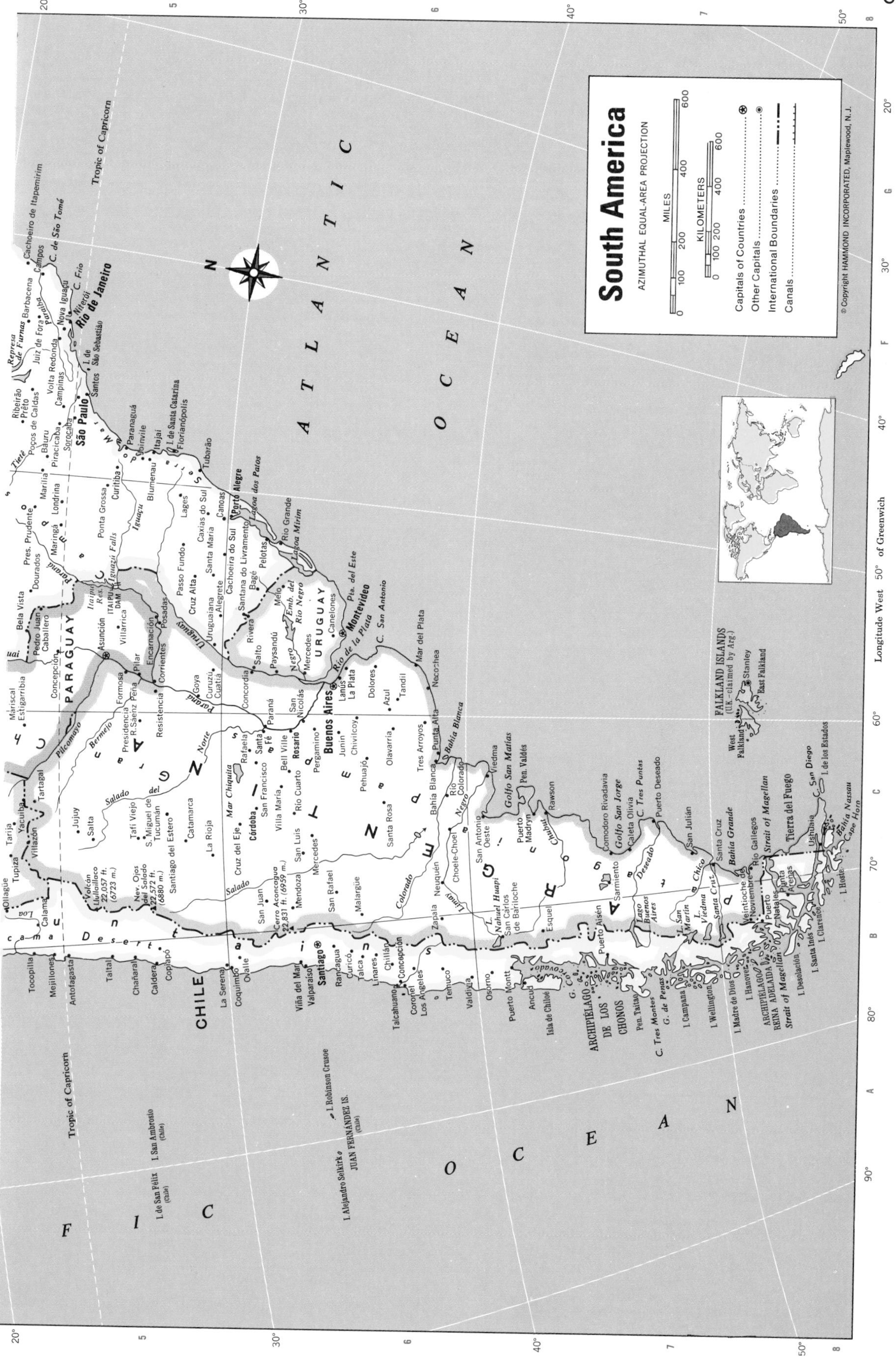

Maroni (riv.) . . . . D 2
Mato Grosso (plat.) . . . . D 4
Meta (riv.) . . . . B 2
Mirim (lake) . . . . D 6
Misti, El (mt.) . . . . B 4
Nahuel Huapi (lake) . . . . B 7
Napo (riv.) . . . . B 3
Nassau (bay) . . . . C 8
Negro (riv.) . . . . C 6
Negro (riv.) . . . . C 3
Negro (riv.) . . . . D 6
Nhamundá (riv.) . . . . D 3
Norte (chan.) . . . . E 2
Ojos del Salado (mt.) . . . . C 5
Orinoco (delta) . . . . C 2
Orinoco (riv.) . . . . C 2
Oyapock (riv.) . . . . D 2
Pampas (plain) . . . . C 6
Pantanal (region) . . . . D 4
Pará (est.) . . . . E 3
Paraguacu (riv.) . . . . F 4
Paraguai (riv.) . . . . D 4
Paraíba (riv.) . . . . E 5
Paraná (riv.) . . . . D 5
Paranatinga (riv.) . . . . D 4
Parecis (mts.) . . . . C 4
Paria (gulf) . . . . C 1
Parnaíba (riv.) . . . . E 3
Paru de Oeste (riv.) . . . . D 3
Pastaza (riv.) . . . . B 3
Patagonia (region) . . . . C 7
Patos (lake) . . . . D 6
Paulo Afonso (falls) . . . . F 3
Phelps (mt.) . . . . C 2
Pilcomayo (riv.) . . . . C 5
Plata (riv.) . . . . D 6
Poopó (lake) . . . . C 4
Purus (riv.) . . . . C 3
Putumayo (riv.) . . . . B 3
Reina Adelaida (arch.) . . . . B 8
Robinson Crusoe (isl.) . . . . B 6
Roosevelt (riv.) . . . . C 3
Roraima (mt.) . . . . C 2
Salado (riv.) . . . . C 6
Salado del Norte (riv.) . . . . C 5
Salto Grande (falls) . . . . B 3
San Antonio (cape) . . . . D 6
San Diego (cape) . . . . C 8
San Félix (isl.) . . . . A 5
San Jorge (gulf) . . . . C 7
San Martín (lake) . . . . B 7
San Matías (gulf) . . . . C 7
Santa Catarina (isl.) . . . . E 5
Santa Cruz (riv.) . . . . B 7
Santa Inés (isl.) . . . . B 8
São Francisco (riv.) . . . . E 4
São Marcos (bay) . . . . E 3
São Roque (cape) . . . . F 3
São Sebastião (isl.) . . . . E 5
São Tome (cape) . . . . F 5
Selvas (forest) . . . . C 3
Sobradinho (res.) . . . . E 3
Sul (chan.) . . . . E 2
Taitao (pen.) . . . . B 7
Tapajós (riv.) . . . . D 3
Teles Pires (riv.) . . . . D 3
Tierra del Fuego (isl.) . . . . C 8
Tietê (riv.) . . . . E 5
Titicaca (lake) . . . . C 4
Tocantins (riv.) . . . . E 4
Tolima (mt.) . . . . B 2
Três Marias (res.) . . . . E 4
Tres Montes (cape) . . . . B 7
Tres Puntas (cape) . . . . C 7
Tucuruí (res.) . . . . D 3
Ucayalí (riv.) . . . . B 3
Urubupungá (dam) . . . . D 5
Uruguay (riv.) . . . . D 5
Valdés (pen.) . . . . C 7
Van Blommenstein (lake) . . . . . . D 2
Vaupés (riv.) . . . . B 8
Venezuela (gulf) . . . . B 1
Viedma (lake) . . . . B 7
Xingu (riv.) . . . . D 3
Yavarí (riv.) . . . . B 3

SOUTH AMERICA

ARGENTINA

Name Population	Ref.
Azul, 43,582	J 11
Bahía Blanca, 220,765	H 11
Buenos Aires (cap.), 9,927,404	H 10
Campana, 51,498	H 10
Catamarca, 88,432	H 9
Chivilcoy, 43,779	H 11
Comodoro Rivadavia, 96,865	G 13
Concepcion del Uruguay, 46,065	J 10
Concordia, 193,618	J 10
Córdoba, 982,018	G 10
Corrientes, 179,590	J 9
Formosa, 195,067	J 9
General Roca, 38,296	G 11
Godoy Cruz, 141,553	G 10
Goya, 47,357	J 9
Jujuy, 124,487	G 8
La Plata, 560,341	J 11
La Rioja, 66,826	G 9
Mar del Plata, 407,024	J 11
Mendoza, 596,796	G 10
Mercedes, 50,856	G 10
Necochea, 50,939	J 11
Neuquén, 90,037	G 11
Olavarria, 63,686	H 11
Paraná, 159,581	J 10
Pergamino, 68,989	H 10
Posadas, 139,941	J 9
Presidencia Roque Sáenz Peña, 49,261	J 9
Punta Alta, 54,375	H 11
Rafaela, 53,152	H 10
Reconquista, 32,442	H 9
Resistencia, 218,438	J 9
Río Cuarto, 110,148	H 10
Río Gallegos, 43,479	G 14
Rosario, 954,606	H 10
Salta, 260,323	G 8
San Carlos de Bariloche, 48,222	F 12
San Francisco, 58,616	H 10
San Juan, 290,479	G 10
San Luis, 70,632	G 10
San Miguel de Tucumán, 496,914	H 9
San Nicolás, 96,313	J 10
Santa Fe, 287,240	H 10
Santa Rosa, 51,689	H 11
Santiago del Estero, 148,357	H 9
Tandil, 78,821	J 9
Trelew, 52,073	G 12
Tres Arroyos, 42,118	J 11
Venado Tuerto, 46,775	H 10
Villa María, 67,490	H 10

BOLIVIA

Name Population	Ref.
Cochabamba, 204,684	G 7
Cobija, 3,650	G 6
La Paz (cap.), 635,283	G 7
Oruro, 124,213	G 7
Potosí, 77,397	G 7
Santa Cruz, 254,682	H 7
Sucre (cap.), 63,625	H 7
Tarija, 38,916	H 8
Trinidad, 27,487	H 6

BRAZIL

Name Population	Ref.
Alagoinha, 77,377	N 6
Anápolis, 160,520	L 7
Aracaju, 288,106	N 6
Araçatuba, 113,486	K 8
Araguari, 73,302	L 7
Arapiraca, 84,133	N 5
Araraquara, 77,202	L 8
Bagé, 66,743	K 10
Bahia (Salvador), 1,496,276	N 6
Barbacena, 69,675	M 8
Barretos, 65,294	L 8
Baurú, 178,861	L 8
Belém, 758,117	L 4
Belo Horizonte, 2,541,788	M 7
Blumenau, 144,819	L 9
Brasília (cap.), 411,305	L 7
Cachoeira do Sul, 59,967	K 10
Cachoeiro de Itapemirim, 84,994	N 8
Campina Grande, 222,229	N 5
Campinas, 566,517	L 8
Campo Grande, 282,844	K 8
Campos, 174,218	M 8
Caruaru, 137,636	N 5
Catanduva, 64,813	L 8
Caxias do Sul, 198,824	K 9
Ceará (Fortaleza), 648,815	N 4
Colatina, 61,057	N 7
Conselheiro Lafaiete, 66,262	M 8

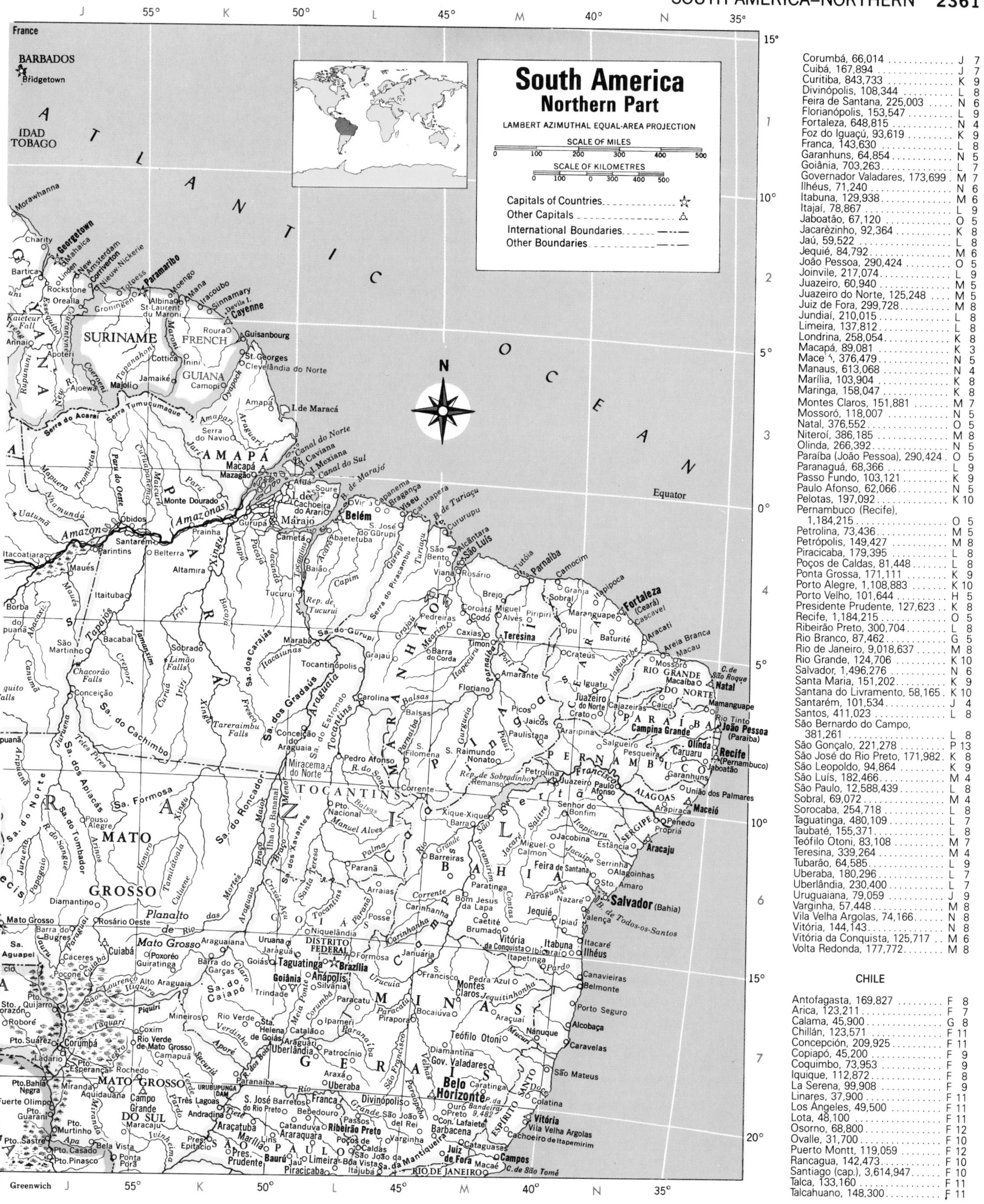
South America
Northern Part
LAMBERT AZIMUTHAL EQUAL-AREA PROJECTION
SCALE OF MILES
0 100 200 300 400 500
SCALE OF KILOMETRES
0 100 0 300 400 500
Capitals of Countries
Other Capitals
International Boundaries
Other Boundaries
ATLANTIC OCEAN
N
Equator
France
BARBADOS
Bridgetown
SURINAME
FRENCH GUIANA
Paramaribo
Cayenne
Georgetown
AMAPÁ
Macapá
Belém
São Luís
Teresina
Fortaleza (Ceará)
Natal
RIO GRANDE DO NORTE
PARAÍBA
João Pessoa (Paraíba)
Recife (Pernambuco)
PERNAMBUCO
ALAGOAS
Maceió
SERGIPE
Aracaju
Salvador (Bahia)
BAHIA
PIAUÍ
MARANHÃO
PARÁ
TOCANTINS
GOIÁS
DISTRITO FEDERAL
Brasília
Goiânia
MINAS GERAIS
Belo Horizonte
ESPÍRITO SANTO
Vitória
MATO GROSSO
Cuiabá
MATO GROSSO DO SUL
Campo Grande
SÃO PAULO
RIO DE JANEIRO
Amazonas
Santarém
Marajó
Greenwich
J K L M N
55° 50° 45° 40° 35°
15° 10° 5° 0° 5° 10° 15° 20°
1 2 3 4 5 6 7

Corumbá, 66,014 .... J 7
Cuibá, 167,894 .... J 7
Curitiba, 843,733 .... K 9
Divinópolis, 108,344 .... L 8
Feira de Santana, 225,003 .... N 6
Florianópolis, 153,547 .... L 9
Fortaleza, 648,815 .... N 4
Foz do Iguaçú, 93,619 .... K 9
Franca, 143,630 .... L 8
Garanhuns, 64,854 .... N 5
Goiânia, 703,263 .... L 7
Governador Valadares, 173,699 .... M 7
Ilhéus, 71,240 .... N 6
Itabuna, 129,938 .... M 6
Itajaí, 78,867 .... L 9
Jaboatão, 67,120 .... O 5
Jacarèzinho, 92,364 .... K 8
Jaú, 59,522 .... L 8
Jequié, 84,792 .... M 6
João Pessoa, 290,424 .... O 5
Joinvile, 217,074 .... L 9
Juazeiro, 60,940 .... M 5
Juazeiro do Norte, 125,248 .... M 5
Juiz de Fora, 299,728 .... M 8
Jundiaí, 210,015 .... L 8
Limeira, 137,812 .... L 8
Londrina, 258,054 .... K 8
Macapá, 89,081 .... K 3
Maceió, 376,479 .... N 5
Manaus, 613,068 .... N 4
Marília, 103,904 .... K 8
Maringa, 158,047 .... K 8
Montes Claros, 151,881 .... M 7
Mossoró, 118,007 .... N 5
Natal, 376,552 .... O 5
Niteroí, 386,185 .... M 8
Olinda, 266,392 .... N 5
Paraíba (João Pessoa), 290,424 .... O 5
Paranaguá, 68,366 .... L 9
Passo Fundo, 103,121 .... K 9
Paulo Afonso, 62,066 .... N 5
Pelotas, 197,092 .... K 10
Pernambuco (Recife), 1,184,215 .... O 5
Petrolina, 73,436 .... M 5
Petrópolis, 149,427 .... M 8
Piracicaba, 179,395 .... L 8
Poços de Caldas, 81,448 .... L 8
Ponta Grossa, 171,111 .... K 9
Porto Alegre, 1,108,883 .... K 10
Porto Velho, 101,644 .... H 5
Presidente Prudente, 127,623 .... K 8
Recife, 1,184,215 .... O 5
Ribeirão Preto, 300,704 .... L 8
Rio Branco, 87,462 .... G 5
Rio de Janeiro, 9,018,637 .... M 8
Rio Grande, 124,706 .... K 10
Salvador, 1,496,276 .... N 6
Santa Maria, 151,202 .... K 9
Santana do Livramento, 58,165 .... K 10
Santarém, 101,534 .... J 4
Santos, 411,023 .... L 8
São Bernardo do Campo, 381,261 .... L 8
São Gonçalo, 221,278 .... P 13
São José do Rio Preto, 171,982 .... K 8
São Leopoldo, 94,864 .... K 9
São Luís, 182,466 .... M 4
São Paulo, 12,588,439 .... L 8
Sobral, 69,072 .... M 4
Sorocaba, 254,718 .... L 8
Taguatinga, 480,109 .... L 7
Taubaté, 155,371 .... L 8
Teófilo Otoni, 83,108 .... M 7
Teresina, 339,264 .... M 4
Tubarão, 64,585 .... L 9
Uberaba, 180,296 .... L 7
Uberlândia, 230,400 .... L 7
Uruguaiana, 79,059 .... J 9
Varginha, 57,448 .... M 8
Vila Velha Argolas, 74,166 .... N 8
Vitória, 144,143 .... N 8
Vitória da Conquista, 125,717 .... M 6
Volta Redonda, 177,772 .... M 8

CHILE

Antofagasta, 169,827 .... F 8
Arica, 123,211 .... F 7
Calama, 45,900 .... G 8
Chillán, 123,571 .... F 11
Concepción, 209,925 .... F 11
Copiapó, 45,200 .... F 9
Coquimbo, 73,953 .... F 9
Iquique, 112,872 .... F 8
La Serena, 99,908 .... F 9
Linares, 37,900 .... F 11
Los Ángeles, 49,500 .... F 11
Lota, 48,100 .... F 11
Osorno, 68,800 .... F 12
Ovalle, 31,700 .... F 10
Puerto Montt, 119,059 .... F 12
Rancagua, 142,473 .... F 10
Santiago (cap.), 3,614,947 .... F 10
Talca, 133,160 .... F 11
Talcahuano, 148,300 .... F 11

Temuca, 197,232 . . . . F 11
Valdivia, 115,536 . . . . F 11
Vallendar, 26,800 . . . . F 9
Valparaíso, 266,726 . . . . F 10
Villarrica, 25,091 . . . . F 11
Viña del Mar, 298,663 . . . . F 10

COLOMBIA

Barrancabermeja, 87,191 . . . . . . F 2
Barranquilla, 661,009 . . . . F 1
Bogotá (cap)., 2,696,270 . . . . F 3
Bucaramanga, 291,661 . . . . F 2
Buenaventura, 115,770 . . . . E 3
Buga, 71,016 . . . . E 3
Cali, 898,253 . . . . E 3
Cartagena, 292,512 . . . . E 1
Ciénaga, 42,546 . . . . F 1
Cúcuta, 219,772 . . . . F 2
Ibagué, 176,223 . . . . F 3
Manizales, 199,904 . . . . E 2
Medellín, 1,070,924 . . . . E 2
Montería, 89,583 . . . . E 2
Neiva, 105,476 . . . . F 3
Palmira, 140,481 . . . . E 3
Pasto, 119,339 . . . . E 3
Pereira, 174,128 . . . . E 3
Popayán, 77,669 . . . . E 3
Santa Marta, 102,484 . . . . F 1
Sincelejo, 68,797 . . . . E 2
Sogamosa, 48,891 . . . . F 2
Tulua, 86,736 . . . . E 3
Tunja, 51,620 . . . . F 2
Villavicencio, 82,869 . . . . F 3

ECUADOR

Ambato, 77,955 . . . . E 4
Babahoya, 28,914 . . . . D 4
Cuenca, 104,470 . . . . E 4
Esmeraldas, 60,364 . . . . D 3
Guayaquil, 823,219 . . . . D 4
Ibarra, 41,335 . . . . E 3
Latacunga, 21,921 . . . . E 4
Loja, 47,697 . . . . E 4
Machala, 69,170 . . . . D 4
Manta, 64,519 . . . . D 4
Pasaje, 20,790 . . . . E 4
Portoviejo, 59,550 . . . . D 4
Quito (cap.), 599,828 . . . . E 4
Riobamba, 58,087 . . . . E 4
Tulcán, 24,398 . . . . E 3

FALKLAND ISLANDS

Stanley (cap.), 1,050 . . . . J 14

FRENCH GUIANA

Cayenne (cap.), 37,097 . . . . K 2
Guisanbourg . . . . K 3
Iracoubo, 483 . . . . K 2
Mana, 623 . . . . K 2
Saint-Georges, 921 . . . . K 3
St-Laurent du Maroni, 5,042 . . . . K 2

GUYANA

Corriverton, 10,520 . . . . J 2
Georgetown (cap.), 63,184 . . . . . J 2
Morawhanna, 292 . . . . J 2
New Amsterdam, 17,782 . . . . J 2

PARAGUAY

Asunción (cap.), 794,166 . . . . J 9
Concepción, 22,866 . . . . J 8
Encarnación, 27,632 . . . . J 9
Fuerte Olimpo, 1,867 . . . . J 8
Mariscal Estigarribia, 5,227 . . . . H 8
San Pedro, 3,515 . . . . J 8
Villarrica, 21,203 . . . . J 9

PERU

Arequipa, 447,431 . . . . F 7
Ayacucho, 68,535 . . . . F 6
Cajamarca, 60,280 . . . . E 5
Callao, 441,374 . . . . E 6
Catacaos, 30,927 . . . . D 5
Cerro de Pasco, 71,558 . . . . E 6
Chiclayo, 280,244 . . . . E 5
Chimbote, 216,406 . . . . E 5
Chincha Alta, 37,475 . . . . E 6
Cusco, 181,604 . . . . F 6
Huacho, 43,402 . . . . E 6
Huancayo, 165,132 . . . . F 6
Huánuco, 52,628 . . . . E 6
Huaráz, 45,116 . . . . E 5
Ica, 111,087 . . . . E 6

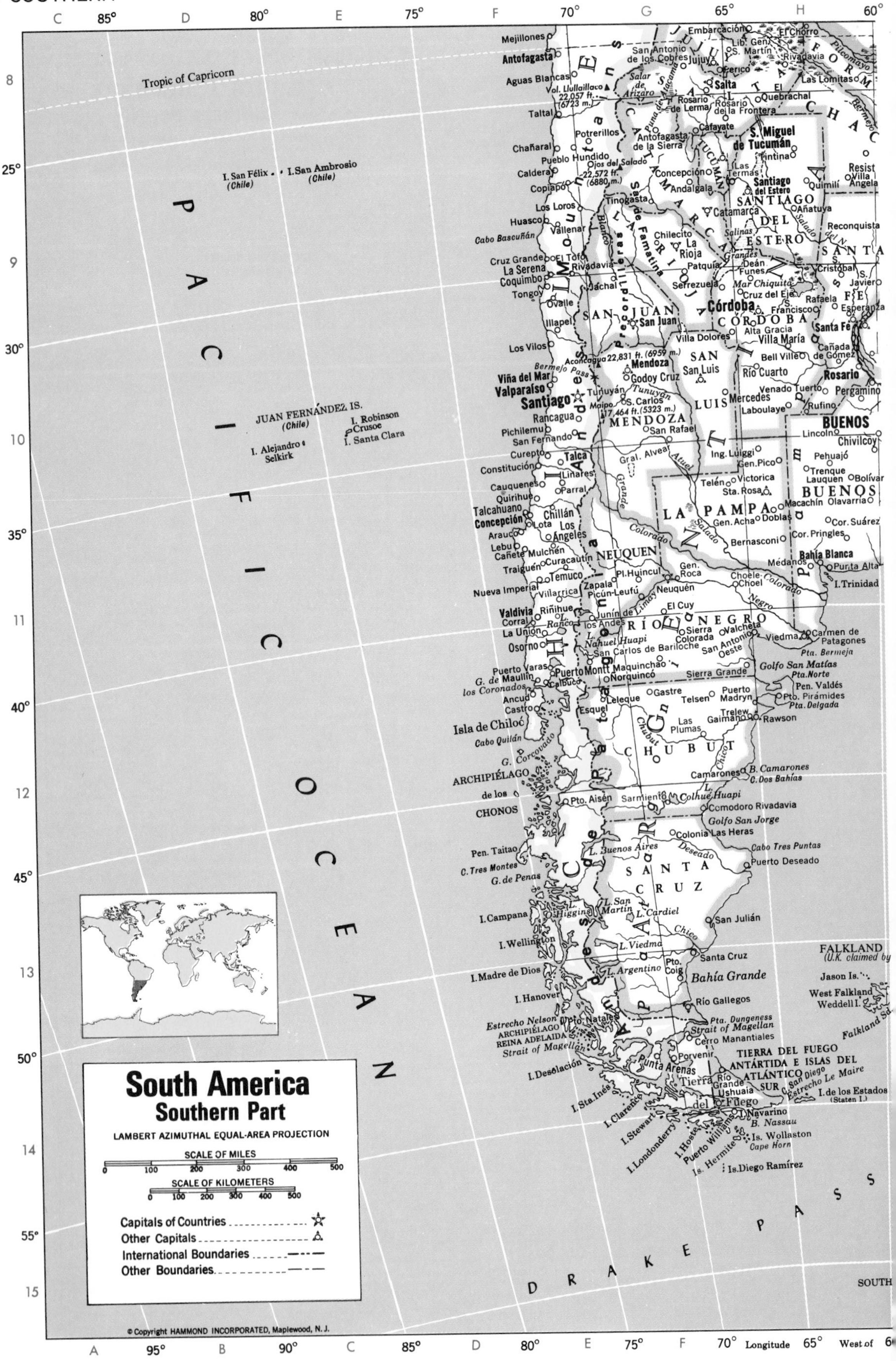

South America
Southern Part

LAMBERT AZIMUTHAL EQUAL-AREA PROJECTION

SCALE OF MILES: 0 100 200 300 400 500

SCALE OF KILOMETERS: 0 100 200 300 400 500

Capitals of Countries ☆
Other Capitals △
International Boundaries
Other Boundaries

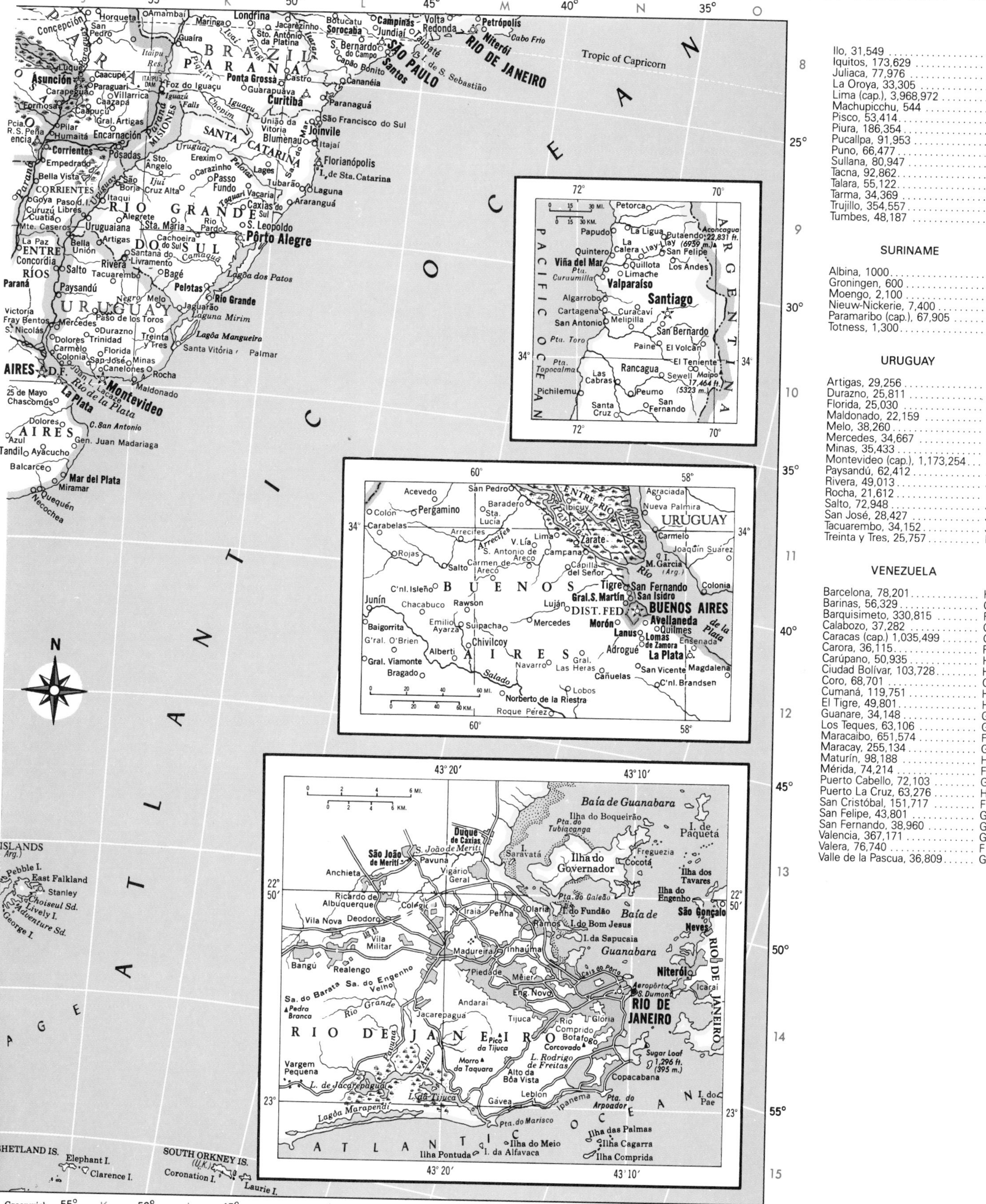

Ilo, 31,549	F	7
Iquitos, 173,629	F	4
Juliaca, 77,976	F	7
La Oroya, 33,305	E	6
Lima (cap.), 3,968,972	E	6
Machupicchu, 544	F	6
Pisco, 53,414	E	6
Piura, 186,354	D	5
Pucallpa, 91,953	E	5
Puno, 66,477	F	7
Sullana, 80,947	D	4
Tacna, 92,862	F	7
Talara, 55,122	D	4
Tarma, 34,369	E	6
Trujillo, 354,557	E	5
Tumbes, 48,187	D	4

SURINAME

Albina, 1000	K	3
Groningen, 600	J	2
Moengo, 2,100	K	3
Nieuw-Nickerie, 7,400	J	2
Paramaribo (cap.), 67,905	K	2
Totness, 1,300	J	2

URUGUAY

Artigas, 29,256	J	11
Durazno, 25,811	J	10
Florida, 25,030	J	10
Maldonado, 22,159	K	11
Melo, 38,260	K	10
Mercedes, 34,667	J	10
Minas, 35,433	K	10
Montevideo (cap.), 1,173,254	J	11
Paysandú, 62,412	J	10
Rivera, 49,013	J	10
Rocha, 21,612	K	10
Salto, 72,948	J	10
San José, 28,427	J	10
Tacuarembo, 34,152	J	10
Treinta y Tres, 25,757	K	10

VENEZUELA

Barcelona, 78,201	H	2
Barinas, 56,329	G	2
Barquisimeto, 330,815	F	2
Calabozo, 37,282	G	2
Caracas (cap.) 1,035,499	G	1
Carora, 36,115	F	1
Carúpano, 50,935	H	1
Ciudad Bolívar, 103,728	H	2
Coro, 68,701	G	1
Cumaná, 119,751	H	1
El Tigre, 49,801	H	2
Guanare, 34,148	G	2
Los Teques, 63,106	G	1
Maracaibo, 651,574	F	1
Maracay, 255,134	G	1
Maturín, 98,188	H	2
Mérida, 74,214	F	2
Puerto Cabello, 72,103	G	1
Puerto La Cruz, 63,276	H	1
San Cristóbal, 151,717	F	2
San Felipe, 43,801	G	1
San Fernando, 38,960	G	2
Valencia, 367,171	G	2
Valera, 76,740	F	2
Valle de la Pascua, 36,809	G	2

AFRICA

CAPITALS

Name	Ref.
Accra, Ghana	B 4
Addis Ababa, Ethiopia	F 4
Algiers, Algeria	C 1
Antananarivo, Madagascar	G 6
Bamako, Mali	B 3
Bangui, Central African Rep.	D 4
Banjul, Gambia	A 3
Bissau, Guinea-Bissau	A 3
Brazzaville, Congo	D 5
Bujumbura, Burundi	F 5
Cairo, Egypt	F 2
Cape Town, South Africa	D 8
Conakry, Guinea	A 4
Dakar, Senegal	A 3
Dar es Salaam, Tanzania	F 5
Djibouti, Djibouti	G 3
Freetown, Sierra Leone	A 4
Gaborone, Botswana	E 7
Harare, Zimbabwe	F 6
Kampala, Uganda	F 4
Khartoum, Sudan	F 3
Kigali, Rwanda	F 5
Kinshasa, Zaire	D 5
Lagos, Nigeria	C 4
Libreville, Gabon	C 4
Lilongwe, Malawi	F 6
Lomé, Togo	C 4
Luanda, Angola	D 5
Lusaka, Zambia	E 6
Malabo, Equatorial Guinea	C 4
Maputo, Mozambique	F 7
Maseru, Lesotho	E 7
Mbabane, Swaziland	F 7
Moroni, Comoros	G 6
Mogadishu, Somália	G 4
Monrovia, Liberia	A 4
N'Djamena, Chad	D 3
Nairobi, Kenya	F 5
Niamey, Niger	C 3
Nouakchott, Mauritania	A 3
Ouagadougou, Burkina Faso	B 3
Porto-Novo, Benin	C 4
Pretoria, South Africa	E 7
Rabat, Morocco	B 1
São Tomé & Príncipe	C 4
Tripoli, Libya	D 1
Tunis, Tunisia	D 1
Windhoek, Namibia	D 6
Yamoussoukro, Ivory Coast	B 4
Yaoundé, Cameroon	D 4

PHYSICAL FEATURES

Name	Ref.
Aden (gulf)	G 3
Agulhas (cape)	D 8
Ahaggar (range)	C 2
Aldabra (isls.)	G 5
Annobon (isl.)	C 5
Ascension (isl.)	A 5
Ashanti (reg.)	B 4
Aswân High (dam)	F 2
Atlantic (ocean)	B 5
Atlas (mts.)	B 1
Bab el Mandeb (strait)	G 3
Bassas da India (isl.)	F 7
Benue (riv.)	C 4
Bette (peak)	D 2
Bijagós (isls.)	A 3
Bioko (isl.)	C 4
Black Volta (riv.)	B 3
Blanc (cape)	A 2
Blue Nile (riv.)	F 3
Bobaomby (Amber) (cape)	G 6
Bodélé (depr.)	D 3
Bojador (cape)	A 2
Bomu (riv.)	E 4
Bon (cape)	D 1
Boyoma (Stanley) (falls)	E 5
Cameroon (mt.)	C 4
Canary (isls.)	A 2
Caprivi Strip (reg.)	E 6
Chad (lake)	D 3
Chech, Erg (des.)	B 2
Congo (riv.)	D 5
Cosmoledo (isls.)	G 5
Cuango (riv.)	D 5
Cuanza (riv.)	D 5
Cubango (riv.)	D 6
Cunene (riv.)	D 6
Cyrenaica (reg.)	E 1
Delgado (cape)	G 6
Desertas (isl.)	A 1
Djado (plat.)	D 2
Edward (lake)	E 5
El Djouf (des.)	B 2
Elgon (mt.)	F 4
Emi Koussi (mt.)	D 3
Eritrea (reg.)	F 3
Europa (isl.)	G 7

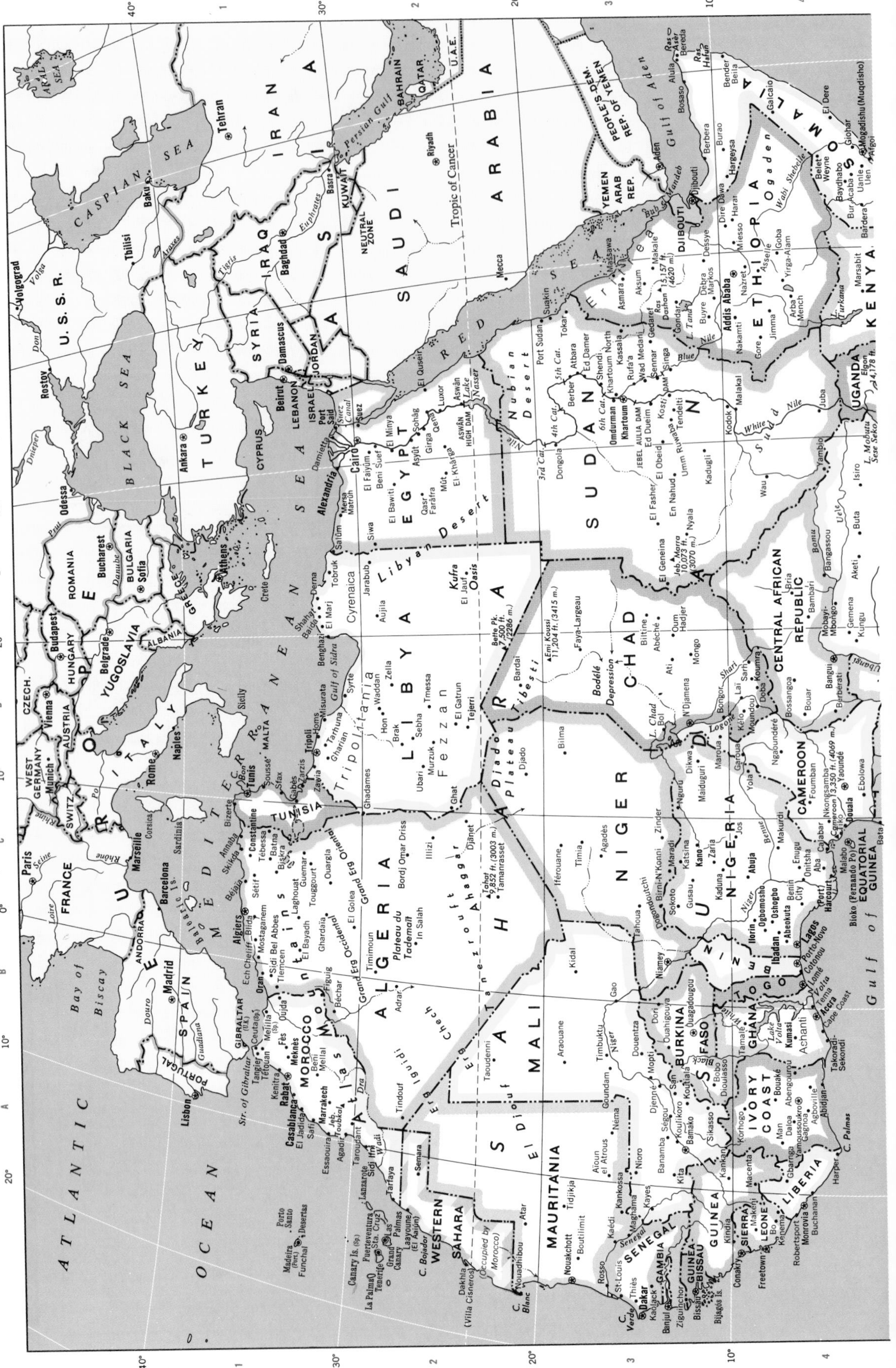

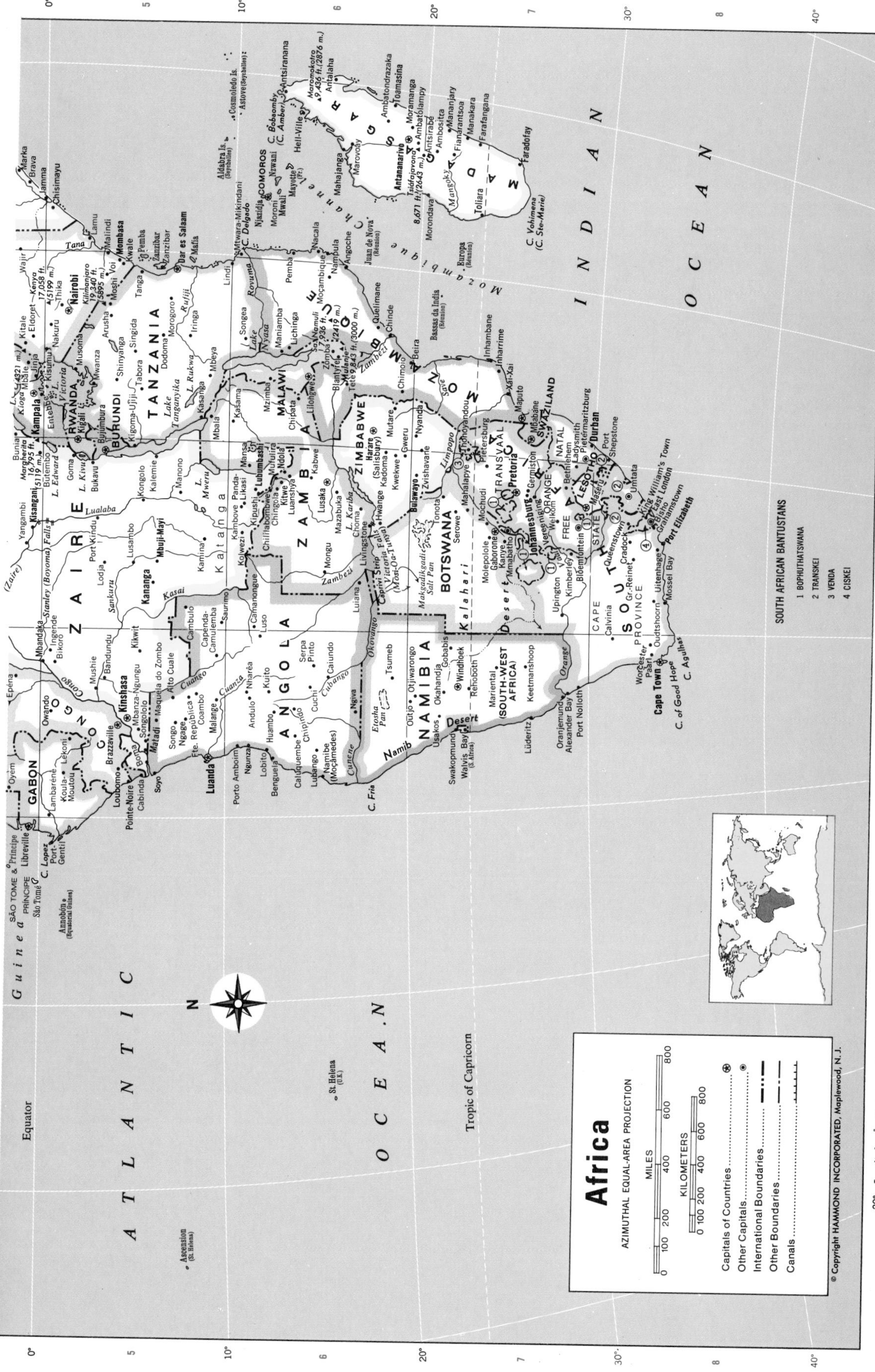

WESTERN AFRICA

ALGERIA

Name	*Population*	*Ref.*
Algiers (Alger) (cap.)	1,365,400	E 1
Annaba (Bône)	255,900	F 1
Batna	112,100	F 1
Blida	160,900	E 1
Constantine	335,100	F 1
Ech Cheliff (Orléansville)	106,100	E 1
Oran	491,900	D 1
Mostaganem	101,600	D 1
Sétif	144,200	F 1
Sidi Bel-Abbes	116,000	D 1
Skikda (Philippeville)	107,700	F 1
Tlemcen	109,400	D 2

BENIN

Name	Population	Ref.
Abomey	50,170	E 7
Cotonou	327,595	E 7
Porto-Novo (cap.)	131,989	E 7

BURKINA FASO

Name	Population	Ref.
Bobo Dioulasso	115,063	D 6
Koudougou	36,838	D 6
Ouagadougou (cap.)	172,661	D 6

CAPE VERDE

Name	Population	Ref.
Mindelo	36,265	A 7
Praia (cap.)	37,480	B 8
Ribeira Grande	1,980	B 7

GAMBIA

Name	Population	Ref.
Banjul (Bathurst) (cap.)	39,476	A 6

GHANA

Name	Population	Ref.
Accra (cap.)	1,420,066	D 7
Cape Coast	51,653	D 8
Kumasi	345,117	D 7
Sekondi-Takoradi	160,868	D 8
Takoradi	58,161	D 8
Tamale	83,653	D 7
Tema	60,767	E 7

GUINEA

Name	Population	Ref.
Conakry (cap.)	525,671	B 7
Kindia	79,861	B 6
Kankdan	85,310	C 6

GUINEA-BISSAU

Name	Population	Ref.
Bissau (cap.)	109,486	A 6
Cacheu	15,194	A 6

IVORY COAST (CÔTE D'IVOIRE)

Name	Population	Ref.
Abidjan	685,828	D 7
Bouaké	173,248	D 7
Daloa	60,958	C 7
Port-Bouet	72,616	D 8
Yamoussoukro (cap.)	35,585	C 7

LIBERIA

Name	Population	Ref.
Buchanan	23,999	B 7
Monrovia (cap.)	166,507	B 7
Tubmanburg	14,089	B 7

MALI

Name	Population	Ref.
Bamako (cap.)	404,022	C 6
Kayes	44,736	B 6
Mopti	53,885	D 6
Ségou	64,890	C 6
Timbuktu (Tombouctou)	20,483	D 5

MAURITANIA

Name	Population	Ref.
Káedi	20,848	B 5
Nouadhibou	21,961	A 4
Nouakchott (cap.)	134,986	A 5

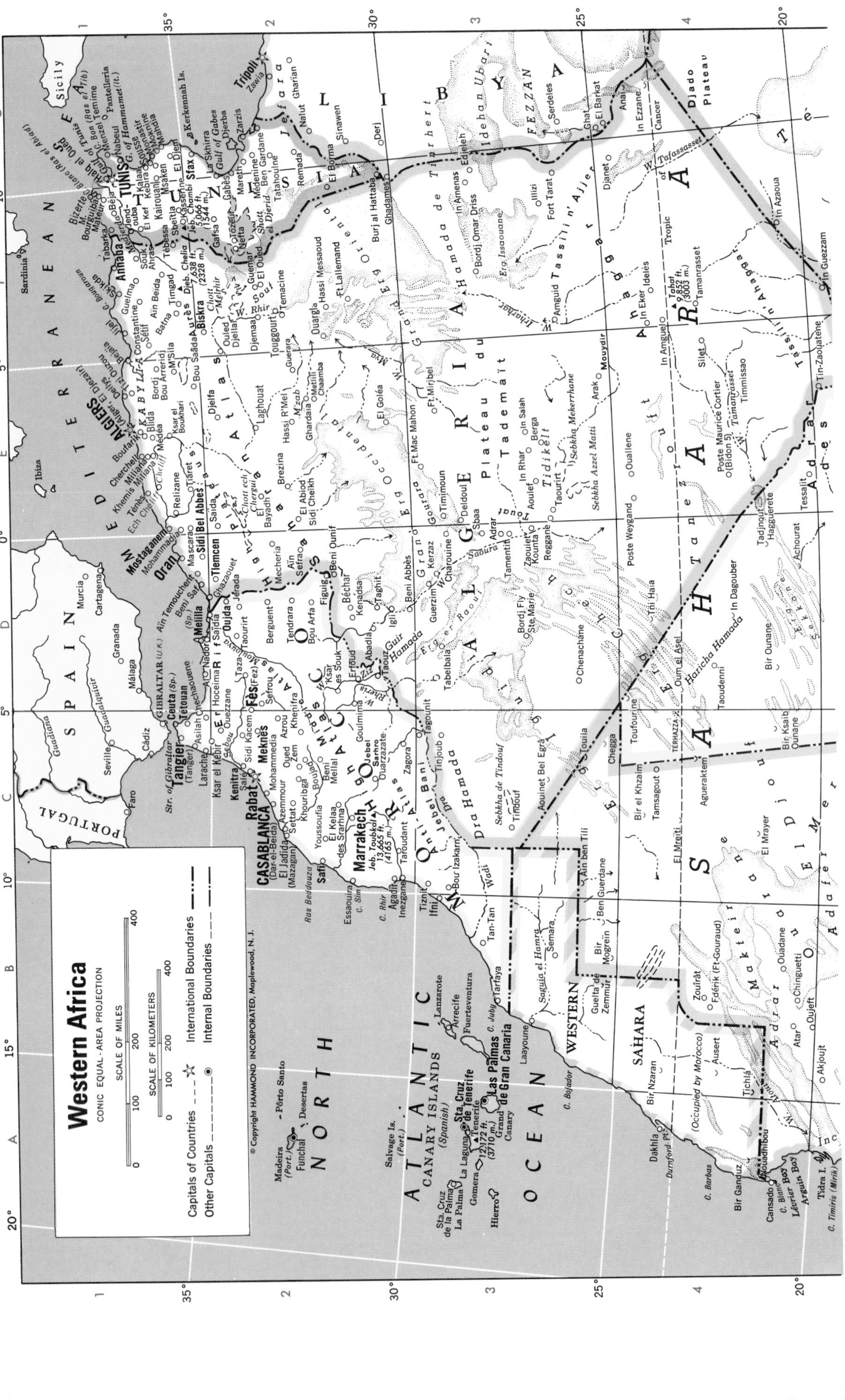

Western Africa

CONIC EQUAL-AREA PROJECTION

SCALE OF MILES: 0 100 200 400

SCALE OF KILOMETERS: 0 100 200 400

Capitals of Countries
Other Capitals
International Boundaries
Internal Boundaries

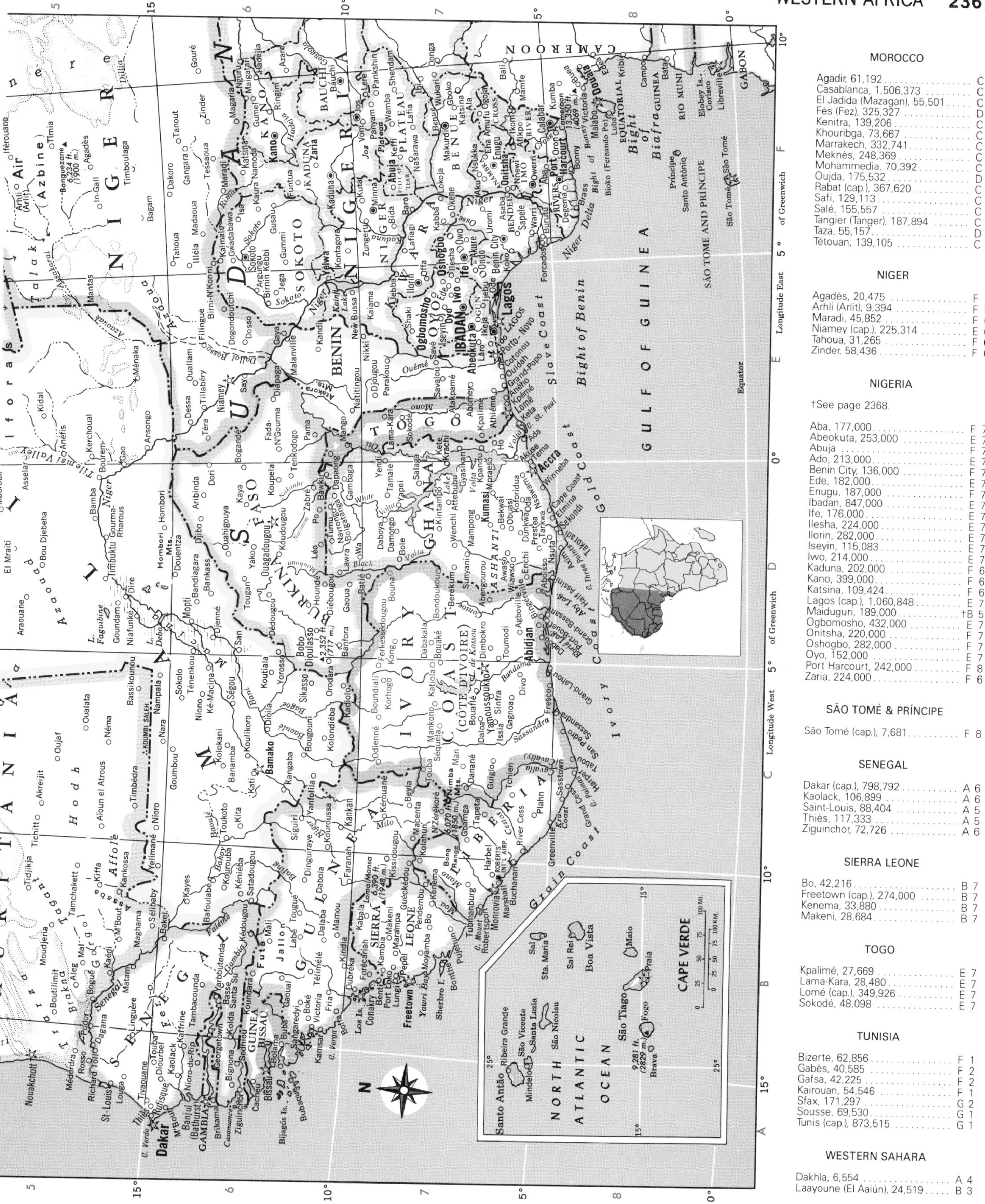

MOROCCO

Agadir, 61,192 . . . . C 2
Casablanca, 1,506,373 . . . . C 2
El Jadida (Mazagan), 55,501 . . . . . C 2
Fès (Fez), 325,327 . . . . D 2
Kenitra, 139,206 . . . . C 2
Khouribga, 73,667 . . . . C 2
Marrakech, 332,741 . . . . C 2
Meknès, 248,369 . . . . C 2
Mohammedia, 70,392 . . . . C 2
Oujda, 175,532 . . . . D 2
Rabat (cap.), 367,620 . . . . C 2
Safi, 129,113 . . . . C 2
Salé, 155,557 . . . . C 2
Tangier (Tanger), 187,894 . . . . . . C 1
Taza, 55,157 . . . . D 2
Tétouan, 139,105 . . . . C 1

NIGER

Agadès, 20,475 . . . . F 5
Arhli (Arlit), 9,394 . . . . F 5
Maradi, 45,852 . . . . F 6
Niamey (cap.), 225,314 . . . . E 6
Tahoua, 31,265 . . . . F 6
Zinder, 58,436 . . . . F 6

NIGERIA

†See page 2368.

Aba, 177,000 . . . . F 7
Abeokuta, 253,000 . . . . E 7
Abuja . . . . F 7
Ado, 213,000 . . . . E 7
Benin City, 136,000 . . . . F 7
Ede, 182,000 . . . . E 7
Enugu, 187,000 . . . . F 7
Ibadan, 847,000 . . . . E 7
Ife, 176,000 . . . . E 7
Ilesha, 224,000 . . . . E 7
Ilorin, 282,000 . . . . E 7
Iseyin, 115,083 . . . . E 7
Iwo, 214,000 . . . . E 7
Kaduna, 202,000 . . . . F 6
Kano, 399,000 . . . . F 6
Katsina, 109,424 . . . . F 6
Lagos (cap.), 1,060,848 . . . . E 7
Maiduguri, 189,000 . . . . †B 5
Ogbomosho, 432,000 . . . . E 7
Onitsha, 220,000 . . . . F 7
Oshogbo, 282,000 . . . . F 7
Oyo, 152,000 . . . . E 7
Port Harcourt, 242,000 . . . . F 8
Zaria, 224,000 . . . . F 6

SÃO TOMÉ & PRÍNCIPE

São Tomé (cap.), 7,681 . . . . F 8

SENEGAL

Dakar (cap.), 798,792 . . . . A 6
Kaolack, 106,899 . . . . A 6
Saint-Louis, 88,404 . . . . A 5
Thiès, 117,333 . . . . A 5
Ziguinchor, 72,726 . . . . A 6

SIERRA LEONE

Bo, 42,216 . . . . B 7
Freetown (cap.), 274,000 . . . . B 7
Kenema, 33,880 . . . . B 7
Makeni, 28,684 . . . . B 7

TOGO

Kpalimé, 27,669 . . . . E 7
Lama-Kara, 28,480 . . . . E 7
Lomé (cap.), 349,926 . . . . E 7
Sokodé, 48,098 . . . . E 7

TUNISIA

Bizerte, 62,856 . . . . F 1
Gabès, 40,585 . . . . F 2
Gafsa, 42,225 . . . . F 2
Kairouan, 54,546 . . . . F 1
Sfax, 171,297 . . . . G 2
Sousse, 69,530 . . . . G 1
Tunis (cap.), 873,515 . . . . G 1

WESTERN SAHARA

Dakhla, 6,554 . . . . A 4
Laayoune (El Aaiún), 24,519 . . . . . B 3

NORTHEASTERN AFRICA

CHAD

Name Population	Ref.
Abéché, 28,100	D 5
Ati, 7,500	C 5
Baibokoum, 5,500	C 6
Bardai	C 3
Bitkine, 5,000	C 5
Bokoro, 6,500	C 5
Bongor, 14,300	C 5
Bousso, 4,500	C 5
Doba, 13,300	C 6
Faya-Largeau, 6,800	C 4
Fianga, 10,000	C 6
Kélo, 16,800	C 6
Koumra, 17,000	C 6
Kyabé, 5,000	C 6
Laï, 10,400	C 6
Mao, 4,900	C 5
Moïssala, 5,100	C 6
Mongo, 8,300	C 5
Moundou, 39,600	C 6
Moussoro, 7,700	C 5
N'Djamena (cap.), 179,000	C 5
Oum Hadjer, 5,600	D 5
Pala, 13,200	B 6
Sarh, 43,700	C 6

DJIBOUTI

Name Population	Ref.
Djibouti (cap.), 96,000	H 5
Obock	H 5

EGYPT

Name Population	Ref.
Abnûb, 39,343	J 4
Akhmim, 53,234	F 2
Alexandria (El Iskandariya), 2,318,655	J 2
Aswân, 144,377	F 3
Asyût, 213,983	J 4
Benha, 88,992	J 3
Beni Mazar, 39,373	J 4
Beni Suef, 118,148	J 3
Biba, 33,074	J 3
Cairo (El Qâhira) (cap.), 5,084,463	J 3
Dairût, 31,624	J 4
Damanhur, 188,927	J 3
Damietta (Dumyât), 93,546	J 3
Disûq, 58,650	J 3
El 'Alamein	E 1
El Faiyûm, 167,081	J 3
El Fashn, 33,506	J 4
El Hammam, 6,588	E 1
El Karnak	F 2
El Khârga, 26,375	F 2
El Mahalla el Kubra, 292,853	J 3
El Mansûra, 257,866	K 3
El Minya, 146,423	J 4
El Quseir, 12,297	F 2
El Wasta, 17,659	J 3
Girga, 51,110	F 2
Giza, 1,246,713	J 3
Helwân	J 3
Idfu, 34,858	F 3
Ismailia, 145,978	K 3
Isna, 34,186	F 2
Kôm Ombo, 44,531	F 3
Luxor, 92,748	F 2
Maghâgha, 40,802	J 4
Mallawi, 74,256	J 4
Manfalût, 41,126	J 4
Mersá Matrûh, 27,857	E 1
Minûf, 55,131	J 3
Mût, 8,032	E 2
Port Said (Bur Sa'id), 262,620	K 3
Qalyub, 62,739	J 3
Qena, 94,013	F 2
Rosetta (Rashid), 42,962	J 2
Salûm, 4,161	E 1
Samalût, 48,146	J 4
Shibin el Kom, 102,844	J 3
Sidi Barrani, 1,574	E 1
Sinnûris, 42,022	J 3
Siwa, 4,999	E 2
Sohâg, 101,758	F 2
Suez, 194,001	K 3
Tahta, 45,242	F 2
Tanta, 284,636	J 3
Zagazig, 202,637	J 3
Zifta, 50,410	J 3

ETHIOPIA

†See page 2371.

Name Population	Ref.
Addis Ababa (cap.), 1,412,575	G 6
Adigrat, 9,400	G 5
Adi Ugri, 12,800	G 5

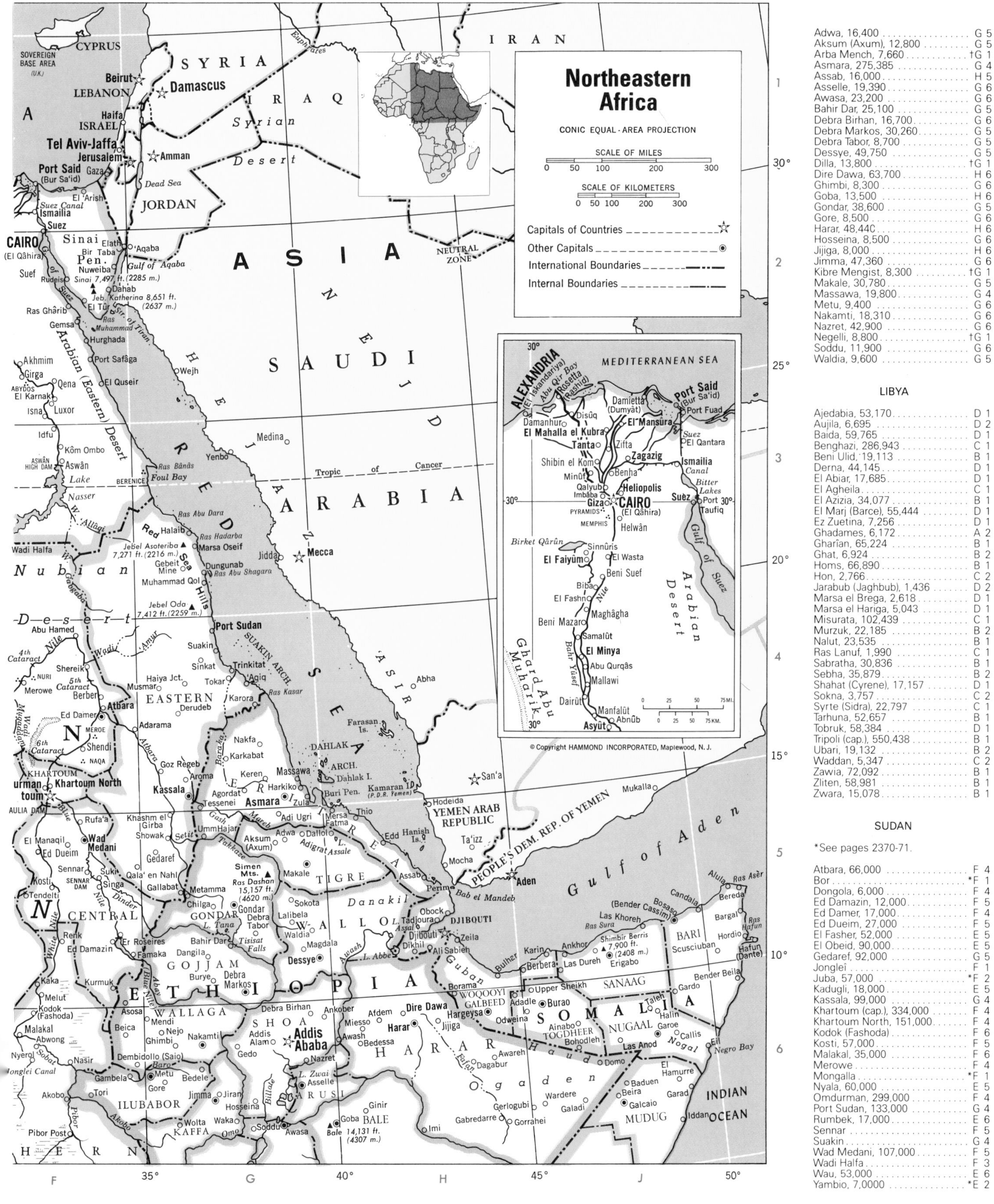

Adwa, 16,400	G 5
Aksum (Axum), 12,800	G 5
Arba Mench, 7,660	†G 1
Asmara, 275,385	G 4
Assab, 16,000	H 5
Asselle, 19,390	G 6
Awasa, 23,200	G 6
Bahir Dar, 25,100	G 5
Debra Birhan, 16,700	G 6
Debra Markos, 30,260	G 5
Debra Tabor, 8,700	G 5
Dessye, 49,750	G 5
Dilla, 13,800	†G 1
Dire Dawa, 63,700	H 6
Ghimbi, 8,300	G 6
Goba, 13,500	H 6
Gondar, 38,600	G 5
Gore, 8,500	G 6
Harar, 48,44C	H 6
Hosseina, 8,500	G 6
Jijiga, 8,000	H 6
Jimma, 47,360	G 6
Kibre Mengist, 8,300	†G 1
Makale, 30,780	G 5
Massawa, 19,800	G 4
Metu, 9,400	G 6
Nakamti, 18,310	G 6
Nazret, 42,900	G 6
Negelli, 8,800	†G 1
Soddu, 11,900	G 6
Waldia, 9,600	G 5

LIBYA

Ajedabia, 53,170	D 1
Aujila, 6,695	D 2
Baida, 59,765	D 1
Benghazi, 286,943	C 1
Beni Ulid, 19,113	B 1
Derna, 44,145	D 1
El Abiar, 17,685	D 1
El Agheila	C 1
El Azizia, 34,077	B 1
El Marj (Barce), 55,444	D 1
Ez Zuetina, 7,256	D 1
Ghadames, 6,172	A 2
Gharian, 65,224	B 1
Ghat, 6,924	B 2
Homs, 66,890	B 1
Hon, 2,766	C 2
Jarabub (Jaghbub), 1,436	D 2
Marsa el Brega, 2,618	D 1
Marsa el Hariga, 5,043	D 1
Misurata, 102,439	C 1
Murzuk, 22,185	B 2
Nalut, 23,535	B 1
Ras Lanuf, 1,990	C 1
Sabratha, 30,836	B 1
Sebha, 35,879	B 2
Shahat (Cyrene), 17,157	D 1
Sokna, 3,757	C 2
Syrte (Sidra), 22,797	C 1
Tarhuna, 52,657	B 1
Tobruk, 58,384	D 1
Tripoli (cap.), 550,438	B 1
Ubari, 19,132	B 2
Waddan, 5,347	C 2
Zawia, 72,092	B 1
Zliten, 58,981	B 1
Zwara, 15,078	B 1

SUDAN

*See pages 2370-71.

Atbara, 66,000	F 4
Bor	*F 1
Dongola, 6,000	F 4
Ed Damazin, 12,000	F 5
Ed Damer, 17,000	F 4
Ed Dueim, 27,000	F 5
El Fasher, 52,000	E 5
El Obeid, 90,000	E 5
Gedaref, 92,000	G 5
Jonglei	F 1
Juba, 57,000	*F 2
Kadugli, 18,000	E 5
Kassala, 99,000	G 4
Khartoum (cap.), 334,000	F 4
Khartoum North, 151,000	F 4
Kodok (Fashoda)	F 6
Kosti, 57,000	F 5
Malakal, 35,000	F 6
Merowe	F 4
Mongalla	*F 1
Nyala, 60,000	E 5
Omdurman, 299,000	F 4
Port Sudan, 133,000	G 4
Rumbek, 17,000	E 6
Sennar	F 5
Suakin	G 4
Wad Medani, 107,000	F 5
Wadi Halfa	F 3
Wau, 53,000	E 6
Yambio, 7,0000	*E 2

CENTRAL AFRICA

ANGOLA

Name	*Population*	*Ref.*
Benguela	40,996	B 5
Caála	8,894	C 5
Cabinda	21,124	B 4
Huambo	61,885	C 5
Kuito	18,941	C 5
Lobito	59,528	B 5
Luanda (cap.)	475,328	B 4
Lubango	31,674	B 5
Malange (Malanje)	31,599	C 4
Namibe (Moçâmedes)	12,076	B 6
Ngunza (Sumbe)	7,911	B 5
Saurimo	12,901	D 4
Uíge	11,972	C 4

BURUNDI

Name	*Population*	*Ref.*
Bujumbura (cap.)	141,040	E 3
Gitega	19,500	F 3

CAMEROON

Name	*Population*	*Ref.*
Bafoussam	62,239	B 1
Bamenda	48,111	B 1
Douala	708,000	A 2
Foumban	33,944	B 1
Garoua	63,900	B 1
Kumba	44,175	A 2
Limbe	27,016	A 2
Maroua	67,187	†B 5
Ngaoundéré	38,992	B 1
Nkongsamba	71,298	B 2
Yaoundé (cap.)	485,184	B 2

†See page 2368.

CENTRAL AFRICAN REPUBLIC

Name	*Population*	*Ref.*
Bambari	31,285	D 1
Bangassou	21,773	D 2
Bangui (cap.)	300,723	C 2
Berberati	27,285	C 2
Bossangoa	25,150	C 1
Bouar	29,528	C 1
Carnot	17,863	C 2

CONGO

Name	*Population*	*Ref.*
Brazzaville (cap.)	298,967	C 3
Djambala		B 3
Impfondo		C 2
Kinkala		B 3
Loubomo	29,600	B 3
Nkayi	30,600	B 3
Ouesso		C 2
Pointe-Noire	141,700	B 3
Sibiti		B 3

EQUATORIAL GUINEA

Name	*Population*	*Ref.*
Bata	27,024	A 3
Malabo (cap.)	37,237	A 2

GABON

Name	*Population*	*Ref.*
Franceville	9,345	B 3
Lambaréné	17,770	B 3
Libreville (cap.)	105,080	A 2
Moanda	10,709	B 3
Mouila	15,016	B 3
Port-Gentil	48,190	A 3
Tchibanga	14,001	B 3

KENYA

Name	*Population*	*Ref.*
Eldoret	18,196	G 2
Isiolo	8,201	G 2
Kericho	10,144	F 3
Kisumu	32,431	F 2
Kitale	11,573	G 2
Lamu	7,403	H 3
Malindi	10,757	H 3
Mombasa	341,148	G 3
Nairobi (cap.)	827,775	G 3
Nakuru	47,151	G 3
Nanyuki	11,624	G 2
Thika	18,387	G 3
Thomson's Falls	7,602	G 2

MALAWI

Name	*Population*	*Ref.*
Blantyre	222,153	F 7
Karonga	11,873	F 5
Lilongwe (cap.)	102,924	F 6
Nkhotakota	10,312	F 6
Nsanje	6,091	G 7

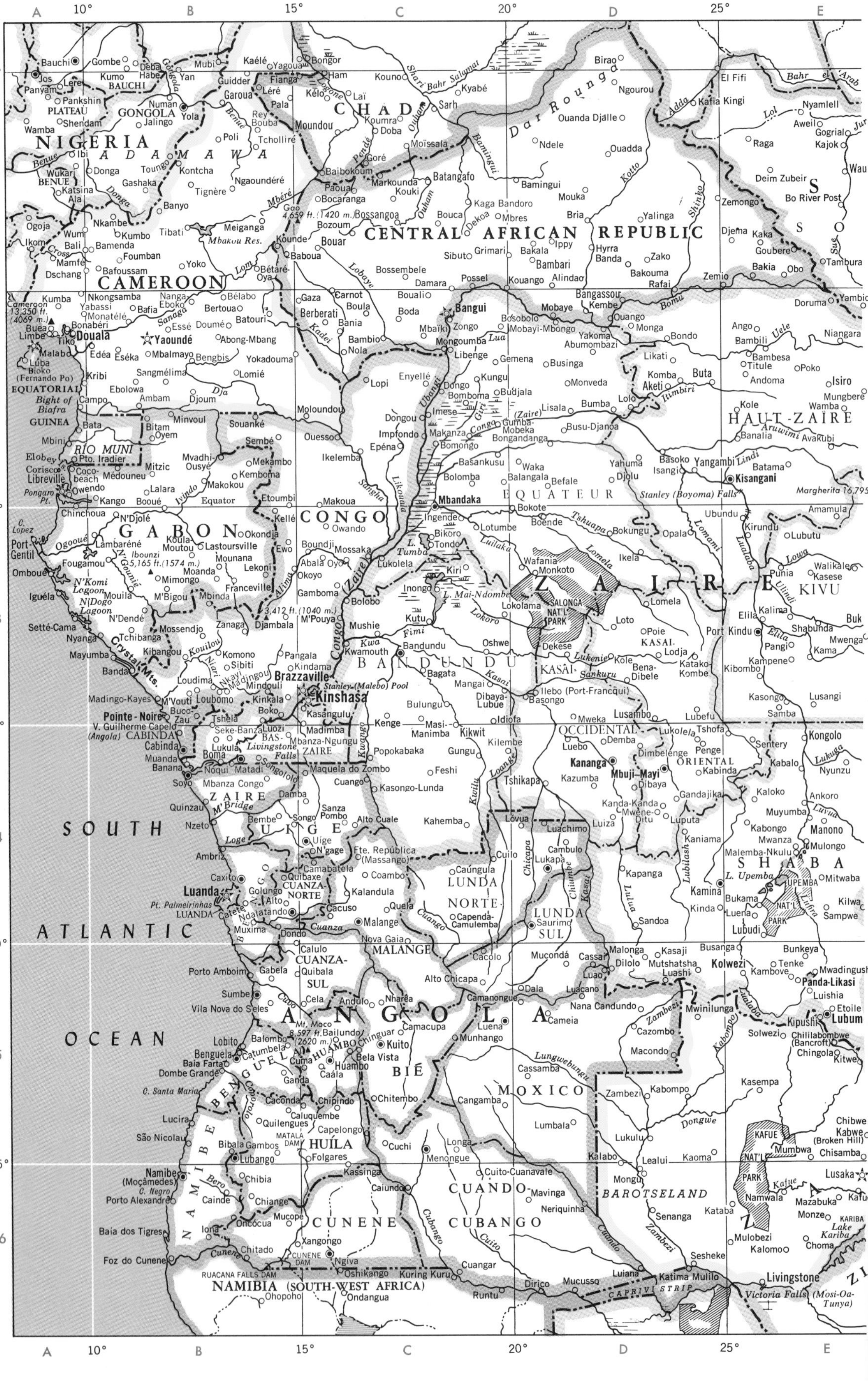

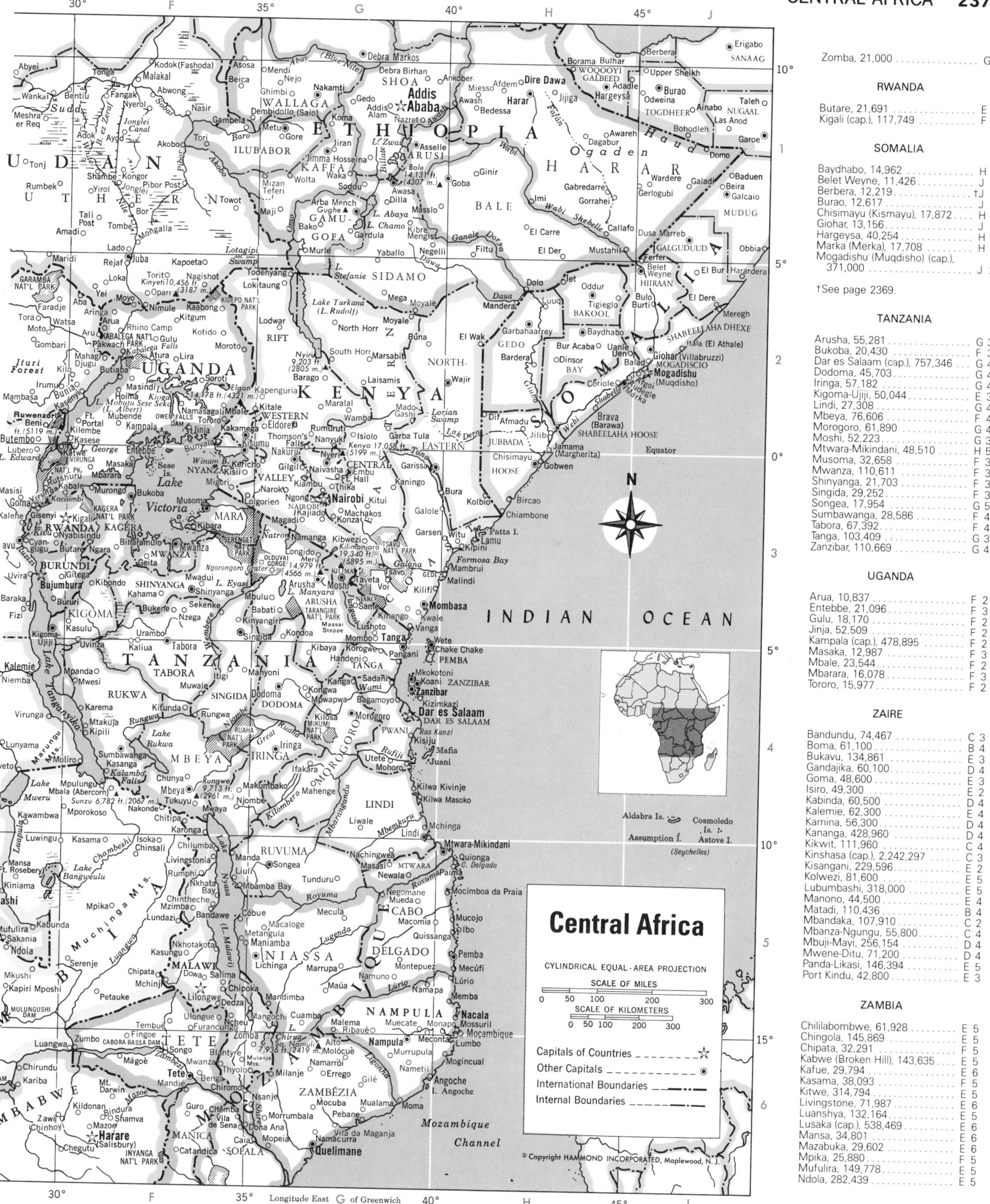

Zomba, 21,000 .... G 7

RWANDA

Butare, 21,691 .... E 3
Kigali (cap.), 117,749 .... F 3

SOMALIA

Baydhabo, 14,962 .... H 2
Belet Weyne, 11,426 .... J 2
Berbera, 12,219 .... †J 5
Burao, 12,617 .... J 1
Chisimayu (Kismayu), 17,872 .... H 3
Giohar, 13,156 .... J 2
Hargeysa, 40,254 .... H 1
Marka (Merka), 17,708 .... H 2
Mogadishu (Muqdisho) (cap.), 371,000 .... J 2

†See page 2369.

TANZANIA

Arusha, 55,281 .... G 3
Bukoba, 20,430 .... F 3
Dar es Salaam (cap.), 757,346 .... G 4
Dodoma, 45,703 .... G 4
Iringa, 57,182 .... G 4
Kigoma-Ujiji, 50,044 .... E 3
Lindi, 27,308 .... G 4
Mbeya, 76,606 .... F 4
Morogoro, 61,890 .... G 4
Moshi, 52,223 .... G 3
Mtwara-Mikindani, 48,510 .... H 5
Musoma, 32,658 .... F 3
Mwanza, 110,611 .... F 3
Shinyanga, 21,703 .... F 3
Singida, 29,252 .... F 3
Songea, 17,954 .... G 5
Sumbawanga, 28,586 .... F 4
Tabora, 67,392 .... F 4
Tanga, 103,409 .... G 3
Zanzibar, 110,669 .... G 4

UGANDA

Arua, 10,837 .... F 2
Entebbe, 21,096 .... F 3
Gulu, 18,170 .... F 2
Jinja, 52,509 .... F 2
Kampala (cap.), 478,895 .... F 2
Masaka, 12,987 .... F 3
Mbale, 23,544 .... F 2
Mbarara, 16,078 .... F 3
Tororo, 15,977 .... F 2

ZAIRE

Bandundu, 74,467 .... C 3
Boma, 61,100 .... B 4
Bukavu, 134,861 .... E 3
Gandajika, 60,100 .... D 4
Goma, 48,600 .... E 3
Isiro, 49,300 .... E 2
Kabinda, 60,500 .... D 4
Kalemie, 62,300 .... E 4
Kamina, 56,300 .... D 4
Kananga, 428,960 .... D 4
Kikwit, 111,960 .... C 4
Kinshasa (cap.), 2,242,297 .... C 3
Kisangani, 229,596 .... E 2
Kolwezi, 81,600 .... E 5
Lubumbashi, 318,000 .... E 5
Manono, 44,500 .... E 4
Matadi, 110,436 .... B 4
Mbandaka, 107,910 .... C 2
Mbanza-Ngungu, 55,800 .... C 4
Mbuji-Mayi, 256,154 .... D 4
Mwene-Ditu, 71,200 .... D 4
Panda-Likasi, 146,394 .... E 5
Port Kindu, 42,800 .... E 3

ZAMBIA

Chililabombwe, 61,928 .... E 5
Chingola, 145,869 .... E 5
Chipata, 32,291 .... F 5
Kabwe (Broken Hill), 143,635 .... E 5
Kafue, 29,794 .... E 6
Kasama, 38,093 .... F 5
Kitwe, 314,794 .... E 5
Livingstone, 71,987 .... E 6
Luanshya, 132,164 .... E 5
Lusaka (cap.), 538,469 .... E 6
Mansa, 34,801 .... E 6
Mazabuka, 29,602 .... E 6
Mpika, 25,880 .... F 5
Mufulira, 149,778 .... E 5
Ndola, 282,439 .... E 5

SOUTHERN AFRICA

BOTSWANA

Name	Population	Ref.
Francistown, 31,100		D 4
Gaborone (cap.), 59,700		D 4
Kanye, 20,300		D 5
Lobatse, 19,000		D 5
Mahalapye, 21,700		D 4
Mochudi, 18,300		D 4
Molepolole, 20,700		D 4
Selebi-Pikwe, 30,200		D 4
Serowe, 23,700		D 4

COMOROS

Moroni (cap.), 20,112 .... G 2
Mutsamudu, 12,518 .... G 2

LESOTHO

Maseru (cap.), 71,500 .... D 5

MADAGASCAR

Ambanja, 12,258 .... H 2
Ambatolampy, 11,539 .... H 3
Ambatondrazaka, 18,044 .... H 3
Ambilobe, 9,415 .... H 2
Ambositra, 16,780 .... H 4
Antalaha, 17,541 .... J 2
Antananarivo (Tananarive) (cap.), 451,808 .... H 3
Antsirabe, 32,979 .... H 3
Antsiranana (Diégo-Suarez), 40,443 .... H 2
Antsohihy, 8,721 .... H 2
Faradofay (Fort-Dauphin), 13,805 H 5
Farafangana, 10,817 .... H 4
Fianarantsoa, 68,054 .... H 4
Majunga, 65,864 .... H 3
Manakara, 19,768 .... H 4
Mananjary, 14,638 .... H 4
Marovoay, 20,253 .... H 3
Moramanga, 10,806 .... H 3
Morondava, 19,061 .... G 4
Sosumav, 10,946 .... H 2
Toamasina (Tamatave), 77,395 .... H 3
Toliara (Tuléar), 45,676 .... G 4
Tsiroanomandidy, 11,444 .... H 3

MAURITIUS

Curepipe, 52,709 .... G 5
Port Louis (cap.), 141,022 .... G 5
Quatre Bornes, 51,638 .... G 5

MAYOTTE

Dzaoudzi (cap.), 196 .... H 2

MOZAMBIQUE

Beira, 130,398 .... F 3
Chibuto, 23,763 .... E 4
Chimoio, 4,507 .... E 3
Inhambane, 4,975 .... F 4
Lichinga, 3,011 .... F 2
Manica, 1,529 .... E 3
Maputo (cap.), 755,300 .... E 5
Moçambique, 1,730 .... G 3
Nacala, 4,601 .... G 2
Nampula, 23,072 .... F 3
Pemba, 3,629 .... G 2
Quelimane, 10,522 .... F 3
Tete, 4,549 .... E 3
Xai-Xai, 5,234 .... E 5

NAMIBIA (SOUTH-WEST AFRICA)

Bethanie, 1,207 .... B 5
Gobabis, 4,428 .... B 4
Grootfontein, 4,627 .... B 3
Keetmanshoop, 10,297 .... B 5
Lüderitz, 6,642 .... A 5
Mariental, 4,629 .... B 4
Omaruru, 2,783 .... B 4
Otavi, 1,814 .... B 3
Otjiwarongo, 8,018 .... B 4
Outjo, 2,545 .... B 4
Rehoboth, 5,363 .... B 4
Runtu (Rundu), 521 .... B 3
Swakopmund, 5,681 .... A 4
Tsumeb, 12,338 .... B 3
Warmbad, 810 .... B 5
Windhoek (cap.), 61,369 .... B 4

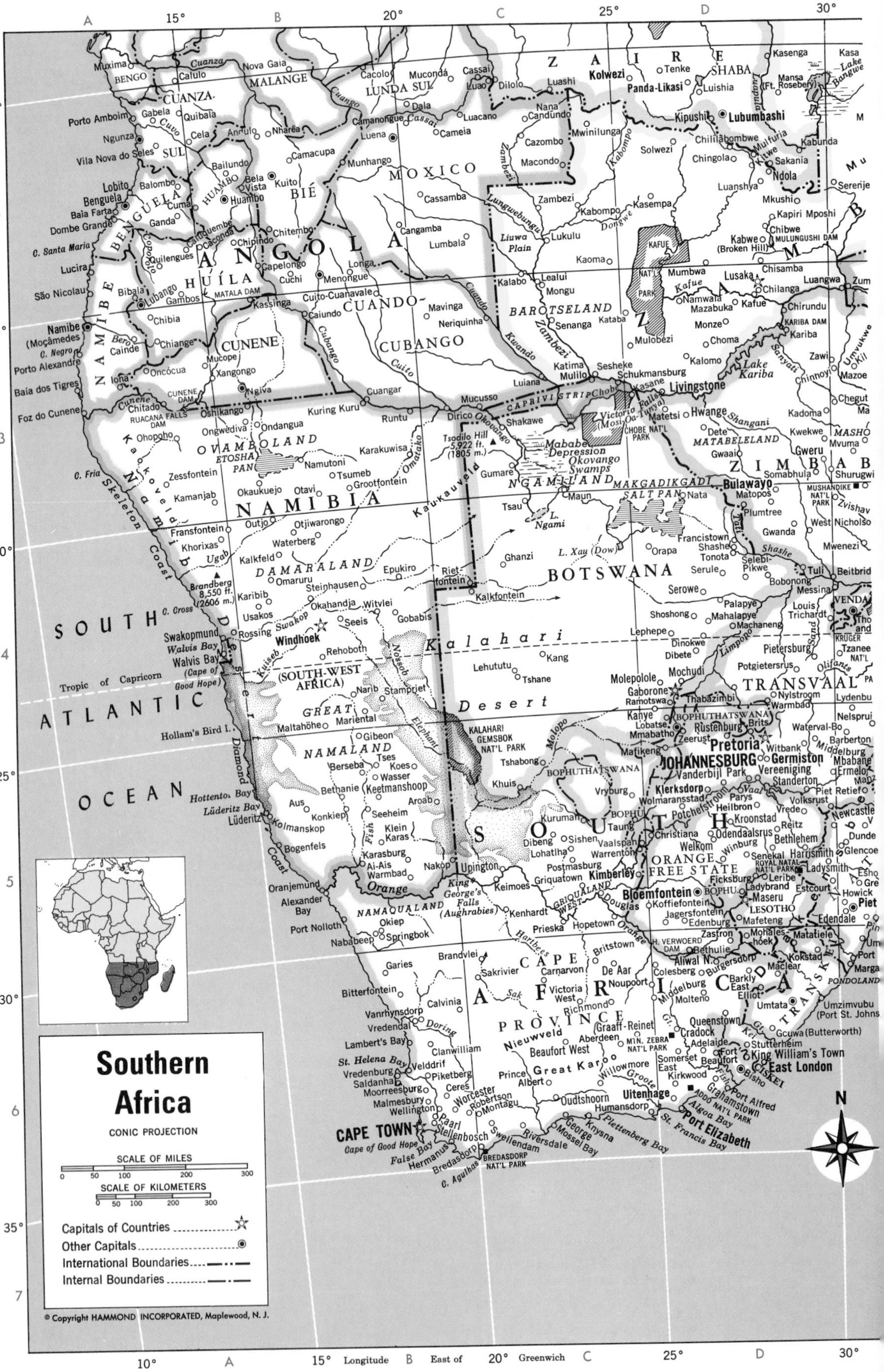

Southern Africa

CONIC PROJECTION

SCALE OF MILES: 0 50 100 200 300

SCALE OF KILOMETERS: 0 50 100 200 300

Capitals of Countries ☆
Other Capitals ◉
International Boundaries —·—
Internal Boundaries —·—

15° Longitude B East of 20° Greenwich C

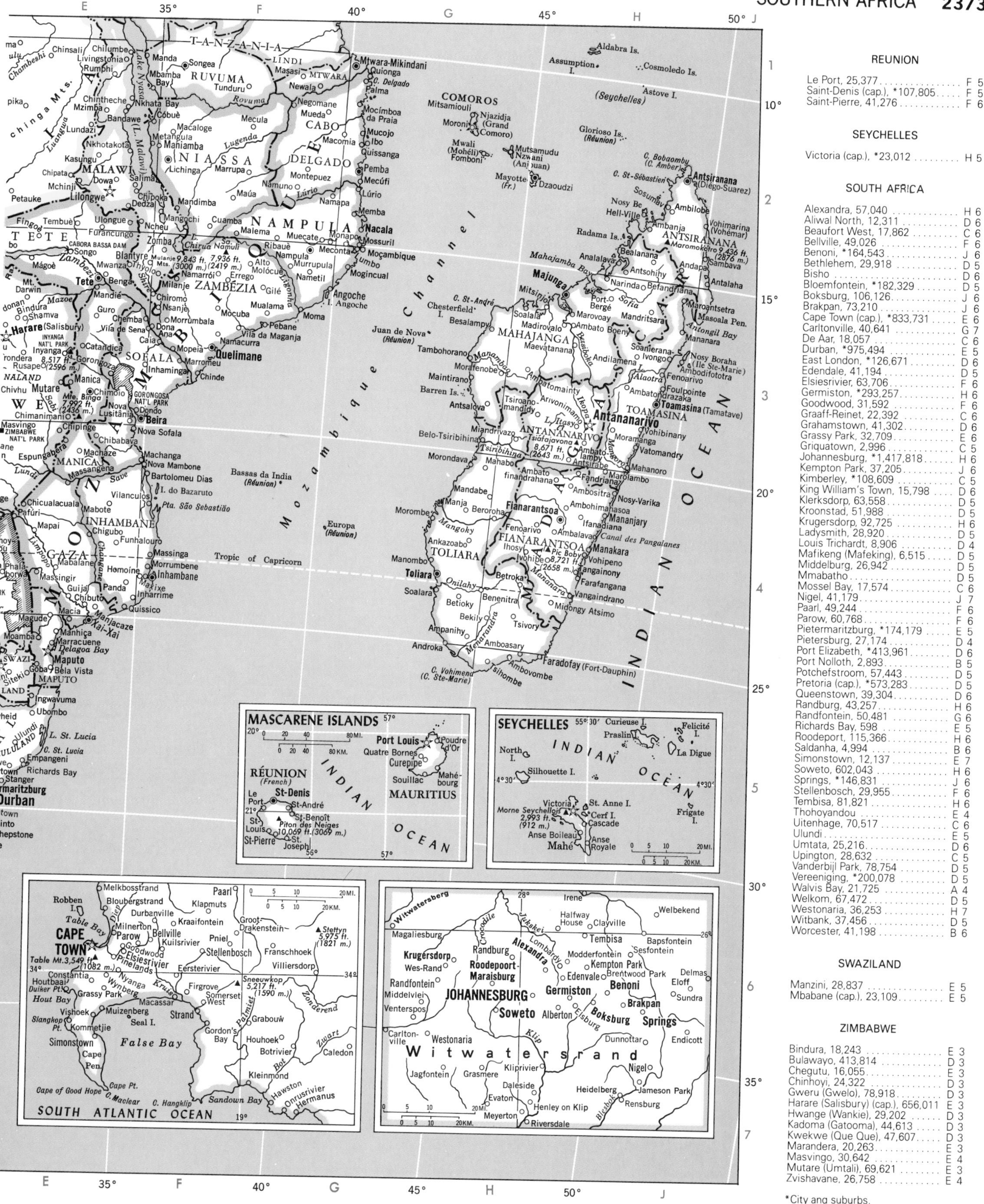

REUNION

- Le Port, 25,377 .... F 5
- Saint-Denis (cap.), *107,805 .... F 5
- Saint-Pierre, 41,276 .... F 6

SEYCHELLES

- Victoria (cap.), *23,012 .... H 5

SOUTH AFRICA

- Alexandra, 57,040 .... H 6
- Aliwal North, 12,311 .... D 6
- Beaufort West, 17,862 .... C 6
- Bellville, 49,026 .... F 6
- Benoni, *164,543 .... J 6
- Bethlehem, 29,918 .... D 5
- Bisho .... D 6
- Bloemfontein, *182,329 .... D 5
- Boksburg, 106,126 .... J 6
- Brakpan, 73,210 .... J 6
- Cape Town (cap.), *833,731 .... E 6
- Carltonville, 40,641 .... G 7
- De Aar, 18,057 .... C 6
- Durban, *975,494 .... E 5
- East London, *126,671 .... D 6
- Edendale, 41,194 .... D 5
- Elsiesrivier, 63,706 .... F 6
- Germiston, *293,257 .... H 6
- Goodwood, 31,592 .... F 6
- Graaff-Reinet, 22,392 .... C 6
- Grahamstown, 41,302 .... D 6
- Grassy Park, 32,709 .... E 6
- Griquatown, 2,996 .... C 5
- Johannesburg, *1,417,818 .... H 6
- Kempton Park, 37,205 .... J 6
- Kimberley, *108,609 .... C 5
- King William's Town, 15,798 .... D 6
- Klerksdorp, 63,558 .... D 5
- Kroonstad, 51,988 .... D 5
- Krugersdorp, 92,725 .... H 6
- Ladysmith, 28,920 .... D 5
- Louis Trichardt, 8,906 .... D 4
- Mafikeng (Mafeking), 6,515 .... D 5
- Middelburg, 26,942 .... D 5
- Mmabatho .... D 5
- Mossel Bay, 17,574 .... C 6
- Nigel, 41,179 .... J 7
- Paarl, 49,244 .... F 6
- Parow, 60,768 .... F 6
- Pietermaritzburg, *174,179 .... E 5
- Pietersburg, 27,174 .... D 4
- Port Elizabeth, *413,961 .... D 6
- Port Nolloth, 2,893 .... B 5
- Potchefstroom, 57,443 .... D 5
- Pretoria (cap.), *573,283 .... D 5
- Queenstown, 39,304 .... D 6
- Randburg, 43,257 .... H 6
- Randfontein, 50,481 .... G 6
- Richards Bay, 598 .... E 5
- Roodeport, 115,366 .... H 6
- Saldanha, 4,994 .... B 6
- Simonstown, 12,137 .... E 7
- Soweto, 602,043 .... H 6
- Springs, *146,831 .... J 6
- Stellenbosch, 29,955 .... F 6
- Tembisa, 81,821 .... H 6
- Thohoyandou .... E 4
- Uitenhage, 70,517 .... C 6
- Ulundi .... E 5
- Umtata, 25,216 .... D 6
- Upington, 28,632 .... C 5
- Vanderbijl Park, 78,754 .... D 5
- Vereeniging, *200,078 .... D 5
- Walvis Bay, 21,725 .... A 4
- Welkom, 67,472 .... D 5
- Westonaria, 36,253 .... H 7
- Witbank, 37,456 .... D 5
- Worcester, 41,198 .... B 6

SWAZILAND

- Manzini, 28,837 .... E 5
- Mbabane (cap.), 23,109 .... E 5

ZIMBABWE

- Bindura, 18,243 .... E 3
- Bulawayo, 413,814 .... D 3
- Chegutu, 16,055 .... E 3
- Chinhoyi, 24,322 .... D 3
- Gweru (Gwelo), 78,918 .... D 3
- Harare (Salisbury) (cap.), 656,011 E 3
- Hwange (Wankie), 29,202 .... D 3
- Kadoma (Gatooma), 44,613 .... D 3
- Kwekwe (Que Que), 47,607 .... D 3
- Marandera, 20,263 .... E 3
- Masvingo, 30,642 .... E 4
- Mutare (Umtali), 69,621 .... E 3
- Zvishavane, 26,758 .... E 4

*City and suburbs.

EUROPE

CAPITALS

Name	Ref.
Amsterdam, Netherlands	E 3
Athens, Greece	G 5
Belfast, N. Ireland	D 3
Belgrade, Yugoslavia	G 4
Berlin, E. Germany	F 3
Bern, Switzerland	E 4
Bonn, W. Germany	E 3
Brussels, Belgium	E 3
Bucharest, Romania	G 4
Budapest, Hungary	F 4
Cardiff, Wales	D 3
Copenhagen, Denmark	F 3
Dublin, Ireland	D 3
Edinburgh, Scotland	D 3
Helsinki, Finland	G 2
Lisbon, Portugal	D 5
London, United Kingdom	D 3
Madrid, Spain	D 4
Moscow, U.S.S.R.	H 3
Oslo, Norway	F 2
Paris, France	E 4
Prague, Czechoslovakia	F 3
Reykjavík, Iceland	B 2
Rome, Italy	F 4
Sofia, Bulgaria	G 4
Stockholm, Sweden	F 3
The Hague, Netherlands	E 3
Tiranë, Albania	F 4
Tórshavn, Faeroe Is.	D 2
Valetta, Malta	F 5
Vienna, Austria	F 4
Warsaw, Poland	G 3

PHYSICAL FEATURES

Name	Ref.
Adriatic (sea)	F 4
Aegean (sea)	G 5
Alps (mts.)	E 4
Apennines (mts.)	F 4
Araks (riv.)	J 5
Atlantic (ocean)	C 4
Azov (sea)	H 4
Balaton (lake)	F 4
Balearic (isls.)	E 5
Balkan (mts.)	G 4
Baltic (sea)	F 3
Barents (sea)	J 1
Ben Nevis (mt.)	D 3
Biscay (bay)	D 4
Black (sea)	H 4
Blanc (mt.), France	E 4
Bornholm (isl.)	F 3
Bosporus (strait)	G 4
Bothnia (gulf)	G 2
Bug (riv.)	G 3
Carpathian (mts.)	G 4
Caspian (sea)	J 4
Caucasus (mts.)	J 4
Channel (isls.)	D 4
Corsica (isl.)	E 4
Crete (isl.)	G 4
Crimea (pen.)	H 4
Danube (riv.)	G 4
Dardanelles (strait), Turkey	G 5
Denmark (strait)	B 2
Dnieper (riv.)	H 3
Dniester (riv.)	G 4
Don (riv.)	J 4
Donets (riv.)	H 4
Douro (riv.)	D 4
Drava (riv.)	F 4
Dvina, Northern (riv.)	J 2
Dvina, Western (riv.)	G 3
Ebro (riv.)	D 4
Elba (isl.)	E 4
Elbe (riv.)	F 3
El'brus (mt.)	J 4
English (chan.)	D 4
Etna (vol.)	F 5
Evvoia (isl.), Greece	G 5
Faeroe (isls.)	D 2
Finisterre (cape)	C 4
Finland (gulf)	G 3
Frisian (isls.)	E 3
Garonne (riv.)	D 4
Geneva (lake)	E 4
Gibraltar (strait)	D 5
Glittertind (mt.)	E 2
Gotland (isl.)	F 3
Great Britain (isl.)	D 3
Guadalquivir (riv.)	D 5
Guadiana (riv.)	D 5
Hardangerfjorden (fjord)	E 3
Hebrides (isls.)	D 3
Hekla (mt.), Iceland	C 2
Hiiumaa (isl.)	G 3
Horn (cape)	B 2
Ibiza (isl.)	E 5
Ii (riv.)	G 2
Il'men (lake)	H 3

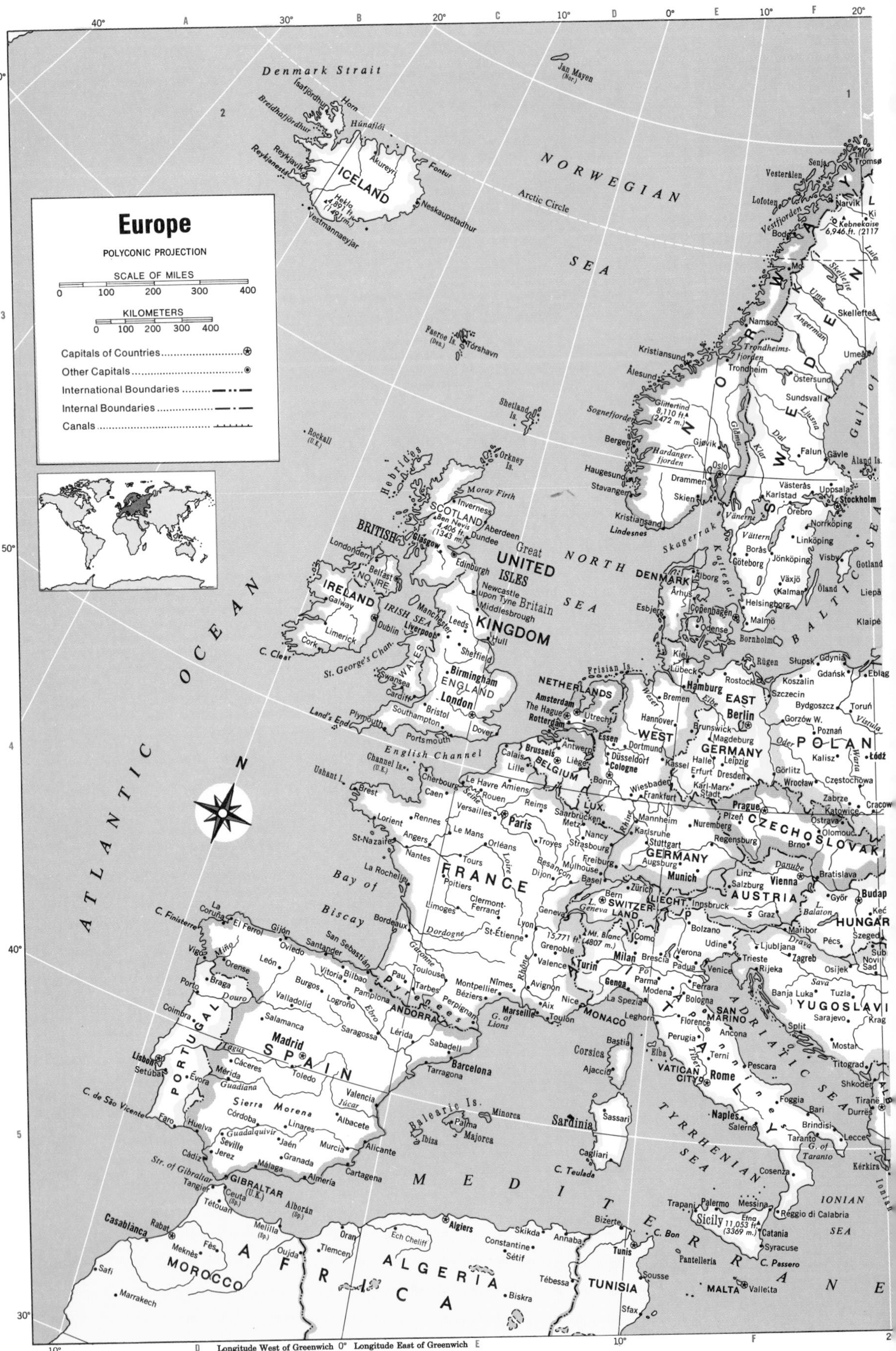

Inari (lake) .... G 2
Ionian (isls.) .... F 5
Ionian (sea) .... F 5
Irish (sea) .... D 3
Jan Mayen (isl.) .... D 1
Júcar (riv.) .... D 5
Kama (riv.) .... K 3
Kanin (pen.) .... J 2
Kattegat (strait) .... F 3
Kebnekaise (mt.) .... F 2
Kemi (riv.) .... G 2
Kerkira (isl.) .... F 5
Kjolen (mts.) .... F 2
Klar (riv.) .... F 2
Kola (pen.) .... H 2
Kolguyev (isl.) .... J 2
Kuybyshev (res.) .... K 3
Ladoga (lake) .... H 2
Land's End (prom.) .... D 3
Lesvos (isl.) .... G 5
Lindesnes (cape) .... E 3
Lions (gulf) .... E 4
Lofoten (isls.) .... F 2
Loire (riv.) .... E 4
Lule (riv.) .... G 2
Majorca (isl.) .... E 5
Marmara (sea) .... G 4
Mediterranean (sea) .... E 5
Mezen' (riv.) .... J 2
Mino (riv.) .... D 4
Minorca (isl.) .... E 4
Moray (firth) .... D 3
Morena, Sierra (mts.) .... D 5
Muonio (riv.) .... G 2
Narodnaya (mt.) .... K 2
Niemen (riv.) .... G 3
Nordkapp (North) (cape) .... G 1
North (sea) .... E 3
Norwegian (sea) .... D 2
Oder (riv.) .... F 3
Oland (isl.) .... F 3
Onega (lake) .... H 2
Orkney (isls.) .... D 3
Oulu (lake) .... G 2
Pantelleria (isl.) .... F 5
Passero (cape) .... F 5
Pechora (riv.) .... K 2
Peipus (lake) .... G 3
Po (riv.) .... E 4
Pripyat' (riv.) .... G 3
Prut (riv.) .... G 1
Pyrenees (mts.) .... D 4
Reykjanesta (cape) .... B 2
Rhine (riv.) .... E 4
Rhodes (isl.) .... G 5
Rhone (riv.) .... E 5
Riga (gulf) .... G 3
Rockall (isl.) .... C 3
Rugen (isl.) .... F 3
Rybinsk (res.) .... H 3
Saaremaa (isl.) .... G 3
Saint George's (chan.) .... D 3
São Vicente (cape) .... C 5
Sardinia (isl.) .... E 4
Sava (riv.) .... F 4
Seine (riv.) .... E 4
Sevan (lake) .... J 4
Shetland (isls.) .... D 2
Sicily (isl.) .... F 5
Sierra Morena (mts.) .... D 5
Siret (riv.) .... G 4
Skagerrak (strait) .... E 3
Skellefte (riv.) .... E 2
Sognefjorden (fjord) .... E 2
Tagus (riv.) .... D 5
Tainaron (cape) .... G 5
Taranto (gulf) .... F 5
Tiber (riv.) .... F 4
Torne (riv.) .... G 2
Trondheimsfjorden (fjord) .... F 2
Tsimlyansk (res.) .... J 4
Tyrrhenian (sea) .... F 4
Ume (riv.) .... F 2
Ural (mts.) .... L 2
Usa (riv.) .... K 2
Ushant (isl.) .... D 4
Vanern (lake) .... F 3
Varangerfjorden (fjord) .... H 1
Vattern (lake) .... F 3
Vesteralen (isls.) .... F 2
Vestfjorden (fjord) .... F 2
Vistula (riv.) .... F 3
Volga (riv.) .... J 4
Warta (riv.) .... F 3
Weser (riv.) .... E 3
White (sea) .... H 2

UNITED KINGDOM

ENGLAND and WALES

Name	Population	Ref.
Bath	79,965	E 5
Birkenhead	123,907	G 2
Birmingham	920,389	F 5
Blackpool	147,854	G 1
Bolton	147,009	H 2
Bournemouth	144,803	F 7
Bradford	280,691	J 1
Brighton	146,134	G 7
Bristol	387,977	E 6
Cambridge	90,440	F 4
Cardiff	273,856	E 5
Coventry	314,124	F 5
Croydon	316,557	H 8
Derby	215,736	F 5
Exeter	95,621	D 7
Gloucester	92,133	E 6
Hastings	74,803	G 5
Huddersfield	123,888	J 2
Hull	268,302	G 4
Ipswich	120,447	J 5
Leeds	448,528	J 1
Leicester	279,791	F 5
Liverpool	510,306	G 2
London (cap.)	6,608,598	H 8
Luton	164,049	G 6
Manchester	449,168	H 2
Merthyr Tydfil	53,843	E 5
Middlesbrough	149,770	F 3
Newcastle upon Tyne	195,454	H 3
Newport	105,374	E 5
Northampton	156,848	F 5
Norwich	122,270	J 5
Nottingham	271,080	F 5
Oxford	98,521	F 6
Plymouth	243,895	C 7
Portsmouth	179,419	F 7
Preston	143,734	G 1
Reading	132,037	G 8
Rochdale	92,704	H 2
Sheffield	477,142	J 2
Southampton	204,406	F 7
Southend-on-Sea	156,683	H 6
Stockton-on-Tees	154,585	F 3
Stoke-on-Trent	252,351	E 4
Sunderland	196,152	J 3
Swansea	167,796	D 5
Wandsworth	255,723	H 8
Wolverhampton	252,447	E 5
Worcester	74,790	F 4
Wrexham	40,272	E 4
York	99,789	F 4

IRELAND

Name	Population	Ref.
Bray	22,853	C 4
Carlow	11,722	C 4
Clonmel	12,407	C 4
Cork	*149,792	B 5
Drogheda	23,247	C 4
Dublin (cap.)	*915,115	C 4
Dundalk	25,663	C 3
Dún Laoghaire	54,596	D 4
Galway	37,835	B 4
Limerick	*75,520	B 4
Sligo	17,232	B 3
Tralee	16,495	B 4
Waterford	*39,636	C 4
Wexford	11,417	C 4

NORTHERN IRELAND

Name	Population	Ref.
Ballymena	28,166	C 3
Belfast (cap.)	295,223	D 3
Larne	18,224	C 3
Lisburn	40,391	D 3
Londonderry	62,697	C 3
Newry	19,426	C 3

SCOTLAND

Name	Population	Ref.
Aberdeen	190,200	F 2
Clydebank	51,656	B 1
Dundee	174,746	E 2
Dunfermline	52,057	E 2
Edinburgh (cap.)	419,187	C 1
Glasgow	762,288	B 1
Greenock	57,324	A 1
Inverness	39,736	D 2
Kirkcaldy	46,314	E 2
Paisley	84,789	A 1
Perth	41,998	E 2
Stirling	38,638	B 1

*Population of city and suburbs.

United Kingdom and Ireland

BONNE PROJECTION

Capitals of Countries ⊛

Canals

NORWAY, SWEDEN, FINLAND and DENMARK

DENMARK

Name	Population	Ref.
Ålborg	114,302	B 3
Århus	181,830	B 3
Copenhagen (cap.)	*1,381,822	C 3
Esbjerg	70,220	B 3
Helsingör	44,068	B 3
Herning	29,522	B 3
Horsens	46,855	B 3
Kolding	41,374	B 3
Naestved	38,455	C 3
Odense	136,646	B 3
Randers	56,672	B 3
Vejle	43,300	B 3

FINLAND

Name	Population	Ref.
Hämeenlinna	41,922	D 2
Helsinki (cap.)	483,051	D 2
Hyvinkää	37,559	E 2
Joensuu	45,180	F 2
Jyváskylá	64,455	E 2
Kemi	26,732	E 2
Kotka	60,577	E 2
Kouvola	31,322	E 2
Kuopio	75,255	E 2
Lahti	94,692	E 2
Oulu	94,869	E 2
Pori	79,223	D 2
Rauma	30,911	D 2
Rovaniemi	30,759	E 1
Savonlinna	28,451	E 2
Tampere	167,028	E 2
Turku	163,526	D 2
Vaasa	53,903	D 2

NORWAY

Name	Population	Ref.
Ålesund	25,085	A 2
Bergen	180,959	A 2
Bodö	27,601	C 1
Drammen	56,863	B 2
Fredrikstad	50,703	B 3
Gjövik	15,681	B 2
Halden	20,740	B 3
Hamar	27,022	B 2
Haugesund	30,170	A 3
Kristiansand	51,284	B 3
Lillehammer	15,416	B 2
Moss	29,665	A 2
Narvik	14,998	C 1
Oslo (cap.)	*642,954	A 1
Porsgrunn	35,304	B 3
Ringerike	30,156	A 1
Sandefjord	31,370	A 2
Sandnes	26,591	B 3
Sarpsborg	39,889	A 2
Skien	28,151	B 3
Stavanger	90,825	A 3
Tonsberg	36,788	A 2
Tromsö	36,268	D 1
Trondheim	127,624	B 2

SWEDEN

Name	Population	Ref.
Borås	187,710	C 3
Borlänge	40,158	C 2
Eskilstuna	66,409	C 3
Gävle	67,454	C 2
Göteborg	690,767	B 3
Halmstad	49,558	C 3
Hälsingborg	215,894	C 3
Jönköping	131,499	C 3
Kalmar	32,049	C 3
Karlskoga	35,425	C 3
Karlskrona	33,414	C 3
Karlstad	51,243	C 3
Kristianstad	30,780	C 3
Linköping	132,839	C 3
Luleå	42,139	D 2
Lund	55,047	C 3
Mölndal	47,248	C 3
Malmö	453,339	C 3
Norrköping	163,206	C 3
Nyköping	30,352	C 3
Örebro	171,440	C 3
Östersund	40,056	C 2
Södertälje	58,408	B 1
Solna	53,992	C 1
Stockholm (cap.)	*1,357,183	B 1
Sundsvall	52,268	C 2
Trollhättan	42,499	C 3
Umeå	49,715	D 2
Uppsala	157,202	C 2
Västeras	147,508	C 3
Växjö	40,328	C 3

*City and suburbs.

GERMANY

EAST GERMANY

Name	Population	Ref.
Berlin, East (cap.),	1,152,529	E 2
Brandenburg,	94,953	E 2
Cottbus,	113,479	F 3
Dessau,	102,529	E 3
Dresden,	516,255	E 3
Erfurt,	211,575	D 3
Frankfurt an der Oder,	80,414	F 2
Gera,	125,383	D 3
Görlitz,	81,399	F 3
Halle,	232,294	E 3
Jena,	103,718	D 3
Karl-Marx-Stadt (Chemnitz),	317,644	E 3
Leipzig,	562,480	E 3
Magdeburg,	289,032	D 2
Neubrandenburg,	79,006	E 2
Plauen,	78,828	D 3
Potsdam,	130,900	E 2
Rostock,	232,506	D 1
Schwerin,	121,175	D 2
Stralsund,	74,947	E 1
Weimar,	63,709	D 3
Zwickau,	122,129	E 3

WEST GERMANY

Name	Population	Ref.
Aachen,	245,000	B 3
Augsburg,	247,148	D 4
Baden-Baden,	48,886	C 4
Bayreuth,	70,957	D 4
Bergisch Gladbach,	101,081	B 3
Berlin (West),	1,869,584	E 2
Bielefeld,	309,964	C 2
Bochum,	393,799	B 3
Bonn (cap.),	293,852	B 3
Bremen,	547,619	C 2
Bremerhaven,	137,769	C 2
Brunswick (Braunschweig),	257,780	D 2
Cologne (Köln),	961,777	B 3
Cuxhaven,	57,888	C 2
Darmstadt,	138,577	C 4
Dortmund,	599,521	B 3
Düsseldorf,	583,445	B 3
Duisburg,	546,566	B 3
Erlangen,	102,730	D 4
Essen,	638,812	B 3
Esslingen am Neckar,	88,782	C 4
Flensburg,	86,601	C 1
Frankfurt am Main,	620,186	C 3
Freiburg im Breisgau,	178,545	B 5
Fürth,	99,680	D 4
Gelsenkirchen,	297,493	B 3
Göttingen,	132,537	D 3
Hagen,	214,069	B 3
Hamburg,	1,623,848	D 2
Hamm,	170,307	B 3
Hannover,	526,253	C 2
Heidelberg,	134,575	C 4
Heilbronn,	111,276	C 4
Hildesheim,	102,355	D 2
Ingolstadt,	90,371	D 4
Kaiserslautern,	98,774	B 4
Karlsruhe,	271,236	C 4
Kassel,	192,338	C 3
Kiel,	248,733	C 1
Koblenz,	112,519	B 3
Krefeld,	223,124	B 3
Leverkusen,	158,494	B 3
Lübeck,	217,225	D 2
Ludwigshafen am Rhein,	158,117	C 4
Mainz,	186,467	C 4
Mannheim,	302,621	C 4
Mönchengladbach,	258,552	B 3
Münster,	272,918	B 3
Munich (München),	1,287,080	D 4
Nuremberg (Nürnberg),	479,035	D 4
Offenbach am Main,	109,246	C 3
Oldenburg,	138,345	B 2
Osnabrück,	156,558	C 2
Paderborn,	110,333	C 3
Pforzheim,	105,217	C 4
Recklinghausen,	119,365	B 3
Regensburg,	132,617	D 4
Reutlingen,	96,046	C 4
Saarbrücken,	190,853	B 4
Salzgitter,	111,770	D 2
Schweinfurt,	51,939	D 3
Siegen,	110,296	C 3
Stuttgart,	573,577	C 4
Trier,	94,683	B 4
Ulm,	99,725	C 4
Wiesbaden,	273,703	B 3
Wilhelmshaven,	99,174	B 2
Wolfsburg,	124,609	D 2
Worms,	73,243	C 4
Würzburg,	129,582	D 4
Wuppertal,	387,951	B 3

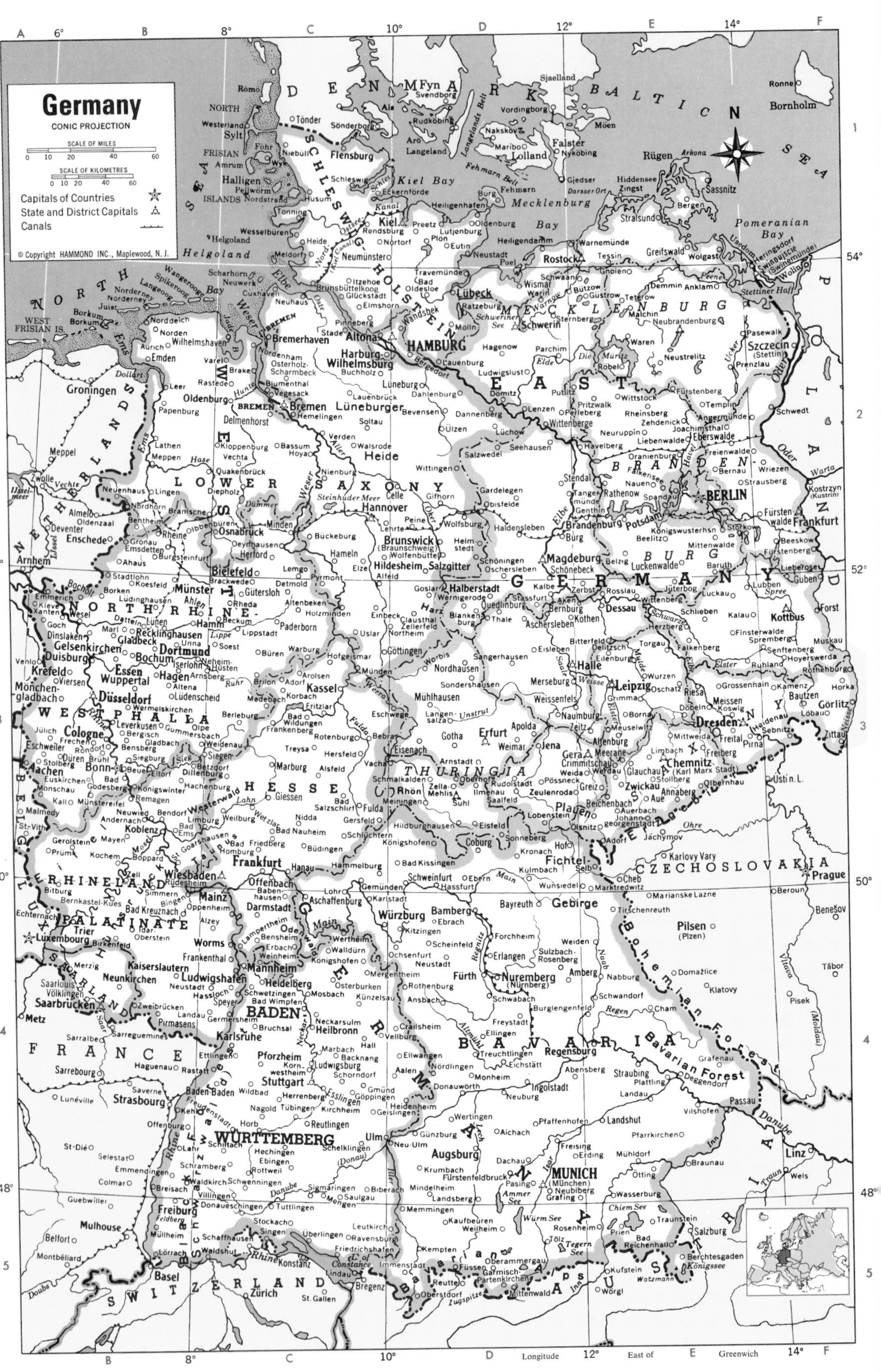

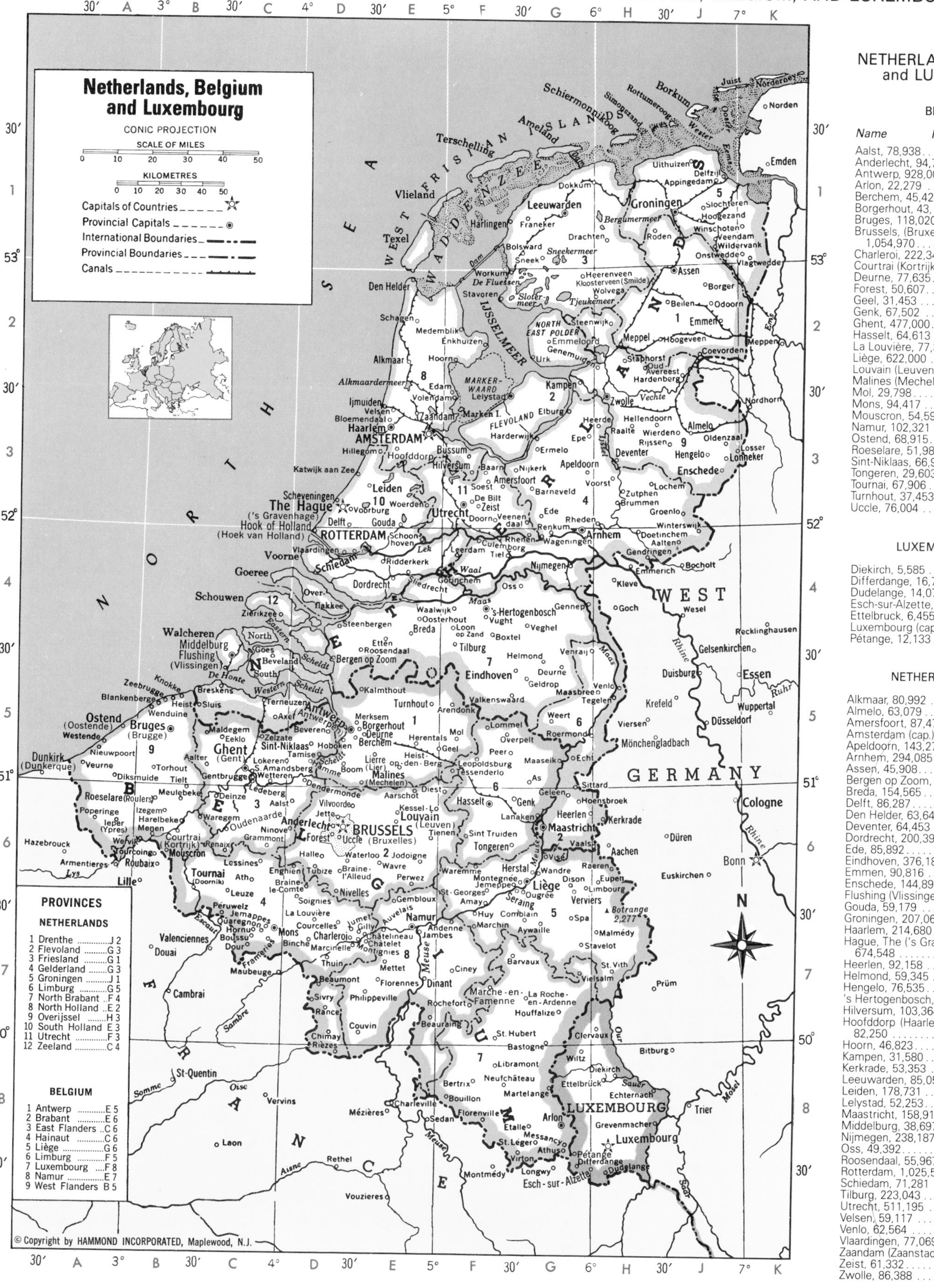

NETHERLANDS, BELGIUM and LUXEMBOURG

BELGIUM

Name	Population	Ref.
Aalst	78,938	C 4
Anderlecht	94,764	D 4
Antwerp	928,000	D 3
Arlon	22,279	G 8
Berchem	45,423	D 5
Borgerhout	43, 521	D 5
Bruges	118,020	B 5
Brussels, (Bruxelles) (cap.)	1,054,970	E 6
Charleroi	222,343	D 7
Courtrai (Kortrijk)	75,917	B 6
Deurne	77,635	D 5
Forest	50,607	D 6
Geel	31,453	F 5
Genk	67,502	G 6
Ghent	477,000	C 5
Hasselt	64,613	F 6
La Louvière	77,326	D 7
Liège	622,000	G 6
Louvain (Leuven)	85,076	E 6
Malines (Mechelen)	77,269	E 5
Mol	29,798	F 5
Mons	94,417	D 7
Mouscron	54,590	B 6
Namur	102,321	E 7
Ostend	68,915	A 5
Roeselare	51,984	A 6
Sint-Niklaas	66,992	D 5
Tongeren	29,603	F 6
Tournai	67,906	B 6
Turnhout	37,453	E 5
Uccle	76,004	D 6

LUXEMBOURG

Name	Population	Ref.
Diekirch	5,585	H 8
Differdange	16,712	G 8
Dudelange	14,074	H 8
Esch-sur-Alzette	25,142	G 8
Ettelbruck	6,455	G 8
Luxembourg (cap.)	78,924	H 8
Pétange	12,133	G 8

NETHERLANDS

Name	Population	Ref.
Alkmaar	80,992	E 2
Almelo	63,079	J 2
Amersfoort	87,471	F 3
Amsterdam (cap.)	938,920	E 3
Apeldoorn	143,276	G 3
Arnhem	294,085	H 4
Assen	45,908	J 2
Bergen op Zoom	45,178	D 4
Breda	154,565	E 4
Delft	86,287	D 3
Den Helder	63,647	E 2
Deventer	64,453	H 3
Dordrecht	200,396	E 4
Ede	85,892	G 3
Eindhoven	376,185	F 5
Emmen	90,816	J 2
Enschede	144,897	J 3
Flushing (Vlissingen)	46,379	C 4
Gouda	59,179	E 3
Groningen	207,060	H 1
Haarlem	214,680	E 3
Hague, The ('s Gravenhage) (cap.)	674,548	D 3
Heerlen	92,158	G 6
Helmond	59,345	G 5
Hengelo	76,535	J 3
's Hertogenbosch	189,067	F 4
Hilversum	103,364	F 3
Hoofddorp (Haarlemmermeer)	82,250	E 3
Hoorn	46,823	E 2
Kampen	31,580	G 3
Kerkrade	53,353	H 6
Leeuwarden	85,058	G 1
Leiden	178,731	E 3
Lelystad	52,253	F 3
Maastricht	158,915	G 6
Middelburg	38,697	B 4
Nijmegen	238,187	G 4
Oss	49,392	F 4
Roosendaal	55,967	E 4
Rotterdam	1,025,585	D 4
Schiedam	71,281	D 4
Tilburg	223,043	F 3
Utrecht	511,195	F 3
Velsen	59,117	E 3
Venlo	62,564	H 5
Vlaardingen	77,069	D 4
Zaandam (Zaanstad)	129,341	E 3
Zeist	61,332	F 3
Zwolle	86,388	H 3

FRANCE

Name	Population	Ref.
Agen, 31,239		D 5
Ajaccio, 48,324		B 7
Albi, 42,724		E 6
Alençon, 30,952		D 3
Amiens, 130,302		D 3
Angers, 135,293		C 4
Angoulême, 45,495		C 5
Annecy, 49,753		G 5
Arras, 41,376		E 2
Auch, 19,543		D 6
Aurillac, 29,704		E 5
Auxerre, 36,504		E 4
Avignon, 75,178		F 6
Bar-le-Duc, 18,406		F 3
Beauvais, 51,542		D 3
Belfort, 51,034		G 4
Besançon, 112,023		G 4
Blois, 46,925		D 4
Bordeaux, 201,965		C 5
Boulogne-Billancourt, 102,582		A 2
Bourg-en-Bresse, 37,582		F 4
Bourges, 74,622		E 4
Brest, 154,110		A 3
Caen, 112,332		C 3
Cahors, 18,204		D 5
Carcassonne, 38,379		D 6
Châteauroux, 51,744		D 4
Chalon-sur-Saône, 53,893		F 4
Chambéry, 49,465		G 5
Charleville-Mézières, 57,814		F 3
Chartres, 36,706		D 3
Chaumont, 26,203		F 3
Clermont-Ferrand, 145,901		E 4
Colmar, 61,560		G 3
Creil, 34,332		E 3
Digne, 12,540		G 5
Dijon, 139,188		F 4
Draguignan, 23,391		G 6
Épinal, 37,228		G 3
Évreux, 45,215		D 3
Foix, 9,212		D 6
Gap, 21,798		G 5
Grenoble, 156,437		F 5
Guéret, 15,456		D 4
La Roche-sur-Yon, 42,026		C 4
La Rochelle, 74,728		C 4
Laon, 26,180		E 3
Laval, 53,582		C 3
Le Havre, 198,700		C 3
Le Mans, 145,976		D 3
Le Puy, 22,806		E 5
Lille, 167,791		E 2
Limoges, 137,809		D 5
Lons-le-Saunier, 19,996		F 4
Lyon, 410,455		F 5
Marseille, 868,435		F 6
Melun, 34,379		E 3
Mende, 10,520		E 5
Metz, 113,236		G 3
Mont-de-Marsan, 25,896		C 6
Montauban, 36,122		D 6
Montpellier, 190,423		E 6
Moulins, 25,096		E 4
Mulhouse, 111,742		G 4
Nancy, 95,654		F 3
Nantes, 237,789		C 4
Nevers, 42,768		E 4
Nîmes, 120,515		E 6
Nice, 331,165		G 6
Niort, 56,256		C 4
Orléans, 81,615		D 4
Paris (cap.), *10,073,059		E 3
Pau, 82,186		C 6
Périgueux, 32,632		D 5
Perpignan, 107,812		E 6
Poitiers, 76,793		D 4
Pontoise, 27,885		D 3
Privas, 9,253		F 5
Quimper, 52,335		A 4
Reims, 176,419		F 3
Rennes, 190,861		C 3
Rodez, 23,858		E 5
Roubaix, 101,488		E 2
Rouen, 100,696		D 3
Saint-Brieuc, 48,259		B 3
Saint-Étienne, 193,938		F 5
Saint-Lô, 21,790		C 3
Strasbourg, 247,068		G 3
Tarbes, 50,306		D 6
Toulon, 177,443		F 6
Toulouse, 344,917		D 6
Tours, 131,265		D 4
Troyes, 62,946		F 3
Tulle, 18,033		D 5
Valence, 66,143		F 5
Vannes, 39,214		B 4
Versailles, 91,014		A 2
Vesoul, 18,257		G 4
Villeurbanne, 115,378		F 5

*City and suburbs.

France

CONIC PROJECTION

SCALE OF MILES 0 20 40 60 80 100

KILOMETRES 0 20 40 60 80 100

Capitals of Countries ⊛

Paris and Environs

Corsica — Same scale as main map

B Longitude 2° West of C Greenwich 0° D 2° E Longitude 4° East of F Greenwich 6° G

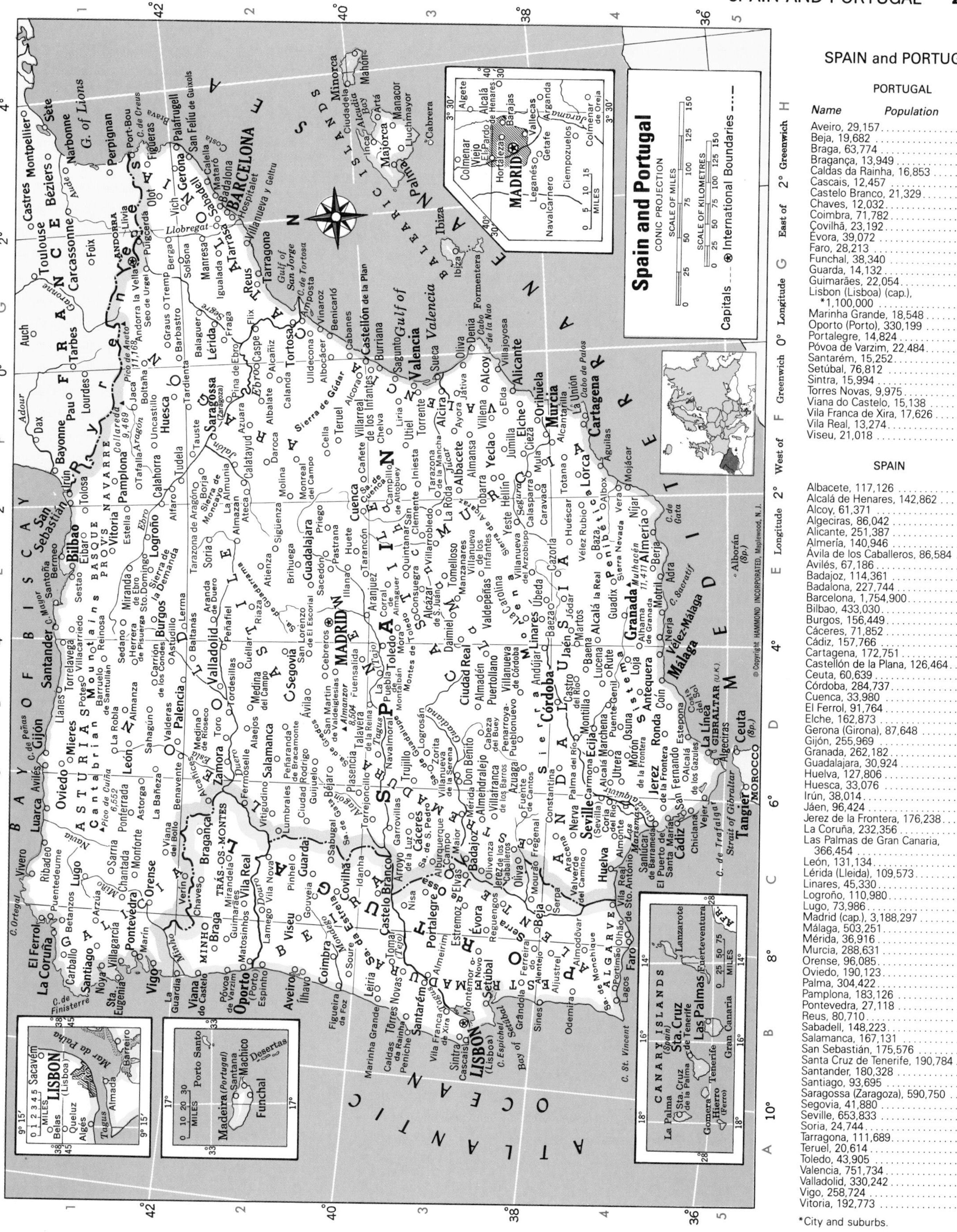

SPAIN and PORTUGAL

PORTUGAL

Name	*Population*	*Ref.*
Aveiro	29,157	B 2
Beja	19,682	C 3
Braga	63,774	B 2
Bragança	13,949	C 2
Caldas da Rainha	16,853	B 3
Cascais	12,457	B 3
Castelo Branco	21,329	C 3
Chaves	12,032	C 2
Coimbra	71,782	B 2
Çovilhã	23,192	C 2
Évora	39,072	C 3
Faro	28,213	B 4
Funchal	38,340	A 2
Guarda	14,132	C 2
Guimarães	22,054	B 2
Lisbon (Lisboa) (cap.)	*1,100,000	A 1
Marinha Grande	18,548	B 3
Oporto (Porto)	330,199	B 2
Portalegre	14,824	C 3
Póvoa de Varzim	22,484	B 2
Santarém	15,252	B 3
Setúbal	76,812	B 3
Sintra	15,994	B 3
Torres Novas	9,975	B 3
Viana do Castelo	15,138	B 2
Vila Franca de Xira	17,626	B 3
Vila Real	13,274	C 2
Viseu	21,018	C 2

SPAIN

Name	Population	Ref.
Albacete	117,126	F 3
Alcalá de Henares	142,862	H 3
Alcoy	61,371	F 3
Algeciras	86,042	D 4
Alicante	251,387	F 3
Almería	140,946	E 4
Ávila de los Caballeros	86,584	D 2
Avilés	67,186	C 1
Badajoz	114,361	C 3
Badalona	227,744	H 2
Barcelona	1,754,900	H 2
Bilbao	433,030	E 1
Burgos	156,449	E 1
Cáceres	71,852	C 3
Cádiz	157,766	C 4
Cartagena	172,751	F 4
Castellón de la Plana	126,464	G 3
Ceuta	60,639	D 5
Córdoba	284,737	D 4
Cuenca	33,980	E 2
El Ferrol	91,764	B 1
Elche	162,873	F 3
Gerona (Girona)	87,648	H 2
Gijón	255,969	D 1
Granada	262,182	E 4
Guadalajara	30,924	E 2
Huelva	127,806	C 4
Huesca	33,076	F 1
Irún	38,014	F 1
Jáen	96,424	E 4
Jerez de la Frontera	176,238	D 4
La Coruña	232,356	B 1
Las Palmas de Gran Canaria	366,454	B 4
León	131,134	D 1
Lérida (Lleida)	109,573	G 2
Linares	45,330	E 3
Logroño	110,980	E 1
Lugo	73,986	C 1
Madrid (cap.)	3,188,297	H 3
Málaga	503,251	D 4
Mérida	36,916	C 3
Murcia	288,631	F 4
Orense	96,085	C 1
Oviedo	190,123	C 1
Palma	304,422	H 3
Pamplona	183,126	F 1
Pontevedra	27,118	B 1
Reus	80,710	G 2
Sabadell	148,223	H 2
Salamanca	167,131	D 2
San Sebastián	175,576	E 1
Santa Cruz de Tenerife	190,784	B 4
Santander	180,328	D 1
Santiago	93,695	B 1
Saragossa (Zaragoza)	590,750	F 2
Segovia	41,880	D 2
Seville	653,833	C 4
Soria	24,744	E 2
Tarragona	111,689	G 2
Teruel	20,614	F 2
Toledo	43,905	D 3
Valencia	751,734	F 3
Valladolid	330,242	D 2
Vigo	258,724	B 1
Vitoria	192,773	E 1

*City and suburbs.

ITALY

Name Population	Ref.
Alessandria, 100,523	B 2
Ancona, 106,498	D 3
Andria, 76,405	F 4
Arezzo, 92,105	D 3
Asti, 77,681	B 2
Bari, 371,022	F 4
Barletta, 75,116	F 4
Belluno, 36,634	D 1
Benevento, 62,636	E 4
Bergamo, 122,142	C 2
Bologna, 459,080	C 2
Bolzano, 105,180	C 1
Brescia, 206,661	C 2
Brindisi, 89,786	G 4
Cagliari, 233,848	B 5
Caltanissetta, 61,146	D 6
Caserta, 66,318	E 4
Catania, 380,328	E 6
Catanzaro, 100,832	F 5
Como, 95,571	B 2
Cosenza, 106,801	E 5
Cremona, 80,929	B 2
Ferrara, 149,453	D 2
Florence (Firenze), 448,431	C 3
Foggia, 156,467	E 4
Forlì, 110,806	D 2
Frosinone, 44,644	D 4
Gela, 66,845	E 6
Genoa (Genova), 762,895	B 2
Gorizia, 41,557	D 2
Grosseto, 69,523	C 3
La Spezia, 115,392	B 2
Latina, 93,738	D 4
Lecce, 91,289	G 4
Leghorn (Livorno), 175,741	B 3
Lucca, 91,246	C 3
Macerata, 43,782	D 3
Mantua (Mantova), 60,866	C 2
Massa-Carrara, 65,687	C 2
Merano, 30,951	C 1
Messina, 260,233	E 5
Milan (Milano), 1,604,773	B 2
Modena, 180,312	C 2
Molfetta, 63,250	F 4
Monza, 110,735	B 2
Naples (Napoli), 1,212,387	D 4
Novara, 102,086	B 2
Nuoro, 35,779	B 4
Padua (Padova), 234,678	C 2
Palermo, 801,782	D 5
Parma, 179,019	B 2
Pavia, 85,029	B 2
Perugia, 142,348	D 3
Pesaro y Urbino, 90,412	D 3
Pescara, 131,330	E 3
Piacenza, 109,039	B 2
Pisa, 104,509	C 3
Pistoia, 92,274	C 2
Potenza, 64,358	E 4
Prato, 100,385	C 3
Ragusa, 64,492	E 6
Ravenna, 138,034	D 2
Reggio di Calabria, 173,486	F 5
Reggio nell'Emilia, 130,376	B 2
Rieti, 43,079	D 3
Rimini, 101,579	D 2
Rome (Roma) (cap.), 2,840,259	D 4
Salerno, 157,385	E 4
San Severo, 49,622	E 4
Sassari, 119,596	B 4
Savona, 75,353	B 2
Siena, 61,989	C 3
Syracuse (Siracusa), 117,615	E 6
Taranto, 249,101	F 4
Terni, 253,912	D 3
Torre Annunziata, 71,068	D 4
Trapani, 71,927	D 5
Trento, 99,179	C 2
Treviso, 87,696	D 2
Trieste, 252,369	E 2
Turin (Torino), 1,117,154	A 2
Udine, 102,021	D 1
Varese, 90,527	B 2
Venice (Venezia), 346,146	D 2
Vercelli, 52,488	B 2
Verona, 265,932	C 2
Vicenza, 114,598	C 2

MALTA

Name Population	Ref.
Valletta, 14,042	E 6

SAN MARINO

Name Population	Ref.
San Marino, 5,410	D 3

VATICAN CITY

Name Population	Ref.
Vatican City, 728	D 4

Italy

CONIC PROJECTION

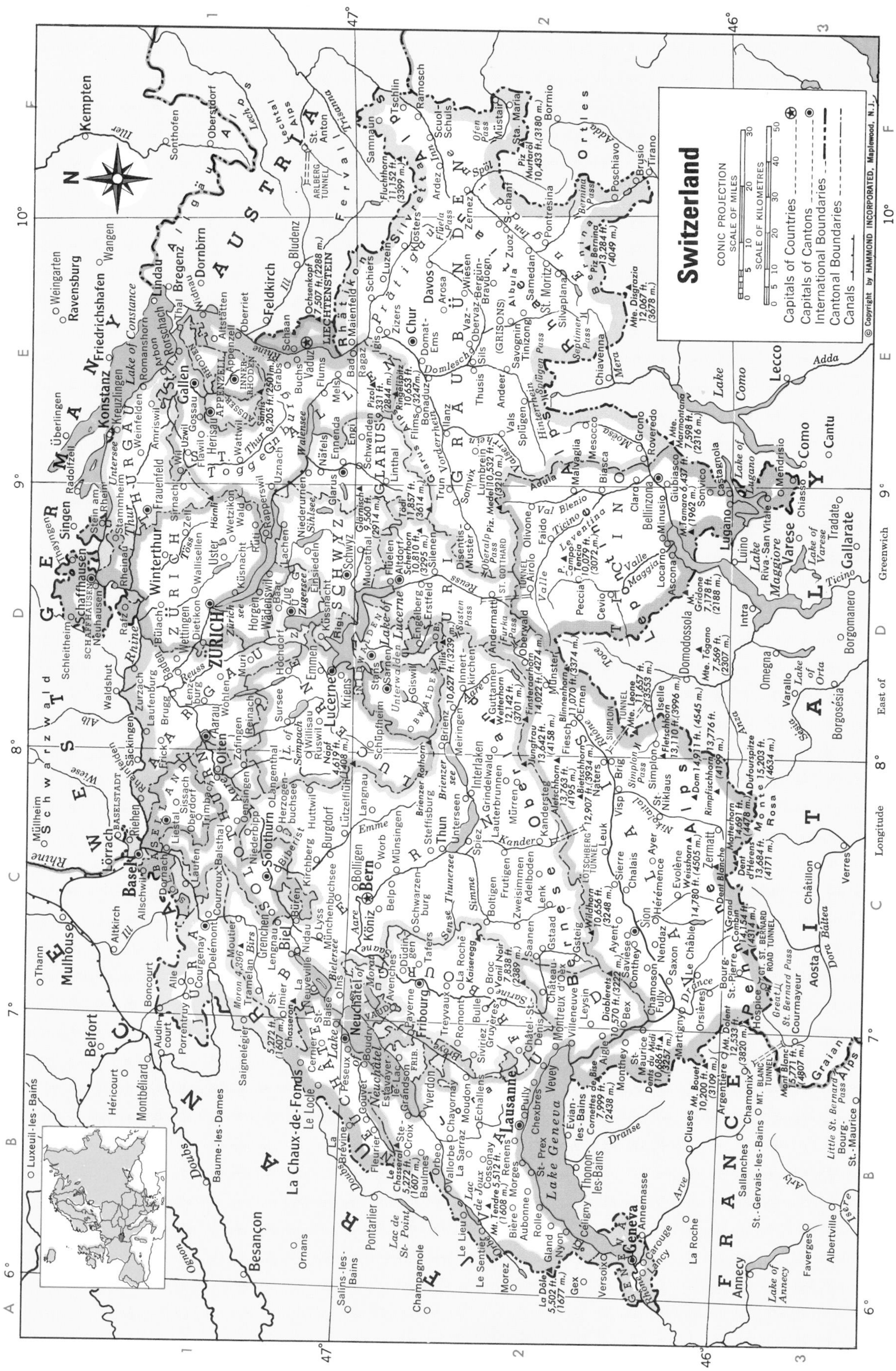

SWITZERLAND and LIECHTENSTEIN

SWITZERLAND

Name Population	Ref.
Aarau, *51,283	D 1
Allschwil, 17,638	C 1
Altdorf, 8,647	D 2
Appenzell, 5,217	E 1
Arbon, *14,846	E 1
Baar, 14,074	D 1
Baden, *68,418	D 1
Basel, *364,813	C 1
Bellinzona, *33,061	D 2
Bern (cap.), *286,903	C 2
Biel, *84,056	C 1
Bolligen, 26,121	C 2
Brugg, 8,635	D 1
Buchs, 8,454	E 1
Bulach, 11,043	D 1
Burgdorf, *18,248	C 1
Carouge, 14,055	B 2
Chiasso, 8,868	D 3
Chur, 32,037	E 2
Davos, 10,468	E 2
Delemont, 11,797	C 1
Dietikon, 22,705	D 1
Emmen, 22,040	D 1
Frauenfeld, 17,576	D 1
Fribourg, *50,575	C 2
Geneva (Genève), *335,401	B 2
Glarus, 6,189	D 1
Gossau, 12,793	E 1
Grenchen, *24,968	C 1
Herisau, 14,160	E 1
Horgen, 15,691	D 1
Interlaken, 4,735	C 2
Koniz, 33,800	C 2
Kreuzlingen, 15,760	E 1
Kriends, 20,409	D 1
Küsnacht, 12,193	D 1
La Chaux-de-Fonds, 37,234	B 1
Lancy, 20,523	B 2
Langenthal, *21,427	C 1
Lausanne, *228,700	B 2
Le Locle, 12,039	B 1
Liestal, *41,341	C 1
Locarno, *39,738	D 2
Lucerne, *156,867	D 1
Lugano, *68,357	D 2
Martigny, 10,478	B 2
Monthey, 10,114	B 2
Montreux, 19,685	C 2
Morges, *18,866	B 2
Neuchâtel, *58,403	C 2
Neuhausen am Rheinfall, 12,103	D 1
Nyon, 11,424	B 2
Olten, *46,946	D 1
Pully, 15,917	B 2
Rapperswil, 8,713	D 1
Renens, 17,391	B 2
Riehen, 21,026	C 1
Romanshorn, 8,329	E 1
Rorschach, *23,112	E 1
Ruti, 9,546	D 1
Saint Moritz, 5,699	E 2
Sankt Gallen, *88,361	E 1
Sarnen, 6,952	D 2
Schaffhausen, *53,562	D 1
Schwyz, 12,194	D 1
Sierre, 11,017	C 2
Sion, 21,925	C 2
Solothurn, *34,733	C 1
Spiez, 9,911	C 2
Stans, 5,180	D 2
Steffisburg, 12,621	C 2
Thun, *66,120	C 2
Uster, 23,702	D 1
Uzwil, 9,133	E 1
Vevey-Montreux, *60,558	B 2
Wadenswil, 15,695	D 1
Wald, 8,185	D 1
Wallisellen, 10,415	D 1
Weinfelden, 8,621	E 1
Wettingen, 19,900	D 1
Wetzikon, 13,469	D 1
Wil, *22,366	E 1
Winterthur, *107,752	D 1
Wohlen, *15,746	D 1
Worb, 9,526	C 2
Yverdon, 20,538	B 2
Zofingen, 9,292	D 1
Zug, *52,162	D 1
Zürich, *706,220	D 1

LIECHTENSTEIN

Name Population	Ref.
Schaan, 4,552	E 1
Vaduz (cap.), 4,614	E 1

*City and suburbs.

Switzerland

CONIC PROJECTION

Capitals of Countries
Capitals of Cantons
International Boundaries
Cantonal Boundaries
Canals

POLAND

Name, Population	Ref.
Będzin, 76,868	B 3
Biała Podlaska, 40,956	F 3
Białystok, 229,651	F 2
Bielsko-Biała, 167,843	D 4
Bolesławiec, 40,049	B 3
Brzeg, 36,298	C 3
Bydgoszcz, 352,424	C 2
Bytom, 237,828	A 3
Chełm, 54,943	F 3
Chorzów, 149,649	B 4
Cracow (Kraków), 722,903	E 3
Częstochowa, 237,713	D 3
Dąbrowa Górnicza, 147,995	B 3
Dzierżoniów, 36,542	C 3
Elbląg, 112,136	D 1
Gdańsk (Danzig), 458,874	D 1
Gdynia, 237,150	D 1
Gliwice, 202,238	A 4
Gniezno, 63,502	C 2
Gorzów Wielkopolski, 109,013	B 2
Grudziądz, 91,081	B 2
Inowrocław, 66,530	D 2
Jastrzębie Zdroj, 97,895	D 3
Jaworzno, 90,712	B 4
Jelenia Góra, 87,131	B 3
Kalisz, 100,340	D 3
Katowice, 363,523	B 4
Kędzierzyn-Koźle, 69,648	D 3
Kielce, 188,822	E 3
Konin, 69,585	D 2
Koszalin, 94,267	C 1
Krosno, 40,436	F 3
Kutno, 42,567	D 2
Legnica, 91,358	C 3
Leszno, 50,393	C 3
Łódź, 843,027	D 3
Łomża, 42,686	F 2
Lubin, 68,002	C 3
Lublin, 308,805	F 3
Mysłowice, 81,660	B 4
Nowa Sól, 39,067	B 3
Nowy Sącz, 65,415	E 4
Nysa, 42,216	C 3
Olsztyn, 140,011	E 2
Opole, 118,196	C 3
Ostrołęka, 39,621	E 2
Ostrowiec Świętokrzyski, 66,814	E 3
Ostrów Wielkopolski, 63,983	C 3
Oświęcim (Auschwitz), 45,245	D 3
Otwock, 47,362	E 2
Pabianice, 70,968	D 3
Piekary Ślaskie, 65,295	B 4
Piła, 61,616	C 2
Piotrków Trybunalski, . 73,691	D 3
Płock, 107,973	D 2
Poznań, 557,992	C 2
Pruszków, 50,293	E 2
Przemyśl, 62,196	F 4
Puławy, 46,313	F 3
Racibórz, 57,182	D 3
Radom, 194,381	E 3
Radomsko, 40,838	D 3
Ruda Śląska, 181,588	B 4
Rybnik, 126,772	D 3
Rzeszów, 125,779	F 4
Siedlce, 57,722	F 2
Siemianowice Śląskie, 78,216	B 4
Sieradz, 31,837	D 3
Skarżysko-Kamienna, 44,281	E 3
Słupsk, 87,517	C 1
Sopot, 51,085	D 1
Sosnowiec, 251,916	B 4
Stalowa Wola, 57,338	F 3
Starachowice, 49,769	E 3
Stargard Szczeciński, 60,457	B 2
Starogard Gdański, 44,842	D 2
Suwałki, 43,237	F 1
Świdnica, 57,807	C 3
Świętochłowice, 59,930	A 4
Świnoujście, 48,292	B 1
Szczecin (Stettin), 389,909	B 2
Tarnobrzeg, 38,477	E 3
Tarnów, 107,139	E 4
Tarnowskie Góry, 68,430	A 3
Tczew, 55,046	D 1
Tomaszów Mazowiecki, 63,923	E 3
Toruń, 180,053	D 2
Tychy, 171,897	B 4
Wałbrzych, 134,299	C 3
Warsaw (cap.), 1,611,565	D 1
Wejherowo, 43,068	D 1
Włocławek, 109,997	D 2
Wodzisław Śląski, 105,906	D 4
Wrocław (Breslau), 621,865	C 3
Zabrze, 196,841	A 4
Zamość, 49,102	F 3
Zawiercie, 63,725	D 3
Zduńska Wola, 39,862	D 3
Zgierz, 53,696	D 3
Zielona Góra, 103,536	B 3
Żyrardów, 37,701	E 2

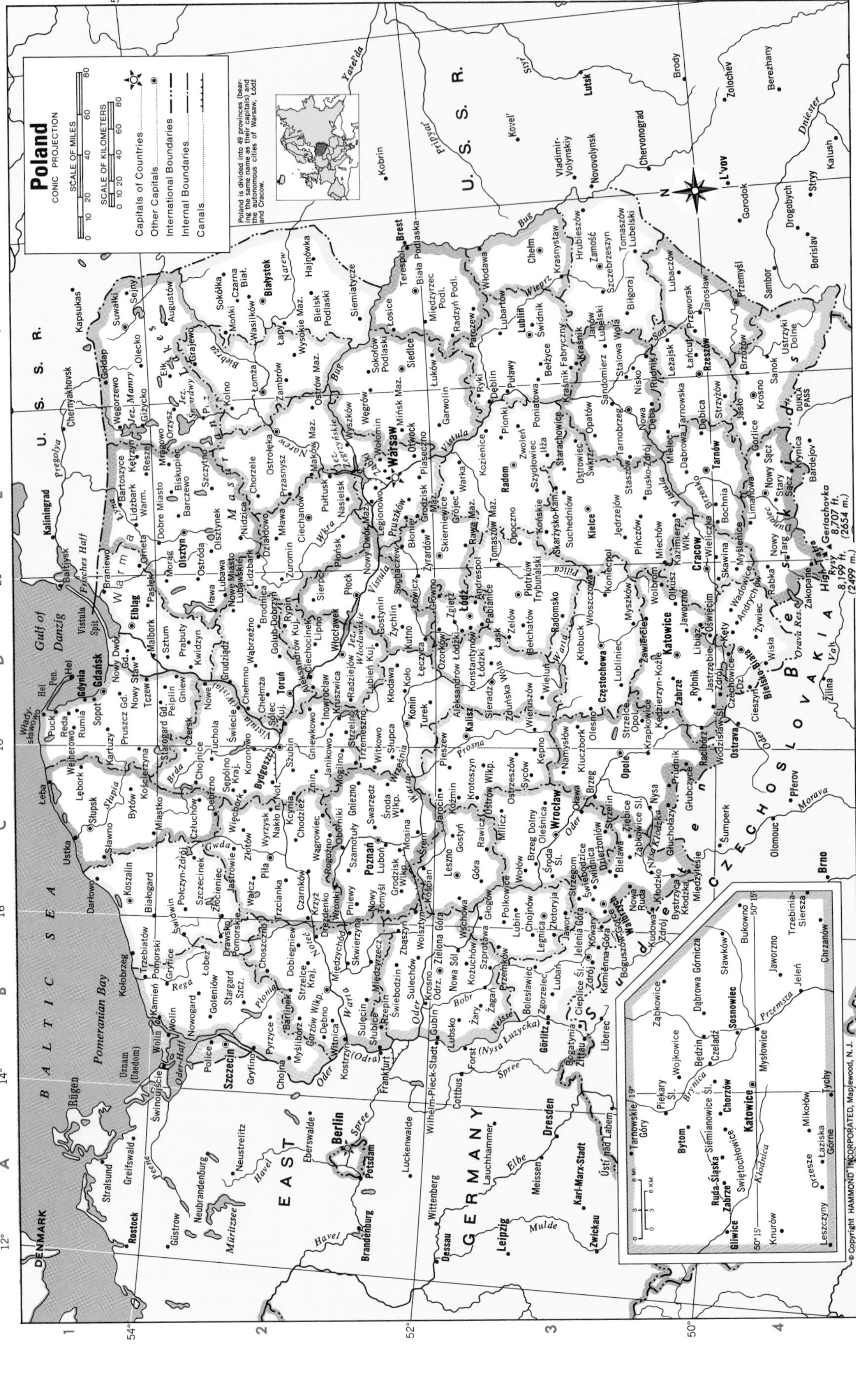

Poland

CONIC PROJECTION

Poland is divided into 49 provinces (bearing the same name as their capitals) and the autonomous cities of Warsaw, Łódź and Cracow.

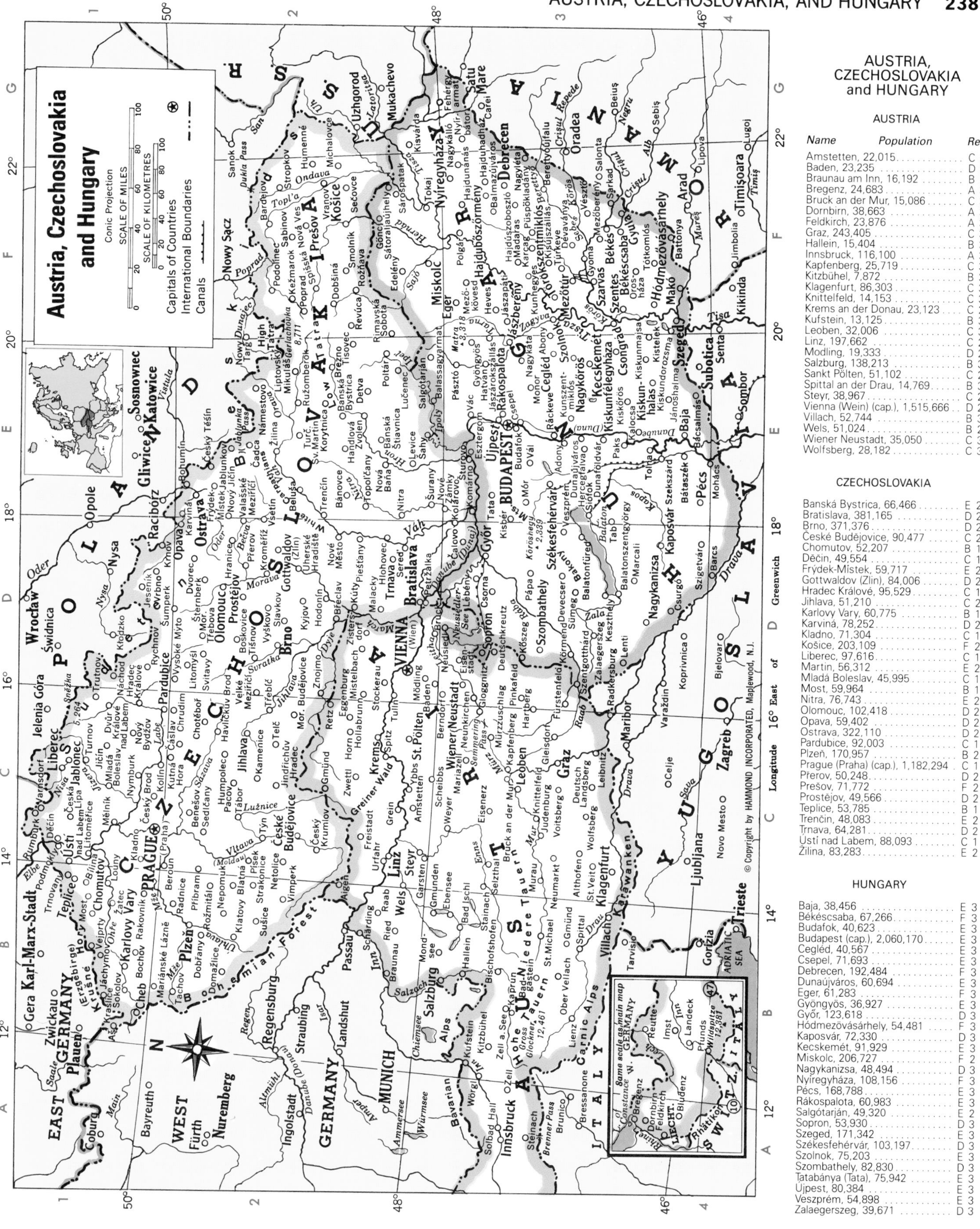

AUSTRIA, CZECHOSLOVAKIA and HUNGARY

AUSTRIA

Name	Population	Ref.
Amstetten, 22,015		C 2
Baden, 23,235		D 2
Braunau am Inn, 16,192		B 2
Bregenz, 24,683		A 3
Bruck an der Mur, 15,086		C 3
Dornbirn, 38,663		A 3
Feldkirch, 23,876		A 3
Graz, 243,405		C 3
Hallein, 15,404		B 3
Innsbruck, 116,100		A 3
Kapfenberg, 25,719		C 3
Kitzbühel, 7,872		B 3
Klagenfurt, 86,303		C 3
Knittelfeld, 14,153		C 3
Krems an der Donau, 23,123		C 2
Kufstein, 13,125		B 3
Leoben, 32,006		C 3
Linz, 197,662		C 2
Modling, 19,333		D 2
Salzburg, 138,213		B 3
Sankt Pölten, 51,102		C 2
Spittal an der Drau, 14,769		B 3
Steyr, 38,967		C 2
Vienna (Wein) (cap.), 1,515,666		D 2
Villach, 52,744		B 3
Wels, 51,024		B 2
Wiener Neustadt, 35,050		C 3
Wolfsberg, 28,182		C 3

CZECHOSLOVAKIA

Name	Ref.
Banská Bystrica, 66,466	E 2
Bratislava, 381,165	D 2
Brno, 371,376	D 2
České Budějovice, 90,477	C 2
Chomutov, 52,207	B 1
Děčín, 49,554	C 1
Frýdek-Místek, 59,717	E 2
Gottwaldov (Zlín), 84,006	D 2
Hradec Králové, 95,529	C 1
Jihlava, 51,210	C 2
Karlovy Vary, 60,775	B 1
Karviná, 78,252	D 2
Kladno, 71,304	C 1
Košice, 203,109	F 2
Liberec, 97,616	C 1
Martin, 56,312	E 2
Mladá Boleslav, 45,995	C 1
Most, 59,964	B 1
Nitra, 76,743	E 2
Olomouc, 102,418	D 2
Opava, 59,402	D 2
Ostrava, 322,110	D 2
Pardubice, 92,003	C 1
Plzeň, 170,957	B 2
Prague (Praha) (cap.), 1,182,294	C 1
Přerov, 50,248	D 2
Prešov, 71,772	F 2
Prostějov, 49,566	D 2
Teplice, 53,785	B 1
Trenčín, 48,083	E 2
Trnava, 64,281	D 2
Ústí nad Labem, 88,093	C 1
Žilina, 83,283	E 2

HUNGARY

Name	Ref.
Baja, 38,456	E 3
Békéscsaba, 67,266	F 3
Budafok, 40,623	E 3
Budapest (cap.), 2,060,170	E 3
Cegléd, 40,567	E 3
Csepel, 71,693	E 3
Debrecen, 192,484	F 3
Dunaújváros, 60,694	E 3
Eger, 61,283	F 3
Gyöngyös, 36,927	E 3
Győr, 123,618	D 3
Hódmezővásárhely, 54,481	F 3
Kaposvár, 72,330	D 3
Kecskemét, 91,929	E 3
Miskolc, 206,727	F 2
Nagykanizsa, 48,494	D 3
Nyíregyháza, 108,156	F 3
Pécs, 168,788	E 3
Rákospalota, 60,983	E 3
Salgótarján, 49,320	E 2
Sopron, 53,930	D 3
Szeged, 171,342	E 3
Székesfehérvár, 103,197	D 3
Szolnok, 75,203	E 3
Szombathely, 82,830	D 3
Tatabánya (Tata), 75,942	E 3
Újpest, 80,384	E 3
Veszprém, 54,898	E 3
Zalaegerszeg, 39,671	D 3

THE BALKAN STATES

ALBANIA

Name	Population	Ref.
Durrës (Durazzo), 53,800		B 3
Korçe, 47,300		C 3
Shkodër, 55,300		B 3
Tiranë (Tirana) (cap.), 206,118		B 3

BULGARIA

Name, Population	Ref.
Burgas, 175,659	D 3
Gabrovo, 75,034	D 3
Kazanlük, 53,607	D 3
Pernik, 87,432	C 3
Pleven, 133,795	D 3
Plovdiv, 362,686	D 3
Ruse, 177,467	D 3
Shumen, 83,525	D 3
Silistra, 58,270	D 3
Sofia (cap.), 1,076,337	C 3
Stara Zagora, 140,312	D 3
Tolbukhin (Dobrich), 86,184	E 3
Varna, 294,494	E 3
Veliko Túrnovo, 56,497	D 3
Yambol, 75,861	D 3

GREECE

Name, Population	Ref.
Athens (cap.), 3,027,331	D 4
Corinth, 22,658	C 4
Dráma, 36,109	C 3
Ioánnina, 44,829	C 4
Iráklion (Candia), 101,634	D 5
Kalámai, 41,911	C 4
Kateríni, 28,808	C 3
Kavála, 56,375	D 3
Khalkís, 44,867	C 4
Khaniá (Canea), 47,338	C 5
Komotini, 34,051	D 3
Lamía, 41,667	C 4
Lárisa, 102,048	C 4
Pátrai, 141,529	C 4
Piraiévs (Piraeus), 196,389	C 4
Ródhos (Rhodes), 40,392	E 4
Salamís, 20,807	F 6
Sérrai, 45,213	C 3
Thessaloníki (Salonika), 406,413	C 3
Vólos, 71,378	C 4

ROMANIA

Name, Population	Ref.
Arad, 172,669	C 2
Bacau, 131,413	D 2
Baia Mare, 112,893	C 2
Brăila, 203,983	C 2
Braşov, 299,172	D 2
Bucharest (Bucureşti) (cap.), 1,960,097	D 2
Buzău, 106,738	D 2
Cluj-Napoca, 274,095	C 2
Constanţa, 279,308	E 2
Craiova, 220,893	C 2
Galaţi, 252,884	D 2
Iaşi, 262,493	D 2
Oradea, 178,407	C 2
Piteşti, 133,179	D 2
Ploieşti, 207,009	D 2
Reşiţa, 90,698	C 2
Satu Mare, 108,152	C 2
Sibiu, 141,981	C 2
Timişoara, 281,320	C 2
Tîrgu Mureş, 129,284	D 2

YUGOSLAVIA

Name, Population	Ref.
Banja Luka, 123,937	B 2
Belgrade (Beograd) (cap.), 1,087,915	C 2
Bitola, 64,467	C 3
Kragujevac, 72,080	C 2
Ljubljana, 224,817	A 2
Maribor, 106,113	A 2
Mostar, 47,821	B 3
Niš, 161,376	C 3
Novi Sad, 170,020	C 2
Osijek, 104,775	B 2
Pančevo, 53,979	C 2
Prilep, 48,045	C 3
Priština, 108,083	C 3
Rijeka (Fiume), 159,433	A 2
Sarajevo, 319,017	B 3
Skopje, 408,143	C 3
Split, 169,322	B 3
Subotica, 100,516	B 2
Titograd, 54,639	B 3
Tuzla, 53,836	B 2
Zagreb, 649,586	A 2
Zenica, 49,522	B 2
Zrenjanin, 60,201	C 2

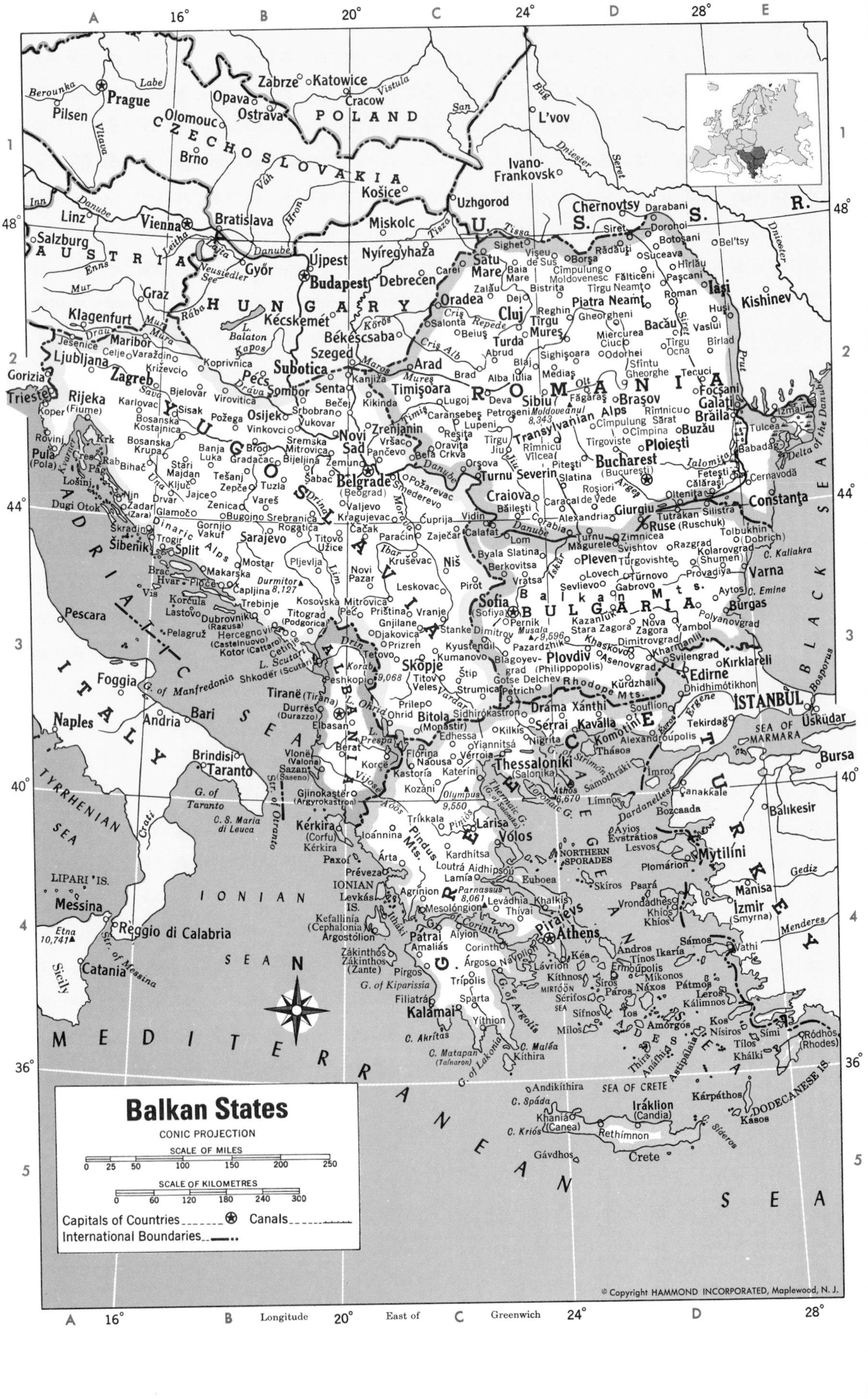

Balkan States

CONIC PROJECTION

SCALE OF MILES: 0 25 50 100 150 200 250

SCALE OF KILOMETRES: 0 60 120 180 240 300

Capitals of Countries ⊛ Canals

International Boundaries

Longitude East of Greenwich

UNION OF SOVIET SOCIALIST REPUBLICS

*See pages 2388-89.
†See page 2387.

Name	Population	Ref.
Abakan	128,000	*K 4
Achinsk	117,000	*K 4
Aginskoye	7,922	*M 4
Akmolinsk (Tselinograd)	234,000	*H 4
Aktyubinsk	191,000	*F 4
Alma-Ata	910,000	*H 5
Ambarchik		*R 3
Anadyr'	7,703	*S 3
Andizhan	230,000	*H 5
Angarsk	239,000	*L 4
Anzhero-Sudzhensk	105,000	*J 4
Archangel (Arkhangel'sk)	385,000	†F 2
Armavir	162,000	†F 6
Artem	69,000	*O 5
Arzamas	93,000	†F 3
Asbest	79,000	*G 4
Ashkhabad	312,000	*F 6
Astrakhan'	461,000	†G 5
Ayan		*O 4
Baku	1,550,000	†H 6
Balashov	93,000	†F 4
Balkhash	78,000	*H 5
Baranovichi	131,000	†B 4
Barnaul	533,000	*J 4
Batumi	123,000	†F 6
Baykonyr		*G 5
Bel'tsy	125,000	†C 5
Belgorod	240,000	†E 4
Belogorsk	63,000	*N 4
Belovo	112,000	*J 4
Berdsk	67,000	*J 4
Berezniki	185,000	†J 3
Birobidzhan	69,000	*O 5
Biysk	212,000	*J 4
Blagoveshchensk	172,000	*N 4
Bobruysk	192,000	†C 4
Borisov	112,000	†C 4
Bratsk	214,000	*L 4
Brest	177,000	†B 4
Bryansk	394,000	†E 4
Bukhara	185,000	*G 5
Chapayevsk	85,000	†G 4
Chardzhou	140,000	*G 6
Cheboksary	308,000	†G 3
Chelyabinsk	1,030,000	*G 4
Cheremkhovo	77,000	*L 4
Chernobyl'		†D 4
Cherepovets	266,000	†E 3
Cherkassy	228,000	†D 5
Cherkessk	91,000	†F 6
Chernigov	238,000	†D 4
Chernogorsk	71,000	*K 4
Chernovtsy	219,000	†C 5
Chimkent	322,000	*H 5
Chirchik	132,000	*H 5
Chita	303,000	*M 4
Daugavpils	116,000	†C 3
Dimitrovgrad	106,000	†H 4
Dnepropetrovsk	1,066,000	†D 5
Donetsk	1,021,000	†E 5
Dudinka	19,701	*J 3
Dushanbe	494,000	*G 6
Dzerzhinsk	257,000	†F 3
Dzhambul	264,000	*H 5
Dzhezkazgan	89,000	*G 5
Ekibastuz	66,000	*H 4
Elista	70,000	†F 5
Engel's	161,000	†G 4
Erivan	1,019,000	†F 6
Fergana	176,000	*H 5
Frunze	533,000	*H 5
Glazov	81,000	†H 3
Gomel'	383,000	†D 4
Gor'kiy	1,344,000	†F 3
Gorlovka	336,000	†E 5
Grodno	195,000	†B 4
Groznyy	375,000	†G 6
Gur'yev	131,000	*F 5
Irkutsk	550,000	*L 4
Ishim	63,000	*H 4
Ivano-Frankovsk	150,000	†B 5
Ivanovo	465,000	†F 3
Izhevsk	549,000	†H 3
Izmail	83,000	†C 5
Kalinin (Tver)	412,000	†D 3
Kaliningrad (Königsberg)	355,000	†B 4
Kaluga	265,000	†E 4
Kamenets-Podol'skiy	81,000	†C 5
Kamensk-Ural'skiy	187,000	*G 4
Kamyshin	112,000	†F 4
Kansk	101,000	*K 4
Karaganda	572,000	*H 5
Karshi	108,000	*G 6
Kaunas	370,000	†B 3
Kazan'	993,000	†G 3
Kemerovo	471,000	*J 4

Kerch, 157,000 .... †E 5
Khabarovsk, 528,000 .... *O 5
Khanty-Mansiysk, 24,754 .... *H 3
Khar'kov, 1,444,000 .... †E 5
Kherson, 319,000 .... †D 5
Khiva, 24,139 .... *F 5
Khmel'nitskiy, 172,000 .... †C 5
Khorog, 12,295 .... *H 6
Kiev, 2,144,000 .... †D 4
Kineshma, 101,000 .... †F 3
Kirov, 390,000 .... †H 3
Kirovabad, 232,000 .... †G 6
Kirovograd, 237,000 .... †D 5
Kiselevsk, 122,000 .... *J 4
Kishinev, 503,000 .... †C 5
Klaipeda (Memel), 176,000 .... †B 3
Kokand, 153,000 .... *H 5
Kokchetav, 103,000 .... *H 4
Kolomna, 147,000 .... †E 4
Komsomol'sk-na-Amure, 264,000 .... *O 4
Konotop, 82,000 .... †D 4
Kopeysk, 146,000 .... *G 4
Kostroma, 255,000 .... †F 3
Krasnodar, 560,000 .... †E 5
Krasnotur'insk, 61,000 .... *G 3
Krasnoyarsk, 796,000 .... *K 4
Kremenchug, 210,000 .... †D 5
Krivoy Rog, 650,000 .... †D 5
Kudymkar, 26,350 .... †H 3
Kurgan, 310,000 .... *G 4
Kursk, 375,000 .... †E 1
Kustanay, 165,000 .... *G 4
Kutaisi, 194,000 .... †F 6
Kuybyshev (Samara), 1,216,000 .... †H 4
Kuznetsk, 94,000 .... †G 4
Kyzyl, 66,000 .... *K 4
Kzyl-Orda, 156,000 .... *G 5
L'vov (Lwow), 667,000 .... †B 4
Leninabad, 130,000 .... *G 5
Leninakan, 207,000 .... †F 6
Leningrad, 4,588,000 .... †D 3
Leninsk .... *G 5
Leninsk-Kuznetskiy, 132,000 .... *J 4
Liepaja, 108,000 .... †B 3
Lipetsk, 396,000 .... †E 4
Lutsk, 137,000 .... †B 4
Magadan, 121,000 .... *P 4
Magnitogorsk, 406,000 .... *G 4
Makeyevka, 436,000 .... †E 5
Makhachkala, 251,000 .... †G 6
Mary (Merv), 74,000 .... *G 6
Maykop, 128,000 .... †F 6
Melitopol', 161,000 .... †D 5
Miass, 150,000 .... *G 4
Michurinsk, 101,000 .... †F 4
Minsk, 1,276,000 .... †C 4
Mogilev, 290,000 .... †D 4
Moscow (Moskva) (cap.), 8,011,000 .... †E 3
Murmansk, 381,000 .... †D 1
Murom, 114,000 .... †F 3
Naberezhnye Chelny, 301,000 .... †H 3
Nakhichevan', 33,279 .... †F 7
Nakhodka, 133,000 .... *O 5
Nal'chik, 207,000 .... †F 6
Namangan, 227,000 .... *H 5
Naryn, 21,098 .... *H 5
Navoi, 84,000 .... *G 6
Nebit-Dag, 71,000 .... *F 6
Nikolayev, 440,000 .... †D 5
Nizhnevartovsk, 109,000 .... *H 3
Nizhniy Tagil, 398,000 .... *G 4
Nordvik-gol'naya .... *M 2
Noril'sk, 180,000 .... *J 3
Novgorod, 186,000 .... †C 3
Novocherkassk, 183,000 .... †F 5
Novokazalinsk, 34,815 .... *G 5
Novokuznetsk, 541,000 .... *J 4
Novomoskovsk, 147,000 .... †E 4
Novorossiysk, 159,000 .... †E 6
Novosibirsk, 1,312,000 .... *J 4
Novyy Urengoy .... *H 3
Nukus, 109,000 .... *G 5
Odessa, 1,046,000 .... †D 5
Okhotsk .... *P 4
Oktyabr'skiy, 88,000 .... †H 4
Omsk, 1,014,000 .... *H 4
Ordzhonikidze, 279,000 .... †G 6
Orel, 305,000 .... †E 4
Orenburg, 459,000 .... †J 4
Orsha, 112,000 .... †D 4
Orsk, 247,000 .... †J 4
Osh, 169,000 .... *H 5
Palana, 2,735 .... *R 4
Pavlodar, 273,000 .... *H 4
Penza, 483,000 .... †F 4
Perm' (Molotov), 999,000 .... †J 3
Pervoural'sk, 129,000 .... *F 4
Petropavlovsk, 207,000 .... *G 4
Petropavlovsk-Kamchatskiy, 215,000 .... *R 4
Petrozavodsk, 234,000 .... †D 2
Pevek .... *S 3
Pinsk, 90,000 .... †C 4
Poltava, 279,000 .... †D 5

Union of Soviet Socialist Republics

CONIC PROJECTION

SCALE OF MILES

0 100 200 300 400 500 600

SCALE OF KILOMETERS

0 100 200 300 400 500 600

Capitals	Boundaries
National	——·——
Union Republic	——·——
A.S.S.R.	——·-·——
Autonomous Oblast	————
Autonomous Okrug	....

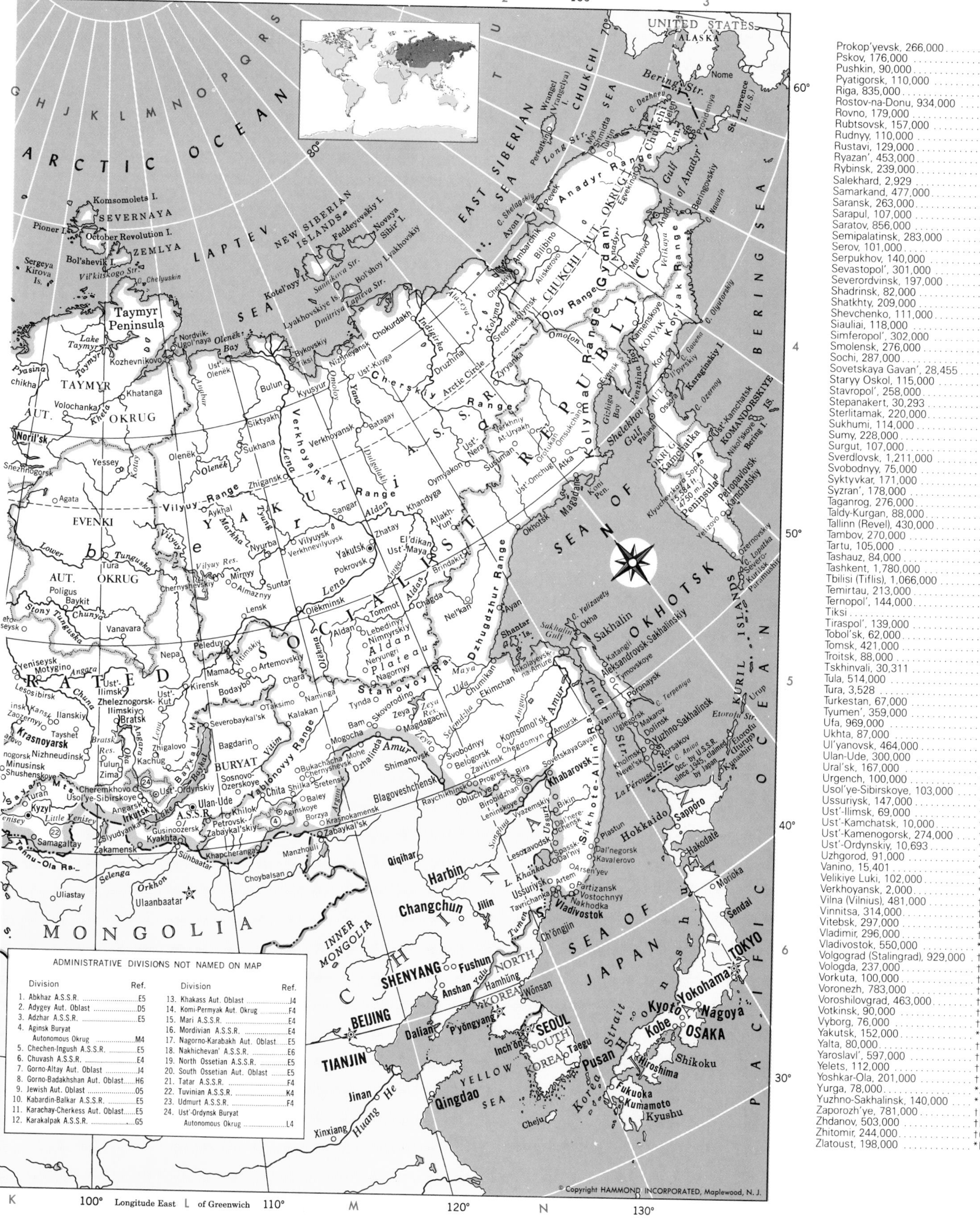

Prokop'yevsk, 266,000 .... *J 4
Pskov, 176,000 .... †C 3
Pushkin, 90,000 .... †D 3
Pyatigorsk, 110,000 .... †F 6
Riga, 835,000 .... †B 3
Rostov-na-Donu, 934,000 .... †F 5
Rovno, 179,000 .... †C 4
Rubtsovsk, 157,000 .... *J 4
Rudnyy, 110,000 .... *G 4
Rustavi, 129,000 .... †F 6
Ryazan', 453,000 .... †E 4
Rybinsk, 239,000 .... †E 3
Salekhard, 2,929 .... *G 3
Samarkand, 477,000 .... *G 6
Saransk, 263,000 .... †F 4
Sarapul, 107,000 .... †H 3
Saratov, 856,000 .... †F 4
Semipalatinsk, 283,000 .... *H 4
Serov, 101,000 .... *G 4
Serpukhov, 140,000 .... †E 4
Sevastopol', 301,000 .... †D 6
Severordvinsk, 197,000 .... †E 2
Shadrinsk, 82,000 .... *G 4
Shatkhty, 209,000 .... †F 5
Shevchenko, 111,000 .... *F 5
Siauliai, 118,000 .... †B 3
Simferopol', 302,000 .... †D 6
Smolensk, 276,000 .... †D 4
Sochi, 287,000 .... †E 6
Sovetskaya Gavan', 28,455 .... *P 5
Staryy Oskol, 115,000 .... †E 4
Stavropol', 258,000 .... †F 5
Stepanakert, 30,293 .... †G 7
Sterlitamak, 220,000 .... †H 4
Sukhumi, 114,000 .... †F 6
Sumy, 228,000 .... †D 4
Surgut, 107,000 .... *H 3
Sverdlovsk, 1,211,000 .... *F 4
Svobodnyy, 75,000 .... *N 4
Syktyvkar, 171,000 .... †H 2
Syzran', 178,000 .... †G 4
Taganrog, 276,000 .... †E 5
Taldy-Kurgan, 88,000 .... *H 5
Tallinn (Revel), 430,000 .... †C 3
Tambov, 270,000 .... †F 4
Tartu, 105,000 .... †C 3
Tashauz, 84,000 .... *F 5
Tashkent, 1,780,000 .... *G 5
Tbilisi (Tiflis), 1,066,000 .... †F 6
Temirtau, 213,000 .... *H 4
Ternopol', 144,000 .... †C 5
Tiksi .... *N 2
Tiraspol', 139,000 .... †D 5
Tobol'sk, 62,000 .... *G 4
Tomsk, 421,000 .... *J 4
Troitsk, 88,000 .... *G 4
Tskhinvali, 30,311 .... †F 6
Tula, 514,000 .... †E 4
Tura, 3,528 .... *L 3
Turkestan, 67,000 .... *G 5
Tyumen', 359,000 .... *G 4
Ufa, 969,000 .... †J 4
Ukhta, 87,000 .... *F 3
Ul'yanovsk, 464,000 .... †G 4
Ulan-Ude, 300,000 .... *L 4
Ural'sk, 167,000 .... *F 4
Urgench, 100,000 .... *G 5
Usol'ye-Sibirskoye, 103,000 .... *L 4
Ussuriysk, 147,000 .... *O 5
Ust'-Ilimsk, 69,000 .... *L 4
Ust'-Kamchatsk, 10,000 .... *R 4
Ust'-Kamenogorsk, 274,000 .... *J 5
Ust'-Ordynskiy, 10,693 .... *L 4
Uzhgorod, 91,000 .... †B 5
Vanino, 15,401 .... *P 5
Velikiye Luki, 102,000 .... †D 3
Verkhoyansk, 2,000 .... *N 3
Vilna (Vilnius), 481,000 .... †B 4
Vinnitsa, 314,000 .... †C 5
Vitebsk, 297,000 .... †D 3
Vladimir, 296,000 .... †F 3
Vladivostok, 550,000 .... *O 5
Volgograd (Stalingrad), 929,000 .... †G 5
Vologda, 237,000 .... †E 3
Vorkuta, 100,000 .... †K 1
Voronezh, 783,000 .... †F 4
Voroshilovgrad, 463,000 .... †F 5
Votkinsk, 90,000 .... †H 3
Vyborg, 76,000 .... †C 2
Yakutsk, 152,000 .... *N 3
Yalta, 80,000 .... †D 6
Yaroslavl', 597,000 .... †E 3
Yelets, 112,000 .... †E 4
Yoshkar-Ola, 201,000 .... †G 3
Yurga, 78,000 .... *J 4
Yuzhno-Sakhalinsk, 140,000 .... *P 5
Zaporozh'ye, 781,000 .... †E 5
Zhdanov, 503,000 .... †E 5
Zhitomir, 244,000 .... †C 4
Zlatoust, 198,000 .... *F 4

ASIA

CAPITALS

Name	Ref.
Abu Dhabi, United Arab Emirates	G 7
Aden, People's Dem. Rep. of Yemen	F 8
Al Kuwait, Kuwait	F 7
Amman, Jordan	E 6
Ankara, Turkey	E 6
Baghdad, Iraq	F 6
Bandar Seri Begawan, Brunei	N 9
Bangkok, Thailand	M 8
Beijing (Peking), China (Mainland)	N 6
Beirut, Lebanon	E 6
Colombo, Sri Lanka	J 9
Damascus, Syria	E 6
Dhaka (Dacca), Bangladesh	L 7
Doha, Qatar	G 7
Hanoi, Vietnam	M 7
Islamabad, Pakistan	J 6
Jakarta, Indonesia	M 10
Jerusalem, Israel	E 6
Kabul, Afghanistan	H 6
Kathmandu, Nepal	K 7
Kuala Lumpur, Malaysia	M 9
Macau, Macau	N 7
Male, Maldives	J 9
Manama, Bahrain	G 7
Manila, Philippines	O 8
Muscat, Oman	G 7
New Delhi, India	J 7
Nicosia, Cyprus	E 6
P'yongyang, N. Korea	O 6
Phnom Penh, Cambodia	M 8
Rangoon, Burma	L 8
Riyadh, Saudi Arabia	F 7
San'a, Yemen Arab Republic	F 8
Seoul, S. Korea	O 6
Singapore, Singapore	M 9
Taipei, China (Taiwan)	O 7
Tehran, Iran	G 6
Thimphu, Bhutan	K 7
Tokyo, Japan	P 6
Ulaanbaatar, Mongolia	M 5
Victoria, Hong Kong	N 7
Vientiane, Laos	M 8

PHYSICAL FEATURES

Name	Ref.
Aden (gulf)	F 8
Aldan (riv.)	P 3
Altai (mts.)	K 5
Altun Shan (range)	K 6
Amami (isls.)	P 7
Amudar'ya (riv.)	H 5
Amur (riv.)	P 5
Anadyr' (gulf)	V 3
Anadyr' (riv.)	U 3
Andaman (isls.)	L 8
Andaman (sea)	L 8
Angara (riv.)	L 4
Aqaba (gulf)	E 7
Arabian (sea)	H 8
Araks (riv.)	F 6
Aral (sea)	G 5
Ararat (mt.)	F 6
Arctic (ocean)	C 1
Argun (riv.)	N 4
Bali (isl.)	N 10
Balkhash (lake)	J 5
Banda (sea)	O 10
Baykal (lake)	N 4
Bengal (bay)	K 8
Bering (sea)	V 4
Bering (strait)	W 3
Black (sea)	E 5
Bonin (isls.)	R 7
Borneo (isl.)	N 9
Brahmaputra (riv.)	L 7
Cannanore (isls.)	J 8
Caspian (sea)	G 5
Celebes (isl.)	N 10
Celebes (sea)	O 9
Chagos (arch.)	J 10
Chang Jiang (Yangtze) (riv.)	N 6
Chelyuskin (cape)	N 2
Christmas (isl.)	M 11
Chukchi (sea)	W 3
Cocos (isls.)	L 11
Comorin (cape)	J 9
Dahana (des.)	F 7
Daito (isls.)	P 7
Da Hingan Ling (Great Khingan) (range)	O 5
Damavand (mt.)	G 6
Diego Garcia (isl.)	J 10
East China (sea)	O 7
East Siberian (sea)	T 2
Engano (cape)	O 8
Etorofu (isl.)	R 5

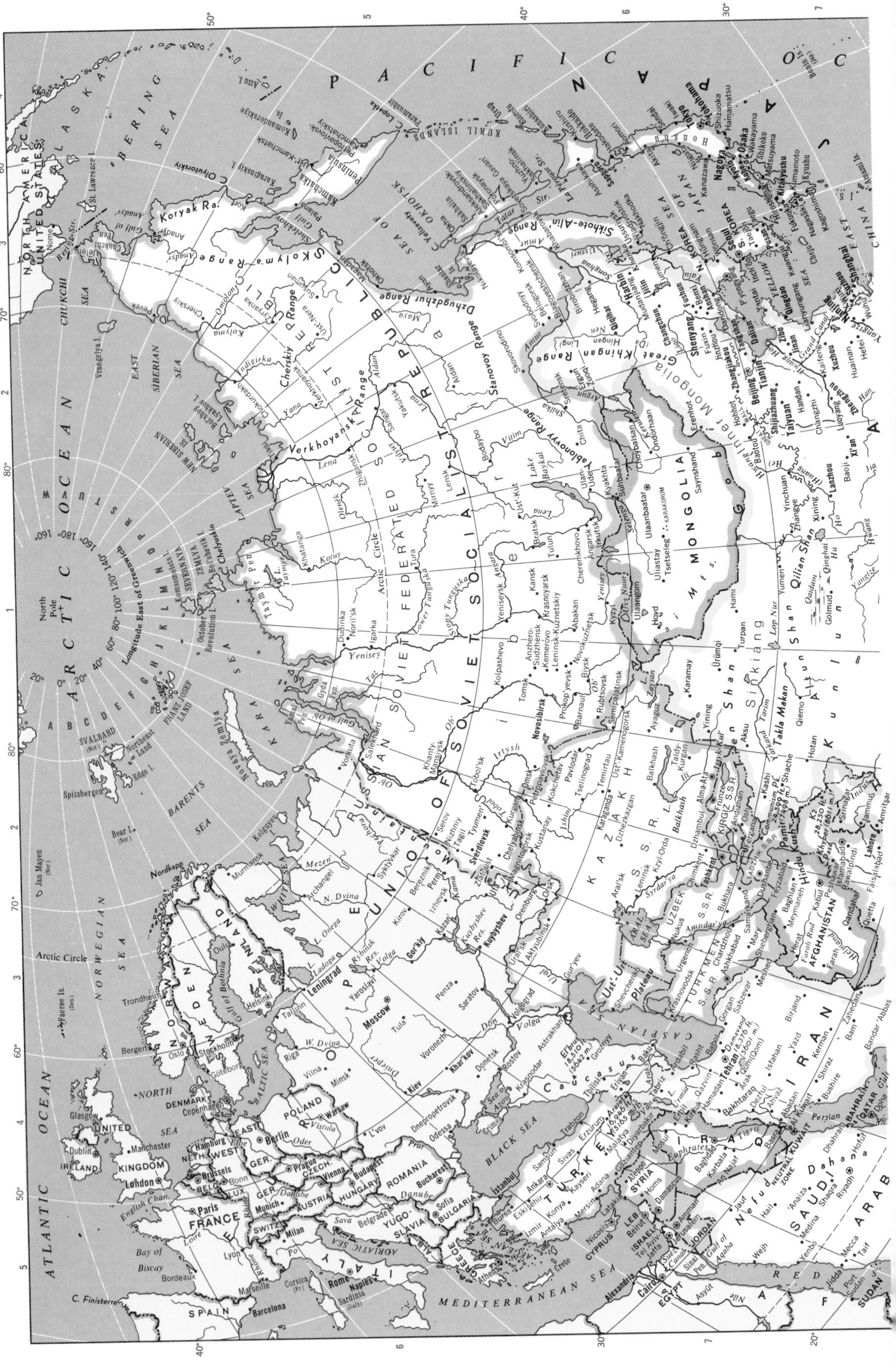

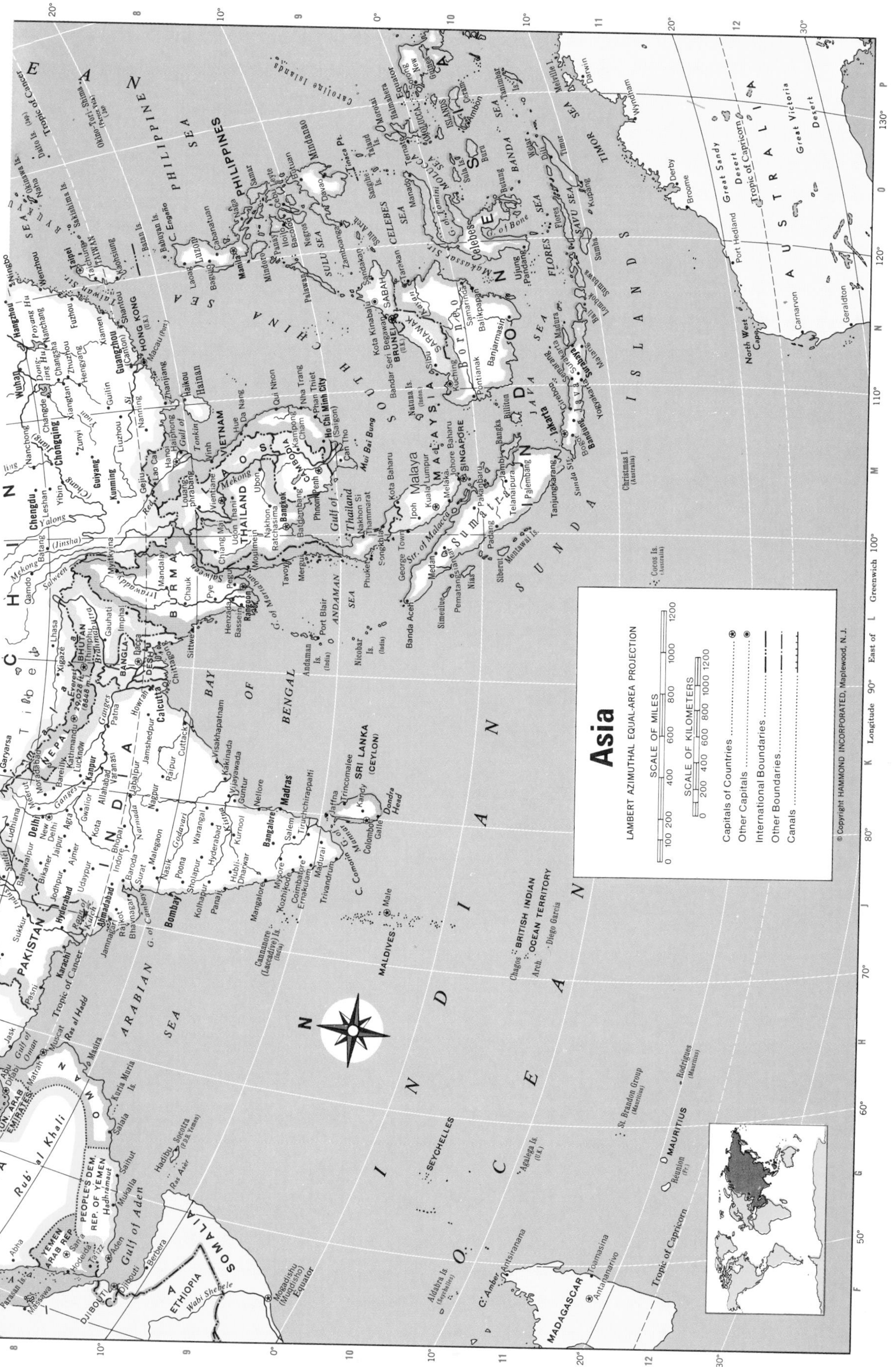

Euphrates (riv.) .... F 6
Everest (mt.) .... K 7
Ganges (riv.) .... K 7
Gobi (des.) .... M 5
Grand (canal) .... N 6
Great Khingan (range) .... O 5
Great Wall .... N 5
Hadhramaut (region) .... F 8
Hainan (isl.) .... N 8
Halmahera (isl.) .... O 9
Helmand (riv.) .... H 6
Himalaya (mts.) .... K 7
Hindu Kush (mts.) .... J 6
Hokkaido (isl.) .... R 5
Honshu (isl.) .... P 6
Huang He (Hwang Ho) (riv.) .... N 6
Ili (riv.) .... J 5
Indian (ocean) .... H 10
Indigirka (riv.) .... R 3
Indus (riv.) .... H 7
Inner Mongolia (region) .... N 5
Irrawaddy (riv.) .... L 7
Irtysh (riv.) .... J 4
Ishim (riv.) .... H 4
Issyk-Kul' (lake) .... J 5
Japan (sea) .... P 6
Java (isl.) .... M 10
Java (sea) .... M 10
Jialing (riv.) .... M 6
Jinsha (Yangtze) (riv.) .... L 7
K2 (mt.) .... J 6
Kamchatka (pen.) .... S 4
Kara (sea) .... H 2
Karakorum (ruins) .... M 5
Kerulen (riv.) .... N 5
Khyber (pass) .... J 6
Kolyma (range) .... S 3
Kunlun (range) .... K 6
Kuria Muria (isls.) .... G 8
Kuril (isls.) .... R 5
Kyushu (isl.) .... P 6
La Perouse (strait) .... R 5
Laptev (sea) .... O 2
Lena (riv.) .... O 3
Leyte (isl.) .... O 8
Lop Nur (lake) .... L 5
Lower Tunguska (riv.) .... L 3
Luzon (isl.) .... O 8
Makassar (strait) .... N 10
Malacca (strait) .... M 9
Malaya (region) .... M 9
Mekong (riv.) .... M 8
Mindanao (isl.) .... O 9
Molucca (isls.) .... O 10
Narmada (riv.) .... J 7
Nefud (des.) .... F 7
New Guinea (isl.) .... P 10
New Siberian (isls.) .... R 2
Nicobar (isls.) .... L 9
Ob' (riv.) .... H 3
October Revolution (isl.) .... K 2
Okhotsk (sea) .... R 4
Okinawa (isls.) .... O 7
Oman (gulf) .... G 7
Pacific (ocean) .... T 5
Persian (gulf) .... G 7
Philippine (sea) .... O 8
Red (riv.) .... M 7
Red (sea) .... E 7
Rub' al Khali (des.) .... G 7
Ryukyu (isls.) .... O 7
Sakhalin (isl.) .... R 4
Salween (riv.) .... L 8
Severnaya Zemlya (isls.) .... M 1
Siberia (region) .... M 4
Sinkiang (region) .... K 5
Socotra (isl.) .... G 8
Songhua (riv.) .... P 5
South China (sea) .... N 8
Stony Tunguska (riv.) .... L 3
Sulu (sea) .... N 9
Sumatra (isl.) .... L 9
Sunda (isls.) .... L 10
Syrdar'ya (riv.) .... H 5
Taiwan (isl.) .... O 7
Takla Makan (des.) .... K 6
Taymyr (pen.) .... L 2
Thailand (gulf) .... M 8
Tibet (region) .... K 6
Tien Shan (range) .... K 5
Tigris (riv.) .... F 6
Timor (isl.) .... O 10
Tobol (riv.) .... H 4
Tonkin (gulf) .... M 8
Urmia (lake) .... F 6
Ural (riv.) .... G 5
Ust'-Urt (plat.) .... G 5
Van (lake) .... F 6
Verkhoyansk (range) .... O 3
Xi (riv.) .... N 7
Yalu (riv.) .... O 5
Yangtze (riv.) .... N 6
Yellow (sea) .... O 6
Yenisey (riv.) .... K 3

NEAR and MIDDLE EAST

BAHRAIN

Name Population	Ref.
Manama (cap.), 108,684	F 4
Muharraq, 37,732	F 4

IRAN

Name Population	Ref.
Abadan, 296,081	E 3
Ahvaz, 329,006	E 3
Amol, 68,782	F 2
Arak, 114,507	E 3
Ardabil, 147,404	E 2
Babol, 67,790	F 2
Bakhtaran (Kermanshah), 290,861	E 3
Bam, 22,000	G 4
Bandar 'Abbas, 89,103	G 4
Bandar-e Anzali (Enzeli), 55,978	E 2
Birjand, 25,854	G 3
Bojnurd, 31,248	G 2
Borujerd, 100,103	E 3
Bushehr, 57,681	F 4
Dezful, 110,287	E 3
Emamshahr, 30,767	G 2
Gorgan (Asterabad), 88,348	F 2
Hamadan, 155,846	E 3
Isfahan, 617,825	F 3
Jahrom, 38,236	F 4
Kashan, 84,545	F 3
Kazerun, 51,309	F 4
Kerman, 140,309	G 3
Khorramabad, 104,928	E 3
Khorramshahr, 146,709	E 3
Khvoy, 70,040	E 2
Mahabad, 28,610	E 2
Maragheh, 60,820	E 2
Meshed, 670,180	H 2
Mianeh, 28,447	E 2
Najafabad, 76,236	F 3
Neyshabur, 59,101	G 2
Qazvin, 138,527	E 2
Qom, 246,831	F 3
Quchan, 29,133	G 2
Rafsanjan, 21,000	G 3
Rasht, 187,203	E 2
Rey, 102,825	F 2
Sabzevar, 69,174	G 2
Sanandaj, 95,834	E 2
Sari, 70,936	F 2
Semnan, 31,058	F 2
Shahreza, 34,220	F 3
Shiraz, 416,408	F 4
Shustar, 24,000	E 3
Tabriz, 598,576	E 2
Tehran (cap.), 4,496,159	F 2
Torbat-e Heydariyeh, 30,106	G 2
Urmia (Reza'iyeh), 163,991	D 2
Zahedan, 92,628	H 4
Zanjan, 99,967	E 2

IRAQ

Name Population	Ref.
Al Falluja, 38,072	D 3
Al Fatha, 15,329	D 2
Al Musaiyib, 15,955	D 3
'Amara, 64,847	E 3
'Ana, 15,729	D 3
An Najaf, 128,096	D 3
An Nasiriya, 60,405	E 3
Baghdad (cap.), *1,745,328	E 3
Ba'quba, 34,575	D 3
Basra, 310,950	E 3
Erbil (Arbela), 90,320	D 2
Habbaniya, 14,405	D 3
Hai, 16,988	E 3
Hilla, 111,338	D 3
Karbala'a, 83,301	D 3
Khanqin, 23,522	D 3
Kirkuk, *183,981	D 2
Kut, 42,116	E 3
Mosul, 264,146	D 2
Ramadi, 28,723	D 3
Samarra, 24,746	D 3
Samawa, 33,473	D 3
Sulaimaniya, 86,822	E 2

KUWAIT

Name Population	Ref.
Al Kuwait (cap.), 78,116	E 4
Mina al Ahmadi	E 4
Mina Saud	E 4

OMAN

Name Population	Ref.
Matrah, 15,000	G 5
Muscat (cap.), 6,208	G 5
Salala, 4,000	F 6
Suwaiq	G 5

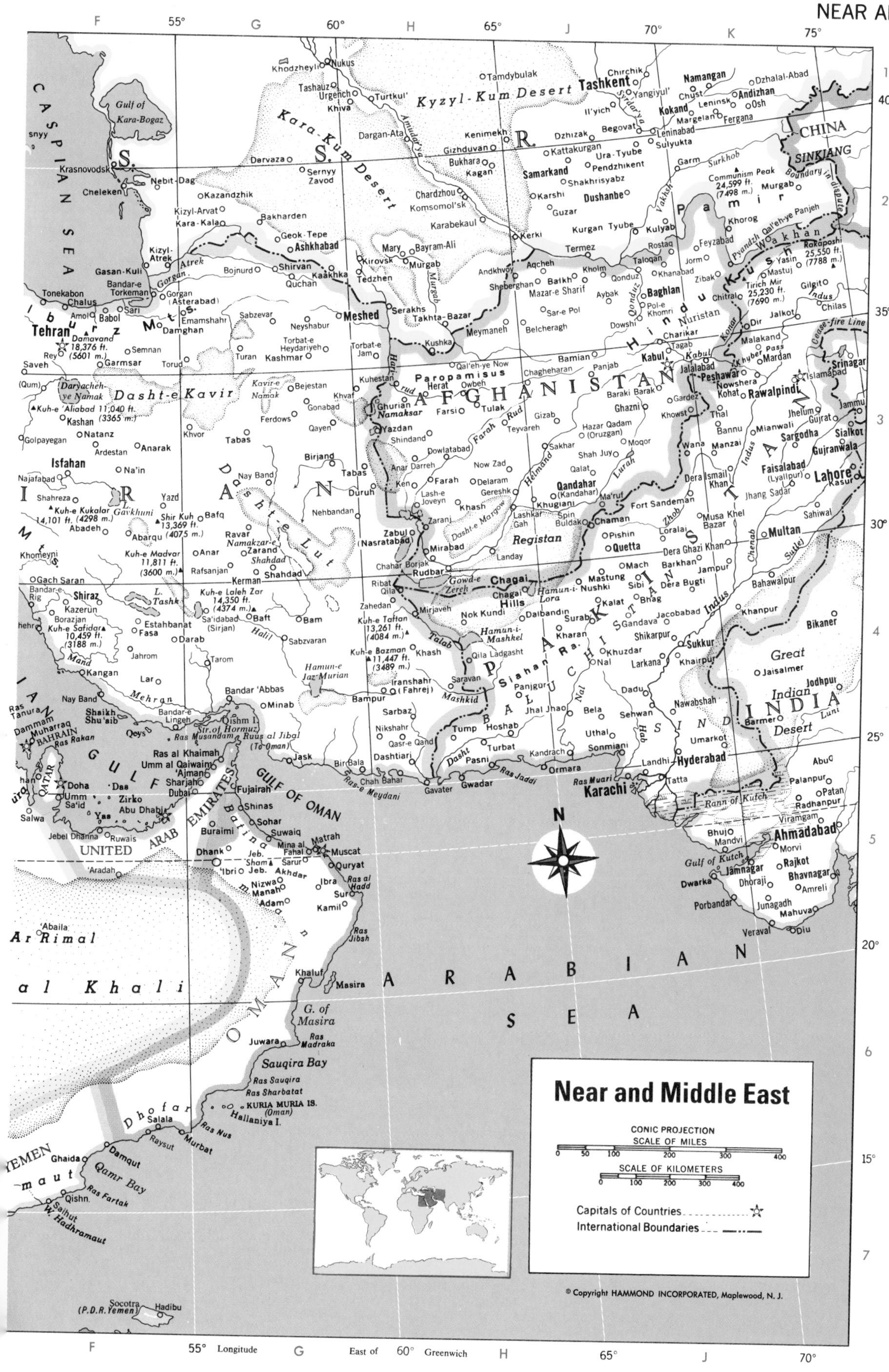

QATAR

Doha (cap.), 150,000 .... F 4
Dukhan .... F 4
Umm Sa'id .... F 5

SAUDI ARABIA

Aba as Sa'ud, 47,501 .... D 6
Abha, 30,150 .... D 6
Abqaiq .... E 4
Abu 'Arish .... D 6
Abu Hadriya .... E 4
'Ain al Mubarrak .... C 5
Al 'Ain .... C 4
Al Birk .... D 6
Al Muadhdham .... C 4
'Ashaira .... D 5
Buraida, 69,940 .... D 4
Dammam, 127,844 .... F 4
Dhaba .... C 4
Dhahran .... E 4
Doqa .... D 6
Hail, 40,502 .... D 4
Hofuf, 101,271 .... E 4
Jabrin .... E 5
Jidda, 561,104 .... C 5
Jizan (Qizan), 32,812 .... D 6
Jubail .... E 4
Jubba .... D 4
Khamis Mushait, 49,581 .... D 6
Khurma .... D 5
Maqna .... C 4
Mecca, 366,801 .... C 5
Medina, 198,186 .... D 5
Mubarraz, 54,325 .... E 4
Muwailih .... C 4
Najran (Aba as Sa'ud), 47,501 .. D 6
Nisab .... D 4
Qadhima .... C 5
Qatif .... E 4
Qizan, 32,812 .... D 6
Rabigh .... C 5
Ras Tanura .... F 4
Riyadh (cap.), 666,840 .... E 5
Taif, 204,857 .... D 5
Tebuk (Tabuk), 74,825 .... C 4
Yenbo (Yanbu) .... C 5

UNITED ARAB EMIRATES

Abu Dhabi (cap.), 347,000 ...... F 5
'Ajman .... G 4
Aradah .... F 5
Dubai .... F 4
Fujairah .... G 4
Ras al Khaimah .... G 4
Ruwais .... F 5
Umm al Qaiwain .... G 4

YEMEN ARAB REPUBLIC

Dhamar, 19,467 .... D 7
El Beida, 5,975 .... E 7
Hajja, 5,814 .... D 6
Hodeida, 80,314 .... D 7
Ibb, 19,066 .... D 7
Marib, 292 .... E 6
Mocha .... D 7
Sa'ada, 4,252 .... D 6
San'a (cap.), 140,339 .... D 6
Ta'izz, 78,642 .... D 7

YEMEN, PEOPLE'S DEM. REPUBLIC OF

Aden (cap.), 285,373 .... E 7
Ahwar .... E 7
Bir 'Ali .... E 7
Ghaida .... F 6
Hadibu .... F 7
Haura .... E 7
Hureidha .... E 6
'Irqa .... E 7
Madinat ash Sha'b .... E 7
Mukalla, 45,000 .... E 7
Saihut .... F 6
Seiyun, 20,000 .... E 6
Shabwa .... E 6
Shibam .... E 6
Shihr .... E 7
Tarim .... E 6
Zinjibar .... E 7

*Metropolitan population.

Near and Middle East

CONIC PROJECTION
SCALE OF MILES
SCALE OF KILOMETERS
Capitals of Countries
International Boundaries

TURKEY, SYRIA, LEBANON and CYPRUS

CYPRUS

Name, Population	Ref.
Famagusta, 38,960	F 5
Larnaca, 19,608	E 5
Limassol, 79,641	E 5
Nicosia (cap.), 115,718	E 5

LEBANON

Name, Population	Ref.
Baalbek, 15,560	G 5
Beirut (cap.), 474,870	F 6
Saida (Sidon), 32,200	F 6
Sur (Tyre), 16,483	F 6
Tarabulus (Tripoli), 127,611	F 5
Zahle, 53,121	F 6

SYRIA

Name, Population	Ref.
Aleppo (Haleb), 976,727	G 4
Baniyas, 19,506	F 5
Damascus (Dimishq) (cap.), 1,251,028	G 6
Deir ez Zor, 92,091	H 5
Dera', 49,534	G 6
Duma, 51,321	G 6
El Bab, 29,930	G 4
El Haseke, 72,532	J 4
El Quneitra, 17,752	F 6
El Rashid (Raqqa), 87,138	H 5
En Nebk, 19,371	G 5
Es Suweida, 43,414	G 6
Hama, 176,640	G 5
Homs, 354,508	G 5
Idlib, 51,334	G 5
Jerablus, 5,502	G 4
Latakia (El Ladhiqiya), 196,791	F 5
Qamishliye, 93,385	J 4
Tadmor (Palmyra), 18,105	H 5
Tartus, 52,589	F 5
Zebdani, 16,368	G 6

TURKEY

Name, Population	Ref.
Adana, 776,000	F 4
Adiyaman, 70,777	H 4
Afyonkarahisar, 88,340	D 3
Akhisar, 68,404	B 3
Aksaray, 77,219	E 3
Altindağ, 422,323	E 2
Ankara (cap.), 2,251,533	E 3
Antakya (Hatay), 109,233	G 4
Antalya (Adalia), 258,139	D 4
Balikesir, 152,402	C 3
Beşiktaş, 219,998	D 6
Beykoz, 115,637	D 5
Beyoğlu, 251,555	D 6
Bursa, 614,133	C 2
Çorum, 96,809	F 2
Denizli, 171,360	C 4
Diyarbakir, 305,259	H 4
Edirne, 86,739	B 2
Elâzığ, 181,523	H 3
Ereğli, 71,171	F 4
Erzincan, 82,133	H 3
Erzurum, 252,648	J 3
Eskişehir, 367,328	D 6
Eyüp, 369,498	D 6
Gaziantep, 466,302	G 4
Iskenderun (Alexandretta), 173,607	G 4
Isparta, 101,784	D 4
Istanbul, 5,494,916	C 2
Izmir (Smyrna), 1,489,817	B 3
Izmit, 236,144	C 2
Kadiköy, 573,261	D 6
Karabük, 95,500	D 2
Kayseri, 378,458	G 3
Kirikkale, 320,745	E 3
Konya, 438,859	E 4
Kutahya, 120,354	C 3
Malatya, 251,257	H 3
Manisa, 126,319	B 3
Maraş (Kahramanmaraş), 212,206	G 4
Mersin, 314,105	F 4
Nazili, 77,568	C 4
Osmaniye, 107,748	G 4
Sakarya, 155,041	D 2
Samsun, 280,068	G 2
Sariyer, 142,523	D 5
Sivas, 197,266	G 3
Tarsus, 160,150	F 4
Tokat, 72,884	G 2
Trabzon (Trebizond), 155,960	H 2
Urfa (Sanliurfa), 206,385	H 4
Uşak, 88,124	C 3
Üsküdar, 467,395	D 6
Van, 121,306	K 3
Zonguldak, 119,125	D 2

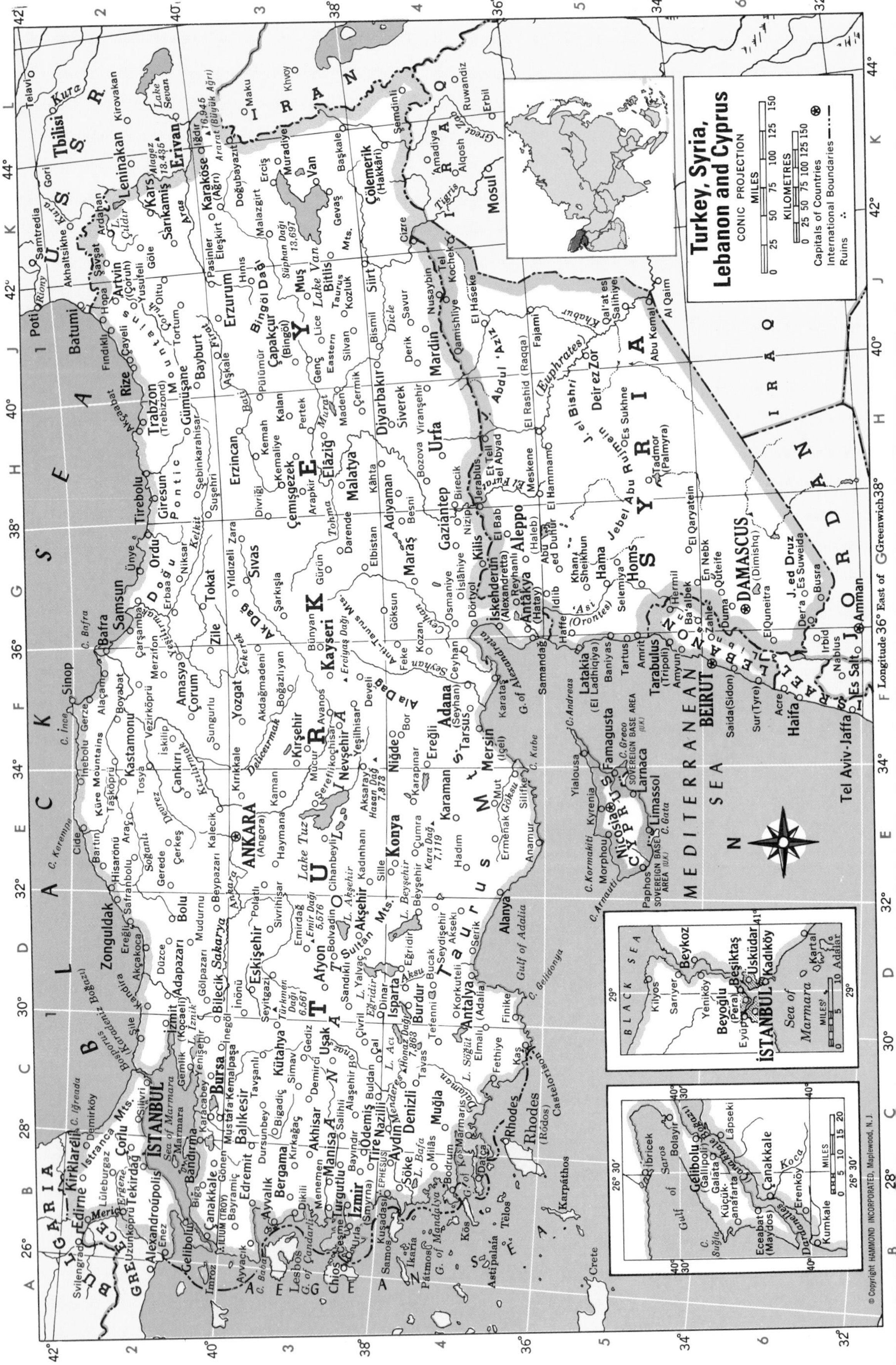

Turkey, Syria, Lebanon and Cyprus

CONIC PROJECTION

Capitals of Countries ⊛
International Boundaries
Ruins ∴

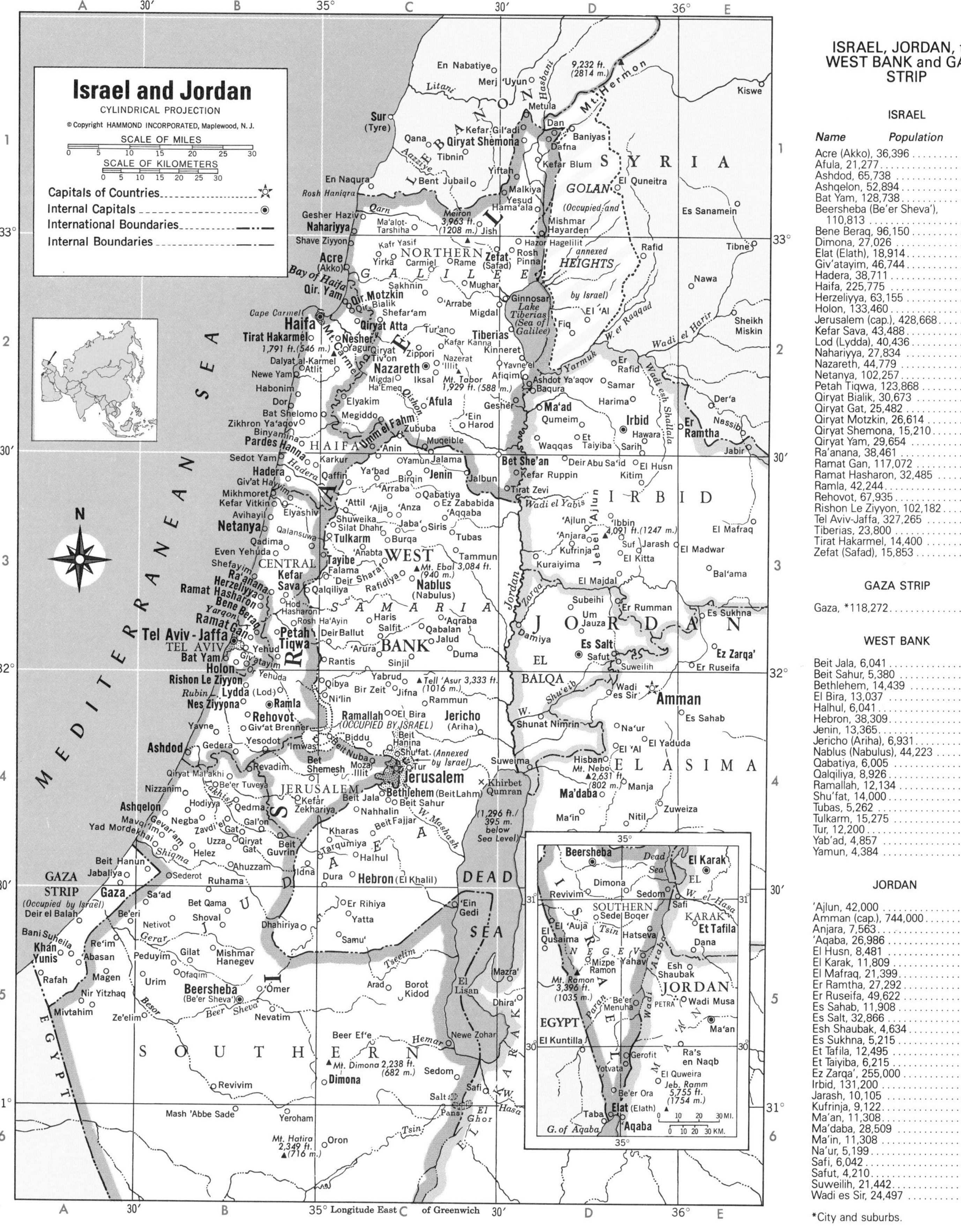

ISRAEL, JORDAN, the WEST BANK and GAZA STRIP

ISRAEL

Name	Population	Ref.
Acre (Akko), 36,396		C 2
Afula, 21,277		C 2
Ashdod, 65,738		B 4
Ashqelon, 52,894		A 4
Bat Yam, 128,738		B 3
Beersheba (Be'er Sheva'), 110,813		B 5
Bene Beraq, 96,150		B 3
Dimona, 27,026		D 4
Elat (Elath), 18,914		D 6
Giv'atayim, 46,744		B 3
Hadera, 38,711		B 3
Haifa, 225,775		B 2
Herzeliyya, 63,155		B 3
Holon, 133,460		B 3
Jerusalem (cap.), 428,668		C 4
Kefar Sava, 43,488		B 3
Lod (Lydda), 40,436		B 4
Nahariyya, 27,834		C 1
Nazareth, 44,779		C 2
Netanya, 102,257		B 3
Petah Tiqwa, 123,868		B 3
Qiryat Bialik, 30,673		C 2
Qiryat Gat, 25,482		B 4
Qiryat Motzkin, 26,614		C 2
Qiryat Shemona, 15,210		C 1
Qiryat Yam, 29,654		C 2
Ra'anana, 38,461		B 3
Ramat Gan, 117,072		B 3
Ramat Hasharon, 32,485		B 3
Ramla, 42,244		B 4
Rehovot, 67,935		B 4
Rishon Le Ziyyon, 102,182		B 4
Tel Aviv-Jaffa, 327,265		B 3
Tiberias, 23,800		C 2
Tirat Hakarmel, 14,400		B 2
Zefat (Safad), 15,853		C 2

GAZA STRIP

Name	Population	Ref.
Gaza, *118,272		A 5

WEST BANK

Name	Population	Ref.
Beit Jala, 6,041		C 4
Beit Sahur, 5,380		C 4
Bethlehem, 14,439		C 4
El Bira, 13,037		C 4
Halhul, 6,041		C 4
Hebron, 38,309		C 4
Jenin, 13,365		C 3
Jericho (Ariha), 6,931		C 4
Nablus (Nabulus), 44,223		C 3
Qabatiya, 6,005		C 3
Qalqiliya, 8,926		C 3
Ramallah, 12,134		C 4
Shu'fat, 14,000		C 4
Tubas, 5,262		C 3
Tulkarm, 15,275		C 3
Tur, 12,200		C 4
Yab'ad, 4,857		C 3
Yamun, 4,384		C 3

JORDAN

Name	Population	Ref.
'Ajlun, 42,000		D 3
Amman (cap.), 744,000		E 4
Anjara, 7,563		D 3
'Aqaba, 26,986		D 6
El Husn, 8,481		D 3
El Karak, 11,809		E 4
El Mafraq, 21,399		E 3
Er Ramtha, 27,292		E 2
Er Ruseifa, 49,622		E 3
Es Sahab, 11,908		E 4
Es Salt, 32,866		D 3
Esh Shaubak, 4,634		D 5
Es Sukhna, 5,215		E 3
Et Tafila, 12,495		E 5
Et Taiyiba, 6,215		D 2
Ez Zarqa', 255,000		E 3
Irbid, 131,200		D 2
Jarash, 10,105		D 3
Kufrinja, 9,122		D 3
Ma'an, 11,308		E 5
Ma'daba, 28,509		D 4
Ma'in, 11,308		D 4
Na'ur, 5,199		D 4
Safi, 6,042		E 5
Safut, 4,210		D 3
Suweilih, 21,442		D 3
Wadi es Sir, 24,497		D 4

*City and suburbs.

INDIAN SUBCONTINENT and AFGHANISTAN

AFGHANISTAN

Name	Population	Ref.
Aybak, 33,016		B 1
Baghlan, 75,130		B 1
Charikar, 25,093		B 1
Farah, 18,797		A 2
Feyzabad, 290,142		C 1
Gardez, 11,415		B 2
Ghazni, 30,425		B 2
Herat, 163,960		A 2
Jalalabad, 56,384		B 2
Kabul (cap.), 905,108		B 2
Lashkar Gah, 26,646		A 2
Mazar-e Sharif, 122,567		B 1
Meymaneh, 54,954		A 1
Qandahar, 178,409		B 2
Qonduz, 107,191		B 1
Sheberghan, 54,870		B 1
Taloqan, 46,202		B 1

BANGLADESH

Barisal, 159,298	G 4
Chittagong, 1,388,476	G 4
Dhaka (Dacca) (cap.), 3,458,602	G 4
Jamalpur, 89,847	F 4
Khulna, 623,184	F 4
Narayanganj, 196,139	G 4
Rajshahi, 171,600	F 4
Rangpur, 166,847	F 3

BHUTAN

Paro, 46,480	F 3
Thimphu (cap.), 81,340	G 3

INDIA

Agartala, 131,513	G 4
Agra, 770,352	D 3
Ahmadabad, 2,515,195	C 4
Aizwal, 31,740	G 4
Ajmer, 374,350	C 3
Aligarh, 319,981	D 3
Allahabad, 642,420	E 3
Amravati, 261,387	D 4
Amritsar, 589,229	C 2
Asansol, 365,371	F 4
Bangalore, 2,913,537	D 6
Bareilly, 437,801	D 3
Baroda (Vadodara), 744,043	C 4
Belgaum, 300,290	C 5
Benares (Varanasi), 793,542	E 3
Bhagalpur, 221,276	F 4
Bhavnagar, 308,194	C 4
Bhopal, 672,263	D 4
Bhubaneswar, 219,419	F 4
Bikaner, 280,356	C 3
Bombay (Greater), 8,227,332	B 7
Calcutta, 9,165,650	F 2
Calicut (Kozhikode), 546,060	D 6
Cawnpore (Kanpur), 1,688,242	E 3
Chandigarh, 421,256	D 2
Cochin, 639,686	D 6
Coimbatore, 917,155	D 6
Cuttack, 326,468	F 4
Darjeeling, 42,873	F 3
Dehra Dun, 293,628	D 2
Delhi, 5,713,581	D 3
Dhanbad, 676,736	F 4
Dharwar-Hubli, 526,493	C 5
Dispur, 1,725	G 3
Durgapur, 305,838	F 4
Durg-Bhilainagar, 490,158	E 4
Erode, 275,103	D 6
Gangtok, 12,000	F 3
Gauhati, 200,377	G 3
Gaya, 246,778	F 4
Ghaziabad, 291,955	D 3
Gorakhpur, 306,399	E 3
Guntur, 367,219	D 5
Gwalior, 559,776	D 3
Hubli-Dharwar, 526,493	C 5
Hyderabad, 2,528,198	D 5
Imphal, 155,639	G 4
Indore, 827,021	D 4
Itanagar, 18,787	G 3
Jabalpur, 757,726	D 4
Jaipur, 1,004,669	D 3
Jammu, 155,338	D 2
Jamnagar, 317,037	B 4
Jamshedpur, 669,984	F 4
Jhansi, 231,332	D 3
Jodhpur, 493,604	C 3
Kakinada 226,642	E 5
Kanpur, 1,688,242	E 3
Kharagpur, 234,931	F 4
Kohima, 21,545	G 3

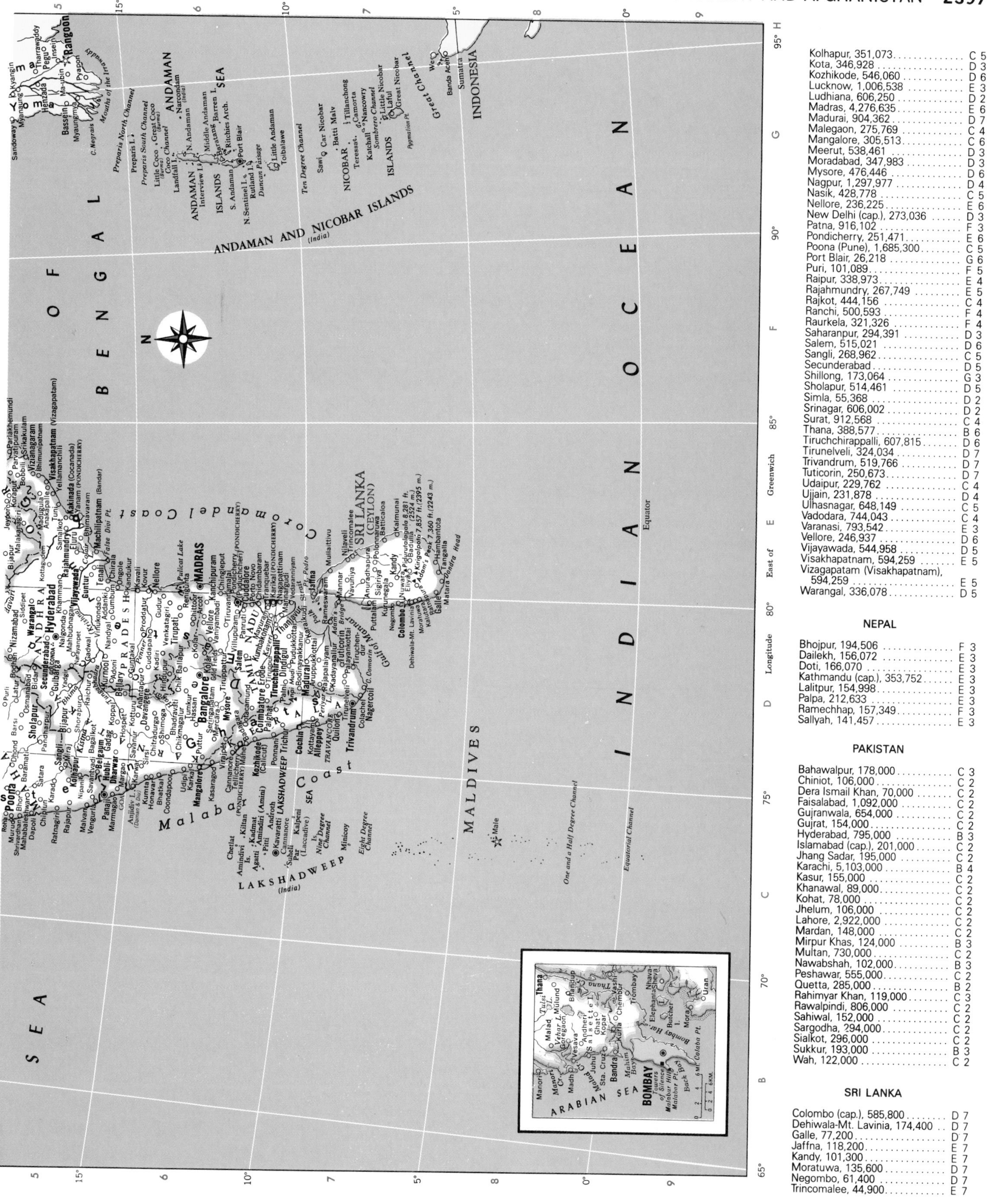

Kolhapur, 351,073	C 5
Kota, 346,928	D 3
Kozhikode, 546,060	D 6
Lucknow, 1,006,538	E 3
Ludhiana, 606,250	D 2
Madras, 4,276,635	E 6
Madurai, 904,362	D 7
Malegaon, 275,769	C 4
Mangalore, 305,513	C 6
Meerut, 538,461	D 3
Moradabad, 347,983	D 3
Mysore, 476,446	D 6
Nagpur, 1,297,977	D 4
Nasik, 428,778	C 5
Nellore, 236,225	E 6
New Delhi (cap.), 273,036	D 3
Patna, 916,102	F 3
Pondicherry, 251,471	E 6
Poona (Pune), 1,685,300	C 5
Port Blair, 26,218	G 6
Puri, 101,089	F 5
Raipur, 338,973	E 4
Rajahmundry, 267,749	E 5
Rajkot, 444,156	C 4
Ranchi, 500,593	F 4
Raurkela, 321,326	F 4
Saharanpur, 294,391	D 3
Salem, 515,021	D 6
Sangli, 268,962	C 5
Secunderabad	D 5
Shillong, 173,064	G 3
Sholapur, 514,461	D 5
Simla, 55,368	D 2
Srinagar, 606,002	D 2
Surat, 912,568	C 4
Thana, 388,577	B 6
Tiruchchirappalli, 607,815	D 6
Tirunelveli, 324,034	D 7
Trivandrum, 519,766	D 7
Tuticorin, 250,673	D 7
Udaipur, 229,762	C 4
Ujjain, 231,878	D 4
Ulhasnagar, 648,149	C 5
Vadodara, 744,043	C 4
Varanasi, 793,542	E 3
Vellore, 246,937	D 6
Vijayawada, 544,958	D 5
Visakhapatnam, 594,259	E 5
Vizagapatam (Visakhapatnam), 594,259	E 5
Warangal, 336,078	D 5

NEPAL

Bhojpur, 194,506	F 3
Dailekh, 156,072	E 3
Doti, 166,070	E 3
Kathmandu (cap.), 353,752	E 3
Lalitpur, 154,998	E 3
Palpa, 212,633	E 3
Ramechhap, 157,349	F 3
Sallyah, 141,457	E 3

PAKISTAN

Bahawalpur, 178,000	C 3
Chiniot, 106,000	C 2
Dera Ismail Khan, 70,000	C 2
Faisalabad, 1,092,000	C 2
Gujranwala, 654,000	C 2
Gujrat, 154,000	C 2
Hyderabad, 795,000	B 3
Islamabad (cap.), 201,000	C 2
Jhang Sadar, 195,000	C 2
Karachi, 5,103,000	B 4
Kasur, 155,000	C 2
Khanawal, 89,000	C 2
Kohat, 78,000	C 2
Jhelum, 106,000	C 2
Lahore, 2,922,000	C 2
Mardan, 148,000	C 2
Mirpur Khas, 124,000	B 3
Multan, 730,000	C 2
Nawabshah, 102,000	B 3
Peshawar, 555,000	C 2
Quetta, 285,000	B 2
Rahimyar Khan, 119,000	C 3
Rawalpindi, 806,000	C 2
Sahiwal, 152,000	C 2
Sargodha, 294,000	C 2
Sialkot, 296,000	C 2
Sukkur, 193,000	B 3
Wah, 122,000	C 2

SRI LANKA

Colombo (cap.), 585,800	D 7
Dehiwala-Mt. Lavinia, 174,400	D 7
Galle, 77,200	D 7
Jaffna, 118,200	E 7
Kandy, 101,300	E 7
Moratuwa, 135,600	D 7
Negombo, 61,400	D 7
Trincomalee, 44,900	E 7

CHINA and MONGOLIA

CHINA

Name	Population	Ref.
Anqing, 449,310		J 5
Anshan, 1,195,580		K 3
Anyang, 501,390		H 4
Baicheng, 276,420		K 2
Baoding, 495,140		J 4
Baoji, 341,240		G 5
Baotou, 1,075,920		G 3
Beihai, 173,740		G 7
Beijing (Peking) (cap.), 5,597,972		J 3
Bengbu, 550,360		J 5
Benxi, 773,730		K 3
Canton (Guangzhou), 3,181,510		H 7
Changchun, 1,747,410		K 3
Changde, 213,890		H 6
Changhua, 185,816		K 7
Changsha, 1,066,030		H 6
Changzhou, 533,940		K 5
Chengde, 326,910		J 3
Chiai, 251,840		K 7
Chongqing (Chungking), 2,673,170		G 6
Dalian, 1,480,240		K 4
Dandong, 545,180		K 3
Datong, 962,470		H 3
Dukou, 497,330		F 6
Fushun, 1,184,940		K 3
Fuxin, 646,580		K 3
Fuzhou, 1,111,550		J 6
Ganzhou, 362,880		H 6
Gejiu, 352,980		F 7
Guangzhou (Canton), 3,181,510		H 7
Guilin, 432,410		G 6
Guiyang, 1,350,190		G 6
Haikou, 263,280		H 7
Handan, 929,530		H 4
Hangzhou, 1,171,450		J 5
Hanzhong, 374,270		G 5
Harbin, 2,519,120		L 2
Hefei, 795,420		J 5
Hegang, 592,470		L 2
Hengyang, 531,730		H 6
Hohhot, 754,120		H 3
Horqin Youyi Qianqi, 174,050		K 2
Hsinchu (Sinchu), 243,218		K 7
Huainan, 1,029,220		J 5
Huangshi, 375,640		J 5
Huzhou, 952,900		K 5
Ji'an, 167,550		J 6
Jiamusi, 540,190		M 2
Jiangmen, 212,450		H 7
Jiaozuo, 484,370		H 4
Jilin, 1,088,420		L 3
Jinan, 1,359,130		J 4
Jingdezhen, 611,030		J 6
Jining, 158,570		H 3
Jinshi, 84,080		H 6
Jinzhou, 599,490		K 3
Jiujiang, 350,190		J 6
Jixi, 781,800		M 2
Kaifeng, 602,230		H 5
Kaohsiung, 1,227,454		J 7
Kaxgar (Kashgar), 256,890		A 4
Keelung, 347,828		K 6
Kunming, 1,418,640		F 6
Lanzhou, 1,364,480		F 4
Leshan, 958,360		F 6
Lhasa, 83,540		D 6
Lianyungang, 397,090		J 5
Liaoyang, 470,020		K 3
Liaoyuan, 771,510		K 3
Liuzhou, 581,940		G 7
Luoyang, 958,360		H 5
Luzhou, 305,220		G 6
Maoming, 412,540		H 7
Mianyang, 768,500		G 5
Mudanjiang, 581,300		M 3
Nanchang, 1,075,710		J 6
Nanchong, 228,340		G 5
Nanjing (Nanking), 2,091,400		J 5
Nanning, 889,790		G 7
Nantong, 402,990		K 5
Neijiang, 270,750		G 6
Ningbo, 478,940		K 6
Peking (Beijing) (cap.), 5,597,972		J 3
Pingdingshan, 470,330		H 5
Pingtung, 189,347		K 7
Qingdao (Tsingtao), 1,172,370		K 4
Qingjiang, 234,750		J 5
Qinhuangdao, 374,210		K 4
Qiqihar (Tsitsihar), 1,209,180		K 2
Quanzhou, 403,180		J 7
Shanghai, 6,320,872		K 5
Shangqiu, 186,760		J 5
Shangrao, 135,160		J 6
Shantou (Swatow), 717,620		J 7
Shaoguan, 370,550		H 7
Shaoxing, 1,091,170		K 5
Shaoyang, 396,600		H 6
Shashi, 238,960		H 5
Shenyang (Mukden), 3,944,240		K 3

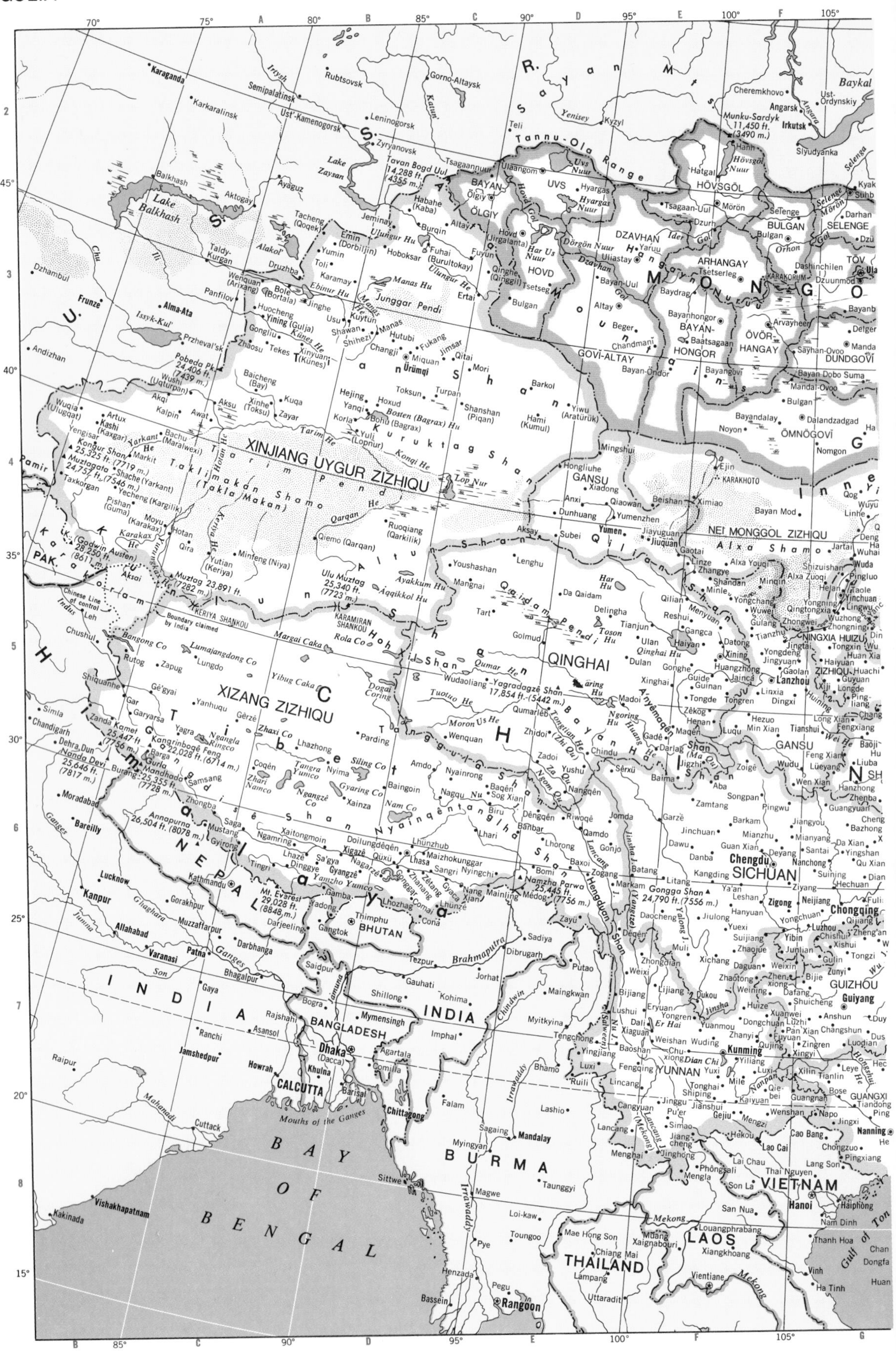

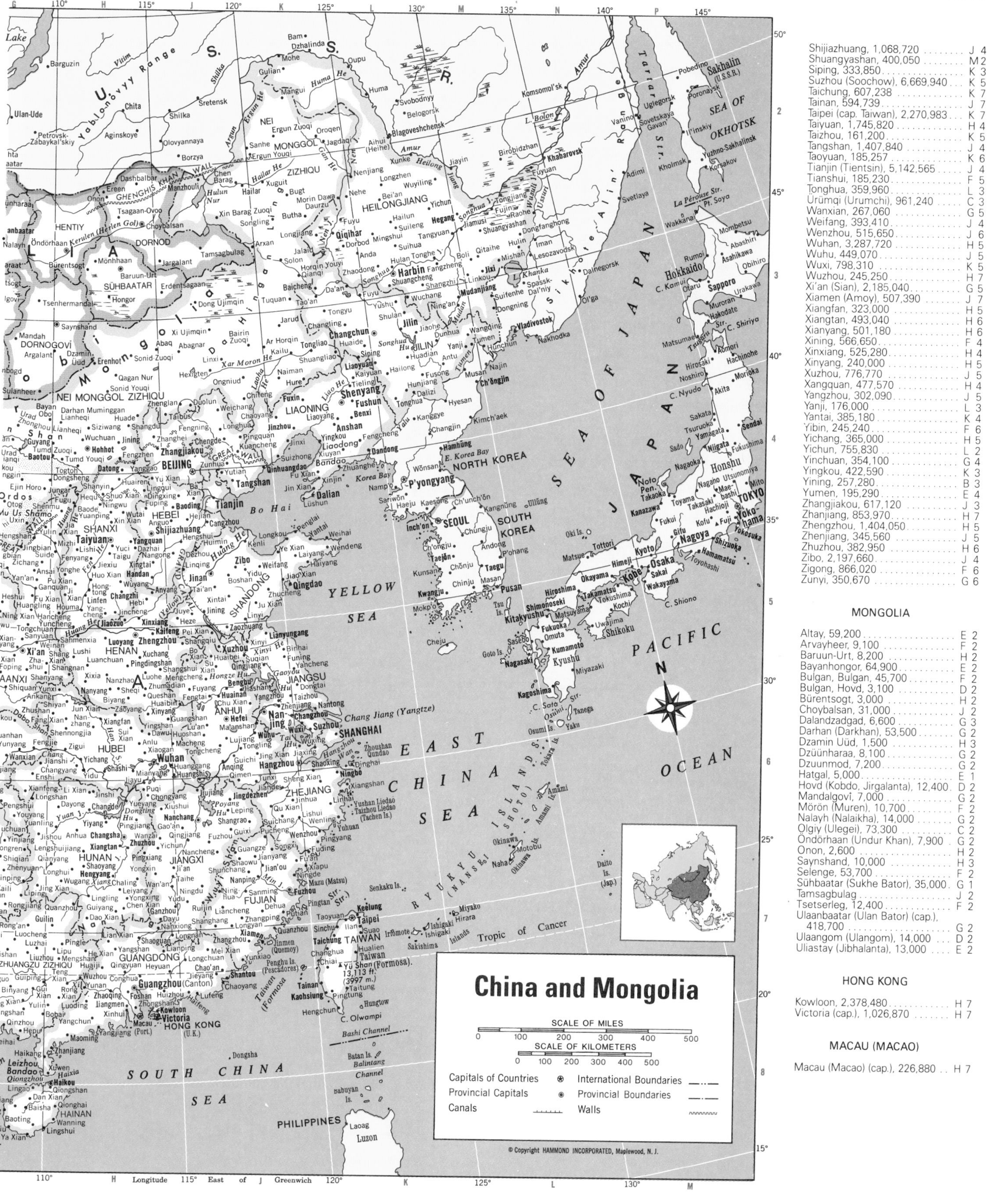

Shijiazhuang, 1,068,720 .... J 4
Shuangyashan, 400,050 .... M 2
Siping, 333,850 .... K 3
Suzhou (Soochow), 6,669,940 ... K 5
Taichung, 607,238 .... K 7
Tainan, 594,739 .... J 7
Taipei (cap. Taiwan), 2,270,983 ... K 7
Taiyuan, 1,745,820 .... H 4
Taizhou, 161,200 .... K 5
Tangshan, 1,407,840 .... J 4
Taoyuan, 185,257 .... K 6
Tianjin (Tientsin), 5,142,565 ..... J 4
Tianshui, 185,230 .... F 5
Tonghua, 359,960 .... L 3
Ürümqi (Urumchi), 961,240 ..... C 3
Wanxian, 267,060 .... G 5
Weifang, 393,410 .... J 4
Wenzhou, 515,650 .... J 6
Wuhan, 3,287,720 .... H 5
Wuhu, 449,070 .... J 5
Wuxi, 798,310 .... K 5
Wuzhou, 245,250 .... H 7
Xi'an (Sian), 2,185,040 .... G 5
Xiamen (Amoy), 507,390 .... J 7
Xiangfan, 323,000 .... H 5
Xiangtan, 493,040 .... H 6
Xianyang, 501,180 .... H 6
Xining, 566,650 .... F 4
Xinxiang, 525,280 .... H 4
Xinyang, 240,000 .... H 5
Xuzhou, 776,770 .... J 5
Xangquan, 477,570 .... H 4
Yangzhou, 302,090 .... J 5
Yanji, 176,000 .... L 3
Yantai, 385,180 .... K 4
Yibin, 245,240 .... F 6
Yichang, 365,000 .... H 5
Yichun, 755,830 .... L 2
Yinchuan, 354,100 .... G 4
Yingkou, 422,590 .... K 3
Yining, 257,280 .... B 3
Yumen, 195,290 .... E 4
Zhangjiakou, 617,120 .... J 3
Zhanjiang, 853,970 .... H 7
Zhengzhou, 1,404,050 .... H 5
Zhenjiang, 345,560 .... J 5
Zhuzhou, 382,950 .... H 6
Zibo, 2,197,660 .... J 4
Zigong, 866,020 .... F 6
Zunyi, 350,670 .... G 6

MONGOLIA

Altay, 59,200 .... E 2
Arvayheer, 9,100 .... F 2
Baruun-Urt, 8,200 .... H 2
Bayanhongor, 64,900 .... E 2
Bulgan, Bulgan, 45,700 .... F 2
Bulgan, Hovd, 3,100 .... D 2
Bürentsogt, 3,000 .... H 2
Choybalsan, 31,000 .... J 2
Dalandzadgad, 6,600 .... G 3
Darhan (Darkhan), 53,500 .... G 2
Dzamin Üüd, 1,500 .... H 3
Dzüünharaa, 8,100 .... G 2
Dzuunmod, 7,200 .... G 2
Hatgal, 5,000 .... E 1
Hovd (Kobdo, Jirgalanta), 12,400 . D 2
Mandalgovĭ, 7,000 .... G 2
Mörön (Muren), 10,700 .... F 2
Nalayh (Nalaikha), 14,000 .... G 2
Olgiy (Ulegei), 73,300 .... C 2
Öndörhaan (Undur Khan), 7,900 . G 2
Onon, 2,600 .... H 2
Saynshand, 10,000 .... H 3
Selenge, 53,700 .... F 2
Sühbaatar (Sukhe Bator), 35,000 . G 1
Tamsagbulag .... J 2
Tsetserleg, 12,400 .... F 2
Ulaanbaatar (Ulan Bator) (cap.), 418,700 .... G 2
Ulaangom (Ulangom), 14,000 ... D 2
Uliastay (Jibhalanta), 13,000 .... E 2

HONG KONG

Kowloon, 2,378,480 .... H 7
Victoria (cap.), 1,026,870 .... H 7

MACAU (MACAO)

Macau (Macao) (cap.), 226,880 .. H 7

JAPAN and KOREA

JAPAN

Name Population	Ref.
Akita, 284,863	E 3
Amagasaki, 523,650	E 4
Aomori, 287,594	F 2
Asahikawa, 352,619	F 2
Chiba, 746,430	F 4
Fukui, 240,962	D 3
Fukuoka, 1,088,588	C 4
Fukushima, 262,837	F 3
Fukuyama, 346,030	D 4
Funabashi, 479,439	H 2
Gifu, 410,357	E 4
Hachioji, 387,178	H 2
Hakodate, 320,154	F 2
Hamamatsu, 490,824	E 4
Higashiosaka, 521,558	E 4
Himeji, 446,256	D 4
Hirakata, 353,358	E 4
Hiroshima, 899,399	D 4
Ichikawa, 364,244	H 2
Iwaki, 342,074	F 3
Kagoshima, 505,360	C 5
Kanazawa, 417,684	D 3
Kawaguchi, 379,360	H 2
Kawasaki, 1,040,802	H 2
Kitakyushu, 1,065,078	C 4
Kobe, 1,367,390	E 4
Kochi, 300,822	D 4
Kofu, 199,262	E 4
Kumamoto, 525,662	C 4
Kure, 234,549	D 4
Kyoto, 1,473,065	E 4
Maebashi, 265,169	E 3
Matsuyama, 401,703	D 4
Mito, 215,566	F 3
Miyazaki, 264,855	C 5
Morioka, 229,114	F 3
Nagano, 324,360	E 3
Nagasaki, 447,091	C 4
Nagoya, 2,087,902	E 4
Naha, 295,778	G 4
Nara, 297,953	F 5
Niigata, 457,785	E 3
Nishinomiya, 410,329	E 4
Oita, 360,478	C 4
Okayama, 545,765	D 4
Omiya, 354,084	H 2
Osaka, 2,648,180	E 4
Otsu, 215,321	F 4
Saga, 163,765	C 4
Sakai, 810,106	E 5
Sapporo, 1,401,757	F 2
Sendai, 664,868	F 3
Shizuoka, 458,341	E 4
Suita, 332,418	E 4
Takamatsu, 316,661	D 4
Takatsuki, 340,720	E 4
Tokushima, 249,343	D 4
Tokyo (cap.), 8,351,893	H 2
Toyohashi, 304,273	E 4
Toyonaka, 403,174	E 4
Urawa, 358,185	H 2
Utsunomiya, 377,746	F 3
Wakayama, 400,802	D 4
Yamagata, 237,041	E 3
Yokohama, 2,773,674	H 2
Yokosuka, 421,107	H 2

NORTH KOREA

Name	Ref.
Ch'ongjin, 306,000	C 2
Haeju, 140,000	B 3
Hamhung, 484,000	B 3
Kaesong, 175,000	B 3
Kimch'aek, 100,000	C 2
Namp'o, 140,000	B 3
P'anmunjom	C 5
P'yongyang (cap.), 1,250,000	B 3
Sinuiju, 300,000	B 2
Wonsan, 275,000	B 3

SOUTH KOREA

Name	Ref.
Cheju, 167,546	B 4
Chinju, 202,753	B 4
Ch'ongju, 252,985	B 4
Chonju, 366,997	B 4
Inch'on, 1,084,730	B 3
Kunsan, 165,318	B 4
Kwangju, 727,627	B 4
Masan, 386,773	C 4
Mokp'o, 221,856	B 4
P'anmunjom	C 5
P'ohang, 201,355	C 3
Pusan, 3,160,276	C 4
Seoul (cap.), 8,366,756	B 3
Taegu, 1,607,458	C 4
Taejon, 651,642	B 3
Ulsan, 418,415	C 4

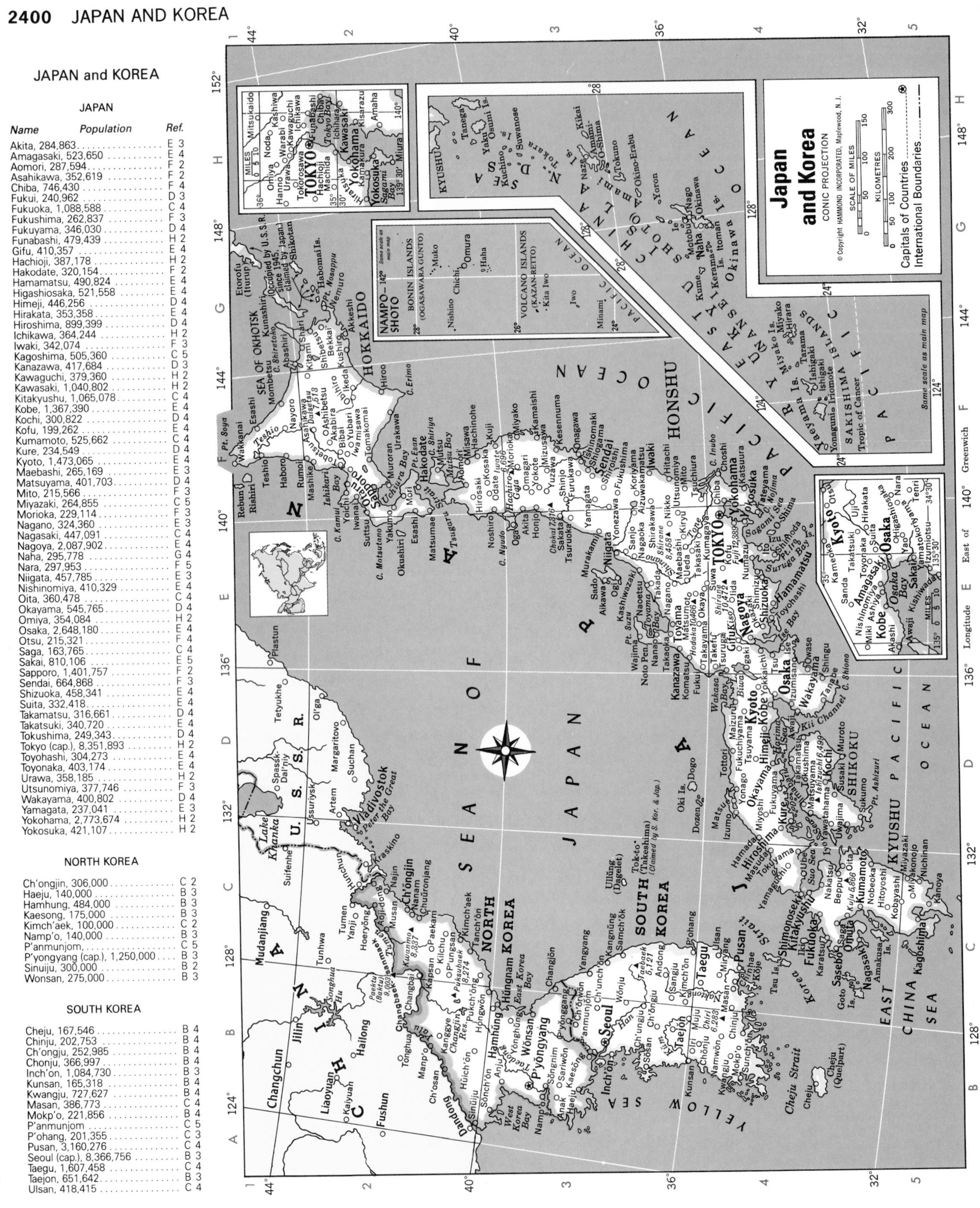

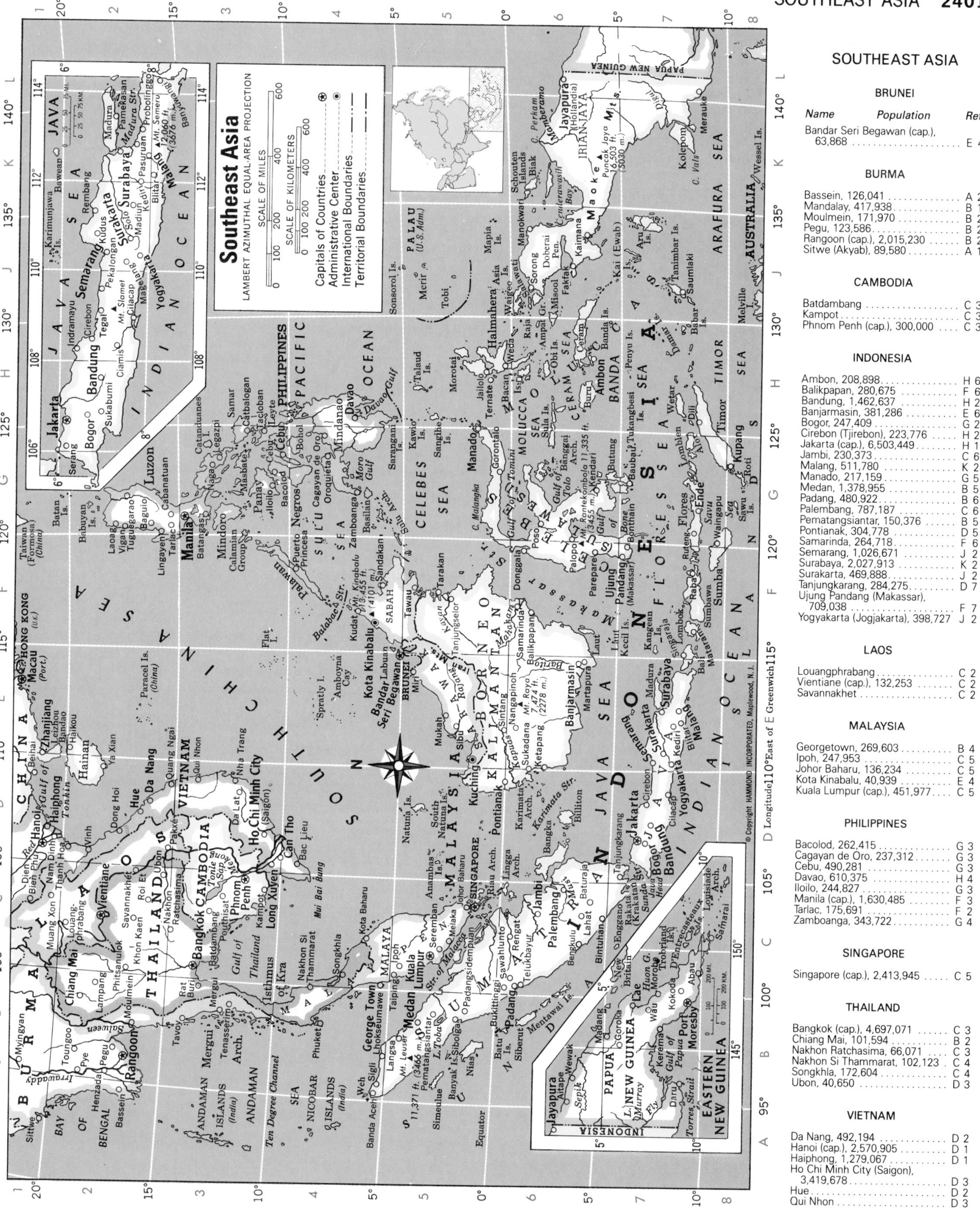

SOUTHEAST ASIA

BRUNEI

Name	Population	Ref.
Bandar Seri Begawan (cap.),	63,868	E 4

BURMA

Name	Population	Ref.
Bassein	126,041	A 2
Mandalay	417,938	B 1
Moulmein	171,970	B 2
Pegu	123,586	B 2
Rangoon (cap.)	2,015,230	B 2
Sitwe (Akyab)	89,580	A 1

CAMBODIA

Name	Population	Ref.
Batdambang		C 3
Kampot		C 3
Phnom Penh (cap.)	300,000	C 3

INDONESIA

Name	Population	Ref.
Ambon	208,898	H 6
Balikpapan	280,675	F 6
Bandung	1,462,637	H 2
Banjarmasin	381,286	E 6
Bogor	247,409	G 2
Cirebon (Tjirebon)	223,776	H 2
Jakarta (cap.)	6,503,449	H 1
Jambi	230,373	C 6
Malang	511,780	K 2
Manado	217,159	G 5
Medan	1,378,955	B 5
Padang	480,922	B 6
Palembang	787,187	C 6
Pematangsiantar	150,376	B 5
Pontianak	304,778	D 5
Samarinda	264,718	F 6
Semarang	1,026,671	J 2
Surabaya	2,027,913	K 2
Surakarta	469,888	J 2
Tanjungkarang	284,275	D 7
Ujung Pandang (Makassar)	709,038	F 7
Yogyakarta (Jogjakarta)	398,727	J 2

LAOS

Name	Population	Ref.
Louangphrabang		C 2
Vientiane (cap.)	132,253	C 2
Savannakhet		C 2

MALAYSIA

Name	Population	Ref.
Georgetown	269,603	B 4
Ipoh	247,953	C 5
Johor Baharu	136,234	C 5
Kota Kinabalu	40,939	E 4
Kuala Lumpur (cap.)	451,977	C 5

PHILIPPINES

Name	Population	Ref.
Bacolod	262,415	G 3
Cagayan de Oro	237,312	G 3
Cebu	490,281	G 3
Davao	610,375	H 4
Iloilo	244,827	G 3
Manila (cap.)	1,630,485	F 3
Tarlac	175,691	F 2
Zamboanga	343,722	G 4

SINGAPORE

Name	Population	Ref.
Singapore (cap.)	2,413,945	C 5

THAILAND

Name	Population	Ref.
Bangkok (cap.)	4,697,071	C 3
Chiang Mai	101,594	B 2
Nakhon Ratchasima	66,071	C 3
Nakhon Si Thammarat	102,123	C 4
Songkhla	172,604	C 4
Ubon	40,650	D 3

VIETNAM

Name	Population	Ref.
Da Nang	492,194	D 2
Hanoi (cap.)	2,570,905	D 1
Haiphong	1,279,067	D 1
Ho Chi Minh City (Saigon)	3,419,678	D 3
Hue		D 2
Qui Nhon		D 3

PACIFIC OCEAN

Name	Ref.
Abaiang (atoll)	H 5
Abemama (atoll)	H 5
Admiralty (isls.)	E 6
Agaña (cap.), Guam, 896	E 4
Ailinglapalap (atoll)	G 5
Aitutaki (atoll)	K 7
Alofi (cap.), Niue, 960	K 7
Ambrym (isl.)	G 7
American Samoa	J 7
Angaur (isl.)	D 5
Apataki (atoll)	M 7
Apia (cap.), W. Samoa, 33,100	J 7
Arno (atoll)	H 5
Arorae (atoll)	H 6
Atiu (isl.)	L 8
Austral (isls.)	L 8
Avarua (cap.), Cook Is.	L 8
Babelthuap (isl.)	D 5
Bairiki (cap.), Kiribati, 1,777	H 5
Baker (isl.)	J 5
Banaba (Ocean) (isl.)	G 6
Banks (isls.)	G 7
Beru (atoll)	H 6
Bikini (atoll)	G 4
Bismarck (arch.)	E 6
Bonin (isls.)	E 3
Bora-Bora (isl.)	L 7
Bougainville (isl.)	F 6
Bounty (isls.)	H 10
Butaritari (atoll)	H 5
Capitol Hill (cap.), No. Marianas, 592	E 4
Caroline (isls.)	E 5
Chichi (isl.)	E 3
Choiseul (isl.)	F 6
Cook (isls.)	K 7
Coral (sea)	F 7
Easter (isl.)	Q 8
Ebon (atoll)	G 5
Efate (isl.)	G 7
Enderbury (isl.)	J 6
Enewetak (Eniwetok) (atoll)	G 4
Erromanga (isl.)	H 7
Espiritu Santo (isl.)	G 7
Fiji	H 8
Fongafale (cap.), Tuvalu	H 6
French Polynesia	L 8
Funafuti (atoll)	H 6
Futuna (Hoorn) (isls.)	J 7
Gambier (isls.)	N 8
Gilbert (isls.)	H 6
Guadalcanal (isl.)	F 7
Guam (isl.)	E 4
Hawaiian (isls.)	J 3
Hivaoa (isl.)	N 6
Honiara (cap.), Solomon Is., 14,942	F 6
Hoorn (isls.)	J 7
Howland (isl.)	J 5
Huahine (isl.)	L 7
Huon (gulf)	E 6
Iwo (isl.)	E 3
Jaluit (atoll)	G 5
Jarvis (isl.)	K 6
Johnston (atoll)	K 4
Kadavu (Kandavu) (isl.)	H 7
Kanton (Canton) (isl.)	J 6
Kapingamarangi (Greenwich) (atoll)	F 5
Kavieng, 4,633	E 6
Kermadec (isls.)	J 9
Kieta, 3,491	F 6
Kingman (reef)	K 5
Kiribati	J 6
Kiritimati (Christmas) (isl.)	L 5
Kolonia (cap.), Micronesia, 5,549	F 5
Koror (cap.), Palau, 6,222	D 5
Kosrae (isl.)	G 5
Kwajalein (atoll)	G 5
Lae, 61,617	E 6
Lau Group (isls.)	J 7
Lavongai (isl.)	F 6
Lifu (isl.)	G 8
Line (isls.)	K 5
Little Makin (atoll)	H 5
Lorengau, 3,986	E 6
Louisiade (arch.)	F 7
Loyalty (isls.)	G 8
Luganville, 4,935	G 7
Madang, 21,335	E 6
Majuro (atoll) (cap.), Marshall Is.	H 5
Makin (Butaritari) (atoll)	H 5
Malaita (isl.)	G 6
Malden (isl.)	L 6
Malekula (isl.)	G 7
Maloelap (atoll)	H 5
Mangaia (isl.)	L 8
Mangareva (isl.)	N 8
Manua (isls.)	K 7
Manus (isl.)	E 6
Marcus (isl.)	F 3
Marianas, Northern	E 4

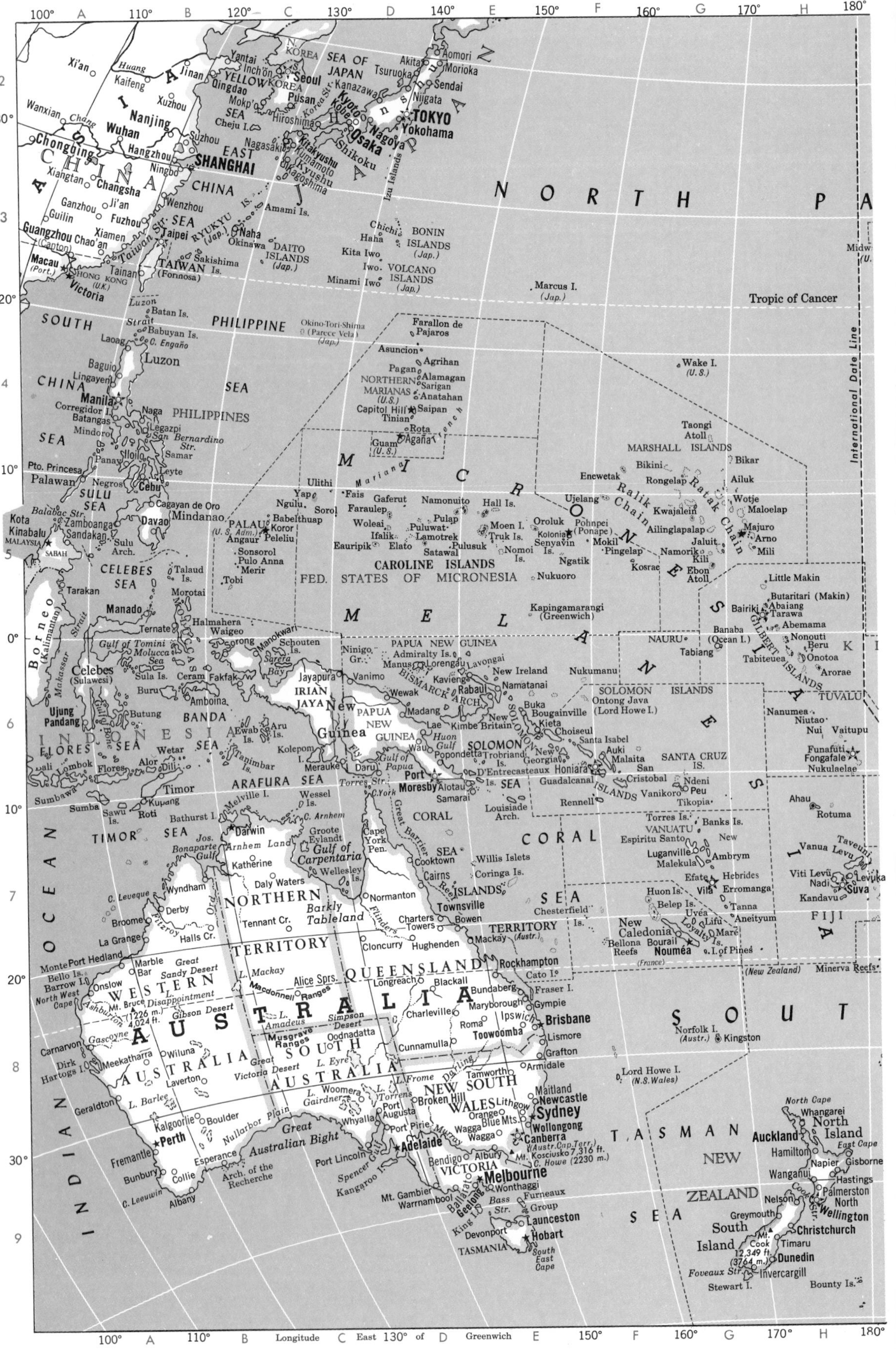

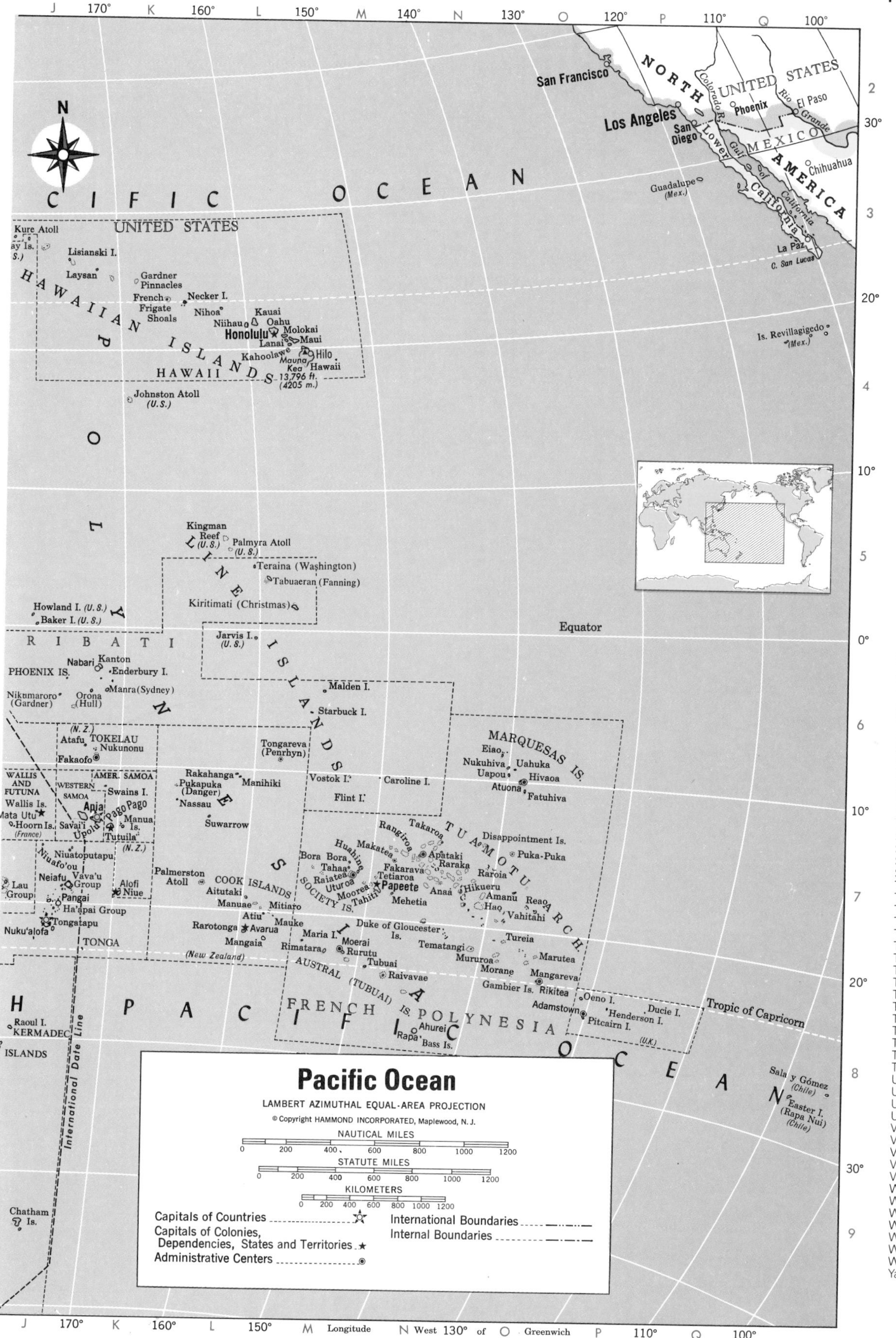
PACIFIC OCEAN
UNITED STATES
HAWAIIAN ISLANDS
HAWAII
Kure Atoll
Lisianski I.
Laysan
Gardner Pinnacles
Necker I.
French Frigate Shoals
Nihoa
Kauai
Niihau
Oahu
Honolulu
Molokai
Lanai
Maui
Kahoolawe
Hilo
Mauna Kea 13,796 ft. (4205 m.)
Hawaii
Johnston Atoll (U.S.)
San Francisco
Los Angeles
San Diego
NORTH AMERICA
UNITED STATES
Phoenix
El Paso
Rio Grande
Colorado R.
MEXICO
Chihuahua
Gulf of California
Lower California
Guadalupe (Mex.)
La Paz
C. San Lucas
Is. Revillagigedo (Mex.)
Kingman Reef (U.S.)
Palmyra Atoll (U.S.)
LINE ISLANDS
Teraina (Washington)
Tabuaeran (Fanning)
Kiritimati (Christmas)
Howland I. (U.S.)
Baker I. (U.S.)
Jarvis I. (U.S.)
KIRIBATI
Equator
PHOENIX IS.
Nabari
Kanton
Enderbury I.
Manra (Sydney)
Nikumaroro (Gardner)
Orona (Hull)
Malden I.
Starbuck I.
TOKELAU
Atafu
Nukunonu
Fakaofo
AMER. SAMOA
WESTERN SAMOA
WALLIS AND FUTUNA
Swains I.
Wallis Is.
Mata Utu
Hoorn Is. (France)
Savai'i
Upolu
Apia
Pago Pago
Manua Is.
Tutuila
Niuatoputapu
Niuafo'ou
Neiafu
Vava'u Group
Alofi
Niue
Lau Group
Pangai
Ha'apai Group
Tongatapu
Nuku'alofa
TONGA
Tongareva (Penrhyn)
Rakahanga
Manihiki
Pukapuka (Danger)
Nassau
Suwarrow
Palmerston Atoll
COOK ISLANDS
Aitutaki
Manuae
Mitiaro
Atiu
Mauke
Rarotonga
Avarua
Mangaia
(New Zealand)
Vostok I.
Caroline I.
Flint I.
MARQUESAS IS.
Eiao
Nukuhiva
Uahuka
Uapou
Hivaoa
Atuona
Fatuhiva
TUAMOTU ARCH.
Disappointment Is.
Puka-Puka
Takaroa
Rangiroa
Makatea
Apataki
Raraka
Fakarava
Raroia
Tetiaroa
Anaa
Hikueru
Amanu
Reao
Hao
Vahitahi
SOCIETY IS.
Huahine
Bora Bora
Tahaa
Raiatea
Uturoa
Moorea
Tahiti
Papeete
Mehetia
Duke of Gloucester Is.
Tematangi
Tureia
Mururoa
Marutea
Morane
Mangareva
Gambier Is.
Rikitea
Maria I.
Moerai
Rimatara
Rurutu
Tubuai
Raivavae
AUSTRAL (TUBUAI) IS.
FRENCH POLYNESIA
Rapa
Ahurei
Bass Is.
Adamstown
Pitcairn I.
Oeno I.
Henderson I.
Ducie I.
(U.K.)
Tropic of Capricorn
Sala y Gómez (Chile)
Easter I. (Rapa Nui) (Chile)
Raoul I.
KERMADEC ISLANDS
Chatham Is.
International Date Line
Pacific Ocean
LAMBERT AZIMUTHAL EQUAL-AREA PROJECTION
© Copyright HAMMOND INCORPORATED, Maplewood, N. J.
NAUTICAL MILES
0 200 400 600 800 1000 1200
STATUTE MILES
0 200 400 600 800 1000 1200
KILOMETERS
0 200 400 600 800 1000 1200
Capitals of Countries
Capitals of Colonies, Dependencies, States and Territories
Administrative Centers
International Boundaries
Internal Boundaries
Longitude West of Greenwich
J 170° K 160° L 150° M 140° N 130° O 120° P 110° Q 100°
30° 20° 10° 0° 10° 20° 30°

AUSTRALIA and NEW ZEALAND

AUSTRALIA

Name	Population	Ref.
Adelaide (cap.), S. Aust.,	882,520	D 8
Albany	15,222	B 6
Alice Springs	18,395	E 4
Ararat	8,336	G 7
Armidale	18,922	J 6
Auburn	46,622	K 4
Bairnsdale	9,459	H 7
Ballarat	35,681	G 7
Bankstown	152,636	K 4
Bathurst	19,640	H 6
Bega	4,388	J 7
Bendigo	31,841	G 7
Blackall	1,609	H 4
Blue Mountains	55,877	J 6
Boulder-Kalgoorlie	19,848	C 6
Bourke	3,326	H 6
Bowen	7,663	H 3
Brisbane (cap.), Queens.,	942,836	K 3
Broken Hill	26,913	G 6
Broome	3,666	C 3
Bunbury	21,749	B 6
Bundaberg	32,560	J 4
Burnie-Somerset	19,994	H 8
Burnside	37,593	E 8
Busselton	6,463	A 6
Cairns	48,557	H 3
Campbelltown	43,084	E 8
Canberra (cap.), Aust.	*220,822	H 7
Carnarvon	5,053	A 4
Cessnock-Bellbird	16,916	J 6
Charleville	3,523	H 5
Charters Towers	6,823	H 4
Clermont	1,659	H 4
Cloncurry	1,961	G 4
Collie	2,667	B 6
Condobolin	3,355	H 6
Cooma	7,978	H 7
Coonamble	3,090	H 6
Cunnamulla	1,627	H 5
Dalby	8,784	J 5
Dandenong	54,962	L 3
Darwin (cap.), N. Terr.	56,482	E 2
Deniliquin	7,354	G 7
Derby	2,933	C 3
Dubbo	23,986	H 6
Echuca	7,943	G 7
Enfield	66,797	D 7
Fairfield	129,557	K 4
Forbes	8,029	H 6
Fremantle	22,484	B 6
Geelong	14,471	G 7
Geraldton	20,895	A 5
Gold Coast	135,437	J 5
Goulburn	21,755	J 6
Griffith	13,187	H 6
Gympie	10,768	J 5
Hamilton	9,751	G 7
Hay	2,958	H 6
Hobart (cap.), Tas.	128,603	H 8
Horsham	12,034	G 7
Hughenden	1,657	G 4
Ingham	5,598	H 3
Innisfail	7,933	H 3
Kalgoorlie	9,145	C 6
Katanning	4,413	B 6
Kempsey	9,037	J 6
Kingaroy	5,134	J 5
Launceston	31,273	H 8
Longreach	2,971	G 4
Mackay	35,361	H 4
Maitland	38,865	J 6
Malvern	43,211	J 6
Mandurah	10,978	B 3
Maryborough	7,858	G 7
Melbourne (cap.), Vic.,	2,578,759	K 2
Mildura	15,763	G 6
Moree	10,459	H 5
Mount Gambier	18,193	G 7
Mount Isa	23,679	F 4
Mount Morgan	2,974	J 4
Naracoorte	4,758	F 7
Narrabri	7,296	J 6
Narrandera	5,813	H 6
Narrogin	4,969	B 6
Nedlands	20,257	B 2
Newcastle	135,207	J 6
New Norfolk	6,243	H 8
Northam	6,791	B 6
Nyngan	2,485	H 6
Parramatta	130,943	K 4
Penrith	108,720	J 6
Perth (cap.), W. Aust.	809,035	B 2
Peterborough	2,575	F 6
Port Augusta	15,566	F 6
Portland	9,353	G 7
Port Lincoln	9,846	E 6
Port Macquarie	19,581	J 6

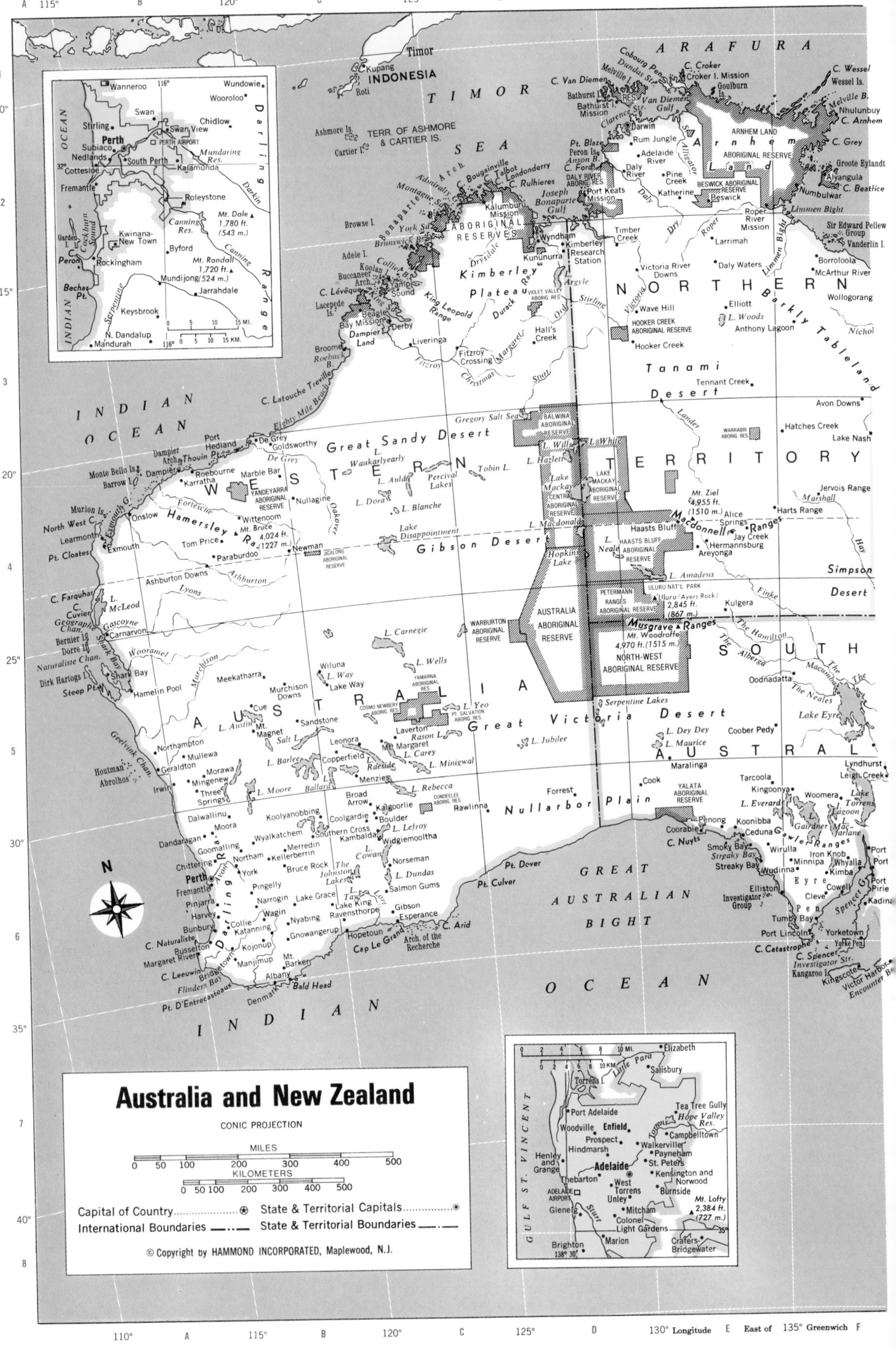

CORAL SEA
CORAL SEA ISLANDS TERRITORY
PAPUA NEW GUINEA
GULF OF CARPENTARIA
QUEENSLAND
NEW SOUTH WALES
VICTORIA
TASMANIA
AUSTRALIAN CAPITAL TERRITORY
TASMAN SEA
Great Barrier Reef
Great Dividing Range
Torres Strait
Bass Strait
Brisbane
Sydney
Melbourne
Canberra
Adelaide
Hobart
Tropic of Capricorn
PORT PHILLIP BAY
PACIFIC OCEAN
NEW ZEALAND
NORTH ISLAND
SOUTH ISLAND
Southern Alps
Auckland
Wellington
Christchurch
Dunedin
Same Scale as main map
Long. East of Greenwich

ANTARCTICA

Name	Population	Ref.
Adare (cape)		B 9
Adélie Coast (region)		C 7
American Highland		B 4
Amery Ice Shelf		C 4
Amundsen (bay)		C 3
Amundsen (sea)		B 13
Amundsen-Scott Station		A 14
Antarctic (pen.)		C 15
Balleny (isls.)		C 9
Banzare Coast (region)		C 7
Barr Smith (mt.)		C 5
Batterbee (cape)		C 3
Beardmore (glacier)		A 8
Bellingshausen (sea)		C 14
Bouvet (isl.)		D 1
Budd Coast (region)		C 6
Byrd Station		A 12
Caird Coast (region)		B 17
Clarie Coast (region)		C 7
Coats Land (region)		B 17
Colbeck (cape)		B 10
Darnley (cape)		C 4
Dart (cape)		B 12
Davis (sea)		C 5
Davis Station		C 4
Drake (passage)		C 15
Dumont d'Urville Station		C 7
Edward VII (pen.)		B 11
Edward VIII (bay)		C 4
Eights Coast (region)		B 14
Ellsworth Land (region)		B 14
Enderby Land (region)		B 3
English Coast (region)		B 15
Executive Committee (range)		B 12
Filchner Ice Shelf		B 16
Ford Ranges (mts.)		B 11
Gaussberg (mt.)		C 5
George V Coast (region)		C 8
Getz Ice Shelf		B 12
Graham Land (region)		C 15
Hobbs Coast (region)		B 12
Hollick-Kenyon (plateau)		B 13
Hope (bay)		C 16
Indian Ocean		C 3
Kemp Coast (region)		C 3
King George (isl.)		C 16
Larsen Ice Shelf		C 16
Lazarev Station		C 1
Levick (mt.)		B 8
Lister (mt.)		B 8
Little America		B 10
Luitpold Coast (region)		B 17
Lützow-Holm (bay)		C 3
Mackenzie (bay)		C 4
Mac-Robertson Land (region)		B 4
Marguerite (bay)		C 15
Marie Byrd Land (region)		B 13
Markham (mt.)		A 8
Mawson (station)		C 4
McMurdo (sound)		B 9
Mirnyy (station)		C 5
New Schwabenland (region)		B 1
Oates Coast (region)		B 8
Palmer (arch.)		C 15
Palmer Land (region)		B 15
Palmer Station		C 15
Peter I (isl.)		B 14
Prince Edward (isls.)		E 2
Price Olav Coast (region)		C 3
Princess Astrid Coast (region)		B 1
Princess Martha Coast (region)		B 18
Prydz (bay)		C 4
Queen Mary Coast (region)		C 5
Queen Maud (mts.)		A 12
Queen Maud Land (region)		B 1
Riiser-Larsen (pen.)		C 2
Ronne Entrance (inlet)		B 15
Ronne Ice Shelf		B 15
Roosevelt (isl.)		A 10
Ross (isl.)		B 9
Ross (sea)		B 10
Ross Ice Shelf		A 10
Sabrina Coast (region)		C 6
Scotia (sea)		D 16
Scott (isl.)		C 10
Scott Station		B 9
Shackleton Ice Shelf		C 5
South Georgia (isl.)		D 17
South Magnetic Pole		C 8
South Orkney (isls.)		C 16
South Polar (plateau)		A 1
South Pole		A 4
South Sandwich (isls.)		D 17
South Shetland (isls.)		D 15
Transantarctic (mts.)		B 17
Victoria Land (region)		B 8
Vincennes (bay)		C 6
Vinson Massif (mountain)		B 14
Walgreen Coast (region)		B 13
Weddell (sea)		C 16
West Ice Shelf		C 5
Wilhelm II Coast (region)		C 5
Wilkes Land (region)		B 7

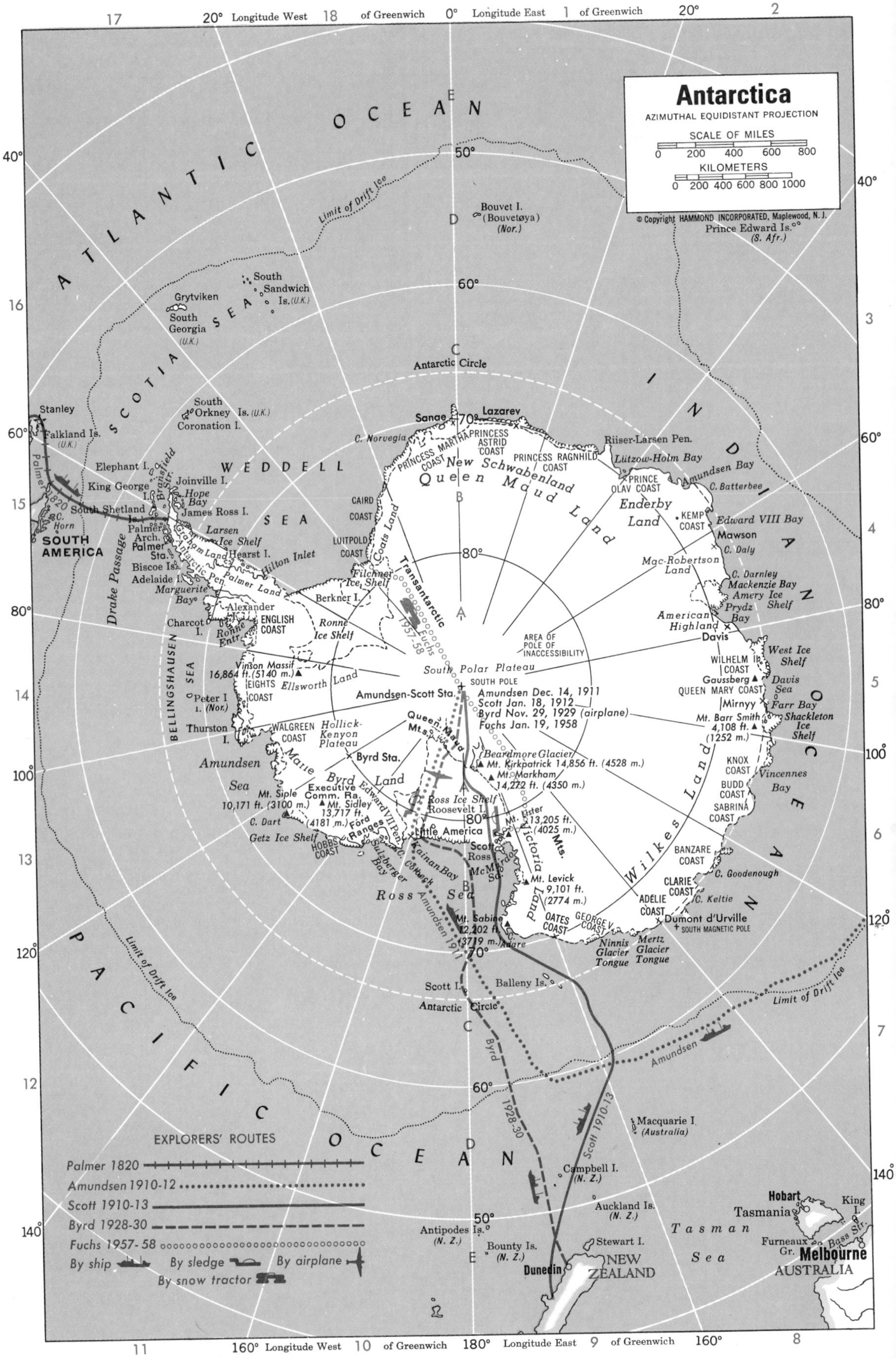

Antarctica

AZIMUTHAL EQUIDISTANT PROJECTION

SCALE OF MILES 0 200 400 600 800

KILOMETERS 0 200 400 600 800 1000

EXPLORERS' ROUTES

Palmer 1820

Amundsen 1910-12

Scott 1910-13

Byrd 1928-30

Fuchs 1957-58

By ship By sledge By airplane

By snow tractor

VOLUME 28

Index

HOW TO USE THE INDEX

The INDEX volume, the key to your *Volume Library,* was produced with the newest high-speed computer equipment. All entries were stored, sorted, and alphabetized with a speed and accuracy unknown to man before the computer age. One hundred hours of hand indexing was completed in less than an hour. Type was produced at speeds up to six million characters (or 700 pages) an hour.

Properly used, this index is a quick, easy guide to the information you seek in *The Volume Library.* As you use it, keep in mind the easy-to-understand format described below.

Page numbers under each entry are preceded by a volume number (1: 35, 39, 106); a semicolon reflects a change of volume number (1: 35, 39, 106; 2: 1345, 1567). Numbers are followed by a letter that indicates the column on the page: *a* refers to the first column; *b* to the second; *c* to the third. This convenient guide will help you pinpoint information quickly and easily.

The computer has alphabetized all entries in a letter-by-letter system. That is, all entries, regardless of punctuation, are arranged in precise alphabetical order; there are no exceptions.

Port Elizabeth (South Africa)
Porter, Cole
  biography
Porter, George
Porter, Katherine Anne
  biography
Porter, William Sidney *see* Henry, O.
Port Etienne (Mauritania)

There are no alphabetical priorities for persons with like names. In the case of persons of rank, such as kings and emperors, all the firsts (I) are listed together, then the seconds (II), thirds (III), and so forth. Descriptive material identifying such persons follows the name in parenthesis.

Henry I (King of Germany)
Henry I (King of England)
Henry II (Duke of Silesia)
Henry II (King of England)
Henry III (King of England)
Henry III (King of France)
Henry IV (Holy Rom. Emp.)

Names beginning with Mac or Mc are also arranged in strict alphabetical order. Mac is located among the general *mac* listings and Mc among the *mc* listings. Spanish and French names preceded by an article, such as *La, Les,* or *Los,* are listed under the article, since the article is part of the name. Arabic names beginning with *ibn* (son of), as ibn Saud, are under *i.* However, Burmese names preceded by the honorary term *U,* as *U* Thant, are indexed under the surname.

Names beginning with prepositions such as *von, van,* or *de* are indexed according to the traditional use of the name. For example, De Gaulle and D'Annunzio are indexed under *d;* Van Gogh under *v.* But Honoré de Balzac, Simone de Beauvoir, and St. Thomas à Becket are all indexed under *b.* Handy cross references are used whenever a listing may be ambiguous.

References to prominent works of art, books, plays, and so forth, are listed under the name of the author (except in the case of anonymous works, which have their own listings).

Wagner, Richard
  biography
  Die Meistersinger
  Lohengrin
  Ring of the Nibelungs

Famous works are cross-referenced to their author: **Iliad** *see* Homer; **Little Women** *see* Alcott, Louisa May; **Importance of Being Ernest** *see* Wilde, Oscar.

ABBREVIATIONS

Afgh.	Afghanistan
Afr.	Africa, African
Ala.	Alabama
Am.	America, American
anat.	anatomy
anc.	ancient
anthro.	anthropology
arch.	architecture
Arg.	Argentina
Ariz.	Arizona
Ark.	Arkansas
astro.	astronautics
astron.	astronomy
bib.	biblical
bot.	botanical, botany
bus.	business
Calif.	California
cer.	ceramics
chem.	chemistry
Colo.	Colorado
Conn.	Connecticut
Czech.	Czechoslovakia
Del.	Delaware
econ.	economics
Emp.	Emperor, Empress
Eng.	England
fin.	finance
Fla.	Florida
form.	former, formerly
Fr.	France, French
Ga.	Georgia
geog.	geography
geol.	geology
Ger.	Germany
govt.	government
Gr.	Greece
il.	illustration
Ill.	Illinois
Ind.	Indian, Indiana
Ire.	Ireland
is.	island, islands
It.	Italian
Kan.	Kansas
Ky.	Kentucky
La.	Louisiana
lang.	language
Leb.	Lebanon
leg.	legend, legendary
lit.	literature
Mass.	Massachusetts
math.	mathematics
Md.	Maryland
meteorol.	meteorology
Mich.	Michigan
mineral.	mineralogy
Minn.	Minnesota
Miss.	Mississippi
Mo.	Missouri
mod.	modern
Mont.	Montana
myth.	mythology
N. Am.	North American
N.C.	North Carolina
N. Dak.	North Dakota
Neb.	Nebraska
Neth.	Netherlands
Nev.	Nevada
N.H.	New Hampshire
N.J.	New Jersey
N. Mex.	New Mexico
N.Y.	New York
oceanog.	oceanography
Okla.	Oklahoma
Oreg.	Oregon
Pak.	Pakistan
Para.	Paraguay
Penn.	Pennsylvania
philos.	philosophy
physiol.	physiology
Port.	Portugal, Portuguese
P.R.	Puerto Rico
print.	printing
pseud.	pseudonym
psych.	psychology
R.I.	Rhode Island
Rom.	Roman
S. Afr.	South Africa
S. Am.	South American
S.C.	South Carolina
Scan.	Scandinavian
sci.	science
Scot.	Scotland
sculp.	sculpture
S. Dak.	South Dakota
St.	Saint
Switz.	Switzerland
tab.	table
Tenn.	Tennessee
Tex.	Texas
U.S.	United States
Va.	Virginia
Venez.	Venezuela
Vt.	Vermont
Wash.	Washington
Wis.	Wisconsin
W. Va.	West Virginia
Wyo.	Wyoming
Yugo.	Yugoslavia
zool.	zoology

VOLUME 28 Index

A

B

C

D

E

F

H

J

K

M

O

T

U

V

Z